Who Was Who in America®

Who Was Who in America®
with world notables

1996-1998
Volume XII

MARQUIS
Who's Who® 121 Chanlon Road
New Providence, NJ 07974 U.S.A.

Who Was Who in America®

Marquis Who's Who®

Senior Managing Director   Paul Canning

Senior Editorial Director   Tom Bachmann

Research Director   Judy Redel

Senior Managing Editor   Fred Marks

Senior Editor   Karen Chassie

Associate Editor   Maurice Brooks

International Standard Book Number   0-8379-0228-2 (14-volume set)
                                         0-8379-0229-0 (volume XII)
                                         0-8379-0230-4 (Index volume)
International Standard Serial Number   0146-8081

Manufactured in the United States of America

Table of Contents

Preface

The publication of Volume XII of *Who Was Who in America* answers an ongoing demand among biographical researchers for the books in the *Who's Who in America* series. *Who's Who in America*, the major component of the series, has continued to advance the highest standards of biographical compilation throughout a century of continuous publication.

The *Was* books (to use the shortened form by which they are perhaps better known) have sought to reflect the history and genealogical heritage of America. These books have inherited the unique characteristics that have made *Who's Who in America* both an internationally respected reference work and a household word here in the country of its origin.

For example, sketches in each *Was* volume have not only been prepared from information supplied by the Biographees themselves, but have been approved personally—and frequently revised—before being printed in a Marquis publication during the subject's lifetime. As with all *Was* volumes, many of these sketches have been scrutinized and revised by relatives or legal representatives of the deceased Biographee.

The preface to the first volume of *Who's Who in America* stated: "The book is autobiographical, the data having been obtained from first hands." It follows that *Who Was Who in America* is also autobiographical to a distinctive degree. In that respect, it is unique among American biographical directories. And although condensed to the style that Marquis Who's Who has made famous, the sketches contain all essential facts.

Most of the sketches in Volume XII are of deceased Biographees from *Who's Who in America*. This volume also contains the sketches of deceased Marquis Biographees whose careers were of regional or international significance and whose listings were in Marquis publications other than *Who's Who in America*. Additionally, this volume includes sketches of some Marquis Biographees who were born in 1896 or earlier, and are believed to be deceased.

Continuously updated, and now published in fourteen volumes containing some 130,000 biographies, *Who Was Who in America* is a vital portion of American history from the early days of the colonies to the present. It is the autobiography of America.

The Editors
New Providence, N.J.
1998

Table of Abbreviations

The following abbreviations and symbols are frequently used in this book.

A Associate (used with academic degrees only)

AA, A.A. Associate in Arts, Associate of Arts

AAAL American Academy of Arts and Letters

AAAS American Association for the Advancement of Science

AACD American Association for Counseling and Development

AACN American Association of Critical Care Nurses

AAHA American Academy of Health Administrators

AAHP American Association of Hospital Planners

AAHPERD American Alliance for Health, Physical Education, Recreation, and Dance

AAS Associate of Applied Science

AASL American Association of School Librarians

AASPA American Association of School Personnel Administrators

AAU Amateur Athletic Union

AAUP American Association of University Professors

AAUW American Association of University Women

AB, A.B. Arts, Bachelor of

AB Alberta

ABA American Bar Association

ABC American Broadcasting Company

AC Air Corps

acad. academy, academic

acct. accountant

acctg. accounting

ACDA Arms Control and Disarmament Agency

ACHA American College of Hospital Administrators

ACLS Advanced Cardiac Life Support

ACLU American Civil Liberties Union

ACOG American College of Ob-Gyn

ACP American College of Physicians

ACS American College of Surgeons

ADA American Dental Association

a.d.c. aide-de-camp

adj. adjunct, adjutant

adj. gen. adjutant general

adm. admiral

adminstr. administrator

adminstrn. administration

adminstrv. administrative

ADN Associate's Degree in Nursing

ADP Automatic Data Processing

adv. advocate, advisory

advt. advertising

AE, A.E. Agricultural Engineer

A.E. and P. Ambassador Extraordinary and Plenipotentiary

AEC Atomic Energy Commission

aero. aeronautical, aeronautic

aerodyn. aerodynamic

AFB Air Force Base

AFL-CIO American Federation of Labor and Congress of Industrial Organizations

AFTRA American Federation of TV and Radio Artists

AFSCME American Federation of State, County and Municipal Employees

agr. agriculture

agrl. agricultural

agt. agent

AGVA American Guild of Variety Artists

agy. agency

A&I Agricultural and Industrial

AIA American Institute of Architects

AIAA American Institute of Aeronautics and Astronautics

AIChE American Institute of Chemical Engineers

AICPA American Institute of Certified Public Accountants

AID Agency for International Development

AIDS Acquired Immune Deficiency Syndrome

AIEE American Institute of Electrical Engineers

AIM American Institute of Management

AIME American Institute of Mining, Metallurgy, and Petroleum Engineers

AK Alaska

AL Alabama

ALA American Library Association

Ala. Alabama

alt. alternate

Alta. Alberta

A&M Agricultural and Mechanical

AM, A.M. Arts, Master of

Am. American, America

AMA American Medical Association

amb. ambassador

A.M.E. African Methodist Episcopal

Amtrak National Railroad Passenger Corporation

AMVETS American Veterans of World War II, Korea, Vietnam

ANA American Nurses Association

anat. anatomical

ANCC American Nurses Credentialing Center

ann. annual

ANTA American National Theatre and Academy

anthrop. anthropological

AP Associated Press

APA American Psychological Association

APGA American Personnel Guidance Association

APHA American Public Health Association

APO Army Post Office

apptd. appointed

Apr. April

apt. apartment

AR Arkansas

ARC American Red Cross

arch. architect

archeol. archeological

archtl. architectural

Ariz. Arizona

Ark. Arkansas

ArtsD, ArtsD. Arts, Doctor of

arty. artillery

AS American Samoa

AS Associate in Science

ASCAP American Society of Composers, Authors and Publishers

ASCD Association for Supervision and Curriculum Development

ASCE American Society of Civil Engineers

ASHRAE American Society of Heating, Refrigeration, and Air Conditioning Engineers

ASME American Society of Mechanical Engineers

ASNSA American Society for Nursing Service Administrators

ASPA American Society for Public Administration

ASPCA American Society for the Prevention of Cruelty to Animals

assn. association

assoc. associate

asst. assistant

ASTD American Society for Training and Development

ASTM American Society for Testing and Materials

astron. astronomical

astrophys. astrophysical

ATLA Association of Trial Lawyers of America

ATSC Air Technical Service Command

AT&T American Telephone & Telegraph Company

atty. attorney

Aug. August

AUS Army of the United States

aux. auxiliary

Ave. Avenue

AVMA American Veterinary Medical Association

AZ Arizona

AWHONN Association of Women's Health Obstetric and Neonatal Nurses

B. Bachelor

b. born

BA, B.A. Bachelor of Arts

BAgr, B.Agr. Bachelor of Agriculture

Balt. Baltimore

Bapt. Baptist

BArch, B.Arch. Bachelor of Architecture

BAS, B.A.S. Bachelor of Agricultural Science

BBA, B.B.A. Bachelor of Business Administration

BBB Better Business Bureau

BBC British Broadcasting Corporation

BC, B.C. British Columbia

BCE, B.C.E. Bachelor of Civil Engineering

BChir, B.Chir. Bachelor of Surgery

BCL, B.C.L. Bachelor of Civil Law

BCLS Basic Cardiac Life Support

BCS, B.C.S. Bachelor of Commercial Science
BD, B.D. Bachelor of Divinity
bd. board
BE, B.E. Bachelor of Education
BEE, B.E.E. Bachelor of Electrical Engineering
BFA, B.F.A. Bachelor of Fine Arts
bibl. biblical
bibliog. bibliographical
biog. biographical
biol. biological
BJ, B.J. Bachelor of Journalism
Bklyn. Brooklyn
BL, B.L. Bachelor of Letters
bldg. building
BLS, B.L.S. Bachelor of Library Science
BLS Basic Life Support
Blvd. Boulevard
BMI Broadcast Music, Inc.
BMW Bavarian Motor Works (Bayerische Motoren Werke)
bn. battalion
B.&O.R.R. Baltimore & Ohio Railroad
bot. botanical
BPE, B.P.E. Bachelor of Physical Education
BPhil, B.Phil. Bachelor of Philosophy
br. branch
BRE, B.R.E. Bachelor of Religious Education
brig. gen. brigadier general
Brit. British, Brittanica
Bros. Brothers
BS, B.S. Bachelor of Science
BSA, B.S.A. Bachelor of Agricultural Science
BSBA Bachelor of Science in Business Administration
BSChemE Bachelor of Science in Chemical Engineering
BSD, B.S.D. Bachelor of Didactic Science
BSEE Bachelor of Science in Electrical Engineering
BSN Bachelor of Science in Nursing
BST, B.S.T. Bachelor of Sacred Theology
BTh, B.Th. Bachelor of Theology
bull. bulletin
bur. bureau
bus. business
B.W.I. British West Indies

CA California
CAA Civil Aeronautics Administration
CAB Civil Aeronautics Board
CAD-CAM Computer Aided Design–Computer Aided Model
Calif. California
C.Am. Central America
Can. Canada, Canadian
CAP Civil Air Patrol
capt. captain
cardiol. cardiological
cardiovasc. cardiovascular
CARE Cooperative American Relief Everywhere
Cath. Catholic
cav. cavalry
CBC Canadian Broadcasting Company
CBI China, Burma, India Theatre of Operations
CBS Columbia Broadcasting Company
C.C. Community College
CCC Commodity Credit Corporation

CCNY City College of New York
CCRN Critical Care Registered Nurse
CCU Cardiac Care Unit
CD Civil Defense
CE, C.E. Corps of Engineers, Civil Engineer
CEN Certified Emergency Nurse
CENTO Central Treaty Organization
CEO chief executive officer
CERN European Organization of Nuclear Research
cert. certificate, certification, certified
CETA Comprehensive Employment Training Act
CFA Chartered Financial Analyst
CFL Canadian Football League
CFO chief financial officer
CFP Certified Financial Planner
ch. church
ChD, Ch.D. Doctor of Chemistry
chem. chemical
ChemE, Chem.E. Chemical Engineer
ChFC Chartered Financial Consultant
Chgo. Chicago
chirurg. chirurgical
chmn. chairman
chpt. chapter
CIA Central Intelligence Agency
Cin. Cincinnati
cir. circle, circuit
CLE Continuing Legal Education
Cleve. Cleveland
climatol. climatological
clin. clinical
clk. clerk
C.L.U. Chartered Life Underwriter
CM, C.M. Master in Surgery
CM Northern Mariana Islands
CMA Certified Medical Assistant
cmty. community
CNA Certified Nurse's Aide
CNOR Certified Nurse (Operating Room)
C.&N.W.Ry. Chicago & North Western Railway
CO Colorado
Co. Company
COF Catholic Order of Foresters
C. of C. Chamber of Commerce
col. colonel
coll. college
Colo. Colorado
com. committee
comd. commanded
comdg. commanding
comdr. commander
comdt. commandant
comm. communications
commd. commissioned
comml. commercial
commn. commission
commr. commissioner
compt. comptroller
condr. conductor
Conf. Conference
Congl. Congregational, Congressional
Conglist. Congregationalist
Conn. Connecticut
cons. consultant, consulting
consol. consolidated
constl. constitutional
constn. constitution
constrn. construction
contbd. contributed
contbg. contributing
contbn. contribution

contbr. contributor
contr. controller
Conv. Convention
COO chief operating officer
coop. cooperative
coord. coordinator
CORDS Civil Operations and Revolutionary Development Support
CORE Congress of Racial Equality
corp. corporation, corporate
corr. correspondent, corresponding, correspondence
C.&O.Ry. Chesapeake & Ohio Railway
coun. council
CPA Certified Public Accountant
CPCU Chartered Property and Casualty Underwriter
CPH, C.P.H. Certificate of Public Health
cpl. corporal
CPR Cardio-Pulmonary Resuscitation
C.P.Ry. Canadian Pacific Railway
CRT Cathode Ray Terminal
C.S. Christian Science
CSB, C.S.B. Bachelor of Christian Science
C.S.C. Civil Service Commission
CT Connecticut
ct. court
ctr. center
ctrl. central
CWS Chemical Warfare Service
C.Z. Canal Zone

D. Doctor
d. daughter
DAgr, D.Agr. Doctor of Agriculture
DAR Daughters of the American Revolution
dau. daughter
DAV Disabled American Veterans
DC, D.C. District of Columbia
DCL, D.C.L. Doctor of Civil Law
DCS, D.C.S. Doctor of Commercial Science
DD, D.D. Doctor of Divinity
DDS, D.D.S. Doctor of Dental Surgery
DE Delaware
Dec. December
dec. deceased
def. defense
Del. Delaware
del. delegate, delegation
Dem. Democrat, Democratic
DEng, D.Eng. Doctor of Engineering
denom. denomination, denominational
dep. deputy
dept. department
dermatol. dermatological
desc. descendant
devel. development, developmental
DFA, D.F.A. Doctor of Fine Arts
D.F.C. Distinguished Flying Cross
DHL, D.H.L. Doctor of Hebrew Literature
dir. director
dist. district
distbg. distributing
distbn. distribution
distbr. distributor
disting. distinguished
div. division, divinity, divorce
divsn. division
DLitt, D.Litt. Doctor of Literature
DMD, D.M.D. Doctor of Dental Medicine
DMS, D.M.S. Doctor of Medical Science
DO, D.O. Doctor of Osteopathy
docs. documents
DON Director of Nursing

DPH, D.P.H. Diploma in Public Health
DPhil, D.Phil. Doctor of Philosophy
D.R. Daughters of the Revolution
Dr. Drive, Doctor
DRE, D.R.E. Doctor of Religious Education
DrPH, Dr.P.H. Doctor of Public Health,
Doctor of Public Hygiene
D.S.C. Distinguished Service Cross
DSc, D.Sc. Doctor of Science
DSChemE Doctor of Science in Chemical
Engineering
D.S.M. Distinguished Service Medal
DST, D.S.T. Doctor of Sacred Theology
DTM, D.T.M. Doctor of Tropical Medicine
DVM, D.V.M. Doctor of Veterinary
Medicine
DVS, D.V.S. Doctor of Veterinary Surgery

E, E. East
ea. eastern
E. and P. Extraordinary and Plenipotentiary
Eccles. Ecclesiastical
ecol. ecological
econ. economic
ECOSOC Economic and Social Council (of
the UN)
ED, E.D. Doctor of Engineering
ed. educated
EdB, Ed.B. Bachelor of Education
EdD, Ed.D. Doctor of Education
edit. edition
editl. editorial
EdM, Ed.M. Master of Education
edn. education
ednl. educational
EDP Electronic Data Processing
EdS, Ed.S. Specialist in Education
EE, E.E. Electrical Engineer
E.E. and M.P. Envoy Extraordinary and
Minister Plenipotentiary
EEC European Economic Community
EEG Electroencephalogram
EEO Equal Employment Opportunity
EEOC Equal Employment Opportunity
Commission
E.Ger. German Democratic Republic
EKG Electrocardiogram
elec. electrical
electrochem. electrochemical
electrophys. electrophysical
elem. elementary
EM, E.M. Engineer of Mines
EMT Emergency Medical Technician
ency. encyclopedia
Eng. England
engr. engineer
engring. engineering
entomol. entomological
environ. environmental
EPA Environmental Protection Agency
epidemiol. epidemiological
Episc. Episcopalian
ERA Equal Rights Amendment
ERDA Energy Research and Development
Administration
ESEA Elementary and Secondary Education
Act
ESL English as Second Language
ESPN Entertainment and Sports
Programming Network
ESSA Environmental Science Services
Administration
ethnol. ethnological
ETO European Theatre of Operations

Evang. Evangelical
exam. examination, examining
Exch. Exchange
exec. executive
exhbn. exhibition
expdn. expedition
expn. exposition
expt. experiment
exptl. experimental
Expy. Expressway
Ext. Extension

F.A. Field Artillery
FAA Federal Aviation Administration
FAO Food and Agriculture Organization (of
the UN)
FBA Federal Bar Association
FBI Federal Bureau of Investigation
FCA Farm Credit Administration
FCC Federal Communications Commission
FCDA Federal Civil Defense Administration
FDA Food and Drug Administration
FDIA Federal Deposit Insurance
Administration
FDIC Federal Deposit Insurance Corpora-
tion
FE, F.E. Forest Engineer
FEA Federal Energy Administration
Feb. February
fed. federal
fedn. federation
FERC Federal Energy Regulatory
Commission
fgn. foreign
FHA Federal Housing Administration
fin. financial, finance
FL Florida
Fl. Floor
Fla. Florida
FMC Federal Maritime Commission
FNP Family Nurse Practitioner
FOA Foreign Operations Administration
found. foundation
FPC Federal Power Commission
FPO Fleet Post Office
frat. fraternity
FRS Federal Reserve System
FSA Federal Security Agency
Ft. Fort
FTC Federal Trade Commission
Fwy. Freeway

G-1 (or other number) Division of General
Staff
GA, Ga. Georgia
GAO General Accounting Office
gastroent. gastroenterological
GATE Gifted and Talented Educators
GATT General Agreement on Tariffs and
Trade
GE General Electric Company
gen. general
geneal. genealogical
geod. geodetic
geog. geographic, geographical
geol. geological
geophys. geophysical
geriat. geriatrics
gerontol. gerontological
G.H.Q. General Headquarters
GM General Motors Corporation
GMAC General Motors Acceptance
Corporation
G.N.Ry. Great Northern Railway

gov. governor
govt. government
govtl. governmental
GPO Government Printing Office
grad. graduate, graduated
GSA General Services Administration
Gt. Great
GTE General Telephone and
ElectricCompany
GU Guam
gynecol. gynecological

HBO Home Box Office
hdqs. headquarters
HEW Department of Health, Education and
Welfare
HHD, H.H.D. Doctor of Humanities
HHFA Housing and Home Finance Agency
HHS Department of Health and Human
Services
HI Hawaii
hist. historical, historic
HM, H.M. Master of Humanities
HMO Health Maintenance Organization
homeo. homeopathic
hon. honorary, honorable
Ho. of Dels. House of Delegates
Ho. of Reps. House of Representatives
hort. horticultural
hosp. hospital
H.S. High School
HUD Department of Housing and Urban
Development
Hwy. Highway
hydrog. hydrographic

IA Iowa
IAEA International Atomic Energy Agency
IATSE International Alliance of Theatrical
and Stage Employees and Moving
Picture Operators of the United States
and Canada
IBM International Business Machines
Corporation
IBRD International Bank for Reconstruction
and Development
ICA International Cooperation Administra-
tion
ICC Interstate Commerce Commission
ICCE International Council for Computers
in Education
ICU Intensive Care Unit
ID Idaho
IEEE Institute of Electrical and Electronics
Engineers
IFC International Finance Corporation
IGY International Geophysical Year
IL Illinois
Ill. Illinois
illus. illustrated
ILO International Labor Organization
IMF International Monetary Fund
IN Indiana
Inc. Incorporated
Ind. Indiana
ind. independent
Indpls. Indianapolis
indsl. industrial
inf. infantry
info. information
ins. insurance
insp. inspector
insp. gen. inspector general

inst. institute
instl. institutional
instn. institution
instr. instructor
instrn. instruction
instrnl. instructional
internat. international
intro. introduction
IRE Institute of Radio Engineers
IRS Internal Revenue Service
ITT International Telephone & Telegraph Corporation

JAG Judge Advocate General
JAGC Judge Advocate General Corps
Jan. January
Jaycees Junior Chamber of Commerce
JB, J.B. Jurum Baccalaureus
JCB, J.C.B. Juris Canoni Baccalaureus
JCD, J.C.D. Juris Canonici Doctor, Juris Civilis Doctor
JCL, J.C.L. Juris Canonici Licentiatus
JD, J.D. Juris Doctor
jg. junior grade
jour. journal
jr. junior
JSD, J.S.D. Juris Scientiae Doctor
JUD, J.U.D. Juris Utriusque Doctor
jud. judicial

Kans. Kansas
K.C. Knights of Columbus
K.P. Knights of Pythias
KS Kansas
K.T. Knight Templar
KY, Ky. Kentucky

LA, La. Louisiana
L.A. Los Angeles
lab. laboratory
L.Am. Latin America
lang. language
laryngol. laryngological
LB Labrador
LDS Latter Day Saints
LDS Church Church of Jesus Christ of Latter Day Saints
lectr. lecturer
legis. legislation, legislative
LHD, L.H.D. Doctor of Humane Letters
L.I. Long Island
libr. librarian, library
lic. licensed, license
L.I.R.R. Long Island Railroad
lit. literature
litig. litigation
LittB, Litt.B. Bachelor of Letters
LittD, Litt.D. Doctor of Letters
LLB, LL.B. Bachelor of Laws
LLD, L.L.D. Doctor of Laws
LLM, L.L.M. Master of Laws
Ln. Lane
L.&N.R.R. Louisville & Nashville Railroad
LPGA Ladies Professional Golf Association
LPN Licensed Practical Nurse
LS, L.S. Library Science (in degree)
lt. lieutenant
Ltd. Limited
Luth. Lutheran
LWV League of Women Voters

M. Master
m. married

MA, M.A. Master of Arts
MA Massachusetts
MADD Mothers Against Drunk Driving
mag. magazine
MAgr, M.Agr. Master of Agriculture
maj. major
Man. Manitoba
Mar. March
MArch, M.Arch. Master in Architecture
Mass. Massachusetts
math. mathematics, mathematical
MATS Military Air Transport Service
MB, M.B. Bachelor of Medicine
MB Manitoba
MBA, M.B.A. Master of Business Administration
MBS Mutual Broadcasting System
M.C. Medical Corps
MCE, M.C.E. Master of Civil Engineering
mcht. merchant
mcpl. municipal
MCS, M.C.S. Master of Commercial Science
MD, M.D. Doctor of Medicine
MD, Md. Maryland
MDiv Master of Divinity
MDip, M.Dip. Master in Diplomacy
mdse. merchandise
MDV, M.D.V. Doctor of Veterinary Medicine
ME, M.E. Mechanical Engineer
ME Maine
M.E.Ch. Methodist Episcopal Church
mech. mechanical
MEd., M.Ed. Master of Education
med. medical
MEE, M.E.E. Master of Electrical Engineering
mem. member
meml. memorial
merc. mercantile
met. metropolitan
metall. metallurgical
MetE, Met.E. Metallurgical Engineer
meteorol. meteorological
Meth. Methodist
Mex. Mexico
MF, M.F. Master of Forestry
MFA, M.F.A. Master of Fine Arts
mfg. manufacturing
mfr. manufacturer
mgmt. management
mgr. manager
MHA, M.H.A. Master of Hospital Administration
M.I. Military Intelligence
MI Michigan
Mich. Michigan
micros. microscopic, microscopical
mid. middle
mil. military
Milw. Milwaukee
Min. Minister
mineral. mineralogical
Minn. Minnesota
MIS Management Information Systems
Miss. Mississippi
MIT Massachusetts Institute of Technology
mktg. marketing
ML, M.L. Master of Laws
MLA Modern Language Association
M.L.D. Magister Legnum Diplomatic
MLitt, M.Litt. Master of Literature, Master of Letters

MLS, M.L.S. Master of Library Science
MME, M.M.E. Master of Mechanical Engineering
MN Minnesota
mng. managing
MO, Mo. Missouri
moblzn. mobilization
Mont. Montana
MP Northern Mariana Islands
M.P. Member of Parliament
MPA Master of Public Administration
MPE, M.P.E. Master of Physical Education
MPH, M.P.H. Master of Public Health
MPhil, M.Phil. Master of Philosophy
MPL, M.P.L. Master of Patent Law
Mpls. Minneapolis
MRE, M.R.E. Master of Religious Education
MRI Magnetic Resonance Imaging
MS, M.S. Master of Science
MS, Ms. Mississippi
MSc, M.Sc. Master of Science
MSChemE Master of Science in Chemical Engineering
MSEE Master of Science in Electrical Engineering
MSF, M.S.F. Master of Science of Forestry
MSN Master of Science in Nursing
MST, M.S.T. Master of Sacred Theology
MSW, M.S.W. Master of Social Work
MT Montana
Mt. Mount
MTO Mediterranean Theatre of Operation
MTV Music Television
mus. museum, musical
MusB, Mus.B. Bachelor of Music
MusD, Mus.D. Doctor of Music
MusM, Mus.M. Master of Music
mut. mutual
MVP Most Valuable Player
mycol. mycological

N. North
NAACOG Nurses Association of the American College of Obstetricians and Gynecologists
NAACP National Association for the Advancement of Colored People
NACA National Advisory Committee for Aeronautics
NACDL National Association of Criminal Defense Lawyers
NACU National Association of Colleges and Universities
NAD National Academy of Design
NAE National Academy of Engineering, National Association of Educators
NAESP National Association of Elementary School Principals
NAFE National Association of Female Executives
N.Am. North America
NAM National Association of Manufacturers
NAMH National Association for Mental Health
NAPA National Association of Performing Artists
NARAS National Academy of Recording Arts and Sciences
NAREB National Association of Real Estate Boards
NARS National Archives and Record Service

NAS National Academy of Sciences
NASA National Aeronautics and Space Administration
NASP National Association of School Psychologists
NASW National Association of Social Workers
nat. national
NATAS National Academy of Television Arts and Sciences
NATO North Atlantic Treaty Organization
NATOUSA North African Theatre of Operations, United States Army
nav. navigation
NB, N.B. New Brunswick
NBA National Basketball Association
NBC National Broadcasting Company
NC, N.C. North Carolina
NCAA National College Athletic Association
NCCJ National Conference of Christians and Jews
ND, N.D. North Dakota
NDEA National Defense Education Act
NE Nebraska
NE, N.E. Northeast
NEA National Education Association
Nebr. Nebraska
NEH National Endowment for Humanities
neurol. neurological
Nev. Nevada
NF Newfoundland
NFL National Football League
Nfld. Newfoundland
NG National Guard
NH, N.H. New Hampshire
NHL National Hockey League
NIH National Institutes of Health
NIMH National Institute of Mental Health
NJ, N.J. New Jersey
NLRB National Labor Relations Board
NM New Mexico
N.Mex. New Mexico
No. Northern
NOAA National Oceanographic and Atmospheric Administration
NORAD North America Air Defense
Nov. November
NOW National Organization for Women
N.P.Ry. Northern Pacific Railway
nr. near
NRA National Rifle Association
NRC National Research Council
NS, N.S. Nova Scotia
NSC National Security Council
NSF National Science Foundation
NSTA National Science Teachers Association
NSW New South Wales
N.T. New Testament
NT Northwest Territories
nuc. nuclear
numis. numismatic
NV Nevada
NW, N.W. Northwest
N.W.T. Northwest Territories
NY, N.Y. New York
N.Y.C. New York City
NYU New York University
N.Z. New Zealand

OAS Organization of American States
ob-gyn obstetrics-gynecology

obs. observatory
obstet. obstetrical
occupl. occupational
oceanog. oceanographic
Oct. October
OD, O.D. Doctor of Optometry
OECD Organization for Economic Cooperation and Development
OEEC Organization of European Economic Cooperation
OEO Office of Economic Opportunity
ofcl. official
OH Ohio
OK Oklahoma
Okla. Oklahoma
ON Ontario
Ont. Ontario
oper. operating
ophthal. ophthalmological
ops. operations
OR Oregon
orch. orchestra
Oreg. Oregon
orgn. organization
orgnl. organizational
ornithol. ornithological
orthop. orthopedic
OSHA Occupational Safety and Health Administration
OSRD Office of Scientific Research and Development
OSS Office of Strategic Services
osteo. osteopathic
otol. otological
otolaryn. otolaryngological

PA, Pa. Pennsylvania
P.A. Professional Association
paleontol. paleontological
path. pathological
PBS Public Broadcasting System
P.C. Professional Corporation
PE Prince Edward Island
pediat. pediatrics
P.E.I. Prince Edward Island
PEN Poets, Playwrights, Editors, Essayists and Novelists (international association)
penol. penological
P.E.O. women's organization (full name not disclosed)
pers. personnel
pfc. private first class
PGA Professional Golfers' Association of America
PHA Public Housing Administration
pharm. pharmaceutical
PharmD, Pharm.D. Doctor of Pharmacy
PharmM, Pharm.M. Master of Pharmacy
PhB, Ph.B. Bachelor of Philosophy
PhD, Ph.D. Doctor of Philosophy
PhDChemE Doctor of Science in Chemical Engineering
PhM, Ph.M. Master of Philosophy
Phila. Philadelphia
philharm. philharmonic
philol. philological
philos. philosophical
photog. photographic
phys. physical
physiol. physiological
Pitts. Pittsburgh
Pk. Park
Pky. Parkway
Pl. Place

P.&L.E.R.R. Pittsburgh & Lake Erie Railroad
Plz. Plaza
PNP Pediatric Nurse Practitioner
P.O. Post Office
PO Box Post Office Box
polit. political
poly. polytechnic, polytechnical
PQ Province of Quebec
PR, P.R. Puerto Rico
prep. preparatory
pres. president
Presbyn. Presbyterian
presdl. presidential
prin. principal
procs. proceedings
prod. produced (play production)
prodn. production
prodr. producer
prof. professor
profl. professional
prog. progressive
propr. proprietor
pros. atty. prosecuting attorney
pro tem. pro tempore
PSRO Professional Services Review Organization
psychiat. psychiatric
psychol. psychological
PTA Parent-Teachers Association
ptnr. partner
PTO Pacific Theatre of Operations, Parent Teacher Organization
pub. publisher, publishing, published
pub. public
publ. publication
pvt. private

quar. quarterly
qm. quartermaster
Q.M.C. Quartermaster Corps
Que. Quebec

radiol. radiological
RAF Royal Air Force
RCA Radio Corporation of America
RCAF Royal Canadian Air Force
RD Rural Delivery
Rd. Road
R&D Research & Development
REA Rural Electrification Administration
rec. recording
ref. reformed
regt. regiment
regtl. regimental
rehab. rehabilitation
rels. relations
Rep. Republican
rep. representative
Res. Reserve
ret. retired
Rev. Reverend
rev. review, revised
RFC Reconstruction Finance Corporation
RFD Rural Free Delivery
rhinol. rhinological
RI, R.I. Rhode Island
RISD Rhode Island School of Design
Rlwy. Railway
Rm. Room
RN, R.N. Registered Nurse
roentgenol. roentgenological
ROTC Reserve Officers Training Corps

RR Rural Route
R.R. Railroad
rsch. research
rschr. researcher
Rt. Route

S. South
s. son
SAC Strategic Air Command
SAG Screen Actors Guild
SALT Strategic Arms Limitation Talks
S.Am. South America
san. sanitary
SAR Sons of the American Revolution
Sask. Saskatchewan
savs. savings
SB, S.B. Bachelor of Science
SBA Small Business Administration
SC, S.C. South Carolina
SCAP Supreme Command Allies Pacific
ScB, Sc.B. Bachelor of Science
SCD, S.C.D. Doctor of Commercial Science
ScD, Sc.D. Doctor of Science
sch. school
sci. science, scientific
SCLC Southern Christian Leadership Conference
SCV Sons of Confederate Veterans
SD, S.D. South Dakota
SE, S.E. Southeast
SEATO Southeast Asia Treaty Organization
SEC Securities and Exchange Commission
sec. secretary
sect. section
seismol. seismological
sem. seminary
Sept. September
s.g. senior grade
sgt. sergeant
SHAEF Supreme Headquarters Allied Expeditionary Forces
SHAPE Supreme Headquarters Allied Powers in Europe
S.I. Staten Island
S.J. Society of Jesus (Jesuit)
SJD Scientiae Juridicae Doctor
SK Saskatchewan
SM, S.M. Master of Science
SNP Society of Nursing Professionals
So. Southern
soc. society
sociol. sociological
S.P.Co. Southern Pacific Company
spkr. speaker
spl. special
splty. specialty
Sq. Square
S.R. Sons of the Revolution
sr. senior
SS Steamship
SSS Selective Service System
St. Saint, Street
sta. station
stats. statistics
statis. statistical
STB, S.T.B. Bachelor of Sacred Theology
stblzn. stabilization
STD, S.T.D. Doctor of Sacred Theology
std. standard
Ste. Suite
subs. subsidiary
SUNY State University of New York
supr. supervisor
supt. superintendent

surg. surgical
svc. service
SW, S.W. Southwest
sys. system

TAPPI Technical Association of the Pulp and Paper Industry
tb. tuberculosis
tchg. teaching
tchr. teacher
tech. technical, technology
technol. technological
tel. telephone
Tel. & Tel. Telephone & Telegraph
telecom. telecommunications
temp. temporary
Tenn. Tennessee
Ter. Territory
Ter. Terrace
TESOL Teachers of English to Speakers of Other Languages
Tex. Texas
ThD, Th.D. Doctor of Theology
theol. theological
ThM, Th.M. Master of Theology
TN Tennessee
tng. training
topog. topographical
trans. transaction, transferred
transl. translation, translated
transp. transportation
treas. treasurer
TT Trust Territory
TV television
TVA Tennessee Valley Authority
TWA Trans World Airlines
twp. township
TX Texas
typog. typographical

U. University
UAW United Auto Workers
UCLA University of California at Los Angeles
UDC United Daughters of the Confederacy
U.K. United Kingdom
UN United Nations
UNESCO United Nations Educational, Scientific and Cultural Organization
UNICEF United Nations International Children's Emergency Fund
univ. university
UNRRA United Nations Relief and Rehabilitation Administration
UPI United Press International
U.P.R.R. United Pacific Railroad
urol. urological
U.S. United States
U.S.A. United States of America
USAAF United States Army Air Force
USAF United States Air Force
USAFR United States Air Force Reserve
USAR United States Army Reserve
USCG United States Coast Guard
USCGR United States Coast Guard Reserve
USES United States Employment Service
USIA United States Information Agency
USMC United States Marine Corps
USMCR United States Marine Corps Reserve
USN United States Navy
USNG United States National Guard
USNR United States Naval Reserve

USO United Service Organizations
USPHS United States Public Health Service
USS United States Ship
USSR Union of the Soviet Socialist Republics
USTA United States Tennis Association
USV United States Volunteers
UT Utah

VA Veterans Administration
VA, Va. Virginia
vet. veteran, veterinary
VFW Veterans of Foreign Wars
VI, V.I. Virgin Islands
vice pres. vice president
vis. visiting
VISTA Volunteers in Service to America
VITA Volunteers in Technical Assistance
vocat. vocational
vol. volunteer, volume
v.p. vice president
vs. versus
VT, Vt. Vermont

W, W. West
WA Washington (state)
WAC Women's Army Corps
Wash. Washington (state)
WATS Wide Area Telecommunications Service
WAVES Women's Reserve, US Naval Reserve
WCTU Women's Christian Temperance Union
we. western
W. Ger. Germany, Federal Republic of
WHO World Health Organization
WI Wisconsin
W.I. West Indies
Wis. Wisconsin
WSB Wage Stabilization Board
WV West Virginia
W.Va. West Virginia
WWI World War I
WWII World War II
WY Wyoming
Wyo. Wyoming

YK Yukon Territory
YMCA Young Men's Christian Association
YMHA Young Men's Hebrew Association
YM & YWHA Young Men's and Young Women's Hebrew Association
yr. year
YT, Y.T. Yukon Territory
YWCA Young Women's Christian Association

zool. zoological

Alphabetical Practices

Names are arranged alphabetically according to the surnames, and under identical surnames according to the first given name. If both surname and first given name are identical, names are arranged alphabetically according to the second given name.

Surnames beginning with De, Des, Du, however capitalized or spaced, are recorded with the prefix preceding the surname and arranged alphabetically under the letter D.

Surnames beginning with Mac and Mc are arranged alphabetically under M.

Surnames beginning with Saint or St. appear after names that begin Sains, and are arranged according to the second part of the name, e.g. St. Clair before Saint Dennis.

Surnames beginning with Van, Von, or von are arranged alphabetically under the letter V.

Compound surnames are arranged according to the first member of the compound.

Many hyphenated Arabic names begin Al-, El-, or al-. These names are alphabetized according to each Biographee's designation of last name. Thus Al-Bahar, Neta may be listed either under Al- or under Bahar, depending on the preference of the listee.

Also, Arabic names have a variety of possible spellings when transposed to English. Spelling of these names is always based on the practice of the Biographee. Some Biographees use a Western form of word order, while others prefer the Arabic word sequence.

Similarly, Asian names may have no comma between family and given names, but some Biographees have chosen to add the comma. In each case, punctuation follows the preference of the Biographee.

Parentheses used in connection with a name indicate which part of the full name is usually deleted in common usage. Hence Chambers, E(lizabeth) Anne indicates that the usual form of the given name is E. Anne. In such a case, the parentheses are ignored in alphabetizing and the name would be arranged as Chambers, Elizabeth Anne. However, if the name is recorded Chambers, (Elizabeth) Anne, signifying that the entire name Elizabeth is not commonly used, the alphabetizing would be arranged as though the name were Chambers, Anne. If an entire middle or last name is enclosed in parentheses, that portion of the name is used in the alphabetical arrangement. Hence Chambers, Elizabeth (Anne) would be arranged as Chambers, Elizabeth Anne.

Where more than one spelling, word order, or name of an individual is frequently encountered, the sketch has been entered under the form preferred by the Biographee, with cross-references under alternate forms.

Who Was Who in America®

AAGAARD, GEORGE NELSON, medical educator; b. Mpls., Aug. 16, 1913; s. George N. and Lucy T. (Nelson) A.; m. Lorna D. Docken, Aug. 26, 1939; children: Diane Louise, George Nelson, Richard Nelson, David Nelson, Steven Nelson. B.S., U. Minn., 1934, M.B., 1936, M.D., 1937. Intern Mpls. Gen. Hosp., 1936-37; successively fellow, instr., asst. prof. internal medicine U. Minn. Med. Sch., 1941-47, assoc. prof., dir. continuing med. edn., 1948-51; prof. medicine, dean Southwestern Med. Sch., U. Tex., 1952-54; dean U. Washington Sch. Medicine, 1954-64, prof. medicine, 1954-78, disting. prof. medicine and pharmacology, 1978—, head div. clin. pharmacology, 1964-79; mem. Nat. Adv. Council for Health Research Facilities USPHS, 1954-58; mem. nat. adv. heart council NIH, 1961-65; mem. spl. med. adv. group VA, 1970-74; chmn. bd. trustees Network for Continuing Med. Edn., 1966-78. Bd. dirs., editorial bd.: Western Jour. Medicine. Mem. Am. Heart Assn. (trustee), Assn. Am. Med. Colls. (pres. 1960-61), AMA (dir., chmn. com. continuing profl. edn. programs 1972), Pharm. Mfrs. Assn. Found. (mem. sci. adv. com. 1967-74), Am. Soc. Clin. Pharmacology and Therapeutics (pres. 1977, Elliott award 1983), N.Y. Acad. Scis., A.A.A.S., Washington, King County med. socs., Alpha Omega Alpha. Died May 7, 1997.

ABBOTT, GEORGE, playwright, director, producer; b. Forestville, N.Y., June 25, 1887; s. George Burwell and May (McLaury) A.; m. Ednah Levis, July 9, 1914 (dec. 1930); 1 dau., Judith Ann; m. Mary Sinclair, Apr. 1946 (div. 1951); m. Joy Valderrama, Nov. 1983. A.B., U. Rochester, 1911, H.H.D., 1961; postgrad., Harvard U., 1912; H.H.D., U. Miami, Fla., 1974. Actor from 1913, appearing at 48th St. Theatre, 1915; appearances include The Misleading Lady, 1913, The Yeoman of the Guard, 1915, The Queen's Enemy, 1916, Daddies, 1918, The Broken Wing, 1920, Zander the Great, 1923, The White Desert, 1923, Hell-Bent for Heaven, 1924, Lazy Bones, 1924, Processional, 1925, Cowboy Crazy, 1926, Those We Love, 1930, John Brown, 1934, The Skin of Our Teeth, 1955, Give My Regards to Broadway, 1991; actor, playwright: (with Winchell Smith) A Holy Terror, 1925; playwright: The Head of My Family, 1912, Man in the Manhole, 1912 (Boston Globe award 1912), (with James Gleason) The Fall Guy, 1925, The Ragged Edge, 1935, (with Richard Rodgers and Lorenz Hart) On Your Toes, 1936, Music Is, 1976; playwright, dir. Broadway shows: (with John V.A. Weaver) Love 'Em and Leave 'Em, 1926, (with Philip Dunning) Broadway, 1926, (with Dana Burnet) Four Walls, 1927, (with Ann P. Bridges) Coquette, 1927, (with Edward E. Paramore Jr. and H. Daab) Ringside, 1928, (with S.K. Lauren) Those We Love, 1930, (with John Cecil Holm) Three Men on a Horse), 1935, The Boys from Syracuse, 1938, Where's Charley?, 1948, (with Richard Bissell and Jerome Robbins) The Pajama Game, 1954 (Best Author Tony award 1955, Donaldson Best Dir. award 1955), (with Douglas Wallop) Damn Yankees, 1955 (Best Author Tony award 1956), New Girl in Town, 1957, (with Jerome Weidman) Fiorello, 1959 (N.Y. Drama Critics Circle award 1960, Best Author Tony award 1960, Pulitzer Prize for drama award 1960), (with Jerome Weidman) Tenderloin, 1960, (with Robert Russell) Flora, the Red Menace, 1965, (with Guy Bolton) Anya, 1965; dir. Broadway shows: Chicago, 1927, Spread Eagle, 1927, (with John Meehan) Bless You, Sister, 1927, Gentlemen of the Press, 1928, Jargnegan, 1928, Poppa, 1928, Louder Please, 1931, The Great Magoo, 1932, Small Miracle, 1934, Page Miss Glory, 1934, Ladies' Money, 1934, Jumbo, 1935, Brother Rat, 1936, Room Service, 1937, Angel Island, 1937, Brown Sugar, 1937, All That Glitters, 1938, What A Life, 1938, The Primrose Path, 1939, Mrs. O'Brien Entertains, 1939, See My Lawyer, 1939, Ring Two, 1939, Two Many Girls, 1939, Sweet Charity, 1942, On the Town, 1944, Billion Dollar Baby, 1945 (Donaldson Best Dir. award 1946), Beggar's Holiday, 1946, High Button Shoes, 1947 (Donaldson Best Dir. award 1948), Out of this World, 1950, Tickets, Please!, 1950, Call Me Madam, 1950, The Number, 1951, Wonderful Town, 1953 (Donaldson Best Dir. award 1953, N.Y. Drama Critics award 1953, Best Musical Tony award 1953), Me and Juliet, 1953, Drink to Me Only, 1958, Once Upon a Mattress, 1959, A Call on Kuprin, 1961, Take Her, She's Mine, 1961, A Funny Thing Happened on the Way to the Forum, 1962 (Outer Critics Circle award 1962, Best Dir. Tony award nominee 1963), Never Too Late, 1962 (Best Dir. Tony award nominee 1963), Fade Out-Fade In, 1964, The Well-Dressed Liar, 1966, Help Stamp Out This Marriage, 1966, Agatha Sue, I Love You, 1966, How Now, Dow Jones, 1967 (Best Dir. Tony award nominee 1968), The Education of Hyman Kaplan, 1968, The Fig Leaves Are Falling, 1968, Three Men on a Horse, 1969, Norman, Is That You?, 1970, Not Now, Darling, 1970, The Pajama Game, 1973, Life with Father, 1974, Music Is, 1976, Winning Isn't Everything, 1978, On Your Toes, 1983, Broadway, 1987; dir., prodr. Broadway shows: (with Philip Dunning) Lilly Turner, 1932, (with Philip Dunning) Twentieth Century, 1932, (with Philip Dunning) The Drums Begin, 1933, (with Philip Dunning) Kill That Story, 1934, Boy Meets Girl, 1935, Sweet River, 1936, The Unconquered, 1940, The White-Haired Boy, 1940, Kiss and Tell, 1943, Get Away Old Man, 1943, A Highland Fling, 1944, Snafu, 1944, (with Richard Myers) Mr. Cooper's Left Hand, 1945, One Shoe Off, 1946, (with Richard Oldrich) It Takes Two, 1947, Barefoot Boy with Cheek, 1947, Look, Ma, I'm Dancing, 1948, Mrs. Gibbons' Boys, 1949, (with Jule Styne) In Any Language, 1952, On Your Toes, 1954; playwright, dir., prodr.: (with Leon Adams and Philip Dunning) Heat Lightning, 1933, (with John Cecil Holm) Best Foot Forward, 1941, (with George Marion Jr.) Beat the Band, 1942, (with Betty Smith) A Tree Grows in Brooklyn, 1951; screenwriter: All Quiet on the Western Front, 1930; dir. films: The Bishop's Candlesticks, 1928, Why Bring That Up?, 1929, Manslaughter, 1930, Secrets of a Secretary, 1931, Stolen Heaven, 1931, My Sin, 1931, Too Many Girls, 1940, Kiss and Tell, 1945; screenwriter, dir., prodr. films: (with Stanley Donen and Richard Bissell) The Pajama Game, 1957, Damn Yankees, 1958; author: (autobiography) Mr. Abbott, 1963, (novel) Try-Out, 1979. Recipient Merit award Soc. Stage Dirs. and Choreographers, 1965, Lawrence Langner award, 1976, Disting. Career Achievement Tony award, 1976, Handel medallion City of N.Y., 1976, JF Kennedy Performing Arts Ctr. honoree, 1983, Spl. Tony award, 1987, Nat. Arts medal NEA, 1990; named to Theatre Hall of Fame, 1972. Clubs: Coffee House, Dutch Treat (N.Y.C.); Indian Creek Country (Fla.); Merriewold (N.Y.). Home: New York N.Y. Died Jan. 31, 1995.

ABBOTT, WILTON ROBERT, aerospace engineer; b. Campbell, Calif., Jan. 19, 1916; s. Ernest A. and Audrey (Keesling) A.; m. Pearl Honeychurch, Sept. 2, 1938; children: Mary Louise, Wilton R., Mark R. B.S., U. Calif.-Berkeley, 1937; postgrad., Stanford U., 1937-38; M.S., Iowa State U., 1942, Ph.D., 1945. Asst. Stanford U., 1937-38; engr. Remler Co., Ltd., San Francisco, 1938-39, Gen. Electric Co., 1939-40; asst. prof. to assoc. prof. Iowa State U., Ames, 1940-46; asst. prof. U. Calif.-Berkeley, 1946-51; research specialist N.Am. Aviation, Downey, Calif., 1951-57; sr. cons. engr. Lockheed Missiles and Space Co., Sunnyvale, Calif., 1957—, chief devel. engr. Agena spacecraft; program chmn. Reliability and Maintainability Symposium, 1970. Contbr. articles to profl. jours.; patentee in field. Trustee Linfield Coll., 1977-92, emeritus, 1992. Recipient cert. of excellence Gemini Agena Target Vehicle Program, 1966. Mem. IEEE (life sr.), Reliability Soc., Systems, Man and Cybernetics Soc. (sr.), Sigma Xi, Eta Kappa Nu, Tau Beta Pi. Office: Bldg 150 70-01 PO Box 504 Sunnyvale CA 94086-0001 Died Feb. 5, 1997.

ABEL, REUBEN, humanities educator; b. N.Y.C., Nov. 25, 1911; s. Louis and Dora (Friedsell) A.; m. Marion Buchman, July 30, 1937; children—Richard L., Elizabeth F. A.B., Columbia U., 1929; J.D., N.Y. U., 1934; M.Social Sci., New Sch., 1941, Ph.D., 1952. Dept. store buyer, 1929-44, 46-48; faculty New Sch. for Social Research, N.Y.C., 1950—; adj. prof. philosophy New Sch. for Social Research Grad. Faculty, 1967-84, chmn. humanities div., 1965-84, assoc. dean, 1972-74; Regional unit chief OPA, 1944-46; pres., treas. Atlas Bedspread Co., Inc., N.Y.C., 1948-61; chmn. Conf. on Methods in Philosophy and Scis., 1966-68, 90-91, sec.-treas., 1950-53. Author: The Pragmatic Humanism of F.C.S. Schiller, 1955, Man Is The Measure, 1976; also articles, revs. encys.; Editor: Humanistic Pragmatism, 1966; founder, editor 12th St: A Quarterly. Mem. Am. Philos. Assn., Am. Assn. U. Profs., Philosophy of Sci. Assn., Internat. Assn. for Philosophy of Law and Social Philosophy, Am. Soc. for Aesthetics, Soc. Philosophy and Psychology, N.Y. Philos. Club. Died 08/08/97.

ABELOFF, ABRAM JOSEPH, retired surgeon; b. N.Y.C., Mar. 19, 1900; s. Samuel and Rebecca Esther (Rogow) A.; m. Gertrude Theresa Kopsch, May 15, 1953; 1 son, Tobias Samuel. A.B., Columbia U., 1922, M.D., 1926. Diplomate: Am. Bd. Surgery. Sub-surg. intern Presbyn. Hosp., N.Y.C., 1926-27; surg. intern Lenox Hill Hosp., 1927-29; research asst. Inst. Pathology U. Freiburg, Germany, 1929; surg. service Frankfurt U., Germany, U. Vienna, Austria, 1930; adj. surgeon Beth Israel Hosp., 1930-37; assoc. surgeon Neurol. Hosp., N.Y.C., 1930-33; asst. adj. surgeon Lenox Hill Hosp., 1930-36, attending surgeon clinic, 1930-36, chief surgeon, 1936-42, adj. attending, 1936-46, assoc. surgeon, 1946-54, attending surgeon, 1954-65, hon. cons. surgeon, 1965—, charge service, 1971; surgeon Lexington Sch. for Deaf, 1947-68; asso. clin. prof. surgery NYU, 1947—. Hon. mem. exec. com., emeritus chmn. med. adv. bd. Am. Jewish Joint Distbn. Com.; adv. bd. Paul Baerwald Sch. Social Work, Parks; past pres., treas., now trustee Physicians Home; bd. visitors Watson Libr. Met. Mus. Art, 1976-94; trustee Columbia U., 1959-65. Col. M.C. AUS, 1942-46; hosp. comdr. 256th Sta. Hosp., 19th Field Hosp., 21st Sta. Hosp., 113th Gen. Hosp., Lawson Gen. Hosp. surg. cons. Persian Gulf Command. Decorated Legion of Merit; Distinctive Service Cross of State of N.Y.; recipient Disting. Service medal Columbia U. Alumni Fedn., 1963; Distinctive Achievement award Stuyvesant High Sch., 1965; Alumni Silver medal Coll. Phys. & Surg., 1969; Meritorious Service Unit citation Lawson Gen. Hosp. Fellow ACS, Brazilian Coll. Surgeons; mem. N.Y. Acad. Medicine, N.Y. Surg. Soc. (past council mem.), AMA, N.Y. State and County med. socs., Assn. Alumni Coll. Phys. and Surg. Columbia U. (pres. 1956-57), N.Y. Hist. Soc. (life). Club: Grolier (N.Y.C.). Died Aug. 15, 1997.

ABERNATHY, JACK HARVEY, petroleum, utility company and banking executive; b. Shawnee, Okla., June 10, 1911; s. George Carl and Carrie (Howell) A.; m. Mary Ann Staig, June 13, 1932 (dec.); children: Jack Harvey, Carrilee Abernathy Bell; m. Virginia Watson, Dec. 21, 1974 (dec. Aug. 1986). B.S. in Petroleum Engring, U. Okla., 1933. Petroleum engr. Sinclair Oil & Gas Co., 1933-34; chief engr., gen. prodn. supt. Sunray DX OIL Co., Tulsa, Okla., 1935-45; pres. Seneca Oil Co., Oklahoma City, 1959-65, Post Oak Oil Co., Oklahoma City, 1966-72; chmn. exec. com., dir. Entex, Inc., Houston, 1972-85; pres., chmn. dir. Big Chief Drilling Co., Oklahoma City, 1946-82; dir. Entex Petroleum, Inc., Houston, Entex Coal Co., Houston, Hinderliter Industries, 1981-85; dir., mem. exec. com. Liberty Nat. Bank & Trust Co., Oklahoma City, 1967-85; dir., chmn. Southwestern Bank & Trust Co., Oklahoma City, 1964—; mem., past chmn. Nat. Petroleum Council, 1957-83; dir., vice chmn. bd. dirs. Gen. Producing and Drilling Co., Houston, 1981-83. Contbr. numerous tech. articles to profl. jours. Bd. dirs. The Benham Group, 1983-94, Oklahoma City Zool. Soc., 1983—, Oklahoma City Art Mus.; trustee U. Okla. Found., Oklahoma City Cmty. Found., Okla. Ednl. TV Authority, Okla. Found. for Excellence. Recipient numerous awards inlcuding Disting. Engring. Grad award Okla. U., 1990.; elected to Okla. State Hall of Fame, 1971, Nat. Petroleum Hall of Fame, 1990. Mem. Mid-Continent Oil and Gas Assn. (dir., past chmn.), Am. Petroleum Inst. (dir., exec. com. 1964-83), Oklahoma City C. of C. (dir. 1963-83), All-Am. Wildcatters, Nat. Soc. Profl. Engrs., Soc. Petroleum Engrs., Internat. Assn. Oilwell Drilling Contractors (pres., bd. dirs.), Sigma Tau, Tau Beta Pi, Pi Epsilon Tau, Beta Gamma Sigma. Presbyterian. Clubs: Men's Dinner, Petroleum (Oklahoma City); Oklahoma City Golf and Country. Home: Oklahoma City Okla. Died Oct. 26, 1996.

ABERNETHY, GEORGE LAWRENCE, philosophy educator; b. West Orange, N.J., Aug. 23, 1910; s. John and Lydia (Johnson) A.; m. Helen Sarah McLandress, Aug. 25, 1936 (dec. 1992); children: Robert John, Jean Helen (Mrs. Thomas H. Poston). AB, Bucknell U., 1932; MA, Oberlin Coll., 1933; PhD, U. Mich., 1936. Prof. philosophy Culver-Stockton Coll., Canton, Mo., 1936-40; prof. philosophy and psychology U. S.D., Vermillion, 1940-46; prof. philosophy Davidson Coll., N.C., 1946—; Richardson prof. Davidson Coll., 1967—, Dana prof., 1974—, emeritus, 1976—; vis. prof. Coll. Charleston (S.C.), 1951; mem. faculty U. N.C. at Charlotte, part-time, 1947-48, Barber-Scotia Coll., Concord, N.C., part-time, 1951-52; mem. regional selection com. Woodrow Wilson Fellowships Found., 1960-62; Ford Found. Faculty fellow Columbia, 1952-53, Cooperative Humanities program fellow U. N.C.-Duke, 1967-68. Author: Pakistan- A Selected Annotated Bibliography, 1957, 60, 68, 74, The Idea of Equality, 1959, Living Wisdom from the World's Relgions, 1965, (with T.A. Langford) Philosophy of Religion, 1962, 2d edit., 68, History of Philosophy, 1965, Introduction to Western Philosophy, 1970; Contbg. editor: Presbyn. Outlook, 1963-75. Recipient Thomas Jefferson award McConnell Found., 1962; recipient Bucknell U. Alumni medal, 1969. Mem. N.C. Philos. Soc. (pres. 1951-52), AAUP, Am. Philos. Assn., So. Soc. Philosophy and

Psychology, Philosophy Discussion Club Charlotte. Democrat. Presbyn. Died Aug. 14, 1996.

ABLON, ARNOLD NORMAN, accountant; b. Ft. Worth, July 12, 1921; s. Esir R. and Hazel (Dreeben) A.; m. Carol Sarbin, July 25, 1962; children: Jan Ellen, Elizabeth Jane, William Neal, Robert Jack. BS, La. State U., 1941; MBA, Northwestern U., 1942. Lectr. acctg. So. Meth. U., 1946-47, Levine's Dept. Stores, 1947-49; acct. Peat, Marwick, Mitchell & Co., 1946-47; sr. ptnr. Arnold N. Ablon and Co., CPAs; owner ANA Properties, Dallas; pres., bd. dir. Ablon Enterprises, Inc.; bd. dir. 1st Continental Enterprises, Inc., Hunsaker Truck Lease, Inc., Dallas Summer Musicals. Mem. fin. com. Dallas Summer Musicals; past trustee Spl. Care Sch., Greenhill Sch., June Shelton Sch., St. Mark's Sch., Lamplighter Sch.; past co-chmn. Parents Ann. Fund, Georgetown U., past v.p. Temple Emanuel; past vice chmn. Greenhill Sch., Lamplighter Sch., past treas.; past chmn. Parents Coun., Georgetown U.; past mem. Parents Coun., Amherst Coll.; adv. bd. Communities Found. for Tex.; co-founder, hon. bd. June Shelton Sch.; mem. rsch. coun. S.W. Med. Sch. U. Tex. Capt. AUS, 1942-45. Mem. AICPA, Tex. Soc. CPAs, Nat. Assn. Accts., Columbian Club, Crescent Club, Masons, Shriners. Home: Dallas Tex. Died June 19, 1995.

ABRAHAMS, ALLEN E., consulting economist; b. Ithaca, N.Y., Nov. 6, 1926; s. Howard Phineas and Florence I. (Blostein) A.; m. Lillian Elaine Sieber; children: Paul, Bruce. BS in Chem. Engring., U. Md., 1949; MS in Indsl. Engring., Stevens Inst. Tech., 1954; PhD in Econs., NYU, 1960. Engr. RCA Corp., Harrison, N.J., 1950-53, Suburban Propane Gas Co., Whippany, N.J., 1953-55; sales mgr. Nat. Ammonia Co., Phila., 1955-60; asst. prof. bus. adminstrn. Oreg. State U., Corvallis, 1960-61; mgr. commercial devel. Witco Chem. Co., N.Y.C., 1961-63; prof. mgmt. Poly. U., Bklyn., 1963-68; exec. dir. Interam. Rsch. Corp., Caracas, Venezuela, 1968-71; v.p. N.Y. Mercantile Exchange, N.Y.C., 1971-79; exec. dir. So. Agronomics, Inc., Waverly, Ala., 1975-94; dir. Vols. in Tech. Assistance, Arlington, Va., 1986-94; corr. Am. Metal Market, N.Y.C., 1972-94; corr. Metall, Berlin, 1979-94; adj. prof. Baruch Coll., CUNY, N.Y.C., 1978-79; mem. adv. com. continuing edn. Atlanta U., 1985. Co-author: Love Again, Live Again, 188; contbr. travel and fin. articles to profl. jours. Dir. Assn. to Revive Grant Park, Atlanta, 1985. Lt. (j.g.) USN, 1944-46, PTO. Recipient Award of Merit, Chem. Industry Assn., 1972; Ampart grantee USIA, Africa, 1983. Mem. Internat. Precious Metals Inst. (dir. 1976-88, cert. of merit 1988), Atlanta Farmers Club (dir. 1985-87), Atlanta Econs. Club. Died Jan. 16, 1994.

ABRAHAMS, JOHN HAMBLETON, retired life insurance company executive; b. Topeka, Aug. 10, 1913; s. John Vanneman and Meliora Clarkson (Hambleton) A.; m. Julia Laval Jencks, Apr. 30, 1938; 1 child, Julia Louise (Mrs. Peter R. Siefert). Ph.B., U. Chgo., 1935; D.B.A. (hon.), Washburn U., Topeka, 1978. With Security Benefit Life Ins. Co., Topeka, 1935—; exec. v.p. Security Benefit Life Ins. Co., 1953-54, pres., chmn. bd., 1954-75, chmn. bd., chief exec. officer, 1975-78, chmn. bd., 1978-95; ret., 1995. Trustee Menninger Found. Served to lt. USNR, 1942-45. Mem. Kan. Assn. Commerce and Industry (pres. 1970), Greater Topeka C. of C. (pres. 1950), Chi Psi. Club: Topeka Country. Died Dec. 15, 1996.

ABZUG, BELLA SAVITZKY, lawyer, former congresswoman; b. N.Y.C., July 24, 1920; d. Emanuel and Esther Savitzky; m. Maurice M. Abzug, June 4, 1944 (dec.); children: Eve Gail, Isobel Jo. BA, Hunter Coll., 1942; LLB, Columbia U., 1947; hon. degree, Hunter Coll., Hobart Coll., Manhattanville Coll. Bar: N.Y. 1947. Pvt. law practice in N.Y.C., 1944-70, 1980—; legis. dir. Women Strike for Peace, 1961-70; mem. 92nd Congress from 19th Dist. N.Y., 1970-72, 93rd-94th Congresses from 20th Dist. N.Y., 1972-76; presiding officer Nat. Commn. on Observance of Internat. Women's Year, 1977; presided Nat. Women's Conf., Houston, 1977; co-chmn. Pres.'s Nat. Adv. Com. for Women, 1978; cable news commentator; spkr. numerous coll. campuses; Congl. advisor to U.S. Del. to UN Conf. on the Decade for Women, Mexico City, 1975; fellow Inst. Politics, John F. Kennedy Sch. Govt., Harvard U., 1987; founder Nat. Women's Polit. Caucus; presided over World Women's Congress for a Healthy Planet, 1991; mem. Internat. Facilitating Com. of Nongovtl. Orgns. and Ind. Sectors, UN Conf. on Environment and Devel., Brazil, 1992; sr. adv. to UNCED sec. gen. for UN Conf. on Environment & Devel., 1992. Editor: Columbia Law Rev.; author: Bella! Ms. Abzug Goes to Washington, 1972, Gender Gap: Bella Abzug's Guide to Political Power for American Women, 1984. Apptd. chair of Commn. on Status of Women by Mayor Dinkins, 1992. Mem. Women Strike for Peace, Nat. Urban League, NOW, Nat. Women's Polit. Caucus, ACLU, Women U.S.A. (pres.), UN Assn. U.S., Women's Environ. and Devel. Orgn. (founder, pres., co-chairperson, co-chair), Ams. for Dem. Action (v.p.), Am. Jewish Congress. Died March 31, 1998.

ACAR, YALCIN BEKIR, civil engineer, soil remediation technology executive, educator; b. Ankara, Turkey, July 7, 1951; arrived in U.S., 1980, naturalized.; s. Mahmut Bedri and Serife Bedriye Acar. BSCE, Robert Coll., Istanbul, Turkey, 1973, MSCE, 1975; PhD in Civil Engring., Bogazici U., Istanbul, 1980. Registered profl. engr., La. Asst. site engr. Companie Industriel et Travaux Emile Blaton, Brussels, 1970, 72; rsch. asst. dept. civil engring. Bogazici U., 1973-75, rsch. assoc. Earthquake Engring. Rsch. Inst., 1975-77, rsch. engr. dept. civil engring-Earthquake Engring. Inst., 1977-80; rsch. engr., Fugro postdoctoral fellow dept. civil engring. La. State U., Baton Rouge, 1980-81, asst. prof., 1981-86, assoc. prof., 1986-92, prof., 1992—; sr. rsch. scientist Norwegian Geotech. Inst., 1993; presenter in field, condr. seminars; mem. com. on physiochem. phenomena in soils Transp. Rsch. Bd., NRC, 1989—. Patentee in field; contbr. articles to profl. jours. Mem. ASCE (publs. com. 1988, environ. geotechnics com. 1989), ASTM (com. on soil and rock), AIChE, U.S. Nat. Soc. Internat. Soc. for Soil Mechanics and Found. Engring. (com. on environ. geotechnics), Assn. Drilled Shaft Contractors, Internat. Geotextile Soc., Masons, Sigma Xi. Republican. Avocations: snow skiing, bicycling, swimming. Died May 9, 1996.

ACCETTOLA, ALBERT BERNARD, orthopedic surgeon, educator; b. N.Y.C., Feb. 4, 1918; s. Vincent and Rose (Andriola) A.; BS, Wagner Coll., 1941; MD, Boston U., 1944; m. Rose Galasso, Mar. 14, 1943 (dec. Apr. 16, 1994); children: Albert Bernard, Paul E., Judith A. Intern, S.I. (N.Y.) Hosp., 1944-45, coordinator intern and resident edn., 1949-58, attending orthopedic surgeon, 1951-87, Emeritus Chief Orthopedics, 1987-97, pres. med. bd., 1968-69, trustee, 1973-85, sr. trustee, 1985-97; resident in orthopedic surgery Bellevue Hosp., N.Y.C., 1945-47, asso. vis. orthopedic surgeon, 1964-88; resident fracture service Milw. County Hosp., 1948; asst. orthopedic surgery Sch. Medicine, Marquette U., Milw., 1948; practice medicine specializing in orthopedic surgery, S.I., 1948-87; assoc. clin. prof. orthopedic surgery Sch. Medicine, NYU, 1964-88; emeritus attending dept. surgery St. Vincent's Med. Ctr., 1994; surgeon collegiate athletics Wagner Coll., S.I., 1949-87, trustee, 1981-93, emeritus trustee, 1993—; assoc. staff mem., orthopedic surgeon Hunterdon Med. Ctr., Flemington, N.J., 1953-77; chmn. pub. health forums Richmond County Med. Soc., S.I. Advance, 1953-54; mem. community adv. bd. USPHS Hosp., S.I., 1965-68; mem. med. adv. bd. Vis. Nurse Assn., S.I., 1954-74; chmn., 1967-74, Served with M.C., AUS, 1944. Recipient Svc. award Wagner Coll., 1957, Achievement award, 1973, inducted into Wagner Coll. Athletic Hall of Fame, 1994, Recognition award for 35 yrs. svc. NYU Sch. Medicine, 1985, Disting. Svc. award Vis. Nurse Assn. S.I., 1988. Diplomate Am. Bd. Orthopedic Surgery, Nat. Bd. Med. Examiners. Fellow A.C.S., Am. Acad. Orthopedic Surgeons; mem. Richmond County (pres. elect 1963-64, pres. 1964-65), N.Y State (chmn. med.-legal and workmen's compensation sect. 1974) med. socs., AMA. Contbr. articles to profl. jours.

ACTON, LLOYD PHELPS, JR., architect; b. Phila., July 11, 1938; s. Lloyd Phelps and Louise Ferguson (Albrecht) A.; div. 1979; children: Ann Elizabeth, Katharine Beall. BArch, Cornell U., 1961. Registered architect, Mass., Conn., Calif., R.I. Mem. staff Shepley, Bulfinch, Richardson & Abbot, Boston, 1962—, assoc., 1969-77, prin., 1977—. Prin. works include Tramway Terminal, Squaw Valley, Calif. (nat. honor award AIA 1970), Francis de Marneffe Libr., Dining Bldg., McLean Hosp., Belmont, Mass. (hon. mention AIA 1990), Corp. Hdqrs. ACP, Phila. (award of excellence Archtl. Woodwork Inst. 1991). Recipient Boy Scouts Am. health care honor awards Dartmouth-Hitchcock Med. Ctr., 1993, Children's Hosp.-Yale U., New Haven, 1994, Hasbro Children's Hosp. R.I., George Mason U. Ctr. Recipient health care honor awards Dartmouth-Hitchcock Med. Ctr., 1993, Children's Hosp.-Yale U., New Haven. Mem. AIA, Boston Soc. Architects, Country Club. Democrat. Episcopalian. Died June 14, 1997.

ADAMKIEWICZ, VINCENT WITOLD, microbiology and immunology educator, researcher; b. Poland, Nov. 27, 1924; came to Can., 1951; s. George and Zofia (Lewicka-Rogala) A.; m. Lidia Maria Gowor, July 11, 1953; children—Pavel, Marek, Tomek, Misio, Macio. B.Sc. in Biology, U. Bristol, 1948, B.Sc. in Chemistry with honors, 1949, M.S. in Pharmacology, 1950; Ph.D. in Exptl. Medicine, U. Montreal, 1954. Asst. prof. biology U. St. Francis Xavier, Antigonish, N.S., Can., 1951-52; chemist F.W. Horner Ltd., Montreal, Que., Can., 1954-56; asst. prof. physiology U. Montreal, 1956-60, assoc. prof., 1960-67, prof. microbiology and immunology, 1967-96. Contbr. numerous articles to profl. jours. Pres. Can. Polish Congress, Que., 1969-71, Can. Polish Welfare Inst., Montreal, 1980-82. With Polish Underground Army, 1942-44; Polish Army under Brit. command, 1945-46. Mem. Am. Physiol. Soc. (emeritus); founding mem. Can. Soc. for Immunology, Can. Pharmacological Soc., Can. Biochem. Soc. Avocation: farming. Died Aug. 30, 1996.

ADAMS, ALVIN PHILIP, aviation management consultant; b. Grand Junction, Colo., Dec. 29, 1905; s. Orson and Letty (Low) A.; m. Elizabeth Miller, May 29, 1929 (div. 1946); children: Nathan, Edith Low, Alvin; m. Shirley Ward, June 30, 1951; 1 dau., Helen Ward. Ph.B., Yale U., 1927. Aviation editor Wall St. Jour., N.Y.C., 1927-29; v.p. Aero Industries, Inc., 1929-34, Nat. Aviation Corp., 1930-34; pres. Western Air Lines (formerly Western Air Express Corp.), Los Angeles, 1934-42, Seaboard Airways, Inc., N.Y.C., 1940-43; v.p. Fairchild Engine & Airplane Corp., N.Y.C., 1942-45, also bd. dirs.; owner Alvin P. Adams & Assocs., Los Angeles, 1944; sr. v.p. Pan Am. World Airways, N.Y.C., 1951-70; aviation mgmt. cons., 1970; pres., chmn. Airbus Industries N.Am., 1974-77. Past mem. exec. com. Nat. Football Found., Internat. Center, N.Y.C.; former trustee Nat. Art Mus. of Sport. Episcopalian. Clubs: Sky (N.Y.C.) (hon., past pres., now dir.), Madison Square Garden (N.Y.C.), Deepdale Golf (N.Y.C.), Yale (N.Y.C.) (past council), Conquistadores del Cielo (N.Y.C.) (life, charter), Boone and Crockett (N.Y.C.). Home and Office: 930 5th Ave New York NY 10021-2651 Died Oct. 2, 1996.

ADAMS, BETTY VIRGINIA, petroleum products company executive; b. Butler, Ga., Jan. 6, 1925; d. William Burton and Martha William (Duckworth) A. B.A., Va. Intermont Coll., 1944, U. N.C., 1946. Chmn., chief exec. officer Fuel Oil & Equipment Co., Inc., Roanoke, Va., 1949—. Roanoke Country Club, Yacht and Country Club (Stuart, Fla.), Amb. Club (Stuart). Died Sept. 8, 1996.

ADAMS, CHARLES RICHARD, manufacturing executive; b. Frederick, Okla., Sept. 4, 1927; s. Oran Bailey and Corin Lucille (Adkins) A.; m. Katie Hennen, Apr. 23, 1949 (dec. Jan. 17, 1989); children: Patrick, Molly Ewing, Cynthia Lawson; m. Janice Marie Whelan, Sept. 22, 1990. Student, Tex. A&M U., 1944-45; BA, Baylor U., 1950. Sales Endo Labs., Dallas, 1951-53; sales Riker Labs., Northridge, Calif., 1953-55, dist. mgr., 1955-59, sales mgr., 1959-61, v.p. mktg., 1961-66, pres., 1966-80; chmn., pres., CEO Chad Therapeutics, Inc., Chatsworth, Calif., 1982-95. With USN, 1945-47. Mem. Health Industry Mfg. Assn., Pharm. Mfg. Assn. (dir. 1970-80). Republican. Methodist. Avocations: wines, food, reading, photography. Home: Northridge Calif. Died Sept. 18, 1995.

ADAMS, DAVID KYLE, architect; b. Washington Court House, Ohio, Mar. 28, 1930; s. Gilbert Gustin and Lois (Kyle) A.; m. Barbara Trueland, Sept. 20, 1957 (div. 1973); children: Deborah, Kimberly, Shawn, Kyle. Student, Muskingum Coll., 1947-49; BArch, Ohio State U., 1953. Project architect Dan A. Carmichael Architect, Columbus, Ohio, 1956-66; prin. David Kyle Adams, Architect, Columbus, 1966-69; v.p. Adams Harder Kincheloe Swearingen, Architects, Columbus, 1969-80; pres. Swearingen/Adams, Inc., Columbus, 1980—. Served to cpl. U.S. Army, 1953-55. Mem. AIA, Ohio Soc. Architects, Beta Theta Pi. Lodge: Optimists (local pres. 1971-72). Avocation: golf. Died Mar. 6, 1997.

ADAMS, DOLPH O., pathologist, educator; b. Montezuma, Ga., Apr. 12, 1939; s. J.F. and Frances O. Adams. AB in Chemistry, Duke U., 1960; MS in Anatomy, Med. Coll. Ga., 1963, MD, 1965; PhD in Exptl. Pathology, U. N.C., 1969. Lic. Ga. State Bd. Med. Examiners, N.C. State Bd. Med. Examiners; diplomate Am. Bd. Pathology. Dir. autopsy svc. Med. Ctr, Duke U., 1972-93, chief, 1978-93; program leader Comprehensive Cancer Ctr., Duke U., Durham, N.C., 1982-92, program dir., 1992-95; dir. grad. studies Med. Ctr., Duke U., Durham, N.C., 1986-89, assoc. prof. immunology, 1986-91, dir. Lab. Cell & Molecular Biology of Leukocytes, 1986—, vice chmn. pathology, 1991-93, prof. pathology, 1981—; vis. prof. The Rockefeller U., N.Y., 1982-83; cons. Ctr. Demographic Studies Duke U., 1973-80, VA Hosp., 1977-82; mem. exec. com. Integrated Program in Toxicology Duke U., Durham, N.C., 1981-90. Editor: (book) Methods for Studying Mononuclear Phagocytes, 1981, Contemporary Topics in Immunobiology, 1984. Major U.S. Army Med. Corps, 1970-72. Recipient Bausch and Lomb Metal award Am. Soc. Clin. Pathology, 1965, Rsch. Recognition award Noble Found., 1985. Mem. Am. Soc. Pathologists, Am. Soc. Cell Biology, Am. Assn. Immunologists, Am. Assn. Cancer Rsch., Soc. Leukocyte Biology (coun. pres. 1990-91), Internat. Endotoxin Soc. (sci. councilor 1994—), IMUTEC Corp. (sci. adv. bd., Ont., 1995—). Achievements include research in the role of macrophages in cellular immunology and tumor biology. Died Aug. 9, 1996.

ADAMS, EVERETT MERLE, sociologist, educator; b. Spencer, Iowa, Dec. 27, 1920; s. Everett Merle and Irma (Beatty) A.; m. J. Clare, June 2, 1943; children: Clare, Douglas, Samuel. AB, Doane Coll., 1942; MA, Harvard U., 1950, PhD, 1963. Instr. sociology Syracuse U., 1950-57; asst. prof. U. N.D., 1957-58; asst. prof. to prof. sociology U. Colo., 1958—, chmn. dept., 1966-70, 76-78, prof. emeritus, 1990; rsch. assoc. Responsive Environments Found., Inc. Served with USAAF, 1942-46.

ADAMS, FRANK M., construction and development company executive. Formerly exec. v.p. Morrison Knudsen Corp., Boise, Idaho; pres., chief oper. officer Morrison Knudsen Corp., Boise, 1989—. Address: Boise ID

ADAMS, JAMES NORMAN, microbiologist; b. Bklyn., Nov. 4, 1932; s. James Thomas and Anna Gertrude (Feldzaman) A.; m. Margie Beatrice McDaniel, Sept. 6, 1955; children—Bruce E., Leah E., Connie J., Thomas M. B.S., U. Ky., 1954; Ph.D., U. Ga., 1961.

Research asst. Okla. State U., Stillwater, 1955-56; research fellow U. Ga., Athens, 1959-62; asst. prof. U. Ga., 1962-63; mem. faculty U. S.D., Vermillion, 1963-75; asst. prof. U. S.D., 1963-67, asso. prof., 1967-71, prof. microbiology, 1971-75, acting chmn., 1970-71; prof., coordinator med. microbiology Sch. Medicine U. S.C., Columbia, 1975-79; pres. Micros Cons., 1979-91; vis. prof. Med. Coll. Ga., 1972, Universidad de los Andes, Merida, Venezuela, 1974, Universidad Nacional Autonoma de Mexico, 1975; adj. prof. biology U.S.C.-Beaufort, 1982; cons. on research Polish Acad. Sci., Wroclaw, Poland, 1976. Cons. editor: The Aquarium Jour, 1961-66; assoc. editor: Biology of Actinomycetes and Related Organisms, 1975-91 ; adv. com.: Bergey's Manual of Determinative Bacteriology, 1966-70; review: Indsl. Microbial Genetics; mem. editorial bd.: Jour. Bacteriology, 1973-79; invited reviewer: Internat. Jour. Systematic Bacteriology, 1969, Canadian Jour. Microbiology, 1972-91 ; contbr. articles to profl. jours. Served with U.S. Army, 1957-61. USPHS career devel. awardee, 1966-75. Fellow Am. Acad. Microbiology; mem. AAAS, Am. Soc. Microbiology, Soc. for Gen. Microbiology, Soc. for Indsl. Microbiology, Genetics Soc. Am., Sigma Xi, Phi Kappa Phi, Tau Kappa Epsilon (U.S.D. chpt. advisor 1967-70). Club: Am. Radio Relay League. Developer conjugation system in bacterial genus Nocardia. Home: Raymond WA Died Nov. 20, 1991, interred Menlo Cemetery, Pacific, WA.

ADAMS, JAMES WILSON, physical education educator; b. Fowler, Ind., Dec. 3, 1928; s. Carl Fain and Zella Orena (Wilson) A.; m. Willonese Kathleen Adams, June 11, 1968; children: Debora T., Shauna K. BS, U. Indpls., 1955; MS, Ind. U., 1961, PEDr, 1974; PhD, Walden U., Mpls., 1982. Basketball coach Morristown (Tenn.) Coll., 1961-63; asst. prin. Englewood High Sch., Chgo., 1963-64; dean students, dir. placement, to prof. phys. edn. Talladega (Ala.) Coll., 1964-68, 69-95, 1st emeritus prof., 1995-96; fin. aid officer Langston (Okla.) U., 1968-69; coordinator coll. prog. Fed. Correctional Inst., Talladega, 1984—; cons. in field; athletic trainer Talladega County Tng. High Sch., 1985—; prof. adminstr. Nat. Youth Sports Prog., Talladega, 1978-89. Author: Kinesiological Workbook, 1980. Adv. bd. N. Talladega County Assn. Retarded, Talladega, 1978; scoutmaster Boy Scouts Am., Talladega, 1976—. With U.S. Army, 1946-49, ETO, 1950-51, Korea. Recipient Vol. Svc. award Fed. Bureau Prisons, 1993, Exemplary Svc. award Inmates and Sta. Fed. Correctional Instn.; named "I" Person of the Yr., U. Indpls., 1989, Educator of Yr. for Exemplary Svc., Ala. Assn. Coll. Adminstrs., 1992. Mem. NEA, AAHPERD, Nat. Coll. Physical Edn. Assn. for Men, Nat. Assn. Collegiate Athletic Dirs. Avocations: hunting, fishing, jogging, gardening, camping. Died Jan. 30, 1996.

ADAMS, JOHN MICHAEL GEOFFREY MANNINGHAM, prime minister of Barbados; b. Barbados, Sept. 24, 1931; s. Grantley Herbert and Grace (Thorne) A.; M.A. in Politics, Philosophy and Econs., Magdalen Coll., Oxford (Eng.) U., 1954, hon. fellow, 1983. Barrister-at-law, Gray's Inn, London, 1958, Queen's counsel; m. Genevieve Turner, June 2, 1962; children—Douglas Philip Grantley, Rawdon John Herbert. Called to bar, 1959; BBC and freelance TV broadcaster and producer, 1952-62; M.P., 1966—, leader Opposition in Barbados, 1971; prime minister of Barbados, 1976—; mem. Privy Council. Asst. sec., then gen. sec. Barbados Labour Party, 1965, chmn., polit. leader, 1971. Mem. Ch. of Eng. Clubs: Union (Bridgetown, Barbados); Reform (London); Masons. Home: Saint George Barbados

ADAMS, JOSEPH ELKAN, automotive manufacturing consultant; b. Cleve., Feb. 26, 1913; s. Samuel A. and Dorothy (Berkson) A.; m. Eleanore Ture, Aug. 30, 1940; children: Stephen Eric, Gail M.; m. Edna Mumaw, Nov. 29, 1986. B.S., Carnegie Inst. Tech., 1934. Asst. to pres. Garland Co., Cleve., 1934-38; gen. mgr. Internat. Molded Plastics, 1938-41; dir. material control White Motor Corp. (formerly White Motor Co.), Cleve., 1945-50; dir. purchasing and planning White Motor Corp. (formerly White Motor Co.), 1950-55, gen. mgr. mfg., 1955, v.p., 1956-59, exec. v.p., 1959-72; now cons. and investor; vice chmn. bd. Gen. Computer Corp., Twinsburg, Ohio, 1977—; spl. asst. for prodn. to v.p. ops. WPB, Washington, 1941-44. Mem. Soc. Automotive Engrs., Mus. Arts Assn. Cleve. (trustee 1989—, exec. com., treas. 1982), Pi Tau Sigma (v.p.), Pi Delta Epsilon, Beta Sigma Rho. Clubs: Mid-Day, Cleve. City, Oakwood. Home: Cleveland OH

ADAMS, MIKE See GEERTS, LEO

ADAMS, OSCAR WILLIAM, JR., state supreme court justice; b. Birmingham, Ala., Feb. 7, 1925; s. Oscar William and Ella Virginia (Eaton) A.; m. Anne-Marie Jones, Jan. 1984; children: Oscar William, III, Gail, Frank T., Kynath, Kevin. A.B., Talladega (Ala.) Coll., 1944; LL.B., Howard U., 1947. Bar: Ala. Practice in Birmingham, 1947-80; ptnr. Adams & Adams, 1980, assoc. justice Supreme Ct. Ala., 1980-93; of counsel White, Dunn & Booker, Birmingham; past instr. Miles Coll. Sch. Law; bd. dirs. Lawyers Com. Civil Rights Under Law. Recipient Winner's award Talladega Coll.; award EEO Commn. Mem. Ala. Law Inst., Ala. Lawyers Assn. (award for outstanding public and profl. service), Nat. Bar Assn. (jud. council), Am. Trial Lawyers Assn., Omega Psi Phi, Phi Beta Boule. Democrat. Methodist. Clubs: Shriners, Elks. Home: Birmingham Ala. Died Feb. 15, 1997.

ADAMS, PHILIP, lawyer; b. Los Angeles, July 18, 1905; s. Thaddeus Lafayette and Lena (Kelly) A.; m. Alice Rahman, 1933 (div.); children: Stephen, Judith, Deborah, Kate; m. Elaine Margaret Anderson, 1968 (wid. 1996). Student, Pomona Coll., 1924-27; JD, Hastings Coll. Law, U. Calif., 1938; LLD (hon.), Ch. Div. Sch. of Pacific, Berkeley, Calif., 1965. Bar: Calif. 1938. Purser Panama Mail S.S. Line, 1928-29; profl. investigator, 1930-38; pvt. practice San Francisco, 1938-95; ptnr. Adams & Romer, San Francisco, 1996—; atty. U.S. Govt., 1942-46. Author: Adoption Practice in California, 1956. Dir. ACLU of No. Calif., 1933-54, Children's Protective Soc., 1939-44, United Cerebral Palsy Assn., San Francisco, 1952-72, Assn. Mental Health, 1952-70, Unitee Bay Area Crusade, 1955-61, United Community Fund, San Francisco, 1957-62, San Francisco State Coll., 1964-69; trustee Ch. Divinity Sch. of Pacific, 1951-76; chancellor Episcopal Diocese Calif., 1960-67; dep. Episcopal Gen. Conv., 1946-70; trustee Grad. Theol. Union, Berkeley, 1959-66, pres. bd., 1963-66. Fellow Am. Acad. Matrimonial Lawyers (dir. No. Calif. chpt. 1968-80), Acad. Calif. Adoption Lawyers (dir. 1988—); mem. ABA (chmn. com. on adoption, family law sect. 1959-60), Calif., San Francisco Bar Assn., Lawyers Club San Francisco (gov. 1956), San Francisco Symphony Assn., Chamber Soloists San Francisco (dir. 1985—), Soc. Genealogists (London). Clubs: Villa Taverna, Commonwealth. Deceased.

ADAMS, RUSSELL B(AIRD), corporate executive; b. Wheeling, W.Va., Dec. 28, 1910; s. Russell Updegraff and Daisy Dell (Hilton) A.; m. Frances Esther Nordin, Oct. 27, 1935; children: Russell Baird, Richard Alan, Marilyn (Mrs. Joseph H. Felter, Jr.), David Anthony. Student, Elliott Bus. Coll., Wheeling, 1926, Bethany Coll., 1926-27, U. Ky., 1927. Office mgr. Bradford Supply Co., 1927-28; clk. John J. McKay, Sistersville, W.Va., 1928-30; various positions in office of chief post office insp. Post Office Dept., 1930-36, apptd. post office insp., 1936; trans. to CAA (later CAB), 1939, serving in various capacities in econ. bur., apptd. dir., 1945, mem. CAB, 1948; Rep. interdept. adv. com. on surplus aircraft disposal, 1944-46; tech. adviser U.S. del. Internat. Civil Aviation Conf., Chgo., 1944, 1st Interim Assembly, Provisional Internat. Civil Aviation Orgn., Montreal, Can., 1946; mem. U.S. Sect. Com. of Internat. Tech. Aerial Legal Experts, 1946; chmn. econ. div. Air Coordinating Com., 1946-50; alternate rep. CAB, 1946-50; mem. Internat. Civil Aviation Orgn. Panel, 1947-50; alternate del. U.S. del. First Assembly Internat. Civil Aviation Orgn., Montreal, Can., 1947; del. U.S. del. commn. on multilateral agreement on comml. air rights in Internat. Air Transport, Geneva, Switzerland, 1947; chmn. U.S. delegation 2d Assembly Internat. Civil Aviation Orgn., Geneva, 1948; signing on behalf of U.S. in accordance with powers given by the pres. Conv. of Internat. Recognition of Rights in Aircraft, 1948; chmn. (U.S. del. Peruvian negotiations), 1948, (Canadian negotiations), 1949, (U.S. Philippine negotiations), 1950, (U.S.-Netherlands negotiations), 1951, 4th Assembly Internat. Civil Aviation Orgn., 1950, U.S.-French Negotiation, Paris, 1951; spl. asst. to Sec. State, 1951; v.p. Pan Am. World Airways, 1951-72. Chmn. Davies Meml. Com. Decorated Grand Offcl. Merit Ordem Soberana Vera Cruz (Brazil). Mem. Sigma Nu. Democrat. Unitarian. Clubs: Met., National Aviation (v.p. 1955-65), Circus Saints & Sinners (bd. govs.), Aero (pres. 1960), Congl. Country, International (Washington) (bd. govs. 1964—, sec. 1965-84, v.p. 1982-84, pres. 1984-88); Burning Tree. Mar. 17, 1996.

ADAMS, THOMAS BOYLSTON, journalist; b. Kansas City, Mo., July 25, 1910; s. John and Marian (Morse) A.; m. Ramelle Frost Cochrane, Jan. 5, 1940; children: John, Peter Boylston, Francis Douglas, Henry Bigelow, Ramelle Frost. Student, Harvard U., 1929-32. Exec. Waltham Watch Co., 1935-41; exec. v.p., also bd. dirs. Sheraton Corp. Am., 1946-63, v.p., 1954-63; treas. Adams Securities Co., 1950-63, pres., 1964-68; publicist Adams Manuscript Trust. Author: A New Nation, 1981; editorial writer Boston Herald, 1932-35; columnist History Looks Ahead, Boston Globe, 1974-91; contbr. articles to newspapers. Anti Vietnam War candidate for Senate, 1966, Ho. of Reps., 1968; del. Dem. Nat. Conv., 1972; chmn. Lincoln Dem. Com., 1972-80; trustee Neuroscies. Research Found., Nat. Humanities Ctr., Bemis Fund, Lincoln, 1974-81; life trustee Lincoln Pub. Library; designator Henderson Fund for Beautification of Boston, 1978—. Served to capt. USAAF, 1942-46. Fellow Am. Acad. Arts and Scis. (treas. 1955-90); mem. Mass. Self-Insurers Assn. (past v.p.), Mass. Hist. Soc. (pres. 1957-75), Colonial Soc. Mass., Tavern Club (Boston), Phi Beta Kappa (pres. Mass. Alpha chpt. 1976). Clubs: Somerset, Tavern (Boston). Died June 4, 1997.

ADAMS, THOMAS BROOKS, advertising consultant; b. Detroit, Sept. 16, 1919; s. Andrew S. and Louise A. (Brooks) A.; m. Mary E. Bryant, Mar. 22, 1945; children: Janis E., Julie A., Kathleen M. BA, Wayne State U., 1941. With Campbell-Ewald Co., Detroit, 1945-84; chmn. bd. Campbell-Ewald Co., 1968-84; bd. dirs. Thyssen, Inc. V.p. United Found.; chmn. Wayne County Stadium Authority.; Trustee Children's Hosp. Mich., Menninger Found.; bd. dirs. Wayne State U. Alumni Fund. Lt. comdr. USNR, 1941-45. Decorated Navy Cross, D.F.C., Air medal. Named Outstanding Young Advt. Man of Yr. N.Y. Assn. Advt. Men and Women, 1955; inductee Advt. Hall of Fame, 1985. Mem. Advt. Council (chmn., dir.). Died Sept. 28, 1997.

ADAMS, THOMAS RANDOLPH, bibliographer, librarian, historian; b. Durham, N.C., May 22, 1921; s. Randolph Greenfield and Helen Newbold (Spiller) A.; m. Virginia Hedges Matzke, Dec. 29, 1951; children: Virginia Hedges, Josephine Lippincott, Eliza Stokes. BA, U. Mich., 1944; MA, U. Pa., 1949. Rsch. asst. Libr. Co. Phila., 1947-48; asst. to curator rare books U. Pa. Libr., Phila., 1948-50, curator rare books, 1950-55; custodian Chapin Libr. Williams Coll., Williamstown, Mass., 1955-57; libr. John Carter Brown Libr. Brown U., Providence, 1957-83, John Hay prof. bibliography, 1983-90, John Hay prof. bibiography emeritus, 1991—, univ. bibliographer, 1983-91, libr. emeritus John Carter Brown Libr., 1991—. Author: American Independence, 1965, American Controversy, 1980; project dir. 6 Vols. European Americana, 1980-95, Mount & Page Publishers of Eighteenth-Century Maritime Books, 1993, (with D.W. Waters) English Maritime Books Printed Before 1801, 1995, (with N. Barker) A New Model for the Study of the Book, 1993. Pres. Bibliog. Soc. Am., N.Y.C., 1978-80; trustee R.I. Hist. Soc., Providence, 1967-78, Mystic (Conn.) Seaport Mus., 1977-93; bd. dirs. Providence Athenaeum, 1968-78, 82-84; mem. coun. Inst. Early Am. History and Culture, Williamsburgh, Va., 1975-78; chmn. draft com. 18th Century Short-Title Catalog, London, 1976-78; chmn. libr. com. R.I. Sch. Design, Providence, 1968-70. Lt. (j.g.) USNR, 1943-46, PTO. Guggenheim fellow, London, 1963, sr. fellow NEH, Oxford, 1971. Mem. Am. Antiquarian Soc., Am. Hist. Soc., Mass. Hist. Soc., Colonial Soc. Mass., Bibliog. Soc., Soc. Nautical Rsch. (London), Club of Odd Vols. (Boston), Grolier Club (N.Y.C.). Episcopalian. Avocations: sailing, fishing. Died Mar. 16, 1996.

ADAMS, WILLIAM JOHN, JR., mechanical engineer; b. Riverdale, Calif., Feb. 9, 1917; s. William John and Florence (Dodini) A.; m. Marijane E. Leishman, Dec. 26, 1939; children—W. Michael, John P. B.S., Santa Clara U., 1937. Registered profl. mech. engr., agrl. engr., Calif. Design and project engr. Gen. Electric Co., Schenectady, 1937-45; project engr. FMC Corp., San Jose, Calif., 1946-47; chief engr. Bolens div., Port Washington, Wis., 1947-53; asst. gen. mgr. Central Engring. Labs., Santa Clara, 1953-71; dir. planning and ventures, advanced products div. Central Engring. Labs., 1971-76, mgr. new bus. ventures, 1976-80, cons. to mgmt., 1980—; regent Santa Clara U., 1986—. Chmn. Santa Clara United Fund drive, 1967, Santa Clara Indsl. Citizens Bd., 1965-66; bd. dirs. Santa Clara County council Boy Scouts Am., 1962—, Santa Clara Valley Sci. Fair, Eagle Scout Assn. Recipient Ignatian award disting. svc. to humanity Santa Clara U., 1990, Inaugural Disting. Engring. Alumnus award Santa Clara U., 1991; inducted into Silicon Valley Engring. Hall of Fame, 1998. Fellow Am. Soc. Agrl. Engrs. (dir. Pacific Coast region); mem. ASME (life, del. Silicon Valley Engring. Coun.), Soc. Automotive Engrs., Joint Coun. Sci. and Math. Edn., Tau Beta Pi, Pi Tau Sigma. Achievements include patents in field U.S., Can., numerous fgn. countries. Died Mar. 26, 1996.

ADAMS, WILLIAM LEE, financial consultant; b. Monterey Park, Calif., Sept. 4, 1945; s. Edward William and Mildred Jeniece (Oakes) A.; m. Lucie Anne Staples, Oct. 17, 1971; children: Randall J., Anthony S., Timothy W. AA in Edn., Chaffey Coll., 1975; BSBA with honors, U. Redlands, 1980. Calif. community coll. (life) credential. Chaplain dir. The Quiet Hour Prison Min., Redlands, Calif.; chaplain, commdr. San Bernardino (Calif.) County Sheriff; paralegal super Michael J. Hemming Atty., Diamond Bar, Calif.; tchr. Clackamas Community Coll., Oregon City, Oreg.; pres. Action Credit Cons., Beavercreek, Oreg.; bd. dirs. Redlands Jr. Acad., 1980-81, Someone Cares Prison Ministry, Lansing, Mich. Author: (manual) How To Colelct Your Money That's Due You, 1978. Bd. dirs. Kiwanis Internat., Loma Linda, Calif., 1978; vol. Calif. Dept. Corrections, Norco, Calif., 1982-86, Riverside (Calif.) Police Dept., 1971-74; reserve deputy San Bernardino County Sheriff, 1983-86. Recipient award of Merit, Soc. Magicians, Hollywood, Calif., 1967. Mem. Magic Castle Inc. Avocations: magician, musician. Died Feb. 14, 1995.

ADELMANN, FREDERICK JOSEPH, philosophy educator; b. Norwood, Mass., Feb. 18, 1915; s. Frederick Michael and Helen Margaret (Casey) A. A.B., Boston Coll., 1937, M.A., 1942; S.T.L., Weston Coll., 1948; Ph.D., St. Louis U., 1955; L.H.D. (hon.), Boston Coll., 1985. Entered Soc. of Jesus; ordained priest Roman Catholic Ch., 1947; instr. math. and physics Army Specialized Tng. Program, Boston Coll., 1942-44, asst. prof. philosophy, 1955-68, assoc. prof. philosophy, 1968-70, prof., 1970-88; chmn. dept., 1955-65; ascetical theology Exerzitienhaus Rottmannshohe, Germany, 1949-50; teaching fellow philosophy, St. Louis U., 1950-54; lectr. philosophy Weston (Mass.) Coll.; adj. prof. philosophy Boston Coll., 1986-88. Author: From Dialogue to Epilogue, 1968, (with others) Guide to Marxist Philosophy, 1972; editor: Demythologizing Marxism, 1969, Authority, 1974, Philosophical

Investigation in the USSR, 1975, Philosophy in the USSR Revisted, 1977, Contemporary Chinese Philosophy, 1982; editor-in-chief: The Quest for the Absolute, 1966. Mem. AAUP, Am. Philos. Assn., Jesuit Philos. Assn., Realist Soc. DIED 04/01/96. .

ADEN, ROBERT CLARK, retired computer information systems educator; b. Paris, Tenn., Jan. 13, 1927; s. Robert Franklin and Esther Lucile (Clark) A.; m. Martha Elizabeth Irby; children: Robert Paul, Martha Lucille. BA, U. N.Mex., 1947; MA, Murray State Coll., 1953; PhD, George Peabody Coll., 1955. Visiting prof. Bemidji (Minn.) State U., 1955; prof., chmn. Bethel Coll. Edn. & Psychology Dept., McKenzie, Tenn., 1955-60; assoc. prof. N. Tex. State U., Denton, 1960-67; prof. edn. Mid. Tenn. State U., Murfreesboro, 1967-68, grad. dean., 1968-81, dir. institutional research, 1978-82, chmn. dept. computer info. systems, 1985-88, prof. computer info. systems, 1982-92, ret., 1992. Cpl. U.S. Army, 1950-52. Mem. NEA, Tenn. Edn. Assn., Phi Delta Kappa, Kappa Delta Pi, Pi Gamma Mu, Beta Gamma Sigma, Phi Kappa Phi (mem. scholarship com. 1990-92, 93-95). Presbyterian. Died Aug. 13, 1997.

ADLER, KURT ALFRED, psychiatrist; b. Vienna, Austria, Feb. 25, 1905; came to U.S., 1935; s. Alfred and Raissa (Epstein) A.; m. Tanya Drucker, Dec. 13, 1958; 1 child by previous marriage, Margot Susanna Gliedman-Adler. PhD, U. Vienna, 1935; MD, L.I. Coll. Medicine, 1941. Intern Kings County Hosp., Bklyn., resident in psychiatry; pvt. practice N.Y.C.; dir., dean Advanced Inst. Analytical Psychotherapy, N.Y.C., 1978—; dir. Alfred Adler Inst. Ottawa, Ont., Can., 1978—; mem. staff, Lenox Hill Hosp., Gracie Sq. Hosp., both N.Y.C.; med. dir., Advanced Ctr. Analytical Psychotherapy, N.Y.C., 1966-78;dir., Adler-Dreikurs Inst., Bowie, Md., 1978-82; pres. bd. dirs., AA Mental Hygiene Clinic, N.Y.C., 1980-88. Contbr. articles to med. publs. Maj. M.C., U.S. Army, 1942-46. Fellow Am. Psychiat. Assn. (life), N.Y. Soc. Clin. Psychiatry, Assn. for Advancement of Psychotherapy; mem. AMA, Internat. Assn. Individual Psychology (pres. 1970-78), N.Y. State Med. Soc., Am. Psychopathol. Assn. Died May 28, 1997.

ADLER, PHILIP, osteopathic physician; b. N.Y.C., Jan. 2, 1925; s. Willie and Ethel (Zichler) A.; m. Ethel Kugler, Sept. 23, 1948 (dec. 1991); 1 dau., Deborah. B.S., N.Y. U., 1944; D.O., Phila. Coll. Osteo. Medicine, 1947. Diplomate: Nat. Bd. Osteo. Medicine and Surgery, Am. Osteo. Bd. Obstetrics and Gynecology. Intern Detroit Osteo. Hosp., 1947-48, resident obstetrics and gynecology, 1948-50, mem. profl. staff, 1950-72, sec. intern/resident tng. com., 1960-63, chmn. dept. obstetrics and gynecology, 1964-67; practice osteo. medicine specializing in obstetrics and gynecology Farmington, Mich., 1950—; med. dir., dir. med. edn. Zieger/Botsford Osteo. Hosp., 1970-76, med. dir., 1970-72; clin. practice ob-gyn. Mich. Med. Clinic, Detroit, 1993; clin. prof. obstetrics and gynecology Mich. State U., Coll. Osteo. Medicine; cons. MIST Program; bd. dirs. Blue Shield of Mich., 1963-69; mem. adv. com. for teaching hosps. for social security studies HEW; mem. Mich. adv. com. Third Nat. Cancer Survey, Fed. Govt.; apptd. by gov. to Mich. State Health Coordinating Com., 1980-83; mem. State Health Coordinating Com. of Mich., 1984-87, vice chmn., 1987; coordinator for clin. clk. Mich. State U. Coll. Osteopathic Medicine, 1983—. Contbr. articles to med. jours. Recipient Walter F. Patenge medal of pub. service Mich. Coll. Osteo. Medicine at Mich. State U., 1973, Medal of Pub. Service Ohio U. Coll. Osteo. Medicine, 1977, medal of Pub. Service Okla. Coll. Osteo. Medicine and Surgery, 1977. Mem. Am. Coll. Osteo. Obstetricians and Gynecologists (life); mem. Am. Osteo. Assn. (trustee 1968—, pres. 1977-78, chmn. dept. ednl. affairs 1976—), Mich. Assn. Osteo. Physicians and Surgeons (trustee 1963-68, pres. 1966-67), Wayne County Assn. Osteo. Physicians and Surgeons (trustee 1955-64, pres. 1961-62), Am. Assn. for Hosp. Med. Assn., Mich. Assn. for Hosp. Med. Edn., Mich. Assn. Regional Med. Programs (profl. adv. com.), Detroit Cancer Club, Carlton Club, B'nai B'rith. DIED 03/18/97. .

ADLER, RICHARD B., electrical engineering educator, science administrator; b. N.Y.C., May 9, 1922; m. Dorothy Gordon; children: Gordon, Nicholas, Lucas. Student, Harvard U., 1939-41; SB, MIT, 1943, ScD, 1949. Instr. MIT, Cambridge, 1949-50, leader solid state and transistor group Lincoln Lab., 1951-53, asst. prof., 1950-55, assoc. prof., 1955-59, prof., 1959—, Disting. prof. elec. engring. and computer sci., 1985—, assoc. dept. head, 1978-89, co-dir. MIT microsystems tech. labs., 1989—. Co-author: 7 textbooks; contbr. papers to profl. publs.; co-producer 16 ednl. films and film coops. Lt. (j.g.) USNR, 1944-46. Recipient Sloan award MIT, 1955, 56; co-recipient Premium award Royal Aero. Soc., 1955. Fellow IEEE (Edn. medal 1986), Am. Acad. Arts and Scis.; mem. Sigma Xi, Tau Beta Pi, Eta Kappa Nu. Home: Concord MA

ADLER, RUTH, editor, journalist; b. Rochester, N.Y., July 10, 1910; d. Mortimer Adler and Ida Lichtenstein. Grad., Smith Coll. Sec. The Times, 1934-46; editor Times Talk, 1947-1980. Avocations: golf, tennis, traveling. Home: Manhattan N.Y. Died Aug. 4, 1997.

ADMIRE, BEN H., lawyer; b. Abilene, Tex., July 13, 1949; s. Charles B. and Marie L. (Haney) A.; m. Charlotte Anne Brown, Nov. 23, 1984; children: James B., David Kyle. BSEE, So. Meth. U., 1971, JD, 1975. Bar: Tex. 1975, U.S. Dist. Ct. (no., ea., we. and so. dists.) Tex., U.S. Ct. Appeals (5th cir.). Assoc. Touchstone Bernays & Johnston, Dallas, 1975-78; mem. Cowles Sorrells Patterson & Thompson, Dallas, 1978-82; ptnr. Strasburger & Price, Dallas, 1982—. Mem. Tex. Assn. Def. Counsel, Dallas Assn. Def. Counsel, Product Liability Adv. Coun., Def. Rsch. Inst. Methodist. Avocations: golf, jogging. Died Nov. 25, 1996.

AGGARWAL, SUNDAR LAL, technology management consultant; b. Jullundur, Punjab, India, Oct. 15, 1922; came to U.S., 1945; s. Basheshar Dyal and Bhagvati (Devi) A.; m. Eleanor Weller, July 23, 1948; children: Vijay, Leila, Sheila. BS with honors, Punjab U., India, 1942, MS with honors, 1943; PhD, Cornell U., 1949. Sci. officer Nat. Chem. Lab., Poona, India, 1950-52; sr. scientist Olin Industries, New Haven, Conn., 1952-54, sect. chief, 1954-57; chem. physics head Gen. Tire & Rubber Co., Akron, Ohio, 1957-62, mgr. basic rsch., 1962-68, mgr. materials rsch., 1968-75; v.p., dir. rsch. GenCorp (formerly Gen. Tire & Rubber Co.), Akron, 1975-87, tech. advisor, 1988; pres. Global Tech. Assocs. Inc., Akron, 1988—; tech. advisor Repsol Quimica, Madrid, 1988, J.K. Industries, New Delhi. 1988; chmn. Gordon Rsch. Confs., 1969; mem. evaluation panel Nat. Bur. Standards, 1976-80; bd. trustees Edison Polymer Innovation Corp., 1986-88. Editor Comprehensive Polymer Sci., 1987—; regional editor Rubber and Plastics Jour., 1985-89; mem. editorial bd. Polymer Jour., 1975—; author or co-author tech. articles on synthetic rubbers and polymers, 1952—; patentee in field. Recipient tech. achievement award Internat. Inst. Synthetic Rubber Producers, 1986. Fellow Plastics and Rubber Inst. (U.K.); mem. Am. Chem. Soc. (Goodyear medal award com. div. chmn. 1982-89), Soc. Plastics Engrs. Democrat. Unitarian. Avocations: World War II history, gardening, photography. Home and Office: Global Polymer Tech Assocs 1200 Brentford Ln Malvern PA 19355-9776 Died Oct. 1, 1996.

AGGER, CAROLYN E., lawyer; b. N.Y.C., May 27, 1909. A.B., Barnard Coll., 1931; M.A., U. Wis., 1932; LL.B. cum laude, Yale U., 1938. Bar: D.C. 1938, U.S. Tax Ct. 1943, U.S. Supreme Ct. 1950, U.S. Ct. Claims 1956, U.S. Ct. Appeals (6th cir.) 1958. Atty., NLRB, 1938-39; atty. tax div. U.S. Dept. Justice, Washington, 1939-43; now ptnr. Arnold & Porter, Washington. Mem. Order of Coif. Died Nov. 7, 1996.

AGNEW, SPIRO THEODORE, former Vice President of U.S.; b. Balt., Nov. 9, 1918; s. Theodore S. and Margaret (Akers) A.; m. Elinor Isabel Judefind, May 27, 1942; children: James Rand, Pamela Lee, Susan Scott, Elinor Kimberly. Student, Johns Hopkins Univ.; LLB, Univ. Balt., 1947; LLD, Univ. Md., Morgan State Coll., Ohio State Univ., Loyola Univ., Univ. Balt., Drexel Univ. Bar: Md. Law sch. instr. U. Balt., 1947-50; Former claims adjuster Lumbermens Mut. Casualty Co.; then personnel dir. Schreiber Food Stores; formerly engaged pvt. practive law Balt. and Baltimore County; then mem. firm Karl F. Steinmann; chmn. Baltimore County Bd. of Appeals, 1958-61; exec. Baltimore County, 1962-66; gov. of Md., 1967-69, vice pres. of U.S., 1969-73, resigned, 1973; chmn. transp. com. Nat. Assn. Counties, 1963. Author: Canfield Decision, 1976, Go Quietly...Or Else, 1980. Officer AUS, 1941-45, 51. Decorated Bronze Star. Mem. Md., Baltimore County bar assns. Republican. Episcopalian. Home: Rancho Mirage Calif. Died Sept. 17, 1996.

AGUZZI-BARBAGLI, DANILO LORENZO, literature educator; b. Arezzo, Italy, Aug. 1, 1924; came to U.S., 1950; s. Guglielmo and Marianna (Barbagli) Aguzzi-B. Dottore in Lettere, U. Florence (Italy), 1949; Ph.D., Columbia U., 1959. Instr., asst. U. Chgo., 1959-64; assoc. prof. Tulane U., New Orleans, 1964-71; prof. U. B.C., Vancouver, 1971-90; Mem. Fulbright-Hayes final scholarship com., 1970—; adviser on scholarship application Can. Council, 1972-75. Author: Critical Edition of Della Poetica of Francesco Patrizi, 3 vols., 1969, 70, 71, 72, Critical Edition of Francesco Patrizi's Lettere ed Opuscoli ineditl., 1975, Critical Edition of Pellegrino Prisciani's Spectacula, 1992; contbr. author: L'umanesimo in Instria, 1983, Contemporaries of Erasmus, 1985, Renaissance Humanism, Foundations, Forms and Legacy, 1988; contbr. articles to profl. jours. Newberry Library fellow Chgo., 1974; Folger Shakespeare Library fellow Washington, 1975. Fellow Am. Philos. Soc.; mem. AAUP, Newberry Libr. Assocs., Dante Soc. Am., Italian Honor Soc. (regional rep.), Accademia Petrarca, Medieval Soc. Am., Renaissance Soc., Am., Modern Lang. Assn., Am. Assn. Tchrs. Italian.

AHEARN, PATRICIA JEAN, lawyer; b. Amarillo, Tex., Sept. 8, 1936; d. Robert Howard and Lottie Mae (Hillin) Bridges; m. Joseph R. Ahearn, Sept. 26, 1955 (div. 1968); children: Joseph Robert Jr., David Christopher, Steven Paul. BA with honors, West Tex. State U., Canyon, 1972; JD with honors, U. Tex., Austin, 1983. Bar: Tex. 1983. Tchr. Amarillo Ind. Sch. Dist., 1972-76; dep. clk. U.S. Dist. Ct., Amarillo, 1976-80; law clk. Tex. Ct. Appeals (7th cir.), Amarillo, 1983-84; pvt. practice Amarillo, 1984-86; lawyer Tex. Edn. Agy., Austin, 1986-89, Tex. Assn. Sch. Bds., Austin, 1989-90, 93—; prin. Henslee, Ryan & Groce, Austin, 1990-92; Speaker in field of edn. for handicapped children; cons. to sch. dists. Contbr. articles on laws for handicapped to various publs. Mem. Tex. Bar Assn. Died Feb. 21, 1997.

AHLERS, B. ORWIN, marketing executive; b. Bremen, Germany, Aug. 10, 1926; came to U.S., 1953, naturalized, 1962; s. Richard G. and Lillie (Pflueger) A.; B.A. summa cum laude, Bklyn. Coll., 1957; M.B.A., N.Y.U., 1959; m. Ellen Roser, Apr. 11, 1959; children—Eve Doris, Suzanne Ellen. With Ferrostaal A.G., Essen, W. Ger., 1950-53; with Ferrostaal Overseas Corp., N.Y.C., 1953-91, pres. Ferrostaal Corp., N.Y.C., 1973-91, also bd. dirs.; pres. Heavy Duty Equipment Inc., Irvington, N.J., also bd. dirs.; pres. Ferrostaal Machine Tool Corp., also bd. dirs.; bd. dirs. Ferrostaal Metals Corp., San Mateo, Calif.; ret. Mem. ASME. Lutheran. Died April 11, 1996.

AHLERS, ELEANOR EMILY, emeritus educator, librarian; b. Seattle, May 16, 1911; d. Francis Richard and Elizabeth Frances (Prior) A. A.B., U. Wash., 1932, M.A., 1957; B.S. in L.S, U. Denver, 1942; student, U. Calif., summer 1948. Tchr., librarian South Bend, Wash., 1932-36, Mt. Vernon, 1936-42; high sch. librarian Everett, Wash., 1942-53; also supr. sch. libraries, 1952-53; asst. prof. library sci., sch. edn. U. Oreg., 1953-57; exec. sec. Am. Assn. Sch. Librarians div. ALA ALA), 1957-61; supr. library services Wash. Dept. Pub. Instrn., Olympia, 1961-66; asso. prof. Sch. Librarianship. U. Wash., 1966-70, prof., 1970-76, emeritus, 1976—; instr. tchr.-librarian courses U. Wyo., summers, 1945, 46, San Jose State Coll., summers 1947, 52; asst. dir. workshop for sch. librarians Central Wash. Coll. Edn., summer 1951; coordinator workshop for sch. librarians U. Oreg., summer 1956; dir. sch. librarians workshop Kans. State Tchrs. Coll., summer 1964. contbr. articles to library and edn periodicals editor bulls in field;. Mem. Am. Assn. Sch. Librarians (pres. 1965-66), ALA, Wash. Sch. Library Assn., Phi Beta Kappa, Pi Lambda Theta, Mortar Board, Kappa Delta. Episcopalian. Died Nov. 22, 1996.

AIKEN, WILLIAM ERIC, securities research executive; b. Cambridge, Mass., Feb. 8, 1935; s. William Edward and Elizabeth (Polson) A.; m. Barbara Joan Rizzi, May 28, 1958 (div. Sept. 1963); 1 dau., Elizabeth Stewart; m. Yvonne P. Kane, June 1, 1985. BA in English, UCLA, 1960. Assoc. editor Bus. Week mag., Los Angeles, Chgo., N.Y.C., 1960-63; editor RIA Investors Service, N.Y.C., 1963-67; mng. editor Electronics mag., N.Y.C., 1967-69; exec. editor Value Line Investment Survey, N.Y.C., 1969-73; assoc. editor Barron's, N.Y.C., 1973-74; freelance writer and editor, N.Y.C., 1974-78; sr. v.p., dir. research Daniels & Cartwright, N.Y.C., 1978-84; founder, chief exec. officer, pub. The Proxy Monitor Inc., 1984—; cons. in field. Contbr. articles to various publs. Served with USMC, 1952-56. Mem. Sigma Delta Chi. Republican. Episcopalian. Club: Princeton (N.Y.C.).

AKERS, SHELDON BUCKINGHAM, JR., electrical and computer engineering educator; b. Washington, Oct. 22, 1926; s. Sheldon Buckingham and Ina (Graham) A.; m. Jean Ellen Daniel, May 30, 1953; children: Janet, Karen, Steven, David. BSEE, U. Md., 1948, MA in Math., 1952. Electronics scientist Nat. Bureau of Standards, Washington, 1948-50, computer engr., 1953-54; radio engr. USCG Hdqrs., Washington, 1950-53; mathematician Avion div. ACF Industries, Alexandria, Va., 1954-56; computer engr. Electronics Lab. GE Co., Syracuse, N.Y., 1956-85; prof. elec. and computer engring. U. Mass., Amherst, 1985-94; adj. prof. Syracuse U., 1975-85. Co-author: Design Automation of Digital Systems, 1974. Grantee Tektronix Corp., 1986, NSF, 1987-89. Fellow IEEE (guest editor jour. 1986); mem. Math. Assn. Am., Sigma Xi. Presbyterian. Home: Atlanta Ga. Died May 5, 1996.

ALBERT, GERALD, sonar manufacturing company executive; b. Bklyn., Feb. 13, 1925; s. Barney and Minnie A.; m. Evelyn Kriegshan, July 4, 1948; children—Bruce M., Steven A. B.E.E., CCNY, 1948; postgrad., Poly. Inst. Bklyn. With EDO Corp. (sonar mfrs.), College Point, N.Y., 1948—; pres. indsl. and govt. products group EDO Corp., 1978-80, pres., chief exec. officer, 1980—, also dir. Mem. Nat. Security Indsl. Assn. (trustee), Acoustical Soc. Am., Am. Def. Preparedness Assn., Am. Helicopter Soc., Am. Soc. Naval Engrs., NAM, Naval War Coll. Found., Soc. Naval Architects and Marine Engrs., U.S. Naval Inst., Flushing (N.Y.) C. of C. DIED 05/22/97. .

ALBRECHT, PAUL ABRAHAM, dean; b. Newton, Kans., Dec. 9, 1922; s. Abraham and Lena (Ratzlaff) A.; m. Bernice Hertha Goertz, June 29, 1947; children: Patricia Kay Senner, Jeanne Elizabeth Anderson. B.A., Bethel Coll., 1947; M.A., U. Chgo., 1949, Ph.D., 1953. Survey dir. Nejelski & Co. Inc. (Mgmt. Counsels), N.Y.C., 1951-53; dir. communication projects Indsl. Relations Center U. Chgo., 1953-55; asst. prof. psychology Whittier (Calif.) Coll., 1955-57; asso. prof. psychology Claremont Men's Coll. and Claremont Grad. Sch., Calif., 1957-62; prof. Claremont Men's Coll. and Claremont Grad. Sch., 1962-68; prof., chmn. grad. faculty in bus. econs. Claremont (Calif.) Grad. Sch.,

1968-71, dean grad. sch., 1972-82, v.p., 1980-82, exec. v.p., exec. dean, 1982-87, C.S. and D.J. Davidson prof. mgmt., 1987—, exec. dean emeritus, 1988—; mgmt. cons. to industry, 1951—; dir. Grad. Record Exams. Bd. Contbr. articles profl. jours. Mem. president's council advisers Bethel Coll.; bd. dirs. Haynes Found. Mem. APA, Nat. Council Univ. Research Adminstrs., Council Grad. Schs. U.S. (dir., chmn. 1980-81), Western Assn. Grad. Schs. (pres.), Western Assn. Schs. and Colls. (sr. accrediting commn., vice chmn.), Am. Assn. Collegiate Schs. Bus. (bd. dirs.), Sigma Xi. Deceased.

ALBRIGHT, LOIS, operetta company executive director; b. Elwood, Ind., May 17, 1904. Student, Chgo. Musical Coll., Berlin Conservatory (scholar), Vienna Conservatory. Concertmaster Nashville Symphony; 1st violinist Gary String Ensemble, 1935; condr. Opera in the Parks, Chgo., Harding U. Choir, South Music Festival, Chgo. Music Festival, Phoenix Symphonic Choir, Phoenix Opera Assn., 1948-53, Ariz. Music Drama Guild, 1954, others; tchr. voice Glendale Community Coll., Phoenix, 1964-72; chmn. music dept. Harding U., Ark., 1935-40; founder, artistic dir. Phoenix Opera Assn., Inc.; exec. dir. Phoenix Oratorio, Opera Singers; lectr. on Hopi lore throughout U.S. to museums, univs., high schs., others; pianist, first concert at age four; concerts in Midwest; soloist with mem. Chgo. Symphony Orch. Hall; tours throughout U.S.; violinist, concerts throughout Midwest; played many chamber music concerts throughout Midwest and East coast; mem. Chgo. Women's Symphony; compositions include Psalm 99, S.A.T.B. with soprano obbligato, Psalm 136, S.A.T.B. with piano, Isaiah 62, S.A.T.B. tenor, mezzo and soprano solos with piano, Revelation 22, S.A.T.B. soprano, tenor mezzo and soprano solos with piano, Psalm 45, soprano or tenor solo, with piano, others; coach Opera for Chgo. Opera Co.; tchr. voice Chgo., Los Angeles, Phoenix, N.Y.C.; founder, artistic dir. Phoenix Opera Assn., Inc.; exec. dir. Phoenix Oratorio/Opera Singers; founder, exec. dir., Viennese Operetta Co. of N.Y., Inc., N.Y.C., 1975-96, pres., condr. at Sun Dial, Sun City, Ariz, 1990; pres. Viennese Operetta Co. Am., Inc., 1989-96, condr. in Sun City, 1990; condr. all performances Lincoln Ctr., toured West Coast, 1982, East Coast, 1983. Author: Saul and the Medium, 1965; composed: Hopitu, folk opera, 1955; presented: Three Opuses, 1987; condr. six performances of Viennase Operetta Co., Phoenix, Sun City, Ariz., 1992, tchr. artist students Met. Opera, N.Y.C., N.Y. C. Opera, 1991-92. Recipient award Internat. Robert Stolz Soc. of Vienna. Mem. N.Y. Singing Tchrs. Assn. (rec. sec. 1959-60), Sun City Symphony Assn. (bd. dirs.). Deceased.

ALDERETE, JOSEPH FRANK, psychiatrist, medical service adminstrator; b. Las Vegas, N.Mex., Sept. 10, 1920; s. Jose P. and Adela R. (Armijo) A.; m. Christine Krajewski, June 24, 1964; children: Joseph Frank, Sarah A. BS in Chemistry and Biology, Tex. Western Coll., 1950; MD, Nat. U. Mex., 1959. Intern USPHS Hosp., Balt., 1959-60; resident in psychiatry USPHS Hosp., Lexington, Ky., 1960-62; sr. resident in psychiatry U. Hosp. U. Okla. Sch. of Medicine, Oklahoma City, Ky., 1962-63; practice medicine specializing in psychiatry Balt., 1963-65, Springfield, Mo., 1965-67, Atlanta, 1968—; staff psychiatrist USPHS Hosp., Balt., 1963-65; chief of psychiat. service U.S. Med. Center for Fed. Prisoners, Springfield, Mo., 1965-67; clin. and research fellow in electroencephalography Mass. Gen. Hosp.-Harvard, Boston, 1967-68; clin. instr. psychiatry Emory U. Sch. of Medicine, Atlanta, 1968-84, asst. prof. medicine, 1986—; chief med. officer, hosp. dir. U.S. Penitentiary Hosp., Atlanta, 1968-78; asst. regional flight surgeon So. Dist., ARTCC, Atlanta, 1978—; evaluation sect. VA Hosp., Decatur, Ga., 1983—; psychiat. cons. to Student Health Office, Okla. State U., Stillwater, 1962-63, U.S. Fed. Reformatory, El Reno, Okla., 1962-63. Contbr. articles to profl. jours. Served with USAF, 1944-48, to capt. AUS, 1948-50. Fellow Am. Acad. Psychosomatic Medicine; mem. AMA, Am. Psychiat. Assn., Am. Soc. Clin. Hypnosis, So. EEG Soc., Am., Internat. acads. of law and psychiatry, Acad. of Psychosomatic Medicine, Atlanta Med. Soc., Clin. Soc. of USPHS, Phi Rho Sigma. Deceased.

ALDRICH, DUANE CANNON, lawyer; b. Ft. Bragg, N.C., Mar. 10, 1943; s. Charles Duane and Elizabeth (Cannon) A.; children: Jessamine Shaw, Abigail Suzanne. AB, Harvard U., 1965, LLB, 1968. Bar: Ga. 1968, D.C. 1977, U.S. Supreme Ct. 1979. Assoc. Kilpatrick & Cody, Atlanta, 1968-74, ptnr., 1974—. Contbr. articles to profl. jours. Mem. ABA, Atlanta Bar Assn., State Bar of Ga., D.C. Bar, Lawyers Club of Atlanta, Capital City Club. Died Dec. 1997.

ALEIXANDRE, VICENTE, author; b. Seville, Spain, April 26, 1898; s. Cirilo and Elvira (Merlo) A.; licence U. Madrid (Spain), 1919. Decorated gran cruz Orden de Carlos III; recipient Nat. Prize Lit., Nobel Prize for Lit. 1977. Fellow Am. Assn. Tchrs. Spanish and Portuguese (hon.); mem. Spanish Acad., Hispanic Soc. Am., Monde Latin Paris Acad., Acad. Scis. and Arts P.R., Málaga Acad., Hispano-Am. Bogotá Acad. Author: Ámbito, 1928; Espadas com Labios, 1932; Pasión de la Tierra, 1935; La Destrucción o el Amor, 1935; Sombra del Paraíso, 1944; Mundo a Solas, 1950; Vida del Poeta: El amor y la poesía, 1950; Poemas Paradisiacos, 1952; Nacimiento Último, 1953; Historia del Corazón, 1954; Algunos Caracteres de la Neuva Poesía Española, 1955; Ocho Poemas de Aleisandre, 1955; Mis Poemas Mejores, 1957; Los Encuentros, 1958; Poemas Amorosos, 1960; Poesías Completas, 1960; Picasso, 1961; Antigua Cas Madrileña, 1961; En Un Vasto Dominio, 1962; María la Gorda, 1963; Retratos con Nombre, 1965; Presencias 1965; Dos Vidas, 1967; Obras Completas, 1968; Poemas de la Consumación 1968; Antología del Mary La Noche, 1971; Poesía Superrealista, 1971; Sonido de la Guerra, 1972; Diá logos del Conocimiento, 1974; Antología Total, 1976; Antología Poética, 1978.

ALEO, JOSEPH JOHN, pathology scientist, educator, academic research administrator; b. Wilkes-Barre, Pa., Oct. 8, 1925; s. Vincent and Martha (Lupino) A.; m. Fannie Ocuto, Aug. 28, 1949; children: Joseph John, James Robert. BS, Bucknell U., 1948; DDS, Temple U., 1953; PhD, U. Rochester, 1965. Commd. dental surgeon USPHS, 1953-54; pvt. practice dentistry Meshoppen, Pa., 1954-60; research fellow U. Rochester, N.Y., 1960-65; assoc. prof., chmn. dept. pathology Temple U., 1965-67, prof., chmn. dept., 1967-70, dean advanced edn. and research, 1970-87; cons., mem. standing coms. NIH, FDA, other gov. agencies, industries; vis. scholar U. Cambridge, 1971-72. Editorial bd., reviewer numerous sci. jours.; pub. over 100 papers, chpts., abstracts; rsch. connective tissue diseases; ascorbic acid transport in health and disease. Served with AUS, 1943-46. Decorated Bronze Star. Fellow AAAS, N.Y. Acad. Sci.; mem. numerous profl., sci., hon. socs. Died Nov. 15, 1997.

ALEPOUDELIS, ODYSSEUS See ELYTIS, ODYSSEUS

ALEXANDER, MYRL EARLY, criminal justice educator; b. Dayton, Ohio, Aug. 23, 1909; s. John Lester and Florence (Early) A.; m. Lorene Shoemaker, Jan. 18, 1934; children: Nancy (Mrs. Robert B. Hibbs), John Alexander. A.B., Manchester Coll., 1930, LL.D., 1956, LL.D., Pacific Luth. U., 1966; L.H.D., Susquehanna U., 1972. Warden's asst. U.S. Penitentiary, Atlanta, 1931; parole exec. U.S. Bd. Parole, Washington, 1937-40; assoc. warden U.S. Penitentiary, Lewisburg, Pa., 1940-43; warden Fed. Correctional Instn., Danbury, Conn., 1943-45; chief prisons Mil. Govt. for Germany, 1945-46; asst. dir. Bur. Prisons, Dept. Justice, Washington, 1947-61, dir., 1964-70; prof. correctional adminstrn., dir. Center for Study Crime, Delinquency and Corrections, So. Ill. U., Carbondale, 1961-64, 70-73; prof. criminal justice U. Fla., Gainesville, 1974-85; U.S. rep., vice chmn. delegation UN Congress on Prevention Crime and Treatment of Offenders, Stockholm, 1965, Kyoto, Japan, 1970; U.S. corr. sect. on social def. UN; spl. cons. various state correctional systems. Author: Jail Administration, 1957. Mem. exec. bd. Ill. Synod, Luth. Ch. in Am., 1961-64, mem. bd. social ministry, 1966-72, mem. Bishop's Commn. Econ. Justice, 1985-87; mem. bd. social ministry Mission in N.Am., 1972-80. Recipient Pres.'s award for distinguished fed. service, 1967. Mem. Am. Correctional Assn. (pres. 1956), Osborne Assn. Democrat. Home: Corpus Christi Tex. Died Jan. 14, 1993.

ALLEN, ANNA FOSTER, librarian; b. West Pittston, Pa., Feb. 20, 1901; d. Henry J. and Mary H. (Ainey) Foster; m. C. Spencer Allen, Sept. 1, 1927. Ph.B., Muhlenberg Coll., 1927; B.L.S., Drexel Inst. Tech., 1931. Asst. ref. libr. Bryn Mawr Coll., 1931-36; circulation libr. Temple U., 1936-66; libr. Lehigh County Hist. Soc., Allentown, Pa., 1967-84; sec. Lehigh County Hist. Soc., 1968-71. Author: Leopold Paul Unger Allentown Artist. Vol. Allentown Hosp., 1967-90; pres. Muhlenberg Coll. Aux., 1971-75, 80-84, fin. sec., 1975-80, treas., 1984-87; mem. coordinating council Allentown Girls Club, 1972-73, Vols. of Am. Day Care Center; mem. Lehigh Valley Com. on Historic Areas; sec. West Park Civic Assn., 1975-84; libr. Luther Crest Libr., 1986-95. Recipient Four Chaplains Legion of Honor award. Mem. Middle Atlantic Regional Archivist Conf. (Community Spirit award 1989). Lutheran. Clubs: Athenaeum (Allentown) (pres. 1972-73, treas. 1975-81), Gamma Delphian (Allentown). Died July 31, 1995.

ALLEN, CATHERINE MACDONALD, artist, communications company executive; b. Winchester, Va., Aug. 8, 1949; d. Douglas Brooke and Nancy Grey (Stevens) A.; m. Howard Goodman, Aug. 24, 1980; children: Aaron, Michael. BA with gen. honors, Am. U., 1971; MFA in Painting, Boston U., 1976. Grad. asst., instr. printmaking Boston U., 1975-76; mem. faculty Mt. Wachusett C.C., Gardner, Mass., 1977-79, Coll. of New Rochelle, 1980-81; dir. core program N.Y. Feminist Art Inst., N.Y.C., 1980-81, bd. dirs., 1980-89, dir. spl. events, 1980-82, dir. visual artists exch., 1983, 87; lectr. Calif. State U., Long Beach, 1991; CEO, Goodman Comm. West, Calabasas, Calif., 1991—. One-woman shows include SOHO 20 Gallery, N.Y.C., 1985, 86, 89; 2-person show John Jay Coll., CUNY, 1994; 3-person show Wade Gallery, L.A., 1990; exhibited in group shows, including Ny Carlsberg Mus., Copenhagen, 1980, Smithsonian Instn., Washington, 1981, Everson Mus., Syracuse, N.Y., 1984, South Bay Contemporary Mus. Art, Torrance, Calif., 1992, L.A. Festival, 1993; represented in permanent collections South Bay Contemporary Mus. Art, Nat. Mus. Women in Arts Libr., Boston U., also corps. Yaddo fellow, 1982, fellow Hand Hollow Found., 1983, Nat. Endowment for Arts, 1989-90. Mem. Coll. Art Assn., Women's Caucus for Art. DIED 06/27/96. .

ALLEN, DURWARD LEON, biologist, educator; b. Uniondale, Ind., Oct. 11, 1910; s. Harley J. and Jennie M. (LaTurner) A.; m. Dorothy Ellen Helling, Sept. 23, 1935 (dec.); children: Stephen R., Harley W., Susan E.; m. Suzanne E. Grieser, Oct. 21, 1985. A.B., U. Mich., 1932; Ph.D., Mich. State Coll., 1937; L.H.D. (hon.), No. Mich. U., 1971; D.A. (hon.), Purdue U., 1985. Game research biologist Mich. Dept. Conservation, 1935-46; wildlife research biologist U.S. Fish and Wildlife Service, Laurel, Md., 1946-50; asst. chief br. wildlife research U.S. Fish and Wildlife Service, Washington, 1951-54; prof. wildlife ecology Purdue U., West Lafayette, Ind., 1954-76, prof. emeritus, 1976-97; mem. Adv. Bd. on Nat. Parks, Monuments and Historic Sites, U.S. Dept. Interior, 1966-72, chmn., 1971-72; chmn. Nat. Sci. Adv. Com. on Fish and Wildlife and Parks, U.S. Dept. Interior, 1975-76; adj. prof. Tex. Tech U., 1982. Author: Michigan Fox Squirrel Management, 1943, Pheasants Afield, 1953, Our Wildlife Legacy, 1954, 62, The Life of Prairies and Plains, 1967, Wolves of Minong, 1979, 93; editor: Pheasants in North America, 1956, Land Use and Wildlife Resources, 1970. Recipient medal of honor Anglers' Club of N.Y., 1956; inducted into Mich. Conservation Hall of Fame, Mich. United Conservation Clubs, 1985; named Sagamore of the Wabash, Ind. Gov., 1983. Fellow AAAS; mem. Wildlife Soc. (hon. life mem., pres. 1956-57, Annual Tech. Publ. award 1946, Annual Conservation Edn. award 1955, Leopold Meml. medal 1968), Am. Soc. Mammalogists, Ecol. Soc. Am., Washington Biologists' Field Club, Am. Inst. Biol. Scis., Am. Forestry Assn. (bd. dirs. 1983-88), George Wright Soc., Wilderness Soc., Outdoor Writers Assn. Am. (Jade of Chiefs award 1968, hon. life mem.), Nature Conservancy, Conservation Found., Nat. Parks and Conservation Assn., Nat. Wildlife Fedn. (ann. sci. award 1985), Ind. Acad. Sci. (named lectr. of yr. 1968), Nat. Audubon Soc. (bd. dirs. 1975-84, Audubon medal 1990), George Bird Grinnell Soc. (charter mem.), Boone and Crockett Club (emeritus), Cosmos Club, Explorers Club, Sigma Xi, Phi Sigma, Xi Sigma Pi, Seminarium Botanicum. Home: West Lafayette Ind. Died Oct. 17, 1997.

ALLEN, GAY WILSON, writer, former English educator; b. Lake Junaluska, N.C., Aug. 23, 1903; s. Robert Henry and Ethel (Garren) A.; m. Evie Allison, July 15, 1929. A.B., Duke U., 1926, M.A., 1928; Ph.D., U. Wis., 1934; D.Lit., Duke U., 1975, U. Wis.-Madison, 1983. Instr. in English Lake Erie Coll., Painesville, Ohio, 1929-31; instr. in English Shurtleff Coll., Alton, Ill., 1934-35, State Univ., Bowling Green, Ohio, 1935-46; prof. English NYU, 1946-69; tchr. summer schs. Harvard, U., Duke U., U. Tex., U. Hawaii; vis. prof. Harvard U., 1969-70, Emory U., 1979. Author: American Prosody, 1935, Literary Criticism: Pope to Croce, (with H. H. Clark), 1941, Walt Whitman Handbook, 1946, Masters of American Literature, (with H. A. Pochmann), 1949, The Solitary Singer. A Critical Biography of Walt Whitman, 1955, Walt Whitman Abroad, 1955, Walt Whitman's Poems, (with C.T. Davis), 1955, Walt Whitman: Evergreen Profile Book, 1959, Walt Whitman as Man, Poet and Legend, 1961, American Poetry, (with Walter Rideout and James K. Robinson), 1965, William James, A Biography, 1967, The World of Herman Melville, 1971; editor: A William James Reader, 1971, Studies in Leaves of Grass, 1972, The New Walt Whitman Handbook, 1975, 2d edit. 1986, (with Roger Asselineau) St. John de Crévecoeur: the Life of an American Farmer, 1987, Waldo Emerson, A Biography, 1981; gen. editor: (with Sculley Bradley) Collected Writings of Walt Whitman, 1961-84, 24 vols.; contbr. articles and reviews to nat., internat. jours. Fellow Rockefeller Found., 1944-45; Guggenheim fellow, 1952-53, 59-60; recipient Los Angeles Times prize for biography, 1982. Fellow Soc. Am. Historians; mem. Internat. Assn. Univ. Profs. English, MLA (Lowell prize 1982), Phi Beta Kappa. Club: P.E.N. Home: Raleigh N.C. Died Aug. 6, 1995.

ALLEN, GINA, author; b. Trenton, Nebr.; d. R.V. and Osa (Hanel) Hunkins; 1 dau., Ginita Allen Wall. B.A., Northwestern U., 1940. Exec. sec. Youth Commn. 3d Jud. Dist., N.Mex., 1956-60; chairwoman N.Mex. Dem. Cen. Com., 1956-59; mem. bd. Golden Gate chpt. NOW, 1970-93; pres. Humanist Assn. San Francisco, 1976-85; sec. Am. Humanist Assn., 1973-77, v.p., 1979-83, sr. humanist counselor, 1972-93, founding chmn. feminist caucus, 1977-86, chmn. div. humanist counseling, 1982-86, exec. coun.div. Humanist Counseling, 1987-93. Author: Prairie Children, 1941, On the Oregon Trail, 1942, Rustics for Keeps, 1948, The Forbidden Man, 1961 (Anisfield Wolf award 1962), Party Girl, 1962, Gold!, 1964, Gold Is, 1969, Intimacy, 1971; (with R.V. Hunkins) Tepee Days, 1941, Trapper Days, 1942, Sod-House Days, 1945; also short stories, articles in popular mags.; mem. editorial bd. Humanist mag., 1983-93. Named to Humanist Counselors AHA Hall of Fame, 1989. Mem. Authors Guild, Internat. Assn. Humanists Educators, Counselors and Leaders (bd. dirs. 1988-92), Vets. Feminist Wars (founding mem.). Unitarian. Home: San Diego Calif. Died Dec. 26, 1993.

ALLEN, HERBERT, investment banker; b. N.Y.C., Feb. 13, 1908; s. Charles and Francis (Mayer) A.; m. Kathleen Heffernan (dec.); children—Herbert Anthony, Susan Kathleen Allen; m. Ethel Strong. D.C.S. (hon.), Ithaca Coll. Ptnr. Allen & Co., N.Y.C., 1927—; dir. emeritus Irvine Co., Newport Beach, Calif. Trustee, v.p. Hackley Sch., Tarrytown, N.Y. Clubs: Deepdale Golf; Indian Creek Golf (Fla.); Mark's (London); Saratoga Golf and Polo; Bal Harbour Club. Died Jan. 18, 1997.

ALLERS, FRANZ, orchestra conductor; b. Czechoslovakia, Aug. 6, 1905; came to U.S., 1938; s. Carl and Paula (Kellner) A.; m. Carolyn Shaffer, 1941 (div. 1961); 1 dau., Carol Frances; m. Janne Furch, 1963. Student, Praha Conservatory, Prague, 1920, Berlin Hochschule für Musik, Berlin, 1923-26. First violinist, Berlin Philharmonic Orch., 1924-25, condr., Muncpl. Theatre, Carlsbad, 1926, Wupperthal, 1927-33, asst. at, Bayreuth Festival, summer 1927, asst., Wagner Festival, Paris, 1929, chief of opera and condr. Philharmonic concerts, Municipal Theatre, Aussig-on-Elbe, 1933-38, condr., Ballet Russe and Ballet Russe de Monte Carlo, London, 1938, toured U.S., South America and Can., musical dir., 1942-44, condr., Met. Opera House, N.Y.C., 1963-76, N.Y. Philharmonic, 1965, Nuremberg Philharmonic, 1967-76, Radio-TV Hilversum-Holland, 1968-79, gen. music dir., State Opera Comique, Munich, guest condr., Opera Munich and Cologne, musical dir., Music Theatre Lincoln Center, N.Y.C., 1964-66, Nat. Symphony, Washington, 1969, 78, 79, 81, 82, 83, 84, 85, Saratoga Festival, 1969-82, 69-86, Wolf Trap Festival, 1974, 77-85, Philharmonic Orch., London, 1970, Ravinia Festival, 1969, 70, 71, 74-82, 85, Holland Opera, 1973, 74, 75, 76, others; condr. radio broadcast concerts, Czech Philharmonic and Radio Corp. of Prague orchs.; U.S. condr.: Day Before Spring, 1945-46, Brigadoon, 1947-49, South Pacific, 1950-51, Paint Your Wagon, 1951-52; film Haensel and Gretel, 1953, Plain and Fancy, 1954-55; musical dir. State Fair Musicals, Dallas, Texas, 1953-56, My Fair Lady, 1956-60 (Antoinette Perry award 1957), tour to, Russia, 1960, Berlin, 1961, Munich, 1962, Vienna, 1963, Geneva, 1968, Brussels, 1969, U.S. tour with, Vienna Tonkuenstler Orch., 1978, 80, Hallmark TV program, 1955-63, also Omnibus, Susskind, Firestone programs, Camelot, 1960-63 (Antoinette Perry award 1961); condr. symphony orchs. of Phila., Chgo., Cleve., Toronto, Cin., Seattle, Denver, Buffalo, Pitts., Mpls., Vancouver, Ottawa and Montreal, Can., 1949-89, also Berlin Philharmonic Orch., 1957, 59, 67, Hamburg Radio Orch., 1958, 59, 62, 64, 65, 66, Munich Radio Orch., 1962-65, Bavaria TV Munich, 1962-69, Radio Oslo, 1962, Cologne Radio Orch., 1965-82, Oslo Philharmonic Orch., 1965, Vienna Tonkuenstler Orch., 1965-95, Vienna Symphony Orch., 1964-68, Opera Geneve, 1968-72, Miami Opera, 1977, 80, 81, 84, Cleve. Opera, 1984, 86, 87, 88, 89, Pacific Coast Opera, 1988, Mich. Opera, 1988; Rec. artist, Columbia RCA Victor, Vanguard, Phillips, Electrola., Eurodisk. Home: Miami Fla. Died Jan. 26, 1995.

ALLIN, ELLWOOD CLIFFORD, protective services official; b. Regina, Sask., Can., June 28, 1933; s. Percy Allin and Margaret (Banks) Middleton; m. Matilda Nellie Erskine, Jan. 22, 1953; children: Heather Evelyn, Brian Douglas, Shelley Marie. Cert. mcpl. mgmt., Banff (Alta., Can.) Ctr.; cert. mcpl. govt., urban mgmt., Western U., London, Ont., Can. Salesman Weston's Bakery, Regina, 1950-57; sr. fire fighter Regina Fire Dept., 1957-77, asst. dep. fire chief, 1977-80, dir. fire support services, 1980-84, fire chief, 1984—. Pres. Srs. Activity Ctr., Regina, 1983—; bd. dirs. Community Health Services, Regina, 1972-77, Luth. Home, Regina, 1976-78, United Way, Regina, 1984. Mem. Internat. Arson Investigators (bd. dirs. Sask. chpt. 1985—), Sask. Fire Chiefs Assn. (pres. 1985-86), Internat. Assn. Fire Chiefs, Can. Assn. Fire Chiefs. Lodge: Optimist (bd. dirs. Regina club 1979—). Avocations: community service, fishing.

ALLING, CHARLES CALVIN, III, oral-maxillofacial surgeon, educator, writer; b. Guthrie, Okla., Dec. 27, 1923; s. Charles Calvin Jr. and Bessie Palmer (Keller) A.; m. Laura Esther Freeland, May 10, 1947; children: Elaine Sue (Mrs. Andrew W. Lilliston Jr.), Rocklin David, Robert Freeland. AB, Ind. U., 1943, DDS, 1946; MS, U. Mich., 1954; DSc (hon.), Georgetown U., 1987. Diplomate Am. Bd. Oral and Maxillofacial Surgery (pres. 1983-84). Prof., chmn. dept. oral surgery U. Ala., Birmingham, 1969-81; oral-maxillofacial surgeon Drs. Alling & Alling, 1981-96; adj. prof. Coll. Dentistry, U. Iowa; cons. ADA, U.S. Army Med. R & D Command, Surgeon Gen., VA; vis. prof. and lectr. Howard U., Georgetown U., Seoul U. Editor, author: Maxillofacial Trauma, 1988, Facial Pain, 3d edit., 1991, Oral Maxillofacial Surgery Clinics North America, 1973, 93, Impacted Teeth, 1993, Lasers in Oral Maxillofacial Surgery, 1997; mem. editorial bd. Oral Surgery, Oral Medicine, Oral Pathology; contbr. chpts. to books, articles to profl. jours. Bd. dirs. Kwang Myung Orphanage and Sch. for Blind, Inchon, Republic of Korea. Col. U.S. Army, 1943-69, ret. Decorated Legion of Merit; Medaslha Le Rene Forte (Brazil); recipient U.S. Army Outstanding Civilian Svc. award, W.F. Harrigan award Bellevue Hosp., Sadi Fountaine award Alameda Med. Instns., Fauchard Disting. Svc. award, W.J. Gies Disting. Svc. award. Fellow Am. Coll. Dentists; mem. ADA, Am. Soc. Oral Surgeons (bd. dirs.), Am., Southeastern, Ala. Internat. Assn. Oral-Maxillofacial Surgeons, Chalmer Lyons Acad. Oral Surgery, 38th Parallel Dental Soc. (charter pres.), Greater Washington Soc. Oral Surgeons (charter pres.), Internat. Assn. Dental Rsch., Pan Pacific Implant Assn., Masons, Shriners, Phi Kappa Phi. Achievements include research on repair of maxillofacial osseous tissues, clinical investigations in facial pain and impacted teeth. Died March 25, 1996.

ALMEIDA, LAURINDO, guitarist, composer; b. Brazil, Sept. 2, 1917; came to U.S., 1947, naturalized, 1961; s. Benjamin and Placedina (Araujo) A.; m. Maria M. Ferreira, May 20, 1944 (dec. Aug. 1970); m. Deltra Eamon, Aug. 3, 1971. Student, Escola Nacional de Muscica do Rio de Janeiro. Owner, operator Brazilliance Music Pub. Co., 1952—. Featured soloist, Stan Kenton Orch., 1947-50, Modern Jazz Quartet, 1964, 92; guitarist motion picture prodns., 1949—; composer over 200 pieces including First Concerto for Guitar and Orch. in three movements, 1979, recorded for Concord Concerto, 1980, mus. scores for TV (Acad. award for Magic Pear Tree, 1970-71); also films Maracaibo, 1956, Goodbye My Lady, 1957; rec. artist, Capitol, World Pacific, Decca, Orion and Concord records. Recipient cert. of appreciation Am. String Tchrs. Assn., award Latin Am. and Caribbean Cultural Soc. (London), 1992, award for worldwide contbn. to musical arts and edn., Sch. of the Arts, Calif. State U., 1994. Mem. ASCAP, AFTRA, Am. Songwriters Assn., Composers Guild Am., Nat. Acad. Rec. Arts and Scis. (bd. govs. classical music, 5 Grammy awards, 14 nominations), Acad. Motion Picture Arts and Scis., Am. Guitar Soc. (Vadah Olcott-Bickford Meml. award). Died August, 1995.

ALMGREN, FREDERICK JUSTIN, JR., mathematician; b. Birmingham, Ala., July 3, 1933; s. Frederick Justin and Sarah Cone (Wright) A.; m. Jean Ellen Taylor, Oct. 6, 1973; children—Robert Frederick, Ann Stewart, Karen Taylor. B.S. in Engring, Princeton U., 1955; Ph.D. in Math, Brown U., 1962. Instr. math. Princeton U., N.J., 1962-63, asst. prof., 1965-68, assoc. prof., 1968-72, prof., 1972-97; scholar Inst. Advanced Study, Princeton, 1963-65, 69, 74-75, 78, 81-82, 85, 92; exch. visitor Steklov Math. Inst., Leningrad, USSR, 1970; vis. scholar Stanford U., 1989. Author: Plateau's Problem, 1966; contbr. numerous articles to math. jours. Served with USN, 1955-58. Alfred P. Sloan fellow, 1968-70; Guggenheim Meml. fellow, 1974-75; NSF grantee, 1962-97. Mem. Am. Math. Soc., Math. Assn. Am., Soc. Indsl. and Applied Math., AAAS. Home: Princeton N.J. Died Feb. 5, 1997; buried Princeton Cemetery.

ALMGREN, HERBERT PHILIP, bank executive; b. Fairfield, Ala., Oct. 22, 1916; s. O. Philip and Lillie (Becker) A.; m. Jean R. Cleaveland, June 10, 1939; children: Caroline C. (Mrs. Douglass N. Ellis Jr.), Nancy B. (Mrs. Robert A. Killam). BS magna cum laude, Springfield Coll., 1938; postgrad., Columbia. Tchr. Rectory Sch., Pomfret, Conn., 1938-40; with Monarch Life Ins. Co. (and predecessor), 1940-63, v.p., 1958-63; with Shawmut First Bank & Trust Co. Hampden County, 1963-97, sr. v.p., 1964-65, pres., 1965-68, pres., chief exec. officer, 1968-79, chmn., chief exec. officer, 1979-81, also dir.; bd. dirs. Am. Pad & Paper Co., Holyoke, Mass., Am. Pad Plus, Daniel O'Connell's. Past chmn. bd. Baystate Med. Center; corporator Springfield Boys Club, Springfield Jr. Achievement. Served to lt. (j.g.) USNR, 1943-46. Mem. Mass. Bankers Assn. (former pres.), Greater Springfield C. of C. (dir., past pres.). Club: The Yacht and Country Inc. (former bd. dirs.). Home: Stuart Fla. Died March 7, 1997.

ALPERT, DANIEL, physicist, educator; b. Hartford, Conn., Apr. 10, 1917; s. Elias and Dora (Prechepa) A.; m. Natalie L. Boyle, Jan. 12, 1942; children—Amy A. Arai, Laura Jane. B.S., Trinity Coll., Hartford, 1937, D.Sc. (hon.), 1957; Ph.D., Stanford, 1942. Research physicist Westinghouse Research Lab., Pitts., 1942-50; mgr. physics dept. Westinghouse Research Lab., 1950-55, asso. dir., 1955-57; prof. physics U. Ill. at Urbana, 1957—; dir. Coordinated Sci. Lab., 1959-65; dean Grad. Coll., 1965-72; dir. Center for Advanced Study; assoc. dir. Computer-Based Edn. Research Lab., 1972-87; dir. Program in Sci., Tech., and Soc., 1986-90; rsch. scientist. Nat. Ctr. for Supercomputing Applications, 1988—. Author articles on ultrahigh vacuum tech., surface physics, computer based edn., sci., tech. and society. Mem. Allegheny County Sch. Bd., 1956-57, Def. Sci. Bd., 1963-72; Trustee Trinity Coll., 1964-89, Inst. Def. Analyses. Recipient Newcomb Cleveland award AAAS, 1954; Gaede-Langmuir award Am. Vacuum Soc., 1980. Mem. Am. Phys. Soc., AAAS, Phi Beta Kappa, Sigma Xi. DIED 01/20/97. .

ALPS, GLEN EARL, printmaker, visual artist, educator; b. Loveland, Colo., June 20, 1914. B.A., U. No. Colo.; M.F.A., U. Wash.; postgrad., U. Iowa. prof. art emeritus U. Wash. Author: works included in numerous art and print books. The Collagraph; represented in permanent collections: Mus. Modern Art, N.Y.C., Phila. Art Mus., Chgo. Art Inst., Los Angeles County Art Mus., Library of Congress, Nat. Mus. Am. Art Smithsonian Instn., Washington, Vivian and Gordon Gilkey Ctr. Graphic Arts, Portland (Oreg.) Art Mus., others; sculpture includes panels, Seattle Public Library, 1960, fountains, Seattle Mcpl. Bldg., 1961, First Christian Ch, Greeley, Colo., 1962, others; numerous exhbns. prints. Tamarind fellow; Ford Found. fellow; recipient Wash. Gov.'s award, U. No. Colo. Trail Blazer Alumnus award, 1985, Hall of Fame award U. No. Colo. Alumni, 1989. Mem. NW Printmakers (pres. 1951-53, 62-64). Died Nov. 3rd, 1996.

ALTER, ELLEN J., lawyer, educator; b. Cambridge, Mass., Feb. 13, 1949; d. Douglas and Sylvia Ann (Green) Chandler; divorced; children: Daniel, Jessica. BA, Brandeis U., 1970; postgrad., Columbia U.; JD, U. Mich., 1974. Bar: Mich. 1974. Ptnr. Hertzberg, Jacob & Weingarten, Detroit, 1983-88, Jaffe, Raitt, Heuer & Weiss, Detroit, 1988-93. Mem. State Bar Mich., Am. Bankruptcy Inst., Oakland County Bar Assn., Detroit Bar Assn. Home: Detroit Mich. Died Sept. 18, 1993.

ALTSHULER, BERNARD, biomathematician; b. Newark, June 22, 1919; s. Max and Mamie (Bampe) A.; m. Lillian Esther Schulsinger, June 11, 1944; children: Jean, Miriam. BS in Engring. Physics, Lehigh U., 1940; PhD, NYU, 1953. Asst. prof. NYU Med. Ctr., 1953-57, assoc. prof., 1957-69, prof., 1969—. Maj. Ordnance Corps, U.S. Army, 1940-46. Fellow NRC, 1946-49. Mem. Am. Math. Soc., Am. Physics Soc., Am. Indsl. Hygiene Soc., Soc. Indsl. and Applied Math. Achievements include research in pulmonary aerosol deposition and cancer risk assessment. DIED 10/04/97. .

AMBROSANIO, ANTONIO, archbishop; b. Naples, Italy, Aug. 18, 1928. Ordained to Roman Cath. ch., 1951. Aux. and vicar Gen. Diocese of Naples; archbishop City of Spoleto-Norcia, Italy, 1988—. Died, Feb. 7, 1994.

AMERMAN, JOHN ELLIS, lawyer; b. Ann Arbor, Mich., Apr. 27, 1944; s. Ellis L. and Thelma R. (Anderson) A.; m. Nancy Lorenzen, July 28, 1967 (div. 1978); children: Victoria L., Elizabeth M.; m. Adel Bracci, June 16, 1979. BA with high honors, Mich. State U., 1965; JD cum laude, U. Notre Dame, 1968. Bar: Mich. 1968, U.S. Dist. Ct. (ea. dist.) Mich. 1968. Assoc. Honigman Miller Schwartz & Cohn, Detroit, 1968-73, ptnr., 1973-96; bd. dirs. Osceola Fin. Corp. and affiliates, Orlando, Fla.; dir. Mateke Hills Safaris Pvt. Ltd., Harare, Zimbabwe. Editor Notre Dame Law Rev., 1966-68. Mem. ABA, Mich. Bar Assn., Detroit Bar Assn., Safari Club Internat. (Tucson), NRA. Republican. Methodist. Avocations: big game and bird hunting, fishing, modern literature. Died Nov. 12, 1996.

AMES, FISHER, retired lawyer; b. Oklahoma City, July 6, 1905; s. Charles Bismark and Elizabeth P. (Allen) A.; m. Jewell Turner, Nov. 5, 1934; children: Judith (Mrs. James P. Rhoads), Sarah (Mrs. Bruce B. Lenz). AB, Harvard Coll., 1926; LLB, U. Okla., 1930. Bar: Okla. 1930. Practiced in Oklahoma City; sr. ptnr. Ames, Daugherty, 1950, of counsel, 1984; ret. Comdr. USNR, 1941-45.

AMOROSO, MARIE DOROTHY, medical technologist; b. Phila., Jan. 16, 1924; d. Salvatore and Clorinda (Gaudio) A. Med. Lab. Tech., Hahnemann Hosp., Phila., 1943; postgrad., Temple U., Phila., 1945-48, U. Pa., Phila., 1947-48, 1950. Registered EEG Technologist; cert. registered EEG Technologist. EEG technician Hahnemann Med. Coll., Phila., 1943-53, Phila. Gen. Hosp., 1953-62; histology technician Temple Med. Coll. Temple U., Phila., 1962-63; allergy technician Harry Rogers, M.D., Phila., 1963; EEG technologist Haverford (Pa.) State Hosp., 1963-85, Irvin M. Gerson, MD, Haverford, 1985-88; EEG technologist to pvt. physician Haverford State Hosp., 1985-88; instr. EEG Osteopathic Med. Ctr. Sch. Allied Health, Phila., 1978-85. Editor: The Eastern Breeze, 1977-79; contbr. articles to profl. jours.; patentee in field. Mem. Am. Soc. Electroneurodiagnostic Technologists Inc., Western Soc. Electrodiagnostic Technologists, So. Soc. Electroneurodiagnostic Technologists Inc., Ea. Soc. EEG and Neurodiagnostic Technicians Assn. (sec. 1977-79), Phila. Regional EEG Technicians Assn. (exec. bd. dirs. 1967, sec. 1969), Ctrl. Soc. Electroneurodiagnostic Technologists, Ea. Assn. Electroencephalographers (subscriber). Avocations: writing musical compositions, poetry. Home: Drexel Hill PA. Died July 19, 1995; interred Saints Peter and Paul Cemetery.

AMOSS, WILLIAM HAMILTON, state senator; b. Balt., Dec. 2, 1936. Student, Harford Community Coll., U. Md., Mo. Sch. Auctioneering. Del. Ho. of Dels., Annapolis, Md., 1975-82; senator Md. State Legislature, Annapolis, 1983-97; mem. State Use Industries Adv. Com., Gov.'s Task Force on Vol. Fire, Rescue and Ambulance Cos., Joint Budget and Audit Com., Joint Com. on Chesapeake Bay Critical Areas, Joint Com. on Pensions Budget and Taxation Com., chmn. subcom. on pensions, mem. subcom. on capital budget; chmn. Protocol Com. With U.S. Army, 1955-58. Mem. Soc. for the Preservation Md. Antiquities, Md. Farm Bur., Md. Auctioneer Assn., Nat. Auctioneer Assn., Jaycees (past dir.). Died Oct. 8, 1997.

ANDERSEN, ERNEST CHRISTOPHER, lawyer; b. Minden, Nebr., Sept. 10, 1909; s. Dines Peter and Marie (Jensen) A.; m. Audrey Etta Robertson, Sept. 10, 1954; 1 dau., Elaine Carolyn Andersen Smith; 1 stepson, Albert Henry Whitaker. JD, U. Denver, 1952, BS in Bus.

Adminstrn., 1956. Bar: Colo. 1954, U.S. Supreme Ct. 1960; CPA, Colo. With U.S. Treasury Dept., Denver, 1935-39; accountant, Denver, 1939-41; with Civilian Prodn. Adminstrn., Denver, 1946-49; dep. state auditor Colo., 1949-51; with U.S. Commerce Dept., Denver, 1951-52; mgmt. cons., Denver, 1953-54; sole practice law, Denver, 1955-56, 69-75; asst. dir. GAO, Los Angeles, 1957-58, Denver, 1959, Washington, 1960-69, cons., 1969-75; sole practice law, Cedaredge, Colo., 1975-86; owner Cedar Crest Farm, 1983—, Stand Sure Press (later Christopher Pub. Co.), 1977—; mem. faculty U. Denver, 1948-56; mcpl. judge Cedaredge, 1977-86; exec. in residence Tulane U., spring 1973. Bd. dirs. Delta Montrose Electric Assn., 1976-84, Colo.-Ute Electric Assn., 1980-84. Served to lt. col. USAR, 1939-62. Recipient Meritorious Service award GAO, 1968. Republican. Presbyterian. Clubs: Masons, Shriners. Died Nov. 14, 1996.

ANDERSON, RALPH ALEXANDER, JR., architect; b. Houston, Jan. 1, 1923; s. Ralph Alexander and Ruby (Ellison) A. B.A. in Arch, Rice Inst., 1943, B.S., 1947. With firm Wilson, Morris & Crain, Houston, 1947-52; partner Wilson, Morris & Crain, 1952-62; partner firm Wilson, Morris, Crain & Anderson, Houston, 1962-72, Wilson/Crain/Anderson/Reynolds, Houston, 1972-78; partner firm Crain/Anderson Inc., Houston, 1978-88, ret., 1988. Prin. works include Spl. Events Centers, U. Tex., Austin, 1977, El Paso, 1977, Kelsey-Seybold Clinic, Houston, 1963, WISH-TV, Indpls., 1966, Western Nat. Bank, Houston, 1967, Houston Post Bldg, 1969. Pres. Contemporary Art Mus. Houston, 1957, Houston Bot. Soc., 1967-68; chmn. Billboards, Ltd., action group, 1967-71. Served with inf. AUS, 1943-45, ETO. Fellow A.I.A. (pres. Houston 1966); mem. Phi Beta Kappa.

ANDERSON, ROBERT, United States ambassador to Dominican Republic; b. Mass., Jan. 6, 1922; m. Elena Fenoaltea; children: Cynthia, Christina, Mark. B.A., Yale U., 1944. Commd. fgn. service officer Dept. State, 1946; transport officer, Shanghai, 1946-47; polit. officer, Nanking, 1947-49; served at Dept. State, Washington, 1949-50; prin. officer, Chiengmai, 1950-51; polit. officer, Bangkok, 1951-52; polit. officer, New Delhi, 1953-55; Ceylon desk officer, Washington, 1955-57; staff asst. bur. Pub. Affairs, Washington, 1957-59; chief reports sect., Bordeaux, 1959-61; comml. policy officer, Paris, 1961, spl. asst. to U.S. ambassador to France, 1962-63; spl. asst. to sec. of state, 1963-65; dep. dir. Office European Affairs, 1965-66; country dir. of France and Benelux, 1966-68; counselor for polit. affairs, Paris, 1968-72; U.S. ambassador to Dahomey, 1972-74; spl. asst. for press relations to sec. of state and spokesman for Dept. State, 1974-76; U.S. ambassador to Morocco, 1976-78; spl. asst. for internat. affairs to comdr.-in-chief, Atlantic and supreme allied comdr. Atlantic, 1978-82; U.S. ambassador to Dominican Republic, 1982-96. Died Apr. 5, 1996. Home: Washington D.C.

ANDERSON, STEPHEN THOMAS, entertainment executive and cinematographer; b. Pasadena, Calif., Apr. 6, 1949; s. Thomas Alton and Barbara Ives; m. D. Kimberly (Gardiner) Smith, Apr. 6, 1993. Student cinema, USC, 1994; BA cinematography, Brooks Inst. Motion Picture, Santa Barbara, Calif., 1995. Field engr. Applicon Inc., Burlington, Mass., 1976-79; asst. systems engr. Pacific Missile Test Ctr. Grumman Data Systems, Port Mugu, Calif., 1979-80; R & D engr. Omnidata Corp., Westlake Village, Calif., 1980-82; engr. STS program Martin Marietta, Vanderberg AFB, Calif., 1982-85; systems design engr. Quintron Systems, Vanderberg AFB, 1985-87; R & D engr. Indsl. Computer Design, Westlake Village, 1987-88; owner Gray Wolf Entertainment, Santa Barbara, Calif., 1992-96. Author: (novel) Medic! Medic!, 1991; film prodr. 3AM Eternal '95; (featured in Santa Barbara Film Festival 1995). Served as medic U.S. Army, 1966-69, Vietnam. Decorated Purple Heart. Mem. Acad. TV Arts and Scis., Soc. of Motion Picture and TV Engrs., The Tech. Coun. of Motion Picture and TV Industry. Achievements include integration of the first complete CAD-CAM link in U.S.; design and development of Net Selectable Jack Sta. communication device, Integration Safety Info. System database mgmt. system; established software verification program for enabling testing of all software used in STS (Shuttle Transp. System) program, of the Facility Checkout and Maintenance Control System. Home: Santa Barbara Calif. Died Jan. 27, 1996.

ANDERSON, STUART LEROY, college chancellor emeritus, clergyman; b. Elmore, Ohio, Jan. 24, 1912; s. George Alfred and Grace Pearl (Longfellow) A.; m. Raezella Tom Klepper, Sept. 25, 1935; children—Philip, Catherine. A.B., Albion Coll., 1933, D.D. honoris causa, 1945; B.D., Chicago Theol. Sem., 1936; M.A., U. Chgo., 1936; Litt.D., Pacific U., 1960. Ordained to ministry Congl. Ch., 1936; minister First Ch., Argo, Ill., 1935-36, Glendale, Calif., 1938- 43, Long Beach, 1943-50; minister youth First Ch., Los Angeles, 1936-37; pres., prof. homiletics Pacific Sch. Religion, Berkeley, Calif., 1950-71; chancellor Pacific Sch. Religion, 1971-77, pres. emeritus, 1977-95; Moderator Los Angeles Assn. Congl.-Christian Chs., 1943-44, Congl. Conf. So. Calif. and S.W., 1949-50, Northern Calif. Congl. Conf., 1952-53; mem. Congl. Commn. on Theol. Edn., 1956-66; mem. nat. com. war victims and reconstrn. Congl. Christian Chs.; mem. Prudential com. Am. Bd. Commrs. for Fgn. Missions, 1943-46, v.p., 1946-53; mem. U.S. Conf. for World Council Chs., 1961-69; asst. moderator for Gen. Synod United Ch. Christ, 1961-63; protestant observer Second Vatican Council, 1965; mem. theol. commn. United Ch. of Christ, 1971-77; Bd. dirs. Rockefeller Bros. Theol. Fellowship Program, 1958-64. Author: A Faith to Live By, 1959. Mem. Tau Kappa Epsilon, Alpha Phi Gamma, Delta Sigma Rho. Clubs: Rotary (Berkeley), U. Calif. Faculty (Berkeley); Commonwealth (San Francisco). Home: Long Beach Calif. Died July 22, 1995.

ANDREOLI, PETER DONALD, lawyer; b. N.Y.C., July 31, 1919; s. Peter E. and Lucy C. (Scannapleco) A.; m. Catherine F. McCarthy, Aug. 25, 1945; children: Peter, Brian, Catherine, Christine, Francine. BS, St. John's U., Bklyn., 1941; LLB, Columbia U., 1947. Bar: N.Y. 1948, U.S. Dist. Ct. (ea. and so. dists.) N.Y. 1961, U.S. Supreme Ct. 1966, U.S. Ct. Appeals (2d cir.) 1975, U.S. Tax. Ct. 1977, U.S. Dist. Ct. (no. dist.) N.Y. 1978, Assoc. Kupfer, Silberfeld, Nathan & Danziger, N.Y.C., 1947-48; asst. dist. atty. New York County (N.Y.), 1948-76, dep. chief rackets bur., 1963-68, chief Criminal Ct. Trial Bur., 1969-70, chief Supreme Ct. Trial Bur., 1970-74, chief Frauds Bur., 1974-76; spl. state prosecutor Onondaga County (N.Y.), 1976-81; sole practice, Pelham, N.Y., 1981—; lectr. Practicing Law, Inst., Battelle Inst.; organized Crime Confs., 1966-68, Econ. Crim Conf., 1975-76, 1st Nat. Symposium in Law Enforcement, 1978. Served to col. USAAF, 1942-45; with USAFR, 1945-79. Decorated D.F.C. with oak leaf cluster, Air medal with 4 oak leaf clusters, Presl. citation (2). Mem. Assn. of Bar of City of N.Y., New York County Lawyers, N.Y. State Bar Assn., Columbia Law Alumni Assn., Xavier Alumni Sodality, Phi Delta Phi. Club: K.C. Mem. editorial bd. St. John's Law Rev., 1941-42. Died Oct. 1997.

AOI, JOICHI, manufacturing company executive; b. Okayama, Japan, Mar. 30, 1926; s. Renichiro and Aeko Aoi; m. Shigeyo Ohne; children: Motoko Takahashi, Yuko Morita, Yoji. BS, Tokyo U., 1948. V.p. Toshiba Corp., Tokyo, 1978-81, sr. v.p., 1981-82, exec. v.p., 1982-84, sr. exec. v.p., 1984-87, pres., CEO, 1987-92, chmn. bd., 1992-96, adv. to bd., 1996—. Decorated officer Nat. Order of Merit (France), 1992; recipient Medal with Blue Ribbon, Japanese Govt., 1990. Mem. Japan Assn. Corp. Execs., Keidanren (vice chmn. 1994—). Died Dec. 28, 1996.

ARAPOV, BORIS ALEKSANDROVICH, composer, educator; b. St. Petersburg, Russia, Sept. 12, 1905; s. Alexander Borisovich and Eliszbeta Ivanovna (Merz) A.; m. Tatiana Pavlovna Todorova, Dec. 2, 1933; children: Margarita, Tatiana. Student, conservatoire, Leningrad, 1923-30. Dozent Conservatoir, Leningrad, 1930-40, prof., 1940—; head dept. instrumentiae Conservatoire, Leningrad, 1951-74, compositons dept, 1974. Author: Analysis of Musical Form, 1956 rev. edit. 1982; contbr. articles to profl. jours.; composer 69 musical works, 1928-91. Recipient Order of Red Banner, 1953, People Artist of the Russian Fed. award Verhovnogo Sovietra of Russian Fedn, 1976, Order Lenin's award Verchovnogo Sovicta USSR, 1986. Mem. Union Soviet Composers (sec. 1977). Avocations: traveling, Western European painting. Died January 27, 1992.

ARCARO, EDDIE (GEORGE EDWARD), sports broadcasting journalist, former jockey, horse trainer; b. Cin., Feb. 19, 1916; s. Pasquale and Josephine (Giancola) A.; m. Ruth Arcaro, 1937; children—Carolyn, Bobbie. Profl. jockey, 1931-62; then commentator horse racing ABC. One of 2 jockeys to ride five Kentucky Derby winners; rider of six Preakness Stakes winners, six Belmont Stakes winners, including Whirlaway, 1941, Triple Crown winner Citation, 1948; only rider to win 2 Triple Crowns. Died Nov. 15, 1997.

ARCHAMBAULT, BENNETT, corporate executive; b. Oakland, Calif.; s. Albert Joseph and May (Smales) A.; m. Margaret Henrietta Morgan; children: Suzanne Morgan, Michele Lorraine, Steven Bennett. Student, Ga. Inst. Tech.; S.B., Mass. Inst. Tech.; LLD (hon.), Ill. Inst. Tech. V.p., gen. mgr. M.W. Kellogg Co., N.Y.C., 1945-54; pres. Stewart-Warner Corp., Chgo., 1954-87; chmn. bd. Stewart-Warner Corp., 1959-90, chmn. emeritus, 1990—; pres. The Archambault Corp., 1982—; former dep. chmn. bd. BTR Inc.; former dir. Kemper Corp., Lumbermen's Mutual Casualty Ins. Co., Am. Motorists Ins. Co., Am. Mfrs. Ins., Harris Trust and Savs. Bank, Harris Bancorp Inc., Trans Union Corp., Fed. Kemper Ins. Co., Lawter Internat., Inc. Life trustee Ill. Inst. Tech. and Mus. Sci. and Industry; bd. dirs. Terra Found. for the Arts, Citizens Against Govt. Waste; hon. mem. Corp. Devel. Com. MIT; former mem. adv. coun. grad. sch. mgmt. Northwestern U., exec. com. Grace Commn. (the Pres.'s Pvt. Sector Survey on Cost Control); former chmn. Ill. Rep. Fin. Com.; former chmn., pres. Ill. Mfrs. Assn.; former dir., regional v.p., mem. exec. com., nominating com. NAM; mem. bd. govs. United Rep. Fund Ill. Decorated Medal Merit U.S.; His Majesty's Medal for Service in Cause of Freedom (Gr. Britain). Mem. Chgo. Club, Econ. Club, Exec. Club, MIT Club (Chgo.), Racquet Club, Saddle & Cycle Club, Glen View Club, Westmoreland Country Club, Fairbanks Ranch Country Club, Comml. Club, L.A. Country Club, Lambda Chi Alpha, Tau Beta Pi. Died July 7, 1996.

ARCHER, KENNETH DAVIDSON, lawyer, insurance executive; b. Chgo., Feb. 15, 1940; s. Martin A. and Madeline D. (Davidson) A.; m. Barbara Elizabeth Clark, Aug. 22, 1970; children: Matthew Clark, Anthony Miles. B.S. with honors, U. Ill., 1961; J.D. cum laude, Harvard U., 1965. Bar: N.Y. State 1966, Ill. 1976. Assoc. firm Shearman & Sterling, N.Y.C., 1965-70; assoc. counsel GAF Corp., N.Y.C., 1970-73; asst. counsel Cerro Corp., Chgo., 1973-75; v.p., gen. counsel, sec. Cerro Corp., 1975-76; v.p. law and adminstrn., sec. Orange and Rockland Utilities, Inc., Pearl River, N.Y., 1976-80; sr. v.p. law and adminstrn., sec. Orange and Rockland Utilities, Inc., 1980-87; sr. v.p., gen. counsel, sec. Home Life Ins. Co., N.Y.C., 1987-92. Bd. dirs. Chgo. Lyric Opera Guild, 1975-76, Bergen Community Coll. Found., 1984-86; trustee Pascack Valley Hosp., Westwood, N.J., 1979-86, pres. bd. trustees, 1981-83; mem. exec. bd. Bergen County council Boy Scouts Am., 1983-86. Mem. ABA, N.Y. State Bar Assn., Assn. of Bar of City of N.Y., Am. Soc. Corp. Secs., Assn. Life Ins. Counsel (legis. com.). Clubs: University, India House (N.Y.C.); Hackensack Golf (Oradell, N.J.); Metropolitan (Washington). Died Apr. 29, 1994.

ARCHER, SYDNEY, chemistry educator; b. N.Y.C., Jan. 23, 1917; s. Samuel and Eva (Cohen) A.; m. Therese Neiman, Jan. 26, 1946; children: Eve, David, Daniel. B.A., U. Wis., 1937; Ph.D., Pa. State U., 1940. Chemist, dir. chemistry div. Sterling-Winthrop Research Inst., Rensselaer, N.Y., 1943-68, assoc. dir., v.p., 1968-73; research prof. medicinal chemistry Rensselaer Poly. Inst., Troy, N.Y., 1973—, dean sch. sci., 1980-85; cons. WHO, Geneva, 1975-85; mem. exec. com. Com. on Problems of Drug Dependence, 1980-84; mem. extramural sci. adv. bd. Nat. Inst. on Drug Abuse, 1991-92. Bd. editors: Medicinal Chemistry Rev., 1981-92. Fellow AAAS; mem. Am. Chem. Soc. (Medicinal Chemistry award 1968), Chem. Soc. (London) (1968), Am. Soc. for Pharmacology and Exptl. Therapeutics, Sigma Xi. DIED 08/22/96. .

ARENA, JAY M., pediatrician, educator; b. Clarksburg, W.Va., Mar. 3, 1909; s. Anthony M. and Rose (Sandy) A.; m. Pauline Elizabeth Monteith, July 10, 1931; children—Rosanne (Mrs. Oscar Green), Jay Morris Jr., Carolyn Jean (Mrs. Harry C. Wood), Mary Margaret (Mrs. Robert Beeching), Katherine (Mrs. Arthur Prosser), Pauline (Mrs. William Myers), Regina (Mrs. Needham Smith). B.A., W.Va. U., 1930; M.D., Duke U., 1932. Intern Strong Meml. Hosp., Rochester, N.Y., 1932, Johns Hopkins Hosp., 1932-33; asst. resident Duke Hosp., 1933-34, resident, 1934-35; instr. pediatrics Vanderbilt U., 1936; asst. prof. pediatrics Duke Hosp., 1936-50, asso. prof., 1951-56, prof., 1956—, prof. community health scis., 1970—; dir. Poison Control Center, 1953—; Duke Arena Chair in pediat. pharmacology and toxicology, 1993; editorial bds. Council Family Health, Clin. Pediatrics, Nutrition Today, Pediatric News, Highlights; mem. adv. bd. Pediatrics Annals.; Chmn. Z 66 standards com. Nat. Standards Inst., 1969—; mem. com. U.S. Consumer Products Safety Commn., 1976-78; pres. Am. Assn. Poison Controls Centers, 1968-70. Author: The Compleat Pediatrician, 1969, (with James W. Hardin) Human Poisoning from Native and Cultivated Plants, 1969, 2d edit., 1973, Poisoning: Toxicology-Symptoms-Treatments, 5th edit, 1986, Dangers to Children and Youth, 1971, (with Miriam Settle) Child Safety is No Accident, 1978, 2d rev. edit. 1987, (with Barbara Echols) The Common Sense Guide to Good Eating, 1978, Davison of Duke: His Reminiscences, 1980, also numerous articles on poisoning and varied pediatric subjects. Recipient Disting. Med. Alumnus award W.Va. U. Sch. Medicine, 1988. Mem. Am. Acad. Pediatrics (exec. bd. 1965-71, pres. 1971-72, Jacobi award 1983), Am. Pediatric Soc., Phi Beta Kappa, Sigma Xi, Alpha Omega Alpha.

ARENDALL, CHARLES BAKER, JR., lawyer; b. Portsmouth, Va., Feb. 13, 1915; s. Charles B. and Kate (Peacock) A.; m. Nan Eager Boone, Oct. 26, 1944; children—Nan Boone McGinley, Lawrence Barclay Manley, Kathryn Baker Weller, Elizabeth Charles Tilney. A.B., U. Richmond, 1935; LL.B. cum laude, Harvard, 1938. Bar: Ala. bar 1938. Asso. firm Smith & Johnston, Mobile, 1938-41; mem. firm Hand, Arendall, Bedsole, Greaves & Johnston (and predecessor), Mobile, 1941-97; Adv. bd. Cumberland Law Sch., Samford U. Trustee Mobile Coll. Fellow Am. Coll. Trial Lawyers; mem. Internat., Am., Ala., Inter-Am., Mobile bar assns., Am. Judicature Soc., Assn. Bar City N.Y., Internat. Assn. Ins. Counsel, Am. Law Inst., Assn. Railroad Trial Counsel, Omicron Delta Kappa, Pi Delta Epsilon, Alpha Psi Omega, Kappa Sigma. Baptist. Clubs: Athelstan, Lakewood, Country. Home: Point Clear Ala. Deceased.

ARENSBERG, CONRAD MAYNADIER, anthropologist, sociologist; b. Pitts., Sept. 12, 1910; s. Charles F. C. and Emily Wright (Maynadier) A.; m. Vivian Garrison, July 14, 1974; children—Emily Maynadier, Margaret Farrell, Cornelius Wright. A.B., Harvard U., 1931, Ph.D., 1934. Jr. fellow Harvard U., 1934-37; with indsl. relations sect. Mass. Inst. Tech., 1937-40; chmn., organizer dept. sociology and anthropology Bklyn. Coll., 1940-42; chmn. sociology Barnard Coll., 1946-50; cons. research in Ruhr, Socialforschungstelle, Dortmund, Germany, 1950-51; research dir. UNESCO

Inst. Social Scis., Cologne, 1952; prof. anthropology Columbia U., 1953—; co-dir. (with Alan Lomax) Cantometrics-Choreometrics Project, 1969-79. Author: Irish Countryman, 1936, Family and Community in Ireland, 1940, Measuring Human Relations, (with Eliot D. Chapple), 1942; editor: Human Orgn, 1946-52, Am. Anthropol. Assn. Manual for Point 4 Workers, 1953, Indsl. Relations Research Assn. Summary Human Relations Research, 1955, (with Karl Polanyi) Trade and Markets in the Early Empires, 1957, (with Solon T. Kimball) Culture and Community, 1965, (with Arthur Niehoff) Introducing Social Change, 1964. Served from capt. to maj. AUS, 1943-45. Mem. Soc. Applied Anthropology (founder), Am. Anthrop. Assn. (pres. 1979-80). Episcopalian. Clubs: Century (N.Y.C.); St. Botolph (Boston). Died Feb. 10, 1997.

ARENT, LORENE LUCILLE, retired secondary education educator; b. Gordon, Nebr., Aug. 6, 1927; d. Phillip Clarence and Louise Linda (Jones) A. BA, Wayne State Coll., 1949; MA, No. U. of Colo., 1956. Cert. tchr., Nebr. Home econs., English tchr. Oakdale (Nebr.) Pub. Schs., 1949-51, Rising City (Nebr.) Pub. Schs., 1951-52; home econs. and geography tchr. Wisner (Nebr.) Pub. Schs., 1952-53; home econs. and English tchr. Wausa (Nebr.) Pub. Schs., 1954-91, ret., 1991. Treas. Congl. United Ch. of Christ Women's Fellowship; sec. Bd. Christian Edn. Mem. NEA, Nebr. State Edn. Assn., Am. Home Econs. Assn., Wausa Edn. Assn. (treas., pres.), Am. Vocat. Assn. (asst. grand warden 1983), Order of Eastern Star (worthy matron 1983-84), Delta Kappa Gamma (treas. 1984-90), Sigma Tau Delta (Pi Beta chpt. 1948), Pi Gamma Mu. Republican. Congregationalist. Avocations: knitting and hand works, gardening, bowling, reading.

ARION, GEORGES JULIEN, retired commercial organization executive; b. Brussels, Aug. 5, 1920; s. Léon Philippe Arion and Marguerite Claeys; m. Suzanne Lapierre de Coussemaker, Aug. 12, 1954; children: Philippe, Pierre. Grad. comml. engr., U. Brussels, 1945; master practitioner, N.Y. Tng. Inst. for NLP, 1990. Asst. sales mgr. L'Oréal, Brussels, 1947; dep. sec. gen. Internat. Orgn. Employers, Brussels, 1948; founder, hon. pres. Etablissements G. Arion S.A., Brussels, 1948-88, Environ. Improvement S.A., Brussels, 1972-88; co-founder, dir. Ctr. Internat. d'Etude du Lindane, Brussels, 1976; founder-pres. Immobiliere Financiere Arion S.A., Brussels, 1982-97; founder Parimo S.A., 1989-97, G. Arion a cie S.C.A., 1992-97. Author poems. Avocations: painting, music, animation of organizations, human sciences. Mem. Soc. Royale d'Economie Politique de Belgique. Died Sept. 23, 1997.

ARMBRECHT, WILLIAM H., lawyer, business executive; b. Mobile, Ala., Nov. 1, 1908; s. William H. and Anna Bell (Paterson) A.; m. Katherine Little, Oct. 8, 1927; children: William H. III, Katherine, Anna Bell, Conrad Paterson, Clara. LL.B., U. Ala., 1932. Bar: Ala. 1932. Practice law Mobile, 1932—; partner Armbrecht, Jackson, DeMouy, Crowe, Holmes & Reeves; dir. emeritus AmSouth Bank N.A. of Ala. Mem. Am. Bar Assn., Ala. Bar Assn., Mobile Bar Assn. (pres. 1954), C. of C., Phi Delta Phi, Alpha Tau Omega. Episcopalian (trustee). Clubs: Kiwanis, Lakewood Country (Point Clear, Ala.); Mobile Country, Athelstan, Propeller, Bienville, Internat. Trade (Mobile).

ARMSTRONG, JOHN KREMER, lawyer, artist; b. Washington, Apr. 15, 1934; s. Stuart Morton and Marion Louise (Kreutzer) A.; m. A.M.E. (Mieke) van Haersma Buma, Apr. 1963; children: Marca Carine van Heloma, Jeb Stuart. BA with honors, Haverford Coll., 1956; postgrad., U. Delhi, 1956-57; LLB, Yale U., 1960. Bar: N.Y. 1961. Assoc. Davies, Hardy and Schenck, N.Y.C., 1960-68; ptnr. Davies, Hardy, Ives and Lawther, N.Y.C., 1968-72, Armstrong and Ulrich, N.Y.C., 1973-81, Cole and Deitz, N.Y.C., 1981-85, Carter, Ledyard & Milburn, N.Y.C., 1985—; lectr. Rotary Club, 1995-96, Am. Law Inst./ABA, 1995, 96, Nat. Health Lawyers Assn., 1996-97. Author: (with others) The Grey Market, 1994; contbr. articles to law revs.; works exhibited N.Y.C., Salisbury and Bar Harbor, Maine; All-ABA, Nat. Health Lawyers Assn., 1996, 97. Trustee Bklyn. Bot. Garden, chmn. bd., 1982-89; trustee Westchester Land Trust, 1991—, Aitken Neurosci. Inst., 1995—; bd. dirs. Netherlands-Am. Amity Trust, 1992-94; bd. regents L.I. Coll. Hosp., 1968-72; fellow Rotary Found., 1956-67. Mem. ABA, N.Y. State Bar Assn. (co-chmn. com. health law 1987-89), Pilgrims Soc., Ch. Club of N.Y. (trustee 1990-94, sec. 1991-94), Sharon Country Club, The Down Town Assn., Phi Beta Kappa. Died Apr. 5, 1997.

ARN, KENNETH DALE, physician, city official; b. Dayton, Ohio, July 19, 1921; s. Elmer R. and Minna Marie (Wannagat) A.; m. Vivien Rose Fontini, Sept. 24, 1966; children—Christine H. Hulme, Laura P. Hafstad, Kevin D., Kimmel R. B.A., Miami U., Oxford, Ohio, 1943; M.D., U. Mich., 1946. Intern Miami Valley Hosp., Dayton, Ohio, 1947-48; resident in pathology U. Mich., 1948-49, fellow in renal research, 1949-50; fellow in internal medicine Cleve. Clinic, 1950-52; pvt. practice specializing in internal medicine, pub. health and vocat. rehab. Dayton, 1952-97; commr. of health City of Oakwood, Ohio, 1953-97; assoc. clin. prof. medicine Wright State U., 1975-97; mem. staffs Kettering Med. Ctr., Dayton, Miami Valley Hosp.; adj. assoc. prof. edn. Wright State U.; field med. cons. Bur. Vocat. Rehab., 1958-97, Bur. Svcs. to Blind, 1975-97; med. dir. Ohio Rehab. Svcs. Commn., 1979-87; mem. Pres.'s Com. on Employment of Handicapped, 1971-97; chmn. med. adv. com. Goodwill Industries, 1960-75, chmn. bd. trustees 1985-87, chmn. rehab. com. 1987-97; mem., chmn. lay adv. com. vocat. edn. Dayton Pub. Schs., 1973-82; exec. com. Gov.'s Com. on Employment Handicapped; bd. dirs. Vis. Nurses Assn. Greater Dayton; chmn. profl. adv. com. Combined Gen. Health Dist. Montgomery County. Trustee Luth. Social Svc. of Miami Valley, 1982-88. Named City of Dayton's Outstanding Young Man, Jr. C. of C., 1957; 1 of 5 Outstanding Young Men of State, Ohio Jr. C. of C., 1958; Physician of Yr., Pres.'s Com. on Employment of Handicapped, 1971; Bishop's medal for meritorious service Miami U., 1972. Mem. AMA, Ohio Med. Assn., Montgomery County Med. Soc. (chmn. com. on diabetic detection 1955-65, chmn. polio com. 1954-58), Nat. Rehab. Assn., Am. Diabetes Assn., Am. Profl. Practice Assn., Am. Heart Assn., Am. Pub. Health Assn., Ohio Pub. Health Assn., Aerospace Med. Assn., Fraternal Order Police, Dayton Country Club, Kiwanis, Royal Order Jesters, Masons (past potentate), Shriners, K.T., Scottish Rite (33 deg.), Nu Sigma Nu, Sigma Chi. Lutheran. Died Nov. 1997.

ARNDT, HELMUT (HOYER), economics scientist, educator; b. Königsberg, Germany, May 11, 1911; s. Gustav Adolf and Louise (Zabeler) A.; children: Claudia, Rolf; m. Maria Haendcke-Hoppe, June 4, 1992. JD, U. Marburg, Germany, 1933; D in Polit. Sci., U. Marburg, 1944; D honoris causa, U. Innsbruck, Austria, 1970. Clk. Rawack & Grünfeld, Berlin, 1937-40, Treuhand A.G., Mannheim, Germany, 1943-45; assoc. prof. U. Marburg, 1946-52; prof. U. Istanbul, Turkey, 1953-54, U. Darmstadt, Fed. Republic Germany, 1954-57; prof. Free U. Berlin, 1957-97, now prof. emeritus; vis. prof. Maxwell Grad. Sch., U. Syracuse, N.Y., 1950-51, U. Heidelberg, Fed. Republic Germany, 1963, U. Leningrad, USSR, 1969, U. South Fla., St. Petersburg, 1973-74; UNESCO adviser U. Istanbul, Turkey, 1970; Leverhulme fellow Oxford (Eng.) U., 1976-77. Author: Capitalism-Socialism, 1976, Economic Power, 1980, Economic Theory vs. Economic Reality, 1984, Full Employment, 1984, Competitive Process, 1986, Textbook of Economic Evolution, 1994, Unemployment in the Market Economy, 1996; editor: On Economic Concentration, 1971. Mem. Am. Econ. Assn., Royal Econ. Soc., European Econ. Assn. Died Oct. 27, 1997.

ARNESON, HAROLD ELIAS GRANT, manufacturing engineer, consultant; b. Mpls., Dec. 18, 1925; s. Theodore John and Ella Marie (Eliason) A.; m. Lorna May Mullen, Nov. 25, 1950 (dec. May 1991); 1 child, Grant. Student, U. Minn. Inst. Tech., 1943-46. Ptnr. Profl. Instruments Co., Mpls., 1947-77; cons. Precision Engring., Ft. Myers Beach, Fla., 1977-95; vis. lectr. Sa388 Paulo U., Saú Carlos U., Santa Catarina U., Brazil, 1988, MIT, Cambridge, Mass., 1994. Patentee in field. With USAF, 1943-45. Grantee UN Devel. Program, 1988. Mem. AAAS, Am. Soc. Precision Engrs., Soc. Mfg. Engrs. Home: Fort Myers Beach Fla. Died May 8, 1995.

ARNOLD, SHEILA, former state legislator; b. N.Y.C., Jan. 15, 1929; d. Michael and Eileen (Lynch) Keddy; coll. courses; m. George Longan Arnold, Nov. 12, 1960; 1 child, Peter; 1 child by previous marriage, Michael C. Young (dec.); stepchildren: Drew, George Longan, Joe. Mem. Wyo. Ho. of Reps., 1978-93, vice chmn. Laramie Regional Airport Bd. Former mem., sec. Wyo. Land Use Adv. Coms.; past pres. Dem. Women's Club, Laramie; past chmn. Albany County Dem. Party; past mem. Dem. State Com.; mem. adv. bd. Wyo. Home Health Care; former mem. Nat. Conf. State Legislatures Com. on Fiscal Affairs and Oversight Com. Recipient Spl. Recognition award from Developmentally Disabled Citizens of Wyo., 1985. Mem. Laramie Area C. of C. (pres. 1982; Top Hand award 1977), LWV (Laramie bd. dirs. 1993-94), Internat. Platform Assn., Faculty Women's Club (past pres.), VFW Ladies Aux. (past pres. Post 2221), Zonta (Laramie bd. dirs.), Laramie Women's Club.

ARNOLD, WILLIAM STRANG, lawyer; b. Yonkers, N.Y., Feb. 5, 1921; s. L.J. and Hazel (Strang) A.; children—Patricia (Mrs. Henry King), Richard L. A.B., U. Ark., 1942, J.D., 1947; LL.M., Columbia, 1948. Bar: Ark, bar 1947. Practice in Crossett and Hamburg, 1948-95; sr. partner Arnold, Hamilton & Streetman.; bd. dirs. First Nat. Bank of Crossett, Ashley County Abstract Co. Mem. Ark. Commn. on Uniform State Laws, Ark. Jud. Disability and Discipline Com., 1989-95; chmn. Ark. Code Rev. Commn., 1983-95. Mem. ABA, Ark. Bar Assn. (past pres.), Am. Coll. Estate and Trust Counsel, Am. Coll. Trial Lawyers, Am. Judicature Soc. Home: Crossett Ark. Died Oct.14, 1995.

ARNSTEIN, SHERRY PHYLLIS, health care executive; b. N.Y.C., Jan. 11, 1930; m. George E. Arnstein, June 22, 1951; BS, UCLA, 1951; MS Communications, Am. U., 1963, DLH honoris causa U. Scis. & Osteopathic Medicine, 1993; LLD (hon.) Phila. Coll. Osteopathic Medicine, 1995; postgrad. in systems dynamics MIT, summer 1976. Washington editor Current mag., 1961-63; staff cons. Pres. Com. on Juvenile Delinquency, 1963-65; spl. asst. to asst. sec. HEW, 1965-67; chief citizen participation advisor Model Cities Adminstrn., HUD, 1967-68; pub. policy cons., Washington, 1968-75; sr. research fellow HHS, Washington, 1975-78; v.p. govt. rels. Nat. Health Coun., Inc., Washington, 1978-85; exec. dir. Am. Assn. Colls. Osteo. Medicine, 1985-95; pres., CEO Arnstein & Assocs., Washington, 1995-97. Author: (with Alexander Christakis) Perspectives on Technology Assessment, 1975; (with Laurence Haspel) A Perspective from Osteopathic Medical Schools; editor: Government Relations Handbook Series, 1979-85, Washington Report Series, 1985. mem. editorial bd. Tech. Assessment Update, 1975-78, The Bureaucrat, 1975-83, Pub. Adminstrn. Rev., 1978-83, Health Mgmt. Quar., 1985; contbr. articles to profl. jours. Bd. dirs. Youth Policy Inst. Recipient Phillips medal Ohio U. Pub. Svcs., 1993. Mem. Cosmos Club (program com.), Capital Hill Club, Nat. Press Club (Washington). Died Jan. 19, 1997; interred Shalom Memorial Park. Home: Washington D.C.

ARONOVITZ, SIDNEY M., federal judge; b. Key West, Fla., June 20, 1920; s. Charles and Ethel (Holtsberg) A.; m. Elinore Richman, Mar. 24, 1943; children—Elaine, Tod, Karen. BA with honors, U. Fla., 1942, JD with honors, 1943. Bar: Fla. 1943. Ptnr. Aronovitz & Haverfield, Miami, 1946-58; sole practice Miami, 1958-61; sr. ptnr. Aronovitz, Silver & Scher, Miami, 1961-68, Aronovitz, Zinn & Silver, Miami, 1968-70, Aronovitz, Silver & Booth, Miami, 1970-76; judge U.S. Dist. Ct. (so. dist.) Fla., 1976—. Commr., City of Miami, 1962-66, vice-mayor, 1965. Served with U.S. Army. Mem. ABA, Am. Judicature Soc., Fla. Bar Assn., Dade County Bar Assn. Died Jan. 8, 1997.

ARROL, JOHN, corporate executive; b. Scotland, Aug. 6, 1923; came to U.S., 1924, naturalized, 1934; s. William and Isabella (Gordon) A.; m. Jane Trice, June 18, 1949 (dec. Sept. 1995); children: Robert, Nancy, David, William. BS in Bus. Adminstrn, Xavier U., 1953; MA, Vanderbilt U., 1964. Cost supr. Ford Motor Co., 1950-57; planning supr. Curtiss Wright Corp., 1957-58; with Avco Corp., 1958-64, asst. controller, 1962-64; corp. controller Globe-Union, Inc., Milw., 1964-70, v.p., controller, 1970-72, chief fin. officer, 1972-73; sr. v.p. finance Rucker Co., Oakland, Calif., 1973-77, NL Industries-Petroleum Services, Oakland, 1977-78; v.p., chief fin. officer, dir. Gardner-Denver Co., Dallas, 1978-79; v.p. fin. and adminstrn. Systron Donner Corp., Concord, Calif., 1980-81, exec. v.p., 1982; chmn., CEO, 1983-86; gen. ptnr. Thorn EMI Venture Fund Ltd., 1983-94; vice chmn. On-Site Technology Inc., Campbell, Calif., 1988-91, Nat. Water Mgmt. Corp., San Jose, Calif., 1988-90; CEO Personics, Inc., 1990-91; bd. dirs. Optical Spltys. Inc., Fremont, Calif., Agts. Referral Group, Inc., Longwood, Fla., Music Writer, Los Gatos, Calif., ERA Advantage Group, Fla., chmn., Longwood; adviser to bd. dirs. Personics Inc., Redwood City, Calif., 1986-91, Gamma Link, Palo Alto, Calif., 1986-96, Life Point Sys. Inc., New Orleans, 1988-96, Judson Steel Co., 1976-77; instr. cost acctg. U. Tenn., 1960-62; instr. bus. adminstrn. Ind. U., 1964; adv. bd. Fin. Ctr. Bank, San Francisco, 1983-92. Author: A Brief Encounter, 1995, First Love: A Rascal at Sea, 1995, Discord in Richland County, 1995, I Love to Dance, 1995, Memories of Mother, 1995, Sir William Arrol, 1995, A Labor Day Bear-Hug, 1995, The Arrol, Arroll, and Arrell Families, 1994, Many Paths, 3 vol. memoirs, 1996, The China Trade, 1996, Remembrances of Jane, 1996, Across Europe In Search of Solace, 1996. Bd. dirs. Dallas Civic Opera, Milw. chpt. ARC; mem. adv. council Sch. Bus., San Francisco State U., 1981-94; mem. adv. bd. Mt. Diablo chpt. Boy Scouts Am., Walnut Creek, Calif., 1983-94; bd. dirs. Calif. Found. for Retarded, 1985-96. Mem. Nat. Assn. Accts., Fin. Execs. Inst., Round Hill Country Club (Alamo, Calif.). Home: Danville Calif. Deceased, Aug. 31, 1996.

ASADE, JIM (JAMES W. ASSAD), director, actor; b. Denbo, Pa., Sept. 12, 1930; s. Rene (Seghi) Assad. MA in Psychology, U. W.Va., 1958; MA in Theater, U. Mo., 1967; student, Royal Acad. Dramatic Art, London. Artistic dir. Mo. Vanguard Theatre, Pa. Arts Co.; dir. theater Avila Coll., Kansas City, Mo., 1970-73; dir. arts co. Pa. State U., University Park, 1978-79; asst. dir. Mo. Repertory Theatre, Kansas City, 1979-80; co-dir. M.F.A. acting program U. Mo., Kansas City, 1979-80; founder, exec. and artistic dir. Am. Heartland Theatre, 1987—. Actor numerous stage appearances including Rumpelstiltskin, Hamlet, Enrico IV, Tartuffe, Becket, The Hasty Heart, The Corn Is Green, The Medium, (film) In Cold Blood, 1968, TV appearances include Hamlet, Arts in Kansas City, Watermelon Boats; dir. numerous stage plays including The Cherry Orchard, 1976, Wings, 1976, The Shadow Box, 1976, Old Times, 1976, The Rainmaker, 1980, Six Characters in Search of an Author, 1980, Nicholas Nickleby (Citation award Ho. of Reps.), 1983, The Death of Joe Egg, 1985, Romeo and Juliet, 1985, Die Kluge, 1985, Hansel and Gretel, 1985, Crimes of the Heart, 1985. Kansas City Trust and Found. grantee. Mem. Actors' Equity Assn., Soc. Stage Dirs. and Choreographers, Am. Guild Mus. Artists, Alpha Psi Omega, Pi Sigma Phi. Died Apr. 14, 1992.

ASCIONE, ALFRED MICHAEL, judge; b. N.Y.C., July 16, 1915; s. Antonio and Annunziata Ascione; m. Joan Petra, March 22, 1942; children: Diane, Joseph. LLB, St. John's Coll., 1940. Bar: N.Y. 1941.

Sole practice N.Y.C., 1941-57; sec. to judge City Ct., N.Y.C., 1946-50; tax commr. Tax Commn., City of N.Y., 1954-57; justice Mcpl. Ct. N.Y.C., 1958-62, Civil Ct. of City of N.Y., 1962-66, N.Y. State Supreme Ct., N.Y.C., 1967—; bd. 1st Jud. Dept., N.Y. State Supreme Ct. Legis. editor St. John's Coll. Law Rev., 1940. Pres. emeritus East Harlem Civic Assn.; former trustee Holy Rosary Roman Cath. Ch.; trustee St. Joseph's Roman Cath. Ch. Served as sgt. USAF, 1942-45. Recipient Rapallo award Columbian Lawyers Assn., 1980. Mem. Am. Justinian Assn. (exec. sec.), Columbian Lawyers Assn. (Rapallo award 1980), N.Y.C. Assn. Supreme Ct. Justices (v.p.), St. John's Law Sch. Alumni Assn. (bd. dirs. 1959—, v.p. 1974-76, pres. 1976-78). Deceased.

ASHBURN, DON RICHARD, retired baseball player, broadcaster; b. Tilden, Nebr., Mar. 19, 1927. Baseball player Phila. Phillies, 1948-59, Chgo. Cubs, 1960-61, N.Y. Mets, 1962; radio broadcaster WOGL-AM, Phila., WPHL-TV, Phila. Named to Baseball Hall Fame, 1995; recipient Nat. League Batting Title, 1955, 58. Died Sept. 9, 1997.

ASHER, FREDERICK, former mail order company executive; b. Chgo., Mar. 6, 1915; s. Louis Eller and Alice (Wormser) A.; m. Frances Reitler, June 30, 1938; children—Frederick Matheson, Alice, Deborah Helene. B.A. cum laude, Dartmouth, 1937; student, Coll. Agr. U. Wis., 1938. Gen. mgr. Louis G. Cowan, Chgo., 1938-41; advt. mgr. Consol. Book Publ. Co., Chgo., 1945-50; pres. Frederick Asher, Inc. (advt.), Chgo., 1950-55, John Plain & Co. (mail order), Chgo., 1955-66; pres., chief exec. officer John Plain & Co. (mail order), 1966-72, Bellwether Devel. Corp., Highland Park, Ill., 1972-84; bd. dirs. Harris Bank Glencoe, Ill., 1958-73, chmn., 1974-95, chmn. emeritus, 1995—. Mem. Chgo. exec. com. Anti-Defamation League, 1952-56; mem. budget reviewing com. Community Fund Chgo., 1957-59; trustee Highland Park Hosp., 1950-72, bd. mgr., 1970-72; bd. dirs. Highland Park Community Chest, 1951-68, pres., chmn., 1955-57; bd. dirs. Immigrants' Service League, 1951-68, pres., 1955-56; bd. dirs. Highland Park Civic Assn., 1952-56, Scholarship and Guidance Assn., 1953-55; adminstrv. bd. Travelers Aid Soc. Chgo.; trustee Lake Forest (Ill.) Acad., 1968-73, 83-87, life trustee, 1992—. Served with AUS, 1944-45. Mem. Mail Order Assn. Am. (dir. 1958-69), Dartmouth Club Chgo. (dir. 1965-67), Nat. Planning Assn. (mem. nat. council 1967-69). Clubs: Mid-America (Chgo.); Lake Shore Country (Glencoe, Ill.); Ojai (Calif.) Valley Country. DIED 09/25/96. .

ASHIN, MARK, English language educator; b. N.Y.C., Mar. 1, 1917; s. Max and Zina (Rudin) A.; m. Alice Elaine Froyd, Jan. 9, 1949; 1 son, Paul. B.A., U. Chgo., 1937, M.A., 1938, Ph.D., 1950. Instr. Mich. State Coll., East Lansing, 1938-41; instr. U. Chgo., 1947-51, asst. prof., 1951-57, assoc. prof., 1957-67, prof. English, 1967-87, prof. emeritus, 1987—; vis. prof. Rochester U., 1961, NYU, 1964; dir. NDEA Special Inst. for Advanced Study in English, 1968; dir. Spl. Summer Session Disadvantaged Students, U. Chgo., 1970, sec. of faculties, 1980—. Served to 2d lt. OSS AUS, 1943-46. Recipient Quantrell Distinguished Teaching award U. Chgo., 1954. DIED 09/06/97. .

ASHMORE, HARRY SCOTT, editor, foundation executive; b. Greenville, S.C., July 27, 1916; s. William Green and Nancy Elizabeth (Scott) A.; m. Barbara Edith Laier, June 2, 1940; 1 dau., Anne Rogers. B.S., Clemson Coll., 1937, LLD (hon.), 1988; Nieman fellow journalism, Harvard, 1941-42; LL.D., Oberlin Coll., 1958, Grinnell Coll., 1963, U. Ark., 1972. Reporter-columnist Greenville (S.C.) Piedmont, 1937-39; polit. writer Greenville News and Charlotte (N.C.) News, 1939-41; asso. editor Charlotte News, 1945-47, editor, 1947; editor editorial page Ark. Gazette, Little Rock, 1947; exec. editor Ark. Gazette, 1948-59, on leave to serve as asst. Stevenson for presdl. campaign, 1955-56; cons. Center for Study Democratic Instns., Fund for Republic, 1959-60; editor in chief Ency. Brit., 1960-63; editor Brit. Perspectives, 1964-68; sr. fellow Center for Study Dem. Instns., 1959-75; exec. v.p., 1967-69, pres., 1969-74; sr. fellow in communications Duke, 1973-74; Howard R. Marsh vis. prof. U. Mich., 1975. Author: The Negro and the Schools, 1954, An Epitaph for Dixie, 1957, The Other Side of Jordan, 1960, The Man in the Middle, 1966, (with William C. Baggs) Mission to Hanoi, 1968, Fear in the Air, 1973, Arkansas: A Bicentennial History, 1977, Hearts and Minds: The Anatomy of Racism from Roosevelt to Reagan, 1982, Unseasonable Truths: The Life of Robert Maynard Hutchins, 1989, Civil Rights and Wrongs: A Memoir of race and Politics, 1994; editor: The William O. Douglas Inquiry, 1978. Bd. dirs. Nat. Com. for an Effective Congress, 1966—; vice chmn. adv. council Am. Civil Liberties Union, 1970-84; bd. dirs. Fund for Republic, 1954-79. Served from 2d lt. to lt. col. 95th Inf. Div. AUS, 1942-45; mem. War Dept. Gen. Staff 1945. Decorated citation for spl. duty as chief staff Task Force Faith, Ruhr Pocket, 1945; Bronze Star with two oak leaf clusters; recipient Sidney Hillman award, 1957; Pulitzer Prize, editorial writing, 1958; Freedom House award, 1958; Lillian Smith award, 1982; Robert F. Kennedy award for Lifetime Achievement, 1996. Home: Valle Verde D-502 900 Calle de los Amigos Santa Barbara CA 93105 Died Jan. 1998.

ASIMOV, STANLEY, newspaper executive; b. Bklyn., July 25, 1929; s. Judah and Anna Rachel (Berman) A.; m. Ruth Sheinaus, Nov. 26, 1955; children—Daniel, Eric, Nanette. B.A., NYU, 1951; M.S. in Journalism, Columbia U., 1952. Reporter, copy editor Newsday, L.I., N.Y., 1952-57, asst. night city editor, 1957-60, night city editor, 1960-62, news editor, 1962-67, asst. mng. editor, 1967-69, asst. to pub., 1969-71, asst. pub., 1971-79, v.p. devel., 1979-86, v.p. editorial adminstrn., 1986—; instr. journalism NYU, N.Y.C., 1954-60; instr. Columbia U. Grad. Sch. Journalism, N.Y.C., 1967-74, adj. asst. prof., 1974-76, adj. assoc. prof., 1976-77; Pulitzer Prize juror, 1979-80. Mem. N.Y. State Publishers Assn. (dir. 1974-77), N.Y. Newspapers Found. (trustee 1979-82, 89—, vice chmn. 1982-87, chmn. 1987-89), Am. Newspaper Publishers Assn. (market research com. 1980-84, industry affairs com. 1984-86, circulation and readership com. 1987-88), Columbia U. Grad. Sch. Journalism Alumni Assn. (pres. 1973-75, Alumni Award, 1980), Atex Newspaper Users Group (pres. 1976-77). Home: Roslyn Heights N.Y. DIED 08/16/95. .

ASPIN, LES, former U.S. secretary of defense, former congressman; b. Milwaukee, Wis., July 21, 1938; s. Leslie and Marie (Orth) A. B.A. summa cum laude, Yale U., 1960; M.A., Oxford (Eng.) U., 1962; Ph.D., MIT, 1965. Mem. staff Sen. William Proxmire, 1960, campaign dir., 1964; staff asst. to Walter Heller; chmn. Pres. Kennedy's Council Econ. Advisers, 1963; mem. 92d-102d Congresses from 1st Wis. dist., Washington, D.C., 1971-93; sec. Dept. Defense, Washington, 1993. Served to capt. AUS, 1966-68. Mem. Jr. C. of C., Am. Legion, Phi Beta Kappa. Episcopalian. Home: Washington D.C. DIED 05/21/95. .

ATCHLEY, DANA WINSLOW, JR., electronics manufacturing company executive; b. N.Y.C., Oct. 27, 1917; s. Dana Winslow and Mary Cornelia (Phister) A.; m. Barbara Welch, Aug. 26, 1939 (div. 1953); children: Dana Winslow III, Mary Babcock, Elizabeth Ross, Sarah Ross; m. Barbara Standish Payne, May 1, 1954; children: Marion Woodward, Abigail Adams (dec.), Cornelia Phister, Katherine Saltonstall. Grad., Loomis Sch., 1935; B.S., Harvard U., 1940. Engr. Hygrade-Sylvania, Inc., 1940-41; govt. sales mgr. electronics div. Sylvania Electric Products, 1945-47; sales mgr. Tracerlab, Inc., 1947-50, dir. engring., 1950-51; tech. coordinator United Paramount Theatres, Inc., 1951-52; pres. Microwave Assocs., Inc., Burlington, Mass., 1952-69, chmn., chief exec. officer, 1969-75, chmn., chmn. exec. com., 1975-77, vice-chmn., 1981-83; vice chmn. M/A-COM Inc., 1978-81, chmn. emeritus, 1983-87. Bd. dirs. Anorexia Bulimia Care, Inc. Served to lt. comdr. USNR, 1941-45. Fellow Radio Club Am. (Sarnoff citation 1985); Mem. IEEE (life), Am. Radio Relay League. Clubs: Appalachian Mountain; Edgartown Yacht (trustee 1980-83). Home: Lincoln Mass. Died Apr. 22, 1995.

ATHA, STUART KIMBALL, JR., retired banker; b. Newark, May 28, 1925; s. Stuart Kimball and Katharine Grosvenor (Dixon) A.; m. Eleanor Hendry, July 6, 1946 (dec. Apr. 1995); children: Stuart Kimball III, Susan Hendry, Peter William; m. Barbara Bingenheimer, Mar. 16, 1996. B.A., Princeton, 1950. With Hanover Bank, N.Y.C., 1950-62; asst. sec. Hanover Bank, 1955-56, asst. treas., 1956-62; asst. sec. Chem. Bank, Co., N.Y.C., 1962; asst. v.p. Chem. Bank, Co., 1962-65, v.p., 1965-71, regional v.p., 1971-72, sr. v.p., 1972-88. Served to 1st lt. USAAF, 1943-46. Clubs: Bd. Room (N.Y.C.); Cannon (Princeton). Home: Russet Rd Valley Cottage NY 10989 Died May 23, 1997.

ATHERTON, ALEXANDER SIMPSON, newspaper executive; b. Honolulu, Mar. 29, 1913; s. Frank Cooke and Eleanore Alice (Simpson) A.; m. LeBurta Marie Gates, Oct. 8, 1941; children—Burta Lee, Frank Cooke II, Marjory Gates. Grad., Tabor Acad., Marion, Mass., 1931; B.A., Dartmouth, 1936. With Hawaiian Trust Co., Honolulu, 1954-66; asst. v.p. Hawaiian Trust Co., 1958-66. Past campaign chmn. Honolulu Community Chest; trustee Atherton Family Found.; bd. dirs. Africare, Inc. Mem. Pacific Club, Adventurers Club, Waialae Country Club, Oahu Country Club, Collectors Club, Outrigger Canoe Club, Theta Delta Chi. Republican. Mem. United Ch. of Christ. Home: Honolulu Hawaii Died July 17, 1996.

ATHNASIOS, ALBERT KAMEL, chemist, science administrator; b. Alexandria, Egypt, Feb. 10, 1935; came to U.S., 1973; s. Hanna and Gemiana Hanna (Tiab) A.; m. Samiha Salama Ibrahim, Nov. 22, 1959; children: Magda Salib and Magid Athnasios. BSc in Chemistry, Alexandria U., 1956; MSc in Chemistry, N.C. State U., 1962. Instr. chemistry faculty sci. Alexandria U., 1956-60; sr. chemist, group leader/mgr. FDA-Egypt, Alexandria, 1963-74; sr. rsch. chemist rsch. labs. Quaker Oats Co., Barrington, Ill., 1974-77; sr. rsch. assoc. tech. ctr. Nabisco Brands, Inc., East Hanover, N.J., 1977-90; dir. R & D Fleischmann's Yeast Inc., Fenton, Mo., 1990-96; cons., 1996—. Contbr. articles to profl. jours. Mem. AAAS, Am. Chem. Soc., Assn. Ofcl. Analytical Chemists, Am. Oil Chemists Soc. (assoc. editor Ofcl. Book of Methods 1985-95, mem. coms. on mycotoxins and uniform methods 1985-90), Internat. Union of Pure and Applied Chemistry, Inst. Food Technologists, Am. Assn. Cereal Chemists, N.Y. Acad. Sci., Sigma Xi (N.C. State U. chpt.). Achievements include patent for process for removal of cholesterol and saturated fatty acids from butter oil, fish oil, egg yolk oil, lard, tallow and other fatty materials; isolation of psoralen and bergapten from fig leaves used for treatment of leukoderma and skin depigmentation. Deceased.

ATKINSON, BILL, designer; b. Utica, N.Y., Feb. 22, 1916; s. J. Harry and Elizabeth Anne (Woolfenden) A.; m. Sylvia Small, 1940; children: Lynn, Gail; m. Jeanne Marie Pagnucco, 1969; stepchildren: Robert, Rachael. B. Arch./Landscape Arch., Cornell U., 1940; postgrad., New Sch. Social Research, 1965, Sch. Visual Arts, N.Y.C., 1966. Spl. asst. to Eero Saarinen, Bloomfield Hills, Mich.; research engr. Chrysler Corp., Detroit, 1942-46; pres., designer Bill Atkinson Ltd., N.Y.C., 1974-95, Atkinson Internat., Ltd., N.Y.C., 1983-95; dir. Glen Mfg. Co., Milw.; cons. to bd. trustees R.I. Sch. Design.; set designer Metro-Goldwyn Meyer, 1938-39; draftsman/designer Architects Edward Stone, Phillip Goodwin, N.Y.C.; designer, renderer Architects McKim, Meade & White, N.Y.C.; pvt. practice architecture and design, Bloomfield Hills, 1946-49; fashion designer, 1950-70; designer, V.P. Glen of Michigan, N.Y.C.; corp. fellow Profit Tech. Inc., N.Y.C.; founder, dir. Environs., 1993. Photographer book series Time-Life, N.Y.C., 1971; designer career apparel Amtrak, N.Y.C., St. Louis, Washington, 1972; originator, designer Hilton Hotel's Rainbow Concept, N.Y.C., St. Louis, Beverly Hills, Calif., 1973; creator pathol. portrait of AIDS for visualization therapy. Bd. dirs. City and Country Sch., N.Y.C.; dir. Wingate Growth Ctr.; rep. UN Conf. on Environment and Devel., Rio de Janeiro, 1992. Co-winner Rome Collaborative in Architecture, 1937; recipient numerous awards including over 50 for graphics and printing, 1952-79; Designer of Yr. award Sports Illustrated, Corduroy Council awards, Made in U.S.A. award for Am. Sportswear, 1965 awards Am. Retailers, Coty award for Am. fashion, 1978, Am. Design award Leather Industries Am., 1979; Flying Colors Fashion award, 1980; winner Silver Medal del Amo Internationale Invitational Competition for Sculpture and Fashion for Yr. 2000. Mem. Council Am. Fashion Designers, Cornell U. Alumni Assn., Sch. Visual Arts Alumni Assn., New Sch. Social Scis. Alumni Assn. Home: Westport Conn. Died Aug. 20, 1995.

ATTEAN, PRISCILLA ANN, state legislator, state official; b. Old Town, Maine, July 3, 1941; d. Elmer Norman Attean and Eunice M. (Lewey) Attean Crowley; m. Francis Leo Kelly, Nov. 8, 1957 (div. 1967); children: Cheryl, Mary, Richard, Maureen, Colleen. Student U. Maine-Orono. Asst. mgr. Pompeii Restaurant, Bridgeport, Conn., 1970-81; cons. Penobscot Nation, Old Town, 1982-84, tribal, state relations officer, 1984-95; mem. Maine Ho. of Reps., Augusta, 1984-95, chmn. Joint Select Com. on Indian Affairs, 1984-95. Mem. census com. Penobscot Nation, Old Town, 1982-84, adult vocat. tng. com., 1985-95, mus. com., 1985-95. Roman Catholic. Avocations: genealogical research, rafting, arts, crafts. Died Feb. 24, 1995. Home: Old Town Maine

ATTEBERRY, WILLIAM DUANE, diversified manufacturing company executive; b. Decatur, Ill., Mar. 24, 1920; s. William Herman and Lucile (Hunter) A.; m. Doris Jean Walker, Dec. 19, 1946; children: William Thomas, James Norman, Thomas Hunter. B.E., U. So. Calif., 1943; DBA (hon.), Ohio No. U., 1993. Engr. P.R. Mallory & Co., Indpls., 1946; v.p. Western Lead Products Co., Los Angeles, 1946-51; engr., prodn. mgr. chems. and metals div. Eagle-Picher Co., Cin., 1951-60; pres. chems. and metals div. Eagle-Picher Industries, Inc., Cin., 1960-65, exec. v.p. corp., 1965-67, pres., 1967-78, chmn. bd., 1978-85, chief exec. officer, 1968-82, also dir., chmn. exec. com.; dir. Fifth-Third Bank Cin., 1st Nat. Bank Joplin, Mo., Empire Dist. Electric Co., Xtek Inc., Kroger Co., Vulcan Materials Co., Western So. Life Ins. Co. Chmn. bd. dirs. Bethesda Hosp., bd. dirs. Joplin YMCA; trustee Ohio No. U., Boys Club Cin.; dir. Greater Cin. Found. Served to capt. USMCR, 1943-46, PTO. Recipient Engring. Alumnus award U. So. Calif., 1979, Great Living Cincinnatian award, 1988. Mem. AIME, Am. Zinc Inst. (bd. dirs., v.p.), Queen City Club (bd. govs. 1981-90, v.p. 1988), Cin. Country Club, Tippecanoe Lake Country Club, Hole-in-the-Wall Golf Club, Naples Yacht Club, Bankers Club, Comml. Club (pres. 1987-88), Sigma Chi. Republican. Presbyterian (trustee). Died Apr. 9, 1997.

ATWATER, JOHN SPENCER, physician; b. Cin., Oct. 12, 1913; s. Carleton William and May (Spencer) A.; m. Laura Virginia Zipplies, July 29, 1939; children: John Spencer, Paul Carleton, Elizabeth Baron. Student, Western Res. U., 1931-32; A.B., Denison U., 1935; student, Ind. U. Sch. Medicine, 1934-36; M.D., Johns Hopkins, 1939; M.S. in Medicine, U. Minn., 1944. Diplomate: Am. Bd. Internal Medicine, Am. Bd. Gastroenterology. Intern medicine U. Chgo. Clinics, 1939-40, asst. resident medicine, 1940-41; fellow Mayo Found., 1941-44; 1st asst. medicine Mayo Clinic, Rochester, Minn., 1943-44; practice medicine specializing in internal medicine and gastroenterology Atlanta, 1946-92; mem. staffs Ga. Bapt. Hosp., Crawford W. Long Meml. Hosp.; asso. chief medicine Ga. Baptist Hosp., 1948-57, acting chief medicine, 1958-60, chief medicine, 1973-77, pres. staff, 1962, mem. exec. com., 1961-64, chmn. exec. com., 1963, chief gastroent. sect., 1948-92; chief dept. medicine Atlanta Hosp., 1968-69, chief medicine, 1969-72, mem. exec. com., 1968-72, chmn. credentials com., 1968-69, mem. utilization rev. com., 1968-69, mem. med. recs. com., 1968, mem. joint conf. com., 1970-72; cons. in gastroenterology Robert T. Jones Meml. Hosp., Canton, Ga., 1962-92, Cobb Gen. Hosp., Austell, Ga., 1968-73; instr. in medicine U. Minn., 1943-44, Emory U., 1946-54, asso. in medicine, 1954-65; cons. internal medicine VA, Ga. Dept. Edn., Fgn. Mission Bd. So. Bapt. Conv., U.S. Dept. State, Chmn. Atlanta Grad. Med. Assembly, 1958-59, exhibit chmn., 1960, mem. advisory com., 1961, mem. emergency care service com., 1964-65; mem. Gov.'s Commn. on Aging, 1959-62, chmn. health com., 1959-62; del. White House Conf. on Aging, 1961; chmn. Gov.'s Conf. on Aging, 1960, Ga. Joint Council to Improve Health Care of Aged, 1959-92; mem. health advisory com. Ga. Commn. on Aging, 1964-92; mem. clin. lab. blood and bank and tissue bank com. Ga. Dept. Pub. Health, 1971-92; Partner Caduceus Properties, 1969-92; dir. So. Gen. Ins. Co., Stuyvesant Ins. Co., Stuyvesant Life Ins. Co., Jersey Ins. Co. N.Y., 1st Ga. Bank, Peoples Am. Bank Atlanta, GAC Corp. Author numerous articles in field, (with others) sci. exhibits at med. meetings, films, TV demonstrations in field. Bd. dirs. Atlanta Boys Club, med. dir., 1953-65, mem. endowment com., 1970-72; bd. dirs. Atlanta Girls Club, vice-chmn., 1957-58, chmn. bd., 1958-59, 3d v.p., 1960; bd. dirs. Atlanta Ballet, 1978-92. Served as lt. M.C. USNR, 1944-46. Recipient Certificate of Appreciation Fulton County Med. Soc., 1960, 63; Aven Citizenship award, 1961; Award of Recognition Atlanta Boys Club, 1966; Keystone Bronze award Boys Clubs Am., 1968, 74; Letter of Appreciation Med. Assn. Ga., 1969; Certificate of Appreciation, 1970; Golden Owl award Case Western Res. U., 1983; Disting. Alumni citation Denison U., 1985. Fellow A.C.P., Am. Geriatrics Soc.; mem. AMA (cons. council med. services 1960-92, chmn. reference com. med. edn. 1969, mem. reference com. fin. med. care 1967, mem. reference com. ins. and med. services 1971, cert. of appreciation 1977), Med. Assn. Ga. (chmn. bd. spl. activities 1961-92, treas. 1962-92, mem. publs. com. jour. 1962-92, mem. exec. com. 1962-92, mem. fin. com. 1962-92, mem. spl. fin., central billing, hdqrs. expansion and bldg. coms., chmn. awards com.), Fulton County Med. Soc. (chmn. com. on aging 1959, 60, 61), 5th Dist. Med. Soc., So. Med. Assn. (past chmn.), Am. Gastroent. Assn., Am. Gastroscopic Soc., Am. Soc. Gastrointestinal Endoscopy, World Congress Gastroenterology, N.Y. Acad. Scis., Am. Heart Assn., Alumni Assn. Mayo Found. Med. Edn. and Research, Mayo Gastrointestinal Alumni Assn., Johns Hopkins Med. and Surg. Soc., U. Chgo. Med. Alumni Assn., Am., Ga. socs. internal medicine, Johns Hopkins Alumni Assn. (past pres. Ga. soc., past nat. v.p.), Atlanta C. of C., SAR, Phoenix Soc., Phi Gamma Delta, Nu Sigma Nu. Baptist. Clubs: Kiwanian (mem. boys and girls work com. 1966-70, fund raising com. 1969-70, vocat. guidance com. 1969, operation drug alert com. 1970-71), Commerce, Atlanta City (charter mem.). Home: Atlanta Ga. Died May 7, 1992.

AUCHINCLOSS, SAMUEL S., electronics executive; b. N.Y.C., Oct. 12, 1903; s. Samuel S. and Anne Stavely (Agnew) A.; m. Dorothy Milburn, Oct. 12, 1927 (div. July 1938); 1 child, Robert Gordon; m. Lydia Knight Garrison, Feb. 19, 1939; children: Philip Sloan, Samuel Sloan. Student, MIT, 1922-25. V.p. N.Y. Quotation Co., N.Y.C., 1930-40, Am. Machine and Foundry, Buffalo, 1946-48; industry officer Marshall Plan, Stockholm, 1948-49; pres. Dewalt Inc., Lancaster, Pa., 1949-57, Tracerlab., Inc., Waltham, Mass., 1957-65; pres., bd. dirs. AMP Inc., Harrisburg, Pa., 1965-72, vice chmn., 1972-75, dir. emeritus, 1975-91. Served to col. Signal Corp., U.S. Army, 1940-46, dep. chief signal officer, 1942-46. Decorated D.S.M., Legion of Merit, Silver Star, Bronze Star with 2 oak leaves. Republican. Club: Links. Home: Sarasota Fla. Died Nov. 1991.

AUER, EDWARD THOMAS, psychiatrist; b. Phila., Jan. 18, 1919; s. William Harper and Anna (Maguire) A.; m. Mary Hedesh, Sept. 23, 1944 (dec.); children: Robert, Thomas, Kenneth, Mary Ann, Edward. B.A., U. Rochester, 1940; M.D., Temple U., 1943. Intern Abington (Pa.) Meml. Hosp., 1943-44, chief resident, 1947-48; fellow psychiatry U. Pa. Med. Sch., 1948-50, mem. faculty, 1950-62, assoc. prof. psychiatry, 1956-62, clin. prof., 1976-89, ret., asst. instr. medicine, 1950-53; practice medicine specializing in psychiatry with Dr. Kenneth Appel & Assos., Phila., 1950-56; with Drs. Edward T. Auer, William T. Donner & Assos., Pa., 1956-62; cons. psychiatry Coatesville VA Hosp., Phila., 1954-56; prof. psychiatry, chmn. dept. neurology and psychiatry St. Louis U. Sch. Medicine, 1962-76, Samuel W. Fordyce prof. psychiatry, 1967-76; chief mental health and behavioral sci. service St. Louis VA Hosp., 1972-76; med. dir. Inst. Pa. Hosp., Phila., 1976-80, ret.; mem. Nat. Task Force Homosexuality, 1967-70; vice chmn. Mental Health Planning Com., St. Louis, 1966-69. Cons. editor: Jour. Human Sexuality; contbr. articles to med. jours. Served to capt. M.C. AUS, 1944-47. Fellow Am. Psychiat. Assn. (chmn. council on emerging issues 1972-75, chmn. task force on sex edn. and sex therapy 1976-82), Am. Coll. Psychiatry, Am. Coll. Psychoanalysts (charter bd. regents 1985-88, chmn. com. invitations to membership 1973-95); mem. AMA, Pa., Phila. med. socs., Group Advancement Psychiatry (dir. 1966-68), Eastern Mo. Psychiat Assn. (pres. 1967-68), So. Psychiat. Assn., AAAS, Sigma Xi, Alpha Omega Alpha. Home: Columbia Md. Died Jan. 23, 1995.

AUERBACK, ALFRED, psychiatrist; b. Toronto, Can., Sept. 20, 1915; came to U.S., 1939, naturalized, 1944; s. Murray M. and Lena (Breslin) A.; m. Molly Loy Friedman, June 21, 1942; children—Norman L., Sandra J., Diana K. Auerback Gleave. M.D., U. Toronto, 1938. Intern Toronto Gen. Hosp., 1938-39; resident French Hosp., San Francisco, 1939-40; resident in neurology and psychiatry U. Calif. Hosp., San Francisco, 1940-42; practice medicine specializing in psychiatry San Francisco, 1943-90; staff psychiatrist Sheppard Pratt Hosp., Towson, Md., 1942-43; staff U Calif.-San Francisco, 1943—, asst. clin. prof., 1953, assoc. clin. prof., 1962, clin. prof., 1970-83, clin. prof. emeritus, 1983—; cons. San Francisco Gen. Hosp., 1953-70; mem. Mental Health Adv. Bd. of San Francisco, 1962-77, chmn., 1967-70; bd. dirs. San Francisco Mental Health Assn., 1981-87; cons. Nat. Adv. Council on Alcohol Abuse and Alcoholism, Washington, 1971-76, Calif. Alcoholic Rehab. Commn., 1955-57; mem. Citywide Alcoholism Adv. Bd., San Francisco, 1972-74; chmn., 1972-73, 1st Pacific Congress of Psychiatry, Melbourne, Australia, 1975; chmn. psychiat. congresses, Tokyo, Jerusalem, 1963, Mexico City, Lima, Rio de Janeiro, Sao Paulo, 1964; chmn. psychiat. congresses Edinburgh, 1965. Editor: Schizophrenia, An Integrated Approach, 1959. bd. dirs., sec. Fontana East Apt. Cooperative, 1985-87. Recipient Royer award U. Calif., 1966, Fromm Inst. award, 1993. Fellow Am. Psychiat. Assn. (life, v.p. 1966), San Francisco Med. Soc. (bd. dirs. 1955), Am., Royal, Royal Australian, New Zealand colls. psychiatrists; mem. No. Calif. Psychiat. Soc. (pres. 1956, award 1990), Am. Assn. Social Psychiatry (councillor 1980-86), Mental Health Assn. (award 1986), Commonwealth Club, Masons, Pi Lambda Phi, Phi Delta Epsilon. Died Mar., 1997.

AULD, DAVID VINSON, civil engineer; b. Washington, Dec. 18, 1907; s. Robert Edgar and Elizabeth (Vinson) A.; m. Saranell Wilson, Nov. 21, 1931; 1 son, David. B.C.E., Princeton U., 1929. Registered profl. engr., D.C., Md. Diplomate Am. Acad. Environ. Engrs. With Govt. D.C., 1929-64, supt., chief engr. water div., 1946-53, dir. dept. san. engring., 1953-64; pvt. practice engring., 1965-77; mem. Interstate Commn. Potomac River Basin, 1953-64, chmn., 1959-61; chmn. Washington Sanitation Conf., 1947-48. Chmn. Talbot County Historic Dist. Commn., 1975-81. Flotilla comdr. USCG Aux., 1967. Recipient Merit citation for outstanding career pub. service Nat. Civil Service League, 1957, Career Service award, 1962. Fellow ASCE; mem. Water Pollution Control Fedn. (life), Am. Water Works Assn. (life, dir. 1954-57, George Warren Fuller award 1962), Am. Pub. Works Assn. (Pub. Works Man of Year award 1961), Washington Soc. Engrs. (dir. 1959-60, award 1962), Princeton Engring. Assn., Hist. Soc. Talbot County (pres. 1971-74, 79-80). Episcopalian. Clubs: Cosmos, City Tavern (Washington); Chesapeake Bay Yacht (gov. 1973-75). Died Mar. 14, 1992.

AUNGST, JOHN WAYNE, JR., historian, preservationist; b. Landisville, Pa., Apr. 26, 1920; s. John Wayne and Adeline D. (Kauffman) A.; m. Margaret C. Wagner, 1941; 1 child, Dora Jo Aungst Bentos. AB, Dickinson Coll., 1948; postgrad., Dickinson Sch. Law, 1948-50. Law clk. Alspach & Wenger, Lancaster, Pa., 1951-53; with U.S. Post Office, Landisville, Pa., 1954-72; trustee Wm. Klein Trust, Elizabethtown, Pa., 1972-84; adminstr. Lancaster County Hist. Soc., Elizabethtown, Pa., 1973-87, dir. emeritus, 1987—; founder, dir. Hist. Preservation Trust Lancaster County, 1966-88, now hon. dir., 1988—, pres., 1973-77; dir. James Buchanan Found., Lancaster, 1976-87, hon. dir., 1988—. Ed. Hand Med. Heritage Found., 1982-87, hon. dir., 1988—; mem. Lancaster County Land Use Adv. Com., 1976—, Lancaster County Records Retention Com., 1978—, Mus. Coun. Lancaster County, 1983—. Sustaining mem. Rep. Nat. Com., 1972—; charter mem. Rep. Presdl. Task Force, 1982—. 1st lt. U.S. Army, 1941-46, PTO. Mem. Am. Assn. State and Local History, Nat. Trust Hist. Preservation, Mid-Atlantic Regional Archives Conf., Soc. Archtl. Historians, Newcomen Soc. N.Am., Decorative Arts Trust, Libr. Co. Phila., Pa. German Soc., Phila. Mus. Art, Victorian Soc. Am., Winterthur Guild, Friends of Am. Philos. Soc., Cliosophic Soc. Lancaster, Boehm's Chapl Soc., Donegal Soc., Elizabethtown Hist. Soc., Ephrata Cloister Assocs., Fulton Opera House Found., Heritage Ctr. Lancaster County, Hist. Soc. Cocalico Valley, Lancaster Pirates, Landis Valley Mus. Assocs., Manheim Hist. Soc., Mount Joy Area Hist. Soc., Sigma Alpha Epsilon, Hamilton (Lancaster), Capitol Hill (Washington), Classic Car of Am., Lincoln Owners, Lincoln Zephyr Owners, Rolls-Royce Owners, Rotary (Lancaster). Deceased Apr. 15, 1988.

AUSTIN, WILLIAM LAMONT, educational consultant, former superintendent of schools; b. Detroit, June 18, 1915; s. William Lamont and Dorcas Sarah (Allen) A.; m. Virginia Martha Holm, June 6, 1942; children—Anne, Frank. A.B., Mich. State U., 1937, M.A., 1946, Ph.D., 1970; LL.D. (hon.), Adrian (Mich.) Coll., 1966. Classroom tchr. Charlotte, Mich., 1938-42; with Bendix Aviation Co., also Naval Bur. Ordnance, 1942-46; mem. faculty N.Y.C. Coll., Columbia and Hunter Coll., 1946-48; supt. sch. Wyoming, Mich., 1948-52, Adrian, 1952-65, 84, Muskegon, Mich., 1965-83; ptnr. Austin, Goldhammer & Howard, Inc., ednl. cons., 1983-84; pres. Am. Assn. Sch. Adminstrs., 1973. Contbr. articles to ednl. jours. Pres., bd. dirs. Lenawee Youth Center; pres. Huron Valley Child Care Center, 1961. Mem. Mich. Assn. Sch. Adminstrs. (pres. 1963). Lodge: Rotary (past local pres., dist. gov.). Died Apr. 20, 1996.

AVRETT, JOHN GLENN, advertising executive; b. Atlanta, Mar. 16, 1929; s. Robert Cary and Annie Berry (Hinton) A.; m. Rosalind Case, Dec. 31, 1972; 1 stepson, Gerald. B.J., U. Ga., 1950. With advt. dept. Rich's Dept. Store, Atlanta, 1950-52; v.p. Foote, Cone & Belding, N.Y.C., 1959-66, Wells, Rich, Greene Inc., N.Y.C., 1966-68; sr. v.p. Sullivan, Stauffer, Colwell & Bayles, Inc., N.Y.C., 1968-69; pres. Marchalk Co., N.Y.C., 1969-71; founder, chmn. bd. Avrett, Free & Ginsberg, Inc., N.Y.C., 1971—. Bd. dirs. Am. for Arts. Recipient profl. awards. Mem. Am. Assn. Advt. Agys. (past bd. dirs., chmn. bd. govs. east region), Am. Advt. Fedn. (past chmn. bd. dirs.), Advt. Club N.Y. (past bd. dirs.), N.Y. Racquet and Tennis Club, River Club, Univ. Club, Sky Club, Met. Opera Club, Creek Club. Methodist. Died Aug. 29, 1997.

AWDRY, WILBERT VERE, children's author, priest; b. Ampfield, Eng., 1911; s. Vere and Lucy Louisa (Bury) A.; m. Margaret Emily Wale, Aug. 1938; children: Christopher, Veronica, Hilary Margaret. BA, St. Peter's Coll., Oxford U., Eng., 1932, MA, 1936; diploma in theology, Wycliffe Hall, Oxford U., Eng., 1933. Ordained priest Ch. of Eng., 1937. Schoolmaster boy's sch. Jerusalem, 1933-36; curate Odiham, Eng., 1936-38, West Lavington, Eng., 1938-40; curate Kings Norton, Birmingham, Eng., 1940-46; rector Elsworth with Knapwell, Eng., 1946-53; vicar Emneth, Eng., 1953-65; officiant Diocese of Gloucester, Eng., 1965—. Writings include: The Three Railway Engines, 1945, Thomas the Tank Engine, 1946, James the Red Engine, 1948, Tank-Engine Thomas Again, 1949, Troublesome Engines, 1950, Henry the Green Engine, 1951, Toby the Tram Engine, 1952, Gordon the Big Engine, 1953, Edward the Blue Engine, 1954, Four Little Engines, 1955, Percy the Small Engine, 1956, Eight Famous Engines, 1957, Duck and the Diesel Engine, 1958, Belinda the Beetle, 1958, The Little Old Engine, 1959, The Twin Engines, 1960, Belinda Beats the Band, 1961, Branch Line Engines, 1961, Gallant Old Engine, 1962, Stepney the Bluebell Engine, 1963, Mountain Engines, 1964, Very Old Engines, 1965, Main Line Engines, 1966, The Small Railway Engines, 1967, Enterprising Engines, 1968, Oliver the Western Engine, 1969, Duke the Lost Engine, 1970, Map of the Island of Sodor, 1971, Thomas the Tank Engine's Surprise Packet, 1972, Tramway Engines, 1972; co-author: (with Peter Long) The Birmingham and Gloucester Railway, 1987, The Island of Sodor, Its People, History and Railways, 1987 editor: The Industrial Archaeology of Gloucestershire, 1973, 75, 83 (with Christopher Cook) A Guide to the Steam Railways of Great Britain, 1979, 84. Died Mar. 21, 1997.

AWTRY, JOHN HIX, lawyer; b. Quitman, Tex., July 29, 1897; s. Emmett and Mary Elizabeth (Williams) A.; m. Nell Catherine Jacoby, Apr. 24, 1922; 1 dau., Nell Catherine Awtry Gilchrist (dec.). J.D., U. Tex., 1921. Bar: Tex. 1920, U.S. Ct. Mil. Appeals, U.S. Supreme Ct. 1922. Mem. Taylor and Awtry, Dallas, 1921-24; pres. John H. Awtry & Co., Dallas, John H. Awtry & Co., Inc.; v.p. Bowes and Awtry, Inc.; pres. First Reins. Co., Hartford, Conn., 1936-41; pres. Reins. Co., Hartford, Fire Reins. Co., 1936-41; served as enlisted man U.S. Army, World War I; commd. maj. JAGC, U.S. Army, 1942, advanced through grades to col. by direct order of Pres. U.S., 1953; chief war fraud office, mem. gen. staff Dept. War, 1946-49; chief contract and procurement br. Commdg. Gen European Command, Heidelberg, Germany 1949-50; mem. army panel War Dept. Bd. Contract Appeals, 1950-53; various other positions Office Army Judge Adv. Gen., Office of Asst. Sec. Army, Hdqrs. Staff of Gen. Omar Bradley, 12th Army Group; ret., 1953; Mem. Pres.'s Republican Task Force. Decorated Bronze Star; Legion of Merit (France); recipient various letters of commendation, including from U.S. Atty. Gen., 1949, JAG, 1950. Life mem. Dallas Bar Assn., Tex. Bar Assn., Fed. Bar Assn., ABA, Judge Adv. Assn. Ret. Officers, Mil. Order World Wars, Assn. U.S. Army, Am. Legion, Ex-Students Assn. U. Tex. (life). Baptist. Clubs: Exchange (first pres. Dallas club 1925-26, first pres. Tex. clubs 1926-27, nat. pres. 1932-33, 34, mem. laws and jurisprudence com. 1966, nat. dir. 1928-36,); Drug and Chem., Downtown Athletic (N.Y.C.); Army and Navy (Washington); Town (life), Scarsdale Golf; Shriners (Leisure World Shrine Club Shriner of Yr. 1985), High Twelve, Masons; Sojourners (life). Republican. Contbr. legal opinions as mem. Bd. Contract Appeals to Commerce Clearing House publs.

AYDELOTTE, WILLIAM OSGOOD, historian; b. Bloomington, Ind., Sept. 1, 1910; s. Frank and Marie Jeannette (Osgood) A.; m. Myrtle Elizabeth Kitchell, June 22, 1956; children: Marie Elizabeth, Jeannette Farley. A.B., Harvard U., 1931; Ph.D., U. Cambridge,

Eng., 1934. Asst. in chmn.'s office Fed. Home Loan Bank Bd., Washington, 1934-36; mem. faculty Trinity Coll., Hartford, Conn., 1937-43, Smith Coll., Northampton, Mass., 1943-45, Princeton U., 1945-47, U. Iowa, Iowa City, 1947-96; prof. history U. Iowa, 1950-96, chmn. dept. history, 1947-59, 65-68, Carver prof., 1976-78, emeritus, 1978-96; vis. prof. Harvard U., Cambridge, Mass., 1966, U. Leicester, Eng., 1971; fellow Center Advanced Study Behavioral Scis., 1976-77; chmn. Midwest sect. selection com. for Marshall scholarships, 1955-60; mem. selection com. for dissertation fellowships Woodrow Wilson Nat. Fellowship Found., Princeton, 1962-68. Author: Bismarck and British Colonial Policy, 1937, rev. edit., 1970, Quantification in History, 1971; Editor: The Dimensions of Quantitative Research in History, 1972, The History of Parliamentary Behavior, 1977; bd. editors: Am. Hist. Rev, 1976-78; contbr. articles to profl. jours. Decorated hon. officer Order Brit. Empire, 1961. Fellow Royal Hist. Soc.; mem. Am. Hist. Assn., AAUP (com. A and exec. com. 1963-66), Social Sci. Research Council (dir. 1964-70), Nat. Acad. Scis., Iowa Acad. Sci., Social Sci. History Assn. (steering com. 1973-96, v.p. 1978-79, pres. 1979-80), Phi Beta Kappa. Clubs: Athenaeum (London); Century (N.Y.C.). Home: Iowa City Iowa Died Jan. 17, 1996.

AYLWARD, THOMAS JAMES, JR., communication arts and theatre educator; b. Milw., Nov. 4, 1923; s. Thomas James and Dorothy (Leary) A.; m. Mary L. Lakeman, Jan. 30, 1954; children: Mary Virginia, Thomas James III, Kathleen Grace, Matthew Maxwell, Peter Richard, Anne Marie, Wendy Spring. B.S., U. Wis., Madison, 1947, M.S., 1949, Ph.D., 1960. Tchr. Shorewood (Wis.) High Sch., 1947-48; instr. U. Md., College Park, 1949-59, asst. prof., 1959-62, asso. prof., 1962-68, prof., 1968-92, prof. emeritus, 1993-97, chmn. dept. communication arts and theatre, 1970-84; interim dean Coll. Arts and Scis., 1971-74; cons. to govt. agys.; cons. mem. College Park Cable TV Com., 1976-95. Producer, dir. numerous radio and TV programs. Chmn. Md. Dance Theatre Inc., 1971-83. Ford Found. fellow in adult edn., 1953-54. Mem. Speech Communication Assn., Internat. Communication Assn., Broadcast Edn. Assn., Phi Kappa Phi, Sigma Circle of Omicron Delta Kappa. Republican. Roman Catholic. Home: Olney Md. Died Jan. 23, 1997; interred Gate of Heaven Cemetery, Silver Spring, MD.

AYRES, RAY MORRIS, business management educator; b. Evanston, Ill., Feb. 20, 1928; s. Raymond Morris and Marjorie (Booth) A. BS, Va. Commonwealth U., 1954, MS, 1969; PhD, U. Md., 1974. Tchr., supr. Richmond Pub. Schs., 1954-66; v.p., gen. mgr. Robert Kline Advt., Richmond, 1966-69; coord., assoc. prof. bus., dir. mgmt. ctr. Va. Commonwealth U., Richmond, 1969-81; assoc. prof. mgmt., dir. ctr. for profl. and exec. devel. U. Tex., Arlington, 1981-91, dir. Small Bus. Inst., 1991-94; cons. Aerospatiale Helicopter Corp., Grand Prairie, Tex., 1984-85, Tuesday Morning, Inc., Dallas, 1985-86, Miller Bus. Systems, Inc., Arlington, Dallas, Houston, 1986-87, Tom's Mech., Inc., Arlington, 1987-89. Past pres., mem. Non-profit Mgmt. Svcs., 1984-92, United Way Metro Tarrant County; mentor Arlington Ind. Sch. Dist., 1990-92; pres., fellow Nat. Coun. for Small Bus. Mgmt. Devel., 1977. With USN, 1946-48. Grantee pilot study Tex. Ednl. Assn., 1985. Mem. Am. Soc. for Tng. and Devel. (chpt. pres. 1974-75, 84-86), Acad. Mgmt., Small Bus. Inst. Dirs. Assn. Avocation: scuba diving. Died Dec. 24, 1994.

AZCARRAGA MILMO, EMILIO, communication company executive; s. Emilio and Laura (Milmo) A. Grad., Culver Mil. Aca., Ind., 1948. Various positions in TV; pres., controlling shareholder Televisa S.A.; owner major Mexican TV stas. Died Apr. 16, 1997.

BABBAGE, JOAN DOROTHY, journalist; b. Montclair, N.J., Jan. 10, 1926; d. Laurence Washburn and Dorothy A. (Davenport) Babbage; m. Vernon H. Ellsworth, Mar. 6, 1971. B.A. in English, Mt. Holyoke Coll., 1948; postgrad. Art Students League, New Sch. for Social Research. Publicist Paramount Internat. Films, N.Y.C., 1952-58; reporter Newark News, 1960-67, food editor, 1967-72; feature writer, reporter Star-Ledger, Newark, 1972—. Author: (with others) Past and Present Lives of New Jersey Women, 1990; contbr. bus. articles to New Jersey Business mag., articles to Official Dog mag. Operator rescue orgn. SaintSaver, N.J., N.Y., Pa.; v.p. jr. group Women's Nat. Republican Club, N.Y.C., 1955. Recipient recommendation award N.J. br. Humane Soc. U.S., PICA Club N.J. award, 1980, Community Media award Assn. Retarded Citizens, Morris County Unit, N.J., 1987, Willard H. Allen Agrl. Communications Media award, N.J. Agrl. Soc., 1988, Communicator of Yr. award N.J. Dept. Agriculture, 1990. Appeared on NBC-TV to demonstrate dog tng. Died Oct. 1996.

BACH, MARCUS, author, educator; b. Sauk City, Wis., Dec. 15, 1906; s. Louis P. and Albertina (Buerki) B.; m. Lorena Ernest, Aug. 17, 1932. Student in music, U. Wis., 1920-22; student, Mission House Coll. and Sem., Plymouth, Wis., 1924-25; AM, U. Ia., 1937, PhD, 1942; Engaged in rsch. and study, Ky., N.M., Cal., Mexico, 1933-35; Engaged in rsch. and study (Rockefeller fellowship in rsch. and creative writing), 1934-36. Instr. dramatic lit. Carleton Coll., Northfield, Minn., 1937; research among Am. religious and folk groups, 1938-40; assoc. dir. and prof. Sch. Religion U. Iowa, 1942-95. To write dramatic spectacles and dramas for centennial observances, including Light of Ages, City of Chgo., 1937, Timothy Alden, Allegheny Coll., Meadville, Pa., 1940, The Path of Faith, Iowa Methodism, 1944; Author: religious and folk plays While Mortals Sleep, 1935, Within These Walls, 1936, Champion of Democracy, 1940, Who is Mrs. Chimpsie?, 1940, Common Ground, 1943, Sunrise By Request, 1944; books They Have Found a Faith, 1946, Report to Protestants, 1948, The Dream Gate, 1949, Faith and My Friends, Of Faith and Learning, 1951, Strange Altars, 1952, The Will to Believe, 1955, The Circle of Faith, 1956, God and the Soviets, 1958, Major Religions of the World, 1959, Adventures in Faith, 1959, Strange Sects and Curious Cults, 1961, Had You Been Born in Another Faith, 1962, The Unity Way of Life, 1963, Let Life Be Like This, 1964, Spiritual Breakthroughs for our Time, 1965, The Power of Perception, 1966, The Wonderful Magic of Living, 1968, The World of Serendipity, 1970, Strangers at the Door, 1971, What's Right With The World, 1973, The Power of Total Living, 1977, I, Monty, 1978, Because of Christmas, 1986, Whispers from Wildlife, 1990, Who Stole My Utopia?, 1992; contbr. to ency. and nat. mags. Founder, dir. Found. for Spiritual Understanding, Internat., Palos Verdes, Calif. Recipient Charles Sergel Nat. Playwriting award for Happy Merger, 1937, Nicholas Copernicus award, 1943. Mem. Am. Acad. Polit. and Social Sci. Commd. Lectr. on interfaith understanding, contemporary religious movements and Am. religious scene with emphasis on America's little-known religions. Home: Palos Verde Est. Cali. Died Mar. 26, 1995.

BACH, MICHAEL KLAUS, biochemist; b. Stuttgart, Wurtenberg, Germany, Oct. 2, 1931; came to U.S., 1947; s. Rudolph D. and Ruth C. (Meyer) B.; m. Shirley Rosenberg, June 20, 1954; children: Mark Allen, David Scott. BS summa cum laude, Queens Coll., 1953; MS in Biochemistry, U. Wis., 1955, PhD in Biochemistry, 1957. Rsch. scientist Union Carbide Chem. Co., South Charleston, W.Va., 1957-60; rsch. assoc., project leader The Upjohn Co., Kalamazoo, Mich., 1960-67; sr. rsch. assoc. The Upjohn Co., Kalamazoo, 1967-70, sr. scientist, project leader, 1970-83, disting. scientist, 1983—; vis. lectr. Harvard Med. Sch., Boston, 1969-70; vis. rsch. scientist Karolinska Inst., Stockholm, Sweden, 1986-87; mem. study sect. allergy and immnology NIH, 1982-86. Author, editor Immediate Hypersensitivity Modern Concepts and Development, 1978; assoc. editor Jour. Immunology, 1978-83, Internat. Journal Immunopharmacology, 1978-89; mem. editorial bd. Revs. Immunology, 1986—; contbr. articles, papers, abstracts to profl. publs. Sec., treas. Chamber Music Soc. Kalamazoo, 1980-86, ACLU, Kalamazoo, 1970; mem. Coun. for a Livable World. Mem. Am. Soc. Biol. Chemistry and Molecular Biology, Am. Assn. Immunologists, Internat. Soc. for Immunopharmacology, Collegium Internat. Allergologicum, Sierra Club, Phi Beta Kappa, Sigma Xi. Avocations: photography, gardening, carpentry, classical music, hiking. Office: The Upjohn Co Kalamazoo MI 49001

BACHER, ROSALIE WRIDE, educational administrator; b. L.A., May 25, 1925; d. Homer M. and Reine (Rogers) Wride; m. Archie O. Bacher, Jr., Mar. 30, 1963. AB, Occidental Coll., 1947, MA, 1949. Tchr. English, Latin, history David Starr Jordan High Sch., Long Beach, Calif., 1949-55, counselor, 1955-65; counselor Lakewood (Calif.) Sr. High Sch., Long Beach, 1965-66; rsch. asst., counselor Poly. High Sch., Long Beach, 1966-67; counselor, office occupational preparation, vocat. guidance sect. Long Beach Unified School Dist., Long Beach, 1967-68; vice prin. Washington Jr. High Sch., Long Beach, 1968-70; asst. prin. Lakewood Sr. High Sch., Long Beach, spring 1970; vice prin. Marshall Jr. High Sch., Long Beach, 1981-87, 1981-87; vice prin. Lindbergh Jr. High Sch., Long Beach, 1987—; counselor Millikan High Sch., Calif., 1988—, Hill Jr. High Sch., Calif., 1988-89; ret. Hill Jr. High Sch., 1989; chmn. vocat. guidance steering com. Long Beach Unified Sch. Dist., 1963—. V.p. Palos Verdes Woman's Club, 1993—, philanthropy com., garden tour chmn.; docent coun. sec. Palos Verdes Art Ctr., 1991—; leader TOPS CA 471, 1992-93. Mem. AAUW, Long Beach Pers. and Guidance Assn. (dir. 1958-60), Long Beach Sch. Counselors Assn. (sec. high sch. segment 1963-64), Phi Beta Kappa, Delta Kappa Gamma (pres., area dir. Delta Psi chpt., Calif. profl. affairs com. chmn. 1972-74), Phi Delta Gamma (pres. chpt. 1977-78, 87-90, nat. chmn. bylaws com. 1980-91, 87-90, nat. conv. com. 1987-88, nat. nominating com. 1989), Pi Lambda Theta (pres. chpt. 1974-76, v.p. So. Calif. coun. 1974-76, sec. 1991), Phi Delta Kappa (sec. Long Beach chpt. 1977-80).

BACKENSTOSS, HENRY BRIGHTBILL, electrical engineer, consultant; b. Washington, Sept. 28, 1912; s. Ross Elwood and Susan Catherine (Brightbill) B.; m. Violet Pentleton, Jan. 23, 1942 (div. 1952); m. Bernadette Humbert, Sept. 24, 1954; 1 child, Martine Susan. BSEE, MSEE, MIT, 1935. Registered profl. engr., Pa., Mass., Conn. Project mgr. Jackson & Moreland, Engrs., Boston, 1945-59; prof. power tech. Am. U. Beirut (Lebanon), 1959-61; spl. cons. Gen. Pub. Utilities Corp., N.Y.C., 1961-62; v.p. Jackson & Moreland Internat., Beirut, 1962-68; v.p. Bray, Backenstoss & Co., Ltd., Beirut, Riyadh & Jeddah, 1968-71; sr. cons. Gen. Pub. Utilities Svc. Corp., Reading, Pa., 1970-77; cons. Devel. Analysis Assocs., Cambridge, Mass., 1977-82; Govt. Saudi Arabia, 1962-69; panelist fuel crisis and power industry IEEE Tech. Conf., 1973. Contbr. articles to profl. publs. Bd. dirs. Reading Symphony Orch. (Pa.), 1975-86, Berks County Conservancy (Pa.), 1984-92, Reading Mus. Found., 1986—, pres., 1988-91, chmn., 1991-95, vice chmn., 1995—. Mem. IEEE (life sr., power sys. engring. com. 1952-87, sys. econs. subcom. 1952-76), Nat. Soc. Profl. Engrs., Pa. Soc. Profl. Engrs., Sigma Xi (assoc.), Tau Beta Pi. Congregationalist. Achievements include research in preparing economic studies leading to bulk power generation at mine-mouth in western Pennsylvania with transmission at 500 kv. to eastern markets; underlying studies and recommendations to Govt. of Saudi Arabia for the kingdom-wide standardization of electric system frequency and voltages. Died Apr. 20th, 1997.

BACKLUND, RALPH THEODORE, magazine editor; b. Hoffman, Minn., Aug. 3, 1918; s. Adolph T. and Grace (Sheppard) B.; m. Caroline Hillman Eckel, May 18, 1956; 1 son, Nicholas Sheppard. A.B. magna cum laude, U. Minn., 1940. Newswriter Sta. WCCO, Mpls., 1946-50; producer news and public affairs CBS, 1950-55; exec. producer public affairs programs CBS Radio Network, 1955-58; asso. editor Horizon, N.Y.C., 1958-64; mng. editor Horizon, 1964-66; spl. asst. for arts Bur. Ednl. and Cultural Affairs, Dept. State, Washington, 1966-69; bd. editors Smithsonian mag., Washington, 1969-76, exec. editor, 1976-87, contbg. editor, 1987. Served with AUS, 1942-46, 51-52. Recipient Heywood Broun award Am. Newspaper Guild, 1948. Episcopalian. Deceased.

BAER, ANDREW RUDOLF, public relations consultant; b. N.Y.C., Feb. 14, 1946; s. Rudolf Lewis and Louise Jeanne (Grumbach) B.; children: David, Jessica. BS, Boston U., 1969, postgrad., 1969-70. With Equitable Life Assurance Co., N.Y.C., 1970-79; assoc. Kekst and Co., N.Y.C., 1979-84, prin., 1984—. Bd. dirs. Rudolf L. Baer Found. for Skin Diseases Inc., N.Y.C., 1977—, pres., 1986—. Mem. Nat. Investor Relations Inst. Deceased.

BAILEY, DAVID ROY SHACKLETON, classics educator; b. Lancaster, Eng., Dec. 10, 1917; came to U.S., 1968; s. John Henry Shackleton and Rosamund Maud (Giles) B.; m. Kristine Zvirbulis, 1994. B.A., Gonville and Caius Coll., Cambridge, 1939, M.A., 1943, Litt.D., 1958; Litt.D. (hon.), U. Dublin, 1984. Fellow Gonville and Caius Coll., 1944-55, praelector, 1954-55, dep. bursar, 1964, sr. bursar, 1965-68, Univ. lectr. Tibetan, 1948-68; fellow, dir. studies in classics Jesus Coll., Cambridge, 1955-64; vis. lectr. classics Harvard U., 1963, prof. Greek and Latin, 1975-82, Pope prof. Latin lang. and lit., 1982-88, prof. emeritus, 1988—; prof. Latin U. Mich., Ann Arbor, 1968-75, adj. prof., 1989—; vis. Andrew V.V. Raymond prof. classics SUNY, Buffalo, 1973-74; vis. fellow Peterhouse, Cambridge, 1980-81, Inst. For Advanced Study, Princeton U., 1986. Author: The Satapancasatka of Matrceta, 1951, Propertiana, 1956, Cicero's Letters, 10 vols., 1965-81, Cicero, 1971, Profile of Horace, 1982, Anthologia Latina I, 1982, Horatius, 1985, Cicero's Philippines, 1986, An Onomasticon to Cicero's Speeches, 1988, Ciceronis Epistulae, 4 vols., 1987-88, Lucanus, 1988, Quintilianus, Declamationes Minores, 1990, Martialis, 1990, Martial, 3 vols., 1993, Back From Exile, 1994, Homoeoteleuton in Latin dactylic poetry, 1994, Onomasticon to Cicero's Letters, 1995, Onomasticon to Cicero's Treatises, 1996, Selected Classical Papers, 1997, others; contbr. articles on Oriental and classical subjects to profl. jours.; editor Harvard Studies in Classical Philology, 1978-84. Recipient Charles J. Goodwin award of merit, 1978; Nat. Endowment for Humanities fellow, 1980-81; Kenyon medal, Brit. Acad., 1985. Fellow Brit. Acad., Am. Acad. Arts and Scis.; mem. Am. Philos. Soc.

BAILEY, DUDLEY, English educator; b. Lamoni, Iowa, Feb. 7, 1918; s. Vaughn Corless and Lida (Hayer) B.; m. Sue Ogden, Apr. 27, 1945; children—Geoffrey Ogden, Paul Fletcher, Jane Barker. B.A., U. Kansas City, 1942, M.A., 1944; Ph.D., U. Ill., 1954. Instr. U. Nebr., 1943-44, 45-46, Wentworth Mil. Acad., 1944-45, U. Kansas City, 1946-48; grad. asst. U. Ill., 1948-54; mem. faculty U. Neb., 1954—, prof. English, 1963-84, prof. emeritus, 1984, chmn. dept., 1962-72; Mem. Nat. Council Accreditation Tchr. Edn., 1966-69. Co-author: Form in Modern English, 1958; Editor: Essays on Rhetoric, 1965, Introductory Language Essays, 1965; editorial adv. bd.: World Book Ency. Dictionary; editorial cons., Oxford Univ. Press. Mem. Coll. Conf. Composition and Communication (chmn. 1968), Nat. Council Tchrs. English (exec. com. 1967-68), Coll. English Assn. (dir. 1963-66), Am. Assn. U. Profs., Modern Lang. Assn., Assn. Depts. English. Democrat. Unitarian. Died Oct. 29, 1997.

BAILEY, RUTH HILL (MRS. A. PURNELL BAILEY), foundation executive; b. Roanoke, Va., Sept. 17, 1916; d. Henry Palmer and Carolyn Ruffin (Andrews) Hill, m. Amos Purnell Bailey, Aug. 22, 1942; children: Eleanor Carol Bailey Harriman, Anne Ruth Bailey Page, Joyce Elizabeth Bailey Richardson, Jeanne

Purnell Bailey Allen. AA Va. Intermont Coll., 1936; student Hollins Coll., 1936-38; BS in Edn., Longwood Coll., Farmville, Va., 1939; postgrad. Ecumenical Inst., Jerusalem, 1979. High sch. tchr. in Va., 1939-48; tour dir. to Europe and Mid. East, 1963-73; participant ednl. study mission to Eng., 1988; syndicated columnist family newspapers, 1954-70; exec. sec. Nat. Meth. Found., Arlington, Va., 1979-82; pres. Va. Conf. Bishop Cabinet Wives, United Meth. Ch., 1963-64; pres. Richmond (Va.) Ministers Wives, 1965-66; chmn. bd. missions Trinity United Meth. Ch., McLean, Va., 1975-79, adminstrv. bd., 1971-79; life mem. United Meth. Women. Div. sec. United Givers Fund, 1964-65; sec. bd. dirs. N.T.M., Inc., 1981—. Recipient Staff award Bd. Higher Edn. and Ministry, United Meth. Ch., 1976, Chaplain Ministry award, 1981. Clubs: Country of Va., Jefferson Woman's.

BAIN, ROBERT ADDISON, American literature educator; b. Marshall, Ill., Sept. 20, 1932; s. Ernest A. and Linda Gail (Clark) B.; m. Bonnie Jean Baker, Dec. 27, 1951 (div. 1981); children: Susan E., Robin Anne, Michael A. B.S. with honors, Eastern Ill. U., 1954; A.M., U. Ill., 1959, Ph.D., 1964. Tchr. Lanphier High Sch., Springfield, Ill., 1954-58; reporter Ill. State Jour., Springfield, 1954-58; teaching asst. U. Ill., Urbana, 1958-64; prof. English U. N.C., Chapel Hill, 1964—, dir. freshman English, 1967-70, asst. dean The Gen. Coll., 1979-82, Bowman and Gordon Gray prof. undergrad. teaching, 1987; vis. prof. U. Alcala de Henares, Spain, 1993; editorial cons. Prentice-Hall, Inc., 1966-78, Scott, Foresman & Co., 1966-79. Author: H.L. Davis, 1974, (introduction) H.L. Davis: Collected Essays and Short Stories, 1986; co-editor, author: The Writer and the Worlds of Words, 1975, Southern Writers: A Biographical Dictionary, 1979, Fifty Southern Writers Before 1900, 1987, Fifty Southern Writers After 1900, 1987, The Cast of Consciousness: Concepts of the Mind in British and American Romanticism, 1987, Contemporary Fiction Writers of the South: A Bio-Bibliographical Sourcebook, 1993, Contemporary Poets, Dramatists, Essayists, and Novelists of the South: A Bio-Bibliographical Sourcebook, 1994; editor: (with George F. Horner) Colonial and Federalist American Writing, 1966, Whitman's and Dickinson's Contemporaries: An Anthology of Their Verse, 1996; mem. editl. bd. So. Lit. Jour., 1975—. Den leader Cub Scouts Am., 1970-72. Recipient Tanner award U. N.C., 1976, Disting. alumnus award Ea. Ill. U., 1989. Mem. N.C.-Va. Coll. English Assn. (pres. 1970-71), Conf. Coll. Composition and Comm. (exec. com. 1971-74), Nat. Coun. Tchrs. English (commn. on composition 1976-79), Southeastern Conf. English in Two-Yr. Coll. (exec. com. 1983-86), S. Atlantic Modern Lang. Assn. Democrat. Baptist. Died July 31, 1996.

BAIRD, RUSSELL MILLER, retired lawyer; b. Chgo., Aug. 4, 1916; s. Frederick Rogers and Ruth Estelle (Miller) B.; m. Martha Steere, Mar. 28, 1942; children: Lindsay Ruth, Scott Rogers, Frederick Rogers II. AB, U. Chgo., 1938; LLB, Harvard U., 1941. Bar: Ill. 1941, U.S. Dist. Ct. (no. dist.) Ill. 1948, U.S. Supreme Ct. 1982. Ptnr., mem. exec. com. Sidley & Austin, and predecessors, Chgo., 1941-88; ret., 1988. Bd. dirs. Chgo. Crime Commn., 1960, Lyric Opera Chgo., 1972-96; mem. vis. com. Div. Sch. U. Chgo., 1963; pres. Mental Health Assn. Greater Chgo., 1962-64. Lt. USNR, 1942-45. Fellow Am. Bar Found.; Ill. Bar Assn., Chgo. Bar Assn. (author Christmas Spirits Gridiron Show 1956-66), Bar 7th Fed. Cir., Internat. Wine and Food Soc. Chgo. (gov. 1964-96), Racquet Club (Chgo.), Bohemian Club (San Francisco), Univ. Club (Chgo.), Midday Club (Chgo.), Crystal Downs Country Club (Frankfort, Mich.), Oak Park (Ill.) Country Club, Legal Club Chgo. (pres. 1961-62), Law Club (Chgo.) (pres. 72-73). Republican. Presbyterian. Died Nov. 5, 1996.

BAISLEY, HARRIET ESTHER, biographical research adviser; b. Bklyn., Jan. 9, 1917; d. William Taylor and Florence (Lindner) B. Student, Campbell Coll., 1950, Duke U., 1952, U. Richmond, 1952-53; LLD (hon.), U. Rome, 1963. Pvt. practice, biographical cons., inventory control Esther's Enterprises, Richmond, Va., 1929-89, owner, mgr., chief exec. officer, 1983—; hwy. inspector State of Va., Richmond, 1961-73. Co-author: The Fly and the Man, 1956, The Word of God, 1960. Named Woman of Yr., 1991. Mem. Am. Mgmt. Assn. Roman Catholic. Avocations: walking, camping, pub. speaking, ednl. rsch.

BAKER, LAVERN, singer; b. Chgo.. Songs include: Tweedlee Dee, Jim Dandy, Bop Ting-a-Ling, Play It Fair, Jim Dandy Got Married, Voodoo Voodoo, I Cried A Tear, Fly Me to the Moon, Saved, See See Rider, Shake a Hand, others; performed in (movie) Rock, Rock, Rock!, 1956, (Broadway) Black and Blue. Recipient career achievement award Rhythm-and-Blues Found., 1990; inductee Rock-and-Roll Hall of Fame, 1991. Died March 1997.

BAKER, LILLIAN L., author, historian, artist, lecturer; b. Yonkers, N.Y., Dec. 12, 1921; m. Roscoe A. Baker; children: Wanda Georgia, George Riley. Student, El Camino (Calif.) Coll., 1952, UCLA, 1968, 77. Continuity writer Sta. WINS, N.Y.C., 1945-46; columnist, free-lance writer, reviewer Gardena (Calif.) Valley News, 1964-76; free-lance writer, editor Gardena, 1971-96; lectr. in field; founder, editor Internat. Club for Collectors of Hatpins and Hatpin Holders, bi-monthly newsletter Points, ann. Pictorial Jour., 1977-96, conv. and seminar coord., 1979, 82, 84, 87, 90, 92. Author: Collector's Encyclopedia of Hatpins and Hatpin Holders, 1976, third printing, 1993, 100 Years of Collectible Jewelry 1850-1950, 1978, rev. edit., 1986, 88, 89, 91, 92, 94, Art Nouveau and Art Deco Jewelry, 1980, rev. edit. 1985, 87, 88, 90, 91, The Concentration Camp Conspiracy: A Second Pearl Harbor, 1981 (Scholarship Category award of Merit, Conf. of Calif. Hist. Socs. 1983), Hatpins and Hatpin Holders: An Illustrated Value Guide, 1983, rev. edit. 1988, 90, 91, 94, Creative and Collectible Miniatures, 1984, rev., 1991, Fifty Years of Collectible Fashion Jewelry: 1925-1975, 1986, rev. edit., 1988, rev., 1991, 94, Dishonoring America: The Collective Guilt of American Japanese, 1988, American and Japanese Relocation in World War II: Fact Fiction and Fallacy, 1989 (Pulitzer prize nomination, George Washington Honor medal Freedom Found., 1991), rev. edit., 1991, The japanning of America: Redress and Reparations Demands by Japanese-Americans, 1991, 20th Century Fashionable Plastic Jewelry, 1992, revised 1994, 95, The Common Doom, 1992, Dishonoring America: The Falisfication of World War II History, 1995; established The Lillian Baker Collection Hoover Archives, 1989; author poetry; contbg. author Vol. VII Time-Life Encyclopedia of Collectibles, 1979; numerous radio and TV appearances. Co-founder Ams. for Hist. Accuracy, 1972, Com. for Equality for All Draftees, 1973; chair S. Bay election campaign S.I. Hayakawa, for U.S. Senator from Calif., 1976; witness U.S. Commn. Wartime Relocation, 1981, U.S. Senate Judiciary Com., 1983, U.S. Ho. Reps. Judiciary Com., 1986, U.S. Ho. Reps. Subcommittee on Appropriations, 1989; guest artist U.S. Olympics, 1984. Recipient award Freedoms Found., 1971, George Washington Honor medal, 1989, Ann. award Conf. Calif. Hist. Socs., 1983, monetary award Hoover Instn. Stanford (Calif.) U., 1985, award Pro-Am. Orgn., 1987, Golden Poet award Internat. Poets Soc., 1989, Editor's Choice award for outstanding achievement in poetry Nat. Libr. Poetry, 1994. Fellow Internat. Biog. Assn. (life); mem. Nat. League Am. Pen Women, Nat. Writers Network, Nat. Writers Club, Soc. Jewelry Historians U.S.A. (charter), Art Students League N.Y. (life), Nat. Historic Soc. (founding), Nat. Trust for Historic Preservation (founding), Ams. for Hist. Accuracy (co-founder), World War II Nat. Commemorative Assn. (adv. bd. 1993-95), The Ctr. for Civilian Internee Rights Inc. (hon.), other orgns. Died Oct., 1996.

BALCH, CLYDE WILKINSON, retired chemical engineer, educator; b. Winterset, Iowa, June 11, 1917; s. Harry C. and Beulah (Wilkinson) B.; m. Mary Jo Mitchell, Apr. 13, 1940; children: Charles M., Thomas S., John R. B.S., U. Md., 1937, M.S., 1938; M.S. in Engring. Sci, U. Toledo, 1958. Phys. chemist U.S. Naval Research Labs., 1938-39; chem. engr. E.I. duPont de Nemours & Co., Inc., 1939-46; v.p. Maumee Chem. Co., 1946-65, dir., 1946-66; prof. chem. engring., chmn. dept. U. Toledo, 1965-68, dean adult and continuing edn., dir. evening sessions, 1967-77; cons., lectr. in field, 1960-83. Bd. dirs. Toledo Goodwill Industries, 1967-82. Named Toledo Engr. of Year, 1962; recipient Gold T Alumni award U. Toledo, 1979. Fellow Am. Inst. Chem. Engrs., Tau Beta Pi, Phi Kappa Phi, Sigma Rho Tau, Sigma Alpha Epsilon, Alpha Chi Sigma, Alpha Phi Omega.

BALDIN, LIONEL SILUAN, consulting engineer; b. St. Petersburg, Russia, May 28, 1907; came to U.S., 1919, naturalized, 1939; s. Siluan F. and Augusta J. (Malkoff) B.; m. Jane M. Campbell, June 21, 1934. B.S. in Elec. Engring, Columbia, 1927, M.S., 1928. Registered profl. engr., N.Y., Conn. Engr. N.Y. Telephone Co., 1928-29; indsl. engr. Arthur Andersen & Co., N.Y.C., 1929-30; with Ford, Bacon & Davis, Inc., N.Y.C., 1935-72; mgr. valuation, report and indsl. dept. Ford, Bacon & Davis, Inc., 1954-63, v.p., 1957-72; also dir.; pres., dir. Norwich & Worcester R.R. Co., 1972-74; cons. engr., 1974-95. Mem. Newcomen Soc. U.S., Sigma Alpha Epsilon, Theta Tau, Epsilon Chi. Home: Norwalk Conn. Died July 8, 1995.

BALLAM, JOSEPH, physicist, educator; b. Boston, Jan. 2, 1917; s. John Joseph and Sarah (Roosov) B.; m. Ethel Hirsh, Dec. 28, 1938; children—John Joseph, Elysa Denise. B.S. in Physics, U. Mich., 1939; Ph.D., U. Calif. at Berkeley, 1951. Physicist Navy Dept., 1940-45; instr., research asso. Princeton, 1951-56; prof. physics Mich. State U., 1956-60; asso. dir., head research div. Stanford Linear Accelerator Center, 1961-82, prof. physics, 1963-87, emeritus, 1987—; rsch. collaborator, guest physicist Brookhaven Nat. Lab., 1955; NRC sr. vis. fellow Imperial Coll., London, 1980-81; sr. vis. scientist Ecole Polytechnique Paliseau, Paris, 1981; cons. to Dir., Superconducting Supercollider Lab., 1989-93; vis. scholar Columbia U., 1991-92. Author articles on cosmic rays, high energy exptl. physics.; Editor proc. VI: Internat. Conf. High Energy Physics, 1956. Ford Found. fellow Geneva, 1960-61; Guggenheim fellow, 1971-72. Fellow Am. Phys. Soc. Died Dec. 14, 1997.

BALLANTINE, IAN, publisher; b. N.Y.C., Feb. 15, 1916; s. Edward James and Stella (Commins) B.; m. Elizabeth Jones, June 22, 1939; 1 son, Richard. A.B., Columbia, 1938; student, London Sch. Econs., 1938-39. Gen. mgr. Penguin Books, Inc., N.Y.C., 1939-45; pres., dir. Bantam Books, Inc., N.Y.C., 1945-52, Ballantine Books, Inc., N.Y.C., 1952-95; pres. Greenwich Press, Trumbull, Conn.; dir. Peacock Press Ltd.; instr. sociology Columbia. Mem. Phi Beta Kappa. Home: New York N.Y. Died Mar. 9, 1995.

BALLEW, NELLIE HESTER, retired secondary school educator; b. Feb. 26, 1914; d. Chester Leon and Ethel (Bell) Crank; 1 child, William Wayne Ballew. BA with high honors, Cen. Meth. Coll., 1936; postgrad., U. Mo., 1938, 40, 42, U. Calif., Berkeley, 1957; MA, San Francisco State U., 1970. Tchr. elem. schs., 1936-38, various high schs., 1938-57; tchr., prin. Avalon (Mo.) Union High Sch., 1938-39; counselor Vallejo (Calif.) Jr. High, 1957-67; counselor Taft (Calif.) Union High Sch., 1967-79, dean, info. officer, 1967-72, attendance officer, info. officer, 1972-74, pub. info. officer, 1974-79; area rep. placement and supervision of fgn. students Ednl. Resource Devel. Trust, L.A., 1981-88; dir. placement of fgn. students World Exch., Putnam Valley, N.Y., from 1990, dist. dir., from 1991; advisor student activities Taft High Sch., 1968-72; mem. coms. and curriculum development Vallejo Jr. High Sch., Taft High Sch., 1944-79. Life mem. PTA, Kern County Calif. Hist. Soc. Recipient Vol. Cert. of Appreciation, Kern County Pub. Health Dept., 1976, Hilltop Convalescent Hosp., 1990, Bakersfield Community House for Srs., 1992. Mem. NEA, Kern County Ret. Tchrs., Calif. Ret. Tchrs., Am. Contract Bridge Club, Soroptimists (life, past pres., sec.), PED Sisterhood (past corresponding sec., recording sec., treas., v.p.), Rebekah Lodge, Civitan Internat. (bd. dirs. Bakersfield 1992), Delta Kappa Gamma. Presbyterian. Home: Reading Calif. Deceased.

BALLINGER, HARRY RUSSELL, artist; b. Port Townsend, Wash., Sept. 4, 1892; s. James Guy and Lourena (Russell) B.; m. Madeline Waters, Feb. 19, 1922; m. Kay Mollison, Oct. 12, 1951. Student, U. Calif., San Francisco, 1910-11, Art Student's League, 1912-13, Acad. Colorossi, Paris, France, 1927; pupil of, Harvey Dunn, 1915-16. Instr. Grand Central Art Sch., 1930-36, Central Conn. Coll., New Britain, 1945-58, Central Conn. Coll. (marine painting classes), Rockport, Mass., 1952-60, U. Hawaii, 1959, 60. Illustrator nat. mags., 1916-17, 19-35; rep. permanent collections, NAD, New Haven Paint and Clay Club, New Britain Mus. Am. Art, Wadsworth Atheneum, Hartford, Conn., Springfield (Mass.) Art Mus., Central Conn. State Coll., Meriden (Conn.) Arts and Crafts Soc., also mural, Plant High Sch., W. Hartford, Conn., ann. exhbns., Allied Artists, Audubon Artists, Nat. Acad. Design, Am. Watercolor Soc., Salmagundi Club, Napier Co., Meriden, Meriden Savs. Bank, Torrington (Conn.) Savs. Bank, one man shows include, New Britain Mus. Am. Art, 1947, Ward Eggleston Gallery, N.Y.C., 1948, Rockport Art Assn., 1951, 53, 55, 58, 61, 65, 68, 71, 74, Marblehead (Mass.) Art Assn., 1954, Choate Sch., 1959, Guild Boston Artists, 1960, Woodmere Art Gallery, Phila., 1962, Central Conn. Coll., 1965, Cayuga Mus. Art, Auburn, N.Y., 1955, U. Conn., 1966, Wisteria Hurst Mus., Chicopee, Mass., 1977, Ellsworth Gallery, Simsbury, Conn., 1977; Author: Painting Surf and Sea, 1957, Painting Boats and Harbors, 1959, Painting Landscapes, 1965, Painting Sea and Shore, 1973, also articles. Recipient numerous watercolor prizes Salmagundi Club; prizes Meriden Arts and Crafts Soc., 1944, 52, 57, 60, 61, 65, 68, 71, 72, 74; prizes Springfield Acad. Artists Assn., 1952, 53, 55, 62, 64, 65, 70, 72, 74; prizes Hudson Valley Art Assn., 1958, 60, 64, 70, 74; prizes Jordan Marsh Co., Boston, 1953, 56, 60; prizes Am. Artists Profl. League, 1961; prizes Rockport Art Assn., 1953, 55, 60 (2), 63, 65, 68, 74; prizes N. Shore Art Assn., 1963, 64, 70, 73, 76; prizes Audubon Artists Ann. Exhbn., 1968, 71; prizes Acad. Artists; prizes Springfield N. Shore Arts Assn.; prizes Rockport Art Assn.; prizes Allied Artists Am., 1976; citation contbn. to Am. art, 1980. Asso. NAD.; Mem. Allied Artists, Audubon Artists, Salmagundi Club, New Haven Paint and Clay Club, Conn. Acad., Kent (Conn.) Art Assn., Springfield Acad. Art, N. Shore Art Assn., Rockport Art Assn., Guild Boston Artists, Acad. Artists Springfield (council 1977—). Died July 3, 1993.

BALSLEY, HOWARD LLOYD, economist; b. Chgo., Dec. 3, 1913; s. Elmer Lloyd and Katherine (McGlashing) B.; m. Irol Verneth Whitmore, Aug. 24, 1947. A.B., Ind. U., 1946, M.A., 1947, Ph.D., 1950; postgrad., Johns Hopkins U., 1947-48, U. Chgo., summer 1948. Asst. prof. econs. U. Utah, Salt Lake City, 1949-50; assoc. prof. econs., dir. Sch. Bus., Russell Sage Coll., Troy, N.Y., 1950-52; asso. prof. econs. Washington and Lee U., Lexington, Va., 1952-54; prof. bus. stats., head dept. bus. and econ. research La. Tech. U., Ruston, 1954-65; prof. bus. adminstrn. and stats. Tex. Tech U., Lubbock, 1965-75; head dept. econs. and fin., prof. econs. and stats. U. Ark., Little Rock, 1975-80; adj. prof. econs. and stats. Hardin-Simmons U., Abilene, Tex., 1980-81; adj. prof. math. U. South Fla., Tampa, 1992. Author: (with James Gemmell) Principles of Economics, 1953, Readings in Economic Doctrines, vols. 1 and 2, 1961, Introduction to Statistical Method, 1964, Quantitative Research Methods for Business and Economics, 1970, (with Vernon Clover) Business Research, 1974, 2d edit., 1979, 3d edit. 1984, 4th edit. 1988, alt. 4th edit. 1992, Basic Statistics for Business and Economics, 1978, Data for Decision: Statistics in a Dynamic Economy, 1989, 2nd edit., 1992, (with James

Conway) Acquiring a Fortune: Financial Novice to Millionaire, 1991. Served with USAAF, 1943-46. Mem. So. Econ. Assn., S.W. Fedn. Adminstrv. Disciplines, Phi Beta Kappa, Beta Gamma Sigma. Home: Bremen Ind. Died Dec. 5, 1996.

BALTZELL, E(DWARD) DIGBY, sociology educator; b. Phila., Nov. 14, 1915; s. Edward Digby and Caroline Adelaide (Duhring) B.; m. Jane Piper, Feb. 21, 1943 (dec. Aug. 1991); children: Eve, Jan Carles; m. Jocelyn Carlson, Apr. 17, 1993. B.S., U. Pa., 1939, LHD (hon.), 1989; LHD (hon.), Kenyon Coll., 1992; Ph.D. in Sociology, Columbia U., 1952; LL.D. (hon.), La Salle Coll., 1981. Prof. sociology U. Pa., Phila., 1947—. Author: Philadelphia Gentlemen: The Making of a National Upper Class, 1958, Protestant Establishment, 1964, Puritan Boston and Quaker Philadelphia: Two Protestant Ethics and the Spirit of Class Authority and Leadership, 1979, Sporting Gentlemen: Men's Tennis from the Age of Honor to the Cult of the Superstar, 1995. Served with USNR, 1942-45. Decorated Air medal; Danforth fellow Soc. for Religion in Higher Edn. Princeton Theol. Sem., 1967-68; Charles Warren research fellow Harvard U., 1972-73; Hardy Chair lectr. Hartwick Coll., 1975; Guggenheim fellow, 1978-79. Fellow Am. Acad. Arts and Scis.; mem. Am. Sociol. Assn., Am. Studies Assn., Ea. Sociol. Soc., Pa. Hist. Soc. Democrat. Episcopalian. Died Aug. 17, 1996.

BANDEIAN, JOHN JACOB, physician, surgeon; b. Gurin, Armenia, Mar. 15, 1912; s. John and Flora (Gureghian) B.; m. Alice M. Kechijian, Apr. 4, 1942; children: Natalie, John Jacob, Stephen H. BS, Harvard U., 1935; MD, Tufts U., 1941. Intern Med. Center Jersey City, 1941-42, Mass. Meml. Hosp., 1942; resident in diseases of chest Trudeau San., Saranac Lake, N.Y., 1943, in oncol. surgery, Pondville State Hosp., Walpole, Mass., 1943-45; fellow gynecology Mass. Gen. Hosp., Boston, 1945-46; surg. resident Beverly (Mass.) Hosp., 1946-48; practice surgery, Holyoke, Mass., 1948—; pres. John J. Bandeian M.D. Assocs., Inc. Vestryman, St. Paul's Ch. Diplomate Am. Bd. Surgery. Fellow ACS; mem. AMA, Mass. Med. Soc. (del.), Hampden Dist. Med. Soc. (pres. 1971-72), New Eng. Cancer Soc., Holyoke C. of C. Republican. Survivor of the Armenian Genocide by the Ottomon Turks. Deceased.

BANKS, EPHRAIM, chemistry educator, consultant; b. Norfolk, Va., Apr. 21, 1918; s. Israel and Ada (Gezunsky) B.; m. Libby Kohl, Mar. 17, 1945 (dec. May 14, 1985); children: Thomas Israel, Jay Lewis. BS, CCNY, 1937; PhD, Poly. Inst. of Bklyn., 1949. Jr. metallurgist N.Y. Naval Shipyard, Bklyn., 1941-46; rsch. fellow Poly. Inst. of Bklyn., N.Y., 1946-49, rsch. assoc., 1949-50; instr. to prof. Poly. Inst. of Bklyn. (now Poly. U.), 1951-87, prof. emeritus, 1987—; cons. Westinghouse, GM, Mallinckrodt Chem., 1966—. Contbr. over 120 articles to profl. publs. including Jour. Am. Chem. Soc., Jour. Electrochem. Soc., Sci., Jour. Solid State Chemistry, Jour. Phys. Soc., Jour. Chem. Physics, and others. With USNR, 1944-46. Weizmann fellow, 1963-64; NSF Faculty fellow, 1971-72. Fellow AAAS, N.Y. Acad. Sci., Mineral. Soc. Am.; mem. Am. Chem. Soc. (mem. exec. com. inorganic div. 1959-62), Am. Phys. Soc., Electrochem. Soc. (assoc. editor jour. 1956-85), Am. Crystallography Assn. Achievements include research in luminescent materials, magnetic oxides, oxide bronzes, high temperature superconductors, semiconducting materials. Died Dec., 1993.

BANKS, JAMES HOUSTON, trade association executive, public relations consultant; b. Waco, Tex., Nov. 3, 1925; s. Elijah Halbert and Eva Virginia (Haralson) B.; m. Mary Virginia Bussey, June 15, 1947; children: Virginia Anne, Janet Lynn Banks Tate. Student, U. Tex., 1943, 46-47, 58, 60. Various newspaper assignments Tex., 1941-53; pub. rels. dir. Tex. State Tchrs. Assn., 1953-54; exec. asst. Gov. Allan Shivers, 1954-57, Gov. Price Daniel, 1957; Austin Corr. Dallas Morning News, 1957-70; campaign publicity dir. U.S. Sen. Lloyd Bentsen, 1970; editor The Tex. Star, 1970-72; publicity dir. Sen. John G. Tower, 1972; exec. asst. Sen. John G. Tower, Austin, 1973-75; pub. rels. dir. Tex. R.R. Assn., Austin, 1975-89; pvt. practice pub. rels. cons., 1989-95; editor Tex. Rys. mag.; free-lance writer and pub. rels. cons., 1958-95. Author: Money, Marbles & Chalk, 1971, Darrell Royal Story, 1973, Gavels, Grit & Glory, 1981, Corralling the Colorado, 1988; Austin corr. Sports Illustrated mag. Mem. legis. com. State Bar Tex., 1984-87; bd. dirs. Travis County Grand Jury Assn., Austin, 1985-92; chmn. Tex. State Libr. and Archives Commn., 1990-91, mem. 1989-95. 1st lt. USAF, 1943-45, 51-52. Recipient numerous writing awards, 1960-95. Mem. R.R. Pub. Relations Assn. (pres. 1982), Assn. R.R. Communicators (v.p. 1981), Assn. R.R. Editors (disting. achievement awards 1976, 77, 78, 80, 81, 82), Football Writers Am., Tex. Sports Writers Assn., Sigma Delta Chi (pres. Austin chpt. 1962). Methodist. Clubs: Austin, Headliners (pres. 1976). Avocations: travel, photography. Home: Austin Tex. Died July 12, 1995.

BARAHAL, HYMAN SAMUEL, hospital administrator, psychiatrist; b. Bereznieza, Russia, May 21, 1905; came to U.S., 1914, naturalized, 1923; s. Oscar and Pearl (Rothman) B.; m. Irene Jaffe, Dec. 24, 1939; children: Paul, Susan. M.B., Wayne State U., 1930, M.D., 1931. Diplomate: Am. Bd. Psychiatry and Neurology. Gen. intern Gorgas Hosp., C.Z., 1930-31; staff psychiatrist Kings Park (N.Y.) State Hosp., 1931; then supervising psychiatrist; clin. dir. Pilgrim State Hosp., West Brentwood, N.Y., 1946-53; asso. dir. Pilgrim State Hosp., 1953-58, acting dir., 1958-64; prof. psychiatry N.Y. Sch. Psychiatry, 1955-94; founder, dir. Hoch Psychiat. Hosp., 1968-94; asso. clin. prof. psychiatry N.Y. State U. Med. Sch. at Stony Brook, 1972-94; psychiatrist Catholic Charities. Contbr. numerous articles to profl. jours., chpts. to books. Served to maj., M.C. AUS, 1942-46. Fellow Am. Psychiat. Assn. (life), Acad. Psychoanalysis; mem. Suffolk County Med. Soc. (chmn. com. on mental health, alcoholism and drug addiction). Home: Brightwaters N.Y. Died Aug. 2, 1994.

BARBA, FRANK PETER, insurance executive; b. N.Y.C., Nov. 7, 1932; s. Louis Frank and Ann (Giannantonio) B.; m. Carolyn Straniero, Apr. 23, 1955; children: LuAnn Markowitz, Paula Soricelli. High sch. grad., N.Y.C.; grad., Mechanic's Inst. of N.Y., 1956, The Am. Coll., 1970, Bronxville Art Sch., 1990, Scarsdale Art Sch., 1994. CLU; registered rep., Nat. Assn. Securities Dealers. Pvt. practice builder N.Y.C., 1952-60; account exec. Met. Life Ins. Co., N.Y.C., 1960-66, sales mgr., 1966-75, dist. mgr., 1975-82; branch mgr. Met. Life Ins. Co., Larchmont, N.Y., 1982-94; instr. Life Underwriters Tng. Coun., Washington, 1971-75, mem. exem. bd. dirs., 1972-75. Bd. dirs. Green Knolls, Green Vale Civic Assn., Eastchester, N.Y., 1973-76, '81-82; town bd. adv., 1973-82; minority hiring rep. Unidos, Inc., N.Y.C., 1972. With USMC, 1950-52. Mem. Nat. Assn. Life Underwriters (Nat. Mgmt. award 1975-88, Nat. Quality award 1961-66, Nat. Sales Achievement award 1961-66), N.Y. Life Underwriters Assn. (bd. dirs. 1972-85), Westchester Life Underwriters (bd. dirs. 1975-86, sec. 1984, v.p. 1985, chmn. sales congress, 1984-85, chmn. Life Ins. Week 1982-83). Roman Catholic. Avocations: reading, water colorist, photography. Home: Scarsdale N.Y. Died Nov. 29, 1994; interred Gate of Heaven Cemetery, Hawthorne, NY.

BARBASH, JACK, economist, educator; b. Bklyn., Aug. 1, 1910; s. Louis and Rose (Titel) B.; m. Kate Hubbelbank, May 27, 1934; children: Louis, Fred, Mark. B.S., NYU, 1932, M.A., 1937. Investigator N.Y. State Dept. Labor, 1937-39; economist NLRB, 1939-40, U.S. Office Edn., 1943-45, WPB, 1943-45, Dept. Labor, 1945-48; research and edn. dir. Amalgamated Meat Cutters Union, 1948-49; economist, staff dir. subcom. labor and labor mgmt. relations U.S. Senate, 1949-53; economist legal dept. CIO, 1953-55; research and edn. dir., indsl. union dept. AFL-CIO, 1955-57; mem. faculty U. Wis., 1957-94, prof. econs., 1959-94, Bascom prof., 1976-94, prof. emeritus, 1981-94; vis. prof. U. Calif. Davis, 1985-90; lectr. cultural affairs U.S. Dept. State, Europe, Asia, Latin Am., 1966-94. Author: Labor Unions in Action, 1948, Practice of Unionism, 1956, Labor's Grass Roots, 1961, American Unions, Structure, Government, Politics, 1967, Trade Unions and National Economic Policy, 1972, Elements of Industrial Relations, 1984, Theories and Concepts in Comparative Industrial Relations, 1988. Mem. Wis. Commn. Status of Women, 1959-62. Recipient Teaching Excellence award U. Wis., 1968. Mem. AAUP (pres. U. Wis. chpt. 1970-71), Indsl. Rels. Rsch. Assn. (exec. bd. 1963-68, pres. 1980), Internat. Indsl. Rels. Assn. (exec. com. 1979-89), Assn. Evolutionary Econs. (pres. 1980). Democrat. Home: Madison Wis. Died May 21, 1994.

BARBOUR, WILLIAM ERNEST, JR., manufacturing executive; b. Evanston, Ill., 1909; s. William Ernest and Mabel Ridgway (Hair) B.; m. Georgiana Whitney, Dec. 16, 1950; children: Alicia Barbour Megowen, Georgiana Barbour Gagnon; m. 2d: Anne King, Dec. 31, 1987. B.S., Mass. Inst. Tech. Cons. in field indsl. instrumentation, 1933-36; with Raytheon Mfg. Corp., 1936-39, Boston Edison Co., 1939-41; pres. Tracerlab, Inc., Boston, 1946-57, Controls for Radiation, Inc., 1957-58; cons. nuclear and magnetic fields, 1965-92; pres. Magnion, Inc., 1960-65; exec. sec. Assn. Nuclear Instrument Mfrs., 1966-92; Dir. QSC Industries, Gen. Aircraft Corp.; Cons. tech. utilization NASA.; Mem. New Eng. Govs. Com. on Atomic Energy, also; Atomic Indsl. Forum.; Mem. alumni council Mass. Inst. Tech.; Mem. council atomic energy Nat. Indsl. Conf. Bd., 1955-92; mem. So. Regional Edn. Bd. Nuclear Energy Devel. Project, 1955-56. Bd. corporators Emerson Hosp., 1968-70. Served with USAAF, 1941-46. Mem. IEEE (adminstrv. com. group on nulcear sci.), Am. Standards Assn. (mem. nuclear standards bd.), Am. Inst. Elec. Engrs. (mem. standards com., Geneva observer 1956, chmn. com. nucleonics 1954-57), Am. Nuclear Soc. (dir. 1954-56), Nat. Pilots Assn., Aircraft Owners and Pilots Assn., Aero Club New Eng. (dir. 1969-92, pres. 1970-71), Concord Country Club, Delta Kappa Epsilon. Home: Concord Mass. Died Nov. 15, 1992.

BARCELO, RANDY, set and costume designer; b. Havana, Cuba, Sept. 19, 1946; s. Ramon and Ondina (Lopez) B. Costume designer: (Broadway prodns.) Ain't Misbehavin', Jesus Christ Superstar, Sergeant Pepper's Lonely Hearts Club Band, A Broadway Musical, The Night that Made America Famous, Lenny, (operas) Mass, L'Histoire du Soldat, Les Troyen, (TV shows) Ailey Celebrates Ellington, Ain't Misbehavin', (films) Fat Chance, The Cop and the Anthem, Welcome to Miami. Recipient Maharam award, Critics Poll award Variety mag. Mem. United Scenic Artists. Home: New York N.Y. Died Dec. 6, 1994.

BARCLAY, CARL ARCHIE, physician; b. Nanticoke, Md., July 30, 1922; s. Souvenir Archie and Viola Victoria (Elsey) B.; m. Mae Neece Hodge, June 4, 1949; children: Carl A. Jr., Kenneth D. BS, Hampton Inst., 1942; MD, Howard U., 1947. Teaching asst. dept. biology Hampton (Va.) Inst., 1942-44; intern Homer G. Phillips Hosp., St. Louis, 1947-48; house physician Edward Meml. Hosp., Oklahoma City, 1948-51; sch. physician Oklahoma City Bd. Edn., 1949-59; pvt. practice family medicine Oklahoma City, 1951-79; staff physician Guthrie (Okla.) Job Corps Ctr., 1971-91; bd. dirs., treas., mng. dir. MDP Investment Fund, Inc., Oklahoma City, 1969-86. Chmn. met. outreach dept. Greater Oklahoma City YMCA, 1971-75. Elected to Hall of Fame Greater Oklahoma City YMCA, 1977; charter mem. Cowboy Hall of Fame and Western Heritage Ctr. Mem. AMA (life membership award 1991), Okla. Med. Assn., Okla. County Med. Assn., Okla. Med. Dental and Pharm. Assn. (pres. 1952-53, life membership award 1983), Oklahoma City Med. Dental Pharm. Soc. (pres. 1962-65), Oklahoma City Clin. Soc., Nat. Med. Assn. (life membership award 1992), Oklahoma City Urban League, NAACP. Democrat. Methodist. Avocation: china painting, photography, cooking, canning. Home: Oklahoma City Okla. Died March 21, 1996; interred Trice Hill Cemetery, Oklahoma City, OK.

BARCO, VIRGILIO, Colombian ambassador; b. Cucuta, Colombia, Sept. 17, 1921; s. Jorge Enrique Barco and Julieta Vargas Duran; m. Carolina de Barco; children: Carolina, Julia, Diana, Virgilio. Student, Nat. U., Bogota, Colombia; BCE, MIT, 1943, postgrad., 1951-54; MS in Social Scis., Boston U., 1952. Sec. pub. works and pub. fin. Norte de Santander, 1943-45; sec. gen., acting minister of communications Republic of Colombia, 1945-46, mem. Ho. of Reps., 1949-51, senator, 1958-66, Minister of Pub. Works, 1958-61, ambassador to U.K., 1961-62, Minister of Agr., 1963-64, acting Minister of Fin., 1964; mayor of Bogota, 1966-69; senator, fgn. relations com., fgn. affairs nat. adv. bd., 1974-78, ambassador to U.S., 1977-80; pres. Republic of Colombia, 1986-90; cons. and lectr. in govt., econs. and politics; Colombian rep. to numerous internat. confs. and seminars including World Bank, IMF, UN, others. Decorated for profl. and govtl. service in numerous countries including Gran Cruz de la Orden de Boyaca, de San Carlos, del Merito Militar Jose Maria Cordoba, al Merito Julio Garavito, Colombia, numerous others; recipient Award for Democracy Inst. of Ams., 1990, Tree of Life award Mayors of the World, 1991. Mem. Colombian Soc. Economists (pres. 1960), Colombian Soc. Civil Engrs. (honor roll), Chi Epsilon, Pi Gamma Mu. Mem. Colombian Liberal Party. Died May 20, 1997.

BARDFIELD, MORTON L., communications executive; b. Boston, June 23, 1930; m. Claire R. Medcalf; children: David, Melissa, Edward. Student, Northeastern U., Saunders Sch., U.S. Army Adv. Signal Sch., USAR R&D Unit MIT. Lic. FAA comml. pilot fixed wing aircraft, FAA comml. pilot lighter-than-air rating, U.S. Coast Guard license, FCC radiotelephone, 1st class, FCC amateur extra-class lic., French Antilles amateur, FCC radio examiner. Pub. info. officer Nat. Guard, 1955-60, H.V. Engring. Corp., Burlington, Mass.; owner U.S. Broadcasting Corp. (WNUS), Springfield, Mass., 1960-65, Bardfield Realty Devel.; sr. field editor Wiley Pub. Co., 1965-80; staff cons. Brookline (Mass.) Police Dept.; comms. chief Suffolk County, Mass., 1975-80; dep. sheriff, capt. Suffolk County, 1980; lt. col. mil. aid-de-camp to commdr. in chief Commonwealth of Mass.; U.S. consular warden for St. Martin State Dept., 1995; founder, mng. dir. E. Caribbean Cellular N.V.; cons. engr. and systems designer; cons., investor in field. Active in non-profit cmty. affairs St. Martin; v.p. Navy League of the U.S.-St. Martin. Mem. IEEE, Am. Fedn. of Police (v.p., comms.), Assn. Pub. Safety Comms. Officers, Cellular Telecomms. Industry Assn., Quarter Century Wireless Assn., Mcpl. Police Science Inst. Babson Coll., St. Maarten Radio Assoc. (founder and pres.). Republican. Avocations: flying, boating, ham radio.

BARGER, JAMES DANIEL, physician; b. Bismarck, N.C., May 17, 1917; s. Michael Thomas and Mayte (Donohue) B.; m. Susie Belle Helm, 1945 (dec. 1951); m. Josephine Steiner, 1952 (dec. 1971); m. Jane Ray Regan, Apr. 21, 1980 (dec. Feb. 1991); children: James Daniel, Mary Susan, Michael Thomas, Mary Elizabeth. Student, St. Mary's Coll., Winona, Minn., 1934-35; A.B., U. N.D., 1939, B.S., 1939; M.D., U. Pa., 1941; M.S. in Pathology, U. Minn., 1949. Diplomate Am. Bd. Pathology; registered quality engr., Calif. Intern. Milw. County Hosp., Wauwatosa, Wis., 1941-42; fellow in pathology Mayo Found., Rochester, Minn., 1941-49; pathologist Pima County Hosp., Tucson, 1949-50, Maricopa County Hosp., Phoenix, 1950-51; chmn. dept. pathology Good Samaritan Hosp., 1951-63; assoc. pathologist Sunrise Hosp., Las Vegas, Nev., 1964-69, chief pathology dept., 1969-81, sr. pathologist, 1981—; former med. dir. S.W. Blood Bank, Blood Services, Ariz., Blood Services Nev.; treas. Commn. for Lab. Assessment, 1988; emeritus clin. prof. pathology U. Nev.

Sch. Medicine, 1988. Served to maj. AUS, 1942-46. Recipient Sioux award U. N.D. Alumni Assn., 1975; recipient disting. physician award NSMA, 1983; ASCP-CAP Disting. Service award, 1985. Mem. AAAS, AMA, Am. Assn. Pathologists, Am. Assn. Clin. Chemists, Am. Assn. History Medicine, Coll. Am. Pathologists (gov. 1966-72, sec.-treas. 1971-79, v.p. 1979-81, pres. 1980-81, historian 1988—, Pathologist of Yr. 1977), Nev. Soc. Pathologists (AMA del. 1990), Am. Assn. Blood Banks, Am. Soc. Quality Control (sr. mem.), Am. Mgmt. Assn., Soc. Advancement Mgmt., Am. Soc. Clin. Pathologists, Am. Cancer Soc. (nat. dir. 1974-80), Nat. Acad. Practice Medicine (dist. practitioner 1984—, del. AMA Ho. Dels. 1989-97), others. Lodge: Knights of St. Lazarus (comdr. 1983).

BARKAN, PHILIP, mechanical engineer; b. Boston, Mar. 29, 1925; s. Philip and Blanche (Seifert) B.; m. Hinda Brody, Sept. 5, 1948 (dec. Aug. 1979); children—Ruth, David; m. Susan Albro Sheehan, July 28, 1991. B.S.M.E., Tufts U., 1946; M.S.M.E., U. Mich., 1948; Ph.D. in Mech. Engring, Pa. State U., 1953. Asst. prof. engring. research Pa. State U., 1948-51; sect. mgr. applied physics and mech. engring. Gen. Electric Co., Phila., 1953-77; prof. mech. engring. Stanford U., 1977-93, emeritus prof., 1993-96; vis. prof. Israel Inst. Tech., Haifa, 1971-72; cons. electric power industry, 1977-96, concurrent engring., 1986-96; bd. dirs. Xerox Inst. for Design Excellence, 1993-96. Contbr. numerous articles to profl. publs. Pres. bd. trustees Middletown (Pa.) Free Library, 1959-61; chmn. bd. trustees Sch. in Rose Valley, 1967-68; Democratic candidate for Middletown Twp. Supr., 1959, 61, 63; pres. Middletown Dem. Club, 1960. Served with USN, 1943-46. Recipient 1st Charles P. Steinmetz medal and award Gen. Electric Co., 1973; Electric Power Research Inst. grantee, 1979. Fellow IEEE; mem. ASME (life, mem. com. on engring. accreditation), NAE, Soc. Mfg. Engrs., Am. Soc. Engring. Educators, Sigma Xi. Patentee in field. Home: Mountain View Calif. Died June 21, 1996.

BARKHUUS, ARNE, physician; b. Copenhagen, Aug. 24, 1906; came to U.S., 1937, naturalized, 1972; s. Carl and Alma (Langkilde) B.; m. Anneli von dem Hagen, Jan. 1941 (dec. 1947); m. Adda von Bruemmer, Feb. 1951. B.A., U. Copenhagen, 1926, M.D., 1933; postgrad., London Sch. Hygiene and Tropical Medicine, 1934, 36-37; Dr.P.H., Johns Hopkins U., 1938. Intern, then resident Blegdamshosp., Copenhagen, 1934, 36; med. officer Brit. Red Cross in Ethiopia, 1935-36; adviser Ministry Health, Caracas, Venezuela, 1938-39; lectr. dept. hygiene U. Calif. at Berkeley, 1940-42; mem. Milbank Meml. Fund, 1942-44; pub. health expert U.S. Fgn. Econ. Adminstrn. Mission to Ethiopia, 1944-45; cons. Def. Dept., 1945-46; with UN Dept. Trusteeship, 1946-55; pub. health expert, chief med. officer for Arab refugees, 1948; dir. health services regional office WHO, S.E. Asia, 1955-59, chief pub. health tng. sect., Geneva, 1959-60; sr. pub. health adminstr. African regional office, 1960-62; chief nat. health planning WHO, Geneva, 1962-68; prof. pub. health practice Columbia U., N.Y.C., 1969-73, adj. prof. pub. health, 1973-83; cons. WHO, AID, in Cambodia, 1968, The Philippines, 1972, Haiti and West Africa, 1974, Chad, 1976. Author: (with Hilleboe and Thomas) Approaches to National Health Planning, 1972; contbr. articles to profl. jours. Mem. Danish Med. Assn., AAAS. Club: Explorers. Died Sept. 28, 1996.

BARLOW, JOEL, retired lawyer; b. Deckerville, Mich., May 15, 1908; s. Luther Stanley and Jae (McKown) B.; m. Eleanor Livingston Poe, Feb. 19, 1936; children: Eleanor Poe, Jae Roosevelt, Grace Bowman. A.B., Alma Coll. (Mich.), 1929, LL.D.; LLB, JD, George Washington U., 1935; LL.D., Norwich U. Bar: D.C. 1935. Ptnr. Covington & Burling, 1944-77; prof. law Columbus U., 1937; adj. prof. George Washington Law Sch. Author articles on fed. taxation. Trustee George Washington U., Corcoran Gallery of Art, Madeira Sch., Greenway, Va. Mem. Nat. Tax Assn-Tax Inst. Am. (pres. 1959, dir.), Am., D.C., N.Y. bar assns., Am. Bar Found., Am. Law Inst., U.S. C. of C. (treas., dir.), Order of Coif, Phi Beta Kappa, Sigma Alpha Epsilon, Phi Delta Phi. Episcopalian. Club: Ocean of Fla.

BARNES, GENE (LEGENE SAGE BARNES, III), photojournalist, writer, director; b. Hollywood, Calif., Nov. 30, 1926; s. Legene Sage Barnes Jr. and Hollis Mildred (George) Donahoe; m. Sheila Stevenson, Dec. 26, 1962; 1 child, Christina. Grad., U.S. Naval Sch. Photography, Pensacola, Fla., 1945; student, Los Angeles City Coll., 1949-51. Freelance portrait photographer Hollywood, Calif., 1949-51; photojournalist NBC News, Burbank, Calif., 1952-65; freelance cameraman, producer, dir. documentaries, Los Angeles, 1965-73; freelance photojournalist, writer Studio City, 1973—. Author: (screenplays) Snowball, 1978, Junkie, Junkman, Treehouse, (with others) Devil in Dixie, 1982, Pillars of Hercules, 1990, (novel) Members of the Club, 1985, (photoessay) West Coast Bureau: Reflections of a Photojournalist, 1987; photojournalist for Huntley-Brinkley News, Sunday Show with John Chancellor, Today Show, Tonight Show, Brinkley Journal, Huntley Reports, Threshold of Space, White Paper; producer, dir.; cameraman: (police tng. films and documentaries) The Chimel Case, Christian Science Youth Convention, The Trouble with Water is People, Contributions of Howard Hughes, California

Test Bureau Study; photographic exhbn. Orland Gallery, Sherman Oaks, Calif., 1994. Served with USN, 1944-46, PTO. Recipient 12 News Pictures of the Yr. awards and Golden Mike awards Press Photographers Assn. Sch. Journalism, U. Mo. Ency. Britannica, Spl. Citation for 1st hand-held sound-on-film, 1959. DIED 09/04/97. .

BARNES, MAE, singer; b. N.Y.C., 1907. Songs include Topsy, On the Sunny Side of the Street, I'm Gonna Sit Right Down and Write Myself a Letter, Sweet Georgia Brown, They Raided the Joint and Took Everybody Down but Me, numerous others; appeared in Runnin' Wild, 1924, Shuffle Along, Ziegfeld Follies, 1950, By the Beautiful Sea, 1954; appeared at Bon Soir, Cerutti, the Little Casino and the Blue Angel, others. Died Dec. 13, 1996.

BARNES, ROBERT MARSHALL, securities firm executive; b. Jersey City, May 3, 1923; s. Frederick Marshall and Mabelle (Sniffen) B.; m. Margaret Carolyn Hickman, July 1, 1944; children: Nancy C., Joanne Barnes Schock, James H., Henry M., William R., Carol M., John H. B.S., U. Pa., 1944, M.B.A., 1944. Registered rep. White Weld & Co., 1947-55; registered rep. Eastman Dillon, Union Securities Co., 1955-61; Midwest mgr. corporate buying dept. Eastman Dillon, Union Securities Co., Chgo., 1961-63; ptnr. Howe, Barnes & Johnson, Inc., Chgo., 1963-67; chmn. bd. Howe, Barnes & Johnson, Inc., 1968-91, chmn. exec. com., 1979-91, chmn. emeritus, 1988-91; corp. mem. N.Y. Stock Exchange, 1965-91, arbitrator, 1984-91; bd. dirs. Investors' Forum TV series, WGN-TV, Chgo., 1965-67. Trustee United Methodist Homes and Services, Chgo., David C. Cook Found.; exec. v.p., trustee Chgo. Assn. Retarded Citizens; bd. dirs. Holy Family Cath. Ch., Chgo., 1975; bd. govs. Midwest Stock Exchange, 1969-70; fin. chmn. Johnson for Mayor, 1979; exec. v.p. Chgo. Assn. Retarded Citizens, 1979-80, pres., 1979-82. Mem. Investment Bankers Assn. Am. (chmn. Central States group 1971-72, nat. bd. govs.), Nat. Assn. Securities Dealers Inc. (nat. bd. govs. 1971-74, chmn. dist. 8 1969, national arbitrator), Bond Club Chgo. (dir.). Methodist (trustee ch. 1971-91). Clubs: Pres.'s (U. Chgo.), Bond (pres. 1973), Econ., Union League (bd. dirs. 1984-87) (Chgo.), Buttonwood (N.Y. Stock Exchange). Home: Glencoe Ill. Died Oct. 9, 1991; interred Bronswood Cemetery, Hinsdale, IL.

BARNETT, FRANK R., think-tank executive.

BARNETT, ROBERT WARREN, diplomat, author; b. Shanghai, China, Nov. 6, 1911; s. Eugene Epperson and Bertha Mae (Smith) B.; m. Patricia Glover, Apr. 26, 1940 (div.); children: Dickson Glover, Robert Warren, Clare (dec.), Eugenia; m. Joan B. Burrows, Dec. 10, 1983. BA, U. N.C., 1933, MA, 1934; M.A. (Rhodes scholar), Oxford U., 1936, M.Litt., 1937; postgrad. (Gen. Edn. Bd. fellow), Yale U., 1937-39, U. Mich., 1938, Universita per Stranieri, Perugia, Italy, 1935, (Corp. fellow), Harvard U., 1959-60. Mem. staff Inst. Pacific Relations; exec. sec. program com. United China Relief, 1941-42; U.S. mem. econs. and reparations coms. Far Eastern Commn. representing U.S. Dept. State, Japan, 1945-49; officer charge China econ. affairs U.S. Dept. State, 1949-51; charge Western European econ. affairs, 1951-54, charge European econ. orgns., 1954-56; econ. counselor U.S. embassy, The Hague, Netherlands, 1956-60; counselor U.S. Mission European Communities, Brussels, 1960-61; dep. dir. fgn. econ. adv. staff. Dept. State, Washington, 1961-62; dep. asst. sec. state for East Asian and Pacific affairs Dept. State, 1963-70; dir. Washington Center, Asia Soc., also; v.p., 1970-79; sr. fellow Asia Soc.; resident assoc. Carnegie Endowment for Internat. Peace, 1979-85. Author: Economic Shanghai: Hostage to Politics, 1941, Orientation Booklet for U.S. Military Personnel in China, 1945; contbr. to: U.S. Economic Foreign Policy, 1948, Day after Tomorrow in the Pacific Region, 1976-82, Pacific Region Interdependencies, 1981; Beyond War: Japan's Concept of Comprehensive National Security, 1984, Wandering Knights, China Legacies Lived and Recalled, 1990. Served from 1st lt. to maj. USAAF, 1943-45, PTO. Decorated Legion of Merit; Order Supreme Merit Indonesia; Rockefeller Found. fellow, 1940-41; Center Internat. Affairs fellow Harvard U., 1959-60. Mem. Coun. Fgn. Rels., Assn. Asian Studies, Am. Rhodes Scholar Assn., Washington Inst. Fgn. Affairs, Cosmos Club, Chevy Chase Country Club, Phi Beta Kappa, Beta Theta Pi. Congregationalist. Died July 25, 1997.

BARNEY, JOHN BRADFORD, legal counsel; b. Bridgewater, Mass., Dec. 18, 1915; s. George William and Carrie (Cole) B.; m. Grace Lucille Larsen, Aug. 19, 1950 (dec. May 1992); children: Mary W., Ann D.; m. Sally Regan, Jan. 21, 1995. AB, Harvard Coll., 1937; cert. in meteorology, MIT, 1943; JD, U. Mich., 1951. Statistician Mass. Rating Bur., Boston, 1937-42; with legal divsn.-trust Northwestern Nat. Bank, Mpls., 1951-55; trust escrow officer Ariz. Title Guaranty & Trust Co., Phoenix, 1955-56; asst. v.p. Canal Nat. Bank, Portland, Maine, 1956-60; assoc. counsel, sec. Union Mutual Life Ins. Co., Portland, 1960-72; v.p., counsel Key Trust Co. Maine, Portland, 1972-94; counsel Key Trust Co. Maine, 4 locations, Maine, 1995—. Treas., sec. Portland Symphony Orch., 1960-66; treas. Children's Theatre, Portland, 1967-71, Maine Econ. Com., Portland, 1972-74. Capt. USAF, 1943-47, lt. col. USAF

ret. Mem. Estate Planning Coun., Chartered Life Underwriters (Maine chpt., pres. 1975-77), Maine Bar Assn. Avocations: golf, volunteer at Rockport Pub. Libr. Died Nov. 7, 1997.

BARON, MELVIN LEON, civil engineer, consultant; b. Bklyn., Feb. 27, 1927; s. Frank and Esther (Hirskowitz) B.; m. Muriel Wicker, Dec. 24, 1950 (dec. Apr. 1993); children: Jaclyn Adele, Susan Gail; m. Ruth Berkowitz, Nov. 6, 1994. B.C.E., CCNY, 1948; M.S., Columbia U., 1949, Ph.D., 1953. Lic. profl. engr., N.Y., Mass. Structural designer Corbett-Tinghir Co., N.Y.C., 1949-50; research assoc. civil engring. Columbia U., 1951-53, asst. prof., 1953-57, adj. assoc. prof., 1958-61, adj. prof., 1961—; chief engr. Paul Weidlinger, N.Y.C., 1957-60, assoc., 1960-64, ptnr., dir. research, 1964—, also bd. dirs.; also v.p. Advanced Computer Techniques Corp., N.Y.C., 1962-66; Formerly chmn. adv. panel engring. mechanics program NSF. Author: (with M.G. Salvadori) Numerical Methods in Engineering, 1952; Editor: Jour. Engring. Mechs. Div. ASCE, 1970-83; Contbr. articles profl. jours. Recipient Spirit of St. Louis Jr. award Am. Soc. M.E., 1958; J. James R. Croes medal ASCE, 1963; Walter L. Huber Research prize, 1966; Arthur M. Wellington prize, 1969; Nathan M. Newmark medal, 1977; Thomas Egelston medal Columbia U. Sch. Engring., 1983, Exceptional Pub. Service medal Def. Nuclear Agy., U.S. Dept. Def., 1985, Townsend Harris medal CCNY, 1988, Lifetime Achievement medal Def. Spl. Weapons Agy., U.S. Dept. Def., 1997. Fellow ASCE (exec. com. engring. mechanics divsn. 1966-69, 72-76, mem. mgmt. group C engring. mechanics divsn. 1972-76, mem. tech. activities com. 1974), ASME, AAAS; mem. N.Y. Acad. Scis., U.S. Nat. Acad. Engring. (chmn. com. computational mechanics), Sigma Xi. Died Mar. 5, 1997.

BARON, SAMUEL, flutist; b. Bklyn., Apr. 27, 1925; s. Jacob and Bella (Deutsch) B.; m. Carol Lynn Kitzes, Dec. 21, 1963; children—Pamela Rachel, David Lazar. Student, Bklyn. Coll., 1940-44; B.S., Juilliard Sch. Music, 1948. Flutist N.Y. Woodwind Quintet, 1948-69, 80—, N.Y. Chamber Soloists, 1958-65, Contemporary Chamber Ensemble, 1962-65; flutist Bach Aria Group, 1965—, dir., 1980—; lectr. flute Yale U., 1965-67; instr. chamber music U. Wis.-Milw., summers 1965-67; cons. N.Y. State Arts Council, 1964; asst. prof. flute and chamber music SUNY Stony Brook, 1966-67, lectr. flute, 1966-71, assoc. prof., 1972-74, prof., 1974—; performing artist in residence Harpur Coll., 1967-69; prof. chamber music Juilliard Sch., 1971—, tchr. flute, 1976—, chair woodwinds, 1995—; vis. prof. Eastman Sch. Music, 1974-75, Sibelius Acad. Helsinki, Finland, summer 1975, Jerusalem Music Ctr., 1988, 89; cons. music program Nat. Endowment for Arts, Washington, 1973-76; dir. Bach Aria Group, 1980—. Performer Sarasota Summer Music Festival, 1974—; Transcribed for: chamber music (J. S. Bach) The Art of the Fugue, 1958; Internat. concert tours auspices, State Dept. to, S.Am., 1956, S.E. Asia and Orient, 1962, Central and South Am., 1969. Decorated officer Order Merit Monisaraphon (Cambodia); recipient disting. award in performing arts Sch. Fine Arts, U. Milw., 1964, Disting. Lifetime Svc. awards Chamber Music Am., 1996, Nat. Flute Assn., 1996. Mem. Nat. Flute Assn. (pres. 1977). DIED 05/16/97. .

BARRETT, CHARLES CLAYTON, real estate and finance consultant; b. Milton, Oreg., Mar. 8, 1918; s. Lawrence Clayton and Capitola (Scott) B.; m. Dorothy Grace Smith, Oct. 6, 1942; children—Barbara Lynn, Jeffrey Scott, Pamela Jean, Bradley Clayton, Mark Douglas. Student, U. Oreg., 1936-39; J.D., John Marshall Law Sch., Chgo., 1949. With Percy Wilson Mortgage & Finance Corp., Chgo., 1940-53, v.p., 1948-53; v.p. Greenbaum Mortgage Co., Chgo., 1953-55; with Franklin Life Ins. Co., Springfield, Ill., 1955-65, v.p. charge real estate dept., 1965; v.p. charge real estate dept. Continental Ill. Bank and Trust Co., Chicago, 1965-74; pres., dir., chief exec. officer Gt. Lakes Mortgage Corp., Chgo., 1974—; now real estate and fin. cons. Chgo.; dir., mem. exec. com. Republic Realty Mortgage Corp.; dir. Marina City Mgmt. Corp., Royal-Conill Corp., Continental Ill. Realty Advisors Co., Builders Capital Ltd., Can., N. Marina Bldg. Corp., Continental Ill. Properties Advisors, Western Builders Capitol Corp. Ltd., Can. Adv. com. Central Bus. Dist. Assn.; capital funds com. United Community Services. Served to maj. ordnance dept. AUS, 1942-46. Mem. Springfield Assn. Commerce and Industry (dir.), Am. Mortgage Bankers Assn., Chgo. Mortgage Bankers Assn. (pres., dir.), Am. Inst. Banking, Ill. Assn. Commerce and Industry, Chgo. Real Estate Bd., Lambda Alpha. Presbyn. (deacon). Clubs: Bankers; Illini Country (Springfield).

BARRINGER, (JOHN) PAUL, transportation executive, retired diplomat and career service executive; b. Stafford, Pa., Feb. 10, 1903; s. Daniel Moreau and Margaret (Bennett) B.; m. Dorothy Allen Pray; 4 children. BS, Princeton U., 1924. With Pa. Co. Banking and Trusts, 1925-35; specialist U.S. govt. securities Brown, Harriman & Co., Guaranty Trust Co. N.Y.C.; sr. ofcl., chief aviation div. Dept. State, Washington, 1946-48, dir. Office Transp. and Communications Policy, 1950-56; charge d'affairs Port-au-Prince, Haiti, 1956-58; charge d'affairs Am. Embassy, Tripoli, Libya, 1958-59, Benghazi-Beida, Libya, 1959-61; sr. fgn. service insp. with rank ambassador Washington, 1962-65; mng. trustee Edn. Career Service, Inc., Princeton, N.J., 1965-75; chmn. bd. dirs. Barringer Crater Co., Princeton, 1975-96, Cass County Iron Co., 1975-96; ret., 1992-96; chmn. U.S. dels. to many Internat. Civil Aviation Orgns. Confs., 1947-55, Internat. Telecommunications Union, Rome, 1949-50, others. Author publs., lectrs. on govt. financing and mktg. securities, basic mil. tng., internat. civil aviation. Served as col. USAAF, 1941-46. Decorated Legion of Merit, Bronze Star (U.S.); Order Flying Cloud, Spl. Order Nun Hui, China. Mem. English Speaking Union (pres. Princeton br. 1965-75), U.S. Polo Assn. (past gov.), Army-Navy Club, Racquet Club, Univ. Barge Club, Princeton Club, Nassau Club. Republican. Died Aug. 15, 1996.

BARRIO, RAYMOND, author, artist; b. W. Orange, N.J., Aug. 27, 1921; s. Saturnino and Angelita (Santos) B.; m. Yolanda Sanchez, Feb. 2, 1957; children: Angelita, Gabriel, Raymond, Andrea, Margarita. B.A., U. Calif. at Berkeley, 1947; B.F.A., Los Angeles Art Center Coll. Design, 1952. Artist, 1950—. Exhibited nationally, art tchr. various colls., San Francisco area, 1965—; Author: The Big Picture, 1967, Experiments in Modern Art, 1968, Selections from Walden, 1968, The Plum Plum Pickers, 1969, Mexico's Art, 1975, The Devil's Apple Corps, 1976, A Political Portfolio, 1985; Columnist Barrio's Estuary, 1980. Served with arty. AUS, 1943-46. DIED 01/22/96. .

BARROW, FRANK PEARSON, JR., retired energy company executive; b. Montgomery, Ala., Nov. 22, 1928; s. Frank Pearson and Kathleen (Hillman) B.; m. Faye Parker, Mar. 1, 1951; children: Frank Pearson, III, Cathy. B.S.C.E., Auburn U., 1951. With Baton Rouge Refinery, Exxon Co., U.S.A., 1951-66; process supt. Baton Rouge Refinery, Exxon Co., 1964-65, mech. supt., 1965-66; exec. v.p. Exxon Enterprises, N.Y.C., 1966-72, 74-77; also dir.; exec. v.p. Esso Libya, 1972-74; pres. Exxon Minerals Co., U.S.A., Houston, 1977-80; project exec. Colony Shale Oil Project, Exxon Co. U.S.A., 1980-82. Congregationalist. Died May 23, 1997.

BARRY, COLMAN JAMES, religious educator; b. Lake City, Minn., May 29, 1921; s. John and Frances (O'Brien) B. B.A., St. John's U., 1942; M.A., Cath. U. Am., 1950, Ph.D., 1953. Joined Order St. Benedict, 1942; ordained priest Roman Cath. Ch., 1947. Sec. Am. Benedictine Rev.; mem. faculty St. John's U., 1953-94, prof. history, 1953-64, pres., 1964-71; exec. dir. Inst. Spirituality, 1977-82; pres. Hill Monastic Manuscript Library, 1982; summer tchr. San Raphael (Calif.) Coll., 1956-59, Cath. U. Am., 1959-64, dean religious studies, 1973-77; vis. prof. ch. history Yale U., 1973; Commn. Jours. Acad. and Profl., 1958; chmn. Nat. Com. Edn. for Ecumenism, 1965; commr. N. Central Assn. Colls., 1966; pres. Assn. Minn. Colls., 1967; Penfield fellow in, Germany, 1950, Soc. Religion in Higher Edn. fellow, 1972. Author: The Catholic Church and German Americans, 1953, The Catholic University of America, IV, 1950, Worship and Work, 1956, Catholic Minnesota, 1958, Readings in Church History, 3 vols., 1959-65, American Nuncio: Cardinal Aloisius Muench, 1969, Upon These Rocks: Catholics in the Bahamas, 1973, Readings in Church History, 1985, A Sense of Place: Saint John's of Collegeville, 1987, A Sense of Place II: Benedictines of Collegeville, 1990; editor: Benedictine Studies, 1958-94; contbr. numerous articles to profl. and religious publs. Mem. Am. Cath. Hist. Assn. (pres. 1976). Home: Collegeville Minn. Died Jan. 7, 1994.

BARSCHALL, HENRY HERMAN, physics educator; b. Berlin, Germany, Apr. 29, 1915; m. Eleanor A. Folsom; two children. A.M., Princeton U., 1939; Ph.D., Princeton, 1940; Dr. rer. nat. h.c., U. Marburg, Germany, 1982. Instr. Princeton U., 1940-41, U. Kans., 1941-43; mem. staff Los Alamos Sci. Lab., 1943-46, asst. div. leader, 1951-52; mem. faculty U. Wis., 1946—, prof. physics, 1950—, chmn. dept., 1951, 54, 56-57, 63-64, Bascom prof., 1973—; prof. emeritus, 1988—; assoc. div. leader Lawrence Livermore Labs., 1971-73; Vis. prof. U. Calif., Davis, 1972-73. Assoc. editor: Revs. Modern Physics, 1951-53; Asso. editor: Nuclear Physics, 1959-72; editor: Phys. Rev. C, 1972-87; mem. editorial bd.: Jour. Phys. and Chem. Reference Data, 1979-84. Fellow Am. Phys. Soc. (chmn. div. nuclear physics 1968-69, mem. coun. 1983-85, sec.-treas. Forum on Physics and Soc. 1988-93, Bonner prize 1965), Am. Acad. Arts and Scis. (Midwest coun. 1992—); mem. Nat. Acad. Sci. (chmn. physics sect. 1980-83), Am. Inst. Physics (chmn. publ. bd. 1980-82, governing bd. 1983-88), NRC (assembly math. and phys. scis. 1980-83). Deceased.

BART, GEORGIANA CRAY, artist, educator; b. Wilkes-Barre, Pa., Oct. 30, 1948; d. William Getamyne and Jean Marie (Milisaukas) Cray; m. Michael Douglas Bart, Dec. 2, 1972; children: Jean Michelle, Marjorie Alison, Michael Douglas William Jr. BA in Fine Arts and Art Edn., Wilkes Coll., 1970; MEd in Art Edn., U. Pitts., 1972; pvt. studies in painting. Tchr. art Wyoming Valley West Sch. Dist., Kingston, Pa., 1971-72; substitute tchr., adult art instr. Pub. Sch. Price Georges County, Md., 1972-76; instr. early childhood edn. dept., tchr. adult art Luzerne County C.C., Nanticoke, Pa., 1976-78; tchr. elem. art Wyoming Valley Montessori Sch., Kingston, 1991-92; substitute tchr. Wyoming Sem. Lower Sch., Forty Fort, Pa., 1984-94; tchr. studio arts U. Scranton, Pa., 1995-96; represented by Laura Craig Galleries, Scranton, Pa., Brazier Fine Art, Richmond, Va., Perry House Galleries, Alexandria, Va., Water Lily, Shavertown, Pa.; mem. Art Jury, Wilkes-Barre, 1977-78. One-woman shows include Sheehy Gallery, Kings Coll., Wilkes-Barre, 1993, Hanover Bank, West Pittston, Pa., 1993, Am. Savs. Bank, Hazelton, Pa., 1994, Doshi Ctr. Contemporary Art, Harrisburg, Pa., 1995, Wilkes U., 1995, AFA Gallery, Scranton, Pa., Art Assn. Harrisburg, 1996, Hazleton Art League, 1996, Bixler Gallery, Stroudsburg, Pa., 1997, Chauncy Conf. Ctr. Galleries Ednl. Testing Svc., Princeton, N.J., 1997, Core State Bank, Wilkes-Barre, Pa., 1997; exhibited in group and juried shows at Wyoming Valley Art League galleries and off-site exhbns., 1989-98 (2nd pl. painting award 1990, 96, Purchase award 1991, Grumbacher gold medallion 1993, 2nd pl. pastel 1994, 96, 3rd pl. painting 1994, 1st pl. pastel 1995, 97,, 2nd pl. pastel 1997, 2nd pl. paintings 1996, 1st pl. painting 1997), Lackawanna Arts Coun., Scranton, Pa., 1989, 90, 91, 92, 93 (2nd pl. painting award 1992, 2nd pl. graphics award 1993), 36th Ann. Nat. Juried Exhbn. of Mamaroneck Artists Guild Westbeth Gallery, N.Y.C., 1994, Nat. Arts Club, N.Y.C., 1994 (Catharine Lorillard Wolf Pres.'s award 1994, Still Life Painting award 1994), 96, Baum Sch. Art, Allentown, Pa., 1994, Susquehanna Art Soc., Selinsgrove, Pa., 1994, AFA Gallery, Scranton, 1995, Salmagundi Club, N.Y.C., 1995—, Perry House Galleries, Alexandria, 1995, Audubon Artists, N.Y.C., 1995, 96, 97, Everhart Mus., Scranton (3d pl. award 1995, 97), Ctrl. Pa. Festival Arts, 1995, Monroe County Arts Coun., Stroudsburg, 1995, Phila. Internat. Contemporary Art Competition, Old City, 1996, Broome St. Gallery summer exhbn., Soho, N.Y.C., 1996, 97, Pocono Manor, Pa., 1994, 95, 96 (1st pl. award pastel 1996, 97), Spaces ISE Art Gallery, N.Y.C., 1996, Allied Artists Am., N.Y.C., 1996, Pastel Soc. Am., N.Y.C., 1996, Catharine Lorillard Wolfe, N.Y.C., 1996, Comtemporary Arts Corridor, 1997, Fowler Gallery, Provincetown, Mass., 1997, La Fond Galleries, Pitts., 1997, Pastel Soc. N.Mex., 1997 (Am. Artist award 1997), Chuck Levitan Gallery, N.Y.C., 1997, several others; represented in permanent pvt. and pub. collections; published in: The Best of Oil, 1996, The Best of Pastel, 1996, Manhattan Arts International, 1996, 97. Set designer pvt. sch. theatrical prodn., Forty Fort, 1993; vol. Am. Heart Assn., 1992-96, Am. Cancer Soc., 1992-95; mem. area Rep. com., Wilkes-Barre, Pa., 1983-85; mem. Everhart Mus., Scranton, Pa. Recipient 1st pl. painting award Moscow County Fair, 1990, 92, 3rd pl. painting award, 1991, 1st pl. painting award, 1992, 3rd pl. drawing award, 1993, Purchase award Hazleton (Pa.) Art League, 1991, 2nd pl. graphics award Wilkes-Barre Fine Arts Fiesta, 1993, honorable mention award Contemporary Gallery, Marywood Coll., Scranton, 1993, Artist Showcase award Manhattan Arts Internat. Mag., 1996-97; Pastel Study scholar Pastel Soc. Am., N.Y.C., 1996. Mem. Nat. Assn. Women Artists, Wyo. Valley Art League, Artists for Art of AFA Gallery, MacDonald Art Gallery, Sordoni Art Gallery, Contemporary Arts Corridor, Doshi Ctr. Contemporary Art, Art Assn. Harrisburg, Salmagundi Club (N.Y.C.), N.Y. Artists Equity Assoc., Inc., Pastel Soc. Am. N.Y.C., Everhart Mus., Am. Soc. Contemporary Artists (N.Y.C.), Orgn. of Ind. Artists, Knickerbocker Artists, Audubon Artists, N.Y.C. Roman Catholic. Avocations: water sports, travel, reading, golf.

BARTA, FRANK RUDOLPH, SR., psychiatrist, neurologist; b. Omaha, Nov. 3, 1913; s. Rudolph J. and Anna (Smejkal) B.; m. Mildred K. Ware, Aug. 12, 1939; children—Frank Rudolph, Nancy and Carol (twins), Richard, Matthew, Michael. A.B., Creighton U., 1935; M.D., Johns Hopkins, 1939. Diplomate Am. Bd. Psychiatry and Neurology. Intern Harper Hosp., Detroit, 1939-40; resident psychiatry Yale Sch. Medicine, 1941-43; resident neurology U. Chgo. Billings Hosp., 1942-43; pvt. practice psychiatry and neurology, 1946—; assoc. prof. psychiatry and neurology Creighton U. Sch. Medicine, 1946-49, prof. psychiatry and neurology, 1949-70, chmn. dept. psychiatry and neurology, 1949-56, prof. emeritus psychiatry and neurology, 1970—; clin. prof. psychiatry Chgo. Med. Sch., 1970-74; attending psychiatrist St. Joseph's Hosp., St. Catherine's Hosp., 1949-67; cons. in psychiatry A.R.C., VA Hosp., Cath. Charities, SAC, 1949-67; med. dir. Mental Health Center LaSalle County, Ottawa, Ill., 1968-73; clin. dir. Tideland Mental Health Center, Washington, N.C., 1973-75; psychiatrist Gulfport div. VA Center, 1975-85. Author: The Moral Theory of Behavior—A New Answer to the Enigma of Mental Illness, 1952; Contbr. articles med. jours. Chmn. personnel bd., City of Omaha, 1959-67. Dir. mental hygiene unit U.S. Army, 1943-46, Fort Bliss, Tex. Fellow ACP (life), Am. Geriatrics Soc., Am. Psychiat. Assn. (life); mem. AMA, Miss. Psychiat. Assn., Nat. Acad. Religion and Mental Health (charter, life mem.), So. Med. Assn. Roman Catholic.

BARTELS, JOHN RIES, federal judge; b. Balt., Nov. 8, 1897; s. William Nicholas and Louise (Reuter) B.; m. Anne Bell Willson, May 3, 1930; children: John Ries, William Gilpin. A.B. cum laude, Johns Hopkins, 1920; LL.B., Harvard, 1923. Bar: N.Y. 1924. Since practiced in N.Y.C.; justice Supreme Ct. N.Y., 1950-51; mem. firm Bartels & Hartung, 1951-59; judge U.S. Dist. Ct., Bklyn., 1959-73, sr. judge, 1974—; mem. N.Y. Law Revision Commn., 1945-50, 52-57; spl. referee appellate div. N.Y. Supreme Ct.; ex-counsel fgn. debt readjustment Govt. Ecuador; former gen. counsel Gen. Acceptance Corp. (and subsidiaries), The Fyr-Fyter Co. (and subsidiaries), Brilhart Plastics Corp. Dir. Bklyn. Council for Social Planning, 1953-58; mem. Mayor's Com. on Puerto Rican Affairs, N.Y.C., 1955-57; Alumni trustee Johns Hopkins, 1953-54; former sec. bd. regents L.I. Coll. Hosp.; former chmn. lay adv. bd. Kings County Hosp. Center; bd. dirs. NCCJ, Brotherhood-in-Action, Bklyn. Boys Club. Named Hon. Citizen Md., 1958; recipient Johns Hopkins U. Disting. Alumnus award, 1967, Plaque Bd. of Judges of Ct. for svcs. as trustee John R. Bartels Libr., 1992; portrait of him presented to him by law clks. of U.S. Dist. Ct. (ea. dist.) N.Y., 1992. Fellow Am. Coll. Trial Lawyers; mem. Am., N.Y. State, Bklyn. bar assns., Assn. Bar City N.Y., N.Y. County Lawyers Assn., Fundacion Internacional Eloy Alfaro, Am. Law Inst., Fed. Bar Council, Am. Judicature Soc., Inst. Jud. Adminstrn., Squadron A Ex-Mems., Harvard Law Sch. Assn. N.Y.C. (v.p.), Omicron Delta Kappa, Delta Upsilon. Republican (past treas. exec. com. Kings County). Conglist. (trustee). Clubs: Harvard, Down Town Assn., Lawyers, Nat. Lawyers, Inc. (hon.). Died Feb. 13, 1997.

BARTELS, MILLARD, lawyer; b. Syracuse, N.Y., Feb. 24, 1905; s. Herman and Jane Agnes (Millard) B.; m. Eulalia Stevens; children—Millard Stevens, Chester Bruce, Jane Lee. A.B., Cornell U., 1927, LL.B., 1929. Bar: Conn. bar 1930. Since practiced in Hartford; gen. counsel Travelers Ins. Cos., Hartford, 1945-69; chmn. ins. exec. com., dir. Travelers Ins. Cos., 1955-70; hon. dir. Hosp. Corp. Am. Mem. Parole Bd., Conn. State Prison, 1953-55; Mem. Town Council of West Hartford, 1939-45, pres., 1943-45; Bd. dirs. Health Ins. Inst., chmn., 1966-67; mem. Cornell U. Council; adv. bd. Cornell Law Sch.; hon. trustee Bishop's Fund, Diocese of Conn., Bushnell Meml. Hall Corp.; regent U. Hartford, 1950-58; former trustee Soc. for Savs. Mem. Am., Conn., Hartford County bar assns., Assn. Life Ins. Counsel (pres. 1957-58), Health Ins. Assn. Am. (pres. 1960-61). Clubs: Hartford (pres. 1956-57), Hartford Golf. DIED 10/16/97. .

BARTHELME, DONALD, architect; b. Galveston, Tex., Aug. 4, 1907; s. Fred and Mary (Anderson) B.; m. Helen L. Bechtold, June 21, 1930 (dec. Mar. 1995); children: Donald, Joan Barthelme Bugbee, Peter, Frederick, Steven. B.Arch., U. Pa., 1930. Pvt. practice Galveston, 1935-36, Houston, 1940-63; designer various firms Dallas and Houston, 1936-40; instr. to profl. U. Houston, 1946-59, 61-73, prof. emeritus, 1973—; William Ward Watkins prof. Rice U., Houston, 1959-61; vis. prof. U. Pa., Tulane U., Rice U. Archtl. works include, St. Rose of Lima Ch. and Sch., Houston, West Columbia Elem. Sch., Tex. (1st award for schs. Sao Paulo 2d Biennial 1954), Adams Petroleum Ctr., Houston, exhibits, Nat. Gallery, Washington, Mus. Modern Art Ctr., N.Y.C. and Sao Paulo, also Dallas, Houston, Aurich, Berlin and Yogoslavia. Emeritus fellow AIA (honor awards 1948), Tex. Soc. Architects (hon. award 1952). Home: Houston Tex. Deceased.

BARTHOLOMEW, ALAN ALFRED, librarian, educator; b. Lancaster, Pa., June 10, 1953; s. Alfred Clinton and Joyce (Studenmund) B.; m. Mary Ellen Shope, June 21, 1975; children: Robert Alan, Daniel Nathan, Lydia Deniz. BA in History with honors, Ursinus Coll., 1975; MS, Drexel U., 1977; MA, Bryn Mawr Coll., 1985, PhD, 1989. Head libr. Tarsus (Turkey) Am. Sch., 1977-89; asst. prof. history Albertus Magnus Coll., New Haven, 1990—, dir. libr. svcs., 1990—, dir. master of arts in liberal studies program; pres. Friends of the Am. Bd. Schs. in Turkey, 1995—. Author: A History of Tarsus American School, 1988. Missionary United Ch. Bd. for World Ministries, 1977-89; mem. Stewardship and Missions Interpretation Dept. Conn. Conf. United Ch. of Christ, 1991—, chairperson, 1993—; mem. Conn. Coun. of Acad. Libr. Dirs. Mem. ALA, Am. Hist. Assn., Am. Soc. of Ch. History, Conn. Libr. Assn., New England Libr. Assn., Assn. of Grad. Liberal Studies, Assn. of Coll. and Rsch. Librs. Democrat. Mem. United Ch. of Christ. Died June 22, 1996.

BARTOCHA, BODO, scientist, educator; b. Wroclaw, Poland, Dec. 26, 1928; came to U.S., 1956, naturalized, 1964; s. Karl and Erna A. (Mevers) B.; m. Elisabeth Kieckhoefer, Nov. 23, 1957. B.S. in Chemistry and Physics, Philipps U., Marburg/Lahn, Germany, 1951, M.S. in Inorganic Chemistry, 1953, Ph.D. in Inorganic Chemistry, 1956. Milton fellow Harvard U., 1956-58; head propellant br. U.S. Naval Ordnance Lab., Corona, Calif., 1958-61; dir. research, acting dir. devel. U.S. Naval Propellant Plant, Indian Head, Md., 1961-64; dep. dir. naval scis. Office Naval Research Br. Office, London, Eng., 1964-66; asst. tech. dir. advanced planning and programs Naval Ordnance Sta., Indian Head, 1966-67; with NSF, Washington, 1967-88, staff assoc., dep. head office planning and policy studies, 1967-70, dep. exec. sec. exec. council, 1970-71, exec. asst. to asst. dir. nat. and internat. programs, 1971, dir. div. internat. programs, 1972-86; cons. in planning, evaluation and tech. forecasting, 1969-71; vis. scholar, assoc. dir. internat. programs U. Ariz., 1986-88, dir. Office Internat. programs, 1988-89, prof. Coll. Agr., 1988-92, adj. prof., 1993—; exec. dir. Tech. Advancement Assn., 1992-94. Author: (with Clinton A. Stone, Francis Narin) The Science of Managing Organized Technology, 1970, Wirtschaftliche und Gesellschaftliche Auswirkungen des

Technischen Fortschritts, 1971, The Education of Engineers and Social Responsibility, 1974; editor: (with M. Cetron) Technology Assessment in a Dynamic Environment, 1970, The Methodology of Technology Assessment, 1972; contbr. (with M. Cetron) articles to profl. jours. Patentee in field. Recipient Meritorious Civilian Service award U.S. Navy, 1966, Disting. Service award NSF, 1978. Fellow AAAS. DIED 05/16/97. .

BARTON, EVAN MANSFIELD, physician; b. Chgo., Nov. 7, 1903; s. Enos Melancthon and Mary C. (Rust) B.; m. Jane Purvis High, Oct. 16, 1937 (dec. 1980); children—Cynthia, Eric McMillan. Grad., Choate Sch., 1920; A.B., Williams Coll., 1924; M.D., Johns Hopkins, 1929. Intern Presbyn. Hosp., Chgo., 1929-30; resident in pathology Presbyn. Hosp., 1931-34; practice medicine, specializing internal medicine Chgo., 1935-96; attending physician Presbyn.-St. Lukes Hosp.; prof. medicine Rush. Med. Coll.; cons. rheumatology VA Hosp., Hines, Ill. Served from maj. to col., M.C. AUS, 1942-46. Fellow A.C.P.; mem. AMA, Am. Coll. Rheumatology, Chgo. Rheumatism Soc., Chgo. Soc. Internal Medicine (pres. 1969), Chgo. Pathol. Soc., Phi Beta Kappa, Phi Gamma Delta, Nu Sigma Nu. Republican. Baptist. Club: Quadrangle. Died Apr. 14, 1996.

BARTON, VICKIE, nursing supervisor, educator; b. Dayton, Ohio, Dec. 19, 1954; d. Arthur LeRoy and MaryJane (Dredge) Siebert; m. Thomas James Barton, Jr., Feb. 8, 1980. AAS, Miami U., 1979; BSN, Miami U., Hamilton, Ohio, 1986; AS, U. Cin., 1975. Cert. ACLS. Relief charge intensive care unit step down Kettering (Ohio) Med. Ctr., relief charge open heart intensive care unit; nursing supr. Sycamore Hosp., Miamisburg, Ohio; instr. nursing Kettering Coll. Med. Arts; ACLS instr. Recipient Peer award, Ruth Ann Busald award for ednl. excellence. Mem. AACN, NAFE. Home: Franklin Ohio Died Apr. 11, 1995.

BARTUNEK, ROBERT RICHARD, physician; b. Cleve., Dec. 3, 1914; s. Emil Arthur and Mae (Friedl) B.; m. Clare Elizabeth Lonsway, Dec. 30, 1943 (dec. July 1975); children: Jean Marie, Robert R., Thomas J.; m. Mary Anne Piotrkowski, July 23, 1978. A.B., Case Western Res. U., 1936, M.D., 1940. Diplomate: Am. Bd. Internal Medicine. Intern St. Alexis Hosp., Cleve., 1940-41; resident St. Alexis Hosp., 1941-42; fellow in medicine Cleve. Clinic., 1946-48; pvt. practice medicine, specializing in gastroenterology Cleve., 1949-91; mem. staff St. Alexis Hosp., 1948-91, dir. gastroenterology, 1949-81, dir. medicine, 1952-61, dir. labs., 1950-62; mem. staff St. Vincent Charity Hosp., Cleve., 1950-96; dir. gastroenterology St. Vincent Charity Hosp., 1960-83, dir. emeritus, 1983-96, dir. medicine, 1966-72, 80-81; assoc. mem. staff emeritus Met. Gen. Hosp.; cons. Marymount Hosp., Garfield Heights, Ohio; faculty mem. Case Western Res. U. Med. Sch., from 1952, up through ranks to assoc. prof., 1980. Mem. med. morals adv. bd. Cleve. Catholic Diocese. Served to lt. col. AUS, 1942-46. Decorated Bronze Star. Fellow Am. Coll. Gastroenterology (pres. 1963-64, Samuel Weiss award 1974), ACP, AAAS (council 1963-76); mem. Am. Geriatric Soc., Am. Soc. Gastrointestinal Endoscopy, Assn. Mil. Surgeons, Internat. Congress of Internal Medicine, Am. Soc. Internal Medicine, Cleve. Diabetes Assn. (dir. 1967-70), AMA, Ohio Med. Assn., Cleve. Acad. Medicine, L'Organisation Mondiale de Gastro-Enterologie (U.S. del. 1963-65), Nu Sigma Nu. Eder-Bartunek Gastroscope designed 1947-48 in Smithsonian Inst., 1971. Home: Beachwood Ohio Died Aug. 9, 1996.

BASKWILL, GEOFFREY RANDALL, travel association executive; b. Mayfield, Staffordshire, Eng., Nov. 22, 1920; arrived in Can., 1941; s. William Henry and Janet (Willshaw) B.; m. Irene E. Gillespie, May 31, 1943 (div. 1970); children: Beverley, Stephen, Deborah; Mary Elizabeth Andrews, Aug. 1, 1982. BSc, U. Leeds, 1939. Sales mgr. H. Hacking Co. Ltd., Vancouver, B.C. and Toronto, Ont., Can., 1946-50; gen. mgr. Sask. (Can.) Wool Products, Moose Jaw, 1950-56; pres. Slater & York Ltd., Moose Jaw, 1956-59; sales mgr. Hacking Agys., Vancouver, 1959-60; mktg. mgr. Frank W. Horner, Vancouver and Montreal, Que., Can., 1960-64; chief exec. officer Ea. Drug Svcs., Halifax, N.S., Can., 1964-69; pres. 500 Selection Svcs., Halifax, 1970-77, Randall Travel Mktg., Halifax, 1977-87, Avanti Travel Ltd., Halifax, 1982-89; exec. dir. Alliance Can. Travel Assns., Ottawa, Ont., 1990—. Alderman City of Moosejaw, 1951-59, police commr., 1958-59, dep. mayor, 1959. Pilot, squadron leader, RAF, 1939-46, ETO. Mem. Assn. Kinsmen Clubs (dist. gov. Sask.), Skal Club (pres.), Rideau Club (Ottawa).

BASSETT, CAROL HOFFER, mathematics educator; b. Scotland, S.D., Mar. 13, 1931; d. Joachim Francis and Clara Belle (Waggoner) Hoffer; m. Charles Walker Bassett, Sept. 15, 1956; children: David Francis, Elizabeth Alice. BA cum laude, U. S.D., 1953, MA, 1955. Tchr. math. Rock Rapids (Iowa) Regional High Sch., 1953-54; asst. instr. math. U. S.D., Vermillion, 1954-55; instr. math. Iowa State U., Ames, 1955-56, Kans. State U., Manhattan, 1956-58; tutor and sub. tchr. math. U. Kans., Lawrence High Sch., 1958-59; instr. math, asst. to chmn. U. Kans., Lawrence, 1959-64; instr. math. Colby Coll., Waterville, Maine, 1974-81, asst. prof. math., 1981-94, assoc. prof. math. emerita, 1994-95. Pres. Averill Sch. Parent/Tchr. Orgn., Waterville, Maine, 1972-73; coord. Colby Coll. Coop. Nursery Sch., Waterville, 1973-74; mem. affirmative action adv. com. Commn. Bd. Edn., Waterville, 1975-76, mem. ednl. devel. com., 1975-76. Mem. AAUP, Am. Math. Soc., Assn. for Women in Math., Math. Assn. Am., Nat. Coun. Tchrs. Math., Phi Beta Kappa (v.p. Colby Coll. chpt. 1983-84, pres. 1984-85, sec. 1985-92, exec. coun. 1992-94). Roman Catholic. Avocations: gardening, snowshoeing. Home: Waterville Maine Died Feb. 5, 1995.

BATES, JACK ALFRED, service executive; b. Columbus, Ohio, Mar. 4, 1923; s. Merritt Allen and Bertha Helen (Lehman) B.; m. Marie Virginia Warriner, Nov. 2, 1946 (div. June 1971); children: Wesley, Daniel, Amy Marie Muccio; m. Betty Maxine Campbell, Nov. 3, 1972. Student, Ohio State U., 1941, Miami U., 1942-43, Franklin U., 1946-47. Pres. Jack Bates Carpet Cleaning, Columbus, 1947-72; pres. Stanley Steemer Internat. Inc., Columbus, 1972-85, chmn. bd., 1985-95. Served as ensign USNR, 1943-46. Republican. Methodist. Home: Dublin Ohio Died Oct. 16, 1995.

BATTEN, JAMES KNOX, newspaper executive; b. Suffolk, Va., Jan. 11, 1936; s. Eugene Taylor and Josephine (Winslow) B.; m. Jean Elaine Trueworthy, Feb. 22, 1958; children: Mark Winslow, Laura Taylor, Taylor Edison. B.S., Davidson Coll., 1957; M. Pub. Affairs, Princeton, 1962. Reporter Charlotte (N.C.) Observer, 1957-58, 62-65; corr. Washington bur. Knight Newspapers, 1965-70; editorial staff Detroit Free Press, 1970-72; exec. editor Charlotte (N.C.) Observer, 1972-75; v.p. Knight-Ridder Newspapers, Inc., Miami, Fla., 1975-80, sr. v.p., 1980-82, pres., 1982-88, pres., chief exec. officer, 1988-89, chmn., chief exec. officer, 1989-95, chmn., 1995—. Trustee Knight Found., U. Miami; co-chair Miami Ptnrs. for Progress. With AUS, 1958-60. Recipient George Polk Meml. award for regional reporting, 1968; Sidney Hillman Found. award, 1968. Mem. Greater Miami C. of C. Methodist. Deceased.

BATTIN, JAMES FRANKLIN, judge, former congressman; b. Wichita, Kans., Feb. 13, 1925; m. Barbara Choate; children: Loyce Battin Peterson, Patricia Battin Pfeiffer, James Franklin. J.D., George Washington U., 1951. Bar: D.C., Mont. Practice in Washington, 1951-52; now in Billings; past dep. county atty.; past sec.-counsel City-County Planning Bd.; past asst. city atty. Billings; then city atty.; mem. Mont. Ho. of Reps., 1958-59; mem. 87th-91st Congresses from 2d Mont. dist., Mont.; resigned when apptd. U.S. dist. judge Mont., 1969; chief judge U.S. Dist. Ct. Mont., Billings, 1978-90, sr. judge, 1990—. Served with USNR, World War II. Mem. Am. Legion, DeMolay Legion of Honor. Presbyterian. Club: Mason (Shriner). Died Sept. 23, 1996.

BAUM, ALVIN JOHN, JR., professional clown, optometrist; b. Birmingham, Ala., June 25, 1918; s. Alvin John and Mildred (Fox) B.; m. Ruth Virginia Marks, Sept. 4, 1943 (div. 1966); children: Barbara, Joanne; m. Charlene Ballingee Wall, Feb. 26, 1971 (div. Oct. 1992). OD, Pa. Coll. Optometry, 1941. Cert. optometrist, Va. Optometrist specializing in contact lenses, Richmond, Va., 1945-96. Contbr. articles to profl. jours. Life mem. Tuckahoe Vol. Rescue Squad, Richmond, 1975; dir. Alvin The Clown (Baum) hosp. shows, Richmond, 1986-96; producer/dir. Patroitism Day Richmond Newspapers, Inc., 1988-91. Pres. Parents Without Partners, chpt. 116, 1970, Meadowbrook Estates Civic Assn., 1991-92. With U.S. Army, 1942-45, USCG aux., 1942-78, lt. col. USAF aux. CAP, 1952-80. Named Ofcl. Ambassador of Mirth Commonwealth of Va., 1987, Hon. Clown Ringling Bros. & Barnum and Bailey's Circus, 1978, Sr. Vol. Hall of Fame, Chesterfield County, Va., 1989, Clown Wall of Fame, Delavan, Wis. Mem. Richmond Optometric Soc. (past pres. 1950), Clown Assn. Richmond (dir.). Republican. Jewish. Clubs: Virginia Alley 3 (pres. 1969-72), Va. C.B. Communicators (past pres. 1986-87). Avocations: professional clown. Died December 22, 1996.

BAY, MELBURN EARL, entertainment professional; b. Bunker, Mo., Feb. 25, 1913; s. Albert Monroe and Edith (Bryson) B.; m. May Doris, May 24, 1918; children: Susan Lynn Banks, William A. Grad. high sch., Desoto Mo. Pres. Mel Bay Pubs., Mel Bay Music Ctr., Mel Bay Enterprises; radio rec. dance bands, theatre orchs. and night clubs, 1934-74; studio operator. Avocation: golfing, fishing.

BAYNE, JAMES WILMER, mechanical engineering educator; b. Balt., Apr. 2, 1925; s. John Ernest and Marie Jeanette (Sullivan) B.; m. Loretta Catherine Schumacher, Aug. 16, 1948; children: Marilyn Bayne Schroeder, Charles, Cathy, John, Kenneth, Lisa, Robert. BSME, U. Ill., 1946, MSME, 1950. From instr. to asst. prof. mech. engring. U. Ill., Urbana, 1946-57, assoc. prof., 1957-68, prof., 1969-96, prof. emeritus, 1985-96, acting head dept. mech. and indsl. engring., 1974-75, assoc. head dept. mech. and indsl. engring., 1970-85. Co-author: Opportunities in Mechanical Engineering. Trustee Holy Cross Ch., 1970-92. Served with USN, 1943-46. Recipient Everitt Undergrad. Teaching Excellence award, 1968, Western Electric-ASEE Outstanding Teaching award, 1972, Pierce award, 1981, Haliburton award, 1985, Disting. Alumni award U. Ill. Dept. Indsl./Mech. Engring., 1985, Coll. Engring. Alumni Honor award U. Ill., 1986. Mem. ASME (exec. com. mech. engring, div., past pres., sec.-treas. U. Ill. br.), Am. Soc. for Engring. Edn. (exec. com.), Assn. Coll. Honor Socs. (pres. 1975-76), U. Ill. Alumni Assn. (Loyalty award 1985), Sigma Tau, Pi Tau Sigma (pres. 1972-75, nat. sec.-treas. 1959-71, editor Condenser 1959-71), Tau Beta Pi, Omicron Delta Kappa, Sigma Chi (Order of Constantine 1986). Roman Catholic. Lodge: KC (grand knight 1958). Avocation: golf. Home: Champaign Ill. Died Dec. 19, 1996; interred St. Boniface, Seymour, IL.

BEACH, MARGARET GASTALDI (MRS. EDWARD WOODBRIDGE BEACH), foundation executive, nurse; b. Placerville, Calif., Aug. 10, 1915; d. Giovanni Batista and Josephine (Bisagno) Gastaldi; student Sacramento City Coll., 1934; grad. Mercy Coll. Nursing, 1938; m. Edward Woodbridge Beach, Feb. 15, 1946 (dec. Aug. 1968); children—Laura G. (Mrs. Robert L. Phillips), Edward Woodbridge, Margaret J. In charge urol. dept. Mercy Hosp., Sacramento, 1938-42; tchr. urology to student nurses, 1943-45. Treas., Germana M. Wilson Meml. Scholarship Found., 1967-93. Mem. Woman's Aux. AMA, Sacramento County Women Med. Soc., Am. Legion Aux., Italian Cultural Soc. Clubs: Carriage Trade, Women of the Moose, Hon. Guild St. Patrick's Day Mummurs.

BEAL, JOHN, actor, director, narrator; b. Joplin, Mo., Aug. 13, 1909; s. Edmund Albert and Agnes Josephine (Harragan) Bliedung; m. Helen Craig, July 13, 1934 (dec. July, 1986); children: Tita Beal Kruger, Tandy Beal Scoville. BS in Econs., Wharton Sch., U. Pa., 1930; student, Art Students League, N.Y.C., 1931, Chouinard Art Sch., Los Angeles, 1935, Sanden Portrait Classes, N.Y.C., 70's, 80's. Ind. actor, narrator, dir., 1930—; founder Actor's Hobby Market, Hollywood and Beverly Hills, Calif., circa 1948. Starred on Broadway in The Voice of The Turtle, The Teahouse of The August Moon, appeared in numerous other stage plays including Another Language, Russet Mantle, Soliloquy, Liberty Jones, Our Town, at Circle in the Sq., N.Y., 1959 and summer stock, 1970, The Front Page, 1968, star Long Day's Journey Into Night, Promenade Theatre and Cherry Ln. Theater, N.Y., 1971, Off-Broadway prodn. To Be Young, Gifted and Black, In The Matter of J. Robert Oppenheimer at Lincoln Ctr., 1969, co-star on Broadway as Dansker in musical Billy, The Iceman Cometh at Long Wharf Theatre, New Haven, 1972; toured with all star cast in The Little Foxes, 1968; performed with Nat. Actors Theatre on Broadway at Belasco Theatre in The Crucible, A Little Hotel on the Side, The Master Builder, 1991-92, The Seagull Lyceum Theatre, Three Men on a Horse, 1993; performances in other cities include No Time for Comedy, The Petrified Forest, The Fourposter, title role in Mr. Roberts, Everyman Today; appeared in regional theatre as Sir Thomas More in A Man for All Seasons, To Grandmother's House We Go, Mass Appeal, 1989; appearances in over 40 films including The Little Minister, Another Language, Les Miserables, My Six Convicts, The Sound and The Fury, starred as Major John Wesley Powell in Ten Who Dared, 1960, Amityville IIID, The Bride, The Firm; TV appearances include U.S. Steel Hour, The Long Way Home on Robert Montgomery Presents (Sylvania award), Bonanza, Loretta Young Show, Studio One, all 1960-61, The Adams Chronicles, chpts. 11, 12, 13, guest star The Waltons, co-star The Legend of Lizzie Borden, other roles in Carl Sandburg's Abraham Lincoln, Kojak, Hawkins, Ark II, The Streets of San Francisco, The Blue Knight, Eleanor and Franklin, The White House Years, Barnaby Jones, Family, A Year in The Life, Buck James, A Place at the Table, The Kid Who Loved Christmas; numerous roles on Voice of America, CBS Mystery Theatre; narrator Tandy Beal's Nutcracker, Listening to the Earth, for Tandy Beal & Co., 1987; inventor transposing aid John Beal's Music Color Wheels, 1940; author, illustrator lyrics and verse books, songs for children; portrait painter. Served as staff sgt. USAF, 1942-45. Democrat. Roman Catholic. Avocations: drawing, painting portraits, writing lyrics, verse books and songs for children, reading, walking. DIED 04/26/97. .

BEAMAN, SOPHIE ANN, nursing administrator, community health educator; b. Zebulon, N.C., July 7, 1939; d. Percy S. and Bettie E. (Adams) Brown; m. Rush L. Beaman; 1 child, Paul L. BS in Nursing, Agrl. and Tech. U. N.C., 1960; MS in Child Psychiat. Nursing, U. Md., 1968. Emergency rm. and admission unit nurse Oak Forest (Ill.) Hosp., 1960-61; rehab. nurse George Washington U. Hosp., Washington, 1961-63; staff nurse Sinai Hosp., Balt., 1963-64, head nurse Ob-gyn. dept., 1964-66; psychiat. nurse therapist children and adolescent svcs. Inner City Comty. Mental Health Clinic, Balt., 1968-70, dir. of clinic, 1970-72, dir. of children and adolescent svc., 1972-76; dir. nursing Walter P Carter Ctr., Balt., 1976-80, Md. Rehab. Ctr., Balt., 1980—; nursing rsch. project Sinai Hosp., Balt. 1967; cons. Social Svc. Child Day Care, Balt. 1969-70; presenter health edn. Comty. Groups, churches etc., Balt., 1980—. Author, editor (newsletter) Vocat. Rehab. Nursing, 1992. Mem. adv. bd. Adolescent Coffee House, Balt., 1969-70; judge Miss Wheelchair, Md., Balt., 1981. Mem. Assn. Rehab. Nursing, Nat. Rehab. Assn. Democrat. Baptist. Died Oct. 7, 1997.

BEAN, CHARLES PALMER, biophysicist, consultant; b. Buffalo, Nov. 27, 1923; s. Barton Adrian and Theresa (Palmer) B.; m. Elizabeth Harriman, Sept. 13, 1947; children: Katherine G., Bruce P., Margaret E., Sarah H., Gordon T. B.A., U. Buffalo, 1947; M.A., U. Ill., 1948, Ph.D., 1952. Research scientist Gen. Electric Co., Schenectady, 1951-85; adj. asso. prof. Rensselear Poly. Inst., Troy, N.Y., 1957-67, adj. prof., 1978-96, disting. prof., 1983-85, inst. prof., 1986-96 inst. prof. emeritus, 1994; adj. prof. SUNY, 1978-96, Union Coll., Schenectady, 1981-96; guest investigator Rockefeller U., N.Y.C., 1973-76. Contbr. articles to profl. jours.; asso. editor: Biophys. Jour., 1974-80. Bd. dirs. Dudley Obs., Albany, N.Y., 1975-90, pres., 1983-90; bd. dirs. Bellevue Research Found., Schenectady, 1973-96. Served with USAAF, 1943-46. Fellow Am. Phys. Soc., AAAS; mem. Biophys. Soc., Scis., Am. Acad. Arts and Scis., Nat. Acad. Sci., Fortnightly Club, Mohawk Golf Club. Patentee in field. Died Sept. 30, 1996.

BEARD, RICHARD LEONARD, education educator emeritus; b. Findlay, Ohio, Dec. 10, 1909; s. Jesse William and Mae (Leonard) B.; m. Reva Leona Coleman, July 3, 1937; children: Elaine Louise Coleman, John Coleman. AB, Findlay Coll., 1936; MA, Bowling Green State U., 1936; PhD, Ohio State U., 1943. Tchr. English Elida (Ohio) Pub. Schs., 1936-37; head English dept. Whitmer High Sch., Toledo, 1937-42; asst., then instr. Ohio State U., 1942-43; asst. prof. edn. Iowa State Tchrs. Coll., 1946-48; prof. edn. Marshall U., Huntington, W.Va., 1948-52; asso. prof. edn. U. N.C., Chapel Hill, 1952-57; head counselor tng. N.C. Coll. at Durham, 1952-56; chmn., prof. edn., counselor edn. dept. U. Va., Charlottsville, 1957-72; prof. edn. U. Va., 1972-80, prof. emeritus, 1980—, acting chmn. dept., 1977-78; lectr. Sta. KXEL, Waterloo, Iowa, 1947-48; TV instr. WUNC, Chapel Hill, N.C., 1954-57; ednl. cons. Served to 1st lt. AUS and USAAF, 1943-46, CBI. Career Service award Va. Personnel and Guidance Assn., 1967. Mem. Am. Personnel and Guidance Assn., Am. Assn. Counselor Edn. and Supervision, Nat. Vocational Guidance Assn., Assn. for Humanistic Edn. and Devel., Phi Delta Kappa. (Disting. Service award Va. chpt. 1966). Club: Colonnade. Died May 6, 1997.

BEATTIE, GEORGE, artist; b. Cleve., Aug. 2, 1919; s. George Hamilton and Mary (Mossman) B.; m. Virginia Lane, Dec. 31, 1943 (dec.); children: George III, Drew. Student, Cleve. Inst. Art. Painter, tchr. Atlanta, 1948-57; chmn. Dept. Creative Drawing Sch. Architecture Ga. Inst. Tech., 1957-67; exec. dir. Ga. Coun. Arts, 1967-75; dir. pub. svc. Art Ga. State U., 1975; vice chmn. Am. Assembly State Art Agys., 1968-69; hon. life mem. bd. dirs. High Mus. Art, hon. bd. dirs. Atlanta Arts Festival. One man shows include High Mus. Art, Atlanta, 1950, 61, Gallery Atlanta, 1952, Grand Ctrl. Moderns Gallery, N.Y.C., 1954, Ga. Inst. Tech. 1954, Columbus Mus. Arts and Crafts, 1956, 63, Hirschl and Adler Galleries, N.Y.C., 1960, Swan Coach House Gallery, Atlanta, 1965, 89, State Capitol Cldg., Atlanta, 1990; exhibited in group shows at Met. Mus. Art, 1952, Nat. Acad. Galleries, N.Y.C., 1955, Smithsonian Instn., 1955, Uffizi Logia, Florence, Italy, 1957, Schneider Gallery, Rome, 1957, Whitney Mus., 1958, 59, coliseum, N.Y., 1959, Swan Coach House Gallery, 1987; represented in permenent collections Whitney Mus., Childe Hassam Purchase, High Mus. Art, Columbus Mus. (Mead Packaging painting of Yr.), Montclair (N.J.) Mus., Temple Collection, Atlanta U. Collection, Larry Aldrich Collection, others; designer set designs Mcpl. Thetre Under Stars, Atlanta, 1954, 55, Opera in the Park, 1965, murals Ga. Agrl. Bldg., Atlanta, Fed. Post Office, Macon, Ga. Sgt. USAF, 1942-45. Recipient Gov's. award visual arts Ga., 1978, artist of excellence award Gov. Ga., 1990; grantee Nat. Inst. Arts and Letters, 1956-57; Fulbright grantee Italy. Deceased.

BECCHETTI, FREDERICK DANIEL, physicist, educator; b. Mpls., Mar. 3, 1943; s. Frederick Daniel and Olga Maxine Becchetti. B.S., U. Minn., 1965, M.S., 1968, Ph.D., 1969. Research assoc. Niels Bohr Inst., Copenhagen, 1969-71; research assoc. Lawrence Berkeley Lab., Calif., 1971-73; asst. prof. U. Mich., Ann Arbor, 1973-76; assoc. prof. U. Mich., 1976-82, prof. physics, 1982—. Contbr. articles to profl. jours. NSF fellow, 1970-71. Mem. IEEE, Am. Phys. Soc., Am. Assn. Physics Tchrs. Democrat. Roman Catholic.

BECK, PAUL ADAMS, metallurgist, educator; b. Budapest, Hungary, Feb. 5, 1908; came to U.S., 1928, naturalized, 1945; s. Philip O. and Laura (Bardos) B.; children—Paul John, Philip Odon. MS, Mich. Coll. Mining and Tech., 1929; ME, Royal Hungarian U. Tech. Scis., 1931; Dr.Min. (hon.), Leoben Inst. Tech., 1979; DSc (hon.), U. Ill., 1991. Metallurgist Am. Smelting & Refining Co., Perth Amboy, N.J., 1937-41; chief metallurgist Beryllium Corp., Reading, Pa., 1941-42; supt. metall. lab. Cleve. Graphite Bronze Co., 1942-45; faculty U. Notre Dame, 1945-51, prof. metallurgy, 1949-51, head dept. metallurgy, 1950-51; research prof. phys. metallurgy U. Ill., 1951-76, prof. emeritus, 1976—. Contbr. to: The Physics of Powder Metallurgy, 1951, Metal Interfaces, 1952, The Sorby Centennial Symposium on the History of Metallurgy, 1963, Recrystallization, Grain Growth and Textures, 1966, Phase Stability in Metals and Alloys, 1966, Order-Disorder Transformations in Alloys, 1974, Noble Metal Alloys, 1986; Editor: Theory of Alloy Phases, 1956, Electronic Structure and Alloy Chemistry of Transition Elements, 1963; co-editor: Magnetic and Inelastic Scattering of Neutrons by Metals, 1968, Magnetism In Alloys, 1972. Recipient U.S. Scientist award Humboldt Found., 1978, Heyn Meml. award German Metall. Soc., 1980. Fellow Metall. Soc. of AIME (Mathewson Gold Medal award 1952, ann. lectr. 1971, Hume-Rothery award 1974), Am. Soc. Metals (Sauveur Achievement award 1976), Am. Phys. Soc., Hungarian Phys. Soc. (hon.); mem. Nat. Acad. Engring. Died March 20, 1997.

BECK, ROBERT ARTHUR, insurance company executive; b. N.Y.C., Oct. 6, 1925; s. Arthur C. and Alma (Wickware) B.; m. Frances Theresa Kenny, Aug. 7, 1948; children: Robert Arthur, Arthur Francis, Kathleen Ann, Stephen Duncan, Theresa Frances. BS summa cum laude, Syracuse U., 1950. Fin. analyst Ford Motor Co., Detroit, 1950-51; salesman Prudential Ins. Co. of Am., 1951-56; mgr. Prudential Ins. Co. of Am., Cin., 1956-57; dir. agy. Prudential Ins. Co. of Am., Jacksonville, Fla., 1957-63; exec. gen. mgr. Prudential Ins. Co. of Am., Newark, 1963-65, v.p., 1965-66; sr. v.p. Prudential Ins. Co. of Am., Chgo., 1966; sr. v.p. Prudential Ins. Co. of Am., Newark, 1967-70, exec. v.p., 1970-73, pres., 1974-78, chmn., chief exec. officer, 1978-86, chmn. emeritus, 1987—, also bd. dirs.; bd. dirs. Campbell Soup Co., Xerox Corp., The Boeing Co., Texaco, Inc. Trustee Syracuse U.; past trustee Renaissance Newark, Inc.; past chmn. Bus. Roundtable; mem., past vice chmn. Bus. Council; past mem. exec. com. Pres. Reagan's Pvt. Sector Survey on Cost Control; past pres. N.J. Hist. Soc.; past vice-chmn. Kennedy Ctr. Corp. Fund Bd.; past chmn. United Way Am., Nat. Ctr. for State Cts., Am. Coll. Mem. Health Ins. Assn. (past chmn.), Life Ins. Mktg. and Rsch. Assn. (past chmn.), Beta Gamma Sigma (past pres., chief exec. officer dir.'s table), Navesink Club, Rumson Club, John's Island Club, Bent Pine Club, Knights of Malta. Died May 4, 1997.

BECK, STANLEY DWIGHT, retired entomology educator, researcher; b. Portland, Oreg., Oct. 17, 1919; s. Dwight William and Eunice (Dodd) B.; m. Isabel Helene Stalker, Aug. 29, 1943; children: Bruce Dwight, Diana Helene, Karen Christine, Marianne Elizabeth. B.S., Wash. State U., 1942; M.S., U. Wis., 1947, Ph.D., 1950; D.Sc., Luther Coll., 1972. Asst. prof. entomology U. Wis., Madison, 1950-57, assoc. prof., 1957-64, prof., 1964-69, W.A. Henry Disting. prof., 1969-88, emeritus, 1989.; chmn. cotton study team Nat. Acad. Sci., Washington, 1973-75; mem. editorial com. Annual Rev. Entomology, 1975-79. Editor, Wis. Acad. Scis., Arts and Leters, 1957-60; author: Simplicity of Science, 1959, Animal Photoperiodism, 1963, Insect Photoperiodism, 1968, (2d edit.), 1980, Modern Science and Christian Life, 1970, Two in the Game, 1993. Chmn. Madison Lutheran Campus Ministry, Wis., 1967-72; mem. Council of So. Wis. Dist., Am. Luth. Ch., 1968-70 and mem. Task Force on Ethical Issues in Medicine, 1975-76; mem. Task Force on Ch. and Disabilities Wis. Conf. Chs., 1980-82. Served to lt. USNR, 1942-45. AAAS fellow, 1964; recipient Founders Meml. award Entomol. Soc. Am., 1962, Disting. Achievement award Wash. State U. Almuni Assn., 1981. Mem. NAS, AAAS, Entomol. Soc. Am. (pres. 1982), Am. Soc. Zoologists, Phi Beta Kappa. Lutheran. Died July 8, 1997.

BECKER, BETTIE GERALDINE, artist; b. Peoria, Ill., Sept. 22, 1918; d. Harry Seymour and Magdalene Matilda (Hiller) B.; m. Lionel William Wathall, Nov. 10, 1945; children: Heather Lynn (dec.), Jeffrey Lee. BFA cum laude, U. Ill., Urbana, 1940; postgrad. Art Inst. Chgo., 1942-45, Art Student's League, 1946, Ill. Inst. tech., 1948. Dept. artist Liberty Mut. Ins. Co., Chgo., 1941-43; with Palenskie-Young Studio, 1943-46; free lance illustrator N.Y. Times, Chgo. Tribune, Saturday Rev. Lit., 1948-50; co-owner, operator Pangaea Gallery/Studio, Fish Creek, Wis.; pvt. tutor, tchr. studio classes. Exhibited one-man show Crossroads Gallery, Art Inst. Chgo., 1973; exhibited group shows including Critics' Choice show Art Rental Sales Gallery Art Inst. Chgo., 1972, Evanston-North Shore exhbns., 1964, 65, Chgo. Soc. Artists, 1967, 71, Union League, 1967, 72, Women in Art, Appleton (Wis.) Gallery Art, Milw. Art Mus., 1986, Neville Pub. Mus., Green Bay, Wis., 1987, Valperine Gallery, Madison, Wis. 1989, 92, Wis. Arts Gallery, Allouez, 1990, 94, North Cen. Coll., Naperville, Ill., 1991, Neville Mus., Green Bay, Wis., 1990, 91, 95-96, Art Works Gallery, Green Bay, 1992, 94, Tria II Gallery, Fish Creek, Wis., Oesterle Gallery, N. Ctrl. Coll., Naperville, 1993, Neville Mus., Green Bay, 1993-94, 96-97, Rabbi Joseph L. Baron Mus., Milw., 1994, Beacon St. Gallery, Chgo., 1995, Paint Box Gallery, Ephraim, Wis., 1995—, Oldtown Gallery, Chgo., 1995, William Bonifas Fine Arts Ctr., Escanaba, Mich., 1996, Chgo. Soc. Artists Oldtown Art Gallery, Chgo., 1996; represented in permanent collection Witte Meml. Mus., San Antonio, Miller Art Ctr., Stugeon Bay, Wis., Neville Mus., Green Bay, Wis.; executed mural (with F. Wiater) Talbot Lab. U. Ill., Urbana, 1940; contbr. articles and illustrations to mags. and newspapers. Active Campfire Girls, Chgo., 1968, 70; art chmn., mem. exec. bd. local PTA, 1959-60; active various art festivals, 1967—. Mem. Chgo. Soc. Artists (rec. sec. 1968-77, print and drawing show), Wis. Arts Coun., N.E. Wis. Arts Coun. (bd. dir.), Alumni Assn. Art Inst. Chgo., Door County Art League, Wis. Women in the Arts, Soc. Exptl. Artists. Republican. Mem. Unity Ch. Died Oct. 23, 1997.

BECKER, HERBERT P., mechanical engineer; b. N.Y.C., Oct. 8, 1920; s. David and Jeanette (Solomon) B.; m. Shirley Schneider, Apr. 13, 1947; children: Eileen Lois, Robert Bruce. BME, CCNY, 1942; MME, NYU, 1948. Registered profl. engr., N.Y., N.H., Mass. Sales engr., dir. A.I. McFarlan, N.Y.C., 1950-58; project engr. Syska & Hennessey, N.Y.C., 1958-64; asst. v.p. Michael Baker Jr. N.Y., N.Y.C., 1964-76; energy systems analyst Pope, Evans & Robbins, N.Y.C., 1976-80, Flack & Kurtz, N.Y.C., 1980-81; prin. H.P Becker, P.E., N.Y.C., 1981-95; energy crisis statement Congrl. Record, Washington, 1973; tchr. HVAC courses Voorhees C.C., NYU, U. Wis., Ctr. Profl. Advancement; lectr. in field. Contbr. numerous articles to profl. jours. With USN, 1943-45. Recipient Energy Engr. of Yr. award Bklyn Engrs. Club, 1990. Fellow ASHRAE (contbg. author handbook 1973-92, Best Jour. Paper award 1974, Crosby Field award 1974, N.Y. chpt. Honoree of Yr. 1995), Assn. Energy Engrs. (Energy Engr. of Yr. 1992). Achievements include research in concept of variable speed pumping systems to the commercial heating ventilating and air conditioning industry. Home: Bronx N.Y. Died Nov. 11, 1995.

BECKER, JOSEPH, information scientist; b. N.Y.C., Apr. 15, 1923; s. Julius and Bella (Mazer) B.; m. Arlene Berlin, Apr. 17, 1945; children: Jane C., Wendy L., William S., Sara E. B.Aero. Engring., Poly. Inst. Bklyn., 1944; M.S. in L.S., Cath. U. Am., 1955. Libr. asst. N.Y. Pub. Libr., 1939-44; electronic data processing Fed. Govt., 1946-66; pres. edn. com. Interuniv. Communications Council, U. Pitts, 1966-70; adj. prof. U. Pitts., 1966-69; adj. prof. libr. sci. UCLA, 1976-95; pres. Becker and Hayes Inc., Pacific Palisades, Calif., 1969-95; pres. Univ. of the World, La Jolla, Calif., 1985-95; lectr. Cath. U. Am., 1960-71; cons. in field. Author: Handbook of Data Processing for Libraries, 1970, Application of Computer Technology to Library Processes, 1973, First Book of Information Science, 1974, A National Approach to Scientific and Technical Information in the U.S., 1976; co-author: (with R.M. Hayes) Information Storage and Retrieval, 1963; editor: Wiley Information Sciences Series, 1963-95, Data Processing Equipment in Libraries Series, 1964-65, Interlibrary Communications and Information Networks, 1971, The Information Society, 1979-95. Tech. dir. computerized library exhibits World's Fair; mem. Nat. Commn. Libraries and Info. Sci., 1971-78, Nat. Archives Adv. Council, 1977-95. Served to capt. AUS, 1944-46. Research fellow computer sci. UCLA, 1960. Fellow AAAS (sec. sect. T-info., computers and communications 1972-77); mem. Assn. Computing Machinery, Am. Cybernetics Soc., Am. Soc. Info. Sci. (pres. 1969), ALA (hon., pres. info. sci. and automation div. 1968), Spl. Libr. Assn. (hon.). Clubs: Army-Navy (Washington), George Town (Washington), Cosmos (Washington); Los Angeles Athletic. Home: Pacific Palisades Calif. Died July 24, 1995.

BECKER, NORBERT V., real estate executive; b. Sublette, Ill., July 29, 1922; s. Justin George and Gertrude (Vincent) B.; m. Evelyn Anderson, Oct. 19, 1955. BS in Chemistry, Loras Coll., 1944. Chemist F.E. Shundler, Joliet, Ill., 1946-55, tech. dir., 1955-59; tech. dir. perlite divsn. Johns Manville, Joliet, 1959-60, plant mgr., 1960-67; plant supt. Johns Manville, Waukegan, Ill., 1967-69; prin. real estate cos., New Lenox and Joliet, Ill., 1970-76; exec. v.p. Will County Assn. Realtors, Joliet, 1976-80, pres., 1980—. Pres. adv. bd. Providence High Sch., New Lenox, 1974-80. With USN, 1944-46. Mem. IFA (pres. N.E. chpt. 1988, 90), Nat. Assn. Realtors, Am. Soc. Assn. Execs., Ill. Assn. Realtors (dist. v.p. 1983), Elks. Republican. Roman Catholic. Avocations: fishing, hunting, traveling, golf, collecting coins and stamps. Died Dec. 22, 1996.

BECKWITH, CHARLES EMILIO, English educator; b. Oberlin, Ohio, June 8, 1917; s. Charles Clifton and Anna (Wilkinson) B.; m. Elizabeth Ungar, Sept. 8, 1951; children—Constance Anne, James Allan, Margaret Andrea; m. Joanne Glossop, Dec. 19, 1971. A.B., U. Calif. at Berkeley, 1948, M.A., 1950; Ph.D., Yale U., 1956. Faculty English Cornell U., 1956-57; mem. faculty Calif. State U., L.A., 1957-96, prof. English, 1964-91, prof. emeritus, 1991-96, chmn. div. lang. arts, 1963-64, chmn. dept. English, 1964-67, 77-80, coord. Am. studies, 1975-77. Publs. editor: Twentieth Century Interpretations of A Tale of Two Cities, 1971; asst. editor: John Gay Poetry and Prose, 1974. Served to 2d lt. AUS, 1942-45. Mem. Calif. State Employees Assn., United Profs. Calif. Democrat. Unitarian. Died Dec. 22, 1996.

BEDNAR, JAMES EDMUND, lawyer; b. Omaha, Oct. 13, 1911; s. James Edmund and Britannia R. (Daughters) B.; m. Rachel A. Hancock, Oct. 15, 1940 (dec. May 1975); 1 dau., Lisa; m. Irene Lowrie, July 31, 1976. A.B., Stanford U., 1932; LL.B., Harvard U., 1935. Bar: Calif. 1936. Pvt. practice Los Angeles, 1937-91; assoc. firm Musick & Burrell, Los Angeles, 1937-49; partner Musick & Burrell, 1949-53, Jones & Bednar, Los Angeles, 1953-91; instr. law Southwestern U., Los Angeles, 1949-65; bd. dirs. Western Air & Refrigeration Inc., 1953-74, Preferred Theatres Corp.

Served with JAG Dept. AUS, 1943-46. Mem. Calif. Bar Assn., ABA, Phi Beta Kappa, Phi Gamma Delta. Methodist. Club: Jonathan (Los Angeles). Home: Marina Del Ray Calif. Died Dec. 6, 1991.

BEDWELL, THEODORE CLEVELAND, JR., physician, association executive; b. Caddo Mills, Tex., Mar. 31, 1909; s. Theodore Clevel and Mary Rebecca (Gary) B.; m. Blanche Elizabeth Harper, June 1, 1935; 1 dau., Beverly Anne. B.S., So. Meth. U., 1931; M.D., Baylor U., 1933; certificate indsl. medicine, Harvard Sch. Pub. Health, 1941; M.P.H., Johns Hopkins U., 1951. Diplomate, Am. Bd. Preventive Medicine and Pub. Health (aviation medicine 1953, occupational medicine 1956). Intern Baylor Hosp., Dallas, 1933-34; gen. practice medicine and surgery Longview, Tex., 1934-35; commd. 1st lt. M.C. U.S. Army, 1935; advanced through grades to maj. gen. USAF, 1963; staff duties various army hosp., 1935-40; grad. (Army Med. Field Service Sch.), 1940; chief indsl. medicine (Army Surgeon Gen. Office), 1940-42; grad. (USAAF Sch. Aviation Medicine), 1942; base surgeon, comdg. officer (USAAF hosps.), 1942-46; dep. surgeon (Air Material Command), 1946-47, surgeon, 1947-48; staff surgeon (5th Air Force), Nagoya, Japan, 1948-50; grad. (Air War Coll.), 1951-52; assigned Office Asst. Sec. Def. Health and Medicine, 1952-53; chief preventive medicine USAF Surgeon Gen.'s Office, 1953-56; dep. surgeon SAC, 1956-59, surgeon, 1959-61; comdr. USAF Aero. Med. Center, 1961, USAF Aero. Med. Center (Aerospace med. div. Air Force Systems Command), Brooks AFB, 1961-66; dir. staff Office Dep. Asst. Sec. Def., Health and Medicine; dep. asst. sec. of def., health and med. Office Dep. Asst. Sec. Def., Health and Medicine, Washington, 1966-68; ret., 1968; chief med. officer Bur. Health Ins., Social Security Adminstrn., Balt., 1968-75; asst. v.p. sci. and profl. relations, dir. med. relations Pharm. Mfrs. Assn., Washington, 1975-79. Decorated D.S.M., Air Force medal with oak leaf cluster; Republic Korea Presdl. citation; recipient Distinguished Alumnus award So. Meth. U., 1966, Spl. Aerospace Medicine Honor Citation AMA, 1964. Fellow Am. Coll. Preventive Medicine (v.p. aviation medicine 1960-61), Aerospace Med. Aesn. (pres. 1964-65), Royal Soc. Health (Eng.); mem. Soc. USAF Flight Surgeons (pres. 1961-62), Am. Pub. Health Assn., Assn. Mil. Surgeons, Internat. Acad. Aviation and Space Medicine, Phi Chi, Alpha Omega Alpha. Died Oct. 11, 1997.

BEECH, OLIVE ANN MELLOR, aircraft company executive; b. Waverly, Kans., Sept. 25, 1903; d. Frank B. and Suzannah (Miller) Mellor; m. Walter H. Beech, Feb. 24, 1930; children: Suzanne Mellor Beech Warner, Mary Lynn Beech Oliver. Ed. pub. schs., Paola; student pvt. schs. and night courses; DSc in Bus. Adminstrn. (hon.), Southwestern Coll., 1954, Wichita State U., 1982; LHD (hon.), St. Mary of the Plains Coll., 1988. Office mgr., bookkeeper Staley Elec. Co., Augusta, Kans., 1921-24; office mgr., sec. to. pres. Walter H. Beech Travel Air Co., Wichita, 1924-29; founder with husband Beech Aircraft Corp., Wichita, 1932, sec., treas., dir., 1932-50, pres., chmn. bd. dirs., 1950-68, chmn. bd., chief exec. officer, 1968-93, also chmn. bd., chief exec. officer subs. orgns.; bd. dirs. Raytheon Co., mem. exec. com., 1980-93; bd. dirs. 4th Nat. Bank and Trust Co., Wichita' participant in panel discussion on Women's Part in War Effort, Am. Bankers Assn. Forum, N.Y.C., 1943. Mem. adv. bd. Nat. Air and Space Mus. of Smithsonian Instn., other aero. mus.; bd. dirs. 4-H Found., United Way Wichita and Sedgwick County, Wichita Symphony Soc., Nat. Jr. Achievement, Met. Wichita Coun., Wichita Area Devel. Bd.; trustee Southwestern Coll., Winfield, Kans., Wichita State U. Endowment Assn., St. Francis Sch. Nursing Coun.; trustee emeritus Wesley Med. Ctr.; chmn. bd. trustees Wichita Art Assn.; nat. trustee Nat. Symphony, 1973-75; bd. dirs. Music Theatre Wichita. Recipient Lady Hay Drummond-Hay trophy, 1952, Dirs.' medal Freedoms Found., Valley Forge, Pa., 1953, Nat. Aviation Flight award, 1968, Meritorious award Nat. Bus. Aircraft Assn., 1969, Disting. Service award Bus. Aviation, 1971, Disting. Service citation U. Kans., 1974, award Wesley Med. Ctr., Wichita, 1977, plaque Pratt & Whitney Aircraft of Can. Ltd., 1978, Wright Bros. trophy and civilian award, 1980, Twin Special award YWCA, 1987; named one of 12 most disting. women U.S. N.Y. Times, 1943, Kansan of the Yr. Native Sons and Daus. of Kans., 1958, one of Am.'s 10 most successful bus. women by nation's bus. and fin. editors, 1970, one of nation's most outstanding women Am. Mothers' Com., 1970, one of 10 highest-ranking women in bus. Fortune mag., 1973, 78, Donor of Yr. Kans. Independent Coll. Fund, 1989; named to Internat. Forest of Friendship Memory Ln., 1978, Aviation Hall of Fame, 1981; laureate Jr. Achievement Nat. Bus. Hall of Fame, 1983; 1st inductee Kans. Aviation Hall of Fame, 1986, Wichita Jr. Achievement Bus. Hall of Fame, 1986; accepted Gold medal on behalf of late Walter H. Beech on his induction Aviation Hall of Fame, 1977; 1st inductee Kans. Bus. Hall of Fame, 1988. Mem. Women's Aero. Assn. (honoree for Disting. Service 1978), Nat. Aero. Assn. (elected Elder Statesman of Aviation 1974), Kans., Wichita (Over the Yrs. award 1963, Uncommon Citizen award 1976) chambers commerce, Am. Inst. Aeros. And Astronautics, Am. Bonanza Soc. (hon.), Soc. Automotive Engrs. (aviation div.), Soroptimists (hon. life dir. Wichita), Wichita Country Club, Wichita Club, Wings Club (Disting. Achievement award 1981). Home: Wichita Kans. Died July 6, 1993.

BEERMAN, HERMAN, physician, editor; b. Johnstown, Pa., Oct. 13, 1901; s. Morris and Fannie (Toby) B.; m. Emma N. Segal, May 13, 1924. A.B., U. Pa., 1923, M.D., 1927, Sc.D. in Medicine, 1935, M Dermatology (hon.), 1988. Diplomate: Am. Bd. Dermatology, 1935. Asst. Dept. Agr., Phila., 1925-26; intern Mt. Sinai Hosp., Phila., 1927-28; resident Hosp. U. Pa., 1929-33, asst. chief dermatology clinic, 1938-65, Abbott fellow in chemotherapeutic research, 1932-46; with U. Pa. Sch. Medicine, 1929-95, prof. dermatology, 1951-70, prof. emeritus, 1970-95; prof. U. Pa. Sch. Medicine (Grad. Sch. Medicine), 1947-67, chmn., 1949-67; assoc. serology Pepper Lab., 1949-95; asst. dir. Inst. Study Venereal Disease, 1939-54; physician out patient dept. Pa. Hosp., 1929-36; hosp. dermatologist, chief Pa. Hosp. (Out-Patient Service B), 1935-45, assoc. dermatologist, 1946-47, dermatologist, head dept., 1947-67, cons. dermatologist, 1967-95; asst. dermatologist radium clinic Phila. Gen. Hosp., 1938-40, dermatologist, 1940-53, active cons. dermatology, 1953-68, hon. cons. in dermatology, 1968-95; cons. lab. Children's Hosp., Phila., 1949-95; cons. VA Hosp., Phila., 1953-66; cons. pathology U.S. Naval Hosp., Phila., 1954-95; cons. dermatology VA Hosp., Coatesville, Pa., 1967-79, USPHS, 1937-95; pvt. practice, Phila., 1933-95; mem. panel venereal diseases subcom. infectious disease, chemotherapy NRC, 1954-95; Sigmund Pollitzer lectr. N.Y. U., 1963; Irving Wershaw Meml. lectr., Israel, 1967; Pusey Meml. lectr. Chgo. Dermatol. Soc., 1968; Ruben Nomland Meml. lectr. U. Iowa, 1968; Samuel M. Bluefarb lectr., Chgo., 1973; treas., trustee Inst. Dermatologic Communication and Education, 1963-95. Editorial bd.: Jour. Investigative Dermatology, 1948-53, Am. Jour. Med. Scis., Internat. Jour. Dermatology, Jour. Cutaneous Pathology, 1978-95; mem. bd. editors sect.: XIII-Dermatology and Syphilology, Excerpta Medica, 1950-75; contbr. articles to profl. jours. Hon. librarian Coll. Physicians of Phila., 1978, 82. Recipient Dean's award for outstanding achievements U. Pa., 1990; H. Beerman fellowship in dermatology established in his honor Sch. Medicine, U. Pa., 1990. Fellow ACP, AAAS, Phila. Coll. Physicians; mem. N.Y. Acad. Scis., Tissue Culture Assn., Med. Club Phila., Am. Acad. Dermatology (dir. 1941-48, 62-67, pres. 1965-67, hon.), Am. Soc. Dermatopathology (hon.; pres. 1965-66), Assn. Profs. Dermatology (dir. 1963-68, pres. 1967-68), Dermatology Found. (past trustee), Am. Dermatol. Assn. (hon.; dir. 1960-65, pres. 1967-68), Pacific Dermatol. Assn. (hon.), Phila. Dermatol. Assn., Brit. Assn. Dermatology (hon. fgn. mem.), Swedish Dermatol. Soc., Soc. Française de Dermatologie et Syphiligraphie (fgn. corr.), Finnish Dermatologic Soc. (hon.), Greek Dermatol. and Venereological Union (hon.), Deutsche Dermatologische Gesellschaft (hon.), Med. Soc. Study Venereal Disease (hon.; Eng.), Soc. Investigative Dermatology (ann. Herman Beerman lecture 1960-95, past pres., dir., sec.-treas. 1950-65, hon., Stephen Rothman award 1985), AMA, Med. Soc. Pa., AAUP, Soc. Investigation Psychosomatic Problems, John Morgan Soc., La Société Dermatol. Danoise (corr.), Am. Venereal Disease Assn. (Thomas Parran award 1974), Solomon Solis-Cohen Med. Lit. Soc. (pres. 1961), Iranian Soc. Dermatology and Venereology (hon.), Sociedad Venezolana De Dermatología, Venereología y Leprología (hon.), Phila. County Med. Soc. (chmn. com. on infectious diseases 1968-95, Strittmatter award 1986), Israeli Dermatol. Soc. (hon.), La Academia Mexicana de Dermatología (hon.), Academia Espanola de Dermatología y Sifilografia, Dermatol. Assn. Poland, Internat. Coll. Exptl. Dermatology, Laboratorio de Investigaciones Leprológicas, Societati Dermatologicae Danicae, Iowa Dermatol. Soc., Asociación Argentina de Dermatología (corr.), Am. Acad. Veterinary Medicine (hon.), Royal Soc. Medicine London (hon.; sect. dermatology), Pa. Acad. Dermatology (hon.), Physiol. Soc. Phila., Phila. Art Alliance, Pub. Health Soc. U. Pa., Phila. Rhuematism Soc., Am. Med. Writers Assn., Athenaeum, Sigma Xi, Phi Lambda Kappa, Alpha Omega Alpha (alumni mem.). Home: Philadelphia Pa. Died Jan. 1, 1995.

BEHLEN, HERBERT PETER, manufacturing company executive; b. Columbus, Nebr., Oct. 15, 1909; s. Frederick Arthur and Ella Sarah (Benthack) B.; m. Ethel Minnie Russell, Apr. 13, 1940 (dec. Aug. 1946); 1 dau., Donna Lee (Mrs Kenneth Kalkowski); stepchildren: James William, Karen Jean (Mrs. David Senften); m. Lois Viola Hickey, Jan. 24, 1948; 1 son, Frederick Michael. Student, U. Nebr., 1934-35. Co-founder Behlen Mfg. Co., Columbus, 1936; former dir., pres.; pres. G.M.W. Corp., Columbus, 1977-92; past pres. Behlen-Wickes Co. Ltd., Brandon, Man., Can.; pres. Columbus Conv. Center, 1972-92; dir. Industries Nebr. Pres. bd. Columbus YMCA, 1960; past dir. adv. bd. St. Mary's Hosp., 1961; past trustee Platte Coll. Found., Columbus, Nebr.; past bd. dirs. Doane Coll., Crete, Nebr. Served with USAAF, World War II. Recipient Legion of Merit award Sec. War for design of aircraft tng. aids, 1945; Nebr. Builder citation U. Nebr., 1977. Mem. Columbus C. of C. (past pres.), Am. Legion, Mo. Valley Orchid Soc. (past pres.). Republican. Conglist. Club: Elks Country. Home: Columbus Nebr. Died March 20, 1992.

BEHLER, ERNST HEITMAR, comparative literature educator; b. Essen, West Germany, Sept. 4, 1928; came to U.S., 1963, naturalized, 1976; s. Philip and Elisabeth (Lammerskoetter) B.; m. Diana Elizabeth Ipsen, Nov. 24, 1967; children—Constantine, Sophia, Caroline. Ph.D., U. Munich, Germany, 1951; post-grad., Sorbonne, Paris, France, 1951-53; Habilitation, U. Bonn, Germany, 1961. Asst. prof. philosophy U. Bonn, 1961-63; prof. Germanics and comparative lit. Washington U., St. Louis, 1963-65; prof. U. Wash., 1965—, chmn. humanities council, 1972-78, chmn. dept. comparative lit., dir. program humanities, 1975—; hon. prof. U. B.C., Can., Vancouver, 1968-73. Author: Die Ewigkeit der Welt, 1965, Friedrich Schlegel, 1968, Japanese transl., 1974, Klassische Ironie, Romantische Ironie, Tragische Ironie, 1972; Editor: Critical Edit. of Friedrich Schlegel, 35 vols, 1958—; Contbr. numerous articles on romantic movement, history of Aristotelianism during Middle Ages, and on lit. criticism to profl. jours. Guggenheim fellow, 1967, 75-76; Am. Philos. Soc. grantee, 1969, 72; Am. Council Learned Socs. fellow, 1970; grantee, 1974. Mem. Am. Comparative Lit. Assn., Ovidianum Societas (Bucharest, Roumania) (honoris causa), Medieval Acad. Am., Am. Soc. Eighteenth Century Studies, Am. Lessing Soc., Modern Lang. Assn. Am. Died Sept. 16, 1997.

BEHRSTOCK, JULIAN ROBERT, publishing consultant, writer; b. Chgo., Dec. 14, 1916; s. Herman and Anne (Joseph) B.; m. Monique Delessert, Sept. 24, 1971; 1 child, Jeremy. B.S. with honors, Northwestern U., 1937. Reporter Paris bur. Time mag. and Paris Herald Tribune, 1937-38; editor Compton's Pictured Ency., Chgo., 1938-41; staff writer Office Emergency Mgmt., Washington, 1941-42; editor U.S. Fgn. Broadcast Info. Service; then successively dir. bur. U.S. Fgn. Broadcast Info. Service, London, Hawaii and Tokyo, 1942-47; dir. free flow info. and book devel. UNESCO, Paris, 1948-76; chief editor UNESCO publs., Paris, 1971-76; book pub. cons., author, 1976-97; mem. internat. adv. bd. British pub. mag. LOGOS; cons. Kodansha Publ., Tokyo, 1952-97. Author: The Eighth Case: Troubled Times at the United Nations, 1987, Countess Mona Bismarck: A Biography, 1989; organizer, head Internat. Book Year, 1972. Trustee Am. Coll. in Paris; adv. bd. Bismarck Found. for Franco-Am. Friendship; mem. lit. jury Noma Award for Pub. in Africa; hon. advisor Asian Cultural Ctr. UNESCO, Tokyo. Recipient Internat. Book award for outstanding services to cause of books, 1977, Alumni Merit award Northwestern U. Alumni Assn., 1988. Mem. Phi Beta Kappa. Died Apr. 13, 1997.

BEISER, GERALD J., retired paper products company executive; b. Hamilton, Ohio, Nov. 11, 1930; s. Ralph M. and Eunice (Platt) B.; m. Delores Joy Reynolds, Oct. 8, 1960; children: Jeffrey Gerald, Jennifer Joy. A.B., Earlham Coll., 1952; M.B.A., U. Mich., 1956. Mgmt. trainee Champion Papers, Hamilton, 1956-60; asst. to v.p. finance Champion Papers, 1960-67; dir. budgets and forecasts U. S. Plywood-Champion Papers Inc. (name later changed to Champion Internat.), 1967-69, spl. asst. to chmn., 1968, dir. fin. planning, 1969-70, treas., 1970-72, v.p., treas., 1972-75, sr. v.p. fin., 1975—; mem. nat. adv. bd. Chem. Bank, N.Y.C., Fairfield County adv. bd. Conn. Nat. Bank; mem. N.Y. adv. bd. Allendale Ins.; bd. dirs. Weldwood Can., Ltd. Served with AUS, 1952-54. Mem. Am. Paper Inst. (chmn. fin. mgmt. com. 1978-80), The Conf. Bd.'s Coun. Fin. Execs., Alpha Kappa Psi. Club: Economic (N.Y.C.). Died Sept. 26, 1996.

BEKEFI, GEORGE, physics educator; b. Prague, Czechoslovakia, Mar. 14, 1925; s. Emerich and Klara (Braun) B. B.Sc., U. Coll., London, 1948; M.Sc., McGill U., 1950, Ph.D., 1952. Lectr. McGill U., Montreal, Can., 1952-55; asst. prof. McGill U., 1955-57; with div. sponsored research MIT, 1957-61, asst. prof. physics, 1961-64, assoc. prof., 1964-67, prof., 1967-95. Recipient Gold medal for Merit in Phys. Scis. Czech Acad. Scis., 1993; Guggenheim fellow, 1972-73. Mem. IEEE (Plasma Sci. and Applications award 1989), Am. Phys. Soc. (chmn. div. plasma physics 1978). Home: Brookline Mass. Died Aug. 17, 1995.

BELK, THOMAS MILBURN, apparel executive; b. Charlotte, N.C., Feb. 6, 1925; s. William Henry and Mary Leonora (Irwin) B.; m. Katherine McKay, May 19, 1953; children: Katherine Belk Morris, Thomas Milburn, Jr., Hamilton McKay, John Robert. BS in Mktg., U. N.C., 1948; DHL, St. Andrews Presbyn. Coll., 1978; D of Pub. Svc., U. N.C.C., 1987. With Belk Stores Services, Inc., 1948—, pres., 1980—; also pres. of most Belk Stores throughout S.E.; bd. dirs. exec. com. Nations Bank Corp.; bd. dirs. Bus. Devel. Corp. of N.C., Jefferson-Pilot Corp., Ruddick Corp. (group of supermarkets, textile and paper cos.). Bd. dirs. Mecklenburg County council Boy Scouts Am., U. N.C. at Charlotte Found., Inc.; bd. dirs. YMCA, pres., 1978-79; gen. chmn. Shrine Bowl of Carolinas, 1963-64, United Appeal, 1959; past pres. United Community Services; past chmn., trustee Montreat-Anderson Coll., 1964-68, St. Andrews Presbyn. Coll., Laurinburg, N.C., 1967-71; trustee Crossnore (N.C.) Sch., Inc., Davidson (N.C.) Coll., 1974—, Endowment Fund, 1975-78, Presbyn. Hosp., Charlotte; trustee U. N.C., Charlotte, 1975-84, chmn. 1982-84; mem. bd. visitors Wake Forest U. Lt. (j.g.), USN, 1943-46. Recipient Green Thumb award Apparel Found. of Am. Apparel Mfrs. Assn., 1989; named Young Man of Yr., Jr. C. of C., 1960, Man of Yr., Charlotte News, 1962, Tarheel of Week, Raleigh News & Observer, 1964, Man of Yr., Delta Sigma Pi, 1962. Mem. Charlotte C. of C. (chmn. 1977), N.C. Citizens for Bus. and Industry (past pres.), Cen. Charlotte Assn. (pres. 1965-66), Mountain Retreat Assn. (past chmn. bd. trustees). Democrat. Clubs: Charlotte Country, Quail Hollow Country, Country of N.C., Biltmore Forest, Grandfather Golf and Country (Linville, N.C.), DeBordieu Club (Georgetown, S.C.). Lodges: Rotary, Masons, Shriners (Charlotte bd. dirs.). Died Jan. 25, 1997.

BELL, CLARENCE ELMO, former state senator; b. Camden, Ark., Feb. 1, 1912; s. Joseph Dudley and Dona (Massengale) B.; A.B., Ouachita Bapt. U., 1934; M.A., U. Ark., 1940; m. Hope Raney, Aug. 16, 1936; children: Joseph Dudley, Beverly (Mrs. William Kinneman), Barbara (Mrs. Richard Blaine). High sch. prin., coach, Parkin, Ark., 1935-39; coach, Marked Tree, Ark., 1939-40; supt. schs., Parkin, 1941-63; with Ark. La. Gas Co., Little Rock, 1963—, dir., 1972—. Named Layman of Yr. in Edn., Ark., 1972; Conservationist of Yr., Ark., 1966. Rotarian. Died April 29, 1997.

BELL, JAMES MILTON, psychiatrist, educator; b. Portsmouth, Va., Nov. 5, 1921; s. Charles Edward and Lucy (Barnes) B. Student, Va. State Coll., 1939-40; BS, N.C. Cen. U. (formerly N.C. Coll.), 1943; MD, Meharry Med. Coll., 1947. Diplomate in psychiatry and child psychiatry Am. Bd. Psychiatry and Neurology (examiner 1980-97), Pan. Am. Med. Assn. (coun. psychiatry sect.); cert. N.Y. State Dept. Mental Hygiene. With Harlem Hosp., N.Y.C., 1947-48; asst. physician to clin. dir. Lakin (W.Va.) State Hosp., N.Y.C., 1948-51; fellow gen. psychiatry Menninger Sch. Psychiatry-Menninger Found., Topeka, 1953-56, tng. child psychiatry, 1957-58; resident Winter VA Hosp., Topeka, 1953-56; asst. sect. chief children's unit Topeka State Hosp., 1956-58; clin. teaching staff Menninger Sch. Psychiatry, 1956-58; clin. dir., psychiatrist Berkshire Farm Ctr. and Svcs. for Youth, Canaan, N.Y., 1959-86, sr. child and adolescent psychiatrist, 1986-97; mem. N.Y. State post-Vietnam planning comm., 1968, vice chmn. subcom. on returning veteran, 1968; clin. asst. to clin. prof. psychiatry Albany Med. Coll., Union U., 1959-97, mem. admission com., 1972-79; psychiatrist-in-charge Albany Home for Children, N.Y., 1959-77; staff psychiatrist Parsons Child and Family Ctr., 1977-97, staff mem. adoption svc. and foster care, 1995-97; asst. dispensary to dispensary psychiatrist Albany Med. Ctr. Clinic, 1960; trainee cons. Albany Child Guidance Ctr. Psychiat. Svc., Inc., 1961. cons. Keller U.S. Army Hosp., U.S. Mil. Acad., West Point, N.Y.; del. White House Conf. on Children, mem. exec. com., gov.'s state wide com., 1970; lectr. in field; spkr. in field worldwide; participant in confs., hosps., state/govt. coms. Contbr. numerous articles to profl. jours. Cons. Astor Home for Children, Rhinebeck, N.Y., 1965; instrnl. staff Frederick Amman Meml. Inst. Delinquency and Crime, St. Lawrence U., 1965-70; cons. adolescence N.Y. State Div. Youth, 1966-76, mem. med. rev. bd., 1974-76; mem. Child Abuse Adv. Coun., Albany; bd. dirs., mem. com. on proposed policy N.Y. Spaulding for Children, v.p., 1988-89; bd. dirs., exec. com. Guold Farm, Barrington, Mass.; life mem. NAACP; hon. life bd. mem. Parsons Child and Family Ctr., Albany, N.Y., 1995-97. Capt. M.C., AUS, 1951-53; col. USAR, 1955-85. Decorated Army Commendation medal, Meritorious Svc. medal, others, Plaque of Appreciation Com. of Physicians of Vol. Child Care Agencies, 1993, N.Y. Capital Dist. Coun. of Child and Adolescent Psychiatry, 1993, hon. Life Bd. Mem. Parsons Child and Family Ctr., Albany, N.Y., 1995; named Disting. Alumnus, Meharry Med. Coll., 1980; Tng. Inst. named in his honor Berkshire Farm Ctr. & Svcs. for Youth, 1996. Fellow AAAS (life), Am. Psychiat. Assn. (life, panelist on child & adolescent psychiatry 1963, chmn. coun. nat. affairs 1973-75, past vice-chmn.), Am. Acad. of Child and Adolescent Psychiatry (life, chmn. com. psychiat. facilities for children and adolescence 1973-75), Am. Orthopsychiat. Assn. (life, past dir.), Am. Soc. Adolescent Psychiatry (life), N.Y. Acad. Scis., Am. Coll. Psychiatrists (past mem. Stanley Dean award com.), Am. Psychopathol. Assn.; mem. AMA, Am. Acad. Polit. and Social Sci., Am. Soc. Addiction Medicine, Black Psychiatrists Am., Group for Advancement of Psychiatry (com. on child psychiatry), Inst. Religion and Health (charter), Coun. for Exceptional Children, Nat. Assn. Tng. Schs. and Juvenile Agys., Assn. N.Y. Educators of Emotionally Disturbed, Med. Soc. State N.Y. (life), Columbia Country med. assns., Child Care Workers (bd. dirs. N.Y.), Assn. Psychiat. Treatment of Offenders, N.Y. State Soc. Med. Rsch., N.Y. Capitol Dist. Coun. Child Psychiatry (pres. 1974), Am. Legion (life), Rotary (ann. participant youth leadership conf., Youth Leadership award 1992), Alpha Omega Alpha. Died Nov. 9, 1997; interred Maplegrove Cemetery, Kew Gardens, NY.

BELL, KENNETH JOHN, chemical engineer; b. Cleve., Mar. 1, 1930; s. Harold Henry and Alma Wilma (Southwick) B.; m. Karen Yvonne McLemore, June 23, 1956; children: Lorna Lyn, Tamra Ann, Craig Ian, Ellen Kym. BS ChemE, Case Inst. Tech., 1951; M ChemE, U. Del., 1953, PhD ChemE, 1955. Registered profl. engr., Okla. Engr. Hanford Ops., Gen. Electric Co., Richland, Wash., 1955-56; asst. prof. chem. engring. Case Inst. Tech., Cleve., 1956-61; assoc. prof. Okla. State U., Stillwater, 1961-67, prof., 1967—, Regents prof. chem. engring., 1977—, Kerr-McGee chair, 1990-94, chair emeritus, 1994—; rsch. engr. Heat Transfer Rsch. Inc., Alhambra, Calif., 1968-69; sr. chem. engr. Argonne (Ill.) Nat. Lab., 1985-96, cons., 1996—; cons. Phillips Petroleum, Dept. Energy, Heat Transfer Research, Inc., numerous other orgns., 1953—. Editor-in-chief Heat Transfer Engring., 1976-96, editor emeritus, 1997—; mem. editorial bd.: Heat Exchanger Design Handbook, 1974—; contbr. over 100 papers, book chpts., monographs to profl. publs. Fellow Am. Inst. Chem. Engrs. (chmn. heat transfer and energy conversion div., Donald Q. Kern award 1978); mem. NSPE, Okla. Soc. Profl. Engrs. (outstanding engr. award 1980), Am. Soc. Engring. Edn. Avocations: collecting fine editions, reading, mineralogy, Swiss philately. Died May 15, 1997.

BELL, MICHAEL DAVITT, history and literature educator; b. Pitts., Mar. 30, 1941; s. Davitt Stranahan and Marian (Whieldon) B.; m. Claudia Swett, 1967 (div. 1975); children—Sophia, Cathleen. A.B., Yale U., 1963; M.A., Harvard U., 1968, Ph.D., 1969. Instr. Princeton U., N.J., 1968-69; asst. prof. English Princeton U., 1969-75; assoc. prof. Williams Coll., Williamstown, Mass., 1975-79; prof. Williams Coll., 1979-81, J. Leland Miller prof. Am. history, lit. and eloquence, 1981—. Author: Hawthorne and the Historical Romance of New England, 1971; (with others) Blacks in America, 1971, The Development of American Romance, 1980, The Problem of American Realism, 1993; editor: Father Bombo's Pilgrimage to Mecca, 1975. Died April 9, 1997.

BELL, SIDNEY, university educator; b. Bklyn., July 14, 1929; s. Edward and Minnie (Iskowitz) B.; m. Edith Labowsky, Jan. 15, 1955; children: Alice, Daniel. BA, Bklyn. Coll., 1952; MA, U. Wis., Madison, 1956, PhD, 1969. Teaching asst. U. Wis., Madison, 1955-59; instr. U. Wis. Extension Ctrs., Racine, Kenosha, Wis., 1959-62; asst. prof. to prof. Concord Coll., Athens, W.Va., 1963—; chmn. social scis. div. Concord Coll., Athens, 1988-92; ret., 1992; mem. faculty adv., coun. to bd. dirs. W.Va. Humanities Found., Charleston, 1979-86; editorial bd. West Va. History, 1982-83. Author: Righteous Conquest, 1972, Regulation, Essential to Capitalism, 1982. Bd. dirs. W.Va. Rainbow Coalition, 1986—, Mercer County Community Action Assn., Princeton, 1966-69, W.Va. Council on Aging, Athens, 1973-75; round table participant W.Va. Humanities Found., Charleston, 1987. Cpl. U.S. Army, 1954-56. Named Associate Danforth Found., 1977-82. Mem. AAUP (pres. W.Va. 1982), ACLU (bd. dirs.), W.Va. Civil Liberties Union, Orgn. Am. Historians, W.Va. Hist. Assn., Common Cause W.Va. (bd. dirs.), W.Va. Consortium for Faculty and Course Devel. in Internat. Studies. Democrat. Jewish. Avocations: hiking, camping, backpacking, carpentry. DIED 12/13/96. .

BELLIN, MILTON ROCKWELL, artist; b. New Haven, Conn., June 6, 1913. BFA, Yale U., 1936. Cert. asst. prin., N.Y. Artist-in-residence Cen. Conn. State U., New Britain, 1937-40; illustrator-designer Houghton Mifflin Pub. Co., Boston, 1936-41; chief confidential designer Gould Aeronaut. Corp., Deep River, Conn., 1941-42; tech. designer Johnson, Cushing & Nevell, N.Y.C., 1942-46; art dir. Cinefects, Inc., N.Y.C., 1946-54, Republic Aviation Corp., Farmingdale, N.Y., 1954-66; asst. prin. High Sch. of Art and Design, N.Y.C., 1966-78; pres. Bellin Studio, N.Y.C., 1978-91; owner studio N.Y.C., Norwich, Conn., 1936—; art dir. Warner Bros. Cinerama, N.Y.C., 1955-56, Thunderbolt-P47 Pilots Assn., Farmingdale, 1964—; art coord. Air France, N.Y.C., Paris, 1975-76. One man show includes New Britain (Conn.) Mus. Am. Art, 1958; painter (mural) Fairfield and Stamford, Conn., 1936-37, Cen. Conn. State U., 1984, Nathan Hale-Slater Meml. Mus., Norwich, Conn., 1984, Farm Fire-Slater Meml. Mus., Norwich, 1991, Nat. Acad. Design, 1994. Photographer Murray Hill Community Com., N.Y.C., 1986-88. Recipient First prize Springfield (Mass.) Art Mus., 1937, Graphic award Mus. Modern Art, N.Y.C., 1940, Sage Allen award Wadsworth Atheneum, Hartford, Conn., 1952, First prize Ridgewood Art Inst., 1986, Harrisburg (Pa.) Art Assn., 1989, Kans. Soc. Pastel award, 1991, Springfield Instn. for Savs. award 74th Springfield Art League, 1993, Frank Nolan Meml. award Conn. Pastel Soc., 1993, Pauline Law Meml. award Allied Artist Am., 1994, Gladys Emerson Cook prize Nat. Acad. Design, 1994, Jurors Print award Erector Sq. Gallery, 1994, Medal of Honor for pastel and graphics Am. Artist Profl. League, 1994, 95, Award Pastel Soc. of the West Coast, 1997. Mem. Conn. Watercolor Soc. (hon. life), Pastel Soc. Am. (bd. dirs. 1981-86), Oil Painters Am., Met. Mus. Art, Audubon Artists, Allied Artists, Print Club Albany, Watercolor Soc. Ala. Avocations: single-engine pilot, photography, model making. Died Oct. 29, 1997.

BELMONT, AUGUST, investment banker; b. N.Y.C., Dec. 30, 1908; s. August and Alice Wall (de Goicouria) B., Jr.; m. Elizabeth Lee Saltonstall, June 16, 1931; children: Alice Lee, August, John Saltonstall, Priscilla; m. Louise Vietor Winston, Feb. 8, 1946. A.B., Harvard U., 1931. With Bonbright & Co., Inc. (investment bankers), N.Y.C., 1932-42; v.p., dir. Bonbright & Co., Inc. (investment bankers), 1942-46; v.p. Dillon, Read & Co. Inc., 1946-62, pres., 1962-70, chmn., 1971-73; pres. Nassau Assos., Inc., 1958-70, chmn., 1971-73; past dir. The Ryland Group, Tex. Gas Transmission Corp., Am. Viscose Corp., U.S. & Fgn. Securities Corp., Rouse Co., Am. Kennel Club (chmn. 1977-79), Cameron Iron Works, Inc., Chemistrand Corp., Congoleum Nairn Co., Great Am. Ins. Co.; spl. asst. to under sec. Navy, 1940. Hon. trustee Presbyn. Hosp., N.Y.C., Am. Mus. Natural History. Served to lt. comdr. USNR, 1942-45; served under comdr. Air Force, Pacific Fleet. Decorated Bronze Star. Clubs: Links (N.Y.C.); Jockey (steward 1978-95, chmn. 1982-83). Home: Easton Md. Died July 10, 1995.

BEMIS, HAL LAWALL, engineering and business executive; b. Palm Beach, Fla., Jan. 30, 1912; s. Henry E. and Elise (Lawall) B.; m. Isabel Mead, June 27, 1942 (div.); children: Elise, Carolyn, Claudia; m. Jeanne Chatham, June 5, 1982. B.S., MIT, 1935. With Campbell Soup Co., 1935-53; mgr., asst. to pres., v.p., dir. Campbell Soup Co., Ltd., 1946-53; organizer, pres. Mariner Corp., 1954-96; v.p. Hosp. Food Mgmt., Inc., 1954-57; sec., treas. Bell Key Corp., 1955-96; v.p. Coral Motel Corp., 1963-96; pres. Jennings Machine Corp., 1957-96; cons. Coopers & Lybrand, 1973-96; dir., mem. exec. and audit coms. Publicker Industries; chmn., dir. Phila. Reins. Corp.; dir. Ott, Hertner, Ott & Assos., Colonial Savs. Bank. Past pres. Commn. Twp. Lower Merion, Pa.; bd. dirs., chmn. Spring Garden Coll.; exec. bd. Com. of 70; chmn. bd. Am. Cancer Soc.; bd. dirs. Delaware Valley area Nat. Council on Alcoholism; adv. bd. Salvation Army; past trustee Haverford Sch.; dir. Phila. Port Corp., West Phila. Corp., Phila. Indsl. Devel. Corp.; trustee United Fund, Young Men's Inst.; pres., trustee Greater Phila. Found.; bd. dirs. Am. Diabetes Assn., M.I.T. Devel. Found., Broad St. So. Com.; mem. corp. bd. Goodwill Industries, Garrett-Williamson Found., chmn. Spring Garden Coll. Served 1st lt. to lt. col. AUS, 1942-45. Decorated Legion of Merit with oak leaf cluster, Bronze Star medal; Croix de Guerre (France). Mem. Greater Phila. C. of C. (past chmn. bd., past pres.), SAR, S.R., Pa. Soc., Newcomen Soc., Mil. Order World Wars, Mil. Order Fgn. Wars, Am. Legion (past comdr.), Tau Beta Pi, Delta Psi. Clubs: Union League (pres.), Racquet, Rittenhouse, Penn, Philadelphia; St. Anthony (N.Y.C.), Merion Golf (Ardmore, Pa.); Merion Cricket (dir.) (Haverford, Pa.); Bachelor's Barge, IV Street, Pine Valley Golf, Sunday Breakfast, Right Angle, Toronto Golf, Royal Canadian Yacht, Brit. Officers. Died Mar. 6, 1996.

BENHAM, DAVID BLAIR, civil engineer; b. Ft. Riley, Kans., Nov. 11, 1918; s. Webster Lance and Margaret Lemon (Drake) B.; m. Betty Louise Prichard, June 29, 1950; children: Barbara Lee, Zan, Nancy Ann, David Blair. Student, Oklahoma City U., 1936-37; B.S. in Engring., U.S Naval Acad., 1941; cert. naval architecture, U.S. Naval Acad., 1942. Registered profl. engr., 25 states. Jr. engr. Benham Engring. Co., Oklahoma City, 1946, design engr., jr. ptnr., 1947-52, sr. and mng. ptnr., 1952-64; sr. and mng. ptnr. Benham-Blair-Poppino-Stealy, Oklahoma City, 1964-67; pres., chmn. bd, chief exec. officer The Benham Group, Oklahoma City, 1967-74, chmn. bd., chief exec. officer, 1974—. Contbr. articles to profl. jours. Ruling elder, trustee Westminster Presbyn. Ch.; mem. Com. of 100 Oklahoma City, Inc.; colleague Kirkpatrick Ctr.; patron mem. Okla. Heritage Assn.; life mem. Okla. Hist. Soc.; trustee U.S. Naval Acad. Found.; mem. nat. adv. bd., chmn. adv. bd. Salvation Army, Okla. and Ark., 1978-79; vice-chmn. Okla. Mental Health Bd., 1958-59; chmn. bd. Okla. Bd. Registration Profl. Engrs., 1964; mem. Okla. Engring. Found. Blue Ribbon Action Com.; sr. active mem. bd. visitors Coll. Engring. U. of Okla.; past bd. visitors Coll. Engring. Okla. State U.; mem. Okla. Environ. Concerns Coun., Univ. Okla. Assocs.; bd. dirs. Am. Heart Assn., Oklahoma City metro Div.; past. bd. dirs. ARC, Oklahoma County chpt.; past. chmn. Easter Seals Telethon, 1981, 82; past trustee U. Ozarks, Clarksville, Ark. Served to lt. comdr. USN, 1941-46. Recipient citation Sec. Navy, World War II, cert. of qualification Nat. Bur. Engring. Registration, 1956; inducted Engring. Hall of Fame Coll. Engring., Okla. State U., 1973, Nat. Cowboy Hall of Fame. Mem. NSPE, ASTM, Am. Acad. Environ. Engrs. (life), Am. Cons. Engrs. Council (chmn. com. of fellows 1989-90), ASCE (life mem., past pres. Okla. sect.), Soc. Am. Mil. Engrs. (nat. dir. 1977-79 Outstanding Service award), Founder Okla. City Post, Okla. Soc. Profl. Engrs., Frontiers of Sci. Found. (Okla. past pres., vice chmn. bd.) Okla. State C. of C. (dir.), Okla. City C. of C. (dir.), Mil. Order World Wars (comdr. Oklahoma City 1979), U.S. Naval Acad. Alumni Assn. (nat. pres. 1975-77), U.S. Naval Acad. Blue and Gold Affiliate, Navy League U.S. (past nat. dir., state pres. Okla. chpt.), Newcomen Soc. N. Am. (honoree 1979), Am. Water Works Assn. (life). Clubs: Queensbury; Economic; Men's Dinner (mem. exec. com.); Oklahoma City Golf and Country; Beacon; Petroleum; Order of Red Red Rose. Lodges: Masons (32 degree), Shriners, Jesters.

BENJAMIN, ALBERT, III, retired naval officer, oil company executive; b. Boston, Mass., June 14, 1904; s. Albert and Etta Melissa (Wolcott) B.; m. Alice Moorhead Jackson, May 25, 1929; 1 son, Albert Jackson. B.S., U.S. Naval Acad., 1926. Commd. ensign U.S. Navy, 1926, advanced through grades to capt., 1943; sr. mil. mem. Army-Navy Mission to Uruguay,

1944; sr. Navy mem. Dept. State-Army-Navy Mission to Argentina, 1945; naval attache, also naval attache for air Am. embassy, Montevideo, Uruguay, 1941-45; asso. editor Am. mag., 1931-41, advt. dir., 1947-51; exec. asst. newspaper rels. This Week mag., N.Y.C., 1952-54; mgr. gen. mktg. div. This Week mag., 1954-56, mgr. sales devel., 1956-59; mgr. Latin Am. div. employee and pub. relations Texaco Inc., Caracas, Venezuela, 1959-60; dir. pub. affairs worldwide Texaco Inc., N.Y.C., 1960-69; mem. pub. info. adv. com. U.S. Navy; mem. nat. adv. bd. Am. Security Council. Contbr. to popular mags. Decorated Legion of Merit; recipient Disting. Service medal N.Y. State. Mem. SAR, Pub. Rels. Soc. Am., U.S. Naval Inst., Navy League, U.S. Naval Acad. Alumni Assn., Mil. Order World Wars, Ret. Officers Assn., U.S. Def. Com., Security and Intelligence Found., Assn. Former Intelligence Officers, Nature Conservancy, Nat. Pks. and Conservation Assn., Dutch Treat Club (N.Y.C.), Chevy Chase Club (Md.), Farmington Club (Va.).

BENJAMIN, THEODORE SIMON, publishing company executive; b. Jacksonville, Fla., Feb. 3, 1926; s. Roy A. and Phyllis M. (Meyer) B.; m. Barbara Joyce Bloch, Sept. 20, 1964; adopted children: Elizabeth J. Sanders, Ellen J.; children by previous marriage—Phyllis A., Jill. Student, N.C. State Coll. Agr. and Engring., Raleigh, 1943; B.A., U. Fla., 1948. Mgr. Leitman Assos., Switzerland and Germany, 1948-49, Tire Mart, Los Angeles, 1949-53; exec. v.p. Benjamin Co., Inc., N.Y.C., 1954-55, 57-82, pres., 1982-96; sales dir. Dell Calif. Corp., Los Angeles, 1956; speaker in field. Democratic Dist. leader, White Plains, N.Y., 1958-64; mem. Dem. City Com., 1960-68, Westchester County Dem. Com., 1964-68; mem. Am. Jewish Com.; chmn. Concerned Citizens for Open Space, Inc. Served with inf. AUS, 1944-46. Decorated Bronze Star medal; annual citizenship award, Ted Benjamin Memorial. Mem. Am. Book Producers Assn., Assn. Am. Pubs., Publishers' Luncheon Club, U. Fla. Alumni Assn., Phi Beta Kappa, Phi Kappa Phi, Phi Eta Sigma, Pi Lambda Phi. Home: White Plains N.Y. Died Dec. 16, 1996.

BENNE, KENNETH DEAN, educator; b. Morrowville, Kans., May 11, 1908; s. Henry and Bertha Alveen (Thrun) B. B.S., Kans. State Coll., 1930; A.M., U. Mich., 1936; Ph.D. (scholar Advanced Sch. Edn.), Columbia U., 1941; L.H.D. (hon.), Lesley Coll., Cambridge, Mass., 1969, Morris Brown Coll., 1971. Tchr. phys. and biol. scis. Concordia (Kans.) High Sch., 1930-35; tchr chemistry Manhattan (Kans.) High Sch., 1935-36; asso. social and philos. founds. edn. Columbia Tchrs. Coll., 1938-41; asso. prof. edn. and research asso. Horace Mann-Lincoln Inst., 1946-48; asst. prof. edn. U. Ill., 1941-46, prof. edn., 1948-53; editor Adult Leadership, 1952-53; Berenson prof. Boston U., 1953-73, prof. emeritus philosophy and human rels., 1973-92; dir. Human Rels. Ctr., 1953-61; pres. Staff and Orgn. Consultation, Inc., 1975-89; v.p. Boston Adult Edn. Ctr., 1957-60; exec. bd. New Eng. Adult Edn. Inst., 1958-69; fellow Nat. Tng. Lab., 1959-92, dir., 1959-62, 66-70. Author: A Conception of Authority, 1943, 71, Education for Tragedy, 1967, From Pedagogy to Anthropogy, 1981, Teach Me to Sing of Winter, 1988, The Task of Post-Contemporary Education, 1990; co-author: Discipline of Practical Judgment, 1943, Mobilizing Educational Resources, 1943, Group Dynamics and Social Action, 1950, Improvement of Practical Intelligence, 1950, Theoretical Foundations of Education, 1952, Social Foundations of Education, 1955, The Planning of Change, 1961, 69, 76, 85, The Educated Man, 1965, The University and the National Future, 1966, Philosophy and Educational Development, 1966, Mid-Twentieth Century American Philosophy, 1974, Educational Reconstruction, 1975, Work, Technology and Education, 1976, Teaching and Learning about Science and Social Policy, 1978, The Social Self, 1983; co-editor: Readings in Foundations of Education, 2 vols., 1941, Essays for John Dewey's Ninetieth Birthday, 1950, Human Relations in Curriculum Change, 1951, Readings in Social Aspects of Education, 1951, T-Group Theory and Laboratory Method, 1963, The Laboratory Method of Changing and Learning, 1975, Society as Educator in an Age of Transition, 1987; editorial bd.: Progressive Edn., 1948-53, Jour. Applied Behavioral Sci., 1963-68; bd. cons. editors: Teachers College Record, 1962-64, Integrativ Therapie, 1973-92. Mem. Mayor's Civic Unity Com., Boston, 1954-59; mem. Commn. Human Relations, 1957-65. Served to lt. comdr. USNR, 1942-46. Recipient Kilpatrick award for disting. contbn. to Am. Philosophy of Edn., 1943, Disting. Alumni award Tchrs. Coll. Columbia U., 1989; Bode Meml. lectr. Ohio State U., 1961; Centennial prof. social scis. U. Ky., 1965. Fellow Nat. Coun. Religion in Higher Edn., Internat. Inst. Arts and Letters, NTL Inst.; mem. Adult Edn. Assn. (pres. 1955-56, publs. com. 1956-59), Soc. for Psychol. Study Social Issues, Am. Philos. Assn., Philosophy of Edn. Soc. (pres. 1950-51), Am. Edn. Fellowship (pres. 1949-52), Internat. Assn. Applied Social Scientists (chmn. bd. 1971-73), Phi Delta Kappa, Phi Kappa Phi, Kappa Delta Pi. Home: Washington D.C. Died Oct. 8, 1992.

BENNETT, CARL MCGHIE, engineering company executive, consultant, army reserve and national guard officer; b. Salt Lake City, Sept. 11, 1933; s. M. Woodruff and Sybil L. (McGhie) B.; m. Ardel Krantz, Aug. 10, 1954; children: Carlene, Matt, Brent, Dale, Hugh, Caren, Teri. BS, U. Utah, 1956; postgrad., U.S. Army Engr. Sch., 1964; M, Command and Gen. Staff Coll., 1974; postgrad., Indsl. Coll. Armed Forces, 1976. Commd. 2d. lt. ROTC U.S. Army, 1953; treas. and office mgr. Hercules Inc. and Data Source Corp., Salt Lake City and Los Angeles, 1963-70; controller Boise Cascade, Los Angeles, 1970-72; corp. controller Griffin Devel. Co., Los Angeles, 1972-75; controller Dart Industries, Dart Resorts, Los Angeles, 1975-78; chief fin. officer Ford, Bacon & Davis, Salt Lake City, 1978-87; pres. B & Assocs., 1987-92; cons. in field, 1992—. Rep. County Del., 1992-94. Lt. col. USAR, 1953-79, col. Utah N.G., 1985-93, AUS, 1993—. Recipient Meritorious Service medal Pres. of the U.S., 1979. Mem. Controllers Council, Nat. Assn. Accts. (v.p., bd. dirs. 1979-85), Inst. Mgmt. Accts. Dec. Feb. 14, 1995.

BENNETT, EDWARD HERBERT, JR., architect; b. Chgo., Dec. 22, 1915; s. Edward Herbert and Catherine (Jones) B.; 1 child, Edward Herbert III; m. Katharine F. Phillips, Nov. 4, 1960; stepchildren: David C. Phillips, Frederick F. Phillips. A.B., Harvard U., 1938, M.Arch., 1950. Mem. firm Schweikher & Elting (architects), Chgo., 1953-54, Elting & Bennett, 1954-56; pvt. practice architecture Chgo., 1956-94; Bd. dirs. Chgo. Regional Planning Assn., 1952-58; vice chmn. Lake County regional planning commn., 1958-60, chmn., 1960-70. Bd. dirs. Lyric Opera of Chgo., 1956-76; trustee Chgo. Art Inst., 1958-85, hon trustee, 1985-94; trustee Chicago Symphony Orch., 1969-78. Served to lt. comdr. USNR, 1940-45. Mem. Chgo. Orchestral Assn., AIA. Clubs: Arts (Chgo.), Chgo. (Chgo.), Cliff Dwellers (Chgo.). Died Dec. 6, 1994.

BENNETT, JOHN F(REDERIC), poet, educator; b. Pittsfield, Mass., Mar. 12, 1920; s. John Frederick and Lauretta (Simpson) Garrigan; m. Elizabeth Mary Owens Jones, Aug. 20, 1960; children: Catherine Jeremy, Jennifer Nora. B.A., Oberlin Coll., 1942; M.A., U. Wis., 1950, Ph.D., 1956. Instr. English Indiana U., Jeffersonville, 1953-58; asst. prof. Beloit (Wis.) Coll., 1958-59; asso. prof. Rockford (Ill.) Coll., 1959-62, prof., 1962-68, chmn. dept., 1960-68; prof. English St. Norbert Coll., DePere, Wis., 1968-70; Bernard H. Pennings Disting. prof. St. Norbert Coll., 1970-91, poet in residence, 1979-91; Mem. faculty adv. com. Ill. Bd. Higher Edn., 1962-68. Author: Melville's Humanitarian Thought: A Study in Moral Idealism, 1956; poetry The Zoo Manuscript, 1968; Griefs and Exultations, 1970, The Struck Leviathan, 1970, Knights and Squires, 1972, Poems from a Christian Enclave, 1976, Echoes from the Peaceable Kingdom, 1978, Seeds of Mustard, Seeds of Tare, 1979, Fire in the Dust, 1980, Beyond the Compass Rose, 1983, The Nixon Rubaiyat, 1984, The Holy Unicorn, 1985, A Book of Trousered Apes, 1987, Beyond These Creatures Dragons Wait, 1988, A Tuning of the Sky, 1989, The Iambic Butterfly Net, 1990, Dinner in the Union Lunch, 1991; co-editor: poetry Beloit Poetry Jour., 1958-72. Served to 1st lt. arty. AUS, 1942-46; ETO, OSS. Recipient Borestone Publs., Devins Meml. award, 1970, Chgo. Book Clinic award, 1970, Printing Industries Am. award, 1970, Midwestern Book of Year award, 1970, Am. Assn. U. Presses Book Competition award, 1970, Soc. Midland Authors Poetry award, 1970, 79; named Notable Wisconsin Author, 1980, Donald B. King Disting. Scholar, 1986. Mem. Melville Soc., Amnesty Internat., Whale Protection Fund., Smithsonian Instn., Am. Mus. Natural History, Greenpeace, DAV, Wilderness Soc., Common Cause, Anti-Defamation League, Audubon Soc., NRA, Sierra Club. Democrat. Episcopalian. Died Nov. 30, 1991.

BENNETT, MARY KATHERINE, mathematics educator; b. Waterbury, Conn., Jan. 30, 1940; d. Thomas Francis and Gertrude (Powell) B. BA, Albertus Magnus Coll., New Haven, 1961; MA, U. Mass., 1965, PhD, 1966. Tchr. Wilby High Sch., Waterbury, 1961-63; J.W. Young rsch. instr. Dartmouth Coll., Hanover, N.H., 1068-70; teaching asst. U. Mass., Amherst, 1963-65, grad. fellow, 1965-66, asst. prof. math., 1966-68, prof., 1970—. Contbr. articles to lattice theory to profl. jours. Mem. Am. Math. Soc., Math. Assn. Am. Died Mar. 15, 1997.

BENNETT, NORMAN E., publisher; b. Saugus, Mass., Aug. 15, 1917; s. Elmer A. and Mildred J. (Smith) B.; m. Eleanor Teel, Dec. 3, 1942; children: Roger, Jeffrey, Alison. Student, N.Y. U., 1937-40. Dir. bus. relations, v.p. Nat. Better Bus. Bur., 1946-51; with P.F. Collier Inc., N.Y.C., 1951-93; sr. v.p. P.F. Collier Inc., 1960-65, pres., 1965-68, chmn. bd., 1968-71; v.p. Crowell-Collier & MacMillan, Inc., N.Y.C., 1961-67; sr. v.p. Crowell-Collier & MacMillan, Inc., 1968-73; chmn. bd. Merit Students Ency., Inc., 1968-71; pres. P.F. Collier Ltd., Toronto, Ont., Can., 1965-68; chmn. P.F. Collier Ltd., 1968-71; chmn. bd. Crowell Internat., 1970-72. Past mem. at large Nassau County council Boy Scouts Am.; Past trustee Oceanside (N.Y.) Pub. Library. Served to lt. col., ord. dept. AUS, 1941-45. Club: Laconia (N.H.) Country. Home: Center Harbor N.H. Died Jan. 5, 1993.

BENNINGHOFF, WILLIAM SHIFFER, educator, plant ecologist; b. Ft. Wayne, Ind., Mar. 23, 1918; s. William Nelson and Edith Esther (Shiffer) B.; m. Gladys Helen Kunst, Apr. 19, 1941 (div. 1968); children: Valerie Anne, Jonathan William; m. Anne Louise Stevenson, June 14, 1969. SB magna cum laude, Harvard, 1940; AM, Harvard U., 1942, PhD, 1948. Botanist U.S. Geol. Survey, Washington, 1948-57; chief sect. U.S. Geol. Survey (Alaska terrain and permafrost sect.), 1953-57; mem. faculty U. Mich., 1957-93, assoc. prof. botany, 1957-60, prof., 1960-88, prof. emeritus, 1988-93; prof. U. Mich. Biol. Sta., Douglas Lake, summers 1957, 61, 63, 66; palynologist Great Lakes Research div. Inst. Sci. and Tech., 1960-63; prof., asst. dir. Bot. Gardens, 1965-66, prof., curator, 1966-93, acting dir., 1975, dir., 1977-86; Mem. com. on polar research, panel on biol. and med. scis. Nat. Acad. Scis., 1962-75, chmn., 1966-71, 1973-75, mem. polar research bd., 1975-77; chmn. aerobiology panel U.S. Nat. Com. for Internat. Biol. Program, 1967, dir. aerobiology program, 1968-72; convenor Internat. Biol. Program aerobiology working group, 1968-74; mem. working group on biology Sci. Com. on Antarctic Research, 1968-71, 74-82, chmn., 1974-80; sec. commn. on aerobiology Internat. Union Biol. Scis., 1973-82; convenor 1st Gordon Research Conf. on Aerobiology, 1980. Asso. editor: Ecological Monographs, 1965-67; Contbr. numerous articles on Pleistocene biogeography, pollen and spores in atmosphere to sci. jours. Served to lt. Commander, USNR, 1942-46, ETO, PTO. Recipient Meritorious Service award Dept. Interior, 1954, Antarctic Svc. medal of U.S.A., 1973, medal for distinguished contbns. to natural sci. U. Hiroshima, Japan, 1974. Fellow AAAS, Geol. Soc. Am., Arctic Inst. N.Am. (gov. 1957-63, 66-71, chmn. research com. 1964-66, vice chmn. bd. 1967-68); mem. Am. Polar Soc. (bd. govs. 1968-93), Bot. Soc. Am., Am. Soc. Limnology and Oceanography, Ecol. Soc. Am., Internat. Soc. Plant Geography and Ecology (v.p. 1963-80), Internat. Assn. for Aerobiology (founding pres. 1974, hon. mem. 1982-93), Sigma Xi. Clubs: Explorers (N.Y.C.); Cosmos (Washington). Home: Ann Arbor Mich. Died Jan. 8, 1993; buried Arlington National Cemetery.

BENNINGTON, NEVILLE LYNNE, biology educator; b. Canton, Ohio, Aug. 8, 1906; s. James William and Leora Bell (Slates) B.; m. Virginia Rebecca Tudor, Apr. 19, 1930; children: James Lynne, Ann Tudor. A.B., Coll. of Wooster, 1928; postgrad., Franz Theodore Stone Inst. Hydrobiology, summers 1928, 29; M.A., Northwestern U., 1930, Ph.D., 1934. Instr. zoology Northwestern, part-time 1934-35, mem. staff summer session, 1948; instr. biology Coll. of Wooster (Ohio), 1936; asst. prof. botany and zoology Beloit (Wis.) Coll., 1937-38, assoc. prof., 1939-40, prof., 1941-42; prof. biology Cornelia Bailey Williams Found., 1943-92; rschr. Oceanographic Labs. Friday Harbor, Washington U., summer 1934; mem. stream survey Ohio Div. Conservation, 1936; biologist in charge lake survey So. area Wis. Wis. Conservation Dept., summer 1946; rsch. cons. Parker Pen Co., 1955-92; head insts. sect. NSF, 1959-60, cons., 1960-92; asst. commr. for profl. edn. state edn. dept. SUNY, 1962-66; div. dir. pre-coll. edn. in sci. NSF, Washington, 1966-68; dir. grants adminstrn. U. Wis., Oshkosh, 1968-73; protocol reviewer Health Scis. Cons. Corp., 1980-92; cons. Health Scis. Cons. Corp., 1980-92. Mem. AAAS, AAUP, Am. Soc. Zoologists, Sigma Xi, Omicron Delta Kappa, Sigma Pi. Research germ cells and reproductive rhythms of fish. Home: Walnut Creek Calif. Died May 10, 1992, Orinda, Fla.

BENSLEY, EDWARD HORTON, pathologist, educator; b. Toronto, Ont., Can., Dec. 10, 1906; s. Benjamin Arthur and Ruth (Horton) B.; m. Catharine Speid, Sept. 9, 1944. B.A. (Fulton scholar 1924, Balmer scholar 1924, Blake scholar 1925), U. Toronto, 1927, B.A. (Wilson scholar, 1926, Bronze medal Brit. Assn. Advancement Sci. 1927), 1927, M.D. (Gold medal 1930), 1930; D.Sc. (hon.), Acadia U., 1964. Diplomate: licentiate Med. Council Can. Jr. intern Montreal Gen. Hosp., 1930-31, resident pathology, 1931-32, mem. staff, 1932—, dir. dept. metabolism and toxicology, 1947-61, chem. pathologist-in-chief, 1947-61, sec. med. bd., 1951-60, cons. physician, 1962—; hon. cons. Royal Victoria Hosp., 1962-67; mem. faculty McGill U., 1932-34, 41—; asst. dir. Univ. Med. Clinic, 1952-57, vice dean faculty medicine, 1961-67, prof. exptl. medicine, 1965-77, hon. lectr. biochemistry, 1956-69, lectr. in history of medicine, 1968—, prof. medicine emeritus, 1977—, hon. Osler librarian, 1979—; cons. metabolism and toxicology Reddy Meml. Hosp., 1950-61; chmn. nutrition panel Def. Research Bd., 1949-52; mem. Canadian Council Nutrition, 1948-58; cons. nutrition Canadian Forces Med. Council, 1957-60; pres. Nutrition Soc. Can., 1961-62. Contbr. numerous articles in fields metabolic diseases, clin. chemistry, nutrition, toxicology, med. history. Bd. curators, past chmn. Osler Library. Served to maj. M.C. Royal Canadian Army, World War II. Decorated Order Brit. Empire. Fellow A.C.P., Royal Coll. Physicians Can., Chem. Inst. Can.; mem. Canadian Med. Assn. (past chmn. com. nutrition), Canadian Soc. Clin. Chemists (past pres.), Osler Soc. (past hon. pres.), Canadian Fedn. Biol. Socs. (past hon. sec.).

BENSON, D. FRANK, neurologist, educator; b. Grand Forks, N.D., Mar. 26, 1928; s. Frank Lawrence and Emily Margaret (Groom) B.; m. Donna Virginia Bagge, Sept. 4, 1948; children: Robert, Vicki, Sonia. BA, U. N.D., 1950, BS in Medicine, 1951; MD, Northwestern U., 1953. Diplomate Am. Bd. Psychiatry and Neurology. Intern Good Samaritan Hosp., Portland, Oreg., 1953-54; gen. practitioner Sweet Home, Oreg.,

1954-56; resident in neurology VA Hosp., San Francisco, 1956-59; neurologist pvt. practice Eugene, Oreg., 1959-64; neurologist, prof. Boston VA Hosp., Boston U., 1964-79; neurologist, prof. UCLA Sch. of Medicine, 1979-95, prof. emeritus, 1995—. Author, co-editor, editor of 153 papers, 82 chpts. and 8 books. Pvt. 1st class U.S. Army, 1946-47, Japan. Recipient Weir Mitchell award Am. Acad. Neurology, 1958, Disting. Alumnus award U. N.D., 1983. Mem. Am. Neurol. Assn., Am. Acad. Neurology, Acad. of Aphasia. DIED 10/12/96. .

BENT, BRIAN EDWARD, chemistry, educator; b. Mpls., Oct. 18, 1960; s. Henry A. and Anne (McKnight) B; m. Stacey Shane, July 28, 1991. BA, Carleton Coll., 1982; PhD, U. Calif., Berkeley, 1986. Postdoctoral fellow AT&T Bell Labs., Murray Hill, N.J., 1986-88; asst. prof. chemistry Columbia U., N.Y.C., 1988-92, assoc. prof., 1992-96. Recipient Presdl. Young Investigator award NSF, 1989-94, Peter Mark Meml. award Am. Vacuum Soc., 1996; fellow Sloan Found., 1992-94; Camille and Henry Dreyfus tchr.-scholar, 1993-98. Mem. Am. Chem. Soc., Am. Phys. Soc., AAAS, Materials Rsch. Soc., Phi Beta Kappa, Sigma Xi. Deceased.

BENTLEY, ANTOINETTE COZELL, insurance executive, lawyer; b. N.Y.C., Oct. 7, 1937; d. Joseph Richard Cozell and Rose (Lafata Cozell) Vila; children: Robert S., Anne W. BA with distinction, U. Mich., 1960; LLB, U. Va., 1961. Bar: N.Y. 1962, N.J. 1971. Assoc. Sage Gray, Todd & Sims, N.Y.C., 1961-65; of counsel Farrell, Curtis, Carlin & Davidson, Morristown, N.J., 1971-73; sec. Crum and Forster Inc., Basking Ridge, N.J., 1973; v.p. Crum and Forster Inc., Morristown, 1975-87, sr. v.p., sec., assoc. gen. counsel, 1987-92; bd. dirs. Smith Barney Shearson Equity and Income Mut. Funds. Mem. policy com. N.J. Future, 1986; trustee Crum and Forster Found., 1979-92; v.p. Mendham Borough (N.J.) Bd. Edn., 1976-79; trustee N.J. Conservation Found., 1983—, pres. 1986-89; trustee Peddie Sch., 1977-80, Morris Mus., 1982—, Drew U., 1989—, Delbarton Sch., 1989—; mem. adv. com. N.J. Trust for Pub. Lands; trustee St. Peter's Coll., 1984-89, mem. bd. regents, 1991—. Recipient award Exec. Women of N.J., 1988. Mem. ABA, N.J. Bar Assn., Order of Coif, Chi Omega. DIED 03/19/97. .

BENZ, EDMUND WOODWARD, SR., retired educator, surgery; b. Nashville, May 8, 1911; s. Max B. Jr. and Angela (L.) Hudson; m. Elizabeth Ann McElroy, June 16, 1945; children: Edmund Jr., Charles (dec.), Angela Yarrott. BA, Vanderbilt U., 1937, D. of Medicine, 1940. From asst. prof., surgery to clin. prof., surgery Vanderbilt U., 1950-83, prof. emeritus, 1983; med. cons. Vocat. Rehab. Svc., Tenn. Dept. Human Svcs., 1983-95. Fellow ACS; mem. Phi Beta Kappa, Alpha Omega Alpha. Home: Nashville Tenn. Died Jan. 28, 1995.

BERCOVITCH, HANNA MARGARETA, editor; b. Chgo., Il., Sept. 5, 1934; d. Sven Victor and Elizabeth (Rubin) Malmquist; m. Sacvan Bercovitch, July 29, 1956 (div. Mar. 1987); 1 son, Eytan. Student, St. Thomas More Coll., 1960, Sir George Williams Coll., Montreal, 1960-61. Acquisition librarian Honnold Library, Claremont, Calif., 1961-62, acting rare book librarian, 1962-63, spl. project staff, 1963-64; asst. editing Partisan Rev., Rutgers U. Congress Monthly, N.Y.C., 1974-75, 78-80; free lance research assoc. Columbia U., N.Y.C., 1965-80; sr. editor Library of Am. Literary Classics, N.Y.C., 1980-86, editor-in-chief, 1986—; guest curator Melville Whitman Exhibit, N.Y. Pub. Libr., 1982. Environ. commr. City of Leonia, N.J., 1971-73. Mem. Grolier Club (N.Y.C.). Died Oct. 25, 1997.

BERG, ERICSON, insurance company executive; b. Haverhill, Mass., Mar. 15, 1942; s. Winfred Emil and Charlotte (Noyes) B.; m. Marcela Emperador, Nov. 27, 1963; children: Christine Anne, Deborah Marie. BA, Tex. A&M U., 1963; MBA, George Washington U., 1970. CPA, Tex. Sr. chem. technician Melpar Inc., Arlington, Va., 1961-65; staff acct. Ernst & Whinney, Washington, 1967-68; v.p., contr. United Svcs. Life Ins. Co., Washington, 1968-72; v.p. acctg. Am. Health & Life Ins. Co., Balt., 1972-75; sr. v.p. fin. ops. Occidental Life Ins. Co., Raleigh, N.C., 1975-77; exec. v.p. ops. McM Corp., Raleigh, 1977-85, pres., chief exec. officer Occidental Life Ins. Co., 1985-89; chmn., pres., chief exec. officer Western Ins. Cos., 1989—. Contbr. articles to profl. publs. Chmn. pastoral coun. Roman Cath. Diocese of Raleigh, pres. devel. com. Ft. Worth Opera Assn.; mem. exec. com. Ft. Worth Opera Assn.; v.p. Ft. Worth Opera Assn.; chmn. council Our Lady of Lourdes Cath. Ch. Mem. Council Life Insurers (chmn. fin. reporting principles com. 1983-85). Mem. AICPA, Tex. Soc. CPAs.

BERG, JEAN HORTON LUTZ, writer; b. Clairton, Pa., May 30, 1913; d. Harry Heber and Daisy Belle (Horton) Lutz; m. John Joseph Berg, July 2, 1938; children: Jean Berg Eselgroth, Julie Berg Blickle, John J. B.S. in Edn, U. Pa., 1935, A.M. in Latin, 1937. Tchr. creative writing Wayne, Pa., 1968-95; speaker in field of creative writing. Author 50 books for children and young people, 1950-95, articles, stories, poems for young people, articles for adults. Former mem. Health and Welfare Bd., Phila.; former chmn. Main Line Parents Council. Recipient U. Pa. Alumni award of merit, 1969, Follett award for beginning-to-read book, 1961, Disting. Alumni award Friends' Cen. Sch., 1978, medallion City of Phila.; named Disting. Dau. of Pa., 1990. Mem. ASCAP, LWV (Disting. Dau. of Pa. award 1990), Authors Guild, Authors League, Nat. League Am. Pen Women, Phila. Childrens Reading Round Table. Died Jan. 17, 1995.

BERGER, DAVID, radio journalist; b. Berlin, July 20, 1916; came to U.S., 1939; s. Paul and Marie (Korngut) B.; m. Mali Scharf, May 24, 1944; children: Myron S., Roger S. Student, N.Y. City Coll., 1940-41, Columbia U., 1946-48, Hunter Coll., 1984-86. Actor, also reporter various radio stas., N.Y.C., 1940-42; reporter, commentator Voice of Am., N.Y.C., 1946-55; writer, producer Sta. WQXR, over 100 other radio stas., U.S., 1955-84; reporter European radio stas. Germany, Luxembourg, 1984—. Vol. various neighborhood and community orgns., N.Y.C., 1980—. Sgt. U.S. Army, 1942-46, ETO. Avocation: photography. DIED 02/02/97. .

BERGER, ERIC, magazine editor; b. N.Y.C., Dec. 18, 1906; s. David and Mary (Friedenberg) B.; m. Isabelle Gronich, Jan. 5, 1935; 1 son, Neil. Student, N.Y. U., 1924-25; LL.B., St. John's Coll., Bklyn., 1928. Reporter Bklyn. Daily Eagle, 1929-31, Bklyn. Times, 1931-33; editor Nat. Sci. Publs., Inc., N.Y.C., 1934-39; free-lance writer and editor, 1940-41; with Scholastic Mags., Inc., N.Y.C., 1941-95; editor Sr. Scholastic, 1941-59, World Week, 1942-43, Lit. Cavalcade, 1948-55; editorial dir. Science World, 1960-70; editorial dir. Science Tchrs. World, 1959-70, dir. sci. dept., 1963-70, editor in chief high sch. div., 1968-70, asso. pub. sch. div., 1970-72, editorial cons., 1973-95. Served with AUS, 1943-45. Recipient Freedoms Found. award for articles on democracy, 1953. Mem. Nat. Assn. Sci. Writers, AAAS. Home: New York N.Y. Died April 30, 1995.

BERGER, FRED ROBERT, philosophy educator; b. Phila., Dec. 1, 1937; s. Harold Allen and Lillian Arlene (Loev) B.; m. Audrey Mendelblatt, June 18, 1960; children: Liv, Daniel. BA, U. Fla., 1959, MA, 1962; post-grad., Oxford (Eng.) U., 1966, U. Oslo, 1967; PhD, U. Calif., Berkeley, 1969. Asst. prof. U. Calif., Davis, 1969-75, assoc. prof., 1975-80, prof. philosophy, 1980—; mem. steering com. Calif. Humanities Project, 1985-86; vis. prof. U. Ariz., Tucson, 1985. Author: Happiness, Justice and Freedom, 1984, Studying Dedutive Logic, 1977; editor: Freedom of Expression, 1980; mem. editorial bd. Ethics jour., 1985—; contbr. articles to profl. jours. Fellow Rockefeller Found. 1980-81, U. Calif., Davis 1976, Am. Scandinavian Found. 1967. Mem. Am. Philos. Assn. (program com. Pacific div. 1973-76), Soc. For Philosophy and Pub. Affairs (nat. bd. 1982—), Soc. for Philosophy of Sex and Love. Democrat. Jewish.

BERGER, OSCAR, artist; b. Presov, Eperjes, Czechoslovakia, May 12, 1901; came to U.S., 1928, naturalized, 1955; s. Henry and Regina (Berger) B.; m. Ann Arany I. Varga, Feb. 9, 1937. Art study, in Europe. Cartoonist; sketched meetings at League of Nations, Geneva, 1925, House of Commons, London, 1935-45, San Francisco Conf. of UN for N.Y. Times and Daily Telegraph, London, 1945, UN confs., 1945-89, UN gen. assemblies, 1946-90; work represented in permanent collections Library of Congress, Nat. Portrait Gallery, Met. Mus., also pvt. collections and museums.; author: Tip and Top, 1933, A La Carte, 1948, Aesop's Foibles, 1949, Famous Faces, 1950, My Victims, 1952, I Love You, 1960, The Presidents, 1968; contbr. to Am., European publs.; portrait subjects include: Winston Churchill, Eleanor Roosevelt, Queen Elizabeth II, Prince Philip of Eng., Bernard Shaw, H.G. Wells, Robert Frost, King Paul I of Greece, Gen. de Gaulle, King Baudouin, King Feisal, Emperor Haile Selassie, Gorbachev, Gromyko, Premier Kruschev, Premier Indira Gandhi, Pope Pius XII, Pope Paul VI, Anna Pavlova, Toscanini, Prof. Einstein, Jacqueline Kennedy Onassis, Pres. Pompidou, Alexei Kosygin, Molotov, Brezhnev, Chancellor Brandt, Gen. Carlos P. Romulo, Premier Golda Meir, Pres. Tito, Anwar Sadat, 12 U.S. presidents, from Calvin Coolidge to George Bush (all portraits drawn from life). Club: Nat. Press (Washington). Died May 15, 1997.

BERLIN, SIR ISAIAH, philosopher, author; b. Riga; b. June 6, 1909; s. Mendel and Marie B.; ed. St. Paul's Sch., London, 1922-28; scholar Corpus Christi Coll., Oxford (Eng.) U., 1928-32; LL.D. (hon.), Hull (Eng.) U.; D. Litt., U. Glasgow, U. Cambridge, U. Oxford, U. East Anglia, U. Columbia, Duke U., Brandeis U., Jerusalem U., U. London, U. Liverpool, New Sch. Social Rsch., Johns Hopkins U., Northwestern U., Sussex U., N.Y. Theol. Sem., CUNY, D.Phil., Tel-Aviv U., Ben Gurion U., Hull U., Colimbia U., Yale U., Dublin U., Toronto U., Bologna U., Athens U.; m. Aline de Gunzbourg, 1956. Fellow, All Souls Coll., Oxford U., 1932-38, 50-67, 75—, New Coll., 1938-50, lectr. philosophy New Coll., 1932-50, Chichele prof. social and polit. theory at univ., 1957-67, pres. Wolfson Coll., 1966-75; vis. prof. Harvard U., 1949, 52, 53, 61, Bryn Mawr Coll., 1952, Princeton U., 1965; Alexander White prof. U. Chgo., 1955; prof. humanities CUNY, 1966-71; first sec. Brit. embassy, Washington, 1942-46, Moscow, USSR, 1945. Mem. com. awards Commonwealth (Harkness) Fellowships, 1961-65, Kennedy Scholarships, 1965-87 ; bd. dirs. Royal Opera House, London, 1955-66, 75-86; trustee Nat. Gallery, London, 1975-1986; bd. govs. U. Jerusalem, 1955-80. Decorated comdr. Order Brit. Empire, 1946; created knight, 1957; recipient Order of Merit, 1971, Agnelli Internat. prize for Ethics, 1987, Erasmus prize, Lippincott prize. Fellow Brit. Acad. (pres. 1974-78); hon. fellow Corpus Christi Coll., New Coll., Wolfson Coll., St. Antony's Coll., Oxford, Wolfson Coll., Cambridge; hon. mem. Am. Acad. Arts and Scis., Am. Acad. Arts and Letters, Am. Philos. Soc. Author books and essays on lit., philosophy, polit. theory, history of ideas, other subjects.

BERMAN, ARTHUR MALCOLM, newspaper editor; b. N.Y.C., Aug. 16, 1935; s. Jack Abraham and Pearl Sarah (Sann) B.; m. Elaine Ruth Kreiner, Sept. 22, 1956; children—Arthur Michael, Tonia Jean, Daniel Adlai. B.A., Antioch Coll., 1957. Reporter Daily News and Sun, Springfield, Ohio, 1957-59; reporter Star News, Pasadena, Calif., 1959-60, Mirror News, Los Angeles, 1960-61; reporter Los Angeles Times, 1962-69, asst. met. editor, 1970-77, suburban editor, 1978-82, View editor, 1983-87, asst. nat. editor, 1987-91, asst. Calendar editor, 1992—. Co-recipient Pulitzer Prize, 1966; Pulitzer Gold Medal, 1969, Best Local News Story award Greater Los Angeles Press Club, 1961, 64, 65, 67. Avocations: running, piloting. Died Nov. 28, 1996.

BERMAN, BERNARD ALVIN, pediatric allergist; b. Boston, Mar. 12, 1924; s. Hyman Isaac and Elsi Marion (Dubbs) B.; m. Lois Deborah Landau, Aug. 27, 1955; children: Susan, Steven, Laura. MD, Tufts U., 1948. Diplomate Am. Bd. Allergy and Immunology, Am. Bd. Pediatrics (chmn. sect. pedicatrics). Intern pediatrics Jewish Hosp., Bklyn., 1949-51; resident pediatrics Children's Hosp., Boston, 1953-55; fellow pediatric allergy Rochester, N.Y., 1956-58; pvt. practice allergy Brookline, Mass., 1957-95; staff Children's Hosp., Boston, 1957, Boston Lying-In Hosp., 1957-95, Beth Israel Hosp., Boston, 1957-95, Mt. Auburn Hosp., Cambridge, Mass., 1957-95, N.E. Med. Ctr., 1958-95; staff St. Elizabeth's Hosp., Boston, 1959-95, mem. allergy clinic, 1965-95, dir. pediatric allergy, 1966-95; cons. pediatrics Chelsea (Mass.) U.S. Naval Hosp., 1959-73; staff Boston Floating Hosp., 1959-95, pres. alumni, 1973-76; dir. allergy clinic Boston City Hosp., 1966-70; asst. pediatrics Sch. Medicine Boston U., 1957-67; sr. clin. instr. pediatrics Sch. Medicine Tufts U., Boston, 1957-66, assoc. clin. prof. pediatrics, 1966-95; regional cons. Children's Asthma Rsch. Inst., Denver, 1959-74; mem. Pres.' Commn. White House Conf. Allergy, 1971. Author textbook; contbr. 70 articles on allergy and immunology to profl. jours. Trustee Krebs Sch., Lexington, Mass., 1970-75. Lt. (j.g.) USNR, 1951-53. Fellow Am. Assn. Clin. Allergy & Immunology, Am. Coll. Allergists (pres. 1974-75), Am. Acad. Allergy, Am. Coll. Chest Physicians, Am. Assn. Cert. Allergists (pres. 1981-82), Am. Acad. Pediatrics (Jerome Glaser Disting. Service award 1988); mem. Internat. Assn. Allergy & Immunology (mem. at large exec. com. 1986-88), New Eng. Pediatrics Soc., New Eng. Soc. Allergy, AMA, Mass. Med. Soc., Norfolk County Med. Soc., Greater Boston Med. Soc. (pres.), Brookline Med. Soc. (pres. 1971), Mass. Allergy Soc. (pres. 1979-81), Nat. Bd. Med. Examiners, Phi Delta Epsilon Grad. Med. Soc. Boston (pres.), Assn. Asthmatic Convalescent Homes (pres., mem. bd. govs.). Home: Brookline Mass. Died June 9, 1995.

BERMAN, PANDRO SAMUEL, motion picture producer; b. Pitts., Mar. 28, 1905; s. Harry M. and Julie E. (Epstein) B.; m. Kathryn Hereford, July 20, 1960; children: Harry Michael, Susan Pamela, Cynthia. Student pub. schs. Asst. dir., asst. cutter F.B.O. Studios, Hollywood, Calif., 1923-28; with R.K.O. Studios, Hollywood, 1928-40; producer R.K.O. Studios, 1930-37, head prodn., 1937-40; producer M.G.M. Studios, 1940-67, Twentieth Century Fox Studio, 1967-70. Films include: What Price Hollywood, 1932, Morning Glory, 1933, The Gay Divorcee, 1934, Of Human Bondage, 1934, Roberta, 1935, Alice Adams, 1935, Top Hat, 1935, Winterset, 1936, Stage Door, 1937, Gunga Din, 1939, Hunchback of Notre Dame, 1940, Seventh Cross, 1944, National Velvet, 1944, Dragon Seed, 1944, Portrait of Dorian Gray, 1945, Three Musketeers, 1947, Madame Bovary, 1948, Father of the Bride, 1950, Ivanhoe, 1951, Knights of the Round Table, 1953, Blackboard Jungle, 1954, Bhowani Junction, 1955, Tea and Sympathy, 1956, Something of Value, 1957, Brothers Karamazov, 1958, Reluctant Debutante, 1959, Butterfield 8, 1960, Sweet Bird of Youth, 1962, The Prize, 1963, Patch of Blue, 1965. Mem. Acad. Motion Picture Arts and Scis. (Irving G. Thalberg award 1977). Jewish. Club: Hillcrest Country. Died July 13, 1996.

BERMAN, SIDNEY, psychiatrist; b. Washington, July 31, 1908; s. Saul and Gertrude B.; m. Claire Richardson, Nov. 23, 1935; 1 dau., Sarah Miriam Berman Schlein. BS, Georgetown U., 1928, MD, 1932. Diplomate Am. Bd. Psychiatry and Neurology, Am. Bd. Child Psychiatry. Intern D.C. Gen. Hosp., 1932-33; jr. med. officer, resident in psychiatry St. Elizabeth's Hosp., Washington, 1933-35; sr. med. officer VA Hosp., Northport, N.Y., 1935-41; Commonwealth Fund fellow in child psychiatry U. Md. Med. Sch. and Hosp., 1941-42; dir. U. Md. Mental Hygiene Clinic, 1942-43, Washington Inst. Mental Hygiene, 1946-48; clin. prof.

psychiatry George Washington U Sch. Medicine, 1948—; Practice medicine specializing in child and adult psychiatry and psychoanalysis Washington, 1948—; sr. adv. staff Children's Hosp. Nat. Med. Ctr., Washington, 1948—; tng. and supervising analyst Washington Psychoanalytic Inst., 1957-80, Washington Assn. Psychoanalytic Edn., 1979-81; cons. Walter Reed Gen. Hosp., 1960-71, NIH, 1953-88. Contbr. articles to med. jours. Founder Nat. Consortium Child Mental Health Svc., 1971; rep. to Congress Mental Health Manpower, 1971-74. Served to maj. M.C. USAAF, 1943-46. Fellow Am. Soc. Physician Analysts (hon.); mem. AMA, Am. Acad. Child and Adolescent Psychiatry (pres. 1969-71), Washington Psychoanalytic Soc. (pres. 1963-65), Washington Psychiat. Soc. (pres. 1962), Med. Soc. D.C., Am. Psychiat. Assn. (Spl. Presdl. commendation 1995), Am. Orthopsychiat. Assn., Am. Psychoanalytic Assn., Internat. Psychoanalytic Assn., Pan-Am. Med. Assn., George Washington U. Club. Jewish. Deceased.

BERNARDIN, JOSEPH LOUIS CARDINAL, archbishop, university chancellor; b. Columbia, S.C., Apr. 2, 1928; s. Joseph and Maria M. (Simion) B. AB in Philosophy, St. Mary's Sem., Balt., 1948; MA in Edn., Cath. U. Am., 1952. Ordained priest Roman Catholic Ch., 1952; asst. pastor Diocese of Charleston, S.C., 1952-54; vice chancellor Diocese of Charleston, 1954-56, chancellor, 1956-66, vicar gen., 1962-66, diocesan consultor, 1962-66, adminstr., 1964-65; aux. bishop Atlanta, 1966-68; pastor Christ the King Cathedral, 1966-68; sec., mem. exec. com. Nat. Conf. Cath. Bishops-U.S. Cath. Conf., gen. sec., 1968-72, pres., 1974-77; archbishop of Cin., 1972-82, Chgo., 1982—; chancellor U. St. Mary of the Lake, Mundelein (Ill.) Seminary; mem. Congregation for Bishops, 1973-78; del., mem. permanent coun. World Synod of Bishops, 1974, 77, 80, 83, 87, 90, 94; mem. Coll. of Cardinals, 1983—, Pontifical Commn. for Revision Code Canon Law, 1983, Congregation for Evangelization of Peoples, 1983-88, Congregation for Sacraments and Divine Worship, 1984—, Coun. for Promoting Christian Unity, 1984—; chmn. ad hoc com. on war and peace Nat. Conf. Cath. Bishops, 1983, chmn. ad hoc com. to assess the moral status of deterrence, 1985-88, chmn. com. for pro-life activities, 1983-89, chmn. com. for marriage and family life 1990-93, chmn. ad hoc com. on structure and function of conf. with U.S. Cath. Conf. Author: Prayer in Our Time, 1973, Let the Children Come to Me: A Guide for the Religious Education of Children, 1976, Called to Serve, Called to Lead: Reflections on the Ministerial Priesthood, 1981, It Is Christ We Preach, 1982, Our Communion, Our Peace, Our Promise, 1984, Christ Lives in Me, 1985, In Service of One Another, 1985, Guidelines on Access to the Sacraments of Initiation and Reconcilation for Developmentally Disabled Persons, 1985, The Challenges We Face Together: Reflections on Selected Questions for Archdiocesan Religious Educators, 1986, A Challenge and A Responsibility: A Pastoral Statement on the Church's Response to the AIDS Crisis, 1986, Growing in Wisdom, Age and Grace: A Guide for Parents in the Religious Education of Their Children, 1988, The Consistent Ethic of Life, 1988, Come Holy Spirit: A Pastoral Statement on the Catholic Charismatic Renewal, 1988, The Family Gathered Here Before You: A Pastoral Letter on the Church, 1989, The Parish in the Contemporary Church, 1992, The Call to Service: Pastoral Statement on the Permanent Diaconate, 1993, A Sign of Hope: A Pastoral Letter on Healthcare, 1995, Building Bridges Between Communities of Faith, 1996. Mem. adv. coun. Am. Revolution Bicentennial, 1975-76, Pres.'s Adv. Com. on Refugees, 1975, pres.'s nat. adv. coun. U. S.C., 1979-90; mem. bd. trustees Cath. U. Am., 1973-81, 89-93, chmn. bd., 1985-88. Recipient Albert Einstein Internat. Peace prize, 1983, U.S. Presdl. medal of Freedom, 1996; named to S.C. Hall of Fame, 1988. Mem. Nat. Cath. Edn. Assn. (chmn. bd. 1978-81), Religious Alliance Against Pornography (founding mem., vice chmn.), Cath. Charities USA Nat. Devel. Task Force. Died Nov. 14, 1996.

BERNEY, JOSEPH HENRY, appliance manufacturing company executive; b. Balt., May 7, 1932; s. Eugene Philip and Blanche (Ney) B.; m. Phyllis Pearlove, Jan. 18, 1956; children: Richard, Philip, Julia, David. BS, U. Pa., 1953; MS, Columbia U., 1954. C.P.A., Va., Wis. Staff acct. Touche, Niven, Bailey & Smart, C.P.A.s, N.Y.C., 1954, A.M. Pullen & Co., C.P.A.s, Richmond, Va., 1954-56; vice chmn. Nat. Presto Industries, Inc., Eau Claire, Wis., 1956-95, also bd. dirs.; officer, bd. dirs. Nat. Holding Investment Co., Canton Mfg. Corp., Jackson Sale & Storage, Presto Mfg. Co., Nat. Pipeline Co. Past pres. Chippewa Valley coun. Boy Scouts Am. Mem. AICPA, Va. Soc. Accts., Wis. Soc. Accts., Beta Gamma Sigma, Delta Sigma Rho. Home: Eau Claire Wis. Died Oct. 8, 1995.

BERNSTEIN, ABRAHAM, state senator; b. N.Y.C., May 1, 1918; s. Samuel and Anna (Cohen) B.; m. Ruth Schub, Dec. 23, 1941 (div. July 1985); m. Gretchen Diamond, Feb. 17, 1989. BS in Social Sci., CUNY, 1935; LLB, Bklyn. Law Sch., 1941. Bar: N.Y., U.S. Ct. Mil. Appeals, U.S. Supreme Ct. Atty. pvt. practice N.Y.C., 1941-54; atty. Bernstein & Koenigsberg, N.Y.C., 1954-71, Bernstein & Bernstein, N.Y.C., 1971-82, Bernstein & Arfa, N.Y.C., 1982—; appeal agt. U.S. Selective Svc. System, N.Y.C., 1942-45; state senator N.Y. State Legislature, Albany, 1961—; Mem. Com. on Banks, Com. on Fin., Con. on Judiciary, Com. on Housing and Community Devel., Com. on Investigations, Taxation and Gov. Ops., Com. on Mental Hygien and Addiction Control, Com. on Vets. Affairs, Spl. Com. on Casino Gambling; sec. Senate TAsk Force on Ct. Re-organization, 1974-75, Com. on Crime, 1977-79, Minority Task Force on Women's Issues. Bd. dirs. Pelham Pkwy. Jewish Ctr., Zionist Orgn. Am., Bronx Park East Chotiner Jewish Ctr., Bronx House; exec. com. officer Bronxboro Citizens Com. on the Aging; mem. adv. coun. Soc. for Children with Emotional Disturbances; treas. Muscular Dystrophy Bronx chpt., 1967, 69, chmn. Bronx mem. campaign, 1965; past chmn. Bronx Joint Def. Appeal, N. Bronx Fedn. Jewish Philanthropies; mem. speaker's com. United Jewish Appeal; bd. govs., speaker's com. Anti-Defamation League; adv. bd. Ctr. for Holocaust Studies Bronx High Sch. Sci. Sgt. U.S. Army, 1943-46. Mem. Bronx County Bar Assn. (com. state legis., com. mcpl. affairs), Nat. Assn. Jewish Legislators (past pres.), Jewish War Vets Post, Am. Jewish Congress, B'nai B'rith (pres. 1960-61).

BERNSTEIN, LOUIS, clergyman; b. N.Y.C., Apr. 2, 1927; s. Sam and Anna (Richman) B.; m. Pearl Moshel, Mar. 13, 1955; children: Sara, David, Sima, Avraham. BA, Yeshiva Coll., 1947; Hebrew Tchrs. degree, Tchrs. Inst., 1947, PhD, 1977; rabbi, Isaac Elchanan Theol. Sem., 1950. Ordained rabbi, 1950. Rabbi Glenwood (N.Y.) Jewish Center, 1950-52, Kissena Jewish Center, Flushing, N.Y., 1954-55, Young Israel of Windsor Park, Bayside, N.Y., 1955-95; prof. Yeshiva U., 1955; mem. edn. staff Camp Massad, N.Y.C., 1946-81, camp dir., 1957-71; pres. Rabbinical Coun. Am., 1972-74, 84-86, 1st v.p., 1992-95; chmn. Israel schs., 1960-95; mem. exec. com. Queens Jewish Community Council, 1971-95; sec. Hapoel Mizrachi Am., 1954-55; v.p. Religious Zionists Am., 1972-75, pres., 1975-81, 88-91, chmn. exec. bd., 1981-88, 91-95; exec. World Zionist Orgn., 1978-95. Editor RCA Rec., 1954-90. Served as chaplain AUS, 1952-54, ETO. Mem. Yeshiva Coll. Alumni Assn. (pres.). Home: Bayside N.Y. Died Mar. 12, 1995.

BERRY, BILL, broadcast executive; b. Harrisburg, Pa., Jan. 3, 1943; s. William Hugh and Verna Gertrude (Fox) B.; m. Penelope Anne Starnes, Jan. 13, 1967 (div. 1977). AS, Harrisburg Area Community Coll., 1969; B in Humanities, Pa. State U., 1971. Sales mgr. Sta. WKVA, Lewistown, Pa., 1971-75; v.p. sales, mktg. Automatic Passenger Counting Systems, Inc., Lewistown, 1975-78; v.p., co-owner Sta. WJUN-AM-FM, Mexico, Pa., 1978—, Stas. WHHO/WKPQ, Hornell, N.Y., 1983—; pres., co-owner Sta. WKZA, Kane, Pa., 1981—; chief exec. officer, co-owner Bilbat Broadcast Bunch, Wilmington, Del., 1984—. Author: The Muffin Modification, 1977. Mem. Pa. Assn. Broadcasters, Rotary. Republican. Avocations: tennis, philately, music, writing, bird-watching.

BERRY, LEONIDAS HARRIS, gastroenterologist, internist; b. Woodsdale, N.C., July 20, 1902; s. Llewellyn L. and Beulah Anne (Harris) B.; m. Opheila Flannagan Harrison, June 27, 1937; 1 child, Judith Berry Griffin; m. Emma Ford Willis, Aug. 7, 1959; stepchildren: Alvin E. Harrison, Frances W. Jackson. BS, Wilberforce U., Ohio, 1924, DSc (hon.), 1945; BS, U. Chgo., 1925, MD, 1930; MS in Pathology, U. Ill., 1933; LLD (hon.), Lincoln U. of Pa., 1983. Diplomate Am. Bd. Internal Medicine and Gastroenterology, Nat. Bd. Med. Examiners. Intern Freedmen's Hosp., Washington, 1929-30; resident internal medicine, gastroenterology Cook County Hosp., Chgo., 1931-35; sr. attending physician, gastroenterologist Cook County Hosp., 1946-74, chief gastrointestinal endoscopy service, 1966-74, emeritus, 1975—; courtesy staff Michael Reese Hosp., Chgo., 1946-63, sr. attending physician, 1963-74; founder, chmn. div. gastroenterology Provident Hosp., Chgo., 1936-70; sr. attending physician Provident Hosp., 1935—, chmn. dept. medicine, 1947-48; spl. dep. for profl.-community affairs, Cook County Hosps, Governing Commn., 1975-79; clin. asst. prof. medicine U. Ill. Med. Sch., 1950-57, clin. assoc. prof., 1957-67; prof. gastroenterology and endoscopy Cook County Grad. Sch. Medicine, 1947—; Fgn. cultural exch. lectr. U.S. Dept. State, East Africa, West Africa, 1965, Japan, Republic of Korea, The Philippines, 1966, Paris, 1970; organizer, coord. med. counseling clinics narcotics Ill. Dept. Health, 1950-59; co-founder, trustee Coun. Bio-Med. Careers, 1962-72; mem. health com. Chgo. Commn. Human Rels., 1947-65, chmn., 1960-65; organizer Flying Black Medics, Chgo. and Cairo, Ill., 1970; mem. 1st nat. adv. coun., regional med. programs on heart disease, cancer and stroke HEW, 1966-68; mem. Berry com. excellence Rush Med. Coll., 1993. Sr. author, editor: Gastrointestinal Panendoscopy (with internat. contributors), 1974, (textbook) Comprehensive, 1974; author: I Wouldn't Take Nothin' for my Journey, Two Centuries of an Afro-American Minister's Family, 1981; contbr. articles to med. publs., books. Inventor Berry Direct Vision Gastro-Biopsy Scope, 1955. Trustee Cook County Grad. Sch. Medicine, 1967-90, life, 1990—; trustee Mary Thompson Hosp., 1965-73; active A.M.E. Ch., also steward, trustee, connectional officer, gen. officer, med. dir., 1948-76, emeritus, 1976—. Served to 1st lt. U.S. Army Med. Res., 1931-41; from capt. to maj. Ill. Res. Militia 1942-47. Recipient resolution of appreciation HEW, 1968; 50th Anniversary cert. U. Chgo. Med. Sch., Disting. Alumni award Wilber Force U., 1987; Disting. Alumnus award of Rush Med. Coll., 1987, Trustee medal of honor, 1991; Alumni Pub. Service award U. Chgo., 1966, Profl. Achievement award, 1978, Daniel Hale Williams Disting. Service award Cook County Physicians Assn., 1969, 40 Yr. Svc. citation A.M.E. Ch., 1977; Leonidas Berry Soc. for Digestive Diseases organized in his honor, 1980. Fellow ACP, N.Y. Acad. Medicine; mem. AMA, Am. Coll. Gastroenterology (master, past. gov., trustee, 1st Clin. Achievement award 1987), Am. Soc. Gastrointestinal Endoscopy (Rudolf Schindler award 1977), Nat. Soc. Gastroenterology France and Chile S.A., Japan Endoscopy Soc. Nat. Med. Assn. (hon. mem. internal medicine sect., Disting. Svc. award 1958, past pres. 1965), NAACP (life, Marshall Bynum Svc. award Chgo. br. 1989), Assn. Study Afro-Am. Life and History, Original Forty Club Chgo. (Man of Year award 1974); pres., founder, Daniel Hale Williams Meml. Med. Soc., Sigma Xi, Alpha Phi Alpha (life), Alpha Omega Alpha (hon.). Died Dec. 4, 1995.

BERRY, WALLACE TAFT, educator, composer, music theorist; b. La Crosse, Wis., Jan. 10, 1928; s. Edward Carl and Louise (George) B.; m. Maxine Cecile Metzner, May 11, 1954. B.Mus., U. So. Calif., 1949, Ph.D., 1956; student, Conservatoire Nat. de Paris, 1953-54. Lectr. music U. So. Calif., 1956-57; instr. U. Mich., 1957-60, asst. prof., 1960-63, asso. prof., 1963-66, prof. music, chmn. dept. music theory, 1966-77; prof., head dept. music U. B.C., Vancouver, Can., 1978-84; prof. U. B.C., 1985—; pub. lectr. ednl. cons. Author: Form in Music, 1966, rev., 1985, Eighteenth-Century Imitative Counterpoint, (with E. Chudacoff), 1969, Structural Functions in Music, 1975, Musical Structure and Performance, 1989; contbr. articles to Jour., Music Theory, Perspectives of New Music, Music Theory Spectrum., Mus. Quar., Coll. Music Symposium; Composer piano, choral, chamber and orchestral works; rec. of works include Trio for Piano, Violin and Cello, String Quartet No. 2, Duo for Flute and Piano, Canto Lirico for Viola and Piano, Duo for Violin and Piano, Sonata for Piano. Served with AUS, 1954-56. Fulbright fellow, 1953-54; recipient U. Mich. Distinguished Faculty Service award, 1963; Am. Acad.-Inst. Arts and Letters composer award, 1978. Mem. Am. Musicol. Soc., Soc. for Music Theory (pres. 1982-85), ASCAP.

BERSHADER, DANIEL, aerophysics educator; b. N.Y.C., Mar. 14, 1923; s. Joseph and Clara (Kosak) B.; m. Ilse Gluckstadt, Mar. 18, 1976 (div. Apr. 1986); children: Brian Kenneth, Lee Karlin. BA, Bklyn. Coll., 1942; MA in Physics, Princeton U., 1946, PhD in Physics, 1948. Rsch. scientist Bell Aircraft Corp., Niagara Falls, N.Y., 1944; rsch. faculty U. Md., College Park, 1949-52; instr. physics Princeton (N.J.) U., 1944-45, rsch. assoc. prof., 1952-56; mgr. gas dynamics dept. Lockheed Missiles & Space Co., Palo Alto, Calif., 1956-64; assoc. prof. aeronautics Stanford (Calif.) U., 1956-64, prof. aerophysics, 1964-95; chmn. faculty senate Stanford U., 1971-72; cons., mem. adv. group for govtl. and pvt. orgns., 1965-95. Editor 4 books on fluid physics; contbr. chpts. to books, articles to encys. and profl. jours. With U.S. Navy, 1944-45. Rsch. grantee NASA, Air Force U.S. Army, NSF, 1965-95. Fellow AIAA, Am. Phys. Soc.; mem. Sigma Xi. Democrat. Jewish. Achievements include measuring optical polarizability of atomic hydrogen ground state; verification of resonant refractivity of sodium vapor; radiative behavior of non-equilibrium shock-heated gases; internal energy transfer in the CO2 molecule; compressible vortex structure and surface interactions. Home: Stanford Calif. Died May 30, 1995.

BERTSCH, FRANK HENRY, furniture manufacturing company executive; b. Mpls., Oct. 2, 1925; s. Herbert Thomas and Eleanor Emma (Tuscany) B.; m. Rita Bertsch, Nov. 7, 1987; children: Jeffrey T., Steven H., Carolyn T. BS in Mech. Engring, Northwestern U., 1947; D of Laws (hon.), U. Dubuque, 1992. With Flexsteel Industries, Inc., Dubuque, Iowa, 1947—, plant engr., 1947-49, plant mgr., 1949-53, v.p., dir. design and devel., 1953-58, pres., 1958-85, chmn. bd., chief exec. officer, 1985-90, chmn. exec. com., 1990—; bd. dirs. Retirement Investment Corp. Bd. dirs. U. Dubuque, Four Mounds Found. With USNR, 1944-46. Recipient Disting. Svc. award Dubuque C. of C., 1964, Man Behind the Boy award Dubuque Boys Club, 1969, Bronze Merit award Jr. Achievement of Am., 1995. Mem. Am. Legion, Dubuque Golf and Country Club, Desert Mountain Club (Scottsdale), Thunder Hills Country Club (Peosta, Iowa). Presbyterian (elder, trustee). Died Oct. 4, 1997.

BETHEA, JOSEPH BENJAMIN, bishop; b. Dillion, S.C., Sept. 9, 1932; s. Rufus E. and Ella (Johnson) B.; m. Shirley Cundiff, June 7, 1958 (dec. 1992); 1 dau., Josefa Elizabeth. BA, Claflin Coll., Orangeburg, S.C., 1953, DH (hon.), 1988; MDiv, Gammon Theol. Sem., Atlanta, 1956, DD (hon.), 1974; DD (hon.), N.C. Wesleyan Coll., Rocky Mount, 1988; DH (hon.), Columbia (S.C.) Coll., 1989; LHD (hon.), Claflin Coll., 1988. Ordained to ministry United Meth. Ch. as deacon, 1954, as elder, 1956. Pastor St. Paul Meth. Ch., Reidsville, N.C., 1961-65; dist. supt. Va. Conf., Richmond, 1965-68; pastor St. Matthews United Meth. Ch., Greensboro, N.C., 1968-72; dir. Black Studies Duke Divinity Sch., Durham, N.C., 1972-77; dist. supt. N.C. Conf. United

Meth. Ch., Rockingham, 1977-83; adminstrv. asst. to bishop N.C. Conf. United Meth. Ch., Raleigh, 1983-86, dist. supt., 1986-88; resident bishop United Meth. Ch., Columbia, S.C., 1988—; lectr. Duke Div. Sch., Durham, N.C., 1980-81; mem. com. relational concerns Coun. Bishops, 1988; mem. exec. com. World Meth. Coun., 1981-88. Author: The Duke Divinity Sch. Re., 1975, 78; contbr. articles to Meth. jours. Vice chmn. Gen. Commn. Religion & Race, 1988, pres. 1992—. Mem. NAACP, Black Methodists for Ch. Renewal, Rotary Internat., Alpha Phi Alpha. Avocations: reading, sports. Died March 12, 1996.

BEUYS, JOSEPH, artist, sculptor; b. Kleve, Germany, May 12, 1921; s. Joseph and Johanna (Hulsermann) B.; student Gymnasium Kleve, Kurstakademic, Dusseldorf; m. Eva Wurmbach, 1959; 2 children. One man shows in galleries throughout Europe including Kranenburg, 1953, 63, Dusseldorf, 1965-66, 69, Vienna, 1966-71, Antwerp, 1968, Eindhoven, 1968, Basel, 1969, 70, Lucerne, 1971, Innsbruck, 1971, Stockholm, 1971; Tate Gallery, London, 1973, London Inst. Contemporary Arts, 1975; Guggenheim Mus., N.Y.C., 1979; group shows include: Fluxus Kunstakademie, Dusseldorf, 1963, Documenta 3, Kassel, W. Ger., 1964, 68, Documenta 5, Kassel, 1972, Biennale di Veneqia, Venice, 1976; prof. Staatliche Kunstakademie, Dusseldorf, 1961-72. Founder German Students Party, Dusseldorf, 1967, Non-Voting Free Referendum Party for Direct Democracy, Com. for Free U., Dusseldorf, 1970-71. Served with German Air Force, 1941-45.

BEVAN, DONALD EDWARD, retired marine science educator, university dean; b. Seattle, Feb. 23, 1921; s. Arthur and Violette B.; m. Tanya L. Potapova, Sept. 8, 1971. B.S., U. Wash., 1948, Ph.D., 1959; postdoctoral student, Moscow U., 1959-60. Sr. fisheries biologist U. Wash., Seattle, 1955-59; lectr., rsch. asst. prof. U. Wash., 1959-61, rsch. assoc. prof, 1961-64, assoc. prof., 1964-66, prof., 1966-86, prof. emeritus, 1986—, assoc. dean Coll. Fisheries, 1977, dean Coll. Fisheries, 1980-81, dir. Univ. Computer Ctr., 1968-69, asst. v.p. research, 1969-77, adj. prof. Inst. Marine Studies, 1973-86, prof. emeritus, 1986—, assoc. dean Coll. Ocean and Fishery Scis., 1984-86; pres., dir. Univ. Book Store, 1977-93; mem. US-USSR Pacific Fisheries Negotiations; chair Snake River Salmon Recovery Team, 1992-96. Author articles and pamphlets in field. Served to capt., arty. U.S. Army, World War II. Decorated Purple Heart, Bronze Star. Mem. North Pacific Region Fisheries Coun. (chmn. sci. and statis. com.), Pacific Fisheries Coun., Marine Tech. Soc., Am. Inst. Fishery Rsch. Biologists, Pacific Fisheries Biologists, Sigma Xi, Phi Sigma. Died May 3, 1996.

BEYER, KARL HENRY, JR., pharmacologist; b. Henderson, Ky., June 19, 1914; s. Karl H. and Lennie M. (Beadles) B.; m. Camille Slobodzian, Nov. 9, 1979; children by previous marriage: Annette Matilda Beyer Mears, Katherine Louise Beyer Cranson. B.S., Western Ky. State Coll., 1935; Ph.M., U. Wis., 1937, Ph.D., 1940, M.D., 1943, Sc.D. (hon.), 1972. Asst. dir. pharmacol. research Sharp & Dohme, 1943-44, dir. pharmacol. research, 1944-50, asst. dir. research, 1950-56; dir. Merck Inst. Therapeutic Research, West Point, Pa., 1956-58; pres. Merck Inst. Therapeutic Research, 1961-66; v.p. life scis. Merck Sharp & Dohme, Research Labs., West Point, 1958-66; sr. v.p. research Merck Sharp & Dohme, Research Labs., 1966-73; vis. prof., guest lectr. U. Wis., 1958, Swedish U. Med. Schs., 1962, Howard U., 1964, Free U. Berlin, 1966; vis. prof. Milton S. Hershey Med. Center, Pa. State U., 1973—, Vanderbilt U. Sch. Medicine, 1973-79, Harvard U. Sch. Medicine, 1985-89; chmn. Cosmetic Ingredient Rev., 1976-86; bd. sci. advisers Merck Inst., 1973-77, 78-82 ; chmn. bd. Phila. Assn. Clin. Trials, 1980. Author: Pharmacological Basis of Penicillin Therapy, 1950, Discovery, Development and Delivery of New Drugs, 1978; contbr. articles to profl. jours. Recipient Gairdner Found. award, 1964; Modern Pioneers in Creative Industry award NAM, 1965; Modern Medicine Disting. Achievement award, 1967; Am. Pharm. Assn. Found. Achievement award, 1967; Disting. Service award Wis. Alumni Assn., 1968; Lasker award, 1975; Torald Sollmann award, 1978; Catell award Am. Coll. Clin. Pharmacology, 1980, Wis. Med. Alumni Citation, 1987; Pharm. Mfrs. Assn. Discoverer's award, 1988. Fellow ACP, AAAS, N.Y. Acad. Scis.; mem. NAS (drug rsch. bd. 1964-70), Am. Chem. Soc., Am. Physiol. Soc., Phila. Med. Soc., Am. Soc. for Pharmacology and Exptl. Therapeutics (pres. 1964-65), Fedn. Am. Soc. Exptl. Biology (pres. 1965-66), Phila. Coll. Physicians, Am. Therapeutic Soc., Soc. Toxicology, Am. Soc. Nephrology, Am. Heart Assn. (hypertension research award 1979, coun. circulation and renal sect.), Heart Assn. Southeastern Pa., Biol. Abstracts (trustee, treas. 1965-69). Died Dec. 2, 1996.

BEYER, ROBERT EDWARD, retired biochemist, educator; b. Englewood, N.J., Feb. 20, 1928; s. Edward I. and Rebecca H. (Lewis) B.; m. Boon Neo Juliana Ong, Aug. 24, 1991. BS, U. Conn., 1950, MS, 1951; PhD, Brown U., 1954. USPHS postdoctoral fellow U. Stockholm, 1954-56; asst. prof. Sch. Medicine Tufts U., 1956-62; asst. prof. enzyme chemistry Inst. Enzyme Rsch. U. Wis., 1962-65; prof. biology U. Mich, Ann Arbor, 1965-93; ret. U. Mich., Ann Arbor, 1994; vis. prof. dept. neurology U. Calif., San Francisco, 1973-74; vis. prof. dept. biochemistry U. Stockholm, 1985-86; vis. scientist biomed. ctr. U. Uppsala, Sweden, 1994; vis. scientist dept. biochemistry U. Bologna, Italy, 1995. Sr. Rsch. fellow NIH, 1958-60, Fogarty Sr. Internat. fellow, 1985-86; recipient Rsch. Career Devel. award NIH, 1960-65. Died May 1, 1997.

BIEDENHARN, LAWRENCE C., JR., physicist, educator; b. Vicksburg, Miss., Nov. 18, 1922; s. Lawrence Christian and Willetta (Lyons) B.; m. Sarah Jeffress Willingham, Mar. 25, 1950; children: John David, Sally Willetta. B.S., M.I.T., 1944, Ph.D., 1949. Research asso. M.I.T., 1949-50; physicist Oak Ridge Nat. Lab., 1950-52; asst. prof. Yale U., 1952-54; assoc. prof. Rice U., 1954-61; prof. physics Duke U., 1961-92, James B. Duke prof. physics, 1989-92, prof. emeritus, from 1993; adj. prof physics U. Tex., Austin, 1992-97; cons. Los Alamos Sci. Lab. Author: (with Pieter Brussaard) Coulomb Excitation, 1965, (with H. Van Dam) Quantum Theory of Angular Momentum, 1965, (with J.D. Louck) Angular Momentum in Quantum Physics: Theory and Application, 1981, The Racah-Wigner Algebra in Quantum Theory, 1981, (with N. Mukunda and H. Van Dam) Relativistic Models of Extended Hadrons Obeying a Mass-Spin Trajectory Constraint, 1982, (with M.A. Lohe) Quantum Group Symmetry and q-Tensor Algebras, 1995; assoc. editor Jour. Math. Physics, 1964-68, 70-74, 79-85, editor, 1985-92; contbr. articles to profl. jours. Served with Signal Corps AUS, 1943-46. Sr. Fulbright fellow, 1958; Guggenheim fellow, 1959; NSF Sr. postdoctoral fellow, 1964-65; Erskine fellow N.Z., 1973; Alexander von Humboldt sr. U.S. scientist award, 1976. Fellow AAAS, Am. Phys. Soc. (Jesse Beams award 1979), Inst. Physics, Phys. Soc. Gt. Britain; mem. AAUP, European Phys. Soc., Am. Math. Soc., Sigma Xi, Kappa Sigma. Died Feb. 12, 1996.

BIENSTOCK, HERBERT, economist, educator; b. N.Y.C., Dec. 25, 1922; s. Nathan and Anna (Flaum) B.; m. June Klein, June 28, 1947; children: Ruth Bienstock Anolik, Joshua E. BBA, CCNY, 1945, PhD (hon.), 1976. Asst. economist U.S. Bur. Lab. Statistics, N.Y.C., 1945-53, liaison to price stabilization bd., 1953-54, asst. regional dir., 1955-62, regional com. labor statistics, 1962-80; alumni merit prof. labor and urban values Queens Coll., CUNY, N.Y.C., 1980-94, dir. ctr. labor and urban programs, rsch. and analysis, 1981-94; adj. prof. L.I. U., Cornell U., Hunter Coll., New Sch., N.Y.C., 1947-73; prof., chair grad sch. dept. indsl. rels. Pace U., N.Y.C., 1973-79. Mem. Gov.'s Job Tng. Coun., N.Y., 1983-88; mem. N.Y.C. Mayor's Coun. on Econ. Advisers, 1993. Recipinet Outstanding Svc. award U.S. Dept. Labor, 1979; citation Gov. of State of N.Y., 1980, N.Y. State Assembly, 1980. Fellow Am. Statis. Assn.; mem. IRRA, Am. Econ. Assn., Indsl. Rels. Rsch. Assn. (past pres.). Died May 30, 1994.

BILBY, KENNETH W., diversified electronic company executive; b. Salt Lake City, Oct. 7, 1918; s. Ralph W. and Marguerite (Mansfield) B.; m. Joanne Herbert Stroud, Oct. 15, 1978; children by previous marriage: Barbara Windsor, Kenneth Mansfield, Marquerite Mansfield, Robert Bryan. B.A., U. Ariz., 1941. Fgn. corr. Europe and Middle East N.Y. Herald Tribune, 1947-50; pub. relations rep. RCA Victor, Camden, N.J., 1950-54; v.p. pub. relations, exec. v.p. NBC, 1954-60; v.p. pub. affairs RCA, 1960-62, exec. v.p. corporate affairs, 1962—; dir. RCA Global Communications, Inc., N.Y. Bank for Savs., exec.-in-residence Harvard Bus. Sch., 1982. Author: New Star in the Near East, 1950. Bd. dirs. Boys' Clubs Am.; trustee, exec. com. South Street Seaport Mus. Served to lt. col. AUS, World War II. Decorated Silver Star medal, Legion of Merit, Bronze Star medal, Combat Infantry Badge; Croix de Guerre; recipient Alumni Achievement award U. Ariz., 1960. Mem. Phi Delta Theta. Clubs: Apawamis (Rye, N.Y.); Blind Brook (Purchase, N.Y.); Shinnecock Hill Golf (Southampton, N.Y.); River (N.Y.C.). Died August 1997.

BILLHARZ, CONSTANCE ELLEN CLARK, speech educator, educational diagnostician; b. Golden City, Mo., July 29, 1921; d. Harley B. and Flossie J. (Mitchell) Clark; m. Roger William Billharz, Jan. 12, 1946; 1 child, Roger Clark. BA, Pace U., 1971; MA, NYU, 1975; MPS, Manhattanville Coll., 1978. Cert. tchr., N.Y. Mem. N.Y. Opera Co., N.Y.C., 1943-46; speech pathologist St. Joseph's Mental Health Clinic, Peekskill, N.Y., 1978-79; speech and lang. pathologist Rye (N.Y.) City Sch. Dist., 1980-82; speech therapist, spl. edn. tchr. Hartsdale Sch., Elmsford, N.Y., 1985-90; adj. prof. speech Westchester C.C., Valhalla, N.Y., 1991-93; ednl. diagnostician, North Tarrytown, N.Y., 1979-93. Mem. New Opera Co., N.Y.C., 1943-46. Mem. Am. Speech, Lang. and Hearing Assn. (cert. clin. competence), N.Y. State Speech, Lang. and Hearing Assn., Westchester Speech, Lang. and Hearing Assn., Westchester Assn. for Children with Learning Disabilities, Am. Arbibtration Assn. Republican. Died Nov. 8, 1993.

BILLINGS, MARLAND PRATT, geologist, educator; b. Boston, Mar. 11, 1902; s. George Bartlett and Helen Agnes (McDonough) B.; m. Katharine Stevens Fowler, Apr. 23, 1938; children: George, Elizabeth. BA, Harvard U., 1923, MA, 1925, PhD, 1927; DSc, Washington U., St. Louis, 1960, U. N.H., 1966. Asst. in geology Harvard U., Cambridge, Mass., 1922-25, instr., 1925-28, asst. prof. geology, 1930-39, assoc. prof. geology, 1939-46, prof. geology, 1946-72, prof. emeritus, 1972-96; chmn. div. geol. scis., Harvard U., 1946-51; assoc. Bryn Mawr Coll., 1928-29; assoc. prof., 1929-30, asst. geologist, U.S. Geol. Survey, 1929-38, 1940-43, assoc. geologist, 1943-44, geologist, 1945; curator Geol. Mus., Harvard U. Author: Geological Map of N.H., Bedrock Geology of New Hampshire, 1956, Structural Geology; contbr. numerous geol. articles. Civilian tech. observer U.S. Army, 1944. Fellow Geol. Soc. Am. (v.p. 1951, 58, pres. 1959, Penrose medal 1987), Mineral Soc. Am.; mem. Am. Acad. Arts. and Scis., Seismol. Soc. Am., Nat. Acad. Scis., AAAS (v.p. 1947), Am. Assn. Petroleum Geologists. Died Oct. 9, 1996.

BILLINGS, WILLIAM DWIGHT, ecology educator; b. Washington, Dec. 29, 1910; s. William Pence and Mabel (Burke) B.; m. Shirley Ann Miller, July 29, 1958. BA, Butler U., 1933, DSc, 1955; MA, Duke U., 1935, PhD, 1936. Instr. botany U. Tenn., 1936-37; instr. biology U. Nev., 1938-40, asst. prof., 1940-43, assoc. prof., 1943-49, prof., chmn. biology dept., 1949-52; assoc. prof. botany Duke U., 1952-58, prof., 1958-67, James B. Duke prof., 1967-97; prin. rsch. assoc. Inst. Arctic Biology, U. Alaska, 1984-97; mem. adv. panels NSF-AEC, Washington, 1954-58; adj. rsch. prof. Desert Rsch. Inst., U. Nev., 1982. Author: Plants and the Ecosystem, 1964, 78, Plants, Man and the Ecosystem, 1970, Vegetation and the Environment, 1974, The Vegetation of North America, 1988; editor Ecology, 1952-57, Ecol. Monographs, 1969; mem. editorial bd. Ecol. Studies, 1975-93, Arctic and Alpine Rsch., 1975-82. Fulbright rsch. scholar, N.Z., 1959, Nev. medal Gov. of State of Nev., 1989. Fellow Arctic Inst. N.Am., Am. Acad. Arts and Scis., Explorers Club; mem. Ecol. Soc. Am. (v.p. 1960, pres. 1978-79, Mercer award 1962, Disting. Svc. award 1981, Eminent Ecologist award 1991), Brit. Ecol. Soc. (hon. fgn. mem.), Bot. Soc. Am. (chmn. ecology sect. 1976, Cert. of Merit 1960), Inst. Arctic and Alpine Rsch. (mem. sci. adv. com. 1975-89). Achievements include research on arctic, alpine and desert ecology. Died Jan. 4, 1997.

BILSKY, MANUEL, educator, philosopher; b. Bklyn., Mar. 25, 1910; s. Harry and Minnie (Haber) B. M.A., U. Mich., 1947, Ph.D., 1951. Asst. prof. U. Chgo., 1949-58; asso. prof. Roosevelt U., Chgo., 1958-60; prof. philosophy Eastern Mich. U., 1960-80, ret., 1980. Author: Logic and Effective Argument, 1956, Patterns of Argument, 1963, (with H.G. Duffield) Tolstoy and the Critics, 1965; also articles, book revs. Served to 1st lt. AUS, 1942-46. DIED 11/12/96. .

BINION, WILLIE CLAYTE, JR., newspaper editor; b. Houston, June 7, 1912; s. Willie Clayte and Mattie (Sayers) B.; m. Sara Dell Newsom, Mar. 28, 1937; children: Clayte III, Jack Russell, Emma Lee (Mrs. David V. Wilson), Tommy Sayers. Student, Southwestern U., Georgetown, Tex., 1929-31, Stephen F. Austin Coll., Nacogdoches, Tex., 1931-32, U. Tex., 1932-35. With Lufkin (Tex.) Daily News, 1937-42, 45-48, mng. editor, 1942, 47-48; mem. pub. relations dept. Jefferson Amusement Co., Beaumont, Tex., 1942-43; with sports copy desk Beaumont Enterprise, 1948-49; with Houston Chronicle, 1949-87, mng. editor, 1965-71, exec. editor, 1971-77, dir., 1968-87; vis. lectr. dept. communications Stephen F. Austin U., 1978-85; mem. journalism jury Pulitzer Prize, 1969, 70; mem. newspapers editors com. U. Tex. Served with USMCR, 1944-46, PTO. Mem. UPI Editors Assn. (pres. 1971), Nat. Tex. AP Mng. Editors Assn. (pres. 1969), Am. Soc. Newspaper Editors, SAR, Sons Republic of Tex., Kappa Sigma, Sigma Delta Chi. Methodist. Clubs: Houston Press; Crown Colony Country (Lufkin). Deceased.

BIRD, AGNES THORNTON, lawyer; b. Wichita Falls, Tex., Sept. 15, 1921; d. Ernest Grady and Ann McNulty (Renfro) Thornton; m. Frank Babington Bird, Mar. 10, 1946; 1 child, Patricia Ann. BS, Tex. Woman's U., 1943; MA, U. Tenn., 1959, PhD, 1967, JD, 1974. Bar: Tenn. 1975. Instr. polit. sci. U. Tenn., 1961-64; asst. prof. Maryville (Tenn.) Coll., 1969-72; ptnr. Bird, Navratil, Bird, Kull & McCroskey, Maryville, 1975-94; mem. Tenn. Human Rights Commn., 1965-68; mem. adv. com. U.S. Civil Rights Commn., Tenn., 1963-72, vice chair, 1968; chair Tenn. Commn. on Status of Women, 1977-79; bd. dirs. Nat. Assn. Commns. on Women, 1977-78. Pres. Tenn. Fedn. Dem. Women, 1964-65; parliamentarian Nat. Fedn. Dem. Women, 1974-85, 87-93; mem. Nat. Assn. Dem. State Chairs, 1976-84; Dem. vice chair and nat. committeewoman State of Tenn., 1976-84; mem. adv. coun. Maryville Coll., 1979-86. Recipient Disting. Alumna award Tex. Women's U., 1980, Annie Selwyn Humanitarian award, 1989; Citizens Rsch. Found. of Princeton, N.J., grantee, 1965. Mem. ABA (com. on immigration 1987-92), Tenn. Bar Assn., Blount County Bar Assn. (treas. 1978-79, pres. 1989), AAUW (pres. Maryville br. 1967-68, chmn. assn. topic com. 1970-72, pres. Tenn. divsn. 1985-87, dir. legal advocacy fund project 1987-91, 92-94, mem. adv. bd. Legal Advocacy Fund 1989-93), Blount Meml. Hosp. Found. (bd. dirs. 1989-94), Blount County C. of C. (bd. dirs. 1994, chair found. bd. 1994—), DAR, Chilhowee Club (pres. 1965-66), Kiwanis. Unitarian. Home: Walland Tenn. Died March 31, 1994.

BIRDSALL, BLAIR, civil engineering executive; b. Newark, May 21, 1907; s. William Adams and Carrie Jane (Mulford) B.; m. Helen S. Burnett, Oct. 15, 1931;

children: Elizabeth Jane Birdsall Evans, William Blair, James Brewster; m. Elizabeth Figueroa, Nov. 28, 1955; stepchildren: Rodolfo Celis, Jose Roberto Celis, Maria Rosario Wirth. B.S.C.E., Princeton, 1929, C.E., 1930. Engr. Voorhees, Gmelin & Walker, N.Y.C., 1930-31; Engr. Port of N.Y. Authority, 1931-32; Engr. Buildings Wallkill (N.Y.) State Prison, 1932-34; Engr. John A. Roebling's Sons Co., Trenton, 1934-65; Steinman, Boynton, Gronquist & Birdsall, N.Y.C., 1965-92; Manag. partner Steinman, Boynton, Gronquist & Birdsall, 1976-88; Engring. cons., Allendale, 1992-97. Recognized worldwide as one of the foremost suspension bridge engineers of the century. Contbr. articles to profl. publs about suspension bridges, cables and wire rope. Recipient Kerensky medal for structural engring., London, 1988, Roebling medal for lifelong achievement Internat. Bridge Conf., Pitts., 1989; named Mr. Bridges, Inst. Bridge Integrity and Safety, 1984; May 24, 1984 proclaimed Blair BirdsallDay by Andrew Stein, borough pres. Manhattan; recip. Key to the City of San Francisco, 1987. mem. ASCE (hon); fellow ASME; ASTM; Internat. Assn. Bridge and Structural Engring.; Internat. Wire Assn.; Am. Soc. Metals. Republican. Presbyterian. Home: Allendale N.J. Died June 25, 1997; New Hurley Cemetery, New Hurley, NY.

BIRKHOFF, GARRETT, mathematician, educator; b. Princeton, N.J., Jan. 10, 1911; s. George David and Margaret (Grafius) B.; m. Ruth Collins, June 21, 1938; children: Ruth W., John D., Nancy C. AB, Harvard U., 1932; postgrad., Cambridge (Eng.) U., 1932-33; hon. degree, U. Nacional Mexico, 1951, U. Lille, 1960, Case Inst. Tech., 1964, Tech. U., Munich, 1986, Tech. H. Darmstadt, 1991. Instr. Harvard U., 1936-38, asst. prof., 1938-41, assoc. prof., 1941-46, prof., 1946-81; cons. to govt. and pvt. industry; Walker-Ames lectr. U. Wash.; Taft lectr. U. Cin., 1947. Author: Survey of Modern Algebra, 1941, 4th edit., 1977, Lattice Theory, 1940, 3d edit., 1967, Hydrodynamics, 1950, rev. edit., 1960; (with E.H. Zarantonello) Jets, Wakes and Cavities, 1957; (with G.C. Rota) Ordinary Differential Equations, 1962, 4th edit., 1989; (with S. Mac Lane) Algebra, 1967, 3d edit., 1988; Source Book in Classical Analysis, 1973; (with R.E. Lynch) Numerical Solution of Elliptic Problems, 1984; mem. editorial bd. Ency. Brit., 1985-88. Chmn. organizing com. Internat. Congress Mathematicians, 1950. Guggenheim fellow, 1948. Mem. AAAS (chmn. sect. 1979), Am. Math. Soc. (v.p. 1958), Math. Assn. Am. (v.p. 1971-72), Am. Acad. Arts and Scis. (v.p. 1966-68), Am. Philos. Soc., Nat. Acad. Sci., Conf. Bd. Math. Sci. (chmn. 1969-70), Soc. Indsl. and Applied Math. (pres. 1967-68), Sociedad Math. Mex. (hon.), Acad. Ciencias Lima. Mem. Soc. of Friends. DIED 11/22/96. .

BISEL, HARRY FERREE, oncologist; b. Manor, Pa., June 17, 1918; s. George Culbertson and Mary Stotler (Ferree) B.; m. Sara Louise Clark, Oct. 30, 1954; children: Jane, Clark, Harold. B.S., U. Pitts., 1939, M.D., 1942. Intern U. Pitts. Med. Center, 1942-43; resident U. Pa., 1948-49, Harvard U. Boston City Hosp., 1949-50; resident physician Meml. Sloan Kettering Cancer Center, 1951-53; cancer coordinator medicine U. Pitts., 1953-63; chmn. div. med. oncology Mayo Clinic, Rochester, Minn., 1963-72; sr. cons. div. med. oncology Mayo Clinic, 1972-83; prof. oncology Mayo Med. Sch., 1967-83; cons. Nat. Cancer Inst. Served to capt. M.C. USNR, 1943-47. Recipient Philip S. Hench Disting. Alumnus award U. Pitts. Sch. Medicine, 1972. Mem. Am. Soc. Clin. Oncology (past pres.), Soc. Surg. Oncology, Am. Assn. Cancer Edn., Am. Assn. Cancer Research. Presbyterian. Club: Rotary. Home: Rochester Minn. Died Sept. 2, 1994.

BISHOP, JOSEPH WARREN, JR., lawyer, educator; b. N.Y.C., Apr. 15, 1915; s. Joseph Warren and Edna Priscilla (Dashiell) B.; m. Susan Carroll Oulahan, May 6, 1950; 1 son, Joseph Warren III. Grad, Deerfield Acad., 1932; A.B., Dartmouth Coll., 1936; LL.B., Harvard U., 1940. Bar: D.C. 1941, N.Y. 1954, Conn. 1963. Spl. asst. to undersec. war, 1940-42; with Office Solicitor Gen., Dept. Justice, 1947-50; asst. to gen. counsel U.S. High Commn. Occupied Germany, 1950-52; dep. gen. counsel, acting gen. counsel Dept. Army, 1952-53; pvt. practice law N.Y.C., 1953-57; prof. law Yale Law Sch., 1957—, Richard Ely prof. law, 1968—; vis. prof. law U. Muenster, West Germany, 1965; faculty Salzburg Seminar Am. Studies, 1967; vis. fellow Clare Hall Cambridge (Eng.) U., 1974; vis. prof. U. Munich, W. Ger., 1980; asst. counsel trustees New Haven R.R., 1961-74; Expert cons. SEC, 1958. Author: Indemnifying and Insuring the Corporate Executive, 2d edit., 1980, Obiter Dicta, 1971, Justice Under Fire: A Study of Military Law, 1974; also articles, book revs. Served with AUS, 1943-46. Recipient Exceptional Civilian Service citation Dept. Army, 1953; Guggenheim fellow, 1974. Club: Century.

BISHOP, LUTHER DOYLE, emeritus management educator; b. Graham, Tex., Oct. 31, 1921; s. Luther Whitfield and Clara Bell (Rowe) B.; m. Nan Alice Schneider, Mar. 15, 1942. Student, Baylor U., 1939-40; B.B.A., U. Tex., 1948, M.B.A., 1950; Ph.D., Ohio State U., 1959. With Clifton Mfg. Co., Waco, Tex., 1940-42, Brown and Root Constrn. Co., Texarkana, Tex., 1942; mgr. vets. dormitories U. Tex., 1948-49, instr. mgmt. dept., 1949-51; mem. faculty U. Okla., Norman, 1951-95; prof. bus. mgmt. U. Okla., 1959-73, David Ross Boyd prof. emeritus mgmt., 1973-95, chmn. dept., 1959-68, 70-72; Grad. asst. in bus. orgn. Ohio State U., 1953-54. Served with USNR, 1942-45. Mem. Acad. Mgmt., AAUP, Nat. Rehab. Assn., Soc. Advancement Mgmt., Southwestern Social Sci. Assn., Beta Gamma Sigma. Home: Norman Okla. Died Apr. 10, 1995.

BISSELLE, MORGAN FITCH, lawyer; b. N.Y.C., Mar. 25, 1908; s. Luther Cleaveland and Lillian (Jones) B.; m. Lucille Florence Marks, Oct. 21, 1933; children: Philip Morgan, Walter Cleaveland. A.B., Colgate U., 1929; J.D., Yale, 1932. Bar: N.Y. bar 1933, U.S. Supreme Ct. bar 1950. Practiced in N.Y.C., 1933-35, Utica, N.Y., 1939-53, New Hartford, N.Y., 1953-73, Hamilton, N.Y., 1973—; confidential clk. Asso. Justice Rowland L. Davis Appellate Div., Supreme Ct., 2d Judicial Dept., Bklyn., 1935-38; mem. firm Hart, Senior & Nichols, 1939-43, Tucker & Bisselle, 1943-65; gen. counsel Utica Mut. Ins. Co., 1943-73, sec., 1968-73. Trustee Savs. Bank of Utica.; Mem. Bd. Edn., New Hartford Central Sch., 1946-53, pres., 1952; mem. New Hartford Planning Bd., 1962-68, Hamilton Zoning Bd. Appeals. Mem. ABA, N.Y. State Bar Assn., Oneida County Bar Assn. (past pres.), Sigma Nu, Phi Alpha Delta. Republican. Baptist. Clubs: Mason. (Utica), Fort Schuyler (Utica). Died Apr. 24, 1991.

BLACK, EMILIE ANNABELLE, physician, government medical institute administrator; b. New Haven, Apr. 14, 1919; d. Lewis Albert and Margaret Anna (Knopf) B.; m. Samuel J. Solt, July 19, 1946; 1 dau., Margaret. BS, George Washington U., 1942, MD, 1945. Intern Garfield Meml. Hosp., Washington, 1945-46; resident in internal medicine Garfield Meml. Hosp., 1946-47; resident Children's Hosp., Washington, 1947-49; practice medicine specializing in pediatrics Bethesda, Md., 1949-66; med. officer D.C. Dept. Pub. Health Child Health Clinics, 1963-68; with NIH, Bethesda, Md., 1968-92; dep. dir. clin. and physiol. program Nat. Inst. Gen. Med. Scis., 1974-76, program dir., 1976-78; asst. dir. Nat. Inst. Gen. Med. Scis. for Clin. Research, 1978-92; cons. in grant adminstrn.; clin. instr. pediatrics George Washington U., 1950-92 ; NIH rep. 3d Internat. Congress on Burn Research, Prague, Czechoslovakia, 1970, White House Conf. on Children, 1970; mem. planning com. Internat. Trauma Symposium, 1970, First World Congress on Pain, Florence, Italy, 1975; participant V Internat. Congress on Burn Injuries, Stockholm, 1978, 6th Internat. Congress on Burn Injuries, 1982. Editor and contbr.: numerous studies and presentations including A Trauma Conference Report, 1974, A Consensus Development Conference on Burn Injuries, 1978, 2d Conference on Burn Injuries, 1980. Vol. Nat. Acad. Scis., Am. Assn. World Health; nat. bd. dirs. Med. Coll. of Pa., 1985-92. Recipient Harvey Stuart Allen award for Disting. Service Am. Burn Assn., 1982, Dir.'s award for disting. service NIH, 1984, G.W.U. Disting. Alumni Achievement award, 1987. Mem. Am. Assn. Surgery Trauma, Internat. Soc. Burn Injuries, Am. Burn Assn. (hon.), George Washington U. Assn., Am. Trauma Soc. (founding mem.), HEW Interagy. Task Force on Burn Ctrs., George Washington U. Alumni Assn. (Disting. Alumni Achievement award 1987). Home: Washington D.C. Died Nov. 18, 1992.

BLACK, NORMAN WILLIAM, federal judge; b. Houston, Dec. 6, 1931; s. Dave and Minnie (Nathan) B.; m. Berne Rose Efron, Feb. 21, 1959; children: Elizabeth Ann, Diane Rebecca. B.B.A., U. Tex., Austin, 1953, J.D. (Frank Bobbitt scholar 1954), 1955. Bar: Tex. 1955. Law clk. to Houston judge, 1956; asst. U.S. atty. Houston, 1956-58, pvt. practice, 1958-76; U.S. magistrate, 1976-79; U.S. dist. judge So. Dist. Tex., Houston, 1979—, now sr. judge; adj. prof. South Tex. Coll. Law. Served with AUS, 1955-56. Mem. Fed. Bar Assn., State Bar Tex., Houston Bar Assn., Houston Philos. Soc. Died July 23, 1997.

BLACK, THEODORE MICHAEL, SR., publisher, consultant; b. Bklyn., Oct. 3, 1919; s. Walter Joseph and Elsie (Jantzer) B.; m. Barbara A. Somerville, Nov. 10, 1956; children: Walter Joseph II, Theodore Michael Jr.; stepchildren: Mrs. Beverly A. Pavlak, Mrs. Dorothy B. Scharkopf. A.B. summa cum laude, Princeton U., 1941; grad., Inf. Officers Candidate Sch., Ft. Benning, Ga., 1943; Litt.D. honoris causa, Siena Coll., Loudonville, N.Y., 1971; LL.D. (hon.), Adelphi U., Garden City, N.Y., 1974, Fordham U., 1978; Pd.D. (hon.), Hofstra U., Hempstead, N.Y., 1974; D.C.L. (hon.), Molloy Coll., Rockville Centre, N.Y., 1975; L.H.D. (hon.), C.W. Post Center, L.I. U., Greenvale, N.Y., 1976, Pace U., 1978, SUNY-Farmingdale, 1986; D.Sc. (hon.), N.Y. Chiropractic Coll., 1984. With Walter J. Black, Inc., 1945-94, v.p., 1952-58, pres., 1958-90, treas., 1958-80, chief exec. officer, 1980-90, chmn. bd., 1990-94; gen. ptnr. Black's Readers Service Co., 1949-58, pres., 1958-90; pres. The Classics Club, Detective Book Club, 1958-90; trustee Roslyn Savs. Bank, 1973-94. Author: Know Your Stamps, 1934, Democratic Party Publicity in the 1940 Campaign, 1941, How to Organize and Run a Citizens' Committee for Your Candidate, 1964, Straight Talk about American Education, 1982. Alumni pres. Class of 1941 Princeton, 1968-73; area chmn. Mercy Hosp. Ball Com., 1966; chmn. county fund drive Nassau Heart Assn., 1967; mem. Nassau-Suffolk com. USO, 1972; staff publicity div. Democratic Nat. Com., 1940; exec. dir. Citizens for Nixon-Lodge, Nassau County, N.Y., 1960; chmn. Citizens for Congressman S.B. Derounian, 1962-64; del. 1967 Constl. Conv.; mem. Port Washington Rep. Club; chmn. Seldin for Congress, 1968; mem. minority research staff N.Y. State Assembly, 1968; dir. Fair Campaign Practices Com., 1971; del. Rep. Nat. Conv., 1980, 1984, 88; mem. Nassau County Bd. Ethics, 1984-91, Fed. Adv. Panel on Financing Elem. and Secondary Edn., 1979-83; pres. Chairmen's Club, 1979-89; exec. com. Alumni Council, Princeton, 1950-63; mem. N.Y. State Bd. Regents, 1969-80, vice chancellor, 1974, chancellor, 1975-80. Served from pvt. to capt., CIC AUS, 1941-45; lt. col. Army Res. ret., 1967. Decorated Bronze Star with cluster (U.S.) Belgian, French Fourragère; recipient medal SAR; Humanitarian award Am. Jewish Com., 1976; John Jay Higher Edn. Public Policy award, 1980; Disting. Service award Nassau-Suffolk Sch. Bds. Assn., 1973; award Poly. Inst. N.Y., 1974; award L.I. Assn. Spl. Edn. Adminstrs., 1975; Man of Yr. award L.I. Advt. Club, 1975; Citizen of Yr. award N.Y. State Soc. Profl. Engrs., 1980; St. John Neumann award Buffalo, 1980, award L.I. Rough Riders (BSA), 1988. Mem. Better Bus. Bur. L.I., M.I. Res. Soc. (chmn. res. affairs 1956-59, pres. 1961-62), Res. Officers Assn. U.S., Assn. U.S. Army, Nat. CIC Assn., 3d Armored Div. Assn., Am. Legion, Battle Normandy Found., Vets. of Battle of Bulge, Phi Beta Kappa. Republican. Roman Catholic. Clubs: Elk, Lion, Port Washington (N.Y.) Yacht; Capitol Hill (Washington); L.I. Advt; Publishers/Lunch (N.Y.C.). Died Mar. 19, 1994.

BLACKBURN, DOUGLAS BRYAN, government official; b. N.Y.C., Nov. 20, 1918; s. Charles Henry and May Elizabeth (Scofield) B.; m. Frances T. Coleman, May 12, 1943; children: Dolores May, Doreen, Douglas Bryan. B.S. in Adminstrv. Engring., Cornell U., 1939. Registered profl. engr., N.J., N.Y., 13 other states. Field engr. Ethyl Corp., Detroit, 1939-42; asst. mgr. Hormiguero (sugar mill), Las Villas, Cuba, 1946-51; engr. Ford, Bacon & Davis, Inc., N.Y.C., 1951-64, So. P.R. Sugar Co., N.Y.C., 1964-65; sr. engr., then v.p. Ford, Bacon & Davis, Inc., 1965-72, pres., 1972-73, chmn. bd., chief exec. officer, 1973-82; dir. Mblzn. Concepts Devel. Ctr., Nat. Def. U., Ft. McNair, Washington, 1982—; dir. Trident Engring. Assos., Stratford Graham Engring. Corp. Served to lt. USNR, 1942-46. Mem. ASME, Am. Mgmt. Assn., Am. Arbitration Assn., Nat. Def. Trans. Assn. (chmn.), Nat., La., Cornell U. socs. profl. engrs., Tau Beta Pi, Pi Kappa Alpha. Republican. Episcopalian. Clubs: Lake Mohawk Country (Sparta), Lake Mohawk Golf (Sparta); City Midday (N.Y.C.), University (N.Y.C.); Mariner Sands Country (Stuart, Fla.). Died Aug. 16, 1997.

BLACKBURN, JOHN LEWIS, consulting engineer; b. Kansas City, Mo., Oct. 2, 1913; s. John Ealy and Lela (Garnett) B.; m. Margaret Bailey, Sept. 12, 1943; children: Susan T., Joan Blackburn Krist, Margot A. Blackburn Jahns. BSEE with high honors, U. Ill., 1935. With Westinghouse Electric Corp., Newark, 1936-78, cons. engr., 1969-78; pvt. practice cons., Bothell, Wash., 1979-97; adj. prof. Poly. Inst. N.Y., 1949-65, Poly. Inst. N.J., Newark, 1958-71; spl. lectr. IEEE Ednl. Activities, 1952-80; affiliate prof. U. Wash., 1988; instr. North Seattle Community Coll., 1988-93. Author, editor: Applied Protective Relaying, 1978; author: Protective Relaying Principles and Application, 1987, Symmetrical Components for Power Systems Engineering, 1993. Trustee, treas. Millington Bapt. Ch., N.J., 1952-69. Recipient Order of Merit award Westinghouse Electric Corp., 1971, Attwood Assocs. award U.S. Nat. Com. Internat. Conf. for Large High Voltage Electric Systems, 1986. Fellow IEEE (life, chmn. publ. dept. Power Engring. Soc. 1972-76, sec., 1977-79, chmn. power system relaying com. 1969-70, Disting. Service award 1978, Outstanding Service award IEEE ednl. bd. 1979, Centennial medal 1984); mem. China Stamp Soc. Inc. (Meritorious Svc. award, treas. 1961-82, dir. 1968-77, pres. 1980-97), Am. Soc. Polar Philatelists (bd. dirs., treas. 1967-97), Sigma Xi, Tau Beta Pi, Eta Kappa Nu, Phi Kappa Phi. Died Feb. 23, 1997. Home: Bothell Wash.

BLACKMAN, LIONEL HART, psychiatrist; b. N.Y.C., Apr. 26, 1923; s. Theodore Abraham and Bessie (Fishman) B.; m. Miriam Roder, Oct. 4, 1945; children: Jerome, Clifford, Daniel, Carol. BS, Tulane U., 1943, MD, 1946; postgrad., Columbia U. Psychiat. Inst., 1951-52, N.Y. Psychoanalytic Inst., 1951-53. Diplomate Am. Bd. Psychiatry and Neurology, Am. Bd. Forensic Psychiatry. Intern Maimonides Hosp., Bklyn., 1946-47; resident Bklyn. State Hosp., Bklyn., 1949-52, sr. psychiatrist, 1949-52; chief psychiatry McCornack Gen. Hosp., Pasadena, Calif., 1951-52; med. dir. Lake Hosp., Lake Worth, Fla., 1973-75; psychiatrist pvt. practice, N.Y.C., 1952-56, New Hyde Pk., N.Y., 1956-71, Palm Beach, Fla., 1971-75, West Palm Beach, 1975-97; lectr. in field. Contbr. articles to profl. jours. Troop chmn. Boy Scouts Am., Roslyn, N.Y., 1960-65; mem. drug com. Mayor's Coun., Roslyn, 1969; physician Civil Def., Roslyn, 1968-70. Capt. AUS, 1947-49. Fellow Pan Am. Med. Soc., Am. Geriatric Soc., Am. Coll. Forensic Psychiatry, Am. Soc. Psychoanalytic Physicians, Am. Psychiat. Assn. (life); mem. AMA, Acad. Psychosomatic Medicine, Fla. Med. Assn. Fla. Psychiat. Soc., Palm Beach County Med. Soc., Palm Beach County Psychiat. Soc., Am. Acad. Psychiatry and Law, So. Psychiat. Assn., Marce Soc., Fla. Acad. Forensic Psychiatry, Internat. Psychiat. Assn. for Advancement Electrotherapy,

Tulane Alumni Club. Jewish. Avocations: tennis, swimming, painting, music. Died Feb. 9, 1997.

BLACKSTONE, HARRY BOUTON, JR., magician, actor; b. Three Rivers, Mich., June 30, 1934; s. Harry Bouton and Mildred Irene (Phinney) B.; m. Arla Gay Blevins, Oct. 14, 1974; 1 child, Bellamie Gay; children by previous marriage: Harry Bouton, III (dec.), Cynthia Caswell, Adrienne Susan, Tracey Irene. Student, Swarthmore Coll., 1951-53; B.A., U. So. Calif., 1958; M.F.A. (Library of Congress fellow), U. Tex., 1961. Appeared as magician in Australia, Eng., France, Japan, Spain and throughout Europe and Far East, 1952-97; The Sahara-Tahoe, The Nugget, The Flamingo, Caesar's Palace, The Sahara and, The Tropicana, Las Vegas, Las Vegas Hilton, Bally's, Orch. Hall, Chgo.; symphony shows include Houston Music Hall, Honolulu Symphony at Blaisdell Ctr., Van Wezel Performing Arts Hall, Sarasota, Fla.; Inland Empire Symphony Orch., 1991, Cin. Pops, 1993; other appearances include Pabst Theatre, Milw., Seattle Opera House, Kansas City Starlight Theatre, Concord Pavillion, Sea World, Magic Mountain, Disneyworld and Disneyland, Calif. Inst. Tech., San Diego State U., Ind. U., Fla. State U.; also in numerous night clubs, theatres, amusement parks and univs. in U.S., including Harrah's Club Reno and Lake Tahoe; appeared at The Tropicana Christmas Extravaganza, 1985-86, Detroit Fox, Orange County Performing Arts Ctr., McCallum Theatre. Star, producer (illusion show) Blackstone (longest running magic show in Broadway history); also appeared on: TV shows Good Morning, America, Hart to Hart, Santa Barbara, Square One TV; television spl. Mandrake, The Magician, Magic, Magic, Magic!, Magical Musical Halloween, Magic!, Search for Houdini, 1987; guest star Miss Am. Pageant, 1996; tech. cons., magic coordinator: spl. film for The Great Houdini's, ABC-TV; host: television spl. The Magic Show, 5 spls for BBC, Internat. Magic award, Disney Night of Magic, 1993; gen. mgr. nat. touring cos. of: Hair; assoc. producer: Smothers Bros. Comedy Hour, CBS, 1969-70; gen. mgr. West Coast cos.: Hair, 1970-72; producer star magic extravaganza at, Harrah's Club, Lake Tahoe, 1971; appeared in: Hocus Pocus at, Fremont Hotel, Las Vegas, 1972; creator magic for Earth, Wind & Fire, New Kids on the Block, Vanilla Ice; author: There's One Born Every Minute, 1976, The Blackstone Book of Magic and Illusion, 1985; designer, builder magical effects for ski shows at, Sea World of, Ohio and, Fla.; magic exhibit Smithsonian Inst. Served with U.S. Army Security Agy., 1953-56. Recipient Star of Magic award, 1979; named U.S. Bicentennial Magician, 1976. Mem. Magic Castle and Acad. Magical Arts and Scis. (bd. dirs. 1994-97, Magician of Yr. 1979, 82), Internat. Brotherhood Magicians, Soc. Am. Magicians (life, amb.), Inner Magic Cir. (gold star), Internat. Coll. Surgeons (hon.). Episcopalian. Died May 14, 1997.

BLAIN, ALEXANDER, III, surgeon, educator; b. Detroit, Mar. 9, 1918; s. Alexander William and Ruby (Johnson) B.; m. Josephine Woodbury Bowen, May 3, 1941; children—Helen Bowen, Alexander IV, Bruce Scott Murray, Josephine Johnson; m. Mary E. Mains, 1968. B.A., Wayne U., 1940, M.D., 1943; M.S. in Surgery, U. Mich., 1948. Diplomate Am. Bd. Surgery. House officer, Halsted fellow in surgery Johns Hopkins U., 1943-46; resident surgeon U. Hosp., Ann Arbor, Mich., 1946-50; instr. surgery U. Mich., 1950-57; chief surgeon 14th Field Hosp., Bad Kreuznach, Fed. Republic Germany; clin. assoc. prof. surgery Wayne State U., 1962-87; surgeon-in-chief Alexander Blain Hosp., Detroit, 1953-78; cons. surgeon Highland Park Gen. Hosp, St. Josephs's Hosp., Blain Clinic, Ostego Meml. Hosp., Gaylord, Mich.; med. dir. The Budd Co., 1977-82; staff periop. St. John Hosp., 1988-92; med. cons. bd. 67 adjudication VA, 1990—; pres. Met. Detroit Family Svc. Assn., 1962-63, Detroit Mus. Soc., 1961-62; staff Harper Hosp., Detroit Deaconess Hosp.; surgeon Detroit Urban Indian Health Ctr., 1982-90. Author: (with F.A. Coller) Indications For and Results of Splenectomy, 1950, Prismatic Papers. and an Ode, 1968, Prismatic Haiku Poems (Remembered Voices), 1973, (poems) Shu Shu Ga, 2d edit., 1983, Clackshant, 1982; contbr. numerous articles to surg. jours.; editorial bd. Rev. Surgery, 1959-79. Mem. Detroit Zool. Park Commn., 1974-82, pres., 1978-82; trustee Alexander Blain Hosp., 1942-67, Ostego Meml. Hosp. Found., Gaylord, Mich., 1976—; bd. dirs. Detroit Zool. Soc., 1972-75, 82—; pres. W.J. Stapleton Found. Health Edn., 1978-84. Served as lt. M.C., AUS, 1942-44, maj., 1955-57. Recipient Wayne State U. Med. Alumni award, 1968. Fellow ACS, N.Y. Acad. Scis.; mem. Internat. Cardiovascular Soc., F.A. Coller Surg. Soc., Am. Fedn. for Clin. Rsch., Cranbrook Inst. Sci., Soc. Vascular Surgery, Am. Thyroid Assn., Soc. Internat. de Chirugie, Mich. Med. Soc. (chmn. surg. sect. 1963), Assn. Clin. Surgery, Pan-Pacific Surg. Assn., Acad. Am. Poets, Am. Poetry Assn., Mich. Poetry Soc., Acad. of Surgery of Detroit, Coun. of Wayne County Med. Soc., Nu Sigma Nu, Phi Gamma Delta. Clubs: Grosse Pointe (fleet surgeon 1986-89), Otsego, Prismatic (pres. 1967), Detroit Racquet (pres. 1976-80), Cardio-Vascular Surgeons (pres. 1961-62), Acanthus, Waweatonong (pres. 1978), Circumnavigators, Witenagemote.

BLAINE, NELL, artist, printmaker; b. Richmond, Va., July 10, 1922; d. Harry Wellington and Eudora Catherine (Garrison) B. Student, Richmond Profl. Inst., 1939-42, Hans Hofmann Sch. Fine Arts, N.Y.C., 1942-44, Art Students League, 1943; student etching, Atelier 17, Stanley W. Hayter, N.Y.C., 1945; student, New Sch. for Social Research, 1952-53; hon. degree, Moore Coll. Art, 1980; Doctorate (hon.), Va. Commonwealth U., 1985. Pvt. tchr. of painting N.Y.C., 1943-49; tchr. adult program Great Neck (N.Y.) pub. schs., 1956; Costume designer for Eleanore Goff, dancer, Studio Theater, N.Y.C., 1949; costume, set designer for Midi Garth, 1956; artistic adviser for Garth concerts Henry St. Playhouse, 92d St. YM-YWHA Dance Center, N.Y.C., 1951, 54, 55. One-woman-shows include, Jane St. Gallery, N.Y.C., 1945, 48, So. Ill. U., Carbondale, 1949, Tibor de Nagy Gallery, 1953, 54, 95, Stewart Rickard Gallery, San Antonio, 1961, Phila. Art Alliance, 1961, Poindexter Gallery, N.Y.C., 1956, 58, 60, 66, 68, 70, 72, 76, Yaddo, Saratoga Springs, N.Y., 1961, Zabriskie Gallery, Provincetown, Mass., 1963, U. Conn., Storrs, 1973, Va. Mus. Fine Arts, 1947, 55, 73, 79, Stagecoach House Gallery, Gloucester, Mass., 1977, Watson/de Nagy Gallery, Houston, 1977, Fischbach Gallery, N.Y.C., 1979, 81, 83, 85, 87, 89, 91, 93, 95, Hull Gallery, Washington, 1979-80, Jersey City Mus., 1981, Alpha Gallery, Boston, 1981, Reynolds Gallery, Richmond, 1982, 92, 94, others; travelling retrospective, N.Y. State, 1974-75; exhibited in group shows including, Art Inst. Chgo., 1944, Va. Mus. of Fine Arts Biennials, Richmond, 1944-53, Riverside Mus., N.Y.C., 1944-57, Va. Mus., 1945, Art of This Century Gallery, 1945, Stable Galleries Anns., N.Y.C., 1954-57, San Francisco Mus. Art, 1960, Whitney Mus. Am. Art, N.Y.C., 1957, 74, Met. Mus., N.Y.C., 1979 (2 shows), 1986, print and Book Exhbn., 1986, prints, 1991; summer festivals on Cape Ann and Cape Cod, Mass., 1943, 54, 58, Mus. Modern Art, N.Y.C., 1956, 68, 74, Wildenstein Gallery, N.Y.C., 1960, Sidney Janis Gallery, N.Y.C., 1984, Nat. Mus. Women in Arts, 1990-91, 91-92, 92, also, Brooks Meml. Art Gallery, Visual Arts Gallery, Corcoran Gallery, Mus. Modern Art, Rome, Copenhagen, Denmark, Seville World Expo, Kansas City Art Inst., Smithsonian Instn., Palais des Beaux-Arts de la Ville de Paris, France, Mus. Modern Art, Tokyo, Japan, 1955, Nat. Inst. Arts and Letters, 1967, 70, 76, 83, 85, 86, 90 (Purchase award Am. Inst. Arts and Letters 1994), U. Tex., Austin, 1974, and others; represented in numerous permanent collections including, Whitney Mus. Am. Art, N.Y.C., Met. Mus. Art, N.Y.C., Mus. Modern Art, N.Y.C., Carnegie Inst., Pitts., Ga. Mus. Art, Athens, Va., Mus. Fine Arts, Richmond, State U. of Iowa Mus., Iowa City, Chase Manhattan Bank Collection, N.Y.C., U. Art Mus., U. Calif. at Berkeley, Slater Meml. Mus., Norwich, Conn., Rose Art Mus., Brandeis U., Waltham, Mass., Bklyn. Mus., Hallmark Internat. Award Collection, Kansas City, Mo., Hirshhorn Mus. and Sculpture Garden, Nat. Mus. Women in Arts, numerous others; author: Nell Blaine Prints/Kenneth Koch Poems, 1953, Nell Blaine Sketchbok, 1986; co-author: (with Marge Piercy) The Earth Shines Secretly: A Book of Days, 1990. Recipient 1st prize Norfolk Mus., 1945, Purchase award Whitney Mus., 1958; 1st Gov.'s Art Award of Va., 1979, Honor award Women's Caucus for Art, 1986, Louise Nevelson award in art Am. Acad. and Inst. Arts and Letters, 1990; Va. Mus. fellow, 1943, 46; Ingram Merrill grantee, 1962, 64, 66; Longview grantee, 1964, 70; Cultural Council Found. grantee, 1972; Rothko grantee, 1973; Guggenheim fellow, 1974-75; Nat. Endowment grantee, 1975-76. Mem. Artists Equity Assn., NAD (academician). DIED 11/14/96. .

BLAIR, GEORGE SIMMS, social science educator; b. Homewood, Kans., May 31, 1924; s. William Horace and Mary (Simms) B.; m. Gloria Jean Barnes, Sept. 10, 1949; children: David Lawrence, Rebecca Lynn. AB, Kans. State Tchrs. Coll., Emporia, 1948, BS in Edn, 1948, MS, 1949; PhD, Northwestern U., 1951. Asst. prof. polit. sci. U. Tenn., 1951-53; asst. prof. polit. sci. U. Pa., 1953-56, asso. prof., 1956-60; asso. prof. govt. Claremont (Calif.) Grad. Sch., 1960-64, prof., 1964-72, Elizabeth Helm Rosecrans prof. social sci., 1972-90; sr. rsch. assoc. Rose Inst. State and Local Govt. Claremont McKenna Coll., 1989-91. Author: (with S.B. Sweeney) Metropolitan Analysis, 1958 (Fruin-Colnon award 1959), Cumulative Voting in Illinois, 1960, American Local Government, 1964, El Gobierno Local en Los Estados Unidos, 1966, American Legislatures, 1967, (with H.I. Flournoy) Legislative Bodies in California, 1967, Government at the Grass Roots, 1977, 81, 86. Bd. editors: Western Polit. Quar, 1964-68. Mem. Claremont City Planning Commn., 1964-71, Scholars for Rockefeller, 1960, 68, Scholars for Nixon, 1960, 68, Scholars for Reagan, 1969-70, 80, 84; bd. dirs. Greater Los Angeles Consortium. Served with AUS, 1943-46, PTO. Mem. Am. Polit. Sci. Assn., Pi Sigma Alpha, Pi Gamma Mu. Republican. Methodist.

BLAIR, WILLIAM TRAVIS (BUD BLAIR), organization executive; b. Canton, Ohio, Dec. 17, 1925; s. George Neely and Helen Irene (Travis) B.; m. Eleanor I. Reid, Mar. 16, 1954; children: Carol Blair Oliver, Timothy R., Anne T. Blair Sisson, Linda Blair Hall. B.A., Ohio Wesleyan U., 1950; grad., Advance Mgmt. Inst. for Assn. Execs., Mich. State U., 1964. Sales rep. Columbus (Ohio) Coated Fabrics, 1950-57; assoc. dir. legis. affairs Ohio C. of C., Columbus, 1958-61, dir. indsl. devel., 1961-77, dir. social legis., 1963-77, dir. legis. affairs, 1973-77, exec. v.p., 1977-80, pres., 1980-87, life dir., 1987-97; sec., mem. exec. com. Ohio Med. Indemnity, Inc., Worthington, 1966-79; pres. Gt. Lakes Indsl. Devel. Coun., 1971. Chmn. bd. mgmt. Ctrl. YMCA. Columbus, 1974; bd. trustees Ctr. of Sci. and Industry, 1962-97; mem. Gov.'s Adv. Coun. on Internat. Trade, 1970-74, Gov.'s Devel. Adv. Coun., 1977-82, Gov.'s Adv. Coun. on Labor/Mgmt. Cooperation, 1984-87, Gov.'s Trade Mission to China, 1979; exec. dir. Ohio Small Bus. and Entrepreneurship Coun., 1993-94. With USCG, 1943-46. Mem. Ohio Commodores (charter), Coun. State C. of C. (sec. treas. 1978, vice chmn. 1979, mem. exec. com., chmn. 1980-82), Ohio Trade Assn. Execs. (dir. 1979-82), SAR, C. of C. Execs. of Ohio (dir. 1978), Ohio Wesleyan U. Alumni Assn. (v.p., Disting. Alumni award, 1997), Jazz Arts Group (bd. dirs. 1989-92), University Club (bd. dirs. 1980-83, v.p. 1982-83), Columbus Athletic Club, York Golf Club, Rotary, Masons, Phi Mu Alpha, Phi Kappa Psi. Presbyterian (Elder, commr. to Presbytery). Home: Columbus Ohio Died Aug. 30, 1997.

BLAKE, JEANNETTE BELISLE, psychotherapist; b. Manchester, N.H., Aug. 1, 1920; d. Emile Henry and Mathilda Cecelia (Martin) Belisle; m. Roland Oscar Royer, Sept. 6, 1937 (div. 1948); 1 child, Dorothy Marie Royer Lyman; m. Albert Willard Blake Sr., Aug. 11, 1979. Cons. Al Blake Advt. Cons., Manchester, N.H., 1959-68; pvt. practice Manchester, 1968-95; founder, dir. N.H. Metaphys. Establishment, Manchester, 1976-95; presenter workshops in field. Recipient medal N.H. Metaphysicians, 1978; cert. Greater Manchester Mental Health Ctr., 1985, 86. Mem. N.H. Assn. for Counseling and Devel., N.H. Assn. of Family Counselors, Am. Assn. of Mental Health Counselors (N.H. br.), Therapeutic Touch Healing (Manchester chpt.), Soc. for Psychic Rsch. of N.H. and Mass. (adv. bd.). Roman Catholic. Avocations: harness horse racing, oil painting, workshops on Holistic health. Home: Manchester N.H. Died Apr. 24, 1995.

BLAKE, JUDITH, sociology educator; b. N.Y.C., May 3, 1926; d. Forrest James and Sylvia (Blake) Kincade; 1 child, Laura Isabelle Davis. BS, Columbia U., 1950, PhD, 1961. Asst. prof. demography to assoc. prof. U. Calif., Berkeley, 1962-69, prof., 1969-72; prof. Grad. Sch. Pub. Policy, Fred H. Bixby prof. Sch. Pub. Health and dept. sociology UCLA, 1976-93, mem. adv. bd. Rand Grad. Sch. Author: Family Size and Achievement, 1989; editor Ann. Rev. Sociology; contbr. articles to prof. jours. Population Coun. fellow, 1954, Guggenheim fellow, 1976-77; Phi Beta kappa vis. scholar, 1976-77. Fellow AAAS (chmn. sect. K 1988-89); mem. Am. Acad. Arts and Scis., Population Assn., Am. (pres 1980), Am. Sociol. Assn. (William J. Goode book award 1989-90, Sociol. Rsch. Assn. (pres. 1978), Am. Pub. Health Assn. Home: Arroyo Grande Calif. Died Apr. 29, 1993.

BLAKE, LAMONT VINCENT, electronics consultant; b. Somerville, Mass., Nov. 7, 1913; s. Earl Clement and Mary Bella (Munro) B.; m. Charline Manees, July 16, 1938 (dec. 1956); children: Donald Earl, Barbara Jean; m. Elizabeth Hannah Cochran, June 17, 1957 (div. 1978); 1 child, David Munro (dec.); m. Betty Ruth Sachs, Oct. 18, 1980. B.S., Mass. State Coll., 1935; M.S. in Physics, U. Md., 1950, postgrad., 1950-53, 63-64. Radio interference investigator Ark. Power & Light Co., Little Rock and Pine Bluff, 1937-40; radar research scientist Naval Research Lab., Washington, 1940-72; sr. scientist Tech. Service Corp., Silver Spring, Md., 1972-85; self-employed radar cons., 1985-94, retired, 1994. Author: Antennas, 1966, revised edit., 1984, Transmission Lines and Waveguides, 1969, Radar Range-Performance Analysis, 1980; contbr. chpt. to Radar Handbook, 1970, rev. edit., 1990; contbr. articles to profl. jours. Recipient Applied Sci. award Research Soc. Am., 1963; Superior Civilian Service award U.S. Navy, 1972. Fellow IEEE; mem. Am. Phys. Soc., Sigma Xi, Sigma Pi Sigma. Died June 17, 1997.

BLANCHARD, CARL RICHARD, architect; b. New Haven, Mar. 17, 1912; s. Carl Russell and Mary (Dann) B.; m. Rachel Estelle Begor, Jan. 8, 1937; children: Mary Ludia (Mrs. James Bradford Kalloch), Susan Anne (Mrs. Mohamed Ahmed Fadl). Cert. in constrn., Pratt Inst., 1933, cert. design, 1934. Job capt. Fletcher Thompson, Bridgeport, Conn., 1937-40; designer Lorenzo Hamilton, Meriden, Conn., 1935-37; individual practice architecture New Haven, 1937—; Dir. New Haven Savs. & Loan Assn.; chmn. New Eng. Council Archtl. Registration Bds., 1975-77; Pres. Conn. Archtl. Registration Bd., 1974-77. Mem. Town Plan Commn., North Haven, Conn., 1970-74; trustee Center Church Home for Aged. Fellow AIA. Republican. Mem. United Ch. of Christ. Club: Quinnipiack. Lodges: Kiwanis; Masons. Died May 16, 1996.

BLANKENHORN, DAVID HENRY, cardiologist; b. Cleve., Nov. 16, 1924; s. Marion Arthur and Martha (Taggart) B.; m. Anne Wood Ramsey, June 15, 1948; children: David, Mary, Susan, John. M.D., U. Cin., 1947; MD (hon.), U. Uppsala, Sweden, 1991. Diplomate: Am. Bd. Internal Medicine. Instr. medicine U. Cin., 1955-57; asst. prof. medicine U. So. Calif., L.A., 1957-61, assoc. prof., 1961-66, prof, 1966-93, dir. cardiology, 1966-80, dir. Atherosclerosis Rsch. Inst., 1980-93; research asst. Rockefeller Inst. Med. Research, 1952-54; pres. Nutrition Sci. Corp. Mem. editorial bd. Jour. Atherosclerosis. Served as capt. M.C. U.S. Army, 1950-52. Commonwealth fellow; recipient Daniel Drake medal U. Cin., 1992. Fellow ACP, Am. Coll. Cardiology, AAAS; mem. Western Assn. Physicians, Am. Heart Assn., Assn. Univ. Cardiologists, Am. Soc. Clin. Nutrition, Alpha Omega Alpha. Home: Pacific Grove Calif. Died May 9, 1993.

BLANTON, FRED, JR., lawyer; b. Muscle Shoals, Ala., July 2, 1919; s. Fred Sr. and Mary (Covington) B.; m. Mercer Potts McAvoy, Aug. 11, 1962. AB, Birmingham-So. Coll., 1939; JD, U. Va., 1942; postgrad., U. Ala., 1946, LLM in Taxation, 1979; postgrad., U. Mich., 1951. Sole practice, Birmingham, Ala., 1946-48, 54-83; prof. Dickinson Sch. Law, Carlisle, Pa., 1948-49; vis. prof. law U. Ala., Tuscaloosa, summer 1949; asst. prof. law U. Va., Charlottesville, 1949-51; assoc. Martin & Blakey, Attys., Birmingham, 1951-54; pvt. practice, Gardendale, Ala., 1983-93, Fultondale, Ala., 1994—. Contbr. articles to profl. jours. Served with USNR, 1942-46. Mem. Ala. Bar Assn. Republican. Episcopalian.

BLASIUS, DONALD CHARLES, retired appliance company executive; b. Oak Park, Ill., June 10, 1929; s. Ervin A. and Frances C. (Critchfield) B.; m. Carle Ann Forslew, Oct. 11, 1952; children: Douglas Charles, Ann Louise. BSBA, Northwestern U., 1951. Various exec. positions McCulloch Corp., 1953-68; various exec. positions J.I. Case Co., 1968-74, v.p., gen. mgr. div., 1970-72, sr. v.p., gen. mgr. div., 1972-74; exec. v.p., chief operating officer Tappan Co., Mansfield, Ohio, 1974-76, pres., chief exec. officer, 1976-84, chmn. bd., chief exec. officer, 1984-86; chmn., chief. exec. officer home products group White Consol. Industries, Inc., Columbus, Ohio, 1986-88; pres. White Consol. Industries, Inc., Cleve., Ohio, 1988-93, retired, 1993; bd. dirs. Ohio Edison Co., Akron, Wolverine Tube Inc., Huntsville, Ala. Died Nov. 1997.

BLASS, GERHARD ALOIS, physics educator; b. Chemnitz, Germany, Mar. 12, 1916; came to U.S., 1949, naturalized, 1955; s. Gustav Alois and Anna (Mehnert) B.; m. Barbara Siegert, July 16, 1945; children—Andrew, Marcus, Evamaria, Annamaria, Peter. Abitur, Oberrealschule Chemnitz, 1935; Dr. rer. nat., Universität Leipzig, 1943. Asst. Institut für Theoretische Physik, Leipzig, 1939-43; research cons. Siemens & Halske, Berlin, 1943-46; dozent math. and physics Oberrealschule, Nuremberg, 1946-47, Ohm Polytechnikum, Nuremberg, 1947-49; prof. physics Coll. St. Thomas, St. Paul, 1949-51; prof. physics U. Detroit, 1951-81, chmn. dept., 1962-71; guest prof. U. Baroda, India, spring, 1967. Author: Theoretical Physics, 1962, "Weil Hiersein viel ist" Poems in German, 1987. Fellow AAAS; mem. Soc. Asian and Comparative Philosophy, Esperanto League N.Am., Sigma Pi Sigma. Roman Catholic. Home: Metamora Mich. Died May 29, 1995.

BLATT, GENEVIEVE, state judge; b. East Brady, Pa., June 19, 1913; d. George F. and Clara (Laurent) B. AB, U. Pitts., 1933, MA, 1934, JD, 1937; LLD (hon.), St. Francis Coll., 1959, Villanova U., 1960, St. Joseph's U., 1964, Barry Coll., 1966, Seton Hill Coll., 1968, LaSalle U., 1970, Elizabethtown Coll., 1974, Dickinson Coll. Law, 1974, York (Pa.) Coll., 1975, St. Charles Sem., 1975, Cedarcrest Coll., 1976, Allentown Coll. of St. Francis de Sales, 1976, Shippensburg U., 1987, Wilson Coll., 1987, Millerville U., 1989, Lock Haven U., 1990, Harrisburg Area Community Coll, 1991. Bar: Pa. 1938. Mem. faculty U. Pitts., 1934-38; sec., chief examiner Pitts. CSC, 1938-42; asst. solicitor City of Pitts., 1942-45; dep. treas., exec. dir. treasury dept. State of Pa., 1945-49, sec. internal affairs, 1955-67; asst. dir. Pres.'s Office Econ. Opportunity, Washington, 1967-68; spl. counsel Shared Services Assn., Daus. of Charity, 1968-71; dir. departmental audits Pa. Auditor Gen.'s Office, 1969; counsel to Morgan, Lewis & Bockius, Attys., 1970-72; judge Commonwealth Ct. Pa., 1972-83, sr. judge, 1983—; founder, exec. dir. Pa. Intercollegiate Conf. on Govt., 1934-72; mem. Pa. Bd. Pardons, 1955-67; sec. Pa. Indsl. Devel. Authority Bd. and Gen. State Authority Bd., 1956-67; Pa. del. to Interstate Oil Compact Commn., 1955-67, vice chmn., 1959-60; mem. weights and measures adv. com. Nat. Bur. Standards, 1960-67; mem. adv. com. women in armed services Def. Dept., 1964-67; mem. Pres.'s Consumer Adv. Council, 1964-66, Pres.'s Commn. on Law Enforcement and Adminstrn. Justice, 1965-67. Bd. dirs. Ctr. for Rsch. in Apostolate, 1972-75, 80-85, mem. adv. coun. Nat. Conf. Cath. Bishops, 1972-75; mem. Nat. Bishops Bicentennial Com., 1974-76; chmn. Harrisburg Diocesan Bicentennial Com., 1974-76; sec. Pa. Dem. Com., 1948-70; Dem. nominee for auditor gen. Pa., 1952; del. Dem. Nat. Convs., 1936-68; Dem. nominee for U.S. Senate, 1964; Dem. nat. committeewoman Pa., 1970-72; fellow Harry S. Truman, Lyndon B. Johnson Librs.; pres. James A. Finnegan Fellowship Found., 1960-89, hon. 1990—. Recipient Disting. Dau. of Pa. award, 1956, Mother Gerard Phelan Gold medal Marymount Coll., 1965, Elizabeth Seton medal Seton Hall Coll., 1960, Pro Ecclesia et Pontifice medal Pope Paul VI, 1966, Louise de Marillac medal St. Joseph's Coll., 1966, Dubois medal Mt. St. Mary's Coll., 1970, St. Thomas More Legal award City of Pitts., 1974, St. Thomas More award City of Phila., 1990, FAME award Greater Phila. Women's Clubs, 1978, Elizabeth Ann Seton medal St. John's U., L.I., N.Y., 1978. Mem. Am. Bar Found., ABA, Pa. Bar Assn., Dauphin County Bar Assn., Am. Judicature Soc., Nat. Assn. Women Judges, Nat. Assn. Women Lawyers, LWV (award 1964), Bus. and Profl. Women, Cath. War Vets. Aux., Nat. Coun. Cath. Women, Nat. Cath. Women's Union, Mortar Bd., Phi Beta Kappa, Delta Sigma Rho, Pi Tau Phi, Pi Sigma Alpha, Beta Sigma Phi, Delta Kappa Sigma. Lodges: Eagles (hon., Liberty Under Law award 1980), Soroptimists (hon.), Equestrian Order of Knights and Ladies of Holy Sepulchre Vatican (comdr. 1978), Altrusa (hon.), Zonta (hon.). DIED 07/04/96. .

BLEIBERG, ROBERT MARVIN, retired financial editor; b. Bklyn., June 21, 1924; s. Edward and Frances (DuBroff) B.; m. Harriet Evans, May 1948 (div. Mar. 1953); 1 dau., Ellen; m. Sally Diane Beverly, Oct. 25, 1956; 1 son, Richard Beverly. B.A., Columbia, 1943; M.B.A., N.Y. U., 1950; D.C.Sc., Hillsdale Coll., 1977. v.p. Dow Jones & Co., Inc. Assoc. editor: Prudden's Digest of Investment and Banking Opinions, N.Y.C., 1946; assoc. editor: Barron's Nat. Bus. and Financial Weekly, N.Y.C., 1946-54; editor, 1955-81, pub., 1980-89, editorial dir., 1981-91. Served with inf. AUS, 1943-45, PTO. Decorated Purple Heart; recipient GBA Alumni Achievement award, NYU, 1981. Mem. N.Y. Soc. Security Analysts., N.Y. Fin. Writers Assn. (Elliott V. Bell award), Mont Pelerin Soc., Econ. Club N.Y., Phi Beta Kappa, Phi Beta Kappa Assos. Died Nov. 4, 1997.

BLINKOV, SAMOUIL, neuropathologist; b. Elisabethgrad, Russia, July 17, 1904; s. Michall and Sophia (Talnovskaya) B.; m. Anna Artarian, 1958. MS, Azerbaijan State U., 1926; PhD, VAK, Moscow, 1941. Resident various neurol. clinics Bakou, Perm, Moscow, 1926-31; asst. dept. neurology Inst. of Physiotherapy, Moscow; from sci. worker to chief clin. dept. and dept./ asst. dir. Brain Inst. of Moscow, 1931-52; leader lab. of neurosurg. anatomy and exptl. neurology Burdenko Inst. of Neurosurgery, 1952-96. Author: Human Brain in Figures and Tables, 1968, Brain Displacements and Deformations, 1971, Atlas of Neurosurgical Anatomy, 1990, others.; contbr. articles to profl. jours. Named Honoured Scientist of Russia, Pres. of Russia, 1994. Died Dec. 3, 1996.

BLOCK, JOSEPH DOUGLAS, utility executive, lawyer; b. Three Lakes, Wis., Apr. 18, 1919; s. Max and Rose (Chaimson) B.; m. Doris Ruth Schoenewald, Sept. 26, 1958. B.A., U. Wis., 1939, J.D., 1941; LL.M., Harvard, 1946. Bar: Wis. bar 1941, Ill. bar 1947, N.Y. bar 1971. Atty. OPA, Washington, 1942, 45-46; practiced in Chgo., 1946-70; partner firm Aaron, Aaron, Schimberg & Hess, Chgo., 1957-70; v.p., gen. counsel Consol. Edison Co. N.Y., Inc., N.Y.C., 1970-73; exec. v.p. Consol. Edison Co. N.Y., Inc., 1973-80, exec. v.p., gen. counsel, 1980-84; counsel Leboeuf, Lamb, Leiby & MacRae, N.Y.C., 1984—; spl. asst. atty. gen. Ill., 1951-53. Served with CIC AUS, 1942-45. Mem. Am., N.Y. State, Wis. Bar Assns., Bar Assn. N.Y.C., Boca Raton Hotel Club, Boca Pointe Country Club, Order of Coif, Phi Kappa Phi. Died Jan. 18, 1997.

BLOOM, BERNARD MORRIS, judge; b. Bklyn., Aug. 21, 1926; m. Helen C. Bloom; children—Gwen Susan, Carrie R. Student, Bklyn. Coll., 1947-49; LL.B., Bklyn. Law Sch., 1952. Bar: N.Y. 1953, U.S. Ct. Mil. Appeals 1956, U.S. Dist. Ct. (ea. and so. dists.) N.Y. 1957, U.S. Customs Ct. 1957, U.S. Supreme Ct. 1963, U.S. Ct. Appeals (2d Cir.) 1966. Assoc. Senator Jeremiah Bloom, N.Y.C., 1953-60; asst. counsel to speaker N.Y. State Assembly, 1957, asst. counsel to minority leader, 1957-60; confidential clk., law sec. Appellate div. N.Y. Supreme Ct., 1960-67; asst. counsel N.Y. State Joint Legis. Com. on Congl. Reapportionment, 1967-68; dep. pub. adminstr. Kings County, N.Y., 1968-71, judge Surrogate's Ct., 1976—; ptnr. Bloom & Epstein, N.Y.C., 1970-76. Mem. Democratic Law Com. Kings County, 1950—; former sec. Young Democrats of Kings County; active Bklyn. Soc. for Prevention Cruelty to Children; trustee, Aauro Law Sch., Isaac Albert Research Inst., Kingsbrook Jewish Med. Ctr., Bklyn. Lawyers div. United Jewish Appeal; bd. dirs. Flatbush br. YMCA, Fedn. Jewish Philanthropies. Served with AUS, 1944-46. Mem. Bklyn. Bar Assn., Kings County Criminal Bar Assn., Bklyn. Coll. Alumni Assn., Am. Judicature Soc., Jewish War Veterans, Bklyn. Lawyers Club, Am. Legion, Nat. Narcotic Officers Assn., ABA, Nat. Rifle Assn. Democrat. Jewish. Lodge: Masons. Deceased.

BLOOMER, JOHN H., lawyer, economist; b. Rutland, Vt., Apr. 13, 1960; s. John H. and Judith Ellen (Wener) B. BA, Williams Coll., 1982; MA, U. Pa., 1985; JD, Rutgers U., 1987. Bar: Pa. 1987, N.J. 1987, U.S. Dist. Ct. Pa. 1987, U.S. Dist. Ct. N.J. 1987, Vt. 1990, U.S. Ct. Appeals (3d cir.) 1991, U.S. Dist. Ct. Vt. 1992. Ptnr. Bloomer & Bloomer, P.C., Rutland; state legislator State of Vermont. Bd. dirs., sec. Rutland Regional Cmty. TV, 1992—; dir., v.p. Rutland H.S. Found., 1992—.

BLOOMFIELD, COLEMAN, insurance company executive; b. Winnipeg, Man., Can., July 2, 1926; came to U.S., 1952, naturalized, 1958; s. Samuel and Bessie (Staniloff) B.; m. Shirley Rosenbaum, Nov. 4, 1948; children: Catherine, Laura, Leon, Diane, Richard. B.Commerce, U. Man., 1948. With Commonwealth Life Ins. Co., Louisville, 1948-51; actuary, sr. v.p. Minn. Mut. Life Ins. Co., St. Paul, 1952-70, exec. v.p., 1970-71, pres., chief exec. officer, 1971-95, chmn. bd., 1977-95; dir. First Bank System, Inc. Bd. dirs. Minn. Orch. Assn.; bd. dirs. St. Paul United Way, Ordway Music Theatre. Fellow Soc. Actuaries. Home: Saint Paul Minn. Died June 16, 1995.

BLOUGH, GLENN ORLANDO, author, educator; b. Edmore, Mich., Sept. 5, 1907; s. Levi and Catherine (Thomas) B. Student, Central Mich. Coll. Edn., 1922-24, LL.D., 1950; B.A., U. Mich., 1929, M.A., 1932; postgrad., Columbia, summers 1935-37, U. Chgo., 1938. Tchr. secondary schs. Mich., 1925-27, 29-31; instr. State Tchrs. Coll., Ypsilanti, Mich., 1932-36; asst. prof. sci. edn. State Tchrs. Coll., Greeley, Colo., 1937-38; instr. U. Chgo., 1939-42; specialist sci. U.S. Office Edn., HEW, Washington, 1947-55; prof. edn. U. Md., 1956—; edn. cons. Nat. Geog. Soc., 1970—. Author: Monkey With A Notion, 1948, Beno The Riverburg Mayor, 1949, The Tree on the Road to Turntown, 1953; Jr. Lit. Guild selections Not Only for Ducks, The Story of Rain, 1954, Lookout for the Forest, 1955, After the Sun Goes Down, 1956, Who Lives in This House, 1957; When You Go to the Zoo, 1957, Young Peoples Book of Science, 1958, Soon After September, 1959, Discovering Dinosaurs, 1959, Who Lives in This Meadow?, 1960, Christmas Trees and How They Grow, 1961, Who Lives at the Seashore, 1962, Bird Watchers and Bird Feeders, 1963, Discovering Plants, 1966, Discovering Insects, 1967, Discovering Cycles, 1973, Elementary School Science and How To Teach It, 1978, 84, 90, also textbooks.; contbr. numerous articles in sci. and popular publs. Served as lt. comdr. USNR, World War II. Recipient Disting. Service to Sci. Edn. citation Nat. Sci. Tchrs. Assn., 1971; Spl. Recognition for contbn. to sci. edn. Council Elementary Sci. Internat., 1971; award for contbn. to lit. of natural history Am. Nature Study Soc., 1980. Mem. NEA, Assn. Supervision and Curriculum Devel., Assn. Childhood Edn., AAUP, Nat. Council Elementary Sci. (pres. 1947), Nat. Sci. Tchrs. Assn. (pres. 1957-58, adviser ednl. policies commn.), Elementary Prins. Assn., Phi Delta Kappa, Phi Sigma. Died Aug. 31, 1995.

BLUETT, THOMAS BYRON, SR., child psychologist; b. Milw., May 29, 1931; s. Byron Walter and Ida Mae (Mineau) B.; m. Daina Lauretta Kubilius, Sept. 21, 1974; children: Thomas Jr., Elizabeth, William, Martha, Dorothea (dec.), Byron. BS, U. Wis., 1953, MS, 1955, PhD, 1971. Lic. psychologist, Wis.; nat. cert. sch. psychologist; listed Nat. Register Health Svc. Providers in Psychology. Counselor Appleton (Wis.) Pub. Schs., 1955-57; psychologist Green Bay (Wis.) Pub. Schs., 1957-65; exec. dir. United Cerebral Palsy, Green Bay, 1965-68; dir. pupil services Cooperative Edn. Service Agy., Wis., 1968-71; child psychologist Pediatrics Beaumont Clin., Green Bay, 1972-95; sec.-treas. Tri-State Testing Svc., Inc., DePere, Wis., 1958-95; child psychologist Sta. WTMJ-TV and Radio, Milw., 1981-95, Sta. WOAI, San Antonio, 1986-95, Sally Jessy Raphael Show, 1989, Montel Williams Show, 1993, Jerry Springer Show, 1993; lectr. child devel. U. Wis., Green Bay, 1968-73. Author, presenter (TV series) In-Charge Parenting, 1982, (book, audio tapes) In-Charge Parenting Kit, 1983; author: Conquering Low Impulse Control, 1984; co-author: Youth Tutoring Youth, 1970. Bd. dirs. United Cerebral Palsy, N.Y.C., 1957-65; exec. dir. Nat. Early Childhood Edn. Fund, Wis., 1971-80; mem. profl. and adv. bd. Wis. Assn. for Children with Learning Disabilities, 1989-95; adult leader Kewaunee County 4-H Club, 1988-95. With U.S. Army, 1953-55, Korea. Grantee Rural Pupil Services, HEW, Washington, D.C., 1969, Early Childhood Edn. , ESEA, Madison, 1970. Fellow Am. Assn. Mental Deficiency, Nat. Assn. Mental Deficiency; mem. Wis. Soc. Clin. Cons. Psychologists (charter, co-chmn. publicity com. 1986-95), Nat. Gen. Psychol. Svcs. Corp., Nat. Assn. Sch. Psychologists (charter), Brown County Clin. Cons. Psychologists (treas. 1985-87), Children and Adults Attention Deficit Disorders S.E. Wis., Elks (handicapped children's chmn. 1958-68), Optimist (youth chmn. 1957-68), Phi Delta Kappa (pres. 1958-60). Roman Catholic. Avocations: fishing, hunting, playing banjo. Home: Algoma Wis. Died Dec. 12, 1995; interred St. Mary's Parish Cemetery, Algoma, WI.

BLUM, JEROME, educator; b. Balt., Apr. 27, 1913; s. Moses and Fannie (Herzfeld) B. A.B., Johns Hopkins U., 1933, Ph.D., 1947. Faculty Princeton U., 1947-81, prof. history, chmn. dept., 1961-67, James Madison preceptor, 1952-55, master Grad. Coll., 1958-78, Henry Charles Lea prof. history, 1966-81; Lawrence lectr. Conn. Coll., 1968; Schouler lectr. Johns Hopkins U., 1974. Author: Noble Landowners and Agriculture in Austria, 1815-1848, 1948, Lord and Peasant in Russia from the Ninth to the Nineteenth Century, 1961, The End of the Old Order in Rural Europe, 1978; co-author: The European World, 1966, Civilizations: Western and World, 1975, European Landed Elites in the Nineteenth Century, 1977, Our Forgotten Past, 1981; Bd. editors: Jour. Modern History, 1956-58; editorial bd.: Jour. Econ. History, 1963-68; Contbr. articles to scholarly jours. Pres. bd. mgrs. N.J. State Home for Girls, 1965-69; chmn. Ad Hoc Com. on Children's Services N.J., 1966-68; bd. dirs. Morrow Assn. on Correction, 1968-71, Citizens Commn. for Children N.J., 1971-73; mem. Mercer County Mental Health Bd., 1972-74; trustee Princeton U. Press, 1966-70. Served from pvt. to capt. F.A. AUS, 1942-46. Guggenheim fellow, 1951-52, 71-72; Shreve fellow Princeton U., 1952, 68; Nat. Endowment for Humanities fellow, 1975-76. Fellow Am.

Acad. Arts and Scis.; mem. Am. Philos. Soc. (Henry Allen Moe prize in humanities 1982), Am. Hist. Assn. (Herbert Baxter Adams prize 1962, Higby prize 1972), Agrl. History Soc. (pres. 1981-82). Jewish. Club: Nassau (Princeton). Home: Baltimore Md. Died May 7, 1993.

BLUM, JOHN LEO, biology educator; b. Madison, Wis., May 2, 1917; s. John E. and Kathryn (Cullen) B.; m. Anna M. Raick, Jan. 25, 1947; children—Colette Blum Meister, Suzanne Blum Martin, Annette Blum Rolfsmeyer. B.S., U. Wis., 1937, M.S., 1939; Ph.D., U. Mich., 1953. From instr. to prof. biology Canisius Coll., Buffalo, 1941-63; mem. faculty U. Wis.-Milw., 1963-95, prof. botany, 1966-85, now emeritus, assoc. dean Coll. Letters and Sci., 1967-69. Author: The Vaucheriaceae, 1972. Pres. Niagara Frontier chpt. Izaak Walton League, 1959-62. Served with AUS, 1943-45. Cole fellow U. Mich., 1952-53. Mem. Wis. Acad. Sci., Arts and Letters, Sigma Xi. Home: Milwaukee Wis. Died Apr. 12, 1995.

BLUME, JACK PAUL, retired lawyer; b. N.Y.C., Jan. 25, 1915; s. Bernard and Carrie (Goldberg) B.; m. Ethel Nelson, Oct. 2, 1941 (dec. 1959); children: Mark (dec.), Laura (Mrs. Marvin Kuperstein). B.S., CCNY, 1934; LL.B., N.Y. U., 1937. Bar: N.Y. 1937, D.C. 1952, also U.S. Supreme Ct. 1952. Pvt. practice N.Y.C., 1937-42; atty., dep. hearing adminstr. OPA, 1942-46; regional atty. FCC, Chgo., 1946; adminstrv. law judge FCC, 1947-51; sr. partner, counsel Fly, Shuebruk, Blume & Gaguine, Washington, 1951-81; founder, 1st chmn., Inst. For Learning in Retirement, Am. U., 1982-84, mem. exec. coun. 1982-89. Co-author: West's Federal Practice Manual, 2d edit, 1970. Bd. dirs. Jewish Social Service Agy., Washington, 1960-95; adv. bd. Opportunities for Older Ams. Fund. Mem. ABA, D.C. Bar Assn., Fed. Communications Bar Assn. (pres. 1974-75), ACLU. Home: Washington D.C. Died July 12, 1995.

BLUMENBERG, RICHARD MITCHELL, cinema and photography educator; b. Gloversville, N.Y., May 26, 1935; s. Ella Olga Sesonski; m. Julia Porcher Wickham Porter, Mar. 1970 (div. Aug. 1982); m. Irena Lane Grant, June 22, 1984; children: Robert John, Joseph Allen. BA, U. Iowa, 1959, MFA, 1963; PhD, Ohio U., 1969. Asst. prof. Slippery Rock (Pa.) State U., 1969-70; prof. cinema and photography So. Ill. U., Carbondale, 1970-97; assoc. producer Optos Ltd., 1969-97; pres. Windmill Prodns., Inc., 1985-97. Assoc. producer, writer (film) America First, 1972 (Edinburgh Film Festival award 1972); author: Critical Focus, 1975, (poems) Mentor Midwest Poets, 1966; contbr. articles to profl. jours. Bd. trustees Univ. Film and Video Found., 1984-97. With U.S. Army, 1954-57. Ohio U. Italian fellow, 1968, Earl Siegfred Arts scholar, 1969; ICA grantee, 1979; recipient travel award Brit. Coun., 1982. Mem. Soc. for Cinema Studies, Univ. Film and Video Assn. (pres. 1984-86). Democrat. Jewish. Avocations: swimming, classical guitar. Died June 11, 1997.

BOBA, IMRE, history educator; b. Gyor, Hungary, Oct. 23, 1919; came to U.S., naturalized, 1956; s. Wladyslaw and Ilona (Faludi) B.; m. Elizabeth Herndon Hudson, Dec. 22, 1954; children—Eleanor, Leslie. Grad., U. Budapest, Hungary, 1946; Ph.D. in History, U. Wash., 1962. Mem. Polish Resistance Movement in Hungary, 1939-45; mem. Polish desk and office of polit. advisor Radio Free Europe, 1952-59; Faculty U. Wash., Seattle, 1962-90; assoc. prof. medieval history U. Wash., 1967-71, prof. history, Russian and East European studies, 1971-90, prof. emeritus, 1990-96. Author: Nomads, Northmen and Slavs, 1967, Moravia's History Reconsidered, 1971, Croat edit., 1986; Hungarian edit., 1996, co-editor: Ungarn-Jahrbuch, Munich; contbg. editor: Dictionary of Political Science, 1963. Mem. Am. Hist. Assn., Am. Assn. for Advancement Slavic Studies. Home: Seattle Wash. Died Jan. 11, 1996.

BOETTCHER, WILFRIED, cellist, conductor, educator; b. Bremen, Germany, Aug. 11, 1929. Studied cello with, Arthur Troester, Hamburg, Pierre Fournier, Paris, Pablo Cassals. Prin. cellist Hannover Opera, 1956-58; prof. cello Vienna Acad. Music, 1958; founded, toured chamber group Die Wiener Solisten, 1959; prof. Hochschule für Musik, Hamburg; chief condr. Hamburg Symphony Orch., 1967-71; guest condr. Germany, Eng., France. Deceased.

BOHANNON, DAVID D., community planner and developer; b. San Francisco, May 23, 1898; s. David Eugene and Elizabeth Jane (Bosch) B.; m. Ophelia E. Kroeger, June 7, 1921; children: Frances B. Nelson, Barbara B. Carleton, David E. Ed. public schs. of Calif. Mfr. metal products, until 1925, in real estate bus. and land devel., 1925—; organizer, pres. David D. Bohannon Orgn.; community planner and developer San Mateo, Calif., 1928—; pres. Hillsdale Devel. Co., 1951—; developer Bohannon Bus. Ctr., Hayward, Calif., Bohannon Indsl. Park, Menlo Park, Bay Center Indsl. Park, San Lorenzo, Mayfair Heights, San Jose, Westwood, Westwood Oaks and Park Westwood, Santa Clara, El Cerrito Manor, Hillsdale, Hillsdale Shopping Center, San Mateo, San Lorenzo Village, Alameda County, Westwood, Napa, Rollingwood, Contra Costa County, Woodside Hills, Woodside, Homeplace, Hillsborough, Montgomery Estates and Tahoe Tyrol, Lake Tahoe, all Calif. Named to Calif. Bldg. Industry Hall of Fame. Mem. Urban Land Inst. (trustee, past pres., mem. past pres.'s adv. bd., Disting. Developer award), Nat. Assn. Home Builders U.S. (past pres., mem. past pres.'s council, named to Housing Hall of Fame), Nat. Assn. Realtors (past v.p.), San Francisco Bay Area Council, Calif. Assn. Realtors (life dir.), Lambda Alpha. Clubs: Commonwealth (bd. govs., past pres.), Bohemian, Peninsula Golf and Country, Eldorado Country, The Vintage, Sharon Heights Golf and Country, Internat. Order St. Hubert (Knight Grand Order), Mzuri Safari, Shikar-Safari Internat, Game Conservation Internat, Ducks Unltd. (sponsor in perpetuity, trustee emeritus), Wildlife Preservation Soc. India, No. Calif. Retriever Trial, Rotary (hon.), Kiwanis (hon.). Recipient nat. recognition for wartime housing activities; credited with unusually large number of wartime pvt. houses and dev. of on-site prodn. techniques. Died Mar. 13, 1995.

BOJAXHIU, AGNES GONXHA See TERESA, MOTHER

BOKE, NORMAN HILL, botanist; b. Mobridge, S.D., Mar. 14, 1913; s. Hans Christian and Elenor (Hill) B.; m. Beulah Esther Brown, Sept. 4, 1948; 1 dau., Janice Sue. A.B., U. S.D., 1934; M.S., U. Okla., 1936; Ph.D., U. Calif. at Berkeley, 1939. Instr. biology U. N.Mex., 1941-42, Johns Hopkins U., 1942-44; mem. faculty U. Okla., Norman, 1945—; George Lynn Cross research prof. botany U. Okla., 1965—. Contbr. articles to profl. jours.; editor: Am. Jour. Botany, 1970-75. Served with USAAF, 1944-45, PTO. Guggenheim Meml. fellow, 1953. Mem. Bot. Soc. Am., Sociedad Mexicana de Cactologia, Torrey Bot. Club, Explorers Club, Phi Beta Kappa, Sigma Xi, Alpha Tau Omega. Author research articles on plant anatomy and morphology, especially Cactaceae. Died Feb. 8, 1996.

BOLEY BOLAFFIO, RITA, artist; b. Trieste, Italy, June 7, 1898; d. Angelo Luzzatto and Olga Senigaglia; came to U.S., 1939, naturalized, 1944; diploma with Joseph Hoffmann, Kunstgewerbe Schule, Vienna, Austria; diploma violin Music Conservatory, Vienna; student of F. Ondricek; m. Orville F. Boley; children: Lucius R., Bruno A. Fashion, textile and interior designer Wiener Werkstatte, Vienna and Milan, Italy; contbr. Harper's Bazaar; murals and displays for Saks Fifth Ave, Bergorf Goodman, Lord & Taylor and throughout U.S., maj. exhbns. collage and assemblage include Mus. of Art, Columbia, S.C., Am. House, N.Y.C., J.L. Hudson Gallery, Detroit, Pen and Brush Club, N.Y.C., Richard Kollmar's Gallery, N.Y.C., Guild Hall Mus., East Hampton, N.Y., James Pendleton Gallery, N.Y.C. Washington Art Assn. Conn., Galerie St. Etienne, N.Y.C., Hudson River Mus., Yonkers, N.Y., Lamborghini Gallery, N.Y.C., 1990; represented in pvt. collections, also represented in European and Am. publs. Recipient Premio Ciglione della Malpensa award for equitation, 1936, Poetry prize Premio di Sorrento, 1965. Mem. arts group ARC, 1942-44. Mem. Composer, Author and Artists Am. Died May 20, 1995.

BÖLL, HEINRICH THEODOR, author; b. Cologne, Germany, Dec. 21, 1917; s. Viktor and Maria (Hermanns) B.; student state schs., Cologne, 1924-37; m. Annemarie Cech, 1942; children: Christoph (dec.), Raimund, René, Vincent. Books include: Der Zug war pünktlich, 1949, Wanderer, kommst du nach Spaooo, 1950, Die schwarzen Schafe, 1951, Wo warst du, Adam?, 1951, Und sagte kein einziges Wort, 1953, Nicht nur zur Weihnachtszeit, 1952, Haus ohne Hüter, 1954, Das Brot der frühen Jahre, 1955, So ward Abend und Morgen, 1955, Unberechenbare Gäste, 1956, Im Tal der donnerden Hufe, 1957, Irisches Tagebuch, 1957, Die Spurlosen, 1957, Dr. Murkes gesammeltes Schweigen, 1958, Billard um halbzehn, 1959, Erzählungen, Hörspiele, Aufsätze, 1961, Ein Schluck Erde, 1962, Ansichten eines Clowns, 1963, Entfernung von der Truppe, 1964, Als der Krieg ausbrach, 1962, Frankfurter Vorlesungen, 1966, Ende einer Dienstfahrt, 1966, Aufsatze, Kritiken, Reden, 1967, Hausfriedens Bruch, 1969, Aussatz, 1969, Gruppenbild mit Dame, 1971, Gedichte, 1972, Erzählungen 1950, 1970, 72, Politische und literanische Schriften, 1973, Die verlorene Ehre der Katharina Blum, 1974, Drei Tage im März, 1975, Berichte zur Gesinnungslage der Nation, 1975, Einmischung erwünscht, 1977, Werke, Band 1-5, 1977, Band 5-10, 1978, Fürsorgliche Belagerung, 1979; Was soll aus dem Jungen bloss werden?, 1981; Vermintes Gelände, 1982; Das Vermä chtnis, 1982. Recipient numerous lit. prizes including: Group 47 prize, 1951, Rene Schickele prize, 1952, Kritikerpreis, 1952/53, So. German Narrator prize, 1953, Eduard Van der Heydt prize, 1957, Charles Veillon prize, 1960, Lit. prize Cologne, 1961, Nobel prize for lit., 1972, Carl von Ossietzky Medal, 1974; hon. prof. numerous univs. Mem. Am. Acad. Arts and Letters (hon.), German Acad. for Lang. and Poetry, PEN (past pres.).

BOMAR, PORTIA HAMILTON, psychoanalyst, clinical psychologist; b. Cleve., July 19; d. Charles Brooks and Marion (Clements) Goulder; m. William P. Bomar, July 1, 1966. B.A., U. Mich., 1923; postgrad. Oxford U. (Eng.), 1923-25; M.A., Columbia U., 1932, Ph.D., 1940. Pvt. practice psychoanalysis and psychotherapy, N.Y.C., 1930-58; dir. teaching clinic Columbia Presbyn. Med. Ctr., N.Y.C., 1942-50; assoc. prof. psychology U. Richmond, Va., 1964-66; lectr. psychology U. Tex.-Austin, 1968-71; mem. faculty Southwestern Grad. Sch. Banking, So. Meth. U., Dallas, 1975-78. Author: When 'Mid This Glory I Was Young, 1980; contbr. articles to profl. jours. Vice-chmn. Human Relations Commn., Ft. Worth, 1968-71; bd. dirs. Tarrant County Hist. Soc. (Tex.), 1968—, Child Study Ctr., Ft. Worth, 1972-78, Tarrant County Mental Health Assn., 1974-76, Casa Manana, Ft. Worth, 1974-76; mem. corp. Eye Research Inst. of Retina Found., Boston. Fellow Am. Psychol. Assn.; mem. Psychical Research Found., Parapsychology Assn., Chi Omega, AAUW. Clubs: Rivercrest Country (Ft. Worth); University, Longboat Key.

BOND, CALHOUN, lawyer, retired; b. Balt., June 29, 1921; s. Henry Marvin and Lala Belle (Jacobs) B.; m. Jane L. Piper, Apr. 14, 1956; children: Calhoun, Jr., James Piper, Louise Cover, Jane Carson. B.A., Washington and Lee U., 1943; LL.B., U. Md., 1949. Bar: Md. 1949. Ptnr. firm Cable, McDaniel, Bowie & Bond, Balt., 1962-91; of counsel McGuire, Woods, Battle & Boothe, 1992—. Mem. Md. Bd. Pub. Welfare, 1959-72, Md. Constl. Conv. Commn., 1965-67; mem. Balt. Bd. Fire Commrs., 1972-79, pres., 1976-79; chmn. bd. dirs. Lafayette Sq. Cmty. Ctr., 1967-68, Md. Commn. on Long-Term Health Care, 1988-92, Md. Commn. on Welfare Policy, 1993-94; trustee Episcopal Ministry for Aging, 1976-93, Balt. City Retirement Sys., 1976-79, Md. Trust for Retarded Citizens, 1982-87; pres. Balt. Assn. for Retarded Citizens, Inc., 1987-89; pres. The Tommy McNulty Found., 1991-94. Comdr. USNR. Fellow Md. Bar Found.; mem. Am., Md., Balt. bar assns., Am. Judicature Soc. (dir. 1980-83). Democrat. Episcopalian. Clubs: Maryland; 14 W. Hamilton St. Deceased.

BOND, GORDON CREWS, college dean; b. Ft. Myers, Fla., Nov. 17, 1939; s. Henry C. and Hazel (Crews) B.; m. Stephanie Johns, Sept. 7, 1974; children: Michael, Annie. BS, Fla. State U., 1962, MA, 1963, PhD, 1966. Asst. prof. history U. So. Miss., Hattiesburg, 1966-67; asst. prof. history Auburn (Ala.) U., 1967-74, assoc. prof., 1974-80, prof., 1980-97, head dept. history, 1985-91, assoc. dean liberal arts, 1991-92, dean Coll. Liberal Arts, 1992-97. Author: The British Invasion of Holland in 1809, 1979. Mem. Rotary Internat. Died Mar. 27, 1997.

BONDI, ENRICO, engineer; b. Budrio, Bologna, Italy, Jan. 17, 1933; s. Renato and Dina (Andreini) B.; m. Bettina Grassani, Apr. 18, 1960; children: Antonella, Marco, Francesca. Cert., A. Righi, 1952; PhD in Mech. Engring., U. Bologna, 1958, cert., 1959. Registered profl. engr., Italy. Steel shop asst. Thyssen Group, Duesseldorf, Fed. Republic of Germany, 1959-60; chief rolling mills project Cogne, S.p.A., Aosta, Italy, 1960-68; mgr. rolling mills project INNSE, S.p.A., Milan, 1968-90; mem. rsch. team Max Planck Inst., Duesseldorf, 1966-67; technology and engring. cons. to various cos., univs., polys., acads.; presenter in field. Patentee in field. Mem. Assn. Italiana di Metallurgia Plastic Deformation Ctr. (v.p. 1986-87, pres. 1988-93). Avocations: photography. Home: Milan Italy Died May 29, 1993.

BONIFACE, JOHN, JR., manufacturing company executive; b. Boston, Dec. 30, 1944; s. John and Priscilla (Goodwin) B.; m. Ann Reese Murray, June 25, 1966; children: Merrilee Ann, Dexter Scott. BS in Mktg., Pa. State U., 1966. Sales rep. Denison div. Abex Corp., Pitts., 1970-77; regional mgr. Denison div. Abex Corp., Mpls., 1977-81; sales mgr. Denison div. Abex Corp., Columbus, Ohio, 1981-86; dir. sales Hagglunds Denison Corp., Columbus, 1986-89; sales mgr. Vickers S.Y.S., Inc. subs. Vickers, Inc., Toronto, Ont., Can., 1989-90, gen. mgr., 1990-91; mgr. mkt. sales Vickers, Inc., Troy, Mich., 1992-94; mem. Toronto Bd. Trade. Capt. U.S. Army, 1966-70, Vietnam. Mem. Nat. Fluid Power Assn. (mem. pub. affairs com. 1985-87), Country Club at Muirfield Village. Republican. Episcopalian. Avocations: golf, boating, fishing. Home: Rochester Hills Mich. Died Dec. 1, 1994.

BONO, SONNY SALVATORE, congressman, singer, composer, former mayor; b. Detroit, Feb. 16, 1935; m. Donna Rankin; 1 child, Christy; m. Cher LaPiere, Oct. 27, 1964 (div.); 1 child, Chastity; m. Susie Coehlo (div.); m. Mary Whitaker, Mar. 1986; children: Chesare Elan, Chianna Maria. Congressman, Calif. 44th Dist. U.S. Ho. of Reps., Washington, 1995—, mem. Nat. Security and Judiciary coms. Songwriter, later artist and repertoire man for Speciality Records; singer with Cher as team Sonny and Cher, 1964-74, co-star The Sonny and Cher Show, 1971-74; now solo night club act; numerous recs., TV, concert and benefit appearances; has appeared on numerous TV series; composer, lyricist, appearance in Good Times, 1966; films include: Escape to Athena, 1979, Airplane II-The Sequel, 1982, Hairspray, 1988; producer film: Chastity, 1969; composer: A Cowboy's Work is Never Done, The Beat Goes On, I Got You, Babe, Needles & Pins, others; TV video Nitty Gritty Hour with Cher, 1992; autobiography: And The Beat Goes On, 1991. Restaurateur; mayor Palm Springs, Calif., 1988-92; ran, defeated U.S. Senate, 1992. Died Jan. 5, 1998.

BOORSTEIN, LUCILLE PAULA, law librarian; b. N.Y.C., July 18, 1927; d. Rueben and Laurette (Goldsmith) Lapidus; m. S.M. Boorstein, Aug. 2, 1947 (div. 1959); children: William S., Amy M., Mark S. BA, NYU, 1948. Legal indexer, mng. editor Matthew Bender & Co., N.Y.C., 1970-84, index mgr., 1975-84; freelance legal indexer N.Y.C., 1984-86; asst. law librarian Mfrs. Hanover Trust, N.Y.C., 1986-87; index mgr. R.R. Bowker, N.Y.C., 1987-89; mng. editor RR Bowker/Martindale-Hubbell, New Providence, N.J., 1989—, Legal Pub. Preview, 1990—. Index editor: Code of Federal Regulations Index, 4 vols., 1991. Mem. Am. Soc. Indexers, Am. Assn. Law Librarians. Avocations: horticulture, cooking. Died Dec. 23, 1996.

BOOTH, GEORGE WARREN, artist, advertising executive; b. Omaha, July 6, 1917; s. George H. and Rae (McGrady) B.; m. Nancy Jane Schuele, Dec. 6, 1968; children: George Geoffrey, Katherine Ellen, Robert Alan. AB with highest honors, Ohio U., 1940, MA, 1942; postgrad. John Huntington Poly. Inst., 1941, Chouinard Sch. Art, 1945-46. Art dir. J. Walter Thompson Co., N.Y.C., 1947-58, Gardner Advt. Co., N.Y.C., 1958-60, Ted Bates Co., N.Y.C., 1960-64. One-man shows include N.Y.C., Calif., Washington, Md., Fla., 1972-96, group shows: NAD, N.Y.C., Am. Water Color Soc., N.Y.C., Allied Artists Am., Calif. Watercolor Soc., Los Angeles, L.A. Mus. Art, San Francisco Mus. Art, Butler Art Inst., others; represented in permanent collections, galleries in N.Y.C., Washington, Palm Beach, Sarasota, Fla., Middleburg, Va.; teaching fellow photography Ohio U., Athens, 1941-42; cons. in field. Animation film dir. with Signal Corps, U.S. Army, 1942-44. Recipient Art Dirs. Club N.Y.'s gold medal, 1954, Kerwin H.Fulton medal, 1954. Mem. Soc. Illustrators N.Y.C., N.Y. Artists Equity, Art Dirs. Club N.Y., Fla. Thoroughbred Breeders Owners Assn., others. Died August 2, 1996. Home: Ocala Fla.

BOOTHE, DYAS POWER, JR., emeritus finance company executive; b. Berkeley, Calif., Dec. 23, 1910; s. Dyas Power and Margaret (Stewart) B.; m. Margaret Kempenich, June 28, 1933 (div. 1966); children: Margaret Joanne Turkington, Barry Power; m. Catherine Causey, 1967; 1 dau., Catherine Elizabeth Lifto. A.B., Stanford, 1931. Pres. Boothe Fruit Co., Modesto, Calif., 1946-59; co-founder and pres. U.S. Leasing Corp., 1952-55; pres. Boothe Leasing Corp., San Francisco, 1954-67; chmn., chief exec. officer Boothe Fin. Corp., Armco-Boothe Corp., to 1972; chmn., chief exec. officer GATX-Boothe Corp., 1967-81, chmn. emeritus; also domestic and fgn. subs. Courier Terminal Systems Inc., Phoenix, 1971-78, chmn. bd., dir., 1971-78; pres., chief exec. officer, trustee IDS Realty Trust, 1976-80; chmn., chief exec. officer IDS Mortgage Corp., 1976-80; pres., chief exec. officer Boothe Holdings, 1981-96; dir. BEI Electronics, Inc., 1983-93, McMahon Fin. Svcs., Inc., 1981-88; chmn. Vacu Dry Co., 1983-95. Trustee Pacific Inst. Pub. Policy Rsch., 1977-94, Schs. of Sacred Heart, San Francisco, 1984-88; regent St. Mary's Coll., Moraga, Calif., 1985-91; adv. bd. Ctr. for Econ. Policy Rsch., Stanford U., 1988-96. Comdr. USNR, 1942-46, PTO. Mem. Delta Tau Delta. Home: Sausalito Calif. Died Sept. 11, 1996.

BORDEN, GEORGE ASA, retired communications educator; b. Elmira Heights, N.Y., June 16, 1932; s. Arthur Leroy and Matilda Catherine (Hartmann) B.; children—Sherrie, Cynthia, Curtis. Student, Bible Inst. Los Angeles, 1950-52, N.Mex. State U., 1955-57; B.A. in Math, U. Denver, 1958; M.A. in Math, 1959, M.A. in Communication Methodology, 1962; Ph.D. in Speech Behavior, Cornell U., 1964. Mathematician Marathon Oil Co., Littleton, Colo., 1959-62; from asst. prof. to prof. Pa. State U., University Park, 1964-75; prof. dept. communication U. Del., Newark, 1975-88, ret., 1988; chmn. dept. U. Del., 1975-78; cons. Augmented Intellect Project of Rome Air Devel. Center; cons. human communication systems Universidad Estatal a Distancia, Costa Rica. Author: (with Gregg and Grove) Speech Behavior and Human Interaction, 1969, Introduction to Human Communication Theory, 1971, (with Stone) Human Communication: The Process of Relating, 1976, La Comunicación Humano: El Proceso de interrelación, 1982; Human Communication Systems, 1985, 2d edit., 1989; Cultural Orientation: An Approach to Understanding Intercultural Communication, 1991; contbr. articles to profl. jours. Served with U.S. Army, 1952-54. Fulbright scholar, Panama and Cen. Am., 1987-90. Mem. Internat. Communication Assn., Speech Communication Assn. Died Nov. 11, 1994.

BORDERS, ELIZABETH ACOSTA, architect; b. El Paso, Tex., Oct. 14, 1949; d. Salomon Acosta Baylon and Betsy Ruth (Horner) Acosta; m. James Buchanan Borders IV, Oct. 16, 1976; children: James Buchanan V, Miaflor Elizabeth. BArch., Tulane U., 1973. Lic. real estate broker, La. Architect Inmobiliaria Del Norte, Juarez, Mex., 1974; sole proprietor, mgr. Tianguis Imports, New Orleans, 1975-80; architect Maison Blanche Co., New Orleans, 1979-81; architect, v.p. Architects Internat., New Orleans, 1982—; cons., New Orleans, 1975—. Prin. works include La Placita Restaurant, Tijuana, Mex., Weekend Residences, Pontchatoula, La. Bd. dirs. Lower Garden Dist. Assn., New Orleans, 1984—; pres. Coliseum Place Condominiums, 1984—. Mem. Architects Internat., Rainbow Cottage Inc., Nat. Assn. Female Execs. Roman Catholic. Clubs: Contemporary Art Ctr. (New Orleans), Women in Mainstream (New Orleans). Avocations: painting; reading; travel.

BORDIN, EDWARD S., psychologist, educator; b. Phila., Nov. 7, 1913; s. Morris and Jennie (Zarovsky) B.; m. Ruth Birgitta Anderson, June 2O, 1941; children—Martha Christine (Mrs. Steven A. Hillyard), Charlotte Anna (Mrs. Sung P. Lin). B.S.C., Temple U., 1935, M.A., 1937; Ph.D., Ohio State U., 1942. Asst. to co-ordinator, also counselor univ. testing bur. U. Minn., 1939-42, acting dir. bur., 1945-46; personnel technician (War Dept.), 1942-45; asso. prof. psychology Wash. State U., 1946-48, U. Mich., Ann Arbor, 1948-55; prof. U. Mich., 1955—. Author: Psychological Counseling, 1955, 2d edit. 1968, Research Strategies in Psychotherapy, 1974; Editor: Jour. Cons. Psychology, 1959-64. Recipient Leona Tyler award, 1985. Mem. Am. Psychol. Assn. (pres. div. counseling psychology 1955), AAAS, Soc. for Psychotherapy Research (pres. 1979, research career award 1985). Spl. personality and vocational choice research theory psychotherapy.

BORG, DOROTHY, educator, author; b. Elberon, N.J., Sept. 4, 1902; d. Sidney C. and Madeleine (Beer) B.; (divorced). A.M., Ph.D., Columbia. Research asso. Am. Inst. of Pacific Relations, 1939-58, E. Asian Research Center, Harvard, 1960-61; sr. research asso. E. Asian Inst., Columbia, 1962—; lectr. Peking (China) Nat. U., 1947. Author: American Policy and the Chinese Revolution, 1925-28, 1947, The United States and The Far Eastern Crisis, 1933-1938, 1964; Co-editor: Pearl Harbor as History: Japanese-American Relations, 1931-1941, 1973, Uncertain Years: Chinese-American Relations, 1947-1950, 1980. Recipient Bancroft prize, 1965, Graebner prize Soc. Historians of Fgn. Relations, 1986. Mem. Am. Hist. Assn., Assn. Asian Studies, Orgn. Am. Historians, Soc. for Historians of Am. Fgn. Relations.

BORST, JOHN, JR., lawyer, electronics corporation executive; b. Berwyn, Ill., Dec. 18, 1927; s. John William and Nellie (Tornga) B.; m. Frances Malone, June 25, 1955 (div.); children: Alicia C., John W., Julia E.; m. Mary Capron, Apr. 26, 1973. BA, U. Chgo., 1948, JD, 1951. Bar: Ill. 1951, U.S. Dist. Ct. (no. dist.) Ill. 1951, U.S. Supreme Ct. 1971. Pvt. practice Chgo., 1951-74; asst. gen. counsel Zenith Radio Corp., Glenview, Ill., 1974-83; gen. counsel Zenith Electronics Corp., Glenview, 1983-85, v.p., gen. counsel, 1985-95. Assoc. editor U. Chgo. Law Rev., 1950-51. Served with U.S. Army, 1946-47. Mem. ABA, Order of Coif. Club: Law (Chgo.). Home: Glen Ellyn Ill. Died Feb. 1, 1995.

BORTON, HUGH, history educator; b. Moorestown, N.J., May 14, 1903; m. Elizabeth Wilbur; children—Anne Carter, Anthony. B.S., Haverford Coll., 1926; M.A., Columbia U., 1932; student, Imperial U., Tokyo, 1931-37; Ph.D., Rijksuniversiteit, Leyden, Holland, 1937; research asst., Inst. Pacific Relations, summer 1938; LL.D., Temple U., 1960, U. Pa., 1961, Haverford Coll., 1969. Mem. faculty Columbia, 1937-57; asso. prof. Japanese and asst. dir. East Asian Inst., 1947-50; prof. Japanese and dir. E. Asian Inst., 1950-57; pres. Haverford Coll., Pa., 1957-67; sr. research asso. East Asian Inst., Columbia U., 1967-95; on leave for govt. duty, 1942-48; mem. faculty War Dept. Sch. Mil. Govt., Charlottesville, Va., 1942; also in various positions with Dept. of State, including chief N.E. Asian Affairs div. and spl. asst. office of dir. Far Eastern Affairs, 1942-48; chmn. U.S. delegation, co-chmn. U.S.-Japan Ednl. and Cultural Conf., Japan, 1962-66; Chmn. U.S. delegation, co-chmn. U.S.-Japan Ednl. and Cultural Conf., Washington, 1963; U.S. del. U.S.-Japan Ednl. and Cultural Conf., 1970, 72; mem. Harvard vis. com. Far Eastern Civilizations; v.p. Japan Soc., Inc.; dir. Am. Friends Service Com.; v.p. Japan Internat. Christian U. Found. Author: Japan Modern Century: Its Political and Social Development, Peasant Uprisings in Japan, 1968, Occupation of Japan, Korea and Mandated Islands, 1945-47, Japan's Modern Century, 1970, America Presurrender Planning for Postwar Japan; co-author: A Selected List of Books and Articles on Japan; Japan between East and West, 1957; editor: Japan 1951; contbr. numerous articles on Japanese history and politics. Decorated 2d Order of Sacred Treasure 1st class Japan; recipient Japan Found. award, 1980. Fellow Internat. Inst. Arts and Letters (life); mem. Assn. Asian Affairs (com. coll. and world affairs), Am. Hist. Assn., Council on Fgn. Relations, Phi Beta Kappa. Home: Conway Mass. Died Aug. 6, 1995.

BOSCAGLIA, CLARA, San Marinese government official. Sec. of state Fin. and Budget, Govt. San Marino, 1994—. Died July 22, 1990.

BOSSERMAN, JOSEPH NORWOOD, architecture educator; b. Harrisonburg, Va., July 12, 1925; s. Joseph Astir and Ethel (Wise) B. B.S., U. Va., 1948; M.F.A., Princeton U., 1952. Designer C. W. Wenger, Harrisonburg, 1948-50, Kenneth Franzheim, Houston, 1952-54; acting asst. prof. architecture U. Va., 1954, asst. prof. architecture, 1954-60, asso. prof., 1960-64; asst. dean Sch. Architecture, 1965, acting dean, 1966, prof., 1966, 81-97, dean, 1967-81; vis. prof. architecture Kingston Sch. Art, Kingston-upon-Thames, Eng., 1960-61; sr. Fulbright prof. Technische Hochschule, Stuttgart, Germany, 1964-65; Bd. dirs. Va. Found. Archtl. Edn., Inc.; bd. govs. Am. Assn. Archtl. Bibliographers. Served with USAAF, World War II, PTO. Fellow Royal Soc. Arts. (Eng.), FAIA; mem. Raven Soc., Alpha Rho Chi, Omicron Delta Kappa. Democrat. Mem. United Ch. of Christ. Clubs: Mason. Clubs: Greencroft (Charlottesville). Died Jan. 27, 1997.

BOTEZ, MIHAI HORIA, diplomat; b. Romania, 1940. PhD in Math., Romania, 1966. Prof., researcher Bucharest U.; amb. of Romania to U.S. Govt. Romania, Washington, 1994-95. Author 5 books; contbr. numerous articles to sci. jours. Died July 11, 1995.

BOURASSA, ROBERT, former Premier of Québec; b. July 14, 1933; s. Aubert and Adrienne (Courville); m. Andrée Simard; children: François, Michelle. BA, Coll. Jean-de-Brébeuf, Montréal, Que., Can., 1953; LLB, U. Montréal, 1956; MA in Econs. and Polit. Sci., Oxford (Eng.) U., 1959; MA in Internat. Taxation and Corp. Law, Harvard U., 1960; PhD (hon.), U. Tel Aviv, 1987. Taxation advisor Dept. Nat. Revenue, 1960-63; prof. econs. and taxation U. Ottawa, Ont., Can., 1961-63; sec., rsch. dir. Bélanger Commn., 1963-65; spl. advisor econ. and fin. Fed. Dept. of Fin.; prof. pub. fin. U. Montréal and Laval U., 1966-69; Premier Province of Que., 1970-76, 85-94; assoc. prof. Chaire Jean-Monet, U. Montreal, 1994-95; vis. prof. Inst. Européen Adminstrn., 1976, U. So. Calif., L.A., 1981, Yale U., New Haven, Conn., 1982; prof. Ctr. Advanced Internat. Studies John Hopkins U., 1978. Author: Bourassa/Québec!, 1970, La Baie James, 1973, Les Années Bourassa: l'intégrale des entretiens Bourassa-St-Pierre, 1977, Deux fois la Baie James, 1981, Power from the North, L'Energie du Nord: la force du Québec, Le Défi technologique, 1985. Re-elected leader of Que. Liberal Party, 1983; 20th recipient Order of Merit of Grads. of U. Montréal. Died Oct. 2, 1996.

BOURDEAU, PAUL TURGEON, insurance company executive; b. Concord, N.H., June 7, 1932; s. Adelard J. and Marie (A.) B.; m. Patricia Shapiro, Sept. 1, 1979; children: Paul, Corinne, Bonnie, Jacqui. B.A., Pa. State U., 1953; M.B.A., U. Hartford, 1970; postgrad., Stanford U., 1980. Gen. mgr. Layman Motor Co., 1956-60; v.p., actuary Travelers Ins. Co., 1960-81; pres. Phoenix Am. Life Ins. Co., Hartford, Conn., 1981-83; sr. v.p. Phoenix Mutual Life Ins. Co., Hartford, 1981-83; pres., chief exec. officer Beneficial Standard Life Ins. Co., Los Angeles, 1983-88, Direct Mktg. Corp. Am., 1983-86; pres. Bourdeau Cons., Pasadena, Calif., 1988—. Contbr. in field; speaker in field. Chmn. organizing com. U.S. Figure Skating Championships, 1977, World Figure Skating Championships, 1981. Served with USN, 1953-56. Fellow Soc. Actuaries; mem. Acad. Actuaries, Soc. C.L.U.s, Phi Beta Kappa. Died Aug. 14, 1996.

BOVILLE, BYRON WALTER, meteorologist; b. Ottawa, Ont., Can., Dec. 14, 1920; married, 1945; 3 children. BA, U. Toronto, 1942; MSc, McGill U., 1958; PhD in Meteorology, 1961. Meteorologist Can. Meteorology Svc., 1942-58; from asst. prof. to prof. meteorology McGill U., 1960-72, chmn. dept., 1968-70; dir. atmospheric processes rsch. br. Atmospheric Environ. Svc., 1972-78; dir. Can. Climate Ctr., 1978-80; World Climate Prog. World Meteorology Orgn., Geneva, 1980-82; chmn., 1986-88; adj. prof. earth & atmospheric sci. York U., 1982—; mem. Can. Nat. Com. Internat. Union Geodesy. & Geophysics, 1956-69 (chmn. 1969—), Internat. Ozone Commn. Working Group on Stratospheric Pollution, UN Environ. Prog. Ozone Coord. Com.; sabbatical leave Meteorology Nat. France, 1970-71; dir. Climate Conf., China, 1980, Latin Am., 1982. Fellow Royal Meteorlogy Soc., Am. Meteorology Soc., Can. Meteorlogy Soc., Sigma Xi. Research in dynamic meteorology, especially on the general circulation and on the stratosphere and interlayer coupling.

BOWDEN, HENRY LUMPKIN, lawyer; b. Atlanta, July 23, 1910; s. John and Mattie (Turner) B.; m. Ellen Marian Fleming, June 30, 1937 (dec. Nov. 1986); children—Mary Lamar Fidler, Anne Turner, Henry Lumpkin. B.Ph., Emory U., 1932, LL.B., 1933, LL.D., 1959; LL.D. (hon.), Clark Coll., 1981. Bar: Ga. bar 1933. Since practiced in Atlanta; assoc. firm William E. Arnaud, 1933-39; partner firm Lokey & Bowden, 1939—; city atty. City of Atlanta, 1963-76; dir. 1st Nat. Bank, Atlanta., 1960-81; Mem. U.S. Regional Loyalty Bd., 1950-52, U.S. Loyalty Rev. Bd., 1952-53. Trustee Emory U.; chmn., 1957-79, Wesleyan Coll., Macon, Ga., Clark Coll., 1959-81. Served from 2d lt. to lt. col. AUS, 1941-46. Recipient Alexander Meiklejohn award AAUP, 1963, Atlanta Shining Light award Sta. WSB and Atlanta Gas Light Co., 1976, award NCCJ, 1982. Fellow Am. Bar Found., Am. Coll. Probate Counsel; mem. Ga. Bar Assn. (pres. 1955-56), ABA, Fed. Bar Assn., Atlanta Bar Assn. (pres. 1947), Inter-Am. Bar Assn., Am. Law Inst., Am. Judicature Soc., Phi Beta Kappa, Phi Delta Theta, Phi Delta Phi, Omicron Delta Kappa. Methodist. Clubs: Capital City (Atlanta), Lawyers (Atlanta), Piedmont Driving (Atlanta); The 10 (Atlanta); Homosassa Fishing (Fla.). Died Feb. 17, 1997.

BOWDEN, WILLIAM LUKENS, state university system executive; b. Paducah, Ky., Sept. 8, 1922; s. Homer Marvin and Gertrude (Lukens) B.; m. Carol Lorraine Morris, Dec. 22, 1948; children: William Breckenridge, Andrew Scott, Marion Lorraine, Joseph

Craig. B.A., Southwestern at Memphis, 1948; M.A., U. Chgo., 1950, Ph.D., 1957; Pd. D. (hon.), Christian Bros. Coll., 1973. Credit reporter Dun & Bradstreet, Birmingham, Ala., 1947; research asst. to dean U. Chgo., Ill., 1948-50; coordinator Richmond Area U. Center, 1950-51; dir. eve. coll. Coll. William and Mary at, Richmond, 1951-52; dir. confs. U. Va., Charlottesville, 1952; dir. Richmond div. U. Va., 1952-58; asso. dir. So. Regional Edn. Bd., Atlanta, 1958-66; adviser Ford Found., Buenos Aires, Argentina, 1966-67; prof. edn., chmn. dept. adult edn. U. Ga., Athens, 1967-68; also mem. grad. sch. faculty U. Ga., 1967-68; vice chancellor U. System Ga., 1968-69; pres. Southwestern at, Memphis, 1969-72; exec. dir. So. Growth Policies Bd., 1972-76; mem. staff Duke U., 1972-76; coordinator So. Assn. Colls. and Schs., Atlanta, 1977-78; pres. Cleve. Inst. Electronics, 1978-81, Jack Eckerd Ednl. Inst., Clearwater, Fla., 1981-84; asst. dir. Ala. Commn. on Higher Edn., Montgomery, 1985—. Mng. editor The Electron. Mem. Tenn./Tombigbee Waterway Devel. Council, So. Growth Policies Bd. Served with USCG/USMC, 1942-46. Mem. Assn. Univ. Continuing Edn., Am. Soc. for Engring. Edn., C. of C. U.S. (com. on edn., employment and tng.), Phi Beta Kappa, Omicron Delta Kappa, Pi Kappa Alpha. Presbyterian (deacon 1960-62, ruling elder 1962—).

BOWERS, GRAYSON HUNTER, building parts manufacturing company executive; b. Frederick, Md., Nov. 18, 1897; s. Grayson Eichelberger and Chrisse Byrd Dell (Firestone) B.; ed. Gettysburg Coll., 1919; m. Isabel Houck, June 6, 1921 (dec. Dec. 1961); children: Grayson Hunter, Charles R., Alice Josephine Bowers Butler; m. 2d, Frances L. Crilly, June 20, 1964. Vice pres. William D. Bowers Lumber Co. and pres. allied corps., Frederick, 1919-96; pres. Fidelity Bldg. & Loan Assn., 1961-80; Mt. Olivet Cemetery Co.; sr. v.p., dir. Fredericktown Bank & Trust Co., 1931-79; dir., officer Lumbermens Merchandising Corp., Wayne, Pa., 1945-70. Alderman, City of Frederick, 1928-34; pres. Bd. Election Suprs., 1934-38, Frederick City Planning Commn., 1943-70; trustee Hood Coll., 1950-74; mem. adv. council Md. Hosp. Constrn., 1968-71. Served to 1st lt. U.S. Army, 1919. Club: Masons. Mem. Frederick County Hist. Soc. (pres. 1965-67, 70-72). Died 1996. Home: Frederick Md.

BOWES, DAVID DWIGHT, ballet company director; b. Sanford, Fla., Aug. 16, 1951; s. Charles Roderick and Elizabeth Fanning (Thurmond) B. BA in Theater with honors, Tulane U., 1973. Dir. N.Y.C. Opera Theater, 1975-79; dir. prodn. Mich. Opera Theater, Detroit, 1979-81, stage dir., 1986; gen. mgr. Orlando (Fla.) Opera Co., 1981-83; gen. dir. Ft. Worth Opera Assn., 1983-85; cons., co-mgr. Tex. Opera Theater, Houston, 1985-86; exec. dir. Sacramento Ballet Assn., 1986-88, San Jose (Calif.) Cleve. Ballet, 1988-93; stage dir. U. Ill. Opera, Champaign, Opera Carolina, Mich. Opera Theatre, Anchorage Theatre. Trans. (opera libretto) The Impressario, 1979. Mem. Mayor's Spl. Task Force on Meml. Auditorium, Sacramento, 1987. Mem. Dance Calif. (v.p. dance bay area 1989-93), Sacramento Area Dance Alliance (bd. dirs. 1986-93), San Jose Arts Round Table (chair 1990-93). Democrat. Episcopalian. Club: Nat. Arts (N.Y.C.). Avocations: cooking, books. Deceased.

BOWLING, JAMES CHANDLER, retired executive, farmer, philanthropist; b. Covington, Ky., Mar. 29, 1928; s. Van Dorn and Belinda (Johnson) B.; m. Ann Jones, Oct. 20, 1951; children: Belinda, Nancy, James Jr., Stephanie. B.S., U. Louisville, 1951, D Bus. Adminstrn. (hon.), 1997; LL.D. (hon.), Murray U., 1976, U. Ky., 1981. With Philip Morris, Inc., N.Y.C., 1948-86, various positions from campus rep. to v.p. sales and corp. relations; then exec. v.p., group v.p.., dir. mktg., sr. v.p., bd. dir. Miller Brewing Co., Seven Up Co., until 1986; bd. dirs., mem. exec. com. Tobacco Inst., Washington., until 1984; sr. adv. bd. Burson-Marsteller, 1986-95; advisor USIA, 1980-92; bd. dirs. Cherokee Farms, Union Trust, Darien, Conn., Centurion, Inc., Centurion Stables, Inc.; chmn. bd. dirs. Pub. Rels. News., 1986-88; chmn. Bowling Investments, Inc. Author: How To Improve Your Personal Relations, 1959. Mem. nat. coun. Boy Scouts Am., 1961-97; trustee Boy Scout Mus.; justice of peace, Rowayton, Conn., 1960-68; chmn. Pub. Affairs Coun., Washington; bd. overseers U. Louisville; bd. dirs., past pres. and chmn. Keep Am. Beautiful, 1966-80; bd. dirs. Nat. Automatic Merchandising Assn., Ky. Ind. Coll. Found., Nat. Tennis Found. Hall of Fame, Sanders Brown Found., Ky. Ctr. Aging, Country Music Hall Fame, 1956, U. Ky. Devel. Coun.; trustee, vice chmn. Berea Coll., Midway Coll. Recipient Kolodny award as outstanding young exec. in tobacco industry, 1963; named U.S. Young Businessman of Year St. John's U., 1967, Outstanding Alumnus U. Louisville, 1970, 86, 90, Kentuckian of Year, 1977; elected to Tobacco Industry Hall of Fame, 1976. Mem. Nat. Assn. Tobacco Distbg. (bd. dirs. exec. mgmt. div.), Pub. Rels. Soc. Am. Sales Execs. Club N.Y., The Kentuckians (past pres.), Laymen's Nat. Bible Assn. (v.p., bd. dirs.), World Press Inst., Lambda Chi Alpha (found. v.p., pres.), Wee Burn Country Club, Union League Club, John's Island Club, Windsor Club. Episcopalian. Died June 24, 1997.

BOWLING, WILLIAM GLASGOW, English educator; b. St. Louis, May 7, 1902; s. William Walter and Mary Susan (Glasgow) B.; m. Violet Whelen, Aug. 3, 1933; 1 son, Townsend Whelen. A.B., Washington U., St. Louis, 1924, A.M., 1925; postgrad., Harvard U., 1930-31. Instr., asst. prof., asso. prof. English, Washington U., 1925-70, prof. emeritus, 1970—, asst. to dean, acting dean, dean Univ. Coll., 1928-42, dean Coll. Liberal Arts, 1942-46, dean of men, 1942-44; civilian adminstr. pre-profl. unit Army Specialized Tng. Program, Washington U., 1943-44, dean admissions, 1946-65, univ. grand marshal, 1960-68, univ. historian, 1965—; part time drama critic St. Louis Times, 1929-30. Contbr. articles to profl. jours. Recipient Washington U. Alumni award for disting. service, 1960. Mem. Am. Assn. Collegiate Registrars and Admissions Officers (hon.; book rev. editor quar. jour. Coll. and Univ. 1955-66), Greater St. Louis Council Tchrs. of English (pres. 1936-39, exec. sec. 1939-41), Washington U. Assn. Lecture Series (exec. sec. 1940-47), St. Louis Audubon Soc. (dir. 1944—, pres. 1950-52), Phi Delta Theta, Omicron Delta Kappa, Phi Delta Kappa. Republican. Episcopalian. Club: University (St. Louis). Died July 1, 1994.

BOWMAN, MONROE BENGT, architect; b. Chgo., Aug. 28, 1901; s. Henry William and Ellen Mercedes (Bjork) B.; m. Louise Kohnmann, Nov. 1944; 1 son, Kenneth Monroe; B.Arch., Ill. Inst. Tech., 1924. Registered architect, Ill., Wis., Ind., Ohio, Colo. Asso., Benjamin H. Marshall, Chgo., 1926; exhibited models and photographs of Bowman Bros. comtemporary designs at Mus. Modern Art, N.Y.C., 1931; pvt. practice architecture, Chgo., 1941-44; asso. Monroe Bowman Assos., Chgo., 1945—; cons. Chgo. Dept. City Planning, City of Sparta (Wis.), Alfred Shaw, Architect. Mem. Navy League U.S. Important works include Boeing Aircraft bldgs., Wichita, Kans., Emerson Electric bldgs., St. Louis, Maytag Co., Newton, Iowa, Douglas Aircraft bldgs., Park Ridge, Ill., Shwayder Bros. bldgs., Denver, Clark Equipment Co., Buchannon, Mich., Radio-TV Sta. WHO, Des Moines, Foote, Cone & Belding offices, Chgo., Burridge Devel., Hinsdale, Ill., Yacht Club and recreational facilities, Lake Bemiji, Minn., United Airlines offices downtown Chgo., Automatic Sprinkler Corp., Chgo., King Machine Tool div. Am. Steel Foundries, Cin., Marine Terr. Apts., Chgo., Dorchester Park Apts., Chgo., Manteno (Ill.) State Hosp., No. Ill. Gas Co. bldgs., LaGrange, Joliet, Streator and Morris, 1340 Astor St. Apt. Bldg., Burnham Center, Chgo., NSF, Green Bank, W.Va., Naval Radio Research Sta., Sugar Grove, W.Va., Columbus Boy Choir Sch., Princeton, N.J., office bldg. and hotel, Charleston, W.Va. Deceased.

BOYD, SAMUEL MATTHEW, retail stores executive; b. Uniontown, Pa., Mar. 12, 1908; s. Eli Jacob and Martha (Albright) B.; m. Mary Kathryn Collins, July 26, 1932; children—Vance Eugene, Maureen Ellen (Mrs. James F. O'Hara), Suzanne Martha (Mrs. Allan Byrne). Grad., Inst. Mgmt., Am. U., 1956. Sales mgr. Collins Electric Co., Springfield, Mass., 1929-45; pres. New Eng. Service Center, Inc., Springfield, 1945-59, Boyd & Parker, Inc. (builders and developers), Springfield, 1948-60, Bailey-Wagner, Inc. (retail furniture-appliance stores), Springfield, 1933—; lectr. merchandising Mass. U. extension, 1938—, Internat. Coll., Springfield, 1956—. Pres. Greater Springfield Vis. Nurses Assn., 1968-69. Mem. Nat. Appliance and Radio-TV Dealers Assn. (pres. 1962-63). Clubs: Longmeadow (Mass.); Mens (pres. 1956).

BOYDEN, ALLEN MARSTON, surgeon, educator; b. Brookings, S.D., Oct. 31, 1908; s. Frank Edson and Maude Eva (Hegeman) B.; m. Margery French Davis, Sept. 19, 1936; children: Frank Davis, Allen Moore, Bradley Hunt. A.B., U. Oreg., 1929; M.D., U. Mich., 1932, M.S. in Surgery, 1936. Diplomate: Am. Bd. Surgery. Surg. house officer Mass. Gen. Hosp., 1932-34; instr. surgery U. Mich. Med. Sch., 1934-37; practice medicine specializing in surgery Astoria, Oreg., 1937-42; head dept. gen. surgery Portland (Oreg.) Clinic, 1948-79; clin. instr. U. Oreg. Med. Sch., 1946, clin. assoc. surgery, 1946-51, asst. clin. prof. surgery, 1951-54, assoc. clin. prof. surgery, 1954-66, clin. prof. surgery, 1966-86, clin. prof. emeritus, 1987-93; chief surg. service St. Vincent Hosp., 1955-58, 68-70, chief staff, 1964 acting dir. surgery, 1983-85, sr. lectr. in surgery, 1979-93 ; mem. exec. com., trustee Oreg. Physicians Service, 1954-66, v.p., 1959. Cons. editor: Surgery Gynecology and Obstetrics, 1966-74. Served from capt. to maj., M.C. U.S. Army, 1942-45. Decorated Bronze Star medal. Fellow AMA, A.C.S. (gov. 1948-63, vice chmn. bd. govs. 1958-59, 2d v.p. 1960-61); mem. Am. Surg. Assn. (2d v.p. 1973-74), Western Surg. Assn. (pres. 1976-77), Pacific Coast Surg. Assn. (pres. 1973-74), North Pacific Surg. Assn., Internat. Surg. Soc., Portland Surg. Soc. (pres. 1958-59), Frederick A. Coller Surg. Soc. (pres. 1955-58), Ore., Multonomah County med. socs., Portland Acad. Medicine (pres. 1965), Soc. Surgery Alimentary Tract, Phi Beta Kappa, Alpha Omega Alpha, Phi Kappa Phi, Nu Sigma Nu, Kappa Sigma. Republican. Unitarian. Clubs: Multnomah Athletic (Portland); Flyfishers of Oreg. Home: Portland Oreg. Died June 18, 1993.

BOYDEN, JOEL MICHAEL, lawyer; b. Muskegon, Mich., Apr. 18, 1937; s. Wilbur B. and Dorothy Elizabeth (Damm) B.; m. Jean Ann Zuiderveld, Apr. 18, 1964; children: Jacquelyn Kay, Kathryn Marie, Dorothy Elizabeth, Joel Michael. BA in Speech, U. Mich., 1959, JD, 1962. Bar: Mich. 1963, Fla. 1964, U.S. Ct. Appeals (6th cir.) 1963, U.S. Supreme Ct. 1968. Law clk. to judge U.S. Dist. Ct. (we. dist.) Mich., 1962-64; assoc. McCobb & Heaney, Grand Rapids, Mich., 1964-66; ptnr. Baxter & Hammond, Grand Rapids, 1966-84, Dykema Gossett, Grand Rapids, 1984-91, Boyden, Waddell, Timmons & Dilley, 1991—; mem. task force on gender bias, Mich. Supreme Ct., 1987-89. Bd. dirs. Kewano coun. Campfire Girls, 1969-73, v.p., 1972-73; bd. dirs. Western Mich. Alliance for Health, 1993—; mem. cen. bd. Grand Rapids YMCA, 1972-76, chmn., 1974-76, mem. met. bd. dirs., 1976-85, 89-92; mem. devel. bd., Porter Hills Found., 1993-96, bd. dirs. 1995—, Found. bd. 1996—; mem. com. visitors U. Mich. Law Sch., 1986-91; bd. deacons Eastminster Presbyn. Ch., 1977-79, elder, clk. session, 1987-90, founding pres. Christ Community Ch. of Grand Rapids, 1992. Named one of Mich.'s 20 Most Influential Pvt. Practitioners During 1989-90, 90-91, Mich. Lawyers Weekly. Fellow Am. Bar Found., Mich. State Bar Found. (chairperson fellows 1989-92, bd. dirs. 1993—), Am. Coll. Trial Lawyers, Am. Bd. Trial Advocates, Internat. Acad. Trial Lawyers, Internat. Soc. Barristers (bd. govs. 1981-88, pres. 1986-87); mem. ABA (ho. of dels. 1974-75, 84-88, sec. litigation sect. 1976-77 coun. mem. 1973-77, legis. com. 1973-78), State Bar Mich. (pres. 1983-84, bd. commrs. 1973-84, dir. Bar Found. 1990—, chmn. Fellows MSB 1992-94), Grand Rapids Bar Assn. (trustee 1974-76), Am. Judicature Soc. (bd. dirs. 1979-83), Am. Counsel Assn. (bd. dirs. 1989-93), Inns of Ct., Torch Club, U. Mich. Pres.'s Club (exec. com. 1981-83), Cen. Mich. U. Pres.'s Club (nat. chairperson 1986—, Centennial award 1993), Rotary (pres. 1992-93 Grand Rapids).

BOYER, RAYMOND FOSTER, physicist; b. 1910. BS in Astronomy, Case Western Res. U., 1933, MS in Physics, 1935, DSc (hon.), 1955. With Dow Chem. Co., Midland, Mich., 1935-75; asst. dir. phys. research lab. Dow Chem. Co., 1945-48, dir. phys. research lab., 1948-52, dir. plastics research, 1952-69, asst. dir. corp. research, 1969-72; ptnr. Boyer and Boyer, Midland, 1975-92; research affiliate Mich. Molecular Inst., 1975-91; appointed 1st rsch. fellow Dow Chem. Co., 1972; vis. prof. Case Western Res. U., 1974, adj. prof., 1979, adj. prof. Cen. Mich. U., 1984-93, Mich. Technol. U., 1986-93; guest Russian Acad. Scis., 1972, 78, 80, 87, Polish Acad. Scis., 1973; Past chmn. Gordon Conf. on Polymers. Contbr. numerous articles to profl. jours. Recipient Swinburne award Plastics Inst., London, 1972; named to Plastics Hall of Fame, 1991. Fellow Am. Phys. Soc. (past chmn. high polymer div.), Mich. Molecular Inst.; mem. NAE, Am. Chem. Soc. (past chmn. high polymer div., Borden award in chemistry of plastics and coatings 1970), Soc. Plastics Engrs. (internat. award in polymer engring. and sci. 1968), N.Y. Acad. Scis. Home: Midland Mich. Died Feb. 23, 1993.

BOYNTON, WYMAN PENDER, retired lawyer; b. Portsmouth, N.H., Oct. 8, 1908; s. Harry Edwin and Helen Catherine (Pender) B.; m. Mildred Elizabeth Ballard, Feb. 1, 1935; children: Elizabeth Ballard Boynton Larsen. BS, MIT, 1931; LLB, U. Mich., 1936. Bar: N.H. 1936, U.S. Dist. Ct. 1946; registered profl. engr. With C.E. Walker & Co., 1931-33; jr. acct. J. Ben Hart, 1934; assoc. Jeremy R. Waldron, 1936-39; ptnr. Waldron & Boynton and successors Boynton, Waldron, Doleac, Woodman & Scott, P.A., Portsmouth, N.H., 1940-86; trustee Portsmouth Coop. Bank, 1946-81, chmn. bd. 1976-81. Asst. scoutmaster, then scoutmaster Boy Scouts Am., 1931-33, mem. troop com. and dist. com. 1936-40, mem. coun. exec. bd. 1951-60, coun. commr., 1953-54, coun. pres. 1957-58; mem. Portsmouth Athenaeum, N.H. Hist. Soc., Soc. for Preservation of New Eng. Antiquities; trustee Portsmouth Hist. Soc., 1940-92, v.p., 1946-85, 87-93, pres., 1985-87, hon. trustee, 1993—; trustee Mark H. Wentworth Home for Chronic Invalids, 1948-81, pres. 1950-81; pres. Chase Home for Children, 1950-77, trustee 1946—; trustee Portsmouth YWCA, 1949-70; pres. Portsmouth Athenaeum, 1977-80; trustee Portsmouth Pub. Libr., 1955-70; trustee N.H. Indsl. Sch., Manchester, 1955-66, chmn. 1958-66; mem. Portsmouth Spl. Water Com., 1958-62; mem. Portsmouth City Mgr. Charter Com., 1947-49; mem. N.H. Hos. of Reps., 1933-34; mem. Portsmouth City Coun., 1937-38; county atty. Rockingham County, 1947-50; mem. Portsmouth Sch. Bd., 1954-58, 62-70; del. Rep. Nat. Conv., Chgo., 1952; mem. N.H. Constl. Conv., 1974. Commd. 2d lt. USAR, 1931, with C.E., 1940-45, ETO, col. res., 1945-61. Decorated Bronze Star; recipient Silver Beaver award Daniel Webster Coun. Boy Scouts Am., 1958, Portsmouth C. of C. Community Svc. award, 1978. Mem. ABA, N.H. Bar Assn., N.H. Soc. Profl. Engrs., NSPE, N.H. Land Surveyors Assn., Soc. Am. Mil. Engrs., Rotary (Paul Harris award 1985), Wentworth Fairways Golf Club. Republican. Congregationalist. Died May 26, 1997.

BOYSEN, HARRY, obstetrician, gynecologist; b. Harlan, Iowa, Aug. 21, 1904; s. Hans and Dorothea (Brodersen) B.; m. Patricia Dougherty, May 4, 1940 (dec. Oct. 1988); children—Gerald, Patricia Anne (Mrs. Thomas P. Lennon). B.S., U. Iowa, 1924, M.D., 1928. Diplomate: Am. Bd. Obstetrics and Gynecology. Intern Highland Hosp., Oakland, Calif., 1928-29; resident obstetrics and gynecology Presbyn. Hosp., Chgo., 1930-32, mem. staff; pvt. practice, from 1945; former clin. prof. obstetrics, gynecology Rush Med. Coll.-Presbyn.-St. Luke's Med. Center; now emeritus; former chmn. div. obstetrics and gynecology Presbyn.-St. Luke's Hosp. Served from lt. comdr. to comdr., M.C. USNR, 1942-45. Fellow A.C.S.; mem. A.M.A., Chgo. Gynecol. Soc. (pres. 1963-64), Am. Coll. Obstetrics and Gynecology, Phi Kappa Psi, Nu Sigma Nu. Clubs: Obstetrics and Gynecology Travel (Wheaton, Ill.), Chicago Golf (Wheaton, Ill.); LaQuinta (Calif.); Country. DIED 12/22/96. .

BOZO, DOMINIQUE, museum director; b. Alencon, France, 1935. Curator, Musé e nat. d'art moderne, 1969-72, redesigned nat. collections, in charge graphics scheme; with Centre nat. d'art et de culture Georges-Pompidou (CNAC), 1972-93, acting dir., 1973-74, dir., 1981-86, 90-93; designer new Musé e Picasso at l'hotel Sale, 1974-93; co-dir. Picasso Retrospective Exhbn., N.Y., 1980. Died Apr. 28, 1993. Home: Paris Cedex France

BRACKLEY, WILLIAM LOWELL, aviation management consultant; b. Laramie, Wyo., July 23, 1919; s. Frank Lowell and Ella Augusta (Ramsel) B.; m. Juanita Jean Potter, May 31, 1946; children: James Thomas, Marc Lowell, Bruce Gene. Student, U. Wyo., 1938-42. Commd. 2d lt. USAF, 1942, advanced through grades to col., 1962; with 457th Bombardment Group, 8th Air Force, 1944; command and staff assignments SAC, 1949-63; dep. comdr. 7101st Air Base Wing, Europe, 1963-66; dep. chief of Staff 14th Air Force Air Def. Command, 1966-68; ret., 1968; asst. mgr. Intercontinental Airport, Houston, 1968-74, mgr., 1974-78; dir. aviation City of Houston, 1978-82; aviation cons., 1982-96. Decorated Legion of Merit, D.F.C., Air medal with 3 oak leaf clusters, others. Mem. Nat. Rifle Assn., Ret. Officers Assn., Masons, Quiet Birdmen, A.A.A.E., A.O.C.I. Home: Houston Tex. Died Aug. 19, 1996.

BRADBURY, NORRIS EDWIN, physicist; b. Santa Barbara, Calif., May 30, 1909; s. Edwin Perly and Elvira C. (Norris) B.; m. Lois Platt, Aug. 5, 1933; children—James Norris, John Platt, David Edwin. B.A., Pomona Coll., 1929, D.Sc., 1951; Ph.D., U. Calif., 1932; LL.D., U. N.Mex., 1953; D.Sc., Case Inst. Tech., 1956. NRC fellow in physics M.I.T., 1932-34; asst. prof. physics Stanford U., 1934-37, assoc. prof., 1937-42, prof., 1942-50; prof. physics U. Calif., 1945-70; dir. Los Alamos Sci. Lab., 1945-70. Contbr. tech. articles to phys. revs., jours. Served with USNR, 1941-45; capt. Res. Decorated Legion of Merit. Fellow Am. Phys. Soc. (Enrico Fermi award 1970); mem. Nat. Acad. Sci. Episcopalian. Died Aug. 20, 1997.

BRADLEY, OWEN, country western musician, recording executive; b. Westmoreland, Tenn., Jan. 1, 1915. Dir. Sta. WSM Radio, Nashville, 1940-58; producer Decca Records, Nashville, 1947-52; chief staff producer MCA Records, Nashville, artist and repertory dir., 1958-68, v.p. Nashville ops., 1968; ind. producer. Album: Big Guitar. Named to Country Music Hall of Fame, 1974; helped define and create Nashville Sound.

BRADY, LYNN ROBERT, pharmacognosist, educator; b. Shelton, Nebr., Nov. 15, 1933; s. Connie E. and Laura M. (Vohland) B.; m. Geraldine Ann Walcott, June 23, 1957. B.S., U. Nebr., 1955, M.S., 1957; Ph.D., U. Wash., 1959. Asst. prof. pharmacognosy U. Wash., 1959-63, asso. prof., 1963-67, prof., 1967-92, chmn. dept., 1972-80, asst. dean, 1982-90, assoc. dean, 1990-92; chmn. conf. Tchrs. Am. Assn. Colls. Pharmacy, 1966-67. Author: (with others) Pharmacognosy, 6th edit., 1970, 7th edit., 1976, 8th edit., 1981, 9th edit., 1987. Fellow Acad. Pharm. Scis. (chmn. sect. pharmacognosy and natural products 1969-70); mem. Am. Pharm. Assn., Am. Soc. Pharmacognosy (hon. mem. 1991, pres. 1970-71), Sigma Xi, Rho Chi, Kappa Psi. Research in fungal constituents, chemataxonomy. Home: Seattle Wash. Died Aug. 20, 1992.

BRAESTRUP, PETER, editor; b. N.Y.C., June 8, 1929; s. Carl Bjorn and Elsebet (Kampmann) B.; m. Angelica Hollins (div. 1985); children: Angelica, Elizabeth Kate, Carl Peter; m. Sandra Cornelia Newing, 1989. BA, Yale U., 1951. Contbg. editor Time Mag., N.Y.C., 1953-55; corr. Time Mag., Chgo., 1955-57; reporter N.Y. Herald Tribune, N.Y.C., 1957-59, N.Y. Times, Washington, 1960-62; corr. N.Y. Times, Algiers, 1962-65, Paris, 1965, Bangkok, Saigon, 1966-68; bur. chief Washington Post, Saigon, 1968-69; nat. staff writer Washington Post, 1969-73; founding editor Wilson Quar., Washington, 1975-89; sr. editor, dir. communications Libr. of Congress, Washington, 1989-97. Author: Big Story, 1977 (Sigma Delta Chi award 1978), (with others) Battle Lines, 1985; editor: Vietnam as History, 1984; project dir. Civilization mag., 1994-97; contbr. articles to profl. jours. Mem. Yale Alumni Publs. Bd., 1975-88, 20th Century Fund Task Force on Mil. Media Rels., 1984-85; chmn. Media Studies Project, Washington, 1987-92. 1st lt. USMC, 1951-53, Korea. Nieman fellow Harvard U., 1960, Woodrow Wilson Internat. Ctr. for Scholars fellow, 1973-75. Mem. Cosmos Club (Washington). Died Aug. 10, 1997.

BRAGNO, EDWARD ALBERT, vintner; b. Chgo., Sept. 30, 1910; s. Francesco and Josephine (Mustari) B.; m. Molly Netcher, Aug. 9, 1947. Student parochial schs., Chgo. Assoc. with wine industry, 1933—; pres. Larkmead Vineyards, Inc., St. Helena, Calif., 1943-46, Salmina Lands, Inc., St. Helena, 1943-46; v.p. Bragno & Co., Chgo., from 1938; pres. Bragno & Co., Riverbank, Calif., Edward A. Bragno & Co., Inc., Bragno World Wines Ltd., Chgo. Bd. dirs., trustee Italian Welfare Council; active Arthritis and Rheumatism Found. Mem. Assoc. Vintners of Middle West (past pres.), Acad. Wine at Bordeaux (Grand Council award). Club: Racquet (Palm Springs, Calif.). Home: Paw Paw Lake Mich.

BRAHTZ, JOHN FREDERICK PEEL, civil engineering educator; b. St. Paul, Jan. 29, 1918; s. John Henry August Brahtz and Charlotte Beatrice Peel; m. Lise Vetter, May 11, 1991. BA, Stanford U., 1939, MS, 1948, PhD, 1951. Registered profl. civil and mech. engr., Calif. Various engring. positions Calif., 1939-53; assoc. prof. UCLA, 1953-57; v.p., dir. engring. J.H. Pomeroy & Co. Inc., San Francisco, L.A., 1957-60; mgr. constrn. scis. dvsn. Stanford Rsch. Inst., Menlo Park, Calif., 1960-63; staff cons. U.S. Naval Civil Engring., U.S. Naval Elec. Labs., Port Hueneme, San Diego, Calif., 1963-70; lectr. UCLA, 1963-70; dir. constrn. systems inst. Calif. State U., San Diego, 1970-73; vis. prof. ocean engring. U. Calif., San Diego, 1986-87; cons. rsch. prof. civil engring. Stanford U., 1987—; cons., mem. gen. ocean engring. panel nat. coun. marine resources and engring. Exec. Office of Pres. U.S., Washington, 1964-68; cons. various orgns., San Francisco, N.Y.C., San Diego, Chgo., 1964—; cons. to Devel. Engring. and Rsch. Inst., Carmel, Calif. Co-author, editor: (books) Ocean Engineering: System Planning and Design, 1968, Coastal Zone Management: Multiple Use with Conservation, 1972; editor (book series) Construction Management and Engineering Series, 1976—; patentee in field. Comdr. USN, WWII, ret. Fellow ASCE (mem. tech. coun. on ocean engring.); mem. Am. Soc. for Engring. Edn., Old Capital Club (Monterey, Calif.), Beach and Tennis Club (Pebble Beach, Calif.), Sigma Xi. Died Nov. 1, 1996.

BRÂNCUSI, PETRE, composer, musicologist, educator; b. Târgu-Jiu, Gorj, Romania, June 1, 1928; s. Vasile and Paulina Brâncusi; m. Maria Brâncusi, July 1950; children: Cristian-Dorel, Valentin. Ed. Ciprian Porumbescu Acad. Music, Bucharest, 1950-55, M.A., 1955, D Musicology, 1975. Mng. dir. Music Pub. House, Bucharest, 1959-62; asst. lectr., reader, prof. Acad. Music, Bucharest, 1959, 62, 70, 76; music dir. Romanian RTV, Bucharest, 1968-72; prin. Ciprian Porumbescu, Acad. Music, Bucharest, 1972-81; pres. Union of Composers, Bucharest, 1977-82; mng. dir. Romanian Opera, Bucharest, 1982-89. Co-author: Music in Romania After August 23, 1944, 1964; Romanian Music History, 1969; Music in Socialist Romania, 1973; George Breazul and the Unwritten History of Romanian Music, 1976; Romanian Music and its Grand Transformations vol. I, 1978, vol. 2, 1980; Monuments of Romanian Musical Culture, Vol. I, 1986, Vol. II, 1988, Vol. III, 1989; Course in History of Romanian Music, Vol. I, 1989. Composer choral poems: Branch Under the Sun; Spring Song; At the Springs of a Dream; I am Leaving, Mother. Rep., Grand Nat. Assembly of the S.R. of Romania, 1975-80. Recipient prize Acad. Romania, 1965, Union Composers Romania, 1969, 73, 76; named Laureate, Nat. Festival Cîntarea României, 1979. Mem. Romanian Composers Union (dir. 1968—), Internat. Assn. Lyric Theatres (leading bd.), Santa Cecilia Acad. (Rome) (corr.). Died Feb. 25, 1995.

BRANDON, DONALD WAYNE, educator, author, essayist; b. Portland, Ore., May 14, 1926; s. Elmer Irving and Edna Louise (Plog) B.; m. Rosemary Vollmar, June 9, 1948; children—Elisabeth, Margaret, Catherine, Jennifer. Student, Reed Coll., 1946-48; A.B., U. Calif. at Berkeley, 1949, M.A., 1950, Ph.D., 1954. Staff writer Portland Oregonian, 1946-48; instr. U. San Francisco, 1953-55; intelligence analyst CIA, Washington, 1955-56; cultural officer Am. embassy, Bonn, W. Germany, 1956-58; faculty U. San Francisco, 1958—, prof. polit. sci., 1966-91, prof. emeritus, 1991—. Author: American Foreign Policy-Beyond Utopianism and Realism, 1966, A Politica Externa Americana, 1966; contbr. chpts. to books, articles, essays and reviews to nat. jours. Served with AUS, 1944-46, ETO. Decorated Combat Inf. Badge, Battle Star (2). Mem. U.S. Tennis Assn. Died June 14, 1996.

BRANDT, RICHARD BOOKER, former philosophy educator; b. Wilmington, Ohio, Oct. 17, 1910; s. Henry and Clara Belle (Guyatt) B.; m. Mary Elizabeth Harris, June 19, 1937 (div. Oct. 1968); children: Richard Charles and Karen Elizabeth. AB, Denison U., 1930, LHD (hon.), 1977; BA, Cambridge U., 1933; Burney student; Stanton student, Trinity Coll., Cambridge, 1933-35; student, Tuebingen U., Germany, 1934-35; Ph.D., Yale, 1936. Mem. faculty Swarthmore (Pa.) Coll., 1937-64, successively instr., asst. prof., asso. prof., 1937-52, prof., 1952-64, chmn. dept. philosophy and religion, McDowell prof., 1957-64; prof., chmn. dept. philosophy U. Mich., Ann Arbor, 1964-77; Sellars Collegiate prof. U. Mich., 1978-81; assoc. Center for Philosophy and Public Affairs, U. Md., 1980-81; vis. prof. Fla. State U., 1982, Georgetown U. Law Ctr., 1982-83, U. Calif., Irvine, 1990. Author: The Philosophy of Schleiermacher, 1941, Hopi Ethics: A Theoretical Analysis, 1954, Ethical Theory, 1959, Value and Obligation, 1961, A Theory of the Good and the Right, 1979, Morality, Utilitarianism and Rights, 1992; also articles in profl. publs. Guggenheim fellow, 1944-45; fellow Center for Advanced Study in Behavioral Scis., 1969-70; sr. fellow Nat. Endowment for Humanities, 1971-72; John Locke lectr. Oxford U., 1973-74. Mem. AAUP, Am. Philos. Assn. (exec. com. Eastern div. 1951-54, v.p. 1965, pres. Western div. 1969-70), Am. Soc. Polit. and Legal Philosophy (pres. 1965-66), Soc. for Philosophy and Psychology (pres. 1979), Am. Acad. Arts and Scis., Phi Beta Kappa. Died Sept. 10, 1997.

BRANSCOMB, ANNE WELLS, communications consultant; b. Statesboro, Ga., Nov. 22, 1928; d. Guy Herbert and Ruby Mae (Hammond) Wells; m. Lewis McAdory Branscomb, Oct. 13, 1951; children: Harvie Hammond, Katharine Capers. BA, Ga. Coll., 1949, U. N.C., 1949; postgrad., London Sch. Econs., 1950; MA, Harvard U., 1951; JD with honors, George Washington, 1962; LLD, U. Notre Dame, 1995. Bar: D.C. 1962, Colo. 1963, N.Y. 1973, U.S. Supreme Ct. 1972. Rsch. assoc. Pierson, Ball and Dowd, Washington, 1962; law clk. to presiding judge U.S. Dist. Ct., Denver, 1962-63; assoc. Williams & Zook, 1963-66; pvt. practice Boulder, 1966-69; assoc. Arnold and Porter, Washington, 1969-72; communications counsel Teleprompter Corp., N.Y.C., 1973; v.p. Kalba-Bowen Assocs. Inc., communication cons., Cambridge, Mass., 1974-77, chmn. bd., 1977-80, sr. assoc., dir., 1980-82; pres. The Raven Group, Concord, Mass., 1986-97; trustee Pacific Telecomm. Coun., 1981-83, 86-93; mem. tech. adv. bd. Dept. Commerce, 1977-81; vis. scholar Yale U. Law, 1981-82; mem. program on info. resources policy Harvard U., 1986—; chmn. program com. Legal Symposium Telecom '87, Internat. Telecomm. Union, 1986-87; adj. prof. internat. law Tufts U., 1987-89; sr. scholar Annenberg Pub. Policy Ctr., Annenberg Sch. Comm., U. Pa., 1994-95. Author: Who Owns Information?, 1994; mem. editl. bd. Info. Soc.; editor: Toward a Law of Global Communications Network; contbg. editor Jour. Comm., 1980-90; contbr. articles to profl. jours. Bd. dirs. Nat. Pub. Radio, 1975-78; vice chmn. Colo. Dem. State Ctrl. Com., 1967-69; del. mem. permanent orgn. com. Dem. Nat. Conv., 1968; trustee, exec. com. Rensselaer Poly. Inst., 1980-89; trustee Telluride Inst., 1994-97. Recipient Alumni Achievement award Ga. Coll., 1980, Belva Lockwood award George Washington U., 1995; Rotary Found. fellow, 1950-51; Inaugural fellow Freedom Forum Media Studies Ctr., Columbia U., 1985. Mem. ABA (nat. conf. lawyers and scientists ABA/AAAS 1985-91, chmn. communications com. sci. and tech. sect. 1980-82, chmn. communications law div. 1982-84, mem. coun. sci. and tech. sect. 1981-85), Am. Polit. Sci. Assn., Internat. Inst. Communications, Internat Intercommunications Union (legal symposium organizer 1983, chmn. program com. 1987), Soc. Preservation of First Wives and First Husbands (pres.), Order of Coif, Valkyries, Phi Beta Kappa, Alpha Psi Omega, Pi Gamma Mu. Died Oct. 2, 1997.

BRANTINGHAM, CHARLES ROSS, podiatrist, ergonomics consultant; b. Long Beach, Calif., Feb. 14, 1917; m. Lila Carolyn Price; children: Paul Jeffery, John Price, Charles Ross, James William. Student, Long Beach City Coll., 1935; D in Podiatric Medicine, Calif. Coll. Podiatric Medicine, 1939, postdoctoral student surgery, 1947. Diplomate Am. Bd. Podiatric Pub. Health. Resident in podiatry Podiatry Clinics, San Francisco, 1939-40; pvt. practice podiatry Long Beach, 1946-56; podiatrist, dir. Podiatric Group, Long Beach, 1956-71, Los Alamitos (Calif.) Podiatric Group, 1971-90; chief podiatry sect., dept. orthopedics Los Alamitos Med. Ctr., 1983-90; ergonomics educator and cons. Nipomo, Calif., 1990-96; adj. prof. Calif. State U., Long Beach, 1972-89; vol. faculty Sch. Medicine U. So. Calif., L.A., 1965-94; cons. Specified Products Co., El Monte, Calif., 1969-91, Armstrong World Industries, Lancaster, Pa., 1983-91, Cert. Carpet Svcs., Lancaster, 1991-94. Contbr. chpts. to books, articles to profl. jours. Patentee in field. Bd. dirs. Diabetes Assn. So. Calif., L.A., 1964-67; cons., bd. dirs. Comprehensive Health Planning Assn., L.A., 1969-72; pub. improvement and adv. cons. Long Beach City Coun. and Office of Mayor, 1957-67. With USN, 1942-46, to lt. comdr. (ret.) USNR. Fellow Am. Assn. Hosp. Podiatrists (pres. 1958-60), Am. Pub. Health Assn. (sect. coun. pres. 1986, Steven Toth award 1982), Am. Soc. Podiatric Medicine, Internat. Acad. Standing and Walking Fitness (pres. 1963-96); mem. Am. Podiatric Med. Assn. (mem. nat. coun. 1953-55, bd. trustees 1957-59, exec. coun. 1957-59, Hall of Sci. award 1973), Calif. Podiatric Med. Assn. (life, pres. 1951), Assn. Mil. Surgeons U.S. (life.), Res. Officers Assn. U.S. (life), Exch. Club (local pres. 1948-49), Ind. Bus. Club (pres. 1958), Nat. Acad. Practice (Disting. Practioner Podiatric Medicine award 1983, Founders Honor Roll 1993). Republican. Mem. LDS Ch. Achievements include patents on special stress reducing floor surface, and ergonomic foot gear. Died Aug. 29, 1996.

BRANTLEY, OLIVER WILEY, retired lawyer; b. Troy, Ala., Oct. 30, 1915; s. James T. and Julia (Wiley) B.; m. Betty Jane Gaston, Jan. 20, 1936; children—Michael Wiley, Elizabeth Ayers (Mrs. William

M. Gresham), Grace Lamar (Mrs. William G. Anderson), Oliver Wiley (dec.). LL.B., U. Ala., 1939. Bar: Ala. 1939. Since practiced in Troy.; solicitor Pike County, 1947-74; Mem. Jud. Commn. Ala., 1972-74, chmn., 1973-74; chmn. Ala. Jud. Inquiry Commn., 1974-75; mem. bd. commrs. Ala. State Bar, 1952-79. Trustee Ala. State Bar Found., 1961-79; Bd. dirs. U. Ala. Law Sch. Found., 1966-80, pres., 1973-74. Served to lt. (j.g.) USNR, 1943-46. Fellow Am. Coll. Trial Lawyers; mem. ABA, Ala. Bar Assn., Pike County Bar Assn., Delta Kappa Epsilon, Phi Delta Phi, Farrah Order Jurisprudence, Farrah Law Soc. (chmn. 1972-73). Episcopalian. Died July 15, 1996.

BRATT, (JOHAN) BERTIL, publisher; b. Borås, Sweden, Jan. 7, 1932; m. Kerstin Mårtensson, Sept. 24, 1957 (div. 1982); children: Gunilla, Kristina; m. Vibeke Siegwarth, Aug. 17, 1983. M. Polit. Sci., Lund U., Sweden, 1959. Mng. dir. Bratt Internat. AB, Lund, 1963—. Died Mar. 17, 1997.

BRATTEN, THOMAS ARNOLD, lawyer, consulting engineer; b. Dayton, Ohio, Sept. 11, 1934; s. Samuel Arnold and Helen Jeannette (Wonderly) B.; m. Glenna Mary Bratten, Apr. 20, 1963; children: Charles, Christina, Thomas. ME, U. Cin., 1957; JD, Chase Coll., Cin., 1968. Bar: Ohio, 1968, Fla., 1968, U.S. Supreme Ct., 1972; cert. civil trial lawyer Fla. Bar, Nat. Bd. Trial Advocacy; Engr. in tng. Gen. Motors Corp., 1953-57, test engr., 1957-59, project engr., 1963-68, sr. project engr., 1968; design engr. Pratt & Whitney Aircraft, 1959-61; gen. mgr. Auto-Technia, Inc., 1961-63; with Pub. Defender's Office, 1968-75, chief trial atty., 1970-72, chief Capital div., 1972-75; ptnr. Campbell, Colbath, Kapner & Bratten, West Palm Beach, Fla., 1969-72; prin. Bratten & Harris, P.A., West Palm Beach, 1973-86; of counsel Easley, Massa & Willits, P.A., West Palm Beach, Fla., 1986-89; spl. master, 1973-85; faculty Nat. Inst. Trial Advocacy, U. Fla., 1978—; nat. panel arbitrators Am. Arbitration Assn., 1970-78. Mem. Palm Beach County Republican Exec. Com., 1971-80, county campaign chmn., 1974. Mem. Fla. Bar Assn. (exec. com. criminal law sect. 1978-81), Acad. Fla. Trial Lawyers, Assn. Trial Lawyers Am., Palm Beach County Bar Assn., Fla. Engring. Soc., Soc. Automotive Engrs., Nat. Acad. Forensic Engrs. (diplomate, v.p.), Pi Tau Sigma. Author: Criminal Lawyers Trial Notebook, 1977, Florida Criminal Procedure, 1981. Inventor, 6 U.S. and 9 fgn. patents.

BRAUDEL, FERNAND, historian, educator; b. Lumeville, France, Aug. 24, 1902; m. Paule Pradel, 1933; two daus. Ed. Lycée Voltaire, Paris, Sorbonne. Prof., Algiers, 1923-32; with Lycées Condorcet and Henri IV, Paris, 1932-35; mem. Faculty of Arts, Sao Paulo, 1935-38; with Ecole Pratique des Hautes Etudes, 1938-39, 1945—; prof. Coll. de France, 1949-72, hon. prof., 1972—; adminstrv. Maison des Sciences de l'Homme, 1963—; mem. Commn. des Archives diplomatiques, 1975—. Author: La Mediterranée et le monde mediterranéen à l'epoque de Philippe II, 1949, 2d edit., 1967, Vol. II, 1973; Navires et marchandises à l'entrée du port de Livourne 1547-1611 (with R. Romano), 1951; Le monde actuel, 1963; Ecrits sur l'historic, 1969; Civilisation materielle et capitalisme, Vol. 1, 1968, Vols. II, III, 1979; Histoire economique et sociale de la France, Vol. III, 1977; La Mediterranée, 1978. Dr.h.c., univs. Sao Paulo, Madrid, Brussels, Geneva, Oxford, Cologne, Warsaw, Florence, Padua, London, Hull, Leiden Norwich, Montreal, Yale U., St. Andrews U., U. Chgo., Cambridge U.

BRAY, OSCAR S., consulting engineer; b. Dover, N.J., Dec. 21, 1905; s. Oscar S. and Bertha (Janner) B.; m. Helen L. Shanley, Jan. 11, 1933; children—Helen Margaret (Mrs. William Allen Jeffers Jr.), Mary Elizabeth (Mrs. Edward Peters Womack). B.C.E., U. Cin., 1932. Surveyman D.L. & W. RR, Hoboken, N.J., 1923-27; constrn. supt. Nat. Park Service, Cold Spring, N.Y., 1934-35; field engr. Nat. Park Service, Boston and Salem, Mass., 1936-38; engr. Nat. Park Service, Washington, 1939-40; structural engr., asst. chief structural engr., project mgr. Jackson & Moreland, Boston, 1941-58; pres., chief engr. Jackson & Moreland Internat., Inc., 1959-68, Bray, Backenstoss, Inc. Ltd., Lynnfield, Mass., 1969-71; v.p. Camp Dresser & McKee Internat. Inc., Boston, 1972-76; cons. Camp Dresser & McKee Inc., 1977-94, sr. cons., 1980-91; lectr. Northeastern U.; guest lectr. U. Ill. Mem. Lynnfield Planning Bd., 1968-75, chmn., 1970; mem. Lynnfield Bd. Appeals, 1977-80, United Engr. Trustees Bd., 1973-83, pres., 1980-81. Served with AUS, 1933. Fellow ASCE (dir. 1964-66, pres. 1971-72), Am. Cons. Engrs. Coun.; mem. Tau Beta Pi, Chi Epsilon (nat. hon. mem.), Sigma Alpha Epsilon. Republican. Presbyterian. Home: Nashville Tenn. Died Jan. 13, 1994; interred Puritan Lawn Memorial Park, Peabody, MA.

BRAYMER, MARGUERITE ANNETTA, optical company executive; b. Camden, N.J., Mar. 25, 1911; d. Arthur Thomas and Annetta May (Sherman) Adams; m. Raymond A. Dodd, Sept. 12, 1931; 1 child, Peter R.; m. Lawrence Braymer, Mar. 25, 1950 (dec.). Student, South Jersey Law Sch., 1929-30. Freelance writer various mags., 1950-54; decorating editor Woman's Day mag., N.Y.C., 1944-53; founder, sec. Questar Corp., New Hope, Pa., 1950-65, pres., advt. dir., 1965-76, chmn., advt. dir., 1976-95; pres., founder Questar Libr. Sci. and Art, Inc., New Hope, 1980-95. Author America's Homemaking Book, 1957, America's Cookbook, 1963. Active Small Bus. Task Force, Washington, 1982-84; trustee New Sch. of Music, Phila., 1973-83, Bucks County Hist. Soc., 1990-95. Recipient Bus. Achievement award, Cen. Bucks C. of C., Bucks County, Pa., 1985. Democrat. Episcopalian. Avocations: gardening, walking, reading, music. Home: New Hope Pa. Died Oct. 27, 1995.

BRECKNER, JANE MCMILLIN, headmistress; b. St. Louis, Dec. 1, 1915; d. Walter Frazer and Margaret Jane (Scott) McM.; m. Kenneth Duus Breckner; 1 child, Marget Breckner Lippincott. Student, Northrup Collegiate Sch., Mpls., 1929-33, U. Minn., 1933-35. From tchr. to headmistress The Wilson Sch., St. Louis, 1945-75; v.p. Mo. chpt. Ednl. Confederation, St. Louis, 1970-71. Author: The Life And Times of My Father, W.F. McMillin, 1988, My Life, Wilson Sch. Mem. NEA (life), DAR (vice regent 1986), Conservationists, Colonial Dames XVII Century (treas., chaplain 1985), Wash. Family Descendants (registrar 1986-92), Jr. League (St. Louis), Colonial Dames of Am. (vice-regent), Daus. Am. Colonists (regent), Colonial Order of the Crown of Charlemagne in U.S.A., Nat. Soc. Magna Charta Dames, others. Prebyterian. Died Aug. 6, 1992.

BREESE, GERALD WILLIAM, sociology educator; b. Horseheads, N.Y., June 4, 1912; s. Bert Minard and Leona (Goodrich) B.; m. Alice Janette Bailey, July 4, 1937 (dec. Feb. 1972); children: Adele Embree, James Bert, Dana Sue Bailey, Brinda Sue Bailey; m. Alice Dodge Osborn Brown, Oct. 18, 1980. A.B., Ohio Wesleyan U., 1935; B.D., Yale U., 1938; Ph.D. (Marshall Field fellow), U. Chgo., 1947. Asst. prof. sociology, dean of men Pacific U., Forest Grove, Oreg., 1938-41; research planner Chgo. Plan Commn., 1942; instr. urban sociology Shrivenham Am. U., Eng., 1945, U. Chgo., 1947; sec. com. on housing research Social Sci. Research Council, 1947-49; asst. prof. sociology Princeton U., 1949-51, assoc. prof., 1951-59, prof., 1959-77, prof. emeritus, 1977-95; dir. bur. urban research, 1950-66; Fulbright prof. Am. U., Cairo, 1954-55; coordinator Ford Found., Delhi Regional Master Plan Cons. Team, New Delhi, 1957-58; vis. lectr. U. Natal, South Africa, summer 1963; vis. fellow Inst. Advanced Studies, Australian Nat. U., 1966; Mem. N.J. Resources Com., 1950-57. Author: Daytime Population of Central Business District of Chicago, 1949, Industrial Land Use in Burlington County, N.J, 1951, An Approach to Urban Planning, 1953, Regional Analysis Trenton-Camden Area, 1954, Industrial Site Selection, 1954, Accelerated Urban Growth in a Metropolitan Fringe Area, 1954, Urbanization in Old and New Countries, 1964, Urbanization in Newly Developing Countries, 1966, Impact of Large Installations on Nearby Areas, 1966, rev., 1968; Editor, contbr.: The City in Newly Developing Countries, 1969; editor: Urban Southeast Asia, 1973, Urban and Regional Planning in the Delhi-New Delhi Area, 1974, Princeton University Land 1752-1984, 1986, Footprints on Edgehill Street—Glimpses of Princeton Life 1684-1990, 1991. Served with AUS, 1942-45. Recipient Demobilization award Social Sci. Research Council, 1946-47. Mem. Am. Inst. Planners, Am., Eastern sociol. socs., Population Assn. Am., Phi Beta Kappa. Home: Hightstown N.J. Died Aug. 25, 1995.

BREITWIESER, CHARLES JOHN, engineer, educator; b. Colorado Springs, Colo., Sept. 23, 1910; s. Joseph Valentine and Ruth (Fowler) B.; m. Irene Louise Kellman, May 29, 1943; children—Diane Louise, Janice Lynn. B.S. in E.E, U. N.D., 1930, D.Sc. (hon.), 1949; student, Chgo. Central Sta. Inst., 1930- 31; M.S., Calif. Inst. Tech., 1933. Instr. engring. and math. U. N.D., 1931; elec. engr. Pub. Service No. Ill., 1930-31; engr. United Sound Products Corp., Los Angeles, 1933-34; cons. engr. and mfg. comml. research Pasadena, Calif., 1934-37; formed C.J. Breitwieser & Co., 1935, C.J. Breitwieser & Co. (co. merged with Bropar Engring. Co. of Los Angeles, forming Caldo Corp. of which became chief engr. and v.p.), 1937; sec.- treas. Conducto-Therm. Corp., Los Angeles, 1939; cons. engr. DeForest Labs.; and chief engr. DeForest Research; with Consol.-Vultee Aircraft Mfg. Co., chief engring. labs. and electronics, 1940-50; v.p. engring., gen. mgr. research and devel. div. Lear, Inc., Santa Monica, Calif., 1954-57; v.p., gen. mgr. Learcal div. Lear, Inc., 1955-57; pres. Metrolog Corp. (subs. Air Logistics Corp.), 1958-60; v.p. engring. and customer relations Air Logistics Corp., 1958-60; pres., chmn. bd. Dominion Devel. Corp., 1960-76; faculty Calif. Pacific U. Sch. Bus. Adminstrn., 1976-84; exec. v.p., gen. mgr. Cubic Corp., San Diego, 1961-73; also dir. Cubic Corp.; dir. Swan Electronics Corp., U.S. Elevator Corp., T Systems Inc., 1975—, Drip Irrigation Products, San Diego; dir. engring. P.R. Mallory & Co., Indpls., 1950-54; cons. engr. Los Angeles Police and Fire depts., 1932- 35; Cons. to Research and Devel. Bd.; staff Global Mgmt. Services, Inc., 1987—, Rancho Santa Fe. Author papers in field. Recipient Sioux award U. N.D., 1989. Fellow Inst. Radio Engrs., mem. Am. Inst. E.E. (mem. com. on electronics), AAAS, American Physics Soc., Nat. Aircraft Standards Com., Sigma Xi, Phi Delta Gamma. Patentee. Died March 13, 1997.

BRENNAN, JAMES THOMAS, radiologist; b. St. Louis, Jan. 12, 1916; s. James Thomas and Ellen Loretta (Hayes) B.; children by previous marriage: Martha Ellen, James Thomas; m. Elizabeth Bast Gagné, Aug. 23, 1975; stepchildren: William Roderick, Philip Bast, Elizabeth Lower. B.A. in Philosophy, U. Ill., 1939; M.D., U. Minn., 1943; M.A. (hon.), U. Pa., 1972. Diplomate Am. Bd. Radiology. Commd. 1st lt., M.C. AUS, 1943; advanced through grades to col. U.S. Army, 1959; intern St. Mary's Group Hosps., St. Louis, 1943; bn. surgeon 101st Airborne div., Europe, 1944-45; engaged in radiation hazard control and radiobiology research Los Alamos Labs., 1948-52; chief biophysics dept. Walter Reed Army Inst. Research, 1952-54; resident radiology Walter Reed Army Hosp., 1954-57; cons. radiol. def. to chief surgeon U.S. Army, Europe, 1957-60; chief radiation therapy Walter Reed Gen. Hosp., 1960-61; dir. Armed Forces Radiobiology Research Inst., 1961-66; ret., 1966; vis. lectr. radiology U. Pa. Med. Sch., Phila., 1966-67; Matthew J. Wilson prof. research radiology U. Pa. Med. Sch., 1967-78, prof. emeritus, 1978-92; cons. in field, 1965-92. Decorated Bronze Star, Legion of Merit, D.S.M. Mem. Radiol. Soc. N.Am., AMA, AAUP, AAAS. Home: Ambler Pa. Died July 5, 1992.

BRENNAN, WILLIAM JOSEPH, JR., retired United States supreme court justice; b. Newark, Apr. 25, 1906; s. William J. and Agnes (McDermott) B.; m. Marjorie Leonard, May 5, 1928 (dec.); children—William Joseph, Hugh Leonard, Nancy; m. Mary Fowler, Mar. 9, 1983. B.S., U. Pa., 1928; LL.B., Harvard, 1931, LL.D. (hon.), 1968; LL.D. (hon.), U. Pa., 1957, Wesleyan U., 1957, St. Johns U., 1957, Rutgers U., 1958, Jewish Theol. Sem. Am., 1964, George Washington U., 1965, U. Notre Dame, 1968, Yale U., 1987, Ohio State U., 1987, Glasgow U., 1989; LLD (hon.), Univ. Coll. Dublin in N.Am., 1990; LLB (hon.), Princeton U., 1986, Columbia U., 1986, Brandeis U., 1986, N.Y. Law Sch., 1986, John Marshall Law Sch., 1986; D Jud. Sci. (hon.), Suffolk U., 1956; DCL (hon.), NYU, 1957, Colgate U., 1957; LittD, U. Miami, 1991. Bar: N.J. bar 1931. Practiced Newark, 1931-49; mem. firm Pitney, Hardin, Ward & Brennan; superior ct. judge, 1949-50, appellate div. judge, 1950-52; justice Supreme Ct. N.J., 1952-56; assoc. justice U.S. Supreme Ct., 1956-90. Served to col. with gen. staff corps AUS, World War II. Decorated Legion of Merit, Medal of Freedom Pres. Clinton, 1993, recipient medal ABA, 1994. Died July 24, 1997.

BRENT, ANDREW JACKSON, lawyer; b. Richmond, Va., Nov. 25, 1918; s. Andrew Jackson and Gussie Millhiser (Reinhardt) B.; m. Virginia Armistead McGuire, Nov. 1, 1941; children: Virginia Armistead (Mrs. Roger P. Hailes), Roberta Harper Peek, Elizabeth Marshall McGuire (Mrs. Peter F. Nostrand), Andrew Mason, Maria Meade (Mrs. W. Brady Jones). LLB, U. Va., 1941; LHD (hon.), Mary Baldwin Coll. Bar: Va. 1940. Pvt. practice Richmond, 1946—; ptnr. Christian, Barton, Epps, Brent & Chappell, 1949—; gen. counsel, sec., dir. Media Gen., Inc.; past chmn., dir. Cen. Va. Ednl. TV Corp.; dir. Denver Post Corp., Richmond Newspapers, Inc., Piedmont Pub. Co., Inc., Winston-Salem, N.C., Tribune Co., Tampa, Fla.; bd. dirs. Productora Nacional de Papel Destintado S.A. de C.V., Mexico City, Fiber-Lam Inc., Garden State Newspapers, Inc. Past pres., bd. dirs. Richmond Area Community Coun., 1963-66; bd. dirs., trustee, former chmn. Richmond Eye and Ear Hosp.; gen. counsel, sec. Richmond Met. Authority; bd. dirs., past chmn. Va. Pub. Telecommunications Coun.; past sec., visitor Va. Commonwealth U.; past pres., trustee Va. Law Found.; life trustee, pres. Collegiate Schs., Va. Commonwealth U. Fund; past chmn., trustee emeritus Mary Baldwin Coll; trustee Naval Intelligence Found.; former pres., trustee George Mason Meml. Soc.; pres., gov. Capital Area Assembly; warden, vestryman Episcopal Ch. Lt. comdr. USNR, 1941-46. Recipient Annual Good Govt. award Richmond First Club, 1965, Disting. Svc. award Va. State C. of C., 1981, Community Svc. award 1989. Fellow ABA, Va. Law Found.; mem. Va. Bar Assn., Richmond Bar Assn., Am. Judicature Soc., SAR of Va., Met. Richmond C. of C. (past pres., dir.), Commonwealth Club (past pres., gov.), Country Club of Va., Downtown Club (past pres., dir.), Omicron Delta Kappa, Phi Alpha Delta, Phi Kappa Psi, Pi Delta Epsilon.

BRESLIN, JAMES E. B., English language educator; b. Bklyn., Dec. 12, 1935; s. James T. and Marion M. (Clancy) B.; m. Glenna Fink, Nov. 23, 1962 (dec. 1980); children: Jennifer, Susannah; m. Ramsay Bell, May 23, 1981. BA, Bklyn. Coll., 1957; MA, U. N.C., 1959; PhD, U. Minn., 1963. Instr. U. N.C., Chapel Hill, 1959, U. Minn., Mpls., 1959-62; asst. then assoc. prof. English U. Calif., Berkeley, 1964-78, prof., 1978-96. Author: William Carlos Williams, An American Artist, 1970, From Modern to Contmeporary: American Poetry, 1945-65, 1984, Something to Say--William Carlos Williams and Younger Poets, 1985. NEH fellow, 1977, Guggenheim Found. fellow, 1986; Am. Philos. Soc. travel grantee, 1986. Mem. Modern Language Assn. Avocation: running. Home: Berkeley Calif. Died Jan. 6, 1996.

BRETT, (PETER) JEREMY (WILLIAM HUGGINS), actor; b. Nov. 3, 1935; s. H.W. and Elizabeth Huggins; m. 1958 (divorced); 1 son; m. 1978; 1 son. Student, Central Sch. of Drama, Eton, Eng. With Nat. Theatre, 1967-71. Performances include (plays) As You Like It,

Love's Labour's Lost, Hedda Gabler, The Merchant of Venice, Macrune's Guevara, Voyage round my Father, Haymarket, Eng., 1972, Design for Living, Phoenix, 1973-74, The Way of the World, Stratford, Ont., 1976, The Tempest, Toronto, 1982, narrator Song, Martha Graham ballet, N.Y.C., 1985, Aren't We All, Broadway, 1985; (films) War and Peace, 1955, My Fair Lady, 1965; (TV) Rebecca, 1978, On Approval, 1980, The Good Soldier, 1981, Macbeth the Last Visitor, 1982, The Barretts of Wimpole Street, 1982, William Pitt the Younger, 1983, The Adventures of Sherlock Holmes, 1984, The Return of Sherlock Holmes, 1986, Florence Nightingale, 1986, Deceptions, 1986, The Secret of Sherlock Holmes, 1989. Club: Woodmen of Arden. Avocation: archery. Home: Beverly Hills Calif. Died Sept. 12, 1995.

BREWER, JOHN ISAAC, obstetrician, gynecologist; b. Milford, Ill., Oct. 9, 1903; s. John H. and Edna (Ishler) B.; widowed, Jan. 1985, ; m. Ruth Russell, June 2, 1928; 1 child, John Vernon. BS, U. Chgo., 1925, MD, 1928, PhD, 1935; student, Bradley U., 1921-24. Diplomate Am. Bd. Ob-Gyn. Instr. to assoc. prof. ob-gyn Northwestern U., Chgo., 1930-48, prof. ob-gyn, 1948-74, prof. emeritus and dept. chmn. ob-gyn, 1974-76; investigator cancer Northwestern U. Sch. Medicine, 1935—; mem. Joint Commn. on Accreditation of Hosps., Chgo., 1959-74, chmn. bd. 1963. Author: Textbook of Gynecology 4th edit., 1967; editor-in-chief Am. Jour. Ob-Gyn, 1959—. Served to lt. col. USAF, 1942-45. Decorated Legion of Merit; named to Sr. Citizen Hall of Fame City of Chgo., Bradley U. Fellow Royal Coll. Obstetricians and Gynecologists; mem. AMA, ACS, Ill. Med. Soc., Chgo. Med. Soc., Am. Bd. Ob-Gyn (bd. dirs. 1974—), Ill. Cancer Soc. (trustee, 1959-74, pres. 1963), Am. Coll. Obstetricians and Gynecologists (pres. 1959), Am. Gynecol. Soc. (pres. 1965), Am. Assn. Obstetricians and Gynecologists (pres. 1969), Am. Gynecol. Club (pres. 1971), Cen. Assn. Obstetrician and Gynecologists (pres. 1952), Chgo. Gynecol. Soc. (past pres., regent Am. Coll. Surgeons 1962-71, Am. Anatomists Assn., Chgo. Pathology Soc., Soc. Pelvic Surgeons, Sigma Xi. Republican. Congregationalist. Club: Flossmoor (Ill.) Country. Avocation: sports. Died January 15, 1997.

BRICKER, SEYMOUR (MURRAY), lawyer; b. N.Y.C., May 19, 1924; s. Harry and May (Glick) B.; m. Darlene M. Mohilef, July 29, 1951 (dec. Mar. 1987); children: Andrea Helene, Phillip Alan, Julie Ellen. Student, U. Okla., 1943-44; AB, U. Calif., Los Angeles, 1947; LLB, U. So. Calif., 1950. Bar: Calif. 1951. Atty. Calif. Jud. Coun., 1951-52; with legal dept. Universal Pictures, 1952-56; ptnr. Cohen & Bricker, 1956-68, Kaplan, Livingston, Goodwin, Berkowitz & Selvin, 1968-81, Mitchell, Silberberg & Knupp, 1982-96; exec. v.p. Ed Friendly Prodns. Inc.; pres. Friendly/Bricker Prodns. Bd. dirs. Acad. TV Arts and Scis. Found. Served with inf. AUS, 1943-46. Fellow ABA Found.; mem. ABA (mem. coun. patent, trademark and copyright sect., past chmn., copyright divsn., past chmn. forum com. on entertainment and sports industries, mem. com. on Bicentennial program), L.A. Copyright Soc. (past pres.), Copyright Soc. U.S. (trustee), Calif. Copyright Conf. (past pres.), Adv. Com. for Comm./Entertainment. Died July 26, 1996.

BRICKFIELD, CYRIL FRANCIS, lawyer, association executive; b. Bklyn., Jan. 30, 1919; m. Ann Jacobsen, Aug. 4, 1951; children: Ann, Edmund Cyril. LLB, Fordham U., 1948; LLM, George Washington U., 1953, SJD, 1957, MS, 1965. Bar: N.Y. 1949, D.C. 1952. Law clk. to chief judge N.Y. Ct. Appeals, 1949-51; counsel judiciary com. U.S. Ho. of Reps., 1951-61; gen. counsel VA, 1961-63, chief benefits dir., 1963-65, dep. adminstr., 1965-67; exec. dir. Am. Assn. Ret. Persons,, 1967-69, 77-87; trustee Am. Assn. Ret. Persons Investment Trusts; hon. pres., spl. counsel Am. Assn. Ret. Persons, 1987-97; chmn. Am. Assn. Ret. Persons Fed. Credit Union, 1987-90, trustee, 1987-90; pres. Fed. Bar Bldg. Corp., 1991-97; pvt. practice law, 1969-75; ptnr. Miller, Singer, Michaelson, Brickfield & Raives, 1975-77; del. U.S. Internat. Treaty Convs. on Patents, Trademarks, Copywrights, 1958-61; pres. Nat. Sr. Citizens Law Center, 1977-79; mem. adv. council White House Conf. on Aging, 1981; pres. Corp. for Older Americans, 1981-97; chmn. Leadership Conf. of Aging Orgns., 1980, 83, 86; U.S. del. UN World Assembly on Aging, 1982; bd. councillors U. So. Calif., 1983-97. Author govt. reports. Trustee Suburban Hosp., Bethesda, Md., 1968-79, 87-93; Maj., pilot USAAF, ETO. Decorated Air medal with 9 oak leaf clusters. Mem. ABA, Am. Assn. Ret. Persons (hon. pres. 1987-97), FBA (pres. 1968, chmn. gen. counsels com., jud. selection com., pres. D.C. chpt.; del. ABA), Bklyn. Bar Assn., Fed. Bar Bldg. Corp. (pres. 1991-97), Bethesda Country Club (pres. 1967, 69), KC, Delta Theta Phi. Died Mar. 14, 1997.

BRIDGES, LLOYD, actor; b. San Leandro, Calif., Jan. 15, 1913; s. Lloyd and Harriet (Brown) B.; m. Dorothy Bridges; children: Beau, Jeff, Lucinda. BA, UCLA. Appeared in stock cos., coll. dramatic prodns., motion pictures, Broadway; motion pictures Miss Susie Slagle's, 1946, Abilene Town, 1945, Canyon Passage, 1946, Ramrod, Trouble with Women, 1947, The Hideout, 1949, Calamity Jane and Sam Bass, 1949, Trapped, 1949, Try and Get Me, 1950, Colt 45, 1950, Rocketship XM, 1950, Whistle at Eaton Falls, 1951, Walk in the Sun, Home of the Brave, White Tower, Plymouth Adventure, 1952, High Noon, 1952, Last of the Comanches, 1953, Tall Texan, 1953, Kid from Left Field, 1953, City of Bad Men, 1953, Limping Man, Pride of the Blue Grass, 1954, Apache Woman, 1955, Wichita, 1955, The Rainmaker, 1958, The Goddess, 1959, Wetbacks, Daring Game, 1968, Deadly Game, 1976, Happy Ending, Silent Night, Holy Night, The Fifth Musketeer, 1979, Airplane, 1980, Airplane II, 1983, The Winter People, 1985, Tucker, 1988, Cousins, 1989, Joe vs. the Volcano, 1990, Hot Shots!, 1991, Honey, I Blew Up The Kid, 1991, Hot Shots! Part Deux, 1993, Blown Away, 1994; TV series Sea Hunt, 1957-61, San Francisco Internat, NBC, Joe Forrester; TV mini-series Roots, 1977, East of Eden, 1981, Nothing Lasts Forever, 1995, The Other Woman, 1995; TV film Do You Take This Stranger?, 1971, Haunts of the Very Rich, 1972, Trouble Comes to Town, 1973, Death Race, 1973, Stowaway to the Moon, 1975, Telethon, 1977, The Great Wallendas, 1978, The Critical List, 1978, Disaster on the Coastliner, 1979, Moviola: This Year's Blonde, 1980, John Steinbeck's East of Eaden, 1981, The Blue and the Gray, 1982, Grace Kelly, 1983, George Washington, 1984, North and South, Book II, 1986, The Devil's Odds, 1987, Tucker, 1987, Winter People, 1987, Cross of Fire, 1989, Leona Helmsley: The Queen of Mean, 1990, Secret Sins of the Father, 1993; TV series The Lloyd Bridges Show, The Loner, San Francisco Airport, Joe Forrester, Paper Dolls, Capital News, 1990, Hart's of the West, 1993. Died March 1998.

BRIMACOMBE, JAMES KEITH, metallurgical engineering educator, researcher, consultant; b. Windsor, N.S., Can., Dec. 7, 1943; s. Geoffrey Alan and Mary Jean (MacDonald) B.; m. Margaret Elaine Rutter, Feb. 6, 1970; children: Kathryn Margaret, Jane Margaret. B of Applied Sci. with honors, U. B.C., 1966; PhD, U. London, 1970, DSc in Engring., 1986; D in Engring. (hon.), Colo. Sch. Mines, 1994. Registered profl. engr., B.C. Asst. prof. metall. engring. U. B.C., Vancouver, Can., 1970-74, assoc. prof., 1974-79, prof., 1979-80, Stelco prof., 1980-85, Stelco/Nat. Scis. and Engring. Rsch. Coun. Can. prof., 1985-91; Alcan chair in materials process engring.; dir. Ctr. for Metall. Process Engring. U. B.C., Vancouver, Can., 1985—; Arnold Markey lectr. Steel Bar Mill Assn., 1981; retained cons. Hatch Assocs., Toronto, 1984-89; cons. over 60 metall. cos. Author: Continuous Casting, vol. II, 1984, The Mathematical and Physical Modeling of Primary Metals Processing Operations, 1988; contbr. numerous articles to profl. jours.; patentee in field. Capt. Can. Air Force, 1961-70. Recipient B.C. Sci. and Engring. Gold medal Sci. Coun. B.C., 1985, Ernest C. Manning Prin. award The Manning Trust, 1987, Izaak Walton Killam Meml. prize in engring. The Can. Coun., 1989, Corp. Higher Edn. Forum award 1989, Commemorative medal for 125th Anniversary of Can. Confedn., numerous awards for publs., Can. Gold medal for sci. and engring., 1997; Can. Commonwealth fellow Nat. Scis. and Engring. Rsch. Coun. Can., 1980; Office Order of Can. Fellow Can. Inst. Mining, Metallurgy and Petroleum Engrs., Can. Acad. of Engring., Royal Soc. Can., Minerals, Metals and Materials Soc. (founding chmn. extraction and processing divsn. 1989-92, extractive metallurgy lectr. 1989, pres. 1993-94); mem. AIME (bd. trustees 1992—, pres-elect designate, Disting. Svc. award), NAE (fgn. assoc.), Metall. Soc. of Can. Inst. Mining and Metallurgy (pres. 1985-86, Alcan award 1988), Iron and Steel Soc. (disting. mem., bd. dirs. 1989-97, Howe Meml. Lectr. 1993, pres. 1995-96), Inst. Materials, Am. Soc. Metals (now ASM Internat., Can. Coun. lectureship 1986, Campbell Meml. lectr. 1996), Iron and Steel Inst. Japan, United Engring. Trust (bd. trustees), Sigma Tau Xi (U. B.C. hon. frat.). Roman Catholic. Avocations: travel, jogging, photography. Died Dec. 16, 1997.

BRINKMAN, GABRIEL, former college president; b. Indpls., Dec. 3, 1924; s. John Henry and Mary Frances (Bartsch) B. Student, Our Lady of Angels Sem., 1943-47, St. Joseph Sem., 1947-51; Ph.D. in Sociology, Cath. U. Am., 1957. Instr. ethics Our Lady of Angels Sem., Cleve., 1955-57; mem. faculty dept. sociology Quincy (Ill.) Coll., 1957-63, prof. sociology, 1970-77, 84-85, pres. coll., 1963-70, 77-83; dir. Franciscan Herald Press, Chgo., 1986—. Author: Social Thought of John de Lugo, 1957. Roman Catholic. DIED 12/31/96. .

BROADHURST, AUSTIN, retired lawyer; b. Springfield, Mass., Nov. 27, 1917; s. Edward Thomas and Bertha Louisa (Bassett) B.; m. Deborah Lowell, Sept. 13, 1942; children—Austin Jr., Martha Broadhurst Lowery., James B., Susan Broadhurst Taylor. A.B., Williams Coll., 1938; LL.B., Harvard U., 1942. Bar: Mass. 1946, U.S. Dist. Ct. Mass. 1950, U.S. Ct. Appeals (1st cir.) 1953. Assoc. Ely, Bartlett, Brown & Proctor, Boston, 1946-51; ptnr. Gaston & Snow, Boston, 1951-92; mng. ptnr. Gaston Snow & Ely Bartlett, Boston, 1983-86, Hutchins & Wheeler, Boston, 1991-92; trustee, v.p. Winchester Savs. Bank, Mass. Chmn. Winchester Sch. Com., 1971-72; trustee Mus. Sci., Boston, Bentley Coll., Waltham, Mass. Served to lt. comdr., USNR, 1942-46. Mem. ABA, Boston Bar Assn. (mem. council 1955-58). Episcopalian. Avocations: tennis, bridge, hiking. DIED 05/14/96. .

BROCHES, ARON, international lawyer, arbitrator; b. Amsterdam, Netherlands, Mar. 22, 1914; s. Abraham and Chaja (Person) B.; m. Catherina J. Pothast, May 2, 1939 (dec. Sept. 1982); children: Ida Alexandra, Paul Elias. LLM, U. Amsterdam, 1936, LLD, 1939; JD, Fordham U., 1942. Legal adviser Netherlands Embassy, also Netherlands Econ. Mission, Washington and N.Y.C., 1942-46; with World Bank, 1946-79, gen. counsel, 1959-79, v.p., 1972-79, mem. pres.'s coun., 1965-79; sec. gen. Internat. Centre for Settlement Investment Disputes, 1967-80, mem. panel arbitrators, 1980—; mem. Internat. Panel Arbitrators, Am. Arbitration Assn.; mem. panels arbitration ctrs. Asian-African Legal Consultative Com., Kuala Lumpur and Cairo; sec. Netherlands del. UN Monetary and Fin. Conf., Bretton Woods, N.H., 1944; sec., legal adviser Netherlands del. inaugural meeting bd. govs. IMF and IBRD, Savannah, Ga., 1946; chief Internat. Bank gen. survey mission, Nigeria, 1953-54; mem. Internat. Council for Comml. Arbitration, 1971—; lectr. Acad. Internat. Law, The Hague, 1959, 72. Author: Commentary on UNCITRAL Model Law on Internat. Comml. Arbitration, 1990; contbr. articles to profl. jours. Trustee Internat. Legal Ctr., 1970-77. Decorated Comdr. Order Orange Nassau Queen of the Netherlands, 1979. Mem. Internat. Law Assn., Am. Soc. Internat. Law, Netherlands Soc. Internat. Law. Avocation: music. Died Sept. 9, 1997.

BROCK, PAUL WARRINGTON, lawyer; b. Mobile, Ala., Feb. 23, 1928; s. Glen Porter and Esther (Goodwin) B.; m. Grace Leigh Blasingame, Sept. 4, 1948 (dec. June 1960); children—Paul W., Bette Leigh, Valerie Grace; m. Louise Morris Shearer, July 6, 1962; children—Louise Shearer, Richard Goodwin. Student, Ala. Poly. Inst., 1944; B.S., U. Ala., 1948, J.D., 1950. Bar: Ala. 1950. Practiced in Mobile, 1953—; mem. Hand, Arendall & Bedsole, 1953-56, Hand, Arendall, Bedsole, Greaves & Johnston, 1956-95, hand, Arendall, L.L.C., 1996—. Served to 2d lt. USAF, 1952-53. Recipient Nat. Balfour award Sigma Chi, 1946-47. Mem. ABA, Internat. Assn. Ins. and Def. Counsel, Assn. Def. Trial Attys., Ala. Bar Assn., Mobile Bar Assn., Am. Coll. Trial Lawyers, Am. Bar Found., Ala. Def. Lawyers Assn. (past pres.), Def. Rsch. Inst. (past pres.), Nat. Assn. R.R. Trial Counsel, Mobile Am. Inn of Ct. (past pres.), Omicron Delta Kappa, Beta Gamma Sigma. Republican. Episcopalian.

BRODERICK, FRANCIS LYONS, historian, educator, lawyer; b. N.Y.C., Sept. 13, 1922; s. Joseph Aloysius and Mary (Lyons) B.; m. Barbara Baldridge, June 12, 1950; children: Thomas, Joseph, James, Ann. Grad., Phillips Acad., Andover, Mass., 1939; AB with high honors, Princeton U., 1943; MA in History, Harvard U., 1947; PhD in History Am. Civilization, Harvard, 1955; JD, Boston Coll., 1989; LLD, Merrimack Coll., 1969; LHD, St. Anselm Coll., 1987. Instr. history Princeton, 1945-46, State U. Ia., 1948-50, Phillips Exeter Acad., 1951-63; dir. Peace Corps, Ghana, 1964-66; dean Lawrence and Downer Colls.; also Gordon R. Clapp prof. Am. studies Lawrence U., Appleton, Wis., 1966-68; chancellor U. Mass., Boston, 1968-72; Commonwealth prof. U. Mass., 1972-87, emeritus, 1988-92; staff N.H. Legal Assistance, Portsmouth, N.H., 1989-91. Author: W.E.B. DuBois: Negro Leader in a Time of Crisis, 1959, Right Reverend New Dealer: John A Ryan, 1963, The Origins of the Constitution, 1964, (with August Meier) Negro Protest Thought in the Twentieth Century, 1966, Reconstruction and the American Negro, 1969, Progressivism at Risk, 1989; Editor: (John Tracy Ellis) The Life of James Cardinal Gibbons, 1963 (Nat. Cath. Book award 1964). trustee St. Anselm Coll. Served to 1st lt. USAAF, 1943-45. Woodrow Wilson fellow, 1945-46. Mem. Am. Cath. Hist. Assn. (pres. 1968), Mass. Hist. Soc. Home: Stratham N.H. Died June 22, 1992.

BRODHEAD, GEORGE MILTON, lawyer; b. Phila., May 23, 1904; s. George M. and Clara (Chaplain) B.; m. Pauline W. Hand, Sept. 13, 1934; children: Anne Foster Brodhead Zehner, Richard Chaplain. A.B., Wesleyan U., Middletown, Conn., 1926; LL.B., U. Pa., 1930. Bar: Pa. 1930. Tchr. Choate Sch., 1926-27; since practiced in Phila.; asso. Rawle & Henderson, 1930-43, partner, 1943-88, ret., 1988. Bd. dirs. Barra Found., Claneil Found., Stephen Watchorn Found.; past dir. Germantown Boys Club. Mem. SR (pres. Pa. soc. 1971-73), Mil. Order Loyal Legion, Soc. War 1812 (past v.p.), Colonial Soc. Pa. (past councillor), Am., Pa., Phila. bar assns., Soc. Sons St. George, Soc. Colonial Wars, Holland Soc. of N.Y., Penn Club, Phi Beta Kappa, Psi Upsilon, Phi Delta Phi. Presbyn. Clubs: Phila. Cricket (Phila.), Union League (Phila.) (pres. 1969-70), Lawyers (Phila.) (pres. 1967-68).

BRONFMAN, PETER FREDERICK, independent investor; b. Montreal, Que., Can., Oct. 2, 1929; s. Allan and Lucy (Bilsky) B.; m. Diane Feldman; m. Theodora Reitsma (div.); children—Linda, Bruce, Brenda; m. Lynda Hamilton. Student, Lawrenceville Sch., 1948; B.A., Yale U., 1952. Sr. chmn. The Edper Group Ltd., Toronto. Home: Toronto Can Deceased.

BROOK, BARRY S., musicologist, foundation administrator. BSS, CUNY, 1939; MA, Columbia U., 1942; Doctor de l'Université, U. Paris, 1959; PhD (Hon.), U. Adelaide, 1974. Fellow CUNY, 1940-42; from instr. to prof. Queens Coll., 1945-89; lectr. Bklyn. Coll., 1945-46; prof. Hunter Coll., CUNY, 1954, exec. officer, prof., 1967-89, disting. prof., 1986-89, disting.

prof. emeritus, dir. Ctr. for Music Rsch. and Documentation, 1989—; adj. prof. Inst. Musicology U. Paris., 1967-68; disting. vis. prof. Eastman Sch. Music U. Rochester, 1973; centenary vis. prof. U. Adelaide, 1974; vis. faculty Aspen Music Sch., 1974; head faculty The Juilliard Sch., 1977-87; cons. in field. Author: (book) La Symphonie Française dans la Seconde Moitié du XVIII Siècle, 1962, The Breikopf Thematic Catalogue, 1762-1787, 1966; editor: Musicology and the Computer: Musicology 1960-2000, 1970, Thematic Catalogues in Music: An Annotated Bibliography, 1972, 2d edit. (with Marvin Paymes), 1997, Giovanni Battista Pergolesi Complete Wotks/Opere Complete, The Symphony 1720-1840: A Comprehensive Collection of Full Scores in Sixty Vols., 1979-85, French Opera in the 17th and 18th Centuries; 75 Vols. Comprising About 100 Full Scores in Facsimile, 1984—, (with Bruce MacIntyre) Joseph Haydn Streich-Trios1 Folge, 1986; contbr. numerous articles to jours. in field. Capt. USAF, 1942-45. Recipient Ford Found. fellow, 1954-55, Guggenheim fellow, 1961-62, 66-67; Fulbright Rsch. scholar, 1958-59; Disting. Flying Cross, Air Medal with 3 Oak Leaf Clusters, Certificate of Valor, Dent medal Royal Music Assn., 1965, Chevalier in the Order of Arts and Letters French Govt., 1972. Fellow Royal Swedish Acad. Music; mem. ASCAP, Am. Musicological Soc. (chmn. Greater N.Y. chpt. 1964-66, chmn. adv. com. on grad. standards 1965-67, mem. coun. 1959-61, 73-76, steering com. 1974-76, bd. dirs. 1975-77, editl. bd. jour. 1989-91), Am. Soc. for Info. Science (exec. com. spl. interest group-arts and the humanities 1968-70), Internat. Assn. Music Libraries, Archives, and Documentation Ctrs. (mem. coun. 1969—, v.p. 1974-77, pres. 1977-80), Internat. Music Coun./UNESCO (exec. com. 1978-84, v.p. 1980-82, pres. 1982-84), Rsch. Ctr. for Musical Iconography (dir. 1972—), Répertoire Internat. d'Iconographie Musicale (pres. commn. internat. mixte 1970—), Répertoire Internat. de Littérature Musicale (pres. commn. internat. mixte 1966—), UMH: The Universe of Music (pres. bd. dirs., editor-in-chief). Died Dec. 12, 1998.

BROPHY, BRIGID, writer; b. London, June 12, 1929; d. John and Charis Weare (Grundy) B.; m. Sir. Michael Levey, June 12, 1954; 1 child, Kate. Student, U. Oxford, 1947-48. Died August 7, 1995.

BROPHY, ROBERT F., seafood company executive. Pres. Icicle Seafoods, Inc. Died Dec. 14, 1994. Home: Seattle Wash.

BROUGHTON, CARL L(OUIS), food company executive; b. Marietta, Ohio, June 22, 1910; s. John H. and Josephine B. (Barnhart) B.; m. Elizabeth Sugden, Aug. 23, 1936; children—Ruth, Mary George W. LL.D. (hon.), Marietta Coll., 1975. Co-founder, pres. Broughton Foods Co., Marietta, 1933-75, chmn. bd., 1975-89, chmn. exec. com., 1989—; chmn. bd. Peoples Bancorp, Inc., Marietta, 1977-91, dir., 1947-94; past mem. exec. com., dir. Marmac Corp., Parkersburg, W.Va. Trustee Marietta Coll., 1950-90, trustee emeritus, 1990—, chmn. bd., 1966-70; trustee Marietta Meml. Hosp., 1946-77, chmn. bd., 1977-78; mem. adv. bd. Ohio Agrl. R & D Center, Agrl. Coll., Ohio State U., until 1989. Served to lt. USNR, 1943-46. Recipient Outstanding Citizens award Marietta Jaycees, 1965, award of merit Ohio State U. Dept. Dairy Tech., 1969, George Washington award of excellence Freedoms Found. Valley Forge, 1988. Mem. W.Va. Dairy Products Assn. (pres. 1958-59, bd. dirs., award for 45 yrs. svc. to dairy industry 1978), Ohio C. of C. (bd. dirs. 1972-84), Marietta Area C. of C. (pres. 1955, bd. dirs. 1953-63, Bus. Man of Yr. award 1989), Ohio Masons (Rufus Putnam Disting. Svc. award 1993), Ohio Thoroughbred Breeders Assn. (pres. 1969-70), Rotary (Marietta pres. 1948-49), Elks. Republican. Died May 10, 1996.

BROWN, BARTON, retired automotive company executive; b. Glen Cove, N.Y., Sept. 21, 1924; s. Andrew Malcolm and Julia Marie (terKuile) B.; m. Priscilla Thomason, May 9, 1953; children—Barbara Kerr Brown Swafford, Suzanne Goree Brown Irwin. S.B., S.M., MIT, 1950. Various positions parent co. and subs. Gen. Motors Corp., 1950-65; mng. dir. Continental div. Gen. Motors Corp., Antwerp, Belgium, 1965-68; dir. staff ops. overseas div. Gen. Motors Corp., N.Y.C., 1968-78; dep. dir. Latin Am. div. Gen. Motors Corp., Detroit, 1978-80, exec. dir. Asia div., 1980-83, v.p., 1983-89. Served as sgt. USAF, 1943-46. Republican. Avocations: sailing; photography; travel. Home: Austin Tex. Died Aug. 4, 1995.

BROWN, BEATRICE, symphony conductor; b. Leeds, Eng., May 17, 1917; came to U.S., 1921, naturalized, 1927; d. Abraham and Sarah (Levinson) B.; m. Morris Rothenberg, Jan. 29, 1961. BA, Hunter Coll., 1937; MA, N.Y.U., 1939. Condr. Chamber Music Assocs., N.Y.C., 1950-53; music dir., condr. Scranton (Pa.) Philharm. Orch., 1963-70, NE Pa. Philharm., 1970-95, Ridgefield (Conn.) Symphony Orch., 1969-95, Western Conn. Symphony Orch., Danbury, 1981-82, Housatonic Chamber Orch., 1982-83; condr. N.Y., N.J., Conn. opera cos.; TV appearances; lectr.; violist symphony orchs., 1944-97, Chamber Music Group, Musique Vivante, Am. Symphony Orch., N.Y. Pops Orch., 1979-97; guest conductor, Brazil, 1989; instr. music Hunter Coll., 1937-43; tchr. music N.Y.C. Pub. Schs., 1944-61; adj. asst. prof. Lehman Coll., 1972-74; tchr. music Bronx High Sch. Sci., N.Y.C., 1970-79; music dir. Conn. Berkshire Music Ctr. scholar, 1948-49; artistic dir. Keeler Tavern Chamber Music Series, 1990-95. Fulbright grantee, 1953-55, Martha Baird Rockefeller grantee, 1957-59, Peace award UN, 1980, Wellington award, 1981; named to Hunter Coll. Hall of Fame, 1972; named One of 100 Disting. Women in Conn., 1976, One of 5 outstanding Women in Ridgefield, Conn., 1979. Mem. Conductors' Guild, Phi Beta Kappa. Died Feb. 11, 1997. Home: Norwalk Conn.

BROWN, FREDERICK HAROLD, insurance company executive; b. Troy, N.Y., Apr. 21, 1927; s. Harold Lamphere and Maida Adelaide (Wooden) B.; m. Mary Lee Lamar, Aug. 12, 1950; children: Deborah Elaine Wright, Frederick Harold. BSME, Bucknell U., 1949. Registered profl. engr., Wis., Pa. With CIGNA and Subs., Phila., 1949-73, from asst. v.p. to v.p., 1970-73; founder, pres., CEO Jersey/Internat. Group, Cherry Hill, N.J., 1973-84; pres., CEO Admiral Ins. Co. subs. W.R. Berkeley Corp., Greenwich, Conn., 1979-84; sr. v.p. W.R. Berkley Corp., Greenwich, 1984-87; from chmn. bd., pres., CEO to chmn. Investors Ins. Holding Corp. and all subs., 1987-94, dir., 1987-95; chmn., pres., treas. Brown/Wright Risk Cons. Inc., Ocean City, N.J.; cons. various ins. cos. Contbr. articles to profl. jours. Mem. Phila. Fire Prevention Com., 1958-68; exec. treas. Camden County (N.J.) Rep. Orgn., 1968-73; clk. bd. chosen freeholders of Camden County, 1969-73; active United Way, Boy Scouts Am. With USNR, 1944-46. Named Citizen of Yr., INA, 1970, Honoree of Yr. N.J. Surplus Lines Assn., 1983. Mem. Soc. Fire Protection Engrs., Nat. Fire Protection Assn., Conf. Spl. Risk Underwriters, Nat. Assn. Ins. Commrs. (surplus lines adv. com.), Nat. Assn. Ind. Insurers (surplus lines com.), U.S. Jaycees (hon. life, Outstanding State V.P. 1961, Outstanding Nat. Dir. 1962), Tavistock Country Club, Kiwanis. Died May 29, 1997.

BROWN, GEORGE ARTHUR, international civil servant; b. St. Elizabeth, Jamaica, July 25, 1922; s. Samuel Austin and Gertrude B.; m. Leila Leonie Gill, 1964; children: Isabel, Alexia. B.S. with honors in econs., London Sch. Econs., 1950; LL.D. (hon.), U. W.I., 1976. Cert. acct. Dir. Central Planning Unit, Jamaica, 1955-62; fin. sec., head Jamaica Civil Service, 1962-67; econ. adviser to Govt. of Jamaica, 1967-72; gov. Central Bank of Jamaica, 1967-77; assoc. adminstr. UN Devel. Programme, N.Y.C., 1978-93. Decorated Order of St. Michael and St. George (Eng.); Order of Jamaica. Fellow Assn. Cert. and Corp. Accts. Roman Catholic. Club: Jamaica (Kingston). Died Mar. 2, 1993. Home: New York N.Y.

BROWN, GLENN HALSTEAD, chemist, educator; b. Logan, Ohio, Sept. 10, 1915; s. James E. and Nancy J. (Mohler) B.; m. Jessie Adcock, May 27, 1943; children—Larry H., Nancy K., Donald S., Barbara J. BS, Ohio U., 1939; MS, Ohio State U., 1941; PhD, Iowa State U., 1951; DSc (hon.), Bowling Green State U., 1972, Ohio U., 1987. Asst. prof. U. Miss., 1941-46, 49-50; instr. Iowa State U., 1946-49; asst. prof. U. Vt., 1950-52; assoc. prof. U. Cin., 1952-60; with Kent (Ohio) State U., 1960-85, prof. chemistry, head dept., 1960-65, dir. Liquid Crystal Inst., 1965-83, fellow Liquid Crystal Inst., 1983-85, dean for research, 1963-69, Regents prof. chemistry, 1968-85, prof. emeritus, 1985-95; Bikerman lectr., 1981. Author: (with F.A. Anderson) Fundamentals of Chemistry, 1944, (with Wollett and Fogelsong) Laboratory Manual for Organic Chemistry, 1944, Record Book for Quantitative Analysis, 1954, (with E. M. Sallee) Quantitative Chemistry, 1963, (with others) Liquid Crystals, 1967, Review of the Structure and Properties of Liquid Crystals, 1970, (with J.J. Wolken) Liquid Crystals and Biological Structures; contbr. articles to sci. jours.; editor: Liquid Crystals 2, Parts I and II, 1969, Photochromism, 1971, Liquid Crystals 3, parts I and II, 1972, Advances in Liquid Crystals, vol. I, 1975, vol. II, 1976, vol. III, 1978, vol. IV, 1979, vol. V, 1982, vol. VI, 1983; editor-in-chief: Jour. Molecular Crystals and Liquid Crystals, 1968-84. Recipient Morley award in chemistry, 1977; Pres.'s award Kent State U., 1980; 8th Internat. Liquid Crystal Conf. dedicated in his hon. Tokyo, 1980; citation for liquid crystal research 9th Internat. Liquid Crystal conf., Bangalore, India, 1982; named hon. chmn. 11th Internat. Liquid Crystal Conf., Berkeley, Calif., 1986; Gov.'s Spl. Recognition for Excellance award Gov. of Ohio, 1986; Glenn H. Brown award initiated by Internat. Liquid Crystal Confs. for best doctoral thesis, 1986; Liquid Crystal Inst., Kent State U. renamed Glenn H. Brown Liquid Crystal Inst., 1986. Fellow Ohio Acad. Sci. (pres. 1960, Disting. Svc. award 1966, Centennial award 1991); mem. AAAS, Am. Chem. Soc. (chmn. Akron sect. 1965, nat. councilor Akron sect., chmn. regional meeting planning com. 1968, Disting. Svc. award Akron sect. 1971), Am. Inst. Chemists (chmn. Ohio 1969-71), Am. Crystallographic Assn., N.Y. Acad. Scis., Sigma Xi (nat. lectureship 1970), Alpha Chi Sigma, Phi Lambda Upsilon, Omicron Delta Kappa. Methodist. Spl. research X-ray structural studies liquids, concentrated salt solutions, photochromism, liquid crystals. Home: Kent Ohio Died Apr. 18, 1995.

BROWN, HELEN BENNETT, biochemist; b. Greenwich, Conn., Oct. 6, 1902; d. John Lansingh and Susan Jessie (Bronson) Bennett; m. John James Brown, June 16, 1928 (div. Jan. 1977); children: Susan Jessica Brown Girardeau, Margaret Bronson Brown Bevington. BA, Mt. Holyoke Coll., 1924; PhD, Yale U., 1930; ScD (hon.), Mt. Holyoke Coll., 1974. Technician dept. pediatrics Grace Hosp., New Haven, Conn., 1924-27; rsch. asst. dept. physiology Yale U., New Haven, Conn., 1927-28; rsch. assoc. dept. pediatrics Western Res. Univ., Cleve., 1928-31; rsch. assoc. Ben Venue Labs., Cleve., 1944-48; staff rsch. div. Cleve. Clinic, 1948-68, dir. dietary rsch., 1958-68, resident emeritus staff in rsch., 1968-95; cons. Am. Heart Assn., Dallas, 1968-77, Nat. Heart, Lung, Blood Inst., Bethesda, 1968-82, AMA, Chgo., 1982-83, Blue Shield Sr. Adv. Com., Cleve., 1983-94. Author ednl. materials on diets, blood lipids, others; sr. editor Heartline, 1972-94. Pres. Nutrition for Greater Cleve., 1979-84; mem. ministry on aging Ohio Episcopal Diocese, Cleve., 1986-90; cons. Judson Retirement Cmty., Cleve., 1984-95. Named Woman of Profl. Excellence, Cleve. Clinic, 1983, Lifetime Achievement award, 1990, Cleve. Career Woman of Achievement, YWCA, 1990. Fellow Coun. on Atheriosclerosis, Coun. on Epidemiology; mem. Am. Inst. Nutrition, Am. Dietetic Assn. (hon. mem.), Am. Heart Assn., NEO Affiliate, Sigma Xi. Home: Cleveland Ohio Died July 30, 1995.

BROWN, JERRY WILLIAM, cell biology and anatomy educator; b. Wichita, Kans., July 4, 1925; s. Jerry I. and Sarah Helen (Lowry) B.; m. Mary Mina MacNair, Aug. 12, 1950; children: Louise Hyde, Margaret Stewart Hildreth, Elizabeth Lowry Brown Bardo. AB, Wichita State U., 1946; MA, U. Kans., 1949, PhD, 1951. Instr. U. Pitts., 1951-56; asst. prof. U. Mo., Columbia, 1956-58, assoc. prof., 1958-64; assoc. prof. cell biology and anatomy U. Ala., Birmingham, 1964-70, prof., 1970-92, prof. emeritus, 1992-97. Contbr. articles to profl. jours. NIH grantee, 1965-66, 68-71. Mem. AAAS, Am. Assn. Anatomists, Soc. for Neurosci., Am. Acad. Neurology, Ala. Acad. Sci., Sigma Xi. Republican. Episcopalian. Avocations: gardening, art history, reading. Home: Birmingham Ala. Died Apr. 14, 1997.

BROWN, J(OSEPH) GORDON, university administrator; b. Terre Haute, Ind., Aug. 25, 1927; s. Joseph H. and Helen (Gordon) B.; m. Patsy Ralston Myers; children: Sheridan Lynn Brown Matthiesen, Karen Sue DeBord, Michael Gordon. Student, U. Ky., 1946-47; B.S., East Tenn. State U., 1950; M.S., U. Tenn., 1957. Prin. Bassel Sch., Alcoa, Tenn., 1950-51, Springbrook Sch., Alcoa, 1951-57; dean men, dir. student activities Emory and Henry Coll., Emory, Va., 1957-60, dean men, assoc. prof. edn., 1960-64; dean men Va. Poly. Inst. and State U., Blacksburg, 1964-68, dean for student services, 1968-77, dean for student programs and services, 1977-79, dir. univ. student devel. services, 1979-82, asst. dir. placement services/alumni, 1982-87, emeritus dean students. Pres. Blacksburg Community Fedn.; bd. dirs. Blacksburg United Fund; adv. com. for Cable TV, Blacksburg Town Council; mem. alumni bd. dirs. East Tenn. State U., 1977-83, v.p., 1979-80, pres., 1981-82. Served with USNR, 1945-46. Mem. Nat. Assn. Student Personnel Adminstrs. (commns. on profl. rels. and fin. aids, Region III Va. state dir., Region III Disting. Svc. citation 1975, 77), Va. Assn. Student Personnel Adminstrs. (past pres., Disting. Svc. citation 1979), So. Assn. Colls. and Schs., Rotary (found. benefactor 1993), Phi Delta Kappa, Phi Eta Sigma, Pi Delta Epsilon, Omicron Delta Kappa, Lambda Chi Alpha. Methodist. Club: Rotary (past pres.). Home: Lakeland Fla. Died July 28, 1993.

BROWN, LOUIS MORRIS, lawyer, educator; b. L.A., Sept. 5, 1909; s. Emil and Anna B.; m. Hermione Kopp, 1937; children: Lawrence David, Marshall Joseph, Harold Arthur. A.B. cum laude, U. So. Calif., 1930; J.D., Harvard U., 1933; LL.D., Manhattan Coll., Riverdale, N.Y., 1977. Bar: Calif. 1933, U.S. Supreme Ct. 1944. Practiced in Los Angeles, 1933-35; with Emil Brown & Co., Dura Steel Products Co., both Los Angeles, 1936-41; counsel RFC, Washington, 1942-44; ptnr. firm Pacht, Warne, Ross and Bernhard, Los Angeles, Beverly Hills, Calif., 1944-47, Irell & Manella, Los Angeles, 1947-69; counsel Irell & Manella, 1969-72; Lectr. in law Southwestern U. Law Sch., Los Angeles, 1939-41, U. Calif. at Los Angeles, 1944-46; lectr. in law U. So. Calif., 1950-51, lectr., adj. prof. law, 1960-74, prof. law, 1974-80, prof. emeritus, 1980-96, acad. dir. program for legal para-profls., 1970-77; mem. planning com. Tax Inst., 1948-69; vis. prof. law Loyola-Marymount Law Sch., Los Angeles, 1977-82; Disting. vis. prof. Whittier Coll. Sch. Law, 1980-85; mem. nat. panel arbitrators Am. Arbitration Assn., 1956-63; chmn. bd. trustees Nat. Ctr. for Preventive Law, U. Denver Coll. Law, 1987-96. Author: Preventive Law, 1950, How to Negotiate a Successful Contract, 1955, Lawyering Through Life: The Origin of Preventive Law, 1986; also case books, articles profl. jours.; co-author: Planning by Lawyers: Materials on a Non-Adversarial Legal Process, 1978, Legal Audit: Internal Corporate Investigations, 1990, Legal View column L.A. Times, 1991-95; editor: Major Tax Problems, 3 vols., 1948-51; mem. Am. Community Symphony Orch., European Tour, 1968; an issue of So. Calif. Law Rev. pub. in his honor, 1975. Mem. com. Jewish Pers. Rels. Bur., Cmty. Rels. Com., 1950-60; pres. Friends of Beverly Hills Pub. Libr., 1960; founder, adminstr. Emil Brown Fund Preventive Law Prize Awards, 1963-85, Hermione and Louis

Brown Found., 1985-96, Client Counseling Competition (named Louis M. Brown Internat. Client Counseling Competition 1993), 1968-73, cons., 1973-74. Recipient Merit award U. So. Calif. Gen. Alumni Assn., 1979, Disting. Svc. award Beverly Hills Bar Found., 1985, Pacem in Terris medal Manhattan Coll., 1991, Disting. Emeritus award U. So. Calif., 1995. Fellow Am. Bar Found., Soc. for Values in Higher Edn.; mem. ABA (chmn. standing com. legal assistance for servicemen 1969-72, mem. accreditation com. sect. legal edn. and admissions to bar 1978-81, ann. Legal Access award named in his honor 1994-96), L.A. County Bar Assn. (chmn. prepaid legal svcs. com. 1970-71, ann. Conflict Prevention award named in his honor 1994-96), Beverly Hills Bar Assn. (pres. 1961, Disting. Svc. award 1981, Life Achievement award 1989), Am. Judicature Soc., Am. Bus. Law Assn., Internat. Assn. Jewish Lawyers and Jurists, Town Hall L.A., Order of Coif. Jewish. Clubs: Mason (mem.), B'nai B'rith, Harvard Southern Calif. Died Sept. 19, 1996.

BROWN, MARY ELEANOR, physical therapist, educator; b. Williamsport, Pa., Jan. 1, 1906; d. Sumner Locher and Mary Kate (Eagles) Brown. Student U. Wis.-Madison, 1927-28; B.A., Barnard Coll., 1931; M.A., NYU, 1941, postgrad., 1942-45, Western Reserve U., 1960-61; postgrad. U. Miami, Miami-Dade Jr. Coll., 1971-72, Cuesta Community Coll., 1977-79. Supervising phys. therapist, rsch. asst. Inst. for Crippled and Disabled, N.Y.C., 1941-46; instr. edn. N.Y.U., 1942-46; phys. therapist Childrens Rehab. Inst., Cockeysville, Md., 1946; organizing dir. phys. edn. State Rehab. Hosp., West Haverstraw, N.Y., 1946-47; phys. therapy cons. Nat. Soc. for Crippled Children and Adults, Chgo., 1947-49; physical therapy cons., dir. prof. svcs., dir. cerebral palsy sch. N.Y. State Dept. Health, Albany, N.Y. and Eastern N.Y. Orthopedic Hosp. Sch., Schenectady, N.Y., 1949-53; chief phys. therapist Bird S. Coler Hosp. for Chronic Diseases, N.Y.C., 1953-54; chief phys. therapist, instr. edn. St. Vincents Hosp. and N.Y.U., 1954-58; chief rsch. assoc. hand rsch. Highland View Hosp., Cleve., 1958-64, cons. on kinesiology, hand rsch., 1964-65; supr. continuing edn. for phys. therapists, asst. prof. phys. therapy Case Western Res. U., Cleve., 1964-68; dir. phys. therapy Margaret Wagner House of Benjamin Rose Inst., Cleve., 1968-70; free lance writer, 1970—; 1st Mary Eleanor Brown lectr. clin. phys. therapy rsch. Inst. Rehab. and Rsch., Tex. Med. Center, Houston, 1979; Adv. bd. Community Svcs. Dept. Cuesta Community Coll., San Luis Obispo, Calif., 1977-92; vol. UN and Univ. for Peace, Costa Rica, 1982—. Author: Therapeutic Recreation and Exercise: Range-of-Motion Activities for Health and Well-Being, 1990; contbr. articles in field to profl jours. Recipient Award of Merit, Case-Western Res. U., 1970; award for clin. rsch. Inst. Rehab. and Rsch., Tex. Med. Ctr., Houston, 1979; Lucy Blair Svc. award Am. Phys. Therapy Assn., 1984, Disting. Alumna award Lancaster Country Day Sch., 1987. Mem. Inst. Gen. Semantics, Internat. Soc. Gen. Semantics, Am. Phys. Therapy Assn. (Catherine Worthingham fellow 1990), Women for Internat. Peace and Arbitration, Found. for Global Community. Died July 24, 1996.

BROWN, MILTON WOLF, art historian, educator; b. Newark, July 3, 1911; s. Samuel and Celia (Harriton) B.; m. Blanche R. Levine, July 15, 1938. B.A., N.Y.U., 1932, M.A., 1935; Ph.D., Inst. Fine Arts, 1949; postgrad., Courtauld Inst., summer 1934, U. Brussels, summer 1937, Harvard, 1938-39. Instr. art dept. Bklyn. Coll., 1946-49, asst. prof., 1949-56, assoc. prof., 1956-60, prof., 1960-70, chmn. dept. art, 1964-71; exec. officer doctoral program in art history City U. N.Y., 1971-79, resident prof., 1979-91, prof. emeritus, 1991—; sr. fellow Williams Coll. Art Mus., 1979-93; Phi Beta Kappa vis. scholar, 1987-88; Samuel H. Kress prof. CASVA Nat. Gallery Art, 1989-90; mem. adv. bd. Archives Am. Art, 1967—, chmn., 1983, 92. Author: Painting of the French Revolution, 1937, American Painting from the Armory Show to the Depression, 1955, The Story of the Armory Show, 1963, 2d edit., 1988, American Art to 1900, 1977; co-author: American Art, 1978; contbg. editor: Ency. Painting, 1955, 100 Masterpieces of American Painting from Public Collections in Washington, D.C., 1983. Served with AUS, 1943-46, ETO. Decorated Bronze Star medal. Mem. Coll. Art Assn. Am., Soc. Archtl. History, Victorian Soc. Died Feb. 6, 1998.

BROWN, ROBERT, manufacturing executive; b. N.Y.C., Jan. 16, 1931; s. Samuel and Dorothy (Keppler) B.; m. Barbara Schwartz, Oct. 8, 1953 (div. 1984); m. Angelika Jansen, Oct. 18, 1986. BBA, CCNY, 1957. CPA, N.Y. Sr. acct. M.R. Feinod & Co., N.Y.C., 1957-61; v.p. ops. Ehrenratch Photo-Optic Industries, Roosevelt Field, N.Y., 1961-65; exec. v.p. BFL Communications, Plainview, N.Y., 1965-74, Seatrain Lines Inc., N.Y.C., 1974-81, Chromalloy Gas Turbine Corp., San Antonio, 1982—. With U.S. Army, 1950-51, Korea. Republican. Avocations: photography, gardening. DIED 06/07/97. .

BROWN, ROGER, professional basketball player; children: Roger Jr., Rodney, Roger 3d, Stacey Hicks, Gail, Destiny, Melissa. Student, U. Dayton. With Gen. Motors, Dayton, Ohio; basketball player Ind. Pacers, Indpls., 1967-75, asst. coach; coach Continental Basketball Assn., Evansville. Active Indpls. City Coun. Mem. three ABA championships, leagues first 10,000 point scorer. Died 1997.

BROWNE, MILLARD CHILD, newspaper editor; b. Sprague, Wash., Feb. 7, 1915; s. Clarence Swain and Irma Josephine (Child) B.; m. Jane Sweet, Aug. 25, 1939; children: Katherine Anne Browne Kunkle, Millard Warren, Jeffrey Child, Barbara Jane Browne Atlas. AB, Stanford U., 1936, MA, 1939; postgrad. (Nieman fellow), Harvard U., 1942-43. Reporter, Columnist, editorial writer Calif. newspapers Santa Paula Chronicle, Santa Ana Jour., Sacramento Union, 1936-42; asso. editor Sacramento Union, 1943-44; editorial writer Buffalo Evening News, 1944-80, chief editorial writer, 1953-66, editorial page editor, 1966-80; sr. mem. Wolfson Coll., Cambridge (Eng.) U., 1980-81. Mem. Nat. Conf. Editorial Writers (pres. 1962-63), Am. Soc. Newspaper Editors, Internat. Press Inst., World Press Freedom Com., Soc. Profl. Journalists, Sigma Alpha Epsilon. Unitarian. Home: Menlo Park Calif. Died July 17, 1996.

BROWNING, RALPH LESLIE, cement company executive; b. Buffalo, Apr. 18, 1915; s. Leslie E. and Bertha L. (Rea) B.; m. Nancy B. Crane, Sept. 6, 1940; children—Peter Crane, Richard Leslie, Pamela (Mrs. David Durrant). A.B., Colgate U., 1937. With Lehigh Portland Cement Co., Allentown, Pa., 1937—; asst. v.p. Lehigh Portland Cement Co., 1951-52, v.p., asst. gen. sales mgr., 1952-55, v.p. of sales, 1955-59, exec. v.p., 1959—; also dir.; dir. Mchts. Nat. Bank, Allentown, Lehigh Realty Co., Allentown. Served as lt. (j.g.) Supply Corps USNR, 1944-46. Mem. Kappa Delta Rho. Republican. Episcopalian. Clubs: Lehigh Country, Livingston, Allentown; Ponte Vedra (Fla.); Saucon Valley Country (Bethlehem, Pa.); University (Chgo.), Tavern (Chgo.); University (Jacksonville, Fla.).

BRUHN, HJALMAR DIEHL, agricultural engineer, educator; b. near Spring Green, Wis., Aug. 5, 1907; s. Aksel Theodor and Emma Bertha (Diehl) B.; m. Janet Helen Weber, Aug. 7, 1938; 1 child, Janet Margaret Bruhn Jeffcott. BS in Agrl. Engring., U. Wis., 1931, BSME, 1933; MSME, MIT, 1937. Registered profl. engr., Wis. Mem. faculty dept. agrl. engring. U. Wis., Madison, 1933-97, chmn. dept., 1962-66, prof. emeritus, 1978-97; cons. H.D. Bruhn and Assocs., Madison, 1978-97; external examiner U. Ibadan, Nigeria, Africa, 1976, 77. Contbr. over 150 articles to sci. jours. Past bd. dirs. Highlands-Mendota Beach Sch., Madison Twp.; pres., bd. dirs. Middleton (Wis.) Sportsmen's Club, 1962-77. Fellow Am. Soc. Agrl. Engrs. (McCormick Case Gold medal 1992, Engr. of Yr. Wis. sect. 1971, Outstanding Paper award 1955, 74); mem. AAAS, NSPE, AAUP, Wis. Soc. Profl. Engrs., Wis. Acad. Scis., Arts and Letters, N.Y. Acad. Sci., Soc. Green. Vegetation Rsch., others. Achievements include development of machinery for pelletting alfalfa, mechanical cherry picking, irrigation and well jetting procedures, mechanical tree-acreage planting, plant protein extraction to feed the world's malnourished. Home: Madison Wis. Died July 1, 1997.

BRUMM, JOSEPH DANIEL, investment banker; b. St. Louis, Aug. 8, 1916; s. Edward and Henrietta (Knehans) B.; m. Virginia Crady, July 13, 1940; children: Gregg Edward, Eric Joseph. Certificate in commerce, St. Louis U., 1939. With Bemis Bros. Bag Co., 1934-41; with Stix, Baer & Fuller Co., St. Louis, 1941-69; sec.-treas. Stix, Baer & Fuller Co., 1957-69, exec. v.p., 1961-69; also dir.; financial v.p., treas., dir. Rich's, Inc., Atlanta, 1969-72; exec. v.p., dir. Zeal Corp., St. Louis, 1972-92; exec. v.p., treas., dir. Guarantee Elec. Co., St. Louis, 1975-92; mem. adv. bd. Liberty Mut. Ins. Co., Mercantile Bank; dir. DePaul Med. Office Bldg. Bd. dirs. Atlanta chpt. Nat. Found. March of Dimes, Boy Scouts Am., Atlanta, Heart Assn.; Bd. dirs. Salvation Army, St. Louis, chmn., 1983-84; mem. hosp. assn. bd. Mo. Bapt. Hosp. Mem. Financial Execs. Inst., Capital City Club, Old Warson Country Club, Mo. Athletic Club, Strathalbyn Farms Club, Wyndemere Country Club (Naples, Fla.). Home: Naples Fla. Died May 21, 1992.

BRUNO, MICHAEL PETER, economist; b. Hamburg, Germany, July 30, 1932; arrived in Israel, 1933; s. Hans W. and Lotte (Samson) B.; children: Yael, Ido, Asa; m. Netta Ben-Porath Bruno, 1993. BA in Econs., Cambridge U., Eng., 1956, MA in Econs., 1960; postgrad., Hebrew U., Jerusalem, 1960-61; PhD in Econs., Stanford U., 1962. Joint dir. rsch. Bank of Israel, Jerusalem, 1957-65; gov. Bank of Israel, 1986-91; lectr. Hebrew U., Jerusalem, 1963-65, sr. lectr., 1965-67, assoc. prof., 1967-70, prof. econs., 1970—; econ. policy adviser to pres. Ministry of Fin., Govt. of Israel, Tel Aviv, 1975-76; chief economist, v.p. The World Bank, Washington, 1993—; vis. prof. Harvard U., Cambridge, Mass., 1965-66, 70-71, 76-77, 81, MIT, Cambridge, 1965-66, 70-71, 76-77, 81; dir. rsch. Falk Inst. Econ. Rsch., Israel, 1973-75; rsch. assoc. Nat. Bur. Econ. Rsch., Cambridge, 1979-81; mem. planning team Israel Stabilization Program, Govt. of Israel, 1985-86; occasional adviser on stabilization programs Govts. of Mexico, Yugoslavia and Poland, 1988-90. Author: Interdependence, Resource Use and Structural Change in Israel, 1962, Crisis, Stabilization and Economic Reform: Therapy by Consensus, 1994; (with J. Sachs) Economics of Worldwide Stagflation, 1985; (with G. Ci-Tella, R. Dornbusch and S. Fischer) Inflation Stabilization: Argentina, Israel, Brazil, Bolivia and Mexico, 1988; (with S. Fischer, E. Helpman and N. Liviatan) Lessons of Stabilization and Its Aftermath, 1991. Recipient Rothschild Found. prize for social sci., 1974, Israel prize, 1993. Fellow Econometric Soc. (mem. coun. 1967-69, pres. 1986-87); mem. Internat. Econ. Assn. (pres. 1992-95). Avocations: hiking, music. Died Dec. 26, 1996.

BRUST, LEO, bishop; b. St. Francis, Wis., Jan. 7, 1916. Student, St. Francis Sem., Wis., Canisianum, Austria, Cath. U., Washington. Ordained priest Roman Catholic Ch., 1942; ordained titular bishop of Sueli and aux. bishop Milw., 1969-95. Home: Milwaukee Wis. Died Jan. 31, 1995.

BRYAN, JOSEPH MCKINLEY, insurance company executive; b. Elyria, Ohio, Feb. 11, 1896; s. Bart and Caroline (Ebert) B.; ed. Mt. Hermon Sch.; LLD (hon.), Belmont Abbey Coll., 1957, U. N.C., Greensboro, 1979, Duke U., 1980; HHD (hon.), N.C. A&T State U., 1977; LHD (hon.), Sacred Heart Coll., 1982; DBA (hon.), Greensboro Coll., 1986; m. Kathleen Marshall Price, Nov. 19, 1927 (dec. 1984); children: Kay (Mrs. Bryan Edwards), Nancy Bryan Faircloth, Joseph McKinley. Mem. N.Y. Cotton Exch., 1923-36; mem. exec. com., sr. v.p., hon. chmn. bd. dirs. Jefferson Standard Life Ins. Co. (now Jefferson-Pilot Life Ins. Co.), 1931-93, mem bd. dirs., mem. exec. com., chmn. bd. dirs., hon. chmn. bd. dirs. Pilot Life Ins. Co., 1948-86, bd. dirs., mem. exec. com., hon. lifetime mem. Jefferson-Pilot Corp., 1968-93; founding pres., chmn. bd., hon. chmn. bd. Jefferson Pilot Communications Co., owner and operator 1st TV station in N.C.; chmn. fin. sect. Am. Life Conv., 1949-50, pres., 1955-56. Chmn. N.C. Bd. Elections, 1960-61; bd. govs. Shriner's Hosp. for Crippled Children, Greenville, 1945-72. Served with U.S. Army, World War I, AEF. Mem. Southeastern Shrine Assn. (past pres.), Sigma Chi. Clubs: Bath and Tennis, Everglades, Greensboro Country, Greensboro City, Sedgefield Country (Greensboro); Rolling Rock (Ligonier, Pa.); Nat. Golf (Augusta, Ga.); Metropolitan (Washington); Lyford Cay (Nassau, Bahamas). Lodges: Masons, Shriners, Rotary. Died Apr., 1995.

BRYANT, ALAN WILLARD, human resources executive; b. Glen Ridge, N.J., Aug. 17, 1940; s. Alan Willard and Clara Sherman (Clark) B.; m. Karen Koenig; children: Hilary Ann, Christopher Bowman. AB, Dartmouth Coll., 1962, MBA, 1963; postgrad., St. Mary's U. Law, San Antonio, 1964-65. Specialist profl. placement spacecraft dept. GE, King of Prussia, Pa., 1965-66; foreman, methods analyst TV dept. GE, Syracuse, N.Y., 1966-67; specialist salaried employment armament dept. GE, Springfield, Mass., 1967-68; specialist profl. and salaried compensation info. systems equipment div. GE, Phoenix, 1968-70; mgr. personnel relations nuclear energy dept. GE, Wilmington, N.C., 1970-72; mgr. relations practices TV receiver products dept. GE, Portsmouth, Va., 1972-76; mgr. employee and community relations meter bus. dept. GE, Somersworth, N.H., 1976-85; mgr. human resources operation GE, San Jose, Calif., 1985-93; v.p. human resources Paramount Pub./Computer Curriculum Corp., Sunnyvale, Calif., 1993—; mem. sr. staff positive mgmt. leadership course GE, Fairfield, Conn., 1981-93, mem. staff exec. assessment and devel., 1987-93; speaker nat. conf. Am. Mgmt. Assn., 1986, U.S.-Japan Inst., 1991. Author in field. Pres., campaign chair United Way of Strafford County, Dover, N.H., 1980-81; founding pres. Strafford Hospice Care, Somersworth, 1982-85; trustee Wentworth Douglass Hosp., Dover, 1982-85. Served to capt. U.S. Army, 1963-65. Recipient Pub. Svc. award Gov. Ariz., 1970, Pub. Svc. award Gov. N.H., 1982, 84. Mem. Soc. for Human Resource Mgmt., Bay Area Human Resource Execs. Coun. (pres. 1992-93), No. Calif. Human Resources Coun., Santa Clara County Mfg. Group Working Coun., Dover C. of C. (pres. 1984-85) Rotary (Disting. Svc. award 1985). Republican. Avocations: sailing, art, civic activities, reading, photography.

BRYANT, HOWARD LOUIS, real estate appraiser and broker, consultant, farmer; b. Drewryville, Va., Dec. 7, 1921; s. Lewis Harum and Bessie Elizabeth (Vick) B.; student U. Va., Va. Commonwealth U.; m. Maude Gertrude Bryant, June 5, 1942; children: Stephen L., Robyn Denise. Owner, operator Merrydale Farm, Boykins, Va., 1941-95, Boykins Hardware Co., also Boykins Tractor & Implement Co., 1947-50; contractor, real estate developer, 1950-62; sr. appraiser Va. Dept. Hwys., 1963-86; pres. Howard L. Bryant and Assocs., Ltd., 1986-95; guest lectr.; mem. adv. bd. Va. Dept. Motor Vehicles; vice chmn. Colonial Heights (Va.) Bd. Zoning Appeals. Mem. Am. Soc. Appraisers (sr. mem.), Assn. Fed. Appraisers, Am. Right of Way Assn., Nat. Assn. Review Appraisers, Lions, Masons, Shriners, Order Eastern Star. Baptist. Died July 18, 1995. Home: Colonial Heights Va.

BUCK, CHRISTIAN BREVOORT ZABRISKIE, independent oil operator; b. San Francisco, Oct. 18, 1914; s. Frank Henry and Zayda Justine (Zabriskie) B.; student U. Calif., Berkeley, 1931-33; m. Natalie Leontine Smith, Sept. 12, 1948; children—Warren Zabriskie Barbara Anne. Mem. engring. dept. U.S. Potash Co. Carlsbad, N.Mex., 1933-39; ind. oil operator, producer

Calif., 1939-79, N.Mex., 1939—; owner, operator farm, ranch, Eddy County, N.Mex., 1951-79; dir. Belridge Oil Co. until 1979; dir. Buck Ranch Co. (Calif.). Served with RAF, 1942-45. Democrat. Episcopalian. Club: Riverside Country (Carlsbad). Died Aug. 17, 1995.

BUCKHOUT, ROBERT, psychology educator; b. Bklyn., Nov. 1, 1935; s. Robert Cushman and Martha Geraldine (Bracken) B.; m. Alice Mae Young, Apr. 29, 1959 (div. June 1968); children: Eileen Elizabeth, Mark Allen. BS, Queens Coll. CUNY, 1957; MS, NC. State U., 1959; PhD, Ohio State U., 1963. Prof. psychology Washington U., St. Louis, 1963-68, U. Calif., Santa Cruz, 1968-69, U. Calif., Berkeley, 1969-70, State U. Calif., Hayward, 1970-72, Bklyn. Coll. CUNY, 1972—; cons. in law and psychology. Dir., Ctr. for Responsive Psychology, N.Y.C., 1973—; editor, pub. Social Action and the Law, 1973—; author: Psychology: The Science of Mental Life, 1973; Psychology and Criminal Justice, 1981; editor: Toward Social Change, 1971. Capt. USAF, 1959-62. NSF grantee, 1980. Fellow Am. Psychol. Assn., Am. Psychol. Soc.; mem. Psychonomic Soc., Am. Psychology Law Soc., N.Y. Acad. Sci., Sigma Xi, Psi Chi. Avocations: photography, jazz piano.

BUCKSBAUM, MARTIN, real estate developer; b. Marshalltown, Iowa, July 31, 1920; s. Louis and Ida Bucksbaum; married; 1 child, Mary. Student, Marshall Coll., 1939. Pres. Cashway Super Markets, Marshalltown, 1950-60; pres. Gen. Mgmt., Des Moines, 1960-92, chmn., 1975-92; chmn., CEO Growth Properties, Inc., Des Moines, 1993-95. Home: Des Moines Iowa Died July 7, 1995.

BUFFA, SEBASTIAN JOSEPH, art history educator, consultant; b. Detroit, May 20, 1954; s. Sebastian Anthony and Betty Marie (Binder) B. Student, Universite de Haute Bretagne Rennes, France, 1976; BA, Western Mich. U., 1977; MA, Columbia U., 1979. Instr. art history Western Mich. U., Kalamazoo, 1979; editor Abaris Books, N.Y.C., 1980-82, cons., 1983-95. Editor: The Illustrated Bartsch vols. 34-38, 1982-84. Avocations: chess, travel, film, hiking. Home: Somerville Mass. Died Sept. 17, 1995.

BUIE, JAMES LANG, electronics consultant; b. Los Angeles, Feb. 21, 1920; s. Claude Lang and Agnes Olive Amelia (Mitchell) B.; m. Esther Ione Winey, May 29, 1941; children: Janet Lynn Buie Reasoner, John Wesley. BEE, UCLA, 1949. Electronics engr. Hoffman Co., Los Angeles, 1949-54; electronics engr., sr. scientist TRW Inc., Redondo Beach, Calif., 1954-77; cons. San Diego, 1978-88. Holder of 22 patents including patent for Transistor-Transistor Logic, which has worldwide application in design of integrated circuits, dielectrically isolated integrated circuits, single-chip parallel multipliers, single-chip analog-to-digital converters and triple-diffused bipolar devices. Lt. comdr. USN, 1940-45, PTO. Decorated D.F.C., 4 Air medals. Fellow IEEE; mem. Eta Kappa Nu, Tau Beta Pi. Democrat. Home: Panorama City California Died Sept. 1988; buried Fort Rosencrans Nat. Cemetery, San Diego.

BULBULIAN, ARTHUR H., biomedical scientist, medical graphics and facial prosthetics specialist; b. Talas, Turkey, Dec. 20, 1900; came to U.S., 1920, naturalized, 1931; s. Hagop C. and Naomi (Iynejian) B.; m. Wilhelmine M. Wilson, Sept. 9, 1944; children—Naomi, Josephine, Rachel. B.S., M.S., Middlebury Coll., 1925, D.Sc. (hon.), 1966; D.D.S., U. Minn., 1931. Asst. Mus. Natural History, U. Ia., 1927-28; instr. Coll. Dentistry, U. Minn., 1931-32; with Mayo Found., Rochester, Minn., 1933-65; asso. prof. med. edn. Mayo Grad. Sch. Medicine, until 1965; dir. Mayo Found. Mus. of Hygiene and Medicine, 1935-65; mem. staff Mayo Clinic, 1935-65, emeritus mem., 1965-96; clin. prof. maxillofacial prosthetics U. Minn. Sch. Dentistry, 1965-96; pvt. practice facial prostheses; pvt. practice facial prostheses; spl. cons. U. Minn. Hosps., Mpls., 1966-67; prepared Mayo Found. exhibit Hall of Sci., A Century of Progress, Chgo., 1933-34; pres. 1st Internat. Symposium on Facial Prosthetics, Arnhem, Netherlands, 1976. Author: textbook Facial Prosthesis, 1945; co-author: (with Dry, Edwards et al) Atlas on Congenital Anomalies of the Heart and Great Vessels, 1948, Facial Prosthetics Textbook, 1973, articles on medical mus. techniques and facial prosthetic methods. Mem. Nat. Resources Planning Bd., 1942-44, mem. com. on conservation culture resources. Recipient Billings Gold medal A.M.A., 1955, 58, 64, Golden plate Am. Acad. of Achievement, 1965, Award of Merit Am. Assn. Inhalation Therapy, 1960, Andrew Ackerman award, 1964; Outstanding Achievement award U. Minn., 1972. Fellow Am. Coll. Dentists; mem. Am. Dental Assn., Assn. Med. Illustrators, Am. Acad. Maxillofacial Prosthetics (pres. 1956-58, dir. 1953-96 , editor jour.), Sigma Xi. Co-inventor (with Lovelace and Boothby), BLB Oxygen Mask for oxygen therapy and high altitude flying; designer A-14 oxygen mask used by USAAF during World War II. Home: Rochester Minn. Died June 23, 1996.

BULLARD, HELEN (MRS. JOSEPH MARSHALL KRECHNIAK), sculptor; b. Elgin, Ill., Aug. 15, 1902; d. Charles Wickliffe and Minnie (Cook) Bullard; student U. Chgo., 1921-29; m. Lloyd Ernst Rohrke, June 11, 1924 (div. Feb. 1931); children—Ann Louise (Mrs. Ross DeWitt Netherton), Barbara Jane (Mrs. Valtyr Emil Gudmundson); m. 2d, Joseph Marshall Krechniak, Jan. 30, 1932 (dec. Feb. 1964); 1 child, Mariana (Mrs. Wilfred Martin). With research dept. L.V. Estes, Inc., Chgo., 1920-22; operator Square D Co., Detroit, 1922-24; researcher Commerce and Adminstrn. library U. Chgo., Detroit, 1924-25, dir. Crossville (Tenn.) Play Ctr., 1949-50. Creator hand-carved dolls, 1949—, wood sculpture, 1959—; exhibited with Nat. Inst. Am. Doll Artists Exhbns., Los Angeles, 1963, Cin., 1964, Washington, 1965, Chgo., 1966, Boston, 1967, New Orleans, 1969, Detroit, 1970, Los Angeles, 1971, Omaha, 1972, Louisville, 1973, Miami, Fla., 1974, Milw., 1975, Watts Bar Dam, Tenn., 1976, Chgo., 1977, N.Y.C., 1979, others until 1987, also craftsmen's fairs, 1954-65, The Club, Birmingham, Ala., 1963, Oak Ridge Art Ctr., 1965, Children's Mus., Nashville, 1967, McClung Mus., Knoxville, 1969; one woman show Tenn. State Mus., 1972, Nashville, Knoxville, Asheville, N.C.; author: Dr. Woman of the Cumberlands, 1953, The American Doll Artist, 1965, Vol. II, 1974, A Bullard Family, 1966, Dorothy Heizer, the Artist and Her Dolls, 1972; Crafts and Craftsmen of the Tennesee Mountains, 1976, (monograph) My People in Wood, 1984, Faith Wick: Doll Artist Extraordinaire, 1986, Cumberland County, 1956-86, Vol. II, 1987, (with husband) Cumberland County's First Hundred Years, 1956. Campaign chmn. Cumberland County unit Am. Cancer Soc., 1947-52. HB Scholarship in the Arts honoree Cumberland County (Tenn.) Arts Coun., 1996. Mem. So. Highland Handicraft Guild (dir. 1957-59), Highland Handicraft Guild, Nat. Inst. Am. Doll Artists (founder, pres. 1963-67, 69-71, chmn. bd. 1977-80, honoree Helen Bullard Scholarship Fund 1995), United Fedn. Doll Clubs (2d v.p. 1977-79), Am. Craftsmen's Coun., Tenn. Folklore Soc., Mensa. Democrat. Unitarian. Died. Oct. 31, 1996.

BULLOCK, EDNA JEANETTE, photographer; b. Hollister, Calif., May 20, 1915; d. Fred A. and Gertrude A. (Chase) Earle; m. Wynn Bullock, 1943 (dec. 1975); children: Barbara Ann Bullock-Wilson, Lynne Harrington-Bullock; 1 stepchild, Mary Wynn Burnat Horner. AA, Modesto (Calif.) Jr. Coll., 1936; B of Edn., UCLA, 1938. Cert. tchr., Calif. Phys. edn., dance tchr. Fresno (Calif.) H.S., 1940-43; from phys. edn. to home econ. tchr. Monterey (Calif.) Peninsula Unified Sch. Dist., 1959-1974; pvt. practice as photographer Monterey, 1976—; lectr. in field. One-women shows include Shado Gallery, Portland, Oreg., 1977, Pacific Grove (Calif.) Art Ctr., 1979, Photo-Synthesis Gallery, Clovis, Calif., 1979, Cafe Balthazar Gallery, Pacific Grove, 1980, Collectors Gallery, Pacific Grove, 1980, Focus Gallery, San Francisco, 1981, San Jose City Coll., 1981, Exposures Gallery, Libertyville, Ill., 1982, Jeb Gallery, Providence, 1982, Ledel Gallery, N.Y.C., 1983, Neikrug Gallery, N.Y.C., 1983, Spectrum Gallery, Fresno, 1985, Vision Gallery, San Francisco, 1985, Photography at Oreg. Gallery, Eugene, 1986, Betty Garland Gallery, San Francisco, 1987, Exposure Gallery, Orleans, Mass., 1987, Olive Hyde Art Gallery, Fremont, Calif., 1987, Foto Galerie, Chincoteague, Va., 1990, G. Ray Hawkins Gallery, Santa Monica, Calif., 1993, Halsted Gallery, Birmingham, Mich., 1993, 95, PhotoZone Gallery, Eugene, 1993, Marjorie Evans Gallery, Carmel, Calif., 1995, F Stops Here Gallery, Santa Barbara, Calif., 1995, S. K. Josefsberg Studio, Portland, Oreg., 1995, Benham Studio Gallery, Seattle, 1996, Palm Beach Photographic Ctr., Delray Beach, Fla., 1996, Southern Vt. Art Ctr., Manchester, 1996, Santa Catalina Sch. Art Gallery, Monterey, Calif., 1997; exhibited in group shows including Stills Gallery, Edinburgh, Scotland, 1988, Dancing Man Gallery, Santa Cruz, 1989, Josephus Daniels Gallery, Carmel, Calif., 1989, Pacific Grove Art Ctr., 1987, 89, 91-92, Imagery Gallery, Lancaster, Ohio, 1992, Grant Gallery, Denver, 1992, Silver Image Gallery, Seattle, 1992, Photographic Image Gallery, Portland, 1993, Scott Nichols Gallery, San Francisco, 1994, Marywood Coll. Contemporary Gallery, Scranton, Pa., 1996, Olive Hyde Gallery, Fremont, Calif., 1997; photographer Combing the Coast I, 1981, Combing the Coast II, 1982, Combing the Coast I and II, 1985, Edna's Nudes, 1995. Bd. dirs. Friends the Arts U. Calif., Santa Cruz, 1983-87, Ctr. for Photographic Art, 1991-94. Recipient Lifetime Achievement award Gov. Pete Wilson State of Calif., 1995; named Local Hero, Coast Weekly, 1996. Democrat. Unitarian Universalist. Avocations: reading, travel, cultural events. Died Dec. 13, 1997.

BULLOCK, HUGH, investment banker; b. Denver, June 2, 1898; s. Calvin and Alice Katherine (Mallory) B.; m. Marie Leontine Graves, Apr. 5, 1933 (dec. Dec. 1986); children: Fleur Weymouth, Fair Alice Bullock McCormick. B.A., Williams Coll., 1921, LL.D., 1957; LL.D., Hamilton Coll., 1954. Investment banker, 1921-96; head Bullock Co., N.Y.C.; pres. Calvin Bullock, Ltd., 1945-62, chmn. bd., chief exec. officer, 1963-85; pres., dir. Bullock Fund, Ltd., Canadian Investment Fund, Ltd., Dividend Shares, Inc., Canadian-Fund, Inc., 1945-85; former chmn., dir. Carriers and Gen. Corp., Nation-Wide Securities Co., Monthly Income Shares; former chmn. or pres. and dir. dozen investment cos. Author: The Story of Investment Companies, 1959. Mem. Marshall Scholarship Regional Com., 1955-58; life trustee, mem. exec. com. Williams Coll., 1961-69; trustee Roosevelt Hosp., 1949-69; hon. trustee St. Lukes Roosevelt Hosp. Center; adv. coun. Grad. Sch. Bus., Columbia U., 1958; chmn. Westminster Abbey Am. Appeal Com. 2d lt., inf. World War I; lt. col. World War II; civilian aide to sec. Army, for First Army Area, 1952-53. Decorated knight grand cross Order Brit. Empire; knight of grace Order of St. John of Jerusalem (v.p. Am. soc.); knight comdr. Royal Order George I, Greece; recipient U.S. Army certificate of appreciation, 1953; James C. Rogerson Cup for Service, Loyalty, Achievement Williams Coll., 1961; Exceptional Service award Dept. Air Force, 1961; Disting. Public Service award Dept. Navy, 1972; Disting. Citizens award City of Denver; Benjamin Franklin fellow Royal Soc. Arts. Mem. Mil. Order Fgn. Wars in U.S., Am. Legion, Pilgrims of U.S. (chmn., pres.), St. George's Soc., New Eng. Soc., English-Speaking Union, Fgn. Policy Assn., Acad. Polit. Sci., Investment Bankers Assn. Am. (gov. 1953-55), Am. Mus. Natural History, Assn. Ex-mems. Squadron A. (gov. 1945-50), Calvin Bullock Forum (pres. 1945-85), Coun. Fgn. Rels., Nat. Inst. Social Scis. (pres. 1950-53), Newcomen Soc., Acad. Am. Poets (chmn.), Ends of Earth (pres.), Gargoyle Alumni Assn., Kappa Alpha. Episcopalian. Clubs: Chevy Chase (Washington), Met. (Washington), Racquet and Tennis (N.Y.C.), Downtown Assn., N.Y. Yacht (N.Y.C.), Bond (N.Y.C.), River (N.Y.C.), Williams, Ch. (N.Y.C.), Union (N.Y.C.), West Side Tennis (Forest Hills, N.Y.), , Denver Country (Colo.), N.Y. Yacht Club, Mount Royal (Montreal), Edgartown (Mass.), Yacht (commodore 1966-67), Edgartown Reading Room, White's (London). Pioneer of investment company movement. Died Nov. 5, 1996.

BULLOUGH, BONNIE, nurse, educator; b. Delta, Utah, Jan. 5, 1927; d. Ruth Uckerman; m. Vern L. Bullough; children: David (dec.), James, Steven, Susan, Robert. BS, Youngstown U., 1954; MS, UCLA, 1962, MA, 1965, PhD, 1968. Nurse Salt Lake City Gen. Hosp., 1947-51, U. Chgo., 1951-54; instr. health Youngstown (Ohio) U., 1956-59; nurse Northridge (Calif.) Hosp., 1959-61; research asst. UCLA, 1962-63, asst. prof. nursing, 1968-72, assoc. prof. nursing, 1972-75; Fulbright lectr., higher inst. nursing Cairo U., United Arab Republic, 1966-67; instr. sociology San Fernando Valley State Coll., Northridge, 1967-68; coordinator grad. program, prof. Calif. State U., Long Beach, 1975-79; prof., dean SUNY, Buffalo, 1980-91, prof. nursing, 1991-93; prof. U. So. Calif., 1993-96. Author: (with Vern Bullough) Poverty, Ethnic Identity and Health Care, 1972, Sin Sickness and Sanity: A History of Sexual Attitudes, 1977, The Care of the Sick: The Emergence of Modern Nursing, 1978, Prostitution: An Illustrated Social History, 1978, Nursing: An Historical Bibliography, 1981, Health Care for the Other Americans, 1982, History, Trends and Politics of Nursing, 1984, Women and Prostitution: A Social History, 1987, Nursing in the Community, 1990, Contraception: Modern Methods of Birth Control, 1990, (with Bullough) Cross Dressing, Sex and Gender, 1993, Encyclopedia of Human Sexuality, 1994; (with others) A Bibliography of Prostitution, 1977, Nursing Issues and Nursing Strategies for the Eighties, 1983, Annotated Bibliography of Nursing Issues, Women and Prostitution: A Social History, 1985, (with George Rosen) Preventive Medicine in the United States 1900-1990: Trends and Interpretation, 1992; author, editor: The Law and the Expanding Nursing Role, 1980; (with Bullough) Expanding Horizons for Nurses, 1977; editor: The Management of Common Human Miseries: A Text for Primary Care Practitioners, 1979; (with Bullough) Issues in Nursing, 1966, New Directions for Nurses, 1971, Cross Dressing Sex and Gender, 1993, Human Sexuality: An Encyclopedia, 1994, Nursing Issues For The Nineties and Beyond, 1994, (with Bullough) Sexual Attitudes: Myths and Realities, 1995; (with Bullough and Marietta Stanton) Nightingale and Her Era: New Scholarship About Women and Nursing, 1990. Recipient Kinsey award for Disting. Sex Rsch., 1994, Syntex Outstanding Nurse Practitioner award, 1992. Fellow Am. Acad. Nursing, Soc. for Sci. Study of Sexuality; mem. APHA, Am. Humanist Assn. Democrat. Home: Northridge Calif. Died Apr. 12, 1996.

BUNDY, HARVEY HOLLISTER, retired bank executive; b. Cambridge, Mass., May 1, 1916; s. Harvey Hollister and Katherine Lawrence (Putnam) B.; m. Edith Southerland Wright, May 29, 1943; children: Harvey Hollister, Harriet Southerland Bundy Burgin, Peter Putnam, Rodman Richards. B.A., Yale U., 1938; M.B.A., Harvard U., 1940. C.P.A., Mass. Accountant Lybrand Ross Bros. & Montgomery (C.P.A.s), Boston, 1940-41; with Gorton Group, Gloucester, Mass., 1946-78; treas. Gorton Group, 1948-78, fin. v.p., 1958-69, exec. v.p., 1969-78; pres., chief exec. officer Bank of New Eng.-North Shore, 1978-84, chmn. bd., 1984-85; chmn. bd. Gloucester Bank and Trust Co., 1986-92; ret., 1992. Mem. Manchester (Mass.) Sch. Com., 1948-54, chmn., 1951-53; agt. Class of '38, Yale Alumni Fund, 1967-71; mem. coms. to visit math. and statistics depts. Harvard Coll., 1970-77; bd. overseers Bates Coll.; trustee Addison Gilbert Hosp., Gloucester. Served to maj. AUS, 1941-46. Mem. Nat. Fisheries Inst. (dir. 1955-63, pres. 1961-62, chmn. bd. 1962-63). Club: Myopia Hunt. Died Feb. 13, 1997.

BUNDY, MCGEORGE, former government official, history educator; b. Boston, Mar. 30, 1919; s. Harvey Hollister and Katharine Lawrence (Putnam) B.; m. Mary Buckminster Lothrop, June 10, 1950; children: Stephen, Andrew, William, James. A.B., Yale, 1940.

Polit. analyst Council Fgn. Relations, 1948-49; vis. lectr. Harvard, 1949-51, assoc. prof. govt., 1951-54, dean faculty arts and scis., 1953-61, prof., 1954-61; spl. asst. to Pres. for nat. security affairs, 1961-66; pres. Ford Found., 1966-79; prof. history NYU, N.Y.C., 1979-89, prof. emeritus, 1989-96; chair com. on reducing the nuclear danger Carnegie Corp. of New York, N.Y.C., 1990-93, scholar-in-residence, 1993-96. Author: (with Stimson) On Active Service, 1948, The Strength of Government, 1968, Danger and Survival, 1988, (with Crowe and Drell) Reducing Nuclear Danger, 1993; editor: Pattern of Responsibility, 1952. Mem. Am. Philos. Soc., Phi Beta Kappa. Died Sept. 16, 1996.

BUNGE, RICHARD PAUL, cell biologist, educator; b. Madison, S.D., Apr. 15, 1932; married, 1956; 2 children. BA, U. Wis., 1954, MS, 1956, MD, 1960. Asst. anatomist U. Wis., 1954-57, instr., 1957-58; from asst. prof. to assoc. prof. anatomy, coll. physicians and surgeons Columbia U., 1962-70; prof. anatomy sch. medicine Washington U., St. Louis, 1970-89; sci. dir. Miami project/paralysis divsn., prof. neurosurg. cell biology anatomy Miami (Fla.) U., 1989—; vis. prof. Harvard Med. Sch., 1968-69; Nat. Multiple Sclerosis Soc. fellow surgeon Coll. Physicians and Surgeonos, Columbua U., 1960-62. Co-author: Peripheral Neuropathy, 2 vols., 2d edit., 1984; co-editor: Spinal Cord Reconstruction, 1983, Current Issues in Neural Regeneration Research, 1988. Recipient Lederle Med. Faculty award, 1964-67. Mem. Am. Assn. Anatomy, Am. Soc. Cell Biology, Am. Assn. Neuropathology, Tissue Culture Assn., Soc. Neuroscience. Achievements include research in biology of cells of the nervous system in vivo and in vitro.

BUNTEN, JOHN WILLIAM, school system administrator; b. Kenilworth, Utah, Aug. 29, 1917; s. John Abner and Martha Ann (Parr) B.; m. Mary Lorene Doty, Jun 24, 1943 (div. Oct. 13, 1943); 1 child, Janice Lorene Auld; m. Lorrene Love Stevenson, Nov. 18, 1973. BS in Agr. Edn., Utah State U., 1939; ME in Vocat. Edn. Adminstrn., Colo. State U., 1951. Tchr. high sch. vocat. agr. Moapa Valley, Nev., 1939-41; supr. edn. and tng. div. VA, Reno, Nev., 1946-48; state supr. agr. edn. State Dept. Edn., Carson City, Nev., 1948-56, state supr. tech. edn., 1958-63; state dir. vocat., tech. and adult edn. Nev. State Bd. Vocat. Edn., Carson City, 1950-71; tchr. edn. educator U. Nev., Reno, 1948-56; sr. program officer Bur. Occupation and Adult Ednl. Region IX/U.S. Dept. Edn., San Francisco, 1971-78; edn. program specialist Western States Br., U.S. Dept. Edn., Washington, 1978-79; chief, so. states br. Bur. Occupation and Adult Edn./U.S. Dept. Edn., Washington, 1979-81, chief program accountability br., 1981-82; commr. Pacific Assn. Schs. and Colls., Newport Beach, Calif., 1992-94; various teaching positions in field. Col. USA, 1941-46, USAR, 1946-78. Recipient Hon. Am. Farmer Degree, FFA, Kansas City, Mo., 1950, Hon. State Homemakers degree State Future Home Makers of Am., Carson City, 1956. Mem. Nat. Assn. State Dirs. Vocat. Edn. (pres. 1970-71, v.p. 1969-70), Nat. Assn. Future Farmers of Am. (bd. dirs. 1974-82), Nev. State Employees Assn. (pres. 1956), Nev. Adult Edn. Assn. (pres. 1961), Am. Assn. Sch. Adminstrs., Am. Vocat. Assn. 9bd. dirs. 1971-72), Nat. Assn. Retired Fed. Employees (v.p. 1989-90), Distributive Edn. Clubs of Am. (life mem.), Indsl. Edn. Clubs of Am. (life mem.), Masons, Phi Delta Kappa, Iota Lama Sigma, Alpha Zeta, Alpha Tau Alpha. Democrat. Presbyterian. Avocations: travel, fishing, hunting, gardening, ednl. cons. Home: Medford Oreg. DIed Oct. 26, 1995.

BURCHESS, ARNOLD A., artist, sculptor, educator; b. Chgo., June 7, 1912; s. Herman Burchess and Annetta Rossiny; m. Aline Thistlethwaite; 1 child, Robert. B.S.S., CCNY, 1934; student George W. Eggers, Robert Garrison. Asst. 3 stone bas-reliefs walls of Radio City, N.Y.C, 1935; lectr./demonstrator Shapes in Clay, Met. Mus. Art, N.Y.C., 1963; chmn. dept. fine art Fashion Inst. Tech., N.Y.C., 1963-73; instr. art Saddleback Coll. (Calif.), 1980-83; vis. prof. sculpture Bowdoin Coll., Maine, 1977. One-man shows include: Van Dimant Gallery, Southampton, N.Y., 1957, Mus. Modern Art, N.Y.C., 1959, Maine Art Gallery, Wiscasset, 1975, Walker Art Mus., Brunswick, Maine, 1978; exhibited in group shows: Riverside Mus., 1955, G.W.V. Smith Mus., Springfield, Mass., 1955, Contemporary Art Gallery, 1955, Birmingham Mus. Art, 1955, Calif. Watercolor Soc., 1955, Delgrado Mus. Art, 1957, Westchester Art Ctr., 1958, U.S. Nat. Mus., 1958, N.Y. City Ctr., 1958, Long Beach Mcpl. Art Ctr. (Calif.), 1957, Ala. Poly. Coll., 1957, Jacksonville Mus. Art (Fla.), 1957, Lauren Rogers Mus. Art, Laurel, Miss., 1957, Challis Gallery, Laguna Beach, Calif., 1983; executed portrait bust in bronze of Edmund Muskie, State Capitol, Augusta, Maine, 1972. Author: Understanding the Human Form, 1981. Featured water colorist Am.-Artist, 1959, 100 Watercolor Techniques, Watson-Guptill, 1968. Mem. Am. Watercolor Soc., Audubon Artists, Ala. Watercolor Soc., Springfield Art League, Calif. Watercolor Soc., New Orleans.

BURGAR, RUBY RICH, college health service nurse; b. Boardman, N.C., Sept. 29, 1908; d. William Hardy and Lena (Carter) Rich; m. William Edward Burgar, June 29, 1935 (div. 1940). Diploma, Baker Sanatorium Sch. Nursing, 1929; BA in Sociology, Occidental Coll., 1955; postgrad., UCLA, 1957-64. RN, Calif. Indsl. nurse Manville-Jenkes Co., Gastonia, N.C., 1929-30; pub. health nurse Hampshire County Dept. Health, W.Va., 1931-32; staff nurse USPHS, San Francisco, 1932-35, Emergency Hosp., Washington, 1940-41, Queen's Hosp., Honolulu, 1941, St. Francis Hosp., San Francisco, 1941, Monterey (Calif.) Hosp., 1941-42; staff nurse, then head nurse Emmons Student Health Svc., Occidental Coll., L.A., 1942-66, nurse dir., 1966-74, relief nurse, 1976-77. Active L.A. chpt. ARC, 1952-91. Staff nurse USN, 1930-31; jr. nurse officer res. USPHS, 1954-74. Recipient Clara Barton medallion ARC, 1977, 40 Yr. pin, 1992; named Vol. of Yr. Am. Bapt. Home, 1992-93. Fellow Am. Coll. Health Assn. (emeritus; Ruth E. Boyington award 1968, Edward E. Hitchcock award 1971, Cert. of Appreciation 1993); mem. ANA, Pacific Coast Coll. Health Assn. (exec. dir. emeritus 1987, Ruby Rich Burgar Svc. award established 1977), Calif. Nurses Assn., Nat. League Nursing (charter), Calif. League for Nursing, L.A. Lung Assn., L.A. County Heart Assn., L.A. Art Mus., Alpha Tau Delta. Presbyterian. Avocations: sewing, knitting, gardening, photography, ceramics. Died May 22, 1996.

BURGESS, ARTHUR HARRY, accountant; b. Sharon, S.C., Oct. 25, 1903; s. Arthur Calhoun and Mary (Love) B.; m. Sara Elizabeth Doll, Nov. 30, 1933; children: Sara Elizabeth Burgess Frazer, Arthur Harry. Student Furman U., 1921-23. Pub. acct., Hickory, N.C., 1928—; chmn. bd. Arthur H. Burgess & Co. Mem. adv. bd. trustees Queens Coll.; elder Presbyn. Ch. Mem. Am. Inst. CPA's, N.C. Assn. CPA's, Sharon Found. CPA's (pres.). Paul Harris fellow. Clubs: Lake Hickory Country (Hickory); Charlotte (N.C.) City.

BURHENNE, HANS JOACHIM, physician, radiology educator; b. Hannover, Germany, Dec. 27, 1925; emigrated to U.S., 1955, naturalized, 1959; s. Adolph and Clara (Ditges) B.; m. Linda Jean Warren, Oct. 20, 1978; children by previous marriage: Mark, Antonia, Yvonne. Matura, Gymnasium, Salzburg, Austria, 1944; M.D. magna cum laude, Maximilian Med. Sch., Munich, 1951. Intern Monmouth Med. Center, Long Branch, N.J.; resident in radiology Peter Bent Brigham Hosp., Boston, 1955-59; instr. Harvard U., 1958-59; chmn. dept. radiology Children's Hosp., San Francisco, 1960-78; clin. prof. radiology U. Calif., San Francisco, 1960-78; prof. radiology U. B.C., 1978-96, head dept. radiology, 1978-91. Author: Sierra Spring Ski Touring, 1971, (with A.R. Margulis) Alimentary Tract Roentgenology, 4th edit., 1989, Biliary Lithotripsy, 1990, Practical Alimentary-Tract Radiology, 1993; editor: Mammography, 1969; editorial Bd. Radiologica Clinica, 1964-90, Oncology, 1973-77, Gastrointestinal Radiology, 1976-96, Western Jour. of Medicine, 1975-79, Radiology, 1983-91, Lithotripsy and Stone Disease, 1988-94. Chmn. bd. dirs. Cathedral Sch., San Francisco, 1976-77; bd. dirs. Sterling-Winthrop Imaging Rsch. Inst., 1989-92. NIH fellow, 1959; recipient Walter B. Cannon medal, 1982, Forsell Lectr. and medal Swedish Acad. Medicine, Stockholm, 1990, Disting. Svc. Gold medal Am. Roentgen Ray Soc., 1995; named Disting. Lectr., U. B.C., 1987. Fellow Am. Coll. Radiology (counselor 1973-77), Royal Coll. Physicians Can., Royal Coll. Surgeons Ireland (hon. faculty radiology); mem. Calif. Radiol. Soc. (pres. 1977-78), Internat. Soc. Radiology (exec. com. 1985-96, chmn. diagnostic radiology 1988-96), Soc. Gastrointestinal Radiologists (pres. 1977), Internat. Soc. Biliary Radiology (pres. 1989-91). Home: Vancouver Can Died June 1, 1996.

BURKE, WILLIAM JAMES, chemist, educator, consultant; b. Lowellville, Ohio, May 24, 1912; s. Sylvester L. and M. Catherine (Saltzman) B.; m. Katharine M. King, June 21, 1940; children: Mary Katharine (Mrs. Frank Noyes), Susan E. (Mrs. Victor Burke), Thomas W.J., D. Kevin. A.B., Ohio U., Athens, 1934; Ph.D., Ohio State U., 1937. Research chemist central chem. dept. E.I. duPont de Nemours & Co., Henry Clay, Del., 1937-46; assoc. prof. Ohio U., Athens, 1946-47; assoc. prof. U. Utah, 1947-50, dept. head, 1949-62, prof., 1950-62; v.p. Ariz. State U., Tempe, 1962-76; prof. chemistry Ariz. State U., 1962-83, prof. emeritus, 1983-94, dean Grad. Coll., 1963-76, dean emeritus Grad. Coll., 1989-94; cons. U.S. Army, 1956-62, 72-75, Monsanto Co., Paragon Optical; mem. ICA team to survey higher edn. in Ethiopia U.S. State Dept., 1959-60; past pres. Western Assn. Grad. Schs, Midwest Assn. Grad. Schs.; mem. exec. com. Nat. Assn. State Univs. and Land Grant Colls., 1969-71; mem. Grad. Record Exam. Bd., 1972-74; chmn. editorial bd. Grad. Programs and Admissions Manual; generalist cons. Nat. Council Archtl. Registration Bd., 1969-72; mem. Nat. Archtl. Accrediting Bd., 1973-78. Contbr. articles to profl. jours. Past pres., dir. Catholic Charities Salt Lake City. Fellow AAAS; mem. Am. Chem. Soc. (vis. assoc. com. on profl. tng. 1959-94, councilor for Central Ariz. sect. 1967-70), Australian Rock Art Research Assn., Am. Rock Art Research Assn., Midwest Conf. on Grad. Study and Research (past chmn.), Phi Beta Kappa, Sigma Xi, Phi Lambda Upsilon, Gamma Alpha, Alpha Chi Sigma, Phi Kappa Phi (pres. Ariz. State U. chpt. 1977-78), Pi Sigma Epsilon. Patentee in field. Home: Tempe Ariz. Died Dec. 18, 1994.

BURKET, RICHARD EDWARD, agriprocessing executive; b. Sandusky, Ohio, Apr. 25, 1928; s. Firm C. and Marie (Bock) B.; m. Carolyn Anne McMillen, Feb. 22, 1951 (div. 1979); children: Leslie, Buffie, Lynn Murphy Burket. B.A., Oberlin Coll., 1950. Tech. sales mgr. Rhoades Equipment Co., Ft. Wayne, Ind., 1954-55; with Chemurgy div. Central Soya Co., Ft. Wayne, Ind., 1955-69; dir. mktg. Chemurgy div. Central Soya Co., Chgo., 1966-69; v.p. protein specialties Archer Daniel Midland Co., Decatur, Ill., 1969-74, v.p., asst. to pres., 1974-80; v.p., asst. to chmn. Archer Daniel Midland Co., Decatur, 1980—; mem. Gov.'s Task Force on Future Rural Agriculture. Bd. dirs. Decatur Area Arts Council, 1972-84; bd. dirs. Macon County United Way, 1974-77, Boys Club, Decatur, 1979-86, Decatur Metro C. of C., 1982-87; mem. Millikin U. Assocs., Macon County Econ. Devel. Found., St. Mary's Hosp. Adv. Bd., Ill. Agriculture Export Adv. Com. Served to 1st lt. U.S. Army, 1974-77. Mem. Inst. Food Technologists, Am. Mgmt. Assn., Soy Protein Council (chmn. 1974-76), Gov.'s Rural Affairs Council, U.S. Sweetener Producers Group, Ill. Agrl. Export Adv. Com., Ill. 4-H Found. Bd. Clubs: Decatur, Decatur Country.

BURKHART, ROBERT EDWARD, English language educator; b. Pitts., Jan. 11, 1937; s. Edward Wendelin and Violet Elizabeth (Reichel) B.; m. Sylvia Carol Davis, June 11, 1966 (div. 1988); 1 child, Heather Ellen; m. Elesha Lillian Pennington, Jan. 28, 1989; 1 child, Jonathan Robert Lowell. BBA, U. Pitts., 1958, MA, 1963; PhD, U. Cin., 1967. Instr. U. Ky., Lexington, 1965-67; asst. prof. Ea. Ky. U., Richmond, 1967-69, assoc. prof., 1969-71, prof., 1971-95, chair dept. English, 1979-86. Author: Shakespeare's Bad Quartos, 1975, (poetry) Places in Time, 1995; co-editor: Perspectives on Our Time, 1970; contbr. articles to profl. and scholarly jours. Exec. com. Concerned Citizens Madison County, Richmond, 1984-87. 1st lt. U.S. Army, 1959-61. Fellow Inst. at Folger Shakespeare Libr., NEH, 1981. Mem. MLA, Shakespeare Assn. Am., Internat. Shakespeare Assn., South Atlantic MLA, Southeastern Renaissance Conf., Ky. Philological Assn. (pres. 1985-86), Ky. Assn. Depts. English (pres. 1984-86), Hemingway Soc., Sigma Tau Delta. Democrat. Avocation: art collecting. Died Sept., 1995.

BURKS, VERNER IRWIN, architect; b. Des Arc, Ark., June 16, 1923; s. Verner Irwin and Leta Beatrice (Burton) B. BArch, Washington U., St. Louis, 1951. Registered architect, Mo., Kans. Ptnr. Burks & Landberg Architects, St. Louis, 1955-76; v.p., sec. Burks & Landberg Architects, Inc., St. Louis, 1976-78; propr. Burks Assoc., Architects and Planners, St. Louis, 1978-95; chmn. Landmarks and Urban Design Commn., City of St. Louis, 1969-77; chmn. condemnation com. St. Louis Bd. Bldg. Appeals, 1962-68; co-chmn. Old Post Office landmark Com., 1963—; 1st v.p. Campbell House Found., 1965-75, hon. dir., 1975—. Jr. warden Christ Ch. Episcopal Cathedral, 1975. Recipient spl. honor award for renovation Christ Ch. Epcopal Cathedral, Guild R eligious Architecture, 1970; designated cathedral architect, 1980; also named architect of New Cthedral of St. Louis (R.C.) 1985, supervised completion of Cathedral's Mosaic Interior, designed and supervised Mosaic Mus. on lower level. Fellow AIA (emeritus). Died Feb. 12, 1998.

BURLANT, WILLIAM JACK, retired chemical company executive; b. Chgo., Oct. 20, 1928; m. Arlene Rosenberg, July 31, 1955; children: Diana, Michael. BS, CCNY, 1949; MA, Bklyn. Coll., 1953; PhD in Chemistry, Poly. Inst. N.Y. Asst. dir. chem. scis. Ford Motor Co., Dearborn, Mich., 1955-79; tech. mgr. Gen. Electric Corp., Columbus, Ohio, 1979-81; dir. Lexington Lab. Kendall Co., Boston, 1981-84; v.p. rsch., prin. scientist GAF Chems. Corp., Wayne, N.J., 1984-93; ret., 1993; mem. adv. bd. NSF. Author: (book) Block and Graft Polymers, 1959; contbr. articles to profl. jours.; patentee in field. Mem. Am. Chem. Soc. Died Mar. 12, 1997.

BURNETT-ZEISEL, HALLIE SOUTHGATE, author, editor; b. St. Louis, Dec. 3, 1907; d. John McKnight and Elizabeth (Baker) Southgate; m. Whit Burnett, 1942 (dec.); children: John Southgate, Whitney Ann Burnett Voss; m. William Zeisel, 1977 (dec. 1981). Co-editor Story mag. Story Press, N.Y.C., 1942-70, Welcome to Life, 1947; sr. fiction editor Prentice-Hall, Inc., N.Y.C., 1958-60; fiction editor Yankee Mag., N.H., 1959-60; assoc. prof. lit. Sarah Lawrence Coll., Bronxville, N.Y., 1960-64; book editor Reader's Digest Book Club, Pleasantville, N.Y., 1965-66; tchr. short story writing N.Y.C. Writers Conf. Wagner Coll., S.I., N.Y., summers 1955-60, Hunter Coll., 1959-61. Author: (short stories, novellas) The Boarders in the Rue Madame, 1966, others; (novels) A Woman in Possession, 1951, This Heart, This Hunter, 1953, The Brain Pickers, 1957, Watch on the Wall, 1965, Daughter-in-Laws's Cookbook, 1969, The Millionaire's Cookbook, 1971, also On Writing the Short Story, 1983, and mag. articles, anthologies; author, editor: (with Whit Burnett) Fiction Writer's Handbook, 1975; editor: (with Whit Burnett) The Fiction of the Forties, 1949, Sextette, Story Nos. 1, 2, 3, 4, 1951-54, The Best College Writing, 1962, Prize College Stories, 1963, The Stone Soldier, 1964, The Modern Short Story in the Making, 1964, Story Jubilee, 1965, Story: The Yearbook of Discovery, 1968-70, Fiction of a Generation, The Tough Ones, Thirteen Tales of Terror. Past mem. Jr. League N.Y.C. Recipient O. Henry prize, 1942. Mem. Woman Pays Club, PEN (past mem. bd. dirs.), Overseas Press Club (N.Y.C.

chpt.), Woman's Club (Raleigh, N.C. chpt.). Episcopalian. Home: Raleigh N.C. Died Sept. 4, 1991.

BURNHAM, LINDEN FORBES SAMPSON, executive president of Guyana; b. Feb. 20, 1923; s. James Ethelbert and Rachel Abigail B.; ed. Queen's Coll., Brit. Guiana; B.A., London (Eng.) U., 1944, LL.B., 1947; LL.D. (hon.), Dalhousie U., N.S., Can., 1977; m. Sheila Bernice Lataste, May 1951; children—Roxane, Annabelle, Francesca; m. 2d, Viola Victorine Harper, Feb. 24, 1967; children—Melanie Abiola, Ulele Imoinda. Called to bar Gray's Inn, London, 1948, created Queen's counsel, 1960, sr. counsel, 1966; pres. West Indian Students' Union, London, 1947-48; co-founder People's Progressive Party, 1949, chmn., 1949-55; mem. Legislature, 1953, 57—; minister edn., 1953; founder People's Nat. Congress, 1957, leader, 1957—; pres. Brit. Guiana Labour Union, 1952-56, 63-65, leader Parliamentary opposition, 1957-64; mayor Georgetown (Guyana), 1959-60, 63-64; premier of Brit. Guiana, 1964-66; prime minister of Guyana, 1966-81, pres., 1980—. Decorated Order of Excellence (Guyana); Order Nat. Flag 1st Class (Democratic People's Republic of Korea). Methodist. Clubs: Guyana Motor Racing (patron), Guyana Sports, Cosmos Sports, Malteenoes Sports, Guyana Chess Assn. (pres.), Demerara Cricket, Georgetown Cricket. Author: A Destiny to Mould, 1970.

BURNHAM, VIRGINIA SCHROEDER, medical writer; b. Savannah, Ga., Dec. 9, 1908; d. Henry Alfred and Natalie Morris (Munde) Schroeder; children: Douglass L., Peter B., Gilliat S. (dec.), William W., Virginia L., Daniel B. Student, Smith Coll., Barnard Coll. V.p., sales mgr., bd. dirs. Conn. Mfg. Co. Inc., Waterbury, 1952-61, pres., chief exec. officer, bd. dirs., 1961-73; pres. Burnham Industries, Watertown, Conn., 1956-59; pres., bd. dirs. NuTip Corp., Waterbury, 1962-64, Maretta Inc., N.Y.C., 1963-65, pres., treas., bd. dirs. Tech., Inc., Waterbury, 1969-73; sec. The Gaylord Hosp., Wallingford, Conn., 1970-81; pres. Tech. Internat. Corp., 1973-75, Tech. Interaction, Med. Cons., Greenwich, Conn., 1975—, The Paper Mill, Inc., 1989-92; dir. Community Mental Health Ctr., Inc., Stamford, Conn., 1974-78; mem. nat. adv. food and drug com. FDA, Dept. Health, Edn., and Welfare, Washington, 1973-76; mem. health rsch. facilities coun. NIH, Washington, 1959-61, nat. adv. heart coun., 1957-60; mem. ad-hoc com. cons. on med. rsch. Subcom. Labor, Health and Welfare, U.S. Senate Appropriations Com., Washington, 1959-60. Co-author: Knowing Yourself, 1992, The Two-Edged Sword, 1990, The Lake With Two Dams, 1993, Since Time Began, 1994; contbr. articles to Am. Health Found. Newsletter, Jour. Sci. Health, Conn. Med. Jour. Mem. adv. coun. steering com. The Episc. Ch. Found., 1970-76, Commn. to Reform the Ct. System, Gen. Assembly, State of Conn., 1974-78, nat. adv. coun. SBA, Washington 1976-77, chmn. dist. adv. coun., Hartford, Conn., 1976-77; pres. Conn. Citizens for Judicial Modernization, Inc., Hartford, 1976-78; mem. Presdl. Task Force on Rehab. of Prisoners, Washington, 1969-70; bd. dirs. Assn. to Unite the Democracies, Washington, 1982—; chmn. dist. adv. coun. Small Bus. Adminstrn., Hartford, 1976-77; pres. Conn. chpt. Am. Health Found., N.Y.C., 1971-73; dir. exec. com. Greater N.Y. Safety Coun., N.Y.C., 1971-79, dir., 1964-79; vice-chmn., dir. Conn. Coun. of Nat. Coun. Crime and Delinquency, Hartford, 1965-73; mem. adv. com. Conn. Regional Med. Program, 1973-76, FDA, Washington and many more civic and health orgns. Decorated Knighthood of Honour and Merit, Sovereign Hospitaler Order of St. John of Jerusalem, Knights of Malta, 1985; recipient Ira V. Hiscock award Conn. Pub. Health Assn., 1986; Silver Key award The Gaylord Hosp., 1970, Disting. Svc. award Conn. Heart Assn., 1960, Conn. Mother of Yr. award Am. Mothers Com., 1951, Cert. of Honor, Conn. Cancer Soc., 1950, Merit award Am. Heart Assn., 1960. Mem. AAAS, APHA, Am. Cancer Soc., Am. Heart Assn., Am. Holistic Med. Found., Am. Women in Sci., Conn. Bus. & Industry Assn., Conn. Pub. Health Assn., Nat. Assn. Mfrs., N.Y. Acad. Sci. Republican. Episcopalian.

BURNS, GEORGE WASHINGTON, botany educator; b. Cin., Nov. 20, 1913; s. George Washington and Caroline (Little) B.; m. Hermine McDonald, June 15, 1942; children: George McDonald, Barbara Lynette, Theodore Scott. AB, U. Cin., 1937; PhD, U. Minn., 1941. Teaching fellow botany U. Minn., 1937-41, instr., 1945-46, faculty, summer sessions, 1948-49; asst. prof. botany Ohio Wesleyan U., 1946-50, assoc. prof., 1950-54, prof. botany, 1954-79, prof. emeritus, 1979-94, chmn. dept., 1954-70, acting v.p., dean, 1957-59, acting pres., 1958-59, v.p., dean, 1959-61; vis. prof. Kerala U., India, 1964, U. Bombay, India, 1965, 66; Cons. State Dept. Edn. Mission to India, AID, summers 1964-67; Head insts. sect. NSF, 1961-62. Author: The Science of Genetics, 1969, 72, 76, 80, 83, 89, The Plant Kingdom, 1974; also articles in tech. jours. Served as lt. USNR, 1942-45. Fellow A.A.A.S., Ohio Acad. Sci. (v.p. 1956-57, sec. 1957-63, pres. 1969-70); mem. Am. Genetic Assn., Am. Soc. Human Genetics, Bot. Soc. Am., Arctic Inst. in N.Am., Sigma Xi. Home: Delaware Ohio Died Apr. 23, 1994; interred Oak Grove Cemetery, Delaware, OH.

BURRIS, KATHRYN ANN, professional association administrator; b. Fredricksburg, Tex., Dec. 1, 1957; d. Bryon Curthburn and Sara Lee (Matthews) Rinehart; m. Charles Anthony Burris, Nov. 4, 1989. BS, Howard Payne U., 1979; diploma, Ranger Jr. Coll., 1982. Cert. Okla. Bd. Nurse Registration and Nursing Edn. Educator Brownwood (Tex.) Home and Sch., 1979-80; critical care nurse Brownwood Regional Hosp., 1981-83; home healthcare nurse Healthcare, Inc., Tulsa, 1983-85; staff nurse Broken Arrow (Okla.) Med. Ctr., 1984-85; state dir. Am. Chronic Pain Assn., Tulsa, 1987-93; exec. dir. Pain Tamers Support Network, Inc., Tulsa, 1993-96; mem. Rehabilitative Adv. Coun. State Okla., 1993—; mem. Assistive Tech. Coun. Okla., 1994—. Feature columnist (newspaper) The Tulsa Tribune, 1988-92; contbg. writer (newsletters) Nat. Chronic Pain Outreach Assn. Lifeline, 1988, Am. Chronic Pain Assn. Chronicle, 1989-93, Pain Tamers Support Network, Inc., 1993—. Make-up artist Brownwood Theater Co., 1980-81, wardrobe dir., 1980; mem. State of Okla. Rehab. Adv. Coun., 1993—, State of Okla. Assistive Tech. Adv. Coun., 1994-95. Mem. Reflex Sympathetic Dystrophy Syndrome Assn. (state dir. 1988—), Fibromyalgia Network. Democrat. Avocations: collectibles, gardening, floral arranging, regional cuisine, cinema. Died Apr. 24, 1996.

BURROUGHS, WILLIAM SEWARD, writer; b. St. Louis, Feb. 5, 1914; s. Perry Mortimer and Laura (Lee) B.; m. Ilse Herzfeld Klapper, 1937 (div. 1946); m. Joan Vollmer, 1946 (dec. 1951); 1 son, William Seward, Jr. (dec. 1981). A.B., Harvard U., 1936; postgrad. in ethnology and archeology; med. student, U. Vienna. Formerly newspaper reporter, pvt. detective, exterminator, now full-time writer. Author: Junkie: Confessions of an Unredeemed Drug Addict, 1953 (pub. as Junky, 1977), The Naked Lunch, 1959 (pub. as Naked Lunch, 1962), (with Brion Gysin) The Exterminator, 1960, (with Sinclair Beiles, Gregory Corso, and Gysin) Minutes to Go, 1960, The Soft Machine, 1961, The Ticket That Exploded, 1962, (with Allen Ginsberg) The Yage Letters, 1963, Dead Fingers Talk, 1963, Nova Express, 1964, Roosevelt After Inauguration, 1964, Valentine's Day Reading, 1965, The White Subway, 1965, Health Bulletin: APO:33: A Metabolic Regulator, 1965, (with Lee Harwood) Darayt, 1965, Time, 1965, (with Claude Pelieu and Carl Weissner) So Who Owns Death TV?, 1967, They Do Not Always Remember, 1968, Ali's Smile, 1969, The Dead Star, 1969, Entretiens avec William Burroughs, 1969, (with Pelieu and Weissner) Fernseh-Tuberkulose, 1969, (with Weissner) The Braille Film, 1970, (with Gysin) Third Mind, 1970, The Last Words of Dutch Schultz: A Fiction in the Form of a Film Script, 1970, The Wild Boys: A Book of the Dead, 1971, (with Pelieu) Jack Kerouac, 1971, Electronic Revolution, 1971, (with Gysin and Ian Somerville) Brion Gysin Let the Mice In, 1973, Mayfair Academy Series More or Less, 1973, Exterminator!, 1973, The Book of Breething, 1974, (with Charles Gatewood) Sidetripping, 1975, (with Eric Mottram) Snack: Two Tape Transcripts, 1975, Port of Saints, 1975, Cobblestone Gardens, 1976, The Retreat Diaries, 1976, Short Novels, 1978, Naked Scientology, 1978, Blade Runner: A Movie, 1979, Doctor Benway: A Variant Passage from "The Naked Lunch", 1979, Ah Pook Is Here and Other Texts, 1979, Cities of the Red Night, 1981, Easy Routines, 1981, Letters to Allen Ginsburg, 1953-1957, 1981, A William Burroughs Reader, 1982, The Place of Dead Roads, 1984, The Burroughs File, 1984, The Adding Machine: Collected Essays, 1985, Queer, 1986, The Cat Inside, 1986, The Western Lands, 1987, Interzone, 1988, The Black Rider (libretto), 1990, Ghost of Chance, 1991, Speed & Kentucky Ham: Two Novels, 1993, The Letters of William S. Burroughs, 1945-1959, 1993, Seven Deadly Sins, 1994, My Education: A Book of Dreams, 1994; screenwriter: (with Gysin) Towers Open Fire, 1963, (with Antony Balch) Bill and Tony, 1966; recs. include Call Me Burroughs, 1965, William S. Burroughs/John Giorno, 1975, You're the Man I Want to Share My Money With, 1981, Nothing Here Now But the Recordings, 1981. Served with AUS, World War II. Died Aug. 5, 1997.

BURROWS, GORDON W., judge, assemblyman; m. Josephine Ramirez; children: Craig A., Gordon A., Paul D. Grad., Yale U.; JD, St. John's U. Ptnr. Woodrow, Burrows & Vaccaro, Yonkers; justice State Supreme Ct., White Plains, N.Y., 1988-96; dep. minority leader Assembly; chmn. Assembly Judiciary com.; elected mem. Yonkers City Coun., Westchester County Bd. of Suprs. With USN. Home: Yonkers N.Y. Died Jan. 10, 1997.

BURTON, DWIGHT LOWELL, educator; b. Carson Lake, Minn., Aug. 9, 1922; s. Benjamin Otis and Beryl (Green) B.; m. Claudia Holland, Feb. 15, 1968; children: Barbara Kay, Christine Beryle. B.S., U. Minn., 1943, M.A., 1947, Ph.D., 1951. High sch. tchr. English Superior, Wis., 1946-47; tchr. English, head dept. U. Minn. High Sch., 1947-52; prof. English edn. Fla. State U., 1952-91, chmn. dept. curriculum and instrn., ret. Author: Literature Study in the High Schools, 1958, rev. edit., 70; co-author: Teaching English in Today's High Schools, 1965, rev. edit., 1970, Teaching English Today, 1975; editor: English Jour., 1955-64; cons. editor: Research in the Teaching of English. Served from pvt. to capt. AUS, 1943-46. Decorated Bronze Star; Croix de Guerre (France); recipient Honor award Adolescent Lit. Assembly, 1981. Mem. Nat. Conf. Research in English, Conf. English Edn. (past chmn.), Nat. Council Tchrs. of English (2d v.p. 1966, Disting. Service award 1970), Phi Delta Kappa, Sigma Tau Delta. Home: Tallahassee Fla. Died Aug. 19, 1995.

BUTA, MARY OPRITZA, retired business education educator; b. Youngstown, Ohio, Jan. 2, 1913; d. Daniel Pamfilie and Marina (Neaga) Opritza; m. Serafin Simon Buta, Mar. 5, 1949 (dec. 1989); 1 child, Mary Jeanette Buta Lomuscio. BS in Edn., Miami U., Oxford, Ohio, 1935; MA in Edn., NYU, 1940; postgrad., Youngstown (Ohio) State U., 1932-33, 73, Westminster Coll., New Wilmington, Pa., 1962. Cert. apprentice pharmacist, Ohio State Bd. Tchr. Bryan High Sch., Yellow Springs, Ohio, 1935-37, Meml. High Sch., Campbell, Ohio, 1937-43, Bliss Coll., Columbus, Ohio, 1944, Struthers (Ohio) High Sch., 1946-49, 53-81; tchr., treas. North High Sch., Youngstown, Ohio, 1952-53; confidential sec. Am. Embassy U.S. State Dept., Bucharest, Romania, 1949-50; dept. chmn. Struthers High Sch., 1976-81. Sponsor Nat. Honor Soc., Struthers High Sch.; active Struthers Girl Scouts, 1962-65. Named One of Outstanding Secondary Educators by Outstanding Secondary Educators of Am., 1973. Mem. AAUW (editor Youngstown chpt. bull. 1968-70), NEA (life), Mahoning Ret. Tchrs. Assn. (sec. 1981-83), Salem Hist. Soc. (life), Ohio Ret. Tchrs. Assn. (life), Nat. Ret. Tchrs. Assn., Office Strategic Svcs. Vets. (life), Raymond Molyneaux Hughes Soc. (personal accomplishmensts recognition cert. Miami U.), FDR Pensioners Club, Carmen Sylva Aux., Frat. Bus. Edn. (hon.), Delta Kappa Gamma Internat. Soc. (Gamma Epsilon chpt. honoring women educators 1974), Delta Pi Epsilon (life, hon. grad. bus. edn. 1948). Mem. Holy Trinity Romanian Orthodox Ch. Avocations: ceramics, memoirs.

BUTCHER, DONALD FRANKLIN, statistics educator, computer scientist; b. Parkersburg, W.Va., June 29, 1937; s. John Franklin and Anna Pearl (Hersman) B.; m. Alice Adelia Rosier, July 24, 1959; children: Dianna Lynn, Daniel Bruce, Damon Scott. B.S., W.Va. U., 1960, M.S., 1962; Ph.D., Iowa State U., 1965. Asst. prof. stats. W.Va. U., Morgantown, 1965-69, assoc. prof., 1970-73, prof., 1973—, chmn. dept. stats. and computer sci., 1973-94; asst. prof. Kans. State U., 1969-70; dir. Math. and Statis. Cons., Inc.; chair bd. dirs. Software Valley Corp., 1985-90, mem., 1991-92; pres. bd. dirs. Software Valley Found., 1986-87; sec. bd. dirs. Software Valley Devel. Bd., 1987-88; mem. Software Valley Policy Com., 1990—. Contbr. articles on statis. methodology, exptl. design, Monte Carlo simulation using digital computers to profl. jours. Mem. Assn. Computing Machinery, Am. Statis. Assn., Biometrics Soc., Sigma Xi, Gamma Sigma Delta, Upsilon Pi Epsilon, Mu Sigma Rho. Republican. Methodist. Died Oct. 9, 1997.

BUTCHER, JAMES WALTER, biologist; b. Pa., Feb. 14, 1917; s. Louis and Mary B.; m. Mary Katharine Culley, June 18, 1944; children: Craig, Mary Helen. B.S., U. Pitts., 1943; M.S., U. Minn., 1949, Ph.D., 1951. With Gulf Research Devel. Corp., 1948, Dept. Agr., 1950-52, Minn. Dept. Agr., 1952-57; mem. faculty Mich. State U., East Lansing, 1957-96; prof. biology Mich. State U., 1965-96, asst., asso. dean research, 1969-74, chmn. dept. zoology, 1974-81, prof., chmn. emeritus, 1981-96; acting dean Mich. State U. (Coll. Natural Sci.), 1973; cons. in field. Author papers in field, rev. articles. Served with USAAF, 1943-47. Fulbright sr. research scholar U. Vienna, 1966-67; grantee fed. and state govts., also industry. Mem. Phi Beta Kappa, Sigma Xi. Home: Saint Augustine Fla. Died May 12, 1996.

BUTLER, EUGENE, editor, publisher; b. Starkville, Miss., June 11, 1894; s. Tait and Dell (Bell) B.; m. Mary Britt Burns, June 11, 1921; children: Eugene Britt, Mary Jean. BS, Miss. Agrl. and Mech. Coll. (now Miss. State U.), 1913, Cornell U., 1915; MS, Iowa State U., 1917. With Progressive Farmer, 1917-95, editor Tex. edit., mgr. Dallas office, pres., 1953-68, chmn. bd. dirs., 1964-84, editor-in-chief emeritus, 1984-95; agrl. info. specialist M.S.A. trip to, Europe, 1952; mem. group educators and journalists selected by Carnegie Endowment for Internat. Peace to make goodwill trip to, S.Am., 1941. Bd. dirs. Hill Jr. Coll. History Complex; mem. Fed. Hosp. Coun., 1951-55, Nation Cotton Adv. Coun., 1962-66. Recipient Hoblitzelle award for advancement Tex. rural life, 1953; award for outstanding contbn. to Tex. agr. Tex. Cottonseed Crushers Assn., 1957; award for profl. writers Am. Seed Trade Assn., 1961; Tex. Fedn. Co-ops. Agrl. Press award, 1962; Nat. award for Agrl. Excellence Nat. Agrl. Mktg. Assn., 1986; Distinguished Service award Nat. Future Farmers Am., 1968; Farm Editor of Year award Tex. Farmers Union, 1975; Centennial award for outstanding contbns. to Tex. agr. Tex. A. and M. U., 1976; Distinguished Service award Miss. State U. Alumni Assn., 1978; named Alumnus of Yr. Miss. State U. Alumni Assn., 1986, also one of ten most disting. grads.; one of 10 grads. chosen to represent Miss. State U. at Nat. Assn. State Univs. and Land Grant Coll.'s 100th anniversary observance. Mem. Tex. Agrl. Workers Assn. (pres. 1940-41, Distinguished Service award 1978), Dallas Agrl. Club (pres. 1935), Tex. Forestry Assn., S.C.V., Phi Kappa Phi, Alpha Zeta, Sigma Delta Chi. Clubs: Dallas Hardware and Implement, Ferndale Fishing. Home: Dallas Tex. Died June 5, 1995.

BUTLER, GEORGE ANDREWS, retired banker; b. Westmont, N.J., Apr. 14, 1928; s. John T. and Kathryn B.; m. Barbara J. Thomas, June 17, 1950; children: Lynn B., William E. Thomas S., Pamela S. BS in Econs, U. Pa., 1950. With First Pa. Banking and Trust Co., 1950-97, exec. v.p., 1968-76, chief adminstrv. officer, 1976-77; exec. v.p. First Pa. Corp., 1973-74, vice chmn., 1975-97, also bd. dirs.; vice chmn., pres., chief oper. officer First Pa. Bank, 1977-79; chmn., pres., chief exec. officer First Pa. Corp., 1979-90; pres. Core States Fin. Corp. (formerly First Pa. Corp.), 1990-91; bd. dir. Gen. Accident Group Cos., CoreStates Fin. Corp. Bd. dirs. Peirce Phelps. With AUS, 1946-47. Mem. Union League Club, Mfrs. Golf and Country Club (Phila.). Died Aug. 22, 1997.

BUTLER, JAMES ROBERT, geology educator; b. Macon, Ga., Apr. 17, 1930; s. Walter Clark and Edna Ruth (Hardwick) B.; m. Gail Ann Sargeant, July 30, 1960 (div. 1980); children: James Robert, Sarah Pace, Erin Gail; m. Elizabeth L. Van Leuven, Oct. 14, 1989. BS, U. Ga., 1952; MS, U. Colo., 1955; PhD, Columbia U., 1962. Lectr. Columbia U., N.Y.C., 1959-60; successively asst. prof., assoc. prof., prof. U. N.C., Chapel Hill, 1960-93, prof. emeritus, 1993—; cons. in field. Contbr. articles to profl. jours. Served to 1st lt. U.S. Army, 1954-56. Fellow Geol. Soc. Am. (chmn. S.E. sect. 1980); mem. Nat. Assn. Geology Tchrs. Democrat. Avocations: travel; hiking. Deceased.

BYRD, JOHN LUTHER, JR., civilian military employee, senior executive service, SES-04; b. Simms, Tex., June 12, 1935; s. John Luther, Sr. and Mary Ethyl (Jacobs) B.; m. Bonny Jane Daugherty, Dec. 31, 1960; 1 child, Randall Duane. BS in Indsl. Engring., Tex. A&M U., 1962. Licensed Professinoal Engineer, State of California, 1970. Ammunition surveillance inspector U.S. Army Red River Arsenal, Texarkansas, Tex., 1955-56, 56-57, U.S. Army Raritan Arsenal, Metuchen, N.J., 1956, U.S. Army Pueblo (Colo.) Ordnance Depot, 1957-59; ammunition sch. instr. U.S. Army Savanna (Ill.) Ordnance Depot, 1959-64, chief mgmt. engring. office, 1964-67, dep. dir. supply and transp., 1966-67; chief ops. U.S. Army Material Command Ammunition Ctr., Savanna, 1967-79; dir. ops. U.S. Army Def. Ammunition Ctr. and Sch., Savanna, 1979-89, dir. ops., sr. exec. svc. Congressional appointment, 1989-95; dir. ops., founder U.S. Army Tech. Ctr. for Explosives Safety, Savanna, 1987-95; dep. exec. dir. for explosives safety for the Army Hdqrs. U.S. Army Material Command, Alexandria, Va., 1987-95, functional chief rep. quality assurance specialist career program, 1991-95; sr. mem. V.P. Al Gore's Nat. Performance Rev. Mgmt. Adv. Coun.; Chairman, Dept. of Defense Joint Ordinance Commanders Group/American Defense Preparedness Assn Global Demilitarization Syposium; Chairman, Dept. of the Army Ordinance and Explosive Waste Task Force, 1995; Chairman, Dept. of Defense Joint Ordinance Commanders Group Large Rocket Motor Demilitarization Adhoc Group, 1995; Director, Dept. of the Army Chemical Stockpile Emergency Preparedness Program, 1993; United States Army Representative, Dept. of Defense, Japan Armament Study Team, 1988; mem. adv. com. Luxembourg Internat. Symposium on Rehab. of Mil. Sites and Demilitarization of Explosive Ordinance; and numerous others. Chmn. Savanna City Planning Commn., 1971-72; mem. Savanna Bd. Edn. Adv. Com., 1980-81; mem. exec. steering com. for biotech. Tex. A&M U. Bioremediation Project. With Army Nat. Guard, Nat. Guard of Iowa. Decoration for Meritorious Civilian Svc. with oak leaf cluster (posthumously); decoration for Meritorious Civilian Svc. Dept. Army, 1981, decoration for Exceptional Civilian Svc. Dept. Army, 1985, Performance Mgmt. and Recognition Sys. Performance awards Dept. Def., 1979-89 (Exceptional Ratings Received), Supr. Civilian Svc. award Dept. Army, 1991, Sr. Exec. Svc. Performance awards U.S. Fed. Govt. Exec. Br., 1989-94 (Exceptional Ratings Received), Joint Logistics Comdrs. cert. of merit Dept. Def., 1994; named to the U.S. Army Ordnance Corps Hall of Fame (posthumously), 1995; The John L. Byrd, Jr. award for Excellence in Demilitarization named in his honor by Dept. Def. Joint Ordnance Comdrs. Group and Am. Def. Preparedness Assn., 1995 and Inaugural award presented to John L. Byrd, Jr. (posthumously), 1995; Named one of Outstanding Young Men of America, 1966. Mem. AARP, Assn. of U.S. Army, Am. Ordnance Assn., Am. Def. Preparedness Assn., Inst. Indsl. Engrs. (sr. mem., charter pres. Blackhawk chpt. 1965—), Texas A&M Alumni Assn., Aircraft Owners and Pilots Assn., Savanna Moose Lodge # 1095, Miss. Masonic Lodge # 385 (past master, 32d degree), Freeport Consistory of Ancient Accepted Scottish Rite, Palisades Amateur Radio Club. Baptist. Avocations: flying (lic. pvt. pilot), singing, playing acoustic guitar, farming,HAM Radio Operator, K9FGH. Died Jan. 19, 1995; interred Sand Hill Cemetery, Simms, TX.

BYRD, RICHARD EDWARD, minister, psychologist; b. St. Petersburg, Fla., Jan. 23, 1931; s. Eldo Lawton and Louise (Parker) B.; m. Helen Mandeville Penn, Aug. 31, 1950; children: Jacqueline Louise, Richard Edward. B.A., U. Fla., 1952; M.S.T., Va. Theol. Sem., Alexandria, 1956; Ph.D., N.Y. U., 1970. Ordained priest Episcopal Ch., 1956; priest-in-charge St. Paul's Ch., Waldo, Fla., also; 1St. Anne's Ch., Keystone Heights, Fla., 1956-57; vicar, then rector Grace Episc. Ch., West Palm Beach, Fla., 1957-60; asst. Trinity Ch., West Palm Beach, 1957-58; founder Ch. of Holy Communion, Hawthorne, Fla., 1957; pres. The Richard E. Byrd Co., Faribault, Minn., 1966—; exec. v.p. Wilson Center for Edn. and Psychiatry, Faribault, 1977-79; also group therapist, individual therapist, supr. group therapy Wilson Center for Edn. and Psychiatry, 1971-75; dir. E.W. Cook Sch. Psychotherapy, 1972-77; past chief exec. Jones & Byrd Inc. (Tng. Cons. Internat.); adj. faculty dept. psychology Antioch Coll., Yellow Springs, Ohio, 1973—, adj. faculty, Columbia, Md., 1976; adj. faculty Am. U., Washington; asso. sec. adult edn. and leadership tng. Exec. Council Episc. Ch., 1961-64; inventor Creative Risk Taking Lab.; cons. tng. Ch. Action Program, St. Martins-by-the Lake, Minnetonka Beach, Minn., 1964-66; vis. lectr. Hamline U.; instr. Cornell Sch. Indsl. Relations. Author: Crises in Faith, 1964, Creative Risk Taking Training Laboratory, Book of Basic Readings, 1967, Communication, 1970, Seize the Times, 1971, A Guide to Personal Risk Taking, 1974, 77, paperback, 1978, Managing Risk in Changing Times, 1982, Love The Customer, sermons from The Marketplace, 1987, How to Stay in Charge-Even with a Consultant, Team Building, 1988, Creative Risk Taking The 1989 Ann.: Developing Human Resources, The Best of Byrdseed, 1990, American Quality: Born Again Handbook of Organizational Consultation,, 1992, Corporate Integrity: Paradise Lost and Regained Business Horizons, 1992, Say the Magic Words, 1993; contbr. articles to profl. jours. Co-founder Greenwich (Conn.) Fair Housing Assn., 1963; 1st chmn. Human Rights Commn., Edina, Minn., 1971; dist. chmn. United Fund, 1971. Recipient Profl. Excellence award ASTD, 1984, 89, Orgn. Devel. Practitioner of Century award OD Network, 1994. Mem. Am., Minn. psychol. assns., Assn. for Creative Change (1st pres.), Internat. Assn. Applied Social Scientists, NTL Inst., Am. Psychol. Assn., 3M Meeting Mgmt. Inst. (bd. dirs.). Died Aug. 21, 1994.

CADE, JOHN A., state senator; b. Charleston, S.C., July 2, 1929. BS, Xavier U., 1953; MBA, Northwestern U., 1954; postgrad., U. Md., 1959-60. Mem. charter bd. County of Anne Arundel, Md., 1962-63, mem. county council, 1965-70; mem. Md. State Senate, from 1975, minority leader, from 1983, chmn. budget and tax subcom. on health, edn./human resources; profl. bus. mgr. Republican. Deceased.

CADORET, MAURICE GERARD, hospital administrator; b. Quebec, Que., Can., Sept. 16, 1924; s. Leo and Mary Anne (Hughes) C.; m. Doris Eva Carbonneau; children—Stephen Anthony, James David. B.Com., Concordia U., Montreal, 1977; cert. in acctg. scis., Laval U., Quebec, 1959; cert. in hosp. orgn. and mgmt., Can. Hosp. Assn., 1964. Various positions Can. Gen. Electric Co., Quebec, 1946-59; comptroller, v.p. Continental Electric Ltd., Quebec, 1959-62; exec. dir. Hospital des Sept Iles, Que., 1962-66, Reddy Meml. Hosp., Westmount, Que., 1966-78, Ste. Anne's Hosp., Ste.-Anne-de-Bellevue, Que., 1978-85, Lakeshore Gen. Hosp., Pointe Claire, Que., 1985—. Fellow Am. Coll. Hosp. Adminstrs., Am. Coll. Healthcare Execs. (regent for Que.); mem. Can. Coll. Health Service Execs. (charter and founding mem.)., Assn. Hosps. Province of Que. Roman Catholic. Avocations: skiing; swimming.

CAEN, HERB, newspaper columnist, author; b. Sacramento, Calif., Apr. 3, 1916; s. Lucien and Augusta (Gross) C.; m. Sally Gilbert, Feb. 15, 1952 (div. 1959); m. Maria Theresa Shaw, Mar. 9, 1963 (div. 1982); 1 son, Christopher; m. Ann Moller, Apr. 20, 1996. Student, Sacramento Jr. Coll., 1934. Daily newspaper columnist San Francisco Chronicle, 1936-50, 1958-97; columnist San Francisco Examiner, 1950-58. Author: The San Francisco Book, 1948, Baghdad-by-the-Bay, 1949, Baghdad 1951, 1950, Don't Call It Frisco, 1953, Herb Caen's Guide to San Francisco, 1957, Only in San Francisco, 1960, (with Dong Kingman) City on Golden Hills, 1968, The Cable Car and the Dragon, 1972, One Man's San Francisco, 1976, The Best of Herb Caen, 1960-75, 1991, Herb Caen's San Francisco-1976-1991, 1992. Served from pvt. to capt. USAAF, 1942-45. Decorated Medaille de la Liberation France, 1949. Democrat. Club: Calif. Tennis. Home: San Francisco Calif. Died Feb. 1, 1997.

CAHILL, JAMES DAVID, lawyer; b. Mpls., June 21, 1924; s. David P. and Maude Elizabeth (Wilson) C.; m. Helen Kathryn Stoltman, June 21, 1947; children: Steven, Mary, Kathleen, Martha, David, Brian, Robert, Barton, Matthew. JD, U. Minn., 1950. Bar: Minn. 1950, N.D. 1984; cert. civil litigation specialist. With claim dept. State Farm Mut. Auto Ins. Co., St. Paul, 1950-55, claim mgr., 1955-58; ptnr. Garrity & Cahill, Moorhead, Minn., 1958-73; sr. ptnr. Cahill, Gunhus, et al., Moorhead, 1973-80; pres. Cahill, Marquirt P.A., Moorhead, 1981-94; pres. Minn. Def. Lawyers Assn., 1969-70, 7th Jud. Dist. Bar Assn., 1968-79. Fellow Am. Coll. of Trial Lawyers; mem. Assn. of Ins. Atty., Am. Bd. of Trial Advocates (diplomate), Fed. of Ins. and Corp. Counsel, Def. Rsch. Inst., Internat. Assn. Ins. Counsel. Avocations: golf, swimming, gourmet foods and restaurants. Home: Fargo N.D. Died Aug. 28, 1994.

CAHILL, WILLIAM JOSEPH, JR., utility company executive; b. Suffern, N.Y., June 13, 1923; s. William Joseph and Sophie A. (Scozzafava) C.; m. Edna Kiernan, Oct. 3, 1953; children: William E., Kathleen, Madeleine. B MechE, Poly. Inst. Bklyn., 1949. Registered profl. engr., N.Y., La., Tex. Engr. Consol. Edison, N.Y.C., 1949-54, 57-60, nuclear plant engr., 1961-68, v.p., 1969-80; engr. Knolls Atomic Power Lab., Schenectady, N.Y., 1954-56; sr. v.p. Gulf State Utilities Co., St. Francisville, La., 1980-88; cons. to pres. Tex. Utilities Co., Dallas, 1988; exec. v.p. TU Electric Co., Dallas, 1989-91, group v.p., 1991-94; exec. v.p., chief nuclear officer N.Y. Power Authority, 1994—; chmn. safety and analysis task force Electric Power Research Inst., Palo Alto, Calif., 1978-80. Inventor, patentee nuclear reactor vessel, self-activated valve, triggerable fuse. Pres. Queens County Young Republicans, (N.Y.), 1952; bd. dirs. Rockland County Assn. for Retarded, 1966-67. Served with AUS, 1942-46. Fellow ASME; mem. Am. Soc. Registered Profl. Engrs., Am. Nuclear Soc. (dir. 1980-81, Walter H. Zinn award for outstanding contbns. to advancement nuclear power 1986), La. Nuclear Soc. (chmn. 1982—), Knights Holy Sepulcher. Republican. Roman Catholic. Club: City (Baton Rouge, La.); Nat. Arts (N.Y.C.).

CAHN, JOSHUA BINION, lawyer; b. N.Y.C., Feb. 11, 1915; s. Edward and Martha (Binion) C.; m. Ruth Hagler Walker, Mar. 6, 1971 (dec. Nov. 1994); children: Deborah (Mrs. T. Richard McIntosh), Nicholas Binion, Martha Cunliffe. A.B., Harvard, 1935; LL.B., Columbia, 1938. Bar: N.Y. State bar 1938. Since practiced in N.Y.C.; assoc. firm Sol A. Rosenblatt & William B. Jaffe, N.Y.C., 1938-43; ptnr. firm Cahn & Mathias (and predecessor firm), N.Y.C., 1950-80; Dir. Masback Inc. Author: Artistic Copyright, 1948; Editor: Columbia Law Rev, 1936-38, What Is An Original Print?, 1961; Contbr. articles to profl. publs. Club: Century Assn. Home: New York N.Y. Died Dec. 14, 1994.

CALAMARAS, LOUIS BASIL, lawyer, association executive; b. Peabody, Mass., Jan. 6, 1908; s. Basil James and Margo (Papalexaton) C.; m. Pauline Spirrison, May 2, 1937; children—Margo, Basil, Georgia. Prep., L'école-Metaxa, Athens, Greece; B.A., Columbia U., 1931; LL.D., Georgetown U., 1934; postgrad. student law and commerce, Northwestern U. Dept. commr. Ind. Securities Commn., 1935-37; supr. Ill. Labor Dept., 1937-40; counsellor Labor Indsl. Relations, 1940-44; exec. sec. Nat. Electronic Distbrs. Assn., 1944-51, exec. v.p., 1951—; mng. dir. Midwest Elec. Distbrs. Assn.; bd. dirs., mem. exec. com. Electric Assn.; dir. Montclare Theatre Corp., Elm Theatre Corp., Geo. A. Davis Co.; trustee Nat. Assn. Wholesalers; mgmt. cons. Lawn and Garden Assn., Suburban Restaurant Assn.; Mem. Wholesalers Adv. Com. to Sec. of Commerce; chmn. Radio-TV Industry FTC Trade Practice Conf.; mem. Electronic Coordinating Com.; established James Calamaras scholarship fund at Ind. U. Law sch. Editor, pub.: Nat. Electronic Distbrs. Assn. Jour; contbr. articles to profl. jours. Chmn. Park-Recreation Bd., Planning Commn., Zoning Bd., Village of Lincolnwood. Recipient Disting. Service award Nat. Elec. Mfrs. Reps. Assn., 1985; named Man of Yr., Radio Electronic Industry, 1955, Man of Yr., Elec. Industry, 1975, Man of Yr., Elec. Industry Golf Club. Mem. Chgo. Exchange, Electric Assn., Am. Acad. Polit. Sci., Phi Delta Theta. Clubs: Variety, Tam O'Shanter Country, Lake Shore Athletic (Chgo.); Ridgemore Country (v.p., dir.), Columbia University, Lake Michigan (exec. dir.), Electric Golf, Tower, Countryside Country. Lodges: Rotary, Masons, KP (Chgo.). Died April 21, 1996.

CALAME, ALEXANDRE EMILE, retired French literature educator; b. Lausanne, Switzerland, Apr. 9, 1913; came to U.S., 1960; s. Jules H. and Hedwig I. (Mittelstenscheid) C.; m. Jeanne M. Burollet, Mar. 29, 1947; children: Isabelle, Beatrice, Mireille, Marianne. D.Lettres, Sorbonne, 1960. Asst. prof. French U. Saarbrucken, W. Ger., 1948-56; assoc. prof. U. Algiers, Algeria, 1956-60; mem. faculty U. Calif., Berkeley, 1960-80; prof. French U. Calif., 1960-80, emeritus, 1980-96, chmn. dept., 1963-68. Author books on seventeenth-century French, 1959-81. Trustee Lycée Français, San Francisco, 1967-78. Decorated chevalier Legion of Honor, comdr. Palmes Academiques. Mem. Am. Assn. Tchrs. French. Died Dec. 27, 1996.

CALHOUN, WALTER BOWMAN, university official; b. Mt. Olive, Miss., May 19, 1917; s. William Sidney and Fannie (Holloway) C.; m. Eva Burnell Linton, Sept. 23, 1946; children—Eva Suzanne, Mai Fran. B.S., Miss. State U., 1938; M.B.A., La. State U., 1939. Mem. staff La. State U. and A&M Coll., 1940-92, comptr., 1958-62, v.p. charge finance, 1962-73, v.p. for employee relations, 1973-92, v.p. emeritus, 1992-95. Treas. La. State U. Found.; mem. exec. bd. Istrouma Area council Boy Scouts Am. Served as aviator USNR, 1942-45. Mem. Am. Legion, Phi Kappa Phi, Beta Gamma Sigma, Beta Alpha Psi, Omicron Delta Kappa. Methodist. Home: Baton Rouge La. Died July 9, 1995.

CALLAHAM, THOMAS HUNTER, former business executive; b. Lynchburg, Va., Nov. 29, 1915; s. Charles Edwin and Celina (Rector) C.; m. Patricia Mae Murphy, Oct. 16, 1953; children: Sandra Colleen (Mrs. Billy C. Herrmann), Thomas Hunter, Kathleen Louise Callaham Millikan, Michael Merriman. B.S., Va. Poly. Inst.,

1937. Accountant Standard Oil Co. N.J., also Godfrey L. Cabot, Inc., Charleston, W.Va., 1937-40; budget officer Office U.S. High Commr. for Germany, 1949-53; budget and programs officer MSA, FOA, ICA, 1953-56; bus. specialist, chief fiscal mgmt., asst. regional dir. for mgmt., regional dir. Ft. Worth regional office Pub. Housing Adminstrn., 1956-66; asst. regional adminstr. HUD, Region V, 1966-72; dir. mgmt. Tulsa Housing Authority, 1972; pres. Callaham & Assocs., Inc., Tulsa, 1973-95. Served with AUS, 1940-49; col. USAR (ret.). Inducted to Ark. Housing Hall of Fame, 1987. Mem. Nat. Assn. Housing and Redevel. Ofcls. (exec. com. 1968-69), Ret. Officers Assn. (pres. chpt. 1986), SAR. Home: Tulsa Okla. Died Feb. 20, 1995.

CALLAWAY, JAMES THORPE, advertising executive; b. St. Louis, Dec. 10, 1937; s. William F. and Rosemary (Thorpe) C.; m. Elizabeth Ann Neal, Sept. 10, 1960; children—David Arthur, John Patrick. B.Journalism, U. Mo., 1959, M.A., 1961. Account exec. Benton & Bowles, Inc., N.Y.C., 1961-64; mgmt. supr. Papert Koenig Lois Inc., N.Y.C., 1965-67; prin., pres. Lois Holland Callaway Inc., N.Y.C., 1967-78, Holland & Callaway Advt., N.Y.C., 1978—. Served to capt. AUS, 1960-67. Mem. Sigma Nu. Democrat. Roman Catholic.

CALLEN, HERBERT BERNARD, physics educator; b. Phila., July 1, 1919; s. Abraham and Mildred (Goldfarb) C.; m. Sara Smith, Jan. 21, 1945; children: Jill Bressler, Jed. B.S. in Edn, Temple U., 1941, M.A., 1942; Ph.D., Mass. Inst. Tech., 1948. With Manhattan Project, N.Y.C., 1944-45; with Guided Missile Project, Princeton, 1945; mem. faculty physics dept. U. Pa., Phila., 1948-93; prof. U. Pa., 1956-93; cons. Sperry Rand Univac, 1950-60; UN cons. Pakistan AEC, 1965; Mem. adv. com. physics NSF, 1966-69, chmn., 1969; mem. adv. com. Nat. Magnet Lab., 1965-68, chmn., 1968; U.S. rep. Commn. on Thermodynamics, Internat. Union Pure and Applied Physics, 1972-78, chmn., 1975-78. Author: Thermodynamics, 1960, also articles. Pres. Am. Profs. for Peace in Middle East, 1976; Bd. dirs. Jewish Community Rels. Coun. Phila., 1970-82. Recipient Elliott Cresson medal Franklin Inst., 1984; Guggenheim fellow, 1972-73. Fellow Am. Phys. Soc. (coun., officer div. solid state physics 1966-69); mem. NAS. Home. Sarasota Fla. Died May 22, 1993.

CALLISON, CHARLES HUGH, conservation organization executive; b. Lousana, Alta., Can., Nov. 6, 1913; came to U.S., 1918, naturalized, 1937; s. Guy A. and Dorinda (Stuart) C.; m. Amelia D. Ferguson, June 7, 1951; children: Charles Stuart, Joyce Marie Melville, Karen Sue (Mrs. Glenn Bater), Bettye Ruth (Mrs. Kenneth Palermo). B.Jour., U. Mo., 1937, D.Sc. (hon.), 1979. Editor Garnett (Kan.) Rev., 1937-38, Boonville (Mo.) Advertiser, 1938-41; editor, info. div. chief Mo. Conservation Commn., 1941-46; exec. sec. Conservation Fedn. Mo., 1947-51; asst. conservation dir., then conservation dir. Nat. Wildlife Fedn., 1951-60; asst. to pres. Nat. Audubon Soc., 1960-66, exec. v.p., 1967-77; founder, dir. Pub. Lands Inst., Denver, 1977-86; founder, dir. Mo. Parks Assn., Jefferson City, 1982-91, treas., 1990-93; chmn. Nat. Resources Coun. Am., 1957-59; mem. organizing and exec. coms. 5th World Forestry Congress, 1960; chmn. legis. com. Internat. Assn. Game, Fish and Conservation Commrs., 1955-59; mem. Fed. Water Pollution Control Advisory Bd., 1961-64; mem. of Pres.-Elect's Task Force on Resources and Environment, 1968; mem. N.Y. State Environ. Bd., 1970-75; legis. rep. Mo. Audubon Coun., 1989-93. Author: Man and Wildlife in Missouri, 1952; co-author: Overlooked in America, 1991; editor: America's Natural Resources, rev. edit., 1967; participating author: Exploring Missouri's Legacy: State Parks and Historic Sites, 1992. Village trustee, 1969-71. Recipient Frances K. Hutchinson medal Garden Club Am., 1974; Audubon medal Nat. Audubon Soc., 1978; Conservation award Dept. Interior, 1980; Disting. Service award Am. Forestry Assn., 1986. Mem. Wildlife Soc., Sierra Club, Wilderness Soc., Am. Ornithologists Union, Sigma Delta Chi, Kappa Tau Alpha. Democrat. Mem. Disciples of Christ. Club: Cosmos (Washington). Home: Jefferson City Mo. Died Feb. 23, 1993.

CALLISTER, MARION JONES, federal judge; b. Moreland, Idaho, June 6, 1921; m. Nina Lynn Hayes, June 7, 1946; children—Nona Lynn Callister Haddock, Lana Sue Callister Meredith, Jenny Ann Callister Thomas, Tamara Callister Banks, Idonna Ruth Callister Andersen, Betty Patricia Callister Carr, Deborah Jean Hansen, Mary Clarice Fowler, David Marion, Nancy Irene Callister Garvin, Michelle Burk, Kimberly Jane Simmons. Student, Utah State U., 1940-41; B.S.L., U. Utah, 1950, J.D., 1951. Bar: Idaho 1951. Dep. pros. atty. Bingham County, Idaho, 1951-52; asst. U.S. atty. Dist. of Idaho, 1953-57, U.S. atty., 1975-76; pvt. practice, 1958-69; judge Idaho Dist. Ct. 4th Jud. Dist., 1970-75; judge U.S. Dist. Ct. Idaho, Boise, 1976—, chief judge, 1981-88, sr. judge, 1989—. Served with U.S. Army, 1944-46. Decorated Purple Heart. Republican. Mormon. Died June 24, 1997.

CALLMER, JAMES PETER, architect; b. Aurora, Ill., May 6, 1919; s. Carl L. and Anna (Hegg) C.; m. Sally-Lee Maxwell Young, Mar. 21, 1944; children—Melinda-Lee, Sally Susanne, Shelley Ann. B.S. in Architecture, U. Ill., 1942. Architect with Justement, Elam, Callmer & Kidd, Washington, 1956-66, Justement & Callmer, Washington, 1966-68, Callmer & Milstead, Washington, 1969-73; asso. Dalton, Dalton, Little, Newport, Inc., Bethesda, Md., 1973-77; constrn. mgr. Eisinger, Kilbane & Assos., Bethesda, 1978-91; Bd. govs. Washington Bldg. Congress, 1968-71; pres. Bd. Examiners and Registrars Architects Washington, 1970-77; chmn. design and decoration com. 1969 Inaugural Com.; Mem. panel arbitrators Am. Arbitration Assn.; past pres. Western Bethesda Community Planning Assn. Prin. works include Nat. Guard Meml. Bldg, Washington, Sibley Meml. Hosp, Washington, Pan Am. Health Orgn, Washington; master plan for Judiciary Sq, Washington. Served to lt. comdr. USNR, 1942-46. Mem. A.I.A. (pres. Washington Met. chpt. 1968), Alpha Chi Rho (v.p. Phi Kappa chpt. 1941). Club: Columbia Country (Bethesda); Cosmos (Washington). Deceased.

CALVIN, MELVIN, chemist, educator; b. St. Paul, Minn., Apr. 8, 1911; s. Elias and Rose I. (Hervitz) C.; m. Genevieve Jemtegaard, 1942; children: Elin, Karole, Noel. BS, Mich. Coll. Mining and Tech., 1931, DSc, 1955; PhD, U. Minn., 1935, DSc, 1969; hon. rsch. fellow, U. Manchester, Eng., 1935-37; Guggenheim fellow, 1967; DSc, Nottingham U., 1958, Oxford (Eng.) U., 1959, Northwestern U., 1961, Wayne State U., 1962, Gustavus Adolphus Coll., 1963, Poly. Inst. Bklyn., 1962, U. Notre Dame, 1965, U. Gent, Belgium, 1970, Whittier Coll., 1971, Clarkson Coll., 1976, U. Paris Val-de-Marne, 1977, Columbia U., 1979, Grand Valley U., 1986. With U. Calif., Berkeley, 1937—; successively instr. chemistry, asst. prof., prof., Univ. prof., dir. Lab. Chem. Biodynamics U. Calif., 1963-80, assoc. dir. Lawrence Berkeley Lab., 1967-80; Peter Reilly lectr. U. Notre Dame, 1949; Harvey lectr. N.Y. Acad. Medicine, 1951; Harrison Howe lectr. Rochester sect. Am. Chem. Soc., 1954; Falk-Plaut lectr. Columbia U., 1954; Edgar Fahs Smith Meml. lectr. U. Pa. and Phila. sect. Am. Chem. Soc., 1955; Donegani Found. lectr. Italian Nat. Acad. Sci., 1955; Max Tishler lectr. Harvard U., 1956; Karl Folkers lectr. U. Wis., 1956; Baker lectr. Cornell U., 1958; London lectr., 1961, Willard lectr., 1982; Vanuxem lectr. Princeton U., 1969; Disting. lectr. Mich. State U., 1977; Prather lectr. Harvard U., 1980; Dreyfus lectr. Grinnell Coll., 1981, Berea Coll., 1982; Barnes lectr. Colo. Coll., 1982; Nobel lectr. U. Md., 1982; Abbott lectr. U. N.D., 1983; Gunning lectr. U. Alta., 1983; O'Leary disting. lectr. Gonzaga U., 1984; Danforth lectr. Dartmouth Coll., 1984, Grinnell Coll., 1984; R.P. Scherer lectr. U. S. Fla., 1984; Imperial Oil lectr. U. Western Ont., Can., 1985; disting. lectr. dept. chemistry U. Calgary, Can., 1986; Melvin Calvin lectr. Mich. Tech. U., 1986; Eastman prof. Oxford (Eng.) U., 1967-68. Author: (with G.E.K. Branch) The Theory of Organic Chemistry, 1940, (with others) Isotopic Carbon, 1949, (with Martell) Chemistry of Metal Chelate Compounts, 1952, (with Bassham) Path of Carbon in Photosynthesis, 1957, (with Bassham) Photosynthesis of Carbon Compounds, 1962, Chemical Evolution, 1969, Following the Trail of Light: A Scientific Odyssey, 1992; contbr. articles to chem. and sci. jours. Recipient prize Sugar Research Found., 1950, Flintoff medal prize Brit. Chem. Soc., 1953, Stephen Hales award Am. Soc. Plant Physiologists, 1956, Nobel prize in chemistry, 1961, Davy medal Royal Soc., 1964; Virtanen medal, 1975, Priestley medal, 1978, Am. Inst. Chemists medal, 1979, Feodor Lynen medal, 1983, Sterling B. Hendricks medal, 1983, Melvin Calvin Medal of Distinction Mich. Tech. U., 1985, Nat. Medal of Sci., 1989, John Ericsson Renewable Energy award U.S. Dept. Energy, 1991. Mem. Britain's Royal Soc. London (fgn. mem.), Am. Chem. Soc. (Richards medal N.E. chpt. 1956, Nichols medal N.Y. chpt. 1958, award for nuclear applications in chemistry, pres. 1971, Gibbs medal Chgo. chpt. 1977, Priestley medal 1978, Desper award Cin. chpt. 1981), Am. Acad. Arts and Scis., Nat. Acad. Scis., Royal Dutch Acad. Scis., Japan Acad., Am. Philos. Soc., Sigma Xi, Tau Beta Pi, Phi Lambda Upsilon.

CAMERON, ELEANOR, author; b. Winnipeg, Man., Can., Mar. 23, 1912; d. Henry and Florence Lydia (Vaughan) Butler; m. Ian Stuart Cameron, June 24, 1934; 1 son, David Gordon. Student, UCLA, 1931-33. Clk. Los Angeles Pub. Library, 1930-36; clk. Los Angeles Sch. Book Depository, 1936-42; spl. librarian advt. Foote Cone & Belding, Los Angeles, 1942-43; research asst. Batten, Barton, Durstine & Osborn, Los Angeles, 1956-58; spl. librarian Dan B. Miner Co., Los Angeles, 1958-59; mem. editorial bd. Cricket Mag., LaSalle, Ill., 1973—, Children's Lit. in Edn., 1982—. Author: The Unheard Music, 1950, The Wonderful Flight to the Mushroom Planet, 1954 (Hawaiian Nene award), A Room Made of Windows, 1971 (Boston Globe Horn-Book award, Focal award 1990, ALA Notable Book), The Court of the Stone Children, 1973 (Nat. Book award 1973, ALA Notable Book), To the Green Mountains, 1975 (finalist Nat. Book award; ALA Notable Book), The Green and Burning Tree: On the Writing and Enjoyment of Children's Books, 1969 (Commonwealth Lit. award 1969), Julia and the Hand of God, 1977 (Focal award, ALA Notable Book), A Spell is Cast (Commonwealth award), Beyond Silence, 1980, That Julia Redfern, 1982 (ALA Notable Book), Julia's Magic, 1984, The Private Worlds of Julia Redfern, 1988, The Seed and the Vision: On The Writing and Appreciation of Children's Books, 1993, others; contbr. numerous magazines. Recipient Kerlin award U. Minn., 1985, Hope S. Dean Mem. award, 1995; named Disting. contbr. to the Field of Children's Lit. Calif. State, L.A., 1965. Mem. Children's Lit. Assn., Save-the-Redwoods League, Sierra Club, Audubon Soc., Wilderness Soc., Authors League. Deceased.

CAMERON, JOHN LANSING, retired government official; b. Sanford, N.C., Sept. 14, 1916; s. William John and Lena (Rosser) C.; m. Beulah Arena Bradley, Sept. 7, 1940; children: William John, Elizabeth Ann (Mrs. Irvin A. Pearce), David Bradley. A.B., Elon Coll., 1937; M.A., U. N.C., 1947, D.Ed., 1965. Dir. school planning N.C. Dept. Pub. Instrn., 1949-59; with U.S. Office of Edn., Washington, 1959-78; dir. facilities devel. staff, dir. ednl. tech. U.S. Office of Edn., 1971-72, acting asso. commr., 1972-73, dir. program devel., 1972-73, dir. ednl. broadcasting facilities program, 1973-78; dir. public telecomm. facilities program Nat. Telecomm. and Info. Adminstrn., Dept. of Commerce, 1978-82; chmn. U.S. del. Internat. Edn. Bldg. Conf., London, 1962, Mexico City, 1966; mem. Continuing Care Community Residents N.C., Inc., 1988—, past pres.; mem. N.C. Adv. Com. on Continuing Care Facilities. Lt. comdr. USNR, 1942-46. Recipient Superior Service award HEW, 1966. Mem. A.I.A. (hon.), Am. Assn. Sch. Adminstrs., Council Ednl. Facility Planners (pres. 1966-67), Phi Delta Kappa. Methodist.

CAMM, JOHN SUTCLIFFE, package manufacturing company executive; b. Jan. 18, 1925; s. Thomas Howard and Mary Ethel Sutcliffe C.; m. Barbara Kathleen Small, 1956; 6 children. Student Wycliffe Coll.; B.A., Bristol U. Schoolmaster, Wycliffe Coll., 1950-53; dir. E.S. & A. Robinson (Holdings), 1963; with DRG (formerly Dickinson Robinson Group Ltd.), 1967—, joint mng. dir., 1972-74, mng. dir., 1974-77, dep. chmn., 1977-78, chmn., chief exec., 1978—; dir. Bristol & West Bldg. Co., Kohler Ltd., S. Africa. Chmn. govs. Wycliffe Coll., 1982.

CAMP, PHILIP WILLIAM, writer, retired farmer, state employee; b. South Kent, Conn., May 30, 1919; s. Raymond Arthur and Anna Catherine (Heinen) C.; m. Marie Anna Neels, Oct. 18, 1942; children: Philip William Jr., Dianne Marie Camp Lang. Grad. high sch., Kent, Conn. Dairy farmer South Kent, 1936-63, beef farmer, 1963-75; prin. Philip W. Camp Real Estate, South Kent, 1966-77; employee food dept. Wassaic (N.Y.) State Sch., 1963-72, Harlem Valley Psychiat. Ctr., Wingdale, N.Y., 1972-74; freelance writer, 1988-97. Author: Stories and Recollections of Kent, 1988, Country Living in Kent, 1989, Old Times and Old Timers, 1990, A Lifetime of Stories, 1991, Remembering Yesterday, 1993, Fond Memories, 1995; columnist local newspaper. Lifetime mem. Merwinsville Hotel Restoration, Gaylordsville, Conn.; mem. Kent Congrl. Ch. Mem. Grange Patrons of Husbandry (mem.), Kent Hist. Soc. Republican. Mem. Congl. Ch. Died Sept. 25, 1997.

CAMPBELL, ALAN KEITH, business educator; b. Elgin, Nebr., May 31, 1923; s. Charles E. and Anna (Schneckloth) C.; m. Linna Jane Owen, Mar. 9, 1945; children: Kimberly Ann, Charles Duncan. AB, Whitman Coll., 1949, LLD (hon.), 1972; MPA, Harvard U., 1950, PhD, 1952; LHD (hon.), Ohio State U., 1979; LLD (hon.), Syracuse U., 1990. Asst. dir. summer sch. Harvard U., 1950-55, instr., 1952-54, vis. lectr., 1957; prof., chmn. polit. sci. dept. Hofstra U., Hempstead, N.Y., 1955-60; dep. comptroller adminstrn. N.Y. State, 1960-61; vis. prof. Columbia U., 1961-62; prof. polit. sci., dir. met. studies program Maxwell Grad. Sch. Syracuse (N.Y.) U., 1961-68, dean Maxwell Sch. Citizenship and Pub. Affairs, 1968-76; dean Lyndon B. Johnson Sch. of Pub. Affairs U. Tex., Austin, 1977; chmn. CSC, Washington, 1977-78; dir. U.S. Office Pers. Mgmt., 1979-80; exec. v.p., vice chmn. ARA Svcs., Inc., Phila., 1980-92; bd. dirs. ARAMARK, Phila., 1980—; exec. prof. Wharton Sch., U. Pa., 1990-93; chmn. Commn. on Social Security "Notch" Issue, 1994-95; chmn. Phila. CSC, 1981; mem. staff N.Y. Commn. on Govtl. Ops., N.Y.C., 1959; mem. faculty Salzburg (Austria) Seminar Am. Studies, 1965; mem. rsch. adv. com. Com. Econ. Devel., 1965-74, chmn. task force on tchr. workforce, 1985-86; mem. com. urban econs. Resources For Future, 1965-70, adv. com. to Sec. HUD, 1967-68, social sci. panel div. behavioral sci. Nat. Acad. Sci., 1971-74; chmn. bd. dirs. Sta. WHYY, 1986—. Author: Case Studies in American Government, 1962, (with Seymour Sacks) Metropolitan America: Governmental Systems and Fiscal Patterns, 1967, The States and the Urban Crisis, 1970, (with Joel Berke and Robert Goettel) Financing Equal Educational Opportunity: Alternatives for State Finance, 1972, (with others) Watergate: Implications for Responsible Government, (with Roy Bahl) Taxes, Expenditures and the Economic Base: The Case of New York City, 1974, The Political Economy of State and Local Government Reform, 1976; contbr. to: Anatomy of a Metropolis, articles to profl. jours.; editor: (with Edwin Bock) Case Studies in American Government, 1962, Carnegie-sponsored Study Large City Schs, 1966—, Carnegie-sponsored Task Force on Teaching as a Profession, 1986-88. Bd. dirs. Thomas Jefferson U., Edn. Testing Svc., 1987—, Inst. Pub. Adminstrn., Nat. Bd. for Profl. Tchg. Stds., 1987—, Pub. and Pvt. Ventures; mem. steering group Nat. Rsch. Coun., Nat. Forum on Future of Children and Their Futures, 1987—; bd. overseers Whitman Coll., Sch. Edn., U. Pa.; vice chmn. bd. dirs. Coun. for

Excellence in Govt.; bd. trustees Syracuse U., 1996—; active various polit. orgns. in past. Ensign CIC, USNR, 1943-46. Recipient Alumnus of Merit award Whitman Coll., 1970, Stockberger award for outstanding achievements in pers. mgmt. Internat. Pers. Mgmt. Assn., 1978, Pub. Service Achievement award Common Cause, 1981, Hubert H. Humphrey Pub. Service award, 1981, Gunnar and Alva Myrdal award for govt. services, 1981; Wayne State U. Volker fellow, 1949, Harvard U. Sheldon Traveling fellow, 1952. Mem. Am. Polit. Sci. Assn., Am. Soc. Pub. Adminstrn., Nat. Assn. Sch. Pub. Affairs and Adminstrn. (exec. coun. 1973—, pres. 1974-75). Nat. Acad. Pub. Adminstrn., Assn. for Pub. Policy Analysis and Mgmt. (pres.-elect 1989-90, pres. 1990-91), Nat. Acad. Human Resources, Phi Beta Kappa.

CAMPBELL, DONALD GUY, journalist, author; b. Brownsburg, Ind., June 27, 1922; s. George Guy and Ella (Menefee) C.; m. Jean Farson, Oct. 15, 1949; children—Scott Guy, Jennifer Lee. A.B. in Journalism, Ind. U., 1948. Reporter, feature writer St. Petersburg (Fla.) Time, 1948-49; writer Nat. Safety Council, 1949-52; reporter Indpls. Star, 1952-54, bus. and financial editor, 1954-65; exec. bus. and financial editor Ariz. Republic, Phoenix, 1965-72; financial editor N.Y. Daily News, 1972-74; columnist Daily Investor, United Feature Syndicate, 1972-79; staffwriter Los Angeles Times, 1979-88; real estate columnist King Features Syndicate, 1968—; chief researcher, writer Dow Theory Trader, 1956-71; editor, pub. Money Views, investment newsletter, 1977-79; hon. lectr. Am. Inst. Fgn. Trade, 1966-72. Contbr. N.Am. Newspaper Alliance, 1967-72; Author: Let's Take Stock, 1959, What Does Daddy Do All Day, 1962, Understanding Stocks, 1965 (Kiplinger Book Club best seller 1965), The Handbook of Real Estate Investment, 1968; contbg. editor Ariz. Hwys. mag., 1984—. Served with AUS, 1942-45, ETO. Mem. Soc. Am. Bus. Writers (v.p.), Author's Guild, Sigma Delta Chi, Phi Gamma Delta. Club: Los Angeles Press.

CAMPBELL, KENNETH, consulting engineer; b. San Francisco, June 1, 1899; s. William Wallace and Elizabeth Ballard (Thompson) C.; m. Margaret Bruce Macon, Nov. 8, 1930; children: Janet Bruce, Elizabeth Wallace, Margaret Macon, Martha Madison; m. 2d Miriam N. Frank, Mar. 16, 1972. Grad., Hotchkiss Sch., Lakeville, Conn., 1917; A.B., Harvard U., 1921, S.B., 1923; D.Sc. (hon.), Bard Coll., 1952. Mem. staff Lick Obs. solar eclipse expdn., Kiev, USSR, 1915; mem. eclipse party Freyburg, Maine, 1932; with various depts. Bethlehem Steel Co., Pa., 1923-26; indsl. engr. Sanderson & Porter, N.Y.C., 1928-33; aircraft power plant research, devel. designer Curtiss-Wright Corp., Wood-Ridge, N.J., 1933-64, dir. research, 1950-55, gen. mgr. research div., 1956-60, chief scientist, 1960-64; cons. Inst. for Def. Analyses, 1964-95, others, 1964-95; chmn. subcom. compressors and turbines NACA, 1940-45; mem. tech. mission to Germany USN, 1945. Contbr. articles to profl. jours.; patentee in field. Served as ambulance driver ARC, 1918, World War I; served as Lt. RAF, 1918-1919. Decorated Croce di Guerra Italy; recipient Wright Bros. medal Soc. Automotive Engrs., 1944, Charles Matthews Manley medal, 1945. Fellow Inst. Aero. Sci.; mem. Soc. Automotive Engrs., Harvard Engrs. and Scientist (past pres.). Episcopalian. Home: Oradell N.J. Died July 10, 1995.

CAMPBELL, WILLARD DONALD, lawyer; b. New Philadelphia, Ohio, June 6, 1901; s. Dr. Howard N. and Eloise (Gray) C.; m. Rosanna L. Vance, Nov. 25, 1936 (dec. Dec. 1965); children—Rosanna Vance (Mrs. Michael Guy), Willard Donald. A.B., Muskingum Coll., 1922; student, U. Pitts., 1922-23, Cornell U., 1924; LL.B. (fellow); J.D., Yale, 1925. Bar: Ohio 1925, Fla. 1926. Acting city solicitor Cambridge, Ohio, 1928-30; pros. atty., 1930-34; mem. Ohio Senate representing 17th, 18th 19th, 28th dists., 1935-37; chief enforcement counsel OPA, Columbus, 1941-46; dir. Bur. Code Revision Oreg., 1946-53; practice law Columbus, 1953-63; chmn. bd. rev. Ohio Bur. Employment Sers., 1963-81; sr. partner Campbell, Potts, Alban & Watson; spl. asst. atty. gen. Ohio, 1957-58; chmn. Ohio Bd. Rev., Bureau Employment Services Ohio.; judge Guernsey Ct. Common Pleas; pros. atty. Guernsey County. Author: Ohio Revised Code, 1953, Accumulated Index Attorney General Opinions, 1959. Chmn. Columbus Park Commn., 1963-71, Columbus Tree Commn., 1972-78; officer, trustee Columbus Zoo, 1985—. Named Fraternalist of Year Ohio Council Fraternal and Service Orgns., 1962. Mem. ABA, Ohio Bar Assn., Fla. Bar Assn., Columbus Bar Assn., Guernsey County Bar Assn., Am. Judicature Soc., Cambridge C. of C. (past dir., v.p.), U.S. Navy League, Athletic Club Columbus, Agonis Club, Mason (32 deg., Shriner), Moose (state pres. 1939-40, supreme councilman 1946-51, supreme prelate 1951, supreme gov. 1953), Phi Delta Theta, Delta Theta Phi, Tau Kappa Alpha (hon.). Presbyterian.

CAMRAS, MARVIN, electrical and computer engineering educator, inventor; b. Chicago, Ill., Jan. 1, 1916; s. Samuel and Ida (Horwich) C.; m. Isabelle Pollack, 1951; children: Robert, Carl, Ruth, Michael, Louis. BSEE, Armour Inst. Tech. (now Ill. Inst. Tech.), 1940; MSEE, Ill. Inst. Tech., 1942, LLD (hon.), 1968. Registered profl. engr., Ill. Mem. staff Armour Rsch. Found. now Ill. Inst. Tech. Rsch. Inst., Chgo., 1940-95, asst. physicist, 1940-45, assoc. physicist, 1945-46, physicist, 1946-49, sr. physicist, 1949-58, sr. engr., 1958-65, sci. adviser electronics div., 1965-69, sr. sci. adviser, 1969-95; rsch. prof. elec. and computer engring. Ill. Inst. Tech., 1986-95; mem. Am. Nat. Standards Inst., 1966-95, chmn. s-4 com., 1966;. Author: Magnetic Tape Recording, 1985, Magnetic Recording Handbook, 1988, others; editor: Inst. Radio Engrs. Trans. on Audio, 1958-63. 500 patents in devel. wire and tape recorders, stereo sound reproduction, motion picture sound, video recorders, others in field. Recipient Disting. Svc. award Ill. Inst. Tech. Alumni Assn., 1948, Achievement award for outstanding contbn. motion picture photography U.S. Camera mag., 1949, John Scott medal Franklin Inst. Phila., 1955, citation Ind. Tech. Coll., 1958, Achievement award I.R.E., 1958, product award Indsl. Rsch. mag., 1966, Merit award Chgo. Tech. Socs., 1973, Alumni medal Ill. Inst. Tech., 1978, Inventor of Yr. award Patent Law Assn., Chgo., 1979, Nat. medal tech. Pres. of U.S., 1990, Am. Ingenuity award Coors Co./Nat. Assn. Mfrs., 1992, Nat. medal of Tech. U.S. Dept. Commerce, 1990; named to Ill. Inst. Tech. Hall of Fame, 1981, Am. Ingenuity Hall of Fame, 1992, Acad. Chgo. Assn. Tech. Socs., 1981, Pioneers of Electronics Foothills Electronics Mus., 1981, Nat. Inventors Hall of Fame Nat. Coun. Patent Law Assns., Patent and Trademark Office, U.S. Dept. Commerce, 1985, Am. Creativity award Found. for a Creative Am., 1993. Fellow IEEE (sec.-treas. 1951-53, Consumer Electronics award 1964, nat. chmn. profl. group on audio I.R.E. 1953-54, Info. Storage award Magnetics Soc. 1990, other awards), Acoustical Soc. Am. (patent rev. bd.), AAAS, Soc. Motion Picture and TV Engrs. (bd. mgrs. Chgo. 1986-88, Hon. Mem. award 1990); mem. NAE, Western Soc. Engrs. (Washington award 1979), Physics Club Chgo. (bd. dirs. 1969-95, pres. 1973-74), Radio Engrs. Club Chgo., Chgo. Acoustic and Audio Group (bd. dirs. 1967-68), Audio Engring. Soc. (cen. v.p. 1972-73, hon. gov. 1970-95, John S. Potts Meml. Gold medal 1969), Midwest Acoustics Conf. (bd. dirs. 1969-95), Sigma Xi (chpt. pres. 1959-60), Tau Beta Pi, Eta Kappa Nu. Home: Glencoe Ill. Died June 23, 1995.

CANIZARO, PETER CORTE, surgeon, educator; b. Vicksburg, Miss., June 30, 1935; s. Peter Joseph and Masie Nona (Ross) C.; m. Sandra Lou Brian, Dec. 21, 1957 (div. 1981); children: Peter, Carolyn, Vincent, Janet; m. Hana Pospisil, Nov. 1, 1982; children: Martin, Anna. B.A., U. Tex.-Austin, 1956; M.D., U. Tex.-Dallas, 1960. Diplomate: Am. Bd. Surgery. Intern Parkland Meml. Hosp., Dallas, 1960-66, resident, 1964-68; asst. prof. surgery U. Tex.-Southwestern, Dallas, 1968-72, assoc. prof., 1972-74; assoc. prof. surgery U. Wash., Seattle, 1974-76; assoc. prof. surgery Cornell U., N.Y.C., 1976-81, prof., 1981-82; prof., chmn. dept. surgery Tex. Tech. U. Health Scis. Ctr., Lubbock, 1982—; mem. Pres.'s Nat. Health Adv. Com., 1972-73, Govs. Task Force on Cancer, Tex. Contbr. articles to profl. jours.; assoc. editor (Circulatory Shock), 1979—, mem. editorial bd. (Tex. Medicine), 1983—. Served to capt. U.S. Army, 1961-63. Recipient Elliot Hochstein Teaching award Cornell U., 1979, William Fyre Teaching award, Tex. Tech, 1983, 84, 86; named Peter C. Canizaro Lectr. Cornell U., 1983; fellow NIH, 1963-64, 71-74; grantee Nat. Inst. Med. Scis., 1974-76. Fellow ACS (chmn. edn. com. 1988); mem. Am. Assn. Surgery of Trauma, Soc. Internationale de Chirurgie, Soc. Surg. Chairmen, Soc. Univ. Surgeons, Shock Soc., Am. Surg. Assn., Halstead Soc. Republican. Roman Catholic.

CANN, WILLIAM HOPSON, former mining company executive; b. Newark, June 17, 1916; s. Howard W. and Ruth (Hopson) C.; m. Mildred E. Allen, Mar. 7, 1942 (dec. 1982); children: William Hopson, Sharon Lee, John Allen, Lawrence Edward; m. Nancy B. Barnhart, Nov. 17, 1984. A.B. magna cum laude, Harvard, 1937; LL.B., 1940. Bar: N.Y. 1941, Calif. 1947. Assoc. Chadbourne, Parke, Whiteside & Wolfe (and predecessors), N.Y.C., 1940-53; asst. to pres. Rockwell Internat. Corp., 1953-60, v.p., sec., 1960-75; coordinator for stockholder relations Cyprus Mines Corp., Los Angeles, 1975-76; corp. sec. Cyprus Mines Corp., 1977-85, ret., 1985. Former mem. adv. bd. Family Svc. of Los Angeles. Served to 1st lt. USAAF, 1942-45. Mem. Am. Soc. Corp. Secs. (past pres.), Phi Beta Kappa. Episcopalian. Club: Rocky Mountain Harvard (Denver).

CANNADY, EDWARD WYATT, JR., retired physician; b. East St. Louis, Ill., June 20, 1906; s. Edward Wyatt and Ida Bertha (Rose) C.; m. Helen Freeborn, Oct. 20, 1984; children by previous marriage: Edward Wyatt III, Jane Marie Starr. AB, Washington U., St. Louis, 1927, MD, 1931. Intern in internal medicine Barnes Hosp., St. Louis, 1931-33, resident physician, 1934-35, asst. physician, 1935-74, emeritus, 1974—; asst. resident Peter Bent Brigham Hosp., Boston, 1933-34; fellow in gastroenterology Washington U. Sch. Medicine, 1935-36, instr. internal medicine 1935-74, emeritus, 1974—; cons. internal medicine Washington U. Clinics, 1942-74; physician St. Mary's Hosp., East St. Louis, 1935-77, pres. staff, 1947-49, chmn. med. dept., 1945-47; physician Christian Welfare Hosp., 1935-77, chmn. med. dept., 1939-53, dir. electrocardiography, 1936-77; dir. electrocardiography Centreville Twp. Hosp., East St. Louis; mem. staff Meml. Hosp., Belleville, Ill., St. Elizabeth Hosp., Belleville; pres. C.I.F. Dir. health service East St. Louis pub. schs., 1936-37; chmn. med. adv. bd. Selective Svc., 1941-45; pres. St. Clair County Coun. Aging, 1961-62; chmn. St. Clair County Home Care Program, 1961-68, St. Clair County Med. Soc. Com. Aging, 1960-70; del. White House Conf. Aging, 1961, 71, 81; mem. Adv. Coun. Improvement Econ. and Social Status Older People, 1959-66; bd. dirs., exec. com. Nat. Council Homemaker Svcs., 1966-73, chmn. profl. adv. com. 1971-73; bd. dirs. St. Louis Met. Hosp. Planning Commn., 1966-70; mem. Ill. Coun. Aging, 1966-74; mem. Gov.'s Council on Aging, 1974-76; mem. Ill. Regional Heart Disease, Cancer and Stroke Com.; mem. exec. com. Bi-State Regional Com. on Heart Disease, Cancer and Stroke; pres. Ill. Joint Council to Improve Health Care Aged, 1959-61; dir. Ill. Coun. Continuing Med. Edn., 1972-77, v.p., 1974-75. Trustee McKendree Coll., 1971-79; adv. bd. Belleville Jr. Coll. Sch. Nursing, 1970-78; bd. dirs. United Fund Greater East St. Louis, 1953-58. Recipient Disting. Service Award Am. Heart Assn., 1957, Disting. Achievement award, 1957; award Ill. Public Health Assn., 1971; Greater Met. St. Louis award in geriatrics, 1976. Diplomate Am. Bd. Internal Medicine. Fellow Am. Coll. Cardiology, Am. Geriatrics Soc., ACP (gov. 1964-70); mem. AMA (ho. dels. 1961-71, mem. aging com.; editorial adv. bd. Chronic Illness News Letter 1962-70, chmn. Ill. delegation 1964-66, mem. council vol. health agys.), Am. (dir. 1956-62, personnel and personnel tng. com. 1956-60), Ill. (pres. 1950-51) heart assns., St. Clair County (pres. 1952, bd. censors 1953-57), Ill. (sec. cardiovascular sect. 1957, chmn. sect., 1958-59; chmn. com. on aging, 1959-69, speaker Ho. Dels. 1964-68, pres. 1969-70) med. socs., Mason, St. Clair Country Club, Palmbrook Country Club (Sun City, Ariz.), Sun Cities Physicians Club, Palmbrook Country Club, Beta Theta Pi, Nu Sigma Nu, Alpha Omega Alpha. Presbyterian. Contbr. articles to med. jours. Deceased. Home: Sun City Ariz.

CANNON, SARAH OPHELIA COLLEY See **PEARL, MINNIE**

CANTOR, BERNARD GERALD, financial executive; b. N.Y.C., Dec. 17, 1916; s. Julius and Rose (Delson) C.; m. Iris Bazel, June 4, 1977; 1 child, Jay S. Student, NYU, 1935-37; DFA (hon.), Holy Cross Coll., 1980, Gonzaga U., 1985; LHD (hon.), Long Island U., 1986. Chmn. bd. Cantor, Fitzgerald, N.Y.C., 1945-96. Mem. bd. regents Pres.'s Coun., Holy Cross Coll., Worcester, Mass., 1980-96; trustee emeritus Met. Mus. Art, N.Y.C., 1985-96; life trustee Los Angeles County Mus. of Art, 1972-85, hon. trustee, 1986-96. Decorated officer Order of Rio Branco (Brazil), French Ministry of Culture's Order of Arts and Letters. Died July 3, 1996.

CANTRALL, IRVING J(AMES), entomologist, educator; b. Springfield, Ill., Oct. 6, 1909; s. Ula J. and Elsie M. (LaRue) C.; m. Dorothy Louise Ransom, Dec. 24, 1932; children: Marion Louise, James Bruce. AB, U. Mich., 1935, PhD, 1940. Asst. Mus. Zoology U. Mich., Ann Arbor, 1935-37, tech. asst. Mus. Zoology, 1937-42, from asst. to prof. Zoology, 1949-77; curator Edwin S. George Res., Ann Arbor, 1949-59; curator insects Mus. Zoology U. Mich., Ann Arbor, 1959-77, curator insects emeritus, 1978-97, prof. emeritus, 1978-97; jr. aquatic biologist TVA, 1942, asst. aquatic biologist, 1942-43; asst. prof. biology U. Fla., Gainesville, 1946-49. Editor Great Lakes Entomologist, 1971-76; contbr. numerous articles on zoology to profl. jours. 1st lt. USAAF, 1943-46. Fellow AAAS; mem. Am. Entomol. Soc., Mich. Entomol. Soc. (pres. 1957-58, editor 1971-76), Soc. for Study of Evolution, Ecol. Soc. Am., Soc. Systematic Zoology, The Orthopterists Soc., Mich. Acad. Sci., Arts and Letters (sec. 1963-65), N.Y. Acad. Sci., Ind. Acad. Sci., Fla. Acad. Sci., Sigma Xi, Phi Kappa Phi, Phi Sigma, Gamma Alpha. Home: Ann Arbor Mich. Died May 9, 1997.

CANTRELL, MARY, mental health association administrator; b. Grafton, W.Va., Jan. 10, 1915; d. John and Olga (Meister) Robinson; 1 child, Suzanne Herbert. BS in Nursing, Baylor U., 1955; MS in Nursing, U. Tex., 1960; doctoral student, North Tex. U. RN. Head nurse St. Elizabeth Hosp., Washington, 1937-40; dir. nursing svc. U. Okla., Norman, 1942-51; dir. nursing edn. Waco (Tex.) VA Hosp., 1952-74; dir. mental health assoc. program McLennan Community Coll., Waco, 1974-85; dir. Heart of Tex. chpt. Mental Health Assn., Waco, 1985—; cons. Community Career Ctr. for Displaced Homemakers, Tex. Coordinating Bd.; nursing cons. Brazos Ctr. for Psychiatry; mem. speakers' pool continuing edn. in the health scis. Baylor U. Med. Ctr., adv. com. faculty tng. project So. Regional Edn. Bd., Coun. for Standards in Human Svc. Edn.; site visitor for So. Regional Edn. Bd. accreditation of mental health programs in colls. and univs. Mem. women's issues forum com. YWCA, Heart of Tex. Coun. Govts. Exec. Health Planning Com., vol. svcs. coun. Waco Ctr. for Youth, Retired Sr. Vol. Program Adv. Bd., Adaptive Living Ctr. Adv. Bd., Cen. Tex. Coun. for the Deaf Adv. Bd., Assn. for the Advancement Community Welfare; past mem. Freeman House Bd., adv. com. Area Agy. on Aging, com. on drug abuse Heart of Tex. Coun. Govts.; mem. Waco YWCA Pathfinder, 1985; elected to Silver Haired Legis., com. chair, mem. exec. com., 1987. Recipient Jr. C. of C. Annual award for community svc., 1986, Gov. of Tex. award for vol. svc. to the handicapped, 1986, Appreciation award VFW, 1988, Miriam Klubok award for outstanding and continuous leadership in the nat. orgn. for human svc. edn., 1989,

Waco Unit Annual award Nat. Assn. Social Workers, 1989; named nominee Tex. Dept. Mental Health-Mental Retardation's Vol. of Yr., Waco Ctr. for Youth, 1986, Tex. Vol. award Waco United Way, 1986. Mem. Tex. Nurses Assn. (past dir., every office except treas., chmn. of every com. Dist. 10, Nurse of Yr. 1990), Am. Nurses' Assn. (past sec., exec. com. on psychiat. nursing practice), Nat. Orgn. Human Svc. Educators (immediate past pres., bd. dirs., Lenore McNeer award 1984), Tex. Mental Health Assn., Tex. Jr. Coll. Tchr.'s Assn., Tex. Orgn. Human Svc. Edn., Nat. Mental Health Assn., Nat. Assn. for Mental Health (staff coun.), Sigma Theta Tau. DIED 05/29/97. .

CAPEHART, HOMER EARL, JR., lawyer; b. Green Bay, Wis., Oct. 29, 1922; s. Homer Earl and Irma (Mueller) C.; m. Harriet Jane Holmes, June 17, 1950; children: Craig Earl, Caroline Mary. A.B., DePauw U., 1945; LL.B., Harvard U., 1948. Bar: Ind. 1948. Pvt. practice Indpls., 1948—; of counsel Krieg, DeVault, Alexander & Capehart, 1952—; dir. Secured Ins. Co., Indpls., 1950-62; pres. Capehart Farms, Inc., 1979—. Bd. dirs. Indpls. Symphony Orch., 1958-61, Ind. State Mus. Soc., 1982-88; bd. dirs. Hist. Landmarks Found. Ind., 1976-85, vice-chmn., 1979-81, chmn., 1981-84; trustee Indpls. Mus. Art, 1987—; mem. Ind. State Student Assistance Commn., 1988-91, vice chmn., 1990-91, Ind. Flood Control and Water Resources Commn., 1953-60, Ind. Environ. Mgmt. Bd., 1974-77; pub. mem. Ind. Air Pollution Bd., 1972-79, chmn., 1974-78; dir. Ind. Friends of Archives, Inc., 1995. Mem. ABA, Ind. Bar Assn., Ind. Bd. Bar Examiners, Indpls. Bar Assn (v.p. 1972-73), Decorative Arts Soc. (pres. 1979-81), SAR (pres. Ind. 1960), Ind. Hist. Soc., Ind. Soc. Pioneers, Indpls. Valley of Scottish Rite (trustee 1990—), Phi Beta Kappa, Beta Theta Pi. Republican. Clubs: Masons (Indpls.) (33 deg.), Literary (Indpls.) (pres. 1976), Exchange (Indpls.) (pres. 1969, nat. dist. dir. 1970-71), Columbia (Indpls.), Woodstock (Indpls.), Contemporary (Indpls.) (pres. 1975), Portfolio (Indpls.) (pres. 1983-84). Died Apr. 28, 1996.

CAPONE, ROBERT, retail store executive; b. N.Y.C., Sept. 11, 1928; s. Ralph and Mae (Josloff) C.; m. Joan Konop, Mar. 12, 1950 (div. Apr. 1984); children: Linda, Claudia, Clifford, Alyson; m. Margaret Ann Quirk; children: Michael, Eileen, Kimberly. BBA, Hofstra U., 1958. Sr. tech. specialist Exxon Corp., N.Y.C., 1944-65; sr. v.p. J.C. Penney Co., Inc., N.Y.C., 1965-95; bd. dirs. Infomat, Dallas. Trustee Nyack Hosp., N.Y., 1986-95. Recipient Silver Plaque Disting. Service in Retailing, Nat. Retail Mchts. Assn., 1974. Republican. Roman Catholic. Home: Nyack N.Y. Died Nov. 1, 1995.

CAPPON, ALEXANDER PATTERSON, English language educator; b. Milw., May 11, 1900; s. John, Jr. and Charlotte Curry (Patterson) C.; m. Dorothy Churchill, Nov. 13, 1922; 1 child, Frances Burney (Mrs. Hardison J. Geer). Student, Milw. State Tchrs. Coll., 1919-20, Harvard, 1921, 1929-31; Ph.B., U. Chgo., 1925, M.A., 1926, Ph.D., 1935. Instr. English U. Tulsa, 1926-27; asso. English lit. U. Wash., 1927-29; lit. editor The New Humanist, 1931-35; instr. English Mont. State. Coll., 1932-33, asst. prof., 1934-37; instr. Western Ill. State Tchrs. Coll., 1934; asso. editor U. Kansas City Rev., 1937, 42-52, editor in chief, 1938-42, 53-70; asst. prof. English U. Kansas City, 1937-41, asso. prof., 1941-45, chmn. dept. English, 1941-44, 48-51, prof. English lang. and lit., 1945-63; prof. English lit., editor in chief Univ. Rev., U. Mo. at Kansas City, 1953-70. Author: About Wordsworth and Whitehead: A Prelude to Philosophy, Aspects of Wordsworth and Whitehead: Philosophy and Certain Continuing Life Problems, 1983; Action, Organism, and Philosophy in Wordsworth and Whitehead, 1985; contbr. articles to profl. pubs. Research on Bertrand Russell. Mem. MLA, AAUP, Phi Kappa Phi. Died Jan. 25, 1997.

CAPPS, WALTER HOLDEN, religion educator; b. Omaha, May 5, 1934; s. Holden Frances and Mildred Linnea (Bildt) C.; m. Lois Ragnhild Grimsrud, Aug. 21, 1960; children: Lisa Margarit, Todd Holden, Laura Karolina. BS, Portland (Oreg.) State U., 1957; BD, Augustana Theol. Sem., Rock Island, Ill., 1960; STM, Yale U., 1961, MA, 1963, PhD, 1965. Prof. religious studies U. Calif., Santa Barbara, 1964—. Author: The Unfinished War, 1982, The Monastic Impulse, 1983, New Religious Right, 1990, Thomas Merton, 1990. Bd. dirs. Pacific Luth. Sem., Berkeley, Calif., 1965-73, La Casa de Maria Retreat Ctr., Santa Barbara, 1966-84; chair Calif. Coun. for Humanities, San Francisco, 1984-87; pres. Fedn. State Humanities Couns., Washington, 1985-87. Lutheran. Died Oct. 28, 1997.

CARAY, HARRY CHRISTOPHER, sports announcer; b. St. Louis, Mar. 1, 1919; s. Christopher and Daisy (Argint) Carabina; m. Dolores Caray, June 8, 1975; children: Harry, Patricia, Christopher, Michelle, Elizabeth. Student pub. schs., St. Louis. Sports announcer St. Louis Baseball, 1944-69, Oakland (Calif.) A's, 1969-70, Chgo. White Sox, 1970-81, Chgo. Cubs, 1982—; broadcaster numerous All-Star, World Series, and Bowl games. Recipient numerous awards which include Nat. Assn. Broadcasters Hall of Fame, 1994, Nat. Baseball Hall of Fame, 1988, Ford C. Frick Award, 1989. Died Feb. 18, 1998.

CARCANI, ADIL, Prime Minister, chairman Council of Ministers of Albania; b. Gjirokastra, May 4, 1922. Asst. commr. of 5th Assault Brigade during nat. war of liberation; various positions in several govt. ministries as asst. minister of commerce, 1948, minister of industry, 1951, asst. minister of the merged ministry of industry and constrn., 1953; minister of industry and mines, 1955; leading mem. of Tirana Communist Party Orgn., 1948, candidate mem. of the Central Com., 1952, full mem., 1956; candidate mem. of Politburo, 1956, full mem., 1961; dep. premier, 1965, 1st dep. premier, 1974-82; mem. parliament, 1946—; mem. gen. council of Albanian Democratic Front, 1967—; chmn., Council of Ministers and Prime Minister, 1982—; chmn. Central Electrification Commn., 1970; head Albanian Econ. Delegations to China, 1968, 75; mem. com. drafting new constrn., 1975. Decorated Order of Freedom First Class, 1962.Died Oct. 13, 1997.

CÁRDENAS, RENÉ, television executive, demographer; b. San Francisco, Feb. 13, 1928; s. Lauro and Maria (Ball) C.; m. Doris F. Marino, June 7, 1952; children: Rene, Kevin, Gregory. PhD in Cultural Anthropology, U. Calif.-Berkeley, 1970. Producer, writer Villa Alegre, Oakland, Calif., 1970-81; mgr. Kingston Trio, 1959-69; with Stanford Research, Inc., 1956, Ampex Corp., San Juan, P.R., 1957-59; pres. BCTV, San Leandro, Calif., 1969-95; adj. prof. sch. edn. U. Mass., Amherst, 1986-95; cons. U.S. Office Edn., 1971-72, Office Mgmt. and Budget, 1972-73, White House, 1974-75, also fed. govt. agys.; disting. vis. scholar broadcast communications art dept. San Francisco State U. Served with USNR, 1941-48. Grantee Exxon USA Found., 1973-76, Ford Found., 1972, Lilly Endowment Found., 1975-76, HUD, 1978, Dept. Labor, 1972-73, Levi Strauss Corp., 1975; named Hon. Col. N.Mex.; Hon. Citizen Okla.; recipient Tex. Silver Spur award, 1975; NEA Humanitarian award, 1974; recognition Calif. State Legislature for outstanding ednl. achievement in broadcasting; 4 Emmys, 1977, 79, 80, 81. Mem. Nat. Acad. TV Arts and Scis. Democrat. Club: Oakland Athletic. Author: Parenting in a Multi Cultural Society, 1980; contbr. numerous articles on edn. of culturally disadvantaged child to profl. jours. Died Sept. 30, 1995. Home: Oakland Calif.

CARLSON, OSCAR NORMAN, metallurgist, educator; b. Mitchell, S.D., Dec. 21, 1920; s. Oscar and Ruth Belle (Gammill) C.; m. Virginia Jyleen Forsberg, July 30, 1946; children: Gregory Norman, Richard Norman, Karen Virginia. B.A., Yankton Coll., 1943; Ph.D., Iowa State U., 1950. Mem. faculty Iowa State U., Ames, 1943-87, prof., sr. metallurgist Ames Lab., 1960-87, emeritus prof., 1987, chmn. dept. metallurgy, chief metallurgy div., 1962-66; vis. scientist Max Planck Inst. for Metallforschung, Stuttgart, Germany, 1974-75, 83. Bd. regents Waldorf Coll., 1964-74, faculty citation, 1971. Fellow Am. Soc. Materials Internat. (chmn. Des Moines 1957-58); mem. AIME, Am. Chem. Soc., Iowa Acad. Scis., Sigma Xi, Phi Kappa Phi. Lodge: Lions. Spl. research metallurgy of vanadium, niobium and yttrium, phase studies alloy systems, deformation behavior metals and alloys, mass transport of solutes in metals. Home: Ames Iowa Died Sept. 10, 1993.

CARLSTON, RICHARD CHARLES, aerospace engineer; b. San Francisco, May 17, 1929; s. Charles Oliver and Gertrude Madeline (Green) C.; m. Margaret Elizabeth Schoenborn, July 19, 1958; children: Donald, Elizabeth, Stuart. BS, U. San Francisco, 1951; MS, U. Mo., Columbia, 1954; PhD in Chemistry, U. Kans., Lawrence, 1957. Registered profl. engr., Calif. Sr. chemist Sperry Gyroscope Co., Great Neck, N.Y., 1957-60; research engr. Grumman Aircraft Co., Bethpage, N.Y., 1960-62; head solid state physics dept. Aerojet Gen. Corp., Azusa, Calif., 1962-64; physicist Office Naval Research, Washington, 1964-68; assoc. prof. metall. engring. Calif. Poly. State U., San Luis Obispo, 1968-72; research group leader EG&G Co., Santa Barbara, Calif., 1972-76; mgr. corrosion program for ICBMsystems TRW Def. and Space Systems Group, Redondo Beach, Calif., 1976-92; mgr. The Trading Post and Serra Stamp Svc. (scout memorabilia and philately); dir. SRA Internat., San Bernardino; exec. search mgr. Serra Assocs., engring. cons. Mem. editorial bd. Electrochem. Soc., 1967-72, chem. abstractor, 1960-65. Cofounder Plainedge (N.Y.) Pub. Libr., 1961; active local Boy Scouts Am., mem. Jamboree staffs, Can., U.S., 1985; exec. bd. Nat. Cath. Com. on Scouting, Internat. Cath. Com. Scouting, 1992—; oblate Order of St. Benedict, Conception Abbey, Roman Cath. Ch. Recipient Wood badge & St. George Bronze Pelican award Boy Scouts Am. Fellow Washington Acad. Scis., Am. Inst. Chemists; mem. Nat. Assn. Corrosion Engrs., Air Pollution Control Assn., Am. Soc. Quality Control, Electrochem. Soc., Am. Soc. Metals, Am. Philatelic Soc., German Philatelic Soc., Philatelic Libr. So. Calif., Arrowhead Stamp Club, KC, Sigma Xi. Republican. Home: San Luis Obispo Calif. Deceased.

CARMACK, GEORGE, newspaper editor; b. Troy, Tenn., Feb. 20, 1907; s. Dan Meacham and Frances (Burnett) C.; m. Bonnie Tom Robinson, Oct. 1943; 1 dau., Judith Anne. Student, Union U., Jackson, Tenn., 1922-24; A.B., U. Tenn., 1927. Reporter, Knoxville Sentinel, 1926-28, Memphis Evening Appeal, 1928-30; city editor Memphis Press-Scimitar, 1930-35; mng. editor, 1935-37; editor Knoxville News-Sentinel, 1937, Houston Press, 1946-64; staff writer Scripps-Howard Newspaper Alliance, 1964-66; editor Albuquerque Tribune, 1966-73; editorial bd., columnist San Antonio Express-News, 1973-75, 80-89, ret., 1989, assoc. editor, 1975-78. Served as pvt. in 6th Cav. 1940; commd. 1942, ETO.; commd. PTO. Mem. Tex. Philos. Soc., Tex. Hist. Assn. Episcopalian. Home: San Antonio Tex. Died Sept. 27, 1995.

CARNÉ, MARCEL ALBERT, film director; b. Aug. 18, 1906; s. Paul and Maria (Racouet) C. Asst. operator Les Nouveaux Messieurs, 1928; asst. to dir. Cagliostro, 1929; mem. editorial staff Cinemagazine; asst. dir. René Clair in Sous les Toits de Paris, 1930; asst. dir. Le Grand Jeu, Pension Minosa, La Kermesse Heroique; dir. films: Jenny, 1936, Drô le de drame, 1937, Quai des brumes, 1938, Le jour se lève, 1939, Les visiteurs du soir, 1941, les enfants du Paradis, 1943 (named Best French Film since the invention of talking pictures), Les portes de la nuit, 1946, La Marie du port, 1949, Juliette ou la clé des songes, 1950, Thérèse Raquin, 1953, L'air de Paris, 1954, Le pays d'où je viens, 1956, Les tricheurs, 1958, Terrain vague, 1960, Du mouron pour les petits oiseaux, 1963, Trois chambres à Manhattan, 1965, Les jeunes loups, 1968, Les assassins de l'ordre, 1970, La merveilleuse visite, 1974, La Bible, 1976, César des Césars, 1979. Decorated grand officier Légion d'honneur, comdr. Ordre des Arts et des Lettres, grand croix Ordre National du Mérite; Recipient Grand Prix de Cinéma, 1958, Médaille de Vermeil, 1972, Grand Prix Oecuménique, Cannes, 1977, Biennale de Venise 1938-53, 82, Praemium Imperiale of Japan Art Assn., 1989, Prix Lumiere, 1990, Film Critic prize Moscow, Golden Globe award San Francisco, 1985, Pik Donatillo Rome, 1991, Prie Grand Siecle Paris, 1995. Author: La vie à belles dents, 1989, 96; contbr. criticisms to profl. jours. Died Oct. 31, 1996.

CARNEY, WILLIAM RAY, lawyer; b. Chgo., Nov. 3, 1940; s. Benedict Frederick and Mary (Eyster) C.; m. Eileen Martin, Dec. 29, 1982; children: Michael Ethan, Diana Marie, Matthew Davis, Cayla Anne. Student, Cornell U., 1958-59; AB, Northwestern U., 1962, postgrad., 1962-63; JD, Loyola U., Chgo., 1967. Bar: Ill., U.S. Dist. Ct. (no. dist.) Ill., U.S. Ct. Appeals (3d, 6th, 7th, and 8th cirs.), U.S. Supreme Ct. Assoc. Bell, Boyd & Lloyd, Chgo., 1967-74; ptnr. Bell, Boyd & Lloyd, Chgo., Dallas and Washington, 1974—; bd. dirs. Computer Overseas Corp., Chgo., W.R. Magnus Inc., Chgo.; bd. advisors, lectr., instr. Litigation Risk Analysis, Menlo Park, Calif.; lectr., instr. Nat. Inst. Trial Advocacy. Mem. Bd. Edn., Northbrook, Ill., 1970-73; chief transition team Gov. Ill., Tollway Commn., 1970; labor negotiator Chgo. Bd. Edn., 1981-82. Fellow Ill. Bar Fedn.; mem. ABA, Ill. Bar Assn., Chgo. Bar Assn., Bar Assn. 7th Jud. Cir. Ct., Chgo. Athletic Assn., Chgo. Downtown Sports Club. Avocation: hunting. Deceased.

CARNOW, BERTRAM WARREN, occupational and environmental health consultant; b. Phila., June 19, 1922; s. Louis H. and Helen (Warren) C.; m. Shirley Ann Conibear, Oct. 31, 1975; children: David Robert, Donald James, Tammi Jo, Rebecca Ann, Kalinka Rose, Tina Lisa. BS in Biology, NYU, 1947; MB, MD, Chgo. Med. Sch., 1951. Diplomate Am. Bd. Preventive Medicine. Intern Cook County Hosp., Chgo., 1951-52; basic sci. resident in cardiology Michael Reese Hosp., Chgo., 1952-53, clin. resident in internal medicine, 1953-55, attending physician internal medicine, cons. chest diseases, 1955-71; dir. Dept. Occupational and Environ. Medicine U. Ill. Sch. Pub. Health, Chgo., 1972-78; dir. residency tng. in occupation medicine U. Ill. Hosp., Chgo., 1982-87, dir. programs in occupational medicine, 1977-87, dir. Great Lake Ctr. for Occupational Safety and Health, 1977-87; pres., sr. scientist Carnow, Conibear, and Assocs., Ltd., Chgo., 1974-88, exec. v.p., 1988-96; pvt. practice in occupational and environ. medicine, Chgo.; prof. occupational medicine U. Ill., Chgo., 1966-92, dept. preventive medicine, 1987-92, environ. and occupational health scis., U.I. Sch. Pub. Health, 1972-92, ; dir. div. occupational medicine Cook County Hosp., 1976-80, Environ. Health Resource Ctr. State of Ill, 1969-77; chmn. com. for rev. of NIOSH criteria documents, Soc. for Occupational and Environ. Health, 1974-80; chmn. NRC panel on SO2, Nat. Acad. Scis., 1974, mem. panel on non-renewable resources, 1974, mem. panel on polycyclic organic matter, 1974; cons. U.S. Congress Subcom. on Investigations and Oversight of the Pub. Works and Transp. Com. on Subcom. on Commerce, Transp. and Tourism of Energy and Commerce Com., Washington, Karolinska Inst., Sweden, NSF, EPA, NAS, City of El Paso, Tex., Minister of Environment City of Toronto, EPA, Senate Commerce Subcom. on Health Effects of Lead, AEC, Ill. Agent Orange Commn., Nat. Inst. Environ. Health Sci., State of Ill., Am. Pub. Health Assn., Acad. Pediatrics, Meat Packer's Union, AFL-CIO, Senate Subcom. on Environment, Sulfates and Intermittent Stack Tech., Pres. Coun. on Environ. Quality, State of Calif., State of Pa., State of N.Y., OSHA, Inst. on Man and Sci., Govt. of Can., B.C. (Can.) Coun. of Indian Chiefs, St. Regis Coun. Akwasame Indians. N.Am. contbg. editor Am. Jour. Indsl. Medicine, assoc. editor, 1980; mem. editorial bd. Jour. Safety Rev., 1975-96; contbr. articles to profl. jours. With USAF, 1942-46. Med. dir. Chgo. Lung Assn., 1970-78; mem. epidemiology com. Am. Heart Assn., 1976, mem. task force on heart disease in industry; mem. epidemiology and statistics task force, Ill.

Cancer Coun., 1978. Grantee NIOSH, 1977-87, State of Ill., 1969-78, Kellogg Found., 1975-78, EPA, NIOSH, 1969-84. Master Am. Coll. Occupational and Environ. Medicine; fellow APHA, Am. Coll. Preventive Medicine, Am. Coll. Epidemiology, Royal Soc. Health, Chgo. Inst. Medicine; mem. AAAS, Am. Coll. Toxicology, Cen. States Occupational Medicine Assn., Am. Assn. Tchrs. Preventive Medicine, Am. Trudeau Soc., Am. Acad. Occupational Health, Ill. Coll. Chest Physicians, Nat. Thoracic Soc., N.Y. Acad. Scis. Home: Barrington Ill. Died Nov. 4, 1996.

CARO, WARREN, theatrical executive, lawyer; b. Bklyn., Feb. 24, 1907; s. Arthur Brinton and Madeline (Davidsburg) C.; m. Nancy Kelly, Nov. 25, 1955 (div. 1965); 1 child, Kelly Caro-Rosenberg; m. Elizabeth Rehill, Dec. 9, 1979. BA, Cornell U., 1927, JD, 1929. Bar: N.Y. 1930, U.S. Supreme Ct. 1932. Sole practice law N.Y.C., 1929-39; asst. gen. counsel Fed. Works Agy., Washington, 1940-42; exec. dir. The Theatre Guild-Am. Theatre Soc., N.Y.C., 1946-67; dir. theatre ops. The Shubert Orgn., N.Y.C., 1967-81; exec. dir. The Theatre Guild-NBC-TV Play Series, N.Y.C., 1949; vis. prof. drama and dir. U. Hawaii, 1955; mem. adv. commn. JFK Ctr. for Performing Arts, Washington; v.p., chmn. bd. trustees Am. Acad. Dramatic Arts; mem. adv. com. Performing Arts Ctr., Cornell U. Served as lt. comdr., aide to Gov. Alaska USCG 1942-45. Recipient 2 Tony awards. Mem. Am. TV Soc. (founder, pres.), Shaw Soc. Am. (founder, lectr.), Internat. Theatre Inst. (founding mem.). Home: Norwalk Conn. Died Jan. 1, 1995.

CARPENTER, JOHN WILSON, III, management consultant, air force officer, educational administrator; b. Starkville, Miss., Aug. 11, 1916; s. John Wilson and Alice Margaret (McBee) C.; m. Dorothy Biglow Goding, June 13, 1939; children: Carol Sue (Mrs. James P. Rogers), John Wilson IV, Jean McBee Carpenter Murray. Student, Okla. State U., 1934, Miss. State U., 1935; B.S., U.S. Mil. Acad., 1939; grad., Air Command and Staff Coll., 1947, Air War Coll., 1954. Commd. 2d lt. USAAF, 1939; advanced through grades to lt. gen. USAF, 1965; vice-comdr. 13th Air Force, 1949-50; plans and programming office, dep. for operations and chief of staff Hdqrs. Air Research and Devel. Command USAF, 1950; vice-comdr. Arnold Air Devel., USAF Center, 1954; insp. gen., chief plans and programming, asst. vice comdr. Air Research and Devel. Command, USAF, 1955, 57-58; comdr. Flight Test Center, USAF, 1959-62; dir. plans, Hdqrs. USAF, 1962-64, asst. dep. chief of staff for plans and operations. (JCS matters), 1964-65; comdr. Air U. Maxwell AFB, Ala., 1965-68; dep. chief staff, personnel Hdqrs. U.S. Air Force, 1968-69; asst. vice chief staff (Hdqrs. U.S. Air Force), 1969-70; supt. Culver Mil. Acad., Ind., 1970-74; pres. Carpenter Assos., Montgomery, Ala., 1974-89, ret., 1989. Decorated D.S.M. with oak leaf cluster, also; Silver Star with two oak leaf clusters; Legion of Merit with two oak leaf clusters; D.F.C. with two oak leaf clusters; Air Medal with oak leaf cluster; Presdl. Citation (U.S., P.I.). Assoc. fellow AIAA; mem. Ret. Officers Assn. (chmn. bd. dirs. 1975-79), Soc. Exptl. Test Pilots (asso.), Order Daedalians, Tau Beta Pi, Sigma Alpha Epsilon. Home: San Antonio Tex. Died Nov. 8, 1996.

CARR, HOWARD ERNEST, retired insurance agency executive; b. Johnson City, Tenn., Oct. 4, 1908; s. William Alexander and Gertrude (Feathers) C.; BS, E. Tenn. State U., 1929; MEd, Duke, 1935; postgrad. U. N.C., 1938-39; m. Thelma Northcutt, June 11, 1937 (dec. Oct., 1972); 1 son, Howard Ernest. Supt., Washington Coll. (Tenn.), 1929-35; ednl. advisor U.S. Office Edn., Ft. Oglethorpe, Ga., 1935-37; prin. Greensboro (N.C.) city schs., 1937-42; dir. activities First Presbyn. Ch., Greensboro, 1946-47; with Jefferson Standard Life Ins. Co., Greensboro, 1947—, spl. rep., 1947-54, supr. agy. Greensboro, 1964, mgr., 1964-67; pres. Everett's Lake Corp. Chmn. Guilford County Bd. Edn., 1950-77; vice chmn. N.C. Gov's Com. Edn., 1956-60; N.C. rep. White House Conf. Edn., 1955. Mem. adv. com. Greensboro div. Guilford Coll., 1958—; head Guilford County Cancer Drive, 1956, bd. dirs. Cancer Soc., 1956—; v.p. N.C. State Sch. Bds. Assn., 1959-61; bd. dirs. Greensboro Jr. Mus., 1956-62, Tannenbaum Sternberger Found. Lt. USNR, 1942-46, asst. head motion picture dept., Washington; to capt., 1951-54, as head motion picture dept; ret. as capt., 1968. Recipient Nat. Quality award Nat. Assn. Life Underwriters, 1948, Nat. Honor award East Tenn. State U., 1993; named Boss of the Year, Lou-Celin chpt. Am. Bus. Woman's Assn., 1967; W.H. Andrews, Jr. award, 1985; named Man of Yr., 1988. Mem. Nat., N.C. (pres. 1964-65; Man of Year award 1969), Greensboro (pres. 1956-57) assns. life underwriters, N.C. Leaders Club, Greensboro C. of C. (chmn. edn. com. 1960-62). Presbyn. (elder). Mason (32 deg.), Kiwanian (pres. Greensboro 1951). Author: History of Higher Education in East Tennessee, 1935.

CARR, ROBERT ALLEN, finance educator; b. L.A., Sept. 28, 1917; s. Harry Newton and Elvaretta (Wilson) C.; m. Ruth Eleanor Holland, Dec. 7, 1946; children: Nancy Ellen, David Allen. AB, San Francisco State Coll., 1951, MA, 1953; PhD, U. So. Calif., 1959. Orgn. and methods examiner VA, San Francisco, 1946-48; instr. Golden Gate Coll., 1952; lectr. U. So. Calif., 1956-57; coord. econ. edn. project Calif. State U., Fresno, 1952-56, asst. prof., 1957-61; assoc. prof. Calif. State U., 1961-66, prof., 1966-83, asst. head div. bus., 1964-65, chmn. dept. fin. and industry, 1965-76, prof. emeritus, 1983-93, coord. Somali project, 1983-88, chmn. emeritus Faculty Assn., 1990-92; cons. economist Fresno Planning Dept., 1962-63; cons. Somali Inst. Devel. Adminstrn. and Mgmt., 1982-83; trustee Fresno Meml. Gardens, 1977-86, chmn., 1978-80. Contbr. articles to profl. jours. Mem. Fresno County Econ. Devel. Adv. Coun., 1977-80, vice chmn., 1978, chmn., 1979-80. Staff sgt. USAAF, 1941-45. Ford Faculty fellow, 1962; E.L. Phillips intern, 1963-64. Mem. AAUP, Am. Western Econs. Assns., Am. Fin. Assn., Western Fin. Assn. (exec. com. v.p. 1966-67, pres. 1967-68), Fin. Mgmt. Assn. (dir. 1970-72, v.p. 1973-74), Soc. Internat. Devel., am. Statis. Assn. (pres. San Joaquin Valley chpt. 1975-77), Regional Sci. Assn. Emeritus and Retired Faculty Assn. of Calif. (mem. state coun. 1990-92). Home: Fresno Calif. Died June 29, 1993.

CARRIGAN, RICHARD ALFRED, environmental scientist, chemist; b. Somerville, Mass., May 11, 1906; married, 1931; 1 child. BS, U. Fla., 1932; PhD in Soil Chemistry, Cornell U., 1948. Supr. analytical chemistry Armour Rsch. Found., Ill., 1951-60; program dir. sci. facility evaluation group divsn. inst. program NSF, 1960-64; staff assoc., 1964-70, program mgr. divsn. inst. devel., 1970-71, program mgr. divsn. advanced environ. rsch. and tech., 1971-78, program mgr. divsn. problem-focused rsch. applications, 1978-79, program dir., 1980-82; sr. sci. assoc. divsn. atmospheric sci. NSF, 1982-94; h.s. tchr., Fla., 1932-33; lab supr. Magnolia Petrol Co., Tex., 1933-38; assoc. chemist experiment station U. Fla., 1938-45, biochemist, 1945-51; prof. soils Coll. Agrl. 1948-51; specialist anal chemistry Union of Burma Applied Rsch. Inst., 1954-55. Recipient Edward A. Flinn award Am. Geophysical Union, 1994. Fellow AAAS, Am. Inst. Chemistry; mem. Am Chem. Soc., Soil Sci. Soc. Am., Am. Geophysical Union (Edward A. Flinn III award 1994). Research in chemistry of minor elements in soils; spectrographic analysis; pasture fertility; chemistry of cobalt in soils; spectroscopy of plasmas; federal grant administration. Died Sept. 23, 1996.

CARROLL, ALBERT, retired corporate executive; b. Phila., Aug. 25, 1914; s. William and Florence (Levy) C.; m. Rhoda Freudenthal, June 20, 1942; children—David William, Barbara Jean. B.S. in Econs, U. Pa., 1936. Advt. copywriter N.W. Ayer & Son, 1936-40; advt. dir. Merck & Co., Inc., Rahway, N.J., 1940-55; v.p. profl. mktg. div. Benton & Bowles, Inc., N.Y.C., 1955-57; v.p. Vick Internat., 1957-60; v.p., spl. products mgr. Lever Bros. Co., N.Y.C., 1960-68; pres. Julius Schmid Inc., N.Y.C., 1968-75, Med. Funding Corp., Westwood, N.J., 1975-79, Wharton Bus. Cons., Inc., White Plains, N.Y., 1979—; retired. Trustee Hartsdale Bd. Edn.; vol. coordinator advt. council Nat. Blood Program, 1952. Served as 1st lt. USAAF, 1943-45. Mem. Assn. Nat. Advertisers (chmn. chem. group 1953), Bus. Publ. Audit (dir. 1952-55), Pharm. Advt. Club (dir. 1953-55), Am. Marketing Assn., Beta Gamma Sigma, Pi Gamma Mu. Club: Maplewood. DIED 10/06/97. .

CARROLL, JOHN HOWARD, sales executive; b. Luttrell, Tenn., Feb. 11, 1927; s. Robert Howard and Clemmie (Seivers) C.; m. Carmen Pinney, Sep. 13, 1947; children: Dale Robert, Barbara Jean, Tracey Lynette. BS in Commerce, Grove City (Pa.) Coll., 1950. Mgr. spl. product sales Superior Steel Corp., Carnegie, Pa., 1958-62; sales engr. Reactive Metals Inc., Niles, Ohio, 1962-65; regional sales mgr. RMI Co., Chgo., 1965-82; v.p. sales TRADCO Inc., Washington, Mo., 1982-90; sales mgr. Murdock Inc., Compton, Calif., 1990-95; pioneer titanium-zirconium projects spl. and rare metals Superior Steel Corp., Carnegie, Pa., 1954-62. Officer Chartiers Valley Jaycees, Carnegie, Pa., 1956-60; leader Boy Scouts Am., Lombard, Ill., 1972-76. Mem. AIAA (sr.), Soc. Mfg. Engrs. (sr.), Zirconia Assn., Air Force Assn., Am. Def. Preparedness Assn. Avocations: music, golf, fishing. Home: Washington Mo. Died Jan., 1995.

CARRUTHERS, IAN DOUGLAS, agrarian development educator; b. London, Aug. 30, 1938; s. William Walker and Kathleen (Irvin) C.; m. Sarah Ann Ladbury, Dec. 31, 1993. BSc, U. London, 1961, PhD, 1976; diploma agrl. econs., Oxford U., 1962. Cons. Pakistan, 1962-67; lectr. Wye Coll., U. London, 1968-82, prof., 1983-96; cons. World Bank, 1976-93, UN FAO, Romillaly, 1971-95; bd. dirs. Commonwealth Devel. Corp., 1991-96. Contbr. articles to profl. jours. Avocation: gardening. Died May 24, 1996.

CARTER, MARGUERITE, publishing executive; b. Seattle, Jan. 31, 1899; d. William Whitfield and Minnie (Stafford) Herring; m. Alan C. McConnell, Sept. 29, 1914; 1 child, Alan Richard. Sec., treas. Alan McConnell & Son, Inc., Indpls., 1928-88. writer syndicated daily newspaper feature, 1928-39. Home: Mooresville Ind. Died Nov. 1988.

CARTER, NANCY HADLEY REID, secondary education educator; b. Jacksonville, Fla., July 25, 1944; d. Hubert Hadley and Emma (Hill) Reid; m. John Frederick Atkins, Feb. 27, 1973 (div. Feb. 1982); 1 child, Margaret Hill Atkins; m. James Hill Carter, June 6, 1987. BS, Blue Mountain (Miss.) Coll., 1967; MEd, U. Ga., 1975. Cert. home economist. Tchr. home econs. and English Clay County High Sch., Green Cove Springs, Fla., 1967-69; tchr. home econs. Hephzibah (Ga.) Jr. High Sch., 1971-73; tchr. reading Hillcrest Bapt. Ch. Sch., Augusta, Ga., 1980-81; tchr. home econs. Kingstree (S.C.) Sr. High Sch., 1982—. Mem. NEA, S.C. Edn. Assn., Am. Home Econs. Assn., S.C. Home Econs. Assn., Am. Vocat. Assn., S.C. Vocat. Assn., S.C. Vocat. Home Econs. Tchrs. Democrat. Baptist. Avocations: stamp collecting, doll collecting, needlework, gardening, reading. Died Apr. 29, 1994.

CASADO, ANTONIO FRANCISCO, real estate executive; b. Puerto Padre, Cuba, Oct. 10, 1913; came to U.S., 1926, naturalized, 1936; s. Miguel and Mercedes (Puig); m. Ardeen Frances Burkett, June 27, 1948; children: Jill Anne, Nancy, Mary Lou (dec.). B.A., Friends U., Wichita, Kans., 1937. Auditor Stanley Spurrier & Co. (C.P.A.s); accountant Boeing Airplane Co., Wichita, 1939-42; sec.-treas, v.p. Casado-McKay Inc. (Realtors and developers), Wichita, 1946-93; ret.; dep. dir. U.S. AID, Paraguay, 1970-72; dir. Wichita Bd. Realtors, 1951-58, pres., 1953. Mem. Kans. Ho. of Reps., 1960-64, Kans. Senate, 1964-70; mem. Wichita City Coun., 1975-86, Mayor of Wichita, 1977, 79, 86. Served with Med. Dept. AUS, 1942-46. Recipient Realtor of Year award, 1962, Lion of Year award, 1964. Mem. Wichita Assn. Home Builders, Masons, Lions. Republican. Methodist. Home: Concordia Kans. Died May 11, 1996.

CASARELLA, EDMOND, sculptor, printmaker; b. Newark, Sept. 3, 1920; s. Domenick Antonio and Natalina (Feliciani) C.; m. Mary Peters, July 21, 1946; 1 child, Demetra. BFA, Cooper Union, 1942; student, Bklyn. Mus. Art Sch., 1949-51. Instr. graphics Bklyn. Mus. Sch., 1956-60, Yale U., New Haven, 1958, 64—, NYU, 1962, Cooper Union, N.Y.C., 1963-70, Hunter Coll., N.Y.C., 1963—, Rutgers U., New Brunswick, N.J., 1964—, Pratt Inst., N.Y.C., 1964—, Finch Coll., 1969-74, Manhattanville Coll., N.Y., 1973-74, Queens Coll., 1980. One-man shows include Speed Mus., Louisville, 1968-69, Landmark Gallery, N.Y., 1977, 80, Sculpture Ctr., N.Y., 1977; group exhbns. include Bklyn. Mus., 1952, 53, Pa. Acad. Fine Arts, Phila., 1953, 59, 63, Libr. Congress, Washington, 1955, 56, 58, Corcoran Gallery Art, Washington, 1955, Mus. Fine Arts, Boston, 1957, Victoria and Albert Mus., London, 1959, Whitney Mus. Am. Art, N.Y.C., 1959, 61, 63, 96, L.A. County Mus. Art, 1963; retrospective exhbns. include Allegheny Coll., 1978, Edward Williams Coll., 1979, Sylvan Cole Gallery, 1988, 89, 90, Bergen Mus., Paramus, N.J., 1993-94, others; permanent collections include Whitney Mus. Am. Art, Bklyn. Mus., Nat. Gallery Art, Canberra, Australia, N.J. State Mus., Trenton, Speed Mus., Libr. Congress, Nat. Gallery, Athens, Greece, Wooster Mus., Mass., Cleve. Mus. With U.S. Army, 1944-46. Fulbright grantee, 1951-52; Guggenheim fellow, 1959-60; recipient Tiffany Graphics award, 1955. Mem. NAD. DIED 02/13/96. .

CASCIERI, ARCANGELO, sculptor, educator, administrator; b. Civitaquana, Italy, Feb. 22, 1902; came to U.S., 1907, naturalized, 1934; s. Corrado and Marie (Trabucco) C.; m. Eda Di Biccari, Sept. 19, 1943. Student, Sch. Arch., Boston Archtl. Ctr., 1922-26, Boston U., 1932-36. Tchr. pvt. classes Boston, 1932-37, Craft Center Sch., Boston, 1939-40; tchr. design New London (Conn.) Jr. Coll., 1941-43; tchr. design Boston Archtl. Ctr., 1936—, head Sch. Architecture, 1937—, also dean, also mem. bd. dirs.; partner with Adio Di Biccari (in studio for sculpture and decorations), Boston and Arlington, 1952—; Mem. Mass. Postsecondary Edn. Commn., 1976—. Sculptor, asst. dir. sculpture and wood carving, W. F. Ross Studio, Cambridge, Mass., 1923-41, sculptor, asst. dir., Schwamb Assos. Studio, Arlington, Mass., 1941-46, sculptor, dir., 1946-52; prin. sculptural works include statues in parts of, Cathedral St. John the Divine, N.Y.C., Washington Cathedral, Cathedral St. John Evangelist, Spokane, Wash., Cathedral Most Holy Redeemer, Cornerbrook, Nfld., Cathedral Mary Our Queen, Balt., Riverside Bapt. Ch., N.Y.C., East Liberty Presbyn. Ch., Pitts., St. George's Sch. Chapel, Newport, R.I., Boston U. Chapel, St. Ignatius Ch., Chestnut Hill, Mass., Shrine Immaculate Conception, Washington, also works at, Boston Coll., Holy Cross Coll., Buffalo Courier Express Bldg., Parlin Jr. High Sch., Everett, Mass., Lexington (Mass.) High Sch., Am. War Meml. World War I at Belleau Woods, France, World war II at Margraten, Holland, exterior, Meml. Auditorium, Lynn, Mass., Boys' Stadium, Franklin Field, Dorchester, Mass., sculpture on fountain, Parkman Plaza, Boston, sculpture, Backus Estate, Pointe Rose, Mich.; author articles. Decorated cavaliere Order Al Merito della Repubblica Italiana; recipient Gold medal citation Nat. Sculpture Soc., 1961; 75th Anniversary citation Boston Archtl. Center, 1964; citation Boston 200, 1975; silver medal Boston U. Alumni Assn., 1976; 1st Visual Communication award New Eng. Sch. Art and Design; also made hon. alumni, 1979; citation Boston 350, 1980. Fellow AIA (chmn. com. collaborative arts); mem. Dante Alighieri Soc. (hon.), Boston Soc. Architects, Mass. Assn. Architects, Assn. Architects and Engrs. Campania Region-Naples (hon.), New Eng. Sculptors Assn. Roman Catholic. Died Jan. 14, 1997.

CASH, FRANK ERRETTE, JR., foreign service officer; b. Oriskany, Va., Mar. 7, 1921; s. Frank Errette and

Libbie (Adamson) C.; m. Naomi Duncan, Dec. 3, 1947; children: Hal Duncan, Susan Hamilton. B.S., Birmingham-So. Coll., 1941, U.S. Mil. Acad., 1944; postgrad., Harvard U., 1951-52. Commd. 2d lt. U.S. Army, 1944, advanced through grades to capt., 1948; served in ETO, World War II; resigned, 1948; joined U.S. Fgn. Service, 1948; assigned Am. consulate gen., Stuttgart, Germany, 1948-51; polit. officer Am. embassy, Bonn, Germany, 1952-55; consul, polit. officer Am. embassy, Manila, Philippines, 1955-57; head dept. univ. tng. and area studies Fgn. Service Inst., State Dept., 1958-60; officer charge German polit. affairs, also dep. dir. Berlin task force State Dept., 1960-63; participant Sr. Seminar in Fgn. Affairs, Fgn. Service Inst., 1963-64; counselor for mut. security affairs Am. embassy, Ankara, Turkey, 1964-68; country dir. for Turkey State Dept., 1968-71; Am. minister, dep. chief mission Am. embassy, Bonn, 1971-77; dep. comdt. for internat. affairs U.S. Army War Coll., 1977-80; dir. U.S. Nat. Security Seminar George C. Marshall Found., 1980-85. Died Nov. 4, 1997.

CASSIDY, CLAUDIA, performing arts critic; b. Shawneetown, Ill.; d. George Peter and Olive (Grattan) C.; m. William John Crawford, June 15, 1929. A.B., U. Ill. Music, dance and drama critic, Chgo. Jour. of Commerce, 1925-41, Chgo. Sun, 1941-42, music, drama critic, Chgo. Tribune, 1942-65, critic-at-large, 1966-69; formerly critic-at-large: weekly program Critic's Choice, WFMT, Chgo.; film critic: weekly program The Chicagoan mag. (now Chicago mag.), 1973-74; contbg. editor monthly column On the Aisle: Chicago mag., 1974-87; spl. commentator: radio Lyric Opera, Chgo. Named to Chgo. Press Club Journalism Hall of Fame, 1980. Died July 21, 1996.

CASTLE, MARIAN JOHNSON, writer; b. Kendall, Ill.; d. Oliver C. and Anna Mary (French) Johnson; m. Edward Carrick Castle, May 24, 1924. Student, Carroll Coll., Millikin U.; Ph.B., U. Chgo., 1920; Litt.D., Carroll Coll., 1950. Publicity work for concert and lectr. tours; gen. sec. Albuquerque YWCA, 1922-23. Author: novel Deborah (serialized in Woman's Home Companion), 1946 (Fiction Book Club choice, reprinted in 7 fgn. countries), The Golden Fury, 1949, also paperback edit. (selection 5 book clubs including alt. selection Lit. Guild), Roxana, 1955, also paperback edit.; Silver Answer, 1960 (made into Talking Books for Blind); Contbr. to: Harper's Mag., Good Housekeeping, Reader's Digest, others. Recipient Alumni Merit award Millikin U., 1962. Mem. Colo. Authors League, Zeta Tau Alpha. Presbyterian. Club: Denver Woman's Press.

CAUTHEN, IRBY BRUCE, JR., language professional, educator; b. Rock Hill, S.C., Aug. 24, 1919; s. Irby Bruce and Ruth (Kimbrell) C.; m. Elizabeth Bagby Greear, Aug. 28, 1954; children: Irby Bruce III, James Noah Greear. B.A., Furman U., 1940, Litt.D., 1980; M.A., U. Va., 1942, Ph.D., 1951. Asst. prof. English Hollins Coll., 1951-54; faculty U. Va., Charlottesville, 1954-94; prof. English U. Va., 1964-87, prof. emeritus, 1987-94, asso. dean, 1958-62, dean coll., 1962-78, asso. dir. summer session, 1958-72; Chmn. regional selection com. Woodrow Wilson Fellowship Found., 1962-72. Editor: Gorboduc, 1970, Two Mementoes from the Poe-Ingram Collection, 1971, (with J.L. Dameron) Edgar Allan Poe: A Bibliography of Criticism, 1827-1967, 1974, Edgar Poe at the University—1826, 1991 ; contbg. editor: The Dramatic Works in the Beaumont and Fletcher Canon, 1966, Dictionary of Literary Biography, 1987, 1991; contbr. articles to profl. jours. Trustee Hollins Coll., 1983-87, bd. overseers, 1991. With AUS, 1942-46, MTO. Decorated Bronze Star; recipient Raven Soc. award U. Va., 1963, Thomas Jefferson award, 1977, Algernon Sydney Sullivan award, 1978. Mem. Bibliog. Soc. U. Va. (v.p. 1961-78, pres. 1978-94), Modern Lang. Assn., Phi Beta Kappa (pres. Va. Beta chpt. 1969-71), Omicron Delta Kappa. Democrat. Presbyn. Clubs: Colonnade (Charlottesville), Greencroft (Charlottesville). Home: Charlottesville Va. Died May 27, 1994.

CAVALLERO, HAZEL HELEN, properties corporation executive; b. Burntmill, Colo., Mar. 18, 1913; d. Walter Merwin and Elizabeth Belle (Donley) Heller; m. John Walter Miller, June 4, 1937 (dec. Dec. 1943); m. Robert Angelo Cavallero, May 10, 1950; 1 child, Robert Clive. BA, U. Ill., 1941; MA, Stanford U., 1950. Pres. CSI, Inc., San Mateo, Calif., 1979—. Bd. dirs. Peninsula Vols., Menlo Park, Calif., 1962-74. Lt. (j.g.) USN, 1943-45. Republican. Episcopalian. Avocation: golf.

CAVERLY, GARDNER A., foundation executive; b. Tuftonboro, N.H., Aug. 2, 1910; s. Arthur L. and Emma (Lamprey) C.; divorced; Children: Martha, Jon Christian, Jefferson Smith, Nathaniel Eaton, James R., Douglas G. B.S., Northeastern U., 1934; postgrad., Harvard U., 1938; LL.D., Nasson Coll., 1973. With Bond & Goodwin Inc., Boston, 1935-38; pres. Sargent-Roundy Corp., Randolph, Vt., 1939-45; with Tucker Anthony & Co., N.Y.C., 1941-44; reorgn. mgr. Rutland R.R., 1949-50, trustee, dir., 1950-57, sr. v.p., 1951-54, pres., 1954-57; exec. v.p. New Eng. Council, Boston, 1957-66; pres. Crotched Mountain Found., Greenfield, N.H., 1967-73; chmn. Crotched Mountain Found., 1973-83; Chmn. N.H. Comprehensive Health Planning Council, 1968-71; mem. corp. Joslin Diabetes Found., Boston; former mem. corp. Northeastern U. Named hon. lt. col. R.I. State Police. Mem. Order DeMolay, Legion of Honor. Clubs: Harvard (Sarasota, Fla.); Harvard Faculty (Cambridge); Ivy League (Sarasota). Home: Laconia N.H. Died July 25, 1996.

CAWL, FRANKLIN ROBERT, JR., marketing consultant; b. Phila., Dec. 6, 1920; s. Franklin Robert and Abigail (Pretlow) C.; m. Florence Rainsford, June 15, 1946; children—Annette Susan, Jeannette Florence. B.S., U. Pa., 1942, M.A., 1948. Instr. mktg. Wharton Sch., U. Pa., 1946-48; with plans dept. Hearst Advt. Service, N.Y.C., 1948-56; instr. mktg. Rutgers U., 1948-56; v.p., dir. mktg. Outdoor Advt., Inc., N.Y.C., 1956-61, Million Market Newspapers, N.Y.C., 1961-65; pres. Inst. Outdoor Advt., 1965-71, Outdoor Advt. Assn. Am., N.Y.C., 1971-78; mktg. cons., 1978-79; pres. F.R. Cawl & Assos., Inc., Searsport, Maine and N.Y.C., 1980-95; dir. Advt. Council; dir., mem. exec. com. Outdoor Advt. Assn. Am. Chmn. bd. Four Winds Hosp. Served with AUS, 1942-46. Mem. Sales Execs. Club, Am. Mktg. Assn., Am. Soc. Assn. Execs., Sigma Phi Epsilon. Club: Waccabuc Country. Home: Searsport Maine Died July 26, 1995.

CECI, ANTHONY THOMAS, executive secretary; b. Wilmington, Del., May 21, 1917; s. Romano and Ersilia (Filichetti) C. Student, U. Del., 1948-51. Exec. sec. Baldwin Locomotive Works, Eddystone, Pa., 1940-46; with VA Hosp., Wilmington, Del., 1946-96, ret., 1976. Recipient Citation, Gov. State of Del., 1975. Republican. Roman Catholic. Avocations: reading, classics, philosophy, political science, current events. Home: Wilmington Del.

CELIBIDACHE, SERGIU, conductor; b. Rumania, July 11, 1912; student Hochsch. für Musik, Berlin; m. Joana Celibidache; 1 child. Condr., Berlin Philharm., 1945-52; art dir., condr. Radio-Sinfonic orchs., Stockholm, Stutgart, 1961—; gen. mus. dir. Stadt München and chief dir. Munich Philharm., 1979—. Decorated knight Order of Vasa (Sweden). Composer symphonies, orchestral suites, piano works. Mem. Acad. Fine Arts. Died Aug. 14, 1996.

CHADWICK, WALLACE LACY, consulting engineer; b. Loring, Kans., Dec. 4, 1897; s. Perley C. and Anna Ruth (Lacy) C.; m. Beulah Dye, Oct. 15, 1921 (dec.); children: Isabelle Ruth (dec.), Marilyn Joyce, Sandra Louise. Student, U. Redlands, 1916-20, D in Engring. Sci. (hon.), 1965. Draftsman, div. engr. hydro electric devels. So. Calif. Edison Co., 1922-27, transmission engr., 1928-31, civil engr., mgr. engring. dept., 1938-51, v.p. engring. and constrn., 1951-62; engr. Met. Water Dist. So. Calif., 1931-37; internat. cons. in field, 1962—; cons. Churchill Falls Project Labrador, 1963-90, Bechtel Group, Bay Area Rapid Transit Project, San Francisco, 1964-78; chmn. bd. engring. cons. James Bay Hydroelectric Project, Que., Can., 1972-89; cons. constrn. mgmt. Washington Metro Area Rapid Transit System, 1975-83; chmn. mgmt. rev. bd. Jubail Ind. City Project, for Bechtel Group, Saudi Arabia, 1977-87, Bechtel Group, South Tex. Nuclear Power Project, Houston Light & Power Co., 1982-88; chmn. Joint Rsch. Coun. Power Plant Air Pollution Control, L.A., 1956-62; mem. U.S. exec. com. Internat. Commn. on Large Dams, 1970-76, gen. reporter 12th Congress, Mexico City, 1976; mem. joint bd. environ. studies NAS and NAE, 1965-69; chmn. ind. panel to rev. cause of Teton Dam failure, 1976. Editor-in-Chief: Devel. Dam Engineering in the U.S., 1988. Trustee U. Redlands, 1937-79, chmn. bd. trustees, 1956-69; mem. City Council, San Marino, Calif., 1963-71. Served with U.S. Army, 1918. Recipient Sprague award, Instrument Soc. Am., 1963, Beavers award, Beavers Heavy Constrn. Org., 1969; named Man of Yr., Engring. News Record, 1978. Fellow IEEE, ASCE (pres. 1964-65, Rickey award); mem. ASME (hon.), NAE.

CHAGALL, MARC, artist; b. Vitebsk, Russia, July 7, 1887; s. Zacharie and Ida (Scherlin) C.; student l'Academie de St. Petersburg; m. Bella Rosenfeld, 1915 (dec.); 1 dau., Ida; m. 2d, Valentine Brodsky, 1952. Ceramist, painter, illustrator, engraver, watercolorist; went to Paris, 1910; painter numerous pictures, including Moi et le Village, 1910-14; exhibited in Berlin, 1914; designer costumes and decorations, also executed murals for Theatre Julif, Moscow, 1919, for Met. Opera House, Lincoln Center, N.Y.C., 1966; returned to Paris, 1923, and made engravings for Ames Mortes (Gogol), 1923; Fables de la Fontaine, 1927; also for the Bible 1956; visited U.S., 1941; designer costumes for ballets: Aleko (Tchaikovsky), The Firebird (Stravinsky); retrospective exhbns.: Mus. Modern Art (N.Y.C.), Art Inst. Chgo. (all 1946), Musé e d'Art Moderne, Paris, 1947; also exhbns. Tate Gallery (London), museums of Amsterdam, Israel, Turin, Zurich, Berne, Basle, represented in permanent collections at Kunstmus., Basel, Nat. Gallery, Berlin, Albright-Knox Gallery, Buffalo, Wadsworth Atheneum, Hartford, Conn., Los Angeles County Mus., Mus. of Art, Phila., Detroit Inst. Arts, Mus. Nat. d'Art Moderne, Paris, Tel Aviv Mus., Russian Mus., Leningrad, Tate gallery, London, Stedelijk Mus., Amsterdam, numerous others. Decorated grand cross Legion d'Honneur, 1977; comdr. Ordre des Arts et des Lettres; grand cross Nat. Order of Merit; recipient Carnegie prize, 1939; Internat. prize for engraving Biennial at Venice, 1948; Wolf prize Israeli Parliament, 1982. Mem. Am. Acad. Arts and Letters (hon.). Author and illustrator: Ma Vie, 1931; illustrator: Mille de une nuits; Contes de Bocace.

CHAKO, NICHOLAS, mathematician, physicist, educator; b. Hotova, Epirus, Albania, Nov. 11, 1910; came to U.S., 1929, naturalized, 1935; s. Kyriacus (Qako) Demetrius and Victoria John (Tako) C.; m. Bernadine van Looy, July 16, 1952; 1 child, Alexander Constantine. M.D., Anatolia Coll., 1925-28, Faculty Sci. and Engring., Paris and Marseille, 1928-29; B.S. and Dr.ès Sc., Sorbonne, Paris, 1966; Ph.D., Johns Hopkins U., 1934; postgrad., Harvard U., 1933-34, 35-36. Postdoctoral fellow U. Mich., Ann Arbor, summer 1933; career prof., head depts. math. and physics State Gymnasium, Scutari, Albania, 1936-37; mem. staff Cruft Lab., Harvard U., Cambridge, Mass., 1938-40; mem. staff spectroscopic lab. MIT, Cambridge, 1940-41; lectr. elec. engring. Ill. Inst. Tech., Chgo., 1941-42; fellow by courtesy U. Chgo., 1941-43; advanced fellow, lectr. Brown U., Providence, summers 1944, 45; assoc. prof. Kans. State Coll., 1946-47, Ala. Poly. Inst., 1947-49; Fulbright prof. U. Utrecht, Netherlands, 1950-51; guest prof. Chalmers U. Tech., Gothenburg, Sweden, 1951-52; spl. lectr. U. Lund, Sweden, spring 1952; research assoc. Inst. Math. Scis., NYU, N.Y.C., 1953-56; prof. physics Adelphia Coll., 1955-56; mem. faculty Queens Coll., Flushing, N.Y., 1956-81; ret., 1981; tech. advisor Signal Corps 6th Service Command, Chgo., 1942; cons. OSS, Washington, 1942-45; mathematician, research engr. Russell Electric Co., Chgo., 1942-46; vis. prof. Inst. Space Studies, N.Y.C., summer 1961; invited lectr. Polish Acad. Scis., Warsaw and U. Athens, Greece, summer 1965; guest lectr. French AEC and exchange prof. U. Paris, 1965-66; lectr. U. Laval, Que., Can., winter 1968. Author: newspaper serial Anglo-Saxon Universities and Education, 1937-40, Contribution a la Theorie de la Diffraction, 1966; contbr. articles to profl. jours. Recipient Ann. prize Royal Soc. Engrs. and Chalmers Alumni Assn., 1952. Fellow Inst. Math. and Applications (U.K.); mem. Am. Math. Soc., Am. Phys. Soc. Mem. Byzantine Ch. Clubs: Harvard of L.I.; Brown (N.Y.C.). Died Mar. 18, 1997.

CHAMBERS, GEORGE MICHAEL, minister of finance and planning Trinidad and Tobago; b. Oct. 4, 1928; student Burke's Coll., Osmond High Sch.; m. Juliana Jacobs, 1956; 1 dau. Parliamentary sec. in Ministry of Fin., Republic of Trinidad and Tobago, 1966, minister of public utilities and housing, 1969, minister of state in Ministry of Fin., Planning and Devel. and minister of state in Ministry of Nat. Security, 1970; minister of nat. security, 1979; minister of fin., planning and devel., 1971-73; prime minister of Trinidad and Tobago, 1981; minister fin. and planning, 1981—. Mem. central exec. People's Nat. Movement, leader, 1981—, mem. gen. council, chmn. investigations com. on disciplinary matters; chmn. bd. World Bank and IMF, 1973. Died Nov. 4, 1997.

CHAMPLIN, MARJORIE WEEDEN, retired secondary education educator, writer; b. Newport, R.I., Mar. 26, 1921; d. Lawrence Weeden and Ena (Eddy) C. BA in English, Wheaton Coll., Norton, Mass., 1943; MA in Classics, Brown U., 1959; postgrad., Harvard U., 1961, 65, 67; MA in English, U. R.I., 1974. Cryptographer Signal Corps U.S. Army, Arlington, Va., 1943-45; reporter, sec. Washington Post, 1945-46; sec. Christian Sci. Monitor, Boston, 1946-49; tchr. English Cranston (R.I.) High Sch., 1958-59; tchr. Latin and French North Kingston (R.I.) High Sch., 1960-70, debating coach, 1965-70, drama coach, 1968-69. Writer to nat. leaders in Congress and State Dept. Mem. AAUW, Conanicut Island Art Assn. Avocations: swimming, walking, listening to news and political programs, writing.

CHANDLER, B. J., educator, superintendent schools; b. Bluffton, Ark., July 23, 1921; s. J.V. and Edna (McCreight) C.; m. E. Ursula Bieder, 1978; children: Brenda (Mrs. Thomas Dexter Barbour), Robert W., Cynthia (Mrs. Patrick Bost), Maria, Michael, Bobby Joe. B.A., U. Tex., 1948, M.Ed., 1949; Ed.D., Columbia, 1951. Asst. prof. edn. U. Va., Charlottesville, 1951-54; asso. prof. U. Va., 1954-56; asso. prof. edn. Northwestern U., 1956-59, prof. edn., 1959-78; dean Northwestern U. (Sch. Edn.), 1963-78, dean emeritus, 1978—; supt. schs. Dardanelle, Ark., 1981—; ednl. cons. State Farm Ins. Cos., 1953-70; cons. Nat. Bd. Med. Examiners, 1978-79, Nat. Sch. Bds. Assn., 1978-80; Co-chmn. Gov's. Com. on Literacy and Learning, 1963-67; cons. River City Ednl. Program, Chgo.; Chmn. adv. council, trustee Aerospace Edn. Found., 1964-69; mem. adv. council Kellogg Found., 1963-65; mem. Gov.'s Task Force on Edn., 1965-67; pres. Ill. Council on Econ. Edn., 1969-73; chmn. Ill. Task Force on Tchr. Edn.; mem. Ill. Tchr. Certification Bd.; Bd. dirs. Films, Inc., Law in Am. Soc. Found., 1971-78, Citizens Sch. Com. Chgo.; mem. Carter-Mondale Task Force on Edn., 1976; trustee Chgo. Y Community Coll., Evanston Roycemore Sch., North Shore Country Day Sch.; mem. adv. com. Ark. Ednl. Reform Study, 1985—. Author: Education and the Teacher, 1961, (with Lindley J. Stiles and John I. Kitsuse) Education in Urban Society, 1962, (with Paul V. Petty) Personnel Management in School Administration, 1955, (with Daniel Powell and William Hazard) Education and the New Teacher, 1971; Gen. editor: Introduction to Teaching, 8 vols, 1969-78, Free Press Series; mem. editorial adv. bd.: Edn. and Urban Society; cons. editor: Standard Edn. Almanac, 1980-81,

Acad. Media, 1980-83; Contbr. articles to profl. jours. Served with USAAF, 1942-44. Fulbright-Hays sr. scholar Rumania, 1975-76; Fulbright-Hays sr. scholar Moscow, spring 1979. Mem. Nat. Cath. Edn. Assn. (dir. 1972), Internat. Council of Scholars (chmn. adv. com. 1979-82).

CHANDLER, DOROTHY BUFFUM, civic worker; b. Lafayette, Ill.; d. Charles Abel and Fern (Smith) Buffum; m. Norman Chandler, Aug. 30, 1922; children: Camilla (Mrs. F. Daniel Frost), Otis. Student, Stanford U., 1919-22; LHD (hon.), U. Calif., U. Judaism, U. Redlands, Hebrew Union Coll.; LLD (hon.), Occidental Coll., Mt. St. Mary's Coll., U. So. Calif.; DFA (hon.), U. Portland, Pepperdine Coll., Loyola Marymount U.; D of Arts (hon.), Art Inst. Los Angeles County. Hon. life chmn. Los Angeles Philharmonic Assn.; chmn. bd. govs. Performing Arts Council, Music Ctr. Los Angeles County; chmn. The Amazing Blue Ribbon of Music Ctr., Music Ctr. Found.; former regent U. Calif.; hon. life trustee Occidental Coll., Calif. Inst. Tech. Recipient Herbert Hoover medal Stanford Alumni Assn., Humanitarian award Variety Clubs Internat., 1974. Died July 6, 1997.

CHANDLER, LOUIS, lawyer; b. Portland, Maine, Apr. 25, 1911; m. Miriam Lourie Chandler, Nov. 21, 1937; children: Carol, Robert, Judith. JD, Boston U., 1934. Bar: Mass. 1934, Maine 1934, U.S. Supreme Ct. 1970, U.S. Dist. Ct. Mass., U.S. Ct. Appeals. Pvt. practice law Boston, 1934-41; hearing officer, acting regional dir. New Eng. War Labor Bd., Boston, 1941-45; ptnr. Stoneman Chandler Miller, Boston, 1945-95; counsel Boston Hotel and Motel Assn., Assoc. Builders and Contractors, Printing Industries New Eng., Retail Fuel Inst., Wholesale Liquor Dealers; guest lectr. Harvard Bus. Sch., 1946, Boston U. Faculty Club, 1948. Hon. vice consul Govt. of Costa Rica, 1956. Mem. ABA, Mass. Bar Assn., Boston Bar Assn., Mass. Hotel and Motel Assn., Pinebrook Country Club (pres. 1977-78). Home: Newton Centre Mass. Died Feb. 27, 1995.

CHAPMAN, G. ARNOLD, Romance languages educator; b. Fresno, Calif., June 26, 1917; s. George Arnold and Marie (Homsy) C.; m. Marguerite M. Nickerson, Aug. 7, 1957; children: John, Anna, Mary. A.B., Fresno State Coll., 1939; M.A., U. Wis., 1941; Ph.D., U.Wis., 1946. Instr. Romance langs. Oberlin Coll., 1945-46; from instr. to prof. Spanish U. Calif., at Berkeley, 1946-87, emeritus prof., 1987-96. Author: The Spanish American Reception of United States Fiction, 1920-1940, 1966; Mexico y el Señor Bryant, un embajador literario en el México liberal, 1984; contbr. articles to profl. jours. Mem. Assn. Tchrs. of Spanish and Portuguese, Philol. Assn. Pacific Coast. Home: Kensington Calif. Died Sept. 2, 1996; interred Sunset View Cemetery, Kensington, CA.

CHAPMAN, GRETEL, art educator; b. Denver, Mar. 11, 1933; d. Edmund Haupt and Affa (Gray) C. BA, Oberlin Coll., 1954; MA, NYU, 1956; PhD, U. Chgo., 1964; MS, Drexel U., 1984. Prof. art, curator Goucher Coll., Balt., 1962-80, So. Ill. U., Carbondale, 1984-97. Author: Mosan Art, 1988; also articles. Fellow Am. Coun. Learned Socs., 1967, A.W. Mellon fellow, 1973-74, fellow Am. Philos. Soc., 1980, 81; rsch. grantee Goucher Coll., 1972, 75, 78, 79. Mem. Coll. Art Assn., Medieval Acad. Am., Internat. Ctr. for Medieval Art, Hagiography Soc. Office: So Ill U Carbondale IL 62901 Died Mar. 5, 1997.

CHATHAM, HUGH G., textile manufacturing executive; b. 1921; student Princeton U. With Chatham Mfg. Co., Elkin, N.C., 1946—, exec. v.p., 1950, pres., 1955, chmn. bd., 1970—, also dir.; dir. N.C. Textile Found. Inc., Bus. Found. N.C., John Motley Morehead Found. Served to lt. USN, 1942-45.

CHAVEZ, EDUARDO ARCENIO, artist; b. Wagonmound, N.Mex., Mar. 14, 1917; s. Cornelio and Beatrice (Martinez) C.; m. Jenne Magafan, July 28, 1941; m. Eva Van Rijn, 1962; 1 dau., Maia. Student, Colorado Springs Fine Arts Center, 1935-38; studied with, Frank Mechau, Boardman Robinson, Peppino Mangravite, Arnold Blanch. Instr. drawing and painting Art Students League N.Y., 1954, summer sch., 1955-58; vis. prof. art Colo. Coll., 1959; asst. prof. art Syracuse U., 1960-61; instr. art Dutchess Community Coll., Poughkeepsie, 1963. Executed murals, post offices, service clubs, schs., hosps., one-man shows, Denver Art Mus., 1938, Asso. Am. Artists N.Y., 1948-49, Ganso Gallery, N.Y.C., 1950, 52-54, Il Camino Gallery, Rome, 1951, Mus. N.Mex., 1954, Alexandre Rabow Gallery, San Francisco, 1954, Annie Werbe Galleries, Detroit, 1957, John Heller Gallery, N.Y.C., 1955, 56, 58, 59, 60, N.Y. State Coll. Tchrs., Albany, 1960; exhibited, Chgo. Art Inst., NAD, Nat. Inst. Arts and Letters, Whitney Mus., Met. Mus., N.Y.C., Pa. Acad. Art, Carnegie Inst., Pitts., Corcoran Bienniel, Washington, Bronx Mus. Art, N.Y., 1988, Colorado Springs Find Arts Ctr., 1989, others; represented in collections, Mus. Modern Art, N.Y.C., Newark Mus. Art, Library of Congress Print Collection, other museums, galleries and pvt. collections; Recipient Pepsi-Cola art prize 1947; mus. collectios: Nat. Acad. Design, Palm Springs Desert Mus., U. Minn. Gallery of Art, Ullrich Mus. of Art. Lathrop prize Print Club of Albany, 1948; Hermine Kleinert award, 1952; Childe Hassam Purchase award, 1953; 1st prize Albany Inst. History and Art, 1966; Louis Comford Tiffany grantee, 1948; Fulbright grantee Italy, 1951; academician NAD; Albany Inst. of Art Sculpture award, 1965, Felton Sculpture award Silvermine Guild of Artists, 1977. Mem. Nat. Soc. Mural Painters (hon.), Woodstock Art Assn. (sec). Home: Woodstock N.Y. Died Jan. 11, 1995.

CHEN, CHRISTOPHER YUN HIAN, infertility specialist, consultant; b. Singapore, Dec. 27, 1939; s. Pow Loke Chen and Soon Hee Choong; 1 child, Adrian. MBBS, U. Singapore, 1964. Head/sr. cons., dir. gamete rsch. ctr. Kandang Kerbau Hosp., Singapore, 1987-93; prin. dir. Christopher Chen Ctr. Reproductive Medicine, Singapore, 1993—; clin. dir. Gleneagles IVF Ctr., Singapore, 1993—; sr. cons. obstetrician/gynecologist Gleneagles Hosp., Singapore, 1993—. Author: Recent Advances in the Management of Infertility, 1988. Scholar U. Singapore, 1959. Fellow ACS, Acad. Medicine (mem. coun. 1990—), Royal Coll. Obstetrics & Gynecology, Royal Australian Coll. Obstetrics and Gynecology, Internat. Coll. Surgeons (pres. Singapore chpt. 1992—). Avocations: reading, hi-fi. Deceased.

CHEN, YUN, government official of People's Republic of China; b. Qingbu, Jiangxi, People's Republic of China, 1905. Joined Chinese Communist Party, 1925, mem. 6th Central Com., 1931, dep. dir. organizing dept., 1937, dir. organizing dept., 1943, dir. peasants dept., 1939, mem. 7th Central Com., 1945, sec. to Secretariat, Central Com., 1954, vice-chmn. party, 1956-69, mem. standing com. Politburo, 1956-69, 78—, mem. 9th-12th Central Coms., 1969—, vice-chmn. 11th Central Com., 1979-81, mem. standing com. 12th Central Com., 1982—; lon Long March, 1934-35; vice-premier State Council, 1949-75, 78-80; minister heavy industry People's Republic of China, 1949-50, minister of commerce, 1956-58; chmn. State Capital Constrn. Com., 1958-61.

CHERKASKY, MARTIN, physician; b. Phila., Oct. 6, 1911; s. Samuel and Sarah (Kosharsky) C.; m. Sarah Griffin, Feb. 3, 1941; children: Marny, Michael, Karl. M.D., Temple U., 1936. Pvt. med. practice Phila., 1939-40; exec. home care dept. Montefiore Hosp., 1947; dir. Med. Group, 1948-51, chief div. social medicine, 1950; dir. Montefiore Hosp. and Med. Center, 1951-75, pres., 1975-81, cons. to hosp. and to bd. trustees, 1981—; Atran prof. dept. community health Albert Einstein Coll. Medicine, 1967-77; cons. N.Y. State Joint Hosp. Rev. and Planning Council; cons. to commr. hosps. N.Y.C. Dept. Hosps., 1961-62; exec. com. Health Research Council of N.Y.C., 1968-74; regional health adv. bd. Region II, Dept. Health, Edn. and Welfare, 1970-72; chmn. profl. adv. com. Joint Distbn. Com., N.Y.C., 1969-78; com. of 100 for Nat. Health Ins., 1969—; dir. Asso. Hosp. Service, 1969—; mem. Gov.'s Steering Com. Social Problems, 1970-72. Editorial bd. jour.: Chronic Diseases, 1957—, Commonwealth and Internat. Library Sci. Tech. and Engring; Contbr. articles to various publs.; Lectr. Served as lt. col. M.C. AUS, 1940-46. Fellow N.Y. Acad. Medicine (chmn. bd. trustees 1990); mem. NAS (sr. mem. inst. medicine 1971—, coun. inst. 1972-74), Am. Pub. Health Assn., Am. Hosp. Assn., Greater N.Y. Hosp. Assn. (past pres.), Assn. Am. Med. Colls. Died Sept., 1997.

CHERNENKO, KONSTANTIN USTINOVICH, Soviet government official; b. Bolshaya Tes, Sept. 24, 1911; ed. CPSU Higher Party Sch. and Kishinev Pedagogical Inst. Mem. Communist Party, 1931—; head dept. dist. com. Young Communist League; head dept. dist. and regional com. Communist Party of Soviet Union, 1929-41, sec. Krasnayarsk Ter. com., 1941-43, sec. Penza Region com., 1945-48; head agitation and propaganda of central com. of Moldavian Communist Party, 1948-56; head sect., dept. agitation and propaganda of central com. CPSU, 1956-60; head sec. of presidium of Supreme Soviet USSR, 1960-65; head gen. dept. of central com. Communist Party of Soviet Union, 1965-83, sec. Central Com., 1976—; dep. to Supreme Soviet, from 1966; chmn. Presidium of the Supreme Soviet of the USSR, 1984—; pres. USSR, 1984—; alt. mem. Politburo, 1977-78, mem., 1978—. Decorated Order of Lenin (2), Hero of Socialist Labour, 1976, Gold medal of Hammer and Sickle, Order of Klement Gottwald, 1982, others.

CHERNOFF, ROBERT, rabbi; b. Bklyn., Sept. 4, 1922; s. Louis and Sarah Dorothy (Grotsky) C.; m. Lea Rosen, Nov. 23, 1943 (dec.); children: Howard, Shira, Frances. Student Yeshivah D'Bklyn., 1939; BA Elysion Coll., 1978, PhD, 1979. Rabbi, Rabbinical Acad. Am., 1972. Ordained rabbi, 1972. Rabbi Congregation Sons of Israel, Chambersburg, Pa., 1974-90, ret., 1990; Pa. state chaplain South Mountain Restoration Ctr., Pa., 1974-95. Author: Shechitah, The Jewish Method of Slaughtering and Attendant Dietary Laws, 1973; Aspects of Judaism, 1975, Some Other Aspects of Judaism, 1987. Recipient Meritorious Service award Dept. Air Force, 1956, Commendation award Dept. Def., 1972. Mem. Am. Assn. Rabbis (nat. sec. 1981, hon. pres.), Greater Carolinas Assn. Rabbis, Chambersburg Area Ministerium, Jewish Chaplains Orgn. Pa. Lodge: Kiwanis (past pres.). Died Jan. 19, 1995. Home: Rockville Md.

CHERNOW, BURT, artist, educator, writer; b. N.Y.C., July 28, 1933; s. Abe and Selma (Schnieder) C.; m. Tamara Sackman, Jan. 1, 1957 (div. July 1970); children: Perrin, Paul, Paige; m. Ann Levy, Dec. 12, 1970. B.S., N.Y. U., 1958, M.A., 1960. Tchr. art pub. schs. Valley Stream, L.I., N.Y., 1958-60, Westport, Conn., 1960-66; prof., chmn. art dept., dir. art museum Housatonic Community Coll., Bridgeport, Conn., 1966-85; prof. emeritus Housatonic Community Coll., Bridgeport, 1985-97; dir. emeritus, founder Housatonic Mus. Art, Bridgeport, Conn., 1985-97; tchr. Mus. Modern Art, N.Y.C., 1967-70, Silvermine Guild, New Canaan, Conn., 1970-79, Stamford (Conn.) Mus., 1967-68; art critic Fairpress, Westport and Stratford (Conn.) News, 1972-73, 78-79, Art New Eng.; art cons., writer Ednl. Directions, Westport, 1968-97; mem. staff Higher Edn. Center for Urban Studies, 1968-71; cons. ABCD Cultural Arts Center, 1970-71; cons., writer Model Cities, Bridgeport, summer 1969; founder permanent art collection Westport Schs., 1964. Author: Milton Avery Drawings, 1973, Paper, Paint and Stuff, 2 vols., 1969, Lester Johnson Paintings, 1974, Contemporary Graphics, 1977, Francisco Zuniga, 1978, Abe Ajay, 1978, Christo, 1978, Will Barnet Paintings, 1980, Gabor Peterdi Paintings, 1982, The Drawings of Milton Avery, 1984, Francisco Zuniga: The Complete Grahics, 1985, Milton Avery: A Singular Vision, 1987, Barkley Hendricks Paintings, 1988, Von Rebay's Kandinskys, 1989, Arman, 1994, Branko Bahunek Paintings, 1995, Harvey Weiss sculpture, 1996, Jean Woodham sculpture, 1996, David Hayes sculpture, 1996; contbg. author: MacMillan Dictionary of Art, 1991; contbr. to profl. jours.; one man shows include, Mus. Art, Sci. and Industry, Bridgeport, 1972, others; exhibited in group shows, N.Y. World's Fair, 1964-65, UNESCO and USIA traveling shows, Ct. Coll., 1989; represented in permanent collection, Jacksonville (Fla.) Mus., Bridgeport Mus., Coll. Art Mus., Hampton, Va., Le Musee de l'art Contemporain, Skopje, Yugoslavia, Housatonic Mus. Art, Bridgeport. Mem. Westport Edn. Assn., 1965-67; bd. dirs. Westport Weston Arts Coun., 1969—, Bridgeport Commn. Arts, 1972—, Art Resources of Conn., 1976-79, ABCD Cultural Arts Ctr. for Arts, 1983-86; pres. Westport Arts Ctr., 1984-86; chmn. Westport Art Adv. Coun., 1993—. Scholar, Conn. Humanities Council; recipient 1st prize Barnum Festival, Bridgeport Mus., 1966. Mem. Appraisers Assn. Am., Nat. Art Edn. Assn. (Conn. Art Assn., exec. com. 1965-67), Westport Art Assn. (exec. com. 1962-64); mem. Silvermine Guild Artists (bd. dirs. 1972-80), Internat. Assn. Art Critics. DIED 06/09/97. .

CHERRY, WALTER LORAIN, electronics executive, engineer; b. Cedar Rapids, Iowa, Jan. 31, 1917; s. Walter Lorain and Laura Fox (White) C.; m. Virginia Ames Ballard, May 31, 1941; children: Walter Lorain, Peter B. Catherine Cherry Moore. B. Chem. Engring., Yale U., 1939. Research engr. Cherry-Burrell Corp., Chgo., 1939-42, Zenith Radio Corp., Chgo., 1946-69; co-founder Cherry-Channer Corp., Highland Park, Ill., 1949-53; founder The Cherry Corp., Waukegan, Ill., 1953-93; founder, pres. Cherry Display Products Corp., Waukegan, 1991-92; bd. dirs., past pres. Midwest Indsl. Mgmt. Assn., Westchester, Ill., 1969-79; bd. dirs. Chicagoland Enterprise Ctr. Holder 41 U.S. patents. Mem. zoning bd. Village of Winnetka, Ill., 1959-71, village caucus, 1958-59, park bd., 1962-68, chmn. 1967-68, planning commn., 1967-68, trustee, 1970-75; assoc. Rehab. Inst., 1978-96; pres. Allendale Sch. for Boys, 1975-79, trustee 1973-96; trustee Ill. Inst. Tech., 1977-96, chmn. bus. and industry devel. coun., 1979-82, vice chmn. devel., 1983-87; trustee Presbyn. Home, 1980-92, Evanston Hosp. 1987-92, 93-94, Winnetka Congl. Ch., 1979-82, Mus. Sci. and Industry; bd. dirs. St. Therese Hosp., 1984-86, vice-chmn., 1986. Served with U.S. Army, 1943-46. Mem. IEEE, Physics Club, Econs. Club, Comml. Club. Republican. Congregationalist. Deceased.

CHIARELLI, JAMES JOSEPH, retired architect; b. Spokane, July 3, 1908; s. Joseph and Josephine (Dematteis) C.; m. Patricia Alice Bradwell, May 3, 1947; children: Randall Gennaro, Diana Maria, Mark Angelo, Teresa Allegra. B. Arch., U. Wash., 1934. Pvt. practice architecture Seattle, 1945-87. Architect: Seattle Center Opera House, 1961, Thomas Burke Meml, Wash. State Museum, 1962, Herzl-Ner Tamid Conservative, Sanctuary, Social Hall and Offices, 1970, Tsimpshean Long House, Metlakatla, Alaska. Chmn. Bd. Adjustment Seattle Planning Commn., 1959-60; chmn. Citizens Recreation and Park Com. King County, Wash., 1957-58; chmn. performing arts div. Cultural Arts Bd. for Century 21 Seattle World's Fair, 1960-62; Trustee St. Martin's Coll. Fellow A.I.A. (pres. Wash. State chpt. 1956-58); mem. Tau Sigma Delta.

CHILD, ARTHUR JAMES EDWARD, food company executive; b. Guildford, Eng., May 19, 1910; s. William Arthur and Helena (Wilson) C.; m. Mary Gordon, Dec. 10, 1955. B.Commerce, Queen's U., 1931, LL.D., 1983; grad., Advanced Mgmt. Program, Harvard, 1956; M.A., U. Toronto, 1960, LL.D., 1984; LL.D., U. Calgary, 1984. Chief auditor Can. Packers Ltd., 1938-52, v.p., 1952-60; pres. Intercontinental Packers Ltd., 1960-66; chmn., chief exec. officer, dir. Burns Foods Ltd., Calgary, Alta., 1966-96; bd. dirs. Imperial Group Windsor, R. Howard Webster Found.; assoc. prof. U. Sask., 1964-65. Author: Economics and Politics in United States

Banking, 1965, (with B. Cadmus) Internal Control, 1953. Hon. col. comms. and electronics br. Can. Forces. Decorated Order of Can., Order of Good Hope, South Africa; named Hon. Col. 5 Signal Regt., South Africa. Fellow Royal Soc. Arts, Chartered Inst. Secs.; mem. Can. Meat Coun. (past pres.), Inst. Internal Auditors (past pres.), Am. Mgmt. Assn., Inst. for Strategic Studies. Home: Calgary Alberta CAN Died July 30, 1996.

CHILDRESS, FAY ALICE, university administrator; b. Annapolis, Md., Nov. 23, 1929; d. John Douglas and Winifred Lee (Stevens) Howard; m. Larry Brownlow Childress, June 7, 1949; children: Patricia, Peter, Mary, Charles. AA, Montgomery Coll., Takoma Park, Md., 1979; BS, U. Md., 1982, M of Gen. Adminstrn., 1992. Program technician NSF, Washington, 1972-78, sr. program technician, 1978-82, adminstrv. officer, 1982-86; asst. to exec. v.p. and equal opportunity officer Cath. U. Am., Washington, 1986-95. Contbr. articles to profl. jours. Mem. steering com. Washington Area Affirmative Action Group, 1988-95; mem. Washington Area Higher Edn. Liaison Group, 1989-95; chief election judge Montgomery County Election Bd., Silver Spring, 1986-92; mem. Seven Oaks-Evanswood Citizens Assn., Silver Spring, 1980-95; vol. Montgomery County Mental Health Assn., Rockville, 1982-84. Mem. Coll. and Univ. Pers. Assn., Montgomery Coll. Alumni Assn. (bd. govs. 1985-87), U. Md. Coll. Alumni Assn. (govt. rels. com. 1992-95), Soc. Human Resource Mgmt., Alpha Sigma Lambda (pres. Tau chpt. 1988-90). Avocations: photography, canoeing, swimming. Home: Silver Springs Md. Died May 19, 1995.

CHIN, MATILDE VALLADOLID, controller, accountant; b. Iloilo, Philippines, Jan. 26, 1941; came to U.S., 1971, naturalized, 1982; d. Pablo Chin and Dulzura Valladolid. BS in Commerce, U. San Agustin, Iloilo, 1960; postgrad., NYU, 1972-76. Adminstrv. asst. A.B. Martinez Constrn., Manila, 1961-64; mgr. import div. Spark Radio Elec. Supply Pioneer Ceramics, Inc., Manila, 1964-67; exec. asst. Frank J. Elizalde, Manila, 1967-68; bookkeeper accounts br. Dept. Mcpl. Affairs, Toronto, Ont., Can., 1968-70; auditor Bur. Taxation, Toronto, 1970-71; various acctg. positions N.Y.C., 1971-84; controller Salpeter Paganucci Internat. Inc., N.Y.C., 1985—. Vol. pledge drive Pub. Broadcasting Service, 1985—; broadcast vol. In Touch Networks, Inc., 1988—. Mem. Nat. Assn. Female Execs. Roman Catholic. Club: Legion of Mary (sec. 1972-79). Avocations: reading, sewing, piano.

CHINN, HERMAN ISAAC, biochemist; b. Connellsville, Pa., Apr. 8, 1913; s. Alex and Anna (Blumberg) C.; m. Rowena Carter, July 22, 1945; children: Susan, Stephen, Nancy. B.S., Pa. State Coll., 1934; M.S., Northwestern U., 1935, Ph.D., 1938. Instr. Med. Sch. Northwestern U., 1938-42; prin. chemist Fla. Bd. Health, 1946-47; chief dept. pharmacology Sch. Aviation Medicine, 1947-55; sci. liaison officer Office Naval Research, London, 1955-57; chief biol. scis. Air Force Office Sci. Research, 1957-60; dep. sci. attache Am. embassy, Bonn, Germany, 1960-63; sci. officer Office Internat. Sci. Affairs, State Dept., Washington, 1963-65; sci. attache Am. embassy, Tehran, Iran, 1965-67; sci. officer State Dept., 1967-71; sci. attache Am. embassy, Stockholm, Sweden, 1971-73, Tel Aviv, 1973-75; sr. scientist Fedn. Am. Socs. for Exptl. Biology, 1976-81. Served to maj. AUS, 1942-46; col. USAF Res. Recipient Sir Henry Wellcome award; Dist. Civilian award USAF; Commendation medal U.S. Army; Superior Honor award Dept. State. Mem. Am. Soc. Pharmacology, Biochem. Soc., Am. Physiol. Soc., Am. Chem. Soc., AAAS, Soc. Exptl. Biology and Medicine, Sigma Xi. Deceased.

CHIRIAEFF, LUDMILLA GORNY, ballet company executive, ballet dancer, choreographer; b. Riga, Latvia, Jan. 10, 1923; d. Alexandre and Catherine (Abrahmoff-Radziwill) Gorny; m. Uriel Luft, Aug. 9, 1962; children: Ludmilla, Catherine; children from previous marriage: Anatasie, Avde, Glebe. Grad., Russian German High Sch., Berlin; LittD (hon.), McGill U., 1982, U. de Montréal, 1982, U. du Québec, 1988. Founder Les Ballets Chiriaeff, Montreal, Que., Can., 1952-58; founder Les Grands Ballets Canadiens, Montreal, 1958, dir., 1958-74; founder L'Academie des Grands Ballets Canadiens, 1958, École supérieure de dansedes Grand Ballets Canadiens (known as École supérieure de danse du Québec since 1980), 1966, Les Compagnons de la danse, 1971, Maison de la danse, 1981; Established ballet program at the École Pierre-Laporte Sainte-Croix, 1975, program extended to Cégep du Vieux-Montréal, 1979. Made debut with Ballets Russes, 1936; soloist, Berlin Opera Ballet, 1939-41, prima ballerina, choreographer, Mcpl. Theater Lausanne, Switzerland, 1945-47. Works choreographed include Artère, Bagatelle (Jeux d'Arleguin), Canadiana, Carnaval des animaux, Cendrillon, Étude, Exercices, Farces (Commedia dell'arte), Fête Hongroise, Horoscope, Initiation à la danse, Kaleidoscope, L'Oiseau phoenix, La fille mal gardée, Les clowns, Les noces, Lully, Mémoires de Camille, Nonagone -- Essai, Paysse, Pétrouchka, Pierre et le loup, Pierrot de la lune, Pulcinella, Quatrième concert royal, Ruse d'amour, Suite canadienne, Une nuit sur la mont chauve, Variations en blanc, Variations sur un thème enfantin. Recipient best prodn. of ballets on TV award Can. Broadcasting Co., 1955, Can. Montreal Ballet Assn. award, 1957, Centennial medal, 1967, medal Order Can., 1969, Parchemin Honorifique de l'Accord, 1969, Concert Soc. award, 1970, Prix Denise Pelletier, 1980, Companion of the Order of Can., 1984; named Grand Officer, Ordre Nat. du Québec, 1985. Mem. Union des Artistes, Can. Actors Equity Assn. Deceased.

CHITTICK, DAVID RUPERT, environmental management consultant; b. Boston, Jan. 2, 1934; s. Rupert Addison and Evelyn Florence (Bradley) C.; m. Eileen Elizabeth Ashley, Oct. 12, 1957; children: Bradley David, Allison Ashley. BSEE, U. Vt., 1955; MS, MIT, 1969. Divestiture v.p. We. Elec. Co., Morristown, N.J., 1983-84; gen. mgr. engring. design and constrn. AT&T, N.Y.C., 1984-86; sr. v.p. Resource Mgmt. Corp. AT&T, Basking Ridge, N.J., 1985-86, engring. v.p., 1986-94; pres., chmn. bd. Industry Coop. for Ozone Layer Protection, Inc., 1990-94; bd. dirs. AT&T Resource Mgmt. Corp., 1987-94, Am. Ridge Ins. Co., 1990-94, Environ. Law Inst., 1991-95. Mem. Stratospheric Ozone Protection Adv. Coun. EPA, 1989-94, Corp. Conservation Coun. Nat. Wildlife Fedn., 1990-94; bd. dirs. World Environ. Ctr., 1991-94, Mgmt. Inst. for Environ. and Bus., 1991-94. A.P. Sloan Fellow, 1969. Mem. Environ. Mgmt. Roundtable (chmn. steering com.), World Environment Ctr., Mgmt. Inst. Environ. & Bus., Aircraft Owners and Pilots Assn. Republican. Episcopalian. Avocations: flying, golf, music. Home: Basking Ridge N.J. Died Nov. 19, 1995.

CHLEBORAD, WILLIAM JOHN, surgeon; b. Omaha, 1929. MD, U. Nebr., 1954. Diplomate Am. Bd. Surgery. Intern Univ. Hosp., Omaha, 1954-55; resident in surgery Omaha VA Hosp., 1966-70. Fellow ACS; mem. AMA. Died Nov. 12, 1996.

CHOLAKIS, CONSTANTINE GEORGE, federal judge; b. Troy, N.Y., Oct. 6, 1930; s. George Nicholas and Katine (Dukas) C.; m. Dassie Michaels, June 16, 1957; children: George D., Catherine, Gregory D. BA in Sociology, Siena Coll., 1955; JD, Albany Law Sch., 1958. Bar: N.Y., 1958. Pvt. practice lawyer Dwyer, Fogarty & Ormsby, Troy, N.Y., 1958-70, Cholakis, Morgan & Lang, Troy, N.Y., 1960-67; asst. dist. atty. County Rensselaer, Troy, 1963-65, 1st asst. pub. defender, 1966-67; sole practitioner Troy, N.Y., 1968-70; dist. atty. County of Rensselaer, Troy, 1968-74, judge county Ct., 1974-77; justice N.Y. Supreme Ct. (3d jud. dist.), Troy, 1978-86; judge U.S. Dist. Ct. (no. dist.) N.Y., Albany, 1986—; asst. dist. atty. County of Rensselear, 1963-65, asst. pub. defender, 1966-67. Served to sgt. USMC, 1951-53, Korea. Republican. Greek Orthodox. Died Dec. 1, 1996.

CHRISTENSEN, ALBERT SHERMAN, federal judge; b. Manti, Utah, June 9, 1905; s. Albert H. and Jennie (Snow) C.; m. Lois Bowen, Apr. 4, 1927; children: A. Kent, Karen D., Krege B. Student, Brigham Young U., intermittently 1923-27; J.D., Nat. U., 1931. Bar: D.C. 1932, Utah 1933. Asst. bus. specialist U.S. Dept. Commerce, 1930-32; practiced in Provo, Utah, 1933-42, 45-54; U.S. dist. judge Dist. of Utah, Salt Lake City, 1954-96; sr. fed. judge, 1972-96; mem. com. on revision laws Jud. Conf. U.S., 1960-68, com. on ct. adminstrn., 1968-75, adv. com. rules of civil procedure, 1972-82, rev. com., 1977-78, jud. ethics com., 1978-82, Temporary Emergency Ct. Appeals, 1972-93; bd. Utah Bar Examiners, 1939-42; chmn. Ad Hoc Com. Am. Inns of Ct. 1983-85. Republican congressional candidate, 1939. Served from lt. to lt. comdr. USNR, 1942-45. Recipient Chmn.'s award Am. Inns of Ct. Found., 1988; Fulbright award Nat. Law Ctr., George Washington U., 1990. Mem. ABA (awarded medal 1990), Utah Bar Assn. (pres. 1951-52, Judge of Yr. award 1977), Utah Jr. Bar Assn. (pres. 1937-38), Utah County Bar Assn. (pres. 1936-37, 47-48). Mem. Ch. Jesus Christ of Latter-day Saints.

CHRISTENSEN, CLYDE MARTIN, plant pathology educator; b. Sturgeon Bay, Wis., Aug. 8, 1905; s. Peter Karl and Christine Ann (Christensen) C.; m. Katherine Wallace Barry, Sept. 27, 1935; children—Sarah Ellen Christensen Nelson, Melanie Barry Christensen Behrendt, Jane Martin Christensen Vance. B.S., U. Minn., 1929, M.S., 1930, Ph.D., 1937; postgrad., U. Halle, Halle an der Saale, Germany, 1932-33. Instr. U. Minn., 1929-37, asst. prof., 1937-46, asso. prof., 1946-48, prof. plant pathology, 1948—, Regents' prof., 1973—; Cons. various grain storage and processing firms. Author: Common Edible Mushrooms, 1943, Common Fleshy Fungi, 1946, The Molds and Man, 1953; Spanish edit. Los Hongos y El Hombre, 1964, (with H.H. Kaufmann) Grain Storage: The Role of Fungi in Quality Loss, 1969, Molds, Mushrooms and Mycotoxins, 1975, E.C. Stakman, Statesman of Science, 1984, (with R.A. Meronuck), Quality Maintenance in Stored Grains and Seeds, 1986; also articles. Fellow Am. Phytopath. Soc., Am. Coll. Allergists (hon.); mem. Am. Soc. Microbiology, Mycol. Soc. Am., Sigma Xi. Died Oct. 12, 1993.

CHRISTINE, VIRGINIA FELD, actress; b. Stanton, Iowa, Mar. 5, 1920; d. George Allen Ricketts and Helga (Ossian) Kraft; m. Fritz Feld, Nov. 10, 1940; children: Steven, Danny. Student, UCLA, 1939-40. Actress appearing in Edge of Darkness, Mission to Moscow, The Killers, Cover Up, High Noon, The Mummy's Curse, Not as a Stranger, Cyrano, The Men, Three Brave Men, Cobweb, Body Snatchers, The Spirit of St. Louis, Johnny Tremaine, Judgement at Nuremberg, Guess Who's Coming to Dinner?, The Prize, Rage to Live, Four for Texas, 300 TV shows; spokeswoman, role of Mrs. Olson TV comml. Proctor & Gamble (Folgers), Cin., 1964-85. Hon. mayor, Brentwood, Calif.; bd. dirs. Family Planning Ctrs. Greater Los Angeles; judge Am. Coll. Theatre Festival. Recipient 1st place award Forensic League, 1937, Hall of Fame award Long Beach City Coll., 1977, citation-cultural award City of Los Angeles, 1979. Democrat. Died July 24, 1996.

CHRISTMAN, JOHN FRANCIS, science administrator, university administrator; b. Terre Haute, Ind., Feb. 17, 1924; s. Fred Garland and Josephine Louise (Vesque) C.; m. Emma Neale Slover, June 7, 1950; children: John Benton, Claudia Anne. B.S. in Chemistry, U. Notre Dame, 1944; M.A., Ind. U., 1946; M.S., U. Tenn., Knoxville, 1948, Ph.D., 1950. Mem. faculty La. State U., Baton Rouge, 1950-66; prof. biochemistry La. State U., 1966, Loyola U., New Orleans, 1966-86; dir. acad. grants Loyola U., 1966-67, v.p. acad. affairs, 1967-68, dir. research, 1968-71, dir. research and grad. studies, 1971-86, prof. emeritus, 1986-95; pres. Aurora Research Inc., 1980-93; research participant biology div. Oak Ridge Nat. Labs., 1954-55; asso. program dir. student and coop. programs NSF, 1964-65; dir. student sci. tng. program, 1959-73; mem. La. Commn. Extension and Continuing Edn., 1966-75. Author: (with J.B. Christman and C.S. Gifford) Mastering the Enhanced ACT, 1991; mem. editorial bd. New Orleans Rev, 1974-86; contbrs. articles to jours. in field. Recipient Spl. Public Service citation U.S. Dept. Commerce, 1979; predoctoral research fellow USPHS, 1948-50. Fellow Am. Inst. Chemists; mem. Am. Chem. Soc. (regional tour speaker 1979-95), Sigma Xi, Delta Epsilon Sigma (nat. pres. 1974-77), Phi Lambda Upsilon, Alpha Chi Sigma (dist. counselor 1954-59), Tau Kappa Epsilon. Democrat. Roman Catholic. Home: New Orleans La. Died Oct. 11, 1995; interred Westlawn Memorial Park, Gretna, LA.

CHRONIC, BYRON JOHN, geologist, educator, consultant; b. Tulsa, June 3, 1921; s. Byron John Chronic and Pansy Lee (Whitehead) Yarbrough; m. Halka Pattison, Aug. 21, 1948 (div. 1981); children: Emily Ann Silver, Felicie Jane Williams, Lucy Marylka Hinze, Susan Elizabeth; m. Carol A. Williams, June 18, 1981. BS with honors, U. Tulsa, 1942; profl. cert. in meteorology, U. Chgo., 1943; MS, U. Kans., 1947; PhD, Columbia U., 1949. Mem. faculty dept. geology U. Mich., 1949-50; mem. faculty dept. geology U. Colo., 1950-80, prof. emeritus, 1980-96; lectr. Edinburgh U., Scotland, 1958-59; prof., chmn. dept. geology Haile Sellassie I Univ., Addis Ababa, Ethiopia, 1965-66; prof. U. P.R., Mayaguez, 1978-79; pres., dir. Frobex Exploration Co., Toronto, 1971-77, Kanexco Exploration Co., Miami, 1971-74, Sastex Exploration Co., Houston, 1985-96; chief geologist Scarth Oil & Gas Co., Amarillo, 1980-81; exploration mgr. Evans Exploration Co., Houston, 1981; sr. geologist Keplinger & Assocs., Houston, 1981-83; chief geologist Nuclear Geophys., Inc., Houston, 1983-84; cons. Petroleum Research Co., Denver, on Microfilm Library of Rocky Mountain region, 1954-58, Denver oil and minerals cos., 1955-75, Pitch Mine, Colo., 1963-64, Jack Grynberg & Assoc., Denver, 1965-72, Oceanic Exploration Co., Australia, 1969-70, U.S. Geol. Survey, Denver, 1970-78, U.S. Park Service, Denver, 1975-78, Petroconsultants, Geneva, Switzerland, 1980, Internat. Petroleum Co., Houston, 1981, Win-Eldrich Mines, Inc., Toronto, 1984-96, Tenneco, Houston, 1984-85; chief geologist Frankenburg, 1991; cons. paleontologist Am. Stratigraphic Co., Denver, 1956-72; cons. micropaleontologist Sirte Oil Co., Libya, 1984; mem. geol. expdn. to Inner Mongolia, 1987; rsch. assoc. Houston Mus. Natural Sci., 1980-96; docent Houston Zoo, 1988-96. Co-author: Prairie, Peak and Plateau, 1972, Upper Paleozoic of Peru, 1952; co-editor: Bibliography of Geology theses, 1959, 60-65; contbr. numerous articles to profl. jours., 1949-96. Served to 1st lt. USAAF, 1942-46; ETO; PTO. Decorated Air Medal with 5 oak leaf clusters; recipient Disting. Svc. award Rocky Mt. Assn. Geologists, 1973; faculty fellow Woods Hole Oceanographic Inst., 1956; sr. fellow emeritus Geol. Soc. London. Fellow AAAS, Geol. Soc. Am. (sr.); mem. Am. Assn. Petroleum Geologists (assoc. editor, del., emeritus), Houston Geol. Soc. (acad. liaison com., Pres.'s award 1991), Rocky Mountain Assn. Geologists (v.p.), Explorers Club (assoc. editor jour.), Soc. Econ. Paleontologists and Mineralogists, Paleontological Soc., Geol. Socs. Malaysia, Greece, Sigma Xi, Sigma Gamma Epsilon, Phi Sigma, Phi Gamma Kappa. Died July 15, 1996.

CHRYSOSTOMOS (GONZÁLEZ-ALEXOPOULOS), archbishop, clergyman, psychologist, educator; b. Apr. 6, 1943. BA, U. Calif.-Riverside, 1964, Calif. State U., San Bernardino, 1971; MA, U. Calif., Davis, 1970, Princeton U., 1974; PhD, Princeton U., 1975. Bishop True Orthodox Ch. of Greece. Preceptor in psychology Princeton U., 1972-75; asst. prof. psychology U. Calif., Riverside, 1975; adj. asst. prof. Christian thought Ashland (Ohio) Theol. Sem., 1981-83; asst., assoc. prof. psychology Ashland U., 1980-83; dir. Ctr. for Traditional Orthodox Studies, Etna, Calif., 1981-85, scholar-in-residence, 1986, acad. dir., from 1986; bishop of Etna; vis. scholar Harvard

Divinity Sch., 1981; vis. assoc. prof. Uppsala U., Sweden, from 1987. Marsden research fellow Oxford U., 1985. Greek Orthodox.

CHRYSSAFOPOULOS, NICHOLAS, civil engineer; b. Istanbul, Turkey, Apr. 23, 1919; came to U.S., 1951, naturalized, 1959; s. John and Despina (Hondropoulos) C.; m. Hanka Wanda Sobczak, Sept. 6, 1956. BSCE, Robert Coll., Istanbul, 1940; MS, U. Ill., 1952, PhD, 1956. Registered profl. engr., Calif., Ill., N.Y., N.J., Mo., Pa., Kans., Fla., Va. Design and constrn. work in Turkey, 1940-51; mem. faculty U. Ill., 1951-59, asst. prof., 1956-59; chief engr., mng. prin., exec. v.p. Woodward, Clyde, Sherard, Kansas City, Mo. and Los Angeles, 1959-68; partner Dames & Moore (cons. engrs.), N.Y.C., 1968-85; regional mgr. for Dames & Moore (cons. engrs.), Latin Am., Boca Raton, Fla., 1978-85; cons. civil engr., 1985-86; v.p. engring. HSce, Inc., 1986-95; adj. prof. civil engring. Fla. Atlantic U., 1989-93; assoc. Transp. Rsch. Bd. Author reports, tech. papers. Served with Turkish Army, 1941-44. Fulbright scholar, 1951-52. Fellow ASCE, Am. Cons. Engrs. Coun.; mem. ASTM, NSPE, Am. Assn. Engring. Socs. (chmn. com. sustainable devel.), Fla. Engring. Soc., PanAm. Fedn. Engring. Socs. (U.S. mem. bd. dirs., chmn. com. on sustainable devel.), Sigma Xi. Greek Orthodox. Home: Boca Raton Fla. Died Sept. 1, 1995.

CHUN, DAI HO, educational consultant; b. Waipio, Hamakua, Hawaii, Jan. 8, 1905; s. Hin and Shee (Kwock) C. BA with honors, U. Hawaii, 1930, MA, 1937; PhD, Ohio State U., 1947; DHL (hon.) U. Hawaii, 1989. Tchr. pub. schs., Hawaii, 1930-41; dir. placement and ednl. vocat. guidance, 1941-42; asst. prof. edn., supr. practice teaching U. Hawaii, Honolulu, 1945-51, assoc. prof. edn., 1951-58, prof., 1958-70, prof. emeritus, 1970-94; dir. Internat. Coop. Center Hawaii, 1956-61; exec. dir. Inst. Tech. Interchage, East-West Center, 1961-69, dir. Tech. and Devel. Inst., 1969-70; internat. ednl., mgmt. and devel. cons., Honolulu, 1970-94; adviser Hawaii Tng. Council, 1968-70, Utah State U. East-West Inst., 1972-75, Taiwan Bur. Tourism, 1971-94; cons. to Pacific Investment Fund, 1957-58, Pacific Mgmt., Ltd., 1957-58; dir. Security Assos. Ltd., Honolulu, 1956-60; trustee Norco Corp. Mem. Gov.'s Commn. on Pub. Edn., 1950-70, on East-West Ctr., 1959-61, on Internat. Visitors, 1961-64; on Peace Corps,, 1962-65, on Tourism, 1969-70; mem. pres.'s club Ohio State U.; mem. Friends of East-West Ctr.; state chmn. 11th Anniversary UN, 1956; bd. mgrs. Mid-Pacific Inst., 1946-47, sec., 1946; mem. Community Chest Steering Com., Honolulu, 1960-61. Served to lt. col. USAAF, 1942-45. Recipient Disting. Service award U. Hawaii Alumni Assn., 1959, Disting. leadership award U. Hawaii Found., 1982, Disting. Svc. award Ohio State U., 1988; named Alumnus of Yr. Mid-Pacific Inst., 1988, Living Legend Ohio State U. Alumni Club Hawaii, 1989; fellow Ohio State U., 1951; research fellow Joint Council on Econ. Edn., 1952. Fellow Progressive Edn. Assn., Internat. Inst. Arts and Letters.; mem. Mensa, AAUP (v.p. Hawaii chpt.1955-56), Internat. Platform Assn., John Dewey Soc., Soc. Internat. Devel., Air Force Assn., Hawaii Union (pres. 1929-30), Phi Beta Kappa (counselor 1953-55), Phi Kappa Phi, Pi Gamma Mu (sec.-treas. 1947), Delta Sigma Rho, Phi Delta Kappa. Lodge: Rotary (dir. 1960-62). Author: Mooneys Problem Check List, 1942; Personal Problems of Adolescent Youth (script and film strip), 1952; Meeting the Manpower Needs of Taiwan's Tourism Industry, 1974; others; editor: Hawaii Plan for Teacher Education, 1949; University High School Curriculum Guide, 1955; Hawaii-U.S.A.: Resources for Technical Assistance, 1958; Hawaii's Training Resources, 1959. Died May 14, 1994; interred Hawaii State Veterans Cemetery, Kaneohe, HI. Home: Kaneohe HI

CHURCH, ALONZO, mathematics and philosophy educator; b. Washington, June 14, 1903; s. Samuel Robbins and Mildred Hannah Letterman (Parker) C.; m. Mary Julia Kuczinski, Aug. 25, 1925 (dec. Feb. 1976); children—Alonzo, Mary Ann, Mildred Warner. A.B., Princeton U., 1924, Ph.D., 1927, D.Sc. (hon.), 1985; D.Sc. (hon.), Case Western Res. U., 1969, SUNY, Buffalo, 1990. Faculty Princeton U., 1929-67, prof. math., 1947-61, prof. math. and philosophy, 1961-67; prof. philosophy and math. UCLA, 1967-90, ret. Author: Introduction to Mathematical Logic, vol. I, 1956; editor: Jour. Symbolic Logic, 1936-79; contbr. articles to math. and philos. jours. Mem. Am. Acad. Arts and Scis., Assn. Symbolic Logic, Am. Math. Soc., AAAS, Nat. Acad. Scis., Brit. Acad. (corr.), Am. Philos. Assn. (pres. Pacific div. 1973-74). Home: Hudson Ohio Died Aug. 11, 1995.

CHURCH, C. HOWARD, artist, educator; b. South Sioux City, Nebr., May 1, 1904; s. Charles Cyrus and Della (Pilgrim) C.; m. Ila Hamer. B.F.A., Sch. Art Inst. Chgo., 1935; student with, John Norton, Wm. P. Welsh, Boris Anisfeld, 1928-32; A.B., U. Chgo., 1938; M.A., Ohio State U., 1939, postgrad., 1939-40. Freelance artist, 1928-33; dir. Morgan Park Sch. Art, Chgo., 1933-36; head dept. art and dir. Mulvane Art Mus., Washburn U., Topeka, 1940-45; head dept. art Mich. State U., East Lansing, 1945-60; prof. art Mich. State U., 1960-72; Mem. Mich. Gov.'s Cultural Commn., 1960-68. Executed mural project for Morgan Park Mil. Acad., Chgo., 1933-36, Canterbury Pilgrims libr. panel; St. Francis and Sir Galahad panels 1934, also exhibited Chgo. Century Progress, 1934; exhibited group and one-man shows, 1982-93, one man print exhbn. Hackley Gallery, Muskegon, Mich., Mich. State U. Gallery, 1960-93; one-man show, 1970. Recipient prizes Kansas Artists, 1940-41, prizes Six State Exhbn. Omaha, 1941, 42; Print Purchase award Mich. Artists Exhbn.; Print Purchase award Mich. Edn. Assn., 1969, 70. Mem. Mich. Acad. Sci., Arts and Letters (Fine Arts medal 1963, 1st purchase award mems. exhbn. 1966), Midwestern Coll. Art Assn. (pres. 1959-60), AAUP, Phi Beta Kappa. Home: East Lansing Mich. Died Jan. 3, 1993.

CIAPPI, MARIO LUIGI CARDINAL, bishop; b. Florence, Italy, Oct. 6, 1909. Ordained Roman Catholic priest, 1932, bishop, 1977. Papal theologian, 1955—; bishop of Misenum, 1977, elected Sacred Coll. Cardinals, 1977; deacon Our Lady of Sacred Heart. Mem. Causes of Saint Congregation, Apostolic Signatura Tribunal. Deceased.

CIMINO, RICHARD ANGELO, broadcasting personality, actor; b. Gilroy, Calif., Dec. 17, 1929; s. Angelo and Laura Maria (Macchione) C.; student Hartnell Coll., 1948-50; m. Enid Lucile Kilburn, Dec. 9, 1962. Program mgr. Sta. KCRA, Sacramento, 1966-68; morning program host Sta. KNEW, Oakland, 1968-72; afternoon program host Sta. KSFO, San Francisco, 1974-77; ptnr. Charles Jewelry; pres. Rick Cimino, Inc.; developer and chief exec. officer Compu-Cast; instr. voice, acting; freelance advt. voice. Served with U.S. Army, 1951-53. Recipient Best Radio Personality award TV-Radio Mirror mag., 1969; 9 CLIO awards, 1976-83, Gold Clio award, 1985; 2 Nat. Acad. TV Arts and Scis. awards, 1981; Gold medal 1982 Internat. Film Festival; Addy award, 1983. Mem. Am. Advt. Fedn. (radio div. chmn. Am. Advt. Best in West awards), AFTRA, Screen Actors Guild, Il Cenacolo, Cousteau Soc., Oceanic Soc., Internat. Platform Assn. Died Nov. 10, 1991; interred Sunset Mem., El Cerrito, CA. Home: El Cerrito Calif.

CLAPP, NORTON, building materials company executive; b. Pasadena, Calif., Apr. 15, 1906; s. Eben Pratt and Mary Bell (Norton) C.; m. Mary Cordelia Davis, July 8, 1929 (dec.); children: James Hayes (dec.), Matthew, Ralph (dec.), Roger (dec.); m. Evelyn Beatrice Booth, Jan. 15, 1941 (dec.); children: William Hayes, Stephen Gilbert; m. Jane Bumiller, Apr. 19, 1952 (div. 1980); m. Jacquline Hazen, Apr. 14, 1984. A.B., Occidental Coll., 1928, LL.D., 1958; Ph.B., U. Chgo., 1928, J.D., 1929; D.C.L., U. Puget Sound, 1958. Bar: Calif. 1929, Wash. 1929. Practiced in Tacoma, 1929-42; chmn. Met. Bldg. Corp., Seattle, 1954-75; pres. Pelican (Alaska) Cold Storage Co., 1947-60, chmn., 1960-77; pres. Boise (Idaho) Payette Lumber Co., 1949-55, Laird Norton Co., bldg. materials, Winona, Minn., 1950-60; chmn. Laird Norton Co., bldg. materials, 1960-95; v.p. Weyerhaeuser Co., 1956-57, chmn. bd., 1957-60, 66-76, pres., 1960-66. Mem. nat. adv. bd., hon. v.p. Boy Scouts Am., nat. pres., 1971-73; trustee U. Puget Sound, Tacoma; life trustee U. Chgo.; trustee Menninger Found. Served as lt. comdr. USNR, 1942-46. Mem. Seattle C. of C. (pres. 1970-71). Republican. Episcopalian. Clubs: Harbor, Rainier, University, Overlake Golf and Country, Yacht, Tennis (Seattle); Tacoma, Country and Golf, Yacht (Tacoma). Home: Medina Wash. Died Apr. 22, 1995.

CLARE, STEWART, research biologist, educator; b. nr. Montgomery City, Mo., Jan. 31, 1913; s. William Gilmore and Wardie (Stewart) C.; m. Lena Glenn Kaster, Aug. 4, 1936. B.A. (William Volker scholar), U. Kans., 1935; M.S. (Rockefeller Research fellow, teaching fellow), Iowa State U., 1937; Ph.D. (Univ. fellow), U. Chgo., 1949. Dist. survey supr. entomology bur. entomology and plant quarantine CSC, 1937-40, tech. cons., 1941-42; instr. meteorology USAAF Weather Sch., 1942-43; research biologist Midwest Research Inst., Kansas City, Mo., 1945-46; spl. study, research Kansas City Art Inst., U. Mo., 1946-49; instr. zoology U. Alta., 1949-50, asst. prof. zoology, lectr.-instr. sci. color, dept. fine arts, 1950-53; interim asst. prof. physiology Kansas City Coll. Osteopathy and Surgery, 1953; lectr. zoology U. Adelaide, S. Australia, 1954-55; sr. research officer and cons. entomology Sudan Govt. Ministry Agr., Khartoum, Sudan and Gezira Research Sta., Wad Medani, Sudan, N.Africa, 1955-56; sr. entomologist and cons. Klipfontein Organic Products Corp., Johannesburg, Union S.Africa, 1957; prof., head dept. biology Union Coll., 1958-59, chmn. sci. div., prof., head biology, 1959-61, spl. study grantee, 1960; prof., head dept. biology Mo. Valley Coll., Marshall, 1961-62; research grantee Mo. Valley Coll., 1961-62; lectr., instr. biology, meteorology, sci. of color Adirondack Sci. Camp and Field Research Sta. at Twin Valleys, SUNY, Plattsburgh, 1962-66; dir. acad. program SUNY, 1963-66, research facilities grantee, 1963-66; Buckbee Found. prof. biology Rockford (Ill.) Coll., lectr. biology evening coll., 1962-63, spl. research grantee, 1962-63; prof., chmn. dept. biochemistry, mem. research div. Kansas City (Mo.) Coll. Osteopathy and Surgery, U. Health Scis., 1963-67; also NIH basic research grantee, 1963-67; prof. biology Coll. of Emporia, Kans., 1967-74; dir. biol. research Coll. of Emporia, 1972-74, prof. emeritus, 1974-92; research biologist, cons., 1974-86, with continuing research, 1986-92; research study grantee, 1967-74, spl. research grantee study in, Arctic, 1970, 72, C. Am. and Mexico, 1973; cons. VITA, 1962-92, Adirondack Research Sta., 1962-66, Nat. Referral Center for Sci. and Tech., other orgns. Contbr. over 100 papers and monographs on capillary movement in porous materials, physiology and biochemistry of arthropoda; numerous local, nat., internat. exhbns. on color, also articles to profl. jours. Mem. adv. bd. Fine Art Registry Soc. N.Am. Artists. Served with USNR, 1943-45. Recipient Certificate of Service Vols. Internat. Tech. Assistance, 1970; Creativity Recognition award Internat. Personnel Research, 1972; Distinguished Achievement and Service awards for edn. and research in biology; Certificate of Merit in Art Internat. Biog. Centre, Cambridge, 1968, 72, 73, 76; Outstanding Service to Community award Am. Biog. Inst., 1975, 76, 77, 79-80; Notable Ams. of Bicentennial Era award, 1976; Book of Honor award, 1978; named Outstanding Educator Coll. of Emporia, 1973; research grantee Alta. Research Council, 1951-53; research facilities grantee U. Alaska, 1970; research facilities grantee No. Research Survey Arctic Inst. N.Am., 1970, 72. Fellow Internat. Biog. Assn. (life), Am. Biog. Inst., Explorers Club, Anglo-Am. Acad. (hon.); mem. N.Y. Acad. Scis. (life), Brit. Assn. Adv. Sci. (life), Am. Entomol. Soc. (life), Nat. Assn. Biology Tchrs., AAUP, Arctic Inst. N.Am., Am. Polar Soc., Inter-Soc. Color Council, Sigma Xi, Phi Sigma, Psi Chi, numerous others. Special research science of color and design of color, history, genealogy, science of photography, art collections. Home: Kansas City Mo. Died Apr. 23, 1992.

CLARK, CLAYTON, electrical engineering educator; b. Hyde Park, Utah, Mar. 9, 1912; s. Arthur B. and Ethel (Shirley) C.; m. Helen Brown, Aug. 23, 1933; children: Carole, Janet. B.S., Utah State U.; E.E., Ph.D., Stanford U. Registered profl. engr., Utah. Prof. elec. engring. dept. Utah State U., Logan, 1937-77, prof. emeritus, 1977-96; dir. Engring. Expt. Sta., 1964-75; program dir. NSF, Washington, 1966-67; cons., 1946-96. Pres. Sunshine Terrace Found., 1988-96. Served to col. U.S. Army, 1940-46. Recipient Disting. Service award Utah State U. Alumni, 1980. Fellow IEEE (Centennial medal 1984); mem. Logan C. of C. (pres. 1971), Sigma Xi, Tau Beta Pi. Republican. Mormon. Lodge: Kiwanis (pres. Logan 1957). Died June 7, 1996.

CLARK, HALLIDAY, marketing executive; b. Bklyn., May 15, 1918; s. David Hatfield and Elizabeth C.H. (Halliday) C.; m. Hazel J. Frost, June 28, 1941; children: Halliday Clark, Jr., Elizabeth F. Kubie, Deborah G. Reinhart. Student NYU, 1938-41; LLB, LaSalle Law Sch., Chgo., 1966; MBA, Calif. Coast U., Santa Ana, 1982, PhD, 1983. Assoc. editor Variety Store Merchandiser Publs., N.Y.C., 1945-48; nat. accounts mgr. Best Foods Inc., N.Y.C., 1948-55; gen. sales mgr. Yale & Towne Mfg. Co., White Plains, N.Y., 1955-63; gen. mgr. Towne Hardware div., N.Y.C., 1963-68; v.p. sales Arrow Fastener Corp., Saddle Brook, N.J., 1968-72; pres., chmn. What to Do County Publs., Chappaqua, N.Y., 1972-78; pres. Halliday Clark & Assoc., Chadds Ford, Penn., 1978—; v.p. sales and mktg. Quaker City Mfg. Co., Sharon Hill, Pa., 1990—; pres., dir. Westchester Sales Execs., White Plains, N.Y., 1955-57; v.p. Sales, Mktg. Execs. Internat., N.Y.C., 1964-67; chmn. bd. UCP of Westchester, Harrison, N.Y., 1965-74. Author, publisher: What to do in Connecticut, 1973; What to do on Long Island, 1975; What to Do in New Jersey, 1976. Pres. bd. visitors Wassaic Devel. Ctr. (N.Y.), 1966-78; mem. U.S. Olympic Adv. Com., 1967-68; pres. Hanover-Pennsbury Assn. Served as capt. USAF, 1942-45, ETO. Recipient Civic Virtue award, UCP of Westchester, 1964. Mem. Scarsdale Alumni Assn. (pres. 1988—). Republican. Episcopalian (lic. lay reader).

CLARK, J(OHN) GRAHAME (DOUGLAS), author; b. July 28, 1907; s. Charles Douglas and Maude Ethel Grahame (Shaw) C.; m. Gwladys Maude White, 1936; 3 children. MA, Cambridge (Eng.) U., PhD, ScD; also 3 hon. degrees. Asst. lectr. archaeology Cambridge U., 1935-46, univ. lectr., 1946-52, Disney prof., 1951-74, head dept. archaeology and anthropology, 1956-61, 68-71, fellow of Peterhouse, 1950-73, master of Peterhouse, 1973-80, hon. fellow, 1980; Munro lectr. Edinburgh U., 1949; Reckitt lectr. Brit. Acad., 1954; Dalrymple lectr. Glasgow U., 1955; G. Grant MacCurdy lectr. Harvard U., 1957; William Evans vis. prof. U. Otago, 1964; Commonwealth vis. fellow, Australia, 1964; Hitchcock prof. U. Calif., Berkeley, 1969; Leverhulme vis. prof. U. Uppsala, 1972; mem. Ancient Monuments Bd., 1954-77. Author: The Stone Age Hunters, 1967, World Prehistory a New Outline, 1969, Aspects of Prehistory, 1970, The Earlier Stone Age Settlement of Scandinavia, 1975, World Preshitory in New Perspective, 1977, Mesolithic Prelude, 1980, The IDentity of Man, 1982, Symbols of Excellence, 1986, Economic Prehistory, 1989, Prehistoric Archaeology at Cambridge and Byond, 1989, Space, Time and Man: A Prehistorian's View, 1992, and many others, (with Stuart Piggott) Preshitoric Societies, 1965; numerous articles. Mem. Royal Commn. on Hist. Monuments, 1957-69; trustee Brit. Mus., 1975-88. With Brit. Army, 1939-45. Decorated comdr. Order Brit. Empire, comdr. Order of Danebrog; recipient Hodgkins medal Smithsonian Instn., 1967, Viking medal Wenner Gren Found., 1971, Lucy Wharton Drexel gold medal Mus. U. Pa., 1974, Chanda medal Asiatic Soc., 1979, Erasmus prize, 1990. Fellow Brit. Acad., German Archaeol. Inst., Royal Soc. Scis. (Uppsala, fgn.); mem. Prehistoric Soc. (hon. editor Proc. 1935-70, pres. 1958-

62), Soc. Antiquaries (v.p. 1959-61, Gold medal 1978); hon. corr. mem. Royal Soc. No. Antiquaries (Copenhagen), Swiss Prehistoric Soc.; hon. mem. Royal Inst. Archaeology, Archaeol. Inst. Asm.; fgn. mem. Finnish Archaeol. Soc., Am. Acad. Arts and Scis. (hon.), Royal Danish Acad. Scis. and Letters, Royal Netherlands Acad. Scis.; fgn. assoc. NAS (U.S.), others. Died Sept. 12, 1995.

CLARK, PEGGY, theatrical lighting designer; b. Balt., Sept. 30, 1915; d. Eliot Round and Eleanor (Linton) C.; m. Lloyd R. Kelley, Jan. 28, 1960. A.B. cum laude, Smith Coll., 1935; M.F.A., Yale U., 1938. Designer theatrical costumes, 1938-96; instr. lighting Lester Polakov Studio & Forum of Stage Design, Inc., 1965-87; lectr. lighting design Smith Coll., 1967-69, Yale Drama Sch., 1969-70; Bd. counselors Smith Coll., 1961-69, pres. class of, 1935, 1970-75, 80-85; mem. adv. com. Internat. Theatre Inst. Designer settings and lighting Gabrielle, 1941, High Ground, 1951, Curtain Going Up, 1952, Agnes de Mille Dance Theatre, 1953-54; designer stage lighting: numerous plays, including Beggar's Holiday, 1946, Song of Norway, 1952; Peter Pan, 1954, Will Success Spoil Rock Hunter, 1955, Kiss Me Kate, 1955, No Time for Sargeants, 1956; designer decor: Stage Door Canteen; tech. dir.: Am. Theatre Wing; lighting and tech. dir.: other plays including Connecticut Yankee, 1942; Brigadoon, 1946, High Button Shoes, 1947, Along Fifth Avenue, 1948, Gentlemen Prefer Blondes, 1949, Pal Joey, 1951, Mr. Wonderful, Auntie Mame, Bells Are Ringing, 1956, N.Y.C. Center Musical Revivals, 1956-58, 63-68, Say Darling, 1957; prodns. Wonderful Town, Carousel, Susannah, at Brussels Internat. Expn., Flower Drum Song, 1958; lighting tech. supr.: Goodbye Charlie, 1959, Bye Bye Birdie, Unsinkable Molly Brown, Under the Yum Yum Tree, 1960, Show Girl, Mary Mary, 1961, Sail Away, 1961, Romulus, 1962, Girl Who Came to Supper, 1963, Around the World in 80 Days, 1963-64, Bajour, Poor Richard, 1965, The Rose Tattoo, 1966; designer lighting: Darling of the Day, 1968, South Pacific, 1968, Rosalinda, 1968, Jimmy, 1969, Last of the Red Hot Lovers, 1969, Sound of Music, 1970, How the Other Half Loves, 1971, The King and I, 1972, Bil Baird's Bandwagon, 1973, Bil Baird's Whistling Wizard and the Sultan of Tuffet, Pinochio, 1973, Jones Beach's Carousel, 1973, Alice in Wonderland, 1974, Winnie the Pooh, Davy Jones' Locker for Bil Baird Theatre, 1976, Student Prince and Merry Widow for Light Opera of Manhattan, 1976, Mlle. Modiste, Grand Duchess, Babes in Toyland, 1978. Recipient Smith medal, Disting. Alumnae award, 1977. Fellow U.S. Inst. Theatre Tech. (vice commr. engring. commn.; Heritage award 1985); mem. United Scenic Artists (rec. sec. 1942-47, trustee 1948-51, pres. 1968-69, v.p. 1974-76, pension and welfare trustee 1970-80, 84-90), ANTA, Illuminating Engring. Soc., Yale Drama Alumni Assn. (Eastern v.p. 1970-77, pres. 1977-83), Woods Hole Protective Assn. (pres. 1978-81). Clubs: French Bull Dog of Am. (pres. 1972-86), Smith (Bklyn., N.Y.C. and Cape Cod); Woods Hole Yacht (sec. 1978-80, vice commodore 1980-81, commodore 1981-83). Died June 19, 1996.

CLARK, ROGER ARTHUR, lawyer; b. Chgo., May 23, 1932; s. Frank Arthur and Alice Rita (Mahoney) C.; m. Kate Dawson, June 24, 1961; children: Alice, Anne, John, Michael. BS, U. Ill., 1954, LLB, 1958. Bar: Ill. 1958, N.Y. 1961, D.C. 1962, U.S. Supreme Ct. 1967. Trial atty. Antitrust div. U.S. Dept. Justice, Washington, 1958-60; assoc. Donovan, Leisure, Newton & Irvine, N.Y.C., 1960-61; sr. ptnr. Rogers & Wells, Washington, 1961—; adj. prof. law Georgetown U., Washington, 1961-67; dir. Cafritz Cos., Washington; spl. counsel U.S. Architect of the Capitol, 1963-64; trustee, gen. counsel Fed. City Coun., Washington, 1969; dir., gen. counsel Fed. City Housing Corp., Washington, 1972-76. Nationalities coord. Citizens for Nixon-Agnew, Washington, 1968; gen counsel 1981 Presidential Inaugural Com. 1st lt. U.S. Army, 1955-57. Mem. ABA, D.C. Bar Assn., Order of the Coif, Chevy Chase Club, Met. Club. Republican. Died April 12, 1997.

CLARK, SHARON KAY, organization administrator; b. Glendale, W.Va., June 23, 1941; d. John and Edna Marie (Shepherd) Callahan; m. Oscar Leroy Clark, Aug. 13, 1959, (dec.); children: John Gregory (dec.), Rebecca Janine. Grad. high sch., Moundsville, W.Va. Exec. dir. Upper Ohio Valley Crisis Hotline, Inc., Wheeling, W.Va., 1989—. Bd. dirs. Wheeling Area Tng. Ctr. for Handicapped, 1980—, Laura Ctr. Inc., 1986—, Nat. Benevolent Assn. Recipient Great Am. Family award U.S. Jaycees, 1982. Mem. Nat. Soc. Fund Raising Execs. Baptist. Club: Pilot.

CLARK, WILLIAM STRATTON, physician; b. Dayton, Ohio, Nov. 24, 1914; s. Clyde Melvin and Hazel Marie (Walker) C.; m. Vivien Ranschburg, June 25, 1971; children: William Stratton, Judith Ann, Robin Walker, James Pennell. BS, U. Dayton, 1934; MD, St. Louis U., 1938. Diplomate: Am. Bd. Internal Medicine. Intern Miami Valley Hosp., Dayton, 1938-39; gen. practice medicine Dayton, 1939-44; asst. in pathology Tulane U., 1944-45; clin. fellow medicine Mass. Gen. Hosp., 1945-48; rsch., tchr. Mass. Gen. Hosp., Med. Sch. Harvard, 1948-53; asst. prof. medicine Western Res. U., 1953-56, assoc. prof. medicine, 1956-58; dir. med. dept. Nat. Found., 1958-64; pres., chief exec. officer Arthritis Found., N.Y.C., 1964-70; assoc. attending physician St. Luke's Hosp., 1971-74, attending physician, 1974-80, cons. physician, 1980-96, acting dir. dept. medicine, 1975-76, dir. dept. medicine, 1977-79, chief div. rheumatic diseases, 1979-85; prof. clin. medicine Columbia U. Coll. Physicians and Surgeons, 1975-84, lectr., 1985-96. Former editor-in-chief: Arthritis and Rheumatism (ofcl. jour. Am. Rheumatism Assn.); contbr. articles to profl. jours. Master Am. Coll. Rheumatology; fellow ACP; mem. AMA, Century Assn. Episcopalian. Home: New York N.Y. Died Sept. 22, 1996; interred Kensico Cemetery.

CLARKE, ALFRED ALEXANDER, sociology educator; b. L.A., Aug. 30, 1923; s. Alfred Alexander Clarke, Sr. and Benita Valentine Talladay; m. Helen Josephine O'Flahavan, Feb. 14, 1954; 1 child, Timothy Alexander. Student, U. Denver, 1945-49; B of Gen. Edn., U. Nebr., 1965; MEd, Westfield State Coll., 1967; MA in Sociology, U. Mass., 1971. Enlisted USAF, advanced through grades to sr. master sgt., comms. specialist, 1942-45, manpower mgmt. technician, 1949-67; film booker RKO Radio Pictures, Denver, 1946-47; prof. sociology Western New Eng. Coll., Springfield, 1971-90, chair dept. human studies, 1974-76, 89-91. Author: (workbook) The Squadron Manpower Role, 1955, (handbook) Intention, Design and Outcome: A First Handbook in Sociological Research, 1995, (book of poetry) Snow Crystal Universe, 1956; co-author: (workbook) Discovering Sociology, 1981; originator/host weekly radio talk show Networking at Western New Eng. Coll., 1986-90; performances include Three Sonatinas for Piano, 1957, Tears, 1957, Prelude and toccata for Harp, 1957, Art of Peace, 1995; art exhbns. include Del Rio Art League Gallery & Libr., Laughlin AFB, Tex., 1959, Western New Eng. Coll., 1992, Tripoli (Libya) C.C., 1992. Rsch. cons. Urban League, Springfield unit, 1972-74, LWV Springfield chpt., 1977-79; cons., mayor, Chicopee, Mass., 1987-91. Mem. AAUP, ASCAP, Am. Sociol. Assn. (convener task group sociol. concepts 1975-78), Am. Cancer Soc. (mem. Springfield unit, pres. 1979-80, bd. dirs. 1978-90, hon. bd. dirs. 1990-97), New Eng. Sociol. Assn. (charter, dir. 1980-81, originator apple award for outstanding contbn. to tchg. sociology 1981-97, pres. 1983-84, archivist 1984-91, apple award for outstanding contbn. to tchg. sociology 1983, pioneer award 1989), Alpha Kappa Delta (area I rep. 1985-91), Psi Chi. Democrat. Home: Springfield Mass. Died Oct. 19, 1997.

CLARSON, JOHN JULIUS, real estate company executive; b. N.Y.C., Feb. 27, 1921; s. John F. and Martha (Nichols) C.; m. Ruth Ann Beck, Apr. 28, 1945; children: Dorothy, John, Donna, Patrick. B.B.A., Pace Coll., 1953. With Champion Internat. Corp., N.Y.C., 1949-77; v.p. fin. services Champion Internat. Corp., 1970-77, v.p. real estate, 1977-95; pres. Champion Realty, Houston, 1977-95; dir. Tex. Commerce Bank, Greens Crossing. Served with AUS, 1942-45. Home: Houston Tex. Died Jan. 13, 1995.

CLASTER, NANCY, actress; b. Balt.; d. L. Edwin Goldman and Rita Strauss; m. Bertram Claster, 1938. BA, Goucher Coll., 1937. Appeared in Romper Room, 1953-64. Home: Baltimore Md. Died 1997.

CLAY, JAMES RAY, mathematics educator; b. Burley, Idaho, Nov. 5, 1938; s. Charles Milton Clay and Dahlia LaRae Carlson; m. Carol Cline Burge, June 12, 1959; children: Thea Patricia, Christine Marie, Terri Susan. Student, U.S. Naval Acad.; BS in Math., U. Utah, 1960; MS in Math., U. Wash., 1962, PhD in Math., 1966. Asst. prof. U. Ariz., Tucson, 1966-69, assoc. prof., 1969-74, prof., 1974-96, assoc. head math. dept., 1969-72; guest prof. U. Tuebingen, Germany, 1972-73, Kings' Coll., U. London, 1973, Technische U. Muenchen, Munich, Germany, 1979-80, 87, U. Edinburgh, Scotland, 1980, U. Stellenbosch, South Africa, 1989, U. der Bundeswehr, Hamburg, Germany, 1990, Nat. Cheng Kung U., Tainan, Taiwan, 1991, Johannes Kepler Universitaet, Linz, Austria, 1994, Klagenfurt (Austria) Universitaet, 1995; postdoctorate dir. Hubert Kiechle, Technische U. Muenchen, 1991-93; lectr. in field. Author: Trigonometry--A Motivated Approach, 1977, Nearrings: Geneses and Applications, 1992; contbr. 50 articles to profl. jours. With USN, 1956-59. Recipient Dist. Sr. U.S. Scientist award Humboldt Found., 1972-73, Am. Men of Sci. Mem. Am. Math. Soc. Mem. LDS Ch. Home: Tucson Ariz. Died Jan. 16, 1996; interred Bingington LDS Cemetery.

CLAYTON, PRESTON COPELAND, lawyer; b. Eufaula, Ala., Sept. 21, 1903; s. Lee Johnston and Caroline E. (Copeland) C.; m. Jewel Gladys Robinson, July 20, 1933; children—Mary Elliott (Mrs. Robert Mack Dixon), Sarah Hunter (Mrs. Thos. S. Lawson, Jr.), Preston Copeland. B.A., U. Ala., 1924; LL.B., Jones Law Sch., 1935. Bar: Ala. 1931. Cotton mcht. Quanah, Tex., 1927-32; pvt. practice in Clayton and Eufaula, 1932-96; assoc. justice Supreme Ct., Ala., 1953-54; instr. econs. U. Ala., 1923-24; dir., atty. Clayton Banking Co., 1946-53; organizer, atty. Pea River Electric Coop., 1937-53, Wiregrass Electric Coop., 1938-42; Breeder Arabian horses. Contbr. articles on Arabian and Barb horses of No. Africa to mags. City atty., Clayton, 1933-39; mem. Ala. Bd. Vets. Affairs, 1946-50; chmn. Barbour County Dem. Exec. Com., 1937-53; mem. Ala. Senate, 1938-53; pres. Ala. Cattlemens Assn. Lt. col. AUS, World War II. Mem. VFW (life), Internat. Arabian Horse Assn. (bd. dirs.), Rotary. Episcopalian. Home: Eufaula Ala. Died June 20, 1996, interred Fairview Cemetery, Eufaula, AL.

CLEMENTS, ROBERT JOHN, educator; b. Cleve., Oct. 23, 1912; s. Earl W. and Mildred (Warner) C.; m. Helen Louise Card, Sept. 3, 1940 (div.); children: Caird Robert, Cleveland Warner; m. Lorna Levant, July 19, 1975; 1 dau., Erin June. A.B., Oberlin Coll., 1934; Ph.D., U. Chgo., 1939; postgrad., U. Bordeaux, U. Florence, Harvard; Litt. D., U. Rome, Italy, 1961; H.H.D., Philathea Coll., Can., 1966. Instr. U. Chgo., 1937-39; instr. U. Ill., 1939-40; instr., asst. prof. Harvard U., 1940-47; prof., chmn. dept. Romance langs., lits. Pa. State U., 1947-54; prof. Romance langs. and lits. Grad. Sch., NYU, 1954-56, prof., chmn. dept. comparative lit., 1956-78, prof. emeritus, 1978-93; lectr. U. Madrid, 1953; univ. asso. Columbia, 1955-93; Fulbright Research scholar, Rome, 1960-61; Mellon prof. lit. U. Pitts., 1968; screening com. for langs. and lit. Fulbright office, Washington, 1965-68; adv. modern lang. editor Ginn & Co., Boston, 1944-57; cons. Juilliard Sch., 1971-84; adv. bd. Nat. Endowment Humanities, 1978. Author: Critical Theory and Practice of the Pléiade, 1942 (rev. as Critical Theory of Pléiade 1968), (co-author) Pennsylvania Curriculum Revision for Modern Languages, 1952, Platonism in French Renaissance Poetry, 1957, The Peregrine Muse; Studies in Renaissance Comparative Literature, 1959, rev., 1968, Picta Poesis, Literary and Humanistic Theory in Renaissance Emblem Books, 1960, Michelangelo's Theory of Art, 1960, Michelangelo, A Self-Portrait, 1962 (rev. as Michelangelo, Self Portrait 1968), Michelangelo Scultore, 1964, The Poetry of Michelangelo, 1964, Renaissance Letters, 1976, Anatomy of the Novella, 1977, Comparative Literature as Academic Discipline, 1978; Corr. editor: (co-author) Boletín de Filología Espanola, Madrid, Romantisches Jahrbuch, Hamburg; asso. editor: (co-author) Gotham Library, 1962-93; co-editor: (co-author) Renaissance Letters, 1976; mem. editorial bd. (co-author) Modern Internat. Drama, 1967-93; contbr. (co-author) chpts. to books and bibliographies, many articles, revs. to profl. periodicals, newspapers.; columnist: (co-author) Literary Scene in Europe, Saturday Rev, 1964-71. Co-organizer Civil Affairs Tng. Program, Harvard, 1940-44. Decorated knight cavaliere ufficiale, Italy). Mem. MLA (chmn. French, Italian, Portuguese, Romance sects.), Am. Council Learned Socs. (mem. editorial bd., Renaissance com. 1944-93), Société des Amis du Louvre, Dante Alighieri Soc., Accademia dell' Arcadia Rome, Mazzini Soc., Mediaeval Acad. Am. (sec. pub. 1940-47), Internat. Assn. for Study of Italian Lang. and Lit. (v.p. 1962-73, co-pres. 1973-79), Am. Comparative Lit. Assn. (adv. bd. 1965-68, 77-80), Am. Assn. Tchrs. Italian (pres. 1960-62), Phi Beta Kappa (nat. bd. 1954-62). Home: Mahopac N.Y. Died Sept. 8, 1993.

COATES, JESSE, retired chemical engineer; b. Baton Rouge, Mar. 12, 1908; s. Charles Edward and Ollie (Maurin) C.; m. Judith Mills Williams, Apr. 16, 1938; children—Judith Mills, Jesse Jr., Victor Maurin (dec.). B.S., La. State U., 1928; postgrad., Mass. Inst. Tech., 1930-31; M.S., U. Mich., 1932, Ph.D., 1936. Mem. La. Bd. for Registration Profl. Engrs. Chemist, treating engr. Nat. Lumber & Creosoting Co., 1928; chemist Internat. Paper Co., 1928-29, Meeker Sugar Refinery, 1930-31, Punta Alegre Sugar Co., 1931; chem. engr. Tex. Pacific Coal & Oil Co., 1932-33, United Gas Pub. Service, 1933-36; asst. prof. chem. engring. La. State U., Baton Rouge, 1936-42; asso. prof. La. State U., 1942-47, prof., 1947-75, chmn. dept., 1955-67, 69-70, Alumni prof., 1969-73, alumni prof. emeritus, 1973-94, ret., 1973; cons. chem. engr. Contbr. articles to profl. jours. Recipient Technol. Accomplishment medal La. Engring. Soc., 1958; Charles E. Coates meml. award Am. Chem. Soc.-Am. Inst. Chem. Engrs., 1958; named Man of Month Chem. Engring. mag., Apr. 1958; Distinguished Service certificate Nat. Council Engring. Examiners, 1977. Fellow Am. Inst. Chemists, Am. Inst. Chem. Engrs.; mem. Am. Chem. Soc., Am. Soc. Engring. Edn., La. Acad. Scis., Sigma Xi, Phi Kappa Phi, Alpha Chi Sigma, Phi Lambda Upsilon, Kappa Alpha. Episcopalian. Home: Baton Rouge La. Died Dec. 21, 1994.

COCHRAN, OLIVE LEIGH MYATT, retired educational administrator; b. Monroe, La., Sept. 8, 1907; d. Webster Andrew and Martha Fidelia (Morton) Myatt; m. Raymond Nevitt Cochran, June 4, 1940 (dec. Jan. 1985); children: Kathleen, Susan. Student, La. State Normal Coll., 1923-25; kindergarten cert., Harris Tchrs. Coll., 1926; BS cum laude, La. State U., 1942; MEd, N.E. La. U., 1962. Tchr. rural schs., Ouachita Parish, La., 1925-27, Georgia Tucker Elem. Sch., Monroe, 1927-43, 55-62; tchr., owner Cochran Nursery Sch., 1949-51; supr. elem. edn. Monroe Sch. System, 1962-67, dir. elem. curriculum, 1967-73; organizer first spl. edn. classes Monroe schs., 1964; supr. spl. edn. Monroe City schs., 1964-73; Active CD. during World War II. Mem. Internat. Reading Assn. (dir. local unit 1970-73), Assn. Childhood Edn. Internat. (br. pres. 1967-71, treas. 1971-83), La. Assn. Childhood Edn. Internat., AAUW, Delta Kappa Gamma, Sigma Tau Delta. Republican. Baptist. Died Oct. 1995. Home: Monroe La.

COCKERHAM, COLUMBUS CLARK, retired geneticist, educator; b. Mountain Park, N.C., Dec. 12,

1921; s. Corbett C. and Nellie Bruce (McCann) C.; m. Joyce Evelyn Allen, Feb. 26, 1944; children: Columbus Clark Jr., Jean Allen, Bruce Allen. B.S., N.C. State Coll., 1943, M.S., 1949; Ph.D., Iowa State Coll., 1952. Asst. prof. biostats. U. N.C., Chapel Hill, 1952-53; mem. faculty N.C. State U., Raleigh, 1953—, prof. stats., 1959-72, William Neal Reynolds prof. stats. and genetics, 1972-96, disting. univ. prof., 1988-96, prof. emeritus, 1991-96; mem. genetics study sect. NIH, 1965-69; cons. adv. com. protocols for safety evaluation FDA, 1967-69. Author papers population and quantitative genetics, plant and animal breeding; editor, assoc. editor: Theoretical Population Biology, 1975-85; editl. bd.: Genetics, 1969-72, Genetic Epidemiology, 1984-90; assoc. editor: Am. Jour. Human Genetics, 1978-80. Served with USMCR, 1943-46. Recipient N.C. award in sci., 1976, Oliver Max Gardner award, 1980, D.D. Mason faculty award, 1983, N.C. State U. Alumni Assn. award, 1986, Superior Svc. award (group award) USDA, 1990, Alexander Quarles Holladay medal, 1994; grantee Nat. Inst. Gen. Med. Scis., 1960-95. Fellow AAAS, Am. Soc. Agronomy, Crop Sci. Soc. Am.; mem. NAS, Am. Soc. Animal Sci., Biometric Soc., Genetics Soc. Am., Genetics Soc. Japan (fgn. hon. mem.), Sigma Xi, Gamma Sigma Delta (award merit 1964), Phi Kappa Phi. Died Nov. 4, 1996.

COE, WARD BALDWIN, JR., retired lawyer; b. Riderwood, Md., Aug. 24, 1913; s. Ward Baldwin and Marguerite Almy (Hall) C.; m. Diana Chittenden, Jan. 18, 1942; children: Diana, Ward III, Henry, Michael. A.B., Princeton U., 1936; LL.B., Harvard U., 1939. Bar: Md. 1939. Since practiced in Balt.; assoc. Ward B. Coe, 1939-41, John R. Norris, 1940; assoc. firm Carman, Anderson & Barnes, 1945-49, Anderson & Barnes, 1949-52; partner firm Anderson, Barnes & Coe, 1952-58, Anderson, Barnes, Coe & King, 1958-63; partner firm Anderson, Coe & King, 1963-83, of counsel, 1984—; ret., 1993; mem. Md. State Bd. Law Examiners, 1963-72, sec., 1963-68; asst. atty. gen., State of Md., 1949-52; mem. Gov.'s Commn. to Revise Annotated Code of Md., 1975-86. Bd. dirs. Balt. Legal Aid Bur., 1947-53, Balt. League for Crippled Children and Adults, 1952-58, Md. Soc. Crippled Children and Adults, 1955-61; trustee Gilman Sch., 1964-67. Served with AUS, 1941; Served with USNR, 1941-45. Fellow Md. Bar Found. (dir. 1977-83, sec. 1979-81); mem. Bar Assn. City Balt., Md. State Bar Assn. Died Nov. 12, 1996.

COFFIN, TRISTRAM, writer, editor; b. Hood River, Oreg., July 25, 1912; s. Clarence Eugene and Lenora (Smith) C.; m. Margaret Avery, June 26, 1933; children: Lynne, Stephen Avery. AB, DePauw U., 1933. Reporter Indpls. Times, 1933-37; asst. to gov. Ind., 1937-41; with Office Facts and Figures, OWI, 1941-44; White House corr. CBS, 1945-47; newspaper columnist, 1948-51, free-lance writer and broadcaster, 1951-68; editor Washington Spectator, 1975-93. Author: Missouri Compromise, 1947, Your Washington, 1954, Not to the Swift, 1961, The Passion of the Hawks, 1964, Mine Eyes Have Seen the Glory, 1964, The Sex Kick, 1966, Senator Fulbright, 1966; contbr. Washington Watch Newsletter, 1968-74. Mem. P.E.N. DIED 05/28/97. .

COFFMAN, WILLIAM EUGENE, educational psychologist; b. Belington, W.Va., June 13, 1913; s. Walter E. and Mary (Thornhill) C.; m. Eloise Clarke, Dec. 21, 1939; children—Mary Eloise Coffman Crocker, Judith Ann Coffman Piché. Student, Potomac State Coll., Keyser, W.Va., 1930-32; B.S. in Edn, Wittenberg U., 1934, Litt.D.(hon.), 1985; M.A., W.Va. U., 1938; Ed.D., Columbia U., 1949. Tchr. Mineral County (W.Va.) Schs., 1934-37, prin., 1937-44; asso. prof. Okla. State U., 1949-52; asst. dir. test devel. div. Ednl. Testing Service, Princeton, N.J., 1952-54; asso. dir. Ednl. Testing Service, 1954-57, dir., 1957-60; dir. research and devel. CEEB Programs, 1960-66, research adviser, 1966-69; E.F. Lindquist prof. ednl. measurement, dir. Iowa Testing Programs U. Iowa, Iowa City, 1969-81, prof. emeritus, 1981—; vis. prof. edn. Syracuse U., 1966; vis. lectr. Princeton Theol. Sem., 1964-69; cons. Nat. Assessment Ednl. Progress, Systems Devel. Corp., Ford Found., Calif. Assessment Program, U.S. Dept. Edn., U.S. Dept. Justice. Author: (with Fred Godshalk, Frances Swineford) The Measurement of Writing Ability, 1966, Developing Tests for the Culturally Different, 1965, Concepts of Achievement and Proficiency, 1970, Testing in the Schools: Historical Perspectives, 1985, Measurement of Thinking Skills: An Historical Perspective, 1988, Educational Measurement in Theoretical and Political Perspective, 1990; editor: Frontiers of Educational Measurement and Information Systems, 1973, (with B. Randhawa) Visual Learning, Thinking and Communication, 1978. contbr.: Educational Measurement, 2d edit. Served with U.S. Army, 1944-45. Recipient Alumni Achievement award Potomac State Coll. of W.Va. U., 1980. Fellow Am. Psychol. Assn.; mem. Am. Ednl. Research Assn., Nat. Council Measurement in Edn. (pres. 1972-73), Alpha Tau Omega.

COGRAVE, JOHN EDWIN, retired judge; b. Washington, Dec. 29, 1929; s. John Roscoe Cograve and Eleanor Frances (Reus) Rosenburg; m. Mary Claire Carpenter, Aug. 23, 1952; children: John, Karen, Joan. LLB, U. Va., 1959. Bar: Va. 1959. Mem. office gen. counsel FAA, 1959-60; mem. office gen. counsel FMC, Washington, 1960-65, dep. gen. counsel, 1965-74, chief adminstrv. law judge, 1974-86, mng. dir., 1986-87; judge Mcpl. Ct., Charles Town, W.Va., 1987-94; ret. Mcpl. Ct., 1994. 1st lt. U.S. Army, 1951-54. Died July 17, 1997.

COHEN, BURTON JEROME, financial service executive; b. Phila., Dec. 8, 1933; s. Alexander David and Esther (Mirrow) C.; m. Jane McDowell, Mar. 16, 1968; children: Paul, Joshua, Douglas, Glen. B.S. in Acctg, Temple U., 1955; student, c. Program, Harvard U. Ops. v.p. Cakemasters, Inc., Phila., 1957-61; mgr. IBM, Phila., White Plains, N.Y., N.Y.C., 1961-70; ptnr. Touche & Ross & Co., N.Y.C., 1970-77; ptnr., nat. dir. fin. and adminstrn. Coopers & Lybrand, N.Y.C., 1977-82; exec.-chief adminstrv. officer Paul, Weiss, Rifkind, Wharton & Garrison, N.Y.C., 1982-96; adj. prof. Columbia U. Grad. Sch. Bus.; lectr. Am. Mgmt. Assn. seminars.; Mem. adv. bd. Borough Manhattan Community Coll. Author: Cost Effective Information Systems, 1971; contbr. to: Info. Systems Handbook, 1975. Served with Fin. Corps U.S. Army, 1955-57. Mem. Fin. Execs. Inst. Club: Masons. Home: New Canaan Conn. Died Feb. 12, 1996.

COHEN, BURTON MARCUS, physician, clinical investigator; b. Elizabeth, N.J., Dec. 13, 1925; s. Philip and Beatrice (Kaufman) C.; AB, Columbia U., 1945; MD, U. Rochester, 1948; ScD (hon.), Inst. Applied Rsch., London, 1972; m. Elaine N. Mohr, Dec. 24, 1950; children: Elizabeth Cohen Hamill, Hugh Philip, Claire Cohen Lerner, Suzanne Jane. Intern, resident Maimonides Hosp., Bklyn., 1948-51; resident physician Strong Meml. Hosp., also asst. medicine U. Rochester, 1950-51; research fellow Columbia U. Research Service, Goldwater Meml. Hosp., asst. medicine Columbia Coll. Phys. and Surg., 1954-58; asst. prof. clin. medicine and clin. preventive medicine N.J. Coll. Medicine, 1959-61, clin. asst. prof. medicine, 1961-63, assoc. prof. clin. medicine, 1963-82; clin. prof. medicine U. Medicine and Dentistry, N.J. Med. Sch., 1982—; gov's task force on phys. edn. dept. environ. and community medicine Robert Wood Johnson Med. Sch., Piscataway, N.J., 1986—; mem. Clean Air commn., N.J., 1988; pres. Burton M. Cohen, M.D.; attending physician Jersey City Med. Center, Univ. Hosp., Newark, 1982—; assoc. dir. White Cardiopulmonary Inst., Pollak Hosp., Jersey City, 1959-63; sr. attending physician Elizabeth Gen. Hosp., chmn. dept. medicine, 1975-77; attending Physician Univ. Hosp., Newark; med. bd. Deborah Hosp., Browns Mills; assoc. U. Rochester. Dir. Clodagh Assos., Ltd., Ireland; active Clean Air Council, Dept. Environ. Protection, State of N.J. Served as midshipman USNR, 1943-44, lt comdr., USPHS, 1952-55; comdr. (sr. surgeon) Res., 1968-79, capt. (med. dir.), 1979—. Fellow Am. Coll. Cardiology. Am. Coll. Chest Physicians, Acad. Medicine N.J., ACP, Royal Soc. Medicine (London), Royal Soc. Health, Internat. Acad. Sci. and Medicine, Am. Coll. Clin. Pharmacology and Chemotherapy (a founding fellow, emeritus), Am. Soc. Clin. Radiology; mem. Union County Heart Assn. (past pres.), Am. Fedn. Clin. Research. Internat. Soc. Internal Medicine, Internat. Cardiovascular Soc. (emeritus), European Soc. Clin. Respiratory Physiology, AAAS, Am. Therapeutic Soc., AAUP, Mil. Surgeons U.S. Soc. Automotive Historians, Res. Officers U.S., N.J. Acad. Sci., John Jay Soc., George Hoyt Whipple Soc. (charter), Soc. Older Grads. Columbia U. Clubs: Columbia University (N.Y.C.), Cornell (N.Y.C.), Rolls-Royce Owners (U.S.), Rolls-Royce Enthusiast, Rolls-Royce and Bentley Drivers (Eng.). Cardiology editor Medecine et Hygiene (Switzerland), 1961-64; editor-in-chief Current Concepts in Pacing. Contbr. articles to profl. jours. Deceased.

COHEN, HENNIG, English educator; b. Darlington, S.C., Aug. 26, 1919; s. David A. and Hilda (Hennig) C.; m. Merrie Lou Conaway, June 16, 1946; children: David, Mark, Jonathan. AB, U. S.C., 1941, MA, 1948; PhD, Tulane U., 1951; MA (hon.), U. Pa., 1971. News editor sta. WCOS, Columbia, S.C., 1945-46; dir. pub. relations U. S.C., Columbia, 1946-56; asst. prof. English U. Pa., Phila., 1957-61, assoc. prof., 1961-65, prof., 1965-74, John Welsh Centennial prof. history and lit., 1974-92, lectr., 1992-96; vis. lectr. Bryn Mawr Coll., 1962-63, Swarthmore Coll., 1963-64, 65; vis. prof. Stanford U., 1968, U. Delhi, 1982, Doshisha U., Kyoto, Japan, 1988, U. Sussex, Eng., 1989; Fulbright prof. Am. studies U. London, 1973-74, U. Budapest, 1978. Author: The South Carolina Gazette, 1953, (with D. Yannella) Herman Melville's Malcolm Letter, 1992; editor: Am. Quar, 1958-70, The Battle Pieces of Herman Melville, 1963, Selected Poems of Herman Melville, 1964, (with William Dillingham) Humor of the Old Southwest, 1964, (with T.P. Coffin) Folklore in America, 1966, The Parade of Heroes, 1978, The American Culture, 1968, The American Experience, 1968, Landmarks in American Writing, 1969, Folklore from the Working Folk of America, 1973, (with James Levernier) The Indians and Their Captives, 1977; (with T.P. Coffin) Folklore of American Holidays, 1986, Israel Potter by Herman Melville, 1991, (with T.P. Coffin) America Celebrates!, 1991; contbr. articles to profl. jours. With USAAF, 1941-45, ETO. Decorated Air medal with five oak leaf clusters.; Guggenheim fellow, 1960, Newberry Library fellow, 1976, Nat. Endowment for Humanities fellow Winterthur Mus., 1980-81. Mem. Melville Soc. (sec. 1968-74, pres. 1975), Am. Studies Assn. (exec. sec. 1956-61), Am. Lit. Assn. (award for profl. svc. 1991), Franklin Inn Club. Jewish. Home: Swarthmore Pa. Died Dec. 12, 1996.

COHEN, HOWARD WILLIAM See **COSELL, HOWARD**

COHEN, JOZEF, psychophysicist, educator; b. Brookline, Mass., July 21, 1921; s. David J. and Dora A. (Levin) C.; m. Huguette Schachnovitch, July 31, 1958. BS, U. Chgo., 1942; PhD, Cornell U., 1945. Susan Linn Sage fellow Cornell U., 1942-45; rsch. staff Psycho-Acoustic Lab. Harvard U., 1945; mem. faculty Cornell U., 1945-48; mem. faculty U. Ill., Champaign, 1948-95, prof. psychology, 1969-91, prof. psychology emeritus, 1991-95, adj. prof. supercomputing applications, 1988-91. Author: Eyewitness Series in Psychology, including Personality Assessment, 1969-72; also articles on history of ideas and sci., theory and applications of Euclidean color space including color TV.; co-discoverer: (with Thomas P. Friden) Euclidean color space, 1974. Recipient Macbeth award Inter-Soc. Color Coun., 1992. Mem. Sigma Xi. Home: Urbana Ill. Died Aug. 18, 1995.

COHN, VIRGINIA S., public relations executive; b. Bklyn.; d. Lewis Henry and Beatrice Rita (Grouse) Saper; m. N. Burton Tretler, Feb. 7, 1940 (div. 1961); children: Amy Tretler Lynn Silverman, Richard Sterling; m. Julian M. Cohn, July 6, 1961 (dec. 1974). Grad. Ann-Reno Inst., N.Y.C., Bklyn. Coll. With various advt. agys., Miami, Fla., 1962-68; dir. advt., pub. relations Modernage, Miami, 1968-69, Bauder Coll., Miami and Ft. Lauderdale, Fla., 1970-84; owner, mgr. Two In Prodn., Miami, 1984-86; dir. mktg. amd pub. info. Hartford Easter Seal Rehab. Ctr., Conn., 1986-92. Contbr. aricles to mags., profl. jours. Mem. Fashion Group Miami (treas. 1974-75), Internat. Soc. Interior Designers, Advt. Fedn. Greater Miami (pres. 1974-75, named Advt. Personality of Yr. 1975), Greater Hartford Advt. Club, Hartford Women's Network, Am. Acad. Advt., Women in Communications (bd. dirs. cen. Conn. chpt., pres. 1989-91), Charter Oak Cultural Ctr. (bd. dirs.), West Hartford Sr. Job Bank, Probus Club Greater Hartford. Avocation: writing. Died July 4, 1992. Home: West Hartford Conn.

COLBY, JEFFREY JOHN, artist; b. S.I., N.Y., Mar. 26, 1956; s. John W. and Rose C. Colby. BFA, U. Tex., 1978; MFA, Sch. of the Art Inst., Chgo., 1980. artist-in-residence Ragdale Found., Lake Forest, Ill., 1983, 88, 90. One person shows include Moody Gallery, Houston, 1983, Kirkland Gallery, Milliken U., Decatur, Ill., 1984, Roy Boyd Gallery, Chgo., 1982, 84, 87, 88, 92, 94, J. L. Becker Gallery, Provincetown, Mass., 1987, Univ. Club. Chgo., 1988, Union League Club, Chgo., 1988, A Montgomery Ward Gallery, U. Ill., Chgo., 1990, Kansas City (Mo.) Artists' Coalition, 1993, State of Ill. Gallery, Chgo., 1994; exhibited in group shows Artemesia Gallery, Chgo., 1979, 80, 85, Ball State U., Muncie, Ind., 1981, 83, 88, Cultural Ctr., Chgo., 1982, Roy Boyd Gallery, Chgo., 1983, 86, 91, Mandeville Gallery, U. Calif., San Diego, 1983, WPA Gallery, Chgo., 1984, Northeastern U. Gallery, Boston, 1984, Foster Gallery, U. Wis., Eau Claire, 1984, Flynn Hall, The Fourth Presbyn. Ch., Chgo., 1984, Lakeview Mus. Arts and Sci., Peoria, Ill., 1985, Quincy (Ill.) Art Ctr., 1985, Rockford (Ill.) Art Mus., 1986, J. L. Becker Gallery, Provincetown, 1988, Janus Gallery, Santa Fe, 1989, Watson Gallery, Houston, 1989, Moody Gallery, Houston, 1985, 90, Hyde Park Art Ctr., Chgo., 1985, 86, 87, 90, 95, Evanston (Ill.) Art Ctr., 1987, 88, 90, State of Ill. Gallery, Chgo., 1991, Charles A. Wustum Mus., Racine, Wis., 1992, Cultural Ctr., Chgo. and South Bend, Ind., 1993, U. Ill. at Chgo. Fed. Res. Bank Chgo., 1994. Ford Found. fellow, 1977, 78, artist's fellow Nat. Endowment for Arts, 1987; Pollack-Krasner Found. Inc. grantee, 1990. Home: Chicago Ill. Died March 31, 1996.

COLEMAN, A. LEE, sociologist, educator; b. Devereux, Ga., Jan. 3, 1913; s. John Amoss and Magnolia (Lee) C.; m. Alberta Louise Nelson, Dec. 11, 1943; children—Nancy Louise, Martha Lee. B.A., Emory U., 1937; M.A., U. N.C., 1940; Ph.D., Cornell U., 1949. Research analyst Govtl. Research Inst., St. Louis, 1938-39; social sci. analyst, farm population, rural life br. U.S. Dept. Agr., Atlanta, also Freeport, Ill., 1939-42, 45-46; grad. asst. dept. rural sociology Cornell U., 1946-49; asst. prof. U. Ky., 1949-53, asso. prof., 1953-57, prof., 1957-78, prof. emeritus, 1978-95, head, later chmn. dept. sociology, 1959-66; cons. So. Regional Council, State Commn. on Human Rights, Civil Rights div. U.S. Dept. Justice, NSF; state adv. com. U.S. Civil Rights Commn., 1963-85. Contbr. profl. jours. Served with AUS, 1942-45. Mem. Am. Sociol. Assn., Rural Sociol. Soc. (pres. 1964-65), So. Sociol. Soc. (pres. 1966-67), North Central Sociol. Soc. Democrat. Home: Lexington Ky. Died June 18, 1995; interred Lexington Cemetery, Lexington, KY.

COLEMAN, ALMAND ROUSE, accounting educator; b. Smithfield, Va., July 16, 1905; s. Archer Almand and Ruby Booth (Rouse) C.; m. Clare Merryman Whitfield, April 13, 1940 (dec. Jan. 1961); children: Lisa Coleman Rose, William Stephen; m. Louise Hudson Foster, May 21, 1962; stepchildren: Emily (Mrs. John Pickering), Edmund Palmer Foster, George William Foster; 1 son,

Charles Almand. AB, Washington and Lee U., 1926, BS in Commerce, 1927, LLD, 1977; MBA, Harvard U., 1934. C.P.A., Va. Asst. to treas. Washington and Lee U., 1926-28; sr. accountant A.M. Pullen & Co., Richmond, Va., 1928-33; acting chief financial analysis and statis. Farm Credit Adminstrn., Washington, 1934-35; asst. trust officer, asst. cashier State Planters Bank and Trust Co., Richmond, 1935-39; assoc. prof. Washington and Lee U., 1939-41, prof. accounting, 1941-55; Disting. lectr. accounting, 1979-83; vis. prof. accounting Harvard Bus. Sch., 1954-55; prof. bus. adminstrn. U. Va. Grad. Sch. Bus., Charlottesville, 1955-72; Charles C. Abbott prof. U. Va. Grad. Sch. Bus., 1972-76, prof. emeritus, 1976-96; vis. prof. bus. adminstrn. Tenn. Tech. U., 1976-78, Disting. vis. prof., 1978-79. Author: Financial Accounting: A General Management Approach, 1970, (with Brownlee and Smith) Financial Accounting for Management, 1980, Financial Accounting and Statement Analysis: A Manager's Guide, 1982; contbr. to bus. and profl. jours. Served to maj. Ordnance U.S. Army, 1942-45; lt. col. Res. 1950-54. U.S. Nat. Masters Track and Field champion, javelin throw (age 80-84, 1988, age 85-89, 1991). Mem. Am. Inst. CPA's (accounting procedure com. 1953-56), Am. Accounting Assn. (v.p. 1956), Financial Execs. Inst., Raven Soc., Phi Beta Kappa. Episcopalian. Died July 19, 1996.

COLEMAN, PAMELA, investment advisor; b. Wichita, Kans., July 17, 1938; d. Clarence William and Emry Regester (Inghram) Coleman; student U. Okla., 1956-57, U. Mo., 1962-65, Wichita State U., 1972-73; children—Cristy Jeanne Coleman, Cathryn Coleman. Teller, Union Nat. Bank, Wichita, 1959, 1st Nat. Bank, Charleston, S.C., 1959-61, 1st Nat. Bank of New London (Conn.), 1961-62; acct., bookkeeper Greenbaum & Assos., Sydney, Australia, 1966-68; pres., chief exec. officer Sweet Peach Prodns. Pty., Ltd., Sydney, 1968-72; fin. mgr. Clarence Coleman Investments, Wichita, 1972-75, registered investment adv., office mgr., 1976—; bd. dirs. Coleman Co., Inc. Formerly active Project Bus. of Jr. Achievement; bd. dirs. Goodwill Industries of Wichita, 1978-80, sec., 1978-79, treas., 1979-80; 1st v.p. Angel Fire Guild, Santa Fe Opera, 1983-84, treas., 1984-85; pres. Guilds of the Santa Fe Opera, 1984-85; 1st v.p. N.Mex. Opera Guilds, Inc., 1984-85. Mem. Midwest Geneal. Soc., DAR, Soc. Mayflower Descs., Daus. Am. Colonists, Nat. Soc. Colonial Dames of Am. (Kans., bd. mgrs. N.Mex. chpt. 1986—). Clubs: Wichita, Wichita Country.

COLLAR, LEO LINFORD, marine transportation company executive; b. Cleve., Nov. 27, 1930; s. Leo Webster and Martha Caroline (Guenther) C.; m. Gail Valine, May 27, 1949; children—Randy L., Gary L., Steven M., Susan L. Student, Golden Gate Coll. With Crowley Maritime Corp., San Francisco, 1948—, exec. v.p., 1975-87, pres., chief operating officer, 1987—; now also pres., dir. Delta Steamship Lines, Inc., subs. Crowley Maritime Corp., New Orleans. Mem. Nat. Maritime Council (vice chmn. 1984—), Council Am. Ship Operators (bd. dirs. 1983—. Republican. Mem. Ch. of the Nazarene. Avocations: boating; fishing; golf. Died 1996.

COLLIER, CLIFFORD WARTHEN, JR., landscape architect; b. Vienna, Ga., Aug. 16, 1927; s. Clifford Warthen and Mary Ellen (Smith) C., m. Martha Mann Thompson, Dec. 15, 1950; children: Ellen Claire, Clifford Cason. Student, N. Ga. Coll.; BFA, U. Ga., 1949, MLA, 1960. Registered landscape architect, W.Va. Asst. to traffic mg. Synthetic Nitrogen Corp., N.Y.C., 1950-54; salesman Frank A. Smith Landscape Co., Atlanta, 1955-57; asst. traffic mgr. L.B. Foster Co., Atlanta, 1955-56; ext. specialist, prof. W.Va. U., Morgantown, 1960-94. Author or co-author 7 reference books on trees, shrubs, vines, groundcovers. V.p., pres. Suncrest Garden, Morgantown; sec., v.p., bd. dirs. Morgantown Civitan Club, 1965-96. With USN, 1946-47. Fellow Am. Soc. Landscape Architects (trustee, Extension Landscape Architect award, 1982); mem. W.Va. Chpt. Soc. Landscape Architects (charter mem., v.p., pres., sec., Recognition awards 1976, 88), W.Va. Garden Club Inc. (bd. dirs., recognition award 1972, life), Sigma Lambda Alpha, Epsilon Sigma Phi. Baptist. Avocations: arts and crafts, gardening, swimming. Home: Morgantown W. Va. Died Apr. 18, 1996.

COLLINS, COPP, federal, corporate, institutional consultant; b. Keokuk, Iowa, Dec. 31, 1914; s. Harrie Richards and Elsie (Parsons) C.; m. Frances Cordelia Truax, Sept. 28, 1940; children: Michael Truax, Nicole Elyse Collins MacArthur, Copp Parsons. B.A., U. Redlands, 1938. Mgr. San Diego bur. UP, asst. Los Angeles bur., 1939-40; flight adminstrn., comml. sales supr. Convair Corp., 1942-47; owner Copp Collins Pub. Relations, San Diego and Beverly Hills, Calif., 1948-51; rep. pub. relations West Coast area MBS, N.Y.C., 1951-53, mgr. pub. relations, 1953-55; mgr. pub. relations Bahrain (Persian Gulf) Petroleum Co. Ltd., 1955-58; asst. to exec. v.p. Burns & Roe, Inc., N.Y.C., 1958-60; cons. pub. relations Copp Collins Assocs., N.Y.C. and Westport, Conn., 1960-61, pres., cons. pub. relations, 1963-67; v.p., dir. pub. relations Chirurg & Cairns, Inc., N.Y.C. and Boston, 1961-62, Friend-Reiss Advt., Inc., N.Y.C., 1962-63; pres. Collins & Lynge, Ltd., N.Y.C. and Norwalk, Conn., 1965-67; dir. mktg. merchandising N.Am. Soccer League, 1967-68; dir. info. Nat. Pro Soccer League, 1967-68; asst. to dir. communications Nixon for Pres.; Nixon-Agnew campaign coms.; asst. to dir. communications Office of Pres.-Elect, Washington and N.Y.C., 1968-69; asst. to sec. USDA, Washington, 1969; cons. pub. affairs Dept. State, 1969-70; cons. spl. asst. to dir. Peace Corps, 1970-71; asst. to sec., S.W. field rep. Dept. Interior, 1971-73; dir. regional ops. Fed. Energy Office; interagy. coordinator, asst. dir. exec. secretariat FEO-Fed. Energy Adminstrn.; cons. Nat. Energy Info. Center, FEA, 1973-75, Office of Energy Programs, Dept. Commerce, 1975-77; cons. energy and minerals div. GAO, 1977-78, Pres.'s Commn. on Coal, 1978-79, Burns & Roe, Inc., Washington, 1979; cons. to dir. Biomass div., cons. to asst. sec. fossil energy Dept. Energy, Washington, 1979-81; fed. and bus. cons., 1986—. Author, princ. investigator: NSF Biosaline Research and Arid Land Sciences: Application of New Scientific Knowledge and Advanced Technologies to the Arid Lands of the World, 1977. Chmn. public relations adv. council to So. Conn. chpts. ARC, 1955; press aide primary campaign Sen. Clifford Case, 1959-60, Ogden Reid for Congress Com., Westchester County, 1962, 64; bd. dirs. Northland Pioneer Coll. Found., Ariz., 1991—. Mem. Redlands U. Alumni Assn. (past chpt. chmn.), Pi Kappa Delta, Alpha Phi Gamma, Kappa Sigma Sigma. Republican. DIED 03/02/97. .

COLLINS, RICHARD JONATHAN, ballet director, author; b. Copdock, Suffolk, Eng., June 9, 1945; came to U.S., 1987; s. Lewis John and Diana Clavering (Elliot) C.; m. Diana Adeline Goedhuis, July 14, 1974 (div. 1987); children: Martha Thalia Daisy, Toby Jonathan Daniel; m. Elizabeth Leah Collins, Sept. 12, 1987; 1 child, Leah Kathryn. BA, Oxford (Eng.) U., 1966. Dancer Bolshoi Bailet, Moscow, 1968-73; dancer, ballet master London Festival Ballet, 1973-87; ballet master Cin. Ballet, 1988-90, artistic dir., 1990—; cons. Backstage at the Bolshoi, BBC-TV, London, 1987; coach to Natalia Makarova, Nat. Video, London, 1986-87. Author: Behind the Bolshoi Curtain, 1974, Minka, 1986; (musical) Cacaphonia, 1987; actor, dancer TV play Dancers, 1985. Mem. McDowell Soc. (hon.). Avocations: music, literature, tennis, travel.

COLLIS, CHARLES THEODORE MILLER, lawyer; b. Paget, Bermuda, Sept. 23, 1932; s. Charles T. and Mary Alfreda (Miller) C.; m. J. Margaret Ross, Apr. 22, 1957; children: John, Graham, Charles. BCom, Dalhousie U., Halifax, Can., 1953; MA, Oxford (Eng.) U., 1955. Bar: Eng. Assoc. Conyers Dill & Pearman, Hamilton, Bermuda, 1956-61, ptnr., 1962-98, sr. ptnr., 1992-98; dep. chmn. Bank of Bermuda, Ltd., Hamilton, 1984-98; chmn. BF&M, Hamilton, 1991-98. Govt. leader Bermuda Senate, 1982-92; min. without portfolio Bermuda Govt., 1982-84, min. for legis. affairs, 1984-87, min. for telecom., 1987-92. Recipient Justice of Peace award Bermuda Govt., 1982, Queen's Counsel award Queen of Eng., Officer of Brit. Empire award Brit. Govt., 1994. Mem. Hamilton C. of C. (pres. 1980-82), Royal Bermuda Yacht Club, R & A Golf Club of St. Andrews, Mid-Ocean Club. Mem. United Bermuda Party. Mem. Ch. of Eng. Avocations: skiing, golf, boating. Died Jan. 26, 1998.

COLQUITT, LANDON AUGUSTUS, mathematics educator; b. Fort Worth, Jan. 25, 1919; s. Fred Augustus and Maude Lena (Pyeatt) C.; m. Betsy Feagan, May 29, 1954; children: Clare E., Catherine A. B.A., Tex. Christian U., 1939; M.A., Ohio State U., 1941, Ph.D., 1948; postgrad., Calif. Inst. Tech., 1942. Asst. instr. math. Ohio State U., 1946-48; mem. faculty Tex. Christian U., 1948-89, prof. math., 1955-89, emeritus, 1989-91, chmn. dept., 1962-79; vis. faculty U. Tex., Austin, spring 1980; sr. nuclear engr. Convair, Fort Worth, summers 1955, 56. Served with USAF, 1942-46, ETO. Fellow AAAS, Tex. Acad. Scis. (past vice chmn.); mem. Am. Math. Soc., Math. Assn. Am., Soc. Indsl. and Applied Math., Phi Beta Kappa, Sigma Xi, Pi Mu Epsilon. Home: Fort Worth Tex. Died Dec. 19, 1991.

COLVIN, LLOYD DAYTON, electrical engineer; b. Spokane, Wash., Apr. 24, 1915; s. George R. and Edna M. Colvin; m. Iris Venita Atterbury, Aug. 11, 1939; 1 child, Joy Victoria. BS, U. Calif., 1938; grad., AUS Command Gen. Staff Coll., Ft. Leavenworth, Kans., 1947, U. Heidelberg, Fed. Republic of Germany, 1955. Registered elec., mech., constrn. and asbestos engr. Elec. engr. Pacific Gas and Electric Co., San Francisco, 1938-40; commd. 2d lt. U.S. Army, 1938, advanced through grades to col., ret., 1961; pres. Drake Builders, Richmond, Calif., 1962—. Co-author: (with Iris Colvin) How We Started Out Building Our Own Home in Our Spare Time and Went On to Make a Million Dollars in the Construction Business, 1967. Mem. Yasme Found. (pres.), various amateur radio clubs.

COMMAGER, HENRY STEELE, retired writer, history educator; b. 1902. Trustee, friends of Cambridge Univ. prof. history Columbia U., N.Y.C., 1938-56; prof. history Amherst Coll., Mass., 1956-72, Simpson lectr., 1972—; v.p. com. on effective Congress Amherst Coll. Author: (with Samuel Eliot Morison) The Growth of the American Republic, 2 vols., 1940, 10th edit. 1987, Theodore Parker: Yankee Crusader, 1936, (with A. Nevins) The Heritage of America, 1939, America: The Story of a Free People, 1943, 1966, Majority Rule and Minority Rights, 1944, The Story of the Second World War, 1945, The Blue and Gray, 1950, 1991, The American Mind, 1950, Living Ideas in America, 1951, Robert E. Lee, 1951, Freedom, Loyalty, Dissent, 1954, Joseph Story, 1956; (with G. Brunn) America, 1942, 1954, (with R.B. Morris) The Spirit of Seventy Six, 1958, rev. edit. 1975, Great Declaration, 1958, Great Proclamation, 1960, Crusaders for Freedom, 1962, History: Nature and Purpose, 1965, Freedom and Order, 1966, Search for a Usable Past, 1967, Was America a Mistake? 1968, The Commonwealth of Learning, 1968, The American Character, 1970, The Discipline of History, 1972, Jefferson, Nationalism and Englightenment, 1975, American Liberty, 1976, The Defeat of America, 1976, The Empire of Reason, 1977; editor: The Documents of American History, 1934, 10th edit. 1988, Tocqueville: Democracy in America, 1946, The St. Nicholas Anthology, 1948, Living Ideas in America, 1951, 1964, Atlas of American Civil War, 1959, Immigration in American History, 1961; Why the Confederacy Lost the Civil War, 1967, Britain Through American Eyes, 1974, The Spirit of Seventy-Six, 1975, Churchill's History of the English-Speaking Peoples, 1987, The Empire of Reason, 1982, The Era of Reform 1830-60, 1982, Fifty Basic Civil War Documents, 1982, North Webster's American Spelling Book, others. Died March 1998.

CONDIT, CARL WILBUR, history educator; b. Cin., Sept. 29, 1914; s. Arthur Thomas and Gertrude (Pletz) C.; m. Isabel Marion Campbell, June 19, 1943; children: Stephen Campbell (dec.), Richard Stuart, Kenneth Arthur. B.S. in Mech. Engring., Purdue U., 1936; M.A., U. Cin., 1939, Ph.D., 1941, L.H.D. (hon.), 1967; L.H.D. (hon.), Knox Coll., 1981; L.H.D., DePaul U., 1983; hon. fellow history sci., U. Wis., 1951-52. Instr. math. and mechanics ordnance tng. div. War Dept., Cin., 1941, War Prodn. Sch., Cin., 1941-42, Engring. Coll., U. Cin., 1942-44; asst. designing engr. bldg. dept. N.Y.C. R.R., Cin., 1944-45; asst. prof. Carnegie Inst. Tech., 1946-47; from instr. to asso. prof. Northwestern U., Evanston, Ill., 1945-46, 47-61; prof. history, art history and urban affairs Northwestern U., 1961-82, prof. emeritus, 1982-97; Research asso. Smithsonian Instn., 1966-67, mem. adv. council, 1973-78. Author: The Rise of the Skyscraper, 1952, American Building Art: The 19th Century, 1960, American Building Art: The 20th Century, 1961, The Chicago School of Architecture, 1964, (with others) Technology in Western Civilization, 1967, American Building: Materials and Techniques, 1968, Chicago 1910-29: Building, Planning, and Urban Technology, 1973, Chicago 1930-70: Building, Planning, and Urban Technology, 1974, The Railroad and the City: A Technological and Urbanistic History of Cincinnati, 1977, The Pioneer Stage of Railroad Electrification, 1895-1905, 1977, The Port of New York: A History of the Rail and Terminal System from the Beginning to Pennsylvania Station, 1980, The Port of New York: A History of the Rail and Terminal System from The Grand Central Electrification to the Present, 1981, (with Sarah Bradford Landau) Rise of the New York Skyscraper 1865-1913, 1996; editor: (with Eugene Ferguson) Technology and Culture, 1962-76. Recipient Abbott Payson Usher prize Soc. for History Tech., 1968; Civil Engring. History and Heritage award ASCE, 1971; Disting. Service award Chgo. chpt. AIA, 1980. Mem. ACLU, History Sci. Soc., Soc. Archtl. Historians (Disting. Achievement award Chgo. chpt. 1982), Soc. History Tech. (exec. coun. 1959-63, Leonardo da Vinci medal 1973). Office: Northwestern U Evanston IL 60208 Died Jan. 4, 1997.

CONE, EDWIN EARL, lumber company executive; b. Portland, Oreg., Aug. 10, 1916; s. Edwin Earle and Emma Louise (Ziegler) C.; m. June Elizabeth Woldt, Jan. 31, 1943; children: Barbara Jean, Richard Bruce, Susan Elizabeth (dec.), Douglas Earl, Gregory Paul. BA, Willamette U., 1941. Ptnr., gen. mgr. Cone Lumber Co., Goshen, Oreg., 1941-88, cons., 1988-95. Mayor City of Eugene, Oreg., 1958-69, councilman, 1953-54; state rep. from Lane County Oreg. State Legis., 1955, 57. Athletic field house, chapel named in honor of him and his wife Willamette U., Salem, Oreg.; orch. pit named in honor of him and his wife Hult Ctr. Performings Arts; endowed chair sch. bus. adminstrn. U. Oreg.; named Eugene's First Citizen, 1974, Boss Yr. Springfield Jaycees, 1979; recipient Bus. Adminstrn. Dean's Award U. Oreg., 1974, Pioneer Award, 1980. Mem. Masons, Al Kader Shrine, Travelers' Century Club, Knights Round Table, Eugene Country Club. Republican. Methodist. Died Feb. 19, 1995.

CONFALONIERI, CARLO CARDINAL, clergyman; b. Seveso, Milan, Italy, July 25, 1893; s. Giuseppe and Maria C. Laureate in Theology, also e dizitto canonico. Ordained priest Roman Catholic Ch., 1916, archbishop, 1941, elevated to Sacred Coll. Cardinals, 1958; pvt. sec. to Pope Pius XI, to Pope Pius XII; transferred to titular archbishopric of Nicopoli, al Nesto, 1950; titular bishop suburban see of Palestrina, 1972; entered order of cardinal bishops and Ostia, 1977; dean Coll. of Cardinals; prefect of Sacred Congregation for Bishops, 1967-73; sub-dean Coll. Cardinals, 1974-77; archpriest of Patriarchal Liberian Basilica, 1977—. Served with Italian Army, 1914-18. Decorated Medal of Merit.

CONGER, KYRIL B., urologist; b. Berlin, Germany, Apr. 11, 1913; s. Seymour Beach and Lucile (Bailey) C.; m. Joy Springer, June 1, 1945; children: Steven B., Kyril B. II, James W. and William T. (twins). A.B., U.

Mich., 1933, M.D., 1936. Instr. urology U. Mich. Hosp., 1941; urologist; med. group Honolulu, 1946-47; prof. urology, dept. head Temple U. Med. Sch. and Hosp., Phila., 1947-82; urologist VA Ctr., Ft. Meyers, Fla., 1982-87; chief urologist VA Outpatient Clinin, Ft. Meyers, Fla., 1987-96; area cons. urology VA Mid-Atlantic State and P.R. Contbr. articles to profl. jours.; Author: Transurethral Prostatic Surgery, 1964. Served from lt. to col. M.C. AUS, 1942-46; urology sect. 298th Gen Hosp. Fellow A.C.S.; mem. Am. Urological Assn., Sigma Xi, Nu Sigma Nu. Home: Fort Myers Fla. Died Sept. 11, 1996.

CONROY, THOMAS HYDE, lawyer; b. Beloit, Kans., Feb. 6, 1922; s. Thomas Emmett and Ida Ruth (Hyde) C.; m. Helen Regina Supple, Nov. 27, 1952; children: Thomas William, Sheila Anne, Regina Marie, Joseph Patrick (dec.). AB, U. Kans., 1945, LLB, 1949. Bar: Kans. 1949. Assoc. Ralph H. Noah, Beloit, 1949-52; city atty. City of Beloit, 1953-55, 67-81; county atty. County of Mitchell, Kans., 1957-65; ptnr. Hamilton & Conroy, 1965; pvt. practice law Beloit, 1965-97; owner, developer Conroy Place, 1965-97. Bd. dirs. Mitchell County Hist. Soc., Inc. 1972-97, 1st v.p., 1972-75, pres., 1975-77; trustee Mitchell County Hosp., 1965-87, pres. 1965-73, Marymount Coll. of Kans., 1983-88. Mem. ABA, Kans. Bar Assn., Am. Legion, Lions, KC (state adv. 1958-59), Phi Kappa, Phi Delta Phi.

CONTA, BART JOSEPH, mechanical engineering educator; b. Rochester, N.Y., Mar. 29, 1914; s. Joseph and Mary (Dalcin) C.; m. Ruth Fletcher, Nov. 26, 1937; children: Fred, Jacquelyn (Mrs. Frank Davidson), Susan; m. Claire Tallman, Mar. 26, 1989. B.S., U. Rochester, 1936; M.S., Cornell U., 1937. Registered profl. engr., N.Y. Instr. Cornell U., Ithaca, N.Y., 1937-40; asst. prof., assoc. prof. mech. engring. Cornell U., 1941-47, prof., 1951-84, prof. emeritus, 1984-93; research engr. Texaco Corp., Beacon, N.Y., 1940- 41; prof. mech. engring. Syracuse U., 1947-51; Ford Found. vis. prof. Universidad del Valle, Cali, Colombia, 1964-65. NSF fellow U. Calif. at Berkeley, 1967-68. Mem. AAAS, AAUP, Soc. for History Tech., Phi Beta Kappa, Sigma Xi, Tau Beta Pi, Pi Tau Sigma, Phi Kappa Phi. Clubs: Statler (past pres.), Tower. Home: Ithaca N.Y. Died Nov. 1, 1993.

CONVERTI, VINCENZO, computer systems company executive; b. Roseto, Italy, Nov. 27, 1925; came to U.S., 1949; s. Rocco and Maria Antoinette (Russo) C.; m. Marjorie Ruth Pefley, Sept. 12, 1951; children: Mark, David, Paul, Cathy. B.S. in E.E., U. Ariz.-Tucson, 1952, M.S. in E.E., 1956. Research engr. Ariz. Computer Research, Phoenix, 1955-59; systems engring. supr. Ariz. Pub. Service, Phoenix, 1959-67, systems engring. mgr., 1967-75, computer service mgr., 1975-85, computer systems mktg. dir., 1985-88; pres. Ariz. Computer Systems Internat., Payson, Ariz., 1988—. Contbr. in field. Fellow IEEE (chmn. power system engring. com. 1980-81). Republican. Died Nov. 27, 1925.

COOGAN, JEANMARIE D., editor; b. Phila., Oct. 26, 1925; d. John J. and Catherine (Dennehey) Dunn; m. Joseph P. Coogan, June 16, 1951; children—Kevin, Nell. A.B., Immaculata Coll., Pa., 1947. Editorial asst. Ladies Home Jour., Phila., 1947-52; editor-in-chief Nursing Mag., Springhouse, Pa., 1973—; v.p. editorial affairs Springhouse Corp., Springhouse, 1984—. Writer short stories for various mags. Mem. Am. Soc. Mag. Editors, Ednl. Press Assn. (recipient Golden Globe 1983), Am. Bus. Press (recipient Neal award 1981, 82, 83, 84). DIED 01/31/97. .

COOK, RICHARD WALLACE, retired aerospace engineer; b. Muskegon, Mich., Aug. 8, 1907; s. Harry James and Rose (Van Dame) C.; m. Helen L. Benson, Dec. 25, 1934. B.S., Mich. State U., 1933. Registered profl. engr., Wis. Marine constrn. Gt. Lakes area, 1933-35; resident engr. in charge constrn. Consoer, Townsend & Quinlan (cons. engrs.), 1935-40; dep. mgr. Oak Ridge operations AEC, 1947-49, mgr., 1949-51; dir. prodn. AEC, Washington, 1951, asst. gen. mgr. mfg., 1954; dep. gen. mgr. AEC, 1954-58; dir. adminstrn. govt. products group Am. Machine and Foundry Co., 1958-59; divisional v.p., dep. group exec., also group exec. Atomic Energy Group, AMF, 1959-61, v.p., dep. group exec. Titan program and govt. products group; dir. AMF Atomics Can., Ltd., 1959-61, dir. atomics and adminstrv. divs., 1962; corporate v.p. spl. products Advance Products Group AMF, 1962-64; asst. dir. research and devel. operations, dep. dir. operations, sci. and engring. Marshall Space Flight Center, NASA, Huntsville, Ala., 1964-69; dep. dir. mgmt. Marshall Space Flight Center, NASA, 1969-73; ret., 1973. Served from 1st lt. to col., Q.M.C., C.E. AUS, 1940-47. Decorations include Legion of Merit, Army Commendation ribbon, Meritorious Service Unit Star; recipient Mich. State U. Centennial award, 1955; AEC Distinguished Service award, 1956; Exceptional Service medal NASA, 1969; Distinguished Service medal NASA, 1973. Mem. ASCE, Phi Kappa Tau, Blue Key, Scabbard and Blade. Club: Elks. Home: Pinehurst N.C. Died Oct. 26, 1992; buried Pinelawn Meml. Park, Pinehurst, N.C.

COOK, WALTER MCQUEEN, lawyer; b. Selma, Ala., Jan. 29, 1915; s. Wlater PItts and Mattie Julia (McQueen) C.; m. Norma Webster Rogers, June 15, 1938; children: Norma McQueen, Julia Cook Melson, Walter, Kathryn Cook Satchfield. Student, U. Ala., 1933, Hill Coll., 1934; LLB, LLM, George Washington U., 1948. Bar: D.C. 1948. Examiner Office of Price Adminstrn., Selma and Mobile, Ala., 1943-47; sr. ptnr. Lyons, Pipes & Cook, Mobile, 1949-82, of counsel, 1982—. Pres. Mobile Azalea Trail, 1952, Am.'s Jr. Miss Pageant, Mobile, 1962, Mobile County Wildlife Assn., 1964, Ala. Wildlife Fedn., Montgomery, 1968, Ala. Wildlife Endowment, Mobile, 1968—. Mem. ABA, D.C. Bar Assn., Ala. Bar Assn., Mobile Bar Assn., Ala. Judicature Soc., Fedn. Ins. Counsel. Club: Athelstan, Mobile Country, Bienville.

COOKE, HARRIET LEVITER, art historian, writer; b. White Plains, N.Y., Feb. 14, 1935; d. Aaron Leon and Anne (Drozin) L.; m. William Barrie Cooke, Feb. 7, 1957 (separated 1964); children: Liadin, Julia. BA, Brandeis U., 1956. Designer Poet's Theater, N.Y.C. and Cambridge, Mass., 1955-56, Ballet Theatre, N.Y., 1956; writer, critic Irish Times, Dublin, Ireland, 1967—, The Guardian, London, 1969—; writer British Broadcasting Corp., Belfast, No. Ireland, 1973; curator Artist's Choice Ulster Mus., Belfast, 1973; critic ArtNews, N.Y., 1970—; writer, critic New Nation, Dublin, 1988—; cons. pvt. and pub. art collections in U.S. and Europe, 1969—. Author: Pictures Don't Lie, 1984; contbr. articles to profl. jours. Recipient First Prize in Painting Young Artists, 1951. Mem. Assn. Internationale des Critiques d'Art, Nat. Union Journalists, Internat. Fedn. Journalists, Fizwilliam Turner Soc., Press Club of London. Jewish. Avocation: reading.

COOKE, JACK KENT, diversified company executive; b. Hamilton, Ont., Can., Oct. 25, 1912; s. Ralph Ercil and Nancy (Jacobs) C.; m. Barbara Jean Carnegie, May 5, 1934 (div.); children: Ralph Kent (dec.), John Kent; m. Jeanne Maxwell Williams, Oct. 31, 1980 (div.); m. Marlena Ramallo, May 5, 1990. Student, Malvern Collegiate. Ptnr. Thomson Cooke Newspapers, 1937-52; pres. Sta. CKEY, Toronto, Ont., Can., 1944-61, Liberty of Can. Ltd., 1947-61, Toronto Maple Leaf Baseball Club Ltd., 1951-64; chmn. bd., pres. Consol. Press Ltd., 1952-61; chmn. Cooke Properties Inc. (Chrysler & Kent Bldgs, N.Y.C.), 1966-97, Jack Kent Cooke Inc., 1976-97, Pro-Football Inc., Washington Redskins, NFL, 1960-97; pres. Calif. Sports, Inc. (Los Angeles Lakers, NBA, Los Angeles Kings, NHL), 1965-79; chmn., CEO Teleprompter Corp., 1974-81; chmn. Cooke Media Group, Inc. (Daily News), Los Angeles, 1985-97, Elmendorf Farm, Inc., Lexington, Ky., 1985-97. Trustee Little League Found. Mem. Nat. Athletic Inst. (bd. dirs.). Died April 6, 1997.

COONEY, ROBERT JOHN, lawyer; b. Chgo., May 30, 1924; s. Harry Michael and Loretta (Gallagher) C.; m. Noreen Walsh, Mar. 17, 1951 (dec. 1978); children: Robert John Jr., John Devitt, Nora Jane; m. Linda Williams Fite, Apr. 27, 1985. Student, St. Mary's Coll., 1941, Loyola U., Chgo., 1946-47; JD, U. Detroit, 1950. Bar: Ill. 1950, U.S. Dist. Ct. (no. dist.) Ill. 1958, U.S. Supreme Ct. 1977. Asst. state's atty. Cook County, Chgo., 1950-58; ptnr. Cooney and Stenn, Chgo., 1958-84, Robert J. Cooney & Assocs., Chgo., 1984-88, Cooney & Conway, Chgo., 1989—. Sgt. U.S. Army, 1942-46. Fellow Am. Coll. Trial Lawyers; mem. ABA, Ill. State Bar Assn., Chgo. Bar Assn., Ill. Trial Lawyers Assn., Lake Geneva Country Club, Saddle & Cycle Club. Democrat. Roman Catholic. Avocations: skiing, golf. Died Feb. 11, 1995.

COOPER, CLARE DUNLAP, civic worker, writer; b. Berkeley, Calif., Nov. 1, 1938; d. Claude and Mathilda (Egger) D.; m. William Secord Cooper, July 22, 1964; children: Constance, Edwin, Emily. AA, Cottey Coll., Nevada, Mo., 1958; BA, U. Calif., Berkeley, 1960; MA, San Francisco State U., 1981. Tchr. drama and English Istanbul, Turkey, 1960-63; pipe organist in concert and in svc. to various chs., 1989-94; writer for local newspapers, Orinda and Lafayette, Calif. Author: (play) Good and Perfect Gifts, 1988; author poems, adaptations and short plays related to teaching. Tchr. music, drama and English as second lang. local schs. and community ctrs., 1970-88. Avocations: music, hiking, cooking, traveling, gardening. Home: Orinda Calif. Deceased.

COOPER, MARIO, artist, educator; b. Mexico City, Nov. 26, 1905; came to U.S., 1915; s. Louis Rodgrigo and Maria (Garfias Hidalgo y Costilla) C.; m. Aileen Whetstine, Feb. 26, 1927 (div. Apr. 1964); children: Vincent, Patricia; m. G. Dale Meyers, Oct. 1964. Student, Otis Art Inst., L.A., 1924, Chouinard Art Sch., L.A., 1925, Grand Cen. Art Sch., N.Y.C., 1927-37; pupil, F. Tolles Chamberlin, Louis Treviso, Pruett Carter, Harvey Dunn; BA, Strategic Air Command, 1989. Staff artist Tracey Locke & Dawson, Dallas, 1925, Honig Cooper Advt., San Francisco, 1926; freelance artist L.A., San Francisco, N.Y.C., 1926-27; visualizer and layout man Batten, Barton, Durstine & Osborne, N.Y.C., 1927-28; instr. illustration, advt. art Columbia U., 1937-41, Grand Cen. Art Sch., 1941-45, Art Students League, 1945, Vets. Class, Soc. Illustrators, 1945-50, Pratt Inst., 1950-57; tchr. watercolor Art Students League, from 1957; inst. watercolor Nat. Acad. Sch. Fine Arts, 1959; guest instr. Mcpl. Mus. Art, Springfield, Mo., 1961, Laguna Beach Art Assn., 1962; lectr. CCNY, 1962-67; art cons. USAF, 1959; pres. U.S. com. Internat. Assn. Plastic Arts, UNESCO, 1976-77. Author: Flower Painting in Watercolor, 1962, Drawing and Painting the City, 1967, Painting with Watercolor, Mario Cooper, 1972, Watercolor by Design, Mario Cooper, 1980; paintings in collection USAF Acad.; illustrator stories by P.G. Woodhouse, Alfred Noyes, Gouverneur Norris, Quentin Reynolds, Clarence Budington Kelland, Agatha Christie, Eric Maria Remarque; represented in permanent collections Met. Mus. Art, N.Y.C., Libr. of Congress, Libr. Royal Soc. Arts, London, NAD, Butler Inst. Am. Art, Reading (Pa.) Pub. Mus., Adelphi Coll.; represented at St. Luke's Hosp., Denver, Madonna and Child; exhibited sculpture Third Internat. Sculpture Phila., 1949, Pa. Acad., 1948-51, Nat. Acad., 1947, 49-51, other water colors various acads. and soc. shows, Exch. Exhbn. Royal Painters in Watercolor, London, 1962, Ichiban Gallery, Tokyo, Fuji Daimaru Gallery, Kyoto, Japan; work represented in permanent collection U.S. Navy. Brig. gen. USAF, 1954, 56. Recipient 1st award NAD, 1956, Samuel F.B. Morse medal, 1967, medal of achievement Inst. Art Mex., 1970, Greathouse medal, 1978, also various gold and 1st awards for sculpture and watercolor. Fellow Royal Soc. Arts (London); mem. NAD, Royal Watercolor Soc. (hon.), Audubon Artists (hon. pres. 1954-58, Gold medal of honor 1974, Silver medal 1979, Ralph Fabri medal 1978), Soc. Illustrators (life), Nat. Sculptors Soc., Artists Guild (v.p. N.Y. chpt. 1936), Am. Watercolor Soc. (pres. from 1959-86, now pres. emeritus, Gold medals of honor 1974, 89), Nat. Acad. (coun. 1973-76), Watercolor Soc. Mex. (hon.), Australian Watercolor Soc. (hon.), Can. Soc. Painters in Water Color (hon.), Century Assn., Officers Club (hon.), Salmagundi Club (hon., medal of honor 1980). Commd. by NASA to document Apollo 10 and Apollo 11 flights to moon at Cape Kennedy, 1969; commd. by EPA to document the environment. Home: New York N.Y. Died July 19, 1995.

COOPER, NELSON JESS, biologist; b. Orwell, N.Y., Mar. 26, 1936; s. Clarence Stephan Cooper and Rosetta Jane (Cronk) Babcock Cooper. AA in Environ. Studies, L.A. City Coll., 1978; BS in Gen. Biology, Calif. State U., L.A., 1983, postgrad., 1983-84, 84-86. Lab. asst., asst. lab. technician Roswell Park Meml. Inst., Buffalo, 1958-60; emergency lab. technician Health Rsch. Inc., Buffalo, 1960-69; tutor biology and math. L.A. City Coll., L.A., 1976-78, tchg. asst. bio-organic chemistry, 1981-82; greenhouse asst. Calif. State U., L.A., 1982, tutor various scis., 1982-91, environ. impact surveyor, 1983, computer programmer, 1988-91; animal health technician USDA, Inglewood, Calif., 1992-97. Author (lab. guide) Electrophoresis of Serum Proteins, 1981, (booklet) Natural History of the Ostrich, 1994. With USAF, 1953-67, Korea. Mem. AAAS, Am. Mus. Natural History, Nat. Audubon Soc. Avocations: landscaping, gardening, astronomy, camping, photography. Died Jan. 13, 1997.

COOPER, PAUL, composer, educator; b. Victoria, Ill., May 19, 1926; m. Christine Ebert, April 30, 1953; 2 children. Studied with Ernest Kanitz, Halsey Stevens & Rogers Sessions, U. So. Calif., BA, 1950, MA, 1953, DMA, 1956; with Nadia Boulanger, Nat. Conservatory Paris & Sorbonne, 1953-54. Performer, 1953—; music critic Los Angeles Mirror, 1952-55, Ann Arbor News, 1959-65; minister music St. Matthews Luth. Ch., North Hollywood, Calif., 1954-55; faculty mem. U. Mich., Ann Arbor, 1955-68, prof. music, 1965-68, chmn. theory dept., 1966-68; prof. of composition U. Cinn. Coll. of Conservatory Music, 1969-74; now Lynette S. Autrey prof. music Rice U., Houston, prof. Shepherd Sch. Music, 1974-96; guest lectr. colls. and univs., 1968-96; composer in residence. Works including six symphonies, 1966, 71, 71, 73-75, 82-83, 87; six concertos, violin and orch., 1967, flute and orch., 1980-81, #2 violin and orch., 1980-82, organ and orch., 1982, saxaphone concerto, 1982, double concerto-violin, viola and orch.; eight instrumental works including Sinfonia for solo piano, 1989 (premiered by John Perry DA Camera Soc., Houston, Oct. 1989), Love Songs and Dances, 1985 (premiered by Cleve. Chamber Orch., 1985), four oratorios, 1970, 72, 76, 83; six string quartets, 1952, 54, 59, 63, 1963-64, 73, 77, six sonatas, 1962-63, 62-63, 62, 62, 64, 65; twelve chamber music pieces for various ensemlbles; 13 vocal/choral works and song cycles including Last Call, 1989 for soprano, flute, clarinet, piano, violin, viola, and cello (premiered DA Camera Soc., Houston, Oct. 1990), five additional keybd. works, 1962-63, 67, 69, 73, 80; author: Perspectives in Music Theory, 1973, Music for Sight Singing, 1980. Guggenheim fellow, 1965, 72; Martha Baird Rockefeller Found. grantee, 1966; recipient citation and award Am. Acad. & Inst. Arts & Letters, 1977. Mem. Music Tchrs. Nat. Assn. (v.p. 1975-77, exec. bd. 1977-96). Home: Houston Tex. Deceased.

COORTS, GERALD DUANE, horticulturist, educator, college dean; b. Emden, Ill., Feb. 3, 1932; s. Ralph Albert and Hannah Tena (Wubben) C.; m. Annette Bosman, Sept. 14, 1957; children: David Jonathan, Charles Frederick, Cynthia Anne. BS (Danforth summer fellow), U. Mo., 1954, MS, 1958; PhD, U. Ill., 1964. Instr. horticulture Purdue U., 1959-61; asst. prof. horticulture U. R.I., 1964-68; assoc. prof. plant and soil sci. So. Ill. U., Carbondale, 1968-72, prof., 1972-85, chmn. dept., 1973-85; prof., dean Coll. Agriculture and Home Econs. Tenn. Technol. U., Cookeville, 1985-94.

Bd. dirs. Jackson County YMCA, 1975-81, Green Earth, Inc., 1974-85; v.p. fin. Tech. Community Symphony Orch., 1990-91, v.p., 1991-92, pres., 1992-93; pres. Bryan Symphony Orch., 1992-93, bd. dirs., 1993-94; mem. tree bd., sec. City of Cookeville, 1991-94. 1st lt. Chem. Corps, U.S. Army, 1954-56. Recipient Obelisk award for outstanding teaching, 1972. Mem. U.S. Jr. C. of C. (chpt. v.p. 1966-67), Am. Soc. Hort. Sci., Am. Soc. Agronomy, Am. Hort. Soc., Coun. Agr. Sci. and Tech., Plant Growth Regulator Soc. Am., Soc. Am. Florists, Farmhouse (chpt. adviser 1986-94), Am. Assn. State Colls. Agriculture and Renewable Resources (pres.-elect 1988-89, pres. 1989-90, bd. dirs. 1990-93, sec. 1993-94, editor newsletter 1991-94), Soil and Water Conservation Soc. (pres. Tenn. coun. chpt. 1989-90), Nat. Resource Conservation Socs. of Tenn. (chmn. 1989-90), Kiwanis (bd. dirs. local chpt. 1983-84, pres. local chpt. 1984-85), Joint Coun. on Food and Agrl. Scis. USDA (nat. higher edn. com. 1991-94, sec. 1992-93), Rotary (bd. dirs. local chpt. 1987-88), Sigma Xi (chpt. pres. 1982-83, 87-88), Alpha Zeta, Gamma Sigma Delta, Pi Alpha Xi, Phi Mu Alpha, Phi Sigma, Phi Kappa Phi, Omicron Delta Kappa (faculty sec. local chpt. 1990-94). Home: Cookeville Tenn. Died June 11, 1994; interred Bellefountaine Cemetery, St. Louis, MO.

COPE, ALFRED HAINES, political scientist, educator; b. Oakbourne, Pa., May 29, 1912; s. Joseph and Ellen (Fussell) C.; m. Ruth Balderston, Aug. 23, 1937; 1 child, Joan. AB, Earlham Coll., 1934; postgrad., U. Chgo., 1939-40; PhD, U. Pa., 1948. Agt. Equitable Life Ins. Co., 1934-36; dir. Am. Friends Service Co., Chgo., 1936-38, War Relief Adminstrn., Spain, 1938-39; adminstrv. asst. U. Pa. Inst. Local and State Govt., 1940-42, instr., 1946-48; sr. adminstrv. aid. U.S. CSC, Phila., 1942-43; asst. prof. Syracuse (N.Y.) U., 1948-51, assoc. prof., 1951-56, asst. dean, prof. citizenship Utica Coll., 1956-60; asst. dean Coll. Liberal Arts Syracuse U., 1960-70; prof. citizenship Coll. Liberal Arts Syracuse (N.Y.) U., 1956-75, prof. polit. sci. Coll. Liberal Arts, 1962-75, univ. registrar and mgr. student data systems, 1970-74, prof. emeritus Coll. Liberal Arts, 1975-97; ad hoc arbitrator Am. Arbitration Assn., Phila., 1946-48. Author: Administration of Civil Service in Cities of the Third Class in Pennsylvania, 1948; (with Fred Krinsky) Franklin Roosevelt and the Supreme Court, 1952, rev. edit., 1969; Current Defense of the U.S., 1954; (with E.E. Palmer) The Dixon Yates Contract and the National Power Policy, 1955; The Basis for a New Legal System, 1973; Managing World Resources, 1975. Pres. bd. dirs. Syracuse Child and Family Svcs., 1963-66; arbitrator Syracuse BBB; trustee Oakwood Sch., Poughkeepsie, N.Y., 1974-90, treas., 1977-84, chmn. fin. com., 1984-87, pres. bd. mgrs., trustee, 1987-89; chmn. fin. com. sect. of Ams., Friends World Com., 1976-81, mem. world fin. group, 1975-81, del. triennial meeting, Gwatt, Switzerland, 1980; mem. Friends Assn. for Higher Edn.; co-clk. Task Force on Peace Studies, 1985-88; mem. ctrl. com. Friends Gen. Conf., 1978-84; chmn. devel. com., mem. exec. pers. and advancement coms.; mem. gen. svcs. com. N.Y. Yearly Meeting Religion Soc. Friends, 1978-81, chmn. com. sharing of world resources, 1981-85; mem. gen. bd. Pendle Hill, Wallingford, Pa., 1982-93; treas., trustee Syracuse Friends Meeting; trustee Lindley Murray Fund, 1984-94, chmn., 1992-94; mem. coord. com. witness sect. N.Y. Yearly Meeting of Friends, 1992-95, mem. sessions com., 1993-96, mem. com. on sufferings, 1994—, mem. fin. svcs. com. 1995—. Capt. AUS, 1943-46. Fellow AAAS; mem. Am. Acad. Polit. Sci., Friends Assn. Higher Edn., Acad. Polit. Sci., Friends Hist. Soc., Geneology Soc. Pa., Chester County Hist. Soc. (life), Phi Delta Kappa. Club: Torch (Syracuse) (pres. 1969-70). Died Aug. 1997.

CORDELL, ROBERT JAMES, retired geologist; b. Quincy, Ill., Jan. 7, 1917; s. Vail R. and Gertrude (Robison) C.; m. Frances Regina Sparacio, Sept. 20, 1942; children: Victor V., David M., Margaret L. B.S., U. Ill., 1939, M.S., 1940; Ph.D, U. Mo., 1949. Instr. U. Mo., Columbia, 1946-47; from instr. to asst. prof. Colgate U., Hamilton, N.Y., 1947-51; rsch. paleontologist, rsch. geologist, sr. rsch. geologist Sun Oil Co., Abilene, Tex., 1951-55; mgr. geol. rsch. Sun Oil Co., Richardson, Tex., 1955-63; sr. sect. mgr., sr. rsch. and profl. scientist Sun Co., Richardson, 1963-77; pres. Cordell Reports Inc., Richardson, 1977-92; mem. exec. bd. Potential Gas com., Colorado Springs, 1976-82. Co-editor: Problems of Oil Migration, 1981; contbr. articles to profl. jours., treatises. Bd. dirs. Richardson Community Concerts Inc., Tex., 1958-70, pres., 1963-64; bd. dirs. Richardson Symphony Inc., 1962-82, pres., 1970-71, chmn. bd., 1971-72; area chmn. James Collins Campaign for U.S. Senate, Richardson, 1982. Fellow AAAS (sr.), Geol. Soc. Am. (sr.); mem. Am. Assn. Petroleum Geologists (gen. chmn. nat. conv. 1975, Spl. Svc. award 1975, co-winner Spl. Pubs. award 1982), Dallas Geol. Soc. (hon. life, pres. 1977-78, Spl. Svc. award 1975, Rsch. Publ. award 1980), Soc. Sedimentary Geology. Episcopalian. Died Feb. 7, 1997.

CORDIER, HUBERT VICTOR, communications educator; b. North Canton, Ohio, Apr. 27, 1917; s. Emery Andrew and Minnie (Lahr) C.; m. Ruth Virginia Roop, Aug. 3, 1940; 1 child, Gary Michael. B.A., Manchester Coll., Ind., 1939; M.A., Mich. State U., 1942; Ph.D., U. Ill., 1955. Tchr., coach Columbia (Ind.) City High Sch., 1939-40; teaching fellow Mich. State U., 1940-42; asst. prof. speech Allegheny Coll., Meadville, Pa., 1946-49; head dept. radio and TV U. Ill. at Urbana, 1949-68; dir. broadcasting, prof. speech U. Iowa, Iowa City, 1968-90; head. div. broadcasting and film. U. Iowa; Bd. dirs., chmn. Nat. Ednl. Radio, Assn. Pub. Radio Stas. Served with USAAF, 1944-46. Mem. Assn. Profl. Broadcasting Edn. (pres., bd. dirs.), Nat. Assn. Ednl. Broadcasters (chmn. publs. com.), Am. Assn. U. Profs., Speech Assn. Am., Radio and TV News Dirs. Assn. Presbyterian. Home: Iowa City Iowa Died Dec. 10, 1990; buried Memory Gardens, Iowa City, IA.

COREY, DAVID See VERNON, DAVID LYLE

COREY, PAUL FREDERICK, author; b. Shelby County, Iowa, July 8, 1903; s. Edwin and Margaret Morgan (Brown) C.; m. Ruth Lechlitner, 1928; 1 dau., Anne Margaret. A.B. in Journalism, U. Ia., 1925. On staff The Economist, Chgo., 1925-26; with Retail Credit Co., N.Y.C., 1926; later with Ency. Brit.; with Real Estate Record and Builders Guide, N.Y.C., 1929-30, Nat. Ency., 1930-31; furniture designer Cavedale Craftsman. Author books, 1936-46; teen-age novel Five Acre Hill, 1946; novel Acres of Antaeus, 1946; juvenile The Little Jeep, 1946; Shad Haul, 1947, Corn Gold Farm, 1948, Homemade Homes, 1951, Milk Flood, 1956, Home Workshop Furniture Projects, 1957, Holiday Homes: A Build-it-yourself Handbook, How to Build Country Homes on a Budget; novel The Planet of the Blind; biography Bachelor Bess: My Sister; Do Cats Think? Notes of a Cat-Watcher, Are Cats People?, 1979; also short stories. Mem. Sci. Fiction Writers Am., Authors Guild. Guerrilla warfare specialist; did work on the subject in connection with First Service Command Tactical Sch., Sturbridge, Mass., 1942. Home: Sonoma Calif. Died Dec. 17, 1992.

CORN, JOSEPH EDWARD, JR., arts management consultant; b. St. Louis, Oct. 20, 1932; s. Joseph Edward and Melba (Goldberg) C.; m. Jane Wu, Feb. 3, 1989; children: Sophia Wu, Jason Joseph. BA, Yale U., 1954. Gen. mgr. August Opera Festival, St. Louis, 1960-64; pres. Theatrical Assocs., St. Louis, 1960-68; mgr. Western Opera Theater, San Francisco, 1969-74, San Francisco Opera, 1972-75; spl. asst. to exec. dir. Met. Opera, N.Y.C., 1975, dir. planning and pub. affairs, 1976-77; mgr. Opera Co. of Phila., 1977-80; dir. opera-mus. theatre program Nat. Endowment for Arts, Washington, 1980-81; exec. v.p., gen. dir. Wolf Trap Found. for Performing Arts, Vienna, Va., 1981-82; exec. prodr. Minn. Opera Co., St. Paul, 1982-86; pres. Arts Pacific, Inc., 1986—; producer Gateway Theater, St. Louis, 1963-66; dir. Performing Arts Office, Washington U., St. Louis, 1964-67; dir. publicity and pub. rels. St. Louis Mcpl. Opera and Entertainment Enterprises, 1967; ind. arts mgmt. cons., 1986—; cons. Opera Am., 1972-80, bd. dirs., mem. exec. com., 1977-80; mem. music adv. panel Nat. Endowment for Arts, 1972-76, mem. fed.-state reassessment steering com., 1976-77, mem. opera/mus. theater adv. panel, 1978-80; mem. performing arts and music adv. panels Calif. Arts Commn., 1973-75; pres. Am. Arts Alliance, 1977-79; trustee Nat. Opera Inst., 1977-80, 82-86; chmn. music adv. com., mem. coun. Yale U., New Haven, 1978-80; v.p. Greater Phila. Cultural Alliance, 1979-80. Bd. dirs. Nat. Com. on U.S.-China Rels., 1982-88, Midwest China Ctr., 1983-91, 1st All-Children's Theater, N.Y.C., 1983-85, Music Theater Group, Lenox Art Ctr., 1983-90, CenterFilms, St. Paul, 1986—, Minn. Ctr. for Arts Criticism, 1985-91, Asia Edn. Network, 1990-94, United Arts, St. Paul, 1991-92, Minn. Ctr. for Arts, Entertainment and the Law, 1993—, Met. Regional Arts Coun., 1993-94; active Ind. Com. on Arts Policy, N.Y.C., 1982-94; v.p. Fourth World Co., 1992—. Died Oct., 1997.

CORNUELLE, HERBERT CUMMING, corporate executive; b. Cin., Mar. 25, 1920; s. Herbert Cumming and Gertrude (Schleitzer) C.; m. Jean Bradbeer, Dec. 20, 1942; children: John, Richard, Bruce, Ann. A.B., Occidental Coll., 1941; postgrad., U. Denver, 1942. With Dole Corp., Honolulu, 1953-63, v.p., 1955-58, pres., dir., 1958-63; exec. v.p., dir. United Fruit Co., Boston, 1963-67, pres., 1967-69; exec. v.p. Dillingham Corp., Honolulu, 1969-70, pres., 1970-81; trustee Campbell Estate, Honolulu, 1982-90. Served to lt. USNR, 1942-45. Mem. Phi Beta Kappa. Clubs: Pacific (Honolulu), Oahu Country (Honolulu). Home: Honolulu Hawaii Died Aug. 20, 1996.

CORREA, GUSTAVO, educator; b. Colombia, Sept. 20, 1914; came to U.S., 1941, naturalized, 1956; s. Urbano and María (Forero) C.; m. Inés, Aug. 20, 1947; children: Amanda, Albert, Patricia. Licenciado, Escuela Normal Superior, Bogota, 1941; Ph.D., Johns Hopkins U., 1947. Nat. dir. secondary edn. Bogota, 1948-50; vis. prof. Spanish, U. Oreg., 1950-51; asso. prof. Spanish, Tulane U., 1951-54, U. Chgo., 1954-56, U. Pa., 1956-59; prof. Spanish, Yale U., 1959-95; Co-editor Hispanic Rev., 1958-60, adv. editor, 1960-95. Author: El espíritu del mal en Guatemala; ensayo de semántica cultural, 1955, La Poesía mítica de Federico García Lorca, 1957, El simbolismo religioso en las novelas de Pérez Galdós, 1962, Realidad, Ficcíon y símbolo en las novelas de Pérez Galdós, 1966, Poesía española del siglo Veinte, Antología, 1972, Antología de la poesía española, 1900-1980 (2 vols.), 1980. Mem. Hispanic Soc. Am., N.Am. Acad. Spanish Lans. Home: Saint Petersburg Fla. Died Feb. 15, 1995.

CORRIGAN, ROBERT EMMETT, psychologist; b. Chgo., Sept. 25, 1920; s. Lawrence Michael and Winifred (Gavin) C.; m. Betty Elise Odenwald, July 22, 1945; children: Robert Emmett, Ward Lawrence, Gavin Joseph. BA, U. Wis., 1947, MA, 1949; PhD, Tulane U., 1954. Project dir. Am. Inst. Rsch., Pitts., 1954-56; human factors specialist Douglas Aircraft Co., Long Beach, Calif., 1956-58; pres. R.E. Corrigan & Assocs., Garden Grove, Calif., 1958; assoc. prof. U. So. Calif., L.A., 1958-61; prof. dept. edn. Orange State Coll., 1960-63; dir. programming svcs. Nat. Edn. Scis. Corp., Anaheim, Calif., 1963-64; v.p. instructional materials div. Litton Industries, Anaheim, 1965-68; pres., chmn. bd. dirs. Inst. of Effective Learning, Inc., Garden Grove, Calif. and New Orleans, 1968-95; chmn. dept. instructional system technology for master's degree program, grad. dept. edn. Chapman Coll., Orange, 1965-69; developer plans and instructional materials Job Corps Camp Atterbury, Indpls., Systematic Approach for Effectiveness tng. programs, 1968-95; installed Systematic Approach for Effectiveness Learner-Centered Mgmt. and Curriculum System in Duval County Pub. Schs., Jacksonville, Fla., 1969-95, Moss Point (Miss.) Sch. System, 1982-95, South Panola Sch. System, Batesville, Miss., 1984-95, schs. in Calif., New Orleans, Tex., Iowa, 1989-95; lectr. UCLA, Tulane U.; cons. USAF air tng. command hdqrs. Randolph AFB, Calif. Dept. Edn., Nat. Def. Edn. Adminstrn. Author: Self-Sufficiency for Our Citizens and Community, 1987, (with Betty O. Corrigan) Demystifying the Building of Competent Learners: What Works and Why!, 1990, (with others) Quality Controlled Schooling: Building a Competitive Workforce and Economy, 1990, Graduates with Competitive Skills: A Blueprint for Predictable Success, 1993; developer, field tester Tutorials in Science (54 titles), 1960-64; author (video) Every Kid Can Be a Winner, Building Successful Learners; contbr. articles to profl. jours.; patentee in field. Chmn. human factors subcom. Gov.'s Indsl. Safety Conf., 1959-61. Dir. tng. Operation PEP (Preparing Ednl. Planners) program, Calif., 1965-69. Served to capt. USAAF, 1941-46; ETO. Decorated D.F.C., Air medal with 7 clusters, Purple Heart; SAFE System cited U.S. Gen. Acctg. Office, 1993-95. Mem. Nat. Soc. Programmed Instrn., Sigma Xi. Democrat. Roman Catholic. Home: New Orleans La. Died Feb. 9, 1995; interred Metairie Cemetery, New Orleans, LA.

CORTISSOZ, PAUL, English language educator; b. N.Y.C., Nov. 9, 1924; s. Alfred and Helen (O'Brien) C.; m. Geraldine Smith, Aug. 27, 1949; children: Anne, Celia Jo, Marie. B.A., Manhattan Coll., 1947; M.A., Columbia, 1949; Ph.D., N.Y.U., 1955. Instr. Manhattan Coll., Bronx, N.Y., 1947-53; asst. prof. Manhattan Coll., 1953-58, asso. prof., 1958-64, prof., 1964-91, head English and world lit. dept., 1963-67, 70-78. Author: (with Francis Davy) Perspectives for College, 1963. Served with USAAF, 1942-45. Recipient Founders Day award N.Y.U., 1955. Mem. Modern Lang. Assn., AAUP. Home: Scarsdale N.Y. Died April 24, 1991; interred Calvary Cemetery, N.Y.

COSELL, HOWARD (HOWARD WILLIAM COHEN), sports journalist; b. Winston-Salem, N.C., Mar. 25, 1918; s. Isidore and Nellie Cohen; m. Mary Edith Abrams, 1944; children: Jill, Hilary. Grad., NYU, 1940; hon. doctorate, Johns Hopkins U., Wilmington Coll., U.S. Sports Acad. Pvt. practice, until 1956; sportscaster ABC, 1956-85; commentator ABC Radio, 1953-92; mem. faculty Yale U., 1974-80; newspaper columnist N.Y. Daily News, 1986-88; lectr. in field; TV talk show host Speaking of Everything, 1988. Appeared in (films) Bananas, The World's Greatest Athlete, Broadway Danny Rose; (TV) Sonny and Cher Show, The Partridge Family; guest host Tonight Show, Dick Cavett Show, Mike Douglas Show, Merv Griffin Show; Dean Martin Show, Flip Wilson Show, Laugh-In, Odd Couple, various Bob Hope specials, various Danny Thomas specials, Sonny Bono Show, David Letterman Show, Sports Reporters, Wall Street Week, Crossfire, Good Morning America; Saturday Night Live with Howard Cosell; commentator ABC's Monday Night Football, 1970-83; author: Cosell, 1973, Like It Is, 1974, I Never Played the Game, 1985, What's Wrong with Sports, 1991; editor NYU Law Rev. Nat. chmn. Multiple Sclerosis, 1976. Served to maj. AUS, World War II. Recipient Bob Considine award St. Bonaventure U., 1984, Order of Leather Helmet NFL Alumni Assn., 1986, Ronald Reagan Media award U.S. Sports Acad., 1986, Sports Journalist of All Time award U.S. Sports Acad., 1987, 2 Emmy award for Sportsbeat by Internat. Radio and TV Soc.; named Broadcaster of Yr. Internat. Radio and TV Soc., 1974; inducted into Jewish Sports Hall of Fame, 1983; scholarship in journalism named in his honor Brown U., 1985; Howard and Mary Edith Cosell Ctr. for Phys. Edn. created in their honor at Hebrew U., Jerusalem, 1985. Mem. ABA (apptd. chmn. elect sports law com. sect. tort and ins. practice 1986), Phi Beta Kappa. Home: New York N.Y. Died Apr. 23, 1995.

COSTAIN, CECIL CLIFFORD, retired physicist; b. Ponoka, Alta., Can., June 16, 1922; s. Henry Hudson and Elida Mary (Eakin) C.; m. Cynthia Hazell Ewing, July 26, 1949; children: Linda Carol, Charles Gordon. B.A. with hons, U. Sask. (Can.), 1941, M.A., 1947; Ph.D., Cambridge U., Eng., 1951. With spectroscopy sect. div. physics NRC Can., Ottawa, Ont., 1951-71; head time and frequency sect. div. physics

NRC Can., 1972-85, part-time elec. and time standards sect., 1985-87; prin. research officer NRC Can. Contbr. numerous articles to profl. jours. Served to lt. comdr. RCNVR, 1942-45. Decorated D.S.C.; Exhbn. of 1851 scholar, 1947. Fellow Royal Soc. Can., IEEE; mem. Can. Assn. Physicists (pres. 1980).

COTTON, DANA MESERVE, educational consultant; b. Wolfeboro, N.H., Oct. 17, 1905; s. Jacob Henry and Sarah Frances (Meserve) C.; m. Margaret Fenner Berry, Dec., 1972; children by previous marriage—John Pierce, Rebecca. A.B., U. N.H., 1928, LL.D., 1968; Ed.M., Harvard U., 1943; postgrad., Columbia Tchrs. Coll., Oxford (Eng.) U.; LL.D., Am. Internat. Coll., 1953, U. N.H., 1970; Ed.D., Tufts U., 1955; L.H.D., New Eng. Coll., 1959; D.Sc., Nasson Coll., 1972. Dir. guidance Maine Dept. Edn., Augusta, 1940-44; asst. to dean admissions, mem. bd. freshman advisers Harvard, 1944-72, sec. faculty edn., 1957-72; acting dean Harvard (Grad. Sch. Edn.), 1971-72; cons. edn. and industry, 1972—; Rec. sec. New Eng. Sch. Devel. Council, 1950-72; mem. edn. com. New Eng. Council, 1954-72, New Eng. Council Econ. Devel., 1949-72; exec. sec.-treas. New Eng. Assn. Colls. and Secondary Sch., 1947-70. Mem. New Eng. Citizens Crime Commn., 1966-72. Episcopalian. Club: Mason.

COUDERT, FERDINAND WILMERDING, lawyer; b. N.Y.C., Feb. 9, 1909; s. Frederic Rene and Alice Tracy (Wilmerding) C.; m. Helen F. Carey, Oct. 14, 1942; dec. Oct. 1971. A.B. magna cum laude, Harvard, 1930, A.M., 1933; LL.B., Columbia, 1937. Bar: N.Y. 1938. Practiced in N.Y.C., 1938—; mem. firm Coudert Bros., 1938-64. Past pres. bd. Brez Found.; bd. dirs., past v.p. Humanities Fund; past sec., bd. dirs. C.T. Loo Chinese Ednl. Fund. Served from 1st lt. to maj. AUS, 1942-46. Fellow Frick Collection.; mem. Soc. Colonial Wars. Clubs: Paris American (past pres.); Century (N.Y.C.), University (N.Y.C.), Sky (N.Y.C.); Union Interalliee (Paris). Died Sept. 15, 1997.

COUSTEAU, JACQUES-YVES, marine explorer; b. St.-André-de-Cubzac, France, June 11, 1910; s. Daniel P. and Elizabeth (Duranthon) C.; m. Simone Melchior, July 11, 1937 (dec. 1990); children: Jean-Michel, Philippe (dec.); m. Francine Triplet, 1992; children: Diane Elizabeth, Pierre-Yves Daniel. Bachelier, Stanislas Acad., Paris, 1927; midshipman, Brest Naval Acad., 1930; DSc, U. Calif., Berkeley, 1970, Brandeis U., 1970, Rensselaer Poly. Inst., 1979, Harvard U., 1979, U. Ghent, Belgium, 1983, U. Valence, 1990; degree (hon.), U. Bucharest, Romania, 1993, Am. U. of Paris, 1994. Founder Groupe d'etudes et de recherches sous-marines, Toulon, France, 1946; founder, pres. Campagnes océanographiques françaises, Marseille, 1950, Centre d'etudes marines avancees (formerly Office Francais de recherches sous-marines), Marseille, 1953; leader Calypso Oceanog. Expdns.; dir. Oceanog. Mus., Monaco, 1957-88, ret., 1988; promoted Conshelf saturation dive program, 1962; sec. gen. Internat. Commn. Scientific Exploration of the Mediterranean, 1966; sec. gen. Internat. Commn. Sci. Exploration Mediterranean leader sci. cruise around the world, 1967, basis for TV series The Undersea World of Jacques-Yves Cousteau; leader expedn. to Antarctic and Chilean coast, 1972, expdn. to Amazon, 1982-84, Mississippi, 1984. Rediscovery of World (Haiti, Cuba, Marquesas Islands, New Zealand, Australia, etc.), 1985-94; lectr., spkr. at numerous worldwide confs. and assns.; chmn. Coun. for the Rights of Future Generations, France, 1993; mem. UN High Level Adv. Bd., mem. World Bank Adv. Group on Sustainable Devel. Films include The Silent World, 1956 (Grand Prix, Gold Palm award Cannes Film Festival 1956, Acad. award Motion Picture Acad. Arts and Scis. for best documentary feature 1957), The Golden Fish, 1959 (Gold Palm award Cannes Film Festival 1959, Acad. award 1959), The World Without Sun, 1965 (Acad. award for best short film 1965), The Secret Societies of Dolphins and Whales, 1994 (Emmy for rsch. documentary 1964); author and producer documentary films which received awards at Paris, Cannes and Venice film festivals; producer over 100 films for TV; TV series include The World of Jacques-Yves Cousteau, 1966-68, The Undersea World of Jacques-Yves Cousteau, 1968-76, Oasis in Space, 1977, The Cousteau Odyssey Series, 1977-81, The Cousteau/Amazon Series, 1982-84; TV spls. include The Tragedy of the Red Salmon, The Desert Whales, Lagoon of Lost Ships, The Dragons of Galapagos, Secrets of the Sunken Caves, The Unsinkable Sea Otter, A Sound of Dolphins, South to Fire and Ice, The Flight of Penguins, Beneath the Frozen World, Blizzard of Hope Bay, Life at the End of the World, (film series) Cousteau's Rediscovery of the World I, 1985-91, Rediscovery of the World II, 1992-94; author: Par 18 mètres de fonds, 1946, La Plongée en scaphandre, 1950, The Silent World, 1952, (editor with James Dugan) Captain Cousteau's Underwater Treasury, 1959, (with James Dugan) The Living Sea, 1963, World Without Sun, 1965, (with Philippe Cousteau) The Shark: Splendid Savage of the Sea, 1970, (with Philippe Cousteau) Life and Death in a Coral Sea, 1971, Diving for Sunken Treasure, 1971, The Whale: Mighty Monarch of the Sea, 1972, Octopus and Squid, 1973, Three Adventures: Galapagos- Titicaca- the Blue Holes, 1973, (20 vol. ency.) The Ocean World of Jacques Cousteau, 1973, Diving Companions, 1974, Dolphins, 1975, Jacques Cousteau: The Ocean World, 1979, A Bill of Rights for Future Generations, 1980, The Cousteau Almanac of the Environment, 1981, Jacques Cousteau's Calypso, 1983, Jacques Cousteau's Amazon Journey, 1984, (with Yves Paccalet) Jacques Cousteau--Whales, 1988; contbr. articles to Nat. Geographic Mag.; co-inventor: (with Emile Gagnan) aqualung, 1943 (with Malavard and Charrier) turbosail system, 1985. Lt. de vaisseau French Navy, WWII. Decorated comdr. legion of Honor, Croix de Guerre with palms, merite Agricole, merite Maritime, officer des Arts et des Lettres; recipient Potts medal Franklin Inst., 1970, Gold medal Grand Prix d'Oceanographie Albert I, 1971, UN Internat. award for the Environment, 1977, Presdl. medal of Freedom, 1985, Founders award Internat. Coun. Nat. Acad. Arts and Scis., 1987, Centennial award Nat. Geog. Soc., 1988, 3d Internat. Catalan prize, 1991, Oceanus award Diving Equipment Mfg. Assn., 1997, Water Watch award Nat. Marine Mfrs. Assn., 1997; inducted into TV Hall of Fame, 1987; recipient James Smithson Bicentennial medal Smithsonian Inst., 1996. Fgn. assoc. NAS U.S.A.; mem. Academie Francaise. Died June 25, 1997.

COWAN, CAROLYN CANNON, retired early childhood education educator; b. Slocomb, Ala., Mar. 28, 1924; d. Warren Denson and Leila (Reese) Cannon; m. Clinard Hartwell Cowan, Sept. 6, 1944; children: Carol Cowan Allen, Patricia Cowan Thompson, Nancy Cowan Swanson. Student, Judson Coll., 1942-44; BA in Edn., U. S.C., Aiken, 1981. Tchr. South Aiken Presbyn. Kindergarten, Aiken, S.C., 1960-68; tchr. First Bapt. Ch. Kindergarten, Aiken, 1968-80, tchr., dir., 1980-92, ret., 1992; past dir. First Bapt. Ch. Kindergarten. Mem. DAR, Town and Country, Cereus Garden Club. Baptist. Avocations: travel, crafts, sewing, reading, painting. Died Dec. 6, 1995.

COWAN, J MILTON, linguist; b. Salt Lake City, Feb. 22, 1907; s. James Brimley and Mabel Vickers (Brown) C.; m. Theodora Mary Ronayne, Sept. 1, 1934; children: J Ronayne, Bruce Milton, Julia. A.B., U. Utah, 1931, A.M., 1932; fellow, U. Calif. at Berkeley, 1932-33; Ph.D., U. Iowa, 1935; student, Univ. of Leipzig, Germany, 1929-30. Rsch. assoc. U. Iowa, 1935-38; asst. prof. German, 1938-41, asso. prof., 1942; dir. intensive lang. program Am. Council Learned Socs., 1942-46; also spl. cons. War Dept. in charge of lang. phase of tng. programs in war and state depts., prof. linguistics, dir. div. modern langs. Cornell U., 1946-72; pres. Spoken Lang. Services, Inc., 1972-93; asso. with Linguistic Inst. sponsored by Linguistic Soc. as prof. or lectr. U. Mich., 1938, 40, U. N.C., 1941, U. Wis., 1944, U. Mich., summer 1948. Author: Pitch and Intensity Characteristics of American Stage Speech; Co-author: Conversational Arabic; Editor: A Dictionary of Modern Written Arabic. Fellow Acoustical Soc. Am.; mem. Am. Council Learned Socs. (dir. 1956-60), Linguistic Soc. Am. (sec.-treas., bus. mgr. pubs. 1939-50, pres. 1966), Sigma Xi. Home: Ithaca N.Y. Died Dec. 20, 1993; buried Lakeview Cemetery, Ithaca, N.Y.

COWEN, ROBERT HENRY, lawyer; b. Williamston, N.C., Jan. 16, 1915; s. Henry Herbert and Jenette (Mobley) C.; m. Sue Henderson, Aug. 6, 1953; children: Robert H., Susan Carol, Sarah Cantrell. JD, LLB, Wake Forest Coll., 1942. Bar: N.C. 1942, U.S. Supreme Ct. 1962. Practiced in Williamston, 1975-95; atty. U.S. Dept. Labor, Richmond, 1945-46; counsel to com. on mcht. marine and fisheries U.S. Ho. of Reps.; U.S. atty. Eastern dist. N.C., 1961-69; counsel, joint com. on printing U.S. Senate, 1969-75. Mayor Town of Williamston, 1947-57, 75-85; mem. N.C. Senate, 1957-58; bd. dirs. N.C. League Municipalities, 1947-49, 78-79. With USNR, World War II. Mem. ABA, N.C. Bar Assn., Jr. C. of C., Am. Legion, Rotary, Roanoke Country Club. Baptist. Home: Williamston N.C. Died Nov. 6, 1995; buried Woodlawn Cemetery.

COX, JOHN THOMAS, retired public relations executive; b. Newport News, Va., Mar. 13, 1921; s. John T. and Grace E. (Johnson) C.; m. Jacquelin G. Sanne, July 13, 1946; 1 child, Donald E. Student, U. Ill., Coll. William and Mary. Sports editor Newport News (Va.) Times-Herald, 1940-41; dir. pub. rels. Coll. william and Mary, Williamsburg, Va., 1947-49, U.S. Naval Acad., Annapolis, Md., 1949-62; dir. devel. and pub. rels. Fairfax Hosp. Assn., Falls Church, Va., 1962-72; dir. pub. and community rels. Suburban Hosp. Assn., Inc., Bethesda, Md., 1972-79, asst. to pres., 1979-83; ret. Suburban Hosp. Assn., Inc., Bethesda, 1986. Writer weekly column Redskins News. Mem. Harden & Weaver's Annual Golf Tournament Com., 1976—; press room aide Annheiser Busch Annual Golf Tournament. With U.S. Army Air Corps, 1942-45. Nominated Fairfax County Citizen of Yr.; inducted Helms Hall of Fame for Coll. Sports Info. Dirs. Mem. PRSA (nat. chmn. task force on health care), Am. Soc. Hosp. Pub. Rels. (bd. dirs., v.p. mid. Atlantic region), Am. Coll. Pub. Rels. Assn., Nat. Assn. Hosp. Devel. (bd. dirs.), Acad. Hosp. Pub. Rels., Montgomery County C. of C., Bethesda-Chevy Chase C. of C., Montgomery County Press Assn., Coll. Sports Info. Dirs. Am. (exec. sec.), Met. Washington Hosp. Pub. Rels. Soc., Va. Hosp. Pub. Rels. Soc., Nat. Press Club, Nat. Com. to Preserve Social Security and Medicare. Republican. Episcopalian.

COX, WINSTON H., television executive; b. Montclair, N.J., 1941. Student, Princeton U., 1963; postgrad. Bus Sch. of Bus., Harvard U., 1965. Chmn., chief exec. officer Showtime Networks Inc., N.Y.C.; bd. dirs. Lifetime Cable TV Network, Crowley Cheese Co., San Jose Giants Baseball, Inc. Trustee Ctrl. Park Conservancy Nat. Parenting Orgn. Mem. Nat. Cable TV Assn. (bd. dirs.). Deceased.

CRAIG, BERNARD DUFFY, lawyer; b. Kansas City, Mo., Nov. 12, 1909; s. John Clarence and Edith Margaret (Duffy) C.; m. Margaret Mary Conrad, June 25, 1938; children: Bernard D. Jr., Jo Anne Craig Fanganello, John E., Kathleen M. Craig Harbert. JD, U. Mo., 1936. Bar: Mo. 1936, U.S. Dist. Ct. (we. dist.) Mo. 1937, U.S. Supreme Ct. 1946, U.S. Tax Ct. 1975. Ptnr. Levy & Kirschner, Kansas City, 1936-50, Granoff, Levy & Craig, Kansas City, 1950-60; ptnr. Levy & Craig, Kansas City, 1961-75, sr. ptnr., 1975-90; of counsel, 1991—. Gen. chmn. Brotherhood Citation Banquet Nat. Conf. Christians and Jews, 1959; nat. dir. Nat. Conf. Christians and Jews, 1966; trustee Pope John XXIII Found., 1964-67, Law Found. U. Mo. at Kansas City, Legal Aid and Defender Soc. of Greater Kansas City, 1964-70, v.p. 1970; mem. St. Joseph Hosp. Adv. Council, 1978—. Decorated Knight of Holy Sepulchere Pope Paul VI, 1965; named hon. Col. Staff Gov. Warren E. Hearnes, 1964-72. Mem. ABA, Mo. Bar Assn., Kansas City Bar Assn. Roman Catholic. Clubs: Kansas City, Blue Hills Country (Kansas City).

CRAIN, DARRELL CLAYTON, JR., physician; b. Washington, Mar. 29, 1910; s. Darrell Clayton Sr. and Annie Augusta (Rau) C.; m. Leslye Louise Moore, July 12, 1934; children: Barbara Jean, Lillian Anne, Darrell Clayton III. MD, George Washington U., 1932. Diplomate Am. Bd. Internal Medicine. Practice medicine specializing in arthritis and rheumatic diseases Washington, 1937-87; founder, sr. physician Arthritis Rehab. Ctr., Washington, 1966-87; founder, dir. Rheumatology Clinic, Georgetown U. Hosp., Washington, 1947-72; clin. prof. Georgetown U. Sch. Medicine, Washington, 1971-87, ret., 1987; cons. in arthritis and rheumatic diseases Office of Surgeon Gen. U.S. Army, Washington, 1947-72, Surgeon Gen. U.S. Pub. Health, Bethesda, Md., 1947-69. Author: Help for Ten Million, 1959, The Arthritis Handbook, 1971; com. chmn. for booklet The Arthritis Primer, 1959. Bd. dirs. Westminster Found. at Annapolis, Md., 1947-91; co-founder Arthritis and Rheumatism Assn. Met. Washington, 1947, pres., 1948-49, bd. dirs., 1948-72; mem. medals subcom. Ofcl. Inaugural Coms., 1980, 84, 88, 92. Maj. U.S. Army, 1942-45, PTO. Fellow ACP, Washington Acad. Scis.; mem. AMA, Acad. Medicine of Washington (pres. 1980-84), Med. Soc. D.C. (pres. 1972). Republican. Presbyterian. Avocation; collecting commemerative U.S. Presdl. Inaugural Medals. Home: Chevy Chase Md. Died July 22, 1995.

CRAIN, GERTRUDE RAMSAY, publishing company executive; m. G.D. Crain Jr. (dec. Dec. 1973); children: Keith, Rance. D in Journalism (hon.), DePauw U., 1987; LHD (hon.), U. Detroit, 1988. Asst. treas. Crain Communications Inc., Chgo., 1942, sec., asst. treas., 1943-62, sec., treas., 1962-74, chmn. bd., 1974-96; bd. dirs. Internat. Advt. Assn., Mag. Pubs. Am., Execs. Club of Chgo., The Nat. Press Found. of Wash., Advt. Coun. of N.Y. Trustee Lincoln Acad. of Ill., James Webb Young Scholarship U. of Ill.; founding mem. Com. of 200, 1982; bd. dirs. Mus. of Broadcast Comm. in Chgo., Northwestern Meml. Hosp. Corp.-Chgo., Mus. of Sci. and Industry. Named to Working Woman Hall of Fame, 1987; named Chicagoan of Yr. Boys and Girls Club of Chgo., 1987, One of Top 60 Women Bus. Owners Saavy Mag., 1987, One of Top 50 Businesswomen Mich. Womans Mag., 1987; recipient Magnificat medal Mundelein Coll., Chgo., 1988. Mem. Internat. Advt. Assn. (bd. dirs.), Mag. Pubs. Am. (bd. dirs.), Nat. Press Found. Washington, Advt. Club N.Y., Execs. Club Chgo. Home: Chicago Ill. Died July 20, 1996.

CRAIN, IRVING JAY, psychiatrist, educator; b. N.Y.C., May 4, 1914; s. Rubin and Bertha (Liphsitz) C.; m. Eleanor Blum, Feb. 16, 1939. BS, Columbia U., 1933; MD, Rush Med. Coll., 1937; MPH, Harvard U., 1942. Diplomate Am. Bd. Psychiatry and Neurology. Intern Israel Zion Hosp., Bklyn., 1937-39; resident in psychiatry Menninger Sch. Psychiatry, Topeka, 1946-48; pvt. practice N.Y.C., 1948-95; asst. clin. prof. psychiatry N.Y. Med. Coll., N.Y.C., 1975-95. Maj. M.C., U.S. Army, 1943-46, ETO. Fellow Am. Psychiat. Assn. (life), Am. Acad. Psychoanalysis, Internat. Philosophers for Prevention Nuclear Omnicide (internat. com. and adv. coun. 1986-95). Avocations: music, golf. Home: New York N.Y. Died May 11, 1995.

CRAMPTON, CHARLES GREGORY, history educator; b. Kankakee, Ill., Mar. 22, 1911; s. Charles C. and Carrie (Beecher) C.; m. Mary Helen Patrick Walters, 1978 (dec. July 1996); children: Patricia, Juanita. A.B., U. Calif. at Berkeley, 1935, M.A., 1936, Ph.D., 1941. Teaching asst. history U. Calif. at Berkeley, 1937-40; spl. agt. FBI, 1943-45; depot historian Calif. Q.M. Depot, Oakland, 1944-45; prof. history U. Utah, 1945-79, Duke research prof., 1972-76, dir. Western History Center, 1966-68; Rockefeller Found. travelling fellow Latin Am., 1941-42, 48-49; vis. prof. U. Panama, 1955. Author: Outline History of the Glen Canyon Region 1776-1922, 1959, Standing Up Country, The Canyon Lands of Utah and Arizona,

1964, Land of Living Rock: The Grand Canyon and the High Plateaus, Arizona, Utah, Nevada, 1972, The Zunis of Cibola, 1977, Ghosts of Glen Canyon: History Beneath Lake Powell, 1986; editor: Yosemite and the High Sierra, 1957; also articles. Mem. Phi Alpha Theta (pres. 1949-50). Home: Saint George Utah Died May 2, 1995.

CRAWFORD, B. BLAIR, lawyer; b. Greenwich, Conn., July 12, 1941; s. Bruce D. and Bettie (Richardson) C.; m. Harriet J. Blasch, Sept. 20, 1966; children: Kimberly, Bruce. BA, Tufts U., 1963; LLB, Rutgers U., 1966. Bar: Conn. 1966, Pa. 1975. Assoc. Day, Berry & Howard, Hartford, Conn., 1966-69; asst. U.S. Atty. Dept. Justice, Hartford, Conn., 1969-72; internat. atty. Westinghouse Electric Corp., Pitts., 1972-80; ptnr. Baskin & Sears, Pitts., 1981-84, Buchanan and Ingersoll, Pitts., 1984—; pres. Pa. Internat. Trade Conf., 1984-85. Contbr. articles to profl. jours. Pres. Highland Park Community Club, Pitts., 1985-86.

CRAY, SEYMOUR R., computer designer; b. Chippewa Falls, Wis., 1925. BSEE, U. Minn., 1950, BS in Math., 1950. Computer scientist Engring. Research Assocs. (later Remington Rand, Sperry Rand Univac div.), St. Paul, until 1957; co-founder Control Data Corp., 1957, computer scientist, 1957-72; founder Cray Research Inc., Mendota Heights, Minn., 1972; chmn. Cray Computer Corp., Colorado Springs, Colo., 1989—. Designer first computer made with transistors, Cray-1, Cray-2, other computer systems.

CREDE, ROBERT HENRY, physician, educator; b. Chgo., Aug. 11, 1915; s. William H. and Ethel (Starke) C.; m. Marjorie L. Lorain, Aug. 29, 1947; children: William, Victoria, Christina. A.B., U. Calif., Berkeley, 1937; M.D., U. Calif., San Francisco, 1941. Diplomate Am. Bd. Internal Medicine. Commonwealth fellow, instr. medicine U. Cin. Coll. Medicine, 1947-49; intern San Francisco City and County Hosp., 1941-42; asst. resident medicine U. Calif. Hosp., San Francisco, 1945-46; chief resident medicine U. Calif. Hosp., 1946-47; mem. faculty Sch. Medicine U. Calif., San Francisco, 1949—; prof. medicine Sch. Medicine U. Calif., 1960-86, vice chmn. dept., 1965-80, asso. dean, 1960-73, 79-89; chmn. div. ambulatory and cmty. medicine Gen. Med. Clinic Sch. Med. U. Calif., 1965-80; prof. emeritus Sch. Medicine U. Calif. (Gen. Med. Clinic.), 1986—. Author articles in field. Served to capt., M.C. AUS, 1942-46. Recipient Guy K. Woodward prize internal medicine U. Calif. Sch. Medicine, 1941, Gold Headed Cane award, 1941. Mem. Am. Geriatrics Soc., Soc. Gen. Internal Medicine, Am. Psychosomatic Soc., Calif. Med. Assn., San Francisco Med. Soc., Soc. Tchrs. Preventive Medicine. Deceased.

CRENNER, JAMES JOSEPH, credit services company executive; b. Pitts., June 22, 1922; s. Michael J. and Edna T. (Schleich) C.; m. Julia Rossell, Nov. 10, 1945; children: Patricia, Constance. Student, U. Pitts., 1946-54. With Dun & Bradstreet, Inc., 1945-82; mgr. offices Dun & Bradstreet, Inc., Erie, Pa., 1955-58, Winston-Salem, N.C., 1955-58; dist. mgr. Dun & Bradstreet, Inc., Rochester, N.Y., Indpls. and Chgo., 1959-69; pres. Nat. Credit Office subs. Dun & Bradstreet, Inc., N.Y.C., 1969; regional mgr., then v.p. Dun & Bradstreet, Inc., Chgo., 1969-71; sr. v.p. ops. Dun & Bradstreet, Inc., N.Y.C., 1972-75; exec. v.p. ops. Dun & Bradstreet, Inc., 1975-76, pres., 1976—, chmn. bd., 1978-82; exec. v.p. parent co. Dun & Bradstreet Corp., 1982-84; now writer and bus. cons.; lectr. in field. Contbr. articles to newspapers and trade jours. Bd. govs., bd. trustees Jersey Shore Med. Ctr. Served with USMC, 1942-45. Mem. Nat. Assn. Credit Mgmt., Sales Exec. Club, Nat. Sales Mgmt. Assn. (accredited speaker). Clubs: Spring Lake Golf (N.J.), Longboat Key Golf (Fla.).

CRENSHAW, DOROTHY W., public relations executive; b. Atlanta, July 29, 1955. BA in English and French, Wesleyan U., 1977. Copywriter, media specialist Simon & Schuster, N.Y.C., 1979-81; account exec. Dorf & Stanton Comm., N.Y.C., 1981-83, account supr., 1983-85, v.p., 1985-86, exec. v.p. and ptnr., 1988; sr. v.p. Edelman Pub. Rels. Worldwide, N.Y.C., 1988-93; exec. v.p. consumer mktg. GCI Group, N.Y.C., 1993—. Mem. Women Execs. in Pub. Rels., Women's Agenda.

CRENSHAW, MARION CARLYLE, JR., obstetrician, educator; b. Lancaster, S.C., Apr. 15, 1931; s. Marion Carlyle and Mabel (Byrd) C.; m. Lillian Ruth Blackmon, Nov. 22, 1979; children: Marion Carlyle III, William, Hugh, Faith. BS cum laude, Davidson Coll., 1952; MD, Duke U., 1956. Intern Duke U. Med. Center, Durham, N.C., 1956-57; resident Duke U. Med. Center, 1957-62, instr. obstetrics and gynecology, 1961-62, assoc., 1964-65, asst. prof., 1965-70, assoc. prof., 1970-71, E.C. Hamblen prof. reproductive biology and family planning, 1971-80, asst. prof. pediatrics, 1971-80, assoc. physiology, 1965-75; prof., chmn. dept. obstetrics and gynecology U. Md. Sch. Medicine, Balt., 1980-95; v.p. U. Md. Med. Faculty Found., 1983-86, pres., 1986-89; pres. U. Md. Hosp. Med. Staff, 1987-88; vis. scholar Physiol. Lab. Cambridge (Eng.) U., 1978-79; mem. Coun. on Residency Edn. in Ob-Gyn., 1985-91; chmn. CITROG, 1987-91; mem. Md. Gov.'s Commn. on Infant Mortality, 1992-95. Editl. bd. mem. Md. Med. Jour., 1994-95; contbr. articles and chpts. to profl. jours. and books. Served with USAF, 1962-64. Mead Johnson fellow, 1960-61, Macy Faculty fellow, 1966-69; Disting. Alumni award Duke U. Sch. Medicine, 1991. Fellow Howard K. Kane-A.F.A. King Obstet. Soc., Am. Coll. Obstetricians and Gynecologists; mem. Am. Gynecol. Soc., F. Bayard Carter Soc. Obstetricians and Gynecologists (treas. 1970-77, v.p. 1977-79, pres. 1985-86), No Name Soc., Soc. Gynecol. Investigation, N.C. Obstetric and Gynecology Soc., N.Y. Acad. Socs., Perinatal Research Soc., So. Perinatal Assn., Soc. Perinatal Obstetricians (dir. 1977-80), Md. Ob-Gyn Soc. (exec. com. 1981-84, pres. 1984-85, chmn. bd. 1985-86), Med. and Chirurg. Faculty Md. (ho. of dels. 1983-84), Balt. City Med. Soc. (credentials com. 1988-95), So. Med. Assn. (editorial bd.), Western Ob-Gyn Soc. (hon.), South Atlantic Assn. Obstetricians and Gynecologists (hon.), Assn. Profs. Gynecology and Obstetrics (exec. com. 1990-92), Splint Soc., Am. Gynecol. Club (exec. com. 1988, pres. elect 1990, pres. 1991), Balt. Monthly Med. Reunion, N.Am. Travel Club, Splint Club (pres. 1994-95), Phi Beta Kappa., Alpha Omega Alpha. Home: Baltimore Md. Died Apr. 22, 1995.

CRIPE, NICHOLAS MCKINNEY, speech educator; b. Goshen, Ind., Jan. 25, 1913; s. Nicholas M. and Eva Letitia (McKinney) C.; m. Dorothy Mae Dunivan, Jan. 19, 1945. A.B., Goshen Coll., 1949; M.A., Northwestern U., 1949, Ph.D., 1953. With Goshen Rubber Co., 1935-42; instr. speech U. Vt., 1949-50; grad. asst. Northwestern U., 1950-52; lectr. speech Grinnell Coll., 1952-53; head dept. speech Butler U., Indpls., 1953-83; prof. speech Butler U., 1954-83, prof. emeritus, 1983-92; pub. speaker, 1946-92. Contbr. articles profl. jours. Candidate for state rep., Ind., 1956; chmn. Marion County (Ind.) Citizens for Kennedy, 1960. Served with inf. AUS, 1942-46. Recipient Baxter award for outstanding teaching Butler U., 1954, Outstanding Prof. award, 1962, Butler medal, 1977; named Ky. col., 1978, Sagamore of Wabash, 1983. Mem. Am. Forensic Assn. (pres. 1961-63), Midwest Forensic Assn. (Ind. pres. 1969-71), Central States Speech Assn., Speech Assn. Am. (legislative assembly 1965-66), Ind. Speech Assn. (pres. 1970-72), Tau Kappa Alpha, Delta Sigma Rho (nat. council 1970-77, nat. sec. 1966-69, nat. pres. 1972-75), Phi Kappa Phi. Home: Indianapolis Ind. Died Dec. 7, 1992.

CRISPIN, MILDRED SWIFT (MRS. FREDERICK EATON CRISPIN), civic worker, author; b. Branson, Mo.; d. Albert Duane and Anna (Harlan) Swift; m. Herbert William Kochs, Dec. 1, 1928 (div. Mar. 1955); children: Susan Kochs Judevine (dec.), Herbert William Jr., Judith Ann (Mrs. Nelson Shaw); m. George Walter King Snyder, Oct. 6, 1962 (dec. 1969); m. Frederick Eaton Crispin, May 20, 1972. Student, Galloway Woman's Coll., 1922-24. Bd. dirs. Travelers Aid Soc., Chgo., 1936-68, nat. dir., 1948-71; founding mem. U.S.O., Chgo., 1944-65, nat. dir., 1951-57; bd. dirs. John Howard Assn., 1958-67, Community Fund Chgo., 1950-56, Welfare Coun. Met. Chgo., 1950-56; chmn. woman's div. Crusade of Mercy, Chgo., 1964. Mem. U.S. Women's Curling Assn. (co-founder 1947, pres. 1950, founder Indian Hill Women's Curling Club, Winnetka, Ill., 1945, chmn. 1945-46), DAR, Daus. Am. Colonists, Town and Country Arts Club (pres. 1957-58, Chgo., Woman's Athletic Club Chgo., Everglades Club (Palm Beach, Fla.), Venice (Fla.) Yacht Club, Coral Ridge Yacht Club (Ft. Lauderdale, Fla.). Republican. Methodist. Died November 20, 1996.

CRITCHFIELD, RICHARD PATRICK, journalist; b. Mpls., Mar. 23, 1931; s. Ralph James and Anne (Williams) C. MS, Columbia U., 1957; student, Leopold Fraenzens U., Innsbruck, Austria, 1968, U. Vienna, Austria, 1958-59, Northwestern U., 1960; HHD (hon.), N.D. State U., 1986. Reporter Cedar Valley Daily Times, Vinton, Iowa, 1955-56; Washington corr. Salt Lake City Deseret News, also other papers Munroe News Bur., Washington, 1957-58; acting asst. prof. U. Nagpur, India, 1960-62; Asian corr. Washington Star, 1963-68; White House corr. Washington Star, Washington, 1968-69, nat. corr., 1971-72; spl. corr. on rural devel. The Economist, London, 1973-94; free-lance writer Los Angeles Times, Asian Wall St. Jour., N.Y. Times, Reader's Digest, Christian Sci. Monitor, Internat. Herald Tribune, Fgn. Affairs, Economist, World Monitor, also others; book reviewer N.Y. Times, Washington Post, Book World, L.A. Times, 1986-94; cons. Am. Univs. Field Staff, 1976-85, AID, Indonesia, 1979, Rockefeller Found., 1980-81, AAAS, 1980; vis. fellow Overseas Devel. Council, 1985-94; keynote speaker Am. Soc. Agronomy, 1981; condr. seminars World Bank, Congressional Staff Speakers Forum, Harvard U., Johns Hopkins U., Tufts U., MIT, Brown U., Dartmouth Coll., U. Calif.-Berkeley, U. Minn., Iowa State U., U. Iowa, Ind. U., Mich. State U., others, 1980-86; condr. workshop on African agr. Sasakawa Africa Assn., Washington, 1992, Cotonou, Benin, 1993; visitor in residence Wadham Coll., Oxford U., 1986; presenter numerous seminars; speaker in field. Author: The Indian Reporter's Guide, 1962, The Long Charade: Political Subversion in the Vietnam War, 1968, The Golden Bowl Be Broken: Peasant Life in Four Cultures, 1974, rev. edit., 1987, Shahhat, an Egyptian, 1978, Villages, 1981, rev. edit., 1983, 91, Those Days: An American Album, 1986, An American Looks at Britain, 1990, rev. edition, 1991, Trees, Why Do You Wait? America's Changing Rural Culture, 1991, The Villagers: Changed Values Altered Lives: The Closing of the Urban-Rural Gap, 1994, (preface) We Have Eaten the Forest, 1994; editor, illustrator: Lore and Legend of Nepal, 1962; (survey) Britain: An Outsider's View, The Economist, 1987; contbr. articles to profl. jours. and newspapers. Served with AUS, 1953-55, Korea. Recipient Alicia Patterson Fund award, 1970-71; Ford Found. grantee, Asia, Africa, Latin Am., U.S., 1972-74, 76-81, 86-87, 90-92, Mex., 1993-94; Inst. Current World Affairs grantee, 1971; Rockefeller Found. humanities fellow, 1978, grantee, 1990-92, MacArthur Found. Prize fellow, 1981. Mem. Explorers Club, Overseas Press Club of N.Y.C. (award best daily reporting Vietnam 1965), Cosmos Club, Commonwealth Club of Calif., Phi Kappa Psi. Home: Berkeley Calif. Died Dec. 10, 1994.

CROCETTI, DINO See MARTIN, DEAN

CROCKETT, GEORGE WILLIAM, JR., congressman, retired; b. Jacksonville, Fla., Aug. 10, 1909; s. George William and Minnie A. (Jenkins) C.; m. Ethelene Jones (dec.); children: Elizabeth Ann Crockett Hicks, George William III, Ethelene C.; m. Harriette Clark, Aug. 1980. A.B., Morehouse Coll., 1931, LL.D., 1972; J.D., U. Mich., 1934; LL.D., Shaw Coll., 1973. Bar: Fla. 1934, W.Va. 1935, Mich. 1944, U.S. Supreme Ct. 1940. Practiced law Jacksonville, 1934-35, Fairmont, W.Va., 1935-39; sr. atty. Dept. Labor, 1939-43; hearings officer Fed. Fair Employment Practices Commn., Washington, 1943; founder, dir. Internat. UAW Fair Employment Practices Dept.; adminstrv. asst. to internat. sec-treas. UAW; assoc. gen. counsel Internat. UAW, 1944-46; sr. mem. firm Goodman, Crockett, Eden and Robb, Detroit, 1950-66; judge Recorder's Ct., Detroit, 1966-78; presiding judge Recorder's Ct., 1974-75; vis. judge Mich. Ct. Appeals, 1979; acting corp. counsel City Detroit, 1980; mem. 96th-101st Congresses from 13th Mich. Dist.; mem. com. fgn. affairs, com. judiciary, select com. on aging, exec. bd. Dem. study group U.S. Congress; mem. Congl. Black Caucus, Congl. Auto Caucus, Congl. Arts Caucus; hon. mem. Congl. Hispanic Caucus. Trustee Morehouse Coll. Mem. Nat. Bar Assn. (founder and 1st chmn. Jud. Council), Nat. Lawyers Guild, N.E.-Midwest Econ. Coalition, Congress For Peace Through Law, Phi Beta Kappa, Kappa Alpha Psi. Democrat. Baptist. Died Sept. 7, 1997.

CROMWELL, NORMAN HENRY, chemist, educator; b. Terre Haute, Ind., Nov. 22, 1913; s. Henry and Ethel Lee (Harkelroad) C.; m. Grace N. Newell, Jan. 29, 1955; children: Christopher Newell, Richard Earl. B.S. with honors (Rea scholar 1932-35), Rose-Hulman Inst., 1935; Ph.D., U. Minn., 1939; DSc (hon.), U. Nebr., 1987. Teaching asst. U. Minn., 1935-39; instr. organic chemistry U. Nebr., Lincoln, 1939-42; asst. prof. U. Nebr., 1942-45, assoc. prof., 1945-48, prof., 1948—, Howard S. Wilson regents prof., 1960-70, chmn. dept. chemistry, 1964-70, exec. dean for grad. studies and research, 1970-72, v.p., dean Grad. Coll., 1972-73, Regents prof. chemistry Grad. Coll., 1973-83, Regents prof. emeritus, 1983—; interim dir. Eppley Inst. for Cancer Research, Med. Center, Omaha, 1979-80, dir., 1981-83; guest dept. chemistry MIT, 1967; hon. research assoc. Univ. Coll., London, 1950-51, 58-59; hon. research assoc. Calif. Inst. Tech., 1958; Am. Chem. Soc. tour lectr., 1952-70; frontiers of chemistry lectr. Wayne State U., 1958; research lectr. U. Coll., Dublin, Ireland, 1958; vis. prof. U. Calif. Med. Center, 1961; Gordon Research Conf. lectr., 1961, conf. discussion leader, 1970, 77; Hungarian Chem. Soc. lectr., 1962, Sigma Xi nat. lectr., 1964; Keynote speaker Nat. Com. Adminstrn. Research Conf., 1970; cons. Parke Davis & Co., 1943-46, Smith, Kline & French Labs., 1946-51, Am. Cancer Soc., 1956-58, Philip Morris, Inc., 1964-79, USPHS, 1952-64, chmn. medicinal chem. study sect., 1960-64; Nat. Cancer Inst., 1964-70; pres. 2d Internat. Congress Heterocyclic Chemistry, Montpellier, France, 1969; plenary lectr. 5th Internat. Congress, Ljubljana, Yugoslavia, 1975; U.S.-India exchange scientist, 1977; dir. coop. coll. tchr. devel. program for Nebr. NSF, 1960-63. Asst. editor: Jour. Heterocyclic Chemistry, 1963-89 (Mar.-Apr. issue 1988 dedicated to Norman H. Cromwell); Contbr. articles to research publs. Mem. bd. Lincoln Bryan Hosp. Fulbright advanced research scholar, 1950-51; Guggenheim Meml. fellow, 1950, 58; recipient Outstanding Alumnus Achievement award U. Minn., 1975, Outstanding Research and Creativity award U. Nebr., 1978, Doc. Elliott award, 1989. Mem. Am. Chem. Soc. (plenary lectr. nat. meeting 1983, 40th Midwest award 1984), Chem. Soc. London, Nebr. Art Assn. (trustee 1958—, v.p. 1971), Sigma Xi, Phi Lambda Upsilon, Sigma Tau, Gamma Alpha, Tau Nu Tau, Alpha Chi Sigma, Alpha Tau Omega.

CROSS, ROBERT BRANDT, emeritus classics educator; b. Stockton, Calif., Dec. 9, 1914; s. LaRue Ackley and Theresa (Brandt) C. A.B. in Greek, UCLA, 1937; M.A. in Greek, U. Calif.-Berkeley, 1939; Ph.D. in Greek, U. So. Calif., 1948. Asst. prof. classical langs. U. So. Calif., Los Angeles, 1948-57; prof. fgn. langs. U. Ark., Fayetteville, 1957-80; emeritus prof. U. Ark., 1980-95. Translator: Milo Rigaud, 1970; writings of E. Yale Dawson in marine biology. Served with USAAF, 1942-45. Mem. Am. Guild Organists, Organ Hist. Soc., Classical Assn. Middle West and South (v.p. for Ark. 1957-80), Sociedade Brasileira De Romanistas, Desert Tortoise Council, Gopher Tortoise Council, The Nature

Conservancy. Democrat. Greek Orthodox. Home: Little Rock Ark. Died Oct. 8, 1995.

CROSSEN, HENRY MORGAN, manufacturing executive; b. Detroit, May 25, 1922; s. Henry Francis and Bernice (Morgan) C.; divorced; children: Carol A. Roderick J., Mark S., Lynne M., Henry Francis II, Scott J. BME, U. Detroit, 1950; MS in Indsl. Mgmt., MIT, 1956. Mfg. exec. stamping div. Ford Motor Co., Dearborn, Mich., 1950-60; v.p. adminstrn. J.I. Case Co., 1960-63; pres., chief exec. officer Crossen Assocs., Ltd., 1963-67; v.p. N.Am. ops. E.W. Bliss Co., 1967-69; chief staff Gulf Western Indsl. Products Co., 1969-70; vice chmn. Thomas A. Miner Assocs., 1970-72; pres., chief exec. officer Beloit Coll. Ctr. Applied Rsch., 1972-74, Rockford (Ill.) Bus. Mgmt. Group, Inc., 1974-78, First Ill. Investment Corp., Rockford, 1978-80, Falls Products, Inc., Genoa, Ill., 1980—, Morgan Mgmt. Group, Inc.; pres., chief exec. officer Bioenergy Nutrients, Inc.; cons. in field. Active Racine (Wis.) United Community Svcs., Inc., 1962-68, pres. 1967-68; bd. dirs. Family Svc. Coun., Racine, 1964-68, Urban league, Racine, 1966-68, Racine C. of C., 1964-66; bd. regents Dominican Coll., 1964-68; mem. Econ. Opportunity Com. Racine County, 1964-65; mem. Racine County Draft Bd., 1964-68; mem. nat. ednl. com. MIT, 1966-67; chmn. Racine Mayor's Adv. Com., 1967-68; chmn. Racine Study Com. on Orgn. Police and Fire Depts., 1967-68. Lt. USAAF, 1942-45. Recipient various pub. svc. awards; Alfred P. Sloan fellow, 1955-56. Mem. Am. Mgmt. Assn., Soc. Sloan Fellows. Roman Catholic. Died Aug. 25, 1992.

CROUCH, FORDYCE WILLIAM, lawyer; b. Curlew, Iowa, Feb. 12, 1914; s. Alfred William and Ida Mae (Nicholson) C.; m. Alice Welch, July 2, 1938; children—Ford William, John Steven, Thomas Nicholson. Student, Ft. Dodge Jr. Coll., 1931-33; B.S., U. Minn., 1935, LL.B., 1937. Bar: Iowa bar 1937, Minn. bar 1938. Practice of law Mpls., 1938—; with M., St. P. & S.S. Ry., Mpls., 1938—; gen. counsel M., St. P. & S.S. Ry., 1957—; v.p., gen. counsel Soo Line R.R. Co., until 1979; ret., 1979. Republican. Conglist. Club: Mpls. Athletic. Died, Feb. 2, 1992.

CROW, WILLIAM CECIL, consultant, former government official; b. Oneonta, Ala., Oct. 4, 1904; s. Mandeville McAlpin and Flora Jane (Brice) C.; A.B., Maryville Coll., 1924; A.M., U. Chgo., 1929; LL.D., Maryville College, 1969; m. Mary Lucille Johnson, July 5, 1935; 1 child, William Cecil. Asst. prof. econs., Auburn U., 1930-35; with U.S. Dept. Agr., 1935-72, successively with Bur. Agrl. Econs., 1935-42, War Food Adminstrn. and Prodn. and Marketing Adminstrn., 1942-53, dir. transp. and facilities research div., and liaison with state depts. of agr. Agrl. Marketing Service, 1953-63, dir. transp. and facilities research div. Agrl. Research Service, 1963-72; cons. food mktg. facilities, equipment, and systems, Africa, Asia, Australia, Europe, N.Am., Central Am., S.Am. Mem. Arlington (Va.) Com. of 100; chmn. Arlington County Pub. Utilities Commn. Trustee Presbytery of Washington. Decorated Chevalier de l'Ordre du Merite Agricole (France); Order of Long Leaf Pine (N.C.); recipient Achievement award Nat. Assn. Produce Market Mgrs., also plaque for exceptional service; Superior Service award U.S. Dept. Agr.; citation Greater Phila. Movement; named Ky. Col. Hon. life mem. Nat. Assn. Refrigerated Warehouses; mem. Am. Agrl. Econs. Assn., AAAS. Presbyterian. Club: Springfield Golf and Country. Author many publs. Died Aug. 22, 1995.

CROWLEY, FREDERICK ALLISON, ophthalmologist; b. Des Moines, Dec. 16, 1911; s. Daniel F. and Rosemary Catherine (Langdon) C.; m. Mildred Kocher, Apr. 5, 1948. B.A., U. Iowa, 1933, M.D., 1937. Diplomate Am. Bd. Ophthalmology. Intern Rochester Gen. Hosp., N.Y., 1937-39; resident in surgery Bklyn. Eye and Ear Hosp., 1939-41; surgeon Gailey Eye Clinic; mem. staff dept. ophthalmology Mennonite Hosp., Bloomington, Ill., 1946-78; surgeon Mennonite Hosp., Bloomington, Ill., 1978-95; dir. Watson Gailey Eye Found., Main Center Corp. Served to maj. U.S. Army, 1942-46. Decorated Bronze star. Fellow A.C.S., Internat. Coll. Surgeons; mem. AMA, Ill. Med. Assn. Home: Bloomington Ill. Died Feb. 5, 1995.

CRUMMER, MURRAY THOMAS, JR., insurance company executive; b. Eldorado, Kans., Aug. 27, 1922; s. Murray Thomas and Bertha Ellen (Sandifer) C.; m. Elliott Downs, Aug. 16, 1952; children—Elizabeth, Ellen, Barbara, Carolyn, Murray Philip. Student, U. Nebr., 1940-43. Underwriter, salesman Central Investment Co. Tex., Dallas, 1946-49; salesman Central Investment Co. Tex., Omaha, 1949-53; various positions United Benefit Life Ins. Co., Omaha, 1953-82; chief investment officer Mut. of Omaha Ins. Cos., 1982-87, ret., 1987. Served as sgt. inf. U.S. Army, 1943-46. Republican. Episcopalian. Died Sept. 9, 1996.

CULLENBINE, CLAIR STEPHENS, lawyer; b. Beardstown, Ill., Nov. 29, 1905; s. Robin James and Victoria (Stephens) C.; m. Jean Williams, Aug. 23, 1930; children: Carol Ann (Mrs. Neal B. Wineman), Robert Stephens. LL.B., Washington U., St. Louis, 1928. Bar: Mo. bar 1928. Practice law St. Louis, 1928-33; local counsel Md. Casualty Co., 1933-35; spl. counsel Asso. Industries of Mo., 1935-36; dir. research, dir. indsl. relations, 1937-43; indsl. relations mgr. Gaylord Container Corp., 1943-48, counsel, 1948-56; dir. Crown Zellerbach Corp. Industry mem. regional, nat. War Labor Bds., World War II. Mem. Calif. Mfrs. Assn. (dir.), Am. Arbitration Assn. (dir.). Club: Burlingame Country. Home: San Mateo Calif. Died Oct. 20, 1993.

CULMER, MARJORIE MEHNE, organization executive; b. Duluth, Minn., Mar. 4, 1912; d. John H. and Nettie (Morey) Mehne; m. Charles U. Culmer, Sept. 4, 1936. B.A., Lawrence Coll., 1933; J.D., Northwestern U., 1947; LL.D., Elmhurst Coll., 1962. Mem. profl. staff Girl Scouts of U.S.A., 1934-40, mem. nat. staff, 1943-44, field com. nat. orgn., 1948-56, vice chmn. orgn. and mgmt. com., 1954-57, chmn. Blue Book (policies) com., 1955-57, dir., 1955—, exec. com., 1956-63, pres., 1957-63, chmn. pub. issues com., 1972-75, mem., 1975-78, chmn. Macy steering com., 1976-78; 1st v.p., chmn. field com. Chgo. orgn., 1953-55, mem. bd., 1952-59, 61—, pres., 1955-57; del. World Conf. Girl Guides and Girl Scouts, Brazil, 1957, Greece, 1960; vice chmn., mem. planning com. World Conf. Girl Guides and Girl Scouts, Denmark, 1963; mem. planning com. World Conf. Girl Guides and Girl Scouts, Japan, 1966, Finland, 1969; mem. planning com., World Com. chmn. World Conf. Girl Guides and Girl Scouts, Can., 1972; mem. World Conf. Girl Guides and Girl Scouts, Eng., 1975, USA, 1984; tech. cons. Ill. Activities for 1970 White House Conf. for Children and Youth, 1968-70; trustee, mem. Nat. Assembly for Social Policy and Devel., 1967-74, Com. Internat. Social Devel., 1969-74; mem. Inter-Am. Seminar, 1958; specialist with Bur. Edn. and Cultural Affairs, Dept. State, India, 1964; mem. com. pub. welfare Welfare Council Met. Chgo., 1964-69; mem. com. Camp Algonquin, 1951-85; forum leader White House Conf. Children and Youth, 1960, mem. nat. com., 1958-60; rep. Internat. Women's Year, 1975. Bd. dirs. United Charities Chgo., 1953—, Family Svc. Com., 1960-63; mem. Legal Aid Com., 1956-64; founder World Found. for Girl Guides and Girl Scouts, bd. dirs. 1971-88, v.p. 1976-88, dir. emerita 1988; trustee Lawrence U., 1962-85, trustee emerita, 1985—, chmn. acad. affairs com., 1984-85; mem. svc. rev. panel Chgo. Community Fund, 1976—. Recipient Distinguished Service award Lawrence Coll., 1959; Merit award Northwestern U., 1960. Mem. ABA, Ill. Bar Assn., Chgo. Bar Assn., Women's Bar Assn. Ill., World Assn. Girl Guides and Girl Scouts (world com. 1963-72, vice chmn. 1966-69, world chmn. 1969-72, hon. Assoc. 1972—), Order of Coif, Mortar Bd., Phi Beta Kappa Assos., Phi Beta Kappa.

CUMMINGS, LARRY LEE, psychologist, educator; b. Indpls., Oct. 28, 1937; s. Garland R. and Lillian P. (Smith) C.; children—Lee Anne, Glenn Nelson. A.B. summa cum laude, Wabash (Ind.) Coll., 1959; postgrad. in psychology (Woodrow Wilson fellow), U. Calif., Berkeley; M.B.A., Ind. U., 1961, D.B.A., 1964. Lic. profl. fishing guide. Asst. prof., then assoc. prof. Grad. Sch. Bus., Ind. U., Bloomington, 1964-67; vis. assoc. prof. Grad. Sch. Bus., Columbia U., 1967-68; mem. faculty U. Wis., Madison, 1968-81; prof. Grad. Sch. Bus. and Indsl. Relations Research Inst., lectr. univ. dept. psychology, 1970-81; dir. Center Study Organizational Performance, 1973-81, H.I. Romnes faculty fellow, 1975-81, Slichter research prof., 1980-81; assoc. dean social scis. Center Study Organizational Performance (Grad. Sch.), 1975-78; Kellogg disting. research prof. orgnl. behavior Kellogg Grad. Sch. Mgmt., Northwestern U., Evanston, Ill., 1981-88; Carlson prof. Carlson Sch. Mgmt. U. Minn., Mpls., 1988-96, prof., 1996-97; CEO, chmn. The Inst., 1997; Ford. Found. sr. research fellow, Brussels, Belgium, 1969-70; vis. prof. Faculty Commerce and Bus. Adminstrn., U., B.C., Vancouver, 1971-72. Co-author: Organizational Decision Making, 1970, Performance in Organizations, 1973, Introduction to Organizational Behavior, 1980; co-editor: Readings in Organizational Behavior and Human Performance, rev. edit., 1973, Research in Organizational Behavior, vol. 2, 1980, vol. 3, 1981, vol. 4, 1982, vol. 5, 1983, vol. 6, 1984, vol. 7, 1985, vol. 8, 1986, vol. 9, 1987, vol. 10, 1988, vol. 11, 1989, vol. 12, 1990, vol. 13, 1991, vol. 14, 1992, vol. 15, 1993, vol. 16, 1994, vol. 17, 1995, vol. 18, 1996, vol. 19, 1997, Publishing in the Organizational Sciences, 1985; cons. editor Irwin series in mgmt. and behavioral scis.; contbr. profl. publs. Bd. trustees Wabash Coll., 1992-97. Woodrow Wilson fellow, 1959-60; fellow Ford Found., 1961-62, summer 1965, grantee; Richard D. Irwin Dissertation fellow, 1963-64; co-recipient McKinsey Found. Mgmt. Research Design award, 1968-69; grantee Richardson Found., 1968-71; grantee Am. Soc. Personnel Adminstrn., 1974-75. Fellow Am. Psychol. Soc. (charter), Acad. Mgmt. (editor jours., bd. govs., v.p., nat. programs chmn., pres., dean of fellow of acad., Disting. Educator award 1995), APA, Am. Inst. Decision Scis. (v.p., exec. bd.); mem. Midwestern Psychol. Assn., Indsl. Rels. Rsch. Assn., Am. Sociol. Assn., Soc. Pers. Adminstrn., Phi Beta Kappa, Sigma Xi, Beta Gamma Sigma, Tau Kappa Alpha, Delta Phi Alpha, Sigma Chi. Home: Edina Minn. Died June 3, 1997.

CUMMINS, EVELYN FREEMAN, retired social agency administrator; b. Beatrice, Nebr., Mar. 24, 1904; d. John Allen and Irene (Townsend) Freeman; m. Paul Otto Cummins, Oct. 8, 1927 (dec. Sept. 1943); 1 child, Beverly Anne (Mrs. Cummins Spangler). Student Nebr. Wesleyan, 1920-23; BA, U. Nebr., 1928; postgrad. U. Chgo., 1934-36, 41; MS, Columbia U., 1946. Tchr. rural Gage County, Nebr., 1921-22, Wilber, Nebr., 1923-25, Lincoln, Nebr., 1925-27; sch. social worker Lincoln, 1930-36; supr. Fla. Dept. Pub. Welfare, Orlando, 1936-42, dist. dir., 1942-45; dir. Nebr. Gov.'s Com. to Study Services to Blind, Lincoln, 1946-47; field rep. Fla. Dept. Pub. Welfare, Jacksonville, 1948-51, appeals officer, 1950-51; exec. dir. Community Coun. Oklahoma City Area, 1952-61; exec. dir. spl. projects Chgo. Community Fund, 1962-63; exec. dir. Family Svc. Assn. La Porte County (Ind.), 1964-89, ret., 1989; lectr. social problems Purdue North Cen.; participant rsch. seminar Non-Profits and Taxation NYU, 1988-89; field supr. Valparaiso U., Loyola U., Jane Addams Sch. Social Work, Chgo. Del. Area II Adv. Coun. on Aging, 1976-80; mem. housing com. Mayor of Michigan City (Ind.), 1973; pres. Community Svc. Coun. Michigan City, 1966-68; chmn. residential campaign United Way Michigan City, 1966-68. Diplomate Conf. Advancement Pvt. Practice in Social Work. Recipient Older Hoosier of Yr., 1989. Mem. DAR, AAUW, NASW, Acad. Cert. Social Workers, Coun. Social Work Edn. Assn., Ind. Coun. Family Svc. Assn., Ind. Home Service Agys. Assn., Ind. Conf. on Social Concerns, Internat. Platform Assn., Nat. Network Social Work Mgrs., Inc., Women in Mgmt., Michigan City C. of C., LaPorte County Coun. on Aging (pres. 1978). Democrat. Methodist. Died Mar. 20, 1996.

CUNNINGHAM, MORRIS, journalist; b. McMinnville, Tenn., July 27, 1917; s. Oscar Lafayette and Jessie Lee (Crawford) C.; m. Helen Henry Morris, Oct. 25, 1947; children: Diane, Morris Frank. Corr., state news editor, state capitol reporter Nashville Tennessean, 1935-43; reporter, news editor A.P., Nashville and N.Y.C., 1943-45; corr. Time, Life, Fortune mags., Nashville, 1945-53; Nashville corr. Memphis Comml. Appeal, 1945-53, Washington corr., 1953-78, bur. chief, 1978-84; mem. adv. com. tng. tchrs. deaf Office Edn., 1962-64; U.S. Del. Internat. Com. on European Migration, Geneva, 1958. Mem. White House Corrs. Assn., State Dept. Corrs. Assn., Overseas Writers, Tenn. Squires, A.G. Bell Assn. for Deaf, Sigma Delta Chi. Methodist. Clubs: Kenwood Golf and Country; National Press (Washington).

CUNNINGHAM, ROBERT MARIS, JR., retired journal editor; b. Chgo., May 28, 1909; s. Robert Maris and Beda (Dickson) C.; m. Deborah Libby, Nov. 24, 1934; children: Dennis, Damon, Margaret, Robert Maris. Ph.B., U. Chgo., 1931. Asst. to pres. Armour (now Ill.) Inst. Tech., Chgo., 1932-34; sales and sales promotion Shell Petroleum Corp., 1934-37; dir. pub. relations Chgo. Blue Cross hospitalization plan, 1938-41; asso. editor Hygeia (pub. by AMA), 1941-45; mng. editor The Modern Hosp. mag., 1945-51, editor, 1951-63, 67-73, pub., 1963-67; editorial dir. The Nations Schools, 1963-67; editorial dir. Coll. and Univ. Bus., 1967-73, pub., 1963-67; pub. The Hosp. Purchasing File, 1963-67; editor Modern Nursing Home, 1964-73, pub., 1964-67; chmn. editorial bd. Modern Healthcare mag., 1974-75, contbg. editor, 1976; contbg. editor Hosps., Jour. Am. Hosp. Assn., 1977—; cons. ACS, 1955-59; editorial cons. Blue Cross and Blue Shield Assn., 1974-90; v.p., dir. F.W. Dodge Corp., 1959-63; bd. dirs. Health Industries Assn., 1966-69, pres. (hon.). Author: Hospitals, Doctors and Dollars, 1961, The Third World of Medicine, 1968, Governing Hospitals, 1976, Asking and Giving, 1980, Wellness at Work, 1981, The Healing Mission and the Business Ethic, 1982; also articles on hosp. and med. subjects. Mem. Psi Upsilon.

CUNY, FREDERICK C., disaster relief executive; b. New Haven, Conn., Nov. 14, 1944. BS, U. Houston, Rice U., 1967. organized relief logistics for post-war Kuwait and So. Iraq; managed aid missions to Kenya and Somalia; restores water service to Sarajevo; rebuilt school systems in Tirana. MacArthur fellow, 1995. Died April 14, 1995.

CURRIE, LEONARD JAMES, architect, planner, educator; b. Stavely, Alta., Can., July 28, 1913; s. Andrew and Florence (McIntyre) C.; m. Virginia M. Herz, Feb. 8, 1937; children: Barbara E., Robert G., Elizabeth A. B.Arch., U. Minn., 1936; M. Arch., Harvard U., 1938, Wheelwright traveling fellow, 1940-41. Apprenticed with Walter Gropius, Marcel Breuer, Cambridge, Mass., 1938-40; archeologist div. hist. research Carnegie Instn. Expdn. to Copan, Honduras, 1941; airport constrn. Pan Am. Airways U.S. Govt., Guatemala and Nicaragua, 1941-42; asst. prof. architecture Harvard, 1946-51; architect Architects Collaborative, Cambridge, Mass., 1946-51; chief tech. aid mission on housing U.S. Govt., Costa Rica, 1951; organized, directed Inter-Am. Housing Center, Bogota, Colombia, 1951-56; prof., head dept. architecture Va. Poly. Inst., 1956-62; dean Coll. Architecture and Art, U. Ill., Chgo., 1962-72; prof. Coll. Architecture and Art, U. Ill., Chgo. Circle, 1972-81; Fulbright Sr. fellow, 1972-73; vis. prof. U. Sains Malaysia, 1972-73; hon. prof. Universidad Nacional de San Antonio Abad, 1977, Universidad Nacional Villarreal, 1977; former partner firm Atkins, Currie and Payne (architects, engrs. and planners); now prin. Leonard J. Currie and Assocs., FAIA, Architect; AID campus planning cons. Central Am. univs., 1964; OECD cons. campus planning and chief adviser on tech. cooperation U. Patras, Greece, 1973-80; Mem. City of Chgo. Cultural Com., 1963-66, Va. Com. on Sch. Bldg. Research, 1956-62; chmn. subcom. on comprehensive community planning, mem. exec. com. Community Improvement Adv. Com. of City of Chgo.; co-promulgator Charter of Machu Picchu, 1977; Bd. mem. Chgo. Sch. Architecture Found. Author: (with Rafaela Espino) Housing in Costa Rica, 1951, Planning of Central American Campuses, 1964, Designing Environments for the Aging, 1977; Contbr. articles to profl. publs.; prin. works include schs. and residences, New Eng., chs., Wesley Found. bldgs., residences in, Va., plan for resort in, W. Va., regional plan, Sogamoso Valley, Colombia, (with others), Six Moon Hill, coop. community, Lexington, Mass., Grad. Center, Harvard; cons., Rockefeller Found. phys. facilities planning, Colombia, 1967, campus planning cons., Nat. U. Nicaragua, 1969-70. Served as officer AUS, 1942-45; ret. lt. col. Res. Decorated Medal of Merit, Colombia, 1956; recipient Disting. Svc. award U. Ill. Alumni Assn., 1982, Test of Time award for Va. residence, 1982; residence named to Va. Landmarks Registry of Historic Places, 1994, Nat. Register of Historic Places, 1994. Fellow Internat. Inst. Arts and Letters, AIA (1st honor award 1963, William C. Nolan award medal Va. Soc. 1993); mem. Sociedad Colombiana de Arquitectos (hon.), Soc. Archtl. Historians, American Inst. Cert. Planners, Inter-Am. Planning Soc.

CURTIS, PHILIP JAMES, lawyer; b. Denver, June 12, 1918; s. Philip C. and Anna J. (Jackson) C.; m. Betty D. Dodds, Mar. 17, 1943; children—Timothy, Anne, Nancy. A.B., Regis Coll., 1939; LL.B., Georgetown U., 1947. Bar: D.C. bar 1947, Ill. bar 1955. Atty. Gen. Counsel's Office, FTC, 1948-53, supr. antimonopoly sect. div. compliance, 1950-53; litigation atty. Zenith Electronics Corp., Glenview, Ill., 1953-57; gen. counsel Zenith Electronics Corp., 1959-70, v.p., gen. counsel, 1970-83, spl. counsel, 1983-87; assoc. firm McConnell, Van Hook & Pashen, 1954-57, McConnell, Freeman, Curtis & McConnell, 1957-70. Author: The Fall of the U.S. Consumer Electronics Industry: An American Trade Tragedy, 1994. Served to maj. AUS and USAAF, 1942-48, ETO. Mem. Am., Ill., Chgo. bar assns., Delta Eta Phi. Died Nov. 14, 1997.

CURTIS, STATON RUSSELL, university dean; b. Portland, Maine, Mar. 19, 1921; s. Clarence Leroy and Eva May (R) C.; m. Ruth Alden, Oct. 17, 1943; children—Sharon Leigh, Martha Gail. B.S., Gorham (Maine) State Coll., 1942; M. Ed., Springfield (Mass.) Coll., 1947. Tchr.-coach pub. schs. Barre, Vt., 1946; faculty chmn. student activities, instr. phys. edn., athletic coach, Brunswick campus U. Maine, 1947-49; dir. Hyde Meml. Rehab. Center and Pine Tree Camp, Bath, Maine, 1949-50; dir. mcpl. recreation Brunswick, Maine, 1950-56; dir. Meml. Union, U. N.H., 1956-60; dean of men, dir. Univ. Union, Boston U., 1960-63, dean of students, 1963-69, dean student affairs, 1969-72, prof. edn., dean phys. devel. programs, 1972-77, prof. edn., internat. rep., 1977-85, prof. and dean emeritus, 1985-95. Served with USNR, 1943-45; lt. comdr. Res. Mem. Eastern Assn. Coll. Deans and Advisers to Students, Lambda Chi Alpha. Home: Kingston N.H. Died Apr. 16, 1995.

DACIUK, MYRON MICHAEL, bishop; b. Mundare, Alta., Can., Nov. 16, 1919; s. Lucas and Ksenia (Bruchkowsky) D. Student in philosophy and theology, Basilian Sem. Mundare, Grimsby, Ont., 1943-45. Ordained priest Ukrainian Catholic Ch., 1945. Priest Ukrainian Cath. Ch., Can., 1945-82; aux bishop Ukrainian Cath. Archeparchy, Winnepeg, Can., 1982-91; bishop Ukrainian Cath. Ch., Winnipeg, Man., Can., 1982-90, Edmonton Eparchy, 1992—; superior Basilian Fathers, Mundare, 1959-64; superior Basilian Fathers, Edmonton, Alta., 1976-79, provincial superior, 1964-70.

DACK, SIMON, physician; b. N.Y.C., Apr. 19, 1908; s. Isidore and Rebecca (Beitch) D.; m. Jacqueline Rosett, Jan. 23, 1949; children: Jerilyn Beth, Leonard. B.S., CCNY, 1928; M.D., N.Y. Med. Coll., 1932. Intern Mt. Sinai Hosp., N.Y.C., 1932-33; research fellow cardiology Mt. Sinai Hosp., 1934-38, clin. staff cardiology, 1938-94, adj. physician cardiology, chief cardiac clinic, 1945-58, attending physician, 1966-94; lectr. cardiology Columbia U.; asso. prof. medicine N.Y. Med. Coll., 1959-94; asso. clin. prof. medicine Mt. Sinai Sch. Medicine, 1966-70, clin. prof. medicine, 1970-76, clin. prof. emeritus, 1976-94; chief cardiac clinics Met. Hosp., N.Y.C., 1955-62; attending vis. physician Met. Hosp., 1962-94; asso. physician in cardiology Mt. Sinai Hosp., N.Y.C., 1958-70; attending physician cardiology Mt. Sinai Hosp., 1970-76, acting chief cardiology, 1972-74, cons. cardiologist, 1976-94; attending physician Flower Fifth Ave. Hosp., 1966-94; hon. prof. medicine U. Santo Tomas, Manila, 1961-94. Editor-in-chief Am. Jour. Cardiology, 1958-82, Jour. Am. Coll. Cardiology, 1982-92; contbr. articles to profl. jours. Served as maj. M.C., AUS, 1942-45. Recipient Disting. Fellow award Am. Coll. Cardiology, 1969; presdl. citation Am. Coll. Cardiology, 1972; Disting. Svc. award Am. Coll. Cardiology, 1994; Jacoby medal Alumni Assn. Mt. Sinai Med. Ctr., 1979, Medicine and Edn. award Alumni Assn. N.Y. Med. Coll., 1987, Lester Gabrilov award for contbns. to medicine Alumni Assn. Mt. Sinai Med. Ctr., 1990. Fellow ACP, Am. Med. Writers Assn. (editorial cons.), Am. Coll. Cardiology (trustee 1952-56, pres. 1956-57, spl. award 1961, Disting. Fellow award 1969, presdl. citation 1972, Disting. Svc. award 1993), N.Y. Cardiol. Soc. (hon.); mem. N.Y. Acad. Scis., AMA, Am. Heart Assn. (coun. on clin. cardiology 1962-94), Am. Fedn. Clin. Rsch., Am. Coll. Chest Physicians, Philippine Heart Assn. (hon.), Alpha Omega Alpha. Home: New York N.Y. Died Feb. 7, 1994.

DADAGLIO, LUIGI, cardinal; b. Sezzádio, Piemonte, Italy, Sept. 28, 1914; s. Francesco Dadaglio and Paloa Sardi. D in Canon and Civil Law, Lateran U., Rome, 1942; D in Canon Law (hon.), Comillas U., Madrid, 1979. Attaché Secretaria of State, Vatican City; sec. in caribean area Nunciatura, 1946-50; diplomatic svc. in U.S., 1950-53, diplomatic svc. in Can., 1953-54, diplomatic svc. in Australia, New Zeland and Pacific Islands, 1954-58, diplomatic svc. Colombia, 1958-60; apostolic in Venezuela Nuntius, 1960-67; amb. in Spain, 1967-80; cardinal Vatican City, 1985; penitentiary major Archpriest of Basilica of St. Mary; Ordained priest Roman Cath. Ch. Mem. Pont Commn. of Vatican State, Sec. of State, Supreme Tribunal of Signatura.

DAFOE, CHRISTOPHER RANDY, marketing, healthcare education professional, diplomat; b. Wilkesboro, N.C., Oct. 26, 1962; s. Alfred Walter Brett and Verna Irene Dafoe. LLB, Somerset, Ilminster,, 1985-89; BEd, York U., North York, Ont., Can., 1991; MEd, Greenwich U., 1992, PhD, 1994; DD (hon.), United Luth. Ch. Sem., Modesto, Calif., 1989. Ordained to ministry Luth. Ch., 1990; incardinated as monsignor Ecumenical Jacobite Orthodox Cath. Ch. of Antioch, 1994; lic. primary/jr. level tchr., psychotherapist, Ark., Ont., Mo., W.Va., Brazil; cert. LCSW, CCSW; registered play therapist. Dir. mktg. Info. Interchange Co. Ltd., Freehold, N.J., 1983-93; regional v.p. Sundance Rehab. Corp., Indpls., 1993—; chair. Profl. Paralegal Assn., Ont., Can., 1985-93; cons. Internat. Mktg. Inst., London, 1989—; consul Repub. Suriname. Named Prince of Medina by Patriarch of Antioch, Baron of San Nicandro by Coun. of Westphalia. Mem. Internat. Lawyers Assn., Internat. Bar Assn., World Jurist Assn., Soc. Psychotherapy and Psychodrama, Notary Assn., Knights Templar (adjutor gen., adjutor 1987-91, Duke of Tyre, 1989), Coun. Seven Sages (H.S.H. sovereign prince, grand master of the order). Avocations: computer science, world peace, live theatre. DIED 10/01/97.

DAHL, HARRY WALDEMAR, lawyer; b. Des Moines, Aug. 7, 1927; s. Harry Waldemar and Helen Gerda (Anderson) D.; m. Bonnie Sorensen, June 14, 1952; children: Harry Waldemar, Lisabeth (dec.), Christina. BA, U. Iowa, 1950; JD, Drake U., 1955. Bar: Iowa 1950, U.S. Supreme Ct. 1965, Fla. 1970, Nebr. 1983, Minn. 1984. Assoc. Steward & Crouch, Des Moines, 1955-59; Iowa dep. indsl. commr. Des Moines, 1959-62, commr., 1962-71; pres., prin. Law Offices of Harry W. Dahl, P.C., 1972-95; of counsel Underwood, Gillis and Karcher, Miami, 1972-77; adj. prof. law Drake U., Des Moines, 1972-96; exec. dir. Internat. Assn. Indsl. Accident Bds. and Commns., 1972-77; pres. Workers' Compensation Studies, Inc., 1974-92, Workers' Compensation Svcs., Inc., 1978-92, Hewitt, Coleman & Assocs. Iowa, Inc., 1975-79; mem. adv. com. Second Injury Fund, Fla. Indsl. Rels. Commn. Author: Iowa Law on Workmen's Compensation, 1975; editor: ABC Newsletter, 1964-77. Bd. counselors Drake U. Law Sch., 1990-93. With USRN, 1945-46. Recipient Adminstrs. award Internat. Assn. Indsl. Accident Bds. and Commns., 1967. Mem. Am. Trial Lawyers Assn. (chmn. workers' compensation sect. 1973), ABA (chmn. workers' compensation com. 1974-76), Iowa Bar Assn. (chmn. workers' compensation com. 1984-89), Fla. Bar (bd. govs. 1988-90), Nebr. Bar Assn., Minn. Bar Assn., Internat. Bar Assn., Am. Soc. Law and Medicine (coun. 1975-82), Iowa Assn. Workers' Compensation Lawyers (co-founder, past pres.), Coll. of Workers Compensation Inc. (co-founder, regent), Swedish Pioneer Hist. Soc., Am. Swedish Inst., Sco. of the Goths (founder, pres.), Des Moines Pioneer Club, East High Alumni Assn. (pres. 1975-76), Grand View Coll. Alumni Assn. (bd. dirs. 1993—), Order of Coif, Masons, Shriners, Sertoma (chmn. bd. dirs. 1974-75). Lutheran. Died May 27, 1996.

DALY, T(HOMAS) F(RANCIS) GILROY, federal judge; b. N.Y.C., Feb. 25, 1931; s. Paul Gerard and Madeleine (Mulqueen) D.; m. Stuart Stetson, Jan. 16, 1960; children: Timothy Francis Gilroy, Matthew M., Loan, Anna L. BA, Georgetown U., 1952; LLB, Yale U., 1957. Bar: Conn. bar 1957, N.Y. bar 1959. Assoc. Simpson Thacher and Bartlett, N.Y.C., 1957-61; asst. U.S. atty. U.S. Dept. Justice, So. Dist. of N.Y., 1961-64; pvt. practice Fairfield, 1964-77; dept. atty. gen. State of Conn., 1967-71; spl. asst. to atty. gen. State of Conn., Conn., 1971-75; dep. state treas. State of Conn., 1976-77, ins. commr., 1975-76; judge U.S. Dist. Ct., Conn., 1977—; chief judge U.S. Dist. Ct. Conn., Bridgeport, 1983-88, mem. subcom. on supporting pers., 1983-87; mem. subcom. jud. stats. and resources com. Jud. Conf., 1987-91; mem. Jud. Coun. Cts. of 2d Cir., 1982-88; bd. dirs. STA-FED Alternative Dispute Resolution, 1993-95. Trustee Leukemia Soc. Am., chmn., 1971; bd. trustees Marist Coll., 1994—; mem. Tapping Reeve's Litchfield Law Sch. Com., 1994—. 1st lt. Rangers, U.S. Army, 1952-54. Recipient Disting. Svc. award Fairfield Jr. C. of C., 1967. Fellow ABA, Conn. Bar Found. (charter fellow James W. Cooper Fellows Program 1994); mem. Conn. Bar Assn., Fed. Bar. Assn., Fed. Judges Assn., Assn. of Bar of City of N.Y., Am. Judicature Soc., Fed. Bar Coun., Am. Legion, Phi Delta Phi. Democrat. Roman Catholic. Died July 11, 1996.

DANDO, GEORGE WILLIAM, professional association executive; b. Balt., May 24, 1935; s. Llewellyn Stewart and Mariester (Anderson) D.; m. Diane Mills, Sept. 1, 1976; 1 child, Ross Stewart. BA, Baylor U., 1960; MDiv, Pitts. Theol. Sem., 1963. Ordained to ministry Presbytery of New Castle, 1963. Pastor 1st Presbyn. Ch., Greenfield, Iowa, 1963-65; commd. ensign USNR, 1962; advanced through grades to lt. comdr. USN, 1969, chaplain, 1965-83, ret., 1983; interim minister Presbytery of Carlisle, Pa., 1984-90; exec. dir. Mil. Chaplains Assn. U.S.A., Washington, 1990—. With U.S. Army, 1957-60. Mem. Kiwanis (lt. gov. Pa. dist. 1989-90).

DANIEL, ELEANOR SAUER, economist, real estate executive; b. N.Y.C., Feb. 8, 1917; d. Charles Peter and Elsie Edna (Dommer) Sauer; m. John Carl Daniel, Dec. 31, 1952; children: Victoria Ann, Charles Timothy. BA magna cum laude (Bardwell fellow), Mt. Holyoke Coll., 1936; MA (Perkins fellow), Columbia U., 1937. Economist, U.S. Steel Co., N.Y.C., 1938; lectr. econs. Bklyn. Coll., 1939-40; with Mut. Life Ins. Co. N.Y., N.Y.C., 1940-74, asst. v.p., 1972-74, sr. econ. adviser, 1972-74; economist Fed. Home Loan Bank, N.Y.C., 1974-75; v.p., dir. Daniel Realty Cos., N.Y.C., 1975-95; pres. Midtown Daniel, 1986-95; former dir., chmn. fin. com. Atlantic City Electric Co.; past chmn. fin. com. Atlantic Energy, Inc.; former mem. bd. mgrs. U.S. Savs. Bank Newark; mem. Pres's. Task Force Fed. Credit Programs, 1968-69; mem. N.J. Gov's. Econ. Recovery Com., 1975-76; mem. econ. adv. bd. U.S. Sec. Commerce, 1971-73; mem. bus. research adv. council U.S. Bur. Labor Statistics, 1966-86. Author: (with J.J. O'Leary and S.F. Foster) Our National Debt and Our Savings; correspondent, author, mem. Am. editorial bd., The London Economist, 1946-52; contbr. articles to profl. jours. Former trustee Blue Shield of N.J., trustee fellow Mt. Holyoke Coll., also past vice chmn., mem. fin. com., trustee; active Nat. Rep. Com. Mem. Am. Econ. Assn., Am. Fin. Assn. (past dir.), N.J. Health Think Tank, Phi Beta Kappa. Died Aug. 26, 1995. Home: East Brunswick N.J.

DANILOVA, ALEXANDRA, ballet dancer, choreographer; b. Peterhof, Russia, Nov. 20, 1903; came to U.S., 1934; d. Dionis and Claudia (Gotovtzeva) D. Ed., Theatrical Sch. Petrograd. Mem. faculty Sch. Am. Ballet; adjudicator Southeastern Ballet Conf., 1960. Mem. Russian State Ballet, Maryinsky Theater, 1922-24, soloist Diaghileff Ballet, 1925, ballerina, 1929, Montecarlo Opera House, 1930-31; star: Oswald Stoll's prodn. Waltzes from Vienna, Alhambra Theatre, London, 1932; ballerina: Oswald Stoll's prodn. Col. de Basil's Ballet Russe, 1933-38; prima ballerina: Oswald Stoll's prodn. Ballet Russe de Monte Carlo, 1938-51; currently head own co. touring various countries, lecture tours, U.S., Europe; guest star: various ballets including Royal Ballet Covent Garden, 1946; star: various ballets including Song of Norway, 1944; Broadway musical Oh Captain, 1958; choreographer Broadway musical, Met. Opera Co.; staged: (with George Balanchine for) Broadway musical Coppelia, N.Y.C. Ballet, 1974, and Los Angeles Ballet, 1980; works for Nijinsky Festival Germany, 1975, for Md. Ballet, 1975; biography: Choura, 1986 (Della Torre Bueno prize 1987). Recipient Capezio Dance award, 1958, Dance mag. award, 1984, Kennedy Ctr. Honors award, 1989, Handel medal, 1989. Greek Orthodox. Died July 13, 1997.

DANTE, HARRIS LOY, history educator; b. Monticello, Ill., Feb. 17, 1912; s. Harris and Myrtle Thread (Loy) D.; m. Margaret June Miller, June 5, 1937; children: Susan Kay (Mrs. Tom Mounkhall), Nancy Jane (Mrs. Victor L. Bennison) John H. B.A. with honors, U. Ill., 1933, M.A., 1941; Ph.D., U. Chgo., 1950. Salesman Standard Oil Co., Chgo., 1933-36; tchr. Thornton (Ill.) Elementary Sch., 1936-38, Burlington (Ia.) Sr. High Sch., 1938-43, Burlington Jr. Coll., 1946-48; lectr. history U. Chgo., 1949-50; asst. prof. history and edn. Kent (Ohio) State U., 1950-52, assoc. prof., 1952-57, prof., 1957-82; cons. U.S. Office Edn., Ohio State Dept. Edn.; Co-dir. comparative edn. seminar to, Finland, USSR, Czechoslovakia and Spain, 1969, to USSR, 1972; mem. evaluation bd. Nat. Council Accreditation Tchr. Edn., 1976—. Co-author: U.S. History, 1967, Teachers Resources Book, 1967, United States History: Search for Freedom, 2 vols, 1974, Recent Ohio History, 1983, U.S. History: Recent Events to 1981, 1984; contbr. articles to Jr. Britannica Ency. and profl. jours. Served to lt. USNR, 1943-46. Recipient President's medal Kent State U., 1971. Mem. Nat. Council Social Studies (dir. 1959-63, 71-76, pres. 1973), Ohio Council Social Studies (pres. 1957, exec. com. 1979-82), Am. Hist. Assn., Orgn. Am. Historians, Ohio Acad. History (chmn. standards com. 1978—), NEA, AAUP (council State Univs. Ohio 1951—, pres. 1961), Phi Delta Kappa, Kappa Delta Pi, Phi Alpha Theta. Died August 7, 1997.

DARITY, EVANGELINE ROYALL, dean, educator; b. Wilson, N.C., June 16, 1927; B.Sc. in Religious Edn., Barber-Scotia Coll., Concord, N.C., 1949; M.Ed., Smith

Coll., 1969; Ed.D., U. Mass., Amherst, 1978; m. William A. Darity; children: William, Janki Evangelia. Various YWCA positions 1949-53; tchr., Egypt, N.C. and Mass., 1953-67; asst. to class deans Smith Coll., Northampton, Mass., 1968-75; v.p. student affairs Barber-Scotia Coll., 1978-79; exec. dir. YWCA, Holyoke, Mass., 1979-81; assoc. dean studies, assoc. dean third world affairs Mt. Holyoke Coll., South Hadley, Mass., 1981-94 ; corp. mem. Community Savs. Bank, Holyoke. Mem. Amherst Town Meeting, 1971-80; mem. adv. bd. Community Adolescent Resource and Edn. Ctr.; trustee Barber-Scotia Coll., Concord, N.C. Mem. AAUW (br. pres. 1971-74, 86-88), Am. Assn. Counseling and Devel., Nat. Assn. Women Deans, Counselors and Adminstrs., LWV, Alpha Kappa Alpha, Phi Delta Kappa. Died Sept. 27, 1994; interred Wildwood Cemetery. Home: Amherst Mass.

DARLINGTON, SIDNEY, educator, electrical engineer; b. Pitts., July 18, 1906; s. Philip Jackson and Rebecca Taylor (Mattson) D.; m. Joan Gilmer Raysor, Apr. 24, 1965; children: Ellen Kerr, Rebecca. B.S. magna cum laude, Harvard U., 1928; B.S. in Elec. Engring, MIT, 1929; Ph.D. in Physics, Columbia U., 1940; D.Sc. (hon.), U. N.H., 1984. Mem. tech. staff Bell Telephone Labs., Murray Hill, N.J., 1929-71; head dept. Bell Telephone Labs., 1960-71; ret., 1971; adj. prof. elec. engring. U. N.H., Durham, 1971—; mem. U.S. commn. VI Internat. Sci. Radio Union, 1959-75, del. gen. assemblies, 1960, 63, 66, 69; cons. in field, 1971—. Author. Recipient Medal of Freedom U.S. Army. Fellow IEEE (Edison medal, 1975, Medal of Honor 1981, CAS Soc. award 1986), AIAA; mem. Nat. Acad. Engring., Nat. Acad. Scis., Phi Beta Kappa, Tau Beta Pi. Club: Appalachian Mountain. Patentee in field. DIED 10/31/97. .

DART, ROBERT, manufacturing executive; b. 1958. Pres., CEO Dart Container, Mason, Mich. Deceased.

DAUB, BERGER ELLIS, real estate agent; b. McKeesport, Pa., Apr. 9, 1927; s. William I. Schuck and Maude Myrtle Schuck Daub; m. Helen Eloise Lawsen; children: Karen L. Daub McKown, Patricia L., Lisa Sue (dec.). Student, Akron U., 1949-51, Franklin U., 1976-77, Columbus State Coll., 1992—. Quality control inspector Westinghouse Electric Corp., Columbus, Ohio, 1960-75; job coord. Ohio Bur. Employment Svc., Columbus, 1980-81; caseworker Franklin County Welfare Dept., Columbus, 1982-83; real estate agt. Century 21 Saxton Real Estate, Columbus, 1976—. Treas. Westwood Civic Assn., West Jefferson, Ohio, 1961-62; bd. dirs. Hardesty Heights Cond Assn., Columbus, 1982-83; chmn. local draft bd., Columbus, 1984-89. With USN, 1945-46. Recipient Recognition for community activities in support of law enforcement Ohio Ho. of Reps., 1979. Fellow KC (4th degree), Am. Legion. Democrat. Roman Catholic. Avocations: wine making, golf, walking, sports.

DAUBEN, WILLIAM GARFIELD, chemist, educator; b. Columbus, Ohio, Nov. 6, 1919; s. Hyp J. and Leilah (Stump) D.; m. Carol Hyatt, Aug. 8, 1947; children: Barbara, Ann. AB, Ohio State U., 1941; AM, Harvard U., 1942, PhD, 1944; PhD (hon.), U. Bordeaux, France, 1980. Edward Austin fellow Harvard U., 1941-42, teaching fellow, 1942-43, research asst., 1943-45; instr. U. Calif. at Berkeley, 1945-47, asst. prof. chemistry, 1947-52, assoc. prof., 1952-57, prof., 1957-92, prof. emeritus, 1992-97; lectr. Am.-Swiss Found., 1962; mem. med. chem. study sect. USPHS, 1959-64; mem. chemistry panel NSF, 1964-67; mem. Am.-Sino Sci. Cooperation Com., 1973-76; NRC, 1977-80. Mem. bd. editors Jour. of Organic Chemistry, 1957-62; mem. bd. editors Organic Syntheses, 1959-67, bd. dirs., 1971-97; editor in chief Organic Reactions, 1967-83, pres., 1967-84, bd. dirs. 1967-97; mem. edit. bd. Steroids, 1989-97; contbr. articles profl. jours. Recipient citation U. Calif., Berkeley, 1990; Guggenheim fellow, 1951, 66, sr. fellow NSF, 1957-58, Alexander von Humboldt Found. fellow, 1980. Fellow Royal Soc. Chemistry, Swiss Chem. Soc.; mem. NAS (chmn. chemistry sect. 1977-80), Am. Chem. Soc. (chmn. div. organic chemistry 1962-63, councilor organic div. 1964-70, mem. coun. publ. com. 1965-70, mem. adv. com. Petroleum Research Fund 1974-77, award Calif. sect. 1959, Ernest Guenther award 1973, Arthur C. Cope scholar 1990), Am. Acad. Arts and Scis., Pharm. Soc. Japan (hon.), Phi Beta Kappa, Sigma Xi, Phi Lambda Upsilon, Phi Eta Sigma, Sigma Chi. Club: Bohemian. Home: Kensington Calif. Died Jan. 2, 1997.

DAUGHERTY, RICHARD BERNARD, lawyer; b. Los Angeles, Aug. 30, 1915; s. Edwin Matthew and Mabel (Dunbar) D.; m. Margaret Amey, Nov. 15, 1941; children: Richard Bernard Jr., Patricia Anne Shallenberger. AB in Econs. and Acctg., Stanford U., 1937; LLB, Harvard U., 1940. Bar: Calif. 1940, U.S. Dist. Ct. (no. dist.) Calif. 1940, U.S. Ct. Claims 1964, U.S. Supreme Ct. 1974. Assoc. Pillsbury, Madison & Sutro, San Francisco, 1940-41, 45-55, ptnr., 1955-91, ret., 1991; gen. atty. Pacific Telephone and Telegraph Co., San Francisco, 1969-79; gen. counsel Presidio Soc., San Francisco, 1978-83. Sec., gen. counsel Ft. Point and Army Museum Assn., San Francisco, 1968-79, pres., 1979-80, bd. dirs., 1979-89; v.p., bd. dirs. Irish Beach Improvement Club, Manchester, Calif., 1970-73; pres., bd. dirs. Irish Beach Water Dist., Manchester, 1975-79. Served to lt. col. U.S. Army, 1941-46. Mem. ABA, Calif. Bar Assn., San Francisco Bar Assn., Harvard Law Sch. Alumni Assn., Beta Theta Pi Alumni Assn. (pres. 1945-47). Republican. Roman Catholic. Clubs: Bohemian, Presidio Officers' (San Francisco). Avocations: swimming, woodworking, gardening. Died Nov. 5, 1996.

DAVID, PAUL THEODORE, political science educator emeritus; b. Brockton, Mass., Aug. 12, 1906; s. Ira E. and Bernice Grace (Harrison) D.; m. Opal Mary Davis, May 31, 1935. Student, Ga. Sch. Tech., 1924-26; AB, Antioch Coll., 1928; AM, Brown U., 1930, PhD, 1933. Instr. econs. Brown U., 1930-31; rsch. fellow Brookings Inst., 1931-32; congl. staff mem. Pub. Utilities Holding Co. Investigation, 1932-33; adminstrv. asst., economist TVA, 1933-36; staff mem. Pres. com. Adminstrv. Mgmt., 1936; sec., asst. dir. U.S. Adv. Com. on Edn., 1936-39; assoc. dir., chief economist Am. youth commn. Am. Council on Edn., 1939-42; mem. econ. staff, fiscal div. Bur. Budget, Washington, 1942-46; alt. U.S. rep. council Internat. Civil Aviation Orgn., Montreal, 1946-50; sr. staff mem. Brookings Instn., 1950-60; prof. govt. and fgn. affairs U. Va., 1960-77, prof. emeritus, 1977-94, dir. Miller Ctr. project to commemmorate 50th Anniversary of Internat. Civil Aviation Orgn., 1993-94; sec. com. to prepare charter for Internat. Civil Aviation Orgn., Conf. on Internat. Civil Aviation, 1944; cons. Fed. Execs. Inst., Charlottesville, 1977-79; fellowship Ctr. for Advanced Study in Behavioral Scis., Stanford, Calif., 1959-60; vis. lectr. Salzburg Seminar in Am. Studies, summer 1963; vis. prof. U. Kent at Canterbury, 1974, U. Tasmania, 1978, Sangamon State U., Ill., 1980-81; cons. commn. rules Democratic Nat. Com., 1969-72. Author: Economics of Air Mail Transportation, 1934, The Politics of National Party Conventions, (with R. M. Goldman and R. C. Bain), 1960, (with Ralph Eisenberg) Devaluation of the Urban and Suburban Vote, Vols. I and II, 1962, Party Strength in the United States 1872-1970, 1972, (with James Ceaser) Proportional Representation in Presidential Nominating Politics, 1980; sr. author Vol. I of Presidential Nominating Politics in 1952; sr. editor other 4 vols. (with Moos and Goldman), 1954; editor: (with D. Everson) The Presidential Election and Transition 1980-81; contbr. numerous articles to profl. jours. Recipient Ford Found. faculty award, 1968-69. Mem. Am. Econ. Assn., Am. Polit. Sci. Assn., Phi Beta Kappa. Democrat. Clubs: Cosmos (Washington); Colonnade (Charlottesville Va.). Home: Charlottesville Va. Died Sept 7, 1994.

DAVIDSON, DALWYN ROBERT, electric utility executive; b. Lorain County, Ohio, Aug. 10, 1918; s. John Francis and Erma Adele (Hayes) D.; m. Georganna Katherine Sharp, Sept. 12, 1942; children: Karen Joy Leech, Dale Wynn, Glenn Kirk. Student, Kent State U., 1936-38; BSEE, Case Western Res. U., 1941. Registered profl. elec. engr., Ohio. Sr. engr. Cleve. Electric Illuminating Co., Cleve., 1952-57, gen. supr., 1957-67, mgr., 1967-74, v.p., 1974-82, sr. v.p., 1982-83, cons., 1983-93. Capt. USAF, 1943-46. Fellow IEEE; mem. Cleve. Engring. Soc. Republican. Methodist. Died Aug. 31, 1996.

DAVIDSON, JOSEPHINE F., newspaper editor; b. El Paso, Tex.; d. Leon Amson and Estelle Therese (Lyon) Rosenfield; m.Herbert Marc Davidson, Jr., Dec. 27, 1947; children: Marc Leon, Julia Rose. BA in Polit. Sci., UCLA, 1943; D of Journalism (hon.), Stetson U., 1994. Reporter Ventura Star Free Press, Calif., 1943-45; reporter News-Journal, Daytona Beach, Fla., sch. editor, food editor, Sunday editor, asst. editor, 1945-85, co-editor, 1985, editor, 1986-95; v.p. News-Journal Corp., Daytona Beach, Fla., 1985-95; mem. jud. nominating commn. for Fla. Supreme Ct., 1994-98; first woman editor UCLA Daily Bruin, 1943. Chmn. Volusia County Student Bicentennial Park, 1974-76; bd. dirs. Fla. Endowment for the Humanities, Tampa, 1984-88, Ctrl. Fla. Cultural Endeavors, Daytona Beach, 1976-95, Seaside Music Theater, Daytona Beach, 1978-95, Civic League, Tiger Bay Club; program chmn. Volusia County Women's Network. Recipient J. Saxton Lloyd award for cmty. svcs. Civic League, 1995; honoree Daytona Beach C.C. Found., 1992, Tippen and Josephine Field Davidson Endowment for Arts. Mem. Am. Soc. Newspaper Editors. Home: Daytona Beach Fla. Died July 18, 1995.

DAVIES, DANIEL R., retired educator; b. Plymouth, Pa., Feb. 21, 1911; s. John R. and Minnie (Kocher) D.; m. Winifred Evans, June 14, 1941 (div. July 1975); children: Catherine, Wendy; m. Nancy Church Edwards, Sept. 9, 1975. A.B., Harvard U., 1933; A.M., Bucknell U., 1943; Ph.D., Columbia U., 1946; Ph.D. (Honorary), NOVA U., 1993. Tchr. Forty Fort (Pa.) High Sch., 1934-44, head dept. English, 1940-44; asst. supt. schs. Briarcliff Manor, N.Y., 1944-45; asst. prof. dept. edn. adminstrn. Columbia, 1945-46, asst. prof. edn., exec. officer div. adminstrn. and guidance, 1946-49; assoc. prof., exec. officer dept. adminstrn. Tchrs. Coll., 1949-50; prof. edn., dir. coop. program in ednl. adminstrn. Tchrs. Coll. (Middle Atlantic region), 1950-59; del. Coop. Center for Ednl. Adminstrn., 1955-59; assoc. dir. Indsl. Mgmt. Work Conf., Columbia U. Sch. Engring., and Indsl. Research Conf., 1955-60; exec. dir. U. Council for Edn. Adminstrn., 1958-59; editorial cons. A.C. Croft Publs., New London, Conn., 1958-60; dir. research and devel. Croft Ednl. Services, 1960-66; v.p. research, devel. and dir. Croft Cons. Services, Tucson, 1966-71; pres. Davies-Brickell Assos., Ltd., 1972-90, Davies-Taylor Assocs., Inc., 1987-90; lectr. U. Ariz., 1962-64; vis. prof. San Diego State, summer 1957, U. N.Mex., summer 1960, Okla. A&M, summer 1963, Tex. A&M, U. Scranton, summer 1964, U. Nebr., summer 1971; mem. Nat. Com. Advancement Ednl. Adminstrn., 1955-57; cons. Lilly Endowment, Inc., 1976-77; head policy cons. Calif. Sch. Bds. Assn., 1976-81; dir. policy services Conn. Assn. Bds. Edn., 1978-88; head policy cons. N.J. Sch. Bds. Assn., 1977-82; spl. cons. on installing Davies-Brickell System in schs., U.S.A., Can., also Am. Schs., France, Holland, Greece, Italy. Author: numerous books including Dynamics of Group Action, 8 vols, 1954; (with V. Anderson) Patterns of Educational Leadership, 1956, (with H.M. Brickell) Davies-Brickell System for School Board Policy Making, 1957, 17th edit., 1988, Calif. edits., 1977-80, Conn. edit., 1978-88, Nebr. edit., 1983-84, Board Policy Letter, 1958-71, (with R.T. Livingston) You and Management, 1958, (translated into Japanese, 1968), (with Margaret Handlong) Teaching of Art, 1962, The Administrative Internship, 1962, (with D.E. Griffiths) Executive Action, 1962-68, (with W.S. Elsbree, Louise H. Nelson) Educational Sec., 1962-67, Catholic Schools Adaptation of the Davies-Brickell System, 1968, (with Father James R. Dineen) New Patterns for Catholic Education, 1968, (with Catherine Davies Armistead) In-Service Education, 1975, Chats in Eternity: Living, Learning and Loving, 1992; weekly columnist Sierra Vista Herald, Bisbee Daily Rev.; contbr. articles to scholarly jours. Pres. bd. dirs. Ariz. Theatre Co., 1976-79; v.p. bd. dirs. Copper Queen Community Hosp., Bisbee, 1985-88, pres., 1988-90; pres., founder, mem. governing bd. The Bisbee Found., Inc., 1986—; pres. Bisbee Coun. on the Arts and Humanities, 1990-91; cons., lectr. Nova U., Scottsdale, Ariz., 1990, 1991, 1993, Ft. Lauderdale, 1992, Washington. Winner Henry Barnard Critical Essay award, 1990; named Citizen of Yr. Bisbee C. of C., 1983; Ford Found. grantee Europe, 1961. Fellow AAAS; mem. NEA, AAUP, Nat. Soc. Study Edn. (contbr. Yearbook 1954), Am. Assn. Sch. Adminstrs., Nat. Conf. Profs. Ednl. Adminstrn. (exec. com., sec.-treas. 1948-58), Phi Delta Kappa. Club: Bisbee Country. Lodge: Bisbee Rotary (pres. 1984-85). Died Aug. 28, 1997.

DAVIES, MARTHA HILL, dance educator; b. East Palestine, Ohio. Studied with Martha Graham; BS, Tchrs. Coll., Columbia U.; MA, NYU; LHD (hon.), Adelphi U., Towson State U., 1981; DFA (hon.), Mt. Holyoke Coll., The Juilliard Sch., 1987; LittD (hon.), Bennington Coll. Dancer Martha Graham Dance Co., N.Y.C.; mem. faculty U. Oreg., Lincoln Sch. Tchrs. Coll.; dir. of dance NYU, N.Y.C., 1930-51; chmn., dance and choreographer Bennington Coll., 1932-51; dir. Bennington Sch. of Dance, 1934-39, Bennington Sch. of Arts, 1940-42; founding dir. Am. Dance Festival, 1948-65; founding chairperson dance dept. Juillard Sch., N.Y.C., 1951—, dir. dance divsn., 1951-85, artistic dir. emeritus, 1985—; bd. dirs. Choreographic Conf., U. NSW, U. Victoria, Australia, 1975-76. Recipient Presdl. citation NYU, 1982, Disting. Svc. award Dance Notation Bur., 1984, Mayor's Honor for Arts and Culture award City of N.Y., 1984, Disting. Svc. medal Tchrs. Coll., Columbia U., 1986, Ernie award Dance USA, 1994. Deceased.

DAVIS, A. ARTHUR, lawyer; b. Sioux City, Iowa, Oct. 12, 1928; s. Edward R. and Isabel (Baron) D.; divorced; children: Pamela Benham, Mark Baron. B.S.S. with honors, Northwestern U., 1950, J.D., 1952. Bar: Iowa 1952, U.S. Circuit Ct. Appeals (8th cir.). 1959, U.S. Ct. Appeals (2d cir.) 1975, D.C. 1968. Practice law Des Moines, 1955—; assoc. Brody, Parker, Roberts, Thoma & Harris, 1955-59; ptnr. Davis, Hockenberg, Wine, Brown, Koehn & Shors and predecessor firms, 1959—; lectr. pub. speaking Drake U., 1955-60; dir. various publicly held corps.; chmn. joint com. Iowa Bar Assn.-Iowa Investment Bankers Assn., 1971-75; mem. U.S. 8th Circuit Judge Nominating Commn., 1978-80. Mem. Des Moines Commn. on Human Rights, 1960-63, U.S. Holocaust Meml. Council, 1980-87; mem. Bd. Edn. Des Moines Ind. Community Sch. Dist., 1963-69, pres., 1966-67; mem. vis. com. Northwestern U. Sch. Law, 1980; mem. Gov.'s Commn. on State and Local Govt., 1964-68, Ins. Commr.'s Spl. Com. on State Regulation, 1967-68; bd. dirs. Planned Parenthood Assn. Iowa, pres., 1976; mem. adv. panel on making govt. work better Democratic Nat. Com., 1981-85; bd. dirs. Iowa Product Devel. Corp., 1983-85, Des Moines Internat. Airport Bd., 1993—; mem. Lt. Gov.'s Iowa Tomorrow Com., 1983-85; state chmn. Iowa Dem. Party, 1985-87, mem. Dem. Nat. Com., 1985-87; bd. of trustees, 1985-87, mem., vice chmn. bd. govs. 1987—, Drake U.; chmn. Boy Scouts Am. Ann. Dinner, 1993. Served to 1st lt. AUS, 1953-55. Recipient Nat. award People to People Program, 1961, Brotherhood award Des Moines chpt. NCCJ, 1981. Mem. Des Moines C. of C. (dir. 1973-75, 80—, pres. 1979, chair Soviet Adv. Bd. 1990—), Corp. for Internat. Trade (bd. dirs. 1991—), J.B. Demos (bd. dirs.), Northwestern U. Law Alumni Assn. (pres. 1977-78), Des Moines Club, Order of Coif, Delta Sigma Rho, Phi Delta Phi, Phi Epsilon Pi. Democrat. Jewish. Deceased.

DAVIS, ARIEL, designer, manufacturer theater lighting equipment; b. Feb. 14, 1912; s. Rual Dennis and Mary Louise (Kitchen) D.; m. Dorothy Jean Harding; children, Ronald, Steven. BS in Physics, Brigham Young U., 1946. Pres. Davis Enterprises, Provo, Uath, Ariel Davis Mfg. Co., Salt Lake City. Patentee numerous stage lighting equipment including Davis Dimmer Switch. Named Outstanding Engr. of Yr. Combined Engring. Councils Utah, 1961. Mem. Illumination Engring. Soc., Nat. Com. Stage Lighting, Theta Alpha Phi. Served as chief petty officer USN, 1943-46, PTO. DIED 02/06/97. .

DAVIS, EUGENIA ASIMAKOPOULOS, food science and nutrition educator, chemist, consultant; b. Chgo., Oct. 15, 1938; d. Efstathios Konstantinos and Marigo (Askounes) Asimakopoulos; m. Howard Theodore Davis, Sept. 18, 1960; children: William Howard, Maria Katherine. BS in Chemistry, U. Chgo., 1959, MS, 1960; PhD in Organic Chemistry, Free U., Brussels, 1967. Rsch. scientist Rsch. Inst. Ill. Inst. Tech., Chgo., 1960-62; rsch. fellow U. Minn., Mpls., 1966-70, rsch. assoc., 1970-71, asst. prof., 1972-78, assoc. prof., 1978-84, prof., 1984—, dir. grad. studies in food sci., 1990-92; sabbatical leave U. Minn., Mpls., France, 1992-93; vis. fellow Tech. U. Compiegne, France, 1992-93; cons. Univ. Rsch. Consortium, Pls., 1985—, Tel-Tech, Mpls., 1990—; bd. dirs., v.p. rsch. Preventative Care Rsch. Inst., Mpls., 1990—. Editor: Food Microstructure Jour., 1981-90; mem. editorial bd. Cereal Chemistry Jour., 1987-90, 93—, Cereal Foods World, 1990—; author: (chpt.) New Frontiers in Food Microstructure, 1983; contbr. articles to profl. jours. Miles Labs. fellow, 1989-90; grantee Agrl. Exptl. Sta., 1972—, Kraft Gen. Food, 1988-92, Borden, 1988-90. Fellow Corn Refiners Assn.; mem. Am. Chem. Soc., Inst. Food Technologists (chmn. carbohydrate div. 1988-90), Am. Assn. Cereal Chemists (bd. dirs. AACC Found.), Royal Microscopical Soc., Am. Home Econs. Assn. Died July 18, 1996.

DAVIS, KATHARINE CLELAND, former law librarian, information specialist, researcher; b. Ft. Myers, Va., Oct. 15, 1907; d. Cleland and Mabel Tillou (Young) D.; m. Alfred Stuart, May 1936 (div.). BA, Wells Coll., Aurora, N.Y., 1930; MFA, Yale U., 1933. Tech. dir. Shubert Corp. Theater, N.Y.C., 1933-34; info. specialist USDA, Washington, 1951-53; asst. to ASTIA after process U.S. Libr. of Congress, 1954-56; asst. law libr. U. Miami, Coral Gables, Fla., 1957-74, Nova U., Ft. Lauderdale, Fla., 1974-76; exec. asst. Loebe Rhodes Investment Co., South Miami, Fla., 1977-81; libr. asst. Drexel, Burnham, Lambert & Sochet, South Miami, Fla., 1981-88; libr. asst. Sochet & Co., South Miami, 1988-90, ret., 1990. Contbr. articles to profl. jours. Charter mem. Rep. Presdl. Task Force, Washington, 1981—; me. High Frontier, Washington, 1983—; reader Rec. for the Blind, 1958-78. Lt. comdr. USN, 1942-46, World War II. Mem. Yale U. Alumni Assn., Actors Equity Assn., Mil. Order World Wars (comdr. 1988-89), Coun. for Inter-Am. Security, State Dept. Watch, Securty and Intelligence, Moral Rearmament Breakthroughs, Accuracy in Media, Friends of Everglades, Yale Club Miami, Wells Club Fla. Avocations: reading, tennis, research on environment. Died 1991.

DAVIS, KINGSLEY, sociologist, educator, researcher; b. Tuxedo, Tex., Aug. 20, 1908; s. Joseph Dyer and Winifred (Kingsley) D.; m. Jane Quinn, Aug. 20, 1936 (div.); children: Jo Ann Daily, Jefferson K.; m. Judith Blake, Nov. 3, 1954 (div. 1977); 1 dau., Laura Isabelle; m. Marta H. Seoane, 1985; 1 child, Austin Alexander Seoane. A.B. in English, U. Tex., 1930; M.A. in Philosophy, 1932; M.A. in Sociology, Harvard U., 1933; Ph.D. in Sociology, 1936. Instr. in sociology Smith Coll., 1934-36; asst. prof. sociology Clark U., 1936-37; assoc. prof., chmn. dept. Pa. State U., University Park, 1937-42, prof., chmn., 1942-44; vis. research assoc. Office Population Research, Princeton U., 1942-44; research assoc. Princeton U., 1944-48, assoc. prof. pub. affairs, 1944-45, assoc. prof. anthropology and sociology, 1945-48; prof. sociology grad. faculty Columbia U., N.Y.C., 1948-55; prof. sociology U. Calif.-Berkeley, 1955-70, chmn. internat. population and urban research, 1956-77, chmn. dept. sociology, 1961-63, Ford prof. sociology and comparative studies, 1970-76, Ford prof. emeritus, recalled, 1976-77; disting. prof. sociology U. So. Calif., Los Angeles, 1977-92; sr. research fellow Hoover Instn., Stanford U., Calif., 1981-92, emeritus sr. rsch. fellow, 1992-97; U.S. rep. Population Commn., UN, N.Y.C., 1954-61; mem. NASA Adv. Council, Washington, 1977-82, Adv. Council Sci. and Tech., Legis Assembly, Sacramento, 1970-71; disting. lectr. SUNY-Stony Brook, 1983. Author: Human Society, 1949, The Population of India and Pakistan, 1951, World Urbanization, 1972; editor: Cities, 1973. Recipient Irene Taeuber award for disting. research in demography, 1979; recipient Common Wealth award for research in sociology, 1979; Oldright fellow, 1931-32; Henry Bromfield Rogers Meml. fellow, 1932-33; Social Sci. Research Council postdoctoral fellow, 1940-41; Carnegie Corp. traveling fellow, 1952; Ctr. Advanced Study Behavioral Scis. fellow, 1956-57, 80-81; NSF sr. postdoctoral fellow, 1964-65. Fellow AAAS (chmn. sect. 1963, 81, v.p. 1963), Am. Sociol. Assn. (pres. 1959 Disting. Career award), Am. Statis. Assn. (liaison mem. council 1968-69); mem. Population Assn. Am. (pres. 1962-63), Sociol. Research Assn. (pres. 1960), AAUP mem. council 1962-65), Am. Eugenics Soc. (bd. dirs. 1953-55), Internat. Union Sci. Study Population (chmn. Am. com. 1967-68), Nat. Acad. Scis., Am. Acad. Arts and Scis., Am. Philos. Soc., World Acad. Art and Sci., Phi Beta Kappa (vis. scholar 1976-77). Home: Stanford Calif. Died Feb. 27, 1997.

DAVIS, MOSHE, historian; b. Bklyn., June 12, 1916; s. William and Ida (Schenker) D.; m. Lottie Keiser, June 11, 1939; children: Zev, Tamar. B.S., Columbia U., 1937; Pd.B., Jewish Theol. Sem. Am., 1937, M.H.L., 1942; Ph.D., Hebrew U. Jerusalem, 1946; L.H.D. (hon.), Hebrew Union Coll.-Jewish Inst. Religion, 1974; D.H.L. (hon.), Jewish Theol. Sem. Am., 1986. Rabbi, 1942; registrar Jewish Theol. Sem. Am., N.Y.C., 1942-45, dean Tchrs. Inst., 1945-50, provost, 1950-63, dir. Am. Jewish History Center, 1953-65, editor Regional History Series, 1963-78, asso. prof. Am. Jewish history, 1956-63, research prof., 1963—; founding head Inst. Contemporary Jewry, Hebrew U., Israel, 1959—; vis. prof. Inst. Contempory Jewry, Hebrew U. Jerusalem, Israel, 1959-63, assoc. prof. Am. Jewish history, 1963-70, Stephen S. Wise prof. Am. Jewish history and instns., 1970—; chmn. Internat. Ctr. for Univ. Teaching Jewish Civilization, 1980-92, chmn. governing coun., 1992—; vis. scholar univs. in Latin Am., U.S., Can., Europe; mem. adv. com. Centre National des Hautes Etudes Juive, Brussels, 1962-75; chmn. Israel Pres.'s Study Circle on World Jewry, 1966-83, Pres.'s Continuing Seminar on World Jewry and State of Israel, 1973-83; committeeman Irving Neuman Hebrew Lit. award Bar Ilan U., Israel; com. J. Machover Trust for Contemporary Jewish History, London; mem. publ. com. Jewish Publ. Soc. Program editor: Eternal Light, NBC-Radio, 1942-52, Frontiers of Faith, NBC-TV, 1951-53; author: (with L. Davis) Land of Our Fathers: Biblical Place-names in America, Guide and Map, 1950, Shaping of American Judaism, 1951, Jewish Religious Life and Institutions, 1953, rev. edit., 1971, (with V. Ratner) Birthday of the World, 1959, Emergence of Conservative Judaism, 1963, From Dependence to Mutuality: The American Jewish Community and World Jewry, 1970, America and the Holy Land, 1995; editor: M.M. Kaplan Jubilee Volumes, 1951, Israel: Its Role in Civilization, 1956, Publications of Study Circle in Home of President of Israel, series I, 1967— series XIII, 1983, Contemporary Jewish Civilization Series, Vol. I, 1970, Vols. II and III, 1971, (with A.J. Karp) Texts and Studies in American Jewish History in Hebrew, Vol. I, 1970, Vols. II, III, 1971, Vol. IV, 1977, Vol. V, 1980, Vol. VI, 1984, The Yom Kippur War—Israel and the Jewish People, 1974, Hebrew vol., 1975, (with Y. Bauer and I. Kolatt) Studies in the History of Zionism, 1976, World Jewry and the State of Israel, 1977, With Eyes Toward Zion, 1977, Zionism in Transition, 1980, Sir Moses Montefiore: American Jewry's Ideal, 1985, Jewish Distinctiveness Within The American Tradition: The Eretz-Yisrael Dimension as Case Illustration, 1986, With Eyes Toward Zion II, 1986, American Christian Devotees in the Holy Land, 1987, (with Y. Ben-Arieh) With Eyes Toward Zion-III, 1991, (with Meir Hovav) The Living Testify; 1994, advisory editor: Teaching Jewish Civilization: A Global Approach to Higher Education, 1995; adv. editor: America and the Holy Land Collection, 1977; mem. adv. bd. Jewish Jour. Sociology, 1966—; project dir. Am.-Holy Land Studies. Recipient Louis LaMed award for Hebrew Lit., 1951, citation B'nai Brith, 1973, Lee M. Friedman Scholar's award, 1977, Israel Knesset Speaker's award, 1987, Samuel Rothberg prize for World Jewish Edn., 1989, medal Jewish Theol. Sem., 1991; Lena Sokolow fellow, 1937-38; Guggenheim fellow, 1956, 59. Mem. Am. Jewish Hist. Soc. (hon. v.p.), World Union of Jewish Studies (hon. mem. exec. coun.). Died Apr. 10, 1996.

DAVIS, PAXTON, novelist, journalist, educator; b. Winston-Salem, N.C., May 7, 1925; s. James Paxton and Emily (McDowell) D.; m. Wylma Elizabeth Pooser, June 6, 1951 (div. 1971); children: Elizabeth Keith, Anne Beckley, James Paxton III; m. Peggy Painter Camper, July 21, 1973. Student, Va. Mil. Inst., 1942-43; AB, Johns Hopkins U., 1949. Reporter Winston-Salem Jour., 1949-51, Richmond (Va.) Times-Dispatch, 1951-52, Twin City Sentinel, Winston-Salem, 1952-53; faculty Washington and Lee U., 1953-76, prof. journalism, 1963-76, chmn. dept., 1968-74; vis. scholar Cambridge U., 1973; fellow Bread Loaf Writers Conf., Va. Ctr. for the Creative Arts, 1983, MacDowell Colony, 1989; adj. prof. Roanoke Coll., 1980. Book editor: Roanoke (Va.) Times & World News, 1961-81; contbg. editorial columnist, 1976-94; Author: Two Soldiers, 1956, The Battle of New Market, 1963, One of The Dark Places, 1965, The Seasons of Heroes, 1967, A Flag at the Pole, 1976, Ned, 1978, Three Days, 1980, Being a Boy, 1988, A Boy's War, 1990 , A Boy No More, 1992. Bd. dirs. Va. State Libr., 1986-90. Served with AUS, 1943-46, CBI. Mem. Phi Beta Kappa, Omicron Delta Kappa. Home: Fincastle Va. Died May 27, 1994.

DAVISON, RODERIC HOLLETT, historian, educator; b. Buffalo, Apr. 27, 1916; s. Walter Seaman and Eloise (Hollett) D.; m. Louise Atherton Dickey, June 18, 1949; children: R. John, Richard H. AB, Princeton U., 1937; AM, Harvard U., 1938, PhD, 1942; DHL (hon.), George Washington U., 1994. Instr. history Princeton, 1940-42, 46-47; faculty history George Washington U., 1947—, prof., 1954-86, prof. emeritus, 1986—, chmn. dept., 1960-64, 69-70; Lectr. diplomatic history Johns Hopkins Sch. Advanced Internat. Studies, 1951-52, 55-58; vis. lectr. Harvard, 1960. Author: The Near and Middle East: An Introduction to History and Bibliography, 1959, Reform in the Ottoman Empire, 1856-1876, 1963, Turkey, 1968, Turkey: A Short History, 1981, 2d edit., 1988, Essays in Ottoman and Turkish History, 1774-1923: The Impact of the West, 1990; contbg. author: The Diplomats 1919-1939, 1953, Guide to Hist. Lit, 1961; mem. adv. bd. editors Middle East Jour, 1954-84; contbr. articles to profl. jours. With Am. Friends Service Com., 1942-44, Civilian Pub. Service Camp, 1944-46. Fellow Social Sci. Rsch. Coun., Nat. Coun. Religion in Higher Edn., Harvard U., 1942, Faculty fellow Fund for Advancement Edn., 1953-54, Guggenheim fellow, 1970-71. Mem. Am. Hist. Assn. (treas. 1974), Middle East Inst. (v.p. 1976-82), AAUP, Soc. for Values, Middle East Studies Assn. (pres. 1974-75), Turkish Studies Assn. (pres. 1980-81), Phi Beta Kappa. Died Mar. 23, 1996.

DAY, EUGENE DAVIS, SR., immunology educator, researcher; b. Cobleskill, N.Y., June 24, 1925; s. Emmons Davis and Alice (McCartey) D.; m. Shirley M. Warner, Sept. 14, 1946; 1 son, Eugene Davis. B.S. in Chemistry, Union Coll., Schenectady, 1949; M.S., U. Del., 1950, Ph.D., 1952. Rsch. assoc. Roscoe B. Jackson Meml. Lab., Bar Harbor, Maine, 1952-54; sr. cancer rsch. scientist Roswell Park Meml. Inst., Buffalo, 1954-58, assoc. cancer rsch. scientist, 1958-62; assoc. prof. immunology Duke U. Med. Ctr., Durham, N.C., 1962-65, prof., 1965-67, prof. immunology and exptl. surgery, 1967-88, prof. emeritus immunology, 1988-96. Author: The Immunochemistry of Cancer, 1966, Foundations of Immunochemistry, 1969, Advanced Immunochemistry, 1972, 2d revised edit., 1990; contbr. articles to profl. jours. Served with AUS, 1943-46. Grantee NIH, 1972-88, Multiple Sclerosis Soc., 1973-82, AEC, 1964-72; Jacob Javits neurosci. investigator awardee NIH, 1984-88. Fellow Am. Soc. Microbiology; mem. Am. Assn. Immunologists, Am. Assn. Cancer Rsch., Am. Soc. Neurochemists, AAAS, Sigma Xi. Died July 22, 1996.

DAY, J(AMES) EDWARD, lawyer, postmaster general; b. Jacksonville, Ill., Oct. 11, 1914; s. James Allmond and Frances (Wilmot) D.; m. Mary Louise, Burgess, July 2, 1941; children: Geraldine (Mrs. James A. Zurn), Molly (Mrs. John Himmelfarb), James Edward (dec.). A.B., U. Chgo., 1935; LL.B. cum laude, Harvard, 1938; LL.D., Ill. Coll., U. Nev. Bar: Ill. 1938, D.C. 1963, Md. 1972. With firm Sidley, Austin, Burgess & Harper, 1939-41, 45-49, 63-72; legal and legislative asst. to Ill. Gov. Adlai Stevenson, Springfield, 1949-50; mem., sec. Ill. Commn. Intergovtl. Coop., 1949-53; commr. ins. Ill., 1950-53; assoc. gen. solicitor Prudential Ins. Co. Am., 1953-56, assoc. gen. counsel, 1956; sr. v.p. charge Western ops. Prudential Ins. Co. Am., L.A., 1957-61; postmaster gen. U.S., 1961-63; ptnr. in charge Washington office Chgo. law firm Sidley and Austin, 1963-73; ptnr. Cox, Langford & Brown, Washington, 1973-96, Squire, Sanders & Dempsey, Cleve. and Washington, 1973-96; chmn. Montgomery County (Md.) Revenue Authority, 1986-91; bd. dirs., mem. exec. com. numerous bus. and ins. corps., 1965-96; spl. counsel Consumer Electronics Group Electronics Industries Assn., 1968-84; gen. counsel 3d Class Mail Assn., 1968-84; vice chmn. Gov.'s Commn. Met. Area Problems, Calif., 1959-61; mem. adv. bd. U.S. Customs Bur., 1966-68; mem. Calif. Gov.'s Bus. Adv. Coun., 1959-61. Author: Bartholf Street, 1946, Descendants of Christopher Day of Bucks County, Pa., 1958, Humor in Public Speaking, 1965, My Appointed Round, 929 Days as Postmaster General, 1965, An Unlikely Sailor, 1990, The Man from Palmyra (A Surgeon's Life), 1993, Farming for Fun, 1994, Carrol Shanks of Prudential, 1995; legis. editor Harvard U. Law Rev.; contbr. articles to legal and ins. publs. V.p. Nat. Capital council Boy Scouts Am.; gen campaign chmn. Los Angeles YMCA, 1959; chmn. adv. com. Md. Ins. Dept., 1966-69; chmn. Dem. Asso., Los Angeles County, 1958-61, Smithsonian Instn. Luncheon Group; alt. del. Dem. Nat. Conv., 1952, del., 1960; trustee Montgomery County Hist. Soc.; trustee, sec. Project Hope, 1974-96; mem. adv. com. Hospitality and Info. Svc. Meridian House Found.; mem. bd. fellows Claremont Coll., Calif., 1958-65; chmn. nat. devel. com. Georgetown U., 1971-78; trustee Hood Coll., Frederick, Md., 1970-77; mem. Clinton preconv. team, 1992; bd. dirs. Population Action Interna. Lt. USNR, 1940-45. Decorated Navy Commendation medal, 3 battle stars. Mem. ABA, Nat. Civil Svc. League (pres. 1964-66), Citizens Conf. State Legislatures (chmn. 1965-70), Nat. Assn. Ins. Commrs. (chmn. Midwestern zone 1950-53), D.C. Bar Assn., Md. Bar Assn., Fed. Bar Assn., Md. Farm Bur., Legal Club Chgo., Nat. Press Club, Phi Kappa Psi. Democrat. Methodist. Home: Washington D.C. Died Oct. 30, 1996; interred Monocacy Cemetery, Beallsville, MD.

DAY, POMEROY, banker; b. Hartford, Conn., June 21, 1906; s. Arthur Pomeroy and Lucy (Bunce) D.; m. Katherine Flateau Long, Feb. 11, 1938 (dec. Sept. 1966); children: Pamela (Mrs. Robert H. Pelletreau, Jr.), Elizabeth (Mrs. Thomas C. Bolton), Roger P., George C.; m. Ella M. Stover, May 1969. AB, Yale U., 1928, LLB, 1931; LLD (hon.), Trinity Coll., 1969. Bar: Conn. 1931. Pvt. practice Hartford, 1931-58; mem. Robinson, Robinson & Cole, 1936-58; pres. Conn. Bank & Trust Co., 1961-66, chmn., 1966-70, chmn. exec. com., 1970-

74; past dir. various corps. Chmn. Hartford chpt. ARC, 1939-42; mem. Conn. Gov.'s Revenue Task Force, 1969-71; trustee Smith Coll., 1951-61; hon. bd. dirs. Hartford Hosp.; hon. trustee Wadsworth Atheneum, pres., 1970-72. Served to lt. col. M.I. AUS, 1942-45. Decorated Bronze Star. Mem. Soc. of Cin. Republican. Episcopalian. Clubs: Hartford (pres. 1955-56), Hartford Golf, Gulf Stream Golf, Gulf Stream Bath and Tennis, Everglades, Ekwanok. DIED 10/12/96. .

DEAN, SIDNEY WALTER, JR., business and marketing executive; b. Boston, May 20, 1905; s. Sidney W. and Marian (Perry) D.; m. Eugenia Serios, Nov. 2, 1963. A.B., Yale U., 1926. With J. Walter Thompson Co., 1927-42; mgr. Trade & Indsl. Dept., dir. media, v.p., 1937-42; exec. v.p., dir. Telecoin Corp., 1945-47; cons. marketing and mgmt., 1947-50; v.p. McCann-Erickson, Inc., 1950-61; pres. Ventures Devel. Co., 1961—; mem. FCC Adv. Com. Cable TV; chmn. N.Y.C. Adv. Com. Telecom.; trustee Met. Ednl. TV Assn., 1954-59, City Club of N.Y., Am. Arbitration Assn., Fed. Grand Jury Assn., Tri-State Regional Planning Commn. Telecom. Com.; dir. Audit Bur. Circulations, 1957-61, Knickerbocker Fed. Savings & Loan Assn., Fluted Paper Products Co., Inc., Marketmath, Inc. Author: Mass Communications in Modern Society, 1948, Planning for Integrated Marketing, 1949, Television in New York: Hitches in the Cable, 1970, Cable Television: Omission by Commission, 1971, Guidelines for Planning a Cable Television Franchise, 1973, others; contbr. numerous articles to Nations Mag., others; cons. in field. Vice chmn. Nat. Businessmen's Council. Served as capt. USAF; with OSS, Lend-Lease Adminstrn. 1943-45. Decorated Bronze Star medal; named to the 105th Congl. Record, Feb. 26, 1997. Mem. Am. Mktg. Assn., Am. Mktg. Assn., Am. Econ. Assn., Nat. Planning Assn., Nat. Cable TV Assn., Nat. Dirs. Am. Dem. Action, Washington Square Assn., Nat. Soc. for the Study of Comm., Yale Club, City Club, Sigma Xi. Democrat. Died Jan. 16, 1997.

DEATON, CHARLES, architect, industrial designer; b. Clayton, N.Mex., Jan. 1, 1921; s. Charles Elmer and Nina Maude (Utter D.; ed. pub. schs.; children—Robert Earle, Claudia, Charlee, Snow. Aircraft illustrator, engr. Lockheed Aircraft Corp., Burbank, Cal., 1941-42, Curtis-Wright Corp., St. Louis, 1942-43; pvt. practice architecture and indsl. design, Chgo. 1943-44, N.Y.C., 1944-49, St. Louis, 1951-55, Denver, 1955—; prin. archtl. works include Wyo. Nat. Bank, Casper, 1962, sculptured house, Denver, 1965, Sports Complex Kansas City, Mo. (asso. with Kivett & Myers), 1967; prin. indsl. design includes bank vault equipment, office furniture, comml. lighting equipment; chief designer Bank Bldg. Corp., St. Louis, 1949-52; tchr. design Franklin Sch. Profl. Arts, N.Y.C., 1946-49. Patentee in field.

DE BARDELEBEN, ARTHUR, lawyer; b. Great Falls, Mont., July 12, 1918; s. John Arthur and Antoinette (Merselis) DeB.; m. Pamela L. Honaker, 1987; children: Suzanne T. Fiedler, Joan T. Ph.D., U. Wis., 1940, LL.B., 1947. Bar: Wis. bar 1947. Since practiced in Park Falls.; Bd. regents U. Wis., 1959-68, pres. bd. regents, 1964-67; bd. regents U. Wis. System, 1974-81; mem. U. Wis. System Task Force Faculty Compensation, 1983-84; mem. spl. adv. com. to Wis. Legis. Council on Wis. Guaranteed Higher Edn. Plan, 1974; mem. Wis. Coordinating Com. Higher Edn., 1959-67, Wis. Higher Ednl. Aids Bd., 1975-78, Fed. Judicial Nominating Commn. Western Dist. Wis., 1979-81; Presdl. elector, 1964. Author: (with Walter P. Metzger, Sanford H. Kadish, Edward J. Bloustein) Dimensions of Academic Freedom, 1969; Mem. bd.: Wis. Law Rev, 1940-41. Served with AUS, 1941-45. Mem. Am. Arbitration Assn. (nat. panel), ABA, 15th Jud. Circuit Bar Assn. (pres. 1959-60), State Bar Wis., Am. Acad. Polit. and Social Sci., Am. Civil Liberties Union. Home: Park Falls Wis. Died Apr. 23, 1993.

DE BEAUVOIR, SIMONE LUCIE ERNESTINE MARIE BERTRANDE, author; b. Paris, Jan. 9, 1908; d. Georges Bertrand and Franç oise (Brasseur) de B.; ed. Paris U. Tchr. various lycé es, 1931-43; author: L'Invité e, 1943, English edit. She Came to Stay, 1949, Am. edit., 1954; Le Sang des Autres, 1945, English and Am. edits. The Blood of Others, 1948; Les Mandarins (Prix Goncourt), 1945, Am. edit. The Mandarins, 1956, English edit., 1957; Tous les Hommes sont Mortels, 1947, Am. edit. All Men are Mortal, 1955; (play) Les Bouches Inutiles, 1954; (nonfiction) Pyrrus et Cineas, 1944; Pour une Morale de l'Ambiguité , Am. edit. The Ethics of Ambiguity, 1948; l'Amé rique du Jour au Jour, 1948, English edit. America Day by Day, 1952; Le Deuxiè me Sexe, 1949, Am. edit. The Second Sex, 1952; Faut-il Bruler Sade'9 , 1951, English and Am. edits. Must We Burn Sade'9 , 1953; Privileges, 1957; La Longue Marche, 1957, Am. and English edits. The Long March, 1958; Memoires d'une Jeune Fille Rangé e, 1958, English edit. The Memoirs of a Dutiful Daughter, 1959; Brigitte Bardot, 1960; La Force de l'Age, La Force des Choses, 1963, English edit. Force of Circumstance, 1965; Une Mort tres Douce, 1964, English edit. A Very Easy Death, 1966; Les Belles Images, 1966; La Femme Rompue, 1968, English edit. The Woman Destroyed, 1969; La Vieillesse, 1970, English edit. The Coming of Age, 1972; Tout compte fait, 1972, English edit. All Accounting Made, 1972; When Things of the Spirit Come First: Five Early Tales, 1982; Adieux: A Farewell to Sartre, 1984. Pres., Ligue de Droit des Femmes, from 1974. Recipient Jerusalem prize, 1975; Sonning prize (Denmark), 1983.

DECOCK, RENÉ JEROME CHARLES, publishing executive; b. Annappes, France, Apr. 13, 1908; s. Jerome and Antoinette (Kerleu) D.; m. Marguerite Delepeleire, Apr. 20, 1936; children: Joöl, Marie-France, Annick, Michèle. Journalist La Voix du Nord, Lille, France, 1948, gen. dir., pres. mgmt. coun., 1949-67, chmn., CEO, 1968-88, permanent rep. to Flemish Press; pres. bd. suprs. La Voix du Nord, La Voix du Nord Investissement, Lille, France, 1988—; bd. dirs. Société Sorecom, Soceété G.B. Affichage; bd. suprs. Norpicom, Comareg Nord; mgr. Telmedia, Telmediacom., Société Nouvell Nord Littoral, Ageconseil. Active French Resistance. Recipient Rosette de la Resistance; named Comdr. Legion of Honor. Died, Jan. 23, 1996.

DEEN, EDITH ALDERMAN, author; b. Weatherford, Tex., Feb. 28, 1905; d. James Harris and Sara (Scheuber) Alderman; m. Edgar Deen, Dec. 30, 1945 (dec.). Student, Tex. U., 1922-23, Columbia U., 1926; student, Tex. Christian U., 1923-24, LittD, 1972; BA, Tex. Woman's U., 1953, LittD, 1959, MA, 1960; LittD (hon.), Pepperdine U., 1987. Woman's editor, daily columnist Ft. Worth Evening Press, 1924-54. Mem. Fort Worth City Council, 1965-67; mem. bd. regents Tex. Woman's Univ., 1951-63. Author: All of the Women of the Bible, 1955, Great Women of the Christian Faith, 1959, Family Living in the Bible, 1963, The Bibl's Legacy for Womanhood, 1970, All the Bible's Men of Hope, 1974, Wisdom from Women in the Bible, 1978. Named Exec. Woman of Year, Zonta Club, 1983; recipient First Lady award Altrusa Club, 1949, Disting. Sr. Citizen award Women's Civic Club, 1974, medal of honor Mary Isham Keith chpt. Nat. Soc. Am. Revolution, 1987. Mem. Tex. Inst. Letters, Women in Communications (Headliner award 1963). Died Jan. 3, 1994.

DEGNAN, THOMAS LEONARD, lawyer; b. Waseca, Minn., Jan. 18, 1909; s. John James and Martha (Kurkowski) D.; m. Nan Glennon, Sept. 24, 1938; children—Nancy, Martha, Denise. Student, St. Mary's Coll., Winona, Minn., 1925-27; J.D., Georgetown U., 1930. Bar: Minn. bar 1930, N.D. bar 1933. With firm Sexton, Mordaunt, Kennedy & Carrol, St. Paul, 1930-38; founder, 1938; sr. ptnr. Degnan, McElroy, Lamb, Camrud, Maddock & Olson, Ltd., Grand Forks, N.D.; now ret.; mem. N.D. Jud. Council, 1961-63, N.D. Med. Center Adv. Bd., 1963-67, N.D. Jud. Survey Commn., 1965-67. Pres. Young Dems., N.D., 1940-44, nat. committeeman, 1944-48; Bd. dirs. St. James High Sch., 1954-56, Grand Forks Indsl. Found.; past pres., bd. dirs. Grand Forks Community Chest. Mem. ABA, N.D. Bar Assn. (pres. 1960-61), First Dist. Bar Assn. (pres. 1957-59), Grand Forks County Bar Assn. (pres. 1952-53), Edward Douglas White Law Club, Pierce Butler Law Club, Grand Forks C. of C. (past pres., dir.), Delta Theta Phi, Elk (past exalted ruler). Deceased.

DE GRAY, JULIAN, pianist, educator, lecturer; b. Harrisburg, Pa., July 15, 1905. BA, Columbia U., 1925. Ind. concert pianist, 1928—; prof. piano U. Miami, Fla., 1928-31, Bennington Coll., 1932-70; pvt. tchr. piano N.Y.C., 1932—; guest prof. U. Minn., 1950-51. London debut, Wigmore Hall, 1928, N.Y.C. debut, Town Hall, 1930; concert tour, The Netherlands, Germany, Austria, 1931, numerous concerts, U.S., 1939-47. Recipient Chappell Gold medal. Mem. Am. Assn. Colls., Am. Matthay Assn. (contbr. to jour.). Home: Cornwall Bridge Conn. DIED 01/24/95. .

DEHNER, DOROTHY, painter, sculptor; b. Cleve.; d. Edward P. and Louise (Uphof) D.; m. David Smith, 1927 (div. 1952); m. Ferdinand Mann, Sept. 9, 1955 (dec.); stepchildren: Irwin Mann, Abigail Mann Thernstrom. Student, UCLA, 1927-31; study and research abroad; BS in Art, Skidmore Coll., 1952, DHL (hon.), 1982. Lectr. Skidmore Coll., 1947, 54; worked Atelier 17, 1952-55; tchr. Indian Hill Music Workshop, Stockbridge, Mass., 1953-54, Barnard Sch. for Girls, N.Y.C., 1954-56; lectr. Rutgers U., N.J., 1987. Exhibited with David Smith, Albany Inst, 1947, retrospective with David Smith at Timmerli Mus., Rutgers U., 1984, Twining Gallery, N.Y.C., 1987; one-man shows include Albany Inst., 1953, Rose Fried Gallery, N.Y.C., 1952, U. Va. Mus. Fine Art, 1954, Chgo. Art Inst., 1955, Willard Gallery, N.Y.C., 1955, 57, 60, 63, 66, 70, 73, Wittenborn's Gallery, 1956, Gres Gallery, Washington, 1959, Parson's-Dreyfuss Gallery, N.Y.C., 1981, A.M. Sachs Gallery, N.Y.C., 1981, 82, 83, 84, Gen. Electric Hdqrs., 1983, 84, Met. Mus. Art, N.Y.C., 1984, Twining Gallery, N.Y.C., 1986, 87, 88, Meulenberg Coll., Allentown, Pa., 1988, Wichita Mus. Art, Pembroke Gallery, Twining Gallery, N.Y.C., Phillips Collection, Washington, 1990, Twining Gallry, N.Y.C., 1990, three works in collection Brit. Mus., London; retrospective exhbns. include Jewish Mus., N.Y., 1965, Marian Locks Gallery, Phila., 1975, Ft. Wayne (Ind.) Mus., 1975, Barbara Fiedler Gallery, Washington, 1980, A.M. Sachs Gallery, N.Y.C., 1981, Wichita Mus. Art, Kans., 1984, 85, Twining Gallery, 1986, 87, AAA Gallery, N.Y.C., 1987; solo retrospective traveling show to 20 colls. and museums, 1953-54, 63-64; exhibited in group shows include Whitney Mus. Am. Art, watercolors, 1951, 52, 53, sculpture, 1960, 63, Bklyn. Mus. Internat. Watercolor show, 1953, 55, 59, Mus. Modern Art, 1952, 54, 59-71, Met. Mus. Art, N.Y.C., 1953, also important museums, U.S.A., France, show, Am. Sculptors Gallery Bernard, Paris, Italy, Holland, Germany, New Sculpture group, Stable Gallery, N.Y.C.; works in permanent collections: Hirshhorn Mus., Washington, Met. Mus., N.Y.C., Dept. State, Columbia, Jewett Art Center, Wellesley Coll., Mpls. Mus., Munson Williams Proctor Inst., Utica, N.Y., Mus. Modern Art, Columbus Gallery Fine Art, Wichita Art Mus., Kans., Hyde Collection, Glens Falls, N.Y., Dresden Mus., German Dem. Republic, Calcutta Mus., India, Cleve Mus. Art, Mus. Palm Beaches, Fla., Phoenix Mus. Art, Seattle Art Mus., Minn. Mus. Art, Newark Mus., Phila. Mus. Art, Storm King Art Center, Mountainville, N.Y., Smithsonian Instn., Washington, Met. Mus. Art, N.Y.C., Mus. Am. Art, Washington; corporate collections include: Gen. Electric Co. Hdqrs., Rockefeller Ctr., AT&T Hdqrs., Chase Manhattan Bank, N.Y.C., 1st Nat. Bank, Chgo., N.Y. Bank for Savs., Bumper Corp., Can.; exhibited in various colls. including Yale U., Boston U., U. Mass., UCLA, British Mus., London, 3 works, 1988; executed bronze relief, Rockefeller Center, bronze sculpture, AT&T hdqrs., N.Y. Med. Coll., Phoenix Mus.; Appeared on radio, NBC; Author: art criticism Archtl. Forum, 1947; foreword John Graham's System and Dialectics of Art, 1971; also poetry. Fellow Tamarind Workshop, 1965; recipient 1st prize for drawing Audubon Ann., 1947; Art U.S.A., 1959; 1st prize for sculpture Kane Meml. Exhbn., Yaddo Found.; Women's Art Caucus award, 1983; honored at U. Cin. Festival for Women Sculptors, Sculptors Conf.; 1 of 9 Am. artists honored at U. Cin. Art Conf., 1987. Mem. Sculptors Guild, New Sculpture group Fedn. Am. Painters and Sculptors.

DEINZER, GEORGE WILLIAM, public welfare organization administrator; b. Tiffin, Ohio, Nov. 1, 1934; s. Harvey Charles and Edna Louise (Harpley) D.;. A.B., Heidelberg Coll., 1956; postgrad., Washington U., 1956-57. Asst. to dir. phys. plant Heidelberg Coll., 1957-58, admissions counselor, 1958-60, dir. admissions, 1960-71, dir. fin. aids, assoc. dir. admissions, 1971-80; exec. dir. Tiffin-Seneca United Way, 1980-85; adminstr. Seneca County (Ohio) Dept. Human Services and Children's Services, 1985—; voting rep. Coll. Entrance Examination Bd., 1963-80; fin. aid cons. Nat. Collegiate Athletic Assn.; cons. Ohio Scholarship Funds, 1960-61. Contbr. articles to profl. jours. Pres., chmn. allocations com., bd. dirs. United Way; pres. lay bd. Mercy Hosp.; treas., bd. dirs. N.W. Ohio Health Planning Assn., co-chmn. steering com., 1984; mem. legis com. Ohio Citizens Coun., 1981-88, human svcs. task force, 1984—; pres. Seneca County Mus. Found.; treas. Tiffin Theatre, Inc.; mem. Seneca Indsl. and Econ. Devel. Corp. Bd., 1983-88; chmn. Tiffin Area Devel. and Pub. Rels. Dirs., 1984—, Charter Rev. Commn., Tiffin, 1990-91; mem. W.S.O.S. Community Action Coun. bd., 19906. Mem. Organ Hist. Soc., Am. Theatre Organ Soc., Nat., Ohio (regional coordinator, treas., state trainer, chmn. needs analysis com.) assns. student fin. aid adminstrs., Ohio Athletic Conf. Fin. Dirs. (past chmn.), Am. Personnel and Guidance Assn., Am. Coll. Personnel Assn., Council Ohio United Way Execs., Farm Bur., Ohio Hist. Soc., U.S. Naval Inst., Buckeye Sheriffs Assn., N.W. Ohio and Ohio Human Service Dirs., Rotary (dir., pres. 1982-83, gen. sec.-elect 1990—), Elks, Beta Beta Beta. Republican. Died Apr. 1993.

DEKKER, MAURITS, publisher, editor; b. Amsterdam, Holland, Mar. 18, 1899; s. Marcus and Elisabeth D.; m. Rozetta Sophia Roos, July 2, 1925 children: Elisabeth Emma, Andrew, Marcel. Degree in Chemistry, Physics and Microbiology, U. Amsterdam 1923; D. honoris causa, N.Y. Poly. Inst., 1982. Pres. founder Dekker & Nordemann, Amsterdam; pres. founder Intersci. Pubs., N.Y.C., 1940-61, Elsevier Pub Co., N.Y.C., 1940-53; v.p. John Wiley, N.Y.C., 1961-64 chmn. Marcel Dekker, Inc., N.Y.C., 1966-90; cons Kodansha, Tokyo, 1966-80. Mem. AAAS, N.Y. Acad Sci. Home: Greenwich Conn. Deceased.

DE KOONING, WILLEM, artist; b. Rotterdam, Holland, Apr. 24, 1904; came to U.S., 1926; s. Leendert and Cornelia (Nobel) de K.; m. Elaine Marie Catherine Fried, Dec. 7, 1943 (dec. 1989). Student, Acad. Fine Arts, Rotterdam, 1916-24. Faculty Black Mountain Coll., N.C., 1948, Yale, 1950-51. painter mural, Hall of Pharmacy, N.Y. World's Fair, 1939; interviewd in popular and profl. publs.; selected one-man shows Egan, N.Y.C., 1948, 51, Sidney Janis, N.Y.C., 1953, 56 59, 62, 72, Allan Stone, N.Y.C., 1966, 71, 72, 94, M Knoedler, N.Y.C., 1967, 69, Paris, 1968, 71, Fourcade N.Y.C, 1974-77, 79, 82-85, Matthew Marks Gallery 1996, 97, Constantine Grimaldis, Balt., 1982, 87, Margo Leavin, L.A., 1986, 87, Galerie Karsten Greve, Paris & Köln, 1990, Salander O'Reilly Galleries, Inc., N.Y.C. 1990, 92, C&M Arts, N.Y.C., 1993-96, 98, Stedelijk Mus., Amsterdam, The Netherlands, 1976, Mus. Modern Art, N.Y.C., 1971, Seattle Art Mus., 1976, 95 96, Guggenheim Mus., N.Y.C., 1978, Carnegie Inst. Pitts., 1979-80, Barbara Mathes Gallery, N.Y.C., 1993 Hirshhorn Mus. and Sculpture Garden, Washington 1993, Caixa Found., Barcelona, Spain, 1994, High Mus Art, Atlanta, 1994, Mus. Fine Arts, Boston, 1994-95 Mus. Fine Arts, Houston, 1995, Guild Hall Mus., East Hampton, N.Y., 1994, San Francisco Mus. Modern Art

1995, Davis Mus. and Cultural Ctr., Wellesley Coll., Mass, 1995, Walker Art Ctr., Minn., 1996, Whitney Mus., N.Y.C., 1996, Kunst Mus., Bonn, 1996, Boymans van Burningen Mus., Rotterdam, 1996; retrospectives: Allan Stone, 1964, Sch. Mus. of Fine Arts, Boston, 1953, Smith Coll. Mus. Art, 1965, Stedelijk Mus., 1968, 83, Tate Gallery, London, 1968-69, 1995, Art Inst. Chgo., 1969, L.A. County Mus. Art, L.A., 1969, Mus. Modern Art, N.Y.C., 1969, Balt. Mus., 1972, Guild Hall Mus., 1981, Whitney Mus. Am. Art, N.Y.C., 1983-84, Louisiana Mus., Humlebaek, Denmark, 1983, Moderna Museet, Stockholm, 1983, Akademie der Kunste, Berlin, 1984, Musée d'Art Moderne, Paris, 1984, Nat. Gallery Art, Washington, 1994, Met. Mus. Art, N.Y.C., 1994-95; group shows include Whitney Annual, 1949-50, 63-64, 65, 67-68, 69-72, Whitney Biennial, 1981, 1987, Venice Biennial 1950, 54, 56; represented in permanent collections: Metropolitan Museum, San Francisco Mus. Modern Art, Tate Gallery, London, Hirshhorn Mus. and Sculpture Garden, Mus. Modern Art, N.Y.C., St. Louis Art Mus., Chgo. Art Inst., Whitney Mus. Am. Art, N.Y.C., Guggenheim Mus., Carnegie Inst., Stedelijk Mus., Australian Nat. Gallery, also numerous pvt. collections. Decorated officer Order of Orange-Nassau (Netherlands), 1979; recipient Logan purchase prize Chgo. Art Inst., 1951, Beckman prize Frankfurt, Fed. Republic Germany, 1984, Kaiser Ring, Goslar, Fed. Republic Germany, 1984, Andrew W. Mellon prize, 1979, Nat. Medal of Arts, 1986, named to Royal Acad. Fine Arts, Stockholm, 1986, Praemium Imperiale of Japan Art Assn., 1989, CAA Disting. Artist award for Lifetime Achievement, 1993. Mem. AAAL (Gold medal for painting 1975), Nat. Inst. Arts and Letters, Royal Acad. of Visual Arts (Nat. Medal of Arts 1986), Acad. der Kunst. Home: New York N.Y. Died Mar. 19, 1997.

DE LA COLINA, RAFAEL, diplomat; b. Tulancingo, Hidalgo, Mexico, Sept. 20, 1898; s. Manuel and Maria (Riquelme) de la C.; m. Ruth Rosecrans, 1920 (dec. 1929); children: Ruth (Mrs. Francis W. Silk), Rafael; m. Amanda Steinmeyer, 1944. M.A., Nat. U. Mexico, 1918; postgrad., Fgn. Service Acad., Mexico, 1918. Held various posts in Consular Service, 1918-34; consul gen. of Mexico, San Antonio, 1934-35, N.Y.C., 1936-43; minister counselor Mexican Embassy, Washington, 1943-44; E.E. and M.P. of Mexico Washington, 1944-48; A.E. and P. of Mexico, 1949-53; permanent rep. to UN, 1953-59; ambassador of Mexico to Can., 1959-62, to Japan, 1962-64; rep. of Mex. to OAS, Washington, 1965-86; ambassador of Mex. to U.S. Washington, 1965-80; ambassador emeritus, 1980-95; Mexican del. Japanese Peace Conf., San Francisco, 1951; chmn. Mexican del. Conf. on Living Resources of Sea, Ciudad Trujillo, Dominican Republic, 1956; acting chmn. Mexican del. to Gen. Assembly of UN, 1953-57; chmn. Mexican dels. Inter-Am. Confs. and Gen. Assemblies Sessions, 1965-95, Meeting of Consultation of OAS, 1965-95, Intelsat, Washington, 1970-71; dean OAS Diplomats, 1979-86. Author books on internat. law.; Contbr. articles to profl. jours. Founder, hon. pres. Mexican Welfare Com., Los Angeles. Decorated Order of Merit Chile; Order Honneur et Merite Haiti; Order of Merit Juan Pablo Duarte Dominican Republic; Order Vasco Nunez de Balboa Panama; Order Rising Sun Japan; Order San Carlos Colombia; Order Libertador Venezuela; Order of Sun Peru; Order Civic Merit Belisario Dominguez Mexican Senate, 1974. Mem. Am. Soc. Internat. Law, Mexican Acad. Internat. Law, Nat. Hist. and Lit. Soc. (Mexico City). Home: Falls Church Va. Died Dec. 27, 1995.

DELACOUR, JEAN-PAUL, civil servant; b. St.-Claude, Jura, France, Nov. 7, 1930; s. Henri and Denise (Brochet) D.; diploma, Inst. Polit. Studies, Paris; grad. Nat. Sch. Adminstrn., 1955; m. Claude Laurence, Sept. 2, 1958; children—Jean-Baptiste, Paul, Pierre (dec.), Antoine, Anne. Adj. insp. finances, 1955, insp., 1957; head office mission fin. councillor, Washington, 1959; tech. advisor to sec. state for interior commerce, 1959-61; head office mission Credit Nat., after 1961, adj. dir., 1968; central dir. Societe Gen., 1973, adj. dir. gen., 1974—; pres.-dir. gen. Sogefim, 1969-77; adminstr. Gen. Alsatian Bank Soc., 1969-78, chmn., 1978-82, adminstr. selected actions, 1970—; prof. Center for Advanced Studies in Banking; adminstr. Cath. Inst. Paris, 1976—, Union des Assurances de Paris, 1970—. Decorated chevalier Lé gion d'Honneur, Nat. Order Merit (France).

DELAMATER, JAMES NEWTON, physician; b. North Plainfield, N.J., Jan. 24, 1912; s. Van Ness and Jacqueline M. (Newton) DeL.; m. Harriet French, Sept. 1, 1934 (dec. Oct. 12, 1973); children: Steven French, Anne Terry, Sarah Van Ness; m. Elizabeth Clark, Oct. 25, 1974. Student, U. Va., 1930-31; AB, Stanford U., 1934, MD, 1938. Intern Los Angeles County Gen. Hosp., 1937-39, resident medicine, 1939-41; individual practice medicine Los Angeles, 1946-80; asst. prof. bacteriology U. So. Calif. Sch. Medicine, 1945, asso. prof., 1946, asso. prof. medicine, asso. dean, 1949-52, clin. prof. medicine, 1952-93; affiliated Huntington Meml., Los Angeles County Gen. hosps.; epidemiologist Los Angeles County Med. Research Found., 1947-93; med. cons. M.C. U.S. Army. Contbr. articles to med. jours. Served from lt. (j.g.) to comdr. M.C., 1941-45. Fellow A.C.P., Los Angeles Acad. Medicine; mem. AMA, AAAS, Am. Geriatrics Soc., Am. Soc. Tropical Medicine and Hygiene, Holland Soc. N.Y., Sigma Xi, Alpha Omega Alpha. Republican. Presbyn. Clubs: University (Pasadena); Hewlett, Toastmasters. Home: Corona Del Mar Calif. Died June 1, 1993.

DELANEY, HAROLD, association executive; b. Phila., Aug. 24, 1919; s. William Y. and Henrietta Pinkney Delaney; BS, Howard U., 1941, MS, 1943, PhD in Chemistry, 1958, LHD (hon.), Towson State U., 1987, Frostburg State U., 1991; LHD (hon.) Maryville U., 1993; m. Geraldine East, Sept. 9, 1946; children: Milton Y., Doyle O. Chemist, Manhattan Project, U. Chgo., 1943-45; asst. prof. chemistry N.C. A&T Coll., 1945-48; instr. chemistry Morgan State Coll., Balt., 1948-69, dean, 1967-69; vice chancellor, asso. provost central adminstrn. SUNY, Albany, 1969-72; v.p. gen. adminstrn. U. N.C., Chapel Hill, 1972-74; pres. Manhattanville Coll., Purchase, N.Y., 1974; assoc. dir. Nat. Inst. Edn., Washington, 1976-77; exec. v.p. Am. Assn. State Colls. and Univs., Washington, 1977-86, exec. v.p. emeritus 1986; spl. asst. to chancellor U. Md. System, 1988-89; acting pres. Chgo. State U., 1989-90; interim pres. Frostburg State U., 1991, Bowie State U., 1992-93. Recipient Disting. Am. award Am. Found. Negro Affairs, 1976. Fellow Am. Inst. Chemists; mem. Am. Chem. Soc., Am. Assn. Higher Edn., Sigma Xi, Phi Beta Sigma. Died Aug. 4, 1994. Home: Silver Spring Md.

DELANO, JACK, photographer, artist, composer; b. Kiev, Russia, Aug. 1, 1914; came to U.S., 1923; s. William and Dries Ovcharov; m. Irene Esser, July 5, 1940 (dec. 1982); children: Pablo, Laura. Diploma, Pa. Acad. Fine Arts, 1937. Photographer-artist Farm Security Adminstrn., Washington, 1940-43, 80-83; film maker Dept. Edn., San Juan, P.R., 1946-53; free lance film maker San Juan, 1953-57; TV dir. WIPR-TV Channel 6, San Juan, 1957-63; gen. mgr. P.R. Radio and TV Service, San Juan, 1963-69; free lance photographer, illustrator, composer, film maker San Juan, 1969—; tech. cons. P.R. Humanities Found., 1977—. Photographer photographs, Library of Congress, 1940-43; illustrator: books The Emperor's New Clothes, 1971; composer: ballet La Bruja de Loiza, 1950, Sinfonietta for Strings, 1985, String Quartette, 1985; film maker: Los Peloteros, 1952. Cresson Travelling scholar Pa. Acad. Fine Arts, 1936; Guggenheim fellow, 1945; UNESCO travelling fellow, 1960; NEH grantee, 1979. Mem. ASCAP. DIED 08/12/97. .

DELEHANTY, EDWARD JOHN, investment company executive; b. Wallingford, Conn., Oct. 14, 1929, s. Robert Thomas and Bertha (Slanec) D.; m. Margaret Marshall, July 18, 1969; children: Marke Cheryl (dec.), Dana Keith, Jeffrey Dean (dec.), Robyn Lee. AB, Clark U., Worcester, Mass., 1951. Agt., agy. supr., regional tng. supr., gen. agt. Paul Revere Life Ins. Co., Worcester, 1951-64; v.p., dir. agys. Boston Mut. Life Ins. Co., 1964-65; v.p., dir. Mut. Fund Assoc., Inc., San Francisco, 1966-68; exec. v.p. Mut. Fund Assoc., Inc., 1968-70; v.p., dir. Putnam Mgmt. Co., Boston, 1970-81; pres. Acadian Fin. Svcs. Inc., 1982-95; mem. exec. com. Putnam Cos., Inc.; dir. Putnam Fin. Services, Inc.; dir., mem. investment com. Putnam Capital Mgmt., Inc., exec. v.p., dir.; pres., dir. Putnam Capital Services, Inc.; sr. v.p., dir. Putnam Adv. Co. Inc.; pres. Acadian Fin. Services, Inc. Mem. alumni com. Clark U., 1962-65; chmn. Maine Coast Meml. Hosp., 1991-93. Mem. Newcomen Soc., Sales and Mktg. Execs. Internat. Club: Commonwealth (San Francisco). Lodge: Masons. Home: Southwest Harbor Maine. Died Oct. 4, 1995.

DELONGA, LEONARD ANTHONY, artist, educator; b. Cannonsburg, Pa., Dec. 18, 1925; s. Raymond Peter and Emma (Bello) DeL.; m. Sandra Katz, Jan. 17, 1954; children: Roy, Beth Alison Senecal. B.A., U. Miami-Coral Gables, (Fla.), 1950; M.F.A., U. Ga., 1952. Asst. prof. Tex. Wesleyan Coll., Ft. Worth, 1954-56, U. Ga., Athens, 1956-64; prof. Mt. Holyoke Coll., South Hadley, Mass., 1964—, David B. Turman Disting. prof., 1981—; cons. Chatham Coll., Pitts., Wellesley Coll., 1978, Hamilton Coll., Clinton, N.Y., 1983. One-man shows, Kraushaar Galleries, N.Y.C., 1954, 67, 70, 74, 77, 78, Mt. Holyoke Coll., 1965-73, group shows include, NAD, 1974, group shows, Nat. Inst. Arts and Letters, 1961; represented in numerous public and pvt. collections. Chair Alumnae Found, Mt. Holyoke Coll., 1979. Served with USAAF, 1944-46. Grantee in field.

DELSON, ROBERT, lawyer; b. N.Y.C., July 18, 1905; s. Louis and Ethel (Naum) D.; m. Marjorie Delson, Dec. 25, 1941; children: Eric, James. B.A., Cornell U., 1926; LL.B., Columbia U., 1928. Bar: N.Y. 1929, D.C. 1971. Assoc. Wise & Seligsberg, 1929-31; assoc., gen. counsel Republic Pictures Corp., 1931-37; assoc. then ptnr. Delson & Gordon, N.Y.C., 1937-80; of counsel Delson & Gordon, 1981-87; dir. Canon, U.S.A., Inc. Contbr. articles to legal jours. Mem. U.S. Com. Inter-Am. Assn. for Democracy and Freedom. AUS, 1942-45. Recipient Great Sign of Honor Pres. Republic of Austria, 1979. Mem. Am. Law Inst., ABA, Internat. Law Assn., Am. Soc. Internat. Law, Am.-Fgn. Law Assn., Consular Law Soc., Maritime Law Assn., Internat. Bar Assn., N.Y. State Bar Assn., N.Y. County Lawyers Assn., Phi Beta Kappa. DIED 05/22/97. .

DE MARGERIE, EMMANUEL JACQUIN, French foreign service officer; b. Paris, Dec. 25, 1927; s. Roland and Melle Jenny (Rabre-Luce) de M.; m. Melle Helene Hottinguer, Oct. 14, 1953; children: Gilles, Laure. Student, Ecole des Roches, Verneuil s/Avre, France, French Lycee, Shanghai, Sorbonne, Paris; diploma Institut d'Etudes Politiques, Paris, grad. Ecole Nationale d'Administrn., Paris. Joined Ministry of Fgn. Affairs Govt. of France, sec. embassy, London, 1954-59, ambassador, 1981-90, 1st sec. embassy, Moscow, 1959-61, dir. East European Affairs, Paris, 1961-67, counsellor embassy, Tokyo, 1967-70, minister counsellor embassy, Washington, 1971-72, undersec. of state, Paris, 1972-74, dir. Mus. of France, 1975-77, ambassador embassy, Madrid, 1977-81. Decorated chevalier de la Legion d'Honneur, Officier de l'Ordre Nationale du Merite, comdr. des Arts et des Lettres, others. Clubs: Garrick, Traveller's, White's, Beefsteak (London). Home: London England

DEMENIL, DOMINIQUE, art collector, philanthropist; b. Paris, Mar. 23, 1908; came to U.S., 1941, naturalized, 1967; d. Conrad and Louise (Delpech) Schlumberger; m. John de Menil, May 9, 1931 (dec.1973); children: Christophe, Adelaide, George, Francois, Philippa. B.A., U. Paris, 1927, postgrad. in math. and physics. Art collector, 1945—; dir. Inst for Arts Rice U., Houston, from 1968; organizer exhbns., 1964—. Trustee Mus. Fine Arts, Houston.; pres. Menil Found., Rothko Chapel, Georges Pompidou Art and Culture Found., Menil Collection Mus. Recipient Nat. medal of Arts, 1986. Died Jan. 1998.

DEMEURE DE LESPAUL, ADOLPHE, petroleum products company executive; b. Sirault, Belgium, Oct. 1, 1929; s. Charles and Adrienne (Escoyez) D.; 1 dau. Student U. Catholique de Louvain. With Petrofinia S.A., Brussels, 1951—, gen. mgr., 1962-67, dir., 1967-69, mng. dir., 1969-73, vice chmn. and mng. dir., 1973-75, vice chmn., chief exec. officer, 1975-79, chmn., chief exec. officer, 1979—.

DEMY, JACQUES, film director; b. Pont Chateau, France, June 5, 1931; s. Raymond and Marie Louise (Leduc) D.;m. Agnes Varda, Jan. 8, 1962, 1 child, Mathieu. Student, Ecole Nat. Photo-Cinema, Paris. Writer, dir.: Lola, 1960, Model Shop, 1968, Lady Oscar, 1978, Parking, 1985. Recipient Palme D'or Cannes, 1964, Prix Louis Dellue, Prix de Liacademie du Cenéma, Prix Du Cinema Français, Ordre nat. de Mérite Chevlier des Arts et Letters.

DENBEAUX, FRED, educator, writer; b. St. Louis, May 8, 1914; s. Ralph and Margaret (Langanke) D.; m. Jane van Voorst, June 9, 1937; children—Mark, Andrea. B.A., Elmhurst (Ill.) Coll., 1936; B.D., Union Theol. Sem., N.Y.C., 1939, S.T.M., 1940. Social worker Bklyn. Children's Aid Soc., 1937-39; ordained to ministry United Presbyn. Ch. USA., 1940; pastor in Rebersburg, Pa., 1940-42; tchr. theology Dana Hall Schs., Wellesley, Mass., 1946-50; faculty Wellesley Coll., 1946—, prof. religion, 1958—, chmn. dept., 1955—, chmn. bd. preachers, 1964—; vis. prof. Brown U., 1960-61; vis. lectr. Trinity Coll., 1962-63. Author: Understanding the Bible, 1958, The Art of Christian Doubt, 1960, Guide to the Old Testament, 1964, Introduction to New Testament, 1965, Guide to the New Testament, 1965, The Premature Death of Protestantism, 1967, also articles. Served as chaplain AUS, 1942-46. DIED 04/27/95. .

DENG XIAOPING, government official; b. Guang'an, Sichuan, China, Aug. 22, 1904; m. Cho Lin; children: Deng Pufang, Deng Chifang, Deng Rong, Deng Maomao. Attended, French Sch., Chungking, Far Eastern U., Moscow. Joined Chinese Communist Party, 1926; dean edn. Chungshan Mil. Acad., Shensi, 1926; polit. commissar 7th Red Army, 1929; chief staff 3d Corps, Red Army, 1930; dir. propaganda dept. 1st Front Army on Long March, 1934-36; polit. commissar Sino-Japanese War; mem. 7th Cen. Com., Chinese Communist Party, 1945; polit. commissar 2d Field Army, People's Liberation Army, 1948-54, chief gen. staff, 1977-80; vice premier, 1952; mem. State Planning Commn., 1952-54; vice chmn. Chinese People's Polit. Consultative Conf., 1953, mem. Standing Com., 1954-59; min. of fin. 1953-54; vice chmn. Nat. Def. Council, 1954-67; 1st sec. East China Bur., Chinese Communist Party, 1949, sec.-gen. Cen. Com., 1953-56, mem. Politburo, 7th Cen. Com., 1955-67, mem. Politburo and Standing Com., sec.-gen. 8th Cen. Com., 1956, mem. 10th Cen. Com., 1973, mem. Politburo, 1974-76, vice chmn. Cen. Com., 1975-82, mem. Standing Com., 1975, vice chmn. mil. affairs com., 1975-76; mem. Politburo, 11th Cen. Com., 1977, mem. 12th Cen. Com., 1982-87, vice chmn. party, 1977, chmn. Nat. Com., from 1978; vice chmn. Nat. Def. Council, 1954-67; removed from office during Cultural Revolution, 1967, removed from office, 1976; chmn. Cen. Mil. Comn., Chinese Communist Party, 1981-89, chmn. Cen. Adv. Com., 1982-88. Avocation: swimming.

DENIS, PAUL, magazine editor; b. N.Y.C., July 1, 1909; s. Nicholas and Amelia (Rozaky) Dejerenis; m. Helen Martin, May 17, 1942; children: Michael Stephan, Christopher Paul. Student, N.Y. U., 1931. Reporter Vaudeville News and Star, 1926-30; asso. editor N.Y. Star, 1930-31, The Billboard, 1931-43; drama reporter and vaudeville columnist N.Y. Post, 1943-45; radio TV editor N.Y. Post Home News, 1946-49; lectr. on radio, TV and show business; columnist N.Y. Daily Compass,

1949-51; columnist, book editor N.Y. Rev., 1951; assoc. editor Why mag., 1951, Academy mag., 1952-53; columnist TV World, TV People, Modern Screen mags., from 1953; TV editor Bklyn. Eagle; radio and TV commentator; editorial dir. daytime TV mags. Sterling's Mags. Inc., 1969-78; founding editor Daytime TV mag., 1982-86. Author: Your Career in Show Business, 1948, Paul Denis' Celebrity Cook Book, 1952, Opportunities in a Dancing Career, 1966, The Jackie Gleason Story, 1956, Super Sound, 1966, Daytime TV Star Directory, 1976, Opportunities in the Dance, 1980, Inside the Soaps, 1985; Contbr. to nat. mags.; columnist Weekly Rev., 1984-86, The Greek Am., 1986—. Del. United Parents Assn., 1957-58; Bd. dirs. Parkinson's Disease Found. Recipient One More River award for promoting tolerance Sta. WNYC, 1947; Gagwriters Inst. award, 1948; Recipient citation Mag. Editors for Equal Rights Amendment, 1979, plaque for outstanding service to daytime TV community 1969 to 1978 Edge of Night, Internat. Club. Mem. Writers Guild Am., Radio Writers Guild, Newspaper Guild Club, Newspaper Guild N.Y., Radio-Television Critics Circle N.Y. (founder, chmn.), Assn. UN, Acad. Television Arts & Scis. Greek-Orthodox. Clubs: Silurians, Lambs. DIED 03/26/97. .

DENNIS, WARD BRAINERD, aerospace company executive; b. Detroit Lakes, Minn., Aug. 28, 1922; s. Fred and Laura (Bergseng) D.; m. Bette Mae Evans, Mar. 16, 1948; children: Karen Christine, Patrick Ward. B. Aero. Scis., U. Minn., 1943; M.S., U. Mich., 1947; postgrad., Johns Hopkins, 1948-50. With Bell Aircraft Co., 1944-45, Cornell Aero. Lab., 1945-46; asst. prof. U.S. Naval Postgrad. Sch., 1947-50; with Rand Corp., 1950-53; with Northrop Corp., 1953-84, v.p. corp. devel. planning, 1963-84. Pres. Great Western council Boy Scouts Am., 1980; bd. dirs. Los Angeles chpt. Soc. Prevention Cruelty to Animals, 1977-80. Home: Fallbrook Calif. Died June 10, 1994; Eternal Hills, Oceanside, CA.

DENNISON, CHARLES STUART, institutional executive; b. N.Y.C., Mar. 21, 1918; s. Charles Stuart and Charlotte (Irwin) D.; m. Carol Frances Krueger, June 6, 1951; children: Laura Hardie, Deborah Irwin. Student, Columbia, N.Y.U. Exec. trainee Gen. Motors Corp., 1935-39; asst. mgr. advt. and sales promotion U.S. Steel Export Co., 1939-42; export sales mgr., acting gen. sales mgr. Willys Overland Motors, Inc., 1946-51; mng. dir. Olin Mathieson Ltd., also E.R. Squibb Ltd., London, Eng., 1951-57; v.p. Chrysler Export Corp., 1957-58; v.p. overseas Internat. Minerals & Chem. Corp., Skokie, Ill., 1958-70; dir. Internat. Minerals & Chem., Ltd., London, Eng., Internat. Minerals & Chem., Ltd. Pty., Australia, Internat. Minerals & Chem., Ltd. (Bahamas), Internat. Minerals & Chem., Ltd. (Can.), Panama, Corommandel Fertilisers, Ltd., Secunderabad, India, Compagnie Senegalaise des Phosphates de Taiba, Dakar, Azufrera Intercontinental S.A. de C.V., Mexico, until 1970; exec. Council Sci. and Tech., Washington; Mem. Pres.'s Sci. Advisory Com. Panel on World Food Supply, 1967; mem. exec. com. FAO Industry Coop. Program, Rome, until 1970; mem. industry adv. com. FAO, Rome; mem. council Soc. for Internat. Devel.; mem. com. on Internat. Devel. Inst., Nat. Acad. Scis.; mem. fgn. relations task force White House Conf. on Youth; mem. com. on tech. Council of Americas, 1973; bd. dirs. Assn. Internat. des Etudiants en Scis. Economiques et Commerciales; adv. mem. U.S. delegation OAS Conf. on Application Sci. and Tech. to Devel. Latin Am.; mem. bd. sci. and tech. for internat. devel. Nat. Acad. Scis., 1973-78; mem. Com. on Environ. Aspects U.S. Materials Policy; chmn. panel role U.S. firms R.D. & E. developing countries Nat. Acad. Scis.; mem. panel on internat. indsl. inst. Nat. Acad. Engring.; mem. com. pub. engring. policy NRC; sr. adviser UN Environment Program; exec. dir. Council Sci. and Tech. for Devel., 1977-96; mem. Scowcroft panel on U.S. Security and Third World Policy Ctr. Strategic and Internat. Studies, 1980-82; dir. Bull. Atomic Scientists; conducted seminars on econ. devel. and environment local univs. and govt. agys. Tokyo, Singapore, Toronto, Can., Kuala Lumpur, Hong Kong, Bankok, also local univs. Trustee Agrl. Devel. Council, to 1974; bd. dirs. Overseas Devel. Council. Served to capt., parachute inf. AUS, World War II. Decorated Bronze Star with V, Combat Inf. badge, Presdl. Unit Citation with oak leaf cluster, combat decoration Royal Wilhelms Order, The Netherlands, Croix de Guerre with fouragerre, Belgium; named comdr. Order Merit Senegal. Mem. AAAS, N.Y. Acad. Scis., English Speaking Union, Council Fgn. Relations. Clubs: Metropolitan (N.Y.C.); American (London). Home: Santa Fe N. Mex. Died May 22, 1996; interred Arlington National Cemetery, Washington, D.C.

DENNSTEDT, FREDERICK DEVERE, retired oil company executive; b. Harmony, Minn., Sept. 23, 1918; s. Frederick William and Ida Henrietta (Bruflodt) D.; m. Marjorie Ernst, July 7, 1948; children: Frederick Ernst, Sara Elizabeth. BChemE, U. Minn., 1948; grad., Advanced Mgmt. Program, Harvard U., 1958. With Esso Standard Oil Co., 1948-61, asst. gen. mgr. Baton Rouge refinery, 1959-61; with Humble Oil & Refining Co. (now Exxon Co. U.S.A.), 1961-64, v.p. mfg. dept., 1962-63, v.p. supply and transp. dept., 1963-64; v.p. refining Humble Oil & Refining Co. (now Exxon Co. U.S.A.), Houston, 1969-79; sr. v.p. Humble Oil & Refining Co. (now Exxon Co. U.S.A.), 1979-83; refining coordinator Standard Oil Co., N.J., 1964-68; logistics ops. mgr., 1968-69. DIED 09/07/95. .

DENVER, JOHN (HENRY JOHN DEUTSCHENDORF, JR.), singer, songwriter; b. Roswell, N.Mex., Dec. 31, 1943; s. Henry John Sr. and Erma Deutschendorf; m. Ann Marie Martell, June 9, 1967 (div., 1983); m. Cassandra Delaney, 1988; children: Zack, Anna Kate, Jesse Belle. Student, Tex. Tech U. With Chad Mitchell Trio, 1965-68; solo rec. and concert artist, 1968-97. Performer TV variety spl. Rocky Mountain Christmas (Emmy award), 1983-97, motion picture Oh, God!, 1977, (narrator) Fire & Ice; TV films include A Christmas Story, 1986, Higher Ground, 1988, The Christmas Gift; appeared in TV documentary: Rocky Mountain Reunion (6 awards), TV drama: Foxfire, 1987; TV specials An Evening with John Denver (Emmy award 1975), John Denver's Christmas in Aspen, 1992; writer: (songs) including Take Me Home, Country Roads, Leaving on a Jet Plane, Rocky Mountain High, Thank God I'm a Country Boy, Annie's Song; (albums) including Rocky Mountain High, 1972, Back Home Again, 1974, Windsong, 1975, John Denver, 1979, Autography, 1980, Seasons of the Heart, 1982, Rocky Mountain Holiday, 1982, It's About Time, 1983, Dreamland Express, 1985, One World, 1986, Rocky Mountain Christmas, 1989, The Flower That Shattered the Stone, 1990, Earth Songs, 1990, Different Directions, 1991, Higher Ground, 1991, John Denver and The Muppets: A Christmas Together, The Wildlife Concert, 1995, John Denver: The Rocky Mountain Collection, 1996; toured USSR, 1984-85. Founder, The Windstar Found., Snowmass, Colo., 1976; mem. Presdl. Commn. on World Hunger, 1978; chmn. Nat. UNICEF Day, 1984. Named Top Male Recording Artist, Record World, 1974-75, Country Music Entertainer of Yr., 1975, Favorite Musical Performer, People's Choice award, 1975, Singing Star of Yr., Am. Guild of Variety Artists, 1975; recipient Golden Apple prize Hollywood Women's Press Club, 1977; 15 gold albums, 8 platinum. Mem. Nat. Space Inst., Save the Children, The Cousteau Soc., Friends of the Earth, The Human/Dolphin Found., European Space Agy. Avocations: aviation, photography. Died Oct. 12, 1997.

DENYS, EDWARD PAUL, education educator; b. Chgo., Aug. 29, 1927; s. Carl Paul and Minna Hilda (Teichmann) D.; m. Loretta Arline Heldt, June 27, 1953; children: Daniel, Scott, Sandra. Student, Sch. of Art Inst., Chgo., 1948-52, 55; BS in Edn., Concordia Coll., River Forest, Ill., 1949; MEd, DePaul U., 1968; PhD, Loyola U., Chgo., 1973. Tchr. St. Stephens Luth. Elem. Sch., Chgo., 1949-53; instr., dept. chmn. Luther High Sch. South, Chgo., 1953-95; instr. Moraine Valley Community Coll., Palos Hills, Ill., 1981-96; vis. instr. No. Mich. U., Marquette, 1975, Am. Inst. Banking, Chgo., 1984-85. Author: Philip Melanchton's Unique Contribution to Education, 1972. Schmidt scholar Loyola U., 1971. Mem. Kappa Delta Pi, Phi Delta Kappa. Lutheran. Avocations: painting, cartooning, music, filming, traveling. Home: Tinley Park Ill. Died Feb. 21, 1996.

DERBER, MILTON, labor and industrial relations educator; b. Providence, June 19, 1915; s. Harry and Sophie (Kalman) D.; m. Zelda Trenner, June 14, 1940; children: Clara Gail, Charles. Student, Springfield (Mass.) Jr. Coll., 1932-33; A.B., Clark U., 1936; A.M., U. Wis., 1937, Ph.D., 1940. Social Sci. Research Council fellow, 1936-39; research asso. 20th Century Fund, 1939-40; economist U.S. Bur. Labor Statistics, 1940-41, 46-47; field examiner NLRB, 1941-42; economist OPA, 1942-43; economist and research dir. Nat. War Labor Bd., 1943-45; coordinator of research Inst. Labor and Indsl. Relations, U. Ill., 1947-58, assoc. prof. labor and indsl. relations, 1947-49, prof., 1949-83, prof. emeritus, 1983—, acting dir., 1951-52; Chief economist Pres.'s Fact-Finding Bds. (Gen. Motors and Pacific Coast Longshore Labor Disputes), 1945-46; vice chmn., project dir. Ill. Gov.'s Adv. Commn. on Labor-Mgmt. Policy for Pub. Employees, 1966; mem. Ill. Office Collective Bargaining, 1974-75, 1976-82. Contbg. author: How Collective Bargaining Works, 1942; Author: Labor-Management Relations under Industry-Wide Bargaining, 1955; co-author: The Local Union-Management Relationship, 1960, Plant Union-Management Relations, 1965, Research in Labor Problems in the United States, 1967, The American Idea of Industrial Democracy, 1865-1965, 1970, Strategic Factors in Industrial Relations Systems: The Metalworking Industry, 1976, Labor in Illinois: The Affluent Years 1945-80, 1989; Editor: Termination Report of Nat. War Labor Board, 1948; Co-editor: Problems and Policies of Dispute Settlement and Wage Stabilization during World War II, 1950, Labor and the New Deal, 1957; Project coordinator: Labor-Management Relations in Illini City, 1953. Fulbright sr. scholar Australia, 1975-76. Mem. Indsl. Relations Research Assn. (editor 1948-50, mem. exec. bd. 1959-61, pres.-elect 1980-81, pres. 1982), AAUP (pres. U. Ill. chpt. 1959-60), B'nai B'rith. DIED 02/19/97. .

DEREN, DONALD DAVID, lawyer; b. Westfield, Mass., Oct. 2, 1949; s. Charles William and Margaret Bernice (Ryan) D.; m. Juanita Maria Marino, Apr. 10, 1982; children: Derek D., Jana L., Dustin M. BBA, Nichols Coll., 1971; JD, Suffolk U., 1974. Bar: Mass. 1974, U.S. Dist. Ct. Mass. 1975, U.S. Ct. Appeals (1st cir.) 1980, U.S. Ct. Internat. Trade 1984. Pub. defender Mass. Defenders Commn., Worcester, 1975-79; assoc. Sullivan & Sullivan, Webster, Mass., 1980; assoc. Collins & Monopoli, Shrewsbury, Mass., 1980-83; pvt. practice, Dudley, Mass., 1983-90; mem. firm Bernardin, Lombardi & Deren, Worcester, 1991—; one of 3 attys. who successfully briefed and argued unconstitutionality of Mass. Death Penalty Statute before Supreme Judicial Ct., 1984. Mem. Town of Dudley Police Evaluating Com., 1981—, Pers. Bd., 1988-90. Recipient Atty. award Mass. Citizens Against the Death Penalty, 1985. Mem. Nat. Assn. Criminal Def. Lawyers, Worcester County Bar Assn., Boston Bar Assn., Bar Advs. of Worcester County, Inc., (bd. dirs. 1986—), Calif. Pub. Defenders Assn., U.S. Parachute Assn. Deceased.

DERGE, DAVID RICHARD, political science educator; b. Kansas City, Mo., Oct. 10, 1928; s. David Richard and Blanche (Butterfield) D.; m. Elizabeth Anne Greene, Sept. 4, 1951 (dec. Mar. 1971); children—David Richard III, Dorothy Anne; m. Patricia Jean Williams, Sept. 2, 1972; children—William David, Mary Jennifer. A.B., U. Mo., 1950; A.M., Northwestern U., 1951, Ph.D., 1955; LL.D., Hanyang U., Korea, 1973. Instr. U. Mo., 1954-56, Northwestern U., summer 1955; mem. faculty Ind. U., 1956-72, prof. polit. sci., 1965-72, dean adminstrn., exec. v.p., 1968-72; pres. So. Ill. U., Carbondale, 1972-74, prof. polit. sci., 1974-96; pres. Behavioral Research Assocs., 1968-96; mem. U.S. Adv. Commn. Internat. Ednl. and Cultural Affairs, 1969-76; White House cons. Exec. Office of President, 1970-72; cons. higher and internat. edn. Dept. Health, Edn. and Welfare, 1971-72; sec., dir. Midwest Univs. Consortium for Internat. Activities, 1967-72; pres. Ill. Joint Council Higher Edn., 1972; bd. dirs. Ill. Ednl. Consortium for Computer Services, 1972; sec. Acad. Assn Midwest Univs. Author: Public Leadership in Indiana, 1969, Institution Building and Rural Development, 1968, The World of American Politics, 1968; also articles. Mem. City Council, Bloomington, Ind., 1963-67. Served with AUS, 1946-48; Served with USNR, 1952-88; comdr. Res., lt. col. CAP., 1987-96. Grantee Social Sci. Research Council, 1957; grantee Eagleton Inst. Practical Politics, 1959; grantee Citizenship Clearing House, 1961; recipient Sigma Delta Chi Teaching award, 1963, Weatherly Distinguished Teaching award Ind. U., 1964, Outstanding Teaching award So. Ill. U., 1987; named Outstanding Young Man Ind. Ind. Jr. C. of C., 1963. Mem. Am. Polit. Sci. Assn., U.S. Naval Inst., Phi Beta Kappa, Pi Sigma Alpha, Alpha Pi Zeta, Alpha Kappa Psi, Phi Delta Kappa, Kappa Sigma. Presbyn. Clubs: Bloomington Squash Racquets, La Table Six. Home: Carbondale Ill. Died Dec. 26, 1996.

DE ST. JORRE, DANIELLE MARIE-MADELEINE, Seychelles government official; b. Mahé, Seychelles, Sept. 30, 1941; d. Henri Jorre and Alice (Corgat) De St. J.; married, 1965 (div. 1983); 3 children. Student, NYU, U. London, U. Edinburgh. Prin. Tchr. Tng. Coll., Seychelles, 1974-76; prin. sec. ministry of fgn. affairs, tourism and aviation Govt. of Seychelles, 1977-79, prin. sec. ministry of planning and external rels., 1983-86, min. of planning and external rels., 1986-92, min. of environment, econ. planning and external rels., 1992-93, min. of fgn. affairs, planning and environment, 1993-97, high commr. in U.K., 1983-85; mem. bd. of govs. World Bank, African Devel. Bank, 1984-97; mem. ctrl. com. Seychelles People's Progressive Front, 1991-97; mem. bd. Internat. Ocean Inst., 1992-97. Author: Apprenons la nouvelle orthographe, 1978, Dictionnaire Créole Seychellois-français, 1982, Lexique de Spécificités de la Langue Française aux Seychelles. Avocations: reading, lexicography, folklore, arts and crafts. Died Feb. 25, 1997.

DESPOL, JOHN ANTON, former state deputy labor commissioner; b. San Francisco, July 22, 1913; s. Anton and Bertha (Balzer) D.; m. Jeri Kaye Steep, Dec. 7, 1937, (dec. 1986); children: Christopher Paul, Anthony John. Student, U. So. Calif., 1931, Los Angeles Jr. Coll., 1929-30. Sec.-treas., council Calif. CIO, Los Angeles, 1950-58, gen. v.p. Calif. Labor Fedn. AFL-CIO, San Francisco, 1958-60; internat. rep. United Steelworkers Am., Los Angeles, 1937-68; with Dempsey-Tegeler & Co., Inc., 1968-70; rep. Bache & Co., 1970-71; commr Fed. Mediation and Conciliation Services, Los Angeles, 1972-73; indsl. relations cons., 1971-76; dep. labor commr. State of Calif., 1976-89; cons., 1989-95; mem. Nat. Steel Panel Nat. War Labor Bd., 1944-45; chmn. bd. trustees Union Mgmt. Ins. Trust Fund, Los Angeles, 1948-68. Mem. Calif. Def. Council, 1939-41, 10th Regional War Manpower Commn., 1942-46; bd. dirs. So. Calif. region NCCJ, 1960-68; bd. dirs. Los Angeles Community Chest, Los Angeles World Affairs Council, 1951-80, Braille Inst. of Am., 1961-95; del. Nat. Democratic Conv., 1948, 52, 56, 60; mem. Los Angeles County Dem. Com., 1942-44; mem. exec. com. Calif. Dem. Com., 1952-56; chmn. Calif. Congl. dist. 1954-56; mem. Calif. Legislative Adv. Commn. to State Legislature, 1956-59; del. Nat. Republican Conv., 1968 bd. dirs. Los Angeles World Affairs Council, 1953-81 Braille Inst. Am., 1961-94; bd. govs. Town Hall, Los Angeles, 1941-44, 67-70, chmn. econ. sect., 1964-65 mem. Los Angeles Coun. Fgn. Rels., 1946-95; mem. Calif. Job Tng. and Placement Coun., 1967-68. Mem. Indsl. Relations Research Assn., Inst. Indsl. Relations Assn. Calif. State Attys. and Adminstrv. Law Judges

Soc. Profl. Dispute Resolution. Died Apr. 4, 1995. Home: Newport Beach Calif.

DESTEVENS, GEORGE, chemist, educator; b. Tarrytown, N.Y., Aug. 21, 1924; s. Samuel and Celeste (Leggin) deS.; m. Ruby, Nov. 30, 1950. B.S., Fordham U., 1950, M.S., 1951, Ph.D., 1953; DSc (hon.), Drew U., 1988. Research chemist Remington Rand, Middletown, Conn., 1953-55; research chemist CIBA Pharm. Co., Summit, N.J., 1955-60; dir. medicinal chemistry CIBA Pharm. Co., 1960-65, dir. chem. research, 1965-67, v.p., dir. research, 1967-70; exec. v.p., dir. research CIBA-Geigy Corp., Summit, 1970-79; prof. chemistry Drew U., Madison, N.J., 1979-95, dir. Charles A. Dana Rsch. Inst. for Scientists Emeriti, 1980-95, chmn. Residential Sch. on Medicinal Chemistry, 1987-95; frontiers in chemistry lectr. Wayne State U., 1961; vis. professorial lectr. medicinal chemistry U. Vienna, 1961, U. Kans., 1964, Weizmann Inst., Israel, 1965, U. Kyoto, Japan, 1965; chmn. award com. CIBA-Geigy-Drew Award in Frontiers in Biomed. Research, 1976-95; mem. research adv. bd. Frito-Lay, 1979-95; chmn. bd. Med. Mark Corp., 1983-95; cons. chem. cos., 1979-95. Author: Diuretics, Chemistry and Pharmacology, 1963, Analgetics, 1965; editor: Medicinal Chemistry Monographs, 1963-95, Medicinal Research Revs, 1981-95; mem. editorial bd.: Organic Preparations and Procedures, 1969-95, Synthetic Reactions, 1971-95, Chemistry in the Economy, 1973; contbr. articles to various publs. Trustee St. Barnabas Med. Center, 1970-95; bd. dirs. N.J. chpt. Huntington's Disease, 1980-95. Served with U.S. Army, 1942-46. Woodrow Wilson vis. fellow, 1986-95; recipient Outstanding Achievement award in sci. Fordham Coll. Alumni Assn., 1966, Walter J. Hartung Meml. award in medicinal rsch. U. N.C., 1979; named to N.J. Inventors Hall of Fame, 1995. Fellow N.Y. Acad. Scis. (research award in chemistry 1961); mem. Am. Chem. Soc. (E.B. Hershberg award 1991), Am. Inst. Chemistry, AAAS, Assn. Research Dirs. (exec. council), Am.-Swiss Found. Sci. Exchange (trustee), Soc. Chem. Industry, Indsl. Research Inst., Sigma Xi, Phi Lambda Upsilon. Clubs: Morris County Golf (Convent Station, N.J.); Summit Tennis. Home: Summit N.J. Died Sept. 5, 1995.

DE STWOLINSKI, GAIL ROUNCE BOYD, music theory and composition educator; b. Sidney, Mont., Nov. 8, 1921; d. Harold Lowell and Alice (Hardenburgh) R.; m. David Robinson Boyd, Sept. 4, 1943 (dec. 1944); 1 son, David Robinson Boyd; m. Louis Charl de Stwolinski, June 15, 1951. MusB, U. Mont., 1943; M in Music Theory, Eastman Sch. Music U. Rochester, 1946, PhD in Music Theory, 1966. Instr. U. Okla., 1946, asst. prof. music theory, 1949-55, assoc. prof., 1955-66, prof., 1966-84, Disting. prof., 1970-84, chmn. dept. music theory and composition, 1953-60; Adviser, cons. in field. Author: Form and Content in Instrumental Music; also articles in mus. jours. Recipient Regents award superior teaching, 1966; named David Ross Boyd prof., 1970; recipient Distinguished Service citation U. Mont., 1974, Disting. Svc. citation U. Okla., 1989. Mem. Okla. Music Tchrs. Assn., Okla. Theory Roundtable, Music Tchrs. Nat. Assn., Music Educators Nat. Conf., AAUP, Coll. Music Soc., Soc. Music Theory, Mortar Bd., Phi Beta Kappa (hon.), Pi Kappa Lambda, Mu Phi Epsilon, Kappa Kappa Gamma. Democrat. Died July 15, 1996.

DEUSS, JEAN, librarian; b. Chgo.; d. Edward Louis and Harriet (Goodwin) D. B.A., U. Wis., 1944; M.S., Sch. Library Service, Columbia U., 1959. Cataloger library N.Y.C. Council Fgn. Relations, 1959-61; head cataloger research library Fed. Res. Bank N.Y., N.Y.C., 1961-68; asst. chief librarian Fed. Bank N.Y., N.Y.C., 1969-70, chief librarian, 1970-85. Author: Banking in the U.S.: An Annotated Bibliography, 1990; editor: Banking and Fin. Collections, Spl. Collections, vol. 2, No. 3, 1983. Mem. U. Wis. Found., 1977—, bd. dirs., 1983—; bd. dirs. Abingdon Square Painters, 1990—. Mem. Spl. Libraries Assn. (assoc. treas. 1967-70, pres. N.Y. chpt. 1971-72, bd. dirs. 1972-76). Episcopalian. Deceased.

DEUTSCHENDORF, HENRY JOHN, JR. See DENVER, JOHN

DEVRIES, BERNARD JERIN, retired architect; b. Chgo., June 21, 1909; s. Christian W.B. and Johana (Zicterman) DeV.; m. Jean Ann Frissel, June 27, 1936 (dec. Aug. 1983); 1 child, Jo-Ann C.; m. Helen I. Johnston, Feb. 22, 1984. Student, Mich. State U., 1929-30; B.S. in Architecture, U. Mich., 1934. Registered architect, Mich., Ill., Ind., Ohio, Mass., Conn., Tex., N.J. Asst. engr. City of Ann Arbor (Mich.), 1934-37; designer Lewis J. Sarvis (architect), Battle Creek, Mich., 1937-38; pvt. practice architecture Bernard J. DeVries (now DeVries Assos., Inc.), architects and planners), Muskegon, Mich., 1938-83; profl. community planner, ret.; architect Gen. Telephone Co. Mich., Master City Plan Muskegon, CBD Redevel. Plan Muskegon, Muskegon Marquette Urban Renewal Project; also schs., churches, indsl. and apt. bldg. complexes. Chmn. Mich. Bd. Registration for Architects; mem. Mich. Bd. Registration for Land Surveyors.; Commr. Muskegon City Planning Commn., 1944-65, chmn., 1947-65; commr. Muskegon Bd. Appeals, 1954-65; charter mem. Muskegon Community Services Planning Council, 1963-70, dir., 1963; founder, charter mem. Lake Michigan Region Planning Council, Inc., 1960-70, vice chmn., 1964, chmn. Mich. delegation, 1961-70; Mem. Nat. Council Archtl. Registration Bds. Co-author: Dunes Area Regional Planning, 1962, Regional Highways and Population Growth Report, 1963. Trustee C.W. Smith Kiwanis Found., 1980—; bd. dirs. Hackley Heritage Assn., 1960-87. Recipient Disting. Service award Jr. C. of C., 1943, hon. mention Am. Gas Assn. Residence Competition, 1939, hon. mention Mich. Sch. Bds. Sch. Design Competition, 1963; 1st place Design award for Branch Bank, Muskegon AIA, 1964; named Muskegon's Mr. Planner Muskegon Chronicle, 1963. Fellow A.I.A. (sec., dir. Western Mich. chpt. 1945-47, v.p. Grand Valley chpt. 1963, pres. 1964); mem. Mich. Soc. Architects (bd. mem. 1967-79, gold medal 1966), Am. Soc. Planning Ofcls., Mich. Soc. Planning Ofcls. (founder, charter dir. 1956, bd. mem. 1967-73, pres. 1970), Mich. Assn. of Professions (charter), Muskegon C. of C. (Builders award 1956). Clubs: Kiwanian (pres. 1952, mem. Legion Honor), Muskegon Century, Muskegon Yacht.

DEW, JESS EDWARD, chemical engineer; b. Okemah, Okla., July 18, 1920; s. Jess Edward and Colleen Avara (Norman) D.; m. Mary Ann Burns, Jan. 3, 1944 (dec. Dec. 1983); children: Anne, Stephen Dodson, David Burns. Student, Okla. Mil. Acad., 1939-41; BS in Chem. Engring., U. Okla., 1943; MS in Chem. Engring., MIT, 1948. Registered profl. engr., Okla. (3709). Asst. chem. engr. Exxon Corp., Baytown, Tex., 1943-47; chem. engr. Amoco Oil Co., Tulsa, 1948-52; v.p. engring. John Deere Chem. Co., Pryor, Okla., 1952-63; gen. supt. John Deere Planter Works, Moline, Ill., 1963-65; v.p. mfg. Arkia Chem. Corp., Helena, Ark., 1965-69; internat. project mgr. Chem. Constrn. Co., N.Y.C., 1969-74; project mgr. Chem. Constrn. Co., Gt. Britain, 1969-71, Argentina, 1971, Saudi Arabia, 1971-72, Algeria, 1972-74; ind. cons. engr., 1974-78; constrn. mgr. W.R. Holway & Assocs., Tulsa, 1978-82; v.p. and gen. mgr. R.L. Frailey, Inc., Tulsa, 1982-86, ret., 1986; pres., bd. dirs. Pryor Indsl. Conservation Co., 1961-63. Contbr. articles to profl. jours. and chpts. to books; patentee in field. Mem. Pryor Mcpl. Utility Bd., 1955-60, Pryor City Council, 1962-63, Rivers and Harbor Commn., Helena, 1966-70; adv. bd. Sacred Heart Acad., 1967-69; bd. dirs. Helena United Fund, 1969; mem. pres.' bd. advisors Rogers State Coll., 1994; chmn. bldg. com. Our Mother of Perpetual Help Cath. Ch. Pryor, 1962-63. Mem. AICHE, ASME, Am. Philatelic Soc., Nat. Eagle Scout Assn., Summit Club Tulsa, Okla. City Golf and Country Club, Okla. City Mem.'s Dinner Club, Elks, Eagles, Moose, Sigma Xi, Beta Theta Pi, Alpha Chi Sigma, Tau Beta Pi. Republican. Roman Catholic. Died May 25, 1996.

DEWITT, JOHN BELTON, conservation executive; b. Oakland, Calif., Jan. 13, 1937; s. Belton and Florence Jeffery D.; m. Karma Lee Sowers, Sept. 17, 1960. BA in Wildlife Conservation, U. Calif., Berkeley, 1959. With U.S. Forest Svc. El Dorado Nat. Forest, 1955-56; ranger naturalist Nat. Park Svc., Yosemite Nat. Park, 1957-58, Mt. Rainer Nat. Park, 1959, Death Valley Nat. Monument, 1960; land law examiner, info. officer, land appraiser Bur. of Land Mgmt., Sacramento, 1960-64; asst. sec. Save-the-Redwoods League, 1964-71; dir. No. Calif. chpt. Nature Conservancy, 1976-77; dir. Tuolumne River Preservation Trust, 1981-85; exec. dir., sec. Save-the-Redwoods League, 1971-95; adv. coun. Trust for Pub. Land, 1975-78, Anza Borrego Desert Com., 1983-93; advisor to U.S. Sec. Interior (4 adminstrns.). Author: California Redwood Parks and Preserves, 1982, 3d edit., 1993. Recipient Nat. Conservation award DAR, 1982, Golden Bear award Calif. State Park & Recreation Commn., 1982, Gulf Oil Conservation award, 1985, Calif. State Park Partnership award, 1995; named hon. Calif. Park Ranger, 1985, Nat. Park Ranger, 1995; hon. recognition Calif. State Assembly, 1995. Mem. Sierra Club (conservation com. 1953-63), Am. Forestry Assn., Nat. Parks Assn., Wilderness Soc., Nat. Audubon Soc. Avocations: fishing, hiking, gardening. Home: Oakland Calif. Died Aug. 24, 1996; buried Mountain View Cemetery, Oakland.

DEXTER, LEWIS, cardiologist; b. Concord, Mass., Mar. 1, 1910; s. Smith Owen and Helen (Denison) D.; m. E. Cassandra Kinsman, Dec. 12, 1941; children—Lewis, Smith Owen, Cassandra Kinsman Short. B.A., Harvard, 1932, M.D., 1936; D.Sc. (hon.), U. Mass. Med. Sch., 1984. Diplomate: Am. Bd. Internal Medicine. Intern Presbyn. Hosp., N.Y.C., 1936-38; staff mem. Peter Bent Brigham Hosp., 1941-95, physician, 1952-95; faculty mem. Harvard Med. Sch., 1941-95; tutor medicine, 1948-76; prof. medicine Peter Bent Brigham Hosp., 1969-76, prof. emeritus hosp. and med. sch., 1976-95; prof. emeritus U. Mass. Sch. Medicine, 1980-90. Recipient James B. Herrick award Am. Heart Assn., 1975, Research Achievement award Am. Heart Assn., 1982, Paul Dudley White award Mass. Heart Assn., 1984; ACP fellow under Dr. Bernardo A. Houssay Inst. Physiology, Buenos Aires, 1940-41. Fellow ACP, Am. Coll. Cardiology; mem. Am. Soc. Clin. Investigation, Assn. Am. Physicians, Am. Heart Assn., Am. Physiol. Soc., Am. Acad. Arts and Scis., Am. Clin. and Climatological Assn., N.Y. Acad. Scis., Assn. Univ. Cardiologists, Brit. Cardiac Soc. (corr.), Interurban Clin. Club; hon. mem. Argentine, Mexican, Peruvian socs. cardiology, Argentine Med. Assn. Home: Walpole Mass. Died Dec. 3, 1995.

DHANAK, AMRITLAL MAGANLAL, engineering educator; b. Bhavnagar, India, July 13, 1925; came to U.S., 1947, naturalized, 1953; s. Maganlal Sojabhai and Nathiben (Valera) D.; m. Harriet Cook, Aug. 28, 1954; children: Eric, Lynn, Michelle. B.Sc., Royal Inst. Sci., Bombay, 1947; B.S., U. Calif. at Berkeley, 1950, M.Engring., 1951, Ph.D., 1956. Asso. mech. engring., research engr. U. Calif. at Berkeley, 1950-56; project engr. Gen. Electric Co., Schenectady, 1956-58; asso. prof. Rensselaer Poly. Inst., Troy, N.Y., 1958-61; prof. mech. engring. Mich. State U., East Lansing, 1961-94; cons. to industry. Sir. Jaswantsinghji scholar U. Bombay, India, 1943-46. Mem. ASME (exec. com. tech. and soc. div. 1974-94), Sigma Xi. Home: East Lansing Mich. Died Dec. 18, 1994.

DIANA, PRINCESS, The Princess of Wales; b. Sandringham, Norfolk, England, July 1, 1961; d. 8th Earl of Spencer and Countess Spencer (now Hon. Mrs. Peter Shand-Kydd); m. Charles, Prince of Wales, July 29, 1981 (div. Aug. 1996); children: William Arthur Philip Louis (Prince William of Wales), Henry Charles Albert David (Prince Henry of Wales). Student, Riddlesworth Hall, Norfolk, Eng., W. Heath Sch., nr. Sevenoaks, Kent, Eng., Chateau D'Oex, Switzerland. Tchr. Young Eng. Kindergarten Sch., London, 1979-81. Pres. The Albany, 1982-97, Wales Craft Coun., 1983-97, Barnardo's, 1984-97, Royal Acad. Music, 1985-97, R.A.D.A., 1989-97, Nat. Meningitis Trust, 1989; hon. col.-in-chief 13th-18th Hussars; col.-in-chief Royal Hampshire Regiment, 1985-97, Light Dragoons, 1992-97; hon. air comdr R.A.F. Wittering, 1985-97. Died Aug. 31, 1997.

DIANIS, WALTER JOSEPH, banker; b. Greenwich, Conn., Aug. 12, 1918; s. Joseph and Susie (Sumka) D.; m. Pauline Frano, Oct. 11, 1942; children: Charles, Thomas. BBA, Iona Coll., 1950; MBA, NYU, 1952; cert., Rutgers U., 1959. Auditor Port Chester Savs. Bank, N.Y., 1936-48; sr. accountant Dusenbury & Hogenauer, Port Chester, 1948-53; 1st sr. v.p. Home Savs. Bank, White Plains, N.Y., from 1953, later pres.; also trustee. Home Savs. Bank. Active Community Chests, Port Chester and White Plains, 1948-57; trustee White Plains YWCA. Served with USCG, 1942-45. Mem. White Plains C. of C. (treas. 1968-72). Lutheran (chief financial officer). Clubs: University (White Plains), Westchester County Assn. (White Plains). Home: Greenwich Conn. Died Nov. 22, 1996.

DI CARLO, FREDERICK JOSEPH, toxicologist, editor; b. N.Y.C., Nov. 24, 1918; s. Amilcare and Anna (Manieri) Di C.; m. Nancy Cucco, Oct. 16, 1943; children: Frederick, Nancy Ann, Paul. BS, Fordham U., 1939, MS, 1941; PhD, NYU, 1944. Instr. chemistry dept. NYU, N.Y.C., 1943-44; rsch. assoc. Squibb Inst. for Med. Rsch., New Brunswick, N.J., 1944-46; head biochemistry divsn. Fleischmann Labs., Stamford, Conn., 1946-60; dir. dept. drug metabolism Warner Lambert Rsch. Inst., Morris Plains, N.J., 1960-77; sr. sci. advisor U.S. EPA, Washington, 1977—; adj. prof. Coll. St. Elizabeth, Convent Sta., N.J., 1968-77; editor Drug Metabolism Rev., Marcel Dekker, Inc., N.Y.C., 1971—; dir. toxicology courses Am. Chem. Soc., Washington, 1981—. Fellow AAAS; mem. Soc. for Leucocyte Biology (hon.). Avocations; travel, reading, tennis. DIED 09/15/97. .

DICKE, ROBERT HENRY, physicist, educator; b. St. Louis, May 6, 1916; s. Oscar H. and Flora (Peterson) D.; m. Annie Henderson Currie, June 6, 1942; children: Nancy Jean Dicke Rapoport, John Robert, James Howard. A.B., Princeton U., 1939; Ph.D., U. Rochester, 1941, D.Sc. (hon.), 1981; D.Sc. (hon.), U. Edinburgh, 1972, Ohio No. U., 1981; DSc. (hon.), Princeton U., 1989. Microwave radar devel. Radiation Lab., MIT, 1941-46; physics faculty Princeton U., 1946-97, Cyrus Fogg Brackett prof. physics, 1957-75, Albert Einstein prof. sci., 1975-84, Albert Einstein prof. sci. emeritus, 1984-97, chmn. physics dept., 1967-70; mem. adv. panel for physics NSF, 1959-61; chmn. adv. com. atomic physics Nat. Bur. Standards, 1961-63; mem. com. on physics NASA, 1963-70, chmn., 1963-66; chmn. physics adv. panel Com. on Internat. Exchange of Persons (Fulbright-Hays Act), 1964-66; chmn. adv. com. on radio astronomy telescopes NSF, 1967, 69; mem. Nat. Sci. Bd., 1970-76; vis. com. Nat. Bur. Standards, 1975-79, chmn., 1979; vis. prof. Harvard U., 1954-55, Inst. Advanced Study, 1970-71; Sherman Fairchild Disting. scholar Calif. Inst. Tech., 1975; Walker Ames prof. U. Wash., Seattle, 1979; Jaynes lectr. Am. Philos. Soc., 1969; Scott lectr. Cambridge U. (Eng.), 1977. Author: (with Montgomery, Purcell) Principles of Micro-wave Circuits, 1948, (with J.P. Wittke) An Introduction to Quantum Mechanics, 1960, The Theoretical Significance of Experimental Relativity, 1964, Gravitation and the Universe, 1970. Trustee Assoc. Univs. Inc., 1980-88. Recipient Nat. Medal Sci., 1970, NASA medal for exceptional sci. achievement, 1973, Cresson medal Franklin Inst., 1974, Michelson Morley award Case Western Res. U., 1987, Pioneer award IEEE Microwave Theory and Techniques Soc., 1991. Mem. NAS (Comstock prize 1973), Am. Philos. Soc., Am. Geophys. Union, Am. Phys. Soc., Am. Astron. Soc. (Beatrice M. Tinsley prize 1992), Am. Acad. Arts and Scis. (Rumford medal 1967), Royal Astron. Soc. (assoc.). Home: Princeton N.J. Died Mar. 4, 1997.

DICKEY, JAMES LAFAYETTE, poet, novelist, filmmaker, critic; b. Atlanta, Feb. 2, 1923; s. Eugene and Maibelle (Swift) D.; m. Maxine Syerson, Nov. 4, 1948 (dec. 1976); children: Christopher Swift, Kevin Webster; m. Deborah Dodson, Dec. 30, 1976; 1 dau., Bronwen Elaine. Student, Clemson Coll., 1942; BA magna cum laude, Vanderbilt U., 1949, MA, 1950. Instr. English Rice Inst. (now Rice U.), Houston, 1950, 1952-54, U. Fla., Gainesville, 1955-56; poet-in-residence Reed Coll., Portland, Oreg., 1963-64, San Fernando Valley State Coll. (now Calif. State U.), Northridge, 1964-65; poet-in-residence U. Wis., Madison, 1966, Milw., 1967; poet-in-residence Wash. U., St. Louis, Mo., 1968; Franklin Disting. Prof. English Ga. Inst. Tech., Atlanta, 1968; poet-in-residence, prof. English U. S.C., Columbia., 1969—; cons. poetry Libr. of Congress, 1966-68, hon. cons. Am. Letters, 1968-71; judge Yale Series of Younger Poets, 1989-96. Author: (poetry) Into The Stone and Other Poems, 1960, Drowning with Others, 1962, Helmets, 1964, Two Poems of the Air, 1964, Buckdancer's Choice, 1965 (Nat. Book award for poetry 1966, Melville Cane award Poetry Soc. Am. 1966), Poems, 1957-1967, 1968, The Eye-Beaters, Blood, Victory, Madness, Buckhead, and Mercy, 1970, Exchanges, 1971, The Zodiac, 1976, The Strength of Fields, 1977, Tucky the Hunter, 1978, Head-Deep in Strange Sounds: Improvisations from the UnEnglish, 1979, Veteran Birth: The Gadfly Poems, 1947-1979, 1980, The Early Motion, 1981, Falling, May Day Sermon, and Other Poems, 1981, The Eagle's Mile, 1981, Puella, 1982, Väermland, 1982, False Youth: Four Seasons, 1983, The Central Motion, 1983, For a Time and Place, 1983, Bronwen, the Traw and the Shape-Shifter, 1986, Summons, 1988, The Whole Motion: Collected Poems, 1992; (novels) Deliverance, 1970 (Prix Medicis Paris 1971), Alnilam, 1987, To the White Sea, 1993; (non-fiction) The Suspect in Poetry, 1964, A Private Brinksmanship, 1965, Spinning the Crystal Ball: Some Guesses at the Future of American Poetry, 1967, Metaphor as Pure Adventure, 1968, Babel to Byzantium: Poets and Poetry Now, 1968, Self-Interviews, 1970, Sorties: Journals and New Essays, 1971, Jericho: The South Beheld, 1974, God's Images: The Bible, a New Vision, 1977, The Enemy from Eden, 1978, In Pursuit of the Grey Soul, 1978, The Water Bug's Mittens, 1980, Starry Place Between the Antlers: Why I Live in South Carolina, 1981, Night Hurdling, 1983, Wayfarer: A Voice from the Southern Mountains, 1988, Southern Light, 1991; (screenplays) Deliverance, 1972; (teleplays) The Call of the Wild, 1976. Served with USAAF and USAF, World War II, Korea. Decorated Air medal, Order of the Palmetto, S.C., 1983; recipient Union League Civic and Arts Found. prize Poetry mag., 1958, Vachel Lindsay prize Poetry mag., 1959, Longview award, 1959, N.Y. Quarterly Poetry Day award, 1977, Levinson prize Poetry mag., 1982; Sewanee Rev. poetry fellow, 1954-55; Guggenheim fellow, 1961-62; Nat. Inst. Arts and Letters grantee, 1966. Mem. Nat. Inst. Arts and Letters, Am. Acad. Arts and Letters, Fellowship of So. Writers, S.C. Acad. Authors, Writer's Guild Am., Nat. Adv. Coun. on the Arts. Died Jan. 19, 1997.

DICKS, JOHN BARBER, educator, physicist; b. Natchez, Miss., Mar. 10, 1926; s. John Barber and Pauline (Merrill) D.; m. Eleanor Ann Burdeshaw, Jan. 5, 1973; children: Pauline, Dunbar.; children by previous marriage—Ian, Ayers Merrill, Agnes, Josephine. B.S., U. South, 1948; Ph.D., Vanderbilt U., 1955. Assoc. prof. Tenn. Technol. U., Cookeville, 1953-54; asst. prof., assoc. prof. U. of South, Sewanee, Tenn., 1954-64; prof. physics U. Tenn. Space Inst., Tullahoma, 1964—, Alumni distinguished prof., 1972—, chief scientist, 1982-87, dir. energy conversion div., 1967-82; pres. Applied Energetics, Inc., 1967—; chmn. steering com. Symposium on Engring. Aspects of Magnetohydrodynamics, 1971; pres. Tenn. Energy Inst., 1980—; chmn. Engring. and Chem. Disposal Inc., 1990—. Contbr. articles profl. jours. Fellow ASME (chmn. energetics div. 1972-73, chmn. synthetic fuels com. 1981-90, bd. dirs. 1985-90, chmn. emerging energy tech. symposium Energy Tech. Conf. Exhbn. 1989-90, chmn. tech. planning com. 1986-90, bd. govt. relations and council on pub. affairs 1985-90, chmn. petroleum div. exec. com. 1987-90, chmn. energy sources tech. conf. and exhbn. 1986-87); assoc. fellow AIAA (asso. editor jour.); mem. U.S. Energy Assn. (bd. dirs., mem. exec. com.1986-90, mem. com. on energy state of union message 1987), Am. Phys. Soc., AAUP (Tenn. state chmn. 1962-64), Sigma Xi, Sigma Pi Sigma.

DICKSON, JOHN R., food products company executive, dairy products company executive; b. 1930. BA, Ashland Coll., 1954. With Loblaw Co., Buffalo, 1954-63, Colonial Foods Inc., 1963-71, Shoprite Foods Inc., Arlington, Tex., 1971-76, Fox Grocery Co., Pitts., 1976-81, Wetterau Inc., St. Louis, to 1986; pres., chief exec. officer Roundy's Inc., Pewaukee, Wis., 1986—, chmn., 1993—. Deceased.

DIETRICH, MARTHA JANE (MARTHA JANE SHULTZ), genealogist; b. Brazil, Ind., Aug. 19, 1916; d. Charles Russell and Florence Delilah (McIntire) Shultz; grad. Ind. State U.; m. E(arl) Donald Dietrich, June 17, 1939; children: Florence Ann Dietrich Harris, Jean Carol Dietrich Litterst, Charles Donald. Clk., CSC, Washington, 1937-43; personnel officer Armed Forces Med. Library, Washington, 1948-54; personnel staffing specialist Navy Dept., Washington, 1954-70, ret., 1970; profl. freelance genealogist, College Park, Md., 1973-88. Cert. Am. lineage specialist; authorized Bd. Cert. of Genealogists, Washington; Author: The Whitenack Family From New Jersey to Kentucky, 1972, Charles Russell Shultz 1876-1959, 1992, Family Reminiscenses, 1992. Mem. Ky. Hist. Soc. (life), Ind. Hist. Soc., Clay County (Ind.) Geneal. Soc. (life), Somerset County (Pa.) Geneal. Soc. (life), Geneal. Soc. Pa., DAR, Nat. Officers Club (bd. dirs. Eastern region 1988-90), DAR, (state registrar 1973-76, state vice regent 1976-79), Md. DAR (state regent 1979-82, hon. state regent 1982-95), Md. State DAR Officers Club, Daus. Am. Colonists (state chmn. 1977-79), Daus. Colonial Wars, UDC (2d v.p. gen. 1988-90), Daus. of 1812, Sons and Daus. of Pilgrims (lt. gov. Md. br. 1980-82, 88-90), Magna Charta Dames, Order Crown of Charlemagne (registrar gen. 1983-86, hon. registrar gen. life 1986), Soc. Ind. Pioneers (life), Order Ky. Cols., Dames of Court of Honor, Clan MacIntyre Assn. (genealogist 1978-84), Daus. Barons of Runnymede, Colonial Dames XVII Century (state pres. D.C. state soc. 1975-77, acting registrar gen. 1974-75, registrar gen. 1975-79, service awards 1977, 78), Soc. Ky. Pioneers, Colonial Daus. Seventeenth Century, Flagon and Trencher (life), Hereditary Order Descendants Twin Territories (life), Palatines to Am., Philippe du Trieux Descendants Assn., Point Lookout Prisoner of War Descendants Assn., Md. Soc. So. Dames (state sec. 1990-92), Kappa Kappa, Kappa Kappa Kappa (Ind.). Episcopalian. Died Apr. 18, 1995. Home: College Park Md.

DI GIOVANNI, JACK LEONARD, newspaper financial executive; b. N.Y.C., Nov. 18, 1935; s. Sebastian and Maria Concetta (Caruso) Di G.; m. Patrina Barone, Jan. 19, 1957; children: Diane Marie, Patricia. B.B.A., CCNY, 1956; M.B.A. with distinction, Pace U., 1975. Fin. exec. Dow Jones & Co., Inc., N.Y.C., 1956-64; fin. exec. N.Y. News Inc., N.Y.C., 1965-87, dir. fin. studies, 1985-86; dir. circulation fin. N.Y. Times Inc., N.Y.C., 1987—; treas. Daily News Charities, N.Y.C., Gaynor News Co., N.Y.C., Daily News Found., N.Y.C., N.Y. News Inc., N.Y.C.; mem. pension coms. N.Y. News Retirement Plans, N.Y.C., 1982; trustee Guild-News Pension Plan, N.Y.C., 1982, Guild-Times Pension and Welfare Funds, N.Y.C., 1989. Treas., trustee Oradell Swim Club, (N.J.), 1978; pres., trustee Oradell Pub. Library, 1982; councilman Borough of Oradell, 1985-88. Mem. Inst. Newspaper Controllers and Fin. Officers. Roman Catholic. Club: UNICO (dir. 1982-86). Lodge: Lions (dir. 1984-89).

DILLON, PAUL, electrical engineering consultant; b. Centre County, Pa., Aug. 18, 1913; s. Frank Wilson and Nancy Mary (Campbell) D.; m. Margaret Adelaide Knight, Mar. 5, 1938; children: Nancy, John, Michael, Ross, Paula, Daisy. Degree in Comm., Mass. Radio Sch., Boston, 1934; BSEE, N.C. State Coll., 1942. Registered profl. engr., Calif. Radio engr. Sta. WEED, Rocky Mount, N.C., 1935-39, State of N.C., Raleigh, N.C., 1939-42; transmitter supr. Sta. WMIT, Mount Mitchell, N.C., 1942-46; chief engr. Sta. WFMY, Greensboro, N.C., 1946-47; chief radio engr. Conservation Dept. State of N.C., Raleigh, 1947-52; applications engr. Collins Radio Co., Dallas, 1952-57; engr. Zumwalt and Vinther, Dallas, 1957-59, Black and Veatch, Dallas, 1960-88; cons. engr. Dillon Design Svcs., Irving, Tex., 1988—. Candidate for City Coun., Irving, 1970. Fellow Radio Club Am.; mem. IEEE, Tex. Soc. Profl. Engrs. (privileged mem.), Quarter Century Wireless Club, Elks. Avocations: amateur radio stations, collecting match books. DIED 11/24/97. .

DILWORTH, JAMES WELDON, lawyer; b. San Antonio, Jan. 1, 1928; s. William H. and Bertie T. Dilworth; m. Marie Miller, Mar. 10, 1945; children: Patricia Ann, Pamela Sue, James Weldon Jr. Student, U. Houston, 1949-51; LL.B., Baylor U., 1953. Bar: Tex. 1953, U.S. Dist. Ct. (so. dist.) Tex. 1954, U.S. Ct. Appeals (5th and 11th cirs.) 1968, U.S. Supreme Ct.1976. Ptnr. Andrews & Kurth, Houston, 1953-94; life mem., counsellor Baylor U. Sch. Law. Mem. Planning and Zoning Commn., Piney Point, Tex., 1973-94. Served as cpl. U.S. Army, 1946-47. Fellow Tex. Bar Found.; mem. ABA, Internat. Bar Assn., Tex. Bar Assn., Houston Bar Assn., Delta Theta Phi (tribune 1953). Republican. Methodist. Clubs: Houston Country, Tex. (Houston). Avocations: golf, hunting; flying; skiing; gourmet cooking. Home: Houston Tex. Deceased.

DILWORTH, JOSEPH RICHARDSON, investment banker; b. Hewlett, N.Y., June 9, 1916; s. Dewees Wood and Edith (Logan) D.; m. Elizabeth Cushing, June 15, 1940; children: Joseph Richardson, Alexandra Cushing, Charles Dewees. AB, Yale U., 1938, LLB, 1942, MA (hon.), 1959, LHD (hon.), 1995; LLD (hon.), Rider U., 1984; DSc (hon.), Rockefeller U., 1993. Bar: Conn. 1942. With buying dept. Kuhn, Loeb & Co., 1946-51, ptnr., 1951-58; with Rockefeller Family & Assocs., 1958-81; chmn. bd. Rockefeller Ctr., Inc., 1966-82, also bd. dirs. Trustee emeritus Inst. for Advanced Study, Met. Mus. Art, Rockefeller U.; trustee Yale U., 1959-86, Col. Williamsburg, 1967-83. Mem. Am. Acad. Arts and Scis., Am. Philos. Soc., Am. Legion, Pilgrims of U.S., Century Assn., Knickerbocker Club, Links, Phi Beta Kappa. Democrat. Deceased.

DINGER, CHARLOTTE, author, publishing executive, consultant; b. East Orange, N.J., Feb. 13, 1930; d. Edward and Alma (Little) Heiss; m. Carl William Dinger Jr., Mar. 10, 1951; children: Carl William III, Jeffrey Edward. Student, Hobart and William Smith Coll., 1947-48, The Berkeley Sch., 1948-49. Asst to art dir. McCann-Erickson Advt., N.Y.C., 1949-51; pres. Carousel Art, Inc., Green Village, N.J., 1983-96; exec. dir. Carousel World Mus., Lahaska, Pa., 1992-96, ptnr., 1992-96; carousel art cons. Sotheby's, N.Y.C., 1988-96, Phillips, N.Y.C., 1985-87. Author: Art of the Carousel, 1983, (chpt.) Time-Life's Encyclopedia of Collectibles, 1979. Mem. internat. adv. bd. Mus. Am. Folk Art, 1990-96; mem. Morris Mus., 1976-96; pres. Parent-Tchr. Orgn., Chatham Twp., N.J., 1964-65; bd. dirs. N.J. State Opera, Newark, 1984-89; bd. trustees Magic Penny Found., 1994-96. Mem. Am. Carousel Soc. (founder, bd. dirs. 1977-90), Morris County Golf Club. Avocations: travel, architecture, photography, swimming, collecting carousel art. Deceased.

DING LING, writer; b. Linli County, Hunan Province, China, 1904; educated Changsha, Shanghai (China) U.; m. Chen Ming, 1942; children Zulin, Zuhui. Began writing short stories, 1927; joined League Left-Wing Writers, 1930, Communist Party, 1931; works banned and house arrested by Kuomintang, 1933; escaped from Nanjing to No. Shanxi to join Mao Tse-Tung's army; worked as journalist till 1942, when sent to work among peasants, being source of epic novel: The Sun Shines Over the Sanggan River (Stalin prize for lit. 1951); dir. Central Lit. Inst., 1949; vice chmn. Writers Assn., 1949; dir. Central Lit. Inst., 1950; dep. Shandong Province, 1st Nat. People's Congress, 1954; dismissed from party posts and banished to Manchuria, 1957; farmed and wrote during next two decades (imprisoned 5 years during Cultural Revolution); restored to public favor, 1979; other works: The Diary of Miss Shafei, In the Water, Mother, When I Was in Xia Village, In Hospital, Comrad Qu Qiubai As I Knew Him; lectured in U.S., 1981.

DIPPLE, ELIZABETH DOROTHEA, language professional, English educator; b. Perth County, Ontario, Can., May 8, 1937; d. Frederick and Sybilla Katherine (Schmidt) D. BA with honors, U. Western Ontario, London, Ontario, Can., 1959; MA, Johns Hopkins U., 1961, PhD, 1963. Asst., assoc. prof. English U. Wash., Seattle, 1963-71; prof. English Northwestern U., Evanston, Ill., 1971—. Author: (book) Plot, 1970, Iris Murdoch: Work for the Spirit, 1982, The Unresolvable Plot: Contemporary Fiction, 1988; contbr. many articles to profl. jours. DIED 11/30/96. .

DISHMAN, LEONARD I., accountant; b. Chgo., May 4, 1920; s. Morris and Jennie (Siegel) D.; m. Frances J. Bernstein, Sept. 26, 1942; children: Ethelynn Dishman Kleiman, Michael. B.S.C., Central YMCA Coll., Chgo., 1942; postgrad., Northwestern U., 1948; DCS (hon.), 1972. Cert. tax advisor, cert. tax acct., cert. tax profl.; enrolled to pracice before IRS. Office mgr. Witco Chem. Co., Chgo., 1947-48; nat. credit mgr. Philip Blum & Co., Chgo., 1948-51; asst. comptroller, office mgr., personnel mgr. Triangle Distbrs. Inc., Chgo., 1951-53; comptroller Lee Shell Co., Chgo., 1953-55; pub. acct. Chgo., 1947—; gen. partner Torrence Assns., Chgo., 1963—; pres. The Ozark Co., Len Ber Ltd.; partner 5700 Co.; bd. dirs. Welstead & Welstead, Inc.; enrolled agt. IRS, 1959—. Co-author: Illinois Wildlife Tutorial for Teachers, 1973. Bd. dirs. Ill. Wildlife Endowment, 1971-82, pres., 1971-73. Mem. Nat. soc. Pub. Accts., Ind. Accts. Assn. Ill. (pres. chpt. 1972-73, state and Chgo. chpt. bd. dirs. 1994-95, pres. Chgo. chpt. 1993-94), Nat. Soc. Tax Profls., Cert. Tax Accts., Accreditation Bd. of Accountancy, No. Ill. Ind. Accts. Assn.

DIVER, WILLIAM, linguistics educator; b. Chgo., July 20, 1921. B.A., Lawrence Coll., 1942; M.A., Harvard U., 1947; Ph.D., Columbia U., 1953. Instr. English Ripon (Wis.) Coll., 1947-49; tchr. Latin Blake Sch., Minn., 1954-55; from asst. prof. to prof. linguistics Columbia U., 1955—. Served from ensign to lt. (j.g.) USNR, 1942-45. Decorated Legion of Merit; Fulbright fellow Italy, 1953-54. Mem. Societe de Linguistique de Paris. Home: New York N.Y. DIED 09/04/95. .

DIVINE, WILLIAM ROBINSON, management consultant; b. Los Angeles, Sept. 13, 1915; s. Thomas J. and Lucy A. (Robinson) D.; m. Leir O. Clifford, Feb. 23, 1941; children: William Robinson, Suzanne (dec.), Phillippe Alvin. B.A., Pomona Coll., 1937; M.A., U. Cin., 1939; J.D., George Washington U., 1947. Bar: D.C. bar 1947. With Bur. Budget, 1941-51, chief mgmt. improvement staff, 1948-51; dir. budget and mgmt. U.S. Regional Office, Paris, France, 1951-54; v.p. Lester B. Knight and Assos. (cons. engrs.), Chgo., 1954-56; asst. comptroller So. Ry. System, 1956-61, comptroller, 1961-70, v.p., 1967-70; v.p. finance Penn Central Transp. Co., 1971-74, fin. adviser, 1974-76; mgmt. cons., 1976-92; prof. bus. and econs. Wingate Coll., N.C., 1980-81, 83-84;; bus. assoc. Greenwich Research Assocs., 1981-89; with Internat. Exec. Svc. Corps, Amman, Jordan, 1987-88; adj. prof. bus. finance and data processing Am. U. Sch. Bus. Adminstrn., 1951-65; mem. orgn. planning council Nat. Indsl. Conf. Bd., 1963-71. Editor: George Washington U. Law Rev, 1946-47. Mem. Fin. Execs. Inst. (pres. Washington chpt. 1965-66), Soc. Advancement Mgmt. (pres. Washington chpt. 1961-62, internat pres. 1964-65, chmn. bd. 1965-66), Am. Mgmt. Assn.,

U.S. C. of C., Phi Beta Kappa, Order of Coif. Home: Bryn Mawr Pa. Died Dec. 8, 1992.

DIXON, JEANE, writer, lecturer, realtor, columnist; b. Medford, Wis., Jan. 5, 1918; d. Gerhart and Emma (von Graffe) Pinckert; m. James L. Dixon, 1939. Founder, chmn. bd. Children to Children Inc., 1964-97; pres. James L. Dixon & Co., Realtors, Washington. Author: My Life and Prophecies, 1969, Reincarnation and Prayers to Live By, 1970, The Call to Glory, 1972, Yesterday, Today and Forever, 1976, Jeane Dixon's Astrological Cookbook, 1976, Horoscopes for Dogs (Pets and Their Planets), 1979, The Riddle of Powderworks Road, 1980, A Gift of Prayer, 1995; syndicated columnist: Horoscope and Predictions, Universal Press Syndicate., featured in Star Mag.; exponent of extrasensory perception (subject of book A Gift of Prophecy), 1988. Chmn. Christmas Seal campaign, Washington, 1968; hon. chairperson, hostess Mystic Ball Cystic Fibrosis Found., 1990-94; pres. exec. adv. coun. United Cerebral Palsy of Washington and No. Va., 1992; mem. disting. citizen adv. bd., 1994. Recipient Loreto Internat. award Loreto Shrine, Italy, 1969; Internat. L'Enfant award Holy Family Adoption League, 1969; named Woman of Year Internat. Orphans, 1968; knight Internat. Order of St. Martin, Vienna; award Md. chpt. Cystic Fibrosis Found., hon. chairperson/hostess Mystic Carnival, 1992; St. John of Jerusalem Internat. Humanitarian Christian Chivalry award; knighted Dame of Humanity; Imperial Byzantine Order of St. Constantine the Great of St. George; Fall Gal award Nat. Saints and Sinners Conv.; Unsung Heroine award Ladies aux. VFW; Golden Lady Humanitarian award AMITA Internat.; Internat. Nostradamus award Internat. Platform Assn.; Leif Erikson Humanitarian award Sons of Norway; First Anglo hon. Navajo princess, 1968; Disting. Am. award (first female) Sales & Mktg. Execs. Met. Washington D.C., 1989; Rep. Senatorial medal of freedom, 1994, Am. Police Hall of Fame. Mem. ASCAP, Nat. League Am. Pen. Women, Internat. Platform Assn. Club: Internat. (Washington). Died Jan. 1997.

DOBBINS, JOHN POTTER, nutritionist, gerontologist; b. Tientsin, Hopeh, China, July 4, 1914; s. John Leslie and Arleta Natalia (Potter) D.; m. Betty Hamilton Brown, Dec. 20, 1939 (div. Dec. 1952), m. Violet Elizabeth Norrman, Oct. 1, 1955; children: Stephen Knightcliffe, Deborah Rose, John Norrman, Michèle Potter. BA, U. Calif., Berkeley, 1935; diplomingenieur, Saxon Inst. Tech., Dresden, Germany, 1938; PhD, Swiss Fed. Inst. Tech., Zurich, 1963. Registered profl. engr., Calif. Chemist Best Foods, Inc., W.P. Fuller & Co., San Francisco, 1935-39; chem. and rsch. engr. N.Am. Aviation, Inc., Inglewood, Calif., 1939-44, sr. rsch. engr., info. specialist, 1945-54; tech. dir., treas. Records Svc. Corp., L.A., 1954-57; student and cons. engr. Contraves AG, Zurich, 1957-63; cons. engr. Bolsey Assocs., others, N.Y.C. and Stamford, Conn., 1964-65; sr. staff scientist Hycon Mfg. Co., Monrovia, Calif, 1966-68; sr. staff scientist electronics div. Rockwell Internat., Anaheim, Calif., 1969-74; ind. cons. engr./scientist San Marino, Calif., 1975-94; v.p. Mariano Rancho Corps., Ventura Calif., 1987-94; mem. adv. Ventura Land & Water co., 1951-56. Author: Thermal Insulation for Jet Engine Exhaust Systems, 1947, Photometrische Bestimmung von Teilchen Grössen, 1967, Acute Viral Disease, 1983, Social Inertia and Cancer, 1983, Cancer, Its Causes, Prevention and Cure, 1985, Is Christianity Current?, 1986. Mem., state actor San Marino City Club, 1976-94; lectr., bd. suprs. Los Angelees County, Calif., 1987; counselor Boy Scouts Am., Dean Sci. Advisors, San Gabriel Valley, 1975-94; chmn., dir. San Marino br. ARC, 1986. Recipient Plaque, City Coun. San Marino, 1979; nominee for Nobel Prize in physiology. Fellow Am. Inst. Chemists, Internat. Acad. Nutrition and Preventive Medicine (cert. 1977); mem. N.Y. Acad. Scis. Republican. Presbyterian. Achievements include six patents; design, construction and operation of world's first microfiche/microcard camera; discovery of statistical law of natural particle size distributions; initiation of liquid-crystal displays (LCDs); successful cure of diabetes (Type II) with dietary chromium, of chicken pox, shingles with lysine ascorbate therapy; first identification of etiology of alcoholism and discovery of its cure through dietary chromium picolinate. Home: San Marino Calif. Died Aug. 19, 1994; interred Sunset View Cemetery, Berkeley, CA.

DOBKIN, IRVING BERN, entomologist, sculptor; b. Chgo., Aug. 9, 1918; m. Frances Berlin, July 1, 1941; children: Jane, Joan, David, Jill. B.S. cum laude, U. Ill., 1940; postgrad., Ill. Inst. Tech., 1941-42. Chmn., pres. Dobkin Pest Control Co., Chgo., 1946-79; pres., dir. Sculptors Guild Ill., 1964-86; lectr. schs. Exhibits include, Art Inst. Chgo., McCormick Pl., Chgo., Old Orchard. Assoc. mem. Smithsonian Instn., Peabody Mus. Natural History, Yale U., Adler Planetarium Assn.; life mem. Art Inst. Chgo., Chgo. Natural History Mus., North Shore Art League, Evanston Art Ctr., Mus. Contemporary Art, Chgo.; pres. Suburban Fine Art Ctr., 1983-84. Served to lt. USN, 1943-46, PTO. Mem. AAAS, AIA, Entomol. Soc. Am., Am. Registry Profl. Entomologists, Fedn. Am. Scientists, Am. Inst. Biol. Scis., Soc. Environ. Toxicology, UN Assn., Oceanographic Soc., Malacology Soc. Am., Sierra Club (assoc.), Chgo. Acad. Sci., Archeol. Inst. Am., Am. Defn. Mineral and Fossil Soc., Calif. Acad. Sci., Am. Schs. Oriental Rsch., Geog. Soc. Am., Nat. Audubon Soc., Ill. Audubon Soc., Am. Indian Affairs Fedn., S.W. Indian Fedn., Nat. Wildlife Soc., Internat. Wildlife Fedn., Save the Redwoods Soc., Wilderness Soc., Nat. Pks. and Conservation Assn., Am. Harp Soc., Chgo. Harp Soc., Archeol. Conservancy, Mid-Am. Paleontology Soc., Nature Conservancy, Chgo. Coun. on Fgn. Rels., UN Fencing Assn., Gen. Secretariat Orgn. U.S., Classical Art Soc., Primative Arts Soc., Internat. Flamenco Soc. (bd. dirs. ensemble Espanol), Ill. Arts Alliance, Explorers Club, Primitive Arts Soc., Lepidoperists Soc. Deceased.

DOCKSTADER, E. STANLEY, construction company executive; b. Elmira, N.Y., Nov. 7, 1923; s. Roy S. and Gertrude (Everts) D.; BCE cum laude, Syracuse U., 1947; m. Ruth Norma Emery, May 11, 1946 (dec.); children: Deborah Ruth, David Stanley. Registered profl. engr., R.I., Pa., W.Va., Ga., N.C. Engr., Am. Bridge Co., Elmira, 1948-50; field engr. Sessinghaus & Ostergaard, Inc., Erie, Pa., 1950-53, project mgr., 1953-58, v.p., 1958-69; gen. mgr. constrn. div. H.H. Robertson Co., Ambridge, Pa., 1969-71; sr. v.p., sec. Sessinghaus & Ostergaard, Inc., Erie, 1972-79; constrn. exec. Gilbane Bldg. Co., Providence, R.I., 1979-84; pres., dir. Sessinghaus & Ostergaard Inc., Erie, 1984-86; pres. Dockstader Constrn. Assocs., 1986—; dir. Erie Constrn. Coun. Mem. Erie Port Commn., 1967-69; vice chmn., dir. N.W. Pa. Rail Authority. Dir. Erie Civic Music Assn. Served with USNR, 1944-46. Mem. Nat. Soc. Profl. Engrs. (life), Am. Arbitration Assn. (arbitrator), Soc. Profls. in Dispute Resolution, Nat. Railway Hist. Soc. bd. dirs. Lakeshore chpt.), Erie Mannerchor, SAR. Mem. Ch. of the Covenant (trustee), Mason (32 deg.), Rotary, Erie Yacht Club, Y Mens Club (past pres.).

DODD, LAMAR, artist, art educator; b. Fairburn, Ga., Sept. 22, 1909; s. Francis Jefferson and Etta Irene (Cleveland) D.; m. Mary Lehmann, Sept. 25, 1930; 1 dau., Mary Irene. Student, Ga. Sch. Tech., 1926-27, Art Students League of N.Y., 1929-33; L.H.D., LaGrange Coll., 1949; A.F.D., U. Cahttanooga, 1959; D.F.A., Fla. State U. Art tchr. Five Point, Ala., 1927-28; asst. mgr. Spivy-Johnson Co., Birmingham, Ala., 1933-37; assoc. prof. art U. Ga., 1937-40, prof., 1940—, head dept. fine arts, 1960—; ant. academician. Exhibited, Whitney Mus. Ann Exhbn., 1937-57, nebr. Ann. Exhbn., 1940, Carnegie Internat., Pitts., 1936, N.Y. World's Fair, 1939-40, San Francisco Fair, 1939; represented permanent collections, Met. Mus., N.Y.C., Telfair Acad., Savannah, High Mus., Atlanta, Pa. Acad. Fine Arts, Whitney Mus. Am. Art, pvt. collections; exhibited one-man show, Corcoran Mus., Washington, 1942, Grnd Central Art Gallery, N.Y., Rochester Meml. Art Gallery, 1949, Witte Meml. Mus., San Antonio, 1951, others; contbr. articles to art jours. Recipient numerous awards and prizes, 1936-57; recipient 2d award, Painting of the Yr. Pepsi-Cola Art Exhbn., 1947, Va. Bienniel Purchase award, 1948, 1st Purchase prize southeastern Art Exhbn., 1949, Nat. Inst. Arts and Letters grantee, 1950, Grumbacher Oil award Fla. Internat. Exhibit, 1952, Edwin Palmer Meml. prize N.A.D., 1953, 1st Transparent Watercolor prize Southeastern Art Assn. Exhbn., 1953, 1st Transparent Watercolor prize Exhbn. am. Art (N.Y. World's Fair), 1940. DIED 09/26/96. .

DODGE, JOHN VILAS, editor; b. Chgo., Sept. 25, 1909; s. George Dannel and Mary Helen (Porter) D.; m. Jean Elizabeth Plate, Aug. 17, 1935; children—Ann, John M., Gerald C., Kathleen. B.S., Northwestern U., 1930; postgrad., U. Bordeaux, France, 1930-31. Editor Northwestern U. Alumni News and ofcl. publs. of Northwestern, 1932-37; exec. sec. Northwestern U. Alumni Assn., 1937-38; asst. editor Ency. Brit.; asso. editor Brit. Book of Year, 1938-43, Ten Eventful Years (4 vol. history 1937-46), 1947; asst. editor Ency. Brit., 1946-50, mng. editor, 1950-60, exec. editor, 1960-64, sr. v.p.-editorial, 1964-65, sr. editorial cons., 1965-70, 72-91, v.p. internat. editorial, 1970-72; editor Brit. World Lang. Dictionary, 1954; Editorial counselor Ency. Universalis, Paris, Japanese Internat. Ency., Tokyo, Enciclopedia Barsa, Mexico City, Enciclopédia Mirador Internacional, Rio de Janeiro. Free-lance writer, 1931-32, Chmn. bd. editors, Ency. Brit. Publs., Inc., 1976-91, Enciclopedia Hispánica, Madrid and Mex. City, 1986-91. Served from pvt. to 1st lt. A.A.A., M.I. AUS, 1944-46. Recipient staff citation War Dept. Mem. Sigma Delta Chi. Home: Northbrook Ill. Died April 23, 1991.

DOHN, GEORGE THOMAS, lawyer; b. Chillicothe, Mo., Nov. 6, 1935; s. George Eckel and Lula Mae (Handley) D.; m. Nancy Lorraine Moore, Oct. 29, 1961 (div. 1971); m. Rita Rae Gardner, June 2, 1972 (div. 1990); children: Kari L., Katrina S., Derek S., Kristin K.; m. Mardi Lundgren, Jan. 6, 1990. AAS, Yakima Valley Coll., 1959; BBA, U. Wash., 1961, LLB, JD, 1963. Bar: Wash. 1963. Assoc. Tunstall & Hettinger, Yakima, Wash., 1963-65; ptnr. Tunstall, Hettinger & Dohn, 1965-72; prin. McArdle, Dohn, Talbott, Simpson & Gibson, P.S., 1973-95, pres., 1982-83, prin., sr. atty. Dohn, Talbott, Simpson, Gibson and Davis, 1989-93, pres. 1991-95; city atty. Ellensburg, Wash., 1964-84, Union Gap, Wash., 1976, Goldendale, Wash., 1979-89, Kittitas, Wash., 1985-86; bd. dirs. Mut. of Enumclaw (Wash.) and Enumclaw Life Ins. Cos., 1985-95, v.p., 1994-95; instr. legal rsch. techniques U. Wash., 1963. Bd. dirs., legal counsel Spring Acres Group Homes, Inc., 1969-76; bd. dirs. Planned Parenthood Assn., Yakima, 1965-75, Yakima County Young Republicans, 1963-65, Yakima Valley C.C. Found. Bd., 1985-95; mem. adv. bd., Wash. Criminal Justice Edn. and Tng. Ctr., 1973-74; mem. legal adv. bd., Wash. Found. Handicapped, 1975-76; mem. YMCA, Yakima; deacon Presbyn. Ch. With USAF, 1953-57. Mem. ABA, Wash. State Bar Assn., Yakima County Bar Assn., U.S. Supreme Ct. Bar Assn., Wash. Assn. Mcpl. Attys. (pres. 1972-73), Am. Arbitration Assn. (arbitrator 1973-95), Nat. Inst. Mcpl. Law Officers, Wash. Govtl. Lawyers Assn., Wash. Def. Trial Attys., Wash. Trial Lawyers Assn., U.S. Supreme Ct. Bar Assn., Def. Rsch. Inst., Nat. Network State Planning Attys., Phi Theta Kappa, Phi Delta Phi, Yakima Ski, Cascadians Mountaineering Club, Yakima Country Club, Hayden Lake Country Club, Washington Athletic Club. Died July 16, 1995.

DOLAN, JOHN F., law educator, consultant; b. Cambridge, Mass., May 14, 1940; s. James F. and Rita (Sivirs) D.; m. Carole A. Ninke, Aug. 29, 1964; children: James, John, Sarah. LLB, U. Ill., 1965. Assoc. Davis, Morgan & Wittersell, Peoria, 1968-75; assoc. prof. law Wayne State U., Detroit, 1975-78, prof., 1978—; vis. prof. law U. Utredht, 1982, U. mich., Ann Arbor, 1984, U. Calif., San Francisco, 1988. Mem. ABA (chair letters of credit subcom. 1988—). Democrat. Roman Catholic.

DOLS, JEROME H., banker, organization consultant; b. Mpls., Aug. 26, 1935; s. Virgil J. and Margaret (Kunde) D.; m. Sandra Johnson, Dec. 30, 1961; children: Barry, Andrea. BBA, U. Minn., 1956, MA, 1958. Orgn. cons. Chase Manhattan Bank, N.Y.C., 1959-71, sr. v.p., dir. orgn. planning, 1971—. mem. mcpl. planning bd., Chatham, N.J., 1974-84. Mem. Conf. Bd. N.Am. (coun. on orgn. and mgmt.), Conf. Bd. Internat. Coun. Orgn. and Mgmt.

DOMAR, EVSEY DAVID, economics educator; b. Lodz, Poland, Apr. 16, 1914; came to U.S., 1936, naturalized, 1942; s. David O. and Sarah (Slonimsky) Domashevitsky; m. Carola Rosenthal, Apr. 16, 1946; children: Erica, Alice. Student, State Faculty of Law, Harbin, Manchuria, 1930-31; B.A., UCLA, 1939; M.A., U. Mich., 1941; postgrad., U. Chgo.; M.A., Harvard U., 1943, Ph.D., 1947. Teaching fellow U. Mich., 1940-41, lectr., summer 1946; teaching fellow Harvard U., 1941-43; economist Bd. Govs. FRS, 1943-46; lectr. George Washington U., summer 1944; asst. prof. econs. Carnegie Inst. Tech., 1946-47; asst. prof. econs., research asso. Cowles Commn., U. Chgo., 1947-48; asso. prof. polit. economy Johns Hopkins U., 1948-55, prof., 1955-58, dir. Russian studies Ops. Research Office, 1949-51; vis. prof. MIT, 1957, prof. econs., 1958-72, Ford prof. econs., 1972-84, Ford prof. emeritus, 1984-97; vis. lectr. U. Buffalo, 1949; vis. asso. prof. Russian Inst., Columbia, 1951-55; vis. Fulbright prof. Oxford U., 1952-53; vis. prof. Stanford, summer 1957, Harvard, 1962, summer 1958, 76, Universidad de Los Andes, Bogota, Colombia, summer 1965, UCLA, summer 1968, Stockholm Sch. Econs., 1972, La Trobe U., Melbourne, Australia, summer 1974, Hebrew U., Jerusalem, 1979; vis. Kathryn Wasserman Davis prof. Slavic studies Wellesley Coll., 1985; vis prof. Brandeis U., 1986-90; disting. exchange scholar People's Republic of China, summer 1981; fellow Harvard Russian Research Center, 1958-97 ; exec. com. Conf. Research in Income and Wealth, 1966-68; cons. Rand Corp., 1951-81; lectr. Centro de Estudios Monetarios Latino- americanos, Mexico City, 1954; cons. fgn. study, research fellowship program Ford Found., 1954-58; chmn. com Slavic grants Am. Council Learned Socs., 1960-62; cons. Brookings Instn., 1956-59, NSF, 1958, 67-69. Author: Essays in the Theory of Economic Growth, 1957, Capitalism, Socialism and Serfdom: Essays, 1989; Contbr. articles profl. jours.; Mem. bd. editors: Am. Econ. Review, 1957-59, Jour. Comparative Econs, 1976-82. Center for Advanced Study in Behavioral Scis. Stanford fellow, 1962-63; John R. Common award Omicron Delta Epsilon, 1965. Fellow Am. Acad. Arts and Scis., Econometric Soc.; mem. Am. Econ. Assn. (disting. fellow; exec. com. 1963-65, v.p. 1970), Royal Econ. Soc., Assn. for Comparative Econs. (pres. 1970), AAUP, Phi Beta Kappa, Pi Gamma Mu, Omicron Delta Epsilon. Home: Concord Mass. Died Apr 1, 1997.

DOMONDON, OSCAR, dentist; b. Cebu City, Philippines, July 4, 1924; Came to U.S., 1954, naturalized, 1956.; s. Antero B. and Ursula (Maglasang) D. ; m. Vicky Domondon. children—Reinelda, Carolyn, Catherine, Oscar. DMD, Philippine Dental Coll., 1951; DDS, Loma Linda U., 1964. Dentist Manila Sanitarium and Hosp., 1952, U.S. Embassy, Manila, 1952-54; pvt. practice dentistry Long Beach, Calif., 1964—; Dentist, Children's Dental Health Center, Long Beach, part-time, 1964-68; past mem. Calif. State Bd. Dental Examiners. Past pres., Filipino Community Action Services, Inc. With AUS, 1946-49, U.S. Army, 1954-60. Fellow Acad. Dentistry Internat., Acad. Gen. Dentistry, Internat. Inst. Community Svc., Acad. Internat. Dental Studies, Internat. Coll. Dentists, Am. Coll. Dentists (life), Acad. Continuing Edn.; mem. ADA (life), Am. Soc. Dentistry Children, Am. Acad. Oral Radiology (award 1964), Internat. Acad. Orthodontists, Am. Soc. Clin. Hypnosis, Am. Endodontic Soc., Western Conf.

Dental Examiners and Dental Sch. Deans, Fedn. of Assns. of Health Regulatory Bds., Calif. Assn. Fgn. Dental Grads. (past pres.), Filipino Dental Soc. (past pres.), Philippine Tech. and Profl. Soc. (v.p.), Am. Acad. Dentistry for Handicapped, Am. Assn. Dental Examiners (life), Nat. Assn. Filipino Dentists in Am. (past pres.), Pierre Fauchard Acad., Knights of Rizal (comdr.), Lions (past pres.), Elks (past chmn. rangers), Masons, Shrine Noble, Am. Legion (comdr. Post 688), Disabled Am. Vets. (comdr. dist. 7, comdr. chpt. 17), VFW (comdr. post 875). Republican. DIED 10/26/97.

DONAT, GEORGE, retired management consultant, business executive; b. Vienna, Austria, June 19, 1920; came to U.S., 1940, naturalized, 1943; s. Lewis and Margaret (Csillagh) D.; m. Glenna Gienty, Oct. 9, 1948; children: Stephanie, Jeffrey M. Grad., Royal Acad. Econs., Budapest, Hungary, 1938; student, George Washington U. Sch. Law, 1950-53. Mem. Allied Control Commn.; sr. investigator Dept. Justice, 1948-50; with Dept. Commerce, 1950-53; with Parke-Davis & Co., 1953-68, dir. comml. devel., 1967-68, dir. European and Can. ops., 1965-67; dep. dir. Bur. Internat. Commerce, Washington, 1962-64; adminstr. bus. and def. services Dept. Commerce, Washington, 1964-65; v.p. E.R. Squibb & Sons, N.Y.C. and Princeton, N.J., 1968-79; pres. ICN Pharms., Inc., Covina, Calif., 1979-80, also bd. dirs.; pres. Geo. Donat Assocs., Inc., Princeton, 1980-86; chmn. bd. Schwarzhaupt Corp., Las Vegas, 1980-86, Rom-Am. Pharm., Las Vegas, 1980-86; leader various profl. seminars. Bd. dirs. Detroit Bd. Commerce, 1965-68, U.S. C. of C., 1965-71, N.J. Trade Expansion Adv. Council, 1975-79; pres. Wrightstown Twp. (Pa.) Civic Assn., 1975-79; bd. dirs. Warsaw Children's Hosp. Found., Wilmington, Del., 1977-83; elected suprs. Wrightstown Twp., 1987. Served with inf. U.S. Army, 1941-45, PTO. Decorated Bronze Star. Clubs: Univ. (Detroit); Nat. Capital Democratic. Home: Newtown Pa. DIED 11/15/95. .

DONNER, MARTIN WALTER, physician; b. Leipzig, Germany, Sept. 5, 1920; came to U.S., 1954; s. Walter T. and Else (Ruehl) D.; m. Adelheid I. Wimmer, Apr. 28, 1951; children—Cornelia, Stephanie, Thomas. M.D., U. Leipzig Med. Sch., 1945. Resident in internal medicine U. Hosp., Leipzig, 1945-50; resident fellow Radiology Center, Cologne, 1950-54; resident Mound Park Hosp. St. Petersburg, Fla., 1954-57; radiologist Johns Hopkins Hosp., Balt., 1957—; asso. prof. radiol. scis. Johns Hopkins Hosp., 1964-68, prof. radiology, 1966—, dir. div. diagnostic radiology, 1967-73, prof. radiol. sci., 1968—, chmn. dept. radiology, 1972-87, radiologist-in-chief, 1972-87, dir. Johns Hopkins Swallowing Ctr., 1980-90; vis. investigator Carnegie Inst., Washington; vis. prof. Free U. of Berlin, State U. Ohio, U. Heidelberg, U. Calif. at San Francisco, Guys Hosp., London, U. Va., Cornell U., Columbia-Presbyn. Hosp., Vanderbilt U., Northwestern U., Royal Soc. Medicine, London, Swedish Soc. Medicine, Radcliffe Infirmary, Oxford U. Editor: Dysphagia; mem. editorial staff Am. Jour. Med. Sci., 1961-68, Johns Hopkins Med. Jour., 1973-76, Investigative Radiology, 1974-79, Radiologica Clinica, 1976-79. Fellow Am. Coll. Radiology; mem. AMA, Radiol. Soc. N.Am., Am. Roentgen Ray Soc., Md. Radiol. Soc., Md. Med. and Chirurgical Faculty, Johns Hopkins Med. Soc., Assn. U. Radiologists, Soc. Gastrointestinal Radiologists, N.Y. Acad. Scis., German Soc. Internal Medicine, German Soc. Radiology (hon.).

DOOHER, M(UREDACH) JOSEPH, editor, writer, publishing consultant; b. Ireland, Oct. 22, 1913; came to U.S., 1923, naturalized, 1938; s. James Francis and Mary Elizabeth (Nixon) D. Grad., St. Benedict's Coll. Prep. Sch., Newark, 1931. Editor Am. Mgmt. Assn., N.Y.C., 1937-56; exec. editor Dun's Rev., N.Y.C., 1956-61; editor indsl. and bus. books McGraw-Hill Book Co., N.Y.C., 1961-71, cons. editor, 1971—. Editor: Rating Employee and Supervisory Performance, 1950, The American Management Association Handbook of Wage and Salary Administration, 1950, The Supervisor's Management Guide, 1949, The Management Leader's Manual, 1947, The Development of Executive Talent, 1952, Effective Communication on the Job, 1956, Selection of Management Personnel, 1957; contbr. essays and verse to Brit. and Am. periodicals. Mem. Indsl. Relations Research Assn. Republican. Roman Catholic.

DOOLITTLE, ROBERT FREDERICK, lawyer; b. Oberlin, Ohio, June 14, 1902; s. Frederick Giraud and Maude (Tucker) D.; m. Gretchen Reller, Oct. 11, 1958. Grad., Ethical Culture Sch., N.Y.C., 1919; A.B. magna cum laude, Harvard, 1923; LL.B., 1930; LL.D., Youngstown State U., 1968. Bar: N.Y. State bar 1932, Ohio bar 1953. Asso. firm Taylor, Blanc, Capron & Marsh, N.Y.C., 1930-32, Cotton, Franklin, Wright & Gordon (name now Cahill, Gordon, Reindel), 1932-42; counsel for Baldwin Locomotive Works (name changed to Baldwin-Lima-Hamilton Corp., Dec. 1950), Phila. 1946-48; v.p. counsel Baldwin-Lima-Hamilton Corp., Phila., 1948-52; asst. gen. counsel, asst. sec. Youngstown Sheet and Tube Co., 1952-59, gen. counsel, corp. sec., 1959-67, v.p., 1964-67, dir., 1967-69; counsel to law firm Baker, Hostetler & Patterson, Cleve., 1967-78. Bd. dirs. World Affairs Coun. Phila., 1951-52; mem. Gov.'s Com. on Water Resources, Ohio, 1954-58; mem. adv. coun. Ohio Water Commn., 1966-67; chmn. adv. coun. task

force on financing State Water Mgmt. Plan, 1966-67; mem. Gov.'s Com. Emergency Resource Planning, Ohio, 1966-67, Planning and Zoning Commn., Gates Mills, Ohio, 1970-75; chmn. Charter Commn., 1972; mem. Ohio Bd. Regents for Higher Edn., 1963-78, vice chmn., 1966-77, chmn., 1977-78; trustee, mem. exec. com. Cleve. Coun. on World Affairs. Lt. col. U.S. Army; assigned by War Dept. to Office Contract Settlement, Exec. Office Pres., 1944, Washington; discharge 1945; asst. gen. counsel, later gen. counsel Office Contract Settlement, 1945-46. Mem. Am. Judicature Soc., ABA, Ohio Bar Assn., Cleve. Bar. Assn., Ohio Mfrs. Assn. (trustee 1955-67, pres. 1965-67, exec. com. 1957-86), Youngstown Symphony Soc. (dir. 1953-67), N.A.M. (edn. policy com.), Am. Iron and Steel Inst., Phi Beta Kappa, Phi Delta Phi. Conglist. Clubs: Chagrin Valley Hunt, Kirtland Country, Union (Cleve.). Deceased.

DORE, FRED HUDSON, retired state supreme court chief justice; b. Seattle, July 31, 1925; s. Fred Hudson and Ruby T. (Kelly) D.; m. Mary Therese Shuham, Nov. 26, 1956; children: Margaret, Fred Hudson, Teresa, Tim, Jane. BS in Fgn. Svc., Georgetown U., 1946, JD, 1949. Bar: Wash. 1949. Pvt. practice Seattle, 1949-77; mem. Wash. Ho. of Reps., 1953-59; state senator Wash. State Senate, 1959-74; judge Wash. State Ct. Appeals, 1977-80; justice Wash. State Supreme Ct., Olympia, 1981-93; chief justice Wash. State Supreme Ct., Olympia, 1991-93; ret., 1993. Died May 16, 1996.

DORFMAN, ISAIAH S., lawyer; b. Kiev, Russia, Mar. 17, 1907; came to U.S., 1913, naturalized, 1931; s. Samuel and Ella (Kite) D.; m. Lillian Schley, Oct. 6, 1934; children: Paul, Tom (dec.), John. Ph.B., U. Chgo., 1927, J.D., 1931. Bar: Ill. 1931. Atty. region 13 NLRB, Chgo., 1937-42; chief spl. litigation unit NLRB, Washington, 1942-43; chief analyst OSS, U.S. Govt., London, Eng., 1943-44; attaché U.S. legation, Stockholm, Sweden, 1944-45; formerly sr. ptnr. Dorfman, Cohen, Laner & Muchin, Ltd. (and predecessor); now of counsel Laner, Muchin, Becker, Dombrow, Levin and Tominberg Ltd.; instr. labor law Law Sch. Nat. U., Washington, 1942-43. Mem. Chgo. Bar Assn. (chmn. com. unauthorized practice law 1966-67), Ill. Bar Assn., ABA, B'nai B'rith. Jewish. Club: Standard (Chgo.).

DORFMAN, MYRON HERBERT, petroleum engineer, educator; b. Shreveport, La., July 3, 1927; s. Samuel Yandell and Rose (Gold) D.; children: Shelley Fonda Dorfman Roberts, Cynthia Renee. B.S., U. Tex., 1950, M.S., 1972, Ph.D., 1975. Registered profl. engr., Tex. Geologist engr. Sklar Oil Co., Shreveport, 1950-56; mgr. prodn. and devel. Sklar Oil Co., 1957-59, partner, 1958-59; owner Dorfman Oil Properties, Shreveport, 1950-71, Austin, Tex., 1971—; prof. petroleum engring. U. Tex., Austin, 1976—, H.B. Harkins prof. petroleum engineering, 1980—, W.A. Moncrief Jr. Centennial chair in petroleum engring., 1983—; dir. Center Energy Studies U. Tex., 1977—, chmn. dept. petroleum engring., 1978-86; dir. Tex. Petroleum Research Commn., Tex. R.R. Commn., 1982-86, Ctr. for Petroleum and Geosystems Engring., 1987—; disting. lectr. Soc. Petroleum Engrs. of AIME, 1978-79, disting. author, 1982-86. Contbr. articles to profl. jours. Pres. Shreveport Community Council, 1966; bd. dirs. Gov.'s Com. Employment Handicapped, 1966-68, La. Youth Opportunity Center, Shreveport, 1966-71, ARC, Caddo Parish, La., 1964-71; pres. La. Mental Health Center, Shreveport, 1967. Served with USNR, 1945-46, PTO. Recipient medal State of Israel, 1963. Fellow Geol. Soc. Am., Geol. Soc. London; mem. Am. Geophys. Union, NAS, Am. Assn. Petroleum Geologists, Soc. Profl. Well Log Analysts, AIME, Shreveport Geol. Soc., Petroleum Club Shreveport, Gas Rsch. Inst. (rsch. coord. coun. 1985-91), Shreveport Jewish Fedn. (pres. 1967), Pi Epsilon Tau., Tau Beta Pi. Club: Shreveport Skeet (pres. 1964).

DORRIS, MICHAEL ANTHONY, anthropologist, writer; b. Louisville, Jan. 30, 1945; s. Jim and Mary Besy (Burkhardt) D.; m. Louise Erdrich, 1981; children: Reynold Abel (dec. 1991), Jeffrey Sava, Madeline Hannah, Persia Andromeda, Pallas Antigone, Aza Marion. B.A. magna cum laude, Georgetown U., 1967; M.Phil., Yale U., 1970. Grad. asst. Yale U., 1969-70; asst. prof. anthropology Johnston Coll., U. of Redlands, 1970-71; asst. prof. Franconia Coll., N.H., 1971-72; prof. Dartmouth Coll., Hanover, N.H., 1972—; founder, chmn. dept. native Am. studies, Dartmouth Coll., 1972-85. Author: Native Americans: 500 Years After, 1975, A Guide to Research in Native American Studies, 1984, (novel) A Yellow Raft in Blue Water, 1987, The Broken Cord, 1989 (Nat. Book Critics Cir. award 1989), Morning Girl, 1992, (stories) Working Men, 1993, Rooms in the House of Stone, 1993, (essays) paper Trail, 1994, Guests, 1994, Sees Behind Trees, 1996, Cloud Chamber, 1996; co-author: (with Louise Erdrich) The Crown of Columbus, 1991, Route 2, 1991; editor Viewpoint, 1967-68, A Sourcebook for Native American Studies, 1977; contbr. articles to profl. and lit. jours. Mem. Native Am. Rights Fund; bd. dirs. Save the Children, 1993-94. Recipient Indian Achievement award, 1985, PEN Syndicated Fiction award, 1988, Christopher award, 1990, Heartland prize, 1990, Sarah Josepha Hale award, 1991, Scott O'Dell award, 1993, Overseas Press Club award, 1993, 94; Danforth grad. fellow 1967, Woodrow Wilson grad. fellow 1967, NIMH

fellow 1970, grantee 1971; Guggenheim fellow 1978, Woodrow Wilson faculty fellow 1980, Rockefeller fellow 1985-86, NEA creative writing fellow 1989. Fellow Soc. Applied Anthropology, PEN Am. Ctr., Author's Guild; mem. Writer's Guild, Am. Anthrop. Assn., Nat. Congress Am. Indians. Died Apr. 11, 1997.

DORSEY, GRAY LANKFORD, law educator emeritus; b. Hamilton, Mo., Feb. 16, 1918; s. Claude Purdue and Mary Alice (Lankford) D.; m. Jeanne DeVall, Jan. 1, 1942; 1 child, Deborah DeVall. Student, Baker U., 1936-38; A.B. in Journalism, U. Kans., 1941; J.D., Yale, 1948, J.S.D., 1950. Bar: Mo. 1956, U.S. Supreme Ct. 1967. Editor, pub. Cameron (Mo.) Sun, 1940-42; mem. faculty Washington U., St. Louis, 1951-97, Charles Nagel prof. jurisprudence and internat. law, 1962-88, Charles Nagel prof. emeritus jurisprudence and internat. law, 1988-97; vis. prof. Nat. Taiwan U., 1952-53; organized World Congress on Equality and Freedom, St. Louis, 1975. Author: Jurisculture: Greece and Rome, 1989, Jurisculture: India, 1990, Jurisculture: China, 1993, Beyond the United Nations: Changing Discourse in International Politics and Law, 1986, American Freedoms, 1987; editor: Equality and Freedom: International and Comparative Jurisprudence, 3 vols., 1977. Lt. USCGR, 1942-46; maj. USAR, 1956-62. Recipient Spurgeon Smithson award Mo. Bar Found., 1985; ACLS fellow, 1948-50. Mem. Internat. Assn. Philosophy of Law and Social Philosophy (pres. 1975-79, hon. pres. Am. sect. 1989-97), Mexican Soc. Philosophy (hon.), U. Carlos Cossio de Argentina Found. (hon.). Achievements include origination and development of Jurisculture as method of analysis and field of study. Home: Chesterfield Mo. Died July 20, 1997.

DORVILLIER, WILLIAM JOSEPH, editor, publisher; b. North Adams, Mass., Apr. 24, 1908; s. Joseph and Aurise (Champagne) D.; m. Mary Elizabeth Johnson, Oct. 1, 1938 (dec. 1979); 1 son, William Clay. Student, N.Y.U. With North Adams Transcript; editor S.Am. desk AP, N.Y.C.; then corr. AP and UPI, Caribbean area; accredited war corr. World War II; editor Puerto Rico World Jour., 1940-43, 44-45, 56-57, Washington corr., 1945-53; accredited correspondent The White House; founder Dorvillier News Letter (weekly bus. and econ. publ.), 1953; founder San Juan Star, 1959, editor, pub., 1959-67; pres., dir. Star Pub., editor, pub., 1959-67; past pres., dir. Star Pub. Corp.; chmn. bd. Dorvillier News Agy., Inc., 1953-79; ret., 1979; news dir. WAPA-TV, 1969-73. (Recipient Pulitzer prize for distinguished editorial writing 1961). Author: Workshop U.S.A., The Challenge of Puerto Rico, 1962. Mem. Sigma Delta Chi. Club: Nat. Press (Washington). Home: Concord N.H. Died May, 5, 1993.

DOUDNA, MARTIN KIRK, English language educator; b. Louisville, June 4, 1930; s. Arthur Bundy and Ruth Edson (Dewey) D.; m. Dorothy Jane Williams, Sept. 15, 1962; children: Jennifer Anne, Ellen Ruth, Sarah Corinne. AB in English, Oberlin (Ohio) Coll., 1952; postgrad., Princeton (N.J.) U., 1952-53; MA in English, U. Louisville, 1959; PhD in Am. Culture, U. Mich., 1971. Writer USAF, Washington, 1959-66; asst. prof. English Mackinac Island (Mich.) Coll., 1966-69; assoc. prof. English U. Hawaii, Hilo, 1971-78, prof. English, 1978—; sec. Hawaii Com. for the Humanities, Honolulu, 1986-88. Author: Concerned About the Planet, 1977; editor: Greene, Transcendentalism (1849), 1981; author: (play) Have You Any Room for Us?, 1975; contbr. articles to profl. jours. With U.S. Army, 1953-55. Rackham fellow U. Mich., 1970; Nat. Endowment for the Humanities, 1976, 83, 88. Mem. Modern Lang. Assn., Thoreau Soc., Phi Beta Kappa. Avocations: swimming, hiking, acting.

DOUGLAS-HOME, CHARLES COSPATRICK, newspaper editor; b. Jan. 9, 1937; s. Henry and Margaret (Spencer) D.-H.; ed. Eton; m. Jessica Violet Gwynne, 1966; 2 sons. Commd. Royal Scots Greys, 1956-57; a.d.c. to Gov. of Kenya, 1958-59; mil. corr. Daily Express, 1961-62; polit. and diplomatic corr., 1962-64; def. corr. The London Times, 1965-70, features editor, 1970-73, home editor, 1973-78, fgn. editor, 1978-81, dep. editor, 1981-82, editor, 1982—; dir. Times Newspapers Ltd., 1982—. Hon. fellow Royal Coll. Music (counselor 1975—). Club: Caledonian. Author: The Arabs and Israel, 1968; Britain's Reserve Forces, 1969; Rommel, 1973; Evelyn Baring: The Last Proconsul, 1978.

DOUGLIS, AVRON, mathematician; b. Tulsa, Mar. 14, 1918; s. Bernard and Minnie (Goldberg) D.; m. Marjorie H. Bergmann; children: Franklin, Carole. BA, U. Chgo., 1938; MA, NYU, PhD, 1949. Office Naval Research fellow Calif. Inst. Tech., Pasadena, 1949-50; asst. prof. NYU, 1950-55, assoc. prof., 1955-56; prof. U. Md., College Park, 1956-88, prof. emeritus, 1988-95. Author: Ideas in Math, 1970; joint author: A Layering Method for Viscous, Incompressible Lp Flows, 1984; contbr. numerous research papers to profl. publs. Served to 1st lt. USAAF, 1942-46, ETO. Mem. Am. Math. Soc., Soc. for Indsl. & Applied Math., Math. Assn. Am., Phi Beta Kappa. Democrat. Jewish. Avocations: theatre, concerts, opera. Home: Silver Spring Md. Died Feb. 15, 1995.

DOWD, MARY-JANE MARTIN, historian; b. Balt., Feb. 4, 1934; d. Philip Cullen and Eva Mary (Shanley) D. BA, Goucher Coll., 1956; MA, Johns Hopkins U., 1959; cert., U. Va., 1972. Archivist Nat. Archives and Records Svc., Washington, 1960-85, with editorial divsn., 1966-68, with records appraisal divsn., 1968-73, assoc. editor, territorial papers br., 1973-74, asst. br. chief projects, sr. archivist, 1978-85; editor, project dir. Fgn. Rels. U.S., 1781-1789 Nat. Archives and Records Adminstrn., Washington, 1985-91, sr. records appraiser, 1991-94; pvt. practice as writer, editor, rschr., 1994—, geneal. and hist. records specialist, 1994—; lectr. Modern Archives Inst., Am. U., 1979; reviewer grant proposals NEH, Washington, 1980-82; dep. to exec. secretariat dir. organizing com. Internat. Coun. Archives, 1965-66, for Extraordinary Archives Congress, Washington, 1966. Author: Index to the American Archivist, vols. 21-30, 1958-67, 1974; assoc. editor: The Territorial Papers of the United States, vol. 28, The Territory of Wisconsin, 1839-1848, 1975; author: Records of the Office of Public Buildings and Public Parks of the National Capital, 1992; editor, project dir.: The Emerging Nation: A Documentary History of the Foreign Relations of the U.S. under the Articles of Confederation, 1780-1789, 3 Vols., 1996; assoc. editor, editl. asst. Am. Archivist, 1962-72. soprano soloist, choir mem. Episcopal Chs. Wheaton, Silver Spring, Kensington, Md., 1960—; mem. Wheaton Parish Liturgical Commn., 1971-72. Fellow Soc. Am. Archivists (editl. bd. 1972-75, chmn. awards com. 1977-80); mem. Am. Hist. Assn., Assn. Documentary Editing, Inst. Early Am. History and Culture (assoc.). Episcopalian. Avocation: vocal music, gardening. Died June 24, 1997.

DOWD, PAUL, chemistry educator; b. Brockton, Mass., Apr. 11, 1936; m. Susan Ramseyer, 1960; children: Katherine, Joseph, Michael. AB, Harvard U., 1958; MA, Columbia U., 1959, PhD in Chemistry, 1962. Lectr. chemistry Harvard U., 1963-64, instr., 1964-66, from lectr. to asst. prof., 1966-70, assoc. prof., 1970-77; prof. chemistry U. Pitts., 1977-96; Alfred P. Sloan Found. fellow, 1970-72. Fellow AAAS; mem. Am. Chem. Soc. (Arthur C. Cope Scholar award 1994). Research in reactive intermediates in organic chemistry; mechanism of action of vitamin B12; free radical rearrangements; mechanism of action of vitamin K; diradicals. Died Nov. 21, 1996.

DOWEIKO, JEANETTE MARIE, orientation and mobility specialist, educator; b. Milw., June 15, 1955; d. Charles Walter and Jean Ann (Krueger) Snyder; m. Harold E. Doweiko, Aug. 4, 1984. BS, U. Wis., Milw., 1978; MA, U. No. Colo., 1980; MS in Edn., No. Ill. U., 1989. Cert. tchr., Minn., Tex. Tchr. visually impaired Dawson (Minn.)-Boyd Sch. Dist., 1984-88; orientation and mobility specialist Ceder River Ednl. Svcs. Coop., Austin, Minn., 1988-91; V.I./O. & M. specialist La Crosse (Wis.) Sch. Dist., 1991—. Mem. Assn. for Edn. and Rehab. Blind and Visually Impaired (cert.), Ill. Assn. Orientation and Mobility Specialists, Kappa Delta Pi. Died Dec. 30, 1996.

DOWLING, JACQUES MACCUISTON, sculptor, painter, writer; b. Texarkana, Tex., Oct. 19, 1906; d. Charles Edward and Viola John (Estes) MacCuiston; m. Thomas Leo Dowling (dec.); 1 child, Mark E. (dec.). Tchrs. cert., Coll. Marshall, 1923; student of art, Loyola U., Frolich's Sch. Fine Art, L.A., NAD, Art Students League, N.Y.C.; Ph.D., Colo. State Christian Coll. One woman shows include Fedn. Dallas Artists, 1950, 52, Rush Gallery, 1958, Sartor's Gallery, 1958, Sheraton-Dallas Hotel, 1960, Dallas Meml. Auditorium, 1960; exhibited in group shows at Dallas Mus. Fine Arts, Mus. of N.Mex., Fedn. Dallas Artists, Sartor's Galleries, Ney Art Mus., Oak Cliff Soc. of Fine Arts, Sartor's Gallery, Shuttles Gallery, Sheraton-Park Internat. Platform Assn., 1966-68, Phillips Mills Art Assn., 1967-74, Yardley Ann. Exhbn., 1968-73, Tinicum Art Festival, 1968, Woodmere Art Gallery (life mem.), 1972-74, others; selected sculpture 1st S.W. ann. show Mus. N.Mex., 1958; represented in permanent collections several corps., many pvt. homes. Recipient 1st Sculpture Fedn. Dallas Artists, pinned (all awards jewels); Recipient Sweepstakes award SW Ann. Art Show, 1953, Hon. Cert. award Dallas Fed. Bus. Assn., 1964, 2 1st awards N.J. Fedn. Womens Clubs, 1972, 2 1st awards, 1974, 1st and 2d awards, 1975, Gold medal Accademia Italia, 1979, Golden Centaur award Accademia Italia, 1982, Gold medal Internat. Parliament (U.S.A.) of Safety and Peace, 1983, Centro Studi e Ricerche delle Nazioni, Parma, Italy, 1986, statue of victory, 1983; Oscar d' Italia, Accademia Italia, 1985; named Cavalier of Arts, Accademia Bedriacense, 1985, many others, including 3 awards for journalism, 1962-63; 2 Golden Flame awards World Parliament (U.S.A.), 1986. Fellow Internat. Inst. Arts and Letters (life); mem. Cousteau Soc. (founding), U.S. Chess Fedn., Am. Contract Bridge League, Internat. Acad. Lit., Arts and Sci. (hon. life mem., Tommaso Campanello with gold medal award 1972), C. of C. South Hunterdon (charter), Woodmere Gallery (life mem.), Order Eastern Star (past grand officer, past matron). Republican. Episcopalian.

DOWNEY, JUAN ANTONIO, artist; b. Santiago, Chile, May 11, 1940; came to U.S., 1965; s. David Gonzalo and Luisa Ester (Alvarado) D.; m. Marilys Belt, Feb. 25, 1969. B.Arch., Universidad Católica de Chile, 1961. asst. prof. Pratt Inst. Sch. Arch. and Media Arts Dept.; artist-in-residence TV Lab., Sta. WNET, N.Y.C., 1978, Synapse, Syracuse U., 1979, WXXI, Rochester, N.Y., 1979. One-man shows Galerie Jacqueline Ranson, Paris, 1968, Corcoran Gallery Art, Washington, 1969-93, Howard Wise Gallery, N.Y.C., 1970-93, Everson Mus. Art, Syracuse, N.Y., 1971-77, Ctr. for Interam. Relations, N.Y.C., 1975, Anthology Film Archives, N.Y.C., 1976, Long Beach (Calif.) Mus., 1976, Whitney Mus., N.Y.C., 1976, 78, Mus. Contemporary Art, Houston, 1976, Museo de Arte Contemporáneo, Caracas, Venezuela, 1977, Galería Adler Castillo, Caracas, 1977, Univ. Art Mus., Berkeley, Calif., 1978, Leo Castelli Gallery, N.Y.C., Mandville Art Gallery, U. Calif., San Diego, 1979, Mandeville Art Gallery, La Jolla, Calif., 1979, The Kitchen, N.Y.C., 1980, San Francisco Mus. Modern Art, 1985, Internat. Ctr. Photography, 1987, Rotunda Gallery, Bklyn., 1988, Inst. Contemporary Art, Boston, 1989, I.C.P. N.Y., 1989; group shows include Venice Biennale, The Pluralist Decade, ICA, Phila., Biennial Exhbn., Whitney Mus., Berlin Film Festival, 1988, Jewish Mus., 1988, Bronx Mus. Art, 1988, Whitney Mus., N.Y.C., 1991, European Media Festival, Osnabruck, Fed. Republic Germany, 1991, Museo de Bellas Artes, Chile, 1991; TV appearances N.Y.C., Chgo., Rochester, N.Y., Boston. Recipient Video award Rockefeller Found., 1981, 90; Guggenheim fellow, 1971-76, fellow MIT, 1973; grantee Nat. Endowment for Arts, 1980-85, 90, 92, N.Y. State Coun. Arts, 1981-85, 89, Rockefeller Found., 1990. Home: New York N.Y. Died June 9, 1993.

DOWNIE, G. ROBERT, retired physiatrist; b. Winthrop, Mass., July 9, 1923. MD, Yale U., 1948. Diplomate Am. Bd. Phys. Medicine and Rehab. Intern Yale U., New Haven, 1948-50; resident in phys. medicine and rehab. New Eng. Med. Ctr., Boston, 1966-68; with Greenville (S.C.) Hosp. Sys. Mem. AMA, Am. Coll. Rehab. Medicine, Am. Acad. Phys. Medicine and Rehab. Home: Greenville S.C. Died Feb. 22, 1995.

DOYLE, DAVID, actor. Appeared in tv shows Charlie's Angels, 1976-81, Murder She Wrote, Love Boat, Fantasy Island, Hart to Hart, (voice) Rug Rats, Lois and Clark, Sunset Beach, (movies) Love or Money, No Way to Treat a Lady, Paper Lion, Vigilante Force, Capricorn One, Coogan's Bluff, The Comeback, (Broadway) Will Success Spoil Rock Hunter?. Died Feb. 26, 1997.

DOYLE, JAMES ALEXANDER, lawyer; b. Thedford, Neb., Jan. 19, 1904; s. John and Hattie (Beckhoff) D.; m. Amelia Brosius, June 9, 1927; children—James Alan, Katherine. Ph.B., Creighton U., 1924; LL.B., U. Nebr., 1933; LL.M., Harvard U., 1942. Bar: Nebr. bar. Ann. Supt. Thomas County High Sch., Thedford, Neb., 1927-30; law clerk to U.S. Circuit Judge, Omaha, 1933-35; prof. law U. Nebr., 1936-43; asst. reviser Nebr. Statute Commn., Lincoln, 1941-43; regional atty. U.S. Dept. of Agr., Lincoln, Nebr., 1943-44, Chgo., 1944-45; asso. solicitor Washington, 1945-48; spl. cons. to solicitor on litigation, 1948; dean Creighton U. Sch. of Law, Omaha, Nebr., 1948-70, dean emeritus, prof. law, 1970-95; also arbitrator in labor disputes. Fellow Harvard Law Sch., 1937-38; Former pres. Legal Aid Soc. Omaha, Inc. Contbr.: articles to Neb. Law Rev. Mem. Nebr. Bar Assn., Am. Arbitration Assn., Order of Coif, Phi Delta Phi, Alpha Sigma Nu. Roman Catholic. Club: Rotary. Home: Omaha Nebr. Died Apr. 27, 1995.

DOYLE, MORRIS MCKNIGHT, lawyer; b. Bishop, Cal., Jan. 4, 1909; s. Guy P. and Helen (McKnight) D.; m. Juliet H. Clapp, Sept. 15, 1934 (dec. 1985); children: Barbara Doyle Roupe, Thomas M.; m. Jean G. Kuhn, May 10, 1986. A.B., Stanford U., 1929; LL.B., Harvard U., 1932; L.H.D., Nat. Coll. Edn., 1965. Bar: Calif. 1932. Asso. McCutchen, Olney, Mannon & Greene, San Francisco, 1932-42; partner McCutchen, Thomas, Matthew, Griffiths & Greene, San Francisco, 1942-58, McCutchen, Doyle, Brown & Enersen, 1958—. Trustee Stanford U., 1959-79, pres. bd. trustees, 1962-65; trustee, chmn. James Irvine Found., 1965-89; dir. Stanford Research Inst.; bd. overseers Hoover Instn. Fellow Am. Bar Found., Am. Coll. Trial Lawyers; mem. Am., Calif. San Francisco bar assns., Bar Assn. City N.Y., Am. Law Inst., Am. Judicature Soc. Clubs: Pacific Union, Bohemian, Commonwealth (San Francisco). Deceased.

DRAGO, RUSSELL STEPHEN, chemist, educator; b. Turners Falls, Mass., Nov. 5, 1928; s. Stephen R. and Lillian (Pucci) D.; m. Ruth Ann Burrill, Dec. 30, 1950; children: Patricia, Stephen, Paul, Robert. BS, U. Mass., 1950; PhD, Ohio State U., 1954. Mem. faculty U. Ill., Urbana, 1955-82, prof. chemistry, 1965-82; prof. chemistry U. Fla., Gainesville, 1982-84, grad. research prof., 1984—. Author: Prerequisites for College Chemistry, 1966, (with N.A. Matwiyoff) Acids and Bases, 1968, Qualitative Concepts from Quantum Chemistry, 1971, Organic Chemistry: A Short Introduction, 1972, Principles of Chemistry, 1974, 2d edit., 1977, (with T.L. Brown) Experiments in General Chemistry, 4th edit., 1977, Physical Methods for Chemists, 1977, 2nd edit., 1992, Problem Solving in General Chemistry I, 1979, Applications of Electrostatic-Covalent Models, 1994; Contbr. articles profl. jours. Guggenheim fellow, 1973-74. Mem. Am. Chem. Soc. (award research inorganic chemistry 1969). Died Dec. 5, 1997.

DRESSER, JESSE DALE, real estate investor; b. San Diego, May 5, 1906; s. Charlwood Fessenden and Ora (Evans) D.; m. Mary A. Goldsworthy, June 9, 1934; children: Dennis T., Brian D., Linda A. Ed. pub. schs. Trainee Union Title Ins. Co., San Diego, 1926; sr. title examiner, chief title officer, v.p. So. Title & Trust Co., San Diego, 1937-51; v.p., chief title officer Security Title Ins. Co., San Diego, 1951-54; asst. to pres. San Diego Fed. Savs. & Loan Assn., 1954-55, v.p., sec., 1955-56, exec. v.p., dir., 1956-70; v.p., dir. Calif. Gen. Mortgage Service, Inc., 1967-70, San Diego Federated Ins. Agy., Inc., 1967-70; real estate investments La Mesa, Calif., 1970-86; ret., 1986. Died Jan. 5, 1995.

DRINKWATER, HERBERT R., mayor; m. Jackie Drinkwater; 2 children. Asst. bus. mgr. Phoenix Union High Sch. and Jr. Coll. System; owner, oper. ind. bus., 1964; mem. Scottsdale (Ariz.) City Coun., 1970-78, chmn. fin. com.; mem. Design Rev. Bd. City of Scottsdale, vice mayor, 1972-73, 76, mayor, 1980—; apptd. to Phoenix adv. coun. U.S. Bur. Land Mgmt.; chmn. Regional Pub. Transit Authority; ex-officio mem. Fiesta Bowl Com.; bd. dirs. No. Trust Co. of Ariz., Mayor's Com. on Employment of Persons with Disabilities. Bd. dirs. Ariz. Heart Inst., Lucky 13 Edn. and Rehab. Ctr., Scottsdale Boys Club, Found. for Handicapped, Ch. of the Beatitudes, Scottsdale Symphony Orch.; co-vice chmn. govt. div. Valley of the Sun campaign United Way; past mem. Scottsdale Adv. Bd., Hospice of the Valley; active Ariz. Acad., Ariz. Sr. Olympics Gold Medal Adv. Group, Camelback Mental Health Found., Scottsdale Sister Cities. Named Nationwide Retailer of Yr., 1968; named Outstanding Young Man, City of Scottsdale, 1972; recipient Disting. Achievement award Ariz. State U. Coll. Pub. Programs, 1986, Disting. Citizen award Boy Scouts Am. Mem. U.S. Conf. Mayors (arts, culture and recreation, energy and environ. standing coms.), League Ariz. Cities and Towns (treas., exec., resolution coms.), Ariz. Mcpl. Water Users Assn., Scottsdale Charros, Ariz. Wildlife Fedn., Paralyzed Vets. Assn. (life mem. Ariz. chpt.), Jaycees (pres. and exec. bd. Scottsdale chpt., internat. senate, adv. bd. Parada Del Sol 1970-74), Lions, Rotary (hon.). Died Dec. 27, 1997.

DROGHEDA, EARL OF (MOORE CHARLES GARRETT PONSONBY), former newspaperman; b. London, Apr. 23, 1910; s. Earl of Drogheda and Kathleen (Pelham-Burn) M.; m. Joan Carr, May 17, 1935; 1 son, Dermot (Viscount Moore). Student, Cambridge U., 1929-30. With Fin. News mag., 1933-45; mng. dir. Fin. Times, Ltd. (merger with Fin. News mag.), 1945-71, chmn., 1971-75; bd. dirs. Henry Sotheran Ltd., Dreyfus Dollar Internat. Fund., Times Newspapers Holdings Ltd. Co-author: (under name Derry Moore) (with Brendan Gill) The Dream Come True, Great Houses of Los Angeles, 1980, (with George Plumtre) Royal Gardens, 1981, (with Sybilla Jane Fowler) Stately Homes of Britain, 1982, (with Henry Mitchell) Washington, Houses of the Capital, 1982, (with Michael Pick) The English Room, 1984, (with Avilde Lees-Milne) The Englishwoman's House, 1984, (with Avilde Lees-Milne) The Englishman's Room, 1986, (with the Marchioness of Salisbury) The Gardens of Queen Elizabeth The Queen Mother, 1988, (with Sarah Hollis) The Shell Guide to the Gardens of England and Wales, 1989. Chmn. Royal Opera House, Covent Garden, 1958-74, Royal Ballet Sch., 1975-82; Asst. sec. Brit. Ministry of Prodn., 1941. Served as capt. Brit. Army, 1939. Mem. Inst. Dirs. (pres. 1975-76).

DRUCKER, BERTRAM MORRIS, emeritus mathematics educator; b. N.Y.C., Oct. 6, 1919; s. Max and Ray (Friedberg) D. A.B., U. N.C., 1940, M.A., 1946, Ph.D., 1953. Instr. U. N.C., 1943-49; grad. fellow Oak Ridge Inst. Nuclear Studies, 1951-53; faculty Ga. Inst. Tech., 1953-93, prof. math., 1962-80, prof. emeritus, 1980-93; dir. Sch. Math., 1962-7O. Home: Columbia S.C. Died Dec. 23, 1993.

DRUCKER, TRUDY, English educator, writer, retired; b. N.Y.C., Dec. 29, 1926; d. Samuel and Sally (Rudich) Jesselson; m. Jules H. Drucker; m. Joseph G. Alam. BS, N.Y.U., 1947; MA, Fairleigh Dickinson U., N.J., 1965; PhD, N.Y.U., 1973. Med. editorial asst. Kessler Inst., West Orange, N.J., 1948-56; med. writer Schering Corp., Bloomfield, N.J., 1956-65; instr. English Fairleigh-Dickinson U., Rutherford, N.J., 1965-67; med. writer Hoffman-LaRoche, Nutley, N.J., 1967-68; prof. English Bergen C.C., Paramus, N.J., 1968-89; editorial cons. Am. Tinnitus Assn., Portland, Oreg., 1970—. Contbg. author: No Walls of Stone, 1993. Mem. North Jersey Humanists, Am. Atheists. Fellow Am. Med. Writers Assn; mem. MLA, AAUP, Nat. Assn. Sci. Writers. Democrat. Avocations: writing, crafts. Died Feb. 16, 1997.

DRURY, ROBERT EDWARD, lawyer; b. Detroit, May 19, 1916; s. John Francis and Theresa (Thomas) D.; m. Lois Lochridge, Oct. 16, 1944; children—Robert J., Diane L., Susan J. Student, Highland Park Jr. Coll., 1933-35; LL.B., J.D., U. Detroit, 1938. Bar: Mich. bar 1938. Practiced in Detroit, 1938-42; investigator Air Force Intelligence, 1942-46; personnel dir. Chrysler Corp., 1946-52; v.p. mfg. Redmond Co., Owosso, Mich.,

1952-61; group v.p. King-Seeley Thermos Co., Ann Arbor, Mich., 1961-72; sec. King-Seeley Thermos Co., 1969-72; also dir.; of counsel Dobson, Griffin & Barense P.C., 1972-95; dir. Bayport State Bank, chmn., 1985-88. Pres. County United Found., 1960-61; dir. A.R.C., 1954-60. Club: Rotarian. Home: Pigeon Mich. Died Mar. 20, 1995.

DUBE, JOHN, retired lawyer; b. Montreal, Que., Can., July 14, 1899; came to U.S., 1926, naturalized, 1945; s. Joseph Edmond and Marie Louise (Quintal) D.; 1 child, John Edmund. BL, BS, Montreal U., 1920, BCL, 1923; licentiate in Civil Law, Paris U., 1924; postgrad., U. Oxford, 1925. Bar: Montreal 1925, N.Y. 1945, apptd. king's counsel 1941, now Queen's counsel 1952, U.S. Supreme Ct. 1960. Assoc. Coudert Bros., N.Y.C. and Paris office, 1926-32, Nice, France, 1933-40; pvt. practice N.Y.C., 1945-89; past pres. Le Moulin Legumes Corp., Wilmington, Del.; past v.p. Bengue, Inc., Union City, N.J.; consul of Monaco, N.Y.C., 1949-71; now consul gen.; dep. permanent observer for Monaco at UN, 1956-71, permanent observer, 1971—. Past trustee Soc. Rehab. Facially Disfigured; co-founder and co-comdr. Anglo-Am. Ambulance Corps., Cannes, France, 1939-40. Decorated Comdr. Order of Grimaldi (Monaco). Mem. ABA, Assn. of Bar of City of N.Y., Internat. Bar Assn., Union Interalliée (Paris), Am. Fgn. Law Assn., Am. Soc. Internat. Law, Soc. Fgn. Consuls, Société de Legislation Comparee. Clubs: Rockefeller Ctr. Luncheon, Sky (assoc.).

DUCANIS, ALEX JULIUS, education educator; b. Pitts., Feb. 18, 1931; s. Alexander J. and Virginia (Vowinkel) D.; m. Anne Keefe Golin. B.S., U. Pitts., 1953, M.Ed., 1954, Ed.D., 1961. Tchr. Lancaster (Pa.) Public Schs., 1956-58; lectr., adminstrv. asst. U. Pitts., 1959-61; research asso. div. research in higher edn. N.Y. State Edn. Dept., Albany, 1961-66; dir. instnl. research SUNY, Binghamton, 1966-69; project dir. Health Sci. Center Feasibility Study, 1967-68; asso. chmn. dept. higher edn. U. Pitts., 1969-95, prof. edn. and health related professions, 1971-95, dir. Inst. Higher Edn., 1970-73, chmn. div. specialized profl. devel. Sch. Edn., 1973-75, dir. program higher edn., 1980-86, prof. adminstrn. and policy studies, 1986-93; prof. emeritus, 1994; cons. Coll. Entrance Exam. Bd., 1966-67, GEAR Corp., 1967, Broome County Social Planning Coun., 1967-68 (div. 1968), Broome County Med. Soc., 1968, Middle Eastern Edn., 1985-87; chmn. doctoral coms. in higher edn., adminstrn. and policy, health professions, ednl in developing countries. Author: (with A.K. Golin) The Interdisciplinary Team: A Handbook for the Education of Exceptional Children, The Interdisciplinary Health Care Team (Book of Yr. award Am. Jour. Nursing 1981); contbr. articles to ednl. jours.; developer (with A.K. Golin) Interprofl. Perception Scale, SCOPE model for improvement of coll. teaching. Chmn. dist. III regional adv. com. Statewide Rehab. Council, 1967-68; bd. dirs. N.Y.-Pa. Health Planning Council, Inc., 1968. Served with AUS, 1954-56. Mem. Am. Ednl. Rsch. Assn., Phi Delta Kappa. Home: Pittsburgh Pa. Died Aug. 26, 1995.

DUCOMMUN, CHARLES EMIL, business executive; b. Los Angeles, Apr. 27, 1913; s. Emil C. and Bescelia (Shemwell) D.; m. Palmer Gross, June 15, 1949 (dec. Apr. 1987); children: Robert Constant, Electra Ducommun dePeyster. A.B., Stanford U., 1935; M.B.A. with distinction, Harvard U., 1942. With Ducommun Inc. (formerly Ducommun Metals & Supply Co.), Los Angeles, 1936-86, dir., 1938-86, sec., 1938-46, treas., 1946, v.p., treas., 1946-50, pres., 1950-78, chmn., 1973-78, chmn. fin. com., 1978-86, chmn. emeritus, 1986—; dir. Ducommun Realty Co., 1938-70, v.p., 1947-70; dir. Farmers & Merchants Nat. Bank of Los Angeles (merged with Security Pacific Nat. Bank 1957), Am. Metal Bearing Co.; adv. dir. Investment Co. Am., 1960-86; mem. adv. com. internat. trade U.S. Dept. Commerce, 1957-60. Mem. Central City Com.; trustee Com. for Econ. Devel., 1958-76; mem. Los Angeles 200 Com., 1978-85, Gov.'s Commn. on Calif. Small Bus., 1950-53, Rep. Nat. Finance Com., 1953-54; chmn. Rep. Finance Com. of Calif., 1953-54; del. Rep. Nat. Conv., 1960, 68; mem. Rep. State Central Com., 1953-56, 64-69; trustee Los Angeles County Mus. Art, 1960-90, v.p., 1974-80, 86—, treas., 1980-86; trustee So. Calif. Area Bldg. Funds; chmn. Stanford Cabinet, 1965-71; del. Japan Calif. Assn., 1965-87; chmn. So. Calif., Invest-in-Am., 1969, now dir., mem.-at-large nat. adv. bd.; past chmn., bd. dirs. Los Angeles Civic Light Opera Assn., Calif. Civic Light Opera Assn., 1979-87; v.p., dir. Am. Ctr. for Mus. Theater and Tng., 1984-87; trustee Claremont Men's Coll. (now Claremont McKenna Coll.); trustee Stanford U., 1961-71, v.p., 1964-70; chmn. Los Angeles Bicentennial Student Art Competition, 1980-81; co-chmn. 1984 Olympics Youth Activities Commn., 1982-84. Lt. USNR, 1942-46; aide to chief staff U.S. Fleet 1944-46. Mem. Los Angeles C. of C. (chmn. fed. affairs com., pres. 1957, treas. 1958, dir. 1952-61), Harvard Bus. Sch. Alumni (exec. council 1953-57), Navy League U.S. (chpt. dir. 1955-60), Stanford Assos. (Gold Spike award 1980), Harvard Bus. Sch. (mem. overseers vis. com. 1962-68, 69-75, Statesman of Yr. So. Calif. 1975), Delta Kappa Epsilon. Club: Lincoln (pres. 1969, bd. govs.).

DUENEWALD, DORIS ANNETTE, publishing executive; b. N.Y.C., Nov. 12, 1921; d. Ralph Martin and Rhoda (Lewis) D.; divorced; children: Laura Aimee Garn, Elizabeth Lewis Garn. BA with honors, Mt. Holyoke Coll., 1942. With prodn. dept. Duenewald-Konecky Printing Corp., N.Y.C., 1946-49; editor in chief, v.p. children's books Grosset & Dunlap, Inc., N.Y.C., 1949-83; pub. Golden Books Western Pub. Co., N.Y.C. and Racine, Wis., 1983—. Bd. dirs. Children's Book Coun., N.Y.C., 1972-75. Mem. Soc. Illustrators. Democrat. Jewish. Avocations: bridge, reading.

DUFFY, JOHN, history educator; b. Barrow-in-Furness, Eng., Mar. 27, 1915; came to U.S., 1928; m. Florence Corinne Cook, 1942; 2 children. B.A., La. State Normal Coll., 1941; M.A., La. State U., 1944; Ph.D. in History, UCLA, 1946. Asst. prof. Northwestern State Coll., 1946-47, 49-53, Southeastern State Coll., 1947-49; from asst. prof. to assoc. prof. history La. State U., 1953-60; from assoc. prof. to prof. pub. health history Grad. Sch. Pub. Health, U. Pitts., 1960-65; prof. history of medicine Coll. Arts and Sci. and Sch. Medicine, Tulane U., 1965-72; Priscilla Alden Burke prof. history U. Md., College Park, 1972-83; prof. emeritus U. Md., 1983-96; Bingham prof. humanities U. Louisville, 1985; clin. prof. emeritus Tulane U. Sch. Medicine, New Orleans, 1989-96; cons. N.Y.C. Health Dept., 1963-69; mem. hist. life sci. study sect. NIH, 1967-70, 91-96, chmn., 1970-71, cons., 1971-96; interim editor Am. Hist. Rev., 1975. Author: Epidemics in Colonial America, 1953, Rudolph Matas History of Medicine in Louisiana, 2 vols., 1958-62, Sword of Pestilence, the New Orleans Yellow Fever Epidemic of 1853, 1966, A History of Public Health in New York City, 1625-1866, 1968, A History of Public Health in New York City, 1866-1966, 1974, The Healers, the Rise of the Medical Establishment, 1976, The Tulane University Medical Center, One Hundred Years of Medical Education, 1984, The Sanitarians, A History of American Public Health, 1990, From Humors to Medical Science: A History of American Medicine, 1993; co-author: Social Welfare in Transition, 1966; editor: Ventures in World Health, The Memoirs of Fred Lowe Soper, 1977. Ford Found. fellow, 1951-52; recipient Arthur Viseltear award APHA, 1992. Fellow La. Hist. Assn.; mem. Am. Hist. Assn., Am. Assn. for History Medicine (pres. 1976-78, Continuing Lifetime Achievement award 1991), Orgn. Am. Historians, So. Hist. Assn. Died June 20, 1996.

DUKAS, PETER, management consultant, educator; b. Lewiston, Maine, Apr. 7, 1919; s. Peter and Katherine (Bezantakos) D.; m. Aphrodite Dukas, June 22, 1950; 1 son, Stephen Peter. BS, U. Chgo., 1950, MBA, 1951. Ops. analyst Brass Rail, N.Y.C., 1951-52; mgr. Mid-City Enterprises, N.Y.C., 1953-54, Prince of Wales Hotel, Can., 1958; mgmt. cons., pres. Manco Assocs., Inc., Tallahassee, 1958—; prof., dir. Sch. Hotel and Restaurant Mgmt., Fla. State U., 1954—; real estate broker, 1980—; Bd. dirs. Nat. Council Hotel and Restaurant Edn. Author: Hotel Front Office Management, 1957, 3d rev. edit., 1970, How To Operate a Restaurant, 1960, How To Organize and Operate a Profitable Restaurant, 1971, Planning Profits in the Food and Lodging Industry, 1975, Guide to Profitable Bar Management, 1975, also articles. Dir. Greek Orthodox Community, Tallahassee, 1961, pres. Ahepa Patmos chpt., dist. gov., 1977-78; Sec. Ahepa Ednl. Found. Bd. Served with USMCR, 1942-46. Recipient numerous awards from motel and restaurant assns. Mem. Internat. Soc. Food Service Cons.'s, AAUP, Am. Hellenic Ednl. Progressive Assn. (dir.), Beta Gamma Sigma. DIED 05/29/95. .

DUKE, HAROLD BENJAMIN, JR., retired holding company executive; b. Washington, Iowa, Jan. 11, 1922; s. Harold Benjamin and Nordica (Wells) D.; m. Maud Barnard Banks, June 11, 1949; children: James Lenox, Harold Benjamin III, Lester Perrin, Charles Banks. B.A., Williams Coll., 1943. With Gates Corp., Denver, 1946-87, mem. exec. com., 1959—, v.p., 1960-73, exec. v.p., 1973-83, pres., 1983-89, vice-chmn., 1987-94, also dir.; ret.; bd. dirs. subs. cos. Gates Corp., A-Bar-A Ranches, Gates Land Co. Mem. Denver Com. on Fgn. Rels., 1967-85; bd. dirs. Boys Clubs Denver, 1960-89; pres., trustee Denver Country Day Sch., Englewood, Colo., 1958-71; trustee Social Sci. Found., U. Denver, 1967-75, pres., 1972-75; trustee Denver Pub. Libr. Friends Found., 1974—, pres., 1976-79, 90-92; nat. bd. dirs. Jr. Achievement, 1986-89; trustee Colo. Nature Conservancy, 1984—, Vail Valley Found., 1983—. With U.S. Army, 1943-45. Decorated Bronze Star medal, Purple Heart. Mem. Nat. Assn. Mfrs. (nat. dir. 1986-88). Republican. Clubs: University, Mile High, Denver Country, Country of Colo, Castle Pines. Deceased.

DULLES, ELEANOR LANSING, diplomatic consultant, retired diplomat, educator; b. Watertown, N.Y., June 1, 1895; d. Allen Macy and Edith (Foster) D.; m. David Blondheim, Dec. 9, 1932 (dec. 1934); children: David Dulles, Ann Dulles Joor. AB (1st New Eng. scholar), Bryn Mawr Coll., 1917, AM (fellow labor and indsl. economics), 1920; postgrad., London Sch. Econs., 1921-22; AM, Radcliffe Coll., 1924, PhD, 1926; Faculté de Droit, U. Paris, 1925-27; LLD, Wilson Coll., 1950, Western Coll., 1957; Dr. honoris causa, Free U. Berlin, 1957; LLD, Mt. Holyoke Coll., 1962; DLitt, Duke U., 1965, Mt. Vernon Coll., 1975, Clarkson Coll., 1979. Relief and reconstrn. Shurtleff Meml. Relief at Paris, 1917; relief work Am. Friends Service Com., 1918-19; asst. personnel mgr. Am. Tube & Stamping Co., Bridgeport, Conn., 1920-21; employment mgr. S. Glemby, N.Y.C., 1920-21; research assoc. Harvard and Radcliffe Bur. Research, France, 1925-27, Switzerland, 1930-32; tchr. Simmons Coll., Boston, 1924-25, 27-28; asst. prof. Bryn Mawr Coll., 1928-30, lectr., 1932-36; research assoc. U. Pa., 1932-36; chief finance div. Social Security Bd., Washington, 1936-42; economist Bd. Economic Warfare, 1942; economic officer Dept. State, 1942-45; fin. attaché Vienna, Austria, 1945-49; with Western European div., Dept. State, 1949-51, Nat. Prodn. Authority, Dept. Commerce, 1951-52; spl. asst. Office of German Affairs, Dept. State, 1952-59; spl. asst. intelligence and research Dept. State, 1959-62, ret.; lectr., vis. prof. Duke U., 1962- 63; prof. Georgetown U., 1963-71; with Center for Strategic Studies, Washington, 1964-67; research fellow Hoover Inst., Stanford, 1967-68; cons. Dept. State, 1970-73, Youth for Understanding, Ann Arbor, Mich., 1969-73; Organizer John Foster Dulles Centennial Program Princeton U., 1985—; mem. Geneva Conf. on Investment Social Security Funds, 1938; rep. U.S. Govt. on Bretton Woods Conf. on IMF, 1944; investigated unemployment ins. Pres. Hoover's Com., 1931. Author: The French Franc, 1928, The Bank for International Settlements at Work, 1932, Depression and Reconstruction, 1934, The Dollar, The Franc and Inflation, 1933; monograph The Evolution of Reparation Ideas, 1932; John Foster Dulles, The Last Year, 1963, Détente, Cold War Strategies in Transition, 1965, Dominican Action, 1965—, Intervention or Cooperation, 1966, Berlin: The Wall Is Not Forever, 1967, American Foreign Policy in the Making, 1968, One Germany or Two The Struggle at The Heart of Europe, 1970, The Wall: A Tragedy in Three Acts, 1972, Eleanor Lansing Dulles—Chances of a Lifetime, a Memoir, 1980; contbr. articles on social security, monetary policy investment, etc. Decorated Grand Cross of Merit (Fed. Republic Germany), Knight's Comdrs. Cross Austria, 1989; recipient Disting. Achievement award Radcliffe Coll., 1955; Carl Schurz plaque, 1957; Ernst Reuter plaque City of West Berlin, 1959; citation for distinction Bryn Mawr Coll., 1960; Tribute of Appreciation Dept. State, 1985; hon. prof. U. Berlin; Lucius D. Clay medal; Centennial medal Harvard Grad. Sch. Arts and Sci., 1991. Mem. P.E.N., Phi Beta Kappa. Clubs: Cosmopolitan (N.Y.C.); Henderson Harbor Yacht; Internat. (Washington). Died Oct. 30, 1996.

DUMBAULD, EDWARD, federal judge; b. Uniontown, Pa., Oct. 26, 1905; s. Horatio S. and Lissa Grace (MacBurney) D.; m. Mary Ellen Whelpley, Jan. 1, 1941. A.B., Princeton U., 1926; LL.B., Harvard U., 1929, LL.M., 1930; Dr. Law, U. Leyden, Netherlands, 1932; LL.D. hon., Findlay Coll., 1981. Bar: Mem. Pa., D.C., U.S. Supreme Ct. bars. Practitioner before ICC, FCC (other adminstrn. agys.); former spl. asst. to atty. gen. U.S., Washington; (charge of litigation under acts regulating transp. and communications); judge Ct. Common Pleas Fayette County, 1957-61; U.S. dist. judge Western Dist. Pa., 1961—; sec. Am. Soc. Internat. Law, 1948-78, hon. v.p., 1979-87, hon. pres., 1988-90. Author: Interim Measures of Protection in International Controversies, 1932, Thomas Jefferson, American Tourist, 1946, The Declaration of Independence and What It Means Today, 1950, The Political Writings of Thomas Jefferson, 1955, The Bill of Rights and What It Means Today, 1957, The Constitution of the United States, 1964, Sayings of Jesus, 1967, Life and Legal Writings of Hugo Grotius, 1969, Thomas Jefferson and the Law, 1978. Democratic county chmn., Fayette County, 1934-36; del. Dem. Nat. Conv., Phila., 1936. Mem. Pa. Bar Assn. (chmn. com. on lawyers referral service). Presbyn. Club: Cosmos (Washington). Lodge: Kiwanis (pres. Uniontown 1955). DIED 09/06/97. .

DUMITRESCU, LUCIEN Z., aerospace researcher; b. Bucharest, Romania, July 28, 1931; arrived in France, 1991; s. Zaharia D. and Natalia V. (Grigoriu) D.; m. Lucia A. Droc, June 21, 1952 (div. 1964); children: Michel-Paul. Dipl.engr., Poly. Inst. Fac. Aeron., Bucharest, 1954; D of Engring., Acad. Scis., Bucharest, 1969. Scientist Inst. Fluid Mechanics, Romanian Acad. Sci., 1952-70; sr. scientist, lab head Inst. of Aeronautics, Romania Ministry of Industry, Bucharest, 1970-80, sr. sci. counselor, 1980-90; prof. U. De Provence, Marseille, France, 1991—; v.p. quality assurance commn. Inst. of Aeronautics, Romanian Ministry of Industry, Bucharest, 1980-90. Author: Research in Shock Tubes, 1969; co-editor: Proc. 19 Internat. Symposium on Shock Waves, 1993; contbr. over 50 articles to profl. publs. Fellow AIAA (assoc.); mem. Internat. Adv. Com. for Shock Tube Symposia. Achievements include devel. of large aerodynamic test facilities; implementation of a quality assurance system for the design and devel. in the Romanian aeron. industry; rsch. on shock waves in gases and aircraft aerodynamics. Deceased.

DUNAVANT, LEONARD CLYDE, state senator; b. Ripley, Tenn., Oct. 29, 1919; s. Harvey Maxie and Chloris Earl (Akin) D.; student Union U., Tenn., Memphis State U.; m. Deloris Anderson, Jan. 5, 1940; children: Janene Dunavant Pennel, Leonard Clyde, Susanne Dunavant Ripski. Alderman City of Millington (Tenn.); mem. Tenn. Ho. of Reps., chmn. fin., ways and means com.; mem. Tenn. Senate, chmn. legis. council pensions and retirement. Served with USNR, World

War II. Mem. So. Regional Edn. Bd. Republican. Methodist. Club: Rotary (past pres.). Died Feb. 28, 1995. Home: Millington Tenn.

DUNBAR, ROBERT STANDISH, JR., animal science educator; b. Providence, Nov. 30, 1921; s. Robert Standish and Lucie (Lowell) D.; m. Mary Agnes O'Grady, Dec. 8, 1941; children: Robert Standish, Barbara Louise (Mrs. John R. Fields). BS, U. R.I., 1949; PhD, Cornell U., 1952. Mem. faculty W.Va. U., 1952-92, prof. statistics, expt. sta. statistician, 1957-63, chmn. dept. animal and vet. sci., 1963-64, dean Coll. Agr. and Forestry, 1964-74, prof. animal sci., 1974-84, prof. emeritus, 1984-92. With U.S. Army, 1942-46. Mem. Gamma Sigma Delta, Alpha Zeta, Phi Kappa Phi. Died Dec. 15, 1992.

DUNCAN, ALASTAIR ROBERT CAMPBELL, philosophy educator; b. Scotland, July 12, 1915; s. Leslie and Jean (Anderson) D.; m. Francoise Pellissier, June 11, 1938; children: Alain, Gregor, Colin. M.A. with 1st class honors in Philosophy, U. Edinburgh, Scotland, 1936; postgrad., Marburg U., Germany, 1936-37; D.Litt., Lakehead U., 1979. Lectr. U. London, Eng., 1938-39; lectr., dir. studies U. Edinburgh, 1945-49; chmn. dept. philosophy Queen's U., Kingston, Ont., Can., 1949-80; prof. emeritus Queen's U., 1980-93, dean faculty of arts and sci., 1959-64; vis. Truax prof. Hamilton Coll., 1974; vis. prof. Sir Wilfred Grenfell Coll., 1982. Author: Practical Reason and Morality, 1957, Moral Philosophy, 1965, On The Nature of Persons, 1990, also articles on philosophy, edn., decision making and Dante.; translator (Vleeschauwer) Development of Kantian Thought, 1962. Served with Brit. Army, 1939-45. Ferguson scholar, 1938. Mem. Royal Inst. Philosophy, Aristotelian Soc., Mind Assn., Canadian Philos. Assn. (pres. 1960-61, 66-67), Dante Soc. N.Am. Club: Cataraqui Golf. Home: Kingston Can. Died Dec. 23, 1993.

DUNCAN, GEORGE HAROLD, broadcasting company executive; b. N.Y.C., Aug. 26, 1931; m. Mary Joan Murphy, Feb. 15, 1958; children: Keith, Kathryn, Patricia. Student, Hofstra Coll., 1949; BA in Govt, Cornell U., 1955. Sales engr. Dewey and Almy Chem. div. W.R. Grace Co., Cambridge, Mass., 1955-56; account exec. Avery-Knodel, Inc., N.Y.C., 1956-58; with Metromedia, Inc., N.Y.C., 1958-86; account exec. Sta. WNEW, 1958-66; v.p., gen. mgr. Sta. WNEW-FM, 1966-69; pres. Metromedia Stereo, 1969-71; exec. v.p. Metromedia Radio, 1971-72, pres., 1972-80; v.p. ops. Metromedia, Inc., 1980-82, pres., dir., 1982-86; pres., owner Encore Communications, Inc., 1986-93; also pres. Buenaventura, Inc., Ventura; past chmn. Radio Advt. Bur. Mem. council Cornell U. With USMC, 1950-51. Mem. Cornell Club, Phi Gamma Delta. Home: Scarsdale N.Y. Died June 10, 1995.

DUNIKOSKI, SARAH BEELS, vocal music educator; b. Oil City, Pa., Dec. 11, 1947; d. Kenneth Woodrow and Kathryn Elizabeth (McClure) Beels; m. Leonard Karol Dunikoski, Jr., June 24, 1972. B.Mus., Westminster Coll., 1969; M.Ed., Pa. State U., 1970. Tchr. vocal music Butler Area Sch. Dist., Pa., 1970-72, Montgomery County Sch. Dist., Rockville, Md., 1972-73, Rumson Bd. Edn., N.J., 1974—; vol. tchr. Rumson Community Edn., 1977-84. Chmn. Greater Red Bank (N.J.) Crop Hunger Walk, 1981-82, recruitment dir., 1983—; ordained deacon Presbyterian Ch. (U.S.A.), 1983; sec. bd. deacons Shrewsbury Presbyn. Ch., N.J., 1985—; pianist Butler Community Theater, 1970. Mem. Nat. Guild Piano Tchrs., NEA, N.J. Edn. Assn., Music Educators Nat. Conf., N.J. Music Educators, Mu Phi Epsilon, Kappa Delta Pi, Delta Zeta. Republican. Presbyterian. Avocations: sailing; horseback riding; tennis; gardening. Dec.

DUNLOP, ROBERT GALBRAITH, retired petroleum company executive; b. Boston, July 2, 1909; s. James B. and Caroline (Cowan) D.; m. Emma L. Brownback, Dec. 4, 1937; children—Barbara E. (Mrs. Robert P. Hauptfuhrer), Richard G. B.S., U. Pa., 1931. C.P.A., Pa. Assoc. with Barrow, Wade, Guthrie & Co., 1931-33; bd. dirs. emeritus Sun Co.; bd. dirs. The Glenmede Corp. Trustee U. Pa. Mem. Sigma Phi Epsilon, Beta Gamma Sigma. Republican. Presbyterian. Home: Bryn Mawr Pa. Died Sept. 20, 1995.

DUNNE, RICHARD EDWIN, III, lawyer; b. Hartford, Conn., Oct. 17, 1950; s. Richard E. Jr. and Jean Alice (O'Leary) D.; children: Anna MacRae, Phoebe Jean. AB, Harvard U., 1972; JD, U. Conn., 1977. Bar: Conn. 1977, D.C. 1978, U.S. Ct. Appeals (4th cir.) 1978, U.S. Dist. Ct. (ea. dist.) Pa. 1982, U.S. Ct. Appeals (9th cir.) 1983, Md. 1983, U.S. Ct. Appeals (11th cir.) 1994. Law clk. to Hon. Alexander Harvey II U.S. Dist. Ct., Balt., 1977-79; assoc. Shipman & Goodwin, Hartford, 1979-80; asst. U.S. atty. U.S. Atty.'s Office, Balt., 1980-83; ptnr. Piper & Marbury, Balt., 1983-88, Hogan & Hartson, Balt., 1988—. Mem. Sergeant's Inn, 4th Cir. Jud. Conf. Democrat. Avocations: aviation, golf, skiing. Died Nov. 26, 1997.

DURENBERGER, DAVID FERDINAND, lawyer; b. St. Cloud, Minn., Aug. 19, 1934; s. George G. and Isabelle M. (Cebulla) D.; children: Charles, David, Michael, Daniel. B.A. cum laude in Polit. Sci, St. Johns U., 1955; J.D., U. Minn., 1959. Bar: Minn. 1959. Mem. firm LeVander, Gillen, Miller & Durenberger, South St. Paul, 1959-66; exec. sec. to Gov. Harold LeVander, 1967-71; counsel for legal and community affairs, corporate sec. H.B. Fuller Co., St. Paul, 1971-78; U.S. senator from Minn., 1978-95, mem. Senate Fin. Com., 1979-95, mem. environ. and pub. works com., 1983-95, mem. labor and human rels. com., 1987-95, mem. ethics com., 1983-84, mem. Senate intelligence com., 1979-87, chair, 1985-87, mem. govt. rels. com., 1979-87, mem. adv. com. intergovtl. affairs, 1980-95; sr. counselor APCO, Washington, 1995; vice chmn. Minn. St. Ethical Pracitces Bd., 1973-77. Chmn. Metro Council Open Space Adv. Bd., 1972-74; chmn. bd. commrs. Hennepin County Park Res. Dist.; vice chmn. Met. Parks and Open Space Bd.; exec. vice chmn. Gov.'s Commn. on Arts; exec. dir. Minn. Constl. Study Commn., Supreme Ct. Adv. Com. on Jud. Responsibility; pres. Burroughs Sch. PTA, Mpls.; chmn. Dakota County Young Republican League, 1963-64; dir., legal counsel Minn. Young Rep. League, 1964-65; co-chmn. State Young Rep. League, 1965; del. State Rep. Conv., 1966, 68, 70, 72; first vice chmn. 1st Dist. Rep. Party, 1970-72; vice chmn. 13th ward Rep. Party Mpls., 1973-74; bd. dirs. Met. Parks Found., Pub. Service Options, Inc., St. Louis Park AAU Swim Club, Minn. Landmarks, 1971-73, Pub. Affairs Leadership and Mgmt. Tng., Inc., 1973-75, U. Minn. YMCA, 1973-75, Community Planning Orgn., Inc., St. Paul, 1973-76, Project Environment Found., 1974-75, Urban Lab., Inc., 1975, Nat. Recreation and Park Assn., Within the System, Inc., 1976-77; trustee Children's Health Center and Hosp., Inc., Mpls.; mem. exec. com. Nat. Center for Vol. Action, Minn. Charities Rev. Council. Served as 2d lt. U.S. Army, 1955-56; capt. USAR, 1956-63. Named Outstanding Young Man in South St. Paul, 1964, One of Ten Outstanding Young Men in Minn., 1965. Mem. ABA, Minn. Bar Assn., 1st Dist. Bar Assn., Corp. Counsel Assn., St. Johns U. Alumni Assn. (pres. Twin Cities chpt. 1963-65, nat. pres. 1971-73), Mpls., St. Paul Area chambers commerce, Gamma Eta Gamma (chancellor 1958-59, v.p. Alumni Assn. 1965-75). Home: Fairfax Va. Deceased.

DURHAM, GEORGE HOMER, educator, church executive; b. Parowan, Utah, Feb. 4, 1911; s. George Henry and Mary Ellen (Marsden) D.; m. Eudora Widtsoe, June 20, 1936; children—Carolyn, Doralee (Mrs. R.H. Madsen), George. A.B., U. Utah, 1932; Ph.D., U. Calif. at Los Angeles, 1939; LL.D., Ariz. State U., 1971, Ind. State U., 1976, State Coll. So. Utah, U. Utah, 1977; D. Pub. Service, Brigham Young U., 1975. Finance div. mgr. Zion's Coop. Merc. Inst., Salt Lake City, 1935-36; fellow, asst. U. Calif., Los Angeles, 1937-39; vis. prof. U. Calif., summer 1950; polit. sci. dept. Utah State Coll., 1939-42, Swarthmore Coll., 1942-43, U. Utah, 1944-60; dir. Inst. Govt., U. Utah, 1946-53, head polit. sci. dept., 1948-53, v.p. univ., 1953-60; pres. Ariz. State U., 1960-69; Utah commr. higher edn. Salt Lake City, 1969-76; research prof. U. Utah, 1976-77; mng. dir. hist. dept. Ch. of Jesus Christ of Latter-day Saints, 1977-85; Mem. Western Interstate Commn. for Higher Edn., 1955-60, 69-76; mem. Ariz. State Bd. Edn., 1960-66; mem. U.S. nat. commn. for UNESCO, 1955-57,59; cons., current affairs analyst KTVT, Intermountain TV Corp., Salt Lake City, 1956-58; mem. lang. adv. devel. bd. U.S. Office Edn., 1959-63; mem. Air Force ROTC adv. panel to sec. air force, 1961-64, Army ROTC Panel, 1968-70; adviser Army Command and Gen. Staff Coll., 1970-73; mem. Bd. Fgn. Scholarships, 1963-66; Bd. dirs. Am. Council on Edn., 1967-70, Ari. Acad., 1964-69, Phoenix Symphony, 1961-69; adv. bd. Utah Symphony, 1969-85, Am. Grad. Sch. Internat. Mgmt. Author: Joseph Smith: Prophet-Statesman, 1944, The Adminstration of Higher Education in Montana, 1958, other monographs.; Contbg. editor: The Improvement Era, 1946-70. Mem. worldwide exec. com. Sunday schs. Ch. of Jesus Christ of Latter-day Saints, 1971-73; pres. Salt Lake Central stake, 1973-76; regional rep. Council of 12, 1976-77; mem. First Quorum of the Seventy, 1977-85. Mem. Am. Polit. Sci. Assn. (exec. council 1949-51), Western Polit. Sci. Assn. (pres 1948), Am. Soc. Pub. Adminstrn. (council 1949-51, v.p. 1952, pres. 1959-60), Nat. Acad. Pub. Adminstrn., Pi Gamma Mu, Pi Sigma Alpha, Phi Kappa Phi. Clubs: Timpanogos, Windsor. Home: Salt Lake City, Utah. Died Jan. 10, 1985.

DUTTON, FREDERIC BOOTH, chemist, educator; b. Cleve., Dec. 24, 1906; s. Charles Frederic and Elma (Booth) D.; m. Faith Kedzie; children—James Kedzie, Diane Hope (Mrs. John B. Haney). A.B., Oberlin Coll., 1928, A.M., 1932; Ph.D., Western Res. U., 1937. Instr. chemistry Baldwin-Wallace Coll., 1931-34, asst. prof., 1934-39, asso. prof., 1941-47; instr. Yale, 1939-40; prof. Olivet Coll., 1941; instr. Cleve. Coll., Western Res. U., 1938-39, summer 1939; asso. prof. chemistry Mich. State U., East Lansing, 1947-50; prof. Mich. State U., 1950-95, head sci. and math. teaching center, 1957-66; dean Lyman Briggs Coll., 1967-73, cons. to provost, 1973-76; Program dir. NSF, 1964-65. Fellow AAAS (sect. sec. 1964-67, sect. chmn., v.p. 1970); mem. Am. Chem. Soc. (sec. Cleve. 1943-46, treas. div. chem. edn. 1952-54, chmn. Mich. U. sect. 1949-95), Nat. Assn. Research Sci. Teaching (pres. 1964-65), Nat. Higher Edn. Assn., Northeastern Ohio Chemistry Tchrs. Orgn. (pres. 1939, 4O, 42), Mich. Sci. Tchrs. Assn. (pres. 1963-64), Nat. Sci. Tchrs. Assn., NEA, Sigma Xi, Alpha Chi Sigma. Home: East Lansing Mich. DIed Aug. 10, 1995.

D'UVA, ROBERT CARMEN, insurance and real estate broker; b. Castelpetroso, Italy, Aug. 25, 1920; s. Gabriele and Bettina D'Uva; m. Josephine C. Del Riccio, Sept. 5, 1948 (dec.);children: Robert Gary, Gary James, James Joseph. Student, Rutgers U., 1946-47, postgrad., 1950-51; BA in Acctg., Seton Hall U., 1949. Spl. rep. Manhattan Life Ins. Co. of N.Y., 1949-95; real estate sales rep. David Cornheim Agy., Newark, 1950-51; pvt. practice ins. and real estate broker Newark, 1951-95; ptnr. Romaine Realty Co., Newark, 1962-83; gen. agt. Md. Am. Gen. Ins. Cos.; pres. Diversified Variable Annuities, Inc., Newark, 1968-95, Del-Gior Corp., Bloomfield, N.J., 1971-95, Diversified Ins. Agy., Inc., Caldwell, N.J., 1973-95. Bd. dirs. Newark Boys Club, pres. Broadway unit, 1967; pres. real estate bd. of Newark, Irvington and Hillside, N.J. Served as cpl. Q.M.C. AUS, 1942-46, PTO. Mem. Nat. Real Estate Brokers Assn., Nat. Security Dealers Assn., N.J. Real Estate Assn., Nat. Assn. Real Estate Bd., Life Underwriters Assn., Ind. Ins. Agts. Assn. Roman Catholic. Lodge: Lions (North Newark) (pres., dep. dist. gov. 1964). Home: West Caldwell N.J. DIed Oct. 17, 1995.

DUVALL, JOANN, retired special education educator; b. Wolfe City, Tex., Apr. 2, 1933; d. Paul Dennis and Mary Emily (Kilgore) Williams; divorced; children: Michele, Joe Dirk. BA, East Tex. State U., 1966; postgrad., Maricopa County Tech. Coll., 1967, Ariz. State U., 1967-88, No. Ariz. U., 1967-88, Rockmont Coll., 1985, Phoenix U., 1988-89. Cert. secondary English tchr., spl. edn.-mentally handicapped tchr., Ariz. Tchr. English lang. Hampton U., 1965; tchr. spl. edn. Isaac Elem. Sch. Dist., Phoenix, 1967-89. Ariz. Dept. Edn. grantee, 1967. Mem. NEA, Nat. Assn. for Female Execs., Ariz. Edn. Assn., Classroom Tchr. Assn. Avocations: writing, reading, dancing, collecting professional books. Home: Phoenix Ariz. Died Apr. 4, 1995.

DWASS, MEYER, mathematician, educator; b. New Haven, Conn., Apr. 9, 1923; s. Israel and Golda (Haz) D.; m. Shirley Labowitz, May 29, 1949; children—Golda, Emily, Michael, Claudia. B.A., George Washington U., 1949; M.A., Columbia U., 1950; Ph.D., U.N.C., 1952. Statistician U.S. Census Bur., Suitland, Md., 1948-50; asst. prof. math. Northwestern U., Evanston, Ill., 1952-58; assoc. prof. Northwestern U., 1958-60, prof., 1960-89, chmn. dept. math., 1978-81; dir. Center for Statistics and Probability, 1975-84; translator Yiddish, 1989-96. Author: First Steps in Probability, 1967, Probability and Statistics, 1970. Served with AUS, 1943-46. Fellow Inst. Math. Stats.; mem. Am. Math. Soc., Am. Statis. Assn., Inst. Math. Stats., Soc. Indsl. and Applied Math., Phi Beta Kappa. Home: Evanston Ill. Died July 15, 1996; interred Menorah Gardens, Broadview, IL.

DWYER, VIRGINIA ALICE, retired telephone company financial executive; b. N.Y.C., May 11, 1921; d. Harold Arthur and Alice Marie (Cullen) D. A.B., U. Rochester, 1943; M.A., N.Y. U., 1953. With Western Electric Co., N.Y.C., 1943-75; chief economist, dir. acctg. research Western Electric Co., 1972-75; asst. treas. AT&T, N.Y.C., 1975-79; v.p., treas. AT&T, 1979-83, sr. v.p. fin., 1984-86; dir. Centennial Ins. Co., Borden Co., Schering Plough Co., Georgia Power Co., Southern Co.; bd. dirs., trustee Atlantic Cos. Trustee U. Rochester, 1979—; trustee St. Vincent's Hosp. Recipient Econ. Equity award Women's Equity Action League, 1980. Mem. Telephone Pioneers Am., Fin. Execs. Inst., Am. Econ. Assn.

DYE, SHERMAN, retired lawyer; b. Portland, Oreg., Nov. 18, 1915; s. Trafton M. and Mary (Ward) D.; m. Jean Forsythe, Dec. 22, 1939; children—Peter S., Kathleen, Richard F., Alice, William T., Mary H. A.B., Oberlin Coll., 1937; LL.B., Case Western Res. U., 1940. Bar: Ohio 1940, U.S. Supreme Ct. 1972. Jr. atty. SEC, Washington, 1940-41; law clk. Tax Ct. U.S., Washington, 1941-42; assoc. mem. firm Baker, Hostetler & Patterson, Cleve., 1942-51; ptnr. Baker & Hostetler, Cleve., 1952-93; ret., 1993. Past trustee, chmn. First Bapt. Ch. Greater Cleve.; past trustee, treas. Am. Cancer Soc., Cleve.; past trustee PACE Assn. With USAF, 1945. Mem. ABA, Ohio Bar Assn., Cleve. Bar Assn. (trustee 1954-57), Soc. Benchers, Order of Coif, Assn. Continuing Edn., Coll. Club of Cleve., Phi Delta Phi. Republican. Baptist. Died June 14, 1997.

DYGERT, HAROLD PAUL, JR., cardiologist; b. Rochester, N.Y., June 21, 1919; s. Harold Paul and Elsie Viola (Howe) D.; m. Helen Adelaine Nelson, Apr. 22, 1944; children: Harold Paul III, William Nelson, Peter Howe. BA, U. Rochester, 1941; postgrad., Alfred U., 1942-43; MD, Syracuse U., 1950. Diplomate Am. Bd. Internal Medicine. Intern Receiving Hosp., Detroit, 1950-51, resident internal medicine, 1951-53, chief resident, 1953-54; instr. medicine Wayne State U., Detroit, 1954-55; mem. staff VA Hosp., Vancouver, Wash., 1955-59; practice medicine specializing in cardiology and internal medicine Vancouver, 1959-95; chmn. Health Care Consortium, 1974-87. Pres. Wash. State Med., Ednl. and Research Found., 1971-73; bd. dirs. Wash.-Alaska Regional Med. Program, 1966-72; participant Manhattan Project, 1943-46. Served with AUS, 1943. Fellow ACP, Am. Coll. Cardiology; mem. AMA (del. 1976-77), Am. Fedn. Clin. Research, Wash. State Med. Assn. (pres. 1973-74), Portland Heart Club (pres. 1975-

77), Wash. State Soc. Internal Medicine (trustee 1976-80). Died Jan. 13, 1995.

DYKSTERHUIS, EDSKO JERRY, ecologist, educator; b. Hospers, Iowa, Dec. 27, 1908; s. Jerry and Jantina (Brouwer) D.; m. Margarett Adeline Cox, Mar. 26, 1933; children: Jantina Kay, Edna Leona, Jerry Edsko. BS in Forestry and Range Sci., Iowa State U., 1932; PhD in Ecology and Soils, U. Nebr., 1945. Range examiner nat. forests U.S. Forest Svc., Utah, Ariz., N.Mex., Tex., Ark. and Mo., 1930, 1933-38; range conservationist U.S. Soil Conservation Svc., Tex., La., Ark. and Okla., 1945-49; chief range conservationist U.S. Soil Conservation Svc., 6 no. plains states, 1949-64; prof. rangeland ecology Tex. A&M U., College Station, 1964-70, prof. emeritus, cons., 1970-91; cons. natural forages U.S. Dept. State, Washington, 1970-91, rangeland classifier, Turkey and Iran, 1973. Author: (monographs) Vegetation of Ft. Worth Prarie, 1946, Vegetation of Texas Cross Timbers, 1948, Ecological Principles in Range Evaluation, 1958. Named Profl. Conservationist Am. Motors Corp., 1977. Mem. Ecol. Soc. of Am. (life, chmn. com. on applied ecology), Soc. for Range Mgmt. (internat. pres. 1968, fellow 1977, chartered life), Soil and Water Conservation Soc. (pres. Tex. chpt. 1948, chartered life), Heritage Edn. & Conservation, Prairies Assn. (Outstanding Svc. award 1987). Home: Bryan Tex. Died Aug. 1991; interred Wyuka Cemetery, Lincoln, NE.

DZUR, MARTIN, minister of national defense Czechoslovakia; b. Plostin, Czechoslovakia, July 12, 1919; ed. W.M. Molotov Mil. Acad., Kalinin, USSR, Mil. Staff Acad. of Armed Forces, USSR. Tech. clk. Slovak Paper Mills, Ruzomberok, 1939-41; joined 1st Czechoslovak Ind. Brigade, Soviet Army, USSR; served in USSR, 1943-45; div. gen. staff officer, state sec.'s A.D.C., A.D.C. to chief mil. office of Pres. of Czechoslovakia, 1945-49; various posts in Army and Ministry of Nat. Def., 1953-58; dep. minister nat. def., 1958-68, minister, 1968; minister nat. def., 1969—; mem. Central Com., Communist Party of Czechoslovakia, 1968—; dep. to Ho. of the People, Fed. Assembly, 1971—. Decorated Order of Labor; Soviet, Czechoslovak and Polish medals including award for Strengthening Friendship in Arms (1st class), Comdr.'s Cross with Star of Order of Polish Revival, Order of Victorious Feb., Order of October Revolution.

EASTMAN, ROBERT EUGENE, electronic engineer, consultant; b. Lincoln, Neb., Sept. 14, 1929; s. Arthur Colgan and Lorraine Mary (Zimmer) E.; m. Dorothy G. Mitchell, Sept. 10, 1949 (div. May 1982); children: John, Ann Marie, Kathleen, Douglas, Caroline, David. AB in Physics and Math., U. Neb., 1956. Assoc. engr. Sperry Gyroscope Co., Great Neck, N.Y., 1956-57; rsch. engr. Schlumberger Well Surveying Corp., Ridgefield, Conn., 1957-58; engr. Electro-Mech. Rsch., Inc., Sarasota, Fla., 1958-61; sr. engr. Beckman Instruments, Inc., Fullerton, Calif., 1961-64; chief engr. Epsco, Inc., Westwood, Mass., 1964-70; v.p., dir. engring., co-founder Interface Engring. Inc., Stoughton, Mass., 1970-82; pres. Eastman Industries Inc., Imperial Beach, Calif., 1982-83; sr. mem. tech. staff GTE, Needham Hts., Mass., 1983-92; prin. engr. Dositec, Inc., Framingham, Mass., 1992-93. Sgt. USAF, 1948-52. Physics scholar U. Neb., 1953-54, 54-55, 55-56. Mem. Lions Club, Am. Legion (svc. officer 1980-82). Republican. Roman Catholic. Achievements include patents in transition detector; in one-shot latch; in AC sample and hold. Home: Raynham Mass. Died Oct. 26, 1993.

EASTON, WILLIAM HEYDEN, geology educator; b. Bedford, Ind., Jan. 14, 1916; s. Harry Thomas and Katharine (Gillen) E.; m. Phoebe Jane Beall, Aug. 10, 1940; children—Phoebe Beall, Robert Bruce, Katharine Louise. B.S., George Washington U., 1937, M.A., 1938; Ph.D., U. Chgo., 1940. With Nat. Park Service, summers 1936, 37, Ark. Geol. Survey, summer 1939, U. Hawaii, summer 1962; with Ill. Geol. Survey, 1940-44; mem. faculty U. So. Calif., 1946-81, prof. geology, 1951-81, prof. emeritus, 1981-96, chmn. dept., 1963-67, acting chmn. dept. French and Italian, 1975-76, 85-86; with U.S. Geol. Survey, 1952-53; cons. geologist, 1950-96. Author: Invertebrate Paleontology, 1960, also articles. Served with USNR, 1944-46. Recipient Publ. award Assn. Engring. Geologists, 1973, Raubenheimer Disting. Faculty award U. So. Calif., 1980; Guggenheim fellow, 1959-60. Fellow Geol. Soc. Am. (chmn. Cordilleran sect. 1965), So. Calif. Acad. Sci.; mem. Am. Assn. Petroleum Geologists (Distinguished lectr. 1955, Teaching award Pacific sect. 1986), Paleontol. Soc. (pres. West Coast br. 1950, pres. 1969), Soc. Econ. Paleontologists and Mineralogists (pres. Pacific sect. 1955), Sigma Xi (Outstanding Service award 1981), Phi Beta Kappa, Phi Kappa Phi, Sigma Gamma Epsilon. Home: Westlake Village Calif. Died July 7, 1996.

EBBITT, KENNETH COOPER, investor; b. Yonkers, N.Y., June 23, 1908; s. Nicholas John and Dora (Cooper) E.; m. Margaret Ann Quinn, May 10, 1936; children: Kenneth Cooper, Nicholas John II, Douglas James, Gordon L. J. BS, Manhattan Coll., 1931. Assoc. Lehman Bros., 1933-45; partner Campbell Phelps & Co., N.Y.C., 1946-47; gen. ptnr. Shelby Cullom Davis & Co., N.Y.C., 1947-82; mem. N.Y. Stock Exchange, 1969-82. Clubs: Westchester Country, John's Island. Home: Vero Beach Fla. Died Sept. 14, 1995.

ECCLES, SIR JOHN CAREW, physiologist; b. Melbourne, Australia, Jan. 27, 1903; s. William James and Mary (Carew) E.; m. Irene Miller, 1928; 9 children; m. Helena Táboríková, 1968. M.B., B.S., Melbourne U., 1925; M.A., Oxford U., 1929, D.Phil., 1929; LL.D., Melbourne U., 1965; D.Sc. (hon.), U. B.C., 1966, Cambridge U., 1960, U. Tasmania, 1964, Gustavus Adolphus, 1967, Marquette U., 1967, Loyola U., 1969, Yeshiva U., 1969, Charles U., Prague, 1969, Oxford U., 1974, U. Fribourg, 1981, U. Torino, 1983, Georgetown U., 1984, U. Tsukuba, Japan, 1986, U. Basel, 1990, U. Madrid, 1992, U. Ulm, 1993. Research fellow Exeter Coll., Oxford U., 1927-34; tutorial fellow Magdalen Coll., 1934-37; dir. Kanematsu Meml. Inst. Pathology, Sydney (Australia) Hosp., 1937-43; prof. physiology Otago U., Dunedin, New Zealand, 1944-51, Australian Nat. U., Canberra, 1951-66; mem. AMA/E.R.F. Inst. Biomed. Research, Chgo., 1966-68; disting. prof. SUNY, Buffalo, 1968-75, emeritus, 1975—. Author: (with others) Reflex Activity of the Spinal Cord, 1932; The Neurophysiological Basis of Mind: The Principles of Neurophysiology, 1953; The Physiology of Nerve Cells, 1957; The Physiology of Synapses, 1964; (with Ito, Szentagothai) The Cerebellum as a Neuronal Machine, 1967; The Inhibitory Pathways of the Central Nervous System, 1968; Facing Reality, 1970; The Understanding of the Brain, 1973; (with Karl Popper) The Self and Its Brain, 1977; (with others) Molecular Neurobiology of the Mammalian Brain, 1978, 2d edit., 1987; (with W. Gibson) Sherrington, His Life and Thought, 1979; The Human Mystery, 1979; The Human Psyche, 1980; (with D.N. Robinson) The Wonder of Being Human: Our Brain, Our Mind, 1984; Evolution of the Brain: Creation of the Self, 1989, How the Self Controls its Brain, 1993. Decorated knight bachelor, 1958, Gold and Silver Stars Order of the Rising Sun, 1986, companion Order of Australia, 1990; recipient Royal medal Royal Soc., 1962, Cothenius medal Deutche Akademie der Naturforscher Leopoldina, Nobel prize in physiology and medicine (with A. L. Hodgkin and A. F. Huxley), 1963, Gold medal Charles U., Prague, 1993. Fellow Royal Soc., 1941, Australia Acad. Sci. (pres. 1957-61); mem. Pontifical Acad. Scis., Am. Philos. Soc. (hon.), Accademia Nazionale del Lincei (fgn. hon.), NAS (fgn. assoc.), Am. Physiol. Soc. (fgn. hon.), ACP (hon.), Am. Acad. Arts and Scis. (fgn. hon.), Max Planck Soc. (hon.). Research, numerous pubs. on the physiology of synapses of the nervous system and chemical transmitters, brain-mind problem. Died May 2, 1997.

ECHIKSON, RICHARD, retail consultant; b. Newark, N.J., Feb. 5, 1929; s. Joseph I. and Pearl (Comando) E.; m. Lenora Greenspan, June 25, 1956 (div. Jan. 1967); children: Andrea, James; m. Florence Roberta Papov, Oct. 18, 1969 (div. July 1992); children: Pamela, Stephen; m. Barbara Pfeiffer, Aug. 2, 1992. BA, Dartmouth Coll., 1950; MBA, Amos Tuck Sch., Hanover, N.H., 1951. Mdse. adminstrv. buyer, exec. training sq. R.H. Macy Inc., N.Y.C., 1951-65; pres. The Fabric Tree Inc., N.Y.C., 1965-78; exec. v.p. W.R. Grace & Co., N.Y.C., 1978-81; chmn. Retail Cons. Inc., Basking Ridge, N.J., 1981—; dir. Met. Pres. Organs., N.Y.C., 1980—, Mgmt. Decisions Lab, NYU Grad. Sch. of Bus., 1980-84, Young Pres. Organs., 1970-80; exec. com. Darthmouth Coll. Class, Hanover, 1960—; class agent Amos Tuck Sch., 1980—. Author: (book) International Council of Shopping Centers, 1988; contbr. articles to mags. Served to 1st lt. USAF, 1951-53, Japan. Mem. Internat. Coun. Shopping Ctrs., Pension Real Estate Assn., NAt. Retail Fedn., Dartmouth Club (N.Y.C., suburban N.J.). Avocations: golf, swimming. DIED 07/10/96. .

EDDISON, JOHN CORBIN, economist; b. N.Y.C., Nov. 4, 1919; s. William Barton and Mary (Corbin) E.; m. Elizabeth Owsley Bole, Feb. 10, 1951; children: Jonathan B., Elizabeth O., Martha C. Grad., St. Paul's Sch., 1938; A.B., Cornell U., 1942, M.S., 1948; Ph.D., MIT, 1955. Personnel asst. E.I. duPont de Nemours & Co., 1947-48; indsl. engr. Campbell Soup Co., 1949-51; indsl. advisor EDA, San Juan, P.R., 1955-56; asst. to rep. in Burma, Ford Found., 1956-57; econ. advisor to Govt. W. Pakistan, Harvard Adv. Group, Lahore, 1958-61, to; Pakistan Planning Commn., Karachi, 1961-63; dep. dir. AID mission to Bolivia, La Paz, 1963-65, Central Am. affairs Dept. State, Washington, 1965-68; dir. Near East affairs AID, 1968-69; econ. adviser to planning dept. Govt. Colombia, Harvard U. Devel. Adv. Service, Bogota, 1969-71; asso. dir. Harvard U. Devel. Adv. Service, Harvard Inst. for Internat. Devel., Cambridge, Mass., 1974-80; exec. v.p. and treas. Warner-Eddison Assocs., Inc., Cambridge, 1980-84; assoc. dir. Ctr. Asian Devel. Studies, Boston U., 1984-85. Author papers, reports. Selectman Town of Lexington, Mass., 1984—, chmn. bd. of selectman, 1986-88, 90. Capt. CE, AUS, 1942-46. Overseas fellow Ford Found., 1953-54. Mem. ACLU, Am. Econ. Assn., Alpha Delta Phi. Episcopalian. Home: Lexington Mass. Died Jan. 22, 1993.

EDEL, (JOSEPH) LEON, biographer, educator; b. Pitts., Sept. 9, 1907; s. Simon and Fannie (Malamud) E.; m. Roberta Roberts, Dec. 2, 1950 (div. 1979); m. Marjorie P. Sinclair, May 30, 1980. MA, McGill U., 1928, LittD, 1963; D.és.L., U. Paris, 1932; DLitt, Union Coll., 1963; D.Litt., U. Sask., 1982; DLitt, Hawaii Loa Coll., 1988. Writer, journalist, 1932-43; vis. prof. N.Y. U., 1950-52, assoc. prof. English, 1953-54, prof. English, 1955-66, Henry James prof. English and Am. letters, 1966-73, emeritus, 1973; citizens prof. humanities U. Hawaii, 1971-78, emeritus, 1978-97; mem. faculty Harvard U., summer 1952, vis. prof., 1959-60; Centenary vis. prof. U. Toronto, 1967; Gauss seminar lectr. Princeton U., 1952-53; vis. prof. Ind. U., 1954-55, U. Hawaii, summer 1955, 69-70, Purdue U., 1970; Alexander lectr. U. Toronto, 1956; Westminster Abbey address Henry James Meml., 1976; vis. prof. Center Advanced Study, Wesleyan U., 1965; vis. fellow Humanities Rsch. Ctr., Canberra, Australia, 1976; Vernon prof. biography Dartmouth Coll., 1977; Bollingen Found. fellow, 1958-61. Author: Henry James: Les années dramatiques, 1932, The Prefaces of Henry James, 1932, James Joyce: The Last Journey, 1947, The Life of Henry James, 5 vols. (The Untried Years, 1953, The Conquest of London and The Middle Years, 1962, The Treacherous Years, 1969, The Master, 1972), Henry James, A Life, 1985; (with E.K. Brown) Willa Cather, A Critical Biography, 1953; The Psychological Novel, 1955, revised, 1959, Literary Biography, 1957; (with Dan H. Laurence) A Bibliography of Henry James, 1957, revised edit., 1985; Henry D. Thoreau, 1970, Henry James in The Abbey, The Address, 1976, Bloomsbury, A House of Lions, 1979, Stuff of Sleep and Dreams, Experiments in Literary Psychology, 1982, Writing Lives, Principia Biographica, 1984, Some Memories of Edith Wharton, 1993. Editor: (writings of Henry James) The Complete Plays, 1949, revised edit., 1990, Ghostly Tales (reissued as Tales of the Supernatural, 1970), rev. edit., 1990, Selected Fiction, 1954, Selected Letters, 1955, American Essays, 1956, revised edit., 1990, The Future of the Novel: Critical Papers, 1956; (with Gordon N. Ray) James and H.G. Wells, Letters, 1958; Complete Tales, 12 vols., 1962-64, HJ: Letters, 4 vols., 1974-84; (with Mark Wilson) Complete Criticism, 2 vols., 1984; (with Lyall H. Powers) The Complete Notebooks, 1987; Henry James Reader, 1965, Selected Letters, 1987. Editor (other authors) Edmund Wilson Papers, 4 vols., 1972-86, Literary History and Literary Criticism, 1965, The Diary of Alice James, 1964. Mem. adv. com. edn. Met. Mus. Centenary, 1969-70; mem. ednl. adv. com. Guggenheim Found., 1967-80. Served as 1st lt. AUS, World War II, 1945; dir. Press Agy. 1945-46, U.S. zone Germany. Decorated Bronze Star; recipient Pulitzer prize in biography, 1963; Nat. Book award for non-fiction, 1963; Nat. Book Critics Circle award for biography, 1985; medal of lit. Nat. Arts Club, 1981; Nat. Inst. Arts and Letters grantee, 1959; elected to Am. Acad. Arts and Letters, 1972; Gold medal for biography Acad.-Inst., 1976; Hawaii Writers award, 1977; Guggenheim fellow, 1936-38, 65-66; Nat. Endowment for Humanities grantee, 1974-77. Fellow Am. Acad. Arts and Scis., Royal Soc. Lit. (Eng.); mem. Nat. Inst. Arts and Letters (sec. 1965-67), W.A. White Psychoanalytic Soc. (hon.), Am. Acad. Psychoanalysis (hon.), Soc. Authors (Eng.), Authors Guild (mem. council, pres. 1969-71), P.E.N. (pres. Am. Center 1957-59), Hawaii Lit. Arts Council (pres. 1978-79), Century Club (N.Y.C.). Home: Honolulu Hawaii Died Sept. 5, 1997.

EDELMAN, HERBERT, actor; b. Bklyn., Nov. 5, 1933; s. Mayer and Jennie (Greenberg) E.; m. Louise Sorel, Dec. 1964 (div.); m. Merrilyn Crosgrove; children: Briana, Jack. Student, Bklyn. Coll., Cornell U. Appeared in (plays) Barefoot in the Park, 1963, Bajour, 1965, Luv, 1967-68, Chapter Two, 1979-80, (films) In Like Flint, 1966, Barefoot in the Park, 1967, The Odd Couple, 1968, I Love You Alice B. Toklas, 1968, The War Between Men and Women, 1972, The Way We Were, 1973, The Front Page, 1974, The Yakuza, 1975, California Suite, 1980, Tora's Dream of Spring, (TV shows) East Side West Side, 1964, The Good Guys, 1968-70, Ladies Man, Strike Force, 1981-82, 9 to 5, 1983-84, Steambath. Served as cpl. U.S. Army. DIED 07/21/96. .

EDWARD, GEORGE See ARCARO, EDDIE

EDWARDS, JOHN HAMILTON, language professional; b. San Francisco, Oct. 16, 1922; s. Henry William and Hilda (Chew) E.; m. Dixie Swaren, July 14, 1947; children—Gregory William, John Steven, Mark Hamilton. B.A., U. Calif. at Berkeley, 1947, Ph.D., 1952; M.A., Columbia, 1948. Instr. English U. Calif. at Berkeley, 1952-54, asst. prof., 1954-59, asst. to v.p., 1959-60; mem. faculty San Francisco State U., 1960—, prof., 1964—, exec. v.p., 1970-72; lectr. ednl. TV KRON-TV, San Francisco, 1962-67. Author: Annotated Index to the Cantos of Ezra Pound, 1957, 71; Editor: The Pound Newsletter, 1954-56. Trustee Lone Mountain Coll., San Francisco, 1968-72; bd. dirs. Am. Civil Liberties Union, No. Calif., 1966-72. Served with OSS AUS, 1944-46. Recipient James D. Phelan award for arts, 1954, Am. Philos. Soc. research awards, 1954, 55. Mem. Modern Lang. Assn., Philol. Assn. Pacific Coast. Home: San Francisco Calif. Died Dec. 24, 1994.

EDWARDS, JOSHUA LEROY, physician, educator; b. Jasper, Fla., Aug. 9, 1918; s. Harry L. and Julia B. (Miller) E.; m. Jeane Perrin, July 7, 1953; children—Julia E., Jean A., Joshua Leroy III. B.S., U. Fla., 1939; M.D., Tulane U., 1943. Diplomate: Am. Bd. Pathology. Intern Bapt. Hosp., New Orleans, 1943-44; practice medicine Lake City, Fla., 1946-48; resident pathology Touro Infirmary, New Orleans, 1948-49; asst. resident lab. pathology N.E. Deaconess Hosp., Boston,

1949-50; chief resident pathology N.E. Deaconess Hosp., 1950-51; teaching fellow pathology Harvard Med. Sch., 1950-51; instr. pathology Duke Sch. Medicine, 1951-52, assoc. pathology, 1951-52; asst. pathology and microbiology; Rockefeller Inst. Med. Research, 1953-55; prof. pathology, chmn. dept. U. Fla. Coll. Medicine, 1955-67; prof. pathology, dir. combined degree program in med. scis. Ind. U., Bloomington, 1967-69; prof., chmn. dept. pathology Ind. U. Med. Center, Indpls., 1969-85, prof. emeritus, 1985-91. Contbr. articles to profl. jours. Served with M.C. AUS, 1944-46. Fellow Coll. Am. Pathologists; mem. Internat. Acad. Pathology, AAAS, N.Y., Fla., Ind. acads. sci., Am. Assn. Pathology, Tissue Culture Assn., Reticuloendothelial Soc., Am., Fla., Ind. med. assns., Am. Soc. Clin. Pathologists, Am. Soc. Cell Biology, Phi Beta Kappa, Sigma Xi, Alpha Omega Alpha. Home: Indianapolis Ind. Died Jan. 14, 1991; buried Crown Hill Cemetery, Indianapolis, IN.

EDWARDS, THOMAS HENRY, JR., construction company executive; b. Montgomery, Ala., Feb. 16, 1918; s. Thomas Henry and Florence Virginia (Cameron) E.; m. Marilyn Rae Myers, Nov. 18, 1943; children: Thomas Henry III, Mary Lynn Edwards Angell. BS in Civil Engring., Auburn U., 1939; postgrad. U. Mich., 1940-41. Registered profl. engr. and land surveyor, Ala. San. engr. W.K. Kellogg Found., Battle Creek, Mich., 1939-40; estimator Algernon Blair Constrn. Co., Montgomery, 1946-47; engr. Tenn. Coal and Iron div. U.S. Steel Corp., Birmingham, Ala., 1947-53; project mgr. Sullivan, Long, Hagerty, Birmingham, 1953-73, v.p., 1973-83. Served with U.S. Army, 1942-45. Mem. Sigma Nu. Republican. Methodist. Lodge: Lions. Died April 12, 1997. Home: Birmingham Ala.

EFRON, SAMUEL, lawyer; b. Lansford, Pa., May 6, 1915; s. Abraham and Rose (Kaduchin) E.; m. Hope Bachrach Newman, Apr. 5, 1941; children: Marc Fred, Eric Michael. B.A., Lehigh U., 1935; LL.B., Harvard U., 1938. Bar: Pa. 1938, D.C. 1949, N.Y. 1967. Atty. forms and regulations div., also registration div. SEC, 1939-40; Office Solicitor Dept. Labor, 1940-42; asst. chief real and personal property sect. Office Alien Property Custodian, 1942-43; chief debt claims sect., also asst. chief claims br. Office Alien Property, Dept. Justice, 1946-51; asst. gen. counsel internat. affairs Dept. Def., 1951-53, cons., 1953-54; partner firm Surrey, Karasik, Gould & Efron, Washington, 1954-61; exec. v.p. Parsons & Whittemore, Inc., N.Y.C., 1961-68; now partner Arent Fox Kintner Plotkin & Kahn, Washington.; dir. UN Assn., nat. chpt. area; mem. internat. rels. vis. com. Lehigh U.; adv. bd. Ctr. for biomedical ethics U. Va.; vis. com. Harvard Sch. of pub. health. Author: Creditors Claims Under the Trading with the Enemy Act, 1948, Foreign Taxes on United States Expenditures, 1954, Offshore Procurement and Industrial Mobilization, 1955, The Operation of Investment Incentive Laws with Emphasis on the U.S.A. and Mexico, 1977. Mem. Com. to Visit Sch. of Pub. Health, Harvard U.; bd. dirs. Ctr. for Biomed. Ethics, U. Va. Lt. USNR, 1943-46. Decorated 1st class comdr. Order of Lion (Finland). Mem. Am., Fed., Inter-Am. bar assns., Am. Soc. Internat. Law, Assn. Bar City N.Y., Bar Assn. D.C., UN Assn. (bd. dirs. nat. capitol area), Phi Beta Kappa. Clubs: Army-Navy (Washington), Cosmos (Washington), Fed. Bar (Washington); Harvard (N.Y.C.), Lotos (N.Y.C.), Univ. (Washington). Died Jan. 4, 1997.

EGGERS, IDAMARIE RASMUSSEN, pharmaceutical manufacturing and research; b. Grand Rapids, Mich., Oct. 19, 1925; d. Nels Peter Victor and Karen Agnes (Feldt) Rasmussen; m. Raymond Frederick Eggers Jr., May 29, 1955; children: Kären Elizabeth Eggers Baird, Raymond Frederick III. BS in Chemistry, U. Mich., 1945, MS, 1946. Chemist Merck & Co. Inc., Rahway, N.J., 1946-57, chem. biol. data coord., 1965-69, sect. head biol. data, 1969-77, mgr. biol. data, 1977-86; agt., broker Ray Eggers Agy., Rahway, 1958-93. Patentee in field. Libr. Rahway Hist. Soc., 1969-75. Scholar Grand Rapids Woman's Club, 1942, U. Mich. Regents, 1944-46. Mem. AAAS, Am. Chem. Soc., Metro Women Chemists, N.Y. Acad. Sci., Rahway C. of C., Rahway Woman's Club (pres. 1988-89, co-pres. 1992-93), N.J. State Fedn. Women's Clubs (6th dist. v.p. 1990-92, 6th dist. internat. rels. chmn. 1992-93). Episcopalian. Avocations: dancing, designing and sewing clothing, genealogy, historic preservation. Died Apr. 3, 1993.

EGGERTSEN, CLAUDE ANDREW, education educator; b. Thistle, Utah, Feb. 25, 1909; s. Claude E. and Helen El Deva (Blackett) E.; m. Nita Wakefield, June 3, 1931 (dec. Oct. 1993); children: Sheary Jill (Mrs. Virgil F. Fairbanks), Claude Wakefield, John Hale. A.B., Brigham Young U., 1930, M.A., 1933; postgrad., Stanford U., 1931; Ph.D., U. Minn., 1939. Tchr. Carbon County (Utah) Sch. Dist., 1931-34; mem. faculty U. Minn., 1934-39, instr. edn., 1935-39; mem. faculty U. Mich., Ann Arbor, 1939-79; prof. edn. U. Mich., 1953-79, emeritus prof. edn., 1979-95, dir. program comparative edn., 1959-79, dir. internat. edn. projects, 1966-79, chmn. social founds., 1952-62, 68-75; Gerald H. Read prof. comparative and internat. edn. Kent (Ohio) State U., 1980-82; vis. faculty mem. Brigham Young U., 1935, U. Colo., 1937, Ohio State U., 1948, San Jose Coll., 1955, UCLA, 1951; hon. vis. prof. U. Sheffield, Eng., 1958, 62; vis. prof. edn., India, 1962, 64; vis. prof. Utah State U.; vis. scholar U. Kyoto, Japan; lectr. comparative edn. U. Hiroshima, U. Kyushu, both Japan, Chinese U. of Hong Kong, summer 1980. Contbr. articles to jours., chpts. to books.; Editor: Studies in the History of Higher Education in Michigan, 1950, Studies in the History of the School of Education, The University of Michigan, 1955, History of Education Jour, 1950-60, Notes and Abstracts in American and International Education, 1962-95. Chmn. bd. trustees Inter-Univ. Internat. Tchr. Edn. Council.; mem. planning com. Ann Arbor Council Chs., 1979-81, chmn., 1982-83. Served to lt. (s.g.) USNR, 1944-46. Decorated Bronze Star medal; recipient Disting. Faculty Gov. award U. Mich, 1992. Fellow Philosophy Edn. Soc., John Dewey Soc.; charter fellow Coll. of Preceptors (London); mem. Nat. Soc. Coll. Tchrs. (sec. 1948-60, co-chmn. history edn. sect. 1948-50), Comparative Edn. Soc. (exec. com. 1959-61, pres. 1963-64, hon. fellow 1986), History Edn. Soc., Am. Ednl. Research Assn., Assn. Ecumenical Edn. (bd. dirs.), UN Assn. of U.S.A. (pres. Mich. div. 1966-70), Phi Delta Kappa, Phi Kappa Phi, Tau Kappa Alpha, Theta Alpha Phi. Clubs: Men's Thursday Luncheon (program chmn.), Nat. Liberal (London). Home: Ann Arbor Mich. Died Feb., 1995.

EHRENSBERGER, RAY, university chancellor; b. Indpls., Dec. 7, 1904; s. Edward H. and Elizabeth (M. Peetz) E.; m. Helen L. Myers, Sept. 21, 1939; children: Betty Ann, Ray. A.B., Wabash Coll., 1929; A.M., Butler U., 1930; fellow, Syracuse U., 1935-36, Ph.D., 1937; grad. student, Ind. U., U. Wis.; LL.D. (hon.), Wabash Coll., 1966, U. Md., 1988. Instr. speech Doane Coll., 1930-32; head speech dept. Franklin Coll., 1932-35; asso. prof. speech U. Md., 1936-39, prof., chmn. dept. speech and dramatic art, 1939-52; dir. U. Md. (European program), Heidelberg, Germany, 1949-50; dean U. Md. (Coll. Spl. and Continuation Studies), 1952-59; dean U. Md. (Univ. Coll.), 1959-70, chancellor, 1970-75, chancellor emeritus, 1975—; dir. Bi-nat. Center, Dept. of State, Ankara, Turkey, 1951-52. Author: (with Elaine Pagel) A Notebook for Public Speaking, 1946. Recipient Exceptional Service award U.S. Air Force, Distinguished Civilian Service medal Dept. Def., Distinguished Pub. Service medal U.S. Army. Mem. Speech Assn. Am., Phi Delta Kappa, Phi Kappa Phi, Sigma Chi, Omicron Delta Kappa, Delta Sigma Rho, Tau Kappa Alpha, Blue Key. Episcopalian. Died Feb. 14, 1997.

EHRLICH, ARNOLD W., magazine editor, writer; b. Phila.; m. Michele Doolan, June 11, 1964; children: Christopher, Elizabeth, Michael. Diploma, Girard Coll., 1940; BA, Johns Hopkins U., 1947. Assoc. editor mag. Tomorrow, N.Y.C., 1949-51; sr. editor mag. Holiday, Phila., 1956-63, mng. editor, 1968-71; sr. editor mag. Show, N.Y.C., 1963-64, Venture, N.Y.C., 1964-67; editor in chief Pubs. Weekly, N.Y.C., 1971-77; sr. editor Atlantic Monthly Press, Boston, 1977-80, Arbor House, N.Y.C., 1981-84; dep. editor mag. Town & Country, N.Y.C., 1984-89. Author: The Beautiful County, 1966; contbr. numerous articles to popular jours. With inf. U.S. Army, 1944, ETO. Decorated Purple Heart. Home: New York N.Y. Died Oct. 3, 1989.

EICHORN, JOHN FREDERICK GERARD, JR., utility executive; b. Boston, Mar. 3, 1924; s. John Frederick Gerard and Hazel (Morris) E. B.S. in Mech. Engring, U. Maine, 1949; postgrad., Northeastern U., 1963-64. Registered profl. engr., Mass. With New Eng. Elec. System, various locations, 1949-71; v.p., regional exec. Mass. Electric div. New Eng. Electric System, North Andover, Mass., 1968-71; exec. v.p. Eastern Utilities Assos., Boston, 1971-72; pres., chief exec. officer Eastern Utilities Assos., 1972-90, chief exec. officer, 1985-89, also trustee; pres. Montaup Electric Co., Somerset, Mass., 1972-85, chmn., 1986-89; pres. EUA Svc. Corp., Boston, 1972-86, chmn., 1986-89, Blackstone Valley Electric Co., Lincoln, R.I., 1975-89, Eastern Edison Co., Mass., 1973-89; pres. EUA Power Corp., Concord, N.H., 1986-87, chmn. 1987-89, EUA Cogenex Corp., Andover, Mass., 1987-89; dir. Conn. Yankee Atomic Power Co., Haddem Neck, Conn., Maine Yankee Atomic Power Co., Wiscasett, Vt. Yankee Nuclear Power Corp., Vernon. Served with AUS, 1942-45. Home: Boston Mass. Died Aug. 19, 1997.

EICKHOFF, HAROLD WALTER, college president, humanities educator; b. Natoma, Kans., Apr. 2, 1928; s. William and Emma (John) E.; m. Rosa Lee Smith, Aug. 19, 1955; children: Sharon Lee, Janet Lee. BA in History, U. Kansas City, 1957, MA in History and Govt., 1958; PhD in History, U. Mo., 1964. Asst. prof. history U. Mo., St. Louis, 1961-64, assoc. prof., dean studies, 1964-69; prof. history, exec. asst. to pres., sec. to bd. visitors Old Dominion U., Norfolk, Va., 1969-74, exec. v.p., 1974-76; prof. history, acad. v.p. Ft. Hays (Kans.) State U., 1976-79; prof. humanities, pres. The Coll. of N.J., 1980—; mem. com. on undergrad. edn. Edn. Commn. States, 1985-87. Mem. bd. overseers Gov.'s Sch., Trenton, 1986—; bd. dirs. Mercer Med. Ctr., Trenton, 1980-97, Mercer County C. of C., Trenton, 1980—; trustee Pennington Sch., 1981-93. With USN, 1948-52, Korea. Recipient Svc. Above Self award Norfolk Rotary Club, 1976, Gov.'s Albert Einstein award for svc. to edn., 1988, N.J. Pride award State of N.J., 1991, Bus. Hall of Fame award for svc. in higher edn. Jr. Achievement, 1992, Citizen of Yr. award Mercer County C. of C., 1993. Mem. Am. Coun. on Edn. (sec. 1986-88), N.J. Governing Bds. Assn., Assn. Am. Colls. Univs. (bd. dirs.). Presbyterian. Avocations: gardening, jogging. Died June 23, 1996.

EISENBUD, MERRIL, engineer, scientist; b. N.Y.C., Mar. 18, 1915; s. Kalman and Leonora (Kopaloff) E.; m. Irma Onish, Jan. 22, 1939; children: Elliott, Michael, Fredrick. BSEE, NYU, 1936; ScD (hon.), Fairleigh Dickinson U., 1960; DHC, Cath. U., Rio de Janiero. Indsl. hygienist Liberty Mut. Ins. Co., 1936-47; faculty Inst. Environ. Medicine, NYU Med. Ctr., 1947-85, prof., dir. lab. environ. studies, 1959-84, prof. emeritus, 1984-97; adj. prof. dept. environ. scis. and engring. U. N.C., 1985-97; adminstr. N.Y.C. EPA, 1968-70; scholar-in-residence Duke U. Med. ctr., Durham, N.C., 1985-97; dir. health safety lab. AEC, 1947-59; mem. Nat. Coun. Radiation Protection and Measurements, 1965-85, dir., 1971-76, hon. mem., 1985-97; mem. expert panel on radiation hazards WHO, 1956-80, N.Y. State Health Adv. Coun., 1975-80. Author: Environment, Technology, and Health, 1979, Environmental Radioactivity, 4th edit., 1987, Environmental Odyssey, 1990. Mem. bd. mgrs. State Cmty. Aid Assn.; mem. adv. coun. Electric Power Rsch. Inst., Inst. Nuclear Power Ops. Recipient Gold medal AEC, 1974, Hermann Biggs medal N.Y. State Pub. Health Assn., Arthur Holly Compton award Am. Nuclear Soc., Power Division Life award Am. Inst. Elec. and Electronic Engrs., Disting. Achievement award Hudson River Environ. Soc., 1985. Fellow AAAS, Health Physics Soc. (pres. 1965-66, Disting. Achievement award 1984), N.Y. Acad. Scis. (hon. life mem., gov., v.p. 1979-80), N.Y. Acad. Medicine; mem. Nat. Acad. Engring., Am. Indsl. Hygiene Assn., Radiation Research Soc., Am. Bd. Health Physics, Brazilian Acad. Scis. (corr.). Club: Cosmos (Washington). Died Aug. 15, 1997.

EISENSTAEDT, ALFRED, photojournalist; b. Dirschau, Germany, Dec. 6, 1898; came to U.S., 1935; s. Joseph and Regina (Schoen) E.; m. Alma Kathy Kaye, 1949. Grad., Hohenzollern Gymnasium, Berlin. Spl. photo reporter Pacific and Atlantic Photos, Berlin office, 1929-35; (this firm taken over with unchanged activities by A.P., 1931); staff photographer Life mag., 1936-95. Author: Witness to Our Time, 1966, The Eye of Eisenstaedt, 1968, Martha's Vineyard, 1970, Witness to Nature, Wimbledon: A Celebration, People, Eisenstaedt's Album, Eisenstaedt's Guide to Photography, 1978, Eisenstaedt-Germany, 1980, Eisenstaedt-Aberdeen, 1984, Eisenstaedt on Eisenstaedt, 1985, Eisenstaedt-Martha's Vineyard, 1988, Eisenstaedt: Remembrances, 1990. Named Photographer of Year Ency. Brit. and; U. Mo., 1951; recipient Culture prize in photography German Soc. for Photography, Cologne, 1962, achievement award Photog. Soc. Am., Lifetime Achievement in Photography award Am. Soc. Mag. Photographers, 1978, Master Photography award Internat. Ctr. Photography, 1988, Arts and Culture Honor award Mayor of N.Y.C., 1988, Nat. Medal of Arts, 1990. Work has covered outstanding events and persons throughout the world. A pioneer in introduction of candid camera technique into news reporting. Home: New York N.Y. Died Aug. 23, 1995.

EJBYE-ERNST, ARNE, journalist; b. Aarhus, Denmark, Dec. 16, 1927; s. Niels and Agnete (Stechhahn) Ejbye-E.; m. Birgit Møller, Jan. 10, 1951; 2 sons. Journalist Danish Labour Press, 1949-56; editor Ny Tid, Aalborg, 1956-59; editor-in-chief Aktuelt, Copenhagen, 1959-64; editor-in-chief Politiken, Copenhagen, 1966-71, editor pub.'s mag., 1972—; lectr., leader Danish Sch. Journalism, 1964-66, dean, 1974-81. Mng. dir., editor-in-chief Ritzaus bur. Nat. Danish News Agy., Copenhagen, 1981—; adviser Danish Newspaper Assn., 1964-66; chmn. Copenhagen Editors Soc., 1962-64, 67-69; author: Mass Communications as Business, 1973; Study of Local Monopoly Press, 1975.

EKANDEM, DOMINIC IGNATIUS CARDINAL, archbishop; b. Obio Ibiono, Nigeria, 1917; s. Paul Ino Ekandem Ubo and Nwa Ibong Umana; D.D., St. Paul's Major Sem., Enugu, 1941, Okpala, 1947; L.L.D., Loyola U., Chgo., 1989; DLitt (hon.), U. Calabar, 1990. Ordained priest Roman Cath. Ch., 1947; priest in Nigeria, 1947-54; consecrated bishop, 1954; bishop of Ikot Ekpene, Akwa Ibom State, 1963-89; chmn. Dept. Social Welfare, Cath. Secretariat of Nigeria, 1970; apostolic adminstr. of Port Harcourt, 1970-73; pres. Episcopal Conf. Nigeria, 1973-79; elevated to Sacred Coll. Cardinals, 1976; cardinal of St. Marcellus, 1976—; archbishop, 1st bishop of Abuja, 1989—; mem. Symposium of Episcopal Conf. of Africa and Madagascar; founding mem. St. Paul's Nat. Missionary Sem., Gwagwalada, Abuja. Decorated Order Brit. Empire; comdr. Order Niger, Order Fed. Republic of Nigeria; named Mission Superior of Abuja, 1981—; recipient 5 chieftancy titles in Nigeria. Mem. Assn. Episcopal Confs. of Anglophone West Africa (pres. 1977), Congregation for the Evang. of Peoples, Pioneer Total Abstinance Assn. Author: Shepherd Among Shepherds, 1979; also articles. 1st black African bishop in West Africa. Died, Nov., 1995.

EKSTRAND, BRUCE ROWLAND, university administrator, psychology educator; b. Chgo., Apr. 30, 1940; s. Rowland Magnus and Helen (Blakeslee) E.; m. Norma Ann Zupansic, June 23, 1962; children—Bradley Cameron, Andrea Helen. B.A., Northwestern U., 1962,

M.A., 1964, Ph.D., 1966. From asst. prof. to assoc. prof. psychology U. Colo., Boulder, 1966-72, prof. psychology, 1972—, chmn. dept. psychology, 1975-80, assoc. vice chancellor for acad. affairs, 1980-82, assoc. vice chancellor for research, dean grad. sch., 1982-83, vice chancellor for research, dean grad. sch., 1984-86, vice chancellor for acad. affairs, dean of faculties, 1986—; mem. Psychol. Scis. Rev. Panel, NIMH, 1978-84. Co-author: The Psychology of Thinking, 1971, Psychology: Its Principles and Meanings, 5th edit., 1985; cons. editor Jour. Exptl. Psychology, Washington, 1970-74. Bd. dirs. Mental Health Ctr. Boulder County, 1977-83, Boulder Community Hosp., 1987-90, Consortium for Sci. Computing, 1983-90, Council Grad. Schs., 1985-86, Ctr. for Rsch. Librs., 1992—, Boulder County United Way, 1994—, Boulder Cmty. Hosp. Found., 1995—; mem. exec. com. Assn. Grad. Schs., 1985-86. Grantee NIMH, 1968-75, NSF, 1973-78. Fellow Am. Psychol. Assn., AAAS; mem. Nat. Council Univ. Research Adminstrs., Am. Psychol. Soc., Rotary (bd. dirs. 1980-81, pres. 1992-93), Sigma Xi. Democrat. Roman Catholic. Avocations: skiing; swimming; tennis; golf. Deceased.

EKSTROM, ROBERT CARL, musician, music educator, choral director, singer; b. Duluth, Minn., Mar. 26, 1917; s. Hans Birger and Hilda Sophia (Nelson) E.; m. Charlotte Virginia Tuttle, Dec. 28, 1940; children: Robert, Virginia, Carol, Richard, Lorrie, Cheryl. Diploma, Duluth Jr. Coll., 1937; BS in Music Edn., U. Minn., 1940, MEd in Music Edn., 1946; EdD in Music Edn., U. So. Calif., 1959. Cert. tchr., Minn., Calif., Ill. Head vocal dept. Sherburn (Minn.) Bd. Edn., 1940-41; instr. music Duluth Pub. Schs., 1941-52, 54-64; prof. music Pasadena (Calif.) City Coll., 1952-54; head music dept. Lindblom Tech. High Sch., Chgo., 1964-95; dir. and soloist Chgo. Choral Soc., 1970-95; mem., oratorio dir. Chgo. Swedish Choral and Symphony Orch., 1964-74; mem., dir. Am. Union Swedish Singers, 1958-95; choir dir. and soloist various chs. Minn., Calif., Ill., 1941-95; music dir. Calif. Bur. Music, Los Angeles, 1951-59, Mayor's Cultural Com., Chgo., 1972-79, State St. Council, Chgo., 1975-79, various musical groups, 1949-95; tenor soloist and singer radio, television, stage, others; recorded with Capitol Records; soloist Great Lakes Bluejacket Choir, 1945-46; as soloist with USN Choir appeared in film Meet Your Navy, 1945; sang at coronation festivities Coronation of Queen Elizabeth II, London, 1953, Luth. World Fedn. Conv., Helsinki, 1963; gave command performance for King of Sweden, Stockholm, 1976; performed in six concert tours of Europe in many countries including Eng., Scotland, France, Germany, Holland, Sweden. Norway, Denmark, Finland, Austria, Italy, Switzerland, Greece, Spain, 1953, 63, 68, 73, 76, 80; sang with choir in more than sixty engagements, Europe, 1963; dir. choir in movie in Athens, 1973; performed in musicals, on radio, on TV, in motion pictures and in numerous personal appearances worldwide. Author: The Male Voice, 1945, Correlation of Music Talent With Intelligence, 1946, Development of the Madrigal, 1947, Comparison of the Male Voice, 1959, Boys Life in Minnesota, 1986. Recipient Singers medal of Merit, Am. Union Swedish Singers, 1974. Mem. Am. Choral Dirs. Assn., Music Educators Nat. Conf., Associated Male Choruses Am. (dir. upper midwest dist., pres. 1949-52). Club: Ill. Athletic (Chgo.). Lodge: Masons (music dir. 1969-95, Meritorious Service award 1980). Home: Chicago Ill. Died July 29, 1995.

EL-AZGHAL, HUSSEIN IBRAHIM, obstetrician, gynecologist; b. Alexandria, Egypt, Sept. 28, 1933; s. Ibrahim El-Azghal Easa and Nefisa Mohammad Mahmoud; m. Aziza Hussein, Feb. 21, 1961; children: Eathar, Ebaa, Amany, Ahmad, Mohammad (dec.). M.B.Ch.B., Ainsham U., 1957, Diploma in Ob-gyn., 1958, Diploma in Gen. Surgery, 1961. House physician/surgeon Ainshan U. Hosp., Cairo, 1957-58, resident dept. ob-gyn., 1958-60, clin. demonstrator in ob-gyn., 1962-64, lectr. in ob-gyn., 1964-72, asst. prof., 1972-78; specialist in ob-gyn. Ministry of Pub. Health, 1960-62; cons. ob-gyn. Riyadh, Saudi Arabia, 1978-97. Contbr. articles to profl. jours. Recipient Gold Medal, Ainshan Faculty Medicine, 1957, Award of Hygiene, 1957. Fellow Royal Coll. Surgeons of Edinburgh, Royal Coll. Obstetrics and Gynecologists London; mem. Royal Coll. Physicians London, Brit. Microsurg. Soc., Fallopius Internat. Soc., Mid. East Fertility Soc., N.Y. Acad. Scis. Avocations: agriculture, horticulture, travel.

EL-BISI, HAMED MOHAMED, scientist; b. Elbagour, Menoufia, Egypt, Mar. 29, 1926; came to U.S., 1950; s. Mohamed Hasan and Ammuna Sultan (Waley) El-Bisi; m. Elizabeth Leigh, Nov. 29, 1952; children: Leila, Kemal, Karim, Tarek, Nadia, Jehann; m. Penelope Ann Baker, Oct. 9, 1992. BSc with honors, U. Ein Shams, Cairo, 1947; MSc, U. Ill., 1951, PhD, 1955. Lectr. U. Ein-Shams, 1955-56; rsch. assoc. U. Ill., Urbana, 1956-58; prof. U. Mass., Amherst, 1958-63; chief microbiology divsn. U.S. Army Natick (Mass.) R & D Ctr., 1963-69; chief rsch. U.S. Army Materiel Command, Alexandria, Va., 1969-75; dep. and acting tech. dir. U.S. Army Natick (Mass.), R & D Ctr., 1975-81, dir sci. and advanced tech. lab., 1981-85; dir. rsch. and lab. mgmt. Office of Asst. Sec. of Army for Rsch., Devel. & Acquisition, Washington, 1985-89; chief scientist Army Rsch. Lab., Watertown, Mass., 1989-97; sci. advisor Mil. Assistance Command, Vietnam, 1968; cons. FDA, Washington, 1971-72, NASA, Washington, 1962-67, NAS, Washington, 1962-63, also several major industrial corps. Chmn. community and regional campaigns, United Fund, 1980-85; bd. govs. Inter-Am. Inst. Advanced Sci., Titusville, Fla., 1983-87; selectman Town of Millis, Mass., 1985; pres. bd. dirs. Shadowalk Home Owners Assn., Fairfax Station, Va., 1986-89; trustee, Bishops Forest Condominium, Waltham, Mass., 1990-95; alumnus Def. UCLA Sci. Seminar; JFK School of Govt., Harvard U. Alumni Counsel; People-to People Internat. Citizen Amb. Program (mem of biosci. & biotech. del. to China, 1990, chmn. of bus. del. to Cairo, Riyadh, & Instanbul, 1993, chmn. of biosci. & biotech. del. to England, Switzerland, & France, 1995). Fellow Sigma Xi, Phi Tau Sigma; mem. AAAS, Am. Acad. Microbiology, Am. Soc. Microbiology, Am. Planetary Soc., Am. Inst. Biol. Scis., Inst. Food Technologists, Soc. Indsl. Microbiology, Sci. Rsch. Soc. Am., Wash. Acad. Sci. Home: Framingham Mass. Died March 9, 1997.

ELIAS, ROBERT GERALD, educational administrator, educator; b. Plains, Pa., Sept. 15, 1934; s. Joseph Michael and Clementine Anne (Dominick) E.; m. Miriam Jeanne Dearden, Sept. 16, 1955; children: Robert David, Amy Jeanne Elias-Barnes. BS in Bus. Edn., Wilkes U., 1956, HLD, 1993; advanced cert. in data processing, N.C. State U., 1965; cert. in data processing, U. Pitts., 1966; MS in Edn., Temple U., 1971. Cert. tchr., supr., adminstr., Pa. Tchr. English lit. and acctg. Shickshinny (Pa.) Sch. Dist., 1955-56, N.W. Joint Sch. Dist., Schickshinny, 1956-63; tchr. acctg. and data processing Wilkes-Barre (Pa.) Area Sch. Dist., 1963-66, supr. data processing, 1966-72; supr. data processing Wilkes-Barre Area Vocat. Tech. Sch., 1972-78, adminstr., 1978—; adj. instr. vocat. edn. Temple U., Phila., 1985—, cons., 1979-80; mem. gen. tech. adv. com. Luzerne County C.C., 1978—; mem. gen. adv. com. Luzerne County Human Resources Devel. Dept., 1978—; mem. Employers' Adv. Coun. N.E., Pa., 1978—; conf. presenter in field; advisor to chief adminstrs. Crestwood, Greater Nanticoke, Hanover, Pittston, Wilkes-Barre area dists., 1978—; sec. profl. adv. coun. Supts. for Vocat. Edn., 1978—. Trustee, chmn. capital improvement fund, mem. adminstrv. bd., mem. pastor-parish rels. com., mem. coun. ministries, Sunday sch. tchr. United Meth. Ch.; mem. adv. com. Greater Wilkes-Barre Area Partnership, Inc.; active Pvt. Industry Coun. Luzerne County, 1982—, Econ. Devel. Coun. Northeastern Pa., 1987—; mem. employer adv. coun. Pa. Job Svc., 1978—; speaker to various civic and community orgns. Recipient cert. of achievement Distributive Edn. Clubs Am., 1979, hon. farmer degree Future Farmers Am., 1980, appreciation recognition DAV Aux., 1980, VA, 1980, Pa. Adv. Coun. for Vocat. Edn., 1983, outstanding svc. award Temple U., 1979, 82. Mem. ASCD, Am. Assn. Sch. Adminstrs., Pa. Assn. Sch. Adminstrs., Coun. Coll. Pres. and Supts., Pa. Sch. Bds. Assn., Nat. Coun. Local Adminstrs., Nat. Assn. Secondary Sch. Prins., Pa. Assn. Secondary Sch. Prins., Coun. Orgns. for Edn., Vocat. Adminstrs. Pa., Am. Vocat. Assn., Pa. Vocat. Assn. Avocations: microcomputer activities, reading, home workshop, church committees.

ELIASSEN, ROLF, environmental engineer, emeritus educator; b. Bklyn., Feb. 22, 1911; s. Olaf and Effie (Albrethsen) E.; m. Mary F. Hulick, Dec. 12, 1941; children: Thomas R., James H. BS, MIT, 1932, MS, 1933, ScD, 1935. Design engr. J.N. Chester Engrs., Pitts., 1935-36; san. engr. Dorr Co., Inc., Chgo., Los Angeles, 1936-39; asst. prof. civil engring. Ill. Inst. Tech., 1939-40; assoc. prof. san. engring. NYU, N.Y.C., 1940-42, prof., 1946-49; design engr. Parsons, Klapp, Brinckerhoff & Douglas, N.Y.C., 1941; chmn. civil engring. dept. Biarritz Am. U., France, 1945; prof. san. engring., dir. Sedgwick Labs San. Sci. MIT, Cambridge, cons. engr., 1949-60, acting head dept. civil engring., 1960-61; prof. civil engring. Stanford U., 1961-73, now Silas H. Palmer prof. civil engring. emeritus; ptnr. Metcalf & Eddy, Inc., Palo Alto, Calif., also Boston, 1961-73, chmn. bd. dirs., 1973-88, chmn. emeritus, 1988—; cons. IAEA, WHO, UN, Exec. Office Pres. of U.S., Calif. Dept. Water Resources, Fed. Power Commn., U.S. Senate Com. on Pub. Works; mem. gen. adv. com. AEC, 1970-75. Contbr. articles to tech. jours. Served to lt. col. C.E., AUS, 1942-46, ETO. Mem. Am. Acad. Arts and Sci., ASCE (hon.), Nat. Acad. Engring., Am. Water Works Assn., Sigma Xi, Tau Beta Pi. Congregationalist. DIED 03/14/97. .

ELIOT, ROBERT SALIM, physician; b. Oak Park, Ill., Mar. 8, 1929; s. Salim and Ruth (Buffington) Elia; m. Phyllis Allman, June 15, 1957; children: William Robert, Susan Elaine. Student, Northwestern U., 1947-48; B.S., U. N.Mex., 1952; M.D., U. Colo., 1955. Intern Northwestern U., Evanston, Ill., 1955-56; resident U. Colo., Denver, 1956-58, fellow cardiology, 1958-60; clin. prof. medicine/cardiology U. Nebr. Coll. Medicine, 1983-96; trainee cardiovascular pathology U. Minn., St. Paul-Mpls., 1962-63, instr., 1963-65, asst. prof., 1965-67; mem. faculty U. Fla., Gainesville, 1967-72, prof. medicine, 1969-72; chief div. cardiology VA Hosp., 1970-72; prof. medicine, dir. Cardiovascular Center U. Nebr. Med. Ctr., Omaha, 1972-81, dir. div. cardiology, 1972-80, chmn. dept. preventive and stress medicine, 1981-83; med. dir. Internat. Stress Found., 1977-96; dir. Nat. Ctr. Preventive and Stress Medicine, 1984-87, Cardiovascular Inst., Swedish Med. Ctr., Denver, 1987-89; cardiol. cons. Cape Kennedy, 1971-77; cons. Kellogg Found., 1978; chmn. Nat. Goals and Objectives for Stress Mgmt. for Surgeon Gen. U.S., 1980-96; dir. Inst. of Stress Medicine, Denver, 1989-90; chmn., dir. Inst. of Stress Medicine, Jackson Hole, Wyo., 1992-96; dir. preventive and rehab. cardiology Heart Lung Ctr., St. Luke's Hosp., Phoenix, 1984-87; cons., lectr. Nat. Def. U., 1985-96; adj. prof. Ariz. State U., nat. and internat. lectr. med. and sci. topics; pres. Alachua County Heart Div., 1969, 70; mem. adv. bd. stress and cardiovascular rsch. ctr. Eckerd Coll., St. Petersburg, Fla., 1980-83; chmn. Bethesda Conf. Com. on Prevention of Coronary Disease in the Occupational Setting, 1980-81; cons., lectr. in field to corps., pub. and profl. orgns. Author: Stress and the Major Cardiovascular Disorders, 1979, From Stress to Strength, How to Lighten Your Load and Save Your Life, 1994, (with D. Breo) Is It Worth Dying For?, 1984; editor: Cardiac Emergencies; mem. editl. bd. Heart and Lung; creator ednl. TV series Heartline to Health; contbr. articles to profl. jours. Served to capt. AUS, 1960-62. Recipient John P. McGovern medal Am. Med. Writer's Assn., 1985, Sci. and Art of Health award Inst. for Advancement of Health, 1989; grantee USPHS, Va, Fla. Heart Assn., Polk Family Charitable Fund, 1995, various pvt. sources. Fellow ACP, Clin. Council Am. Heart Assn., Am. Coll. Cardiology (mem. continuing edn. com., Mountain States coordinator for continuing edn., mem. long range planning com., mem. exec. com. gov. Nebr., vice chmn. bd. govs. 1976-77, chmn. bd. govs. 1977-78, trustee 1977-83, prevention com. 1987-91), N.Y. Acad. Scis.; mem. AMA, Ariz. Med. Assn., Colo. Med. Assn., Cen. Soc. Clin. Investigation, Biophys. Soc., Acad. Behavioral Medicine Research (charter), Soc. Behavioral Medicine (charter), Interstate Postgrad. Med. Assembly (pres. 1982), Alpha Omega Alpha, Phi Sigma, Phi Rho Sigma. Research on effects of changes in blood-oxygen transport and their role in producing or in treating heart disease, mechanisms causing heart attacks and sudden death, role of stress in heart disease. Home: Wilson Wyo. Died May 28, 1996.

ELISCU, FRANK, sculptor; b. N.Y.C., July 13, 1912; s. Charles Henry and Florence (Kane) E.; m. Mildred Norman, May 3, 1942; 1 child, Norma Eliscu Banas. Student, Beaux Arts Inst. Design, Pratt Inst., 1930-33. One-man shows include exhbn. sculpture, Mexico, 1955; works represented in Bookgreen Gardens, S.C., portrait busts, Aero. Hall of Fame, other works in Stevens Inst., Cornell Med. Sch., Olin Hall, N.Y., Heismann Meml. Trophy, Naiad; fountain figure, N.Y.C., Heroic; Atoms for Peace figure, Ventura, Calif., Headley Mus., (The Astronauts), Lexington, Ky., Steuben Glass Co., (Noach), St. Christopher's Chapel, N.Y.C., Soc. Medallists, (Sea Treasurer), "Once Upon a Time" bronze sculpture for Elmhurst Pub. Lib. Sculpture Garden, Adm. Alan Shephard bronze statue for Air Space Mus.; designer Presdl. Eagle for Oval Rm., The White House, also reverse side of ofcl. inaugural medal, 1974; other works include Chase of the Sea Urchin, Sarasota, Fla., 1980, Holocast, Orlando, Fla., 1981, Bronze Grille, James Madison, Libr. of Congress, Washington, 1981, Pieta, Cath. Ctr., Venice, Fla., CARING, The Mus. of Caring Inst., Washington; author: Direct Wax Sculpture. Recipient Edith S. Moore prize, 1948, Bennet prize Nat. Sculpture Soc., Henry Hering award, 1960, Caring award Caring Inst., Washington, Ellen Speyer prize for Noah's Ark, NAD. Fellow Sculpture Soc. (pres. 1967-70); mem. Archtl. League N.Y. (v.p. sculpture, silver medal 1958), Sculpture Ctr. N.Y. Home: Naples Fla. Died June 19, 1996.

ELLENOFF, THEODORE, lawyer; b. N.Y.C., Apr. 13, 1924; s. Solomon and Sadie (Klausner) E.; m. Lois Claire Schwartz, Sept. 10, 1955; children: Gregory D., Douglas S., Debra S. BS, NYU, 1947; LLB, Harvard U., 1948. Bar: N.Y. 1949, U.S. Dist Ct. N.Y. 1949. Ptnr. Gartenberg & Ellenoff, N.Y.C., 1952-70, Squadron, Ellenoff, Plesent & Lehrer, N.Y.C., 1970—; sec. Voit Corp., Rochester, N.Y., 1958—, bd. dirs. Pres. Am. Jewish Com., N.Y.C., 1986-89. Served to 1st lt. USAF, 1953-56. Mem. ABA, Assn. of the Bar of the City of N.Y., N.Y. State Bar Assn. Clubs: Harvard (N.Y.C.); Stamford Yacht (Conn.). Lodge: Knights of Pythias (chancellor/comdr.). Avocations: sailing, collecting American craft. DIED 04/09/95. .

ELLIOTT, BYRON KAUFFMAN, lawyer, business executive; b. Indpls., May 5, 1899; s. William Frederick and Effie (Marquardt) E.; m. Helen Alice Heissler, July 15, 1938 (dec. 1973); children: Barbara (Mrs. John D. Niles), Kent, David. AB cum laude, Ind. U., 1920, LLD, 1955; LLB, Harvard, 1923; LHD, Northeastern U., 1971. Bar: Ind. 1921. Began practice in Indpls.; asst. atty. gen. Ind., 1925; elected judge Superior Ct., Indpls., 1926-29; pres. Curtiss Flying Service of Ind., 1927-29; mgr., gen. counsel Am. Life Conv., 1929-34; pres. Am. Service Bur., 1929-33, chmn. bd., 1933-34; with John Hancock Mut. Life Ins. Co., 1934-69, gen. counsel, 1936, v.p., gen. counsel, 1937-47, exec. v.p., 1947-57, pres., 1957-65, chmn. fin. com., 1961-69, chmn. bd., 1963-69; trustee Provident Instn. Savs., 1950-70; dir. Arthur D. Little Co., 1949-69, Pullman Co., 1950-64, Am. Research and Devel. Co., 1952-70, 1st Nat. Bank of Boston, 1960-69, Boston Edison Co., 1961-69. Author booklets, articles ins. law. Resident mem. Mass. Hist. Soc.; mem. Nat. Commn. Coop. Edn.; trustee

Wellesley Coll., 1951-69, Ind. Coll. Funds Am., Boston Mus. Sci., 1952-70, Fed. City Council, Washington, Tufts Civic Edn. Center, French Library in Boston, Hosp. Research and Edn. Trust Am. Hosp. Assn., 1960-69; bd. overseers Boston Symphony Orch.; chmn. bd. trustees, chmn. corp. Northeastern U., 1960-72; bd. dirs. Ind. U. Found., World Wildlife Fund, 1964-70, Boston Opera Assn., World Affairs Council Boston, 1950-68; nat. chmn. Ind. U. Sesquicentenniel Fund, 1970; gen. chmn. United Fund Greater Boston, 1960; bd. advisers Nat. Fund for Med. Edn.; chmn. devel. fund Cape Cod Conservatory of Music and Art, 1975-79; mem. corp. Peter Bent Brigham Hosp. Served as 2d lt. CAC, World War I. Recipient Disting. Alumni Service award Ind. U., 1981, Lifetime Achievement award Northeastern U., 1987. Fellow Am. Acad. Arts and Scis.; mem. ABA, Am. Law Inst. (life), Am. Judicature Soc., Council Fgn. Relations, Assn. Life Ins. Counsel (pres. 1949-50), Mass. Charitable Fire Soc., Mass. Com. Catholics, Protestants and Jews (exec. com. 1957-60), Inst. Life Ins. (dir., chmn. 1965-66), Am. Legion, Mil. Order Loyal Legion, Pilgrims, S.A.R., Soc. Colonial Wars, Bostonian Soc., U.S. C. of C. (mem. task force on econ. growth), Ind. Pioneers, Scribes, Comml. Club (pres. 1950-52), Harvard Club, Brookline Country Club, Algonquin Club, St. Botolph Club (Boston), Tavern Club (Chgo.), Dramatic Club (Indpls.), Masons (33 degree), Beta Theta Pi, Sigma Delta Chi, Sigma Delta Kappa. Republican. Presbyterian. Died Nov. 30, 1996.

ELLIS, ALBERT TROMLY, applied mechanics educator; b. Atwater, Calif., Apr. 22, 1917; s. Walter Harwood and Mabel (Tromly) E.; m. Helen Margaret Hyder; children: Kathryn, James. BEE, Calif. Inst. Tech., 1943, MS in Physics, 1947, PhD in Mech. Engring., 1953. Lic. profl. elec. engr., Calif. Rsch. engr. Columbia U., N.Y.C., 1944-46; rsch. engr. Calif. Inst. Tech., Pasadena, 1947-49, sr. rsch. fellow, 1950-54, assoc. prof., 1954-66; prof. U. Calif., San Diego, 1967-85, prof. emeritus, 1985—; sr. visitor Cambridge U., Eng., 1964-65, 1974; vis. fellow Oxford U., Eng., 1984, 86. Contbr. articles to profl. jours. Served with Signal Corps, U.S. Army, 1943-44. Recipient numerous grants NSF, Office of Naval Research. Republican. Presbyterian. Deceased.

ELLIS, CALVERT N., former college president; b. Zion City, Ill., Apr. 16, 1904; s. Charles Calvert and Emma Read (Nyce) E.; m. Elizabeth Olier Wertz, June 18, 1929; children: Elizabeth Anne, David Wertz. A.B., Juniata Coll., Huntingdon, Pa., 1923, LL.D., 1963; B.Th., M.A., Princeton, 1927; Ph.D., Yale U., 1932; D.D., Bethany Bibl. Sem., 1950; LL.D., Manchester Coll., 1956, Bridgewater Coll., 1965. Instr. Lewistown (Pa.) High Sch., 1923-24, Wilson Coll., Chambersburg, Pa., 1927-28; asst. prof., prof. bibl. studies and philosophy Juniata Coll., Huntingdon, Pa., 1931-43; pres. Juniata Coll., 1943-68, pres. emeritus, 1968-95; mgr. D.M. Wertz Orchards, Waynesboro, Pa., 1940-60; dir. Penn Central Nat. Bank, Huntingdon, 1946-87, chmn. bd., 1978-81; mem. adv. com. AID, 1966-69; cons. higher edn., 1968-95. Author: The Conception of Revelation in the Dialectic Theology, 1932. Trustee J.C. Blair Hosp., Huntingdon, 1945-65; chmn. Gen. Brotherhood Bd., Elgin, Ill., 1948-54, 66-67; adv. com. higher edn. Edn. Compact States, 1966-68; adviser Com. on Edn. and Labor, Ho. of Reps., 1944-47, chmn. commn. on legislation; adviser Assn. Am. Colls., 1961-64, chmn. bd., 1969. Mem. Middle States Assn. Colls. and Secondary Schs. (pres. 1965). Church of the Brethren. Clubs: Skytop (Pa.); University (Sarasota, Fla.); University (N.Y.C.). Home: Lancaster Pa. Died Apr. 7, 1995.

ELLIS, EVA LILLIAN, artist; b. Seattle, June 4, 1920; d. Carl Martin and Hilda (Persson) Johnson; m. Everett Lincoln Ellis, May 1, 1943; children: Karin, Kristy, Hildy, Erik. BA, U. Wash., 1941; MA, U. Idaho, 1950; M in Painting (h.c.), U. delle Arti, 1983. Assoc. dir. art Best & Co., Seattle, 1943; dir. Am. Art Week, Idaho, 1949-55; mem. faculty dept. art U. Idaho, 1946-48; dir., tchr. Children's Art Oreg., 1966-71; mem. faculty aux. bd. U. Wash., Seattle, 1987-95, faculty chair, 1988-95; freelance artist, 1943-46; lectr. in art, New Zealand, 1971-73. Author: A Comparison of the Use of Color of Old and Modern Masters, 1950; works include: Profilo d'Artisti Contemporanei Premio Centauro D'Oro, 1982; exhbns. shows include Henry Gallery, U. Wash., 1941, Immanuel Gallery, N.Y.C., 1943-46, Rackham Gallery, U. Mich., 1956-64, Detroit Inst. Art, 1959, Kresge Gallery, 1959-64, Portland Art Mus., 1967, Corvallis Art Ctr., Oreg., 1966, U. Idaho, 1946-56, U. Canterbury, N.Z., 1979, Boise Mus., 1949-55, CSA, 1972, 79, small gallery, Sydney, Australia, 1971-73, Survey of New Zealand Art, 1979, Shoreline Mus., Seattle, 1981, N.Z. Embassy, London, 1979, Karlshamn Art Soc., Sweden, 1979, Italian Acad. Art, 1982, Palos Verdes (Calif.) Art Ctr., 1982, Swedish Embassy, 1982, Aigantighe Gallery, N.Z., 1983; represented in permanent collections U. Calif.-Berkeley, U. Wash., Calif. Forest Products Lab., 1991; portrait commns. U.S.A. and Japan; pvt. commns. Wash., Calif., N.Y., Engl., Sweden, 1986-92; guest appearances on NBC-TV, N.Y.C. Counselor Cancer Soc.; active Girl Scouts U.S., People to People Friendship Worldwide, 1943-90, Art in Embassies Abroad Program, U.S., 1980-90; elected to Acad. of Europe, 1980; mem. sister com. Christ Ch., New Zealand and Seattle, 1981-83; chair '41 Class Reunion U. Wash.; chmn. scholarship drive for fgn. students U. Wash., Seattle, 1992; mem. Painting Commns. U.S. and Japan. Recipient awards Acad. Art and Sci., 1958-66, Ann Arbor Women Painters, diploma with gold medal, Italian Acad. Art, 1980, hon. diploma fine art, 3 Nat. awards Nat. League Profl. Artists, N.Y.C.; World Culture prize, 1984; Internat. Peace award in Art, 1984; Internat. Art Promotion award, 1986, others. Fellow I.B.C. (Cambridge, Eng. chpt.); mem. Mich. Acad. Art and Sci., Nat. League Am. Pen Women, Nat. Mus. Women in Arts (charter mem.), Royal Overseas League (London), Fine Arts Soc. Idaho, Canterbury Soc. Art New Zealand, Copley Soc. Fine Arts (Boston), Inst. D'Arte Contemporanea Di Milano (Italy), Women's Caucus for Art, Nat. Slide Registry of Artists (New Zealand and Australia), Alpha Omicron Pi. (featured in nat. mag.), Scandinavian Club (pres. 1977-95), Faculty Wives Club (pres. 1979). Died April 15, 1995. Home: Seattle Wash.

ELLIS, JOHN TAYLOR, pathologist, retired educator; b. Lufkin, Tex., Dec. 27, 1920; s. John Taylor and Rowena (McCurdy) E.; m. Marian A. Caldwell, Dec. 26, 1942; children: Evelyn Floy, George Caldwell, John Taylor. BA, U. Tex., 1942; MD, Northwestern U., 1945. Diplomate Nat. Bd. Med. Examiners, Am. Bd. Pathology. Rotating intern St. Luke's Hosp., Chgo., 1945-46, asst. resident in pathology, 1946; rsch. asst. William Buchanan Blood Ctr. Baylor Hosp., Dallas, 1948; resident in pathology N.Y. Hosp., N.Y.C., 1948-49; prof., chmn. dewpt. pathology Emory U., N.Y.C., 1962-67; asst. in pathology Med. Coll. Cornell U., N.Y.C., 1948-49, instr. in pathology, 1949-50, asst. prof., 1950-56, assoc. prof., 1956-62, prof., chmn. dept. pathology, 1968-94, prof. emeritus, 1994—, David D. Thompson prof. emeritus; attending pathologist, pathologist in chief N.Y. Hosp., 1968-94; attending pathologist Meml. Sloan-Kettering Cancer Ctr., N.Y.C., 1973-94; chief pathology dept. pathology N.Y. Downtown Hosp., N.Y.C., 1991-94; attending pathologist N.Y. Hosp. Med. Ctr., Queens, 1994-97, hon. staff, 1997—; mem. adv. bd. Office of Chief Med. Examiner, N.Y.C., 1988—. Capt. USMC, 1946-48. Recipient Milton Helpern Meml. award. Milton Helpern Libr. Legal Medicine, 1989. Mem. AMA, Am. Soc. Investigative Pathology, Coll. Am. Pathology, Assn. Pathology Chmn., Internat. Acad. Pathology, Arthur Purdy Stout Soc., Harvey Soc., N.Y. Path. Soc. Democrat. Avocation: bird watching.

ELLIS, KENT, radiologist, consultant; b. Grand Rapids, Mich., June 22, 1921; s. Luther Edward and Dorothy (Groman) E.; m. Barbara Janet Koehler, June 10, 1950; children—Stephen Mark, Karen, Kent Bradford. BS, Yale U., 1942, MD, 1950. Diplomate: Am. Bd. Radiology. Intern Walter Reed Army Hosp., Washington, 1950-51; resident radiology Columbia Presbyn. Med. Center, 1952-54, attending radiologist, 1955-92, cons. in radiology, 1992—; prof. radiology Columbia Coll. Physicians and Surgeons, 1958-92, prof. emeritus, 1992—; Cons. USPHS, Yale Med. Sch., Inter-Soc. Commn. for Heart Disease Resources, N.Y. Heart Assn. Contbr. articles to profl. jours. Served to lt. USNR, 1943-46. Fellow Am. Coll. Radiology, Radiol. Soc. N.Am.; mem. Med. Soc. State N.Y. (chmn. sect. radiology 1968-69), Assn. Univ. Radiologists, AAUP, N.Am. Soc. Cardiac Radiology (v.p. 1975-76, pres. 1976-77), N.Y. Roentgen Soc. (v.p. 1974-75, pres. 1975-77), Fleischner Soc. (sec. 1977-80, pres. 1981-82), Am. Heart Assn. (chmn. council on cardiovascular radiology 1980-82, dir. 1980-83), Am. Roentgen Ray Soc., St. Anthony Hall. Presbyterian. DIED 12/01/96. .

ELLIS, ROBERT GRISWOLD, engineering company executive; b. Kokomo, Ind., Dec. 28, 1908; s. Ernest Eli and Ethel (Griswold) E. AB, Ind. U., 1934; m. Rachel O. Burckey, Oct. 27, 1984. Mem. staff Ind. U., Bloomington, 1930-34; researcher Blackett-Sample-Hummert Inc., Chgo., 1934, asst. mgr. merchandising, 1935-36; prodn. mgr. Harvey & Howe, Inc., Chgo., 1936-37; Chgo./Midwest dist. mgr. L.F. Grammes & Sons, Inc., Allentown, Pa., 1937-45; with Ellis and Co., Chgo. and Park Ridge, Ill., 1945—, pres., chief engr., 1948—, mng. dir., chief engr. Ellis Internat. Co., Chgo. and Park Ridge, Ill., 1965—, chief engr. Ellis Engring. Co., Park Ridge, 1969—. Chmn. Citizens Com. for Cleaner and More Beautiful Park Ridge, 1957-60; mem., treas. bd. trustees 1st United Meth. Ch., Park Ridge, 1974-77. Recipient Civic Achievement award City of Park Ridge, 1959. Mem. Soc. Automotive Engrs., Armed Forces Communications and Electronics Assn. (life, disting.), Ind. U. Alumni Assn. (life), Quartermaster Assn. (pres. Chgo. chpt. 1957-58), Ind. Acad. Sci., Am. Powder Metallurgy Inst., Ill. Acad. Sci., Mfrs. Agts. Assn. Great Britian and Ireland, Internat. Union Comml. Agts. and Brokers, Am. Logistics Assn., Am. Soc. Metals, Indiana Soc. of Chgo., Union League (veteran), Varsity Club (pres. Chgo. 1957), Ind. U. Alumni (life, pres. Chgo. 1956-57), Emeritus of Ind. U., Internat. Trade. Republican. Deceased.

ELLIS, WELDON THOMPSON, JR., management specialist, consultant, author; b. Portsmouth, Va., Oct. 17, 1909; s. Weldon Thompson and Ruth (Phillips) E.; m. Nancy Sanford Pobst, Sept. 16, 1936; children: Weldon Thompson III (dec.), Nancy Meredith. BS, Va. Poly. Inst., 1930, MS, 1931; MArch, Harvard U., 1933; postgrad., Vanderbilt U., 1987; PhD in Psychology, Kennedy-Western U., 1991. Pvt. practice architecture, 1933-34; site planner City Planning Commn., Nashville, 1934-35; adminstrv. asst. Tenn. Valley Commn., Nashville, 1935-36; exec. dir. Tenn. State Planning Commn., Nashville, 1936-39; chief, adminstr. planning divsn. Commonwealth of Va., Richmond, 1939-42; adminstrv. analyst U.S. Bur. Budget, 1942, asst. budget and planning officer, 1943-48; chief fed. govt. br. Office CD Planning Office Sec. Def., Washington, 1948-49; adminstrv. analyst orgn. divsn. Hdqrs. USAF, Washington, 1949-50, dep. dir. manpower and orgn., 1950-55; exec. sec. commn. manpower and pers. USAF, 1955; staff dir. House Subcom. Manpower and Pers. Mgmt. House Post Office and Civil Svc. Com., Washington, 1956-57; chief pub. adminstrn. advisor to Govt. of Bolivia, 1957-59, Govt. of Pakistan, 1959-60; sr. staff Brookings Instn., 1960-61; cons. U.S. Commr. Edn., 1961-62; dep. exec. dir. Nashville Housing Authority, 1962-64; mgmt. engr. Edwin A. Keeble Assocs., Nashville, 1964-66; mgmt. cons. on computerized mgmt. USN, 1966-68; cons. Office Energy Mgmt., Nat. Resource Planning Bd., 1941-42, cons. community devel., 1942; mem. bd. for correction of mil. records USAF, 1950-55; professorial lectr. mgmt. George Washington U., 1956; asst. planning office Tenn. Dept. Mental Health, 1974; asst. to dir. Nashville Vet. Hosp., 1975; cons. rejuvenation Internat. Med. Ctr., El Paso, Tex., 1990-91. Author: Japan and I, 1986, Breaking the Space and Time Barrier via the Unified Field, 1988, A Synergistic Model of the Universe, 1989, Integrative Psychology an Outgrowth of The Juarez Experiment, 1992; contbr. articles on human rels., mgmt., sci.; inventor, patentee in field. Mem. Hoover Commn. Study Paperwork Mgmt., Hoover Commn. Work Group on Bus. Machines, Mayor's Health and Hosp. Com., Nashville, Tenn. Commn. On Aging; bd. dirs. Nashville Mental Health Assn.; dir. Nashville Coun. Community Agys.; active Westminster Presbyn. Ch. Capt. AUS, 1942-47. Mem. SAR, Am. Inst. Planners (past pres. Washington chpt.), Armed Forces Mgmt. Assn. (founding, pres.), Nat. Def. Assn. (life), Pan Am. Assn. (bd. dirs. Tenn. chpt.), Am. Def. Preparedness Assn. (hon., life), Nashville Com. Fgn. Rels., Internat. Platform Assn., Am. Soc. Pub. Adminstrs., Am. Acad. Polit. and Social Scis., No. VA (reg. planning commn. 1948-53, airport study commn. 1957), Nashville C. of C. (ctrl. city devel. com.), Va. Poly. Inst. German Club, Friends of Music, Rotary, Tau Beta Pi.

ELLISON, THORLEIF, consulting engineer; b. Lyngdal, Norway, May 13, 1902; s. Andreas Emanuel and Gemalie (Svensen) E.; CE, Christiania Coll. Tech., 1924; postgrad. George Washington U., U. Va.; m. Reidun Ingeborg Skonhoft, Jan. 1, 1932; children: Earl Otto, Thorleif Glenn, Sonja Karen. Came to U.S., 1928, naturalized, 1933. Supervising engr. GSA, Washington, 1948-57; supervising airport and airways svc. engr. FAA, 1957-61; chief airways engring. AID, Iran, Pakistan, Turkey, 1961-67; cons. engr., Washington and Va., 1971-82; supervising structural engr. for reconstrn. of The White House, 1949-52; mission dir. Bethlehem, Israel, Holy Land Christian Mission, Kansas City, 1968-71. Recipient U.S. Navy commendation, 1945. Active Christian Bus. Men's Com., Washington, Boy Scouts Am. Registered profl. engr. Mem. Nat. Soc. Profl. Engrs. (dir.), Sons of Norway (pres. Washington chpt.), Norwegian Soc. (treas.). Presbyterian (ruling elder).

ELMENDORF, WILLIAM WELCOME, anthropology educator; b. Victoria, B.C., Can., Sept. 10, 1912; s. William Judson and Mary (Johnson) E.; m. Eleanor Gerlough, Oct. 12, 1940; children: William John, Anthony Daniel. B.A., U. Wash., 1934, M.A., 1935; Ph.D., U. Calif. at Berkeley, 1949. Teaching asst. U. Calif. at Berkeley, 1940-42; instr., then asst. prof. anthropology U. Wash., 1946-57; teaching asso. Northwestern U., 1950-51; lectr., then asso. prof. Wash. State U., 1957-65; mem. faculty U. Wis., 1963—, prof. anthropology, 1964-81, prof. emeritus, 1981—; vis. prof. anthropology U. Calif.-Davis, 1982-84, research assoc., 1984—; profl. cons. Skokomish Indian Claims Case, 1956. Author: The Structure of Twana Culture, 1960, 2d edit., 1992, Skokomish and Other Coast Salish Tales, 1961, Lexical and Cultural Change in Yukian, 1968, Twana Narratives, 1993. Served to capt. AUS, 1942-46, 51-52. Fellow Am. Anthrop. Assn., Am. Ethnol. Soc.; mem. Linguistic Soc. Am., Central States Anthrop. Soc., Northwest Anthrop. Conf. (pres. 1958), Sigma Xi. Died Oct. 13, 1997.

ELMER, CARLOS HALL, publisher, photographer; b. Washington, July 22, 1920; s. Charles Percival and Dorothy Winslow (Hall) E.; m. Wilma Virginia Hudson, Jan. 29, 1943; children: Frank Hudson, Elizabeth Anne. BA, Ariz. State U.; MA, UCLA, 1947. Sect. head, asst. div. head, div. head U.S. Naval Ordnance Test Sta. (now U.S. Naval Weapons Ctr.), China Lake, Calif., 1947-57; instrumentation salesman Traid Corp., Encino and Glendale, Calif., 1957-72; instrumentation salesman L-W Internat., Inc., Woodland Hills, Woodland Hills and Simi Valley, Calif., 1972-90; travel photographer, Kingman, Ariz., China lake, Scottsdale, Ariz., 1940-93; owner, mgr. Carlos Elmer Pub. Co. Scottsdale and Kingman, 1967-93; chmn. 9th Internat. Congress on High-Speed Photography, Denver, 1970. Author: Carlos Elmer's Arizona, 1967, The Glorious Seasons of Arizona, 1971, London Bridge in Pictures, 1971, Arizona in Color, 1973, Mohave County, Arizona,

U.S.A., 1974, Grand Canyon Country, 1975, Colorful Northern Arizona, 1977, Hoover Dam, Lake Mead and Lake Mohave, 1978, Laughlin in Color, 1989; contbg. editor Ariz. Hwys. mag., 1984-93. Capt. AUS, 1942-46, PTO. Fellow Soc. Motion Picture and TV Engrs., Soc. Photo-Optical Instrumentation Engrs., Am. Soc. Mag. Photographers. Republican. Presbyterian. Died May 22, 1993.

ELMORE, STANCLIFF CHURCHILL, lawyer; b. Washington, Sept. 6, 1921; s. John Archer and Doris Ernestine (Churchill) E.; m. Betty Buchanan, June 12, 1948; children—Stancliff Churchill, Maralyn Ann. Student, Washington and Lee U., 1939-42; LL.B., George Washington U., 1950. Bar: D.C. bar 1950, Md. bar 1960. Counsel U.S. Ho. of Reps. Appropriations Com., subcoms. mil., public works, 1952-53; partner firm Lambert, Furlow, Elmore & Heidenberger, Washington, 1961-79, Williams, Myers and Quiggle, Washington and Montgomery County, Md., 1979-86; counsel Casey, Scott & Canfield, Washington, 1987—; gen. counsel Southeastern U.; legal counsel, lawyer mem. D.C. Real Estate Commn., 1966-74. Served with AUS, 1942-46. Mem. Am. Law Inst. Republican. Episcopalian. Club: Chevy Chase. Home: Washington D.C. DIED 11/01/95. .

ELSBREE, JOHN FRANCIS, banker; b. Methuen, Mass., Apr. 19, 1912; s. Leslie Francis and Beatrice (Roberts) E.; m. Ida Letitia Brooks, Aug. 13, 1938; children: Janet Elaine Elsbree Amoling (dec.), John Francis, Marjorie Evelyn Elsbree Evans, David Brooks, Ruth Elizabeth Elsbree McDermott. Student, Harvard U., 1928-30, Am. Inst. Banking, 1933-45, Stonier Grad. Sch. Banking, 1955-57. With Webster & Atlas Nat. Bank, Boston, 1930-48; auditor Webster & Atlas Nat. Bank, 1945-48; asst. auditor Rockland-Atlas Nat. Bank, Boston, 1948-51; auditor Rockland-Atlas Nat. Bank, 1951-57, asst. v.p., 1957-61; asst. v.p. State St. Bank & Trust Co., Boston, 1961-62; v.p. State St. Bank & Trust Co., 1962-75, sr. v.p., 1975-77, gen. auditor, 1964-77; v.p., gen. auditor State St. Boston Corp., 1970-74, sr. v.p., gen. auditor, 1974-77; past lectr. Am. Inst. Banking, Northwestern U., No. New Eng. Sch. Banking, NABAC Sch. at U. Wis. Author: Social, Economic and Political Causes and Effects of Commercial Bank Mergers, 1957, The Elsbree Family in America, 1992; contbr. articles to profl. publs. Treas. Boston Latin Sch. Assn., 1955-77, asst. treas., 1977-89. Semi-finalist Am. Inst. Banking Nat. Debate Contest, 1950, 53, 54, John F. Elsbree Day proclaimed in his honor, City of Boston, 1989. Mem. Greater Boston Bankers Assn., Am. Inst. Banking (past assoc. councilman, nat. debate chmn., host chpt. chmn. nat. conf. 1986), Inst. Internal Auditors (dir. New Eng. chpt., past chpt. pres., gen. chmn. internat. conf. 1976), Bank Administrn. Inst. (chartered bank auditor, cert. internal auditor, gen. chmn. regional conv. 1967, past pres. Boston chpt., state, dist. dir. 1970-71, chmn. bd. regents). Episcopalian. Home: Boston Mass. Died Apr. 24, 1994.

ELSEN, ALBERT EDWARD, art history educator; b. N.Y.C., Oct. 11, 1927; s. Albert George and Julia Louise (Huseman) E.; m. (div.); children: Matthew, Nancy, Katherine. AB, Columbia, 1949, MA, 1951, PhD, 1955; DFA (hon.), Dickinson Coll., 1980. Asst. prof. art history Carleton Coll., Northfield, Minn., 1952-58; asso. prof. Ind. U., Bloomington, 1958-62; prof. Ind. U., 1963-68; prof. art history Stanford U., 1968-95, Walter A. Haas prof. art history, 1976-95. Author: Rodin's Gates of Hell, 1960, Purposes of Art, 1962, 2d edit., 1968, 3d edit., 1974, 4th edit., 1981, Rodin, 1963, The Partial Figure in Modern Sculpture, From Rodin to 1969, Seymour Lipton, 1970, The Sculpture of Henri Matisse, 1971, Paul Jenkins, 1973, Origins of Modern Sculpture: Pioneers and Premises, 1974, (with John Merryman) Law, Ethics and the Visual Arts, 1979, 2d edit., 1987, Modern European Sculpture 1918-1945, 1979, In Rodin's Studio, 1980; editor, contbr. Rodin Rediscovered, 1981, The Gates of Hell by Auguste Rodin, 1985, Rodin's Thinker and the Dilemmas of Modern Public Sculpture, 1986. Served to sgt. maj. AUS, 1945-46, ETO. Recipient Richard W. Lyman award Stanford U. Alumni Assn., 1989; Fulbright fellow, 1949-50, Guggenheim fellow, 1966-67, Nat. Endowment for Humanities sr. fellow, 1973-74. Mem. Coll. Art Assn. (dir. 1966-70, pres. 1974-76). Home: Stanford Calif. Died Feb. 2, 1995.

ELTON, GEOFFREY RUDOLPH, historian, educator; b. Tübingen, W. Ger., Aug. 17, 1921; s. Victor Leopold and Eva (Sommer) Ehrenberg; m. Sheila Lambert, Aug. 30, 1952. BA, U. London, 1943, PhD, 1949; MA, U. Cambridge, 1949, LittD, 1960; LittD (hon.), U. Glasgow, 1980, U. Newcastle, 1981, U. Bristol, 1981, U. London, 1985, U. Göttingen, 1987; LLD (hon.), U. Cambridge, 1992. Asst. in history U. Glasgow, 1948-49; asst. lectr., U. Cambridge, 1949-54, lectr., 1954-63, reader Tudor studies, 1963-67, prof. English constl. history, 1967-84, Regius prof. modern history, 1983-88 . Served with Inf. and Intelligence Corps, 1944-46. Created knight, 1986. Fellow Brit. Acad. (publs. sec. 1981-90), Royal Hist. Soc. (pres. 1973-77); mem. Selden Soc. (pres. 1984-86), Eccles. Hist. Soc. (pres. 1984-85), Am. Acad. Arts and Scis. (fgn. mem.). Author: Tudor Revolution in Government, 1953, and numerous other books. Died Dec. 4, 1994. Home: Cambridge Eng.

ELY, NORTHCUTT, lawyer; b. Phoenix, Sept. 14, 1903; s. Sims and Elizabeth (Northcutt) E.; m. Marica McCann, Dec. 2, 1931; children: Michael and Craig (twins), Parry Haines. A.B., Stanford U., 1924, J.D., 1926. Bar: Calif. 1926, N.Y. 1928, D.C. 1932, U.S. Supreme Ct. 1930. Practice law N.Y., 1926-29, D.C. and Calif., 1933-97; exec. asst. to Sec. Interior, Washington, 1929-33; chmn. tech. adv. com. Fed. Oil Cons. Bd., Washington, 1931-33; represented Sec. Interior in negotiation of Hoover Dam power and water contracts, 1930-33; counsel to Gov. of Okla. in negotiating Interstate Oil Compact, 1934-35; co-executor of estate of ex-Pres. Herbert Hoover, 1964-68; spl. counsel Colo. River Bd. of Calif., 1946-76 and various Calif. water and power agys.; spl. Asst. Atty. Gen. State of Calif., 1953-64 in Ariz. v. Calif.; mem. nat. Petroleum Council, 1968-76; counsel in 7 U.S. Supreme Ct cases involving rights in Colo., Columbia, Cowlitz, Niagara Rivers and fed. natural resource statutes; legal advisor to Ruler of Sharjah in boundary disputes with Iran, Umm al Qawain, and internat. arbitration of boundary with Dubai; counsel to Swaziland in internat. river dispute with Republic of South Africa and to Mekong Commn. (U.N.) in settling principles for devel. of Mekong Basin; counsel to govts. and cos. in determination of seabed boundaries in Gulf of Thailand, Mediterranean, East China, South China, Caribbean seas, Persian Gulf; represented U.S. Mining cos. in enactment of Deepsea Hard Minerals Act, & subsequent reciprocal internat. recognition of mining leases; gen. counsel Am. Pub. Power Assn., 1941-81; counsel L.A., So. Calif. Edison Co. in renewal of Hoover Power contracts, 1980-97; counsel from time to time to Govts. of Saudi Arabia, Turkey, China, Algeria, Malagasy Republic, Ethiopia, Grenada, Thailand on mining and petroleum legis.; mem. U.S. del. to UN Conf. on application of Sci. and Tech. for Benefit Less Developed Areas, 1963, UN Conf. on mineral legislation, Manila, 1969, Bangkok, 1973; mem. bd. overseers Hoover Instn.; trustee Herbert Hoover Found., Hoover Presdl. Libr. Assn. Author: Summary of Mining & Petroleum Laws of the World, Oil Conservation Through Interstate Agreement, The Hoover Dam Documents; co-author Law of International Drainage Basins, Economics of the Mineral Industries. Mem. adv. bd. Ctr. Ocean Lawys Policy, U. Va. Fellow Am. Bar Found. (life); mem. ABA (chmn. natural resource sect. 1973-74, ho. dels. 1974-80, regulatory reform com.), Calif. State Bar Assn., D.C. Bar Assn., Am. Law Inst. (life), Internat. Law Assn. (chmn. Am. br. com. on deep sea mineral resources 1970-79), Internat. Bar Assn., Sigma Nu, Phi Delta Phi, Sigma Delta Chi. Republican. Clubs: Bohemian (San Francisco); California (L.A.); Metropolitan, Chevy Chase, University (Washington); Fortnightly (Redlands, pres. 1989); Redlands Country. Home: Redlands Calif. Died May 26, 1997; interred Redlands, CA.

ELYTIS, ODYSSEUS (ODYSSEUS ALEPOUDELIS), poet, essayist; b. Hercaleon, Crete, Greece, Nov. 2, 1911. Attended, U. Athens, 1930-33, U. Paris, 1948-52; D in Philosophy (hc), U. Thessaloniki, 1975; Dr (hc), U. Paris; DLitt (hon.), U. London, 1981. Program dir. Nat. Broadcasting Inst., 1945-47, 53-54; art critic, literary critic Kathimerini, 1946-48; advisor Art Theatre, 1955-56, Greek Nat. Theatre, 1965-68; rep. for Greece at Recontres Internat. de Geneve, 1948, Congrès de l'Association des Critiques d'Art, 1949, Incontro Romano della Cultura, 1960; mem. Nat. Theatre Adminstrv. Council, Consultative Com. of Greek Nat. Tourist Orgn. on Athens Festival. Author: (poetry) Prasanatolismi, 1939, O Ilias o Protos, Mazi me tis Parallayes pano se mian Ahtida, 1943, Asma Iroiko ke Penthimo yia ton Hemeno Anthipolohago tis Alvanias, 1945, To Axion Esti, 1959 (Nat. Poetry prize 1960, Nat. Book award 1960), Exi ke Mia Tipsis yia ton Ourano, 1960, To Fotodendro ke i Dekati Tetarti Omorfia, 1971, O Ilias o Iliatoras, 1971, Thanatos ke Anastasis tou Konstantinou Paleologou, 1971 To Monogramma, 1972, Ta Ro tou Erota, 1972, Clear Days: Poems by Palamas and Elytis in Versions by Nikos Tselepides, 1972, Villa Natacha, 1973, O Fillomantis, 1973, Ta Eterothali, 1974, The Sovereign Sun: Selected Poems, 1974, Maria Nefeli, 1978, Selected Poems, 1981, Tria Piimata me Simea Evkerias, 1982, Imerologio enos Atheatou Apriliou, 1984, O Mikros Naftilos, 1985, What I Love: Selected Poems of Odysseus Elytis, 1986, Krinagoras, 1987, Ta Elegia tis Oxopetras, 1991; (other) O Zagrafos Theofilos, 1973, Anihta Hartia, 1974, I Mayia tou Papadiamanti, 1976, Anafora ston Andrea Embiriko, 1980, To Domatio me tis Ikones, 1986, Ta Dimosia ke ta Idiotika, 1990, I Idiotiki Odas, 1990, En Lefko, 1992; translator: Defteri Graphi, 1976, Sappho-Anasinthesi ke Apodosi, 1985, Ioannis I Apokalipsi, 1985. Served to 2d lt. Greek Army, World War II. Recipient Nobel Prize for lit., 1979, Benson medal Royal Soc. Lit., 1981; decorated Order of the Phoenix, 1965, Grand Comdr. Order of Honour, 1979, commandeur dl l'Ordre des Arts et des Lettres, 1984, commandeur de la Legion d'Honneur, 1989. Mem. Internat. Assn. Art Critics, Société Europeénne de Culture. Home: Athens Greece Died March 18, 1996.

EMERSON, WILLIAM STEVENSON, retired chemist, consultant, writer; b. Boston, Mar. 25, 1913; s. Natt Waldo and Marion (Stevenson) E.; m. Flora Millicent Carter, Dec. 12, 1958. AB, Dartmouth Coll., 1934; PhD, MIT, 1937. DuPont fellow U. Ill., Urbana, 1937-38, instr. chemistry, 1938-41; rsch. chemist Monsanto Co., Dayton, Ohio, 1941-44, rsch. group leader, 1944-51, asst. dir. cen. rsch. dept., 1951-54, asst. dir. gen. devel. dept. St. Louis, 1954-56; mgr. cen. rsch. dept. Am. Potash & Chem. Corp., Whittier, Calif., 1956-60; sr. staff assoc. Arthur D. Little, Inc., Cambridge, Mass., 1960-72, ret., 1972. Author: Guide to the Chemical Industry, 1983. Contbr. numerous articles to profl. jours. Patentee in field. Mem. Am. Chem. Soc. (chmn. Dayton sect. 1952), Am. Ornithologists Union, Am. Birding Assn., Phi Beta Kappa, Sigma Xi, Phi Lambda Upsilon, Delta Kappa Epsilon, Alpha Chi Sigma. Republican. Club: Chemists (N.Y.C.). Avocations: fly fishing; birding; golf; squash; reading; philately. Died Oct. 15, 1997.

EMILIANI, CESARE, geology educator, author; b. Bologna, Italy, Dec. 8, 1922; came to U.S., 1948; s. Luigi and Maria (Manfredini) E.; m. Rosita Manzanares, June 28, 1951; children: Sandra, Mario. D in Geology, U. Bologna, 1945; PhD in Geology, U. Chgo., 1950. Geologist Soc. Idrocarburi Nazionali, Florence, Italy, 1946-48; research assoc. U. Chgo., 1950-56; faculty U. Miami, Fla., 1957-93, prof. geology, 1963-93, chmn. dept. geology, 1967-92; pres. Internat. Acad. Scis., 1993—. Author: Dictionary of the Physical Sciences, 1987, The Scientific Companion 1988, Earth Science, 1989, Planet Earth, 1992; editor: The Oceanic Lithosphere, 1981. Recipient Vega medal, Sweden, 1983, Agassiz medal NAS, 1989. Fellow AAAS, Am. Geophys. Union; mem. Sigma Xi. Research on oxygen isotopic analysis of pelagic microfossils from deep-sea sediment cores. Died July 20, 1995.

EMINHIZER, EARL EUGENE, theologian, educator; b. Greenville, S.C., May 22, 1926; s. Eugene Lawrence and Mary Elmyra (Couch) E.; m. Lillian Marcia Downs, July 16, 1955; children: Catharine Marcia (dec.), Eugene Elwood (dec.), Eugene Lawrence II. BA, Furman U., 1948; BS in Edn., Youngstown (Ohio) Coll., 1951; BD, Chozer Seminary, Chester, Pa., 1955, ThM, 1956; ThD, Calif. Sch. Theology, 1968. Tchr. McCormick (S.C.) Schs., 1949-50, Bracevill Schs., Newton Falls, Ohio, 1950-51; instr. religion Denison U., Grandville, Ohio, 1956-57; tchr. Southington (Ohio) Schs., 1957-65; prof. Youngstown State U., 1958-92. Contbr. articles to profl. jours. Bd. dirs. Lake to River Health Care Coalition, 1976, Goodwill Industries, Youngstown, 1979-95, Easter Seals Soc., Youngstown, 1982-95, Ohio Rehab. Svcs. Commn., Columbus, 1979-95. Grantee Youngstown State U., 1978, 85. Mem. NEA, Ohio Edn. Assn., Am. Soc. Ch. Historians, So. Hist. Assn., Am. Assn. Am. Profs., Nat. Assn. Bapt. Profs. of Religion, Orgns. Am. Historians, Ohio Acad. of Religion, Ohio Philos. Assn., Masons, Phi Kappa Phi. Baptist. Avocation: photography. Home: Columbus Ohio

EMMONS, DONN, retired architect; b. Olean, N.Y., Oct. 4, 1910; s. Frederick E. and Mary (Fogarty) E.; m. Nancy Pierson, Apr. 4, 1942; children—Zette, Luli, Andrew; m. Audrey Durland, Oct. 29, 1960. Student, Cornell U., 1928-33, U. So. Calif., 1934; LLD (hon.), U. Victoria, B.C., Can., 1988. With office William W. Wurster, architect, San Francisco, 1938-42; ptnr. Wurster, Bernardi & Emmons, San Francisco, 1945-63; prin. Wurster, Bernardi & Emmons, Inc., 1963—, pres., 1969; ret., 1985; cons. architect Bay Area Rapid Transit, 1964-67, U. Calif.-Berkeley, 1968—, U. Victoria, B.C., Can., 1974—, Office Fgn. Bldgs., U.S. Dept. State, 1979-82; speaker Symposium on Waterfront Planning, Yokohama, 1986. Prin. works include Golden Gateway Redevel. Project, San Francisco, Ghirardelli Sq., San Francisco, Capitol Towers Redevel. Project, Sacramento, Bank of Am. world hdqrs., San Francisco, Merritt Coll., Oakland, Woodlake and Oakcreek Apt. Projects, master plan for San Francisco Civic Ctr., master plan for South Miami Beach bus. dist. Mem. Potomac River Task Force for Rehab. of River. Served to lt. comdr. USNR, 1942-45. Recipient over 100 awards for excellence in design. Fellow AIA (pres. No. Calif. chpt. 1953-54). Died Sept. 7, 1997.

ENDO, SHUSAKU, author; b. Tokyo, Mar. 27, 1923; s. Tsunehisa E. and Iku (Takei) E.; m. Junko Okada, Sept. 3, 1955; 1 son, Ryunosuke. B.A., Keio U., 1948; student French lit., Lyon U., France, 1950-53. Writings include: (fiction) Aden made, 1954, Shiroi hito, 1955 (Akutagawa prize 1955), Kiiroi hito, 1955, Aoi chiisano budō, 1956, Umi to dokuyaku, 1958 (pub. as The Sea and Poison, 1972), Kazan, 1959 (pub. as Volcano, 1978), Obaka-san, 1959 (pub. as Wonderful Fool, 1974), Otoko to kyukanchō, 1963, Watashi ga suteta onna, 1963, Aika, 1965, Ryugaku, 1965 (pub. as Foreign Studies, 1989), Chimmoku, 1966 (pub. as Silence, 1969; Tanizaki prize 1967, Gru de Oficial da Ordem do Infante dom Henrique 1968), Taihen daa, 1969, Shikai no hotori, 1973, Iesu no shōgai, 1973 (pub. as A Life of Jesus, 1978), Yumoa shōsetsu shu, 1973, Waga seishun ni kui ari, 1974, Kuchibue o fuku toki, 1974 (pub. as When I Whistle, 1979), Sekai kikō, 1975, Hechimakum, 1975, Endō Shusaku bungaku zenshu (11 vols.), 1975, Kitsunegata tanukigata, 1976, Gutara mandanshu, 1978, Juichi no iro garasu, 1979 (pub. as Stained Glass Elegies, 1985), Marie Antoinette, 1979, Samurai, 1980, Onna no issho, 1982, Akuryō no gogo, 1983, Sukyandaru, 1986 (pub. as Scandal, 1988), Hangyaku (2 vols.), 1989, Deep River, 1995; (plays) Ōgon no kuni, 1969 (pub. as The Golden Country, 1970), Bara no yakata, 1969; (other writings) Furansu no daigakusei,

1953, Seisho no naka no joseitachi, 1968, Korian vs. Manbō, 1974, Ukiaru kotoba, 1976, Ai no akebono, 1976, Nihonjin wa kirisuto kyō o shinjirareru ka, 1977, Kirisuto no tanjō, 1978, Ningen no naka no X, 1978, Rakuten taishō, 1978, Kare no ikikata, 1978, Ju to jujika, 1979, Shinran, 1979, Sakka no nikki, 1980, Chichioya, 1980, Kekkonron, 1980, Endō Shusaku ni yoru Endō Shusaku, 1980, Meiga Iesu junrei, 1981, Ai to jinsei o meguro dansō, 1981, Okuku e no michi, 1981, Fuyu no yasashisa, 1982, Watakushi ni totte kami to wa, 1983, Kokoro, 1984, Ikuru gakkō, 1984, Watakushi no aishita shōsetsu, 1985, Rakudai bōzu no rirekisho, 1989, Kawaru mono to kawaranu mono: hanadokei, 1990. Recipient Sancti Silvestri, Pope Paul VI, 1970, Noma prize, 1980, Order of Culture, 1995. Died Sept. 29, 1996.

ENFIELD, FRANKLIN D., geneticist; b. Woolstock, Iowa, Dec. 26, 1933; s. Clyde and Ann Mary (Wernet) E.; m. Maxine Ann Miller, Aug. 14, 1955; children: Mark, Marsha Enfield Chizek, Kathy. B.S., Iowa State U., 1955; M.S., Okla. State U., 1957; Ph.D., U. Minn., 1960. Asst. prof. U. Minn., Mpls., 1960-65; asso. prof. U. Minn., 1965-70, prof. genetics, 1970-96, dir. grad. studies in genetics, 1971-76; mem. adv. panel population biology and physiol. ecology NSF, 1987-89; vice chmn. Gordon Rsch. Conf. on Quantitative Genetics and Biotech., 1991, chmn. 1993. Contbr. sci. articles to profl. jours. NIH, USDA and NSF grantee, 1963-96; Genetics Soc. travel grantee to USSR, 1978. Mem. Sigma Xi, Phi Kappa Phi, Gamma Sigma Delta, Alpha Zeta, Phi Eta Sigma. Lutheran. Home: Stillwater Minn. Died Aug. 6, 1996; interred Stillwater Rutherford Cemetery.

ENGELBERT, ARTHUR FERDINAND, university dean; b. St. Johnsburg, N.Y., Dec. 18, 1903; s. Ferdin and Anna (Fetzer) E.; m. Ruth B. Bunt, Aug. 14, 1930; 1 dau., Carol (Mrs. Ervin S. Palmer). Student, Concordia Coll., 1922-24, Concordia Theol. Sem., 1924-27; M.A., U. Pitts., 1929, Ph.D., 1935; postgrad., Duke, 1941, U. Chgo., 1949. Asst. pastorate Immanuel Lutheran Ch., Braddock, Pa., 1927-31; grad. asst. U. Pitts, 1929-30, instr. modern langs., 1930-31; prof., head dept. modern langs. Mt. Union Coll., Alliance, Ohio, 1931-59; dean Coll. Liberal Arts, Washburn U., Topeka, 1959-92; acting pres. Coll. Liberal Arts, Washburn U., 1961, also v.p. for acad. affairs.; Coordinator liberal arts com. N. Central Assn. Colls. and Secondary Schs., 1951-56. Contbr. articles to edn. jours.; Editorial bd.: Soc. for Acad. Achievement. U.S. rep. of Danish Internat. Student Com.; Chmn. Alliance chpt. ARC, 1956-58; mem. planning council for Shawnee County Health Facilities Commn. Mem Am. Assn. Acad. Deans, Acad. Deans Kan. Colls. and Univs. (pres. 1968-69), Tau Delta Pi, Psi Kappa Omega. Clubs: Rotarian, Sagamore, Fortnightly. Home: Topeka Kans. Died Dec. 3, 1992.

ENGELBRECHT, RICHARD STEVENS, environmental engineering educator; b. Ft. Wayne, Ind., Mar. 11, 1926; s. William C. and Mary Elizabeth (Stevens) E.; m. Mary Condrey, Aug. 21, 1948; children: William, Timothy. A.B., Ind. U., 1948; M.S., M.I.T., 1952, Sc.D., 1954. Teaching asst. Ind. U. Sch. Medicine, Indpls., 1949-50; research asst. M.I.T., Cambridge, 1950-52, instr., 1952-54; asst. prof. U. Ill., Urbana-Champaign, 1954-57, assoc. prof., 1957-59, prof. environ. engring., 1959—; dir. Advanced Environ. Control Tech. Research Center, 1979-91; Ivan Racheff prof., 1987; cons. EPA, WHO; mem. Ohio River Valley Water Sanitation Commn., 1976—, chmn., 1980-82, 93. Named Ernest Victor Balsom Commemoration Lectr., 1978; recipient Eric H. Vick award Inst. Pub. Health Engrs., U.K., 1979; George J. Schroepfer award Ctrl. States Water Pollution Control Assn., 1985; Benjamin Garver Lamme award Am. Soc. Engring. Edn., 1985, Founders' award Assn. Environ. Engring. Prof., 1993, Order of the Sacred Treasure, Gold Rays with Neck Ribbon, Nat. Decoration from Emperor of Japan, 1993. Mem. AAAS, NAE, Internat. Assn. Water Quality (hon., pres. 1980-86), Am. Water Works Assn. (George W. Fuller award 1974, Publ. award 1975), Water Environment Fedn. (Eddy medal 1966, Arthur Sidney Bedell award 1973, pres. 1978, hon. mem. 1986, Fair medal 1987), Am. Soc. Microbiology, Abwasser Technische Vereinigung (hon., Germany).

ENIKOLOPOV, NIKOLAI SERGEEVITCH, chemist; b. Stepanakert, USSR, Mar. 13, 1924; s. Sergei Danilovitch and Genofia Aslanovna (Gukasian) E.; m. Shirmazan Madlen Grigorievna, 1948; children: Sergei, Grigori. Grad., Polytech. Inst., Erevan, 1945. Cert. chemist-technologist. Lab. worker Inst. Chemistry Armenian Acad. Sci., Erevan, 1945-46; from jr. to sr. researhcer to head lab. Inst. Chem. Physics USSR Acad. Sci., Moscow, 1946-82; dir. Inst. Synthetic Polymeric Materials Russian Acad. Sci., Moscow, 1982-93; prof., chair Moscow Physicotech. Inst., 1962-93; chmn. Sci. Coun. on Synthetic Materials Praesidium of Russian Acad. Scis., 1978-93. Contbr. articles to profl. jours. Dep. chmn. Soviet Peace Fund, Moscow, 1989-91, adv. com., 1991-93. Recipient Lenin prize Moscow, 1980, Kargin prize USSR Acad. Sci., Moscow, 1985. Achievments include patents in field. Died, Jan. 22, 1993.

ENNES, MARK RAYMOND, financial consultant; b. Lebanon, Mo., Mar. 4, 1952. BA, Valparaiso (Ind.) U., 1974. Fin. cons., v.p. Merrill Lynch, Merrillville, Ind., 1981—; continuing edn. instr. Purdue U. North Ctrl.; bd. dirs. Lake Tippecanoe Property Owners Inc., Leesburg, Ind. Bd. dirs., vice chmn. Valparaiso (Ind.) Lakes Area Conservancy Dist., 1989—; pres. Hillcrest Improvement Assn., Valparaiso, 1982—; mem., alumni chmn. cmty. campaign Valparaiso U., 1988—. Mem. Valparaiso U. Alumni Assn., Bond Club Chgo., Valparaiso Sunrise Kiwanis (past pres.). Lutheran. Avocations: skiing,scuba, sailing, photography, reading. Deceased.

ENRIQUE Y TARANCON, VICENTE CARDINAL, cardinal; b. Burriana, Castellon, June 14, 1907; s. Manuel E. Urios and Vicenta T. Fandos. Ed. Seminario Conciliar Rortosa, Tarragona and Universidad Pontificia Valencia. Adminstrv. asst. Vinaroz, 1930-33, Archpriest, 1938-43; Archipriest, Villarreal, 1943-46; Bishop of Solsona, 1946-64; gen. sec. Spanish Bishopric, 1956-64; Archbishop of Ovopie, 1964-69; Archibishop of Toledo, Primate of Spain, 1969-71; Archbishop of Madrid, 1971-83; elevated to Sacred Coll. Cardinals, 1969; mem. Sacred Congregations for Bishops, Divine Worship and Reform of Canon Law; mem. Spanish Acad., 1969. Author: La Renovación Total de la Vida Cristiana, 1954, Los Seglares en la Iglesia, 1958, Sucesores de los Apostoles, 1960, La Parroquia, Hoy, 1961, El Misterio de la Iglesia, 1963, Ecumenismo y Pastoral 1964, La Iglesia en el Mundo de Hoy, 1965, El Sacerdocio a la Luz del Concilio Vaticano II, 1966, La Iglesia del Posconcilio, 1967, La Crisis de Fe en el Mundo Actual, 1968, Unidad y pluralismo en la Iglesia, 1969, Liturgia y lengua del pueblo, 1970, El magisterio de Santa Teresa, 1970. Avocations: musical composition; classical music. Died Nov. 29, 1994. Home: Castellan de la Plana Spain

ENTWISLE, GEORGE, physician; b. Bolton, Eng., May 27, 1922; came to U.S., 1923, naturalized, 1936; s. Nathan and Edith (Wilkinson) E.; m. Doris Helen Roberts, Aug. 31, 1946; children—Barbara, Beverly, George. B.S., U. Mass., 1944; M.D., Boston U., 1948. Diplomate: Nat. Bd. Med. Examiners, Am. Bd. Internal Medicine. Intern Evans Meml. Hosp., 1948-49, fellow physiology, 1949-51, asst. resident medicine, 1951-52, resident medicine, 1952; lectr. physiology, then instr. medicine Boston U. Sch. Medicine, 1952-56; faculty U. Md. Sch. Medicine, 1956-86, prof. preventive medicine, 1958-86, ret., chmn. dept., 1958-71. Served with AUS, 1943-44, 52-54. Fellow A.C.P., Am. Coll. Preventive Medicine, Am. Pub. Health Assn., Council on Epidemiology of Am. Heart Assn.; mem. Md. Rehab. Assn. (pres. 1963-64), Assn. Tchrs. Preventive Medicine (pres. 1967-68, Distinguished Service award 1977, editor newsletter 1971-78), Mass., Balt. med. socs., Med and Chirurg. Faculty Md., Am. Fedn. Clin. Research, Sigma Xi. Home: Baltimore Md. Died Dec. 24, 1990.

ENTZEROTH, ROBERT ELLEARD, architect; b. St. Louis, Jan. 24, 1926; s. Elleard Colburn and Erma (Braun) E.; m. Barbara Elizabeth Ingold, Aug. 18, 1950; children—Lee Catherine, Lyn Suzanne, Julie Ann. B.Arch., Washington U., St. Louis, 1951. Architect Harris Armstrong (Architect), St. Louis, 1949-51, Murphy & Mackey, St. Louis, 1951-52, 53-54; partner in charge design Smith-Entzeroth, St. Louis, 1955-86; dir. design SMP/Smith-Entzeroth, St. Louis, 1986—; vis. prof. archtl. design Washington U. Sch. Architecture; mem. Mo. Bd. Architects, Profl. Engrs. and Land Surveyors. Prin. works include Pierre Laclede Center, Clayton, Mo., Coll. Center of Principia Coll, University City Pub. Library, Washington U. Chemistry and Engring. Labs, Safeco Ins. Co. Offices, St. Louis, Nashville, Chgo., Mo. State Office Bldg, St. Louis, Alumni House Principia Coll, AAA Hdqrs. Bldg, St. Louis County, Interco Corp. Tower, renovation of west wing St. Louis Art Mus. Served with USNR, 1944-46. Recipient numerous archtl. design awards including Archtl. Forum, 1961, Am. Fedn. Arts, 1968, 40 under 40 Exhbn. of Architects' Works, 1968; LeBrun Traveling fellow, 1952. Fellow AIA. Mem. United Ch. Christ. Club: St. Louis.

EPLEY, MARION JAY, oil company executive; b. Hattiesburg, Miss., June 17, 1907; s. Marion Jay and Eva (Quin) E.; m. Dorris Glenn Ervin, Feb. 12, 1934; children: Marion Jay III, Sara Perry (Mrs. Richard H. Davis). LL.B., Tulane U., 1930. Bar: La. 1930. Practiced in New Orleans, 1930-42, 45-47; gen. atty. Texaco, Inc., New Orleans, N.Y.C., 1948-58; v.p., asst. to chmn. bd. Texaco, Inc., N.Y.C., 1958-60; sr. v.p. Texaco, Inc., 1960-61, exec. v.p., 1961-64, pres., 1964-70, chmn. bd., 1970-71; also dir., chmn. bd. Dormar Ltd., 1986-88. Served to lt. USNR, 1942-45. Decorated officer Ordre de la Couronne, Belgium. Mem. ABA, La. Bar Assn.

EPSTEEN, CASPER MORLEY, physician, educator; b. East Chicago, Ind., May 6, 1902; s. Hyman and Sarah Ida (Goodman) E.; m. Aline Gertrude Grossman, Sept. 26, 1934; children: Lynn, Robert. B.Sc., U. Ill., 1923, M.D., 1925; D.D.S., Loyola U. Chgo., 1930. Diplomate: Internat. Bd. Surgery. Intern Michael Reese Hosp. and Med. Center, Chgo., 1925-26; now sr. attending surgeon; preceptorship with Dr. Truman W. Brophy, 1926-29; practice medicine specializing maxillofacial and plastic surgery Chgo., 1926-95; cons. Weiss Meml. Hosp., Jackson Park Community Hosp. and Med. Center, Central Community Hosp.; clin. prof. maxillofacial and plastic surgery Chgo. Med. Sch., 1960-84, clin. prof. emeritus, 1984-95. Author: Tice's Practice of Medicine, 1948; Guest editor: Am. Jour. Surgery, Dec. 1952; editorial asso.: Internat. Jour. Surgery. Served to lt. col. AUS, 1942-46. Guest of honor 1st Internat. Congress Maxillofacial Surgeons, Venice, Italy, 1971; recipient hon. mention for research salivary glands Am. Soc. Plastic and Reconstructive Surgeons, 1953; Honor award Michael Reese Hosp. and Med. Ctr., 1955; Honor award Louis A. Weiss Meml. Hosp., 1960; Internat. Book Honor Hall of Fame Am. Biographical Inst., 1986. Fellow Ill. Soc. for Med. Research, Ednl. and Sci. Found. Ill. Med. Soc.; mem. Am. Soc. Maxillofacial Surgeons (founder mem.; pres. 1960, Leadership award 1960, Distinguished award 1966, Presdl. Achievement award 1982), Chgo. Med. Soc. (pres. 1962-63, award merit 1963, founder ann. clin. conf., Testimonial of Appreciation 1978, Biog. Roll of Honor award 1983), Ill. Med. Soc. (1st v.p. 1968), AMA, Am., Internat. colls. surgeons, World Med. Assn., Internat. Assn. Burn Injuries, Chgo. Natural History Mus. (life), Am. Burn Assn., Art Inst. Chgo. Clubs: Quadrangle (Chgo.), Executive (Chgo.). Home: Chicago Ill. Died Aug. 19, 1995.

EPSTEIN, JOSEPH, philosophy educator; b. N.Y.C., Jan. 19, 1917; s. Isador and Ida (Snofsky) E.; m. Lucille Goldberger, June 22, 1940; children: Joshua Morris, Samuel David. B.S., CCNY, 1939; Ph.D., Columbia U., 1951; M.A. (hon.), Amherst Coll., 1961. Physicist research and devel. U.S. Army Signal Corps. Labs., 1942-44; physicist research and devel. Fed. Telephone & Radio Corp., Newark, 1944-46; from lectr. to asst. prof. Columbia U., 1946-51; faculty Amherst Coll., Mass., 1952-71; prof. philosophy Amherst Coll., 1961-71, Crosby prof. philosophy, 1976-93; vis. prof. philosophy Yale U., 1966-67; mem. consulente aggregato Centro Superiore di Logica e Scienze Comparate, Bologna, Italy, 1972-93. Editor: Alexandrian Editions, 1960, Rene Descartes: A Discourse on Method and Other Works, 1965, (with Gail Kennedy) The Process of Philosophy, 1967; contbr. articles to profl. jours. Rockefeller Found. grantee, 1958; Ford Humanities grantee, 1972. Mem. AAUP, Am. Philos. Assn., Am. Assn. Physics Tchrs., Mind Assn. N.Y. Acad. Scis., Sigma Xi. Patentee in field. Home: Amherst Mass. Died May 23, 1993.

EPSTEIN, LAURA, social work educator, consultant; b. Chgo., Oct. 31, 1914; d. Ellik and Rose (Kwatnez) E. A.M., U. Chgo., 1936. Cert. Acad. Cert. Social Workers. Field instr. social work U. Chgo., 1967-70, asst. prof., 1970-72, assoc. prof., 1972-76, prof., 1976—; vis. prof. Wilfred Laurier U., Waterloo, Ont., Can., 1980-82; cons. W.Va. Dept. Social Welfare, Charleston, 1982, Villemarie Community Service, Montreal, Que., Can., 1982. Author: Helping People: The Task Centered Approach, 1980, 2d rev. edit., 1988, Talking and Listening: Guide to the Helping Interview, 1985, Brief Treatment: A New Look at the Task-Centered Approach, 1992; editor: (with William J. Reid) Task Centered Casework, 1972, Task Centered Practice, 1977. Mem. Council on Social Work Edn. (del. 1980-83), Nat. Assn. Social Workers. Jewish. Died Sept. 18, 1996.

ERDOS, PAUL, mathematician; b. Budapest, Hungary, Mar. 26, 1913; s. Louis and Anne (Wilhelm) E. Ed. Budapest U. Corr. mem. Hungarian Acad. Scis., Budapest, 1956-62, mem., 1962—. Author: (with Surányi) Válogatott Fejezetak a Számé lmeletból; (with J. Spencer) Probabilistic Methods in Combinations, 1974; Editor (with G. Katona) Theory of Graphs, 1969. Editor in chief: Periodica Mathematica. Recipient Cole prize, U.S., 1951, Kossuth prize, 1958, Wolf prize, 1983. Mem. Royal Dutch Acad., Australian Acad. Scis. Died Sept. 20, 1996.

ERICKSON, FRANK WILLIAM, composer; b. Spokane, Wash., Sept. 1, 1923; s. Frank O. and Myrtle L. (Leck) E.; m. Mary A. Smith, Aug. 15, 1981; children by previous marriage—William, Richard, Christian. Mus.B., U. So. Calif., 1950, Mus.M., 1951. Rep. Bourne Co. (music pubs.), 1952-58; lectr. U. Calif., Los Angeles, 1958; prof. music San Jose (Calif.) State U., 1959-61; owner Frank Erickson Publ., Oceanside, Calif., 1996. Composer, arranger, 1961-96; works include 1st Symphony for Band, 1954, 2d Symphony for Band, 1959, Toccata for Band, 1957, Air for Band, 1956, Balladair, 1956, Double Concerto for Trumpet, Trombone and Band, 1951, Fantasy for Band, 1955, Concerto for Alto Saxophone and Band, 1961, Sonatina for Band, 1962, Rhythm of the Winds, 1964, Citadel, 1964, Blue Ridge Overture, 1976, Overture Jubiloso, 1978, 3d Symphony for Band, 1984, Aria Cantabile, 1990, Time and the Winds, 1991, Festiva Musica, 1991, The Tide Rises, The Tide Falls, 1992, Misty Rain, Softly Falling, 1992; pub. Ballad for Peace, Shadow of Condor, Fantasy on Mexican Folk Tunes, Fantasy on Nordic Themes, "A" is for Allegro, "B" is for Baroque, "C" is for Chorale, (CD) Frank Erickson Band Classics, and other arrangements of Percy Grainger tunes. Served with USAAF, 1942-46. Mem. ASCAP, Nat. Band Assn. (life), Acad. Wind and Percussion Arts (elected 1986), Phi Mu Alpha Sinfonia, Pi Kappa Lambda. Home: Oceanside CA Died Oct. 21, 1996.

ERICKSON, LEROY, state senator, farmer; b. DeLamere, N.D., May 15, 1926; s. Ed and Agnes (Martinson) E.; grad. high sch.; m. Lila Moxness, Nov. 10, 1946; children—Marsha Susag, Kim Mund. Rep. N.D. Legislature, 1967-68, 73-80, N.D. Senate, 1981-84; grain farmer, DeLamere. Del., N.D. Constnl. Conv., 1972; twp. supr., 1952-54; mem. County Sch. Reorgn. Bd., County Spl. Edn. Bd.; dir. S.E. Mental Health; active PTA, Farm Bur. Task Forces. Recipient Sparkplug award for communication for agr., 1981. Mem. Farm Bur., Internat. Flying Farmers, N.D. Stockmen's Assn. (legis. rep.), Aircraft Owners and Pilots Assn. Republican. Lutheran. Club: Milnor Satellite.

ESLICK, LEONARD JAMES, philosopher, educator; b. Denver, Nov. 8, 1914; s. Theodore Parker and Leila (Van Natta) E.; m. Florence Elizabeth Weber, May 3, 1935. A.B., U. Chgo., 1934; M.A., Tulane U., 1936; Ph.D., U. Va., 1939. Instr. philosophy Drake U., Des Moines, 1939-42; tutor St. John's Coll., Annapolis, Md., 1943-48; asso. prof. St. Louis U., 1948-57, prof., 1957-91; vis. prof. U. Va. at Charlottesville, 1961, U. Ill. at Urbana, 1965, U. Notre Dame, 1968. Asso. editor: Modern Schoolman, 1950-91 ; editorial Bd.: Process Studies, 1970-91 ; Contbr. articles on metaphysics, Plato, A.N. Whitehead to philos. jours., books. Served with AUS, 1942. Mem. Am. Philos. Assn., Mo. Philos. Assn. (pres. 1958-59), Metaphys. Soc. Am., Cath. Commn. Intellectual and Cultural Affairs, Phi Beta Kappa. Home: Saint Louis Mo. Died Apil 6, 1991; interred Resurrection Cemetery, St. Louis, MO.

ESSEX, HARRY J., screenwriter, novelist; b. N.Y.C., Nov. 29, 1915; s. Wolfe Wilhelm and Sarah (Bratter) E.; m. Lee Berman, June 22, 1945; children: David, Sarah Madlene. BBA, St. Johns U., 1936. Screenwriter Columbia Studio, Hollywood, Calif., 1945-50, RKO Pictures, Hollywood, 1950-55, Universal Pictures, Universal City, Calif., 1955-65; screenwriter Warner Bros., Burbank, Calif., 1955-60, script writer, story editor, 1968-97; writer Metro Goldwyn Mayer, Culver City, Calif., 1960-65. Writer numerous NBC-TV films including Hostage Flight, 1987, (TV series) Untouchables, Playhouse 90; scenarist: (films) The Lonely Man, 1956, Man and Boy, 1973, The Amigos, 1974, Sons of Katie Elder, 1964, He Walked by Night, 1948, It Came from Outer Space, 1953; playwright: (Broadway prodns.) Something For Nothing, 1954, Neighborhood Affair, 1960, One for the Dame, 1961, Twilight, 1980; play prodns. Dark Passion, 1970, Fatty, 1985; owner, head writer Target the Corruptors, 1961-62; author: (novels) I Put My Right Foot In, 1954, Man and Boy, 1971, Marina, 1981. Served as cpl. AUS, 1942-45. Recipient Theatre Guild award for playwriting, 1940, Venice Festival award, 1949; named to Western Hall of Fame, 1950. Mem. Dramatists League, Writers Guild Am. West, Acad. Motion Picture Arts and Scis., Dirs. Guild. Democrat. Jewish. Avocation: sailing. Deceased.

ESSLINGER, NELL DANIEL, singer, choral director, writer; b. Huntsville, Ala., June 13, 1903; d. William Francis and Blanche (Russell) E.; m. Raymond G. Miller, Aug. 18, 1979. Vocal cert., Agnes Scott Coll., 1922; BA, U. Ala., 1954; MMus., U. Ill., 1962. Dir. Huntsville Music Study Club Chorus, 1938-39, 48-50, Male Chorus, 1948, Tri-Choral, 1950, Music Appreciation Club, 1950; dir., instr. voice Koch Sch. Music, Rocky River, Ohio, 1963-64; tchr. voice Baldwin Wallace Coll., Berea, Ohio, 1965-66; tchr. voice, choral dir. N.E. State Jr. Coll., Rainsville, Ala., 1966-69; owner, CEO The Notation Press, Ala., 1965-96. Debut Carnegie Hall Chambers, N.Y., 1925; ch. and oratorio soloist, 1919-39, guest soloist Waldorf Astoria, N.Y., 1924, 25, Kenilworth Inn, Battery Park Inn, Ashveville, N.C., 1926; appeared in theatre prodns. ADrienne, 1924, Roxy's Gang, N.Y., 1925; radio shows Mr. Naftzeger's Morning Hour, N.Y., The House by the Side of the Road, others; author: (textbook) Revised Notation, 1965, 87 (award for Creative Achievement Ga. Sci. and Tech. Commn. 1968), The Variety of Voice, 1989; also poetry; composer (songs) Immortal, 1996, All for Alabama, 1996. Recipient awards Ala. Writers Conclave, Ala. State Poetry Soc., 1989-90. Mem. Ala. Assn. Inventors, Huntsville Music Study Club (hon. life), Bus. and Profl. Women's Club (charter Rainsville, Ala.), Alpha Epsilon Rho. Died Aug. 1, 1996.

ETCHART, FERDINAND J., food products executive. Mgr. Admiral Packing Co., Glendale, Ariz., 1964-72; now pres. Everkrisp Vegetables, Inc. Died, 1995.

ETTINGER, RICHARD PRENTICE, publishing company executive; b. N.Y.C., Sept. 27, 1922; s. Richard Prentice and Elsie (Davis) E.; m. Sharon Whitaker, May 1, 1971; children: Deborah, Pamela, Heidi, Barbara, Wendy, Richard Prentice, Ronene, Jean, James, Christian, Leland, Matthew. AB, Dartmouth Coll., 1944; LittD, Whittier Coll., 1973. Field rep. coll. div. Prentice-Hall, Inc., 1947-50, Western div. mgr., 1951-54, asst. to pres., 1955, dir., 1951-58, 82-96; pres. Wadsworth Pub. Co., Belmont, Calif., 1957-64; chmn. Wadsworth Pub. Co., 1964-77, Dickenson Pub. Co., Los Angeles, 1968-77, Allyn & Bacon, Inc., Boston, 1980-81, HDL Communications; bd. trustees Ednl. Found. Am., Westport, Conn. Mem. bd. visitors UCLA Grad. Sch. Mgmt., 1975-84, UCLA Sch. Medicine, 1983-89; bd. dirs. U. Calif. Irvine Found., 1986-91, The Earth Circle Found.; trustee Whittier (Calif.) Coll., 1970-76, Nat. Fitness Found., 1986-89; mem. bd. overseers Dartmouth Med. Sch., 1976-79; pres. Native Am. Preparatory Sch., 1988-96, Ettinger Found., 1980-96, Pres.' Cir., NAS, 1990-96. Mem. SAR, Belmont C. of C. (pres. 1969-70), U.S. Yacht Racing Assn., Stanford Sailing Assn. (trustee 1977-81), Indian Harbor Yacht Club, Newport Harbor Yacht Club. Republican. Episcopalian. Home: Santa Fe N. Mex. Died Apr. 26, 1996.

EUTON, MICHAEL FRED, landscape architect; b. Houston, Aug. 10, 1938; s. William Robert and Lillie Bertha (Wischer) E.; student U. Tex., Austin, 1956-59, Massey Bus. Coll., Houston, 1972. Sales mgr. Civic Reading Club, Houston and San Antonio, 1960-62; designer Davis Landscape Service, Houston, 1962-66; landscape architect Mike Euton Landscape Service, Barker, Tex., 1966—, City of Katy (Tex.), 1975-80; founder, pres. Teutonic Internat., 1985; lectr. in field. Exec. com. Democratic Party Harris County (Tex.), 1966-68; del. Harris County Dem. Conv., 1960-80, 84, Tex. State Dem. Conv., 1960, 64, 68, 72, 74; precinct election judge, 1976; mem. U.S. Senator William A. Blakley's Harris County Campaign Staff, 1961; active campaigns J. Evetts Haley for Gov., 1956, W. Lee O'Daniel for Gov., 1956, Dolph Briscoe for Gov., 1968, 72, 74, Bill Clements for Gov., 1978, George Wallace for Pres., 1968, 72, Lloyd Bentsen for Pres., 1976, Reagan for Pres., 1976, John Connally for Pres., 1980, Dems. for Reagan, 1980; Jesse Jackson for Pres., 1984, Reagan-Bush campaign, 1984; active numerous campaigns for U.S. Senate and Ho. of Reps. from Tex., 1957—; mem. Rep. Presdl. Task Force, 1984, 85; active Dems. for Eisenhower, 1956, Dems. for Goldwater, 1964; mem. U.S. Olympic Com., 1980; ex post facto mem. Katy Horizons Com., 1980, 81; mem. horizons com. Tri County Am. Revolution Bicentennial Commn., 1976; mem. Statue of Liberty-Ellis Island Centennial Commn., 1983; mem. Presdl. Task Force, 1984, 85. Recipient U.S. Presdl. Achievement award, 1983; U.S. Presdl. Achievement award for environ. protection, 1985; cert. of appreciation Vietnam Vets. Meml. Fund, 1983; cert. of recognition Republican Congl. Com., 1985; Presdl. cert. of merit for environ. protection, 1985. Mem. Tex. Soc. Landscape Architects, Tex. Farm Bur., Barker Heritage and Preservation Soc. (charter mem., sec. 1976, pres. 1977-78, chmn. bd. 1979—), Native Plant Soc. Tex. (charter), Teutonic Internat. (founder, pres. 1986—), Katy C. of C., U. Tex. Ex-students Assn., C. of C. (life), Nat. Rifle Assn. Club: One-Hundred (Houston). Died May 4, 1988.

EVANS, EDWIN CHARLES, consultant, former manufacturing executive; b. Waterford, N.Y., May 23, 1910; s. Edwin Bernard and Sarah (Slavin) E.; m. Renette Wendell, July 22, 1944. Student, Rensselaer Poly. Inst., 1930-31, Siena Coll., 1939-40, Harvard Grad. Sch. Bus. Adminstrn., 1949. Civil engr. N.Y. State Engring. Dept., 1928-34; with Behr-Manning div. (now Abrasive and Tape divs.) Norton Co.), Troy, N.Y., 1934-68; beginning as mem. sales analysis dept., successively staff purchasing dept., asst. purchasing agt., purchasing agt., asst. to v.p. charge engring. and Behr-Manning div. (now Abrasive div.) Norton Co.), 1955-59; gen. mgr. Behr-Manning div. (now Abrasive and Tape divs.) Norton Co.), 1959-68, pres., 1961-68; cons. N.Y. State Dept. Commerce, 1970-94, asst. dep. commr., 1972-75; v.p. Norton Co., Worcester, Mass., 1961-68. Bd. dirs. Samaritan Hosp.,; trustee Albany Med. Coll. of Union U. Mem. Harvard Bus. Sch. Assn. Club: Troy Country. Home: Troy N.Y. Died Sept. 6, 1994.

EVANS, ERNEST PIPKIN, JR., municipal official; b. St. Petersburg, Fla., Mar. 6, 1944; s. Ernest Pipkin and Carrie (McLeod) E. BS, U. Md., 1972. Chief investigator U.S. Senate Com. on Small Bus., Washington, 1967-74; asst. dir. Com. on Fed. Paperwork, Washington, 1975-77; spl. asst. Dept. Justice Immigration and Naturalization Svc., Washington, 1977-80; sr. ptnr. Ernest Evans & Assocs., Washington, 1980-90; pres. Stonewall Broadcasting Co., Elkton, Va., 1986—; spl. asst. Office of the Mayor, Washington, 1991—; bd. dirs. Am. Internat. Mgmt. Co., Washington. Producer: (radio series) Our Community, Our World, 1989; (radio advt. campaign) Small Market Broadcasters, 1989 (hon. mention). Mem. Dem. Com., Page County, Va., 1990, Gertrude Stein Dem. Club, Washington, 1994. Recipient Reader's Digest cert. of merit, 1965. Mem. Assn. Former Senate Aides, Congl. Correspondents Club, Human Rights Campaign Fund., Lambda Legal Defense Fund. Episcopalian.

EVANS, GERARD ERWIN, retired obstetrician and gynecologist; b. Bklyn., 1922. MD, N.Y. Med. Coll., 1945; BS, U. Ark., 1942. Diplomate Am. Bd. Ob-Gyn. Intern Cumberland Hosp., Bklyn., 1945-46, 48, resident in ob-gyn., 1948-52. Fellow ACS, ACOG; mem. AMA. Died Aug., 1997.

EVARTS, HAL GEORGE, JR., author; b. Hutchinson, Kans., Feb. 8, 1915; s. Hal George and Sylvia (Abraham) E.; B.A., Stanford U., 1936; m. Dorothea Van Dusen Abbott, June 28, 1942; children—Virginia Leland, William Abbott, John Van Dusen. Reporter, Evening Tribune, San Diego, 1935, Call Bull., San Francisco, 1939; reporter, writer Occidental Pub. Co., San Francisco, 1938; writer N.Y. Herald Tribune, European edit., Paris, 1939-40; author novels, including: Treasure River, 1964; The Talking Mountain, 1966; Smugglers' Road, 1968; Mission to Tibet, 1970; The Pegleg Mystery, 1972; Bigfoot, 1973; author biographies: Jedediah Smith, 1958; Jim Clyman, 1959; author anthology: Fugitive's Canyon, 1955, From Skunk Ranch to Hollywood, 1989; contbr. numerous short stories to nat. mags., including Saturday Evening Post, Esquire, Collier's, Am., This Week; tchr. creative writing at workshops. Served with inf. U.S. Army, 1943-45. Recipient Charlie May Simon award for children's lit. Ark. State Sch. Council, 1976, Spl. award Mystery Writers Am., 1964, 68. Mem. Western Writers Am. (v.p. 1959-60, Spl. award 1973), Zeta Psi.

EWERS, JOHN CANFIELD, museum administrator; b. Cleve., July 21, 1909; s. John Ray and Mary Alice (Canfield) E.; m. Margaret Elizabeth Dumville, Sept. 6, 1934; children: Jane (Mrs. Robinson), Diane (Mrs. Peterson). AB, Dartmouth Coll., 1931, DSc, 1968; MA, Yale U., 1934; LLD, U. Mont., 1966; DLitt (hon.), Mont. State U., 1994. Field curator Nat. Park Service, Washington, Morristown, N.J., Berkeley, Calif., Macon, Ga., 1935-40; curator Mus. Plains Indian, Browning, Mont., 1941-44; assoc. curator ethnology U.S. Nat. Mus., Smithsonian Instn., Washington, 1946-56; planning officer U.S. Nat. Mus., Smithsonian Instn., 1956-59, asst. dir. Mus. History and Tech., 1959-64, dir., 1964-65; sr. scientist U.S. Nat. Mus., Smithsonian Instn. (Office Anthropology), 1965-79; now ethnologist emeritus U.S. Nat. Mus., Smithsonian Instn. (Dept. Anthropology); research assoc., hon. trustee Mus. Am. Indian Heye Found., N.Y.C., 1979-90; mus. planning cons. Bur. Indian Affairs, 1948-49, Mont. Hist. Soc., 1950-54; cons. Am. Heritage, 1959. Author: Plains Indian Painting, 1940, The Horse in Blackfoot Indian Culture, 1955 (reprinted in Classics of Smithsonian Anthropology Series, 1980), The Blackfeet: Raiders on the Northwestern Plains, 1958, Artists of the Old West, 1965, Indian Life on Upper Missouri, 1968, Murals in the Round: Painted Tipis of the Kiowa and Kiowa-Apache Indians, 1978, Plains Indian Sculpture, 1986; editor: Adventures of Zenas Leonard, Fur Trader, 1959, Crow Indian Medicine Bundles, 1960, Five Indian Tribes of the Upper Missouri, 1961, O-Kee-pa, A Religious Ceremony and Other Customs of the Mandans, (George Catlin), 1967, Jean Louis Berlandier's Indians of Texas in 1830, 1969, Jose Francisco Ruîz, Report on the Indian Tribes of Texas in 1828, 1972, Indian Art in Pipestone, George Catlin's Portfolio in the British Museum, 1979; editor Jour. Washington Acad. Scis, 1955-56; mem. editorial bd.: The American West, 1965-70; contbr. articles to profl. publs. Served with USNR, 1944-46. Recipient 1st Exceptional Svc. medal Smithsonian Instn., 1965, award for rsch. and publs. in Am. Indian art Native Am. Art Studies Assn., 1989, gold medal for contbn. to history of Am., West Buffalo Bill Hist. Ctr., 1991, award for disting. svc. Am. Assn. Mus., 1996. Fellow Am. Anthrop. Assn., Rochester Mus. Arts and Scis.; mem. Western History Assn. (hon. life, prize for disting. writing 1985), Am. Indian Ethnohist. Conf. (pres. 1960-61), Anthrop. Soc. Washington. Clubs: Cosmos (Washington); Explorers (N.Y.C.). Died May 7, 1997.

EWING, ROBERT, lawyer; b. Little Rock, July 18, 1922; s. Esmond and Frances (Howell) E.; m. Elizabeth Smith, May 24, 1947; 1 child, Elizabeth Milbrey. BA, Washington and Lee U., 1943; LLB, Yale U., 1945. Bar: Conn. 1945. Assoc. Shipman & Goodwin, Hartford, Conn., 1945-50; ptnr. Shipman & Goodwin, Hartford, 1950-94, of counsel, 1994-97; asst. pros. atty. West Hartford, Conn., 1953-55; dir., asst. sec. H.W. Steane Co. Inc., Rocktide Inc.; dir., pres. Still Pasture Corp. Mem. U.S. Constitution Bicentennial Commn. Conn., 1986-91; incorporator Hartford Hosp., Hartford Conservatory; bd. dirs. Travelers Aid Soc. Hartford, 1951-57, treas., 1954-57; bd. dirs. Greater Hartford chpt. ARC, 1974-97, chmn., 1977-79, mem. exec. com., 1977-96, blood svcs. com., 1986-91; chmn. ARC Blood Svcs. Conn. region, 1989-92, Ea. Ops. Adv. Coun., 1988-91; bd. dirs. Family Svc. Soc., 1961-65, Conn. Pub. Expenditure Coun., 1986-91, Old State House, 1991-97, Conn. Coalition Against Gun Violence, 1993-96, mem. adv. bd., 1996—, Knox Parks Found., 1994-97; trustee Watkinson Libr. Trinity Coll., 1989-92; life trustee Old State House. Fellow Am. Bar Found.; mem. ABA, Conn. Bar Assn. (chmn. fed. practice com. 1976-79, exec. com. corp. sect. 1981-85), Hartford County Bar Assn., Am. Law Inst., Conn. Hist. Soc. (standing com. 1954-77, trustee 1978-97, chmn. adminstrv. com. 1980-88, v.p. 1982-89, chmn. pers. com. 1987-89, pres. 1989-92), Newcomen Soc. N.Am., Rotary (pres. Hartford 1966-67, Paul Harris fellow 1988), Twentieth Century Club (pres. 1975-76), Hartford Club (counsel 1975-90, bd. govs. 1991-97, sec. 1994-97), Old Guard of West Hartford, Mory's Assn., Dauntless Club. Congregationalist. (sr. deacon 1972-75). Died 1997.

EYNON, THOMAS HENRY, broadcasting executive; speech educator; b. Providence, Sept. 30, 1928; s. Thomas Benjamin Eynon and Ivy Rita (Robertshaw) Dubrotsky; separated; children: Thomas Mark, Wendy, Marisa. B.A., Saginaw Valley State U., 1973; M.A., Central Mich. U., 1976. News anchorman Sta. WSUN-TV, St. Petersburg, Fla., 1953-55, Sta. KIVA-TV, Yuma, Ariz., 1955-56; news anchorman Sta. WNEM-TV, Saginaw, Mich., 1956-60, news dir., 1960-72, community affairs dir., from 1972; pres. Tom Eynon & Assocs., Saginaw, from 1980. Served with USAF, 1946-53. Recipient Sch. Bell award NEA, 1972, Addy award

Flint Advt. Fedn., 1980, Addy award Advt. Fedn. Saginaw Valley; U. Chgo. fellow, 1982. Republican. Club: Elf Khurafeh. Lodges: Shriners, Masons. Avocation: golf. Deceased. Home: Saginaw Mich.

EYSENCK, HANS JURGEN, psychology educator; b. Berlin, Mar. 4, 1916; s. Eduard Anton and Ruth (Werner) E.; m. Margaret Davies, 1938 (div. 1950); 1 son, Michael; m. Sybil Giuletta Rostal, Sept. 30, 1950; children: Gary, Connie, Kevin, Darrin. BA, U. London, 1938, PhD, 1940, DSc, 1964. Rsch. psychologist Mill Hill Hosp., London, 1942-48; reader Inst. of Psychiatry, London, 1948-55; prof. U. London, 1955-83, prof. emeritus, 1983-97; dir. Personality Investigations, Publs. and Svcs., London, 1975-97; founder Behaviour Rsch. and Therapy. Author 84 books, 1094 articles; founder, editor Personality and Individual Differences. Fellow Am. Psychol. Assn., Brit. Psychol. Soc.; mem. Internat. Soc. for Study of Individual Differences (pres. 1983-85), German Soc. Psychology, Dulwich Tennis Club. Died Sept. 4, 1997.

EYSTER, WILLIAM BIBB, lawyer; b. Decatur, Ala., June 21, 1921; s. Charles Harris and Katharine C. (Bibb) E.; m. Ann J. Kimbrough, May 29, 1948; children—Katharine Ann, William B. B.A. with honors, U. South, 1941; postgrad., Law Sch., U. Va., 1941-42; LL.B., U. Ala., 1947. Bar: Ala. Sr. ptnr. Eyster, Key, Tubb, Weaver & Roth and predecessors, Decatur, 1947-95; dir., chmn. local bd. AmSouth Bank Decatur, AmSouth Bancorp, AmSouth Bank, N.A. Past v.p. Decatur C. of C. Served with USNR, 1942-46. Fellow Am. Coll. Trial Lawyers; mem. ABA, Ala. Bar Assn., Morgan County Bar Assn. Episcopalian. Home: Decatur Ala. Died June 2, 1995.

FACKLER, WALTER DAVID, economist, educator; b. Aitkin, Minn., Aug. 27, 1921; s. Leonard D. and Ruth (Wanous) F.; m. Hazel Shepardson, May 24, 1951; children: Mark Duval, Neil Evan, Paul Leonard. AB with distinction and spl. honors, George Washington U., 1950; postgrad., John Hopkins U., 1951-54. Accountant Pub. Service Co. of Ind., 1939-42; asst. prof. econs. George Washington U., Washington, 1950-56; asst. to dean faculties George Washington U., 1953-56, dir. fgn. service rev. program, 1950-54; instr. polit. economy Johns Hopkins, 1952-54; asst. dir. dept. econ rsch. U.S. C. of C., Washington, 1956-59; sr. economist Cabinet Com. on Price Stability for Econ. Growth, Washington, 1959-60; asso. prof. bus. econs. U. Chgo. Grad. Sch. Bus., 1960-62, prof., 1962-91, prof. emeritus, 1991-93, assoc. dean, 1962-69, acting dean, 1968-69, dir. mgmt. programs, 1970-87; bus. and govt. cons., 1950-93, lectr., 1950-93. Contbr. articles to profl. publs. Served to capt. AUS, 1942-46. Decorated Bronze Star. Mem. Am. Econ. Assn., Am. Statis. Assn., Econ. Club (Chgo.), Univ. Club (Chgo.), Quadrangle Club (Chgo.), Phi Beta Kappa. Home: Chicago Ill. Died July 22, 1993.

FAHIM, MOSTAFA SAFWAT, reproductive biologist, consultant; b. Cairo, Egypt, Oct. 7, 1931; came to U.S., 1966; s. Mohamed and Amna (Hussin) F.; m. Zuhal Fahim, Feb. 23, 1959; 1 child, Ayshe. B.S. in Agrl. Chemistry, U. Cairo, 1953; M.S., U. Mo., 1958, PhD in Reproductive Biology, 1961. Research assoc. Sch. Medicine, U. Mo., Columbia, 1966-68, asst. prof., 1968-71, assoc. prof., 1971-75, prof., 1975—, chief reproductive biol. rsch., 1971-87, dir. Ctr. Reproductive Sci. and Tech., 1987—; prof. environ. trace substances rsch. U. Mo., Columbia, 1981—; cons. in field. Contbr. articles to profl. jours.; patentee in field. Mem. Am. Pub. Health Assn., Mo. Pub. Health Assn., Nutrition Today Soc., Internat. Andrology Soc., Internat. Toxicology Soc., Am. Coll. Clin. Pharmacology, Am. Soc. Pharmacology and Exptl. Therapeutics, Internat. Fertility Soc., Am. Fertility Soc., Fedn. Am. Socs. Exptl. Biology, N.Y. Acad. Scis., Soc. Environ. Geochemistry and Health, Soc. Study Reprodn., AAAS, Sigma Xi, Gamma Alpha. Achievements include patents for Minerals in Bioavailable Form, for Composition and Process for Promoting Epithelial Regeneration, for Intraprostatic Injection of Zinc Ions for Treatment of Inflammatory Conditions and Benigh and Malignant Tumors of the Prostate, for Method of Inhibiting Generation, Maturation, Motility and Viability of Sperm With Minerals in Bioavailable Form, for Chemical Castration.

FAIMAN, ROBERT NEIL, academic administrator; b. Excelsior, Minn., June 25, 1923; s. Clarence C. and Henrietta (Baker) F.; m. Eunice A. Kessler, Mar. 12, 1944; children: Robert Neil Jr., John Charles. BSEE, N.D. State Coll., 1947; MSEE, U. Wash., 1948; PhD, Purdue U., 1956. Registered profl. engr., Ohio. Asso. elec. engring. U. Wash., 1947-48; from asst. prof. to prof. N.D. State Coll., 1948-58, chmn. dept., 1951-58; engr., engring. scis. program NSF, 1957-59; dean Coll. Tech., dir. Engring. Expt. Sta. U. N.H., 1959-67, v.p. research, 1967-74; acad. dir. Air Force Inst. Tech., Wright-Patterson AFB, Ohio, 1974-90, dir. emeritus, 1990-94. Mem. N.H. Bd. Registration for Profl. Engrs., 1971-74. Served with USAAF, 1943-46; maj. Res. ret. Recipient Alumni Achievement award N.D. State U., 1966. Fellow AAAS; mem. IEEE (sr., life), Am. Soc. Engring. Edn. (life), Soc. Profl. Engrs. (life), Air Force Assn., Rotary (Paul Harris fellow), Sigma Xi, Tau Beta Pi, Eta Kappa Nu, Phi Kappa Phi. Lodge: Rotary (Paul Harris fellow). Home: Durham N.H. Died Dec. 12, 1994; interred Memorial Garden, Durham , NH.

FAIRBURN, ROBERT GORDON, business executive; b. Cleve., July 2, 1911; s. William Armstrong and Louise (Ramsay) F.; m. Mary Whitwell, July 15, 1933; children: Anne, Louise Fairburn Lumley; m. Margaret Taylor Watson, July 2, 1951; 1 son, Robert Gardner; m. Eileen Baker Rickard, Aug. 12, 1972. A.B., Princeton U., 1932. With Berst-Forster-Dixfield Co., N.Y.C., 1932-47, pres., gen. mgr., 1942-47; dir. Diamond Match Co., 1941-57, pres., 1947-57; (Diamond Match Co. merged with Gardner Board & Carton Co. to become Diamond Gardner Corp. 1957; Diamond Gardner Corp. merged with U.S. Printing & Lith; chmn. bd., dir. Diamond Nat. Corp., to 1961, Keyes Fibre Co., N.Y.C., 1961-78; dir. Arcata Co., 1978-83; trustee Atacra Liquidating Corp., 1983-85; pres. William Gordon Corp.; co-owner, treas. H.R. Dunham Co., Waterville, Maine, 1975-84. Chmn. bd., trustee Thomas Coll., Waterville, 1974-80, trustee, 1980-84; trustee Marine Research Soc. of Bath, Maine, 1972-92. Mem. Masters of Fox Hounds Assn. Am. Presbyterian. Clubs: Princeton Quadrangle; Spring Valley Hounds (New Vernon, N.J.); Carmel Valley (Calif.) Golf and Country. Home: Carmel Calif. Died Sept. 26, 1992.

FAISON, EDMUND WINSTON JORDAN, marketing educator; b. Rocky Mount, N.C., Oct. 13, 1926; s. Nathan Marcus and Margery Lucille (Jordan) F.; m. Lois Harger Parker; children: Charles Parker, Dorothy Anne, Barbara Jeane, Edmund Jr., Diane, Carol. A.B. in Psychology, George Washington U., 1948, M.A., 1950, Ph.D., 1956. Rsch. asst. NRC, Washington, 1948-49; mgr. exptl. lab. Needham, Louis and Brorby, Chgo., 1955-56; account exec. Leo Burnett Co., 1957-58; v.p. Market Facts, Inc., Chgo., 1959; pres. Visual Rsch. Internat., Zurich, Switzerland, 1960-63; adviser AID, Dept. State, Latin Am., 1963-68; prof. bus. adminstrn. U. Hawaii, Honolulu, 1968-89; chmn. mktg. dept. U. Hawaii, 1975-82; chmn. bd. Scandata Hawaii, Inc., East-West Rsch. and Design, Inc.; vis. prof. London Grad. Sch. Bus. Studies, 1974-75. Author: Advertising: A Behavioral Approach for Managers, 1980; editorial bd. Jour. of Mktg, 1958-63; contbr. articles to profl. jours. With USN, 1944-46, USAF, 1950-54. Mem. Am. Psychol. Assn., Soc. Consumer Behavior, Am. Mktg. Assn. (pres. Honolulu chpt. 1973-74), Acad. Mktg. Sci., Acad. Mgmt., Am. Acad. Advt., Am. Assn. Public Opinion, Sales and Mktg. Execs. Internat., Advt. Rsch. Found., Japan-Am. Soc., Honolulu Advt. Fedn., Market Rsch. Soc. (U.K.), C. of C. of Hawaii, Japanese C. of C., Hawaii Visitors Bur., Small Bus. Assn. Hawaii, Honolulu Acad. Arts, All-Industry Packaging Assn. (chmn. 1961), European Packaging Fedn. (U.S. rep. 1961), World Packaging Orgn., Sigma Xi, Pi Sigma Epsilon, Pacific Club, Oahu Country Club, Kaneohe Yacht Club, Rotary. Home: Kailia Hawaii Died Jan. 26, 1989.

FALK, MYRON, fundraising consultant; b. New Orleans, May 8, 1906; s. Gustave Falk and Margurite Rodriguez; m. Roberta Gilkison, Sept. 2, 1934 (dec. 1980); 1 child, Elizabeth Falk Jones. BA, Tulane U., 1931, postgrad., 1932. Case worker New Orleans Dept. Pub. Welfare, 1932; exec. dir. Baton Rouge area Fed. Bur. Transients, 1933-36; field rep., sr. cons. La. State Dept. Pub. Welfare, 1936-41; dep. dir. La. Civilian Def. Office, 1941-42; exec. dir. Comty. Chest of Baton Rouge, 1944-52; organizer, exec. dir. United Givers Fund of Baton Rouge, 1952-64; dir. western region United Way of Am., N.Y., 1964-72; sr. fundraising cons. United Way of Am., Alexandria, Va., 1972-74; pvt. practice fundraising cons., 1974-78; organizer La. Coun. Migratory Labor and Transients, 1938-41, exec. sec., 1938-41; cons., dep. civilian def. coord. and evacuation officer State of La., 1952; vis. prof. Sch. Social Welfare, La. State U., 1952-64; organizer Comty. Fund for Arts, Baton Rouge exec. dir., 1988-89. Author several pamphlets; contbr. articles to profl. jours. Civilian def. coord. 5-state region 8th Svc. Command, Dallas, evacuation officer La., 1942-44; exec. dir. Baton Rouge Area Found., 1978-88, exec. dir. emeritus, 1990; dist. SCORE rep., La., 1982, 83; mem. adv. bd. Hospice Found. Baton Rouge, Found. Hist. La., Vols. Pub. Schs., Epilepsy Assn. Greater Baton Rouge, Cmty. Fund Arts, Arts Coun. Greater Baton Rouge, Cystic Fibrosis Stair Climb Com.; bd. dirs. ARC, Coun. Aging Baton Rouge Area, Consumer Edn. Found., YMCA. Recipient Cert. Disting. Svc. Pub. Edn., Phi Delta Kappa, 1989, Golden Rule award J.C. Penney Co., 1990, Spirit Giving award Nat. Soc. Fund Raising Execs., 1993, Humanitarian award Arthritis Found., 1994, Golden Apple award Vols. in Pub. Schs., 1994. Mem. Am. Assn. Social Workers (Baton Rouge chpt. pres 1938, nat. bd. dirs. 1946-48), United Way Retirees Assn. (nat. bd. dirs.), La. Conf. Social Welfare (pres. 1939), Rotary. DIED 06/17/97. .

FANUCCI, JEROME BENEDICT, aerospace and mechanical engineering; b. Glen Lyon, Pa., Oct. 7, 1924; s. Benjamin and Celia (Lanuti) F.; m. Janice C. Bavitz, Jan. 26, 1952; children: Jerome Paul, Karen Marie. B.S. in Aero. Engring., Pa. State U., 1944, M.S., 1952, Ph.D., 1956. Aero. engr. Eastern Aircraft Corp., Trenton, N.J., 1944-45, Republic Aviation Corp., Farmingdale, N.Y., 1947-49; asst. prof. aerospace engring. Pa. State U., 1956-57; research engr. Gen. Electric Aerospace Sci. Lab., Phila., 1957-59; sr. research scientist Plasma and Space Applied Physics Lab., RCA, Princeton, N.J., 1959-64; prof. aerospace engring. W.Va. U., Morgantown, 1964-91; chmn. dept. W.Va. U., 1964-81, prof. mech. and aerospace engring., 1981-90, prof. emeritus, 1990-91; indsl. cons. Contbr. articles profl. jours. Served with USAAF, 1946-47. Fellow AIAA (assoc.); mem. Am. Radio Relay League, Sigma Xi, Sigma Gamma Tau, Pi Tau Sigma. Co-designer first STOL aircraft using circulation control wing. Home: Morgantown W. Va. Died May 18, 1991.

FARKAS, PHILIP FRANCIS, musician, music educator; b. Chgo., Mar. 5, 1914; s. Emil Nelson and Anna (Cassady) F.; m. Margaret Groves, May 11, 1939; children—Carol, Lynn, Jean Ann, Margaret. Studied with, Louis Dufrasne, Chgo. Civic Orch.; Mus.D. (hon.), Eastern Mich. U., 1978. Disting. prof. music Ind. U., 1960-84, disting. prof. emeritus, 1984-92. Solo hornist, Kansas City Philharm., 1934-36, Chgo. Symphony Orch., 1936-41, 47- 60, Cleve. Orch., 1941-45, 46-47, Boston Symphony Orch., 1945-46; French horn player symphony orch., radio, other orchestras; author: The Art of French Horn Playing, 1956, The Art of Brass Playing, 1962, A Photographic Study of 40 Virtuoso Horn Players' Embouchures, 1970, The Art of Musicianship, 1976; editor: French Horn Excerpts from the Modern French Repertoire. Home: Bloomington Ind. Died Dec. 21, 1992.

FARLEY, JAMES THOMAS, hospital administrator; b. Chgo., Apr. 12, 1925; s. Thomas Walter and Nona F. (Kelly) F.; m. Mary Jean Powers, Oct. 4, 1947; children—James Thomas, Mary Margaret, Michael, Thomas, Patricia, Donal Joseph (dec.). B.S.A., Loyola U., Chgo., 1950; M.S. in Hosp. Adminstrn, Northwestern U., 1956. Vice pres. Meml. Sloan-Kettering Cancer Center, N.Y., 1964-68; pres. St. John Hosp., Detroit, 1968-84; Cons. NIH, 1969-70. Contbr. articles to profl. jours. Trustee St. Vincents Hosp., N.Y.C., 1967-68; trustee, treas. Hilton Head Hosp., 1987-93. Served with USAAF, 1943-46. Fellow Coll. Hosp. Adminstrs.; mem. Am., Mich. hosp. assns., Soc. Hosp. Adminstrv. Assos., Knights Malta. Club: Grosse Pointe. Home: Hilton Head S.C. Died Sept. 24, 1993.

FARLEY, LLOYD EDWARD, retired education educator, freelance writer; b. Nebr. Sand Hills nr. Broken Bow, Nebr., June 20, 1915; s. Arthur L. and Effie (Tyson) F.; A.B., Kearney State Coll. (currently U. Nebr.), 1945; M.A., Stanford U., 1947, Ed.D., 1950; Litt.D., William Woods U., 1982. Tchr. elem. and secondary schs., also adminstr., 1937-41, 47-51; ednl. specialist U.S. Govt., Washington, Anchorage, Edwards AFB, Calif., 1952-60; prof. edn. U. Alaska, Anchorage, 1960-64; Louis D. Beaumont Distinguished prof. edn., head div. social sci., Marshall faculty William Woods Coll., Fulton, Mo.; chmn. dept. edn. Westminster and William Woods Colls., Fulton, 1964-80, prof. edn. emeritus, 1980-95; vis. prof. St. Cloud State U., summers 1968-72, Aeromed. Inst., FAA, 1980-91. Served to maj. AUS, 1941-46. Named Hon. Tchr. Korea; recipient Centennial medal William Woods Coll. Mem. Nat. Assn. Tchr. Educators, Internat. Council on Edn. for Teaching, Kiwanis, Phi Delta Kappa, Kappa Delta Pi (hon. mem., named Outstanding Educator). Methodist. Died June 22, 1995. Home: Fulton Mo.

FARMER, WALTER INGS, interior designer; b. Alliance, Ohio, July 7, 1911; s. Fred Elihu and Alice Matilda (Putland) F.; m. Renate M. Wichelmann, June 15, 1947 (div. 1966); 1 child, Margaret C. BA, BArch, Miami U., Oxford, Ohio, 1935; LHD (hon.), Miami U., Ohio, 1973. Designer A.B. Closson, Jr. Co., Cin., 1935-42; style coordinator Foley's, Houston, 1946-49; designer, owner Greenwich House Interiors, Cin., 1949-97; lectr. Cin. Art Mus., 1936-70, Columbus (Ohio) Art Mus., 1949-60; instr. U. Cin., 1950-67; designer, trustee Martin D'Arcy Art Gallery Loyola U., Chgo. Author: In America Since 1607, 1987; author numerous papers. Mem. Commn. for Protection and Salvage Artistic and Hist. Monuments in War Areas U.S. State Dept., 1945-46; founder, 1st pres. bd. Contemporary Art Mus., Houston, 1945-49; founder Walter I. Farmer Mus., Miami U., 1978; chairperson O'Byronville Bus. Assn., 1971-73; mem. spl. com. for Park Bd. City of Cin. Served to capt., U.S. Army, 1942-45, ETO, ret. col. res. Recipient S.M. Hexter award, 1963, Factory's Top Plants of Yr. award, 1967, Designer's Choice award F. Schumacher and Co., 1972; Disting. Alumni award Alliance High Sch., 1989. Mem. AIA (affiliate), Am. Soc. Interior Design (state bd. govs., pres.), Inst. Practicing Designers, Soc. Archtl. Historian, Soc. Colonial Wars, Cin. Art Mus. (life), Taft Mus. (life), Mil. Order World Wars, Print and Drawing Circle (pres.), Literary Club (trustee, v.p., pres.), Delta Phi Delta, Phi Mu Alpha. Republican. Episcopalian. Avocation: collecting art, gardening, music, genealogy. Died Aug. 9, 1997.

FARR, LEE EDWARD, physician; b. Albuquerque, Oct. 13, 1907; s. Edward and Mabel (Heyn) F.; m. Anne Ritter, Dec. 28, 1936 (dec.); children: Charles E., Susan A., Frances A.; m. Miriam Kirk, Jan. 12, 1985. BS, Yale U., 1929, MD, 1933. Asst. pediatrics Sch. Medicine, Yale U., 1933-34; asst. medicine Hosp. of Rockefeller Inst. Med. Rsch., 1934-37, assoc. medicine, 1937-40; dir. research Alfred I. duPont Inst. of Nemours Found., Wilmington, Del., 1940-49; vis. assoc. prof.

pediatrics Sch. Medicine, U. Pa., 1940-49; med. dir. Brookhaven Nat. Lab., 1948-62; prof. nuclear medicine U. Tex. Postgrad. Med. Sch., 1962-64, prof. nuclear and environ. medicine Grad. Sch. Bio-Med. Scis., U. Tex. at Houston, 1965-68; chief sect. nuc. medicine U. Tex.-M.D. Anderson Hosp. and Tumor Inst., 1962-67, prof. environ. health U. Tex. Sch. Pub. Health, Houston, 1967-68; head disaster health svcs. Calif. Dept. Health, 1968, chief emergency health svcs. unit, 1968-70, 1st chief bur. emergency med. services, 1970-73; Lippitt lectr. Marquette U., 1941; Sommers Meml. lectr. U. Oreg. Sch. Med., Portland, 1960; Gordon Wilson lectr. Am. Clin. and Climatol. Assn., 1956; Sigma Xi nat. lectr., 1952-53; guest scientist Institut fur Medizinder Kernforschungsanlage, Julich, Germany, 1966; Brookhaven Nat. Lab. lectr., 1990. Mem. NRC adv. com. Naval Med. Res., 1953-68; chmn. NRC adv. com. Atomic Bomb Casualty Commn., 1953-68; mem. adv. com. Naval Res. to Sec. of Navy and CNO, 1968-72; NRC adv. com. on medicine and surgery, 1965-66, exec. com., 1962-65; Naval Research Mission to Formosa, 1953; tech. adviser U.S. delegation to Geneva Internat. Conf. for Peaceful Uses Atomic Energy, 1955; mem. N.Y. Adv. Com. Atomic Energy, 1956-59; mem. cholera commn. SEATO Conf., Bangkok, 1960; mem. AMA Com. Nuclear Medicine, 1963-66; mem. com. med. isotopes NASA Manned Spacecraft Ctr., 1966-68; mem. expert adv. panel radiation WHO, 1957-79; mem. Calif. Gov.'s Ad Hoc Com. Emergency Health Service, 1968-69; mem. sci. adv. bd. Gorgas Meml. Inst., 1967-72; numerous other sci. adv. bds., panels; cons. TRW Systems, Inc., 1966-70, Consol. Petroleum Co., Beverly Hills, Calif., 1946-70. Mem. alumni bd. Yale, 1962-65, mem. alumni fund, 1966-76, agent alumni fund 1994-96; with 1929 class coun. 1994-96. With USNR, 1942-46; capt. (M.C.) USNR, ret. Recipient Mead Johnson award for pediatric research, 1940, Gold Cross Order of Phoenix, Greece, 1960, Verdienstkreuz 1st class Fed. Republic Germany, 1963; named Community Leader in Am., 1969, Disting. Alumni Yale U. Med. Sch., 1989. Diplomate Nat. Bd. Med. Examiners, Am. Bd. Pediatrics. Fellow AAAS, Royal Soc. Arts, Am. Acad. Pediatrics, N.Y. Acad. Scis., Royal Soc. Health, Am. Coll. Nuclear Medicine (disting. fellow); mem. Soc. Pediatric Research, Soc. Exptl. Biology, Harvey Soc., Am. Pediatric Soc., Soc. Exptl. Pathology, Am. Soc. Clin. Investigation, Radiation Research Soc., AMA (mem. council on sci. assembly 1960-70, chmn. 1968-70), Med. Soc. Athens (hon. mem.), Alameda County Med. Assn., Sigma Xi, Alpha Omega Alpha, Phi Sigma Kappa, Nu Sigma Nu, Alpha Chi Sigma. Club: Commonwealth (San Francisco). Author articles on nuclear medicine, protein metabolism, emergency med. services, radioactive and chem. environ. contaminants, environ. noise. Died July 16, 1997.

FARRELL, EUGENE GEORGE, editor; b. Bklyn., Feb. 12, 1905; s. Stephen Andrew and Anna Louise (Kronholm) F.; m. Margaret Frances Reidy, 1928 (dec. 1951); children—Stephen John (dec.), Francis Xavier, Peter Michael; m. Lois Jane Fegan, 1952. A.B. cum laude, U. Notre Dame, 1928. With L.I. Daily Press, Jamaica, N.Y., 1928-38, sports editor, 1937, city editor, 1938; editor L.I. Star, L.I. City Star-Jour., Long Island City, N.Y., 1938-41; city editor, mng. editor Newark Star-Ledger, 1942-48; editorial asst. to pub. Harrisburg Patriot and News, Pa., 1948-51; founding editor Sunday Patriot-News, 1949; editor Jersey Jour., 1951-70, exec. editor, 1970-75; travel writer Motor Club Am. News, 1974-89. Vice chmn. N.J. Pub. Market Commn., 1960-62, chair 1963; chmn. bd. mgrs. Jersey City Med. Ctr., 1962-67. Mem. Am. Soc. Newspaper Editors, Aviation and Space Writers Assn., Am. Assn. Travel Editors, N.J. Press Assn., U.S. Power Squadrons (Life, rear comdr., chmn. nat. publis. 1974-79), N.Y. Press Club, Little Ship (London) Club, Knights of Columbus, Sigma Delta Chi (life). Roman Catholic. Died Dec. 22, 1996; interred Holy Family Cemetery, Harrisburg, PA.

FARRIOR, JOSEPH BROWN, otologist; b. Tuscaloosa, Ala., Dec. 22, 1911; married; 2 children. B.S., U. Fla., 1932; M.D., Tulane U., 1936; M.S. in Otolaryngology, U. Mich., 1942. Diplomate: Am. Bd. Otolaryngology. Intern Tampa (Fla.) Gen. Hosp., 1936-37; resident in otolaryngology Roosevelt Hosp., N.Y.C., 1937-38; resident and instr. U. Mich. Med. Sch., 1938-42; cons. otology New Orleans Ear, Nose and Throat Hosp., 1945-48; asst. prof. Tulane U. Med. Sch., 1946-48; vis. surgeon Charity Hosp., New Orleans, 1947-48; practice medicine specializing in ear surgery Tampa, Fla., 1948-95; mem. staff St. Joseph's, Tampa Gen. hosps.; clin. prof. otolaryngology U. South Fla. Med. Sch., 1972-77, founding chmn. and clin. prof. otolaryngology emeritus, 1977-95, chief dept., 1972-75; Wherry Meml. lectr., 1976; Disting. Alumnus lectr. Tulane U. Med. Sch., 1976; Francis E. LeJeune Meml. lectr., 1978; otologist Oschner Clinic, 1946-48. Author papers in field. Served as officer M.C. AUS, 1942-45. Fellow Am. Acad. Ophthalmology and Otolaryngology (Gold medal 1973, Presdl. citation 1982), A.C.S., Am. Laryngol., Rhinol. and Otol. Soc., Otosclerosis Study Group (pres. 1965-66); mem. Am. Otol. Soc. (award of Merit 1981, Guest of Honor 1984, pres. 1981-82), Triological Soc. (v.p. So. sect. 1975), AMA (Billings Gold medal 1959, 69), So. Med. Assn., Fla. Med. Assn., Centurian Club (pres. 1966, life), Fla. Soc. Ophthalmology and Otolaryngology; corr. mem. various fgn. med. assns. Clubs: Palma Ceia Golf and Country, Tampa Yacht and Country, Tampa Rotary. Died May, 1995.

FATT, IRVING, optometry and bioengineering educator; b. Chgo., Sept. 16, 1920; s. David and Annie Lily (Arkin) F.; married; 1 child, Lois Fatt White. BS in Chemistry, UCLA, 1947, MS, 1948; PhD, U. So. Calif., 1955. Sr. research chemist Standard Oil Co., La Habra, Calif., 1948-52, group supr., 1952-57; mem. faculty U. Calif., Berkeley, 1957—, prof. physiol. optics and engring. sci., 1962-63, Miller Research prof. engring., 1962-67, asst. dean, 1964-69, acting dean, 1975-78, prof. emeritus, 1983—; cons. Berkeley, 1983—; Kinsey lectr. Contact Lens Assn. Ophthalmologists, 1988. Patentee in field. Served to 1st lt. USAAF, 1942-46. Recipient Herschel medal Internat. Soc. Contact Lens Specialists, 1985, Ruben medal Internat. Soc. Contact Lens Rsch., 1988, Dallos medal Contact Lens Mfg. Assn., 1989, gold medal Brit. Contact Lens Assn., 1994; rsch. career grantee Petroleum Fund, 1957. Mem. Biomed. Engring. Soc., Am. Acad. Optometry (Prentice medal 1984, Founders award 1984), U.K. Biol. Engring. Soc. Clubs: Berkeley Faculty, Berkeley Yacht. DIED 10/05/96. .

FAULK, ELIZABETH HAMMOND, psychologist; b. Jacksonville, Fla., May 18, 1925; d. John Harrison and Cornelia Annette (Noble) F. BA, Conn. Coll., 1947; MA, U. Fla., 1950, PhD, 1955; postgrad., Columbia U. Diplomate Am. Bd. Clin Psychology. Staff Menninger Clinic, Topeka, Kans., 1961; psychology svc. VA Hosp., Topeka, 1961-65; chief clin. psychologist Juvenile Ct. Psychiatric Clinic, Miami, Fla., 1965; sr. clin. psychologist/dir. psychol. tng. Guidance Ctr., Daytona, Fla., 1965-68; pvt. practice, pres. Psychol. & Cons. Svcs., Inc., Boca Raton, Fla., 1968-90, Deerfield Beach, Fla., 1990-94; cons., 1994—; founder Elizabeth H. Faulk Found. Ctr. for Group Counseling, 1971-73. Vestry mem. St. Gregory's Episcopal Ch., Boca Raton, 1975-77. Fellow in clin. psychology, Menninger Found., 1959-61, U. Fla., 1953-55, Harriet B. Lawrence prize Conn. Coll., 1993; named Outstanding Clin. Psychologist of the Yr., Fla. Psychol. Assn., 1981, nominated Jr. League Woman of Yr., 1993. Fellow Kans. Psychol. Assn.; mem. Am. Psychol. Assn., Am. Group Psychotherapy Assn., Am. Acad. Psychotherapists, Palm Beach Psychol. Assn. (pres. 1970), Fla. Psychol. Assn. (Lifetime Contribution award, 1994), Soroptimist (pres. 1975, 83, Woman of the Yr. 1974, Dedicated Svc. award, 1994). Episcopalian. Avocations: tennis, golf, boating. DIED 01/02/95. .

FAUST, JOHN WILLIAM, JR., electrical engineer, educator; b. Pitts., July 25, 1922; s. John William and Helen (Crowther) F.; m. Mary Claire Barton, June 7, 1947; children: Mary Faust Baumert, Elizabeth Wickham Kemp, John William III, Charles Barton, Ann Louise Faust Spires, Susan Bosley Roselle, Helen Crowther, Thomas McCullough. BSChemE, Purdue U., 1943; MA, U. Mo., 1949, PhD, 1951. Research scientist Westinghouse Research Labs., Pitts., 1951-63; mgr. materials characterization lab. Westinghouse Research Labs., 1963-65, project mgr. crystal growth, 1965-67; prof. materials sci. Pa. State U., State College, 1967-69; prof. elec. and computer engring. U. S.C., Columbia, 1969-93, disting. prof., 1992-93; mem. faculty senate; assoc. chmn. dept. U. S.C., Columbia, 1990-95, grad. dir. dept., 1989-92; disting. prof. emeritus U. S.C., 1994-95; faculty senator U. S.C., Columbia, 1989-91; disting. lectr. Naval Rsch. Labs., 1979, rsch. physicist, 1980-81; cons. Wright-Patterson Air Force Rsch. Ctr., 1957, Corning Glass Rsch. Labs., 1968-70, semicondr. div. Dow Corning, 1967-69, Gen. Tel. & Tel. Labs., 1968, materials div. Sylvania, 1968-70, Langley Air Force Rsch. Labs., 1970, Air Force Materials Lab., Wright-Patterson AFB, 1977, Borg-Warner Corp., 1982-84, Silaq Corp., 1979-80, Morgan Semicondr. Corp., 1982-88; co-chmn. Internat. Com. on Silicon Carbide, 1969-75; chmn. tech. adv. panel on solar energy S.C. Ho. of Reps., 1979-90. Editor: The Surface Chemistry of Metals and Semiconductors, 1960, Marcel Dekker, Inc., 1967-71, Silicon Carbide-1973, 1974; contbr. articles to profl. jours.; patentee in field. Vol. Food Program for Needy. Served with USNR, 1942-46. Recipient Outstanding Prof. of Yr. award IEEE. Fellow Am. Inst. Chemists; mem. AAAS (councilor 1967-69), Minerals, Metals and Materials Soc., Electrochem. Soc. (editorial com. 1971-91, div. editor jour. 1971-91), Am. Phys. Soc., Am. Soc. Metals, Internat. Com. on Crystal Growth, Am. Assn. for Crystal Growth, Internat. Soc. Hybrid Microelectronics, Am. Chem. Soc., Materials Rsch. Soc., Robert Burns Soc., Sigma Xi, Eta Kappa Nu, Tau Beta Pi. Home: West Columbia S.C. Died Apr. 23, 1995.

FAWCETT, HOWARD HOY, chemical health and safety engineer, consultant; b. McKeesport, Pa., May 31, 1916; s. Harry Garfield and Ada (Deetz) F.; m. Ruth Allen Bogan, Apr. 7, 1942 (dec. Oct. 1986); children: Ralph Willard, Harry Allen. BS in Indsl. Chemistry, U. Md., 1940; postgrad. U. Del., 1945-47. Registered profl. engr., Calif. Rsch. chemist Manhattan project E.I. DuPont de Nemours & Co., Inc., Chgo., Hanford, Wash., 1944-45, rsch. and devel. chemist organic chemistry div., Deepwater, N.J., 1945-48; cons. engr. GE, Schenectady, N.Y., 1948-64; tech. sec. com. on hazardous materials Nat. Acad. Scis.-NRC, Washington, 1964-75; staff scientist, project mgr. Tracor Jitco, Inc., Rockville, Md., 1975-78; sr. chem. engr. Equitable Environ. Health, 1978-81; pres., sr. engr. Fawcett Consultations, Inc., 1981—; mem. adv. com. study on socio-behavioral preparations for, responses to and recovery from chem. disasters NSF, 1977-82; adj. prof. Fed. Emergency Mgmt. Agency Acad., 1983—; cons. to industry and govt. agys. Author Am.-Can. supplement Hazards in Chemical Lab., 1983, Hazardous and Toxic Materials, Safe Handling and Disposal, 1984, 2d edit., 1988; co-editor: Safety and Accident Prevention in Chemical Operations, 1965, 2d edit., 1982, (with others) Hazards in the Chemical Laboratory, 4th and 5th edits.; mem. editorial adv. bd. Jour. Safety Rsch., 1968—, Transp. Planning and Tech., 1972—; N.Am. regional editor Jour. Hazardous Materials, 1975—; guest editor: Jour. Hazardous Materials, 1994; also book chpt. Chief radiol. sect. Schenectady County CD, 1953-63; bd. dirs. Safety sect. Schenectady C. of C., 1957-64; tech. advisor Hazmat Emergency Response Team, Montgomery County, Md., 1988—. Deacon Warner Meml. Presbyn. Ch., Kensington, Md., 1990—. Recipient Disting. Svc. to Safety citation Nat. Safety Coun., 1966, Cameron award, 1962, 69, Profl. Svc. award, 1992. Fellow Am. Inst. Chemists; mem. Am. Chem. Soc. (sec. com. chem. safety, chmn. council com. on chem. safety 1974-77, chmn. div. chem. health and safety 1977-79, 91, vice-chair, 1990-91, chair, 1991—, councilor 1980-82, archivist, 1984—, author audio course on hazards of materials 1977, CHAS award 1993), ASTM (membership sec. 1972—, sub-chmn. D-34 com.), Am. Inst. Chem. Engrs. (com. on occupational health and safety 1977—, editor newsletter 1988-89), Internat. Platform Assn., Am. Indsl. Hygiene Assn. (dir. Balt.-Washington chpt. 1975-77), Nat. Inst. Standards and Tech. (com. assistance 1993), Alpha Chi Sigma (contbr. video tapes on chemical hazards). Deceased.

FAY, ALBERT HILL, building materials executive; b. Bklyn., Aug. 19, 1911; s. Albert Hill and Clara (Constable) F.; m. Leona May Anderson, Sept. 4, 1934. B.Arch., Columbia, 1934, M.S., 1935. Product mgr., then prodn. mgr. Flintkote Corp., 1936-50; advt. mgr. Asbestone Corp., New Orleans, 1950-53; dir. product mgmt. Nat. Gypsum Co., Buffalo, 1953-65; v.p. mktg. Nat. Gypsum Co., 1965-69, v.p. research and mktg., 1969-76; pres. Constrn. Mktg. Services, 1977—; mem. bldg. research adv. bd. Nat. Acad. Sci., 1974-79. Past trustee Niagara Frontier Housing Devel. Corp.; Trustee Nat. Council of Housing Industry, 1969-75, vice chmn., 1970-72; Bd. dirs. Brand Names Found., Better Bus. Bur. Western N.Y., 1978-83. Served to lt. USNR, 1944-46. Consultative mem. Nat. Inst. Bldg. Scis.; mem. Nat. Home Improvement Council (pres. 1971-73, dir.), Asbestos Cement Products Assn. (pres. 1962-74), Asbestos Information Assn. N.Am. (pres. 1972-73). Deceased.

FEAVER, JOHN CLAYTON, philosopher, educator; b. Fowler, Calif., June 24, 1911; s. Ernest Albion and Agnes Katherine (Hansen) F.; m. Margaret Storsand, June 21, 1936; children: John Hansen, Katherine Elaine, Margaret Ellen. A.B., Fresno State Coll., 1933; student, San Francisco Theol. Sem., 1934; B.D., Pacific Sch. Religion, 1936; Ph.D., Yale U., 1949. Asst., then assoc. prof. philosophy Berea Coll., 1941-51; Kingfisher Coll. prof. philosophy religion and ethics U. Okla., 1951-81, emeritus, 1981—, David Ross Boyd prof. philosophy, 1959-81, emeritus, 1981—; chmn. exec. com. Coll. Liberal Studies U. Okla., 1961-73; chmn. exec. com. S.W. Center Human Relations Studies, 1971-81. Co-editor: Religion in Philosophical and Cultural Perspective, 1967. Dir. Scholar-Leadership Enrichment Program, 1977-87. Recipient. Disting. Service citation U. Okla., 1979; Disting. Prof. Philosophy, U. Sci. and Arts of Okla., 1987—. Mem. Am. Philos. Assn., Southwestern Philos. Soc. (pres. 1960), Soc. Philosophy Religion, Am. Acad. Religion, AAUP, Phi Beta Kappa, Omicron Delta Kappa. Died July 14, 1995.

FEDERICI, TONY, state legislator, small business owner; b. St. Helens, Oreg., Mar. 21, 1937; s. Nickolas and Rose (Albrizio) F.; m. Nancy Alice Weeks, July 10, 1965; children: Nick, Catherine. BA, U. Oreg., 1963. Science instr. Salem Pub. Schs., Oreg., 1963-65; owner Tony's Shoes, St. Helens, 1965-95; mem. Oreg. State Legislature, 1993-95. City councilman City of St. Helens, 1980-88; port commr. Port of St. Helens, 1988-92. With U.S. Army, 1960-62. Mem. Western Ind. Shoe Enterprises (pres. 1979, chmn. 1980), St. Helens Lion Club (pres. 1972-95). Democrat. Roman Catholic. Avocations: symphony, opera, drama, musical comedy. Home: Saint Helens Oreg. Died Aug. 30, 1995; interred Columbia Memorial Gardens.

FEHRENBACHER, DON EDWARD, retired history educator; b. Sterling, Ill., Aug. 21, 1920; s. Joseph H. and Mary (Barton) F.; m. Virginia Ellen Swaney, Feb. 9, 1944; children: Ruth Ellen Fehrenbacher Gleason, Susan Jean Fehrenbacher Koprince, David Charles. B.A., Cornell Coll., 1946; M.A., U. Chgo., 1948, Ph.D., 1951; M.A., Oxford U., 1967; D.H.L. (hon.), Cornell Coll., 1970. Asst. prof. history Coe Coll., Cedar Rapids, Iowa, 1949-53; asst. prof. history Stanford U., 1953-57, assoc. prof., 1957-62, prof., 1962-66, William R. Coe prof. Am. history, 1966-84, prof. emeritus, 1984—; Harmsworth prof. Am. history Oxford U., 1967-68; Harrison prof. history Coll. William and Mary, 1973-74; tchr. Rutgers U., summer 1959, Northwestern U., 1964, Harvard U., 1967, U. B.C., 1970; Commonwealth Fund lectr. U. London, 1978; Walter Lynwood Fleming lectr. La. State U., 1978; Seagram lectr. U. Toronto, 1981; Lamar lectr. Mercer U., 1987. Author: Chicago Giant: A Biography of Long John Wentworth, 1957, Prelude to Greatness: Lincoln in the 1850s, 1962, The Era of Expansion, 1969, The Dred Scott Case: Its Significance in American Law and Politics, 1978 (Pulitzer prize in history 1979), The South and Three Sectional Crises, 1980, Slavery, Law and Politics, 1981, Lincoln in Text and Context, 1987, Constitutions and Constitutionalism in the Slaveholding South, 1989, Sectional Crisis and Southern Constitutionalism, 1996; editor: History and American Society: Essays of David M. Potter, 1973, The Impending Crisis (David M. Potter), 1976, Freedom and Its Limitations in American Life (David M. Potter), 1976, Abraham Lincoln: Speeches and Writings, 2 vols., 1989, Lincoln: Selected Speeches and Writings, 1992, Recollected Words of Abraham Lincoln, 1996; contbr. articles to profl. jours.; adviser Ken Burns film series The Civil War, 1990. Served to 1st lt. USAAF, 1943-45. Decorated D.F.C., Air medal with 3 oak leaf clusters.; recipient Diploma of Honor, Lincoln Meml. U., 1991, Lincoln prize Gettysburg Coll., 1997; Guggenheim fellow, 1959-60, 84-85; NEH fellow, 1975-76; Huntington Library fellow, 1985-86. Mem. Abraham Lincoln Assn. (Logan Hay medal 1989), Am. Acad. Arts and Scis., Am. Hist. Assn. (pres. br. 1983-84), So. Hist. Assn., Am. Soc. Legal History, Am. Antiquarian Soc. Died Dec. 13, 1997.

FEIKEMA, FEIKE See MANFRED, FREDERICK FEIKEMA

FEISS, CARL LEHMAN, retired urban planning educator; b. Cleve., June 18, 1907; m. Alleen Kelly, Oct. 10, 1941. BFA, U. Pa. Sch. Architecture, 1931; fellow, Cranbrook Acad. Art, Bloomfield Hills, Mich., 1932-35; MA in City Planning, MIT, 1938. Asst. prof., dir. planning and housing div. Columbia U., N.Y.C., 1936-41; dir. City Planning Commn., Denver, 1942-46; chief planning and engring. br. Divsn. of Slum Clearance Urban Redevel. U.S. Housing & Home Fin. Agy., Washington, 1950-55; cons. personal svcs. planning, renewal and preservation, 1956-71; cons. Conn. Devel. Commn., V.I. govt., San Juan Housing Authority, P.R., Hist. Savannah Found., City of Charleston, S.C., TVA, Mid-Cumberland Coun. Govts., Nashville, Inter-Am. Housing Ctr., Bogota, Colombia, Tampa Bay Regional Planning Coun., St. Petersburg, E. Cen. Fla. Regional Planning Coun., Titusville, Palm Beach County Area Planning Bd., West Palm Beach, Fla., White House Conf. on Children and Youth, 1963, White House Conf. on Natural Beauty, 1965; dir. Urban Studies Ctr., chmn. dept. urban and regional planning Coll. Architecture, U. Fla., 1971-83. Tech. editor, author: With Heritage So Rich, 1966; co-author, editor: Historic Savannah, 1968; contbr. articles to Progressive Architecture, Jour. Am. Planning Assn., other tech. and profl. jours. Trustee Nat. Trust for Hist. Preservation, Washington, 1960-71 (Honor award 1981); co-founder, trustee 1000 Friends of Fla., 1985. Recipient Conservation Svc. award U.D. Dept. Interior, 1976. Fellow AIA (Presdl. citation 1988), U.S./Internat. Coun. Monuments and Sites; mem. Am. Inst. Cert. Planners, Cosmos Club (Washington). Avocation: travel. Died Oct. 10, 1997.

FEIST, LEONARD, trade association administrator; b. Pelham, N.Y., Dec. 12, 1910; s. Leo and Bessie (Meyer) F.; m. Mary Regensburg, Dec. 6, 1937; children—Linda S., Betsy. Grad., Worcester Acad., 1928; B.A., Yale, 1932; postgrad., Columbia U., 1933-34; Mus. Doc. (h.c.), Peabody Inst. Conservatory Music, 1976. Sec. Leo Feist, Inc., 1932-35; pres. Century Music Pub. Co.-Mercury Music Corp., 1936-56, Assoc. Music Pubs., Inc., 1956-64; exec. v.p. Nat. Music Pubs. Assn., N.Y.C., 1965-76; pres. Nat. Music Pubs. Assn., 1976-84; Pres. Seaview Assn., N.Y., 1954-56. Contbr. articles to mags. Served with AUS, 1944-46. Mem. Nat. Music Council (dir. 1963-66, treas. 1966-71, pres. 1971-76, chmn. bd. 1976-79), Music Pubs. Assn. U.S. (pres. 1952-54), Nat. Acad. Popular Music (v.p. 1969-84), Copyright Soc. U.S. (v.p. 1974-78), Am. Music Conf. (dir. 1978-84), Am. Copyright Council (dir. 1983), Phi Mu Alpha (hon. life), Sigma Alpha Iota (nat. arts associated mem.). Died Nov. 18, 1996.

FELD, LIPMAN GOLDMAN, former lawyer, former credit agency executive; b. Kansas City, Mo., Jan. 16, 1914; s. Emel and Celia (Goldman) F.; m. Anne Brozman, Apr. 30, 1942; children: Robert David, Celia Anne (Mrs. Terry Harms). BS cum laude, Harvard, 1935; JD, U. Mo., 1935-38. Bar: Mo. 1938. Assoc. Butler Disman, Kansas City, 1938-41; v.p., counsel Century Acceptance Corp., Kansas City, 1946-79, sr. v.p., 1973-79; v.p. CenCor Inc., Kansas City, 1968-79; counsellor to ofcl. child learning facilities, income tax offices, colls. of med. and dental assts., profl. practice mgmt. services, temporary labor centers, consumer finance offices; lectr. Mo. Dept. Corrections and Human Resources. Author: Harrassment and Other Collection Taboos, 1976, Bad Checks and Fraudulent Identity, 1978; contbr. numerous articles profl. jours. Capt. AUS, 1941-46. Died Jul. 23, 1994.

FELD, NICHOLAS, foreign service officer; b. Vicksburg, Miss., Dec. 5, 1915; s. Nicholas and Mabel (Philips) F.; m. Cora Helene Hochstein, Dec. 27, 1949; 1 child, Evelyn Dana. A.B., Harvard U., 1936, postgrad., 1937-38. Apptd. fgn. service officer, unclassified, vice consul career, sec. Diplomatic Service; assigned vice consul Diplomatic Service, Zurich, Switzerland, 1939, Basel, 1939; with Fgn. Service Officers Tng. Sch., Dept. State, Washington, 1940; vice consul Madras, India, 1940; 3d sec. Pretoria, Union South Africa, 1944, 2d sec., 1945; commd. consul, 1948; consul Dar-es-Salaam, Tanganyika Ty., East Africa (now Tanzania), 1948, Geneva, 1950; officer in charge West, Central and East African affairs Office African Affairs, Dept. State, 1951; consul Singapore, 1954-56; officer in charge trusteeship affairs Office Dependent Area Affairs, Dept. State, 1956-60; counselor Budapest, Hungary, 1960-62; chief, jr. officer personnel Dept. State, Washington, 1963-65; acting dir. Office West African Affairs, 1965; dep. dir. Office Inter-African Affairs, Bur. African Affairs, Dept. State, 1965; country dir. Office East African Affairs, Bur. African Affairs, Dept. State, Kenya, Tanzania, Seychelles and Uganda, 1967; U.S. adviser Entente Guaranty Fund, Abidjan, Ivory Coast, 1969. Club: Harvard of Cape Cod (v.p. 1980-81, pres. 1981-83). DIED 09/28/95. .

FELDER, RODNEY OTTO, college president; b. Redwood, N.Y., May 25, 1927; s. Otto and Pearl Maybelle (Lambert) F. B.S. SUNY-Albany, 1949; M.A., Columbia U., 1953, Ed.D., 1957. Tchr. public schs., Worcester, N.Y., 1949-50, Morristown, N.Y., 1950-52; instr. Santa Barbara City Coll., 1953-55; chmn. bus. and econs. Finch Coll., 1955-59, asst. dean, 1959-60, dean, 1960-69, v.p., 1969-70, pres., 1970-77; pres. Finch Coll. Mus. Art, 1969-77, Upsala Coll., 1977—; vis. prof. econs. UCLA, 1962; mem. N.J. Dept. Higher Edn. Master Planning Com. Contbr. numerous bus. and econ. articles to profl. jours., 1952-62. Bd. dirs. Ind. Coll. Fund N.J.; numerous radio, TV appearances on pvt. colls.; Past pres. Council Lutheran Ch. in Am. Colls. Served with U.S. Army, 1945-47. Mem. Assn. Ind. Colls. and Univs. N.J. (exec. com.).

FELLERS, JAMES DAVISON, lawyer; b. Oklahoma City, Apr. 17, 1913; s. Morgan S. and Olive R. (Kennedy) F.; m. Margaret Ellen Randerson, Mar. 11, 1939; children: Kay Lynn Fellers Sturm, Lou Ann Fellers Street, James Davison. AB, U. Okla., 1936, JD, 1936; LLD (hon.), Suffolk U., 1974, William Mitchell Coll. Law, 1976; LL.D. (hon.), San Fernando Valley U., 1976; DHL (hon.), Okla. Christian Coll., 1974; LLD (hon.), Oklahoma City U., 1991. Bar: Okla. 1936. Practiced in Oklahoma City; of counsel Fellers, Snider, Blankenship, Bailey & Tippens; mem. U.S. Com. Selection of Fed. Jud. Officers, 1977-79; mem. bd. Nat. Legal Aid and Defender Assn., 1973-76; bd. dirs. Am. Bar Endowment, 1977-92; mem. adv. bd. Internat. and Comparative Law Center. Trustee Southwestern Legal Found.; hon. consul Belgium, for Okla., 1972-87. Served to lt. col. USAF, 8 campaigns, 1941-45, ETO, MTO. Decorated Bronze Star, knight Order of Crown (Belgium); recipient Hatton W. Sumners award, 1975, Disting. Svc. citation U. Okla., 1976, Jour. Record Law Day award, 1990, Okla. Bar Disting. Svc. as a Lawyer award, 1991, Atty. Recognition award Ctrl. Okla. Assn. Legal Assts., 1995; selected as Outstanding Young Man, Oklahoma City C. of C., 1948; named to Okla. Hall of Fame, 1982. Fellow Am. Coll. Trial Lawyers, Am. Bar Found., Okla. Bar Found., Nat. Jud. Coll. (dir. 1967-70); mem. ABA (nat. chmn. jr. bar conf. 1946-47, gov. 1962-65, chmn. ho. of dels. 1966-68, pres. 1974-75), Barra Mexicana (hon.), Can. Bar Assn. (hon.), Internat. Bar Assn., Inter-Am. Bar Assn., Minn. Bar Assn. (hon.), Okla. Bar Assn. (pres. 1964), W.Va. Bar Assn. (hon.), Am. Judicature Soc., Am. Law Inst. (life, ALI-ABA com. continuing profl. edn. 1947-49, 73-75), Inst. Jud. Adminstrn., Internat. Assn. Def. Counsel (v.p. 1955-56), Nat. Conf. Bar Pres.'s, World Peace through Law Center, Fellows of Young Lawyers Am. Bar (hon. chmn. 1977-79), Oklahoma City C. of C. (dir. 1976), Phi Kappa Psi. Episcopalian. Died April 3, 1997.

FERGUSON, JOHN HENRY, political science educator; b. Lexington, Nebr., Aug. 22, 1907; s. Leonard Calvin and Dicie Shirley (Sipes) F.; m. Ruth Arvilla Benton, June 10, 1930 (dec. Oct. 1976); children: Milton O., Richard B., David J., Rachel A. (Mrs. Rider); m. Eleanor Ely Mackey, June 26 1977. A.B., Nebr. Central Coll., 1929; M.A., U. Pa., 1932, Ph.D., 1937. Prin., tchr. Monroe (Nebr.) High Sch., 1929-30; dir. boys work Friends Neighborhood Guild, Phila., 1930-34; instr. polit. sci. Pa. State U., 1934-37, asst. prof., 1937-41, assoc. prof., 1941-47, prof., 1947-66, prof. emeritus, 1966-97, head dept. polit. sci. Inst. Pub. Adminstrn., 1947-48, 1963-65, dir. Social Sci. Research Ctr., 1953-55, dir. Inst. Pub. Adminstrn., 1959-65, dean sch. politics New Sch. Social Research, 1948-49; vis. prof. U. Nebr., summer 1948; dir. program evaluation Office Gov. of Pa., 1955-56, sec. of adminstrn., 1956-59, budget sec., 1957-59; vis. lectr. U. Pa., 1966-77. Author: American Diplomacy and the Boer War, 1939, (with Dr. Dean E. McHenry) The American System of Government, 14th edit., 1981, The American Federal Government, 14th edit., 1981, Elements of American Government, 9th edit., 1971, (with Dr. Charles F. LeeDecker) Municipally Owned Waterworks in Pennsylvania, 1948, Municipally Owned Electric Plants in Pennsylvania, 1950, (with Drs. Dean E. McHenry and E.B. Fincher) American Government Today, 1951, (with David L. Cowell) The Minor Courts of Pennsylvania, Politics Quaker Style (1624-1718), 1995. Co-dir. research Pa. Constl. Conv., 1967-68; pres. Better Govt. Assocs., Inc., 1967-77; sr. asso. Berger Assos., 1976-81; exec. dir. Commonwealth Compensation Commn., 1976-80; mem. bd. Pub. Service Inst., chmn., 1963-73; bd. dirs. Lincoln U., 1960-72; dir. Civilian Public Service Camp, Gatlinburg, Tenn., 1943-44; adminstrv. asst. Am. Friends Service Com., 1944-45, exec. bd., 1950-56, 57-60. Recipient Hall of Fame award William Penn Coll., 1980. Mem. Am. Polit. Sci. Assn. (exec. council 1951-53), Pa. Polit. Sci. Assn. (pres. 1958-60), Am. Soc. Pub. Adminstrn. (award for disting. achievement 1958). Mem. Soc. of Friends. Home: State College Pa. Died May 12, 1997.

FERMAN, IRVING, lawyer, educator; b. N.Y.C., July 4, 1919; s. Joseph and Sadie (Stein) F.; m. Bertha Paglin, June 12, 1946; children: James, Susan Glicksman. B.S., N.Y.U., 1941; J.D., Harvard, 1948. Bar: La. 1948, D.C. 1974. Partner Provensal, Faris & Ferman, New Orleans, 1948-52; dir. Am. Civil Liberties Union, Washington, 1952-59, Am. Civil Liberties Clearing House, 1952-54; exec. vice chmn. Pres.'s Com. Govt. Contracts, 1959-60; v.p. Internat. Latex Corp., 1960-66; pres. Piedmont Theaters Corp., 1966-69; adj. asso. prof. mgmt. NYU Grad. Sch. Bus., 1964-68; adj. prof. law Howard U., 1968-69, prof. law, 1969-86, prof. emeritus, from 1986; dir. Project for Legal Policy, 1976-97; vis. prof. law Am. U., 1971-72; mem. Am. Com. Cultural Freedom, 1954; mem. Com. of Arts and Scis. for Eisenhower, 1956; mem. citizens adv. com. U.S. Commn. on Govt. Security, 1957; chmn. Police Complaint Rev. Bd., 1965-73; mem. Dept. HEW Reviewing Authority, 1969-79; chmn. Interdisco Ltd., London, 1986-97; bd. dirs. Control Fluidics, Inc., Greenwich Conn., D.C. Housing Fin. Agy. Contbr. to books and revs. Mem. bd. dirs. New Orleans Acad. Art, 1948-51. Served from cadet to 1st lt. USAAF, 1942-46. Mem. ABA, La. Bar Assn., D.C. Bar Assn., New Orleans Bar Assns., Army-Navy Country Club (Arlington, Va.), Army-Navy Club (Washington), Harvard Club (N.Y.C.), Caterpillar Club (N.Y.C.). Jewish. Home: Washington D.C. Died March, 1997.

FERRAR, ROBERT L., economist, educator; b. Cleve., May 3, 1938; s. Sam L. and Mary (Capasso) F.; m. Joyce P. Ferrar, July 11, 1959; children: Brian, Paul, Jason, Corey. BSBA, Kent State U., 1965; MS in Econs., U. Oreg., 1967, PhD in Econs., 1969. Asst. prof. econs. Allegheny Coll., Meadville, Pa., 1969-71; asst. prof. labor rels. Cleve. State U., 1971-76; assoc. prof. econs. Am. U., Cairo, Egypt, 1973-75; prof., chair of bus. Lorain (Ohio) Coll., 1976-80; dean Sch. of Bus. Sinclair Coll., Dayton, Ohio, 1980-85, prof. econs., 1990-95. Contbr. numerous articles to profl. jours. Child rights advocate for various parent, foster parent and adoption groups, Cleve. and Dayton. Danforth fellow. Home: Dayton Ill. Died Dec. 7, 1994; buried Pleasant Grove, Murphysboro, IL.

FERRIS, BENJAMIN GREELEY, JR., retired physician, environmental researcher, educator; b. Watertown, Mass., Jan. 24, 1919; s. Benjamin Greeley and Margaret (Wright) F.; m. Sarah Brooks Upham, Dec. 20, 1942 (dec. Oct. 13, 1979); children: Pamela Upham Barneby Farmer, Margaret Upham Zimmermann, Katharine Wright Goddard, Patience Brooks Sandrof, Sarah Elizabeth Di Monda; m. Stefana Puleo, Dec. 7, 1980. A.B., Harvard U., 1940, M.D., 1943; Dr. h.c., U. Bordeaux II, 1983. Diplomate: Am. Bd. Pediatrics, Am. Bd. Preventive Medicine. Rsch. fellow Harvard U., Boston, 1948-50; assoc. in physiology Harvard U., 1950-53, asst. prof., 1953-58, assoc. prof. environ. health and safety, 1958-71, prof., 1971-89, prof. emeritus, 1989-96; dir. environ. health and safety Univ. Health Svc., 1958-96, chief, 1988; cons. medicine Mass. Gen. Hosp.; cons. environ. health Children's Med. Center; sr. cons. internal medicine Lemuel Shattuck Hosp., Boston, 1955-56; vis. prof. U. B.C., Can., 1974-78; lectr. medicine Tufts U., Boston, 1965-96. Editor emeritus Safety Report, Am. Alpine Club; contbr. articles to profl. jours. Served with M.C. U.S. Army, 1945-47. Fellow Am. Pub. Health Assn.; mem. AAAS, Am. Physiol. Soc., Am. Epidemiol. Soc., Royal Soc. Medicine (affiliate), Sigma Xi. Clubs: Am. Alpine, Appalachian Mountain, Harvard, St. Botolph. Died Aug. 1, 1996.

FERRY, WILBUR HUGH, foundation consultant; b. Detroit, Dec. 17, 1910; s. Hugh Joseph and Fay (Rutson) F.; m. Jolyne Marie Gillier, Oct. 23, 1937 (div. 1972); children: Lucian (stepson), Dennie LaTourelle, Fay Ferry Christiansen, Robin; m. Carol Underwood Bernstein, 1973; stepchildren: Katherine Andre, John. A.B., Dartmouth Coll., 1932; L.H.D., Starr King Sch., Berkeley, Calif., 1969. Instr. Choate Sch., 1932-33; newspaperman, 1933-35, 37-41; dir. publicity Eastern Air Lines, 1936; chief investigator in N.H. for OPA, 1942-44; cons. ILO, 1940-44; dir. pub. relations CIO-Polit. Action Com., 1944; partner Earl Newsom & Co., 1945-54; v.p. Center Study Democratic Instns., 1954-69, cons., 1969—; U.S. rep. European Nuclear Disarmament, 1981; dir. Exploratory Project on the Conditions of Peace and Peace System Project, 1984—, DJB Found. Author: The Corporation and The Economy, 1959, The Economy Under Law, 1961, Caught on the Horn of Plenty, 1962, What Price Peace, 1963, Masscomm as Educator, 1966, Farewell to Integration, 1967, Tonic and Toxic Technology, 1967, The Police State Is Here, 1969, The Zaca Manifesto, 1980; editor: Warming Up for Fifty Years, 1982, Letters from Tom, 1983. Deceased.

FEST, THORREL BROOKS, former speech educator, consultant; b. Audubon, Iowa, Aug. 23, 1910; s. Albert F. and Augusta (Boers) F.; m. C. Lucille Etzler, June 5, 1934; children: Stephen, Bruce. BA, State Coll. Iowa (now No. Iowa U.), 1932; MPh, U. Wis., 1938, PhD, 1952. Tchr. secondary schs. Griswold and Spencer, Iowa, 1939-40; asst. prof. U. N.D., 1940-44, Albion Coll., 1940-44; staff Manhattan Project, 1944-45; mem. extension faculty U. Tenn., 1945; asst. prof. U. Colo., 1945-53, assoc. prof., 1953-58, prof., 1958-79, prof. emeritus, 1979-96; acad. dean U. Colo. (Semester at Sea Program), 1979, chmn. dept. speech communication, 1960-68, 83-84; vis. prof. Western State Coll., 1957, U. Hawaii, 1959, 63, Syracuse U., 1961; vis. lectr. U. New South Wales, Australia, spring 1970, summer 1975, Autonomous U. of Giadalajara, 1961-75; sr. vis. fellow Caulfield Inst. Tech., Melbourne, Australia, 1980-81, 86, Western Australia Inst. Tech., Perth, 1956-71, U.S. C. of C., 1959-76, Colo. Divsn. Wildlife, B.C. Tchrs. Fedn., 1968-77, Colo. Tax Commn., 1965-75; v.p. Nat. Ctr. Communication Arts and Scis., 1965-78, program dir., 1966-75; pres. Fest Farms, Inc., 1947-79, 89-96; cons. Conservation Family of Ill., 1991. Author: (with Martin Cobin) Speech and Theater, 1964, Registry of Communications Research, 1970, (with R.V. Harnack and B.S. Jones) Group Discussion: Theory and Technique, 2d edit, 1977, (with J. Robbins) Cross Cultural Communications and the Trainer, 1976; also profl. articles. Bd. govs. Nat. Installment Bankers Inst., 1972-79; mem. adv. com. Alexander Hamilton Bicentennial Commn., 1956-58; chmn. bd. trustees Intercultural Sch. Rockies, 1968-71; mem. internat. founding com. Center for Audio Visual Instrn. via Satellite, 1968-79; pres. U. Colo. Ret. Faculty Assn., 1990. Recipient Disting. Svc. award U. Colo., 1971, Disting. Alumni award No. Iowa U., 1978; honored by Internat. Comm. Assn., Spring 1995. Fellow Internat. Inst. Arts and Letters (hon.), Societé Internationale pour le Dévelopment Des Organisations (hon.); mem. Nat. U. Extension Assn., Nat. Collegiate Players, Am. Forensic Assn., Adult Edn. Assn., Speech Communication Assn. (emeritus, com. on ret. 1992-96, chair 1982, legis. coun. 1955-57, exec. coun. 1957-60, chmn. com. on curricula and certification 1963-66, legis. 1963-65, 67-69), Canadian Speech Assn., Colo.-Wyo. Acad. Sci., Am. Edn. Theatre Assn., AAUP (pres. chpt. 1960-62), Colo. (pres. state conf. 1962-64), Western (v.p.), Ctrl., So. Speech Assns., Colo. Speech and Drama Assn. (Disting. Contbn. award 1981), Indsl. Communication Coun., Indsl. Relations Rsch., Assn., Nat. Soc. Tng. and Devel., Internat. Communication Assn. (nat. coun. 1955-62, nat. pres. 1960-61), Internat. Soc. Gen. Semantics (program at ann. conv. 1995), Izaak Walton League, Delta Sigma Rho (editor Gavel 1949-53, nat. pres. 1953-57, Disting. Alumni award 1972), Lambda DeltaLambda, Kappa Delta Pi, Theta Alpha Phi. Died Dec. 21, 1996.

FEY, RUSSELL CONWELL, urban and regional planning educator; b. Lincoln, Nebr., Mar. 12, 1926; s. Harold Edward and Golda Esper (Conwell) F.; m. Patricia Marian Baker, Aug. 23, 1952; children: Sarah, David, Ellen. AB, Hiram Coll., 1948; postgrad., U. Ill., 1951, 52; M of City Planning, U. Calif., Berkeley, 1958; MA, U. Calif., Riverside, 1982. Cert. Am. Inst. Cert. Planners. Assoc. planner planning dept. City Tacoma, Wash., 1954-55; assoc. redevel. planner Richmond (Calif.) Redevel. Agy., 1955-56; land use planner Fresno (Calif.)-Clovis Area Planning Commn., 1956, 57; sr. planner Planning Dept., Modesto, Calif., 1958-61; planning dir. Planning Dept., Modesto, 1962-69; lectr. U. Calif. Extension, 1962-63; prof. urban and regional planning Calif. State U., Fresno, 1969-94, chmn. dept. urban and regional planning, 1975-78, 82, emeritus, 1995-96; cons. City of Sanger, Calif., 1958, City of Riverbank, Calif., 1960, City of Orange Cove, Calif., 1972; pres. planning dept. League Calif. Cities, 1968-69; cons. historic preservation inventory City of Reedley, Calif., 1984, City of Tulare, Calif., 1987, Calif. Dept. Transp., 1992. Exhibited photographs and watercolor paintings at various shows, 1969-96. Moderator Coll. Cmty. Congregational Ch., 1976-78; mem. Planning Commn., Fresno, 1977-79; chmn. Historic Preservation Commn., Fresno, 1990-91, 94-95; bd. dirs. Calif. Preservation Found., 1988-89, Self Help Housing, Inc., Visalia, Calif., 1984-90, Habitat for Humanity, Fresno, 1985-87, Fresno City-County Hist. Soc., 1986-93; mem., vice chmn. Fresno County Hist. Landmarks Commn., 1986-94; mem. tower dist. specific plan com., Fresno, 1990-91, Fulton-Lowell specific plan com., Fresno, 1994-96. Sgt. U.S. Army, 1944-46, ETO. Mem. Am. Planning Assn. (mem.-at-large Calif. chpt. 1962-63, v.p. Calif. chpt. 1964-65, dir. ctrl. sect. Cal. chpt. 1967-68), Ctrl. Calif. Photographers Guild (pres. 1986-88). Democrat. Avocations: watercolor painting, photography, sketching. Home: Fresno Calif. Died Apr. 4, 1996; interred Belmont Memorial Park, Fresno, CA.

FIALKOW, PHILIP JACK, academic administrator, medical educator; b. N.Y.C., Aug. 20, 1934; s. Aaron and Sarah (Ratner) F.; m. Helen C. Dimitrakis, June 14, 1960; children: Michael, Deborah. BA, U. Pa., 1956; MD, Tufts U., 1960. Diplomate: Am. Bd. Internal Medicine, Am. Bd. Med. Genetics. Intern U. Calif., San Francisco, 1960-61, resident, 1961-62; resident U. Wash., Seattle, 1962-63, instr. medicine, 1965-66, asst. prof., 1966-69, assoc. prof., 1969-73, prof. medicine, 1973—, chmn. dept. medicine, 1980-90, dean Sch. Medicine, 1990—, v.p. for med. affairs, 1992-96; chief med. svc. Seattle VA Ctr., 1974-81; physician-in-chief U. Wash. Med. Ctr., Seattle, 1980-90; attending physician Harborview Med. Ctr., Seattle, 196-96; cons. Children's Orthopedic Hosp., Seattle, 1964-96. Contbr. articles to profl. jours.; mem. editorial bds. profl. jours. Trustee Fred Hutchinson Cancer Research Ctr., Seattle, 1982-90. Recipient NIH Merit award, Mayo Soley award for achievement in research; NIH fellow, 1963-65; NIH grantee, 1965-96. Fellow ACP; mem. AAAS, Am. Soc. Clin. Investigation, Assn. Am. Physicians, Am. Soc. Human Genetics (bd. dirs. 1974-77), Assn. Am. Med. Colls. (at large, coun. deans 1993-96), Am. Soc. Hematology, Inst. Medicine, Alpha Omega Alpha. Died 1996.

FIELSTRA, HELEN ADAMS, education educator; b. Elkhorn, W.Va., Feb. 26, 1921; d. Fred Russell and Clara Sue (Williams) Adams; m. Edmond T. Dooley, Jr., Nov. 15, 1941 (div. 1948); 1 dau., Dereth Dooley Pendleton; m. Clarence Fielstra, Jan. 1, 1956. A.B., UCLA, 1950; M.A., Stanford U., 1954, Ed.D., 1967. Tchr. Santa Monica (Calif.) Unified Sch. Dist., 1947-50; elem. coordinator San Diego County Schs., 1950-52; lectr. edn. Stanford U., 1953-54, UCLA, 1957-58; gen. elementary supr. Burbank (Calif.) Unified Sch. Dist., 1954-56, Beverly Hills (Calif.) Unified Sch. Dist., 1959-61; asst. prof. edn. Calif. State U., Northridge, 1961-67; assoc. prof. Calif. State U., 1967-70, prof., 1970—; sec.-treas., editor Fielstra Publs., Inc., Pacific Palisades, Calif.; sec.-treas. Hadco, Inc., Los Angeles.; Tng. coordinator Office Econ. Opportunity Tng. and Devel. Center, 1965-66; cons., speaker curriculum devel. and instructional supervision, 1952—; prin. investigator U.S. Office Edn. Project Tchr. Edn. for Disadvantaged, 1968-70; dir. interdisciplinary social sci. projects NSF, 1972-83; dir. Western Regional Center Edn. Devel. Center, 1974-76; chief cons. early childhood edn. Listener Corp. Author: (with L.G. Thomas, A. Coladarci, Lucien Kinney) Perspective on Teaching, 1961, (with Clarence Fielstra) Africa With Focus on Nigeria, 1963, Relationship Between Selected Factors and Pupil Success in Elementary School Foreign Languages Classes; also various monographs, curriculum guides, 2 ednl. films. Trustee, mem. exec. com. Calif. State U. Found., Northridge, 1970-72. Recipient Disting. Prof. award Calif. State Univ. and Coll. System, 1969, certificate of service Asso. Students Calif. State U., Northridge, 1970. Mem. Nat. Soc. for Study Edn., Am. Ednl. Research Assn., Nat. Council Social Studies (mem. publs. bd. 1970-72), Calif. Tchrs. Assn. (life), NEA (life), Congress of Faculty Assns. (founder), Assn. Supervision and Curriculum Devel., Stanford U. Alumni Assn., Calif. Assn. Supervision and Curriculum Devel. (chmn. state com. on supervision in structure public edn.), Calif. Council on Edn., AAUP, Calif. Higher Edn. Assn. (dir. 1970-74, pres. 1973-74), Calif. Coll. and U. Faculty Assn. (pres. chpt. 1969-70, state pres. 1972-73), Delta Zeta, Pi Lambda Theta, Delta Kappa Gamma (pres. Beta Eta chpt. 1960-62). Democrat. Clubs: Stanford (Los Angeles County); Palisadian Woman's.

FILES, GORDON LOUIS, lawyer, judge; b. Ft. Dodge, Iowa, Mar. 5, 1912; s. James Ray and Anna (Louis) F.; m. Kathryn Thrift, Nov. 24, 1942; children: Kathryn Lacey, James Gordon. A.B. in Polit. Sci. with honors, UCLA, 1934; LL.B., Yale U., 1937. Bar: Calif. 1937, U.S. Supreme Ct. 1957. Law clk. U.S. Ct. Appeals (8th cir.), 1937-38; enforcement atty. Office Price Adminstrn., 1942; ptnr. Freston & Files, Los Angeles, 1938-59; judge Los Angeles Superior Ct., 1959-62; assoc. justice 2d dist., div. 4 Calif. Ct. Appeal, 1962-64, presiding justice, 1964-82, adminstrv. presiding justice, 1970-82; arbitrator, referee and mediator, 1982-86; mem. Jud. Council Calif., 1964-71, 73-77; mem. governing com. Ctr. for Jud. Edn. and Research, 1981-82; mem. bd. govs. State Bar Calif., 1957-59. Mem. bd. editors Yale Law Jour., 1935-37. Served to lt. USN, 1942-45. Fellow Am. Bar Found.; mem. ABA, Am. Judicature Soc., Inst. Jud. Adminstrn., Los Angeles County Bar Assn. (trustee 1952-56), Calif. Judges Assn. (exec. com. 1971-72), Am. Legion, Order of Coif, Phi Beta Kappa, Phi Delta Phi. Democrat. Clubs: Chancery (pres. 1972-73) (L.A.); Valley Hunt (Pasadena). Died Jan. 12, 1995. Home: Pasadena Calif.

FINE, STANLEY SIDNEY, pharmaceuticals and cosmetics executive; b. N.Y.C., Sept. 26, 1927; s. Morris and Sophie (Brajer) F.; m. Eleanor D. Baker, July 21, 1955 (dec. 1972); children: Lauren Allison Caban, Stephen Sidney (dec.); m. Astrid E. Merget, June 8, 1984 (div. Apr. 1987); m. Li L. Yang, July 31, 1991. Student, NYU, 1944-45; B.S., U.S. Naval Acad., 1949; postgrad., Coll. William and Mary, 1955-56, U. Va., 1956-57; MBA, Am. U., 1959; postgrad., Harvard U., 1963-65, UCLA, 1993—. Commd. ensign U.S. Navy, 1949, advanced through grades to rear adm., 1972; comdg. officer USS Hawk, 1954-56, Polaris Program, 1956-59, USS Lowe, 1961-63; comdr. Escort Divsn. 33, 1963; comdg. officer USS Ingraham, 1965-67; br. head Navy Material Command, Washington, 1967-68; exec. asst., naval aide to asst. sec. Navy, 1968-70; study dir. Center for Naval Analysis Navy Dept., Washington, 1970; dep. dir. Navy Program Info. Center, 1970-71; br. head OPNAV, 1971; spl. asst. to dir. Navy Program Planning, Washington, 1971-72; dep. chief Programs and Fin. Mgmt.; comptr. Naval Ship Systems Command, Washington, 1972-73; dir. fiscal mgmt. divsn. Office Chief Naval Ops., Washington, 1973-78; dir. budget and reports Navy Dept., 1975-78; ret., 1978; sr. v.p. United-Guardian, Inc. (AMEX), Hauppauge, N.Y., 1979—, also bd. dirs.; v.p., bd. dirs. New Energy Leasing Corp., McLean, Va.; bd. dirs. Bell Industries, Inc. (NYSE); cons. GAO. Co-author: The Federal Budget: Cost Based in the 1980's, 1979, The Military Budget on a New Plateau: Strategic Choices for the 1990's; contbr. articles to profl. jours. and other publs.; lectr., TV commentator on def. and fed. budget issues. Mem. presdl. transition team Dept. Commerce, 1980-81; bd. dirs. Bronx High Sch. of Sci. Found., N.Y.C., 1987-91; dir. Com. for Nat. Security, 1987-92, Montgomery County Fiscal Affairs Com., 1987-88, Coun. for Econ. Priorities, 1993—. Decorated D.S.M., Navy Commendation medal, Legion of Merit with gold star; recipient outstanding Mgmt. Analyst award Am. Soc. Mil. Comptrollers, 1971, cert. of recognition and appreciation Montgomery County, Md. Mem. Naval Inst., World Affairs Coun. D.C., Naval Acad. Alumni Assn., Harvard U. Bus. Sch. Alumni Assn. Democrat. Jewish. Avocation: collecting ancient Roman coins. Home: Beverly Hills Calif. Deceased.

FINETTE, FLORENCE, nurse educator; b. Aurora, Ill., July 4, 1906; d. Frank Monroe and Anna (Madden) Durham; m. Carl G. Finette, Aug. 2, 1938. Student, St. Charles Sch. Nursing, Aurora, 1923-26; BS, DePaul U., 1941; MS, U. Chgo., 1947, also postgrad. work. Instr. St. Charles Sch. Nursing, Aurora, 1927-29; dir., edn. dir. St. Mary Sch. Nursing, Kakakee, Ill., 1929-34; edn. dir., acting dir. Garfield Park Sch. Nursing, Chgo., 1934-39; edn. dir. St. Joseph Mercy Sch. Nursing, Aurora, 1939-44; instr. Loyola U., Chgo., 1944-47; chmn., prof. nursing DePaul U., 1947-72; Mem. health edn. commn. Ill. Bd. Higher Edn.; mem. adv. bd. Aurora U. Mem. citizens adv. bd. Aurora U., 1980—. Mem. Nat. League Nursing, Am. Nurses Assn. (past mem. exec. com. of educators, adminstrs. sect.), Ill. League Nursing (pres. 1955-59, dir.), Chgo. League Nursing (pres. 1941-45), Ill. Hosp. Assn. (hon.), AAUP, Am. Adult Edn. Assn. Died Nov. 25, 1992.

FINK, EUGENE RICHARD, security company executive, lawyer; b. N.Y.C., Feb. 27, 1944; s. William and Anne (Kimsorofsky) F.; m. Sheila Barbara Boodish, Jan. 14, 1968; children: Zachary Evan, Jason Alexander. BS, NYU, 1966; JD, U. Tulsa, 1969. Bar: N.Y., 1970. Assoc. Booth, Lipton & Lipton, N.Y.C., 1970-72; exec. Nat. Kinney Corp., N.Y.C., 1972-75; v.p. Holmes Protection, Inc., 1974-75; pres. Winfield Security Corp., N.Y.C., 1975—; guest lectr. John Jay Coll. of Criminal Justice. Apptd. chmn. N.Y. State Security Guard Adv. Coun. Mem. Am. Soc. Indsl. Security, Nat. Assn. Security Cos. (1st vice chmn. 1995—), Assn. Lic. Detectives of N.Y. State (v.p. 1993—), Princeton Club. Deceased.

FINK, LYMAN ROGER, retired manufacturing executive; b. Elk Point, S.D., Nov. 14, 1912; s. Willis James and Helen (Black) F.; m. Frances Louise Kelly, Dec. 17, 1937; children—William R., Patricia H., James W. B.S., U. Calif. at Berkeley, 1933, M.S., 1934, Ph.D., 1937. Mgr. electronics lab. Gen. Electric Co., 1947-49, mgr. engr. radio and TV dept., 1949-55, mgr. research application dept., 1955-57, gen. mgr. X-ray dept., 1957-59, gen. mgr. atomic products div., 1959-63, v.p., 1962-63; v.p. Otis Elevator Co., 1963-66; v.p., chief tech. officer The Singer Co., 1966-68, group v.p., 1968-70; exec. v.p., dir. Church's Fried Chicken, Inc., 1970-73; pres. Diversitek Co., 1973-89; Dir., v.p. Atomic Indsl. Forum, 1961-63; trustee S.W. Research Inst., 1976-89. Recipient Charles A. Coffin award Gen. Electric Co., 1948. Fellow IEEE; mem. N.Y. Acad. Scis., AAAS, Sigma Xi, Phi Beta Kappa, Tau Beta Pi, Kappa Delta Rho. Club: Oak Hills Country (San Antonio). Deceased.

FINNEY, ROSS LEE, composer; b. Wells, Minn., Dec. 23, 1906; s. Ross Lee and Caroline (Mitchell) F.; m. Gretchen Ludke, Sept. 3, 1930; children—Ross Lee, Henry C. Student, U. Minn., 1924-25; B.A., Carleton Coll., 1927, L.H.D., 1957; postgrad., Harvard U., 1929; studies with Nadia Boulanger, 1928, Alban Berg, 1932, student of Roger Sessions, 1935, Francesco Malipiero, 1937; Mus.D., New England Conservatory of Music. Prof. music Smith Coll., 1929-48, Mt. Holyoke Coll., 1940-44; chmn. dept. mus. theory Hartt Sch. Music, Hartford, 1941-42, Amherst Coll., 1946-47; dir. Northampton Chamber Orch.; prof. U. Mich., Ann Arbor, 1949-74, emeritus, 1974-97. Composer in residence, U. Mich., 1948-74, emeritus, from 1974, composer in residence, Am. Acad. in Rome, 1960; composer Piano Sonata, 1933, First String Quartet, 1935, Second String Quartet, 1936, Piano Trio, 1938, Eight Poems by Archibald MacLeish, 1935-37, Sonata for Viola and Piano, 1937, Bleheris, 1937, Fantasy for Piano, 1939 Third String Quartet, 1940, Slow Piece, 1940, Pole Star for This Year, 1939, Symphony Communique, 1942, Third Piano Sonata, 1942, Hymn, Fuguing and Holiday 1943, Duo for Violin and Piano, 1944, Pilgrim Psalms 1945, Fourth Piano Sonata, 1945, Poor Richard, 1946 Nostalgic Waltzes, 1947, 4th String Quartet, 1947, Six Spherical Madrigals, 1947, Violin Concerto, 1933-47 Three Love Songs, 1948, Piano Quartet, 1948, Piano Concerto, 1948, 5th String Quartet, 1948, 2d Sonata for

Cello and Piano, 1950, 6th String Quartet, 1950, Sonata for Violin and Piano, 1951, 36 Songs; chamber music, 1952, Immortal Autumn, 1952, Variation for Piano, 1952, Piano Quintet, 2d Sonata for Viola and Piano, 3d Sonata for Violin and Piano, 1953, song Piano Trio, 1954, 7th String Quartet, Inventions for Piano, Variations for Orchestra, Fantasy for Solo Cello, all 1957, Fantasy for solo violin, command Yehudi Menuhin, String Quintet, commd. by Coolidge Found., all 1958, 2d Symphony, commd. by Koussevitsky Found., Edge of Shadow, commd. by Grinnell Coll., 1959, 8th String Quartet, commd. by U. Ala., 3d Symphony, 1960, 2d Piano Quintet, commd. by U. S.C., 1961, Still are New Worlds, May Festival, Ann Arbor, 1962, Sonata quasi una fantasia, Quincy (Ill.) Art Festival, 1961, Three Pieces for Strings, Winds, Percusion and Tape Recorder, 1962, Divertimento, 1963, Divertissement, commd. by Bowdoin Coll., 1964, Three Studies in Fours, commd. by Poznon Ensemble, 1965, Concerto for Percussion and Orch, commd. by Carleton Coll., 1965, Nun's Priest's Tale, commd. by Dartmouth Coll., 1965, The Martyr's Elegy, commd. U. Mich. Sesquicentennial, 1966, Symphony Concertante, commd. by Kansas City Philharmonic, 1967, Organ Fantasies, 1967, 32 Piano Games, 1968, 2d Concerto for Piano and Orch, 1968, The Remorseless Rush of Time, for Chorus and 13 Instruments, commd. Wis. State U., 1969, Summer in Valley City, for Concert Band, commd. U. Mich. Band, 1969, 24 Inventions for Piano, 1970, 2 Acts for 3 Players; clarinet, percussion and piano, commd. G. LaBlanc Corp., 1970, Landscapes Remembered, 1971, Spaces; for large orch., commd. N.D. Council Arts, 1971, transcribed for symphonic band, commd. U. Mich. Bands, 1985, Symphony No. 4, commd. for Balt. Symphony Orch., 1972, 2d Concerto for Violin and Orch, 1973, 2 Ballades for Flutes and Piano, 1973, Variations on a Memory, 1975, 7 Easy Pieces for Percussion, 1975, Narrative for Cello and Orch, 1975, Concerto for String, 1976, Skating on the Sheyenne for Concert Band, commd. by Bklyn. Coll., 1977, Earthrise for Chorus, Soli and Orch, commd by U. Mich. Sch. Music Centennial, 1978, Youth's Companion, 5 Piano Pieces, 1980, Chamber Concerto, 1981, 2 Studies for Saxophone and Piano, 1981, Hexechord for Harpsicord, 1983, Narrative in Retrospect, 1984, Weep Torn Land, opera, 1984, Divertimento for Oboe, Percussion and Piano, 1987, Narrative in Argument, 1987, Computer Marriage Comic Opera, 1991, others; author: The Game of Harmony, 1947, Thinking About Music: The Collected Writings of Ross Lee Finney, 1991, Profile of a Lifetime, A Musical Autobiography of C.F. Peters, 1992; editor-in-chief: Smith Coll. Music Archives, 1935-48; edited, for same: XII Sonatas for Violin and Figures Bass, by Francesco Geminiani, 1935; editor, Valley Music Press. Chief Paris office Interdeptl. com. OSS, 1944-45. Decorated Purple Heart; recipient Conn. Valley prize, 1935, Boston Symphony award, 1955, Acad. Arts and Letters award, 1956, Brandeis Creative Arts award, 1967; fellow Johnson Found., 1927, Pulitzer Found., Guggenheim Found., 1939, 47; Rockefeller grantee, 1956. Mem. Am. Musicol. Soc., Nat. Inst. Arts and Letters, Am. Acad. Arts and Scis., Phi Beta Kappa, Pi Kappa Lambda, Phi Mu Alpha. Died Feb., 1997.

FINNEY, SELMA, retired adult education educator; b. Arcadia, Mich., Mar. 21, 1906; d. John Alfred and Mary Isabella (Lawson) Carlson. BA, U. Mich., 1932; MA, U. Detroit, 1942; postgrad., Mich. State U., 1972. conductor workshops in field. Author: Beginning Reading Series for Adults, 1971-72. Counselor Svc. Corps of Ret. execs., Detroit, Traverse City, 1977—. Recipient Disting. Svc. for Teaching Adults award Mich. Assn. Pub. Sch. Adult Edn., 1970. Republican. Methodist. Avocations: photography, knitting. Deceased.

FISCH, MAX HAROLD, educator; b. Elma, Wash., Dec. 21, 1900; s. William F. and Bessie J. (Himes) F.; m. Ruth A. Bales, June 12, 1927 (dec. July 1974); children: Emily J. Fisch Maverick, Margaret E. Fisch Karl, William B. A.B., Butler U., 1924; Ph.D., Cornell U., 1930; LHD (hon.), Ind. U., 1985, Butler U., 1985. Instr. philosophy Cornell U., 1926-28; asst. prof. philosophy Western Res. U., 1928-43; curator rare books U.S. Army Med. Library, 1942-45, chief history of medicine div., 1946; prof. philosophy U. Ill. at Urbana, 1946-69, prof. emeritus, 1969-95, assoc. Center Advanced Study, 1961, 62, 63, 67; vis. prof. SUNY, Buffalo, 1969-70, U. Fla., 1970-71; vis. univ. prof. Tex. Tech U., 1973-75; vis. prof. U. Chgo., winter 1955, Keio U., Tokyo, 1958-59; Fulbright research prof. U. Naples, Italy, 1950-51; Matchette lectr. Purdue U., 1956, adj. prof. philosophy Ind. U.-Purdue U. Indpls., 1975-91; George Santayana Fellow Harvard University, 1960, honorary research assoc. in philosophy, 1966-67; mem. adminstrv. bd. Internat. Assn. Univs., 1950-55. Mem. adv. bd.: Works of William James, 1973-91 ; Bd. editors: Jour. History Medicine and Allied Scis, 1946-57; gen. editor: Writings of Charles S. Peirce, 1975-83, sr. editor, 1983-89; author, editor, translator numerous books and articles. Pres. C.S. Peirce Bicentennial Internat. Congress, 1976; pres. Charles S. Peirce Found., 1977-91. Decorated knight Order of Merit Italian Republic, 1976. Mem. Am. Philos. Assn. (chmn. 1956-58, pres. Western div. 1955-56), History Sci. Soc. (council 1951-53, del. Am. Council Learned Socs. 1955-58), Charles S. Peirce Soc. (pres. 1960-61), Semiotic Soc. Am. (v.p. 1977-78, pres. 1978-79); fgn. mem. Nat. Soc. Scis., Letters and Arts, Naples, Italy. Home: Los Angeles Calif. Died Jan. 6, 1995.

FISH, HAMILTON, JR., congressman; b. Washington, D.C., June 3, 1926; s. Hamilton and Grace (Chapin) F.; m. Julia Mackenzie (dec. Mar. 1969); children: Hamilton III, Julia Alexandra, Nicholas S., Peter L.; m. Billy Laster Cline, Apr. 3, 1971 (dec. May 1985); m. Mary Ann Knauss, Dec. 31, 1988. AB, Harvard U., 1949; LLB, NYU, 1957; postgrad., John F. Kennedy Sch. Pub. Adminstrn.; LLD (hon.), Mercy Coll., 1989, Marist Coll., 1978, St. Thomas Acquinas Coll., 1981; LHD (hon.), Mt. St. Mary Coll., 1989. Bar: N.Y. Vice consul to Ireland, 1951-53; with firm Alexander and Green, N.Y.C., 1957-64; practice law Poughkeepsie and Millbrook, N.Y., 1964—; mem. 91st-103rd Congresses from 21st (now 19th) N.Y. dist., Washington, D.C., 1969—; ranking mem. House Judiciary Com., Washington. Mem. Franklin Delano Roosevelt Meml. Commn., Environ. and Energy Study Conf., Congl. Caucus for Women's Issues, N.E.-Midwest Coalition, N.Y. State Congl. Del.; co-chmn. ad hoc Congl. Com. for Irish Affairs; exec. com. Congl. Human Rights Caucus; chmn. N.Y. State Rep. Congl. Del.; adv. com Clearinghouse on the Future. Recipient Disting. Pub. Servant award NYU Sch. Law, 1974, Walter White award NAACP, 1989, Congl. Civil Liberties award ACLU, 1990, Eleanor Roosevelt Valkill medal, 1990, Ea. Paralyzed Vets. Assn. award, 1990, Pub. Policy award Computer and Bus. Mfrs. Assn., 1990. Mem. N.Y. State Bar Assn., Dutches County Bar Assn., Soc. Cin., Jewish Fedn. Greater Orange County, Am. Legion, VFW, S.R., Soc. of Friendly Sons of St. Patrick of Putnam County, Order of Red Men, Masons, Elks. Republican. Died July 23, 1996.

FISHER, CLARKSON SHERMAN, federal judge; b. Long Branch, N.J., July 8, 1921; s. Albert Emmanuel and Katherine Morris (Sherman) F.; m. Mae Shannon Hoffmann, Dec. 26, 1949; children—Albert James, Clarkson Sherman, Scott Laurus, Daniel Russell. LLB cum laude, U. Notre Dame, 1950; LLD (hon.), Seton Hall U., 1988. Bar: N.J. bar 1951. Law clk., atty. Jacob Steinbach, Jr. (Atty. at Law), Long Branch, 1950, 51; atty. Edward F. Juska (Lawyer), Long Branch, 1951-58; ptnr. Juska & Fisher (Counsellors at Law), Long Branch, 1958-64; Monmouth County (N.J.) Ct. judge, 1964-66; judge N.J. Superior Ct., 1966-70; judge U.S. Dist. Ct., Dist. of N.J., 1970-79, chief judge, 1979-87, sr. judge, 1987-97. Trustee Central Jersey Bank & Trust Co.; Atty. Long Branch Planning Bd., Patrolmen's Benevolent Assn., Long Branch, Monmouth County, and Bayshore (N.J.); Mem. West Long Branch Fire Co. 2, 1955-97 , West Long Branch Bd. Adjustment, 1958; mem. Borough Council, West Long Branch, 1959-64; N.J. State assemblyman from Monmouth County, 1964; Trustee Monmouth Coll., West Long Branch, 1971-76. Served to staff sgt. Signal Corps, also Inf. AUS, 1942-45. Mem. ABA., N.J. Bar Assn., Monmouth County Bar Assn. (trustee 1962-64), Am. Legion, Holy Name Soc. (pres. chpt. 1960), VFW. Home: West Long Branch N.J. Died July 27, 1997.

FISHER, EVERETT, lawyer; b. Greenwich, Conn., May 23, 1920; s. Henry Johnson and Alice Gifford (Agnew) F.; m. Catherine Gray Marshall, Aug. 21, 1943 (dec. Sept. 1997); children: Catherine Field, Emily Trenholm Griswold. Grad., Phillips Acad., 1937; BA, Yale U., 1941, LLB, 1948. Bar: Conn. 1948, N.Y. 1949. Assoc. Littlefield, Miller & Cleaves, N.Y.C., 1948-51; ptnr. Pullman, Comley, Marshall & Parker, Greenwich, 1951-58, Parker, Badger & Fisher, 1958-72, Badger, Fisher, Cohen & Barnett, 1972-88, Badger, Fisher & Cohen, 1988-90; of counsel Whitman & Ransom, 1990-93, Whitman Breed Abbott & Morgan, Greenwich, 1993-95, Epstein Fogarty Cohen & Selby, Greenwich, 1995-96, Fogarty, Cohen, Selby & Nemiroff, Greenwich, 1997—; past trust bd. dirs. Union Trust Co.; past bd. dirs., sec., mem. exec. com. Times Mirror Mags., Inc. Past chmn. Bd. Estimate and Taxation, Greenwich; past mem. Town of Greenwich Retirement Bd.; bd. dirs., v.p. Greenwich Boys' and Girls' Club; trustee Internat. Coll., Beirut, Lebanon; trustee Round Hill Community Ch. Mem. ABA, Internat. Bar Assn., State Bar of Conn., Am. Coll. Trust and Estate Counsel, Phi Delta Phi. Republican. Clubs: Pine Valley Golf (Clementon, N.J.); Royal and Ancient Golf (St. Andrews, Scotland); Round Hill (Greenwich, dir., past pres), Field (Greenwich); Yale (N.Y.C.); Royal St. George's Golf (Sandwich, Eng.); Honourable Company of Edinburgh Golfers (Muirfield, Scotland); U.S. Seniors Golf Assn. (sec., gov.). Died Sept. 15, 1997.

FISHER, MILTON NATHAN, manufacturing company executive; b. Newark, Nov. 25, 1921; s. Davis and Maria (Rapaport) F.; B.S. in Bus. Adminstrn., U. Fla., 1946; m. Berna Braunstein, June 9, 1946; 1 son, Jerome Peter. Pres., dir. Panelfab Internat. Corp., Miami, Fla., 1951—, Decor Internacional de Cuba, 1958-59, Dicoa Corp., 1958—, Panelfab Pacific, Inc., 1965—, Panelfab P.R., Inc., 1967—; dir. Nihon Panelfab, Ltd., Japan, Panelfab Europe, Ltd.; chmn. regional export expansion council U.S. Dept. Commerce; chmn. Fla. Export Council; mem. Adv. Com. for Trade Negotiations; mem. adv. com. on the Future Fla. Ho. of Reps.; mem. high tech. task force U.S. Trade Rep.; bd. dirs. So. Center Internat. Studies. Past pres., dir. Internat. Center, Greater Miami, Fla.; bd. dirs., past chmn. ARC; chmn. Fla. Tax Coalition; mem. bd. exec. advisors U. Miami Coll. Bus. Adminstrn.; vice chmn. Fla.-Korea Econ. Cooperation Com., Inc. Served to maj. USAAF, 1942-45. Decorated D.F.C., Air medal with 3 oak leaf clusters; named Fla. Internat. Businessman of Yr., 1976; recipient Bill Pallot Internat. Achievement award Internat. Ctr. of Fla., 1983. Mem. SE U.S.-Japan Assn. (past chmn. Fla. del.), Coral Gables C. of C. (pres.), Tau Epsilon Phi, Beta Alpha Psi, Beta Gamma Sigma. Clubs: Bankers (Miami), Masons.

FISHER, RAYMOND G., management consultant, former manufacturing company executive; b. Heber City, Utah, June 30, 1911; s. John David and Maude (Van Wagoner) F.; m. Ruth Bitner, July 27, 1935; 1 son, Stephen Bitner. B.S. with honors, U. Utah, 1934; postgrad., George Washington U., 1936-38, Am. U., 1938-39. Asst. chief munitions br. WPB, 1940-42, asst. to prodn. vice chmn., 1942-43; dir. program control div. Combined Chiefs Staff, 1943-44; adv. mil. programs Office of War Moblzn. and Reconversion, 1944-45; dir. reports and statistics Office of Mil. Govt. for Germany, 1945-46; asst. to bd. dirs. RFC, 1946; economist Rockefeller Office, 1946-52; on leave as asst. prodn to dir. Def. Moblzn., 1951; dir. econ. research Continental Can Co., 1952-58, v.p. mktg., 1958-62, v.p., gen. mgr. flexible packaging, 1962-65, v.p., gen. mgr. central metal div., 1965-67, group v.p. diversified products group, 1967-71, exec. v.p., 1971-73, vice chmn., 1974-76, chmn. exec. com., 1976-77; bus. cons., 1977-94; chmn. Europemballage Corp.; dir. Continental Can Co., Continental Can Co. Can., Tee-Pak, Inc.; Adv. formulation European Recovery Program, 1948, Point Four Program, 1949-50. Mem. nat. adv. council U. Utah.; Trustee Inst. for Future. Served as capt. AUS, 1944. Decorated Medal of Freedom. Mem. Am. Statis. Assn., Indian Harbour Club, Greenwich Country Club, Jonathans Landing Golf Club (Jupiter, Fla.), Owl and Key, Pi Kappa Alpha. Home: Greenwich Conn. Died Feb. 6, 1994.

FISHER, SEYMOUR, psychologist, educator; b. Balt., May 13, 1922; s. Sam and Jean (Miller) F.; married; children: Jerid, Eve. MA, U. Chgo., 1943, PhD, 1948. Chief psychologist Elgin (Ill.) State Hosp., 1949-51; rsch. psychologist VA Hosp., Houston, 1952-56; assoc. prof. Baylor Coll. Medicine, Houston, 1957-61; prof. SUNY Health Sci. Ctr., Syracuse, 1961—. Author: The Female Orgasm, 1973, Development and Structure of the Body Image (vols.1 and 2), 1986, Sexual Images of the Self, 1989; co-author (with Roger Greenberg): The Scientific Credibility of Freud's Theory and Therapy, 1977, The Limits of Biological Treatments for Psychological Distress, 1989. Mem. APA. DIED 12/05/96. .

FISHER, WALTER DUMMER, economist, educator; b. Chgo., Sept. 17, 1916; s. Walter Taylor and Katharine (Dummer) F.; m. Marjorie Smith, Dec. 21, 1948; children: Andrew, Carol, Dorothy. AB, Harvard U., 1937; PhD, U. Chgo., 1943. Asst. economist U.S. Surplus Mktg. Adminstrn., Washington, 1940-42; instr. econs. U. Calif. at Berkeley, 1946-48, asst. prof., 1948-51; asst. prof. Kans. State U., Manhattan, 1951-54; assoc. prof. Kans. State U., 1954-57, prof., 1957-67; prof. econs. Northwestern U., Evanston, Ill., 1967-85, prof. emeritus, 1985-95; cons. Pullman Bank, Chgo., 1951-53, Rand Corp., Santa Monica, Calif., 1958-62; vis. prof. U. Louvain, Belgium, 1971-72; dir. Nat. Bur. Econ. Research, N.Y.C., 1967-83. Author: Clustering and Aggregation in Economics, 1969, Statistics Economized, 1981; Contbr. articles to profl. jours. Served to capt. USAAF, 1943-46. Faculty rsch. fellow Social Sci. Rsch. Coun., 1954-57; Guggenheim fellow, 1960-61. Fellow Econometric Soc.; mem. Am. Statis. Assn. Home: Evanston Ill. Died Apr. 14, 1995.

FISSINGER, EDWIN RUSSELL, music educator, composer; b. Chgo., June 15, 1920; s. Paul Clevel and Isabel (Sweney) F.; m. Cecile Patricia Monette, Feb. 27, 1943; children: Edwin Monette, Laura. MusB, Am. Conservatory of Music, Chgo., 1947, MusM, 1951; D in Mus. Arts, U. Ill., 1962. Instr. music Am. Conservatory of Music, Chgo., 1947-54; instr. music U. Ill., Urbana, 1954-57; chmn. dept. U. Ill. (Chgo. Circle campus), 1957-67; prof., chmn. dept. music N.D. State U., Fargo, 1967-85; dir. concert choir N.D. State U., 1967-85; cons. in field. Composer: To Everything There Is a Season, 1976, Lux Aeterna, 1983, Babylon, 1976, Something has Spoken to Me in the Night, 1979, Flowers and Love, 1987,At the Cry of the First Bird, 1989, In Paradisum, 1989, The Splendor Falls on Castle Walls, 1990, Dover Beach, 1990. Served with USAAF, 1942-44. Decorated Purple Heart; recipient Kimball award for composition, 1950. Mem. Am. Choral Dirs. Assn., Music Educators Nat. Conf. Home: Fargo N.D. Died Oct. 16, 1991; interred Holy Cross, Fargo, ND.

FITCH, DAVID ROBNETT, finance educator; b. Brookfield, Mo., Dec. 10, 1921; s. Donald Colt and Helen Morton (Robnett) F.; m. Doris Griffin Stephenson, Aug. 1, 1952; children: Cynthia, Robin, Susan. B.A. in Econs., Tex. A&M U., 1942; M.S. in Econs., U. Wis., 1948; Ph.D., U. Okla., 1956. C.L.U., Tex. Assoc. prof. Tex. A&M U., College Station, 1949-56; prof. Tex. A&M U., 1956-60; prof., chmn. dept. finance, ins. and real estate North Tex. State U., Denton, 1960-83, prof. emeritus, 1983-94. Served to capt. F.A. AUS, 1942-47. Mem. Am. Finance Assn.,

Am. Econ. Assn., Am. Risk and Ins. Assn., Assn. C.L.U.s, Southwestern Finance Assn. (pres.), Phi Delta Theta, Delta Sigma Pi, Beta Gamma Sigma. Home: Denton Tex. Died Feb. 7, 1994.

FITZGIBBON, JOHN FRANCIS, philosophy educator; b. Rock Island, Ill., Sept. 12, 1923; s. James Francis and Gertrude Marie (Schikan) F.; m. Elizabeth Jane Burke, Sept. 1, 1951; children: Elizabeth, John, Margaret, Mara, Timothy. A.B., St. Mary's of Barrens, 1946; A.M., St. Louis U., 1950; Ph.D., U. Notre Dame, 1956. Instr. U. Notre Dame, 1953-54; instr. Georgetown U., 1955-57, asst. prof., 1957-58; asst. prof. St. Ambrose U., Davenport, Iowa, 1958-60, assoc. prof., 1960-66, prof., 1966-90, prof. emeritus, 1990-92, chmn. dept. philosophy, 1967-74, 75-81; chmn. div. philosophy and theology St. Ambrose Coll., 1969-79; participant Coun. on Religion and Internat. Affairs seminars, 1967, 68, Am. Maritain Assn. seminar, 1980, Internat. Conf. on Religious Liberty, Washington, 1985; presented paper 2d World Congress of Christian Philosophy, Monterrey, Mex., 1986, Inter-Am. Congress of Philosophy and Tech., Mayaguez, P.R., 1988. Author: Ethics: Fundamental Principles of Moral Philosophy, 1983. Pres. Rock Island chpt. Citizens for Ednl. Freedom, 1963-64; mem. Davenport (Iowa) Cath. Interracial Council, 1959-70, R.I. County Interracial Council, 1965-70. Mem. AAUP (chpt. pres. 1960-61, 62-63, 68-70), Am. Maritain Assn., Metaphys. Soc. Am., Iowa Philos. Assn., Soc. for Medieval and Renaissance Philosophy. Home: Rock Island Ill. Died Nov. 30, 1992; interred Calvary Cemetery, Rock Island, IL.

FITZPATRICK, FRANCIS JAMES, lawyer; b. N.Y.C., Apr. 29, 1916; s. Francis James and Susan Clemens (Tompkins) FitzP.; m. Ethel Marie Peters, Mar. 2, 1956. AB, Duke U., 1938; postgrad., Harvard U., 1939-40; JD, Cornell U., 1947. Bar: Iowa 1951, N.J. 1954. Exec. trainee U.S. Fidelity & Guaranty Co., N.Y., 1940-41; counsellor Western Electric Co., Kearny, N.J., 1942-45; pvt. practice Orange, N.J., 1954-95. With M.C., U.S. Army, 1941-42. Mem. ABA, N.J. State Bar Assn., Essex County Bar Assn., Am. Judicature Soc., Cornell Law Student Assn. (sec.-treas.), Cornell U. Law Assn., Duke U. Met. Alumni Assn., Duke U. Glee Club & Chapel Choir, Delta Theta Phi (pres.), Am. Legion (former judge adv. Orange), Sigma Alpha Epsilon. Methodist. Home: Westfield N.J. Died Oct. 20, 1995.

FITZPATRICK, PETER, lawyer; b. Hilltown, No. Ireland, June 26, 1906; came to U.S., 1907; s. James and Mary Ann (McCrickard) F.; m. Alma Berard, July 19, 1937; children: James, Maureen, Elaine, Michael, Joseph, Barbara, Yvonne, Robert, Thomas, Rita, Colleen, John, William, Dorothy, Catherine, Margaret. BA, Loras Coll., 1926; JD, Chgo. Kent, 1933, LLM, 1934. Bar: Ill. 1933, U.S. Supreme Ct. 1956, U.S. Ct. Appeals (7th cir.) 1955, U.S. Dist. Ct. (no. dist.) Ill. 1933. dep. commr. Local Liquor Control Commn., Chgo., 1967—; hearing commr. Mayor's License Commn., Chgo., 1967—. Chair Chgo. Commn. on Human Rels., 1967-90. Fellow Am. Coll. of Trial Lawyers; mem. Chgo. Bar Assn., Ill. State Bar Assn. (pres. 1965-66). Democrat. Roman Catholic. DIED 07/31/96. .

FLACCUS, EDWARD, retired biology educator; b. Lansdowne, Pa., Feb. 3, 1921; s. Louis William and Laura Lynne (Kimball) F.; m. Sarah Emlen, Mar. 15, 1947; children: Jennifer Ann, Christopher Edward, Lynnette Marie. B.S., Haverford Coll., 1942; M.S., U. N.H., 1952; Ph.D., Duke U., 1959. Relief worker Am. Friends Service Com., Germany(British Zone), 1946-47; tchr. High Mowing Sch., Wilton, N.H., 1948-50, Loomis Sch., Windsor, Conn., 1951-55; asst. assoc. prof. U. Minn.-Duluth, 1958-68; vis. scientist Brookhaven Nat. Lab., Upton, N.Y., 1968-69, SUNY-Stony Brook, 1968-69; prof. biology Bennington (Vt.) Coll., 1969-86, ret., 1986. Author: North Country Cabin, 1979. Served with Civilian Pub. Service, 1942-46. Recipient Student Faculty award U. Minn., 1961; NSF fellow, 1957-58. Fellow AAAS; mem. Ecol. Soc. Am., Bot. Soc. Am., N.Y. Acad. Sci., Am. Inst. Biological Scis., New England Bot. Club, Sigma Xi. Quaker. DIED 09/07/96. .

FLAGLER, ROBERT LOOMIS, global export company executive, consultant; b. Chgo., Dec. 17, 1940; s. Holland Joseph and Frances (Loomis) F.; m. Stephanie Eggleston, Nov. 19, 1963(div. 1969); children: Holland Flagler Black, R. Stephen. BA, U. Miss., 1964. V.p., adminstrv. officer, dir. Telemation, Inc., Glenview, Ill., 1970-79; pres., dir. OCENCO, Inc., Northbrook, Ill., 1979-81, Frysinger Constrn. Co., Inc., Delray, Fla., 1985-87; prin. Flagler & Assocs., Inc., Wellington, Fla., 1987-94; bd. dirs. Energo, Inc., Bakersfield, Calif., Ptnrs. in Golf., Inc., Boca Raton, Fla., Blitz Corp., Phoenix, Wis. Ednl. Industries, Inc., Lake Geneva; nat., internat. cons. in field, Winneka, Ill., Boca Raton, 1981-94. Coauthor, editor: Suicide Prevention Manual, 1980 (Washington Pub. Svc. award 1980). Mem. govs. staff Miss. U.S. Bicentennial Com., 1963-94; staff mem. Boy Scouts Am., Glencoe, Ill., 1967-71; commr. Ptnrs. in Edn., 1991-94, Rep. Nat. Agenda Commn., Washington, 1993; dir. Fla. Coun. Art, 1992-94; del. Rep. Platform; mem. Rep. Senatorial Com.; active Salvation Army. Lt. USCG, 1959-60. Mem. Am. Assn. Investors, Nat. Soc. Pub. Accts., Nat. Golf Found., Internat. Videotape Producers Assn. (dir., pres. 1975-80), Internat. Global Leaders, U. Miss. Com. of 100 (life, commr. 1987-94), Assn. Bank Officers. Republican. Episcopalian. Avocations: social work, raquetball, computers, education. Deceased.

FLAMMERION, HENRI, publisher; b. Paris, Apr. 1, 1910; s. Charles and Madeleine (Engel) F.; m. Pierrette Chenelot, Oct. 20, 1945; children—Charles-Henri, Alain, Jean-Noel. Grad. Ecole Alsacienne, Paris; Licence (hon.), Faculte de Droit, Paris; diploma (hon.), Ecole Sciences Politiques, Paris. With Librairie Flammarion, Paris, 1933—, now chmn. bd. Vice pres. Syndicat des Editeurs, Paris, 1966-69. Decorated comdr. Legion d'Honneur, comdr. Arts et Lettres.

FLEESON, WILLIAM, medical educator; b. Sterling, Kans., May 21, 1915; s. William H. and Eva Lynn (Seward) F.; m. Beatrice Riedel, Mar. 26, 1943; children—William, Breck, Lucinda, Peter, Elizabeth. A.B. (Summerfield scholar), U. Kans., 1937; M.D., Yale U., 1942; postgrad. Advanced Mgmt. Program, Harvard U., 1964. Diplomate: Am. Bd. Psychiatry and Neurology. Intern U. Hosps., Mpls., 1942-43; assoc. psychiatrist Manhattan Project, Oak Ridge, 1945-46; assoc. psychiatrist, dir. child guidance div. Minn. Psychiat. Inst., Mpls., 1946-55; staff psychiatrist Elizabeth Kenny Inst., Mpls., 1953-56; Nat. Found. fellow U. Minn., Mpls., 1956; asst. prof. psychiatry and phys. medicine U. Minn., 1957-61; MEND coordinator Coll. Med. Scis., 1959-63; lectr. Law Sch., 1960-63; assoc. prof. psychiatry Med. Sch. (1961-63); asst. dean Coll. Med. Scis., 1960-63; prof. psychiatry Sch. Medicine, U. Conn., Farmington, 1963-82; assoc. dean Sch. Medicine, U. Conn., 1963-74, acting clin. dir. dept. psychiatry, 1979-80, assoc. chmn., 1980-82, prof. emeritus, 1982—; lectr. Sch. Medicine, U. Conn. (Sch. Social Work), 1967-75; acting head dept. psychiatry U. Conn., 1967-68; acting chief psychiatry VA Med. Ctr., Newington, Conn., 1983-84; sr. staff psychiatrist VA Med. Ctr., 1984-95; lectr. psychiatry Sch. Medicine, Yale, 1965-74; supr. psychotherapy Inst. for Living, Hartford, Conn., 1965-67; fellow Bur. Health Resources Devel. program Center for Ednl. Devel., U. Ill., 1974-75; vis. prof. psychiatry Free Catholic U., Lille, France, 1975-80; cons. to probate courts. Contbr.: book revs. to Sci. Books. Cons. psychiatry child study div. Mpls. Bd. Edn., 1957-63. Served to capt. AUS, 1943-46. USPHS fellow child psychiatry Judge Baker Guidance Center, Boston, 1950-51. Fellow Am. Psychiat. Assn. (life); mem. Assn. Am. Med. Colls. (sec.-treas. Northeastern group for student affairs 1970-72, chmn. 1972-73), Conn. Psychiat. Soc. (coun. 1966-68). Home: West Hartford Conn. Died Nov. 13, 1995.

FLEISCHMAN, LAWRENCE ARTHUR, art dealer, publisher, consultant; b. Detroit, Feb. 14, 1925; s. Arthur and Stella (Granet) F.; m. Barbara Greenberg, Dec. 18, 1948; children: Rebecca, Arthur, Martha. Student, Purdue U., 1942-43; BS, U. Detroit, 1948; LHD, St. John's U., 1978. Pres. Lawrence Investment Co., Detroit, 1949-66, Lawrence Advt. Agy., Detroit, 1950-60; dir. Ind. Newspaper, Inc., Detroit, 1952-60, WITI, Channel 6, Milw., 1952-59; pres., owner Kennedy Galleries, N.Y.C., 1966—; dir. Hartwell Hedge Fund, N.Y.C., 1966-72; founder, pres. Archives Am. Art, 1952-66, dir., 1967—; mem. Fine Arts Commn., USIA, 1956-62; advisor Fine Arts Commn., White House, 1960-62, 64-66; pres. Detroit Arts Commn., 1962-66; treas. Soc. Arts and Crafts Sch., Detroit, 1953-66; bd. dirs. Mannes Coll. Music, N.Y.C., 1967-71, Skowhegan Sch. Painting and Sculpture, Maine and N.Y., 1968-83; v.p. Com. Religion and Art of Am., N.Y.C., 1972—; mem. president's coun. Met. Mus. Art, chmn. Philodores Soc., 1988; mat. trustee Balt. Mus. Art.; chmn. Caryatids, British dept. of Greek and Roman Antiquities, London; nat. trustee Balt. Mus. Art. Editor Am. Art Jour., 1969—. Chmn. Am. Friends of Brit. Mus., London, 1991; mem. vis. com. dept. Greek and Roman, Mus. Fine Arts, Boston, 1991. Served with AUS, 1943-46, ETO. Recipient Spl. Resolution award City of Detroit, 1966, Art award Lotus Club, N.Y.C., 1967; Copley medal Nat. Portrait Gallery, 1978; decorated knight Order of San Silvestre Pope Paul VI, 1978; fellow Morgan Library, N.Y.C., 1968. Mem. Pa. Acad. Fine Arts (life), Pa. Hist. Soc. (life), Art Dealers Assn. Am. (bd. dirs.), Am. Antiquarian Soc. Died Jan. 31, 1997.

FLEMING, JOHN GUNTHER, law educator; b. Berlin, July 6, 1919; came to U.S., 1960; m. Valerie Joyce Beall, Apr. 16, 1946; children: Anthony, Barbara, Colin, Stephen. BA, Oxford U., Eng., 1939, MA, 1941, PhD, 1948, DCL, 1959, LLD, 1985. Bar: Eng. 1947. Lectr. in law King's Coll., London, 1946-48; prof., dean faculty law Australian Nat. U., 1949-60; prof. law U. Calif., Berkeley, 1957-58, 60-90, Shannon Cecil Turner prof. law, 1974-90, prof. emeritus, 1990; Goodhart prof. Cambridge U., 1987-88. Author: Introduction to the Law of Torts, 1967, 2d edit., 1986, The American Tort Process, 1988, Law of Torts, 9th edit., 1997; editor in chief: Am. Jour. Comparative Law, 1971-87. With Royal Armoured Corps, Brit. Army, 1941-45. Fellow Brasenose Coll., Oxford U. (hon.), Brit. Acad.; mem. Am. Law Inst., Internat. Acad. Comparative Law, Internat. Assn. Legal Sci. (pres. 1980-82). Home: Richmond Calif. Died Sept. 22, 1997.

FLEMING, RUSSELL, JR., utility company executive, lawyer; b. New Brunswick, N.J., Aug. 20, 1938; s. Russell and Margaret Olga (Kebly) F.; m. Cheryl Hall; children: Eileen, Russell III. AB, Rutgers U., 1960; JD, Columbia U., 1963. Bar: N.J. 1964. Assoc. Sailer and Holzapfel, Elizabeth, N.J., 1965-70; ptnr. firm Sailer and Fleming, Elizabeth, N.J., 1965-73; ptnr. Elizabethtown Gas Co., 1970-73, exec. v.p., gen. counsel, 1980-85; chief oper. officer, pres. svc. div. NUI Corp., Bridgewater, N.J., 1985, pres. svc. div., 1986, gen. counsel, 1975-88; ptnr., dir. Theodore Barry & Assocs., N.Y.C., 1988-89, Putnam Hayes and Bartlett, Inc. (econ. and mgmt. counsel), N.Y.C., 1989-90; sr. v.p. N.Y. State Electric and Gas Corp., Binghamton, 1990-94; gen. atty. Elizabethtown Water Co., 1973-80; v.p., gen. counsel NUI Corp., 1975-85; exec. com. Associated Gas Distbrs., 1979-85; counsel boroughs of, Milltown and Middlesex, 1969, 73. Pres. Milltown Bd. Edn., 1968-69; sec. Middlesex County Charter Study Commn., 1973; bd. dirs., br. pres. YMCA, Raritan Valley, N.J., 1971-73; trustee St. Peter's Med. Ctr., New Brunswick, 1982-83. Served to capt. USAR, 1963-65. Named Outstanding Young Man of Yr. Milltown (N.J.) Jaycees, 1968. Mem. ABA, N.J. Bar Assn. (chmn. pub. utility law sect. 1975), Fed. Energy Bar Assn., Am. Gas Assn. (legal sect., mng. com. 1978-86, chmn. fed. regulatory affairs 1984-86), Assoc. Gas Distbrs. (exec. com. 1979-86, bd. dirs. 1991-94). Home: Stillwater Okla. Died Aug. 31, 1994; interment Sunset Memorial Gardens, Stillwater, OK.

FLEMING, WILLIAM DAVID, stockbroker; b. San Mateo, Calif., July 8, 1910; s. William J. and Maude (Lockie) F.; m. Barbara Trotter, Oct. 20, 1934; children—Gerald S., Richard D. Student, pub. schs. With Blyth & Co., San Francisco, Los Angeles, 1929-45; with Walston & Co., Inc., Los Angeles, 1945-52; partner Walston & Co., Inc., N.Y.C., 1952-57; sr. v.p. Walston & Co., Inc., Chgo., 1957-64; pres. Walston & Co., Inc., N.Y.C., 1964-74; with Shearson/Lehman Bros., Newport Beach, Calif., 1974-85. Home: Corona Del Mar Calif. Died Dec. 14, 1994.

FLINT, EMILY PAULINE RIEDINGER, editor; b. N.Y.C., Apr. 1, 1909; d. Louis and Emma Therese (Schaufele) Riedinger; m. Paul H. Flint, Aug. 18, 1935; 1 son, Paul H. A.B., Barnard Coll., 1930; M.A., Tufts U., 1932; B.S., Columbia Sch. Library Service, 1935; L.H.D. (hon.), New Eng. Coll., 1967; D.Litt (hon.), Franklin Pierce Coll., 1969. Teaching fellow English Tufts Coll., 1930-32; instr. Tufts U. Writers' Workshop, summer 1954; library staff Mt. Vernon (N.Y.) Pub. Library, 1932-34, Columbia Library, 1934-35; humanities librarian Mass. Inst. Tech., 1935-44; editorial asst. Atlantic Monthly, 1945-47, research editor, 1948-51, mng. editor, 1951-70, contbg. editor, 1970-73; editor Peabody Museum, Harvard U., 1970-76; pres. Creative Editing, Inc., 1970-88; assoc. editor Alma Mater mag., 1971-74; isntr. div. journalism Boston U., 1948-51; lectr. editorial procedures Simmons Coll., 1975, spl. instr. in communications, 1977-78. Editor: (with Edward Weeks) Jubilee: 100 Years of the Atlantic, 1957, The Lithographs of Ture Bengzt, 1978, Every Child a Wanted Child, The Work of Clarence J. Gamble, M.D. in the Birth Control Movement, 1978, Creative Editing and Writing Handbook, 1980; editorial cons.: History of the Harvard Medical Unit at Boston City Hospital, 1915-1973, 2 vols., 1982. Trustee Medford (Mass.) Pub. Library, 1954-84; trustee Franklin Pierce Coll., 1972-95, vice chmn. bd., 1977-79, chmn. bd., 1979-87; alumna trustee Barnard Coll., 1965-69. Recipient Citizen of Yr. award Medford C. of C., 1984, Outstanding Service to the Coll. award Franklin Pierce Coll. Alumni Assn., 1989. Club: Zonta (Woman of Achievement award Medford 1984). Died Mar. 16, 1995.

FLOCH, HERVÉ ALEXANDRE, medical biologist; b. Lambezellec, France, Oct. 3, 1908; s. Herve Marie and Jeanne (Le Rouzic) F.; m. Lucie Henry; children: Therese, Herve Henri, Daniele. M.D., Faculté de Medecine de Bordeaux, 1932. Asst. Colonial Hosp., scholar Pasteur Inst., Paris, from 1938; mil. physician, medicin col., until 1956; dir., founder Pasteur Inst. Cayenne, French Guiana (br. Pasteur Inst., Paris), 1940-66; dir. Pasteur Inst. Pointe à Pitre, Guadeloupe, 1969-71; chief Anti-Mosquito Svc. and Leprosy Svc., French Guiana, 1940-66, Guadaloupe, 1969-71; chief lab. Inst. Pasteur, Paris, 1956-73; biologist chief Lab. Svc. Hosp. Morlaix, France, 1974-79; prof. microbiology Faculty Odontology, Brest, 1978-85; malariologist and pathologist WHO. Author over 918 publs. to profl. jours. Mem. French Acad. Medicine (6 prizes), French Acad. Sci. (Prix Muteau, grand prix Etancelin 1974), French Acad. Overseas Sci., other sci. socs. Rsch., publs. on leprology, promoter use of D.D.S. in treatment of leprosy, malariology, epidemiology, entomology, acarology, parasitology, mycology, virology, bacteriology, biology and tropical pathology; studies on tropical alimentation-nutrition habitat. Died Feb., 1996.

FLOOD-STOLLER, JOAN ELIZABETH, critical care nurse; d. Raymond Gabriel Flood and Anna Annoinette Augresani; m. Leslie Stoller, Feb. 8, 1964; children: Cheryl Ann R. Cole. RN, Laboure Coll., Boston, 1984; BS, Boston U., 1975; BSN, U. Mass., 1987. Formerly ICU-CCU nurse Lee Meml. Hosp., Ft. Myers, Fla. Medicare clin. coord. Healthpark Care Ctr., Ft. Myers

1994-97. Mem. Amnesty Internat. Mem. ANA, Sigma Theta Tau. Died Jan. 2, 1997.

FLORIT, ERMENEGILDO CARDINAL, clergyman; b. Fagagna, Italy, July 5, 1901; ed. Seminario Diocesano di Udine, Pontificia U. Lateranense, U. Gregoriana. Ordained priest Roman Catholic Ch., 1925; chaplain, Palmanova, 1927-29; canon of San Marco, 1933; prof. theology Pontificia U. Lateranense, 1929-51, pro-rector, 1951-54; pro-rector Pontificium Institutum Utriusque Juris, 1951-54; domestic prelate to His Holiness, 1950—; coadjutor archbishop of Florence, Italy, 1954-62, archbishop, 1962-77; elevated to Sacred Coll. Cardinals, 1965. Mem. Pontifical Commn. on Bishops, Diocesan Orgn. for Ecumenical Council, 1960—, Pontifical Commn. for Revision Code Canon Law, 1965—. Mem. Cath. Bibl. Assn. Am. Author books on Bibl. culture, including Il Metodo della Storia delle Forme. Founder Lateranum mag.

FLUOR, JOHN ROBERT, chemical engineer; b. Santa Ana, Calif., Dec. 18, 1921; s. Peter E. and Margaret (Fischer) F.; grad. U. So. Calif., 1946; m. Lillian Marie Breaux, May 17, 1944; children—John Robert II, Peter. With Fluor Corp., 1946—, successively mgr., v.p. and gen. mgr. mfg., v.p. in charge mfg., exec. v.p., 1952-62, pres., 1962-68, chief exec. officer, 1962—, chmn., 1968—, also dir.; dir. Calif. Canadian Bank, Tex. Commerce Bancshares, Santa Anita Operating Co., Santa Anita Realty Enterprises; trustee Pacific Mut. Trustee, U. So. Calif., James Irvine Found.; campaign chmn. United Way Los Angeles County, 1977, pres., 1977—, chmn., 1978 -; chmn. devel. mem. Boy Scouts Am., 1977—. Served as 1st lt. USAAF, 1941-45. Recipient MOLES award for outstanding achievement in constrn., 1982. Mem. NAM (dir.), Am. Mgmt. Assn., Am. Petroleum Inst., Am. Inst. Chem. Engrs., Calif. Thoroughbred Breeders Assn. (dir.). Roman Catholic. Clubs: California, Bohemiam, San Gabriel Country; Sky (N.Y.C.); Eldorado Country, Vintage (Palm Desert, Calif.); Los Angeles Country.

FLYNN, JOHN ALLEN, lawyer; b. Riverside, Ill., Jan. 12, 1945; s. William and Marian Rae (Gustafson) F.; m. Georgette A. Kaleiki, Dec. 31, 1988; children: Judson John, Erin Courtney. AB, Stanford U., 1966; JD, U. Calif., San Francisco, 1969. Bar: Calif. 1970, U.S. Dist. Ct. (no. and ea. dists.) Calif. 1970, U.S. Ct. Appeals (9th cir.) 1970, U.S. Supreme Ct. 1975. Assoc. Graham & James, San Francisco, 1969-75, ptnr., 1976-97; now ptnr. Flynn Delich & Wise; lectr. in field. Mem. ABA, Maritime Law Assn. (mem. com. on practice and procedure 1983—), San Francisco Bar Assn. (chmn. admiralty com. 1978—). Roman Catholic. Club: San Francisco Press. Died Feb. 14, 1997.

FOA, JOSEPH VICTOR, aeronautical engineer, educator; b. Turin, Italy, July 10, 1909; came to U.S., 1939, naturalized, 1944; s. Ettore and Lelia (DellaTorre) F.; m. Lucy Bouvier, June 27, 1942; children: Lelia, Sylvana, Eugenie, Gay. D in Mech. Engring., Politecnico di Torino, 1931; D in Aero. Engring., U. Rome, 1933. Project engr. Piaggio Aircraft Co., Italy, 1933-35, 37-39; chief engr. Caproni Engring. Ctr., Studi Caproni, Italy, 1935-37; project engr. Bellanca Aircraft Corp., 1939-40; cons., chief engr. Am. Aeromarine Co., 1942; head aero. design rsch. Curtiss Wright Corp., 1943-45; head propulsion br. Cornell U. Aero. Lab., 1945-52; prof. aero. engrng. Rensselaer Poly. Inst., 1952-70, head dept., 1958-67; prof. engring. and applied sci. George Washington U., 1970-89; cons. to aircraft cos.; originator cryptosteady flow concept and theories, new concepts in aero. and marine propulsion, lift augmentation, high-speed ground transp., heating and air conditioning; patentee in field. Author and co-author sci. books and articles. Recipient devel. award and cert. for exceptional service Navy Ordnance Dept., 1945. Cert. of appreciation Dept. Army, 1951. Home: Bethesda Md. Died March 31, 1996.

FOLEY, DANIEL EDMUND, real estate development executive; b. St. Paul, Mar. 1, 1926; s. Edward and Gerry (Fitzgarld) F.; student U. Minn., 1941-43; m. Paula Evans, Apr. 1, 1946. Chmn. bd. Realty Ptnrs. Ltd., Los Angeles; pres. Alpha Property Mgmt. Served with AUS, 1943-46.

FOLSOM, FRANKLIN BREWSTER, author; b. Boulder, Colo., July 21, 1907; s. Fred Gorham and Mary Elvira (Elwell) F.; m. Mary Letha Elting, Sept. 1, 1936; children: Michael Brewster, Rachel Alice Folsom Moll. Student, Dartmouth Coll., 1924-25; B.A., U. Colo., 1928, Oxford U., 1932; M.A., Oxford U., 1963. Instr. Swarthmore Coll., 1928-30; editor Hunger Fighter, 1934-35; exec. sec. League Am. Writers, 1937-42, New York Council Am.-Soviet Friendship, 1943; dir. adult edn. Downtown Community Sch., 1945; staff writer Tass, 1946-47; free lance writer, 1948-95; chmn. Council on Interracial Books for Children, 1965-69; vis. lectr. U. Colo., 1987. Author: America's Ancient Treasures, 1971, (with Mary Elting Folsom) 3d edit., 1983, 4th edit., 1993, Red Power on the Rio Grande: The Native American Revolution of 1680, 1973, 2d edit., 1989, Life and Legend of George McJunkin: Black Cowboy, 1974, Give Me Liberty: America's Colonial Heritage, 1974, Some Basic Rights of Soviet Citizens, 1983; (with Connie Fledderjohan) The Great Peace March: An American Odyssey, 1988, Impatient Armies of the Poor: The Story of Collective Action by the Unemployed, 1808-1942, 1991, Days of Anger, Days of Hope: A Memoir of the League of American Writers 1937-1942, 1994; numerous others.; contbr. articles to numerous periodicals. Bd. dirs. Great Peace March for Global Nuclear Disarmament, 1986-88. Served with U.S. Mcht. Marine, 1945-46. Recipient Harriet Monroe poetry award, 1937, Follett award, 1974, Spur award, 1974, Norlin award Alumni U. Colo., 1974, Eugene M. Kayden award Univ. Press of Colo., 1990, Colo. Book Author award, 1991; Macdowell Colony fellow; Rhodes scholar, 1930-33. Mem. So. Am. Archeology, Authors Guild, Soc. Children's Book Writers, Colo. Archaeol. Soc., Colo. Authors League (Top Hand award, 1975, 79, 83, 91), Archaeol. Soc. N.J. (v.p. 1968-72). Home: Boulder Colo. Died Apr. 30, 1995.

FONTES, PATRICIA J., educational psychologist; b. Providence, Dec. 10, 1936; d. Manuel William and Conceicao Elizabeth (Sousa) F. BS in Edn., Boston U., 1957; MEd, Boston Coll., 1965, PhD, 1968. Tchr. Warwick (R.I.) pub. schs., 1957-59; religious sister/superior Sisters of Our Lady of Providence, 1959-65; asst. prof. U. R.I., Kingston, 1968-69; asst./assoc. prof. Salve Regina Coll., Newport, R.I., 1969-72; cons. psychologist Girl Scouts of R.I., Inc., Providence, 1972-73; research fellow Ednl. Research Ctr., St. Patrick's Coll., Dublin, Ireland, 1973-88; cons. psychologist Girl Scouts R.I., Providence, 1989-92; prof. CEFOPE, U. Minho, Braga, Portugal, 1992—; lectr. in field. Author: Equality in Primary Teaching 1985; contbr. articles to profl. jours. Boston U. scholar, 1953-57; Boston Coll. fellow, 1965-68; Inst. for Portuguese Lang. and Culture grantee, 1982. Mem. APA, Am. Ednl. Rsch. Assn., Nat. Coun. on Measurement in Edn., Internat. Coun. Psychologists (sec.-gen. 1991-94), Internat. Assn. Applied Psychology. Roman Catholic. Avocations: biking, mountain walking, travel, gardening, reading, cooking.

FORCE, ROLAND WYNFIELD, anthropologist, museum executive; b. Omaha, Dec. 30, 1924; s. Richard Erwin and Edna Fern (Collins) F.; m. Maryanne Tefft, Sept. 16, 1949. B.A., Stanford U., 1950, M.A. in Edn., 1951, M.A. in Anthropology, 1952, Ph.D. in Anthropology, 1958; D.Sci. (hon.), Hawaii Loa Coll., 1973. Acting instr. Stanford U., 1954; assoc. in ethnology Bernice P. Bishop Mus., Honolulu, 1954-56, dir., 1962-76, dir. emeritus, 1976-96, holder C.R. Bishop Disting. chair in Pacific studies, 1976-77; dir. Mus. Am. Indian, Heye Found., N.Y.C., 1977-86, pres., dir., 1986-90, pres., dir. emeritus, 1990-96; curator oceanic archeology, ethnology Field Mus. of Natural History, Chgo., 1956-61. Served with C.E. and Infantry AUS, 1943-46. Fellow Am. Anthrop. Assn., AAAS, Pacific Sci. Assn. (hon. life, mem. council 1966-77); mem. Sigma Xi. Deceased.

FORD, GEORGE HARRY, language professional, educator; b. Winnipeg, Man., Can., Dec. 21, 1914; s. Harry and Gertrude (Burgess) F.; m. Patricia Murray, May 4, 1942; children: Leslie Margaret, Harry Seymour. B.A., U. Man., 1936; M.A., U. Toronto, 1938; Ph.D., Yale U., 1942. Lectr. U. Man., 1945-46; asso. prof. U. Cin., 1946-54, prof., 1954-58; vis. prof. U. Chgo., 1948, Johns Hopkins U., 1949, U. B.C., 1953; prof. English, U. Rochester, 1958-94, chmn. dept., 1960-72, Joseph H. Gilmore prof., 1969. Author: Keats and the Victorians, 1945, Dickens and His Readers, 1955, Double Measure: D.H. Lawrence, 1965, The Making of a Secret Agent, 1978; editor: Dickens' David Copperfield, 1958, Hard Times, 1966, 2d edit., 1990, Bleak House, 1977, The Dickens Critics, 1962, The Norton Anthology of English Literature, 4th edit., 1979, 5th edit., 1985, 6th edit., 1992, Victorian Fiction, A Second Guide to Research, 1978. Served from lt. to capt. Can. Army, 1942-45. Guggenheim fellow; Huntington Library fellow; Wilbur Cross medal Yale U., 1983. Fellow Am. Council Learned Socs.; mem. Internat. Assn. Profs. English, Literary Club Cin., Pundit Club, Dickens Fellowship (pres. 1975), N.Y. Council Humanities, Internat. Assn. Study of Time (pres. 1979), Am. Acad. Arts and Scis. Episcopalian. Home: Rochester N.Y. Died Dec. 6, 1994.

FORD, JOSEPH, retired superior court judge; b. Easton, Mass., May 18, 1914; s. Joseph L. and Margaret E. (Malloy) F.; children—Carolyn Ford Howell, Richard B. J.D., Northeastern U., 1938, LL.M., 1941. Bar: Mass. 1938, U.S. Dist. Ct. Mass. 1941, U.S. Ct. Appeals (1st cir.) 1946, U.S. Supreme Ct. 1953. Ptnr. Bingham, Dana & Gould, Boston, 1942-62, of counsel, 1986—; superior ct. judge Boston, 1962-84; appellate div. of ct., 1978-84; lectr. trial practice Suffolk U., 1976-90; adj. prof. Boston U. Law Sch., 1977-87, New Eng. Sch. Law, 1976-92. Mem. Mass. Crime Commn., 1953-55. Served to lt. (j.g.) USNR, 1944-46. Mem. ABA, Am. Law Inst., Mass. Bar Assn., Boston Bar Assn. (spl. asst. dist. atty. 1985-97), Nat. Dist. Atty. Assn. Roman Catholic. DIED 02/26/97. .

FORD, LEE ELLEN (LEOLA FORD), scientist, educator, retired lawyer; b. Auburn, Ind., June 16, 1917; d. Arthur W. and Geneva (Muhn) Ford; BA, Wittenberg Coll., 1947; MS, U. Minn., 1949; PhD, Iowa State Coll., 1952; JD, U. Notre Dame, 1972. Bar: Ind. 1972. CPA auditing, 1934-44; assoc. prof. biology Gustavus Adolphus Coll., 1950-51; prof. and head biology dept. Anderson (Ind.) Coll., 1952-55; vis. prof. biology U. Alta. (Can.), Calgary, 1955-56; assoc. prof. biology Pacific Luth. U., Parkland, Wash., 1956-62; prof. biology and cytogenetics Miss. State Coll. for Women, 1962-64; chief cytogeneticist Pacific N.W. Rsch. Found., Seattle, 1964-65; founder, dir. Canine Genetics Consulting Svc., Parkland, Wash., 1963-69; pvt. practice, Ind., 1972-92. Founder, sponsor, trainer guide dogs for adult and child blind, mentally and physically handicapped Companion Collies for the Adult, Jr. Blind, 1955-65; founder, dir., rschr. Genetics Rsch. Lab., Butler, Ind., 1955-75, cons. cytogenetics, 1969-75; legis. cons., 1970-79; dir. chromosome lab. Inst. Basic Rsch. in Mental Retardation, S.I., 1968-69; founder, dir., rschr. Legis. Bur. U. Notre Dame Law Sch., 1969-72, editor New Dimensions in Legis., 1969-72; editor Butler Record Herald, 1972-76; founder, dir., writer Ind. Interreligious Commn. on Human Equality, 1976-80; exec. asst. to Gov. Otis R. Bowen, Ind., 1973-75; founder, sponser, bd. dirs. Ind. Commn. on Status Women, 1973-74; bd. dirs. Ind. Coun. Chs.; founder, editor, writer Ford Assocs. pubs., 1972-86; mem. Pres.'s Adv. Coun. on Drug Abuse, 1976-77. Admitted to Ind. bar, 1972. Adult counselor Girl Scouts U.S., 1934-40; founder, sponsor, bd. dirs. Ind. Task Force Women's Health, 1976-80; mem. exec. bd., bd. dirs. Ind.-Ky. Synod Lutheran Ch., 1972-78; bd. dirs., mem. coun. St. Marks Luth. Ch., Butler, 1970-76; mem. social svcs. pers. bd., 1970-76; mem. DeKalb County (Ind.) Sheriff's Merit Bd., 1983-87; founder, dir., pres. Ind. Caucus for Animal Legis. and Leadership, 1984-87. Mem. AAUW, AAAS, Genetics Soc. Am., Am. Human Genetics Soc., Am. Genetic Assn., Am. Inst. Biol. Scis., Am. Soc. Zoologists, La. Acad. Sci., Miss. Acad. Sci., Ind. Acad. Sci., Iowa Acad. Sci., Bot. Soc. Am., Ecol. Soc. Am., ABA (bd. dir.), Ind. Bar Assn. (bd. dir.), DeKalb County Bar Assn. (bd. dir.) Bar Assn., Humane Soc. U.S. (bd. dir. 1970-88), DeKalb County Humane Soc. (founder, bd. dirs. 1970-86), Ind. Fedn. Humane Socs. (bd. dir. 1970-84), Nat. Assn. Women Lawyers (bd. dir.), Bus. and Profl. Women's Club, Nat. Assn. Rep. Women (bd. dir.), Women's Equity Action League (bd dir.), Assn. So. Biologists, Phi Kappa Phi. Club: Altrusa. Author: Lee's 7 Lives, 1992; founder, editor: Breeder's Jour., 1958-63; numerous vols. on dog genetics and breeding, guide dogs for the blind. Contbr. over 4000 sci., popular and rsch. publs. on cytogenetics, dog breeding and legal topics; contbr. articles to Am. Kennel Club Gazette, 1970-81, also others; Pioneer in research of identifying and isolating monoploid chromosomes in humans, corn, and other plants and animals by use of cytology to give hybrid monoploid seeds quicker corn yeild; pioneer in identifying and separating cytologically individual chromosomes in corn plants, oats, wheat, barley, animals; pioneer work in genetics which laid the foundation for later DNA research. Died July 18, 1997.

FORDHAM, JEFFERSON BARNES, lawyer, educator; b. Greensboro, N.C., July 8, 1905; s. Christopher Columbus and Maggie Shepherd (Barnes) F.; m. Rebecca Jane Norwood, Sept. 6, 1930 (dec. 1962); children: Robert, William; m. Rita Ennella, Mar. 21, 1964. A.B., U. N.C., 1926, A.M., J.D. with honors, 1929, LL.D., 1953; J.S.D., Yale, 1930; LL.D., Franklin and Marshall Coll., 1960; L.H.D., U. Pa., 1970. Bar: N.Y., N.C., Ohio, Pa., Utah bars. Sterling Research fellow Yale Law Sch., 1929-30; mem. law faculty W.Va. U. and faculty editor W.Va. Law Quar., 1930-35; spl. asst. to U.S. Sec. Labor, 1935; asso. law firm Reed, Hoyt & Washburn, N.Y.C., 1935-38; rev. counsel U.S. PWA, Washington, 1938-39; counsel, chief bond atty. U.S. PWA, 1939-40; prof. law La. State U., 1940-46, Vanderbilt U., 1946-47; dean, prof. law Ohio State U., 1947-52; dean, prof. law U. Pa., 1952-70, univ. prof. law, 1970-72, dean, prof. emeritus, 1972-94; prof. law U. Utah, 1972-94, distinguished prof. law, 1974-94; prof. emeritus; Edward Douglass White lectr. La. State U., 1954; Benjamin N. Cardozo lectr. Assn. Bar City N.Y., 1957; William H. Leary lectr. U. Utah, 1971. Author: Local Government Law, rev. edit, 1986; co-author: Coursebook on Legislation; Contbr. legal publs. Mem. Pres.'s Adv. Panel on Conflicts of Interest and Ethics in Govt., 1961, Utah Constituional Revision Com., until 1987; co-chmn. Utah Joint Legis. Com. on Energy Policy, 1976. Served with USNR, 1942-45. Recipient Distinguished Service award Yale Law Alumni, 1968, U. N.C. Sch. Law, 1969, U. Pa. Law Alumni, 1970; Jefferson B. Fordham professorship established at U. Pa. Law Sch., 1973; Fordham Forum established at U. Utah Coll. Law, 1985. Mem. Am. Bar Assn. (chmn. sect. municipal law 1949-51, 1st chmn. sect. individual rights and responsibilities 1966-68), Am. Law Inst. (council), Assn. Am. Law Schs. (pres. 1970), Phi Beta Kappa, Phi Kappa Phi, Order of Coif. Democrat. Home: Salt Lake City Utah Died June 24, 1994.

FORKERT, CLIFFORD ARTHUR, civil engineer; b. Verona, N.D., Oct. 16, 1916; s. Arthur Louis and Bessie (Delamater) F.; grad. N.D. State Coll., 1940; postgrad. M.I.T.; m. Betty Jo Erickson, July 1, 1940; children: Terry Lynn Forkert Williamson, Michael, Debra Edwards. Hwy. engr., N.D., Tex., 1937-40; hydraulic engr. Internat. Boundary Commn. Tex. on Rio Grande and Tributaries, 1940-43; constrn., topographic and cons. engr., Calif. 1946—; now civil engr., prin. Clifford A. Forkert, Civil Engr.; pres. Calif. Poly. Pomona Assos. Capt. USMCR, 1943-46. Registered civil engr.

Calif., Oreg., Ariz., profl. engr., Nev., Ariz.; lic. land surveyor, Nev., Ariz. Mem. Am. Congress and Mapping (life), ASCE (life), Land Surveyors Assn. Calif. (dir.), Alumni Assn. N.D. State Coll. Died Mar. 29, 1995.

FORKIN, THOMAS S., lawyer; b. Berkeley Twp., N.J., Dec. 20, 1937; s. Thomas Francis and Sally Marie (Johnston) F.; m. E. Syvonne Keffer, June 27, 1964; children: Thomas J., Keith A., Tracey S. B.A. in English, Villanova U., 1959, LL.B., 1962. Bar: N.J. 1963, U.S. Dist. Ct. N.J. 1963, U.S. Supreme Ct. 1966, U.S. Ct. Appeals (3d cir.) 1970. Pres., sr. atty. Forkin, McShane, Manos & Rotz, P.A., Cherry Hill, N.J., 1972-96; lectr. Villanova U. Sch. Law, 1969-87, Burlington County Coll., 1974-75. Co-author: Tax Strategies in Divorce, 1987; contbr. articles to legal publs. Recipient Villanova U. Alumni medal 1989; selected The Best Lawyers in Am., Family Law, 1983, 87, 89-90, 93-94, 94-95. Life mem. bd. consultors Villanova U. Law Sch., 1979-96. Fellow Am. Acad. Matrimonial Lawyers (v.p. 1973-77, bd. govs. 1977-80), Internat. Acad. Matrimonial Lawyers; mem. N.J. Acad. Matrimonial Lawyers, Burlington County Bar Assn. (chmn. family law sect. 1976, 80-82), Camden County Bar Assn. (chmn. family law sect. 1975), N.J. Bar Assn. (chmn. family law sect. 1977, exec. com. 1987-88, 90-91, 93-95, supreme ct. family practice com. 1990-96), ABA. Republican. Roman Catholic. Clubs: Union League (Phila.); Metropolitan (Chgo.); Tavistock Country (Haddonfield, N.J.). Died Oct. 3, 1996.

FÖRSTER, WERNER RUDOLF MARIA, pharmacologist, consultant; b. Brüx, Czechoslovakia, Aug. 20, 1919; arrived in Germany, 1945; s. Josef and Wilhelmine (Liebig) F.; m. Liese Herbrich; children: Walter, Günter, Reinhard, Ulrike. MD, U. Prague and Mainz, 1948; D habilitatus medicinae, Medical U., Magdeburg, Germany, 1961. Asst. dept. pharmacology U. Mainz, 1948-52; sr. physician dept. pharmacology BASF, Ludwigshafen, 1952-57, U. Jena, Germany, 1957-59, Med. U. Magdeburg, 1959-66; head dept. pharmacology Martin-Luther U. Halle-Wittenberg, Halle, Germany, 1966-83; prof. of pharmacology Martin-Luther U., Halle, 1969; prof. emeritus, 1983, scientific cons., 1992-95. Author; editor: Drug Therapy for General Practitioners, 1989; editor: Prostaglandins and Thromboxanes, 1981. Recipient Nat. prize for Sci., 3d Class of German Dem. Republic, 1979. Mem. German Soc. Cardiology, German Soc. Prevention and Rehab. of Cardiovascular Diseases, N.Y. Acad. Sci., Hungarian Soc. Cardiology (hon.). Died Nov. 16, 1997.

FORTENBACH, RAY THOMAS, retired lawyer; b. Chgo., Apr. 27, 1927; s. Ray J. and Mary Lee (Shively) F.; m. Marie Septer, Aug. 31, 1951; children: Karen, Karl, Kurt. B.A., U. Louisville, 1947; LL.B., U. Houston, 1954. Bar: Tex. 1954, U.S. Supreme Ct. 1971. Partner firm Childs, Fortenbach, Beck & Guyton, Houston, 1956-82; of counsel Childs, Fortenbach, Beck & Guyton, 1982-87; sole practice Houston, 1987-90; of counsel Margraves & Schueler, 1991-92; ret., 1992. Served with USCGR, 1945-46. Recipient Outstanding Alumnus of Yr. award U. Houston Coll. Law, 1971, Pres.'s award for meritorious service, 1976. Mem. ABA, Tex. Bar Assn., Houston Bar Assn., U. Houston Alumni Assn. (pres. 1974-75) U. Houston Law Alumni Orgn. (bd. dirs., mem. exec. com. 1985-89, trustee 1982-90, trustee emeritus, life 1990—). Roman Catholic. Clubs: River Oaks Country. Died June 18, 1997.

FORTNA, LIXI, state legislator; b. Austerlitz, Moravia, Czechoslovakia, July 1, 1913; came to U.S., 1939; d. Felix Redlich von Wezek and Marianne Loew; m. Peter Wenzel, May 26, 1936 (div. 1944); children: Victor, Rosi; m. Floyd W. Fortna, Nov. 13, 1947. LLD, U. Prague, Czechoslovakia, 1936. Office mgr. Sugarbush Ski Area, Warren, Vt., 1958-82; supr. U.S. War Damage Commn., Manila, 1947-50; mem. Ho. of Reps. State of Vt., Montpelier, 1982—; bd. dirs. Cen. Vt. Solid Waste Mgmt. Plan, Barr, Valley Med. Ctr., Waitsfield, Vt. Selectman Town Govt., Warren, pres. "Smart" Ski Municipalities Assn., Montpelier; chairperson Rep. Caucus. With USAF, 1950-54. Mem. Rotary. Roman Catholic. Avocation: recycling. Home: Warren VT DIED 10/13/95. .

FOSS, HARLAN FUNSTON, religious education educator, academic administrator; b. Canton, S.D., Oct. 10, 1918; s. Hans and Thea (Hokenstad) F.; m. Beatrice Naomi Lindaas, Sept. 2, 1943; children—Richard John, Kristi Marie, Marilyn Jean. B.A., St. Olaf Coll., 1940; B.Th., Luther Theol. Sem., 1944; Th.M., Princeton Theol. Sem., 1945; Ph.D., Drew U., 1956; postgrad., Mansfield Coll. Oxford (Eng.) U., 1967, Pontifical Inst. and Gregorian U., Rome, 1974. Ordained to ministry Luth. Ch., 1944. Pastor Mt. Carmel Luth. Ch., Milw., 1944-47; mem. faculty St. Olaf Coll., Northfield, Minn., 1947-95; assoc. prof. religion St. Olaf Coll., 1954-56, prof., 1957-95, v.p., dean coll., 1979-80, pres., 1980-85. Mem. Northfield Bd. Edn., 1959-66, treas., 1960-61, chmn., 1961-66. Decorated Knight 1st class Order St. Olav (Norway); Ezra Squire Tipple fellow, 1951-52. Mem. AAUP, Am. Acad. Religion, Norwegian-Am. Hist. Assn., Blue Key. Republican. Club: Lion. Home: Northfield Minn. Died Dec. 20, 1995.

FOSTER, FRANCES, actress; b. Yonkers, N.Y., June 11, 1924; d. George Henry and Helen Elizabeth (Lloyd)

Brown Davenport; m. Morton Goldsen, Sept. 11, 1982; m. Robert Standfield Foster, Mar. 29, 1941 (dec.); 1 son, Terrell Robert. Student, Am. Theatre Wing, N.Y.C., 1949-52. Artist in residence CCNY, N.Y.C., 1973-77; actress Negro Ensemble Co., N.Y.C., 1967-86. Appeared in plays throughout the world including, Munich Olympics, 1972; World Theatre Festival, London, 1969, Australia, 1977; (films) Malcolm X, Crooklyn, Clockers; (Broadway) Having Our Say. Recipient Obie award, 1985. Mem. SAG, AFTRA, Actors Equity Assn. (councillor 1953-67). Democrat. DIED 06/17/97. .

FOSTER, WALTON ARTHUR, broadcasting executive; b. San Angelo, Tex., Aug. 26, 1927; s. Arthur Rambo and Katie (Walton) F.; m. Arla Vee Bishop, Feb. 17, 1950; 1 child, Walton Arthur II (dec.). AA, San Angelo Coll., 1948. Mem. staff Sta. KGKL, San Angelo, 1944-46; gen. mgr. Stas. KTXL-AM-FM and KTXL-TV, San Angelo, 1947-54; mem. staff Stas. KGKO, KLIF, Dallas, 1954-56, Sta. KTRK-TV, Houston, 1954-56; founder, pres. Stas. KWFR-AM-FM, KIXY-AM-FM, Solar Broadcasting Co., San Angelo, 1954-78; founder Stas. KHOS-AM-FM, KYXX-AM-FM, The Foster Broadcasters, Inc., Sonora and Ozona, Tex., 1974-89; founder, CEO Stas. KIXY-FM and KXQZ-AM, Foster Comms. Co., Inc., San Angelo, 1984-95. 1st violin San Angelo Symphony Orch., 1947; bd. dirs. United Blood Svcs., chmn. Concho Valley chpt. ARC, 1988-89; bd. dirs. Ret. Srs. Vol. Program,. San Angelo Civic Theatre, San Angelo Conv., Coliseum and Auditorium; trustee St. Johns Hosp. and Health Ctr. Found.; chmn. San Angelo Zoning Bd. Adjustment. Mem. San Angelo C. of C. (vice-chmn. City Planning Commn. 1994), SAR, Phi Theta Kappa. Home: San Angelo Tex. Died Feb. 4, 1995.

FOUSHEE, GERALDINE GEORGE, municipal county government official, detective; b. Newark, Aug. 14, 1947; d. Clarence Milton and Anna Mae (Smith) George; m. Joseph Edward Foushee, Aug. 14, 1966; children: Chere Michele, Kyle Edward. AS in Edn. magna cum laude, Essex County Coll., 1976; BA in Polit. Sci. magna cum laude, Rutgers U., 1981, M in Social Work, Adminstrn., Policy and Planning magna cum laude, 1993. Cert. tchr., sch. social worker, N.J.; lic. social worker, N.J. Computer keypunch operator Continental Ins. Co., Newark, 1965-66; computer verification operator Blue Cross/Blue Shield of N.J., Newark, 1966; tech. asst., adminstrv. asst., acting coordinator learning resource ctr. Essex County Coll., Newark, 1968-79; investigator field claims, adjustor Hartford Ins. Group, Randolph, N.J., 1979-81; police officer Newark Police Dept., 1981-84; detective fugitive warrant squad Sheriff's Office Essex County, Newark, 1984-86; exec. sec. Alcoholic Beverage Control Bd. City of Newark, 1986—; spl. instr. Newark Police Acad., 1986—; pres., CEO Axiom Consultants, Vintage Security Inc. Mem. adv. bd. Div. of Youth and Family Services, Newark, 1986—; apptd. mem. Supreme Ct. Task Force, Essex Vicinage Adv. Com. on Minority Concerns by the HOn. Chief Justice Robert Wilentz, N.J. Supreme Ct.; life mem. Met. Bapt. Ch., Newark. Recipient Merit award State of N.J. Tng. Commn., 1981, Law Enforcemnt award City of Newark Mayor James Sharpe, 1986, Service award Lions Club, Hillside, N.J.; named Police Officer of Month, Woman of Yr., Grace Reformed Bapt. Ch., 1987. Mem. Internat. Assn. Women Police (Cert. of Merit award 1984), Nat. Orgn. Black Law Enforcement Execs., Nat. Black Alcoholism Council, North N.J. Women in Police, Nat. Council Negro Women (Woman of Yr. 1987), Nat. Black Police Assn., Safety Officers Coalition, Essex County Coll. Alumni Assn., Baton's Inc. (chairwoman com. 1986-87), Fraternal Order Police (bd. dirs. 1982-84, Police Officer of Month 1982), Bronze Shields, Inc. (fin. sec 1982-86, Police award 1981, Achievement award 1987), Alpha Sigma Lambda. Democrat. Avocations: horseback riding, skiing, swimming, skating, abstract art. Died Jan. 27, 1997.

FOUTY, WILLIAM JOSEPH, surgeon; b. Columbus, Ohio, June 25, 1929; s. William Perry and Ruth Lillian (Johnson) F.; m. Mary Lena Wrenn, July 2, 1965; children: Patrick, Jennifer, Scott. BSc, Ohio State U., 1952, MD, 1957. Diplomate Am. Bd. Surgery. Intern, then resident in surgery San Diego Naval Hosp., 1957-63; commd. ensign M.C., USN, 1956, advanced through grades to capt., 1971; mem. attending staff Ct. Lakes (Ill.) Naval Hosp., 1963-65; mem. attending staff Nat. Naval Med. Ctr., Bethesda, 1965—, chmn. dept. surgery, 1973—, program dir. gen. surgery, 1973—; chmn. dept. surgery, program dir. gen. surgery, dir. residency program Washington Hosp. Ctr., 1977—; acting chmn. dept. surgery Uniformed Svc. U. Health Scis., 1976-77, also program dir. gen. surgery; cons. govt. agys. Mem. editorial bd. Am. Jour. Surgery. Fellow ACS; mem. Chesapeake Vascular Soc.

FOWKE, EDITH MARGARET FULTON, author, English language educator emeritus; b. Lumsden, Sask., Can., Apr. 30, 1913; d. William Marshall and Margaret (Fyffe) Fulton; m. Franklin George Fowke, Oct. 1, 1938. Student, Regina Coll., 1929-31; B.A. with high honors in English and History, U. Sask., 1933, M.A. in English, 1938; LL.D. (hon.), Brock U., 1974, U. Regina, 1985; D.Litt., Trent U., 1975, York U., 1982. Editor Western Tchr., Saskatoon, Sask., 1937-45; assoc. editor

Mag. Digest, Toronto, Ont., 1945-50; freelance writer CBC Radio, 1950-71; assoc. prof. English, York U., Downsview, Ont., 1971-77; prof. York U., 1977-83, prof. emeritus, 1983-96. Author: Folk Songs of Canada, 1954, Folk Songs of Quebec, 1957, Songs of Work and Freedom, 1960, Canada's Story in Song, 1960, Traditional Singers and Songs from Ontario, 1965, More Folk Songs of Canada, 1967, Lumbering Songs from the Northern Woods, 1970, Sally Go Round the Sun, 1969, Canadian Vibrations, 1972, Penguin Book of Canadian Folk Songs, 1974, Folklore of Canada, 1976, Ring Around the Moon, 1977, Folktales of French Canada, 1979, Sea Songs and Ballads from Nineteenth Century Nova Scotia, 1981, Riot of Riddles, 1982, Singing Our History, 1985, Tales Told in Canada, 1986, Red Rover, Red Rover: Children's Games Played in Canada, 1988, Canadian Folklore, 1988, A Family Heritage: The Story and Songs of LaRana Clark, 1994, Legends Told in Canada, 1994, Black Cats and Shooting Stars, 1995; editor: Songs and Sayings of an Ulster Childhood by Alice Kane, 1983, Can. Folk Music Jour., 1971-96; co-editor: Bibliography of Canadian Folklore in English, 1982, Explorations in Canadian Folklore, 1985. Decorated Order Can. Fellow Am. Folklore Soc., Royal Soc. Can.; mem. Writer's Union Can. (life), English Folk Dance and Song Soc., Can. Soc. Children's Authors, Illustrators and Performers, Folklore Studies Assn. Can. (life), Can. Soc. Traditional Music (hon. pres.). Home: Toronto Can. Died Mar. 29, 1996.

FOWLER, ELIZABETH MILTON, real estate executive; b. Watertown, Fla., Jan. 11, 1919; d. Arthur Wellington and Mattie Jean (Hodges) Milton; m. Albert L. Fowler, Jr., Aug. 6, 1948; children: Patricia Dawn Cecilia, Richard Gordon Sean. Student Bowling Green Bus. U., 1938-39; Cultural HHD (hon.), World U. Roundtable, 1988. Sec. to dir. Workmen's Compensation Div., Fla. Indsl. Commn., Tallahassee, 1940-41; sec. to supt. div. Gibbs Ship Yard Repair, 1942-44; sec. to elec. engrs. Reynolds, Smith & Hills, Architects and Engrs., 1946-49; sec. to pres. Aichel Steel Corp., Jacksonville, Fla., 1949-50; adminstr. office mgr. for prin., vice-prin. Am. Dependent Sch., Moron Air Base, Spain, 1961-63; owner, mgr. Elizabeth Properties, Jacksonville, 1956-69. Chmn. ways and means com. Chattanooga High Sch. PTA, 1956-57; asst. den mother Cub Scout Troop, 1970; block worker Gov. Reagan's Presdl. Campaign. Recipient Spl. Appreciation award Eglin AFB, Fla., 1969. Mem. Nat. Assn. Female Execs., Am. Security Council (nat. adv. bd.), Dade County Crimewatch Orgn. Republican. Avocations: art and interior design, horseback riding, collecting fine porcelain, reading, politics and world affairs. Died Sept. 3, 1996. Home: Miami Fla.

FOWLER, RICHARD GILDART, physicist; b. Albion, Mich., June 13, 1916; s. Rufus Alexander and Ethel Alberta (Gildart) F.; m. Frances Miriam Holmes, Aug. 26, 1939; children: Lynne Carol, Nancy Barbara, Patricia Ann, Richard Gerald. A.B., Albion Coll., 1936; M.S., U. Mich., 1939, Ph.D., 1942; postgrad., Christ Ch., Oxford, Eng., 1953-54, U. Zurich, 1968-69; postgrad. (NATO fellow), U. Giessen, Ger., 1971. Rsch. asst. Dow Chem. Co., 1936-38; grad. rsch. asst. U. Mich., 1938-42, rsch. physicist, 1943-46; asst. prof. physics N.C. State Coll., 1942; asst. to assoc. to prof. U. Okla., Norman, 1946-61; rsch. prof. U. Okla., 1961-80, prof. emeritus, 1980—, chmn. dept. physics, 1955-59, 66-68; chmn. U. Okla. (Sch. Engring. Physics), 1948-53, 55-62; v.p. U. Okla. (Research Inst.), 1962-64; chmn. physics fellowship panel NSF, 1959-61. Assoc. editor: Physics of Fluids, 1964-68, Jour. Quant. Spect. Rad. Transfer, 1980-83, Jour. Sci. Exploration, 1986-88, Proc. Okla. Acad. Sci., 1984-87; physics cons.: World Book Ency., 1966-84. Carroll fellow U. Sydney, Australia, 1963; Fulbright lectr., 1963; Guggenheim fellow Oxford U., 1952-53. Fellow Okla. Acad. Scis., Am. Phys. Soc. (chmn. fluid dynamics div. 1968), Inst. Physics; mem. AAAS, AAUP, Am. Inst. Physics (regional counsellor 1964-66), Phi Beta Kappa, Sigma Xi, Sigma Pi Sigma (hon.), Sigma Tau, Delta Tau Delta, Gamma Alpha. Died Oct. 1992.

FOX, ELEANOR MAE COHEN, lawyer, educator, writer; b. Trenton, N.J., Jan. 18, 1936; d. Herman and Elizabeth (Stein) Cohen; children: Douglas Anthony, Margot Alison, Randall Matthew. BA, Vassar Coll., 1956; LLB, NYU, 1961. Bar: N.Y. 1961, U.S. Dist. Ct. N.Y. 1964, U.S. Supreme Ct. 1965. Editor high sch. textbooks Cambridge Book Co., N.Y.C., 1956-57; editor labor service publ. Bur. Nat. Affairs, Washington, 1957-58; assoc. Simpson Thacher & Bartlett, 1962-70, partner, 1970-76, of counsel, 1976—; assoc. prof. law NYU, 1976-78, prof., 1978—, dir. Root-Tilden program, 1979-81, assoc. dean Law Sch., 1987-90, Walter Derenberg prof. trade regulation, 1994—; lectr. on antitrust and competition policy, domestic, internat. and comparative; mem. Pres. Carter's Nat. Commn. Rev. Antitrust Laws and Procedures, 1978-79; mem. adv. bd. Bur. Nat. Affairs Antitrust and Trade Regulation Reporter, 1977—coun. fgn. rels., 1993—; trustee NYU Law Ctr. Found. 1974-92; trustee Lawyers' Com. Civil Rights Under Law, 1988—; mem. Coun. Fgn. Rels., 1993—; mem. internat. competition policy adv. com. to advise the U.S. Atty. Gen., 1998—. Author: (with Byron E. Fox) Corporate Acquisitions and Mergers, Vol. 1, 1968, Vol. 2, 1970, Vol. 3, 1973, Vol. 4, 1981, rev. edit., 1998; (novel) W.L., Esquire, 1977, (with G. Bermann, R

Goebel, W. Davey) European Community Law, Cases and Materials, 1993, supplement, 1998; (with Lawrence A. Sullivan) Antitrust—Cases and Materials, 1989, supplement, 1995; (with J. Fingleton, D. Neven, P. Seabright) Competition Policy and the Transformation of Central Europe, 1996; bd. editors N.Y. Law Jour., 1976—, Antitrust Bull., 1986—; mem. adv. bd. Antitrust Law and Econs. Rev., 1988—, Rev. Indsl. Orgn., 1990—, EEC Merger Control Reporter, 1992—, Gaceta Juridica de la CE y de la Competencia, 1992—; contbr. articles to legal jours. Fellow Am. Bar Found., N.Y. Bar Found.; mem. ABA (chmn. merger com. antitrust sect. 1974-77, chmn. publs. com. 1977-78, chmn. Sherman Act com. 1978-79, mem. council antitrust sect. 1979-83, 90-94, vice chmn. antitrust sect. 1992-94, chair NAFTA Task Force, 1993—), N.Y. State Bar Assn. (chmn. antitrust sect. 1978-79, mem. exec. com. antitrust sect. 1979-83), Fed. Bar Council (trustee 1974-76, v.p. 1976-78), Assn. of Bar of City of N.Y. (v.p. 1989-90, exec. com. 1977-81, chmn. trade regulation com. 1973-76, lawyer advt. com. 1976-77, chmn. com. on U.S. in a global economy, 1991-94), Am. Law Inst., Assn. Am. Law Schs. (chmn. sect. antitrust and econ. regulation 1981-83), NYU Law Alumni Assn. (bd. dirs. 1974-79, 87-91), Am. Fgn. Law Assn. (v.p. 1979-82).

FOX, SAMUEL J., rabbi, educator; b. Cleve., Feb. 25, 1919; s. Joseph and Yetta (Mandel) F.; m. Edith Phyllis Muskin, Jan. 25, 1942; 1 child, Joseph Raphael. BA, Yeshiva U., 1940, rabbi, 1941; MA, Butler U., 1946; PhD, Harvard U., 1959. Ordained rabbi Union Orthodox Jewish Congregations Am., 1941. Rabbi United Hebrew Congregation, Indpls., 1941-51, Congregation Chevra Tehillim, Lynn, Mass., 1951-94; prof. theology Merrimack Coll., North Andover, Mass., 1970-95; pres. Orthodox Rabbinical Coun., Boston, 1950-95, Mass. Coun. Rabbis, Boston, 1950-95. Author: Hell in Jewish, 1958; profucer TV program Massachusetts Rabbis, 1960; columnist Why Because, 1942. Bd. dirs. Value of Life Com., Boston, 1952. Mem. AAUP, Coll. Theology Soc. Home: Lynn Mass. Died Dec. 26, 1994.

FRAME, JAMES SUTHERLAND, mathematics educator; b. N.Y.C., Dec. 24, 1907; s. James Everett and Jean Herring (Loomis) F.; m. Emily Bogert Boyce, June 25, 1938; children: Barbara Eger, Paul S., Roger E., Lawrence H. AB summa cum laude, Harvard U., 1929, MA, 1930, PhD, 1933. Instr. Harvard U., Cambridge, Mass., 1930-33; traveling fellow, 1933-34; instr., asst. prof. Brown U., Providence, R.I., 1934-42; assoc. prof., dept. head Allegheny Coll., Meadville, Pa., 1942-43; prof. math. Mich. State U., East Lansing, 1943-77, dept. head, 1943-60, prof. engring. rsch., 1963-77, prof. emeritus, 1977-97; with Inst. Advanced Study, Princeton, 1950-51; mem. Univ. Devel. Commn., Bangkok, 1968; cons. Ford Found., Bangkok, 1970, Institut für Quantenchemie Free Univ. Berlin, 1972; vis. prof. Technische Hochschule Aachen, Fed. Republic Germany, 1981. Co-author: General Mathematics, 1939; author: Solid Geometry, 1948, Buildings and Facilities for the Mathematical Sciences, 1963; contbr. articles to profl. jours. Mem. Bd. Edn. East Lansing, 1948-52; chmn. sanctuary bldg. com. Edgewood United Ch., 1963-66. Recipient Distig. Faculty award Mich. State U., 1967; mem. People to People math. delegation to Peoples Republic of China, 1983. Mem. AAUP (mem. nat. coun. 1948-51), Am. Math. Soc., Math. Assn. Am. (bd. govs. 1950-52, 58-60, Disting. Svc. award Mich. 1989, Yueh-Gin Gung and Charles Y. Hu Disting. Svc. to Math. award 1994), Mich. Acad. Scis., Arts and Letters (pres. 1958-59), Harvard Club Ctrl. Mich. (pres. 1968-69), Kiwanis (pres. East Lansing chpt. 1969), Phi Beta Kappa (chpt. pres. 1974-75), Sigma Xi (chpt. pres. 1974-75), Phi Kappa Phi (chpt. pres. 1958-59), Pi Mu Epsilon (founder jour. 1949, sec.-treas. 1951-54, v.p. 1954-57, pres. 1957-66, C.C. MacDuffee award 1966). Home: East Lansing Mich. Died Feb. 27, 1997.

FRANCIS, JOSEPH A., clergyman; b. Lafayette, La., Sept. 30, 1923; s. Joseph and Mabel (Coc) F. BA, Cath. U. Am., MA; postgrad., Xavier U., New Orleans, Loyola U., Mt. St. Mary's Coll. Ordained priest Roman Catholic Ch., 1950; asst. dean students St. Augustine Sem., 1951-52; asst. dir. Holy Rosary Inst., 1952-60; adminstr. Immaculate Heart of Mary Parish, 1950, Holy Cross, Austin, Tex., 1960-61; instr. Pius X High Sch., 1961-62; founder, prin. Verbun Dei High Sch., Watts, Calif., 1962-67; provincial superior, 1967-73, titular bishop of Valiposita, aux. bishop of Newark, 1976-97; trustee Immaculate Conception Sem., Mahwah, N.J.; bd. overseers Harvard Div. Sch.; bd. trustees Divine Word Coll., Epworth, Iowa; bd. dirs. Am. Bd. Cath. Missions, Cath. Relief Services. Mem. Black Priests' Caucus (past pres.), Nat. Office for Black Catholics (dir.), Conf. Maj. Superiors of Men (past pres.), Nat. Cath. Conf. Interracial Justice (dir.). Died Sept. 1, 1997.

FRANCOEUR, LEOPOLD, engineering company executive; b. St. Anne de Bellevue, Que., Can., Oct. 29, 1927. B. Commerce, McGill U., Montreal, Can.; C.A., Inst. Chartered Accts., Que. Chartered acct., Can. Comptroller div. Hawker Siddeley Can., Inc., Montreal, 1965-78; corp. comptroller Hawker Siddeley Can., Inc., Toronto, 1978-81, v.p. fin., 1981-91; dir. Hawker Siddeley Can. Inc., Toronto, Racair, Toronto, CGTX Inc., Montreal, Dosco Overseas Engring. Ltd., Tuxford, Eng., CanCar Inc., Atlanta, Kockums CanCar Corp., Atlanta. Mem. Ordre des Comptables Agrees du Quebec, Inst. Chartered Accts. Ont. Home: Mississauga Can Deceased 1991.

FRANKL, VIKTOR E., psychiatrist, author; b. Vienna, Austria, Mar. 26, 1905; s. Gabriel and Elsa (Lion) F.; m. Eleonore Katharina Schwindt, July 18, 1947; 1 dau., Gabriele Vesely. M.D., U. Vienna, 1930, PhD, 1949; 28 hon. doctoral degrees, U.S., Latin Am., South Africa, Europe, Israel, 1970-96. Editor jour. Man in Everyday Life, 1927; founder, head Youth Counseling Centers, Vienna, 1928-38; staff Neuropsychiatric Univ. Hosp., 1930-38; diplomate neurology and psychiatry, 1936—; head neurol. dept. Rothschild Hosp., Vienna, 1940-42; head Neurol. Poliklinik Hosp. of Vienna, 1946-70; assoc. prof. neurology and psychiatry U. Vienna, 1947-55, prof., 1955—; Distinguished prof. logotherapy U.S. Internat. U., San Diego, 1970—; vis. prof. Harvard Summer Sch., 1961, So. Meth. U., 1966, Stanford U., 1971-72, Duquesne U., 1972; founder sch. logotherapy or existential analysis. Lectr., U.S. and fgn. countries. Author: The Doctor and the Soul, from Psychotherapy to Logotherapy, 1955, Man's Search for Meaning, an Introduction to Logotherapy, 1962 (named 1 of 10 most influential books in Am. Libr. of Congress), Psychotherapy and Existentialism, 1967, The Will to Meaning, Foundations and Applications of Logotherapy, 1969, The Unconscious God, Psychotherapy and Theology, 1976, The Unheard Cry for Meaning, Psychotherapy and Humanism, 1978, Recollections, An Autobiography, 1997, others pub. Portuguese, German, Polish, Japanese, Dutch, Spanish, Italian, Swedish, Norwegian, Danish, French, Chinese, Hebrew, Greek, Serbo-Croatian, Finnish, Korean, Slovene, Afrikaans, Russian, Hungarian, Czech, Bulgarian, Icelandic; Editor: (with V.E. von Gebsattel, J. H. Schultz) Ency. of Psychotherapy (5 vols.). Trustee The Am. Austrian Found. Recipient Albert Schweitzer award, 1977, Cardinal Innitzer award, 1977, Theodor Billroth medal, 1980, City of Vienna Ring of Honor, 1980, World Congress of Logotherapy award, 1980, Oskar Pfister award Am. Psychiat. Assn., 1985, Lifetime Achievement award, 1987, Gt. Cross of Merit with star (Germany), 1983, Goethe medal, 1994, Gt. Cross of Merit with Star (Austria), 1995, numerous others; named Hon. Citizen of Austin, Tex., 1976, Hon. Citizen of Vienna, Austria, 1995. Mem. Austrian Med. Soc. for Psychotherapy (founder, pres. 1950—), Austrian Soc. for Psychiatry Neurology (hon.), Austrian Acad. Scis. (hon.). Imprisoned in concentration camps, 1942- 45. Died Sept. 2, 1997.

FRANKLIN, MARGARET LAVONA BARNUM (MRS. C. BENJAMIN FRANKLIN), civic leader; b. Caldwell, Kans., June 19, 1905; d. LeGrand Husted and Elva (Biddinger) Barnum; m. C. Benjamin Franklin, Jan. 20, 1940 (dec. 1983); children: Margaret Lee (Mrs. Michael J. Felso), Benjamin Barnum. B.A., Washburn U., 1952; student, Iowa State Tchrs. Coll., 1923-25, U. Iowa, 1937-38. Tchr. pub. schs. Union, Iowa, 1925-27, pub. schs., Kearney, Nebr., 1927-28, Marshalltown, Iowa, 1928-40; advance rep. Redpath-Vawter-Chautauquas, 1926, Associated Chautauquas, 1927-30. Mem. Citizens Adv. Com., 1965-69; mem. Stormont-Vail Regional Ctr. Hosp. Aux.; bd. dirs. Marshalltown Civic Theatre, 1938-40, pres. 1938-40; bd. dirs. Topeka Pub. Libr. Found., 1984-92; mem. Park Ave. Christian Ch., N.Y.C.; 1st sec. beautification com. City of Topeka, 1951. Recipient Waldo B. Heywood award Topeka Civic Theatre, 1967, Vol. Svc. award Topeka Pub. Libr., 1991. Mem. DAR (state chmn. Museum 1968-71), AAUW (50+ Yr. mem.), Gemini Group of Topeka, Topeka Geneal. Soc., Topeka Civic Symphony Soc. (dir. 1952-57, Svc. Honor citation 1960), Doll Collectors Am., Shawnee County Hist. Soc. (dir. 1963-75, sec. 1964-66), Stevengraph Collectors Assn., Friends of Topeka Public Libr. (dir. 1970-79, Disting. Svc. award 1980), PEO Sisterhood, Philanthropic and Ednl. Orgn. (pres. chpt. 1956-57, coop. bd. pres. 1964-65, chpt. honoree 1969), Native Sons and Daus. Kans. (life), Nonoso, Topeka Stamp Club, Western Sorosis Club (pres. 1960-61), Minerva Club (2d v.p. 1984-85), Woman's Club (1st v.p. 1952-54), Knife and Fork Club, Alpha Beta Gamma. Republican. Home: Topeka Kans. Died Sept. 11, 1997; interred Mt. Hope Cemetery, Topeka, KS.

FRASER, GEORGE BROADRUP, lawyer, former educator; b. Washington, May 9, 1914; s. George B. and Florence M. (Hillyard) F.; m. Phebe E. Bandy, Dec. 20, 1965 (dec. Nov. 1989). AB, Dartmouth Coll., 1936; LLB, Harvard U., 1939; LLM, George Washington U., 1941. Bar: D.C. 1939, Okla. 1952. Practiced in Washington, 1939-41; assoc. atty. Boise regional office, VA, Idaho, 1946; acting prof. law, then prof. law U. Idaho, 1946-49; prof. law U. Okla., 1949-84, Boyd prof., 1959-84, Murrah prof. law, 1981, prof. emeritus, 1984-95; vis. prof. George Washington U., summers 1948, 51, 58, U. Ill., 1959-60; vis. prof. law U. Mich., spring 1964, Hastings Coll. Law, U. Calif.-San Francisco, 1966. Contbr. articles to profl. jours., chpts. in books. Lt. comdr. USNR, 1941-45. Mem. ABA, Okla. Bar Assn. (Golden Gavel award 1983), Cleveland County Bar Assn., Order of Coif, Phi Delta Phi. Home: Norman Okla. Died Sept. 20, 1995.

FRAUENS, MARIE, editor, researcher; b. Kansas City, Mo., July 10, 1902; d. Frank Henry and Amanda Margaret (Stansch) F. AA, Kansas City (Mo.) Jr. Coll., 1921; BJ, U. Mo., 1924; MA, Columbia U., 1947; postgrad., Naval Res. Officers Sch., Washington, 1955-64, Indsl. Coll. Armed Forces, 1964. Instr. swimming, Kansas City, 1919-21; rschr. Mo. State Hist. Soc., 1922-24; teaching prin., dir. extra curricular newspaper and dramatics club Wardell (Mo.) High Sch., 1924-27; math. editor Row Peterson and Co., Evanston, Ill., 1927-35; chief editor high sch. program McGraw-Hill Book Co., N.Y.C., 1935-43; commd. lt. (j.g.) USNR, 1943, advanced through grades to permanent commn. as lt. comdr., 1949, liaison officer U.S. Navy-U.S. Armed Forces Inst., 1943-44, tng. officer Bur. Ordnance, 1944-47; tech. writer Naval Res. Tng. Publs. Project, 1947-49; ret. from Res., 1965; tng. dir. John I. Thompson and Co., Washington, 1949-57; tech. writer Dept. Navy, Washington, 1957; adminstrv. officer Office of Sec. Def., Washington, 1958-69; freelance editor, rschr., Washington, 1969-86, Kansas City, Mo., 1986—, messages of Gov. Ky. to gen. assembly for Ky. Hist. Soc., 1974-76; editor The Machine Gun, Vol. II, Part VII for Lt. Col. George Chinn, USMC, 1952; editor reports for, also exec. sec. Spl. Com. Adequacy of Range Facilities, Dept. Def., 1958; completed authentic restoration of 1882 town house on Capitol Hill, 1980. Active first aid, health courses ARC, 1917-18; girls' advisor YWCA, Kansas City, 1921; counselor Chgo. settlement house, 1930-35; active Red Cross Fund, D.C., 1949; mem. bd. dirs. Naval Gun Factory Welfare and Recreation Assn., 1947-49; mem. work group to develop Interagy. Sci. and Engring. Exhibit The Vision of Man, Office Sec. Def., 1963-65. Decorated mil. medals. Mem. Naval Res. Assn., Ret. Officers Assn., Res. Officers Assn., Naval Order U.S., Am. Def. Preparedness Assn., Union Cemetery Hist. Soc., Nat. Trust Hist. Preservation, Pi Gamma Mu. Contbr. to Commn. Implications of Armed Services Ednl. Programs. Author manuals, pamphlets in field of naval ops. Avocation: genealogical and historical rsch.

FREDRICKS, ANTHONY THEO, retired lawyer; b. Georgetown, Idaho, Aug. 10, 1910; s. Charles Henry and Louella Marie (Sorensen) F.; m. Edna Nellie Pershall, Apr. 14, 1934 (dec. July 1945); children: Shirley Fay, Edna Thea, Darylann; m. Epha Jane Sutcliffe, Aug. 12, 1969 (dec. June 1995). Tchr.'s Cert., U. Idaho So. Br., Pocatello, 1931; JD, George Washington U., 1938. Bar: D.C. 1938, Mont. 1938, U. S. Dist. Ct. D.C. 1938, U.S. Ct. Appeals 1938, Idaho 1945, U.S. Dist. Ct. Idaho 1945, U.S. Supreme Ct. 1947. Spl. agt. Div. Investigations, Washington, 1938-41; referee in bankruptcy U.S. Dist. Ct. for Mont., 1941-42; assoc. counsel Reconstruction Fin. Corp., Washington, 1942-44; organizer, dir. Fed. Rent Control for Idaho, Boise, 1944-47; Idaho state counsel FNMA, Boise, 1947-51; sr. mem. law firm Boise, 1947-72; mem. Am. Bd. Arbitration, 1968. Patentee of over-snow vehicle, U.S., 1961, Norway, 1961, Fed. Republic of Germany, 1961, remote control scaffold, U.S., 1971, brakeable swivel casters, U.S., 1976. Recipient Cert. of Achievement, United Inventors and Scientists of Am., 1976, 50 Yrs. Practice of Law Meritorious Svc. award State of Idaho, 1995. Mem. Inter-american Bar Assn. Avocations: inventing, woodworking, real estate development. Died Nov. 30, 1996.

FREEDBERG, SYDNEY JOSEPH, museum curator, fine arts educator; b. Boston, Nov. 11, 1914; s. Samuel and Lillian (Michelson) F.; m. Anne Blake, Jan. 15, 1942 (div. 1950); 1 child, William Blake; m. Susan Pulitzer, Apr. 10, 1954 (dec. June 1965); children: Kate Pulitzer, Nathaniel Davis; m. Catherine Blanton, June 24, 1967; 1 child, Sydney Joseph. AB summa cum laude, Harvard U., 1936, AM, 1939, PhD, 1940. Mem. faculty Harvard U., 1938-40, 53-97, prof. fine arts, 1960-83, Arthur Kingsley Porter prof., 1979-83, prof. emeritus, 1983-97; prof. in residence Harvard U. Ctr. Renaissance Studies, 1973-74, 80-81; chmn. dept. Harvard U., 1959-63, Walter Channing Cabot fellow, 1973-76, mem. faculty coun., 1974-77, chmn. univ. mus. coun., 1977-80; chief curator Nat. Gallery, Washington, 1983-88; asst. prof., then assoc. prof. art Wellesley Coll., 1946-54; mem. adv. coun. Guggenheim Found., 1978-86; spl. rschr. 16th-century Italian art. Author: Parmigianino, His Works in Painting, 1950, Painting of the High Renaissance, 1961, Andrea del Sarto, 1963, Painting in Italy, 1500-1600, 1971, Circa 1600, 1983. Vice chmn. Nat. Exec. Com. for Rescue of Italian Art, 1966-74; bd. dirs. Save Venice, Inc., 1970-90; adv. coun. Sistine Restoration, 1987-94, pres., 1991-94; chmn. I. Tatti Coun., 1990-93. Maj. AUS, 1942-46. Guggenheim fellow, 1949-50, 54-55, Am. Coun. Learned Socs. fellow, 1958-59, 66-67, NEH sr. fellow, 1973-74; decorated Order Brit. Empire, Grand Officer Order of Star of Italian Solidarity, Grand officer Order of Merit of Italian Republic; recipient faculty prize Harvard U. Press, 1961, Morey Book prize Coll. Art Assn., 1965, Nat. Medal Arts, 1988, Galileo Galilei prize, 1995. Fellow Am. Acad. Arts and Scis., Accademia Clementina (Bologna), Ateneo Veneto, (Venice); mem. Phi Beta Kappa. Home: Washington D.C. Died May 6, 1997.

FREEDMAN, JAY MICHAEL, automobile care company executive, lawyer; b. Chgo., Aug. 25, 1939; s. Nathan and Adele (Klong) F.; m. Barbara Picker, Jan. 17, 1963 (div. 1972); children: Joel L., Lee, Keith; m. Nancy J. Biddick, Nov. 12, 1972; 1 child, Mark. BA, Mich. State U., 1960; JD, U. Wis., 1963; DJP, U. Johannesburg, 1969. Bar: Ill. 1963, Wis. Assoc. Freeman, Liebling & Adelman, Chgo., 1963-65; ptnr.

McCarty, Watson, Hootman & Freedman, Chgo., 1965-69, Freedman & Michaels, Chgo., 1969-74; sole practice Chgo., 1974-80; chief exec. officer Broken Bow Corp., Chgo., 1980-81, L.G.I.C., Inc., L.A., 1981-87, Infotech Mgmt. Svcs., Inc., Long Island City, N.Y., 1983; chmn. Autocare Am., Inc., Denver, 1988—; cons., bd. dirs. Guarantee Ins. Agy. Inc., Skokie, 1967—; cons. Cogenco Corp., Denver, 1986-87, PPS Corp., New Orleans, 1987-88, Anchor Fin., L.A., 1988-90; chmn. bd. Fuji Electrocell Corp., 1989—. Author: (novel) Fever of Violence, 1971. Kapp Found. fellow, 1962. Avocations: flying, sailing, travel, hybrid gardening.

FREEMAN, IRA HENRY, author, journalist; b. N.Y.C., Aug. 12, 1906; s. Arthur J. and Rachel (Abrams) F.; m. Beatrice Oppenheim, Sept. 21, 1937. B.Litt., Columbia U., 1928. Staff writer N.Y. Times, 1928-61; now free-lance writer. Instr. journalism CCNY, 1950-51; corr. Yank (army weekly), U.S., Europe and Middle East, 1943-45. Author: White Sails Shaking, 1949, Out of the Burning, 1960, (with Beatrice Freeman) Careers and Opportunities in Journalism, 1965; contbr. to: Yank, the GI Story of the War, 1947, Great Reading from Life, 1960, The Death Penalty in America, 1964, Detail and Pattern, 1969; also contbr., illustrator numerous articles, mainly on travel, and short stories in nat. mags. Recipient George Polk award for nat. reporting L.I.U., 1951; on honor roll Best Short Stories, 1941. Mem. Am. Newspaper Guild (charter). L.I. Mandolin and Guitar Orch., Classical Mandolin Soc. Am. Died Jan. 12, 1997.

FREEMAN, LARRY LEROY, insurance agent; b. Kalamazoo, Mich., May 7, 1934; s. Kenneth C. Freeman and Lillian M. (Stevens) Delamater; m. Jo Ann Stratton, Apr. 12, 1954; 1 child, Terri Lynn. Grad. high sch., Portland, Oreg., 1952. CLU. Agt. State Farm Ins., Kalamazoo, 1960-94; ins. adv. com. Ferris State Coll., Big Rapids, Mich., 1975-79. Mem., bd. dirs. Kalamazoo Jaycees, 1962-69. With U.S. Army, 1954-56. Mem. Kalamzaoo Assn. Life Underwriters (pres. 1970-71), Mich. Assn. Life Underwriters (regional v.p., state edn. dir. 1972-75), Kalamazoo Assn. CLUs (pres. 1975-76). Republican. Avocations: golf, reading, sports, travel. Home: Kalamazoo Mich. Died Mar. 16, 1994.

FREIDBERG, SIDNEY, lawyer, real estate development company executive, author; b. N.Y.C., Jan. 20, 1914; s. David and Tillie (Friedman) F.; children: David, Emily. BS, NYU, 1933; JD, Yale U., 1936. Bar: N.Y. 1936, D.C. 1945. Assoc. Phillips, Nizer, Benjamin, Krim, 1936-42; practice law N.Y.C., 45-68; ptnr. Freidberg, Rich & Blue, N.Y.C., 1945-62, Posner, Fox, Arent & Freidberg, Washington, 1945-54; research and analysis div. OSS, 1942-43; counsel printing and pub. div. WPB, Washington, 1943-45; counsel Ho. of Reps. select com. on newsprint and paper supply, Washington, 1948-49; commr. Fgn. Claims Settlement Commn. U.S., Washington, 1968-70; exec. v.p., gen. counsel Nat. Corp. for Housing Partnerships, Washington, 1970-77; counsel firm Arent, Fox, Kintner, Plotkin & Kahn, Washington, 1977-84; pres. Morningside Heights Property Assn., 1960-62; bd. dirs. SPI, Inc. Contbr. articles to profl. jours. Mem. alumni bd. visitors N.Y. U., 1959-61; bd. dirs. Nat. Housing Conf., Inc., 1979-83, Planned Parenthood of Met. Washington, Inc., 1979-86, Preterm, Inc., 1983-85; bd. dirs., sec.-treas. Nat. Minority Purchasing Council, Inc., 1977-81. Mem. Am., Fed., D.C., N.Y. State, City N.Y. bar assns., Am. Soc. Internat. Law, World Assembly Judges, World Peace Through Law Center, D.C. C. of C. (dir., counsel 1979-80), Phi Beta Kappa. Democrat. Clubs: Cosmos, Nat. Press, Yale (N.Y.C. and Washington). Home: Pelham N.Y. Died Aug. 31, 1995.

FRENZEL, HUGH NEUMANN, petroleum geologist, consultant; b. Madison, Wis., Apr. 21, 1918; s. Harry Morton and Iva Florence (Neumann) F.; m. Dorothy Helen Chambers; children: Arthur Chambers, Hugh Robert, Ann, Thomas Neumann. BA, U. Wis., 1940, MA, 1942. Geologist Standard Oil Co. Tex., Carslbad, 1946-48; dist. geologist Standard Oil Co. Tex., Midland, 1948-52; geologist Ryon, Hoyes and Burke, Midland, 1952-54; geologist Ralph Lowe, Midland, 1954-60, chief geoloist, 1960-74; chief geoloist Flag-Redfern Oil Co., Midland, 1974-76, v.p. exploration, 1976-80; v.p. exploration Bison Exploration, Midland, 1981-83; pvt. cons. Midland, 1983—. Contbr. numerous articles to profl. publs. Staff sgt. USAF, 1941-45. Decorated Legion of Merit. Fellow Geol. Soc. Am.; mem. Am. Assn. Petroleum Geologists (hon. 1982, chmn. Ho. of Dels. 1974-75, Sidney Powers Meml. award 1989), Soc. Econ. Paleontologists and Mineralogists. Republican. Episcopalian.

FRESCOLN, KATHARINE PITMAN, emeritus history educator; b. Swarthmore, Pa., May 9, 1917; d. John Himes and Katharine Elsie (Anders) Pitman; m. Joseph Wright Frescoln, Jan. 6, 1942. AB, Wittenberg U., 1965; MA, W.Va. U., 1966, PhD, 1971. Social studies tchr. sch. Parsons, W.Va., 1963-65; instr., asst. prof., assoc. prof. history Shepherd Coll., Shepherdstown, W.Va., 1967-75, prof., 1975-85, prof. emeritus, 1985—. Contbr. articles to profl. jours. Samuel Sprecker scholar, 1959. Mem. DAR, Am. Hist. Assn., Am. Assn. for Advancement Slavic Studies, N.Am. Conf. on Brit. Studies, Soc. for Descendants of Schwenkfelder Exiles, Phi Alpha Theta (internat. councillor 1980-82).

FREUND, GERALD, foundation administrator; b. Berlin, Oct. 14, 1930; came to U.S., 1940, naturalized, 1946; s. Kurt and Annelise (Josephthal) F.; m. Jane Bicker Shaw Trask, Sept. 1956 (div. Sept. 1970); children: Jonathan Gerald, Matthew Trask, Andrew Josephthal; m. Peregrine White Whittlesey, Dec. 31, 1976. B.A. magna cum laude, Haverford Coll., 1952; D.Phil., Oxford (Eng.) U., 1955. Research asst. Inst. Advanced Study, Princeton, 1956-57; fellow Council Fgn. Relations, 1957-59; asst. prof. Haverford Coll., 1958-60; from asst. dir. to assoc. dir. social scis., humanities, arts Rockefeller Found., 1960-69; asst. to pres. Yale, 1969-70; exec. v.p. Film Soc. of Lincoln Center, 1970-71; dean humanities and arts, prof., dir. Hunter Arts, Hunter Coll., 1971-80; v.p., dir. Prize Fellows Program, John D. and Catherine T. MacArthur Found., Chgo., 1980-84; dir. for planning Nat. Task Force on the Individual Artist, Am. Council Arts; dir. Whiting Writers' Awards, Whiting Found., 1984—; pres. Pvt. Funding Assocs., 1985—, Pro Bono Ventures, Inc., 1994—; exec. dir. Harlem Ednl. Activities Fund, 1989-94; sr. cons. Lila Wallace-Reader's Digest Fund, 1990-91; cons. Washington Ctr. of Fgn. Policy Rsch., 1959-60, Annenberg Ctr., Phila., 1970-71, Performing Arts Program, N.Y. State Coun. on Arts, N.Y.C., 1973, Arts, Edn. and Americans Project, 1975-77, Inst. Advanced Mus. Studies, Montreux, Switzerland, 1975-77, Dartmouth Coll., 1978-79, John and Catherine MacArthur Found., 1979-80, Inst. Study World Politics, 1980, 83, Esther A. and Joseph Klingenstein Fund, Inc., 1983-85, N.Y. Inst. Visual History, Nat. Found. Advancement in the Arts, Teagle Found., Heinz Family Found., Dorothy and Lillian Gish Trust, MacDowell Colony; lectr., TV and radio activities; mem. Charter Revision Commn., Stamford, Conn., 1964-65, planning commn. cons., 1965-67; exec. dir. Harlem Ednl. Activities Fund, 1989-94. Author: German Russian Relations, 1917-1926, 1957, 1958, Germany Between Two Worlds, 1961, Narcissism and Philanthropy, 1996; contbg. editor: Worldview. Mem. Com. on Orgn. of Peace, 1963-77; mem. exec. com., chmn. Manhattan Theatre Club; v.p. Dem. Party, North Stamford, Conn., 1962-64; trustee Woodstock (Vt.) Country Sch., 1962-81, pres. bd., 1972-75; mem. bd. Nat. Book Com., until 1975; bd. dirs. Inst. Current World Affairs, N.Y.C., until 1975, Fund for Artists Colonies; mem. Am. Com. East-West Accord, Washington; bd. dirs. Poets' House, 1984-94, Fund for Artists' Colonies, 1983-89, Creative Alternatives of N.Y., 1985-90, N.Y. Eye and Ear Infirmary, 1986, Fund for Peace, 1986, exec. com. 1990—, Global Kids, 1995, Austen Riggs Ctr., 1995; bd. dirs. Imagination Workshop, Inc., co-chmn. bd., 1977-78. Rsch. fellow St. Anthony's Coll., Oxford U., England, 1955-56. Mem. Nat. Aphasia Assn. (bd. dirs. 1991—), Coun. Fgn. Rels. (fellowship com., libr. com.), Phi Beta Kappa. Clubs: Lotos, Century Assn. Died May 14, 1997.

FRICKE, WILLIAM GEORGE, JR., metallurgist; b. Pitts., May 10, 1926; s. William George and Elsie Elizabeth (Kustes) F.; m. Betty Joan Semelsberger, Aug. 7, 1948; children: William, Dianne, James, Dana. BS, Pa. State U., 1950, MS, 1951; PhD, U. Pitts., 1962. Fellow ALCOA, Alcoa Ctr., Pa., 1952-95; adjunct faculty Pa. State U., New Kensington, 1965. Author: The Baby Maker, 1987. Lay asst. Southwest Pa. Synod Ev Luth. Ch. in Am., Pitts., 1968-95. Recipient Templin award ASTM, 1954. Mem. Am. Soc. Metallurgy Internat. (com. mem. 1948-95), Metall. Soc. AIME, Microbeam Analysis Soc., Internat. Soc. Stereology, Sigma Xi (com. mem. 1955-95), Am. Legion, VFW. Democrat. Home: Alcoa Center Pa. Died Feb. 25, 1995; interred Greenwood Memorial Park.

FRIEDLAENDER, ALEX SEYMOUR, allergist; b. Schenectady, N.Y., Oct. 31, 1911; s. Leo Isadore and Frances (Levine) F.; m. Eileen Berman, Feb. 6, 1942; children: Gary E., Linda Friedlaender Goss, Howard E. BA, Wayne U., 1932, MD, 1936, MS in Pathology, 1938. Diplomate Am. Bd. Allergy and Immunology. Attending staff Sinai Hosp. of Detroit, 1954-94; ret.; gen. practice medicine specializing in allergies West Bloomfield, Mich.; clin. asst. prof. internal med. Wayne U. Coll. Med. 1945-76. Contbr. articles to profl. jours. Maj. AUS, WW II. Fellow Am. Acad. Allergy, Am. Coll. Allergists, Am. Assn. Clin. Immunology and Allergy (pres. 1971, exec. sec. 1975-77, Disting. Clinician award 1983), Am. Coll. Physicians (subspecialty council 1976-85); Life mem. AMA, Am. Acad. Dermatology, Mich. Allergy Soc. (pres. 1961-62), Am. Soc. Internal Medicine, Mich. Med. Soc., Wayne County Med. Soc., Oakland County Med. Soc. Lodge: Masons. Avocations: swimming, computer science. Home: Bloomfield Hills Mich. Died July 3, 1995.

FRIEDMAN, HERBERT, psychology educator; b. Bklyn., Oct. 13, 1933; m. Ina Doris Malawista, Sept. 7, 1959; children: David, Mara. AB, Bklyn. Coll., 1954; MA, U. Conn., 1956, PhD, 1960. Instr. U. Conn., Storrs, 1958-59; postdoctoral fellow Duke U., Durham, N.C., 1960-61, rsch. assoc., 1961-63; from asst. prof. to assoc. prof. College of William and Mary, Williamsburg, Va., 1964-73, prof. psychology, 1973—, chair dept. psychology, 1988-94. Author: Introduction to Statistics, 1972, Understanding and Improving Behavior, 1975, Doing Your Best on the S.A.T., 1987, The Psychology Major's Handbook, rev., 1992; contbr. articles to profl. jours. Mem. AAAS, Am. Psychol. Soc., Psychonomic Soc., Eastern Psychol. Assn., Va. Acad. Sci., Sigma Xi. Deceased.

FRIEDMAN, MELVIN, geology educator, college dean; b. Orange, N.J., Nov. 14, 1930; s. Leonard and Hannah Lillian (Sholk) F.; m. Deborah Friedman, June 13, 1954 (dec. Feb. 1992); children: Barry David, Cheryl Anne; m. Rose P. VanArsdel, June 26, 1993. BS (Henry Rutgers scholar), Rutgers U., 1952, MS, 1954; PhD, Rice U., 1961. Field geologist Geologic Survey of Nfld., 1952-54; geologist Shell Devel. Co., Houston, 1954-58, project leader, 1958-65, research assoc., sect. leader, 1965-67; assoc. prof. geology Tex. A&M U., College Station, 1967-69, prof., 1969—, Mollie B. and Richard A. Williford prof. petroleum geology, 1992-96, dir. Ctr. for Tectonophysics, 1979-82, assoc. dean Coll. Geoscis., 1982-83, dean, 1983-91, dean emeritus, prof. emeritus, 1996—; chair Sampling of the Earth's Continental Crust, 1988-91; rschr., cons. in field; co-editor-in-chief Tectonophysics (internat. jour.), 1980-94, hon. editor, 1994—. Contbr. numerous articles to profl. jours. Past pres. Congregation Beth Shalom College Station; bd. dirs. B'nai-B'rith Hillel Found. (Tex. A&M U.). Recipient Rsch. award Intersociety Com. on Rock Mechanics, 1968-69, Faculty Disting. Achievement award Tex. A&M U., 1975, Geoscis. and Earth Resources Disting. Achievement award Tex. A&M U., 1989. Fellow Geol. Soc. Am., AAAS; mem. Am. Geophys. Union, Sigma Xi. Phi Kappa Phi., Phi Beta Kappa. Club: Briarcrest Country (Bryan, Tex.). DIED 03/11/97. .

FRIEDMAN, MELVIN JACK, language professional, literature educator; b. Bklyn., Mar. 7, 1928; s. Julian and Edith (Block) F.; m. H. Judith Zervitz, Oct. 12, 1958; children: Jennifer, James. AB, Bard Coll., 1949; MA, Columbia U., 1951; PhD (Am. Council Learned Socs. fellow 1953, Jr. Sterling fellow 1953-54), Yale, 1954. Instr. English U. Md., 1956-59, assoc. prof. English and comparative lit., 1962-66; instr., asst. prof. English U. Wis.-Madison, 1959-62; prof. comparative lit. and English U. Wis., Milw., 1966-95, prof. emeritus, 1995—; assisted in establishing programs in Am. studies in India for State Dept., 1960; mem. fellowship com. NEH, 1973, 87; mem. selection com. Ritz Paris Hemingway award, 1985—; guest prof. U. Hannover, Fed. Republic. Germany, 1977, J.W. Goethe U. Frankfurt, Fed. Republic Germany, 1986; disting. vis. humanist U. Colo., Boulder, 1987; mem. adv. com. Beckett Internat. Found., U. Reading, Eng. Author: Stream of Consciousness: A Study in Literary Method, 1955, (with others) Calepins de Bibliographie Samuel Beckett, 1971, William Styron, 1974 (French transl. in Fer de Lance 1977-78); editor: Configuration Critique de Samuel Beckett, 1964, (with Lewis A. Lawson) The Added Dimension: The Art and Mind of Flannery O'Connor, 1966, 2d edit., 1977, (with August J. Nigro) Configuration Critique de William Styron, 1967, (with John B. Vickery) The Shaken Realist: Essays in Modern Literature in Honor of Frederick J. Hoffman, 1970, Samuel Beckett Now: Critical Approaches to His Novels, Poetry and Plays, 1970, 2d edit., 1975, (with Irving Malin) William Styron's The Confessions of Nat Turner: A Critical Handbook, 1970, The Vision Obscured: Perceptions of Some Twentieth-Century Catholic Novelists, 1970, (with Rosette C. Lamont) The Two Faces of Ionesco, 1978, Samuel Beckett sect. of Critical Bibliography of French Literature: The Twentieth Century, 1980, (with Beverly L. Clark) Critical Essays on Flannery O'Connor, 1985, (with Thomas L. Scott) Pound/The Little Review: The Letters of Ezra Pound to Margaret Anderson, 1988, (with François Jost) Aesthetics and the Literature of Ideas: Essays in Honor of A. Owen Aldridge, 1989, (with Janet E. Dunleavy and Michael P. Gillespie) Joycean Occasions, 1991, (with Ben Siegel) Traditions, Voices, and Dreams: The American Novel Since the 1960s, 1995; (with Beverly L. Clark) Critical Essays on Carson McCullers, 1996; assoc. editor Yale French Studies, 1951-53; editor Wis. Studies in Contemporary Literature, 1960-62, Comparative Literature Studies, 1962-66; asst. mng. editor Modern Lang. Jour., 1963-70; mem. editorial bd. Jour. of Popular Culture 1970—, Renascence, 1972—, Studies in the Novel, 1973—, Fer de Lance, 1976—, Jour. Am. Culture, 1978—, Studies in American Fiction, 1979—, Contemporary Lit., 1981—, Jour. Beckett Studies, 1982—, Arete, 1983—, Internat. Fiction Rev., 1985—, Essays in Graham Greene, an Ann. Rev., 1985—, Yiddish, 1986—, Jour. Modern Lit., 1988—, Studies in Am. Jewish Lit., 1990—; contbr. articles to profl. jours. Served with U.S. Army, 1954-56. Fulbright fellow to Lyon France, 1950-51; vis. sr. fellow U. East Anglia, 1972; Fulbright sr. lectr. U. Antwerp, 1976; Canterbury vis. fellow U. Canterbury, N.Z., 1985; Fulbright Short-Term sr. scholar, Australian Nat. U., Canberra, 1992. Mem. MLA (sec., chmn. Comparative Lit. 5 group 1964-66, sec., chmn. English 11 group 1972-74, sec. chmn. 20th century English lit. div. 1977-78, del. assembly 1986-89, chmn. Anglo-Irish lit. discussion group 1995), Am. Assn. Profs. Yiddish (v.p. 1986-87, pres. 1987-89), Internat. Comparative Lit. Assn., Am. Comparative Lit. Assn., Brecht Soc., Popular Culture Assn. Am. Com. for Irish Studies, PEN Am. Ctr., Phi Kappa Phi. Died Mar. 25, 1996.

FRIEDMAN, SOL, inventor, writer; b. N.Y.C., June 10, 1922; s. Marcus and Ida (Wolf) F.; m. Rose Schenkerman, July 19, 1945 (dec. 1981); children: Miles, Alan; m. Paula Jacobson, Sept. 17, 1982. Student, Cooper Union U., N.Y.C., 1945-47. Profl. inventor Sol Friedman and Assocs., N.Y.C., 1950—. Inventor toys and games, including Operation Orbit, 1960 (donated to Smithsonian Inst. Air and Space Mus.), Johnny Astro, 1967 (Boys Toys of Yr., Nat. Assn. Toy Retailers U.K. 1967), Baby Party, Walt Disney World. Sgt. U.S. Air Corps Army, 1942-45. Recipient Presdl. citation Pres. Harry S Truman, 1994, cert. of merit Eleanor Roosevelt Dem. Club, Monsey, N.Y. DIED 09/12/97. .

FRIEDMAN, STEPHEN, motion picture producer; b. N.Y.C., Mar. 15, 1937; s. Irving and Dorothy (Lipsious) F. B.S., U. Pa., 1957; LL.B., Harvard U., 1960. Bar: N.Y. 1958. Atty. Herzfeld & Rubin, N.Y.C., 1958-59, Columbia Pictures, N.Y.C., 1960-63, Ashley Famous Agy., N.Y.C., 1963-67, Paramount Pictures, Los Angeles, 1967-69; chmn. bd. Kings Road Prodns., Century City, Calif., 1979—. Producer: Last Picture Show, 1971, Lovin Molly, 1973, Slap Shot, 1977, Fast Break, 1979, Little Darlings, 1978, Hero at Large, 1980, Bloodbrothers, 1978, Eye of the Needle, 1981, All of Me, 1984, Creator, 1985, Enemy Mine, 1985, The Best of Times, 1986, The Big Easy, 1987. Mem. Acad. Motion Picture Arts and Scis., Bar Assn. State N.Y. DIED 10/04/96. .

FRIEDRICH, OTTO ALVA, writer, editor; b. Boston, Feb. 3, 1929; s. Carl Joachim and Lenore (Pelham) F.; m. Priscilla Boughton, Apr. 13, 1950; children: Elizabeth Charlotte, Margaret Emily, Nicholas Max, Amelia Anne, Charles Anthony (dec.). A.B. magna cum laude, Harvard, 1948. Mem. copy desk Stars & Stripes, 1950-52; with United Press in Paris and London, 1952-54; with telegraph desk N.Y. Daily News, 1954-57; mem. fgn. dept. Newsweek, 1957-62, asst. fgn. editor, 1959-62; fgn. editor Sat. Eve. Post, 1962-63, asst. mng. editor, 1963-65, mng. editor, 1965-69; free lance writer, 1969-71; sr. editor TIME, 1971-80, sr. writer, 1980-95. Author: (novels) The Poor in Spirit, 1952, The Loner, 1964; non-fiction Decline and Fall, 1970 (George Polk Meml. award); Before the Deluge, 1972, The Rose Garden, 1972, Going Crazy, 1976, Clover, 1979, The End of the World, 1982, City of Nets, 1986, Glenn Gould: A Life and Variations, 1989, The Grave of Alice B. Toklas, 1989, Olympia: Paris in The Age of Manet, 1992; (with wife) juveniles The Easter Bunny That Overslept, 1957; Clean Clarence, 1959, Sir Alva and the Wicked Wizard, 1960, The Marshmallow Ghosts, 1960, The Wishing Well in the Woods, 1961, Noah Shark's Ark, 1961, The Christmas Star, 1962, The April Umbrella, 1963, The League of Unusual Animals, 1965; also numerous articles and short stories. Home: Locust Valley N.Y. DIed Apr., 1995.

FRIENDLY, FRED W., journalist, educator; b. N.Y.C., 1915; m. Ruth W. Mark; children by previous marriage—Andrew, Lisa, David; stepchildren—Jon Mark, Michael Mark, Richard Mark. Student, Cheshire Acad., Nichols Jr. Coll.; L.H.D. (hon.), Grinnell Coll., U. R.I.; hon. degree, Brown U., Carnegie-Mellon U., Columbia Coll., Chgo., Columbia U., Duquesne U., N.Y. Law Sch., U. So. Utah, Coll. Wooster, U. Utah; LHD (hon.), New Sch. for Social Rsch., 1992. Broadcast producer, journalist WEAN radio, Providence, 1937-41; pres. CBS News, N.Y.C., 1964-66; Edward R. Murrow prof. emeritus broadcast journalism Columbia U. Grad. Sch. Journalism, dir. Seminars on Media and Soc.; adviser on communications Ford Found., 1966-80. Began career in radio, 1938; wrote, produced and narrated: radio series Footprints in the Sands of Time, later at, NBC, Who Said That; quiz based on quotations of famous people; collaborated (with Edward R. Murrow), in presenting oral history of 1932-45 (recorded by Columbia Records under title I Can Hear It Now); I Can Hear It Now-The Sixties; (with Walter Cronkite) CBS radio series Hear It Now; also CBS TV Series See It Now; past exec. producer: (with Edward R. Murrow) CBS TV show CBS Reports; (Recipient George Peabody awards for TV prodn.); Author: (with Edward R. Murrow) See It Now, 1955, Due to Circumstances Beyond Our Control, 1967, The Good Guys, The Bad Guys, The First Amendment, 1975, Minnesota Rag, 1981, (with Martha J.H. Elliott) The Constitution: That Delicate Balance, 1984. Dir. Michele Clark Program for minority journalists, Columbia U., 1968-75; mem. bd. visitors Calif. Inst. Tech., 1970-75, Nat. Def. U., 1984-86; commr. Charter Revision Commn. for City of N.Y., 1986-90. Served with AUS, 1941-45, CBI. Decorated Legion of Merit and 4 battle stars; recipient DeWitt Carter Reddick award, 1980, numerous awards schs. journalism; Disting. vis. prof. Bryn Mawr Coll., 1981, vis. prof. Yale U., 1984, Montgomery fellow Dartmouth Coll., 1986. Mem. Am. Assn. U. Profs., Assn. for Edn. in Journalism. Died March 1998.

FRIESEN, GORDON ARTHUR, health care consultant; b. Rosthern, Sask., Can., Jan. 21, 1909; emigrated to U.S., 1951, naturalized, 1962; s. Abraham James and Eliza (Friesen) F.; m. Jane Helen Fuller, July 25, 1947; children: Mary Jane, Sarah Elizabeth. LL.D., George Washington U.; D. Adminstrn. (hon.), North-and Open U., Toronto, Ont., Can. Bus. mgr. Saskatoon City Hosp., 1929-37; adminstr. Belleville Gen. Hosp., Ont., Can., 1937-41, Kitchener-Waterloo Hosp., Ont., 1946-51; prin. cons. sr. hosp. adminstr. United Mine Workers Hosps. in Appalachia, 1951-54; founder Gordon A. Friesen Internat., Inc., Washington, 1954—; vis. lectr. Sch. Hosp. Adminstrn., St. Louis U., Health Services Planning and Design Program, Columbia George Washington U. Grad. Sch., C.W. Post U., U.S. Army Med. Field Service Sch., U.S. Naval Sch. Hosp. Adminstrn., Nat. Naval Center; cons. surgeon gen. U.S. Navy.; Mem. adv. council, lectr. Xavier U., Cin. Contbr. articles to profl. jours. Served with RCAF, 1941-46. Gordon A. Friesen chair in health svcs. adminstrn. established in his honor George Washington U., 1989; recipient numerous Modern Hosp. of Month awards, Gerard B. Lambert 1st prize award for accomplishments in improved patient care and reduced hosp. costs; Gold medal Govt. of Costa Rica. Fellow Am. Coll. Hosp. Adminstrs., Royal Soc. Arts, Royal Soc. Health; hon. fellow Am. Acad. Med. Adminstrs.; hon. mem. Costa Rican Hosp. Assn. (hon. pres.); mem. Internat. Hosp. Fedn., Am. Assn. Hosp. Planning, Am. Hosp. Assn., Canadian Coll. Health Service Execs.; life mem., founder Sask. Hosp. Assn. (hon. life), Luther Rice Soc. Club: Cosmos.

FRIST, THOMAS FEARN, internist; b. Meridian, Miss., Dec. 15, 1910; m. Dorothy Cate, 1935; children: Thomas Fearn, Robert Armistead, William Harrison, Dorothy Frist Boensch, Mary L. Frist Barfield. BS, U. Miss., 1929; MD, Vanderbilt U., 1933. Diplomate: Am. Bd. Internal Medicine. Intern U. Iowa, 1933-35; asst. clinician Vanderbilt U., 1935-37;, 1940-93; emeritus The Frist Clinic, Nashville, 1993—; past pres. staff Nashville Gen. Hosp.; past pres., mem. exec. com. St. Thomas Hosp.; co-founder, past pres. Hosp. Corp. Am., 1968-71; vice-chmn. bd., chief med. svcs.; founder, vice-chmn. bd. Am. Retirement Corp., past chmn. Pres.'s Com. on Aging, Washington. Founder, past chmn. bd. Park Manor Presbyn. Apts. for Elderly; founder, past chmn. bd. Cumberland Heights Found. for Rehab. Alcoholics; founder, bd. dirs. Med. Benevolence Found.; bd. dirs. Montgomery Bell Acad., Nashville; hon. trustee Rhodes Coll., Memphis. Served to maj. USAAF, World War II. Fellow ACP; mem. Southeastern Clin. Club (past pres.), Tenn. Heart Assn. (past pres.), Nashville Soc. Internal Medicine (past pres.), Sigma Alpha Epsilon, Belle Meade Country Club, Lago Mar Golf Country Club.

FROMSON, ANTOINETTE DUVAL, civic worker; b. Chgo., May 22, 1925; d. Ralph A. and Yvonne (Duval) Brown; Barnard Coll., 1947; m. Howard A. Fromson, Oct. 12, 1946 (div. Mar. 1991); children—Michele Yvonne, Michael Erik, Timothy Arthur, Brett Duval. Plaintiff, Women vs. Conn., legal action about the right of women to control their bodies, 1969; convenor, 1st chmn. Conn. Women's Polit. Caucus, 1970; organizer Westport-Weston (Conn.) chpt. NOW, 1972, organizer, convenor, pres. Southwestern conn. chpt., 1974-78; del. Conn. Democratic Conv., 1974; mem. Weston Town Dem. Com., 1972-74; bd. dirs. Westport YMCA, bd. trustess; bd. dirs. Conn. Planned Parenthood, Five Town Found., Greater Norwalk Community Coun.; lifetime mem. Nature Conservancys, Arlington, Va., Weston (Conn.) Hist. Soc. Mem. Unitarian-Universalists Women's Fedn., Barnard Alumni Assn., Nature Conservancy Arlington (life), Weston Hist. Soc. (life), Cedar Point Yacht Club, Aspetuck Valley Country Club, Fairfield Organic Gardening Club. Democrat. Unitarian. Died July 21, 1995.

FROST, EARLE WESLEY, lawyer, judge; b. Blue Rapids, Kans., July 11, 1899; s. John and Myrtle Mary (Pulleine) F.; m. Esther C. Houston, June 24, 1930; children: Earle W. Jr., Sylvia Elaine. BS, Kans. State U., 1920; LLB, Columbia U., 1923. Bar: Mo. 1923. Asst. pros. atty. Jackson County, Mo., 1926; spl. asst. solicitor USDA, 1930-33; judge Mcpl. Ct., Kansas City, Mo., 1940-67; pvt. practice Kansas City, to 1984; retired, 1984; Bd. dirs. Helping Hand Inst. Kansas City, Mo., pres. 1975-77; chmn. traffic ct. div. Nat. Safety Coun., 1942-43, 54-55; mem. enforcement com. Pres.'s Highway Safety Confs., 1946-67. Author, pub.: The Descendant of John Frost, Jr. and Rebecca York Frost of Jackson County, Missouri, The Long and Doub Families of North Carolina and Their Midwestern Descendants, The Yorkshire Pulleine-Dunn Family in the U.S.A. and Their English Ancestry; contbr. articles to legal jours. Mem. ABA (chmn. com. on improvement in traffic cts. 1943-47, mem. coun. sect. jud. adminstrn. 1947-52, vice chmn. 1952), Cosmopolitan Internat. (pres. Kansas City chpt. 1941, internat pres. 1946-47), Lawyers Assn. Kansas City, Kansas City Bar Assn., Mo. Bar Assn., Phi Delta Phi, Pi Kappa Delta, Sigma Phi Epsilon (nat. pres. 1945-46). Died Feb. 10, 1997.

FUENNING, SAMUEL ISAIAH, sports medicine research director; b. Ft. Morgan, Colo., Sept. 20, 1916; s. Albert Julius and Elizabeth Johanna (Muenzinger) F.; m. Lillian Mary Brown; children: Elizabeth Jane, Gretchen Ann, James Albert, Thomas Samuel, Jon William. BSc, U. Nebr., 1940, MSc, 1941; MD, U. Nebr., Omaha, 1945. Med. dir. U. Nebr., Lincoln, 1946-75; med. dir. rsch. dept. sports medicine U. Nebr., Lincoln, 1975-96; pres. Am. Coll. Health Assn., Washington, 1960-61, v.p. liason, 1962-76; mem. vis. com. Harvard U. Bd. Govs., Boston, 1965-70; prof. Family Wellness U. Nebr., Lincoln, 1970-75; chmn. Gov.'s Coun. Physical Fitness and Sports, Lincoln, 1980. Bd. dirs. Nebr. Lung Assn., Nebr. Inter Agy., Lincoln, Omaha. Named to Nebr. chpt. Nat. Football Hall of Fame, Lincoln, 1981. Mem. ACHA (Hitchcock award 1964, Ruth Boynton award 1968), Nebr. Med. Assn. (chmn. health edn. com.) Lancaster County Med. Assn. (chmn. program com. 1970), Lincoln C. of C. (Leadership award 1968), Welcom (Leadership award), Sigma Xi. Avocations: mountain climber, jogging, photography, travel. Home: Lincoln Nebr. Died Oct. 25, 1996.

FUKUI, KENICHI, chemist; b. Nara, Japan, Oct. 4, 1918; s. Ryokichi and Chie Fukui; m. Tomoe Horie, 1947; 2 children. Student, Kyoto Imperial U. Researcher synthetic fuel chemistry Army Fuel Lab., 1941-45; lectr. in fuel chemistry Kyoto Imperial U., 1943-45; asst. prof. Kyoto U., 1945-51, prof., 1951-82; pres. Kyoto Inst. Tech. (formerly Kyoto U. Indsl. Arts and Textile Fibres), 1982-88; dir. Inst. for Fundamental Chemistry, 1988—; councillor Kyoto U., 1970-73, dean faculty engring., 1971-73; councillor Inst. Molecular Sci., 1976-93; chemist U.S.-Japan Eminent Scientist Exch. Programme, 1973. Contbr. articles to profl. jours. Chmn. exec. com. 3d Internat. Congress Quantum Chemistry, Kyoto, 1979. Sr. Fgn. Scientist fellow NSF, 1970; fgn. assoc. NAS; recipient Japan Acad. medal, 1962, Nobel Prize for chemistry, 1981, Order of Culture award, 1981; named Person of Cultural Merits, 1981. Mem. Am. Acad. Arts, Scis. and Humanities, Japan Acad., Pontifical Acad. Scis., Chem. Soc. Japan (v.p. 1978-79, pres. 1983-84), Royal Soc. (London, fgn. mem.), Royal Instn. Gt. Britain (hon.), Academia Europaea (fgn. mem.), Korean Acad. Sci. and Tech. (hon. fgn. mem.).

FULLER, RICHARD HARRISON, industrial engineering educator; b. San Francisco, Mar. 15, 1928; s. Harry Samuel Fuller and Elizabeth Tatom; m. Leilani Baggott, Jan. 15, 1960 (dec. Sept. 1970); m. Lorna Apple, Dec. 15, 1971. BSEE, Calif. Inst. Tech., 1952; MSEE, MIT, 1954; PhD, UCLA, 1963. Dir. R & D Gen. Precision, Glendale, Calif., 1963-68; gen. mgr. Sperry Rsch. Ctr., Sudbury, Mass., 1968-77; v.p. corp. tech. Emerson Electric, St. Louis, 1977-80; v.p. digital tech. Gen. Instrument, N.Y.C., 1980-86; dean The Gordon Inst., Wakefield, Mass., 1986-90; asst. chair indsl. engring. dept. U. Cen. Fla., Orlando, 1990—. Contbr. articles to profl. jours.; holder 15 patents. Fellow IEEE. Avocations: swimming, skiing, sailing.

FULLER, SAMUEL (MICHAEL), scriptwriter, film director; b. Worcester, Mass., Aug. 12, 1912; m. Christa Lang, July 25, 1967; 1 dau., Samantha. Crime reporter N.Y. Evening Jour., N.Y. Graphic, San Diego Sun. Writer, dir.: (films) I Shot Jesse James, 1949, The Baron of Arizona, 1950, The Steel Helmet, 1951, Fixed Bayonets, 1951, Park Row, 1952, Pickup on South Street, 1953 (Bronze Lion award Venice Film Festival 1953), (with Jesse L. Lasky, Jr.) Hell and High Water, 1954, (with Harry Kleiner) House of Bamboo, 1955, Run of the Arrow, 1956, China Gate, 1957, Forty Guns, 1957, Verboten!, 1959, The Crimson Kimono, 1959, Underworld U.S.A, 1961, (with Milton Sperling) Merrill's Marauders, 1962, Shock Corridor, 1963, The Naked Kiss, 1964, Caine, 1967, (with John Kingsbridge) Shark, 1970, Dead Pigeon on Beethoven Street, 1972, The Big Red One, 1980, (with Curtis Hanson) White Dog, 1982, Thieves After Dark, 1983, The Street of No Return, 1991; screenwriter: (with Edmund Joseph) Hats Off, 1937, (with Ethel Hill and Harvey Fergusson) It Happened in Hollywood, 1937, (with Wellyn Totman, Jack Townley, and Charles Francis Royal) Gangs of New York, 1938, (with Helen Deutsch) Shockproof, 1949, (with Ted Sherdeman, Eugene Ling, and James Poe) Scandal Sheet, 1952, (with Russell Hughes) The Command, 1954, (with Harold Medford) Capetown Affair, 1967, (with Millard Kaufman) The Klansman, 1974; author: (novels) Burn, Baby, Burn!, 1935, Test Tube Baby, 1936, Make Up and Kiss, 1938, The Dark Page, 1944, The Naked Kiss, 1964, Crown of India, 1966, Shock Corridor, 1966, 144 Piccadilly, 1971, Dead Pigeon on Beethoven Street, 1974, The Big Red One, 1980, The Rifle, 1981, Pecos Bill and the Soho Kid, 1986, Quint's World, 1988; actor: (films) House of Bamboo, 1955, Pierrot le fou, 1965, Brigitte et Brigitte, 1966, The Last Movie, 1971, The Young Nurses, 1973, The American Friend, 1977, Scott Joplin, 1977, 1941, 1979, All Night Long, 1981, Hammett, 1982, White Dog, 1982, The State of Things, 1983, Slapstick of Another Kind, 1984, Return to Salem's Lot, 1987, China Sea, 1989, Sons, 1989, Street of No Return, 1991. Served with inf. U.S. Army, World War II. Decorated Silver Star, Bronze Star. Died Oct. 30, 1997.

FULTON-CALKINS, PATSY JO, educational administrator, writer; b. Ft. Worth, Sept. 14, 1934; d. Roy and Thyra Pearl (Smith) LaFaver; m. Stanley R. Fulton (div. June 1987); 1 child, Paul Alan Foust. BBA, North Tex. State U., 1965, MEd., 1969, PhD, 1975. Tchr. Irving (Tex.) High Sch., 1965-70; instr. Mountain View Coll., Dallas, 1970-77; div. chairperson Cedar Valley Coll., Lancaster, Tex., 1977-80, v.p. instr., 1980-82; v.p. instr. El Centro Coll., Dallas, 1982-84; pres. Brookhaven Coll., Dallas, 1984-91; chancellor Oakland Community Coll., Bloomfield Hills, Mich., 1991—; bd. dirs. Town North Bank, Dallas; cons. Evergreen Coll., Washington, 1987—. Author: Exploring Human Relations, 1982, General Office Procedures for College, 1983, Procedures for the Professional Secretary, 1985, General Office

Procedures and Technology for Colleges, 1994, Procedures for the Office Professional, 1995' contbr. articles to profl. jours. Mem. Tex. Jr. Coll. Tchrs. Assn., Am. Mgmt. Assn., Tex. Bus. Edn. Assn. (sec. 1974, historian 1975, treas. 1976), Metrocrest and Farmers Branch C. of C. (chmn. bd. 1984—), Bookhaven Country Club, Beta Gamma Sigma, Delta Pi Epsilon (treas. 1975). Democrat. Baptist. Avocations: hiking, swimming, reading, travel.

FUNK, ARVILLE LYNN, lawyer; b. Corydon, Ind., Dec. 11, 1929; s. Herman E. and Elsie (McMonigle) F.; m. Rosemary E. Springer, Aug. 25, 1956; children—Cynthia Lynn, Mark Andrew (dec.). B.A. in History, Ind. Central Coll., 1955; M.S. in Edn., Butler U.; J.D., Ind. U., 1963. Bar: Ind. 1963. Head history dept. Perry Central Jr. High Sch., Indpls., 1955-61; head history dept. Perry East Jr. High Sch., Indpls., 1961-65; ptnr. O'Bannon Funk & Simpson and predecessor firm, Corydon, 1965—; atty. Crawford County, City of Corydon; gen. counsel Ind. Toll Bridge Commn., 1969-83; instr. history Purdue U. extension. Author: Tales of Our Hoosier Heritage, 1965, 66; Harrison County in Sesquicentennial Year, Indiana's Birthplace, 1966; Our Historic Corydon, 1967; Pioneers of Harrison County, 1967; Hoosiers in the Civil War, 1968; A Sketchbook of Indiana History, 1969; The Morgan Raid in Indiana and Ohio, 1971; Squire Boone in Indiana, 1973; Historical Almanac of Harrison County, 1974; Revolutionary War Era in Indiana, 1975; Revolutionary War Soldiers in Harrison County, 1975; A Hoosier Regiment in Dixie, 1978; The Battle of Corydon, 1976; The Hoosier Scrapbook, 1981, also articles in profl. jours.; editor: Teaching Indiana History, 1962-64. Hist. advisor Ind. Dept. Conservation, 1961-80; publs. chmn. Marion County Civil War Centennial Commn., 1961-65; chmn. Harrison County Bicentennial Commn.; del. Ind. Republican State Conv., 1966, 68, 70, 74, 82, 84, 86; pres., bd. dirs. N.Am. Indian Found., 1966-67; pres. bd. trustees local Methodist Ch. Served to capt. AUS, 1947-48, 50-52. Recipient Nat. Classroom Tchrs. medal Freedom Found., 1962. Mem. ABA, Ind. Bar Assn., Harrison County Bar Assn. (pres.), Ind. Hist. Soc., Harrison County Hist. Soc. (bd. dirs.), C. of C. (bd. dirs.), Ind. Central Coll. Alumni (bd. dirs.), Phi Delta Phi. Lodge: Rotary (bd. dirs.).

FUNK, ELLA FRANCES, genealogist, author; b. Domino, Ky., Apr. 7, 1921; d. Roy William and Edna Rene (Cummins) Roach; m. Eugene Boyd Funk, June 20, 1942; children: Susan Teresa, Eugene Boyd. B of Liberal Studies, Mary Washington Coll., 1982. Exec. sec. Lang. Labs., Inc., Bethesda, Md., 1969-70; office mgr. legal firm Donovan Leisure Newton & Irvine, Washington, 1970-76; genealogist, hist. researcher, writer, 1976—; class lectr., bd. dirs. Mary Washington ElderStudy Program; vol. Assn. Preservation Va. Antiquities; mem. Presbyn. Ch., Fredericksburg, Va. Named Exec. of Week, Sta. WGMS, Washington, June 1975; recipient Blue Ribbon winner for poem Va. Fedn. Women's Clubs, 1994. Life mem. Nat. Geneal. Soc.; mem. Hist. Fredericksburg Found., DAR, Alpha Phi Sigma, Sigma Phi Gamma. Club: Woman's (Fredericksburg, Va.). Lodge: Order Eastern Star. Author: Cummins Ancient, Cummins New, vol. 1, 1978, vol. 2, 1980, Joseph Funk, a biography, 1984, Benjamin's Way, 1988, (short stories) Christmas In The Abbey, 1988 (ribbon winner 1989), Dangerous Mission (Va. Fedn. Women's Clubs ribbon 1991), The Phobia (Va. Fedn. Women's Clubs ribbon 1994), My Son and the Westwind (Women's Club blue ribbon 1996), (poem) The Good Ship (ribbon 990), Sounds From The Night (Women's Club red ribbon 1997). Died Oct. 6, 1997. Home: PO Box 711 Charlottesville VA 22902-0711

FUNKE, LEWIS BERNARD, drama editor; b. Bronx, N.Y., Jan. 25, 1912; s. Joseph and Rose (Keimowitz) F.; m. Blanche Bier, July 5, 1938; children: Phyllis Ellen, Michael Jeffrey. A.B., N.Y. U., 1932. Free-lance writer, sports dept. N.Y. Times, 1928-32, staff sports writer, 1932-44, gen. news staff, movie dept., 1944, drama editor, asst. drama critic, 1944-73, asst. cultural news editor, 1970-73; former adj. lectr. Queens Coll., N.Y.C.; disting. vis. prof. Sch. Theater, Fla. State U., Tallahassee, 1973-80; pub. relations cons. Eugene O'Neill Meml. Theater Center, 1973-86. Author articles various nat. mags.; co-author: Actors Talk About Acting, 1962, Max Gordon Presents, 1963, A Gift of Joy, 1965; author: The Curtain Rises, 1971, Playwrights Talk About Playwriting, 1975, Actors Talk About Theater, 1977; contbg. editor: The Exec. Jeweler, 1980-83. Home: Delray Beach Fla. Died June 26, 1992.

FUSON, WAYNE EDWARD, sports editor; b. Terre Haute, Ind., Mar. 2, 1925; s. David Emorest and Grace Leona (Bruner) F.; m. Carolyn Joan Bare, June 2, 1946; children: Bonnie Fuson Toth, Wayne F., Jay K., Craig A. LLD (hon.), Ind. State U., 1988. Reporter Terre Haute Star, 1944-46; copy editor, sports writer Indpls. News, 1946-51, sports editor, columnist, 1951-96. Founding dir. Associated Press Sports Editors, 1975, pres. 1978-79; founding dir. Ind. Basketball Hall of Fame, 1965, dir. emeritus, 1992-96; bd. dirs. GTE North Sr. Classic, Indpls., 1989-96. Named Sportswriter of Yr., Nat. Sportswriters and Sportscasters, 1975. Mem. Indpls. Athletic Club Found. (bd. dirs. 1992-96). Avocation: amateur radio. Died Sept., 1996.

FUTAS, ELIZABETH DOROTHY, library and information studies educator, program director; b. N.Y.C., May 8, 1944; d. Bart and Eleanore Rhoda (Tabak) F. BA, Bklyn. Coll., 1965; MA, U. Minn., 1966; postgrad., Queens Coll., 1968-71; PhD, Rutgers U., 1980. Grad. asst. U. Minn., Mpls., 1965-66; cataloguer Ford Found., N.Y.C., 1967-68; reference bibliographer Queens Coll., N.Y., 1968-74, 76-77; adj. faculty Rutgers U., New Brunswick, N.J., 1975-76; asst. prof. Emory U., Atlanta, 1977-83, assoc. prof., 1983-85; adj. prof. U. Wash., Seattle, 1985, North Tex. State U., 1992; dir., prof. grad. sch. libr. and info. studies U. R.I., Kingston, 1986-95, acting dean Coll. Arts and Scis., 1990; adj. prof. U. North Tex., 1992; cons. Smith Coll. Librs., Northampton, Mass., 1993-94; chmn. mgmt. com. Dept. State Libr. Svc., Providence, 1986-88. Author 5 books on libr. sci.; editor RQ Jour., 1987-91; mem. editl. bd. Collection Bldg., 1978-95, Audiofile, 1994-95; contbr. articles to profl. jours. Regents scholar Brooklyn Coll., 1961-65. Mem. ALA (councilor 1978-88, 92-95, exec. bd. 1984-88), Coun. Deans and Dirs. (chair 1989-90), R.I. Libr. Assn., N.H. Libr. Assn., Phi Kappa Phi. Home: Wakefield R.I. Died Feb. 6, 1995.

GADBOIS, RICHARD A., JR., federal judge; b. Omaha, June 18, 1932; s. Richard Alphonse Gadbois and Margaret Ann (Donahue) Bartlett; children from previous marriage: Richard, Gregory, Guy, Geoffrey, Thomas; m. Vicki Cresap, May 14, 1993. A.B., St. John's Coll., Camarillo, Calif., 1955; J.D., Loyola U., Los Angeles, 1958; postgrad. in law, U. So. Calif., 1958-60. Bar: Calif. 1959, U.S. Dist. Ct. (cen. dist.) Calif. 1959, U.S. Supreme Ct. 1966. Dep. atty. gen. Calif., 1958-59; ptnr. Musick, Peeler & Garrett, L.A., 1959-68; v.p. Denny's Inc., La Mirada, Calif., 1968-71; judge Mcpl. Ct., L.A., 1971-72, Superior Ct., L.A., 1972-82, U.S. Dist. Ct. (cen. dist.) Calif., L.A., 1982-96. Decorated knight Order of Holy Sepulchre (Pope John Paul II). Mem. ABA, Los Angeles County Bar Assn. (trustee 1966-67), State Bar Calif. (profl. ethics com. 1965-70). Republican. Roman Catholic. Died Oct. 2, 1996.

GAFFNEY, JOHN FRANCIS, state congressman; b. Atlantic City, Mar. 23, 1934; s. John Fasio and Marie Bernadet (Cooney) G.; m. Judith Ann Brangenberg, Sept. 19, 1957 (div. Aug. 1985); children: Lynn, Patricia, Virginia, Kathleen; m. Carol Laura Crane, Sept. 21, 1985; children: Laurie, Amy. Land surveyor Atlantic Electric, Pleasantville, N.J., 1959-68, asst. engr., 1968-82, svc. rep., 1982-89; exec. dir. Greater Mainland C. of C., Pleasantville, 1990-92; mem. N.J. State Assembly, 1992-95. Councilman, City of Linwood, N.J., 1974-75, mayor, 1975-79; freeholder Atlantic County, N.J., 1979-92; pres. South Jersey Freeholders Assn., Northfield, 1988-89. Sgt. U.S. Army, 1957-59. Mem. Friendly Sons of St. Patrick. Republican. Roman Catholic. Avocations: golf, tennis, skiing. Died 1995.

GAILEY, FRANKLIN BRYAN, retired biology educator; b. Atlanta, Oct. 18, 1918; s. James Herbert and Edna (Bryan) G.; m. Sara Helen Clark, July 31, 1948; children: David Clark, Carol Bryan, Patricia Lowe, Mark Alan. B.S. in Chemistry, Ga. Inst. Tech., 1940; M.S., U. Wis., 1942, Ph.D. in Biochemistry, 1946. Instr. biology, chemistry Lees Jr. Coll., Jackson, Ky., 1946-48; mem. faculty Berea (Ky.) Coll., 1948-89, prof. biology, 1957-95, chmn. dept., 1957-82; Research participant Oak Ridge Inst. Nuclear Studies, summers 1954, 55, U. Ill., summer 1966, U. Ky., 1966-67. Fellow AAAS; mem. Sigma Xi, Phi Kappa Phi. Mem. Ch. of Christ, Union, also Berea Friends Meeting. Home: Berea Ky. Died Oct. 26, 1995.

GAIRDNER, JOHN SMITH, securities investment dealer; b. Toronto, Ont., Can., July 25, 1925; s. James A. and Norma Ecclestone (Smith) G.; m. Ivy Jane Brothwell, Nov. 30, 1946; children—John Lewis (dec.), Robert Donald, Brenda Leigh. Grad., Appleby Coll., Oakville, Ont., 1942; student, U. Toronto, 1942-43. Clk. Gairdner & Co., Ltd., Toronto, 1945-48, dir., 1948-55; v.p., dir. Gairdner & Co., Ltd. (now Security Trading Inc.), Toronto, 1955-58, pres., 1958-66, chmn. bd., dir., 1965-74; pres., bd. dirs. Joronda Resources Ltd., 1991-94; chmn. Security Trading Inc., Toronto, 1974-91. Bd. govs. Appleby Coll. Served with RCAF, 1943-45. Mem. Zeta Psi. Deceased.

GALLAGHER, JAMES WES, journalist; b. San Francisco, Oct. 6, 1911; s. James and Chispa (Howard) G.; m. Betty L. Kelley, June 1, 1946; children—Brian, Jane, Christine. B.A., U. San Francisco, 1931; ed., La. State U., 1935. Reporter Baton Rouge State Times, 1935; reporter Rochester Democrat and Chronicle, N.Y., 1935-36; with A.P., 1937-76; editor A.P., Buffalo, 1937-39, Albany, 1939, N.Y.C., 1939; became fgn. corr. A.P., 1940, chief mil. staff African invasion, 1942; chief invasion staff for A.P., France, 1944; acting chief A.P. (Paris Bur.), 1945; chief bur. in A.P. (Paris Bur.), Germany, 1945-51; gen. exec. A.P., N.Y.C., 1951-54; asst. gen. mgr. A.P., 1954-62, gen. mgr., 1962-76, pres., 1972-76; chmn. A.P., Ltd.; pres. Press Assn., Inc., La Prensa Asociada, City News Assn., A.P. Can., World Wide Photos, Inc.; dir. A.P. Norway, A.P. Belgium, pres., gen. mgr., 1972-76; ret., 1976; dir. Gannett Co., 1976-83, chmn. mgmt. continuity com. Author: Back Door to Berlin, 1943. Pres. Santa Barbara Boy's Club, 1981-84. Recipient William Allan White award, 1967, George Polk award L.I. U., 1969, Carr Van Anda award Ohio U., 1969, Peter Zenger award Ariz. U., 1969, Medal of Honor U. Mo., 1976; named One of Outstanding Young Men in U.S., U.S. C. of C., 1945. Fellow Sigma Delta Chi (Deadline Club Hall of Fame 1975). Clubs: Overseas Press; Birnam Wood (Santa Barbara, Calif.). Home: Santa Barbara Calif. Died Oct. 11, 1997.

GALLARDO, JOSÉ MARÍA, museum director; b. Buenos Aires, Aug. 1, 1925; s. Gallardo Angel León and Demarchi de Gallardo Maria Luisa; m. Vayo Juana de Jesus; children: Juana Maria, José Maria, Maria Aurelia Trinidad, Maria del Espiritu Santo. Bachiller, Colegio Champagnat, Buenos Aires, 1943; Licenciado Ciencias Naturales, U. Buenos Aires, 1950, Dr. Ciencias Biológicas, 1983. Investigator, scientist Argentine Mus. Natural Scis., Buenos Aires, 1946-71, dir. cargo, 1971-73, dir. titular, 1973-96; prof. Catolica U. Argentina, Buenos Aires, 1971-81, U. Buenos Aires, 1981-96; investigator prin. CONICET, Buenos Aires, 1961. Author: Anfibios de los Alrededores de Buenos Aires, 1974, Reptiles, 1977, Anfibios Argentinos, 1987, Anfibios y Reptiles del Partido de Magdalena, 1987. Rsch. fellow Harvard U., 1959; sci. fellow N.Y. Zool. Soc., 1974. Mem. Históricas de la Manzana de las Luces (pres. 1984-96), Acad. del Plata, Soc. Sci. Argentina Buenos Aires, Acad. Argentina de Ciencias del Ambiente (pres.), Acad. Nat. de Geografia, Assn. Herpetólogica Argentina (v.p.). Died Oct. 12, 1994.

GAMBLE, WILLIAM BELSER, JR., retired physician; b. Andrews, S.C., Apr. 17, 1925; s. William Belser and Anna (Moyd) G.; m. Margaret Florence DuBose, June 7, 1947 (dec.); children: William Belser III, Richard Ervin, Heather Margaret; m. Archer Lee Hannah, Nov. 7, 1992. BS, U. S.C., 1945; MD, Med. Coll. S.C., 1948; MPH, U. N.C., 1972. Diplomate Am. Bd. Pediatrics, Am. Bd. Allergy and Clin. Immunology. Intern Roper Hosp., Charleston, S.C., 1948-49; resident pediatrics, teaching fellow Med. Coll. S.C., Charleston, 1953-56; assoc. clin. prof. pediatrics Med. Univ. S.C., Charleston, 1963-95; practice pediatrics sub-specializing in pediatric allergy and immunology Charleston, 1956-87; state epidemiologist State Dept. Health and Environ. Control, Columbia, S.C., 1972-93, immunization and communicable disease cons., 1972-93, chief bur. preventive health svcs., 1988-89; chief pediatrics Roper Hosp., Charleston, S.C., 1986-88; adj. prof. epidemiology and statis. Sch. Pub. Health, U. S.C., Columbia, 1989-93; dist. med. dir. Waccamaw Pub. Health Dist., 1989-94. Contbr. articles on communicable diseases in U.S., Latin Am. and Can. to profl. jours. Past bd. dirs. Charleston County Mental Health Assn., Charleston County Tb Assn., ARC, Georgetown County. Served with M.C., U.S. Army, 1951-53. Recipient J. Marion Sims award S.C. Pub. Health Assn., 1991; named to 1992 Centennial Roll of Honor, Med. U. S.C. Fellow Am. Acad. Allergy, Am. Acad. Pediatrics (infectious disease com. 1987-90), S.C. Soc. Allergy and Clin. Immunology (charter pres.), Southeastern Allergy Assn., Rotary (past pres.), Phi Beta Kappa, Alpha Kappa Kappa, Kappa Sigma, Alpha Omega Alpha, Delta Omega. Presbyterian (past elder). Home: Johns Island S.C. Died Aug. 8, 1995.

GANDHI, INDIRA NEHRU, prime minister India; b. Allahabad, India, Nov. 19, 1917; d. Jawaharlal and Kamala (Koul) Nehru; student schs. Switzerland, India, Eng., Somerville Coll., Oxford (Eng.) U.; D.Litt. (hon.), Andhra U., 1963; hon. drs. Agra, Bangalore, Vikram, El Salvador, Buenos Aires, Waseda, Oxford, Moscow, Charles, Punjab, Gurukul Kangri, Nagpur, Poona, Baghdad, Visva Bharati univs.; D.Sc. (hon.), Soviet Acad. Scis., 1976; m. Feroze Gandhi, Mar. 26, 1942 (dec.); children—Rajiv, Sanjay (dec.). Disciple of Gandhi; formed Vanar Sena children's orgn. to help Indian Nat. Congress during non-cooperation movement; worked among untouchables popularizing hand-spun cloth and Indian-made goods; active student movement India, Eng.; mem. Indian Nat. Congress 1938—, mem. working com., 1955—, central election com., 1955—, central parliamentary bd., 1958—, pres Congress, 1959-60, 78—; prime minister India, 1966-77 80—, minister external affairs, 1967-69, fin., 1969-70 home affairs, 1970-73, info. and broadcasting, 1971-74 atomic energy, 1967-77, space, 1972-77, electronics 1973-77, planning, 1975-77, def., 1975, 80-82; ofcl. hostess Prime Minister Nehru, 1947-64. Vice chmn. Central Social Welfare Bd., 1953-57; chmn. Citizens' Central Council, 1962; mem. Nat. Def. Council, 1962; exec com. Nat. Def. Fund, 1962; life patron Indian Council Child Welfare; v.p. Internat. Council Child Welfare mem. Indian del. UNESCO, 1960-64 also mem. exec bd. UNESCO; mem. integration council Indian Nat Congress, Nat. Inst. women; founder, pres. Kamala Nehru Vidayalaya; chmn. Bal Bhavan Bd., Children's Nat. Mus.; founder, chmn. Bal Sahyog, New Delhi 1954—; chmn. Sangeet Natak Akademi, 1965-72 Acharye Visva-Bharati, 1966-77; pres. Dakshina Bharat Hindi Pracher Sabha; pres. Nehru Meml. Fund and Nehru Meml. Mus. and Library Soc.; patron various insts., socs.; pres. Himalayan Mountaineering Inst. Tibetan Homes Found.; pres. bd. trustees Kamala Nehru Meml. Hosp.; trustee Kasturba Ghandi. Meml Trust, Gandhi Smarak Nidhi; chmn. Swarj Bhavan Trust. Recipient Mother's award, U.S.A., 1953 Howland Meml. prize Yale U., 1960; Diploma c

Honour Argentine Soc. for Protection of Animals, 1971; various other awards. Mem. Fed. Film Socs. India (v.p.).

GANTER, GLADYS MARIE, retired Latin language educator; b. Hamilton, Ohio, May 24, 1908; d. William Edward and Mary Barbara (Schultheiss) G. AB, Capital U., Columbus, Ohio, 1931; student, Middlebury Coll., 1933, Miami U., Oxford, Ohio, 1940; AB, Xavier U., 1940. Latin and English tchr. Fairfield (Ohio) Sch., 1931-33; Latin, English and comparative language tchr. Roosevelt Jr. High Sch., Hamilton, Ohio, 1935-37; Latin, English tchr. Hamilton (Ohio) Sr. High Sch., 1937-59, Garfield Sr. High Sch., Hamilton, 1959-71; latin and English critic tchr. Miami U., 1937-59; private tutor, Hamilton, 1935-71. Mem. Salvation Army, 1987—. Mem. YMCA, AAUW, Nat. Tchrs. Assn., Ohio Edn. Assn., Chaps, Tri-Fi, Women's Club, DAR, Kappa Sigma Theta (pres. Capital U. chpt.). Lutheran. Avocations: reading, theater, usic, ballet, travel, European tours.

GARDNER, WALTER, artist; b. Liverpool, Eng., May 7, 1902; s. Herman G. and Lily (Cuddy) G.; m. Emilie Roland, Nov. 1, 1937 (dec. June 1947); m. Jane Beckwith, Aug. 1948. Elementary edn., Eng.; student, Pa. Acad. Fine Arts, 1921-25. Phila. Cresson traveling scholar, 1924. Exhibited at, Whitney Mus., N.Y.C., Artists for Victory Show, Met. Mus., N.Y.C., Corcoran Gallery, Washington, Chgo. Art Inst., Detroit Inst. Art, Va. Mus. Fine Arts, Richmond, Pa. Acad.; Executed murals, post offices at, Honesdale, Pa., Phila. (Sta. O), Berne, Ind., Municipal Ct. Phila. Recipient purchase prize Wanamaker Regional Art Exhibit, 1934; fellowship prize Pa. Acad., 1938. Died Jan. 24, 1996.

GARNER, SAMUEL PAUL, accounting educator, author; b. Yadkinville, N.C., Aug. 15, 1910; s. Samuel W. and Ila Jane (Hoots) G.; m. Ruth Bailey, Aug. 25, 1934; children: Thad Barclay, Walter Samuel, Sarah Jane. A.B., Duke U., 1932, A.M., 1934; postgrad., Columbia U., 1936; Ph.D., U. Tex., 1940; D.Ec. (hon.), Busan Nat. U., 1966; LL.D., U. Ala., 1971. C.P.A., Ala., Tex. Faculty Duke U., 1934-35, Miss. State Coll., 1935-37, U. Tex., 1937-39; assoc. prof. accounting U. Ala., University, 1939-43, prof., 1943-71, head dept. accounting, 1949-55; dean Coll. Bus. Adminstrn. U. Ala., 1954-71; Mem. Knight & Garner (C.P.A.s, University), 1942-49; bd. dirs. emeritus First Fed. Savs. & Loan Assn., Hardins Bakery, Inc.; bd. dirs. O. Bowers Co., Tide Clean, Inc., Tuscaloosa, Ala., cons. edn. to comptr. gen. U.S., 1955-61; cons. grad. edn. U.S. Office Edn., 1965-70; cons. mgmt. edn. U.S. Dept. Def., 1965-70; fin. cons. City of Tuscaloosa, 1940-96; Comer lectr. U. Ga., 1957; Price Waterhouse Found. lectr. Ga. State U., 1964; Disting. faculty lectr. Tex. Western Coll., 1963, U. S.D., 1963, East Carolina Coll., 1965, Va. Poly. Inst., 1966, Tex. Tech. U., 1970, Tex. A&M U., U. Tenn., 1972, Ala. A&M U., 1973, Fla. Atlantic U., 1975, Fla. Internat. U., 1973, Western Carolina U., 1976, Appalachian State U., 1975, Judson Coll., 1977, Santa Clara U., 1978, Wollongong U., 1980, others; U.S. del. internat. mgmt. and acctg. congresses, 1957-96; condr. spl. ednl. assignments U.S. State Dept. and other agys. in Turkey, 1958, Far East, 1960, 66, 68-69, 72, 80, 86-90, Europe, 1957, 60-61, 63-85, 86, 88-95, S.Am., 1962, 65, 75, 81-82, 90, Africa, 1964, 73, 82; adv. bd. Internat. U. Contact for Mgmt., Holland, 1964-72; U.S. Coun. Internat. Exch. Commerce Students; hon. dir. Yong-You Inst. for Acctg. Ednl. Rsch., Beijing, China, 1990. Author: (with G.H. Newlove) Elementary Cost Accounting, 1941, rev. edit., 1949, Spanish edit., 1952, Advanced Accounting, Vol. I, 1951, Vol. II, 1950, Advanced Accounting Problems, Book I, 1951, Advanced Accounting Problems, Book II, 1950, Handbook of Modern Accounting Theory, 1955, Education for the Professions, 1955, Readings in Cost Accounting, Budgeting and Control, 1955, rev. edit., 1960, Evolution of Cost Accounting to 1925, 1954, Japanese edit., 1956; co-editor: (with Ken Berg) Readings in Accounting Theory, 1966, Readings on Accounting Development, 1978; (with Atsuo Tsuji) Studies in Accounting History, 1995; editl. adv. bd. Mgmt. Internat. mag., 1964-70; editl. bd. Acctg. Rev., 1968-70, Essays in Internation Business, annual, 1967-70; contbr. articles to profl. jours. Recipient Dow-Jones award, 1976; inducted into Ala. Bus. Hall of Fame, 1992. Fellow Acad. Internat. Bus. (historian 1974-93); mem. AICPA, Am. Acctg. Assn. (life, pres. 1951, exec. com. 1948, 51-54, chmn. com. internat. rels. 1966-67, 1st Internat. Svc. award 1990, disting. prof. 1993, chmn. com. profl. stats. 1960-62), Nat. Assn. CPA Examiners (chmn. com. acctg. edn. 1960-61), Am. Coll. CLUs (coun. ednl. advisors 1961-69), U.S. Coun. Internat. Progress in Mgmt. (nat. bd. dirs. 1960-69), Acad. Acctg. Historians (co-founder, life, trustee 1975-78), Fed. Govt. Accts. Assn. (adv. com. rels. with univs.), Fin. Execs. Inst. (nat. com. edn. 1956-70), Am. Assn. Collegiate Schs. Bus. (pres. 1964-65), Internat. Assn. Acctg. Edn. and Rsch. (pres. 1985-88), Soc. Expert Accts. (corr. mem.), France, Nat. Assn. Accts., Ala. Soc. CPAs (sec.-treas. 1949-58, Disting. Svc. award 1988), University Club, Sigma Alpha Epsilon, Phi Beta Kappa, Beta Gamma Sigma (nat. exec. com. 1961-66, presdl. citation 1991), Beta Alpha Psi (Disting. Svc. award 1975), Omicron Delta Kappa, Pi Tau Chi, Omicron Delta Epsilon, Alpha Kappa Psi (trustee found., Found. award 1962), Pi Gamma Mu, Phi Beta Delta. Baptist. Died Oct. 16, 1996.

GARRISON, MARION AMES, mechanical engineer, oil tool company executive; b. Indpls., July 20, 1907; s. Charles C. and Ella J. (Hilligoss) G.; m. Meriam Kathleen Goode, Aug. 23, 1933; 1 dau., Charlotte Ann. M.E., U. So. Calif., 1929. Pvt. practice bottom hole oil tool design Los Angeles, 1945-55; chief engr. Eastman Oil Well Survey Co., Denver, 1955-57, Empire Oil Tool Co., Denver, 1957—. Mem. Am. Inst. M.E., Delta Sigma Rho, Sigma Phi Epsilon. Patentee in fluid mechanics, bottom hole oil tools; inventor linkage type automotive power steering. Died May 3, 1993.

GARVER, OLIVER BAILEY, JR., bishop; b. L.A., July 19, 1925. BS, UCLA, 1945; MBA, Harvard U., 1948; STB, Episc. Theol. Sch., Cambridge, Mass., 1962; DD, Ch. Div. Sch. Pacific, 1987. Ordained to ministry Episcopal Ch. as deacon, 1962, as priest, 1963. With Lockheed Aircraft Corp., 1948-59; curate St. Alban's, L.A., 1966-72; urban assoc. Ch. of the Epiphany, L.A., 1966-72; canon to the ordinary Staff Bishop Rusack, 1973-85; consecrated bishop suffragan Diocese of L.A., 1985-89; bishop in residence Harvard Sch., 1989—. With USNR, 1943-46. Mem. Phi Beta Kappa, Beta Gamma Sigma. Deceased.

GARVEY, ROBERT ROBEY, JR., former government official; b. Elkin, N.C., Feb. 16, 1921; s. Robert Robey and Rose Edna (Brown) G.; m. Nancy Douglas Maclay, June 15, 1945; children: Robert Michael, Jean Maclay, Lee Beasley, William Sinclair. Student, Davidson Coll., 1938-41; sr. exec. program, Fed. Exec. Inst., 1975. Gen. mgr. Dennis, Inc., Winston-Salem, N.C., 1945-54; exec. dir. Old Salem, Inc., Winston-Salem, 1955-60, Nat. Trust for Historic Preservation, Washington, 1960-67; exec. sec. Adv. Council on Historic Preservation, 1967-76, exec. dir., 1976-86; asst. sec. Nat. Park Found., 1968-71; Nat. Park Service liaison officer Am. Revolution Bicentennial Commn., 1968-71; mem. internat. com. Nat. Assn. Housing and Redevel. Ofcls., 1963-86; v.p. Internat. Council of Monuments and Sites, 1965-75; cons. on cultural property UNESCO; mem. U.S. nat. commn. for UNESCO, 1974-79, vice chmn., 1976-79; mem. landscape and archaeologists com. on Philae project Govt. of Egypt. Served to maj. USMCR, 1942-45. Decorated DFC, Air medal with silver star; recipient N.C. Pub. Svc. award, 1978, Disting. Alumnus award Davidson Coll., 1982, Presdl. rank of Meritorious Exec., 1981, Louise duPont Crowningshield award, 1991. Home: Emerald Isle N.C. Died Dec. 28, 1996; interred Arlington National Cemetery.

GATES, LARRY, actor; b. St. Paul, Sept. 24, 1915; s. Lloyd Roland and Marion Douglas (Wheaton) G.; m. Tania Wilkof, Aug. 2, 1959 (dec. Sept. 1961); m. Judith Seaton, Apr. 11, 1963. Student, U. Minn., 1933-38. Mem. Barter Theatre, Abingdon, Va., 1946-47; mem Webster Shakespeare Co., N.Y.C., 1950-51; councillor Actors' Equity Assn., N.Y.C., 1952-62. Appeared in Broadway play Bell, Book and Candle, 1951, The Love of Four Colonels, 1952, The Teahouse of the August Moon, 1953, First Monday in October, 1979, Poor Murderer, 1976, A Case of Libel, 1963 (nominated for Tony award); mem. nat. tour The Gin Game, 1982; appeared in The Missiles of October, The Lou Grant Show, Backstairs at the White House; (films) The Invasion of the Bodysnatchers, Cat on a Hot Tin Roof, Some Came Running, The Sand Pebbles, In the Heat of the Night. Vice chmn. Democratic Town Com., Cornwall, Conn., 1958-81; Democratic candidate for Conn. senate, 1972; chmn. Cornwall Recreation Commn., 1966-77; vice chmn. Housatonic River Commn., Warren, Conn., 1978. Served to maj. C.E. AUS, 1941-49, PTO. Recipient Outstanding Achievement award U. Minn., 1976, Emmy award for outstanding supporting actor in drama series Guiding Light, 1985. Mem. AFTRA, SAG, Soc. Stage Dirs. and Choreographers, Episcopal Actors' Guild (councillor N.Y.C. 1977-96), Players Club N.Y.C. Home: West Cornwall Conn. Died Dec. 12, 1996.

GATTULLO, MARIO, educator; b. Zurig, Switzerland, May 29, 1933; s. Giuseppe and Helen (Maag) G.; m. Rosalia Mustacchia, May 9, 1959; children; Francesca, Chiara. Maturita classical, Leonardo Da Vinci, Catania, Italy, 1951; degree in philosophy, Univ. Catania, 1959. Univ. asst. Univ. Bologna, Bologna, Italy, 1960-69, assoc. prof., 1969-76, prof., 1976-91; dir. Inst. of Pedagogy Bologna, 1976-82, dir. dept. edn. Bologna, 1982-86, Ednl. Rsch. Ctr. Bologna, 1987-91. Author: Didattica e Docimologia, 1967, Problemi Di Politica Scolastica, 1978, La Scuola Italiana Dal 1945 al 1983, 1986, Misurare E Valutare L'apprendimento nella scuola media, 1989. City counselor, Bologna, 1990-91. Recipient Archiginnasio D'Oro City Coun., 1992, Sigillo D'Oro Univ. Bologna, 1996. Mem. Italian Soc. Pedagogy (pres. 1989-91). Avocations: chess, hiking. Died Nov. 9, 1991.

GAULL, GERALD EDWARD, nutritionist, scientist, educator, food company executive; b. Boston, Sept. 17, 1930; s. Samuel and Alice Charlotte (Berkowitz) G.; children: Erik, Stephen; m. F. McSherry Heffernan, Nov. 18, 1984. BA in Philosophy with Honors, U. Mich., 1951; MD, Boston U., 1955. Jr. and sr. resident in pathology Peter Bent Brigham Hosp., Boston, 1955-57; NIH postdoctoral rsch. fellow Harvard U., 1957-59; jr. resident pediatrics Babies Hosp., N.Y.C., 1960-61; NIH rsch. fellow in metabolism U. Coll. Hosp., London, 1961-62; sr. resident in pediatrics Children's Hosp. Med. Ctr., Boston, 1963-64; NIH rsch. fellow in neurochemistry Med. Rsch Coun. Lab., Eng., 1964-65; rsch. assoc. Columbia U., 1965-67; attending pediatrician Babies Hosp., N.Y.C., 1965-67; chief dept. pediatric rsch. N.Y. State Inst. for Rsch. in Mental Retardation, 1967-76; chief dept. nutrition and human devel. N.Y. State Inst. Rsch. in Devel. Disabilities, 1976-84; assoc. prof. pediatrics Mt. Sinai Sch. Med., 1967-74, prof., 1974-84; assoc. attending, then attending pediatrician Mt. Sinai Hosp., 1967-84; adj. prof. Rockefeller U., 1978-80; clin. prof. pediatrics U. Chgo., 1985-88; adj. prof. pediatrics Northwestern U., Evanston, Ill., 1987-92; v.p. nutritional scis. The NutraSweet Co., Deerfield, Ill., 1984-92; rsch. prof., dir. Ctr. for Food and Nutrition Policy and The Ceres Forum Georgetown U., Washington. Author/editor: Biology of Brain Dysfunction, 1973-75, Natural Sulfur Compounds, 1980, Nutrition in the 90's, 1991, New Technologies and the Future of Food and Nutrition, 1991, The Emerging Global Food System: Public and Private Sector Issues, 1993; contbr. articles to profl. jours. Served with U.S. Army, 1961-62. Recipient Borden award Am. Acad. Pediatrics, 1978, St. Ambrosiano Gold medal City of Milan (Italy), 1983; Andelot fellow in Biochemistry Harvard U., 1958. Mem. Am. Soc. Biol. Chemistry and Molecular Biology, Soc. Pediatric Rsch., Am. Soc. Nutritional Scis., Am. Soc. Clin. Nutrition, Am. Pediatric Soc., Internat. Brain Rsch. Orgn., Am. Coll. Nutrition, Internat. Soc. Rsch. Human Milk and Lactation, Cosmos Club. Achievements include patents on infant milk formula, human nutritional compositions containing taurine and vitamins and/or minerals.

GEERTS, LEO (MIKE ADAMS), writer; b. Doel, Antwerp, Belgium, Feb. 18, 1935; s. Gerard and Anna (Huygen), G.; m. Rika Heymans, 1962; children: Hank, Ina. Licentiate in Philosophy, Catholic U., Louvain, Belgium, 1958. Literary critic De Nieuwe Mag., Brussels, 1964-84; TV presenter Flemish TV, Belgium, 1970-75; editor Streven Mag., Belgium, 1975—; Tchr. Catholic Schs., Belgium, 1964—. Author: Leoders, 1975, Pagadders, 1982, Dada-ders, 1984; palys Ballad of Blood and Tears, 1977, Free Belgium, 1980, The Fair of Bloof, 1982; opera Ulrike an Antique Tragedy, 1979, The Mentor, 1988, Een Held die Armoe Zaait, 1988, Sapfo's Lief, 1991. Named Knight in Leoplod's order, 1987, Officer, 1989. Mem. P.E.N. Club.

GEHR, MARY, illustrator, painter, printmaker; b. Chgo.; d. Francis Lycett and Ruth Nettie (Mead) G.; m. Bert Ray, Oct. 14, 1950. Student, Smith Coll., Art Inst. Chgo., 1946-53, Inst. Design, Ill. Inst. Tech., 1962. Designer, book illustrator, 1954—; lectr. Art Inst. Chgo., 1979-82. One-man shows include Joseph Faulkner-Main St. Galleries, Chgo., 1964, 65, 67, 69, 70, Helenic Am. Union, Athens, Greece, 1971, Jacques Baruch Gallery, Chgo., 1973, 75, Art Rental and Sales Gallery, Art Inst. Chgo., 1954-80, A. Montgomery Ward Gallery U. Ill. Chgo., 1986, Princeton (N.J.) U., 1995; group exhbns. include Best Books of Midwest, 1954-55, 66-67, Art Inst. Chgo., Galerie Schwarze, Vienna, 1975, Loyola U., Chgo., 1995, others; represented in permanent collections Art Inst. Chgo., Bklyn. Mus., Phila. Mus., Free Libr. Phila., Libr. of Congress, many pvt., corp. collections; author, illustrator: The Littlest Circus Seal, 1952; illustrator numerous others. Recipient prizes for etchings. Mem. Am. Ctr. for Design, Arts Club Chgo. Democrat. Episcopalian.

GEIS, NORMAN WINER, lawyer; b. St. Paul, July 13, 1925; s. Alexander Winer and Shirley (Magid) Winer; m. Dorothy Bockman, Oct. 17, 1954; children: Deborah, Nancy, Carolyn (dec.), Sarah. AB with honors, U. Chgo., 1947, JD, 1951. Bar: Ill. 1950. Mng. editor U. Chgo. Law Review, 1949-50; practice in Chgo., 1951-96; counsel firm Miller, Shakman, Hamilton Kurtzon & Schlifke; advisor Nat. Conf. Commrs. Uniform State Laws spl. drafting coms. for Uniform Condominium Act, 1976-77; advisor Uniform Planned Community Act, 1978-80; adv. Nat. Conf. Commrs. Model Real Estate Coop. Act, 1979-80, Uniform Common-Interest Ownership Act, 1982, Uniform Land Security Interest Act, 1985; adv. Am. Law. Inst. Restatement of Servitudes, 1993-96; adj. prof. John Marshall Law Sch., 1989-90. Author: Condominiums, Planned Communities and Other Forms of Common-Interest Ownership, 1987; co-chmn. joint editl. bd. on Uniform Real Property Acts of ABA/Am. Coll. Real Estate Lawyers/Nat. Conf. Commrs. on Uniform State Laws, 1991-96; contbr. articles on condominium and homeowner assn. law and mortgage financing law to legal jours. Chmn. Highland Park (Ill.) Bd. Zoning Appeals, 1983-85. With inf., AUS, 1943-45. Decorated Purple Heart, Bronze Star medal. Mem. ABA (chmn. com. on condominiums, coops, homeowners assns. 1978-80, sec. real property divsn., sect. real property probate/trust law 1981-83), Ill. State Bar Assn. (real estate sect.), Chgo. Bar Assn. (chmn. real property law com. 1970-71, mem. condominium subcom. 1966-68, mem. exec. coun. 1972-96), Am. Coll. Real Estate Lawyers (gov. 1980-83, sec. 1983-85, v.p. 1985-86, chmn. uniform real property acts com. 1989-95), Anglo-Am. Real Property Inst. (gov. 1985-89), Mid-Day Club Chgo., Pi Lambda Phi. Home: Deerfield Ill. Died Aug. 27, 1996.

GEISMER, ALAN STEARN, lawyer; b. Cleve., May 10, 1917; s. Eugene L. and Mollie (Stearn) G.; m. Barbara Peck, Aug. 2, 1942; children: Alan Stearn Jr., Martha Geismer Ostrum, Mollie R. A.B. magna cum laude, Harvard U., 1938, LL.B., 1941. Bar: Ohio 1941. Clk. to justice Supreme Ct. Ohio, 1941-42; with firm Hahn, Loeser, Freedheim, Dean & Wellman, Cleve., 1946-51, 52-91; ptnr. Hahn, Loeser and Parks and predecessor firms, 1955-91, of counsel, 1970-91. Sec., dir. Child Welfare League Am., 1954-62; hon. life trustee, past pres. Jewish Children's Bur. Cleve. and Bellefaire, Ohio; mem. Shaker Heights (Ohio) Bd. Edn., 1957-67, pres., 1964-66; hon. life trustee, past sec. Musical Arts Assn. operating Cleve. Orch.; past trustee Cleve. Welfare Fedn.; past trustee, v.p. Cleve. Guidance Center. Served to capt. CIC, AUS, 1942-46, 51-52. Mem. ABA, Ohio Bar Assn., Cleve. Bar Assn., Harvard Club (past pres. Cleve.), Rowfant Club (mem. emeritus), Phi Beta Kappa. Home: Cleveland Ohio Died Dec. 26, 1991; interred Mayfield Cemetery, Cleveland, OH.

GELBART, ABE, mathematician, educator; b. Paterson, N.J., Dec. 22, 1911; s. Wolf and Pauline (Landau) G.; m. Sara Goodman, July 2, 1939 (dec. Nov. 23, 1988); children: Carol Marie (Mrs. Ivan P. Auer), Judith Sylvia (dec.), William Michael, Stephen Samuel; m. Mona Siegel, Mar. 4, 1990. B.Sc., Dalhousie U., 1938, LL.D. honoris causa, 1972; Ph.D. in Math, MIT, 1940; D.Sc. (h.c.), Bar-Ilan U., Israel, 1985. Asst. MIT, 1938-40; instr. math. N.C. State Coll., 1940-42; research asso. Brown U., 1942; asso. physicist NACA, Langley Field, Va., 1942-43; asst. prof. to prof. math. Syracuse U., 1943-58; dir. Inst. Math., Yeshiva U., 1958-59; dean Belfer Grad. Sch. Sci., 1959-70, dean emeritus, 1970-94, disting. univ. prof. math., 1968-94; vis. disting. prof. math. Bard Coll. and fellow Bard Coll. Center, 1979-94, David and Rosalie Rose Disting. prof. natural sci. and math., 1983-94; lectr., Sorbonne, Paris, 1949; vis. prof. U. So. Calif., 1951; mem. Inst. Advanced Study, Princeton, 1947-48, 77-81; Fulbright lectr., Norway, 1951-52; mem. directorate math. scis. USAF Office Sci. Research.; vice chmn. bd. dirs., chmn. sci. adv. bd. Daltex Med. Scis., Inc., 1983-94; mem. adv. bd. Inst. for Thinking and Learning, Pace U., 1982-94; founding dir. series, lectures Bard Coll. Scis., 1979-94. Editor: Scripta Mathematica, 1957-94; co-developer theory of pseudo-analytic functions. Trustee, chmn. acad. sci. com. Bar-Ilan U., Israel, 1982-94. Recipient Bard medal, 1981; spl. award of recognition U. Pa. Sch. Nursing; chair in math. named in his honor Bar-Ilan U., 1983; Internat. Rsch. Inst. Math. Scis. Bar-Ilan U. renamed Gelbart Internat. Rsch. Inst. Math. Scis., 1990; appointed fgn. mem. Acad. Tech. Scis. Russian Fedn., 1992. Mem. Am. Math. Soc., Math. Assn. Am., Acad. Ind. Scholars (trustee 1982-94), Russian Acad. Tech. Sci. (fgn.), City Athletic Club, Cosmos Club, Sigma Xi. Home: New York N.Y. Died Sept. 7, 1994.

GELDMACHER, ROBERT CARL, engineering educator; b. Elgin, Ill., Apr. 22, 1917; s. Walter Carl and Emma (Goers) G.; m. Theresa Julia Swanberg, Sept. 27, 1941; children: Ann Marie (Mrs. Peter A. Alicandri), Cecily Louise, Mary Ellen (Mrs. James A. Goble). B.E., No. Ill. U., 1942; M.S., Purdue U., 1946; Ph.D., Northwestern U., 1959. Instr. Naval Tng. Sch., Purdue U., 1943-45, research asst., 1945-47, from asst. prof. to assoc. prof. engring. sci., 1947-60; prof. engring. sci., assoc. dean sch. Engring. and Sci., NYU, 1960-66; Anson Wood Burchard prof. Stevens Inst. Tech., 1966-83, head dept. elec. engring., 1966-76, prof. emeritus, 1983-97; pres., chief exec. officer Sundale Software Corp., 1983-89, chmn. bd. dirs., 1989-96; cons. Dept. Def., 1952-97. NSF Sci. Faculty fellow, 1958-59. Mem. Am. Soc. Engring. Edn., Am. Phys. Soc., AAAS, IEEE, Math. Assn. Am., Soc. Indsl. and Applied Math., AAUP, Sigma Xi, Tau Beta Pi. Rsch. in magneto-elasto-dynamics, combinatorics. Died Dec. 25, 1997.

GELERNT, IRWIN M., surgeon, educator; b. N.Y.C., Sept. 27, 1935; s. Lipman and Ray (Samuels) G.; married, June 11, 1960; children: Lee, Alicia, Michelle. BS, CCNY, 1957; MD, SUNY, N.Y.C., 1961. Diplomate Am. Bd. Surgery. Intern Bellevue Hosp. Cornel Med. Svc.; attending surgeon Mt. Sinai Hosp., N.Y.C., 1962-67, pres. attending staff, 1985-87; clin. prof. of surgery Mt. Sinai Sch. Medicine, N.Y.C., 1987—, dean for hosp. and med. affairs; pres. med. bd. Mt. Sinai Hosp. Contbr. articles to profl. publs., chpts. to books. Trustee Manhattan Country Sch., N.Y.C., 1978-84. Named Physician of Yr., Nurses Assn. of Mt. Sinai Hosp., 1991. Fellow ACS, Am. Coll. Gastroenterology; mem. Found. Ileitis and Colitis (Man of Yr. 1983), Phi Beta Kappa, Alpha Omega Alpha. Died 1997.

GENEEN, HAROLD SYDNEY, communications company executive; b. Bournemouth, Eng., Jan. 22, 1910; came to U.S., 1911, naturalized, 1918; s. S. Alexander and Aida (DeCruciani) G.; m. June Elizabeth Hjelm, Dec. 1949. B.S. in Accounting. and Fin., NYU, 1934; grad., Advanced Mgmt. Program, Harvard U.; LL.D. (hon.), Lafayette Coll., PMC Colls. C.P.A., N.Y., Ill. Accountant and analyst Mayflower Assocs., 1932-34; sr. accountant Lybrand, Ross Bros. & Montgomery, 1934-42; chief accountant Am. Can Co., 1942-46; controller Bell & Howell Co., Chgo., 1946-50, Jones & Laughlin Steel Corp., Pitts., 1950-56; exec. v.p., dir. Raytheon Mfg. Co., Waltham, Mass., 1956-59; pres. ITT, 1959-73, chief exec., 1959-77, dir., 1959-83, chmn. bd., 1964-79, chmn. exec. com., 1974-80, chmn. emeritus, 1980—, also dir. fgn. subs., affiliated cos.; adv. com. Uptown br. Bankers Trust Co. Author: (with Alvin Moscow) Managing, 1984. Bd. dirs. Internat. Rescue Con.; mem. nat. council Salk Inst. Biol. Studies, from 1977; treas. Voice Found. Decorated grand officer Order of Merit Peru; comdr. Order of the Crown, Belgium; Grand Cross of Civil Merit; Grand Cross of Isabella Cath. Mothers of the Americas, Spain; co-recipient 5th Ann. Communications award ICD Rehab. and Research Center, 1976. Mem. Am. Inst. C.P.A.s, Financial Execs. Inst., Soc. C.P.A.s N.Y., Internat. C. of C. (trustee U.S. council). Episcopalian. Clubs: Duquesne (Pitts.); Oakmont Country, Braeburn Country, The Links, Oyster Harbors, Union League (N.Y.C.); Harvard (Boston).

GEOFFEY, RUTH, director activities, artist; b. Brno, Czechoslovakia, July 2, 1915; came to U.S., 1951; d. Theodor and Else (Moser) Huber; m. Joseph Reiner (dec.). BA in Fine Arts, UCLA, 1968. Fashion designer Berlin, 1935-38; freelance illustrator Shanghai, 1939-40; head art dept. Manila-Am. Sch., 1945-62; freelance artist L.A. and San Francisco, 1968-80; dir. activities and programs Aldersly, 1984-94. Mem. Marin Watercolor Sco., AAUW. Jewish. Avocations: painting. Home: San Rafael Calif. Died Sept. 21, 1994.

GEORGE, EDWIN ORDELL, utility executive; b. Petoskey, Mich., Feb. 9, 1905; s. Edward Daley and Ethel (Brott) G.; m. Florence E. Watchpocket, June 6, 1931; 1 dau., Julie Ann George Pope. Student, Alma Coll., 1925; AB, Knox Coll., 1928; postgrad., U. Ill., 1929, Wayne State U., 1938; LL.D., No. Mich. U., 1966. With Detroit Edison Co., 1929—, comml. office clk., supr. tng., asst. supr. comml. office div., supr. comml. office div., asst. comml. mgr., comml. mgr., mgr. sales, 1929-56, v.p., 1956-65, sr. v.p., 1965-67, exec. v.p. for mktg., 1967, pres., 1967-70, dir., 1967—; trustee emeritus 1st Fed. Mich. Bd. dirs., past pres. Detroit Ednl. TV Found.; pres. Traffic Improvement Assn. Oakland County; bd. dirs., v.p. Overseas Adv. Assn., Inc.; bd. dirs., past pres. Detroit Area council Boy Scouts Am.; trustee Detroit Sci. Ctr., Oakland U. Found., United Hosp.; trustee emeritus, mem. exec. com. Alma Coll.; trustee emeritus, mem. bd. control, past chmn. No. Mich. U.; mem. exec. bd., past pres. Greater Mich. Found.; pres. Detroit and Wayne County Tb Found.; mem. Great Lakes Sports Commn., 1987—. Recipient Disting. Alumnus award Knox Coll. Mem. World Soc. Ekistics, Newcomen Soc. N.Am., Pi Kappa Delta, Pi Gamma Nu. Presbyterian (trustee). Clubs: Detroit Athletic (past pres., dir.), Detroit; Circumnavigators (past pres. Mich. br.), Oakland Hills Country. Lodge: Rotary (past pres. Detroit).

GERALD, ELIZABETH BART, painter, designer; d. Edmund Henry and Elsie Augusta (Sprules) Bart; m. John Doby Gerald, Nov. 10, 1930; children: Antonia Bart, John Bart. Student, Cleve. Sch. Art, Sch. Hans Hoffman, W. Ger., Sch. Andre L'Hôte, Paris, Julien Acad., Paris. One woman shows include Cordier-Ekstrom, N.Y., 1977-78, Meredith Long, Houston, 1979, Washington Art Gallery Conn., 1973; group shows include exhibits in Can., U.S., France. Represented in permanent collections Houston Mus. Fine Art, Albright-Knox Gallery, Buffalo, Bklyn. Mus., Cleve. Mus., Cranbrook, Mus., Mich., High Mus., Atlanta, Newark Mus., Vassar Coll. of Art, Whitney Mus. Am. Art, and others. Patentee in field. Mem. Artists Equity.

GERBER, HEINZ JOSEPH, computer automation company executive; b. Vienna, Austria, Apr. 17, 1924; came to U.S., 1940; s. Jacques and Bertha (Spielmann) G.; m. Sonia Kanciper, 1952; children—David Jacques, Melisa Tina. B.S. in Aero. Engring., Rensselaer Poly., 1943, Dr. Engring. (hon.), 1981; Dr. Engring. (hon.), U. New Haven, 1990, U. of Hartford, 1996. Engr. Hamilton Standard, Windsor Locks, Conn., 1947-51, pres., chmn. bd., 1948-96; pres., chmn. bd. Gerber Sci. Inc., South Windsor, Conn.; chmn. bd. Gerber Optical, Inc., Gerber Sci. Products Inc., Gerber Garment Tech. Inc., Gerber Systems Corp. Holder 677 U.S. and fgn. patents issued and pending. Hon. trustee Rensselaer Poly. Inst., Hartford Grad. Ctr. Recipient Eli Whitney award Conn. Patent Law Assn., 1980, Holden medal The Clothing and Fottwear Inst., 1983, Sci. and Tech. award ORT, 1988, Companion Membership award Textile Inst., 1993, Nat. medal of Tech., 1994, Conn. medal of Tech., 1995, Award Smithsonian's Nat. Mus. of Am. History, 1994. Mem. Nat. Acad. Engring. (elected 1982, Lifetime Achievement award in entrepreneurial mgmt. 1989), Conn. Acad. Sci. and Engring. (elected 1983). Died Aug. 8, 1996.

GERENTZ, SVEN THURE, news agency executive; b. Visby, Sweden, Sept. 3, 1921; s. Thure and Elin (Hemstrom) G.; m. Kerstin Blix, Sept. 14, 1945; children: Martin, Anna. Licentiate in Econs., PhD Stockholm Sch. Econs. Sec. Swedish Bd. of Trade, Stockholm, 1945-52; sec. Stockholm C. of C., Stockholm, 1952-57; gen. mgr. Assn. Swedish Automobile Mfrs., Stockholm, 1957-59; dep. gen. mgr. Svenska Dagbladet, Stockholm, 1960-62, gen. mgr., 1962-73, editor-in-chief, 1969-73; gen. mgr. Tidningarnas Telegrambyrå, Stockholm, 1974-86; chmn. Nat. Swedish Rd. Adminstrn., Borlange, 1982-92. Author: The Stockholm Mercantile Marine Office 1748-1948, 1948, Individuals, Families and Blocs, 1994. Mem. Stockholm Club of Mchts. (chmn. 1980-85), Stockholm C. of C. (hon., vice chmn., 1982-91q). Died Jan. 13, 1997.

GERRY, ROGER GOODMAN, retired oral surgeon; b. Far Rockaway, N.Y., Feb. 26, 1916; s. Bernard Abraham and Edith Rose (Goodman) G.; m. Peggy Newbauer, Nov. 6, 1944. AB, U. N.C., 1936; DMD, U. Louisville, 1940; Diplomate Am. Bd. Oral and Maxillofacial Surgery. Commd. lt. (j.g.) Dental Corps., USN, 1941, advanced through grades to capt., 1955; ret. 1965; dir. dental and oral surgery svc. Mt. Sinai Hosp. Svcs., City Hosp. Ctr., Elmhurst, N.Y., 1965-81; attending oral surgeon, head divsn. oral surgery Mt. Sinai Hosp., N.Y.C.; prof. oral surgery Mt. Sinai Sch. Medicine, CUNY. Author: Catalogue of Japanese Ceramics, 1961; contbr to profl jours., Dictionary of Art; contbr. to spl. exhbn. in collection of Japanese Ceramics Met. Mus. Art, 1989-90. Chmn. planning bd. Roslyn, N.Y., 1960-72; pres. Roslyn Preservation Corp., 1964-95, Roslyn Landmark Soc., 1964-95; trustee Bryant Libr., Village Roslyn, N.Y., Preservation League of N.Y. State. Recipient Howard C. Sherwood award Soc. for Preservation Long Island Antiquities, 1976, Nat. Trust Historic Preservation award, 1982, Ann. award Victorian Soc. in Am., 1985, Honor award N.Y. State Preservation League, 1993. Fellow Internat. Am. Coll. Dentists, Internat. Assn. Oral Surgeons, Met. Mus. Art (life), Brit. Assn. Oral and Maxillofacial Surgeons (hon.); mem. Am. Assn. Oral and Maxillofacial Surgeons, Am. Acad. Oral Pathology (emeritus), Am. Dental Assn. (hon.), Soc. Archtl. Historians, Japan Soc. Died May 12, 1995.

GERSHBEIN, LEON LEE, chemist, educator; b. Chgo., Dec. 22, 1917; s. Meyer and Ida (Shutman) G.; m. Ruth Zelman, Sept. 30, 1956; children: Joel Dan, Marcia Renee, Carla Ann. SB, U. Chgo., 1938, SM, 1939; PhD; Northwestern U., 1944. Rsch. assoc. Northwestern U., Evanston, Ill., 1944-47; asst. prof. biochemistry U. Ill. Med. Sch., Chgo., 1947-53; assoc. prof. biology Ill. Inst. Tech., Chgo., 1953-57, adj. prof., 1957-94; pres., dir. Northwest Inst. Med. Rsch., Chgo., 1957-94; dir. labs. Northwest Hosp., Chgo., 1957-86. U. Chgo. scholar, 1936-38; recipient Merit award Chgo. Chromatography Discussion Group, 1978; citations Ill. State Acad. Scis., 1975-79. Fellow Nat. Acad. Clin. Biochemistry; mem. AAAS, Am. Chem. Soc., Am. Inst. Chemists, Am. Oil Chemists Soc., Ill. Acad. Sci., Soc. Exptl. Biol. Medicine, Soc. Applied Spectroscopy, Am. Phys. Soc., Am. Fedn. Clin. Rsch., Am. Assn. Cancer Rsch., Contbr. numerous articles to profl. jours. Died Dec. 7, 1994. Home: Wilmette Ill.

GERSHINOWITZ, HAROLD, chemist, former oil company executive; b. Bklyn., Aug. 31, 1910; s. Louis and Mamie (Leibowitz) G.; m. Mary Piesman, June 14, 1935. BS, CCNY, 1931; AM, Harvard U., 1932, PhD, 1934. Research assoc. Columbia U., 1935-36, Harvard U., 1936-38; research technologist Shell Oil Co., 1938-40, dir. mfg. research, 1940-45, dir. exploration, prodn. research div., 1945-50, v.p. in charge exploration, prodn. tech. div., 1950-52, cons. to pres., 1965-66; pres., dir. Shell Devel. Co., 1953-62; research coordinator, chmn. research council, dir. Royal Dutch Shell Group of Cos., 1962-65; vis. fellow Princeton (N.J.) U., 1935-36; cons. Orgn. for Econ. Cooperation and Devel., 1966-70; Chmn. environ. studies bd. Nat. Acad. Scis-Nat. Acad. Engring., 1967-70; affiliate mem. faculty Rockefeller U., 1967-78, adj. prof., 1979-82. Mem. exec. bd. Council on Environment of N.Y.C., 1973-76. Fellow AAAS; mem. N.Y. Acad. Scis., Am. Chem. Soc., Phi Beta Kappa, Sigma Xi. Clubs: Explorers, Harvard of N.Y, Princeton of N.Y. DIED 07/24/96. .

GERST, ELIZABETH CARLSEN (MRS. PAUL H GERST), university dean, researcher, educator; b. N.Y.C., June 10, 1929; d. Rolf and Gudrun (Wiborg) Carlsen; A.B. magna cum laude, Mt. Holyoke Coll., 1951; Ph.D., U. Pa., 1957; m. Paul H. Gerst, Aug. 3, 1957; children—Steven Richard, Jeffrey Carlton, Andrew Leigh. Instr. physiology Grad. Sch. Medicine, U Pa., 1955-57, Cornell U. Med. Coll., N.Y.C., 1957-58; instr. Columbia Coll. Physicians and Surgeons, N.Y.C. 1959-61, asst. prof., 1961—, dir. Center Continuing Edn. in Health Scis., 1978-87, asst. dean continuing edn., 1984-87, spl. lectr., 1987—, dir. Office Med. Edn. N.Y. Acad. Med., 1987—; Authors: (with others) The Lung, Clinical Physiology and Pulmonary Function Tests, 1955, rev. edit., 1962. Pres. Citizen's Ednl Council Tenafly, 1972-73; mem. Citizens Long-Range Planning Com., Tenafly Bd. Edn., 1973-77, chmn. supt search, edn., tchr. hiring, personnel coms.; vice chmn Tenafly Environ. Commn., 1972-77; trustee Tenafly Nature Center, 1972-80; bd. dirs., chmn. environ quality Tenafly LWV, 1971-78; v.p. Bergen County LWV, 1973-75. Porter fellow Am. Physiol. Soc., 1956-57. Mem. Middle States Assn. Colls. and Schs. (team Commn. on higher edn., 1984—), Soc. Med. Coll. Dirs of Continuing Med. Edn., Am. Physiol. Soc. (task force Women in Physiology 1973-75), N.Y. County Med. Soc (com. on continuing med. edn. 1978—), Physiol. Soc Phila., Harvey Soc., Biophys. Soc., Alliance Continuing Med. Edn., N.Y. Acad. Scis., AAAS, Phi Beta Kappa Sigma Xi, Sigma Delta Epsilon. Unitarian. Died Dec 28, 1994.

GESMER, HENRY, lawyer; b. Quincy, Mass., Apr. 1, 1912; s. Abraham Meyer and Esther Frances (Zide) G.; m. Bessie Nathanson, Nov. 24, 1940; children: Linda Schrank Ohlhausen, Gabriel Myles, Ellen Frances Gesmer Hyde. BS, Harvard U., 1933, JD, 1936. Bar: Mass. 1936, U.S. Dist. Ct. Mass. 1937. Sr. ptnr. Brown, Rudnick, Freed & Gesmer, Boston, 1959—; hon. dir. USTrust, Boston. Hon. trustee Combined Jewish Philanthropies, Boston, 1965—; trustee Soc. Law Libr., Boston, 1988-96; pres. assoc. Harvard U., Cambridge, Mass., 1987; past pres. Jewish Family and Children's Svcs., Jewish Ctrs. Assoc. Greater Boston. Brandeis U. fellow, Waltham, Mass., 1988—. Mem. ABA, Mass. Bar Assn., Boston Bar Assn., Mass. Trial Lawyers Assn. Democrat. Jewish. Died May 26, 1997.

GETMAN, FRANK NEWTON, business consultant; b. Ilion, N.Y., Nov. 5, 1910; s. George B. and Bertha (Myers) G.; m. Dorothy D. Etheridge, Nov. 4, 1941 (dec. July 20, 1979); 1 son, Willard E. A.B., Cornell U., 1932, J.D., 1934. Bar: N.Y. bar 1934. With firm Alfeld, Sowers & Herrick, N.Y.C., 1934-37; atty. Vick Chem. Co., N.Y.C., 1937-42; atty., sec. William S. Merrell Co., Cin., 1946-49; v.p., asst. gen. mgr. William S. Merrell Co., 1949-55, pres., gen. mgr., 1957-62; exec. v.p. Hess & Clark, Inc., Ashland, O., 1955-56; pres. Hess & Clark, Inc., 1956-57, 60-61; v.p. Richardson-Merrell, Inc. (formerly Vick Chem. Co.), N.Y.C., 1959-61; exec. v.p. Richardson-Merrell, Inc. (formerly Vick Chem. Co.), 1961-75; dir. Fifth Third Union Trust Co., Cin., 1959-65. Mem. coun. Cornell U., 1963-69; bd. dirs. Nat. Multiple Sclerosis Soc., 1975-80, mem. nat. adv. coun., 1980-92. Maj. USAAF, 1942-46. Mem. Delray Dunes Country Club (Delray Beach, Fla.), Lambda Chi Alpha. Presbyterian. Home: Boynton Beach Fla. Died Oct. 4, 1992.

GEWIRTZ, JACOB, social science researcher; b. N.Y.C., Apr. 11, 1926; arrived in Eng., 1961; s. Joseph Chaim and Frieda (Horowitz) G.; m. Agathe Hajnal-Konyi, Sept. 18, 1958; children: Deborah, Jonathan, Sharon. BA, Syracuse U., 1949; JD, U. Pa., 1952. Bar: N.Y., 1953. Official Jewish Agy. for Israel, Jerusalem, 1957-59; lit., features editor The Jewish Chronicle, London, 1964-71; exec. dir. Jewish def. and group relations com. Bd. of Deps. of British Jews, London, 1974-86; hon. sr. rsch. fellow The City Univ., London, 1987—; mem. exec. bd. Trades Adv. Council, Eng., 1976, Joint Com. Against Racism, Eng., 1979, Friends of Tel Aviv Univ., Eng., 1987—; cons. Bd. of Deps. of British Jews, 1987—. Served with U.S. Army, 1945-47. Avocation: birdwatching. DIED 09/29/96. .

GIBBONS, JOSEPH JOHN, builders supply company financial executive; b. Wheatland, Wyo., Mar. 18, 1906; s. Michael and Edith (D'Arcy) G.; m. Hazel M. Bisson, Jan. 1, 1930; children: Betty Louise (Mrs. Donald G. Smith), Albert J., Robert J. Ph.B., U. Chgo., 1930; student, Northwestern U., 1931-33, DePaul U. Law Sch., 1933-35. C.P.A., Ill. Office mgr. George Hardin Constrn. Co., Chgo., 1927-35; exam. agt. IRS, 1935-40; sr. tax accountant Arthur Andersen and Co. (C.P.A.'s), Chgo., 1941; tax supr. U.S. Steel Corp., Duluth, Minn. and Pitts., 1941-50; mgr. tax and ins. dept. Mine Safety Appliances Co., 1950-52; with Blaw-Knox Co., 1952-69, treas., 1967-68, v.p. finance, 1968-69; pres. Corde Co., 1967-69; treas. Blaw Knox Can. Ltd., 1967-69; controller Cleve. Builders Supply Co., 1969-71. Mem. Am. Inst. C.P.A.s, Tau Kappa Epsilon, Alpha Kappa Psi. Presbyn. (elder). Club: Deerfield Country. Died April 4, 1996.

GIBBONS, RONALD JOHN, microbiologist, educator; b. N.Y.C., Dec. 10, 1932; s. Ronald John and Martha Edith (Smith) G.; m. Marcia E. Day, Aug. 29, 1959; children: Sarah J., John A., David P. B.S., Wagner Coll., 1954; M.S., U. Md., 1956, Ph.D., 1958; Dr. Odontology (hon.), U. Goteborg, 1977; Dr. Medicine (hon.), U. Utrecht, 1981. Sr. staff mem., head dept. microbiology Forsyth Dental Ctr., Boston, 1958-91, dir., 1991-95; clin. prof. oral biology Harvard U. Sch. Dental Medicine, Boston, 1958-95. Contbr. articles to sci. jours. Recipient USPHS Career Devel. award, 1964-68, Disting. Scientist award Am. Assn. Dental Rsch., 1992. Mem. AAAS, Internat. Assn. for Dental Rsch. (award for basic rsch. in oral sci. 1967, for basic rsch. in dental caries 1990, for disting. scientist 1992), Am. Soc. Microbiology, Sigma Xi. Deceased.

GIBSON, ALEXANDER DRUMMOND, conductor; b. Motherwell, Scotland, Feb. 11, 1926; s. James McClure and Wilhelmina (Williams) G.; m. Ann Veronica Waggett, Feb. 21, 1959; children: James, Philip, John, Claire. Student, Glasgow U., Scotland, Royal Coll. Music, Scoland, Accademia Chigiano, Siena, Italy, Mozarteum, Salzburg, Austria; D, U. Stirling, 1972, U. York, 1991; D (hon.), Open U., 1978; MusD (hon.), Newcastle U., 1990. Prin. condr., dir. music Scottish NAt. Orch., 1959-84, hon. pres., 1984-95; founder, artistic dir. Scottish Opera, 1962-85, music dir., 1985-87, founder, condr. laureate, 1987-95; prin. guest condr. Houston Symphony Orch., 1981-83; repetiteur, asst. condr. Sadler's Wells Opera, 1951-52, staff condr., 1954-57, musical dir., 1957-59; asst. condr. BBC Scottish Orch., Glasgow, Scotland,1952-54. With Royal Signals, 1944-48. Recipient St. Mungo prize, 1970, Arnold Bax Meml. medal, 1959, Sibelius medal, 1978, Musician of Yr. award ISM, 1976, Brit. Music Yr. Book, 1980. Mem. Garrick Club, Oriental Club. Home: Edinburgh Scotland Died Jan. 14, 1995.

GIBSON, CHARLES COLMERY, former rubber manufacturing executive; b. Edwards, Miss., Sept. 12, 1914; s. William Bayne and Anna (Colmery) G.; m. Margaret Eaton, Nov. 4, 1939; children—William Bayne II, John Clark. A.B., Harvard, 1937, grad. Advanced Mgmt. Program, 1953. With Goodyear Tire & Rubber Co., Akron, Ohio, 1937-73, v.p., 1956-73. Trustee John S. and James L. Knight Found., 1975—. Served from ensign to lt. comdr. USNR, WWII. Died June 22, 1997.

GIBSON, DAVID ARGYLE, lawyer; b. Austin, Tex., Apr. 10, 1934; s. Benjamin Argyle and Virginia Claire (Ratlif) G.; m. Yahne Peto, 1981; children: Diane, Laura, Julie. B.S., U. Houston, 1955, J.D., 1957. Bar: Tex. 1957; Cert. in family, civil trial and criminal law Tex. Bd. Legal Specialization. Asst. dist. atty. Harris County, Tex., 1957-59; practiced law Houston, 1959—; mem. firm Engel, Groom, Miglicco and Gibson, 1975—; Lectr. U. Houston Law Sch., 1975—; pres. Tex. Bill of Rights Found., 1974-75. Chmn. Democratic County Com., 1966-67; bd. dirs. Gulf Coast Legal Found., 1980—. Mem. Houston Bar Assn., Assn. Trial Lawyers Am., Cert. Civil Trial Lawyers Assn. (pres. 1981-82), Tex. Assn. Civil Trial Specialists, Am. Arbitration Soc. (arbitrator 1970—), Gulf Coast Family Lawyers Assn. (pres. 1987-88, David A. Gibson award of excellence 1990).

GIDDINGS, J. CALVIN, chemistry educator. Disting. prof. dept. chemistry U. Utah, Salt Lake City. Author: Dynamics of Chromatography, Chemistry, Man, and Environmental Change, Unified Separation Science. Recipient award in chromatography and electrophoresis Am. Chem. Soc., 1967, award in analytical chemistry, 1980, award in separations sci. and tech., 1986, William H. Nichols medal, 1991, Martin award The Chromatography Soc., London, 1988. Died Oct. 24, 1996.

GIESECKE, G(USTAV) ERNST, education educator emeritus; b. Marble Falls, Tex., Sept. 13, 1908; s. Walter C. and Ulrika (Matern) G.; m. Louise Helene Bittner, Sept. 17, 1943; children—Mark Ernst, Helene Louise Ebrill. A.B., Stanford U., 1931, A.M., 1934, Ph.D., 1938; LL.D., U. Toledo, 1962. Teaching asst. German Stanford U., 1932-37; instr. and asso. in German, counselor student personnel bur. U. Ill., 1937-42, supr. counseling in residence halls, 1946, asst. dean liberal arts sch., asst. prof. German, 1946; asst. dean U. Ill. (Galesburg (Ill.) undergrad. div.), asst. prof. German, 1946-49; dean sch. applied arts and scis. N.D. State U., Fargo, 1949-53; v.p. Tex. Tech. U., Lubbock, 1953-59; prof. higher edn., asso. dean Grad. Sch. Edn., U. Chgo., 1959-65; univ. prof., provost U. Toledo, 1965-70; prof. humanities, acting v.p. acad. affairs Sangamon State U., Springfield, Ill., 1970-71; prof. higher edn., dir. ednl. relations Sangamon State U., 1971-76, prof. emeritus, 1976-95; planning cons. to alt. system of higher edn. in, Ill., 1976-95; founder N.D. Inst. for Regional Studies, 1950, exec. sec., 1950-53, dir. summer session, 1950-53; Mem. SW adv. com. Inst. Internat. Edn., 1958-59; mem. visitation and appraisal com. Nat. Council Accreditation Tchr. Edn., 1963-66; cons., examiner N. Central Assn. Colls. and Secondary Schs., 1960-72; chmn., dir. Midwest Fulbright Terminal Conf., 1964; chmn. Mayor's com. on the Young Citizen and the Ballot, 1956-58; mem. Tex. adv. com. conservation edn., 1956-59; chmn. Lubbock Internat. Affairs Com., 1954-59; mem. research adv. com. Tex. Commn. Higher Edn., 1956-59; chmn. Mental Health Week in Lubbock, 1958; co-dir. Ill. observance 75th anniversary of creation of first jr. coll., Joliet, 1974-77; mem. research adv. council Ill. Community Coll. Bd., 1972-81; mem. liaison com. Am. Assn. Community and Jr. Colls. Council Univs. and Colls. and Nat. Council State Dirs. Community and Jr. Colls., 1976-78; head study tour, guest Fed. Republic Germany, 1958, Yugoslavia, 1974, USSR, 1976, Taiwan, 1981. Author: N.D. Inst. for Regional Studies, Fargo, 1952, An Alternative System of Higher Education in Illinois, 1973; Contbr. articles to profl. publs.; Founder: Community Coll. Frontiers, Quar, 1972. Trustee Toledo Ednl. Television Found., 1967-70; pres. Springfield Local Devel. Corp., 1980-95. Served as lt. USNR, 1942-46. Fellow Inst. Internat. Edn. Germany, 1931-32. Mem. Ill. Community Coll. Faculty Assn. (life), Am. Ednl. Research Assn. (mem. com. 1967-70), West Tex. C. of C. (dir. 1957-58). Home: Springfield Ill. Died Jan. 4, 1995.

GIESEKE, ELMER W. (JAKE GIESEKE), mining consultant; b. Concordia, Mo., 1927. BS in Metallurgical Engring., U. Mo. With U.S. Bur. Mines, Rolla, Mo.; from truck driver to chief chemist Potash Co. Am., Carlsbad, N.M.; with United Feldspar and Minerals, Spruce Pine, N.C.; with rsch. dept. Am. Cyanamid Co., Stamford, Conn., field work; cons. on kyanite oper. Contbr., supr. chpt. to Mineral Processing Handbook. Recipient Howard N. Eavenson award Soc. Mining, Metallurgy and Exploration, 1996. Achievements include design of flocculant system to remove coal from water, development of ilmenite, apatite, kyanite, iron ore, glass sands, etc. processes, sulfonates in nonmetallic flotation industry, patents for reagents in several non-metallic minerals systems. Deceased.

GILES, HOMER WAYNE, lawyer; b. Noble, Ohio, Nov. 9, 1919; s. Edwin Jay and Nola Blanche (Tillison) G.; m. Marcia Ellen Hurt, Oct. 3, 1987; children: Jay, Janice, Keith, Tim, Gregory. A.B., Adelbert Coll., 1940; LL.B., Western Res. Law Sch., 1943, LL.M., 1959. Bar: Ohio 1943. Mem. firm Davis & Young, Cleve., 1942-43, William I. Moon, Port Clinton, Ohio, 1946-48; pres. Strabley Baking Co., Cleve., 1948-53; v.p. French Baking Co., Cleve., 1953-55; law clk. 8th Dist Ct. Appeals, Cleve., 1955-58; ptnr. Kuth & Giles, Cleve., 1958-68, Walter, Haverfield, Buescher & Chockley, Cleve., 1968—; pres. Clinton Franklin Realty Co., Cleve., 1958—, Concepts Devel., Inc., 1980—; sec. Holiday Designs, Inc., Sebring, Ohio, 1964—; trustee Teamster Local 52 Health and Welfare Fund, 1950-53; mem. Bakers Negotiating Exec. Com., 1951-53. Contbr. articles to profl. publs.; editor: Banks Baldwin Ohio Legal Forms, 1962. Troop com. chmn. Skyline council Boy Scouts Am., 1961-63; adviser Am. Security Council; trustee Hiram House Camp, Florence Crittenton Home, 1965; chmn. bd. trustees Am. Econ. Found., N.Y.C., 1973-80, chmn. exec. com., 1973-80; mem. Heritage Found. Served with AUS, 1943-46, ETO. Mem. Am. Bar Assn., World Law Assn. (founding), Am. Arbitration Assn. (nat. panel), Com. on Econ. Reform and Edn. (life), Inst. Money and Inflation, Speakers Bur. Cleve. Sch. Levy, Citizens League, Pacific Inst., Phila. Soc., Aircraft Owners and Pilots Assn., Cleve. Hist. Soc., Mus. Modern Art, Met. Mus., Mercantile Libr,, Delta Tau Delta, Delta Theta Phi. Unitarian. Clubs: Cleve. Skating, Cleve. Econ., Harvard Bus., The City, Cleve. City, Cleve. Econs.

GILL, BRENDAN, writer; b. Hartford, Conn., Oct. 4, 1914; s. Michael Henry Richard and Elizabeth (Duffy) G.; m. Anne Barnard, June 20, 1936; children: Brenda, Michael, Holly, Madelaine, Rosemary, Kate, Charles. AB, Yale U., 1936. Contbr. The New Yorker, 1936—, film critic, 1961-67, drama critic, 1968-87, architecture columnist, 1987-97. Author: Death in April and Other Poems, 1935, The Trouble of One House, 1950 (Nat. Book award 1951), The Day the Money Stopped, 1957 (adapted into play with Maxwell Anderson, 1958), La Belle, 1962, (with Robert Kimball) Cole: A Book of Cole Porter Lyrics and Memorabilia, 1971, Fat Girl, 1971, Tallulah, 1972, The Malcontents, 1972, Ways of Loving, 1974, Here At The New Yorker, 1975, New York Custom House on Bowling Green, 1976, Lindbergh Alone, 1977, (with Dudley Witney) Summer Places, 1977, (with Derry Moore) The Dream Come True, 1980, Wooings, 1980, John F. Kennedy Center for the Performing Arts, 1982, A Fair Land to Build In: The Architecture of the Empire State, 1984, Many Masks: A Life of Frank Lloyd Wright, 1987, A New York Life: Of Friends and Others, 1990; editor: Happy Times by Jerome Zerbe, 1973, States of Grace, Eight Plays by Philip Barry, 1975, Letters to Phil: Memories of a New York Boyhood, 1848-1856, 1982, Flatiron: A Photographic History of the World's First Steel Frame Skyscraper, 1903-1989, 1990, Late Bloomers, 1996. Chmn. Warhol Found. for Visual Arts; chmn. emeritus Inst. for Art and Urban Resources, N.Y., Landmarks Conservancy of N.Y.; bd. dirs. Film Soc. Lincoln Ctr., MacDowell Colony, Mcpl. Art Soc., Whitney Mus. Am. Art, N.Y.C., Pratt Inst. Art, N.Y.C., MacDowell Colony. Mem. AAAL, Irish Georgian Soc., Victorian Soc. Am. Club: Century Assn. (N.Y.C.). Died Dec. 27, 1997.

GILLER, ROBERT MAYNARD, physician; b. Chgo., Sept. 14, 1942; s. Edward M. and Lillian (Katz) G. Student, U. Ill., 1960-63, MD, 1967; postgrad., Columbia U., 1979—. Intern U. Ill., 1967-68; resident in internal medicine Cornell Hosp., N.Y.C., 1968-69, pvt. practice medicine specializing in preventive medicine, 1974-96; mem. faculty New Sch. Social Rsch., 1975-96. Author: A Guide for Health, 1982, Medical Makeover, 1986, Maximum Metabolism, 1989, Natural Prescriptions, 1994. With U.S. Army, 1969-71. Fellow Am. Coll. Preventive Medicine, Internat. Acad. Preventive Medicine, Am. Acad. Family Physicians; mem. AMA (Physician Recognition award 1982, 90, 96). Home: New York N.Y. Died Oct. 19, 1996.

GILLESPIE, ALEXANDER JOSEPH, JR., lawyer; b. N.Y.C., Sept. 2, 1923; s. Alexander Joseph and Catharine (Allen) G.; m. Elizabeth Margaret Roth, Dec. 4, 1944; children: Robert Daniel, James Edward, William Gerard, Patricia Elise, Anne Marie. A.B. magna cum laude, Dartmouth Coll., 1943; J.D., Fordham U., 1957. Credit mgr. cosmetic div. Vick Chem. Co., 1946-50; dist. sales mgr. Avco Mfg. Co., 1950-54; assoc. atty. Breed, Abbott & Morgan, 1957-60; asst. gen. counsel ASARCO Inc. (formerly Am. Smelting & Refining Co.), N.Y.C., 1960-68; sec. ASARCO Inc. (formerly Am. Smelting & Refining Co.), 1968-69, sec., gen. counsel, 1969-86, v.p., 1972-77, sr. v.p., sec., gen. counsel, 1977-84, vice chmn., gen. counsel, 1984-86, vice chmn., dir., 1984-89; of counsel Breed, Abbott & Morgan, N.Y.C., 1989-93; arbitrator Nat. Assn. Security Dealers, Am. Arbitration Assn. Mem. adv. bd. S.W. Legal Found., Parker Sch. Internat. Law, Columbia U.; bd. dirs. Bruce Mus. Inc., Round Hill Assn. Lt. (j.g.) USNR, 1943-46, PTO. Mem. ABA, N.Y. State Bar Assn., Conn. Bar Assn., N.Y. County Lawyers Assn., Americas Soc., The Corp. Bar Fairfield and Westchester Counties, Assn. Gen. Counsel, Yale Club, Stanwich Club.

GILMER, B. VON HALLER, retired educator, industrial psychologist; b. Draper, Va., June 15, 1909; s. Beverly Tucker and Willie Sue (Graham) G.; m. Ellen Conduff, Aug. 23, 1934; 1 child, Nancy Tucker. BS, King Coll., 1930; MS, U. Va., 1932, PhD, 1934. Instr. psychology King Coll., Bristol, Tenn., 1934-36; asst. prof. psychology Carnegie Inst. Tech. (now Carnegie-Mellon U.), 1936-42, prof. psychology, dept. head, 1947-76; prof. psychology Va. Poly. Inst. and State U., 1976-84; asso. prof. psychology U. Va., 1946-47; vis. prof. U. Calif-Berkeley, 1964-65; adviser U.S. Office Edn., 1949-51; cons. USAF, 1950-51. Author: 18 books on psychology, including Industrial and Organizational Psychology, 4th edit, 1977, Applied Psychology, 1975; also numerous research publs.; edited family genealogy book. Bd. dirs. Pitts. Child Guidance Center, Inc., 1952-94, Mental Health Soc. Allegheny County, 1954-94, Sta. WQED Pitts.; mem. bd. visitors King Coll., 1970-76. Served from 1st lt. to maj. USAAF, 1942-46. Recipient Nat. Author award Am. Soc. Tng. and Devel., 1966. Fellow Am. Psychol. Assn. (mem. edn. and tng. bd. 1955-57), Eastern Psychol. Assn.; mem. So. Soc. Philosophy and Psychology (pres. 1948), Va. Psychol. Assn. (award for disting. contbns. to applied psychology 1986), Pitts. Psychol. Assn. (dir. 1950-51), Sigma Xi, Phi Kappa Phi, Phi Sigma Pi. Presbyn. Died Sept. 1, 1994.

GINGRAS, GUSTAVE, physician; b. Outremont, Que., Can., Jan. 18, 1918; s. Gustave and Augusta (Descaries) G.; m. Rena MacLean, July 13, 1948 (dec. 1983); m. Camille De La Chevrotière, Jan., 1988. BA, Bourget Coll., Rigaud, Que., 1936; MD, U. Montreal, 1943; LLD (hon.), Sir George Williams U., 1967, U. Winnipeg, 1970, U. Western Ont., 1971, McMaster U., 1982, U. P.E.I., 1987; DM (hon.), U. Sherbrooke, 1973; DCL (hon.), Bishop's U., 1974; DSc (hon.), St. Mary's U., 1984; DSc, DM, U. Paris, 1988. Diplomate: Am. Bd. Phys. Medicine and Rehab. Founding exec. dir. Rehab. Inst. Montreal, 1949-76; chief of service, phys. medicine and rehab. Queen Mary Vets. Hosp. and D.V.A. Montreal Dist., Can., 1945-76; chancellor U. P.E.I. (Can.), Charlottetown, 1974-82, chancellor emeritus, 1993; dir. rehab. svcs., med. dir. Rehab. Centre, P.E.I. Dept. Health, 1977-81; mem. Can. Forces Med. Coun., 1973-92 , chmn., 1984; life gov. Cerebral Palsy Assn. Que., hon. v.p. Can. Nat. Inst. for Blind, 1975-92 ; mem. Can. Social Scis. and Humanities Rsch. Coun., 1978-84 , mem. exec. bd., 1983-84; mem. sci. and tech. com. CBC, 1979-81; appointed Hon. Physician to Queen Elizabeth II, 1982; cons. med. rehab. WHO, 1955-84; prof. phys. medicine and rehab. Faculty of Medicine, U. Montreal, 1954-76, emeritus prof. medicine, 1977—; past mem. numerous adv. coms. in field; pres. St. John Ambulance Council P.E.I., 1981-91. Contbr. numerous articles to profl. publs. pres. P.E.I. Hosp. Assn., 1980-84. Served with R.C.A.M.C., 1941-46. Decorated companion Order of Can., Order of Compassion, Can. Centennial medal; knight of justice Order St. John of Jerusalem; Knight Grace of Malta; cavaliere Order St. Agatha Republic of San Marino; Order Cedar of Lebanon; officer of Order of Ouissam Alouite (Morocco); recipient Silver medal of Internat. Coop., 1965; Humanitarian award B'nai Brith, 1966, Albert Lasker award Internat. Soc. Rehab. of Disabled, 1969, Outstanding Citizen award Montreal Citizenship Council, 1970, Royal Bank of Can. award, 1972, medal of Honour, Pharm. Mfrs. Assn. Can., 1973, F.N.G. Starr award Can. Med. Assn., 1978, Province Que. Hosp. Assn. award, 1980, Keith Armstrong award Can. Rehab. Coun. for the Disabled, 1977, Commemorative medal 125th Anniversary Confedn. Can., 1992, medal honor Faculty Medicine U. Montreal, 1993, medal of Honor Les Plus Grands Invalides de Guerre, France, 1992; named hon. col. 35th Med. Co. N.S., 1990. Fellow Royal Coll. Physicians Can., Am. Acad. Phys. Medicine and Rehab., Internat. Coll. Surgeons, Am. Geriatric Soc.; mem. Can. Med. Assn. (pres. 1972-73), Can. Assn. Phys. Medicine and Rehab. (past pres.), Can. Coll. Health Svc. Execs., L'Association des medecins de langue française du Canada, Fedn. des medecins specialistes de Que., Med. Coun. P.E.I., P.E.I. Hosp. Assn. (pres. 1989), Med. Soc. P.E.I., Royal Soc. Medicine, Internat. Med. Soc. Paraplegia, Internat. Rehab. Medicine Fedn. (past pres.), Internat. Soc. Prosthetics and Orthotics, Sociedad Colombiana de Medicina Fisica y Rehabilitacion (corr.), Heraldry Soc. Can., Can. R.R. Hist. Assn.; hon. mem. AMA, Def. Med. Assn. (hon. v.p.), World Fedn. Health Profls., (commr.) Can. Red Cross Soc., phys. medicine and rehab. socs. of Italy, Venezuela, Uruguay, Mex., Spain, Argentina, France, Belgium, and Brazil. Deceased.

GINSBERG, ALLEN, poet, photographer, musician; b. Newark, June 3, 1926; s. Louis and Naomi (Levy) G. AB, Columbia U., 1948. With various cargo ships, 1945-56; book reviewer Newsweek, N.Y.C., 1950; market rsch. cons. N.Y.C. and San Francisco, 1951-53; instr. U. B.C., Vancouver, Can., 1963; co-founder, co-dir. Kerouac Sch. of Disembodied Poetics, Naropa Inst., Boulder, Colo., 1974-83, dir. emeritus, from 1983; disting. prof. Bklyn. Coll., 1986-97; resident lectr. Va. Mil. Inst., 1991-97; founder, treas. Com. on Poetry Found., 1966-97; organizer Gathering of the Tribes For a Human Be-In, San Francisco, 1967. Assoc. with early Beat Generation prose-poets, 1945-97; actor: motion picture PullMy Daisy, 1961, Guns of the Trees, 1962, Couch, 1964, Wholly Communion, 1965, Allen for Allen, 1965, U.S.A. Poetry: Allen Ginsberg and Lawrence Ferlinghetti, 1966, Joan of Arc, 1966, Galaxie, 1966, Chappaqua, 1966, Herostratus, 1967, The Mind Alchemists, 1967, Don't Look Back, 1967, Renaldo and Clara, 1978, Fried Shoes, Cooked Diamonds, 1978, This is For You, Jack, 1984; narrator: film Kaddish, NET, 1977; author: (poetry) Howl and Other Poems, 1955, Siesta in Xbalba and Return to the States, 1956, Empty Mirror, 1961, Kaddish and Other Poems, 1961, Reality Sandwiches, 1963, A Strange New Cottage in Berkeley, 1963, The Change, 1963, (with William Burroughs) The Yage Letters, 1963, Kral Majales, 1965, Wichita Vortex Sutra, 1966, TV Baby Poems, 1967, Airplane Dreams, 1968, (with Alexandra Lawrence) Ankor Wat, 1968, Scrap Leaves, 1968, Wales: A Visitation, 1968, The Heart is a Clock, 1968, Message II, 1968, Planet News: Poems 1961-67, 1968, Indian Journals, 1970, For the Soul of the Planet is Waking..., 1970, The Moment's Return: A Poem, 1970, Notes After an Evening with William Carlos Williams, 1970, Ginsburg's Improvised Poetics, 1971, Declaration of Independence for Dr. Timothy Leary, 1971, New Year Blues, 1972, Open Head, 1972, Bixby Canyon Ocean Path Word Breeze, 1972, Iron Horse, 1972, The Fall of America: Poems of these States, 1973 (Nat. Book award for poetry 1974), The Gates of Wrath: Early Rhymed Poems 1948-51, 1973, Allen Verbatim, 1974, Sad Dust Glories: Poems During Work Summer in Woods, 1974, Gay Sunshine Interview: Allen Ginsberg with Allen Young, 1974, The Vision of the Great Rememberer, 1974, First Blues, 1975, To Eberhart from Ginsberg: A Letter About Howl, 1976, The Dream of Tibet, 1976, (with Jack Kerouac) Take Care of My Ghost, Ghost, 1977, Journals Early 50's Early 60's, 1977, Mind Breaths, Poems 1972-1977, 1978, As Ever: Correspondence A.G. and Neal Cassady 1948-68, 1978, Poems All Over the Place: Mostly Seventies, 1978, Careless Love: Two Rhymes, 1978, Mostly Sitting Haiku, 1979, Composed on the Tongue, Literary Conversations, 1967-77, 1980, Straight Hearts Delight: Love Poems and Selected Letters, 1980, Plutonian Ode and Other Poems 1977-1980, 1982 (L.A. Times Book prize for poetry 1982), Collected Poems, 1947-80, 1984, Many Loves, 1984, Old Love Story, 1986, White Shroud: Poems 1980-85, 1986, Annotated Howl, 1986, Your Reason and Blake's System, 1989, The Hydrogen Jukebox (libretta), 1990, Allen Ginsberg: Photographs, 1990, Snapshot Poetics, 1993, Cosmopolitan Greetings Poems, 1986-1992, 1994, Journals 1954-1958, 1995, Selected Poems 1947-95, (illus. by Eric Drooker) Illuminateed Pours, 1996; recs. include Songs of Innocence and of Experience by William Blake Tuned by Allen Ginsberg, 1970, First Blues: Songs, 1982, Birdbrain, 1981, The Lion For Real, 1989; Holy Soul Jelly Roll Poems and Songs, 1949-93, 1994, Rhino Records; (opera) Hydrogen Jukebox Philip Glass Music Allen Ginsberg: Libretta; collaborated with Timothy Leary on works concerning anti-war new-consciousness movement, (with Paul McCartney, Lenny Kaye, Philip Glass) Ballad of The Skeletons, 1996, (with Kronos Quartet, Music by Lee Hyla) Howl USA, 1996. Gay activist. Decorated chevalier l'Ordre des Arts et de Lettres (France); Guggenheim fellow in poetry, 1965-66, NEA fellow, 1986, Am. Acad. Arts and Scis. fellow, 1992; NEA grantee, 1966; recipient Woodbury Poetry prize, Nat. Inst. Arts and Letters award, 1969, Nat. Arts Club Honor medal for lit., 1979, Golden Wreath prize, 1986, Gold medal Poetry Soc. Am., 1986, Manhattan Borough Pres. Dinkens' award for arts excellence, 1989, Lifetime Achievement award Before Columbus Found., 1990, Harriet Monroe Poetry award U. Chgo., 1991. Mem. PEN (v.p. Am. chpt. 1987-88), Am. Inst. Arts and Letters. Buddhist. Home: New York N.Y. Died Apr. 5, 1997; interred B'nai Israel, Elizabeth, NJ.

GINSBERG, EDWARD, lawyer; b. N.Y.C., May 30, 1917; s. Charles and Rose G.; m. Rosalie Sinek, Aug. 11, 1941; children—William, Robert. B.A. with honors, U. Mich., 1938; J.D., Harvard, 1941; D.H.L., Hebrew Union Coll., 1972. Bar: Ohio bar 1941. Former sr. partner law firm Ginsberg, Guren & Merritt; former exec. v.p. and trustee U.S. Realty Investments; past partner N.Y. Yankees Am. League baseball club; past dir. El Al Israel Air Lines, Chgo. Bulls Nat. Basketball Assn., First Israel Bank & Trust Co. N.Y.; counsel Dinn, Hochman & Potter, Cleve. Past pres., mem. exec. com., nat. campaign cabinet United Jewish Appeal, formerly gen. chmn.; v.p. Jewish Telegraphic Agy.; former chmn. Am. Jewish Joint Distbn. Com., now hon. pres.; v.p. Hebrew Sheltering and Immigrant Aid Soc.; life trustee United Israel Appeal, Jewish Community Fedn. Cleve., Mt. Sinai Hosp., Jewish Convalescent Home Cleve. With USAAF. Hon. fellow Hebrew U., Jerusalem. Mem. Cleve. Bar Assn. (life), Ohio State Bar Assn., Phi Kappa Phi, Phi Sigma Delta. Jewish religion (pres. temple). Died Jan. 3, 1997.

GINSBERG, LEWIS ROBBINS, lawyer; b. Chgo., May 7, 1932; s. Maurice Jesse and Zelda (Robbins) G.; m. Linda Cox, June 16, 1973; children: Aaron, Brenda, Stephen. AB, U. Chgo., 1953, JD, 1956. Bar: Ill. 1956. Assoc. Lederer, Livingston, Kahn & Adsit, Chgo., 1956, 60-63; corp. atty. Maremont Corp., Chgo., 1963-66; assoc. firm McDermott, Will & Emery, Chgo., 1966-69, ptnr., 1969-89; pvt. practice Chgo., 1990-93; ptnr. Much Shelist Freed Denenberg & Ament, P.C., Chgo., 1994-95. Contbr. articles to profl. jours. Bd. dirs. Ravenswood Hosp. Med. Ctr., Chgo., 1981-88. Capt. U.S. Army, 1957-60. Mem. Order of Coif. Democrat. Jewish. Died Oct. 3, 1997.

GINSBURG, MARCUS, lawyer; b. Marietta, Ohio, Feb. 16, 1915; s. Louis and Dora (Brachman) G.; m. Martine Heilbron, Feb. 23, 1949; children: Harold Heilbron, Robert L. Student, Marietta Coll., 1932-33; A.B., U. Mich., 1936; J.D., Harvard U., 1939. Bar: Md. 1939, Tex. 1940. Assoc. Simon & Wynn, 1939-42; ptnr. Simon, Wynn, Sanders & Jones, 1945-51; mng. ptnr. McDonald, Sanders, Ginsburg, Newkirk, Gibson & Webb, 1951-90, of counsel, 1990; of counsel McDonald Sanders, 1991—. Pres. United Fund and Community Services, Fort Worth, 1962, Tarrant County Community Council, 1966-67, Traveller's Aid Soc., Fort Worth, 1953-54; vice chmn. city solicitations commn., 1963-67; past trustee Am. Jewish Congress; past v.p. Nat. Community Relations Adv. Council; mem. U.S. nat. commn. UNESCO, 1959-64, exec. com., 1963-64, steering com., 1964, chmn. pub. info. com., 1962-64; past v.p., treas. Children's Mus. Fort Worth; mem. Nat. Budget and Consultation Com., 1966—; mem. exec. com. Community Trust Fund of Tarrant County; trustee Retina Research Found.; bd. dirs. Modern Art Mus. of Fort Worth, trustee Community Trust of Ft. Worth. Served to 2d lt. USAAF, 1942-45. Decorated Army Commendation medal; recipient award excellency United Fund Fort Worth, award Fort Worth Traveller's Aid Soc. Fort Worth Community Council, Humanitarian award Nat. Jewish Hosp., 1989. Mem. Harvard Law Sch. Assn. (life mem., pres. Tex. 1955-56, nat. v.p. 1956-57, dir. 1978), Assn. Life Ins. Council, Tex. Assn. Bank Attys., Nat. Assn. Coll. and Univ. Attys., Newcomen Soc. N.Am., Confrerie des Chevaliers du Tastevin (commandeur N.Tex. chpt.), Pi Lambda Phi. Clubs: Shady Oaks Country. DIED 09/05/96. .

GIOVANNITTI, LEN, writer; b. N.Y.C., Apr. 16, 1920; s. Arturo and Carrie (Zaikaner) G.; m. Sara Steinberg, Aug. 28, 1943 (div. May 1977); children: David, Nina. B.S., St. John's U., 1942. Labor journalist, 1946-58; asst. prof. Inst. Film and TV, Sch. Arts, N.Y. U., 1978. Free-lance writer, 1959- 61, tv documentary writer, 1961-62; writer, dir., producer: NBC News, 1962-70; producer, writer, dir.: The Decision of Japan to Surrender, 1965; producer, writer: NBC TV documentaries Lyndon Johnson's Texas, 1966, The Am. Alcoholic, 1968; assoc. producer NBC TV documentaries, NBC, White Paper programs The Death of Stalin, 1963, The Rise of Khrushchev, 1963; asso. producer: NBC TV documentaries Cuba: The Bay of Pigs, 1964, Cuba: The Missile Crisis, 1964; assoc. producer: NBC TV documentaries The Decision to Drop the Bomb, 1965; writer: ABC TV documentaries Winston Churchill: The Valiant Years, 1961, Walking Hard, 1962; producer, writer: ABC TV documentaries Black Business in White America, ABC News, 1972; The Energy Crisis (NBC White Paper), 1973, And Who Shall Feed This World?(NBC White Paper), NBC News, 1974; Author: Sidney Hillman: Labor Statesman, 1948; novel The Prisoners of Combine D, 1957 (ALA liberty and justice award 1958); history The Decision to Drop the Bomb, 1965; novel The Man Who Won The Medal of Honor, 1973, novel The Nature of the Beast, 1977. Served with USAAF, 1942-45. Recipient Lasker Med. Journalism award, 1969, Ohio State U. award, 1969, Peabody award, 1975. Mem. PEN, Authors Guild, Writers Guild Am. East. Died March 27, 1992.

GITTLIN, ARTHUR SAM, industrialist, banker; b. Newark, Nov. 21, 1914; s. Benjamin and Ethel (Bernstein) G.; m. Fay Lerner, Sept. 18, 1938; children: Carol Franklin, Regina (Mrs. Peter Gross), Bruce David, Steven Robert. BCS, Newark U., 1938. Ptnr. Gittlin Bag Co. (name now changed to Gittlin Cos. Inc.), Livingston, N.J., No. Miami, Fla., N.Y.C., 1935-40; v.p., dir. Gittlin Bag Co., 1954—, chmn. bd., 1963—; v.p., dir. Abbey Record Mfg. Co., Newark, 1958-60; chmn., treas. Packaging Products & Design Co. (now PPD Corp.), Newark and Glendale, Calif., 1959-71, chmn. exec. com., treas., 1972—; chmn. Pines Shirt & Pajama Co., N.Y.C., 1960-85, Pottsville Shirt & Pajama Co. (Pa.), 1960—, Barrington Industries, N.Y.C., 1963-72, First Peninsula Calif. Corp., N.Y.C., 1964-68, Peninsula Savs. and Loan, San Francisco and San Mateo, Calif., 1964-68, Wall-co Imperial, Miami, Fla., 1965-87, Levin & Hecht, Inc., N.Y.C., 1966-72, Wallco of San Juan (P.R.), Brunswick Shirt Co., N.Y.C., 1966-72, Fleetline Industries, Garland, N.C., 1966-72, All State Auto Leasing & Rental Corp., Beverly Hills, Calif., 1968-72, Packaging Ltd., Newark, 1970-76, Kans. Plastics, Inc., Garden City, 1970-76, Bob Cushman Distbrs., Inc. (now Wallpapers Inc.), Phoenix, 1972-87, Wallpaper Supermarkets, Phoenix, 1976-80, Wallco Internat. Inc., Miami, 1976, Overwrap Equipment Corp., Fairfield, 1978-86, GCI Ala. Inc., Birmingham, 1981—; chmn. Wallpapers Inc., Oakland, Calif., 1982-86, Portland, Oreg., Honolulu, Denver, L.A. and Phoenix, 1982-86; pres. Covington Funding Co., N.Y.C., 1963—; vice chmn. bd. Peninsula Savs. and Loan Assn., San Mateo and San Francisco, 1964-67, chmn., 1967-68; chmn. bd., treas. Bob Cushman Painting & Decorating Co. (now Wallco West), Phoenix, 1972-86; treas., dir. Flex Pak Industries, Inc., Atlanta, 1973-76, Ploy Plax Films, Inc., Santa Ana, Calif., 1973-76; sec., chmn. exec. com. Zins Wallcoverings, Newark; v.p., bd. dirs. JKG Printing & Graphics, Boca Raton, Fla., 1994—; ptnr. Benjamin Co., Livingston, N.J., Laurel Assocs. (Md.), Seaboard

Realty Assocs., Miami, 1980—, GHG Realty Assocs., N.Y.C., 1980, Parkway Assocs., Miami, 1987—; ptnr., investors cons. Mission Pack, Inc., L.A.; vice chmn., dir., chmn. exec. com. Falmouth Supply, Ltd., Montreal, Que., Can., Ascher Trading Corp., Newark, Aptex, Inc., Newark; v.p., dir. JKG Printing and Graphics, Boca Raton, Fla., 1994—; bd. dirs., fin. cons. Ramada Inns, Phoenix; bd. dirs., fin. cons. Aztar Corp., Phoenix; bd. dirs. Harris Paint & Wall Covering Super Marts, Miami, Morgan Hill Mfg. Co., Reading, Pa., Douglas Gardens Home for the Aged, Miami. Chmn. N.C. com. B'nai B'rith, 1940; treas. N.C. Fedn. B'nai B'rith Lodges, 1941-43, v.p., 1943-44, pres., 1944-47; mem. com. to rev. dept. banking and ins. N.J. Commn. on Efficiency and Economy in State Govt., 1967-69; trustee Benjamin Gittlin Charity Found., Newark, BAMA Master Retirement Program, Hillel Found. at Rutgers U., Temple Emanuel, Miami, hon. v.p., bd. dir.; founders bd. Miami Gardens Home Aged. Mem. Greenbrook Country Club (Caldwell, N.J.), B'nai B'rith. Jewish (trustee Temple Emanuel, Miami, 1987—). Deceased.

GIUS, JULIUS, retired newspaper editor; b. Fairbanks, Alaska, Dec. 31, 1911; s. Julius and Mary (Sarja) G.; m. Elizabeth Gail Alexander, Aug. 24, 1940; children—Gary Alexander, Barbara Gail. Student, U. Puget Sound, 1930-33. Reporter Tacoma (Wash.) Times, 1929-35; founding editor Bremerton (Wash.) Sun, 1935-60; editor Ventura (Calif.) Star-Free Press, 1960-87; also editorial dir. John P. Scripps Newspapers, 1961-85. Mem. Am. Soc. Newspaper Editors, Sigma Delta Chi. Clubs: Elk, K.C, Rotarian. Died Oct. 18, 1996.

GLASIER, ALICE GENEVA See KLOSS, GENE

GLASS, WILLIAM EVERETT, physician; b. Amarillo, Tex., May 14, 1906; s. William P. and Gertrude (Compton) G.; m. Margaret H. Quam, Nov. 21, 1931; children—William Lewis, Cynthia Anne Paige. B.S., U. Ill., 1928, M.D., 1931. Diplomate: Am. Bd. Psychiatry and Neurology. Staff physician Worcester (Mass.) State Hosp., 1931-36; city physician Marlboro, Mass., 1936-37; asst. supt. Grafton (Mass.) State Hosp., 1938-47; hosp. insp. Boston Dept. Mental Health, 1947-48; supt. Taunton (Mass.) State Hosp., 1948-73; instr. psychiatry Tufts U. Med. Sch., 1939-48; dir. clinics Bristol County Mental Health Inst., 1949-65; cons. psychiatry Sturdy Meml. Hosp., Attleboro, Mass., 1960-95, Union, Truesdale hosps., Fall River, Mass., 1960-95, Morton Hosp., Taunton, 1967-95. Fellow AMA, Am. Psychiat. Assn.; mem. Mass. Med. Soc., Mass. Soc. Research Psychiatry, New Eng. Soc. Psychiatry (past pres.), Am. Soc. Clin. Hypnosis. Club: Rotarian. Home: Taunton Mass. Died Jan. 14, 1995.

GLASSER, OTTO JOHN, former business executive, former air force officer; b. Wilkes-Barre, Pa., Oct. 2, 1918; s. Leo George and Lillian (Cave) G.; m. Norma Mayo, Sept. 11, 1943 (dec.); children: Charlene Lee, Carole Jeanne; m. Eugenia Kolakowski, May 12, 1990. E.E., Cornell U., 1940; M.S. in Elec. Engring, Ohio State U., 1947. Test engr. Gen. Electric Co., 1940-41; commd. 2d lt. U.S. Army, 1941; advanced through grades to lt. gen. USAF, 1969, dir. Atlas and Minuteman programs, 1954-59, asst. dep. chief staff research and devel. Hdqrs., 1966-69, dep. chief staff research and devel., 1969-73; v.p. internat. Gen. Dynamics Corp., St. Louis, 1973-76; v.p. internat. Washington, 1976-85, v.p. govt. relations, 1985-86, ret., 1986. Decorated D.S.M. Legion of Merit, Air Force Commendation medal, Legion d'Honneur France). Died Feb. 26, 1996.

GLEASON, JOHN MARTIN, community development consultant; b. N.Y.C., May 10, 1907; s. James S. and Letitia (Haydock) G.; m. Margaret Nicholson, Oct. 15, 1929; children: Nancy (Mrs. Nancy G. Scrantom), John Martin. Student, Columbia, 1927, N.E. Traffic Officers Tng. Sch., Harvard U., 1936, Northwestern Traffic Safety Inst., 1936, Northwestern Exec. Officers Tng. Sch., 1938-41, Rutgers U., 1940, Yale, 1941, 43; grad., FBI Nat. Acad., 1944. Cadet engr. Conn. Light & Power Co., 1927-30; with Greenwich (Conn.) Police Dept., 1930-56, beginning as patrolman, successively detective, sgt., lt., capt., chief of police, 1930-54, town chief adminstrv. officer, 1954-56; nat. dir. Boys' Clubs of Am., 1956-69, also bd. dirs.; coord. community devel. action plan Greenwich, 1969-71; instr. FBI Acad., Washington, 1945-55; guest lectr. Northeastern U., Northwestern U., Yale, Columbia; mem. adv. com. N.Y. U. Grad. Sch. Pub. Adminstrn.; Chmn. state and local ofcls. Nat. Hwy. Safety Commn.; pub. safety specialist U.S. Army in, Germany, 1949, Office U.S. High Commr. for, Germany, Office Polit. Affairs, 1951; mem. Atty. Gen.'s Conf. Organized Crime, Washington; staff Pres.'s Hwy. Safety Conf.; gen. chmn. traffic sect., mem. exec. com. Nat. Safety Council, Chgo.; police cons. U.S. Office Civil Def.; nat. com. Uniform Traffic Laws and Ordnances, 1947-95; exec. v.p. Putnam Hill Apts. Inc. Mem. Citizens Adv. Com. on Fitness Am. Youth.; rep. non-govtl. orgn. UN, for Boys' Clubs of Am.; bd. dirs. ARC, Conn. Assn. Mental Health, Community Chest; pres. Greenwich Safety Council, 1965-70; mem. Pres.'s Task Force on Crime and Law Enforcement, 1969-95. Recipient spl. honor diploma Cuban Soc. Police Sci. and Criminalistics, 1949; diploma of honor Bd. Traffic Control, Fed. Republic Germany, 1952. Mem. Internat. Assn. Chiefs Police (pres. 1950, life mem. exec. com.), N.E. Chiefs Police Assn. (dir.), Internat. Assn. Identification, Conn. Police Assn. (life mem.), Nat. Safety Council, Detective Endowment Assn., Nat. Law Enforcement Assns., Greenwich Taxpayers Assn., Jr. C. of C., Nat. Inst. Social Sci. N.Y.C., Nat. Assn. Realtors, Conn. Assn. Realtors, Greenwich bds. realtors. Clubs: K.C. (Greenwich), Kiwanis (Greenwich), Boat and Yacht (Greenwich), Rotary (Greenwich) (hon.), Kiwanis (Greenwich) (charter); Union League (N.Y.C.); Harpoon, The 13 (pres.). Home: Charleston S.C. Died Jan. 10, 1995.

GLEASON, RALPH NEWTON, economic development consultant; b. Townville, S.C., Jan. 5, 1922; s. Arthur Bryan and Clara Belle (McAdams) G.; m. Marjorie Nelle Little, Apr. 4, 1942; children: Ralph Newton Jr., Delno Rex, Charles Stanley, Edward Dean, Cindy Ann. BS with honors, Clemson Coll., 1942; certificate, Internat. Corr. Schs., 1957, U.S. Dept. Agr. Grad. Sch., 1957; MS, Ohio State U., 1963; cert., Grad. Realtors Inst., 1992. Lic. real estate agt., S.C. Statis. adviser to South Korean interim govt., 1947-48; food and econ. adviser ECA, Seoul, Korea, 1949-50; chief food and fertilizer div. Sino-Am. Joint Commn. Rural Reconstrn., Taipei, Taiwan, 1950-56; agrl. programs officer Near East South Asia FOA, Washington, 1957-58; dep. chief agriculturist Tech. Cooperation Mission to India, New Delhi, 1958-62; chief food and agr. div. Econ. Mission to Turkey, 1963-68; dep. dir. Agr. and Rural Devel. Service Office War on Hunger, Washington, 1968-70; dep. asso. dir. food and agr. AID, South Vietnam, 1970-75; econ. devel. cons., 1975-96; gen. mgr. Gleason Properties, Anderson, 1989-96; with Vance Wells Realty, 1993-96. Mem. dels. UN Food and Agr. Agy. Confs.; bd. dirs., treas. Taipei Am. Sch., 1950-56; bd. dirs. Ponderosa Parks-Lake Hartwell, 1974-93. Served to maj. AUS, 1942-47, ETO, Korea. Decorated Silver Star, Bronze Star. Mem. Am. Fgn. Svc. Assn., Blue Ridge Rural Electric Co-op, Phi Kappa Phi, Alpha Zeta. Lodge: Mason. Died Mar. 2, 1996.

GLOTH, ALEC ROBERT, retail grocery executive; b. Spokane, Wash., Mar. 26, 1927; s. Erich Carl and Ella L. (Felsch) G.; m. Catharine E. Seabloom, May 26, 1954; children: A. Stephen, Rebecca J. Parlet. Grad., Stanford exec. program Boise State U., 1975. With Albertson's, 1951—; v.p. mktg. Albertson's, Boise, Idaho, 1972-74, v.p. store planning, 1974-76, dist. mgr., 1976-77; v.p., div. mgr. Albertson's, Spokane, Wash., 1977-79; sr. v.p., regional mgr. Albertson's, Boise, 1979-81, sr. v.p. store planning, 1981—. Active Boy Scouts Am., Eagle Scout; bd. dirs. Discovery Ctr. Idaho. With U.S. Army, 1954-56. Mem. Am. Mgmt. Assn., Food Mktg. Inst. Republican. Methodist. Clubs: Exchange, Hillcrest Country, Spokane. Lodge: Elks. Deceased.

GLUECK, HELEN IGLAUER, physician; b. Cin., Feb. 4, 1907; d. Samuel Iglauer and Helen R. Ransohoff; 1 child, Charles. BA, Wisc. U., 1929; MD, Cin. U., 1934. Instr. U. Cin. Dept. Med., 1945-59; asst. prof. U. Cin. Dept. Med. Hematol, 1959-65; prof. U. Cin. Dept. Med. Hematol., 1965-78; prof. emeritus U. Cin. Depts. Med. and Pathology, 1979-95; dir. coagulation research; dir. rsch. U. Cin., Dept. Pathologist, 1956-95. Contbr. 91 articles to profl. jours. Bd. mem. Hebrew Union Coll., Cin. 1972-95. Fellow Am. Coll. Physicians, mem. Internat. Thrombosis and Hemostasis. Jewish. Avocations: gardening, travelling, reading, golf, archaeology. Home: Cincinnati Ohio Died Aug. 8, 1995.

GLYNN, WILLIAM THOMAS, JR., entrepreneur, lawyer; b. Newark, Feb. 6, 1921; s. William T. Marie (Grant) G.; m. Jean Patricia Bagger, June 20, 1953; children: William T. III, Diane P., Thomas M., Denis C., Michael C., Timothy G., Sharon A., Kathleen T. BBA, St. Bonaventure (N.Y.) Coll., 1943; JD, Fordham U., 1950. Bar: N.J. 1949, N.Y. 1952, Fed. Dist. Ct. 1949. Acct. various orgns., 1946-52; v.p., treas. Wah Chang Corp. (now Teledyne, Inc.), N.Y.C., 1952-69; exec. v.p. Benilite Corp., N.Y.C., 1969-79; pres. Multi Resources Internat., N.Y.C., 1969-81; chmn. Hitox Corp., Corpus Christi, Tex., 1974-83; chmn., pres. Applied Microwave Devices Corp., Belmar, N.J., 1983-90; pres. GMK Resources, Inc., Wall, N.J., 1990—, DMN, Inc., Wall. Mayor, commr. Allenhurst, N.J., 1970-80, 84-88; pres. bd. edn., Allenhurst, 1966-70; mem. planning bd., bd. adjustment, Allenhurst, 1980-84. With U.S. Army, 1943-46, ETP, with USAR, 1951-66. Avocations: golf, sports.

GODDU, ROLAND JEAN-BERCHMANS, college dean; b. Holyoke, Mass., Aug. 1, 1936; s. Jean-Berchmans and Irene Marie (Quenneville) G.; m. Priscilla Lillian Moquin, June 30, 1962; children: Christopher Roland, Teresa Alice, Caroline Irene. AA, Oblate Coll., 1956, AB, 1959; MEd, U. Mass., 1962; EdD, Harvard U., 1966. Asst. dir. MA in Teaching programs Harvard U., Cambridge, Mass., 1964-66; dir. MA in Teaching programs Trinity Coll., Washington, 1966-68; dean Sch. of Edn. The Cath. U. of Am., Washington, 1968-70; exec. dir. New Eng. Program in Tchr. Edn. Inc., Durham, N.C., 1970-79; dean Coll. of Edn. Northeastern U., Boston, 1978-80; dean School of Edn. Rollins Coll., Winter Park, Fla., 1980-84; dir. R&D edn. Harcourt Brace Jovanovich Inc., Orlando, Fla., 1984-88; CEO Commonwealth & Canney Ltd., Durham, N.H., 1988-90; sr. fellow Edn. Devel. Assocs., Durham, N.H., 1988-93; dean Sch. of Edn. and Profl. Studies Coll. of Boca Raton, Fla., 1990-92; assoc. commr. for tchr. edn. and cert., exec. sec. Edn. Profl. Stds. Bd., Ky. Dept. Edn., 1993-95; bd. dirs. Nat. Adv. Com. on the Edn. of the Deaf, Washington, 1967-80. Author: Networks, 1977; creator Places of Learning map, 1986, interactive videodisc in Math & Reading & Instrn., 1984-88. Bd. dirs. Atlantic Ctr. for the Arts, New Smyrna Beach, Fla., 1984-89. Recipient Cert. of Appreciation U.S Office Edn., 1980. Mem. National Counsel for Accreditation for Teacher Education (unit accreditation bd.), Am. Edn. Rsch. Assn., Phi Delta Kappa. Home: Boca Raton Fla. Died Sept. 25, 1995.

GODUNOV, ALEXANDER BORIS, ballet dancer, actor; b. Sakhalin Island, USSR, Nov. 28, 1949; came to U.S., 1979; s. Boris Ilaryion and Lydia Nicolaivna (Studensova) G.; m. Ludmilla Vlasova, Oct. 1971 (div.). Student, Riga Music Sch., 1958-67, Riga Choreography Sch., 1967, Stella Adler Acting Sch., after 1981. Dancer, actor various cos., USSR and U.S., 1967—. Dancer with Igo Moiseyev's Young Ballet Co., 1958-66; prin. dancer Bolshoi Dance Co., 1967-79, Am. Ballet Theater, N.Y.C., 1979-82, premier dancer, 1980-82; TV appearance in Godunov: The World to Dance In, 1983-84; appeared in movies Anne Karenina, 1975, Witness, 1985, The Money Pit, 1986, Die Hard, 1988, The Runestone, 1992, Waxwork Two: Lost in Time, 1992, North, 1994; freelance guest artist numerous world tours. Recipient Gold medal Moscow Internat. Compeition, 1973. DIED 05/18/95. .

GOE, GERALD LEE, organic chemist, research director; b. Kansas City, Mo., Aug. 17, 1942; s. Tom A. and Lucille (Bauer) G.; m. Mary Ellen Stapleton; 1 child, Jason Andrew. BS, U. Mo., 1963; PhD, MIT, 1967. Postdoctoral fellow Iowa State U., 1967-69; asst. prof. U. Notre Dame, 1969-73; sr. rsch. chemist Reilly Industries, Inc. (formerly Reilly Tar & Chem. Corp.), Indpls., 1973-77, assoc. dir. rsch., 1977-80, dir. rsch., 1980—. Author: (audio course) Applications of Orbital Symmetry, 1974; contbr. articles to profl. jours.; patentee in field. Fellow NSF, 1964-66, NIH, 1966-67. Mem. AAAS, Am. Chem. Soc., Soc. Chem. Industry, Phi Beta Kappa, Sigma Xi, Alpha Chi Sigma. Avocations: fishing, fly-tying.

GOFF, JAMES ALBERT, medical center administrator, civil engineer; b. Hyannis, Mass., Sept. 16, 1941; s. James Satterlee and Evelyn Cornelia (Williams) G.; m. Gail Dorothy Smith, Aug. 24, 1963; children—James Satterlee II, Melissa Anne. B.S.C.E., U. Ill., 1963; M.H.A., U. Minn., 1972. Registered profl. engr., Ill. Asst. hosp. dir. VA Med. Ctr., Spokane, Wash., 1972-73; asst. dir. field ops. VA Central Office, Washington, 1973-74, asst. dir. field ops., San Francisco, 1974-75; dep. exec. asst. VA Med. Dist. 27, San Francisco, 1975-76; asst. dir. VA Med. Ctr., Cleve., 1976-79; dir. VA Med. Ctr., Boise, Idaho, 1979-96. Bd. dirs. Statewide Health Coordinating Council, Boise, 1980-87, Idaho Health Systems Agy., Boise, 1980-87, Boise chpt. ARC, 1981-87, Univ./Community Health Scis. Assn., Boise, 1981-96, v.p., 1984-96; bd. dirs. United Way of Ada County, Idaho, 1984-85; adj. regent Am. Coll. Healthcare Execs., 1984-85, regent for Idaho chpt., 1985—. Served to capt. U.S. Army, 1964-67. Fellow Am. Coll. Hosp. Adminstrs. (regent for Idaho 1985-96); mem. Idaho Hosp. Assn. (bd. dirs. 1987-96), Fed. Health Care Execs. Alumni Assn., Fed. Exec. Council (pres. Boise chpt. 1983), Sr. Execs. Assn. (sr. exec. VA chpt. 1981-96). Episcopalian. Lodge: Rotary. Died 1996.

GOFORTH, WILLIAM CLEMENTS, lawyer; b. Danville, Va., July 10, 1937; s. Henry Earl and Naomi Rivers (Hill) G.; m. Bonita May Karlstrom, Dec. 4, 1971. BA, U. S.C., 1959, MA, 1960; JD, Am. U., 1978. Bar: Va 1979, N.C. 1979, U.S. Dist. Ct. (ea. dist) Va 1979, U.S. Ct. Appeals (4th cir.), 1979, U.S. Ct. Appeals (fed. cir.) 1993, U.S. Ct. Mil. Appeals 1984, U.S. Ct. Vets. Appeals 1991, U.S. Supreme Ct. 1982. Commd. 2d lt. USAF, 1959, advanced through grades to lt. col., 1980; spl. agt. USAF Office Spl. Investigation, Washington, 1960-80; staff atty. Def. Privacy Bd. Sec. of Def., Washington, 1980-84; sole practice Alexandria, Va., 1984-95; cons. Office Sec. of Def., Washington, 1985, N.G. Bur., 1986, Bur. Pub. Dept., 1989; mem. com. on legal edn. and admission to bar Va. State Bar, 1986-89, bd. govs. gen. practice sect., 1988-95, chair, 1991-92, 94-95. Mem. ATLA, ABA (chmn. govt. access-privacy com., adminstr. law sect. 1984-85, vice chmn. solo and small firms and milit. law coms. gen. practice sect. 1992-95), Fed. Bar Assn., Va. Trial Lawyers Assn., Va. Bar Assn., N.C. Bar Assn., Nat. Orgn. of Vet. Advocates, Am. Soc. Access Profls. (v.p. 1982-83, bd. dirs. 1991-93, Outstanding Achievement award 1982), Assn. Fed. Investigators (cert.), Assn. Record Mgrs. (award 1976), U. S.C. Alumni Assn., Am. U. Alumni Assn. (alumni rels. com. 1984-89), VFW, Am. Legion, Ret. Officers Assn., Veitnam Vets. Am., Former OSI Spl. Agts. (exec. dir.), Masons, Shriners. Avocations: coin collecting, stamps. Died Aug. 3, 1995.

GOGLIA, GENNARO LOUIS, mechanical engineering educator; b. Hoboken, N.J., Jan. 15, 1921; s. Fred Goglia and Rose (Coppola) G.; m. Lieselotte Pause, Oct. 4, 1942; children: Diann, Linda. B.S., U. Ill., 1942; M.S., Ohio State U., 1950; Ph.D., U. Mich., 1959. Registered profl. engr., Ohio, Mich. Jr. engr. Rochester Ordnance Dist., N.Y., 1942- 44; devel. engr. Gen. Electric Co., 1945-47; tech. writer Detroit Edison Co., 1951-54; engring. cons. Overhead Heaters Co., Detroit, 1957-58; instr. Ohio State U., 1947-51; asst. prof. U. Detroit, 1951-59; assoc. prof., acting head mech. engring. dept. N.C. State Coll., 1961-62; prof., head dept. mech. engring. U. Maine, Orono, 1962-64; prof., head power and energy conversion Old Dominion Coll., Norfolk, Va., 1964; prof., chmn. dept. thermal engring. Old Dominion Coll., 1965-71, 72-73, asst. dean engring., 1971-72, prof., chmn. mech. engring., 1973-79, Eminent prof. and chmn. mech. engring., 1979-84, Eminent prof., 1984-86, emeritus prof., 1986-94; co-dir. Am. Soc. Engring. Edn.-NASA Langley Research Center Summer Faculty Insts., 1967-79; cons. NASA, 1966-79; dir. research projects NSF. Contbr. articles to profl. jours. Recipient Disting. Faculty award Old Dominion U., 1983; DuPont research grantee, 1960; Am. Soc. Engring. Edn.-NASA postdoctoral fellow, summers 1965-66. Fellow ASME (cert. award 1963, chmn. Norfolk group 1966-67); mem. Am. Soc. Engring. Edn., Sigma Xi (chpt. pres. 1966-67), Tau Beta Pi, Pi Tau Sigma, Phi Kappa Phi. Home: Norfolk Va. Died Nov. 23, 1994.

GOIZUETA, ROBERTO CRISPULO, food and beverage company executive; b. Havana, Cuba, Nov. 18, 1931; came to U.S., 1964; s. Crispulo D. and Aida (Cantera) G.; m. Olga T. Casteleiro, June 14, 1953; children: Roberto S., Olga M., Javier C. BS, BChemE, Yale U., 1953; degree (hon.), U. Notre Dame, 1995. Process engr. Indsl. Corp. Tropics, Havana, 1953-54; with tech. dept. Coca-Cola Co., Havana, 1954-61; asst. to sr. v.p. Coca-Cola Co., Nassau, Bahamas, 1961-64; asst. to v.p. R&D Coca-Cola Co., Atlanta, 1964-66, v.p. tech. R&D, 1966-74, sr. v.p., 1974-75, exec. v.p., 1975-79, vice chmn., 1979-80, pres., COO, 1980-81, chmn. bd., CEO, 1981—; bd. dirs. SunTrust Banks, Inc., Ford Motor Co., SONAT Inc., Eastman Kodak; trustee Emory U., 1980—, The Am. Assembly, 1979—, Boys and Girls Clubs Am., Robert W. Woodruff Arts Ctr., 1990—. Recipient Svc. to Democracy award Am. Assembly, 1990, Equal Justice award NAACP Legal Def. Fund, 1991, Disting. Pub. Svcs. award Advt. Coun., 1994. Mem. Bus. Coun., Bus. Roundtable Policy Com., Points of Light Initiative Found. Died Oct. 18, 1997.

GOLAND, MARTIN, research institute executive; b. N.Y.C., July 12, 1919; s. Herman and Josephine (Bloch) G.; m. Charlotte Nelson, Oct. 16, 1948; children—Claudia, Lawrence, Nelson. M.E., Cornell U., 1940; LL.D. (hon.), St. Mary's U., San Antonio. Instr. mech. engring. Cornell U., 1940-42; sect. head structures dept. research lab., airplane div. Curtiss-Wright Corp., Buffalo, 1942-46; chmn. div. engring. Midwest Research Inst., Kansas City, Mo., 1946-50; dir. for engring. scis. Midwest Research Inst., 1950-55; v.p. Southwest Research Inst., San Antonio, 1955-57; dir. Southwest Research Inst., 1957-59, pres., 1959—; pres. S.W. Found. Biomed. Rsch. (formerly S.W. Found. Rsch. & Edn) San Antonio, 1972-82; dir. Nat. Bancshares Corp. Tex., 1972-87; chmn. subcom. vibration and flutter NACA, 1952-60; chmn. research adv. com. on aircraft structures NASA, 1960-68, chmn. materials and structures group, aeros. adv. com., 1979-82; sci. adv. com. Harry Diamond Labs., U.S. Army Materiel Command, 1955-75; adv. panel com. sci. and astronautics Ho. of Reps., 1960-73; mem. adv. bd. on undersea warfare Dept. Navy, 1968-70, chmn., 1970-73; mem. spl. aviation fire reduction com. FAA, 1979-80; sci. adv. panel Dept. Army, 1966-77; chmn. U.S. Army Weapons Command Adv. Group, 1966-72; mem. materials adv. bd. NRC, 1969-74; vice-chmn. Naval Research Adv. Com., 1974-77, chmn., 1977; dir. Nat. Bank Commerce, San Antonio, 1969-90; dir. Engrs. Joint Council, 1966-69; mem. adv. group U.S. Armament Command, 1972-76; mem. sci. adv. com. Gen. Motors, 1971-81; mem. Nat. Commn. on Libraries and Info. Scis., 1971-78; chmn. NRC Bd. Army Sci. and Tech., 1982-89; chmn. Commn. Engring. and Tech. Systems, NRC, 1980-86. Editor: Applied Mechanics Review, 1952-59; editorial adviser, 1959-84. Bd. govs. St. Mary's U., San Antonio, 1970-76, 85-94; pres. San Antonio Symphony, 1968-70, chmn. bd., 1970-71; bd. dirs. So. Meth. U. Found. Sci. and Engring., Dallas, 1979-90; trustee Univs. Rsch. Assocs., Inc., 1979-84; mem. Tex. Nat. Rsch. Lab. Commn., 1986-91. Recipient Spirit of St. Louis Jr. award ASME, 1945, Jr. award, 1946, Alfred E. Noble prize ASCE, 1947, Outstanding Civilian Svc. award U.S. Army, 1972, 88, Nat. Engring. award, 1985, W.W. McAllister Patriotism award, 1986, Herbert Hoover medal, 1987, Citation, Air Force Assn., 1996; named Employer of Yr. Nat. Employee Svcs. and Recreation Assn., 1993. Fellow AAAS, Am. Inst. Aeros. and Astronautics (pres. 1971); hon. mem. ASME (dir., mem. bd. tech., mem. tech. devel. com., v.p. communications); mem. NAE, Soc. Automotive Engrs., C. of C. (bd. dirs.), Sigma Xi, Tau Beta Pi. DIED 10/29/97. .

GOLAY, FRANK HINDMAN, retired economist; b. Windsor, Mo., July 2, 1915; s. Frank Leslie and Alice (Hindman) G.; m. Clara Ruth Wood, Oct. 23, 1945; children: Frank Hindman, John Wood, David Clark, Jane White. B.S. in Edn, Central Mo. State Coll., Warrensburg, 1936; M.A. in Econs, U. Chgo., 1948, Ph.D., 1951; LL.D., Ateneo de Manila U., 1966. Economist internat. div. Fed. Res. System, 1950-52; mem. faculty Cornell U., Ithaca, N.Y., 1953-85; prof. econs. Cornell U., 1962-80, prof. Grad. Sch. Bus., 1983-85, chmn. dept., 1963-67, assoc. dir. Cornell Southeast Asia program, 1961-70, dir., 1970-76; vis. lectr. U. London Sch. Oriental and African Studies, 1965-66; dir. London-Cornell Project, 1968-70, Cornell Philippines Project, 1967-74; vis. prof. sch. econs. U. Philippines, 1973-74. Author: The Philippines: Public Policy and National Economic Development, 1961; editor: The Santo Tomas Story (A.V.H. Hartendorp), 1964; editor, contbr.: American Assembly, The U.S. and The Philippines, 1966; co-author: Land and People in 1990: Philippine Rice Needs, Output and Input Requirements, 1967, Underdevelopment and Economic Nationalism in Southeast Asia, 1969, 1980's Project, Diversity and Development in Southeast Asia, 1977. Served to lt. comdr. USNR, 1941-45. Decorated Silver Star medal with gold star, Bronze Star; Fulbright fellow, 1955-56; Guggenheim and Social Sci. Research Council fellow, 1960-61; Nat. Endowment for Humanities fellow, 1977-78. Mem. Assn. Asian Studies (pres. 1985-86), Asia Soc. (chmn. Philippines council 1964-67), Nat. Acad. Scis. (Pacific sci. bd. Philippines com.).

GOLDBERG, HAROLD H., finance company executive. Sr. v.p., chmn. corp. ratings com. Moody's Investors Svc., Inc., N.Y.C.

GOLDEN, ALFRED, pathologist; b. N.Y.C., Aug. 4, 1908; s. Bernard and Rheba (Dryer) G.; m. Libby Siegel, Sept. 8, 1955; children—David Alfred, Frederick Leonard. B.S., U. Wis., 1930, M.S., 1932; M.D., Washington U., St. Louis, 1938. Diplomate Am. Bd. Pathology. Assoc. prof. pathology U. Tenn., Memphis, 1946-48, U. Buffalo, 1948-55; dir. labs. Jennings Meml. Hosp. and Blain Meml. Hosp., Detroit, 1955-72, St. Vincent Med. Ctr., Toledo, Ohio, 1972-77; cons. pathologist Takoma Park Gen. Hosp., Md., 1942-46; cons. to hosps. and med. ctrs., Detroit, 1955-72. Contbr. articles to profl. publs. Bd. dirs., pres. Physicians for Social Responsibility, Phoenix, 1981—. Served to lt. col. USMC, 1941-46. Fellow Am. Coll. Pathologists, ACP, Am. Soc. Clin. Pathologists; mem. Am. Cancer Soc. (v.p., bd. dirs. Ariz. div. 1984—), Scottsdale Ctr. for Arts. Club: Mens League (Scottsdale, Ariz.) (bd. dirs. 1982—).

GOLDMAN, ROBERT HURON, lawyer; b. Boston, Nov. 24, 1918; s. Frank and Rose (Sydeman) G.; m. Charlotte R. Rubens, July 5, 1945; children: Wendy Eve, Randolph Rubens. A.B., Harvard U., 1939, LL.B., 1943. Bar: N.Y. State 1945, Mass. 1951. Practiced in N.Y.C., 1945-50, Lowell, Mass., 1951—; law clk. Judge Learned Hand, U.S. Ct. Appeals, 1943-44; partner firm Goldman and Curtis (and predecessor firms), 1951—; columnist Lowell Sun. Sun and The Lowell Sun, 1954-78; v.p., assoc. pub. Malden (Mass.) Evening News, 1969-86, Medford (Mass.) Daily Mercury, 1969-86, Melrose (Mass.) Evening News, 1969-86; mem. adv. bd. Baybank iddlesex, 1966-84; radio commentator on internat. affairs, 1954-86. Author: A Newspaperman's Handbook of the Libel Law of Massachusetts, 1966, rev., 1974, The Law of Libel—Present and Future, 1969; Editor: Harvard Law Review, 1943. Chmn. Greater Lowell Civic Com., 1952-55, Lowell Hist. Soc., 1957-60, Lowell Devel. and Indsl. Commn., 1959-60; Del. Republican State Conv., 1960-62; Bd. dirs. Boston World Affairs Council, 1960-82. Named Citizen of Year Greater Lowell Civic Com., 1956. Mem. ABA (mem. nat. com. on consumer protection 1972-73, Sherman Act com. 1973—), Mass. Bar Assn. (chmn. bar-press com. 1973-76), Middlesex County Bar Assn., Lowell Bar Assn., Boston Bar Assn., Phi Beta Kappa. Club: Harvard (dir. Lowell 1968—). Office: 4th Ave Fl 144 Lowell MA 01854-2706

GOLDOWSKY, SEEBERT JAY, surgeon; b. Providence, R.I., June 6, 1907; s. Bernard Manuel and Antoinette (Lotary) G.; m. Gertrude Nisson. AB, Brown U., 1928; MD, Harvard U., 1932. Diplomate Am. Bd. Surgery. Intern Beth Israel Hosp., Boston, 1932-34; resident neurosurgery Boston City Hosp., 1934; resident surgery Mt. Sinai Hosp., N.Y.C., 1935; surgeon-in-chief Miriam Hosp., 1960-64, R.I. Hosp., Providence; emeritus lectr. surgery Brown U. Author: Yankee Surgeon: The Life and Times of Usher Parsons, MD 1788-1868, 1988, A Century and a Quarter of Spiritual Leadership: The Story of the Congregation of the Sons of Israel and David, 1989; editor-in-chief R.I. Med. Jour., 1961-88. Recipient Charles L. Hill award R.I. Med. Soc., 1990, Founders Day award Soc. of Friends of Touro Synagogue Nat. Hist. Shrine, 1997. Mem. AMA, ACS, Internat. Coll. Surgeons. Home: Providence R.I. Died Nov. 5, 1997; Interred Temple Beth-El Cemetery, Providence, RI.

GOLDSTEIN, DAVID GARSON, electro-optical executive, marketing professional; b. Rochester, N.Y., Oct. 25, 1914; s. Samuel Isahia and Ida Dora (Steinborg) G.; m. Jenette Glazer, June 18, 1944; children: Alben, Ferne, Stafford, Benson, Darice, Julian, Jackie, Jeremy. BS, U. Rochester, 1938, MS in Optical Engring., 1942. Optical engr. Ilex Optical Co., Rochester, 1938-40; pres. Elgeet Optical Co., Rochester, 1946-67; pres. D.O. Industries, Rochester, 1967-91, chmn. bd., 1991-94; pres. Amarel Precision Optics, Rochester, 1980-86. Treas. United Jewish Appeal, Rochester, 1950-52. Mem. Optical Soc. (pres. Rochester chpt. 1989-90), Soc. Photog. Engrs., Rochester C. of C., Eastman Mus. Jewish. Avocations: golf, tennis, reading, photography, international travel.

GOLDSTEIN, MENEK, neurochemistry educator; b. Poland, Apr. 8, 1924; s. Jacob and Ceylia (Hirsch) G. PhD, U. Berne, Switzerland, 1955; D Medicine (hon.), Karolinska Inst., 1982. Rsch. asst. in biochemistry U. Berne, 1953-56; rsch. staff mem. Worcester Found. for Exptl. Biology, 1956-57; researcher in biochemistry NYU Med. Ctr., N.Y.C., 1957-58, instr. biochemistry, 1958-59, asst. prof., 1960-63, assoc. prof., 1963-69, prof. neurochemistry, physiology and biophysics, 1969—. Contbr. articles to profl. jours. Recipient medal Hellenic Geratric Soc., 1980; Robert and Adele Blank Lectureship award, 1986, R. & J. Bendheim fellowship Parkinson Disease Assn., 1986, Sarah L. Poiley Meml. award N.Y. Acad. of Sci. Mem. Am. Soc. Biol. Chemists, Am. Soc. Pharmacology and Exptl. Therapeutics, Soc. for Neurosci., Am. Coll. Neuropsychopharmacology. Died Oct. 18, 1997.

GONZALEZ, PANCHO See GONZALEZ, RICHARD A.

GONZALEZ, RICHARD A. (PANCHO GONZALEZ), professional tennis player; b. Los Angeles, May 9, 1928; s. Manuel A. and Carmen (Alire) G.; divorced; children: Richard, Michael, Danny, Christina, Andrea; m. Betty Steward, Dec. 31, 1972; 1 child, Jeanna Lynn.; m. Rita Agassi, Mar. 31, 1984; 1 child, Skylar Richard. Profl. tennis player, participant profl. tennis championships, 1953-60; tournament chmn., 1971, participant sr. grand master tournaments. Served with USNR, 1945-47. U.S. champion,1948, 49; winner Davis Cup, 1949. Home: Las Vegas Nev. Died July 3, 1995.

GONZÁLEZ-ALEXOPOULOS See CHRYSOSTOMOS

GOODMAN, CHARLES MORTON, architect; b. N.Y.C., Nov. 26, 1906; s. Harris and Jennie (Blomsten) G.; m. Charlotte K. Dodge, June 30, 1934; 1 child, Lynn Lelah; m. Dorothy M. Sopchick, Oct. 30, 1980. Student, U. Ill., 1925-28; B.S., Armour Inst. Tech., 1934. Registered architect, Va. Designing architect Treasury Dept., Washington, 1934-37; designer Washington Nat. Airport, Fed. Bldg., New Orleans, U.S. Govt. Group, N.Y. World's Fair; pvt. practice architecture, 1937—; head architect Air Transport Command, 1942-45; architect Am. U., Washington, 1946-50, Hollin Hills Community, Alexandria, Va., 1948-68, Officer's Club, Andrews AFB, Washington, Shopping Ctr., Lafayette, Ind., River Park, S.W., Washington, 1963, Reston, Hickory Cluster, 1964, Reston N. Golf Club, 1965, Houston House Tower, 1965, Westgate Research Park, McLean, Va., 1964-73, Nat. Hdqrs. Machine Tool Builders Assn., McLean, Va., 1971, Westpark Office and Residential Park, McLean, Va., 1970-73; cons. architect Nat. Homes Corp., Reynolds Metals Co., Tecfab Corp. Prin. works include No. Va. Regional Park Authority Hdqrs.; Greenbriar Sch., Chantilly, Va.; Forest Edge Sch., Reston, Va.; Mitre Corp. Bldg., Planning Research Corp. Bldg., Western Union Bldg., TRW Bldg., Systems Devel. Corp. Bldg., Lincoln Bldg., Westgate Corp. Hdqrs., Frederick Bldg., Brunswick Bldg., Polk Bldg., Culpeper Bldg., Garfield Bldg., Van Buren Bldg. (all McLean, Va.); The Commons Apt. Complex, Fairfax County, Va., expanded Nat. Hdqr. Machine Tool Builders Assn., McLean, 1981-82, Dickenson Bldg., McLean, 1983; work represented in A Guide to the Architecture of Washington, D.C., 1965, Architecture in Virginia, 1968; co-author: Life for Dead Spaces, 1963. Mem. tech. services adv. com., bldg. research adv. bd. Nat.Acad. Scis., 1958-60. Recipient biennial archtl. award Washington Bd. Trade 1944, 48, 50, 55, 57, 64, 66, 69; Architect of Yr. award SW Research Inst., 1951; Gold medal Art Dirs. Club, Washington, 1960; Centennial honor Rice U., 1962; 1st Honor award FHA, 1964. Fellow AIA (Test of Time award Va. Soc. 1981, 83, Outstanding Achievement in Profession of Architecture award N. Va. chpt. 1982); mem. Assn. Engrs. and Architects in Israel, Am. Hort. Soc., Am. Craftsman's Council, Nat. Wildlife Fedn., Am. Forestry Assn., Nat. Council Archtl. Registration Bds., Ill. Inst. Tech. Alumni Assn. (Profl. Achievement award 1986), Washington Bd. Trade, Nat. Audubon Soc. Died Oct. 29, 1992.

GOODMAN, LINDA, author; b. Richmond, Va.; d. Robert Stratton and Mazie (McBee) Kemery; grad. high sch.; m. William Herbert Snyder (dec.); children—Melissa Anne, James, John Anthony, Sarah Elizabeth, William Dana; m. 2d, Sam O. Goodman (dec.); children—Jill Kemery, Michael Aaron. Writer-broadcaster Letter From Linda radio shows WAMP (NBC), Pitts.; writer Emphasis and Monitor for NBC network radio; continuity chief WHN Radio, N.Y.C. Author: Sun Signs, 1968, Venus Trines at Midnight, 1970, Love Signs, 1978, Love Poems, 1979, Star Signs, 1987, Gooberz, 1989. Mem. Assn. for Research and Enlightenment, Virginia Beach, Va. Speech writer for Whitney Young and Nat. Urban League. Named Dau. of Year, W.Va. Soc. Washington, 1971. Mem. AFTRA, Authors League Am., Nat. Writer's Union N.Y.

GOODMAN, MILES, composer. Scores include (films) Slumber Party '57, 1976, Skatetown, U.S.A., 1979, Lookin' to Get Out, 1982, Jinxed, 1982, The Man Who Wasn't There, 1983, Table for Five, 1983, Footloose, 1984, Teen Wolf, 1985, About Last Night..., 1986,

Little Shop of Horrors, 1986, La Bamba, 1987, Real Men, 1987, The Squeeze, 1987, Like Father Like Son, 1987, Dirty Rotten Scoundrels, 1988, K-9, 1989, Staying Together, 1989, Opportunity Knocks, 1990, Funny About Love, 1990, Vital Signs, 1990, Problem Child, 1990, He Said, She Said, 1991, What About Bob?, 1991, The Super, 1991, Housesitter, 1992, The Muppet Christmas Carol, 1992, Indian Summer, 1993, Sister Act 2: Back in the Habit, 1993, Getting Even with Dad, 1994, Blankman, 1994, (TV movies) A Last Cry for Help, 1979, Having It All, 1982, The Face of Rage, 1983, High School, U.S.A., 1983, An Uncommon Love, 1983, A Reason to Live, 1985, Poison Ivy, 1985, Space, 1985, Children of the Night, 1985, Thompson's Last Run, 1986, Passion Flower, 1986, Blind Justice, 1986, Americangeisha, 1986, Outback Bound, 1988, The Travelling Man, 1989, Money, Power, Murder, 1989, For Richer, For Poorer, 1992, Indecency, 1992. Deceased.

GOODSELL, JAMES NELSON, journalist; b. Evanston, Ill., June 7, 1929; s. Nelson Jesse and Jean (Wilson) G.; m. Alice Louise Forn, Aug. 26, 1953 (div.); children: Paul Nelson, Amy Jean, Victoria Louise; m. Rhoda Merle Ford, July 24, 1982. BA, Principia Coll., 1951; MA, Mex. City Coll., 1953; PhD, Harvard U., 1966. Reporter The Chgo. Sun, 1947, The Cin. Post, 1955-56; reporter The Christian Sci. Monitor, Boston, 1957-62, Latin Am. editor, 1962-85; editorial advisor Sta. WGBH-PBS, Boston, 1984; anchor, editor Monitor Radio The Christian Sci. Monitor, Boston, 1985-87, Latin Am. corr., World Monitor, 1987-89, anchor, editor El Monitor de Hoy (TV), 1989-92; dir. Maria Moors Cabot awards Columbia U., 1993-96; ptnr. PanAm. Cons. Assocs., Boston and Miami, Fla., 1993-96; James L. Knight chair U. Miami, 1994-96. Editor: The Quest for Change in Latin America, 1969, Castro's Personal Revolution, 1973. Cpl. U.S. Army, 1953-55. Recipient Maria Moors Cabot award Columbia U., 1968, Peabody award, 1985, Emmy nomination, 1988. Mem. Am. Hist. Assn., Lat. Am. Studies Assn., Conf. on Latin Am. History, Coun. of the Ams., Royal Soc. of Arts, Coun. on Fgn. Rels., Inter-Am. Press Assn. (Fgn. Corr. award 1969, 72, 82), Overseas Press Club (Fgn. Corr. award 1967, 70), Sigma Delta Chi (Fgn. Corr. award 1966). Home: Morro Bay Calif. Died Feb. 1, 1996.

GOODSON, WALTER KENNETH, clergyman; b. Salisbury, N.C., Sept. 25, 1912; s. Daniel Washington and Sarah (Peeler) G.; m. Martha Ann Ogburn, July 12, 1937; children: Sara Ann (Mrs. Larry M. Faust), Walter Kenneth, Nancy Craven Richey. AB, Catawba Coll., 1934, LHD; student, Duke Div. Sch., 1934-37, D.D., 1960; D.D., High Point (N.C.) Coll., 1951, Birmingham-So. Coll., Athens Coll., Shenandoah Coll., Campbell U., 1985; L.H.D., St. Bernard Coll.; LL.D., U. Ala. Ordained to ministry Methodist Ch., 1939; pastor in Western N.C. Conf., 1935-64; bishop Birmingham area, 1964-72, Richmond area, 1972-80; now bishop-in-residence Duke U. Divinity Sch., Durham, N.C.; Del. World Conf. Meth. Ch., Oxford, Eng., 1951, Lake Junaluska, N.C., 1956, London, 1966, Denver, 1971, Dublin, 1977; mem. Meth. World Council; bd. dirs. Meth. Com. Overseas Relief, 1964-72; mem. (Mission Team to Gt. Britain), 1962, study team to, France and Berlin, 1962; chmn. finance com. bd. missions United Meth. Ch., 1968-72, pres. commn. on religion and race, 1968, pres. gen. bd. discipleship, 1972-80, also pres. council bishops United Meth. Ch., Southeastern Jurisdiction, 1976, pres. council on ministries, 1976. Pres. J.B. Cornelius Found., 1946-64; Trustee Duke Endowment, Brevard Coll., Duke U., Shenandoah Coll. Clubs: Rotarian, Mason (32 deg.). Home: Winston Salem N.C. Died Sept. 17, 1991.

GOODSPEED, STEPHEN SPENCER, university administrator; b. Berkeley, Calif., Nov. 15, 1915; s. Thomas Harper and Florence (Beman) G.; m. Grace Frances Halloran, May 12, 1938; 1 son, Roger Halloran. A.B., U. Calif. at Berkeley, 1937, Ph.D., 1947. Instr. U. Calif. at Santa Barbara, 1946-49, asst. prof., 1949-55, asso. prof., 1955-60, prof., 1960—, asst. to chancellor, 1958-60, vice-chancellor, 1960-78, emeritus, 1979—; summer faculty U. Calif. at Berkeley, 1942, U. Calif. at Los Angeles), 1950, 59; cons. 4th Army and Western Def. Command, 1942, Civil Disturbance Orientation Seminar, Ft. Gordon, Ga., 1970, Calif. Specialized Tng. Inst., San Luis Obispo, 1972, 77, Nat. Security Seminar, Carlisle Barracks, Pa., 1974; radio commentator, 1946-49. Author: Nature and Function of International Organization, 1967; Contbr. articles to profl. jours. Mem. Standard Oil Co. Calif. Faculty Seminar, 1954; mem. U.S. Army War Coll. Strategy Seminar, 1965; Vice pres., trustee Laguna Blanca Sch.; bd. dirs. Nat. Council on Alcoholism, Montecito Water Dist., UN Assn. Santa Barbara County, Calif., United Way, Center for Law Related Edn. Served from ensign to lt. USNR, 1942-46. Recipient Distinguished Service award Alpha Delta Phi, 1966. Mem. Am., Western polit. sci. assns., Pan-Am. Inst. History and Geography, Pacific Coast Athletic Assn. (1st pres.), C. of C. (bd. dirs.), Alpha Delta Phi, Pi Sigma Alpha. Clubs: Valley (pres.), Santa Barbara.

GOOKIN, WILLIAM SCUDDER, hydrologist, consultant, deceased; b. Atlanta, Ga., Sept. 8, 1914; s. William Cleveland and Susie (Jaudon) G.; m. Mildred Hartman, Sept. 4, 1937; children: William Scudder Jr., Thomas Allen Jaudon. BSCE, Pa. State U., 1937. Registered profl. engr. and hydrologist. Engr. U.S. Geol. Survey, Tucson, 1937-38; inspector City of Tucson, 1938-39; steel designer Allison Steel Mfg. Co., Phoenix, 1939-40; engr. Bur. Reclamation, various locations, 1940-53; chief engr. San Carlos Irrigation and Drainage Dist., Coolidge, Ariz., 1953-58; chief engr. Ariz. Interstate Stream Commn., Phoenix, 1956-62, state water engr., 1962-68; adminstr. Ariz. Power Authority, Phoenix, 1958-60; cons. engr. Scottsdale, Ariz., 1968—; mem. exec. com. Cen. Ariz. Project Assn., Phoenix, 1985—. Contbr. articles to profl. jours. Dem. committeeman State of Ariz., 1979-84; Ariz. mem. Com. of 14, Western States Water Coun.; episcopal lay reader. Served to 2d lt. C.E., U.S. Army, 1938-42. Fellow Am. Soc. Civil Engrs.; mem. NSPE (outstanding engr. project 1988), Nat. Water Resources Assn. (small projects com.), Colo. River Water Users' Assn., State Bar Ariz. (assoc.), Assn. Western State Engr. (pres.), Am. Legion, Culver Legion, Order of the Engr., Mason, Chi Epsilon.

GOOSTREE, ROBERT EDWARD, political science and law educator; b. nr. Clarksville, Tenn., Sept. 23, 1923; s. William Lee and Lucy (Frech) G.; m. Jane Rogers, July 16, 1955; children—Laura, Frederic, Samuel. A.B., Southwestern at Memphis, 1943; M.A., State U. Ia., 1948, Ph.D., 1950; J.D., Am. U., 1962. Instr. polit. sci. U. Ia., 1946-50; instr. polit. sci. U. Md., 1951-53; asst. prof. Am. U., 1953-56, assoc. prof., 1956-60, prof., 1960-71; asst. dean Am. U. (Sch. Govt.), 1958-62, acting dean, 1962-63, prof. law and govt., 1963-71, acting dean law sch., 1970-71; prof. Capital U. Law Sch., Columbus, Ohio, 1971-93; prof. emeritus, 1993-96, dean, 1971-79; cons. John F. Kennedy Center for Performing Arts, Washington, 1964-71. Contbr. articles to legal jours. Mem. Reynoldsburg (Ohio) City Charter Commn., 1978-79; pres. League of Ohio Law Schs., 1984-85. Served with AUS, 1943-46. Mem. ABA, Fed. Bar Assn., Am. Polit. Sci. Assn. Home: Reynoldsburg Ohio Died Dec. 21, 1996.

GORDON, M. MICHAEL, judge; b. San Francisco, Dec. 21, 1911. B.A., St. Ignatius Coll., 1931; J.D., U. San Francisco, 1935. Bar: Tex. 1935. Sole practice, Houston, 1935—; assoc. judge Houston Mcpl. Ct., 1962—; v.p. Am. Acad. Jud. Edn., 1971-75; bd. dirs. Nat. Ctr. State Cts., 1971-78; bd. dirs. Houston Bd. Pub. Welfare, 1946-58; pres. Houston Juvenile Delinquency and Crime Commn., 1958-59. Recipient award for reducing juvenile delinquency Disneyland, 1965; Allstate Safety Crusade award, 1966; Hon. mention Brit. Parliament, 1967. Mem. ABA, State Bar Tex., Am. Judges Assn. (pres. 1969-70, Award of Merit 1976), Am. Judicature Soc. (dir. 1969-70, Centennial Jud. award 1972), Inst. Jud. Adminstrn.

GORDON, MARGARET SHAUGHNESSY, economist, educator; b. Wabasha, Minn., Sept. 4, 1910; d. Michael James and Mary (O'Brien) Shaughnessy; m. Robert Aaron Gordon, Aug. 15, 1936 (dec. 1978); children: Robert James, David Michael. B.A., Bryn Mawr Coll., 1931; M.A., Radcliffe Coll., 1933, Ph.D., 1935; student, London Sch. Econs., 1933-34. Instr. Wellesley Coll., 1935-36; research fellow Harvard-Radcliffe Bur. Internat. Research, 1936-39; head research unit Export-Import office OPA, Washington, 1942-43; asst. research economist Inst. Indsl. Relations, U. Calif. at Berkeley, 1950-54, asso. dir., 1954-77, lectr. econs., 1965-77; Mem. Calif. Gov.'s Commn. on Employment and Retirement of Older Workers, 1959-60; mem. Personnel Bd., City of Berkeley, 1961-65, 70-75; asso. dir. Carnegie Commn. on Higher Edn. (name later changed to Carnegie Council on Higher Edn.), 1969-79; mem. Pres.'s Commn. on Income Maintenance Programs, 1968-69; cons. unemployment ins. U.S. Bur. Employment Security, 1962-66; adv. com. research devel. U.S. Social Security Adminstrn., 1965-68, chmn., 1966-67. Author: Employment Expansion and Population Growth, 1954, The Economics of Welfare Policies, 1963, Youth Education and Unemployment Problems: An International Perspective, 1979, Social Security Policies in Industrial Countries: A Comparative Analysis, 1988; editor: Poverty in America, 1965, (with E.F. Cheit) Occupational Disability and Public Policy, 1963, Higher Education and the Labor Market, 1974; mng. editor: Indsl. Relations, 1961-63, 65-66. Mem. council, City of Berkeley, 1965-69; bd. dirs. Consumers Coop. of Berkeley, 1980-87. Mem. Am. Econ. Assn., Indsl. Relations Research Assn.

GORDON, ROBERT EDWARD, university administrator; b. N.Y.C., June 20, 1925; s. Lewis Francis and Claire (McEvoy) G.; m. Catherine Tigner, Sept. 16, 1948; children: Claire Catherine, Martha Lee. A.B., Emory U., 1949; M.S., U. Ga., 1950; Ph.D., Tulane, U., 1956; LLD, U. Notre Dame, 1989. Curator Highlands (N.C.) Museum Biol. Sta., 1949-50; mem. faculty N.E. La. State Coll., 1954-58, U. Notre Dame, South Bend, Ind., 1958-96; prof. biology U. Notre Dame, 1966-90, prof. emeritus, from 1990, chmn. dept., 1964-67; assoc. dean U. Notre Dame (Coll. Sci.), 1967-71, v.p. for advanced studies, v.p. rsch., dean grad. sch., 1971-89; Mem. working party sci. publs. UNESCO, Phila., 1963, Paris, France, 1964; mem. panel primary publs. U.S.-Japan Coop. Sci. Program, Tokyo, 1965, 67; mem. sci. info. coun. NSF, 1969-72, chmn., 1971-72; biomed. communications study sect. NIH, 1967-71; mem. U.S. Nat. com. for F.I.D., 1969-71, U.S. Nat. Com. for Internat. Union Biol. Socs., 1969-75; chmn. bd. council biol. scis. information NAS-NRC, 1967-68; bd. overseers Fermi Lab, 1987-90. Editor: Am. Midland Naturalist, 1958-64; sect. editor: Biol. Abstracts, 1963-69; Contbr. articles to profl. jours. Trustee Biol. Abstracts, 1973-79, pres., 1978; trustee Univs. Rsch. Assn., 1983-87; mem. Grad. Record Exam. Bd., 1982-86; trustee Argonne Univs. Assn., 1973-83, v.p., 1979; mem. exec. com. AFGRAD, African Am. Inst., 1986-89; bd. dirs. Assn. Cath. Colls. and Univs., 1980-85; bd. dirs. Coun. Grad. Schs., 1982-86, chmn., 1984-85. With M.C. AUS, 1944-46. Fulbright scholar, Ecuador, 1988. Fellow AAAS (council 1964-70), Herpetologists League; mem. Am. Inst. Biol. Sci. (nat. lectr. 1960-65, mem. at large bd. govs. 1968-77, v.p. 1975, pres. 1976), Am. Soc. Icthyologists and Herpetologists, Am. Soc. Naturalists, Council Biology Editors (sec. 1963-69), Ecol. Soc. Am., Herpetological Soc. Japan, Soc. Study Amphibians and Reptiles (chmn. 1971), Explorers Club, Sigma Xi. Died June 2, 1996.

GORDON, SAUL WOLFE, technology educator; b. N.Y.C., June 6, 1942; s. Jerome and Lea Gordon; m. Holly Lester, Aug. 30, 1964; children: David, Michael, Matthew. BS, Buffalo State U., 1964; MA, NYU, 1967; postgrad., Hofstra U., Farmingdale U. Tchr. tech. Amityville (N.Y.) Pub. Schs., 1964—, dept. chmn. jr. high sch., 1967-91, dean students jr. high sch., 1972-74. Scoutmaster troop 43 Bay Shore, N.Y., Boy Scouts Am., 1980-94. Mem. N.Y. State Tech. Edn. Assn., N.Y. State United Tchrs., Amityville Tchrs. Assn. (pres., v.p.). Avocations: camping, photography. Deceased.

GORDON, VIVIAN VERDELL, African and Afro American studies educator. BS in Physics and Social Sci., Va. State U., 1955; MA in Sociology, U. Pa., 1957; PhD in Sociology, U. Va., Charlottesville, 1974. Social worker, child welfare divsn. The Women's Christian Alliance Child Welfare Agency, Phila., 1956-57; rsch. asst., edn. and social sci. analyst, congressional reference svc. Libr. of Congress, Washington, 1957-63; organizer, assoc. dir. Upward Bound Project of UCLA, L.A., 1966-67; dir., ednl. participation in cmtys. program Calif. State Coll., L.A., 1967-69; instr. in sociology Sch. of Continuing Edn. U. Va., Charlottesville, Va., 1971-73; asst. prof. dept. sociology, chairperson program in African studies U. Va., Charlottesville, 1974-79, assoc. prof., dept. sociology, 1979-84; assoc. prof., chairperson dept. African and Afro American studies SUNY, Albany, N.Y., 1985-86, assoc. prof. dept. African and Afro American studies, 1987-92, prof., 1992-95; coord. rsch. spl. study Ho. Reps. Com. on Edn. and Labor, Washington, 1957-63; vis. assoc. prof. dept. black studies, Wellesley Coll., Mass., 1986-87; lectr. in the field. Author: The Self-Concept of Black Americans, 1977, Lectures: Black Scholars on Black Issues, 1979, Black Women, Feminism, Black Liberation: Which Way?, 1985, rev. edit. 1987, Kemet and Other Ancient African Civilization, 1991, Black Women in a Typical Town: Perceptions of Self and Role, 1991, African American Family Patterns. Essays on Vital Topics, 1991, Understanding Prisons and the Justice System. A Discussion for Youthful Readers, 1991; author: (with others) Confusion By Any Other Name. Essays on the Negative Impact of the Blackman's Guide to Understanding the Blackwomen, 1990; TV appearances: Young Broadcasting of Albany, Inc. WTEN TV, 1990-91, CBS News Nightwatch, 1990, Channel 3 Boston, 1990, KYW TV Phila., 1990, Channel 13, 1990, ABC 20/20, 1991, BBC, 1991; teaching tapes: Targeting the Minority Aged, 1991, Maintaining Positive Black Male-Female Relationships, 1990, Teaching About African and African American Experience from an Afrocentric Perspective, 1989, Issues of Race and Racism, 1989; spl. news features: Dallas Times Herald, 1990, Newsweek Mag., 1990, N.Y. Times, 1990, USA Today, 1990; editorial bd. The Negro Educational Review, 1980-83, Jour. of Black Studies, 1984-89, editor 1984-89; contbd. numerous articles to profl. jours. Recipient Outstanding Teaching award Students of SUNY, 1988, Outstanding Svc. award Black Women's Week, 1988, 89, Outstanding Contributions award Delta Sigma Theta, 1989, Martin Luther King award U. Va., 1990; Summer Rsch. grant U. Va., 1977-78, Nat. Inst. Mental Health Rsch. grant, 1980-83, Carter G. Woodson Inst., U. Va. grant, 1982-83. N.Y. State African Am. Rsch. Inst. grant, 1988, N.Y. State African Am. Rsch. Inst., Dept. African and African Am. Studies of SUNY, Affirmative Action Com. of SUNY grant, 1991. Mem. Assn. Black Sociologist, Assn. Black Women Historians, Internat. Black Women's Congress (charter mem.), Nat. Coun. Black Studies (mem. at large, exec. bd. coord., chair com. on student affairs), Blacks in Government (mem. at large exec. bd). Home: Albany N.Y. Died Mar. 15, 1995.

GORDON, WALTER, architect; b. Buffalo, Sept. 8, 1907; s. Walter William and Florence (Green) G.; m. Margaret Murray, July 4, 1936. B.S., Princeton U., 1930, M.F.A. in Architecture, 1932; spl. student, Yale U., 1936-37, U. Paris, France, 1934. Curator San Francisco Mus. Art, 1937-39; asst. dir. Portland (Oreg.) Art Mus., 1939-41; practicing architect Portland, 1946-58; dean Sch. Architecture, U. Oreg., 1958-62; faculty mem. Reed Coll., 1962-65; sr. partner Gordon & Hinchliff, architects, 1962-72; prin. Walter Gordon, architect, 1972—; design cons. Portland Devel.

Commn., 1962-76, Eugene Renewal Agy., 1972-80, Salem (Oreg.) Renewal Agy., 1973-82; mem. Gov.'s Adv. Com. for Preservation Yaquina Head, 1977-80, Oreg. Bd. Architect Examiners, 1956-58, Portland Art Commn., 1955-57, Oreg. Capitol Planning Commn., 1959-68. Prin. works include Southwest Hills Libr., Portland, Alpha Phi sorority house, Corvallis, Oreg. libr., dormitories, faculty residence Marylhurst Coll., Portland, Pub. Libr., Toledo, Oreg., visitor's lodge, infirmary Trappist Abbey, Lafayette, Oreg., parish hall, chapel Sacred Heart Ch., Newport, Oreg., numerous residences, Pacific N.W. Trustee Portland Art Mus., 1947-51. Fellow A.I.A. (mem. nat. edn. com. 1960-62); mem. Phi Beta Kappa. Clubs: City of Portland (v.p. 1971-72), University. DIED 04/05/97. .

GORHAM, DONALD R., clinical psychologist; b. Kalamazoo, May 23, 1903; s. Adelbert Leroy and Emma Louise (Rogers) G.; m. Elizabeth Ann Young, June 23, 1926; children: Ann Emily, Janet Susan; m. Rosemary Steele, Sept. 1, 1985. B.Th., Colgate U., 1926, M.A., 1927; scholar, U. Pa., 1929-30, Ph.D., 1934. Prof., dir. Sch. Edn., Eastern Bapt. Theol. Sem., 1931-43; prof. edn. and psychology Keuka Coll., 1943-50; clin. psychologist VA Neuro-psychiat. Hosp., Waco, Tex., 1950-59; prof. clin. psychology (part time) Baylor U., 1950-59; cons. The Hogg Found., 1957-58; research psychologist VA Hosp., Perry Point, 1959-69; chief psychol. service VA Center, Bath, N.Y., 1969-70; cons. and ltd. pvt. practice, 1970—; cons. N.Y. Dept. Social Services Office of Disability Determinations; mem. Md. Bd. Examiners in Profl. Psychology. Author: books including Understanding Adults, 1948, Proverbs Test, 1954, (with J.E. Overall) Brief Psychiatric Rating Scale, 1961; Contbr. articles to profl. jours. Fellow Internat. Council Psychology, Am. Psychol. Assn.; mem. Md. Psychol. Assn. Interam. Soc. Psychology. Deceased.

GORLIN, RICHARD, physician, educator; b. Jersey City, June 30, 1926; s. Sol George and Henrietta (Bernfeld) G.; m. Florence; children by previous marriage: Wendy, William, Douglas. M.D., Harvard U., 1948. Diplomate Am. Bd. Internal Medicine, Nat. Bd. Med. Examiners. Intern Peter Bent Brigham Hosp., Boston, 1948-49; resident Peter Bent Brigham Hosp., Boston, 1948-52, mem. staff, 1953-74, sr. assoc. medicine, 1960-66, physician, dir. cardiovascular unit, 1967-74, chief cardiovascular div., 1969-74; cons. physician VA Hosp., Bronx, N.Y., 1974-97; faculty Harvard Med. Sch., 1949-74, asst. prof. medicine, 1961-67, assoc. prof., 1968-74; physician-in-chief Mt. Sinai Hosp. and Med. Ctr., N.Y.C., 1974-92; sr. v.p. Mt. Sinai Med. Ctr., N.Y.C., 1992-97; prof., chmn. dept. medicine Mt. Sinai Med. Sch., 1974-92; George Baehr prof. medicine Mt. Sinai Med. Ctr., 1992-97; med. dir. Mt. Sinai Health System, 1994-97; hon. asst. St. Thomas Hosp., London, 1952-53; officer in charge cardiopulmonary lab. U.S. Naval Hosp., Portsmouth, Va., 1957-60; lectr. internal medicine Chelsea (Mass.) Naval Hosp., 1957-74; vis. lectr. numerous internat. colls. including Rogers lectr. U. Wis., Madison; McArthur lectr. U. Edinburgh, Scotland, R.T. Hall Trust lectr., Australia; Centennial lectr. U. Ill. Med. Sch., Chgo.; Lewis Meml. lectr. Stanford Sch. Medicine; Merck, Sharpe & Dohme vis. lectr. Yale U., 1971; prin. lectr., vis. prof. U. Cin. Med. Sch.; Sir James Wattie prof., N.Z., 1972; George Fahr lectr. U. Minn., 1974; Fried Meml. lectr., 1976, Avila Berger lectr., 1981, George Cecil Clarke Meml. lectr., 1981; Laurence B. Ellis Meml. lectr. Harvard U. Med. Sch., 1982; vis. prof. St. Vincent's Hosp., Worcester, Mass., 1983; James V. Warren lectr. Ohio State U. Sch. Medicine, 1983; F. Mason Sones lectr. Cleve. Clinic Fedn., 1983; Macklin lectr. Portsmouth Naval Hosp. (Va.), 1983; Lewis Conner lectr. Am. Heart Assn., 1985, exec. com. thrombosis council, 1972-97; Louis N. Katz lectr. Michael Reese Hosp. U. Chgo., 1986; Henry Jackson lectr. New Eng. Cardiovascular Soc., Boston, 1987; Paul Dudley White lectr. AHA, 1988; Irwin Callen lectr. Miami Heart Inst., 1991; Henry I Russek lectr. ACC, 1991; Isadore Rosenfeld lectr. New York Hosp., 1992; Lawrence Green lectr. Brigham and Women's Hosp., Boston; John Sampson vis. prof. U. Calif., San Francisco, 1990; mem. cardiovascular program study sect. NIH, 1964-68, tng. grant com., 1969-72, task force coronary artery disease, 1972-97; chmn. digitalis intervention trial NHLBI, DVA, 1990-97, Va. Coop. Study number 287, Vasodilators in chronic heart failure II 1985; task force coronary artery disease Internat. Study Group Research in Cardiac Metabolism; spl. cons. U. Ill. Med. Sch., 1968; cons. in field; mem. steering com. coop. study in cardiac catheterization Nat. Heart Inst., 1963-97; research allocations com. Mass. Heart Assn., 1965-70; trustee Heart Research Found.; Rose Weiss lectr. Lahey Clinic Med. Ctr., Burlington, Mass., 1990; Louis F. Bishop lectr. ACC, 1993, J. V. Warren lectr., VHEFT I, II, III; Survival and Ventricular Enlargement Study, chair data monitoring and policy bds.; thrombolysis in myocardial infarction VII, 1992. Mem. editl. bd. Am. Jour. Cardiology, 1964-70, Am. Jour. Med. Scis., 1967, Circulation, 1970, Am. Jour. Medicine, 1973, Catheterization and Cardiovascular Diagnosis; editor-in-chief Primary Cardiology, 1975-95; contbr. articles to profl. jours. Pres. Freedom Inc., 1957; officer in charge cardiopulmonary lab. U.S. Naval Hosp., Portsmouth, Va., 1957-60. Lt. comdr. USNR, 1954-56. Recipient Cummings Humanitarian award, 1963, Ignaz Semmelweis Gold medal, 1980, Maimonides award, 1985, Disting. Achievement award Am. Heart Assn., 1987, Med. Sci. award Heart Rsch. Found., 1990, Glorney-Raisbeck award and lectr., 1994, James B. Herrick award Am. Heart Assn., 1995; Bower traveling scholar ACP, 1960; Moseley traveling fellow, 1952-53; Nat. Heart and Lung Inst. grantee, 1956-76. Master ACP; fellow Am. Coll. Cardiology (v.p.); mem. Am. Fedn. Clin. Rsch. (nat. councillor 1960-64), New Eng. Cardiovascular Soc. (pres. 1967-68), Mass. Heart Assn. (pres. elect 1973-74), Brit. Cardiac Soc. (corr. mem.), Argentine Cardiac Soc., Assn. Am. Physicians, Am. Soc. Clin. Investigation, Am. Physiol. Soc., Royal Soc. Medicine (U.K.), Assn. Univ. Cardiologists, Am. Clin. and Climatol. Assn., Cardiac Muscle Soc., N.Y. Heart Assn. (pres. 1985), N.Y. Cardiol. Soc. (pres. 1987). Clubs: Harvard (N.Y.C.), Badminton and Tennis (Boston); Appalachian Mountain. Home: Bedford Hills N.Y. Died Oct. 16, 1997.

GORMAN, MARGARET MARY, psychology consultant and educator; d. Vincent A. and Margaret (Thomser) G. BA in English, Trinity Coll., 1939; MA in Philosophy, Fordham U., 1952; PhD in Ednl. Psychology, Cath. U., 1958. Mem. Soc. of Sacred Heart. Tchr. Acads. of the Sacred Heart, 1942-56; prin. parochial sch. St. Katherine's Sch., Torresdale, Pa., 1957-59; chmn. dept. psychology, prof. psychology Newton Coll. of the Sacred Heart, 1959-75; psychol. cons. U.S. Army, Ft. Monmouth, N.J., 1962-90, USAF, Montgomery, Ala., 1967—; adj. prof. psychology, theology Boston Coll., 1981—. Bd. dirs. Newton Community Svc. Ctr., 1969-77, pres., 1974-76; commr. Newton Human Rights Commn., 1970-74, chair, 1972-74; trustee Mass. Sch. Profl. Psychology, 1976—, chair bd. trustees, 1978—. Fellow Mass. Psychol. Assn. (sec. 1968-71, bd. dirs. 1973-75); mem. APA (divsn. 36 religious issues), Soc. for Psychol. Study of Social Issues, Assn. for Moral Edn. Avocation: walking. Office: Boston Coll Chestnut Hill MA 02167

GORNICK, ALAN LEWIS, lawyer; b. Leadville, Colo., Sept. 23, 1908. AB, Columbia U., 1935, JD, 1937. Bar: N.Y. 1937, Mich. 1948. Assoc. Baldwin, Todd & Young, N.Y.C., 1937-41, Milbank, Tweed, Hope & Hadley, 1941-47; asso. counsel charge tax matters Ford Motor Co., Dearborn, Mich., 1947-49; dir. tax affairs, chmn. tax com., tax counsel Ford Motor Co., 1949-64; lectr. tax matters NYU, Inst. Fed. Taxation, 1947-49, ABA and Practicing Law Inst. (courses on fundamentals in fed. taxation), 1946-55, Am. Law Inst. (courses in continuing legal edn.), 1950; spl. lectr. sch. bus. adminstrn. U. Mich., 1949, 53. Author: Estate Tax Handbook, 1952, Arrangements for Separation or Divorce, Handbook of Tax Techniques, 1952, Taxation of Partnerships, Estates and Trusts, rev. edit, 1952; adv. editor Nat. Tax Jour., 1952-55; contbr. articles on tax matters to profl. jours. Exec. bd. Detroit area council Boy Scouts Am., chmn. fin. com., 1960; pres. Mich. Assn. Emotionally Disturbed Children, 1962-65; v.p. Archives of Am. Art; mem. Mich. Heart Assn., Columbia Coll. council Columbia U., N.Y.C., Founder's Soc. Detroit Inst. Art; trustee Council on World Affairs, Detroit; trustee, past pres. Detroit Hist. Soc.; mem. Bd. Zoning Appeals City Bloomfield Hills, 1980-89. Recipient Gov.'s Spl. award State Colo., 1952. Mem. World Bar Assn. for Peace through Law, ABA (council tax sect. 1957-58), Detroit Bar Assn., N.Y. City Bar Assn. (chmn. subcom. estate and gift taxes 1943-47), Am. Law Inst., Tax Inst. Inc. (pres. 1954-55), U.S. C. of C., Empire State C. of C., Council on Fgn. Relations, Nat. Tax Assn. (exec. com.), Internat. Fiscal Assn. (council, nat. reporter 6th Internat. Congress Fiscal Law, Brussels 1952), Internat. Law Assn., World assn. Lawyers (founding mem.), Assn. Ex-Mems. Squadron A, Nat. Fgn. Trade Council (mem. com. taxes 1950), Automobile Mfrs. Assn. (chmn. com. on taxation 1960-62), Tax Execs. Inst. (pres. 1956-57), Fedn. Alumni Columbia (bd. dirs. 1946), Class 1935 Columbia Coll. (pres.), N.Y. Adult Edn. Council (bd. dirs. 1939-45), Detroit Hist. Soc. (trustee, pres. 1983-85), Bloomfield Hills (Mich.) Country Club, Detroit Club, Detroit Athletic Club, Church Club (N.Y.C.), Columbia U. Alumni Club of Mich. (pres. 1950—), Otsego Ski Club (Gaylord, Mich.), Little Club (Gulfstream, Fla.), Everglades Club (Palm Beach, Fla.), Phi Delta Phi. Died Feb. 26, 1998.

GOTTMANN, JEAN, geographer, educator; b. Kharkov, Russia, Oct. 10, 1915; s. Elie and Sonia (Ettinger) G.; m. Bernice Adelson, Aug. 11, 1957. Bacc. Lettres, U. Paris, 1932, D. Et. Sup. in History and Geography, 1934, Docteur es Lettres, 1970; LL.D., U. Wis., 1968; M.A, Oxford U., 1968; D.Sc., So. Ill. U., 1969; D.Litt., U. Liverpool, 1986. Asst. dept. geography Sorbonne, Paris, 1937-40; several times mem. Inst. Advanced Study, Princeton, N.J., 1942-65; cons. Bd. Econ. Warfare, FEA, 1942-44; instr. Princeton U., 1943; lectr., assoc., then assoc. prof. Johns Hopkins U., 1943-48; adviser French Ministry Nat. Economy, Paris, 1945-46; dir. studies and research, dept. social affairs UN, N.Y.C., 1946-47; research assoc. Conseil National de la Récherche Scientifique, Paris, 1948-51; prof. Institut d'Etudes Politiques, U. Paris, 1948-60, École des Hautes Etudes en Sciences Sociales, Paris, 1960-83; prof. geography Oxford (Eng.) U., 1968-83, prof. emeritus, 1983-94; research dir. study of megalopolis Twentieth Century Fund, N.Y.C., 1956-61; vis. prof. Columbia U., 1949, 56, U. Geneva, 1950, U. Durham, Eng., 1951, Hebrew U., Jerusalem, 1956, 79, 83, U. Pitts., 1962, So. Ill. U., 1964, Laval U., 1964, U. Calif., Berkeley, 1966, 79, U. Wis.-Milw., 1968, 79, U. Va., 1971, U. Hong Kong, 1973, Brandeis U., 1977, U. B.C., 1981, U. Rome, 1981, 84, 89, 93, U. Tsukuba, Japan, 1982, U. of Verona, 1993; first Elkins prof. U. Md., 1982; fellow Hertford Coll., Oxford, 1968-94, hon. fellow, 1993-94; Hanna Disting. vis. prof., Mich. State U., 1991. Author: L'Amerique, 1949, A Geography of Europe, 1950, Virginia at Midcentury, 1955, Megalopolis, 1961, The Significance of Territory, 1973, The Coming of the Transactional City, 1983, La Citta Invincibile, 1984, Megalopolis Revisited, 1987, Since Megalopolis, 1990; editor: Centre and Periphery, 1980, Urban Growth and Politics, 1990 (with C. Muscara) La Citta Prossima Ventura, 1991; editorial bd.: Ekistics, Athens, 1965-92, Sistema Terra, Rome, 1992-94. Chmn. commn. on regional planning Internat. Geog. Union, 1949-52, rsch. com. on polit. geography Internat. Polit. Sci. Assn. (IPSA), 1975-94; trustee Research Group European Migration Problems, The Hague, Netherlands, 1952-70; bd. govs. U. Haifa (Israel), Institut d'Etudes Americaines, Paris, 1966-80; bd. mgmt. Town Planning Rev., Liverpool, Vaughan Cornish Bequest, Oxford, 1970-82. Recipient Charles P. Daly medal Am. Geog. Soc., 1964; Bonaparte-Wyse award Paris Geog. Soc., 1962, Grand Prix, 1984; Keys to City of Yokohama Japan; decorated chevalier Légion d'Honneur; chevalier Palmes Académiques (France). Fellow Royal Geog. Soc. (London) (recipient Victoria medal 1980, v.p. 1981-84), Brit. Acad.; mem. World Soc. for Ekistics (pres. 1971-73), Am. Geog. Soc. (hon.), Assn. Am. Geographers, Inst. Brit. Geographers, Internat. Polit. Sci. Assn. (chmn. polit. sci. rsch. com. 1976-94), Assn. de Géographes Français, Assn. Française de Science Politique, Royal Netherlands Geog. Soc. (hon.), Am. Acad. Arts and Scis. (fgn. hon.), Societa Geografica Italiana (hon.), Ateneo Veneto, Societe de Geographie de Liege (hon.), United Oxford and Cambridge University Club (London). Home: Oxford Eng. Died Feb. 28, 1994.

GOTTSCHALK, CARL WILLIAM, physician, educator; b. Salem, Va., Apr. 28, 1922; s. Carl and Lula (Helbig) G.; m. Helen Marie Scott, Nov. 22, 1947 (dec. June 1988); children: Carl S., Walter P., Karen E.; m. Susan K. Fellner, May 25, 1996. BS, Roanoke Coll., 1942, ScD, 1966; MD, U. Va., 1945; Docteur honoris causa, University of Mons-Hainout, Belgium, 1992. Intern, asst. resident, resident in medicine Mass. Gen. Hosp., Boston, 1945-52; research fellow physiology Harvard U., 1948-50; fellow U. N.C. Med. Sch., Chapel Hill, 1952-53; faculty U. N.C. Med. Sch., 1953-92, Kenan prof. medicine and physiology, 1969-92, disting. rsch. prof. medicine and physiology, 1992—; established investigator Am. Heart Assn., 1957-61, career investigator, 1961-92; Bowditch lectr., 1960, Harvey lectr., 1962; Mem. physiology study sect. NIH, 1961-65; mem. research career award com. Nat. Inst. Gen. Med. Scis., 1965-69, mem. physiology tng. com., 1970-73, mem. med. scientist tng. com., 1973; chmn. com. chronic kidney disease Bur. Budget, 1966-67; adv. com. biol. and med. scis. NSF, 1967-69, vice chmn., 1968, chmn., 1969; mem. Nat. Adv. Gen. Med. Scis. Council, 1977-80, Nat. Arthritis, Diabetes and Digestive and Kidney Diseases Adv. Council, 1982-86; lectr. The Dr. Richard Bright Soc., 1995. Author books and papers on physiology of kidney. Mem. adv. com. Burroughs Wellcome Fund for Clin. Pharmacology, 1980-93, Student Sci. Enrichment Adv. Com., 1996-98; pres. Children's Theatre N.C., 1967-68. Served to capt. M.C., AUS, 1946-48. Recipient N.C. award, 1967, Modern Medicine Distinguished Achievement award, 1966, Horsley Meml. prize U. Va., 1956, Homer W. Smith award N.Y. Heart Assn., 1970, David Hume award Nat. Kidney Found., 1976, O. Max Gardner award U. N.C., 1978; Gottschalk lectr. in basic scis. named in his honor N.C. Med. Sch., 1992; charter mem. Salem H.S. Hall of Fame, 1996. Mem. ACP, NAS, AAUP (coun. 1970-73), Assn. Am. Physicians, Am. Physiol. Soc. (Robert W. Berliner award 1993, Carl W. Gottschalk Disting. Lectureship of Renal Physiology sect. established 1993), Am. Soc. Clin. Investigation, Am. Clin. and Climatol. Assn., Soc. Exptl. Biology and Medicine, Inst. Medicine of NAS, Internat. Soc. Nephrology (hon. mem., A.N. Richards award 1990), Am. Soc. Nephrology (coun. 1971-77, pres. 1975-76), Am. Acad. Arts and Scis., Phi Beta Kappa, Sigma Xi, Alpha Omega Alpha. Died Oct. 15, 1997.

GOULD, DENNIS JAY, lawyer; b. San Francisco, Aug. 30, 1942; s. William Adolph and Mildred Anna (Noy) G. AB, U. Calif., Davis, 1964; JD, U. Calif., San Francisco, 1967. Bar: Calif. 1967. Assoc. Downey Brand Seymour & Rohwer, Sacramento, 1968-71; ptnr. Crosby Heafey Roach & May, Oakland, Calif., 1971—; adj. prof. law Kennedy U., Orinda, Calif., 1975-76; lectr. Continuing Edn. of B ar U. Calif., Berkeley, 1975-88, cons. editor, 1978-82. Co-author: California Decedent Estate Practice, 1986, Durable Power of Attorney Handbook, 1988. Pres. U. Calif. Alumni Assn., Davis, 1982-84, Easter Seal Soc. Alameda County, Oakland, 1984; chmn. bd. trustees Easter Seal Found. Alameda County, 1980; bd. dirs. Easter Seal Soc. Calif., San Francisco, 1986—. 1st lt. U.S. Army, 1964-67. Fellow Am. Coll. Probate Counsel; mem. ABA, Calif. Bar Assn., Alameda County Bar Assn., Merchants Exchange Club (San Francisco), Lakeview Club (Oakland). Republican.

GOULD, SAMUEL B., academic adminstrator; b. N.Y.C.; m. Laura Ohman Gould (dec. 1989); 1 child, Richard. Student, Oxford U., Cambridge U.; grad., Bates Coll.; AM, NYU, 1936. Staff Boston U., asst. to the pres., 1950; pres. Antioch Coll., 1954-59; chancellor U. Calif., Santa Barbara, 1959-62; pres. Ednl. TV for the Met. Area Inc., SUNY, 1964-70. Lt. comdr. USN. Home: Sarasota Fla. Died 1997.

GOULD, SYD S., publisher; b. Boston, Dec. 16, 1912; s. Charles M. and Cecelia (Duke) G.; student Coll. William and Mary, 1934; m. Grace Leich, May 22, 1938; 1 child, Nancy Hamilton (Mrs. Lucien M. Gex, Jr.). Radio bus., Buenos Aires, Argentina, 1934, 36; advt. dept. Call-Chronicle Newspapers, Allentown, Pa., 1936-42; v.p. adv. dir. Baytown Sun, Tex. 1943-55; pub.-owner Cleveland Daily Banner, Tenn., 1955-94; pres. Cleveland Newspapers, Inc., 1956-67; exec. v.p. So. Newspapers, Inc., 1963-69; pres. Syd S. Gould Assocs., 1966-94, Bolivar Newspapers, Inc., 1967-94, Ironton Tribune Corp. Ohio, Franklin Newspapers, Inc., La., Comet-Press Newspapers, Thibodaux, La., Milton Newspapers, Inc., Fla. Mem. Regional Small Bus. Adv. Council. Sec., Bradley County (Tenn.) Indsl. Devel. Bd., 1961-94; bd. dirs. Providence Hosp.; pres. Bradley County Heart Assn., 1960-61. Served with USNR, World War II. Recipient Disting. Eagle Scout award Boy Scouts Am., 1983. Mem. Newspaper Advt. Execs. Assn., Tenn. Press Assn., Bur. Advt., Am. Newspaper Pubs. Assn., So. Newspapers Pubs. Assn., Gulf Coast Conservation Assn., USCG Aux., U.S. Power Squadron, U.S. Naval Inst., Navy League, Eagle Scout Assn., Sigma Delta Chi. Episcopalian. Clubs: Bayou Country, Mobile Big Game Fishing, Isle Dauphine Country, Capitol Hill, Yachting of Am., Internat. Trade, Bienville, Athelstan, Commodore, Bay Point Yacht, Inc. Died Sept. 25, 1994.

GOUR, BETTY, dance instructor, choreographer; b. Chgo., July 10, 1914; d. Andre Anastus and Marie Luclla (Weeden) G. Studies with George Balanchine, Edna McRae, Anatole Vilzak, others. Dancer Chgo. Civic Opera Ballet, 1929-34, Am. Ballet Co. and Met. Opera Ballet, 1935-36; dancer, capt. of touring group Chester Hale Tex. Comets, 1937-40; dancer Broadway prodn. Frederika Imperial Theatre, 1937; dancer Phila. Ballet, 1940-44, Am. Jubilee New York's World's Fair, N.Y.C., 1940; dancer Nat. Co. of Oklahoma, 1944-53, ballet mistress, 1946-53; instr., choreographer stage play Oklahoma West Berlin, Fed. Repubic Germany, 1951, Paris, 1955; instr. of choreography movie version of Oklahoma, 1954, staged various prodns., 1953-58; instr., owner dance studio Chgo., 1958-64; ballet mistress Ruth Page's Chgo. Opera Ballet, 1957-59; prof. in dance Butler U., Indpls., 1964-86, assoc. prof. emeritus, 1986—, choreographer Oklahoma, 1990—; instr. ballet Dance Kaleidoscope, Indpls., 1987—; choreographer Chgo. Nat. Auto Show, 1957-58, Chgo. World's Fair of Music and Sound, 1962, Nat. Boat Show, 1963, 20 ballets for the Butler Ballet, 1964-86, Nat. Arts and Letters Competition, 1990. Avocations: teaching specialized teacher's class in ballet, writing autobiography and instruction books on ballet and vaudeville. DIED 12/07/96. .

GOVE, DOROTHY BERYL, civic worker; b. Haverhill, Mass., Apr. 14, 1905; d. Maurice Leslie and Minnie Evelyn (Tilton) McDaniel; m. William Lionel Gove; children—Inez Beryl Gove Riley, Barbara Evelyn, William Lionel, Donna Ilene Gove Matthews. Student Hall Hosp. Nurses Tng.; grad. Lincoln Inst. Practical Nursing, 1952. Lic. practical nurse, Mass. Treas., sec., founder Pioneer Nursing Assn., Malden, Mass,, 1950-60; treas., founder WWI Vets., Woburn, Mass., 1944-60; vol. ARC, Mass., 1952-59; girl scout leader Boston council Girl Scouts U.S.A., 1942-54; leader, founder 4-H, Woburn, 1942-55; mem. Mayor's Dem. race, Woburn, 1943; vol. Health and Rehab. Services Hillsborough County, Tampa, Fla., 1979—(Vol. of Yr. 1986, 87); vol. James A. Haley Vets. Hosp., Tampa, 1979—(1,000 hour pin for vol. services 1988); officer DAV orgns., Brandon, Fla.; nat. aux. commdr. Wm. L. Gove Sr. Veterans Inc., Valrico, Fla., 1979-87. Mem. D.A.V., Aux. (life), Marine Corps League in Fla. (hon.), Angus R. Goss detachment Marine Corps League aux., 1987, Wm. L. Gove Sr. Vets. Aux. (life, founder), Brandon C. of C. Lodges: Women of Moose (founder aux.), Order Eastern Star. Died March 1990.

GOWAN, ARTHUR MITCHELL, university dean; b. Cleghorn, Iowa, Dec. 1, 1910; s. William and Annie (Mitchell) G.; m. Marjorie Mace, June 19, 1940; children—Barbara (Mrs. Donald K. Watkins), Sandra (Mrs. Gary R. Kirk). B.A., U. No. Iowa, 1932; M.A., U. Ia., 1939; Ph.D., Iowa State U., 1947. Adminstr. secondary sch. Nevada, Iowa, 1932-42; supr. math. U.S. Naval Tng. Sch., Iowa State U., 1942-44; asst. to dean of engring. Iowa State U. at Ames, 1944-46, asst. registrar, 1946-51, registrar, 1951-65, dean admissions and records, 1965—; Ford Found. cons. Nat. Engring. U., Lima, Peru, 1965. Mem. Ames City Planning Commn., 1970—. Mem. Am. Assn. Collegiate Registrars and Admissions Officers, Am. Assn. Higher Edn., Phi Kappa Phi, Phi Mu Epsilon. Club: Kiwanian (lt. gov. Nebr.-Iowa dist. 1965).

GRACE, J. PETER, specialty chemicals and specialized health care company executive; b. Manhasset, N.Y., May 25, 1913; s. Joseph and Janet (Macdonald) G.; m. Margaret Fennelly, May 24, 1941. Student, St. Paul's Sch., Concord, N.H., 1927-32; BA, Yale U., 1936; LLD (hon.), Mt. St. Mary's Coll., Manhattan Coll., Fordham U., Boston Coll., U. Notre Dame, Belmont Abbey, Stonehill Coll., Christian Bros. Coll., Adelphi U., Furman U., Rider Coll., Mt. St. Vincent Coll., Barry U.; D Latin Am. Rels., St. Joseph's Coll.; DSc, Clarkson Coll.; DCS (hon.), St. John's U.; LHD (hon.), Fairleigh Dickinson U., Canisius Coll.; LLD (hon.), Assumption Coll., The Citadel, Stevens Inst. of Tech., Ala. A&M U., Barry U. With W.R. Grace & Co., Boca Raton, Fla., 1936-95; sec. W.R. Grace & Co., N.Y.C., 1942, dir., 1943-95, v.p., 1945, pres., CEO, 1945-81; chmn., CEO W.R. Grace & Co., Boca Raton, Fla., 1981-92, chmn., 1993-95; bd. dirs. Chemed Corp., chmn., 1993—; bd. dirs. Milliken & Co., Omnicare Inc., Roto-Rooter, Inc., Stone & Webster Inc., Nat. San. Supply Co.; dir. emeritus Ingersoll-Rand Co.; hon. dir. Brascan Ltd.; trustee emeritus Atlantic Mut. Ins. Co., Atlantic Reins. Co.; bd. dirs., trustee Centennial Ins. Co. Pres., bd. dirs. Cath. Youth Orgn. of Archdiocese of N.Y.; bd. dirs. Boys Clubs Am.; pres., trustee Grace Inst.; mem. pres.'s com. Greater N.Y., corp. grants com., trustee emeritus, Notre Dame U.; chmn. coun. nat. trustees Nat. Jewish Ctr. for Immunology and Respiratory Medicine, Denver; chmn. Pres.'s Pvt. Sector Survey on Cost Control in Fed. Govt., 1982-84; co-chmn. Citizens Against Govt. Waste; trustee U.S. Coun. for Internat. Bus.; bd. govs. Thomas Aquinas Coll.; chmn. adv. com. Americares Found. Decorated Knight Grand Cross, Equestrian Order Holy Sepulchre of Jerusalem; decorated by govts. of Colombia, Chile, Ecuador, Panama, Peru. Mem. Newcomen Soc., Knights of Malta (pres., bd. councillors), Links, Meadow Brook Club, Pacific Union Club, Everglades Club, Lotus Club, River Club. DIED 04/19/95. .

GRAHAM, ALEXANDER STEEL, cartoonist; b. Glasgow, Scotland, Mar. 2, 1917; m. Winnifred Margaret Bird, Nov. 9, 1944; children: Neil, Arran Graham Field. D iploma in Drawing and Painting, Glasgow Sch. Art, 1939. Free lance cartoonist, 1945—; syndicated cartoonist: Fred Basset strip, 1964—, cartoon collections published in over 10 books of Punch drawings, 37 books of Fred Basset strips; series in the New Yorker (The Eavesdropper), 1961.

GRAHAM, KENNETH L. (KEN GRAHAM), speech educator emeritus, actor, director; b. Coffeyville, Kans., Apr. 25, 1915; s. Ethan L. and Maud (Huff) G.; m. Barbara Louise Fowler, Dec. 15, 1945 (dec. July 1969); children: Greg Fowler Graham, Sherry Lynn Graham Nelson. BA, State U. Iowa, 1936; MA, Northwestern U., 1939; PhD, U. Utah, 1947. Tchr. speech and drama Watertown (S.D.) High Sch., North Kansas City (Mo.) High Sch.; dir. Sch. of Theatre, Cain Park Theatre, Cleveland Heights, Ohio, summers 1941, 42, 46, 47; instr. speech, communication theater arts dept. U. Minn., from asst. prof. to assoc. prof. to prof., 1948-80, prof. emeritus, 1980-96, also chmn. theater arts dept.; founder Ken Graham and Assocs., Inc. Actor (TV and radio commls.) United Bldg. Ctrs., Gen Mills, N.W. Airlines, Met. Fed. Bank, Saxon Paints, and others, (TV spls.) The Chicago Story, Sarah T.-Portrait of a Teen-Age Alcoholic, (theater prodns.) About Time, Two by Two, Foxfire, The Tavern, Carousel, The Kingfisher, The Caine Mutiny Court Martial, Blithe Spirit, Broadway Bound, and others; also numerous advt. print/films. Served with USNR, 1942-45. Fellow Am. Theatre Assn. (exec. sec., treas. 1946-58, 2d v.p. 1962, 1st v.p. 1963, pres. 1964); mem. Actors Equity Assn., Screen Actors Guild, AFTRA, Nat. Theatre Conf., Citizens League Mpls., Beta Theta Pi. Unitarian. Died Feb. 8, 1996.

GRAHAM, ROBERT KLARK, lens manufacturer; b. Harbor Springs, Mich., June 9, 1906; s. Frank A. and Ellen Fern (Klark) G.; A.B., Mich. State U., 1933; B.Sc. in Optics, Ohio State U., 1937; O.D. (hon.), 1987; hon. Dr. Ocular Sci., So. Calif. Coll. Optometry, 1988; children (by previous marriage)-David, Gregory, Robin, Robert K., Janis, Wesley; m. Marta Ve Everton; children: Marcia, Christie. With Bausch & Lomb, 1937-40; Western mgr. Univis Lens Co., 1940-44, sales mgr., 1945-46; v.p., dir. research Plastic Optics Co., 1946-47; pres., chmn. bd. Armorlite, Inc., 1947-78; lectr. optics Loma Linda U.; assoc. prof. So. Calif. Coll. Optometry, 1948-60. Co-founder (with Hermann J. Muller) Repository for Germinal Choice; trustee Found. Advancement of Man; bd. dirs. Inst. for Research on Morality; bd. dirs. Intra-Sci. Research Found., v.p., 1980; founder Graham Sci. Ctr., Escondido. Recipient Herschel Gold medal Germany, 1972, Feinbloom award Am. Acad. Optometry, 1987, Glenn Fry medal Physiol. Optics, 1992; named Disting. Alumnus, Ohio State U., 1987. Fellow AAAS; mem. Am. Inst. Physics Profs., Optical Soc. Am., Am. Acad. Optometry, Rotary Club, Mensa, Sigma Xi. Republican. Author: The Evolution of Corneal Contact Lenses; The Future of Man; also articles in sci. publs. Inventor variable focus lens, hybrid corneal lens; directed devel. hard resin lenses. Died Feb. 13, 1997. Died Feb. 13, 1997. Home: Escondido Calif.

GRANT, RHODA, biomedical researcher, educator, medical physiologist; b. Hopewell, N.S., Can., Jan. 12, 1902; d. James William and Marjorie Madelein (Cruickshank) G. BA in Biology and Chemistry with honors, McGill U., Montreal, 1924, MA in Biochemistry, 1930, PhD in Exptl. Medicine cum laude, 1932. Biochemistry rsch. technician Med. Lab., Royal Victoria Hosp., McGill U., Montreal, 1925-29; demonstrator in physiology Banting & Best Med. Rsch. Inst., U. Toronto, Ont., Can., 1933-35; researcher on hearing Physiology Dept., McGill U., Montreal, 1936; asst. prof. physiology Med. Coll., Dalhousie U., Halifax, N.S., Can., 1937-38; teaching and rsch. faculty appointee dept. physiology McGill U., 1939-47; rsch. assoc. clin. sci. med. Coll. U. Ill., Chgo., 1948-61; rsch. assoc. pathology med. Coll. U. Ill., 1961-66; participant in Internat. Symposium on Gastric Cancer, Nat. Cancer Inst./NSF, Japan, 1969. Contbr. articles to profl. jours., med. texts, physiol. handbook. Fellow Royal Soc. Medicine (Eng.); mem. Can. Physiol. Soc., Am. Physiol. Soc., Sigma Xi. Avocation: research and writing on biblical truth in the context of science and history. Home: Lansing Mich. Died Nov. 7, 1994.

GRAPPELLI, STEPHANE, jazz violinist; b. Paris, Jan. 26, 1908; s. Ernest and Anna (Hanocke) G.; 1 daughter. With Django Reinhardt, organizer Quintette du Hot Club de France, 1934; frequent tours and recordings; recordings include Afternoon in Paris, At the Winery, 1980, Satin Doll, 1982, How Can You Miss, 1989, Live At Carnegie Hall, 1989, 85 And Still Swinging: Live at Carnegie Hall, 1993, Stephane Grappelli & Jean-Luc Ponty, 1995, Stephane Grappelli & Eddy Louiss, 1996, Live at the Blue Note, 1996, numerous others; 1st U.S. appearance at Newport, R.I., Jazz Festival, 1969;concert appearances and recordings with Yehudi Menuhim; Carnegie Hall debut in 1974, 80th birthday concert, 1988, 85th birthday concert, 1993. decorated chevalier of the Nat. Order of the Legion of Honor; named to Downbeat Hall of Fame, 1983.

GRASSIE, JOSEPH ROBERTS, real estate developer; b. Buenos Aires, Argentina, Oct. 3, 1933; (parents Am. citizens); s. Joseph Flagg and Vida Clarissa (Roberts) G.; m. Josette Krespi, Mar. 23, 1958; children: Yvonne Gail, Scott Roberts. Student, U. Chgo., 1953-54, 57-58, B.A. in Polit. Sci., 1958, M.A., 1960. Mgmt. cons. state and local govt. Pub. Adminstrn. Service, Chgo., 1959-64; chief tech. assistance group AID, State Dept., 1965-68; dep. mgr. City of Grand Rapids, Mich., 1968-70; city mgr. City of Grand Rapids, 1970-76, City of Miami, Fla., 1976-80; pres. Gamma Investments, Miami, Fla., 1981, Worsham Bros. Co., Inc., 1981-95. Trustee Grand Valley Found., Govtl. Affairs Inst., Hist. Mus. So. Fla., Miami Mus. Science; chmn. corp. campaign Greater Miami Opera Assn. Served with USMCR, 1955-56. Mem. Internat. City Mgmt. Assn., Am. Soc. Pub. Adminstrn. Home: Miami Fla. Died June 28, 1995.

GRAY, BARRY SHERMAN, radio commentator; b. Red Lion, N.J., July 2, 1916; s. Manuis Joseph and Dora (Horowitz) Yaroslaw; m. nancy Kellogg-Hess, Sept. 5, 1986; children: Melodie, Michael N., Dora Grace. Grad. high sch., L.A. Broadcaster Sta. KMTR, L.A., 1937, Sta. KGFJ, L.A., 1937, Sta. KOYL, Salt Lake City, 1939, Sta. KMPC, L.A., 1940-41, Sta. WOR, Mutual, N.Y., 1945-47, Sta. WKAT, Miami, Fla., 1947-48, Sta. WMIE, Miami, 1949, Sta. WMCA, N.Y.C., 1950-89; weekly columnist Our Town Newspaper Sta. WOR, N.Y.C., 1989-97, broadcaster, 1989-97. Author: My Night People, 1975; contbr. travel articles to: New York Times; contbg. editor: Diversion mag. Served to lt. col. AUS. Recipient Legion of Honor, N.Y. Police Dept., 1953, Michael award, 1953, award English Speaking Union, 1956. Mem. AFTRA, Screen Actors Guild, NRA (life), Commanderie de Bordeaux, Arms and Armor Club, Met. Mus. N.Y., Sigma Delta Chi. Home: New York N.Y. Died Jan., 1997.

GRAY, HOPE DIFFENDERFER, industrial specialist; b. Los Angeles, Dec. 28, 1917; d. Herbert and Florence (Immerman) Anker; B.A., U. Redlands, 1938; M.B.A., George Washington U., 1976; Ph.D. in Systems Acquisition Mgmt., Pacific Western U., 1982; m. Henry Earl Diffenderfer, Dec. 26, 1938 (dec. 1988); children: Niccole, Pieter, Deborah, Kenneth, William; m. Murray Gray, 1989. Counselor, tchr. Seoul (Korea) Fgn. Sch., 1958-61; contract photographer, writer AID, U.S. Dept. State, Sierra Leone, W. Africa, 1962-67; adminstr., tchr. Am. Sch. of Vientiane, Laos, 1967-70; with TRACOR, Inc., Washington, 1970-71; mgr. Fed. Women's Program, Washington Navy Yard, 1975-77; indsl. specialist Naval Air Systems Command, Washington, 1972-78; team chief Navy audit team for cost/schedule control of major naval aviation contracts, 1978-84; navy rev. dir. for contractors' cost/schedule control systems Asst. Sec. of the Navy, Washington, 1984-89; vol. Ednl. Publs.; with Am. Natural Hygiene Soc., since 1989. Mem. Nat. Contract Mgmt. Assn., Am. Inst. Indsl. Engrs., Federally Employed Women, Inc., Inst. Cost Analysis, Am. Assn. Fgn. Service Women, Phi Beta Kappa, Pi Kappa Delta, Alpha Phi Gamma, Phi Delta Gamma. Contbr. articles to jours. and mags. Died June 9, 1995.

GRAY, JOHN EDMUND, chemical engineer; b. Woonsocket, R.I., Apr. 13, 1922; s. John Joseph and Alice (Naylor) G.; m. Mary Lightbody, Dec. 3, 1944 (div. 1982); children: Jane Elizabeth Gray Redmond, John Carlton, Jeffrey Naylor. BSChemE, U. R.I., 1943.

Rsch. engr. Westinghouse Electric Corp., Bloomfield, N.J., 1943-46; sr. design engr. engring. div. GE, Hanford, Wash., 1946-47; head materials sect. atomic power dept. Gen. Engring. and Cons. Lab., Schenectady, 1948-49; materials adminstr. Naval Reactors br. AEC, U.S. Navy, 1949-50; dir. tech. and prodn. div. U.S. AEC (Savannah River Plant), S.C., 1950-54; project mgr. Shippingport Atomic Power Sta., Duquesne Light Co., Pitts., 1954-60; pres., chmn., chief exec. officer NUS Corp., Rockville, Md., 1960-72; energy cons. Ford Found. Energy Policy Project, 1972-73, MIT Ctr. for Policy Alternatives, 1973, Edison Electric Inst., 1974-77; chmn., chief exec. officer Internat. Energy Assocs. Ltd., Washington, 1976-85; chmn. IEA of Japan Co., Ltd., Tokyo, 1982—, IEAL Energie Cons., Bonn., 1985-90, Integrex, Inc., Alexandria, Va., 1993—; bd. dirs. ERC Internat., pres., 1985-90, vice chmn., 1988-90; chmn., CEO ERC Environ. and Energy Svcs. Co., 1988-90; bd. dirs. Energy Resources Internat., Washington, Abacus Controls, Inc., Somerville, N.J., Gallagher Marine Svcs., Alexandria, Versar Inc., Alexandria, Scientech Inc., Idaho Falls, Idaho, Integrated Resources Group, New Orleans, Ocean Farming, Inc., Alexandria; chmn. bd. mgrs. P&H Marine Safety Inc., 1995—. Author: Energy Policy: Industry Perspectives, 1975; (with others) Energy Research and Development, 1975, Nuclear Fuels Policy, 1976, International Cooperation on Breeder Reactors, 1978, Nuclear Power and Nuclear Weapons Proliferation, 1978, U.S. Energy Policy and U.S. Foreign Policy in the 1980s, 1981, U.S.-Japan Energy Relationships in the 1980s, 1981, Annual of Review of Energy, 1985, Energy Supply and Use in Developing Countries: A Fresh Look at Western (OECD) Interests, 1986, U.S. and Japan Energy Policy Considerations for the 1990s, Energy Imperatives for the 1990s, Global Climate Change, 1991, Energy Technology Cooperation for Sustainable Development, 1992, Basic Policies for the Development of Energy Policies for Russia and Ukraine, 1993, The Magic of Atomic Power, 1993, (Japan Energy Forum award Best Book Yr. 1993), Cooperative Russian-Ukrainian-Japanese-U.S. Recommendations on Energy Pricing, Taxation and Investment for the Russian Federation, 1995. Trustee U. R.I. Found., 1983—, Atlantic Coun. Found., 1986—; trustee Cathedral Choral Soc., 1988-94, v.p., 1991; bd. dirs. Atlantic Coun. U.S., 1976—, vice chmn., 1985—, chmn. energy policy com., 1979—; chmn. U.S.-Japan Energy Cons., 1981—, U.S.-Japan-Newly Ind. States Coop. Approach to Energy Policies for NIS, 1992-95; mem. steering com. Nat. Working Group on Drugs and Addictions Policy, 1994-96. With U.S. Army, 1945-46. Recipient Award for Excellence in Sci. and Tech. U. R.I. Alumni Assn., 1993; named to Hall of Fame, U. R.I. Sch. Engring., 1997. Mem. AAAS, AIChe, Am. Nuclear Soc., U.S. Energy Assn. (bd. dirs. 1985-94, chmn. 1990-92, chmn. USEA-U.S. govt. oversight com. for NIS ctrl. Europe and developing countries programs 1991-94), Internat. Nucl. Energy Acad., Am Soc. Macro Engring. (bd. dirs. 1989—), World Energy Efficiency Assn. (bd. dirs., exec. com. 1993—), U.S. Nat. Acad. of Engring., Univ. Club (Washington). Died Oct. 20, 1997.

GRAYSON, DAVID D., diversified financial services executive; b. 1920. Various mgmt. positions First Investors' Cos., N.Y.C., 1962-68, officer, 1968-94, pres. Home: New York N.Y. Died Feb. 24, 1994.

GREANEY, PATRICK JOSEPH, electronics industry executive; b. N.Y.C.; s. John Joseph and Julia (Dore) G.; m. Susan Kleinermann; children: Kathleen M., Patrick J. Jr., John M. BEE, Manhattan Coll., Riverdale, N.Y.; MBA, Iona Coll., New Rochelle, N.Y. With Philips Electronics, N.Y.C., 1971-97, corp. v.p., 1983-90; pres., COO Cellular Vision USA, N.Y.C., 1997. Mem. IEEE, Ridgewood Country Club (N.J.), Union League Club (N.Y.). Deceased.

GREEN, DAVID, insurance company executive; b. N.Y.C., Mar. 31, 1899; s. Joseph and Sarah (Rosenstein) G.; m. Jeannette Katchen, Mar. 25, 1926 (dec. Oct. 1985); children: Joan (Mrs. Michael Miron) (dec.), Alice (Mrs. Robert Fried). Naval Engr., Lehigh U., 1922; J.D., Rutgers U., 1926. Bar: N.J. 1926. Practiced in Newark, 1926-46; incorporator Motor Club of Am. Ins. Co., Newark, 1928; bd. dirs. Motor Club of Am. Ins. Co. (name changed to MCA Ins. Co.), 1926-89, pres., 1954-89, pres. emeritus, 1989—; pres., dir. Motor Club Am.; pres., dir. emeritus Motor Club Am., 1989-90; ret. Motor Club Am. Trustee N.J. State Safety Council. Served with U.S. Army, 1918; from lt. to lt. comdr. USNR, 1942-45. Recipient Service award Def. Research Inst., 1968; Lehigh U. Alumni Assn. award, 1972; Man of Year award Ins. Brokers Assn. N.J., 1975. Mem. ABA (publs. vice chmn., assoc. editor Forum 1966-67), VFW (life), Fedn. Ins. and Corp. Counsel (pres. 1964-65, chmn. bd. 1965-66, Man of Yr. award 1974, pres. emeritus 1982—), N.J. Bar Assn., Essex County Bar Assn., Nat. Assn. Ind. Insurers (Gov. 1953, 89—, hon. past chmn. 1989—), Nat. Conf. Lawyers (past chmn.), N.J. Spl. Joint Underwriting Assn. (bd. dirs.), N.J. Property Liability Ins. Guaranty Assn., N.J. Ins. Underwriting Assn. (past chmn. bd.), N.J. Auto Full Inst. Underwriting Assn. (bd. dirs.), Am. Legion, Masons, Kiwanis (past pres.), Pi Lambda Phi (Big Pi award 1995). Republican. Jewish. Lodges: Masons, Kiwanis (past pres.).

GREEN, MARGUERITE, history educator; b. Chgo., Sept. 2, 1922; d. Edward A. and Mary (Prindeville) G. BA, Barat Coll., 1943; MA, Cath. U. Am., 1953, PhD, 1956; postgrad., U. Mich., 1964, Sophia U., Tokyo, 1966, U. Minn., 1972, U. London, 1973; grad., Theol. Union, U. Calif-Berkeley, 1984. Joined Religious of Sacred Heart, 1944; tchr. high sch. Acad. Sacred Heart, Chgo., 1946-49; prof. history and Am. studies Barat Coll., Lake Forest, Ill., 1949-83; chmn. dept. history Barat Coll., 1958-83; staff World Without War Council, Berkeley, Calif., 1984-88; mem. Cath. Social Service Legis. Team, San Francisco, 1984-88. Author: The National Civic Federation and the American Labor Movement, 1900 to 1925, 1956; editor: Peace Archives: A Guide to Library Collections, 1986, Americans and World Affairs: A Guide to Organizations and Institutions in Northern California, 1988. Nat. Endowment for Humanities scholar, 1975. DIED 08/26/97. .

GREENBAUM, SIDNEY, English language educator; b. London, Dec. 31, 1929; s. Lewis and Nellie (Bernknopf) G. BA in Hebrew and Aramaic with honors, U. London, 1951, MA, 1953, postgrad. cert. in edn., 1954, BA in English with honors, 1957, PhD, 1967; HHD (hon.), U. Wis., Milw., 1989. Primary sch. tchr. London, 1954-57, head h.s. English dept., 1957-64; tutor in adult evening courses Goldsmith's Coll., U. London, 1963-66; instr. English Univ. Coll., U. London, 1967-68, Quain prof. of English lang. and lit., 1983-90, dir. Survey of English Usage, 1983—, dean faculty of arts, 1988-90; assoc. prof. U. Wis., Milw., 1970-72, prof. English, 1972-83; dean faculty of arts London U., 1986-88; vis. asst. prof. English U. Oreg., Eugene, 1968-69; vis. prof. U. Wis., Milw., 1969-70, Hebrew U. Jerusalem, 1972-73, Univ. Coll., London, 1991-95, rsch. prof., 1995—. Writings include: Studies in English Adverbial Usage, 1969, Verb-Intensifier Collocations in English: An Experimental Approach, 1970, (with Randolph Quirk) Elicitation Experiments in English: Linguistic Studies in Use and Attitude, 1970, (with Quirk, Geoffrey Leech and Jan Svartvik) A Grammar of Contemporary English, 1972, (with Quirk) A Concise Grammar of Contemporary English, 1973, Acceptability in Language, 1977, (with Leech and Svartvik) Studies in English Linguistics, 1980, The English Language Today, 1984, (with Quirk, Leech and Svartvik) A Comprehensive Grammar of English Language, 1985, (with Charles Cooper) Studying Writing: Linguistic Approaches, 1986, (with Janet Whitcut) Guide to English Usage, 1988, Good English and the Grammarian, 1988, A College Grammar of English, 1989, (with Quirk) A Student's Grammar of the English Language, 1990, An Introduction to English Grammar, 1991, Oxford English Grammar, 1996, Comparing English Worldwide: The International Corpus of English, 1996; editor: (with Whitcut) The Complete Plain Words (Ernest Gowers), 1986; editor series (with Cooper) Written Communication ann., 1984-91, Studies in English Language, 1987—. Club: Reform Club. Jewish. Died May 28, 1996.

GREENE, DAVID MASON, retired English language educator; b. Washington, Mar. 16, 1920; s. David Thomas and Eliza Beverley (Mason) G.; m. Helen Mildred Howard, June 10, 1944; 1 child, Dana Mason. Student, Corcoran Art Sch., 1938; BA, San Diego State Coll., 1951; MA, U. Calif., Berkeley, 1952, PhD, 1958. Lectr. English U. Calif., Berkeley, 1955-57; instr. Pa. State U., 1957-58; asst. prof. Lehigh U., Bethlehem, Pa., 1958-64, assoc. prof., 1964-69, prof., 1969-88, ret., 1988; writer on music. Reviewer Fanfare and Am. Record Guide. Mem. Phi Beta Kappa, Omicron Delta Kappa, Phi Mu Alpha Sinfonia. Democrat. Died Feb. 25, 1997.

GREENE, GLEN LEE, minister; b. Clarks, La., Nov. 12, 1915; s. Columbus C. and Roxie S. (Byrd) G.; m. Grace Lois Prince, Nov. 22, 1938; children: Glen Lee, Roxie Greene St. Martin, Jerry Prince. BA, La. Coll., 1939; BD, New Orleans Bapt. Theol. Sem., 1948, ThD, 1950. Ordained to ministry So. Bapt. Conv., 1934. Pastor Pollock (La.) Bapt. Ch., 1938-40; pastor Long Leaf (La.) Bapt. Ch., 1940-42, 1st Bapt. Ch., Paris, Mo., 1942-44, Gonzales (La.) Bapt. Ch., 1944-53, Oak Ridge (La.) Bapt. Ch., 1953-87; Protestant chaplain State Colony and Tng. Sch., Pineville, La., 1938-42; ofcl. historian La. Bapt. Conv., 1973-87. Author: History of the Baptists of Oak Ridge, 1960, Masonry in Louisiana, 1962, The History of Southern Baptist Hospital, 1969, rev. edit., 1976, House Upon a Rock: About Southern Baptists in Louisiana, 1973, Louisiana Baptist Historical Atlas, 1975. Sec. Oak Ridge Dem. Exec. Com.; mem. United Fund Com. Recipient plaque La. Bapt. Hist. Soc., 1979. Mem. Lions, Masons (worshipful master Brookville lodge). Home: Oak Ridge La. Died Apr. 28, 1991; interred Oak Ridge Baptist Cemetery, Oak Ridge, LA.

GREENFIELD, JONATHAN, lawyer; b. Jamaica, N.Y., Mar. 15, 1940. BS, Coll. of Holy Cross, 1962; JD, Stanford U., 1971. Bar: Calif. 1972. Atty. Ware & Freidenrich, Palo Alto, Calif. Mem. ABA (mem. litigation, antitrust law sects.), State Bar Calif., Bar Assn. San Francisco, Palo Alto Bar Assn. DIED 10/14/95. .

GREGORY, BOBBY LEE, science administrator, electrical engineer; b. Allen, Okla., Sept. 30, 1938; s. Jessie Lee and Sylvia Sylvoy (Caldwell) G.; m. Margaret E. Brown, July 15, 1961; children: Gwen, Ginger, Elizabeth. BS, Carnegie Inst. Tech., 1960, MS, 1961, PhD, 1963. With Sandia Nat. Lab., Albuquerque, 1963-88, dir. microelectronics, 1981-88; dir. Microelectronic Lab. Polaroid Corp., Cambridge, Mass., 1988—; vis. asst. prof. Carnegie Mellon U., 1969; mem. microelectronics adv. bd. Jet Propulsion Lab., 1988—, sci. adv. bd. USAF, 1989—. Assoc. editor jours. Solid State Cirs. Soc. IEEE, Solid State Electronics Soc. of IEEE, 1978-81; contbr. articles to profl. jours. Fellow IEEE. Republican. Home: Boston Mass. DIED 12/04/94. .

GREGORY, WILLIAM EDGAR, psychologist; b. Steelville, Mo., Nov. 13, 1910; s. Edward Clark and Rilla Frances (Edgar) G. m. Ella Virginia Sausser, Mar. 10, 1937 (dec. 1953); 1 child, William Edgar Jr.; m. Muriel Holden Van Gilder, June 10, 1956 (dec. 1995). BA, Colo. Coll., 1933; postgrad., U. Chgo., 1933-36; BD, Chgo. Theol. Sem., 1936; PhD, U. Calif., Berkeley, 1955. Ordained to ministry United Ch. of Christ, 1937. Asst. min. Jefferson Park Congl. Ch., Chgo., 1934-36; editorial assoc. Advance, Boston, 1936-37; pastor West Congl. Ch., Concord, N.H., 1937-39; acting supt. Ft. Berthold Indian Mission, Elbowoods, N.D., 1939-40; chaplain U.S. Army, 1940-45; dir. ministry svcs. pers. and vets. San Francisco Coun. of Chs., 1945-47; dir. rsch. N. Calif. Coun. of Chs., San Francisco, 1947-48; prof. psychology Coll. of Pacific, Stockton, Calif., 1938-81; prof. emeritus U. Pacific, Stockton, 1981—; instr. U. Md. abroad, Verona, Italy, 1965. Mem. APA, Am. Sociol. Assn., Am. Anthropol. Assn., Soc. for Sci. Study Religion, DAV. Democrat. Avocation: travel. Deceased.

GRENLEY, PHILIP, urologist; b. N.Y.C., Dec. 21, 1912; s. Robert and Sara (Schrader) G. BS, NYU, 1932, MD, 1936. Diplomate Am. Bd. Urology; m. Dorothy Sarney, Dec. 11, 1938; children: Laurie (Mrs. John Hallen), Neal, Jane (Mrs. Eldridge C. Hanes), Robert. Intern, Kings County Hosp., Bklyn., 1936-38, resident, 1939; resident in urology L.I. Coll. Hosp., Bklyn., 1939-41; pvt. practice medicine specializing in urology, Tacoma, Wash., 1946-90, ret., 1990; urologist Tacoma Gen. Hosp., St. Joseph Hosp., Tacoma, Good Samaritan Hosp., Puyallup, Wash.; pres. med. staff St. Joseph Hosp., Tacoma, 1968-69, mem. exec. bd., 1950-54, 67-68; cons. urologist to Surgeon Gen., Madigan Army Med. Ctr., Tacoma, 1954-87, VA Hosp. at American Lake, 1953-80, USPHS McNeil Island Penitentiary, 1955-82, Good Samaritan Rehab. Ctr., Puyallup, 1960-90; med. cons. State of Wash. Dept. Soc. and Health Svcs., 1990-94; chief of urology 210th Gen. Hosp., Ft. Jackson Regional Hosp., Ft. McClellan Regional Hosp., 1941-46; lectr. in sociology U. Puget Sound, Tacoma, 1960-94. Trustee Wash. Children's Home Soc., 1951-60, Charles Wright Acad., 1961-69, Wash. State Masonic Home, 1984-94; trustee Pierce County Med. Bur., 1949-51, 59-61, 71-73, pres., 1973-74, mem. exec. bd., 1975-77; mem. Lakewood adv. commn. TAE Pierce County Coun., 1992-94. With AUS, 1941-46. Fellow ACS; mem. Am. Urol. Assn., AMA, Wash., Pan Am. med. assns., Pierce County Med. Soc., Masons, Shriners (med. dir. 1965-78, imperial coun. 1982-85, potentate 1983), Royal Order Jesters (dir. 1986, 87), Lions, Elks, Red Cross of Constantine (viceroy 1994). Died Apr. 11, 1994. Home: Tacoma Wash.

GRIFFETH, PAUL LYMAN, educator; b. Sturgis, Mich., Aug. 3, 1919; s. Shirley C. and Edna M. (Kaechele) G.; m. Phyllis Mae Dean, Jan. 17, 1942; children: Gary Dean, Lindsey Jo. B.A., Mich. State U., 1941; M.A., U. Iowa, 1955; Ph.D., 1958. Officer Walstrom-Griffeth Co., Harbor Springs, Mich., 1946-52; asst. dean men U. Iowa, 1953-56, dean men, 1956-58; dean students Western Mich. U., Kalamazoo, 1958-66; v.p. student services Western Mich. U., 1966-70, prof. counselor edn. and counseling psychology, 1970-84, chmn. dept. counselor edn. and counseling psychology, 1980-84; pres. Coun. Mich. Guidance Pers. Orgns., 1962. Past pres. Constance Brown Speech and Hearing Ctr.; bd. dirs. First Savs. and Loan Assn., 1962-88. Served with USNR, 1941-46. Mem. Sigma Nu, Omicron Delta Kappa, Phi Delta Kappa. Presbyterian (elder). Club: Kiwanis. Home: Kalamazoo Mich. Died July 28, 1994; interred Fort Custer National Cemetery.

GRIFFIN, CLAIBOURNE EUGENE, university dean, chemistry educator; b. Rocky Mount, N.C., Oct. 15, 1929; s. Claibourne Eugene and Virginia (Perry) G.; m. Dorthella L. McArthur, June 14, 1972. Student, Phillips Andover Acad., 1946-47; B.A., Princeton, 1951; M.S., U. Va., 1953, Ph.D., 1955. USPHS fellow Cambridge U., 1955-57; instr. U. Pitts., 1957-58, asst. prof., 1958-62, asso. prof., 1962-66, prof. dept. chemistry, 1966-69; adj. sr. fellow Mellon Inst., 1966-69; prof., chmn. dept. chemistry U. Toledo, 1969-74; dean grad. studies and research, prof. chemistry U. Akron, 1974-77, dean arts and scis., prof. chemistry, 1977—, assoc. v.p. for rsch. and grad. studies, 1991—; adj. prof. chemistry Bowling Green State U., 1973-74; cons. Stauffer Chem. Co., 1962-82. Contbr. articles to profl. jours. Mem. Sigma Xi, Phi Lambda Upsilon. DIED 05/30/97. .

GRIFFIN, DEWITT JAMES, architect, real estate developer; b. L.A., Aug. 26, 1914; s. DeWitt Clinton and Ada Gay (Miller) G.; m. Jeanmarie Donald, Aug. 19, 1940 (dec. Sept. 1985); children: Barbara Jean Griffin Holst, John Donald, Cornelia Caulfield Claudius, James DeWitt (dec.); m. Vivienne Dod

Kievenaar, May 6, 1989. BA, UCLA, 1936-38; B.A., U. Calif., 1942. Designer Kaiser Engrs., Richmond, Calif., 1941; architect CF Braun & Co., Alhambra, Calif., 1946-48; pvt. practice architecture Pasadena, Calif., 1948-50; prin. Goudie & Griffin Architects, San Jose, Calif., 1959-64, Griffin & Murray, 1964-66, DeWitt J. Griffin & Assocs., 1966-69; pres. Griffin/Joyce Assocs., Architects, 1969-80; chmn. Griffin Balzhiser Affiliates (Architects), 1974-80; founder, pres. Griffin Cos. Internat., 1980—; founder, dir. San Jose Savs. and Loan Assn., 1965-75, Capitol Services Co., 1964-77, Esandel Corp., 1965-77. Pub. Sea Power mag, 1975-77; archtl. works include U.S. Post Office, San Jose, 1966, VA Hosp, Portland, 1976, Bn. Barracks Complex, Ft. Ord, Calif., 1978. bd. dirs. San Jose Symphony Assn., 1973-84, v.p. 1977-79, pres. 1979-81; active San Jose Symphony Found., 1981-86, v.p. 1988-90; bd. dirs. Coast Guard Acad. Found., 1974-87, Coast Guard Found., 1987-90; founder, bd. dirs. U.S. Navy Meml. Found., 1978-80, trustee, 1980—; trustee Montalvo Ctr. for Arts, 1982-88. Served to comdr. USNR, 1942-46, 50-57. Recipient Navy Meritorious Pub. Svc. medal, 1971, Disting. Service medal Navy League of U.S., 1973; Coast Guard Meritorious Pub. Svc. medal, 1975; Navy Disting. Pub. Svc. medal, 1977; Coast Guard Disting. Pub. Svcs. medal, 1977. Fellow Soc. Am. Mil. Engrs.; mem. AIA (emeritus), U.S. Naval Inst., Navy League U.S. (pres. Santa Clara Valley coun. 1963-66, Calif. state pres. 1966-69, nat. dir. 1967—, exec. com. 1968—, pres. 12th region 1969-71, nat. v.p. 1973-75, nat. pres. 1975-77, chmn. 1977-79), U.S. Naval Sailing Assn., Naval Order of U.S., Wash. Athletic Club (Seattle), St. Francis Yacht Club, Commonwealth of San Francisco Club, Conf. de la Chaine des Rotisseurs, Phi Gamma Delta. Republican. Congregationalist. Died Sept. 5, 1997.

GRIFFIN, EDDIE, education educator; b. Perry, Ga., Oct. 28, 1946; s. Marvin and Ruby Irene (Phillips) G. BS in Edn., Ga. So. U., 1968; MEd, U. Ga., 1973, EdS, 1976; PhD, Ga. State U., 1985. Cert. biology and gifted sci. tchr., adminstr., supr., Ga. Tchr. biology Fayette County Sch. System, Fayetteville, Ga., 1968-70; head biology and physics dept. Houston County Sch. System, Perry, Ga., 1970-81; tchr. gifted program Gwinnett County Pub. Schs., Lawrenceville, Ga., 1981-88; asst. prof. edn. Lander Coll., Greenwood, S.C., 1988—; mem. People to People Biology Edn. Delegation, People's Republic China, summer 1988. Recipient STAR Tchr. award Perry C. of C., 1975, 76, 78, 80. Mem. NEA, NSTA (conv. presenter), Nat. Assn. Biology Tchrs. (conv. presenter), Nat. Assn. for Rsch. in Sci. Teaching, Nat. Coun. Tchrs. Math., Assn. for Edn. Tchrs. Sci., S.C. Sci. Coun., Phi Delta Kappa, Kappa Delta Pi. Died Jan. 2, 1993.

GRIFFIN, W(ILLIAM) L(ESTER) HADLEY, shoe company executive; b. Edwardsville, Ill., May 17, 1918; s. Ralph D. and Julia (Hadley) G.; m. Phoebe M. Perry, Apr. 1, 1942; children: Dustin H. II, Lockwood Perry, Peter Burley. AB, Williams Coll., 1940, LLD (hon.), 1987; LLB, Washington U., 1947, LLD (hon.), 1990. Bar: Mo. 1947. Counsel Wohl Shoe Co., St. Louis, 1947-51; asst. sec. treas. Wohl Shoe Co., 1950-51; sec. Brown Shoe Co. (name changed to Brown Group, Inc. 1972), St. Louis, 1954-64; v.p. Brown Shoe Co. (name changed to Brown Group, Inc. 1972), 1964-66, exec. v.p., 1966-68, pres., 1968-72, chief exec. officer, 1969-82, chmn. bd., 1972-85, pres., 1972-79, chmn. exec. com., 1971-94, also hon. dir.; retired, 1994; chmn. bd. Fed. Res. Bank St. Louis, 1983-87. Trustee (life), former chmn. bd. Washington U., 1983-88; hon. mem. Smithsonian Nat. Bd., 1983-84, chmn.; trustee Williams Coll., 1975-80; life trustee St. Louis Symphony Soc., former pres.; pres. United Fund Greater St. Louis, 1973, campaign chmn., 1972; former pres. St. Louis Civic Progress. Served from ensign to lt. USNR, 1941-45; as lt. comdr. 1951-52, Korea. Fellow Am. Acad. Arts Scis.; mem. Am. Footwear Industries Assn. (past chmn.). Republican. Died Nov. 9, 1997.

GRIFFING, JOSEPH BRUCE, genetics educator; b. Tempe, Ariz., Feb. 24, 1919; s. John B. and Anna M. (Kelly) G.; m. Penelope M. Scott, Sept. 1, 1950; children—Cynthia, Steven, Joan, Deborah. B.S., Ia. State U., 1941, M.S., 1947, Ph.D., 1948; Roosevelt fellow, U. San Marcos, Lima, Peru, 1941-42; NRC fellow, U. Cambridge, Eng., 1953-55. Instr. genetics Iowa State U., 1947-48, asst. prof., 1948-53; prin. research officer plant industry Commonwealth Sci. and Indsl. Research Orgn., Australia, 1955-57; sr. research fellow Commonwealth Sci. and Indsl. Research Orgn., 1957-59, sr. prin. research scientist, 1959-65, chmn. genetic sect., 1960-62; Mershon prof. genetics Ohio State U., 1965-88, chmn. dept., 1967-84. Bd. dirs. Ohio State U. Research Found. Served with AUS, 1943-46. Chilean-Pan.-Am. fellow, 1942. Mem. Genetics Soc. Am., Am. Soc. Naturalist, AAAS, Ohio Acad. Sci., Sigma Xi, Gamma Sigma Delta. Home: Columbus Ohio Died Dec. 1, 1994.

GRIFFITH, EDWIN CLAYBROOK, economist, educator; b. Hague, Va., May 24, 1915; s. Richard Lee and Sarah Lee (Brown) G.; m. Mary Owen Hill, Dec. 28, 1940; children—Martha Anne, Richard Lee III. A.B., Hampden-Sydney Coll., 1936; M.A., U. Va., 1939, Ph.D., 1940. Instr. govt. Marshall (Va.) High Sch., 1936-37; instr. econs. Berea Coll., summer 1940; prof. econs. U. Ga., 1940-46; faculty Washington and Lee U., Lexington, Va., 1946-80, prof., 1950-80, prof. econs. emeritus, 1980—, head dept., 1959-80. Labor arbitrator Fed. Mediation and Conciliation Service, 1950-87; pres. Community Chest, Lexington, 1956-57; mem. planning commn. Lexington, 1957-62, chmn., 1957-60; mem. Lexington Sch. Bd., 1960-71, chmn., 1968-71; hon. chmn. Lexington United Fund, 1968; pres. Stonewall Jackson Hosp., Lexington, 1964-68. Mem. So. Econs. Assn., Va. Social Sci. Assn., Phi Beta Kappa, Omicron Delta Kappa, Beta Gamma Sigma. Episcopalian (vestryman). Lodge: Lions (past pres. Lexington). Died Nov. 21, 1992.

GRIFFITH, WILLIAM SAMUEL, adult education educator; b. Johnstown, Pa., Nov. 25, 1931; s. Samuel Nelson and Myrtle Irene (Hess) G.; m. Beverly Ann Breland, Aug. 21, 1964; children: Thomas Nelson, Kathryn Ann, Rebecca Leigh. BS in Dairy Sci., Pa. State U., 1953; MS in Dairy Sci., La. State U., 1955; PhD in Adult Edn., U. Chgo., 1963. Asst. farm dir. Sta. KDKA, Pitts., 1952; rsch. assoc. La. State U., Baton Rouge, 1954; asst. prof. Va. Poly. Inst., Blacksburg, 1955-62; asst. prof. U. Chgo., 1963-67, assoc. prof., 1968-77; vis. lectr. U. Wis., Madison, 1979; prof. U. B.C., Vancouver, Can., 1977-96; vis. lectr. N.C. State U., Raleigh, 1971, 88, Pa. State U., University Park, 1989; chmn. Commn. of Profs. of Adult Edn., 1969-71. Sr. editor (book series): Handbook of Adult Education in the U.S., 1980-81; mem. editl. com. Jour. Extension, 1970-76; cons. editor Adult Edn. Quar., 1968-96, Adult Basic Edn., 1990-96. Bd. dirs. Planned Parenthood Fedn., Ottawa, Ont., Can., 1989-94; pres. Point Roberts (Wash.) Registered Voters' Assn., 1993-96; charter mem. Rep. Presdl. Task Force, 1989-96. Rsch. grantee Adult Edn. Assn. U.S.A., 1980, Fulbright sr. rsch. grantee, Australia, 1972-73; travelling fellow Brit. Coun., Eng., 1982. Mem. Am. Assn. Adult and Continuing Edn. (pres. 1990-91), N.W. Adult Edn. Assn. (pres. 1986-87, Meritorious Svc. award 1988), Ill. Adult Edn. Assn. (pres. 1969-70, rsch. to practice award 1980), N.Y. Acad. Scis., Lion's Paw Alumni Assn., Sigma Xi (U. B.C. chpt. sec.-treas. 1992-96), Phi Delta Kappa. Lutheran. Avocations: playing the organ, gardening, hiking, travel. Home: Point Roberts Wash. Died Aug. 12, 1996.

GRIMALDI, PASCHAL QUIRINO, elementary and secondary education educator; b. Mt. Vernon, N.Y., Jan. 21, 1931; s. Quirino and Fortunata (Fava) G.; m. JoAnn Cilento (dec.); children: Elaine, Paul, Mindy (dec.); m. Helen Michelini. BS, Manhattan Coll., N.Y.C., 1952; MS in Med. Sci., U. Bridgeport, Conn., 1976. Cert. specialist in chemistry Am. Soc. Clin. Pathologists; cert. nuclear med. technologist; cert. clin. chemist, elem. and secondary tchr. Asst. prof. clin. chemistry Orange County Community Coll., Middletown, N.Y., 1974-84; tchr. math., chemistry and physics Stamford (Conn.) Cath. High Sch., 1985-86; dir. lab. for applied math. and phys. sci. Greenwich (Conn.) High Sch., 1986-88; nuclear med. technician DIANON Systems Inc., Stratford, Conn., 1989; tchr. Mr. "G"ee! Elem. Math.-Sci. Children's Program, Greenwich, 1986-93. Author: Our World; contbr. article to profl. publ. Lt. USNR, 1952-60. Grantee Clay-Adams Corp., Helena Labs. Mem. Am. Assn. for Clin. Chemistry (com.), Downstate Soc. Med. Technologists, Am. Chem. Soc., Nat. Sci. Tchrs. Assn. Home: Greenwich Conn. Died Nov. 5, 1993.

GRIMES, MARGARET WHITEHURST, medievalist, educator; b. New Bern, N.C., Oct. 12, 1917; d. Robert Emmet and Margaret Edna (Ervin) Whitehurst; m. Alan Pendleton Grimes, May 16, 1942; children: Margaret, Alan P. Jr., Katherine E., Peter E. BA, U. N.C., 1938; MA, Mich. State U., 1967, PhD, 1969. Instr. Mich. State U., E. Lansing, 1969-71, asst. prof. humanities, 1971-75, instr., 1969-71, assoc. prof., 1975-80, prof., 1980-86, prof. emeritus, 1986-97; chmn., organizer Medieval Studies Consortium, Mich. State U., E. Lansing, 1991-97. Contbr. articles to profl. jours.; presenter to medieval studies groups. Mem. Medieval Assn. Midwest, Dante Soc. Am., Medieval Acad. Am., Mich. State U. Dante Soc. (chmn., founder 1985). Democrat. Avocations: tutoring gifted students, writing, family. Died Sept. 17, 1997.

GRIMLAND, JOHN MARTIN, JR., accountant, organization official; b. Clifton, Tex., May 11, 1917; s. John Martin and Mayme (Gollihar) G.; BS in Commerce, Tex. Christian U., 1939, LLD (hon.), 1979; m. Phyllis Montgomery, Nov. 1, 1947; children: Diane, Donna Jean, Norma Gayle. With Universal C.I.T. Corp., 1940-42, IRS, 1946-47; pub. accountant, Midland, Tex., 1947-51, C.P.A., 1951-95; ptnr. KMG Main Hurdman, 1968-83, cons., 1983-87; acct., Midland, 1987-95; bd. dirs. Dawson Geophysical Co. Mem. Optimist Internat., 1949-95, gov. Dist. 7, 1957-58, internat. v.p., 1958-59, chmn. internat. pub. relations com., 1959-62, internat. pres., 1962-63, chmn. internat. cmty. svc. com., 1966-69; treas. Midland Symphony Assn., 1960-62, pres. 1963-65; pres. Midland United Fund, 1969, Indsl. Found. of Midland, 1971-74. Trustee Tex. Christian U., 1972-93, Midland Meml. Hosp., 1976-80; pres. Midland YMCA, 1980-82, mem. exec. com., 1979-83. Served to lt. USNR, World War II. C.P.A., Tex. Mem. AICPA, Tex. Soc. CPA's (Disting. Pub. Svc. award 1970), Tex. Christian U. Alumni Assn. (pres. 1965-66, recipient Valuable Alumnus award 1989), Midland C. of C. (pres. 1970). Methodist (chmn. adminstrv. bd. 1961-62, trustee 1983-93, chmn. bd. trustees 1983-84, mem. 1985-93). Club: Midland Country (dir. 1982-85, pres. 1984, bd. gov. Midland Meml. Found., 1990-95, sec., 1992-95). Died Feb. 2, 1995. Home: Midland Tex.

GRIST, CLARENCE RICHARD, chemist, precious metals investor; b. High Point, N.C., Dec. 17, 1932; s. James Wiley and Margaret Hazel (Ewell) G. BA, Bridgewater Coll., 1957; postgrad., U. Richmond, 1961, U. W.Va., 1963, U. Tenn., 1963-64. Chemist FDA, Washington, 1957-58; pvt. practice Rockville, Md., 1967-68; clk. letter sorting machine operator City Post Office U.S. Postal Svc., Washington, 1968-92. With U.S. Army, 1954-56, Germany. Mem. Am. Chem. Soc. (assoc.), N.Y. Acad. Scis., Chem. Soc. Washington, D.C., Washington Tennis Found. (top seed 1968-91, one trophy), Masons (master of the veils 1962-65). Democrat. Methodist. Achievements include product development for future manufacturing.

GROSS, KENNETH E., retired radiologist, medical educator; b. Newark, Oct. 5, 1919. MD, U. Pa., 1943. Diplomate Am. Bd. Radiology. Intern Dartmouth Hitchcock Med. Ctr., 1944, resident in radiology, 1947-48; resident in radiology New Eng. Deaconess Hosp., Boston, 1949-50; clin. prof. U. Wash. Sch. Medicine. Fellow Am. Coll. Radiology, Am. Acad. Pediat. Radiology; mem. Am. Roentgen Ray Soc., Radiol. Soc. N.Am., Soc. Pediat. Rsch.

GROSS, PAUL, pathologist, educator; b. Berlin, June 8, 1902; s. Martin and Julia (Baumgarten) G.; m. Dorothy J. Mulac, Aug. 4, 1930; children: Julianne Gross Sauvageot, Paul James, Peter Martin, John Edwin. A.B., Western Res. U., 1924, M.D., 1927, M.A. (Crile research fellow pathology 1928-29), 1929. Intern St. Vincent's Charity Hosp., Cleve., 1927-28; resident pathology Cleve. City Hosp., 1929-31; pathologist St. Vincent's Charity Hosp., 1931-35; vol. asst. to Prof. Erdheim, Vienna, Austria, 1931-32; pathologist West Pa. Hosp., Pitts., 1935-44, St. Joseph's Hosp., Pitts., 1944-54; dir. research lab. Indsl. Health Found., Mellon Inst., also sr. fellow Inst., 1948-68, adv. fellow, 1968-97; adj. prof. pathology indsl. diseases Grad. Sch. Pub. Health. U. Pitts., 1960-68; research prof. Grad. Sch. Pub. Health, U. Pitts., 1968-71, adj. prof., 1971-76; disting. research prof. pathology Med. U. S.C., 1971-76, adj. prof., 1976-97. Author: (with T.F. Hatch) Pulmonary Deposition and Retention of Inhaled Aerosols, 1964, (with D.C. Braun) Toxic and Biomedical Effects of Fibers with Special Reference to Asbestos, Man-Made Vitreous Fibers and Organic Fibers, 1983; also numerous articles. Recipient Adolph G. Kammer merit in authorship award Indsl. Med. Assn., 1967. Fellow ACP; mem. Am. Coll. Chest Physicians, Indsl. Med. Assn., Coll. Am. Pathologists, Am. Thoracic Soc., Am. Indsl. Hygiene Assn. (hon.), Am. Assn. Pathologists and Bacteriologists, Internat. Acad. Pathology, Am. Soc. Clin. Pathologists, AMA, Am. Soc. Exptl. Pathology. Achievements include special research in chronic pulmonary diseases. Died Jan. 16, 1997.

GROSS, SIDNEY W., neurosurgeon, educator; b. Cleve., Aug. 28, 1904; s. Joseph and Frieda (Weiss) G.; m. Bobbie Bruce, 1983; 1 son by previous marriage, Samuel. A.B., Western Res. U. (now Case Western Res. U.), 1925, M.D., 1928. Diplomate: Am. Bd. Neurol. Surgery. Intern Michael Reese Hosp., Chgo., 1928-29; resident Neurol. Inst., N.Y.C., 1929-31; asst. neurosurgery Washington U., St. Louis, 1931-33; vol. Neuropath. Lab. U. Chgo., 1933; neurosurgeon Mt. Sinai Hosp., Cleve., 1933-34; now emeritus prof. neurosurgery Mt. Sinai Sch. Medicine, N.Y.C.; emeritus dir. dept. neurosurgery City Hosp., Elmhurst, N.Y.; dir. emeritus dept. neurosurgery Mt. Sinai Med. Ctr., N.Y.C.; prof. neurology U. So. Fla. Coll. Medicine, 1978-79; sr. neurosurg. cons. Tampa (Fla.) VA Hosp., 1978-79; cons. Wadsworth VA Hosp., L.A., 1980-95; neurosurgeon Serra Meml. Health Ctr., Sun Valley, Calif.; clin. prof. neurology UCLA Sch. Medicine, 1981-95. Author: Diagnosis and Treatment of Head Injuries, 1940; Contbr. numerous articles to profl. jours. Served with AUS, World War II; chief neurosurg. sect. Halloran Gen. Hosp. maj. M.C. U.S. Army, 85th Evacuation Hosp., 180th and 116th gen. hosps., ETO. Fellow A.C.S., N.Y. Acad. Medicine; mem. Am. Neurol. Assn., Am. Assn. Neurol. Surgeons, N.Y. Soc. Neurosurgery (sec.), Phi Beta Kappa, Alpha Omega Alpha. Home: Santa Monica Calif. Died April 25, 1995.

GROSSCHMID-ZSOGOD, GEZA BENJAMIN, economics educator; b. Budapest, Hungary, Oct. 29, 1918; came to U.S., 1947, naturalized, 1950; s. Lajos de Grosschmid and Jolan de Szitanyi; m. Leonora Martha Nissler, Nov. 8, 1946; 1 child, Pamela Ann. J.U.D., Royal Hungarian Pazmany Peter U., Budapest, 1943. Adminstrv. asst. German mission UNRRA, 1946-47; mem. faculty Duquesne U., 1948-89, prof. econs., 1955-89; dir. Duquesne U. (Inst. African Affairs), 1959-70; dir. Duquesne U. (African Lang. and Area Center), 1960-74, acting acad. v.p., 1970-71, acad. v.p., 1971-75, chmn. div. economic scis., 1978-89; prof. emeritus, 1989-92; cons., field reader U.S. Office Edn., 1965-89. Author: (with others) Principles of Economics, 1959, Louis the Great King of Hungary and Poland, 1986; also numerous monographs, translations, articles, book revs. Served with Royal Hungarian Army, 1944-45. Decorated knight of obedience Sovereign Mil. Order Malta, also grand cross; grand cross of justice Constantine Order St. George; Nat. Order Valor Fed. Republic of Cameroon; knight comdr. with star Order St. Gregory Great Holy See; officer Order of Equatorial Star (Gabon); knight Nat. Order Zaire; officer Order of Lion (Senegal); comdr. Order of Sts. Maurice and Lazarus (Italy). Mem. Duquesne Club, Middlesex County Cricket Club, Squash Racquets Assn., Athenaeum, Marylebone Cricket Club (London), Royal Forth Yacht Club (Edinburgh, Scotland), Met. Club (Washington), Army and Navy Club (Washington), Jockey Club (Vienna), Royal Malta Yacht Club. Republican. Roman Catholic. Home: Pittsburgh Pa. Died Nov. 27, 1992.

GROSSMAN, MAURICE, psychiatrist, educator; b. Phila., Dec. 5, 1907; s. Abraham and Sarah (Bernstein) G.; m. Mollie Froman, Nov. 15, 1938 (div. 1953); children: Paul, Kaye, Carl, Roy. BS, U. N.C., 1927; MD, Jefferson Med. Coll., 1931. Diplomate Am. Bd. Psychiatry and Neurology. Chief rehab. VA Med. Ctr., Palo Alto, Calif., Roseburg, Oreg., Brentwood, Calif., Augusta, Ga., Waco, Tex.; asst. clin. dir. VA Med. Ctr., Roanoke, Va.; pvt. practice, Palo Alto; tng. in psychoanalysis San Francisco Psychoanalytic Inst., 1949-54; asst. clin. prof. psychiatry U. Calif., San Francisco, 1950-59; clin. prof. psychiatry emeritus Stanford (Calif.) U. Sch. Medicine, 1959—; mem. staff psychiat. divsn. Stanford U. Med. Ctr.; mem. U.S. Consultative Com. on Rehab., Calif. Consultative Com. on Rehab., 1950-65. Contbr. chpts. to med. books. Maj. M.C., AUS, 1942-45. Fellow AAAS, Am. Psychiat. Assn. (life, chmn. task force on confidentiality)), Calif. Psychiat. Assn. (co-founder, 1st moderator Calif. dist. 1964-66); mem. No. Calif. Psychiat. Soc. (pres. 1960-61, Outstanding Achievement award 1983), Mid Peninsula Psychiat. Soc. (pres. 1963-64). DIED 10/19/96. .

GROSSMANN, WALTER, librarian, history educator; b. Vienna, June 5, 1918; came to U.S., 1939, naturalized, 1941; s. Otto and Valerie G.; m. Maria Schweinburg, Oct. 6, 1945; children—John, Carol, Barbara. B.A., Yankton (S.D.) Coll., 1941; M.A., Harvard, 1943, Ph.D., 1951; M.S., Simmons Coll., Boston, 1962. Asso. prof. history Simmons Coll., 1947-52; asst. librarian book selection Harvard, 1952-64, lectr. history and lit., 1961-64, Archibald C. Coolidge bibliographer, 1964-66; prof. history U. Mass., Boston, 1966-86; prof. emeritus U. Mass., 1986-92, dir. libraries, 1969-84; vis. lectr. McGill U. Sch. Library Sci., 1966-78. Author: Johann Christian Edelmann: From Orthodoxy to Enlightenment, 1976; editor: Edelmann Sämtliche Schriften, 12 vols, 1969-87. Guggenheim fellow, 1964-65; Humboldt Gesellschaft fellow, 1970. Mem. Am. Hist. Assn., MLA, ALA, Soc. 18th Century Studies, Société Européenne—de Culture. Home: Conway Mass. Died May 29, 1992.

GROVE, KATHRYN MOWREY, church lay worker; b. Harrisburg, Pa., Jan. 11, 1914; d. D. Floyd and Eva (Shearer) Mowrey; AB cum laude, Lebanon Valley Coll., 1934; m. D. Dwight Grove, July 11, 1939; children: David, Carol (Mrs. Ronald W. Miller). Tchr. high sch., New Cumberland, Pa., 1934-39. Missionary, Evang. U.B. Ch., Sierra Leone, West Africa, 1939-41; mem. bd. Christian edn. East Pa. Conf., 1957-62, children's work council, 1957-62; v.p. Pa. Council Chs., 1964-68; mem. fgn. student com., dept. united ch. women Greater Phila. Council Chs., 1960-64; pres. Women's Soc. World Service, Phila. 3d Ch., 1964-67; pres. East Pa. Conf. br. Women's Soc. World Service, 1957-62, mem. gen. program com., 1957-62, mem. com. leadership edn., 1963-67, dept. health and welfare, 1963-67, mem. nat. council, 1963-68; pres. Gen. Women's Soc. World Service; sec. jud. council United Methodist Ch., 1968-76; trustee Eastern Pa. Conf. United Meth. Ch., 1976-82; mem. bus. and fin. com. Pa. Council Chs. Founder Jr. Story League, New Cumberland, 1936, Jr. Civic Club, 1936; pres. Phila. Story League, 1955-57; chmn. 20th biennial conv. Nat. Story League, Phila., 1964; pres. Birney Sch. P.T.A., Phila., 1960-61; speaker various ch. meetings, conv. confs. Contbr. articles to religious publs. Mem. women's planning com. Japan Internat. Christian U. Found., Inc. Trustee, Lebanon Valley Coll., 1968—, Christ United Meth. Ch. Mem. AAUW, Pa. Folklore Soc., Elfreth's Assn. Republican. Mem. Order Eastern Star. Contbr. articles to religious publs.

GRUBER, ALAN RICHARD, insurance company executive; b. N.Y.C., Nov. 2, 1927; s. Abraham and Esther Lucille (Hiller) G.; m. Harriet C. Mandel, Nov. 7, 1948; children: James Mark, Marian Amy Gruber Montgomery, Steven Bennett. S.B., M.I.T., 1945, S.M., 1946; M.A., Harvard U., 1948. Treas., mgr. engring. Nuclear Devel. Corp. Am., White Plains, N.Y., 1948-57; div. mgr. Marquardt Corp., Van Nuys, Calif., 1958-61; exec. v.p. Capital for Tech. Industries, Inc., Santa Monica, Calif., 1961-64; dir. corp. planning Xerox Corp., Stamford, Conn., 1965-70; v.p. corp. devel. Heublein Inc., Farmington, Conn., 1970-72; pres. Triumph Am. Inc., N.Y.C., 1972-75; v.p. Internat. Basic Economy Corp., N.Y.C., 1975-76; chmn., pres. Orion Capital Corp., N.Y.C., 1976-82, chmn., chief exec. officer, 1982-92, chmn. exec. and investment coms., 1997; chmn. Guaranty Nat. Corp., Englewood, Colo.; trustee Neuberger & Berman Family of Equity Mutual Funds, N.Y.C.; dir. Trenwick Group, Stamford, Conn. (formerly Trenwick, Ltd., Hamilton, Bermuda); mem. SEC Adv. Com. on Tender Offers, 1983-97. Recipient Corp. Leadership award MIT, 1987. Mem. Am. Econs. Assn., N.Y. Soc. Security Analysts, Assn. Corp. Growth. Clubs: Harmonie, Econ. (N.Y.C.); Metropolis Country (White Plains), Troon Golf and Country Club (Scottsdale). Died Apr. 17, 1997.

GRUNWALD, ARNOLD PAUL, communications executive, engineer; b. Berlin, Dec. 7, 1910; came to U.S., 1952, naturalized, 1957; s. Richard Michael and Hedwig (Bamann) G.; m. Grete Marie Gwinner, Dec. 29, 1945; children: Eva Dubowski, Peter. Degree in physics and math., Univ., Munich, 1933; degree in engring., Tech. Univ., Munich, 1945. Chief engr., gen. mgr. Wehoba GmbH, Weilheim, Germany, 1946-49; engr. Capital Engring. Co., Chgo., 1952-58; assoc. engr. Argonne (Ill.) Nat. Lab., 1958-77, chmn. Argonne Senate, 1971-72; cons., pres. Rsch. for Braille Communication, Chgo., 1977—; cons. Am. Found. for Blind, N.Y.C., 1973-76, divsn. for blind Libr. Congress, Washington, 1970; cons. engr. Chisholm, Boyd & White, Chgo., Ethicon Inc., Chgo.; participant internat. confs. on engring., social and ethical issues. Contbr. articles to profl. jours. V.p., edn. chmn. Parents of the Blind, Chgo., 1957-67; group discussion leader World Federalists, Chgo.; lectr. Union of Concerned Scientist, Argonne; ptnr. Pub. Citizen Ptnrs. Recipient Letter of Commendation, Pres. U.S., 1976, One of 100 Most Significant Products award Indsl. Rsch. mag., 1969; Hew grantee U.S. Dept. Health, Edn. and Welfare, 1969-75, grantee State of Ill., 1992-93. Mem. Fedn. Am. Scientists, Nat. Fedn. of the Blind, Sigma Xi. Achievements include U.S. and foreign patents in several fields. Deceased.

GUANDOLO, JOHN, lawyer; b. Beaver County, Pa., Sept. 11, 1919; s. Vincent and Tommasina (Meta) G.; m. Elizabeth Wade, Feb. 13, 1942; 1 son, Joseph Wade. A.B. in Econs, U. Ill., 1940; J.D., U. Md., 1943; transp. courses, Northwestern U., 1962. Bar: D.C. 1944, Md. 1952, Ill. 1956, Mo. 1962, U.S. Supreme Ct. 1949, U.S. Ct. Appeals (D.C. cir.) 1944, U.S. Ct. Appeals (5th and 11th cir.) 1981, U.S. Ct. Appeals (3d cir.) 1983, U.S. Ct. Appeals (9th cir.) 1984, U.S. Ct. Appeals (fed. cir.) 1982, U.S. Dist. Ct. D.C. 1944, U.S. Dist. Ct. Oreg. 1955, U.S. Dist. Ct. (no. dist.) Ill. 1956, U.S. Ct. Mil. Appeals 1956, U.S. Claims Ct. 1957, U.S. Ct. Internat. Trade 1980. Trial atty. Dept. Justice, 1948-56; gen. atty. Rock Island R.R., 1956-57; practice law specializing in transp. and antitrust law Washington, 1957-62, 63—; commerce atty. M.P. R.R., 1962-63; gen. ptnr. Macdonald, McInerny, Guandolo, Jordan & Crampton, Washington, 1963-87; counsel McCarthy & Durette, P.C., Washington, 1987-88, Lalos & Keegan, Washington, 1988-92, Miller, Hamilton, Snider, Odom & Bridgeman, Washington, 1992-95; pvt. practice Washington, 1995—; lectr. Am. U., 1967-73. Co-author: Federal Procedure Forms, Vol. 1, 1949, author 3 vols., 1961, also supplements; co-author: Regulation of Transportation, 1964, Transportation Regulation, 1972, 79, 83; author: Transportation Law, 1965, 73, 79, 83, (with others) Coordinated Transportation: Problems and Requirements, 1969; also articles; editor-in-chief: Practitioners Jour., 1959-75. Mem. ABA, Fed. Bar Assn., D.C. Bar Assn., Assn. for Transp. Law, Logistics and Policy, Transp. Lawyers Assn., Maritime Adminstrn. Bar Assn., Univ. Club. DIED 12/23/96. .

GUARINO, JOHN RALPH, physician, scientist, educator; b. N.Y.C., Aug. 17, 1915; s. Joseph J. and Marie (Ferrara) G.; m. Kathleen Paff, Aug. 2, 1947; children: Christopher John, Joseph Charles, Edward James. B.S., L.I. U., 1937; M.D., Coll. Physicians and Surgeons, Boston, 1943. Diplomate: Am. Bd. Internal Medicine. Intern Wyckoff Hosp., Bklyn., 1943-44; resident in internal medicine VA Hosp., Buffalo, N.Y., 1955-57; practice medicine Westford, Mass., 1947-52; research on simplified artificial kidney, 1947-52; inaugurated artificial kidney service Harlem Hosp., N.Y.C., 1952-53; chief artificial kidney service Harlem Hosp., 1952-53, L.I. Coll. Medicine Hosp., 1952-53; asst. chief medicine VA Hosp., Livermore, Calif., 1959-69; chief medicine VA Hosp., Poplar Bluff, Mo., 1969-72, Topeka, Kans., 1972-74; cons. VA Hosp., Boise, Idaho, 1974—; clin. asst. prof. medicine U. Wash., 1977-79, clin. assoc. prof., 1979-83, clin. prof., 1983—; cons. dialysis and treatment uremia, 1952—, guest lectr. nephrology, 1952—, physical diagnosis, 1983—. Contbr. articles on internal medicine to profl. jours. Served to capt., M.C. USAF, 1953-55. Presdl. Medal of Freedom award nominee, 1982-83. Fellow Am. Coll. Physicians (Laureate award 1993); mem. Am. Soc. Artificial Internal Organs (charter), Mass. Med. Soc., AMA. Pioneer in development of artificial kidney, lung and heart; developed auscultatory percussion method of chest examination, auscultatory percussion exam. of head to detect intracranial masses, auscultatory percussion exam. of urinary bladder to detect urinary retention, auscultatory percussion exam. of abdomen to detect ascites; inventor of pneumatic blood treating apparatus; co-inventor of apparatus for dialyzing fluids, diagnostic apparatus utilizing low-frequency sound waves. Died Mar. 8, 1995.

GUDJÓNSSON, HALLDÓR KILJAN See **LAXNESS, HALLDÓR KILJAN**

GULINO, ATEO LOUIS, specialty chemical company executive; b. Cin., Feb. 12, 1917; s. Emil G. and Celeste (Ragnetti) G.; m. Virginia P. Plogsted, Apr. 17, 1941; children: Denis G., Talia C. B.A., U. Cin., 1950. With DuBois Chems., Cin., 1940-70, exec. v.p., 1969-70; sr. v.p. Chemed Corp., Cin., 1970, exec. v.p., 1970—; pres. Total Group, Cin., 1982—. Pres. Cin. Speech and Hearing Ctr., 1970-74; trustee Cin. Symphony Orch., Good Samaritan Hosp., Cin. Clubs: Hyde Park Golf and Country (trustee), Queen City (trustee 1970—), Banker's (trustee 1975—).

GULLEDGE, JACK, retired religious editor; b. Monroe, La., Jan. 14, 1924; s. William J. and Naomi S. (Cole) G.; m. Shirley O., Apr. 10, 1943; children—Gregory Joel, Steven Shelby, Julie Ann. B.A., Ouachita Bapt. U., 1949; B.D., Southwestern Bapt. Theol. Sem., Ft. Worth, 1952. Ordained to ministry So. Bapt. Conv. Pastor Bapt. chs. in Ark. and Ariz., 1947-69; chaplain, pub. relations and devel. staff Scottsdale Meml. Hosp., Ariz., 1970-74; editor. Bapt. Sunday Sch. Bd. of So. Bapt. Conv., Nashville, 1974-89. Author: Horray for Grandparents, 1978, Ideas for Effective Worship, 1979, Sermons and Services for Special Days, 1979, The Senior Years: Getting There, Being There, 1983, Ideas & Illustrations for Inspirational Talks, 1986; co-author: Treasury of Clean Jokes for Senior Adults, 1989. Affiliate Bapt. hosps., Jacksonville, 1962-74, affiliate Bapt. Children's Home, Monticello, Ariz., 1960-62; trustee Bapt. Hosp. of Phoenix, 1963-69, Grand Canyon Coll., Phoenix, 1964-69. Served to sgt. U.S. Army, 1943-46, Korea. Republican. DIED 02/18/97. .

GUNDERSON, RICHARD L., insurance company executive; b. 1933. BSME, S.D. State U., Brookings, 1958; MBA, Northwestern U., 1961. V.p. investments St. Paul (Minn.) Cos., 1961-74, v.p. and asst. to the pres., 1974-76; pres. Western Life Ins. Co., St. Paul, 1976-85; pres., CEO Aid Assn. Luths., Appleton, Wis., 1985—. With U.S. Army, 1954-57.

GURIN, SAMUEL, biochemist, educator; b. N.Y.C., July 1, 1905; s. Morris and Rose (Zwinig) G.; m. Celia Zall, June 14, 1930; children—Robert N., Richard S. B.A., Columbia, 1926, M.S., 1930, Ph.D., 1934; NRC fellow, U. Ill., 1935-37; D.Sc., LaSalle Coll., 1965, Phila. Coll. Pharmacy, 1961, U. Fla., 1979. Prof. biochemistry U. Pa., 1951-68, chmn. dept., 1954-62, dean Med. Sch., 1962-68; prof. biochemistry Med. Sch. and dept. biol. scis. U. Fla., Gainesville, 1970-85; dir. Cornelius Vanderbilt Whitney-U. Fla. Marine Biol. Labs., 1972-78; mem. metabolism panel NRC; study section physiol. chem. NIH, council nat. inst. gen. med. sci.; scientific counselors bd. Nat. Inst. Arthritis and Metabolic Disorders. Editorial bd.: Jour. Biol. Chemistry. Mem. Am. Soc. Biol. Chemists, Am. Chem. Soc.

GURNEY, EDWARD JOHN, lawyer, senator; b. Portland, Maine, Jan. 12, 1914; s. Edward J. and Nellie (Kennedy) G.; m. Leeds Dye, May 1979; children—Jill, Sarah. B.S., Colby Coll., 1935; LL.B., Harvard, 1938; LL.M., Duke, 1948. Bar: N.Y. bar 1939, Fla. bar 1949. Practiced law in N.Y.C., 1938-41, Winter Park, Fla., 1948-96; mem. 88th-90th congresses from 11th Dist. Fla., U.S. Senate from Fla., 1969-75; City commr., Winter Park, 1952-58, mayor, 1961-62. Served to lt. col. AUS, 1941-46, ETO. Decorated Silver Star medal, Purple Heart. Mem. Am., Fla., N.Y. bar assns. Home: Winter Park Fla. Died May 14, 1996.

GURY, JEREMY, writer, advertising executive, artist; b. N.Y.C., Mar. 2, 1913; s. Abraham and Rebecca (Silverman) G.; m. Louise Hutchison, Feb. 24, 1950 (dec. Oct. 1986; children: Michael Collister, Melissa Jeremie. MA with 1st honors, Columbia U., 1935; PhD fellowship, Can. Contbg. editor The Spur, N.Y.C.; mng. editor Stage Mag., N.Y.C., 1936; sr. script writer We the People, 1937; copy chief Ferry Hanley Advt. Agy., N.Y.C., 1938-41; copy dir. Donahue & Coe, N.Y.C., 1941-47; sr. writer Ted Bates & Co., N.Y.C., 1948-53; creative supr., v.p. Ted Bates & Co., 1956-59, v.p., 1959-95, creative dir., 1959-68, chmn. planning bd., 1965-67, dep. chmn. bd. dirs., creative services, 1968-71, creative cons., 1972-95; creative dir. Benton & Bowles, N.Y.C., 1953-56; exec. dir. Quadrant Communications, Inc., 1973-75; creative cons. Mktg. Corp. Am., 1978-79; adv. bd. Software Technology Group, Inc.; advisor Harvard Grad. Sch. Design. Author: (with Aldous Huxley) They Still Draw Pictures, (with Reginald Marsh) The Round and Round Horse, 1943; play The Hither and Thither of Danny Dither, 1956, (with Hilary Knight) The Wonderful World of Aunt Tuddy, 1958; Author, librettist: (with William Schuman) The Mighty Casey, 1953, 2d edit., 1983. Hon. trustee Inst. Internat. Edn.; creative dir. N.Y. Statue of Liberty Centennial Commn., 1983; chmn. Somers Meml. Com., 1987. Aide to surgeon gen. U.S. Army, 1941-44; polit. campaign cons. D.D. Eisenhower, 1952, L.B. Johnson, 1968, A. Ribicoff, 3d term, E.G. Muskie, 1968. Mem. English Grad. Union. Home: Staatsburg N.Y. Died Nov. 28, 1995.

GUSSOW, ALAN, artist, sculptor; b. Bronx, N.Y., May 8, 1931; S. Don and Betty (Gussow) G.; m. Joan Dye, Oct. 21, 1956; children: Adam Stefan, Seth James. A.B., Middlebury Coll., 1952; postgrad.,

Cooper Union, 1953. Instr. in painting and drawing Parsons Sch. Design, N.Y.C., 1956-68; vis. artist and sr. lectr. U. Calif., Santa Cruz, 1975; vis. prof. Queens Coll., CUNY, 1983; univ. scholar Iowa State U., 1984; vis. prof. Middlebury Coll., Vt., 1986; artist-in-residence Am. Acad. in Rome, 1986; adj. asoc. prof. Pace U., Pleasantville, N.Y., 1977; project dir. Artists-in-Residence in Palisades Interstate Park, 1975-78; co-dir. Internat. Shadow project, 1985; Regents prof. U. Calif., Santa Cruz, 1990, mem. art and environ. studies bd., 1992; lect.r. Richard Jones Meml. U. of Tasmania, Hobart, Australia, 1991; organizer Pukamani for Reuben Tam, Monhegan, Maine, 1992. Author: A Sense of Place: The Artist and the American Land, Saturday Review Press, 1972, The Artist as Native: Reinventing Regionalism, 1993; contbr. articles on landscape beauty and preservation to various publs.; one-man shows include Peridot Gallery, N.Y.C., 1962-72, Portland Mus. Art, Maine, 1971, Washburn Gallery, N.Y.C., 1973-80, MB Modern, N.Y.C., Neruda's Garden Odes, 1996; group shows include Joslyn Art Mus., Omaha, 1973, Sheldon Meml. Art Gallery, Lincoln, Nebr., 1973, Am. Acad. and Nat. Inst. Arts and Letters, N.Y.C., 1977; represented in permanent collections Va. Mus., Richmond, Corcoran Gallery of Art, Washington, Sheldon Meml. Art Gallery, Lincoln, Albany Inst. History and Art, N.Y.; sculptural installations Pukamani for Reuben Tam, Maine Coast Artists Gallery Rockport, Tam Studio, Monhegan Island, Maine, 1991; guest curator Babcock Galleries, N.Y.C., 1993; co-curator Rediscovering the Landscape of the Americas, Gerald Peters Gallery, Santa Fe, 1996. Del. to Democratic Nat. Conv., 1972; founding trustee Edward Hopper Landmark Preservation Found., Nyack, N.Y., 1971—; founding trustee Artists for Environment Found., 1971, chmn. bd., 1971-74; trustee America the Beautiful Fund, 1970—, pres., 1979; trustee Friends of the Earth, v.p., 1976, pres. 1986-87, chmn. bd. 1988-90, pres. found., 1980-86, Friends of the Earth/Action. Recipient Prix de Rome, 1953-55; Edward John Noble Found. grantee, 1974. DIED 05/05/97. .

GUSTAFSON, RALPH BARKER, poet, educator; b. Lime Ridge, Que., Can., Aug. 16, 1909; s. Carl Otto and Gertrude Ella (Barker) G.; m. Elisabeth Renninger, Oct. 4, 1958. BA, MA, Bishops U., 1930, DCL (hon.), 1977; BA, MA, Oxford U., Eng., 1933; DLitt (hon.), Mt. Allison U., 1973, York U., 1991. Music master Bishops Coll. Sch., 1930; master St. Alban's Boys Sch., Ont., 1934; with Brit. Info. Services, 1942-46; prof., univ. poet Bishop's U., Lennoxville, Que., 1963-79; music critic Canadian Broadcasting Corp., 1960—; Mem. various award juries Can. Council; rep. Can. poet to U.K., 1972, Can. poet to USSR, 1976, Can. poet to Washington, 1977, Can. poet to Italy, 1981, 82; prof. emeritus Bishop's U., 1992. Author: poetry The Golden Chalice, 1935, Alfred the Great, 1937, Epithalamium in Time of War, 1941, Lyrics Unromantic, 1942, Flight into Darkness, 1944, Rivers among Rocks, 1960, Rocky Mountain Poems, 1960, Sift in an Hourglass, 1966, Ixion's Wheel, 1969, Theme and Variations for Sounding Brass, 1972, Selected Poems, 1972, Fire on Stone, 1974, Corners in the Glass, 1977, Soviet Poems, 1978, Sequences, 1979, Gradations of Grandeur, 1982, Landscape with Rain, 1980, Manipulations on Greek Themes, 1988, Conflicts of Spring, 1981, The Moment is All: Selected Poems, 1944-83; Directives of Autumn, 1984, At the Ocean's Verge (selected poems U.S.), 1984; Impromptus, 1984, Twelve Landscapes, 1985, Winter Prophecies, 1987, Collected Poems, (Vols. I & II), 1987, 94, Celestial Corkscrew, 1990, Shadows in the Grass, 1991; (essays) Plummets and Other Partialities, 1987, Configurations at Midnight, 1992, Tracks in the Snow (collected poems vol. III), 1994; short stories The Brazen Tower, 1975, The Vivid Air, 1980; editor: Anthology of Canadian Poetry, 1942, A Little Anthology of Canadian Poetry, 1943, Canadian Accent, 1944, The Penguin Book of Canadian Verse, 1958, rev. edit., 1967, 75, 84; A Literary Friendship: The Correspondence of Ralph Gustafson and W.W.E. Ross, 1985. Decorated Order of Can.; recipient Gov. Gen.'s award for poetry, 1974, A.J.M. Smith award Mich. State U., 1974, Queen's Silver Jubilee medal, 1978, Commemorative medal for 125th Anniversary of Confedn. of Can., 1992, award of merit Bishop U., 1992; Sr. fellow Can. Coun., 1959-60; Winter Prophecies: The Poetry of Ralph Gustafson documentary film made of his works Nat. Film Bd. Can., 1989, A Poetics of Place: The Poetry of Ralph Gustafson, 1990, Poetry award Soc. for Promotion of English Lang. Lit. Mem. Keble Assn., Oxford (life), League Can. Poets (life), Writers Union Can. Died May 29, 1995.

GWINN, WILLIAM DULANEY, physical chemist, educator, executive, consultant; b. Bloomington, Ill., Sept. 28, 1916; s. Walter E. and Allyne (Dulaney) G.; m. Margaret Boothby, July 11, 1953; children—Robert B., Ellen, Kathleen. A.B., U. Mo., 1937, M.A., 1939; Ph.D., U. Calif. at Berkeley, 1942. Teaching asst. U. Calif., Berkeley, 1939-42, mem. faculty, 1942-97, prof. phys. chemistry, 1955-79, prof. emeritus, 1979-97; rsch. prof. Miller Rsch. Inst., 1961-62; pres. Environ. Conversion Tech., Inc., El Cerrito, Calif., 1992-97; vis. prof. chemistry U. Minn., Mpls., 1969-70; cons. several energy-related fields. Assoc. editor: Jour. Chem. Physics, 1962-64. Guggenheim fellow, 1954; Sloan fellow, 1955-59; recipient citation merit U. Mo., 1964. Fellow Am. Phys. Soc.; mem. Am. Chem. Soc., Phi Beta Kappa, Sigma Xi, Pi Mu Epsilon. Achievements include spl. rsch. on molecular structure, microwave spectroscopy, quantum mechanics, direct digital control, rsch. and consulting in several energy-related fields. Home: El Cerrito Calif. Died May 5, 1997.

HAAS, FREDERICK PETER, lawyer; b. Yonkers, N.Y., Oct. 16, 1911; s. John George and Margaret Mary (McDevitt) H.; m. Mary Helen Parke, Feb. 8, 1941 (dec. Aug. 1982); children: Susanne Phyfe (Mrs. Bruce W. Harned), Margaret McDevitt, Harriet Parke (Mrs. Ralph Levesque); m. Anne Webb Sargent, Feb. 18, 1984. Grad., Phillips Acad., Andover, Mass., 1931; B.A., Yale, 1935, LL.B., 1938. Bar: N.Y. bar 1939. Asso. firm Webster & Garside, N.Y.C., 1938-46; partner firm Webster & Sheffied (and predecessors), N.Y.C., 1946-65; counsel, dir. Liggett Group, Inc. (and predecessors), N.Y.C., 1965-76; v.p. Liggett Group, Inc. (and predecessors), 1967-76; ret., 1976; pres. Tobacco History Corp., Durham, N.C., 1976-83; past dir. Paddington Corp., N.Y.C., Austin-Nichols, N.Y.C., Nat. Oats Co., Inc., Brite Industries, Inc., Earl Grissmer Co., Inc. Served to lt. USNR, 1943-46. Fellow Am. Coll. Trial Lawyers; mem. Am., N.Y. State bar assns., Assn. Bar City N.Y. (sec. 1949-51). Club: Yale (N.Y.C.). DIED 09/28/97. .

HAAS, WALTER J., professional baseball team executive; S. Walter A. Jr. and Evelyn (Danzig) H.; m.; 3 children. Former pres. Goldmine Records; exec. v.p. Oakland (Calif.) A's, Am. League, 1980-88, chief oper. officer, 1988-89, former pres., former chief exec. officer, now chmn., COO. Trustee Evelyn and Walter A. Haas, Jr. Fund, Marin County Day Sch. Died 1995.

HABBEN, CAROL, professional baseball player. Grad. h.s., Midland Pk., N.J. Player Rockford (Ill.) Peaches All-Am. Girls Profl. Baseball League, 1951-52, player Kalamazoo (Mich.) Lassies, 1953. Mem. All-Am. Girls Profl. Baseball League championship team, 1953. Died Jan. 1997.

HABER, EDGAR, physician, educator; b. Berlin, Germany, Feb. 1, 1932; came to U.S., 1939, naturalized, 1944; s. Fred Siegfried and Dorothy Judith (Bernstein) H.; m. Carol Avery, Nov. 16, 1958; children: Justin, Graham, Eben. AB, Columbia U., 1952, MD, 1956; MA (hon.), Harvard U., 1968; MA, U. Oxford, 1991. Diplomate: Am. Bd. Internal Medicine. Intern in medicine Mass. Gen. Hosp., Boston, 1956-57; asst. resident in medicine Mass. Gen. Hosp., 1957-58, resident in medicine, 1961-62, asst. in medicine, 1963-64, asst. physician, 1965-68, physician, 1969-97, chief cardiac unit, 1964-88; assoc. Lab. Cellular Physiology, Nat. Heart Inst., Bethesda, Md., 1958-61; hon. clin. asst. cardiac dept. St. George's Hosp., London, Eng., 1962-63; instr. medicine Harvard Med. Sch., Boston, 1963-64, assoc. in medicine, 1964-65, asst. prof., 1965-68, assoc. prof., 1968-71, prof., 1971-90, clin. prof., 1990-91, prof., 1991-97; Elkan R. Blout prof., dir. div. biol. scis. Harvard Sch. Pub. Health, Boston, 1991-97, dir. Ctr. for Prevention of Cardiovascular Disease, 1991-97; pres. Squibb Inst. for Med. Research, Princeton, N.J., 1988-90, Bristol-Myers Squibb Pharm. Rsch. Inst., N.J., 1990-91; sr. physician Brigham & Women's Hosp., Boston, 1992-97; fellow Lincoln Coll., Oxford, 1992-97; mem. study sect. allergy and immunology NIH, 1965-68, vice chmn. panel on heart and blood vessel diseases, 1972-73, mem. arteriosclerosis task force, 1978; mem. task force on immunology and disease Nat. Inst. Allergy and Infectious Disease, 1972-73; mem. tissue and organ biology interdisciplinary cluster President's Biomed. Research Panel, 1975; mem. U.S. del. to U.S.-USSR Health Exchange, 1975; chmn. CIBA award com. Council for High Blood Pressure Research, 1980-81; vis. prof. Stanford U., 1967, 78, 85, Emory U., 1971, U. Ala., 1971, 76, 86, Mayo Clinic, 1972, U. Calif., San Francisco, 1972, Los Angeles, 1987, Am. U., Beirut, Lebanon, 1972, Duke U., 1976, U. Miss., 1978, U. Tex., Dallas, 1982, Chinese Acad. Med. Scis., Beijing, 1982, Monash U., Melbourne, Australia, 1983, Royal Postgrad. Med. Sch., London, 1984, U. Queensland, Brisbane, Australia, 1985, Dartmouth Coll., 1986, SUNY, Syracuse, 1987; sr. physician Brigham Women's Hosp., Boston, 1992-97; vis. scholar McGill U., Montreal, 1984; guest lectr. Biol. Soc. and Cardiol. Soc., Copenhagen, Denmark, 1971; WHO lectr., Santiago, Chile, 1973; Jennifer Jones Simon lectr. in med. scis. Calif. Inst. Tech., 1974; Alpha Omega Alpha lectr. La. State U., 1975; George C. Griffith sci. lectr., 1975; Centennial lectr. Meharry Med. Sch., 1976; John Kent Meml. lectr. Stanford U., 1978; Ives lectr. Soc. of Fellows, Scripps clinic and Research Found., 1979; Bunn Meml. lectr. Youngstown Hosp. Assn., N.E. Ohio Univs., 1979; John J. Sampson lectr. Mt. Zion Hosp. and Med. Center, San Francisco, 1979; 1st internat. lectr. Internat. Soc. and Fedn. of Cardiology, 1980; Pfizer lectr. Southwestern U., 1980, Clin. Research Inst., Montreal, Can., 1981, Plenary lectr. Japanese Soc. Hypertension, 1981, Berry Meml. lectr., Chandigarh, India, 1982; 1st George Pickering lectr. Brit. Hypertension Soc., 1983; 7th ann. Irvine Page lectr. Cleve. Clinic Found., 1984; Sommer Meml. lectr. U. Oreg., 1985; lectr. William Goldring Meml. NYU, 1985; lectr. R.T. Hall Lectureship of Cardiac Soc. Australia and New Zealand, 1986; lectr. Joseph A. Nicholson Lecture in Cardiology at Tufts U., 1987; lectr. James B. Herrick Lecture of Chgo. Heart Assn., 1987, 17th ann. Arvilla Berger lectr. N.Y. Cardiological Soc., 1990; bd. dirs. Ctr. for Prevention Cardiovascular Disease. Co-author: Digitalis, 1974, The Future of Antibodies in Human Diagnosis and Therapy, 1976; co-editor: The Practice of Cardiology, 1980; editor: Scientific American Molecular Cardiovascular Medicine, 1995; editor-in-chief: Hypertension, 1983-88; mem. editorial bd. Jour. Clin. Investigation, 1969-70, Immunochemistry, 1970-74, Jour. Immunology, 1971-73, Clin. Immunology and Immunopathology, 1971-89, new Eng. Jour. Medicine, 1979-81, Herz, 1980-97, Circulation, 1978-81, Hybridoma, 1980-97, Circulation Rsch., 1981-84, Jour. Hypertention, 1982-88. Trustee Boston Biomed. Research Inst., Inc. Served with USPHS, 1958-62. Named One of 10 Outstanding Young Men Boston Jr. C. of C., 1966; recipient medal of excellence Columbia U., 1976, Grand Sci. award Phi Lambda Kappa, 1984, Otsuka award for Outstanding Rsch., Internat. Soc. Heart Rsch., 1985, Rsch. Achievement award Am. Heart Assn., 1986, Dupont Specialty Diagnostic award Clin. Ligand Assay Soc., 1988, CIBA award for Hypertention Rsch., Am. Heart Assn., 1989, Joseph Mather Smith prize Coll. Physicians & Surgeons Columbia U., 1991. Fellow Am. Coll. Cardiology (Disting. Scientist award 1991), Am. Acad. Arts and Scis., AAAS; mem. NAS (Inst. Medicine), Royal Soc. Medicine (London), Am. Soc. Biol. Chemists (membership com. 1971-73), Mass. Med. Soc., Am. Assn. Immunologists, Am. Soc. Clin. Investigation (nominating com. 1972, councillor 1975), Am. Fedn. Clin. Research, Brit. Soc. Immunology, Assn. Am. Physicians, Internat. Soc. Hypertension (Volhard Prize 1980), Am. Heart Assn (fellow council on clin. cardiology, research com. 1970-76, v.p. for research 1973-74, pub. policy and govt. relations working group 1973-74, George E. Brown meml. lectr. 1973), Internat. Union Immunological Socs. (chmn. edn. com. 1971-73), New Eng. Cardiovascular Soc. (pres. 1978-79), Assn. Univ. Cardiologists (v.p. 1979-80, pres. 1980-81), Phi Beta Kappa, Alpha Omega Alpha. Club: Harvard (Boston). Home: Salisbury N.H. Died Oct. 13, 1997.

HABERMAN, FREDERICK WILLIAM, educator; b. Duquesne, Pa., May 11, 1908; s. Louis Henry and Maude (McLaughlin) H.; m. Helen Louise Power, June 16, 1934; children—Frederick William IV, Ann Marwood (Mrs. Gene L. Armstrong). A.B., Allegheny Coll., 1930, A.M., U. Wis., 1936; Ph.D., Cornell U., 1947. Tchr. Harborcreek (Pa.) High Sch., 1930-32; instr. Allegheny Coll., 1932-36, asst. prof., 1942-43; instr. Princeton, 1938-42; mem. faculty U. Wis., Madison, 1947—; successively asst. prof., asso. prof. U. Wis., 1949-52, prof., 1952-79, Andrew T. Weaver prof. communication arts, 1973-79, Andrew T. Weaver prof. emeritus, 1979—; chmn. dept. speech, 1954-70. Author: (with James W. Cleary) A Bibliography of Rhetoric and Public Address, 1947-61, 1964, Nobel Lectures—Peace, 3 vols, 1972; Editor: (with others) An Historical Anthology of Select British Speeches, 1967; Contbr. (with others) essays to profl. jours. and books. Mem. bd. edn. Joint dist. 1, towns of, Middleton and Madison, Wis., 1951-54. Served to lt. USNR, 1943-46. Mem. AAUP, Speech Communication Assn., Central States, Wis. speech communication assns., Phi Kappa Phi, Delta Sigma Rho, Phi Delta Theta. DIED 05/10/95. .

HACKER, HILARY BAUMANN, bishop; b. New Ulm, Minn., Jan. 10, 1913; s. Emil and Sophia (Baumann) H. Student, Nazareth Hall, St. Paul, Minn., 1928-32, St. Paul Sem., 1932-38; J.C.B., Gregorian U., Rome, Italy, 1939. Ordained priest Roman Cath. Ch., 1938; asst. pastor Ch. of Nativity, St. Paul, June-Oct. 1938; asst. pastor Ch. of Most Holy Trinity, Winsted, Minn., 1939-41; vice chancellor Archdiocese of St. Paul, June-Sept. 1941, chancellor, 1941-45, vicar gen., 1945-56; bishop Bismarck, N.D., 1956-82; asst. pastor Ch. of Christ the King, Mandan, N.D., 1982-87.

HACKLER, LOYD, association executive; b. Cloud Chief, Okla., Mar. 23, 1926; m. Norma Conley; 3 children. BA in Psychology cum laude, Okla. State U., 1949. Writer, reporter, editor newspapers Okla., N.Mex., Tex., 1949-65, assoc. dir. info. VA, Washington, 1965; asst. press sec. to Pres. Johnson, 1966-69; pres. Mgmt. Cons., Inc., 1969-71; adminstrv. asst. to Senator Lloyd Bentsen, 1971-75; pres. Am. Retail Fedn., Washington, 1975-86, vice chmn. 1986— ; owner, operator cattle farm, Kearneysville, W.Va., 1971—; bd. dirs. 70001 Ltd.-The Youth Employment Co., Washington, Space Svcs., Inc., Houston, Fortune Energy, Dallas, FAM Prodns., Houston, Century Nat. Bank, Washington, Va. Farm and Recreation, Washington, Crownblock Oil & Gas Ltd., Tyler, Tex. Named one of 100 Most Influential in Washington, Washingtonian Mag.

HAGAN, WALLACE WOODROW, geologist; b. Griggsville, Ill., Feb. 3, 1913; s. Warren L. and Mabel Rea (Bruner) H.; m. Mary Elizabeth Levan, Nov. 30, 1940; children: Elizabeth Annette, Karen Rea. B.S., U. Ill., 1935, M.S. (grad. scholar), 1936, Ph.D. (grad. fellow), 40-41), 1942; postgrad., U. Mo., summer 1937. Cert. profl. geologist, Ind., Ky. Park geologist Mesa Verde Nat. Park, summer 1935; field asst. Geol. Soc. Am. studies, summers 1935, 36; asst. petroleum geologist J.V. Wicklund Devel. Co., Detroit, 1937-39; cons. geologist Greenville, Ky., Urbana, Ill., 1939-40; geologist charge ground water sect., div. geology Ind. Dept. Conservation, 1942-44; geologist Sohio Petroleum Co.,

1945-48, Felmont Oil Corp., 1948-52; cons. geologist Owensboro, Ky., 1952-58; dir., state geologist Ky. Geol. Survey U. Ky., 1958-78, state geologist emeritus Ky. Geol. Survey, 1978—; cons. geologist, 1978—; mem. topographic mapping com. Ky. C. of C., 1947-51; mem. adv. bd. Ky. Geol. Survey, 1952-58, ex officio mem., 1958-78, mem., 1978—, chmn. legis. com., 1990; Am. Assn. State Geologists rep. to Dept. Interior Geol. Survey div. com. water data for pub. use, Washington, 1968-78; rep. gov. of Ky. research com. Interstate Oil Compact Commn., 1958-94, 94-96, chmn. research com., 1965-66; bd. dirs. Ky. Conservation Congress, also mem. natural resources devel. com. and mineral resources subcom., 1961-64; chmn. quality water com. Ky. Water Resources Study Commn., 1959; rep. gov. Ky. Nat. Water Research Symposium, 1961; mem. research and policy adv. com. Ky. Water Resources Research Inst., 1964-78, mem. fed.-state adv. council, 1973-78; mem. adv. council Inst. for Mining and Mineral Research, U. Ky., 1972-78; mem. Ky. Water Resources Council; mem. subcom. on Maxey Flats radioactive waste disposal site Ky. Sci. and Tech. Commn., 1971-75; mem. adv. com. on underground injection wastewaters Ohio River Valley Water Sanitation Commn., 1970-78; mem. mineral resources subcom. Lower Mississippi Region Comprehensive Study, 1970-76; ex-officio mem. Ky. Devel. Cabinet, 1973-78; mem. adv. bd. Maxey Flats Nuclear Waste Disposal Site Decommissioning Plan, 1983-84; mem. adv. bd. dept. geological sci. Coll. Arts & Scis. U. Ky., 1993—. Contbr. articles to profl. jours. Mem. 1st United Meth. Ch., Lexington, 1959—, pres. Meth. Men, 1965-66, 90-92, v.p., 1989, chmn. nominations com. Lexington dist., 1990. Recipient John Wesley Powell award U.S. Geol. Survey, Dept. Interior, 1972; Dr. Wallace Woodrow Hagan scholarship fund established by Maj. Gen. Richard C. Hagan U. Ky., 1989. Fellow Geol. Soc. Am. (vice chmn. S.E. sect. 1957); mem. Am. Assn. Petroleum Geologists (dist. rep. Great Lakes chpt. 1954, mineral econs. symposium com. 1969-72, Ky.-Tenn. soc. del. to nat. convs. 1984-86, mem. nomination and election com. ho. of dels. 1986, Pub. Svc. award 1982), Geol. Soc. Ky. (pres. 1966-67, hon. life mem., 1978—), Ind.-Ky. Geol. Soc. (hon., exec. officer 1955-56(, Lexington Geol. Soc., Assn. Am. State Geologists (statistician 1963-66, v.p. 1966-67, pres. 1968-69, chmn. liaison com. 1966-68, hon. 1978—), Am. Inst. Profl. Geologists (mem. adv. bd. 1983-84, pres. Ky. sect. 1982-83, lobbyist to Ky. Gen. Assembly 1984, 86), Ky. Acad. Sci. (Disting. Scientist of Yr. 1977), Ky. Oil and Gas Assn. (hon. life emeritus), Rotary (polio plus campaign com. 1987-88). Methodist (ofcl. bd., vice chmn. 1974, chmn. edn. commn. 1979-81, transp. and bus. com. 1990-92, adminstrv. bd. 1990-92). Club: Rotarian (chmn. invocation com. 1982-87, Paul Harris fellow 1985—). Died July 18, 1997.

HAGELSTANGE, RUDOLF, author; b. Nordhausen/Harz, Germany, Jan. 4, 1912; s. Wilhelm and Helene (Struchmann) H.; m. Karola Dittel, 1939; 5 children. Ed. Humanistisches Gymnasium, Nordhausen. Journalist, 1935-40; war corr., 1940-45; author, 1945—. Author: (poetry) Es spannt sich der Bogen, 1943; Venezianisches Credo, 1945; (poetry) Strom der Zeit, 1948; Meersburger Elegie, 1950; Ballade vom verschutteten Leben, 1951; (poetry) Zwischen Stern und Staub, 1953; Tragodie des Orpheus, 1955; Die Nymphe von Fiesole, 1957; Die Nacht, 1954; Es steht in unserer Macht, 1953; How do you like America/, 1957; Lied der Muschel, 1958; Spielball der Gotter, 1959; Nacht Mariens, 1959; Viel Vergnugen, 1960; Holdigung, 1960; Romisches Olympia, 1961; Lied der Jahre, 1961; Reise nach Katmandu, 1962; Farbiges Deutschland, 1962; Die Puppen in der Puppe (Eine Russlandreise), 1963; Corazon (Gedichte aus Spanien), 1973; Zeit fur ein Lachein-Heitere Prosa, 1966; Der schielende Lowe (U.S.A.), 1967; (poetry) Der Krak in Prag, 1969; Altherrensommer, 1969; Alleingang, 1970; (Poetry) Gesprache uber Baume, 1971; Venus im Mars, 1972; (poetry) Gas der Elemente, 1972; (anthology) Funf Ringe, 1975; Reisewetter, 1975; Tranen gelacht—Steckbrief eines Steinbocks, 1976; Und es geschah zur Nacht, 1978; Spiegel des Narziss, 1979; Der sachsische Grossvater, 1979; Trias, 1980; Das Haus (Der Aufstieg Balsers), 1981; Menschen und Gesichter, 1982; Flaschenpost, 1982; Hausfreund bei Kalypso, 1983., Der Niedergang, 1983. Recipient German Critics' prize, 1952, German Schiller Stiftung, 1955, Julius Camps prize, 1958, Grosses Verdienstkreuz, 1959, Olympic Diploma, 1964. Mem. Munich Bavarian Acad., Darmstadt Acad. Speech and Poetry, PEN.

HAHN, EMILY, author; b. St. Louis, Mo., Jan. 14, 1905; d. Isaac Newton and Hannah (Schoen) H.; m. Charles R. Boxer, Nov. 28, 1945; children: Carola, Amanda. B.S., U. Wis., 1926; postgrad., Columbia U., 1928-29, Oxford U., 1934-35. Mining engr. Deko Oil Co., St. Louis, 1926; courier Santa Fe, 1927-28; instr. geology Hunter Coll., N.Y.C., 1929-30; with Red Cross in, Belgian Congo, 1930-31; instr. English, writing Customs Coll., Shanghai, China, 1935-38, Chungking, China, 1940; instr. Customs U., Hong Kong, 1941. Writer of stories and scenarios, N.Y.C. and Hollywood, also travels and newspaper work in, Eng., Continent and North Africa, 1931-32; Author: books including China To Me, 1943, Hongkong Holiday, 1946, China A to Z, 1946, Picture Story of China, 1946, Raffles of Singapore, 1946, Miss Jill, 1947, England to Me, 1949, Purple Passage, 1950, Love Conquers Nothing, 1952, Chiang Kai-Shek, 1955, Diamond, 1956, The Tiger House Party, 1959, China Only Yesterday, 1963, Indo, 1964, Africa to Me, 1964, Animal Gardens, 1967, Times and Places, 1970, On the Side of the Apes, 1971, Once Upon a Pedestal, 1974, Mabel, 1977, Look Who's Talking, 1978, Love of Gold, 1981, Eve and the Apes, 1988. Home: New York N.Y.

HALE, ARNOLD WAYNE, religious educator, army officer, clergyman, psychotherapist; b. Colome, S.D., Sept. 2, 1934; s. Archiebald William and Alvena Lucille (Williams) H.; m. Mary Alice Mauricio, Nov. 30, 1962; 1 child, Alexander; children by previous marriage: Colleen, Zola; stepchildren: Charles, Marlow. BA, U. S.D., 1959; MEd, Our Lady of the Lake U., 1971, MEd, 1973; BS, U. State of N.Y., Albany, 1976; AA, Austin Comm. Coll., 1979; ministerial cert. Gospel Ministry Inst., 1981; DD (hon.), Gospel Ministry Ctr., 1981; diploma ministerial studies, Berean Coll., 1983; ThD, Reeves Christian Seminary, 1984, D of Ministry, 1990; PhD, Christian Bible Coll., 1994. Ordained to ministry Gospel Ministry Ctr. Full Gospel Ch. in Christ, Victory New Testament Fellowship Internat., 1983. Infantryman, U.S. Army, 1953-55, commd. lt., 1959, advanced through ranks to maj., 1973, served in various staff and mgmt. positions with Med. Service Corps, 1959-67, med. adviser Mil. Assistance Command, Vietnam, 1967-68, ednl. tng. officer, U.S. Army Med. Tng. Ctr., Ft. Sam Houston, Tex., 1968-73, hosp. comdr., Ft. Campbell, Ky., 1973-75, med. adviser Tex. Army N.G., Austin, 1975-77, ret., 1977; librarian Thorndale/Milano Independent Sch. Dists., Milam County, Tex., 1977-78; instr. psychology Austin Community Coll., 1977-79; librarian, dist. test adminstr. Austwell-Tivoli Ind. Sch. Dist., Tex., 1979-81; adult probation officer Travis County (Tex.), 1981-82; founding min.-counselor Chaplain Biblio Edn. Counseling Ministry, 1983—; counselor, min. Ministries United, Christ For The Nations Min. Fellowship, Internat. Charismatic Bible Ministries. Decorated Bronze Star; recipient Duke of Paducah award, 1975, Experienced Pastoral Counselor award Inst. Experienced Pastoral Counselors, 1981, Commemorative medal of honor Am. Biog. Inst., 1985, Appreciation plaque Messengers of Great King, 1994, Faithful Svc. cert., Trinity Ch. of Assemblies of God, 1996, Appreciation cert., Ministries United, 1996, Order of Merit, Nat. Rep. Senatorial Com., 1996. Mem. ALA (bibliotherapy discussion group), NEA, Am. Pers. and Guidance Assn., Christians United for Israel, Am. Assn. Christian Counselors, PTL Club, Nat. Chaplains Assn., Internat. Platform Assn., Tex. Jr. Coll. Tchrs. Assn., CAP (maj., med. advisor, chaplain), Ret. Officers Assn. (life), N.G. Assn. Tex. (life), Mil. Order World Wars, Assn. U.S. Army, U.S. Armor Assn., Inst. of Experienced Pastoral Counselors (diplomate advanced Christain pastoral counselor), Internat. Assn. of Christian Pastoral Counselors (diplomate 1987), United Assn. of Christian Counselors Internat. (diplomate), Full Gospel Biblio Counseling Ministry Soc. (diplomate 1989), Am. Acad. Clin. Family Therapists (supervising clin. therapist), Christian Assn. Psychol. Studies, Am. Assn. Marriage and Family Therapy (clin. mem.), Am. Legion (life), VFW (life). Club: Masons (Fed. Republic West Germany). Lodge: Lions. Died Nov. 1997.

HALE, HAMILTON ORIN, retired lawyer; b. Crystal Lake, Ill., Sept. 15, 1906; s. Alva Harry and May Gale (Hamilton) H.; m. J. Elizabeth Hale, June 29, 1946; children: Jean, Hamilton, Jamie. B.S., U. Ill., 1931; J.D., Northwestern U., 1931. Bar: Ill. 1931, N.Y. 1940, D.C. 1965. Practiced in McHenry County, Ill., 1931; assoc. firm Pruitt & Grealis, Chgo., 1932-40; ptnr. firm Pruitt, Hale & MacIntyre, N.Y.C., 1940-48; founder Hale & Stimson (Hale, Russell & Gray), N.Y.C. and Washington, 1948-86; mem. firm Joslyn & Green, Woodstock, Ill., 1970-77; mem. Wardell & Johnson, 1977-88; ret., 1988; Dir. emeritus USAir, Inc.; faculty lectr. on air law Northwestern U. Law Sch., 1934-35. Mayor Village of Roslyn Estates, 1963-67; trustee Village of Bull Valley; chmn. McHenry County Pub. Bldg. Commn.; v.p. bd. trustees Buckley Country Day Sch., N.Y. Decorated knight of Order of St. Olav Norway). Mem. Am., Ill. bar assns., Order of Coif, Theta Chi, Phi Alpha Delta. Republican. Methodist. Club: Woodstock (Ill.) Country. Died Sept. 30, 1994.

HALE, MASON ELLSWORTH, JR., museum curator; b. Winsted, Conn., Sept. 23, 1928; s. Mason Ellsworth and Lillian (Swanson) H.; m. Beatrice Wilde, Apr. 19, 1952; children: Janet Arlene, Sandra Louise, Robert Alan. BS, Yale U., 1950; MA, U. Wis., 1951, PhD, 1953. Asst. prof. biology U. Wichita, 1953-55, W.Va. U., 1955-57; assoc. curator div. cryptograms, dept. botany Mus. Natural History Smithsonian Instn., Washington, 1957-62, curator, 1962—, chmn. dept. botany, 1968-70; field exploration Arctic Can., 1950, Mexico, 1960, Pacific area, 1964-65, India and Sri Lanka, 1974-78, Antarctica, 1980-84, South Africa, 1986-88; spl. rsch. taxonomy and chemistry lichenized fungi. Author: Lichen Handbook, 1961, Biology of Lichens, 1961, How To Know the Lichens, 1969, 2d edit., 1979, (with M. Cole) Lichens of California, 1988. Mem. Am. Soc. Plant Taxonomists, Am. Bryological Soc., Jam. Am. Soc., Explorers Club, Phi Beta Kappa, Sigma Xi.

HALEVY, SIMON, physician, educator; b. Bucharest, Romania, June 5, 1929; came to U.S., 1963, naturalized, 1970; s. Meyer Abraham H. and Rebecca (Landau) H.; m. Hilda M. Valdes, 1968; 1 child, Daniel Abraham. M.D., U. Bucharest, 1953. Diplomate: Am. Bd. Anesthesiology. Intern Univ. Hosp., Coltzea, Romania, 1952-53; resident Univ. Hosp., 1953-54; practice medicine specializing in anesthesiology, 1955—; instr. anesthesia Postgrad. Inst. Medicine, Bucharest, 1955-57; chief lab. in anesthesia Postgrad. Inst. Medicine, 1957-60; preparator, instr. anatomy U. Bucharest Med. Sch., 1950; attending anesthesiologist Univ. Hosp., Fundeni, Bucharest, 1960-63; intern Community Hosp., Glen Cove, N.Y., 1964-65; resident Mt. Sinai Hosp., N.Y.C., 1965-67; asst. prof. anesthesiology Mt. Sinai Sch. Medicine, 1967-68; asst. prof. Albert Einstein Coll. Medicine, 1969-74; assoc. prof. Coll. Physicians and Surgeons, Columbia U., 1974-75; prof. SUNY, 1976—; asst. attending anesthesiologist Mt. Sinai Hosp. Services and Bronx Mcpl. Hosp. Center, 1967-71, attending anesthesiologist, 1973-74; attending anesthesiologist, assoc.-anesthesiologist-in-chief, dir. obstet. anesthesiology and anesthesia rsch. Nassau County Med. Center, 1976—; Chmn. com. on sci. exhibits and posters Postgrad. Assembly in Anesthesiology, N.Y.C., 1971-80. Mem. editorial bd.: Microcirculation, Urgences Médicales; co-editor: Cardiovascular Actions of Anesthetics and Drugs Used in Anesthesia; contbr. articles to sci. jours. Fellow Am. Coll. Anesthesiologists; mem. AMA, Am. Soc. Anesthesiologists, Deutsche Gesellschaft für Anaesthesiologie und Intensivmedizin, Société Française d'Anesthesie et de Réanimation, Association Internationale des Anesthésiologistes d'Expression Française (v.p., mem. adminstrv. council), N.Y. Acad. Scis., AAAS, Am. Soc. Pharmacology and Exptl. Therapeutics. DIED 09/18/95. .

HALL, LUTHER EGBERT, JR., retired lawyer; b. New Orleans, Nov. 14, 1926; s. Luther Egbert and Louisiana (Heard) H.; m. Marie Grehan, Aug. 5, 1950; children: Wendel, Patricia, Terrell, Clayton, Robert. B.B.A., Tulane U., 1950, LL.B., 1952. Bar: La. 1952, U.S. Supreme Ct. 1971. Assoc. Curtis, Foster & Dillon, New Orleans, 1952-54; asst. city atty. City of New Orleans, 1954-56; atty. Pan Am. Petroleum Corp., 1956-62; assoc. Jones, Walker, Waechter, Poitevent & Carrere & Denegre, 1962-67, ptnr., 1967-91; pvt. practice, 1991—; pres. Biloxi Marshlands Corp., 1980-95, also bd. dirs. Served with USN, 1944-46. Mem. Phi Delta Phi. Republican. Roman Catholic. Club: Boston. Died Sept. 23, 1996.

HALL, ROBERT HOWELL, federal judge; b. Soperton, Ga., Nov. 28, 1921; s. Instant Howell, Jr. and Blanche (Mishoe) H.; m. Janice Kay Wren, July 15, 1982; children: Carolyn C., Patricia A., Howell A. B.S. in Commerce, U. Ga., 1941; LL.B., U. Va., 1948; LL.D. (hon.), Emory U., 1973. Bar: Ga. 1948, U.S. Supreme Ct 1948. Prof. law Emory U., 1948-61; asst. atty. gen. Ga., 1953-61; head criminal div. Ga. Law Dept., 1959-61; judge Ga. Ct. Appeals, Atlanta, 1961-74; justice Ga. Supreme Ct., Atlanta, 1974-79; judge U.S. Dist. Ct. (no. dist.) Ga., 1979-95; chmn. Jud. Council Ga., 1973-74, Gov.'s Commn. on Jud. Processes, 1971-73. Author 3 legal texts, also articles. Served with AUS, 1942-46; lt. col. Res. ret. Recipient Leadership award Harvard Law Sch. Assn. Ga., 1971; Golden Citizenship award Fulton Grand Jurors Assn., 1975. Fellow Am. Bar Found.; mem. ABA (ho. of dels. 1971-73, chmn. com. Nat. Inst. Justice 1976-80, mem. exec. com. nat. conf. fed. trial judges 1991-95), Am. Judicature Soc. (bd. dirs. 1964-95, pres. 1971-73, Harley award 1974), Nat. Ctr. State Cts. (adv. coun. 1971-77, bd. dirs. 1977-79), Fed. Judges Assn. (v.p. 1983-87, pres. 1987-89, bd. dirs. 1983-94), Jud. Conf. Com. on Adminstrv. Office, Inst. Ct. Mgmt. (trustee 1976-86), Atlanta Lawyers Club, Delta Tau Delta, Delta Sigma Phi, Phi Delta Phi. Home: Atlanta Ga. Died Oct. 14, 1995.

HALL, WILLIAM STONE, retired mental health official; b. Wagener, S.C., May 1, 1915; s. Henry F. and Mary (Gantt) H.; m. Oxena Elizabeth Gunter, June 29, 1940; children: William Stone, Carol Lynn, Richard F. M.D., Med. U. S.C., 1937; student, Sch. Mil. Neuropsychiatry, 1944, Columbia U., 1947, U. Chgo., 1959. Diplomate: Am. Bd. Neurology and Psychiatry. Intern Columbia (S.C.) Hosp., 1937-38; mem. staff S.C. State Hosp., Columbia, 1938-52; supt. S.C. State Hosp., 1952-69, Pineland State Tng. Sch. and Hosp., 1953-66, Palmetto State Hosp. (name now Crafts-Farrow State Hosp.), 1952-66; commr. mental health S.C. Dept. Mental Health, 1963-85, ret., 1985; clin. prof. psychiatry Med. U. S.C., 1957-95; clin. prof. psychiatry U. S.C., 1957-75, Disting. lectr., 1985-95; mem. Presdl. Task Force on Mentally Handicapped, 1970; chmn. planning com. Surg. Gen.'s Conf. State and Ter. Mental Health Authorities, 1971, 72; liaison mem. Nat. Adv. Mental Health Council, Nat. Inst. Mental Health, 1972-73; mem. Gov.'s State Health Planning Council, 1973-74, Gov.'s Social Devel. Policy Council, 1973-74; mem. coordinating council S.C. Commn. on Aging, 1974-85; mem. S.C. Adv. Council for Comprehensive Health Planning, 1967-75, 1st vice chmn., 1972, 73; councillor, accreditation council for psychiat. facilities Joint Commn. on Accreditation Hosps., 1973-79; mem. Gov.'s Com. on State Employees and their Employment, 1973-85, S.C. Statewide Health Coordinating Council,

1976-85, S.C. Gov.'s Interagy. Coordinating council on Early Childhood Devel. and Edn., 1980-85, S.C. Pretrial Intervention Adv. Com., 1980-85. Trustee United Community Fund, 1968-71; bd. dirs. United Way of Midlands, 1976-80; adv. bd. Remotivation Technique Orgn., 1972-75. Served as maj. M.C. AUS, 1942-46. Recipient disting. svc. plaque S.C. Mental Health Assn., 1960, Orgnl. award S.C. Vocational Rehab. Assn., 1969, Ann. Disting. Svc. award S.C. dept. Am. Legion, 1970, Disting. Svc. award S.C. Hosp. Assn., 1972, Disting. Alumnus award Med. U. S.C., 1974; named to S.C. Hall of Fame, 1975; S.C. Dept. Mental Health ctr. for intensive treatment, rsch. and edn. named in his honor William S. Hall Psychiat. Inst., 1964; William S. Hall Diagnostic Ctr. named in his honor Fenwick Hall, Charleston, 1984; William S. Hall chair neuropsychology and behavioral science named in his honor U. S.C. Sch. Medicine, 1993. Fellow Am. Psychiat. Assn. (life, nominating com. 1968, chmn. program com. 12th Mental Hosp. Inst. 1960, com. certification in adminstrv. psychiatry 1972-80, pres. S.C. dist. br. 1957), Am. Coll. Psychiatrists (charter), Am. Coll. Mental Health Adminstrn.; mem. Am. Hosp. Assn. (chmn. governing council psychiat. hosp. sect. 1971), AMA (com. on nursing 1966-73), S.C. Mental Health Assn., Columbia Med. Soc. (pres. 1958), Assn. Med. Supts. Mental Hosps. (pres. 1964, 65, meritorious service award 1971), Nat. Assn. State Mental Health Program Dirs. (v.p. 1968, 69, pres. 1970, 71), S.C. State Employees Assn. (bd. dirs. 1968-76, v.p. 1971-73, pres. 1973-75, Outstanding State Employee 1967), Am. Assn. Psychiat. Adminstrs. S.C. Med. Assn. Baptist (deacon). Club: Rotarian. Home: Columbia S.C. Died Apr. 10, 1995.

HALSTEAD, JOHN G. H., educator, diplomat, consultant; b. Vancouver, B.C., Can., Jan. 27, 1922; s. Frank Henry and Minnie Williams (Horler) Halstead; m. Jean McAllister Gemmill, June 20, 1953; children: Ian (dec.), Christopher. BA, U. B.C., 1943; BSc, London Sch. Econs., 1950; PhD (honoris causa), U. Augsburg, 1994. Career diplomat Dept. External Affairs, Can., 1946-82, asst., then dep. under sec. of state, 1970-75, ambassador to Bonn, Fed. Republic Germany, 1975-80; ambassador NATO, Brussels, 1980-82; disting. rsch. prof. Sch. Fgn. Svc. Georgetown U., Washington, 1983-89; Paul Martin prof. internat. affairs and law U. Windsor, 1987-88; adj. rsch. prof. Sch. Internat. Affairs Carleton U., Ottawa, 1990—; Skelton-Clark fellow dept. polit. studies Queen's U., Kingston, 1994—; chief adviser to spl. joint com. Parliament Reviewing Can. Fgn. Policy, 1994; lectr. Can. Fgn. Svc. Inst., 1992—. Author: Labor of Love: A Review of Canadian Studies Programs in the United States, 1991, The Troubled Partnership in Transition, 1992, A New Germany in a New Europe, 1992, Collective Security, 1993, Atlantic Community or Continental Drift?, 1993, External Affairs Today, 1995, Canadian Cultural Policy in Germany, 1995, Preventive Diplomacy and Escalation Management, 1995, European Security: What's in it for Canada?, 1996. Bd. dirs. Atlantic Coun. Can., Can. Coun. for European Affairs. Lt. Royal Can. Navy, 1943-46. Recipient Peace prize Assn. German Vets., 1989, Order of Can., 1996. Mem. Can. Inst. Internat. Affairs, Can. Inst. Strategic Studies, UN Assn. of Can., Assn. Can. Studies in the U.S., Assn. Can. Studies in Germany, Assn. Can. Studies in Can.

HALVA, ALLEN KEITH, legal publications consultant; b. Willow River, Minn., Jan. 23, 1913; s. Edward and Frances R. (Allen) H.; m. Julia M. Halva, Oct. 25, 1941; children—Barbara Jo Halva Kachmarzinski, Kurt Edward. Student Pasadena Jr. Coll. and L.A. City Coll., 1931-32; LLB cum laude, Calif. Assoc. Colls., 1935; LLM, L.A. U. Applied Edn., 1950, S.J.D., 1951. Bar: Calif. 1936, Minn. 1941. With West Pub. Co., 1942-82; law book editor; ret.; legal publs. cons. Active Children's Home Soc., Sr. Coalition. Mem. State Bar Calif., Minn. State Bar Assn., Ramsey County Bar Assn., Am. Judicature Soc., Am. Security Council, Nat. Taxpayers Union, Am. Assn. Retired Persons, Am. Diabetes Assn., Met. Sr. Fedn. Presbyterian. Club: Hospitaller Order of St. John of Jerusalem. Died Nov. 30, 1997.

HAM, JAMES MILTON, engineering educator; b. Coboconk, Ont., Can., Sept. 21, 1920; s. James Arthur and Harriet Boomer (Gandier) H.; m. Mary Caroline Augustine, June 4, 1955; chidren: Peter Stace, Mary Martha, Jane Elizabeth (dec.). B.A.Sc., U. Toronto, 1943; S.M., MIT, 1947, Sc.D., 1952; D.ès Sc.A., U. Montreal, 1973; D.Sc., Queen's U., 1974, U. N.B., 1979, McGill U., 1979, McMaster U., 1980; LL.D., U. Man., 1980, Hanyang U., Seoul, Korea, 1981, Concordia Coll., 1983; D.Eng., N.S. Tech. U., 1980, Meml. U., 1981, U. Toronto, 1991; D Sacred Letters, Wycliffe Coll., U. Toronto, 1983; DSc, U. Guelph, 1992. Lectr., housemaster Ajax div. U. Toronto, 1945-46; rsch. assoc. MIT, 1949-51, asst. prof. elec. engring., 1951-52; mem. faculty U. Toronto, 1952-88, head elec. engring., 1964-66, dean faculty applied sci. and engring., 1966-73, chmn. research bd., 1974-76, dean grad. studies, 1976-78, pres., 1978-83, prof. sci., tech. and pub. policy, 1983-88, prof. and pres. emeritus, 1990—; adv. to pres. Can. Inst. for Advanced Research, Toronto, 1988-90; v.p. Can. Acad. Engring., 1988-89, pres., 1990-91; fellow New Coll., 1962; vis. scientist U. Cambridge (Eng.) and USSR, 1960-61; dir. Shell Can. Ltd.; fellow Brookings Instn., 1983-84; chmn. Indsl. Disease Standards Panel, 1985-87. Author: (with G.R. Slemon) Scientific Basis of Electrical Engineering, 1961, Royal Commission on Health and Safety of Workers in Mines, 1976. Bd. govs. Ont. Res. Fedn. Served with Royal Canadian Navy, 1944-45. Decorated Officer Order of Can., 1980; recipient Sci. medal Brit. Assn. Advancement Sco., 1943; Centennial medal Can., 1967; Engring. Alumni medal, 1973; Engring. medal Assoc. Profl. Engrs. Ont., 1974, Gold medal, 1984; Queen's Jubilee medal, 1977; Order of Ont., 1989; confederation medal, Can. 1992. Fellow Engring. Inst. Can. (Sir John Kennedy medal 1983), IEEE (McNaughton medal 1977), Can. Acad. Engring.; mem. Sigma Xi. Died Sept. 16, 1997.

HAMEISTER, LAVON LOUETTA, farm manager, social worker; b. Blairstown, Iowa, Nov. 27, 1922; d. George Frederick and Bertha (Anderson) Hameister; B.A., U. Iowa, 1944; postgrad. N.Y. Sch. Social Work, Columbia, 1945-46, U. Minn. Sch. Social Work, summer 1952; M.A., U. Chgo., 1959. Child welfare practitioner Fayette County Dept. Social Welfare, West Union, Iowa, 1946-56; dist. cons. services in child welfare and pub. assistance Iowa Dept. Social Welfare, Des Moines, 1956-58, dist. field rep., 1959-64, regional supr., 1964-65, supr., specialist supervision, adminstrn. Bur. Staff Devel., 1965-66, chief Bur. Staff Devel., 1966-68; chief div. staff devel. and tng. Office Dep. Commr., Iowa Dept. Social Services, 1968-72, asst. dir. Office Staff Devel., 1972-79, coordinator continuing edn., 1979-86; now mgr. Hameister Farm, Blairstown, Iowa. Active in drive to remodel, enlarge Oelwein (Iowa) Mercy Hosp., 1952; active in devel. mental health ctrs. in N.E. Iowa in 1950's. Mem. Bus. and Profl. Women's Club (chpt. sec. 1950-52), Am. Assn. U. Women, Nat. Assn. Social Workers (chpt. sec.-elect 1958-59), Am. Pub. Welfare Assn., Iowa Welfare Assn., Acad. Cert. Social Workers. Lutheran. Died July 29, 1996.

HAMILTON, T. EARLE, educator, honor society executive; b. Savannah, Ga., June 10, 1905; s. Homer Francis and Catherine Clitheral (Langford) Hartwell; m. Juanita Vivian Adams, Aug. 2, 1933; children: Earle Hartwell, Charles Lee, Helen Catherine (Mrs. Paul A. Anthony). A.B., So. Methodist U., 1927, A.M., 1929; Ph.D. in Spanish and Classics (advanced fellow), U. Tex., Austin, 1940. Tchr. Garland (Tex.) High Sch., 1927-29, Highland Park High Sch., Dallas, 1929-37; instr. classical and Romance langs. Tex. Tech U., Lubbock, 1940-43; asst. prof. Tex. Tech U., 1943-45, assoc. prof., 1945-55, prof., 1955-71, prof. emeritus, 1971-96; vis. prof. Spanish, Tex. Woman's U., Saltillo, Mex., 1945; vis. prof. Spanish and classics Austin Coll., 1962-63; cons. Houston Pub. Sch. Sys., 1953, Angelo State U., 1967-68; co-author grd. reading exams in Spanish, Ednl. Testing Svc., Princeton, N.J., 1966-67. Editor: El Cardenal de Belen (Lope de Vega), 1948, Sigma Delta Pi, A History: The First 75 Years, 1995; editor South Ctrl. MLA Bull., 1953-56, assoc. editor, 1965-67; contbr. articles to profl. jours., various anthologies; presented numerous papers at regional, nat. and internat. profl. meetings. Recipient award Sigma Delta Chi, 1965. Mem. MLA (life), South Ctrl. MLA (hon. life), Tex. Fgn. Lang. Assn. (hon. life, co-founder, pres. 1958, founder, editor Bull. 1953-57), Am. Assn. Tchrs. Spanish and Portuguese (life), NRA (life), Masons (32d degree), Eta Sigma Phi, Sigma Delta Pi (nat. v.p. 1950-59, nat. pres. 1959-68, 72-78, nat. pres. emeritus 1978-96, nat. hon. pres. 1979-96, Order of Don Quijote 1963, del. to Assn. Coll. Honor Socs. 1966-86, Meritorious Svc. award 1986), Sigma Delta Mu (founder, nat. pres. 1979-92). Methodist. Home: Columbus Tex. Died Oct. 2, 1996.

HAMMING, RICHARD WESLEY, computer scientist; b. Chgo., Feb. 11, 1915; s. Richard J. and Mabel G. (Redfield) H.; m. Wanda Little, Sept. 5, 1942. B.S., U. Chgo., 1937; M.A., U. Nebr., 1939, Ph.D. in Math, 1942. With Manhattan Project, 1945-46; with Bell Telephone Labs., 1946-76; mem. faculty Naval Postgrad. Sch., Monterey, Calif., 1976—; adj. prof. computer sci. Naval Postgrad. Sch., 1976—. Author books, papers in field. Recipient Eduard Rhein Found. prize, 1996. Fellow IEEE (Piore award 1979, $10,000 prize medal named in his honor 1986, 1st recipient of same 1988); mem. Assn. Computing Machinery (Turing prize 1968), Nat. Acad. Engring., Am. Math. Assn., AAAS. Died Jan. 7, 1998.

HAMMOND, HAROLD FRANCIS, association executive; b. Lynch, Nebr., June 1, 1908; s. Edward Francis and Lydia (Kallstrom) H.; m. Gertrude Rouse, Oct. 10, 1931; children: Harold Edward, Susan Winslow. Student, Parsons Coll., Fairfield, Iowa, 1926-27; B.C.E., U. Mich., 1930; M.S., Harvard U., 1931. Registered profl. engr., N.J., D.C. Traffic engr. Gov. Mass. Com. St. and Hwy. Safety, 1931-34; traffic analyst Traffic Audit Bur., N.Y.C., 1934-35; dir. traffic and transp. div. Nat. Conservation Bur., 1935-44; mgr. Washington office Am. Transit Assn., 1944-47; asst. mgr. transp. and communication dept. U.S. C. of C., Washington, 1947-48; mgr. dept., 1948-55; exec. v.p., dir. Transp. Assn. Am., Washington, 1955-62; pres., dir. Transp. Assn. Am., 1962-73, sr. advisor, 1973-76; chmn. Nat. Cargo Security Council, 1971-85; transp. cons. (Naval Operating Base), Norfolk, Va., also; (Office Def. Transp.), 1940-44; former mem. adv. council fed. reports (Bur. Budget); mem. transp. adv. council (Dept. Commerce), 1952; former chmn. Harriman Safety Awards Com. Author traffic and transp. manuals.; Co-editor: Traffic Engineering Handbook. Mem. county council, Montgomery County, Md., 1949-53, pres., 1953-54. Harold F. Hammond ann. scholarship fund established in his honor, 1994. Mem. Nat. Inst. Traffic Engrs. (past pres.), Am. Soc. Traffic and Transp. (founder), Eno Found. Transp. (bd. dirs.), Univ. Club (Washington), Congl. Country Club (Washington), Sea Pines Club (Hilton Head Island, S.C.). Republican. Presbyterian. Home: Potomac Md. Died Apr. 2, 1995.

HANCOCK, KENNETH G., chemist, science foundation director; m. Diane K. Hancock, three children. BSc chemistry, cum laude, Harvard U., Cambridge, 1963; Ph.D. chemistry, U. Wisconsin, Madison, 1968. Asst. to tenured assoc. prof. Dept. Chemistry, U. California, Davis, 1968-1977; program dir., acting dir., deputy dir., chemistry division National Science Foundation, Washington, D.C., 1977-90; dir., chemistry division NSF, 1990-93. Mem. Am. Chemical Soc; fellow Am. Assn. for the Advancement of Science; mem. ed. bd. Chemical & Engineering News. Home: Washington D.C.

HANCOCK, THOMAS, machinery manufacturing executive; b. Bloomington, Wis., Aug. 21, 1913; s. Herbert and Helen (Weeks) H.; m. Lena Vogel, Aug. 21, 1942; children: David G., Thomas C., Pamela E. D. Laws (hon.), Viterbo Coll. Asst. to v.p. Trane Co., La Crosse, Wis., 1945-51; v.p. charge sales Trane Co., 1951-53, exec. v.p., dir., 1953-63, pres., 1963-94, chief exec. officer, 1966, chmn., chief exec. officer, 1968-78; dir. Employers Ins. of Wausau, Wis., Tenneco Inc., Houston, Northwest Bancorp., Mpls., No. Engraving Corp., Sparta, Wis., Norplex Corp., La Crosse, No. Trust Bank of Fla., Miami; chmn., chief exec. officer Wausau Ins. Cos., 1985; pres., bd. dirs. Air Conditioning & Refrigeration Inst. Chmn. La Crosse Redevel. Authority; bd. dirs. St. Francis Hosp.; pres. U. Wis.-La Crosse Found.; mem. coun. U. Chgo. Grad. Sch. Bus.; vestryman Christ Episcopal Ch. Lt. comdr. USNR, 1942-45. Recipient Disting. Alumnus award U. Wis.-La Crosse; Pres.'s award La Crosse C. of C. Mem. NAM (bd. dirs.), Wis. Assn. Mfrs. and Commerce (bd. dirs.), Mpls. Club, Chgo. Club, Mid-Am. Club, LaCrosse Club, LaCrosse Country Club, John's Island Club (Vero Beach, Fla., bd. dirs.). Home: Vero Beach Fla. Died Dec. 10, 1994.

HANNA, GORDON, newspaperman; b. Jack County, Tex., Feb. 22, 1920; s. John Grey and Ethyl (Wood) H.; m. Annie Lou Guidry, Apr. 22, 1941; children—Judith, Harriet. Student, Tex. Technol. Coll., 1936-39. Reporter Port Arthur (Tex.) News, 1939-42; reporter Houston Press, 1943-44, reporter, legislative corr., 1946-48, city editor, 1949-54; mng. editor Comml. Appeal, Memphis, 1954-59; editor Evansville (Ind.) Press, 1959-68, Comml. Appeal, Memphis, 1969-75; gen. editorial mgr. Scripps-Howard Newspapers, 1976-83; v.p. E.W. Scripp Co., 1976-83; dir., 1976-87; v.p., dir. E.W. Scripps Co., 1976-83. Served with USAAF, 1944-45. Died Dec. 31, 1995.

HANNA, THOMAS LOUIS, philosopher, educator, author; b. Waco, Tex., Nov. 21, 1928; s. John Dwight and Winifred (Beaumier) H.; m. Susan Taff, May 12, 1950; children—Mary Alice, Michael John, Wendell France.; m. Eleanor Camp Criswell, June 25, 1974. B.A., Tex. Christian U., 1949; B.D., U. Chgo., 1954, Ph.D., 1958. Dir. Jean de Beauvais Club, U. Paris, France, 1951-52; chmn. dept. philos. and religious thought Hollins Coll.; also dir. Hollins Abroad, Paris, 1961-62; writer-in-residence Duke, 1964-65; prof., chmn. dept. philosophy U. Fla., 1965-73, prof., 1973-90; dir., prof. Humanistic Psychology Inst., 1973-75; founder, dir. Novato Inst. for Somatic Research and Tng., 1975-90. Author: The Thought and Art of Albert Camus, 1958, The Bergsonian Heritage, 1963, The Lyrical Existentialists, 1963, Bodies in Revolt: A Primer in Somatic Thinking, 1970, The End of Tyranny: An Essay on the Possibility of America, 1975, Explorers of Humankind, 1979, The Body of Life, 1980, Somatics, 1988; founder, editor: Somatics, 1976-90. Fellow Am. Council Learned Socs., 1968-69. Mem. Somatics Soc. (founder, pres.). Home: Novato Calif. Died July 29, 1990; interred Oakwood Cemetery, Waco, TX.

HANOLD, TERRANCE, lawyer, food industry executive, capital management adviser; b. Mpls., June 22, 1912; s. Robert Arter and Dena (Tillotson) H.; m. Ruth Lorraine Evarts, June 17, 1939; children—Ruth Lorraine, John Terrence, Robert Evarts, Dena Gail, Thomas Tillotson, David Comstock, Lee Hinckley, Dennis Patrick. A.B., U. Minn., 1934, LL.B., 1936. Bar: Minn. bar 1936. Law sec. to chief justice Minn. Supreme Ct., 1936-38; pvt. practice law Mpls., 1938-44; legal counsel Mpls. Star & Tribune Co., 1944-46; with Pillsbury Co., Mpls., 1946-75; atty., asst. sec., treas., asst. gen. counsel Pillsbury Co., 1946-56, treas., 1956-58, treas., controller, 1958-59, treas., prin. financial officer, 1959-60, v.p. finance, 1960-63, exec. v.p. internat. ops. and finance, 1963-67, pres., 1967-73, chmn. exec. com., 1973-75, dir., 1961-75; sr. vis. lectr. Carnegie Mellon Grad Sch. Indsl. Mgmt., 1977-79; adj. prof. U. Minn. Law Sch., 1981-87. Contbr. articles to profl. jours. Mem. food adv. com. Cost of Living Council, 1973-74; chmn. Food and Drug Law Inst., 1974-75, Council

Better Bus. Burs., 1974-76; trustee Com. Econ. Devel., Minn. Symphony, Mpls. Inst. Arts, Inst. Ecumenical and Cultural Research, Council on Religion and Internat. Affairs, Minn. Med. Found. Clubs: Minakahda, Minneapolis Alumni. DIED 01/28/96. .

HANSEN, LEROY JOHN, retired magazine editor; b. Eagle River, Wis., Mar. 10, 1922; s. Harry Forest and Angeline Barbara (Renk) H.; m. Michiko Iwata, June 15, 1954; children—Dane John, Mark Roy, Teresa Ann. Student, U. Wis., 1940-43; B.A. in Journalism, U. So.Calif., 1948. With Riverside Press-Enterprise, Calif., 1948; with UP and UPI, 1948-65; div. news editor in UP and UPI, Asia, 1958-62; with U.S. News & World Report, Washington, 1965-85; fgn. editor U.S. News & World Report, 1979-85; now ret. Served with USMC, 1943-46.

HANSON, EARL DORCHESTER, biology educator; b. Shahjahanpur, India, Feb. 15, 1927; came to U.S., 1942; s. Harry Albert and Jean (Dorchester) H.; m. Carlota Ferne Kinzie, June 10, 1948 (div. 1973); children: Mardi Jean, Stanley Royce, Kenric Mark; m. Evelyn Schenker, Jan. 4, 1975 (div. 1991). A.B., Bowdoin Coll., 1949; Ph.D., Ind. U., 1954. Teaching fellow Ind. U., 1954; from instr. to asst. prof. Yale U., 1954-60; assoc. prof. Wesleyan U., Middletown, Conn., 1960-63; prof. biology Wesleyan U., 1963-82, Fisk prof. natural sci., 1972-93, prof. biology and sci. in soc., 1982-93; mem. Commn. Undergrad. Edn. in Biol. Scis., 1962-67, chmn., 1965-67; mem. regional bd. examiners Woodrow Wilson Fellowships, 1964-65; mem. discipline com. for biology Coll. Entrance Exam. Bd., 1974-76; mem. life scis. panel Coun. for Internat. Exchange of Scholars, 1981-84; vis. prof. Lewis & Clark Coll., 1989-90. Author: Animal Diversity, 3d edit, 1972; co-author: Biology: The Science of Life, 1979; Editor: (with others) The Lower Metazoa, 1963, The Origin and Early Evolution of Animals, 1977, Understanding Evolution, 1981. Served with USMCR, 1945-46. Recipient Harbison award for distinguished teaching, 1970; Fulbright fellow, 1960-61, 78-79; Guggenheim fellow, 1960-61. Mem. AAUP, AAAS, Am. Inst. Biol. Scis. (bd. govs. 1970-74), Soc. Protozoologists, Fedn. Am. Scientists, Nat. Assn. Sci. Tchrs., Nat. Assn. Sci., Tech. and Soc., Internat. Soc. Environ. Ethics. Home: Higganum Conn. Died Oct. 26, 1993.

HANSON, MAURICE FRANCIS (MAURY HANSON), magazine publisher and editor; b. Phila., Oct. 14, 1907; s. Michael Francis and Sarah (O'Neill) H.; m. Margaret Ellen Hixon, Oct. 28, 1939; children: Robert Hixon, Michael Francis, Barbara Hanson (Mrs. Charles Eliot Pierce, Jr.). B.A., Yale, 1930. Fgn. corr., columnist Consol. Pubs. Newspapers, 1930-32; account exec., dept. head Benton & Bowles, Inc., 1932-38; with J. Walter Thompson Co., 1938-43, 46-60, v.p., 1947-60; cons. to Yale pres. A. Whitney Griswold, 1960-62; pub. relations cons. Gen. Motors Corp., 1963-67; founder, editor, pub. The Nutmegger mag. of Conn., Greenwich, 1967-89; dep. dir. OWI, 1943-46. Author: Pierpont the Foxhound, 1939, College Reunion, 1955. Recipient Yale medal for outstanding service to univ., 1975. Republican. Clubs: Round Hill (Greenwich); Royal and Ancient Golf (St. Andrews, Scotland). Home: Greenwich Conn. Died Mar. 10, 1997.

HANSON, RAYMOND LESTER, lawyer; b. San Francisco, Nov. 2, 1912; s. Raymond O. and Hilda (Beavis) H.; m. Eleanor E. Quandt, June 15, 1935; children: E. Lynne Dilling, Christine H. Cabot. AB, Stanford U., 1933; JD, U. Calif. Hastings Coll. Law, 1936; LLD (hon.), Whitworth Coll., 1977; LHD (hon.), Coll. of Idaho, 1980. Bar: Calif. bar 1936, U.S. Supreme Ct. bar 1956. Ptnr. firm Hanson, Bridgett, Marcus, Vlahos & Rudy, San Francisco, 1957-82; retired, 1982; mem. vol. adv. com. atty. gen. Calif., 1972-84, asst. dist. atty., City and County of San Francisco, 1937-38, columnist, lectr. on trusts and estate planning. Elder, trustee Calvary Presbyn. Ch., San Francisco, 1939-41; ruling elder United Presbyn. Ch. in U.S.A., 1939-75; pres. bd. of ch. extension Presbytery of San Francisco, 1946-49, moderator, 1953; justice Permanent Jud. Commn., Supreme Ct. of denomination, 1952-61; chmn. bd. San Francisco Theol. Sem., 1974-84; chmn., mem. worship and music com. First Presbyn. Ch. of San Mateo, 1959-64; past pres., sec. Pacific Med. Center, Inc.; past pres. No. Calif. Presbyn. Homes, Inc.; past chmn. bd., dir. San Francisco Met. YMCA; pres., bd. dirs. Goodwill Industries San Francisco, 1972-73; bd. dirs. U. Calif. Hastings Coll. Law; mem. asso. bd. San Francisco council Boy Scouts Am.; pres. Fellowship Forum, Palo Alto, Calif., 1987; mem. adv. bd. Golden Gate U. Center for Tax Studies; active U. Calif. Alumni Council, 1970-71; trustee Oreg. Shakespeare Festival, 1982-96, Ashland. Served to lt. USNR, 1943-46. Recipient award of year for outstanding and distinguished service U. Calif. Hastings Coll. Law, 1975. Fellow Am. Coll. Probate Counsel (chmn. subcom. on adminstrn. estates, uniform probate code com. 1972); mem. Am. Judicature Soc., Nat. Assn. Coll. and Univ. Attys., Lawyers Club of San Francisco, San Francisco Estate Planning Council, ABA (state chmn. com. on charitable trusts 1972), Calif. Bar Assn. (chmn. com. on conf. resolution 1967-69), San Francisco Bar Assn. (past dir., past chmn. estate and trust law sect., chmn. publs. com. 1969-70), Am. Assn. Homes for Aging, Internat. Acad. Estate and Trust Law (academician). Clubs: Kiwanis Internat. (past chmn. boys and girls work com. Calif.-Nev.-Hawaii Dist., past pres. San Francisco). Died July 17, 1996.

HARDENBURG, ROBERT EARLE, horticulturist; b. Ithaca, N.Y., July 27, 1919; s. Earle Volcart and Aline (Crandall) H.; m. Jean Marie Swett, Oct. 2, 1943; children: Kathryn, Mary Ann. BS, Cornell U., 1941, MS, 1947, PhD, 1949. Assoc. horticulturist USDA, Beltsville, Md., 1949-53, horticulturist, 1953-58, sr. horticulturist, 1958-61, prin. horticulturist, 1961-67, lab. chief, 1971-81; pvt. practice cons. Venice, Fla., 1981-90; ret., 1981-95. Author: Commercial Storage of fruits, Vegetables and Nursery Stocks, 1986; also 135 other rsch. publs. Maj. U.S. Army, 1941-46. Fellow Am. Soc. Hort Scis. (sect. chmn. 1972-73); mem. Produce Mktg. Assn. (life bd. dirs. 1960-62, Disting. Svc. award 1963), Refrigeration Rsch. Found. (mem. sci. adv. coun. 1974-91, Cert. Appreciation 1991), Rotary (dir., editor Venice, Fla. 1981-95), Lions (treas. College Park, Md. chpt. 1955-62). Republican. Methodist. Achievements include research on handling, transportation, storage and packaging of fruits, vegetables and nursery stocks.

HARDY, ALISTER (CLAVERING), zoologist; b. Nottingham, Eng., Feb. 10, 1896; s. Richard H.; M.A., D.Sc., Exeter Coll., Oxford (Eng.) U.; LL.D. hon.), U. Aberdeen (Scotland), D.Sc. (hon.), U. Southampton (Eng.), U. Hull (Eng.); m. Sylvia Lucy, 1927; 2 children. Oxford U. biol. scholar Stazione Zoologica, Naples, Italy, 1920; asst. naturalist dept. fisheries Brit. Ministry Agr. and Fisheries, 1921-24; chief zoologist to Discovery Expdn., 1924-28; prof. zoology and oceanography Univ. Coll., U. Hull, 1928-42; Regius prof. natural history U. Aberdeen, 1942-45, Gifford lectr., 1963-65; Linacre prof. zoology Oxford U., 1946-61, prof. zool. field studies, 1961-63, founder, dir. religious experience research unit Manchester Coll., 1969-76, prof. emeritus U. Oxford, 1976—; fellow Merton Coll., Oxford U., 1946-63, now hon. fellow; hon. fellow Exeter Coll., Oxford U. Served to capt. Brit. No. Cyclist Bn., 1915-19. Recipient Sci. medal Zool. Soc., 1939, Pierre Lacomte du Noüy prize, 1968; Christopher Welch biol. research scholar, 1920. Author: The Open Sea, Part I, The World of Plankton, 1956; The Open Sea, Part II, Fish and Fisheries, 1958; The Living Stream, 1965; The Divine Flame, 1966; Great Waters, 1967; (with R. Harvie and A. Koestler) The Challenge of Chance, 1973; The Biology of God, 1975; The Spiritual Nature of Man, 1979; Darwin and The Spirit of Man, 1984.

HARDY, DAVID, lawyer, corporate executive; b. Los Angeles, May 15, 1924; s. Rex Giffen and Dorothy Field (Simpson) H.; m. Constance Parrette (div. 1969); children: Francesca, David Kimberley, Robert Paul; m. Charlotte Broomberg (div. 1976); m. Jane Myers, 1977; stepchildren: Bradley and Lauren Myers. Student, UCLA, 1942-44, 46-47; BA, U. Calif.-Berkeley, 1948, JD, 1950. Bar: Calif. 1951. V.p. Kaiser Steel Corp., 1969-73; lawyer, exec. Affiliated Kaiser Cos, Oakland, Calif., 1948-73; v.p. Kaiser Industries Corp., 1962-71; ptnr. Millikan & Hardy, Pasadena, Calif., 1973-76; asso. gen. counsel McKesson Corp., 1976-79, dep. gen. counsel, 1979-87; of counsel Buchman & O'Brien, San Francisco, 1987—. Served to lt. (j.g.) USNR, 1943-46. Mem ABA (chmn. com. corporate counsel sect. of bus. law 1983-87); Mem. San Francisco Bar Assn., State Bar Calif., Order of Coif. DIED 12/21/96. .

HARGROVE, JOHN R., federal judge. BA, Howard U., 1947; LLB, U. Md., 1950. Sole practice, Balt., 1950-55; asst. U.S. atty. Dist. Ct. Md., Balt., 1955-57, dep. U.S. atty., 1957-62; assoc. judge People's Ct, Balt., 1962-63; ptnr. Howard & Hargrove, Balt., 1963-68; assoc. judge Municipal Ct., Balt., 1968-71; adminstrv. judge Dist. Ct., Balt., 1971-74; assoc. judge Balt. Circuit Ct., Balt., 1974-84; judge, U.S. Dist. Ct. Md., Balt., 1984—, now sr. judge. Served with AUS, 1943-46. Died April 1, 1997.

HARLOW, JAMES GINDLING, JR., utility executive; b. Oklahoma City, May 29, 1934; s. James Gindling and Adalene (Rae) H.; m. Jane Marriott Bienfang, Jan. 30, 1957; children: James Gindling III, David Ralph. B.S., U. Okla., 1957, postgrad., 1959-61; degree (hon.), Okla. City U., Okla. Christian U. Sci. and Arts. Research analyst Okla. Gas and Electric Co., Oklahoma City, 1961-63; div. auditor Okla. Gas and Electric Co., 1963-65, adminstrv. asst., 1965-66, asst. treas., 1966-68, treas., 1968-69, sec.-treas., 1969-70, v.p., treas., 1970-72, exec. v.p., treas., 1972-73, pres., 1973-76, pres., chief exec. officer, 1976-82, chmn., pres., CEO, 1982-95, chmn., CEO, 1995-96, also bd. dirs.; bd. dirs. Mass. Mut. Life Ins. Co., Fleming Cos., Inc., Oklahoma City, AEGIS, Jersey City. Pres. Missouri Valley Electric Assn., 1977-78; bd. dirs. Edison Electric Inst., 1988-96, exec. com., 1988-96, vice chmn., 1989-91, chmn., 1990-91; bd. dirs. State Fair of Okla.; trustee Okla. Zool. Soc., Oklahoma City U.; bd. govs. Kirkpatrick Ctr., pres. 1987-90; pres. Allied Arts Found., 1982-84; chmn., trustee U. Okla. Found., Inc., 1986-96. Served with USNR, 1957-59. Inducted into Okla. Hall of Fame, 1987. Mem. U.S. C. of C. (bd. dirs. 1978-84), Okla. C. of C. (bd. dirs. 1973-96, pres. 1980), Oklahoma City C. of C. (pres. 1976, vice chmn. econ. devel. 1992, chmn. Oklahoma City Pub. Sch. Found. 1991-93), Okla. Soc. Security Analysts, Petroleum Club, Oklahoma City Golf and Country Club, Econ. Club of Okla. (pres. 1986-87), Men's Dinner Club, Beacon Club. Home: Oklahoma City Okla. Died June 1, 1996; interred Rose Hill Burial Park, Oklahoma City, OK.

HARLOW, LEROY FRANCIS, organization and management educator emeritus, author; b. Seattle, Oct. 20, 1913; s. Milton N. and Ruby Blanche (Robinson) H.; m. Agda Sophie Gronbech, June 28, 1939; children: Steven G., John G., Christine G. Harlow Allie, Thomas G., David G., Peter G., Julia G. Harlow Doolittle. Student, Cameron Jr. Coll., 1931-32; B.S., Iowa State U., 1938; M.A. (Rockefeller Found. fellow), U. Minn., 1943. Assoc. engr. U.S. Pub. Works Adminstrn., Omaha, 1938-39; field asst. U.S. Social Security Bd., Des Moines and Lincoln, Nebr., 1939-42; assoc. budget examiner U.S. Bur. Budget, Washington, 1942-43; city mgr. City of Sweet Home, Oreg., 1943-45, City of Albert Lea, Minn., 1946-47, City of Fargo, N.D., 1947-49, City of Daytona Beach, Fla., 1952-55; staff cons. Public Adminstrn. Service, Chgo., 1945-46; dir. Minn. Efficiency in State Govt. Commn., St. Paul, 1949-51; village mgr. Village of Richfield, Minn., 1951-52; sr. assoc. Booz, Allen & Hamilton (mgmt. cons.), Chgo., Manila, San Francisco, 1955-61; dir. N.Mex. Revenue Structure Study Com., Santa Fe, 1961-63, Greater Cleve. Tax Policy Study Commn., 1963-64; exec. sec. Cuyahoga County Mayors and City Mgrs. Assn., Cleve., 1964-67; dir. Utah Local Govt. Modernization Study, Salt Lake City, 1968-73; prof. emeritus orgn. and mgmt. Brigham Young U., Provo, Utah, 1967-95; mgmt. assoc. Coalition to Improve Mgmt. in State and Local Govt., 1988-95; vis. prof. U. Utah, Bitburg and Spangdahlem, Germany, 1975. Author: Handbook for the Study of State Government Administration, 1950, How to Achieve Greater Efficiency and Economy in Minnesota's Government, 1951, Opportunities for Improving the New Mexico Revenue System, 1962, Guides to Tax Policy Decisions in Greater Cleveland, 1964, Implementing the Metropolitan Desk Concept, 1966, Local Government Modernization Study, 5 vols., 1970, Utah Local Government Finance Study, 5 vols., 1973, Twelve Model Optional Plans of County Government, 12 vols, 1973, Helping Utah's Local Governments Help Themselves, 1973, Without Fear or Favor: Odyssey of a City Manager, 1977, Servants of All: Professional Management of City Government, 1981, Charter of Utah County, State of Utah, 1986, Democracy Efficiently at Work: Better Government for All—A How-to Book, 1992; contbr. articles to profl. jours. Served with U.S. Army, 1933-34. Recipient Disting. Faculty award Brigham Young U. Sch. Mgmt., 1978. Mem. Am. Soc. Pub. Adminstrn. (pres. N.E. Ohio chpt. 1966, Cen. Utah chpt. 1968, cert. of merit 1967), Am. Polit. Sci. Assn., Acad. Polit. Sci., Internat. City/County Mgmt. Assn., Nat. Civic League, Govtl. Rsch. Assn. (nat. award for disting. rsch. 1965, nat. award for effective presentation of govt. rsch. 1970), Soc. Am. Mil. Engrs., Internat. Platform Assn., Ctr. for Study of the Presidency, Commonwealth Club, Phi Kappa Phi. Mem. LDS Ch. Home: Provo Utah Died May 4, 1995.

HARMAN, ALEXANDER M(ARRS), retired state justice; b. War, W.Va., Feb. 7, 1921; s. Alexander M. and Rose Sinclair (Brown) H. Student, Concord Coll., Athens, W.Va., 1938-41, LLD (hon.), 1970; LLB, Washington and Lee U., 1944, LLD (hon.), 1974; grad., Nat. Coll. State Trial Judges, 1965. Bar: Va. 1943. Sole practice Pulaski, Va., 1944-64; ptnr. Gilmer, Harman & Sadler, 1952-64; judge 21st Jud. Cir., 1964-69; justice Supreme Ct. Va., 1969-79, sr. justice, 1980-86; atty. Town of Pulaski, 1944-46; substitute trial justice, 1945-47; mem. Va. Com. Constl. Revision, 1968. Chmn. Pulaski County Devel. Authority, 1962-64; chmn. bd. zoning appeals, Pulaski, 1958-64; pres. N.R.V. Indsl. Found., 1963-82; chmn. Battle for Gov. Com. Pulaski County, 1949, Va. Bd. Elections, 1955-64, Pulaski County Dem. Com., 1960-64; mem. finance com. Va. Dem. Central Com., 1956-64, 19th Dist. Dem. Senatorial Com., 1956-64. DIED 10/31/96. .

HARNACK, ROBERT SPENCER, education educator; b. Milw., Oct. 22, 1918; s. Elmer Frank and Carolyn (Woppert) H.; m. Dorothy Helen Scherbarth, Sept. 5, 1942; children: Robert Spencer, William James. Ph.B., U. Wis., 1941, Ph.M., 1946, Ph.D., 1951. Curriculum coordinator pub. schs. Milw., 1951-54; mem. faculty State U. N.Y. at Buffalo, 1954-95, prof. curriculum devel., 1954-95, chmn. dept., 1965-75. Author: The Use of Electronic Computers to Improve the Individualization of Instruction Through Unit Teaching, 1965, Developing and Using Micro-computer-based Resource Units, 1983, The Grundtvig Culture, 1983. Served with USNR, 1941-45. Mem. Assn. Supervision and Curriculum Devel. (dir. N.Y. chpt. 1965-68), United Univ. Profs., N.Y. State United Tchrs. Home: Williamsville N.Y. Died Apr. 22, 1995.

HARPER, EDWARD J., clergyman; b. Bklyn., July 23, 1910; s. John Edward and Josephine (Realander) H. Student, St. Marys Coll., North East, Pa., 1928-33, St. Mary's Coll., Annapolis, 1933-34, Mt. St. Alphonsus Maj. Sem., 1934-40. Ordained priest Roman Catholic Ch., 1939; missionary P.R., 1941-46, Dominican Republic, 1946-50; dean Mayaguez, P.R., 1950-56; superior Vice Province of San Juan Redemptorist Fathers, 1956-60; prelate V.I., 1960; bishop, 1960-90; 1st residential bishop Diocese of St. Thomas, 1977-85, vicar gen., 1985-90. Pres. Citizens for Drug Edn., Inc., 1968-

90, Cath. Community Conscious Corp.; bd. dirs. V.I. Council on Alcoholism. Mem. bd. Econ. Devel. Council V.I. K.C. (charter). Died Dec. 2, 1990.

HARRIMAN, PAMELA DIGBY CHURCHILL, diplomat, philanthropist; b. Farnborough, Eng., Mar. 20, 1920; came to U.S., 1959, naturalized, 1971; d. Edward Kenelm and Constance Pamela Alice (Bruce) Digby;m. Randolph Churchill, 1939; 1 son, Winston Spencer; m. Leland Hayward, May 4, 1960; m. W. Averell Harriman, Sept. 27, 1971. JD (hon.) Columbia U., Coll. William & Mary. With Ministry of Supply, London, 1942-43; with Churchill Club for Am. Servicemen, 1943-46; journalist Beaverbrook Press, Europe, 1946-49; U.S. amb. to France, Paris, 1993—; U.S. observer to Coun. of Europe, 1996; chmn., founder Democrats for the 80s, 1980-90 and Democrats for the 90s, 1991; nat. co-chair Clinton-Gore Presdl. Campaign, 1992; bd. dirs. Commn. on Presdl. Debates, 1987-93; mem. Nat. Com. Dem. Party, 1989-93; past hon. trustee, past hon. mem. exec. com. Brookings Instn.; mem. Council on Fgn. Rels.; past trustee Rockefeller U., Coun. Nat. Gallery Art, Winston Churchill Found. U.S.; past adv. council W. Averell Harriman Inst. for Russian Studies; past mem. bd. friends Kennan Inst. for Advanced Russian Studies; past vice chmn. Atlantic Council, past bd. dirs. Mary W. Harriman Found., also various philanthropic founds. Named Dem. Woman of Yr., Woman's Nat. Dem. Club 1980; Commandeur Arts & Lettres. Died Feb. 5, 1997.

HARRIS, HARRY, human genetics educator; b. Manchester, Eng., Sept. 30, 1919; came to U.S., 1976; s. Soloman and Sarah Harris; m. Muriel Hargest, Aug. 22, 1948; 1 child, Toby. M.D., Cambridge U., Eng., 1943, M.A., 1946; Dr. Honoris Causa, U. Rene Descartes, Paris, 1976. Prof., head. dept. biochemistry Kings Coll., London, 1960-65; prof., head dept. human genetics Univ. Coll., London, 1965-76; prof. human genetics U. Pa., Phila., 1976-94. Author various books on human genetics; contbr. articles to sci. jours. Served to lt. RAF, 1944-47. Fellow Royal Soc. London; mem. Nat. Acad. Sci. (fgn. assoc.), Am. Soc. Human Genetics (William Allen Meml. award 1968), Genetics Soc. (U.S.A.), Genetics Soc. (U.K.), Biochem. Soc. (U.K.). Home: Newtown Square Pa. Died July 17, 1994.

HARRIS, OREN, retired federal judge; b. Belton, Ark., Dec. 20, 1903; s. Homer and Bettie Lee (Buloock) H.; m. Ruth Ross, May 9, 1934; children: Carolyn Marie, James Edward. BA, Henderson State U., 1929; LLB, Cumberland U., 1930; LLD (hon.), Ouachita State U., 1988. Bar: Ark. 1930, U.S. Supreme Ct. 1943. Dep. pros. atty. Union County, Ark., 1933-36; pros. atty. 13th Jud. Circuit, 1936-40; mem. 77th-89th congresses from 4th Dist. Ark.; chmn. com. on interstate and fgn. commerce, chmn. spl. investigatory com. on regulatory agys., judge U.S. Dist. Ct. for Eastern and Western Dists. Ark., 1966-76, sr. judge, 1976-92; ret., 1992; mem. budget com. Fed. Judiciary, 1973-85; mem. Jud. Conf. U.S., 1971-74. Del. Democratic Nat. Conv., 1944, 52, 56, 60. Recipient Saturday Rev. award, 1960; Public Service award Air Freight Forwarders Assn., 1960; award of merit Air Traffic Control Assn., 1962; Disting. Public Service citation Western Ry. Club, 1962; Joint Chiefs of Staff Nat. Transp. award Nat. Def. Transp. Assn., 1962; Presdl. citation Pioneer Nat. Broadcasting Assn., 1963; Presdl. citation APHA, 1963; Albert Lasker Svc. award, 1964; George Washington award Good Govt. Soc., 1965; Oren Harris Chair of Transp. established at U. Ark., 1970. Mem. Am. Bar Assn., Ark. Bar Assn., Ark. Bar Found., Sigma Alpha Epsilon. Baptist. Clubs: Lions (Ark. dist. gov. 1939-40), Jaycees (life), Masons (33 deg.), Shriners, K.P. DIED 02/05/97.

HARRIS, ROBERT JENNINGS, political scientist, educator; b. Wilson County, Tenn., Oct. 25, 1907; s. Robert Jennings and Lucy (Talley) H.; m. Martha Dashiel Baxter, June 10, 1937. A.B. magna cum laude, Vanderbilt U., 1930; A.M. (polit. sci. scholar), U. Ill., 1931; Ph.D., Princeton U., 1934. Asst. and fellow in politics Princeton, 1931-34; instr. polit. sci. U. Cin., 1934-36; asst. prof. govt. La. State U., 1936-38, assoc. prof., 1938-43, prof., 1943-54, chmn. dept., 1941-54; prof. polit. sci. Vanderbilt U., 1954-63, chmn. dept., 1962-63; prof. polit. sci., dean faculty arts and sci. U. Va., 1963-68, James Hart prof. govt., prof. history, 1968-78, James Hart prof. emeritus, 1978—; vis. prof. Vanderbilt U., summer 1946, U. Minn., summer 1947, U. N.C., summer 1948, Columbia, 1957-58; Edward Douglass White lectr. La. State U., 1959; spl. staff Library of Congress, 1950. Author: The Judicial Power of the United States, 1940, The Quest for Equality: The Constitution, Congress and the Supreme Court, 1960, (with others) Continuing Crisis in American Politics, 1963; also articles, book reviews in profl. jours.; bd. editors Jour. of Politics, 1945-48, editor, 1939-45; assoc. editor: Am. Polit. Sci. Rev, 1951-53; adv. bd. editors: Va. Quar. Rev, 1964-78; collaborator: Constitution of the United States: Analysis and Interpretation, 1953. Mem. AAUP (nat. council 1961-64), Am. Polit. Sci. Assn. (v.p. 1950), So. Polit. Sci. Assn. (pres. 1947), Phi Beta Kappa. Club: Colonnade. Died Mar. 12, 1992.

HARRIS, VINCENT CROCKETT, mathematics educator; b. Mpls., Jan. 26, 1913; s. Jesse Brownell and Virginia Case (Crockett) H.; m. Blanche Peterson Hanson, Jan. 3, 1945; children: Jacqueline Jones Parker, Diane Harris Smith. BA cum laude, Northwestern U., 1933, MA, 1935, PhD, 1950; postgrad., U. Wis., 1935-38, U. Minn., summers 1932, 37, U. Kans., summer 1957. Acct. Wells Lamont Corp., 1938-41; instr. Northwestern U., 1946-50; asst. prof., asso. prof., prof. San Diego State U., 1950-76, prof. emeritus, 1976-93; Summer faculty Ariz. State U., 1961, U. Mo., 1962, Northwestern U., 1963; vis. prof. U. Alta., spring 1976; instr. Pace program Cen. Tex. Coll., Jan.-Feb., 1989-90. Contbr. articles to profl. jours. Served to lt. USNR, 1942-46, PTO. Mem. Math. Assn. Am. (chmn. So. Calif. sect. 1966-67), Math. Assn. (Eng.), A.A.A.S., Fibonacci Assn., Soc. Am. Magicians, Internat. Brotherhood Magicians, Navy League, Phi Beta Kappa, Sigma Chi. Methodist. Home: San Diego Calif. Deceased.

HARRISON, HORACE HAWES, banker; b. Richmond, Va., Nov. 8, 1924; s. A.E. Willson and Anne Sterling (Hawes) H.; m. Sallie M. Labouisse, Feb. 18, 1949; children: Sally Cameron (Mrs. Thomas H. Lewis), Anne Hawes (Mrs. Alex S. Murchison). B.A., Yale U., 1948; grad., Stonier Grad. Sch. Banking, 1956, Mgmt. Program, U. Va. Grad. Sch. Bus., 1958. With United Va. Bank/State Planters (and predecessors), Richmond, 1948-72; pres. UVB Service Corp., 1971-72; exec. v.p. United Va. Bankshares, Inc. (now Crestar Fin. Corp.), 1973-79; exec. v.p. adminstrn. United Va. Bank (now Crestar Bank), 1980-85. Mem. Richmond Tax Study Commn., 1971-72; bd. dirs. Richmond Symphony, 1973-75; mem. exec. com., bd. dirs. Hollywood Cemetary Co.; pres. Family and Children's Service Richmond, 1967-68; trustee Va. Council Health and Med. Care, 1969-71, Sch. for Bank Adminstrn., U. Wis., 1972-75; treas. All Sts. Episcopal Ch., Linville, N.C. Served to 1st lt. AUS, 1942-46. Mem. Bank Adminstrn. Inst. (dir.-at-large 1969-71, nat. 1st v.p. 1973-74, nat. pres. 1974-75), Va. Bankers Assn., Soc. Colonial Wars (gov. 1982-84), Soc. of Cin., The Richmond German, Soixante Plus, Berzelius Club, Country Club of Va., Linville Golf Club, Delta Kappa Epsilon. Home: Richmond Va. Died Mar. 8, 1995.

HARROLD, ORVILLE GOODWIN, retired mathematics educator; b. Chgo., Sept. 2, 1909; s. Orville Goodwin and Estelle (Pancake) H.; m. Gladys Estelle Buell, June 30, 1934; children: Phillip (dec.), Jeffrey. AB with gt. distinction, Stanford U., 1931, MA, 1932, PhD, 1936. Instr. math. Oreg. State Coll., Corvallis, 1937-39; NRC research fellow U. Va., 1939-40; instr. math. Northwestern U., Evanston, Ill., 1940-42; asst. prof. math. La. State U., Baton Rouge, 1942-43, Pomona Coll., Claremont, Calif., 1943-46; lectr. math. Princeton (N.J.) U., 1946-47; prof. U. Tenn., Knoxville, 1947-64, head dept., 1961-64; prof. Fla. State U., Tallahassee, 1964-79, chmn. dept., 1964-74, prof. emeritus, 1979—; lectr. U. Mich. Conf. Math. Topology, Ann Arbor, 1940, Waseda U., Tokyo, 1971; cons. Union Carbide Corp., 1949-61. Co-author: Basic Topology, 1975; contbr. articles to profl. jours. Guggenheim fellow, 1958. Fellow AAAS; mem. Am. Math. Soc. (assoc. sec. southeastern sect. 1964-76), Math. Assn. Am., Set Theoret Topology Inst., 3-Dimensional Topology Inst., Colloquia Mathematica Societatis, Topology Conf., Woodrow Wilson Fellowship Bd (regional selectional com.), NRC (regional devel. com., research fellow 1939-40), Sigma Xi, Phi Beta Kappa. Democrat. Unitarian. Avocations: reading, studying psychology.

HARROP, MARGARET, retired nursing educator; b. Labelle, Idaho, July 22, 1929; d. Joseph and May (Miller) H. Diploma Latter Day Saints Hosp., Idaho Falls, 1950; B.S.N., U. Utah, 1962; M.S., Niagara U., 1971; profl. diploma, 1983. Supr. nursing Latter Day Saints Hosp., Idaho Falls, 1950-51; hosp. adminstr. Oneida County, Malad City, Idaho, 1951-55: supr., dir. practical nursing Latter Day Saints Hosp., Idaho Falls, 1955-60; asst. dir. nursing edn. James Ewing Hosp., N.Y.C., 1963-68; prof. advanced nursing Niagara U., Niagara U., 1968-90, ret. 1990. cons. nursing dept. Roswell Park Meml. Inst., 1972-80; asst. rsch. prof. natural sci. oncology Roswell Park Divsn. SUNY, Buffalo, N.Y., 1974-80. Prodr., host Listen Up!, Access Cable TV, 1991—. Crown Zellerback Found. grantee, 1960. Mem. Am. Nurses Assn., N.Y. State Nurses Assn., Am. Cancer Soc. (Nat. Leadership award, 1993), Oncology Nursing Socs., Sigma Theta Tau, Alpha Sigma Lambda

HARSHAW, DAVID HARE, headwear company executive; b. Phila., Mar. 6, 1904; s. Edward and Margaret Lyons (Jamison) H.; m. Frances Darlington Drewes, 1930; children: David Hare, Adele Drewes Smith; m. June Weaver French, 1974. B.S. in Econs, U. Pa., 1926; postgrad., Temple U. Law Sch., 1927-28; D.Sc., Stetson U., 1955. With U.G.I. Contracting Co., 1926-29, United Engrs. and Constrn. Co., 1929-35; with John B. Stetson Co., 1935-85, sec., treas., 1942, v.p. and treas., 1945, pres., dir., 1966-85, vice chmn., 1966—; dir. Am. Mut. Ins. Co. Bd. dirs. Greater Phila. Partnership, bd. dirs., v.p. Am. Missionary Fellowship; past pres. YMCA, Phila.; bd. dirs., past pres. Jefferson Park Hosp.; trustee Stetson U., Deland, Fla. Mem. Pa. C. of C. (past pres.), Phi Kappa Tau. Republican. Mem. Plymouth Brethren Meeting. Clubs: Union League (Phila.), Philadelphia Country (Phila.).

HART, GEORGE PHILIP PARLEYNS, transportation executive, solicitor; b. Oxford, Eng., Feb. 18, 1935; s. William Ogden and Dorothy Eileen (Churcher) H.; m. Dena Belle, Mar. 21, 1965 (dec. 1976); children: Mary, Dorothy; m. Bodil Rud-Peterson, Apr. 21, 1978. JD, U. Oxford, 1958. Solicitor Supreme Ct., 1961. Asst. solicitor Slaughter and May, London, Eng., 1961-63; legal sec. Fedn. Civil Engring. Contractors, London, 1963-66; solicitor Turriff Constrn. Corp. Ltd., Warwick, Eng., 1966-69; sec. The Bath & Portland Group Ltd, Bath, Eng., 1969-85; dir. The Bath & Portland Group Ltd., Bath, Eng., 1982-85; sec. NFC plc, Bedford, Eng., 1986—. Chmn. Stonar Sch. Ltd., Bath, 1980—. The Law Soc., Eng., Bedfordshire Golf Club. Avocations: golf, walking, skiing.

HARTELL, JOHN, artist, retired art educator; b. Bklyn., Jan. 30, 1902; s. John and Madeline (Engskjen) H.; m. Sylvia Muller, Sept. 10, 1928; children: Mari Hartell Quint, Karin Hartell Cattarulla. BArch, Cornell U., 1925; pograd., Royal Acad. Fine Arts, Stockholm, 1926-27. Instr. architectur Clemson (S.C.) U., 1927-28; assoc. prof. U. Ill., Urbana, 1928-30; prof. architecture Cornell U., Ithaca, N.Y., 1930-68; prof. art Cornell U., Ithaca, 1939-68, chmn. art dept., 1939-59, prof. emeritus, 1968—; mem. McDowell Colony, Peterborough, N.H., summers 1929-30. One-man shows Kraushaar Galleries, 1943—, Cornell U., Dallas Mus. Fine Arts, Hofstra U., Lehigh U., Meml. Art Gallery, Rochester, N.Y., Munson-Williams-Proctor Inst., Syracuse Mus. Fine Arts, also others; exhibted in group shows Albright Knox Gallery, Birmingham Mus., Butler Inst. Am. Art, Carnegie Inst., Art Inst. Chgo., Cin. Mus., St. Louis Art Mus., Indpls. Mus. Art, Walker Art Ctr., Whitney Mus. Am. Art, numerous others; represented in permanent collections in univs., cos., pvt. collections. Recipient award Ill. Wesleyan U., 1950, N.Y. State Fair, 1951, Munson-Williams-PRoctor Inst., 1952, Cortland County Fair, 1952, Meml. Art Gallery, 1953. Democrat. Avocations: baseball, fiction. Home: Ithaca N.Y. DIED 10/12/95. .

HARTLEY, JAMES MICHAELIS, aerospace systems, printing and hardwood products manufacturing executive; b. Indpls., Nov. 25, 1916; s. James Worth and Bertha S. (Beuke) H.; m. E. Lea Cosby, July 30, 1944; children: Michael D., Brent S. Student Jordan Conservatory of Music, 1934-35, Ind. U., Purdue U., Franklin Coll. With Arvin Industries, Inc., 1934-36; founder, pres. J. Hartley Co., Inc., Columbus, Ind., 1937—; founder, pres. Hartley Group, 1989—. Inventor of and patent on a prerotation system for transport-size aircraft landing gear. Pres. Columbus Little Theatre, 1947-48; founding dir. Columbus Arts Guild, 1960-64, v.p., 1965-66, dir., 1971-74; musical dir., cellist Guild String Quartet, 1963-73; active Indpls. Mus. of Art; founding dir. Columbus Pro Musica, 1969-74; dir. Regional Arts Study Commn., 1971-74; v.p. Ind. Coun. Rep. Workshops, 1965-69, pres., 1975-77; pres. Bartholomew County Rep. Workshop, 1966-67. Served with USAAF, 1942-46. Mem. AAAS, Am. Legion (life), NAM, Nat. Fedn. Ind. Bus., N.Y. Acad. Scis., Planetary Soc., Air Force Assn., Nat. Space Soc., U.S. C. of C., Phi Eta Sigma (honoris causa). Achievements include invention, patent prerotation system for transport-size aircraft landing gear. Deceased.

HARTLEY, RICHARD GLENDALE, professional society administrator; b. Bennet, Nebr., Feb. 16, 1926; s. Charles Lynn and Hazel Myra (Williams) H.; m. Wynona Elaine Smutz, Oct. 27, 1962; 1 child, Patricia Hartley Young. Student, U. Nebr., 1945-46, Hastings (Nebr.) Coll., 1947-48. Mgr. Mt. Pleasant (Iowa) C. of C., 1959-62; mgr. Kearney (Nebr.) C. of C., 1962-67; mgr. membership Greater Kansas City (Mo.) C. of C., 1967-68; exec. v.p. Kansas City (Kans.) Area C. of C., 1968-72; mng. dir. Missouri Valley Electric Assn., 1972-96. Revised, edited jour.: Evaluating Chamber Mgmt. Opportunities, 1966. Served with AUS, 1944-45, 52-61. Mem. Am. Soc. Assn. Execs. Died May 11, 1996.

HARTMANN, HUDSON THOMAS, agriculturist, educator; b. Kansas City, Kans., Dec. 6, 1914; s. Dale and Violet (Thomas) H.; m. Dorothy Henson, Sept. 23, 1940 (dec. 1977); children—Carol Robinson, Don, Marilyn, Lawrence. m. Hazel Manning, Nov. 25, 1978. B.S., U. Mo.-Columbia, 1939, M.S., 1940; Ph.D., U. Calif.-Berkeley, 1947. Asst. prof. U. Calif.-Davis, 1947-54, assoc. prof., 1954-60, prof., 1960-80, prof. emeritus agrl. research, 1980-94. Author: Plant Propagation, 1959, 5th edit., 1990; Plant Science, 1981, 2d edit., 1988. Fulbright research grantee, 1960, 64, 69. Fellow Am. Soc. Hort. Sci.; mem. Internat. Plant Propagators Soc. (editor 1974-92). Democrat. Died Mar. 2, 1994. Home: Davis Calif.

HARTSOUGH, WALTER DOUGLAS, physicist; b. Merced, Calif., Sept. 17, 1924; s. Douglas John and Josephine Mary (Oneto) H.; m. Patricia Meta Fain, June 24, 1945; children—Linda Anne, Marian Jane, Joan Marie, Michael David. A.B. in Physics, U. Calif., Berkeley, 1944, postgrad., 1946-48. Mem. staff Lawrence Berkeley Lab., U. Calif., 1946-87, physicist, bevatron group leader, 1958-73, assoc. dir., staff sr. scientist, div. head engring. and tech. services, 1973-85, assoc. dir., staff sr. scientist, div. head facilities mgmt. and tech. services div., 1985-86, dir. office minority outreach programs, 1986-87, assoc. dir. emeritus, 1987-96;

mem. U.S.-People's Republic China Joint Com. High Energy Physics, 1979-87, White House Sci. and Tech. Adv. Com., Historically Black Colls. and Univs., 1985-89; mem. steering com. LBL-Jackson State U. Consortium, 1981-87; mem. adv. com. Ana G. Mendez Ednl. Found. Consortium, 1983-87; bd. dirs., v.p. Nationwide Techs., Inc., Oakland, Calif., 1988-91. Author papers, reports in field. Served with USNR, 1942-46. Democrat. Roman Catholic. Home: Orinda Calif. Died Sept. 26, 1996.

HARWARD, NAOMI MARKEE, retired social worker and educator, volunteer; b. Neponset, Ill., Feb. 25, 1907; d. Joshua Waite and Josephine (Eldridge) Markee; m. Albert Harward, Dec. 25, 1936 (dec. Dec. 1979); children: Alfred, Phyllis Ann, Paulina. BA in History and Polit. Sci., Northwestern U., 1929; BD, Garrett Bibl. Inst., Evanston, Ill., 1931; MA in Religious Edn., U. Chgo., 1934, MA in Social Svc. Adminstrn., 1941. Group worker, dir. primary children South Chgo. Communityy Ctr., 1931-33; caseworker, chmn. placing Joint Svc. Bur., Chgo., 1934-36; supr. field work Sch. Soc. Svc. Adminstrn., U. Chgo., 1936-40; dir. rsch. project Works Progress Adminstrn., Chgo., 1940-41; from caseworker to dist. asst. dir. ARC, Chgo., 1941-44; from lectr. to prof., dir. undergrad. social welfare Ariz. State U., Tempe, 1955-76, prof. emeritus, 1976—; frequent lectr. Ariz. State U., nat. confs. and pub. meetings; mem. adv. bd. Ariz. Area 1 Agy. on Aging, Phoenix, 1980-86; dir. health care forum County Bd. Suprs., Phoenix, 1988—. Officer numerous local action and vol. groups; co-founder Ariz. chpt. Gray Panthers, former mem. nat. bd. dirs., vice chmn., founder, chmn. nat. task force on disability, 1986—; state chmn. Mecham Recall, 1987-88; mem. exec. com. Ariz. Health Care Campaign; participant Ariz. Town Hall, 1985—, Ariz. Women's Town Hall, 1988—; mem. nursing home aids consortium bd. Ariz. Dept. Edn., 1985—; chmn. Coalition for Improved Long Term Care, 1976-85; mem. Tempe Ad Hoc Com. on Mobile Homes, 1985-86, regional conf. Fed. Highway Adminstrn., Calif. facilitator section on sr. drivers, 1993. Recipient Adv. of Yr. award Ctr. for Law in Pub. Interest, 1986, "Women Helping Women" award Soroptomists of Mesa, 1989, Lifetime Achievement award Ariz. Dist. 27 Dem. Party; grantee Vocat. Rehab. Adminstrn., 1966-67, NIMH, 1969-76. Mem. NASW (past officer, chmn. nursing home com. Ariz. chpt. 1976-82, award 1980, 87, 89), Acad. Cert. Social Workers, Am. Pub. Welfare Assn., Ariz. Civil Liberties Union (Disting. Citizen of Yr. award 1987), AFSCME (ret. mem.), Ch. Women United. Methodist. Avocation: gardening.

HATTEM, ALBERT WORTH, physician; b. High Point, N.C., May 20, 1951; s. Henry Albert and Stella Jane (Penfield) H.; m. Deborah Elaine Bellew, Nov. 9, 1974. BA, U. S.C., 1985, MD, 1989. Diplomate Nat. Bd. Med. Examiners. Officer McColl (S.C.) Police Dept., 1970-71; mgr. Norris Ambulance Svc., Spartanburg, S.C., 1971-72; spl. events mgr. Coca-Cola Co., Spartanburg, 1972-73; tng. officer, paramedic Emergency Med. Svcs., Spartanburg, 1973-76; tng. coord. emergency med. svcs. divsn. S.C. Dept. Health, Columbia, 1976-83; intern U. Tenn. Med. Ctr., Knoxville, 1989-90, resident in ob-gyn., 1990-93; obstetrician-gynecologist Paradise Valley Women's Care, Las Vegas, Nev., 1993-94; med. dir. Russellville (Ky.) Women's Ctr., 1995—; clin. assoc. prof. Vanderbilt U. Sch. Nursing. Mem. faculty S.C. Heart Assn., Columbia, 1981-89; adv. coun. S.C. Emergency Med. Svcs., Columbia, 1983-89. Fellow ACOG (jr.), ACS (assoc.); mem. AMA (v.p. student sect. 1985-86), Am. Med. Student Assn. (chpt. v.p. 1985-86), Am. Fertility Soc., Soc. Laparoscopic Surgeons, Am. Assn. Gynecologic Laparoscopists, N.Am. Menopause Soc., Logan County Med. Soc., Logan County Health Bd., Hon. Order Ky. Colonels. Avocations: home computers, record collecting, boating, sailing.

HAUCK, FREDERICK ALEXANDER, nuclear scientist, philosopher; b. Dec. 28, 1894; s. Louis J. Hauck. With Lincoln Bank; from worker to chmn. bd. Max Wocher & Son Co., 1915-37; pres. Transvaal Mining Co., Cumpas, Mex., Continental Mineral Processing, Sharonville, Fla., 1948. Recipient Haley Space Flight award Am. Inst. Aeronautics and Astronautics, 1989. Died May 9, 1997.

HAVILAND, CAMILLA KLEIN, lawyer; b. Dodge City, Kans., Sept. 13, 1926; d. Robert Godfrey and Lelah (Luther) Klein; m. John Bodman Haviland, Sept. 7, 1957. AA, Monticello Coll. 1946; BA, Radcliffe Coll., 1948; JD, Kans. U., 1955. Bar: Kans. 1955. Assoc. Calvert & White, Wichita, Kans., 1955-56; sole practice, Dodge City, 1956-97; probate, county and juvenile judge Ford County (Kans.), 1957-77; mem. Jud. Coun. Com. on Probate and Juvenile Law. Mem. adv. bd. Salvation Army, U. Kans. Sch. Religion, Sch. Anthropology Wichita State U. Recipient Nathan Burkan award ASCAP, 1955. Mem. Ford County Bar Assn. (pres. 1980), S.W. Kans. Bar Assn. (pres. 1968, bd. dirs. 1994—), Kans. Bar Assn., ABA, C. of C., Order of Coif, PEO, Phi Delta Delta. Democrat. Episcopalian. Clubs: Prairie Dunes Country (Hutchinson, Kans.), Soroptimists. Contbr. articles to profl. jours. Died Apr. 11, 1997.

HAWKINS, DONALD MERTON, lawyer; b. Manhattan, Kans., June 19, 1921; s. Floyd and Madge (Thompson) H.; m. Lucille Bilsborough, Dec. 25, 1942; children: Frances Elizabeth Hawkins Lossing, Shirley Lorraine Hawkins Lowe, Richard Henry, Rebecca Susan Hawkins Swanson. Student, U. Mich., 1943; A.B., U. Chgo., 1946, J.D., 1947. Bar: Ill. 1947, Ohio 1948. Ptnr. Fuller & Henry (and predecessors), Toledo, 1952-98. Pres. Toledo Area Coun. Chs., 1968-69, Toledo Dist. Meth. Union, 1966-70; del. Gen. Conf. United Meth. Ch., 1972; pres. coun. fin. and adminstrn. West Ohio Conf. United Meth. Ch., 1972-76, trustee, 1978-87, chmn. bd. trustees, 1979-87, mem. bd. pensions, 1992-98; trustee Goodwill Industries Toledo, 1957-81, sec., 1963-68, v.p., 1968-72, pres., 1972-75. Served to 1st lt. USAAF, 1943-46. Fellow Am. Bar Found. (life), Ohio State Bar Found. (life); mem. ABA, Ohio State Bar Assn., Toledo Bar Assn., Am. Judicature Soc., Order of Coif, Toledo Club, Kappa Sigma. Died Jan. 2, 1998.

HAWKINS, ERICK, dancer, choreographer; b. Trinidad, Colo.. Student, Sch. Am. Ballet, N.Y.C. Mem. Am. Ballet Co., N.Y.C., 1935-37, Ballet Caravan, N.Y.C., 1936-39; guest dancer Martha Graham Co., N.Y.C., 1938, lead dancer, 1939-51; dancer, choreographer Erick Hawkins Dance Co., N.Y.C., 1951-94. Appeared in Theatre des Nations Festival, Paris, France, 1963, Joyce Theater, N.Y.C., 1978-94, Kennedy Ctr., Washington, 1987; choreographer: Show Piece, 1937, Liberty Tree, 1940, Yankee Bluebritches, 1940, Trickster Coyote, 1941, John Brown, 1945, Stephen Acrobat, 1947, The Strangler, 1948, Openings of the Eye, 1953, Here and Now with Watchers, 1957, Sudden Snake-Bird, 1960, Eight Clear Pieces, 1960, Early Floating, 1962, Spring Azure, 1962, To Everybody Out There, 1964, Geography of Noon, 1964, Lords of Persia, 1965, Naked Leopard, 1965, Cantilever, 1966, Dazzle on a Knife's Edge, 1966, Tightrope, 1968, Black Lake, 1969, Of Love, 1971, Angels of the Inmost Heaven, 1972, Classic Kite Tails, 1972, Dawn Dazzled Door, 1972, Greek Dreams with flute, 1973, Meditation on Orpheus, 1975, Hurrah!, 1975, Death is the Hunter, 1975, Parson Weems and the Cherry Tree, 1975, Ah Oh, 1977, Plains Daybreak, 1979, Avanti, 1980, God the Reveller, 1987, Cantilever Two, 1988, New Moon, 1991, Intensities of Space and Wind, 1991, Each Time You Carry Me This Way, 1993, Many Thanks, 1994. Recipient Dance Mag. award, 1979, Samuel H. Scripps Am. Dance Festival award, 1988, Nat. Medal of the Arts, 1994. Home: New York N.Y. Died Nov. 23, 1994.

HAY, ELOISE KNAPP, English language educator; b. Chgo., Nov. 19, 1926; d. G. Prather and Lucy (Norvell) Knapp; m. Stephen Northup Hay, June 11, 1954; children: Catherine, Edward. BA, Elmira Coll., 1948; PhD, Radcliffe Coll., 1961; DLitt (hon.), Elmira Coll., 1994. Tchg. fellow Harvard U., Cambridge, Mass., 1950-54; asst. prof. English U. Ill., Chgo., 1961-64; lectr. dept. English U. Calif., Santa Barbara, 1967-70; prof. English U. Delhi, India, 1970-71; acting assoc. prof., religious studies U. Calif., Santa Barbara, 1975-77, asst. prof. English, 1977-80, assoc. prof. English, 1980-82, prof., 1982-96; mem. English lit. adv. com. Coun. for Internat. Exch. of Scholars, Washington, 1983-85, 88. Author: The Political Novels of Joseph Conrad, 1963, 2d edit., 1981, T.S. Eliot's Negative Way, 1982; contbr. articles on other lit. subjects including Hawthorne, Dickens, James, Kipling, Forster, and Proust. Mem. U. Calif. Santa Barbara Sr. Women's Coun. Radcliffe (Bunting) Inst. fellow, 1964-66; sr. fellow NEH, 1974-75; recipient Disting. Teaching award U. Calif.-Santa Barbara Alumni, 1981. Mem. MLA Am. (mem. exec. com. on late 19th-early 20th-century lit. 1979-84, chmn. com. 1984), Phi Bet Kappa. Democrat. Roman Catholic. Home: Santa Barbara Calif. Died Apr. 30, 1996.

HAYDEN, RALPH FREDERICK, accountant, financial consultant; b. N.Y.C., Jan. 15, 1922; s. Fred T. and Thrya (Ohlson) H.; m. Gloria McCormick, Feb. 27, 1943; children—Craig O., Glen R. BBA, Pace U., 1951. Sr. ptnr. Hayden & Hayden (accts. and auditors), Huntington, N.Y., 1941-96; exec. v.p., chief fin. officer, sec., treas., dir. King Kullen Grocery Co., Inc., Westbury, N.Y., 1948-88; ret. King Kullen Grocery Co., Inc., Westbury, 1988. Contbr. articles to profl. jours. Pres. Old Chester Hills Civic Assn., 1962-64, Goose Bay Civic Assn., 1975-76; pres. L.I. YMCA, 1976-81, then trustee emeritus, bd. dirs.; dir. at large, chmn. Suffolk County Co-op. ext., 1968-76; bd. dirs. L.I. Arthritis Found., L.I. Com. for Crime Control, 1972-82, Bi-County Devel. Corp., 1972-88; mem. Suffolk County Rep. Com., 1958-77; vice-chmn. Suffolk County Airport Adv. Com., 1976-82; former trustee Friends of the Arts; trustee emeritus, past chmn., L.I. Ednl. T.V., CH # 21, Sta. WLIW; former corp. mem., profl. support bd. Vanderbilt Mus. With USCGR, 1942-45. Mem. Empire State Assn. Pub. Accts., Nat. Soc. Pub. Accts., Aviation Coun. L.I. (treas. 1971-87), USCG Aux., N.Y. Soc. Ind. Accts., C.W. Post Tax Inst., Real Estate Inst., Acctg. Inst., Huntington C. of C., Am. Legion, Met. Club (N.Y.C.). Home: Huntington N.Y. Died Sept. 14, 1996.

HAYES, CHARLES A., congressman; b. Cairo, Ill., Feb. 17, 1918; children: Barbara Delaney, Charlene Smith. Internat. v.p.; dir. Region #412 United Food & Comml. Workers Internat. Union, AFL-CIO & CLC,

1968-83; mem. 98th-102nd Congresses from 1st dist. Ill., 1983—; dist. dir. Dist. #41 UPWA, 1954-68; field rep., exec. v.p. Coalition Black Trade Unionists; v.p. Ill. State AFL-CIO, Operation PUSH, Chgo.; exec. bd. Chgo. Urban League; mem. Ill. State Commn. Labor Laws.

HAYES, JAMES L(OUIS), management consultant, educator; b. Binghamton, N.Y., Sept. 25, 1914; s. James Charles and Margaret (Sullivan) H.; m. Pauline Jacobus; children: Elizabeth, James C. AB, Bernard's Coll. 1936; MA, St. Bonaventure U., 1938; hon. degree, Theil Coll., 1970, St. Joseph's Coll., 1976, U. Cin., 1977, D'Youville Coll., 1978, Am. Grad. Sch. Mgmt., 1978, Nichols Coll., 1981, St. Bonaventure, 1982, U. Cin., 1977. Instr. in social studies St. Bonaventure U., Olean, N.Y., 1936-38, prof. economics, 1941-59; dean sch. bus. adminstrn. Duquesne U., Pitts., 1959-70; exec. v.p. devel. Am. Mgmt. Assns., N.Y.C., 1970-71, pres., chief exec. officer, 1971-82, chmn. bd. trustees, chief exec. officer, 1982, chmn. bd. trustees, 1982-84; chmn. bd. Human Resource Services, Inc., N.Y.C., 1984-89; chmn. dept. bus. adminstrn. St. Bonaventure U., Olean, 1941-59; bd. dirs. Crossland Savs., Chattem, Inc., Graphic Industries, Inc.; cons. The Echo Design Group, 1987-89; trustee St. Bonaventure U., Olean, 1987-89, The Juran Found., Inc., 1987-89. Contbr. articles to profl. jours. Bd. dirs. Greater N.Y. Council Boy Scouts of Am., 1987-89. Recipient Silver Beaver award Boy Scouts of Am., 1955, St. George award Boy Scouts Am., Outstanding Civilian award U.S. Army, 1962, Taylor Key award Soc. for Advancement of Mgmt., 1976, Golden Gavel award Toastmasters Internat., 1981, Kenneth David Kaunda award for Humanism Pan Am./Pan African Assn. United Nations, 1981, Profl. Mgr. citation Soc. for Advancement of Mgmt., 1966, Orders of Cedars of Lebanon decoration Lebanese Govt., Commander Order of Leopold II decoration Govt. of Belgium, 1985; named an Honorary Assoc. Japan Mgmt. Assn., 1985. Fellow Acad. Mgmt., Internat. Acad. Mgmt., Am. Mgmt. Assns. Republican. Roman Catholic. Clubs: Union League, Duquesne, Fed. City. Lodge: Knights of Malta. Avocations: stamp collecting, electronics. Home: New York N.Y. Died May 1989; interred Carvary Cemetery, Neptune, NJ.

HAYES, JOHN MARION, civil engineer; b. Wingate, Ind., May 18, 1909; s. William Lucas and Margaret Eliza (Gallaher) H.; m. Coye Matilda Cunningham, June 22, 1935; children: Marian Sue Hayes Jernigan, Julia Kethleen Hayes Casey. BSCE, Purdue U., 1931; MS, U. Tenn., 1944, D in Civil Engring., 1946. Structural engr. TVA, Knoxville, Tenn. and Chattanooga, 1935-46; dist. bridge engr. U.S. Bur. Pub. Rds., Little Rock, 1946-48; assoc. prof. Purdue U., West Lafayette, Ind., 1948-58; prof. structural engr. Purdue U., West Lafayette, 1958-75, prof. emeritus, 1975—. Recipient Outstanding Engring. Alumnus award U. Tenn., 1975. Fellow ASCE (hon., dir. dist. 9 1964-66, v.p. zone III, 1969-70, Outstanding Civil Engr. Ind. sect. 1988), NSPE, Am. Concrete Inst., AAAS, Am. Welding Soc., ASTM, Am. Soc. Engring. Edn., Am. Inst. Steel Constrn. Inc. (Spl. Citation award 1971), Ind. Sci. Engring. Found. Inc., SAR (pres. Ind. Soc. 1990-92, nat. trustee 1992-94), Lions, Chi Epsilon Sigma Xi. Republican. Methodist. Avocations: traveling, languages, reading, photography.

HAYES, WALTER HAROLD, civic worker, retired federal agency administrator; b. Balt., July 5, 1907; s. Walter Paschall and Elizabeth (Link) H.; m. Isabella Mallory, Nov. 9, 1935 (dec. July 1984); 1 child, Anne Hayes Hume. B.A., Duke U., 1928, M.A., 1930. Reporter Roanoke Times, Va., 1929-33; reporter, columnist, feature writer Roanoke World-News, 1933-42; N.C. State dir. U.S. Office War Info., 1942; pub. info. officer Richmond br. VA, 1946-49; editor Rural Electrification News, Rural Electrification Adminstrn., Washington, 1949-51; editorial chief U.S. Office Price Stabilization, 1951-53; chief of publs. Office of Info. for the Armed Forces, Dept. Def., 1953-67, ret., 1967. Head St. Johns County br. ARC, Fla., 1976-77. Served to lt. USN, 1942-45. Recipient Outstanding Citizenship award Am. Heritage Found., 1961, Freedoms Found. award, 1967, Meritorious Achievement award Mil. Order of World Wars. Mem. St. Augustine Hist. Soc., Washington Duke U. Club, Phi Kappa Sigma.

HAYES, WAYLAND JACKSON, JR., toxicologist, educator; b. Charlottesville, Va., Apr. 29, 1917; s. Wayland Jackson and Mary Lula (Turner) H.; m. Barnita Donkle, Feb. 1, 1942; children: Marie Hayes Sarneski, Maryetta Hayes Hacskaylo, Lula Hayes McCoy, Wayland III, Roche del Hayes Moser. BS, U. Va., 1938, MD, 1946; MA, U. Wis., 1940, PhD, 1942. Diplomate Acad. Toxicol. Scis. Chief vector-transmission investigations USPHS, Savannah, Ga., 1947-48; chief toxicology sect. USPHS, 1949-60, Atlanta, 1960-67; chief toxicologist USPHS, 1967-68; prof. biochemistry Vanderbilt U. Sch. Medicine, Nashville, 1968-93; Vol. assoc. prof. pharmacology Emory U., Atlanta, 1962-68; cons. WHO, 1950-91 , NAS-NRC, 1964-86. Author: Clinical Handbook on Economic Poisons, 1963, Toxicology of Pesticides, 1975, Pesticides Studied in Man, 1982; editor: (with Edward R. Laws Jr.) Handbook of Pesticide Toxicology, 1991; mem. editorial bd. Jour. Pharmacology and Exptl. Therapeutics, 1962-64, Food and Cosmetics Toxicology, 1967-78, Toxicology and Applied Pharmacology, 1978-89; mem. editorial bd.

Archives Environ. Health, 1965-72, editor, 1976-85; editor Essays in Toxicology, 1972-76; contbr. sci. papers to profl. lit. Served with AUS, 1943-46. Recipient Meritorious Service medal USPHS, 1964. Mem. Soc. Toxicology (charter, pres. 1971-72, ambassador of toxicology award 1985, merit award 1989), Am. Soc. Pharmacology and Exptl. Therapeutics, Am. Soc. Tropical Medicine and Hygiene, Am. Conf. Govt. Indsl. Hygientists. Home: Nashville Tenn. Died Jan. 4, 1993.

HEAD, HUGH GARLAND, JR., lawyer; b. Atlanta, Dec. 3, 1905; s. Hugh Garland Sr. and Carrie Lulla (Morse) H.; m. Jessie Ella Grover, Mar. 13, 1928; children: Hugh Garland III, William LeVert, Douglas Arthur. LLB, Atlanta Law Sch., 1937; postgrad., Oxford (Eng.) U., 1943. Bar: Ga. 1937, U.S. Dist. Ct. (so., mid. and no. dists.) Ga., 1937; U.S. Supreme Ct., 1956. Asst. city atty. Atlanta, 1945-46, sole practice, 1945—; Contbr. articles to legal jours. Served to maj. U.S. Army, 1942-45, lt. col. Res. ret. Decorated Mem. British Empire. Recipient Bronze medal Inst. Continuing Legal Edn., Ga., 1973. Fellow Internat. Acad. Trial Lawyers (hon., bd. govs. 1971-72); mem. Am. Trial Lawyers Assn. (lifetime faculty, bd. govs. 1975-81, Disting. Lectr. citation 1965), Ga. Trial Lawyers Assn. (pres. 1958, named life mem. bd. govs. 1974), ABA (speaker nat. conv. 1968), Ga. Bar Assn. (Honor Roll award 1980), Atlanta Bar Assn. (exec. com. 1958), SAR (nat. trustee 1960-64, Good Citizenship Bronze medal 1963), The Belli Soc. (trustee). Clubs: Atlanta Athletic, Ft. McPherson Golf, Lawyers. Lodge: Masons. Died Dec. 4, 1994.

HEALY, ROBERT EDWARD, retired advertising executive; b. Bklyn., Aug. 15, 1904; s. Walter F. and Florence D. (Davis) H.; m. Lilie Rose, Aug. 3, 1927 (div. Jan. 1957); children: Lilie Jane, Patricia Anne, Robert Edward (dec.); m. Wayne Clark, Jan. 11, 1957; children: Edward Walter, James Davis. Grad., Dwight Prep. Sch., N.Y.C., Pace Inst., N.Y.C.; D.C.S (hon.), Pace Coll. Asst. to v.p. in charge sales promotion Johns-Manville Co., 1928-33; brand advt. mgr. Colgate-Palmolive Co., 1939-42, gen. advt. mgr., 1942-46, became v.p. in charge advt., 1946; dir., v.p., treas. McCann-Erickson, Inc., 1952-53, gen. mgr. N.Y. office, 1954, exec. v.p. charge, 1955-58, mem. fin. com., 1956-62, vice chmn. bd., 1958-61; chmn. McCann Erickson Corp. (Internat.), 1956-58; pres. Inter-public (S.A.), Geneva, Switzerland, 1962-65; exec. v.p. Interpub. Group of Cos., Inc., 1965-67, pres., chief exec., 1967-72, mem. exec. com., 1967-77, chmn. bd., 1968-73, hon. chmn., 1973-83. Home: Palm Beach Gardens Fla. Died Sept 18, 1993.

HEBSON, ANN See LEVY, ANN PORTER HELLEBUSCH

HECKER, BRUCE ALBERT, lawyer; b. Phila., Aug. 20, 1919; s. Louis and Mary (Golden) H.; m. Mindelle Schulman, Dec. 24, 1921; children—Lynn and Deborah (twins). B.A., NYU, 1939; J.D. cum laude, Harvard U., 1942. Bar: N.Y. 1946, U.S. Ct. Appeals (2d cir.) 1947, U.S. Dist. Ct. (so. dist.) N.Y. 1946, U.S. Dist. Ct. (ea. dist.) N.Y. 1950, U.S. Supreme Ct. 1952. Assoc. Sullivan & Crommwell, N.Y.C., 1945-54; sr. ptnr. Shea & Gould, N.Y.C., 1954-88; of counsel Gray, Cary, Ware & Freidenrich, San Diego, 1992-96; spl. counsel N.Y. State Bar Assn., 1972-73; dir. Doubleday & Co., Binney & Smith Inc., Tetra-Pack USA; author, lectr. in field. Served to lt. USNR, 1942-45. Fellow Am. Coll. Trial Lawyers; mem. ABA, Am. Judicature Soc., Assn. of Bar of City of N.Y., Fed. Bar Assn. Club: Harvard (N.Y.C.). Home: Solana Beach Calif. Died Jan. 15, 1996.

HECKSCHER, AUGUST, journalist, author, foundation executive; b. Huntington, N.Y., Sept. 16, 1913; s. Gustav Maurice and Louise (Vanderhoef) H.; m. Claude Chevreux, Mar. 19, 1941; children: Stephen August, Philip Hofer, Charles Chevreux. BA, Yale U., 1936; MA, Harvard U., 1939; LLD, Fairleigh Dickinson U., 1962; LHD, NYU, 1962, Temple U., 1964, Brandeis U., 1964; LittD, C.W. Post Coll., 1963, Adelphi Coll., 1963; DHL, Parsons Sch. Design, 1987. Govt. instr. Yale U., 1939-41; editor Auburn (N.Y.) Citizen-Advisor, 1946-48; editorial writer, chief editorial writer N.Y. Herald Tribune, 1948-56; dir. Twentieth Century Fund, 1956-67; mem. editorial bd. The Am. Scholar. Author: These Are The Days, 1936, A Pattern of Politics, 1947, The Politics of Woodrow Wilson, 1956, Diversity of Worlds (with Raymond Aron), 1957, The Public Happiness, 1962, When La Guardia Was Mayor (with Phyllis Robinson), 1979, Alive in the City—Memories of an Ex-commissioner, 1974, Open Spaces: The Life of American Cities, 1977, St. Paul's: The Life of A New England School, 1981, Woodrow Wilson, 1991. Spl. cons. on arts for Pres. Kennedy, 1962-63; art commr. City of N.Y., 1957-62, pks. commr., 1967-71; past chmn. bd. dirs. Internat. Coun. Mus. of Modern Art, 1958-63, Nat. Repertory Theatre Found.; trustee Internat. House, St. Paul's Sch.; past trustee Lavanburg Found.; mem. governing bd. Yale U. Press.; v.p. Mcpl. Arts Soc.; mem. N.Y. State Coun. on the Arts; vice-chmn. bd. dirs. Urban Am.; past pres. Woodrow Wilson Found.; chmn. bd. trustees New Sch. Social Rsch., 1966-68. Recipient Joseph Henry medal Smithsonian Instn., 1990; decorated officer French Legion of Honor, Moroccan Order of Quissam Alouit; Jonathan Edwards Coll. fellow. Fellow AAAS; mem. AIA (hon.), Century Assn., Coun. Fgn. Rels., ACLU (past bd. dirs.), Phi Beta Kappa. Home: New York N.Y. Died April 5, 1997.

HEHMEYER, ALEXANDER, lawyer; b. N.Y.C., Oct. 20, 1910; s. Frederick William and Catherine Enole (Schrader) H.; m. Florence Isobel Millar, 1936 (dec. 1967); children: Alexander Millar, Christine McKesson; m. Sheila Mary Vought, 1968. B.S., Yale U., 1932; LL.B., Columbia U., 1935. Bar: N.Y. 1936, Ill. 1968. Asso. Cravath, Swaine and Moore, N.Y.C., 1935-40, 44-46; asst. to chmn. Time, Inc., 1940-43; legal-econ. cons. Fgn. Econ. Adminstrn., 1943-44; partner firm Paul, Weiss, Rifkind, Wharton & Garrison, N.Y.C., 1946-67; exec. v.p., gen. counsel, dir., mem. exec. com. Field Enterprises, Inc., Chgo., 1967-75; counsel Isham, Lincoln & Beale, Chgo., 1976-82; v.p., dir. Gahagan Dredging Corp., 1953-70; dir., mem. exec. com. Am. Heritage Pub. Co., Inc., 1954-69; dir. AM. Research Bur., 1965-69, Field Creations, Inc., Field Communications Corp., Field Enterprises Endl. Corp., Field Enterprises Realty Corp., FSC Paper Corp., Manistique Pulp & Paper Co., Met. Printing Co., P.H.S. Fin. Corp., World Book Life Ins. Co., Field Enterprises Charitable Corp.; mem. mgmt. bd. Kaiser Broadcasting Co., Field Newspaper Syndicate, 1967-75. Author: Time for Change, 1943. Vice chmn., counsel U.S. Econ. Missions to West Berlin, 1952, Gold Coast, 1954; trustee, chmn. Midwest adv. bd. Inst. Internat. Edn., 1972-92; trustee Kent (Conn.) Sch., 1963-84; mem. adv. council Peace Corps, 1982-84; pres. Internat. Vis. Ctr., Chgo., 1989-91; pres. N.Y. Young Republican Club, 1944-46. Fellow ABA; mem. Ill., Chgo. bar assns., Assn. Bar City N.Y., Chgo. Council Fgn. Relations (past vice chmn., mem. exec. com.), Phi Gamma Delta. Clubs: Commercial, Chicago, Racquet, Saddle and Cycle (Chgo.), Yale (N.Y.C.). Home: Chicago Ill. Died Feb. 16, 1993.

HEIMAN, MAXWELL, judge, lawyer; b. Hartford, Conn., Apr. 24, 1932; s. David and Mary (Berman) H.; m. Sylvia P. Dress, Aug. 18, 1957; children: Deborah J., Scott D. BA, U. Conn., 1954; JD, Boston Coll. Law, 1957. Bar: Conn. 1957, U.S. Dist. Ct. Conn. 1958, U.S. Ct. Appeals (2d cir.) 1961, U.S. Supreme Ct. 1963, U.S. Tax Ct. 1974. Assoc. Bracken and Burke, Hartford, 1957-65; ptnr. Furey, Donovan & Heiman, P.C., Bristol, Conn., 1965-87; judge Conn. Superior Ct., 1987-90, Conn. Appellate Ct., 1990—; alt. mem. Judicial Review Coun., 1995—. Editor Conn. Criminal Procedure; contbr. articles to profl. jours. Mem. Republican Town Com., Newington, Conn., 1963-73, Conn. Bar Examining Com., 1996—; mem. Newington Bd. Edn., 1969-73, 74-75; bd. dirs. Hartford Legal Aid Soc., 1979—. Fellow Am. Bar Found. (adv. rsch. com.), Conn. Judges Assn. (v.p. 1992-93, pres. 1993-94), Am. Coll. Trial Lawyers; mem. ABA (ho. of dels. 1980—, chmn. steering com., nominating com., bd. govs. 1987-90, standing com. selection compensation and tenure of judges 1990—, judges adv. com. standing com. on ethics and profl. liaibility), Conn. Bar Assn. (past pres.), Hartford County Bar Assn. (past pres.). Jewish. DIED 11/05/97. .

HEINEN, ERWIN, accountant; b. Comfort, Tex., Mar. 17, 1906; s. Hubert and Else (Strohacker) H.; m. Emily Blanton Plummer, June 25, 1929; children—Nancy Blanton (Mrs. Arnold Earl Luetge), Hubert Plummer. B.B.A., U. Tex., 1927. With Ernst & Whinney (C.P.A.'s), Houston, 1927—; partner Ernst & Whinney (C.P.A.'s), 1948-69, cons., 1969—; former chmn. accounting faculty assos. U. Tex. Sch. Bus. Adminstrn. Vice pres. Houston Grand Opera Assn., 1958-69; treas. Music Guild, 1963-68; bd. mgrs. Harris County Hosp. Dist., 1971-73; Past bd. dirs. Houston Symphony Soc.; trustee Bd. Edn. Houston Ind. Sch. Dist., 1973-77, pres., 1977; former treas. Houston Mus. Fine Arts; chmn. Cultural Arts Council of Houston. Mem. Am. Inst. C.P.A.'s, Tex. Soc. C.P.A.'s, So. States Conf. C.P.A.'s (past pres.), Nat. Accountants Assn., Houston C. of C. (vice chmn. cultural arts com.). Episcopalian. Clubs: River Oaks Country, Houston, Houston Rotary (past pres., (dist. gov.) 1970-71), Harvard Business School (dir.). Home: Houston Tex. DIED 04/09/95. .

HEINRICH, ROSS RAYMOND, geophysicist, educator; b. St. Louis, Dec. 12, 1915; s. Edward Ernst and Mary R. (Busch) H.; m. Marie Frances McKinnon, June 3, 1948; children: Ross Thaddeus (dec.), Christopher Edward, Anita Marie, Victoria Margaret. AB, U. Mo., 1936; MS, St. Louis U., 1938, PhD, 1944. With St. Louis U., 1936-97, successively grad. fellow geophysics, instr., asst. prof., asso. prof., 1936-51, prof., 1951-80, prof. emeritus, 1981-97, dir. dept. geophysics and geophys. engring., 1956-63, acting dean Inst. of Tech., 1968-71, chmn. dept. earth and atmospheric scis., 1975-80; cons. ground vibration problems, 1938-80; mem. St Louis County Explosives Control Adv. Bd., 1964-75; trustee Univ. Corp. Atmospheric Rsch., 1960-71. Mem. Soc. for Mining, Metallurgy and Exploration, Inc., Am. Meteorol. Soc., Am. Geophys. Union, Geol. Soc. Am., Am. Soc. Engring. Edn., Seismol. Soc. Am., Phi Beta Kappa, Sigma Xi. Died Dec. 18, 1997.

HEINTZ, JACK, publishing company executive; b. Chenoa, Ill., Jan. 19, 1907; s. Michael Matthew and Ida Luella (Thayer) H.; m. Mary Louise Keller, June 4, 1927; 1 child, Michael (dec.). Student, Ill. Wesleyan U. Dept. store mgr., 1928-33, dist. mgr. ins. firm, 1933-36, radio sales mgr., 1936-37; radio sta. mgr. WCBS, 1937-43; radio cons. The Copley Press, Inc., 1946-47, v.p., dir., 1958—, Hawaii resident mgr., officer, rep., 1964-74; v.p., gen. mgr. KSDO radio sta., 1946-54; v.p., gen. mgr. KCOP-TV, 1954-58, radio and TV gen. cons., 1957; pub. Ill. State Jour., Ill. State Register, 1958-64; dir. Radio Sta. KGU, Honolulu.; ret. Profl. e'glomisé artist; exhibited works in several one-man shows. Trustee Lincoln Coll., Lincoln Library; bd. dirs. Cerebral Palsy Found. Served as lt. USNR, 1943- 46. Mem. Navy League, Assn. Honolulu Artists, Pacific Club, Honolulu Club, Sangamon Club, Island Bay Yacht Club, Masons (33d degree, Scottish Rite), Tau Kappa Epsilon. Republican. Episcopalian. Died Nov. 25, 1996.

HELD, WALTER W., artistic director, management consultant; b. Natrona Heights, Pa., May 10, 1954. MusB, W.Va. U., 1976. Asst. devel. dir. Cleve. Ballet, 1977-81; devel. dir. Chautauqua (N.Y.) Instn., 1981-83; exec. dir. Ea. Music Festival, Greensboro, N.C., 1983-95; instr. arts mgmt. program U. N.C., Greensboro, 1988-90; music panalist N.C. Arts Coun., Greensboro, 1988-90; co-chmn. music festivals panel Nat. Endowment Arts, Washington, 1990, music overview panel, 1991; freelance mgmt. cons., 1983-95. Mem. adv. bd. Greensboro African Am. Arst Festival, 1991. Mem. Am. Symphony Orch. League, Opera Am., Am. Coun. on Arts, Arts Advocates N.C., Assn. Symphony Orchs. N.C. Deceased July 1995.

HELLER, DOUGLAS MAX, aerospace consultant, former research executive; b. Dover, Kent, Eng., Feb. 23, 1918; came to U.S., 1947; s. William Max and Dorothy (Watt) H.; m. Patricia Short, Apr. 23, 1941; children: Susan Patricia, Wendy Anne, Jennifer Jane. BS in Physics, Royal Coll. Sci., London, 1939. Sci. staff Hirst Labs. GEC, North Wembley Middlesex, Eng., 1939-47; with Bendix Corp., 1947-66; rsch. engr., then asst. chief rsch. radio div. Balt., 1947-50, chief engr. comml. products, 1950-54; dir. engring., then asst. gen. mgr. missile sect. Mishawaka, Ind., 1954-59; asst. group. exec. products div. South Bend, Ind., 1959-61; asst. gen. mgr., then gen. mgr. radio div. Balt., 1961-65, group mgr. radio and field engring., 1966-84; rsch. dir. Martin Marietta Aerospace Co., Balt. and Bethesda, Md., 1984-91; pres. Max Heller Assocs. Inc., Sarasota, Fla., 1984-91. Patentee in field. Fellow IEEE, AIAA (assoc.), Inst. Physics of U.K.; mem. Royal Coll. Sci. (assoc.), Am. Phys. Soc., Kenwood Club (Bethesda, Md.); The Meadows Country Club. Republican. Episcopalian. Home: Sarasota Fla. Died June 14, 1991.

HELLMANN, SIGMUND JEHUDO, community center administrator; b. Shanghai, Peoples Republic of China, Oct. 24, 1928; came to U.S., April, 1948; s. Benjamin and Rachel (Bergman) H.; m. Michelle Silverman Cooley, Aug. 28, 1983 (div. May 1985); children: Dvorah R. Hellmann Kaufman, Benjamin N., Joel J. AB, Hamilton Coll., 1951; MS in Social Service, Boston U., 1955. Exec. dir. JYC Camps, Phila., 1966-72, Jewish Community Ctr. R.I., Providence, 1972-77; assoc. exec. dir. Jewish Ctrs. Assn., Los Angeles, 1977-83; exec. dir. Mittleman Jewish Community Ctr., Portland, Oreg., 1983—. Mem. Assn. Jewish Ctr. Workers (nat. pres. 1974-76, nat. exec. bd.), Am. Camping Assn. (Phila. chptr. pres., 1970-72), Acad. Cert. Social Workers (cert.), Nat. Assn. Social Workers (cert.). Democrat. Avocations: soccer, volleyball, racquetball, tennis.

HELMSLEY, HARRY B., real estate company executive; b. N.Y.C., 1909; m. Leona M. Pres., chief exec. officer Helmsley-Spear, Inc., N.Y.C.; chmn., pres., chief exec. officer Helmsley Enterprises, Inc. (parent co.), N.Y.C. Died Jan. 4, 1997.

HEM, JOHN DAVID, research chemist; b. Starkweather, N.D., May 14, 1916; s. Hans Neilius and Josephine Augusta (Larsen) H.; m. Ruth Evans, Mar. 11, 1945; children: John David Jr., Michael Edward. Student, Minot State Coll., 1932-36, N.D. State U., 1937-38, Iowa State U., 1938; BS, George Washington U., 1940. Analytical chemist U.S. Geol. Survey, Safford, Ariz., 1940-42, 43-45, Roswell, N.Mex., 1942-43; dist. chemist U.S. Geol. Survey, Albuquerque, 1945-53; rsch. chemist U.S. Geol. Survey, Denver, 1953-63, Menlo Park, Calif., 1963-94; rsch. advisor U.S. Geol. Survey, 1974-79, mem. water rsch. adv. com., 1984-94. Author: Study and Interpretation Chemistry of Natural Water, 3d rev. edit., 1985; contbr. articles to profl. publs., chpts. to books. Recipient Meritorious Svc. award U.S. Dept. Interior, 1976, Disting. Svc. award U.S. Dept. Interior, 1980, Sci. award Nat. Water Well Assn., 1986, O.E. Meinzer award Geol. Soc. Am., 1990, Special award Internat. Assn. Geochemistry and Cosmochemistry, 1992. Mem. Am. Chem. Soc., Am. Geophys. Union, Am. Water Works Assn., Geochem. Soc., Soc. Geochemistry and Health. Democrat. Lutheran. Achievements include wide usage of the results of research in aqueous chemistry of aluminum, manganese and iron. Home: Palo Alto Calif. Died Dec. 27, 1994.

HEMENS, HENRY JOHN, lawyer; b. Montreal, Que., Can., June 16, 1913; s. Sidney John and Margaret Ann (O'Brien) H.; m. Sarah Ann Wright, Nov. 4, 1939; children: Mary-Margaret, John, Paul, Eileen. B.A., Loyola Coll., Montreal, 1932; B.C.L., McGill U., Montreal, 1935; postgrad., U. Paris, 1935-36; LL.D., Concordia U., 1982. Called to Que. bar 1935, created Queen's counsel 1956. Mem. legal dept. DuPont Can. Inc., Montreal, 1939-54; gen. counsel DuPont Can. Inc., 1954-62, sec., 1962-69, v.p. and sec., 1969-77, dir., 1971-78, cons., 1977-85; counsel Harris, Allain, Thomas, Mason, Montreal, 1977-87; of counsel Hemens, Cornish, Levac, Quesnel & Hindle, Montreal, 1988-90; mcpl. judge Town of Rosemere, Que., 1965-76. Mayor Town of Rosemere, 1955-59; chancellor, bd. govs. Concordia U., 1974-81, chancellor emeritus, 1989—. Mem. Assn. Can. Gen. Counsel, Can. Mfrs. Assn., Can. C. of C. Roman Catholic. Clubs: Order of Malta, St. James, Lorraine Golf.

HEMSING, ALBERT E., public affairs adviser; b. Barmen, Germany, Feb. 27, 1921; s. Paul and Josephine (Ferder) H.; m. Esther Davidson, Dec. 27, 1944; 1 child, Josephine Claudia. B.S.S., CCNY, 1942; M.A., NYU, 1947. With East and West Assn., 1942-43, OWI, 1943-46, State Dept., 1946-47; ind. documentary film producer, 1947-51; with ECA, Paris, 1951-55; chief overseas operations div. USIA, Washington, 1955-58; press officer then pub. affairs officer U.S. mission Berlin, 1958-64; counselor of embassy pub. affairs Bonn, Germany, 1964-67; dep., then asst. dir. USIA, in charge of Western Europe, 1969-71, insp. gen., 1971-73; minister-counselor pub. affairs Am. embassy, New Delhi, 1973-76; mem. Bd. Internat. Broadcasting, 1976-77; dir. Am. Inst., Freiburg, Germany, 1978-83; research assoc. Edward R. Murrow Ctr., Fletcher Sch., Tufts U., 1984-86; advisor German Marshall FUND U.S., 1986-88; mem. State Dept. Sr. Seminar Fgn. Policy, 1967—; mem. bd. examiners Fgn. Svc., 1970-73; lectr. CCNY, 1946-51, Am. U., 1956-58. Co-author, dir.: (with Esther Hemsing) documentary The Yellow Star (Acad. award nomination 1981); writer, producer: Top Secret—The July 20, 1944 Revolt Against Hitler, 1980. Recipient Meritorious Honor award USIA. Mem. Am. Fgn. Service Assn., Overseas Press Club Am., Phi Beta Kappa. Died Mar. 18, 1997.

HENDEL, FRANK J(OSEPH), chemical and aerospace engineer, educator, technical consultant; b. Sambor, Poland, Dec. 2, 1918; came to U.S., 1950, naturalized, 1955; s. Emil and Henrietta (Sprecher) H.; children: Anna H. (Mrs. Gary Carrillo), Emily E. (Mrs. Edward Winfield), Erica F. Ph.D., P.E. Tech. U. Lwow, 1941. Chief chem. engr. Wigton-Abbott Corp. (engrs. and constructors), Plainfield, N.J., 1950-56; head chem. engring. Aerojet Gen. Corp., Azusa, Calif., 1956-61; staff scientist, space div. N.Am. Aviation, Downey, Calif., 1961-64; mem. tech. staff Jet Propulsion Lab., Calif. Inst. Tech., Pasadena, 1964-67; prof. aerospace sci. and aero. engring., dept. aero. and mech. engring. Calif. Poly. State U., San Luis Obispo, 1967-85, prof. emeritus, 1985-89; with Space Systems div. Gen. Dynamics Corp., San Diego, 1986-89, tech. cons., 1989-90; ret.; cons. Nat. Acad. Sci., 1961-63, Space and Missile Test Ctr., Vandenberg AFB, 1968-75; mem. faculty Inst. Aerospace Safety and Mgmt., U. So. Calif., 1970-73; lectr. aerospace, propulsion and ordnance systems UCLA Extension, 1964-67, researcher Laramie (Wyo.) Energy Tech. Ctr., U.S. Dept. Energy, 1977-78; aero. engr. Flight Test Ctr., Edwards AFB, Summer 1980; research specialist Lockheed Missile and Space Co., Sunnyvale, Calif., summers 1981, 82; gen. engr. U.S. Navy Pacific Missile & Test Ctr., Point Mugu, summer 1983; project engr. United Techs., San Jose, Calif., summer 1984. Abstractor: Chem. Abstracts, 1952-82; contbr. articles to profl. jours. and books; designer presentations on Liquid Rocket Boosters on Space Shuttles. Polyglot San Diego Aerospace Mus., 1989-92. Fellow AIAA (assoc., chmn. symposium on alt. fuel resources 1976, mem. tech. com. on elec. propulsion, subcom. on space missions 1988-91); mem. NSPE, Am. Soc. Engring. Edn. Achievements include design and engring. of several chem., indsl. pyrotechnics and ordnance for space vehicles and missiles.

HENDON, ROBERT CARAWAY, retired transportation and manufacturing company executive, consultant; b. Shelbyville, Tenn., Jan. 13, 1912; s. William Oscar and Anna Bertha (Caraway) H.; m. Ruth Perham, Apr. 23, 1936 (dec. Mar. 1988); children: Robert Caraway, Elizabeth Anne Hendon McGinn. B.A. in Journalism, U. Mont., 1931, J.D., 1934. Bar: Mont. and Tenn. 1934. Gen. practice law Monterey, Tenn., 1934; spl. agt., spl. agt. in charge FBI, 1935-39, insp., adminstrv. asst. to dir., mem. exec. com., 1939-47; exec. rep. to pres. Ry. Express Agy., N.Y.C., 1947; various exec. positions Ry. Express Agy. (later REA Express), 1947-50; asst. to pres., dir. personnel Mathieson Chem. Corp., 1950-52; v.p. personnel and indsl. relations REA Express, 1953-55, v.p. operations, 1955-64, v.p. exec. dept., 1964-68; dir. REA Leasing Corp., 1961-68, pres., 1964-67, vice chmn. bd., 1967-68; pres., dir. TOFC Leasing Corp., 1965-68, REA Express-Seven Arts Transvision, Inc., 1965-68; dir., chmn. exec. com. Fast Service Shipping Terminals, Inc., 1961-68; v.p. Consol. Freightways Inc., 1968-77; dir., mem. exec. com., chmn. nominating, exam. and auditing, mgmt. devel. and compensation coms. Manhattan Life Ins. Co.; dir., mem. exec. com., chmn. auditing, nominating, mgmt. devel. and exec. compensation coms. Manhattan Life Corp.; dir., chmn. exec. com., chmn. auditing com. Manhattan Nat. Life Ins. Co. (name formerly No. Nat. Life Ins. Co.). Author: Frontiers in Labor-Management Problems, 1956, Seniority. First In, Last Out, 1958; also articles. Del. Atty. Gen.'s Conf. on Juvenile Delinquency, 1936; mem. U.S. Com. for Security of War Info., 1942; mem. prevention com. Assn. Am. Railroads, 1947-50; mem. manpower com. Mfg. Chem. Assn., 1950-53; trustee emeritus, mem. exec. com., past pres. U. Mont. Found., Center for Environ. and Resource Analysis; bd. dirs., chmn. awards com. Nat. Safety Council, 1963-68. Recipient Distinguished Service award U. Mont., 1967. Mem. Soc. Former Spl. Agts. FBI, Transp. Assn. Am. (policy implementation and facilitation coms. 1969-77), Internat. Assn. Chiefs of Police (life mem.), Nat. Def. Transp. Assn., Phi Sigma Kappa, Sigma Delta Chi. Episcopalian (former vestryman, warden). Clubs: University (Larchmont, N.Y.) (past pres.); Grizzly Riders Internat. (Mont.) (founding mem., former pres.). Home: Mc Lean Va. Deceased.

HENDRICKSON, ROBERT AUGUSTUS, lawyer; b. Indpls., Aug. 9, 1923; s. Robert Augustus and Eleanor Riggs (Atherton) H.; m. Virginia Reiland Cobb, Feb. 3, 1951 (div. 1980); m. Zita Davisson, May 12, 1981; children—Alexandra Kirk, Robert Augustus III. Cert., Yale U., 1943, U. Besancon, France, 1945, U. Sorbonne, France, 1946; JD, Harvard U., 1948. Bar: Ind. 1948, N.Y. 1949, U.S. Supreme Ct. 1959, Fla. 1971, U.S. Ct. Internat. Trade 1978. Assoc. Lord, Day & Lord, N.Y.C., 1948-52; law asst. to Surrogates of N.Y. County, 1952-54; ptnr. Lovejoy, Wasson, Lundgren & Ashton, 1967-76; counsel Coudert Bros., N.Y.C., 1977-78, ptnr., 1979-86; counsel Citibank N.A., 1986-87; ptnr. Eaton & Van Winkle, N.Y.C., 1987-94, counsel, 1995—; chmn., bd. dirs. Hendrickson Asset Mgmt. Assistance Cons.; vis. prof. U. Miami, Coral Gables, Fla., 1976; mem. sec. of State's Adv. Group on Trusts, 1983—; trade rep. U.S. Sec. of Commerce Industry Sector Adv. Com. on Services in Trade, 1985-87. Author: Interstate and International Estate Planning, 1968, The Future of Money, 1970, The Cashless Society, 1972, Hamilton I 1757-1789, 1976, Hamilton II 1789-1804, 1976, The Rise and Fall of Alexander Hamilton, 1981, Changing the Situs of a Trust, 1981, 94, Estate and Trust Accounting, 1994; prodr. The Ramayana, 1975; writer, cons. TV film An Empire of Reason, 1989; playwright Clash of Ambitions, 1996; contbr. articles to profl. jours. Bd. dirs., sec. Mental Health Assn., N.Y.C. and Bronx Counties, 1964-76; trustee, Hosp. Chaplaincy, 1960-85, Internat. Ctr. Disabled, 1968—, Anne S.K. Brown Mil. Collection Brown U., St. Hilda's and St. Hugh's Sch., 1968-81, Clinton Hall Assn., 1987—, Carl Duisberg Soc., C.D.S. Internat., Inc., 1976—; chmn., CEO CDS Internat., Inc., 1983-87; chmn. Republic Aerospace Co., 1986-87; founder, chmn. Hamiltonian Inst., 1990—. 1st lt. U.S. Army, 1942-46, 51. Decorated Bronze Star, Purple HEart with oak cluster; Yale U. regional scholar, 1941-42, Phelps Assn. scholar, 1942, Officer's Cross of Order of Merit, 1st Class (Bundesverdienst-Kreuz erst Klasse), Fed. Republic Germany, 1987; recipient Alexander Hamilton award N.Y.C. Bowling Green Assn., 1989, Am. Fgn. Law Assn. Disting. Svc. award, 1996. Mem. ABA, SAR, N.Y. State Bar Assn. (founder, editor-in-chief N.Y. Internat. Law Rev. 1987-88, sect. of internat. law and practice), Am. Coll. Trust and Estate Counsel, Ind. Bar Assn., Assn. of Bar of City of N.Y., Fla. Bar, Consular Law Soc. (pres. 1982-83, chmn. 1983-85), Am. Fgn. Law Assn. (v.p. 1982, pres. 1983-87, Pub. Svc. award 1996), Internat. Acad. Estate and Trust Law (exec. coun.), Am. Coll. Trust and Estate Coun., Am. Soc. Internat. Law, Am. br. Internat. Law Assn., Maritime Law Assn. of U.S., Bankruptcy Lawyers Bar Assn., N.Y. Commerce and Industry Assn. (chmn. com. trusts 1964-68), Union Internat. des Avocats, Inst. Mgmt. Cons. Inc., Assn. Mgmt. Cons. Inc., Century Assn., Union Club, Racquet and Tennis Club, Sky, Colonial Wars, Sons of the Revolution (bd. of mgrs. 1990—), Pilgrims of the U.S., The Church (pres. 1977-79), Dutch Treat Club (N.Y.C.). Republican. Episcopalian. Deceased.

HENLEY, J. SMITH, judge; m. Dorothy Henley; children: Jane K., Wordna S. Henley Deere; Referee in bankruptcy, Western Dist. Ark., 1943-45 assoc. gen. counsel, FCC, 1954-56; dir. Office of Adminstrv. Procedure, Dept. Justice 1956-58; judge U.S. Dist. Cts. (ea. and we. dists.) Ark., 1958-75; judge, U.S. Ct. Appeals (8th cir.), Harrison, Ark., 1975-82, sr. judge, 1982—; mem. Judicial Conf. Subcom. on Supporting Personnel, 1975-77, Adv. Com, on Appelate Rules, 1978-84. Mem. ABA, Am. Judicature Soc., Ark. Bar Assn.

HENNEMAN, ELWOOD, educator, neurophysiologist; b. Washington, Dec. 22, 1915; s. Harry Edwin and Rubina (Raihle) H.; m. Karel Van Syckel Toll, Dec. 30, 1950 (dec.); children—Cyrena Van Syckel (dec.), Abby Hastings. A.B., Harvard, 1937; M.D., McGill U., 1943. Intern Royal Victoria Hosp., Montreal, 1943-44; house officer Montreal Neurol. Inst., 1944; fellow physiology Johns Hopkins Sch. Medicine, 1946-47; research asst. Ill. Neuropsychiat. Inst., Chgo., 1947-49; vis. investigator Rockefeller Inst. Med. Research, N.Y.C., 1949-51; asst. prof. physiology Johns Hopkins Sch. Medicine, 1951-55; mem. faculty Harvard Med. Sch., 1955—, prof. physiology, 1969—, chmn. dept. physiology, 1971-74, 78-79; neurophysiologist Mass. Gen. Hosp., Boston, 1960-96; Mem. radiobiology panel Pres.'s Space Sci. Bd., 1971—; vis. prof. physiology U. Bern (Switzerland) Med. Sch., 1987-88; Mayo lectr., 1985; Philip Bard lectr. Johns Hopkins U., 1989; Grass lectr., 1989. Mem. editorial bd.: Am. Jour. Physiology, 1960-63, Jour. Neurophysiology, 1964-70, Physiol. Rev, 1965-66; sect. editor neurophysiology: Am. Jour. Physiology, 1962-63; asso. editor: Exptl. Neurology, 1979—. Served to lt. USNR, 1944-46. Recipient medal College de France, 1976, Wakeman award, 1986; Guggenheim fellow, 1949-50. Mem. Am. Acad. Arts and Scis., Am. Physiol. Soc., Internat. Brain Research Orgn., Soc. for Neuroscis., AAAS, Belgian Soc. Electromyography and Clin. Neurophysiology (hon.), Sigma Xi. Clubs: Longwood Cricket (Chestnut Hill, Mass.); Badminton and Tennis (Boston). Died Feb. 22, 1996.

HENNING, EDWARD BURK, museum curator; b. Cleve., Oct. 23, 1922; s. Harold and Marguerite (Burk) Wagner; m. Margaret Revacko, Dec. 31, 1942; children: Eric M., Lisa A. Henning Puzder, Geoffrey A. B.S. magna cum laude, Western Res. U., 1949; cert., Cleve. Inst. Art, 1949; postgrad., Acad. Julian, Paris, 1949-50; M.A., Western Res. U., 1952. Instr. Cleve. Mus. Art, 1951-53, asst. curator edn., 1953-56, asso. curator edn., 1956-58, asst. to dir., 1958-70, curator contemporary art, 1970-72, curator modern art, 1972-78, chief curator modern art, 1978-85, research curator, 1985-93; adj. prof. art history Case Western Res. U., Cleve., 1967-93; cons. in field. Author: Paths of Abstract Art, 1960, Fifty Years of Modern Art, 1966, The Spirit of Surrealism, 1979, Creativity in Art and Science, 1987; contbr. articles to profl. jours. Served with U.S. Army, 1942-46. Mem. Coll. Art Assn., Am. Assn. Museums, New Orgn. Visual Arts. Home: Cleveland Ohio Died Apr. 18, 1993.

HENNING, HAROLD WALTER, dentist, athletic association executive; b. Lockport, N.Y., Feb. 25, 1919; s. Harold Walter and Erna (Kandt) H. B.A., North Central Coll., 1941, L.H.D. (hon.), 1984; D.D.S. cum laude, Chgo. Coll. Dental Surgery, 1949; postgrad., U. Ill., Ohio State U. Sci. tchr. Roseville, Ill., 1941-42; gen. practice dentistry Naperville, Ill., 1949-88; Amateur coach N. Central Coll., Naperville, 1948-62; bd. govs. Nat. Amateur Athletic Union, 1954—, mem. fgn. relations com., 1954-88; pres. Central Assn., 1965-66; chmn. U.S. men's swimming com., 1959-65; bd. dirs. U.S. Olympic Com., 1969-88, exec. com., 1972-88, chmn. internat. relations com., 1984-88, chmn. swimming com., 1959-65; mem. organizing com. Pan Am. Games, Chgo., 1959, dir. aquatic competition, 1959; sec.-treas. Amateur Swimming Union Ams., 1963-71, pres., 1971-75; del. Fedn. Internationale Natation Amateur, 1964-88, hon. sec., 1968-72, pres., 1972-76; chmn. exec. com. Olympic Men's and Women's Swimming Trials, 1972, 76; dir. Olympic Games, charge swimming, diving and water polo events, 1972, 76; mgr. U.S. Olympic Swimming Team, Tokyo, 1964; founding pres. U.S. Aquatic Sports, 1980-82; bd. dirs. Los Angeles Organizing Com. Olympic Games, 1984, U.S. Pan Am. Team, Mex., 1955 coach mgr. U.S. Teams to, Guatemala and Japan, 1954-62; ofcl., referee various internat. games, 1952-68 founder World Aquatic Championships, 1973, 75, 78 82, 86; pres. Internat. Swimming Hall of Fame, 1983. Mem. Naperville Bd. Edn., 1954-59. Served with USNR, 1942-45. Decorated 1st Order Sports Egypt recipient award Internat. Amateur Athlete, 1964, Ill Gov. Athletic medallion, 1968; R. Max Ritter medallion, 1976; Prize Eminence award Fedn. Internationale Natation Amateur, 1976; Gold medal for distinguished services in sports Republic of China, 1976; Silver Medal Order Internat. Olympic Com.; named to Helms Hall of Fame, 1964, Internat. Swimming Hall of Fame, 1979 Olympic Shield award U.S. Olympic Com., 1984; Joe Rogers sculpture award Nat. YMCA, 1985. Fellow Internat. Coll. Dentists; mem. Am., Ill. dental assns. West Suburban, Far West study clubs, Fedn. Dentaire Internationale, Acad. Gen. Dentistry. Clubs: Masons Rotary.

HENSON, PAUL HARRY, transportation executive; b Bennet, Nebr., July 22, 1925; s. Harry H. and Ma (Schoenthal) H.; m. Betty L. Roeder, Aug. 2, 1946 children: Susan Irene Flury, Lizbeth Henson Barelli. BSEE, U. Nebr., 1948, MS, 1950; hon. doctorates U. Nebr., Ottawa U., Bethany Coll., U. Mo., U. Kans. Registered profl. engr., Nebr. Engr. Lincoln (Nebr.) Tel. & Tel. Co., 1941-42, 45-48, div. mgr., 1948-54, chief engr., 1954-59; v.p. Sprint Corp., Kansas City, Mo 1959-60, exec. v.p., 1960-64, pres., 1964-73, chmn 1966-90, also bd. dirs., 1959-95; chmn. bd. Kansas City So. Industries, Inc., 1990—; also bd. dirs.; bd. dirs Duke Power, Hallmark Cards; pres. Kansas City Equity Ptnrs., L. P. Trustee Midwest Rsch. Inst., Tax Found U. Nebr. Found., Childrens Mercy Hosp., Greater Kansas City Cmty. Found. With USAAF, 1942-45. Mem. NSPE, IEEE, U.S. Telephone Assn. (bd. dirs 1960-76, pres. 1964-65) Kansas City Country Club River Club, Kansas City Club, Eldorado Country Club Old Baldy Club, Mission Hills Country Club, Masons Shriners, Sigma Xi, Eta Kappa Nu, Sigma Tau, Kappa Sigma (Man of Yr. 1987). Died Apr. 12, 1997.

HERB, RAYMOND GEORGE, physicist, manufacturing company executive; b. Navarino, Wis., Jan. 22 1908; s. Joseph and Annie (Stadler) H.; m. Anne Williamson, Dec. 26, 1945; children—Stephen, Rebecca Sara, Emily, William. PhD in Physics, U. Wis Madison, 1935, DSc (hon.), 1988; PhD (hon.), Lund U

1993. Assoc. prof. U. Wis., Madison, 1941-45, prof., 1945-61, Charles Mendenhall prof., 1961-72; chmn. bd., pres. Nat. Electrostatics, Middleton, Wis., 1965-98. Contbr. articles to profl. jours. Recipient Disting. Svc. Citation Coll. Engring. U. Wis., 1994. Fellow Am. Phys. Soc. (Tom W. Bonner award 1968); mem. NAS. Home: Middleton Wis. Deceased.

HERINGTON, CECIL JOHN, classics educator; b. Isleworth, Middlesex, Eng., Nov. 23, 1924; came to U.S., 1960; s. Cecil Edward Eede and Celia Mary (Hewes) H.; m. Helen Janet Rose, June 12, 1948 (dec. 1968); children: David, Christina, Clare; m. Sara Mack, May 25, 1985. B.A., U. Oxford, Eng., 1948, diploma in classical archaeology, 1949, M.A., 1960; MA, Yale U., 1972; DHL (hon.), Adelphi U., 1994. Lectr. Manchester U., Eng., 1949-55, Exeter U., Eng., 1956-60; vis. lectr. Smith Coll., Northampton, Mass., 1960-62; assoc. prof. U. Toronto, Ont., Can., 1962-65; prof. U. Tex., Austin, 1965-70, Stanford (Calif.) U., 1970-72; Talcott prof. Greek Yale U., New Haven, 1972-86, 88-92, prof. emeritus, 1992; Arts and Scis. prof. Duke U., Durham, N.C., 1986-88; vis. Paddison prof. classics U. N.C., Chapel Hill, 1995-96. Author: Athena Parthenos, 1955 (Cromer prize for Greek 1958), Older Scholia on Prometheus, 1972, Poetry into Drama, 1985, Aeschylus, 1986. With RAF, 1943-46. Guggenheim fellow, 1968-69; Sather lectr. classical lit., U. Calif., Berkeley, 1978; Martin classical lectr. Oberlin Coll., 1991. Mem. Hellenic Soc. (London), Classical Assn. Can., Am. Philol. Assn. (bd. dirs. 1986-89), Elizabethan Club. Died Mar. 29, 1997.

HERMAN, ROBERT, physics educator; b. N.Y.C., Aug. 29, 1914; s. Louis and Marie (Lozinsky) H.; m. Helen Pearl Keller, Nov. 24, 1939; children: Jane Barbara, Lois Ellen, Roberta Marie. BS cum laude, CCNY, 1935; MA, Princeton U., 1940, PhD, 1940; hon. degree in engring., U. Karlsruhe, 1984. Fellow physics dept. CCNY, 1935-36, instr. physics, 1941-42; research asst. Moore Sch. Elec. Engring., U. Pa., 1940-41; supr. chem. physics group, physicist, asst. to dir. Applied Physics Lab., John Hopkins U., 1942-55; cons. physicist GM Research Labs., Warren, Mich., 1956, asst. chmn. basic sci. group, 1956-59, dept. head theoretical physics dept., 1959-72, traffic sci. dept., 1972-79; prof. physics Ctr. for Studies in Statis. Mechanics U. Tex., Austin, 1979-84, prof. civil engring., 1979—, L.P. Gilvin Centennial prof. in civil engring., 1982-84, L. P. Gilvin Centennial prof. emeritus, 1986—; vis. prof. U. Calif., Santa Barbara; Patterson lectr. Northwestern U., 1993; Reuben Smeed Meml. lectr. U. Coll., London, 1983; mem. Assembly Math. and Phys. Scis. NRC, 1977-80, mem. Commn. on Engring. and Tech. Sys., 1980-83, mem. com. on sociotech. sys. NRC, com. on resources for math. scis., 1981-84, infrastructure innovation com., 1987—; cons. in field. Assoc. editor: Revs. of Modern Physics, 1953-56, Ops. Rsch. Soc. Am., 1960-74; founding editor: Transp. Sci., 1967-73; author: (with Robert Hofstadter) High Energy Electron Scattering Tables, (with Ilya Prigogine) Kinetic Theory of Vehicular Traffic; contbr. articles to profl. jours.; sculpture/small exotic wood exhibits include Nat. Acad. Sci. and Engring., Washington, 1994, U. Tex., Austin, 1995, Northeastern Woodworkers Expo, Saratoga Springs, N.Y., 1995, Belmont U., Nashville, 1996. Recipient numerous awards including Naval Ordnance Devel. award, 1945, Lanchester prize Johns Hopkins U. and Ops. Rsch. Soc. Am., 1959, medal Université Libre de Bruxelles, 1963, Townsend Harris medal CCNY, 1963, Magellanic Premium Am. Philos. Soc., 1975, Prix Georges Vanderlinden Belgian Royal Acad., 1975, Award in Phys. & Math. Scis., N.Y. Acad. Scis., 1981, Transp. Sci. Lifetime Achievement award ORSA, 1990, Henry Draper medal NAS, 1993, ORSA/TIMS John Von Neumann OR Theory prize, 1993, Roy W. Crum Disting. Svc. award Transp. Rsch. Bd.-NRC, 1993; named Republic of China lectr. Nat. Sci. Coun., 1990. Fellow Am. Phys. Soc., Nat. Acad. Scis. India (fgn.), Washington Acad. Sci., Franklin Inst. (John Price Wetherill gold medal 1980); mem. NAE, Am. Acad. Arts and Scis., Ops. Rsch. Soc. Am. (pres. 1980-81, Philip McCord Morse Meml. lectr. 1989-91, George E. Kimball medal 1976), Washington Philos. Soc., Phi Beta Kappa, Sigma Xi. Achievements include prediction of present temperature of the residual cosmic black-body radiation, a vestige of the initial explosion of the Big Bang Universe; use of high energy electron scattering resulting in theories on proton and neutron charge structure; research on the existence of definite electron trapping states in solids; development of theory of influence of vibration-rotation interaction on the intensity of infrared molecular spectra; development of a theory of the stability and flow of single lane traffic; development of a kinetic theory of multi-lane traffic flow and a two-fluid model of urban traffic. DIED 02/15/97. .

HERMANIUK, MAXIM, archbishop; b. Nowe Selo, Ukraine, Oct. 30, 1911; emigrated to Can., 1948, naturalized, 1954; s. Mykyta and Anna (Monczak) H. Student philosophy and theology, Louvain, Belgium, 1933-35, Beauplateau, Belgium, 1935-39; ThD, Oriental Philology and History, 1943; postgrad., Maitre Agrege Theol., 1947; DD (hon.), U. St. Michael's Coll., Toronto, Can., 1988. Joined Redemptorist Congregation, 1933, ordained priest, 1938; supr. vice provincial Can. and U.S., 1948-51; consecrated bishop, 1951; aux. bishop Winnipeg, Man., Can., 1951; apostolic adminstr., 1956, archbishop met., 1956-92, archbishop emeritus, 1992-96; editor Logos, 1993-96; first editor Logos, 1993-96, Ukraine Theol. Rev., 1950-51; mem. Vatican II Coun., 1962-65, Secretariat for Promoting Christian Unity, Rome, 1963; prof. moral theology, sociology and Hebrew, Beauplateau, 1943-45; prof. moral theology and holy scripture Redemptor Sem. Waterford, Ont., Can., 1949-51; mem. Pontifical Commn. for Revision of Kodex of Oriental Canon Law, 1983; mem. Coun. Secretariat for The Synod of Bishops, Rome; elected for preparation of Ius Speciale As Tempus, 1993, Ukranian Cath. Ch. Author: La Parabole Evangelique, 1947, Our Duty, 1960. Co-founder, mem. Ukrainian Relief Com., Belgium, 1942-48; co-founder 1st pres. Ukrainian Cultural Soc., 1947, organizer Ukrainian univ. students orgn., Obnova, Belgium, 1946-48, Can., 1953; mem. joint working group Cath. Ch. and World Council Chs., 1969; mem. council to Secretariat Synod of Bishops, Rome, 1977, 83. Decorated Order of Can., 1982. Mem. World Congress Free Ukrainians, Taras Shevchenko Sci. Soc., Ukrainian Hist. Assn., KC. Home: Winnipeg Can Died May 3, 1996.

HERMENS, FERDINAND ALOYS, political science educator; b. Nieheim, Federal Republic of Germany, Dec. 20, 1906; came to U.S., 1935; s. Joseph Adam and Theresia (Hoffmeister) H.; m. Mary Ruth Roberts, Aug. 28, 1937; 1 child, Mary Theresa Hermens Harderling. Diploma in Econs., U. Bonn, Fed. Republic Germany, 1928, PhD in Econs., 1931. Asst. prof. econs. Cath. U. Am., Washington, 1935-38; assoc. prof. politics U. Notre Dame, South Bend, Ind., 1938-46, prof. politics, 1946-59; dir. Seminar Polit. Sci. and Rsch. Inst. U. Cologne, Fed. Republic of Germany, 1959-72, fellow Woodrow Wilson Internat. Ctr. for Scholars, 1972-73; vis. prof. Am. Univ., Washington, 1978-89; vis. prof. Cath. U. Am., Washington, 1989—. Author: Demokratie und Kapitalismus, 1931, Der Staat und die Weltwirtschaftskrise, 1936, Democracy or Anarchy? A Study of Proportional Representation, 2d edit., 1972, The Representative Republic, 1958. Presenter testimonies in polit. sci. field to Congress. Recipient Grand Order of Merit of the Fed. Republic of Germany, Cologne, 1971. Mem. Am. Polit. Sci. Assn., Internat. Polit. Sci. Assn., Polit. Sci. Acad. Avocation: swimming. Deceased.

HERNDON, CHARLES HARBISON, retired orthopaedic surgeon; b. Dublin, Tex., Dec. 12, 1915; s. G. Perkins and May (Williams) H.; m. Kathryn Blair, Apr. 14, 1944; children: Charles Laylin, David Newcomb. B.A., U. Tex., 1937; M.D., Harvard, 1940. Diplomate: Am. Bd. Orthopaedic Surgery (mem. bd. 1960-66, chmn. exam. com. 1961-64, pres. 1964-66). Rotating surg. intern Univ. Hosps., Cleve., 1940-41; jr. orthopaedic surgeon Am. Hosp., Oxford, Eng., 1942; Gerard Beekman fellow orthopaedic surgery Hosp. Spl. Surgery, N.Y.C., 1945-46; resident in orthopaedic surgery Hosp. Spl. Surgery, 1946-47; mem. faculty Case-Western Res. U. Sch. Medicine, 1947-97, Rainbow prof. orthopaedic surgery, 1961-82, Rainbow prof. emeritus orthopaedic surgery, 1982-97; dir. dept. orthopaedic surgery Univ. Hosps., Cleve., 1953-82, Rainbow Hosp., Cleve., 1952-82; sr. cons. orthopaedic surgery Cleve. VA Hosp., 1956-82; assoc. orthopaedic surgeon Highland View Hosp., 1953-82; pres. Musculoskeletal Transplant Found., 1988-91. Contbr. numerous articles to profl. jours., chpts. in books. Mem. profl. adv. bd. Ohio Services Crippled Children, 1959-80; skeletal system com. NRC-Nat. Acad. Scis., 1958-67, chmn., 1962-67; Trustee Jour. Bone and Joint Surgery, 1969-74, treas., 1971-74. Served to maj. M.C. AUS, 1942-45, ETO. Mem. AMA, Am. Surg. Assn., A.C.S. (2d v.p. 1973-74), Am. Acad. Orthopaedic Surgeons (pres. 1968, exec. com. 1967-71), Orthopaedic Research Soc. (pres. 1957, exec. com. 1954-60), Am. Orthopaedic Assn., Internat. Soc. Orthopaedic Surgery and Traumatology, Am. Rheumatism Soc., Cleve. Orthopaedic Club (pres. 1963-64), Ohio Orthopaedic Soc. (sec.-treas. 1956-57), Clin. Orthopaedic Soc., Assn. Orthopaedic Chmn. (pres. 1974-75), Council Med. Spltys. Soc. (pres. 1976). Died July 27, 1997.

HERRELL, WALLACE EDGAR, physician, editor; b. Marshall, Va., Oct. 1, 1909; s. Bennett Frost and Bessie (Ballard) H.; m. Margaret Harwick, Jan. 18, 1936; children: Stephen, John, Sarah (Mrs. J. Brady Foust). M.D., U. Va., 1933; M.S., U. Minn., 1937. Intern Virginia Mason Hosp., Seattle, 1933-34; resident Mayo Found., Rochester, Minn., 1934-37; instr. medicine Mayo Found. Grad. Sch. U. Minn., 1938-43, asst. prof. medicine, 1943-47, asso. prof., 1947-52, prof., 1952-53; cons. in medicine Mayo Clinic, 1938-53, head sect. in medicine, 1946-53; cons. medicine Lexington (Ky.) Clinic, 1953-67; clin. prof. medicine U. Ky., 1961-92; editor-in-chief Clin. Medicine and Med. Digest publs., Northfield, Ill., 1967-74; Instr. U.S. Army Med. Center, Washington, 1948-49. Author: Penicillin and Other Antibiotic Agents, 1945, Erythromycin, 1955, Lincomycin, 1969; Contbr. chpts. to textbooks, over 200 articles to med. jours.; Editorial bd.: Am. Review of Microbiology, 1947-52, MD Med. mag, 1956-85. Mayo Found. fellow, 1934-37; Recipient Distinguished Service award U.S. Jr. C. of C., 1943. Mem. AMA, ACP (life), AAAS, Am. Soc. Clin. Investigation, Central Soc. Clin. Research, Am. Fedn. Clin. Research, Am. Med. Writers Assn., Alumni Assn. Mayo Found., U. Va. Alumni Assn. (life), Minn. Soc. Internal Medicine (hon.), Omaha Mid-West Clin. Soc. (hon.), Am. Soc. Clin. Pharmacology and Therapeutics, Zumbro Valley Med. Soc., Minn. State Med. Assn., Am. Soc. Microbiology, Thomas Jefferson Soc. U. Va., Sigma Xi, Alpha Omega Alpha, Phi Chi. Episcopalian. Clubs: Rochester Golf and Country (Rochester), University (Rochester); Thoroughbred Am. (Lexington). Home: Rochester Minn. Died Apr. 7, 1992.

HERRIOT, JAMES (JAMES ALFRED WIGHT), veterinary surgeon, author; b. Oct.3, 1916; s. James Henry and Hannah Wight; m. Joan Catherine Danbury, 1941; 2 children. Ed. Glasgow Vet. Coll.; D.Litt. (hon.), U. Heriot-Watt, 1979; DVSc (hon.), Liverpool, 1983. Practice veterinary medicine, Thirsk, Yorks, Eng., 1940-95. Author: If Only They Could Talk, 1970, It Shouldn't Happen to a Vet, 1972, All Creatures Great and Small, 1972, Let Sleeping Vets Lie, 1973, All Things Bright and Beautiful, 1973, Vet in Harness, 1974, Vets Might Fly, 1976, Vet in a Spin, 1977, James Herriot's Yorkshire, 1979, The Lord God Made Them All, 1981, The Best of James Herriot, 1982, James Herriot's Dog Stories, 1985, Every Living Thing, 1992, James Herriot's Cat Stories, 1994; (also juvenile books) Moses the Kitten, 1984, Only One Woof, 1985, The Christmas Day Kitten, 1986, Bonny's Big Day, 1987, Blossom Comes Home, 1988, The Market Square Dog, 1990, Oscar, Cat-about-Town, 1990, Smudge, the Little Lost Lamb, 1991; numerous translations. Served with RAF, World War II. Decorated Order Brit. Empire. Mem. Royal Coll. Vet. Surgeons, Brit. Vet. Assn. Deceased. Home: Thirsk Eng.

HERSHEY, ALFRED DAY, geneticist; b. Owosso, Mich., Dec. 4, 1908; s. Robert Day and Alma (Wilbur) H.; m. Harriet Davidson, Nov. 15, 1945; 1 son, Peter. B.S., Mich. State U., 1930, Ph.D. in Chemistry, 1934, D.M.S., 1970; D.Sc. (hon.), U. Chgo., 1967. Asst. bacteriologist Washington U. Sch. Medicine, St. Louis, 1934-36; instr. Washington U. Sch. Medicine, 1936-38, asst. prof., 1938-42, asso. prof., 1942-50; mem. staff, genetics research unit Carnegie Inst. of Washington, Cold Spring Harbor, N.Y., 1950-62; dir. Carnegie Inst. of Washington, 1962-74; ret., 1974. Contbr. articles to profl. jours. Recipient Nobel prize in Medicine (joint), 1969; Albert Lasker award Am. Pub. Health Assn., 1958; Kimber Genetics award Nat. Acad. Scis., 1965. Mem. Nat. Acad. Scis. Home: Syosset N.Y. Died May 22, 1997.

HERSHKOVITZ, PHILIP, zoologist; b. Pitts., Oct. 12, 1909; s. Abe and Bertha (Halpern) H.; m. Anne Pierrette Dode, Sept. 15, 1945; children: Francine, Michal Dode, Mark Alan. BS, U. Mich., 1938, MS, 1940. Mem. zool. expdn. Ecuador, Upper Amazon region, 1933-37, Colombia, Columbia, 1941-43, 48-52; mem. zool. expdn. Suriname, 1961-62, Peru, 1980-81, Brazil, 1984, 86-89; asst. curator mammal divsn. Field Mus. Natural History, Chgo., 1947-54, assoc. curator, 1954-56, curator, 1956-61, rsch. curator, 1961-74, curator emeritus, 1974—. Contbr. articles to profl. jours. with U.S. Army, 1943-46. Walter Rathbone Bacon Travelling scholar Smithsonian Inst., 1941-43, 46-47. Mem. Am. Soc. Mammalogists (hon.), Am. Soc. Primatologists (disting. primatologist award 1991), Explorer's Club (corresponding). DIED 02/15/97. .

HERZBRUN, DAVID JOSEPH, retired advertising executive, consultant; b. N.Y.C., Jan. 9, 1927; s. Arthur O. Herzbrun and Lillian (Howards) Herzbrun Katz; m. Ellen Louise Cohn, Nov. 12, 1950; children: Andra Paula Herzbrun Barrand Horton, Douglas Alan, Jane Emily Herzbrun Nevins Glidden. B.A., Marlboro Coll., 1949. Creative dir. Doyle Dane Bernbach, Dusseldorf, Germany, 1961-64; Creative dir. Ogilvy & Mather, N.Y.C., 1965-67; pres. Herzbrun, McManus, Westport, Conn., 1970-73; co-creative dir. HBM, Boston, 1975-80; exec. creative dir. Europe, J. W. Thompson, Frankfurt, Fed. Republic Germany, 1981-82; sr. v.p. internat. Doyle Dane Bernbach, N.Y.C., 1983-85; exec. v.p., creative dir. Saatchi & Saatchi Compton, N.Y.C., 1985-87, also bd. dirs., 1987; cons., ptnr. Cannon Communications, St. Helena Island, S.C., 1987-93. Author: Playing in Traffic on Madison Avenue, 1990, Copywriting by Design, 1996; contbr. articles to profl. jours. Creative dir. Humphrey for Pres. campaign, Washington, 1968, Dukakis for Gov. campaign, Boston, 1974; cons. Rockefeller campaign, N.Y.C., 1970, Republican Nat. Com., Washington, 1980. Recipient Grand prize Internat. Commls. Festival, Cannes, France, 1963, Hatch award New Eng. Advt. Club, 1971-81, more than 200 advt. awards, 1959-97. Mem. One Club (Silver award 1978), Dataw Island Club (Beaufort, S.C.), Dataw Island Yacht Club. Unitarian. Avocations: writing poetry, translating German poems, sailing, golf. Died Nov. 8, 1997.

HERZOG, CHAIM, former president of Israel; b. Belfast, No. Ireland, Sept. 17, 1918; emigrated to Israel, 1935; s. Issac Halevy and Sarah (Hillman) H.; m. Aura Ambache, 1947; 4 children. Ed., Wesley Coll., Dublin, London U., Cambridge U.; LLB, Hebron Yeshiva; Doctorate (hon.), Yeshiva U., 1977, Jewish Theol. Sem., 1977, Bar Ilan U., 1978, Georgetown U., U. Liberia, 1984, Hebrew U., Jerusalem, 1985, Weizmann Inst. Sci., Israel, 1985, U. Haifa, Israel, 1986, Ben Gurion U., Beer-Sheva, Israel, 1986, Brandeis U., 1987, Haifa Inst. Tech., 1989, York U., Toronto, Ont., Can., 1989, U.

Buenos Aires, 1989, Tel-Aviv U., 1993. Admitted as barrister-at-law, advocate, 1941; head security dept. Jewish Agy., 1947-48; mil. naval and air attaché Israeli embassy, Washington, 1950-54; comdg. officer Jerusalem Dist., 1954-57; chief of staff So. Command, 1957-59; dir. Mil. Intelligence, 1948-50, 59-62; 1st mil. gov. for West Bank Israel Def. Forces, 1967; polit. and mil. broadcaster during Six Day War, 1967, Yom Kippur War, 1973; A.E. and P. from Israel to UN, 1975-78; former leadership bur. Israel Labour Party; mem. Knesset, 1981-83; pres. Israel, 1983-93; polit. and mil. publicist for Israeli, Brit. and U.S. periodicals; regular radio and TV commentator, Israel and abroad; former dir. Israeli Discount Bank, Tel Aviv, N.Y.C., Israel Aircraft industries, Indsl. Devel. Bank of Israel; dir. holding Indsl. Devel. Bank of Israel (IDBI), Slim Fast Corp., U.S.A.; mem. adv. bd. Hollinger Inc., Toronto; mng. dir. G.U.S. Industries, 1962-72; sr. ptnr. Herzog, Fox and Neeman, Advocates, 1972-83. Author: Israel's Finest Hour, 1967, Days of Awe, 1973, The War of Atonement, 1975, Who Stands Accused?, 1978, The Arab-Israeli Wars, 1982, Heroes of Israel, 1989, Living History, 1996; co-author: Battles of the Bible, 1978. Mem. internat. adv. bd. Inst. Internat. Studies, Stanford (Calif.) U. Maj. Brit. Army, WWII; maj. gen. Res. Israeli Army. Decorated knight comdr. Brit. Empire; named Hon. Fellow U. Coll. London, Hon. Bencher Hon. Soc. Lincoln's Inn; recipient Silver medal Charles U., Prague;. Mem. World ORT Union (past pres.). Died Apr. 17, 1997.

HESSEL, ALEXANDER, retired engineering educator; b. Vienna, Austria, Oct. 19, 1916; s. Adolf and Jetti (Goldenberg) H.; m. Miriam Levy, Jan. 18, 1948; children: Judith, Nomi Katz. MS in Physics, Hebrew U., Jerusalem, 1938-43; DEE, Poly. Inst. Brooklyn, 1960. Rsch. engr. Israely Min. Def., Israel, 1948-51, 53-56; rsch. assoc. Microwave Rsch. Inst., Brooklyn, N.Y., 1958-60; rsch. asst. prof. Poly. Inst. Brooklyn, N.Y., 1960-62, assoc. prof., 1962-67; prof. Poly. U. (formerly Poly. Inst. Brooklyn), N.Y., 1967-87, prof. emeritus, 1987—. Contbr. over 50 articles to profl. jours. Fellow IEEE (life, best paper award 1974); mem. Sigma Xi. DIED 02/11/97. .

HESSER, HELEN ELIZABETH, elementary and secondary school educator; b. Gladerwater, Tex., Dec. 12, 1935; d. Milton Dysert and Katie Matilda (Durham) Brewer; m. Garland Wayne Hesser, Jan. 1, 1956 (dec. Apr. 1987); children: Sheila Carol, Sheena Sue (dec.), Marvin Ray. AA, Tyler (Tex.) Jr. Coll., 1977; BS in Edn., U. Tex., Tyler, 1979; MEd, Stephen F. Austin State U., Nacogdoches, Tex., 1985. Cert. tchr., Tex., S.D., Alaska. Kindergarten tchr. Tyler Pub. Schs., 1980-86; spl. edn. tchr. Brownsboro (Tex.) Pub. Schs., 1986-91, Little Wound Sch., Pine Ridge Reservation, Kyle, S.D., 1991-95; tchr. mid. sch. history and lang. arts, h.s. lang. arts Heritage Christian Sch., Cadillac, Mich., 1995-96; tchr. Sandusky Christian Sch., Sandusky, MI, 1996—; naturalist Custer State Park, S.D., 1990; selected participant The Mammoth Trek, Chadron (Nebr.) State Coll., 1991, 92. Sunday sch. tchr. Sharps Corner Bapt. Ch., Porcupine, S.D., 1992-95. Mem. Internat. Reading Assn., Alpha Delta Kappa. Avocations: photography, country crafts, hiking, travel, reading. Deceased.

HEUSER, OSCAR EDWARD, marketing professional; b. Ardmore, Okla., Nov. 25, 1922; s. George John Heuser and Velma Violenta (Deardorff) Connell; m. Mary Bolin White, Jan. 27, 1945 (dec. Dec. 1996); children: Ronald Wayne, Debra Leigh. BS in Bus., Okla. City U., 1976, MEd, 1978, MBA, 1979. Announcer and newscaster KSWO Radio, Lawton, Okla., 1941-42; flight instr. Page Aviation/Cimarron Field, Yukon, Okla., 1943-44; copywriter Lowe Runkle Co., Oklahoma City, 1952-55; exec. v.p. Long Runkle Co., Oklahoma City, 1972-81, pres., 1981-87; vice-chmn. Runkle-Moroch Co., Oklahoma City, 1987-88; chmn., CEO Mid-America Mktg. Comms., Oklahoma City, 1988-96; exec. dir. Sales and Mktg. Execs. Internat. Acad., Oklahoma City, 1993-96; trustee, exec. dir. sales and mktg. execs. Internat. Acad. of Achievement, Oklahoma City, 1992-96; bd. dirs. Epworth Villa Retirement Comm., Oklahoma City; adj. faculty Okla. City U., 1980-96; guest participant Nat. Security Seminar, Army War Coll., Carlisle Barracks, Pa., 1995. State chmn. Okla. Com. for Employer Support of the Guard and Res., Office of the Asst. Sec. of Def., Okla. and Arlington, Va., 1994-96. Capt. USAF, 1944-52, ETO; lt. col. USAFR. Named Outstanding Young Man of Oklahoma City, Okla. Jaycees, 1954; recipient George Washington Honor medal Freedom's Found., 1994, Friend of Immunization award Okla. State Dept. Health, Oklahoma City, 1996. Mem. Rotary (Paul Harris fellow 1980, gov. dist. 5750 1991-92), Okla. Sales and Mktg. Execs. Assn. (past bd. dirs. 1989-96). Avocations: travel, reading, photography. Home: Oklahoma City Okla. Died Dec. 3, 1996.

HEWITT, JOHN STRINGER, nuclear engineer; b. Kincardine, Ont., Can., Feb. 5, 1939; s. Albert Edwin and Mabel Priscilla (Stringer) H.; m. Alice Marlene Morton, July 7, 1962. BSc in Engring. Physics, Queen's U., Kingston, Ont., 1961; MSc, U. Birmingham, U.K., 1962, PhD, 1966. Lic. profl. engr., Ont. Asst. prof. chem. engring. and applied chemistry U. Toronto, 1969-75, assoc. prof. chem. engring., 1975-82, assoc. dean Faculty of Applied Sci. and Engring., 1981-84, prof. applied nuclear studies, 1982-87; v.p. technologies ECS Power Systems, Inc., Ottawa, Ont., 1987-89; pres., cons. Stringer Hewitt Assocs., Inc., Ottawa, Ont., 1990—; tech. devel. mgr. Can. Space Sta., Can. Space Agy., Ottawa, 1990-93; sr. tech. adv. Nat. Res. Can., Ottawa, 1993—; vis. scientist Chalk River Nuclear Labs., Atomic Energy of Can., Chalk River, Ont., 1978-79; cons. Tech. Adv. Panel on Nuclear Safety, Ontario Hydro, Toronto, 1990-93, R&D Adv. Panel to Atomic Energy of Can., Ltd., Ottawa, 1991-93. Contbr. articles to profl. jours. Pres. Carleton Condominium Corp. #250, Ottawa, 1990-93; chmn. Metro Toronto Sci. Fair Com., 1973, judge, 1974, 77, 83, 84; coord. United Appeal Campaign, U. Toronto, 1970, 71, 83, 84. Athlone fellow Brit. Bd. Trade, Birmingham, 1961-63; NRC scholar, 1963-65. Fellow Can. Nuclear Soc. (founding mem., pres. 1983-84); mem. Can. Pugwash Group (treas. 1990—), Sci. for Peace (founding mem., dir. 1981-86). Achievements include patents on measurement of slurry consistencies (Can. and U.S.), nuclear reactor plant, and nuclear reactor cooling system. Deceased.

HEWITT, THOMAS EDWARD, financial executive; b. West Lafayette, Ind., Sept. 7, 1939; s. Ernest Edward and Katherine (Thelen) H.; BA, Dartmouth Coll., 1961, MBA, 1962; CPA, Ill.; m. Jeraldine Lee Spurgeon, June 16, 1962; children: Debora Lynn, Laura Jean, Gregory Spurgeon. Staff acct. Ernst & Young, Chgo., 1966-67, acct. in charge, 1967, sr. acct., 1967-69; contr. Thorne United Inc., Addison, Ill., 1969-70, sec.-treas., 1970; supr. Ernst & Young, Chgo., 1971-76; contr. Waterloo (Iowa) Industries, Inc., 1976-79, v.p. fin., 1979-90, exec. v.p., 1991-92; v.p., CFO, sec. and treas. Cupples Co. Mfrs., St. Louis, 1993—, bd. dirs., 1993—. Treas., Salvation Army, Waterloo, 1977-78, 80-82, Cedar Valley United Way, 1983-87, Covenant Med. Ctr., 1986-91, St. Francis Hosp., 1986-89, vice chmn. Covenant Med. Ctr., 1992, chmn., 1992-93; assoc. campaign chmn. United Way of Black Hawk County, 1981, 82; spl. project chmn. Chgo. Jaycees, 1969; trustee Westminster United Presbyterian Ch., 1984-86, vice-chmn., 1985; bd. dirs. Wheaton Franciscan Svcs., Inc., Iowa, 1992-93. Capt. USMC, 1962-66. NROTC regular scholar, 1957-62. Mem. AICPAs, Mo. Soc.CPAs, Inst. Mgmt. Accts., Sunnyside Country Club (treas. 1984, pres. 1985, trustee, 1986-88), Greenbriar Hills Country Club. Died Oct. 28, 1997.

HEWITT, WILLIAM FRANCIS, biomedical consultant; b. Chgo., May 25, 1914; s. William Francis and Ada Alice (Monroe) H.; m. Jerene Grobee; June 25, 1977; children: Alice, Alan, Meredith, Rosalie, Scott, Willa, Mike. AB, Princeton U., 1935; MS, U. Chgo., 1937, PhD, 1942. Diplomate Am. Bd. Sexology; cert. sex counselor, sexologist Am. Coll. Sexologists. Mem. teaching and rsch staff U. Chgo., 1940-42, Coll. Osteo. Physicians and Surgeons, 1943-46, Smith Kline and French Labs., 1946-48, Howard U., 1948-52, Des Moines Still Coll. Osteopathy and Surgery, 1952-57, 60-62, Mead Johnson Labs., 1957-59, Ohio No. U., 1962-65, Norwich-Eaton Pharms., Norwich., N.Y., 1965-77; ptnr. Words Inc. and Whittier (Calif.) Press, 1977—; sex cons., Whittier, 1977—; supr., trainer, mem. speaker's bur. L.A. Sex Info. Helpline, 1980—; tchr. Planned Parenthood, N.Y., 1975-76. sex cons., Whittier, 1977—. Vol. sex info. helpline L.A. Free Clinic, 1978. Mem. Am. Med. Writers Assn. (active fellowship award 1974, med. writing faculty 1974—), Mensa, (chmn. sex advice panel, spl. interest group 1979—), Soc. Exptl. Biol. Medicine, Soc. Social Responsibility Sci., Assn. Sexologists, Writers Club Whittier, Soc. for Sci. Study of Sex, Am. Assn. of Religious Counselors, Sigma Xi, Nu Sigma Nu, Kappa Psi, Rho Chi. Quaker.

HEXTER, JACK H., historian, educator; b. Memphis, May 25, 1910; s. Milton J. and Alma (Marks); m. Ruth Mullin, Mar. 29, 1942; children—Christopher, Eleanor, Anne, Richard. BA, U. Cin., 1931; MA, Harvard U., 1933, PhD, 1937; LittD (hon.), Brown U., 1964, U. Cin., 1978, U. East Anglia, England, 1978; LHD, Washington U., 1973; LLD (hon.), Portland U., 1974. Tchr. U. Cin., 1936, Harvard U., 1937, MIT, 1938, Queens Coll., 1939-57; mem. faculty Washington U., St. Louis, 1957-64, prof. history, 1957-64, chmn. dept., 1957-60, Disting. historian in residence, 1978-86, John M. Olin prof. history of freedom, 1986-90, dir. Ctr. for history of freedom, 1985-89, emeritus dir., 1990-96; prof. history Yale U., 1964-67, Charles J. Stillé prof., 1967-78; dir. Yale Ctr. for Parliamentary History, 1965-85; assoc. seminars Columbia U., 1948-96; founder Troops to Tchrs. Project, 1991; initiator of legis. in edn. PL103-160, 1991-93. Author: The Reign of King Pym, 1941, More's Utopia: The Biography of an Idea, 1952, Reappraisals in History, 1961, The Judaeo-Christian Tradition, 1966, The History Primer, 1971, Doing History, 1971, The Vision of Politics on the Eve of the Reformation, 1973, On Historians, 1979; also articles; co-author: Western Civilization, 1968; translator: The Monarchy of France (Claude de Seyssel), 1981; co-author, editor: Parliament and Liberty from the Reign of Elizabeth to the English Civil War, 1992; assoc. editor Jour. Brit. Studies, 1961-74, Jour. History of Ideas; co-editor: Utopia, Complete Works of Thomas More, 1965; gen. editor: The Traditions of the Western World, 1967; editorial dir. The Making of Modern Freedom, 1985-89. Trustee Danforth Found., 1973-78. Served with AUS, 1942-46. Guggenheim fellow, 1942, 47, 79; Social Sci. Research Council grantee, 1947, 71; Yaddo fellow, summer 1949; Fulbright Research fellow, 1950, 59-60; Ford fellow, 1953-54; fellow Ctr. Advanced Study in Behavioral Scis., 1966-67; fellow Inst. for Advanced Study, 1975-76; Mellon fellow Nat. Humanities Center, 1981-84. Mem. New Eng. Hist. Assn. (pres. 1970-71), Am. Conf. Brit. Studies (pres. 1973-75), Royal Hist. Soc., Am. Acad. Arts and Scis. (council 1979-82), Am. Philos. Soc. Home: Saint Louis Mo. Died Dec. 8, 1996; interred Bellefountaine Cemetery, St. Louis.

HEYBORNE, ROBERT LINFORD, electrical engineering educator; b. McCornick, Utah, Apr. 17, 1923; s. Robert Leigh and Junetta (Nielsen) H.; m. Denese Theobald, Aug. 21, 1942; children: Linford, Brenda. B.S. in Elec. Engring., Utah State U., 1949, M.S., 1960; Ph.D. in Elec. Engring., Stanford U., 1967. Chief engr. So. Utah Broadcasting Co., 1949-51, asst. mgr., dir. news, 1953-57; prof. elec. engring. Utah State U., 1957-69; dean U. Pacific Sch. Engring., Stockton, Calif., 1969-90; cons. elec. engring. to industry; lectr. NSF Vis. Scientist Program, 1966-67. Contbr. articles to profl. jours. Mem. San Francisco Bay Area Rels. with Industry Com., 1969-90; chmn. Calif. Engring. Liaison Com., 1974. Served with USNR, 1942-46, 51-52. Recipient Disting. alumni award Utah State U., 1979, Honor award Cons. Engrs. Assn. Calif., 1985, 87, 90; named Prof. of Year, Utah State U., 1962, Outstanding Engring. Prof., Phi Kappa Phi, Outstanding Engring. Prof., Sigma Tau Logan, 1967, Engr. of Year, No. Calif. Engrs. Coun., 1972; NSF sci. faculty fellow, 1963-65. Fellow AAAS; mem. IEEE, Am. Soc. Engring. Edn. (chmn. Rocky Mountain sect. 1969, nat. developing colls. com. 1969-73, chmn. Pacific S.W. sect. 1975, nat. chmn. coop. edn. div. 1977-78, nat. dir. rels. with industry div. 1974-77, accreditation processes com. 1978-81, chmn. coun. of sects. Zone IV 1982-84, v.p. for member affairs 1988-90, Nat. Clement J. Freund award 1986, Alvah K. Borman award 1983), Am. Geophys. Union, Internat. Sci. Radio Union, Sigma Xi, Tau Beta Pi. Club: Rotary. Home: Stockton Calif. Died Oct. 13, 1996; interred Cherokee Memorial Park.

HEYDE, NORMA LEE, singer, music educator; b. Herrin, Ill., Dec. 31, 1927; d. Charles LaRue and Callie (Logan) Swinney; m. John Bradley Heyde, Aug. 24, 1947. MusB, U. Mich., 1949, MusM, 1950; grad. cert. in lieder and oratorio, Mozarteum, Salzburg, Austria, 1956. Mem. voice faculty U. Mich. Sch. Music, Ann Arbor, 1950-54, Eastern Mich. U., Ypsilanti, 1954-57; instr. music lit. York Coll. Pa., 1969; artist, tchr. in residence Transylvania Music Camp, Brevard, N.C., 1950-54; assoc. prof. music Salisbury (Md.) State U., 1971-87; dir. music 1st Presbyn. Ch., Milford, Del., 1958-66; artist, tchr. voice Franklin and Marshall Coll., Lancaster, Pa., 1988—; soprano artist various orchs. and choral socs. Nat. Gallery of Art, Washington, 1950-88. Benefit recitalist Meml. Hosp., Civic Ctr., Marion, Ill., Milford Libr., York Symphony Assn., 1960-90, Habitat for Humanity Project, York, Pa., 1993. Oliver Ditson scholar U. Mich., 1946-50, James L. Babcock scholar, 1946-50. Mem. Nat. Assn. Tchrs. Singing, Music Tchrs. Nat. Assn. (adjudicator music competitions), Music Educators Nat. Conf., AAUP, PEO, Phi Kappa Phi (emeritus life), Pi Kappa Lambda, Mu Phi Epsilon. Deceased.

HEYDEMANN, JULIUS, radiologist, educator; b. Bruehl, Germany, June 19, 1911. MD, Free U., Berlin, 1937. Diplomate Am. Bd. Radiology. Intern Norwegian Luth. Deaconess Hosp., Bklyn., 1938-39; resident in radiology N.Y. Postgrad. Med. Sch., 1939-41; resident Bronx Hosp., N.Y.C., 1941; resident in roentgenology City Hosp. N.Y., N.Y.C., 1941-42; med. staff Ingalls Meml. Hosp., Harvey, Ill.; acad. faculty U. Ill. Coll. Medicine, Chgo. Mem. AMA, Am. Coll Radiology, Radiol. Soc. N.Am. DIED 03/11/97. .

HEYER, PAUL OTTO, college president, architect; b. Brighton, Eng., July 8, 1936; came to U.S., 1960; s. Albert Otto and Ivy Winifred (Winter) H.; m. Juliet Ruth Attree, Dec. 23, 1969. B.Arch., Brighton Coll. Art, 1958; M.Arch., U. Mich., 1961; M.Arch. in Urban Design, Harvard U., 1962. Registered architect, N.Y., U.K. Architect Yorke, Rosenberg & Mardall, London 1959-60, Edward Durell Stone, N.Y.C., 1961-62, Oskar Stonorov, Phila., 1962-63, Edward Durell Stone N.Y.C., 1963-64, Paul Heyer Architects, N.Y.C., 1965-97; prof. architecture Pratt Inst., Bklyn., 1968-89, co-chmn. Grad. Architecture, 1979-82, acting dir., 1981-82 dean, 1982-89; pres. N.Y. Sch. Interior Design, N.Y.C. 1989-97. Author: Architects on Architecture: New Directions in America, 1966, Architects on Architecture New Directions in America, rev. edit., 1977, reissued 1994, Mexican Architecture: The Work of Abraham Zabludovsky and Teodoro Gonzalez de Leon, 1978 American Architecture: Ideas and Ideologies in the Late 20th Century, 1993, Abraham Zabludovsky 1979-93 1993, Urban Essays/Ensayos Sobre Urbanismo, 1995. Fulbright Found. scholar, 1960; English Speaking Union fellow, 1960; Albert Kahn Found. fellow, 1960; Graham Found. fellow, 1968-69. Mem. AIA, Royal Inst. Brit Architects, Coll. Architects Nuevo Leon, Mex. (disting mem. Internat. Recognition award profl. merit 1990) Colombian Soc. Architects (hon. 1993). Home: Millbrook N.Y. Died Feb. 22, 1997.

HEYN, ERNEST V., author, editor; b. N.Y.C., Oct. 30, 1904; s. Herbert Alexander and Frieda (Senner) H.; m. Ethel Kenyon, May 1, 1942; children: Susan (Mrs. Willard F. Lochridge III), Dalma. Ed., Trinity Sch., Horace Mann Sch.; grad. magna cum laude, Princeton U., 1925; postgrad., U. Berlin, Germany. Founder, editor Modern Screen mag., 1931; editor Radio Mirror, 1935, Photoplay, 1938, Liberty mag., 1942; founder, editor Sport mag.; editor True Story mag.; editor-in-chief True Story mag. all Macfadden publs., 1948-51; editor Am. Weekly, 1951-59, Family Weekly, Suburbia Today, 1959-64; assoc. pub., editor-in-chief Popular Sci. Monthly, 1964-71, ret., 1970. Author: A Century of Wonders, 100 Years of Popular Science, Fire of Genius, Inventors of the Past Century; Author: (with Alfred W. Lees) Popular Science Leisure Homes, Do-It-Yourself Projects for your own Back Yard; (with Herbert Shuldiner) Popular Science Book of Gadgets; (with Evan Powell) Popular Science Book of Home Heating and Cooling; (with Daniel Ruby) Home Alternate Energy Projects, (with Alfred W. Lees and Morton Schultz) What's Wrong With My Car?, Alfred Lees and Ernest V. Heyn: Popular Sciences Decks and Sunspaces; editor: My Most Inspiring Moment, Twelve Sport Immortals, My Favorite True Mystery. Served with AUS, 1942-45. Mem. Sigma Delta Chi. Presbyterian. Clubs: Dutch Treat, Deadline, Overseas Press, New Eng. of N.Y; Princeton (N.Y.C.). Died July 1, 1995.

HEYREND, PATRICIA MAY, individual, marriage and family therapist; b. N.Y.C., Aug. 27, 1940; d. Arthur Owen and Violet Agnes (Colvin) Williams; m. Leonard Gerald Rightmeier Jr., Aug. 27, 1962 (div. Jan. 1975); children: Larry Brent, Mona Rochelle; m. F. LaMarr Heyrend, June 30, 1979. BSW, U. Kans., 1962; MSW, U. Utah, 1977. Cert. social worker. Caseworker Dept. Pub. Assistance, Payette, Idaho, 1965-71; developer, operator Group Home and Shelter Home, 1971-75; social work cons. child protection-youth rehab. units Region IV, Dept. Health and Welfare, 1977-81; pvt. practice social work Boise, Idaho, 1986-95; staff coord. Parents United, 1983-86; instr. Boise State U. Sch. Social Work, 1985, 87-88; supr. child protection and adoption svcs. Region IV, Idaho Dept. Health and Welfare, 1981-86; pvt. practice part-time, Boise, 1977-86. Mem. Ada County Med. Soc. Aux., Boise, 1990-95. Recipient Outstanding Leadership award HHS, Idaho, 1985. Mem. NASW (Social Worker of Yr. Idaho Central chpt. 1985). Avocations: travel, needlepoint, knitting, reading. Died July 31, 1995.

HIBBERT, WILLIAM ANDREW, JR., surgeon; b. Pensacola, Fla., June 15, 1932; s. William Andrew and Blanche Marie (Blair) H.; children: Andy III, Blair, Reb Stuart. BS, U. of South, 1953; MD, Emory U., 1957. Diplomate Am. Bd. Surgery, recert., Am. Bd. Colon and Rectal Surgery, recert. Intern, Duval Med. Center, U. Fla., Jacksonville, 1957-58; resident in gen. surgery Grady Meml. Hosp., Emory U., Atlanta, 1958-62; fellow in colon-rectal surgery Ochsner Found. Hosp., New Orleans, 1962-63, Baylor U. Med. Center, Dallas, 1964-65; practice medicine specializing in colon-rectal surgery, Austin, Tex., 1965-96; mem. staff St. David, Seton, Brackenridge hosps.; instr. Tulane U. Med. Sch., New Orleans, 1962-64; sr. surgeon gen. surgery svc. USPHS, 1963-64; cons. U. Tex. Student Health Center. Bd. govs. Shrine Burn Hosp., Galveston, Tex.; past chmn. bd. trustees Ben Hur Shrine Temple; past vol. People to People; med. amb. to China and Russia. Chmn. fin. bd., bd. dirs. Austin Scottish Rite Learning Ctr. Fellow ACS, Am. Soc. Colon and Rectal Surgeons, Am. Soc. Gastrointestinal Endoscopists, Am. Soc. Laser Surgery, Soc. of Am. Gastrointestinal Endosopic Surgeons, Internat. Soc. Univ. Colon and Rectal Surgeons, Southwestern Surg. Congress; mem. Tex. Med. Assn., Tex. Colon-Rectal Soc. (past pres.), mem. Pan Am. (past chmn. colon-rectal sect.), So. Med. Assn. (past sect. chmn.), Pan Pacific Surg. Soc., Tex. Soc. Gastrointestinal Endosopists, Royal Soc. Medicine (hon.). Club: Austin Rotary Downtown (Paul Harris fellow). Lodges: Masons, Shriners (potentate 1985, past. dov. imperial shrine Burn Hosp., past chmn. rsch. com., past rep. Imperial Council Shrine North Am.), Royal Order of Jesters (past dir.), Order of DeMolay (Legion of Honor), Scottish Rite (Knight Comdr.). Contbr. articles to med. jours.; past assoc. editor So. Med. Jour. Died Nov. 8, 1996.

HIBBS, CLYDE W., retired environmental sciences educator, consultant; b. Independence, W.Va., July 19, 1922; s. Samuel Jacob and Regina Anna (Kincaid) H. BS, W.Va. U., 1944, MS, 1949; MA, U. Mich., 1955, PhD, 1957. Vocat. agriculture tchr. Ravenswood (W.Va.) High Sch., 1944-52; soil conservationist USDA, Ann Arbor, Mich., 1953-56; prof. conservation U. Wis., Stevens Point, 1956-60; coord. outdoor edn. N.J. colls. N.J. Dept. Edn., Branchville, 1960-61; sci. tchr. N. Plainfield High Sch., Plainfield, N.J., 1961-62; prof. conservation and earth sci. Glassboro (N.J.) State Coll., 1962-64; prof. natural resources Ball State U., Muncie, Ind., 1964-90; adj. prof. sanitary engring. Rutgers U., New Brunswick, N.J., 1964; founder dept. natural resources Ball State U., Muncie, 1965-79; rsch. com. chair Environ. Edn. Bibliography, 1975-77; vis. prof. environ. studies Alderson-Broaddus Coll., Philippi, W.Va., 1992-93; cons., advisor in field. Establishment coord. Juanita Hults Environ. Learning Ctr., Albany, Ind., 1987-90, chmn. adv. com., 1987-90; alternate supr. Delaware County Soil Conservation Dist., Muncie, 1987-89; program coord. E. Ctrl. Ind. Sci. Fair, Ball State U., Muncie, 1989-92. Recipient Creative Programming award Nat. Univ. Ext. Assn., 1971, Key Man award Conservation Edn. Assn., 1977. Fellow Soil Conservation Soc. Am. (chair environ. edn. divsn. 1975-76), Ind. Acad. Sci. (chair soils sect. 1970); mem. N.Am. Assn. Environ. Edn. (global studies com. 1992), Nat. Wildlife Fedn., Conservation Edn. Assn. (v.p. 1972-74), Natural Resource Def. Coun., Environ. Edn. Assn. Ind. (pres. 1967-71). Deceased.

HICKS, CLAYTON S., franchise owner. B.B.A., Boston U., 1929. With Hotel Statler, Boston, 1929-36; sales mgr. Providence Biltmore, 1936-43; gen. mgr. Hotel Touraine, Boston, 1943-48; owner, mgr. Kendall Hotel, Framingham, Mass., 1948-62; pres. P.C. Hicks Catering Co., Lynn, Mass., 1959-63; exec. v.p. Northeast Motel Corp., 1962-64; with Howard Johnson Co., Danbury, Conn., 1966-67; owner Howard Johnsons Motor Lodge, Southington, Conn., 1965—. Chmn. ARC, Framingham, 1958-59; corporator Framingham Union Hosp., 1954—, Framingham Savs. Bank, 1955—. Recipient 1972 Golden Innkeeper award Conn. Hotel and Motel Assn., 1972. Mem. Framingham C. of C., Hotel Sales Mgmt. Assn. N.E. (pres. 1939), Hotel Sales Mgmt. Assn. Internat. (pres. 1941-43), Mass. Hotel and Motel Assn. (dir. 1945-47), Conn. Hotel and Motel Assn. (pres. 1970), New Eng. Innkeepers Assn. (pres. 1972), Am. Hotel and Motel Assn. (dir. representing Conn. 1970-78, exec. com. rep. New Eng. 1971, 75, 77).

HICKS, DAVID, interior decorator, designer, author; b. Mar. 25, 1929; s. Herbert H.; m. Lady Pamela Carmen Louise Mountbatten, 1960; 3 children. Ed. Charterhouse; Central Sch. Arts and Crafts, London. Dir. David Hicks Internat. Mktg., David Hicks Ltd.; assoc. offices in Brussels, Geneva, Munich, W.Ger., Paris, Tokyo, Sydney, Australia; master Salters' Co., 1977-78. Interiors for: Helena Rubinstein, Queen Elizabeth II, His Royal Highness, The Prince of Wales, Govt. of New South Wales, Brit. Steel Corp., Aeroflot Offices, Marquess of Londonderry, library in Brit. embassy, Washington, others; designer fabrics, carpets, furniture, women's wear, others; author: David Hicks on Decoration, 1966; David Hicks on Living—with taste, 1968; David Hicks on Bathrooms, 1970; David Hicks on Decoration—with fabrics, 1971; David Hicks on Decoration—5, 1972; David Hicks Book of Flower Arranging, 1976; David Hicks Living with Design, 1979; David Hicks Garden Design, 1982. Recipient Design award CoID (now Design Council), 1970. Fellow Royal Soc. Arts.Died Apr. 1998. Home: Oxfordshire England

HICKS, MARSHALL M., labor union administrator; b. New Tazwell, Tenn., Nov. 28, 1931; s. Horace M. and Lena M. (Essary) H.; m. Marjorie A. Carr-Hicks, Sept. 4, 1952; children: Marcia, James, Mary, Judy. P-res. local 258, Adrian, Erie, Mich., 1955-67; v.p. Mich. State Utility Coun., Jackson, 1960-63, sec./ treas., 1963-67, pres., 1967-70; regional dir. Utility Workers Union Am., Midwest, 1970-71; sec./ treas. Utility Workers Union Am., Washington, 1971-91, nat. pres., 1991—; pres. Jackson County AFL-CIO, 1968-70. County chmn. Jackson County Dem. Commn., 1967-71. Sgt. U.S. Army, 1949-52. Deceased.

HIDALGO, EDWARD, lawyer, former secretary of navy; b. Mexico City, Oct. 12, 1912; came to U.S., 1918, naturalized, 1936; s. Egon and Domitila (Hidalgo) Kunhardt; m. Belinda Bonham; children: Joanne, Edward, Richard, Tila. B.A. magna cum laude, Holy Cross Coll., 1933; J.D., Columbia U., 1936; civil law degree, U. Mexico Law Sch., 1959. Bar: N.Y. 1936, Mexico 1959, D.C. 1976. Law clk. 2d Circuit Ct. Appeals, N.Y., 1936-37; assoc. Wright, Gordon Zachry & Parlin, N.Y.C., 1937-42; mem. Eberstadt Com. on Unification of Mil. Services, Washington, 1945; spl. asst. to Sec. of Navy James Forrestal, Washington, 1945-46; partner Curtis, Mallet-Prevost, Colt & Mosle, 1946-48; founder, sr. partner Barrera, Siqueiros & Torres Landa, Mexico City, 1948-65; spl. asst. to Sec. of Navy Paul H. Nitze, Washington, 1965-66; partner Cahill, Gordon & Reindel, Paris, 1966-72; spl. asst. econ. affairs to dir. USIA, Washington, 1972; gen. counsel Congl. liaison USIA, 1973-76; asst. sec. manpower, res. affairs installations, logistics U.S. Navy Dept., Washington, 1977-79; sec. U.S. Navy Dept., 1979-81; mem. Pres.'s Commn. Aviation Security and Terrorism, 1989-90; cons. to Mexican Govt. on N. Am. Free Trade Agreement, 1991-93. With USNR, 1942-45. Decorated Bronze Star, Royal Order of Vasa (Sweden); Order of Aztec Eagle (Mex.). Roman Catholic. Clubs: Chevy Chase, Met. Home: Mc Lean Va. Died Jan. 21, 1995.

HIGASHI, GENE I., epidemiologist; b. Gardena, Calif., Nov. 6, 1938; s. Kay Kastsutaro and Takeko (Ogo) H.; m. Elizabeth Lee, Aug. 20, 1966; 1 child, Misao. BA, Swarthmore Coll., Pa., 1960; MD, Yale U., New Haven, 1964; SCD, Johns Hopkins U., Baltimore, 1973. Cert. Anatomic Pathology, Md., Conn., Pa. Head, immuuno pathology unit U.S. Naval Morich, Cairo, Pa., 1962-72; asst. prof. pathology Yale U. Sch. Medicine, New Haven, 1972-74; head, immunology Div. U.S. Haven Med. Res. Unit 3, Cairo, Pa., 1974-75; head, immunology dept. U.S. Haven Med. Res. Unit 3, Cairo, Pa.; assoc. prof. epidemic U. Mich., 1979-83, prof. epidemionology, 1984--; cons. Numerous 1985. Intent-Applier Invention Vaccine Dept. 1986. With USNR 1969-72, Egypt. Recipient numerous research awards. Fellow Indian Soc. Malariology and Infectious Dis., mem. Soc. Tropical Medicine and Hygiene, Am. Assn. Immunologists, Am. Soc. Parsiologists, Royal Soc. Tropical Medicine and Hygiene, Am. Assn. for Advancement & Sci.

HILDRETH, CLIFFORD, retired economist, educator; b. McPherson, Kans., Dec. 8, 1917; s. George W. and Lillian Belle (Huenergardt) H.; m. Mary Louise McGee, Jan. 1, 1942; children: Richard, Robert, Susan, Mary. A.B., U. Kans., 1939; M.S., Iowa State U., 1941, Ph.D., 1947. Asst. prof., then assoc. prof. econs. Iowa State U., 1946-48; asst. prof., then assoc. prof. econs and mem. Cowles Commn., U. Chgo., 1949-52; prof. agrl. econs. N.C. State U., 1953-55; prof. agrl. econs. Mich. State U., 1955-58, prof. econs., head dept., 1958-60, prof. econs. and agrl. econs., 1960-64; prof. econs., statistics and agrl. econs. U. Minn., 1964-88, prof. emeritus, 1988—; Fulbright lectr. U. Tokyo, Hitotsubashi U., Keio U., Tokyo, Japan, 1970; mem. com. nat. stats. Nat. Acad. Sci., 1975-81; cons. U.S. Treasury Dept., 1951-52, U.S. Air Force, 1954-56, Fed. Power Commn., 1963-65, Fed. Comm. Commn., 1968-72, Fed. Reserve Bd. Com. on Monetary Stats., 1974-76; fellow Ctr. Advanced Study Behavioral Scis. Standord, Calif., 1961-62; courtesy prof. econs. U. Oreg., 1988—; writings and corr. placed in spl. collections dept. Duke U. William R. Perkins Libr. Author: (with Frank Jarrett) A Statistical Study of Livestock Production and Marketing, 1955; The Cowles Commission in Chicago, 1939-55, 1986. Served to lt. USNR, 1943-46. Fellow Econometrics Soc., Am. Statis. Assn. (editor jour. 1960-65, v.p. 1968-69, pres. 1973), Inst. Math. Statistics; mem. Am. Econ. Assn., Am. Agrl. Econ. Assn. DIED 08/15/95. .

HILL, ISAAC WILLIAM, newspaper editor, writer, public relations counselor; b. Opelika, Ala., Aug. 8, 1908; s. Isaac W. and Laura (Jones) H.; m. Catherine H. Dawson, June 25, 1932 (dec. Sept. 1974); children: Catherine R., Joyce E.; m. Louise B. Andrews, June 22, 1979. A.B., Washington and Lee U., 1929. Reporter-editor Mobile (Ala.) Press, 1929-30; deskman Washington Evening Star, 1930-37, city editor, 1937-49, news editor, 1949-54, asst. mng. editor, 1954-62, mng. editor, 1962-68, assoc. editor, 1968-73; Washington corr. Editor and Pub. mag., 1974-81; book editor Island Packet newspaper, Hilton Head Island, S.C., 1983-87; lectr. newspaper personnel Am. Press Inst., Columbia, 1955-73. Co-author: Mirror of War, 1961; also short stories and articles in popular mags. Mem. Am. Soc. Newspaper Editors (dir. 1972-73), AP Mng. Editors Assn. (pres. 1967), Newspaper Comics Council, Lambda Chi Alpha, Pi Delta Epsilon, Sigma Delta Chi. Clubs: Nat. Press (Washington), Chevy Chase (Washington). Home: Hilton Head Island S.C. Died Mar. 8, 1993; interred Magnolia Cemetery, Mobile AL.

HILL, JAMES STEWART, engineering executive; b. Washington, Dec. 2, 1912; s. Hugh Stewart and Isabel (Burch) H.; m. Elizabeth Barbara Metzger, June 1, 1936; children: Noel Edward, Hugh Stewart, Gary William, Dawn Elizabeth. BEE, Case Western Res., 1934. Registered profl. engr., Ohio. Staff engr. United Broadcasting Co., Cleve., 1934-44; chief engr. United Broadcasting Co., Akron, Ohio, 1944-50; research engr. United Broadcasting Co., Cleve., 1950-53; v.p. Smith Electronics Corp., Cleve., 1953-58; staff engr. Jansky & Bailey, Georgetown, D.C., 1959-60; engring. mgr. Atlantic Research Corp., Alexandria, Va., 1960-64; research engr. Genisco Tech. Corp., College Park, Md., 1965-69; cons. engr. RCA Service Co., Springfield, Va., 1969-78; pres. EMXX Corp., Springfield, Va., 1978—; cons. Martin Marietta Aerospace Corp., Denver, 1979-81; mem. simulated space shuttle flight NASA Ames Research Ctr., Sunnyvale, Calif., 1977. Author: RFI Handbook, 1971, EMC Handbook Volume 6, 1975, Guide to FCC Equipment Authorization, 1985, Reference Book on FCC Authorizations, 1987. Recipient Silver Plaque Alpine Tourist Commn., 1965, citation Lincoln Continental Owners Club, 1969, citation EMC Symposium and Exhibition, Montreaux, Switzerland, 1977. Fellow IEEE (electromagnetic compatibility soc. bd. dirs. 1963—, Cumming award 1983, Centennial medal 1984), Theta Chi. Republican. Episcopalian. Lodges: 6 Napoleons of Balt., Masons. Avocations: photography, classic cars. Home: Hudson Ohio Died Oct. 30, 1988.

HILL, JOHN DEKOVEN, architect; b. Cleve., May 19, 1920; s. John deKoven and Helen Elizabeth (Muckley) H.; m. Heloise Fichter, 1957; 1 son, Christopher deKoven. Taliesin fellow, Frank Lloyd Wright Sch. Architecture, 1938-42. Assoc. of Frank Lloyd Wright, 1942-59; editorial dir. House Beautiful mag., 1953-63; dir. Joel Design Projects, N.Y.C., 1956-63; mem. Taliesin Architects, from 1959. Designer domestic and comml. bldgs. and interiors, writer, critic architecture and aesthetics, recent designs include restoration of bldgs. by Frank Lloyd Wright. Trustee, sec. Frank Lloyd Wrigth Found., 1963-88, hon. chmn. bd., from 1993. also: Taliesin Spring Green WI 53588 Died June 25, 1996.

HILLMAN, STANLEY ERIC GORDON, former corporate executive; b. London, Eng., Oct. 13, 1911;

came to U.S., 1951, naturalized, 1957; s. Percy Thomas and Margaret Eleanor Fanny (Lee) H.; m. May Irene Noon, May 2, 1947; children: Susan, Deborah, Katherine. Educated, pvt. schs., Eng. With Brit.-Am. Tobacco Co., Ltd., London, Shanghai, 1933-47; dir. Hillman & Co., Ltd., Cosmos Trading Co., FED Inc., U.S.A., Airmotive Supplies Co. Ltd., Hong Kong, 1947-52; v.p. Gen. Dynamics Corp., 1953-61; v.p., group exec. Am. Machine & Foundry Co., N.Y.C., 1962-65; v.p., dir. Gen. Am. Transp. Corp., 1965-67; pres., vice chmn., dir. IC Industries, 1968-78; bankruptcy trustee Chgo., Milw., St. Paul & Pacific R.R., 1978-79; chmn., pres., chief exec. officer Conrail Corp., 1989; bd. dirs. Bandag Corp. Clubs: Chgo., Mid Am.; Onwentsia (Lake Forest, Ill.); Royal Poinciana (Naples, Fla.). Home: Lake Forest Ill. Died Aug. 14, 1995.

HINDLE, EDWARD FRANCIS, lawyer; b. Providence, Sept. 28, 1918; s. William and Elizabeth (Turbitt) H.; m. Grace Marie McDonald, Nov. 28, 1942; children: Natalie Hindle Parry, Edward F. Jr., Lyn Hindle Crispino, Denise Hindle Camara. AB cum laude, Harvard U., 1940, JD, 1947; MBA (hon.), Bryant Coll., 1992. Bar: R.I. 1947, U.S. Dist. Ct. R.I. 1948, U.S. Supreme Ct. 1986. Assoc. Edwards & Angell, Providence, 1947-55, ptnr., 1955-88, of counsel, 1989-95. Pres. R.I. Bar Assn., Providence, 1972, R.I. Bar Found., Providence, 1986-88; trustee Bryant Coll., Smithfield, R.I.; pres. Big Bros. of R.I., Providence, 1965; treas. Gilbert Stuart Meml., North Kingstown, R.I., 1965-75. Capt. U.S. Army, 1941-45. Fellow Am. Coll. Trial Lawyers. Home: East Greenwich R.I. Died Nov. 20, 1995; interred St. Ann's Cemetery, Cranston, RI.

HINSHAW, DONALD GRAY, music publisher; b. Boonville, N.C., Aug. 23, 1934; s. Evan Willard and Rosella (Sizemore) H. BA in Music, Davidson Coll., 1955; M of Sacred Music, New Orleans Sem., 1958. Music tchr. Jonesville (N.C.) Pub. Sch., 1955-56; music dir. First Bapt. Ch., Wilson, N.C., 1958-64; prof. of music Barton Coll., Wilson, 1959-64; mgr. Ligett & Myers, Durham, N.C., 1964-67, La Perla, Manila, Phillipines, 1967-68; choral editor Carl Fisher, Inc., N.Y.C., 1968-75; pres., chief exec. officer Hinshaw Music, Inc., Chapel Hill, N.C., 1975—, Hindon Pubs. Inc., Chapel Hill, 1975—, Chapel Hill Music, Inc., 1980—. Composer, Arranger, Editor: 28 titles vocal and choral music, 1965—. Treas. Ch. Music Pubs. Assn., 1980-82; trustee Westminster Choir Coll., Princeton, N.J., 1982-86; nat. winner Take Pride in Am., Washington, 1988. Named Col. Commonwealth of Ky., 1971. Mem. ASCAP, SESAC, Nat. Music Pubs. Assn., Am Choral Conductors Assn., Broadcast Music, Inc., Phi Mu Alpha Singonia. Died Dec. 30, 1996.

HINSHAW, VIRGIL GOODMAN, JR., philosopher, emeritus educator; b. LaGrange, Ill., Nov. 3, 1919; s. Virgil Goodman and Eva (Piltz) H.; m. Alene Kinsey Pryor, June 12, 1950; children: Stephen, Sally. BA, Stanford U., 1941; MA, State U. Iowa, 1942, Princeton U., 1943; PhD, Princeton U., 1945. Asst. State U. Iowa, Iowa City, 1941-42; instr. philosophy Ohio State U., Columbus, 1946-47; asst. prof. Ohio State U., 1947-53, assoc. prof., 1953-60, prof., 1960-81, prof. emeritus, 1981-95, dir. grad. studies, 1968-71, vice chmn., 1971-80; cons. Office Naval Rsch., 1958-59, 62, Army Rsch. Office, 1963, Congress Neurol. Surgeons, 1964, Wright Patterson AFB, 1983, Battelle Meml. Inst., 1989-95. Contbr. articles to profl. jours. Bd. dirs. Arthritis Found. Cen. Ohio. Mem. Am. Philos. Assn., Assn. Symbolic Logic, AAAS, AAUP, Philosophy of Sci. Assn., Ohio Coll. Assn. (sect. pres. 1955-58), N.Y. Acad. Scis., Assn. Princeton U. Grad. Alumni. (governing bd. 1975-87, honoris causa 1987-95), Phi Beta Kappa. Democrat. Methodist. Home: Columbus Ohio Died July 22, 1995.

HINZ, JOHN, English and American literature educator; b. N.Y.C., May 24, 1923; s. Hans and Anna (Borell) H.; m. Dorothy Rose Melvin, May 5, 1945 (div. Jan. 1973); children: John, Mark. BA, CCNY, 1944; MA, Columbia U., 1947, PhD, 1959. Tutor, instr., asst. prof., assoc. prof. dept. English, CCNY, 1946-67; vis. asst. Am. studies prof. Leopold Franzens U., Innsbruck, Austria, 1967-68; prof. Am. studies, dean humanities Richmond Coll. (now Coll. of S.I.), N.Y., 1968-79; prof. English, U. South Fla., St. Petersburg, 1979-94, campus dean, 1979-86; vis. Fulbright prof. Karl Franzens U., Graz, Austria, 1961-62. Contbr. articles to profl. jours. Bd. dirs. Goodwill Industries, St. Petersburg, ARC, St. Petersburg. 2d lt. USAAF, 1943-46. Mem. MLA, Nat. Assn. Scholars, St. Petersburg Yacht Club, Phi Beta Kappa. Roman Catholic. Avocations: reading, travel, music. Died 1996.

HITCHCOCK, J. GARETH, retired judge; b. Putnam County, Ohio June 10, 1914; s. Roy C. and Laura (Adam) H.; m. Helen M. Eck, June 10, 1941 (dec. Oct. 1972); children—James Edward, David Louis; m. 2d, Ruth E. Fessel, Aug. 18, 1973. LL.B., Ohio State U., 1939, J.D., 1969. Bar: Ohio 1939, U.S. Dist. Ct. (no. dist.) Ohio 1945, U.S. Dist. Ct. (no. dist.) Ind. 1960, U.S. Supreme Ct. 1960, U.S. Ct. Appeals (7th cir.) 1960. Sole practice, Paulding, Ohio, 1939-40; spl. agt. FBI, 1940-42; sole practice, Port Clinton, Ohio, 1946-51; protection chief Joseph Horne Co., Pitts., 1951-57; investment sales Federated Investors Inc., Pitts., 1957-59; practice, Paulding, Ohio, 1959-60; judge Common Pleas Ct. Paulding County (Ohio), 1960-86. Served with AUS, 1942-46. Mem. Ohio State Bar Assn. (bar activities com. 1963-80, com. jud. adminstrn. and legal reform 1981—), Paulding County Bar Assn., N.W. Ohio Bar Assn., Am. Judicature Soc., Judge Advocates Assn., Ohio Common Pleas Judges Assn., Soc. Former Spl. Agts. of FBI, Am. Legion (life), VFW (life). Republican. Episcopalian. Club: Kiwanis (lt. gov. 1970-71). Contbr. articles to profl. jours.

HITCHNER, DELL GILLETTE, political scientist, educator; b. Kansas City, Mo., Aug. 31, 1914; s. F.G. and Ouida M. (Kelley) H.; m. Kathleen D. Enlow, Sept. 3, 1938; children: Camilla (Mrs. C.H. Fulton), Nancy (Mrs. Gary A. Uderitz), Stuart. A.B., U. Wichita, 1936; A.M., U. Mo., 1937; Ph.D., U. Wis., 1940. Mem. faculty Coe Coll., 1940-44, asst. prof., 1943-44; asso. prof. U. Wichita, 1946; asst. prof. U. Wash., Seattle, 1947-51; asso. prof. polit. sci. U. Wash., 1951-63, prof. polit. sci., 1963-80, prof. emeritus, 1980-92, acting exec. officer, 1957-59; vis. prof. U. Nebr., 1946, U. Utah, 1952; U.S. specialist Am. Embassy, London, 1956-57; vis. mem. London Sch. Econs. and Polit. Sci., 1957. Author: (with W.H. Harbold) Modern Government, 1962, 3d edit., 1972, (with C. Levine) Comparative Government and Politics, 1967, 2d edit., 1981; contbr. articles to profl. jours. Sec. Seattle Com. on Fgn. Relations, 1948-64. Served as sgt. inf. AUS, 1944-46, PTO. Mem. Am. Polit. Sci. Assn., Pacific N.W. Polit. Sci. Assn. (pres. 1967-68), AAUP. Republican. Home: Edmonds Wash. Died Mar. 20, 1992.

HJELLUM, JOHN, retired lawyer; b. Aurland, Sogn, Norway, Mar. 29, 1910; s. Olav Iversen and Belle (Ohnstad) H.; m. Helen Jeanette Fodness, May 12, 1935; children: Janice Ann, Joan Mae, John II. LL.B., J.D., U. N.D., 1934. Bar: N.D. 1934. Since practiced in Jamestown, N.D. (ret.); mem. firm (ret.) Hjellum, Weiss, Nerison, Jukkala, Wright & Paulson; investigator fed. violations Dept. Justice, 1934; asst. states atty. Stutsman County, N.D., 1943-45; states atty., 1948-50; sec. N.D. Broadcasting Co., 1950-62; sec. bd. dirs. N.Am. Uranium, Inc., 1954-69. Chmn. N.D. Eisenhower for Pres. group, also N.D. Citizens for Eisenhower-Nixon; vice chmn. Stutsman County Republican Orgn., 1955-58; mem. Stutsman County Central Com., 1958-62; del. Rep. Nat. Conv., 1952; trustee Jamestown Coll., 1967-75; chmn., trustee N.D. Ind. Coll. Fund, 1957-68. Served with CIC, AUS, 1944-45. Fellow Internat. Acad. Trial Lawyers (dir. 1969-75, 78-84); mem. ABA, Internat. Bar Assn., N.D. Bar Assn. (pres. 1957-58), 4th Jud. Dist. Bar Assn. (pres. 1949-50), Stutsman County Bar Assn. (pres. 1940-41, 49-50), Am. Legion, VFW, Order of Coif (hon.), Lambda Chi Alpha, Phi Delta Phi, Kappa Kappa Psi. Methodist (chmn. bd. 1946-76). Club: Masons. DIED 12/09/96. .

HOADLEY, JOSEPH E., retired physician; b. Cainsville, Mo., Jan. 12, 1913; s. Archie Guy Hoadley and Ada Pontius; m. Frances Louise Ross, Aug. 30, 1943; children: Frank R., Jeannette, David Allen, Clyde J. BS in Chemistry, Park Coll., Parkville, Mo., 1938; MD, St. Louis Sch. Medicine, 1943. Tchr. Campbell County Sch. Sys., Gillette, Wyo., 1933-35; med. officer U.S. Army/Tripler Gen. Hosp., Honolulu, 1945-46; chief med. staff Gillette Hosp., 1947-53, 53-79; mem. med. staff VA Hosp., Sheridan, Wyo., 1980-92. Author, pub.: The Homestead Doctor, 1995. Pres. Wyo. divsn. Am. Cancer Soc., Gillette, 1956-59; mem. Campbell County Hosp. Bd., Gillette, 1975-79, Northeastern Wyo. Mental Health Bd., Campbell County, 1976-79. Recipient Svc. award N.E. Mental Health Assn., 1979, Campbell County Meml. Hosp., 1979. Mem. Internat. Coll. Surgeons, Masons, Shriners, Lions. Baptist. Avocation: flying. Died June 15, 1997.

HOBBS, VIVIAN LEE, lawyer; b. Washington; d. Moses Edward and Frances Ann (Scribner) Hobbs; children: Jason Michael, Gregory James, Jennifer Ann. BS summa cum laude, U. Md., 1978; JD summa cum laude, Georgetown U., 1981. Bar: D.C. 1981. Ptnr. Arnold & Porter, Washington, 1981—; mem. adv. coun. on employee welfare and pension benefit plans U.S. Dept. Labor; mem. steering com. D.C. chpt. W.E.B. Mem. ABA (employee benefits com. 1985—, chair new welfare benefits legis. subcom. 1992-94), D.C. Bar Assn. (chmn. welfare plan subcom. 1988-90). Died June 23, 1997.

HOCHBERGER, BERNADETTE M., secondary education educator, counselor; b. Summit, N.J., May 18, 1945; d. Benjamin Joseph and Marie Catherine (Valenti) Nuzzio. BS, Fairleigh Dickinson U., Madison, N.J, 1969; MA, Seton Hall U., 1986, EdS, 1994. Cert. elem. tchr., N.J., secondary English tchr., N.J., elem., secondary counseling, N.J. Tchr. English Mother Seton Regional High Sch., Clark, N.J., 1969-71; tchr., counselor Millburn (N.J.) Middle Sch., 1971—; bd. dirs., counselor Quality Writing Inst., Millburn; mem. project curriculum com. Millburn Bd. Edn., 1991—. Active PTA, Millburn, 1971—. Mem. Am. Counseling Assn., Nat. Coun. Tchrs. English, Nat. Middle Sch. Assn., Am. Assn. Counseling and Devel., Assn. Supervision and Curriculum Devel., N.J. Tchrs. English, Middle Sch. Counseling Assn., N.J. Psychological Assn., N.J. Counseling Assn., Essex County Counseling Assn., Jr. League, Alpha Delta Kappa (pres. 1973-75), Kappa Delta Phi, Phi Delta Kappa. Republican. Roman Catholic. Avocations: chess, classical movies, opera, basketball. Died Nov. 2, 1995.

HODDY, RAYMOND ARTHUR, industrial consultant; b. Corning, Ohio, Aug. 31, 1921; s. Arthur H. and Mary Elizabeth (Lutz) H.; m. Audrey Mae Wing, June 23, 1944; children: George Raymond, Jerry Robert, Mary Elizabeth, Martha Ann. Student in elec. engring., Ohio State U., 1938-41. Design engr. A.G. Redmond Co., Owosso, Mich., 1941-42; mfg. engr. Universal Electric Co., Owosso, 1942-71; pres. Universal Electric Co., 1971-77, also dir.; gen. mgr. Ray-O-Vac. div. ESB Inc., 1974-77; exec. v.p. ESB Inc., Phila., 1977-79; also dir. ESB Inc.; indsl. cons., 1979-94. Vice chmn. Tall Pine council Boy Scouts Am., 1950-70; chmn. adv. bd. Salvation Army, 1955-70. Recipient Silver Beaver award Boy Scouts Am., 1964, Meritorious citation Salvation Army, 1965. Mem. Tau Beta Pi. Republican. Methodist. Club: Hiawatha Sportsman's. Patentee electric motors. Home: Holland Mich. Died July 21, 1994.

HOEBEL, EDWARD ADAMSON, anthropologist, educator; b. Madison, Wis., Nov. 16, 1906; s. Edward Charles and Kathryn (Arnold) H.; m. Frances Elizabeth Gore, June 20, 1930 (dec. July 1962); 1 son, Bartley Gore; m. Irene Holth, Aug. 26, 1963; 1 dau., Sue Dunbar (dec.). A.B., U. Wis., 1928; student, Cologne, Germany, 1928-29; A.M., NYU, 1931; Ph.D., Columbia, 1934. Instr. sociology NYU, 1929-35, asst. prof. sociology and anthropology, 1935-41, assoc. prof. 1941-48; lectr. anthropology, dept. psychiatry Sch. Medicine, NYU, 1946-48; vis. prof. various schs.; prof., head dept. anthropology U. Utah, 1948-54, dean Univ. Coll., 1953-54; prof. anthropology, chmn. dept. U. Minn., 1954-68, Regent's prof., 1966-72, emeritus, 1972-93, adj. prof. law, 1972-81; Fulbright prof. Oxford (Eng.) U., 1956-57, Cath. U., The Netherlands, 1970; Research fellow Lab. Anthropology, Santa Fe; dir. Social Sci. Research Council; adv. panel social sci. research NSF, 1958-60; sr. specialist Inst. Advanced Study, East-West Center Cultural and Tech. Interchange, Honolulu, 1964-65; mem. Minn. Gov.'s Commn. Human Relations, 1955-64; behavioral scis. panel Nat. Inst. Gen. Med. Sci., 1962-66; spl. officer Dept. State, ACDA, 1969-73; Conf. Bd. for Internat. Exchange Persons NRC, 1966-70; Research fellow Columbia U. Council Research in Social Scis., Am. Council Learned Socs.; fellow Center Advanced Studies Behavioral Scis., 1960-61; mem. conf. bd. on internat. exchange of scholars, NRC, 1956-60. Author: several books, including (with K.N. Llewellyn) The Cheyenne Way: Conflict and Case Law in Primitive Jurisprudence 1941; (with others) Social Meaning of Legal Concepts Inheritance, 1948, Man in the Primitive World: An Introduction to Anthropology, 1949, (with E. Wallace) The Comanches, 1952, The Law of Primitve Man: A Study in Comparative Legal Dynamics, 1954, The Cheyennes: Indians of the Great Plains, 1961, rev. edit. 1978, Anthropology: The Study of Man, 1966, rev. 1972, (with E.L. Frost) Social and Cultural Anthropology, 1975, The Plains Indians: A Critical Bibliography, 1978, (with Thomas Weaver) Anthropology and the Human Experience, 1979; also articles, revs. in legal, hist. and anthrop. jours.; Assoc. editor: Law and Soc. Rev, 1969-73, Jour. Natural Law, 1960-65, Am. Indian Quar, 1972-80. Trustee Sci. Mus. Minn. Fellow Ctr. for Advanced Study Behavioral Sci., Palo Alto Calif., 1960-61. Fellow AAAS; mem. Am. Philos. Soc. Am. Ethnol. Soc. (pres. 1946-48), Am. Anthrop. Assn. (pres. 1956-57), Assn. Am. Indian Affairs (dir. 1945-56), Am. Philos. Soc., Explorers Club, Alpha Kappa Lambda, Alpha Kappa Delta, Phi Kappa Phi. Club: Skylight. Home: Saint Paul Minn. Died July 23, 1993.

HOFFMAN, WALTER EDWARD, judge; b. Jersey City, July 18, 1907; s. Walter and Ella Adele (Sharp) H.; m. Evelyn Virginia Watkins, Apr. 6, 1939 (dec.); m. Helen Caulfield, Nov. 6, 1971; children: Carole Hoffman Hancock, Walter Edward. BS in Econs., U. Pa., 1928; postgrad. in law, Coll. William and Mary, 1928-29; LLD, 1985; LLB, Washington and Lee U., 1931, LLD 1970. Bar: Va. 1929, U.S. Dist. Ct. (ea. dist.) Va. 1930, U.S. Supreme Ct. 1945. Assoc. Rumble & Rumble, Norfolk, Va., 1931-35; ptnr. Breeden & Hoffman, Norfolk, 1935-54; judge U.S. Dist. Ct. Va., Norfolk, 1954-74, sr. judge 1974-96; instr. Coll. William and Mary, 1933-40, asst. prof. law, 1940-42, vis. prof., 1977-78, chmn. adv. com. on criminal rules, 1978-84, mem. standing com. on rules and practice, 1984-87; judge temp. emergency Ct. Appeals, 1977-93, chmn. Conf. Met. Chief Judges, 1977-86. Recipient Herbert Harley award Am. Judicature Soc., 1976, Devitt award for disting. svc. to cause of adminstrn. of justice, 1983. Mem. ABA, Va. State Bar Assn., Cosmopolitan Club of Norfolk (pres. 1953), Norfolk Yacht and Country Club, Masons, Shriners (past potentate). Methodist. Died Nov. 21, 1996.

HOFFMANN, HEINZ, East German official; b. Mannheim, Germany, Nov. 28, 1910; student Acad. Gen. Staff, USSR. Mem. Community Party of Germany, 1930, Socialist United Party of Germany, 1946—; apprentice fitter, 1925-28; ofcl. Communist Youth Orgn. 1926-30; emigrated to USSR, 1935; fought in Spanish Civil War; returned to USSR; sec. Berlin regional com. Socialist United Party, 1947-49; v.p. German Central Adminstrn. of Interior-Gen. Insp. of German People's

Police, 1949-50; head tng. dept. Ministry of Interior, until 1952; lt.-gen. People's Police and dep. minister of interior, 1952-55; lt.-gen. Nat. People's Army, 1956-59, col.-in-chief, 1959-61, gen., 1961—; dep. minister of nat. def., 1956-60, minister, 1960—; mem. People's Chamber of German Democratic Republic, 1950—; mem. Central Com. Socialist Unity Party, 1952—, mem. Politburo, 1973—. Decorated Held der D.D.R., Karl-Marx-Orden, Banner der Arbeit, Red Banner (USSR), Leinorden (USSR), also others.

HOFFMANN, MALCOLM ARTHUR, lawyer; b. N.Y.C., Nov. 26, 1912; s. Abraham A. and Minna (Newmark) H.; m. Anna Frances Luciano, Apr. 13, 1939 (dec. Feb. 1980); children: Gertrude Nina Hoffmann Bolter, Jessica Ann Hoffmann Davis. BA magna cum laude, Harvard U., 1934, LLB, 1937. Bar: N.Y. 1938, U.S. Supreme Ct. 1943, U.S. Dist. Ct. (so. and ea. dist.) N.Y., U.S. Dist. Ct. Conn., U.S. Ct. Appeals (1st, 2d, 3d, 5th, 11th and D.C. cirs.). Atty. Nat. Labor Relations Bd., 1939-43; spl. atty. appellate sect. criminal div. Dept. Justice, 1943, spl. asst. to U.S. Atty. Gen. U.S. antitrust div., 1944-55; assoc. Rosenman, Colin, Kaye, Petschek, Freund & Emil, 1955-59; of counsel Greenbaum, Wolff & Ernst, N.Y.C., 1959-60; prin. Law Firm of Malcolm A. Hoffmann, N.Y.C., 1960—; lectr. Practising Law Inst., 1957—; mem. faculty Joint Com. on Continuing Legal Edn., Am. Law Inst., ABA, 1966; lectr. trade problems Am. Mgmt. Assn., 1967-71; lectr. antitrust sect. meeting ABA, Honolulu, 1967, lectr. litigation sect. meeting, San Francisco, 1976. Author: Government Lawyer, 1955, Lawyers Heritage, 1956, (with M.L. Ernst) Back and Forth, 1966, The Long Canoe, 1995; editor: Hoffmann's Antitrust Law and Techniques, 3 vols., 1963; co-editor: Monopolies, Markets and Mergers; contbr. articles to profl. jours. Chmn. bd. Hoffmann Sch., Inc., 1968-87. Fellow Am. Bar Found, Fellows of Am. Bar Found. (life); mem. ABA (vice chmn. com.), World Assn. Lawyers (founder), Am. Judicature Soc., Internat. Bar Assn., Fed. Bar Assn., N.Y. State Bar Assn. (past chmn. com., exec. com.), Assn. of Bar of City of N.Y. (past chmn. subcom.), Fed. Bar Coun. (past sec. trade regulation com. 1963—), Harvard Talk Club (chmn.).

HOGAN, HENRY LEON, III, business executive, retired air force officer; b. Cin., Feb. 7, 1920; s. Henry Leon and Helen (Bolan) H.; m. Anne Surkamp, June 1, 1943; children: Robin Hogan Brosseau, Christine Hogan Dopson, James A., Patricia Hogan Revers, Elizabeth Hogan Barksdale. BS, U.S. Mil. Acad., 1943; grad., Nat. War Coll., 1960. Enlisted pvt. inf. U.S. Army, 1938; commd. 2d lt. USAAF, 1943; advanced through grades to maj. gen. USAF, 1965; pilot 483d Bombardment Group Italy, World War II; exch. officer Royal Air Force Coll., 1949-50; mil. aide to secs. of USAF, 1953-55; dep. comdt. cadets U.S. Air Force Acad., Colo., 1955-59; dep. comdr. maintenance, vice comdr. 68th Bombardment Wing, Lake Charles, La., 1960-62; wing comdr. 384th Bombardment Wing, Little Rock, 1962-63; asst. to chmn. Joint Chiefs of Staff, Washington, 1963-65; comdr. 810th Air div. SAC, Minot, N.D., 1965-68; dep. dir., then dir. pub. affairs USAF, Washington, 1968-72; exec. v.p. Circulation, Inc., Melbourne, Fla., 1973-87; v.p. Cert. Audit of Circulations, Inc. Decorated D.S.M., Legion Merit with oak leaf cluster, D.F.C., Air medal with four oak leaf clusters. Died Apr. 13, 1996.

HOGAN, JAMES DONALD, electronics executive; b. North Chicago, Ill., Dec. 28, 1927; s. Joseph Francis and Victoria Rose (Istok) H.; m. Joan Ruth Frintz, May 3, 1953; children: Craig, Phillip, Sheila. BEE, U. Ill., Urbana, 1948, MS, 1953. Seismologist Shell Oil Co., Houston, 1948-51; engr. Hughes Aircraft Co., Los Angeles, 1953-54; mem. tech. staff Ramo-Wooldridge (now TRW Inc.), Los Angeles, 1954-61; v.p. Logicon Inc., Los Angeles, 1961-70, sr. v.p., 1970-89. Patentee digital systems and computers. Mem. U. Ill. Pres.'s council, 1984—. Recipient Bronze Tablet honors award U. Ill., 1948. Mem. IEEE. Republican.

HOGAN, WILLIAM JOSEPH, financial executive; b. St. Louis, Aug. 2, 1902; s. Joseph and Johanna (Grainey) H.; m. Verna L. Coultas, July 12, 1925 (dec.); 1 child, William J.; m. Jean Miller, Aug. 27, 1955; 1 child, Mary Elizabeth. Student, St. Louis U., 1920-26, LL.D. (hon.), 1980. Mem. controller's staff Firestone Tire & Rubber Co., Akron, Ohio, 1929-43; treas., controller, dir. H.J. Heinz Co., Pitts., 1943-47; v.p., treas. AM. Airlines, Inc., N.Y.C., 1947-54; sr. v.p. fin. AM. Airlines, Inc., 1954-58, exec. v.p., chmn. fin. com., dir., 1958-67; chmn. fin. com., exec. v.p., dir. Interpub. Group Cos., 1968-74, chmn. audit and compensation coms., dir., 1974-85; pres., dir. Victory Carriers, Inc., 1968-78; chmn. audit and compensation coms., dir. Raytheon Co., 1961-86; fin. cons., dir., chmn. fin. com. Pan Am. Airways, 1971-80; dir. Intercontinental Hotels Corp., 1971-82. Knight of Malta; recipient Alumni Achievement award St. Louis U., 1963. Mem. Winged Foot Golf Club.

HOGG, ROZALIA CRUISE, genealogist; b. Bluefield, W.Va., Dec. 31, 1931; d. George Mortimer and Beulah Grove (Fleshman) Cruise; m. Edward Welford Hogg, Jr., June 20, 1953 (dec. 1972); children: Gayle Hogg Wells, Alice Ann Hogg Conaty, Nancy Hogg Pinry. Student, Madison Coll., Harrisonburg, Va., 1951-53; BA in History, Mary Baldwin Coll., 1978. Kindergarten tchr. Ft. Meade, Md., 1953-54; tour guide Woodrow Wilson Birthplace, Staunton, Va., 1978-80, P. Buckley Moss Mus., Waynesboro, Va., 1990; genealogist Patrick County, Va., 1985—; bd. advisors Bluefield State Coll. Pres. Women of Ch., 1st Presbyn. Ch., Waynesboro, 1983-85; bd. dirs. Augusta County Hist. Soc., 1987-91, Bluefield State Coll., 1992—; vice chmn. Waynesboro Hist. Commn., 1986-91. Mem. Rosecliff Garden Club (pres. 1973-74), Va. Mus. Fine Arts, Sigma Sigma Sigma, Phi Alpha Theta. Presbyterian. Avocations: art (painting), needlework, travel, reading. Home: Williamsburg Va. Died Jan. 9, 1996.

HOLBERG, RALPH GANS, JR., lawyer; b. Mobile, Nov. 5, 1908; s. Ralph G. and Lillian (Frohlichstein) H.; m. Amelia Schwarz, Feb. 16, 1938; children: Ralph G. III, Robert S. J.D., U. Ala., 1932. Bar: Ala. 1932. Since practiced in Mobile; now sr. counsel Holberg and Holberg P.C. Contbr. articles to hist. and profl. jours. Pres. Mobile Bay Area chpt. ARC, 1954-55; chmn. Southeastern area council, 1957-58; life bd. dirs. emeritus Mobile Bay Area chpt., Ala. nat. v.p., 1960-61, mem. nat. bd. govs., 1965-68, 68-71; chmn. bd. Mobile County Bd. Pensions and Security, 1947-77; bd. dirs. Mobile Gen. Hosp., 1963-67, chmn., 1965-67; mem. Ala. State Docks Adv. Bd., 1962-69, 3d Army Area Adv. Com., Gov. Ala. Com. Adult Edn. Negroes, 1949; chmn. Mobile Pub. Library Bd., 1954-55; past appeal agt. local selective service bd.; pres. Estate Planning Council Mobile, 1971-72; pres. Hon. Fellows Mobile Coll., 1972-73; mem. nat. adv. council Nat. Multiple Sclerosis Soc., 1973-87; alt. Mobile Hist. Devel. Commn., 1973-76; pres. Old Shell Rd. PTA, 1954-55; pres., Ala. Jr. C. of C., 1935; mem. bd. Mobile Community Chest and Council, 1965-71; trustee Mobile YWCA, 1978-80; bd. dirs. Gordon Smith Ctr., 1973-85. Served to lt. USNR, 1944-46. Recipient Disting. Svc. Key, Mobile Jaycees, 1938, J.N. Carmichael Meml. award 1984; named Mobilian of Yr., 1963; ann. vol. svcs. award named in his honor Mobile Bay Area chpt. ARC, 1986. Fellow The Am. Coll. Trust and Estate Counsel; mem. ABA, Ala. Bar Assn., Mobile Bar Assn. (pres. 1942), VFW, Ala. Hist. Assn. (exec. com. 1981-85), Ala. Jud. Coll. Faculty Assn. (hon.), SCV, Am. Legion (post comdr. 1947-48), Mobile Jaycees (pres. 1934), Mobile Area C. of C. (dir. 1962-65, 71-74, 81), Mobile Hist. Preservation Soc. (dir. 1974-77), Mobile's Azalea Trail (pres. 1934-35), Navy League (judge advocate Mobile council 1979-92), Am. Council Judaism (nat. adv. bd. 1955-85), Spring Hill Ave. Temple (pres. 1947-48), Mobile Exch. Club (charter, pres. 1938), Internat. Trade Club, Touchdown Club (past mem. bd.), Country Club of Mobile, Rotary (hon. Mobile club 1989), Zeta Beta Tau (pres. Psi chpt. 1932). Home: Mobile Ala. Died April 7, 1997.

HOLCOMBE, WILLIAM JONES, manufacturing company executive; b. 1925. Group v.p. De Laval Turbine Inc., 1960-65, pres., chief exec. office, 1965-72; group v.p. Transamerica Corp., 1972-75; chmn. bd. dirs., CEO, pres. Teton Inc., 1976-86; chmn., CEO, pres. Imo Industries, Inc., Lawrenceville, N.J., 1986-92; chmn. bd. Imo Industries, Lawrencevile, N.J., 1992-93; cons. in field Norco, Calif., 1993-95. Home: Yorba Linda Calif. Died Dec. 28, 1995.

HOLDEN, JAMES STUART, federal judge; b. Bennington, Vt., Jan. 29, 1914; s. Edward Henry and Mary Anstiss (Thayer) H.; m. Helen Elizabeth Vetal, Mar. 3, 1941; children: Susan (Mrs. Spaeth), Peter Vetal, James Stuart. A.B., Dartmouth Coll., 1935, LL.D. (hon.), 1985; LL.B., Union U., 1938. Bar: Vt. 1938. Practice in Bennington, 1938-41, 46-48; state's atty. Bennington County, 1946-48; chmn. Vt. Pub. Service Commn., 1948-49; superior judge State, 1949-56; assoc. justice Supreme Ct. Vt., 1956-63, chief justice, 1963-72; U.S. dist. judge for Dist. of Vt., 1972-84, sr. U.S. dist. judge for, 1984-96; chmn. Vt. Statutory Revision Commn., 1957-62; chmn. provisional com. to establish Nat. Ctr. for State Cts., 1971; standing com. Rules of Practice and Procedure, Jud. Conf. of the U.S. Trustee Vt. State Library, 1959-69. Served to maj. 43d Inf. Div. AUS, 1941-46. Mem. 43d Inf. Div. Vets. Assn. (past comdr.), Am., Vt. bar assns., Conf. Chief Justices (vice chmn. 1969-70, chmn. 1971), Am. Judicature Soc., Inst. Jud. Adminstrn., Am. Law Inst. Protestant Episcopalian. Died Nov. 18, 1996.

HOLDEN, RANDALL LECONTE, music educator, stage director; b. Bronxville, N.Y., Dec. 4, 1943; s. Randall LeConte and Ruth Isabella (May) H.; m. Pamela Harris, Sept. 3, 1966. AB, Colby Coll., 1965; MA, U. Conn., 1966; MM, U. Wash., 1968, DMA, 1970. Asst. prof. Ariz. State U., Tempe, 1971-76; assoc. prof. U. Louisville, 1976-85, prof., 1985-95; prodn. mgr. Ky. Opera, Louisville, 1977-91. Mem. Nat. Opera Assn. (pres. 1988-89, 94-95). Died May 17, 1995.

HOLDEN, WILLIAM P., manufacturing company executive; b. N.Y.C., Sept. 5, 1933; s. Nicholas and Agnes (McNamara) H.; m. Jean Anne Peter, Sept. 3, 1960; 1 son, Gregory. B.B.A., Pace U., 1962. Budget dir. Reeves Bros., Inc., N.Y.C., 1956-63; asst. to pres. Comfy, Inc. (subs. Reeves Bros. Inc.), N.Y.C., 1963-67; group controller Dorr-Oliver Inc., Stamford, Conn., 1967-69; corporate controller Dorr-Oliver Inc., 1969-73, treas., corporate controller, chief financial officer, 1973-76, v.p. finance, 1976-81, v.p. internat., 1981-82; v.p. chief fin. officer, sec. Moore Spl. Tool Co.,-Inc., 1982-87; with Impact Mgmt. Cons. Ltd., 1988—. Served with USAF, 1952-56. Mem. Financial Execs. Inst. (dir. So. Conn. chpt. 1976, 81, pres. So. Conn. chpt. 1979), MAPI Fin. Council III. Deceased.

HOLLISTER, CHARLES WARREN, history educator, author; b. Los Angeles, Nov. 2, 1930; s. Nathan and Carrie (Cushman) H.; m. Edith Elizabeth Muller, Apr. 12, 1952; children: Charles Warren (dec.), Lawrence Gregory, Robert Cushman. A.B., Harvard U., 1951; M.A., UCLA, 1957, Ph.D., 1958. Mem. faculty U. Calif.-Santa Barbara, 1958-97, prof. history, 1964-97, chmn. dept., 1967-70; vis. rsch. fellow Merton Coll., Oxford U., Eng., 1965-66; vis. fellow Australian Nat. U., 1978, 93-97; lectr. Oxford U., 1965, Cambridge U., Eng., 1966, U. Ghent, Netherlands, 1966, U. Leyden, Netherlands, 1966, U. Utrecht, Netherlands, 1966, U. Bologna, Italy, 1967, U. Melbourne, Australia, 1978, 93, U. Sydney, Australia, 1978, U. Auckland, New Zealand, 1978, 93, Univ. Coll., Dublin, Ireland, 1986, U. Toronto, 1988, U. Victoria, 1990, Ariz. Ctr. for Medieval and Renaissance Studies, 1995. Author: Anglo-Saxon Military Institutions, 1962, Medieval Europe, 8th edit., 1997, The Military Organization of Norman England, 1965, The Making of England, 7th edit., 1996, Roots of the Western Tradition, 6th edit, 1996, The Impact of the Norman Conquest, 1969, The Twelfth-Century Renaissance, 1969, (with Judith Pike) The Moons of Meer, 1969, Odysseus to Columbus, 1974, (with others) Medieval Europe: A Short Sourcebook, 1982, 3d edit., 1997, Monarchy, Magnates, and Institutions in the Anglo-Norman World, 1986, Anglo-Norman Political Culture and the Twelfth-Century Renaissance, 1997. Served to 2d lt. USAF, 1951-53. Recipient Triennial Book prize Conf. Brit. Studies, 1963, E. Harris Harbison award for disting. teaching, Princeton, 1966, Walter D. Love meml. prize, 1981. Fellow Royal Hist. Soc., Medieval Acad. of Am., Medieval Acad. Ireland; mem. Pacific Coast Conf. Brit. Studies (pres. 1968-70), N.Am. Conf. Brit. Studies (pres. 1985-87), Charles Homer Haskins Soc. (pres. 1982-90), Am. Hist. Assn. (exec. coun. Pacific Coast br. 1968-71, v.p. 1989-90, pres. 1990-91, v.p. for teaching 1974-76, chmn. program com. 1984), Medieval Assn. Pacific (exec. coun. 1971-73, pres. 1989-91). Home: Santa Barbara Calif. Died Sept. 14, 1997; buried Goleta Cemetary, Santa Barbara, Calif.

HOLLYWOOD, JOHN MATTHEW, electronics consultant; b. Red Bank, N.J., Feb. 4, 1910; s. Maurice L. and Olga Caroline (Aul) H.; m. Veronica M. Whitney (dec.). BSEE, MIT, 1931, MSEE, 1932. Registered profl. engr., Conn. Engr. Electron Rsch. Labs., N.Y.C., 1933-35, Ken-Rad Tube & Lamp Corp., Owensboro, Ky., 1935-36; sr. engr. CBS Labs., N.Y.C., 1936-43; cons. Radio Rsch. Lab. of Harvard, Eng., 1943-45, Naval Rsch. Lab., Washington, 1945-46, Airborne Instruments Lab., Mineola, N.Y., 1946-49; sci. advisor to pres. CBS Labs., N.Y.C., 1949-72; advisor to pres. Goldmark Communications Corp., Stamford, Conn., 1972-79; pvt. practice cons. Red Bank, 1979-97. Contbr. articles to profl. jours.; reviewer Audio Engring. Soc.; holder 14 patents. Fellow IEEE. Republican. Methodist. Avocation: amateur radio, music. Home: Red Bank N.J. Died Feb. 24, 1997; buried Mount Olive Cemetery.

HOLM, ROBERT ARTHUR, environmental scientist; b. Waukegan, Ill., Sept. 19, 1935; s. Robert and Adele (Gummerus) H.; BS with honors in Chem. Engring., U. Ill., 1958; MS in Chem. Engring., U. Del., 1961, PhD, 1962. Cert. mod. exec. mgmt., 1974; m. Lillian M. Partenheimer, Feb. 2, 1957; children: Anne, Karen, Rachel. Sr. rsch. assoc. Fabric Rsch. Labs., Dedham, Mass., 1962-65; process engr., rsch. assoc., dir div. indsl. and environ. systems Inst. of Paper Chemistry, Appleton, Wis., 1965-74; mgr. product devel. Huyck Felt, Rensselaer, N.Y., 1974-75; mgr. process devel. Erving (Mass.) Paper Mills, 1975-77, tech. dir., 1978-80, dir. environ. resources, 1980-81; assoc. prof. Coll. Environ. Scis. and Forestry SUNY-Syracuse, 1982-95; owner, cons. Holm Assocs.; owner AI Assocs., information services; sec.-treas. Keynet Assocs. Editor, pub. The Naturist Gazette. Cert. wastewater treatment plant operator, Mass. Mem. Am. Assn. Nude Recreation, Mensa, The Naturist Soc., TAPPI. Author: Mathematical Models in the Pulp and Paper Industry, 1983; co-editor: Modelling and Control of Kraft Production Systems, 1975. Died May 21, 1996.

HOLMES, EPHRAIM PAUL, career officer; b. Downsville, N.Y.; m. Nancy Sellers Holmes (dec. 1995); children: Diane H. Fletcher, Ephraim Paul Jr. Grad., Naval Acad., Annapolis, Md., 1930; postgrad., Naval Postgrad. Sch., 1938; studied, Naval War Coll. Commd. ensign USN, 1943, advanced through grades to comdr. in chief, 1967; ret., 1970; tchr. Armed Forces Staff Coll., Norfolk, Va.; dir. Navy program planning for the Chief of Naval Ops. Fifth-highest ranking naval officer. Home: Williamsburg Va. Died 1997.

HOLTZ, GARY LYNN, obstetrician-gynecologist, educator; b. Ann Arbor, Mich., 1949. MD, Wayne State U., 1975. Intern St. Joseph Mercy Hosp., Ann Arbor, 1975, resident ob-gyn., 1975-78; fellow reproductive endocrinologist Med. U. S.C. Hosp.,

Charleston, 1978-80; ob-gyn. East Cooper Cmty. Hosp., Mt. Pleasant, S.C., 1987—; clin. assoc. prof. Med. U. S.C., 1987—. Mem. ACOG, SART, SRE, SRS, Am. Fertility Soc.

HONIG, MERVIN, artist, art conservator; b. N.Y.C., Dec. 25, 1920; s. Joseph and Frances (Flaum) H.; m. Rhoda Sherbell, Apr. 28, 1956; 1 dau., Susan. Student with, Francis Criss, Amadee Ozenfant, Hans Hofmann; B.A., Bklyn. Coll., 1973; postgrad., Hofstra U., 1974—. Apprentice Bklyn. Mus., 1956-58, Keck Studio, 1956-58; asst. Mus. Modern Art, 1958; lectr. conservation of paintings Hofstra U., 1972-90 , Channel 21, L.I., N.Y., 1976-77; mem. faculty New Sch., 1975-90; tchr. Art Students League, 1989. Exhibited one-man shows at: Kingsworthy Art Gallery, N.Y.C., 1961, County Art Gallery, Westbury, N.Y., 1963-65, Grace Gallery, N.Y.C., Community Coll., 1968, Westbury Meml. Pub. Library, 1969, Frank Rehn Gallery, N.Y.C., 1970, Nassau Community Coll., 1971, New Sch. Assocs., N.Y.C., 1978, Bergen Mus. Art and Sci., Paramus, N.J., 1984, Bronx Mus. Arts, 1986, retrospective exhbn., Nat. Art Mus. of Sport, N.Y.C., 1977-78, William Benton Mus. Art, Storrs, Conn., 1985,, Manhattan East Gallery of Fine Art, N.Y.C., 1990, Country Art Gallery, Locust Valley, N.Y., 1990; exhibited in group shows at: Met. Mus. Art, 1944, Carnegie Inst., 1945, Los Angeles County Mus., 1945, Wm. Rockhil Nelson Gallery, Kansas City, 1945, Whitney Mus. Artists Ann., 1949, Bklyn. Mus., 1960, Nat. Acad. Galleries, 1963, 77, 78, 79, 80, 81, 82, 83, 86, 88, 89, 90, Wadsworth Atheneum, Conn. Acad. Fine Arts, 1965-66, Soc. 4 Arts, 1965, Jersey City Mus. Ann. Exhbn., 1966, Locust Valley Art Show, 1966 (1st prize), Am. Vets. Soc., 1966 (Meml. Gold medal), Purdue U., 1966, Butler Inst. Am. Art, Youngstown, Ohio, 1967, 69, Nat. Art Mus. Sport, N.Y.C., 1968, 69, Audubon Artists Ann., 1968-85, 86, 88, 89, Spectrum Gallery, N.Y.C., 1977, Queens Mus., 1978, Port Washington Library, 1978, L.I. Artists, 1978, Allied Artists Am., 1978-85, 86-89, C.W. Post Art Gallery, 1981, The Eye on Sport, CUNY, N.Y.C., 1983, Islip Art Mus., 1983, Pensacola (Fla.) Mus. Art, 1982, Owenboro (Ky.) Mus. Fine Art, 1982, Phila. Coll. Art, 1984, Guild Hall Mus., East Hampton, N.Y., 1986, Audubon Artists ann., 1986, 87. Allied Artists Am., 1986, 87, Castle Gallery Coll. New Rochelle, N.Y., 1987, Nat. Acad. Design Ann. Exhbns., N.Y.C., 1985, 87; represented in permanent collections: Okla. Mus. Art, Oklahoma City, Colby Coll. Art Mus., Met. Mus. Art, N.Y.C., Okla. Mus. Art, Emily Lowe Gallery/ Hofstra Mus.-Hofstra U., Colby Coll. Art Mus., Met. Mus. Art, Nassau County Mus., Siena Hts. Coll., William Benton Mus. Art, NAD, N.Y.C., also pvt. collections: Author papers on art conservation. Bd. advisors Nassau County Mus., 1978; trustee Nat. Art Mus. Sport, 1978. Recipient Bronze medal, hon. mention Am. Vets. Soc. Artists, 1968, also Gold medal; award of excellence Mainstream '70; award of excellence Grover M. Hermann Arts Center, 1970; prize Knickerbocker Artists, 1978; Samuel Morton Meml. award Audubon Artists, 1983; Silvermine Guild Artists award, 39th Art of N.E. U.S.A. Conn. Competition and Exhbn., 1988, others. Mem. Internat. Inst. Conservation Historic and Artistic Works, Coll. Art Assn. Am., Audubon Artists N.Y. (corr. sec. N.Y.C. 1977), Nat. Academician, L.I. Hist. Soc., Allied Artists Am. (dir. oil, Antonio Cirino Meml. award 1989), (v.p. 1980-83), Nassau Council Contemporary Art (sec. 1973-74), Nassau County Mus. Fine Art (advisor, bd. dirs. 1979-87). Home: Westbury NY Died Oct. 14, 1990.

HOOBLER, SIBLEY WORTH, physician, educator; b. N.Y.C., Apr. 30, 1911; s. Bert Raymond and Madge (Sibley) H.; m. Catherine Oppmann, Nov. 11, 1976; children by previous marriage: Raymond, Patricia. A.B., Princeton U., 1933; Sc.D., Johns Hopkins, 1937, M.D., 1938, D.H.L. (hon.), 1985. Mem. faculty U. Mich. Med. Sch., 1945-76, prof. internal medicine, 1959-76, prof. emeritus, 1977-94; clin. prof. emeritus internal medicine Case Western Res. U. Med. Sch.; also adj. staff Cleve. Clinic Found., 1976-85. Author: Hypertensive Diseases, 1959, Adventures in Medicine, 1991, also articles. Served to capt. M.C. AUS, 1942-46. Fellow ACP; mem. Am. Heart Assn. (chmn. high blood pressure council 1963-64), Soc. Exptl. Biology and Medicine, Am. Physiol. Soc., Central Soc. Clin. Research, Am. Soc. Clin Investigation, Am. Soc. Clin. Pharmacology and Therapeutics. Home: Cleveland Ohio Died Jan. 25, 1994.

HOOPER, EDITH FERRY, museum administrator; b. Detroit, Nov. 30, 1909; d. Dexter Mason and Jeannette (Hawkins) Ferry; m. Arthur Upshur Hooper, June 22, 1945; children: Jeannette Williams, Kate Gorman, Queene Ferry. B.A., Vassar U. Indsl. design dept. asst. Mus. Modern Art, N.Y.C., 1939-40; clk. U.S. Procurement Office, Detroit, 1941-43; asst. Roeper City and Country Schs., Detroit, 1944; trustee Balt. Mus. Art., 1957-95, pres. bd., 1973-75, accessions com., 1977-95. Bd. dirs. Friends Art Gallery, Vassar Coll., Poughkeepsie, N.Y., 1974-76; pres. bd. trustees Bryn Mawr Sch., Balt., 1965-71, chmn. bldg. com., 1971-73; pres. DM Ferry Jr. Trustee Corp. (found.), Balt., 1973. Presbyterian. Clubs: Cosmopolitan (N.Y.C.), Hamilton St. (Balt.). Died May 27, 1995. Home: Baltimore Md.

HOPSON, DAN, law educator, educational administrator; b. Phillipsburg, Kans., Sept. 23, 1930; s. Daniel Ashton and Ruth (Whitaker) H.; m. Phyllis Ann Gray, Nov. 23, 1956; children: Daniel Gray, Christopher Paul, Bruce Edward. Student, La. State U., 1947-48; A.B., U. Kans., 1951, LL.B., 1953; LL.M., Yale U., 1954; postgrad., Cambridge U., 1954-55. Bar: Kans. 1953. Asst. prof. law U. Kans., Lawrence, 1955-59, assoc. prof., 1959-63, prof., 1963-67; research assoc. Yale U., New Haven, 1959-60; prof.law Ind. U., Bloomington, 1967-80, asoc. dean faculties, 1974-789; dean, prof. law So. Ill. U., Carbondale, 1980-85; arbitrator Am. Arbitration Assn. and Fed. Mediation and Conciliation Service, 1963-85. Author: (with Quintin Johnstone) Lawyers and Their Work, 1967; contbr. articles to law jours. Mem. ABA, Ill. Bar Assn., Jackson County Bar Assn., Council Juvenile Ct. Judges (assoc.), Order of the Coif, Phi Beta Kappa, Pi Sigma Alpha, Phi Alpha Delta, Phi Delta Theta. Episcopalian. Home: Carbondale, Ill. Died June 16, 1985.

HORAN, STEPHEN FRANCIS, technical writer, insurance agent; b. Denver, June 15, 1933; s. Daniel Stephen and Rose Bridget (Shanley) H.; m. Mary Ann Theresa Perito, Dec. 28, 1957; children: Seanna, Dana, Michelle, Annette, Stephen Jr., Christine, David. Diploma, Interior Command Sch., Gt. Lakes, Mich., 1953, Mech. Design & Draft Sch., Denver, 1956; postgrad., U. Denver, 1957. Sr. tech. writer Missile Systems Corp., Denver, 1961-62; sr. tech. publs. engr. Martin Marietta Co., Denver, 1962-64; chief editorial br. Dugway Proving Ground U.S. Army, Utah, 1964-65, chief svcs. div. Dugway Proving Ground, 1965-68; tech. publs. editorial supr. Deseret Test Ctr. U.S. Army, 1968-73; tech. publs. writer Tropic Test Ctr. U.S. Army, Ft. Clayton, C.Z., Panama, 1973-75; tech. publ. ed. supr. Desert Test Ctr., Dugway Proving Ground, 75-78; tech. manuals writer Missile Command U.S. Army, Huntsville, Ala., 1978-81; tech. publs. writer, editor Communications Security Log U.S. Army, Ft. Huachuca, Ariz., 1981-92; pres. Success Achievement Ctr., Tucson, 1987-93; Amway distributor Horan & Assocs. Amway Distribution, 1992-93. Author Tour of Historic Ft. Douglas, 1976. Coach, Dugway Youth Activities, 1968-72, 75-78; pres. Dugway Parish Council, 1975, Dugway Booster Club, 1976. With USN, 1951-54. Mem. Soc. Tech. Writers and Pubs., Author's Resource Ctr., Toastmasters, KC. Roman Catholic. Home: Tucson Ariz. Died Mar. 13, 1993; interred Holy Hope Cemetery.

HORGAN, PAUL, writer, educator; b. Buffalo, Aug. 1, 1903; s. Edward Daniel and Rose Marie (Rohr) H. Student, N.Mex. Mil. Inst., 1919-23; Litt.D., Wesleyan U., 1956, So. Meth. U., 1957, Notre Dame U., 1958, Boston Coll., 1958, N.Mex. State U., 1962, Coll. Holy Cross, 1963, U. N.Mex., 1963, Fairfield U., 1964, St. Mary's Coll., 1976, Yale U., 1977; D.H.L., Canisius Coll., 1960, Georgetown U., 1962; Litt.D., D'Youville Coll., 1965, Pace U., 1968, Loyola Coll., Balt., 1968, Lincoln Coll., 1968, St. Bonaventure U., 1970, Cath. U., 1973; L.H.D., LaSalle Coll., 1971, U. Hartford, 1987. Prodn. staff Eastman Theatre, Rochester, N.Y., 1923-26; librarian N.Mex. Mil. Inst., Roswell, 1926-42; asst. to pres. N.Mex. Mil. Inst., 1947; sr. fellow Center Advanced Studies, Wesleyan U., Middletown, Conn., 1959-61; dir. Center Advanced Studies, Wesleyan U., 1962-67, sr. fellow in letters, 1967-68, adj. prof. English, 1967-71, prof. emeritus, 1971-95, author in residence, 1971-95; lectr. Grad. Sch. Letters, U. Iowa, Feb.-June 1946; lectr. English, Saybrook Coll., Yale U., 1969; hon. trustee Aspen Inst. Humanistic Studies, scholar in residence, 1968, 70, 71, 73; past mem. Nat. Coun. Humanities; mem. nat. adv. bd. Ctr. for the Book, Libr. of Congress, 1978-95; past mem. bd. of judges Book of Month Club. Author: (juvenile) Men of Arms, 1931, (novels) The Fault of Angels, 1933 (Harper prize), No Quarter Given, 1935, (novel) Main Line West, 1936, From the Royal City, 1936, (hist. sketches) The Return of the Weed, 1936, (short stories) A Lamp on the Plains, 1937, (history) New Mexico's Own Chronicle, (with Maurice Garland Fulton), 1937, (novel) Far from Cibola, 1938, (short stories and sketches) Figures in a Landscape, 1940, (novella) The Habit of Empire, 1941, (libretto) A Tree on the Plains, An American Opera (music by Ernst Bacon 1942), (play) Yours, A. Lincoln, (novel) The Common Heart, 1942, (novella) The Devil in the Desert, 1952, One Red Rose for Christmas, 1952, (history) Great River: The Rio Grande in North American History (Pulitzer prize, Bancroft prize, Tex. Inst. Letters award, 1954), (fiction) Humble Powers, 1954, (novella) The Saintmaker's Christmas Eve, 1955, (history) The Centuries of Santa Fe, 1956, (novel) Give Me Possession, 1957, (film narration) Rome Eternal, 1959, (novel) A Distant Trumpet, 1960, (biography) Citizen of New Salem, 1961, (collected novels) Mountain Standard Time, 1962, (history) Conquistadors in North American History, 1963, (juvenile) Toby and the Nighttime, 1962, (novel) Things as They Are, 1964, (poetry) Songs after Lincoln, 1965, (biography) Peter Hurd: A Portrait Sketch from Life, 1965, (novel) Memories of the Future, 1966, (short stories) The Peach Stone, 1967, (novel) Everything To Live For, 1968, (history) The Heroic Triad, 1970, (novel) Whitewater, 1970, (criticism) Maurice Baring Restored, 1970, (biography) Encounters with Stravinsky, 1972, rev. edit., 1989, (criticism) Approaches to Writing, 1973, rev. edit., 1988, (biography) Lamy of Santa Fe, His Life and Times (Pulitzer prize, Tex. Inst. Letters award, 1975), (novel) The Thin Mountain Air, 1977, (biography) Josiah Gregg and His Vision of the Early West, 1979, (novel) Mexico Bay, 1982, (selected writings) Of America East and West, 1984, (hist. sketches) Under the Sangre de Cristo, 1985, (comic verse) The Clerihews of Paul Horgan, 1985, (drawings) Writer's Eye: Field Notes and Water Colors, 1988, A Certain Climate: Essays in History, Arts and Letters, 1988, (novel) The Richard Trilogy, 1990, (biographical sketches) Tracings, 1993, (satirical drawings) Publisher's List, 1994; articles, fiction to mags.; exhbns. field drawings for research. Chmn. bd. Santa Fe Opera, 1958-69, mem., 1969-95; mem. adv. bd. John Simon Guggenheim Found., 1963-69; pres. bd. dirs. Roswell Mus., 1948-55; mem. bd. Roswell Pub. Library, 1958-62, hon. mem., 1962-95; hon. life fellow Sch. Am. Research; fellow Pierpont Morgan Library, 1974-95, mem. council, 1975-79, 82-83, life fellow, 1977-95; trustee Assocs. Yale U. Library, 1976-79; bd. dirs. Witter Bynner Found., 1972-79; founding trustee Lincoln County (N.Mex.) Heritage Trust, 1976-95. Served from capt. to lt. col. AUS, 1942-46; recalled temp. active duty gen. staff Dept. Army, 1952, Washington. Created knight of St. Gregory, 1957; Guggenheim fellow, 1947-48, 58; Hoyt fellow Saybrook Coll., Yale U., 1965; asso. fellow Saybrook Coll., 1966-95; Decorated Legion of Merit; recipient Tex. Inst. Letters awards, 1955, 71, 76; Campion award of Catholic Book Club, 1957; Cath. Book award Cath. Press Assn., 1965, 68; Laetare medal U. Notre Dame, 1976; Bronze medal Smithsonian Instn., 1980; Copley medal Nat. Portrait Gallery, 1981; Baldwin medal Wesleyan U., 1982, James L. McConaughy Meml. award, 1986; medal Washington Coll., 1985; Robert Kirsch award Los Angeles Times, 1987; Roswell Mus. addition named after him; N.Mex. Mil. Inst. library named after him. Fellow Am. Acad. Arts and Scis., Conn. Acad. Arts and Scis.; mem. Am. Cath. Hist. Assn. (pres. 1960), Wesleyan Writers Conf. (adv. bd.), Am. Acad. Arts and Letters, Soc. Am. Historians, Athenaeum Club (London), Phi Beta Kappa (orator 1973, hon. Alpha of Conn. chpt.). Roman Catholic. Home: Middletown Conn. Died Mar. 8, 1995.

HORN, ALAN STUART, pharmaceutical chemistry educator; b. Portsmouth, Eng., May 26, 1943; s. Leonard and May Emily (Pharoah) H.; m. Heide Sohn (dec. 1989); children: Mark, Nina. Grad. Royal Inst. Chemistry, U. Salford, Eng., 1966; PhD in Organic Chemistry, U. Cambridge, Eng., 1969. Rsch. fellow Johns Hopkins Med. Sch., Balt., 1969-71; head organic synthesis Allergan Pharms., Santa Anna, 1971; staff scientist, assoc. prof. dept. pharmacy U. Cambridge, 1971-76; pharm. chemist U. Groningen, Netherlands, 1976-80; prof. pharm. chemistry U. Groningen, 1980—; chmn., Groningen Ctr. Drug Rsch., 1986-88. Editor: The Neurobiology of Dopamine, 1978, X-Ray Crystallography and Drug Action, 1984; European editor, Drug Design and Delivery jour., 1987—. Mem. Royal Dutch Chem. Soc. (chmn. medicinal chemistry sect.), Royal Dutch Soc. Advancement of Pharmacy.

HORNBEIN, VICTOR, architect; b. Denver, Oct. 26, 1913; s. Samuel and Rose (Frumess) H.; m. Ruth Kriesler, Mar. 20, 1947; children: Victoria Ann, Peter. Student, Atelier Denver, Beaux-Arts Inst. Design, 1930-35. Practice as Victor Hornbein, architect, 1940-60; with firm Victor Hornbein and Edward D. White, Jr., Denver, 1960-76; partner Victor Hornbein and Edward D. White, Jr., 1960-76; prin. Victor Hornbein & Assos., Denver, 1976-80; partner Victor Hornbein & John James, 1980-82; prin. Victor Hornbein, Architect, 1982—; vis. lectr. U. Denver, 1949-52, U. Colo., 1958-59, 68, 75, mem. design rev. bd., 1969-73; design adv. panel region 8 Gen. Services Adminstrn., 1967-70; vol. faculty U. Colo. Sch. Architecture, 1989-90. Major works include: conservatory and edn. bldg. Denver Bot. Gardens, 1966-71, conservatory and edn. bldg. Porter Library, Colo. Women's Coll., Denver, 1962, Bethesda Hosp., Denver, 1970, René Spitz Children's divsn. Ft. Logan Mental Health Center, Denver, 1965, housing for elderly, 1973, Sanctuary Wellshire Presbyn. Ch., 1980, Orchid and Bromeliad House, Denver Bot. Gardens, 1980, Wellshire Presbyn. Ch., 1985. Pres. Met. Council Community Services, 1957; bd. advisors Wright-Ingraham Inst. 1972—, trustee, 1974—, chmn. bd. trustees, 1975-82. Served with AUS, 1942-45. Decorated Bronze Star; recipient Modern Architecture Preservation League 1st Ann. Lifetime Achievement award, 1995. Fellow AIA (pres. Colo. Central chpt. 1971, Silver medal Western Mountain region 1981). Home: Denver Colo. Died July 17, 1995.

HORNER, HARRY, art director, performing arts designer; b. Holic, Czechoslovakia, July 24, 1910; came to U.S., 1935, naturalized, 1940; s. Felix and Gisela (Kohn) H.; m. Betty Arnold Pfaelzer, Sept. 22, 1938 (dec.); m. Joan Frankel, 1952; children: James, Christopher, Tony. Ed., Dept. Architeture, U. Vienna, 1928-33, Acad. of Theater, Vienna, 1930-32, Max Reinhardt's Sem. pres. Enterprises Films Can., 1964-94; mng. dir. Anglo Enterprise Films, London, 1966. Joined Max Reinhardt Theatre Co., Vienna and Salzburg Festivals in U.S., asst. to Max Reinhardt on pageant The Eternal Road, 1936; designer pageants for: N.Y.C. R.R., Cleve. 1937, N.Y. World's Fair, 1939-40; designer numerous Broadway plays and musicals including Our Town (with William Cameron Menzies), 1938, World We Make, Lady in the Dark, The World of Christopher Blake

1947, Joy to the World, Me and Molly, 1948, Herod, Family Portrait, Star and Garter, Little Foxes, Stage Door Canteen; designer Winged Victory for USAF, 1949; prodns. designed for motion pictures include: Our Town, 1940, A Double Life, The Heiress, 1948 (Acad. award 1949), Separate Tables, Born Yesterday, Wonderful Country, The Hustler (Acad. award), They Shoot Horses, Don't They?, 1969 (Acad. award nominee), Who is Harry Kellerman?, 1970, Lady Sings the Blues, 1971, Up the Sandbox, 1972, Black Bird, 1974, Harry and Walter are Going to New York, 1975, Audrey Rose, 1976, The Driver, 1977, Moment by Moment, 1978, The Jazz Singer; motion picture dir. 20th Century Fox Films, 1951-94; dir. films: Beware My Lovely, Red Planet Mars, Vicki, New Faces, Life in the Balance, Step Down To Terror, Lonesome Gun, Wild Party Man From Del Rio ; opera designer and dir. San Francisco Opera, Met. Opera, N.Y. Festival, Vancouver Festival, Hollywood Bowl including Dialogues of the Carmelites, 1957, David, 1956, Magic Flute, 1956, Joan at the Stake, Am. premier new opera Midsummer Nights Dream; designer Idiot's Delight, Ahmanson Theatre, 1970, (L.A. Drama Critics award best stage design), also Time of the Cuckoo, 1974; TV prodns. include Omnibus, Cavalcade, Reader's Digest, Author's Playhouse, Four Star Theatre, Gunsmoke, Revue Prodns., Dupont Theatre; producer, dir. TV series Royal Canadian Mounted Police; also dir. TV series Gunsmoke. Served with USAAF, 1943-45. Recipient award for best moving picture script on a peace theme League of Nations, 1932. Mem. Screen Dirs. Guild, United Scenic Artist Union, Soc. Motion Picture Art Dirs., Acad. Motion Picture Arts and Scis., Canadian Dirs. Guild. Jewish. Home: Pacific Palisades Calif. Died Dec. 5, 1994.

HORNER, J. RICHARD, lawyer; b. Shreveport, La., Aug. 14, 1947; s. J. Frederick and Dorothy (Burks) H.; m. Rebecca Reid, Nov. 12, 1986; 1 child, Stephanie Ann. BBA, Tex. A&M U., 1969, MBA, 1970; JD with honors, U. Tex., 1977. Bar: Tex. 1978, U.S. Dist. Ct. (no. dist.) Tex. 1978. Assoc., ptnr. Shank, Irwin & Conant, Dallas, 1978-86; ptnr. Hughes & Luce, Dallas, 1986-90, Fulbright & Jaworski, Dallas, 1990—. Capt. USAF, 1970-75. Mem. Dallas Energy Fin. Group, Phi Delta Phi. Avocation: ranching.

HORTON, LARRY BRUCE, lawyer, financial consultant; b. Topeka, Kans., Mar. 23, 1942; s. Halbert Greenleaf and Alberta (Rinehart) H.; m. Alison Jean Shirk, Sept. 5, 1964 (div. 1983); children: Margot Lyn Parsons, Michele Rene Horton; m. Madeline Mary Fiduccia, June 30, 1984; stepchildren: James Earl Dickman, Suzanne Dickman Noel. BS, Washburn U., Topeka, 1970; JD, Washburn U., 1974. Bar: Kans. 1974, U.S. Ct. Mil. Appeals 1974, U.S. Supreme Ct. 1982, Va. 1984, U.S. Tax Ct. 1984. Police officer Topeka Police Dept., 1964-65; warehouseman/supr. Goodyear Tire & Rubber Co., Topeka, 1965-74; mil. lawyer U.S. Army Judge Advocate Gen.'s Corps, 1974-84; sole practice Charlottesville, Va., 1984-87; co-founder, exec. v.p., gen. counsel, fin. planner Horton Fin. Svcs., Inc., Charlottesville, 1987-93; pvt. practice estate planning law Charlottesville, 1987-93. With U.S. Army, 1960-63, 74-84, lt. col. Res. Mem. ABA, Va. State Bar Assn., Charlottesville/Albemarle Bar Assn., Judge Advocates Assn., Kans. Bar Assn., Res. Officers Assn., Inst. Cert. Fin. Planners (assoc.), VFW, SAR. Republican. Roman Catholic. Died Aug. 10, 1993.

HOUNSHELL, CHARLES DAVID, retired political science educator; b. Rural Retreat, Va., Dec. 19, 1920; s. David Washington and Florence Earhart (Brown) H.; m. Elizabeth Jane Yoak, Oct. 9, 1944; children: Jeffrey David (dec.), William Douglas, Elizabeth Anne. A.B., Emory and Henry Coll., 1942, LL.D., 1968; Ph.D., U. Va., 1950; Ford Faculty fellow, Princeton, 1953-54. Instr. polit. sci. U. Va., 1948-50; mem. faculty Emory U., 1950-66, asso. prof. polit. sci., 1955-66; asso. dean Emory U. (Coll. Arts and Scis.), 1960-66; dean Newcomb Coll.; prof. polit. sci. Tulane U., New Orleans, 1966-69; pres. Birmingham-So. Coll., Birmingham, Ala., 1969-71; spl. asst. to pres., prof. polit. sci. U. Ala., 1971-72; vice chancellor adminstrn. U. N.C. at Greensboro, 1972-80, prof., 1972-86, prof. emeritus, 1986-93; Chmn. region VI Woodrow Wilson Nat. Fellowship Found., 1957-66, nat. rep., 1962-63, mem. nat. com., 1966-67, chmn. region XII, 1967-69; sec.-treas., editor proc. So. Univ. Conf., 1971-77; panelist Nat. Endowment for Humanities, 1976, 78. Author: The Legislative Process in Virginia, 1951; Book rev. editor: Jour. Politics, 1960-62. Served to lt. USNR, 1942-46; capt. Res. Philip Francis du Pont sr. fellow, 1947-48; research fellow, 1948; summer research scholar Duke Commonwealth Studies Center, 1957; research grantee Emory U. Research Com., 1952, 55, 60; research grantee U. Center in Ga., 1955. Sr. fellow Acad. for Ednl. Devel.; mem. Am. Polit. Sci. Assn., So. Polit. Sci. Assn. (exec. council 1954-57, v.p. 1957), Phi Beta Kappa, Omicron Delta Kappa. Democrat. Methodist. Home: Greensboro N.C. Died Jan. 11, 1993.

HOUSE, CHARLES STAVER, judge; b. Manchester, Conn., Apr. 24, 1908; s. Herbert Bissell and Sophia (Staver) H.; m. Virginia Mabel Brown, Aug. 5, 1938; children: Carolyn, Arthur, Elizabeth. Grad., Williston Acad., 1926; A.B., Harvard U., 1930, LL.B., 1933; LL.D., Suffolk U., 1975. Bar: Conn. 1933. Ptnr. Day, Berry & Howard, Hartford, Conn., 1936-53; judge Conn. Superior Ct., 1953-65; assoc. justice Conn. Supreme Ct., 1965-71, chief justice, 1971-78, state trial referee, 1978-90, ret., 1990; vice chmn. Conn. Jud. Council, 1964-65, chmn., 1965-71; chmn. Jud. Rev. Council, 1970-71; vice chmn. Nat. Adv. Com. on Criminal Justice Standards and Goals, 1975-76; chmn. Nat. Conf. Chief Justices, 1975-76. Chmn. Manchester Bd. Edn., 1943-53; Rep. Conn. Gen. Assembly, 1939, state senator, 1947, 49; Republican leader Senate, chmn. legislative council, 1949, asst. state's atty., 1942-46; legal adviser Gov. Lodge, 1951-53; Hon. trustee Manchester Meml. Hosp. Fellow Am. Bar Found.; mem. Am., Conn. bar assns. Congregationalist. Lodge: Masons. Died Nov. 8, 1996.

HOWARD, GEORGE SALLADÉ, conductor, music consultant, educator; b. Reamstown, Pa., Feb. 24, 1903; s. Hayden H. and Florence (Salladé) H.; m. Sadako Takenouchi, Apr. 5, 1957. Mus.B. with honors, Ithaca Conservatory, 1925; A.B., Ohio Wesleyan U., 1929; Mus.B., Chgo. Conservatory Music, 1934, Mus.M., 1935, Mus.D., 1939; M.A., N.Y. U., 1936; Mus. D. (hon.), Ithaca Coll., 1984. Dean Ernest Williams Sch. Music, Bklyn., 1935-36; dir. music, condr. bands Pa. State Tchrs. Coll., 1936-39; dir. bands, orch. and chorus sch., dir. music in extension Pa. State Coll., 1939-42; commd. capt. U.S. Army, 1942; advanced through grades to col. USAF, 1951; organizer, condr. music programs Greenland, Iceland, Newfoundland, 1942-43; comdg. officer, condr. Ofcl. Army Air Forces Band, Washington, 1944; chief music and radio br. AAF Hdqrs., 1946; established, organized AAF Band Sch., 1946; chief bands and music USAF; condr. USAF (USAF Band and Symphony Orch.), 1947; condr. USAF Band on tour, U.S., Can., Eng., Scotland, Wales, Ireland, Germany, Austria, Norway, Denmark, Libya, Iceland, Azores, Japan, Korea, P.I., Cambodia, others; condr. command performances Buckingham Palace, Royal Palace of Cambodia, The White House; ret. USAF, 1963; distinguished prof. music Troy (Ala.) State U., 1974—; vis. prof., dir. wind ensemble U. Houston, 1977; music cons. (rank of insp.) Met. Police Dept., Washington, 1973—; condr. Met. Police Band, Washington, 1963-73, Air Force Village Voices, San Antonio, 1977—; guest condr. Goldman Band, 1961-75, hon. life mem., 1973; hon. comdr. Tokyo (Japan) Youth Symphony Orch., Tex. Longhorn Band U. Tex., 1975. Clarinetist, Patrick Conway Band, 1922-27, soloist, 1927-29, condr., Ohio Wesleyan U. Band, 1925-29, dir. music, condr., Mooseheart Band, 1929-35; author: Ten Minute Self-Instructor for Pocket Instruments, 1943, The Big Serenade, 1961, (autobiography) A Symphony in the Sky, 1991; composer: Niece of Uncle Sam, 1944, American Doughboy, 1945, My Missouri, 1945, General Spaatz March, 1947, The Red Feather; theme song, Community Chest, Official March of the Washington Evening Star, Official March of the Central Canada Exhibition, Official March Pacific Nat. Exhbn, Vancouver, B.C., Alfalfa Club March, Cougar's Victory, Bachelors of the Sky, others. Chmn. John Philip Sousa Meml., Kennedy Center for the Performing Arts, Washington. Decorated Legion of Merit with cluster U.S.; Guarde Republique medal; comdr. Order of Nonsaraphon Cambodia, Star of the Order, gold medal Sudler Found.; recipient Gold record for furthering Japanese-Am. rels. thru music Nippon-Columbia Co., 1962; named to Hall of Fame for Disting. Band Condrs.; established the Col. George S. Howard Citation of Mus. Excellence for mil. bands, the John Philip Sousa Found.; honored with dedication of Howard Hall, John Philip Sousa Found., 1994. Mem. ASCAP, Nat. Assn. Composers and Condrs. (citation for contbn. Am. music), Am. Bandmasters Assn. (pres. 1956-57, elected hon. life pres. 1986), Tex. Bandmasters Assn. (hon. life), Nat. Band Assn. (pres. 1970-74), Phi Mu Alpha, Pi Kappa Lambda, Phi Kappa Tau, Kappa Kappa Psi, Phi Beta Mu. Club: Alfalfa (Washington).

HOWARD, KINGSTON LEE, hotel management services company executive; b. Hartford, Conn., Aug. 25, 1929; s. Raymond Herbert and Lucille (Dunn) H.; m. Jean Murphy, Feb. 11, 1956; children: Kingston Lee, Deborah Lynn. B.A., Trinity Coll., Hartford, 1953; M.B.A., Harvard U., 1955. V.p., gen. mgr. Brigham's, Inc., Cambridge, Mass., 1955-67; asst. to pres., coord. internat. devel. Howard Johnson Co., N.Y.C., 1967-69; founder, pres. Internat. Mgmt. Services Co., Lexington, Mass., 1969-73, 74-77, 78-93; chief oper. officer Imperial Hotels Corp., Arlington, Va., 1987-88; pres., dir. Days Inn Am., Inc., Atlanta, 1973-77; chmn., CEO Eco Internat. Inc., Norwich, Vt. Chmn. Lexington Bicentennial Com., 1970-73; mem. Lexington Republican Town Com., 1962-68; pres. Com. for Am. Monument in Meaux Inc. Served with AUS, 1950-52. Mem. Am. Hotel and Motel Assn. (bd. dirs., cert. hotel adminstr., chmn. econ. lodging coun.), Nat. Restaurant Assn., Harvard Club (N.Y.C.), Peachtree Club (Atlanta), Masons (Lexington). Republican. Episcopalian. Home: Boston Mass. Died Aug. 1993.

HOWARD, MEL, film producer, educator; b. Bklyn., Feb. 17, 1935. AB, Bklyn. Coll., 1955; postgrad., Columbia U., N.Y.C., 1956. Assoc. dir. Am. Film Inst., 1967-69; head grad. div. Inst. Film & TV NYU, 1974-76; chmn. broadcast and film Boston U., 1990-93; pres. New Voices/New Visions Films; bd. dirs. Planet Ctrl., TV. Co-assoc. prodr. (films) Night of the Generals, Quackser Fortune Has A Cousin In The Bronx, Renaldo and Clara, Washington Affair, Snapshots (also dir.), The Chosen, The Goodbye People, Beat Street, He Makes Me Feel Like Dancing, Rented Lips, The Boost, (theatre) Plough And The Stars, Raisin In The Sun (Broadway), Once There Was A Russian (Broadway); prodn. exec. (films) Twelve Chairs, Night Visitor, First Love, Ice, Switch, The Pawnbroker, Glen and Randa, The Swimmer, THe Happening, The Group, A Thousand Clowns, 5 Heartbeats; actor in films and theatre including leads in Hester Street and Snapshots; head european prodn. for UMC Pictures, Horizon Pictures, Sam Speigel. Fellow Sundance Inst.; mem. Actors Studio, Dirs. Unit. DIED 07/12/96. .

HOWARD, NEIL, performing arts organization administrator; b. The Dalles, Oreg., Feb. 14, 1940; s. Harold A. and Arvilla L. (Kretzer) H.; 1 child, Patrick. Student, U. Oreg., 1958-61, 63-64, Ea. Oreg. Coll., 1961-62. Mgr. Nederlander Orgn., N.Y.C., 1972—; lectr. in field. Mem. Assn. Theatrical Press Agts. and Mgrs. DIED 04/29/96. .

HOWE, RICHARD ESMOND, JR., music educator; b. Murray, Utah, Apr. 30, 1927; s. Richard Esmond and Louise (Hill) H.; m. Agnes Jensen, May 31, 1949 (dec. Feb. 1990); 1 dau., Mary Katherine. Student, U. Utah, 1946; B.S. in Music, Juilliard Sch. Music, 1951, M.S. in Music, 1952; student, U. Florence, Italy, 1952-53; D.Mus. Arts, Eastman Sch. Music, 1956. Mem. faculty Grinnell (Iowa) Coll., 1956-73, prof. music, 1963—, chmn. dept., 1959-62, 65-67, 70-72, chmn. div. humanities, 1971-72; dean San Francisco Conservatory Music, 1973-88. Contbr. articles to mus. jours. Served with USNR, 1945-46. Fulbright grantee Italy, 1952-53, 53-54. Spl. research keyboard music of Baldassare Gallupi.

HOWELL, ALFRED HUNT, former banker; b. Wyoming, Ohio, July 17, 1912; s. Alfred Corey and Florence Alice (Hunt) H.; m. Ruth Rea, Sept. 17, 1938 (dec. Mar. 1993); children: Ann (Mrs. A. Joseph Armstrong), Alfred Hunt, Henry Parish. A.B., Princeton U., 1934; M.A., M.Phil., Columbia U., 1978, PhD, 1993. With Bethlehem Shipbldg. Corp., Quincy, Mass., 1934-37; with Citibank, N.Y.C., 1937-72. Author: Who Made You? Theology, Science and Human Responsibility, 1989. Dir. YMCA Greater N.Y., 1950-84, pres., 1963-66, now emeritus; trustee Nat. Coun. YMCAs, now emeritus; chmn. state exec. com. YMCA of N.Y. State, 1950-96; trustee The Frick Collection, 1972-87, now emeritus, Am. Univ. Beirut, 1967-82, treas, 1978-84, trustees AUB Found., 1985-96, pres., treas.; bd. dirs. Cleveland H. Dodge Found., v.p. With USNR, 1942-45, ETO, PTO. Decorated Order of Cedars Lebanon; Recipient Order of Red Triangle YMCA Greater N.Y., 1966. Mem. Middle East Studies Assn., Century Club, Grolier Club (pres. 1968-72). Home: Kennett Square Pa. Died Apr. 23, 1996.

HOWELL, ROBERT WAYNE, agronomy educator; b. Houlka, Miss., Nov. 26, 1916; s. Raleigh Wayne and Frances Ethel (Stacy) H.; m. Elizabeth Virginia Blair, Sept. 25, 1940; children: Jacqueline Howell Choate, Richard James, Wayne Davis. Student, George Washington U., 1934-37; B.S., Miss. Coll., 1949; M.S., U. Wis., 1951, Ph.D., 1952. Clk., adminstrv. asst. U.S. Dept. Agr., Washington, Cheyenne, Wyo., Ithaca, N.Y., 1934-43; bus. mgr. Pineapple Research Inst., Hawaii, 1947; plant physiologist U.S. Regional Lab., Urbana, Ill., 1952-65; leader soybean investigations U.S. Dept. Agr., Beltsville, Md., 1965; chief oilseed and indsl. crops research br. U.S. Dept. Agr., 1966-71; prof. agronomy U. Ill., Urbana, 1971-93, chmn. dept., 1971-82; sr. advisor FAO project Heilongjiang Acad. Sci., Harbin, China, 1982-84; research cons. Ill. Soybean Program Oper. Bd., 1982-90. Editor: Crop Science, 1969-71. Served to capt. AUS, 1943-46. Recipient award of merit Am. Soybean Assn., 1972. Fellow Am. Soc. Agronomy, AAAS; mem. Crop Sci. Soc. Am., Am. Soc. Plant Physiologists, Am. Soybean Assn. (hon. life), Sigma Chi. Home: Urbana Ill. Died Nov. 22, 1993.

HOWES, BARBARA, poet, author; b. N.Y.C., May 1, 1914; d. Osborne and Mildred (Cox) H.; m. William Jay Smith, Oct. 1, 1947 (div. June 1965); children: David E., Gregory Jay. B.A., Bennington Coll., 1937. Editor: Chimera quar., N.Y.C., 1943-47; author: (poetry) The Undersea Farmer, 1948, In the Cold Country, 1954, Light and Dark, 1959, Looking up at Leaves, 1966, The Blue Garden, 1972, A Private Signal: Poems New and Selected, 1977, Moving, 1983, Collected Poems 1945-90; editor: 23 Modern Stories, 1963, From the Green Antilles: writings of the Caribbean, 1966, The Sea-Green Horse: short stories for young people, (with G.J. Smith), 1970, The Eye of the Heart: Stories from Latin America, 1973 (Christopher award); author: (short stories) The Road Commissioner & Other Stories (with block prints by Gregory Smith), 1983. Guggenheim fellow, 1955; recipient Brandeis U. Creative Arts poetry grant, 1958, Nat. Inst. Arts and Letters lit. award, 1971, Golden Rose award New Eng. Poetry Soc., 1973; Christopher award, 1974; Bennington award for outstanding contbns. to poetry, 1980. Home: North Pownal Vt. Died Feb. 24, 1996.

HOWES, BENJAMIN DURWARD, III, mergers and acquisitions executive; b. L.A., Oct. 31, 1922; s. Durward and Maxine (Eccleston) H.; m. Cynthia Marble,

May 25, 1951; children: Cynthia Marble, Dana Belinda, Melisa Sanborn (dec.), Durward IV, Mary Devin, Daryl Brett, Briant Davidson. Student, Stanford U., 1941-42; BSBA, U. So. Calif., 1943. With B.D. Howes & Son, retail jewelers, Pasadena, Santa Barbara, Newport Beach,, Calif., also Hawaii, 1946-89, pres., 1957-89, chmn. bd. dirs., 1981-88; founder The Howes Cos., 1988-95; founder, vice chmn., bd. dirs. Brookside Savs. & Loan, Pasadena; chmn. bd. dirs. Jewelry Industry Coun., 1970-71. Pres. Pasadena-Altadena Community Chest, 1960, 61; trustee, exec. com. Republican Assos. Served to lt. (j.g.) USNR, World War II. Recipient Disting. Service award as Outstanding Young Man in Pasadena U.S. Jaycees, 1957. Mem. World Bus. Coun., Young Pres. Orgn. (chmn. San Gabriel chpt. 1964-65), Chief Execs. Orgn., Retail Jewelers Am. (pres. 1963-65), Calif. Retail Jewelers Assn. (pres. 1950), Calif. Jr. C. of C. (v.p. 1949), Pasadena Jr. C. of C. (pres. 1951-52), Pasadena C. of C. (v.p.), L.A. Area C. of C. (bd. dirs., v.p. 1971), L.A. Breakfast Panel (founder, past pres.), Pasadena Tournament of Roses Assn., U. So. Calif. Alumni Assn. (mem. bd. govs.), Rotary (pres. Pasadena chpt. 1967-68, bd. dirs.). Episcopalian. Home: Pasadena Calif. Died Sept. 27, 1995.

HOWORTH, LUCY SOMERVILLE, lawyer; b. Greenville, Miss., July 1; d. Robert and Nellie (Nugent) Somerville; m. Joseph Marion Howorth, Feb. 16, 1928. A.B., Randolph-Macon Woman's Coll., 1916; postgrad., Columbia U., 1918; J.D. summa cum laude, U. Miss., 1922. Bar: Miss. 1922, U.S. Supreme Ct. 1934. Asst. in psychology Randolph-Macon Woman's Coll., 1916-17; gauge insp. Allied Bur. Air Prodn., N.Y.C., 1918; indsl. research nat. bd. YWCA, 1919-20; gen. practice law Howorth & Howorth, Cleveland, Greenville and Jackson, Miss., 1922-34; U.S. commr. So. Jud. Dist. Miss., 1927-31; assoc. mem. Bd. Vet. Appeals, Washington, 1934-43; legis. atty. VA, 1943-49; v.p., dir. VA Employees Credit Union, 1937-49; assoc. gen. counsel War Claims Commn., 1949-52, dep. gen. counsel, 1952-53, gen. counsel, 1953-54; ptnr. James Somerville & Assocs. (overseas trade and devel.), 1954-55; atty. Commn. on Govt. Security, 1956-57; pvt. practice law Cleveland, Miss., 1958-97; mem. nat. bd. cons. Women's Archives, Radcliffe Coll.; mem. lay adv. com. study profl. nursing Carnegie Corp. N.Y., 1947-48; chmn. Miss. State Bd. Law Examiners, 1924-28; mem. Miss. State Legislature, 1932-36, chmn. com. pub. lands, 1932-36; treas. Com. for Econ. Survey Miss., 1928-30; mem. Research Commn. Miss., 1930-34. Editor: Fed. Bar Assn. News, 1944; assoc. editor: Fed. Bar Assn. Jour., 1943-44; editor: (with William M. Cash) My Dear Nellie-Civil War Letters (William L. Nugent), 1977; contbr. articles profl. jours. Keynote speaker White House Conf. on Women in Postwar Policy Making, 1944, at conf. on opening 81st Congress. Recipient Alumnai Achievment award Randolph-Macon Woman's Coll., 1981, Lifetime Achievmenet award Schlesinger Libr. of Radcliffe Coll., 1983; named for her outstanding lifetime achievments by Senate Concurrrent Resolution, adopted by Senate and Ho. of Reps., 1984; recipient Excellence medal Miss. U. for Women, 1989. Mem. AAUW (nat. dir., 2d v.p. 1951-55, mem. found. 1960-63), Nat. Fedn. Bus. and Profl. Women's Clubs (nat. dir.; rep. to internat. 1939, chmn. internat. conf. 1946), Nat. Assn. Women Lawyers, Miss. Library Assn. (life), Miss. Hist. Soc. (dir. 1982-97 , Merit award 1983), DAR, Daus. Am. Colonists, Am. Legion Aux. (past sec. Miss. dept.), Assembly Women's Orgns. for Nat. Security (chmn. 1951-52), Phi Beta Kappa, Pi Gamma Mu, Phi Alpha Delta, Alpha Omicron Pi (Wyman award 1985), Delta Kappa Gamma, Omicron Delta Kappa, Phi Kappa Phi (hon.). Democrat (del. nat. conv., 1932). Methodist. Club: Soroptimist (Washington). Home: Cleveland Ohio Died Aug. 23, 1997; interred Memorial Cemetery, Greenville, MS.

HOWREY, EDWARD F., lawyer; b. Waterloo, Iowa, Sept. 6, 1903; s. Benjamin J. and Ada C. (McStay) H.; m. India Pickett Lilly, Aug. 28, 1992. A.B., U. Iowa, 1925; J.D. with honors, George Washington U., 1927, LL.D. (hon.), 1980. Bar: D.C., Iowa bars 1927, Va 1938. With U.S. Dept. Justice, 1927-29; asso. Sanders, Childs, Bobb & Wescott, Washington, 1929-37; partner successor firm Sanders, Gravelle, Whitlock & Howrey, 1937-53; chmn. FTC, 1953-55; practice law Washington, 1955—; ptnr. Howrey & Simon. Fellow Am. Coll. Trial Lawyers, Am. Bar Found.; mem. Am. Soc. Internat. Law, Internat. Bar Assn., Am. Judicature Soc., Acad. of Polit. Sci., English Speaking Union, Am. Bar Assn., Phi Kappa Psi, Phi Delta Phi, Order of Coif. Republican. Episcopalian. Clubs: Metropolitan (Washington), Chevy Chase (Washington), Fairfax Hunt, Middleburg Tennis (Va.), Cheyenne Mountain Country Club (Colo. Springs). Died Apr. 11, 1996.

HOWSE, ERNEST MARSHALL, columnist, author, clergyman; b. Twillingate, Nfld., Can., Sept. 29, 1902; s. Charles and Elfreda (Palmer) H.; m. Esther Lilian Black, Sept. 17, 1932; children: Margery (Mrs. Raymond Dyer), David C. Napier, George Arthur. Student, Meth. Coll., St. John's, Nfld., 1919-20, Albert Coll., Belleville, Ont., Can., 1924-25, Dalhousie U., Halifax, N.S., 1929; B.A., Pine Hill Div. Hall, Halifax, 1931; S.T.M., Union Sem., N.Y., 1932; Ph.D. in History, U. Edinburgh, Scotland, 1934; D.D., United Coll., Man., 1948, Laurentian U., 1964, Pine Hill Div. Hall, 1966, Victoria U., Toronto, Ont., 1967; D. Litt., Nfld. Meml. U., 1965. Ordained to ministry United Ch. Can., 1931. Pastor Beverly Hills (Calif.) Presbyn. Ch., 1934-35, Westminister United Ch., Winnipeg, Man., 1935-48, Bloor Street United Ch., Toronto, 1948-70; free lance journalist, weekly columnist Toronto Star, 1970-79; Participant, newspaper corr. 1st Assembly World Council Chs., Amsterdam, Holland, 1948, 2d Assembly, Evanston, Ill., 1954, 3d Assembly, New Delhi, 1961; press rep. 4th Assembly, Uppsala, Sweden, 1968, 5th Assembly, Nairobi, Kenya, 1974; del. 1st Muslim-Christian convocation, Bhamdoun, Lebanon, 1954; Christian co-pres. Continuing Com. on Muslim-Christian Cooperation, 1955-64; pres. Toronto conf. United Ch. Can., 1961-62; moderator United Ch. Can., 1964-66; mem. Exec. World Meth. Council; Canadian del. 1st World Conf. Religion and Peace, Japan, 1970. Author: Our Prophetic Heritage, 1945, The Law and the Prophets, 1947, Saints in Politics, 1952, 2d edit., 1960, 3d edit., 1971, Story of the English Bible, 1952, Spiritual Values in Shakespeare, 1955, paperback edit., 1964, The Lively Oracles, 1956, People and Provocations, 1965; (Autobiography) Roses in December, 1982; also weekly feature articles syndicated in Canadian newspapers, articles in mags. and other periodicals. Named hon. citizen Seoul, Korea, 1965; recipient Award of Merit with medallion City of Toronto, 1980. Mem. Internat. Meth. Hist. Soc. (v.p. 1966). Club: Empire (dir., hon. chaplain). Home: Willowdale Can. Died Feb. 1, 1993.

HOYER, HARVEY CONRAD, college president, clergyman; b. Clay Co., S.D., July 21, 1907; s. Gust and Johannah (Norder) H.; m. E. Margaret Larson, Sept. 3, 1930; children: Gustav Adolph, Helen JoAnn, Ruth, Marcus Conrad, Bernard Eric. Student, U. S.D., 1925-28; A.B., Augustana Coll., 1931, D.D., 1950; B.D., Augustana Theol. Sem., 1936. Ordained to ministry Luth. Ch., 1936; grad. sch. tchr. S.D., 1926-29; prin. Mission Hill Sch., S.D., 1931-32; pastor Central Luth. Ch., Madison, Wis., 1936-40, Calvary Luth. Ch., Chgo., 1940-42; pres. Ill. Conf. Luther League, 1938-42; v.p. Augustana Synod Luther League, 1940-42; exec. sec. Div. Am. Missions, Nat. Luth. Council, 1942-60; asso. exec. sec. div. home missions Nat. Council Chs. of Christ in U.S.A., 1960-64, asso. exec. sec. dept. for councils of chs., 1965-70; asso. exec. dir. Commn. Regional and Local Ecumenicism, 1970-72; pres. Luther Coll., Teaneck, N.J., 1974-75. Author, co-author: books, pamphlets, latest Go Into all the World, 1951, Ministering to People-on-the-move, 1952, Mission Fields U.S.A, 1956, Heritage and Horizons in Home Missions, 1960, Ecumenopolis-USA, 1971, Forward Together: A Guide to Creative Leadership, 1992; also articles.; Editor: Am. Missions Together, 1946-60, Redeeming the Time, 1949, Christ for the Moving Millions, 1955, Adventuring in American Missions, 1955, Church Planning for Mission in Today's World, 1967, Ecumenopolis, U.S.A, 1971, Aging and the Response of Faith, 1981. Organizer Luth. Ch.'s ministry to temp. def. communities, 1942, Nat. Luth. Council's dept. chmn. for Christian approach to Jewish people, 1946, Christian Ministry to Nat. Parks, Nat. Council of Chs., 1957-60; chmn. Price County (Wis.) Commn. on Aging, 1978; chmn. adv. com. Area Agy. on Aging, 1977-78; chmn. adv. com. to Wis. Bur. on Aging, 1978-79; chmn. personnel and fin. com. Wis. Coalition on Aging Groups, pres., 1979-81. Mem. Assn. Council Secs. (v.p. 1964-65, editor Jour.). Died Aug. 3, 1996. Buried Lakeside Cemetery Phillips, Wisc.

HOYT, F(RANK) RUSSELL, professional society administrator; b. Lowell, Mass., Dec. 7, 1916; s. Frank Russell and Ethel (Rivet) H.; m. Helen Elizabeth Tallmadge, Jan. 24, 1945; children: Alan James, Deborah. B.A., Oberlin Coll., 1939; cert., Yale U. Bur. Hwy. Traffic, 1941. Accredited airport exec. Traffic safety engr. Mass. Safety Council, Boston, 1941-42; airport and airline mgr. Pan Am. Grace Air Lines, Quito, Ecuador, 1946-48, LaPaz, Bolivia, 1948-50; sr. ops. supt. Pan Am. Grace Air Lines, Chile, 1950-54; asst. to chief pilot Pan Am. Grace Air Lines, Miami, Fla., 1954-59; exec. v.p. Am. Assn. Airport Execs., Washington, 1960-84; exec. sec. N.E. chpt. Am. Assn. Airport Execs., 1984—, mgr. spl. projects, 1984—; mem. (cons.) White House Com. on Aviation Noise Abatement, Washington, 1960; mem. NASA adv. com. Aviation Safety Reporting System, 1979-83; cons. Transport Can., Ottawa, Bolivian Govt. Served with USAAF, 1941-45. Recipient Disting. Service Achievement award FAA, 1983; recipient Disting. Service Achievement award NASA, 1980. Mem. Am. Assn. Airport Execs. Clubs: Nat. Aviation (Washington), Aero (Washington). Died Feb. 7, 1997.

HOYT, MONTY, car purchase consultant; b. Balt., Sept. 13, 1944; s. E. Palmer and Helen May (Lininger) H.; m. Kathryn Lee Hamilton, Sept. 7, 1968 (div. Apr. 1985); children: Kimberly Anne, Murray Palmer; m. Marcia A. Carpenter, Mar. 19, 1988; children: Jessica Ann, Brian Robert. BA, U. Denver, 1967; BA, MA, Oxford U., Eng., 1969. Corr. Christian Sci. Monitor, Boston, 1970-75; sr. sports analyst Pres. Commn. on Olympic Sports, Washington, 1975-76; ptnr. Am. Sports Devel. Svc., Arlington, Va., 1976-80; mng. editor Newstrack Exec. Tape Svc., Denver, 1981-83; pres. Cassette Communications, Denver, 1983-89; editor, mgr. media rels. AT&T, Basking Ridge, N.J., 1988-96; owner Car-Search of Am., Phoenix, 1997—. Author, host PBS TV show Showtime on Ice, 1980; contbr. over 500 articles Christian Sci. Monitor, 1970-75. Mem. 1964 U.S. Olympic Team, U.S. World Figure Skating Team, 1962-64, U.S. Men's Figure Skating Champion, 1962. Named one of Outstanding Young Men Am., 1971; Marshall scholar Oxford U., 1967-69. Mem. U.S. Figure Skating Assn. (bd. dirs. 1983-86, internat. judge 1984-96), Morris County C. of C., Phi Beta Kappa. Office: 3712 E Turney Ave Phoenix AZ 85018-4012 DIED 10/09/97. .

HUANG, EDWIN I-CHUEN, physician, environmental researcher; b. Lin-Lin, Hunan, China, Sept. 10, 1933; came to U.S., 1970, naturalized, 1976; s. Chu-Ouh and Wan-Lan (Chaing) H.; m. Zhao-Lin Wu; children: David, Sherman, Jennifer. Student, Nat. Def. Med. Ctr., China, 1951-53; MD, Nat. Def. Med. Coll., Taipei, China, 1960; MPH, U. Tex., 1971. Resident in gen. practice, pediatrics Taiwan, China, 1960-66; staff physician Chaiyi (China) Christian Hosp., 1964-66; staff physician occupational medicine Air Am./Air Asia Inc., Southeastern Asia, 1966-69; intern Kenmore Mercy Hosp., Buffalo, 1973-74; staff physician USPHS Hosp., Clinton, Okla., 1974-76; staff physician dept. correction and rehab. Ga. Diagnostic Ctr., Jackson, 1977; attending physician Walton County Hosp., DeFuniak Springs, Fla., 1978-79; pres. Countryside Med. Clin., Inc., DeFuniak Springs, 1978-79; staff physician VA Med. Ctr., Bath, N.Y., 1979—; coord. Agt. Orange project VA Med. Ctr., Bath., 1979—, Ionizing Radiation program, 1979—. Author: Emotional Stress and Psycho-somatic Disorders, 1971, A Collection of 48 Selected Papers Published from 1980 to 1983, 1985; co-author: The Death of Chaing Kai-Shek, 1975, English-Chinese Aerospace Science/Technology Dictionary, 1977; contbr. articles to profl. jours. Chmn. bd. trustees Chaing Tzu Ming Edn. Foun., Bath, 1987; sustaining mem. Republic Nat. Com., Washington, 1986—; hon. fellow Truman Libr. Inst., Mo., 1976; mem. Am. Mus. Natural History, 1980—, The Smithsonian Assn., 1985—, U.S.-China People's Friendship Assn., 1975—, Soc. Asian Am. Culture Affairs. Served with Chinese Air Force, 1962-63. Named Hon. Prof. Heng Yang Med. Coll. (China), 1992. Mem. AMA, AIAA, APHA, Am. Coll. Physicians (assoc.), Am. Def. Preparedness Assn., Am. Chinese Med. Soc., Am. Acad. Family Physicians, Am. Naval Inst., Chinese Med. Assn., Aero. and Astronautical Soc. Republic of China, Fla. Med. Assn., Walton County Med. Soc., Aerospace Med. Assn., Nat. Geog. Soc., Acad. Polit. Sci., Air Force Assn., So. Tier Chinese Assn., Assn. for Asian Studies, VA Physician Assn., Planetary Soc., Nat. Space Soc., Air & Space Soc., Western Returned Student Assn. (China, hon.). Republican. Mem. Christian Ch.

HUBBARD, JOHN BARRY, lawyer, business consultant, banker; b. Sweetwater, Tex., Mar. 16, 1917; s. John Howard and Shirley (McCarty) H.; m. Virginia Marie Olsen, Dec. 10, 1943; children—Carol Ann (Mrs. Sam Houston Lane III), Virginia Sue Tarlton, Jean Ellen (Mrs. Jackie D. Warren), John Barry. BBA, U. Tex., 1939, LLB, 1940. Atty., former spl. agent U.S. dept. justice FBI, 1940-53; banker, 1953-80. Treas., bd. dirs. various civic orgns. Mem. Tex. Tarrant County bar Assns. Mem. Christian Ch. Home: Fort Worth Tex. Died Jan. 31, 1995.

HUBERT, BERNARD, bishop; b. Beloeil, Que., Can., June 1, 1929. Ed., U. Ottawa, Columbia U. Ordained priest Roman Catholic Ch., 1953; bishop of St. Jerome, 1971-77; coadjutor bishop Saint-Jean-de-Que., 1977-78; bishop St.-Jean-de-Que., now St.-Jean-Longueil, 1978-96; pres., Can. Conf. Catholic Bishops. Home: Lonqueuil Can Died Feb. 2, 1996.

HUCKER, CHARLES OSCAR, author, former Chinese studies educator; b. St. Louis, June 21, 1919; s. Edward Christian and Katie (Bond) H.; m. Myrl C. Henderson, Feb. 12, 1943. B.A. with high honors, U. Tex., 1941; Ph.D. with honors, U. Chgo., 1950; H.H.D. (hon.), Oakland U., 1974. Instr. U. Chgo., 1950-54, asst. prof., 1954-56; assoc. prof. U. Ariz., 1956-58, prof., 1958-61; prof. history and area studies Oakland U., Rochester, Mich., 1961-65; prof. Chinese and history U. Mich., Ann Arbor, 1965-83, prof. emeritus of Chinese, prof. emeritus of history, Williams emeritus prof., 1984—; chmn. dept. Far Eastern langs. and lits. U. Mich., 1965-71; Cons. U.S. Office Edn., 1960, 65, 66, Ford Found., 1962-63; mem. com. on studies Chinese civilization, chmn. subcom. polit. instns. Am. Council Learned Socs., 1963-69; cons. or vis. lectr. various colls. and univs.; mem. del. of Ming-Ch'ing historians to China from Am. Acad. Sci., 1979. Author: Chinese History: A Bibliographic Review, 1958, The Traditional Chinese State In Ming Times, 1961, China: A Critical Bibliography, 1962, The Censorial System of Ming China, 1966, Some Approaches to China's Past, 1973, China's Imperial Past, 1975, China to 1850: A Short History, 1978, The Ming Dynasty: Its Origins and Evolving Institutions, 1978, A Dictionary of Official Titles in Imperial China, 1985, (play) Mums, 1990, (with others) Chinese Thought and Institutions, 1957, Confucianism in Action, 1959, An Introduction to Chinese Civilization, 1973, Chinese Ways in Warfare, 1974, Dictionary of Ming Biography, 1976; Editor: Chinese Government in Ming Times: Seven Studies, 1969; Contbr.: articles to Ency. Americana, Ency. Britannica, Cambridge History of China, profl. jours. Served to maj. USAAC, 1942-46, PTO. Decorated Bronze Star;

postdoctoral fellow Rockefeller Found., 1952-54; sr. fellow NEH, 1968-69; honored by creation of Charles O. Hucker professorship in Dept. Asian Langs. and Cultures, U. Mich., 1986. Mem. Phi Beta Kappa, Phi Alpha Theta. Died Nov. 14, 1994.

HUDACEK, GEORGE C., tax specialist; b. Wheeling, W.Va., Nov. 24, 1942; s. Prince Albert and Angela Teresa (Lisak) H.; m. Judith M. Marsh, May 9, 1944; 1 child, Jessica R. BS, W.Va. U., 1965; AS, W.Va. No. U., 1991. Loan officer Budget Fin. Co., San Francisco, 1965-67; trust, tax officer Wells Fargo Bank, San Francisco, 1968-70, Bank of Calif., San Francisco, 1971-84; tax cons. Putney and Barton, Walnut Creek, Calif., 1984-85; pres., CEO Pay Less Taxes, Wheeling, W.Va., 1985-96; bd. dirs. Wheeling Cycle and Marine, Blakley and Buturla Engring., Caldwell, Idaho; pres. Black Diamond Investment Club, 1947-94; tax cons. Buckley, Inc., San Francisco, 1985-94. Comptr. no. W.Va. Coun. 4 Good Polotics, 1991-94; fund raiser United Way, 1985-95; v.p. bd. advisors St. Ladislaus Ch., 1990-95. Named Hon. Adm. Cheery River Navy of W.Va., 1990. Mem. Soc. Enrolled Agts., Polish, Athletic, Polit. Club (rec. sec. 1992-95), Bikers Am. (treas. 1992-95), Kain Club, Ind. Order Loyal Am., Jet Ski Club (treas. 1992-95), W.Va. U. Alumni Assn. (social chmn. Wheeling chpt. 1985-95). Roman Catholic. Avocations: investments, football, travel, politics. Home: Algonquin Ill. Died Dec. 4, 1996.

HUDSON, GEORGE ELBERT, retired research physicist; b. Pitts., Apr. 25, 1916; s. George Elbert, Jr. and Mary Jane (Wilson) H.; m. Olive Gallant, June 24, 1939 (div. Apr. 1979); children: George, Brian, Nancy; m. Jeanne M. Yacques, Sept. 19, 1984. B.S., George Washington U., 1938; Sc.M., Brown U., 1940, Ph.D., 1942. Vis. prof. physics Georgetown U., 1943-44; asso. prof. physics N.Y. U., 1946-49, prof. physics, 1949-63; physicist Taylor Model Basin, U.S. Navy, 1942-46; dir. research Smyth Research Assos., 1956-57; cons. Naval Ordnance Lab., 1957-59, Brookhaven Nat. Lab., 1958-61, Woods Hole Oceanographic Instn., 1959-61, Avco Corp., 1961-62, Nat. Bur. Standards, 1962-63; asst. chief radio physics div. Nat. Bur. Standards, Boulder, Colo., 1963-67; cons. time and frequency div. Inst. Basic Standards, Nat. Bur. Standards, 1967-70; sr. research cons. Naval Ordnance Lab., 1970-80; Adj. prof. physics Denver U., 1965-69. Contbr. articles to physics and math. profl. publs. Fellow Am. Phys. Soc., AAAS; mem. Washington Philos. Soc. (pres. 1973-74), Planetary Soc., Sigma Xi, Sigma Pi Sigma, Delta Tau Delta. Club: Cosmos (Washington).

HUDSON, HALBERT AUSTIN, JR., retired manufacturing engineer, consultant; b. Orange, Va., Dec. 20, 1923; s. Halbert Austin and Lillian Naomi (Cook) H.; m. Dorothy Alma Keilholz, Aug. 25, 1945; children: Janis Lee Hudson Bamberger, Paul Frederick. M in Engring., U. Cin., 1949. Registered profl. engr., Wis. Apprentice Cin. Milicron Co., 1942-49; signal engr. So. Ry. System, Knoxville, Tenn., 1950-53; indsl. engr., mech. mgr., project engring. mgr., tech. mgr. Procter & Gamble Co., Cin. and Green Bay, Wis., 1953-83; ret., 1983; ind. cons. engr. Green Bay, 1983—; v.p. Green Bay Water Commn., 1967-77. Scoutmaster Cin. area Boy Scouts Am., 1953-59; vol. driver elderly transport ARC, Green Bay, 1983-90, mem. sec. bd. dirs., 1986-88. Capt. U.S. Army, 1942-46, ETO. Decorated Bronze Star medal, Purple Heart medal, Combat Infantryman badge. Mem. NSPE, Assn. Energy Engrs. (chpt. pres. 1986-87), Green Bay Engring. Soc. (b.p. 1972), U. Cin. Alumni Assn., Infantry Officer Candidate Sch. Alumni Assn., Mil. Order of Purple Heart, DAV, 90th Infantry Divsn. Assn., Am. Legion, Vets. of the Battle of the Bulge, Kiwanis Golden K., Pi Tau Sigma. Methodist. Achievements include patent for a milling machine arbor vibration dampener. Deceased.

HUEBNER, GEORGE J., JR., environmental engineering executive; b. Detroit, Mich., Sept. 8, 1910. BS, U. Mich., 1932; DSc (hon.), Bucknell U., 1969. Lab. engr. engring divsn. Chrysler Corp., 1931-36; asst. chief engr. Plymouth divsn., 1936-39; asst. to dir. rsch. engring. divsn. Chrysler Corp., 1939-45, chief engr. rsch., 1945-52; exec. engr. Missile Br. Engring., 1952-53, exec. engr., rsch. engring. staff, 1953-64, dir. rsch., 1964-75. Author numerous pubs. Patentee in field. Fellow Soc. Automotive Engrs. (pres. 1975); mem. Nat. Acad. Scis., Sigma Xi. Died Oct. 4, 1996.

HUFFHINES, KATHY SCHULZ, film critic; b. Akron, Ohio, June 16, 1943; d. Frederick Charles and Nancy (Ayres) Schulz; m. Robert Huffhines (div. 1973). BA in English, Stanford U., 1965; MAT in English Edn., Harvard U., 1966; MA in English, Boston Coll., 1972. English tchr. Boston Coll., Chestnut Hill, Mass., 1968-80; film critc The Real Paper, 1980-81, The Cambridge Express, 1981-88; film writer Boston Herald, 1984-86; columnist Boston Phoenix, 1986-87; film critic Detroit Free Press, 1987—. Editor: Foreign Affairs: A Video Guide to Foreign Films, 1991. Mem. Nat. Soc. Film Critics.

HUFFMAN, GEORGE GARRETT, geology educator; b. Winterset, Iowa, Feb. 13, 1916; s. Walker Garrett and Leota Marie (Greenfield) H.; m. Jane Irene Avery, July 9, 1941; children—Randall Avery, Laurence Marshall, Janice Carol. B.A. with high distinction, U. Iowa, 1940, M.S., 1941; Ph.D. (Lydia Roberts fellow), Columbia, 1945. Geologist Texaco, Inc., Corpus Christi, Tex., 1943-46; faculty U. Okla., Norman, 1946—, prof. geology, 1955—, adviser, seminar dir. Bachelor LIberal Studies program, 1966-81; geologist Okla. Geol. Survey, summers 1949-82; vis. scholar Okla. Coll. Liberal Arts, 1967-68; cons. geologist Cities Service Co., 1957-63, Jet Oil, 1970. Author: Laboratory Syllabus in Physical Geology, 1955, 60, Laboratory Syllabus in Historical Geology, 1955; 6 Okla. Geol. Survey bulls. and guidebooks, Kan. Geol. Soc. Field Conf. guidebooks, 1960, 64. Recipient Outstanding Teaching award U. Okla., 1955; Lowden prize in geology. Fellow Geol. Soc. Am.; mem. Am. Assn. Petroleum Geologists, Phi Beta Kappa (pres. Okla. U. 1972-73), Sigma Xi (pres. Okla. U. 1958-59). Presbyn. (deacon 1954-57, trustee 1957-60, elder 1960-63). Club: Lion (pres. Norman 1968-69, zone chmn. 1969-70).

HUGGINS, CHARLES BRENTON, surgical educator; b. Halifax, N.S., Can., Sept. 22, 1901; s. Charles Edward and Bessie (Spencer) H.; m. Margaret Wellman, July 29, 1927; children: Charles Edward, Emily Wellman Huggins Fine. BA, Acadia U., 1920, DSc (hon.), 1946; MD, Harvard U., 1924; MSc, Yale U., 1947; DSc (hon.), Washington U., St. Louis, 1950, Leeds U., 1953, Turin U., 1957, Trinity Coll., 1965, U. Wales, 1967, U. Mich., 1968, Med. Coll. Ohio, 1973, Gustavus Adolphus Coll., 1975, Wilmington (Ohio) Coll., 1980, U. Louisville, 1980; LLD (hon.), U. Aberdeen, 1966, York U., Toronto, 1968, U. Calif., Berkeley, 1968; D of Pub. Service (hon.), George Washington U., 1967; D of Pub. Service (hon.) sigillum magnum, Bologna U., 1964. Intern in surgery U. Mich., 1924-26, instr. surgery, 1926-27; with U. Chgo., 1927—, instr. surgery, 1927-29, asst. prof., 1929-33, assoc. prof., 1933-36, prof. surgery, 1936—, dir. Ben May Lab. for Cancer Research, 1951-69, William B. Ogden Disting. Service prof., 1962—; chancellor Acadia U., Wolfville, N.S., 1972-79; Macewen lectr. U. Glasgow, 1958, Ravdin lectr., 1974, Powell lectr., Lucy Wortham James lectr., 1975, Robert V. Day lectr., 1975, Cartwright lectr., 1975. Trustee Worcester Found. Exptl. Biology; bd. govs. Weizmann Inst. Sci., Rehovot, Israel, 1973—. Decorated Order Pour le Mérite Germany; Order of The Sun Peru; recipient Nobel prize for medicine, 1966, Am. Urol. Assn. award, 1948, Francis Amory award, 1948, AMA Gold medals, 1936, 40, Société Internationale d'Urologie award, 1948, Am. Cancer Soc. award, 1953, Bertner award M.D. Anderson Hosp., 1953, Am. Pharm. Mfrs. Assn. award, 1953, Gold medal Am. Assn. Genito-Urinary Surgeons, 1955, Borden award Assn. Am. Med. Colls., 1955, Comfort Crookshank award Middlesex Hosp., London, 1957, Cameron prize Edinburg U., 1958, Valentine prize N.Y. Acad. Medicine, 1962, Hunter award Am. Therapeutic Soc., 1962, Lasker award for med. research, 1963, Gold medal Virchow Soc., 1964, Laurea award Am. Urol. Assn., 1966, Gold medal Worshipful Soc. Apothecaries of London, 1966, Gairdner award Toronto, 1966, Chgo. Med. Soc. award, 1967, Centennial medal Acadia U., 1967, Hamilton award Ill. Med. Soc., 1967, Bigelow medal Boston Surg. Soc., 1967, Disting. Service award Am. Soc. Abdominal Surgeons, 1972, Sheen award AMA, 1970, Sesquicentennial Commemorative award Nat. Library of Medicine, 1986; Charles Mickle fellow, 1958. Fellow ACS (hon.), Royal Coll. Surgeons Can. (hon.), Royal Coll. Surgeons Scotland (hon.), Royal Coll. Surgeons England (hon.), Royal Soc. Edinburgh (hon.), La Academia Nacional de Medicina (Mexico, hon.); mem. NAS (Charles L. Meyer award for cancer research 1943), Am. Philos Soc. (Franklin medal 1985), Am. Assn. Cancer Rsch., Can. Med. Assn. (hon.), Alpha Omega Alpha. Died Jan. 12, 1997.

HUGGINS, WILLIAM See **BRETT, (PETER) JEREMY**

HUGHES, EDWARD HUNTER, former magazine editor; b. Ashland, Ky., Aug. 20, 1921; s. Paul Jones and Jessie Lee (Owens) H.; m. Mary J. Stanford, Jan. 15, 1955 (dec.); m. Penelope Maugham, Aug. 25, 1975. A.B., Centre Coll. Ky., 1943; M.A., Harvard, 1947. Reporter Washington bur. Wall Street Jour., N.Y.C., 1947-50, reporter Europe, Middle East and Africa areas, 1950-53, fgn. editor, 1953-54; chief Africa bur. Time Inc., N.Y.C., 1954-56, chief Fed. Republic of Germany and Ea. Europe burs., 1956-59, writer, 1959-62, sr. editor, 1962-68, chief Middle East bur., 1968-70. Served with AUS., 1944-45, ETO. Home: London Eng. Died July 25, 1992.

HUGHES, JOHN EDWARD, sociology educator; b. Phila., Mar. 1, 1922; s. John Thomas and Ann Pauline (Garrity) H.; m. Gertrude Nash, Sept. 22, 1945 (dec. Oct. 1959); children—Mary Susan Wilson-Hughes, Irene A. Hughes Murdock, Jennifer. B.A., Temple U., 1948; M.A., U. Pa., 1949, Ph.D., 1960. Instr. sociology U. Pa., 1949-53; asst. prof. sociology U. Notre Dame, 1953-61; Assoc. prof. Villanova U., 1961-67, prof., 1967-86, chmn. dept., 1961-86, prof. emeritus, 1986-95. Served with U.S. Army, 1943-45. Decorated Purple Heart, Bronze Star. Fellow Am. Sociol. Soc.; mem. Am. Catholic Sociol. Soc. (pres. 1961), Pa. Sociol. Soc. (pres. 1968). Home: Bryn Mawr Pa. DIed Jan. 3, 1995.

HULL, EDWARD WHALEY SEABROOK, freelance writer, consultant; b. Washington, Mar. 10, 1923; s. Edward Seabrook III and Hortense Carver (Marshall) H.; m. Nellie Phinizy Fortson, June 25, 1944; children: Edward, John, Thomas, Nellie Phinizy Hull Price. Student, Union Coll., Schenectady, 1939-42; M Marine Affairs, U. R.I., 1970; PhD in Marine Sci., U. S.C., 1987. Chief copy boy Times-Herald, Washington, 1947; corr. Washington Bur., McGraw-Hill, 1948-51; editor Whaley-Eaton Fgn. Letter, Washington, 1951-53; bur. chief McGraw-Hill World News, London, 1954-56; assoc. editor Missiles & Rockets mag., Washington, 1956-58; ea. rep. Diversey Engring., Inc., Washington, 1958-60; editor, pres., dir. Nautilus Press, Inc., Washington, 1960-73; pres., dir. Intel, Inc., Washington, 1964-67; editor, pub. Geo-Marine Technology, 1964-67, Geo Marine Tech., Washington, 1964-67; cons. Washington, S.C., 1969-85; freelance writer, Yonges Island, S.C., 1987—; dir. S.C. Writers Workshop, Columbia and Charleston, 1991-92. Author: Rocket to the Moon, 1958, The Bountiful Sea, 1964; editor: Peenemunde to Canaveral (D.K. Kuzel), 1962; editor Pegasus, 1995—; contbr. numerous articles on rocketry, space flight, oceanography, also others, to profl. publs. 1st lt. USMCR, 1942-45, PTO. Decorated Air medal; fellow Woodrow Wilson Internat. Ctr. for Scholars, 1970-71. Mem. Nature Conservancy, Appalachian Trail Conf., Wilson Ctr. Assocs. (assoc.), Nat. Press Club (Washington), Poetry Soc. of S.C. (exec. bd. 1994-96 dir. 1994-96). Democrat. Episcopalian. Avocations: photography, canoeing, woodworking, fishing, orchids.

HUMBER, WILBUR JAMES, psychologist; b. Winnipeg, Man., Can., June 21, 1911; came to U.S., 1922; s. Arthur W. and Annie Humber; m. Jean Adriansen, May 25, 1946; children: Philip, Scott, Michael. BA, Macalester Coll., 1930; MA, U. Chgo., 1937; PhD, U. Minn., 1942. Diplomate clin. psychology. Dean Kalamazoo (Mich.) Coll., 1941-43; prof. Lawrence U., Appleton, Wis., 1943-46; psychologist Rohrer, Hibler & Replogle, Chgo., 1947-52; sr. ptnr. Humber, Mundie & McClary, Milw., 1952—; bd. dirs. Hopkins Savs. & Loan, Milw., Pope Sci. Corp., Menomonee Falls, Wis. Co-author: Development of Human Behavior, 1951, Introduction to Social Psychology, 1968; editl. bd. Jour. of Consultation. Bd. dirs. Lakeside Children Ctr., Milw., 1966-86; pres. Wis. Mental Health Assn., Milw., 1962-63. Fellow APA, N.Y. Acad. Sci., AAAS; mem. Wis. Psychol. Assn. (founder, 1st pres., Disting. Contbn. award 1984), Milw. Club, Milw. Country Club. Congregationalist. Avocations: tennis, writing, travel. Died Jan. 22, 1998.

HUMPHREY, JOHN SPARKMAN, insurance company executive; b. Birmingham, Ala., Sept. 15, 1941; s. Roosevelt and Doris (Camp) H.; m. Doris Jane Davenport, Mar. 29, 1969; children: Heather Elaine, Holly Lynn (dec.). BSBA, U. Tenn., 1963. Claims rep. Liberty Mut. Ins. Cos., Nashville, 1965-69; claims supr. Liberty Mut. Ins. Cos., Atlanta, 1970-74; regional claims mgr. Am. Res. Ins. Brokers, Atlanta, 1974-79; claims cons. Bellefonte Reins. Co., Cin., 1980-83, asst. v.p., 1983-84, v.p., 1984-86; asst. v.p. Balis and Co., Inc.-Reins., Phila., 1986-88, v.p., 1988-93. With USCGR, 1964-70. Mem. Pa. Def. Inst., Escess-Surplus Lines Claim Assn. Presbyterian. Home: Philadelphia Pa. Died Mar. 29, 1993.

HUNGERFORD, HERBERT EUGENE, nuclear engineering educator; b. Hartford, Conn., Oct. 3, 1918; s. Herbert Eugene and Doris (Emmons) H.; m. Edythe Lugene Green, Nov. 4, 1949. B.S. in Physics, Trinity Coll., Hartford, 1941; M.S. in Physics, U. Ala., 1949; Ph.D. in Nuclear Engring., Purdue U., 1964; part-time grad. student, U. Tenn., 1951-55, Wayne State U., 1956-61. Tchr. sci. Brent Sch., Baguio, Philippines, 1941; tchr. math. Choate Sch., 1945-46; head physics dept. Marion Mil. Inst., 1946-48; grad. instr. U. Ala., 1948-49; physicist Oak Ridge Nat. Lab., 1950-55; shielding specialist, head shielding and health physics sect. Atomic Power Devel. Assocs., 1955-62; research assoc. Purdue U., 1963-64, assoc. prof., 1964-68, prof. nuclear engring., 1968-83; prof. emeritus, 1983—; on leave Argonne Nat. Lab., 1977-78; adj. prof. mech. engring. Fla. Inst. Tech., 1984-91; cons. in field; v.p., sec., bd. dirs. Hungerford Nuclear, Inc., Vero Beach, Fla., 1984-92; sci. columnist Vero Beach Sun newspaper, 1993-94. Author chpts. in books, articles. Prisoner of War, 1941-45. Mem. Am. Nuclear Soc. (sec. shielding and dosimetry div. 1960-62, div. vice chmn. 1969-70, div. chmn. 1970-71, mem. standards com. 1959-82, Presdl. citation for meritorious svc. 1993), Am. Phys. Soc., Lafayette Organ Soc. (pres. 1971-72), Amateur Organists Assn. Internat., Health Physics Soc., Am. Assn. Physics Tchrs., Kiwanis (bd. dirs. 1966-68, Presdl. citation 1970), Sigma Xi, Sigma Pi Sigma. Episcopalian (vestryman 1965-68). Club: Kiwanis (dir.) (1966-68). Achievements include invention of lattice model stochastic radiation transp.; pioneering use of serpentine and calcium borate as high temperature shield materials. Died June 13, 1996.

HUNT, CHARLES BUTLER, geologist; b. West Point, N.Y., Aug. 9, 1906; s. Irvin Leland and Annie (Butler) H.; m. Alice Parker, Oct. 20, 1930; children: Eugene Parker, Anne Butler Hunt Casimiro. AB, Colgate U., 1928; postgrad., Yale U., 1928-30. With U.S. Geol. Survey, 1930-53, 55-61; prof. geography Johns Hopkins

U., Balt., 1961-73; pvt. practice Salt Lake City, 1973—; exec. dir. Am. Geol. Inst., 1953-55; mem. adv. panel earth sci. div. NSF, 1960-63, chmn., 1962-63, mem. divisional com. math. and phys. sci., 1964-65; vis. prof. N.Mex. State U., 1973-74; vis. scholar U. Utah. Author: (descriptive geology texts) Mt. Taylor New Mexico, 1938, Pike Co., Kentucky, 1938, Henry Mountains, Utah, 1953, Colorado Plateau, 1956, La Sal Mountains, Utah, 1958, Colorado River, 1968, Death Valley, California, 1968; (textbooks) Physiography of the United States, 1967, Natural Regions of the United States and Canada, 1974, Surficial deposits of the United States, 1986; editor G.K. Gilbert field notes about Lake Bonneville, 1982, about the Henry Mtns., Utah, 1988; also articles on storage nuclear wastes, historical archeology of tin cans and bottles, military geology in WW II. Mem. Phi Beta Kappa, Sigma Xi. Home: Gibson Island Md. Died Sept. 3, 1997.

HUNT, FRANK BOULDIN, architect, water color artist; b. Morrill County, Nebr., July 19, 1915; s. Frank Neal and Sylvia Sybil (Ball) H.; m. Isabel Jean Phillips, Sept. 6, 1950; m. Donna Henderson Thomas, Dec. 27, 1955. Student, U. Nebr., 1934-35, U. Calif., Berkeley, 1937-38. Draftsman and designer firms in Calif., 1938-42, 46-48; partner Kitchen and Hunt (Architects), San Francisco, 1948-62; pres. Kitchen and Hunt (Architects), 1962-73, Hunt and Co. (Architects), San Francisco, 1973-75; dir. Hunt and Co. (Architects), 1975-81; v.p., dir. Kennedy/Jenks Engrs., San Francisco, 1975-86, Ecker Co., San Francisco, 1966-82. Prin. works include library expansion, residence halls, Crocker Nuclear Lab. at U. Calif., Davis, 1954-65, facilities for VIII Olympic Winter Games, Squaw Valley, Calif., 1956-60; cons.: U.S. Olympic Tng. Center, 1978-80; facilities for Pacific No. Region Eastman Kodak Co., San Francisco, 1956-58, water treatment plants, Marin County (Calif.) Municipal Water Dist., 1957-73; F.B. Hunt Residence, 1958-60; mausoleums at Mountain View Cemetery, Oakland, Calif., 1958-60, 74-76, 80-81; Donner Animal Bioradiol. Lab, Lawrence Berkeley (Calif.) Lab, 1961-64, 76; music classroom bldg., Calif. State U., Hayward, 1963-66, Reno-Sparks (Nev.) Joint Water Pollution Control plant, 1965-67, 77-82, San Francisco Bay Area Rapid Transit Dist. stas. at North Berkeley, Oakland West, South Hayward, Union City, Fremont, 1965-73, Santa Clara County (Calif.) water treatment plants and related facilities, 1966-73, Maintenance and Ops. Center, United Air Lines, San Francisco Internat. Airport, 1969-72, 76-86, Pacific No. Region distbn. center, Eastman Kodak Co., San Ramon, Calif., 1967-69, Kern County (Calif.) water treatment plant, 1973-76, Central Marin San. Agy. Treatment Plant, San Rafael, Calif., 1980-84, Palace Hotel rehab., San Francisco, 1979-85. Served to lt. USNR, 1942-46. Recipient numerous design awards; archtl. models of Blyth Olmpic Arena, F.B. Hunt residence, related material at Mus. Calif., Oakland. Fellow AIA; mem. Eastbay Watercolor Soc., Phi Gamma Delta. Died Jan. 22, 1997.

HUNT, JACOB TATE, special education educator emeritus; b. Sweetwater, Tenn., Aug. 22, 1916; s. Samuel Lon and Grace Viola (Beals) H.; m. Harriet Elizabeth Durnell, June 17, 1944; 1 child, Steven Craig. B.A., Maryville (Tenn.) Coll., 1938; M.S., U. Tenn., 1941; Ph.D., U. Calif. at Berkeley, 1950; Ford Found. postdoctoral fellow, U. Ill., 1956-57. Tchr. pub. schs. Tenn., 1938-40, Wash., 1940-42; instr. U. Calif. at Berkeley, 1946-48; asst. prof. Western Res. U., 1948-51; asst., then asso. prof. U. N.C., 1951-57; prof. U. Ariz., 1957-64, U. Wash., 1964-68; prof. spl. edn., chmn. div. exceptional children U. Ga., 1968-84, prof. emeritus, 1984; summer vis. prof. U. Wash., 1952, 63, 64, U. Ill., 1956, U. Colo., 1960, 61, U. Calif. at Berkeley, 1962; Mem. study commn. exceptional children Western Interstate Commn. Higher Edn., 1958-60; mem. Ga. Coordinating Com. Exceptional Children, 1969-96; cons. Saguaro Sch. Asthmatic Children, United Cerebral Palsy Assn., HEW. Author: Mentally Retarded Children, 1969; editor High Sch. Jour, 1952-56, Rev. Edn. Research, 1965-69, Education and Training of the Mentally Retarded, 1978-83; asso. editor Exceptional Children, Jour. Spl. Edn., Scientia Paedagogica Experimentalis, 1967-84. Bd. dirs. Pima Assn. Mental Health, 1960-64. Served with USNR, 1942-45. Grantee edn. handicapped U.S. Office Edn., 1964-77. Mem. Am. Ednl. Research Assn. (exec. com. 1959-64, chmn. editorial com. 1965-69), Council Exceptional Children (bd. dirs. 1978-83, editorial com. 1978-83), Am. Psychol. Assn., Internat. Reading Assn., Phi Kappa Phi, Phi Delta Kappa. Presbyterian. Died Aug. 3, 1996.

HURD, CUTHBERT C., computer company executive, mathematician; b. Estherville, Iowa, Apr. 5, 1911; s. Harland Corwin and Olive Grace (Long) H.; m. Bettie Jane Mills, June 20, 1941; children: Steven, Diana, Susan, Elizabeth, Victoria. A.B., Drake U., 1932, LL.D., 1967; M.S., Iowa State Coll., 1934; Ph.D., U. Ill., 1936. Asst. prof. math. Mich. State Coll., 1936-42; dean Allegheny Coll., 1945-47; tech. research head Union Carbide & Carbon Corp., Oak Ridge, 1947-49; cons.; dir. applied sci. dept. IBM, 1949-53, dir. applied sci. div., 1953-55, dir. electronic data processing machines, 1955-56, dir. automation research, 1956-60, dir. control systems, 1961-62, cons., 1962-83; chmn. bd. Computer Usage Co., Inc., N.Y.C., 1962-74; chmn. Solar Energy Research, 1974-76, Cuthbert Hurd Assos., 1974, Picodyne Corp., 1978-83, Quintus Computer Systems, 1984-89, Nu Thena Corp., 1990-92; chmn. sci. bd. Cambridge Rsch. Assocs., 1992-96; chief scientist Northpoint Software Ventures, Inc., 1993-96; Mem. adv. com. Ctr. Computer Scis. and Tech., Inst. Applied Tech., Nat. Bur. Standards; mem. computation com. NRC; chmn. computer sci. adv. com. Stanford U.; mem. adv. coun. to depts. econs. and sociology Princeton U.; vis. scholar Stanford U., 1986-96; chmn. sci. bd. Cambridge Rsch. Assocs., 1992-96; computer pioneer IEEE, 1988. Trustee Drake U.; mem. devel. bd., life fellow Mass. Inst. Tech. Served as lt. comdr. USCGR, 1942-45. Fellow AAAS; mem. Inst. Mgmt. Scis. (past v.p., founder), Am. Math. Soc., Am. Meteorol. Soc., Biometric Soc., Am. Soc. Quality Control, Am. Statis. Assn., Assn. Computing Machinery (council), Econometric Soc., English Speaking Union, Indsl. Math. Soc., Inst. Math. Statistics, Math. Assn. Am. (com. on profl. opportunities), N.Y. Acad. Sci., Operations Research Soc. Am., Soc. Advancement Gen. Systems Theory, Soc. Indsl. and Applied Math., Phi Beta Kappa, Sigma Xi, Phi Kappa Phi. Clubs: University (N.Y.C.), Metropolitan (N.Y.C.), Univ. (N.Y.C.); Stanford Faculty. Home: Portola Valley Calif.

HURST, JAMES WILLARD, law educator; b. Rockford, Ill., Oct. 6, 1910; s. James Dominick and Mabel (Weinert) H.; m. Frances Wilson, Aug. 20, 1941; children: Thomas Robert, Mary Deborah. A.B., Williams Coll., 1932, LL.D., 1974; LL.B., Harvard U., 1935, research fellow, 1935-36; M.A., Cambridge (Eng.) U., 1967; LL.D., U. Fla., 1980, Ripon Coll., 1981. Bar: Ill. 1936, Wis. 1951. Law clk. Justice Brandeis, U.S. Supreme Ct., Oct. term, 1936; instr. law U. Wis., 1937-38, asst. prof., 1938-41, asso. prof., 1941-46, prof. law, 1946-97; vis. prof summer sessions law schs. Northwestern, 1939, 40, Stanford, 1950, 62, U. Utah, 1952, U. Fla., 1978; Pitt prof. Am. history and instns. U. Cambridge, Eng., 1967-68, fellow Trinity Hall, 1967-68. Author: books pertaining to law including The Law Makers, 1950, Law and the Conditions of Freedom, 1956, Law and Social Process in U.S. History, 1960, Law and Economic Growth, 1964, Justice Holmes on Legal History, 1964, The Legitimacy of the Business Corporation, 1970, The Law of Treason in the United States, 1971, A Legal History of Money in the United States, 1973, Law and Social Order in the United States, 1977, Law and Markets in U.S. History, 1982, Dealing with Statutes, 1982; contbr. to books pertaining to law including Supreme Court and Supreme Law, 1954, Law in American History (Fleming and Bailyn), 1971; also various law revs. Staff gen. counsel's office Bd. Econ. Warfare, 1942-43. Served as lt. USNR, 1943-46. Mem. Am. Philos. Soc., Wis. Hist. Soc., Am. Acad. Arts and Scis, Phi Beta Kappa, Phi Delta Phi, Order of Coif. Democrat. Conglist. Home: Madison Wis. Died June 18, 1997.

HUSTON, JOHN ALBERT, retired manufacturing company executive; b. Birmingham, Mich., May 4, 1920; s. Joseph Clark and Clara Amanda (Maynard) H.; m. Mary McClellan Barnhardt, Oct. 7, 1950; children: John A., Margaret G., James M. (dec.). A.B., U. Mich., 1941, J.D., 1947. Bar: N.Y. 1948. With firm Chadbourne, Parke, Whiteside & Wolff (and predecessors), N.Y.C., 1947-59; with Sperry Gyroscope Co. (div. Sperry Corp.), N.Y.C., 1959-68; v.p. legal Sperry Gyroscope Co. (div. Sperry Corp.), 1963-68; asst. gen. counsel Sperry Corp., 1968-71, v.p. law, 1971-79, sr. v.p. law, 1979-81, sr. v.p., gen. counsel, 1981-85. Trustee Devereux Found., 1974-84; bd. dirs. Charles E. Culpeper Found., 1978-92, Mid. Atlantic Legal Found., 1979-84, Lincoln Ctr. Inst., 1982-95. With AUS, 1942-45. Mem. Phi Beta Kappa, Order of Coif. Clubs: N.Y. Athletic.

HUTCHENS, JOHN OLIVER, physiologist, educator; b. Noblesville, Ind., Nov. 8, 1914; s. Bernayse E. and Della M. (Moore) H.; m. Eleanore M. Mothersill, June 3, 1939; children: Margaret A., Judith M., Helen Louise. A.B., Butler U., 1936; Ph.D., Johns Hopkins U., 1939. Nat. research fellow biol. sci., dept. biol. chemistry Harvard Med. Sch., 1939-40; Johnston scholar biology Johns Hopkins U., 1940-41; instr. physiology U. Chgo., 1941, asst. prof. physiology, 1946, asso. prof., 1946-52, prof., 1952-73, chmn. dept., 1946-58, dir. toxicity lab., 1946-48, prof. pharmacology and physiology, 1972-82, prof. emeritus, 1982-93, assoc. dir. toxicity lab., 1972-73, dir. toxicity lab., 1973-80; temp. sci. liaison officer Office Naval Research, London, 1954; cons.-examiner North Central Assn. Colls. and Secondary Schs., 1967-93. Contbg. author: Handbook of Biochemistry, 1968. Mem. corp. Marine Biol. Lab. Capt. AUS, 1944-46. Fellow AAAS, N.Y. Acad. Scis.; mem. AAUP, Biochem. Soc. (Britain), Soc. Gen. Physiologists, Chem. Warfare Assn., Am. Physiol. Soc., Soc. Exptl. Biology and Medicine, Quadrangle Club, Phi Beta Kappa, Sigma Xi, Phi Kappa Phi, Gamma Alpha, Phi Eta Sigma. Methodist. Home: Corpus Christi Tex. Died May 19, 1993; interred Crown Hill Cemetary, Indpls., Ind.

HUTCHESON, HAROLD LEO, retired educator; b. Castana, Iowa, Sept. 26, 1916; s. Leslie G. and Sadie (Moss) H.; m. Hazel Z. Moore, Dec. 11, 1943; children: Gayle Jolon, Rex Allison; m. 2d, Dolores J. Rock, May 12, 1984. B.A., Nebr. State Coll., 1948; M.A., U. Nebr., 1954, D.Ed., 1957. High sch. sci. tchr. Oakdale, Nebr., 1948-49; prin. high schs., 1949-50; supt. schs. Atkinson, Nebr., 1951-55; instr. sch. adminstrn. U. Nebr., 1955-57; dir. tchr. edn. Nebr. State Coll., Peru, 1957-59; v.p. for devel. and services, dean Coll. Edn., U. Wis., Platteville, 1959-72; vice chancellor U. Wis., 1972-76, prof., 1976-86; Inaugurated project PITCH, program tng. tchrs. for culturally deprived children, 1963; planned coll. campus Richland Center, Wis., 1965; inaugurated Assn. for Excellence, 1971; mem. Wis. Sch. Health Council, 1965-92, Wis. Vocat. Edn. Adv. Council, 1963-92. Pres. city council, Peru, 1958; Exec. bd. Wis. PTA, 1965-92; chmn. Platteville Community Chest, 1963; First pres. bd. dirs. Grant County (Wis.) Guidance Center, 1960-62; bd. dirs. U.S. Grant council Boy Scouts Am. Served as officer C.E. AUS, 1941-46. Recipient Patriotic Civilian Ser. citation U.S. Army, 1973. Mem. Phi Eta Sigma, Alpha Psi Omega, Phi Kappa Phi, Pi Gamma Mu, Pi Kappa Delta, Lambda Delta Lambda, Kappa Delta Pi. Home: Platteville Wis. Died Dec. 13, 1992.

HUTCHINSON, GEORGE EVELYN, biology and zoology educator; b. Cambridge, Eng., Jan. 30, 1903; came to U.S., 1928; naturalized, 1941; s. Arthur and Evaline D. (Shipley) H. Student, Greshams Sch., Holt Norfolk, U. Cambridge, Eng. Sr. lectr. zoology U. Witwatersrand, Republic of South Africa, 1926-28; instr. advancing to Sterling prof. zoology Yale U., 1928—; cons. in biogeochemistry Am. Mus. Natural History, N.Y.C., 1946—. Author: The Clear Mirror, 1936, The Itinerant Ivory Tower, 1953, The Enchanted Voyage and Other Studies, 1962, The Kindly Fruits of the Earth, 1979; also numerous sci. papers on aquatic insects, limnology, biogeochemistry, ecological and evolutionary theory. Recipient Daniel Giraud Elliot Medal, NAS, 1984.

HUTSON, JEAN BLACKWELL (MRS. JOHN O. HUTSON), librarian; b. Summerfield, Fla., Sept. 7, 1914; d. Paul Douglass and Sarah Frances (Myers) Blackwell; m. John O. Hutson, June 3, 1950 (dec. 1957); 1 child, Jean. Student, U. Mich., 1931-34; B.A., Barnard Coll., 1935; B.S., Columbia U., 1936; L.H.D. (hon.), King Meml. Coll., Columbia, S.C., 1977. Librarian N.Y. Pub. Library, 1936-84; br. librarian Woodstock Br., 1948; curator Schomburg Collection, 1948-72; chief Schomburg Center for Research in Black Culture, 1972-80, asst. dir. collection mgmt. and devel., 1980-84; ret., 1984; lectr. CCNY, 1962-70, adj. asso. prof., 1970-73; asst. librarian U. Ghana, 1964-65; lectr. Columbia Tchrs. Coll., 1969. Pres. Harlem Cultural Council, 1984—; sec. bd. dirs. Harlem Neighborhoods Assn.; mem. Jack and Jill Found.; mem. adv. bd. Martin Luther King Ctr., 1975—; vice chmn. bd. dirs. Cen. Harlem Meals on Wheels, 1986—. Recipient Camp Minisink community service award, 1952, Who's Who award 7th Ave. Assn., 1954, various awards Assn. for Study Negro Life and History, 1955, 66, 71, Distinguished Service award Caucus of Black Legislators N.Y. State, 1971, Community Service award Kappa Omicrom chpt. Omega Psi Phi, 1976, Lewis-Schuyler-Wheatley Arts and Letters award Delta Sigma Theta, 1976. Mem. ALA, NAACP, Nat. Urban League Guild, Mcpl. Art Soc., African Studies Assn., Delta Sigma Theta.

HYER, WILLIAM GLASSER THOMAS, fine arts company executive; b. Denver, July 12, 1921; s. John Walter and Margurite Harriet (Glasser) H.; m. Nancy Eleanor Pinkett, June 27, 1946; children: Sally Thomas, Richard Pinkett Glasser. Student, U. Denver, 1939-41; AB, Stanford U., 1944; GJ, Northwestern U., Evanston, Ill., 1946. Radio, tv producer TV Airshows, Chgo., 1946-55; v.p., dir. programming Foote, Cone & Belding, Chgo., 1955-71; pres. Fine Arts Internat., Ltd., Chgo., 1971—. Bd. govs. Nat. Acad. TV Arts & Scis., Chgo., 1969-71; bd. dirs. ARC, Chgo., 1969-71; trustee Latin Sch. of Chgo., 1961-67; pres. Old Town Triangle Assn., 1963, Menomonee Club for Boys and Girls, Chgo., 1961. Mem. Broadcast Pioneers (life), Soc. Profl. Journalists, Chgo. Hist. Soc. (life), Art Inst. Chgo. (life), Newberry Libr. (assoc.), Saddle and Cycle Club. Avocations: reading, writing, fine woodworking, photography. Deceased.

IBUKA, MASARU, electronics executive; b. Nikko, Japan, Apr. 11, 1908. BS, Waseda U., Tokyo, DSc (hon.), 1979; DSc (hon.), Brown U., 1994; HHD (hon.), Mindanao State U., Marawi City, The Philippines, 1982. Sr. mng. dir., founder Tokyo Tsushin Kogyo K.K. (former name of Sony Corp.), Tokyo, 1946; pres. Tokyo Tsushin Kogyo K.K. (name changed to Sony Corp. 1958), Tokyo, 1950-71; chmn. Sony Corp., Tokyo, 1971-76, hon. chmn., 1976-94, chief tech. advisor, 1994—; lifetime trustee Japan Com. Econs. Devel., 1967—; chmn. The Railway Tech. Research Inst., 1987—. Inventor modulated light transmission system, 1933. Chmn. bd. Early Devl. Assn., 1969—. Recipient Medal of Honor with Blue Ribbon, His Majesty Emperor of Japan, 1960, First Class Order of Sacred Treas., 1978 First Class Order of Rising Sun with Grand Cordon, 1986; named Comdr. First Class of Royal Order of Polar Star, His Majesty King of Sweden, 1986; designated Person of Cultural Merits of the Japanese Govt., 1989, Order of Cultural Merits, 1992. Fellow IEEE (life, Founders medal); mem. Royal Swedish Acad. Engring. Scis. (fgn.), Nat. Acad. Engring. (fgn.

assoc.), Japan Inst. Invention and Innovation (pres. 1972-91), Japan Audio Soc. (pres. 1979—).

ICELAND, WILLIAM FREDERICK, engineering consultant; b. N.Y.C., Sept. 29, 1924; m. Mildred U., Feb. 1, 1947; children: Stanley Allen, Edward Harold. BEE, NYU, 1949. Sr. engr. Fed. Telecommunications Labs., Nutley, N.J., 1949-54; sr. rsch. specialist Air Reduction Co., Union, N.J., 1954-63, Rockwell Internat., Downey, Calif., 1963-91; engr. cons. S.I. Ent., Los Alamitos, Calif., 1991-95; chmn. and guest speaker various tech. confs. Contbr. articles to profl. jours.; 18 patents in electronics, lasers and composite material joining. With U.S. Army, 1943-45. Mem. Am. Welding Soc. (past chmn., Dist. Merit Cert. award 1983), Toastmasters Internat., Rockwell Mgmt. Assn. (exceptional svc. award 1973). Avocations: music, aerobics. Home: Los Alamitos Calif. Died Jan. 12, 1995.

IDLER, DAVID RICHARD, biochemist, marine scientist, educator; b. Winnipeg, Man., Can., Mar. 13, 1923; s. Ernest and Alice (Lydon) I.; m. Myrtle Mary Betteridge, Dec. 12, 1956; children: Louise, Mark. BA, U. B.C., Vancouver, 1949, MA, 1950; PhD, U. Wis., 1953; DSc (hon.), U. Guelph, 1987. With Fisheries Research Bd. of Can., 1953-71; dir., investigator in charge of steroid biochemistry Halifax (N.S.) Lab., 1961-69; Atlantic regional dir. research Halifax (N.S.) Lab., Halifax, 1969-71; dir. Marine Sci. Research Lab.; dir., prof. biochemistry Meml. U. Nfld., St. John's, 1971-87, J.L. Paton research prof., prof. biochemistry, 1987-95, rsch. prof., 1995—; mem. editorial bd. Steroids, 1963—, Gen. and Comparative Endocrinology, 1966-92, Endocrine Rsch. Comms., 1974—, Can. Jour. Zoology, 1979-82; mem. bd. corr. editors Jour. Steroid Biochemistry, 1981-92; mem. Fisheries Res. Bd. Can., 1972-75, Can. Nat. Sportsman's Fund Grants Com., 1981-84; chmn. bd. dirs. Bay d'Espor Salmon Hatchery Ltd., 1984-89; mem. Fisheries Lic. Appeals Bd., Nfld., 1994—. Editor: Steroids in Nonmammalian Vertebrates, 1982; mem. editl. bd. Steroids, 1963—, Gen. and Comparative Endocrinology, 1966-92, Endocrine Rsch. Comms., 1974—, Can. Jour. Zoology, 1979-82; mem. bd. corr. editors Jour. Steroid Biochemistry, 1981-92; contbr. articles to some 250 publs. With RCAF, 1942-45. Decorated DFC. Fellow Royal Soc. Can.; mem. AAAS, European Soc. Comparative Endocrinologists (founding), Can. Biochem. Soc., Zool. Edn. Trust (pres. 1987-88), Am. Chem. Soc., Am. Zool. Soc., Endocrine Soc., N.Y. Acad. Scis. Died Dec. 21, 1996.

IFILL, O. URCILLE, religious organization administrator. Gen. sec. A. M. E. Ch., Phila.

IGASAKI, MASAO, JR., retired utilities company executive, controller; b. Los Angeles, May 24, 1925; s. Masao and Aiko (Kamayatsu) I.; m. Grace Kushino, June 5, 1948; children: David, Paul. B.S. in Bus. Adminstrn., Northwestern U., 1949; M.B.A., U. Chgo., 1963. C.P.A., Ill. With Peoples Gas Light & Coke Co., Chgo., 1949-87; auditor Peoples Gas Light & Coke Co., 1966-69, asst. v.p., asst. controller, 1969-70, asst. v.p., 1970-76, asst. v.p., controller, 1976-77, v.p., controller, 1977-81, v.p., 1981-87; v.p., controller Peoples Energy Corp., 1981-87. Scoutmaster, Boy Scouts Am., 1964-67; trustee Mt. Sinai Hosp., Chgo., 1980-87; bd. dirs. Chgo. Civic Fedn., 1982-87; bd. govs. Chgo. Heart Assn., 1984-87. Served with U.S. Army 1944-46. Mem. United Ch. Christ. Home: San Diego Calif. Died Feb. 20, 1996; interred El Camino Memorial Park.

IGNATOW, DAVID, poet; b. Bklyn., Feb. 7, 1914; s. Max and Yetta (Wilkenfeld) I.; m. Rose Graubart, July 20, 1940; children: David, Yaedi. Ed. pub. schs., Bklyn.; DLitt (hon.), L.I. U., 1987. Assoc. editor Am. Scene mag., 1935-37; lit. arts editor N.Y. Analytic, 1937; editor Beloit (Wis.) Poetry Jour., 1949-59; poetry editor The Nation, 1962-63; guest editor Chelsea, N.Y., 1962; co-editor, 1968; editor-at-large Am. Poetry Rev., 1973-76; instr. poetry workshop New Sch. Social Research, N.Y.C., 1964; vis. lectr. U. Ky., 1965-66; lectr. English, U. Kans., 1966—; vis. lectr. Vassar Coll., 1967-68; adj. prof. Southampton Coll. of L.I. U., 1967-68; also Columbia poet-in-residence York Coll., CUNY, 1969-84; adj. prof. NYU. Author: Poems, 1948, The Gentle Weight Lifter, 1955, Say Pardon, 1962, Figures of the Human, 1964, Earth Hard, Selected Poems, 1968, Rescue the Dead, 1968, Poems: 1934-1969, 1970, Notebooks: 1934-1971, 1973, (poems) Facing the Tree, 1975, Selected Poems, 1975, Tread the Dark, 1978, Whisper to the Earth, 1981, Leaving the Door Open, 1984; New and Collected Poems, 1970-1985; prose Open Between Us, 1980, The One in the Many: A Poet's Memoirs, 1988, Despite the Plainness of the Day: Love Poems, 1990, Shadowing the Ground, 1991, Selected Letters, 1992, Against the Evidence: Selected Poems, 1934-1994, 1993, I Have a Name, 1996, The End Game and Other Stories, 1996, Gleanings: Uncollected Poems of the 50s and 60s, 1997. Recipient Nat. Inst. Arts and Letters award, 1964, Shelley Meml. award, 1966, CAP award, 1976, Bollingen award, 1977, Josephine Miles award Oakland Pen Club, 1992, John Steinbeck award, 1995, William Carlos Williams prize, 1997; Rockefeller Found. grantee, 1968, Nat. Endowment for Arts grantee, 1970; Wallace Stevens fellow Yale U., 1977, Guggenheim fellow, 1968, 73. Mem. Poetry Soc. Am. (pres. emeritus 1977, Robert Frost Silver medal 1992), Walt Whitman Birthplace Assn. (poet in residence 1987, mem. exec. bd. 1989-97). Died Nov. 17, 1997.

ILLIG, CARL, lawyer; b. Houston, Sept. 10, 1909; s. Carl and Olive (Kirlicks) I.; m. Lillian Elizabeth Horlock, Apr. 27, 1933; children: Elaine (Mrs. Franklin B. Davis), Carol (Mrs. Simeon T. Lake III), Dale. B.A., Rice Inst., 1930; LL.B., U. Tex., 1933; grad., Advanced Mgmt. Program, Harvard U., 1959. Bar: Tex. 1933. Practiced in Galveston, Tex., 1933-34; practiced in Houston, 1967-89, ret., 1989; partner Illig, Brill and Dewitt, 1969-70; with Humble Oil & Refining Co., 1934-67, assoc. gen. counsel, 1961-67. Chmn. budget com., trustee Houston-Harris County United Fund, 1957-58; chmn. Houston Community Council, 1960; mem. Tex. Water Devel. Bd., 1971-76; bd. govs. Rice U., 1970-74, gov. adviser, 1974-95; mem. Harvard Bus. Sch. Alumni Council, 1966-69. Recipient Most Outstanding Fifty-Yr. Lawyer award Tex. Bar Found., 1991. Mem. ABA (chmn. sect. natural resources law 1964-65, mem. ho. of dels. 1966-68), Tex. Bar Assn. (chmn. sect. corp. banking and bus. law 1959-60), Houston Bar Assn., State Bar Tex., Houston Philos. Soc., Assn. Rice Alumni (pres. 1952-53), Houston C. of C. (chmn. water supply and conservation com. 1969-70), Phi Beta Kappa. Club: Houston Country. Home: Houston Tex. Died Apr. 10, 1995.

ILUTOVICH, LEON, organization executive; b. Odessa, Russia; s. Jacob and Leah (Plotycher) I.; m. Rebekka Landau. Ed., Law Sch., Warsaw (Poland) U. Mem. nat. exec. bd. Gen. Zionist Youth Movement Hanoar Hazioni, Poland, 1933-36; mem. cen. com. Zionist Student Fedn. of Poland, 1933-36; sec. provisional representation of Polish Jewry, dir. Warsaw office Jewish mem. Polish Parliament, 1937; mem. cen. com. Maccabi Sports Orgn. Poland, 1937; sec. gen. Orgn. Gen. Zionists Poland, 1938-39; mem. inter-party refugee bd., Far Ea. coms. Jewish Agy. for Palestine, World Jewish Congress, 1940-46; assoc. exec. dir., then exec. dir. Zionist Orgn. Am., exec. vice chmn., nat. sec., 1947-84, mem. nat. exec. com., 1984-97, also hon. v.p.; founder Kfar Silver Edn. Ctr. in Israel; mem. gen. coun. World Zionist Orgn.; del. to Zionist congresses; mem. Am. sect. World Jewish Congress; trustee United Israel Appeal; founder, mem. exec. com. World Union Gen. Zionists; v.p. Fedn. Polish Jews of U.S.; mem. internat. bd. World Fedn. Polish Jews; chmn. Polish Jewry Meml. Forest in Israel; mem. nat. exec. com. Am. Fedn. Holocaust Survivors; nat. bd. dirs. Am. Friends Beth Hatefutsoth. Mem. editorial bd.: Am. Zionist mag., 1964-85. Mem. Am. Arbitraiton Assn. (nat. panel), Hebrew Lang. and Culture Assn. Died Feb. 15, 1997.

INGLIS, DAVID RITTENHOUSE, physicist; b. Detroit, Oct. 10, 1905; s. William and Carolyn Clay (Rittenhouse) I.; m. Dorothy Rosalind Kerr, Mar. 26, 1934; 1 son, John Lockwood. A.B., Amherst Coll., 1928, D.Sc. (honoris causa), 1963; D.Sc., U. Mich., 1931; D.Sc. (honoris causa), U. Ill., 1974; student, U. Afloat, U. Heidelberg, Germany, 1927. Instr. Ohio State U., 1931-34, asst. prof., 1934; research asso. U. Leipsig, Fed. Inst. Tech., Zurich, 1932-33; asst. prof. U. Pitts., 1934-37, Princeton U., 1937-38; asso. Johns Hopkins U., 1938-41, asso. prof., 1941-49; sr. physicist Argonne Nat. Lab., 1949-69; prof. physics U. Mass., 1969-75, prof. emeritus, 1975—; physicist OSRD, 1942, Ballistics Research Lab., Aberdeen Proving Ground, 1943; with theoretical div. Los Alamos Sci. Lab., 1943-46; vis. prof. U. Calif. at Berkeley, 1955-56, U. Grenoble, France, 1964; physicist European Orgn. Nuclear Research, Geneva, 1957-58; professorial lectr. U. Chgo., 1965-68. Author: Dynamic Principles of Mechanics, 1949, Nuclear Energy: Its Physics and Its Social Challenge, 1972, Wind Power and Other Energy Options, 1978, To End the Arms Race: Seeking a Safer Future, 1986; contbr. articles to profl. jours. Fellow Am. Phys. Soc. (Leo Szilard award for physics in pub. interest 1974), Fedn. Am. Scientists (chmn. 1959-60), Phi Beta Kappa, Sigma Xi, Alpha Delta Phi. Died Dec. 3, 1995.

INGRAM, LAWRENCE WARREN, retired editor, publisher; b. Mt. Moriah, Mo., June 19, 1921; s. Earl Russell and Ella Elizabeth I.; m. Irene Farrell, Oct. 11, 1942. AA, George Washington U., 1947; B of Journalism, U. Tex., 1949. Research asst. Pres.'s Commn. on Higher Edn., Washington, 1946-47; editor Tex. State Parks Bd. mag., 1947-49; city editor, mng. editor, exec. editor Temple (Tex.) Daily Telegram, 1949-56, exec. editor, editor, 1961-72; with Denver Post, 1956-61, asst. city editor, 1958-59, radio-TV editor, 1959-60, editorial writer, 1960-61; pres. Stillhouse Hollow Pubs., Inc., Temple, Tex., 1973-88; editor, pub. Belton Jour., 1973-81; editor, bus. mgr. S.W. and Tex. Water Works Jour., Temple, 1977-88; pub. Vestnik, Temple, 1981-84. Dir. Temple Literacy Coun., Temple Child Help, Inc. With U.S. Army, 1942-45. Mem. Wildflower Country Club. Died Dec. 26, 1994. Home: Temple Tex.

INGRAM, ROBERT PALMER, magazine publisher; b. Norfolk, Va., July 21, 1917; s. Robert Palmer and Margaret (Wible) I.; m. Mary Elizabeth Renfro, Sept. 30, 1949; children: Marsha Jill Ingram Reynolds, Robert Palmer III. Student, Washington and Lee U., 1935-36, U. Pitts., 1936-37. Salesman Anchor Hocking Glass Corp., Grand Rapids, Mich., 1942-45, Kansas City, Mo., 1945; pres. Robert P. Ingram & Co., Kansas City, 1946-97, Ingram Investment Co., Mo., 1964-97, LaSalle Leasing Co., Mo., 1971-97, Stas. KXTR and KBEA, Mission, Kans., Kansas City Bus Advt. Co.; pub. The Independent mag., 1983-97, Vanguard Airlines Mag., 1996-97, Corp. Report/Kansas City mag., 1987-97, Ingram mag., Kansas City, 1989-97; chmn. Ingram Media, LLC, 1995-97; pub. Vanguard Airlines Mag., 1996-97, Custom Pub. by Ingram's, L.L.C., 1996-97; chmn. Ingram Media, L.L.C., 1996-97, Ingram Properties, LLC, 1997; bd. dirs. Rubbermaid Inc., Harzfelds, Inc., Am. Cablevision of Kansas City, HDCIC; trustee Conservatory of Music, U. Mo.; hon. consul to Belgium, 1969; dean consular corps, Greater Kansas City Consular Corps, 1987-97. Mem. capital requirements for pub. schs. com., Kansas City, 1969; chmn. fin. com. Jackson County Reps., 1966; trustee U. Mo., Kansas City, M.W. Rsch. Inst.; pres. Downtown, Inc., 1970-72; bd. dirs. Civic Coun. Greater Kansas City, 1990-97. Mem. Nat. Alliance Businessmen (met. chmn. 1969), Man of Month Fraternity (pres. 1991-97), Kansas City C. of C. (past pres.), Am. Royal Assn. (bd. govs.), 711 Club, Kansas City Club, Carriage Club (Kansas City), River Club (Kansas City), Gov.'s Club (Palm Beach, Fla.), Fifth Ave. Club (N.Y.C.). Died Oct. 1997.

IREY, NELSON SUMNER, pathologist; b. Lewisburg, Pa., July 18, 1911; s. Philip Musser and Blanche Sarah (Sechler) I.; B.S., U. Pitts., 1935, M.D., 1938; m. Mary Ellen Sproat, Dec. 21, 1940; children—Ellen Jane, Janet Kathryn, Mary Sarah, Nelson Sumner. Commd. 2d lt. M.C., U.S. Army, 1940, advanced through grades to col.; resident in pathology Fitzsimons Gen. Hosp., Denver, 1946-47, Letterman Gen. Hosp., San Francisco, 1948; chief pathology service Valley Forge (Pa.) Gen. Hosp., 1949-50, 97th Gen. Hosp., Frankfurt, W. Ger., 1950-54, Letterman Gen. Hosp., 1954-60; comdg. officer 65th Med. Group, Korea, 1960-61; chief pathology service Walter Reed Gen. Hosp., 1961-65; ret., 1965; chmn. dept. environ. and drug induced pathology Armed Forces Inst. Pathology, Washington, 1965-97; clin. prof. pathology George Washington U. Sch. Medicine, Uniformed Services U. Health Sci. Diplomate Am. Bd. Pathology. Fellow Am. Soc. Clin. Pathologists, Coll. Am. Pathologists, A.C.P., Am. Acad. Forensic Scis.; mem. Washington Soc. Pathologists (pres. 1969), Soc. Pharmacological and Environ. Pathologists (pres. 1974), Internat. Acad. Pathology, Drug Info. Assn. Baptist. Contbr. chpts. to med. books, articles to profl. jours.; editorial bd. Jour. Environ. Pathology and Toxicology, Drug Nutrient Interaction. Deceased. Office: Armed Forces Inst Pathology Washington DC 20306

IRSAY, ROBERT, professional football team executive, construction company executive; b. Chgo., Mar. 5, 1923; s. Charles J. and Elaine (Nyrtia) I.; m. Harriet Pogorzelski, July 12, 1946 (div. 1988); m. Nancy Clifford, June 17, 1989; children: Thomas, James. BSME, U. Ill., 1941. Pres. Robert Irsay Co., Skokie, Ill., 1952-78, Colt Constrn. and Devel. Co., Skokie, 1978—, Balt. Football Club, Inc., 1972-84; pres. Indpls. Colts, 1984-97, also treas.; dir. Mich. Ave. Nat. Bank, Chgo., 1970-76. Bd. dirs. Clearbrook Ctr. for Handicapped, Rolling Meadows, Ill., 1982-83; bd. dirs. Troubled Children's Found., Hialeah, Fla., 1982-83. Served to lt. USMC, 1941-46, PTO. Named to Ind. Football Hall of Fame, 1997. Died Jan. 14, 1997.

IRVING, GEORGE WASHINGTON, JR., health science association administrator; b. Caribou, Maine, Nov. 20, 1910; s. George Washington Sr. and Adelaide Louise (Butman) I.; m. Frances Catherine Connell, June 4, 1938; children: George Washington III, Mary Constance Fitzpatrick. BS, George Washington U., 1933, MA, 1935, PhD, 1939; postgrad., USDA Grad. Sch., 1933-35, U. Ill., 1937. Rsch. fellow George Washington U. Med. Sch., 1935-38; rsch. fellow Med. Coll. Cornell U., N.Y.C., 1938-39; asst. in chemistry Rockefeller Inst. Med. Rsch., N.Y.C., 1939-42; head protein rsch. USDA, New Orleans, 1942-44; div. head USDA, Beltsville, Md., 1944-47; asst. chief Bur. of Chemistry USDA, Washington, 1947-54, br. chief agrl. mktg. svc., 1954, dep. adminstr. agrl. rsch. svc., 1954-64, assoc. adminstr. agrl. rsch. svc., 1964-65, adminstr. agrl. rsch. svc., 1965-71; rsch. assoc. Fed. Am. Soc. Exptl. Biology, Bethesda, Md., 1972-85; lectr. in antibiotics USDA Grad. Sch., Washington, 1946-52; lectr. in biochemistry George Washington U. Med. Sch., 1947-53; exec. v.p. Agrl. Rsch. Inst., Bethesda, 1982-84; v.p. Internat. Life Sci. Inst., Washington, 1985-87; freelance cons. in field; v.p., mem. grad. coun. George Wash. U., 1956, mem. governing bd., 1959-60; chmn. sci. adv. bd. Sugar Rsch. Found., N.Y., 1967-71; lectr. in field; trustee Nutrition Found., N.Y., 1965-84, chmn. bd., 1983-84; mem. food additives com. NRC, 1985-89; dir. Friends Agr. Rsch., Beltsville, 1985—; mem. adv. bd. Emeritus Scis. Mathematicians, Engrs., 1990-95; dir. Friends of Agrl. Rsch., Beltsville, 1980—. Contbr., co-contbr. numerous articles to profl. jours. and books; patentee in field. Witness U.S. Congress, Washington, 1947-71; vol. sci. tchr. D.C. Pub. Schs., 1990-95; primary lectr. 1st Internat. Congress of Food Sci. and Tech., London, 1962, 3d Congress, Washington, 1970. Fellow AAAS (v.p., chair agr. sect. 1962, mem. at large 1963-67), Wash. Acad. Sci. (del rep. Inst. Food Tech. 1946-48, Phys. Scis. award 1946, pres. 1955), Alpha Chi Sigma (pres. Washington chpt. 1948-49, assoc. editor nat. mag. Indpls. 1970-84, Svc. award 1968, Man of Yr. 1975); mem. Am. Chem. Soc. (cons. 1978-88), Chem. Soc.

Wash. (pres. 1953, Svc. award 1973), Am. Soc. Biochemistry and Molecular Biology, Am. Inst., Chemists, Toastmasters, Cosmos Club (pres. 1974-75), Sigma Xi, Tau Kappa Epsilon. Republican. Roman Catholic. Avocations: bridge, cabinet-making, photography, travel. Died Dec. 27, 1997.

IRVING, ROBERT, aerospace engineer; b. Bradford, Pa., Sept. 6, 1925; s. Ralph Edison and Dorothy Lovina (Hogarth) I.; children—Conrad Paul, Ronald John, Frank Thomas, George Michael, Diane Elizabeth, James Charles, Dorothy-Jean Rebekah. B.S.N.S., Brown U., 1946; M.S.E.E., U.S. Naval Postgrad. Sch., 1954; M.S.M.S., Calif. State U., Northridge, 1975. Served as enlisted man U.S. Marine Corps., 1943-44; served U.S. Navy, 1944-46, commd. ensign, 1946, advanced through grades to lt. comdr., 1957; various assignments including U.S.S. Randolph, U.S.S. Macon, U.S.S. Philippines Sea, also Polaris program, ret., 1964; staff engr. Bunker-Ramo Corp., Canoga Park, Calif., 1964-66; sr. staff engr. Hughes Aircraft Co., Canoga Park, Calif., 1966—; adv. First State Bank. Contbr. articles to profl. jours.; patentee in field. Fellow AAAS; mem. Marine Tech. Soc., IEEE, Inst. Navigation, U.S. Naval Inst., Internat. Oceanographic Found., Ret. Officers Assn., Soc. Naval Engrs., Sigma Xi. DIED 10/15/95. .

IVANHOE, ICLE See IVES, BURL

IVES, BURL (ICLE IVANHOE), singer, actor; b. Hunt, Ill., June 14, 1909; s. Frank and Cordella (White) I.; m. Dorothy Koster, Apr. 1971; 1 son, Alexander. Student, Eastern Ill. State Tchrs. Coll., 1927-30, N.Y. U., 1937-38. With CBS, 1940-42. Made Columbia concerts annual country-wide concert tour as solo concert artist presenting folksongs and ballads; appears on radio and TV; makes theatrical appearances, tours and; stars in own co., every summer, also world tours; participated in: film productions including Smoky, 1946, Green Grass of Wyoming, 1948, Station West, 1948, So Dear to My Heart, 1948, Sierra, 1950, East of Eden, 1955, The Big Country, 1958 (Motion Picture Acad. award), Cat on a Hot Tin Roof, 1958, Day of the Outlaw, 1959, Our Man in Harvard, 1959, Robin and the Seven Hoods, 1964, Just You and Me, Kid, 1979, Earthbound, 1981; and numerous other motion pictures; appeared in: musical productions including Showboat; plays including Cat on a Hot Tin Roof; appeared on: TV program The Bold Ones, 1970-72; TV series Roots, 1977, Crackerly, The Lawyers, Captains and The Kings, New Adventures of Heidi; former recording artist TV program, Columbia and Decca, now records for MCA, recordings include, the Best of Burl Ives, 1961, Sings Little White Duck and Other Children's Favorites, 1989; hist. song series, Ency. Britannica; author: autobiography Wayfaring Stranger, 1948, Burl Ives Song Book, 1953, Sailing on a Very Fine Day, 1955, Tales of America, 1954, Burl Ives' Book of Seas Songs, Burl Ives Book of Irish Song, Song in America, 1961, A Wayfaring Stranger's Notebook: Albad, The Oaf, 1966. Recipient Motion Picture Acad. award for The Big Country. Mem. Am. Fedn. TV and Radio Artists, Writers Guild, Am. Fedn. Musicians, Screen Actors Guild. Democrat. Travelled throughout 46 states as troubadour, collecting and singing Am. folk songs, approximately 500 songs. Home: Anacontes Wash. Died Apr. 15, 1995.

IVORY, CECIL AUGUSTUS, lawyer, judge; b. Charlotte, N.C., June 28, 1947; s. Cecil Augustus and Emily (Richardson) I. BA, Lincoln U., Pa., 1969; JD, George Washington U., 1972. Bar: N.Y. 1974, U.S. Dist. Ct. (so. and ea. dists.) N.Y. 1974, U.S. Supreme Ct. 1983. Mem. staff Office of Dist. Atty., Queens, N.Y., 1972-74; asst. atty. gen. N.Y. Dept. Law, N.Y.C., 1974-85; judge N.Y. State Workers' Compensation Bd., 1985-86. Bd. dirs. Bowery Residence Com., N.Y.C., 1978-86; trustee A.L. Richardson Scholarship Fund, Charlotte, 1983-86; adviser Dem. Orgn., Bronx, 1984. Mem. Macon B. Allen Bar Assn., Third World Lawyers Caucus (corr. sec. 1983). Democrat. Presbyterian. Deceased Oct. 1986. Home: Los Angeles Calif.

JACK, HOMER ALEXANDER, minister; b. Rochester, N.Y., May 19, 1916; s. Alexander and Cecelia (Davis) J.; m. Ingeborg Kind, June 14, 1972; children: Alexander, Lucy Jack Williams. B.S., Cornell U., 1936, M.S., 1937, Ph.D., 1940; B.D., Meadville Theol. Sch., 1944, D.D., 1971. Ordained to ministry Unitarian Assn., 1949; minister Universalist Ch., Litchfield, Ill., 1942, Unitarian Ch., Lawrence, Kans., 1943; exec. dir. Chgo. Council Against Racial and Religious Discrimination, 1944-48; minister Unitarian Ch., Evanston, Ill., 1948-59; assoc. dir. Am. Com. on Africa, 1959-60; exec. dir. Nat. Com. for Sane Nuclear Policy, 1960-64, mem. nat. bd., 1965-84; chmn. Non-Govtl. Orgn. Com. on Disarmament, UN Hdqrs., 1973-84; dir. Div. Social Responsibility, Unitarian Universalist Assn., 1964-70; sec.-gen. World Conf. Religion and Peace, N.Y.C., 1970-84, emeritus 1984-93; minister Lake Shore Unitarian Soc., Winnetka, Ill., 1984-87; pres. Unitarian Fellowship for Social Justice, 1949-50; vice chmn. Ill. div. ACLU, 1950-59. Editor: Wit and Wisdom of Gandhi, 1951, To Albert Schweitzer, 1955, The Gandhi Reader, 1956, Religion and Peace, 1966, World Religion and World Peace, 1968, Religion for Peace, 1973, Disarmament Workbook: The UN Special Session and Beyond, 1978, World Religion/World Peace, 1979, Religion in the Struggle for World Community, 1980, Disarm: Or Die, 1983, Albert Schweitzer on Nuclear War and Peace, 1988. Bd. dirs. Dana Greeley Found. for Peace and Justice, 1986-93; bd. dirs. Albert Schweitzer Fellowship, 1974-93. Recipient Thomas H. Wright award City of Chgo., 1958; Niwano Peace prize, 1984, Adlai Stevenson award, 1985, Minns Lectrs., 1987, Defender of Peace award Sarvodhaya Peace Movement, India, 1988, Holmes/Weatherly award, 1989. Home: Swarthmore Pa. Died Aug. 5, 1993.

JACKENDOFF, NATHANIEL, finance educator; b. N.Y.C., Feb. 24, 1919; s. Harry and Bella (Brainin) J.; m. Elaine Muriel Flanders, Apr. 4, 1943; children: Ray Saul, Harry Alan, Samuel Jay. B.S.S., Coll. City N.Y., 1938; M.A., U. Ill., 1939, Ph.D., 1948. Asst. prof. econs. Washington and Jefferson Coll., 1948-50; asst. prof. to prof. fin. Temple U., 1950-89, prof. emeritus, 1989-97; Dir. SBA Research Project, 1959-60; econ. cons. U.S. Naval War Coll., Newport, R.I., 1962. Author: The Use of Financial Ratios by Small Business, 1961, A Study of Published Industry Financial and Operating Ratios, 1962, Money, Flow of Funds and Economic Policy, 1968. Served to tech. sgt. USAAF, 1943-45. Fulbright research scholar Spain, 1969. Mem. Am. Econ. Assn., Am. Fin. Assn. Jewish. Home: Belmont Mass. Died Jan. 14, 1997.

JACKSON, DONALD DEAN, historian; b. Glenwood, Iowa, June 10, 1919; s. Marion Dean and Eula Frances (Woods) J.; m. Mary Catherine Mayberry, Oct. 6, 1943; children: Robert Woods, Mark Richard. BS, Iowa State U., 1942; MA, U. Iowa, 1947, PhD, 1948. Editor U. Ill. Press., Urbana, 1948-68; prof. history U. Va., Charlottesville, 1969-76; cons. Colorado Springs, Colo., 1976—. Author: Archer Pilgrim, 1942, Custer's Gold, 1966, Valley Men, 1983, Voyages of Steamboat Yellow Stone, 1985; editor: Black Hawk: an Autobiography, 1955, Letters of Lewis and Clark Expedition, 1962, rev. edit., 1978, Journals of Zebulon Pike, 1966, Expeditions of John C. Fremont, 1970-73, Diaries of George Washington, 1976-79; editor (papers) Papers of George Washington, 1968-76. Served to lt. (j.g.) USNR, 1942-46. Recipient Award of Merit, Am. Assn. State and Local History, 1967. Mem. Western History Assn. (Award of Merit, 1979), Am. Antiquarian Soc., Orgn. Am. Historians.

JACKSON, EVERETT GEE, painter, illustrator; b. Mexia, Tex., Oct. 8, 1900; s. W.B. and Fanny (Eubank) J.; m. Eileen Dwyer, July 21, 1926; 1 child, Jerry Gee Jackson Williamson. Student, Tex. A&M Coll., 1919-21, Art. Inst. Chgo., 1921-23; A.B., San Diego State Coll., 1929; A.M., U. So. Calif., 1934. Faculty Sul Ross State Tchrs. Coll., Alpine, Tex., 1929; prof. art San Diego State U., 1930-63; tchr. U. Costa Rica, 1962; painter, illustrator, 1926-95; adv. bd. to pres. San Diego State U. Illustrator: Miller, Mexico Around Me, 1937, Louis Untermeyer, Paul Bunyan, 1945, Ugly Duckling; Popol Vuh, 1954, Conquest of Peru, 1956, American Chimney Sweeps, 1958, Ramona, Helen Hunt Jackson, 1960, Estudio de Evaluation de la Academia de Bellas Artes, Universidad de Costa Rica, 1963, American Indian Legends, 1971; author, illus. Burros and Paintbrushes, 1985, Its A Long Road To Comondu, 1987, Four Trips to Antiquity, 1991, Goat Tails and Doodlebugs-A Journey Toward Art, 1993; exhbns. include, Instituto Nacional de Antropologia e Historia at El Museo del Carmen, San Angel, Mexico City, 1979, retrospective, San Diego Mus. Art, 1984, San Diego Mus. Man, 1988, San Diego State U., 1991. Recipient citation Ltd. Edits. Club; named with wife Mr. and Mrs. San Diego, Rotary, 1992. Mem. AAUP, Fine Arts Soc. San Diego (trustee; founding chmn. Latin-Am. arts com.), San Diego Mus. Art. Home: San Diego Calif. Died Mar. 4, 1995.

JACKSON, LEWIS ALBERT, university official; b. Angola, Ind., Dec. 29, 1912; s. Albert and Cora (Beverly) J.; m. Violet Burden, Sept. 17, 1938; children: Joyce Harlene, Robert Lewis. B.S., Marion (Ind.) Coll., 1939; M.A., Miami U., Oxford, Ohio, 1948; Ph.D., Ohio State U., 1950. Tchr. Grant County (Ind.) Pub. Schs., 1936-40; contractor-flight instr. Chgo. Sch. Aeros., 1940; dir. tng. div. aeros. Tuskegee Inst., 1940-46; tchr. Gary (Ind.) Pub. Schs., 1946; faculty Cen. State U., Wilberforce, Ohio, 1946-66, 67-94, prof. edn., dir. student personnel, 1950-57, dean coll., 1957-60, v.p., dean adminstrn., 1961-66, acting pres., 1965-66, chmn. dept. ednl. adminstrn. and guidance, 1967-69, dir. grad. studies, 1969-70, pres. univ., 1970-72, asst. to pres., 1972-73; assoc. prof. dept. aviation Ohio State U., 1966-67; v.p. for adminstrn. Sinclair Community Coll., Dayton, Ohio, 1973-79; now self-employed in aviation and investments; mem. tech. edn. com. Ohio Bd. Regents, cons. to evaluate programs, summer 1968; chmn. aviation com. Dayton-Miami Valley Consortium Colls. and Univs., 1968; mem. home econs. com. Ohio Dept. Vocational Edn.; sch. survey team Lincoln Heights Sch. Dist., 1961; mem. examining teams N. Central Assn. Colls. and Secondary Schs., 1973-77; evaluation bd. Nat. Council Accreditation Tchr. Edn., 1973-77; mem. citizens adv. com. on aviation FAA, 1975-77. Editor sect. in: Jour. Human Relations, 1952-57. Recipient Disting. Alumnus award Marion Coll. Alumni Assn., 1983, Frontier award First Frontier, Inc., 1989, Pioneer, Achievement, Trail Blazer award Links, Inc., 1990, award State of Ohio-FAA, 1992. Mem. Conf. Deans Edn. State Univs. Ohio (sec. 1959, chmn. 1960), NEA, Am. Indsl. Arts Assn., Ohio Ednl. Assn., AAUP, Beta Kappa Chi, Phi Delta Kappa. Home: Xenia Ohio Died Jan. 8, 1994.

JACKSON, PATRICIA LEE (MRS. CLIFFORD L. JACKSON), psychologist; b. N.Y.C.; d. Albert George and Lisbeth P. (Lee) Scharf; B.A., Barnard Coll.; M.A., Ph.D., Tchrs. Coll. Columbia U.; m. Clifford L. Jackson. Dir. psychol. testing R. H. Macy & Co., Inc., 1941-49; employment dir. Alexander's Dept. Stores, Inc., Bronx, N.Y., 1949-52; asst. prof. psychology Hunter Coll., N.Y.C., 1951-66, asso. prof., 1966-77, coordinator of counseling services, 1959-71; research dir. Klein Inst. for Aptitude Testing, Inc., N.Y.C., 1953-59, asst. v.p., 1957-59; pvt. practice in psychotherapy, 1964—. Trustee Alfred Adler Inst.; v.p. bd. trustees Ch. of Healing Christ (Emmet Fox Ch.), N.Y.C. Mem. AAAS, Am. Assn. Counseling & Devel., Am. Psychol. Assn., Am. Statis. Assn., Am. Group Psychotherapy Assn., N.Y. Soc. Clin. Psychologists. Author articles in field. Deceased.

JACKSON, ROBERT JOHN, industrial engineer; b. L.A., Dec. 24, 1922; s. John M. and Ona Blanche (Hill) J.; m. Ethel K. Beecher, Dec. 1, 1950; children: Kathryn, Bradley, Diane, Margaret, Shirley, Kelly, Riley. AA, Pasadena Coll., 1958. Supr. assembly dept. Lockheed Aircraft Co., Burbank, Calif., 1941-51; time standards engr. Bendix Pacific Co., North Hollywood, Calif., 1951-53; indsl. engr. Walsco Electronic Co., Los Angeles, 1953-55; methods and time standards engr. Lockheed-Calif. Co., Burbank, 1955-69, dir. hours rep., 1969—. Dir. Modal Investment Co., Eagle Rock, Calif., 1955-56. Served with AUS, 1944-46; PTO. Decorated Purple Heart with oak leaf cluster, Bronze Star, Silver Star. Mem. Am. Inst. Indsl. Engrs. Lodge: Masons.

JACOB, HERBERT, political science educator; b. Augsburg, Germany, Feb. 10, 1933; came to U.S., 1940, naturalized, 1946; s. Ernest I. and Annette (Loewenberg) J.; m. Lynn Susan Carp, Aug. 19, 1968; children: Joel Benjamin, David Samuel, Jenny Ellen, Michael Max. AB, Harvard U., 1954; MA, Yale U., 1955, PhD, 1960. Mem. faculty Tulane U., 1960-62; mem. faculty U. Wis.-Madison, 1962-69, prof., 1967-69; prof. polit. sci. Northwestern U., Evanston, Ill., 1969-84, 85-96, chmn. dept., 1974-77; Hawkins disting. prof. polit. sci. U. Wis., Madison, 1984-85; vis. prof. Johns Hopkins U., 1972; prin. investigator Govtl. Responses to Crime Project, 1978-81; vis. fellow Center for Socielegal Research, Oxford U., 1981. Author: Law and Politics in the U.S., 2d edit., 1995, Law, Court, and Politics in Comparative Perspective, 1996; editor: Law and Politics Book Review, 1991-96. Mem. Human Rels. Commn. Evanston, 1971-73. With AUS, 1955-57. Recipient Emil H. Steiger award U. Wis., 1964; NSF faculty fellow, 1967-68; fellow Ctr. for Advanced Studies in Behavioral Scis., 1973-74, Ctr. for Socio-legal Research, Oxford U., 1981. Mem. Law and Society Assn. (pres. 1981-83). Home: Evanston Ill. Died Aug. 29, 1996.

JACOB, HERBERT, economics educator; b. Frankfurt, Germany, Feb. 25, 1927; s. Otto Christian Wilhelm and Margaret Emma Klara; m. Marlies Yvonne Brovot, July 11, 1957; children: Uwe, Imke, Maik. Degree in Bus., U. Frankfurt, 1951, degree in Econs., 1951, PhD in Polit. Sci., 1954; PhD, Habl., U. Cologne, 1955; PhD (hon.), U. Rostock, 1996, U. Istanbul, 1981. Asst. prof. U. Cologne, 1954-59; assoc. prof. Technische Hochschule, Munich, Germany, 1959-60; prof. U. Hamburg, Germany, 1960—, dean sch. econs., 1964-65. Author: Allgemein Betriebswirtschaft, 1969, 5th edit., 1988, Preispolitik, 1971, Investment Rechnung, 1977, 4th edit., 1994, Preisbildung in der Industriegesellschaft, 1985, others; contbr. over 100 articles to profl. jours. Recipient medal Wirtschafts U., Helsinki, Finland, 1985. Mem. Assn. Hochschullehrer für Betriebswirtschaft (pres. 1964-66).

JACOBI, JOHN EDWARD, sociology educator; b. Mansfield, Ohio, Feb. 4, 1907; s. Edward Walter and Josephine (Munhall) J.; m. Carrie Anna Baumann, Dec. 29, 1933; children—John Edward, Susan Jane Jacobi Sherman. B.A., Lehigh U., 1929; Ph.D., N.Y. U., 1933. Prof. sociology, dean Tusculum Coll., Greeneville, Tenn., 1941-46; prof. sociology Albright Coll., Reading, Pa., 1946-48, Lehigh U., Bethlehem, Pa., 1948-62; lectr. Boston Coll., 1965-68; prof. sociology State U. Coll., Oneonta, N.Y., 1968-91; head dept. State U. Coll., 1970-73; vis. prof. N.Y. U., summers 1946, 48, 49; dir. local area research and demonstration project Mass. Com. Children and Youth, 1962-68; co-dir. inter-disciplinary research team Lehigh U., 1957-60. Author: Meeting the Needs of Children and Youth in a Regional Area, 1968, Meeting the Needs of Children and Youth in an Urban Community, 1968, Meeting the Needs of Children and Youth in Massachusetts Communities, 1968, A Professor's Odyssey, 1976; Co-editor: An Introduction to the Social Sciences, 1954. Mem. nat. youth program com. YMCA, 1959-65. Rockefeller fellow, 1930-33. Mem. Am., Eastern sociol. socs., Pi Gamma Mu, Beta Gamma Sigma, Lambda Chi Alpha. Home: Oneonta N.Y. Died June 11, 1991.

JACOBS, BERNARD B., theater executive; b. N.Y.C., 1916. Grad., NYU, 1937, Columbia U. Law Sch., 1940.

Pres. Shubert Orgn., N.Y.C., Shubert Found., N.Y.C. Recipient Columbia Law Sch. Disting. Achievement award, 1995, Labor-Mgmt. award Union Label and Svc. Trades Dept. AFL-CIO; inducted into the Theater Hall of Fame, 1994. Mem. League Am. Theatres and Producers (v.p., bd dirs.). Died Aug. 27, 1996.

JACOBS, DONALD WARREN, dentist; b. Waynesburg, Pa., Apr. 6, 1932; s. Donald Ray and Nellie Fayette (Church) J.; m. Diane Jeanette Marshall, June 28, 1958; children: Donald Marshall, Carol Anne Jacobs Nagle. BS, Waynesburg Coll., 1953; DDS, U. Pitts., 1961. Pvt. practice York, Pa., 1963-95. Author: Implant Materials, 1961, Esthetic Dentistry, 1970. Lt. (j.g.) USN, 1953-57; lt. Dental Corps USN, 1958-63. Recipient Presidential Achievement award Pres. of U.S., Washington, 1980. Fellow Acad. Gen. Dentistry, Internat. Coll. Dentists, Am. Coll. Dentists, Royal Soc. Health, Pierre Fauchard Acad.; mem. ADA, Pa. Dental Assn. (del. chmn. coms. 1972-83), York County Dental Soc. (pres.), Fifth Dist. Dental Soc. (pres.), York C. of C., Tall Cedars of Lebanon, Masons, Shriners, Delta Sigma Phi, Psi Omega. Republican. Presbyterian. Avocations: golf, hunting, fishing. Home: York Pa. Died July 15, 1995.

JACOBS, HELEN HULL, tennis player, writer; b. Globe, Ariz., Aug. 6, 1908; d. Roland Herbert and Eula (Hull) J. Student, U. Calif.-Berkeley, 1926-29, William and Mary Coll., 1942. Designer sports clothes, N.Y.C., London. Author: Modern Tennis, 1932, Improve Your Tennis, 1936, Beyond the Game: An Autobiography, 1936, Barry Cort, 1937, Tennis, 1941, By Your Leave, Sir: The Story of a WAVE, 1943, Storm Against the Wind, 1944, Laurel for Judy, 1945, Adventure in Blue Jeans, 1947, Gallery of Champions, 1949, Center Court, 1950, Judy, Tennis Ace, 1951, Proudly She Serves: The Realistic Story of a Tennis Champion Who Becomes a WAVE, 1953, Golf, Swimming and Tennis, 1961, The Young Sportsman's Guide to Tennis, 1961, Famous American Women Athletes, 1964, Better Physical Fitness for Girls, 1964, Courage To Conquer, 1967, The Tennis Machine, 1972, Famous Modern American Women Athletes, 1975, Beginner's Guide to Winning Tennis, 1975, The Savage Ally, 1977; contbr. articles to mags. Served to lt. comdr. USNR, 1949-52, comdr. USNR, 1959-68. Recipient Tennis Immortal award Tennis Writers Assn. Am., 1968; named to N. Calif. Tennis Hall of Fame, Nat. Tennis Hall of Fame, Intl. Tennis Hall of Fame, San Francisco Bay Area Sports Hall of Fame, U. Calif. Athletic Hall of Fame, Coll. William and Mary Athletic Hall of Fame. Hon. mem. Eugene Field Soc., English Speaking Union (London), Nat. Geog. Soc., Mark Twain Soc., Jr. League (Oakland-East Bay), Women's Athletic Club (Oakland) San Francisco Press Club, Calif. Writers Club, Berkeley Tennis Club, All England Lawn Tennis and Croquet Club (Wimbledon, Eng.), Nice (France) Tennis Club, Calif. Tennis Club, Kappa Alpha Theta. Episcopalian. Nat. jr. tennis champion, 1924-25; champion U.S. women's singles and doubles, 1932, U.S. singles champion, 1933, champion U.S. singles, doubles and mixed doubles, 1934; champion U.S. singles, doubles, 1935 (1st to win single championship 4 times successively); 6 times Wimbledon finalist; Wimbledon singles champion, 1936; mem. Am. Wightman Cup team for 13 successive years, 1927-39. Home: East Hampton N.Y. Died June 2, 1997; interred Memorial Garden of St Luke's Episcopal Church.

JACOBS, HENRIETTA MARIE, early childhood educator, consultant; b. Polk, Nebr., Dec. 13, 1920; d. Wilbur Arnold and Henrietta Martha (Whitacre) Refshauge; m. Vernon Frederick Jacobs, July 11, 1943; children: Randall Alan, Jonathan Frederick, Martin Karl. BS in Edn., U. Nebr. Kearney, 1943; postgrad., Tulsa U., 1965, 67, Pepperdine Coll., 1970, UCLA, 1971, U. Mo. St. Louis, 1978, 79. Instr. vocat. home econs. Minden (Nebr.) H.S., 1944-45; instr. Tulsa Pub. Schs., 1963-67; tchr. Downey (Calif.) Ind. Sch. Dist., 1968-71; dir. social svcs. Tabitha Home, Lincoln, Nebr., 1971-75; instr., dir. early childhood edn. Kansas City (Mo.) Pub. Schs., 1976-80; dir. First Luth. Ch. Pre-Sch., Omaha, 1981-84; cons. Omaha, 1984—. Mem. AAUW, Women of Evang. Luth. Ch. Am. (Syndocial Constn. com. 1986-87, instr., bd. dirs.), Midland Women, P.E.O. (pres. Nebr. chpt. DY 1995-97). Avocations: choral singing, violinist, genealogy, interior decorating. Died Oct. 13, 1997.

JACOBS, LEON, medical research administrator; b. N.Y.C., Mar. 26, 1915; s. Samuel and Evelyn (Rosenthal) J.; m. Eva Eisenberg, Nov. 28, 1946; children: Jonathan H., Alice E., Abby M. B.A., Bklyn. Coll., 1935; M.A., George Washington U., 1938, Ph.D., 1947. Zoologist, protozoologist NIH, 1937-43, 46-59; chief Lab. Parasitic Diseases NIH, Bethesda, Md., 1959-64, acting sci. dir. Nat. Inst. Allergy and Infectious Diseases, 1965, sci. dir. div. Biologics Standards, 1966-67, assoc. dir. collaborative research, 1969-78, dir. Fogarty Internat. Ctr. for Advanced Study in Health Scis., 1978-79; dep. asst. sec. for sci. HEW, Washington, 1967-69; sci. dir. Nat. Soc. Med. Research, Washington, 1981-84; bd. dirs. Gorgas Meml. Inst., 1967-89, chmn., pres., 1983-92; mem. WHO Expert Panel on Parasitic Diseases, 1969-79; lectr. Johns Hopkins U., Case Western U.; vis. prof. U. Ariz., 1979, 80, U. So. Fla., 1980-83. Contbr. numerous chpts., articles on parasitic diseases, revs. to profl. publs. Served with U.S. Army, 1943-46. Recipient Arthur S. Flemming award U.S. Jr. C. of C., 1954, Biol. Sci. award Washington Acad. Sci, 1954, Barnet Cohen award Md. Soc. Bacteriology, 1956, Disting. Service medal USPHS, 1966, Superior Service award HEW, 1968; named Disting. Alumnus, Bklyn. Coll., 1955, Disting. Alumnus, George Washington U., 1967; Fulbright scholar, 1960-61; Guggenheim fellow, 1960-61. Mem. Am. Soc. Parasitologists (editor 1955-58, Henry B. Ward medal 1963, pres. 1978), Am. Soc. Tropical Medicine and Hygiene (v.p. 1970), Helminthological Soc. Washington (pres. 1950), Am. Assn. Immunologists, Soc. Protozoology, Tropical Medicine Soc. Washington (pres. 1971), AAAS, Sigma Xi. Home: Washington D.C. DIED 10/03/95. .

JACOBS, ROBERT, education educator emeritus; b. Murphysboro, Ill., July 17, 1913; s. Arthur Clarence and Zylphia May (Porter) J.; m. Oma Lee Corgan, Aug. 13, 1939; children: Robert Corgan, Janice Lee, Lawrence James, Linda May Jacobs Wineberg. B.Ed., So. Ill. U., 1935; M.A., U. Ill., 1939; Ed.D., Wayne State U., 1949. Pub. sch. tchr., adminstr. Wood River, Ill., 1935-42; personnel staff Ford Motor Co., 1945-46; asst. instr. Wayne U., 1946-47; asst. dir. Ednl. Records Bur., N.Y.C., 1947-51; dir. counseling, prof. edn. Tex. A. and M. Coll., 1951-54; ednl. measurements adviser, dep. chief edn. div. U.S. Operations Mission to Ethiopia, FOA, 1954-56; regional edn. adviser S.E. Asia U.S. Operations Mission, Thailand, 1956-58; chief Far East program div. Office Edn., ICA, 1958-61; chief edn. div. Office Ednl. and Social Devel. AID, 1961-62; prof. edn., dean internat. service div. So. Ill. U., Carbondale, 1962-67, prof. emeritus, 1974—; regional edn. adviser Office Regional Devel. Affairs, Am. Embassy, Bangkok, and cons. S.E. Asian Ministers of Edn. Orgn., Bangkok, 1967-74; continuing edn. cons. SEAMEO; ednl. cons., writer, lectr., 1974—; vis. prof., extension lectr. U. Ark., U. Ala., Rutgers U., U. Addis Abada, George Washington U.; numerous surveys and evaluations edn. programs abroad, including, Korea, Cambodia, Syria, Nigeria, India, Congo., Chile, Colombia; mem. internat. adv. com. Edn. Rec. Bd., 1967-74. Served with AUS, 1942-45. Recipient of Meritorious Svc. citation ICA, 1959, Meritorious Svc. citation AID, 1966, Meritorious Honor award Dept. State, 1968. Mem. NEA, Nat. Soc. Study Edn., AARP, Phi Delta Kappa. Methodist. DIED 06/26/95. .

JACOBY, GEORGE V., electrical engineering consultant, technical advisor; b. Esztergom, Hungary, Feb. 26, 1918; came to U.S., 1950; s. Gabor and Gabriella (Prigl) J.; m. Paula B. Busa, Oct. 2, 1941; 1 son, Charles G. Dipl. Ing. Elec. Engring., Royal Hungarian U. Tech. Scis., Budapest, 1941, postgrad. in bus. adminstrn. and econs. Registered profl.engr., Pa. Design enhr. W.T. LaRose & Assocs., Troy, N.Y., 1950-53; research engr. Honeywell-Brown Instruments, Phila., 1953-58; devel. engr. RCA Electronic Data Processing, Camden, N.J., 1958-68; leader RCA Computer Systems, Marlboro, Mass., 1968-71; mgr. advanced rec. Sperry Univac-ISS, Blue Bell, Pa., and Santa Clara, Calif., 1971-83; sr. profl. cons. Magnetic Peripherals of Control Data Corp., Santa Clara, 1983-94. Patentee in field. Recipient Outstanding Contbr. award ISS-Sperry Univac., Santa Clara, 1978; recipient Invention award ISS-Sperry Univac., Santa Clara, 1980. Fellow IEEE. Roman Catholic. Home: Los Altos Calif. Deceased Dec. 29, 1994.

JAECKEL, RICHARD, actor; b. Long Beach, N.Y., Oct. 10, 1926. Actor: (feature films) Guadalcanal Diary, 1943, Sands of Iwo Jima, 1949, Battleground, 1949, The Gunfighter, 1950, Sea Hornet, 1951, Hoodlum Empire, 1952, My Son John, 1952, Come Back, Little Sheba, 1952, Big Leaguer, 1953, Sea of Lost Ships, 1953, Shanghai Story, 1954, Violent Men, 1955, Platinum High School, 1960, The Young and the Brave, 1963, Apache Ambush, 1965, The Dirty Dozen, 1967, The Devil's Brigade, 1968, The Green Slime, 1969, Sometimes a Great Notion, 1971, Ulzana's Raid, 1972, Pat Garret and Billy the Kid, 1973, The Outfit, 1974, Chosen Survivors, 1974, The Drowning Pool, 1975, Part II: Walking Tall, 1975, Twilight's Last Gleaming, 1977, All the Marbles, 1981, Starman, 1984, (TV series) Frontier Circus, 1961-62, Banyon, 1972-73, Firehouse, 1974, Salvage I, 1979, At Ease, 1983, Spencer: For Hire, 1986-87, (TV episodes) U.S. Steel Hour, Playhouse 90, Gunsmoke, others, (TV movie) Firehouse, 1972. Mem. Screen Actors Guild, AFTRA. Died June 14, 1997.

JAFFE, IRVING, lawyer; b. N.Y.C., Aug. 20, 1913; s. Max Elias and Annie (Shill) J.; m. Alice Cardin Bein, Aug. 30, 1936; children: Matthew Ely, Daniel Paul. BS, CCNY, 1933; LLB, Fordham U., 1935. Bar: N.Y. 1936, U.S. Dist. Ct. (so. dist.) N.Y. 1939, (ea. dist.) N.Y. 1940, U.S. Supreme Ct. 1944, U.S. Ct. Appeals (D.C. cir.) 1946, D.C. 1948, U.S. Dist. Ct. D.C. 1948, U.S. Ct. Appeals (2d cir.) 1958, (1st cir.) 1977, U.S. Claims Ct. 1982, U.S. Ct. Appeals (fed. cir.) 1982. Pvt. practice N.Y.C., 1936-42; atty. U.S. Dept. Justice, Bd. Immigration Appeals, Washington, 1942-44, trial atty. claims div., 1944-46; chief trail atty. Office of Alien Property, 1946-49, chief trial atty., chief spl. litigation sec., 1950-67, dep. asst. atty. gen., 1967-78; ptnr. Wasserman & Jaffe, Washington, 1949-50, Quarles & Brady, Washington, 1978-81, Pettit & Martin, Washington, 1981—; lectr. in field; appointed Appellate Mediator by U.S. Ct. Appeals (D.C. cir.), 1987—. Recipient Dept. Justice Disting. Svc. award, 1971, Spl. Commendation, 1976. Mem. ABA, D.C. Bar Assn. (ethics com. 1976-79), Nat. Lawyers Assn., Fed. Bar Assn. (chmn. pub. contract sect., jud. conf. d.c. cir.), Am. Arbitration Assn. (comml. nat. panel, adv. com. appellate procedure D.C. cir.), Indian Spring Country, B'nai B'rith. Democrat. Jewish.

JAFFE, LEO, motion picture executive; b. N.Y.C., Apr. 23, 1909; m. Anita. BCS, NYU, 1931. Former pres., chief exec. officer and chmn. bd. Columbia Pictures Industries, Inc., now chmn. emeritus; chmn. motion picture and TV sect. U.S. Info. Agy.; bd. dirs. Contel Cellular Corp., Braille Inst. Coachilla Valley, Calif. Past Industry chmn. United Jewish Appeal, Federated Charities, NCCJ; bd. dirs. Will Rogers Meml. Hosp., San Juan Racing Assn., Beth Abraham Hosp. and, Home for Aged; hon. chmn. bd. trustees Nat. Found. March of Dimes, N.Y.C., trustee nat. bd; chmn. Am. Cinema Award Found., 1992-93. Named commendatore, Republic of Italy, Grande Ufficiale in Italy, Knight of Malta of St. John of Jerusalem; recipient N.Y.C. medals of honor; Brandeis U. fellow; fellow, mem. pres.'s council, life trustee NYU; recipient Dean Madden Meml. award, 1977, Jean Hersholt Humanitarian award Acad. Motion Picture Arts and Scis., 1978, Israel Prime Minister's medals of honor, 1978, U.S. medals of honor Bond Sales Drive; Gold award NCCJ, 1981; U.S. Govt. Achievement award U.S.-Israel Assn., 1986, Gloria Swanson Humanitarian award Motion Pictures Awards Com., 1991, Lifetime Achievement award Friars Found., 1991, Walk in the Street Tablet award, 1994; Leo Jaffe Theatre named in his honor NYU Sch. Arts; named Man of Yr. Am. Technion U. Soc., 1987. Mem. Motion Picture Pioneers (dir., Man of Year award 1972), Motion Picture Assn. Am. (dir.), Hampshire Coutry Club, Friars, Tamarisk Country Club, Palm Springs Stroke Ctr. (dir.), Springs Country Club, Delta Mu Delta, Alpha Phi Sigma, Alpha Sigma Phi. Died Aug. 20, 1997.

JAGAN, CHEDDI, Guyanese government official; b. Plantation, Port Mourant, Berbice, Mar. 22, 1918; m. Janet Rosenberg, 1943; 2 children. Attended, Queen's Coll., Guyana, Howard U., Washington, YMCA (now Roosevelt) Coll., Chgo., Northwestern U. Dental Sch., Chgo. Mem. legis. coun., 1947-53; leader People's Progressive Party, 1950; min. agr., lands and mines, leader House Assembly, 1953; min. trade and ind., 1957-61; leader, chief min. PPP Majority Party, 1957-61; first premier, min. devel. planning British Guiana, 1961-64; leader opposition, 1964-73, 1976-92; pres. Guyana, 1992—; gen. sec. PPP, 1970—; pres. Guyana Peace Coun.; hon. pres. Guyana Agrl. and Gen. Worker's Union. Author: Forbidden Freedom, 1954, Anatomy of Poverty in British Guiana, 1964, (autobiography) The West on Trial, 1966, West Indian State Pro-Imperialist or Anti-Imperialist, 1972, The Struggle for a Socialist Guyana, 1976, Trade Unions and Nat. Liberation, 1977, The Caribbean Revolution, 1979, The Caribbean, Whose Backyard, 1985. Avocation, tennis.

JAKOWATZ, CHARLES V., engineering educator; b. Kansas City, Kans., Feb. 6, 1920; s. Louis and Pauline (Steinmetz) J.; m. Roberta Townley, June 27, 1947; children: Judy, Charles V. B.S. in Elec. Engring., Kans. State Coll., 1944, M.S. in Elec. Engring., 1947; Ph.D., U. Ill., 1953. Registered profl. engr., Kans. lic. amateur radio operator. Asst. prof. elec. engring. U. Ill., 1948-53; communications engr. research lab. Gen. Electric Co., 1953-63, liaison scientist, 1963-65; dean and prof. Coll. Engring., Wichita State U., 1965-79, prof. elec. engring., 1980-87, dean emeritus engring., 1987-90; adj. prof. Rensselaer Poly. Inst., 1956-65. Contbr. articles to profl. jours. Bd. dirs. Midwest Med. Research Inst. Served to lt. (j.g.) USNR, 1944-45. Recipient Disting. Elec. Engring. Alumnus award U. Ill., 1972, Disting. Svc. award Wichita State U., 1978, Disting. Svc. award Coll. Engring., Kans. State U., 1982; named to Engring. Hall of Fame, 1989. Mem. IEEE, Math. Assn. Am., Am. Soc. Engring. Edn., Nat. Soc. Profl. Engrs., Kans. Engring. Soc., Sigma Xi, Tau Beta Pi, Phi Kappa Phi, Eta Kappa Nu, Phi Mu Epsilon, Sigma Tau. Patentee in field. Home: Wichita Kans. Died April 10, 1990; interred Sunset Cemetery, Manhatten, KS.

JAKSIC, DJURA, conductor; b. Karlovac, Yugoslavia, Apr. 30, 1924; s. Stojan and Katarina J.; student Prague Conservatoire and Charles U., 1945-48; Mus.B. in Conducting, Acad. Music, Zagreb, 1949; m. Ilic Slobodanka, July 21, 1962; children—Tihomir, Dusan. Condr., Radio Belgrade Orch., 1950-53; asso. condr. Belgrade Philharm. Orch., 1953-66; prin. condr. Chamber Orch. Pro Musica Belgrade, 1967—, also artistic dir.; tours Austria, Belgium, Bulgaria, Denmark, France, Gt. Britain, Holland, Italy, Spain, Hungary, Germany, Norway, USSR, Turkey, Switzerland, Rumania, Czechoslovakia; artistic dir. Nat. Opera and Ballet, Belgrade, 1977-80; high councilor for music Republic of Serbia, 1981-84. Bd. dirs. Acad. Music, Inst. Musicology, Radio Belgrade, Kolarac Peoples U.; pres. bd. festival Marble and Sound; mem. artistic commune Kresimir Baranovic. Recipient prize City of Belgrade for musical excellence, 1976, 81. Mem. Internat. Fedn. Musicians (exec. com. 1965-69), Assn. Serbian Performing Artists (awardee 1975), Writers Club, Cultural Workers Club. Author: On the Symphony

Orchestra, 1953; editor-in-chief Pro Musica, 1964—, Musical Culture in Serbia, 1969; Two Symphonies of Amando Ivancic, 1984; essays on Vivaldi, Telemann, Berg, Britten; contbr. over 200 articles for Yugoslav Music Cyclopaedia, 1958-74. Died July 1, 1991.

JAMES, EARL EUGENE, JR., aerospace engineering executive; b. Oklahoma City, Feb. 8, 1923; s. Earl Eugene and Mary Frances (Godwin) J.; m. Barbara Jane Marshall, Dec. 15, 1945 (dec. Feb. 2, 1982); children: Earl Eugene III, Jeffrey Allan; m. Vanita L. Nix, Apr. 23, 1983. Student Oklahoma City U., 1940-41; BS, U. Okla., 1945; postgrad. Tex. Christian U., 1954-57; MS, So. Meth. U., 1961. Asst. mgr. Rialto Theatre, 1939-42; with Consol. Vultee Aircraft Co., San Diego, 1946-49; with Convair, Ft. Worth, 1949-89, group engr., 1955-57, test group engr., supr. fluid dynamics lab., 1957-81, engring. chief Fluid Dynamics Lab., 1981-89. Asst. dist. commr. Boy Scouts Am., 1958-59; adviser Jr. Achievement, 1962-63; mem. sch. bd. Castleberry Ind. Sch. Dist. (Tex.), 1969-83; chmn. bd. N.W. br. YMCA, 1971. Served to lt. (j.g.) USNR, 1942-46; PTO. Author/editor over 1000 engring. reports. Fellow AIAA (assoc.); mem. Air Force Assn. (life), U.S. Naval Inst. (assoc.), Gen. Dynamics Mgmt. Assn., Nat. Mgmt. Assn., Okla. U. Alumni Assn. (life), Tex. Congress Parents and Tchrs. (hon. life), Pi Kappa Alpha, Alpha Chi Sigma, Tau Omega. Methodist. Democrat. Clubs: Squaw Creek Golf, Camera. Lodge: Elks. Deceased.

JANSS, WILLIAM CLUFF, resort development executive; b. Los Angeles, June 9, 1918; s. Edwin and Florence (Cluff) J.; m. Anne Searls, Dec. 10, 1940 (dec. 1972); children: Suzanne Ferguson, Mary Daenzer, William Cluff Jr.; m. Glenn Candy Cooper, June 16, 1973. BA, Stanford U., 1940. Chmn. Sun Valley (Idaho) Co., 1968-77; dir. Aspen (Colo.) Ski Corp., 1955-65; trustee Aspen Inst., 1955-65; dir. Janss Investment Co., Thousand Oaks, Calif., 1978-93; bd. dirs. Manville Corp., Denver, 1978-89. Mem. U.S. Olympic Ski Team, 1940; mem. Coun. Mus. Modern Art, 1980-96, Nat. Com. Phillips Collection, 1981-96; trustee U.S. Ski Edn. Found. Park, Utah, 1981-96, U.S. Ski Edn. Fedn., 1981-96. With USAF, 1943-45. Named to Nat. Ski Hall of Fame, 1979. Club: Bohemian (San Francisco). Died Dec. 4, 1996.

JAQUES, LOUIS BARKER, pharmacologist; b. Toronto, Ont., Can., July 10, 1911; s. Robert Herbert and Ann Bella (Shepherd) J.; m. Helen Evelyn Delane, May 15, 1937 (dec. May 1987); 1 child, Mary Jaques Hall; m. Georgina Merrick Powell, Nov. 16, 1991 (dec. Dec. 1993). BA, U. Toronto, 1933, MA, 1935, Ph.D., 1941; D.Sc., U. Sask., 1974. Faculty U. Toronto, 1934-46; faculty U. Sask., Saskatoon, 1946—; prof. physiology, head physiology, pharmacology U. Sask., 1946-71; W.S. Lindsay prof. U. Sask. (Coll. Medicine), 1972-79; emeritus prof. physiology, research assoc. dentistry U. Sask. (Coll Dentistry), 1979—; ofcl. Can. rep. Council and Gen. Assembly Internat. Union Physiol. Scis., Leyden, 1962. Author: The Prayer Book Companion, 1963, Anticoagulant Therapy; Pharmacological Principles, 1965; also numerous articles. Fellow N.Y. Acad. Sci., Royal Soc. Arts, Royal Soc. Can., Internat. Soc. Hematology; mem. Am. Physiol. Soc., Am. Soc. Pharmacology and Exptl. Therapeutics. Rsch. on metabolism and action of anticoagulant and related drugs basic to use of these compounds. Died May 1997.

JARMAN, DEREK, film director; b. Eng., 1942. Co-dir.: Sebastiane, 1977, Aria, 1987; dir. (films) Jubilee, 1979, The Tempest, 1980, In The Shadow of the Sun, 1981, Angelic Conversations, 1985, Caravaggio, 1986, The Last of England, 1987, War Requiem, 1988, The Garden, 1990, Edward II, 1991, Wittgenstein, 1993. Died.

JARRARD, JERALD OSBORNE, food industry executive; b. Mt. Washington, Mo., Oct. 12, 1917; s. Frank Lewis and Mary Minerva (Osborne) J.; m. Deena Morgan, Sept. 29, 1978; children: Sharon Louise, Jerry Michael, Janeece Rene (Mrs. Anthony Swainey). Student, Kansas City Jr. Coll., 1935-36, 38-39; LL.B. magna cum laude, U. Mo., 1947. Bar: Mo. 1947. With Trans World Airlines, 1942-60, dir. labor relations, 1957-60; v.p. indsl. relations Eastern Airlines, 1960-63; v.p. personnel Am. Airlines, Inc., 1963; regional v.p. sales and services Am. Airlines, Inc., N.Y., 1964-66; system v.p. sales and services Am. Airlines, Inc., 1966-68; pres. Contract Food Services div. Marriott Corp., Washington, 1968-78; sr. corp. v.p., spl. asst. to pres. Marriott Corp., 1978-82. Editor: U. Mo. Law Rev, 1944-46. Mem. Mo. Integrated Bar, Inst. Radio Engrs., Am. Soc. Travel Agts., Newcomen Soc. N. Am., Nat. Restaurant Assn., Nat. Rifle Assn., Sales Execs. Club, Phi Delta Phi. Methodist. Clubs: Pinnacle (N.Y.C.), Wings (N.Y.C.); Congressional (Washington); Isla del Sol (St. Petersburg, Fla.). Home: Saint Petersburg Fla. Deceased April 19, 1995.

JARRETT, CHARLES EDWARD, accountant; b. Terre Haute, Ind., July 29, 1924; s. Isaac Edward and Eliza May (France) J.; m. Mary Frances Seiler, Apr. 8, 1944; children—Susan Elizabeth, Barbara Jane, Charles Edward. B.S. in Acctg., Ind. U., 1948; cert. exec. devel. program U. Mich., 1959; M.B.A. in Procurement and Contracting, George Washington U., 1971. C.P.A., Ind., Ohio, Va., Fla., Calif.; C.I.A., C.P.C.M., C.C.A. Pub. acct. Dieterle and Thompson, C.P.A.s, Bloomington, Ind., 1948-49; auditor U.S. Air Force, various locations, 1949-65; br. chief hdqrs. Def. Contract Audit Agy., Washington, 1965-67; procurement specialist Office Sec. Def., Washington, 1967-76; owner, mgr. Charles Edward Jarrett, C.P.A., Tallahassee, 1976-83; dir. Coopers & Lybrand, Govt. Contract Services Group, San Diego, 1983-88, Jaycor, San Diego, 1988-91; cons. on pricing and preparing proposals for govt. contracts. Served with U.S. Army, 1943-44. Fellow Nat. Contract Mgmt. Assn; mem. Am. Inst. C.P.A.s, Calif. Inst. C.P.A.s, Inst. Internal Auditors, Inst. Cost Analysts, Assn. Govt. Accts. Prin. Deceased 1991. Home: San Diego Calif.

JASPEN, NATHAN, educational statistics educator; b. N.Y.C., Oct. 21, 1917; s. Jacob J. and Sarah (Kantor) J.; m. Helen G. Shulman, June 11, 1944; children: David, Robert, Sandra Hughes, Daniel, Richard. B.S., CCNY, 1942; M.A., George Washington U., 1944; Ph.D., Pa. State U., 1949. Occupational analyst USES, Washington, 1942-47; rsch. fellow Pa. State U., 1947-49, asso. prof., 1949-52; dir. stats. automation Nat. League Nursing, N.Y.C., 1952-59; also cons.; asso. prof. NYU, 1959-62, prof. ednl. stats., 1962-82, prof. emeritus, 1982—, chmn. dept. ednl. stats., 1963-80, chmn. dept. math., sci. and statis. edn., 1980-82; cons. Am. Pub. Health Assn., USPHS, Bd. Coop. Edn. Services, Westchester, Bd. Jewish Edn. N.Y. Contbr. articles to profl. jours. Fellow AAAS, Am. Psychol. Assn.; mem. AAUP, Am. Ednl. Research Assn., Am. Statis. Assn., Assn. Computing Machinery, Inst. Math. Stats., Math. Assn. Am., Psychometric Soc., Sigma Xi, Pi Mu Epsilon, Psi Chi. Died Jan. 7, 1996.

JASTRUN, MIECZYSLAW, author; b. Oct. 29, 1903; grad. Jagiellonian U., Cracow, Poland, 1928. Tchr. secondary schs., Lodz, 1928-39; tchr. clandestine edn., Lwow, 1939-40, Warsaw, 1941-44; sub-editor Kuznica, Lodz, 1945-49. Recipient numerous awards and citations including Gold Cross of Merit, 1946, Order of Banner of Labour 1st Class, 1949, State Prize 1st class, 1950, 55, Commdr. Cross of Order of Polonia Restituta, 1954, Medal of 30th Anniversary of People's Poland, 1974. Author: Between Word and Silence; Essays, 1960; Larger than Life; Poems, 1960; Piekna Choroba, 1961; Schene Krankheit, 1961; (novel) Beautiful Illness; Mediterranean Myth; Essays, 1962; Intonatienen, 1962; Zone of Fruits, 1964; Poetry and Truth; Essays, 1966; Poezje (selection of poems), 1966; In Broad Daylight, 1967; (biographic novel) Mickiewicz, 1967; Poezje wybrane (selection of poems), 1968; Signs of Memory-poems, 1969; Freedom of Choice-essays, 1969; (poems) The Isle; Starry Diamond, 1971; (essays) Eseje Wybrane, 1971; Eseje mit Srodziemnomorski, Wolnosc Wyboru, Historia Faustia, 1973; Walk o Slowo (fighting for a Word), 1973; Wyspa (Isle poems), 1973; Blysk obrazu (poems), 1975; Poezje Zebrane, 1976; Scena Obrotowa (poems), 1977; Podroz do Grecji (voyage in Greece), 1978.

JAYEWARDENE, JUNIUS RICHARD, former president of Sri Lanka; b. Colombo, Ceylon, Sept. 17, 1906; s. E.W. and Agnes Helen Jayewardene; m. Elina B. Rupesinghe, 1935; 1 child. Student Royal Coll., Univ. Coll. Law Coll. of Colombo. Mem. Colombo Municipal Council, 1940, State Council, 1943; hon. sec. Ceylon Nat. Congress, 1940-47; mem. Ho. of Reps., 1945-77, leader, 1953-56; minister of fin., 1947-53, of agr. and food, 1953-56, of fin., info., broadcasting, local govt. and housing, 1960; dep. leader of opposition, 1960-65; minister of state, parliamentary sec. to minister def., external affairs and planning, 1965-70; leader opposition, 1970-77; prime minister of Sri Lanka, 1977-78; minister of aviation, 1978, pres. of Sri Lanka, 1978-88; minister of def. and plan implementation, 1979-88, minister of higher edn., Janatha estate devel., state plantations, 1981-88, minister of power, from 1982, minister of energy, 1982-88; del. numerous internat. confs. Hon. trustee Anakarika Dharmapala Trust; hon. treas. United Nat. Party, 1947-48, v.p., 1953, sec., 1972, leader, 1973-75, 75-90. Author: Some Sermons of the Buddha; Buddhist Essays; (speeches) In Council; Buddhism and Marxism; Selected Speeches. Died Nov. 1, 1996.

JEANES, LINCOLN DOUGLAS, JR., neurosurgeon; b. Shreveport, Feb. 13, 1931; s. Lincoln Douglas Jeanes and Hazel Graves Goins; m. Nina Crisman Vann; children: Lincoln Douglas, Lisa Vann. BA with highest honors, U. Tex., 1952; MD, Harvard Med. Sch., 1960. Diplomate Am. Bd. Neurol. Surgery. Intern surg. Balt. City Hosp., 1959-60; resident neurosurgery Johns Hopkins Hosp., Balt., 1960-66; pvt. practice neurosurgery Austin, Tex., 1966-67, Corpus Christi, Tex., 1967-71, Minot, N.D., 1971-73, San Diego, 1973-78; emergency medicine physician Ft. Stewart Winn Army Hosp., Hinesville, Ga., 1990; physician clinic medicine Primary Care Clinic, Naval Hosp., Jacksonville, Fla., 1990-94. Lt. (j.g.) USN, 1952-55, Korea. Mem. Navy League, Am. Legion, Phi Beta Kappa. Libertarian. Methodist. Avocations: cycling, military history. Died Oct. 31, 1996.

JEFFRIES, CARSON DUNNING, physicist, educator; b. Lake Charles, La., Mar. 20, 1922; s. Charles William and Yancey (Dunning) J.; m. Elizabeth Dyer, Sept. 15, 1945 (div. 1976); children: Andrew, Patricia; m. Elizabeth Olivia Eielson, Feb. 28, 1990. B.S., La. State U., 1943; Ph.D., Stanford U., 1951. Research assoc. Radio Research Lab., Harvard U., 1943-45; research asst. Stanford U., 1946-50; instr. Physikalisches Institut der Universitat, Zurich, Switzerland, 1951; mem. faculty U. Calif. at Berkeley, 1952—, prof., 1963—; dir. AEC and Office Naval Rsch. projects in solid state physics, 1953—; faculty sr. scientist Lawrence Berkeley Lab., 1978—. Author: Dynamic Nuclear Orientation, 1963, Electron Hole Droplets in Semimconductors, 1983; contbr. articles to profl. jours.; also profl. sculptor. Sr. Postdoctoral fellow NSF, Oxford (Eng.) U., 1958; Sr. Postdoctoral fellow Harvard, 1965-66; Fulbright prof. France, 1959. Fellow Am. Phys. Soc., Am. Acad. Arts and Scis.; mem. NAS.

JELAVICH, BARBARA, history educator; b. Belleville, Ill., Apr. 12, 1923; m. Charles Jelavich, Sept. 27, 1944; children—Mark, Peter. Ph.D., U. Calif.-Berkeley, 1948. Asst. prof. history Ind. U., Bloomington, 1962-64; assoc. prof. Ind. U., 1964-67, prof., 1967-84, disting. prof., 1984—. Author: Russia and the Rumanian National Cause, 1858-1859, 1959, Russia and Greece during the Regency of King Othon, 1832-1835: Russian Documents on the First Years of Greek Independence, 1962, Russland 1852-1871. Aus den Berichten der bayerischen Gesandtschaft in St. Petersburg, 1963, A Century of Russian Foreign Policy, 1964, (with Charles Jelavich) The Balkans, 1965, Japanese transl., 1982, Russia and the Greek Revolution of 1843, 1966, The Habsburg Empire in European Affairs, 1969, The Ottoman Empire, the Great Powers, and the Straits Question, 1870-1887, 1973, St. Petersburg and Moscow: Tsarist and Soviet Foreign Policy, 1814-1974, 1974, (with Charles Jelavich) The Establishment of the Balkan National States, 1804-1920, 1977, History of the Balkans: Eighteenth and Nineteenth Centuries, 1983, History of the Balkans: Twentieth Century, 1983, Russia and the Formation of the Romanian National State, 1821-1878, 1984, Modern Austria: Empire and Republic 1815-1986, 1987, Russia's Balkan Entanglements 1806-1914, 1991; editor: (with Charles Jelavich) Russia in the East, 1876-1880; The Russo-Turkish War and the Kuldja Crisis as Seen through the Letters of A.G. Jomini to N.K. Giers, 1959, (with Charles Jelavich) The Education of a Russian Statesman: The Memoirs of Nicholas Karlovich Giers, 1962, 82, (with Charles Jelavich) The Balkans in Transition, 1963, 74; contbr. articles to profl. jours. Home: Bloomington Ind. DIED 01/14/95. .

JENKINS, LAWRENCE EUGENE, retired aeronautics company executive; b. Salt Lake City, Mar. 12, 1933; s. Lawrence Eugene Sr. and Grace (Crabbe) J.; m. Roberta Catherine Muirhead, Dec. 27, 1957; children: William Robert, Julie Ann Jenkins Kowalik, Mark Fraser. BS in Elec. Engring., U. Utah, 1955, MS in Elect. Engring., 1957. Engring. mgr. space systems div. Lockheed Missiles and Space Co., Sunnyvale, Calif., 1963-71; asst. gen. mgr., chief engr. Lockheed Missiles and Space Co., 1971-72, v.p., spl. assignment, 1972-79, v.p., advanced program devel., 1979-81; v.p., gen. mgr. Lockheed Austin div. Lockheed Missiles and Space Co., Tex., 1981-87, v.p., 1987-88; Chmn. group on engring. IEEE, 1968-69; bd. dirs. Republic Bank, Austin, Fed. Reserve Bank Dallas, San Antonio. Bd. dirs. Austin Symphony, 1983-90, Capital Club, 1984-88, Better Bus. Bur., Austin, 1984-87; chmn. Gov.'s Task Force on Vocat. Edn., 1987, Gov.'s Select Com. on Edn., 1988-89; chmn. Tex. Higher Edn. Coord. Bd., Austin Comm. Coll. Found., 1991-94, trustee, 1989; bd. dirs. Austin C. of C., 1982-88, chmn. 1987. Recipient Silver Knight of Mgmt. award Nat. Mgmt. Assn., 1970, Significant Achievement award U.S. Air Force, 1977; Stanford-Sloan exec. fellow, 1965-66. Fellow AIAA (spacecraft tech. com. 1967-69); mem. Nat. Acad. Engring., Sigma Xi, Tau Beta Pi. Lodge: Masons. Avocation: philately. Died Apr. 5, 1996.

JENNINGS, BURGESS HILL, mechanical engineering educator; b. Balt., Sept. 12, 1903; s. Henry Hill and Martha (Burgess) J.; m. Etta M. Crout, Nov. 7, 1925; 1 son, Robert Burgess. B.E., Johns Hopkins, 1925; M.S., Lehigh U., 1928, M.A., 1935. Test engr. Consol. Gas & Electric Co., Balt., 1925; mem. faculty Lehigh U., 1926-40; prof. dept. mech. engring. Northwestern U., 1940—, ret. prof. emeritus, chmn. dept., 1943-57, assoc. dean, 1962-70; research investigator U.S. OSRD, 1942-45; dir. research labs. Am. Soc. Heating, Refrigerating and Air Conditioning Engrs., Cleve., 1957-60; cons. and gen. research and writing relating to refrigeration, air conditioning and energy usage, 1930—. Author: Heating and Air Conditioning, 1956, Environmental Engineering, 1970, The Thermal Environment, 1978; co-author: Internal Combustion Engines, 1944, Gas Turbine Analysis and Practice, 1953, Air Conditioning and Refrigeration, 1958; also articles on engring., heating and air conditioning. Recipient Richards Meml. award in Mech. Engring., 1950; Merit award Chgo. Tech. Socs. Council, 1963; Worcester Reed Warner medal, 1972. Fellow ASHRAE (pres. 1948-49, F. Paul Anderson medal 1981); mem. ASME (hon.), Nat. Acad. Engring., Am. Soc. Lubricating Engrs. (v.p. 1947-50), Am. Soc. Engring. Edn., Internat. Inst. Refrigeration (v.p. 1958-67), Sigma Xi, Pi Tau Sigma (pres. 1948-50), Tau Beta Pi. Died June 6, 1996.

JENS, ARTHUR MARX, JR., insurance company executive; b. Winfield, Ill., June 26, 1912; s. Arthur M. and Jeanette Elizabeth (Vinton) J.; m. Elizabeth Lee Shafer, Aug. 14, 1937; children: Timothy Vinton, Christopher Edward, Jeffrey Arthur. BS, Northwestern U., 1934; JD, Kent Coll. Law, Ill. Inst. Tech., 1939. Bar: Ill. 1939. Ins. underwriter, claim mgr. Continental Casualty Co. and Royal Globe Group, Chgo., 1934-39; sec., asst. treas. TWA, Kansas City, Mo., 1939-47; v.p., pres., chmn. bd. Fred S. James & Co. Inc., Chgo., 1947-76, hon. chmn. bd., 1947-76; dir. Airline Service Corp. and all TWA subs., Comml. Resources Corp.; founder, dir. 6 First Security Banks of DuPage County; chmn. Jenson Corp. Life gov. Central DuPage Hosp.; mem. Ill. Gov.'s Panel on Racing. Contbr. articles to air transp. and ins. jours. Mem. Ill. State Bar Assn., ABA, Nat. Assn. Ins. Agts. and Brokers (dir.), Chgo. Golf Club (past pres.), Mid-Day Club (trustee), Chgo. Club (Rm. 19), Thunderbird Country Club (Rancho Mirage, Calif.). Republican. Presbyterian. Home: Chicago Ill. Died April 13, 1989; interred Forest Hill Cemetery.

JENSEN, JAMES LESLIE, chemistry educator, dean; b. Tulare, Calif., Oct. 17, 1939; s. Lester Eugene and Mabel Irene (Brown) J.; m. Nancy Ruth Peterson, Aug. 13, 1960; children: Randall Mark, Linda Suzanne. BA in Chemistry, Westmont Coll., 1961; MA in Chemistry, U. Calif., Santa Barbara, 1963; PhD in Organic Chemistry, U. Wash., 1967. Instr. chemistry Westmont Coll., Santa Barbara, Calif., 1962-64, U. Wash., Seattle, 1968; from asst. prof. to prof. Calif. State U., Long Beach, 1968—, assoc. dean Sch. Natural Scis., 1983-93, dean Coll. Nat. Scis. and Math., 1993—; vis. scientist Brandeis U.-W.P. Jencks Lab., Waltham, Mass., 1974-75; vis. prof. U. Calif. Irvine, 1981-82; chmn. various univs. and schs. dept. coms.; lectr. over 40 univs. and profl. confs., U.S., U.K., France, Italy, Sweden. Reviewer NSF, Jour. Am. Chem. Soc., Jour. Organic Chemistry; contbr. 25 articles to profl. jours. Weyerhauser fellow, U. Wash., 1966-67; scholar Westmont Coll., 1957-58, 60-61; recipient Merit award Long Beach Heart Assn., 1970, Disting. Service award Am. Heart Assn., 1971; grantee: NSF, NIH. Mem. AAAS, Am. Sci. Affiliation, Internat. Union of Pure and Applied Chemistry, Am. Chem. Soc. (organic div.), Royal Soc. Chemistry (organic chemistry div., fast reactions groups), Nat. Assn. for Sci., Tech., Soc., Sigma Xi, Phi Beta Kappa, Phi Lambda Upsilon. Republican. Died Aug. 21, 1995.

JENSSON, OLAFUR, physician, educator; b. Reykjavik, Iceland, June 16, 1924; s. Jens Palsson Hallgrimsson and Sigridur Olafsdottir; m. Erla Gudrun Isleifsdottir, May 1, 1953; children: Arnfridur, Isleifur, Sigridur. MD, U. Iceland, 1954, D of Med. Sci., 1978. Specialist in hematology and clin. cytology Ministry of Health, Iceland, 1959—; dir. Blood Bank Nat. Univ. Hosp., Iceland, 1972—, prof. medicine, 1990—. Editor Icelandic Med. Jour., 1965-71. Chmn. Icelandic Soc. Blood Donors, Reykjavik, 1981-92. Mem. Am. Assn. Blood Banks, Royal Soc. Medicine (U.K.), Am. Soc. Human Genetics, Internat. Soc. Amyloidosis, Icelandic Med. Soc., European Soc. Human Genetics (bd. dirs. 1966—). Avocations: genetics, anthropology, history, politics, economy.

JERISON, MEYER, mathematics educator; b. Bialystok, Poland, Nov. 28, 1922; came to U.S., 1929, naturalized, 1933; s. Elia Israel and Esther (Rasky) J.; m. Miriam Schwartz, Aug. 5, 1945; children—Michael, David. B.S., Coll. City N.Y., 1943; M.S., Brown U., 1947; Ph.D., U. Mich., 1950. Physicist NACA, 1944-46; lectr. Case Inst. Tech., 1945-46; research asso. U. Ill. at Urbana, 1949-51; from asst. to assoc. prof. Purdue U., 1951-60, prof., 1960—, chmn. div. math. scis., 1969-75, prof. emeritus, 1991—; research engr. Lockheed Aircraft Corp., 1952. Author: (with Leonard Gillman) Rings of Continuous Functions, 1960. Mem. Am. Math. Soc. (editor bull. 1980-85), AAUP, Math. Assn. Am. (com. on undergrad. program in math. 1968-71, gov. 1981-84), Phi Beta Kappa, Sigma Xi. Died Mar. 13, 1995.

JERNIGAN, VERLAND HENRY, retired newspaper writer; b. Hillsboro, Tenn., Mar. 4, 1911; s. Marion Marlin and Theora Addie (Gentry) J.; m. Verna Lee Thomas, Nov. 12, 1932; children: Virginia Sue Jernigan Bryan, Thomas Marlin. Lic. real estate agt., ins. and stock broker. Newspaper writer and printer Murfreesboro, Tenn. and Hopkinsville, Ky., 1930-42; freelance writer, 1942-76; freelance writer, photographer Southeastern Outdoor Press Assn., 1964-96; freelance writer, columnist Manchester (Tenn.) Newspaper, 1948-84; columnist The Independent, Manchester, 1990—. Author: History of TOWA 1942-90. Pres. Manchester Football Team, 1929, Manchester Golf Assn., 1970, Manchester Golf Course. Recipient Cartter Patton award Tenn. Conservation League, 1964, Tom Rollins award Southeastern Outdoor Press Assn., 1974; named to Ctrl. H.S. Hall of Fame. Mem. Southeastern Outdoor Press Assn. (life; pres. 1971-73), Tenn. Outdoor Writers Assn. (life; pres. 1967, 1st place black and white photo award 1988, 89, 2d place color photo award 1988), Tenn. Conservation League (life; pres. 1963), Outdoor Writers Assn. Am. (bd. dirs. 1979 81), Tenn. Hist. Soc., Masons, NRA (life). Methodist. Avocations: fishing, hunting, golfing, writing, travel.

JESURÚN, HAROLD MÉNDEZ, obstetrician-gynecologist, educator; b. San Juan, P.R., Dec. 24, 1915; s. Willy and Esterlinda (Méndez) J.; m. Dolores López y Piñero, May 17, 1947; children: Carlos Antonio, John Alberto, Maria Celeste, Richard James. B.A., Columbia U., 1937; M.D., U. Mich., 1940. Diplomate: Am. Bd. Ob-Gyn. Intern, Kings County (N.Y.) Hosp., Bklyn., 1940-41; commd. 1st lt. M.C., U.S. Army, 1941, advanced through grades to col., 1959; area med. dir. Brit. Guiana, 1942-43; malariologist New Guinea, 1943-44; chief provincial health officer Taegu, Korea, 1945-46; exec. officer, chief cholera control officer Korea, 1946; asst. resident Fitzsimmons Gen. Hosp., Denver, 1947-48; resident to chief sr. resident Brooke Gen. Hosp., San Antonio, 1948-50; asst. chief ob-gyn service, 1952-55; chief ob-gyn William Beaumont Gen. Hosp., El Paso, Tex., 1950-51, Percy Jones Gen. Hosp., Battle Creek, Mich., 1951-52, U.S. Army Hosp., Ft. Ord, Calif., 1952, Rodriguez Army Hosp., San Juan, 1955-58; chief ob-gyn, chief instr. ob-gyn Letterman Gen. Hosp., San Francisco, 1958-62; chief ob-gyn service, dep. comdr. U.S. Army 97th Gen. Hosp., Frankfurt, Germany, 1962-66; chief ob-gyn service, asst. chief profl. service Madigan Gen. Hosp., Tacoma, 1966-67; ret. Madigan Gen. Hosp., 1967; program dir. ob-gyn St. Michael Hosp., Newark; and asso. clin. prof. N.J. Coll. Medicine and Dentistry, 1967-69; clin. dir. ob-gyn R.E. Thomason Gen. Hosp., El Paso, 1969-73; project dir. Family Planning, OEO, El Paso, 1970-73; clin. investigator Am. Women's Health Program, Temple U., 1972-73; prof. ob-gyn U. Tex.-Houston, 1973-81; clin. prof. ob-gyn Tex. Tech. U. Med. Sch., 1981-94; asst. prof. obstetrics Baylor Med. Sch., 1954-55; ob-gyn cons. U.S. Army Europe, 1962-66; cons. 6th U.S. Army Area, San Francisco, 1958-62. Contbr. numerous articles to profl. jours., chpt. to An Introduction to Gerontology and Geriatrics. Bd. dirs., pres. El Paso chpt. Am. Cancer Soc., 1971-72, bd. dirs. Houston chpt., 1975. Decorated Bronze Star, Army Commendation medal, Legion of Merit; recipient Physician's Recognition award AMA, 1969. Fellow ACS, Am. Coll. Obstetricians and Gynecologists; mem. AAAS, Soc. Med. Cons. to Armed Forces, Houston Ob-Gyn Soc., Tex. Assn. Ob-Gyn, Am. Assn. Tropical Medicine and Hygiene, Bishop Alonso Manso Soc. (v.p. 1957-58), Assn. Mil. Surgeons, El Paso County Med. Soc., Am. Med. Soc. Vienna (Austria) (life), Phi Rho Sigma (v.p. Zeta chpt. 1939-40). Home: El Paso Tex. Died Mar. 18, 1994.

JETER, LOREN EUGENE, SR., retired bulding contractor; b. Carterville, Ill., Feb. 16, 1909; s. Leonard Franklin and Ella Leonora (Hicks) J.; m. Bessie Marie Sizemore, Sept. 1, 1931 (dec. Apr. 1939); children: Loren Eugene Jr., Harold Leon, Lloyd Gordon; m. Jeanette Feltl Hoff, Feb. 12, 1983. ert. cement mason. Constr. laborer Internat. Hod Carriers, Bldg. and Common Laborers Unio Am., Royalton, Ill., 1926-30; coal miner Clayton Coal Co., Denver, 1935-40; cement mason AFL-CIO Union, Cahmpaign, Urbana, Ill., 1941-61; councilman, bd. dirs. City of Nelson, Ill., 1961-62, mayor, 1963-65; administr. Amboy (Ill.) Hosp., 1965; owner, operator, cement mason Longmont (Colo.) Auto Ct., 1966-79; bldg. contractor Longmont, 1969-79. Author, pub.: Who Am I A Jeter Family Saga. Pres. Com. on Pub. Edn., Lee County, Ill., 1956-62; exec. bd. mem. Polit. Edn. in the 16th Congl. Dist. Ill., 1956-62. Mem. SAR, Operative Plasterers and Cemet Mason (50 yr. golden pin). Avocations: fly tying, fly fishing.

JOHNSON, ALVIN HAROLD, musicology educator; b. Virginia, Minn., Apr. 18, 1914; s. Ernest and Rena (Sanden) J.; m. Anita Leonard, Apr. 8, 1944 (dec. 1977); children—David, Timothy, Gwendolyn. B.A., U. Minn., 1936; Ph.D., Yale, 1954; M.A. (hon.), U. Pa., 1968. Instr. Yale U., New Haven, 1950-54, asst. prof., 1954-60; assoc. prof. Ohio State U., Columbus, 1960-61; assoc. prof. musicology U. Pa., Phila., 1961-82, assoc. prof. emeritus, 1982—. Author: (with others) Art of Music, 1960; contbr. articles to profl. jours. Trustee Swathmore Presbyterian Ch., 1980-82. Served to lt. USN, 1942-45. Mem. Am. Musicol. Soc. (treas. 1970—, exec. dir. 1978—, hon. mem. 1985). Democrat.

JOHNSON, (FRANCIS) BENJAMIN, actor; b. Foraker, Okla., June 13, 1918; s. Benjamin John and Ollie (Workmon) J.; m. Carol Elaine Jones, Aug. 31, 1941. Student pub. sch. rancher, Sylmar, Calif., 1966-96. Star: Mighty Joe Young, 1949, Wagonmaster, 1950, Wild Stallion; others film appearances include: Fort Defiance, 1941, Rio Grande, 1950, Shane, 1953, War Drums, 1957, Ten Who Dared, 1960, One Eyed Jacks, 1961, Will Penny, 1968, Undefeated, 1969, Wild Bunch, 1969, Chisum, 1970, Something Big, 1971, The Last Picture Show, 1971 (named Best Supporting Actor 1972), The Getaway, 1972, Junior Bonner, 1972, Corky, 1972, The Train Robbers, 1972, Kid Blue, 1973, Dillinger, 1973, The Sugarland Express, 1974, Bite the Bullet, 1975, Hustle, 1975, Breakheart Pass, 1976, The Town that Dreaded Sundown, 1977, The Greatest, 1977, Grayeagle, 1978, The Swarm, 1978, Terror Train, 1980, The Hunter, 1980, Ruckus, 1981, Tex, 1982, Soggy Bottom U.S.A., 1982, Champions, 1983, Tresspass, 1983, Red Dawn, 1984, Ballet Black, 1985, Let's Get Harry, 1987, Cherry 2000, 1988, Dark Before Dawn, 1988, Back to Back, 1990, The Last Ride, 1989, My Heroes Have Always Been Cowboys, 1991, Radio Flyer, 1992, Angels in the Outfield, 1994; co-star TV series the Monroes, 1966-67; appeared in TV movies of week The Red Pony, 1973, Runaway!, 1973, Blood Sport, 1973, Locusts, 1974, The Savage Bees, 1976, Louis L'Amour's "The Shadow Riders", 1982, Wild Horses, 1985, Stranger on My Land, 1988, The Chase, 1991, Bonanza: The Return, 1993, Bonanza: Under Attack, 1995; miniseries: The Sacketts, 1979, Wild Times, 1980, Dream West, 1986. Home: Westlake Village Calif. Died April 8, 1996.

JOHNSON, CHARLES EDGAR, education educator; b. Rochester, N.Y., July 6, 1919; s. Mason Frank and Ethel Clithero (Lyons) J.; B.S., SUNY, Geneseo, 1946; M.A., UCLA, 1948; M.Ed., U. Ill., 1950, Ed.D., 1952; m. Rita Irene Boyd, July 19, 1963. Tchr., Mt. Morris, N.Y., 1946-47, Geneseo, N.Y., 1948-49; asst. prof. U. Kans., Lawrence, 1951-55; assoc. prof. U. Ill., Urbana, 1955-65; prof. edn. U. Ga., Athens, 1965-85, prof. emeritus, 1985-96, assoc. dir. Research and Devel. Ctr., 1965-68, dir. Ga. Ednl. Models, 1968-75,Ga. Tchr. Assessment Project, 1976-81; ednl. researcher Spencer Press, Chgo., Grolier Inc., N.Y.C., 1958-62; vis. prof. U. P.R., 1963-64; cons. tchr. edn. Ministry of Edn., Indonesia, 1980, 82. Served with AUS, 1941-46. Recipient Cert. of Merit, U. Ga., 1980. Mem. Am. Edn. Research Assn., Assn. Supervision and Curriculum Devel., Phi Delta Kappa (v.p. U. Ga. chpt. 1986-88), Kappa Delta Pi (tchr. educator award for excellence 1979). Baptist. Clubs: Elks, Masons. Designer competency based tchr. edn. program model and Ga. tchr. performance assessment instruments; contbr. numerous articles in field to profl. jours.; editor Holiday Series, Garrard Pub. Co., Champaign, Ill., 1962-96. Died Apr. 7, 1996. Home: Athens Ga.

JOHNSON, DORA MYRTLE KNUDTSON, principal; b. Bryant, S.D., Sept. 4, 1900; d. Knudt Guttorm and Margit Knudtson; m. Arthur Johnson, Jan. 31, 1949 (dec. Aug. 1949); 1 stepdaughter, Doris Miller. BA, St. Olaf Coll., 1923; MA, U. Wash., Seattle, 1941. Sr. high sch. tchr. math. Gaylord (Minn.) Sch. Dist., 1923-26, Madison (S.D.) Sch. Dist., 1926-43; dean of girls Madison (S.D.) Sch. Dist., S.D., 1932-41; prin. Madison (S.D.) Sch. Dist., 1941-43; high sch.tchr. math. Kansas City (Mo.) Sch. Dist., 1943-49; dean of women Mo. Christian Coll., Columbia, 1950-58; cons. AAUW, Kansas City, 1969-71. Editor: A History of the Mo. Div. of AAUW, 1946-76. Mem. AAUW (state pres. Madison, S.D., state chmn., fellowship found. Kansas City 1963-67, state pres. Kansas City 1967-69, nat. com. for ednl. found. D.C. chpt. 1971-75, honorary life mem. 1989, Significant Svc. award 1989), Internat. Assn. of Univ. Women (Ednl. Found. award), Internat. Rels. Coun., Friends of Art. Democrat. Lutheran. Home: Kansas City Mo. Deceased.

JOHNSON, ELIZABETH KATHARINE, transportation executive, civic volunteer; b. Bend, Oreg., Jan. 12, 1951; d. Samuel S. and Elizabeth Avery (Hill) J.; m. John Christopher Helm, Sept. 6, 1986. Grad., Carleton Coll., 1974, Lewis & Clark Law Sch., 1977. Sr. recognizance Multnomah County Cir. Ct., Portland, Oreg., 1974-77; chief exec. officer TransWestern Helicopters, Inc., Scappoose, Oreg., 1978—. Bd. dirs. WIN-PAC, 1990—, S.S. Johnson Found., San Francisco and Redmond, Oreg., 1972—, Oreg. Symphony Assn., 1986-90, Bd. of Oreg. Mil. Mus. Found., 1986—, Planned Parenthood of Columbia and Williamette area, 1987—, Oreg. Mus. Sci. and Industry, 1985-88, N.W. Film Study Coun., 1982-88, Oreg. Sch. Arts and Crafts, 1980-81, Thousand Friends of Oreg., 1976-78, Christie Sch., 1977-79, St. Helens Hosp., 1988-90, William Temple House, 1989-90; bd. dirs. Oreg. Pub. Broadcasting Found., 1987—, sec./treas; bd. dirs., exec. v.p. Doernbecher Children's Hosp. Found., 1986—; treas. Whirly-Girls, Inc., 1987—; mem. Portland Downtown Heliport Citizen Adv. Com.; chmn. com. Grantmakers Oreg. and S.W. Wash.; mem. Oreg. Tourism Alliance; dir. Oreg. Episc. Sch., 1990—; mem. adv. bd. Loaves and Fishes Ctrs., 1989—; apptd. to Columbia County Econ. Devel. Com., 1986—; trustee Pacific Crest Outward Bound Sch., 1986-87. Named one of 100 Most Powerful Women, Oreg. Mag., 1981. Mem. NRA, Nat. Aeronautic Assn., Am. Pilot's Lobby, Helicopter Assn. Internat., Profl. Helicopter Pilots Assn., Internat. Women's Forum, Am. Helicopter Soc., Oreg. Pilot's Assn., Oreg. Hist. Soc., N.W. Antique Airplane Club, Asian Arts Coun., N.W. Rotorcraft Assn., Ninety-Nines Inc., Portland Art Assn., Friends of the Zoo, Oreg. High Desert Mus., Scappoose City Club, Multnomah Athletic Club, Wings, Town Club, Nat. Soc. Colonial Dames. Republican. Episcopalian. Avocation: pistol shooting. Capt of U.S.A. Women's Helicopter Team, USSR, 1978. DIED 10/22/97. .

JOHNSON, FERD, cartoonist, color artist; b. Spring Creek, Pa., Dec. 18, 1905; s. John F. and Bessie A. Johnson; m. Doris Lee White, Feb. 24, 1930; 1 child, Thomas. Student, Chgo. Acad. Fine Arts, 1923. Color artist, Chgo. Tribune, 1923, asst. to, Frank Willard (Moon Mullins), 1923-58; sports illustrator: Westbrook Pegler, 1925-30; cartoonist: Texas Slim; syndicated, Tribune Media Svcs. 1925-27, 40-58, Moon Mullins, 1958-91; oil paintings represented in various So. Calif. galleries. Mem. Nat. Cartoonist Soc., Comics Coun. Home: Corona del Mar Calif. Died Oct. 14, 1996.

JOHNSON, GLENN WALTER, JR., manufacturing corporation executive; b. Albuquerque, May 24, 1921; s. Glenn Walter and Myrtle M. (Reynolds) J.; m. Harriet E. Schwindt, Oct. 26, 1970; children by previous marriage: Kristina, Mitzi A., Glenn Walter III. Grad. magna cum laude, Stanford U., 1947. Pilot Pan-Am. Airways,

Miami, Fla., 1945-46; sales engr., regional sales mgr., plant mgr., gen. mgr., v.p. AGA div. Elastic Stop Nut Co., Elizabeth, N.J., 1947-59; exec. v.p. parent co. Elastic Stop Nut Co., Union, N.J., 1967, pres., 1968; sr. v.p. Amerace Corp., N.Y.C., 1969-74, exec. v.p., 1974-83; pres. Aircast Inc., Summit, N.J., 1983—. Patentee in field. Served with USAAF, 1943-45. Decorated Air medal. Mem. Phi Beta Kappa, Phi Gamma Delta. Club: Baltusrol Golf (Springfield, N.J.). Died Jan. 23, 1997.

JOHNSON, JACK THOMAS, political science educator; b. Burlington, Iowa, July 16, 1915; s. James H. and Emily L. (Holihan) J.; m. Lavelda Hall, Mar. 10, 1977. BA, State U. Iowa, 1935, MA, 1936, PhD, 1938. Asst. in instrn. State U. Iowa, 1936-40, instr. polit. sci., 1940-42, asst. prof., 1942-47, assoc. prof., 1947-51; asst. adminstr. tng. and edn. Office FCDA, 1951-53; provost Hofstra Coll., 1953-57, v.p., 1957-62; vis. prof. polit. sci. N.M. Western Coll., 1962-63; dir. Bur. Govt. Research, Ind. State U., 1964-65; asso. dir. Inst. Higher Edn., Tchrs. Coll., Columbia, 1965-68; asso. dean arts and scis. Ind. State U., 1968-70, dir. spl. gen. edn. projects, 1974-75, prof. polit. sci., 1975-87, prof. emeritus, 1987-95. Author: A Railroad to the Sea, 1939, Peter A. Dey, 1939, A Handbook for Iowa Mayors, 1943, Iowa Government, 1951, The Changing Mission of Home Economics, 1968; Contbr. profl. jours. Mem. Gov.'s Bd. Incorporators for U. So. Ind., 1984-85; mem. GTE North's Consumer Cons. Panel, 1983-89. Served to ensign USNR, 1944-46. Rockefeller Found. fellow, 1946. Mem. Phi Beta Kappa, Pi Gamma Mu, Omicron Delta Kappa, Alpha Tau Omega, Pi Delta Epsilon, Sigma Kappa Alpha. Home: Terre Haute Ind. Died Aug. 22, 1995; interred Roselawn, Terre Haute, IN.

JOHNSON, JESSIE JONES, newspaper columnist, writer; b. Alleghany County, N.C., Mar. 24, 1924; d. Mack Astor and Lula Delta (Billings) Jones; m. Peter Dexter Johnson Sr., Oct. 3, 1943 (Sept. 1978); children: Peter Dexter Jr., Carol Osborne Johnson Haigh, William Todd. AB in English, U. N.C., 1949; postgrad., Cornell U., 1957, SUNY, Albany, 1959, Skidmore Coll., 1982, 84. Columnist Schenectady (N.Y.) Gazette, 1950-55; mag. feature writer Niskayuna (N.Y.) Bull., 1957-81; pub. rels. dir. Bellevue Women's Hosp., Niskayuna, 1967-75; med. scriptwriter Sta. WGY Radio, Niskayuna, 1970-77; newspaper columnist The Blue Ridge Sun, Sparta, N.C., 1990-93; corr. sec. Women's Press Club of N.Y. State, Albany, 1970-71; pres. Internat. Toastmistress, Schenectady, 1965; 3d v.p. AAUW, Schenectady, 1969. Author: History of Alleghany County, N.C., 1983, History of Grayson County, Va., 1996; editor: History of Niskayuna, N.Y., 1976; contbr. hist. and geneal. articles to Alleghany Hist. Soc., 1981-97, Grayson County Hist. Soc., 1995-97. Bicentennial chmn. Town of Niskayuna, 1974-80; mem. assoc. Nat. Trust for Hist. Preservation, Washington; mem. Met. Mus. Art, N.Y.C., N.C. Preservation Trust, Raleigh, N.C., Scott and Zelda Fitzgerald Mus., Montgomery, Ala., 1993-97. Recipient 1st pl. award for feature story N.C. Roundtable, 1981, 82, 3d pl. award for short story, 1982. Mem. Women's Press Club. Home: Sparta N.C. Died Oct. 17, 1997; buried New Hope Cemetary.

JOHNSON, LAWRENCE, JR., history educator; b. Sintra, Portugal, Aug. 23, 1921; s. Lawrence and Gwladys (Rawes) J.; married; children: Caroline, Lawrence III. BGE, U. Omaha, 1963; MA, U. Maine, 1968; PhD, Temple U., 1975. Commd. U.S. Army, advanced through ranks to lt. comdr.; history prof. Union Coll., Cranford, N.J., 1971-86; retired U.S. Army; adj. prof. history Phila. Coll. Textile and Sci., 1986—. Bd. dirs., pres. St. Anthony Ednl. Found., Ithaca, N.Y., 1987-92. Mem. Phila. Club, Penn Club. Democrat. Episcopalian. Avocations: rowing, tennis. DIED 02/23/95. .

JOHNSON, LOWELL FERRIS, consumer products executive, consultant; b. Butler, N.J., Sept. 21, 1912; s. George F. and Eliza (James) J.; m. Josephine Herche, July 7, 1939 (dec. Jan. 1964); children: Don W., Joy C. Johnson; m. Beverly Herman, Sept. 25, 1965 (dec. June 1979). B.S., N.J. State U., 1934; Ed.M., Rutgers U., 1938; postgrad., N.Y. U; LL.D., Coll. of the Ozarks, 1977, Trenton State Coll., 1988. Mem. staff N.J. State Legislature, 1934-41; mem. faculty Rutgers U., 1941-45; with Am. Home Products Corp., N.Y.C., 1945-94, mem. ops. com., 1957-94, v.p. indsl. relations, 1959-61, v.p., 1961-77, cons., 1977-94; chmn. bd. AHPC Coordinated Bargaining Trust; v.p., bd. dirs. Citizen's Realty Co.; exec. com., trust com., bd. dirs. United Nat. Bank; bd. dirs. Mid Jersey Savs. and Loan Assn., Bankers Nat. Life Ins. Co.; v.p., bd. dirs. United Nat. Bancorp; pres., bd. dirs. LOR, Inc.; former spl. lectr. Rutgers U., Columbia U., NYU, George Washington U., U. Balt. Mem. mgmt. team U.S. Dept. State Mission to Guatemala, 1961; mem. Mayor's Labor-Mgmt. Adv. Com., N.Y.C.; mem. adv. com. Social Welfare Center, Columbia U.; also affiliated bus. fellow Grad. Sch. Bus.; chmn. bd. govs. Mulhlenberg Regional Med. Ctr.; bd. dirs. Internat. Coun. for Operation Enterprise; chmn. bd., chmn. exec. com., mem. internat. com., nat. fund raising chmn. Am. Heart Assn.; trustee, vice chmn. bd. N.J. State Coll.; bd. dirs. Nat. Health Coun., Am. Fedn. for Aging Rsch.; v.p., mem. exec. com. U.S.O.; councilman North Plainfield (N.J.) City Coun.; chmn. Gantt Gold Medal Award Bd.; bd. dirs. Huntington Found., Muhlenberg Hosp. Found.; chm. bd. Lowell F. Johnson Found., 1992-94. Recipient Boss of Yr. award N.Y. chpt. Nat. Secs. Assn., 1959, Disting. Alumnus award N.J. State Coll., Gold Heart award Am. Heart Assn., Disting. Svc. award N.J. Heart Assn., cert. of appreciation Coun. for Internat. Progress in Mgmt. U.S., Lowell F. Johnson award Muhlenberg Regional Med. Ctr., William Augustus Muhlenberg award Muhlenberg Hosp. Found, Outstanding Svc. award State of N.J., Mgr. of Yr. award Lockheed Electronics Mgmt. Assn., resolution of commendation N.J. State Senate, Community award for A Life Worthwhile project, Alumni award Sch. Bus. Trenton State Coll., 1988. Mem. N.J. C. of C. (chmn. mgmt.-employee relations com.), Commerce and Industry Assn. (chmn. state and local affairs com, mem. council), U.S. C. of C., Council State Chambers Commerce U.S., Soc. Advancement Mgmt., Am. Arbitration Assn. (nat. labor panel), Am. Mgmt. Assn. (life; v.p., trustee, exec. com., chmn. human resources council, Disting. Service award 1979, Man of Yr. award 1980, pres.'s council 1979-94), NAM (mem. labor relations policy com.), Nat Indsl. Conf. Bd., N.Y. Indsl. Relations Assn. (past pres.), N.J. Hosp. Assn. (coun., Spl. Recognition award 1991), Internat. Platform Assn., Lowell F. Johnson Found. (chmn. bd.), Phi Delta Kappa. Clubs: Plainfield Country, Vanderbilt Athletic, T.D. of N.Y. Home: North Plainfield N.J. Died Oct. 29, 1994.

JOHNSON, MARVIN MELROSE, industrial engineer, consultant; b. Neligh, Nebr., Apr. 21, 1925; s. Harold Nighram and Melissa (Bare) J.; m. Anne Stuart Campbell, Nov. 10, 1951; children: Douglas Blaikie, Harold James, Phyllis Anne, Nighram Marvin, Melissa Joan. B.S., Purdue U., 1949; postgrad., Ill. Inst. Tech., 1953; M.S. in Indsl. Engring, U. Iowa, 1966, Ph.D., 1968. Registered profl. engr., Iowa, Mo., Nebr. Quality control supr., indsl. engr. Houdaille Hershey, Chgo., 1949-52; indsl. engr. Bell & Howell, Chgo., 1952-54; with Bendix Aviation Corp., Pioneer Ctrl. Divsn., Davenport, Iowa, 1954-64, successively chief indsl. engr., staff asst., supr. procedures and systems, reliability engr. Pioneer Cen. div., 1954-64; indsl. engring. cons., Bendix Aviation Corp. (Pioneer Central div.), Alcoa, Brunswick, Rapid City, S.D., 1964—; lectr. indsl. engring. State U. Iowa, 1963-64; instr. U. Iowa, 1965-68; assoc. prof. U. Nebr., 1968-73, prof., 1973-88, emeritus prof., 1988-96; vis. prof. S.D. Sch. Mines and Tech., 1989-91, Ervin Pietz prof., 1991; U.S. AID adviser mgmt. engring. and food processing, Kabul, Afghanistan, 1975-76; vis. prof. indsl. engring. U. P.R., Mayaguez, 1982-83. Editor The Johnson Reporter, 1980-88. Served with AUS, 1943-46, ETO. Fellow Inst. Indsl. Engrs.; mem. ASME (life), Ops. Rsch. Soc., Sigma Xi, Tau Beta Pi, Pi Tau Sigma, Alpha Pi Mu. Presbyterian. Died April 16, 1996; buried Laurel Hill Cemetery, Neligh, NE.

JOHNSON, NORMAN, music director, opera producer, educator; b. Oneida, N.Y., Nov. 12, 1928; s. James Kenneth and Mildred (Sevy) J.; m. Matilda Nickel, Dec. 31, 1962. BS, Juilliard Sch. Music, 1950, MS, 1951. Assoc. condr. Oratorio Soc. N.Y., N.Y.C., 1955-64; mem. conducting staff Central City (Colo.) Opera Festival, Denver, 1962-70; mem. conducting faculty Peabody Conservatory Music, Balt., 1964-68; artistic dir. Denver Lyric Opera, 1967-72; condr. Winston-Salem (N.C.) Symphony Chorale, 1975-80; dir. opera N.C. Sch. Arts, Winston-Salem, 1968-96; founder, artistic dir. Piedmont Opera Theatre, Winston-Salem, 1976-82, gen. dir., 1982-96; coach Met. Opera Nat. Co., 1965; co-dir. Met. Opera Dist. Auditions, 1982-94; music dir. N.C. Summer Festival, Winston-Salem, 1973, Manhattanville Summer Opera Workshop, Purchase, N.Y., 1979-80; condr. Agnes De Mille's Heritage Dance Theater, Winston-Salem, 1973; guest condr. various orchs., opera cos., 1974-96; artistic dir. Greensboro Opera Co., 1994. Performed at Instanbul Internat. Festival, Turkey, 1987, Appalachian Summer Festival, 1989; translator: (operas) Hansel and Gretel (Humperdinck), The Daughter of the Regiment (Donizetti); rec. artist for Riverside and SMC Records. Mem. Cmty. Adv. Bd. Sta. WFFD, Winston Salem, 1984-88. Mem. Am. Fedn. Musicians. Home: Winston Salem N.C. Died Sept. 10, 1996.

JOHNSON, ROBERT IVAR, scientific consultant; b. Chgo., Aug. 18, 1933; s. Ivar Carl and Anna Elina (Wirkula) J. Diploma, Wright Coll., 1953; A.B., Northwestern U., 1957; postgrad., U. Mich., 1958-59. Research asst. Dearborn Obs., Northwestern U., 1953-54, 57; planetarium tech. Adler Planetarium and Astron. Mus., 1953-55, asst. dir., acting dir., 1959, dir., 1960-66; staff Mus. Expdn. Observation Total Solar Eclipse, 1954, 63; dir. Kansas City Mus. History and Sci., 1966-70; exec. v.p., asst. sec., asst. treas., dir. Envirco, Inc., Northbrook, Ill., 1970-72; ptnr., exec. v.p. Tomorrow's Products Co., 1972-73; dir. spl. projects Bus. Communications Am., Tampa, Fla., 1989, dir. advanced projects, exec. bd., 1990-93; br. writer, ednl. publs. and spl. svcs. NASA, 1989-93; spectrographic observer U. Mich., 1958-59; adult edn. faculty Central YMCA, Chgo., 1959-61; lectr. astronomy Chgo. Acad. Scis., 1959-66, Chgo. Tchrs. Coll., 1960-66; spl. lectr. astronomy Ind. U., 1960-65; cons. Field Enterprises Ednl. Corp., 1960-66, Hubbard Sci. Co., 1961, Replogle Globe Co., 1962-63, 68, Compton's Ency., 1961-73, No. Ill. U., 1961-65, Ency. Brit. Films, Inc., 1962-64, McGraw-Hill, Inc., 1963, Mus. Sci. and Tech., Tel Aviv, 1965-70, Rand McNally & Co., 1966, NSF Earth Sci. Curriculum Project, 1966, Coll. Am. Pathologists, 1970, 73-76, 79-85, MCR, Inc., 1972-76, McCrone Research Inst., 1972-83, Frank J. Corbett, Inc., 1972-75, Johnson & Johnson Advt., 1972-83, Dynamic Mktg. Programs, Inc., 1972-73, McCrone Assos., Inc., 1972-77, Yunker Industries, Inc., 1977-93, Clay Engring. & Mfg. Co., 1977-90, Sci. Teaching Aids Co., Inc., 1977-86, Sonoscan Inc., 1977-83, F.E. Fryer Co., Inc., 1978-83, Andreas Assos., Inc., 1979-80; Scott Abbott Mfg. Co., 1978-86, Tech. Mktg. Group Ltd., 1979-86, Intermatic, Inc., 1979-83, others; dir. NSF Summer Inst. in Astronomy, 1963, 64, 66; partner TBM Investments Co., 1964-65; tech. cons. Follett Pub. Co., 1966-68; mem. citizens adv. com. for natural scis. Lake Forest Coll., 1961-66; bd. advisers World Book Ency. Sci. Service, 1964-66; program adv. bd. Inter-Univ. Center, 1966-73; mem. Am. Nat. ICOM Com. Edn. and Cultural Action; cons. astronomy and allied scis., planetarium design and ednl. films prodn. various orgns., Greater Tampa C. of C., Com. of 100, 1985-88, U. So. Fla., The Living Ctr. for Biblical and Archeol. Studies, 1985-87, Hillsborough County Med. Assn., 1985-86, Marketech Advt. and Design, 1985-86, HLA Advt. and Pub. Relations, 1985-87, Sensidyne, Inc., 1985-86, CGM Services, Inc., 1985-90, LA Force Enterprises, Inc., 1985-89, LA Force Mktg. Group Ltd., Inc., 1986-93; cons. editor Slack Inc., Thorofare, N.J., 1989-93; writer NASA Tech. Briefs, 1990-93. Author: Teachers Guide for the Celestial Globe, 1961, Astronomy-Our Solar System and Beyond, 1963, Galaxy Model Study Guide, 1963, The Story of the Moon, 1963, rev. edit., 1968, 2d revision, 1971, Celestial Planetarium Guide Book, 1964, Meteorite Kit Study Guide, 1968, Sundials, 1968, Cataract Surgery-Before and After: A Patient's Views, 1987-88; editor: Insight, 1972-77, Techniques, Instruments and Accessories for Microanalysts: A User's Manual, 1972-83; editorial bd.: Space Frontiers, 1962-66; contbr. articles to profl. jours., other publs. Sci. fair judge high sch. div. Chgo. Bd. Edn., Parochial Schs., 1959-66; mem. U.S. com. for ednl. and cultural affairs Internat. Council Museums, 1966-70; mem. fine arts com. Ill. Sesquicentennial Commn., 1967-68; mem. Model Cities Com., Liberty Meml. Exhbn. Com., 1967-70, both Kansas City; mem. Regional Health and Welfare Council, 1967-70, Kansas City Assembly on U.S. and Eastern Europe, 1968, NSF panel Summer Inst. for Secondary Schs., 1968-76; mem. Midwest Mus. Conf., 1964-70, fin. com., 1967-70; mem. spl. events com. Kansas City Jewish Community Center, 1968-70; mem. Twin Lakes Bicentennial Com., 1976; v.p. Lakewood Sch. Parent Tchr. Orgn., 1976-77, pres., 1977-78, 80; bd. govs. Bacchus Cultural and Ednl. Found., 1968-70; mem. biomed. devices subcom. Fla. High Tech. and Industry Coun., 1990—. Served with AUS, 1955-56; intelligence analyst Chgo.-Gary Nike Def. Hdqrs. Recipient certificate for service Gary (Ind.) Pub. Schs., 1959; Indsl. Research 100 award, 1973; named One of 10 Outstanding Young Men Chgo. Jr. C. of C. and Industry, 1961. Fellow AAAS; mem. Am. Astron. Soc. (co-chmn. com. spl. events 1964), Chgo. Astron. Soc., Internat. Platform Assn., Chgo. Planetarium Soc., Chgo. Physics Club (dir., pres. 1960-66), Royal Astron. Soc. Can., Assn. Sci. Mus. Dirs., Chgo. Geog. Soc., Adult Edn. Council Greater Chgo. (speakers bur., dir.), Am. Assn. Museums (chmn. planetarium sect. 1962-66, program chmn. 1966), Northwestern U. Alumni Assn., Nat. Adult Edn. Assn. (tours com. 1966), Golf (Ill.) Civic Assn., Mu Beta Phi (hon.). Clubs: Execs. (Chgo.); Carriage. Home: Tampa Fla. Died Jan. 1993.

JOHNSON, U. ALEXIS, diplomat; b. Falun, Kans., Oct. 17, 1908; s. Carl Theodore and Ellen Irene (Forsse) J.; m. Patricia Ann Tillman (dec. 1981); children: Judith Ann, Stephen Tillman, William Theodore Kim, Jennifer Ellen; m. Dode Fee, Aug. 19, 1989 (dec. 1994). AB, Occidental Coll., 1931, LLD (hon.), 1954. Fgn. service officer Dept. of State, Washington, 1935-77; ambassador Dept. of State, Prague, Czechoslovakia, 1953-58, Bangkok, Thailand, 1958-61; dep. under sec. Dept. of State, Washington, 1961-64, under sec., 1965-66; ambassador Dept. of State, Tokyo, Japan, 1966-69; under sec. Dept. of State, Washington, 1969-73, ambassador at large, 1973-77; vice chmn. Atlantic Coun. U.S., Washington, 1984-97; chmn. Washington Inst. Fgn. Affairs, 1984-97. Author: Right Hand of Power, 1984; coauthor: China Policy for the Next Decade, 1984, The Common Security Interests of Japan, the U.S., and NATO, 1981. Recipient Disting. Service award, Pres. Nixon, 1971, Disting. Hon. award, Sec. of State, 1977, Disting. Pub. Service, Sec. of Def., 1977, Rockefeller Pub. Service award, Princeton U., 1965, Order of the Rising Sun, Japanese Emperor, 1982. Died Mar., 1997.

JOHNSRUD, RUSSELL LLOYD, surgeon, insurance company executive; b. Portland, Oreg., June 4, 1909; s. Joseph Andreus and Mignonette Josephine (Fleischer) J.; m. Barbara Faire Pittock, Apr. 18, 1939 (dec. Mar. 1991); children—Georgiana Johnsrud Rathman, Nancy Johnsrud Dudley, Stephen Russell; m. Frances M. Rogers, Sept. 25, 1991. B.A., U. Oreg., 1930, IM.D., 1933. Diplomate: Am. Bd. Surgery. Intern U. Oreg. Med. Sch. Hosps., 1933-34; resident St. Luke's Hosp., San Francisco, 1934-35; practice medicine specializing in surgery Portland, 1935-76; asst. prof. surgery U. Oreg., 1952—; dir. Blue Cross of Oreg., Portland, 1949-79, vice chmn., 1965-79; dir., treas. Gearhart Condominium

Mgmt. Co., Oreg., 1973-79, v.p., 1979-80; mem. staff St. Vincent Hosp.; mem. staff, dir. Med. Center Hosp., 1961-76. Served to comdr. USNR, 1939-45, PTO. Mem. ACS, AMA, North Pacific Surg. Assn., Portland Surg. Soc. (pres. 1957-58), Nu Sigma Nu, Alpha Omega Alpha. Clubs: Multnomah Athletic (Portland), Arlington (Portland), Waverley Country (Portland); Charbonneau Golf and Country (Wilsonville, Oreg.). Died Feb. 9, 1992.

JOHNSTON, DAVID TOWNSEND, commodity broker; b. Richmond Hill, N.Y., Feb. 12, 1921; s. Alexander S. and Ruth J.; 1 son, Peter A. B.S. in Econs, Wharton Sch., U. Pa., 1942. Asst. v.p. commodity dept. Merrill Lynch, Pierce, Fenner & Smith, N.Y.C., 1946-68; sr. v.p. commodities, dir. E.F. Hutton & Co. Inc., N.Y.C., 1968—; dir. E.F. Hutton London Ltd.; mem., past chmn. bd. govs. Commodity Exchange, Inc.; mem. Chgo. Bd. Trade, Coffee, Sugar and Cocoa Exchange, Inc.; N.Y. Cotton Exchange, Winnipeg Commodity Exchange, Mpls. Grain Exchange. Trustee Northfield Mt. Hermon Sch., N.Y.C., Mission Soc. Served to lt. USNR, 1942-45. Mem. Futures Industry Assn. (past chmn. bd. dirs.), Nat/Futures Assn. (vice chmn., dir.). Clubs: Ridgewood (N.J.); Country.

JONES, BARCLAY GIBBS, regional economics researcher; b. Camden, N.J., June 3, 1925; s. Barclay Gibbs Jones and Kathryn (Prince) Preston; m. Anne Van Syckel Tompkins, June 8, 1957 (dec. Jan. 22, 1994); children: Barclay Gibbs, Louise Tompkins. BA, U. Pa., 1948, BArch, 1951; MRP, U. N.C., 1955, PhD, 1961. Registered architect, N.C. Community planner Citizens Coun. on City Planning, Phila., 1951; from instr. to asst. prof. Dept. City Regional planning U. Calif. at Berkeley, 1956-61; from assoc. prof. to prof. Dept. City Regional Planning Cornell U., 1961—; program dir. Cornell Inst. for Social and Econ. Rsch., 1983—; exec. com. mem. Nat. Ctr. for Earthquake Engring. Rsch., Buffalo, 1989-91, rsch. com. mem. 1991—. Editor Protecting Historic Architecture and Museum Collections from Natural Disasters, 1986; contbr. articles to profl. jours. Bd. dirs. Archtl. Rsch. Ctrs. Consortium, Inc., 1980—; chair Ithaca City Landmarks Preservation Commn., N.Y., 1984-91, vice chair, 1992-94; pres. Historic Ithaca and Tompkins County, Inc., 1979-81, bd. dirs., 1975-81; bd. dirs. Nat. Preservation Inst., Inc., 1984—. With U.S. Army, 1943-46. Decorated Purple Heart; recipient Pub. Svc. award Nat. Park Svc., U.S. Dept. Interior, 1988, Disting. Planning Educator award Am. Collegiate Sch. Planning, 1990; fellow U.S. Internat. Coun. on Monuments and Sites, 1986. Mem. AIA, AAAS, AAUP, Am. Inst. Cert. Planners, Am. Planning Assn., Am. Statis. Assn., Earthquake Engring. Rsch. Inst., Nat. Trust Historic Preservation, N.E. Regional Sci. Assn. (pres 1975-76, 87-88), Am. Econ. Assn., Regional Sci. Assn. (coun. 1976-80, pres. 1983, archivist 1984—), Soc. Archtl. Historians, Urban Regional Info. Systems Assn. (pres. 1966-69), Phi Kappa Phi. Republican. Episcopalian.

JONES, BEN, retired steel company executive; b. N.Y.C., Jan. 27, 1912; s. Adolf and Rose (Gelbaum) J.; m. Esther M. Kasle, Jan. 24, 1937; children: Judith, Linda, Karen, David. BS, NYU, 1933. Exec. in tng. Henshaw Furniture Co., N.Y.C., 1932-36; salesman Kasle Steel Corp., Detroit, 1937-38, various adminstrv. positions, 1938-45, various exec. positions, currently vice chmn., 1945—. Author: These, Them and Those, 1973; (autobiography) A Piece of Time, 1987, Silvered Glass, 1992. Chmn. budget com. United Found., Detroit, 1972. Recipient 2nd place award in poetry Am. Poetry Assn., 1988, 1989; recipient of Citation of Excellence for Sculpture, Internat. Art Horizons, 1989. Mem. Steel Svc. Ctr. Inst. (pres. 1953-54), Franklin Hills Country Club (v.p., bd. dirs.). Avocations: photography, sculpting, writing. Home: Franklin Mich. DIED 09/15/95. .

JONES, BOB, JR., academic administrator, educator, lecturer, minister; b. Montgomery, Ala., Oct. 19, 1911; s. Bob and Mary Gaston (Stollenwerck) J.; m. Fannie May Holmes, 1938; children: Bob III, Jon Edward, Joy Estelle. Grad., Bob Jones Coll., 1930; M.A., U. Pitts., 1932; student, U. Chgo., U. Ala., Northwestern U.; Litt.D. (hon.), Asbury Coll., Wilmore, Ky., 1935, Chung-ang U., Seoul, Korea, 1972; L.H.D., John Brown U., Siloam Springs, Ark., 1941; LL.D., Houghton Coll., 1943; D.D., Northwestern Schs., Mpls., 1950; S.T.D., Midwestern Bible Coll., Pontiac, Mich., 1974. Acting pres. Bob Jones Coll., 1932-47; pres. Bob Jones U., 1947-71, chmn. bd. trustees, 1964-97, chancellor, 1971-97; Shakespearean authority and interpreter. Minister, lectr., radio speaker; author: All Fullness Dwells, How to Improve Your Preaching, As the Small Rain, Inspirational and Devotional Verse, Wine of Morning, Ancient Truths for Modern Days, Revealed Religion: Paintings by Benjamin West, Prologue: A Drama of Jon Hus, Showers Upon the Grass, Heritage of Faith, Old Testament Sermons (4 vols.), Rhyme & Reason, Daniel of Babylon, Cornbread and Caviar; contbr. writings to various religious and profl. periodicals; editor: Faith for the Family, 1973-86. Col. Gov's. Staff, S.C.; Col. Gov's. Staff, Tenn.; Col. Gov's. Staff, Ala.; recipient Order of Palmetto State of S.C.; Silver Good Citizenship medal Birmingham chpt. SAR. Mem. Gospel Fellowship Assn. (pres. bd.), Internat. Cultural Soc. Korea (hon.). Died Nov. 12, 1997.

JONES, CLAIBORNE STRIBLING, zoologist; b. Petersburg, Va., Dec. 20, 1914; s. Claiborne Turner and Elizabeth (Stribling) J.; m. Annie Goodwyn Boisseau, June 12, 1940; children—Anne Goodwyn, Maria de Saussure, Elizabeth Claiborne. A.B., Hampden-Sydney Coll., 1935; M.A., U. Va., 1940, Ph.D., 1944. Faculty U. N.C., 1944—, prof. zoology, 1956-84, prof. emeritus, 1984—; assoc. dean Gen. Coll., 1958-65, asst. vice chancellor, 1965-66, asst. to chancellor, 1966-73, vice chancellor for bus. and finance, 1973-77, exec. asst. to chancellor, 1977-80, spl. asst. to chancellor, 1980-84. Mem. Am. Soc. Zoologists, Phi Beta Kappa, Sigma Xi, Omicron Delta Kappa, Pi Kappa Alpha. Democrat. Episcopalian. DIED 03/23/96. .

JONES, HARRY WILLMER, lawyer, educator; b. N.Y.C., Mar. 4, 1911; s. Harry and Leona May (Coffin) J.; m. Shirley O'Neal Coggeshall, Nov. 21, 1935 (dec. 1955); m. Alice Neuburger Katz, July 11, 1956 (dec. 1984); m. Jean Brown Kinney, Jan. 21, 1990. Student, Westminster Coll., Fulton, Mo., 1929-31; LL.B., Washington U., St., Louis, 1934, A.B., 1937; postgrad., Oxford U., Eng.; postgrad. (Rhodes scholar), 1934-35; LL.M., Columbia, 1939; LL.D., Jewish Theol. Sem. Am., 1967; L.H.D., Villanova U., 1972. Bar: Mo. bar 1934, Calif. bar 1946. Part-time law practice, lecture series on public and internat. affairs, 1935-38; instr., asst. prof. law Washington U., 1935-39; vis. lectr. in law Columbia, 1939-40, Stanford, summer 1940; asso. prof. law U. Calif., 1940-41, prof., 1946; prof. law Columbia, 1947-57, Cardozo prof. jurisprudence, 1957-79, Cardozo prof. emeritus, 1979-93; prof. law U. Chgo., 1963-64; dir. research Am. Bar Found., 1963-64; with O.P.A., Washington, 1941-43; successively as head, research and opinion unit, chief appellate litigation branch, asst. gen. counsel, dir. food enforcement div.; vis. prof. Columbia, summer 1947; vis. prof. law U. Delhi, Inda, 1968; Phi Beta Kappa vis. scholar, 1981-82; Chmn. O.D.M. shipbldg. industry panel, summer 1952; research dir. Am. Assembly, 1953; faculty Salzburg Seminar in Am. Studies, summers 1955-59. Author: (with N.T. Dowling, E.W. Patterson and R.R. Powell) Materials for Legal Method, 1952, Economic Security for Americans, 1954, Legal Realism and Natural Law (Riverside lectures), 1956, Cases on Contract, (with E.W. Patterson and G.W. Goble), 1957, The Courts, The Public and The Law Explosion, 1965, (with E.A. Farnsworth, William F. Young) Cases and Materials on Contracts, 1965, Law and the Social Role of Science, 1966, The Efficacy of Law, 1969, Political Separation and Legal Continuity, 1976, Legal Institutions Today, 1976, (with J.M. Kernochen and A.W. Murphy) Legal Method: Cases and Text Materials, 1980; Editor in charge of dept. legislation: Am. Bar Assn. Jour, 1948-51; directing editor: Univ. Textbook Series. Trustee W.E. Meyer Research Inst. Law, 1957-73. Served as asst. counsel Bur. Aercs. and counsel for Bur. Aeronautics gen. rep., Western Dist., with rank of lt. (j.g.) and lt. comdr. USNR, 1943-46; cons. on legis. research and drafting problems for conl. and state legis. coms. Recipient Alumni citation Washington U., 1958, Alumni citation Westminster Coll., 1960; Henry M. Phillips award for jurisprudence, 1976. Mem. Am. Law Inst., Am. Philos. Soc., Am. Acad. Arts and Scis., Am. Bar Assn., Am. Bar Found., Order of Coif, Phi Delta Theta, Phi Delta Phi. Democrat. Presbyterian. Home: Gaylordsville Conn. Died Apr. 6, 1993.

JONES, LILLIE AGNES, retired elementary education educator; b. Leroy, Iowa, Nov. 25, 1910; d. Orace Wesley and Lorena Floy (Buffum) Davis; m. John Hammond Jones, May 27, 1938 (dec. Aug. 1994); children: John Harry, Mary Agnes Jones Edwards. BA, Colo. State Coll. Edn., 1937. Cert. elem. tchr., Colo. Elem. tchr. Weld County Sch. Dist. 8l, Kersey, Colo., 1930-34, Weld County Sch. Dist. 12l, Erie, Colo., 1934-38, Longmont (Colo.) Pub. Schs., 1955-59, Adams County Sch. Dist. 12, Thornton, Colo., 1959-67, Littleton (Colo.) Pub. Schs., 1967-69; Farmington (N.Mex.) Pub. Schs., 1969-76, ret., 1976; cataloger Longmont Pub. Libr., 1953-55. Kersey High Sch. scholar, 1928. Mem. AAUW (life, past treas. Longmont), Nat. Ret. Tchrs. Assn., N.Mex. Ret. Tchrs. Assn. (life), Pub. Employees Retirement Assn., Colo. Ret. Sch. Employees Assn., Alpha Delta Kappa (rec. sec. Farmington 1975-76, sec. Sun City, Ariz. 1980, historian 1982). Democrat. Avocations: travel, reading, crafts, sports. Deceased.

JONES, OKLA, II, judge; b. 1945. BA, So. U., 1968; JD, Boston Coll. Sch., 1971. With Douglas, Nabonne & Wilkerson, New Orleans, 1976-79, White, Jones & Lombard, New Orleans, 1982-86; judge Civil Dist. Ct. foe Parish of Orleans, 1991-94; dist. judge U.S. Dist. Ct. (ea. dist.), La., 1994—. Died no info.

JONES, REGINALD VICTOR, physicist, natural philosophy educator; b. Sept. 29, 1911; s. Harold Victor and Alice Margaret (May) Jones; m. Vera Margaret Cain, Mar. 21, 1940; children: Susan, Robert, Rosemary. MA, PhD, Oxford (Eng.) U., 1934, fellow (hon.), 1968, 81; DSc (hon.), Strathclyde U., Eng., 1969, Kent U., Eng., 1980; D. Univ. (hon.), York U., Eng., 1976, Open U., 1978, Surrey U., Eng., 1979, Bristol U., 1979, Westminster Coll., 1992. Chartered physicist, chartered engr., Eng. With Royal Air Force, 1936-46; chief sci. intelligence Air Ministry, London Scottish mil., 1939-46, ret., 1946; prof. natural philosophy U. Aberdeen, Scotland, 1946-81, prof. emeritus, 1981—; dir. Centre for Policy Studies, London, 1982-88; vis. prof. U. Colo., 1982. Author: The Wizard War, 1978, Future Conflict and New Technology, 1981, Some Thoughts on Star Wars, 1985, Instruments and Experiences, 1988, Reflections on Intelligence, 1989; contbr. articles to profl. jours. Pres. Crabtree Found., 1958; active European Conv. Human Rights, 1970; gov. Dulwich Coll., 1965-79; life gov. Haileybury Coll., 1978; chmn. Safety in Mines Rsch. Bd., 1960-63. Decorated companion Order Brit. Empire, companion Order of Bath (Eng.), Companion of Honor; recipient Medal for Merit, Pres. Truman, 1946, Merit of Freedom medal with Silver Palm U.S. Govt., 1947, 48. Fellow Royal Soc. (v.p. 1971-72); hon. fellow Balliol Coll. Oxford U., Wadham Coll. Oxford U., Inst. Elec. Engrs., Inst. Measurement and Control, Royal Soc. (v.p. 1971); mem. Electronics Rsch. Coun. (chmn.), Mins. Aviation and Tech., Brit. Nat. Com. for History of Sci., Medicine, and Tech., Athenaeum Club (London), Spl. Forces Club (London).

JONES, ROXANNE HARPER, state legislator; b. N.C., May 3, 1928; d. Gilford and Mary (Bruton) Harper; m. James H. Jones, 1957 (dec.); children: Patricia Hill, Wanda. Student pub. schs. Bd. dirs. Pa. Minority Bus. Devel. Authority, Pa. Legis. Black Caucus, 1985-96, Pa. Intra-Govtl. Long Term Care Coun.; mem. urban affairs and housing com., minority chmn. pub. health and welfare com., mem. aging and youth com., mem. consumer protection and professional licensure com. Pa. State Senate, 1985-96. Recipient Nat. Welfare Rights Orgn. Leadership award Nat. Welfare Rights Orgn., 1972, Woman of Yr. award Zeta Phi Beta, 1985, Achievement cert. Nat. Coun. Negro Women, 1985. Bd. dirs. Ams. for Democratic Action;mem. United house of prayer; mem. children's health adv. coun. Pa. Trauma Systems Found., 1985-96; co-chmn. Coalition Concerned Citizens; exec. dir. Phila. Citizens in Action; mem. Allegheny West Found. Mem. Apostolic Ch. Died May 19, 1996. Died May 19, 1996. Home: Philadelphia Pa.

JONES, RUTH ELAYNE, speech and hearing pathologist; b. Grand Rapids, Mich., July 15, 1920; d. Francis A. and Harriet E. (Madison-Wright) Housler; m. John Arthur Jones, Aug. 5, 1950; children: Jeannine, Joni. Student, Western Mich. U.; AB in Speech and Hearing, Whittier Coll., 1950; postgrad., U. Wis., Milw., 1939, U. Calif., 1955, U. So. Calif., 1959, Wayne State U.; MA, U. Mich., 1960. Tchr. elem. and physical edn. Royal Oak (Mich.), Des Moines, 1939-41; audiometrist Montebello (Calif.) Unified Sch. Dist., 1942-50; head cons. Hearing Impaired, Whittier, Calif., 1950-59; cons. San Juan Capistrano, San Clemente, Calif., 1966; county cons. Lake County, Lakeport, Calif., 1965-66; head of speech and hearing program Mt. Eden Hayward (Calif.) Unified Sch. Dist., 1959-67; master therapist San Jose (Calif.) State Coll., 1968; speech and hearing cons. Napa (Calif.) Unified Sch. Dist., 1972-79; speech therapist Fremont Community Clin., 1968-72; pvt. practice Fairfield, Calif. Author: For Speech Sake; (poems) River of Life, 1988 (Gold award), So Much For Nothing. Vol. convalescent homes, Carson City, Nev., 1982-85, suicide prevention; vol. RSVP program for sr. citizens hearing impaired classes, 1982-85. Recipient Spl. Hon. award Calif. State Fedn., San Francisco, 1978, Hon. Award Napa Union Sch. Dist., 1979, also awards for poetry. Mem. Am. Speech and Hearing Assn. (charter mem., cert. clin. competence); Coun. for Exceptional Children, Internat. Platform Assn., Beta Sigma Phi. Club: Univ. Women's (Whittier, Calif.). Died April 4, 1992.

JONES, VINCENT STARBUCK, retired newspaper editor; b. Utica, N.Y., Dec. 4, 1906; s. William Vincent and Susan B. (Starbuck) J.; m. Nancy van Dyke Parsons, May 25, 1940; children: Suzanne Cansler, Margot Mabie. A.B., Hamilton Coll., 1928; postgrad., Harvard U., 1929-30; LL.D., Hamilton Coll., 1971. Reporter Utica Daily Press, 1928-29, night city editor, 1930-37, city editor, 1937-38, mng. editor, 1938; mng. editor Utica Observer-Dispatch, 1938-42; exec. editor Utica Observer-Dispatch and Utica Daily Press, 1942-50; dir. news and editorial office Gannett Newspapers, 1950-55, exec. editor, 1955-70, v.p., 1965-70; trustee Gannett Found., exec. v.p., sec., 1970-75; Lectr. Am. Press Inst., 1946-68; lectr., writer newspaper readership, readability, photography; dir. Kent State U. photo short course, 1952. Directed, edited: The Road to Integration (Pulitzer prize citation 1964). Mem. Utica City Planning Bd., 1946-50; v.p. St. Luke's Meml. Hosp., Utica, N.Y., 1950; bd. govs. Genesee Hosp., Rochester, 1957-93; treas. Gannett Newspaper Carrier Scholarships, Inc., 1967-75; bd. dirs. Rochester Civic Music Assn., 1954-62; trustee Monroe Community Coll., Rochester, 1961-78, chmn., 1969-74; trustee Internat. Mus. Photography at George Eastman House, Rochester, chmn., 1974-77; bd. overseers Sweet Briar Coll., 1968-75; past trustee Hamilton Coll. Recipient distinguished service medal Syracuse Journalism Sch., 1969. Mem. N.Y. State AP Assn. (pres. 1947), Am. Soc. Newspaper Editors (dir. 1962-70, pres. 1968-69), Asso. Press Mng. Editors Assn. (dir. 1949-56, pres. 1955), N.Y. State Soc. Editors (pres. 1962-63), Internat. Press. Inst. (chmn. Am. com. 1965-68), Nat. Press Photographers Assn. (Sprague award 1954), Rochester Inst. Tech. Inst. of Fellows, Sigma Delta Chi, Psi Upsilon. Episcopalian. Clubs: Genesee Valley (Rochester.), Country (Rochester.). Home: Rochester N.Y. Died Feb. 15, 1993.

JONG, ANTHONY, public health dentist, educator; b. Hong Kong (mother Am. citizen);, Aug. 1, 1938; s. Goddard S. and Lily (Fung) J.; m. Patricia May Westwater, Dec. 14, 1985; children: Jessica Westwater, Alexander Robert Westwater. B.S., CCNY, 1960; D.D.S., NYU, 1964; M.P.H., Harvard U., 1966; certificate, Sch. Dental Medicine, 1968; D.Sc. in Dentistry, Boston U., 1976. Diplomate: Am. Bd. Dental Public Health. Intern Jewish Meml. Hosp., N.Y.C., 1964-65; resident Mass. Dept. Public Health, 1966-67; dental supr. Project Head Start, Boston, 1966; dir. dental services Boston Maternity and Infant Care Project, 1968-69; dir. Boston Maternity, Infant Care and Children and Youth Projects, 1969-70; asst. dean student affairs Harvard Sch. Dental Medicine, 1971-73; prof., chmn. dept. dental care mgmt. Boston U. Sch. Grad. Dentistry, 1973—, asst. dean postdoctoral studies, 1978-80, assoc. dean for acad. affairs, 1980—; Research fellow Harvard Sch. Dental Medicine, 1966-68, research assoc., 1968-69, asst. prof. dental ecology, 1969-73; cons. Boston Head Start Health Services, 1966-70; mem. dental health research and edn. adv. com. U.S. Dept. HEW, 1971-73. Editor: Dental Pub. Health and Community Dentistry, 1981, Community Dental Health, 2d edit., 1988; contbr. articles to profl. jours. and chpts. to textbooks. Recipient USPHS Research Career Devel. award, 1969. Mem. Am. Pub. Health Assn. (mem. dental sect. council 1974-77, chmn. dental sect. 1978-79, governing council 1979-83), Mass. Pub. Health Assn. (chmn. dental sect. 1971-72), Am. Assn. Dental Schs. (council of faculties 1979-86, chmn. preventive and community dentistry sect. 1981-82, chmn. practice adminstrn. sec. 1987-88), ADA, Am. Assn. Pub. Health Dentistry, Omicron Kappa Upsilon (treas.-sec. 1972-74).

JORDAN, ELLEN RAUSEN, law educator, consultant; b. Denver, Feb. 6, 1943; d. Joseph and Sarah (Ratner) Rausen; m. Carl Parsons Jordan, Aug. 20, 1967; children: Daniel Victor, Timothy Julian. BA, Cornell U., 1964; JD, Columbia U., 1972. Bar: Md. 1972. Analyst Nat. Security Agy., Ft. Meade, Md., 1964-66; programmer Bankers Trust Co., N.Y.C., 1966-69; sole practice, Cumberland, Md., 1972-75; asst. prof. law U. Ga., Athens, 1976-79, assoc. prof., 1980-85, prof., 1985-91, assoc. dean Sch. of Law, 1983-86; dean Sch. of Law, U. Calif., Davis, 1991-92; prof. of law, 1992-96; vis. asst. prof. U. Va., Charlottesville, 1979-80; cons. U.S. Dept. Justice, Washington, 1980-81, Adminstrv. Conf. of U.S., Washington, 1982-83; acting assoc. v.p. academic affairs, U. Ga., 1986-88. Contbr. articles to profl. jours. Legal History fellow U. Wis., 1983. Mem. ABA, Assn. Am. Law Schs (exec. com. 1986-89), Am. Law Inst., Phi Beta Kappa, Phi Kappa Phi. Died Aug. 9, 1996. Home: Davis Calif.

JORDY, WILLIAM HENRY, art history educator; b. Poughkeepsie, N.Y., Aug. 31, 1917; s. Elwood Benjamin and Caroline May (Hill) J.; m. Sarah Stoughton Spock, July 25, 1942. B.A., Bard Coll., 1939, L.H.D., 1968; postgrad., Inst. Fine Arts, NYU, 1939-42; Ph.D., Yale U., 1948; DFA, RISD, 1993. Instr., then asst. prof. art and Am. civilization Yale U., 1948-55; faculty Brown U., Providence, 1955—; prof. art Brown U., 1960—, chmn. dept., 1963-66, 76-77. Author: Henry Adams, Scientific Historian, 1952, American Buildings and Their Architects, 2 vols., 1972; editor: (with Ralph Coe) Montgomery Schuyler, American Architecture and Other Writings, 1961, (with Wim de Wit and David Zanten) Louis Suillivan, The Function of Ornament, 1986; cons.: Arts of the United States, 1960; contbr. articles to profl. jours. Mem. Coll. Art Assn., Soc. Archtl. Historians, Victorian Soc. Died Aug. 1997.

JORGENSEN, WILLIAM ERNEST, retired librarian; b. Heber, Utah, Oct. 13, 1913; s. George Michael and Mary Annette (Jackman) J.; m. Margaret Louise Boyle, May 25, 1940; children: Robert Ernest, Barry Steven, Mollie Ann. B.A. summa cum laude, U. Idaho, 1938; certificate librarianship, U. Calif. at Berkeley, 1940; M.A., Oreg. State U., 1942. Engring. librarian Oreg. State U., 1940-42; supr. tech. data sect., frequency change dept. So. Calif. Edison Co., 1945-46; chief librarian research library Naval Electronics Lab. Center, San Diego, 1946-74; dir. Research Info. Services, 1974-94; John Cotton Dana lectr. U. Calif. at Los Angeles, 1964; Mem. investment bd. Coronado Mgmt. Corp., 1970-72; Mem. inter-library task group San Diego Ednl. Resources Project, 1960-74; library com. Fine Arts Soc., San Diego, 1965-67; chmn. 10th Mil. Librarians Workshop, 1966; mem. Navy Research Library Council W. Coast, 1955-74; expert examiner U.S. Civil Service Examiners for So. Calif. Navy Labs., 1951-68; mem. Com. for Asso. Sci. Libraries San Diego, 1963-74; adv. council edn. for Librarianship U. Calif., Berkeley, Los Angeles, 1965-68; mem. San Diego Met. Area Library Council, 1973-74; vice chmn. library com. U. Calif. at San Diego Sch. Medicine Assos., 1974-77, treas., 1977-78. Author: The Use of a Technical Library, 1942, Naval Electronics Laboratory Reliability Bibliography, 1956-58, Navy Electronics Laboratory and the Point Loma Military Reservation, A Collection of Historical Photographs, 1966; Editor: procs.: Tenth Military Librarians Workshop, 1966; Contbr. articles to profl. jours. Bd. dirs. San Diego chpt. ACLU, 1971-73. Served to lt. comdr. USNR, 1942-45; comdr. Res. ret. Mem. Calif. Library Assn. (pres. Palomar dist. 1963, councilor 1967-70), Spl. Libraries Assn. (chmn. engring. sect. 1950), U. Calif. Schs. Librarianship Alumni Assn. (pres. 1963), San Diego Writers Assn., Phi Beta Kappa, Phi Kappa Phi. Home: Carmel Calif. Died 1994.

JORRE DE ST. JORRE, DANIELLE MARIE-MADELINE, diplomat, government official; b. Victoria, Mahe, Seychelles, Sept. 30, 1941; d. Henri and Alice (Corgat) de St. J.; m. Marcel d'Offay (div.); children: Cedric d'Offay, Anne-Laure d'Offay, Jean-Remy d'Offay. MA with honors, U. Edinburgh, Scotland, 1965; postgrad. cert. in edn., U. London, 1966; PhB, U. York, U.K., 1972. Tchr. French Streathan Hill and Clapham, U.K., 1967-69; tchr. French and English, head French dept. Seychelles Coll., 1969-71; prin. Tchr. Tng. Coll., Seychelles, 1974-76; prin. edn. officer Ministry Edn., Seychelles, 1976-77; prin. sec. Ministry Fgn. Affairs, Tourism and Aviation, Seychelles, 1977-79, Ministry Edn. and Info., Seychelles, 1980-82, Ministry Planning and External Rels., Seychelles, 1982-86; amb. to France, U.K., Can., Cuba, Germany, Greece and USSR Seychelles, 1983, 84, 85; sec. of state Ministry Planning and External Rels., Seychelles, 1986, min., 1989-92; min. Ministry of Environ., Econ. Planning and External Rels., Seychelles, 1992-93, Ministry Fgn. Affairs, Planning and Environ., Seychelles, 1993—; gov. for Seychelles Bd. Govs. World Bank and African Devel. Bank, 1984—; bd. dirs. Internat. Ctr. Ocean Devel.; chair Seychelles Nat Printing Co., 1977-82, Nat. Bookshop, 1977-82, Nat. Consultancy Svcs., 1983-88, Seychelles Hotels Ltd., Nat. Monument Bd., Devel. Bank Seychelles, 1988-91; v.p. E. African region Adv. Com. on Protection of the Sea, 1994; mem. head del. various internat. confs.; mem. various world confs. on creole langs. Author: Apprenons la Nouvelle Orthographie, 1978, Dictionary Creole Seychellois/ Francais, 1982, Lexique des Specificites de la Langue Francaise aux Seychelles, 1989. Mem. cen. exec. com. Seychells People's Progressive Front, 1991—. Mem. Com. Internat. Creole Studies (v.p. 1984—), Bannzil Kreol (pres. 1986—). Avocations: reading, lexicography, folklore. Died Feb. 25, 1997.

JOSSELSON, FRANK, lawyer; b. Cin., Sept. 27, 1944; s. Jack Bernard and Beatrice Elaine (Lichtenstein) J.; m. Linda Mae Mustard, 1968 (div. 1986); children: Laura, David. Bar: Ohio 1969, Oreg. 1973, U.S. Dist. Ct. (so. dist.) Oreg., U.S. Ct. Appeals (6th and 9th cirs.). Law clk. to Hon. Anthony J. Celebrezze U.S. Ct. Appeals (6th cir.) Ohio, 1969-71; asst. atty. gen. Office Atty. Gen. Ohio, Columbus, 1971-73; assoc. Stoel, Rives, Portland, Oreg., 1973-75; ptnr. Griffith, Bittner, Abbott & Roberts, Portland, 1975-83, Josselson, Potter & Roberts, Portland, 1983-98. Editor: Oreg. Land Use Bd. Appeals Decisions, 1981-82, Oreg. Land Conservation & Devel. Commn. Decisions, 1981; assoc. editor, editor-in-chief Oreg. Real Estate & Land Use Digest, 1978-88; recent case editor Cin. Law Rev., 1968-69. Mem. Met. Svc. Dist. charter com., 1991-92. Mem. ABA, Oreg. State Bar (exec. com., real estate and land use sect.), Ohio State Bar, Multnomah County Bar Assn. Died Feb. 9, 1998.

JOVA, JOSEPH JOHN, foundation executive, consultant, ambassador; b. Newburgh, N.Y., Nov. 7, 1916; s. Joseph Luis and Maria Josefa (Gonzalez-Cavada) J.; m. Pamela Johnson, Feb. 9, 1949; children: Henry Christopher, John Thomas, Margaret Ynes Grunberg. A.B., Dartmouth, 1938; grad. sr. seminar on fgn. policy, Fgn. Service Inst., 1959; L.H.D., Mt. St. Mary Coll., 1973; LL.D., Dowling Coll., 1973. With Guatemala div. United Fruit Co., 1938-41; fgn. service officer Dept. State, 1947-77; vice consul Basra, 1947-49; 2d sec., vice consul Tangier, 1949-52; consul Oporto, 1952-54; 1st sec. Lisbon, 1954-57; officer-in-charge French-Iberian affairs, 1957-58, asst. chief personnel, 1959-60, chief personnel operations div., 1960-61; dep. chief of mission Santiago, Chile, 1961-65; ambassador to Honduras Tegucigalpa, 1965-69; ambassador to OAS Washington, 1969-74; ambassador to Mexico, 1974-77; pres. Meridian House Internat., 1977-89; pres. emeritus, 1989-93; chmn. Dept. State Mgmt. Reform Task Force, U.S. dels. to Inter-Am. Coun. on Edn., Sci. and Culture at Panama, 1972, Mar del Plata, 1973, UN Econ. Commn. for Latin Am., Santiago, 1971, UN Econ. Commn. Latin Am. Population Conf., Mexico, 1974; vice chmn. U.S. del. to gen. assembly OAS, 1970, 71, 72, 73, chmn. Inter-Am. com. culture, 1983-88; bd. dirs. First Am. Bank of Washington. Contbr. articles to profl. jours. Trustee Mt. St. Mary's Coll., Pan-Am. Devel. Found., pres., 1989-93; trustee Friends of OAS Mus. of Latin Am. Art, v.p., 1986-93, Textile Mus., Georgetown U. Libr. Lt. USNR, 1942-47. Named Knight Malta-Am. Assn., Comdr. Order of Leopold II of Belgium, Grand Cross Order of Isabel the Cath. of Spain, Order of Morazan, Honduras, Constantinian Order St. George, Order of Aztee Eagle Mexico, Order of Orange-Nassau (Netherlands), Order of Bernardo O'Higgins, Chile; recipient Presdl. Mgmt. Improvement award, 1970, Am. Acad. Diplomacy award, 1986, T.A. Cunningham award New Orleans Internat. House, 1975, Wilbur J. Carr award U.S. Dept. State, 1977, certs. appreciation for work at Meridian House, Sec. of State, 1989, Dir. of U.S.I.A., City Coun. Washington; awarded Fgn. Service Cup, 1988. Mem. Mexican Acad. Internat. Law (pres. Am. chpt.), U.S. Fgn. Svc. Assn., Ctr. Inter-Am. Rels., Inst. Hispanic Culture of Spain, Asociacion de Hidalgos a Fuero de España, Nat. Hispanic Quincentennial Commn. Soc., Sulgrave, Internat. Club of Washington, Chapultepec Golf, Dacor House, Sigma Phi Epsilon. Roman Catholic. Home: Washington D.C. Died Mar. 31, 1993.

JUBANY ARNAU, NARCISO CARDINAL, archbishop; b. Santa Coloma de Farnes, Spain, Aug. 12, 1913. Ordained priest Roman Cath. Ch., 1939; formerly prof. law Barcelona Sem.; served on Ecclesistical Tribunal; titular bishop of Ortosia, also aux. of Barcelona, 1956; bishop of Gerona, 1964-71; archbishop of Barcelona, 1971-96; elevated to Sacred Coll. of Cardinals, 1973; archbishop dimissionary, 1990. Died Dec. 26, 1996.

KABUA, IMATA, President republic of the marshall islands; b. Jabor Island, Jaluit Atoll, Nov. 17, 1928. Attended, Mauna Olu Coll., Hawaii; PhD (hon. causa), U. Taiwan. Chief clerk Marshall Islands Coun. of Iroji, 1951-58; mem. First Marshall Islands Congress, 1958-63; senator for Marshall Islands Congress of Micronesia, 1963-78; pres. Senate of the Marshall Islands, 1963-70; elected M.P., 1979; pres. Govt. of the Marshall Islands, 1980—; founder, leader Polit. Movement for Marshall Islands Separation from Micronesia, 1972-78; delegate Marshall Islands Constl. Conv., 1978-79. Died Dec. 20, 1996.

KACZMAREK, LEON, linguist, researcher; b. Wanne, Westfalen, Germany, Mar. 12, 1911; s. Jan and Maria (Kosmala) K.; m. Zofia Lubawa, Dec. 24, 1938; children: Urszula, Cyryl, Bozydar, Ewa. MA, Adam Mickiewicz U., Poznań, Poland, 1935, PhD, 1952. Asst. Poznań Univ., 1934-36, elder asst., 1936-39; docent Maria Curie Sklodowska U., Lublin, 1954-66, assoc. prof., 1966-73, full prof., 1973-81, prof. emeritus, 1981—, head Polish lang. dept., 1954-70, dean of art faculty, 1956-58, head logopedic dept., 1970-88, dir. Polish Lang. Inst., 1973-75; pres. Polish Logopedic Soc., Lublin, 1963-89. Author: Speech Formulation, 1953, Our Child Acquires Speech, 1988; co-author: Dictionary of Student Jargon, 1974, 2d edit., 1994; editor Logopedia-Culture of the Word of Mouth, 1960-83. Active Soc. Child Friend, Warsaw, 1970. Decorated comdr.'s cross Poland Restitution Order; recipient medal Poznan U., 1934; named Tchr. of Merit of Polish People's Republic, State Bd., Warsaw, 1978. Mem. Polish Linguistic Soc. (hon.), Societas Linguistica Europea, Polish Neurolinguistic Soc., Polish Assn. of the Deaf, Poznań Soc. Sci. Avocations: theatre, music. Died Oct. 26, 1996.

KAHANE, HENRY, educator, linguist, medievalist; b. Berlin, Germany, Nov. 2, 1902; came to U.S., 1939, naturalized, 1945; s. Arthur and Paula (Ornstein) K.; m. Renée Toole, Dec. 5, 1931; children: Roberta, Charles. Student univs., Berlin, Rome and Greifswald, 1922-30; Ph.D., U. Berlin, 1932; Ph.D. renewal, Humboldt U., 1982; PhD (hon.), Freie U., Berlin, 1988; D.Litt. (hon.), U. Ill., 1977; alumnus, Am. Sch. Classical Studies, Athens. Departmental asst. Romance linguistics U. Berlin, 1932; lectr. U. Florence, Italy, 1934-38; research asst. U. So. Calif., 1939-41; mem. faculty U. Ill.-Urbana, 1941-92; now prof. linguistics, also prof. Center Advanced Study, acting dir., 1971-72; mem. U.S. Nat. Com. for Byzantine Studies, 1981. Author: (mostly in coop. with wife) Italian Placenames in Greece, 1940, Spoken Greek, 1945-46, Descriptive Studies in Spanish Grammar, 1954, Development of Verbal Categories in Child Language, 1958, Lingua Franca in the Levant, 1958, reissue 1988, Structural Studies on Spanish Themes, 1959, The Krater and the Grail, 1965, reissue, 1984; Glossary of Old Italian Portolani, 1967, Linguistic Relations between Byzantium and the West, 1976, Graeca et Romanica: Scripta Selecta, 3 vols., 1979-86; also articles. Assoc. editor: Romance Philology, 1947-83. Guggenheim fellow, 1955, 62; recipient Silver award Acad. of Athens, 1977; fellow Dumbarton Oaks Research Inst., 1985. Fellow Am. Acad. Arts and Scis.; mem. Linguistic Soc. Am. (pres. 1984), MLA, Arthurian Soc., Am. Name Soc., Wolfram von Eschenbach Gesellschaft, Dictionary Soc. N.Am. Home: Urbana Ill. Died Sept. 11, 1992.

KAHN, HERMAN BERNARD, construction company executive; b. Cleve., Feb. 12, 1923; s. Myron Bernard and Bessie (Shur) K.; m. Revera C. Tolochko, Aug. 1, 1948 (div. Feb. 1970); children: Meryl Denise, David Geoffrey.; m. Gerda Moore, June 10, 1983. BS in Gen. Engring, N.C. State U., 1949. Lic. real estate broker. Ptnr. M.B. Kahn Constrn. Co., Columbia, S.C., 1949-74; pres. M.B. Kahn Constrn. Co., Inc., 1965-76, Kahn Southern, 1976-77, Kahn-Lockwood, Inc. (gen. contractors), 1977-92; owner, prin. broker KLI. Mem. adv. bd. S.C. Fire Marshall, 1969-79, UN Day com., 1969-74; bd. dirs. Columbia Music Festival Assn., 1981-86, Columbia Lyric Opera, 1979-89 (treas.1986-89); pres. Opera Guild of Greater Columbia, 1984-86. With AUS, 1943-46. Mem. Am. Inst. of Constructors. Jewish. Died March 18, 1997; interred Hebrew Benevolent Cemetery, Columbia, S.C.

KAITSCHUK, JOHN PAUL, bishop; b. Red Bud, Ill., Dec. 31, 1937; s. Walter E. and Bine (Nielsen) K.; m. Janet Nay, June 18, 1965; children: Jennifer, James. BA, Carthage Coll., 1959, DD (hon.), 1988; MDiv, Northwestern Luth. Theol. Sem., Mpls., 1962; D of Ministry, Drew U., 1980. Ordained to ministry Luth. Ch. in Am., 1962. Missionary Luth. Ch., Madison,

Ind., 1962-65; pastor Resurrection Luth. Ch., Madison, 1965-70, Salem Luth. Ch., Indpls., 1970-76, Trinity Luth. Ch., Olney, Ill., 1976-87; bishop Cen./So. Ill. synod Evang. Luth. Ch. in Am., Springfield, 1987—; mem. death penalty task force Evang. Luth. Ch. in Am., Chgo., 1990; chair judicatory execs. Ill. Conf. Chs., Springfield, 1990—. Pres. adv. com. Mayor's Commn. on Youth, Madison, 1965-70; vice-chair bd. dirs. Opportunity Ctr. Southeastern Ill., 1978-84; mem. East Richland Bd. Edn., Olney, 1985-87; exec. dir., bd. dirs. Luth. Social Svcs. Ill., Des Plaines, 1987—; bd. dirs. Luth. Sch. Theology, Chgo., 1991—. Deceased.

KALAMAROS, EDWARD NICHOLAS, lawyer; b. Williamsport, Ind., July 5, 1934; s. Nicholas John and Margaret Louise (Riley) K.; m. Marilyn Jane Foster, June 14, 1958; children: Alexander, Philip, Anastasia, Timothy. BS in Commerce, U. Notre Dame, 1956, LLB, 1959, JD, 1969. Bar: Ind. 1959. Chief dep. prosecutor 60th Jud. Cir. of Ind., 1963-67; pvt. practice South Bend, 1960—; pres. Edward N. Kalamaros & Assos., P.C., 1971—; U.S. govt. appeal agt. SSS, 1967-71, adviser to registrants, 1971-75; mem. St. Joseph County Tax Adjustment Bd., 1970-73; bd. dirs. Tower Fed. Bank, 1986-88. Author: (ICLEF Vols.) Special Problem Areas, Indiana Workmen's Compensation, 1981, 3d edit. 1983, Administrative Law—Worker's compensation and occupational Desease Cases, 1983; contbr. articles to profl. jours. Past deacon, elder, trustee Presbyn. Ch.; bd. dirs. Coun. for Retarded of St. Joseph County, 1966-72, 72-78; bd. dirs., sec. Alcoholism Coun.; pres. bd. edn. St. Joseph H.S., 1975-81; bd. dirs. Madison Ctr., 1989-91, Ind. Opera North, 1990-94, Notre Dame U. Snite Mus. Art, 1992—, South Bend Regional Mus. Art, 1994—, South Bend Entertainment, Inc., 1993-96. With Ind. N.G. and USAR, 1960-66. Fellow Ind. Bar Found. (Am. Citizenship Com. 1985-95); mem. ABA, St. Joseph County Bar Assn., 7th Fed. Cir. Bar Assn., Am. Arbitration Assn. (panel of arbitrators), Lawyers and Pilots Bar Assn., Am. Judicature Soc., Def. Rsch. Inst., Internat. Assn. Indsl. Accident Bds. and Commns., Am. Trial Lawyers Assn., Ind. Trial Lawyers Assn., Ind. Def. Lawyers Assn., Comml. Law League, Masons (32 deg.), Shriners, Macatawa Bay Yacht Club, South Bend Press Club (hon.), Columbia Club. Died Sept. 1, 1996.

KALKIN, GARY, marketing executive; b. N.Y.C., Mar. 29, 1950. MA, NYU, 1972. V.p. publicity Walt Disney Pictures, Burbank, Calif., 1985-87, v.p. domestic mktg., 1987-89, sr. v.p. domestic mktg., 1989—. Mem. Acad. Motion Picture Arts and Scis. Home: West Hollywood Calif. DIED 01/06/95. .

KALLO, ROBERT MAX, chemistry educator; b. San Francisco, Oct. 6, 1923; s. Max Karl and Emma Antoinette (Piaggio) K.; m. Cora Elizabeth Hermann, Feb. 2, 1947; children: Diane Cynthia, Janet Roberta. BS, U. Calif., Berkeley; PhD, U. Calif. Instr. chemistry Calif. State U., Fresno, 1950-53, asst. prof., 1953-56, assoc. prof., 1956-60, prof., 1960—. Author: Elements of Physical Chemistry, 1975. Mem. Calif. Sect. Am. Chem. Soc. (assoc.). Avocation: studying Russian lang.

KALMAN, SUMNER MYRON, pharmacology educator; b. Boston, Nov. 14, 1918; s. Max Manuel Kalman and Bessie Jane Richmond; m. Anneliese Friede Friedsam, Oct. 29, 1952; children: Susan, Stephanie. AB, Harvard U., 1940; MD, Stanford U., 1950. Lic. physician, Calif. Intern Mt. Zion Hosp., San Francisco, 1950-51; postdoctoral fellow Stanford (Calif.) U., 1951-52, instr. pharmacology, 1954-67, prof., 1967—; dir. drug assay lab. Stanford U. Hosp., 1973-80; postdoctoral fellow Carlsberg Lab., Copenhagen, 1952-53, U. Copenhagen, 1953; vis. lectr. bacteriology and immunology Harvard U. Sch. Medicine, 1961-62; cons. U.S. FDA, 1972-75. Co-author: Principles of Drug Action, 1974, Drug Assay: Strategy of Therapeutic Drug Monitoring, 1980. Chmn. med. bd. Planned Parenthood Assn. of Santa Clara County, Calif., 1971-72, bd. dirs. 1969-72; mem. air conservation com. Am. Lung Assn., Santa Clara and San Benito Counties, Calif., 1974-75. Recipient Research Career award USPHS, Stanford U., 1959-69; named Tour Speaker of Yr. Southwest Sect. Am. Chem. Soc., 1969; Graham fellow Stanford U., 1954-59. Mem. Am. Soc. Biol. Chemists, Am. Soc. Pharmacology and Exptl. Therapeutics, Soc. Gen. Physiologists, Calif. Assn. Toxicologists, Instituto de Investigaciones Citológicas. Democrat. Jewish. Avocations: squash, skiing, martial arts.

KALMUS, ALLAN HENRY, public relations executive; b. N.Y.C., Nov. 7, 1917; s. Nathaniel I. and Louise (Simson) K.; m. Jane Waring, Sept. 9, 1944 (div. 1968); children: Susan Jane Partier, John Allan; m. Ellin Silberstein, May 16, 1969; stepchildren: James Silberstein, John Silberstein, Barbara Keezell. B.A. magna cum laude, Harvard U., 1939; M.S., Columbia Grad. Sch. Journalism, 1940. News editor, pub. relations dir. Radio Sta. WQXR, N.Y.C., 1942-43; publicity dir. NBC-TV, N.Y.C., 1944-52, Lever Bros. Co., N.Y.C., 1952-54; owner, pres. Kalmus Corp., N.Y.C., 1954-97; lectr. Columbia U. Grad. Sch., N.Y.C. Trustee Harry S. Truman Library Found. Mem. Pub. Rels. Soc. Am., Internat. Radio and TV Soc., Overseas Press Club Am., Broadcast Pioneers, Acad. TV Arts and Scis., Sunningdale Country Club (Scarsdale, N.Y.), Yale Club of N.Y., Phi Beta Kappa. Died Mar. 12, 1996.

KAMPEN, EMERSON, chemical company executive; b. Kalamazoo, Mar. 12, 1928; s. Gerry and Gertrude (Gerlofs) K.; m. Barbara Frances Spitters, Feb. 2, 1951; children: Douglas S., Joanie L., Lampen Dubham, Laura L. Jampen Shiver, Emerson II (dec.), Deborah L. Kampen Smith, Cynthia S. Kampen Van Zelst, Pamela E. Kampen Mayes. B.S. in Chem. Engring., U. Mich., 1951; grad. (hon.), Purdue U., 1990. Chem. engr Gt. Lakes Chem. Corp., West Lafayette, Ind., 1951-57, plant mgr., 1957-62, v.p., 1962-67, sr. v.p., 1968, exec. v.p., 1969-71, pres., 1972—, chief exec. officer, 1977—; pres., chief exec. officer, chmn. bd. GLCD, Inc., Ark., 1988, also bd. dirs.; bd. dirs. GLCD, Inc., Bio-Lab, Inc., Decatur, Ga.; pres., dir. GLI, Inc., Newport, Tenn., GHC (Properties) Inc.; bd. dirs. WIL Rsch. Labs., Inc., OSCA, Inc., Lafayette Life Ins. Co., Ind. Nat. Bank, Huntsman Chem. Corp., Salt Lake City, Pub. Svc. Ind., Plainfield, QO Chems., Inc., Chgo., Pentech Chems., Inc., Chgo.; chmn. bd. E/M Corp., Hydrotech Chem. Corp., Great Lakes Chem. (Europe) Ltd.; pres. Ark. Chems.; mem. listed co. adv. com. Am. Stock Exchange. Mem. corp. advising group Huntington's Disease Soc. Am., N.Y.C.; Ind. United Way Centennial Commn.; trustee Ind. U., Bloomington, Purdue U., West Lafayette; bd. dirs. Jr. Achievement Greater Lafayette Inc., Lafayette Art Assn. Found. Inc., Purdue Rsch. Found., West Lafayette, Lafayette Symphony Found.; dir., v.p. Hoosier Alliance Against Drugs, Indpls. Capt. USAF, 1953. Recipient Bronze medal Wall Street Transcript, 1980, 86, Gold medal, 1983, 85, 88, 90, 92, 93, Silver medal, 1989, 91, Man of Yr. award Nat. Huntington's Disease Assn., 1984, Kavaler award Chem. Mktg. Reporter, 1992, Bronze Medal award Fin. World Mag., 1992, 93, Winthrop-Sears award Chemist's Club, 1993; co-recipient Gold medal Wall Street Transcript, 1984; named 5th Most Involved CEO Chief Exec. Mag., 1986, Sagamore of the Wabash, 1988, Industrialist of Yr., Ind. Bus. Mag., 1991, CEO of Yr., Fin. World Mag., 1992; inductee Ind. Acad., 1992. Fellow Am. Inst. Chemists; mem. Soc. Chem. Industry, Nat. Asn. Mfrs. (bd. dirs.), Chem. Mfrs. Assn., Ind. C. of C. (bd. dirs.), Greater Lafayette C. of C., Ind. Acad., Lafayette Country Club, Skyline Club (Indpls.), Elks, Rotary. Avocations: golf; family events. Home: West Lafayette Ind. Deceased.

KAMPSCHROR, LESLIE DEAN, government official, lawyer; b. Clendive, Mont., Nov. 6, 1932; s. Christopher Henry and Mary Margaret (Sullivan) K.; m. Nancy Iris Arrants Quinn, Oct. 31, 1929 (div. 1961); children: Susan, Richard, Kevin, Tracy, Lisa, John, Dana. BS in Aero. Engring., U. Ill., 1961, JD, 1964. Bar: D.C., Va. Patent examiner U.S. Patent Office, Washington, 1964-65; accident report writer, investigator-in-charge Nat. Transp. Safety Bd., Washington, 1970-79, hearing officer, chief engring. div., 1979-85, dir. Bur. Tech., 1985-95. With USAF, 1954-58, pilot Vietnam, 1968-69, brig. gen. Res., 1978-85. Mem. D.C. Bar Assn., Va. Bar Assn. Avocation: flying. Home: Manassas Va. Deceased March 26, 1995.

KANTOROVICH, LEONID VITALJEVICH, mathematician, economist; b. Leningrad, Russia, Jan. 19, 1912; s. Vitalij M. and Pauline G. (Saks) K.; Prof., Leningrad U., 1934, Sc.D., 1935; Doctor (hon.), univs. Glasgow, Grenoble, Nice, Helsinki, Sorbonne, Cambridge, Varsovie, Phila., Calcutta, others; m. Natalia V. Iljina, Mar. 11, 1938; children—Ien, Vsevolod. Instr., then prof. Inst. Indsl. Constrn. Engring., 1930-39; instr., then prof. Leningrad U., 1932-60; head dept. Math. Inst., USSR Acad. Scis., 1948-60, head math.-econs. dept. at inst. at Siberian br., 1961-71; head research lab. Inst. Nat. Economy Control, Moscow, 1971-76; head dept. sci. Inst. Systems Studies, Moscow, 1976—; prof., head chair computer math. Novosibizu U., 1961-71; mem. State Com. Scis. and Techniques, 1975—. Served with Russian Army, 1941-48. Decorated Order Honor, Order Trade Red Banner, Order Lenin; recipient State prize, 1949; Lenin prize, 1965; Nobel prize in econs., 1975. Mem. USSR Acad. Scis.; fellow Econometric Soc. (council); hon. mem. Hungarian Acad. Scis., Am. Acad. Arts and Scis., Nat. Acad. de Ingen. Mex., Yugoslavian Acad. Arts and Sci. Author books on math. and econs., 1931—, latest being Optimal Solution in Economics, 1973; Essays on Optimal Planning, 1976; Functional Analyze, 1977; also numerous other publs. in field.

KAPLAN, HELEN SINGER, physician, researcher; b. Vienna, Feb. 6, 1929; came to U.S., 1939; d. Phillip Sigmund Singer and Sofie (Lanzi) Liebo; m. Harold I. Kaplan, 1952 (div. 1970); children: Phillip, Peter, Jennifer K. D'Addio; m. Charles Philip Lazarus, Nov. 2, 1979. MA, Columbia U., 1953, PhD, 1955; MD, N.Y. Med. Coll., 1959.

KAPLAN, STANLEY ABRAHAM, lawyer, educator; b. Chgo., July 17, 1910. PhB, U. Chgo., 1931, JD, 1933; LLM, Columbia U., 1935. Bar: Ill. 1934, U.S. Supreme Ct., 1951. Ptnr. Gottlieb and Schwartz, Chgo., after 1934, counsel, to 1978; ptnr. Reuben & Proctor, Chgo., 1978-82; of counsel Isham, Lincoln & Beale, Chgo., 1982-86; sole practice, Chgo., 1986-91; prof. law U. Chgo., 1960-78; chief reporter corp. governance project Am. Law Inst., 1980-84. Author: (with Blum) Corporate Readjustments and Reorganizations; editor Legal Ethics Forum of ABA Jour., 1976-85. Served to lt. col. USMCR, 1942-46. Mem. ABA, Ill. State Bar Assn., Chgo. Bar Assn. (bd. mgrs. 1947-49, chmn. securities law com. 1950-51, chmn. corp. law com. 1978-79, Chgo. Council Lawyers, Soc. Am. Law Tchrs., Anti Defamation League (exec. bd. Chgo. div.), Order of Coif, Phi Beta Kappa. Clubs: Standard, Lincoln Park Tennis Assn., Adventurer's, Chgo. Mountaineering. Died July 1991.

KAPLAN, STEPHEN, parapsychologist; b. Bronx, N.Y., Sept. 19, 1940; m. Roxanne Salch. BA in Sociology, CCNY, 1967, MS in Communication Skills, 1970; MA in Liberal Studies, SUNY, Stony Brook, 1972; PhD in Sociology, U. S.W., 1977; DD (hon.), 1st Ch. Research, 1970. Founder, dir. Parapsychology Inst. Am., Elmhurst, N.Y., 1971—; instr. parapsychology, occult scis. Forest Hills Adult divsn. N.Y.C. Bd. Edn., 1974-94; instr. parapyschology SUNY, Stony Brook, 1974—; lectr. UN Assembly, 1978, humerous univs. and colls., including Hunter Coll., CUNY, Adelphi U., Miami Dade C.C., LaGuardia Coll., U. Va., Arcadia U., N.S., Can., also network TV Japan, Tokyo, Rome, South Korea; appeared on over 2000 radio programs, over 130 TV programs. Author: (with others) The True Tales of the Unknown series, books, 1, 2 and 3, 1994, The Amityville Horror Hoax, 1974-95, The Island of Ghosts and Strangest Phenomena, 1971-95, Vampires: From Sunset to Sunrise, 1971-95; contbr. numerous articles to non-fiction publs. Recipient Parapsychology Hall of Fame award, 1982, Internat. Hypnosis Hall of Fame award, 1987, Einstein award, 1980, Sir Arthur Conan Doyle award, 1983; named Amityville horrors expert. Home: Maspeth N.Y. DIED 06/09/95. .

KAPRELIAN, EDWARD K., mechanical engineer, physicist; b. Union Hill, N.J., June 20, 1913; s. Karnig and Haiganoosh (Tatarian) K.; m. Lucy Ainilian, Feb. 29, 1936; children: Charles E., Harold R., Helen Kaprelian Ward. M.E., Stevens Inst. Tech., 1934; law student, George Washington U., 1937-38; postgrad. in physics, 1943-44. Registered profl. engr., N.J., Md. Patent examiner for U.S. Patent Office, 1936-42; physicist Bd. Econ. Warfare, 1942-45; patent adviser U.S. Army Signal Corps, 1945-46; chief photo br. Signal Corps Engring. Labs., Ft. Monmouth, 1946-52; dir. research and engring. Kalart Co., Plainville, Conn., 1952-55; pres. Kaprelian Research & Devel. Co., Simsbury, Conn., 1955-57; dep. dir. research U.S. Army Signal Research & Devel. Lab., Ft. Monmouth, 1957-62; tech. dir. U.S. Army Ltd. War Lab., Aberdeen Proving Ground, Md., 1962-67; v.p., tech. dir. Keuffel & Esser Co., 1968-73; pres. Kaprelian Research and Devel., Mendham, N.J., 1973-97; Mem. NRC-Nat. Acad. Scis., 1957-66. Author; patentee in field. Lt. col. Signal Corps, U.S. Army Res. Recipient Stevens Inst. Tech. award 1986, Exceptional Civilian award U.S. Army, 1963. Fellow Soc. Photog. Scientists and Engrs. (past pres.), Am. Photog. Hist. Soc. (past pres.); sr. IEEE; mem. ASME, Optical Soc. Am., Phys. Soc. (London), Soc. Motion Picture and TV Engrs., Royal Photog. Soc. (Eng.), N.Y. Patent Law Assn., AAAS, N.Y. Acad. Sci., Sigma Xi, Tau Beta Pi. Home: Mendham N.J. Died July 21, 1997.

KARABA, FRANK ANDREW, lawyer; b. Chgo., Jan. 23, 1927; s. Frank and Katherine (Danihel) K.; m. Alice June Olsen, June 2, 1951; children: Thomas Frank, Stephen Milton, Catherine Alice. BS with highest distinction, Northwestern U., 1949, JD, 1951. Bar: Ill. 1951. Teaching assoc. Northwestern U. Law Sch., 1951-52; law sec. Ill. Supreme Ct., 1952-53; assoc. firm Crowley, Barrett & Karaba, Chgo., 1953-60; ptnr. Crowley, Barrett & Karaba, 1960-75, mng. ptnr., 1975-95; sr. counsel Crowley, Barrett & Karaba Ltd., 1995-96; bd. dirs. A&R Printers, Inc., Lyrick Corp.; asst. counsel Emergency Commn. on Crime. Pres. 7th Av. P.T.A., 1964-66; Bd. dirs. La Grange Little League, 1964-67, pres., 1968. Served with USNR, 1945-46. Mem. ABA, Ill. Bar Assn., Bar. Assn. (bd. mgrs. 1962-63), Order of Coif. Presbyn. (elder). Clubs: Legal, Law. Home: La Grange Ill. Died August 16,1996.

KARAMANLIS, CONSTANTINE G., lawyer, Greek government official; b. Prote, Macedonia, Mar. 8, 1907; m. Amalia Kanelopoulos (div.). Law degree, U. Athens. Admitted to bar, 1932. Pvt. practice law Serres, Greece, 1932—; mem. Parliament for Serres, 1935-36, 46, 50, 74-80; minister of public works, 1946, 52-54, minister of transp., 1948, minister of social welfare, 1948-50, minister of nat. def., 1950, minister of communications and public works, 1954-55; founder, leader Nat. Radical Union, 1955; prime minister of Greece, 1955-58, 58-61, 61-63, 74-80; self-imposed exile in France, 1963-74; founder, leader New Democracy Party, 1974-80; pres., 1980-85, 90-94. Recipient Grand Cross of George I, Commanders Cross of the Order of the Redeemer, the Legion of Honor, of Merit (Austria), of the Belgian Crown, of Orange-Nassau (Netherlands) Charlemagne, 1978, Shuman, 1980, Gold medal Onassis Found., 1981. Died April 1998.

KARKUT, EMIL JOSEPH, manufacturing company executive; b. Garfield, N.J., Mar. 15, 1916; s. Louis and Anna (Fryc) K.; m. Margaret Louise Bryant; children: Kristin, Kathleen Karkut Rittenhouse, Dianna Colman, Dorothy Kuerth. BSCE, Syracuse U., 1941. Sales trainee Carrier Corp., Syracuse, N.Y., 1941-42; v.p.

Barden Corp., Danbury, Conn., 1946-66, pres., 1976-81; exec. v.p. Kaydon Corp., Muskegon, Mich., 1966-68; group v.p. MPB Corp., Keene, N.H., 1969-76; pres. Mekar-Inc., Sandy Hook, Conn., 1982-95; chmn. bd. dirs. N.H. Ball Bearing Inc., Peterborough, N.H., 1986-93. Served to capt. USAAF, 1943-46. Decorated Army Commendation medal. Mem. Anti Friction Bearing Mfg. Assn. Roman Catholic. Died Aug. 8, 1997.

KARPOWITZ, ANTHONY VICTOR, college dean emeritus; b. Feb. 24, 1907; s. Anton and Alexandra (Koscinski) K.; m. Ilse Alma Bennewitz, Dec. 27, 1937 (dec.); children: Anthony Karl, Susan Marie Herrmann, Claudia Ann Preysz. BEd, Milw. State Tchrs. Coll., 1936; MEd, Marquette U., 1942. Apprentice in printing, journeyman printer, 1924-31; tchr. social studies, printing, art, photography Milw. Area Tech. Coll., 1936-41, tchr. trainer, 1946-76, chmn. apprentice div., 1953-76, dean, 1968-76, dean emeritus, from 1976; mem. pres.'s coun. Marquette U., Milw., 1985-92; coord. chmn. Graphic Communications Workshop, Milw., 1958-76. Supporting mem. Haggerty Mus. Art at Marquette U., West Bend (Wis.) Gallery Fine Arts; at-large del. Rep. Presdl. Task Force, Washington. Recipient Ben Franklin Printer of Yr. award Graphic Arts Industries, 1974; named to U. Wis.-Milw. Athletic Hall of Fame, 1977, Wis. Apprenticeship Hall of Fame, Dept. Industry, Labor and Human Rels., 1983. Mem. Internat. Graphic Arts Edn. Assn. (pres. 1964-65, Pres.'s medal 1965, Elmer G. Voight award 1966), Am. Vocat. Assn. (life), Milw.-Racine Club of Printing House Craftsmen (v.p.), Rotary Internat., West Bend Country Club, Cedar Lake Yacht Club, Phi Delta Kappa, Kappa Delta Pi. Roman Catholic. Deceased.

KASTENBAUM, ABRAHAM, social worker; b. N.Y.C., June 22, 1906; s. Harry and Sarah (Strahl) K.; m. Naomi Berman, Aug. 7, 1947. BSEd, NYU, 1933, MSEd, 1936; MSW, U. Minn., 1952. Cons. on aging Community Health and Welfare Council of Hennepin County, Mpls., 1970-72; producer, host, moderator Sr. Citizen's Forum Sta. KMSP-TV 9, Mpls., 1973—. Active Minn. Bd. on Aging, St. Paul, 1978—. Served with U.S. Army, 1943-45, ETO. Recipient Outstanding Community Service award Minn. Dept. Human Services, 1986, Outstanding Profl. Community Involvement award Am. Coll. Health Care Adminstrs., 1986, Success Over 60 award Sr. Options Health Futures Inst., 1985, Good Neighbor award WCCO Radio-Northwest Airlines, 1985, Spl. Services to Older Minnesotans Minn. Bd. on Aging, 1982, Justice award Hennepin County Bar Assn., 1975-76, The Better Life award Am. Nursing Home Assn., 1975. Mem. Nat. Council on the Aging, Nat. Assn. Social Workers (cert.), Minn. Gerontol. Soc., Am. Assn. Jewish Ctr. Workers, Am. Soc. Aging, Mid-Am. Congress on Aging. DIED 08/15/97. .

KATZ, MILTON, legal educator, public official; b. N.Y.C., Nov. 29, 1907; s. Morris and Clara (Schiffman) K.; m. Vivian Greenberg, July 2, 1933; children: John, Robert, Peter. A.B., Harvard U., 1927, J.D., 1931; LL.D., Brandeis U., 1972. Bar: N.Y. 1932, Mass. 1959. Mem. anthrop. expdn. across Central Africa for Peabody Mus., Harvard, 1927-28; various ofcl. posts with U.S. Govt., 1932-39; prof. law Harvard, 1940; leaves of absence, 1941-46, 48-50, Henry L. Stimson prof. law, also dir. internat. legal studies, 1954-78, dir. internat. program in taxation, 1961-63; Sherman Fairchild Distinguished vis. scholar Calif. Inst. Tech., 1974; John Danz lectr., cons. program social mgmt. tech. U. Wash., 1974; Phi Beta Kappa distinguished vis. scholar, 1977-78; Disting. prof. law Suffolk U. Law Sch., 1978-95; solicitor WPB, 1941-43; U.S. exec. officer Combined Prodn. and Resources Bd., 1942-43; with OSS, 1943-44; U.S. spl. rep. in Europe; with rank AEP, 1950-51; chief U.S. del. Econ. Commn. for Europe, 1950-51; chmn. Def. Financial and Econ. Com. North Atlantic Treaty, 1950-51; v.p. Ford Found., 1951-54, cons., 1954-66; cons., asst. sec. edn. HEW, 1967; cons., chmn. energy adv. com. Office Tech. Assessment, 1974-95, Nat. Endowment Humanities, 1974-95; Pres. Cambridge Community Services, 1959-61; chmn. com. manpower White House Conf. Internat. Cooperation, 1965; chmn. com. on life scis. and social policy Nat. Acad. Sci.-NRC, 1968-75; mem. panel tech. assessment Nat. Acad. Sci., 1968-69; mem. adv. bd. Consortium on Competitiveness and Cooperation, U. Calif., 1986-95. Author: Cases and Materials in Administrative Law, 1947, Government Under Law and the Individual, (with others), 1957, (with Kingman Brewster, Jr.) Law of International Transactions and Relations, 1960, The Things That Are Caesar's, 1966, The Relevance of International Adjudication, 1968, The Modern Foundation: Its Dual Nature, Public and Private, 1968, (with others) Man's Impact on the Global Environment, 1970, Assessing Biomedical Technologies, 1975, Technology, Trade and the U.S. Economy, 1978, Strengthening Conventional Deterrence in Europe—A Proposal for the 1980s, 1983, Contribution to the Positive Sum Strategy: Harnessing Technology for Economic Growth, 1986; also articles. Trustee Case Western Res. U., 1967-80, Brandeis U.; mem. corp. Boston Mus. Sci.; mem. vis. com. humanities MIT, 1970-73; mem. adv. bd. energy lab. MIT, 1974-85; chmn. bd. trustees Carnegie Endowment Internat. Peace, 1970-78, Internat. Legal Center, 1971-78; trustee, mem. exec. com. World Peace Found.; pres. Citizen's Research Found., 1969-78; co-chmn. Am. Bar Assn.-AAAS Com. on Sci. and Law; mem. com. on tech. and internat. econ. and trade issues Nat. Acad. Engring. Served with USNR, 1944-46, MTO, ETO; lt. comdr. Res. Decorated Legion of Merit; comdr.'s cross Fed. Republic Germany)., Order of Merit. Fellow Am. Acad. Arts and Scis. (pres. 1979-82); mem. Harvard Alumni Assn. (dir. 1952-55). Died Aug. 9, 1995.

KATZ, SOL, physician; b. N.Y.C., Mar. 29, 1913; s. Samuel and Bessie K.; m. Beatrice Guzewich Paul, Nov. 16, 1946; children—Paul, Rita, Judith. B.S. magna cum laude, CCNY, 1935; M.D. magna cum laude, Georgetown U., 1939, Sc.D. (hon.), 1978. Diplomate: Am. Bd. Internal Medicine. Intern Georgetown U., Hosp., Washington, 1939-40; resident D.C. Gen. Hosp., Washington, 1940-42; pulmonary fellow D.C. Gen. Hosp., 1942-45, chief div. pulmonary diseases, 1946-59; chief med. service VA Hosp., Washington, 1959-70; dir. pulmonary disease div. Sch. Medicine, Georgetown U., Washington, 1970-78; prof. pulmonary medicine Sch. Medicine, Georgetown U., 1978—, Nehemiah and Naomi chmn. pulmonary disease, 1988—; professorial lectr. in medicine Sch. Medicine, George Washington U.; hon. vis. cons. Brompton Hosp., London, 1974-75, vis. prof., 1981; cons. in pulmonary diseases NIH, Walter Reed Army Hosp. Former asso. editor Am. Family Physician; contbr. writings in field to profl. publs. Recipient commendation for outstanding med. achievement VA, 1962. Mem. ACP (John F. Maher Meml. Laureate award), Am. Coll. Chest Physicians, Am. Thoracic Soc. (Disting. Achievement award 1995), Brit. Thoracic Assn., Am. Fedn. Clin. Rsch., So. Soc. Clin. Investigation, Brompton Hosp. Assn., Internat. Union Against Tb, Med. Soc. D.C. (Disting. Svc. award 1970), Phi Beta Kappa, Alpha Omega Alpha. Condr. rsch. in chemotherapy of Tb. DIED 08/10/97. .

KATZ, STEVEN EDWARD, psychiatrist, state health official; b. Phila., Aug. 10, 1937; s. Benjamin R. and Charlotte (Tomkins) K.; m. Marjorie A. Billstein, June 12, 1960; children: Barri L. Stryer, Stacey J. Herron. BA, Cornell U., 1959; MD, Hahnemann U., 1963. Cert. psychoanalyst, Columbia U., 1972. Diplomate Am. Bd. Psychiatry and Neurology. Intern Montefiore Hosp., Bronx, N.Y., 1963-64; resident Columbia U. N.Y. Psychiat. Inst., N.Y.C., 1966-69; dir. edn. dept. psychiatry Roosevelt Hosp., N.Y.C., 1971-74, assoc. dir., 1974-78; med. dir. dept. psychiatry Bellevue Hosp., N.Y.C., 1979-83; vice-chmn. dept. psychiatry NYU Med. Ctr., 1980-83, prof. psychiatry, 1987—, exec. vice-chmn. dept. psychiatry, 1987-94; commr. N.Y. State Office of Mental Health, Albany, 1983-87; dir. psychiatry Bellevue Hosp., 1987-91, dir. health policy NYU Med. Ctr., 1987-93, med. dir. dept. psychiatry, Tisch Hosp., 1992-94; clin. prof. psychiatry Albany Med. Coll., 1984-87; exec. v.p., med. dir. Jackson Brook Inst., Maine, 1994—, acting pres., CEO, 1997, bd. dirs., 1997; med. dir. Integrated Physician Svcs., Inc., 1994—; clin. prof. Sch. Medicine U. Vt., 1994—; exec. v.p., chief med. officer Cmty. Care Sys., Wellesley, Mass., 1996-97, chief med. officer, 1996—, pres., 1997, bd. dirs., 1997—; acting pres., CEO Jackson Brook Inst., 1997; bd. dirs. Cmty. Care Sys., 1997. Contbr. articles to profl. jours., publs. and book chpts. Bd. dirs. Facilities Devel. Corp., Albany, 1983-87, Am. Mental Health Fund, 1983—, League Ctr., N.Y.C., 1988—, Vis. Nurse Svc., N.Y.C., 1992—; mem. Bd. Profl. Med. Conduct N.Y. State Health Dept., Albany, 1994—; bd. dirs. York Shelter, Alfred, Maine, 1995—, Cmty. Care Sys. of Maine, 1995-97, Viburnum, Inc., 1995-97, Charles River Health Mgmt., Inc., 1997, Charles River Hosp., Inc., 1997, Charles River Hosp.- West, 1997, Monhegan Health Mgmt. Corp., 1997—. Capt. U.S. Army, 1964-66. Recipient Pub. Svc. award N.Y. Psychol. Soc., 1984, Pub. Svc. award Suffolk County Mental Health Assn., 1984, Exceptional Achievement award N.Y. State Office Mental Health, 1985, Governing Bd. award Crotona Park Cmty. Mental Health Ctr., 1985, Pub. Svc. award N.Y. State Psychol. Assn., 1986, Pub. Svc. award for outstanding achievement Am. Assn. for Affirmative Action, 1986, Alexander P. Braile award, 1986, Horace M. Kallen Disting. Cmty. Svc. award Am. Jewish Congress, 1987, William E. Byron award N.Y. State chpt. Assn. Mental Health Adminstrs., 1987; Cert. of Recognition Hosp. Assn. N.Y., 1991. Fellow Am. Psychiat. Assn. (commendation 1983), Am. Coll. Psychiatry (chair fin. com. 1996-97, chair membership com. 1997—); mem. AMA, Group for Advancement of Psychiatry, Am. Assn. Psychiat. Adminstrs. (Disting. Psychiat. Adminstr. award N.Y. regional chpt. 1990), Hosp. Assn. of N.Y. State (cert. of recognition 1991). Democrat.

KAUFFMAN, MARK, photographer; b. Los Angeles, Sept. 3, 1922; s. Mitchell and Anna (Bearman) K.; m. Anita Jansson, May 18, 1948; children: Linda, Yvonne, Lenita, Sylvia Ann. Grad. vocational photography, John C. Fremont Sch., 1940; MS (hon.), Brooks Inst. of Photography. Photographer Life mag., Los Angeles, Chgo., 1941-46; Far East, China Life mag., 1946-47, London, 1948-49, Paris, 1950, Washington, 1950-57, London Bur. Time Life, 1957-61; photography editor Playboy mag., 1971-76, 78-86, 86-90; lectr. Calif. Poly. State U., San Luis Obispo, Calif., 1986-92. Winner first place U. Mo. Sch. Journalism News Pictures Contest, 1951; recipient Grand award Whitehouse Photographers Assn., 1953; 1st place award color photography Ency. Brit. and Nat. Press Photographers Assn., 1959; named Photographer of Year by U. of Mo. and Ency. Brit.

KAUFMAN, FRANK ALBERT, federal judge; b. Balt., Mar. 4, 1916; s. Nathan Hess and Hilda (Hecht) K.; m. Clementine Alice Lazaron, Apr. 22, 1945; children: Frank Albert, Peggy Ann (Mrs. Fred Wolf III). AB summa cum laude, Dartmouth Coll., 1937; LLB magna cum laude, Harvard U., 1940; LLD (hon.), U. Balt., 1984. Bar: Md. 1940. Atty. Offices Gen. Counsel Treasury, Lend Lease Adminstrn. and FEA, 1941-42, 45; lend lease rep. Turkey, 1942-43; bur. chief Psychol. Warfare Allied Forces Hdqrs. and SHAEF, 1943-45; assoc. Frank, Skeen and Oppenheimer, Balt., 1945-47; ptnr. Frank, Bernstein, Conaway, Kaufman & Goldman, 1948-66; judge U.S. Dist. Ct. Md., 1966—; lectr. U. Balt., 1948-61, U. Md., 1953-54; mem. Commn. on Mgmt. and Labor Rels., State of Md., 1960, Commn. on Uniform Comml. Code, 1961, Commn. on Health Problems, 1968; chmn. Commn. on Sentencing Criminal Cases, 1962-66; bd. advisors U. Balt. Law Sch., until 1992. Bd. dirs. Am. Jewish Com., 1960-70, Balt. chpt., 1948-70, Park Sch., Balt., 1956-66, Sinai Hosp. Balt., 1957-75, Balt. chpt. NCCJ, 1950s, Balt. Hebrew Congregation, 1940s-50s, Bat. Jewish Coun., 1954-66, Jewish Family and Children's Svc., Balt., 1946-54, Goucher Coll., 1957-85, trustee emeritus, 1985—; active Harvard U. Law Sch. Assn. and Fund, 1945-60s, Jewish Charities and Welfare Fund, 1953-54, Jewish Welfare Bd., 1965-67, Md. Ptnrs. Alliance, 1965-72, Good Samaritan Hosp., Balt., 1967-73; trustee emeritus, Md. Inst. Coll. Art. Mem. ABA (bd. govs. 1982-85, chair jud. div. 1990-91), Fed. Bar Assn., Md. Bar Assn., Balt. Bar Assn., Am. Law Inst., Am. Judicature Soc. (bd. dirs. 1985-88), Fed. Judges Assn. (v.p. 1987-93), Suburban Club (bd. dirs. 1941-42, 53-60, pres. 1956-60), Rule Day Club, Wrangler Club, Law Roundtable, Hamilton Street Club (chair steering com. 1989-92), Order of Coif, Phi Beta Kappa.

KAUNITZ, HANS, physician, pathologist; b. Vienna, Austria, Oct. 20, 1905; came to U.S., 1941; s. Arpad and Elsa (Hohenberg) K.; m. Esther Beckwith, Apr. 7, 1943. MD, U. Vienna, Austria, 1930. Lic. physician, N.Y. Supervising physician Vienna U. Hosp., 1932-38; assoc. prof. of medicine U. of Phillipines, Manila, 1938-40; from asst. prof. to clin. prof. Columbia U., N.Y.C., 1956-75. Contbr. numerous articles to profl. jours., sci. papers to meetings, confs. Recipient Presidential Merit medal Pres. of Phillipines, Presidential Hon. medal, Austria, 1961. Mem. Pirquet Soc. (Disting. Mem. award 1970), Am. Oil Chem. Soc. (Achievement award 1971, Alton Bailley medal 1981, Hans Kaunitz Student award 1988). Died Nov. 27, 1996.

KAUS, OTTO MICHAEL, lawyer; b. Vienna, Austria, Jan. 7, 1920; came to U.S., 1939, naturalized, 1942; s. Otto F. and Gina (Wiener) K.; m. Peggy A. Huttenback, Jan. 12, 1943; children: Stephen D., Robert M. B.A., UCLA, 1942; LL.B., Loyola U., Los Angeles, 1949. Bar: Calif. 1949. Pvt. practice L.A., 1949-61; judge Superior Ct. Calif., 1961-64; assoc. justice Calif. Ct. Appeal (2d appellate dist., div. 3), L.A., 1965-66; presiding justice Calif. Ct. Appeal (div. 5), 1966-81; assoc. justice Supreme Ct. Calif., San Francisco, 1981-85; ptnr. Hufstedler & Kaus, L .A., 1986-95; sr. of counsel Morrison & Foerster, L.A., 1995-96.; mem. faculty Loyola U. Law Sch., 1950-75, U. So. Calif., 1974-76. Served with U.S. Army, 1942-45. Mem. Am. Law Inst., Phi Beta Kappa, Order of Coif. Home: Los Angeles Calif. Died Jan., 1996.

KAWAGUCHI, MASAAKI, informatics educator; b. Osaka, Japan, Sept. 21, 1928; s. Bumpei and Kimi (Hijikata) K.; m. Akiko Imanaga, Feb. 5, 1956; children: Hiroshi, Akira. BS, Osaka U., 1951, DSc, 1956, D in Engring., 1967. Rsch. assoc. Kyoto (Japan) U., 1952-59, Tokyo U. Edn., 1959-61; assoc. prof. Osaka U., Toyonaka, Japan, 1961-73; prof. Nat. Lab. High Energy Physics, Tsukuba, Japan, 1973-78, Kobe (Japan) U., 1978-92, Kansai U., Takatsuki, Japan, 1994—; dir. Info. Processing Ctr. Kobe U., 1983-87. Author: Research of Particles (in Japanese), 1967, Introdution to Computer Science (in Japanese), 1983, Physical Review D, 1988. Pres. Kawaguchi Fellowship Found. for Children of Traffic Victims, Osaka, 1971—. Mem. Am. Phys. Soc., Phys. Soc. Japan. Avocations: music, butterfly collection, bird watching. Died June 19, 1995.

KAYE, JEROME, accountant; b. N.Y.C., Jan. 10, 1923; s. Harry and Goldie (Harfen) K.; m. Harriet Phyllis Nagin, Mar. 16, 1946 (div. 1975); children: Billie Nora, Lenard Wayne, Bradley Steven. BA, Bklyn. Coll., 1943; MBA, CUNY, 1948. Acct. S.M. Kanarick & Co., N.Y.C., 1943-49; pvt. practice pub. acctg. Lynchburg, Va., 1949-65, 78-86; exec. v.p. Fed. Sweets & Biscuit Co., Clifton, N.J., 1965-70; pres. Universal Devel. Corp., Richmond, 1970-78; pvt. practice pub. acctg. Richmond, Va., 1978-86; v.p., dir. Womack, Burke and Co., Richmond, 1986-90; sr. assoc. Goodman & Co., Richmond, 1990-92; v.p., dir. LaLonde, Wooding & Kaye, Richmond, Va., 1992-96; mem. Va. State Bd. for Accountancy, 1991-96, chmn., 1994-96. Pres. Agudath Sholom Congregation, 1953-54; active Lynchburg Jewish Community Coun., 1959-66; chmn., pres. com. employment of physically handicapped Lynchburg, 1955-56; treas., dir. Beth Ahabah Congregation, Richmond, 1982-85; pres., dir. Beth Sholom

Home Va., Richmond, 1987-89; vice chmn. bd. govs. Beth Sholom Geriatric Svcs. Va., 1990-91. Mem. Va. State Bd. for Accountancy, Va. Soc. CPAs, N.Y. State Soc. CPAs. Died June 30, 1996.

KEANE, STEVEN EDWARD, lawyer; b. Aberdeen, S.D., Oct. 25, 1915; s. Stephen Edward and Freda (Host) K.; m. Geraldine Ellen Cox, Jan. 17, 1942; children: Stephen Edward, John Patrick, Kevin Gerard, Mary Elizabeth. Student No. State Tchrs. Coll., Aberdeen, S.D., 1932-34; LLB, Marquette U., 1937. Bar: Wis. 1937, U.S. Dist. Ct. (ea. and we. dists.) Wis. 1937, U.S. Ct. Appeals (7th cir.) 1956, U.S. Supreme Ct. 1956. Assoc. Foley & Lardner and predecessors, Milw., 1937-47, ptnr., 1947—. Bd. dirs. emeritus St. Mary's Hosp., Milw., 1962—, Chmn., 1965-67; bd. dirs. Better Bus. Bur., Milw., 1968—, Seton Health Care Found., Milw., 1983—, chmn. bd., 1988—; trustee emeritus Marquette U., Milw., 1969—, chmn. bd. trustees and exec. com., 1971-73; co-chmn. Wis. region NCCJ, 1971—; bd. dirs. Sacred Heart Sch. Theology, Milw., 1982—. Served to lt. j.g. USNR, 1943-46. Recipient Brotherhood award NCCJ, 1968; named Alumnus of Yr., Marquette U., 1970. Fellow Am. Coll. Trial Lawyers (elected 1959, chmn. Wis. Fellows 1972-73), Am. Bar Found.; mem. Milw. Bar Assn. (pres. 1968), State Bar Wis. (Charles L. Goldberg Disting. Svc. award 1988), ABA (chmn. Sherman Act com. and mem. council Antitrust Sect. 1965-69, mem. standing com. on fed. judiciary 1979-84, resource devel. council 1983—, ho. of dels. 1970-80), Bar Assn. Seventh Fed. Cir., Am. Law Inst. (life), Am. Judicature Soc., Am. Arbitration Assn., U.S. Supreme Ct. Hist. Soc. (chmn. Membership Com. Wis.), Marquette U. Alumni Assn. (dir. 1963-69), Marquette U. Law Alumni Assn. (dir., chmn. 1957-58). Republican. Roman Catholic. Clubs: Univ., Ozaukee Country. Deceased.

KEATING, LARRY GRANT, electrical engineer, educator; b. Omaha, Jan. 15, 1944; s. Grant Morris and Dorothy Ann (Kauffold) K.; m. Barbara Jean Merley, Dec. 21, 1968. LLB, Blackstone Sch. Law, 1968; BS, U. Nebr., 1969; BS summa cum laude, Met. State Coll., 1971; MS, U. Colo., Denver, 1978. Chief engr. broadcast electronics 3 radio stas., 1965-69; coord. engring. reliability Cobe Labs., Lakewood, Colo., 1972-74; quality engr. Statitrol Corp., Lakewood, Colo., 1974-76; instr. electrical engring. U. Colo., Denver, 1976-78; from asst. prof. to prof. Met. State Coll., Denver, 1978-96, chmn. dept., 1984-95; cons. Transplan Assocs., Boulder, Colo., 1983-84. 1st lt. U.S. Army, 1962-70. Recipient Outstanding Faculty award U. Colo., Denver, 1980, Outstanding Alumnus award Met. State Coll., 1985. Mem. IEEE (sr.), Instrument Soc. Am. (sr.), Order of the Engr., Am. Soc. Engring. Edn., Nat. Assn. Radio and Telecomm. Engrs. (cert. engr.), Eta Kappa Nu (fellow), Tau Alpha Pi, Chi Epsilon. Avocations: skiing, astronomy. Died 1996.

KEATING, LOUIS CLARK, language educator; b. Phila., Aug. 20, 1907; s. Louis Alcloma and Blanche Augusta (DeYoung) K.; m. Lucille Elizabeth Tate, July 23, 1936; children: Richard Clark, Geoffrey Tate, Anne Elizabeth. A.B., Colgate U., 1928; A.M., Harvard U., 1930, Ph.D., 1934; postgrad., Sorbonne, 1932-33, Middlebury Spanish Sch., summers 1928, 29, Heidelberg U., summer 1931, Centro de Estudios Historicos, summer 1933. Saltonstall travelling scholar Harvard U., 1932-33; instr. Romance langs. Colgate U., 1928-29; asst. prof. Spanish Macalester Coll., 1934-36; asst. prof. Romance langs. Monticello Coll., 1936-37; assoc. Romance langs. U. Ill., 1937-39; asst. prof. Romance langs. George Washington U., 1939-40, assoc. prof., 1940-46, prof., exec. officer dept. Romance langs., 1946-57; vis. prof. U. Tenn., summer 1947; resident dean U. Md. Grad. Fgn. Study Center, Paris, 1949-50; head dept. Romance langs. U. Cin., 1957-60; edn. adviser USOM, Peru, 1960-62; prof. Romance langs. U. Ky., Lexington, 1962-91; chmn. dept. modern fgn. langs. U. Ky., 1963-66; vis. prof. U. Calgary, Alta., Can., 1969-70; staff Chapman Coll. World Campus Afloat, spring 1967, fall 1974. Author: Studies on the Literary Salon in France, 1550-1615, 1941, Critic of Civilization, Georges Duhamel, 1965, Tierra de los Incas, 1966, Andre Maurois, 1969, Du Bellay, 1971, Etienne Pasquier, 1972, Audubon, The Kentucky Years, 1976; translator, editor: Arriaga, P.J. de Extirpation of Idolatry, 1968; translator (with Keller): Don Juan Manuel, The Book of Count Lucanor and Patronio, 1977, (with R. Keating) Meilland: A Life in Roses, rev. edit., 1984; articles, revs. in lang. jours. Mem. Arlington County (Va.) Sch. Bd., 1953-57, chmn. bd., 1956-57. Served to capt., Signal Corps AUS, 1943-46. Decorated officier d'Academie (France). Mem. AAUP, MLA, Am. Assn. Tchrs. French, Fed. Schoolmens Club, Phi Beta Kappa. Presbyn. Home: Lexington Ky. Died Aug. 30, 1991.

KECK, WILLIAM, architect; b. Watertown, Wis., Dec. 1, 1908; s. Fred George and Amalie (Henze) K.; m. Stella M. McLeish, Oct. 23, 1937; 1 child, Margaret M. Student, Northwestern Coll., 1926-27; BS, U. Ill., 1931. Draftsman, specifications writer G.F. Keck, Chgo., 1931-42; site planner, specifications writer U.S. C.E., Chgo., 1942-43; ptnr. George Fred Keck & William Keck, architects, Chgo., 1946—; v.p., dir. Keck Furniture Co., Watertown. Prin. works include Kunstadter House, Highland Park, Ill., 1953, Prairie Cts. Housing Project, Chgo., Blair House, Lake Bluff, Ill., 1958, Hirsch House, Highland Park, 1963, Child Care Ctr., Chgo., Harper Sq. Housing Projects, Chgo., 1970; pub.: Keck & Keck (Robert Boyce) 1994. Bd. dirs. Hyde Park Neighborhood Club, S.E. Chgo. Commn. Lt. USNR, 1943-46. Honored at 4th Ann. Conf. of Am. sect. Internat. Solar Energy Soc., 1979; recipient 1st Ill. medal in architecture U. Ill., 1980. Fellow AIA; mem. Alpha Rho Chi. Home: Chicago Ill. DIED 05/25/95. .

KEEGAN, GEORGE JOSEPH, JR., institute executive, former air force officer; b. Houlton, Maine, July 4, 1921; s. George Joseph and Beatrice M. (Bailey) K.; divorced; children: George Joseph III, Elizabeth Anne. BA, Harvard U., 1944; MA, George Washington U., 1965; postgrad., Nat. War Coll., 1965. Commd. 2d lt. USAF, advanced through grades to maj. gen.; chief Air Force Intelligence, 7th Air Force, Vietnam, 1967-69; dep. chief plans and ops. Hdqrs. Air Force Logistics Command, 1970-71; chief Air Force Intelligence, Hdqrs. USAF, Washington, 1971-77; ret., 1977; exec. v.p. U.S. Strategic Inst., Washington, editor Strategic Rev., 1977-78; founder, pres. Inst. Strategic Affairs; vice chmn. Coalition for Peace through Strength, 1980-93; faculty, lectr. Western Monetary War Coll., Ft. Collins, Colo., 1985-93. Founder Soviet Military Thought series. Bd. dirs. Internat. Security, Washington, 1987-93. Decorated D.S.M. with oak leaf cluster, Legion of Merit with 3 oak leaf clusters, Air medal with 2 oak leaf clusters, DFC; D.S.C. (Republic of Vietnam). Home: Fort Washington Md. Died Mar. 3, 1993.

KEELAN, KEVIN ROBERT, priest; b. Elizabeth, N.J., Mar. 4, 1921; s. Patrick Joseph and Ellen Cecelia (McNesby) K. Student, Seton Hall U., 1940-42; BA, St. Francis Coll., 1945; STL, Cath. U. Am., 1949; PhL, St. Thomas U., Rome; HHD (hon.), U. Steubenville, 1987; D Pedagogy (hon.), St. Francis Coll., 1991. Joined Third Order Regular of St. Francis, Roman Cath. Ch., 1942, ordained priest, 1949. Instr. philosophy, dean students St. Francis Coll., Loretto, Pa., 1951-53; pres. St. Francis Coll., 1956-59; asst. prof. philosophy, dean U. Steubenville, Ohio, 1953-56, pres., 1959-62, chmn. bd. trustees, exec. v.p., 1966-69, pres., 1969-74; minister provincial Province Most Sacred Heart Jesus, 1962-66; pastor St. John the Evangelist Ch., Pitts., 1977-86, St. Francis Sem., Toronto, Ont., Can., 1986-88; parochial vicar St. Gabriel Parish, Marlboro, N.J., 1988-91; chaplain St. Francis Convent Motherhouse, Sisters of St. Francis, Pitts., 1991—; bd. trustees St. Francis Coll., 1984—. Recipient Porter W. Averill award Thomas Jefferson High Sch., 1955, Poverello medal Founders Assocs. Coll. of Steubenville, 1975. Lodges: K.C., Ancient Order Hibernians. Deceased.

KEENEY, ARTHUR HAIL, physician, educator; b. Louisville, Jan. 20, 1920; s. Arthur Hale and Eugenia (Hail) K.; m. Virginia Alice Tripp, Dec. 27, 1942; children—Steven Harris, Martha Blackledge Heyburn, Lee Douglas. B.S., Coll. William and Mary, 1941; MD, U. Louisville, 1944; MS, U. Pa., 1952, DSc, 1955; DSc honoris causa, Bellarmine Coll., 1996. Diplomate Am. Bd. Ophthalmology (assoc. examiner 1960-84, hon. M in Ophthalmic Optics 1992). Intern Louisville Gen. Hosp., 1944-46; resident in ophthalmology Wills Eye Hosp., Phila., 1949-51, ophthalmologist in chief, 1965-73; dir. ophthalmology research U. Louisville, 1952-65, asst. prof. ophthalmology, 1958-63, assoc. prof., 1963-65, prof., dean Sch. Medicine, 1973-80, Disting. prof. ophthalmology, dean emeritus, 1980—; prof., chmn. ophthalmology Temple U., 1966-72; profl. adv. com. Nat. Soc. Prevention of Blindness, 1964-78, dir., 1981-84, exec. com., 1984, regional rep., 1984-86, v.p., 1986-87; Alvaro lectr. S.Am. Univs., 1960; sec.-treas. Nat. Com. Research in Ophthalmology and Blindness, 1964-78; vision study sect. neurol. and sensory disease control program Nat. Ctr. Chronic Disease Control, USPHS, 1966-69; med. cons. Project Head Start, 1968-96; chmn. com. on ophthalmic Standards Am. Nat. Standards Inst., 1970-85; chmn. Ky. med. rev. bd. driver limitation program State of Ky., 1974-96; med. adv. bd. Recording for Blind, 1976-80, Nat. Aid to Visually Handicapped, 1970-79; hon. pres. 2d symposium Internat. Congress Diagnostic Ultrasound in Ophthalmology, Czechoslovakia, 1967; pres. 4th Internat. Congress Ultrasonography in Ophthalmology, Phila., 1968. Author: Chronology of Ophthalmic Development, 1951, Ocular Examination: Basis and technique, 1970, 2d edit., 1976; co-author: Dictionary of Ophthalmic Optics, 1995; editor: (with V.T. Keeney) Dyslexia: Diagnosis and Management of reading Disorders, 1968, (with K. Gitter, D. Mayer and L.K. Sarin) Ophthalmic Ultrasound, 1969; assoc. editor Am. Jour. Ophthalmology, 1965-81, cons. editor, 1981-96; mem. editl. bd. Investigative Ophthalmology, 1969-73, Ophthalmology Excerpta Medica, 1974-96, Sight Saving, 1982-86; contbr. articles to profl. jours., chpts. in books. Mem. Phila. Dist. Bd. Health and Welfare Coun., 1967-69, Nat. Coun. to Combat Blindness, 1967-84; mem. adv. bd., assoc. trustee U. Pa. Sch. Social Work, 1968-73; exec. bd. dirs. Old Ky. Home coun. Boy Scouts Am., 1976-79; life trustee James Graham Brown Found., 1978—; bd. dirs. Louisville Orch., 1963-65, Pa. Assn. for Blind, 1965-68, Am. Found. for Blind, 1975-78, The Lighthouse, N.Y.C., 1995—. Served to capt. MC, AUS, 1942-47. Recipient Laureate award Younger Women's Club, 1964, Allstate Safety Crusade award, 1965, Patrick R. O'Connor Meml. award, 1983, 11th Howe medal U. Buffalo, 1973, 21st Beverly Myers Nelson award Am. Bd. Opticianary, 1974, Meritorious Service award Am. Nat. Standards Inst., 1985, Ednl. Achievement award Ky. Med. Assn., 1986, Faculty Dist. Service award U. Louisville, 1987, Disting. Alumnus award U. Louisville Med. Sch. Alumni Assn., 1988, Spirit of Excellence award Ky. Mil. Inst. Alumni Assn., 1992. Fellow Am. Ophthal,. Soc., Am. Acad. Ophthalmology (life, chmn. com. ophthalmic instruments and devices 1977-85, Sr. Merit award 1984, v.p. 1985-87), Coll. Physicians of Phila., Pa. Acad. Ophthalmology and Otolaryngology (v.p. 1973), Am. Soc. Ophthalmic Ultrasound (hon.); mem. AMA, AAAS, Columbian Soc. Ophthalmology, Ky. Eye, Ear, Nose and Throat Soc. (pres. 1958), Hellenic Ophthal. Soc., Joint Commn. Allied Health Pers. in Ophthalmology (v.p. 1985-87, pres. 1987-89), Louisville Acad. Ophthalmology, Ky. Acad. Eye Physicians and Surgeons (pres. 1984), Ky. Surg. Soc., Ill. Soc. Ophthalmology and Otolarynology, Salmagundi Club, Pendennis, Louisville Country Club. Home: Louisville Ky. Died Oct. 1, 1996; interred Cave Hill Cemetery, Louisville, KY.

KEGEL, HERBERT, conductor; b. Dresden, Germany, Sept. 29, 1920; s. Frita and Martha (Missbach) K.; ed. Orch. Sch. of Saxon State Music Sch. and Conservatory; m. Celestina; 1 son, Bjö rn. Band leader Volkstheater, Rostock, Germany, 1946-49; leader Radio Choir, Leipzig, Germany, 1949-78; leader Grossen Rundfunkorchesters, Leipzig, 1949-53; condr. - Rundfunk-Sinfonieorchesters, Leipzig, 1953-60, chief condr., 1960-78; chief condr., leader Dresden Philharm., 1977-90; tchr. Leipzig Music Sch., 1975-77. Recipient numerous awards including Art prize of German Democratic Party, 1959, Nat. Prize German Democratic Republic, 1961, awards music critics of Chile, 1967, Chile Art prize, 1968, Arthur Nikisch prize City of Leipzig, 1974. Died Nov. 20, 1990.

KEIGLER, JOHN E., aerospace engineer; b. Baltimore, Md., July 10, 1929; s. Arthur L. and Eliese E. (Doering) K.; m. Irene Tanis, 1955; children: Eliese A., Arthur L., John E. Jr., Elizabeth I., Janice M., James T. BE, Johns Hopkins U., 1950, MS in Elec. Engring., 1951; PhD, Stanford U., 1958. Aerospace rsch. scientist Ames Lab., NACA, Moffett Field, Calif., 1956; rsch. assoc. Stanford (Calif.) Electronics Labs., 1956-57; mgr. satellite system engring. RCA Astro Electronics, Princeton, N.J., 1958-71, mgr. comml. satellites, 1972-83; chief scientist GE Astro Space Div., Princeton, 1984-91; ret., 1991; mem. communications adv. com. NASA, 1980-83; cons. NRC, 1984-89; mem. Nat. Assn. for Search and Rescue, 1985-90. Contbr. articles to aerospace jours.; satellite design patentee. Trustee Dutch Neck (N.J.) Ch., 1965-68; councilman Boy Scouts Am., Princeton, 1968-70; vestry All Saints Ch., Princeton, 1982-85; Rep. committeeman, Princeton, 1984-86. Active duty USNR, 1951-55; comdr. USNR, ret. Recipient David Sarnoff medal RCA, 1976. Fellow IEEE (chmn. subcom. 1986-89), AIAA (tech. chmn. 1976-77, Aerospace Communications award 1990); mem. Internat. Acad. Astronautics, Electronic Industries Assn. (chmn. satellite telecom. com. 1975-79). Episcopalian. Avocation: light plane pilot. Died, Oct. 5, 1992.

KEITH, BRIAN MICHAEL, actor; b. Bayonne, N.J., Nov. 14, 1921; s. Robert Lee and Helena (Shipmen) K.; m. Victoria Lei Aloha Young, 1968; children: Michael, Mimi, Bobby, Daisy. Student pub. schs., L.I., N.Y. Pres. Miguel Prodns., Inc. (TV prodn., real estate, agr., and minerals co.). Appeared in summer stock, Broadway, films and TV, 1945—; on stage in Heydey, 1946, Mister Roberts, 1948, Darkness at Noon, 1951, Out West of Eighth, 1951, Moon is Blue, 1951, The Emperor of Babylon, 1952, Da, 1978; films Arrowhead, 1952, Jivaro, 1953, Alaska Seas, 1953, Tight Spot, 1954, Violent Men, 1954, Bamboo Prison, 1955, Five Against the House, 1955, Storm Center, 1956, Hell Canyon Outlaws, 1956, Nightfall, 1956, Chicago Confidential, 1957, Hell's Highway, 1957, Desert Hell, 1957, Villa Rides, 1957, Run of the Arrow, 1957, Dino, 1957, Fort Dobbs, 1958, Sierra Baron, 1958, Ten Who Dared Mustangers, 1959, The Young Philadelphians, 1959, Ten Who Dared, 1960, The Deadly Companions, 1961, The Parent Trap, 1961, Moon Pilot, 1962, Savage Sam, 1963, The Raiders, 1964, Those Calloways, 1965, A Tiger Walks, 1964, The Pleasure Seekers, 1964, The Hallelujah Trail, 1965, Tenderfoot, 1964, Rare Breed, 1966, The Russians Are Coming-The Russians Are Coming, 1966, Way...Way Out, 1966, Nevada Smith, 1966, Reflections in a Golden Eye, 1967, With Six You Get Egg Roll, 1968, Krakatoa, East of Java, 1968, Gaily, Gaily, 1969, Suppose They Gave a War and Nobody Came, 1970, McKenzie Break, 1970, Scandalous John, 1971, Something Big, 1971, The Yakuza, 1975, The Wind and the Lion, 1975, Joe Panther, 1976, Nickelodeon, 1976, Hooper, 1978, Meteor, 1979, Moonraker, 1979, The Mountain Men, 1980, Charlie Chan and The Curse of the Dragon Queen, 1981, Sharkey's Machine, 1982, Death Before Dishonor, 1987, Young Guns, 1988, After the Rain, 1988, Welcome Home, 1989; TV series include Crusader, 1955-56, The Westerner, 1960, Family Affair, 1966-71, The Little People, 1972-73, The Brian Keith Show, 1973-74, Archer, 1975, Hardcastle and McCormick, 1983-86, Pursuit of Happiness, 1987, Heartland, 1989, The Secrets of Lake Success, 1993; TV movies include: Second Chance, 1972, The Zoo Gang,

1975, The Loneliest Runner, 1976, The Quest, 1976, In the Matter of Karen Ann Quinlan, 1977, How the West Was Won, 1977, Centennial, 1978, The Seekers, 1979, Power, 1979, The Chisholms, 1979, Moviola, 1980, World War III, 1982, Cry for the Strangers, 1982, The Alamo: Thirteen Days to Glory, 1987, Perry Mason: The Case of the Lethal Lesson, 1989, Lady in a Corner, 1989, The Gambler Returns: Luck of the Draw, 1991. Chmn. Hawaii unit Am. Lung Assn. Served with USMC, 1941-45, PTO. Decorated Navy Air medal. Mem. Actor's Equity Assn., Screen Actors Guild, AFTRA, Dirs. Guild Am. Roman Catholic. Club: Outrigger Canoe (Honolulu). Died June, 1997.

KELLAM, RICHARD B., judge; b. 1909. Bar: Va. bar 1934. Chief judge, sr. U.S. dist. judge U.S. Dist. Ct. for Va. Eastern Dist., Norfolk. Died 1997.

KELLER, ALFRED SAMUEL, cinematographer, professional society executive; b. Monongahela, Pa., Apr. 13, 1911; s. Frank Perry and Maude Hannah (Watson) K.; m. Winifred Kirk Kirkham, Apr. 12, 1936; children—Valerie, Elizabeth Ann. Student, UCLA, 1928-31. Night film loader Columbia Pictures Corp., Hollywood, Calif., 1929-31; asst. cinematographer Columbia, Republic Pictures, Hollywood, Calif., 1932-42; dir. photography Republic Pictures, RKO Pictures, Hollywood, Calif., 1943-55; pres. Western Electromotive Inc., Los Angeles, and Culver City, Calif., 1957-75; exec. dir. Am. Soc. Cinematographers, Hollywood, 1980-86; councillor Soc. Photog. Scientists and Engrs., Hollywood, 1976-80; mem. student films exec. com. Acad. Motion Picture Arts and Scis., Beverly Hills, Calif., 1975—. Dir. and cinematographer Lucky Piece, 1951; co-producer, cinematographer The Professor, 1949, Morass, 1933. Contbr. articles to profl. jours. Dir. photography Los Angeles County Sheriff's Dept., 1978-79. Served to 1st lt. U.S. Army ROTC, 1925-31. Recipient award of Appreciation, Los Angeles Film Tchrs. Assn., 1983, Dialight Corp., 1975. Mem. Am. Soc. Cinematographers (dir., sec. 1980-89, Appreciation award 1981), Internat. Photographers Guild, Internat. Alliance Theatrical Stage Employees and Motion Picture Operators of the U.S. and Can., Soc. Photog. Scientists and Engrs., Acad. Motion Picture Arts and Scis., Soc. Motion Picture and TV Engrs., Western Photog. Collectors Assn. Club: Hollywood Assocs. Avocations: cinematography; collecting antique cinemachinery; aviation; railroads. Died Sept. 1989.

KELLER, CHRISTOPH, JR., bishop; b. Bay City, Mich., Dec. 22, 1915; s. Christoph and Margaret Ely (Walter) K.; m. Caroline P. Murphy, June 22, 1940; children: Caroline, Cornelia, Cynthia, Kathryn, Christoph, Elisabeth. Grad., Lake Forest (Ill.) Acad., 1934; B.A., Washington and Lee U., 1939, D.D., 1973; student, Grad. Sch. Theology, U. South, 1954, D.D., 1968; certificate spl. work, Gen. Theol. Sem., N.Y.C., 1957; S.T.D. (hon.), Gen. Theol. Sem., 1968. Planter Alexandria, La., 1940-95; pres. Deltic Farm & Timber Co., El Dorado, Ark., 1948-51; exec. v.p. Murphy Corp., El Dorado, 1951-54, dir., 1948-89; ordained priest P.E. Ch., 1957; rector Harrison, Ark.; also charge missions in Eureka Springs and Mountain Home, Ark., 1957-61; rector St. Andrews Episcopal Ch., Jackson, Miss., 1962-67; dean St. Andrews Cathedral, Jackson, until 1967; bishop coadjutor Diocese of Ark., 1967-70, diocesan bishop, 1970-81; exec. council Episc. Ch., 1976-82; chmn. Episcopal Ch. Bldg. Fund, 1982-87; dep. Gen. Conv. P. E. Ch., 1958, 61, 64, 67. Pres. La. Aberdeen Angus Breeders Assn., 1947, La. Delta Council, 1950; chmn. United Fund, El Dorado, 1952; mem. Madison Parish (La).) Sch. Bd., 1952-53; Trustee All Saints Jr. Coll., Vicksburg, Miss., 1949-51, 67-81, U. South, 1973-77; bd. dirs. Washington and Lee U., Lexington, Va., 1981-86, Gen. Theol. Sem., N.Y.C., 1981-89, The Living Ch., 1988-90. Served as officer USMCR, World War II. Mem. Phi Kappa Alpha (bd. dirs. 1989-90). Home: Alexandria La. Died May 19, 1995.

KELLER, JOHN RICHARD, insurance company executive; b. Harrisburg, Pa., June 1, 1924; s. Frank Landis and Clemens (Benchoff) K.; m. Janice Marie Taylor, Sept. 1, 1946; children: David Richard, Robert Alan, Nancy Marie. BS in Econs., Franklin and Marshall Coll., 1950. Crewchief traffic survey Pa. Dept. Highways, Harrisburg, 1950-52; underwriter Retailers Mutual Ins. Co., Harrisburg, 1952-57, asst. sec.-treas., 1957, sec.-treas., 1957-69; ptnr. City Ins. Agy., Harrisburg, 1957-69; pres., CEO Yorktowne Mut. Ins. Co., York, Pa., 1975-86, chmn. bd. dirs., 1986-95, ret., 1995; past mem. bd. dirs. Mut. Svc. Orgn. Trustee, deacon Augsburg Luth. Sch., 1959-70, Lakeside Luth. Ch., Harrisburg, 1970-96. With USN, 1942-46. Mem. Nat. Assn. Mut. Ins. Cos., Pa. Ass. Mut. Ins. Cos. (pres. 1982-83, bd. dirs. 1971-75), Am. Legion, Franklin and Marshall Coll. Alumni Assn., Sparks Club (co-chmn. edn. com. 1963), Embers Club (pres. 1974), Masons, Shriners. Republican. Avocations: hunting, fishing, photography, gardening. Died Jan. 7, 1997.

KELLEY, CLARENCE MARION, lawyer; b. Kansas City, Mo., Oct. 24, 1911; s. Clarence Bond and Minnie (Brown) K.; m. Ruby Pickett, 1940 (dec. 1975); children: Mary Kelley Dobbins, Kent Clarence; m. Shirley Ann Dyckes, Oct. 3, 1976. BA, Kansas U., 1936; JD, U. Mo., Kansas City, 1940. Bar: Mo. 1940, U.S. Supreme Ct. 1977. Spl. agt. U.S. FBI, various cities, 1940-65; dir. U.S. FBI, Washington, 1973-78; chief of police Kansas City, 1965-73; chief exec. officer, chmn. Clarence Kelley & Assocs., Kansas City, 1982-90. Author: Clarence M. Kelley, 1987. Life bd. dirs. Salvation Army; life elder Country Christian Ch.; horse racing commr. State of Mo. Lt. (J.g.) USN, 1944-46. Mem. Internat. Assn. Chiefs of Police (life), Mo. Peace Officers Assn. (life), Met. Chiefs and Sheriffs Assn. (life), Rotary of Kansas City (life). Home: Kansas City Mo. Died Aug. 5, 1997; interred Mt. Washington Cemetery, Kansas City, MO.

KELLEY, NOBLE HENRY, former psychologist, educator; b. Thamesville, Ont., Can., Aug. 10, 1901; s. Isaac Wesley and Louisa (Ross) K.; m. Ethel B. Patterson, July 9, 1927; 1 child, Alan Douglas. AA, Graceland Coll., 1931; AB, State U. Iowa, 1933, AM, 1935, PhD, 1936. Lic. psychologist; Diplomate Am. Bd. Profl. Pyschology (sec. treas., exec. officer 1951-70, trustee 1950-74, Disting. psychologist citation 1972). Eastman rsch. fellow dept. psychology U. Iowa, 1936-37; 1st asst. prof. dept. psychology U. Louisville, 1937-43, assoc. prof., 1943-46, prof., head. dept., 1946-51, clin. psychologist, dir. Psychol. Svcs. Ctr., 1946-51; prof., chmn. dept. psychology, dir. psychol. svcs. So. Ill. U., Carbondale, 1951-60, rsch. prof. psychology, 1960-69, emeritus prof., 1969—; mem. adv. bd. Inst. Juvenile Rsch., 1957-65; mem. Ill. Psychiat. Tng. and Rsch. Authority, 1957-65; chmn. adv. com. supt. pub. instrn., Ill., 1954-61; pres. Conf. State Psychol. Assns., 1949-51. Author: Work Book for General Psychology, 1940, A Manual for General Psychology, 1942. Fellow APA (edn. and tng. bd. 1956-59, coun. of reps. 1955-58, 63-65, pres. divsn. cons. psychology 1966-67, Spl. award for disting. contbns. 1974), Acad. Clin. Psychology; mem. AAUP, Assn. Midwestern Coll. Psychiatrists and Clin. Psychologists (pres. 1948-49), Midwestern Psychol. Assn., Ill. Psychol. Assn. (pres. 1957, bd. examiners 1959-63), Fla. Psychol. Assn. (Disting. Svc. award 1977), Lions, Sigma Xi, Alpha Epsilon Delta, Lambda Chi Alpha (named to Alumni Hall of Fame 1996). Unitarian-Universalist. Died January 28, 1997.

KELLOGG, EDMUND H., law educator. Assoc. dean Vt. Law Sch., prof. population law and hist. preservation. Author: (with Norman Williams) Readings in Historic Preservation and Vermont Townscape, 1977. Bd. dirs. Planned Parenthood of No. New Eng., Vt. Land Trust. Home: South Royalton Vt. Died Apr. 9, 1993.

KELLY, JOHN PATRICK, educator; b. Sigourney, Iowa, Sept. 30, 1924; s. John Walter and Vena (Wraight) K.; m. Jean Ann Donohue, June 14, 1947 (dec. 1971); children: Michael, Camilla, Carol; m. Gretchen Louise Bullington, Jan. 6, 1979. B.A., U. Iowa, 1948, M.A., 1953, Ph.D., 1959; B.Mortuary Sci., Coll. Mortuary Sci., St. Louis, 1950. Mem. faculty U. Nev., Reno, 1955-95; prof. elem. edn. U. Nev., 1968-83, prof. emeritus, 1983-95. Co-editor: Basic Reading; Contbr. articles to profl. jours. Served with USNR, 1943-46. William H. Carpenter fellow, 1950; Kellogg Found. fellow, 1965. Mem. Nat. Council Tchrs. English, Internat., Western Region Coll. reading assns., Am. Radio Relay League, Sierra Nevada Amateur Radio Soc., Amateur Radio Emergency Services, Sagebrush Radio Relay Services, Phi Delta Kappa, Phi Delta Theta. Clubs: Elks, K.C. Home: Reno Nev. Died April 13, 1995.

KELLY, WILLIAM R., employment agency executive; b. 1905; married. Grad., U. Pitts., 1925. With Kelly Services, Inc., 1946—; chmn. Kelly Svcs., Inc., Troy, Mich., 1965—, also bd. dirs.

KEMELMAN, HARRY, author; b. Boston, Nov. 24, 1908; s. Isaac and Dora (Prizer) K.; m. Anne Kessin, Mar. 29, 1936; children—Ruth (Mrs. George Rooks), Arthur Frederick, Diane (Mrs. Stephen R. Volk). A.B., Boston U., 1930; M.A., Harvard U., 1931. Tchr. Boston pub. schs., 1935-41, eve. div. Northeastern U., 1938-41; chief job analyst and wage adminstr. Boston Port Embarkation, 1942-49; free-lance writer, 1949-63; tchr. Franklin Inst., Boston, 1963-64, State Coll., Boston, 1964-96. Author: Friday the Rabbi Slept Late, 1964, Saturday the Rabbi Went Hungry, 1966, The Nine Mile Walk, 1967, Sunday the Rabbi Stayed Home, 1969, Commonsense in Education, 1970, Monday the Rabbi Took Off, 1972, Tuesday the Rabbi Saw Red, 1973, Wednesday the Rabbi Got Wet, 1976, Thursday the Rabbi Walked Out, 1978, Conversations with Rabbi Small, 1981, Someday the Rabbi Will Leave, 1985, One Fine Day the Rabbi Bought a Cross, 1987, The Day the Rabbi Resigned, 1992, That Day, The Rabbi Left Town, 1996. Recipient Edgar award for best first novel, 1965; Faith and Freedom Communications award, 1967. Mem. Author's League. Home: Marblehead Mass. Died Dec. 15, 1996.

KEMPNER, ROBERT MAX WASILII, lawyer, political scientist; b. Freiburg, Germany, Oct. 17, 1899; came to U.S., 1939, naturalized; s. Walter K. and Lydia (Rabinowitsch) K.; m. Ruth Hahn (Benedicta Maria); children: Lucian Walter, André Franklin. Student of law, polit. sci., pub. adminstrn., criminology, Univs. of Berlin, Breslau, Freiburg (Germany); student polit. sci., pub. adminstrn., criminology (Dr. of Law and Pub. Adminstrn.); PhD (hon.), U. Osnabrück. Prof. e.H. Senate Berlin; asst. to state atty. Berlin, 1926, judge mcpl. ct., 1927; superior govt. counselor chief legal adviser of Prussian police system of 76,000 men; (recommended suppression of Nazi party and prosecution of Hitler for high treason, fired and expatriated by Hitler), Ministry of Interior, Berlin; judge civil service tribunal Ministry of Interior, 1928-33; lectr. German Acad. Politics Sch. Social Work, Police Inst., Berlin, 1926-33; counselor internat. law and migration problems, 1934-35; Pres. and prof. polit. sci. Fiorenza Coll., Florence, Italy, and Nice, France, 1936-39; research asso. and asst. Inst. Local and State Govt., U. Pa. (research on machinery of European dictatorships under Carnegie and Carl Schurz grants), 1939-42; expert to Fed. courts, espionage and fgn. agt. trials; expert cons. Dept. Justice, OSS and to sec. of War on legal, polit., police and intelligence techniques of European dictatorships and fgn. orgns., 1942-45; U.S. staff prosecutor Nuremberg trials against Goering, Frick et al; research dir. U.S. prosecution, 1945-46; dep. U.S. chief of counsel for war crimes, chief prosecutor of German Reich cabinet mems., state secs. and diplomats investigation of Holocaust, 1946-49; expert cons. in internat. law; atty. indemnification matters and prosecution of war criminals, 1951-93; cons. Reichstag fire trial, 1960; cons. to Israel Govt. in Eichmann case, 1961; vis. prof. Erlangen; lectr. schs., colls., univs. and pvt. orgns. Author several books, primarily on Germany, 1931-93, The Judgment in The Wilhelmstrassen Case, 1950, German Police Administration, 1953, Eichmann and Accomplices, 1961, SS Under Crossexamination, 1964, 86, The Warren Report in German Language, 1964, Edith Stein and Anne Frank-Two of Hundred thousand, 1968, The Third Reich under Crossexamination, 1969, The Murder of 35,000 Berlin Jews, 1971, American Courts in Germany, The Missed Hitler Stop, 1983, Memoirs: Prosecutor of an Epoch, 1983, The Kempner Bibliography, 1987; contbr. to profl. jours. Decorated German Grand Cross of Merit with star Fed. Republic Germany, Cross of Polonia Restituta.; recipient medal with Star and Schulterband, Fed. Republic Germany; medal Charles U., Prague, Carl von Ossietzky medal, Wilhelm Leuschner medal; named hon. prof. emeritus Senate Berlin. Fellow U. Jerusalem.; Mem. Am. Polit. Sci. Assn., Am. Soc. for Internat. Law, German Bar. Home: Lansdowne Pa. Died Aug. 15, 1993.

KEMPNER, WALTER, retired physician; b. Berlin, Germany, Jan. 25, 1903; came to U.S., 1934, naturalized, 1941; s. Walter and Lydia (Rabinowitsch) K. M.D., U. Heidelberg, Germany, 1926. Intern medicine U. Heidelberg, 1926-27; research asst. and asso. to Dr. Otto Warburg, Kaiser Wilhelm Inst. for Cellular Physiology, 1927-28, 33-34; asst. physician dept. medicine Berlin U. Sch. Medicine, 1928-33; with Duke Sch. Medicine, 1934—, asso., then asst. prof., asso. prof., 1934-51, prof., 1952-72, prof. emeritus, 1972-92; ret., 1992. Contbr. articles to profl. jours. Recipient Ciba award Am. Heart Assn., 1975. Fellow ACP; mem. AMA, Am. Physiol. Soc. Originator rice diet in treatment hypertensive and arteriosclerotic vascular disease, heart and kidney disease, vascular retinopathy, diabetes mellitus and obesity. DIED 09/27/97. .

KENDALL, WILLIAM DENIS, medical electronic equipment company executive; b. Halifax, Yorkshire, Eng., May 27, 1903; came to U.S., 1923, naturalized, 1957; s. Joe Willie and Sarah Alice (Fell) K.; m. Margaret Burden, May 22, 1952. Student, Halifax Tech. Coll., 1966-69; Ph.D., Calif. Western U., 1974. Chartered engr. Asst. chief insp. Budd Mfg. Co., 1929; dir. mfg. Citroen Motor Co., Paris, France, 1929-38; mng. dir. Brit. Mfg. & Research Co., mfr. aircraft cannons and shells, Grantham, Eng., 1938-45; cons. to Pentagon on high velocity small arms, 1940-45; exec. v.p. Brunswick (N.J.) Ordnance Plant, 1952-56; dir., v.p. operations Mack Trucks Co., 1952-55; pres., dir. Am. Marc, Inc., Los Angeles, 1955-61; pres. Dynapower Systems and Dynapower Medonics, Los Angeles, 1961-73; chmn., chief exec. Kendall Med. Internat., Inc., Los Angeles, 1973-88; chmn. Steron Products Inc., 1983-88; partner rheumatoid arthritis clinic, London; dir. A.M. Byers Co., Pitts. Patentee in field. Mem. Churchill's War Cabinet Gun Bd., 1941-45, M.P., Grantham div. Kesteven and Rutland, 1942-50; councillor Grantham Town Council, 1945-52; Bd. govs. Kings Sch., Grantham, 1942-52. Served with Royal Fleet Aux., 1919-23. Decorated chevalier Oissam Alouite Cherifien; honoured by King George VI for heroic conduct in World War II; freeman City of London, 1942-95; mem. Worshipful Co. Clockmakers. Fellow Royal Soc. Arts (London), Inst. Mech. Engrs., Inst. Automotive Engrs. Mem. Religious Soc. Friends (Quaker). Clubs: Mason (Pacific Palisades, Cal.) (32 deg., Shriner), Riviera Country (Pacific Palisades, Cal.); United British Service (Lowestoft, Eng.), Royal Norfolk and Suffolk Yacht (Lowestoft, Eng.). Home: Los Angeles Calif. Died July 29, 1995.

KENDREW, JOHN COWDERY, molecular biologist, former academic administrator; b. Oxford, Eng., Mar. 24, 1917; s. Wilfrid George and Evelyn May Graham (Sandberg) K. B.A., Trinity Coll., Cambridge U., 1939, M.A., 1943, Ph.D., 1949; Sc.D., 1962, 1962. With Ministry Aircraft Prodn., 1940-45; sci. adv. allied air comdr. in chief S.E. Asia, 1944; dep. chmn. Med. Rsch. Coun. Lab. for Molecular Biology Cambridge (Eng.) U., 1947-75; fellow of Peterhouse, Cambridge U., 1947-75 (hon. fellow 1975); reader Davy-Faraday Lab., Royal

Instn., London, 1954-68; dir.-gen. European Molecular Biology Lab., Heidelberg, Germany, 1975-82; pres. St. John's Coll., Oxford U., 1981-87 (hon. fellow 1987). Editor in chief Jour. Molecular Biology, 1959-87. Mem. council UN U., 1980-86, chmn., 1983-85. Decorated knight bachelor and comdr. Order Brit. Empire; recipient (with Max Perutz) Nobel prize in chemistry, 1962; Trinity Coll. Cambridge U. hon. fellow, 1972. Fellow Royal Soc., 1960; fgn. asso. Nat. Acad. Scis. (U.S.); fgn. hon. mem. Am. Acad. Arts and Scis.; hon. mem. Am. Soc. Biol. Chemists; mem. Brit., Am. biophys. socs., Internat. Orgn. Pure and Applied Biophysics (pres. 1969), Internat. Council Sci. Unions (sec. gen. 1974-80, pres. 1983-88). Achievements include determination, in work with myoglobin, of structure of a protein in general outline and atomic detail; observation of alpha-helix arrangement of the polypeptide chain, thereby confirming Pauling's earlier description. Died Aug. 23, 1997.

KENLY, F. CORNING, JR., financial consultant; b. Lake Forest, Ill., Feb. 21, 1915; s. F. Corning and Ruth (Farwell) K.; m. Miriam Little, May 21, 1941; children: M.B. Kenly Earle, David F., F. Corning, III. B.S., Harvard U., 1937; postgrad., Harvard U. Bus. Sch., 1964. Loan adminstr. Harris Trust & Savs. Bank, Chgo., 1938-39; fin. exec. Household Finance Corp., Chgo., 1940-41; sr. v.p. investments New Eng. Mut. Life Ins. Co., Boston, 1948-80; v.p., dir. NEL Equity Fund, Inc., NEL Growth Fund, Inc., NEL Retirement Equity Fund, Inc., 1970-80; pres., dir. NEL Income Fund, Inc., NEL Cash Mgmt. Account, NEL Tax Exempt Bond Fund, 1970-80; mem. real estate adv. com. Citibank (N.A.), N.Y.C.; mem. adv. bd. Boston Bay Capital Co., Boston, 1980-86; bd. assocs. R.T. Madden Co., N.Y.C., 1980-86. Trustee Cardigan Mountain Sch., Harvard Advocate; overseer Boston Mus. Sci. Lt. comdr. USNR, 1941-46. Mem. Boston Security Analysts Soc., Harvard Bus. Sch. Assn. of Boston. Clubs: Economic (Boston); Essex County (Manchester), Birnam Wood (Santa Barbara, Calif.). DIED 05/04/97. .

KENSIL, JAMES LEWIS, former professional football team executive; b. Phila., Aug. 19, 1930; s. Lewis Martin and Kathryn Beatrice (Rush) K.; m. Catherine Tighe, Jan. 2, 1954; children: Michael, Joseph, Mary Jo, Daniel. B.A., U. Pa., 1952. Newsman AP, N.Y.C., 1952, Columbus, Ohio, 1954-56; sports writer AP, N.Y.C., 1956-61; dir. pub. relations Nat. Football League, N.Y.C., 1961-67; exec. dir. Nat. Football League, 1968-77; pres. N.Y. Jets Football Club Inc., 1977-90, retired. Served with AUS, 1952-54. Died Jan. 16, 1997.

KENYON, JANE JENNIFER, poet, writer; b. Ann Arbor, Mich., May 23, 1947; d. Reuel Baldwin and Pauline Celeste (Miller) K.; m. Donald Hall, Apr. 17, 1972. BA, U. Mich., 1970, MA, 1972. Author: (poetry) From Room to Room, 1978, The Boat of Quiet Hours, 1986, Let Evening Come, 1990, Constance, 1993, New and Selected Poems, 1996; translator: Twenty Poems of Anna Akhmatova, 1985. Recipient Sara Teasdale award Wellesley Coll., 1991, gift St. Botolph Club, 1991, Frederick Bock prize Poetry, 1993, PEN/Voelcker award for poetry, 1994; creative writing fellow Nat. Endowment for the Arts, 1981, N.H. Coun. on Arts, 1984; Guggenheim grantee, 1992. Democrat. Congregationalist. Avocations: flower gardening, hiking. Died Apr. 22, 1995.

KENYON, KYLE, lawyer; b. Wyeville, Wis., Mar. 22, 1924; s. Charles Martin and Harriet (Shookman) K.; m. Xena Cade Kenyon, June 9, 1951; children: Charles, Kathleen, Elizabeth, John, Helen. LLB, U. Wis., 1952, JD, 1966. Bar: Wis. 1952, U.S. Dist. Ct. (we. dist.) Wis. 1977. Pvt. practice, Tomah, Wis., 1952—; family ct. commr. Monroe County, Toman, 1993—. Mem. Wis. Ho. of Reps., 1956-70. With AUS, 1943-46, PTO. Mem. Wis. Bar Assn., Monroe County Bar Assn. (pres. 1973-74), Modern Woodmen am. (state pres. 1954—), VFW (comdr. 1954-55), Am. Legion (40 and 8), Masons, Shriners, Rotary. Republican. Avocation: politics.

KERN, HARRY FREDERICK, editor; b. Denver, July 1, 1911; s. Harry F. and Alice (Robertson) K.; m. Janet Campbell Mackenzie, Dec. 27, 1939; children—Rosemary Annand, Nathaniel Robertson. Student, Harvard, 1930-35. Joined Newsweek, 1935, became asst. editor, 1937, asso. editor, 1941, war editor, 1942; sr. editor internat. affairs Newsweek mag., N.Y.C., 1950-56; also editor-in-chief internat. edits. Newsweek mag., 1950-56; pres. Fgn. Reports, 1956. Decorated Order Sacred Treasure Japan; Order of Merit Lebanon). Mem. Council Fgn. Relations. Clubs: Knickerbocker (N.Y.C.); Met. (Washington); Travellers (Paris). Home: Bethesda Md. Died May 12, 1996; interred Rockville Cemetery.

KERR, FRANCES MILLS, psychology educator; b. Atlanta, Oct. 21, 1919; d. William Morton and Nina (Walker) Mills; m. Oliver Wendell Kerr, Aug. 12, 1946; children—Judith Nina, Oliver Wendell. A.B., Livingstone Coll., 1939; M.A., State U. Iowa, 1943. Instr. child devel. Tuskegee Inst. (Ala.), 1943-46; dir./coordinator early childhood programs USAF, Tokyo, 1953-56; dir. early childhood program Episcopal Ch., Washington, Yellow Springs, Ohio, 1956-59; prof. psychology Mount Holyoke Coll., South Hadley, Mass., 1960—; cons. Headstart, Holyoke, Mass., 1966-69; Danforth assoc. Danforth Assocs. Program, 1971—. Trustee, Concord (Mass.) Acad., 1975-77, hon. trustee, 1977—; trustee Holyoke (Mass.) Hosp., 1978—; ARC, Holyoke, 1979—, Holyoke Chicopee Mental Health Assn., 1966—; bd. dirs. Vanguard Savs. Bank, Holyoke, 1972—; bd. dirs. Western Mass. Council Girl Scouts U.S.A., 1982—. Mem. Nat. Assn. Edn. Young Children, Western Mass. Assn. Edn. Young Children, Alpha Kappa Alpha. Democrat. Episcopalian. Died May 7, 1996.

KERR, WALTER F., retired drama critic, author; b. Evanston, Ill., July 8, 1913; s. Walter Sylvester and Esther (Daugherty) K.; m. Jean Collins, Aug. 16, 1943; children: Christopher, Colin, John, Gilbert, Gregory, Katharine. B.S. in Speech, Northwestern U., 1937, M.A., 1938, L.H.D., 1962; LL.D., St. Mary's, Notre Dame; D.Litt., LaSalle, 1956, Fordham U., 1965, Notre Dame U., 1968, U. Mich., 1972. Instr. speech and drama Cath. U., Washington, 1938-45; assoc. prof. drama Cath. U., 1945-49; drama critic Commonweal, 1950-52, N.Y. Herald Tribune, 1951-66, N.Y. Times, 1966-83; specialist drama theory and criticism, ret., 1983. Dir., writer profl. theatre Sing Out, Sweet Land, 1944, Touch and Go (George Abbott), King of Hearts (Elaine Perry); author: (plays) Touch and Go, Sing Out, Sweet Land; (books) How Not to Write a Play, 1955; Criticism and Censorship, 1957, Pieces at Eight, 1958, The Decline of Pleasure, 1962, The Theatre in Spite of Itself, 1963, Tragedy and Comedy, 1967, Thirty Plays Hath November, 1969, God on the Gymnasium Floor, 1971, The Silent Clowns, 1975, Journey to the Center of the Theater, 1979, also articles. Recipient George Jean Nathan award, 1964; Dineen award Nat. Cath. Theatre Conf., 1966; Iona award, 1970; Campion award, 1971; Laetare medal, 1971; award Nat. Inst. Arts and Letters, 1972; Pulitzer prize for criticism, 1978; elected to Theater Hall of Fame, 1982; Walter F. Kerr theater named in his honor, 1989. Mem. N.Y. Critics' Circle (pres. 1955-57), Soc. Profl. Journalists. Club: Players (hon.). Deceased.

KERST, DONALD WILLIAM, physicist, retired educator; b. Galena, Ill., Nov. 1, 1911; s. Herman Samuel and Lilian (Wetz) K.; m. Dorothy Birkett, Aug. 1940; children: Marilyn Elizabeth Kerst-Sipe, Stephen Marshall. BA, U. Wis., 1934, PhD, 1937, DS (hon.), 1961; DS (hon.), Lawrence Coll., 1942; Dr. honoris causa, U. São Paulo, Brazil, 1953; D.Sc., U. Ill., 1987. Instr. physics U. Ill., 1938-40, asst. prof., 1940-42, assoc. prof., 1942-43, prof., 1943; war work Los Alamos, 1943-45; tech. dir. Midwestern Univs. Research Assn., 1953-57; with John Jay Hopkins Lab. for Pure and Applied Sci., Gen. Atomic div. Gen. Dynamics Corp., 1957-62; E.M. Terry prof. physics U. Wis., 1962-80, prof. emeritus, 1980-93. Winner Comstock prize Nat. Acad. Scis. for devel. betatron, 1945, John Scott award, 1946, John Price Wetherill medal Franklin Inst. for devel. of betatron, 1950. Mem. AAAS, Am. Acad. Arts and Scis., Nat. Acad. Scis., Am. Phys. Soc. (chmn. plasma physics div. 1972, Maxwell prize for plasma physics, 1984, R.R. Wilson prize for particle accelerator devel. 1987), Inst. Nav. Home: Vero Beach Fla. Died Aug. 19, 1993.

KESTER, LENARD, artist; b. N.Y.C., May 10, 1917; s. Human and Yetta (Kalfus) K. Student pub. schs. Exhibited one-man shows, art galleries and museums, U.S., maj. nat. exhbns.; executed: Mayo Clinic mural, 1953; paintings in permanent collections, Bklyn., Toledo, Boston, Denver, Balt., Springfield, Mo. museums, U. Miami, also, Calif. State Fair, Everson Mus.; pvt. collections.; Designer stained glass window, Billy Rose Mausoleum. Recipient numerous prizes, awards; awarded Life mag. commn., 1947, Albert Dorne award, 1964, Mario Cooper award, 1966; Tiffany Found. fellow, 1949. Mem. Am. Watercolor Soc. (Windsor and Newton award 1959), Soc. Western Artists; asso. N.A.D. (Obrig prize 1959, Saltus gold medal). DIED 01/13/97. .

KEULKS, GEORGE WILLIAM, university dean, chemistry educator; b. East St. Louis, Ill., Apr. 2, 1938; s. George and Meta June (Krug) K.; m. JoAnn Marco, Aug. 27, 1960; children: Gavin Wade, Catherine Danielle, Amy Elizabeth, Laura Ashley. BA, Washington U., St. Louis, 1960; MS, U. Ark., 1962; PhD, Northwestern U., 1964. Chemist Monsanto Co., summers, 1959-60; rsch. chemist Gulf Rsch. and Devel. Co., Pitts., 1964-65; mem. summer session faculty Johns Hopkins U., 1966; asst. prof. chemistry U. Wis., Milw., 1966-71, assoc. prof., 1971-74, prof., 1974-97, chmn. dept. chemistry, 1972-74, assoc. dean natural scis., 1974-75, acting dean Grad. Sch., 1975-76, dean Grad. Sch., 1976-97, dean rsch., 1986-97; cons. in chemistry. Contbr. articles to profl. jours. NSF grantee, 1974-85. Mem. AAAS, Am. Chem. Soc., Catalysis Club Chgo., Catalysis Soc. N.Am., Nat. Council Univ. Research Adminstrs., Nat. Assn. State Univs. and Land-Grant Colls., Sigma Xi, Phi Lambda Upsilon. Methodist. Died Nov. 11, 1997.

KEY, DONALD, art critic; b. Iowa City, Jan. 30, 1923; s. Philip R. and Lola (Diehl) K.; m. Patricia Anne Miller, May 11, 1947; 1 son, Theodore Allen. B.A. in Journalism, U. Iowa, 1950. Asst. to editor, fine arts columnist Cedar Rapids (Ia.) Gazette, 1950-59; art editor Milw. Jour., 1959-72. Author: Future Unknown; Contbr. articles to profl. jours. Served with AUS, 1942-46, ETO. Mem. Theta Xi, Sigma Delta Chi. Club: Milwaukee Press. DIED 05/24/96. .

KEY, KERIM KAMI, historian, educator; b. Istanbul, May 21, 1913; came to the U.S., 1939; s. Huseyin Kami and Azize (Gafar) Key; m. Elizabeth Miller, Mar. 30, 1946. BS, Robert Coll., 1932; MA in History, U. Calif., Berkeley, 1940; PhD, Am. U., 1950. Fgn. affairs officer, econ. U.S. Dept. State, U.S. Dept. Commerce, Washington, 1945-73; assoc. prof. mgmt. Howard U., Washington, 1974-77; mem. adv. bd. Am.-Turkish Friendship Coun.; historian Friendship Heights Village Coun. Bicentennial Com. on Constn. of U.S.A., 1987-92, Chevy Chase, Md.; adj. prof. Am. U., 1950-85, Southeastern U., 1978-94, Benjamin Franklin U., 1986-88; cons. Walden U., 1970-90. Author: Turkish Historiography, 1958; contbr. articles to profl. jours. Lt. Turkish Army, 1934-36, sgt. U.S. Army, 1942-45, capt. USAFR, 1949-54. Mem. Middle East Inst., Assembly Am. Turkish Assns., Am. Turkish Assn. Washington, Md. Am. Turkish Assn., Vets. OSS (life). Avocation: Turkey and Central Asian affairs. Home: Chevy Chase Md.

KEYSER, E. GLEN, nutritional biochemist; b. Bellaine, Ohio, Dec. 24, 1929; s. James Wesley and Mary Helen (Greenlee) K; m. Nancy Louise Kessler Keyser, Dec. 31, 1954; children: Gregory Alan, Laurel Susan Graham, Diane Louise, Christopher Jon, Kevin Glen, Karen Elizabeth Quinn. BS in Agrl. Bus., The Ohio State U., Columbus, 1956; MS in Extension Edn., Mich. State U., E. Lansing, 1959; MS in Poultry Nutrition, U. Ark., Fayettesville, 1968; PhD in Nutritional Biochemistry, The Ohio State U., Columbus, 1971. Cert. profl. Agronomist, crop scientist, soil scientist Am. Soc. Agronomy, Madison, Wis., 1984—; cert. profl. microbiologist Am. Soc. Microbiology, Washington, 1984—; dir. rsch. and mktg. A.O. Smith Herostore Products, Co., Arlington Heights, Ill., 1972-77; dir. rsch. Agrl. Labs. Inc., Columbus, Ohio, 1977-85; rsch. chmn. bd. Bio-One Internat., Grove City, Ohio, 1986—. Inventor in field. Sch. bd. Southwestern City Sch., Grove City, Ohio, 1969-79; exec. com. Opera Columbus, 1982—. Sgt. USAF, 1947-51, Washington. Fellow Urania Lodge # 311. Lutheran. DIED 11/14/96. .

KHALILI, MARYLOUISE DALLAL, management and marketing educator; b. Harlingen, Tex., Sept. 13, 1937; d. Tewfik Gabrial and Minerva (Laham) Dallal. BS in Bus., Central State U, 1961; MS in Bus., Calif. State U., Long Beach, 1971; PhD in Bus., U. Okla., 1990; cert. in communications, U. Hawaii, 1972. High sch. tchr. Okla., Calif. and Kans., 1961-71; dir. family planning Govt. of Iran, Tehran, 1972-76; prof. Oklahoma City U., 1976—; cons. Shifting Gears Unltd., Oklahoma City, 1985—; realtor ERA Bob Linn & Assocs., Oklahoma City, 1985—. Author: Sign of the Times, 1975. Vol. Planned Parenthood Am., Oklahoma City, 1976—, United Cerebral Palsy, Oklahoma City, 1989—, Mar. of Dimes, Oklahoma City, 1976-81; organizer Ptnrs. for Excellence in Edn., Okla., 1985—; campaigner Okla. Dems., 1987-88; vol. Salvation Army, Jesus Ho., Meals on Wheels. Mem. various mgmt. orgns., Delta Pi Epsilon (v.p. 1979-81, pres. 1981-82). DIED 06/30/96. .

KIBIRA, JOSIAH MUTABUZI, bishop; b. Kashenye, Bukoba, Tanzania, Aug. 28, 1925; s. S. Kibira Isayax and Esteria Muhingo Mukahite; diploma Tchr. Tng. Coll., Tabora, 1949; cert. in theology Kirchliche Hochschule, U. Bielefeld, 1960; diploma in theology U. Hamburg (W.Ger.), 1961; S.T.M., Boston U., 1964; Th.D. (hon.), U. Uppsala (Sweden), 1974, U. Erlangen, 1980; D.D. (hon.), St. Olaf Coll., Northfield, Minn., 1978, Bethany Coll., 1981; m. Martha Mukajuna Jeremiah, Nov. 25, 1951; 9 children. Tchr., Kahororo Secondary Sch., Bukoba, 1950-57; ordained to ministry Lutheran Ch., 1961; pastor of Evang. Luth. Ch. in Tanzania, N.W. Diocese, Bukoba, 1960-64, consecrated bishop, 1964; mem. Faith and Order Commn., World Council Chs., 1961—, central com., 1968—; mem. scholarship com. Luth. World Fedn., 1960, chmn. commn. ch. coop., 1970, pres., 1977—. Author: Ebarua ya Askofu, 1964; Aus Einer Africanischen Kirche, 1960; Clan, Church and the World, 1974.

KILBORNE, WILLIAM SKINNER, retired business consultant; b. Stockbridge, Mass., Sept. 1, 1912; s. Robert Stewart and Katharine (Skinner) K.; m. Elizabeth Briggs, June 25, 1935; children: William Skinner, Benjamin Briggs, Allerton Wright, Katharine Skinner Kilborne Cornwell.; m. Virginia G. Wylie, June 29, 1974. B.A., Yale U., 1935; M.B.A., Harvard U., 1937. With William Skinner & Sons, 1937-53, v.p., 1942-53, trustee, 1947-61; dir. Lexington Lumber Co., 1938-43; dir. Internat. Silk Assn., 1948-53, v.p., 1951-53; spl. asst. to Sec. of Commerce, 1953-57; bus. research B.F. Goodrich Co., 1958-60; v.p. Casey & Kilborne, Inc., N.Y.C., 1960-62; pres. William S. Kilborne, Inc., 1962-74; v.p. John Moynahan & Co., Inc., 1963-66; chmn. Harkil Corp., 1969-75; bus. cons., corp. growth, 1975-85. Mem. Nat. Def. Exec. Res., 1958-70; v.p. 15th Assembly Dist. Rep. Club, N.Y.C., 1939-41; mem. New York County Rep. Com., 1940-41, Mercer County Rep. Com., 1978; bd. dirs. Nat. Fedn. Settlements, 1941-42, 44-46; trustee N.Y. Sch. Social Work, 1952-53, hon.

trustee, 1953-59; bd. dirs. Lenox Hill Neighborhood Assn., 1939-50, pres., 1941-46; bd. dirs. Morningside Community Ctr., 1945-53, Union Settlement, 1966-80, Princeton unit Rec. for Blind, 1981-93. Mem. Mayflower Soc. Presbyterian. Clubs: Yale of Princeton (pres. 1978-83). Home: Hightstown N.J. Died Feb. 13, 1995.

KILGORE, WILLIAM JACKSON, philosopher, educator; b. Dallas, Apr. 30, 1917; s. Rather Bowlin and Clara (Cole) K.; m. Barbara Schmickle, Dec. 4, 1943; 1 dau., Barbara (Sally B.) Kilgore Pendleton. AB, Baylor U., 1938; PhD, U. Tex., 1958; postgrad., Columbia U., 1949. Prof. philosophy Baylor U., 1949—, chmn. dept., 1959-87, J. Newton Rayzor, Sr. Disting. prof. philosophy, 1976—; asst.prof. philosophy U. Tex., summer 1958; organizer, pres. Centennial Symposium on Ortega y Gasset World Congress of Philosophy, 1983; vis. lectr. philosophy Summer Inst., U. Warsaw, Poland, 1990, Nat. Philosophy Congress, India, 1991, 92, at internat. congresses and univs. Author: Alejandro Korn's Interpretation of Creative Freedom, 1958, Una evaluación crítica de la philosofía de Alejandro Korn, 1961, One America, Two Cultures, 1965, An Introductory Logic, 1968, 2d edit., 1979; also articles in English, Portuguese, French and Spanish.; translator An Introduction to the Philosophy of Understanding of Andrés Bello, 1983. Pres. sect. on ethics and problems of freedom XIII Internat. Congress of Philosophy, Mexico City, 1963; pres. sect. on art and communication Inter-Am. Congress of Philosophy, Brazilia, 1972. Grantee Danforth Found., 1957-58, Am. Coun. Learned Socs., 1961, 86, Argentine Philos. Soc., 1986, 89 Internat. Acad. Philos. Sci., 1989; Fulbright grantee, 1984, Mex. Philos. Assn. grantee, 1984; hon. prof. Universidad Nacional Pedro Henriquez Urena, Santo Domingo. Mem. Am. Philos. Assn., Southwestern Philos. Assn. (pres. 1963-64), AAUP (2d v.p. 1968-70, nat. coun. 1962-65, 68-70, pres. Tex. conf. 1965), Tex. Philos. Soc., Inter-Am. Soc. Philosophy (exec. com. 1977-91, pres. 1981-85), Interam. Soc. Psychology, Peruvian Philos. Soc. (hon.), N.Am. Soc. for Social and Polit. Philosophy, Indian Philos. Congress, Soc. for Iberian and Latin Am. Thought (pres. 1976), Philos. Congress India. Deceased.

KILHAM, WALTER H., JR., architect; b. Brookline, Mass., Apr. 29, 1904; s. Walter Harrington and Jane (Houston) K.; Louise Collins, Jan. 23, 1943 (div. 1976); children: Leslie, Timothy, Eleanor, Amy Edna. AB, Harvard U., 1925, MArch, 1928. With Raymond Hood, architect, 1928-29, Rockefeller Ctr. Architects, 1929-32, Wallace K. Harrison, architect, 1933-37; ptnr. Van der Gracht & Kilham, assoc. architects, 1937-42; assoc. Morris & O'Connor, 1943-44; ptnr. O'Connor & Kilham, 1944-69, Kilham, Beder and Chu, 1969-76, ret. Arch. Carrol Coll. Libr., Zone Two Contructing Quartermaster, 1941; chief site planning sect. N.Y. dist. U.S. Engrs., 1942-43; other works include Firestone Libr. Princeton U., home office bldg. Phoenix Ins. Co., Hartford, Conn., libr. U. Louisville, Nat. Libr. Medicine, Barnard Coll. Libr., Bethesda, Md., Robert Frost Libr. Amherst Coll., 1965, joint venture post war expansion U.S. Mil. Acad., West Point, N.Y., from 1964, Conn. Coll. Libr.; author: Raymond Hood, Architect, 1973. Trustee Beaux Arts Inst. Design, 1947-49. With Mass. NG, 1921-25, also Res., 1925-35. Wheelwright fellow Harvard U., 1938. Fellow AIA (past pres. N.Y. chpt., Arnold Brunner scholar N.Y. chpt. 1969); mem. NAD, Fine Arts Fedn. N.Y. (pres. 1955-57), Nat. Sculptors Soc., Am. Craftsmens Coun. (trustee), Travelers Club (Boston), Century Assn. (N.Y.C.). Home: Kent Conn. Died Feb. 9, 1997.

KILLINGER, GEORGE GLENN, criminologist, psychologist; b. Marion, Va., Mar. 13, 1908; s. James Peter and Lena (Kelly) K.; m. Grace Davis, June 29, 1935; children: Robert Peter, Evangeline, George Evan. A.B., Wittenberg Coll., 1930, LL.D., 1953; Ph.D., U. N.C., 1933. Diplomate: in clin. psychology Am. Bd. Examiners in Profl. Psychology. Research asst. Mooseheart Lab. for Child Research, summers 1929-31; instr. psychology U. N.C., 1930-33; asst. personnel dir. Mathieson Alkali Works, 1933-34; psychologist and spl. asst. to personnel dir. TVA, Knoxville, 1934-36; dir. out-patient and social service Southwestern State Hosp., Marion, Va., 1936-37; psychologist USPHS, Fed. Reformatory, Chillicothe, Ohio, 1937-38; supr. edn. U.S. Penitentiary, Atlanta, 1938-40; asst. asso. warden U.S. Penitentiary, 1940-41; supr. edn. U.S. Bur. Prisons, Washington, 1941-43; chief psychobiol. activites War Shipping Adminstrn., 1943-47; chmn. clemency and parole bd. Office of Sec. Army, Washington, 1947-48; chmn. U.S. Bd. of Parole, Dept. Justice, Washington, 1948-53; mem. U.S. Bd. of Parole, Dept. Justice, 1953-60; lectr. George Washington U., 1953-54; prof. dept. criminology and corrections Fla. State U., 1960-65; founding dir., dean emeritus Inst. Contemporary Corrections and Behaviorsl Scis., Sam Houston State U., Huntsville, 1965-77, Piper Disting. prof., 1968, prof. emeritus of criminal justice, 1992-93; chmn. Tex. Bd. Pardons and Paroles, 1977-80, vice chmn., 1980-86. Author: Personality Disorders, 1946, Prison Work as a Post-War Career, 1946, The Psychobiological Program of the War Shipping Administration, 1947, Penology, The Evolution of the American Correctional System, 1973, 2d edit., 1979, Corrections in the Community, 1974, 2d edit., 1978, Issues in Law Enforcement, 1975, Probation and Parole, 1976, 2d edit., 1985, 3d edit., 1990, Corrections and Administration, 1976, Introduction to Juvenile Delinquency, 1977; cons. editor Criminal Justice series Harcourt Brace Jovanovich, Inc, 1978-93. Contbr. numerous sci. articles to tech. and professional publs. Mem. Tex. Commn. on Law Enforcement Standards and Edn., Nat. Task Force on Corrections; mem. Tex. Bd. Pardons and Paroles, Austin, 1977-93. Served as lt. comdr., commd. officer USPHS, 1943-47; scientist dir. USPHS Res. Recipient E.R. Cass Achievement award Am. Correctional Assn., 1980; U.S. Dept. labor research grantee, 1966. Fellow Am. Psychol. Assn., AAAS; mem. Am. Prison Assn., Am. Assn. Adult Edn., USPHS Res. Officers Assn., Ednl. Found., Inc., Nat. Probation Parole Assn. (adv. council 1952-54), Wittenberg Alumni Assn. (past pres. Washington), Am. Legion, Alpha Psi Delta, Phi Mu Alpha, Psi Chi, Pi Kappa Alpha, Alpha Kappa Delta. Democrat. Lutheran. Clubs: Kiwanis (N.Y.C.), Advt. (N.Y.C.); Kenwood Golf and Country (Washington), Touchdown (Washington), Univ. (Washington); Warwick (Houston); Huntsville (Tex.). Home: Huntsville Tex. Died Oct. 21, 1993.

KILPATRICK, ROBERT DONALD, retired insurance company executive; b. Fairbanks, La., Feb. 5, 1924; s. Thomas David and Lula Mae (Crowell) K.; m. Faye Hines, May 29, 1948; children: Robert Donald, Kathleen Spencer, Lauren Douglas, Tracy Crowell, Thomas David. B.A., U. Richmond, 1948; postgrad., Harvard U. Grad. Sch. Bus., 1973; received honorary degrees from, Univ. Hartford, Univ. Richmond (Va.), Trinity Coll. (Conn.). With Conn. Gen. Life Ins. Co. (subs. CIGNA Corp.), Hartford, 1954-82, pres., chief exec. officer; also bd. dirs., 1976-82; pres. CIGNA Corp., 1982-85, co-chief exec. officer, 1982-83, chmn., chief exec. officer, 1983-89; bd. dirs. United Cos. Fin. Corp., Kuhlman Corp.; trustee U. Richmond.; mem. The Bus. Coun. Died Jan. 27, 1997.

KIMBLE, SERUCH TITUS, JR., retired internist; b. Washington, Feb. 21, 1921; s. Seruch Titus and Harriet Louise (Zebley) K.; m. Helen Louise Matchett, Jan. 15, 1949; children: Claudia, Kathryn, Stephen, Henry, David, Richard, Robert. AB, George Washington U., 1942, MD, 1944. Diplomate Am. Bd. Internal Medicine. Intern Presbyn. Hosp., Chgo., 1944-45; med. resident Suburban Hosp., Bethesda, Md., 1945-46, VA Hosp., L.A., 1950-51, Mt. Alto VA Hosp., Washington, 1951-52; pvt. practice internal medicine Washington, 1947-50, Silver Spring, Md., 1953-88; attending internist Washington Adventist Hosp., Takoma Park, Md., 1954-88, Holy Cross Hosp., Silver Spring, 1963-88, Suburban Hosp., Bethesda, 1948-88; ret., 1988; councillor Med. and Chirurgical Faculty of State of Md., 1968-74, mem. peer rev. com., 1978-81; ptnr. Forest Glen Med. Ctr., Silver Spring, 1966-95; pres. med. staff Washington Adventist Hosp., 1972-74, trustee, 1976-79; physician in charge of med. processing first POW's from North Korea, 1953. Author: The Kimble Family From Z to A, 1984, Kimbles of Bucks County, Pennsylvania and Cecil County, Maryland, 1994; contbr. author: Geriatric Medicine, 2d edit., 1950; contbr. articles to profl. jours. Mem. Adv. Com. on Health Facilities, Montgomery County, Md., 1968-69; pres. Civitan Club, Silver Spring, 1960-61, 84-85; bd. dirs. Jubilee Assn. of Md., inc., Montgomery County, 1991-93. Capt. Med. Corp U.S. Army, 1946-47, 52-53. Fellow ACP (life); mem. Montgomery County Med. Soc. (pres. 1966-67), George Washington U. Med. Alumni Assn. (chmn. class of '44 50th reunion 1994). Republican. Methodist. Achievements include research on hypothyroidism, premenstrual tension, fat embolism, breast cancer. Avocations: farming, philately, American naval medical history. Died Dec. 10, 1997.

KIMBROUGH, WILLIAM WALTER, III, psychiatrist; b. Cleve., Sept. 26, 1928; s. William Walter and Wilhelmina Grace (Champion) K.; student Cornell U., 1945-46; BS, U. Mich., 1948, MD, 1952; m. Jo Ann Greiner, July 6, 1953; children: Elizabeth, Douglas. Intern, Ohio State U. Health Ctr., Columbus, 1952-53; resident U. Chgo. Clinics, 1955-56, Ypsilanti (Mich.) State Hosp., 1956-59; assoc. psychiatrist U. Mich. Health Ctr., Ann Arbor, 1959-61; practice medicine specializing in psychoanalytic psychiatry, Ann Arbor, 1961—; cons. atty. gen. U.S., 1974—, Ctr. for Forensic Psychiatry, 1958—, Brighton Found. for Alcoholism, 1961—, Washtenaw County (Mich.) Community Mental Health Svcs., 1978—, Mich. Dept. Social Svcs., 1978—, Mich Dept. Mental Health, 1989—; reviewer Mich. Peer Rev. Orgn.; clin. dir. Livingston County (Mich.) Community Mental Health Svcs., 1983-85, Mich. Dept. Corrections, 1985-88; exec. com. Northville Regional Psychiatric Hosp.; pres. Northville (Mich.) Psychiat. Assn., 1991-93; pres. Physicians for Mercy, 1995—. Capt. USPHSR, 1953—. Recipient Physicians Recognition awards AMA, 1972-97. Fellow Am. Acad. Psychiatry and Law, Am. Soc. Psychoanalytic Physicians; mem. AAAS, Am. Acad. Psychotherapists, Am. Psychiat. Assn. (life), Ann Arbor Psychiat. Assn., Northville Psychiat. Assn. (pres. 1991-93), Am. Acad. Psychiatrists in Alcoholism and Addiction (founding mem.), Mich. Psychiat. Soc. (com. on legislation and govt. affairs), N.Y. Acad. Sci., Hon. Order Ky. Cols., Sigma Alpha Epsilon, Phi Rho Sigma. Clubs: Ann Arbor Town, Ann Arbor Racquet, Univ., Travis Pointe Country (Ann Arbor); Little Harbor (Harbor Springs, Mich.), Round Table (Plymouth, Mich.). Died July 23, 1997.

KIMM, DOROTHY ALLENE, elementary education educator; b. Casey, Iowa, Mar. 13, 1931; d. W.J. and Matilda M. (Mowry) Madsen; m. James Wilson Kimm, Aug. 16, 1952; children: Mary, Jill, Tobias J. Cert., U. No. Iowa, 1951; BS, Drake U., 1968, MS in Edn., 1979. Cert. tchr., Iowa. Tchr. 6th grade Marengo (Iowa) Pub. Schs., 1951-52; bookmobile libr. Polk County Supt. Schs., Des Moines, 1952-53; tchr. 4th and 6th grades Muscatine (Iowa) Pub. Schs., 1959-61; tchr. 6th grade Urbandale (Iowa) Pub. Schs., 1961-62, West Des Moines (Iowa) Community Schs., 1975-95. Author: The Book of Kimm, 1982. Mem. NEA, Iowa State Edn. Assn., West Des Moines Edn. Assn., Delta Kappa Gamma (pres. Beta Epsilon chpt. 1990-91). Presbyterian. Home: West Des Moines Iowa Died Aug. 26, 1995.

KING, JOHN WILLIAM, judge; b. Manchester, N.H., Oct. 10, 1918; s. Michael J. and Anna (Lydon) K.; m. Anna MaLaughlin, Oct. 13, 1945. A.B., Harvard U., 1938; M.A., Columbia U., 1941, LL.B., 1943; LL.D.; M.A. (hon.), Dartmouth Coll.; LL.D., St. Anselm's Coll., U. N.H., Columbia U.; Dr. Civil Laws (hon.), New Eng. Coll.; Dr. Pub. Adminstrn., Franklin Pierce Coll., Suffolk U. Bar: N.Y. 1942, N.H. 1945. Pvt. practice N.Y.C., 1943- 48; former sr. partner King, Nixon, Christy & Tessier (attys.); now assoc. justice Superior Ct. of N.H., 1969-79; assoc. justice Supreme Ct. N.H., 1979-80, chief justice, 1980—; chmn. profl. conduct com. N.H. lawyers; instr. bus. law St. Anselm's Coll., Manchester, 1948—; mem. N.H. Constl. Conv., 1956; chmn. Manchester delegation N.H. Legislature, 1957; mem. sub-com. legislative counsel, 1957, minority leader, 1959-62, gov., N.H., 1963-69. Editor: N.H. Bar Jour, 1958-69. Mem. N.H. ballot law commn., 1952-54, sec. charter revision commn., Manchester, 1954-55, mem. salary adjustment commn., 1957—, chmn. ward line commn., 1957—; chmn. N.H. Accreditation Commn. on Cts., 1971—; chmn. Council of State Ct. Reps. of Nat. Center for State Cts., 1975, 76; past pres. J.F. McElwain Manchester Employees' Credit Union, 1956—; bd. dirs. N.H. Tb. Soc.; trustee St. Anselm's Coll. Recipient Robert Frost award Plymouth State Coll., 1987, Charles Holmes Pettee award, U. N.H. Mem. Am., N.Y. State, N.H., Manchester bar assns., Bar Assn. City N.Y., Am. Judicature Society (dir. N.H. chpt., Herbert Harley award). Clubs: Elk. (Manchester), Eagle (Manchester), K.C. (Manchester), Canadian (Manchester), Raphael (Manchester), Manchester Press (Manchester), Belgium (Manchester), Manchester Turnverein (Manchester). Died Aug. 9, 1996.

KING, JONATHAN, architectural researcher, educator, b. N.Y.C., Dec. 31, 1925; s. Gordon Congdon and Carol Therese (Weiss) K.; m. Cynthia Bregman. B.A., Columbia U., 1949. Assoc. editor G.P. Putnam's Sons N.Y.C., 1949-52; staff assoc. Fund Advancement Edn Ford Found., 1952-58; sec. treas. Ednl. Facilities Labs., Inc., N.Y.C., 1958-67; v.p., treas. Ednl. Facilities Labs. Inc., 1967-70; sr. v.p. in charge systems bldg. Caudill Rowlett Scott (architects, engrs., planners), Houston 1970-76; adj. prof. architecture Rice U., Houston, 1973-76; prof. architecture U. Mich., Ann Arbor, 1976-87 prof. architecture emeritus U. Mich., 1987—; dir. archtl research lab. U. Mich., Ann Arbor, 1976-82; chmn Archtl. Rsch. Ctrs. Consortium, 1976-78; mem. coun Cornell U. Coll. Architecture, Art and Planning, 1973-77; Fulbright lectr. Royal Danish Acad. Fine Arts 1983; dir. CRSS Ctr., vis. prof. Tex. A&M U. Coll Architecture, College Station, 1992-97. Prin. author project dir. The Michigan Courthouse Study, 7 vols. 1981-82; contbr. editor Central: Papers on Architecture 1985-86; articles to Sat. Rev. Archtl. Design; Harvard Bus. Rev.; others. Chmn. Beaufort County Dem. Party 1990-92. Served with AUS, 1943-46, PTO. Recipient Am. Builder Mag. award for innovations in bldg., 1965 research citation Progressive Architecture, 1983. Mem AIA (hon.). Died Nov. 19, 1997.

KING, JOSEPH PAUL, finance executive; b. N.Y.C. Nov. 14, 1941; s. Herbert Frederick and Eunice Lauretta (Warren) K.; m. Olga C. King, Dec. 29, 1968 (div.) children—Cristina H., Spencer F. BA, Brown U., 1963 With Morgan Guaranty Trust Co., N.Y.C., 1963-78 v.p., 1972-78; first v.p. Smith, Barney Real Estate Corp 1978-84; sr. v.p.-fin. Security Capital Corp., 1984-86, sr v.p. Benjamin Franklin Savs. Assn., 1986-89; exec. v.p Krofft Entertainment Group, 1989—. Served to lt. U.S Army, 1965-71. Clubs: Univ. (N.Y.), Creek (Locus Valley, N.Y.), Houston City.

KING, PATRICIA MILLER, library administrator historian; b. Bklyn., July 26, 1937; d. Donald Knox and Amy Beatrice (Heyliger) Miller; m. Samuel W. Stein Jan. 2, 1978 (dec. May 1988); 1 child by previous marriage, Victoria Elizabeth King. A.B., Radcliffe Coll. 1959, A.M., 1961; Ph.D., Harvard U., 1970. Teaching asst. Harvard U., 1965-70; asst. prof. Wellesley Coll. Mass., 1970-71; dir. research Haney Assocs., Concord Mass., 1971-73; dir. Schlesinger Library, Radcliffe Coll 1973—, dir. projects. Contbr. articles to profl. jours. Bd. dirs. Nat. Coun. for Rsch. on Women, N.Y.C. 1983-92, Database Task Force, 1986-90, treas., 1988-89 chmn. bd., 1989-92, fin. com., 1992—; trustee Boston Heart Found., 1988—. Grantee in field. Mem. Mass Hist. Soc., Am. Antiquarian Soc., Orgn. Am. His torians, Am. Hist. Assn., Berkshire Conf. of Women Historians. Died May 3, 1994.

KINGREY, BURNELL WAYNE, college dean emeritus; b. Worthington, Minn., Sept. 12, 1921; s. Harold Raymond and Iva (Goodrich) K.; m. Patricia Abbott, June 3, 1945; children—Michael, Jean, Karel. A.A., Worthington Jr. Coll., 1941; D.V.M., Iowa State U., 1944, M.S., 1955. Diplomate Am. Coll. Vet. Internal Medicine. Pvt. practice vet. medicine Lena, Ill., 1944-53; faculty Iowa State U., 1953-63, prof., head dept. vet. medicine and surgery, 1955-63; dir. clinics Vet. Research Council, 1958-63; dean Sch. Vet. Medicine, U. Mo., 1963-73, dean emeritus, 1977-95; pres. Double Crown Ranches, Inc., 1973-95; dir. vet. edn. and services program Old West Regional Commn., Billings, Mont., 1977-95; ICA cons. to, Argentina and Chile, 1961; AID cons. to San Carlos U., Guatemala, 1962, India, 1968; cons. Sch. Vet. Medicine, Bogotá, Colombia, 1969, U. Wis. Bd. Regents, 1973; chmn. Bd. of Scientific Advisors Merck Inst., 1974-95; chmn. external examiners Miss. State U., 1979-95; mem. North Central Coll. and Univ. Accreditation Team, 1976. Mem. Lena Sch. Bd., 1952-63. Recipient Disting. Service award U. Mo., 1976; Stange award Iowa State U., 1979. Mem. AMVA (adv. manpower study 1977-78), Wyo. Vet. Med. Assn., Am. Assn. Vet. Clincians, Am. Acad. Sci., Am. Legion, Phi Kappa Phi, Delta Psi Omega, Gamma Sigma Delta, Phi Zeta, Alpha Zeta, Sigma Xi. Clubs: Rotarian, Mason. Home: Douglas Wyo. Died Jan. 4, 1995.

KINGSLEY, SIDNEY, playwright; b. N.Y.C., Oct. 22, 1906; s. Dr. Robert and Sonia (Kirshner) K.; m. Madge Evans, July 25, 1939 (dec. 1981). Student, Townsend Harris Hall, 1920-24; B.A., Cornell, 1928; D.Litt., Monmouth Coll., 1978, Ramapo State Coll., 1978. Author: plays Men in White, 1934, The Patriots, 1943; author, dir.: plays Dead End, 1936, Ten Million Ghosts, 1937, The World We Make, 1939, Detective Story, 1949, Darkness at Noon, 1951, Lunatics and Lovers, 1954, Night Life, 1962; (Awarded Pulitzer prize for best American play 1934, Theater Club medal for best play 1934, 36, 43, Drama Critics Circle award for best play 1943, 51, N.Y. Newspaper Guild front page award 1943, Page One Citation 1949, Federated Women's Club award, Cath. Dial award 1943, Edgar Allen Poe award for play, film 1949, Donaldson award for outstanding achievement in theater, Am. Acad. Arts and Letters award of merit medal for outstanding drama 1951, Yeshiva U. award achievement in theatre 1965), Dead End, Command Performance at the White House. Named to Theatre Hall of Fame, 1983; recipient Cert. of Achievement Cornell U., 1985, Gold Medal for Drama Am. Acad. and Inst. of Arts and Letters, 1986, William Inge award for lifetime achievement in Am. theatre Independence (Kans.) Community Coll., 1988. Mem. Dramatists Guild (pres. 1961-69), N.J. Motion Picture and TV Authority (chmn. 1976-80). Home: Oakland N.J. Died Mar. 20, 1995.

KINSEY-CALORI, JOANNE, broadcasting firm executive; b. McKeesport, Pa., Sept. 3; d. George Morris and Pauline Vivian (Anderson) Kinsey; B.A., M.A. Ohio State U., 1976; Ph.D., Harvard U., 1982; children—Paula Christine, Kevin Kinsey. Reporter, Sta. WOSU, Ohio State U., Columbus, 1969-70; communications asst. dept. continuing edn. Ohio State U., 1970-72, pub. relations dir. Coll. Adminstrv. Sci., 1974-75, acting asst. prof. communications, psychology, 1971-76; editor Columbus region Internat. Harvester Corp., 1973-77; pres. Profl. Broadcasting Services, Redondo Beach, Calif., 1976—, also Paris, London, Lisbon, Washington; international cross-cultural photographer, writer, comm. cons. Photography showings London, Paris, Washington. Pres. PTA, Marburn, Ridgeview, Whetstone schs., Columbus, 1965-70; campaign mgr. Republican party, Franklin County, 1965-68. Recipient spl. award for outstanding community service Columbus Pub. Schs. Mem. Nat. Acad. TV Arts and Scis., Women in Communications (Los Angeles chpt.), Pacific Pioneer Broadcasters, So. Calif. Wine Writers (charter mem.), Archaeology Soc. Columbus, Jr. League, Mirrors and Chimes, Phi Beta Kappa, Phi Kappa Phi. Presbyterian. Clubs: Worthington Music, Clintonville Women's, Columbus Players.

KINTNER, WILLIAM ROSCOE, political science educator emeritus; b. Lock Haven, Pa., Apr. 21, 1915; s. Joseph Jennings and Florence (Kendig) K.; m. Xandree M. Hyatt, June 15, 1940 (dec.); children: Kay Caldwell, Jane Kintner Hogan, Gail Kintner Markou, Carl H.; m. Faith Childs Halterman, Aug. 28, 1987. B.S., U.S. Mil. Acad., 1940; Ph.D., Georgetown U., 1949. Commd. 2d lt. U.S. Army, 1940, advanced through grades to col., 1956; inf. bn. co., Korean War; mem. sr. staff CIA, 1950-52; mem. planning staff NSC, 1954; mem. staff spl. asst. to Pres., 1955; cons. Pres.'s Com. to study U.S. Assistance Program (Draper Com.), 1959; chief long-range plans strategic analysis sect. Coordination Group, Chief of Staff, U.S. Army, 1959-61; ret., 1961; prof. political sci. Wharton Sch., U. Pa., Phila., 1961-65; dep. dir. Fgn. Policy Research Inst., Phila., 1961-69; dir. Fgn. Policy Research Inst., 1969-73, pres., 1976; Am. ambassador to Thailand, 1973-75; cons. Dept. Def., NSC, Stanford Research Inst.; fellow Hudson Inst.; sr. adviser Ops. Research Office, Johns Hopkins U., 1956-57; mem. acad. bd. Inter-Am. Def. Coll., 1967-72; mem. Bd. Fgn. Scholarships, 1970-73; civilian faculty adv. com. Nat. War Coll., 1970-72; mem. adv. bd. Naval War Coll., 1985; bd. mem. U.S. Peace Inst., 1986—. Author: The Front is Everywhere, 1950, (with George C. Reinhardt) Atomic Weapons in Land Combat, 1953, The Haphazard Years, 1960, (with others) Forging a New Sword, 1958, Protracted Conflict, 1959, A Forward Strategy for America, 1961, Building the Atlantic World, 1963, (with Joseph Z. Kornfeder) The New Frontier of War, 1962, Peace and the Strategy Conflict, 1967, (with Harriet Fast Scott) The Nuclear Revolution in Soviet Military Affairs, 1969, (with Wolfgang Klaiber) Eastern Europe and European Security, 1971, (with Harvey Sicherman) Technology and International Politics, 1975, (with John F. Copper) A Matter of Two Chinas: The China-Taiwan Issue in U.S. Foreign Policy, 1979, Arms Control: The American Dilemma, 1987; editor: Orbis, 1969-73, 76—; editor, contbr.: Safeguard: Why the ABM Makes Sense, 1969, Soviet Global Strategy, 1987; contbr. articles to profl. jours. Trustee Freedom House, N.Y.C.; mem. bd. Gen. Ch. of New Jerusalem, Bryn Athyn, Pa.; mem. adv. com. World Affairs Council, Phila. Decorated Legion of Merit with oak leaf cluster, Bronze Star with oak leaf cluster. Mem. Coun. Fgn. Rels., Am. Polit. Sci. Assn., Pa. Soc., Coun. Am. Ambs., U.S. Inst. Peace (bd. dirs.). Died Feb. 1, 1997.

KIRBO, CHARLES HUGHES, retired lawyer, former presidential adviser; b. Bainbridge, Ga., Mar. 5, 1917; s. Ben and Ethel (West) K.; m. Margaret LeGette, May 20, 1951; children: Charles Hughes, Susan Ray, Betsy Anne, Katherine. LL.B., U. Ga., 1939. Bar: Ga. 1939. Ptnr. King & Spalding, Atlanta, from 1960, now ret.; chief of staff Ga. Gov. Jimmy Carter, 1970-74; adviser to Pres. Jimmy Carter. Served to maj. U.S. Army, World War II. Died Sep. 3, 1996.

KIRBY, WILLIAM MURRAY MAURICE, medical educator; b. Springfield, S.D., Nov. 21, 1914; s. William McLeod and Era R. (Keeling) K.; m. Georgiana H. Dole, Apr. 12, 1944; children: Barbara Dole, Philip Keeling, Richard Murray. B.S., Trinity Coll., Hartford, Conn., 1936; M.D., Cornell U., 1940. Diplomate: Am. Bd. Internal Medicine (bd. 1961-67). Intern N.Y. Hosp., 1940-41; resident in medicine Stanford Hosp., 1941-44; instr. medicine Stanford Sch. Medicine, 1947-49; mem. faculty U. Wash. Med. Sch., 1949—, prof. medicine, 1955—; Mem. med. adv. bd. FDA, 1964—. Author chpts. in textbooks on infectious diseases, also numerous articles. Served with U.S. Army, 1944-47. Mem. A. Soc. Clin. Investigation, Assn. Am. Physicians.

KIRCHNER, EDWIN JAMES, retired food company executive; b. Keokuk, Iowa, July 4, 1924; s. Edwin William and Gertrude Ann (Breheny) K.; m. Wilma Bernice Johnson, Apr. 21, 1944; children: Linda Kirchner, Karen Ann Kirchner Porreca, Patrick Adam. Grad. high sch. Accounting Union Electric Power Co., Keokuk, 1942-48; with Hubinger Co., Keokuk, 1948-83; adminstrv. asst. to v.p. finance Hubinger Co., 1960-67, asst. v.p., asst. treas., asst. sec., 1967-69, treas., 1969-76, asst. sec., 1969-73, v.p., 1973-79, mgr. spl. projects, 1979-83, ret., 1983, also dir., 1969-76; sec.-treas. Keokuk Grain Inspection Service, 1970-72, v.p., 1972-75, also dir. Mem. Keokuk Cath. Sch. Bd., 1972-78, pres., 1972-75, mem. long range planning com., 1977-86; bd. dirs. South Lee County (Ia.) chpt. ARC, 1965-71, chpt. chmn., 1969-71; mem. exec. com. lay adv. bd. St. Joseph Hosp., 1972-75; trustee Keokuk Area Hosp., 1975-77; trustee, treas. Tri-State Health Care Found., 1981-85; commr. Low Rent Housing Authority, 1981-85. Served with USAAF, 1943-46, ETO; Served with USAAF, MTO. Clubs: K.C. (treas. 1965-72), Elk. Died Oct. 30, 1992.

KIRK, GRAYSON LOUIS, retired political science educator, retired universtiy president, trustee; b. Jeffersonville, Ohio, Oct. 12, 1903; s. Traine C. and Nora (Eichelberger) K.; m. Marion Louise Sands, Aug. 17, 1925; 1 child, John. Mem. B.A., Miami (Ohio) U., 1924, LL.D., 1950; M.A., Clark U., 1925; postgrad., Ecole Libre des Sciences Politiques, Paris, 1928-29; Ph.D., U. Wis., 1930; postgrad., London Sch. of Econs., 1936-37; hon. degrees from over 35 U.S. and fgn. colls. and univs., 1950—. Mem. faculty U. Wis., 1929-40; mem. faculty Columbia U., N.Y.C., prof. govt., 1943-47, Bryce prof. history internat. relations, 1959-72, provost, 1949-50, v.p., provost, 1950-51, pres., trustee, 1953-68, pres., trustee emeritus, 1968-97, prof. emeritus, 1972-97. Author of several works in internat. rels. field; editor: (with R.P. Stebbins) War and National Policy: a Syllabus, 1942; contbr. to Yale U. Law Rev. Trustee emeritus Asia Found., Asia Soc., Inst. Internat. Edn.; trustee, v.p. Tinker Found.; chmn. emeritus bd. Am. Soc. French Legion of Honor; fellow Social Sci. Rsch. Coun., 1936-37; mem. secretariat staff Dumbarton Oaks Conf., 1944; exec. officer 3d Commn., San Francisco Conf., 1945. Named comdr. Order Orange-Nassau, Netherlands, 1952; hon. knight comdr. Order Brit. Empire, 1955; grand officer Legion of Honor, 1956; Grand Ufficialato dell Ordine al Merito della Repubblica, Italy, 1956; Assoc. Knight Order of Hosp. of St. John Jerusalem, 1959; medal Order of Taj, Iran, 1961; cross of grand officer Order George I, Greece; Order Sacred Treasure, 1st class Japan; commandeur de 1er Ordre des Palmes Academiques France). Mem. Am. Philos. Soc., Coun. Fgn. Rels. (former pres.), Acad. Arts and Scis., Pilgrims (v.p.), Phi Beta Kappa, Phi Kappa Tau. Died Nov. 21, 1997.

KIRK, PAUL, architect; b. Salt Lake City, Nov. 18, 1914; s. Spencer B. and Malvina Zoe (Blair) K.; m. Helen Catherine Richardson, Feb. 16, 1939; children: Christopher Paul, Hannah Jo. BArch, U. Wash., 1932-37. Registered architect, Wash. Prin. Paul Kirk Architect, Seattle, 1939-45; ptnr. Chiarelli & Kirk, Seattle, 1945-50; prin. Paul Hayden Kirk AIA, Seattle, 1950-56, Paul Hayden Kirk, FAIA & Assocs., Seattle, 1956-60; ptnr. Kirk, Wallace, McKinley, AIA & Assocs., Seattle, 1968-78; prin. Paul Hayden Kirk FAIA, PSC; vis. critic Cornell U. Sch. Architecture, Ithaca, N.Y., jury for Nat. Conf. Ch. Architecture, jury for City Hall competition FHA, Wash. Former bd. dirs. Community Psychiat. Clinic, Pinel Mental Hosp. Found.; bd. dirs. Community Devel. Council, Seattle chpt. AIA; chmn. Gov. Com. Factory-Built Housing; mem. Hist. Seattle Preservation and Devel. Authority, Gov. Com. on Employment for Handicapped, Seattle, Mayor's Com. on Opportunities for Handicapped, Seattle. Named to U. Wash. Hall of Fame, 1986, U. Wash. Alumni Legends, 1987. Fellow AIA (past treas., former bd. dirs. Wash. state chpt., chmn. nat. com. aesthetics, chmn. Architect/Engr. Selection Com.); mem. Portland Devel. Commn. (mem. design adv. council), FHA (adv. com. honor awards for residential design), Jury for Nat. Conf. Ch. Architecture, Jury for City Hall Competition, AIA (past treas., former bd. dirs Wash. state chpt, chmn. nat. com. aesthetics), Forward Thrust Com. on Quality in Urban Design (chmn.), Gen. Services Adminstrn. (mem. design adv. commn.), Tau Sigma Delta, Alpha Rho Chi. Home: Kirkland Wash. DIED 05/22/95. .

KIRK, WEIR RICHARD, health services executive; b. Terre Haute, Ind., Feb. 18, 1920; s. C. Weir and Etta Barbara (Zimmerman) K.; m. Marvel B. Dickson, June 13, 1951; children: Vicki Marie, Jeanine Gayle, Patti Richelle, Terri Sue, Richard Brian, Michael Wayne. BS in Edn., Ind. State Teachers Coll., 1940, MS, 1953. Adminstr. Crawford Meml. Hosp., Robinson, Ill., 1962-64, Riley County Hosp., Wharton Manor, Manhattan, Kans., 1953-62; dir. membership Am. Coll. Hosp. Adminstrs., Chgo., 1964-82; exec. dir. Assn. Mental Health Adminstrs., Chgo., 1984-87, Am. Coll. of Addiction Treatment Adminstrs., 1984-87; dir. devel. credentialing Am. Coll. Healthcare Execs., Chgo., 1985-87, cons., 1987—. Author: Your Future in Hospital Administration, 1963, Aim For a Job in a Hospital, 1968, Your Future in Hospital Work, 1971, Your Future in Hospital and Health Services Administration, 1976, Exploring Careers in Health Services Administration, 1982; contbr. articles to profl. jours. Mem. Community Chest Pub. Rels. Com., Lafayette, Ind., 1942-43, mem. com. on youth Oak Park (Ill.) Twp. chmn., 1973; coord. Post-War Planning Commn., Jeffersonville, Ind., 1943-44; mem. pub. info. com. Allen County Cancer Soc., Ft. Wayne, Ind., 1948-49; prodn. mgr. Community Theatre, Terre Haute, 1951-52; bd. dirs. Riley County Mental Health, 1954-60, pres., 1958-60; active Boy Scouts Am., West Lafayette, Ind., River Forest, Ill., Irvine, Tex., 1942-87; bd. dirs. Crawford County Tuberculosis and Health Assn., Robinson, Ill., 1963-64, Bethesda Luth. Home, Watertown, Wis., 1965-83; mem. Bd. Health, Oak Park, Ill., 1986—; founding bd. dirs. Midwest Ctr. for U.S.-USSR Initiatives, 1988-91; mem. alumni adv. coun. Ind. State U., Terre Haute, 1977-80, Univ. Futures Forum, 1979-80, acad. planning workshop, 1977. Served to sgt. U.S. Army, 1944-46, ETO, to lt. (hon.) USN, 1982. Recipient Disting. Alumni award Ind. State U., 1983, Humanitarian award Nat. Assn. Health Services Execs., 1983; honoree Weir Richard Kirk Day, City of Chgo., Sept. 16, 1986. Fellow Am. Coll. Hosp. Adminstrs.; mem. Am. Hosp. Assn., Nat. Com. Health Credentialing Agencies, Kans. Hosp. Assn., Blue Cross Rels. Com. Luth. Hosp. Assn. Kans., Ill. Hosp. Assn., Profl. Exam Svc. (founder, bd. dirs. 1971-77), Rotary (bd. dirs. Oak Park chpt. 1989—, bd. dirs. Manhattan chpt. 1958-61, Robinson, Ill. chpt. 1962-64), Optimists (bd. dirs. Terre Haute chpt. 1950-52, pres. 1952-53). Lodges: Rotary (bd. dirs. Manhattan chpt. 1958-61, Robinson, Ill. chpt. 1962-64), Optimists (bd. dirs. Terre Haute chpt. 1950-52, pres. 1952-53). Home: Oak Park Ill. Died Aug. 4, 1993.

KIRKENDALL, WALTER MURRAY, physician, educator; b. Louisville, Mar. 31, 1917; s. Charles Allen and Margaret C. (Caplinger) K.; m. Margaret Jane Allen, Mar. 31, 1948; children: William Charles, James Allen, Matthew John, Thomas Murray, David Edwin, Nancy Jane, Mary Margaret, Kathryn Ann, Joseph Howard, Michael Bruce. MD, U. Louisville, 1941. Diplomate Am. Bd. Internal Medicine and Nephrology. Rsch. asst. anatomy Coll. Medicine, U. Louisville, 1938-39; intern Univ. Hosps., Iowa City, 1941-42, resident in internal medicine, 1946-49; jr. asst. resident internal medicine Gen. Hosp., Louisville, 1945-46; staff mem. State U. Iowa Hosps., 1949-72; asst. dept. internal medicine, then assoc. Coll. Medicine, U. Iowa, 1949-51, successively asst. prof., clin. assoc. prof., assoc. prof., 1951-59, prof., 1959-72, dir. cardiovascular rsch. labs., 1958-70, dir. renal-hypertension-electrolyte div., 1970-72; chief med. svcs. VA Hosp., Iowa City, 1952-58, cons. in medicine, 1958-72; prof. medicine Med. Sch., U. Tex., Houston, 1972-91, chmn. dept. internal medicine, 1972-76; dir. med. svcs. Hermann Hosp., 1972-76, dir.

hypertension div., 1976-91; mem. med. adv. bd., chmn. Coun. High Blood Pressure Rsch., Am. Heart Assn., 1967-69; mem. exec. com. Undergrad. Cardiology Tng. Programs, Nat. Heart Inst., 1969-72. Contbr. articles to profl. jours. Served from 1st. lt. to maj. M.C., U.S. Army, 1942-46. Recipient Bierring award Iowa Tb and Health Assn., 1966; named Internist of Yr. Iowa Soc. Internal Medicine, 1971. Fellow ACP, Am. Coll. Cardiology; mem. AAAS, AAUP, AMA, Am. Fedn. Clin. Rsch. (counselor Midwestern sect. 1955-57), Cen. Soc. Clin. Rsch., Cen. Clin. Rsch. Club, Am. Coll. Chest Physicians (Louis Mark lectr. 1963, gov. Iowa chpt. 1964), Internat., Am. socs. nephrology, Internat. Soc. Cardiology, Am. Clin. and Climatol. Assn., Soc. Exptl. Biology and Medicine, So. Soc. Clin. Investigation, N.Y. Acad. Scis., Assn. Profs. Medicine, Am., Houston socs. internal medicine, Nat. Kidney Found., Am. Coll. Pharmacology and Chemotherapy, Am. Soc. Pharmacology and Exptl. Therapeutics, Tex. Med. Assn., Harris County Med. Soc., Sigma Xi, Alpha Omega Alpha, Phi Chi. Home: Houston Tex. Died July 13, 1991.

KIRSCHNER, HEINRICH, judge; b. Cologne, Germany, Jan. 7, 1938; s. Heinrich and Elisabeth K.; m. Edelgard Klisch, 1968; 3 children. Magistrate North Rhine-Westfalia, 1965-70; civil servant Fed. Ministry Justice, 1971-75, 79-89; law asst. EC Commn., 1975-79; judge EC Ct. of First Instance, Luxembourg, 1989—. Died Feb. 6, 1997.

KIRSTEIN, ISABELLA JOHANNA, research company executive; b. Bethulie, Republic of South Africa; d. Jan Adriaan and Isabella Johanna (Janse v. Rensburg) Grobbelaar; m. Jan Gysbert Kirstein, Feb. 4, 1972 (dec. 1977). BA with honors, U. Orange Free State, Bloemfontein, Republic of South Africa. Mng. dir. Internat. Consumer Rsch. (Pty) Ltd., 1959-66, Media and Communications Rsch., 1966-69, IPRA, 1969-73; exec. chmn. IMS Internat. SA, Hillbrow, Republic of South Africa, 1973-89, Decision Surveys Internat. (Pty) Ltd., 1989—. Named Bus. Woman of Yr., 1968-69. Fellow Royal Statis. Soc.; mem. Fedn. Bus. and Profl. Women's Club (chmn. ad hoc com.), Soroptomists.

KLABOSH, CHARLES JOSEPH, aerospace research and development executive; b. Manchester, Conn., Mar. 11, 1920; s. Kasimeraz and Veronica (Christana) Klebosas; m. Lois Thaney Heiser, Oct. 6, 1958. BS in Aero. Engring., U. Mich., 1953; postgrad., U. Houston, 1962-68, U. North Fla., 1983-86. Sales engr. Pratt and Whitney Aircraft, East Hartford, Conn., 1941-43, 48-52; mgr., flight test USAF, Dayton, Ohio, 1953-55; sr. design engr., nuclear power plants Gen. Electric, Co., Evendale, Ohio, 1955-59, 61; sr. devel. engr., gasturbine power plants Am. Airlines, Inc., Tulsa, 1960; advanced space programs engr. NASA, Houston, 1961-67, mgr., lunar ops., 1967-72, space shuttle systems devel. engr., 1973-74; owner, exec. Charles Klabosh, Co., Jacksonville, Fla., 1974—. Inventor space shuttle remote manipulator system, 1974. With USAF, 1943-47. Mem. AIAA, AAAS, IEEE, N.Y. Acad. Sci., Soc. for Indsl. and Applied Math.

KLACSMANN, JOHN ANTHONY, retired chemical company executive; b. West New York, N.J., Oct. 6, 1921; s. Joseph J. Klacsmann and Anna Elizabeth (Schmiedeberg) Goessling; m. Betty Birdsey, Sept. 23, 1944; children—Steven B., Peter G., John Anthony. B.S., Yale U., 1942, M.A., 1944, Ph.D., 1947. Asst. to lab. dir. Union Carbide Corp., Oak Ridge, 1944-46; with E.I. duPont de Nemours & Co., 1947—, v.p., gen. mgr. fabrics and finishes dept., 1973-75, v.p., gen. mgr. internat. dept., 1975-78; v.p. internat. Wilmington, Del., 1978-81; ret., 1981; dir. DuPont Can. Inc.; exec. v.p. Clean Sites, Inc., 1985-86, sr. adv. to pres., 1986—. Trustee Christ Episcopal Ch. Found., pres., 1993-95; bd. dirs. Jacksonville Symphony Assn.; Mayo Reader Adv. Bd. Fellow Am. Inst. Chemists, Fla. Inst. Chemists (treas. 1988-95); mem. Am. Chem. Soc., AAAS, Marsh Landing Club, Sigma Xi, Ponte Vedra Club, The Ladge & Bath Club. Republican. Died Sept. 16, 1997.

KLAUHS, HELLMUTH, banker; b. Vienna, Austria, Mar. 27, 1928; s. Hugo and Hermine Klauhs; m. Lucia Klauhs, July 14, 1950; children: Harald, Helga, Ilse. LLD, U. Vienna, 1952. Mem. Fed. Ministry of Justice, Vienna, 1946-52; sec. Fed. Austrian Econ. Chamber, Vienna, 1952-57, dept. head Credit & Ins. Enterprises, 1985-88; dep. sec. gen. Assn. Rural Copps., Vienna, 1957-64, pres., 1978-88; mem. of the exec. bd. Genossenschaftliche Zentralbank AG, Vienna, 1964-68, dep. chief, exec. dir., 1968-69, chief exec. dir., 1969-88; mem. governing bd. Austrian Nat. Bank, Vienna, 1961-64, 69-88, gov., 1988—; mng. dir. Raiffeisen Bausparkasse GesmbH, Vienna, 1961-73. Mem. Vienna Inst. Comperative Econ. Studies (v.p.), Austrian Inst. Econ. Rsch. (v.p.), Ôsterreichische Bankwissenschaftliche Gesellschaft (v.p.).

KLEEMAN, WALTER BENTON, JR., interior and furniture designer, consultant, author; b. Cin., Sept. 25, 1918; s. Walter Benton Kleeman and Elsa Morgenroth; m. Elizabeth Fleming Blake, June 17, 1949 (div. Jan. 1968); children: Christopher, Elissa. BS in Commerce, U. N.C., 1940; PhD in Interior Ergonomics, Union Grad. Sch., 1972. Chief interior designer, v.p., sec. People's Outfitting Co., Inc., Springfield, Ohio, 1945-61; chief interior designer, pres., prin. Kleemans Contract Interiors, Springfield, Ohio, 1961-74; assoc. prof. interior design Western Ky. U., Bowling Green, 1974-80; pres., chair The Worldport Corp., Springfield, Ohio, 1958-95, South Limestone Corp., Springfield, Ohio, 1961-86; adj. prof. Union Grad. Sch., Cin., 1975—, vis. prof. U. Colo.-Boulder, Denver, 1980-81, Disting. vis. prof. interior design U. Del., Newark, 1987-88; cons. in field; forensic cons. and expert witness for lawyers in 23 states. Author: What is a Furniture Store?, 1943, The Challenge of Interior Design, 1981, Interior Design of the Electronic Office: The Comfort and Productivity Payoff, 1991 (Joel Polsky prize 1992); contbg. editor The Designer, 1976-91; U.S. corr. Facilities newsletter; design editor Wood & Wood Products mag., 1984-90; contbg. editor Designers West/World, 1992-93; contbr. articles to profl. jours. Fellow Am. Soc. Interior Designers (nat. treas. 1968-70, chair environ. rsch. coun., rep. to interprofl. consortium on environ. and behavior 1975-78); mem. Am. Soc. Furniture Designers, Constrn. Specifications Inst., Environ. Design Rsch. Assn., Interior Design Educators Coun., Nat. Forensic Ctr., Ergonomics Soc. (Eng.), Internat. Assn. for Study of People and Their Surroundings (Eng.), Internat. Interior Design Assn., Human Factors and Ergonomics Soc. (com. to revise 1988 Am. Nat. Standards Inst. standard for visual display terminal workstations 1992—). Selected by U.S. Dept. of State and U.S. Info. Agy. to represent Am. interior design in Moscow, 1975; 1st non-Soviet interior designer to visit Tsniiep Zhilischa, the Gosstroy Ctrl. Rsch. and Design Inst. in Moscow. Died Oct. 13, 1997.

KLEENE, STEPHEN COLE, retired mathematician, educator; b. Hartford, Conn., Jan. 5, 1909; s. Gustav Adolph and Alice Lena (Cole) K.; m. Nancy Elliott, Sept. 2, 1937 (dec.); children: Paul Elliott and Kenneth Cole (twins), Bruce Metcalf, Pamela Lee; m. Jeanne M. Kleene, Mar. 17, 1988. AB, Amherst Coll., 1930; PhD, Princeton U., 1934. Instr. math., researcher Princeton U., 1930-35; from instr. math to assoc. prof. U. Wis., Madison, 1935-48, prof., 1948-64, Cyrus C. MacDuffee prof. math., then prof. emeritus, chmn. dept. math., 1957-58, 60-62; vis. prof. Princeton U., 1956-57; mem. Inst. Advanced Study, 1939-40,div. math. NRC, 1956-58; pres. Internat. Union History and Philosophy Sci., 1961. Author: Introduction to Metamathematics, 1952, (with Richard E. Vesley) The Foundations of Intuitionistic Mathematics, 1965; Logic, 1980; 2 other books; cons. editor Jour. Symbolic Logic, 1936-42, 46-49, editor, 1950-62; contbr. articles to profl. jours. Lt. comdr. USNR, 1942-46. Recipient Nat. medal Sci. NSF, 1990; Guggenheim fellow U. Amsterdam, 1950; NSF grantee U. Marburg, 1958-59. Fellow AAAS; mem. Phi Beta Kappa, Sigma Xi (pres. Wis. chpt. 1951-52). Achievements include climbing Mt. Everest. Deceased.

KLEHS, HENRY JOHN WILHELM, civil engineer; b. Dornbusch bez Stade, Germany, Dec. 7, 1910; s. Frederick and Anna (Mahler) K.; B.S., U. Calif., 1935; m. Clodell Peters, July 17, 1948; came to U.S., 1920, naturalized through father, 1922. Engr. So. Pacific Transp. Co., 1936-75, supr. hazardous materials control, until 1975; ret., 1975. Mem. Calif. Fire Chiefs Assn., Internat. Assn. Fire Chiefs, Steuben Soc. Am., Am. Ry. Engring Assn., ASCE. Died Dec. 17, 1996.

KLEIBER, CARLOS, conductor; b. Berlin, July 3, 1930; s. Erich K.; married; 2 children. Studied in Switzerland. Raised in S.Am.; condr. Theater am Gartnerplatz, Munich, 1953, debut in Potsdam, 1954, Deutsche Oper am Rhein, Dusseldorf, 1956-64, Zurich Opera, 1964-66, Wurttemberg State Theater, Stuttgart, 1966-68, Bavarian State Opera, Munich, 1968-73, Vienna State Opera, 1973; guest condr. Bayreuth Festival, 1974, Covent Garden, Berlin and Vienna Philharm. Orchs.; Am. debut San Francisco Opera, 1977. Recordings. Died Oct., 1994.

KLEIMAN, JOSEPH, engineer, consultant, retired life sciences company executive; b. Grand Rapids, Mich., Oct. 1, 1919; s. Jacob and Bessie (Targowitch) K.; m. Shirley Ruth Present, Aug. 30, 1942; children: Richard Neil, Robert, William. BS in Engring, U. Mich., 1941, MS, 1942. Engr. Reeves Instrument Corp., N.Y.C., 1946-51; v.p., gen. mgr. Belock Instrument Corp., College Point, N.Y., 1951-58; v.p., gen. mgr. Whittaker Gyro (div. Telecomputing Corp.), Los Angeles, 1958-59, exec. v.p. corp., 1959-64; v.p. corp. devel. Whittaker Corp., 1964-67, sr. v.p., 1967-84, dir., 1958-84; dir. Yardney Elec. Corp., 1983-85, Diagnostic Products Corp., 1979—, Syncor, Inc., 1985—, Computone, Inc., 1987-88, Z-Seven Fund, 1989—. Officer Union Am. Hebrew Congregations, 1975-87, 93—. Mem. NSPE, Calif. Soc. Profl. Engrs., Sigma Xi, Phi Lambda Upsilon, Iota Alpha. Jewish. DIED 01/06/96. .

KLEIN, RICHARD, botany educator; b. Chgo., Mar. 17, 1923; s. Harry and Grace (Flora) K.; m. Deana Tarson, Sept. 13, 1947. BS, U. Chgo., 1947, MS, 1949, PhD, 1951. Curator N.Y. Bot. Garden, Bronx, 1953-67; prof. U. Vt., Burlington, 1967—; cons. Time-Life Corp., N.Y.C., 1960-64, Union Carbide Corp., Westchester, N.Y., 1962-66. Author: Research Methods in Plant Science, The Green World, 1st and 2d edit., Discovering Plants, Principles of Plant Science. With U.S. Army, 1942-46. Recipient Bausch & Lomb Sci. medal Bausch & Lomb Corp., 1950; U. scholar U. Vt., 1989. DIED 09/04/97. .

KLEIN, WILLIAM MCKINLEY JR., museum director. CEO, pres., exec. dir. Nat. Tropical Botanical Garden, Lawai, Hawaii. Died Feb. 12, 1997.

KLEINZELLER, ARNOST, physiologist, physician, emeritus educator; b. Ostrava, Czechoslovakia, Dec. 6, 1914; s. Arnold and Josefa (Schongut) K.; m. Lotte Reuter, Apr. 2, 1943; children: Anna, Jana. M.D., U. Brno, Czechoslovakia, 1938; Ph.D., U. Sheffield, Eng., 1939-41; Rockefeller fellow, Cambridge U., Eng., 1942; D.Sc., Czechoslovak Acad. Sci., 1959; M.A. (hon.), U. Pa., 1973. Head lab. cell metabolism State Inst. Health, Prague, Czechoslovakia, 1945-48; mem. faculty Tech. U., Prague, 1948-52, Charles U., Prague, 1952-55; head lab. cell metabolism Czechoslovak Acad. Sci., Prague, 1956-66; vis. prof. dept. physiology U. Rochester (N.Y.) Sch. Medicine and Dentistry, 1966-67; prof. physiology U. Pa. Med. Sch., 1967-85, prof. emeritus, 1985-97; vis. prof. dept. biochemistry U. Cambridge, Eng., 1980; mem. exec. com. Internat. Cell Research Orgn., 1962-67, chmn. panel IV, 1962-68; mem. U.S. nat. com. Internat. Union Physiol. Scis., 1975-81, sec., 1975-78. Author: (with Vrba and Malek) Manometric Methods, 1954, (with Kotyk) Membrane Transport and Metabolism, 1961, (with Malek, Longmuir, Cerkasov and Kovac) Manometric Methods, 1964, Exploring the Cell Membrane: Conceptual Developments, 1995; editor: Biochem. Biophys. Acta, Current Topics in Membranes; rsch. in metabolic processes in cells and tissues; mechanism of fatty acid formation in yeast cells; transport of electrolytes and sugar across cell membranes; history of science (membrane phenomena). Med. Research Council fellow, 1943-44. Fellow Phila. Coll. Physicians; mem. Internat. Soc. Cell Biology (exec. com. 1964-68), Czechoslovak Nat. Com. Biol. Scis. (hon. sec. 1961-66), Biochem. Soc. Gt. Britain, Am. Physiol. Soc., Soc. Gen. Physiologists (councillor 1977-79), Biophys. Soc., Am. Soc. Cell Biology, Academia Leopoldina, Gt. Britain Physiol. Soc., AAAS (com. sci. freedom and responsibility 1982-85). Died Feb. 1, 1997.

KLESTADT, LOTHAR, import/export company executive; b. Buren, Germany, Dec. 28, 1917; came to U.S., 1937; s. Rudolf and Ida (Alexander) K.; m. Berta Merker, May 3, 1953; children: Gary L., Alan R., Peter W. BS in Traffic Mgmt., NYU, 1944. Export clk. S. Stern Steiner & Co., Inc., N.Y.C., 1937-38; import entry clk. Kramer & Hauser, Inc., N.Y.C., 1938-41; asst. traffic mgr. The Sweets Co. of Am., Inc., Hoboken, N.J., 1941; export traffic mgr. Panatlantic, Inc., N.Y.C., 1941-46; v.p., exec. v.p., pres. Trans-World Shipping Corp., N.Y.C., 1946—. Mem. Nat. Customs Brokers and Forwarders Assn. of Am. (bd. dirs. 1972-93), N.Y. Freight Forwarders and Brokers Assn. (bd. dirs. 1974—, pres. 1983-84), NYU Club (bd. govs. 1980-90, chmn. 1988-90). Died Dec. 13, 1996.

KLINE, GORDON MABEY, chemist, editor; b. Trenton, N.J., Feb. 9, 1903; s. Manuel Kuhl and Florence (Campbell) K.; m. Dorothy Beard, Mar. 15, 1926; 1 child, Ann Linthicum (Mrs. Robert True Cook). A.B., Colgate U., 1925; M.S., George Washington U., 1926; Ph.D., U. Md., 1934. Research chemist N.Y. State Dept. Health, 1926-27; research chemist Picatinny Arsenal, 1928-29; chemist, phys. sci adminstr. Nat. Bur. Standards, Washington, 1929-69, chief organic plastics sect. Nat. Bur. Standards, 1935-51, chief div. polymers, 1951-63, cons., 1964-69; tech. editor Modern Plastics Mag., 1936-90, tech. editor emeritus 1991—; editorial dir., cons. Modern Plastics Ency., 1936-90; tech. investigator with U.S. Army, ETO, 1945; chmn. tech. com. on plastics Internat. Standardization Orgn., ann. meetings, N.Y.C., 1951, Turin, Italy, 1952, Stockholm, 1953, Brighton, Eng., 1954, Paris, 1955, The Hague, Netherlands, 1956, Burgenstock, Switzerland, 1957, Washington, 1958, U.S. del., Munich, 1959, Prague, 1960, 84, Turin, 1961, Warsaw, 1962, London, 1963, Budapest, 1964, Bucharest, 1965, Stockholm, 1966, 86, Phila., 1968, Prague, 1969, Paris, 1970, Moscow, 1971, Baden-Baden, 1972, Montreux, 1973, Tokyo, 1974, Pugnochiuso, Italy, 1975, Ottawa, 1976, London, 1977, Madrid, 1978, Budapest, 1980, Orlando, Fla., 1981, 90, The Hague, 1983, Warsaw, 1984; sec. div. plastics and polymers Internat. Union Pure and Applied Chemistry, 1951-59, vice chmn., 1959-63, chmn., 1963-67, mem. macro-molecules div., 1967-75; observer for ISO, 1976-86; plastics adv. council, Princeton, 1957-65. Editor: Analytical Chemistry of Polymers, Part I, 1959, Parts II and III, 1961; Contbr. articles profl. jours. Recipient Honor award Am. Inst. Chemists, Washington sect., 1952, Exceptional Service Gold medal Dept. Commerce, 1953, award Standards Engrs. Soc. 1964, Rosa award Nat. Bur. Standards, 1965, Meritorious Service award Am. Nat. Standards Inst., 1987; charter mem. Plastics Hall of Fame, 1973. Mem. ASTM (award of merit 1954; D-20 award of excellence 1986), Am. Chem. Soc., Am. Inst. Chemists, Soc. Plastics Engrs., Soc. Plastics Industry, Soc. Plastics Pioneers, Phi Beta Kappa, Sigma Xi. Clubs: Cosmos (Washington); Chemists (N.Y.C.).

KLINE, STEPHEN JAY, mechanical engineer, educator; b. L.A., Feb. 25, 1922; s. Eugene Field and Shed (Lowman) K.; m. Naomi Jeffries, July 10, 1977; chil dren: David M., Mark D., Carolyn R. BA, Stanford U., 1943, MS, 1949; ScD, MIT, 1952. Research analyst N. Am. Aviation, 1946-48; mem. faculty Stanford (Calif.) U., 1952-92; ret., 1992—; prof. mech. engring. Stanford (Calif.) U., 1961—, chmn. thermoscis. div., 1961-73, prof. values, tech. sci. and soc., 1970-92; cons. Gen. Electric, Gen. Motors, United Technology, DuPont, Brown Boveri. Author: Siminitude and Approximation Theory, 1965, Computation of Turbulent Boundary Layers, 1968, Conceptual Foundations for Multidisciplinary Thinking, 1995; editor: Evaluation of Complex Turbulent Flows, 1981. Served with AUS, 1943-46. Recipient George Stephenson medal Instn. Mech. Engrs. Britain, Bucraino medal Italian Film Soc., 1965; named individual who has contributed most to fluid mechanics in 20th century Japanese Soc. Mech. Engrs. Fellow ASME (hon. life, past chmn. fluid mechanics com. fluids engring. div., Melville medal 1959, Fluids Engring. award 1975, Centennial award 1980); mem. AAAS (life), NAE. Died Oct. 23, 1997.

KLINGEL, MARTIN ALLEN, investment company executive; b. Urbana, Ill., Aug. 27, 1941; s. Allen Barclay and Mary Margaret (Oldham) K.; children: Katherine A., Martin A. Jr. BS in Mktg. with honors, U. Ill., 1964. CLU. Life underwriter Northwestern Mut. Life Ins. Co., Milw., 1963-85; pres., CEO Martin A. Klingel Interests, Urbana and Houston, 1985-95; pres. Nat. Mini Warehouses, Urbana, 1973-95, K & M Inc., Urbana, 1976-95; bd. dirs. Busey Bank, Urbana, First Busey Corp., Urbana, First Busey Secruities, Inc., Urbana, First Busey Trust & Investment Co., Urbana, Fresh Foods Corp. of Am., Spokane. Mem. U. Ill. Varsity I Men's Assn., U. Ill. Pres.'s Coun. Republican. Presbyterian. Died Sept. 14, 1995.

KLIVINGTON, KENNETH ALBERT, research administrator; b. Cleve., Sept. 23, 1940; s. Albert Cecil and Evelyn Louise (Groom) K.; m. Karen Jensen, Jan. 4, 1968 (div. Sept. 1975); 1 child, Jason; m. Marie Rose Lopez, Nov. 17, 1975. SB, MIT, 1962; MS, Columbia U., 1964; PhD, Yale U., 1967. Asst. rsch. neuroscientist U. Calif., San Diego, 1967-68; dir. R & D Fisher/Jackson Assocs., N.Y.C., 1968-69; vis. rsch. scientist U. Calif., San Diego, 1973; sr. staff officer Nat. Acad. Scis., Washington, 1975-76; program officer & adminstr. Alfred P. Sloan Found., N.Y.C., 1969-81; v.p. R & D, dir. rsch. Electro-Biology, Inc., Fairfield, N.J., 1981-84; asst. to pres. Salk Inst., San Diego, 1984-93; v.p. sci. Fetzer Inst., Kalamazoo, Mich., 1993—; cognitive sci. evaluator The Pew Charitable Trusts, Phila., 1993-94; cons. in field; fellow, chmn. rsch. adv. com. Fetzer Inst., Kalamazoo, 1990-93. Author: Science of Mind, 1989, The Brain, Cognition and Education, 1986; contbr. articles to profl. jours. Mem. Soc. for Neurosci., Cognitive Sci. Soc., Electrochem. Soc., Internat. Brain Rsch. Orgn. Achievements include discovery of evoked resistance shift in brain.

KLOSS, GENE (ALICE GENEVA GLASIER), artist; b. Oakland, Calif., July 27, 1903; d. Herbert P. and Carrie (Hefty) Glasier; m. Phillips Kloss, May 19, 1925. A.B., U. Calif., 1924; student, Calif. Sch. Fine Arts, 1924-25. Illustrator: The Great Kiva (Phillips Kloss), 1980; One-man shows Sandzen Meml. Gallery, Lindsborg, Kans., Albany Inst. History and Art, 1953, Tulsa, Scottsdale, Ariz., Albuquerque, 1956, Findlay Galleries, Chgo., 1957, Mus. N.Mex., 1960, W. Tex. Mus., 1964, Mus. Arts and Scis., Grand Junction, Colo., 1967, Mus. Okla., 1970, Brandywine Galleries, Albuquerque, 1971, Bishop's Gallery, 1972, Gallery A, Taos, N.Mex., 1973, Wichita (Kans.) Art Assn., 1974, Pratt Graphic Center, N.Y.C., 1976—, Muckenthaler Cultural Center, Los Angeles, 1980, Mus. of Tex. Tech U., 1984, Corcoran Gallery, Washington, 1989; exhibited in Three Centuries Art U.S., Paris, 1938; exhibited 3-man show, Pratt Graphic Center, N.Y., 1975; represented in collections, Library Congress, Carnegie Inst., Smithsonian Instn., N.Y. Pub. Library, Met. Mus., Pa. Acad. Fine Arts, Chgo. Art Inst., Corcoran Gallery, Washington, San Francisco Mus., Honolulu Acad. Fine Arts, Dallas Mus., Mus. N.Mex., Tulsa U., Kans. State Coll., Pa. U. John Taylor Arms Meml., Met. Mus., Peabody Mus., Mus. Tokyo, Auchenback Found. for Graphic Arts, San Francisco, Nat. Gallery, U. N.Mex. Mus., Copley Library, La Jolla, Calif., others; executed 1953 membership prints for, Albany Print Club and for Soc. Am. Graphic Artists, gift plate for, Print Makers of Calif., 1956; exhibited with, Audubon Soc., 1955; etcher, painter in oil, watercolor. Recipient Eyre Gold medal Pa. Acad. Fine Arts, 1936; asso. mem. award Calif. Soc. Etchers, 1934; honorarium Cal. Soc. Etchers, 1940, 41, 44; 3d award oils Oakland Art Gallery Ann., 1939; Purchase prize Chgo. Soc. Etchers, 1940; best black and white Tucson Fine Arts Assn., 1941; 1st prize Print Club, Phila., 1944; Purchase prize Library Congress, 1946; 1st prize prints N.Mex. State Fair, 1946; Ann. Exhibit Meriden, Conn., 1947; Open award Calif. Soc. Etchers, 1949-51; Henry B. Shope prize Soc. Am. Etchers, 1951; hon. mention, 1953; 1st prize prints Arts and Crafts Assn., Meriden, Conn., 1951; 1st prize Chgo. Soc. Etchers, 1952; Phila. Sketch Club prize, 1957; Fowler purchase prize Albany Print Club, 1959; purchase prize, 1961; Annoymous prize NAD, 1961. N.A. Mem. NAD, Soc. Am. Graphic Artists, Print Club of Albany, Phila. Water Color Club, MBLS (adv.). Subject of book Gene Kloss Etchings (Phillips Kloss), 1981. Died June 24, 1996.

KNAPP, JOHN MERRILL, educator; b. N.Y.C., May 9, 1914; s. John Harold and Lillian (Merrill) K.; m. Elizabeth-Ann Campbell, Feb. 21, 1944; children—Joan, Phoebe. A.B., Yale, 1936; M.A., Columbia, 1941; Mus.D., Westminster Choir Coll., 1970. Tchr. history Thacher Sch., Ojai, Calif., 1936-38; asst. dir. Yale Glee Club, 1938-39; mem. faculty Princeton U., 1941-42, 46-82, prof. music, 1961-82, dir. Glee Club, 1941-42, 46-52, asst. dean coll., 1955-58, dean, 1961-66. Author: The Magic of Opera, 1972, (with Winton Dean) Handel's Operas 1704-1726, 1987 (Yorkshire Post book award 1988); editor: Selected List of Music for Mens Voices, 1952, (Handel) Amadigi, 1972. Former trustee Hun Sch., Westminster Choir Coll., Hotchkiss Sch. Served with USNR, 1942-46. Recipient Handel prize German Democratic Republic, 1985. Mem. AAUP, various Internat. and Am. musicol. socs., Coll. Music Soc., Halle Händel Soc. (exec. bd., v.p.), Göttingen Handel Soc. (exec. com.). Died Mar. 7, 1993.

KNIGHT, GEORGE LITCH, minister; b. Rockford, Ill., Jan. 2, 1925; s. Bradley Jay and Grace (King) K. BA, Centre Coll. Ky., 1947, DD, 1968; BD, Union Theol. Sem., N.Y.C., 1951. Ordained to ministry Presbyn. Ch., 1951. Asst. min. West Side Presbyn. Ch., Ridgewood, N.J., 1951-56, co-pastor, 1956-57; min. Lafayette Ave. Presbyn. Ch., Bklyn., 1957-67, 68-89, Old 1st Presbyn. Ch., Newark, 1967-68; lectr. in Christian edn., evangelism and music, 1975-95; tchr. New Brunswick (N.J.) Sem., 1957-63, Bibl. Sem., N.Y.C., 1960-63, Union Sem. Sch. Sacred Music, N.Y.C., 1967-71; moderator Presbytery of N.Y.C., 1963; founder Clarence Dickinson Libr. Sacred Music and Art, William Carey Coll., Hattiesburg, Miss., 1970. mem. editorial com.: 1955 Presbyterian Hymnal; contbr. articles to religious jours. Co-founder Clergy Concerned for a Better Ft. Greene, Bklyn., 1964. Fellow Hymn Soc. Am. (founder The Hymn quar.); mem. Am. Guild Handbell Ringers (founder 1954). Died Oct. 6, 1995.

KNISKERN, MAYNARD, editor, writer; b. Schenectady, N.Y., Nov. 5, 1912; s. Henry Parsons and Hermia Loraine (Maynard) K.; m. Ora Lazenby, Oct. 11, 1945. Student, U. Miami, Fla., 1932-33; L.H.D., Wittenberg U., 1970. Free-lance writer, 1933-36, newspaper and mag. editorial writer, 1936-39; editor: Cranston (R.I.) Herald, 1939-42, Springfield (Ohio) Sun, 1946-77. Air ops. officer and combat corr. USNR, 1942-46. Recipient citizenship medal for journalistic activities VFW, 1940. Mem. Pi Delta Epsilon. Anglican. DIED 08/18/97.

KNOEBEL, LEON KENNETH, physiology educator; b. Shamokin, Pa., Dec. 7, 1927; s. Leon Earl and Bertha Mae (Honicker) K.; m. Paula Delphine Hawkins, Oct. 29, 1966. BS, Pa. State U., 1950, MS, 1952; PhD, U. Rochester, 1955. Asst. prof. physiology Ind. U., Indpls., 1955-62, assoc. prof. physiology, 1962-70, prof. physiology, 1970—. Contbr. articles to profl. jours. With U.S. Army, 1946-47. Avocations: gardening, shell collecting.

KNOWLES, MALCOLM SHEPHERD, education educator; b. Livingston, Mont., Aug. 24, 1913; s. Albert Dixon and Marian (Straton) K.; m. Hulda Elisabet Fornell, Aug. 20, 1935; children: Eric Stuart, Barbara Elisabeth Knowles Hartl. A.B., Harvard U., 1934; M.A., U. Chgo., 1949, Ph.D., 1960; D.Sc. (hon.), Lowell Tech. Inst., 1975; D. Pedagogy (hon.), Nat. Coll. Edn., 1984; D. Edn. (hon.), Regis Coll., 1986; D. Adminstrn., Northland Open U., 1986; D. Edn. (hon.), Mont. State U., 1988; LHD, Empire State U., 1991; LHD (hon.), U. N.H., 1992. Dep. adminstr. Nat. Youth Adminstrn. Mass., Boston, Boston, 1935-40; dir. adult edn. YMCA, Boston, 1940-43; dir. USO, Detroit, 1943-44; exec. sec. YMCA, Chgo., 1946-51; exec. dir. Adult Edn. Assn. U.S., Chgo., 1951-59; prof. edn. Boston U., 1959-74; prof. edn. N.C. State U., 1974-79, ret., prof. emeritus, 1979; adj. prof. edn. U. Ark., 1991—; mem. Task Force on Lifelong Edn., UNESCO Inst. Edn., 1972—; dir. Leadership Resources, Inc., 1962-67, Project Assos., Washington, 1967-79, Data Edn., Inc., Waltham, Mass., 1971-74; cons. on tng. Democratic Nat. Com., 1956-60; cons. U.S. Catholic Conf., Mass. Dept. Mental Health, NIMH, Overseas Edn. Fund, Nat. Council Chs., Coll. Bd., Future Directions for a Learning Soc., Girl Scouts U.S.A., U.S. depts. Labor, Justice, Post Office, HEW, Free Univ. Network, Urban League (various schs. and univs., others.). Author: Informal Adult Education, 1950, (with Hulda Knowles) How to Develop Better Leaders, 1955, Introduction to Group Dynamics, 1995, rev., 1973, The Adult Education Movement in the U.S., 1962, Higher Adult Education in the U.S., 1969, The Modern Practice of Adult Education: Andragogy vs. Pedagogy, 2d edit., 1980, The Adult Learner: A Neglected Species, 1973, rev., 1984, Self-directed Learning: A Guide for Learners and Teachers, 1975, A History of Adult Education in the U.S. 1977, Adragogy in Action, 1984, Using Learning Contracts, 1986, The Making of an Adult Educator, 1989, Designs for Adult Learning, 1995; contbr. articles to profl. jours.; host; TV series The Dynamics of Leadership, NET, 1962, And Now We Are People, Group W Network, 1969. Served with USNR, 1944-46. Recipient Delbert Clark award W. Ga. Coll., Carrollton, 1967; Nat. Tng. Labs. Inst. for Applied Behavioral Sci. fellow, 1969—. Mem. ASTD, AAUP, Adult Edn. Assn. U.S., Authors Guild. Died Nov. 27, 1997.

KNOWLTON, CHARLES WILSON, lawyer; b. Columbia, S.C., July 26, 1923; s. Benjamin Almy and Alice Elizabeth (Wilson) K.; m. Mildred Yates Brown, Apr. 9, 1949; children: Charles Wilson, Mildred Yates, Robert Yates, Frank Burkhead. B.A., U. S.C., 1943; LL.B., Harvard U., 1949. Bar: S.C. bar 1949. Individual practice law Columbia, 1949-50; sr. partner firm Boyd, Knowlton, Tate & Finlay (now Sinkler & Boyd), Columbia, 1952—; cons. to joint legis. com. rewriting S.C. Bus. Corp. Act; cons. to joint legis. com. revising S.C. banking laws; lectr. U. S.C.; former chmn. S.C. Supreme Ct. Com. on Character and Fitness; mem. Columbia adv. bd. S.C. Nat. Bank. Contbr. articles to legal jours. Warden, vestryman Trinity Episcopal Ch., 1964-69; mem. Zoning Bd., Columbia, 1955-65; pres. United Way of Midland, 1977, also bd. dirs., com. chmn.; former pres. Crippled Childrens Assn.; former pres., bd. dirs. U. S.C. Ednl. Found.; bd. dirs. Columbia Urban League, Central Carolina Found.; mem. adv. bd. Providence Hosp., U. S.C. Law Sch. Served with USNR, 1943-46, 51-52. Recipient Algernon Sydney Sullivan award U. S.C., 1967; recipient Disting. Service award U. S.C. Ednl. Found., 1982. Mem. Internat. Bar Assn., Am. Bar Assn. (banking law com.), S.C. Bar Assn. (former chmn., mem. exec. com., former chmn. com. on ethics and profl. responsibility, DuRant award for Disting. Pub. Service), Richland County Bar Assn. (former pres.), Am. Coll. Probate Counsel, Am. Judicature Soc., Am. Law Inst., S.C. Law Inst., U.S. Jud. Conf. 4th Circuit, Forest Lake Club, Palmetto Club (former dir.), Columbia Ball Club (former pres.), Tarantella Club (former pres.), Kosmos, The Forum, Phi Beta Kappa.

KNUDTZON, HALVOR, JR., business executive; b. Choteau, Mont., Nov. 20, 1926; s. Halvor and Esther I. (Clearman) K; m. Esther D. Kreuger, Sept. 20, 1947; children: Debrah, David. BA in Acctg., U. Wash., 1949. CPA. Ptnr. Halvor Knudtzon & Assocs., CPA's, 1949-69; contr., sec.-treas. Pay N Pak Stores, Inc., Kent, Wash., 1969-85, also bd. dirs.; exec. v.p. fin., treas., bd. dirs. The Simpson & Fisher Cos., Inc., Seattle, 1986-91, Westminster Lace Ltd., 1986-91, The Yankee Peddler Ltd., 1986-91; mgr. inventory control, ins. coord. Eagle Hardware, Inc.; cons. Kent, Wash., 1992—; also bd. dirs. all cos. With USNR, 1944-46. DIED 09/20/97.

KOCH, WILLIAM HENRY, elementary education educator; b. Denver, Pa., Apr. 13, 1941; s. William A. and Ruth G. (Burd) K.; m. Katie M. Sumler; children: William, Kevin, Yolanda, Erica, Omar. BE, U. Miami, Fla., 1971, MEd, 1974; postgrad., U. Miami, St. Thomas U., Barry U. With Dade County Schs., Miami, 1971-95, acad. excellence tchr., 1985-86, lead tchr., 1987-89; with bur. of professionalization, 1989-91, Saturn coord., 1991-95; apptd. mem. com. of edn. to adv. com. on computer edn. Dept. of Edn., 1990; chmn. sch. based mgmt. Dade County Pub. Schs., 1987, SBM Speaker's Bur., 1988-91; rsch. linker, 1988-90; coord. state sch. G-1, 1989-95. Del. AFT, Washington, 1980-95, Fla. Nat. Conv., Miami, 1987, Tiger Cope Polit. Conv., Miami, 1988. Named Tchr. of Yr., Coun. Math. Tchrs., 1983. Mem. United Tchrs. of Dade County (County Computer Teacher of Yr. 1988), Svc. award 1978-95), Fla. Reading Assn., Phi Delta Kappa. Democrat. Avocations: genelogy, traveling. Home: Miami Fla. Died Sept. 5, 1995.

KOELLE, GEORGE BRAMPTON, university pharmacologist, educator; b. Phila., Oct. 8, 1918; s. Frederick Christian and Emily Mary (Brampton) K.; m. Winifred Jean Angenent, Feb. 6, 1954; children: Peter Brampton, William Angenent, Jonathan Stuart. BS, Phila. Coll. Pharmacy and Sci., 1939, DS (hon.), 1965; PhD, U. Pa., 1946; MD, Johns Hopkins U., 1950; Dr. Med. (hon.), U. Zurich, Switzerland, 1972. Bio-assayist LaWall & Harrisson, 1939-42; asst. prof. pharmacology Coll. Phys. and Surg., Columbia U., 1950-52; prof. pharmacology Grad. Sch. Medicine, U. Pa., 1952-59; chmn. dept. physiology and pharmacology, dean Grad. Sch. Medicine U. Pa., 1957-59, chmn. dept. pharmacology Med. Sch., 1959-81, disting. prof., 1981—; spl. lectr. U. London, 1961; vis. lectr. U. Brazil, 1962, Polish Acad. Scis., 1979; vis. prof., Guggenheim fellow U. Lausanne, 1963-64; vis. prof. pharmacology, chmn. dept. Pahlavi U., Shiraz, Iran, 1969-70; cons. McNeil Labs., 1951-66, Phila. Gen. Hosp., 1953-65, Valley Forge Army Hosp., 1954-71, Army Chem. Corps, 1956-60, Phila. Naval Hosp., 1957-65; vis. lectr. pharmacology Phila. Coll. Pharmacy and Sci., 1955-57; vis. prof. Mahidol U., Bangkok, Thailand, 1978; Mem. pharmacology study sect. USPHS, 1958-62, chmn. pharmacology study sect., 1965-68; sec. gen. Internat. Union of Pharmacology, 1966-69, v.p., 1969-72; mem. bd. sci. Counselors Nat. Heart Inst., NIH, USPHS, 1960-64, mem. nat. adv. neurol. diseases and stroke council, 1970-75; mem. com. on toxicology NIH, 1996. Assoc. editor: Remington's Practice of Pharmacy, 1951; mem. editorial bd. Pharmacol. Revs, 1955-63; chmn., 1959-62; hon. editorial adv. bd. Biochem. Pharmacology, 1958-72; editorial adv. bd. Internat. Jour. Neurosci, 1970-75; editorial com. Ann. Rev. Pharmacology, 1959-65; editorial bd. Internat. Ency. Pharmacology and Therapeutics; editor: Cholinesterases and Anticholinestrerase Agents, 1963; contbr. articles on pharmacology to profl. jours. Trustee Phila. Coll. Pharmacy and Sci., Found. for Vascular-Hypertension Research; mem. bd. mgrs. Wistar Inst. Served to 1st lt. Med. Adminstrn. Corps AUS, 1942-46. Recipient Abel prize in pharmacology Am. Soc. Pharmacology and Exptl. Therapeutics, 1950; Travel award XVIIIth Internat. Physiol. Congress, Copenhagen; Borden undergrad. research award, 1950; U. Turku Meml. medal, 1972; U. Helsinki Meml. medal, 1984; Sr. Internat. fellow CNRS, Ecole Normale Superieure, Paris, 1986-87. Fellow AAAS (v.p. 1971), N.Y. Acad. Scis., Am. Coll. Clin. Pharmacology (hon.); mem. NAS (del. to USSR 1989), Am. Soc. Pharmacology and Exptl. Therapeutics (pres. 1965-66, plenary lectr. 1981, Torald Sollmann award 1990), Histochem. Soc., Harvey Soc., Soc. Biol. Psychiatry, John Morgan Soc., Sydenham Coterie, Sons Copper Beeches, Brit. Pharmacol. Soc., Biol. Soc. Chile (hon.), Internat. Neurochem. Soc., Soc. for Neurosci., Pharmacol. Soc. Peru (hon.), Pharmacol. Soc. Japan (hon.), Shakespeare Soc. Phila., Sigma Xi, Alpha Omega Alpha. Died Feb. 1, 1997.

KOENIG, GOTTLIEB, mechanical engineering educator; b. Gottschee, Yugoslavia, Apr. 14, 1940; came to U.S., 1952; s. Ernst and Aloisia (Kump) K.; m. Berta Poje, June 25, 1966; children: Robert G., Elizabeth A. BSME, The Cooper Union, 1967; MSME, NYU, 1968, PhD, 1976. Lic. profl. engr., N.Y. Prof. aircraft design Acad. Aeronautics, Flushing, N.Y., 1960-67; chmn. aircraft design dept. Acad. Aeronautics, Flushing, 1970-73, chmn. techs. dept., 1973-76, assoc. dean acad. affairs, 1976-82; prof., chmn. dept. mech. and indsl. engring. N.Y. Inst. Tech., Old Westbury, N.Y., 1982—; adj. asst. prof. SUNY-Maritime Coll., Bronx, 1976-82; accreditation vis. Accrediting Bd. for Engring. and Tech. for AIAA Tech., 1989—. Contbr. articles to Profl. Jour. Proceedings. Recipient Cooper Union Alumni award The Cooper Union, 1967, Nat. Def. Edn. Act fellowship NYU, 1967-70. Mem. AIAA, ASME, Am. Soc. for Engring. Edn., Soc. Automotive Engrs. Roman Catholic. DIED 08/17/97. .

KOH, PUN KIEN, retired educator, metallurgist, consultant; b. Shanghai, People's Republic China, Jan. 31, 1914; came to U.S., 1936, naturalized, 1949; s. Tse-Zan and Shun-Pao (Wang) K.; m. Jean Sie, Jan. 24, 1940; children: Robert, Jessica Koh Lewis. BSME, Nat. Chiao-Tung U., Shanghai, 1935; DSc in Phys. Metallurgy, MIT, 1939. Rsch. fellow Engring. Inst., Academia Sinica, Kumming, Yunan, People's Republic China, 1940-43; rsch. assoc. with rank asst. prof. dept. metallurgy MIT, Cambridge, 1943-45; head materials rsch. Engring. Rsch. Labs. Standard Oil Co. (Ind.), Whiting and Chgo., 1945-60; assoc. dir. rsch. Allegheny Ludlum Steel Corp., Brackenridge, Pa., 1960-66; rsch. engr. Homer Labs., Bethlehem (Pa.) Steel Corp., 1966-81; prof. mech. engring. Tex. Tech U., Lubbock, 1966-81; tech. advisor Metal Industries Rsch. Inst. Ministry Econ. Affairs, Taiwan, Republic of China, 1981-89; cons. nuclear power dept. Taiwan Power Co., 1981-85; metall. cons. cen. elec. works Ministry Econ. Affairs, Kumming, 1971-73; adj. prof. mech. engring. Tsing-Hua U., Taiwan, 1941-43; cons. on noise pollution control China Petroleum Corp., Taiwan, 1978-85; cons. China Caprolactum (Nylon 6) Corp., Maoli, Rep. of China, 1973-78, China Copper and Gold Mining and Refining Corp., Taiwan, 1976-80. Contbr. articles to profl. jours. Fellow Am. Inst. Chemists, N.Y. Acad. Scis.; mem. AIME, ASTM, Am. Soc. Metals, Electron Microscopic Soc. Am. (sec. Phila. chpt. 1964), Sigma Xi. Republican. Achievements include successfully setting the pilot production of popular hydrogenation catalyst, namely, pyrophoric and non-pyrophoric grades of powdered Raney Nickel catalysts; started to recycle pig waste by using E-coli bacteria in the activated sludge arobic process and found that this processfor treating biomass can be further accomplished through future improvement in the better choice of bacteria for the mitosis and the additional use of proper enzymes and catalysts. DIED 12/06/94. .

KOHL, JOHN CLAYTON, emeritus civil engineering educator; b. N.Y.C., June 22, 1908; s. Clayton C. and Margaret (Williams) K.; m. Gladys V. Mitchell, July 10, 1935; children: John Clayton, Atlee Mitchell. Student, Oberlin Coll., 1925-27; B.S.E., U. Mich., 1929; M.A. (hon.), U. Pa., 1973. Registered profl. engr., Pa. With Cin. Union Terminal Co., 1929-30; mem. faculty Carnegie Inst. Tech., 1930-37; with Pitts. Plate Glass Co. and subs. Pitts. Corning Corp., 1937-46; prof. civil engring., dir. Transp. Inst., U. Mich., 1946-66; on leave as asst. adminstr. HHFA, 1961-66; exec. v.p. Am. Transit Assn., Washington, 1966; exec. sec., div. engring. Nat. Acad. Scis.-NRC, 1966-68; sr. asso. Wilbur Smith & Assos., Washington, 1968-70; commr. N.J. Dept. Transp., 1970-74; prof. civil and urban engring. U. Pa., Phila., 1974-76; prof. emeritus U. Pa., 1976-93; Trustee Phila., Balt. and Washington, and Del. railroads, 1974-78; sr. vis. fellow Princeton U., 1976-81. Author: (with Atlee M. Kohl) The Smart Way to Buy a Business, 1986; sr. assoc. editor Woodland Pubs., 1986-88; contbr. articles to profl. jours. Mem. Mich. Commn. Intergovtl. Relations, 1954-58; vice chmn. truck adv. bd. Mich. Pub. Service Commn., 1957-61; mem. Tristate Transp. Commn. N.Y., 1961-66, 70-74, chmn., 1970-71; mem. Delaware Valley Regional Planning Commn., Phila., 1970-74, vice chmn., 1973; chmn. Govs. Transp. Com., 1970-73; mem. transp. research adv. com. Dept. Agr., 1957-61; mem. Pres.'s Policy Adv. Com. for D.C., 1963-66; exec. com., chmn. transp. com. Delaware Valley Council, 1976-79; exec. com., co-chmn. transp. com. Penjerdel Council, 1979-82. Served to lt. USNR, 1944-45. Recipient Distinguished Faculty award U. Mich., 1961. Mem. ASCE (pres. Mich. 1956, Civil Govt. award 1979), Am. Soc. Transp. and Logistics (founder mem.), Transp. Research Forum, Transp. Research Bd. (asso.), Tau Beta Pi, Phi Kappa Phi, Chi Epsilon. Home: Irving Tex. Died Mar. 18, 1993; buried Sparkman-Hillcrest Cemetery, Dallas, Tex.

KOHLMEYER, IDA RITTENBERG, artist; b. New Orleans, Nov. 3, 1912; d. Joseph and Rebecca (Baron) Rittenberg; m. Hugh Bernard Kohlmeyer, Mar. 15, 1934; children: Jane Louise (Mrs. Henry Lowentritt), Jo Ellen (Mrs. Raoul Bezou). B.A., Tulane U., 1933, M.F.A., 1956; student, Hans Hofmann Sch. Art, Provincetown, R.I., 1956. mem. faculty art dept. Newcomb Coll., Tulane U., New Orleans, 1956-64; vis. asso. prof. fine arts La. State U., New Orleans, 1973-74. One-man shows include Delgado Mus. Art, New Orleans, 1956, 66, 67, 74, Tulane U., 1959, 64, 85, Sheldon Meml. Art Gallery, Lincoln, Nebr., 1967, Marion Koogler McNay Art Inst., San Antonio, 1968, Ft. Wayne (Ind.) Mus. Art, 1968, High Mus. Art, Atlanta, 1972, Mary Ryan Gallery, N.Y.C., Arthur Roger Gallery, New Orleans; traveling retrospective: Mint Mus., Charlotte, N.C., Cheekwood Mus. Art, Nashville, Tenn., Okla. Art Ctr., Ft. Wayne Mus. Art, Montgomery Mus. Art, New Orleans Mus. Art, 1983-85, Columbus Mus. Arts and Scis., Ga., 1984, Tucson Mus. Art, 1986, Contemporary Art Ctr., Cin., 1987, Ashville Mus. of Art, N.C., 1994; exhibited in group shows, Wooster Art Mus., Bertha Schaeffer Gallery, N.Y.C., Harvard U., Yale U., Toledo Mus. Fine Arts, Cleve. Inst. Art, Denver Art Mus., Va. Mus. Arts, Richmond, La Jolla (Calif.) Mus. Art, Moore Coll. Art, Phila., Pratt Graphics Center, N.Y.C., Ft. Worth Art Mus., La Jolla Mus. Contemporary Art, Painting in the South: Va. Mus., Tucson Mus. of Art, 1988, Art Mus. S.E. Tex., Beaumont, 1990, Morris Mus. Art, Augusta, Ga., 1996, Springfield (Md.) Mus., 1996, Mobile (Ala.) Mus. Art, 1997, Longue View Gardens, New Orleans, 1997; represented in permanent collections, New Orleans Mus. Art, Rochester Meml. Art Gallery, Rochester, N.Y., Addison Gallery Am. Art, Phillips Acad., Andover, Mass., Okla. Art Center, Oklahoma City, Columbus (Ga.) Mus. Art, Jewish Mus., N.Y.C., Met. Mus. Art, N.Y.C., Tyler (Tex.) Art Inst. Centro-Artistico, Baranquilla, Colombia, Mus. Fine Arts, Houston, High Mus. Art, Atlanta, Sheldon Meml. Art Gallery, Lincoln, Nebr., Ind. State U., Terre Haute, Nat. Collection Fine Arts, Washington, Emory U., Atlanta, Marion Koogler McNay Art Inst., San Antonio, Corcoran Gallery Art, Washington, Birmingham (Ala.) Mus. Art, Milw. Art Center, Hunter Mus. Art, Chattanooga, Ill., State U., Normal-Bloomington, Nat. Mus. of Women in the Arts, Washington, San Francisco Mus. Modern Art, Bklyn. Mus., Mint Mus. Art, Charlotte, N.C., Asheville Art Mus. Recipient award Artists's Ann., New Orleans Mus. Art, 1957, 58, 60, 65, 73, Mayor's Art award, New Orleans, 1984, Governor's Art award, La., 1992, First Annual Strength in Age award, La. Geriatric Ctr., 1992, Outstanding Achievement in Visual Arts award Nat. Women's Caucus for Art, 1980; Chautauqua Nat. Exhbn. award, 1962, 28th Corcoran Biennial Am. Art award, Washington, 1963, 67, Artists Ann. award High Mus. Art, Atlanta, 1963, 66; named Woman of Distinction Birmingham-So. U., 1995. Died Jan. 24, 1997.

KOHN, GERHARD, psychologist, educator; b. Neisse, Germany, Nov. 18, 1921; s. Erich and Marie (Prager) K.; m. Irena M. Billinger, Feb. 9, 1947; children: Mary, Eric. B.S., Northwestern U., 1948, M.A., 1949, Ph.D., 1952; postgrad. U. So. Calif., 1960. Diplomate Am. Bd. Forensic Examiners (fellow), forensic psychology. Instr., Northwestern U., 1947-49; instr., counselor, dir. pub. relations Kendall Coll., Evanston, Ill., 1947-51; psychologist, counselor Jewish Vocat. Services, Los Angeles, 1951-53, Long Beach Unified Sch. Dist., Calif., 1953-61; instr. Long Beach City Coll., 1955-61; asst. prof. psychology Long Beach State U., 1955-56; counselor, instr. Santa Ana Coll., Calif., 1961-65; prof. Calif. State U., Fullerton, 1971-72; lectr. Orange Coast Coll., 1972-75; asst. clin. prof. psychiatry U. Calif.-Irvine; dir. Reading Devel. Ctr., Long Beach, 1958-88, Gerhard Kohn Sch. Ednl. Therapy, 1967-85; exec. dir. Young Horizons; pvt. practice psychology, 1958—; for juvenile diversion program Long Beach Area, 1982—; cons. HEW, Bur. Hearing and Appeals, Social Security Adminstrn., Long Beach/Orange County B'nai B'rith Career and Counseling Svcs. (cons. to Long Beach Coun.), Long Beach Coun. of Parent Coop. Nursery Sch., Orange County Headstart, Orange County Coop. Pre-Schs.; mem. police complaint commn. City of Long Beach; commr. Long Beach Coalition Police Complaint Commn. With AUS, 1942-47. Mem. NEA, Am. Pers. and Guidance Assn., Nat. Vocat. Guidance Assn., Am. Psychol. Assn., Calif. Psychol. Assn. (dir. 1976-79, 91-94, sec. 1980-81), Orange County Psychol. Assn. (dir., pres. 1974), Long Beach Psychol. Assn. (pres. 1985, 86, 93, 94, 95, sec. 1989, treas. 1991, chmn. govtl. affairs com., dir. 1996), L.A. County Psychol. Assn. (treas., sec.), Calif. Assn. Sch. Psychologists, Elks, Kiwanis, Phi Delta Kappa, Psi Chi.

KOHN, HENRY IRVING, radiologist, educator; b. N.Y.C., Aug. 19, 1909; s. Washington Irving and Fanny (Brownstein) K.; m. Linda Hansen, Oct. 22, 1961; children: Mari Annabel, Lars Sebastian. A.B., Dartmouth Coll., 1930; Ph.D. in Gen. Physiology, Harvard U., 1935, M.D., 1946. Diplomate Am. Bd. Radiology (therapy). Traveling fellow Gen. Edn. Bd. at univs., Stockholm and Cambridge, Eng., 1935-37; instr., then asst. prof. physiology and pharmacology Duke Med. Sch., 1937-43; intern Bellvue Hosp., N.Y.C., 1946-47; commd. officer USPHS; serving successively in Balt., Oak Ridge Nat. Lab. and U. Calif.-San Francisco, 1947-53; clin. prof. exptl. radiology, also research radiologist in radiol. lab. U. Calif.-San Francisco, 1953-63; Alvan T. and Viola D. Fuller-Am. Cancer Soc. prof. radiology Harvard Med. Sch., 1963-68, David W. Gaiser prof. radiation biology, 1968-76, prof. radiation biology, 1976-79, prof. emeritus, 1976—; dir. Center for Human Genetics Harvard Med. Sch. 1971-76, Shields Warren Radiation Lab., New Eng. Deaconess Hosp., 1964-79; mem. ad hoc com. nuclear and alternative energy systems Nat. Acad. Scis., 1975-79; sci. sect. adv. com. biology and med. AEC, 1958-62; cons. UN Sci. Commn. Effects Atomic Radiation, 1957; mem. RBE ad hoc com. Internat. Commn. Radiol. Protection, 1960-61; mem. radiation study sect. NIH, 1965-69; chmn. Bikini Atoll Rehab. Com., 1982-88; referee Rongelap Reassessment Project, 1987-89. Asso. editor: Radiation Research, 1957-61. Mem. Brookline (Mass.) Town Meeting, 1971-81. Mem. Am. Physiol. Soc., Radiation Research Soc. (council 1962-65). Died December, 1996.

KOLCHIN, E. R., mathematician; b. N.Y.C., Apr. 18, 1916; s. Morris and Betty (Steinreich) K.; m. Kate Weil, June 14, 1940; children: Peter R., Ellen. AB, Columbia U., 1937, PhD, 1941. From instr. to prof. math. Columbia U., N.Y.C., 1946-86, prof. emeritus, 1986—, vis. prof. Tchrs. Coll., 1990; vis. prof. Bucknell U., Lewisburg, Pa., 1986-87, Rutgers U., New Brunswick, N.j., 1987-88. Author: Differential Algebra and Algebraic Groups, 1973, Differential Algebraic Groups, 1985; contbr. articles to profl. jours. Lt. USNR, 1943-46, PTO. Fellow Gugenheim Meml. Found., Paris, 1954-55, N.Y.C., 1961-62, NSF, Paris, 1960-61. Fellow AAAS, Am. Acad. Arts and Scis.; mem. Am. Math. Soc. Died Nov. 9, 1991.

KOLIN, ALEXANDER, retired biophysics researcher; b. Odessa, Russia, Mar. 12, 1910; came to U.S., 1934; s. Rudolph and Luba (Gershberg) K.; m. Renée Bourcier, 1951. Student, Inst. Tech. and U. Berlin, Berlin, 1929-33; PhD in Physics, German U. Prague, Czechoslovakia, 1934. Rsch. fellow in biophysics Michael Reese Hosp., Chgo., 1935-37; physicist to hosp. Mt. Sinai Hosp., N.Y.C., 1938-41; rsch. fellow NYU Med. Sch., N.Y.C., 1941-42, asst. prof. physics, 1945; instr. CCNY, 1941-44; instr. Columbia U., N.Y.C., 1944-45, rsch. assoc., 1941-46; assoc. prof. U. Chgo., 1947-56; prof. UCLA 1956-77, prof. emeritus, 1977—. Author: Physics, Its Laws, Ideas, Methods, 1951; inventor electromagnetic flow meter, method of analysis isoelectric focusing, also others; discoverer electromagnetophoresis phenomenon. Recipient John Scott medal City of Phila., 1965, Albert F. Sperry medal Instrument Soc. Am., 1967, Alexander von Humboldt award Fed. Republic Germany, 1977; rsch. grantee Office Naval Rsch., NIH, also others 1954—. Mem. AAAS, Am. Phys. Soc., Am. Physiol Soc., Biophys. Soc., Electrophoresis Soc. (hon. life Founders' award 1980), Sigma Xi (pres. UCLA chpt 1966-67). Avocations: playing violin, chamber music writing, shopwork. DIED 04/21/97. .

KOLIQI, MIKEL CARDINAL, archbishop; b. Shkodre, Albania. Parish priest, vicar general Archdiocese of Shkodre, 1936-91; created and proclaimed cardinal, 1994. Died Jan. 28, 1997.

KOLODNER, IGNACE IZAAK, mathematician, educator; b. Warsaw, Poland, Apr. 12, 1920; came to U.S. 1943, naturalized, 1944; s. Israel and Brucha (Gornostajski) K.; m. Ethel Zelnick, June 10, 1948 (div. 1968) children: Richard David, Paul Robert; m. Dorothy Chiavetta Thomas, Apr. 15, 1968 (div.); 1 child, Eva Maria. Student, U. Nancy, France, 1937-39; diploma in engring., U. Grenoble, France, 1940; PhD, NYU, 1950. Instr. Washington Sq. Coll. NYU, 1949-52; mem. staff Courant Inst. Math. Scis., N.Y.U., 1948-56; instr. Stevens Inst. of Tech., Hoboken, N.J., 1950-53; prof. math. U. N.Mex., 1956-64; prof. math. Carnegie-Mellon U., 1964—, head dept., 1964-71, prof. emeritus, 1991—. Fulbright fellow Universidad de la Republica Montevideo, Uruguay, 1967; Sussman vis. prof. Technion, Haifa, Israel, 1973; adj. prof. U. Pitts., 1973-74 76-77; cons. Lawrence Radiation Lab., U. Calif. Livermore, 1958-67, Sandia Corp., Albuquerque, 1956-66; Vis. mem. Math. Rsch. Ctr. U. Wis., Madison, 1962 Sch. Math. Study Group, Stanford U., 1964, Courant Inst. Math. Scis., NYU, 1969; nat. lectr. Siam, 1960-61 80-83. Author: Integral Equations, Differential Equations and Boundary Value Problems, 1972, Lectures on Calculus in Banach Spaces, 1977, Elements of Analysis 1985, Calculus of One Variable, 1989; contbr. numerous articles to profl. jours. Served with C.E. AUS, 1944-46. NSF grantee, 1957-60, 62-65, 71-78, OOR grantee 1957-61, ONR grantee, 1965-69. Mem. AAUP, Am. Math. Soc., Am. Phys. Soc., Math. Assn. Am., Soc. Indsl. and Applied Math., Soc. Natural Philosophy. Democrat.

KOŁOS, WŁODZIMIERZ, chemistry educator; b. Pinsk, Poland, Sept. 6, 1928; s. Pawel and Elzbieta (Saszko) K.; m. Maria Wozna, Oct. 3, 1952; children: Anna, Robert. MS in Chemistry, U. Poznan, 1951

PhD in Physics, U. Warsaw, 1953; D (hon.), A. Mickiewicz U., 1992. Rsch. asst. U. Poznan (Poland), 1950-51, U. Warsaw (Poland), 1951-53; asst. prof., assoc. prof. Inst. Physical Chemistry, Polish Acad. Scis., Warsaw, 1953-62; prof. U. Warsaw, 1962—. Contbr. over 130 papers to scientific jours. Recipient A. Jurzykowski Found. award, 1986, A.V. Humboldt Found. award, 1994. Mem. Polish Acad. Scis., Polish Chem. Soc. (hon., medal 1974), Internat. Acad. Quantum Molecular Sci. (medal 1968), Acad. Europea.

KONE, RUSSELL JOSEPH, advertising agency executive, film producer; b. Hartford, Conn., Mar. 3, 1929; s. Alfred and Pauline (Glazer) K.; m. Barbara Joan Josephs, Aug. 21, 1955; children: Andrew Scott, Susan Elizabeth. BA, U. Hartford, 1954. Exec. producer Televideo Prodns., Inc., N.Y.C., 1962-73; pres., chief exec. officer Atrium Films, Inc., N.Y.C., 1973-78; v.p. McCann-Erickson, Inc., N.Y.C., 1983-85, William Esty Co. Inc., N.Y.C., 1985-87, Wells, Rich, Greene, Inc., N.Y.C., 1978-83, 87-91; v.p., sr. mgmt. cons. GMA Group, N.Y.C., 1991-95. Capt. USAF, 1948-52, Korea. Recipient trophy Internat. Broadcast awards, 1970, Cleo Advt. awards, 1970. Mem. Dirs. Guild Am. Republican. Jewish. Avocations: flying, photography, skeet shooting, sailing. Home: Ardsley N.Y. Died Mar. 1, 1995.

KONHAUSER, JOSEPH DANIEL EDWARD, mathematics educator; b. Ford City, Pa., Oct. 5, 1924; s. Daniel Stephen and Elizabeth (Salaba) K.; m. Aileen Holz, Aug. 19, 1948; children: Daniel Scott. B.S. in Physics, Pa. State U., 1948; M.A. in Math, 1951, Ph.D., 1963. Instr. dept. math. Pa. State U., 1949-55; sr. engr. HRB-Singer, Inc., State College, Pa., 1955-61; staff mathematician HRB-Singer, Inc., 1961-64; asso. prof. math. U. Minn., 1964-68, asso. dir. coll. geometry project, 1966-68; asso. prof. math. Macalester Coll., St. Paul, 1968-70; prof. Macalester Coll., 1970—. Producer: films Curves of Constant Width, 1966, Equidecomposable Polygons, 1968; editor Pi Mu Epsilon jour., 1984—. Served with USNR, 1944-46.

KOOPMAN, RICHARD, J.W., electrical engineer educator retired; b. St. Louis, June 24, 1905. BS, U. Mo., 1928, PhD, 1942; MS, Yale U., 1933. Samuel C. Sachs. prof. emeritus elec. engring. Washington U., St. Louis, Mo. 1st Samuel C. Sachs Prof. Elec. Engring., St. Louis U., 1972; recipient Disting. Svc. award St. Louis Elec. Bd. Trade, 1973, Faculty award Alumni Assn., Washington U., 1973. Fellow IEEE, (1st Paper prize AIEE, 1937, Award of Honor, St. Louis section, 1982); mem. Engrs. Club of St. Louis (hon. mem. 1972), Tau Beta Pi, Sigma Xi, Etta Kappa Nu. Deceased.

KOPEL, DAVID, psychologist, educator; b. Czestachowa, Poland, Feb. 22, 1910; came to U.S., 1913, naturalized, 1924; s. Joseph and Shandel Mary (Motel) K. B.S., Northwestern U., 1930, MS, 1934, PhD, 1935; postgrad., Wiener Psychoanalytischen Vereinigung, Austria, 1948-49, U. Chgo., 1950-52, Psychoanalytic Psychology Study Group, 1955-70. Diplomate: Am. Bd. Profl. Psychology (clin. psychology). Research and teaching asst. Northwestern U., 1933-34, psychologist, instr., 1934-38; sch. psychologist Evanston (Ill.) Pub. Schs., 1935-37; faculty psychology and edn. Chgo. State U. (formerly Chgo. Tchrs. Coll.), 1938-43, 49—, dir. Grad. Sch., 1954-61, coordinator internat. summer study tours, prof. psychology and edn., 1958-76, emeritus, 1976—; supt. U.S. Dependents Schs. System, Austria, 1946-47; specialist tchr. edn. U.S. Allied Commn., Austria, 1947-49; summer faculty Columbia U., 1938, Alameda (Calif.) Guidance Center, 1941, Ohio State U., 1942, U. Ill., 1950; cons. Gary (Ind.) and Chgo. Pub. Schs., Chgo. Psychol. Inst., Temple Sholom, Chgo., U.S. Dept. Edn.; dir. Northwestern U. Psycho-Edn. Clinic, Chgo., 1950-51; pvt. practice psychotherapy, 1952—. Author: (with Paul A. Witty) Diagnostic Child Study Record and Manual, 1936, Reading and the Educative Process, 1938, Mental Hygiene and Modern Education, 1939; contbr.: Progress in Clin. Psychology, 1953; co-editor Ill. Schs. Jour., 1966-68; contbr. articles to profl. jours. 1st lt. AUS, 1943-46, lt. col. USAR, 1949-63. Decorated Army Commendation medal and campaign ribbons. Fellow APA; mem. Ill. Psychol. Assn. (treas.), Assn. for Humanistic Psychology, AAUP (pres. Chgo. State U. chpt.), Internat. Reading Assn. (pres. Chgo. chpt.), Internat. Soc. Gen. Semantics (pres. Chgo. chpt.), Chgo. Psychol. Assn. (pres.), Psychoanalytic Psychol. Study Group (co-convener, chmn.), Internat. House Assn., U. Chgo. (bd. dirs.). Mem. KAM Isaiah Israel Cong. DIED 10/20/97. .

KORN, WALTER, writer; b. Prague, Czechoslovakia, May 22, 1908; came to U.S., 1950, naturalized, 1956; s. Bernard and Clara (Deutsch) K.; m. Herta Klemperer, Dec. 24, 1933. Dr.Comm., Charles U., Prague, 1938; postgrad. London Sch. Econs., 1949-50; cert. systems and procedures Wayne State U., 1957; cert. polit. sci. New Sch., N.Y.C., 1972-73. Dir. mktg. Kosmos Works, Prague, 1934-39; contract mgr. Cantic Switches, Chester, Eng., 1941-44; dir. UN Relief and Rehab. Adminstrn., U.S. Zone Occupation, Germany, 1945-47; country dir. Orgn. for Rehab. and Tng., Geneva, 1948-49; contract mgr. Royal Metal Mfg. Co., N.Y.C., 1951-55; bus. mgr. J. Cmty. Ctr., Detroit, 1956-59; dir. adminstrn. Am. Joint Distbn. Com., Tel Aviv, 1960-64; exec. asst. Self Help/United Help, N.Y.C., 1965-69; housing mgmt. cons. Exec. Dept. Divsn. Housing and Cmty. Renewal, State N.Y., N.Y.C., 1970-76; lectr. housing for aged and housing fin., 1958-74; lectr. Brit. Allied Council, Liverpool, Eng., 1942-44. Nat. field rep. United Jewish Appeal, 1968—; mem. Vols. for Internat. Tech. Assistance, 1968-71. Capt. Czechoslovakian Army, 1938. Mem. Acad. Polit. Sci., Acad. Polit and Social Sci., Am. Judicature Soc., Amnesty Internat., World Affairs Coun., Princeton Club of N.Y., Commonwealth Club of Calif., Press Club (San Francisco), Masons. Author: On Hobbies, 1936, Earn as You Learn, 1948, Learn As You Earn, 1949, The Brilliant Touch, 1950, Modern Chess Openings, 14th edit., 1997, America's Chess Heritage, 1978, American Chess Art, 1975, Moderne Schach Eroeffnungen I and II, 1968, 91, The Art of Chess Composition, 1995, 2d edit., 1996; contbr. essay on chess to Ency. Britannica, 1974.

KOROLKOVAS, ANDREJUS, pharmaceutical chemistry educator; b. Siauliei, Lithuania, Aug. 27, 1923; arrived in Brazil, 1927; naturalized, 1961; s. Vasilius and Agafija (Semenova) K.; m. Ruzena Maglovsky, Aug. 17, 1944; children: Sonia (dec.), Miriam Mirna. B in Pharmacy-Biochemistry, U. São Paulo, 1961, PhD in Pharmacy-Biochemistry, 1966; postdoctoral, U. Mich., 1969-70. Asst. prof. U. São Paulo, 1962-66, asst. prof. doctor, 1966-70, free-dozent prof., 1970-73, assoc. prof., 1973-80, prof., 1980-96; prof. grad. courses at 4 Brazilian univs., 1971-90, 2 L.Am. univs., 1974-88; cons. FAPESP, CNPq, FINEP, CAPES, 1978-92; mem. Brazilian Pharmacopeia; cons. to 4 Brazilian ministries, 1978-96; referee 4 Brazilian jours., 1972-96. Author: Essentials of Molecular Pharmacology, 1970 (pub. also in Japanese and Portuguese), Grundlagen der molekularen Pharmakologie, 1974, Essentials of Medicinal Chemistry, 1976 (pub. also in Japanese, Spanish, Portuguese, Taiwan), Pharmaceutical Analysis, 1984, Essentials of Medicinal Chemistry, 2 edit., 1988, Guanabara Therapeutic Dictionary, 1994; sci. editor Brazilian jour., 1991-96; contbr. over 250 articles to profl. jours. Vital Brazil medal Instituto Butantan, 1965, John R. Reitemeyer Prize Interam. Press Soc., 1967, ABIFARMA Prize, 1975, J. Reis Sci. Pub. award, 1988. Mem. Am. Chem. Soc. Achievements include synthesis of potential drugs for schistosomiasis, malaria, and Chagas' disease, synthesis of prodrugs of schistosomicidal, antimalarial, and anti-Chagas' disease agents, molecular orbital calculations to elucidate the mechanism of action of some antiparasitic drugs, pharmaceutical analyses of new drugs. Home: São Paulo Brazil Died Mar. 19, 1996.

KOSSMANN, CHARLES EDWARD, cardiologist; b. Brooklyn, N.Y., Apr. 20, 1909; s. Edward and Anna (Seidel) K.; m. Margaret Musgrave, Dec. 28, 1946; children: Michael Musgrave Kossmann, Margaret Olive Kossmann Dunklin. BS, NYU, 1928, MD, 1931, DMS, 1938. Asst. in medicine U. Mich. Sch. of Medicine, Ann Arbor, 1934; asst. in medicine to prof. medicine NYU Sch. of Medicine, N.Y.C., 1934-67; prof. medicine U. Tenn. Coll. of Medicine, Memphis, 1967-76, prof. medicine emeritus, 1976-93; hon. physician to vis. physician Bellevue Hosp. 3rd Med. Div., N.Y.C., 1931-67, cons. physician, 1968-93, NY VA Hosp., 1964-67, Memphis VA Hosp., 1968-88; assoc. attending physician NYU Hosp., 1949-59, attending physician, 1955-67, staff physician, City of Memphis Hosp., 1968-88, cons. physician 1988-93, staff physician U. Tenn. Hosp., Memphis, 1975-91, chief cons. in cardiology Cen. Office VA, Washington, 1951-55; mem. Sci. Adv. bd. Chief Staff USAF, 1952-56; cons. Nat. Heart and Lung Inst. Div. of Regional Med. Programs, Bethesda, 1966-73. Author: Flight Surgeon's Handbook, 1943, History of Electocardiographic Leads, 1988, Long Q-T Interval and Syndromes, 1987, Pericardiocentesis, 1980, Changing Views of Coronary Disease, 1976, Intraventricular Block, 1973, Electrocardiography Standards for Computers, 1970, Heart and Circulation, 1965, Vector Analysis in Acute Intarction, 1963, many others; editor: Flight Surgeon's Reference File, 1945, (with others) Advances in Electrocardiography, 1958; contbr. articles to profl. jours. Col. USAF, 1941-46. Named Disting. scholar St. Andrews Acad., 1980; numerous tng. grants Nat. Heart and Lung Inst., 1952-76. Fellow AMA, Am. Coll. Cardiology, N.Y. Acad. Scis., N.Y. Acad. Medicine; mem. ACP (master 1981), Assn. of Am. Physicians, Am. Heart Assn. (ctrl. com. 1958-60), Am. Soc. for Clin. Investigation, Soc. for Biology and Exptl. Medicine, Sociedad Mexicana de Cardiologica, Assn. U. Cardiologists, Sigma Xi. Died Dec. 27, 1993.

KOTTKE, FREDERICK EDWARD, economics educator; b. Menominee, Mich., Sept. 6, 1926; s. Edward Frederick and M. Marie (Braun) K.; BS, Pepperdine U., 1950; postgrad, U. Wis., 1950-52; MA, U. So. Calif., 1957, PhD, 1960; m. Lillian Dorathy Larson, Aug. 27, 1950; children: Karin Lee, Kurt Edward. Lectr., Pepperdine U., 1952-53; asst. prof. U. So. Calif., 1956-63; assoc. prof. econs., chmn. dept., speaker of gen. faculty Stanislaus State Coll., Calif. State U., Turlock, Calif., 1963-68, prof., also chmn. div. arts and scis., 1968-95, prof. emeritus econs., 1992-95; pres. KK Economic Consultants, Inc.; independent tax adviser, managerial adviser, 1960-95; speaker in field. Chmn., Stanislaus County United Crusade, 1964-65; pres., Stanislaus State Coll. Found., 1972; trustee Emanuel Med. Ctr., 1974-95; v.p. Good Shepherd Lutheran Ch., 1985-89. Served with USNR. 1943-46. Recipient Pologrammatic award Pepperdine Coll., 1952, Outstanding Prof. award Calif. State U., Stanislaus, 1987-88. Haynes Found. Postgrad. Research award U. So. Calif., 1959. Mem. Am., Western econ. assns., Nat. Tax Assn. (com. for fed. taxation 1989-90), Am. Finance Assn., C. of C., Omicron Delta Epsilon. Lodge: Kiwanis. Author: An Economic Analysis of Toll-Highway Finance, 1956, An Economic Analysis of Financing an Interstate Highway System, 1959; contbr. to econ. newsletter. Died Aug. 20, 1995. Home: Turlock Calif.

KOTTMAN, ROY MILTON, college dean; b. Thornton, Iowa, Dec. 22, 1916; s. William D. and Millie J. (Christensen) K.; m. Wanda Lorraine Moorman, Dec. 31, 1941; children: Gary Roy, Robert William, Wayne David, Janet Kay. B.S. in Agr, Iowa State U., 1941, Ph.D., 1952; M.S. in Genetics, U. Wis., 1948; LL.D. (hon.), Coll. of Wooster, 1972. Asst. prof. animal husbandry Iowa State U., 1946-47; grad. research asst. U. Wis., 1947-48; mem. faculty Iowa State U., 1949-58, prof. animal husbandry, asso. dean agr., 1954-58; dean Coll. Agr., Forestry and Home Econs., dir. Agrl. Expt. Sta. W.Va. U., 1958-60; dean Coll. Agr. and Home Econs., Ohio State U.; also dir. Ohio Agrl. Research and Devel. Center, 1960-82; dir. Ohio Coop. Extension Service, 1964-82; v.p. Agrl. Adminstrn., 1982; acting assoc. dir. Nev. Agr. Expt. Sta., 1982-83; dir. BancOhio Corp., 1978-80, Swift Ind. Corp., 1981-85; mem. exec. com. sci. adv. bd. DNA Plant Tech. Corp., 1982-89; cons. to Chancellor Univ. P.R., Mayaguez, 1984-85; devel. officer Coll. Agr., Ohio State U. Devel. Fund, 1985-92. Mem. Ohio Soil and Water Conservation Commn., 1960-82; mem. Central Ohio Water Advisory Council, 1976-82; bd. dirs. Ohio 4-H Found., 1964-82, Farm Film Found., 1973-80; mem. agr. higher edn. projects com. Nat. Sci. Found., 1975-80, Friends NACAA Scholarship Com., 1976-80, Ohio Agrl. Mus. Com., 1977-82, Gov.'s Task Force on Gasohol, 1979-80; trustee Farm Found., 1978-88; v.p. Agrl. Research Inst., 1980-81, hon. life mem., 1983. Recipient FFA Am. Farmer Degree, 1977; named to Ohio Agr. Hall of Fame, 1983. Mem. Ohio Turf Grass Fedn. (hon.), Exec. Order Ohio Commodores, Sigma Xi, Gamma Sigma Delta, Alpha Gamma Sigma (hon.), Alpha Zeta, Phi Kappa Phi, Pi Kappa Phi (future policy com. 1976-80), Phi Zeta (hon.), Delta Theta Sigma (hon.), Alpha Gamma Rho (hon.). Presbyterian. Clubs: Rotary (hon.), Nat. Dairy Shrine. Home: Dublin Ohio Died June 4, 1994; interred Union Cemetery, Columbus, OH.

KOVAC, FREDERICK JAMES, tire company executive; b. Akron, Ohio, Apr. 26, 1930; s. John B. and Mary (Kerlosky) K.; m. Ellen June Cole, June 30, 1963; children: Bradford Cole, J. Bartley. BS in Chemistry, U. Akron, 1952, MS in Polymer Chemistry, 1955, JD, 1962; postgrad., Northwestern U. Bar: Ohio 1962. Mgr. tire reinforcing systems Goodyear Tire and Rubber Co., Akron, 1966-73, mgr. task force on innovation, 1973-75, mgr. retail market strategy, 1975-77; dir. internat. tech. ctr. Goodyear Tire and Rubber Co., Luxembourg, 1977-80; corp. v.p. Goodyear Tire and Rubber Co., Akron, 1980—; bd. dirs. Malaysian Rubber Research Bd. Author: Tire Technology, 1978; contbr. numerous articles to profl. jours.; patentee in field. Named life mem. Automotive Hall Fame, 1985. Fellow; Plastics & Rubber Inst.; mem. ABA, Am. Chem. Soc., Soc. Automotive Engrs., World Future Soc. Republican. DIED 10/29/96. .

KRAEHE, MARY ALICE, retired librarian, educator; b. Mpls., Oct. 1, 1924; d. Laurence and Elizabeth (Folds) Eggleston; m. Enno Edward Kraehe, May 25, 1946; children: Laurence Adams, Claudia. BA, U. Minn., 1945; MS, U. Ky., 1963. Libr. asst. U. Ky. Libr., Lexington, 1956-64; out-of-print libr. U. N.C., Chapel Hill, 1964-68, U. Va. Libr., Charlottesville, 1970-94, asst. prof., 1974-94, African bibliographer, 1976-94; ret., 1994; book reviewer African Book Pub. Record, 1983-95. Author: African Languages, a Guide to the Library Collection of the University of Virginia, rev. edit., 1986. Mem. ALA, LWV, Archives Librs. Com. (sec. exec. bd. 1981-85, vice chmn. 1986-87, chmn. 1987-88). African Studies Assn., Southeastern Regional Seminar African Studies, Coop. Africana Microfilm Project (bd. dirs. 1990-92), Colonial Dames, Kappa Kappa Gamma, Beta Phi Mu. Club: Blue Ridge Swim (sec. 1977-83). Died Aug. 26, 1995; interred Univ. of VA Cemetery. Home: Charlottesville Va.

KRAFCISIN, MICHAEL HARRY, communications executive, consultant; b. Chgo., Mar. 4, 1958; s. Michael John and Josephine Lucy (Szela) K. Student, Loyola U., Chgo., 1976-77. Ops. mgr., programmng cons., rec. engr. The FM 100 Plan, Chgo., 1976-81; ops. mgr., programmng cons. Bonneville Broadcasting System, Palatine, Ill., 1981-84; dir. client svcs. Bonneville Broadcasting System, Northbrook, Ill., 1984-85, 89—; gen. mgr. Stas. WSEX/WCBR-FM, Chgo., 1986-89. Ill. State scholar, 1976.

KRAFT, OTTO FRITZ, investment advisor, artist; b. Elizabeth, N.J., Mar. 13, 1929; s. Otto Kraft and Elizabeth C. (Vadder) Kerken; m. Patricia C. McCabe, Dec. 27, 1952 (div. July 1970); children: Roger, Mitchell, Gregory; m. Jacquelyn Hebert, Sept. 15, 1970 (div. Feb. 6, 1980; children: Jaime Irene, Otto F. II; m. Shirley Meyers Lund, Oct. 24, 1984. BS, Rutgers U.,

1953, postgrad., 1953-54; cert. fin. planner, Coll. for Fin. Planning, Denver, 1994. Cert. fund specialist, v.p., gen. mgr. The Torit Corp., St. Paul, 1965-72; nat. sales mgr. Ulmer Pharm. Co., Mpls., 1963-65; dist. mgr. J. B. Roerig & Co. divsn. Pfizer, Mpla., 1958-63; v.p., gen. mgr. McKesson Co. divsn. Narco, Sylvania, Ohio, 1972-73; CEO, v.p. F&F Koenig Kramer divsn. Dentsply Internat., Cin., 1973-76; group v.p. Dentsply Internat., Haileah, Fla., 1976-79; cons. O. F. Kraft Mgmt., Mpls., 1980-81; v.p. New Hermes Inc., N.Y.C., 1981-83; pres. O. F. Kraft Mgmt. Assoc., Inc., Elizabeth and Edison, N.J., 1983-88; sole prop. O. F. Kraft Fin. Svcs., Tequesta, Fla., 1987—. One man exhbns. include Rue Third Gallery, N.Y.C., Capp Towers Gallery, Mpls., Old Log Theatre Gallery, Excelsion, Minn., Temple of Aaron Fine Arts Gallery, St. Paul, Albert Lea Arts Ctr., Cinderella City Art Gallery, Denver; permanent collection St. Jude Cath. Ch. Treas. Heritage Oaks Homeowners Assn., 1995; mem. Rep. Club, Stuart, Fla., 1992-95, Health Facilities Authority, Martin County, Fla., 1995; mem. bd. trustees Help the Hungry at Home, Blowing Rocks Music Festival, Tequesta, Fla., 1996-97. Mem. Internat. Assn. Fin. Planning (pres. 1995), Inst. Cert. Fin. Planners, Am. Legion, Bonnette Hunting and Fishing Club. Died Sept. 23, 1997.

KRAINIK, ARDIS, opera company executive; b. Manitowoc, Wis., Mar. 8, 1929; d. Arthur Stephen and Clara (Bracken) K. BS cum laude, Northwestern U., 1951, postgrad., 1953-54, DFA (hon.), 1984; LHD (hon.), DePaul U., 1985, Loyola U., 1986, U. Wis., 1986; DFA (hon.), St. Xavier Coll., 1986, Knox Coll., 1987, Columbia Coll., Chgo., 1988, Lake Forest Coll., 1989, Roosevelt U., 1989; LLD (hon.), Albion Coll., 1990; D Mus. Arts (hon.), U. Ill., Chgo., 1990; LHD (hon.), No. Ill. U., 1990; HHD (hon.), Lewis U., 1991; MusD (hon.), Ind. U. N.W., 1992, Barat Coll., 1993; LHD honoris causa, Lawrence U., 1993; DFA (hon.), St. Mary's Coll., 1994. Tchr. drama, pub. speaking Horlick High Sch., Racine, Wis., 1951-53; exec. sec., office mgr. Lyric Opera, Chgo., 1954-59; asst. mgr. Lyric Opera, 1960-75, artistic adminstr., 1975-80, awd. mgr., 1981-97, gen. dir., 1987-97; bd. dirs. No. Trust Co. Trustee Northwestern U., mem. women's bd., mem. adv. coun. Kellogg Sch. Mgmt.; mem. governing bd. Ill. Arts Alliance; bd. dirs. Opera Am.;. Recipient commendator Italian Order Merit, 1983, Ill. Order Lincoln, 1985, Appdt. Rector, 1993, Grand Decoration of Honor in Silver, Republic of Austria, 1994, Alumni Merit award Northwestern U., 1986, award of Achievement Girl Scouts U.S., 1987, Dushkin Svc. award Music Ctr. of North Shore, 1987, Thomas de Gaetani award U.S. Inst. for Theatre Tech., 1990, Bravo award Rosary Coll., 1991, Career Svc. award Arts Mgmt. News Svc., 1992, Edward Moss Martin award Union League Club, 1993, Crystal award Chgo. Drama League, 1994, Exemplary Woman award Women in Charge, 1994, Sara Lee Frontrunner award 1994, Friendship award European Union, 1994, award Abraham Lincoln Ctr., 1995, Women of Achievement award Antidefamation League, 1995, Govt. of France/officier des L'ordre de Arts et Lettres, 1996; named to Crain's Chgo. Bus./Top 100 Business Women in Chgo., 1996, Exec. of Yr., 1990, Tribute to Chgo. Women Honoree Midwest Women's Ctr., 1986, one of Chicagoans of Yr. Boys and Girls Club, 1987. Mem. Ill. Arts Alliance (governing bd.), Internat. Assn. Opera Dirs., Opera Am. (bd. dirs.), Chgo. Hist. Soc. Guild, Northwestern U. Women's Bd., Northwestern U. Assocs., Northwestern U. Kellogg Sch. Mgmt. (adv. coun.), Mortar Bd., Econ. Club (bd. dirs.), Comml. Club (past pres.), Lake Geneva Country Club, Pi Kappa Lambda. Christian Scientist. Died Jan. 18, 1997.

KRAMER, AARON, English educator emeritus, poet, author; b. Bklyn., Dec. 13, 1921; s. Hyman and Mary (Click) K.; m. Katherine Kolodny, Mar. 10, 1942: children: Carol, Laura. BA, Bklyn. Coll., 1941, MA, 1951; PhD, NYU, 1966. Instr. English Adelphi U., L.I., N.Y., 1961-63, asst. prof., 1963-66; lectr. Queens Coll., Flushing, N.Y., 1966-68; assoc. prof. English Dowling Coll., Oakdale, N.Y., 1966-70, prof., 1970-91, prof. emeritus, 1991—. Author or translator: The Glass Mountain, 1946, Poetry and Prose of Heine, 1948, Denmark Vesey, 1952, The Tinderbox, 1954, Serenade, 1957, Tune of the Calliope, 1958, Moses, 1962, Rumshinsky's Hat, 1964, Rilke: Visions of Christ, 1967, The Prophetic Tradition in American Poetry, 1968, Melville's Poetry, 1972, On the Way to Palermo, 1973, The Emperor of Atlantis, 1975, (with Siegfried Mandel) Ingeborg Bachmann: Fifteen Poems, 1976, O Golden Land, 1976, Death Takes a Holiday, 1979, Carousel Parkway, 1980, In Wicked Times, 1983, The Burning Bush, 1983, In the Suburbs, 1986, A Century of Yiddish Poetry, 1989, Indigo, 1991, Border Incident: Selected Poems (in Russian), 1996, Majestic Room (in Bulgarian), 1996; translator, editor: Dora Teitelboim: Selected Poems, 1995, Poetry the Healer, 1973, Life Guidance Through Literature, 1991; editor: On Freedom's Side, 1972; poetry editor: West Hills Rev.; A Walt Whitman Jour. (1978-85); editl. bd. mem. Jour. Poetry Therapy. Recipient award N.Y. State Poetry Day Com., 1954, Reynolds Lyric award Lyric mag., 1961, 69, William Oliver song award William E. Oliver Award Com., 1968, Hart Crane Meml. award Hart Crane and Alice Crane Williams Meml. Fund, 1969, various awards ASCAP, prize Los Altos Filmmaker's Festival, 1965, awards All Nations Poetry Contest Triton coll., 1974, 76, 77, 78, award Young Composer Contest Nat. Fedn. Mus. Clubs, 1976, prize Eugene O'Neill Theater Ctr., 1983, Bklyn. Coll. alumni Lifetime Achievement award, 1996; Meml. Found. Jewish Culture fellow, 1978; NEH grantee, 1993; Poetry in Translation: the Second First Art, a festschrift vol. in honor of Aaron Kramer, 1996. Mem. ASCAP, Assn. Poetry Therapy (exec. bd. 1969-85), Walt Whitman Birthplace Assn. (trustee 1980-85), P.E.N. Am. Ctr., Internat. Acad. Poets, Edna St. Vincent Millay Soc., e.e. cummings Soc. Home: Oakdale N.Y. Died Apr. 7, 1997.

KRAMER, ANDREW W., computer engineer consultant; b. Chgo., Apr. 10, 1893. BSEE, Ill. Inst. Tech., 1916. Cons. editor Tech. Publ. Co. Mem. Am. Nuclear Soc. (spl. award 1975).

KRAMER, RUTH, accountant; b. N.Y.C., June 20, 1925; d. Isidore and Sarah (Heller) Kleiner; m. Paul Kramer, Oct. 27, 1946; children: Stephen David, Lynne Adair. BA, Bklyn. Coll., 1946. Registered pub. acct., N.Y. Tchr. elem. sch. N.Y.C. Bd. Edn., 1946-50; acct. Lichtenstein & Kramer, N.Y.C., Lynbrook, N.Y., 1954; jr. ptnr. Paul Kramer & Co., Lynbrook, 1954-56, ptnr., 1956-65, mng. ptnr., 1965—; cons. Nassau County (N.Y.) Dist. Attys. Office, 1956-65; expert witness acctg. matters Nassau County Grand Juries, 1956-65; bd. dirs. Flinch & Bruns Funeral Home, Inc.; mem. IRS liaison com. Bklyn. Dist., 1965-76; mem. N.Y. State Bd. for Pub. Accountancy, 1982-89. Troop leader Girl Scouts U.S., 1947-48; chmn. Tri-Town sect. Anti Defamation League, 1952-53; active Heart Fund; pres. Lynbrook Women's Rep. Club, 1956-58; treas. Assembly Candidates Campaign Com., 1964; mem. Nassau County Fedn. Rep. Women, Syosset Woodbury Rep. Club. Named Woman in Acctg., local TV channel, 1974. Mem. Nat. Soc. Pub. Accts. (del.), Empire State Assn. Pub. Accts. (Meritorious Service award, 2d v.p., 1975-76, 1st v.p. 1977-78, pres. 1978-79, Pres.'s award, 2d past pres. exec. bd. 1979-80, 1st past pres. exec. bd. 1981-82, pres. Nassau County chpt. 1962-63, 75-76, state bd. dirs. 1980—, Woman of Yr. award 1982), Tax Inst. C.W. Post Coll., Acctg. Inst. C.W. Post Coll. Clubs: Am. Jewish Congress, Lynbrook Pythian Sisters (past chief).

KRANZ, NORMAN, advertising executive; b. Chgo., July 17, 1924; s. Irving and Mollie (Diamond) K.; m. Ruth Shapera, Nov. 4, 1951; children—Roberta Suzanne, Philip Lee. Student, Haverford Coll., 1943-44; B.S. in Journalism, U. Ill., 1948. Advt. prodn. mgr. Kencliffe, Breslich, Chgo., 1948-52; asst. to pres. Delta Advt. Co., Chgo., 1952-57; creative dir. food sales promotion Armour & Co., Chgo., 1957-62; asst. sales promotion mgr. Helene Curtis Industries, Chgo., 1962-64; collateral supr. Compton Advt. Co., Chgo., 1964-65; v.p., assoc. creative dir. J. Walter Thompson Co., Chgo., 1965-90; cons. svc. J. Walter Thompson Co., 1990—. With USAAF, 1943-46. DIED 06/09/96. .

KRANZBERG, MELVIN, history educator; b. St. Louis, Nov. 22, 1917; s. Samuel and Rose (Fitter) K.; married, 1943; children: Steven, John; m. Louise Clark Catlett, 1985. AB, Amherst Coll., 1938; MA, Harvard U., 1939, PhD, 1942; LHD (hon.), Denison U., 1967; LittD (hon.), Newark Coll. Engring., 1968, No. Mich. U., 1972; DEng (hon.), Worcester Poly. Inst., 1981, Colo. Sch. of Mines, 1989; LHD (hon.), Amherst Coll., 1983. Adminstrv. asst. service trades br. OPA, 1941-42; instr. history, tutor Harvard, 1946; instr. humanities Stevens Inst. Tech., 1946-47; asst. prof. history Amherst Coll., 1947-52; mem. faculty Case Western Res. U., 1952-72, prof. history, 1959-72, dir. grad. program history sci. and tech., 1963-72; Callaway prof. history tech. Ga. Inst. Tech., 1972-88, emeritus, 1988—; adj. prof. sem. tech., social change, Columbia U., 1962-72; Harris Found. lectr. Northwestern U., 1970; Mellon lectr. Lehigh U., 1975; mem. tech. assessment panel Nat. Acad. Scis., 1968-69, mem. com. survey materials sci. and engring., 1971-72; chmn. hist. adv. com. NASA, 1967-69, 84-87, mem. nat. adv. council, 1984-87; vice chmn. U.S. Nat. Com. History and Philosophy Sci., 1970-71, chmn., 1972-73; v.p. Internat. Coop. History Tech. Com., Internat. Union History Sci., 1968-89, hon. pres., 1989—; mem. Goddard prize essay com. Nat. Space Club, 1966-74; history com. Am. Inst. Aeros. and Astronautics, 1965-66; mem. hon. com. 1st Internat. Film Festival on Human Environment; U.S. State Dept. specialist, India, 1975, S.E. Asia, 1976, Africa, 1979, W. Ger., 1982; mem. adv. com. program sci., tech. and human values NEH, 1975-77; chmn. adv. panel div. policy research and analysis NSF, also div. sci. resources studies, 1977-80; mem. panel on engring. interactions with soc., NRC, 1983-85; mem. internat. adv. bd. Edelstein Ctr. History and Philosophy of Sci., Tech. and Medicine, Hebrew U., Jerusalem, 1988—; mem. rev. com. Goldwater Scholarship Program Ednl. Testing Svc., 1989—; mem. history adv. panel Lawrence Livermore Nat. Lab., 1992-93; mem. adv. com. Cohen Inst. History and Philosophy of Sci. and Ideas, Tel Aviv U., 1993—. Author: The Siege of Paris, 1870-71, 1951, 1848, A Turning Point, 1959, (with others) By the Sweat of Thy Brow, 1975; Technology in Western Civilization, 2 vols, 1967, Technology and Culture: An Anthology, 1972, Technological Innovation, 1978, Energy and the Way We Live, 1979, Ethics in an Age of Pervasive Technology, 1980, Bridge to the Future: A Centennial Celebration of the Brooklyn Bridge, 1984, Technological Education/Technological Style, 1986, Innovation at the Crossroads between Science and Technology, 1989; co-editor: Monograph Series in History of Technology, 1963-77; editor-in-chief: Technology and Culture Quar. Jour, 1959-81; adv. editor: Knowledge, Sci., Tech. and Human Values, Philosophy of Tech., Technology and History; Studies in Comparative Internat. Development; Engring. Edn.; guest editor Am. Scientist, 1986: contbr. to profl. jours. Trustee Charles Babbage Inst.; hon. trustee Birmingham Hist. Soc., 1993—. Served with AUS, 1943-46. Decorated Bronze Star, Combat Inf. badge, three battle stars; recipient Spl. Rsch. Day citation Case Western Res. U., 1970, Apollo Achievement award NASA, 1969, Spl. Recognition award Am. Indsl. Arts Assn., 1978, Roe medal ASME, 1980, Jabotinsky Centennial medal Israel, 1980, J.D. Bernal award Soc. for Social Studies of Sci., 1991; Melvin Kranzberg Professorship established in his honor Ga. Inst. Tech., 1988; other honors include Vol. 12, Nos. 1-3 Lex et Scientia (Internat. Jour. Law and Sci.) devoted to his 1975 Mellon lectures at Lehigh U., 1976, June 1983 issue dedicated to him jour. Culture Technique by Centre de Recherche sur la Culture Technique, France, book titled In Context: History and the History of Technology--Essays in Honor of Melvin Kranzberg published by Lehigh U. Press, 1989; named to Internat. Acad. History of Sci., 1994. Fellow AAAS (v.p. 1966, sect. chmn. 1978-79, chmn. com. sci. and pub. policy 1978-81), Royal Soc. Arts; mem. Soc. History Tech. (sec. 1958-74, pres. 1983-84, Leonardo da Vinci medal 1968), Soc. French Hist. Studies (v.p. 1959), Czechoslovak Acad. History of Sci. and Tech. (hon. fgn. mem.), Am. Soc. Engring. Education (chmn. humanistic social div. 1957-58, edit. adv. bd. 1987-90, Olmsted award liberal edn. div. 1991), Am. Hist. Assn. (chmn. congl. fellowships com. 1982-83, chmn. AHA-NASA fellowship com. 1985-88), Nat. Assn. Sci., Tech. and Soc. (bd. dirs. 1988-92, hon. life mem. 1992—), Phi Beta Kappa (lectr. 1981-90), Sigma Xi (nat. lectr. 1967, 68, 90, 91, Bicentennial lectr. 1975-77, bd. dirs. 1971-80, nat. exec. bd. 1972-88, pres. 1979-80, sci. and soc. com. 1982-90, long range planning com. 1986-90, guest editor Centennial issue 1989). Died Dec. 6, 1995.

KRASNER, LOUIS, concert violinist; b. Cherkassy, Russia, June 21, 1903; came to U.S., 1908, naturalized, 1914; s. Harry and Sara (Lechovetzky) K.; m. Adrienne Galimir, Oct. 10, 1936; children: Elsa, Vivien, Naomi. Diploma, New Eng. Conservatory Music, 1922, MusD (hon.), 1981; MusD (hon.), Syracuse U., 1986; postgrad. study, Berlin, Paris, Vienna. Hon. prof. Accademia Filarmonica of Bologna, Italy; prof. violin and chamber music Syracuse U., 1949—, now prof. emeritus; faculty mem. Internat. String Congress, 1960-64; now New Eng. Conservatory Music, Boston; emeritus prof. U. Mass., 1981; vis. prof. U. Miami, Coral Gables, 1976; now mem. faculty Tanglewood Music Ctr.; mus. dir. Syracuse Friends Chamber Music; music cons. WCNY-FM (Nat. Pub. Radio); Regent's lectr. U. Cal. at La Jolla, 1971; faculty Inst. Advanced Mus. Studies, Switzerland, 1973; Mem. music panel Nat. Endowment for Arts, 1966—. Condr. U. Symphony Orch., 1955—; participant ann. series chamber music concerts pub. schs., Syracuse; 1st perfomances of: Berg and Schoenberg concertos, others; chmn., editor 1964 string symposium, Berkshire Music Center, Tanglewood, 1963-64; editor: String Problems, Players and Paucity, 1965; concert appearances, Europe and U.S.; soloist with orchs. of Vienna, Rome, Berlin, Paris, London, BBC; appeared with Boston Symphony, N.Y. Philharmonic and others; concertmaster Mpls. Symphony, 1944; recs. Columbia, GM and Continuum records. Recipient R.I. Gov.'s award for excellence in arts, 1968, Samuel Simons Sanford medal Yale U. Sch. Music, 1983, Hist. Recording Record of Yr. award Gramaphone Mag., London, 1991. Mem. Am. String Tchrs. Assn. (founder, past pres. N.Y. chpt., Disting. Svc. award), Internat. Alban Berg Soc. (v.p. 1983, 95), Mass. Cultural Coun. (Commonwealth award Artist category 1995). Home: Newton Mass. Dec. May 4, 1995.

KRASNER, OSCAR JAY, business educator; b. St. Louis, Dec. 3, 1922; s. Benjamin and Rose (Persov) K.; BS in Pub. Adminstrn., Washington U., St. Louis, 1943; MA in Mgmt. with honors, U. Chgo., 1950; MS in Quantitative Bus. Analysis, U. So. Calif., 1965, DBA in Mgmt., 1969; m. Bonnie Kidder, June 4, 1944; children: Bruce Howard, Glenn Evan, Scott Allan, Steve Leland, Michael Shawn, Bettina Jeanine. Mem. staff Exec. Office of Sec., U.S. Dept. Navy, 1944-56; supervising cons. Bus. Research Corp., Chgo., 1956-57; mem. staff flight propulsion div. Gen. Electric Co., Cin., 1957-61, mgr. VTOL project planning, 1959-61; exec. adviser long range planning space div. N.Am. Rockwell Corp., Downey, Calif., 1962-64, dir. tech. resources analysis exec. offices, 1964-70; pres. Solid State Tech. Corp. Calif., 1968-71; prof. mgmt. Pepperdine U., Los Angeles, 1970-92; pres. Rensark Assocs., 1976-92; founder Rsch. Inst. Spl. Entrepreneurs, 1992—. Active community orgns.; mem. nat. adv. bd. Nat. Congress Inventor Orgns., 1983-84; bd. dirs. Long Beach (Calif.) JCC, 1969-70; People-to-People del. to Peoples' Republic China, 1987, Russia, 1991. Served with Anti-Aircraft, AUS, 1942-44. Recipient Edwin M. Appel prize Price-Babson Inst. for Entrepreunrial Edn., 1990. Mem. Am. Acad. Mgmt., MBA Internat. (chmn. 1976-77), AIAA, AAAS, World Future Soc., Beta Gamma Sigma.

KRENSKY, HAROLD, retired retail store executive, investor; b. Boston, Apr. 7, 1912; s. Philip and Katherine (Bladd) K.; m. Adele Falk, July 5, 1936; 1 child, Jane Paula. LL.B., Boston U., 1935; D.H.L., Lab. Inst. Merchandising, 1982. Bar: Mass. 1937. With Hearst Publs., 1935-42; mdse. mgr. R.H. White's, Boston, 1942-47; sr. v.p. charge merchandising and publicity Bloomingdale's, N.Y.C., 1947-59; chmn. bd., mng. dir. Bloomingdale's, 1967-69; exec. v.p. William Filene's Sons Co., Boston, 1960-63; pres. William Filene's Sons Co., 1963-65, chmn. bd., chief exec. officer, 1965-66; v.p. Federated Dept. Stores, Inc., 1965-69, group pres., 1969-71, dir., 1969-82, vice chmn., 1971-73, pres., 1973-80, chmn. exec. com., 1980-82; investor, 1982-94; dir. Data Port Mgmt.; trustee Liberty Asset Mgmt. Co. Trustee Boston U.; bd. dirs. Fashion Inst. Tech. Recipient award Tobe Coburn Sch., 1969, award N.Y. Fashion Designers, 1970, Humanitarian award Nat. Jewish Hosp., 1976, Alumnus award Boston U., 1980. Home: New York N.Y. Died Dec. 25, 1994.

KRESH, PAUL, author, editor; b. N.Y.C., Dec. 3, 1919; s. Samuel and Jean (Feinsilver) K.; m. Florence Werner, Apr. 1, 1940 (div. Oct. 1943). Student, New Coll., Columbia U., 1936-37; B.A., CCNY, 1939. Publicist Nat. Jewish Welfare Bd., 1941-45; publicity dir. Am. ORT Fedn., 1945-46; asst. publicity dir. Coun. Jewish Fedns. and Welfare Funds, 1946-47; writer, publicist Nathan C. Belth Assos., 1947-50; motion picture dir., asst. publicity dir. United Jewish Appeal, 1950-59; pub. relations dir. Union Am. Hebrew Congs., 1959-67; editor Am. Judaism, 1960-67; v.p., rec. dir. Spoken Arts Records, 1967-71; rec. exec. Caedmon Records, 1971-72; pub. relations dir. United Jewish Appeal Greater N.Y., 1972-74; creative dir. United Jewish Appeal-Fedn. Jewish Philanthropies, 1974-81; communications cons., 1981—; dir. Artists and Repertoire in N.Am., Listen for Pleasure, Ltd., 1986-87; publicist, sr. assoc. Richard Cohen Assocs., 1988-90; contbg. editor Jewish Week, 1990—; contbg. editor Am. Record Guide, 1958-61, Stereo Rev., 1961-80; book reviewer Sat. Rev., 1960-70; spoken word commn. White House Record Libr. Commn., 1979—; spoken word critic and music record N.Y. Times, 1973—, Musical Heritage Rev., 1980—, High Fidelity, 1984-89, Musical Am., 1984-88, Ovation mag., 1988-89, Classical Music mag., 1989-91. Author: The Power of the Unknown Citizen, 1968, Isaac Bashevis Singer: The Magician of West 86th Street, 1979, Isaac Bashevis Singer: The Story of a Storyteller, 1984, An American Rhapsody: The Story of George Gershwin, 1988; also critical essays, revs., articles; editor: American Judaism Reader, 1967, Spoken Arts Treasury of 100 Modern American Poets Reading Their Poems, 1969; scriptwiter radio sta. WNYC, 1940-42; dir., scriptwriter weekly radio series Jewish World, 1973-74, World of Jewish Music, 1982-83 (Armstrong award 1982); prodr., host daily radio series The Story Dept., Sta. WQXR-AM, 1989-90; panelist 1st Hearing, 1984—; writer, dir. ednl. filmstrips and spoken-word rec.; prodr., rec. dir. Listening Library: George Orwell-A Portrait in Sound, 1988, Short Stories of Katherine Mansfield, High Spirits by Robertson Davies, Virginia Woolf-A Portrait in Sound, 1989; contbg. editor: Audiofile Mag., 1995—; contbr. articles, cons. on spl. projects Victorian Mag., 1995—. Recipient Ohio State U. award for radio scripts Adventures in Music, 1940, 41, for Adventures in Judaism 1965, 66, 67, 68, Golden Eagle award for film script The Day the Doors Closed, Council Internat. Nontheatrical Events 1965, Chris award Columbus Film Festival for May It Be, 1975, On the Brink of Peace 1980, Bronze medal Internat. TV and Film Festival for Broken Sabbath 1974, Silver medal for Commitment 1976, Armstrong award Ohio state award for Jewish World Radio Series 1975, Emmy award for Outstanding individual craft 1979-80; award Religious Heritage Found., 1968; silver medal Internat. Film and TV Festival, N.Y.C., 1972; award best organizational newspaper Council Jewish Fedns., 1972. Fellow MacDowell Colony-Va. Ctr. for Creative Arts.; mem. Nat. Acad. Rec. Arts and Scis. (v.p., gov.), Nat. Acad. TV Arts and Scis., Am. Soc. Journalists and Authors, Nat. Soc. Lit. and Arts, Authors Guild, P.E.N. Am. Center, Writers Guild Am., Audio Pubs. Assn. (v.p.). Avocations: tropical fish, photography, music. Address: For Estate of Mr. Paul Kresh 520 W 110th St Apt 5A New York NY 10025-2073 Deceased.

KRESS, GEORGE F., packaging company executive; b. Green Bay, Wis., Sept. 15, 1903; s. Frank F. and Louise (Schmidt) K.; m. Marguerite Christensen, Nov. 10, 1926; children—James, Marilyn Kress Swanson, Donald. B.A., U. Wis., 1925. With Green Bay Packaging Inc., 1933—, chmn. bd., 1963-95, hon. chmn., 1995—. Trustee Charitable, Ednl. and Sci. Found. of Wis. Med. Soc.; pres., chmn. bd. Green Bay affiliate Am. Found. Counseling Services, Inc.; mem. Brown County Republican Com. Mem. Ch. of Christ. Clubs: Milw., N.Y. Yacht, Great Lakes Cruising, Mackinac Island Yacht, Sun Valley Ski, Elks. Died Dec. 8, 1997.

KRIEBLE, ROBERT H., corporation executive; b. Worcester, Pa., Aug. 22, 1916; s. Vernon K. and Laura (Cassel) K.; m. Nancy Brayton, Sept. 3, 1939; children: Frederick B., Helen Krieble Fusscas. Student, Haverford Coll., 1935; Ph.D. in Chemistry, Johns Hopkins U., 1939; D.Sc. (hon.), Trinity Coll., Hartford, Conn., 1974. Francis P. Garvin fellow Dept. Chemistry, Johns Hopkins Sch. Higher Edn., 1935-39; research chemist Socony Vacuum Oil Co., 1939-43; various positions with Gen. Electric Co., 1943-56; v.p. Loctite Corp., 1956-64, pres., chief exec. officer, 1964-76, chmn., 1976-80, chmn., chief exec. officer, 1980-86, ret., 1986; pres. Krieble Inst., 1989—. Patentee in field of silicones, anaerobic adhesives and petrochems. via air oxidation. Hon. trustee Johns Hopkins U., Balt.; bd. dirs. Inst. for Polit. Economy, Free Congress Rsch. and Edn. Found., Ronald Reagan Presdl. Found., Hoover Instn., Mont Pelerin Soc., Inst. for Rsch. on the Econs. of Taxation, Citizen's Democracy Corp. (presdl. appointment), Heritage Found.; bd. dirs. Jamestown Found.; adv. bd. dirs. Empower Am.; founding chmn. Krieble Inst. Recipient Comml. Devel. Assn. Honor award, 1974, Am. Eagle award in Pub. Affairs, 1979, Winthrop-Sears medal-Entrepreneur of Yr. Chem. Industry Assn., 1979, Adhesives and Sealants Coun. award, 1982, Freedom award Nat. Fedn. Am. Hungarians, 1990, Ashbrook award Am. Conservative Union and John Ashbrook Ctr. for Pub. Affairs, 1996; 1st recipient Krieble Inst. Freedom and Democracy award, 1991. Mem. Phila. Soc., Univ. Club, Phi Beta Kappa, Sigma Xi. Died May 8, 1997.

KRIMM, MARTIN CHRISTIAN, electrical engineer, educator; b. Shively, Ky., Dec. 15, 1921; s. Martin C. Sr. and E. Verlee (Boling) K.; m. Helenora Magdalyn Schenk, Feb. 11, 1946; children: Marsha Lee, Sharon Cecilia, David Leslie, Timothy Wilson. MSEE, U. Ky., 1962. Contractor Louisville, 1945-50, 56; design engr., cons. Am. Standard Rsch., Louisville, 1954-56; asst. prof. elec. engring. U. Ky., Lexington, 1957-90, VPA prof. emeritus, 1991—; areas of interest include electric power engring. and machines, electrobiology and psychobiocybernetics; profl. witness. Contbr. numerous broad-based articles for engring. edn. to profl. jours. With USN, 1942-45. Mem. AAUP, People's Med. Soc., HALT, Tau Beta Pi, Eta Kappa Nu. Died Sept. 12, 1996.

KRISCH, JOEL, motel executive; b. Roanoke, Va., June 23, 1924; s. Samuel J. and Miriam (Weinstein) K.; m. Nancy Jane Scher, Jan. 2, 1950; children: Kathryn Jane Krisch Oelschlager. Student, Va. Poly. Inst., 1941-43. bd. dirs. Sidney's, Inc., Roanoke. Partner bus. firm Roanoke, 1946-57, exec. officer motel corps., 1957-62; pres. Am. Motor Inns, Inc., Roanoke, 1962-85, Krisch Hotels, Inc., Roanoke, 1985—; dir. Sidney's, Inc., Roanoke, Va. Poly. Inst., State U. Ednl. Found., Airline Passengers Assn., Dallas. Served with AUS, 1943-45. Mem. Roanoke Valley C. of C. (dir.). Jewish. Clubs: Masons (Shriner); Hunting Hills Country (Roanoke); B'nai B'rith. DIED 10/08/95. .

KRIST, PETER CHRISTOPHER, former petroleum company executive; b. Ansonia, Conn., Aug. 23, 1919; s. Nicholas and Mary (Vasil) K.; m. Vede Makarion, Nov. 3, 1946; children—David P., Robert P. A.B. magna cum laude in Psychology, Dartmouth Coll., 1942. Dir. Wage and salary adminstrn. Am. Overseas Airlines, N.Y.C., 1946-47; dir. labor relations Wage and salary adminstrn. Am. Overseas Airlines, 1947-48; labor relations rep. Am. Airlines, Inc., N.Y.C., 1948-51; asst. to v.p. indsl. relations Bendix Corp., N.Y.C., 1951-52; mgr. personnel adminstrn. Bendix Corp., 1952-53; dir. wage and salary adminstrn. Ry. Express Agy. Inc., N.Y.C., 1953-55; dir. personnel adminstrn. Ry. Express Agy. Inc., 1955-60; mgr. employee communications, corp. employee relations dept. Mobil Oil Corp., N.Y.C., 1960-61; employee relations adviser Mobil North and Southeast Europe (Internat. Div.), London, 1961-66; gen. mgr. corp. employee relations dept. Mobil North and Southeast Europe (Internat. Div.), N.Y.C., 1966-69; v.p. employee relations Mobil North and Southeast Europe (Internat. Div.), 1969-77, sr. v.p. employee relations, 1977-84, also dir.; prin. Krist Assocs., 1984—; chmn. Great American Tire Co., Del. Corp., N.Y.C., 1994—. Bd. dirs. Westport-Weston United Way; bd. dirs. at large-ptnr. relations com. United Way of Tri-State, 1960-65; mem. bus. adv. council NAACP Spl. Contbn. Fund, 1971—; mem. commerce and industry council Nat. Urban League, Inc., 1973—; mem. labor mgmt. com. Nat. Council on Alcoholism, 1974—; former bd. dirs. Unemployment Benefits Adv.; bd. dirs., mem. coms. Nat. Soc. to Prevent Blindness; bd. dirs., treas. Citizens Crime Commn. N.Y.C.; Trustee John E. Gray Inst.; Bd. dirs. Regional Plan Assn. Served to maj. AUS, 1942-46. Clubs: Marco Polo, Dartmouth (N.Y.), Yale.

KROGER, WILLIAM SAUL, obstetrician-gynecologist; b. Chgo., Apr. 14, 1906; s. Charles Mandel and Rose (Ziskin) K.; m. Jimmy Louise Burton, Sept. 15, 1952; children: Carol Lynn, Deborah Sue, Lisa Robin, William Saul. B.M., Northwestern U., 1926, M.D., 1930. Cert. Am. Bd. Med. Hypnosis. Intern, St. Francis Hosp., Evanston, Ill., 1930-31; resident in obstetrics and gynecology Chgo. Lying-in-Hosp., 1931-32; instr. dept. gynecology U. Ill. Sch. Medicine, Chgo., 1940-44; asso. prof. gynecology Chgo. Med. Sch., 1950-60; practice medicine specializing in psychiatry, psychosomatic medicine, hypnosis and sex therapy, 1960—; cons. psychiatrist City of Hope, Duarte, Calif.; clin. prof. anesthesiology UCLA Sch. Medicine; lectr. in field; condr. seminars and symposia worldwide; cons. NIMH; cons. FBI. Author: (with S.C. Freed) Psychosomatic Gynecology, 1951, (with E. Bergler) Kinsey's Myth of Female Sexuality, 1954, Childbirth With Hypnosis, 1961, Thanks Doctor, I've Stopped Smoking, 1962, Clinical and Experimental Hypnosis, 1963, rev. edit., 1977, Psychosomatic Obstetrics, Gynecology and Endocrinology, 1960, (with W.D. Fezler) Hypnosis and Behavior Modification: Imagery Conditioning, 1976; former mem. editorial bd. jours. in psychosomatics, hypnosis and sexual behavior.; mem. editorial bd. West Jour. Surg. On-Gyn.; formerly cons. editor Jour. Mental Imagery; adv. editor: Internat. Jour. Clin. and Exptl. Hypnosis. Fellow Am. Psychiat. Assn. (life assoc.); mem. Am. Psychosomatic Soc. Acad. Psychosomatic Medicine (co-founder, past pres., award of merit 1957), Am. Pain Soc., Internat. Soc. Clin. and Exptl. Hypnosis (co-founder, Best Book award 1963, Raginsky award for leadership and achievement in field of hypnosis 1969, 80, award of merit 1958, award of recognition 1987, award 1989), Am. Soc. Clin. Hypnosis (co-founder, past v.p., award 1988), Soc. for Sci. Study Sex (co-founder), Portland Acad. Hypnosis (hon.), Am. Acad. Psychotherapists, Am. Assn. Study of Headache, Internat. Soc. Comp. Med., Inst. Comp. Med. (co-founder). Club: Century West (Los Angeles). Died Dec. 12, 1996.

KRÓWCZYŃSKI, LESZEK, pharmaceutics educator; b. Kraków, Poland, Aug. 8, 1925; s. Stanisław and Maria (Szynalik) K.; m. Halina Siedlanowska, June 5, 1965; 1 child, Anna. M Pharmacy, Jagellonian U., Cracow, Poland, 1949; D Pharmacy, Med. Acad., Cracow, 1950; D Honoris Causa, Med. Acad., Lublin, Poland, 1995. Asst. Jagellonian U., 1945-52; sci. worker Pharm. Inst., Warsaw, Poland, 1952-57, chief dept. pharm. tech., 1957-64; asst. prof. Med. Acad., Lublin, Poland, 1954-57; prof. pharmaceutics and biopharmaceutics Coll. Medicine Jagellonian U., Cracow, 1965-95, prof. emeritus, 1995-96; mem. Commn. for Drug Registration, Warsaw, 1992—; mem. Polish Pharmacopoea Commn., Warsaw, 1969—; mem. sci. coun. Inst. Drug Rsch., Warsaw, 1981-91. Mem. editl. bd. Die Pharmazie, 1989—, Acta Polniae Pharmaceutica, 1958-92, Polish Pharmacy, Farmacja Polska, 1968—; author, editor: Practice of Drug Dispensing, 1970, 4th edit., 1994 (award of Polish Ministry of Health 1978, 92); editor: elements of Clinica Pharmacy, 1982, 2d edit., 1988 (award of Polish Ministry of Health 1983); author: Elements of Pharmaceutical Technology (in Polish), 1979, 3d edit., 1977, Extended-Release Dosage Forms, 1987, Dispensing for Medical Students, 1993. Named to Officer of Cross of Poland Revival Order, 1976; recipient Meritorious Tchr. of Polich People's Republic, 1980. Mem. Polish Acad. Scis. (pres. com. on drug rsch. 1975—), Internat. Pharm. Fedn. (v.p. 1984-92), Hungarian Pharm. Soc. (hon.), Czechoslovak Pharm. Soc. (hon.), German Dem. Republic Pharm. Soc. (hon.), USSR Pharm. Soc. (hon.), Romanian Pharm. Soc. (hon.), Polish Pharm. Soc. (hon.), Bulgarian Pharm. Soc. (hon.). Died July 15, 1996.

KRUCKS, WILLIAM, electronics manufacturing executive; b. Chgo., Dec. 26, 1918; s. William and Florence (Olson) K.; m. Lorraine C. Rauland, Oct. 23, 1947; children: William Norman, Kenneth Rauland. BS, Northwestern U., 1940; postgrad., Loyola U., Chgo., 1941-42. Auditor Benefit Trust Life Ins. Co., Chgo., 1940-42; chief tax acct., asst. to comptroller C.M., St.P.&P. R.R., Chgo., 1942-56; asst. comptroller, dir. taxation, asst. treas. C. & N.W. Ry., Chgo., 1956-58, treas., 1968-75; asst. treas. N.W. Industries, Inc., 1968-72; chmn. bd., chief exec. officer, pres. Rauland-Borg Corp., Skokie, Ill., chmn. bd., pres. Rauland-Borg (Can.) Inc., Mississauga, Ont., Can., 1975-95, R-B Acquisition Corp., Skokie, 1989-95; dir. ATR Mfg. Ltd., Hong Kong, 1986-95. Bd. dirs. Civic Fedn. Chgo. Mem. Am. Electronics Assn., Nat. Tax Assn., Tax Execs. Inst., Ill. C. of C., Internat. Bus. Coun. Mid Am., Tower Club, Exec. Club, Union League Club, Internat. Trade Club. Republican. Congregationalist. Home: Winnetka Ill. Died Sept. 29, 1995.

KRUEGER, ROBERT BLAIR, lawyer; b. Minot, N.D., Dec. 9, 1928; s. Paul Otto and Lila (Morse) K.; m. Virginia Ruth Carmichael, June 3, 1956 (div. 1987); children: Lisa Carmichael, Paula Leah, Robert Blair. A.B., U. Kans., 1949; J.D., U. Mich., 1952; postgrad., U. So. Calif., 1960-65. Bar: Kans. 1952, Calif. 1955, D.C. 1978. Practiced in Los Angeles, 1955-87; assoc. O'Melveny & Myers, 1955-59; ptnr. Nossaman, Krueger & Marsh and predecessor firms, 1961-83, Finley, Kumble, Wagner, Heine, Underberg, Manley, Myerson & Casey, 1983-86; sr. internat. counsel Lewis, D'Amato, Brisbois & Bisgaard, San Diego, 1988-96; adj. prof. natural resource law U. So. Calif. Law Ctr., 1973-83; mem. Govs. Adv. Commn. on Ocean Resources, 1966-68, Calif. Adv. Commn. on Marine and Coastal Resources, 1968-73, chmn., 1970-73; mem. adv. coun. Inst. on Marine Resources, U. Calif., 1966-74; adv. coun. Commn. of the Californias, 1977-91; mem. Nat. Security Coun. Adv. Com. on Law of Sea, 1972-82, chmn. internat. law and rels. subcom., 1972-82; U.S. del. to UN Seabeds Com., 1973, 3d UN Law of Sea Conf., 1974-82; cons. energy and natural resources policy to UN, fgn. govts., UN Ctr. on Transnat. Corps.; vice chmn. Calif. Senate Task Force Waste Mgmt., 1988-89; spl. counsel waste legis. Calif. Senate, 1989-90; mem. exec. bd. Law of Sea Inst., U. Hawaii, 1977-83; mem. Nat. Adv. Com. on Oceans and Atmosphere, 1986-88; fellow U. So. Calif. Inst. Marine and Coastal Studies, 1977-96; mem. policy com. Outer

Continental Shelf Adv. Bd. U.S. Dept. Interior, 1987-89. Author: Study of Outer Continental Shelf Lands of the United States, 1968, The United States and International Oil, 1975, World Petroleum Policies Report, 1981; also articles on energy and natural resources.; Asst. editor: Mich. Law Rev., 1951-52; editor: Los Angeles Bar Bull., 1961-63; bd. editors: Calif. Bar Jour., 1962-68. Mem. com. visitors U. Mich. Law Sch.; charter founder Los Angeles Mus. Contemporary Art. 1st lt. USMCR, 1952-54. Fellow Am. Bar Found.; mem. ABA (chmn. spl. com. on energy law 1979-83, chmn. coord. group on energy law 1983-86), Am. Soc. Internat. Law, San Diego County Bar Assn., Internat. Bar Assn., Marine Corps Mus. Hist. Soc. (bd. dirs.), Barristers Calif. Club, Univ. Club (L.A.), Chancery Club, La Jolla Beach and Tennis Club, Met. Club, Tau Kappa Epsilon, Phi Alpha Delta. Republican. Home: La Canada Flintri Calif. Died Sept. 11, 1996.

KRUGER, HAYES, physical education educator; b. Mt. Vernon, N.Y., Aug. 1, 1924; s. Frederich Wilhelm and Wanda (Manthey) K.; m. Anna Snow, Nov. 29, 1952 (div. June 1973); children: Daniel, Cindy, Kevin; m. Jane Harriet Wine. BS, Springfield (Mass.) Coll., 1950, MPE, 1961. Elem. phys. edn. tchr. West Hartford (Conn.) Pub. Schs., 1950-70; prof., phys. edn. James Madison U., Harrisonburg, Va., 1970—; aquatics dir. Newington, Conn. Parks and Recreation Dept., 1957-67; dir., owner JMV Gymnastics Sch., Harrisonburg, 1972—; cons. Gerstung Publs., Baltimore, 1990—. Author: Movement Education in Physical Education, 1977, Pre-School Teacher's Guide, 1989; inventor swim aid, 1990. With U.S. Army, 1943-46, ETO. Mem. Am. Alliance for Health, Phys. Edn., Recreation and Dance (chmn. elem. phys. edn. 1969). Democrat. Avocations: reading, jogging, swimming. DIED 02/11/96. .

KRUGMAN, SAUL, physician, educator, researcher; b. N.Y.C., Apr. 7, 1911; s. Louis and Rachel (Cohen) K.; m. Sylvia Stern, Feb. 18, 1940; children—Richard David, Carol Lynn. Student, Ohio State U., 1929-32; M.D., Med. Coll. Va., 1939. Intern, then resident Cumberland, Willard Parker and Bellevue hosps., N.Y.C., 1939-41, 46-48; teaching and med. research N.Y. U.-Bellevue Med. Center, 1948-95, asso. prof. pediatrics, 1954-60, prof., 1960-95, chmn. dept., 1960-75; dir. pediatric service Bellevue Hosp., 1960-75, Univ. Hosp., 1960-75; Mem. Commn. Viral Infections, 1960-72; mem. nat. adv. council Nat. Inst. Allergy and Infectious Diseases, 1965-69, chmn. infectious disease adv. com., 1971-73; mem. com. on viral hepatitis NRC, 1973-76; chmn. panel on viral and rickettsial vaccines Bur. Biologies, FDA, 1973-79. Co-author: Infectious diseases of Children, 9th ed., 1985; contbr. more than 200 articles on infectious diseases to med. jours. NIH rsch. fellow, 1948-50; recipient 40-plus awards nat. and internat. including 1st Dr. Albert Sabin award German Social Pediatric Soc. Fellow Am. Acad. Pediatrics; mem. Nat. Acad. Sci. (spl. advisor in infectious diseases to Min. of Health, Taiwan 1980's), Am. Pediatric Soc. (pres. 1972-73), Soc. Pediatric Rsch., N.Y. Acad. Medicine (chmn. pediatric sect. 1960-61, several awards), Am. Epidemiol. Soc., Pediatric Infectious Disease Soc. (awards), Harvey Soc., Assn. Am. Physicians (The Lasker award), Am. Acad. Arts and Scis. (hon.). Achievements include developed first hepatitis B vaccine. Home: New York N.Y. Died Oct. 26, 1995.

KUBELIK, RAFAEL JERONYM, conductor, composer; b. Bychory, Czechoslovakia, June 29, 1914; s. Jan and Marianne (v. Szell) K.; m. Ludmila Bertlova, 1942 (dec. 1961); 1 child, Martin; m. Elsie Jean Morison, 1963. Absolutorium in Composition & Conducting, Prague Conservatoire Music, Czechoslovakia, 1933, Absolutorium in Violin, 1934; D (hon.), Am. Conservatory Music, Chgo., 1952. Conductor Czech Philharm. Orch., Prague, 1936, dir. music, 1941-48; dir. music Nat. Opera, Brno, Czechoslovakia, 1939-41, Chgo. Symphony Orch., 1950-53, Covent Garden Opera, London, 1955-58, Symphony Orch. Bavarian Radio, Munich, 1961-79, Met. Opera, N.Y.C., 1973-74. Compositions include various operas, requiems, symphonies, concertos, songs, music for piano and violin; musical recs. include His Master's Voice, Deutsche Grammophon, Orfeo. Named to Grosses Bundesverdienstkreuz, Fed. Republic of Germany, Bavarian Order of Merit, Chevalier de l'Ordre de Daneborg, Denmark, Comtur Istrucao Publica, Portugal, Commandeur de l'Ordre des Arts et Lettres, France; recipient Gold Karl Amadeus Hartmann medal, Munchen Leuchtet City of Munich, Golden Gustav Mahler medal, Vienna, Mahler medal Bruchner Soc. Am., Bruckner medal Italian Assn. Anton Bruckner, Vienna and Genoa, Golden Carl Nielsen medal, Copenhagen, Medal City of Amsterdam, Golden Key City Cleve. Mem. Bavarian Acad. Fine Arts, London Royal Acad. Music, Royal Swedish Acad. Music. Died Aug. 11, 1996.

KUBLY, HERBERT, author, educator; b. New Glarus, Wis., Apr. 26, 1915; s. Nic H. and Alda (Ott) K.; m. Emily Florence Hill, Oct. 28, 1989; 1 adopted child, Alexander. B.A., U. Wis., 1937. City desk reporter Pitts. Sun-Telegraph, 1937-39, edn. editor, art critic, 1939-42; reporter, feature writer N.Y. Herald-Tribune, 1942-44; critic, music editor Time mag., 1945-47; nat. sec. Dramatists Guild Am., 1947-49; assoc. prof. speech, dir. Playwright's Workshop, U. Ill., 1949-53; lectr. Columbia U., 1962-64, New Sch. Social Research, 1962-64; prof. English San Francisco State Coll., 1964-68; prof. English U. Wis., Parkside, 1969-84, prof. emeritus, 1984-96; restaurant reviewer Wis. Mag., Sunday Milw. Jour., 1969-86. Author: American in Italy, 1955, Easter in Sicily, 1956, Varieties of Love, 1958, Italy, 1961, The Whistling Zone, 1963, Switzerland, 1963, At Large, 1964, Gods and Heroes, 1969, The Duchess of Glover, 1975, Native's Return, 1981, The Parkside Stories, 1985; plays Men to the Sea, 1944, Inherit the Wind, 1946, The Cocoon, 1954, Beautiful Dreamer, 1956, The Virus, 1969, Perpetual Care, 1974; contbr. articles and stories to nat. mags. Recipient Rockefeller grant for creative writing, 1947-48; MacDowell Colony fellow, 1947-48, 56-62; Fulbright grant for study humanities in Italy, 1950-51; Nat. Book award for non-fiction, 1956; U. Wis. citation for Distinguished Service as Playwright, Author, Tchr., 1962; 1st award Wis. Council for Writers, 1970, 76; recipient citation for disting. contbrs. to lit. Wis. State Legislature, 1982. Fellow Wis. Acad. Sci., Arts and Letters (Disting. Contbn., to Lit. award 1982); mem. Edward MacDowell Assn., Authors League Am., Dramatists Guild Am., Wis. Acad. Sci., Arts and Letters, Pi Epsilon Delta, Theta Chi. Democrat. Home: New Glarus Wis. Died Aug. 7, 1996.

KUCINSKI, LEO, musician, educator; b. Warsaw, Poland, June 28, 1904; Came to U.S., 1914, naturalized, 1921.; s. Ludwik and Carrie (Sokolowska) K.; m. Ethel Thompson June 20, 1928 (div. Aug. 1969); 1 child, Lenore; m. Irene Kucinski, Aug. 1972. Student, Juilliard Grad. Sch., 1930-31; MusB, Morningside Coll., 1935, MusD with honors, 1957. Head string dept. Morningside Coll., Sioux City, Iowa, 1925-50; condr. Lincoln (Nebr.) Symphony Orch., 1932-42, Sioux City Symphony Orch., 1935-77; ret., 1979; dir. Mcpl. Band Sioux City, 1929-79; guest condr. Mpls. Symphony, Omaha, El Paso (Tex.), Shreveport (La.), Guadalajara (Mex.), Wayne State, Nebr., Le Mars, Iowa, Can. orchs.; v.p. Am. Symphony Orch. League, 1946-48; violin soloist; cons. in field. Author book on Brahms; contbr. articles to profl. jours. 1st lt AUS, 1942-45. Decorated Bronze Star; recipient Sertoma Disting. Citizen, Outstanding achievement in music award, Iowa Gov.'s Music award, 1973. Mem. Am. Bandmasters Assn., Sioux City Kiwanis (civic award medal), Masons, Elks, Phi Mu Alpha, Phi Beta Mu. Republican. Lutheran. Home: 219 Cook Dr Sioux City IA 51104-4039

KUGELMAN, IRWIN JAY, civil engineering educator; b. Bklyn., Feb. 15, 1937; s. Samuel Solomon and Sylvia (Habas) K.; m. Ruth Lillian Cariski, Aug. 28, 1958; children: Sylvia E., Harold M., Elizabeth A., Maura J. BSCE, Cooper Union U., 1958; SM in Sanitary Engring., MIT, 1960, ScDCE, 1963. Cert. engr.-in-tng., N.Y. Jr. and asst. civil engr. City of N.Y., 1958-59; rsch. asst. MIT, Cambridge, Mass., 1960-61; asst. prof. civil engring. NYU, N.Y.C., 1962-65; rsch. scientist Am. Standard Corp., Piscataway, N.J., 1965-70; rsch. sanitary engr. U.S. EPA, Cin., 1970-82; dir. environ. studies, prof. civil engring. Lehigh U., Bethlehem, Pa., 1982-96, chair dept. civil engring., 1985-94, prof. civil engring., 1982-96; cons. Alexander Potter Assoc., N.Y.C., 1963-64, Hydrotechnic Corp., N.Y.C., 1964-65; bd. dirs. ACT Corp., Allentown, Pa.; mem. environ. engring. peer panel U.S. EPA, 1979-96. Author numerous engring. reports, design manuals; contbr. over 100 articles to tech. jours. Fin. sec., v.p. No. Hills Synagogue, Cin., 1971-81; v.p. Bur. Jewish Edn., Cin., 1975-81. Mem. ASCE (dept. chair coun. 1990-93, Water Environ. Fedn. (asst. chair rsch. com. 1986-91), Am. Water Works Assn., Am. Chem. Soc. Achievements include patents in field. Died Mar. 30, 1996.

KUHNER, ARLENE ELIZABETH, English language educator, reviewer, academic administrator; b. Victoria, B.C., Can., May 1, 1939; d. Theodore Foort and Gladys Virginia (Evans) Huggins; m. Robert Henry Kuhner, Dec. 17, 1971; children: Mary Kathleen, Gwynne Elizabeth, Benjamin David. BA in English, Seattle U., 1960; postgrad., U. Calif., Berkeley, 1960-61; MA in English, U. Wash., 1966, PhD in English, 1978. Editor English dept. U. Wash., Seattle, 1964-66; instr. Seattle U., 1966-69, asst. prof., 1969-72; mem. adj. faculty Anchorage Community Coll., 1972-81, tchr., 1981-87; assoc. prof. U. Alaska, Anchorage, 1987-90, chair women's studies dept., 1989-93, prof., chair English dept., 1990-93, assoc. dean for acad. program & curriculum, prof. English, 1993-96. Contbr. numerous papers to profl. confs. Contbg. mem. Oreg. Shakespeare Festival; nat. assoc. Folger Shakespeare Libr., Washington, 1987-96; ptnr. in conscience Amnesty Internat., 1985-96; bd. dirs. Tudor Community Sch., Anchorage, 1975-77. Woodrow Wilson Found. fellow, 1960; Western State Project grantee, 1986, 87, various others. Mem. MLA, Women's Caucus for Modern Langs., Nat. Coun. Tchrs. of English, Renaissance Soc. Am., Nat. Women's Studies Assn., N.W. Women's Studies Assn., Philos. Assn. of the Pacific Coast, Assn. for Can. Studies in U.S., Marlowe Soc. Am., Margaret Atwood Soc., Phi Kappa Phi. Democrat. Roman Catholic. Avocations: reading, travel. Died July 1, 1996.

KUIPER, NICOLAAS HENDRIK, mathematician, educator; b. Rotterdam, The Netherlands, June 28, 1920; s. Koos and Martha (Kolle) K.; m. Agnete Kramers, June 4, 1947; children: Pieter Nicolaas, Anna Suzanne, Niels Jacob. PhD, U. Leiden, The Netherlands, 1946; Dr. honoris causa, Brown U., 1984. Tchr. Inst. Hogere Burger Sch., Dordrecht, 1942-47; asst. Inst. for Advanced Study, Princeton, N.J., 1947-49; maths. instr. Tech. U., Delft, 1949-50; prof. Agrl. U., Wageningen, 1950-61, U. Amsterdam, 1961-71; dir. Inst. des Hautes Etudes Sci., Bures-sur-Yvette, France, 1971-85, prof., 1985—; internat. mem. consultative com. Internat. Congress Mathematicians, Nice, 1970; mem. exec. com. Internat. Mathematicians' Union, 1970-74. Recipient Netherlands Math. Soc. prize, 1941, Alexander von Humboldt prize, 1986; named Chevalier Légion d'Honneur, 1981, Knight of the Order of the Netherlands Lion, 1985. Avocation: piano. Office: Inst des Hautes Etudes Sci, 35 route de Chartres, Bures-sur-Yvette 91440, France Died, Dec. 1994.

KUPPERMAN, HELEN SLOTNICK, lawyer; b. Boston; d. Morris Louis and Minnie (Kaplan) Slotnick; B.A., Smith Coll.; postgrad. Royal Acad. Dramatic Art, London; J.D., Boston Coll., 1966; m. Robert H. Kupperman, Dec. 23, 1967; 1 dau., Tamara. Bar: Mass. 1966, D.C. 1986. Atty., advisor NASA, Washington, 1966-73, sr. atty., 1973-77, asst. gen. counsel for gen. law, 1977-86, assoc. gen. counsel, 1986, spl. asst. gen. counsel space station, 1986-87, chairperson contract adjustment bd., 1974-87, exec. v.p. Robert H. Kupperman & Assocs. Inc., 1987—; adj. fellow space policy study Ctr. Strategic and Internat. Studies, 1987-88; rep. on U.S. delegation to legal subcommittee of UN Com. on Peaceful Uses of Outer Space, 1977-87. Recipient NASA Sustained Superior Performance award, 1977, Exceptional Service medal, 1983, NASA Ses Bonus, 1980, 85, Space Station Task Force Group Achivement award NASA, 1984. Mem. U.S. Assn. of Internat. Inst. Space Law (sec. 1981, bd. dirs. 1989—), ABA, Fed., Mass., D.C., Boston bar assns., Internat. Women Lawyers Assn., Am. Astronautical Assn. (gen. counsel 1986-87). Jewish. Bus. editor Boston Coll. Indsl. and Comml. Law Rev., 1965-66. Deceased.

KURALT, CHARLES BISHOP, writer, former television news correspondent; b. Wilmington, N.C., Sept. 10, 1934; s. Wallace Hamilton and Ina (Bishop) K.; m. Suzanna Folsom Baird, June 1, 1962; children by previous marriage: Lisa Bowers White, Susan Guthery Bowers. B.A., U. N.C., 1955. Reporter, columnist Charlotte (N.C.) News, 1955-57; writer CBS News, 1957-59, corr., 1959-94; corr., host. CBS News Sunday Morning, 1979-94. Author: To the Top of the World, 1968, Dateline America, 1979, On the Road with Charles Kuralt, 1985, Southerners, 1986, North Carolina Is My Home, 1986, A Life on the Road, 1990, Charles Kuralt's America, 1995. Recipient Ernie Pyle meml. award, 1956, George Foster Peabody broadcasting award, 1969, 76, 80, 13 Emmy awards, 4th estate award Nat. Press Club, 1994, spirit of liberty award People for the American Way, 1994, award DuPont-Columbia, 1995; named to Hall of Fame, Acad. TV Arts and Scis., 1996; named broadcaster of yr. Internat. Radio-TV Soc., 1985.

KUREK, DOLORES BODNAR, physical science and mathematics educator; b. Toledo, Dec. 14, 1935; d. James J. and Veronica Clara (Gorajewski) Bodnar; m. Arnold John Kurek, Aug. 30, 1958; children: Kerry, Darrah, Michele, James, Ursula. BS, Mary Manse Coll., 1958; MEd, U. Toledo, 1968, doctoral candidate. Chemistry, physics and math. tchr. St. Ursula Acad., Toledo, 1961-75; sci. tchr. McAuley H.S., Toledo, 1975-78; chemistry tchr. St. Francis de Sales H.S., Toledo, 1978-83; instr. math. and chemistry Owens Tech. Coll., Toledo, 1980-86; instr. chemistry, physics and astronomy Lourdes Coll., Sylvania, Ohio, 1983-86, assoc. prof. phys. sci., 1986-95; instr. math. U. Toledo, 1986-95; pres., chmn. judging, co-dir. N.W. Dist. Sci. Day, Toledo, 1975-95; regional dir. Women of Sci., Toledo, 1987-95; bd. dirs. Toledo Jr. Sci. Humanities Symposium, Toledo; dir. Copernicus Planetarium, Lourdes Coll., 1990-95; v.p. edn. Tech. Soc. Toledo, 1989-95; pres. Tech. Found. Toledo, 1991-95; dir. field-based earth sci. program for mid. sch. tchrs. grant Ohio Bd. Regents, 1992. Inventee in field; contbr. articles to profl. jours. Mem. Toledo Mus. of Art, 1987-95, Toledo Zool. Soc., 1988-95. Grantee Internat. Conf. on Chem. Edn., 1994; Mary Manse scholar, 1954-58; named One of 100 Women Sci. Exemplars in Ohio, Women in Sci., Engring. and Math. Consortium Ohio, 1988, Woman of Toledo, St. Vincent Med. Ctr., 1988; recipient award for tchg. excellence and campus leadership Sears Roebuck Found., 1991. Mem. Am. Chem. Soc. (James Conant Bryant award 1980, 81), Ohio Acad. Sci. (Acker award 1980), Nat. Sci. Tchrs. Assn., Soc. for Coll. Sci. Tchrs., Am. Assn. Physics Tchrs., Mensa, Astron. Soc. Pacific, Gt. Lakes Planetarium Assn., Phi Delta Kappa (newsletter editor 1984-86). Roman Catholic. Avocations: aerobics, running, crossword puzzles, swimming. Died June 2, 1995.

KURNICK, ALLEN ABRAHAM, retired biochemist, nutritionist; b. Kaunas, Lithuania, Mar. 15, 1921; came to U.S., 1938; s. Harry and Rose (Narver) K.; m. Nita Binder, Sept. 6, 1942 (dec. May 1979); children: Eileen R. Kurnick Laudau, Marc B.; m. Younghi Kim, Apr. 15, 1983; 1 child, Kimberley Kim Joseph. BS, Calif. State U., 1953; MS, Tex. A & M U., 1955, PhD, 1957. Asst. prof. dept. poultry sci. U. Ariz., Tucson, 1957-59, prof., head poultry sci. dept., 1959-62, mem. grad. faculty, 1959-62; mgr. tech. svcs. chem. div. Hoffmann-

LaRoche, Pasadena, Calif., 1962-66; mgr. tech. svcs. chem. div. Hoffmann-LaRoche, Nutley, N.J., 1966-80, gen. mgr., v.p. chem. div., 1980-81, v.p., dir. rsch. nutrition and vitamin divsn., 1981-86; ret., 1986. Contbr. numerous articles to profl. publs. Bd. dirs. Animal Health Inst., Washington, 1977-80, Internat. Poultry Sci. Assn., 1976-8; mem. nutrition coun. Am. Feed Mfrs., 1976. Cpl. USAF, 1943-46. NIH fellow, 1955-57. Fellow AAAS; mem. Am. Chem. Soc., Am. Inst. Nutrition. Avocations: golf, photography, travel. Home: Carlsbad Calif. Died March 21, 1995.

KURTEV, BOGDAN JORDANOV, chemistry educator, researcher; b. Sliven, Bulgaria, June 16, 1917; s. Jordan Stoychev and Ivanka Hadjitodorava (Stancheva) K.; m. Gavrila Dinova Daskalova, July 26, 1959; children: Vanya Bogdanova, Dino Bogdanov. Diploma for Higher Edn. in Chemistry, Sofia U., Bulgaria, 1940; PhD in Scis., Higher Inst. Chem. Tech., Moscow, USSR, 1950. Cert. Organic Chemistry. Asst. prof. Sofia U., Bulgaria, 1940-51, assoc. prof., 1951-61, prof., 1961-74; dir. Inst. Chemistry, Bulgarian Acad. Scis., Sofia, Bulgaria, 1958-60, Inst. Organic Chemistry, Bulgarian Acad. Scis., Sofia, Bulgaria, 1960-88; academician sec. dept. chem. scis. Bulgarian Acad. Scis., Sofia, Bulgaria, 1962-72; v.p. Bulgarian Acad. Scis., Bulgaria, 1971-73; dir. United Ctr. Chem. Scis., Bulgarian Acad. Scis., Sofia, Bulgaria, 1972-88; academician Bulgarian Acad. Scis., Sofia, Bulgaria, 1974—. Contrb. to over 150 profl jours.; patentee 10 inventions; devel. rsch. in chem. sci. for past 30 years. Recipient Kiril i Metodii award Parliament of Bulgaria, 1963, Zaslugil Dejatel na Naukata award State Coun. of Bulgaria, 1970, Naroden Dejatel no Naukata award State Coun. Bulgaria, 1976, Dimitrovska Nagrada award Parliament of Bulgaria, 1982. Mem. Union of Bulgarian Scientists, Assn. Chemists. Bulgarian Socialist Party. Eastern Orthodox. Home: Kompl Iztok, Gagarin 5 Block 5, 1113 Sofia Bulgaria Died Dec. 5, 1995.

KURTZ, SAMUEL MORDECAI, architect; b. Russia, Feb. 21, 1904; came to U.S., 1904, naturalized, 1919; s. Louis and Nadia (Form) K.; m. Mary G. Weisthal, Sept. 3, 1928 (dec. May 21, 1981); children: Gerald Norman, Elliot Robert. Grad. diploma in architecture, Cooper Union Inst., 1925; certificate archtl./engring. design, Columbia U., 1927; certificate, CCNY, 1929, N.Y. U., 1942. Registered architect, N.Y., Fla. Assoc. archtl. firm York & Sawyer, N.Y.C., 1926-47; prin. Samuel M. Kurtz, N.Y.C., 1947-54; assoc. archtl. firm Kiff, Voss & Franklin, N.Y.C., 1954-71; pvt. practice archtl. cons. N. Miami Beach, Fla., 1971; spl. cons. to Charles Giller & Assocs. (Architects), Miami, 1972-76; mem. N.Y.C. Mayor's Panel of Architects, 1950-70; mem. archtl. engring. selection bd. Bd. Higher Edn., N.Y.C., 1968-69; mem. Code Enforcement Bd., City of North Miami Beach, 1982-86; mem. planning and Zoning Bd. City of North Miami Beach, 1986-93. Fellow AIA; mem. N.Y. chpt. AIA (Rutkins award 1966, treas. 1968), S.Fla. chpt. AIA, N.Y. Soc. Architects (pres. 1967-68), N.Y. State Assn. Architects (awarded spl. citation 1968), Am. Arbitration Assn. (nat. panel arbitrators 1950-70). Home: Miami Fla. Died July 15, 1993.

KUTTNER, STEPHAN GEORGE, legal history educator; b. Bonn, Germany, Mar. 24, 1907; s. George and Gertrude Hedwig (Schocken) K.; m. Eva Susanne Illch, Aug. 22, 1933; children: Ludwig, Andrew (dec.), Susanne, Angela, Barbara, Thomas, Michael, Francis, Philip; came to U.S., 1940, naturalized, 1945; LLB, U. Frankfurt, Germany, 1928; JUD, U. Berlin, 1930; SJD (hon.), U. Bologna, Italy, 1952; JCD (hon.), U. Louvain, Belgium, 1955; LLD, Holy Cross Coll., 1956, Loyola Coll., Balt., 1960, LaSalle Coll., Phila., 1962; Hon. Dr., U. Paris, 1959, U. Genoa, 1966, U. Milan, 1967, U. Salamanca, 1968, U. Strasbourg, 1970, U. Montpellier, 1972; LHD, Cath. U. Am., 1972, U. Madrid, 1978; LLD, U. Cambridge, Eng., 1978, Lateran U. Rome, 1989; STD (hon.), Wurzburg, 1982, others. Asst. Sch. Law, U. Berlin, 1929-32; rsch. assoc. Vatican Library, 1934-40, hon. assoc., 1955-96; assoc. prof. Pontifical Inst. Law, Rome, 1937-40; vis. prof. history of canon law Cath. U. Am., Washington, 1940-42, prof., 1942-64; Riggs prof. Roman Cath. studies Yale U., 1964-70, prof. law, 1970-77, prof. law emeritus, 1977-96; dir. Robbins Collection U. Calif.-Berkeley, 1970-89; pres. Inst. Rsch. and Study in Medieval Canon Law, 1955-91, chmn., bd. dirs., 1991-95; Walker Ames prof. history U. Wash., 1949; assoc. mem. All Souls Coll., Oxford, Hilary and Trinity, 1951; chmn. Internat. Congress Medieval Canon Law, Bologna, 1952, Louvain, 1958, Boston, 1963, Strasburg, 1968, Toronto, 1972, Salamanca, 1976, Berkeley, 1980, Cambridge, Eng., 1984; hon. cons. Roman and canon, law Library Congress, 1943-70; mem. Pontifical Commn. for the Revision of the Code of Canon Law, 1967-83, Pontifical Commn. Hist. Scis., 1965-90. Author: Repertorium der Kanonistik, 1937; The History of Doctrines and Ideas of Canon Law in the Middle Ages, 1980, rev. 1992; Medieval Councils, Decretals, and Collections of Canon Law, 1980, rev. 1992; Gratian and the Schools of Law, 1983, Studies in the History of Medieval Canon Law, 1991. Co-founder, editor Traditio, 1943-71; editor Seminar, 1953-56, Monumenta Juris Canonici, 1965-96, Bull. Medieval Canon Law, 1971-95; mem. editorial bd. various Am. and fgn. learned jours. Author monographs, pamphlets, booklets in English and other langs. Guggenheim fellow, 1956, 67; recipient prize for disting. achievement in humanities Am. Council Learned Socs., 1959. Fellow Medieval Acad. Am. (pres. 1974), Am. Acad. Arts and Scis., Am. Philos. Soc.; corr. fellow Acad. Gottingen, Acad. Sci. Bologna, Brit. Acad., Bavarian Acad. Munich, Acad. Lincei Rome, Acad. Lisbon, Royal Hist. Soc., Order Pour le Merite for Arts and Scis., Institut de France; mem. Cath. Hist. Assn. (pres. 1958), Soc. d'Histoire de Droit de Paris, Canon Law Soc. (v.p. 1963), Associazione Internationale di Diritto Canonico (v.p. 1973), Am. Cath. Commn. on Cultural Affairs (chmn. 1963), Phi Beta Kappa. Died Aug. 12, 1996. Home: Berkeley Calif.

KUVSHINOFF, NICOLAI VASILY, painter, sculptor; m. Bertha Horne. Exhibited in group shows at Cimaise de Paris Galerie, 1956, 57, La Galerie Norval, Paris, 1957, Smith Tower Gallery, Seattle, 1960, World's Fair, Seattle, 1962, 63, Wash. Capitol Mus., Olympia, 1965, Cath. Ctr. Art Gallery, Balt., 1967, Kupsick Art Gallery, 1969 and numerous others; represented in permanent collections Seattle Art Mus., Phoenix Art Mus., Santa Fe Art Mus., Tacoma Art Mus., Miami (Fla.) Art Mus. and many others; represented in numerous pub. and pvt. collections in France, Brazil, India, Can., Alaska, Japan, Tangier and U.S.; author: (books) Art Book, 1959, Drawings, 1966. Home: Seattle Wash. Died Mar. 17, 1997.

KVAMME, HELGE, insurance company executive; b. Bergen, Norway, Sept. 4, 1938; s. John K. and Astrid (Clemmentsen) K.; m. Marianne Knoph; children: Fredrik, Anne-Lise. Degree Real Artium, Bergen Katedralskole, 1957; degree Studenfag Diplom, Bergen Handelsgymnasium, 1958; instr. military tng., Military Recruit Sch., 1958-60; JD, Oslo U., 1966. Dep. judge Baerum, 1966; lectr. law faculty Oslo U., 1968; claims mgr. Norges Brannkasse, 1974; dep. mng. dir. Uni Forsikring, Oslo, 1977; dep. mng. dir. Norske Folk and Norge Brannkasse, 1982, pres. pos., 1986; various pos. on bds. of dirs. cos. Contbr. articles to profl. jours. Avocations: being with family, skiing, jogging, cycling, literature. Home: Stavanger Norway Deceased.

KVASIL, BOHUMIL, physicist, academy president; b. Planany, Czechoslovakia, Feb. 14, 1920. Degree, Czech. Tech. U., 1947; prof. Charles U., 1958; academician Czech. Acad. Sci., 1973. Dean, Faculty of Elcktrotech., Czech. Tech. U., Prague, 1954, Faculty of Nuclear Physics and Engring., 1960, rector, 1968; v.p. Czechoslovak Acad. Scis., Prague, 1977; dir. Inst. Physics, Acad. Sci., Prague, 1979; pres. Czechoslovak Acad. Scis., Prague, 1981—. Author: Theoretical Fundamentals of Centimetre Waves-Length Technique, 1957; Fundamentals of Quantum Electronics, 1964; Selected Problems of Radioelectronics, 1969. Mem. Central Com. Comunist Party, 1961; bd. chmn. Central Com. Nat. Front, 1976; rep. Fed. Assembly of Nations, 1971; mem. Govt. Com. for Sci. and Tech. Devel., 1976. Recipient Klement Gottwald State award, 1971; medal of Work Merits, 1975; Gold medal S.I. Vavilov, 1981. Mem. Acad. Sci. USSR, Acad. Sci. Bulgaria, Acad. Sci. German Democratic Republic.

KVINNSLAND, BJARNE, insurance company executive; b. Aakrehamn, Rogaland, Norway; s. Sivert Monrad and Else (Housken) K.; m. Ida Rönnevig, Aug. 20, 1960; children: Bjarne Sivert, Svein, Else Birgitte. BA in Commerce, U. Manchester, Eng., 1959; postgrad., Mercer U., Macon, Ga., 1960. Sales mgr. Thoresen Car Ferries, Southampton, Eng., 1964-68, gen. mgr., 1968-70; gen. mgr. Storebrand, Oslo, Norway, 1970-78; pres. Europeiske Reiseforsikring A/S, Oslo, 1978—; chmn. Euro-Alarm A/S, Copenhagen, 1992—, Euro-Ctr. A/S, Copenhagen, 1985—. Mem. Internat. Assn. European Travel Insurers (pres. 1995—), Kolsås Rotary Club (pres. 1982-83). Died Mar. 8, 1996.

KWIAT, JOSEPH J., English literature and American studies educator; b. N.Y.C.; s. Jacob and Sadie (Miller) K.; m. Janice M. Enger; children: Judith, David. PhB in English, U. Chgo.; MA in English, Northwestern U.; PhD in Am. Studies, U. Minn. Instr. English U. Nebr.; mem. faculty U. Minn., Mpls.; prof. English and Am. studies, adj. prof. comparative lit. and religious studies U. Minn.; co-founding mem. program in Am. studies, U. Minn.; lectr., cons. Am. lit. and Am. studies in U.S., Europe, Middle and Far East; lifetime hon. mem. and mem. U.S. adv. com. Am. Studies Rsch. Ctr., Hyderabad, India; cons. Nat. Endowment for Arts; mem. adv. com., rsch. fellow Am. Coun. Learned Socs.; mem. adv. com. in Am. studies and screening com. in Am. lit. Com. on Internat. Exch. of Persons Conf. Bd., Assn. Rsch. Couns., Fulbright Com.; mem. bd. advisors East Lynne (N.J.) Drama Co.; cons. NEH; Fulbright prof. U. Tübingen, Germany, U. Innsbruck, Austria, U. Stuttgart, Germany; vis. mem. St. Catherine's Coll., Cambridge (Eng.) U.; U.S. Dept. State lectr. and cons. Am. lit. and studies, Japan and India; cons. Am. studies for Am. and fgn. univs. Author: America's Cultural Coming of Age; co-editor: Studies in American Culture, (monograph) Literature and the Other Arts, (MLA monograph) Relations of Literature and Other Arts; editor-in-chief: Series in American Studies; contbr. numerous articles to profl. publs., topics including interrelationships between Am. lit. and other arts, Am. culture and soc., Thoreau, 20th century Am. drama, soc. and fgn. backgrounds, Am. social, intellectual and cultural lit. and thought since 1890, especially tradition of New England Transcendentalism. Served with USAAF, World War II. Recipient disting. teaching awards in U.S. and abroad; research grantee U. Minn. Mem. MLA, AAUP, Fulbright Alumni Assn., Am. Studies Assn., European Assn. Am. Studies, German Soc. Am. Studies, Canadian Assn. Am. Studies, Playwright's Ctr. Died Mar. 3, 1997.

L'ABBÉ, GERRIT KAREL, chemist; b. Oostende, Belgium, Dec. 13, 1940; s. Bertram L'abbé and Marie-Rose Coenegrachts; m. Christianne Platteau, Aug. 17, 1967; children: Annick, Caroline. Lic. in Chemistry with highest honors, U. Leuven, Belgium, 1963; Dr. in Sci., U. Leuven, 1966. Postdoctoral fellow Erlangen, Fed. Republic Germany, 1967-68, Boulder, Colo., 1969-70; docent U. Leuven, 1972-75, prof. chemistry, 1975-77, prof. ordinarius, 1977-96; rsch. dir. U. Leuven, 1972-96. Contbr. 200 articles to profl. jours. Recipient Belgian-BP prize, 1959, P. Bruylants prize Chemici Lovanienses, 1966, bieninial prize Jour. Industrie Chimique Belge, 1968, award Japan Soc. for Promotion Sci., 1979, EuChem award European Cmtys. Chemistry Coun., 1993; Alexander von Humboldt fellow, 1967-68, Fulbright rsch. fellow, 1969-70, fellow Nat. Fund for Sci. Rsch., 1963-72. Fellow Brit. Royal Soc. Chemistry (chartered); mem. Am. Chem. Soc., Internat. Soc. Heterocyclic Chemistry, Belgian Royal Acad. Sci. (J.S. Stas medal 1966, Laureate 1972), Flemish Chem. Soc. (Breckpot prize 1983), Internat. Order of Merit. Died Aug. 27, 1996.

LACHENBRUCH, DAVID, editor, writer; b. New Rochelle, N.Y., Feb. 11, 1921; s. Milton Cleveland and Leah Judith (Herold) L.; m. Gladys Kidwell, Dec. 12, 1941; 1 child, Ann Leah Lachenbruch Zulawski. BA, U. Mich., 1942. Corr. Variety, also Detroit Times, 1940-42; reporter, asst. city editor, then wire editor Gazette & Daily, York, Pa., 1946-50; assoc. editor TV Digest with Consumer Electronics, Washington, 1950-58; mng. editor TV Digest with Consumer Electronics, 1959-68; editorial dir. TV Digest with Consumer Electronics, N.Y.C., 1968—; v.p. Warren Pub., Inc., Washington, 1962—. Adv. editor: Academic American Encyclopedia, 1989—; columnist Electronics Now mag., Video mag.; co-author: The Complete Book of Adult Toys, 1983; contbr. articles to consumer mags.; contbg. editor: N.Y. Times Ency. of TV; author: Videocassette Recorders—The Complete Home Guide, 1978, A Look Inside Television, 1985; cons. Acad. Am. Ency. Served with AUS, 1942-45. Inducted Video Hall of Fame, 1993. Mem. White House Corrs. Assn., Union Internat. de la Presse Electronique. DIED 11/03/96. .

LACHMAN, LAWRENCE, business consultant, former department store executive; b. N.Y.C., Jan. 9, 1916; s. Charles and Dorothy (Rubin) L.; m. Judith Lehman, Apr. 8, 1945; children: Robert Ian, Charles Scott. BS summa cum laude, NYU, 1936. Controller James McCreery & Co., N.Y.C., 1938-46; treas., dir. Citizens Utilities Co., Stamford, Conn., 1946-47; treas. Bloomingdale's, N.Y.C., 1947-53; v.p. personnel and ops. Bloomingdale's, 1953-58, exec. v.p. adminstrn. and personnel, 1958-64, pres., chief exec. officer, 1964-69, chmn. bd., chief exec. officer, 1969-78; chmn. bd., chief exec. officer Bus. Mktg. Corp., 1978-80; bd. dirs. DFS Group Ltd., ADVO, Inc. Trustee NYU, 1974-90. Served to maj. USAAF, 1942-46. Decorated Bronze Star; French Legion of Honor; recipient Madden award N.Y. U., 1969. DIED 10/07/97. .

LADD, DAVID LOWELL, government official, lawyer, educator; b. Nauvoo, Ill., Sept. 18, 1926; s. David Mills and Anna Laura (Lowe) L.; m. Ann Weaver, 1966. Student, Kenyon Coll., 1944; B.A., U. Chgo., 1949, J.D., 1953. Bar: Ill. 1953, Ohio 1970, D.C. 1984. Practiced law in Chgo., 1953-61, 63-69, Dayton, 1969-78; U.S. commr. patents, 1961-63; adj. prof. law Ohio State U., 1971-77, U. Miami, Fla., 1974-77; vis. prof., 1977-78, research prof. law, 1978-79, prof. law, 1979-80; co-dir. Olin Found. program in law and econs. Law and Econs. Center, 1978-80; Register of Copyrights and asst. Librarian of Congress for Copyright Services, Washington, 1980-94. Served with AUS, 1945-46. Mem. Am. Bar Assn., Am. Intellectual Property Assn., Chgo. Patent Law Assn., Copyright Soc. U.S.A. Episcopalian. Clubs: Quadrangle (Chgo.); Dayton Racquet, Cosmos. Home: Alexandria Va. Died Oct. 12, 1994.

LAFONTANT-MANKARIOUS, JEWEL (MRS. NAGUIB S. MANKARIOUS), diplomat, lawyer; b. Chgo., Apr. 28, 1922; d. Cornelius Francis Stradford and Aida Arabella Carter; m. John Rogers, 1946 (dissolved 1961); 1 child, John W. Rogers Jr.; m. H. Ernest Lafontant, 1961 (dec. 1976); m. Naguib Soby Mankarious, Dec. 17, 1989. AB in Polit. Sci., Oberlin Coll., 1943; JD, U. Chgo., 1946; LLD (hon.), Cedar Crest Coll., 1973; D Humanitarian Svc. (hon.), Providence Coll., 1973; LLD (hon.), Ea. Mich. U., 1973; LHD (hon.), Howard U., 1974; LLD (hon.), Heidelberg Coll., 1975, Lake Forest Coll., 1977, Marymount Manhattan Coll., 1978, Oberlin Coll., 1979; LHD (hon.), Governor's State U., 1980, LLD (hon.), 1980; citation for pub. svc., U. Chgo., 1980; LLD (hon.), Chgo. Med. Sch., 1982, Loyola U. of Chgo., 1982, Roosevelt U., 1990. Bar: Ill. 1947. Asst. U.S. atty., 1955-58; sr. ptnr. Lafontant, et al., Chgo., 1961-83, Vedder, Price, Kaufman & Kammholz, Chgo., 1983-89; dep. solicitor gen. U.S. Dept. State, Washington, 1972-

75, amb.-at-large, U.S. coord. for refugee affairs, 1989-93; ptnr. Holleb & Coff, Chgo., 1993—; bd. dirs. Mobil Corp., Continental Bank, Foote, Cone & Belding, Equitable Life Assurance Soc. U.S., Trans World Corp., Revlon, Inc., Ariel-Capital Mgmt., Harte-Hanks Communications, Inc., Pantry Pride, Inc., Revlon Group, Howard U.; past dir. Jewel Cos., Inc., TWA, Hanes Corp.; past mem. U.S. Adv. Commn. Internat. Edn. and Cultural Affairs, Nat. Coun. Minority Bus. Enterprises, Nat. Coun. on Ednl. Rsch.; past chmn. adv. bd. Civil Rights Commn.; mem. Pres.'s Pvt. Sector Survey Cost Control; pres. Exec. Exchange; past U.S. rep. to UN. Bd. editors: Am. Bar Assn. Jour. Former trustee Lake Forest (Ill.) Coll., Oberlin Coll., Howard U., Tuskegee Inst.; bd. govs. Ronald Reagan Presdl. Found.; mem. Martin Luther King, Jr., Fed. Holiday Commn.; dir. Project Hope; chmn. Ill. adv. com. U.S. Civil Rights Commn.; mem. bd. overseers Hoover Instn.; mem. nat. adv. bd. Salvation Army. Recipient Howard B. Shepard award Protestant Found., Little Flowers Sem. Soc., Svc. award U.S. Dept. Justice, Humanitarian award Opportunities Industrialization Ctrs. of Am., Inc., Candace award Nat. Coalition of Black Women, Adlai A. Stevenson II award for svc. and support UN, Par Excellence Svc. award People United to Save Humanity, Disting. Svc. award Interracial Coun. for Bus. Opportunity, 1988, Woman of Distinction award Nat. Conf. for Coll. Women Student Leaders and Women of Achievement, 1988, Abraham Lincoln Marovitz award B'nai Brith, 1989, Disting. Svc. to Law and Soc. award Ill. Bar Found., 1989, cert. of recognition Vietnamese Community Leaders in U.S., 1990, Wiley A. Branton Issues Symposium award 1991, United Charities Legal Aid Soc. award, 1991, Spl. Recognition award Assyrian Am. Nat. Found., 1992, Chgo. Chpt. of Links, Inc. award, 1992, CARE Humanitarian award, 1994, Luminary award Girl Scouts U.S., 1995, Raoul Wallenberg award Am. Com. for Shaare Zedek Med. Ctr., Jerusalem, 1995, others; named Hon. Citizen of Abilene, Tex., 1991; named one of One Hundred Most Influential Black Ams., Ebony Mag., 1973-74, one of Crain's Chgo. bus. One Hundred Most Influential Women, 1996. Fellow Internat. Acad. Trial Lawyers; mem. NAACP (sec. Chgo. br.), ACLU (bd. dirs.), Chgo. Bar Assn. (bd. govs., Earl B. Dickerson award 1995), Comml. Club, Econs. Club (past bd. dirs.), Rotary (hon.), Cosmospolitan C. of C. (chairperson 1996 benefit).

LAIRD, ALAN DOUGLAS KENNETH, mechanical engineering educator; b. Victoria, Can., Aug. 8, 1914; came to U.S., 1946, naturalized, 1955; s. George Alexander and Edna A (Foy) L.; m. Joyce Kathleen Morris, Nov. 3, 1941; children: William George, John Douglas, Linda Margaret. B.A.Sc. in Mech. Engring, U. B.C., 1940; M.S., U. Calif. at Berkeley, 1949, Ph.D., 1951. Engr. Def. Industries Ltd., Montreal, 1941-45, Leek and Co., Vancouver, Can., 1945-46; mem. faculty U. Calif. at Berkeley, 1948-80, prof. mech. engring., 1964-80, prof, emeritus, 1980-96, dir. Sea Water Conversion Lab., 1968-80, dir. emeritus Sea Water Conversion Lab., 1980-96. Mem. ASME, Pi Tau Sigma. Home: 860 Sibert Ct Lafayette CA 94549-4925 Died Feb. 11, 1996.

LAKE, I. BEVERLY, SR., state supreme court justice. BS cum laude, Wake Forest U., 1925; LLB, Harvard U., 1929; LLM, Columbia U., 1940, SJD, 1947. Bar: N.C. 1928, U.S. Supreme Ct. 1954, U.S. Dist. Ct. (ea., mid. and we. dists.) N.C., U.S. Ct. Appeals (4th cir.). Pvt. practice Raleigh, 1929-32, 55-65, 78-86; dist. rationing atty. U.S. Office Price Adminstrn., 1943-45; staff atty. U.S. Nat. Prodn. Authority, 1951; asst. atty. gen. N.C., 1950-55, supreme ct. justice, 1965-78; prof. law Wake Forest U., 1932-51, Campbell U., 1978; vis. prof. law Duke U., 1945-46, U. Fla., 1947. Mem. ABA, N.C. State Bar, Wake County Bar Assn., N.C. Bar Assn. Democrat. Home: Raleigh N.C. Died April 1996; interred Wake Forrest Cemetery.

LALUMIA, JOSEPH, philosophy educator, historian; b. Robertsdale, Pa., May 24, 1916; s. John and Josephine (Insalaco) L.; m. Janice Helen Vtracek, Aug. 28, 1976; children from previous marriage: John Daniel, Catherine Louise, Claudia Sue. BA, St. Bernard's Sem., 1941; PhD, Cornell U., 1951. Prof. Kent State U., Ohio, 1950-56, Hofstra U., Hempstead, N.Y., 1956-76, 79—; dean Urbana Coll., Ohio, 1976-79. Author: The Ways of Reason, 1966; contbr. articles to philosophy and history jours. Democrat. Roman Catholic. Avocations: antiques, chess.

LAMANNA, CARL, microbiologist; b. Bklyn., Dec. 1, 1916; s. Frank and Margaret (Ottavi) L.; m. Ruth Weed, June 6, 1942; children: Carla Susan, Roger Weed. B.S., Cornell U., 1936, M.S., 1937, Ph.D., 1939. Research asst. Cornell U., 1936-39; mem. faculty Wash. State U., 1940-41, Oreg. State U., 1941-42, La. State U., 1942-43; with Fed. Security Agy. and War Dept., 1943-48; assoc. prof. Johns Hopkins U. Sch. Hygiene and Public Health, 1948-57; sci. dir. Naval Biol. Lab. U. Calif., Berkeley, 1957-61; dep. chief, sci. advisor Army Research Office, Arlington, Va., 1961-74; assoc. dir. pharm. research and testing Bur. Drugs, FDA, Washington, 1975-85; World Health Orgn. prof. public health microbiology U. Philippines, 1954-55; developer Scientists' Bill of Rights. Author: (with M.F. Mallette) Basic Bacteriology and Its Biological and Chemical Background, 4th edit, 1973; contbr. articles to profl. jours. Recipient Exceptional Civilian Service award War Dept., 1946, Meritorious Civilian Service award, 1966. Fellow AAAS, N.Y. Acad. Scis., Washington Acad. Scis., Am. Acad. Microbiology; mem. Am. Soc. Microbiology, Soc. Exptl. Biology and Medicine. DIED 11/12/97. .

LAMBERT, WILLIAM G., journalist, consultant; b. Langford, S.D., Feb. 2, 1920; s. William G. and Blanche (Townsend) L.; m. Jean Kenway Mead, July 7, 1945; children: Kathryn, Heather Lambert Oxberry. Nieman fellow journalism, Harvard U., 1959-60. Reporter, news editor Enterprise-Courier, Oregon City, Oreg., 1945-50; reporter The Oregonian, Portland, 1950-59; anchor, news dir. KPTV, Oreg. Television, Inc., Portland, 1961-62; corr. Time mag., 1962-63; assoc. editor, staffwriter Life mag., N.Y.C., 1963-71; staff corr. Time-Life News Service, 1971-73; free-lance journalist, 1973; staff writer, cons. Phila. Inquirer, 1974-90; freelance journalist, libel litigation cons., 1990—; cons., U.S. commr. edn. Office of Edn., Washington, 1962. Served in U.S. Army, WWII, PTO, to maj. Res., ret. Decorated bronze star. Recipient Pulitzer prize for local reporting, 1957, Heywood Broun award, 1957, award for mag. reporting Sigma Delta Chi, 1967, Worth Bingham prize for distinguished reporting, 1967, Heywood Brown award, 1969, George Polk award for mag. reporting Abe Fortas articles, Sigma Delta Chi award, Nat. Headliners Club award, Page One award, 1970, Pa. Bar Assn. award, Phila. Bar Assn. award, Phila. Sigma Delta Chi award, AP Mng. Editors award (Pa.), 1981.

LAMOREAUX, JOYCE, educational institute executive; b. Dec. 26, 1938. Officer SW Steel Rolling Mills & Affiliates, L.A., 1963-72; founder Chela Ctr., Pompano, Fla., 1972-75; exec. v.p. Word Masters, Inc., Seattle, 1975-85; pres. OMNIESS, Inc., 1986-92, OMNI Learning Inst., 1975—; cons. in field; lectr. in field. Author: Philosopy of Holism, The Power of Intuition, Multidimensional Health Care, Psychoneuroimmunology: The Role of Flower Essences, Natural Vibrational Healing, 1990; co-author: Intuitive Management Workbook; contbr. articles to profl. jours.; holder patent pending in vibrational medicine process. DIED 08/21/95. .

LANDA, WILLIAM ROBERT, foundation executive; b. Jersey City, Dec. 4, 1919; s. G.B. and Henrietta (Elder) L.; m. Anne E. Longley, June 24, 1939; children: Susanne (Mrs. J.B. Moliere), Stephen R., Scott W., Richard W. Student, Ohio U., 1937-39. Salesman Sterling Drug, Inc., 1942-44; asst. export mgr. Taylor, Pinkham & Co., Inc., 1944-52; export mgr. Bates Fabrics, Inc., 1952-55; pres. Burlington Export Co., N.Y.C., 1955-62; v.p. Burlington Mills Corp., 1957-62, Burlington Industries, Inc., Greensboro, N.C., 1959-62, Warner Bros. Co., Bridgeport, Conn., 1962-66; pres. Warner Bros. Co. (Warner Bros. Internat.), 1962-66; exec. v.p. Turner Jones & Co., 1966-67, pres., 1967-68; group v.p. internat. Genesco, Inc., N.Y.C., 1968-70; v.p. Farah Mfg. Co., 1970-74; pres., dir. Holguin & Assos. Inc., El Paso, Tex., 1978-81; pres. Western Mktg. Corp., El Paso, 1981-85; spl. asst. to pres. Free/Congress Research and Edn. Found. Inc., Washington, 1986-89; dir. Affiliated Mfrs., Inc., North Branch, N.J., AMI-PRESCO; hon. consul of Belgium for West Tex. and State of N.Mex., 1981-86; Mem. Gen. Arbitration Council Textile Industry; mem. Nat. Export Council, 1965-66; cons. Internat. Mktg., 1988—. Decorated chevalier Order of Crown Belgium). Mem. Commerce and Industry Assn. N.Y., Internat. Execs. Assn., U.S. C. of C. (spl. adv. com. on internat. trade), Am. Arbitration Assn., Beta Theta Pi. Presbyterian. Died Apr. 8, 1997.

LANDISMAN, MARK, geophysicist, educator; b. N.Y.C., Apr. 30, 1928; s. David and Rosa Landisman; m. Celia Turk, Aug. 3, 1960; children: Andrew Michael, Jessica, Carole Elizabeth. AB, Columbia U., 1949, PhD, 1959. Rsch. scientist Columbia U. at Lamont Geol. Obs., oceanographic cruises and geophys. field sites, 1949-64; prof. geophysics U. Tex. at Dallas, Richardson, 1964—; adj. prof. So. Meth. U., 1964—; vis. assoc. prof. U. Minn., 1962-63; vis. prof. U. Karlsruhe (Fed. Republic Germany), 1967; UNESCO expert in seismology Internat. Inst. Seismology and Earthquake Engring., Tokyo, 1972; invited contbr., keynote speaker internat. symposia on geophys. theory and computers. Contbr. articles to profl. jours. Bd. dirs., exec. sec., v.p., mem. exec. com. Heard Mus. and Wildlife Sanctuary, McKinney, Tex., 1978—. Mem. AAAS, Am. Geophys. Union, Am. Phys. Soc., Acoustical Soc. Am., European Assn. Exploration Geophysicists, Geol. Soc. Am., Seismol. Soc. Am., Seismol. Soc. Japan, Royal Astron. Soc. (U.K.), Dallas Geophys. Soc., U.S. Geodynamics Com., Sigma Xi. Achievements include development of first computer programs for gravity and magnetic signatures of two-dimensional models, seismic ray-mode duality, computation of global tremors from severe earthquakes, frequency-time analysis of multiply dispersed signals, generalized inversion models from inaccurate and incomplete data, seismic refraction-reflection and electrical properties of relatively wet earthquake-prone zone in the earth's crust; research in field of oceanographic precision depth recorder early seismic surface wave demarcation of global plate tectonic asthenosphere. Died May 4, 1995.

LANE, BURTON (BURTON LEVY), composer; b. N.Y.C., Feb. 2, 1912; s. Lazarus and Frances Levy; m. Marion Seaman, June 28, 1935 (div. 1961); 1 dau.; m. Lynn Daroff Kaye, Mar. 5, 1961. Student, High Sch. of Commerce; studied piano with Simon Bucharoff. Former staff composer for Remick Music Pub. Wrote music for 2 songs in Three's a Crowd, 1930; 1 song in The Third Little Show, 1931; entire score for 9th edit. Earl Carroll's Vanities, 1931; 2 songs in Singin' the Blues, 1931; 1 song in Americana, 1932; composed mus. scores for Hold on to Your Hats, 1940, Laffing Room Only (also lyricist), 1944, Finian's Rainbow, 1947, On a Clear Day You Can See Forever (Tony nomination, Grammy award with Alan Jay Lerner 1965 Carmelina, 1979 (Tony nomination); songs for motion pictures including Dancing Lady, 1933, Babes on Broadway, 1941, Royal Wedding, 1951, Give a Girl a Break, 1953, On a Clear Day You Can See Forever, 1966; animated film Heidi, 1979; composer music for Junior Miss, TV, 1958; composer songs in revue Mighty Fine Music!, off-Broadway, 1983; songs include Everything I Have is Yours, Tony's Wife, Moments Like This, There's A Great Day Coming Mañana, On a Clear Day, The Lady's In Love With You, I Hear Music, Too Late Now, When I'm Not Near The Girl I Love, I Love The Girl I'm Near, Come Back To Me, How Are Things In Glocca Morra?, Look To The Rainbow, How Could You Believe Me When I Said I Love You When You Know I've Been A Liar All My Life, Says My Heart, Stop!, You're Breaking My Heart, (I Like New York In June) How About You?, It's Time For A Love Song, In Our United State, Old Devil Moon, What Did I Have That I Don't Have, One More Walk Around The Garden. Recipient 2 Acad. Award nominations, award for Finian's Rainbow, Essex Symphony Soc. 1947, Mercer Lifetime Achievement award, Richard Rodgers Lifetime Achievement award ASCAP, 1992; inducted into Theatre Hall of Fame, 1993. Mem. ASCAP (bd. dirs.), Am. Guild Authors and Composers (pres. 1957-67, Sigmund Romberg award), Songwriters Hall of Fame (dir.). Died Jan. 5, 1997.

LANG, H. JACK, advertising executive, author; b. Cleve., June, June 24, 1904; s. Hascal Charles and Rosetta (Stettiner) L.; m. Frances Wise, Aug. 10, 1935; children: Wendy, John. BA, Antioch Coll., 1928. Founder, pres. Lang, Fisher Stashower Inc. (name changed to Liggett-Stashower Inc. 1988), Cleve. Author: The Wit and Wisdom of Abraham Lincoln, 1941, Lincoln's Fireside Reading, 1965, Two Kinds of Christmases, 1965, The Rowfant Manuscripts (named one of best books of yr. Am. Inst. Graphic Arts 1979), newspaper syndicated feature and book Letters of the Presidents (George Washington medal Freedoms Found.), 1964; Lincoln's Log Cabin Library (George Washington medal Freedoms Found.), 1965, Letters in American History, 1982, Dear Wit: Letters From the World's Wits, 1990; editor: The Wolf Mag. of Letters, 1934-96; collector autograph letters. Past trustee Planned Parenthood Cleve., Antioch U., Yellow Springs, Ohio; trustee Mt. Sinai Hosp., Cleve., 1947-60, hon. trustee, 1973-96; past mem. exec. com. ARC, Cleve. Lt. col. USAAF, 1942-46. Named to Hall of Fame Cleve. Advt. Club, 1977. Mem. Manuscript Soc., Western Res. Hist. Soc., Rowfant Club (fellow). Died Aug. 30, 1996.

LANGE, VICTOR, foreign language educator, author; b. Leipzig, Germany, July 13, 1908; came to U.S., 1932, naturalized, 1943; s. Walter and Theodora (Schellenberg) L.; m. Frances Mary Olrich, Feb. 23, 1945; children: Dora Elizabeth, Thomas Victor. Student, Thomasschule Leipzig, 1919-28, Oxford U., 1928, Sorbonne, 1929, U. Munich, 1929-30, U. Toronto; MA (Gertrude Davis exchange fellow 1930-31); Ph.D., U. Leipzig, 1934; H.L.D., Monterey Inst., 1978. Dir. Akademische Auslandsstelle, U. Leipzig, 1931-32; lectr. German, Univ. Coll., Toronto, 1932-38; asst. prof. German Cornell U., 1938-41, assoc. prof., 1941-45, prof., 1945-57; prof. German lit. Princeton U., 1957—, John N. Woodhull prof. modern. langs., 1968-77, emeritus, 1977—; hon. prof. Free U., Berlin, 1962—; vis. prof. U. Calif.-Davis, Smith Coll., U. Chgo., Berkeley, U. Cologne, U. Heidelberg, Munich, Columbia U., U. Mich., NYU, CUNY, Yale U., La Jolla, etc.; examiner in chief for German Coll. Entrance Exam. Bd., 1942-50; external examiner U. Hong Kong, 1979; vis. prof. U. Auckland, New Zealand, 1974; Guggenheim fellow, 1950-51, 67, McCosh fellow, 1966-67, Fulbright lectr., Australia, 1969, Phi Beta Kappa vis. scholar, 1968-69, Nat. Endowment Humanities sr. fellow, 1973-74; fellow Humanities Research Centre, Canberra, Australia, 1977. Author: Die Lyrik und ihr Publikum im England des 18. Jahrhunderts, 1936, Kulturkritik und Literaturbetrachtung in Amerika, 1938, Modern German Literature, 1945, Goethe's Craft of Fiction, 1953, Contemporary German Poetry, 1964, The Reader in the Strategy of Fiction, 1973, Mann: Tradition and Experiment, 1976, (with W.R. Amacher) New Perspectives in German Literary Criticism, 1979, The Classical Age of German Literature, 1982, Goethe's Faust II, 1980, Ilyrische Betrachtungen. Essays und Aufsätze aus dreissig Jahren, 1989, Goethe-Studien, 1990, Bilder, Ideen, Begriffe, 1991; editor: Deutsche Briefe, 1940, The Sorrows of Young Werther, 1949, Goethe's Faust, 1950, Great German Short Stories, 1952, Lessings Hamburg Dramaturgy, 1962, Goethe's Wilhelm Meister, 1962, German Classical Drama, 1962, Goethe: Twentieth Century Views, 1968, Humanistic Scholarship in America, 1968, Goethes Werke, 1972; Munich edition Goethes Werke, vols. 6, 1 and 2, 1986; Goethe, 1992;

trans.: Edith Wharton's Ethan Frome, 1948; editorial bd.: Rev. of Nat. Lits., Comparative Lit., 20th Century Lit.; contbr. to lit. jours. Decorated comdr.'s cross Order of Merit (German Fed. Republic); recipient Gold medal Goethe Inst., 1966, Friedrich-Gundolf prize German Acad. Lang. and Lit., 1966, Chancellor's citation U. Calif., 1985, Golden Goethe medal Weimar, 1993, Festschrift Aspekte der Goethezeit, editor T. Ziolkowski, 1977. Mem. Internat. Assn. Germanists (pres. 1965-70), Am. Soc. 18th Century Studies (pres. 1975-76), Goethe Soc. N.Am. (pres. 1980-89), Am. Assn. Tchrs. German, Modern Humanities Research Assn., German Acad. (Darmstadt), Am. Comparative Lit. Assn., Goethe Gesellschaft Weimar, Phi Beta Kappa. DIED 06/29/96. .

LANSKY, ZDENEK JOHN, mechanical engineer; b. Trnava, Czechoslovakia, Jan. 26, 1922; came to U.S., 1922; s. Emanuel Victor and Vlasta Christina (Hrdina) L.; m. Sylvia Albina Koral, Oct. 3, 1945; children: John, Donald. BSME, Ill. Inst. Tech., 1944, MS, 1954; DEng (hon.), Milw. Sch. Engring., 1975. Registered profl. engr., Ill., Ohio. Asst. chief insp. Soreng Manegold Corp., Chgo., 1939-45; R & D engr. Stewart Warner Corp., Chgo., 1946-54; v.p., tech. dir. Parker Hannifin Corp., Cleve., 1954-87. Author: Industrial Pneumatic Control, 1986; co-author: Zero Downtime Pneumatics, 1993; editor 10 vol. series; contbr. 40 articles to profl. jours. Mem. vis. com. engring. sch. Lehigh U., Bethlehem, Pa., 1984-95. Lt. USN, 1945-46, PTO. Recipient Ann. Achievement award Nat. Fluid Power Assn., Milw., 1974, Disting. Achievement award Fluid Power Soc., Milw., 1981, Achievement award Nat. Conf. on Fluid Power, Chgo., 1988. Fellow Soc. Automotive Engrs. (tech. bd. 1982-86); mem. U.S. Power Squadron (pilot, lt.), Bent Tree Country Club. Home: Sarasota Fla. Died Aug. 20, 1995.

LAPIDES, JACK, urologist, medical educator; b. Rochester, N.Y., Nov. 27, 1914; s. Harry and Emma (Seldow) L.; m. Alice Jean Hatt, June 1948 (dec. Oct. 1971); m. Roberta de Vries Stadt, Sept. 1975 (dec. June 1993). B.A., U. Mich., 1936, M.A., 1938, M.D., 1941. Diplomate: Am. Bd. Urology. Rockefeller Research asso. fellow physiology U. Mich. Grad. Sch., 1936-38; intern U. Mich. Hosp., 1941-42, asst. resident surgery, 1946-47, resident sect. urology, dept. surgery, 1947-50; research fellow urology U. Chgo., 1947; USPHS postdoctorate fellow Nat. Cancer Inst., 1948-50; instr. urology U. Mich. Med. Sch., 1950-52, asst. prof. surgery, 1952-55, asso. prof., 1955-64, prof. surgery sect. urology, 1964-84, prof. emeritus surgery, 1984—, head sect. urology, 1968-83; chief sect. urology Wayne County Gen. Hosp., 1950-83, VA Hosp., 1952-83. Author: Fundamentals of Urology, 1976; Contbg. author chpts. in numerous med. texts, also articles. Served with USAAF, 1942-46. Recipient award for disting. achievement U. Mich. Med. Ctr. Alumni Soc., 1994. Mem. Soc. Pediatric Urology, Washtenaw County Med. Soc., Fla. Urol. Soc., AMA, ACS, Am. Urol. Assn., Am. Assn. Genitourinary Surgeons, Pan-Am. Med. Assn., Phi Beta Kappa, Sigma Xi, Phi Eta Sigma, Phi Sigma, Phi Kappa Phi, Alpha Omega Alpha (Paul Zimskind award 1987, Ramon Guiteras award 1987, Pediatric Urology medal 1989, Premier F. Brantley Scott award 1993). Died Nov. 14, 1995.

LA PLANTE, JAMES GAMELIN, insurance company executive; b. Vincennes, Ind., Aug. 13, 1921; s. J.B.E. and Harriet (Jessup) LaP.; m. Margaret MacLaurin, Sept. 10, 1947; children: Lauren Margaret Younger, James Gamelin. B.A., Washington and Lee U., 1943; M.B.A., Stanford, 1948. Asst. treas. Indsl. Indemnity Co., San Francisco, 1964-67; treas. Indsl. Indemnity Co., 1967-71, v.p., treas., 1971-72, sr. v.p., treas., 1972-86; dir., treas. Indsl. Underwriters Ins. Co., San Francisco, 1967-86, 255 Calif. Corp., San Francisco, 1967-86, Indsl. Underwriters, Inc., San Francisco, 1969-86, Indsl. Ins. Co., San Francisco, 1970-86, Indsl. Ins. Co. Hawaii, Ltd., 1971-86, Indsl. Indemnity Alaska, 1972-86, Indsl. Indemnity N.W., 1972-86, Indsl. Indemnity Life Ins. Co., 1972-86, Calif. Ins. Co., 1978; retired, 1986. Served to lt. USNR, 1943-46. Mem. Financial Execs. Inst. (pres. San Francisco chpt. 1977-78), Ins. Accountants Statis. Assn., Soc. Ins. Accountants, Phi Kappa Psi. Clubs: Foothills Tennis and Swim (Palo Alto, Calif.); Profits Unlimited (Atherton, Calif.); Bohemian, Pacific Union (San Francisco); Menlo Country (Redwood City, Calif.) (pres. 1983-85). Home: Portola Vally Calif. Died Feb. 11, 1994.

LARKIN, PETER ANTHONY, zoology educator, university dean and official; b. Auckland, New Zealand, Dec. 11, 1924; arrived in Can., 1929; s. Frank Wilfrid and Caroline Jane (Knapp) L.; m. Lois Boughton Rayner, Aug. 21, 1948; children: Barbara, Kathleen, Patricia, Margaret, Gillian. BA, MA, U. Sask., Can., 1946, LLD (hon.), 1989; DPhil (Rhodes scholar), Oxford U., 1948; DSc (hon.), U. B.C., 1992. Bubonic plague survey Govt. of Sask., 1942-43; fisheries investigator Fisheries Rsch. Bd. Can., 1944-46; chief fisheries biologist B.C. Game Commn., 1948-55; asst. prof. U. B.C., 1948-55, prof. dept. zoology, 1959-63, 66-69; Dir. Pacific Biological Station, 1963-66; also dir. fisheries Inst. Animal Resource Ecology, 1955-63, 66-69, head dept. zoology, 1972-75, dean grad. studies, 1975-84, assoc. v.p. rsch., 1980-86, v.p. rsch., 1986-88, univ. prof., 1969-96; hon. life gov. Vancouver Pub. Aquarium; mem. Can. nat. com. Sci. Com. on Problems of Environment, WHO, 1971-72; mem Killam selection com. Can. Can., 1974-77; mem. Sci. Coun. Can., 1971-76, Nat. Rsch. Coun. Can., 1981-84, Can. Com. on Seals and Sealing, 1981-86, Can. Inst. Advanced Rsch., 1982-85, Nat. Scis. and Engring. Rsch. Coun. Can., various govtl. rsch. coms.; mem. Internat. Ctr. for Living Aquatic Resources Mgmt., 1977, chmn. bd. dirs., 1991-93; bd. dirs. B.C. Packers, 1980-96; mem. bd. govs. Internat. Devel. Rsch. Coun., Can., 1987-93; mem. Nat. Sci. Eng. Rsch. Coun. Can., 1987-93; pres. Rawson Acad., 1988-91; commr. B.C.Utilities Commn., 1993-96; mem. interim gov. coun. U.N.B.C., 1991-93. Contbr. articles to profl. jours. Pres. B.C. Conservation Found., 1987-90; temporary commr. B.C. Utilities Commn., 1993-96; trustee Vancouver Hosp., 1994-95. Recipient centennial medal Govt. Can., 1967, silver jubilee medal, 1977, Can. Sport Fishing Inst. award, 1979, Murray A. Newman conservation award Vancouver Aquarium, 1996; Nuffield Found. fellow, 1961-62. Fellow Royal Soc. Can.; mem. Internat. Limnol. Assn., Am. Fisheries Soc. (award of excellence 1983, Carl R. Sullivan conservation award 1993), B.C. Natural Resources Conf. (pres. 1954), B.C. Wildlife Fedn., Can. Soc. Zoologists (pres. 1972, Fry medal 1978), Can. Assn. Univ. Rsch. Adminstrn. (pres. 1979), Am. Inst. Fisheries Biologists (outstanding achievement award 1986), Sci. Coun. B.C. (career achievement award 1995), Order of Can., 1995, Order of B.C., 1996. Home: Vancouver CAN Died July, 1996.

LARKIN, PHILIP (ARTHUR), author, librarian; b. Coventry, Eng., Aug. 9, 1922; s. Sydney and Eva (Day) L.; B.A., St. John's Coll., Oxford, 1943, M.A., 1947; D.Litt. (hon.), U. Belfast, U. Leicester, U. Warwick, Sussex U., St. Andrews U. Various posts pub., coll. univ. libraries, 1943-54; librarian U. Hull, Yorkshire, Eng., 1955—. Decorated comdr. Brit. Empire; companion of Lit.; recipient Queen's Gold Medal for poetry, 1965; Loines award poetry, 1974; A.C. Benson silver medal, 1975; Shakespeare prize, 1976. Mem. Am. Acad. Arts and Scis. (fgn., hon.). Author: Jill, 1946; A Girl in Winter, 1947; (poems) The North Ship, 1945; The Less Deceived, 1955; The Whitsun Weddings, 1964; All What Jazz, 1970; High Windows, 1974; (essays) Required Writing, 1983. Editor: The Oxford Book of Twentieth-Century English Verse, 1973.

LARSEN, ARTHUR HOFF, educator; b. Boston, Mar. 9, 1907; s. Peter Marinus and Eleonora (Pedersen) L.; m. Faith Elaine Herrick, Aug. 5, 1933; 1 son, Richard Herrick. B.Ed., U. Wis., Ph.M., 1931, Ph.D., 1939; postgrad., U. Chgo., 1934; LL.D. (hon.), Ill. State U., 1974. Prin. state graded sch. Siren, Wis., 1929-30; tchr. math. York Community High Sch., Elmhurst, Ill., 1931-35; mem. faculty Ill. State U., Normal, 1935-94; prof. edn. Ill. State U., 1935-65, head dept. edn. and psychology, 1945-49, v.p. univ., dean faculty, 1949-65, Disting. prof. higher edn., 1965-72, prof. emeritus, 1972-94; Former pres. bd. Bank of Ill., Normal; mem. adv. council Asso. Orgns. Tchr. Edn., 1961-64; adv. council Degree Granting Instns. in, Ill., 1962-76. Mem. Ill. Council on Aging, 1974-83. Mem. NEA, Ill. Edn. Assn., Am. Ednl. Research Assn. Methodist. Home: Bloomington Ill. Died Dec. 13, 1994.

LARSEN, LOUIS ROYTER, retired electronics company executive, consultant; b. Phila., July 4, 1916; s. Lauritz and Anna (Royter) L.; m. Eugenia Riddell Jacobs, Oct. 20, 1944; children: Louis Royter, Eric Risor, Peter Christian, Geoffrey Stang. B.S. in Econs., U. Pa., 1949, M.B.A., 1956. Instr. U. Pa., 1949-51; with Sprague Electric Co., North Adams, Mass., 1951-86; contr. Sprague Electric Co., 1967-85, cons. internat. div., 1985-86; independent cons., 1986—. Served with USAAF, 1942-45. Mem. Nat. Assn. Accts. Died Nov. 10, 1997.

LASKER, EDWARD, lawyer; b. Chgo., May 15, 1912; s. Albert D. and Flora (Warner) L.; m. Cynthia S. Palmer, Nov. 1963; children by previous marriage: Albert, Lawrence, Steven. Grad., Phillips Exeter Acad., 1929; B.A., Yale U., 1933; LL.B., UCLA, 1955. Bar: Calif. 1955. Engaged as account exec., v.p. charge radio, 1st v.p., gen. mgr. Lord & Thomas, 1933-41; spl. asst. to sec. navy, 1941-42, motion picture producer, 1946- 52; counsel firm McKenna & Filling, L.A.; dir. Philip Morris, Inc., 1961-80, dir. emeritus, 1980-83, mem. adv. bd., 1983-84; dir. Gt. Western Fin. Corp., 1956-85; asst. chief disciplinary referee Calif. State Bar, 1976-77, mem. disciplinary bd., 1978-80. Trustee Pomona Coll., hon. 1985-92; del. Democratic Nat. Conv., 1956, 60. Served from lt. (j.g.) to lt. comdr. USNR, 1942-45. DIED 07/11/97. .

LASLETT, LAWRENCE JACKSON, physicist; b. Boston, Jan. 12, 1913; s. William Lawrence and Emily Mary (Jackson) L.; m. Barbara Elizabeth Bridgeford, Feb. 25, 1939; children: Lawrence J. Jr., Emily B., Helen M. BS, Calif. Inst. Tech., 1933; PhD in Physics, U. Calif., 1937. Instr. dept. physics U. Mich., Ann Arbor, 1939-40, Ind. U., Bloomington, 1939-41; prof. Iowa State U., Ames, 1953-55; vis. scientist MIT Rsch. Radiology Lab., Cambridge, Mass., 1942-45; vis. rsch. scientist U. Ill., Urbana, 1955-56, U. Wis., Madison, 1956-57. Mem. AAAS, Am. Phys. Soc. Died May, 1993.

LA SOR, WILLIAM SANFORD, clergyman, biblical studies educator emeritus; b. Phila., Oct. 25, 1911; s. William Allan and Sara (Lewis) La S.; m. Elizabeth Granger Vaughan, June 16, 1934; children: William Sanford, Elizabeth Ann La Sor Kirkpatrick, Frederick Eugene, Susanne Marie La Sor Whyte. A.B., U. Pa., 1931; Th.B., Princeton Sem., 1934, Th.M., 1943; M.A., Princeton U., 1934; Ph.D. (Dropsie fellow in Assyriology), Dropsie U., 1949; Th.D., U. So. Calif., 1956. Lic. comml. pilot (inactive). Ordained to ministry Presbyterian Ch., 1934; pastor First Presbyn. Ch., Ocean City, N.J., 1934-38, Green Ridge Presbyn. Ch., Scranton, Pa., 1938-43; prof., chmn. dept. religion Lafayette Coll., 1946-49; prof. O.T., Fuller Theol. Sem., Pasadena, Calif., 1949-77; sr. prof. O.T. Fuller Theol. Sem., 1977-80, prof. emeritus, 1980—; vis. prof. Israel-Am. Inst., 1962, UCLA, 1981; mem. Pre-Holy Year Ecumenical Pilgrimage, 1974; Comdg. officer Naval Res. Chaplain Co., Los Angeles, 1968-70; pres. bd. dirs. Tokyo Evangelistic Ctr.; leader Holyland Tours. Author: Hebrew Handbook, 1951, Dead Sea Scrolls, 1956, Great Personalities of the Old Testament, 1959, Great Personalities of the New Testament, 1961, Handbook of New Testament Greek, 1964, 2d edit., 1973, Daily Life in Bible Times, 1966, Men Who Knew God, 1970, Men Who Knew Christ, 1971, Church Alive!, 1972, Dead Sea Scrolls and the Old Testament, 1972, Israel, 1976, Handbook of Biblical Hebrew, 2d edit, 1980, The Truth About Armageddon, 1982; co-author: Old Testament Survey, 1982, rev. edit., 1991; author, photographer: documentary film Ghana Miracle in Black, 1964; editor: Bibliographie, Revue de Qumrân, 1960-65; assoc. editor: International Standard Bible Encyclopedia, 1961-88; contbr. articles to profl. jours. honored by Festschrift, Biblical and Near Eastern Studies, Essays in Honor of William Sanford La Sor (editor Gary A. Tuttle), 1978. Served as chaplain USNR, 1943-46, Res. 1946-70. Fellow Am. Assn. Theol. Schs., 1961-62. Mem. Am. Assn. Profs. Hebrew, Soc. Bibl. Lit. and Exegesis (pres. Pacific Coast region 1983-84), Internat. Orgn. for Study of O.T., Soc. O.T. Scholars (Brit.), Inst. Bibl. Research, Mil. Chaplains Assn. (pres. So. Calif. chpt. 1967-69), Alpha Sigma Phi. Republican.

LASSEN, NIELS ALEXANDER, neuroscience educator; b. Copenhagen, Dec. 7, 1926; s. H.C.A. and Johanne A. Lassen; m. Edda Sveinsdottir, 1955-76 (div. 1976); children: Henrik A., Anders, Jens A, Christian A.; m. Birgitte Busk, 1981. MD, Copenhagen U., 1951, PhD, 1952. Chief physician Dept. Clin. Physiology and Nuclear Medicine Bispebjerg Hosp., Copenhagen, 1962-89; prof. neuroscience Danish Med. Rsch. Coun., 1989—. Contbr. more than 690 sci. papers to profl. publs. Named Hon. Doctor at Copenhagen U., Lund U., Lille, U., Toulouse U.; recipient various foundation prices Novo-Nordic, 1968, Jahre, 1977, Klein, 1990, Lundbeck, 1994, George Heresy award Soc. Nuclear Medicine, 1990. Mem. Acad. Sci. (Denmark). Died Apr. 30, 1997.

LASSER, DAVID, space pioneer, writer; b. Balt., Mar. 20, 1902; s. Leonard and Lena (Jaffe) L.; m. Florence Glassberg, Aug. 26, 1927 (div. Sept. 1937); 1 child: Daniel Joseph; m. Helen Gerber, Oct. 1937 (div. 1947); m. Amelia Tolbert, Dec. 23, 1963. BS in Engring., MIT, 1924. Engr. Rossendale-Reddaway Co., Newark, 1924; mgr. prodn. Halperin Mills, Bklyn., 1925-26; mng. editor Gernsback Pubs., N.Y.C., 1927-34; pres. Workers Alliance Am., Washington, 1935-40, Am. Security Union, Washington, 1940-41; asst. dir. plant productivity div. War Prodn. Bd., Washington, 1942, dir. office Labor Adv. Coms., 1944-47, spl. labor advisor, sec. commerce, 1947-48; asst. to pres. Internat. Union Elec., Radio and Machine Workers AFL-CIO, Washington, 1950-69; cons. Dept. State, various countries, 1968-72. Author: Conquest of Space, 1931, Private Monopoly: The Enemy at Home, 1945; contbr. articles to profl. jours. V.p. Ctr. Continuing Edn. San Diego State U., 1979-82. Served as sgt. U.S. Army, 1918-19. Fellow AIAA (Founder award 1981); mem. AAAS, DAV. Home: San Diego Calif. Died May 6th, 1996.

LASSWELL, MARY (MRS. DUDLEY WINN SMITH), author; b. Glasgow, Scotland, Feb. 8, 1905; d. William Robinson and Mary Clyde (Caskey) Lubbock; m. Clyde Lasswell, Jan. 3, 1938; m. Dudley Winn Smith, Feb. 3, 1964. B.S., U. Tex., 1930. Columnist: Houston Chronicle, 1959-64; Author: Suds in Your Eye, 1942 (Broadway play dramatized by Jack Kirkland, 1943), High Time, 1944, Mrs. Rasmussen's Book of One Arm Cookery, 1946, Bread for the Living, 1948, One on the House, 1949, Walt for the Wagon, 1951, Tooner Schooner, 1953, (with Bob Pool) I'll Take Texas, 1958, Let's Go For Broke, 1962, Tio Pepe (wrote words, music, libretto for musical comedy 1968), 1963, Biography John Henry Kirby, 1966, Mrs. Rasmussen's Book of One Arm Cookery With Second Helpings, 1970; also wrote: lyrics, music, and book for mus. Lonely Star set in Republic of Texas, 1951; Editor, compiler: lyrics, music, and book for mus. Rags and Hope; wrote books, lyrics, music: mus. play Suds, 1984, Gone to Texas! G.T.T.!, 1985. Mem. Tex. Civil War Centennial Commn. Mem. Authors League Am., Dramatists Guild, Tex. Inst. Letters, Daus. Republic Tex., ASCAP, Theta Sigma Phi. Episcopalian.

LAUBENSTEIN, VERNON ALFRED, state agency administrator; b. Fredonia, Wisc., Mar. 17, 1933; s. Edwin R. and MArtha (Parlow) L.; m. Barbara Jean Swanson, Oct. 15, 1960; children: Jeffrey, Elizabeth, Katherine, Scott, Suzanne. BA, Ripon (Wisc.) Coll., 1954; MBA, Ind. U., 1955. Contracts and compliance mgr. Kemper Group, Long Grove, Ill., 1957-88; mgmt. ops. analyst State Of Ill., Chgo., 1988—; township supr. Schaumburg Twp., Hoffman Estates, Ill., 1969—. Pres. Twinbrook YMCA, Schaumburg, 1970-71, Twp. Suprs. of Ill., Astoria, 1988-89, Rep. Orgn. of Schaumburg, 1967-68; bd. dirs. Suburban Cook-DuPage Health Sys. Agy., Oak Park, Ill., 1976-81, Twp. Suprs. of Ill., Astoria, 1981—. 1st lt. MSC U.S. Army, 1955-57. Recipient Twinbrook award Twinbrook YMCA, 1975, Friend of Elk Grove-Schaumburg Twp. Mental Health Ctr. award, 1983. Republican. Lutheran. Avocations: fishing, camping, politics. Home: For Estate of Mr Vernon Laubenstein 125 Westover Ln Schaumburg IL 60193-1154 Died July 15, 1997.

LAUGHLIN, J. FRANCIS, state legislator; b. Cochituate, Mass., Feb. 9, 1928; 3 children. Student, Wentworth Inst., Boston, 1947. Carpenter, ret.; rep. dist. 41 N.H. Ho. of Reps., Manchester; mem. labor, indsl. and rehabilitative svc., pub. protection, and vet. affairs coms., N.H. Ho. of Reps. Mem. Mont Royal Club, Fish & Game Club, Am. Legion (Sweeney Post No. 2). Died Jan. 8, 1996.

LAUGHLIN, JAMES, publishing company executive, writer, lecturer; b. Pitts., Oct. 30, 1914; s. Henry Hughart and Marjory (Rea) L.; m. Margaret Keyser, Mar. 13, 1942 (div. 1952); children: Paul, Leila; m. Ann Clark Resor, May 19, 1956 (dec. Nov. 1987); children; Robert (dec.), Henry; m. Gertrude Huston, Dec. 5, 1991. A.B., Harvard U., 1939; Litt.D. (hon.), Hamilton Coll., 1969, Colgate U., 1978; H.H.D. (hon.), Duquesne U., 1980; L.H.D., Yale U., 1982, Brown U., 1984, Bellarmine Coll., 1987, St. Joseph's Coll., Hartford, 1993. Founder New Directions (now New Directions Pub. Corp.), N.Y.C., 1936; pres. New Directions (now New Directions Pub. Corp.), 1964-97, Intercultural Publs., Inc; pub. Perspectives, USA and Perspectives supplements The Atlantic Monthly Jour.; cons. Indian So. Langs. Book Trust, Madras, 1955; vis. Regents prof. U. Calif., San Diego, 1974; Ida Bean vis. prof. U. Iowa, 1981; chmn. creative writing panel Inst. Internat. Edn. Conf. on Arts Exchange, 1956-97; adj. prof. English, Brown U., 1983, 85. Author: Some Natural Things, 1945, A Small Book of Poems, 1948, The Wild Anemone and Other Poems, 1957, Selected Poems, 1960, The Pig, 1970, Thomas Merton and James Laughlin: Selected Letters, 1977; In Another Country, 1978, Stolen and Contaminated Poems, 1984, The House of Light, 1986, Selected Poems, 1986, The Owl of Minerva, 1987, Pound as Wuz, 1987, William Carlos Williams and James Laughlin: Selected Letters, 1989, The Bird of Endless Time, 1990, Kenneth Rexnoth and James Laughlin: Selected Letters, 1991, Random Essays, Random Stories, 1991, The Man in the Wall, 1993, Delmore Schwartz and James Laughlin: Selected Letters, 1993, Collected Poems, 1994, Ezra Pound and James Laughlin: Selected Letters, 1994, (novella) Angelica, 1993, Collected Poems, 1994, Phantoms, 1995, The Country Road, 1995, Heart Island, 1996, The Secret Room, 1997; profiled in New Yorker; contbr. mags. and books; collector lit. mags. (little mag. type); active prodn. documentary films on modern poets, 1983-97. Bd. dirs. Goethe Bi-Centennial Found., 1949, Aspen (Colo.) Inst. Humanities, 1950; mem. Nat. Citizens Commn. for Internat. Cooperation, U.S. Nat. Commn. for UNESCO, 1960-63, Nat. Commn. for Internat. Coop. year, 1966; past trustee Allen-Chase Found.; mem. vis. com. German Princeton U.; mem. vis. com. dept. Romance langs. Harvard U.; co-trustee Merton Legacy Trust, 1969-97; trustee Rosenbach Found., Phila., to 1981. Decorated chevalier Legion of Honor; hon. fellow Coll. Five, U. Calif., Santa Cruz, 1972-97; recipient Disting. Svc. award Am. Acad. Arts and Letters, 1977, award for pub. PEN, 1979, Carey-Thomas citation Pubs. Weekly, 1978, Conn. Arts Comn. award, 1986, Nat. Book Found. medal for Disting. Contbn. to Am. Letters, 1992. Mem. AAAL (elected), Am. Acad. Arts and Scis., Alta Ski Lifts Co. (formerly Salt Lake City Winter Sports Assn.; dir. 1939-97, v.p. 1958), Alta Lodge Co. (v.p. 1948-58, pres. 1958-59), PEN, Asia Soc. (chmn. publs. com. 1959-67), Century Assn. (N.Y.C.), Harvard Club of N.Y.C. Died Nov. 12, 1997.

LAWLESS, LAWRENCE, lawyer; b. Evanston, Ill., June 4, 1926; s. Benjamin Wharrie and Marjorie Josephine (Matlock) L.; m. Sue Rovelstad, May 1, 1953 (div.); children—Leslie Ann Lawless Young, Lisbeth, Patrick Benjamin. B.S., U. Ill., 1950, LL.B., 1951. Bar: Ill. 1951, U.S. Supreme Ct. 1970, U.S. Ct. Appeals (7th cir.) 1955, U.S. Dist. Ct. (no. dist.) Ill. 1955, U.S. Dist. Ct. (no. dist.) Miss. 1979. Assoc., IC Industries, Inc., Chgo., 1952-55, atty. Ill. Central R.R., Chgo., 1955-63, gen. atty., 1966-69, local atty., Cook County, Ill., 1963-66, asst. v.p. IC Industries, Chgo., 1969, pres. subs. Ill. Center Corp., 1970-72, Mid-Am. Improvement Corp., 1970-72, corp. counsel IC Industries, 1972—; incorporator, 1st village atty. Village of Park Forest South (Ill.); magistrate Cir. Ct. Cook County, 1961-65; atty. Rich Twp., 1965-80. Served to 1st lt. AUS, 1944-46, 51-52; ETO, Korea. Mem. ABA, Fed. Bar Assn. (chmn. corp. counsels com. 1979-81), Ill. Bar Assn., Chgo. Bar Assn., Nat. Assn. R.R. Trial Counsel (past pres. Ill. div.), Assn. Trial Lawyers Am., Ill. Trial Lawyers Assn., Phi Alpha Delta, Lambda Alpha. Club: Chicago Yacht.

LAWYER, VERNE, lawyer; b. Indianola, Iowa, May 9, 1923; s. Merrill Guy and Zella (Mills) L.; m. Sally Hay, Oct. 5, 1946; 1 dau., Suzanne; m. Vivian Jury, Oct. 25, 1959; children: Michael Jury, Steven Verne. LL.B., Drake U., 1949. Bar: Iowa 1949, U.S. Dist. Ct. (no. and so. dists.) Iowa, U.S. Supreme Ct. 1957, U.S. Ct. Appeals (8th cir.). Practice law Des Moines, 1949—; speaker Govs. Safety Conf., 1987-88. Author: Trial by Notebook, 1964; co-author: Art of Persuasion in Litigation, 1966, How to Defend a Criminal Case from Arrest to Verdict, 1967, The Complete Personal Injury Practice Manual, 1983. Mem. Iowa Aeros. Commn., 1973-75; trustee ATL Roscoe Pound Found., 1965-71, fellow, 1973. Recipient Outstanding Law Alumni award Phi Alpha Delta, 1964. Fellow Internat. Acad. Trial Lawyers (chmn. aviation & space law com. 1970, ABA ad hoc com. to study court congestion 1973), Am. Coll. Trial Lawyers, Am. Bar Found., Am. Bd. Trial Advocates (treas. Iowa chpt. 1989), Internat. Soc. Barristers; mem. ABA (com. on trial techniques 1969-70; state membership chmn. sect. of ins., negligence and compensation law 1972-75; tort and ins. practice sect., com. on aviation litigation 1983-84), Iowa Bar Assn. (uniform instrn. com. 1962, rules com. 1965, chmn. Iowa rules of civil procedure 1968-69, spl. commn. fed. practice 1971-78, spl. automobile reparations com. 1972—), Polk County Bar Assn., Am. Trial Lawyers Assn./before 1962 the Nat. Assn. Claimant's Compensation Attys. (v.p. Iowa chpt. 1956-57, assoc. editor NACCA law jour., 1961, panelist and del. European conv., Dublin, 1957, .nat. sec. 1963-64, 67-68, bd. govs. 1962-63, com. on internat. membership 1957, nat. conv. com. 1952, co-chmn. tort sect. 1962-63, nat. seminar chmn. 1964-65, 66-67, chmn. nat. speakers bur. 1964-65, govt. liability com. 1971, rules com. of ins. negligence compensation law 1970, com. on trial techniques 1969-70, Iowa Key Man legis session 1969, guest statutes com. 1970, chmn. comml. tort litigation 1970, membership chmn. for Iowa 1972-74, aviation sect. 1971—, automobile accident reparations com. 1971—, trial advs. scholarship com. 1973—, nat. council pub. affairs), Iowa Acad. Trial Lawyers (sec.-treas. 1962—, editor Newsbulletin, 1962, editor Verdict Summary 1970—, editor Acad. Alert, editor Court Says 1978—), Iowa Trial Lawyers Assn., Blackstone Inn of Ct. (sec.-treas. 1989), Law Sci. Acad. Am., Lawyer-Pilots Bar Assn., Am. Judicature Soc., World Peace Through Law Ctr., Trial Lawyers Assn. Des Moines, N.Y. State Trial Lawyers Assn., Calif. Trial Lawyers Assn., Assn. Trial Lawyers Am., Okla. Trial Lawyers Assn., Tex. Trial Lawyers Assn., Am. Bar Found., Melvin M. Belli Soc. (trustee, bd. dirs.), Phi Alpha Delta, Sigma Alpha Epsilon.

LAXNESS, HALLDÓR KILJAN (HALLDÓR KILJAN GUDJÓNSSON), writer; b. Reykjavík, Apr. 23, 1902; s. Gudjon H. Helgason and Sigridur Halldórsdóttir; m. Ingibjörg Einarsdóttir, May 1, 1930; 1 child, Einar; m. Audur Sveinsdóttir, Dec. 24, 1945; children: Sigridur Halldorsdóttir, Gudny Halldórsdóttir. PhD (hon.), Aabo U., Finland, 1968; DLitt Islandcarum (hon.), U. Iceland, 1972; D. honoris causa, U. Edinburgh, Scotland, 1977; PhD (hon.), Eberhaard-Karis-U., Tubingen, Fed. Republic Germany, 1982. Author: (fiction) Barn náttúrunnar, 1919, Nokkrar sögur, 1923, Undir Helgahnúk, 1924, Vefarinn mikli frá Kasmír, 1927, Salka Valka (2 vols.), 1931-32, Fótatak manna, 1933, Sjálfstoett fólk (2 vols.), 1934-35 (pub. as Independent People, 1945), Thódur gamli halti, 1935, Heimsljós (2 vols.), 1955 (pub. as World Light, 1969), Gerska aefintyrid, 1938, Sjö töframenn, 1942, Islandsklukkan, 1943, Hid ljósa man, 1944, Eldur í Kaupinhafn, 1946, Atómstödin, 1948 (pub. as The Atom Station, 1961), Gerpla, 1952 (pub. as The Happy Warriors, 1958), Brekkukotsannáll, 1957 (pub. as The Fish Can Sing, 1966), Ungfrúin góda og Husid, 1959, Paradísarheimt, 1960 (pub. as Paradise Reclaimed, 1962), Sjöstafakverid, 1964 (pub. as A Quire of Seven, 1974), Kristnihald undir Jökli, 1968 (pub. as Christianity at the Glacier, 1972), Gudsgjafathula, 1972, Seiseijú, mikil ósköp, 1977, Dagar hjá múnkum, 1987; (plays) Straumrof, 1934, Snaefrídur Íslandssól, 1950, Silfurtúnglid, 1954, Strompleikurinn, 1961, Prjónastofan Sólin, 1962, Dúfnaveislan, 1966 (pub. as The Pigeon Banquet, 1973), Úa, 1970, Nordanstulkan, 1972; (poetry) Kvaedakver, 1930; (other writings) Kathólsk vidhorf, 1925, Althydubókin, 1929, Í austurvegi, 1933, Dagleid á fjöllum: greinar, 1937, Vettvangur dagsins, 1942, Sjálfsagdir hlutir, 1946, Reisubókarkorn, 1950, Heiman eg fór, 1952, Dagur í senn, 1955, Gjörningabók, 1959, Skáldatími, 1963, Upphaf mannúdarstefnu, 1965, Íslendíngaspjall, 1967, Vínlandspúnktar, 1969, Innansveitarkronika, 1970, Yfirskygdir stadir, 1971, Thjódhátidarrolla, 1974, Í túninu heima, 1975, Úngur eg var, 1976, Sjömeistarasagan, 1978, Grikklandsárid, 1980, Vid heygardshornid, 1981, N. Tryggvadóttir: Serenity and Power, 1982, Og árin lída, 1984, Af menníngarástandi, 1986, Sagan af braudi nu dyra, 1987 (pub. as The Bread of Life, 1987); editor: Grettissaga, 1946, Laxdaela saga, 1973; translator: A Farewell to Arms (Hemingway), Candide (Voltaire), works of Gunnar Gunnarsson, numerous other novels, plays, collections. Commandeur de l'Ordre des Arts et des Lettres, France; recipient Literature prize Internat. Peace Movement, 1953, Nobel Prize for literature, 1955; Sonning prize Copenhagen U., 1969; hon. citizenship Gent Belgium, 1958, Mosfellsoer, Iceland, 1972. Mem. Samfundet Sverige Island, Literarische Freundeskreis, Saarbrucken, Icelandic Literary Soc., Writers' Union Iceland, Union Icelandic Artist, Kungliga sallskapet (Sweden), Deutsche Akademie der Kunste (Berlin), Akademie der Wissenschaften und der Literatur in Mainz, Prix internat. de la paix, Grand Cross of Icelandic Order of Falcon, Kamendör med stora korset av Kungl (Nordstjarneorden, Sweden). Avocations: music, walking tours. Died Feb. 8, 1998.

LAYDE, DURWARD CHARLES, chemistry educator; b. La Crosse, Wis., Dec. 29, 1912; s. Joseph B. and Anna (Garvey) L.; m. Mary Agnes Lee, Nov. 20, 1943; children: Margaret, Michael, Thomas, Peter, Joseph. BA, St. Norbert Coll., 1933; PhD, U. Wis., 1940. Mem. faculty U. Wis. System, 1939-93; faculty U. Wis., Milw., 1956-81; prof. chemistry, 1963-81; prof. emeritus U. Wis., 1981-93, asso. chmn., 1970-74, chmn., 1974-76. Author: Experiments in Qualitative Analysis, 1962, (with Daryle H. Busch) Introduction to Qualitative Analysis, 1961. Mem. AAAS, Am. Chem. Soc., Sigma Xi, Phi Lambda Upsilon. Roman Catholic. Home: Milwaulkee Wis. Died June 22, 1993.

LAYTON, WILLIAM ISAAC, mathematics educator; b. Cameron, Mo., Sept. 26, 1913; s. Joseph Evening and Mary Rebecca (Leighton) L.; m. Eva James Wade Layton, Mar. 28, 1941; children: Mary Layton Wells, Gay Layton Aycock. BS, U. S.C., 1934, MS, 1935; PhD, Vanderbilt U., 1948. Cert. tchr., S.C., Fla., Ga. Math. tchr. Greer High Sch., Greer, S.C., 1935-36, Rome High Sch., Rome, Ga., 1937-39; math. dept. head Albany Sr. High Sch., Albany, Ga., 1939-40; math. tchr. Peabody Demonstration, Nashville, Tenn., 1940-41; math. and engring. drawing tchr. Amarillo Coll., Amarillo, Tex., 1941-46; math. dept. head Austin Peay State Univ., Clarksville, Tenn., 1946-48; assoc. prof. math. Auburn (Ala.) U., 1948-49; dean of instrn. Frostburg (Md.) State Coll., 1949-50; chmn. math. and stat. Stephen F. Austin State U., Nacogdoches, Tex., 1950-79; math prof. Newberry (S.C.) Coll., 1979-92, prof. emeritus, 1992-96, chmn. math., computer sci. and physics, 1982-92, acting chair dept. math., computer sci. and physics, 1992-93. Author: An Analysis of Certification Requirements for Teachers of Mathematics, 1949, (with others) College Algebra, 1956, Mathematics of Finance, 1958, College Arithmetic, 1959, 2d edit., 1971, Essential Business Mathematics, 1977; contbg. author to The Mathematics Teacher. Pres., founder East Tex. Council of Tchrs. of Math. Recipient Alumni Disting. Prof. award Stephen F. Austin State Univ., 1976, Meritorious Svc. award Nat. Coun. Tchrs. Math., 1984, Fifty Yrs. Teaching award, 1987; named Prof. of Yr., Newberry Coll., 1988, 92. Mem. Am. Math. Soc. (pres. Tex. sect.), Math. Assn. Am., S.C. Coun. Tchrs. Math., S.C. Acad. Sci., Rotary (pres. S.C. 1987), Phi Beta Kappa, Sigma Xi, Phi Delta Kappa, Pi Mu Epsilon. Presbyterian. Died April 19, 1996.

LEACH, LUNA BOWDOIN, social services educator; b. Grapeland, Tex., July 19, 1902; d. James Edmon and Alice (Nixon) Bowdoin; m. Cliff M. Leach, Mar. 27, 1956. BS, Fla. State Coll., 1926; cert., Columbia U. Sch. of Social Work, 1936; MA, NYU, 1937. Assoc. prof. U. Conn., Hartford; assoc. prof., asst. prof. Wash. State U., Seattle; assoc. exec. sec. Greater Hartford Community Coun.; social svcs. educator, ret.; mem. adv. bd. dirs. Spl. Welfare Assembly of Am.; apptd. twice to Gov.'s Child Day Care Coun.; active curriculum com. Acad. Liaison Com. Contbr. articles to numerous profl. jours. Contbr. sch. of social work U. of Columbia. Recipient Recognition award; Nat. Rsch. Coun. fellow. Mem. Acad. Cert. Social Workers (cert.), Nat. Coun. Social Welfare, Am. Assn. Social Workers (pres. Conn. chpt.). Avocation: children, families, and legislation affecting them.

LEAGUE, ELLAMAE ELLIS, retired architect, small business owner; b. Macon, Ga., July 9, 1899; d. Joseph Oliver and Susie (Choate) E.; m. George Forest League; children: Jean, Joseph Choate. Student, Fontainbleau Sch. Fine Arts, 1928. Registered architect, Ga. Pvt. practice, 1934-1975. Bd. dirs. forty yrs. Macon Little Theatre. Fellow AIA (ret. 1975); mem. State Orgn. Architects (1st pres., several nat. coms. and design). Republican. Methodist.

LEAKEY, MARY DOUGLAS, archaeologist, anthropologist; b. Feb. 6, 1913; d. Erskine Edward and Cecilia Marion (Frere) Nicol; m. Louis Seymour Bazett Leakey, 1936 (dec. 1972); 3 sons. Ed. pvt. schs.; D.Sc. (hon.), U. Witwatersrand, 1968, Western Mich. U., 1980, U. Chgo., 1981, Yale U., 1976, U. Cambridge, 1987; D.Litt. (hon.), U. Oxford, 1981, Emory U., 1988, Mass. U., 1988, Brown U., 1990, Columbia U., 1991. Former dir. Olduvai Gorge Excavations. Author: Olduvai Gorge, Excavation in Beds I and II, 1971, Africa's Vanishing Art, Disclosing the Past; also articles; editor: (with J.M. Harris) Laetoli, A Pliocene Site in North Tanzania, (with D.A. Roe) Olduvai Gorge, Excavations in Beds III and IV. Joint recipient (with L.S.B. Leakey) Prestwich medal of Geol. Soc. London; recipient Nat. Geog. Soc. Hubbard medal, Centennial award, 1988; Gold medal Soc. Women Geographers; Lineus medal Stockholm, 1978; Stopes medal Geol. Assn. London,

1980; Bradford Washburn prize Boston Mus. of Sci., 1980; Elizabeth Blackwell award Hobart and Smith Coll., 1980. Mem. Royal Swedish Acad. Scis. (hon.), Am. Acad. Arts and Scis. (assoc.), Nat. Acad. Sci. (fgn.). Home: Nairobi Kenya Died March 1998.

LEARY, TIMOTHY, psychologist, author; b. Springfield, Mass., Oct. 22, 1920; s. Timothy and Abigal (Ferris) L.; m. Rosemary Woodruff, Dec. 12, 1967; m. Barbara Chase, Dec. 18, 1978; children: Susan, John Busch, Zachary; remarried Rosemary Woodruff, Mar. 21, 1995. Student, Holy Cross Coll., 1938-39, U.S. Mil. Acad., 1940-41; AB, U. Ala., 1943; MS, Wash. State U., 1946; PhD in Psychology, U. Calif. at Berkeley, 1950. Asst. prof. U. Calif. at Berkeley, 1950-55; dir. psychol. research Kaiser Found., Oakland, Calif., 1955-58; lectr. Harvard, 1959-63; first guide League Spiritual Discovery, 1964—; pres., producer Futique Inc. (electronic books), 1985—; psychol. cons. to mgmt., 1953-63; cons. Mass. Dept. Corrections, 1961-63, Afghanistan Export Assn., 1966-69; Interactive Software Cons., Xor, 1981, Electronic Arts, 1981, Activision, 1986, Epyx, 1988, Autodesk, 1989; keynote speaker Ars Futura, Barcelona, Spain, 1989, Siggraph, Dallas, 1990, Ars Electronica, Linz, Austria, 1990, Cyberthon, San Francisco, 1990, Cyberarts, Pasadena, Libertian Party Nat. Conv., Chgo., Design Forum Symposium, Matsue, Japan, 1991, Am. Humanist Psychology Conv., 1993, Lalapaloosa Festival, 1993; founder Conscious-Net Electron Bulletin Bd., 1994. Producer: Psychedelic Celebrations, 1965-66; writer, actor: (film) Turn On, Tune In, Drop Out, 1967, Volcano of Love, 1991; author: Social Dimensions of Personality, 1950, Interpersonal Diagnosis of Personality, 1950, Multi-level Assessment of Personality, 1951, Psychedelic Experience, 1964, Psychedelic Reader, 1965, Psychedelic Prayers, 1964, High Priest, 1968, Politics of Ecstasy, 1968, The Psychology of Pleasure, 1969, Jail Notes, 1970, Confessions of a Hope Fiend, 1973, Neurologic, 1973, Terra II, 1973, The Intelligence Agents, 1978, Exo-Psychology, 1979, What Does Women Want?, 1979, Changing My Mind, 1982, Flashbacks: An Autobiography, 1983, 1983, Infopsychology, 1987, The Cybernetic Societies of the 21st Century, 1987, Greatest Hits, 1990, Virtual Reality and Telepresence, 1991, Chaos & Cyber Culture, 1994, The Adventures of Huck Getty, 1994, High Priest, 1995, Design for Dying, 1995, Quality of Life Manual, 1995; actor: (film) Cheech & Chong's Nice Dreams, 1981, Return Engagement with G. Gordon Liddy, 1984, Hard Knocks, Showscan, 1987, Moonlighting, 1988, Medium Rare, 1988, Imagine with John Lennon, 1989, Fatal Skies, 1989, Shocker, 1989, Chamelion Blue, 1990, Chill Me, Thrill Me, 1991, Roadside Prophets, 1991, Super Force, 1991, Ted and Venus, 1991, Banana Chip Love, 1991, Volcano of Love, 1992, Roadside Prophet, 1992, Ted and Venus, 1992, Sex Police, 1993, Cyberpunk with Billy Idol, 1993, Brisco County Jr., 1994, (with Retinalogic) Chaos Engineering, 1994; (recordings) Give Peace a Chance, 1969, (with J. Lennon) Seven Up, 1973, (with Jimi Hendrix) You Can Be Anything This Time Around, 1970, TranceFormation (with Psychic TV), 1992, Brain Exchange (with Hyperdelic Video), 1992, How to Operate Your Brain, 1993, With Retinalogic, 1993, (with Richard Chase) Five Generations that Changed American Culture in the 20th Century, 1994, Gilocopter (with Ministry), 1994, (with Aileen Getty) Dying is a Team Sport, 1994; designer interactive computer programs Mind Mirror, Life Adventure, 1985, Head Coach Master Mind; designer reactive videoware program for Mental Fitness, software program Neuromancer, 1986, Intercom Ednl. Software, 1989; designer CD Rom program Wonderland Park, World Wide Web Site. Candidate for gov., Calif., 1969-70; mem. Alcor Cryonics Life Extension Found., 1991; sponsor Cyberspace Room, Digital Hollywood Conv., 1996. Recipient Lifetime Achievement award Acad. Interactive Arts & Scis., 1995. Mem. AFTRA, Screen Actors Guild, Am. Courseware Assn. (pres. 1989), Hemlock Soc. Died May 31, 1996, cremated.

LEBER, LESTER, advertising agency executive; b. Newark, June 11, 1913; s. David and Hattie Leber; m. Ruth Schwarz, Mar. 29, 1940 (div. 1968); m. Magdalena Maurer, July 15, 1968; children: Frederick, Laura Wood, Daniel. BA, Columbia U., 1934. Various positions Grey Advt., N.Y.C., 1935-52; founder, hon. chmn. Leber Katz Ptnrs., N.Y.C., 1952-72. Columnist: Saturday Evening Post, 1950, Tide, 1952, Advertising Age, 1960. Served with USN, 1943-45; Pearl Harbor. DIED 08/27/96. .

LE DUAN, secretary-general Vietnamese Communist Party; b. Quang Tri Province, Central Vietnam, Apr. 4, 1907. Sec. with local rys., Hanoi; imprisoned for polit. activity, 1931-36, 40-45; mem. Communist Party Indochina; prominent in Viet Minh resistance, 1946; commr. mil. hdqrs., S. Vietnam, 1952; sec. Lao Dong Central Com. for So. Region, 1956; sec. gen. Lao Dong Party, 1959, 1st sec., 1960—; mem. Nat. Def. Council, dep. Nat. Assembly, Socialist Republic Vietnam, 1976—, also sec.-gen. Communist Party Vietnam; sec., mem. central com. Lao Dong Politburo; leader various dels. party meetings. Author articles.

LEE, FREDERICK YUK LEONG, obstetrician-gynecologist, educator; b. Honolulu, Sept. 18, 1937; s. Harold K.L. and Frances Y. (Sugai) L.; m. Linda Scott Partridge, June 21, 1974; children—Suelin K.O., David K.F., Catherine K.Y.; children by previous marriage—Mark K.C., Michelle Y.C., Monica Y.Y. Student, U. Hawaii, 1955-58; M.D., Tulane U., 1962. Diplomate Am. Bd. Ob-Gyn, Am. Bd. Laser Surgery. Rotating intern Charity Hosp., New Orleans, 1962-63, resident ob-gyn., 1966-69, instr., chief resident, 1968-69; mem. faculty Tulane U. Sch. Medicine, 1969-78, John Rock prof. reproductive physiology dept. ob-gyn., 1974-78, clin. prof., 1978-92, dir. sec. reproductive physiology, 1975-78, program dir. studies infertility and fertility, 1973-78, dir. ultra-sound unit, 1974-78; assoc. prof. clin. dept. ob-gyn. U. Nev. Sch. Medicine, Las Vegas, 1991—; active staff Valley Hosp. Med. Ctr., U. Med. Ctr. So. Nev., 1991—, Humana Sunrise Hosp. Las Vegas Surgical Ctr., Lakeside Hosp., Metairie, 1978-87, courtesy staff, 1987-91; staff Elmwood Med. Ctr. Hosp., Metairie, 1987-91, Doctors Hosp. of Jefferson, Metairie, 1988-91. Contbr. articles to med. jours. Served to capt. M.C. USAF, 1962-66. Recipient Sidney K. Simon Meml. prize Tulane U. Med. Sch., 1962; fellow USPHS, 1969-70. Fellow ACS, Am. Coll. Obstetricians and Gynecologists; mem. Conrad G. Collins Soc., Soc. Gynecol. Surgeons, Am. Fertility Soc., Am. Inst. Ultrasound in Medicine, Cen. Assn. Obstetricians and Gynecologists, Am. Soc. Laser Medicine and Surgery, Nev. State Med. Soc., Clark County Med. Soc., Clark County Ob-gyn. Soc., Gynecol. Laser Soc., Omega Internat Inst. (bd. dirs. 1988-90), Am. Assn. Gynlaparoscopists, Sigma Xi. Avocations: hunting, fishing. Deceased.

LEE, WILLIAM STATES, retired utility executive; b. Charlotte, N.C., June 23, 1929; s. William States and Sarah (Everett) L.; m. Janet Fleming Rumberger, Nov. 24, 1951; children: Lisa, States, Helen. BS in Engring. magna cum laude, Princeton U., 1951. Registered profl. engr., N.C., S.C. With Duke Power Co., Charlotte, 1955-94, engring. mgr., 1962-65; v.p. engring. Duke Power Co., 1965-71, sr. v.p., 1971-75, exec. v.p., 1976-77, pres., chief operating officer, 1978-82, chmn., CEO, 1982-94, also dir., mem. mgmt. and fin. coms.; retired, 1994; bd. dirs. Liberty Corp., J.P. Morgan Co., Morgan Guaranty Trust Co., Knight-Ridder, Tex. Instruments. Bd. dirs. United Cmty. Svcs., Found. of the Carolinas; trustee Queen's Coll., U. N.C., Charlotte Found., Presbyn. Hosp. Found. With C.E. USNR, 1951-54. Named Outstanding Engr. N.C. Soc. Engrs., 1969. Fellow ASME (George Westinghouse gold medal 1972, James N. Landis medal 1991), ASCE; mem. Nat. Acad. Engring., Nat. Soc. Profl. Engrs. (Outstanding Engr. award 1980), Edison Electric Inst. (dir. econs. and fin. policy com., dir.), Charlotte C. of C. (chmn. 1979), Am. Nuclear Soc., Phi Beta Kappa, Tau Beta Pi. Presbyn. (ruling elder). Died July 10, 1996.

LEFF, ARTHUR, retired administrative law judge; b. N.Y.C., Mar. 19, 1908; s. Isadore Isaac and Bessie (Mansion) L.; m. Miriam Kapit, Feb. 23, 1934; 1 dau., Joanna (Mrs. Mark Pinsky). A.B., Cornell U., 1929, LL.B., 1930. Bar: N.Y. 1931. Practice in N.Y.C., 1931-42; adminstrv. law judge NLRB, SEC, Fed. Res. Bd., 1943-63; chief counsel to chmn. NLRB, 1963-70, asso. chief adminstrv. law judge, 1970-80, chief adminstrv. law judge, 1980-82; mem. Adminstrv. Conf. U.S., 1972-74. Mem. Am., Fed. bar assns., Conf. Adminstrv. Law Judges, Fed. Execs. League. Died Sept. 8, 1996.

LEGGET, ROBERT FERGUSON, civil engineer; b. Liverpool, Eng., Sept. 29, 1904; s. Donald and Mercy (Thomson) L.; m. Lillian S. d. S.A. Free, Feb. 28, 1931; 1 child, David. B.E. with honors, U. Liverpool, 1925, M.E., 1927; LL.D. (hon.), McMaster U., 1961, Queen's U., 1966, U. N.B., 1969, U. Toronto, 1969, Glasgow U., 1971; D.Sc. (hon.), Waterloo U., 1963, Western U, 1969; D.G.Sc. (hon.), Charles U., Prague, 1969; D.Eng. (hon.), Liverpool U., 1971, Nova Scotia Tech. Coll., 1972; D.Sc. (hon.), Clarkson Coll. Tech., 1972, Sir George Williams U., 1972; D.Eng. (hon.), Carleton U., 1974. Asst. engr. C.S. Meik and Buchanan, Westminster, Eng., 1925-29; resident engr. Power Corp. Can. Ltd., 1929-32; engr. Can. Sheet Piling Co. Ltd., Montreal, 1932-36; lectr. civil engring. Queen's U., 1936-38; asst. prof. civil engring. U. Toronto, 1938-43, assoc. prof., 1943-47; dir. div. bldg. research NRC, 1947-69. Author: Geology and Engineering, 1939, 3d edit., 1983, Rideau Waterway, 1955, 2d edit., 1986, Standards in Canada, 1970, Railways of Canada, 1973, Cities and Geology, 1973, Ottawa Waterway, 1975, Canals of Canada, 1976, Canadian Railways in Pictures, 1977, The Seaway, 1979; (with C.P. Disney) Modern Railroad Structure, 1949; (with P.F. Karrow) Handbook of Geology in Civil Engineering, 1983; editor: Soils in Canada, 1961, (with T.W. Fluhr) Reviews in Engineering Geology Vol. 1, 1962, Geology under Cities, Vol. 5, 1982, Glacial Till, 1976; contbr. numerous papers on engring. and research of soil mechanics to profl. jours. Decorated officer, companion Order of Can. Recipient Julian C. Smith medal, 1971, Medaille d'or, Can. Coun. Profl. Engrs., 1972, Logan Gold medal Geol. Assn. Can., 1972, Leo B. Moore Gold medal Standards Engrs. Soc., 1974, Dumont Gold medal Geol. Soc. Belgium, William Smith medal Geol. Soc. London, 1977, Sir John Kennedy medal Engring. Inst. Can., 1978, Royal Bank award, 1989. Hon. fellow Inst. Civil Engrs. (London), Royal Archtl. Inst. Can., Royal Soc. Edinburgh; mem. ASCE (hon.), Assn. Profl. Engrs. Ont., ASTM (pres. 1965-66), Geol. Soc. Am. (pres. 1966), Internat. Council Bldg. Research (pres. 1966-69), Can. Acad. of Engring. (founding pres. 1987), Nat. Acad. Engring. (fgn. assoc.). Home: Ottowa Can. Deceased.

LEHANE, LOUIS JAMES, consulting company executive; b. Wilmington, Del., Apr. 18, 1930; s. Louis Anthony and Naomi Joan (Minors) LeH.; m. Janet Mae Zehfuss, Oct. 7, 1955; children: Kimberly LeHane Rohr, Pamela LeHane Pezewski, Lori, Leslie LeHane Stamp. BS, LaSalle U., 1954; MS, U. Pitts., 1955. Prodn. mgr. Kaiser Aluminum and Chem. Corp., Erie, Pa., 1955-58; dir. mgmt. devel. Continental Can Co., N.Y.C., 1958-71; exec. v.p. Thinc Group, Inc., N.Y.C., 1971-75; v.p. human resources Austin Industries, Dallas, 1975-77; pres. Thinc Cons. Group Internat., N.Y.C., 1977-80, LeHane Cons., Inc., Leesburg, Va., 1980-95; speaker, presenter seminars in field. Contbr. articles to profl. publs. Co-chair United Way, Leesburg, 1985-89. With USN, 1950-52, Korea. Ida Horne Burchefield fellow, 1954. Mem. Assn. Outplacement Cons. Firms (pres. 1987-89, bd. dirs. 1985-90), Army and Navy Club, N.Y. Athletic Club, Purcellville Golf and Country Club. Republican. Episcopalian. Avocations: big game fishing, writing. Home: Leesburg Va. Died June 2, 1995; interred Church of Our Savior, Oatlands, VA.

LEHMAN, ROBERT NATHAN, ophthalmologist, educator; b. Lancaster, Pa., Oct. 22, 1911; s. Harry Nathan and Mable May (Shenk) L.; m. Clara May Hileman, Apr. 24, 1938; 1 dau., Mary Dorcas. B.S., Franklin and Marshall Coll., 1933; M.D., Temple U., 1937. Intern Temple U. Hosp., 1937-39, resident, 1947-48; resident Walter Reed Hosp., Washington, 1948-50, Armed Forces Inst. Pathology, Washington, 1950-51; chief ophthalmology VA Hosp., Pitts., 1954-78; prof. ophthalmology U. Pitts. Med. Sch., 1954-78, lectr. pathology, 1966-78. Contbr. articles to profl. jours. Served with AUS, 1939-54. Decorated Bronze Star; Croix de Guerre (2) France). Mem. ACS, Am. Acad. Ophthalmology, Pitts. Ophthal. Soc., Ea. Ophthal. Pathology Soc., Univ. Club (Pitts.). Home: Los Angeles Calif. Died Aug. 23, 1996.

LEHMANN, FREDERICK GLIESSMANN, university administrator; b. Hinsdale, Ill., Nov. 1, 1930; s. Frederick William and Hermine Barbara (Gliessmann) L.; m. Betty Ann Ferguson, Sept 13, 1952 (div. 1984); children: Karl F., Pamela J., Karen L., Andrew W. SB, MIT, 1951. Cert. Inst. for Ednl. Mgmt., Harvard Bus. Sch., 1973. Adminstrv. staff member MIT, 1953-54; prodn. dept. mgr. Procter & Gamble Co., Kansas City, Kans., 1954-59; asst. sec. MIT Alumni Assn., Cambridge, Mass., 1959-62, sec., 1962-73; advanced to fin. v.p. MIT Alumni Assn., 1973-77; dir. devel. Boston U., 1977-79; exec. dir. devel. & pub. affairs The Rockefeller Univ., 1979-84; v.p. for instl. advancement N.Y. Med. Coll., Valhalla, 1984-89; dep. v.p. for devel. Columbia U., N.Y.C., 1989-95; cons. Nat. Acad. Scis., Washington, 1982-84, devel. div. visiting com., Carnegie-Mellon Univ., Pittsburgh, 1965-68. Trustee, Boxford (Mass.) Town Lib., 1969-78; mem. gov.'s adv. coun. on comprehensive health planning, Boston, 1971-77. 1st lt. USAF, 1951-53. Recipient, U.S. Steel Award 1978, Time/Life Award, 1977. Mem. AAAS, N.Y. Acad. Scis., Assn. Am. Med. Colls./GIA (steering com. 1992-93), MIT Alumni Ctr. N.Y. (exec. com./govs. 1978-95), Unnamed Soc., Harvard Club N.Y.C. Avocations: skiing, sailing, photography. Home: Littleton Colo. Died Nov. 15, 1995.

LEIS, WINOGENE B. (MRS. HENRY PATRICK LEIS, JR.), professional association executive; b. Clay, W.Va., Feb. 27, 1919; d. Gruder L. and Daisy M. (Young) Barnette; RN cum laude, Kanawha Valley Hosp., 1939; m. Henry Patrick Leis, Jr., Jan. 8, 1944; children: Henry Patrick III, Thomas Frederick. Nurse, Kanawha Valley Hosp., 1939-43. Decorated lady comdr. Equestrian Order Holy Sepulchre Jerusalem. Mem. Woman's Aux. Internat. Coll. Surgeons (corr. sec. N.Y. State surg. div. 1955-57, v.p. 1961-63, pres. 1963-67; pres. U.S. sect. 1970, dir. 1970-94, pres. Internat. Body 1977-78, bd. govs. 1978-94, chairperson rsch. and scholarship com. 1990-94), Flower Fifth Avenue Hosp. Woman's Aux. (dir. 1956-59, 69-94), Woman's Aux. N.Y. Acad. Scis., Woman's Aux. N.Y. State Med. Soc., Woman's Aux. Cabrini Med. Ctr., Woman's Aux. Westchester County Med. Ctr., Woman's Aux. Lenox Hill Hosp., Woman's Aux. So. Med. Assn., Cath. Women's Guild, Ocean Dunes Club, Surf Golf and Beach Club. Republican. Roman Catholic. Died Nov. 14, 1994. Home: Myrtle Beach S.C.

LEJEUNE, JEROME JEAN LOUIS MARIE, geneticist, physician; b. Montrouge, Seine, France, June 13, 1926; s. Pierre Ulysse and Marcelle (Lermat) L.; m. Birthe Bringsted; children: Anouk, Damien, Karin, Clara, Thomas. Student, Stanislas Coll., Paris. Attending Nat. Sci. Rsch. Ctr., Paris, 1952-63, dir., 1963-64; chief svc. Hopital Enfants Malades, Paris, 1964-94; prof. fundamental genetics Faculty Medicine Necker-Enfantsmalades, Paris, 1969-94; Inst. Progenese, Paris. Recipient Kennedy prize, 1962, Znanie diploma, 1964, William Allen Meml. award, 1969, Feltrinelli prize, 1984. Mem. Royal Soc. Medicine (London), Am. Acad. Arts and Scis., Pontifical Acad. Scis., Royal Acad. Scis. (Stockholm), Acad. Moral and Polit. Scis., Nat. Acad. Medicine (Paris). Roman Catholic. Home: Paris France Died Apr. 3, 1994.

LEKAI, LASZLO CARDINAL, archbishop of Esztergon; b. Zalalovo, Zala dist., Hungary, Mar. 12, 1910; s. Gyula and Julianna (Freiler) Lung.; Ph.D., Collegium Germanico-Hungaricum, Rome, 1936. Ordained priest Roman Catholic Ch., 1934; chaplain Veszprem (Hungary) Sem., 1936, lectr. in theology, 1937-44; Episcopal sec., 1944-47; Episcopal dir.; parish priest from 1948; dean of Balatonlelle, Zalaszentivan, Badacsonytomaj, Hungary, 1948-74; titular bishop Girus Tarasii (Hungary), 1972; apostolic adminstr. Diocese Veszprem, 1972, Archdiocese Esztergom (Hungary), 1974-76; archbishop of Esztergom and primate of Hungary, 1976—; elevated to Sacred Coll. of Cardinals, 1976; head Bishop's Conf. Hungary. Decorated Order of Ruby Studded Banner (Hungary); recipient Man of Conscience award, U.S., 1979. Contbr. sermons to religious jours. Home and

LELAND, LAWRENCE, insurance executive; b. C., Can., Nov. 13, 1915; Children: Jeanne L. Corbin, James F. Leland, Barbara B. Leland, Marjorie L. McElfresh, Marilyn L. Philbrook, David H. Leland. AB, Earlham Coll. CLU. Asst. supt. agys. Am. United Life Ins. Co., 1948-58, agy. v.p., 1958-67, dir., 1962-67; from sr. v.p., mem. operating com. to exec. v.p. Nat. Life Ins. Co., Montpelier, Vt., 1967-80; ret. Nat. Life Ins. Co., 1980; dir. Nat. Life Investment Mgmt. Co., Inc.; pres., dir. Equity Service, Inc., Adminstrv. Services, Inc.; exec. com. Audit Nat. Life Ins. Co. Trustee Earlham Coll., 1958-67, acting pres., 1984-85, hon. life trustee, 1985—; mem. Vt. Employment Security Bd.; bd. visitors Guilford Coll., 1980-85. Recipient Outstanding Vol. award Earlham Coll. Mem. Gen. Agts. and Mgrs. Assn., Central Vt. Life Underwriters Assn., Lafayette (Ind.) Life Underwriters Assn. (past pres.), Masons, Ind. Leaders Club, Meridian Hills Country Club. Mem. Soc. of Friends. Died Aug. 10, 1996.

LEMELSON, JEROME H., inventor; b. 1923. MSc degrees in aeronautical, industrial engineering, New York U., N.Y.C. Holder more than 450 patents. Achievements include nearly 500 patents.

LEMKE, PAUL ARENZ, botany educator; b. New Orleans, July 14, 1937; s. Paul A. and Glory Ann (Schellinger) L.; m. Joy Faye Owens, 1963 (div. 1982); children: Paul Arenz, Anne Wellesley. B.S., Tulane U., 1960; M.A., U. Toronto, 1962; Ph.D., Harvard U., 1966. Instr. Tulane U., New Orleans, 1962-63; sr. scientist Eli Lilly & Co., Indpls., 1966-72; assoc. prof. Carnegie-Mellon U., Pitts., 1972-79, sr. fellow, 1972-79; prof. Auburn (Ala.) U., 1979—; head dept. botany, plant pathology and microbiology Auburn U., 1979-85; cons. Marcel Dekker Pub., 1974—, E.R. Squibb & Sons, 1975-76, Schering Corp., 1987-90; dir. Am. Genetics, Inc., Denver, 1982-86. Editor: Viruses and Plasmids in Fungi, 1979, Applied and Environmental Microbiology, 1982, Applied Microbiology and Biotechnology, 1985, The Mycota, 1994; author: (with others) Plasmids of Eukaryotes, 1986; patentee in field. Recipient Humboldt Found. award, 1978, Charles Porter award Soc. Indsl. Microbiology, 1982, Charles Thom award, 1994; named annual lectr. Mycological Soc., 1994; Woodrow Wilson fellow, 1960. Fellow Am. Acad. Microbiology; mem. Soc. for Indsl. Microbiology (pres. 1979-80, Charles Porter award 1982, Charles Thom award 1994), Mycol. Soc. Am. (ann. lectr. 1993), Gordon Rsch. Conf. (coun. 1980), Am. Inst. Biol. Sci. (governing bd.), Am. Soc. Microbiology (chmn. fermentation and biotech. div. 1982), Univ. Club, Lions, Phi Beta Kappa. Republican. Roman Catholic.

LEMOYNE, IRVE CHARLES, career officer; b. Brownsville, Tex., June 28, 1939; s. McPherson and Doris (Grimm) LeM.; m. Elizabeth Gzeckowicz, June 11, 1961; children: Irve Charles Jr., Elizabeth Christian. BS in Indsl. Mgmt., Ga. Inst. Tech., 1961; MS in Mgmt., Naval Postgrad Sch., Monterey, Calif., 1972. Commd. ensign USN, 1961, advanced through grades to rear adm., 1991; div. officer USS Massey (DD 778), Mayport, Fla., 1961-62; student underwater demolition team tng. U.S. Naval Amphibious Base, Little Creek, Va., 1962-66, ops. officer Underwater Demolition Team 22, 1963 -66; exec. officer SEAL Team 1 U.S. Naval Amphibious Base, Coronado, Calif., 1966-69; commdg. officer Underwater Demolition Team 11, Coronado, Calif., 1969-71; student Naval Postgrad. Sch., Monterey, 1971-72; spl. warfare project officer Naval Sea Systems Command, Washington, 1972-75; asst. to spl. warfare mission and resource officer OPNAV Staff, The Pentagon, Washington, 1975-77; student Nat. War Coll., Washington, 1977-78; commdg. officer Inshore Undersea Warfare Group One, Coronado, 1978-79; chief staff officer Naval Spl. Warfare Group 1, Coronado, 1979-81; spl. asst. Dep. chief Naval Material for Resources Mgmt., Arlington, Va., 1981-82, chief ops. div., 1982-83; comdr Naval Sp. Warfare Group 1, Coronado, 1983-85; fellow Chief Naval Ops. Strategic Study Group, Naval War Coll., Newport, R.I., 1985-86; br. head Naval Spl. Warfare Plans and Policy Dep. Chief Naval Ops. for Plans, Policy and Ops., Washington, 1986-87; comdr. Naval Spl. Warfare Command, Naval Amphibious Base, Coronado, 1987-89; dir. resources U.S. Spl. Ops. Command, MacDill AFB, Fla., 1989-93, dep. commander-in-chief, 1993-96. Decorated Legion of Merit with two gold stars, Bronze Star with gold star and Combat V, Meritorious Svc. medal with two gold stars, Defense Distinguished Service Medal. Mem. U.S. Naval Inst. Episcopalian. Avocations: beekeeping, windsurfing. Home: Tampa Fla. Deceased.

LENHER, SAMUEL, chemical manufacturing executive; b. Madison, Wis., June 19, 1905; s. Victor and May (Blood) L.; m. Irene Kirkland, Dec. 14, 1929; children: John K., Ann B. (Mrs. A.L. Robinson, Jr.), George V. B.A., U. Wis., 1924, D.Sc., 1959; Ph.D., U. London, 1926; D.Sc., U. Del., 1961. Internat. Edn. Bd. fellow Berlin, 1927; NRC fellow U. Calif., 1928; with E. I. duPont de Nemours & Co., Wilmington, Del., 1929-78; successively research chemist, tech. adviser organic chems. dept., supt. develop. Chambers works, mgr. Chambers works, asst. gen. mgr. organic chems. E. I. duPont de Nemours & Co., 1929-55; v.p., dir. mem. exec. com., 1955-70, dir., 1955-78; commr. Farmers Bank of State of Del., 1976-81. Mem. sec.'s cons. med. research and edn. HEW, 1957-58; adv. com. for Pub. Health Service personnel study, 1961, sec.'s task force environmental health and related problems, 1966-67; mem. gen. tech. adv. com. Office Coal Research, Dept. Interior, 1960-66; mem. research mgmt. adv. panel com. sci. and astronautics U.S. Ho. Reps., 1964-75; patent adv. com. U.S. Patent Office, 1965-68; mem. summer study on space applications Nat. Acad. Scis.-NASA, 1968; pres. Welfare Council Del., Inc.; adv. council Patent, Trademark and Copyright Research Inst., George Washington U., 1965-70; bd. mgrs. Wistar Inst. Anatomy and Biology, 1959-71, v.p., 1961-71; lifetime trustee Johns Hopkins, 1959-77, trustee emeritus, 1977; trustee Wis. Alumni Research Found., 1957-83, trustee emeritus, 1983-92; trustee U. Del., 1963-86, trustee emeritus, 1986-92, chmn., 1972-82; trustee Tower Hill Sch., 1948-66, Johns Hopkins Hosp., 1967-77; trustee, mem. corp. Marine Biol. Lab., Woods Hole, 1967-76; trustee U. Del. Research Found., 1954-75, trustee emeritus, 1975-92, pres., 1955-66; dir., mem. exec. com. United Community Fund No. Del., Inc., 1956-73, pres., 1968-70. Fellow Univ. Coll., London, 1966; Poly. Inst. N.Y. Fellow AAAS, N.Y. Acad. Scis.; mem. Synthetic Organic Chem. Mfgs. Assn. U.S. (pres. 1955), Am. Chem. Soc., Soc. Chem. Industry (vice chmn. Am. sect. 1963, chmn. 1964), Am. Inst. Chem. Engrs., Am. Philos. Soc. Unitarian. Clubs: Wilmington, Wilmington Country (dir. 1965-73). Home: Hockessin Del. Died Dec. 17, 1992.

LE PELLEY, GUERNSEY, editorial cartoonist, writer; b. Chgo., May 14, 1910; s. Franklin and Ardria (Miner) LeP.; m. Maxine Gillis, Sept. 10, 1938; children: Lynn, Richard. Student, Principia Coll., 1928-29, Chgo. Art Inst., Evanston (Ill.) Acad. Fine Art, Northwestern U., Northeastern U.; BA, Harvard U. Writer Highland Park (Ill.) Press, 1930-33, Sta. WFAA, Dallas, 1933-34; freelance writer, artist, 1932—; author daily comic strip Tubby Christian Sci. Monitor, 1935-81, editorial cartoonist, 1961-81, ret., 1981. Author off-Broadway plays including Love is Too Much Trouble, 1946, To Blush Unseen, 1951, Absolutely Murder, 1954. Cofounder Sharon (Conn.) Playhouse, 1946. With USAAF, World War II. Mem. Assn. Am. Editorial Cartoonists (past adv. bd.), Quiet Birdmen, Dramatists Guild.

LERNER, INA ROSLYN, executive administrator; b. Woodbury, N.J., Jan. 19, 1938; d. Jacob and Reba Docktor (Goodman) Goldman; m. Norman C. Lerner, Sept. 6, 1959; children: Sheila Beth, Julie Anne. BA, Marymount U., 1975. Pres. Ina R. Lerner Cons., Fairfax, Va., 1978-85; assoc. Fac Technology Inc., Vienna, Va., 1985—; exec. adminstr. Black & Decker/Planning Rsch. Corp., McLean, Va., 1987—; career advisor Women's Ctr. of No. Va., 1988. Mem. ambassador com. Fairfax C. of C., Vienna, 1988—. Mem. Va. Assn. Female Execs. (adv. com., 1989), NAFE, Sailing Club of Washington. Avocations: skiing, sailing, theatre, travel. Home: Fairfax Va. Deceased.

LERNER, NATHAN BERNARD, artist; b. Chgo., Mar. 15, 1913; s. Louis Alexander and Ida Lerner; m. Kiyoko Asai, July 1, 1968; children: Michael John, Amy Elizabeth. Student, Nat. Acad. Art, Chgo., 1931, Art Inst. Chgo., 1933-34; B.S., Sch. Design in Chgo., 1941. Head of photo workshop Sch. of Design in Chgo., 1941-43; head of product design workshop, dean of faculty and students Inst. of Design, Chgo., 1945-49; ednl. dir. Inst. of Design, 1946-47; prof. U. Ill., Chgo., 1967-72; pres. Lerner Design Assos., 1949-72. One man shows include Chgo. Mus. Sci. and Industry, 1974, Bauhaus Archives, Berlin, 1975, Pentax Gallery, Osaka, Japan, 1976, Harry Lunn Gallery, Washington, 1977, Frumkin Gallery, Chgo., 1977, G.R. Hawkins Gallery, Los Angeles, 1977, Chgo. Hist. Soc., 1983, Photog. Gallery Internat., Tokyo, 1984, Ill. State Mus., Springfield, Chgo. Cultural Ctr., Ind. State U., Terre Haute, 1974, Bradley U., Peoria, Ill., 1973, Frumkin Gallery, Chgo., 1975, New York, 1976, Inst. of Contemporary Art, Boston, 1978, Augustana Mus., Rockford, Ill., 1987, The Photographers Gallery, London, 1988, Valparaiso U. Mus., 1989, U. Iowa Mus., 1993, Milw. Mus. Fine Art, 1995; represented in permanent collections Art Inst. Chgo., Mus. Modern Art, N.Y.C., Met. Mus. Art, N.Y.C., Mus. Fine Arts, Houston, Mus. Modern Art, Paris, Bibliotheque National, Paris, Eastman House, Rochester, Bauhaus Archive, Berlin, Mpls. Art Inst., Mus. Contemporary Art, Chgo., Nihon U., Tokyo, Seattle Mus. Art, Monterey (Calif.), Inst. Art, Amon Carter Mus., Fort Worth Israel Mus., Jerusalem, Kyoto Mus. Art, Japan, San Francisco Mus. Art, Ill. State Mus. Art, Internat. Ctr. Photography, N.Y.C., Ctr. for Creative Photography, Tucson, Santa Fe Mus. Fine Arts, Milw. Art Mus., Smart Gallery, Chgo., Les Recontres D'Arles, France, Tokyo Met. Mus. Ill. Arts Council grantee 1977-78. Mem. Artists Guild Chgo., Art Inst. Chgo. Alumni Assn. Patentee in field. Died Feb. 8, 1997.

LEROY, MAURICE, linguist; b. Jan. 23, 1909; s. Georges and Charlotte (Huet) L.; m. Alice Molinghen, July 8, 1909; children: Claude, Michel. Diploma, Nat. Sch. Oriental Langs., Paris; student, Sch. Practical High Studies, Sorbonne, Paris; Doctor in Philosophy and Letters, U. Brussels; Doctorate (hon.), U. Clermont-Ferrand, France. Prof., rector U. Brussels, 1945-79; mem. Royal Acad. Belgium, Brussels, 1963—, sec., 1975-84. Author: Les Grands Courants de la linguistique moderne, 1977, Introduction á laGrammaire Comparée des Langues Indo-Européenes, 1973. Capt. Belgium Army, 1939-45, POW. Recipient Grand Cross of the Order of the Crown, Belgium, 1986, numerous civil and military awards. Mem.Royal Soc. Letters, Acad. Nat. Lincei, Austrian Acad. Sci., Inst. France, Acad. Inscriptions et Belles Lettres, Mediterranean Acad. Sci.

LESAR, HIRAM HENRY, lawyer, educator; b. Thebes, Ill., May 8, 1912; s. Jacob L. and Missouri Mabel (Keith) L.; m. Rosalee Berry, July 11, 1937 (dec. Oct. 1985); children: James Hiram, Albert Keith, Byron Lee; m. Barbara Thomas, Feb. 12, 1987. AB, U. Ill., 1934, JD, 1936; JSD, Yale U., 1938. Bar: Ill. 1936, Mo. 1954, U.S. Supreme Ct. 1960. Asst. prof. law U. Kans., 1937-40, asso. prof., 1940-42; sr., prin. atty. bd. legal examiners U.S. CSC, 1942-44; assoc. prof. law U. Mo., 1946-48, prof., 1948-57; prof. law Washington U., St. Louis, 1957-72, dean Sch. Law, 1960-72; founding dean, prof. law So. Ill. U., Carbondale, 1972-80, interim pres. univ., 1974, acting pres., 1979-80, disting. service prof., 1980-82, prof. emeritus, 1982-97, vis. disting. svc. prof., 1983-97; disting. vis. prof. McGeorge Sch. Law, 1982-83; vis. prof. law U. Ill., summer 1947, Ind. U., summer 1952, U. So. Calif., summer 1959, U. N.C., summer 1961, NYU, summer 1965. Author: Landlord and Tenant, 1957; Contbr. to: Am. Law of Property, 1952, supplement, 1977, also, Dictionary Am. History, Ency. Brit. Bd. dirs. Legal Aid Soc., St. Louis and St. Louis County, 1960-72, pres. 1966-67; mem. Human Rels. Commn., University City, Mo., 1966-71, chmn., 1966, 67; bd. dirs. Land of Lincoln Legal Assistance Found., 1972-82, pres., 1982, vice chmn., 1988-97; mem. Fed. Mediation and Conciliation Svc., other arbitration panels; bd. dirs. Bacone Coll., 1981-87; trustee Lincoln Acad. Ill., 1987-97. Lt. comdr. USNR, 1944-46. Recipient Pres.' award Mo. Bar, 1968; named Laureate Lincoln Acad. of Ill., 1985. Fellow Am. Bar Found., Ill. Bar Found.; mem. ABA, AAUP, FBA, Am. Arbitration Assn., Am. Law Inst., Ill. Bar Assn., Mo. Bar Assn., St. Louis Bar Assn., Am. Judicature Soc., Univ. Club St. Louis, Yale Club Chgo., Rotary Internat., Jackson Country Club, Masons, K.T., Shriners, Order of Coif, Phi Beta Kappa, Phi Kappa Phi, Phi Delta Phi (hon.). Baptist. Died Aug. 4, 1997.

LESCAZE, LEE ADRIEN, editor; b. N.Y.C., Dec. 8, 1938; s. William Edmond and Mary (Hughes) L.; m. Rebecca Giraud Hughes, Mar. 25, 1967; children: Alexandra Hughes, Miranda Mary, Adrien William. A.B., Harvard, 1960. With Washington Post, 1963—, asst. fgn. editor, 1965-67, Saigon corr., 1967-68, Hong Kong corr., 1970-73, fgn. editor, 1973-74, nat. editor, 1975-77, N.Y. corr., 1977-80, White House corr., 1980-82, asst. mng. editor, 1982-92; weekend editor The Wall Street Jour., 1995—. Deceased.

LESHER, MARGARET, newspaper publisher, songwriter; b. San Antonio, Tex., May 4, 1932; d. Lloyd Elmo Lisco and Dovie Deona (Maynard) Lisco Welch; m. William Jarvis Ryan (dec.); children: Patricia Ryan Simmonds, Wendi Ryan Alves, Jill Ryan Heidt, Roxanne Ryan Gibson; m. Dean Stanley Lesher, Sr., Apr. 2, 1973 (dec.); m. Collin T.C. Thorstenson, Nov. 7, 1996. Dir. cmty. svcs. Contra Costa Times Newspaper, Walnut Creek, Calif., 1973-94; chmn. bd. Lesher Comm., Inc., Walnut Creek, 1974—; pres., ceo, Dean and Margaret Lesher Found. Composer, lyricist gospel song Margaret Lesher Album, 1976 (So. Calif. Motion Picture Coun. Bronze Halo award 1982); author 14 published poems. Regent Holy Names Coll., Oakland, Calif., 1979-86; chief of protocol Contra Costa County, 1980—; dir. Bay Area Sports Hall of Fame, San Francisco, 1982—; bd. overseers U. Calif., San Francisco, 1983-90; bd. dirs. Yosemite Fund; mem. San Francisco Host Com., 1983—, Internat. Host Com. of Calif., 1983-86, Nat. Reading Initiative Coordinating Coun., 1988—; dir. emeritus Alameda-Contra Costa Regional Parks Found.; developed Contra Costa County Citizen Recognition Awards Program with County Police Chiefs Assn.; founded Contra Costa Literacy Alliance; commr. Port of Richmond, Calif., 1983-86; chmn. adv. bd. Crisis Nursery of Bay Area, Concord, 1983-86; adv. bd. Oakland A's Baseball Team, 1984-85, (Battered Women's) Alternatives, 1983—; pres. bd. dirs. Mt. Diablo Hosp. Found., 1980-81; bd. dirs. Contra Costa Council, 1984-90; mem. adv. bd. Las Trampas Sch. Mentally Retarded, chmn., 1984-90; trustee Oakland Symphony Orch., 1985-86; host Informed Viewer pub. svc. program Sta. KFCB-TV. Recipient Spl. Merit award State of Calif., 1982, Charles E. Scripps award Outstanding Contbn. in the Promotion of Literacy, 1988, 2 Internat. Silver Angel awards, 1st pl. for lit. program Calif. Newspaper Pub.'s Assn., 1988; named Calif. Assembly Woman of Yr. Mem. Am. Newspaper Pub. Assn. (ednl. svcs. com. 1988—), Gospel Music Assn., ASCAP, Nat. TV Acad. Arts & Scis., Calif. Cattlemen's Assn., Cancer of the Prostate Cure, Walnut Creek Rotary. Republican. Christian. Avocation: horses.

LESLY, PHILIP, public relations counsel; b. Chgo., May 29, 1918; m. Ruth Edwards, Oct. 17, 1940 (div. 1971); 1 son, Craig.; m. Virginia Barnes, May 11, 1984. BS magna cum laude, Northwestern U., 1940. Asst. to news editor Chgo. Herald & Examiner, 1935-37; copywriter advt. dept. Sears, Roebuck & Co., Chgo., 1940-41; asst. dir. publicity Northwestern U., 1941-42; account exec. Theodore R. Sills & Co. (pub. rels.), Chgo., 1942; v.p. Theodore R. Sills & Co. (pub. rels.), 1943, exec. v.p., 1945; dir. pub. rels. Ziff-Davis Pub. Co., 1945-46; exec. v.p. Harry Coleman & Co. (pub. rels.), 1947-49; pres. Philip Lesly Co. (pub. rels.), Chgo., 1949—; lectr. pub. rels., pub. opinion to bus. and sch. groups. Co-author: Public Relations: Principles and Procedures, 1945, Everything and the Kitchen Sink, 1955; author: The People Factor, 1974, Selections from Managing the Human Climate, 1979, How We Discommunicate, 1979, Overcoming Opposition, 1984, Bonanzas and Fool's Gold, 1987; bimonthly Managing the Human Climate; editor: Public Relations in Action, 1974, Public Relations Handbook, 3d rev. edit., 1967, Lesly's Public Relations Handbook, 1971, rev. edit., 1978, 83, Lesly's Handbook of Public Relations and Communications, 1991, 2d edit., 1997; contbr. articles to bus. publs. Recipient Gold Anvil award Pub. Relations Soc. Am., 1979; voted leading active practitioner Pub. Relations Reporter Survey, 1978. Mem. Pub. Rels. Soc. Am., Phi Beta Kappa. DIED 04/28/97. .

LESOURD, LEONARD EARLE, publisher, editor; b. Columbus, Ohio, May 20, 1919; s. Howard Marion and Lucile (Leonard) LeS.; m. Evelyn Chester, Aug. 21, 1948 (div. Mar. 1959); m. Catherine Marshall, Nov. 14, 1959 (dec. Mar. 1983); m. Sandra Jean Simpson, June 22, 1985; children: Linda, Chester, Jeffrey. BA, Ohio Wesleyan U., 1941. Editor Guideposts mag., N.Y.C., 1946-74; pub. Chosen Books, Grand Rapids, Mich., 1974-92; chmn. Breakthrough, Inc., Lincoln, Va., 1980-94; elder First Presbyn. Ch., Delray Beach, Fla., 1968-77, New Covenant Presbyn. Ch., Pompono Beach, Fla., 1977-81; v.p. Prebyn. Reformed and Renewal Ministries, Oklahoma City, 1977. Author: Skybent, 1944, Strong Men, Weak Men, 1990, (with Catherine Marshall) My Personal Prayer Diary, 1978; editor: Touching the Heart of God, 1990. Pres. PTA, Carmel, N.Y., 1956. 1st lt. USSAC, 1945. Mem. Fellowship Christian Athletes (sec., bd. dirs. 1970-76). Republican. Home: Lincoln Va. Died Feb. 5, 1996.

LESTER, RICHARD ALLEN, economist, educator; b. Blasdell, N.Y., Mar. 1, 1908; s. Garra Kimble and Jessie Isabel (Holmes) L.; m. Doris Margaret Newhouse; children: Margaret Wing, Harriet Tarver, Robert A. PhB, Yale U., 1929; AM, Princeton (N.J.) U., 1930, PhD, 1936. With Princeton U., 1931-32, 34-38, prof., 1945-74, prof. emeritus, 1974—; assoc. dean Woodrow Wilson Sch., 1966-68; dean faculty Princeton U., 1968-73, rsch. assoc. Indsl. Rels. sect., 1973—; asst. prof. U. Wash., Seattle, 1938-40; from asst. to assoc. prof. Duke U., Durham, N.C., 1940-45; br. chief War Prodn. Bd. and War Manpower Commn., Washington, 1941-42; manpower cons. Office of Sec. of War, Washington, 1943-44; chmn. N.J. Employment Security Coun., Trenton, 1954-64; N.J. chmn. Pub. Employer-Employee Rels. Study Commn., Trenton, 1974-75; trustee Tchrs. Ins. and Annuity Assn., N.Y.C., 1959-63; v.p. Princeton U. Press, 1969-72. Author: Monetary Experiments, 1939, As Unions Mature, 1958, Economics of Labor, 2d edit., 1964, Labor Arbitration, 1984, Wages, Benefits and Company Employment Systems, 1988. Elected mem. Princeton Borough Coun., 1958-61; trustee Ctr. for Analysis Pub. Issues, Princeton, 1970-83; vice chmn. Pres.'s Commn. on Status of Women, Washington, 1961-63. U.S. Dept. Labor Merit award, 1968. Mem. Indls. Rels. Rsch. Assn. (pres. 1956), Am. Econ. Assn. (exec. com. 1951-53, v.p. 1961), Nat. Acad. Social Ins. Democrat. Avocations: swimming, fishing. Died Dec. 30, 1997.

LEVA, MARX, lawyer; b. Selma, Ala., Apr. 4, 1915; s. Leo and Fannie Rose (Gusdorf) L.; m. Shirley Pearlman, Oct. 31, 1942; children: Leo Marx, Lloyd Leva Plaine. B.S., U. Ala., 1937, LL.D., 1978; LL.B., Harvard U., 1940. Bar: Ala. 1940, U.S. Supreme Ct. 1946, D.C. 1950. Law clk. to Justice Hugo Black, U.S. Supreme Ct., 1940; sr. atty. O.P.A., 1941; acting regional atty. for Mich. and Ohio WPB, 1942; counsel to fiscal dir. of Navy, 1946, spl. asst. to sec. of navy, 1947; spl. asst. and gen. counsel to Sec. Def., 1947-49; asst. sec of def. (legal and legis.), 1949-51; ptnr. Fowler, Leva, Hawes & Symington, 1951-67, Leva, Hawes, Symington, Martin & Oppenheimer, 1967-85, Leva, Hawes, Mason & Martin, 1985-90; of counsel Robins, Kaplan, Miller & Ciresi, 1990-93; Chmn. civilian-mil. review panel for spl. com. U.S. Senate, 1957; mem. Pres.'s Commn. to Rev. Fgn. Aid, 1958-59, Pres.'s Com. on Def. Establishment, 1960-61. Note editor: Harvard Law Rev, 1939-40; overseer, 1950-55. Served with amphibious forces USNR, 1943-44, ETO. Decorated Bronze Star with combat disting. device; named Outstanding Young Man In Govt., Washington Jr. C. of C., 1949. Died Feb. 2, 1997.

LEVERTOV, DENISE, poet; b. Ilford, Essex, Eng., Oct. 24, 1923; came to U.S., 1948, naturalized, 1955; d. Paul Philip and Beatrice A. (Spooner-Jones) Levertoff m. Mitchell Goodman, Dec. 2, 1947 (div. 1975); 1 child, Nikolai. Ed. privately; Litt.D. (hon.), Colby Coll., 1970, U. Cin., 1973, St. Lawrence U., 1984, Bates Coll., 1984, Allegheny Coll., 1987, St. Michael's Coll., 1987, Mass. Coll. of Art, 1989, U. Santa Clara, 1993. Tchr. YMCA-YWCA Poetry Ctr., N.Y.C., 1964; vis. lectr. Drew U., Madison, N.J., 1965, CCNY, 1965, Vassar Coll., Poughkeepsie, N.Y., 1966-67, U. Calif., Berkeley, 1969; vis. prof. MIT, Cambridge, 1969-70; scholar Radcliffe Inst. Ind. Study, 1964-65, 66-67; artist-in-residence Kirkland Coll., Clinton, N.Y., 1970-71; Elliston lectr. U. Cin., spring 1973; prof. Tufts U., Medford, Mass., 1973-79, Stanford U., Calif., 1981-93; prof. emeritus, 1993—; poet-in-residence Brandeis U., Waltham, Mass., 1981-83; A.D. White Prof. at Large Cornell U., Ithaca, N.Y., 1993—. Author: The Double Image, 1946, Here and Now, 1957, Overland to the Islands, 1958, Five Poems, 1958, With Eyes at the Back of Our Heads, 1959, The Jacob's Ladder, 1961, O Taste and See, 1964, City Psalm, 1964, Psalm Concerning the Castle, 1966, The Sorrow Dance, 1967, A Tree Telling of Orpheus, 1968, A Marigold from North Vietnam, 1968, Three Poems, 1968, In the Night: A Story, 1968, The Cold Spring and Other Poems, 1969, Embroideries, 1969, Relearning the Alphabet, 1970, Summer Poems, 1969, A New Year's Garland for My Students, 1970, To Stay Alive, 1971, Footprints, 1972, The Poet in the World, 1974, The Freeing of the Dust, 1975, Chekov on the West Heath, 1977, Modulations for Solo Voice, 1977, Life in the Forest, 1978, Collected Earlier Poems 1940-60, 1979, Pig Dreams: Scenes from the Life of Sylvia, 1981, Wanderer's Daysong, 1981, Light Up the Cave, 1981, Candles in Babylon, 1982, Poems 1960-1967, 1983, Oblique Prayers, 1984, El Salvador: Requiem and Invocation, 1984, The Menaced World, 1984, Selected Poems, 1986, Poems 1968-1972, 1987, Breathing the Water, 1987, A Door in the Hive, 1989, Evening Train, 1992, New and Selected Essays, 1992, Tesserae, 1995; translator: Selected Poems of Guillevic, 1969, Black Iris: Selected Poems of Jean Joubert, 1988; translator, editor: (with Edward C. Dimock, Jr.) In Praise of Krishna: Songs from the Bengali, 1967; editor: Out of the War Shadow: An Anthology of Current Poetry, 1967. Recipient Bess Hokin prize Poetry mag. 1959, Longview award 1961, Harriet Monroe Meml. prize 1964, Inez Boulton prize Poetry mag. 1964, Morton Dauwen Zabel Meml. prize Poetry mag., 1965, Lenore Marshall Poetry prize 1976, Elmer Holmes Bobst award in poetry 1983, Shelley Meml. award Poetry Soc. of Am., 1984, Robert Frost medal, 1990, Lannan award, 1993; Am. Acad. and Inst. of Arts and Letters grantee, 1965; Guggenheim fellow, 1962; NEA Sr. Fellowship, 1990. Mem. Am. Inst. Arts and Letters, Academie Mallarmé (corr.).

LEVI, JULIAN HIRSCH, lawyer, educator; b. Chgo., July 25, 1909; s. Gerson Baruch and Elsa (Hirsch) L.; m. Marjorie Reynolds, Sept. 16, 1938; children: William Gerson, Kay Levi Pick. Ph.B. with honors, U. Chgo., 1929, J.D. cum laude, 1931; LL.D. (hon.), John Marshall Law Sch., Chgo., Lake Forest (Ill.) Coll., 1967. Bar: Ill. 1931. Ptnr. Wilhartz & Hirsch, Chgo., 1931-46; officer Reynolds Pen Co., also Reynolds Printasign Co., Chgo., 1946-52; exec. dir. S.E. Chgo. Commn., 1952-80; prof. urban studies U. Chgo., 1962-80; vis. prof. Hastings Coll. Law, U. Calif., San Francisco, 1978-79, 79-80; prof. Hastings Coll. Law, U. Calif., 1981-97; founder, chmn. Pub. Law Rsch. Inst., 1984-97; dir. Hyatt Corp., 1977-79, Elsinor Corp., 1979-97; chmn. Chgo. Plan Commn., 1973-79; sec. Am. Council Edn., 1971-72; vice chmn. White House Task Force Cities, 1967; adv. to architect of Capitol, Washington, 1976-97. Author: Municipal and Institution Relations in Boston, 1964, Financing Education and the Effect of Tax Laws, 1975; chmn. editorial adv. bd.: Urban Affairs Reporter, 1972-82. Trustee Michael Reese Hosp., Chgo., 1967-80, Calif. State Libr. Found., 1992-97. Recipient Rockefeller Public Service award Princeton U., 1977, Alumni Svc. medal U. Chgo., 1989. Mem. ABA, Am. Law Inst., Am. Soc. Planning Ofcls., Chgo. Bar Assn., Order of Coif, Phi Beta Kappa. Jewish. Clubs: Tavern, Arts, Quadrangle (Chgo.). Home: San Francisco Calif. Died Oct. 16, 1996.

LEVIN, BERTRAM, physician, educator; b. Chgo., May 2, 1920; s. Max and Rose (Tenenbaum) L.; m. Lucille Marian Rusky, May 28, 1950; children: Elliot Marc, Karen Ruth, Diane Rebecca. B.S., Central YMCA Coll., 1941; M.D., U. Ill., 1944. Diplomate: Am. Bd. Radiology. Intern Michael Reese Hosp., Chgo., 1945; resident radiology Michael Reese Hosp., 1948-50; Nat. Heart Inst. trainee U. Minn., 1952-53; clin. instr. radiology Med. Sch., 1952-53; clin. asst. prof. radiology Chgo. Med. Sch., 1955-61, asso. prof., 1961-69; prof. radiology Pritzker Sch. Medicine, U. Chgo., 1969—; dir. dept. diagnostic roentgenology Michael Reese Hosp. and Med Center, Chgo., 1954-87, chmn. emeritus, 1987—; vis. prof. radiology Hebrew U.-Hadassah Med. Sch., Jerusalem, 1975-76, 78, 81, 87. Mem. editorial adv. bd., RNM Images. Pres. dist. council Chgo. Bd. Edn., 1970-71; Bd. dirs. Council Jewish Elderly, Drexel Home Aged, Bernard Horwich Jewish Community Center, Midwest region Jewish Welfare Bd. Served from 1st lt. to capt. AUS, 1945-47. Fellow Chgo. Roentgen Soc., Am. Coll. Radiology; mem. Radiol. Soc. N.Am., Interam. Radiol. Soc., Inst. Medicine Chgo., N.Y. Acad. Scis., A.A.A.S., Assn. U. Radiologists, Am. Roentgen Ray Soc. Mem. B'nai B'rith. DIED 04/05/96. .

LEVIN, PAUL JOSEPH, evangelist; b. Rock Island, Ill., Oct. 13, 1914; s. Peter and Hulda (Vromberg) L.; m. Dorothy Hayslip, Mar. 17, 1936 (dec. Oct. 1994). DD (hon.), San Francisco Bapt. Sem., 1969. Radio evangelist 41 stas., throughout U.S., 1957—; pres., founder Bible Tracts, Inc., Carlock, Ill., 1938—; bd. dirs. Bill Rice Ranch, Murfreesboro, Tenn., 1956-96. Author: Pre Wedding Days, 1935, One Step at a Time, 1976, and numerous tracts; recorded albums with Bob Findley, 1933-1975. Republican. Avocation: baseball. Deceased, Sept 7, 1996.

LEVINE, GARY, history, criminology, and sociology educator; b. Kingston, N.Y., Feb. 3, 1938; s. Morris and Rose (Scheid) L.; m. Jia Wang; children: Jonathan, Benjamin. AA, Orange County (N.Y.) C.C., 1957; BA, Hartwick Coll., 1959; MA, SUNY, Albany, 1962, Syracuse U., 1963; PhD, St. John's U., 1971. Mgr. Scrap Metal Co., Kingston, 1962-69; lectr. history St. John's U., Jamaica, N.Y., 1968-70; instr. history SUNY, New Paltz, 1970; assoc. prof. social scis. Columbia-Greene C.C., Hudson, N.Y., 1970-72, prof., 1973-96, prof. emeritus, 1996; state sect. dir. Mufon, N.Y., 1974-77, state dir., 1978-96, cons. sci. & tech., adv. bd., 1994-96. Author: The Car Solution: The Steam Engine Comes, 1974, Anatomy of a Gangster: Jack "Legs" Diamond, 1979, Jack "Legs" Diamond: Anatomy of a Gangster, 1995. Mem. Am. Soc. Phys. Rsch., Soc. History Tech., Soc. History Medicine, Catskill Valley Hist. Soc. Avocation: photography. DIED 02/12/96. .

LEVY, ANN PORTER HELLEBUSCH (ANN HEBSON), author, artist; b. Montgomery, Ala., Dec. 20, 1925; d. Charles Merle and Lucille Jarvis (Atherton) Hellebusch; m. William John Hebson Sr., June 8, 1947 (div. 1968); children: William John Jr., Annie Laurie Hebson Sandler, Andrew Campbell; m. Robert S. Levy, July 31, 1976; stepchildren: Patricia Anne, John Robert. BA in English and Journalism with honors, Grinnell Coll., 1947. Social worker State of Iowa, Grinnell, 1947-49; columnist Louisville, 1949-58; feature writer U. Miami, Coral Gables, Fla., 1967-69; news dir. Mary Baldwin Coll., Staunton, Va., 1969-70; writer-producer Ky. Ednl. TV, Lexington, 1970-72; pres. HLF Graphic Art Works, Lexington, 1978—. Author: A Fine and Private Place, 1958, The Lattimer Legend, 1961 (Macmillan Fiction Award 1961, New York Times Best Seller 1962); author TV documentary Images and Things, 1972; numerous other TV scripts; contbr. articles to mags., newspapers; exhibits of painted silk art include Speed Mus., Louisville, Chrysler Mus., Norfolk, Va., Headley Mus., Lexington; exhibited one-man show Lexington Art League, 1986. Mem. Lexington Council for the Arts, 1986—. NEA Creative Fellow, 1977. Mem. Women in Communications, Ky. Artists and Craftsmens' Guild, Am. Crafts Council, Fibre Arts Group, Lexington Arts League, Phi Beta Kappa. Democrat. Episcopalian. Clubs: Cen. Ky. Women's; Louisville Arts. Avocations: painting, travel, reading, music, theatre.

LEVY, BURTON See LANE, BURTON

LEVY, WALTER JAMES, oil consultant; b. Hamburg, Germany, Mar. 21, 1911; s. Moses and Bertha (Lindenberger) L.; m. Augusta Sondheimer, Apr. 11, 1942 (dec.); children: Robert Alan (dec.), Susan Clementine. Student, U. Heidelberg, 1929-30, U. Berlin, 1930-31, U. Kiel, 1931-32. Asst. to editor Petroleum Press Bur., London, Eng., 1936-41; free lance economist N.Y.C., 1941-42; chief petroleum sect. OSS, Washington, 1942-45; asst. office intelligence research Dept. State, 1945-48, cons., also Pres. com. fgn. aid, 1948; chief oil br. ECA, 1948-49, cons., 1949-51; econ. cons., 1949—, NSRB, 1950; pres. Materials Policy Commn., 1951; cons. policy planning staff Dept. State, 1952-53, ICA, 1956-57; cons. office Under Sec. and Asst. Secs., 1960-80, Office Civil and Def. Moblzn., 1960, European Econ. Community, 1970; fgn. econ. adviser Socony-Vacuum Oil Co., 1948; adviser to Mr. Harriman on mission to Iran, 1951; Petroleum adviser U.S. del. Council Fgn. Ministers meeting, 1947; mem. U.S. del. of Austrian Treaty Commn., 1947, State Dept. del. for oil discussions with U.K., 1946, U.S. del. trade discussion with Sweden, 1945, U.S. world programming group on petroleum, 1945; mem. enemy oil com. Joint Chiefs Staff, 1943-45; oil adviser to spl. emissary of Pres. Kennedy to Pres. of Indonesia, 1963; Mem. adv. council to Sch. Advanced Internat. Studies Johns Hopkins U. Author (Oil Strategy and Politics, 1941-81 1982); Contbr. articles to profl. publs. Recipient spl. plaque in grateful appreciation for invaluable contbr. to welfare U.S., Sec. State, 1968; decorated Dato Setia haila Jasa Sultan Brunei, 1968; Order of Taj Iran, 1969; hon. companion Order St. Michael and St. George, Eng.; insignia of comdr.'s cross Order of Merit Fed. Republic of Ger., 1979; President's certificate of merit. Mem. Council on Fgn. Relations. Died Dec. 10, 1997.

LEWIS, HELEN PHELPS HOYT, association executive; b. Lakewood, N.J., Dec. 27, 1902; d. John Sherman and Ethel Phelps (Stokes) Hoyt; m. Byron Stookey, May 11, 1929 (dec. Oct. 20, 1966); children: John Hoyt, Lyman Brumbaugh, Byron; m. Robert James Lewis, Aug. 5, 1971 (dec. May 17, 1988). A.B., Bryn Mawr Coll., Pa.) Coll., 1923; M.A., Union Theol. Sem. of Columbia U., 1925. Bd. mgrs. Christodora Settlement House, N.Y.C., 1927-38; 1st v.p. Christodora Settlement House, 1929-38; nat. bd. YWCA, 1927-30; mem. women's adv. council N.Y. Bot. Garden, 1952-93; mem. nursing com. Columbia Presbyn. Med. Center, N.Y.C., 1944-54; trustee Columbia Presbyn. Med. Center, 1969-78, hon. trustee, 1978-93; mem. women's aux. Neurol. Inst., N.Y.C., 1939-93, chmn., 1949-54; mem. women's exec. com., chmn. com. hosp. auxs. United Hosp. Fund, 1951-64, vice chmn. women's campaign com., 1961-62, chmn. women's subcom. distbn., 1963-65, vice chmn. women's exec. com., 1963-64. Mem. Colonial Dames Am. (dir. 1951-56, chmn. scholarship com. 1949-51, pres.-gen. 1953-56), Daus. Cincinnati. Republican. Presbyterian. Clubs: Darien (Conn.); Garden (pres. 1935-38), Millbrook Garden (past pres.), Garden Club Am; Colony (N.Y.C.) (gov. 1954-76, sec. 1956-59, sec., v.p. 1969-71, pres. 1972-76, chmn. membership com. 1956-71). Home: New York N.Y. Died June 4, 1993.

LEWIS, IRVING JAMES, community health educator, health policy analyst, public administrator; b. Boston, July 9, 1918; s. Harry and Sarah (Bloomberg) L.; m. Rose Helen Greenwald, June 15, 1941; children—Deborah Ann, Amy Rebecca, William David. AB, Harvard U., 1939; AM, U. Chgo., 1940. With U.S. Govt., 1942-70; dep. chief internat. div. Bur. Budget, 1959-65; dept. head Intergovtl. Com. European Migration, Geneva, 1957-59; chief health and welfare div. Bur. Budget, 1965-67; dep. asst. dir. Bur., 1967-68; dep. adminstr. health services and mental health adminstrn. HEW, 1968-70; prof. community health Albert Einstein Coll. Medicine, Bronx, N.Y., 1970-86, prof. emeritus, 1986; cons. to fed. and state govts. Co-author: The Sick Citadel, A Study of Academic Medicine, 1983; author articles on health policy and fin. Served with CIC AUS, 1 943-46. Recipient Exceptional Svc. award Bur. Budget, 1964; Ann. Career Svc. award Nat. Civil Svc. League, 1969; Brookings Instn. rsch. fellow, 1941; WHO summer fellow, 1977. Assoc. fellow N.Y. Acad. Medicine (com. on medicine and society, chmn. ann. health conf. 1985); mem. APHA, Med. Health and Rsch. Assn., Assn. Am. Med. Colls., Am. Vets. Com. (pres. Washington 1949), Inst. Medicine/NAS, Harvard Club (Washington). Jewish (pres. temple). Home: Silver Spring Md. Died Sept. 15, 1996.

LEWIS, WELBOURNE WALKER, JR., lawyer; b. Lewisburg, Tenn., Jan. 11, 1915; s. Welbourne Walker and Jessie (Culbertson) L.; m. Esther Phillips, July 26, 1975; children by previous marriage—Welbourne Walker III, H. Hunter, Berton B. A.B., Dartmouth, 1936; J.D., Harvard U., 1939. Bar: Ohio 1939. Since practiced in Dayton; asso. Smith, Schnacke & Compton, 1939-45; mem. Smith & Schnacke, 1945-75; chmn. Master Consol., Inc., 1950-67; sec. Mead Corp., Dayton, 1952-64, gen. counsel, 1958-75, dir., 1959-75. Former mem. bd. dirs. Dayton dept. ARC; former trustee Dayton Pvt. Sch. Found. Mem. Phi Beta Kappa, Delta Tau Delta, Delta Sigma Rho. Episcopalian (former trustee, mem. planning com. Diocese So. Ohio, former mem. diocesan standing com., former sr. warden). Club: Dartmouth (Dayton). Died Jan., 1996.

LEWIS, WILLIAM SCHEER, electrical engineer; b. Mt. Vernon, N.Y., Feb. 7, 1927; s. Perley Linwood and Nellie Cora (Scheer) L.; m. Jane Alexander, Feb. 4, 1950 (div. 1972); children: Christopher A., Pamela Scheer Shaw, David Robert; m. Barbara Johnson, June 24, 1972. SB, MIT, 1950, SM, 1950. Registered profl. engr. Mass, N.Y. Sales engr. Gen. Electric Co., Erie, Pa., 1950-53, Morrissey Tractor Co., Burlington, Mass., 1953-56, Hubbs Engine Co., Cambridge, Mass., 1956-57; mgr. contract div. Payne Elevator Co., Cambridge, 1957-69; sales mgr. diversified systems Otis Elevator Co., N.Y.C., 1969-72, mktg. analyst/gen. sales, 1972-73; mgr. vertical transp. Jaros, Baum & Bolles, N.Y.C., 1973-91, ptnr., 1978-91, ret., 1991—. Author: (handbooks) Materials Handling, Freight Elevators, 1985, Building Structural Design-Vertical Transportation, 1987; editor: (monograph) Tall Buildings—Vertical and Horizontal Transportation, 1978. Trustee Mt. Ascutney Hosp. and Health Ctr., Windsor, Vt., 1995—, Am. Precision Mus., Windsor, 1994—, chmn. 1995—; active Wayland (Mass.) Bd. Assessors, 1954-69, chmn., 1963-69. Recipient 1st prize award N.Y. Assn. Consulting Engrs., 1987, Honor award Am. Consulting Engrs. Council, 1987. Mem. ASME. Republican. Unitarian. Avocations: white water canoeing, hunting, fishing, photography. Died Nov. 10, 1995.

LEXAU, HENRY, editor; b. St. Paul, Feb. 8, 1928; s. Ole Hendrijk and Anne (Haas) L.; m. Eileen O'Hara, Oct. 18, 1952; children—Catherine, Margaret, Daniel, John, Elizabeth, Benjamin. B.A., Coll. St. Thomas, 1949. Asst. editor Catholic Digest, St. Paul, 1949-72, mng. editor, 1972-75, editor, 1975—; editor Catholic Digest Book Club, 1978—, A Treasury of Catholic Digest, 1986. Served with U.S. Army, 1950-52. Decorated Bronze Star. Roman Catholic. Home: Saint Paul Minn. DIED 09/29/95. .

LEYMASTER, GLEN R., former medical association executive; b. Aurora, Nebr., Aug. 7, 1915; s. Leslie and Frances (Wertman) L.; m. Margaret Hendricks, June 20, 1942; children: Mark H., Mary Beth, Lynn F. A.B., U. Nebr., 1938; M.D., Harvard, 1942; M.P.H., Johns Hopkins U., 1950. Intern, asst. resident, resident Harvard Med. Service, Boston City Hosp., 1942-44; mem. faculty Johns Hopkins Med. Sch., 1944-48; instr., asst. prof. bacteriology Sch. Pub. Health and Hygiene, 1946-48; asso. prof. pub. health, instr. medicine U. Utah Sch. Medicine, 1948-50, prof., head dept., preventive medicine, asst. prof. medicine, also dir. univ. health service, 1950-60; adviser med. edn.- preventive medicine ICA, Bangkok, Thailand, 1956-58; asso. sec. council med. edn. and hosps. AMA, Chgo., 1960-63; pres., dean Women's Med. Coll. Pa., 1964-70; dir. dept. undergrad. med. edn. AMA, 1970-75; exec. dir. Am. Bd. Med. Spltys., Evanston, Ill., 1975-81; ret. exec. dir., 1981. Contbr. articles to profl. jours. Mem. AMA, Ill. Med. Assn., Inst. Medicine Chgo., Phi Beta Kappa, Sigma Xi, Alpha Omega Alpha. Died July 2, 1997.

LIBERMAN, IRA L., real estate broker; b. Richmond, Va., June 21, 1926; s. Morris Joseph and Dora (Sharove) L.; m. Frances Sour, Sept. 26, 1953; children—Barbara Janet, Lynn Dora, Leslie Ann. B.S., U. Va., 1949. With Richmond Tomato Repacking Co., Va., 1949; with Duke City Lumber Co., Inc., Albuquerque, 1949-85; pres., chmn., chief exec. officer Duke City Lumber Co., Inc., 1974-85; assoc. real estate broker Vaughan and Co., 1985-91, Berger Briggs Real Estate & Ins., Albuquerque, 1991-96; nat. chmn. Western Wood Products Assn., 1985-86. Bd. dirs. Albuquerque Indsl. Devel., Albuquerque Symphony Orch., State Girl Scout Council. Served with USAF, 1944-46. Mem. Albuquerque Bd. Realtors, S.W. Pine Assn. (past pres.), Fed. Timber Purchasers Assn. (past pres.), Nat. Forest Products Assn. (dir.). Clubs: Four Hills Country, Crossroads Flying. Lodge: Masons. Died May 1996.

LICHTENSTEIN, ROY, artist; b. N.Y.C., Oct. 27, 1923; s. Milton and Beatrice (Werner) L.; m. Isabel Wilson, June 12, 1949 (div.); children: David, Mitchell; m. Dorothy Herzka, Nov. 1, 1968. BFA, Ohio State U., 1946, MFA, 1949; DFA (hon.), Calif. Inst. Arts., 1977, Ohio State U., 1988, Bard Coll., 1989. Instr. Ohio State U., 1946-51; asst. prof. SUNY-Oswego, 1957-60, Douglass Coll., Rutgers U., 1960-63. Pop art and other themes derived from comic strip techniques; one-man shows include Leo Castelli Gallery, N.Y.C., 1962, 63, 65, 67, 71, 72, 73, 74, 75, 77, 79, 81, 83, 85, 86, 87, 89, 92, Galerie Ileana Sonnabend, Paris, 1963, 65, 70, 75, Pasadena (Calif.) Art Mus., 1967, Walker Art Ctr., Mpls., 1967, Stedelijk Mus., Amsterdam, 1967, Tate Gallery, London, 1968, Guggenheim Mus., N.Y.C., 1969, Nelson Gallery, Kansas City, Mo., 1969, Mus. Contemporary Art, Chgo., 1970, Centre National D'Arte Contemporain, Paris, 1975, and traveling to: Nationalgalerie Staatliche Museum Kulterbesitz, Berlin, Seattle Art Mus., 1976, Inst. Contemporary Art, Boston, 1979, Portland Ctr. for Visual Arts, 1980, St. Louis Art Mus., 1981, Fundacion Juan March, Madrid, 1982, Walker Art Ctr., Mpls., 1986, 'The Drawings of Roy Lichtenstein', Mus. Modern Art, N.Y.C., 1987, and traveling to: Mus. Overholland, Amsterdam, 1987, Tel Aviv Mus., Israel, 1987, Schirn Kunsthalle, Frankfurt, 1988, Mus. Modern Art, Oxford, Eng., 1988, Corcoran Gallery of Art, Washington, 1988; group shows include Whitney Mus. Am. Art, N.Y.C., 1966, 67, 68, 70, 72, 73, 74, 75 (Downtown), 77, 78, 80, 82, 83, 84, 85, 87, Mus. Modern Art, N.Y.C., 1966, 67, 68, 74, 76, 80, 85, 88, Solomon R. Guggenheim Mus., N.Y.C., 1965,76, Venice Biennale, 1966, Corcoran Gallery Art 36th Biennale, Washington, D.C., 1978, Solomon R. Guggenheim MUs., N.Y.C., 1965, 76, Hirschorn Mus., Washington, 1980, Bklyn. Mus. Art, N.Y.C., 1981, Nat. Mus. Am. Art, Smithsonian Inst., Washington, 1984, Palacio Velazquez, Madrid, Spain, 1991, Galerie Martine Queval, Paris, 1992, Galerie Joachim Becker, Paris, 1992; represented in permanent collections: Mus. Modern Art, N.Y.C., Whitney Mus. Am. Art, N.Y.C., Corcoran Gallery Art, Washington, Hirschorn Mus. and Sculpture Garden, Washington, Libr. Congress, Washington, Nat. Gallery Art, Washington, Chgo. Art Inst., Smithsonian Inst., Washington, Victoria and Albert Mus., London, Seibu Art Mus., Tokyo, Ludwig Mus., Cologne, Stedelijk Mus., Amsterdam, Norton Simon Mus., Pasadena, Yale U., New Haven, Walker Art Ctr., Mpls., San Francisco Mus. Modern Art, Albright Knox Gallery, Buffalo; created outside wall for Circarama, N.Y. State Pavillion, N.Y. State World's Fair, 1963, large Painting for Expo '67, Montreal, 1967, Brushstroke Murals for Dusseldorf U. Med. Ctr., 1970, 'Mermaid' (NEA grantee), pub. sculpture for Theatre Performing Arts in Miami Beach, Fla., 1979, 'Brushstrokes in Flight', Port Columbus Airport, Columbus, Ohio, 1984, 'Mural with Blue Brushstroke', Equitable Life Assurance Bldg. with Whitney Mus. Art, 1985, 'Coups de Pinceau', Caisse des Depots and Consignations, Paris, 1988, Tel Aviv Mus. Art, Tel Aviv, 1989. With AUS, 1943-46. Recipient Skowhegan medal for painting, 1977. Mem. Am. Acad. and Inst. Arts and Letters. Died Sept. 29, 1997.

LIEBERMAN, HARVEY MICHAEL, hepatologist, gastroenterologist, educator; b. N.Y.C., Feb. 24, 1949; s. Louis and Ellie (Miller) L.; m. Lewette Alexandra Fielding, Nov. 24, 1985. BA magna cum laude, NYU, 1972, MD, 1976. Intern Bronx (N.Y.) Mcpl. Hosp./Albert Einstein Coll. Medicine, N.Y.C., 1976-77, jr. and sr. resident, 1977-79; fellow in gastroenterology and liver disease Albert Einstein Coll. Medicine, 1979-81, rsch. assoc. Liver Rsch. Ctr., 1983; asst. prof. Albert Einstein Coll. Medicine, Bronx, N.Y., 1984-86; dir. gastroenterology Gouverneur Hosp., N.Y.C., 1986-90; asst. chief gastroenterology Lenox Hill Hosp., N.Y.C., 1992—, founding dir. liver clinic, 1992—; dir. hepatology program, 1994—; ednl. coord. Lenox Hill Hosp., N.Y.C., 1995—; clin. asst. prof. NYU Sch. Medicine, 1986-93, clin. assoc. prof., 1993—; prin. investigator Liver Rsch. Ctr. Albert Einstein Coll. Medicine, 1984-87, vis. scientist, 1992—; med. adv. bd. Crohn's and Colitis Found. of Am., Am. Liver Found., N.Y. chpts., 1987—; researcher in molecular biology of hepatitis B virus and relationship to viral infection and liver cancer. Author: Relationship of Hepatitis B Viral Infection in Serum to Viral Replication, 1983. Recipient Clin. Investigator award NIH, 1984-87. Fellow ACP, Am. Coll. Gastroenterology, N.Y. Acad. Gastroenterology (pres. 1990-91). Achievements include development of assay to measure DNA of hepatitis B virus directly in serum; first to note its greater sensitivity in measuring active viral replication liver disease compared to conventional serological tests. Died Apr. 1995.

LIEBERMAN, MELVYN, biology educator; b. Bklyn., Feb. 4, 1938; married; 2 children. BA in Zoology, Cornell U., 1959; PhD in Physiology, SUNY Downstate Med. Ctr., 1965. Lectr., lab in instr., dept. biology Queens Coll., CUNY, 1960, 63-64; teaching asst. dept. physiology SUNY Downstate Med. Ctr., Bklyn., 1960-64; postdoctoral fellow dept. embryology Carnegie Inst. Washington, Balt., 1964-65, Inst. de Biofisica, U. Federal do Rio de Janeiro, Brazil, 1965-67; postdoctoral fellow div. biomed. engring. Duke U., Durham, N.C., 1967, rsch. assoc. dept. physiology and pharmacology, 1967-68; asst. prof. Duke U. Med. Ctr., Durham, N.C., 1968-73, assoc. prof., 1973-78, prof. dept. physiology, 1978-88, dir. dept. grad. studies, 1977-80, prof. dept. cell biology, 1988—, dir. grad. studies, 1988-90; assoc. prof. medicine, mem. integrated toxicology program, 1989—; spl. asst. to exec. v.p. Duke U. Med. Ctr., Durham, N.C., 1990-95, spl. asst. to sr. v.p. rsch. adminstr., 1995-96, mem. Heart Ctr., 1988—, mem. Comprehensive Cancer Ctr., 1992—, dir. univ. assocs. program, 1992—; prof. dept. biomed. engring., 1993—; Internat. Affairs Commn., 1994—; coordinator U.S.-Japan Coop. Sci. Program Conf., Tokyo, 1974, 88, U.S.-Brazil Coop. Sci. Program Conf., Rio de Janeiro, 1980, Gordon Conf.-Muscle, 1979; vis. investigator Jan Seammerdam Inst., U. Amsterdam, Netherlands, 1975; cons. Macy Found., 1970, NIH, 1972—, physiology study sect., 1980-84, Rsch. Tng. Rev. Comm., 1990-94, NSF, 1974—, others; mem. rsch. rev. com. N.Y. Heart Assn., 1980-85; mem. cardiovascular rsch. study com. Am. Heart Assn., 1987-90; Howard Hughes Predoctorate Fellowship Evaluation, 1994—; participant numerous sci. symposia; mem. basic Sci. coun. Am. Heart Assn., 1963, established investigator, 1971-76, pub. rev. com., 1989-93, Rsch. Program and Evaluation Commn., 1995—; rsch. rev. subcom. N.C. Heart Assn., 1972-75, chmn., 1975-76, pub. affairs com., 1988-91, rsch. com., 1993—; microstructure com., N.C. Bd. Sci. and Tech., 1989-93, Task Force on Intellectual property and licensing govt. univ. industry rsch. roundtable, 1991-93, Indsl. Liaison program, Rsch. Triangle Univs., 1991-93; acad. adv. coun. Indsl. Rsch. Inst., 1994—, Pres.'s adv. coun., Houston Advanced Rsch. Ctr., 1995—. Co-editor: Development and Physiological Correlates of Cardiac Muscle, 1975, Excitable Cells in Tissue Culture, 1981, Normal and Abnormal Conduction of the Heart, 1982, Electrogenic Transport: Fundamental Principles and Physiological Implications, 1984; assoc. editor Am. Jour. Physiology, Cell, 1981—; mem. editorial adv. bd. Experientia, 1982-90, Physiol. Revs., 1985-91, Molecular Cell Biochemistry, 1991—; editorial cons. contbr. numerous articles to profl. jours. Recipient founders award, 1975, achievement award N.C. Heart Assn., 1984, Cecil Hall award Electron Microscopy Soc. Am., 1989. Mem. AAAS, AAUP, Am. Heart Assn., Am. Physiol. Soc. (Porter devel. com. 1974-77, ednl. materials rev. bd. 1975-77, internat. physiol. com. 1993, chmn. 1994-95, councillor cell and gen. physiol. sect. 1984-87, chmn. 1987-88, 91-95, sect. adv. com. 1992-95), Am. Soc. Cell Biology, Biophys. Soc., Cardiac Muscle Soc., Internat. Soc. Heart Rsch. (councillor 1993—), N.Y. Acad. Sci., N.C. Heart Assn., Physiol. Soc., Soc. Gen. Physiologists (sec. 1969-71, rep. NRS 1971-74, pres. 1981-82, publs. com. 1982-85), Physiol. Soc. (U.K.), Sigma Xi. DIED 10/14/97. .

LIEBESKIND, HERBERT, chemistry educator, emeritus university dean; b. N.Y.C., Nov. 24, 1921; s. Irving and Irene (Bauman) L.; m. Ruth Feldman, Sept. 5, 1943 (div. 1981); children—Jan M., Nina S. Liebeskind Aronovitz; m. Nelida Sanchez, June 14, 1982. B.A., N.Y. U., 1941. Teaching fellow NYU, 1941-43, asst. instr., 1943-45; instr. Cooper Union, N.Y.C., 1945-48; asst. prof. Cooper Union, 1948-59, assoc. prof., 1959-66, prof. chemistry, 1966—, asst. dean, 1968-70, dir. admissions, registrar, 1970-72, dean admissions and records, 1972-87, prof. emeritus, 1987—; vis. lectr. Stevens Inst. Tech.,

1953-55; vis. assoc. prof. Yeshiva U., 1961-62. Contbr.: Ency. Americana. Pres. Bay Terrace Jewish Center, Bayside, N.Y., 1964-65. Mem. N.Y. Acad. Scis., Am. Chem. Soc., A.A.A.S., Am. Soc. Engring. Edn., AAUP, Chemistry Tchrs. Club N.Y. (pres. 1961-62, Oscar R. Foster award 1969), Phi Beta Kappa, Phi Lambda Upsilon. Club: Mem. B'nai B'rith (past bd. dirs. Bay Terrace Lodge). DIED 04/01/96. .

LIEDERMAN, AL, editorial cartoonist; b. Rochester, N.Y., Sept. 26, 1911; s. Samuel and Eva (Buff) L.; m. Lee Kleinman, Mar. 8, 1937; children: Carole, Russell. Former editorial cartoonist, Rochester Eve. Jour., Syracuse (N.Y.) Jour. and Am., N.Y. Post, L.I. Press, cartoons syndicated by, Rothco Cartoons, editorial cartoonist, Feature Assocs.; Creator of: syndicated cartoon panel All Stars, 1956, cartoons rep., Syracuse U. Archives, Albert T. Reid Cartoon Collection, U. Kans.; contbr. gag cartoons for newspapers and mags. Author: Li'l Leaguer, 1960, comic strip Double Duty, Am. Internat. Syndicate, 1987. Recipient award Nat. Found. Hwy. Safety, 1972, 74, Page One award N.Y. Newspaper Guild. Mem. Soc. Editorial Cartoonists, Nat. Cartoonist Soc. Baseball Writers Assn., Am. Artists and Writers Assn., Cartoonists Assn. Home: Merrick N.Y. Died Dec. 5, 1992.

LIEM, CHANNING, political science educator, former diplomat; b. Ulyul, Korea, Oct. 30, 1909; s. Posung and Posun (Yu) L.; m. Popai Lee, Jan. 29, 1940; children: Edith (Mrs. Young Jo Sul), G. Ramsay, Paul L. B.S., Lafayette Coll., 1934; M.A., Princeton, 1943, Ph.D., 1945. Postdoctoral fellow Yale, 1954-55; dir. Korean Ch. and Inst., N.Y.C., 1936-41; cons. Far Eastern affairs U.S. Office Censorship and War Information, N.Y.C., 1942-45; instr. Princeton, 1946-48; Korean affairs adviser U.S. Mil. Gov. in Korea, Seoul, 1948-49; prof. polit. sci. Chatham Coll., 1949-60; prof. polit. sci. State U. N.Y. Coll. of New Paltz, also chmn., prof. polit. sci. Asian studies, prof. emeritus, 1978—; ambassador Republic Korea to UN, 1960-61; spl. envoy to Republic Korea to Southwestern African Republics, Cameroun, Dahomey, Congo, Ivory Coast, Togo, Ghana, Senegal, 1961; adviser Nat. Com. for Def. Democratic Rights, Republic Korea, 1972—. Author: America's Gift to Korea: Life of Philip Jaisohn, 1952, Civilization of East Asia, 1973, The First Korean American, 1984, The Korean War: An Unanswered Question, 1992; contbr. articles to profl. publs.; Editor: Voice of the Korean People. Trustee Korean Edn. Found. Am., 1944-55; hon. chmn. bd. dirs. Philip Jaisohn Found. Recipient Humanitarian award Nat. Achievement Clubs, 1953; Ford faculty fellowship Chatham Coll., 1954-55; citation for meritorious service Republic Korea, 1961. Mem. Am. Polit. Sci. Assn., Internat. Mark Twain Soc. (hon.), Union Overseas Koreans for Democracy and Unification (sr. chmn.). Club: Princeton (N.Y.C.).

LIGHTSEY, GEORGE RODNEY, chemical engineering educator; b. Laurel, Miss., Jan. 17, 1943; s. John Sharp and Elsia Ray (Williams) L.; m. Mary Jane Webb, Mar. 29, 1964; children: Anne Kathleen, Beth Marie. BSChemE, Miss. State U., 1965; MSChemE, La. State U., 1967, PhDChemE, 1969. Registered profl. engr., Miss. Polymer engr. NASA, Cleve., 1969-71; rsch. engr. Proctor and Gamble Corp., Memphis, 1971-73; asst. prof. chem. engring. Ga. Inst. Tech., Atlanta, 1973-75; prof. chem. engring. Miss. State U., Starkville, 1975—; pres. Lightsey Engring., Ltd., Starkville, 1978—; vis. lectr. in chem. engring. U. Auckland, New Zealand, 1981; Erskind fellow in chem. engring., U. ChristChurch, New Zealand, 1986; rsch. leader in field. Leader Girl Scouts of Am., Starkville, 1976-83; coach Girls' Sports, Starkville, 1978-84. Capt. U.S. Army, 1970-71. Recipient Cert. of Recognition, NASA, 1977, 93, Award of Excellence, 1983, Tech. Achievement award, 1985, Faculty Achievement award, 1989; named to Alumni Hall of Fame, Theta Tau Profl. Engrs., 1994. Mem. AIChE (Forest Products Divsn. award 1986), ASTD, Soc. Plastic Engrs. (session chmn. 1973-95), Miss. Acad. Scis., TAPPI. Achievements include 4 patents in preparation of polyimides, apparatus for microwave treatment of cellulose, design of biomass hydrolysis process, anti-flare-up device for kerosene heaters. Died Sept. 15, 1995.

LILIENTHAL, JAMES RICHARD, engineer; b. N.Y.C., Aug. 14, 1916; s. August Beekman and Mathilda (Schreiner) L.; m. Elizabeth Haworth, May 27, 1944; children—Marguerite, Richard B., James H., Ann E. Student, Coll. City N.Y., 1933-34; BS in Naval Architecture and Marine Engring., Webb. Inst. Naval Architecture, 1938. Registered profl. engr., N.Y., N.Mex. Chief engr. Stability Meter Corp., N.Y.C., 1938-40; product engr. Sperry Gyroscope Co., N.Y.C., 1940-47; group leader Los Alamos Sci. Lab., 1947-67, asst. div. leader, 1967-77; mem. nat. adv. coun. Atomic Libr. and Tech. Found., Inc., Washington, 1990-95. Mem. Los Alamos Town Coun., 1948-49; mem. bd. assocs. St. John's Coll., Santa Fe, 1966-72; chmn. bd. trustees Mesa Pub. Library, Los Alamos, 1953-55. Fellow Am. Nuclear Soc. (hon. life; nat. v.p., pres. 1972-73, past dir.); mem. N.Y. Acad. Scis. (emeritus). Home: Los Alamos N. Mex. Died Sept. 8, 1995.

LILJA, SVEN INGVAR, marine industry executive; b. Helsingborg, Sweden, May 4, 1936; s. Claes Emil and Syster Ella (Tengvall) L.; divorced; children: Kristin, Asa, Bo, Ollegard, Karin; m. Maria Helena, Aug. 16, 1986; children: Rebecca, Alexandra. Master Mariner, Marine Acad., Malmoe, Sweden, 1958; LLM, U. Lund, Sweden, 1963. Asst. judge Sweden, 1964-66; co. atty. Port Authority of Gothenburg, Sweden, 1966-67, Grangesberg Co., Stockholm, 1968-73; co. atty. Salen Shipping Co., Stockholm, 1973-74, gen. mgr. Tanker div., 1975-79; v.p. Det Norske Veritas, Oslo, 1980-84; sr. v.p. DNV East Med. & BS, Greece, 1986-96; with bus. devel. DNV Divsn. Americas, N.J., 1996—. Mem. The Marine Club (Piraeus), The Yacht Club of Greece, Ekali Club, Stockholm Shipping Lodge. Mem. The Conservative Party. Christian Protestant. Avocations: architectural design, yachting. Deceased.

LILLICH, RICHARD B., law educator; b. 1933. AB, Oberlin Coll., 1954; LLB, Cornell U., 1957; LLM, JSD, NYU, 1960. Bar: N.Y. 1957, D.C. 1980. Pvt. practice N.Y.C., 1957-60; vis. asst. prof. Ind. U., 1960; asst. prof. Syracuse U., 1960-63, assoc. prof., 1963-67, prof., 1967-69; prof. U. Va., 1969-96, Fla. State U., 1996; legal cons. U.S. Naval War Coll., 1964-78, chair internat. law, 1968-69; vis. prof. NYU, 1977, Fla. State U., 1992, Ga. U., 1994, St. Louis U., 1995. Ford fellow, Eng., 1963, Guggenheim fellow, Eng., 1966-67, Sr. fellow NEH, Eng., 1974-75, Thomas Jefferson vis. fellow Downing Coll., Eng., 1980-81, vis. fellow All Souls Coll., Eng., 1987, vis. fellow Max Planck Inst., Heidelberg, 1993. Mem. Internat. Law Assn. (exec. coun., chmn. internat. com. on human rights law and practice), Am. Soc. Internat. Law (exec. coun. 1966-72, 73-76, 82-85), Procedural Aspects of Internat. Law Inst. (pres.). Home: Tallahassee Fla. Died Aug. 3, 1996.

LIMAN, ARTHUR LAWRENCE, lawyer; b. N.Y.C., Nov. 5, 1932; s. Harry K. and Celia L.; m. Ellen Fogelson, Sept. 20, 1959; children: Lewis, Emily, Douglas. A.B., Harvard U., 1954; LL.B., Yale U., 1957. Bar: N.Y. bar 1958. Asst. U.S. atty. So. Dist. N.Y., 1961-63, spl. asst. U.S. atty., 1965; with firm Paul, Weiss, Rifkind, Wharton & Garrison, N.Y.C., 1957-61, 63-97, ptnr. Paul, Weiss, Rifkind, Wharton & Garrison, 1966-97; chief counsel N.Y. State Spl. Commn. on Attica, 1972; chmn. Legal Action Center, N.Y.C., 1975; v.p. Legal Aid Soc., N.Y.C., 1973; pres. Legal Aid Soc., 1983-85; chmn. Gov. N.Y. Adv. Commn. Adminstrn. Justice in N.Y. State, 1981-83; mem. N.Y. State Exec. Adv. Com. Sentencing, 1977; mem. adv. com. civil rules U.S. Jud. Conf., 1980-85; mem. commn. on reduction costs and delay U.S. 2d Cir., 1976-80; bd. dirs. Continental Grain Co., Equitable Life Assurance Soc. U.S.; chmn. bd. dirs. Capital Defenders Office, 1995-97; chmn. mayor's com. on appointments, 1990-93; chief counsel U.S. Senate select com. on secret mil. assistance to Iran and the Nicaraguan Opposition, Washington, 1987. Contbr. articles to legal jours.; bd. editors: Nat. Law Jour, 1979-97. Bd. overseers Harvard U., 1988-94. Fellow Am. Coll. Trial Lawyers, Am. Bar Found.; mem. ABA, N.Y. State Bar Assn., Bar Assn. City N.Y. (exec. com., Lawyers Com. Civil Rights Under Bd. Overseers, Harvard U., 1988-94). Home: New York N.Y. Died July 17, 1997.

LIMPRECHT, HOLLIS JOYCE, retired magazine executive, editor; b. Diller, Nebr., Dec. 8, 1920; s. Elwood George and Elma Joyce (Clark) L.; m. Marjorie Mabel Edwards, July 4, 1943; children: Joseph Allen, Jane Ellen. A.B., U. Nebr., 1943. Med. writer World Herald, Omaha, 1953-58, mag. editor, 1960-84, exec. asst. to pres., 1984-86; mng. editor Daily News, Norfolk, Nebr., 1958-60; vis. prof. Baylor U., Waco, Tex., 1984; adj. asst. prof. U. Nebr. Med. Ctr., Omaha, 1970-84; lectr. in field. Author: (with others) Go Big Red, 1966, (with others) Portrait of a Winner, 1972, A Chance To Live, 1973, The Kiewit Story, 1980, History of the World Herald, 1985, A Century of Miracles: History of Nebraska Methodist Hospital, 1989; co-author: Boys Town: Revolution in Youth Care, 1992. Served to capt. U.S. Army, 1943-46, 51, 52. Decorated 2 Bronze Stars, Purple Heart; recipient Disting. Reporting award Am. Polit. Sci. Assn., Jour. award AMA, Commendation award Soc. Survivors of Holocaust, Hon. Alumnus award Creighton U., Journalism award NCCJ, Profl. Newswriting award Nebr. Sigma Delta Chi, Lifetime Achievement award U. Nebr. at Omaha. Mem. VFW, Omaha Press Club (pres. 1979-80), Am. Legion, U. Nebr. Alumni Assn. Republican. Methodist. Lodge: Elks. Avocations: farming; travel; hiking. Home: Omaha Nebr. Died Dec. 6, 1992; buried Arlington Nat. Cemetery.

LINDBERG, HELGE, aviation consultant; b. London, Sept. 17, 1926; arrived in Norway, 1936; s. Carl Andreas and Sigrid Kristine (Bay) L.; m. Kerstin Hildegard Sjunnesson, Oct. 23, 1970; children by previous marriage: Sigrid Kristine, Carl Andreas. Grad., Treiders Handelsskole, Oslo, 1944. With Scandinavian Airlines System, 1946-91; dist. mgr. Scandinavian Airlines System, Arabian Gulf, 1958; asst. regional mgr. Scandinavian Airlines System, Middle East, 1959-60; traffic sales mgr., dep. mng. dir. Scanair Charter Co. subs. Scandinavian Airlines System, Copenhagen, 1961-68; div. mgr. Scandinavian Airlines System, Finland and Eastern Europe, 1969-72; v.p. industry assn. affairs Scandinavian Airlines System, Stockholm, 1973-75, v.p. passenger mktg., 1976-78, exec. v.p. comml., 1979-83, chief oper. officer, 1983-86; dep. pres. Scandinavian Airlines System Group, Stockholm, 1986-91; chmn. Scanavia Aviation Cons., Stockholm, Sweden, 1993—; chmn. Scandinavian Air Tour Prodn., Stockholm, 1976-79, AMADEUS Global Travel distbn., Madrid, 1988-91; bd. dirs. Nymann & Schultz Travel Agy., Stockholm, 1976-91, Widerøe's Airline, 1986—, Oslo, Diners Nordic A/S, 1986-94, Bennett Scandinavia Travel Bur., Oslo, 1988-91; mem. traffic com. Internat. Air Traffic Assn., Geneva, 1973-74, chmn., 1975-76; mem. European Pratt & Whitney Adv. Bd., Paris, 1993—; chmn. Scanavia Aviation Cons., Oslo, 1994—. Bd. dirs. World Wildlife Fund, 1986-92. Mem. Assn. European Airlines (chmn. comml. and air polit. com. 1981-83), Scandinavian Multi Access System for Travel Agts. (chmn. 1983-85).

LINDENBAUM, JOHN, science educator. Prof. Columbia U., N.Y.C. Recipient Corson medal Franklin Inst., 1996.

LINDER, P. SCOTT, construction company executive; b. 1923; married. BSME, U. Fla., 1943. With USAF, 1943-52; chmn. Linder Indsl. Machinery Co., 1953—; chmn., CEO Scotty's Inc., 1988—; dir. First Fidelity Bank NA, Gen. Tel. Co. Fla., Fla. Progress and Environ. Corp. Deceased.

LINDLEY, AUDRA, actress; b. Los Angeles, Sept. 24, 1925; d. Bert and Bessie (Fisher) L.; married; children: John, Elizabeth, Alice, William, Bert. Appeared Broadway plays, including Take Her She's Mine, 1962, A Case of Libel, 1964, Spofford, 1968, Handy Dandy, 1985, Elba, 1983; summer theatre appearance The Chic Life, Westport, Conn., 1970 (Straw Hat award); appeared in numerous live TV dramas, 1950's, including, Kraft Show, Robert Montgomery Presents, Playhouse 90; TV series Bridget Loves Bernie, 1972, Fay, 1975, Doc, 1974, Three's Company, 1976-78; appeared as Liz Mathews: TV series Another World, 1964-69; appeared as Helen Roper: TV series The Ropers, 1979-80; TV movie Pearl, 1978, Skyward Christmas, 1981, Dangerous Affection, 1987; movies Taking Off, 1971, The Heartbreak Kid, 1973, When You Comin' Back Red Ryder, 1979, Cannery Row, 1982, Best Friends, 1982, Desert Hearts, 1986, Sunday Drive, 1986; guest appearances on various TV shows. Mem. Screen Actors Guild, AFTRA, Actors Equity. Democrat. Died Oct. 16, 1997.

LINDSAY, MICHAEL FRANCIS MORRIS, liberal studies educator; b. London, Feb. 24, 1909; s. Alexander Dunlop and Erica Violet (Storr) L.; m. Hsiao-li Li, July 1941; children: Erica Susan, James Francis, Mary Muriel. BA, Oxford U., 1931, MA, 1935; postgrad., U. Vienna, 1931. Tchr. econs. and contemporary history Workers Ednl. Assn. South Wales, 1934-36; asst. dir. Indsl. Survey South Wales, 1936-37; prof. Yenching U., Peiping, China, 1937-41; tech. advisor communications dept. Shansi-Ch'ahar-Hopei Mil. Dist., 1942-44; vis. lectr. Far East area programme, 1946-47; lectr. econs. Univ. Coll., Hull, Eng., 1948-51; sr. fellow, reader dept. internat. rels. Australian Nat. U., Canberra, 1951-59; vis. prof. Calif. State Coll., L.A., 1966, Ball State U., Muncie, Ind., 1971-72; prof. Far Eastern studies Am. U., Washington, 1959-74; vis. prof. St. Olaf and Carleton Colls., 1976. Author: The Unknown War: North China 1937-1945, 1975, What's Wrong With Communism, 1976; contbr. articles to profl. jours. With Chinese mil., 1941-45. Died Feb. 13, 1994.

LINK, ARTHUR STANLEY, history educator, editor; b. New Market, Va., Aug. 8, 1920; s. John William and Helen Elizabeth (Link) L.; m. Margaret McDowell Douglas, June 2, 1945; children: Arthur Stanley, James Douglas, Margaret McDowell, William Allen. A.B. with highest honors, U. N.C., 1941, Ph.D., 1945; postgrad., Columbia U., 1944-45; MA, Oxford (Eng.) U., 1958; LittD, Bucknell U., 1961, Bethany Coll., 1994; U. N.C., Washington and Lee U., 1965; LHD, Washington Coll., 1962, Eastern Ill. U., 1983, Northwestern U., 1984; L.H.D., Monmouth Coll., N.J., 1993; HHD. (hon.), Davidson Coll., 1965, Westminster Coll. (Pa.), 1984. Instr. N.C. State Coll., 1943-44; instr. Princeton U., 1945-48, asst. prof., 1948-49; mem. (Inst. Advanced Study), Princeton, 1949, 54-55; assoc. prof. Northwestern U., 1949-54, prof., 1954-60; prof. Princeton U., 1960-65, Edwards prof. Am. history, 1965-76, George H. Davis '86 prof. Am. history, 1976-91, prof. emeritus, 1991—; disting. adj. prof. Am. history U. N.C., Greensboro, 1992—; historian Bowman Gray Sch. Medicine, 1993—; Albert Shaw lectr. Johns Hopkins, 1956; Harmsworth prof. Am. history Oxford U., 1958-59; Commonwealth Fund lectr. U. London, 1977; mem. Nat. Hist. Publs. Commn., 1968-72; pres. Nat. Commn. on Social Studies in Schs., 1987-90. Author: Wilson: The Road to the White House, 1947, (with R. W. Leopold and Stanley Coben) Problems in American History, 1972, Woodrow Wilson and the Progressive Era, 1954, 63, 88, (with William B. Catton and William A. Link) American Epoch, 2 vols., 1986, Wilson: The New Freedom, 1956, Wilson the Diplomatist, 1957, Wilson: The Struggle for Neutrality, 1914-15, 1960, La Política de los Estados Unidas en América Latina, 1960, (with D.S. Muzzey) Our American Republic, 1963, Our Country's History, 1964, Woodrow Wilson, A Brief Biography, 1963, Wilson: Confusions and Crises, 1915-1916, 1964, Wilson: Campaigns for Progressivism and Peace, 1916-17, 1965; editor: (with R.W. Patrick) Writing Southern History, 1967, The Growth of American Democracy, 1968, Woodrow Wilson, A Profile, 1968, The Impact of World War I, 1969, (with W.M. Leary, Jr.) The Diplomacy of World Power: The United States, 1889-1920, 1970, (with Stanley Coben) The Democratic Heritage: A History of the United States, 1971, The Higher Realism of Woodrow Wilson and Other Essays, 1970, (with William M. Leary, Jr.) The Progressive Era and the Great War, 1978, Woodrow Wilson: Revolution, War, and Peace, 1979, Woodrow Wilson and a Revolutionary World, 1913-1921, 1982, (with Richard L. McCormick) Progressivism, 1983, (with W.A. Link) The Twentieth Century: An American History, 1991, Brother Woodrow: A Memoir of Woodrow Wilson (Stockton Axson), 1993; editor: Papers of Woodrow Wilson, 69 vols., 1966-94; editor, sr. writer: A Concise History of the American People, 1984, The American People: A History, 1987; translator, editor: Paul Mantoux, The Deliberations of the Council of Four, 2 vols., 1992; mem. bd. editors Jour. So. History, 1955-58, 63-66, Jour. Am. History, 1967-70; contbr. articles to popular and profl. jours. Trustee Westminster (Pa.) Coll., 1971-82, Warren Wilson Coll., 1993—. Recipient Bancroft prize for biography, 1957, 61; Guggenheim fellow, 1950-51; hon. fellow Jagiellonian U., Cracow, Poland. Fellow Am. Acad. Arts and Scis., Soc. Am. Historians; mem. Am. Philos Soc. (Thomas Jefferson medal 1994), Am. Hist. Assn. (pres.-elect 1983-84, pres. 1984), So. Hist. Assn. (v.p. 1967-68, pres. 1968-69), Orgn. Am. Historians (pres.-elect 1983-84, pres. 1984-85), Nat. Coun. Chs. (v.p. 1963-66), Mass. Hist. Soc. (corr.), Assn. Documentary Editors (pres. 1978-79), Soc. Colonial Wars, Nassau Club, Cosmos Club, Phi Beta Kappa.

LINKE, RUSSELL DEAN, academic administrator, educator; b. Angaston, Australia, Feb. 20, 1948; s. Leonard Roy and Elvira Blondina (Krollig) L. BS with hons., Flinders U., 1970; Diploma in Edn., Monash U., Victoria, Australia, 1987, PhD, 1973. Lectr. sci. edn. Toorak Tchrs. Coll., Victoria, 1971-73; rsch. fellow in edn. Faculty of Edn. Monash U., Victoria, 1973-74; rsch. fellow in med. edn. Sch. of Medicine Flinders U., Adelaide, South Australia, 1976-80, sr. lectr. Ednl. Rsch. Unit, 1976-80; dir. acad. planning Tertiary Edn. Authority of South Australia, Adelaide, 1980-85; sr. rsch. fellow Social Justice Project Australian Nat. U., Canberra, 1986, exec. sec. Rev. of Engring., 1987-88; counsellor Nat. Bd. of Employment, Edn., Tng., Canberra, 1988-89; dean and prof. edn. Faculty of Edn. U. Wollongong, NSW, Australia, 1989-93; dep. vice chancellor and prof. edn. The Flinders U. of South Australia, Adelaide, 1993-95; active numerous profl. coms. including Joint Ministerial Adv. Com. on U. of New Eng. Network and Needs for Higher Edn. in No. NSW, 1992, Adv. Coun. on Tchr. Edn., 1992-93, numerous coms. for Tertiary Edn. Authority of South Australia, 1981-85, South Australian Health Commn., Sr. Secondary Assessment Bd. of South Australia, Edn. Dept. of South Australia, others; presenter workshops in field; cons. in field. Theme editor: Australian Sci. Tchrs. Jour., 1974; joint editor: Research in Science Edn., Vol. 4, 1974; Australian editor: Jour. of Biol. Edn., 1978-86; editorial cons: Australian Jour. of TAFE Rsch. and Devel., 1987-88; contbr. articles to profl. jours. and conf. proceedings. Mem. Australian Assn. for Environ. Edn. (found. v.p. 1978-82, pres. 1982-84, del. to seminars), Australian Sci. Edn. Rsch. Assn., Higher Edn. Rsch. and Devel. Soc. Australasia. Avocations: photography, music. Died, 1995.

LIPPERT, ALBERT, health service executive; b. Bklyn., Apr. 23, 1925; s. Hyman and Becky (Shapiro) L.; m. Felice Sally Mark, June 21, 1953; children: Keith Lawrence, Randy Seth. B.B.A., Coll. City N.Y., 1949. Asst. buyer Goldrings, 1949-51; buyer, mdse. mgr. Mangel Stores Corp., 1951-67; v.p. Weight Watchers Internat., Inc., Manhasset, N.Y., 1967-68; chmn. bd.. pres. Weight Watchers Internat., Inc., 1968-79, chmn. bd., from 1979, chief exec. officer, 1979-81; treas., past dir. W.W. Twenty First Corp. Active City of Hope; active Mr. and Mrs. League, Grand St. Boys Club. Served with AUS, 1943-46, ETO. Named Man of Yr., N.Y. Council Civic Affairs, 1968. Club: Sands Point Golf. Died March 1998.

LITCHFIELD, JOHN THOMAS, JR., physician; b. Mpls., Aug. 29, 1912; s. John Thomas and Agnes A. (LeDuc) L.; m. Ann E. Sliwka, Oct. 16, 1937; children—John Thomas III, Barbara Ann. BS, U. Minn., 1935, MB, 1936, MD, 1937. Instr. dept. pharmacology and exptl. therapeutics Johns Hopkins Med. Sch., 1937-43; asst. prof. dept. pharmacology U. Minn., 1943-45; group leader, asst. dir., then dir. pharm. rsch. chemotherapy div. Stamford Rsch. Labs., Am. Cyanamid Co., 1945-54; dir. exptl. therapeutics rsch. sect. Lederle Labs. div., 1955-63, dir. research, 1963-68; cons. Nat. Library Medicine and U.S. Dept. Agr., 1969-70; dir. extramural and clin. research Bur. Drugs FDA, 1970-71; med. asso. Kremers-Urban Co.; Mem. Commn. on Drug Safety; cons. to council on drugs A.M.A., Nat. Library Medicine, U.S. Dept. Agr. Fellow N.Y. Acad. Scis., A.A.A.S.; mem. Soc. Toxicology, Am. Soc. Pharmacology and Exptl. Therapeutics, Soc. Exptl. Biology and Medicine, Canadian Assn. for Research in Toxicology, N.Y. State Soc. Med. Research, Drug Information Assn., Sigma Xi.

LITTLE, BILL, food products executive; b. 1928. With Stadelman Fruit INc., 1965—. Died Apr. 1997.

LITTLE, GERALDINE CLINTON, poet, English literature educator; b. Portstewart, Northern Ireland, Sept. 20, 1923; came to U.S., 1925; d. James R. and Louise M. (Corr) Clinton; m. Robert Knox Little, Sept. 26, 1953; children: Rory K., Timothy Howard, Rodney Clinton. BA in English, Goddard Coll., 1971; MA in English, Trenton State Coll., 1976. Lic. English tchr. Adj. prof. Rutgers U., Camden, N.J., 1985, Trenton (N.J.) State Coll., 1986-87; adj. prof. English lit. Burlington County Coll., Pemberton, N.J., 1978—. Author: (poetry books) Women: In the Mask and Beyond, 1991, A Well-Tuned Harp, 1989, More Light, Larger Vision, 1992 (lst pl. merit books 1992); (verse play) Heloise and Abelard, 1990; (prose study) Out of Darkness, 1993, plus 25 other books. Singer Choral Arts Soc. of Phila., 1981—. Mem. P.E.N., Poetry Soc. Am. (v.p. 1986-87), Haiku Soc. Am. (pres. 1985). Avocations: music, reading. DIED 03/07/97. .

LITTLEJOHN, ANGUS CHISHOLM, banker; b. Marshall, Tex., Oct. 23, 1916; s. Angus C. and Regina (Scully) L.; m. Mercedes Daly, Sept. 28, 1946; children—Angus Chisholm, Mercedes Guevara, Robert Duncan. Student, Dartmouth, 1935-37; LL.B., U. Va., 1941. Bar: Va. 1941. Mng. partner Littlejohn e Cia (and predecessor, investment advisers), Rio de Janeiro and Sao Paulo, Brazil, 1946-64; co-founder Solidor, Inc., 1951, Tudor Ltd., 1953, Anhanguera Corp., 1955, Constanta, Inc., 1960; mng. dir. internat. div. U.S. Trust Co., N.Y.C., 1964-66; pres. Deltec Securities Corp., N.Y.C., 1966-68; also dir.; pres. U.S. Trust Co. (Internat. Corp.), N.Y.C., 1969-74; dep. chmn. Carbomin Internat. Corp. and ICM Group of Cos., 1976-79, also dir.; dir. Leckie Smokeless Coal Co., ICM Mo., G & W Carbomin Coal Co., Colton Creators Investments, ICM Steel Corp., Exchange Nat. Bank Chgo., Republic Mgmt. Corp., Brazilian Mining and Dredging Co. Bd. dirs. Am. C. of C., Brazil and Sao Paulo, 1952-60, Arts Council, Glen Cove, N.Y., N.Y. Coll. Osteo. Medicine, Westbury, N.Y. Served as officer USNR, 1942-45. Clubs: University (N.Y.C.); Piping Rock (Locust Valley, N.Y.); The Pilgrims.

LIU HAISU (PAN JIFANG), painter, calligrapher, poet; b. Changchow, China, Mar. 16, 1896; s. K.F. Liu and Hoong Shu-Yih; m. Hsia J-Chiao; children: Liu Fou-T'Tun, Liu Pao, Liu Ling, Liu Ying-Lun, Liu Qiu, Liu Hung, Liu Tsan. Founder, dir. Acad. of Shanghai of Arts, China, 1912-52; pres. East China Acad. Arts, 1953-58; pres. and chief examiner of Kiansou Provincial Exhbn., 1924; pres., 1st class prof. Nanking Acad. Arts, 1979-84; gen. rep. for organizing famous modern Chinese Painting exhbns. in Germany, Sino-German Joint Conf., Berlin, 1931; lectr. China Inst., Frankfurt, Germany, 1934; guest lectr. various European cities including Berlin and Dü sseldorf, Germany, Amsterdam, Netherlands, Geneva, London, Prague, Czechosolovakia; one-man shows of paintings include Tokyo, 1927, 84, Prussian Mus., Berlin, 1934, China Inst., Frankfort, Ger., 1931, Klinmann Gallery, Paris, 1931, Bruet Gallery, 1935, New Burlington Gallery, London, 1935; numerous group shows including exhbns. Switzerland, 1929, Egypt, 1929, Belgium, 1930, Italy, 1930, Germany, 1934, New Britain Gallery, London, 1935, Salon des Tuileries, Paris, 1930, Salon'd'Autaume, Paris, 1931, Klinmann Gallery, Paris, 1931, various exhbns. in Jakarta, 1939., Singapore, 1940, Shanghai, 1957, 80, 82, Peking, 1979, 82, Nanking, 1979, Hong Kong, 1977, 81; represented in permanent collections: Klinmann Gallery, Bruet Gallery, East Mus., Berlin, Asahi Kinbun Gallery, Tokyo. Recipient Silver Cup award Emperor of Japan, 1927, Prize of Honour, Internat. Exposition Centinary Nat. Independence, Belgium, 1930; diploma of merit, Italy U. Arts, Italy, 1981, 82; Gold medal artistic merit Internat. Parliament for Safety and Peace, U.S.A., 1982; recognized as Le Maitre de la Renaissance Chinoise, 1931. Mem. Internat. Arts Assn., Accademia Italia delle Arti (life), Nat. Joint Men of Letters and Artists Assn. (commr.). Author: (books on history of painting) including: Later Stage Impressionists and Shih-Tao, 1928; Shih-Tao and his View-points on Arts, 1934; On the Six Principles about Chinese Paintings, 1931; Theory of Paintings, 1931; On Modern Paintings, 1936; A General Statement on Sources of Chinese Traditional Painting, 1936; editor Fine Arts monthly, 1918, Arts Weekly, 1924. Deceased. Home: Shanghai China

LO BELLO, NINO, author, journalist; b. Bklyn., Sept. 8, 1921; s. Joseph and Rosalie (Moscarelli) Lo B.; m. Irene Helen Rooney, Feb. 22, 1948; children: Susan, Thomas. BA, Queens Coll., 1947; MA, NYU, 1948. Reporter and columnist Ridgewood (N.Y.) Times, 1946-50; instr. sociology U. Kans., 1950-55; Rome corr. Bus. Week mag., 1959-62, N.Y. Jour. Commerce, 1962-64; European editor corr. Opera Is My Hobby Syndicated Radio Show, 1960—; bus. news writer N.Y. Herald Tribune, 1964-66; Vienna corr. 103 U.S. and Can. dailies, 1966—; vis. prof. sociology Denison U., Ohio, spring 1956; vis. prof. journalism U. Alaska, summer 1974; writer in Italy, Austria, Switzerland, France, Germany, Eng. Author: The Vatican Empire (N.Y. Times Best Seller List), 1968, The Vatican's Wealth, 1971, Vatican, U.S.A., 1972, European Detours, 1981, The Vatican Papers, 1982, Guide to Offbeat Europe, 1985, English Well Speeched Here, 1986, Guide to the Vatican, 1987, Der Vatikan, 1988, Vatikan im Zwielicht, 1990, The Danube: Here And There, 1992, Travel Trivia Handbook of Oddball European Sights, 1992, A Catholic's Encyclopedia of Vatican Trivia and Papal Oddities, 1997; contbr. articles to mags. and jours.; editor The New Gazette, Vienna, 1980-81; columnist "From Here to Nostalgia" Times Newsweekly, N.Y.C., 1994—. With USAAF, 1942-46. Recipient Goldener Rathausmann award for Outstanding Fgn. Reporting, Vienna, 1974, Silver decoration (Austria), 1988, Gold plaque Austrian Nat. Tourist Office, 1988; named Alumnus of Yr., Grover Cleveland High Sch., Queens, N.Y., 1977. Mem. Overseas Press Club Am., Am. Soc. Journalists and Authors, Fgn. Press Club Vienna (bd. dirs.). Died April 12, 1997.

LOCKETT, HAROLD JAMES, physician, psychiatrist; b. Wilmington, Del., July 17, 1924; s. Jesse and Annie Lessie (Colbert) L.; m. Betty Jean Griffin, June 11, 1950 (dec. Aug. 1980); 1 child, Chérie Robin. AB, Ind. U., 1948; MD, Meharry Med. Coll., 1952. Diplomate Am. Bd. Psychiatry and Neurology, Am. Bd. Child Psychiatry. Intern L.A. County Gen. Hosp., 1952-53; resident in psychiatry U. Mich. Med. Ctr., Ann Arbor, 1953-56; resident fellow in child psychiatry Hawthorn Ctr., Northville, Mich., 1956-58, staff psychiatrist, 1958-72, asst. dir., 1972-90, dir., 1990-94; psychiatrist, 1958-94; clin asst. prof. U. Mich. Med. Sch., Ann Arbor, Wayne State U. Med. Sch.; pvt. practice in psychiatry, Ann Arbor, 1958-94; cons. to numerous sch. systems. Contbr. articles to profl. jours. Pres. Ann Arbor Bd. Edn., 1969-71, trustee, 1965-71; bd. dirs. Ann Arbor chpt. ACLU, Spaulding for Children, 1969-94; mem. adv. bd. Mich. Theater Found. Fellow Am. Acad. Child Psychiatry, Am. Orthopsychiatric Assn.; mem. Am Psychiat. Assn., Nat. Med. Assn., Black Psychiatrists Am. Democrat. Avocations: tennis, art objects, paintings, African artifacts, skiing. Died Oct. 1994.

LOEB, JOHN LANGELOTH, banker, broker; b. St. Louis, Nov. 11, 1902; s. Carl Morris and Adeline (Moses) L.; m. Frances Lehman, Nov. 18, 1926; children: Judith Loeb Chiara, John Langeloth, Ann Loeb Bronfman, Arthur Lehman, Deborah Loeb Brice. Student, Dartmouth Coll., 1920-21; SB cum laude, Harvard U., 1924, LLD (hon.), 1971. With Am. Metal Co. (Pitts. office), 1924-26, 26-28, Wertheim & Co., 1929-30; ptnr. Loeb, Rhoades & Co. Inc., N.Y.C., 1931-55, sr. ptnr., 1955-77, chmn., 1977-79; chmn. fin. com. Loeb, Rhoades, Hornblower & Co., 1978-79; vice chmn. Loeb Ptnrs. Corp., N.Y.C., 1980—, also bd. dirs.; gov. N.Y. Stock Exchange, 1951-54; adv. com. on internat. bus. problems State Dept., 1967-69, 70—. Hon. trustee Montefiore Hosp.; chmn., CEO Jacob and Valeria Langeloth Found.; bd. overseers Harvard U., 1962-68; hon. gov. N.Y. Hosp.; trustee, hon. chmn. Inst. Fine Arts, NYU. With Treasury Dept., Office War Moblzn., 1942-44, Washington. Mem. Coun. Fgn. Rels., N.Y. C. of C., SAR, Sky Club, Century Country Club (White Plains, N.Y.), Harvard Club, Lyford Cay Club. Died Dec. 8, 1996.

LOESCH, HARRISON, lawyer, energy and natural resources consultant; b. Chgo., Mar. 10, 1916; s. Joseph B. and Constance (Harrison) L.; m. Louise Mills, June 19, 1940 (dec. Feb. 1986); 1 child, Jeffrey Harrison; m. Agnes Sands Johnson, Sept. 10, 1988. A.B., Colo. Coll., 1936; postgrad., U. Denver, 1936-37; LL.B., Yale U., 1939. Bar: Colo. 1939, U.S. Supreme Ct. 1969. Assoc. firm Moynihan, Hughes & Knous, Montrose, Colo., 1939-42; partner firm Strang & Loesch, 1945-51, Strang, Loesch & Kreidler, 1951-56, Loesch & Kreidler, 1956, then Loesch, Kreidler and Durham, until 1969; asst. sec. for pub. land mgmt. Dept. Interior, 1969-73; minority counsel Senate Interior Com., 1973-76; v.p. govt. relations Peabody Coal Co., St. Louis, 1976-81; energy and natural resources cons., 1981-85; ptnr. Craft & Loesch, Washington, 1986—; chmn. bd. dirs. First Mountain State Bank of Montrose. Mem. sch. bd. Montrose Dist. 1, 1955-61. Served to maj. USAAF, 1942-45. Decorated oak leaf cluster. Mem. ABA, Colo. Bar Assn. (sr. v.p. 1955-56, pres. 1961-62), Midwestern Colo. Bar Assn. (pres. 1956-57), Army-Navy Country Club, Elks, Rotary, Kappa Sigma, Phi Alpha Delta. Republican. DIED 11/11/97. .

LOEW, RALPH WILLIAM, clergyman, columnist; b. Columbus, Ohio, Dec. 29, 1907; s. William Louis and Wilhelmina (Bauer) L.; m. Genevra Maxine Uhl, June 8, 1939; children—Carolyn Maxine, Janet Elaine. A.B., Capital U., 1928; M.Divinity, Hamma Div. Sch., Springfield, Ohio, 1931; D.D., Wittenberg U., 1947; L.H.D., Susquehanna U., 1972, Wagner Coll., 1974; LL.D., Hartwick Coll., 1979. Ordained to ministry Luth. Ch., 1931. Pastor Millerburg (Ohio) Luth. Parish, 1931-37; asso. pastor Luth. Ch. Reformation, Washington, 1937-44; pastor Holy Trinity Luth. Ch., Buffalo, 1944-75; Del. Luth. World Fedn., Lund, Sweden, 1947, Helsinki, Finland, 1968; Knubel-Miller lectr. United Luth. Ch., 1955; lectr. Retreat for Chaplains, Nat. Luth. Council, Berchtesgaden, Germany, 1956; Brit-Am. exchange preacher, 1966, 72; participant Long Range Planning Conf., India, 1968; pres. bd. fgn. missions United Luth Ch. Am., 1956-60, mem. exec. council, 1962-66, pres. bd. world missions, 1970-72, chmn. div. world missions and ecumenism, 1972-76; dir. dept. religion Chautauqua Instn., 1973-84; pres. ct. adjudication

Luth. Ch. Am. Author: The Hinges of Destiny, 1955, The Church and the Amateur Adult, 1955, Confronted by Jesus, 1957, Lutheran Way of Life, 1966, Christmas in the Shadows, 1968, He is Coming Soon, 1972; Contbr.: weekly column From My Window, Buffalo Courier-Express, 1952-82; syndicated column Finding The Way, 1960-67. Pres. Buffalo and Erie County Coun. Chs., 1950-51, Comty. Action Orgn., Buffalo and Erie County; pres. bd. trustees Margaret L. Wendt Found.; trustee Chautauqua Instn., 1988-92; pres. WNY Grantmakers, 1988-90; bd. trustees Habitat for Humanity Internat.; founder Habitat for Humanity, Buffalo, 1974. Recipient Chancellor's medal U. Buffalo, Notable Sermon award Life mag., 1957, numerous others. Home: Buffalo N.Y. Died Mar. 5, 1996; interred Forest Lawn, Buffalo, NY.

LOFERSKI, JOSEPH JOHN, electrical engineering educator; b. Hudson, Pa., Aug. 7, 1925; s. Andrew and Mary (Kochuba) L.; m. Sylvia Sweeda, Aug. 27, 1949; children: Marianne Fleury, Patricia Seal, Joseph, Barbara, Michael, Sharon. BS in Physics, U. Scranton, 1948; MS, U. Pa., 1949, PhD, 1953. Rsch. physicist RCA Labs., 1953-60; faculty Brown U., 1961-97, prof. engring., 1966-97, dean of engring., 1968-74, assoc. dean Grad. Sch., 1980-83; dir. R.I. Ctr. for Thin Film and Interface Rsch., 1987-97; pres. Solamat, Inc., E. Providence, 1977-83; sci. counsellor U.S. Embassy, Warsaw, 1985-87; mem. U.S./Poland Joint Commn. for Sci. and Tech. Coop., 1988-91; U.S./Poland Nat. Acad. Scis. Exch. fellow Inst. Nuclear Rsch., Swierk, 1974-75; mem. New Eng. Energy Congress, 1978-79; mem. organizing coms. 25 IEEE Photovoltaic Conf., 1956-96, Internat. Photovoltaic Confs., 1984-97; gen. chmn. Fifth Internat. Conf. on Solid Films and Surfaces, 1990; cons. in field; lectr. on solar photovoltaic energy, sci. and tech.; vis. chaired prof. Nat. Tsing Hua U., Hsinchu, Taiwan, 1994-96. Mem. editl. bd. Energy Conversion, 1972-97, Jour. Solar Energy Materials, 1978-92, Jour. Solar Energy Materials and Solar Cells, 1992, Progress in Photovoltaics, 1992-97, Ency. of Applied Physics, 1990-97; contbr. numerous articles to profl. jours. Served with AUS, 1944-46. Recipient Freeman award Providence Engring. Soc., 1974; named to Internat. Solar Hall of Fame, 1989. Fellow AAAS, IEEE (William Cherry award 1981); mem. Sigma Xi, Tau Beta Pi. Home: Providence R.I. Died Jan. 20, 1997.

LOGAN, HOMER HARRELL, engineering geologist; b. Coahoma, Tex., July 23, 1933; s. Benjamin Franklin and Mabel (Hood) L.; m. Lucille Legg, Sept. 5, 1959; children: Deborah Reneé, John Randolph, Franklin Phillip. BA in History, Tex. Tech U., 1971; MS in Geology, Tex. Christian U., 1984. Registered geologist, Ga. Geologist Fed. Power Commn., Washington, 1964-65, Internat. Boundary & Water Commn., Del Rio, Tex., 1965-69, U.S. Army Corps Engrs., Ft. Worth, 1973-76, USDA Svcs., Ft. Worth, 1976—; state geologist USDA Soil Conservation Svc., Ft. Worth and Temple, Tex., 1987-88; regional geologist USDA Soil Conservation Svc., Ft. Worth, 1988—. With USNR, 1956-58. Named Fiddler of the Yr., two local country music award shows, 1992. Mem. Assn. Engring. Geologists (chair Tex. sect. 1978-80), Assn. Ground Water Scientists and Engrs., Assn. State Dam Safety Ofcls. Avocation: fiddler player in bands. Died Nov. 9, 1993.

LOKEY, HAMILTON, retired lawyer; b. Atlanta, Aug. 30, 1910; s. Hugh Montgomery and Rebecca Crawford (Hamilton) L.; m. Muriel Ann Mattson, July 18, 1944; children—Hamilton Jr., William Mattson, Fletcher, Ann Montgomery, Rebecca Hazel. A.B., U. Ga., 1931, LL.B., 1933. Bar: Ga. bar 1933, U.S. Supreme Ct. bar 1938. Asso. firm Harold Hirsch & Marion Smith, Atlanta, 1933-37; individual practice law Atlanta, 1937-39; ptnr. Lokey & Bowden, Atlanta, 1939-95; mem. Ga. Gen. Assembly, 1953-56; practising lawyer in residence U. Ga. Law Sch., 1977; chmn. Ga. State Bd. Bar Examiners, 1974-78. Served with USN, 1942-45, 50-52. Mem. Am., Ga., Atlanta bar assns., Lawyers Club Atlanta, Internat. Assn. Ins. Counsel, Am. Coll. Trial Lawyers, Internat. Acad. Trial Lawyers, Am. Judicature Soc., World Assn. Lawyers, Phi Beta Kappa, Phi Kappa Phi. Democrat. Episcopalian. Club: Piedmont Driving. Home: Atlanta Ga. Deceased.

LOLLAR, COLEMAN AUBREY, JR., magazine editor, columnist; b. Birmingham, Ala., Feb. 22, 1946; s. Coleman Aubrey and Vera (Wingard) L. BA in Journalism, U. Ala., Tuscaloosa, 1968. Assoc. editor Metro. Mag., N.Y.C., 1970-72; editorial dir. Communications Internat., N.Y.C., 1972-79; editor Frequent Flyer Mag., N.Y.C., 1979-87; contbg. editor, consumer columnist Travel & Leisure Mag., N.Y.C., 1987-93. Author: Islands of the Mediterranean, 1972, Tunisia, 1972, monthly column Travel & Leisure Mag., N.Y.C.; freelance journalist and columnist. Tchr. U.S. Peace Corps, Sierra Leone, 1968-70. Recipient Japan Nat Writers award Japanese Govt., 1975, Eugene DuBois award, N.Y. Airline Pub. Relations Assn., 1984, writing award Pacific Area Travel Assn., 1992. Mem. Soc. Am. Travel Writers, N.Y. Travel Writers Assn. (v.p.), Am. Soc. Mag. Editors. Democrat. Home: Gulf Shores Ala. Died June 8, 1993.

LOMBARDO, JOSEF VINCENT, educator, artist, author; b. N.Y.C., Nov. 6, 1908; s. Raphael and Amalia (Tanzill) L.; m. Beatrice-Anne Silvy, Nov. 28, 1935; children: Dr. Jovin Carmyn Silvy, Dr. John Wynne, Dr. James Jovin. Diploma, Assoc. Art Studios, 1923, Cooper Union for Advancement of Sci. and Art, 1926; BFA, NYU, 1931, BA, 1939; MA, Columbia U., 1932, PhD, 1949, vis. scholar, 1950, post-doctoral scholarship, 1950-51; LittD, U. Florence, 1934, grad. fellow, 1932, Univ. Medal, 1950; Am. fellow, Accademia di Belle Arti, Florence, 1933; fgn. study, France, Italy and Eng., 1929, 1932-34; LLD (hon.), Villanova U., 1951. Mem. dept. art Bklyn. Coll., 1937-38; chmn. dept. art Queens Coll., 1938-42; mem. dept. art NYU, 1944; mem. dept. art Columbia U., 1946-49, prof. fine art, diploma, dir. fine arts, 1950, now prof. emeritus fine arts; chmn. adv. com. fine arts Carlton Pub. Corp., N.Y.C., 1945-49; Special asst. examiner fine arts Bd. Edn., N.Y.C., 1944; art cons. Prang Co. (pubs.), N.Y.C., 1951—, dir. art, N.Y. State Dept. Edn., 1951; vis. lectr. on Michelangelo Cambridge (Eng.) U., 1976, Accademia Petrarca, Italy, 1976; chmn. coll. scholarship com. L.I. Savings Bank, N.Y. Author: Santa Maria del Fiore: Arnolfo di Cambio, 1934, Attilio Piccirilli (1866- 1945), Life of an American Sculptor, 1944, Chaim Gross, Sculptor, 1949, Michelangelo: New Discoveries, 1976, (with others) Italian Culture in the Twentieth Century, 1952, Michelangelo: The Pietà and other Masterpieces, 1965, Michaelangelo: New Discoveries, 1976, Michelangelo: New Findings and Critical Analyses, 2 vols., 1990-91, also articles fgn. mags., sects. of books and ency. Mem. Community Planning Bd. 6, Forest Hills, N.Y.; Trustee Queens Mus., N.Y. State Sci. Found., Nat. Italian Am. Found. Recipient Gold medal U. Florence, 1934; Carnegie grantee, 1936-39; Columbia Research grantee, 1968; Dartmouth Found. research grantee, 1976. Mem. Met. Mus. Art, Italian Am. Coalition (pres.), United Fedn. Coll. Tchrs. (exec. bd.), Profl. Staff Congress (CUNY), Renaissance Soc. Am., Soc. Archtl. Historians. Apptd. by Italian Ministry Edn. as ofcl. rep. U. Florence at installation of Dwight D. Eisenhower as 13th pres. Columbia; apptd. ofcl. del. U. Florence and personal rep. Rettore to bicentennial anniversary Columbia, 1954.

LONDON, ADELE, poet; b. Brussels, Aug. 25, 1930; came to U.S., 1952; d. Charles and Helen (Hecht) Lubin; m. Ed F. London, Sept. 17, 1960; 1 child, Alan Lewis. Student, U. Belgium. Underwriter Ins. Co., L.A., 1952-60; writer of short stories in English and French, 1960—, French poet, 1950— ; provider readings for French groups in Calif. and Can., 1952. Author: Maintenant et Jadis, 1992, Sentiments, 1994; poems written in French publs., translated into English, 1993-94. Pres. L.A. PTA, 1972-74; other sch. offices. Mem. Alliance Francaise, 1939 Club. Avocations: travel, photography. Died May 25, 1997.

LOPEZ, MARLENE, chief executive officer, Bronx Psychiatric Center; b. South Amboy, N.J., Aug. 1, 1939; d. Frank and Antoinette (Charoullo) L.; 1 child, Sean. BA, Livingston Coll., 1974; MSW, Rutgers U., 1975, PhD, 1986. Asst. fed. liaison N.J. Dept. Human Services, Trenton, 1975-76; program devel. specialist N.J. div. Mental Health, Princeton, 1976-77; asst. hosp. adminstr. Marlboro Psychiat. Hosp., N.J., 1977-87; chief exec. officer Ancora Psychiat. Hosp., Hammonton, N.J., 1981-86; N.Y.C. regional dir. N.Y.C. Office Mental Health, 1986—, CEO, Bronx Psychiat. Ctr., 1988; faculty mem. Einstein Med. Sch., Bronx, 1988. Sec. League Women Voters, Madisontownship, N.J., 1965. Mem. Nat. Assn. Mental Health Adminstrn., N.Y.C. Faculty Dirs. Assn. (N.Y.C. rep.), Assn. Hispanic Mental Health Profls. Avocations: yoga instr., cyclist, tennis, skiing. Home: New York N.Y. DIED 04/02/95. .

LÓPEZ-MORILLAS, JUAN, Spanish and comparative literature educator; b. Jaén, Spain, Aug. 11, 1913; came to U.S., 1935; s. Emilio López-Morillas and Teresa Ortiz; m. Frances Mapes, Aug. 12, 1937; children: Martin, Consuelo, Julian. BLitt, U. Madrid, 1929; PhD, U. Iowa, 1940; LHD (hon.), Brown U., 1979. Asst. prof. romance langs. U. Iowa, Iowa City, 1940-43; asst. prof. Spanish Brown U., Providence, 1943-47, assoc. prof. Spanish, 1947-51, prof. Spanish and comparative lit., 1951-65, Alumni/Alumnae Univ. prof., 1965-73, William R. Kenan prof. humanities, 1973-78, prof. emeritus, 1978—, chmn. dept. Spanish and Italian, 1960-67, chmn. dept. comparative lit., 1967-71; prof. Spanish and comparative lit. U. Tex., Austin, 1978-79, Ashbel Smith prof., 1979-89, prof. emeritus, 1989—; vis. scholar U. Ctr. in Va., 1976-77. Author: El Krausismo español, 1956, Intelectuales y espirituales, 1961, Hacia el 98, 1972, Racionalismo pragmatico, 1988; editor, translator books; contbr. articles to profl. jours. Decorated Order of Isabella the Catholic by King Juan Carlos of Spain, 1985; grantee Am. Coun. Learned Socs., Am. Philos. Soc.; Phi Beta Kappa vis. scholar, 1966-67; Guggenheim fellow, 1950-51, 57-58. Mem. Internat. Assn. Hispanists (pres. 1980-83), Hispanic Soc. Am., MLA (mem. exec. com. 1981-85), Academia Norteamericana de la Lengua Española, Royal Spanish Acad. (corr.). Democrat. Avocations: travel, photography. Deceased.

LORANT, STEFAN, author; b. Budapest, Hungary, Feb. 22, 1901; came to U.S., 1940, naturalized, 1948.; m. Laurie Jean Robertson, 1963 (div. 1978); children: Christopher Stefan, Mark Imre. Ed., Acad. of Econs., Budapest, 1919; LLD, Knox Coll., 1958; MA, Harvard U., 1961; LHD (hon.), Syracuse U., 1985; D (hon.), Bradford U., Eng., 1989. Editor Das Magazin, Leipzig, 1926, Bilder Courier, Berlin, 1926-27, Münchner Illustrierte Presse, Munich, 1928-33, Weekly Illustrated, London, 1934, Lilliput, London, Eng., 1937-40, Picture Post, London, 1938-40. Author: Wir vom Film, 1928, I Was Hitler's Prisoner, 1935, Chamberlain and the Beautiful Llama, 1940, Lincoln: His Life in Photographs, 1941, The New World, 1946 (Carey-Thomas award 1946), F.D.R.: A Pictorial Biography, 1950, The Presidency: The History of Presidential Elections from Washington to Truman, 1951, Lincoln: A Picture Story of His Life, 1952, The Life of Abraham Lincoln, 1954, The Life and Times of Theodore Roosevelt, 1959, The Glorious Burden: The American Presidency, 1968, Sieg Heil!: An Illustrated History of Germany from Bismarck to Hitler, 1974, Pete: The Life of Peter F. Flaherty, 1978, My Years in England: Fragment of an Autobiography, 1982, The Years Before Hitler 1918-1933, 1991; editor: Pittsburgh: The Story of an American City, 1964. Recipient Literary award (Pitts.), 1965. Died Nov. 14, 1997.

LORBER, VICTOR, physiology educator; b. Cleve., Apr. 22, 1912; s. Samuel Zachary and Anna (Elconin) L.; m. Friedel Melanie Mundstock, Mar. 12, 1937; children—Ruth (Fox), Peter, Margaret. B.S., U. Chgo., 1933; M.D., U. Ill., 1937; Ph.D., U. Minn., 1943. Intern Michael Reese Hosp., Chgo., 1937-38; resident in surgery U. Minn. Hosp., Mpls., 1939-40; asst. prof. physiology U. Minn., 1943, prof., 1952—; assoc. prof. biochemistry Western Res. U., 1946-51, prof., 1951-52; career investigator Am. Heart Assn., 1951-77. DIED 02/20/96. .

LORD, JACK, actor, director, producer, painter; b. N.Y.C., Dec. 30, 1930; s. William Lawrence and Ellen Josephine (O'Brien) Ryan; m. Marie de Narde, Apr. 1, 1952. BS in Fine Arts, NYU, 1954. pres. Lord and Lady Enterprises, Inc., 1968—. Works exhibited in galleries, museums including Corcoran Gallery, Nat. Acad. Design, Whitney Mus., Bklyn. Mus., Met. Mus. Art, N.Y.C., Library of Congress, Brit. Mus., London, Bibliotheque Nationale, Paris, Mus. Modern Art, N.Y.C., Met. Mus. Art, Brit. Mus., Bklyn. Mus., Bibliotheque Nationale, Paris, Fogg Mus., Harvard U., Santa Barbara (Calif.) Mus. Art, John and Mable Ringling Mus. Art, Sarasota, Fla., Grunwald Graphic Arts Found., UCLA, Brooks Meml. Art Gallery, Memphis, Cin. Art Mus., Atkins Mus. Art, Kansas City, Mo., Fine Arts Gallery, San Diego, Colby Coll. Art Mus., Waterville, Maine, Ga. Mus. Art, U. Ga., Atlanta, DePauw U. Art Mus., Greencastle, Ind., Chouinard Art Inst., Los Angeles, Free Library Phila., Columbia U., N.Y.C., Lycoming Coll., Williamsport, Pa., Rutgers U., New Brunswick, N.J., U. Maine, Orono; represented in permanent collections, Dartmouth Coll., Hanover, N.H., Colgate U. Library, Hamilton, N.Y., Simmons Coll., Boston, Kalamazoo Inst. Arts, U. N.C., Chapel Hill, Evansville (Ind.) Mus. Arts, Massillon (Ohio) Mus., Hebrew Union Coll., Cin., N.Y.C., Los Angeles, Jerusalem, Flint (Mich.) Inst. Arts, Lehigh U. Coll. Arts, Bethlehem, Pa., Birmingham (Ala.) Mus. Art, Case Western Res. U., Cleve., Coll. of Wooster (Ohio), Calif. Inst. Arts; Broadway appearances include Traveling Lady, Cat on a Hot Tin Roof, Flame-Out, The Illegitimist, (TV shows) Stoney Burke (star); producer, star of 280 hours in 12 yrs. of series Hawaii Five-O; creator (TV series) The Hunter; creator, dir., producer: (TV film) M Station: Hawaii, 1980; writer (original screenplay) Melissa, 1968; dir. episodes Hawaii Five-O; appeared in feature films The Court Marshall of Billy Mitchell, Williamsburg, The Story of a Patriot, Tip on a Dead Jockey, God's Little Acre, Man of the West, The Hangman, Walk Like a Dragon, Dr. No, Ride to Hangman's Tree, Doomsday Flight; leading TV roles include Omnibus, Playhouse 90, Goodyear Playhouse, Studio One, U.S. Steel Hour, Have Gun Will Travel, Untouchables, Naked City, Rawhide, Bonanza, Americans, Route 66, Gunsmoke, Stagecoach West, Dr. Kildare, Greatest Show on Earth, Combat, Chrysler Theater, 12 O'Clock High, Loner, Laredo, FBI, Invaders, Fugitive, Virginian, The Man from UNCLE, High Chaparral, Ironside, Alcoa Theatre, Loretta Young Show, The Millionaire, Checkmate, Climax, Kraft, Philco, Danger, Suspense, The Web, You Are There, Lineup, Grand Hotel, Kraft Suspense Theatre. Served as 2d officer U.S. Merchant Marines. Recipient St. Gauden's Artist award, 1948, Fame award, 1963, Spl. Law Enforcement award, Am. Legion, 1973, Adminstr.'s award VA, 1980, Legend in His Own Time award State of Hawaii, 1980; named to Cowboy Hall of Fame, 1963. Mem. SAG, Dirs. Guild Am. Avocations: running, swimming, sculling, water color, oil painting. Deceased.

LORINCZI, GEORGE GABRIEL, lawyer; b. Budapest, Hungary, Apr. 15, 1929; came to U.S., 1948, naturalized, 1952; s. Eugene and Jane (Szende) L.; m. Ruth N. Kaufman, Jan. 15, 1949 (div. 1968); children—Kathryn Ann, Thomas E.; m. Rhonda Goodkin, Aug. 30, 1969 (dec. 1975); children—Seth D., Stacey M.; m. Irene Gilbert, May 5, 1976. Certificate, U. Paris, 1947; B.A., U. Mich., 1950; J.D., Marquette U., 1953. Bar: Wis. 1953, D.C. 1974. Ptnr. Lorinczi & Weiss, Milw., 1953-73, Sutherland, Asbill & Brennan, Washington, 1973-76, Stroock & Stroock & Lavan, 1976—; lectr. Marquette U., 1955-73; mem. legal com. U.S.-USSR Trade and Econ. Coun., 1975—; mem. various coms. U.S.-Hungarian Bus. coun., 1985—.

Contbr. articles to profl. jours. Bd. dirs. Internat. and Comparative Law Center, Southwestern Legal Found., 1975; chmn. Gov. Wis. Commn. Human Rights, 1965-67. Mem. Am. Bar Assn. (chmn. standing com. unauthorized practice law 1968-70), Internat. Bar Assn (ea. European forum coun. 1991—), Cosmos Club. Died Mar. 21, 1997.

LOTTERMAN, HAL, artist, educator; b. Chgo., Sept. 29, 1920; s. Cesel and Bess L. B.F.A., U. Ill., 1945; M.F.A., State U. Iowa, 1946. Instr. art Tex. Christian U., Ft. Worth, 1946-47, State U. Iowa, Iowa City, 1947-50; instr. art Toledo Mus. Art, 1950-56; assoc. prof. art U. Wis., Madison, 1965-72; prof. U. Wis., 1972-87, prof. emeritus art, 1987-95. Exhbns. include, Corcoran Biennial, 1955, 57, Carnegie Internat., 1952, Nat. Acad., 1954-60, Pa. Acad., 1949, 53, 57, 59, Met. Mus. Art, 1950, Balt. Mus., 1955, Oakland Mus., 1950, State U. Iowa, 1946, 48, 50, 57; represented in permanent collections, Butler Inst. Am. Art, Akron Art Inst., Wright Art Center, State U. Iowa, Ball State U., Ohio U., Toledo Federated Art Socs., Art Inst. Zanesville, Ohio. Served with U.S. Army, 1942-44. Home: Madison Wis. Died Mar. 8, 1995.

LOUCKS, RICHARD NEWCOMB, III, music educator emeritus; b. Pomona, Calif., Aug. 24, 1919; s. Richard Newcomb Jr. and Zeke Kinsworthy (Brunson) L.; m. Marian Edith Kirk, Aug. 19, 1949; children: Warren Frazier (dec.), Allen Frazier, David Brunson. BA, Pomona Coll., 1942; MA, U. Rochester, 1948, PhD, 1960. Successively instr., asst. prof., assoc. prof., prof. music Pomona Coll., Claremont, Calif., 1948-89, prof. emeritus, 1989-95. Author: Arthur Shepherd, American Composer, 1980. Capt. U.S. Army, 1942-45, PTO. Mem. Am. Musicological Soc. Avocation: clavichord maker. Home: Claremont Calif. Died Mar. 10, 1995.

LOUIS, JOHN (JEFFRY), JR., former ambassador; b. Evanston, Ill., June 10, 1925; m. Josephine Peters, Oct. 10, 1953; children: Kimberly, Tracy, John III. Grad., Deerfield Acad., Mass., 1943; student, Northwestern U., 1943, 46; B.A., Williams Coll., 1947; M.B.A., Dartmouth Coll., 1949. Account exec. Needham, Louis & Brorby, Inc., Chgo., 1952-58; dir. internat. mktg. Johnson's Wax, Racine, Wis., 1958-61; chmn. bd. KTAR Broadcasting Co., Phoenix, 1961-68, Combined Communications Corp., Chgo., 1968-81; ambassador to U.K., 1981-83. Trustee Evanston Hosp., Northwestern U. Served with AUS, 1943-45. Mem. Old Elm Club (Highland Park, Ill.), Pine Valley Golf Club (Clementon, N.J.), Augusta Nat. Golf Course (Ga.). Deceased.

LOUTH, EDWIN VERNON, economist, educator; b. Akron, Ohio, Aug. 15, 1920; s. Roland Lawrence and Stella Marie (Mouser) L.; m. Ruth Louise Paul, Aug. 11, 1956; children: Kevin, Gary, Kathy, Bryan, Jacquelyn, Mary. BS in Fin., U. Akron, 1948, postgrad., 1950-51; MS in Mktg., Ohio State U., 1950; cert., Alexander Hamilton Inst., South Bend, Ind., 1960. Economist Studebaker-Packard, Inc., South Bend, 1955-57; asst. to pres. Mercedes-Benz Sales, Inc., South Bend, 1956-65; dir. mktg. rsch. Mercedes-Benz, N.A., Montvale, N.J., 1965-71; gen. mgr. imports & distbn. Nissan Motors, L.A., 1971-75; gen. sales mgr. Downtown L.A. Motors, 1975-83; cons. to automobile industry L.A., 1983—. Ensign USN, 1942-46, World War II. Mem. Am. Mgmt. Assn., Am. Acad. Polit. & Social Scis., Nat. Indsl. Conf. Bd., Pepperdine Assocs., Tau Kappa Epsilon (chmn. local bd.). Roman Catholic.

LOW, PHILIP FUNK, soil chemistry educator, consultant, researcher; b. Carmangay, Alta., Can., Oct. 15, 1921; came to U.S., 1940; s. Philip and Pearl Helena (Funk) L.; m. Mayda Matilda Stewart, June 11, 1942; children—Roseanne, Jeannine, Philip, Lasca, Lorraine, Martin. B.S., Brigham Young U., 1943; M.S., Calif. Inst. Tech., 1944; Ph.D., Iowa State U., 1949. Soil chemistry faculty, agronomy dept. Purdue U., West Lafayette, Ind., 1949-97, prof. soil chemistry, 1955-92, prof. emeritus, 1992-97; cons. Exxon Prodn. Rsch. Co., Houston, 1960-80, Cold Regions Rsch. Lab., U.S. Army, Hanover, N.H., 1962-67, Battelle, Pacific N.W. Labs., 1980-81, U.S. Salinity Lab., Riverside, Calif., summer 1962; hon. prof. Zhejiang Agrl. U., Hangzhou, Peoples Republic of China, 1987-97. Cons. editor Soil Sci., 1957-97, Geoderma, 1981-88, Jour. Colloid and Interface Sci., 1993-97; assoc. editor Clays and Clay Minerals, 1960-66; contbr. articles to profl. jours.; patentee in field. Pres., Indpls. Stake, Ch. of Jesus Christ of Latter Day Saints, 1959-73; regional rep. Ind. Regions, Ch. of Jesus Christ of Latter Day Saints, 1977-83; bd. dirs. Opera de Lafayette, 1984-85. Served to 1st lt. Air Corps, U.S. Army, 1943-45. Recipient Ann. Research award Purdue chpt. Sigma Xi, 1960, Disting. Visitor award to Australia, Fulbright Ednl. Exchange Program, 1968, Disting. Service award Brigham Young U., 1976, Herbert Newby McCoy Research award Purdue U., 1980; Thurburn Vis. fellow U. Sydney, 1983. Fellow Am. Soc. Agronomy (bd. dirs.), Soil Sci. Soc. Am. (pres.-elect 1971-72, pres. 1972-73, bd. dirs. 1971-74, Soil Sci. Achievement award 1963, Bouyoucus Disting. Career award 1984, Soil Sci. Disting. Svc. award 1993); mem. Clay Minerals Soc. (Disting. Mem. award 1992), Internat. Soc. Soil Sci., Internat. Assn. for Study Clay, Nat. Acad. Scis. Avocations: collecting art, classical music, hiking, collecting crystal, jade, ceramics. Home: West Lafayette Ind. Died Jan. 14, 1997; interred Grandview Cemetery, W. Lafayette, IN.

LOWRY, OLIVER HOWE, pharmacologist, biochemist; b. Chgo., July 18, 1910; married Adrienne Clark, 1935; children: Susan, Emily, Charles, Stephen, John. BS, Northwestern U., 1932; MD and PhD in Biochemistry, U. Chgo., 1937; DSc (hon.), Wash. U., 1981. Oliver H. Lowry lectr. prof. exptl. instr. biochemistry Harvard Med. Sch., 1937-42; mem. staff Pub. Health Rsch. Inst., N.Y., 1942-44, assoc. chief divsn. physiology and nutrition, 1944-47; prof. pharmacology Wash. U., 1947-79, head dept., 1947-76, dean, 1955-58, emeritus disting. prof. pharmacology Sch. Medicine, 1979—; Commonwealth Found. fellow Carlsberg Lab., Copenhagen U., 1939. Recipient Borden award Assn. Am. Med. Colls., 1955. Mem. NAS, Am. Soc. Pharmacology and Exptl. Therapeutics, Am. Soc. Biol. Chemistry, Am. Chem. Soc. (Midwest award 1962, Scott award 1963), Histochem. Soc., AAAS, Harvey Soc., Am. Acad. Arts and Scis., Royal Danish Acad. Sci. Deceased.

LUBAR, ROBERT, magazine editor; b. N.Y.C., Oct. 10, 1920; s. George H. and Helen (Gang) L.; m. Patricia Raney, Aug. 2, 1947; children—John, Nicholas, Stephen, Andrew. A.B., Columbia U., 1940, M.S. in Journalism, 1941. Writer N.Y. Times, 1942-43; contbg. editor, then fgn. corr. Time mag., 1946-58; asso. editor Fortune mag., 1958-60, mem. bd. editors, 1960-64, 80-85, asst. mng. editor, 1964-70, mng. editor, 1970-80. Trustee N.Y. State Higher Edn. Services Corp., 1976-77. Mem. Council Fgn. Relations. Club: University. Home: New York N.Y. DIED 04/01/95. .

LUBINSKI, ARTHUR, research engineer; b. Antwerp, Belgium, Mar. 30, 1910; naturalized U.S. citizen.; married; 2 children. Candidate in engring., U. Brussels, 1931; student, Ing CM & E, 1934. Research engr. Barnsdall Research Corp., 1947-50; spl. research assoc. Marine and Arctic Ops. Group research ctr. Amoco Prodn. Co., 1950-75; pvt. tech. cons. Tulsa, 1975—; mem. panel drill tech., Mohole Project Phase I, AMSOC Com., NAS; cons. Mohole Project Phase II, Brown & Root; lectr., U. Tex., 1960-67; tech. evaluation bd. & tech asst. bd., Deep Sea Drilling Project, Scripps Inst. Oceanography, 1967-70. Recipient Disting. Achievement award Offshore Tech. Conf., 1976. Mem. ASME, AIME, NAE (mem. panel energy and resources, com. ocean engring. 1967—), Am. Petroleum. Inst., Belgium Engring. Assn., Belgium. Fedn. Engring. Assns., Internat. Assn. Drilling Contractors. DIED 05/03/96. .

LUCEY, CHARLES TIMOTHY, journalist, author; b. Corry, Pa., Apr. 2, 1905; s. Bartholomew and Jessie (Connors) L.; m. Catherine O'Toole, July 15, 1929; nine children. Grad., Corry (Pa.) High Sch., 1923. Reporter Erie Dispatch-Herald, 1923-26, Toledo News-Bee, 1926-29, Irish Independent, also Universal News Service, Dublin, Eire, 1931-32; Washington corr. N.Y. World-Telegram, 1938-44; chief polit. writer, chief corr. Scripps-Howard Newspapers, 1944-61; assignments in Europe, MidEast, Asia, South Am., Ctrl. Am.; editor Trenton Times Newspapers, 1961-68. Author: Ireland and the Irish, 1970, Harp and Sword: 1776: The Irish in the American Revolution. Bd. dirs. Am. Irish Found., pres., 1975-94. Recipient Raymond Clapper award for distinguished Washington correspondence, 1952. Clubs: Gridiron (Washington); Hibernian United (Dublin). Home: Thurmont Md. Died July 5, 1994.

LUDWIG, JOHN HOWARD, environmental engineer; b. Burlington, Vt., Mar. 7, 1913; s. Rudolf Frederick and Emily Henrietta (Sikora) L.; m. Gilda Mary Silva, Nov. 9, 1946; children—Howard Russell, Robert William. B.S. in Engring, U. Calif., Berkeley, 1934; M.S. in Engring, U. Colo., 1941; M.S. in Indsl. Hygiene, Harvard U., 1956, Sc.D. in Indsl. Hygiene, 1958. Registered profl. engr., Calif., Oreg. Engr. Bur. Reclamation, Denver, 1936-39; Engr. C.E., Portland, 1939-43, Sacramento, 1949-51; engr. water pollution USPHS, Washington, 1951-55; dir. research and devel. EPA, Washington, 1955-69; asst. commr. Nat. Air Pollution Control Adminstrn., 1969-70, asso. commr., 1970-72; cons. environ. engring. to fgn. and internat. agys., 1972-95; U.S. del. Econ. Commn. for Europe, Geneva, 1969-72, Orgn. for Econ. Co-op. and Devel., Paris, 1969-72, NATO Com. on Challenges of Modern Soc., Brussels, 1969-72. Contbr. articles to profl. jours. Mem. Santa Barbara Environ. Quality Bd., 1973-75. Served to capt. USAAF, 1943-46. Recipient Commendation medal HEW, 1963, Superior Service award, 1967; Gold medal for Exceptional Service EPA, 1971; Gordon Fair award Am. Acad. Environ. Engrs., 1973; named Distinguished Engring. Alumnus U. Colo., 1976. Mem. Nat. Acad. Engrs., Cosmos Club, ASCE, Am. Meteorol. Soc., Am. Acad. Environ. Engrs., Phi Beta Kappa, Sigma Xi, Tau Beta Pi, Chi Epsilon, Delta Omega. Home: Santa Barbara Calif. Died Feb. 17, 1995.

LUDWIG, PATRIC E., health care group executive; b. Mpls., Jan. 18, 1939; s. Roy and Gertrude (Anderson) L.; m. Carol Elizabeth Grasley, Oct. 29, 1960; children: Jana Kaye, David James, Mark Thomas. BS in Engring., U. Mich., 1962, MBA, 1963. Assoc. dir. Community Systems Found., Md., 1963-67, Hosp. Assn. N.Y. State, 1967-74; formerly pres. Mich. Hosp. Assn., Lansing, from 1974; now pres., chief exec. officer Bronson Healthcare Group, Kalamazoo, Mich.; mem. Mich. Health Planning Adv. Coun., 1975-76, Mich. Statewide Health Coordinating Coun., 1976-83; cons. Nat. Ctr. Health Svcs. R&D, HEW, from 1972; chmn. Co-author: Management Engineering for Hospitals, 1970. Chmn. trustees Community Systems Found., 1969-70, 72; mem. placement commn. Mich. Commn. for Blind Employer, 1980—. Recipient Outstanding Svc. award Community Systems Found., 1972. Mem. Am. Hosp. Assn., Am. Soc. Assn. Execs. (cert. assn. exec.), Am. Pub. Health Assn., Hosp. Mgmt. Systems Soc. (Outstanding LIt. award 1971), State Hosp. Assn. Execs. Forum, Lay Adminstrs. Mut. Benefit Soc., Mich. Health Econs. Coalition, Orgn. Execs. Mich., Lansing C. of C., Hosp. Adminstrs. Study Soc., Rotary, Capitol Club. Deceased.

LUENING, OTTO, composer, conductor, flutist, educator; b. Milw., June 15, 1900; s. Eugene and Emma (Jacobs) L.; m. Ethel Codd, Apr. 19, 1927 (div.); m. Catherine Brunson, Sept. 5, 1959. Student, State Acad. Music, Munich, 1915-17; diploma, Mcpl. Conservatory Music, Zurich, Switzerland, 1919; student, U. Zurich, 1919-20; D.Mus. (hon.), Wesleyan U., 1963, Wis. Conservatory of Music, 1979; D.Mus (hon.), U. Wis.-Milw., 1985; D.F.A. (hon.), U. Wis.-Madison, 1977; Litt.D. (hon.), Columbia U., 1981. Assoc. prof. U. Ariz., 1932-34; chmn. music dept. Bennington (Vt.) Coll., 1934-44; dir. music Bennington Sch. of Arts, 1940-41; assoc. prof., chmn. music dept. Barnard Coll., 1944-48; prof. music Columbia and Barnard Coll., 1948-68, prof. emeritus of music, 1968-96; music chmn. Sch. Arts Columbia U., 1968-70; prof. Joline Found., 1947-64; mus. dir. Brander Matthews Theatre, Columbia U., 1944-59; mem. composition faculty Juilliard Sch., N.Y.C., 1971-73; co-dir. Columbia-Princeton Electronic Music Center, 1959-80; Bennington Coll. Disting. Hadley fellow, 1975; vis. composer U. S.C., 1978, U. Wis., Kenosha-Parkside, 1979, 80, 81, 82, N.Y. U., 1979, Bklyn. Coll., 1981; commd. N.Y. Philharmonic, BMI, NEA, McKim Fund at Library of Congress; Phi Beta Kappa vis. scholar and hon. mem., 1966; spl. cons. Silver Burdett Co.; mem. ednl. advisory com. Guggenheim Found., 1964-69; life mem. Nat. Inst. Arts and Letters, v.p., 1953; mem. music com. Yaddo, 1936, 37, 38, 40, 47; mem. exec. com. New Music Quar. Records; mem. advisory com. Fed. Music Project in Vt.; mem. Vt. Music Library Com.; co-founder Am. Music Ctr. N.Y.C., chmn., 1940-60; bd. dirs. Vt. Symphony Orch., 1939; founder, mem. Am. Composers Alliance, pres., 1945-51; co-founder Composer's Recs., Inc., pres., 1968-70, chmn. bd., 1970-75, co-pres., 1975-77; bd. mem. Am. Composers Orch., 1974-94 composers Forum; mem. exec. bd. League of Composers, 1943; bd. dirs. Internat. Soc. Contemporary Music, 1974-81; nat. chmn. Am. composition Nat. Fedn. Music Clubs, 1943; mem. com. Soc. for Publ. Am. Music, 1945, Com. on Contemporary Music in U.S.A., Music Educators Nat Conf., 1943; U.S. del. Internat. Composers Conf., Stratford, Ont., 1960; U.S. music advisory com UNESCO, 1953-96; guest lectr. Bourges Internat. Music Festival. Flutist, condr. operetta and symphony orchs., Munich and Zurich, 1915-20; conducted first all-Am opera performance, Chgo., 1922; coach, exec. dir. opera dept., Eastman Sch. Music, 1925-28, asst. condr., later condr., Rochester Am. Opera Co., guest condr., Am Opera Co., N.Y.C., 1928; assoc. condr. N.Y. Philharm Symphony Chamber Orch., 1936; guest condr. Vt Symphony Orch., 1978, 85, Res Musica Balt., 1984, Internat. Festival of the Americas, Miami, 1984, vis composer, trustee Am. Acad. in Rome, composer-in-residence, 1958, 61, 65; vis. composer Peabody Inst Music, 1977, composer-in-residence, 1977-79; vis. composer, Bennington Coll. summer workshops, 1977-79 composer-in-residence Chamber Music Conf. and Composers' Forum, Bennington, 1988, Skaneateles Festival 1991, Cin. Conservatory, Canonical Studies and Fanfare for Those We Have Lost for Wind Orch., 1993, Green Lake, Wis., 1993; retrospective concert and exhbn. of composers' collection, N.Y. Pub. Libr. of Performing Arts at Lincoln Ctr. for 90th Birthday ; other 90th Birthday performances include Sage City (Vt.) Symphony, New Paltz, N.Y., Conn. Early Music Festival, concert at Merkin Hall by Goodman Chamber Choir, N.Y.C.; commission performance Symphonic Fantasia #10, Woodstock Chamber Orch. performances at Eastman Sch. Music, New Eng. Conservatory for 90th Birthday; also appeared as composer and flute soloist; appeared (with Ethel Luening) in concerts, U.S., Can. and Europe, 1928-41; author: The Odyssey of an American Composer: Autobiography 1980; (with others) The Development and Practice of Electronic Music, 1975; contbr.: The Liberation of Sound, 1972, On the Wires of Our Nerves, 1989; also articles; composer over 300 works in various musical forms, many compositions played by Am., fgn symphony orchs., chamber music socs. and soloists recs., Composer Recs. Inc.; also published: (in collaboration with Vladimir Ussachevsky) pioneer works for tape recorder including Rhapsodic Variations, Poem in Cycles & Bells, Concerted Piece for tape recorder and orch., taped electronic music solos and with orch.; recs include Orchestra Works, 1917-92, 1994. Named hon alumnus U. Wis., Parkside, 1981; named in his honor Otto Luening Day, N.Y.C., 1995; recipient David Bispham medal Am. opera, 1993, award Nat. Inst. of Arts and Letters, 1946, citation for outstanding achievements and contbns. to edn. and music Wis. Senate and Ho. of Reps., 1965, 76, Thorne Music Fund Found. award, 1972, citation Nat. Assn. Composers and Condrs., 1966, Am. Composers Alliance Laurel Leaf award, 1970, Laurel Wreath award, 1985, award NEA, 1974, 77, medallion and citation Wis. Acad. Scis., Arts and Letters, 1977, Creative Arts award and medal for music Brandeis U., 1981, Nat. Music Coun. Am. Eagle award, 1985, BMI citation, 1985, citation for svc. and dedication League Composers and Internat. Soc. for Contemporary Music, 1986, citation by Electro-Acoustic Soc. in U.S., Busoni award Busoni Found., 1991, proclamation and commendation Mayor of Milw. and Gov. of Wis., 1995; Guggenheim fellow, 1930-32, 74-75. Mem. N.Y. Acad. Scis. Clubs: Columbia U., Faculty, Century Assn. (N.Y.C.). Broadcasts and concerts in honor of 75th, 80th, 83d, 85th, 90th and 95th birthdays, N.Y.C., Milw., Munich, San Francisco, L.A., Houston, Washington, Boston, Denver, Louisville, Cologne (Germany), Bourges (France), Moscow, London, The Netherlands. Home: New York N.Y. Died Sept. 3, 1996.

LUHRING, JOHN WILLIAM, former bank executive; b. Los Angeles, Sept. 11, 1912; s. Otto August and Lillian Louise (Fritz) L.; m. Josephine Ferentzy, Nov. 12, 1958; children by previous marriage: Karen Maria, John Dietrich. J.D., Southwestern U., 1934, LL.D., 1974; grad., Pacific Coast Sch. Banking, 1950. Bar: Calif. 1936. With Union Bank, Los Angeles, 1931-74, trust counsel, gen. atty., 1931-43, asst. cashier, 1943-45, asst. v.p., 1945-53, regional v.p., 1953-63, v.p. charge So. Calif. dept. Bus. Devel. Div., 1960-63, regional v.p. Wilshire Center regional head office, 1963-67, regional v.p., gen. mgr. hdqrs. banking office, 1967-69, exec. dir. pub. affairs, 1969-74; past dir., mem. exec. com. Harbor Ins. Co.; dir. sec., former pres. Third Laguna Hills Mut.; exec. dir. Friends of Cultural Center, Inc., Palm Desert, Calif., 1974-79. Mem. adv. com. YWCA, 1955-60; mem. investment com. YMCA, 1951-74; past pres. bd. commrs. Dept. Water and Power; dir. Met. Water Dist. So. Calif., 1962-67; pres. Community TV So. Calif., 1967-72; mem. Nat. Adv. Com. Oceans and Atmosphere, 1972-76; pres., dir. Golden Rain Found. Laguna Hills; chmn. Airport Adv. Assos., 1964-74; pres. adv. council Liberty Park; pres. William H. Parker Meml. Scholarship Found, 1966-74; mem.-at-large Los Angeles council Boy Scouts Am., 1950-74; Bd. dirs. ARC, 1951-64, 66-68, exec. com., 1956-64; treas.; bd. dirs. Braille Inst., 1960-75, Vets. Service Center, 1950-60; bd. dirs., past pres. U.S.O., 1964-66, trustee Resthaven Sanitarium, 1956-58; trustee, chmn. exec. com. Southwestern U., pres., chmn. bd., 1974—80; bd. dirs. Saddleback Community Hosp. Found., 1980-83, also bd. dirs. hosp., 1981—83; chmn. bd. dirs. Aliso Viejo Housing Opportunities Corp., 1982—. Decorated knight Order St. Lazarus Jerusalem. Mem. ABA, Los Angeles Bar Assn., State Bar Calif., Beverly Hills Wine and Food Soc., Chevaliers du Tastevin (grand officer), Commanderie de Bordeaux, Wine and Food Soc. So. Calif. (past chmn. bd. govs.), L.A. C. of C. (past dir., chmn. aerospace com.), Founding Friends Harvey Mudd Coll., Ephebian Soc., Alpha Phi Gamma. Died Aug. 9, 1996.

LUKAS, J. ANTHONY, journalist; b. N.Y.C., Apr. 25, 1933; s. Edwin Jay and Elizabeth (Schamberg) L.; m. Linda Healey, Sept. 18, 1982. BA magna cum laude, Harvard U., 1955; postgrad., Free U. Berlin, 1955-56; hon. degree, Northeastern U., 1986, Colby Coll., 1987. Reporter, city hall corr. Balt. Sun, 1958-62; mem. staff N.Y. Times, 1962-72, assigned to the Congo,, 1962-65, assigned to India,, 1965-67, assigned to N.Y.C.,, 1967-68; roving nat. corr. N.Y. Times, Chgo., 1969-70; staff writer Sunday mag., N.Y.C., 1970-72; Nieman fellow Harvard U., 1968-69, fellow Inst. Politics, 1976-77; vis. fellow NYU, 1991; fellow Yale U., 1973-78; adj. prof. journalism Sch. Pub. Comm., Boston U., 1977-78; adj. prof. Columbia U. Sch. of the Arts, 1995; vis. lectr. Yale U., 1973; adj. lectr. Kennedy Sch. Govt., Harvard U., 1979-80; cons. Hastings Ctr., 1979-80; mem. steering com. Reporter's Com. on Freedom of Press, 1970-84; mem. exec. com. PEN Am. Ctr., 1977-83; judge gen. non-fiction Am. Book Awards, 1983, 86, Pulitzer Prize, 1988; mem. study group urban sch. desegregation Am. Acad. Arts and Scis., 1977-78; mem. exec. bd. N.Y. Coun. Humanities, 1986-88; mem. faculty Wesleyan Writers Conf., 1986, New Orleans Writers Conf., 1991, N.Y. State Summer Writers Inst., 1987-88. Contbg. editor: New Times mag., 1973-75; sr. editor: More Journalism Rev., 1972-77, assoc. editor, 1977-78; mem. editorial bd. Book-of-the Month Club, 1989-94, The Am. Prospect; contbr. articles to Gentlemen's Quar., Rolling Stone, Atlantic, Harpers, Saturday Rev., The Nation, New Republic, Psychology Today, Esquire, Reader's Digest, New York, others, 1958—; host radio program: In Conversation, Sta. WOR, N.Y.C., 1973-74; author: The Barnyard Epithet and Other Obscenities: Notes On The Chicago Conspiracy Trial, 1970, Don't Shoot—We Are Your Children, 1971, Nightmare: The Underside of the Nixon Years, 1976, Common Ground: A Turbulent Decade in the Lives of Three American Families, 1985, Big Trouble, 1997. Mem. exec. bd. N.Y. Coun. Humanities, 1986-88; mem. Com. for Pub. Justice, 1972-88. With AUS, 1956-58. Recipient George Polk Meml. award L.I. U., 1967, Pulitzer prize for local spl. reporting, 1968, Page One award N.Y. Newspaper Guild, 1968, Mike Berger award Columbia Sch. Journalism, 1968, Am. Book award, 1985, Pulitzer prize for gen. non-fiction, 1986, Nat. Book Critics Circle award, 1986, Robert F. Kennedy Book award, 1986, Polit. Book of Yr. award The Washington Monthly, 1986; named Literary Lion N.Y. Pub. Libr., 1986; Guggenheim fellow, 1979-80. Fellow Soc. Am. Historians; mem. Author's Guild (sec. 1989-91, pres. 1997—), Signet Soc., Phi Beta Kappa, Harvard Club, St. Botolph Club (Boston), The Century Assn. Died June 5, 1997.

LUNDBERG, FERDINAND EDGAR, author; b. Chicago, Ill., Apr. 30, 1902; s. Otto Ferdinand and Hannah (Svendsen) L.; m. Elizabeth Young, Sept. 19, 1944; children: Randolph Horner, Laurence Young. Student, Chgo. City Jr. Coll., 1921-23; BS, Columbia U., 1948, MA, 1956. Journalist Chgo. Daily Jour., 1924-26, U.P.I., 1926-27; fin. writer N.Y. Herald Tribune, 1927-34; economist WPB and War Shipping Adminstrn., 1941-45; editor Twentieth Century Fund, N.Y.C., 1946-51; adj. prof. social philosophy NYU, 1952-65; vis. prof. Carnegie Inst. Tech., 1956-57; lectr. Finch Coll., Bklyn. Acad. Arts and Scis.; sec. Conf. on Methods in Philosophy and Scis., New Sch. Social Rsch., N.Y.C., 1958-62; sec. Com. for Cultural Freedom, 1939-41. Author: Imperial Hearst, 1936, America's Sixty Families, 1937, Modern Woman: The Lost Sex, 1947, The Treason of the People, 1953, The Coming World Transformation, 1963, The Rich and the Super-Rich, 1968, Scoundrels All, 1968, The Rockefeller Syndrome, 1975, Cracks in the Constitution, 1980, The Myth of Democracy, 1989, The Natural Depravity of Mankind, 1994, (published posthumously) Does God Exist?, 1995; editor: Medical Studies in Merchant Seaman, 1943. Fellow Am. Sociol. Assn.; mem. Am. Philos. Assn., Am. Assn. U. Profs. Home: Chappaqua N.Y. Died Mar. 1, 1995.

LUPINO, IDA, actress, movie and television director; b. London, Feb. 4, 1918; d. Stanley and Constance (O'Shea) L.; m. Louis Hayward, 1938 (div.); m. Collier Young; m. Howard Duff, Oct. 1951; 1 dau., Bridget Mirella. co-owner (with Collier Young); Filmakers Co., until 1980; now retired. Motion pictures include: The Gay Desperado, 1936, Sea Devils, 1937, Life Begins at Eight Thirty, Lady and the Mob, 1939, Adventure of Sherlock Holmes, 1939, They Drive by Night, 1940, Not Wanted, 1940, The Sea Wolf, 1941, Ladies in Retirement, 1941, Lone Wolf Spy Hunt, High Sierra, 1941, Out of the Fog, 1941, Moontide, 1942, The Hard Way, 1942, Thank Your Lucky Stars, 1943, Forever and a Day, 1943, Hollywood Canteen, 1944, In Our Time, 1944, Pillow to Post, 1945, Devotion, 1946, Escape Me Never, 1947, The Man I Love, 1947, Deep Valley, 1947, Road House, 1948, Lust for Gold, 1949, Woman in Hiding, 1950, Fever Fear, 1950, Outrage, 1950, On Dangerous Ground, 1951, Beware, My Lovely, 1952, Jennifer, 1953, The Bigamist, 1953, Private Hell 36, 1954, Women's Prison, 1955, Big Knife, 1955, While the City Sleeps, 1956, Junior Bonner, 1972, The Devil's Rain, 1975, The Food of the Gods, 1976; star: Four Star Playhouse, 3 yrs; TV series Mr. Adams and Eve, 1956-58; TV movies include: Women in Chains, 1972, I Love a Mystery, 1973, The Letters, 1973, others. Home: North Hollywood Calif. Died Aug., 1995.

LUSTGARTEN, IRA HOWARD, lawyer; b. N.Y.C., July 31, 1929; s. Louis and Florine Josephine (Van Mindeno) L.; m. Rhoda Manne, Oct. 24, 1954; children: Lise Anne, Nancy Ellen. AB, NYU, 1950; LLB, Columbia U., 1958. Bar: N.Y. 1958, Fla. 1978, U.S. Dist. Ct. (so. dist.) N.Y. 1959, U.S. Ct. Claims 1985, U.S. Ct. Appeals (fed. cir.) 1986. Assoc. Proskauer Rose Goetz Mendelsohn, N.Y.C., 1958-68, ptnr., 1968-79; ptnr. Willkie Farr & Gallagher, N.Y.C., 1979—; former lectr. law Columbia U. Served to lt. USNR, 1951-55. Mem. ABA, Am. Law Inst., Am. Coll. Probate Counsel Found. (past pres.), Am. Coll. Probate Counsel, N.Y. Bar Assn. (past chmn. trusts and estates law sect.), Assn. of Bar of City of N.Y. (former chmn. trusts, estates, and surrogate cts.), Pub. Adminstrs. N.Y. (adm. bd. oversee), Fla. Bar Assn., Internat. Acad. Estate and Trust Law, N.Y. (legis. adv. com. to rev. law of trusts and estates). Died Oct. 12, 1997.

LYLE, JAMES PALMER O'NEIL, artist; b. Corpus Christi, Tex., Nov. 9, 1943; s. James Palmer O'Neil and Hester Margaret (Singleton) L.; m. Veronique Francoise Avril, Nov. 17, 1986. BFA, U. Ariz., 1967; MFA, Tulane U., 1969; student, Schuler Sch. Fine Art, Balt., 1986-90. Owner Lyle Studio, Augusta, Ga., 1993-95; asst. prof. Augusta Coll., 1971-73; guest lectr., tchr. Girl's Inc., Augusta, 1992-94; works in collections at Shearson-Lehman, Augusta, Le Cafe Du Teau, Augusta, Old Govt. House, Augusta, Port Royal, Augusta, Morris Mus. Art, Augusta, Musee Hotel Baudy, Giverny, France, Genstar Stone Products, Hunt Valley, Md., Sea Heritage Found., Glen Oaks, N.Y., Sun Papers, Inc., Balt., Fed. Res. Bank of Richmond, Mairie de Biarritz, France, others. Group shows include Prince Royal Gallery, Alexandria, Va., 1989, J.R. Leigh Gallery, Tuscaloosa, Ala., 1989, Pinehurst Galleries, 1990, Left Bank Art Gallery, St. Simmons, Ga., 1990, Georgetown U., 1991-92, Butler Gallery, Buffalo, 1992, Port History Mus., Phila., 1992, Ellis Island Mus., 1992, John F. Kennedy Mus., Boston, 1992, Phoebus Gallery, Athens, Greece, 1992-93; solo shows include Palais des Festivals, Biarritz, France, 1993. Bd. dirs. Broad St. Artist Row, Augusta, 1993-95, Main St. Augusta, 1994-95. Recipient Collector's Choice Juror's award Savannah, Ga., 1993, Best Artist of Augusta, Augusta Mag., 1992, 93, 94; Lila Wallace Reader's Digest Internat. fellow, 1992. Mem. Aiken Artist Guild (v.p. 1994-95), Am. Artist Registry, Balt. WAtercolor Soc. (signature mem.), Knickerbocker Artist, Acad. Artist, Salmagundi Club. Avocations: boating, gardening, snow skiing. Home: Augusta Ga. Died Mar. 14, 1995.

LYNCH, SISTER MARY DENNIS, librarian; b. Phila., Apr. 23, 1920; d. J. Raymond and Ida A. (Teal) L. A.B., Temple U., 1941; B.S. in L.S., Drexel U., 1942; M.S. in L.S., Cath. U., 1956; M.A., Villanova U., 1970, St. Charles Sem., 1980. Joined Soc. Holy Child Jesus, 1942; tchr., libr. Sch. Holy Child Jesus, Sharon Hill, Pa., 1942-45, 53-62, Summit, N.J., 1945-47; tchr. social studies West Phila. Cath. Girls High Sch., 1947-53; libr. Rosemont (Pa.) Coll., 1962—, lectr. methods of social studies, 1963-71, chmn. Am. studies com., 1970-73, lectr. polit. sci., 1973-87, lectr. New Testament, 1987—; instr. libr. sci. dept. Villanova U., 1964-65; mem. ednl. adv. bd. St. Charles Borromeo Sem., 1968-76, 78-87; bd. dirs. Tri-State Coll. Libr. Coop., 1967—, pres., 1980-81, exec. sec., 1967-70; trustee PALINET, 1978-81, 83-86, 90—, v.p., 1986; mem. Pa. State Libr. Bibliog. Access Study Adv. Com., 1977-78. Mem. ALA, Cath. Libr. Assn. (nat. exec. coun. 1975-79, 81-87, pres. 1983-85, adv. coun. 1985—), Pa. Libr. Assn. (chairperson coll. and rsch. sect. 1975-76, parliamentarian 1977-88), Assn. Coll. and Rsch. Librs. (pres. Del. Valley chpt. 1987-88), Cath. Libr. Assn. (v.p. Newman chpt. 1987-89, pres. 1989—), OCLC Users Coun. (del. 1978-83, 88-89, exec. com. 1982-83, del. 1988-89), Am. Acad. Polit. and Social Scis., Acad. Polit. Sci., Am. Studies Assn., Nat. Cath. Ednl. Assn., Nat. Coun. Social Studies, Beta Phi Mu.

LYNN, MIKE See SYNAR, MICHAEL LYNN

LYRINTZIS, CONSTANTINOS COSTAS, aerospace engineering educator; b. Athens, Sept. 22, 1960; came to U.S. 1983; s. Sotirios and Angeliki (Christodoulopoulou) L. Dipl., Nat. Tech. U., Athens, 1983; MS, Columbia U., N.Y.C., 1984; PhM, Columbia U., 1985, PhD, 1987. Rsch. asst. Columbia U., 1984-87; prof. aerospace engring. San Diego State U., 1987—; cons. in field. Contbr. articles to profl. jours. Mem. AIAA, ASCE, ASME, Am. Assn. Engring. Edn., Tech. Chamber of Greece, Am. Hellenic Progressive Assn., Sigma Xi. Christian Orthodox. Avocations: chess, soccer, volleyball, stock market. DIED 08/15/96. .

LYTHCOTT, GEORGE I., pediatrician; b. N.Y.C., Apr. 29, 1918. MD, Boston U., 1943. Intern Boston City Hosp., 1943-44, resident in pediat., 1944-46; dean CUNY Med. Sch., 1953-91; pvt. practice cons. pediat. Tappan, N.Y., 1991—; assoc. dean urban cmty. health affairs U. Wis., 1969-74, assoc. vice-chancellor health sci., prof. pediat., 1974-77. With USAF, 1951-53. Mem. Inst. Med.-Nat. Acad. Sci., Am. Pub. Health. Deceased.

LYTLE, ANDREW NELSON, author, editor; b. Murfreesboro, Tenn., Dec. 26, 1902; s. Robert Logan and Lillie Belle (Nelson) L.; m. Edna Langdon Barker, June 20, 1938; children—Pamela, Katharine Anne, Lillie Langdon. A.B., Vanderbilt U., 1925; student, Baker's 47 Workshop, Yale Sch. of Drama, 1927-28; Litt.D. (hon.), Kenyon Coll., 1965, U. Fla., 1970, U. South, 1973; L.H.D., Hillsdale Coll., 1985. Prof. history U. of South, also mng. editor Sewanee Rev., 1942-43, prof. English, editor, 1961-73, ret., 1973; Lectr. U. Iowa Sch. Writing, 1946, lectr., acting head, 1947; lectr. creative writing U. Fla., 1948-61; leader humanities div. internat. seminar Harvard, summer 1954; tchr. Vanderbilt U., Nashville, spring 1974, U. Ky., Lexington, 1976. Author several books, 1930—; latest titles The Velvet Horn, 1957, A Novel, Novella and Four Stories, 1958, the Hero With the Private Parts, 1966, A Wake for the Living, a family chronicle, 1975, Southerners and Europeans, essays in a time of disorder, 1989, From Eden to Babylon, essays, 1990, Kristin: A Reading by Andrew Lytle, 1992; editor: latest titles Craft and Vision: The Best Fiction from the Sewanee Review, 1971; contbr. articles, verse, fiction to various publs. Guggenheim fellow for creative work in fiction, 1940-41, 41-42, 60-61; Kenyon Rev. fellow for fiction, 1956; recipient Nat. Found. Arts and Humanities award, 1966-67, prize Lyndhurst Found., 1985; Brown fellow U. of South, fall 1978, 81-82; prize Ingersoll Found., 1986. Mem. Assn. Little Mags. Am. (officer), So. Acad. Letters, Arts and Scis., Council Lit. Mags.,The Fellowship of Southern Writers (founding fellow), Phi Beta Kappa, Kappa Alpha (Southern). Episcopalian. Died December 12, 1995.

MACDONALD, DONALD STONE, international resources executive, educator; b. Boston, Mar. 28, 1919; m. Jean Carroll Macdonald; 1 child, Thomson Stone. BSBA, MIT, 1938; MA in Polit. Sci., Harvard U., 1960; PhD in Polit. Sci., George Washington U., 1978. Fgn. svc. officer U.S. Dept. State, 1947-69; prin. staff Ops. Rsch., Inc., Carlisle Barracks, Pa., 1969-71; cons. U.S. Dept. State, 1969-75; prof. polit. sci. East Stroudsburg (Pa.) U., 1971-80; coord. adv. area studies, Korea, Foreign Svc. Inst. U.S. Dept. State, 1982-93; rsch. prof. Korea studies Sch. Foreign Svc., Georgetown U., Washington, 1984-89; sr. assoc. Sr. Internat.

Resources, Inc., Washington, 1989-93; internat. rels. officer Hdqs. U.S. Forces Korea, 1975-77; dir. Office of Intelligence Coord., U.S. Dept. State, 1980-83. Author: The Koreans: Contemporary Politics and Society, 1990; editor Mid-Atlantic Bull. of Korean Studies, 1984—; contbr. articles to profl. jours. Bd. dirs. Harbour Sq. Owners, Inc., 1987-90, S.W. Neighborhood Assy., 1982-86. Recipient Citation Comdr.-in-Chief, UN Command, 1977, John Jacob Rogers medal U.S. Dept. of State, 1983; Fulbright scholar, 1990-91. Mem. AAUP, ACLU, Am. Fgn. Svc. Assn., Am. Polit. Sci. Assn., Asia Soc., Assn. for Asian Studies (pres. Mid-Atlantic region 1984-85), Common Cause, Diplomatic and Consular Officers Retired, Internat. Studies Assn., Kings Chapel, Korean-Am. Assn., Royal Asiatic Soc., Smithsonian Resident Assocs., VFW, Rotary, Pi Sigma Alpha. Republican. Home: Washington D.C. Died Aug. 29, 1993.

MACDONALD, H. MALCOLM, government educator; b. San Francisco, May 21, 1914; s. George Childs and Helena (Zaun) M. B.A., U. San Francisco, 1935; M.A., Harvard U., 1937, Ph.D. (Savage scholar), 1939. Instr. U. Tex., 1938, U.S. Naval Acad., 1945-46; asst. prof. U. Tex., Austin, 1946; assoc. prof. U. Tex., 1946, prof., 1953—, chmn. dept., 1953-66; dean ad interim U. Tex. (Coll. Arts and Scis.), 1967, chmn. dept. govt., 1971-75; mil. coordinator U. Tex. (Office Pres. U.), 1948—; Johnson vis. prof. Pomona Coll. and Claremont Grad. Center, 1965; vis. prof. So. Meth. Sch. Law, 1963; vis. lectr. U. San Francisco, 1939; Mem. Sec. Navy Bd. Ednl. Policy, 1962-65, Bur. Naval Personnel Task Force Edn., 1964-66, Legislative Internship Com., Tex., 1964-69. Author: (with Webb, Lewis, Straus) Readings in American Government, 5th edit, 1968, Readings in American National Government, 1964, The Intellectual in Politics, 1966; Book rev. editor: Social Sci. Quar, 1946—; Contbr. articles to profl. jours. Bd. dirs. Clan Donald Ednl. Trust. Served to capt. USNR, 1941-45. Recipient Internat. Relations award St. Mary's U., 1966; Excellence in Teaching award U. Tex., 1958. Fellow Royal Econ. Soc.; mem. Southwestern Polit. Sci. Assn. (past pres.), Southwestern Social Sci. Assn., Am. Soc. Polit. and Legal Philosophy, Assn. Nat. ROTC Colls. and Univs. (past pres.),. Clubs: Army and Navy (Washington); Town and Gown (Austin). DIED 07/05/97. .

MACGREGOR, WALLACE, consulting mineral economist, author; b. N.Y.C., Nov. 27, 1917; s. Alexander and Isabelle (Bradley) M.; m. Mabel Evans, Sept. 11, 1939; children: Joan W. (Mrs. Frank Marino), Barbara, Margaret, Catherine (Mrs. Paul A. Nancarrow). M.B.A., Harvard, 1947. With Am. Export Lines, 1935-42; cons. engr. Coverdale & Colpitts, N.Y.C., 1947-50; asst. treas., then treas. Climax Molybdenum Co., N.Y.C., 1950-57; pres. Climax Molybdenum Co., 1960-66; v.p. Consol. Toronto Devel. Corp., 1958-59, Homestake Mining Co., 1959-60, Am. Metal Climax, Inc., N.Y.C., 1960-66; sr. exec. v.p., 1966-67; also dir.; v.p Kaiser Aluminum & Chem. Corp., Oakland, Calif., 1967-69; exec. v.p. Kaiser Aluminum & Chem. Corp., 1969-72; dir. Diamond-Shamrock Corp., 1983-90, Homestake Mining Co., 1977-89; cons. mine fin. and orgn., 1973—. Served with USNR, 1942-45; lt. comdr. Res. Mem. Am. Inst. Mining, Metall. and Petroleum Engrs., Mining and Metall. Soc. Am. Presbyn. Clubs: Harvard (N.Y.C.); Bohemian (San Francisco). DIED 04/07/95. .

MACGUIGAN, MARK RUDOLPH, judge; b. Charlottetown, P.E.I., Can., Feb. 17, 1931; s. Mark Rudolph and Agnes Violet (Trainor) MacG.; m. Patricia Alice Dougherty, Dec. 26, 1987; children from previous marriage: Ellen, Mark, Thomas, Beth, Buddy. BA summa cum laude, St. Dunstan's U., Charlottetown, 1951; MA, U. Toronto, 1953, PhD, 1957; LLB, York U., Toronto, 1958; LLM, Columbia U., 1959, JSD, 1961; LLD (hon.), U. Prince Edward Island, Charlottetown, 1971, St. Thomas U., Fredericton, N.B., Can., 1981, U. Windsor, Ont., 1983, Law Soc. of Upper Can., Toronto, 1983, York U., 1996. Bar: Ont., Prince Edward Island, Newfoundland, Queen's Counsel-Ont. Asst. prof. law U. Toronto, 1960-63, assoc. prof. law, 1963-66; prof. law Osgoode Hall Law Sch., York U., Toronto, 1966-67; dean of law U. Windsor, Ont., 1967-68; mem. parliament for Windsor-Walkerridge House of Commons Can., Ottawa, 1968-84; joint chmn. spl. joint commn. on constn. of Can. Parliament of Can., Ottawa, 1970-72, 78; parliamentary sec. Min. of Manpower and Immigration, Ottawa, 1972-74, Min. of Labor, Ottawa, 1974-75; vis. assoc. prof. law NYU, N.Y.C., summer 1966; chmn. Justice Com., Ottawa, 1975-79, Sub-Com. on Penitentiaries, Ottawa, 1976-77; critic solicitor-gen., 1979; Sec. State for External Affairs, Govt. of Can., Ottawa, 1980-82, min. of justice and atty. gen., 1982-84; judge, Fed. Ct. Appeal, Ottawa, 1984—; founding dir. Can. Civil Liberties Assn., Toronto, 1996, chair, 1966-67; pres. Can. Sect.-Internat. Commn. of Jurists, 1988-90; founding dir. Parliamentarians for World Order, 1977. Author: (law casebooks) Jurisprudence: Readings and Cases, 2d edit., 1966, Cases and materials on Creditors' Rights, 2d edit., 1967, (monograph) Abortion, Conscience and Democracy, 1994. Recipient Tarnopolsky medal for human rights Internat. Commn. of Jurists-Can. Sect., 1995. Mem. Internat. Law Assn., Can. Inst. for the Adminstrn. of Justice, Can. Judges'

Conf., Can. Bar Assn., Cercle Universitaire. Roman Catholic. Avocations: walking, bridge.

MACHADO, DAVID, conductor; b. Cabo Verde, Minas Gerais, Brazil, Apr. 16, 1938; s. Joaquim Augusto and Yolanda (Jordão) M.; m. Helena Rodrigues Silva, (div. Dec. 1984); 1 child, Claudia; m. Vera Nardelli Campos; children: Marcelo, Denise, Guilherme. Student composition, Sem. Music Pro Arte, São Paulo, Brazil, 1961; M in Conducting, State Acad. Music, Freiburg, Fed. Republic Germany, 1966; hon. diploma, Chigiana Acad., Siena, Italy, 1963, merit diploma, 1966. Cert. master in orchestra conducting. Resident conductor Teatro Massimo, Palermo, Italy, 1966-76; chief conductor Scilian Symphony Orch., Palermo, 1972-78; music dir. Teatro Mcpl., São Paulo, 1974-76, Porto Alegre (Brazil) Symphony Orch., 1978-82, Rio de Janeiro Youth Symphony Orch., 1982-95, SODRE, Montevideo, Uruguay, 1987; tchr. conducting State U. Minas Gerais, Belo Horizonte, Brazil, 1983-95; choir dir. Cantoria ARS Sacra, São Paulo, 1958-61, Mark Ch., Freiburg, 1964-66; conferencist U. Palermo, 1975-78; tchr. conducting U. Rio de Janeiro, 1982-84. Revisor: (opera score) Rosaura, 1967; composer Three Brazilian Songs, 1958 (best composition 1988). Recipient Premio Firenze Aidem, 1965, Premio Cantelli Cantelli Found., 1965, 67; decorated Order Santos Dumont State Minas Gerais, 1988; named Best Conductor APCT, 1961, 65, 75. Avocations: cooking. Died Nov. 25, 1995.

MACHINIS, PETER ALEXANDER, civil engineer; b. Chgo., Mar. 12, 1912; s. Alexander and Catherine (Lessares) M.; m. Fay Mezilson, Aug. 5, 1945; children: Cathy, Alexander. BS, Ill. Inst. Tech., 1934. Civil engr. Ill. Hwy. Dept., 1935-36 engr., estimator Harvey Co., Chgo., 1937; project engr. PWA, Chgo., 1938-40; supervisory civil engr. C.E., Dept. Army, Chgo., 1941-78; asst. to exec. dir. Chgo. Urban Transp. Dist., 1978-84; sr. civil engr. Parsons Brinckerhoff, 1985-93; partner MSL Engring. Cons., Park Ridge, Ill., 1952-93. Apptd. by gov. Civil Def. Adv. Coun. Ill., 1967-93. Served with USAF, also C.E., U.S. Army, 1943-45; ETO; lt. col. Res. ret. Registered profl. engr., Ill. Recipient Emeritus Club award Ill. Inst. Tech., 1989. Fellow Soc. Am. Mil. Engrs. (past pres. Chgo. chpt.); mem. ASCE (life, presenter tech. papers), Nat. Soc. Profl. Engrs. (life, nat. chmn. sessions program com.), Am. Congress Surveying and Mapping, Assn. U.S. Army, Ill. Engring. Coun., Mil. Order World Wars (life). Greek Orthodox (ch. trustee). Died July 6, 1993. Home: Chicago Ill.

MACLEAY, DONALD, lawyer; b. Tacoma, Dec. 27, 1908; s. Lachlan and Mabel (Nye) M.; m. Elizabeth Hall Fesser, Jan. 27, 1934; children: Donald, Linda Dewell, Murdo Lachlan. Student, Hill Mil. Acad., Portland, Oreg., 1922-24, Phillips Acad., Andover, Mass., 1924-25; J.D., U. Colo., 1931. Bar: Colo., Ill., D.C. 1931-33. Com. prevention, punishment of crime Chgo. Assn. Commerce, 1931-32; pvt. practice, 1933—; with Esch, Kerr, Woolley, Taylor & Shipe (and successor firm Kerr, Shipe & Macleay).; ptnr., now counsel Macleay, Lynch, Gregg & Lynch (and predecessor firms), Washington, 1946—. Served to lt. USNR, 1943-45. Mem. Am., D.C., Maritime Adminstrv. bar assns., Am. Judicature Soc., Assn. Transp. Practitioners, Maritime Law Assn. U.S., Clan Stewart Soc. in Am. (pres. 1980-85), Phi Delta Phi, Chi Psi. Episcopalian. Clubs: University, St. Andrews Soc. (pres. 1986) (Washington); Belle Haven Country (Alexandria, Va.); Fairfax Rod and Gun (Manassas, Va.). Home: Falls Church Va. DIED 10/18/94. .

MACLEOD, JOHN DANIEL, JR., religious organization administrator; b. Robbins, N.C., Mar. 16, 1922; s. John Daniel Sr. and Sarah Cranor (McKay) MacL.; m. Helen Frances Boggs, Sept. 18, 1945 (dec. Aug. 1990); children: Sarah MacLeod Owens, Mary Marget MacLeod Silberstein, John Daniel III, William Boggs. AB, Davidson (N.C.) Coll., 1942; MDiv, Union Theol. Sem., Richmond, Va., 1945, ThM, 1949, PhD, 1952; DD (hon.), St., Andrews Presbyn. Coll., Laurinburg, N.C., 1992. Ordained to ministry Presbyn. Ch., 1945. Pastor Carolina Beach (N.C.) Presbyn. Ch., 1945-48, Brett-Reed Presbyn. Ch., Sweet Hall, Va., 1949-53, Keyser (W.Va.) Presbyn. Ch., 1953-63; exec. Appomattox Presbytery, Lynchburg, Va., 1963-67, Norfolk (Va.) Presbytery, 1967-76, Westminster Presbytery, St. Petersburg, Fla., 1976-81, Synod of N.C., Raleigh, 1981-88; interim exec. Coastal Carolina Presbytery, Fayetteville, 1991-93, Holston Presbytery, Kingsport, Tenn., 1993; interim parish assoc. White Meml. Presbyn. Ch., Raleigh, N.C., 1994; interim exec. Western N.C. Presbytery, Morganton, 1995, interim assoc. exec., 1996-97, interim pastor Trinity Presbyn. Ch., Starkville, Miss., 1997; mem., chmn. various local and nat. Presbyn. Ch. Coms. Trustee Warren Wilson Coll., 1985-89, N.C. Presbyn. Hist. Soc., 1981-97, Mary Baldwin Coll., 1960-68, Davis and Elkins Coll., 1955-61, Massanetta Springs Conf. Ctr., 1956-62, Barium Springs Children's Home, 1995-97, Black Mtn. Home for Children, 1995-97; active Mineral County Redevel. Commn., Keyser, 1960-63; mem. N.C. Gov's. Adv. com. on Citizen Affairs, Raleigh, 1983-84; bd. advisors Wake Forest U. Div. Sch., 1991-96. Nominee moderator Presbyn. Ch. USA Gen. Assembly, 1987, moderator Synod of Va., 1969, Synod of Mid-Atlantic, 1990. Fellow Soc. Antiquaries (Scotland); mem. St. Andrews

Soc. (Southern Pines, N.C. chpt., bd. dirs. Tampa, Fla. chpt. 1976-81), N.C. Scottish Heritage Soc. (pres. 1992—), Clan MacLeod Soc. (chaplain, bd. dirs. 1994). Democrat. Avocations: genealogy, history, travel. Home: Raleigh N.C. Died July 8, 1997.

MACMORRIS, DAVID, diversified electronics company executive; b. Trenton, N.J., May 24, 1923; s. John Wesley and Martha (Hendricks) MacM.; m. Jeanne Peruse, July 5, 1947; children: Margaret, Susan Coffin, Ellen MacMorris Scott, Nancy MacMorris Adix. BSME, Iowa State U., 1949. Sales engr. Veeder-Root Inc., Hartford, Conn., 1950-54; applications engr. Reaction Motors, Denville, N.J., 1954-58; with Sundstrand Corp., Rockford, Ill., 1958—; area rep. Sundstrand Corp., Washington, 1958-63; mgr. mktg. Sundstrand Corp., Denver, 1963-66; program mgr. Mark-48 powerplant Sundstrand Aviation, 1966-69, mgr. mktg., new products, 1969-72, mgr. mktg., engine systems, 1972-74; mgr. mktg., power systems Sundstrand Aviation Electric Power, 1974, gen. mgr. advanced tech. group, 1974-78, v.p., gen. mgr. advanced tech. group, 1978, v.p. gen. mgr. advanced tech. group Aviation Ops., 1978-85; exec. v.p Sundstrand Corp., Rockford, Ill., 1985—, also bd. dirs. Trustee Rockford Meml. Corp., 1985—. Served as cpl. U.S. Army, 1943-46. Mem. Nat. Security Indsl. Assn. (trustee), Aerospace Industries Assn., Am. Def. Preparedness Assn., Pi Tau Sigma (hon.), Tau Beta Pi (hon.). Club: Rockford Country. Avocations: tennis, golfing, skiing. DIED 02/14/96. .

MACNAUGHTON, ALEXANDER DOUGLAS, theology educator; b. New Haven, July 10, 1913; s. Norman and Kathleen (Chalk) MacN.; m. Thelma Broadrick, May 19, 1944; children: N. George, Thomas D., John W., Jean K. B.A., Adrian Coll., 1934, D.H.L., 1979; M.S., U. Mich., 1938; postgrad., Harvard U. 1940-41; B.D., Yale U., 1943; Ph.D., U. Chgo., 1956. Tchr., Otisville (Mich.) Pub. Schs., 1935-36; ordained to ministry Methodist Ch., 1943; minister to students Wesley Found., Ohio U., 1943-45; dir. Student Christian Found., So. Ill. U., 1945-48; pastor Meth. Ch., Hoytville, Ohio, 1951-56; prof. religion Defiance (Ohio) Coll., 1956-61; prof. religion Adrian (Mich.) Coll., 1961-83, chmn. dept. philosophy and religion, 1966-77; bd. dirs. Mich. Intercollegiate Athletic Assn. Author: The Methodist Church in Michgian: The Twentieth Century, 1976. Mem. state adv. bd. Office of Services to the Aging, State of Mich., 1984. Mem. Ohio Colls. Assn. (sec. religion sect. 1961-62), Am. Acad. Religion (sec. Midwest region 1971-72, membership chmn. 1972-73, v.p., program chmn. 1973-74, pres. 1975-76). Home: Adrian Mich. Died May 28, 1991.

MACRAE, EDITH KRUGELIS (MRS. DUNCAN MACRAE, JR.), biologist, educator; b. Waterbury, Conn., Jan. 24, 1919; d. Peter Charles and Ezabel (Natkevicius) Krugelis; m. Duncan MacRae, Jr., June 24, 1950; 1 child, Amy Frances. B.S., Bates Coll., 1940; M.A., Columbia, 1941, Ph.D., 1946. Instr. zoology Vassar Coll., 1945-47; Donner Found., also Am. Cancer Soc. fellow Carlsberg Lab. Copenhagen, Denmark, 1947-49; research asso. Osborn Zool. Lab., Yale, 1949-51; instr. biology Mass. Inst. Tech., 1951-53; research zoologist U. Calif. at Berkeley, 1953-56; asst. prof. anatomy U. Ill., Chgo., 1957-64; asso. prof. U. Ill., 1964-66, prof., 1966-72, acting head and chmn., 1969-70; vis. prof. anatomy U. N.C., Chapel Hill, 1971-72; prof. anatomy U. N.C., 1972-89, prof. emerita, 1989-95. Contbr. articles sci. jours. Recipient Raymond B. Allen Instructorship award U. Ill. Med. Sch., 1964; CCB Excellence in Teaching award U. N.C. Med. Sch., 1976, 86; Guggenheim fellow, 1964-65. Mem. A.A.A.S., Am. Soc. for Cell Biology, Electron Microscope Soc. Am., Am. Assn. Anatomists, Southeastern Electron Microscopy Soc. (pres. 1978-79), Am. Soc. Zoologists, N.Y. Acad. Scis., Phi Beta Kappa, Sigma Xi. Home: Chapel Hill N.C. Died Oct. 7, 1995.

MACY, PATRICIA ANN, technical director; b. Washington, Aug. 20, 1955; d. William James and Carmen (Dols) M. BA in Communications and Bus., Am. U., 1977. Dir. Cable News Network, Washington and Atlanta, 1979-81; tech. dir. ABC News, Washington, 1981—. Tech. dir. TV news programs: Good Morning America, This Week With David Brinkley, World News Tonight, Nightline, Weekend News, The Health Show. Mem. NATAS (Emmy nomination 1981), Women in Radio and TV, Nat. Assn. Broadcast Engrs. and Technicians, Chi Omega. Democrat. Avocations: horseback riding, fitness training. Deceased.

MADIGAN, EDWARD R., former secretary of agriculture; b. Lincoln, Ill., Jan. 13, 1936; m. Evelyn M. George, 1955; children: Kimberly, Kellie, Mary Elizabeth. Grad., Lincoln Coll., 1955, LHD (hon.), 1975; JD (hon.), Millikin U., Ill. Wesleyan U. Mem. Ill. Ho. of Reps., 1967-72, 93d-102nd Congresses from 15th Ill. dist., 1973-91; former mem. House Energy and Commerce Com.; former ranking Rep. House Agr. Com.; sec. agr. Dept. Agr., Washington, 1991-93. Recipient Outstanding Legislator award Ill. Assn. Sch. Supts., 1968, Outstanding Pub. Service award Lincoln Coll. Alumni Assn. Mem. Ill. Jaycees (past v.p.), Lincoln C. of C. Lodges: Elks, Kiwanis. Home: Lincoln Ill. Died Dec. 7, 1994.

MAGAW, ROGER WAYNE, construction company executive; b. Beaver, Ohio, Feb. 8, 1933; s. Cecil Elsworth and Thelma Mae (Howerton) M.; m. Virginia May Burdette, July 2, 1955; children: Wayne Robert, Rex Roger. BS, W.Va. State Coll., 1960. V.p. labor rels. Williams Power Corp., Nitro, W.Va., 1959—; bd. dirs. mgmt. chmn. Nat. Maintenance Agreements Policy Com., Washington, 1983—. Chmn. Putnam County Vocat. Adv. Com., W.Va., 1968-90. Served with U.S. Army, 1953-55. Mem. Am. Welding Soc., Nat. Assn. Constrn. Boilermaker Employers (pres., bd. dirs. 1983-87), Putnam County C. of C. (chmn., bd. dirs. 1985-87). Republican. Methodist. Lodges: Masons, Shriners. Avocations: motor home camping, farming. Home: RR 2 Box 112 Hurricane WV 25526-9683 Died Nov., 1997.

MAGG, FRITZ, cellist, educator; b. Vienna, Austria, Apr. 18, 1914; came to U.S., 1938; s. Paul Julius and Helene (Zimmermann) M.; m. Natasha Elizabeth Kugel; 1 child, Kyril; m. Kari Miller, 1989. Student, Hochschule Für Musik, Cologne, Germany, 1932-33, Hochschule Für Musik, Berlin, 1933-34, Ecole Norwale de Musique, Paris, 1936. Ind. rec., concert artist, soloist, 1934—; prin. cellist Vienna Symphony Orch., 1934-36, New Friends of Music Orch., N.Y.C., 1938-40, Met. Opera Orch., N.Y.C., 1947-48; prof. cello, chamber music Ind. U., Bloomington, 1948-87, chmn. string dept., 1950-83; mem. Gordon String Quartet, 1940-47, Berkshire String Quartet, 1948-85. Writer, performer (video series) Cello Sounds of Today, 1984; author: Essentials of Cello Technique, 1965. V.p. Eva Janzer Cello Ctr., Ind. U. Served as sgt. USAAF, 1943-46. Mem. Am. String Tchrs. Assn. DIED 07/20/97.

MAGGAL, MOSHE MORRIS, rabbi; b. Nagyecsed, Hungary, Mar. 16, 1908; came to U.S., 1950, naturalized, 1960; s. David and Ester (Fulop) Gelberman; m. Rachel Delia Diamond, July 8, 1951; children: Davida Elizabeth DeMonte, Michelle Judith Weinstein, Elana Ilene Weinfeld. BA, Nat. Rabbinical Sem., Budapest, Hungary, 1933, Rabbinical degree, 1934; postgrad., U. Zurich, Switzerland, 1935, Hebrew U., Jerusalem, 1936, PhD (hon.), Ben Franklin Acad., Washington, 1979; DDW (hon.), The New Sem., N.Y.C., 1988. Rabbi Temple Meyer-David, Claremont, N.H., 1951-52, Temple Beth Aaron, Billings, Mont., 1952-54, Alhambra (Calif.) Jewish Center, 1955-57, Temple Beth Kodesh, Canoga Park, Calif., 1959-61, Congregation Ahavath Israel, Hollywood, Calif., 1966-70, Temple Emanu-El, Las Vegas, Nev., 1988-94; civilian chaplain USAAF Base, Great Falls, Mont., 1952-54; Editor Hebrew weekly Iton Meyuhad, Tel Aviv, 1940-47; asso. editor Heritage newspaper, Los Angeles, 1958-60; lectr. Free Enterprise Speakers Bur., Coast Fed. Savs. & Loan Assn., 1971-76; instr. adult edn. class Temple Beth Sholom, Las Vegas, 1990-94; mem. U.S. Congl. Adv. Bd. Author: Acres of Happiness, 1968, The Secret of Israel's Victories: Past, Present and Future, 1983; editor Voice of Judaism, 1960-94. Pres. Beverly Hills Zionist Orgn., 1973-77; exec. v.p. So. Pacific Region, 1973-94; mem. Los Angeles-Eilat Sister City Com.; Mem. Speakers Bur. of Com. for Re-election of Pres., 1972; hon. lt. col. New Spirit of 76 Found.; mem. nat. adv. bd. Ben Franklin Acad., Inst. Advanced Studies.; Calif. chmn. Spirit of '76 Found. Served with Israel Def. Army, 1948-49. Recipient Nat. Sermon Contest award Spiritual Moblzn., 1952, citation Crusade for Freedom, 1952, Am. Patriot award Ben Franklin Soc., 1981; named to Los Angeles Bicentennial Com. Speakers Bur. for Am. Revolution Bicentennial Adminstrn., 1975; Hon. sheriff Yellowstone County Mont., 1954; hon. adviser to Cecil B. DeMille for film The Ten Commandments, 1954. Mem. Nat. Jewish Info. Service (founder, pres. 1960-94), Town Hall of Calif., World Affairs Council, Internat. Visitors Program. Democrat. Club: Greater Los Angeles Press. Home: Las Vegas Nev. Died Jan. 21, 1994.

MAGNESS, BOB JOHN, telecommunications executive; b. Clinton, Okla., 1924; married. Grad., South Western State Coll., 1949. Chmn. Tele-Communications, Inc., Denver; chmn. Community Tele-Communications, Inc.; bd. dirs. Republic Pictures Corp., WestMarc Communications, United Artists Communications, Inc. Died Nov. 15, 1996.

MAHAFFAY, WILLIAM EDWARD, mechanical engineer; s. James W. and Ida (Hyink) M.; m. Carolyn Dahlquist, Oct. 15, 1935; 1 son, John W. BS, Northwestern U., 1933. Registered engr., Ind. Various positions Internat. Harvester Co., 1935-42; plant engr. Internat. Harvester Co. (Refrigeration div.), 1942-45, chief engr. advanced engring sect., 1945-51; exec. engr. Whirlpool Corp., St. Joseph, Mich., 1951-53; dir. engring. and rsch. Whirlpool Corp., 1953-56, v.p. engring. and rsch., 1956-65, group v.p., 1965-70; dir. Robbins Myers, Dayton, Ohio, 1970-87, Ranco Inc., Columbus, Ohio, 1970-87; engring. cons.; adj. prof. U. Mich., 1970; vis. prof. Purdue., 1970; Life regent Northwestern U.; tech. adv. com. Purdue U. Mem. ASHRAE, ASME, Acacia, Northwestern U. Alumni Assn., Instrument Soc. Am., Union League Club (Chgo.), Paradise Valley Country Club, Lomas Santa Fe Country Club, (Solana Beach, Calif.), Sigma Xi, Tau Beta Pi, Pi Tau Sigma.

MAHONEY, J. DANIEL, federal judge; b. Orange, N.J., Sept. 7, 1931; s. Daniel Vincent and Louisa (Dunbar) M.; m. Kathleen Mary O'Doherty, Oct. 22, 1955; children: J. Daniel, Kieran Vincent, Francis Kirk, Mary Louisa, Eileen Ann, Elizabeth Anne. B.A. magna cum laude, St. Bonaventure U., 1952; LL.B. (Kent scholar), Columbia U., 1955. Bar: N.Y. 1960. Asso. firm Simpson Thatcher & Bartlett, N.Y.C., 1958-62; partner firm Wormser, Keily, Alessandroni, Mahoney & McCann, N.Y.C., 1965-74, Windels, Marx, Davies & Ives, N.Y.C., 1974-86; state chmn. N.Y. Conservative Party, 1962-86; judge U.S. Ct. Appeals (2d cir.), Milford, Conn., 1986—; elected to Electoral Coll., 1980; dir. Nat. Rev., Inc., N.Y.C., 1972-86. Author: Actions Speak Louder, The Story of the New York Conservative Party, 1967. Mem. adv. coun. Pace U., 1985-87; dean's adv. coun. Hofstra U. Sch. Law, 1982-90; bd. fellows Poly. Inst. N.Y., 1981-91. Lt. (j.g.) USCGR, 1955-58. Roman Catholic. Home: Huntington Conn. Died Oct. 23, 1996.

MAISEL, MICHAEL, clothing executive; b. Newark, Oct. 19, 1947; s. Irving and Betty (Markin) M.; m. Arlette Bernstein, Oct. 18, 1980; children: Ian Albert, Alicia Beth, Noah Shawn, Bette Gabrielle, Melissa Ann, Eunice Blanca. B.S. in Mktg., B.A. in Gen. Bus. Adminstrn., Ariz. State U., 1969. Asst. sales mgr. Mid-Atlantic Shoe Co. div. Beck Industries, N.Y.C., 1969-71; dir. imports Felsway Corp., Totowa, N.J., 1972-73; exec. v.p. Carber Enterprises, N.Y.C., 1973-80; v.p. S.R.O. div. Caressa, N.Y.C., 1980-84; pres. Sandler of Boston, N.Y.C., 1984-85, chmn. bd., 1986—; v.p. Lowell Shoe, Inc., Hudson, N.H., 1992-93; v.p. Selby, U.S. Shoe, Cin., 1993—; cons. in field. Mem. 210 Shoe Industry (life), Nat. Shoe Retailers Assn. (bd. dirs.), Nat. Shoe Mfrs. Assn. Republican. Jewish. Designer Carber's shoe, displayed in Met. Mus. Art; nominated for Coty design award, 1974-78; recipient Friendship award City of Cin. Human Rels. Commn., 1994.

MAJEWSKI, STANISLAW, banker; b. Czelabinsk, Apr. 11, 1915; s. Jozef Majewski and Zofia (Donalska) Majewska; m. Wanda Majewska/Suska, Dec. 26, 1940; children—Ewa, Hanna, Elzbieta. M.A. in Law, Uniwersytet Jagiellonski, Cracow, Poland, 1937. Pres., Nat. Polish Bank, Warsaw, 1965-68, 80—, dep. pres., 1975-80; undersec. state Fin. Ministry, Warsaw, 1965-68, minister fin., 1968-69; v.p. Council Ministers, Warsaw, 1969-71; Polish rep. Council Mut. Econ. Assistance, Moscow, USSR, 1971-75. Recipient Order of Banner of Labour 2d Class, Council of State, Warsaw, 1964, Order of Bannker of Labour 1st Class, 1969, Officer's Cross of Order of Polonia Restituta, 1979. Mem. Polish United Workers' Party.

MALENBAUM, WILFRED, economist, emeritus educator, consultant; b. Boston, Jan. 26, 1913; s. Harry and Bertha (Brandwyn) M.; m. Josephine J. Orenstein, Feb. 26, 1950 (dec. 1965); children: Bruce, Roxanne, Ronald; m. Gloria B. Balaban, Oct. 31, 1976 (div. 1981). A.B., Harvard U., 1934, A.M., 1935, Ph.D., 1941; postgrad., London Sch. Econs., 1937, Inst. Econs., Oslo, 1938. Instr. econs. Harvard U., 1938-41; chief food and agr. sect. OSS, 1941-45; chief div. internat. and functional intelligence Dept. State, 1946-48, chief div. investment and econ. devel., 1948-53; tech. specialist 1st UNRRA conf., Atlantic City, 1943; U.S. mem. Combined Working Party, London, Algiers, Rome, 1944-45; U.S. del. London Conf. on Food and Agrl. Stats., 1945; tech. cons. FAO, WHO; specialist Meeting on Urgent Food Problems, 1946; adviser U.S. del. Interim Commn. of Internat. Trade Orgn., Geneva, 1948; dir. India project Ctr. for Internat. Studies; also vis. prof. econs. MIT, 1953—; in India directing MIT rsch. project, 1955-56; prof. econs. U. Pa., 1959-83, prof. emeritus, 1983—; indsl. cons., 1983—; vis. prof. U. Hawaii, 1961, Harvard U., 1964, Hebrew U. Jerusalem, 1980; chair internat. econs. Heidelberg U., spring 1966; cons. Govt. India, 1963; U.S. del. Colombo Plan Conf., Karachi, Pakistan, 1952, SEATO, Baguio, Philippines, 1960; cons. tech. assistance-internat. health AID; mem. U.S. Council Internat. Health, 1971—; prin. investigator Nat. Commn. on Materials Policy, 1972-73, NSF resch.project on fgn. demand for raw materials, 1975—; mem. com. on resources and the environment NAS, 1973-75; exch. scientist Coun. Sci. and Indsl. Rsch. (India), NSF, 1971, 72; cons. WHO, Geneva, 1976, 77; faculty Semester at Sea, Internat. Inst. Seaboard Edn., fall 1984-85. Author: The World Wheat Economy, 1885-39, 1953, India and China; Development Contrasts, 1956, East and West in Indian Development, 1959, Prospects for Indian Development, 1962, Modern India's Economy: Two Decades of Planned Growth, 1971, Materials Requirements in the United States and Abroad in the Year 2000, 1973, World Demand for Raw Materials in 1985 and 2000, 1978, The Power of Health, 1981, Modern Economic Growth in India and China: The Comparison Revisited, 1950-80, 1982, (with others) The Encyclopedia of Asian History, 1987. Ford Found. grantee, 1973; Smithsonian Instn. sr. fellow India, 1977-78; recipient Detur award, 1931; Rogers Traveling fellow, 1937-38; David A. Wells prize, 1943. Mem. Am. Econ. Assn., Am. Farm Econ. Assn., Assn. Asian Studies, Asia Soc., Soc. Internat. Devel., Phi Beta Kappa, Sigma Alpha Mu. DIED 08/23/96.

MALESKA, EUGENE T., school administrator, author, editoructor; b. Jersey City, Jan. 6, 1916; m. Jean M. Merletto (dec. 1983); children: Merryl, Gary; m. Carol Atkinson, 1991. A.B., Montclair State Coll, 1937, M.A., 1940; Ed.D., Harvard U., 1955; LL.D. (hon.), Montclair State Coll., 1963. Tchr. jr. high schs., N.J., N.Y.C., 1937-46; asst. to prin. Pub. Sch. 169, N.Y.C., 1946-52; prin. Pub. Sch. 192, N.Y.C., 1952-55, Jr. high sch. 164, N.Y.C., 1955-58; prin., coordinator tchr. recruitment Hdqrs. Bklyn., 1958-62, asst. supt. schs. in charge of tchr. recruitment, 1962-63; asst. supt. schs. Dist. 11, Bronx, N.Y., 1964-67; assoc. dir. Ctr. for Urban Edn., N.Y.C., 1967-70; community supt. Dist. 8, Bronx, 1970-73; crossword puzzle editor New York Times, 1977-93; instr. Hunter Coll., 1947-51; lectr. City Coll., 1952-62; instr. U. Vt., 1960, 61; lectr. Baruch Sch., 1967, dir. internship programs, 1973-74; cons. social studies series Noble and Noble, 1972-73. Author: (poetry) Sun and Shadow; co-editor: Junior Crossword Puzzle Book, Educational Crosswords (series), Crosstalk, 1993; co-author: The Story of Education, 1962, 65; Three Voices, 1967, A Pleasure In Words, 1981, Across and Down: Inside The Crossword Puzzle World, 1984, Spell-Write Workbook, 1974; crossword puzzle constructor New York Times, several nat. mags., Dell Puzzles, 1943-93; sole editor: Simon and Schuster's Crossword Book of Quotations, 17 vols., 1976-84, Cryptic Puzzles, 1981-87, Simon and Schuster Crossword Puzzle Book, 1984-93, Children's Word Games and Crossword Puzzles, 1986-93, Times Toughest Puzzles, 1988, 89; author: Maleska's Favorite Word Games, 1989; contbr. articles to profl. jours.; various TV, radio interviews. Recipient Human Rels. award Spanish-Am. Coun. N.Y.C., 1956, Disting. Svc. to Pub. Edn. award N.Y. Acad. Pub. Edn., 1993; Harvard Grad. Sch. Edn. scholar, 1953; Harvard Grad. Sch. Edn. fellow, 1954. Mem. Assn. for Supervision and Curriculum Devel., Am. Ednl. Research Assn., NEA, Am. Assn. Sch. Adminstrn., N.Y. State Council Sch. Dist. Adminstrs., Assn. Asst. Supts. N.Y.C., N.Y. State Assn. Suprs. and Curriculum Devel., Nat. Assn. Secondary Sch. Prins., Harvard U. Grad Sch. Educators Alumni Assn., Nat. Authors' Guild, Montclair State Coll. Alumni Assn. (exec. bd.), Acad. Pub. Edn., Poetry Soc. Am., Kappa Delta Phi, Phi Delta Kappa (Outstanding Achievement Citation Beta Epsilon chpt. 1959). N.Y.C. Pub. Sch. (P.S. 174, Bronx) named after him. Home: Wareham Mass. Died Aug. 3, 1993.

MALLARY, ROBERT, sculptor; b. Toledo, Dec. 2, 1917; s. Benjamin E. and Laura (Grossman) M.; m. Margot Handrahan, Oct. 29, 1942; children: Michelle, Michael, Martine, Dion. Certificate, La Escuela de las Artes del Libro, Mexico D.F., 1939. mem. faculty U. N.M., 1955-59, Pratt Inst., 1959-67; prof. art U. Mass., Amherst, 1967—. Exhbt. One-man shows, San Francisco Mus. Art., 1944, one-man shows, Crocker Art Gallery, Sacramento, 1944; Calif. Exhibitors Gallery, Los Angeles, 1951, Santa Barbara Mus. Art, 1952, Gumps, San Francisco, 1953, Fine Arts Gallery San Diego, 1953, Urban Gallery, N.Y.C., 1954, Coll. Fine Arts, U. N.M., 1956, Jonson Gallery, Albuquerque, 1957-59, Santa Fe, 1958, Allan Stone Gallery, N.Y.C., 1961, 62, 66, Los Angeles Mus. Art, 1951, 53, 54, Colorado Springs Fine Art Center, 1953, Denver Art Mus., 1955, exhibited in group shows, Denver Art Mus., Sao Paulo, Brazil, 1955, 63, Mus. Modern Art, 1959, 61, 65, Gt. Jones Gallery, N.Y.C., 1959, Guggenheim Mus., 1960, Whitney Mus. Am. Art, 1960, 62, 64, 66, 68, Pace Gallery, Boston, 1960, Stable Gallery, N.Y.C., 1960, Martha Jackson Gallery, N.Y.C., 1961, Inst. Contemporary Art, Houston, 1961, 62, Am. Fedn. Art, Riverside Mus., N.Y.C., 1961, Paris, 1962, Exhbt., Seattle Worlds Fair, 1962, Carnegie Inst., 1962, Denver Mus. Fine Arts, 1962, Art Inst. Chgo., 1962, Allan Stone Gallery, 1961, 62, 66, N.Y. State Coll., Potsdam, 1969; represented in permanent collections, Mus. Modern Art, rep., Whitney Mus. Am. Art, Maremont Found., Smith Coll., Brandeis U., Womens Coll. of U. N.C., U. Tex., Kalamazoo Art Center, U. Cal. at Berkeley, Roswell (N.M.) Mus., Los Angeles Mus. Art, U. N.M., Santa Fe, Drew Coll., N.J.; commd. by, N.Y. Worlds Fair, 1963-64, collaborator (with Dale Owne), mural, Beverly Hilton Hotel, Beverly Hills, Cal., 1955; Dir.: Arstecnica: Interdisciplinary Center for Art and Tech. Guggenheim grantee, 1964-65; fellow Tamarind Workshop, 1962. Mem. Computer Arts Soc., Siggraph/ACM. Research in computer art and computer-supported studies in aesthetics; projects in art and tech.; aesthetics of surface mine reclamation; application of computer-aided design techniques to large-scale environ. sculpture and landscape design; devel. of library of art-oriented computer-graphic programs, subroutines and tutorial exercises for dedicated and time-sharing systems; creative work with computer-graphic paint and image-processing systems and research-and-development projects in computer and video stereographic projection; assemblage relief sculpture; and in stereoscopic projection, in assemblage relief sculpture, and in self-referential and self-documenting installations. Died Feb. 10, 1997.

MALLINSON, GEORGE GREISEN, education educator emeritus; b. Troy, N.Y., July 4, 1917; s. Cyrus James and Mathilda (Greisen) M.; m. Jacqueline V. Buck, Aug. 21, 1954; children: Cyrus James, Virginia Alice, Charles Evans, Carolyn Louise. B.A., N.Y. State Coll. Tchrs., Albany, 1937, M.A., 1941; Ph.D., U. Mich., 1947, Burke Aaron Hinsdale scholar, 1947-48. Tchr. sci. Whitesboro, N.Y., 1937-40, Eden, N.Y., 1940-42; dir. sci. edn. Iowa State Tchrs. Coll., 1947-48; prof. psychology, sci. edn. Western Mich. U., Kalamazoo, 1948-54; dean Grad. Coll. Western Mich. U., 1954-77, disting. prof. sci. edn., 1977-88, disting. univ. prof.

emeritus, 1988-94. Author: Science in Daily Life, 1953, General Physical Science, 1960, Science in Modern Life, 1969, Science, 1-6, 1965, 68, 72, 75, Science: Understanding Your Environment, 1-6, 1978, 81, Silver Burdett Science, 1984, 85, 87, 89, Silver Burdett Science Horizons, 1991, 93; editor Newsletter Mich. Sci. Tchrs. Assn., 1954-63, School Science and Math, 1957-82; contbr. articles to profl. jours. Treas. Mich. Found. for Blind and Visually Impaired, 1985-92; mem. Gov. Mich. Sci. Adv. Bd., 1958-62; mem. regional adv. bd. Social and Rehab. Svc., 1971-73. Recipient Disting. Alumnus award SUNY, Albany, 1969, Disting. Svc. award Western Mich. U., 1981, Disting. Alumnus award Edn. Alumni Soc., U. Mich., 1990. Mem. Nat. Assn. Rsch. Sci. Teaching (pres. 1953), Mich. Sci. Tchrs. Assn. (pres. 1954), AAAS (coun.), Am. Soc. Engring. Edn., Nat. Sci. Tchrs. Assn., Nat. Assn. Biology Tchrs., Sch. Sci. and Math. Assn. (George G. Mallinson annual award for disting. svc. established in his honor 1988), Am. Edn. Rsch. Assn., Mich. Coun. Coll. Pres. (chmn. sci. study com. 1957-61), Mich. Acad. Sci., Arts and Letters (v.p. 1968- 70, pres. 1970-71), Coun. of Cen. States Univs. (chmn. coun. 1965-67, pres. bd. dirs. and corp. 1970, 71-73, 77-88, pres. 1983-84, dir. Decline in Sci. and Math. Study 1982-86), Am. Assn. Workers for Blind (dir. 1968-73, chmn. publs. bd. 1974-84, pres. Mich. chpt. 1974, pres. Midwest region 1975-76, C. Warren Bledsoe publs. award 1982). Home: Kalamazoo Mich. Died June 26, 1994; interred Fort Custer National Cemetery.

MALONE, JAMES L., lawyer, diplomat; b. Los Angeles, Calif.. BA magna cum laude, Pomona Coll., 1953; JD, Stanford U., 1959. Bar: Calif. 1961, U.S. Supreme Ct. 1970, D.C. 1977. Lectr. law, asst. dean Law Sch. UCLA, 1961-67; prof., dean-elect Coll. Law Willamette U., Salem, Oreg., 1967-68; vis. prof. Law Sch. U. Tex., 1969; atty. Fed. Maritime Commn., 1970-71; asst. gen. counsel, then gen. counsel Arms Control and Disarmament Agy., 1971-76, acting dir., 1981; atty. Doub and Muntzing, Washington, 1978-81; asst. sec. oceans and internat. environ. and sci. affairs Dept. State, Washington, 1981-85; Navy Chair Prof. of Internat. Law Naval Postgrad. Sch., Monterey, Calif., 1987-90; pvt. practice, 1990-96; U.S. rep. with personal rank of amb. Conf. of Com. on Disarmament, 1976-77; spl. rep. of Pres. for Law of Sea, 1981-85; chmn. U.S. del. and amb. for Law of Sea Conf., 1981-82; adv. bd. Ctr. for Oceans Law and Policy U. Va. Sch. Law. Contbr. articles to profl. jours. Pres. World Affairs Coun. of Monterey Bay Area; trustee Monterey Inst. of Internat. Studies. Lt. U.S. Army, 1954-56. Mem. State Bar Calif., D.C. Adv. Coun. (chmn.), S.W. Ctr. for Environ. Rsch. and Policy, Coun. Am. Ambs., Rotary Internat., NMMI Alumni (bd. dirs.), Met. Club (Washington), Capitol Hill Club (Washington), Order of Coif, Phi Beta Kappa. Home: Monterey Calif. Died Sept. 10, 1996.

MALONEY, JOHN FREDERICK, marketing and opinion research specialist; b. Watertown, N.Y., Apr. 28, 1913; s. John Francis and Grace (Gott) M.; m. Lucia Howard McKellar, Apr. 27, 1940; children—John Frederick, Robert McKellar, Bonnie Hartman, Lucia Willard. Grad., Mt. Hermon Sch., 1931; A.B., Princeton, 1935. With Gallup Poll, 1935-38; v.p. Peoples Research Corp., 1939-40; research analyst Young & Rubicam, 1940; Eastern mgr. Nat. Opinion Research Center, 1941; devel. analyst Curtis Pub. Co., 1946; research dir. internat. and U.S. Reader's Digest, 1946-66, corp. research dir., 1966-70; exec. v.p. Reader's Digest Found., 1970-71; cons. Advt. Research Found., N.Y.C., 1972-87; exec. dir. Council of Am. Survey Research Orgns., 1976-79; ret.; Pres. World Assn. Pub. Opinion Research, 1952-53, Market Research Council, 1958-59; chmn. research com. Mag. Pubs. Assn., 1961-65; vice chmn. tech. com. Advt. Research Found., 1956-70. Chmn. Westchester County Social Agys., 1953-57; v.p. Nat. Social Welfare Assembly, 1964-68; nat. chmn. Princeton Ann. Giving, 1968-69; vice-chmn. Princeton U. Fund, 1968-69; pres. United Way Westchester, 1968-71, Princeton Class 1935, 1970-75; chmn. Westchester County adv. com. N.Y. State Urban Devel. Corp., 1970-86; chmn. adv. com. Westchester Community Found., 1981-86. Lt. comdr. USNR, 1941-45; comdg. officer destroyer escort. Decorated Commendation medal. Mem. Am. Mktg. Assn. (pres. N.Y. chpt. 1960, v.p. internat. div. 1972-73). Conglist. (chmn. bd. deacons 1962-63). Clubs: Princeton (N.Y.C.), Coffee House (N.Y.C.). Home: Chappaqua N.Y. Died Feb. 14, 1997.

MALOZEMOFF, PLATO, mining executive; b. Russia, 1909. BS, U. Calif., Berkeley, 1931; MS, Mont. Sch. Mines, 1932. Metall. engr. Pan-Am. Engring., Berkeley, 1933-39; mgr. of mines of pvt. co.'s Argentina and Costa Rica, 1939-42; mining analyst OPA, Washington, 1942-45; with Newmont Mining Corp., N.Y.C., 1945-87, chief exec. officer, 1954-85, chmn. emeritus, 1985-97. Bd. dirs. Boys' and Girls' Clubs Am., Tolstoy Found., Inc., South Am. Gold and Copper Co., Inc.; dir., trustee Am. Mus. Natural History; mem. James Madison coun. Libr. of Congress. Died Aug. 8, 1997.

MALSKY, STANLEY JOSEPH, physicist; b. N.Y.C., July 15, 1925; s. Joseph and Nellie (Karpinski) M.; m. Gloria E. Gagliardi, Oct. 15, 1965; 1 son, Mark A. B.S., NYU, 1949, M.A., 1950, M.S., 1953, Ph.D., 1963. Nuclear physicist Dept. Def., 1950-54; chief physicist VA, 1954-73; from instr. to asst. prof. physics NYU, 1960-64; adj. asso. prof., then prof. radiol. sci.

Manhattan Coll., Bronx, N.Y., 1960-74; non-resident research collaborator med. div. Brookhaven Nat. Labs., Upton, N.Y., 1962-68; research prof. radiology NYU Sch. Medicine, N.Y.C., 1975-77; pres. Radiol. Physics Assn., White Plains, N.Y., 1965—, Therapy Physics Services, 1980—, Sigmasel Dosimetry, 1986—; bd. trustees Doggs Ferry Hosp., N.Y. Contbr. chpts. to books. Served with U.S. Army, 1945-46. Recipient James Picker Found. award, 1963-67; Founder's Day award NYU, 1964; Leadership award Manhattan Coll., 1969; AEC grantee, Bureau of Radiological Health grantee, Nat. Cancer Inst. grantee. Fellow Am. Public Health Assn., AAAS, Royal Soc. Health; charter mem. Am. Assn. Physicists in Medicine, Health Physics Soc., Sigma Xi, Sigma Pi Sigma, Phi Delta Kappa. Roman Catholic. Died Dec. 18, 1992.

MANAHAN, MADELINE, state legislator; b. Richford, Vt., July 27, 1914; m. Leon J. Manahan (dec.); 3 children. BS, U. Vt., 1936, MA, 1937. Vt. state rep., 1994—, ret. sch. tchr. Mem. NEA, Ret. Tchrs. Assn., Delta Kappa Gamma. Died Dec. 23, 1996.

MANDEL, LEON, III, author; b. Chgo., July 31, 1928; s. Leon Jr. Mandel and Edna (Horn) Seligmann; m. Olivia Eskridge, June 12, 1953; children: Leon, Olivia. Student, Columbia U., 1949, Cornell U., 1950-54, U. Calif., Hastings, 1960. Editor Belmont (Calif.) Courier Bull., 1963, Competition Press, San Francisco, 1964-67; mng. editor Car and Driver Mag., N.Y.C., 1967-68, editor, 1968-71; sr. editor Motor Trend, L.A., 1971-74; editor in chief Crain Communications/Auto Week, Detroit, 1983-87, v.p., pub., 1987—; auto editor Sta. KTVN-TV, Reno, Nev., 1976-82; instr. mag. journalism Truckee Meadows Community Coll., 1980; cons. SRI Internat. Author: Speed with Style: The Autobiography of Peter Revson, 1974, Driven: The American Four-Wheeled Love Affair, 1977, Murder So Real (pseudonym Al Bird), 1978, Fast Lane Summer, 1981, William Fisk Harrah: The Life and Times of a Gambling Magnate, 1982, American Cars, 1982. Mem. Detroit Athletic Club.

MANDEL, SIEGFRIED, English language educator; b. Berlin, Germany, Dec. 20, 1922; came to U.S., 1933, naturalized, 1938; s. Nathan and Pauline (Scheinmann) M.; m. Dorothy Isaacs, Feb. 3, 1946 (dec. 1995); children: Elise Judith, Theodore Scott. B.A., Bklyn. Coll. 1946; M.A., Columbia U., 1947; Ph.D., U. Denver, 1967. Part-time instr. Poly. U. N.Y., 1948-55; sr. editor Inst. Econ. Affairs, N.Y.C., 1952-53; writer, editor Asso. Transp., Inc., 1954-55; book rev. columnist Newsday, 1954-55; lectr. N.Y.U., 1955; from instr. to assoc. prof. Poly. Inst. Bklyn., 1955-62; mem. faculty U. Colo., Boulder, 1962-93, prof. English and comparative lit., 1965-91, chmn. dept. English in engring., 1969-70, dir. grad. studies, dept. English, 1977-79, dir. comparative lit. program, 1988-91, prof. emeritus, 1991-93; vis. prof. Am. studies U. Hawaii at Manoa, Honolulu, 1981-82; indsl. lectr. writing workshops Internat. Tel. & Tel Corp., 1959-60. Editor, contbg. author: Writing in Industry, 1959, (with D.L. Caldwell) Proposal and Inquiry Writing, 1962, Modern Journalism, 1962, Rainer Maria Rilke: The Poetic Instinct, 1965, (with Aaron Kramer) Rainer Maria Rilke: Visions of Christ, 1967, Contemporary European Novelists, 1968, Dictionary of Science, 1969, Writing for Science and Technology, 1970, Group 47: The Reflected Intellect, 1973; editor, translator: Lou Andreas-Salomé: Nietzche in His Works, 1988, Ibsen's Heroines, 1985, Karl Kerényi: Excursions of a Hellenist, Homer, Nietzsche, and Kazantzakis; contbr. articles and book revs. to profl. jours.and ency. yearbooks. Served with AUS, 1943-46. Faculty fellow lit. research U. Colo., 1968-69, 75-76; recipient Eugene M. Kayden nat. translation prize, 1983. Mem. MLA, Am. Comparative Lit. Assn., Georg-Groddeck Soc., Rilke-Gesellschaft, N.Am. Nietzsche Assn. Home: Lexington Ky. Died May 26, 1993.

MANDINO, OG, author; b. Boston, Dec. 12, 1923; s. Silvio and Margaret T. (Lee) M.; m. Bette L. Lang, Dec. 9, 1957; children: Dana, Matthew. Student, Bucknell Jr. Coll., 1941. Sales mgr. Combined Ins. Co., Chgo., 1960-65; sales rep. Met. Life Ins. Co., Boston, 1948-60; exec. editor Success Unlimited mag., Chgo., 1965-72; pres. Success Unltd., Inc., Chgo., 1972-76; pres. Matt-Dana Ltd., 1974—, also dir. Author: A Treasury of Success Unlimited, 1967, The Greatest Salesman in the World, 1968, (with Edward R. Dewey) Cycles, The Mysterious Forces That Trigger Events, 1970, U.S. in a Nutshell, 1971, The Greatest Secret in the World, 1972, The Greatest Miracle in the World, 1975, (with Buddy Kaye) The Gift of Acabar, 1978, The Christ Commission, 1980, The Greatest Success in the World, 1981, Og Mandino's University of Success, 1982, The Choice, 1984, Mission: Success!, 1986, The Greatest Salesman in the World, Part II, End of the Story, 1988, A Better Way to Live, 1990, The Return of the Ragpicker, 1992, The Twelfth Angel, 1993, The Spellbinder's Gift, 1994, Secrets For Success and Happiness, 1995, The Greatest Mystery in The World, 1997. Served to 1st lt. USAAF, 1942-45. Decorated D.F.C., Air medal with 5 oak leaf clusters; recipient Master of Influence award Nat. Speakers Assn., 1996. Mem. Authors Guild, Authors League, Nat. Speakers Assn., Internat. Speakers Hall of Fame. Home: Antrim N.H. Died Sept. 3 , 1996; interred Maplewood Cemetery.

MANELI, MIECZYSLAW, political science, law educator; b. Poland, 1924; children: Elizabeth, Lester. MA in Econs., Law, Warsaw U., 1949, PhD in Law, 1953. Prof. law, chmn. Inst. Polit.-Juridical Doctrines Warsaw U., 1954-68, vice dean, 1956-62, dean, 1963-64; polit. adv. to pres. Indonesia Govt., 1964; prof. law and polit. sci. Queens Coll., CUNY, Flushing, N.Y., 1968-94; co-founder, editor-in-chief Politics and Morality, 1986-94. Author: The Activity of a Socialist State, 1957, The Funcions of the State, 1963, Art of Politics, 1967, Machiavelli, a Monograph, 1968, Foundations, 1968, History of Political and Juricical Ideas, 1968, War of the Vanquished, 1971, Juridical Positivism and Human Rights, 1981, Freedom and Tolerance, 1984; columnist Law and Life, 1957-68. Co-chmn. European Juridical Commn. to Prosecute Nazi Jurists, 1958-68. Served with Polish Underground, WWII; imprisoned Majdanek and Auschwitz concentration camps. Mem. Am. Humanist Assn. (dir. 1985-94). Home: Jackson Heights N.Y. Died Apr. 9, 1994.

MANES, JOHN DALTON, hospital administrator, anaesthesiologist; b. Winnipeg, Man., Can., Oct. 29, 1920; s. John Harold and Elizabeth (Dalton) M.; m. Jean Julia Diggins, Aug. 28, 1946 (dec. 1970); children: Maureen Jean, John William; m. Wilda Ann Suffel, Nov. 7, 1975. B.Sc., McGill U., 1948, M.D., C.M., 1951. Anaesthesiologist Holy Cross Hosp., Calgary, Alta., Can., 1954-86, med. dir., 1967-76, exec. dir., 1976-86; with Bentley Gen. Hosp., Alta., Can., 1986-95; exec. dir. Can. Assn. Med. Clinics, 1967-73. Contbr. articles to profl. jours. Capt. Can. Army, 1940-45. Recipient Queen's Silver Jubilee medal Queen Elizabeth II, 1977. Mem. Can. Med. Assn., Can. Anaesthesia Assn. Progressive Conservative. Roman Catholic. Clubs: Calgary Golf and Country, Glencoe. Avocations: photography, welding, computers. Died Sept. 28, 1995.

MANFRED, FREDERICK FEIKEMA (FEIKE FEIKEMA), writer; b. Doon, Iowa, Jan. 6, 1912; s. Feike Feikes Vi and Aaltje (Van Engen) Feikema; m. Maryanna Shorba, Oct. 31, 1942 (div. Oct. 1978); children: Freya, Marya, Frederick Feikema. AB, Calvin Coll., Grand Rapids, Mich., 1934; student, Nettleton Comml. Coll., Sioux Falls, S.D., 1937; corr. student, U. Minn., 1941-42. Engaged in various work traveling in U.S., 1934-37; reporter Mpls. Jour., 1937-39; editor Modern Medicine, 1942-43; writer-in-residence Macalester Coll., 1949-52, U. S.D., 1968-83; cons. humanities Augustana Coll., Sioux Falls, S.D., 1984-94. Author: The Golden Bowl, 1944, Boy Almighty, 1945, This Is The Year, 1947, The Chokecherry Tree, 1948, Lord Grizzly, 1954, Morning Red, 1956, Riders of Judgement, 1957, Conquering Horse, 1959, (stories) Arrow of Love, 1961, Wanderlust (trilogy including The Primitive, The Brother, The Giant), 1962, Scarlet Plume, 1964, The Man Who Looked Like the Prince of Wales (in paperback The Secret Place), 1965, (poems) Winter Count, 1966, King of Spades, 1966, (stories) Apples of Paradise, 1968, Eden Prairie, 1968, Conversations, 1974, Milk of Wolves, 1976, The Manly-Hearted Woman, 1976, Green Earth, 1977, (reminiscence) The Wind Blows Free, 1979, Sons of Adam, 1980, (poems) Winter Count II, 1987, (essays) Prime Fathers, 1988, The Selected Letters of Frederick Manfred, 1932-54, 1989, Flowers of Desire, 1989, No Fun On Sunday, 1990, Of Lizards and Angels, 1992, Duke's Mixture, (misc.) Duke's Mixture, 1994; contbr. articles and stories to mags. Recipient Mark Twain Lit. award, 1981, recipient $1000 fiction grant-in-aid AAAL, 1945; U Minn. Rockefeller Found. Regional Writing fellowship 1944-46; Field Found. fellowship, 1948-49; Andreas Found. fellowships, 1949, 52; McKnight Found. fellow 1958-59; Huntington Hartford Found. fellow, 1963-64 Avon Found. fellow, 1958-59. Mem. PEN, Author's League Am., Soc. Midland Writers (v.p.), Players Club (N.Y.C.). Home: Luverne Minn. Died Sept. 7, 1994.

MANLEY, MICHAEL NORMAN, government official; b. St. Andrew, Jamaica, Dec. 10, 1924; s. Norman Washington and Edna (Swithenbank); children: Rachael Sarah, Joseph, Natasha, David. BSc in Econs. with honors, London U., 1949; LLD (hon.), Morehouse Coll., 1973; student, Jamaica Coll., Kingston, 1935-43. Freelance journalist BBC, London, 1949-51; assoc editor Pub. Opinion Kingston, 1951-52; staff mem., organizer Nat. Workers Union, Kingston, 1952—; elected mem. People's Nat. Party, Kingston, 1952; mem. Jamaican senate Kingston, 1962-67; v.p. People's Nat. Party Kingston, 1967, mem. parliament Central Kingston 1967-83, 89-97, pres. 1969-97; prime minister Govt. of Jamaica, Kingston, 1972-80, 89-97, opposition leader 1980-83; pres. Nat. Workers Union, 1984-89; vis. lectr Columbia U., 1984; v.p. Socialist Internat., 1979; chmn socialist Internat. Econ. Commn., 1983; mem. Caribbean Labour Congress, Sugar Industry Labour Welfare Bd., Sci. Rsch. Coun., Pensions Authority, Labour Adv Coun.. Author: The Politics of Change, 1974, A Voice at the Workplace, 1973, Search for Solutions, 1977 Jamaica: Struggle in the Periphery, 1982, Global Challenge, 1985, Up the Down Escalator, 1987, A History of West Indies Cricket, 1988, Poverty of the Nations Reflections on Underdevelopment and the World Economy, 1991. Served with RAF, 1943-45. Decorated Order of Liberator (Venezuela), Order Mexican Eagle Order José Martí (Cuba); recipient Jaliot Curie Peace prize, UN anti-apartheid award. Mem. Machado Employees Union (pres.), Caribbean Bauxite and

Mineworkers Fedn. (pres. 1964-72), Jamaica Clerical Workers Assn. Methodist. Died Mar., 1997.

MANN, ARTHUR, historian, educator, writer; b. Bklyn., Jan. 3, 1922; s. Karl and Mary (Koch) Finkelman; m. Sylvia Blut, Nov. 6, 1943; children: Carol Ruth, Emily Betsy. B.A. summa cum laude, Bklyn. Coll., 1944; M.A., Harvard U., 1947, Ph.D., 1952. Tutor, Bklyn. Coll., 1946; from instr. to asst. prof. MIT, 1948-55; from asst. prof. to prof. Smith Coll., 1955-66; prof. Am. history U. Chgo., 1966-93, Preston and Sterling Morton prof. Am. history emeritus and faculty fellow div. social scis., 1990-93; vis. prof. Columbia U., U. Mass., Williams Coll., U. Mich., U. Wyo., Harvard U., Salzburg (Austria) Seminar Am. Studies. Author: Yankee Reformers in the Urban Age, 1954, Growth and Achievement, Temple Israel, 1854-1954, 1954, La Guardia, A Fighter Against His Times, 1882-1933, 1959, The Progressive Era, 1963, rev. edit., 1975, La Guardia Comes to Power, 1933, 1965, Immigrants in American Life, 1968, rev. edit., 1974, (with Harris and Warner) History and the Role of the City in American Life, 1972, The One and the Many: Reflections on the American Identity, 1979; editor: series The University of Chicago Press Documents in American History; adv. editor Am. History, U. Chgo. Press; editorial cons.: Social Service Rev. U.S. Dept. State lectr., Venezuela, 1970, USIA lectr., Fiji, Indonesia, Malaysia, N.Z., Singapore, 1974, Portugal, Germany, Yugoslavia, Romania, 1976, Hong Kong, Japan, 1979. Served with AUS, 1943-46. Recipient Alumni award of merit Bklyn. Coll., 1968, Outstanding Scholarship award LaGuardia Archives, 1987; Fellow Am. Council Learned Socs., 1962-63; Fulbright-Hays sr. scholar Australia, 1974. Mem. Am. Hist. Assn., Orgn. Am. Historians, Soc. Am. Historians. Home: Chicago Ill. Died Feb. 7, 1993.

MANN, HAROLD W., agricultural products executive; b. 1908. Pvt. practice with father Delano and Salinas, Calif., 1919-45; with Mann Packaging Co., Inc., 1945—, now chmn. bd. Died 1996.

MANNERS, ROBERT ALAN, anthropologist; b. N.Y.C., Aug. 21, 1913; m. Margaret D. Hall, July 6, 1943 (div. July 1955); children: Karen Elizabeth, John Hall; m. Jean I. Hall, Sept. 12, 1955; children: Stephen David, Katherine Dora. B.S., Columbia U., 1935, M.A., 1939, Ph.D., 1950. Instr. U. Rochester, 1950-52; lectr., asst. prof., asso. prof., prof. Brandeis U., Waltham, Mass., 1952-96; Ralph Levitz prof. anthropology Brandeis U., 1973-80, Ralph Levitz prof. emeritus, 1980-96, chmn. dept. anthropology, 1963-68, 78-79; vis. prof. Columbia U., summer 1956, Harvard U., summer 1967, Ibero-Am. U., Mexico, 1969-70; mem. social sci. subcom. NIH, 1965-69; Bd. dirs. Research Inst. For Study Man. Co-author: People of Puerto Rico, 1956; editor: (with James Duffy) Africa Speaks, 1961, Process and Pattern in Culture, 1964, The Kipsigis of Kenya, 1967, (with David Kaplan) Theory in Anthropology: A Sourcebook, 1968 and Culture Theory, 1972, Southern Paiute and Chemehuevi: An Ethnohistorical Report, 1974, An Ethnological Report on the Hualapai Indians of Arizona, 1975, Havasupai Indians: An Ethnohistorical Report, 1975; editor-in-chief Am. Anthropologist, 1974-76; contbr. articles to jours. Served to capt. AUS, 1942-46. Fellow Am. Anthrop. Assn.; mem. N.E. Anthrop. Assn. (pres. 1978-79). Home: Newton Centre Mass. Died July 12, 1996.

MANNING, RALPH KENNETH, JR., law educator, writer; b. Everett, Mass., July 5, 1922; s. Ralph Kenneth Sr. and Francéna Betsy (Durgin) M.; m. Barbara Cannell, May 17, 1946; children: David Peter, Stephen Dale, Dwight Kevin. BS, Northeastern U., 1947; JD, Boston U., 1950, LLM, 1951, ThM, 1972. Bar: Mass. 1951, U.S. Dist. Ct. Mass. 1952, U.S. Ct. Mil. Appeals 1956, U.S. Supreme Ct. 1956. Prof. law Cumberland Sch. of Law Samford U., Birmingham, Ala., 1973—; prof. law Ahmadu Bello U., Zaria, Nigeria, 1979-80; fellow U. Denver, 1982-83; fellow dept. politics Princeton (N.J.) U., 1987; fellow U. Kent, Canterbury, Eng., 1989; cons. John Hancock Ins. Co., Boston, 1957-67; researcher Inst. Advanced Legal Studies, U. London, 1980; vis. scholar Georgetown U. Law Ctr., 1992-93; affiliated prof. dept. religious studies Temple U., 1993—. Author: Group Insurance Form Book, 1965; contbr. articles and essays to legal and religious jours. Mem. Com. on Jud. Ethics, Montgomery, Ala., 1974-85, Vestavia Hills Libr. Bd., 1993—; arbitrator Nat. Futures Assn., Chgo., 1984—; chmn. legis. subcom. Adminstrv. Law Com., Montgomery, 1977-79; cons. Birmingham Police Dept., 1982; adj. minister Pilgrim Congl.-UCC Ch., Birmingham, 1985—. Sgt. U.S. Army, 1943-46, 1st lt., 1950-51. NSF fellow U. Denver, 1972-73, NEH fellow Princeton U., 1987. Mem. ABA, Can. Law Tchrs. Assn., Soc. Am. Law Tchrs., Soc. Christian Ethics (chmn. law and religion sect.), Phi Kappa Phi (pres. Samford U. chpt. 1991-92). Democrat. Avocations: sports, philately, reading. Died Jan. 16, 1997.

MANNONI, RAYMOND, retired university administrator; b. Pittsburg, Kans., July 11, 1921; s. Espartero and Mary Katherine (Scalet) M.; m. Karen Whittet, June 2, 1956; 1 dau., Barbara Gwen. BS, Kans. State U., 1944; MEd, U. Mich., 1946; postgrad., Northwestern U., 1947-48; MusD in Edn., Chgo. Mus. Coll., 1956. Dir. bands U. Tulsa, 1946-48; 1st horn Tulsa Symphony Orch., 1946-48; dir. bands, instr. music Kans. State Tchrs. Coll., Emporia, 1949-50; prof. music, dean Coll. Fine Arts, U. So. Miss., Hattiesburg, 1960-80; chmn. div. fine arts U. Guam, Mangilao, 1981-85; Cons. music edn. dept. Lyon & Healy, Chgo., 1949-50; nat. adv. bd. LeBlanc Music Educators, 1958-68. Co-author: Music Theory for Beginners, 1956. Served with USN, World War II; maj. USAR, ret. Recipient Alumni certificate U. So. Miss., 1954-55; award of merit Nat. Fedn. Music Clubs, 1962. Mem. Music Educators Nat. Conf. (life), Nat. Ret. Tchrs. Assn., Ret. Officers Assn. (life), Res. Officers Assn. (life), DAV (life), Masons, Shriners, Elks, Phi Kappa Phi, Phi Delta Kappa, Kappa Kappa Psi, Alpha Psi Omega, Chi Omicron Gamma, Phi Mu Alpha Sinfonia, Phi Kappa Lambda, Omicron Delta Kappa. Died 01/15/95.

MANOOGIAN, ALEX, manufacturing company executive; b. 1901. With Providence Screw Machine Co., Brown-McLoren Screw Products Co., Packard Motor Car Co., 19924-28; ptnr. Masco Screw Products Co., 1928-29; chmn., pres., chief exec. officer Masco Corp., Taylor, Mich., 1929—, chmn. emeritus, 1985—, also bd. dirs. Died July 1996.

MANSFIELD, EDWIN, economist, educator; b. Kingston, N.Y., June 8, 1930; s. Raymond and Sarah M.; m. Lucile Howe, Feb. 21, 1955; children: Edward, Elizabeth. AB, Dartmouth Coll., 1951; MA, Duke U., 1953, PhD, 1955; cert. diploma, Royal Statis. Soc., 1955; MA (hon.), U. Pa., 1971. Asst. prof., assoc. prof. econs. Carnegie-Mellon U., 1955-60, 62-63; vis. assoc. prof. econs. Yale U., New Haven, 1961-62; vis. prof. econs. Harvard U., Cambridge, Mass., 1963-64, Calif. Inst. Tech., Pasadena, 1967-68; prof. econs. U. Pa., Phila., 1964-97; dir. Ctr. Econs. and Tech. U. Pa., 1985-97; guest prof. Chalmers U. Tech. Gothenburg, Sweden, 1983, Nat. Technol. U., 1989-95; cons. Exec. Office Pres. of U.S., U.S. Dept. Commerce, U.S. Gen. Acctg. Office, U.S. Dept. Labor, HHS, NSF, Nat. Inst. Edn., Fed. Power Commn., Inst. for Def. Analysis, SBA, FTC, U.S. Army, Ford Found., RAND Corp., Can. Royal Commn., New Zealand Rsch. Inst., Nat. Inst. Standards and Tech., Internat. Fin. Corp., World Bank, others; mem. Gov.'s Sci. Adv. Com., 1965-66; chmn. U.S.-USSR Working Party on Sci. and Tech., 1974-75; panelist Nat. Bur. Standards/NAS, 1974-76; bd. examiners Grad. Record Exam, 1975-76; econ. adv. com. U.S. Bur. Census, 1982-85; Nat. Tech. Medal Com., 1984-87; chmn. vis. com. Rensselaer Poly. Inst., 1986-91; mem. adv. com. Ctr. for Drug Devel., U. Rochester, 1976-83. Author: The Economics of Technological Change, 1968, Industrial Research and Technological Innovation, 1968, Defense, Science and Public Policy, 1968, Research and Innovation in the Modern Corporation, 1971, The Production and Application of New Industrial Technology, 1977, Monopoly Power and Economic Performance, 4th edit., 1978, Technology Transfer, Productivity and Economic Policy, 1982, Managerial Economics and Operations Research, 5th edit., 1987, Economics, 7th edit., 1992, Economics USA, 5th edit., 1998, Managerial Economics, 1999, 4th edit., 1996, Microeconomics, 9th edit., 1997, Statistics, 5th edit., 1994, (with Elizabeth Mansfield) The Economics of Technical Change, 1993, Applied Microeconomics, 2d edit., 1997, Leading Economic Controversies, 4th edit., 1998, Innovation, Technology, and the Economy, 1995, others; editor Jour. of the Am. Statistical Assn., 1964-67, Am. Economist, 1969-90, Jour. of Econ. Edn., 1982-90, Review of Industrial Organization, 1984-97, IEEE Transactions on Engring. Mgmt., 1985-97, Managerial and Decision Econs., 1988-92, Univ. Wis. series on tech. change, 1984-88, Pub. Rsch. Quar., 1993-97, Essential Macroeconomics, 1998, Essential Microeconomics, 1998, and others. Fulbright fellow, 1954-55, Ford Found. rsch. fellow, 1960-61, Ctr. for Advanced Study Behavioral Scis. fellow, 1971-72; NSF grantee, 1962; recipient Cert. Appreciation U.S. Sec. Commerce, 1979, Publ. award Patent Law Assn., 1984, Honor award Nat. Tech. U., 1992, Citation Classic award Inst. for Sci. Info., 1992, Spl. Creativity award NSF, 1994, Hall of Fame award Prentice Hall, 1995, Enterprise award Kenan Charitable Trust, 1996. Fellow Econometric Soc., Am. Acad. Arts and Scis.; mem. AAAS (sci., engring. and pub. policy com. 1981-84), Am. Econ. Assn., Royal Statis. Soc. (cert.), Phi Beta Kappa. Home: Wallingford Pa. Died Nov. 17, 1997.

MARAMAN, WILLIAM JOSEPH, nuclear engineering company executive; b. El Paso, Tex., May 19, 1923; s. William Minor and Katherine (Hawkins) M.; m. Katherine Ann Thorpe, Oct. 12, 1948; children: Katherine Ann, Linda Susan. BS in Chem. Engring., U. Tex., Austin, 1944; MS, U. N.Mex., 1960. Registered profl. engr., N.Mex. Staff mem. Los Alamos (N.Mex.) Nat. Lab., 1946-56, group leader, 1956-79, div. leader, 1979-83; dir. TRU Engring. Co., Inc., Santa Fe, 1984-96; tech. mgr. LANL Plutonium Facility, Los Alamos, 1969-79; cons. in field. Patentee in field. Income tax preparer Am. Assn. Ret. Persons, Los Alamos, 1985-92. Lt. (j.g.) USN, 1944-46, PTO. Died Oct. 23, 1996.

MARASCUILO, LEONARD ANTHONY, education educator; b. St. Paul, Dec. 11, 1930; s. Luca and Anna (Valenty) M. BA, U. Minn., 1952, MA, 1954; PhD, U. Calif., Berkeley, 1962. Statistician Nekoosa (Wis.) Papers, 1952-54; from instr. to prof. edn. U. Calif., Berkeley, 1962-86. Author: Nonparametric Statistics, 1977, Multivariate Statistics, 1983; contbr. articles to profl. jours. Served with U.S. Army, 1954-56. Mem. Am. Edn. Research Assn. (Palmer O. Johnson award 1970), Am. Statis. Assn., Nat. Council on Measurement in Edn., Am. Evaluation Assn., Phi Beta Kappa.

MARCHAIS, GEORGES, political organization leader; b. La Hoquette, June 7, 1920; s. Rene and Germaine (Boscher) M.; m. Paulette Noetinger, 1941 (div.); 3 children; m. Liliane Garcia; 1 child. Metal worker France, 1935-51; sec. Metal-workers Union, Issy-le-Moulineaux, 1946, Union des syndicats de travailleurs de la metallurgie de la Seine, 1953-56; mem. French Communist Party, 1947-97, mem. Cen. Com., 1956, Polit. Bur., 1959, sec. Cen. Com., 1961, dep. sec.-gen., 1970, sec.-gen., 1972—; dep. for Val-de-Marne, Nat. Assembly, 1973, 78, 81, 86, 88; mem. European Parliament, 1979-89, candidate for pres., 1981. Author: Qu'est-ce que le parti communiste français, 1970, Le défi démocratique, 1973, La politique du parti communiste français, 1974, Parlons franchement, 1977, L'espoir au present, 1980, Communistes et chrétiens, communistes ou chrétiens, 1977; co-author: Les communistes et les paysans, 1972, Democratie, 1990. Died Nov. 16, 1997.

MARCHAND, NATHAN, electrical engineer, corporation president; b. Shawinigan Falls, Que., Can., June 20, 1916; came to U.S., 1917; s. Harry and Rebecca (Shapiro) M.; m. Ernesta Jaros, Sept. 30, 1938; children: Mary Ann Marchand McLure, Anthony, Babette Marchand Pachence, Bonnie Jean Marchand Thomas. BEE, CCNY, 1937; MEE, Columbia U., 1941; postgrad., Poly. Inst. N.Y., 1949-51. Profl. engr., Conn. Sr. engr. Internat. Tel. & Tel., Nutley, N.J., 1941-45; lectr. Columbia U., N.Y.C., 1943-47; cons. to industry Sylvania, Internat. Tel. & Tel., U.S. Army, USAF, 1945-49; pres. Marchand Electronic Labs., Inc., Greenwich, Conn., 1949—; cons. U.S. Army R & D Command, St. Louis, 1976-86, U.S. Army Troop Support and Aviation Readiness Command, 1976-86, USAF, Cape Kennedy, Fla., 1951-54, various others; chmn. spl. com. for micro-navigation and position location systems U.S. Army Lab, Ft. Monmouth, N.J. Author: Ultra High Frequency Techniques, 1942, Ultrahigh Frequency Transmission and Radiation, 1947, Frequency Modulation, 1948; author Antenna Section, bd. editors Data for Radio Engrs., Internat. Tel. & Tel. publ., 1st-5th edits., 1943-68—; contbr. numerous tech. papers and articles to profl. jours.;. Lt. (j.g.) USN, 1943. Fellow IEEE (founder, 1st chmn. Info.-Theory Group); mem. Sigma Xi, Eta Kappa Nu, Tau Beta Pi. Republican. Avocations: pvt. pilot, sailing. DIED 01/02/96. .

MARCHETTI, PETER LOUIS, real estate executive; b. Richmond, Va., Nov. 7, 1937; m. Peter Louis and Marietta (Marroni) M.; m. Bonny Sherrill Jenkins, Nov. 27, 1965; children: Rebecca Terrahe, Alison Karen. BA in Liberal Arts, Belmont Abbey Coll., 1958; BS in Edn., N.C. State U., 1963; postgrad., NYU, 1965-66. Lic. real estate broker. System analyst R.H. Macy's, N.Y.C., 1966-67; project mgr. N.Y. Daily News, N.Y.C., 1967-69; pres., founder Computer Mind Corp., N.Y.C., 1963—; cons. McDonnell Douglas Automation, St. Louis, 1974-76; property mgr. Coll. Mgmt. Co., N.Y.C., 1985-88; real estate broker Marchetti Realty, Suffern, N.Y., 1988—; com. chmn. Rockland County Bd. Realtors, Pearl River, 1991-92. 1st v.p. Adirondack Apt. Assn., Gloversville, N.Y., 1990—; lt. Rockland Taxpayers Assn., Rockland County, 1991-92. Mem. Nat. Apt. Assn. Republican. Roman Catholic. Avocations: coin collecting, gardening, hiking, fishing, boating. Died Feb. 1, 1993.

MARELLA, PAOLO CARDINAL, archpriest Basilica of St. Peter; b. Rome, Jan. 25, 1895. Ordained priest Roman Catholic Ch., 1918; aide in Congregation for Propagation of the Faith; on staff apostolic del., Washington, 1923-33; ordained titular archbishop of Doclea, 1933; apostolic del. to Japan, 1933-48, to Australia, N.Z. and Oceania, 1948-53; nuncio to France, 1953-59; cardinal, 1959; entered order of cardinal bishops as titular bishop of Porto and Santa Rufina, 1972; pres. Secretariat for Non-Christians, 1967-73; archpriest of St. Peter's Basilica, sub-dean Coll. Cardinals, Rome, 1977—; mem., hon. pres. Commn. Sacred Art in Italy.

MARGOLIS, GEORGE, pathologist, medical educator; b. Montgomery, W.Va., Dec. 12, 1914; s. Simon and Sara Reba (Blumberg) M.; m. Anne Maria McCabe, Sept. 23, 1950; children: Susan, George McCabe, Joshua David, Dan Leo. A.B., Johns Hopkins U., 1936; M.D., Duke U., 1940; M.A. (hon.), Dartmouth, 1966. Cert. Am. Bd. Neuropathology, Am. Bd. Pathologic Anatomy, Am. Bd. Clin. Pathology. Intern pathology Duke Med. Sch., 1940-41, instr. pathology, 1940-44, asst. resident pathology, then resident, 1941-44, from asst. prof. to assoc. prof. pathology, 1947-55, prof. pathology, 1955-59; prof. pathology, chmn. dept. Med. Coll. Va., Richmond, 1959-63; prof. pathology Dartmouth Med Sch., 1963-82, prof. emeritus, 1982-96, minority affairs officer, 1969-82, founding and sr. editor alumni mag., 1975-85; v.p., exec. dir., dir. Prescription for Survival Prodns., 1983-96; founder neuropathology Dartmouth U., Med. Coll. Va., Duke U.; creator Donald Love Meml. (Citation), Duke U. Med. Sch., 1994. Editor: med. alumni mag. Emeritus exec. dir. Prescription for Survival; steering com. Nuclear Arms Forum, Westport-Weston, Conn.; regional rep. Duke U. Med. Sch., 1964-90; mem. alumni schs. com. Johns

Hopkins U., 1963-96, class agt.; bd. dirs. A Better Chance, Ridgefield, Conn., Nuclear Arms Freeze, Ridgefield chpt.; trustee, chairperson rsch. and devel. dept. Falk Found. Excellence; co-founder, bd. dirs., treas. West Conn. chpt. Nat. Adv. Council Veterans for Peace; former bd. dirs. Planned Parenthood, Upper Valley, N.H., N.H. Civil Liberties Union, Parents and Tchrs. for Social Responsibility; co-founder N.H. chpt. Physicians for Social Responsibility, 1979, chmn., 1979-82, nat. ho. of dels., 1982-85, mem. steering com. Fairfield County, Conn. chpt., 1985-96; mem. cerebrovascular disease coun. Am. Heart Assn.; mem. editorial bd. Archives of Pathology, 1960-65; mem. cerebrovascular disease subcom. Nat. Inst. Neurolog. Diseases and Blindness, 1962-64; mem. cerebral aneurysm subcom., 1960-64; mem. pathology study sect., Nat. Inst. Gen. Med. Scis., 1956-59. Served to maj. M.C., AUS, 1944-47, ETO. Recipient Disting. Alumni award Duke U. Med. Ctr., 1983, citation for svc. A Better Chance, 1993; Collection for Cross-Cultural Medicine and Minority Affairs named in his honor, Dartmouth med. Sch., 1993. Home: Ridgefield Conn. Died Apr. 25, 1996.

MARGOLIS, LEO, marine biologist; b. Montreal, Que., Can., Dec. 18, 1927; m. Ruth Anne Lall; children: Rhonda Lee, Robert Allan, Murray Howard, Conrad Anton. B.Sc., McGill U., 1948, M.Sc., 1950, Ph.D., 1952. Rsch. scientist Pacific Biol. Sta., Can. Dept. Fish and Oceans, Nanaimo, B.C., 1952-67, head various rsch. divs., 1967-81, head fish health and parasitology sect., 1981-90, sr. scientist, 1990—; co-chmn. Can. Com. on Fish Diseases, 1970-73; mem. com. on biology and rsch. Internat. North Pacific Fisheries Commn., 1971-93, sr. Can. scientist, 1976-93, advisor Can. sect., 1976-93; advisor Fed.-Provincial Fish Com., 1969, 70, 78; mem. Can. Del. North Pacific Anadromous Fish Commn., 1993—, chmn. com. sci. rsch. and stats., 1993-95; mem. editl. referees com. Bull. Internat. North Pacific Fisheries Commn., 1976-84; mem. adv. bd. sci. info. and publs. Fisheries and Oceans Can., 1979-83; mem. aquatic sci. rsch. evaluation com. Sci. Coun. B.C., 1979-88, chmn., 1986-88; adj. prof. Simon Fraser U., 1983—; cons. Internat. Devel. Rsch. Ctr., 1986; mem. nat. tech. com. Can. Fish Health Protection Regulations, 1990—; mem. sci. adv. com. N.B. Aquaculture Consortium, 1991—; mem. external adv. com. BSc in Biology program Malaspina Coll., 1992—. Assoc. editor Can. Jour. Zoology, 1971-81, Jour. World Aquaculture Soc., 1986—; mem. editl. bd., editl. cons. Jour. of Parasitology, 1977-93; mem. adv. bd. Amphipacifica, Jour. of Systematic Biology, 1993—; editl. advisor Diseases of Aquatic Organisms Jour., 1994—; author 3 books; editor 6 books; contbr. articles on parasites and diseases of fishes and other aquatic animals, and on biology of salmon to various profl. jours. Pres. B.C. Amateur Hockey Assn., 1963-66, hon. v.p., 1968-88, life mem. 1988—, Diamond Stick award, 1989, Can. Amateur Hockey Assn. Order of Merit, 1990. Decorated officer Order of Can.; recipient Commemorative medal 125th Anniversary Confedn. Can., 1992, Gold medal Profl. Inst. Pub. Svc. of Can., 1995. Fellow Royal Soc. Can.; mem. Can. Soc. Zoologists (coun. mem. parasitology sect. 1977-78, recognition com. 1985-88, 93-95, 2d v.p. 1988-89, 1st. v.p. 1989-90, pres. 1990-91, recognition com. 1991-94, chmn. 1991-93, bd. trustees Zool. Edn. Trust 1988-93, chmn. 1990-91, R.A. Wardle lectr. award 1982), Atlantic Can. Soc. Parasitologists (hon.), Am. Soc. Parasitologists (in memoriam com. 1982, pub. responsibilities com. 1988, chmn. nominating com. 1992-93, coun. 1994—, Disting. Svc. award 1995), Can. Fedn. Biol. Socs. (bd. dirs. 1990-91), Am. Fisheries Soc. (awards com. 1975-76), Wildlife Disease Assn., Aquaculture Assn. Can., World Aquaculture Soc., Asian Fisheries Soc., Brit. Soc. for Parasitology (hon.). Died Jan. 13, 1997.

MARION, WILLIAM FRANCIS, lawyer; b. York, S.C., Oct. 8, 1923; s. John Alexander and Mary (Burnet) M.; m. Elizabeth A. Marshall, May 5, 1945; children—Helen Bruton, Mary Burnet, William Francis, Alexander Douglas. A.B., U. S.C., 1943, LL.B., 1945. Bar: S.C. bar 1945. Since practiced in Greenville; sr. partner firm Haynsworth, Perry, Bryant, Marion & Johnstone (and predecessors), 1958-95; Dir. Greenville div. S.C. Nat. Bank. Permanent mem. 4th Circuit Jud. Conf. Served with USMCR, 1943. Fellow Am. Coll. Trial Lawyers; mem. Internat. Assn. Ins. Counsel, Am. Judicature Soc., ABA, S.C. Bar Assn. (chmn. com. unauthorized practice 1964), Greenville Bar Assn., Alpha Tau Omega. Episcopalian. Clubs: Torch (Greenville), Greenville Country (Greenville), Poinsett (Greenville) (govs. 1955-57, pres. 1957); Palmetto (Columbia, S.C.). Home: Greenville S.C. Died Feb. 27, 1995.

MARKIEWICZ, ALFRED JOHN, bishop; b. Bklyn., May 17, 1928. Student, St. Francis Coll., Bklyn., Immaculate Conception Sem., Huntington, N.Y. Ordained priest Roman Cath. Ch., 1953, ordained titular bishop of Afufenia and aux. bishop of Rockville Centre, N.Y., 1986. Ordained priest Brooklyn, 1953; ordained titular bishop of Afufenia and aux. bishop New York, 1986—; vicar for Nassau Diocese of Rockville Centre. Deceased.

MARKS, ARNOLD, journalist; b. Phila., Aug. 4, 1912; s. Morris M. and Esther (Joel) M.; m. Isabelle Ruppert, Oct. 3, 1942 (dec.); 1 son, Rupert William Joel (dec.); m. Emi Seligman Simon. B.A., U. Wash., 1935; M.S., Columbia U., 1939. Editor Pasco (Wash.) Herald, 1946; with Oreg. Jour., Portland, 1946-78; drama, TV, entertainment editor Oreg. Jour., 1948-58, entertainment editor, 1958-78, ret., 1978, freelance writer. Served with AUS, 1942-46. Mem. Sigma Delta Chi, Sigma Alpha Mu. Club: University (Portland). also: 2393 SW Park Pl Portland OR 97205-1056 Deceased.

MARMON, DENNIS CARL, accountant, auditor; b. Kew Gardens, N.Y., Dec. 20, 1949; s. Carmine Alphose and Marie (Tersigni) M.; m. Phyllis Theresa Marmon, May 24, 1981; 1 child, Karla Denise Marmon; student SUNY, Farmingdale, 1968-70; A.A.S. magna cum laude, Nassau Community Coll., 1971; B.B.A., Adelphi U., 1973. Acct., Electronic Systems div. Gen. Instruments Corp., Hicksville, N.Y., 1973-75, Exxon Internat., Exxon Corp., N.Y.C., 1975-76; acct./auditor N.Y. State Dept. Taxation and Fin., Mineola, 1976-85, assoc. tax auditors program, 1978-83; active Citrus County Sch. Vol. Program, 1989—, IRS Vita Vol. program, 1991—. Mem. Inst. Mgmt. Acctg. (profl.), Assn. Spl. Tax Auditors N.Y. State. Republican. Roman Catholic. Club: Rockville Centre Advanced Intermediates Tennis League (N.Y.); Beverly Hills (head of calling com. 1990—), Beverly Hills Lions (head calling com. 1990—).

MAROTZ, GUENTER WERNER, engineer, educator; b. Berlin, July 4, 1930; s. Fritz Ludwig and Elisabeth Gertrud (Brischke) M.; m. Marianne Kaethe Kicherer, Sept. 17, 1960; children: Martin, Joachim, Anette. Diploma, U. Stuttgart, Fed. Republic Germany, 1956, D Engring., 1963, cert. univ. educator, 1968. Rsch. engr. Hydraulic Lab., U. Stuttgart, 1960-63; head of lab., prof. Inst. Gen. Hydraulics, U. Stuttgart, 1963-97; dean Faculty Civil Engring. U. Stuttgart, 1970-72. Author: Asphalt in Hydraulics, 1963, Underground Water Storage, 1968; chief editor, Jour. Wasserwirtschaft, 1977-97; contbr. numerous articles, rsch. papers to sci. publs. Mem. Internat. Assn. Hydraulic Rsch., Verein Deutscher Ingenieure, Deutscher Verband für Wasserwirtschaft und Kulturbau, Baden-Württ Wasserwirtschaftsverband, Germania Club (acad. com. 1965-72). Died Apr., 1997.

MARQUARDT, DONALD WESLEY, statistician, researcher; b. N.Y.C., Mar. 13, 1929; s. Kurt C. and Amelia P. (Moller) M; m. Margaret E. Rittershaus, Sept. 13, 1952; children: Paul E. (dec.), Joan N. A.B., Columbia U., 1950; M.A., U. Del., 1956. Rsch. engr./mathematician E.I. du Pont de Nemours & Co., Inc., Wilmington, Del., 1953-57, rsch. project engr./sr. mathematician, 1957-64, cons. supr., 1964-72, cons. mgr. engring. dept., 1972-89; mgr. quality mgmt. and tech. ctr., 1989-91; pres. Donald W. Marquardt and Assocs., Inc., Wilmington, Del., 1991—; mem. NRC eval. panel for applied math. for Nat. Bur. Standards, 1981-84; mem. Am. Nat. Standards Inst. com. on quality assurance, vice chmn., 1983, chmn., 1984, dir., 1985-92, 95—, chmn. mgmt. com., 1992-95; rep. to Internat. Orgn. Standardization tech. com. on quality mgmt. and quality assurance, internat. chmn. Strategic Planning Adv. Group, 1993-95, chmn.'s adv. group, 1995—; nat. chmn. U.S. tech. adv. group, head of U.S. delegation, 1989—; adj. prof. U. Del., 1983-91; part time faculty mgmt. sci. Penn State U., 1993—; sr. examiner Malcolm Baldrige Quality Award, 1988; mem. Nat. Rsch. Coun. MS 2000 Com., 1988-91. Mem. editorial bd. Communications in Stats., 1977-83; assoc. editor: Jour. Bus. and Econ. Stats., 1982-85, Technometrics, 1974-80; contbr. articles to profl. jours. Served with U.S. Army, 1951-52. Fellow Am. Statis. Assn. (pres. 1986, Founders award 1995), AAAS, Am. Soc. for Quality Control (Youden prize 1974, Shewell prize 1984, Shewhart Medalist 1986); mem. Internat. Statistical Inst. (elected mem. 1989), Am. Inst. Chem. Engrs., Sigma Xi. Presbyterian. Rsch. on quality mgmt. systems, quality tech., non-linear estimation, analysis of unequally-spaced time series. Died July 5, 1997.

MARR, DAVID FRANCIS, television announcer, former professional golfer, journalist; b. Houston, Dec. 27, 1933; s. David Francis and Grace Anne (Darnell) M.; m. Caroline Elizabeth Dawson, Sept. 25, 1972; children by previous marriage: Elizabeth S., David Francis III, Anthony J. Student, Rice U., 1950-51, U. Houston, 1951-52. Profl. golfer, 1953—, tour player, 1960-72, part-time tour player, 1973—; golf announcer ABC Sports, 1970-91, BBC Sports, 1992—, NBC Sports, 1995—; dir. Nabisco-Dinah Shore Tournament, 1981-86. Elected to Coll. Golf Hall of Fame, 1977, Tex. Golf Hall of Fame, 1981; named to Ryder Cup Team, 1965. Mem. Profl. Golfers Assn. (nat. champion 1965, Player of Year 1965), AFTRA. Roman Catholic. Clubs: Lochinvar Golf (Houston); Houston City; Champions Golf (Houston); Brae-Burn Country; Loch Lomond (Scotland). Capt. Ryder Cup Team, 1981. Died Oct. 5, 1997.

MARSH, HELEN UNGER, retired educational administrator; b. Grenada, Miss., May 4, 1925; d. John Waugh and Hortense (Baker) Unger; m. Loren C. Marsh, Sept. 4, 1950 (div. Dec. 1981); children: Keith S., Douglas L., Charlene M., Margaret Marsh Woods. AB, Bob Jones U., 1947; MA, Northwestern U., 1950; EdD, Ball State U., 1975. Cert. profl. adminstr., supr., secondary tchr., supt., Ind. Intermittent instr. speech and English Ball State U., Muncie, Ind., 1961-83, mem. adv. bd. for lab. expts., 1987-93; tchr. lang. arts Southside High Sch., Muncie, 1963-74, dept. chmn., 1974-76, dir. guidance, 1976-83; supr. lang. arts and guidance Muncie Community Schs., 1983-87, dir. rsch. and univ. rels., 1987-93; ret., 1993, 1994; judge nat. writing contest Nat. Coun. Tchrs. English, 1974-80; proposal writer Eli Lilly Found.; student placement coord., rschr. coord. Ball State U. and Muncie Community Schs.; community projects coord. Muncie Community Schs.; cons. Brainbow Learning Ctr. Writer, editor, coord. Muncie Community Schs. publs. Bd. dirs. univ. div. Ind. U., Bloomington, 1984-87; bd. dirs. East Ctrl. Ind. Area Libr. Svc., 1987-95; chmn. edn. div. Shakespeare Festival, Ind. Com. for Humanities, Muncie, 1987; chair Mayor's Steering Com. for Muncie/Delaware County History, 1994-95; cons. Brainbow, Inc., 1993-94; assoc. Minn. Cultural Ctr.. Mem. AAUW, Am. Econ. Rsch. Assn., Assn. for Lifelong Learning, Muncie Bus. and Profl. Women's Club (treas. 1980-82, pres. 1982-84), Delaware County Ret. Tchrs. Assn. (sec. 1993-94). Republican. Methodist. Avocations: investing, reading. Home: Muncie Ind. Died Sept. 7, 1995.

MARSHALL, JOHN, professional society administrator; b. Sandwich, Mass., June 30, 1917; s. Walton H. and Vira F. (Stowe) M.; m. Anna Silk, May 11, 1961. BA cum laude, Williams Coll., 1939; Diploma, Sorbonne U., Paris. Trainee Am. Tobacco C., Va., 1939-41; asst. to sr. v.p. European dept. Singer Sewing Machine Co., Europe, Near East and Africa, 1946-56; past pres. Amateur Astronomers Assn., CEO; lectr. in field. Contbr. articles to profl. jours. Lt. comdr. USN, 1941-45, ETO. Recipient Excellence in French Studies award Govt. of France, 1939, Amateur Astronomers medal, 1985. Mem. N.Y. Acad. Scis. Died Jan. 30, 1997.

MARSHALL, J(ULIAN) HOWARD, JR., lawyer; b. Balt., Apr. 18, 1922; s. Julian Howard and Eleanor (Jones) M.; m. Penelope Stewart Spurr, Apr. 11, 1953; children: Edward A., Clinton S., Julia H., Margaret B., Alexander S. AB, Princeton U., 1943; JD, Harvard U., 1949. Bar: Md. 1949, N.Y. 1949. Assoc. Root, Ballantine, Harlan, Bushby & Palmer, N.Y.C., 1949-55; assoc. Wickes, Riddell, Bloomer, Jacobi & McGuire, N.Y.C., 1955-58, ptnr., 1958-78; ptnr. Morgan, Lewis & Bockius, N.Y.C., 1979-88, ret., 1988. Chmn. Irvington (N.Y.) Planning Bd., 1966-89. Served to capt. arty. U.S. Army, 1943-45, PTO. Mem. ABA, N.Y. State Bar Assn., Assn. of Bar of City of N.Y., Internat. Bar Assn. Republican. Episcopalian. Died Mar. 11, 1997.

MARSHALL, WILLIAM, JR., architect; b. Ashland, Ky., Nov. 24, 1925; s. William and Lee (Powers) M.; m. Joan Goodyear Ellingston, June 16, 1951; children—William III, Jenefer, Charles, Elizabeth, Christopher. Student, Va. Mil. Inst., 1943-44; B.S., U. Va., 1949; postgrad., Columbia, 1949-50. Designer, draftsman, 1950-53; architect Lublin, McGaughy & Assos. (Architects and Cons. Engrs.), Norfolk, Washington, 1953-55; architect, partner Lublin, McGaughy & Assos. (Architects and Cons. Engrs.), 1955-60; pres. MMM Design Group, Architects and Cons. Engrs. Norfolk, Va., Washington, Houston, Frankfort, Germany, Athens, Greece, 1960-84, William Marshall Assocs. Ltd., 1984—. Prin. works include United Va. Bank, Norfolk, 1970, Kirn Meml. Library, Norfolk, 1962, Ministry of Def. Hdqrs, Riyadh, Saudi Arabia, 1976, New City of Brega, Libya, 1980, Kuwait Ministry of Def. Interior Design Project, 1976. Mem. profl. uni[t] United Comty. Fund, Norfolk, 1962-71, mem. ad hoc com. to establish city planning dept., Norfolk, 1961-62, mem. citizens adv. com. to mayor, 1962-68, chmn. codes sub-com., 1962-68, mem. exec. com., 1962-68; mem. adv. com. bldg. constrn. curriculum Norfolk State Coll. 1968—; trustee Hermitage Found., 1974—, pres., 1985-95; trustee AIA Rsch. Corp., 1075. With AUS, 1944-46. Fellow AIA (pres. Tidewater sect. Va. chpt. 1964-65, pres. Va. chpt. 1969-70, v.p. nat, pres. Va. chpt. 1971, mem. exec. com. 1974-75, bd. dirs. 1974-75, chmn. commn. govt. affairs 1972-73, commr. spl. assessment program 1973-74, 1st v.p. 1974, chmn. planning com. 1974, pres. 1975—); mem. Am. Inst. Steel Construction (archtl. awards of excellence jury 1974), Am. Iron and Steel Inst. (honor awards jury 1975), Prestressed Concrete Inst. (chmn. honor awards jury 1975), Va. Assn. Professions (bd. dirs. 1970-71, regional v.p. 1970), Downtown Norfolk Assn. (bd. dirs. 1966-72). DIED 11/08/97. .

MARTIN, BARNEY, investment executive; b. St. Louis, Oct. 30, 1925; s. John Cunningham and Margaret Burrage (Bills) M.; m. Virginia Ann Wheeler, Oct. 2[?] 1954. BS in Marine Engring., U.S. Naval Acad., 1946. Lic. naval aviator. Commd. ensign USN, 1946, advanced through grades to capt., 1976; commdr. Task Force 157 Washington, 1967-71; dir. U.S. Naval Investigative Svc., 1973-76; pres. LBCA Investments Inc., Long Beach, Calif., 1976—; gen. ptnr. Delta Devel. [?] San Diego, 1976—. Chmn. Pub. Interest Com., Rancho Sante Fe, Calif., 1989—; co-chmn. Pres.'s Assocs. Planning Com., Zool. Soc. San Diego, 1991—. Recipient (2) Legions of Merit awards. Mem. Rancho Sante Fe Golf Club, Univ. Club (San Diego). Republican. Home: PO Box 2589 Rancho Santa Fe CA 92067-2589 DIED 04/25/96. .

MARTIN, BOYD ARCHER, political science educator emeritus; b. Cottonwood, Idaho, Mar. 3, 1911; s. Archer Olmstead and Norah Claudine (Imbler) M.; m. Grace Charlotte Swingler, Dec. 29, 1933; children: Michael Archer, William Archer. Student, U. Idaho, 1929-30, 35-36, B.S., 1936; student, Pasadena Jr. Coll., 1931-32, U. Calif. at Los Angeles, summer 1934; A.M., Stanford, 1937, Ph.D., 1943. Rsch. asst. Stanford U., 1936-37, teaching asst., 1937-38; instr. polit. sci. U. Idaho, 1938-39; acting instr. polit. sci. Stanford U., 1939-40; John M. Switzer fellow, summer 1939-40; chief personnel officer Walter Butler Constrn. Co., Farragut Naval Tng. Center, summer 1942; instr. polit. sci. U. Idaho, 1940-43, asst. prof. polit. sci., 1943-44, asso. prof. polit. sci., 1944-47; prof., head dept. social sci., asst. dean coll. letters and sci. U. Idaho, 1947-55, dean, 1955-70, Borah Distinguished prof. polit. sci., 1970-73, prof., dean emeritus, 1973—; vis. prof. Stanford U., summer 1946, spring 1952, U. Calif., 1962-63; affiliate Center for Study Higher Edn., Berkeley, 1962-63; mem. steering com. N.W. Conf. on Higher Edn., 1960-67, pres. conf., 1966-67; mem. bd. Am. Assn. of Partners of Alliance for Progress; chmn. Idaho Adv. Coun. on Higher Edn.; del. Gt. Plains UNESCO Conf., Denver, 1947; chmn. bd. William E. Borah Found. on Causes of War and Conditions of Peace, 1947-55; mem. Commn. to Study Orgn. Peace; dir. Bur. Pub. Affair Rsch., 1959-73, dir. emeritus, 1973—; dir. Martin Peace Inst., 1970—. Author: The Direct Primary in Idaho, 1947, (with others) Introduction to Political Science, 1950, (with other) Western Politics, 1968, Politics in the American West, 1969, (with Sydney Duncombe) Recent Elections in Idaho (1964-70), 1972, Idaho Voting Trends: Party Realignment and Percentage of Voters for Candidates, Parties and Elections, 1890-1974, 1975, In Search of Peace: Starting From October 19, 1980, 1980, Why the Democrats Lost in 1980, 1980, On Understanding the Soviet Union, 1987; editor: The Responsibilities of Colleges and Universities, 1967; contbr. to: Ency. Britannica, 1990, 91; also articles. Mem. Am. Polit. Sci. Assn. (exec. council 1952-53), Nat. Municipal League, Am. Soc. Pub. Adminstrn., Fgn. Policy Assn., UN Assn., AAUP, Western Polit. Sci. Assn. (pres. 1950), Phi Beta Kappa, Pi Gamma Mu, Kappa Delta Pi, Pi Sigma Alpha. Died Jan. 8, 1998.

MARTIN, CHARLES ELMER, artist; b. Chelsea, Mass., Jan. 12, 1910; s. Charles and Barbara (Cady) Mastrangelo; m. Florence J. Taylor, June 2, 1934; 1 son, Jared Christopher. Painting supr. teaching div. Fed. Art Project, 1933-37; under contract to New Yorker mag., 1937—; art cartoonist PM, 1939-42; tchr. painting Bklyn. Mus. Art Sch., 1965. Author, illustrator children's books including Island Rescue, 1984, For Rent, 1985; illustrator: Noah's Ark, 1974, Jonah and the Whale, 1976, Island Winter, Summer Business, Sam Saves the Day; one man shows include Rockland Found., 1951, Ruth White Gallery, N.Y.C., 1955, 60, Bklyn. Mus., 54-65, Graham Gallery, 1973, continual exhibit Nicholls Gallery, N.Y.C.; represented permanent collections Met. Mus., Mus. City of N.Y., Libr. of Congress, Syracuse U., Princeton U. Mus., Portland Mus., Maine; cover designs for nat. mags., including 210 for New Yorker under initials C.E.M. Served with Office War Info., 1942-44, ETO. Died June 16, 1995.

MARTIN, CHRISTOPHER MICHAEL, physician, laboratory administrator; b. N.Y.C., Sept. 25, 1928; s. Christopher William and Genevieve (Grennon) M.; m. Phyllis Marie Walsh, Oct. 16, 1954; children: Eileen Margaret, Christopher Walsh, Marianne. AB, Harvard Coll., 1949, MD, 1953. Intern Boston City Hosp., 1953-54, resident, 1956-57; sr. asst. surgeon NIH, Bethesda, Md., 1954-56; rsch. fellow Med. Sch. Harvard U., Boston, 1957-59; assoc. prof. medicine Seton Hall Coll. Medicine, Jersey City, 1959-65; prof. medicine and pharmacology Sch. Medicine Georgetown U., Washington, 1965-70; sr. dir. med. affairs Merck Sharp & Dohme Rsch. Labs., West Point, Pa., 1970-78, exec. dir. infectious diseases, 1978—. Contbr. articles to profl. jours., chpts. to books. Sr. asst. surgeon USPHS, 1950-54. Grantee USPHS-NIH, 1960-65. Fellow Infectious Diseases Soc.; mem. Am. Soc. Microbiology, Am. Soc. Pharmacology and Exptl. Therapeutics, Harvard Club, Phi Beta Kappa, Alpha Omega Alpha. Roman Catholic. Avocation: photography. DIED 04/15/97. .

MARTIN, CLARENCE EUGENE, JR., lawyer; b. Martinsburg, W.Va., Sept. 10, 1909; s. Clarence E. and Agnes G. (McKenna) M.; m. Catherine duBois Silver, June 6, 1942; 1 son, Clarence Eugene III. A.B., Cath. U. Am., 1931, LL.B., 1934. Bar: W.Va. bar 1934. Since practiced in Martinsburg; chmn. bd. Mchts. & Farmers Bank. Mem. W.Va. State Senate, 1950-70. Served as lt. USNR, World War II. Fellow Am. Coll. Trial Lawyers, Am. Bar Found.; mem. ABA, Am. Bd. Trial Advs., West Va. State Bar (pres. 1954-55), W.Va. Bar Assn. (pres. 1962-63), Berkeley County Bar Assn., Am. Judicature Soc., Internat. Assn. Ins. Counsel, Am. Law Inst.

MARTIN, DEAN (DINO CROCETTI), actor, singer; b. Steubenville, Ohio, June 17, 1917; m. Elizabeth Ann McDonald, 1940 (div. 1949); children: Craig, Claudia, Gail, Deanna; m. Jeanne Bieggers, 1949 (div.); children: Dean Paul (dec.), Ricci, Gina; m. Cathy Hawn, 1973. Ed. high sch. Successively employed odd jobs, Weirton,, W.Va.; welterweight boxer, appeared with Jerry Lewis on stage and in films. Amateur dance band singer; singer with Ernie McKay's band, later in night clubs; formed comedy team with Jerry Lewis, 1946; appeared in night clubs, theatres, radio and TV programs, also motion pictures; former star weekly TV show, NBC; appeared in motion pictures including: My Friend Irma Goes West, 1949, At War with the Army, 1950, That's My Boy, 1951, The Stooge, 1952, Jumpin' Jacks, The Caddy, 1953, Scared Stiff, 1953, Money From Home, 1953, Living It Up, 1954, Three Ring Circus, 1954, You've Never Too Young, 1955, Artists and Models, 1955, Pardners, 1956, Hollywood or Bust, 1956, Ten Thousand Bedrooms, 1957, Sailor Beware, 1957, Young Lions, 1958, Rio Bravo, 1959, Some Came Running, Career, 1959, Who Was That Lady?, 1960, Bells Are Ringing, 1960, Ocean's 11, 1960, Ada, 1961, Who's Got the Action, 1962, Who's Sleeping in my Bed, 1963, Toys in the Attic, 1963, What A Way to Go, 1964, Robin and the Seven Hoods, 1964, Kiss Me, Stupid, 1964, Son of Kate Elder, 1965, Rough Night in Jericho, 1967, Silencers, 1966, Murderers Row, 1966, The Ambushers, 1967, How to Save a Marriage, 1968, The Wrecking Crew, 1969, Airport, 1970, Texas Across The River, Something Big, 1972, Showdown, 1973, Mr. Ricco, 1975, Cannonball Run, 1981, Cannonball Run II, 1984; TV shows include: Dean Martin Celebrity Roasts, 1976, 78, Dean Martin Christmas Specials, 1975, 78, 80, Dean's Place, 1976; recorded albums including Memories Are Made of This. Recipient Golden Globe award. Home: Beverly Hills Calif. Died Dec. 25, 1995.

MARTIN, EDGAR THOMAS, telecommunications consultant, lawyer; b. Princeton, W.Va., May 1, 1918; s. Edgar Frank and Delia Florence (Nowlin) M.; m. Hannelore Elisabeth Trucksaess, Jan. 12, 1952. BS, Va. Poly. Inst., 1938, MS, 1953; grad., Royal Air Force Coll., Cranwell, 1941; MA, Am. U., 1957; JD, George Washington U., 1957, M of Forensic Sci., 1977; LLM, Georgetown U., 1959; grad., U.S. Army Command and Gen. Staff Coll., 1963, Indsl. Coll. Armed Forces, 1963. Bar: Va. 1958, U.S. Ct. Mil. Appeals 1959; registered profl. engr., Va., 1939. Chief lab. technician Va. Poly. Inst. Elec. Engring. Dept., 1938-40; elec. engr. Radford Ordnance Works, 1940-41, chief radio sect., 1946-48, chief telecommunications br., 1948-49; office of mil. govt. for Germany; communications specialist Office High Commr., Germany, 1949-52; chief cen. frequency staff, 1952-54, chief engr., 1954-58; engring mgr., Broadcasting Svc. (Voice of Am.) USIA, 1958-75; telecomm. cons., 1975-96. 2d lt. USAR, 1940, U.S. Army, 1941-46, lt. col. USAR, 1946, col. USAR, 1961, col. AUS ret. 1978. Fellow IEEE; mem. ABA, Am. Acad. Forensic Sci., Am. Soc. Internat. Law, Va. Trial Lawyers Assn., Soc. Bibl. Lit., Am. Soc. for Legal History, Soc. for Mil. History, U.S. Commn. on Mil. History, Nat. Lawyers Club, Army Navy Club, Am. Fgn. Svc. Assn., Nat. Mil. Intelligence Assn. Died Aug. 21, 1996.

MARTIN, HAROLD HARBER, author, magazine writer, columnist; b. Commerce, Ga., Sept. 17, 1910; s. Gabriel Pierce and Mary Edna Augusta (Harber) M.; m. Boyce Lokey, Apr. 23, 1935 (dec. July 10, 1988); children: Marian Hamilton Martin Harrison, Harold Harbour, John Pierce, Nancy Boyce Martin Sparks. A.B. in Journalism, U. Ga., 1933. Sports and feature writer Atlanta Georgian and Sunday Am., 1932-39; feature writer, columnist Atlanta Constn., 1939-74; contbr. to Harper's, Collier's, Liberty, Sat. Eve. Post, 1944-50; asso. editor Sat. Eve. Post, 1951-53, contbg. editor, 1958-63, editor at large, 1964-69; lectr. journalism Ga. State U., Atlanta, 1972-94. Author: (with Gen. M. B. Ridgway) Soldier, 1956, Father's Day Comes Once a Year and Then it Always Rains, 1960, Starlifter, 1972, Ralph McGill, Reporter, 1973, Three Strong Pillars, 1974, History of Georgia, 1977, Atlanta Mayor William B. Hartsfield, 1978, This Happy Isle, 1978, Harold Martin Remembers a Place in the Mountains, 1979; humor Cats, Dogs, Children and Other Small Creatures, 1980; A Good Man, A Great Dream: D.W. Brooks of Gold Kist, 1982, Atlanta and Environs A Chronicle of Its People and Events, Years of Change and Challenge, 1940-1976, 1987. Mem. F.D. Roosevelt Warm Springs Meml. Commn.; bd. dirs. St. Judes House, Atlanta, pres., 1976; bd. dirs. Ga. Coop. Services for the Blind, Decatur. Served to capt. USMCR, 1943-45. Decorated Bronze Star; recipient award for non-fiction Southeastern Writers Assn., 1979. Mem. Newcomen Soc. Am., Sigma Delta Chi (Distinguished Service award and Bronze medal 1958). Episcopalian. Club: Nat. Press (Washington). Home: Atlanta Ga. Died July 10, 1994.

MARTINEZ, MIGUEL ANGEL, Spanish language educator; b. Santiago, Oriente, Cuba, July 5, 1930; cme to U.S., 1962; s. Lorenzo Eligio and Isabel Maria (Cosera) M.; m. Mercedes Herrera, Dec. 20. 1953; children: Miguel Angel, Maria Angeles, Jorge Luis. BA, U. Oriente, 1952; MA, Loyola U., Chgo., 1965; PhD., Northwestern U., 1969. Spanish instr. St. Xavier Coll., Chgo., 1964-65; from instr. to asst. prof. Loyola U., Chgo., 1965-72, assoc. prof., 1972—. Contbr. articles to profl. jours. Republican. Roman Catholic. Office: Loyola U Dept Modern Langs & Lits 6525 N Sheridan Rd Chicago IL 60626-5385 Died Feb. 13, 1995.

MARTINEZ-O'FERRALL, JOSÉ A., public health physician, retired air force officer; b. San Juan, P.R., Oct. 30, 1936; s. Jose I. Martinez and Basilia O'Ferrall; m. Ana C. Carrillo, Dec. 27, 1964; children: Ana Celeste, Rebeca Beatriz, Jose Nicolas. BS in Math., U. P.R., 1955, MD, 1959; MPH, U. Calif., Berkeley, 1967; grad., Flight Surgeon Sch., Brooks AFB, Tex., 1960, Sch. Aerospace Medicine, Brooks AFB, Tex., 1969, Air War Coll., Maxwell AFB, Ala., 1973. lectr., presenter in field. Intern Mercy Hosp., Buffalo, 1960; commd. capt. USAF, 1960, advanced through grades to col., 1975; chief of aviation medicine Ben Guerir Air Base, Morocco, 1960-61; chief of profl. svcs. and aviation medicine Zaragoza Air Base, Spain, 1961-64; chief of aerospace medicine Davis-Monthan AFB, Tucson, 1964-66; amb. health clinic med. dir. Bien Hoa, Vietnam, 1969-70; resident in preventive and aerospace medicine Brooks AFB, San Antonio, 1967-69, Scott AFB, Belleville, Ill., 1968-69; hosp. comdr., med. dir. Altus AFB, Altus, Okla., 1970-72; command surgeon, dir. base med. svcs. USAF So. Command, Albrook AFB, Canal Zone, 1973-76; team chief USAF Med. Inspection, Norton AFB, Calif., 1976-78; comdr., med. dir. USAF Med. Ctr., Clark Air Base, The Philippines, 1978-80; dep. surgeon USAF Air Tng. Command, Randolph AFB, Tex., 1980-81; vice comdr. Wilford Hall USAF Med. Ctr., Lackland AFB, Tex., 1981-85; hosp. comdr., med. dir. Laughlin AFB, Del Rio, Tex., 1985-88; med. cons. USAF Mit. Pers. Ctr., Randolph AFB, 1988-90; ret., 1990; preventive medicine cons. Al-Hada Armed Forces Hosp., Taif, Saudi Arabia, 1990-95; prev. medicine cons. Al-Hada Armed Forces Hosp., Taif, Saudi Arabia, 1991-95; apptd. by USAF Surgeon Gen. to represent U.S. Medicine in the Air Forces of Ams., Ecuador, Dominican Republic, Bolivia, Chile, Argentina and Colombia; lectr. in field. Contbr. numerous articles to med. jours. Decorated Legion of Merit with oak leaf cluster, Bronze Star with V for valor, Bronze Star, Air Medal with oak leaf cluster, Meritorious Svc. medal, Air Force Commendation medal; Gallantry Cross with palm (Vietnam); Republic of Vietnam Campaign medal; Vietnamese Honor medal; Vietnam Svc. medal; recipient George Washington medal Freedom Found., 1971, 73; scholar U. P.R., 1952-59; fellow NIH, summer 1956. Fellow Am. Coll. Preventive Medicine (assoc.), Aerospace Med. Assn. (assoc.); mem. AMA, Assn. Mil. Surgeons U.S., Soc. Hosp. Epidemiology Am., U.S.-Mex. Border Health Assn., Soc. USAF Flight Surgeons, Air Force Assn., Fed. Med. Exec. Inst. (life), Soc. Med. Grads. U. P.R. Sch. Medicine, Phi Chi Med. Fraternity. Died Aug. 1997.

MARUYAMA, YOSH, physician, educator; b. Pasadena, Calif., Apr. 30, 1930; s. Edward Yasaki and Chiyo (Sakai) M.; m. Fudeko Tsuji, July 18, 1954; children: Warren H., Nancy C., Marian M., Karen A. AB, U. Calif., Berkeley, 1951; MD, U. Calif., San Francisco, 1955. Diplomate Am. Bd. Radiology. Intern San Francisco Hosp., 1955-56; resident Mass. Gen. Hosp., Boston, 1958-61; James Picker advanced acad. fellow Stanford U., 1962-64; asst. prof. radiology Coll. Med. Scis., U. Minn., Mpls., 1964-67, assoc. prof., 1967-70, dir. div. radiotherapy, 1968-70; prof., chmn. dept. radiation medicine Coll. Medicine, U. Ky., Lexington, 1970-92, dir. Radiation Cancer Ctr., 1975-92; prof. radiation oncology Wayne State U.; dir. clin. neutron therapy Gershenson Oncology Ctr., Detroit, Mich., 1993—; bd. dirs. Markey Cancer Ctr.; cons. VA Hosp., Lexington; examiner Am. Bd. Radiology; mem. spl. study sect. Nat. Cancer Inst., Bethesda, Md.; mem. Panel Transplutonium Rsch., Nat. Rsch. Coun.; convener Internat. Neutron Therapy Workshop, 1985, 90; disting. oncology lectr. Wayne State U., 1993. Author: CF-252 Neutron Brachytherapy: Advance for Bulky Localized Cancer Therapy, 1984; assoc. editor: Applied Radiology, Endocuriether. Hypertherm. Oncology; editor: New Methods in Tumor Localization, 1977, (with others) CF-252 Brachytherapy and Fast Neutron Beam Therapy: Proceedings of the Workshop, 1986, Internat. Neutron Therapy Workshop, 1991; contbr. articles to profl. jours. Served with M.C. AUS, 1956-58. Am. Cancer Soc. fellow, 1960-61; recipient Nat. award Ky. div. Am. Cancer Soc., 1988. Fellow Am. Coll. Radiology (commn. on radiation therapy and patterns of care study), Royal Soc. Medicine; mem. AAAS, Am. Radium Soc., Am. Cancer Soc. (pres. Ky. div.), Am. Endocurietherapy Soc., Cell Kinetics Soc., Soc. Exptl. Biol. Medicine, Am. Assn. Cancer Rsch., European Soc. Therapeutic Radiology and Oncology, N.Am. Hyperthermia Group, Radiol. Soc. N.Am., Am. Soc. Therapeutic Radiology and Oncology, Soc. Chmn. Acad. Radiation Oncology Programs, Soc. Radiology Japan, Am. Assn. Immunologists, Southeastern Cancer Rsch. Assn. (bd. dirs.), Southeastern Cancer Group, Southwestern Oncology Group, Ky. Med. Assn., Order Ky. Cols., Minn. Acad. Scis., N.Y. Acad. Scis., Japan Soc. N.Y., Japan Club Bluegrass (pres.), Shodan Judoka, Kodokan Inst. (Tokyo), Spindletop Hall Club (Lexington), Sigma Xi (chpt. pres.), Phi Beta Kappa, Alpha Omega Alpha. Home: Grosse Pointe Mich. DIED 01/11/95. .

MASIP, ARGILAGA RAMON, food products executive; b. Barcelona, Nov. 28, 1940; m. Maria Teresa Nebot Marcobal; 2 children. Degree in econs., U. Barcelona. With market studies, advt., and sales divsns., then comml. mgr. Nestlé, gen. mgr., 1975-78, bd. dirs., 1978—, v.p., 1981-86, gen. mgr., 1986, v.p., 1986-91; pres., chmn. bd. dirs. Nestlé, Espana, Spain, 1991—; pres. and COO foods divsn. Nestlé S.A., Vevey,

Switzerland, 1992—; mem. adv. coun. Repsol S.A., 1994—; bd. dirs. Caixa d'Estalvis i Pensions de Barcelona-La Caixa, 1995—. Avocations: golf, tennis. Died Sept. 16, 1996.

MASON, DAVID DICKENSON, statistics educator; b. Abingdon, Va., Jan. 22, 1917; s. William Thomas and Eva (Dorton) M.; m. Virginia Louise Pendleton, Oct. 28, 1944; children: Marjorie F., David P. B.A., King Coll., 1936; M.S. (Acad. Merit fellow), Va. Poly. Inst., 1938; postgrad., Ohio State U., 1939-40; Ph.D., N.C. State U., 1948. Asst. soil scientist Va. Poly. Inst., 1938-39; asst. prof. soils Ohio State U., 1947-49; prin. biometrician Dept. Agr., Beltsville, Md., 1949-53; prof. stats. N.C. State U., 1953-62, prof., head dept. stats., 1962-81, emeritus prof. and head, 1981-97; head Inst. Stats., 1962-81, emeritus head, 1981-97; Sr. cons. United Fruit Co., Boston, 1957-71. Contbr. articles to profl. jours. Instl. rep. So. Regional Edn. Bd. com. statistics, 1963-81, chmn., 1973-75; Bd. dirs. Triangle Univs. Computation Center Corp., chmn., 1968-70. Served with AUS, 1941-45. Fellow Am. Statis. Assn., Am. Soc. Agronomy, Soil Sci. Soc. Am.; mem. Biometric Soc., Sigma Xi, Phi Kappa Phi, Gamma Sigma Delta. Presbyn. (elder, deacon). Club: Rotarian. Home: Raleigh N.C. Died Jan. 26, 1997.

MASONER, PAUL HENRY, counseling educator; b. Middletown, Ohio, Mar. 25, 1908; s. Paul and Emma Martha (Hayes) M.; m. Lorraine Carr, 1983; children: Paul, David, Linda; stepchildren: Elisabeth Carr-Jones, Phillip Carr, Jr. Student, Capital U., 1926-28; B.A. in English, Ohio State U., 1930, M.A. in Sociology, 1931; postgrad., Wilmington Coll., summer 1931; Ph.D. in Counseling, U. Pitts., 1949; postgrad., U. London, Eng., summers 1964, 66; D.Litt. (hon.), Hanyang U., Seoul, Korea, 1978. Tchr. English Central High Sch., Uhrichsville, Ohio, 1930-32; tchr. social scis. Bellevue High Sch., Pitts., 1932-34; counselor, vice prin. Bellevue High Sch., 1934-43, acting prin., 1943-44; adminstrv. head Engring. and Sci. Mgmt. War Tng. Center, Bellevue, Pa., 1942-44; sr. analyst Nat. Def. Research Com., U. Pa., 1944-45; counselor, lectr. psychology Vets. Counseling Center, U. Pitts., 1945-46; instr. Vets. Counseling Center, U. Pitts. (Sch. Edn.), 1946-48, asst. prof., 1948-50, asso. prof., 1950-51, prof., 1953-96, asst. dean, 1952-54, acting dean, 1954, dean, 1955-73, dean emeritus, 1973-96, Univ. prof., 1973-96; Mem. adv. com. Learning Research and Devel. Center, Pitts., 1965-73; cons. scholarship aid programs; ednl. cons. to sch. systems, colls., univs., ednl. orgns., govt. agys., others; mem. accreditation teams Middle States Assn. and Nat. Council for Accreditation of Tchr. Edn., 1954-75; mem. adv. com. Pa. Grad. Tchr. Edn., 1964-70; mem. Pa. Curriculum Commn., 1964-70, Com. of One Hundred Citizens for Better Edn., 1963-67; mem. council Nat. Council Accreditation Tchr. Edn., 1968-70; mem. Nat. Adv. Council Edn. Professions Devel., 1970-73; mem. exec. bd. Nat. Reading Center, Washington, 1970-73; Extensive fgn. travel and study. Contbg. author: Standards for the 60's, 1962, Counseling: Selected Readings, 1962, Changes in Teacher Education: An Appraisal, 1964; author: Design for Teacher Education, 1964, An Imperative: A National Policy for Teacher Education, 1972, Evaluación de Sistemas de Communicación Educativa, 1980. Bd. dirs. Falk Elementary Sch., Pitts., 1955-73, Westminster Found., 1964-66, Pitts. Council of Chs., 1964-66; pres. bd. trustees Robert Morris Coll. Recipient Outstanding Service to Edn. award Commonwealth of Pa., 1962, Effective Leadership to Tchr. Edn. award, 1964. Fellow Coll. Preceptors (hon., Eng.); mem. NEA, AAUP, AASA, We. Pa. Scholarship Assn. (exec. sec. 1950-70), Pa. State Edn. Assn. (exec. coun. 1966-68), We. Pa. Edn. Conf. (chmn. 1955-70), Pa. Schoolman's Club (pres. 1963), Pa. Assn. Liberal Arts Colls. for Advancement of Tchg. (pres. 1959), Am. Pers. and Guidance Assn., Nat. Vocat. Guidance Assn. (profl.), Am. Assn. Sch. Adminstrs. (profl.), Internat. Coun. Edn. for Tchg. (trustee 1973-76, pres. 1976-86), Am. Assn. Colls. Tchr. Edn. (pres. 1970-71), Civic Club Allegheny County (Pa.), Allegheny Roundtable (pres. 1964-70), Omicron Delta Kappa, Delta Pi Epsilon (hon.), Iota Lambda Sigma (hon.), Phi Delta Kappa, Kappa Phi Kappa. Conglist. Clubs: Cosmos (Washington); University (Pitts.). Home: Pittsburgh Pa. Died Oct. 15, 1996.

MASTROIANNI, MARCELLO, actor; b. Fontana Liri, Italy, Sept. 28, 1924; s. Ottone and Ida (Irolle) M.; ed. U. Rome; m. Flora Carabella, 1950; 1 child, Barbara; 1 child with Catherine Deneuve, Chiara. Cashier, Eagle Lion Films, Rome, 1944; debut U. Rome stage prodn. Angelica, 1948; appeared in films including: Una Domenica d'Agosto, 1949, Le Notti Bianche, 1957, I Soliti Ignoti, 1958, Beli' Antonio, 1960, La Dolce Vita, 1960, La Notte, 1961, A Very Private Affair, 1961, Divorce—Italian Style, 1961, 8 1/2, 1963, Family Diary, 1963, Yesterday, Today and Tomorrow, 1964, Fantasmi a Roma, 1964, Casanova 70, 1965, Marriage-Italian Style, 1965, The Organizer, 1965, The 10th Victim, 1965, Ciao Rudy, 1966, Lo Straniera, 1967, Viaggio di G. Mastorna, 1967, Shout Louder, I Don't Understand, L'Etranger, 1967, The Man with the Balloons, 1968, Diamonds for Breakfast, 1968, Leo the Last, 1970, The Priest's Wife, 1970, Drama of Jealousy, (prize for best actor Cannes 1970), 1970, Sunflower, 1970, The Pizza Triangle, 1970, What?, 1972, La Grande Bouffe, 1973, Salut L'Artiste, 1973, Massacre in Rome, 1973, Tuche Pas la Femme Blanche, 1974, Allonsanfan, 1975, Gangster Doll, 1975, Down the Ancient Stairs, 1975, The Sunday Woman, 1976, A Special Day, 1977, Bye Bye Monkey, 1978, Stay as You Are, 1979, La Cite des Femmes, 1979, Blood Feud, 1981, The New World, 1981, Gabriella, 1982, Nuit de Varennes, 1983, Allonsanfan, 1985, Macasoni, 1985, Ginger and Fred, 1986, Dark Eyes (best actor Cannes Film Fest.), 1987, Intervista, 1987, The Beekeeper, 1988, The Two Lives of Martin Pascal, Splendor, 1989, What's the Time (Best Actor Venice Film Festival), 1989, The Hesitant Step of the Stork, 1991, Everybody's Fine, 1991, A Fine Romance, Used People, 1992, The Beekeeper, 1993, The Children Thief, 1994, I Don't Want To Talk About It, 1994, Ready to Wear (Prêt-à-Porter), 1994. Recipient Silver ribbon Italian Film Critics, 1958, 61, European Film award, 1988. Died Dec. 18, 1996.

MATHER, ALLEN FREDERICK, lawyer; b. Kansas City, Mo., Apr. 28, 1922; s. William Frederick and Alberta (Stephenson) M.; m. Patricia T. Mitchell, June 23, 1972; children—Allen Frederick, Nathaniel J., J. Miles Mitchell (dec.). A.B., Colgate U., 1943; LL.B., Harvard, 1949. Bar: Calif. bar 1953. With Agrl. Council of Calif., Sacramento, 1950-57; exec. sec. Agrl. Council of Calif., 1954-57; gen. counsel Sunkist Growers, Los Angeles, 1958-66; pres. Sun-Maid Raisin Growers of Calif., Kingsburg, 1966-72, Sunland Marketing, Inc., Menlo Park, Calif., 1971-72, First Nat. Bank Fresno, Calif., 1973-77; mem. firm Wild, Carter, Tipton & Oliver, 1977-84; mng. partner Agribus. Group, 1977—. Mem. Calif. Industry and World Trade Commn., 1969—; pres. Sequoia council Boy Scouts Am., 1969—. Served with USNR, 1943-46. Mem. Dried Fruit Assn. (dir.), Fresno C. of C. (dir.), Colgate Alumni Club, Harvard Bus. Sch. Alumni Club. Club: Sunnyside Country (Fresno). Died Jan. 4, 1997.

MATHIS, JANET, elementary special education educator; b. Arlington, Tex., Nov. 21, 1959; d. Harvey C. Jr. and Mary J. (Hedrick) Scoggins; m. Robert A. Mathis, July 2, 1981; 1 child, R. Oliver. BS, E. Tex. State U., 1981; MEd with honors, Tex. Woman's U., 1987. Cert. spl. edn. tchr., guidance assoc., ednl. diagnostician, Tex.; cert. in mental retardation. Tchr., spl. ednl. tchr. Dallas Ind. Sch. Dist., 1981-88, resource room tchr., 1988-91; tchr. content mastery and resource room Garland Ind. Sch. Dist., 1991—. Mem. Tex. State Tchrs. Assn., Assn. Tex. Profl. Educators, Coun. for Exceptional Children. DIED 08/29/97. .

MATTESON, ROBERT ELIOT, former college administrator; b. St. Paul, Sept. 13, 1914; s. Charles Dickerman and Adelaide Gridley (Hickcox) M.; m. Jane Elizabeth Paetzold, June 21, 1940; children: Adelaide (Mrs. David Elliott Donnelley), Robert Eliot, Fredric L., Sumner W., Elizabeth C. BA, Carleton Coll., Northfield, Minn., 1937; intern, Nat. Inst. Pub. Affairs, 1937-38; MA, Harvard U., 1940; student, Nat. War Coll., 1964-65; D Pub. Svc. (hon.), Northland Coll., 1991. Instr. polit. sci. Carleton Coll., 1940-42; dir. Stassen research staff, Republican presdl. nomination, 1946-48; asst. to pres. U. Pa., 1948-52; asst. dir. Fgn. Operation Adminstrn., Washington, 1953-55; dir. White House Disarmament Staff, 1955-58; asst. to Sherman Adams, White House, 1958; mem. bd. nat. estimates CIA, 1959-62; dir. policy planning staff U.S. Disarmament Adminstrn., 1961; dir. research council, dir. program planning staff, sr. adviser ACDA, 1962-67; dep. CORDS, II Corps, Vietnam, 1967-68; dir. Office Internat. Tng., AID, Washington, 1968-71, Fgn. Affairs Exec. Seminar, Dept. State, 1971-72, Sigurd Olson Environmental Inst. Northland Coll., Ashland, Wis., 1972-74; Mem. planning bd. Nat. Security Council, 1955-58; dep. dir. U.S. Disarmament delegation, London, 1956-57; adviser to U.S. delegation Fgn. Ministers Conf., Geneva, 1957, Summit Meeting and Geneva 10 Nation Disarmament Talks, Paris, 1960, 18 Nation Disarmament Talks, 1962, Geneva; mem. adv. bd. Wis. Environ. Edn. Council, 1972-76; mem. Wis. Wild Resources Adv. Council, 1974-78, Wis. Snowmobile Council, 1974-76; chmn. Pres.'s Adv. Com. on Quetico-Superior, 1976-78; bd. dirs. Duluth-Superior Area Ednl. TV, 1977-81, Environ. Learning Center Minn., 1977-79, Minn. Sci. Mus., St. Paul, 1972-94, Minn. Hist. Soc., 1981-94. Trustee Northland Coll., 1974-75; chmn. bd. Glenview Found., 1981-94. Served with 80th Inf. Div., 3d Army AUS, 1943-46, ETO. Decorated Combat Infantry badge, Silver Star for capture of Nazi Gestapo chief SS Gen. Kaltenbrunner; inducted into Carleton Coll. Athletic Club Hall of Fame, 1991; Littauer fellow, 1938-40. Mem. Assn. Governing Bds. Am. Colls. and Univs. (bd. mentor 1976-94), Minn. Environ. Balance Assn., Internat. Inst. Strategic Studies. Clubs: Harvard of Minn; Explorers (N.Y.C.); Mill Reef (Antigua). Home: Saint Paul Minn. Died Jan. 24, 1994.

MATTHEWS, WILLIAM PROCTER, English educator; b. Cin., Nov. 11, 1942; s. William P. and Mary Elizabeth (Sather) M.; m. Marie Murray Harris, May 4, 1963 (div. 1973); children: William, Sebastian. B.A., Yale U., 1965; M.A., U. N.C., Chapel Hill, 1966. Instr. English Wells Colls., Aurora, N.Y., 1968-69; asst. prof. Cornell U., 1969-74; asso. prof. U. Colo., 1974-78; prof. English U. Wash., Seattle, 1978-83, CCNY, 1983-97; bd. dirs. Asso. Writing Programs, 1977-80, pres., 1979-80; mem. lit. panel Nat. Endowment Arts, 1976-79, chmn., 1978-79. Author: Ruining the New Road, 1970, Sleek For the Long Flight, 1972, Sticks and Stones, 1975, Rising and Falling, 1979, Flood, 1982, A Happy Childhood, 1984, Foreseeable Futures, 1987, Blues If You Want, 1989, Curiosities, 1989, Selected Poems and Translations, 1992, Time and Money, 1995 (Nat. Book Critics' Cir. award 1995), The Mortal City: 100 Epigrams of Martial, 1995. Fellow Nat. Endowment Arts, 1974, 83, Guggenheim Found., 1980-81, Ruth Lilly prize, 1997. Mem. Poetry Soc. Am. Died Nov. 12, 1997.

MAXWELL, JOHN RAYMOND, artist; b. Rochester, N.Y., Nov. 3, 1909; s. Herbert F. and Esther Helen (Donovan) M.; m. Phyllis Mitchell Custer, Sept. 9, 1968. Student, Rochester Inst. Tech., U. Rochester, Provincetown Workshop; studied with nationally known artists including V. Candell, L. Manso, C. Peters, and A. Clements. Past pres. Nat. Advt. Agy., Phila., N.Y.C., L.A. Arts in oil, watercolor, acrylic. Exhbns. include Nat. Acad. of Design, Am. Watercolor Soc., Toledo Mus., Ohio, Richmond Mus., Va., Norfolk Mus., Va., Smithsonian Instn., Art Inst. Chgo., Lehigh U., San Francisco Palace Legion Honor, Corcoran Gallery, Rutgers U., U. Pa., William Penn Mus., Harrisburg, Pa.; represented in permanent collections Phila. Mus. Art, Nat. Acad. Design, Butler Inst. Am. Art, Wichita State U., Allentown (Pa.) Art Mus., U. Pa. Sci. Ctr., Lehigh U., Am. Coll., Phila., Woodmere Mus., Phila.; represented in pvt. collections in U.S., Can. and abroad; work featured in several books on contemporary painting; works reviewed in newspapers and jours.; contbr. articles on art and artists to nat. mags. Recipient Dana medals Pa. Acad. Fine Arts, Soc. Painters Casein and Acrylic, Purchase prizes Butler Inst. Am. Art, Woodmere Mus. Mem. NAD (Altman prize), Am. Watercolor Soc. (silver and bronze honor medals, other prizes), Audubon Artists, Allied Artists Am., Nat. Soc. Painters in Watercolor & Acrylic, Phila. Sketch Club (Gold medals). Died March 13, 1997.

MAXWELL, MARGARET WITMER, musician, editor; b. Irwin, Pa., Jan. 9, 1918; d. Charles Kendrick and Winona (Harrison) W.; m. Paul Russell Maxwell, Jan. 8, 1954 (dec. Oct. 1973); 1 child, James Witmer. MusB, U. Rochester, 1939; MEd, Lehigh U., 1969. cert. music tchr., Pa., Mass., N.Y. Feature writer Gannett Newspapers, Rochester, N.Y., 1945-52; staff mem. Fred Waring Enterprises, Delaware Water Gap, Pa., 1952-55; editor Mus. Jour., N.Y.C., 1953-56; tchr. music, English various pub. schs., Stroudsburg, Pa., Cape Cod, Mass. and Rochester, N.Y., 1956-76, ret., 1976; organist, choir dir. various chs., Pa., N.Y., Mass. N.J. and Fla., 1940—. Contbr. numerous articles to mags., newspapers. Mem. Am. Guild Organists, Sigma Alpha Iota (nat. editor, nat. exec. bd. 1979—). Republican. Presbyterian.

MAXWELL, VINCENT OLUOMA, chief justice; b. Rivers State, Nigeria, Aug. 15, 1926; arrived in Kiribati, Oct. 1985; s. Maxwell and Lucy Diana (Amadienweya) O.; m. Beryl Hazelene Dawes, July 2, 1960; children: Vincent Oluoma Jr., Allan, David. LLB, U. London, 1964, LLM, 1973. Bar: Eng. 1965, Wales 1965, Nigeria 1966, Jamaica 1971. Lawyer Nigeria, 1966-68; barrister Eng., 1965, 69-70; counsel Govt. Jamaica, Kingston 1971-74; resident magistrate Govt. Belize, Copozal 1975-78; master registrar Govt. Botswana, Lobaste 1979; high ct. judge Nigerian Judiciary, Rivers, 1979-84 chief justice Govt. Kiribati, Betio Tarawa, 1985-90; adjudicator immigration appeals Lord Chancellors Jud Dept., London, 1990-93; lectr. Coll. Sci. and Tech. Kingston, 1972-73. Cpl. RAF, 1950-55. Mem Honorable Soc. Inner Temple (hon.), Univ. Coll. Old Student (life), Nigerian Bar Assn., England and Wales Bar Assn., Jamaican Bar Assn., Royal Commonwealth. Anglican. Avocations: swimming, walking, reading Deceased.

MAZA, HERBERT, political scientist, retired university president; b. N.Y.C., Jan. 4, 1918; s. Julius and Tillie (Sherman) Maza; m. Hannah Maza (dec.); children: Sarah, Jonathan, Suzanne; m. Michelle Seguin. Student, Yale U.; BA, Columbia U.; MA Harvard U.; cert., Inst. Hautes Etudes Internat. Geneva; PhD, U. Aix, Marseilles, France; DHL, Am Coll. of Greece, 1996. Lectr. in polit. sci. Vassar Coll. N.Y., 1947-49, CUNY, N.Y.C., 1947-49; polit. sci analyst U.S. Dept. State, 1950-53; lectr. Princeton U. 1953-54, U. Geneva, 1953-54; dir. edn. USAF, Scotland 1954-56; asst. coord. Dept. Health, Edn. and Social Security, 1956-58; pres. Inst. Am. Univs., France and Eng., 1957-83; cons. to pres. Am. Coll. of Greece, 1983-85. Author: Neuf Meneurs Internationaux, 1965; assoc editor New Goliards; contbr. articles to profl. jours. Hon. mem. action com. St. Victor and St. Baume Pks. Fellow Coll. of Preceptors, London, Eliot Coll. Rutherford Coll., U. Kent, Eng.; named Officer des Palmes Académiques; recipient U.S. Medals, WWII medal City of Aix-En-Provence. Mem. AAUP, Am Assn. Univ. Adminstrs. (internat.), Internat. Edn. Assn (trustee, chmn. European coun.), Assn. Internat. Colls and Univs. (sec.-gen.), Assn. pour la Protection des Demeures Anciennes, Acad. Aix-En-Provence (corr.) Acad. Vaucluse (corr.), Acad. Mediterranéene (corr.) Con. Econ. and Social Studies de Martigues (hon.), Internat. Assn. Univ. Pres. (exec. mem.). Avocations gardening. DIED 06/02/97. .

MAZELIS, MENDEL, plant biochemist, educator, researcher; b. Chgo., Aug. 31, 1922; s. Jacob and Anna (Brvarnick) M.; m. Noreen Beimer, Mar. 24, 1969; 1 son, Jacob Russell. B.S., U. Calif.-Berkeley, 1943, Ph.D., 1954. Jr. research biochemist U. Calif.-Berkeley, 1954-55; research assoc., instr. U. Chgo., 1955-57; assoc. chemist Western Regional Research Lab., Albany, Calif., 1957-61; asst. prof. U. Calif.-Davis, 1961-64, assoc. prof., 1964-73, prof., 1973-91, prof. emeritus, 1991—. Served to lt. (j.g.) USN, 1943-46. Mem. Am. Soc. Plant Physiologists, Am. Soc. Biochemists and Molecular Biologists, Biochem. Soc. London, Phytochem. Soc. N.Am., Phytochem. Soc. Europe, Inst. Food Technologists.

MAZUR, THEODORE T., surgeon; b. Yankton, S.D., 1919. MD, Harvard Med. Sch., 1945. Diplomate Am. Bd. Surgery. Intern Henry Ford Hosp., Detroit, 1945-46; resident in gen. surgery Des Moines VA Hosp., 1949-52; with Burlington Med. Ctr., Iowa. Fellow Am. Coll. Surgery; mem. AMA. Home: Burlington Iowa Died May 29, 1997; buried Dudley Cemetery, Stickney, S.D.

MC ADAMS, RONALD EARL, geologist; b. Tulia, Tex., Aug. 6, 1910; s. Earl A. and Laura Ann (Hutchinson) McA.; m. Lucy Grace Harris, Aug. 24, 1927; children—Elizabeth Ann, John Harris. B.A., Tex. A&M U., 1932; M.S., Tex. A. and M. Coll., 1935. Field geologist Shell Oil Co., 1936-42, dist. geologist, 1946-47; exploration mgr. Shell Oil Co., Tulsa, 1947-53, Denver, 1954; mgr. exploration and land, head office Shell Oil Co., N.Y.C., 1955-57; v.p. exploration Shell Oil Co., 1957-70; cons. petroleum geologist, 1970-76; chmn., chief exec. officer McAdams, Roux and Assocs., Inc., ind. oil and gas exploration and producing (merged with Plains Petroleum), 1977-90; ind. oil and gas operator, 1990-95. Served from 1st lt. to lt. col. AUS, 1942-45, ETO. Decorated Bronze Star with oak leaf cluster. Fellow Geol. Soc. Am.; mem. Am. Assn. Petroleum Geologists, Am. Inst. Profl. Geologists, Tau Beta Pi, Cherry Hills Country Club, Champions Golf Club (Houston), Denver Petroleum Club, Castle Pines Golf Club (Castle Rock). Home: Englewood Colo. Died May 5, 1995.

MC BRIDE, RAYMOND ANDREW, pathologist, physician, administrator, educator; b. Houston, Dec. 27, 1927; s. Raymond Andrew and Rita (Mullane) McB.; m. Isabelle Shepherd Davis, May 10, 1958 (div. 1978); children: James Bradley, Elizabeth Conway, Christopher Ramsey, Andrew Gore. B.S., Tulane U., 1952, M.D., 1956. Diplomate: Am. Bd. Pathology. Surg. intern Jefferson Davis Hosp., Baylor U. Coll. Medicine, Houston, 1956-57; asst. in pathology Peter Bent Brigham Hosp., Boston, 1957-60; sr. resident pathologist Peter Bent Brigham Hosp., 1960-61; resident pathologist Free Hosp. for Women, Brookline, Mass., 1959; asst. resident pathologist Children's Hosp. Med. Center, Boston, 1960; teaching fellow pathology Harvard Med. Sch., Boston, 1958-61; research trainee Nat. Heart Inst., NIH, HEW, 1958-61; spl. postdoctoral fellow Nat. Cancer Inst., HEW, McIndoe Meml. Research unit Blond Labs., East Grimstead, Sussex, Eng., 1961-63; asst. attending pathologist Presbyn. Hosp., N.Y.C., 1963-65; asst. prof. pathology Coll. Physicians and Surgeons, Columbia U., 1963-65; research asso. Mt. Sinai Hosp., N.Y.C., 1965-68; assoc. prof. surgery and immunogenetics Mt. Sinai Sch. Medicine, N.Y.C., 1965-68; career scientist Health Research Council City N.Y., 1967-73; attending pathologist Flower and Fifth Ave. Hosps., N.Y.C., 1968-78, Met. Hosp. Center, N.Y.C., 1968-78; prof. pathology N.Y. Med. Coll., 1968-78; prof. pathology Baylor Coll. Medicine, Houston, 1978-96, emeritus prof. pathology, 1996—; attending pathologist Harris County Hosp. Dist., Ben Taub Gen. Hosp., Houston, 1978-96; chief pathology svcs. Harris County Hosp. Dist., 1988-96; assoc. staff Meth. Hosp., Houston, 1978-81, active staff to hon. emeritus, 1981-96, 96—; vis. grad. faculty Tex. A & M U., College Station, 1979—; clin. prof. pathology U. Tex. Grad. Sch. Biomed. Scis., Galveston, 1982—, U. Tex. Med. Br., Galveston, 1982—; prof. pathology Libero Istituto Universitario Campus Bio-Medico, Rome, 1993—; adj. prof. dept. stats. Rice U., Houston; mem. sci. com. Libero Istituto Universitario Campus Bio-Medico, Rome, 1991—; exec. dean N.Y. Med. Coll., Valhalla, 1973-75; exec. dir., COO, bd. dirs. Westchester Med. Ctr. Devel. Bd., Valhalla, 1974-76. Mem. editorial bd. Jour. Immunogenetics, Exptl. and Clin. Immunogenetics, European Jour. Immunogenetics; contbr. articles to profl. jours. Bd. dirs. Westchester Artificial Kidney Found., Inc., 1974-78, Westchester Med. Ctr. Libr., 1974-78, Westchester div. Am. Cancer Soc., 1973-78, Magnificat House, 1989-92, Found. for Life, Nat. Bd. Cath. Campaign for Am., 1989—, Tuxedo Libr., 1976-78; co-chmn. Westchester Burn Ctr. Task Force, 1975-76. Grantee Health Research Council, N.Y.C., 1963-73; Grantee Am. Cancer Soc., 1971-72; Grantee NIH, USPHS, 1964—; Grantee NSF, 1965-68. Fellow Royal Soc. Medicine; mem. Transplantation Soc., Soc. for Organ Sharing, Am. Soc. Extpl. Pathology, Reticuloendothelial Soc., AAAS, Am. Assn. Pathologists and Bacteriologists, Soc. for Investigative Pathology, Am. Assn. Immunologists, AAUP, AMA, Tex. Med. Assn., Harris County Med. Soc., Tex. Soc. Pathologists, Coll. Am. Pathologists, Am. Assn. Clin. Pathologists, Houston Acad. Medicine, Houston Soc. Clin. Pathologists, Assn. Am. Med. Colls., Fedn. Am. Scientists, Am., N.Y. cancer socs., Soc. Health and Human Values, Am. Acad. Med. Ethics, Alpha Omega Alpha (hon. med. soc.). Republican. Roman Catholic. Club: Tuxedo (Tuxedo Park, N.Y.). Achievements include research on relationship between genes of the major histocompatibility complex and the ability to regress tumors induced by different groups of avian sarcoma retroviruses; haptencarrier relationship between erythrocyte isoantigens providing a strategy for the production of antibodies to weakly immunogenic differentiation antigens; complementation of MHC and non-MHC genes in the ability to regress avian sarcoma retrovirus induced tumors; demonstration that the induction of skin graft tolerance in adult inbred mouse strains by means of parabiosis is accompanied by lymphold cell chimerism; development of an assay for quantitation of isoimmune plaque forming cells in a non-hemolytic system.

MC BRYDE, F. WEBSTER, geographer, ecologist, consultant; b. Lynchburg, Va., Apr. 23, 1908; s. John McLaren and Flora O'N. (Webster) McB. B.A., Tulane U., 1930, LL.D. (hon.), 1967; Ph.D., U. Calif., Berkeley, 1940; postgrad. (rsch. fellow) U. Colo., 1930-31, Clark U., 1931-32; m. Frances Van Winkle, July 23, 1934; children: Richard Webster, Sarah Elva, John McLaren. Geographer-photographer 4th Tulane Expdn. across Cen. Am. Maya Area, 1927-28; geology teaching asst. Tulane U., 1929-30, U. of Utah-Smithsonian Uinta Ute Expdn., No. Utah, 1931; field fellow Clark U.-Carnegie Inst., Washington, Guatemala, 1932; rsch. fellow Middle Am. Rsch. Inst., Tulane U., 1932-33; teaching asst. geography U. Calif., Berkeley, 1933-35, 37; predoctoral field fellow social sci. Social Sci. Rsch. Coun. N.Y., Guatemala and El Salvador, 1935-36; instr. geography Ohio State U., 1937-42, UCLA, 1940; field fellow in natural scis.NRC, Washington, also Berkeley, Guatemala, Mexico, 1940-41; expert cons., sr. geographer M.I., War Dept., Washington, 1942-45; lectr. geography Western Res. U., 1944; dir. Peruvian office Inst. Social Anthropology, Smithsonian Instn., Washington, Lima, 1945-47; dir., organizer and writer of curriculum Inst. Geography, U. San Marcos, Lima, 1945-47; spl. rep. Inst. Andean Rsch., Lima, 1947-48; lectr. Fgn. Svc. Inst., Dept. State, 1949-53; prof. geography U. Md., 1948-59, cons. prof., 1959-63; chief geographer office of coord. Internat. Stats. U.S. Bur. Census, Washington and Latin Am., 1948-56; geographer, com. on 1950 Census of Ams., Inter-Am. Statis. Inst., cons. all Am. nations, 1948-51; chief U.S. Census Mission, tech. advisor 1st Nat. Census of Ecuador, Quito, 1949-51; dir. regional planning Gordon A. Friesen Assocs., Inc., San José, Costa Rica nat. master hosp. plan, 1956-58; survey dir., sr. author survey report, Greater Southeast Washington, D.C. Cmty. Hosp., 1958-59; on contract to Exec. Rsch. Inc., N.Y.C., presdl. campaign advisor Pres. Villeda Morales, Honduras, 1957; U.S. rep., electoral advisor to Pres. Ydigoras Fuentes, Guatemala, 1958-64; pres. F.W. McBryde Assocs., Inc., Washington and Guatemala, 1958-64; founder-pres. Inter-Am. Inst. Modern Langs., Guatemala, 1962-66; Latin Am. cons. Inst. Modern Langs., Washington, 1962-66; chief phys. and cultural geography br., natural resources div. Inter-Am. Geodetic Survey, U.S. Army, Fort Clayton, C.Z., 1964-65; field dir. Bioenviron. Program, Atlantic-Pacific Interoceanic Sea-Level Canal Studies in Panama and Colombia (AEC contract), 1965-70, field dir. U.S. Army, Natick, Mass., Andean ecology project, S.Am., 1967-69, dir. project devel. program, Cen. Am. and Mex., 1968-69; cons. in ecology Battelle Meml. Inst., Columbus, Ohio, 1970-95; founder-dir. McBryde Ctr. for Human Ecology, 1969-95; cons. in human ecology and Latin Am., Transemantics, Inc., Washington, 1970-95; with UN Devel. Program, ecologist (tourism), expert Jamaica, W.I., 1971; hydrology ecologist, expert Parana River Nav. Improvement Project, Argentina, 1972; ecol. cons. Battelle Meml. Inst., Panama and Brazil, 1972; U.S. Bur. Census geography adviser to Govt. of Honduras on cartography for 1973 population census, 1972; Battelle cons., procedural analysis in internat. project devel., 1972; ecologist World Bank environ. impact analysis Bayano River Hydroelectric Project, one-man mission to Panama; Battelle cons., ecologist, prin. investigator and field coord., environ. impact study Darien Gap Hwy., Panama-Colombia for U.S. Dept. Transp., 1973; cons. Enviro Plan. Chesapeake Bay ecology; expert ecologist (biology) Engr. Agy. for Resources Inventories, C.E., U.S. Army, Washington, 1974; dir. recruitment, dir. internat. bus. intelligence, 1975-80, dir. Geog. Rsch. div. Transemantics, Inc., Washington, 1975-95; cons. geographer Census Office, Govt. of Honduras, 1981; cons. ecologist UN Tech. Cooperation and Devel., Cerro Colorado Copper Mine, Panama, 1981. Mem. nat. adv. bd. Am. Security Coun.; state advisor U.S. Congl. Adv. Bd., Am. Security Coun. Found.; charter founder Ronald Reagan Rep. Ctr., Washington, 1988, founder Pres. Trust Rep. Nat. Com., 1988, mem. Chmns. Coun., 1993; charter mem. Pres. Bush's Rep. Presdl. Task Force, 1989; charter mem. Rep. Presdl. Trust, 1992, Free Enterprise Coun., Rep. Nat. Com., 1994-95; mem. Rep. Senatorial Inner Circle, 1992-95; sponsor Nat. Rep. Congl. Com., 1994-95; at-large-del., Rep. Party Platform Planning Com., rep. Potomac area, Md., founding prodr., GOP-TV, 1994; charter sponsor Conservative TV Network; advisor U.S. Nat. Strategy Commn., 1993-95; sponsor Nat. Rep. Congressional Com.; charter mem. Free Enterprise Coun. Rep. Nat. Com., 1994-95. Fellow Explorers Club (life); mem. AAAS (life), Am. Anthrop. Assn., Am. Cartographic Assn., Am. Congress on Surveying and Mapping, Am. Geog. Soc., Assn. Am. Geographers (life, formerly Am. Soc. for Profl. Geographers founding pres., sec.(1 yr.), treas., meetings coord., editor publs. 1943-45, creator 8 regional divs. in U.S., 9 quasi-socs. in U.S. and Can.), Am. Geophys. Union (life), Am. Inst. Biol. Scis., Conf. Latin Americanist Geographers, Arctic Inst. N.A., Assn. Tropical Biology, Chesapeake Bay Found., Am. Soc. Photogrammetry and Remote Sensing, Ecuadorian Inst. Anthropology and Geography (founder dir. 1950-52, hon. dir. 1952-95), Inter-Am. Coun. (organizing sec. 1953-59, pres. 1959-62), N.Y. Acad. Scis., Washington Acad. (adv. bd. 1981-95), Lima Geog. Soc., Oceanography Soc. (charter mem.), Soc. Am. Archeology, Soc. Am. Mil. Engrs., Soc. for Med. Anthropology, N.Am. Cartographic Info. Soc., Guatemalan Soc. Geography and History, Internat. Oceanographic Found., Nature Conservancy Internat. Program, Mexican Soc. Geography and Stats., U.S. Naval Inst., World Wildlife Fund, Nat. Wildlife Fedn. (world assoc.), Phi Beta Kappa, Sigma Nu, others. Episcopalian. Author: Solola, 1933; Cultural and Historical Geography of Southwest Guatemala, 1947, Spanish , 1969, 2 vols. transl. by Francis Gall, Guatemala, 1969, Greenwood reprint (English), 1971; (with P. Thomas) Equal-Area Projections for World Statistical Maps, 1949; founding editor Profl. Geographer; contbr. numerous articles to profl. jours. Achievements include patent for equal-area designs and methods of constructing original projections for world maps, wherein median representations between true overall global linear scale (equidistance), true azimuth (indicated by directional bearings of intersecting graticule lines, hence shape of terrestrial features), and equivalence (or true relative size of land and water bodies on the map) are plotted to attain the closest similarity to earth features in all dimensions, which are completely true only on the spherical surface of the terrestrial globe; discovery of origin of beans (phaseolus vulgaris and p. lunatus) in western Guatemala and Chiapas; of maize varieties; development of new system of biological/ecological classification keyed to environmental factors, of new micro-geodemographic planning techniques employing data graphics plotted on thematic maps, especially useful in hospital, health, and economic surveys; research in Mayan and Andean archeology, ecology, on tectonic and seismic determinants and geomorphology. Died June 3, 1995. Home: Potomac Md.

MCBURNEY, GEORGE WILLIAM, lawyer; b. Ames, Iowa, Feb. 17, 1926; s. James William and Elfie Hazel (Jones) McB.; m. Georgianna Edwards, Aug. 28, 1949; children: Hollis Lynn, Jana Lee McBurney-Lin, John Edwards. B.A., State U. Iowa, 1950, J.D. with distinction, 1953. Bar: Iowa 1953, Ill. 1954, Calif. 1985. With Sidley & Austin and predecessor, Chgo., 1953-96, ptnr., 1964-93, counsel, 1994-96; resident ptnr. Singapore, 1982-84. Editor-in-chief: Iowa Law Rev., 1952-53. Mem. Chgo. Crime Commn., 1966-84; trustee Iowa Law Sch. Found., 1988-96, Old People's Home of City of Chgo., 1968-83, sec., 1967-69, exec. v.p., 1969-74, pres., 1974-82, hon. life trustee, 1983-96; hon. life trustee Georgian, Evanston, Ill., trustee, counsel, 1976-82, v.p., 1980-82. Served with inf. AUS, 1944-46. Fellow Am. Coll. Trial Lawyers, Am. Bar Found. (life); mem. ABA, State Bar Calif., L.A. County Bar Assn., Fed. Bar Assn., Bar Assn. 7th Fed. Cir., Am. Judicature Soc., Am. Arbitration Assn. (panelist large complex dispute resolution program), Assn. Atty. Mediators (So. Calif. chpt.), Assn. Bus. Trial Lawyers, The Ctr. for Internat. Comml. Arbitration L.A. (bd. dirs., exec. v.p.), Nat. Coll. Edn. (bd. assocs. 1967-84), U.S. C. of C. (govt. and regulatory affairs com. on coun. on antitrust policy 1980-82), L.A. Complex Litigation Inn of Ct., Law Soc. Singapore (hon.), Western Ctr. on Law and Poverty (bd. dirs. 1992-96), L.A. Union League Club (vet.), Mid-Day Club Chgo., Law Club (life), Legal Club Chgo., Am. Club, Cricket Club, Town Club Singapore, Phi Kappa Psi, Omicron Delta Kappa, Delta Sigma Rho, Phi Delta Phi. Republican. Presbyterian. Died Aug. 5, 1996.

MCCALLUM, KENNETH JAMES, university dean, chemistry and chemical engineering educator; b. Scott, Sask., Can., Apr. 25, 1918; s. James Alexander and Alice (Fines) McC.; m. Christine Chorneyko, Sept. 20, 1950 (dec. 1971); children: Patricia Jean, Douglas James; m. Erika Connell, Aug. 16, 1974. B.Sc., U. Sask., 1936, M.Sc., 1939; Ph.D., Columbia U., 1942. Jr. research officer NRC Can., 1942-43; mem. faculty U. Sask., from 1943, prof. chemistry and chem. engring., from 1953, head dept. chemistry and chem. engring., from 1959, dean grad. studies, from 1970. Assoc. editor: Jour. Chem. Physics, 1947-50; research, publs. (in cement chemistry, electron affinities, radioisotope exchange reactions, chem. effects transformations, radiation chemistry). Fellow Royal Soc. Can., AAAS, Chem. Inst. Can. (dir. sci. affairs 1961-64, pres. 1968-69). Home: Saskatoon Can. Died March 16, 1997.

MC CAMY, JAMES LUCIAN, former political science educator; b. Knoxville, Tenn., June 10, 1906; s. James Lucian and Ida Winfield (Mullendore) McC.; m. Julia Texie Boggess, July 17, 1931; children—Keith, Colin. B.A., U. Tex., 1929, M.A., 1932; Ph.D., U. Chgo., 1938. Reporter Austin (Tex.) Am., 1925-28; editor, publicity dir. Tex. Ex-Students Assn., Austin,

1928-32; tchr. Am. govt. U. Tex., 1932-33; fellow, research asst. dept. polit. sci. U. Chgo., 1933-34; prof. of govt. Bennington Coll., 1934-39, 1941-42; asst. to sec. of agr. U.S. Dept. Agr., 1939-41; asst. to dir. Bd. Econ. Warfare, 1942-43; exec. dir. Bur. Areas, Fgn. Econ. Adminstrn., 1943-45; econ. adviser U.S. Forces, Austria, 1945; dir. Office of World Trade Policy, also dep. dir. for policy Office of Internat. Trade U.S. Dept. Commerce, 1946; prof. polit. sci. U. Wis., 1947-71; ret., 1971; Knapp vis. scholar to U. Wis. Centers, 1967-68, chmn. dept., 1948-52; Brittingham prof. Inst. for Environ. Studies, 1970-71; chmn. Wis. Seminar on Quality of Environment, 1967; distinguished vis. scholar Milton Coll., 1969; mem. Wis. Bd. Ethics, 1973-74; U.S. del. to Internat. Inst. Agr., Rome, 1940; adviser to U.S. delegations at meetings of Internat. Bank and Monetary Fund, Savannah, 1946; 2d and 3d sessions of UNESCO Lake Success, 1946; staff mem. Pub. Library Inquiry, Social Sci. Research Council, 1947-48. Author: Government Publicity, 1939, Governmental Publications for the Citizen, 1949, The Administration of American Foreign Affairs, 1950 (Freedom House-Willkie award), American Government, 1957, Science and Public Administration, 1960, Conduct of the New Diplomacy, 1964, The Quality of the Environment, 1972; Asso. editor: Am. Polit. Sci. Rev, 1952-55; Contbr. articles to profl. jours. Mem. Am. Polit. Sci. Assn. (past v.p.). Died Dec. 14, 1995.

MCCANDLESS, J(ANE) BARDARAH, retired religion educator; b. Dayton, Ohio, Apr. 16, 1925; d. J(ohn) Bard and Sarah Catharine (Shuey) McC. BA, Oberlin Coll., 1951; MRE, Bibl. Sem., N.Y.C., 1953; PhD, U. Pitts., 1968. Dir. Christian edn. Wallace Meml. United Presbyn. Ch., Pitts., 1953-54, Beverly Heights United Presbyn. Ch., Mt. Lebanon, Pa., 1956-61; instr. religion Westminster Coll., New Wilmington, Pa., 1961-65, asst. prof., 1965-71, assoc. prof., 1971-83, prof. religion, 1983-94, prof. emeritus, 1994-97, chair dept. religion and philosophy, 1988-92; leader Christian edn. workshops Presbytery of Shenango, Presbyn. Ch. (U.S.A.), 1961-97, Synod of Trinity, 1972, 76. Author: An Untainted Saint...Ain't, 1978; contbr. articles to profl. jours., Harper's Ency. Religious Edn. Mem. session New Wilmington Presbyn. Ch., 1977-79. Mack grantee Westminster Coll., 1962-63, Faculty rsch. grantee, 1972, 78, 90. Mem. Religious Edn. Assn., Assn. Profs. and Researchers in Religious Edn. (mem. exec. com. 1978-80), Soc. for Sci. Study Religion, Phi Beta Kappa, Pi Lambda Theta. Deceased.

MCCANN, DAVID ANTHONY, publisher; b. N.Y.C., June 13, 1929; s. Patrick Joseph and Helen Clare (McCauley) McC.; m. Carol Louis Gerard, Oct. 8, 1960; children—Peter Gerard, Anthony David, Ellen Agusta. B.A., St. Johns Coll., 1950. Sales staff Comic Weekly, N.Y.C., 1951-60; sales staff Good Housekeeping Mag., N.Y.C., 1960-68, N.Y. mgr., 1968-69, Eastern mgr., 1969-71; v.p., pub. House Beautiful Mag., N.Y.C., 1971-76, Town and Country Mag., N.Y.C., 1977-83; v.p., pub. Connoisseur Mag., N.Y.C., 1983—. Democrat. Roman Catholic. Club: Lloyd Neck Bath (Lloyd Harbor, NY). Died Feb. 14, 1997.

MCCARTHY, MARGARET WILLIAM, music educator; b. Brockton, Mass., Nov. 20, 1931; d. William Francis and Julia Margaret (O'Brien) McC. MusB, Manhattanville Coll., Purchase, N.Y., 1953; MusM, Pius XII Inst., Florence, Italy, 1954; MusD, Boston U., 1965. Joined Sisters of St. Joseph of Boston, 1954. Music specialist St. Thomas Sch., Jamaica Plan, Mass., 1959-61; music prof. Regis Coll., Weston, Mass., 1961—; adv. bd. Sisters of St. Joseph Office of Peace & Justice, Brighton, Mass., 1987-89. Editor: More Letters of Amy Fay, 1986; contbr. articles to profl. jours. Active Weston (Mass.) Cultural Coun., 1989-93, Beyond War, Wellesley, Mass., 1990-92, Found. for a Global Community, 1992—. Radcliffe Rsch. Support grantee Radcliffe Coll., 1983, 87, Mass. Coun. on Arts and Humanities grantee, 1984, Travelto-Collection grantee NEH, 1987, Summer Seminar grantee, 1975. Mem. Sonneck Soc., Am. Musicological Soc., Internat. Soc. for Music Edn., Sigma Alpha Iota. Democrat. Roman Catholic. Avocations: reading, walking, museums, spectator sports. Died Dec. 6, 1996.

MC CARTY, RAYMOND M., lawyer, poet; b. Council Bluffs, Iowa, July 27, 1908; s. Cecil and Eva Frances (Wilson) M.; student S.W. Mo. State Tchrs. Coll., 1931-33; LL.B., So. Law U., Memphis, 1948, Memphis State U., 1967; m. Margaret Esther Burton, Mar. 23, 1942 (div. Mar. 31, 1995). Chief clk. State Social Security Commn., Springfield, Mo., 1937-39; admitted to Tenn. bar 1948; with U.S. Army C.E., Memphis, 1939-72, chief planning and control br. Real Estate div., 1953-72; pvt. practice law, Memphis, 1972-90 . Served with AUS, 1942-43. Recipient Countess d'Esternaux Gold medal award for poetry, 1950. Mem. Poetry Soc. Tenn. (hon. mem., organizer 1953, 1st pres., poet laureate 1977-78), World Poetry Soc. Intercontinental (Disting. citation for Poetry 1970, honoree Mid-South Poetry Festival 1983), Avalon World Arts Acad. (hon.), Ala. Writers Conclave, Nat. Fedn. State Poetry Socs., Acad. Am. Poets, Ala. State Poetry Soc., Am. Legion, Tenn. Bar Assn., Fed. Bar Assn. (sec. Memphis chpt. 1971-72), Nat. Assn. Ret. Fed. Employees. Baptist (deacon, chmn. deacons 1965-66). Author: Harp in a Strange Land, 1973; Trumpet in the Twilight of Time, 1981; The Wandering Jew, 1984; contbr. poems to profl. jours. and poetry mags.

MC CARTY, ROBERT LEE, lawyer; b. New London, Conn., Mar. 1, 1920; s. Robert Patrick and Lyda (Griser) McC.; m. Eileen Joan Noone, Sept. 1, 1945; children: Michael N., Patrick J., Charles Barry. B.S., Bowdoin Coll., 1941; LL.B., Yale U., 1948; LL.M., Georgetown U., 1953. Bar: D.C. 1948, U.S. Supreme Ct 1953, Va. 1976. Assoc. Northcutt Ely, 1948-54; mem. Ely, McCarty & Duncan, 1955-60; ptnr. McCarty and Wheatley, 1961-67, McCarty & Noone, 1968-80, McCarty, Noone & Williams, 1981-87, Heron, Burchette, Ruckert & Rothwell, Washington, 1987-90, Ritts Brickfield & Kaufman, Washington, 1990-92, Brickfield, Burchette & Ritts, Washington, 1993—; mem. Adminstrv. Conf. U.S., 1972-74; mem. edn. appeals bd. U.S. Dept. Edn., 1978-83. Contbr. chpts. to books. Pres. bd. dirs. Belle Haven Citizens Assn., 1959-60. Served with USAAF, 1942-46; Served with USAF, 1951-53; col. Res. Decorated D.F.C. (2), Air medal with 3 oak leaf clusters, Army Commendation medal. Fellow Am. Bar Found.; mem. ABA (chmn. sect. adminstrv. law 1966-67), (sect. del. to ho. dels. 1968-70), Fed. Bar Assn., D.C.Bar Assn., Va. Bar Assn. Roman Catholic. Clubs: University (Washington), Belle Haven Country (Va.). Died Nov. 18, 1997.

MCCLAFFERTY, JOHN JOSEPH, clergyman; b. N.Y.C., Apr. 9, 1906; s. John and Margaret (Moran) McC. AB, Cathedral Coll., 1927; grad., St. Joseph's Sem., 1930; AM, Cath. U. Am., 1932; diploma, N.Y. Sch. Social Work, 1936; LLD, Loyola U., L.A., 1947. Cert. social worker, N.Y. State. Ordained priest Roman Catholic Ch., 1930, apptd. papal chamberlain, 1943; apptd. Domestic Prelate, 1953, Protonotary Apostolic, 1965; asst. dir. div. social action Catholic Charities, N.Y.C., 1936-41; dir. div. social research Catholic Charities, 1941-47; Dean Nat. Cath. Sch. of Social Service, Catholic U. Am., 1947-55, asst. to rector for univ. devel., 1955-63; pastor St. Peter's Ch., S.I., 1963-66, St. Francis de Sales Ch., N.Y.C., 1966-81; pastor emeritus St. Francis de Sales Ch., 1981-95; chaplain Carmel Richmond Nursing Home, S.I., N.Y., 1982-95; Exec. sec. Nat. Legion Decency, 1936-47; mem. bd. consultors Ch. of the Air CBS, 1940-47; bd. advisors Radio Chapel MBS, 1941-47; bd. dirs. Casita Maria Settlement, 1941-47; com. discrimination N.Y. State War Council, 1942-44; Am. del. to Pan-Am. Congress, Caracas, Venezuela, 1948; del. 3d Congress of Inter-Am. Cath. Social Action Confederation, Rio de Janeiro, Brazil, 1948; Mem. Point Four Mission to Colombia, S.A., 1951. Editor: Cath. U. of Am. Bull, 1956-63. Mem. nat. exec. fact-finding coms. Mid-Century White House Conf. on Children and Youth, 1950; Del. White House Conf. Children and Youth, 1960. Served as capt. (chaplain) 5th regiment of N.Y. Guard, 1941-43; col. (chaplain) Hdgrs. N.Y. Guard, 1943-49. Recipient Univ. Pres.'s medal Cath. U. Am., 1988. Fellow Royal Soc. Health; mem. Nat. Assn. Social Workers, Acad. Cert. Social Workers. Home: Staten Island N.Y. Died July 31, 1995.

MC CLAIN, WILLIAM HAROLD, German language and literature educator; b. Cleve., July 22, 1917; s. William Harry and Helen (Newman) McC. A.B., Western Res. U., 1939; M.A., U. Wis., 1940, Ph.D., 1943. Vice consul Office U.S. Polit. Adviser, SHAEF, State Dept., 1945-46; instr., then asst. prof. German Harvard U., 1946-53; mem. faculty Johns Hopkins U., 1953—, prof. German, 1962—, chmn., 1972-83; emeritus prof., 1983—; prelaw advisor Johns Hopkins U., 1986—. Author: Wie sie es sehen, 1952, Deutsch, 1957, Between Real and Ideal, 1963, Karl Gutzkows Briefe an Costenoble, 1971, Traditions and Transitions, 1972, Friedrich Gerstäckers Briefe an Costenoble, 1974, Friedrich von Bodenstedts Briefe an Hermann Costenoble, 1977, L. Mühlbachs Briefe an Costenoble, 1981; also articles; editor: Modern Lang. Notes, 1953—, gen. editor, 1981—. Trustee Julius Hofmann Fund, 1958—. Fulbright rep., 1965; recipient Lindback award for disting. teaching Johns Hopkins U., 1962, Heritage award, 1981, Disting. Alumni citation Western Res. U., 1968; Recipient spl. teaching award Johns Hopkins U. Class of '82, 1982. Mem. AAUP, MLA, Goethe Soc. Md. (pres. 1954-56), Am. Assn. Tchrs. German (pres. Md. 1956-58), Humanities Research Assn., German Soc., Kafka Soc., Soc. for History of Germans in Md. (chmn. editorial com. 1989—), Phi Beta Kappa (pres. Alpha chpt. 1978-79, del. 1984—), Delta Phi Alpha.

MC CLELLAND, JAMES CRAIG, lawyer; b. New Alexandria, Pa., Sept. 8, 1901; s. James Craig and Cora Blanche (Barnhart) McC.; m. Eleanor May Hamilton, June 15, 1929 (dec. July 1964); children—Louise (Mrs. Gerhard Urban), James Craig, Jr.; m. Marjorie Brown Hilkert, Mar. 29, 1969. B.A., Coll. Wooster, 1923; LL.B., Western Res. U., 1926. Bar: Ohio bar 1926. Pvt. practice Cleve., 1926-96; mem. firm Boer, Mierke, McClelland & Caldwell (and predecessor firms), 1926-82; of counsel Wilson Caldwell, 1982-96. Counsel Berea City Sch. Dist., Southwest Gen. Hosp. Mem. ABA, Ohio Bar Assn. (past mem. council of dels.), Cleve. Bar Assn. (past mem. exec. com.), Order of the Coif, Delta Sigma Rho. Home: Chagrin Falls Ohio Died May 9, 1996.

MCCLINTON, OBIE BURNETT, country western musician; b. Senotobia, Miss., May 28, 1942; m. Jo Ann; 1 child, Drexel. Grad., Rust Coll., 1966. Songs include: Don't Let the Green Grass Fool You, My Whole World is Falling Down, 1972, Something Better, 1974, Honky Tonk Tan; albums include: Country, Obie from Senatobie, Live at Randy's Rodeo. Served with USAF. Deceased.

MC CLOSKEY, ROBERT JAMES, former diplomat; b. Phila., Nov. 25, 1922; s. Thomas and Anna (Wallace) McC.; m. Anne Taylor Phelan, July 8, 1961; children: Lisa Siobhan, André Taylor McCloskey. B.S. in Journalism, Temple U., 1953; postgrad., George Washington U., 1958-59. Engaged in hotel work, 1945-50, newspaper reporter, 1952-55; joined U.S. Fgn. Svc., 1955; assigned Hong Kong, 1955-57; publs. officer State Dept., 1957-58; press officer Office of News, 1958-60; assigned U.S. Mission to UN 15th Gen. Assembly, 1960-62; spl. asst. Bur. Pub. Affairs, State Dept., 1962-63; dep. dir. Office News, 1963-64, dir., 1964-66, dep. asst. sec. of state, 1966-69; dep. asst. sec., spl. asst. to sec. for press rels. Office Press Rels., 1969-73; amb. to Republic of Cyprus, 1973-74; amb.-at-large U.S. State Dept., 1974-75, amb.-at-large, asst. sec. state for congl. rels., 1975-76; amb. to The Netherlands, 1976-78, amb. to Greece, 1978-81; ombudsman Washington Post, 1981-83; sr. v.p. Cath. Relief Svcs., Washington, 1984-89; editor Mediterranean Quar., Washington, 1988-90; bd. dirs. Anatoia Coll., Boston, 1981-96. Bd. dirs. Am. Acad. Diplomacy. Staff sgt. USMC, 1942-45. Home: Chevy Chase Md. Died Nov. 28, 1996; buried Arlington National Cemetery.

MCCLURE, DOUG (DOUGLAS OSBORNE MCCLURE), actor; b. Glendale, Calif., May 11, 1935; s. Donald Reed and Clara (Barker) McC.; m. Faye Parker; children: Tane Mae, Valerie Diane; m. Diane Furnberg, Aug. 27, 1979. Student, Santa Monica City Coll., 1954-56, UCLA, 1956-57. Actor: (films) The Enemy Below, The Unforgiven, Because They're Young, Gidget, The Lively Set, Shenandoah, Beau Geste, Nobody's Perfect, The Longest Hundred Miles, King's Pirate, The Land That Time Forgot, What Changed Charlie Farthing, At The Earth's Core, The People That Time Forgot, Warlords of Atlantis, Strange Companion, Humanoids from the Deep, The House Where Evil Dwells, Cannonball II, 52 Pick Up, Omega Syndrome, Tape Heads, (TV series) Men of Annapolis, (TV movies) The Death of Me Yet, Terror in the Sky, Satan's Triangle, Shirts/Skins, Death Race, The Judge and Jake Wyler, Playmates, Birdmen of Beckstad, Death Flight of the Maiden, Wild and Woolly, (TV miniseries) Roots, The Rebels, (plays) The Roast , Come Blow Your Horn, A Thousand Clowns, Boeing-Boeing, Lone Star; star: (TV series) Overland Trail, Checkmate, The Virginian, The Men from Shiloh, Search, The Barbary Coast, Out of This World, 1987-95; guest appearances on TV shows include Fantasy Island, Manimal, Automan, Scarecrow and Mrs. King, Hardcastle & McCormick, The Master, Too Close for Comfort, Simon & Simon, Cover Up, Half Nelson, Family Theatre, The Fall Guy, Magnum P.I., Airwolf, Crazy Like a Fox, Murder She Wrote, Alfred Hitchcock, B.L. Stryker, Zorro, Evening Shade. Matlock; (TV movie of the Week) Battling for Babies. Winner Ben Johnson Pro Celebrity Team Roping Competition, 1986. Avocations: rodeo, tennis, golf, swimming, painting Western theme watercolors. Home: Sherman Oaks Calif. Died Feb. 5, 1995.

MCCOMBS, ROLLIN KOENIG, radiation oncologist; b. Denver, Aug. 17, 1919; s. Curtis and Emma Elizabeth (Koenig) McC.; m. Judy Louise Bacon, Sept. 20, 1952; children: David, Daniel, Susan, Kathleen, Michael. BA in Chemistry, U. Colo., 1941, MA in Physics, 1944; MD, Stanford U., 1954. Diplomate Am. Bd. Radiology, Am. Bd. Nuclear Medicine. Research fellow, assoc. physician Donner Lab. Med. Physics, Berkeley, Calif., 1954-57; resident VA Hosp., Long Beach, Calif., 1957-67, staff; dir. radiation oncology Long Beach Community Hosp., 1967-86; instr. physics U. Colo., Boulder, 1942-48; asst. clin. prof. radiology U. So. Calif. Sch. Medicine, Los Angeles, 1978-84, assoc. clin. prof. radiology, 1984-88. Contbr. articles to profl. jours. Recipient Chmn's. award U. So. Calif. Sch. Medicine, 1983. Mem. Am. Coll. Radiology, Am. Assn. Physicists in Medicine, Sigma Xi, Phi Beta Kappa. Democrat. Presbyterian. Avocations: electronics, model railroading, target and trap shooting.

MCCONNELL, FLORENCE LEONARD, court administration professional; b. Callaway, Va., Mar. 19, 1931; d. William Marshall and Fannie Lera (Prillaman) Mullins; m. Robert W. Leonard, June 24, 1950 (div. 1983); children: Susan Gail Leonard Little, William Ralph, Molly Marie; m. Edward B. McConnell, Oct. 21, 1984; stepchildren: Annalee, Edward B. Jr., Marilyn, Barbara, William. Grad. high sch., Newport News, Va. Sec. guidance office Williamsburg (Va.)/James City County Schs., 1975-77; exec. sec. to exec. dir. Nat. Ctr. State Cts., Williamsburg, 1977-79, adminstrv. asst. to exec. dir., 1979-88, asst. to pres., 1988-90, sec., bd. dirs., 1980-90; ret., 1990. Past bd. dirs., exec. com. Newport News Operatic Soc., Wednesday Morning Music Club. Mem. Kingsmill Women's Social Club, Kingsmill Book Club. Presbyterian. Home: Williamsburg Va. Died May 1991.

MC CONNELL, JOHN WILKINSON, labor relations educator, labor arbitrator, former socio-economics educator; b. Phila, Oct. 18, 1907; s. John and Lucy (Wilkinson) McC.; m. Harriet Hawley Barlow, July 29, 1933; children: Janet (Mrs. John Alexander), Kathleen (Mrs. David Mervin), Grace (Mrs. Alfred Clark), Judith Ann (Mrs. Henry Sondheimer), John C. B.A., Dickinson Coll., 1929, D.Sc., 1959; Ph.D., Yale U., 1937; LL.D., U. R.I., 1967, Ricker Coll., 1968, U. N.H., 1971. Instr. Am. U. at Cairo, 1929- 32; instr. Yale U., 1935; research asso. Inst. Human Relations, 1934-37; asst. prof. econs. and sociology Am. U., Washington, 1937-39; prof. sociology N.Y. U., 1939-46; prof. indsl. and labor relations Cornell U., 1946-63, dean grad. sch., 1955-59, dean sch. indsl. and labor relations, 1959-63; dir. research in indsl. retirement, 1959-97; pres. U. N.H., 1963-71; counselor to coll. Ithaca (N.Y.) Coll., 1971-75, lectr., 1975; adj. prof. labor econs. Cornell U., 1971-97 ; dir. research Twentieth Century Fund, 1951-54; Fulbright lectr. in, India, 1953-54; Pub. mem. region II Nat. War Labor Bd., 1943-46, Nat. WSB, 1950-52; mem. Fgn. Service Grievance Bd., Dept. State, 1974-82; cons. pension and retirement systems, mem. human resources research adv. bd. USAF, 1948-53, Social Security Adminstrn.; mem. adv. council Nat. Inst. Child Health and Human Devel., NIH, 1965-69; mem. labor arbitration panel N.Y. State Mediation Service; mem. Fed. Mediation and Conciliation Service; pub. mem. minimum wage bd., P.R., 1956-97, chmn., 1960, 1968; chmn. study group on edn. of fgn. students Land-Grant Coll. Assn., 1961. Author: Evolution of Social Classes, 1942, Basic Teachings of Great Economists, 1943, (with Robert Risley) Economic Security, 1951, (with others) America's Needs and Resources, 1955, (with John Corson) Economic Needs of Older People, 1955, Ideas of the Great Economists, 1980; contbr. articles to profl. jours. Pres. bd. dirs. Tompkins Community Hosp., 1984-86, v.p., 1986-94. Recipient Outstanding Svc. medal Army Dept., 1967, with oak leaf cluster, 1971, Alumni award of Petee medal U. N.H., 1995; named to Hall of Fame, U. N.H., 1989. Mem. Nat. Acad. Arbitrators, Am. Arbitration Assn., Indsl. Relations Research Assn. (dir. 1951-54), Phi Beta Kappa, Phi Kappa Phi, Omicron Delta Kappa, Pi Gamma Mu. Methodist. Home: Trumansburg N.Y. Died Feb. 19, 1997; buried Grove Cemetery, Johannesburg, N.Y.

MCCONNELL, JOSEPH H., television executive; b. Chester, S.C.; m. Elizabeth Bernard; children: Elizabeth Eells, Ted M. Lowance, Catherine Russell.. Grad., Davidson Coll., 1927; JD, Va. Law Sch., 1931. Pres. NBC, 1949-52, Colgate-Palmolive Co., 1953-55, Reynolds, 1963-71; chmn. Comm. Satellite Corp., 1970-79. Home: Atlanta Ga. Died 1997.

MCCORD, DAVID (THOMPSON WATSON), writer; b. N.Y.C., Nov. 15, 1897; s. Joseph Alexander and Eleanore Baynton (Reed) McC. AB, Harvard U., 1921, AM, 1922, LHD (hon.), 1956; LittD (hon.), Northeastern U., 1954, U. N.B., Can., 1963, Williams Coll., 1971, Keene State Coll., 1983, Skidmore Coll., 1986; LLD (hon.), Washington and Jefferson Coll., 1955; LHD (hon.), Colby Coll., 1968, Framingham State Coll., 1975, Fitchburg State Coll., 1986; D of Art, New Eng. Coll., 1956; EdD, Suffolk U., 1979; DCL, Simmons Coll., 1983. Mem. drama staff Boston Evening Transcript, 1923-28; editor alumni bull. Harvard U., Cambridge, Mass., 1940-46, instr. advanced writing courses, summers 1963, 65-66, hon. curator Poetry Room and Farnsworth Room, Harvard Coll. Library, hon. assoc. Dudley House; mem. com. on Dictionary Am. Biography, Am. Council Learned Socs.; 3 time judge Shelley award; lectr. Lowell Inst., 1950; staff mem. Bread Loaf Writers' Conf., 1958, 60, 62, 64; vis. prof. Framingham State Coll., 1974. Several one-man water color shows. Author: Oddly Enough, 1926, Floodgate, 1927, Stirabout, 1928, Oxford Nearly Visited, 1929, The Crows, 1934, Bay Window Ballads (illustrated by John Lavalle), 1935, H.T.P.-Portrait of a Critic, 1935, Notes on the Harvard Tercentenary, 1936, An Acre for Education, 1938, Twelve Verses from XII Night, 1938, And What's More, 1941, On Occasion, 1943, About Boston, 1948, A Star by Day, 1950, Poet Always Next But One, 1951, The Camp at Lockjaw (illustrated by Gluyas Williams), 1952, Far and Few; poems for children, illustrated by Henry B. Kane, 1952, The Old Bateau, 1953, As Built With Second Thoughts, 1953, Odds Without Ends, 1954, The Language of Request, 1961, Take Sky, 1962, The Fabrick of Man, 1963, In Sight of Sever; Harvard essays, 1963, Sonnets to Baedeker, 1963, All Day Long, 1966, Every Time I Climb a Tree (illustrated by Marc Simont), 1967, Notes from Four Cities, 1969, Poem for the Occasion, 1970, For Me to Say, 1970, Pen, Paper and Poem, 1971, Mr. Bidery's Spidery Garden, 1972, Away and Ago, 1974, The Star in the Pail (illustrated by Marc Simont), 1975, One At A Time, 1977, Speak Up, 1980, All Small, 1986. Editor: Once and For All, 1929, What Cheer, 1945, Arthur Griffin's New England Revisited, 1967, Stow Wengenroth's New England, 1969; Mem. usage panel: Am. Heritage Dictionary; Contbr. to mags., encys. Exec. dir. Harvard U. Fund Council, 1925-63; hon. trustee Boston Ctr. for Adult Edn., Boston Athenaeum, New Eng. Wildflower Soc., Peter Bent Brigham Hosp., Boston; trustee Charity of Edward Hopkins; trustee emeritus New Eng. Coll.; overseer Old Sturbridge Village, Mass., Perkins Inst. for Blind; bd. dirs. Assoc. Harvard Alumni, 1965-68; councilor Harvard Soc. Advanced Study and Research, 1967-72; mem. overseers vis. com. dept. astronomy Harvard U. Served with F.A. U.S. Army, 1918. Recipient Golden Rose, New Eng. Poetry Club 1941, William Rose Benet award 1952, Sarah Josepha Hale medal 1962, Nat. Inst. Arts and Letters grantee, 1961, 1st nat. award for excellence in poetry for children Nat. Council Tchrs. English 1977, Alumni medal Harvard U., 1984; Nat. Book Award nominee (2); Guggenheim fellow, 1954; Kipling fellow Marlboro Coll.; Benjamin Franklin fellow Royal Soc. Arts, London; Littauer Found. grantee, 1981. Fellow Am. Acad. Arts and Scis.; mem. Colonial Soc. Mass., Soc. of Cin. (N.H.), Internat. P.E.N., Am. Alumni Council, Mass. Hist. Soc., Phi Beta Kappa (poet Harvard 1938, Tufts 1938, 78, Coll. William and Mary 1950, M.I.T. 1973, Colby Coll. 1979). Republican. Episcopalian. Clubs: Harvard (Boston), St. Botolph (Boston) (past pres.), Tavern (Boston) (past pres.), of Odd Volumes (Boston); Faculty; Signet (Cambridge); Century (N.Y.C.). Home: Boston Mass. Deceased.

MC CORMICK, HOPE BALDWIN (MRS. BROOKS MCCORMICK), former political party executive; b. N.Y.C., July 9, 1919; d. Alexander Taylor and Loise (Bisbee) Baldwin; m. Brooks McCormick, June 26, 1940; children: Martha McCormick Hunt (dec.), Brooks II, Mark B., Abby D. McCormick O'Neil. Student, Ethel Walker Sch., Simsbury, Conn. Mem. Ill. Ho. of Reps., 1965-67. Past mem. women's bd. Children's Meml. Hosp.; bd. dirs. Lyric Opera, 1979-93, mem. women's bd., 1978-93; founder, past pres. Ill. Epilepsy League; mem. women's bd. Rush-Presbyn.-St. Luke's Hosp., Art Inst. Chgo., Field Mus. Natural History, U. Chgo.; Past chmn. women's div. United Republican Fund, 1957-61, bd. govs., 1957-65; pres. Rep. Citizens Com. of 9th Congl. Dist., 1961-66; mem. Rep. Nat. Com. from Ill., 1964-72, vice chmn., 1972; Past bd. dirs. Chgo. Pub. Sch. Art Soc.; past trustee Chgo. Latin Sch.; trustee Chgo. Hist. Soc., Ill. Children's Home and Aid Soc., Mus. Sci. and Industry, Chgo. Symphony Orch.; past bd. dirs. Lincoln Park Zool. Soc. Republican. Home: Chicago Ill. Died 1993.

MC CORMICK, KENNETH DALE, retired editor; b. Madison, N.J., Feb. 25, 1906; s. John Dale and Ida Pearl (Wenger) McC.; children: Dale, Kevin; m. Anne Hutchens, 1968; 1 son, John Bradley. A.B., Willamette U., 1928. With Doubleday and Co., Inc., 1930-92, successively clk., mgr., bookshop, promotion mgr. pub. house, reader in editorial dept., chief asso. editor, 1938, editor in chief, 1942-71, v.p., 1948-71, sr. cons. editor, 1971-92; lectr. on books. Contbr. to Publishers' Weekly. Democrat. Conglist. Clubs: Century Assn, Coffee House, Dutch Treat. Died June 27, 1997.

MC COY, SETH, tenor; b. Sanford, N.C., 1928; m. Jane Gunter. Grad., N.C. Agrl. and Tech. Coll., 1950; student, Pauline Thesmacher at Music Sch. Settlement, Cleve., Antonia Lavanne, N.Y.C. Soloist with Robert Shaw Chorale, 1963-65, Bach Aria Group, 1973-80, N.Y. Philharm., Boston Symphony, Phila. Orch., Chgo. Symphony, Cleve. Symphony, Pitts. Symphony, San Francisco Symphony, Los Angeles Philharm., Nat. Symphony of Washington, others; mem. Bach Aria Group, 1973—; prof. voice Eastman Sch. Music, Rochester, N.Y., 1982—; appearances at Carmel (Calif.) Bach Festival, Ravinia Festival, Blossom Music Festival, Cleve., Berkshire Festival, Radio and TV Orch. of Madrid, Hamburg (Fed. Republic of Germany) Philharm., P.R. Symphony Orch., others; European debut at Aldeburgh Festival, 1978; recs. for RCA and Vanguard, CRI, Am. Bicentennial Collection, including Brahms' Liebeslieder Walzer, Rachmaninoff—Monna Vanna, 1991; Met. opera debut as Tamino in The Magic Flute, 1979, Am. premiere Krzysztof Penderecki's Utrenja with Phila. Orch., world premiere Scott Joplin's Treemonisha with Atlanta Symphony, Am. premiere A Steffani's Tassilone, N.Y.C. Served with inf. U.S. Army, Korea. Recipient Albert Schweitzer medal for artistry, 1988. Died Jan. 22, 1997.

MCCULLOUGH, DAVID L., urologist; b. Chattanooga, 1938. MD, Bowman Gray, 1964. Intern U. Hosps. Case Western Reserve U., Cleve., 1964-65, resident in surgery, 1965-66; fellow urology Baylor U. Coll. Medicine, Houston, 1968-69; resident in urology Mass. Gen. Hosp., Boston, 1969-72; chief urologist N.C. Bapt. Hosp., Winston-Salem, 1983—; prof., chmn. urology Bowman Gray, Winston-Salem; past pres. Am. Bd. Urology. Mem. ACS, AMA, Am. Urol. Assn. (pres.-elect southeastern sect.), Am. Assn. Genitourinary Surgeons (sec.-treas.), Clin. Soc. Urol. Surgeons.

MCCUNE, SHANNON, geographer, emeritus educator; b. Sonchon, Korea, Apr. 6, 1913; s. George Shannon and Helen (McAfee) McC.; m. Edith Blair, June 30, 1936; children: Antoinette McCune Bement, Shannon McCune Wagner, George Blair. B.A., Coll. of Wooster, 1935; M.A., Syracuse U., 1937; Ph.D., Clark U., 1939, LL.D., 1960; LL.D., U. Mass., 1962, Eastern Nazarene Coll., 1966. Instr., asst. prof. Ohio State U., Columbus, 1939-47; econ. intelligence officer Bd. Econ. Warfare-Fgn. Econ. Adminstrn., 1942-45; asst. prof. to prof. Colgate U., Hamilton, N.Y., 1947-55; provost U. Mass., Amherst, 1955-61; dir. Dept. Edn., UNESCO, Paris, 1961-62; civil adminstr. Ryukyu Islands, 1962-64; staff asso. Office of Pres., U. Ill., Urbana, 1964-65; pres. U. Vt., Burlington, 1965-66; research prof. U. Vt., 1966-67; dir. Am. Geog. Soc., 1967-69; prof. geography U. Fla., Gainesville, 1969-79; prof. emeritus U. Fla., 1979-93. Author: Korea's Heritage, A Regional and Social Geography, 1955, Korea: Land of Broken Calm, 1965, The Ryukyu Islands, 1975, Views of the Geography of Korea, 1935-60, 1980, Islands in Conflict in East Asian Waters, 1984, Intelligence on the Economic Collapse of Japan in 1945, 1989. Recipient medal of freedom; U.S. Presidential award, 1946; Pandit Madan Mahan Malaviya medal Nat. Geog. Soc. India, 1950; Founder's award Hampshire Coll., 1970; Disting. Alumni award Coll. of Wooster, 1976; Korea-U.S.A. Centennial award, 1982; decorated Order of Culture Eun-Gwan (Republic of Korea), 1985. Mem. Assn. Am. Geographers (v.p. honors award), Phi Beta Kappa, Sigma Xi, Phi Kappa Phi. Mem. United Ch. of Christ. Club: Masons. Died Jan. 1993.

MCCURDY, RICHARD CLARK, engineering consultant; b. Newton, Iowa, Jan. 2, 1909; s. Ralph Bruce and Florence (Clark) McC.; m. Harriet Edith Sutton, Sept. 11, 1933; children: Gregor, Richard, Carolyn, Robert. A.B., Stanford U., 1931, E.M., 1933. With engring. and prodn. div. Shell Oil Co., 1933-47; with prodn. mgmt. Shell Caribbean Petroleum Co., 1947-50; gen. mgr. Shell Group Companies, Venezuela, 1950-53; pres. Shell Chem. Co., N.Y.C., 1953-65; dir. Shell Oil Co., mem. exec. com., 1959-69, pres., chief exec. officer, 1965-69; assoc. adminstr. orgn. and mgmt. NASA, Washington, 1970-73; cons. NASA, 1974-82. Trustee United Seamans Service, 1954-70, Stanford U., 1965-70; trustee Hood Coll., 1968-86, trustee emeritus, 1986—, hon. trustee, 1987—; trustee Rensselaer Poly. Inst., 1974-86, hon. trustee, 1986—. Recipient Disting. Service medal NASA, 1972. Mem. Mfg. Chemists Assn. (dir. 1955-65, chmn. bd. 1961-62, chmn. exec. com. 1964-65), Am. Inst. Mining, Metall. and Petroleum Engrs., Am. Phys. Soc., Am. Petroleum Inst., N.Y. Yacht Club, Noroton (Conn.) Yacht Club (commodore), Cruising of Am. (commodore 1980-82), Beta Theta Pi. Home: Contentment Island Darien CT 06820

MCCUSKER, MARY LAURETTA, library science educator; b. Sillery, Que., Can., Jan. 18, 1919; came to U.S., 1938, naturalized, 1942; d. Albert James and Laura (Cleary) McC. B.A., Western Md. Coll., 1942; M.S.L.S., Columbia U., 1952, D.L.S., 1963. Joined Order of Preachers, Roman Catholic Ch., 1961; librarian Annapolis (Md.) High Sch., 1942-44, McDonogh Mil. Sch., 1944-47; asst. prof. Iowa State Tchrs. Coll. (now No. Iowa U.), Cedar Falls, 1948-59; vis. prof. library sci. U. Minn., Mpls., summers, 1958-59; assoc. prof. Sch. Library Sci. Rosary Coll., 1963-67, dir., prof. Grad. Sch., 1967-81, prof. emeritus, rsch. assoc., 1981-94, dean grad. sch., 1969-81, prof. emeritus, from 1994. Contbr. articles to profl. jours. Continuing Edn. grantee World Book Ency., 1994. Mem. ALA, Assn. Libr. and Info. Sci. Edn., Nat. Cath. Libr. Assn. (pres. No. Ill. chpt. 1987-89, chair acad. sect. No. Ill. chpt. 1992-97, v.p. pres.-elect 1995-97), Ill. Libr. Assn., Ill. Sch. Libr. Media Assn. (chair awards com. 1990-91, 94-95, co-chair cert. and stds. com. 1995-97), Chgo. Libr. Club, Sch. Libr. Assn. Died Feb. 24, 1997.

MCDANIEL, RAYMOND LAMAR, newspaper editor; b. Natalbany, La., Dec. 15, 1925; s. Franklin Pierce and Mattie (Stilley) McD.; m. Eugenia Hastings, Nov. 10, 1951; 1 son, Raymond Lamar. Student, Southeastern La. U., 1942-43; B.S., La. Tech. U., 1949. State editor Shreveport Times Pub. Co., La., 1950-53; legis. corr. Shreveport Times Pub. Co., 1953-58, city editor, 1958-68, exec. editor, 1968-74, editor, 1974-87. Chmn. bd. dirs. Bapt. Message; bd. dirs. Salvation Army. Served with USMCR, 1943-46. Mem. Sigma Delta Chi, Pi Kappa Alpha, Gamma Psi. Baptist (deacon, dir. ch.). Club: Rotary. Home: Shreveport La. Died Nov. 22, 1991.

MCDONALD, JAMES CHARLES, industrial engineer; b. Hannibal, Mo., Mar. 29, 1955; s. James Charles Pershing and Frances Lee (Dillender) McD.; m. Amy Elaine Saussele, May 21, 1977; children: Trevor Thomas, Graham Paul, Derek Lee. AA, Hannibal-La Grange Coll., 1975; BS in Indsl. Engring., U. Mo., 1977, MBA, 1984. Methods engr. McDonnell-Douglas, St. Louis, 1977-78; indsl. mfg. engr. Watlow Industries, Hannibal, Mo., 1978; mgr. Watlow Industries, Hannibal, 1986; pvt. practice cons. Hannibal; plant. supt. Watlow Industries, Hannibal, Mo., 1987-90, total quality and ops. support mgr., 1990-91; asst. prof. human resource mgmt. Quincy (Ill.) U., 1991—; bus. courses instr., Culver Stockton Coll., Canton, Mo. Bd. dirs. Data Processing Adv. Com. Hannibal, Mo. Hannibal Community Theatre (v.p. 1979). Mem. Inst. Indsl. Engrs., Am. Mgmt. Assn., Am. Soc. Quality Control, Beta Gamma Sigma. Avocations: hiking, photography, music.

MC DONALD, MARSHALL, holding company executive; b. Memphis, Mar. 30, 1918; s. Marshall and Nadine (Hardin) McD.; m. Florence Harris, Jan. 10, 1952 (dec. Nov. 1963); m. Lucille Smoak Collins, May 7, 1965 (dec. Sept. 1980); m. Barbara Hatcher Poole, Dec. 31, 1983; children: Mary Linda Caton, Charles M. Collins, Cynthia Langston, Marshall III, Roger Collins, Davis, James D. BS in Bus. Adminstrn, U. Fla., 1939, LLB, 1941; MBA, U. Pa., 1947. Bar: Fla. 1941, Tex. 1949; CPA, Tex. Acct. Houston, 1947-49, atty., 1950-52; treas. Gulf Canal Lines, 1953-54; pres. Investment Co. Houston, 1955-58; v.p. Sinclair Oil & Gas Co.,

Tulsa, 1959-61; v.p., gen. mgr. Oil Recovery Corp., Tulsa, 1962-63; asst. to pres. Pure Oil Co., Palatine, Ill., 1964-65; dir. affiliated cos. Union Oil Co., Los Angeles, 1966-68; pres. Sully-Miller Contracting Co., Los Angeles, 1968-71; pres., chief exec. officer Fla. Power & Light Co., Miami, 1971-79, chmn., chief exec. officer, 1979-83, chmn. bd., 1983-86; pres., chief exec. officer FPL Group, Inc. (parent co.), Juno Beach, Fla., 1984-88, chmn. bd. dirs., 1988-90; ret. FPL Group, Inc. (parent co.), Juno Beach, 1990. With AUS, 1941-46. Mem. Alpha Tau Omega. Democrat. Presbyterian. Lodge: Masons. DIED 06/07/97. .

MC DONNELL, JOHN THOMAS, energy consultant, former oil and gas company executive; b. Tulsa, Jan. 5, 1926; s. John Thomas and Louise (Gallo) McD.; m. Dorothy Henry, June 19, 1948; children—Kevin Robert, Lisa Anne McDonnell Raynolds. Student, Villanova U., 1943-44; B.S. in Chem. Engring, U. Okla., Norman, 1946. Vice pres. Iberian Gulf Oil Co., Madrid, 1967-69; pres. Iberian Gulf Oil Co., 1969-70, Warren Petroleum Co., Tulsa, 1970-75; v.p., exec. rep. Gulf Oil Exploration & Prodn. Co., Houston, 1976-83; energy cons. Houston, 1983-94. Bd. dirs. Houston Symphony; met. chmn. Nat. Alliance of Businessmen, 1976-77. Mem. Interstate Natural Gas Assn. Am., Mid-Continent Oil and Gas Assn., Am. Inst. Chem. Engrs., Natural Gas Supply Com., Am. Petroleum Inst. Republican. Episcopalian. Club: Lakeside Country (Houston). Deceased.

MC GARRAH, ROBERT EYNON, business administration educator; b. Scranton, Pa., July 16, 1921; s. Henry Stanley and Jane May (Eynon) McG.; m. Barbara Anne Moore, Oct. 20, 1943; children: Robert Eynon, Anne Louise, Douglas Moore. B.S., Lafayette Coll., 1943; M.S., Princeton, 1948; Ph.D., Cornell U., 1951. Instr. Princeton, 1946-48; from instr. to asso. prof. indsl. engring. Cornell U., 1948-58; asso. prof. bus. adminstrn. Harvard Grad. Sch. Bus. Adminstrs., 1958-63; prof. Imede Mgmt. Devel. Inst., U. Lausanne, Switzerland, 1963-65; asst. dir. def. research and engring., internat. programs Office Sec. of Def., 1966-68; v.p. Logistics Mgmt. Inst., 1965-66; dir. Center Bus. and Econ. Research, 1968-72; prof. mgmt. Sch. Bus. Adminstrn., U. Mass., Amherst, 1968-95; cons. in field, 1948-95; Faculty fellow U.S. Gen. Acctg. Office, Washington, 1974-75; expert in mgmt. edn. UN-Internat. Labor Orgn. Project on Mgmt. Devel., Nigeria, West Africa, 1978; cons. programs indsl. devel. State of Mass., 1983-85. Author: Production and Logistics Management, 1963, Four Volume Production Casebook Series, 1964, Productivity Management, 1982, Defense-industrial Policies, 1982, Manufacturing for the Security of the United States, 1990; also papers. Trustee Moses Brown Preparatory Sch. Served with USNR, 1943-46, 51-53; mem. Am. com. on U.S.-Soviet Relations, 1983-95. Fellow New Eng. Bd. Higher Edn., 1974-78, 80. Mem. Inst. Mgmt. Scis., AAUP, Am. Inst. Indsl. Engrs., Phi Kappa Phi. Home: Amherst Mass. Died July 8, 1995.

MCGARRY, EUGENE L., university official; b. West Chicago, Ill., June 9, 1930; s. Joseph C. and Rose (Gorgal) McG.; m. Jetta F. Grubbs, June 11, 1955; 1 son, Michael. B.A., Cornell Coll., 1952; M.A., Northwestern U., 1956; Ph.D., U. Iowa, 1961. Asst. prof. social scis. U. Minn., Mpls., 1960-62; asst. prof., advisement coordinator, asso. prof. and asso. dean edn., prof. and dean edn. Calif. State U., Fullerton, 1962-71; asso. v.p. acad. adminstrn. Calif. State U., 1971-77, dir. Univ. Learning Ctr., 1977-92, chmn. tchr. edn., 1983-84; ret., 1992. Served with AUS, 1952-54. Died Aug. 7, 1996.

MCGINTY, JOHN, marketing consultant; b. Neosho, Mo., Dec. 5, 1911; s. Abner Crawford and Blanche (Hale) McG.; m. Glenella Florence Davison, July 15, 1934; children: Marilyn McGinty Stewart, Marjorie McGinty Kilpatrick, Maureen, John Edward, Melanie McGinty Tate, Melinda. BCS, Drake U., 1932; LLB, City Coll. Law, St. Louis, 1936; DHL (hon.), Drury Coll., 1988. Bar: Mo. 1936. Mgr. closing div. Fed. Land Bank of St. Louis, 1933-44; with Ralston Purina Co., St. Louis, 1944-73; editor sales publs., mgr. publs., sales promotion mgr. Ralston Purina Co., 1944-59, v.p. and dir. sales promotion, 1959-63, v.p., dir. advt. and sales promotion, 1963-69, v.p., dir. mktg. services, 1969-73; meeting cons. for firms including Ralston Purina, DeLaval Separator Co., Monsanto Co., Babcock Industries Inc., Mktg. Intercontinental, Hudson Foods, Inc., 1973-96; chmn. bd. Christian Bd. Publs., St. Louis, 1955-89. Author: How to Raise the Level of Giving in Your Church, 1978. Trustee Disciples Div. House, U. Chgo., Drake U., 1966-74; chmn. bd. trustees Drury Coll., 1970-73, life trustee. Home: Saint Louis Mo. Died June 3, 1996.

MCGOWIN, NICHOLAS STALLWORTH, lawyer; b. Chapman, Ala., May 17, 1912; s. James Greeley and Essie (Stallworth) McG.; m. Elizabeth Brittain Smith, Apr. 21, 1945; children: Nicholas Stallworth (dec.), Peter H., Elizabeth. A.B., U. Ala., 1933; postgrad., Pembroke Coll., Oxford U., Eng., 1933-34; LL.B., Harvard, 1937. Bar: Ala. bar 1937, Pa. bar 1939. Practice in Greenville, Ala., 1937-39, Phila., 1939-41, Washington, 1941-42, Mobile, Ala., 1946-95; asso. Drinker, Biddle & Reath, 1939-41; mem. legal staff Brit. Purchasing Commn., 1941-42; mem. firm Thornton & McGowin, 1956-91; Chmn. Ala. Fulbright Scholarship Com., 1951-72. Pres. Mobile Symphony, 1956-58; chmn. bd. trustees Lyman Ward Mil. Acad., Mobile Public Library, 1969-70. Served to lt. comdr. USNR, 1942-45, PTO. Decorated Order of Vasa Sweden, Order of North Star. Mem. ABA, Ala. Bar Assn. (chmn. real property, probate and trust sect. 1970-71), Mobile Bar Assn. (pres. 1974), Phi Beta Kappa, Delta Kappa Epsilon. Clubs: Country (Mobile), Athelstan (Mobile); Boston (New Orleans). Home: Mobile Ala. Died May 19, 1995.

MCGUIRE, DELBERT, journalism educator; b. Altus, Okla., Aug. 24, 1917; s. Clinton F. and Ella (Stevens) McG.; m. Virginia Wright, Feb. 6, 1942; 1 son, Delbert Allen. B.J., U. Tex., 1947, M.J., 1948; Ph.D., U. Ia., 1966. Reporter, sub-editor Austin Am.-Statesman, 1945-47; editor So. Florist and Nurseryman, Ft. Worth, 1948-50, Automatic World, Ft. Worth, 1948-52; assoc. prof. journalism N. Tex. State U., 1950-61; prof., head journalism dept. Tex. A.&M. U., 1961-67; vis. prof. journalism U. N.C., 1967-68; prof., chmn. tech. journalism Colo. State U., Ft. Collins, 1968-93. Author: Technical and Industrial Journalism, 1957; editorial cons., 1974-93; contbr. articles to profl. jours. Pres. Found. on Aging, Larimer County, Colo., 1987-93. Served with USAAF, 1942-45. Mem. Am. Council for Edn. in Journalism, Am. Soc. Journalism Sch. Adminstrs. (chmn. newspaper div. 1970-71, pres.-elect 1971-72), A.P. Mng. Editors, Sigma Delta, Chi. Deceased April 11, 1993.

MC HENDRIE, DOUGLAS, lawyer; b. Trinidad, Colo., Mar. 9, 1906; s. Andrew Watson and Frances East (Hamilton) McH.; m. Frances Reed Scott, Aug. 31, 1940; children: Margret Hamilton, Andrew Graig. A.B., Colo. Coll., 1927; postgrad., Harvard Law Sch., 1927-28; B.A. (Rhodes scholar Colo.), Oxford U., 1930, B.C.L., 1931. Bar: Colo. 1932. With McHendrie & Shattuck, Trinidad, 1932-35; with firms Grant, Ellis, Shafroth & Toll (and successor firms), Denver, 1935—; now of counsel Grant, McHendrie, Haines & Crouse; Mem. Colo. Bd. Bar Examiners, 1948-57, chmn., 1957-68; pres. Denver Library Commn., 1961-64. Trustee Colo. Coll., 1964-70, 72-84; trustee Colo. Acad., 1964-69, also past pres. Served to capt. USAAF, 1942-44; capt. OSS AUS, 1944-46. Fellow Am. Bar Found.; mem. ABA, Colo. Bar Assn. (pres. 1958-59), Am. Judicature Soc., Phi Beta Kappa, Phi Gamma Delta. Clubs: University (Denver), Mile High (Denver), City (Denver). Office: One United Bank Center Denver CO 80203 DIED 04/29/97. .

MCILHONE, JOHN THOMAS, educational administrator; b. Montreal, Que., Can., Jan. 26, 1911; s. Robert Emmett and Ellen Eva (O'Rourke) McI.; B.A., Loyola Coll., Montreal, 1933; M.A., U. Montreal, 1939, B.Ed., 1940, Ph.D., 1942; m. Dorothy Agnes Quinn, June 20, 1942; children: Anne Marie (Mrs. R. Marc Huberdeau), Quinn. Prof. edn. St. Joseph's Coll., Montreal, 1939-40, 45-48; lectr. Marian Polis Coll., 1948-61; dir. English schs. Montreal Cath. Sch. Bd., 1948-69, dep. dir. gen., 1967-73; dir. gen. Mt. St. Patrick Corp., Montreal, 1973-93. Ednl. cons. Montreal Cath. Sch. Commn., 197393; mem. Royal Commn. Enquiry into Edn., 1961-66; co-founder, tenured prof. Thomas More Inst., 1946-62. Active charity campaigns; trustee Loyola Coll., Concordia U.; bd. dirs. Canadian Cath. Trustees; bd. dirs. Mt. St. Patrick Inc., pres., 1985. Served to comdr. RCAF, 1940-45. Decorated comdr. Cross of Merit, Order of Malta. Recipient Coronation medal Govt. Can., 1952, Centennial medal, 1967; named comdr. Order of Sch. Merit, Que. Province, 1956. Mem. Can. (life), Nat. Cath. edn. assns., Can. Coll. Tchrs. (Ignace Bourget award 1992), Phi Delta Kappa. Club: Mount Stephen (Montreal). Contbr. articles to profl. jours. Died May 1993. Home: Westmount Can.

MCILWAINE, DEBORAH, state legislator; b. Bronxville, N.Y., Nov. 26, 1923; m. John C. McIlwaine; 4 children. BA, Smith Coll., 1944; MA, Middlebury Coll., Vt., 1973; MEd, U. Bridgeport, 1978; MSW, Fordham U., 1982. Ret. social worker, 1986; mem. N.H. Ho. Reps, mem. children, youth and juvenile justice com.; mediator Youth and Family Mediation; bd. dirs. Burch House. Del. No. County Coun. Mem. Nat. Assn. Social. Workers, Soc. Am. Friends (facilitator alternatives to violence workshops). Democrat. Avocations: music, hiking, skiing, yoga, swimming. DIED 07/01/96. .

MCKEE, PENELOPE MELNA, library director; b. New Liskeard, Ont., Can., Dec. 31, 1938; d. Melvin Hugh and Violet Mary (Hooton) Olimer; m. Arthur Donald McKee, Mar. 5, 1960 (div. 1985); children: Suzanne, Carolyn, Stephen. BA with honors, U. Toronto, Can., 1960, BLS, 1961, MLS, 1980; diploma, Coll. Applied Arts and Tech., 1976. Cert. mcpl. mgr., Ont. Mcpl. Mgmt. Devel. Bd. Fine arts libr. North York Pub. Libr., Ont., Can., 1961-63, reference libr., 1969-74; reference libr. Toronto Montessori Schs., Thornhill, Ont., 1974-76; cons. Grolier Pub., Toronto, 1976; libr. supr. Toronto Pub. Libr., 1977-80; dir. Aurora Pub. Libr., Ont., Can., 1980-86, Peterborough Pub. Libr., Ont., Can., 1986-90, Edmonton Pub. Libr., Alta., Can., 1990—; adj. assoc. prof. U. Alta., Edmonton, 1992—; cons. Edmonton Cath. Sch. Bd., 1992. Contbr. articles to profl. jours. Vice chmn. Project Hostel, Aurora, 1986-89; bd. dirs. Friends of Trent Severn Waterway, Peterborough, 1990; active Edmonton Centennial Celebrations Com., 1992. Russell scholar U. Toronto, 1956. Mem. Canadian Libr. Assn., Ontario Libr. Assn. (pres.), Libr. Assn. Alta., Alta. Pub. Libr. Dirs. Coun. (chair), Rotary Club of Downtown Edmonton (pub. rels. chmn. IVT Woman of Vision 1995, ABI Woman of Yr. 1995). Avocations: reading, music, curling, canoeing. Died May, 1997.

MC KELVEY, JEAN TREPP, industrial relations educator; b. St. Louis, Feb. 9, 1908; d. Samuel and Blanche (Goodman) Trepp; m. Blake McKelvey, June 29, 1934. AB, Wellesley Coll., 1929; MA, Radcliffe Coll., 1931, PhD, 1933. Mem. faculty Sarah Lawrence Coll., 1932-45, N.Y. State Sch. Indsl. and Labor Rels., Cornell U., Ithaca, N.Y., 1946—; from asst. prof. to assoc. prof. indsl. rels. N.Y. State Sch. Indsl. and Labor Rels., Cornell U., 1946-49, prof., 1949—; vis. prof. Sch. Law Cornell U., 1977-78; mem. pub. panel, hearing officer, arbitrator Nat. War Labor Bd., 1944-45; mem. inquiry into Rochester Transit dispute N.Y. State Bd., 1952; mem. pub. adv. com. to sec. of labor, 1953; mem. N.Y. State Bd. Mediation, 1956-66; mem. presdl. emergency bd. on ry. shopcrafts dispute, 1964, ry. signalmen dispute, 1971; mem. Fed. Svc. Impasses Panel, 1970-90. Author: The Uses of Field Work in Teaching Economics, 1939, AFL Attitudes Toward Production, 1952, Dock Labor Disputes in Great Britain, 1953, Fact Finding in Public Employment Disputes, 1969, Sex and the Single Arbitrator, 1971. Editor: The Duty of Fair Representation, 1977; The Changing Law of Fair Representation, 1985, Cleared For Takeoff: Airline Labor Relations Under Deregulation, 1988; also several vols. on arbitration. Alumnae trustee Wellesley Coll., 1946-53. Mem. Nat. Acad. Arbitrators (past pres.), Am. Fedn. Tchrs. (mem. pub. rev. bd. 1969-73), UAW (pub. rev. bd. 1957—), Indsl. Rels. Rsch. Assn., Phi Beta Kappa. Died Jan. 5, 1998.

MCKINLEY, (JENNIFER CAROLYN) ROBIN, writer; b. Warren, Ohio, Nov. 16, 1952; d. William and Jeanne Carolyn (Turrell) McK; m. Peter Dickinson, Jan. 3, 1992. Student, Dickinson Coll., 1970-72; BA, Bowdoin Coll., 1975, PhD (hon.), 1986. Editor, transcriber Ward and Paul, Washington, 1972-73; rsch. asst. Rsch. Assocs., Brunswick, Maine, 1976-77; tchr., counselor pvt. secondary sch., Natick, Maine, 1978-79; edit. asst. Little, Brown & Co., Boston, 1979-81; barn mgr. horse farm Holliston, Mass., 1981-82; clerk Books of Wonder, N.Y.C., 1983—; freelance reader, copy and line editor, 1983—. Author: Beauty: A Retelling of Beauty and the Beast, 1978 (Horn book Honor list citation 1978), The Door in the Hedge, 1981, The Blue Sword, 1982 (Best Young adult books citation ALA 1982, Newbery Honor citation 1983), The Hero and the Crown, 1984 (Horn book honor list citation 1985, John Newbery medal 1985), The Outlaws of Sherwood, 1988, Rowan, 1992 (Best Young adult books citation ALA 1992), My Father is in the Navy, 1992, Deerskin, 1993 (Best YOung adult books citation ALA 1993, Best Adult books for young adults citation ALA 1993), A Knot in the Grain and Other Stories, 1994; contbr. Elsewhere Vol. II, 1982, Vol. III, 1984, Faery, 1985, Writers for Children, 1988; editor, contbr.: Imaginary Lands, 1985 (World Fantasy award Best Anthology 1986); adapter: Jungle Book Tales, 1985, Black Beauty, 1986, The Light Princess, 1988.

MC KINNEY, MONTGOMERY NELSON, advertising executive; b. Chgo., June 20, 1910; s. William Ayer and Roberta (Montgomery) McK.; m. Virginia Dickey, Nov. 2, 1957; children by previous marriage: Jane McKinney McDonald, William; children: Beth McKinney, Robert. BA, Oberlin Coll., 1934, HHD (hon.), 1989. Treas., with sales, advt. and sales promotion depts. Kitchen Art Foods, Inc., Chgo., 1934-40; v.p. Earle Ludgin & Co., Chgo., 1940-55; account supr. Leo Burnett Co., Inc., Chgo., 1956; v.p. Doyle Dane Bernbach, Inc., Los Angeles, 1957-69, sr. v.p. client services, 1969-75; exec. v.p., dir. client services Chiat/Day, Inc., Los Angeles, 1975-76, chmn. bd., 1976-83; chmn. Doyle Dane Bernbach/West, Los Angeles, 1983-86, DDB Needham West (merger Doyle Dane Bernbach and Needham, Harper and Steers), Los Angeles, 1986-87; vice chmn. Kresser, Craig, 1988—; mem. faculty Inst. Advanced Advt. Studies, 1964-68. Chmn. campaign Winnetka (Ill.) Community Chest, 1950, pres., 1952; trustee John Thomas Dye Sch., Bel Air, Calif., 1966-75, pres., 1973-75; trustee Oberlin Coll., 1971-85, emeritus trustee, 1986— ; trustee, chmn. fin. com. Winnetka Congregational Ch., 1950-56. Served to lt. USNR, 1944-46. Recipient silver medal Am. Advt. Fedn., 1983. Mem. Am. Assn. Advt. Agys. (gov. So. Calif. council 1972-76, sec.-treas. 1972, vice chmn. 1973, chmn. 1974-75, nat. dir. 1981-83), West States Assn. Advt. Agys. (dir. 1978-83, Advt. Leader of Yr. 1980), Los Angeles Advt. Club. Methodist (trustee 1970-74, vice chmn. 1973-74). Clubs: Riviera Country (Pacific Palisades, Calif.); Los Angeles Athletic. Home: Santa Monica Calif. DIED 07/00/95. .

MC LAREN, MALCOLM GRANT, IV, ceramic engineering educator; b. Denver, July 22, 1928; s. George W. and Evelyn (Hodgson) McL.; m. Barbara Stephen, Sept. 23, 1950; children: Malcolm Grant, George, Thomas, Michael. B.S., Rutgers U., 1950, M.S., 1951, Ph.D., 1962. Research asst. Rutgers U., New Brunswick, N.J., 1950-54, mem. faculty, 1962-96, prof. ceramics, chmn. dept. ceramics, 1969-94, dir. Inst. for Engineered Materials, 1987-96; chief ceramist Paper Makers Importing Co., Easton, Pa., 1954-55; v.p., dir. Paper Makers Importing Co., 1957-62; hon. life prof. Tsing Hua U., Beijing, China, 1992. Author articles in field. Served to 1st lt. USAF, 1955-57. Recipient Gardner award Rutgers U., 1970; Man of Yr. award Associacão Brasiliera de Cerâmica, 1978; Dr. Harvey Wiley medal FDA, 1984; Ann. award Ceramic Assn. N.J.; Outstanding Engr. award Rutgers U., 1989. Fellow Am. Ceramic Soc. (Disting. life, v.p. 1974, pres. 1979-80, Albert Victor Bleininger award 1979, Founders award Phila. sect. 1983), Brit. Inst. Ceramics; mem. Am. Soc. Engring. Edn., Ceramic Ednl. Coun. (pres.), Internat. Ceramic Fedn. (pres. 1989-90), The Acad. Ceramics (pres., bd. trustees 1993-96), Associacão Brasiliera de Cerâmica (hon. life), Cap and Skull Rutgers U., Sigma Xi, Phi Lambda Upsilon, Phi Gamma Delta, Tau Beta Pi, Keramos. Died Apr. 13, 1996.

MC LEMORE, ROBERT HENRY, petroleum engineer, consultant; b. Dallas, Feb. 28, 1910; s. Edward Eugene and Margaret (Butler) Mc L.; m. Ethel Ruth Ward, June 30, 1935. B.S., Tex. A & M Coll., 1933. Div. engr. Sun Oil Co., Dallas, 1933-41; exec. v.p., gen. mgr. Welex Jet Services, Ft. Worth, 1946-53; cons. engr., 1953-55; v.p., gen. mgr. Turbo Drill div. Dresser Industries, Dallas, 1955-57; pres., dir. Otis Engring. Corp., 1957-75; dir. Halliburton Co., 1968-75; councilor Tex. A & M U. Research Found. Served from lt. to col. USAAF, 1941-45. Mem. Soc. Petroleum Engrs. (treas. 1960-63, pres. 1970, dir. 1969-72, DeGolyer Disting. Service medal 1976), Mid Continent Oil and Gas Assn., Am. Petroleum Inst., Independent Producers Assn. Am., AIME (hon. mem.; dir. 1969-72, v.p. 1971, Roger McConnell Engring. Achievement award 1975). Clubs: Petroleum; Engrs. (Dallas); Northwood Country. Home: Dallas Tex. Died Apr. 16, 1995.

MCLEOD, WALTON JAMES, JR., lawyer; b. Lynchburg, S.C., Aug. 7, 1906; s. Walton James and Pauline (Mullins) McL.; m. Rhoda Lane Brown, Feb. 2, 1935; children: Walton James III, Peden Brown, William Mullins, Thomas Gordon III. BA, Wofford Coll., 1926, LLD, 1988, LLB, U. S.C., 1930. Bar: S.C. 1930, U.S. Dist. Ct., U.S. Ct. Appeals (4th cir.) 1937, U.S. Supreme Ct. 1936. Ptnr. Jefferies & McLeod, Walterboro, S.C., 1930-40, Jefferies, McLeod & Unger, Walterboro, 1940-54, Jefferies, McLeod, Unger & Fraser, Walterboro, 1954-76, McLeod, Fraser & Unger, Walterboro, 1976-85, McLeod, Fraser & Cone, Walterboro, 1985-94; city atty. Walterboro; mem. vice chmn. S.C. Hwy Commn. 1946-50. Mem. nat. exec. com. Young Dems., 1938-42, S.C. Dem. exec. com., 1960-88; Dem. chmn. Colleton County, 1950-60; temporary chmn. state conv., 1976; trustee Walterboro pub. schs., 1936-46, Wofford Coll., 1954-66. Served to lt. comdr. USNR, 1942-46. Recipient Disting. Alumni award Wofford Coll., Durant Disting. Svc. award S.C. Bar Found. Fellow Am. Bar Found., Am. Coll. Trial Lawyers, Am. Coll. Trust and Estate Counsel; mem. ABA (ho. of dels. 1950-70, state del. 1950-64, bd. govs. 1964-67, chmn. resolutions com. 1961-62), Am. Law Inst., S.C. Bar Assn. (pres. 1969-70), Colleton County Bar Assn. (pres. 1962), Jud. Conf. U.S. Ct. Appeals 4th Cr., Am. Judicature Soc., U.S.C. Law Sch. Assn. (former pres.), Am. Legion (comdr. S.C. 1949-50, nat. exec. com. 1951-52), Masons, Shriners, Kappa Alpha, Phi Delta Phi. Methodist. Home: Walterboro S.C. Died Nov. 10, 1994.

MC MANUS, PHILIP DANIEL, business executive; b. Chgo., Apr. 15, 1916; s. Jackson B. and Isabelle (Lewis) McM.; m. Arvada Belle Roche, July 6, 1935; children: Marilyn McManus Osborn, Bonnie McManus Ruggles, Philip Daniel, Kerry. B.A., U. Chgo., 1943, M.B.A., 1946. With A.O. Smith Corp., 1947-63; corp. controller A.O. Smith Corp., Milw., 1947-60; gen. mgr. meter and service sta. equipment div. A.O. Smith Corp., Erie, Pa., 1960-63; v.p. Eagle-Picher Industries, Inc., Cin., 1963-69; group v.p. Eagle-Picher Industries, Inc., 1969-73, exec. v.p., 1973-79; also dir., pres. Ohio Rubber Co. div. Eagle-Picher Industries, Inc., Willoughby, Ohio, 1965-69; chmn. bd. McDonough Co., Parkersburg, W.Va., 1979-82; pres., chief exec. officer, dir. Stearns & Foster, 1982-84; dir. Standard Register, Valley Industries Co.; chmn. bd. Bolen Leather Products Co. Mem. Fin. Execs. Inst. Am. (past dir. Milw. chpt.). Clubs: Cin. Country, Queen City. Home: Cincinnati Ohio Died Aug. 30, 1995.

MC MURRIN, STERLING MOSS, philosophy educator; b. Woods Cross, Utah, Jan. 12, 1914; s. Joseph W. and Gertrude (Moss) McM.; m. Natalie Barbara Cotterel, June 8, 1938; children: Gertrude Ann, Joseph Cotterel, Sterling James, Natalie Laurie, Melanie. A.B., U. Utah, 1936, M.A., 1937, LL.D., 1961; Ph.D., U. So. Calif., 1946, LL.D.; LL.D., Clark U., Del. State Coll., 1962, Pepperdine Coll., 1967; D.Litt., U. Puget Sound, 1963; D. Hum. Litt., Westminster Coll., 1985. Asst. prof. philosophy U. So. Calif., 1946-48; prof. philosophy U. Utah, Salt Lake City, 1948-64; dean Coll. Letters and Sci. U. Utah, 1954-60, acad. v.p., 1960-61, Ericksen disting. prof., 1964-87, E.E. Ericksen Disting. prof. emeritus, 1987-96, provost, 1965-66, U. Marshall dean Grad. Sch., 1966-78, prof. philosophy edn., 1968-83, prof. history, 1970-96, adj. prof. philosophy, 1979-96; vis. scholar Columbia U., 1952-53, Union Theol. Sem., 1952-53; Ford fellow Princeton U., 1952-53; U.S. commr. edn., 1961-62; cons. to Am. Tel. & Tel. Co., IBM Corp., Com. for Econ. Devel., Fund Advancement Edn., D.C. Commn. Licensure, Office Sci. and Tech. Exec. Office Pres. Author: (with James L. Jarrett) Contemporary Philosophy, 1954 (with B.A.G. Fuller) A History of Philosophy, 2 vols., 1955, Religion, Reason, and Truth, 1983; co-author: Toward Understanding the New Testament, 1990, History of the Tanner Lectures on Human Values, 1991, The Crisis of Western Culture, 1994 (with Jackson Newell) Conversations with Sterling McMurrin, 1996; editor: The Schools and the Challenge of Innovation, 1969, Functional Education for Disadvantaged Youth, 1971, The Conditions for Educational Equality, 1971, Resources for Urban Schools: Better Use and Balance, 1971, On the Meaning of the University, 1976, The Tanner Lectures on Human Values, Vol. I, 1980, Vol. II, 1981, Vol. III, 1982, Vol. IV, 1983, Vol. V, 1984, Vol. VI, 1985, Vol. VII, 1986, Vol. VIII, 1988, Values at War, 1983, Liberty, Equality and Law, 1987; contbr. monographs, articles, revs. on philosophy, religion and end. to profl. jours. Mem. U.S. Commn. UNESCO, 1961-62; mem. Bd. Fgn. Scholarships, 1961-62; exec. bd. Nat. Cultural Center; chmn. Fed. Commn. on Instructional Tech.; adviser, chancellor U. Teheran, 1958-59; v.p. 25th Internat. Congress on Edn., Geneva, Switzerland, 1962; mem. U.S. dels. on edn. and cultural affairs to, Washington, Chile, Japan, 1962; chmn. Mountain States and Midcontinent manpower adv. coms. U.S. Dept. Labor, 1965-68; mem. higher commn. Northwest Assn. Secondary and Higher Schs., 1964-73; sr. commr. Western Assn. Schs. and Colls., 1974-77; mem. Grad. Record Exam. Bd., 1974-79; Bd. dirs. Agy. for Instrnl. Television, 1974-78; trustee Carnegie Found. Advancement Teaching, Am. U. of Rome; adv. com. for philosophy Princeton U.; mem. bd. nat. humanities ctr. Yale U., mem. nat. bd. fellowships and associateships NRC, 1974-77; trustee Tanner Lecture Trust, 1977-89, Westminster Coll., 1986-91; dir. Tanner Lectures on Human Values, 1978-87; bd. dirs. Utah Humanities Endowment, 1977-83. Recipient Coll. of Humanities award U. Utah, 1992. Mem. Am. Philos. Assn. (v.p.), Mountain Plains Philos. Assn. (pres.), Nat. Assn. State Univs. and Land-Grant Colls. (com. on fed. legislation), Phi Beta Kappa, Phi Kappa Phi (Rosenblatt prize 1984, 1st Gov.'s Award in Humanities 1988). Home: Salt Lake City Utah Died Apr. 6, 1996.

MCNALLY, ALEXANDER CAMPBELL, wine authority, consultant; b. Indpls., June 29, 1934; s. Edwin Mongan and Dorothea Lauretta (Campbell) McN.; m. Tina Mahar, Apr. 28, 1962; children: Daniel, Alexander. BA, Princeton U., 1956; MBA, Harvard U., 1958, PhD, 1958. Mng. dir. Alexis Lichine & Cie., Bordeaux, France, 1959-62; internat. wine dir. Heublein, Inc., Hartford, Conn., 1962-87; chmn. bd., chief exec. officer McNally Found., 1988—. Author: Wines and Spirits of the World, 1972, What Every Man and Woman Should Know about Wine, 1979. Mem. Rep. Nat. Com., Washington, 1986—; trustee Hartt Sch. Music. Recipient Tilden Fine Arts award Princeton U., 1956. Mem. Princeton Assn. Cen. Conn. (bd. dirs.), Harvard-Radcliffe Assn. of Conn., Conf. des Chevaliers du Tastevin (grand chef du protocole 1975—), Phi Beta Kappa. Methodist. Avocations: boating, music, wine tasting. Died June 11, 1997.

MCPHERSON, JOHN BARKLEY, aerospace consultant, retired military officer; b. Virginia, Minn., Oct. 4, 1917; s. Barkley John and Anna (Holmgren) McP.; m. Leota Irene Wilson, July 16, 1940; children—Kenneth, Sue McPherson Cain, Shirley McPherson Curs, Robin McPherson Rohrback. B.C.E., U. Ariz., 1940. Commd. 2d lt., cav. U.S. Army, 1940; advanced through grades to lt. gen. USAF, 1968; assigned (B-29s, World War II, PTO); comdr. Walker AFB, Roswell, N.Mex., 1950-52; dir. faculty (Air War Coll.), 1955-56; dep. comdr. (5th Air Div. Morocco), 1956-58; comdr. (379th Bomb Wing), Homestead AFB, Fla., 1958-59, (823d Air Div.), Homestead AFB, 1959-62, (810th Air Div.), Minot AFB, N.D., 1962-64; vice dir. ops., joint staff (Joint Chiefs Staff), 1964-67, vice dir. joint staff, 1967-68, asst. to chmn., 1968-70; comdt. (Nat. War Coll.), 1970-73; ret., 1973; cons. Martin Marietta Aerospace, 1973-85; mem. Sr. Govt. Rev. Panel, 1985-91. Decorated D.S.M. with two oak leaf clusters, Legion of Merit, Bronze Star; recipient Gen. H.S. Vandenberg Aerospace Edn. award, 1984; Centennial medallion award U. Ariz., 1989, Disting. Citizen award, 1995; named Outstanding Young Man of Yr., Roswell, 1951. Mem. Air Force Hist. Found. (pres. 1974-83), Air Force Assn., Nat. Space Club, Order of Daedalians, Theta Tau, Kappa Sigma. Died June 23, 1997.

MC QUADE, WALTER, author; b. Port Washington, N.Y., May 1, 1922; s. Walter P. and Theresa (Dwyer) McQ.; m. Ann Aikman, Nov. 25, 1950; children—Molly Elizabeth, Benjamin Barr, Kate Maud. B.Arch., Cornell U., 1947. Writer Archtl. Forum mag., 1947-64; architecture and design critic The Nation, 1959-65, Life mag., 1970-74; bd. editors Fortune mag., 1964-85; contbg. editor Connoisseur Mag., 1985-91; vis. critic Yale U. Sch. Architecture, 1962; mem. N.Y.C. Planning Commn., 1967-72. Author: Schoolhouse, 1958, Cities Fit To Live In, 1971, Stress, 1975, The Longevity Factor, 1979, Architecture in the Real World, 1985. Served with AUS, 1942-46. Ford Found. fellow, 1960; co-recipient Grand prize Milan Trennale, 1960; recipient Howard Blakeslee award Am. Heart Assn., 1972; Penney award U. Mo., 1972. Fellow AIA (Architecture Critics' medal 1974). Roman Catholic. Home: Great Neck N.Y. Died Dec. 26, 1994.

MCQUILLEN, HARRY A., publishing company executive. Formerly with Prentice-Hall; former dir. mktg. services Coll. div. McGraw-Hill; former editor-in-chief Coll. div. CBS Pub., pres. Ednl. and Profl. Pub. div., 1983-87; group v.p. Gen. Pub. Group Macmillan Inc., N.Y.C., 1987-88, v.p., 1988; pres. Macmillan Pub. Co., 1988-91; pres., CEO K-III Mag Corp., N.Y.C., 1991—; pres. K-III Media Group, N.Y.C., 1994—; exec. v.p. K-III Comms. Corp., 1995—, COO, 1997—. June 30, 1997.

MC WHORTER, HEZZIE BOYD, former collegiate athletic commissioner, English language educator; b. Cochran, Ga., May 8, 1923; s. Hezzie and Mary (Durham) McW.; m. Marguerite Antley, Nov. 14, 1964; children: Carol (Mrs. Joel Pittard), William David Volk, Julie (Mrs. John McClusky), Hamilton Boyd. B.S., U.S. Naval Acad., 1945; M.A., U. Ga., 1949; Ph.D., U. Tex., 1960. Mem. faculty U. Ga., Athens, 1949-72; prof. English, dean Coll. Arts and Scis. U. Ga., cons. athletics to Pres., 1986-92; commr. Southeastern Conf., 1972-86. Served with USN, 1945-47, 51-53. Named to North Ga. Coll. Disting. Alumni Hall of Fame, 1978; State of Ga. Sports Hall of Fame, 1980. Mem. Nat. Collegiate Athletic Assn. (dist. v.p., council 1968-72), Southeastern Conf. (sec. 1967-72), Phi Kappa Phi. Mem. Christian Ch. (elder). Home: Athens Ga. Died July 23, 1994.

MEDEARIS, DONALD NORMAN, JR., physician, educator; b. Kansas City, Kans., Aug. 22, 1927; s. Donald Norman and Gladys (Sandford) M.; m. Mary Ellen Marble, Aug. 25, 1956; children: Donald Harrison, Ellen Sandford, John Norman, Jennifer Marble. AB, U. Kans., 1950; MD, Harvard U., 1953. Diplomate: Am. Bd. Pediatrics. Intern internal medicine Barnes Hosp., St. Louis, 1953-54; resident pediatrics Children's Hosp., Cin., 1954-56; rsch. fellow pediatrics Harvard U. rsch. div. infectious diseases Children's Med. Ctr., Boston, 1956-58; from asst. to assoc. prof. pediatrics and microbiology Johns Hopkins Sch. Medicine, Balt., 1959-65; Joseph P. Kennedy Jr. Meml. Found. Sr. Rsch. Scholar in Mental Retardation, 1960-65; prof. pediatrics U. Pitts. Sch. Medicine, 1965-74, chmn. dept., 1965-69, dean, 1969-74; med. dir. Children's Hosp., Pitts., 1965-69; prof. pediatrics Case Western Res. U., Cleve., 1974-77; dir. pediatrics Cleve. Met. Gen. Hosp., 1974-77; Charles Wilder prof. pediatrics Harvard U. Med. Sch., 1977-95, Charles Wilder disting. prof. pediatrics, 1995-97; chief Children's Svc. Mass. Gen. Hosp., Boston, 1977-95; mem. Pres.'s Commn. on Study Ethical Problems in Medicine and Biomed. and Behavioral Rsch., 1979-82. Contbr. articles to profl. jours., texts. Vestry Trinity Ch., Boston, 1983-87. Served with USNR, 1945-46. Mem. Am. Acad. Pediatrics, Am. Pediatric Soc., Infectious Disease Soc. Am., Inst. Medicine/Nat. Acad. Sci., Alpha Omega Alpha. Died Sept. 29, 1997.

MEECE, VOLNEY, retired newspaper reporter, association administrator; b. Tonkawa, Okla., Jan. 23, 1925; s. Charles Walter and Maude Belle (Barclay) M.; m. Mattie Lou Barker, June 13, 1966; children: Pamela Kay, Robin Renee, Michelle Dawn. A.A., No. Jr. Coll., 1948; BA, U. Okla., 1950. Sports reporter Daily Oklahoman & Times, Oklahoma City, 1950-52; sports columnist Oklahoma City Times, 1952-84; sports reporter Daily Oklahoman, 1984-91; exec. dir. Football Writers Assn., Edmond, Okla., 1973—. Author: 13 Years of Winning Oklahoma Football Under Bud Wilkinson, 1960. Served with USAF, 1943-46. Recipient Jake Wade award Coll. Sports Info. Dirs. Am., 1974; Contbr. to Football award Nat. Okla. chpt. Football Found. Hall of Fame, 1990, Oklahoma City 89ers Baseball Hall of Fame, 1988. Mem. Am. Football Coaches Assn. (hon.), Football Writers Assn. (pres. 1971-72, exec. dir. 1973), U.S. Basketball Writers Assn., U. Okla. Football Lettermen's Assn. (hon.), Coll. Sports Info. Dirs. Am. Avocations: jazz; swimming. Home: Edmond Okla.

MEERS, HENRY W., investment banker; b. Joliet, Ill., July 12, 1908; s. Robert and Mary (Cullen) M.; m. Evelyn Huckins; children: Henry Weber, Albert Huckins, Robert. A.B., U. Ill., 1930. With Halsey, Stuart & Co., Chgo., 1930-35, Harriman, Ripley & Co., 1936-42; resident partner White, Weld & Co., 1946-72, vice chmn., 1972-78; mng. dir. Merrill Lynch & Co. Investment Banking Group, Chgo., 1978-97; dir. Merrill Lynch Trust Co., Chgo., 1992-97; dir. DuKane Corp., 1962-97; chmn. bd. govs. Assn. Stock Exchange Firms, 1968-69; bd. govs. Midwest Stock Exchange, 1957-60, N.Y. Stock Exchange, 1970-71. Del. Nat. Rep. Conv., 1984, alt. del., 1988; bd. dirs. Nat. Recreation Park Assn. Found.; mem. Chgo. Crime Commn.; chmn. Modern Cts. Ill., 1970, Met. Cursade Mercy, 1967; life trustee U. Cgho., Chi. Internat. House; life trustee, chair Chgo. Ednl. TV Sta.-WTTW, PBS, 1978-89; life trustee Lake Forest Acad.; trustee Lake Forest Coll., 1968-76; bd. dirs. Children's Meml. Hosp., chmn., 1970-75; chair bd. trustees Latin Sch. Chgo., 195-658; bd. dirs. U. Ill. Found.; mem. citizens bd. Loyola U.; chmn. Chgo.

coun. Boy Scouts Am., 1952-56; mem. Ill. Compensation Rev. Bd., 1985-96; chair Internat. House, U. Chgo. Commdr. USNR, 1942-46. Recipient Man of Yr. award NCCJ, 1969, Founders award, 1992. Mem. Investment Analysts Soc., Ducks Unltd. (nat. trustee 1980-90), Chgo. Club, Comml. Club Chgo., Links Club, Onwentsia Club, Old Elm Club, Seminole Golf Club, Shore Acres Club, Bohemian Club, The Island Club, Phi Beta Kappa. Died Aug. 1997.

MEIER, BEN, state official; b. Napoleon, N.D., Aug. 1, 1918; s. Bernhardt and Theresia (Hilzenderger) M.; m. Clara Kaczynski, Dec. 30, 1944; children: Lynn, Bernie. Student, Dakota Bus. Sch., 1943, U. Wis. Sch. Banking, 1947-48. Asst. cashier Stock Growers Bank, Napoleon, 1945-47, Gackle State Bank, N.D., 1947-49; pres. Bank of Hazelton, N.D.; pres., dir. Mandan Security Bank, N.D., 1959-70; sec. state N.D. Bismarck, 1955-89. Crusade chmn. N.D. Heart Assn., 1969, N.D. Cnacer Soc., 1970. Recipient N.D. Nat. Leadership Excellency award. Mem. N.D. Bankers Assn., Nat. Assn. Secs. State (pres. 1967), Nat. Assn. State Contractors Licensing Agys. (v.p. 1969-70), Sons of Norway. Republican. DIED 10/02/95. .

MEIERHENRY, WESLEY CARL, educator; b. Arlington, Nebr., Nov. 12, 1915; s. Carl H. and Anna (Niederdeppe) M.; m. Delsie Boschult, June 10, 1936; children: Dwight, Kent, Redge. Student, Western Union Coll., 1932-34; B.Sc., Midland Coll., 1936; M.A., U. Nebr., 1941, Ph.D., 1946; D. of Humanitarian Svc., Bishop Clarkson Coll., 1989. Tchr. high sch., coach, supt. schs. Republican City, Nebr., 1936-43; supr. corr. study, extension div. U. Nebr., Lincoln, 1943-46; asst. prof. sch. adminstrn. U. Nebr. (Tchrs. Coll.), 1946-52, assoc. prof., 1952- 57, prof. ednl. adminstrn., history and philosophy of edn., 1957-90, asst. dean, 1959-68, chmn. dept. adult and continuing edn., 1968-84; vis. prof. San Jose (Calif.) State Coll., 1950-51, U. Mass., Amherst, 1961, U. P.R., Rio Piedras, 1966, U. Colo., Boulder, 1968, Colo. State U., Fort Collins, 1969, 70, 71. Editor: Enriching the Curriculum through Motion Pictures, 1952, Media and Educational Innovation, 1966, Planning for Evaluation of Special Education Programs, 1970; Co-editor: Trends in Programmed Instruction, 1964, Educational Media Theory into Practice, 1969. Mem. UNESCO Nat. Commn., 1968-73, exec. com., 1969-70, 70-71; mem. Nat. Adv. Com. for Deaf, 1970-74; mem. adv. com. Model Secondary Sch. for Deaf, 1970-76, 83-86; mem. publs. bd. U. Wis./Sears Roebuck Found. IGE Tchr. Edn. Project, 1973-76; trustee Midland Coll., 1946-49. Recipient Midland Coll. Alumni Citation award, 1959, Disting. Svc. award Adult and Continuing Edn. Assn. Nebr., 1978; inducted into Arlington Edn. Found. Hall of Fame, 1989. Mem. NEA (TEPS commn. 1969-72), Assn. Ednl. Communications and Tech. (pres. 1967-68, Disting. Svc. award 1980), Am. Ednl. Rsch. Assn., Adult Edn. Assn. Am., Missouri Valley Adult Edn. Assn. (sec. 1980-82, Outstanding Adult Educator of Nebr. award 1982), Nebr. State Ednl. Assn., Midland Luth. Coll. Alumni Assn. (pres. 1970-71), Kiwanis, Phi Delta Kappa. Presbyterian (trustee 1956-59, elder 1988-89). Home: Lincoln Nebr. Died Jan. 3, 1990.

MEIKLE, THOMAS HARRY, JR., retired neuroscientist, foundation administrator, educator; b. Troy, Pa., Mar. 24, 1929; s. Thomas H. and Elizabeth (MacMorran) M.; m. Jane T. Germer, Aug. 26, 1966 (div. 1983); children: David Andrew, Sarah Elizabeth; m. Jacqueline Winterkorn, Sept. 27, 1986. A.B., Cornell U., 1951, M.D., 1954. Intern Jefferson Hosp., Phila., 1954-55; clin. fellow Inst. Neurology, London, Eng., 1957-58; research fellow Inst. Neurol. Scis., U. Pa., Phila., 1958-61; instr., asst. prof., assoc. prof., prof. anatomy Cornell U. Med. Coll., N.Y.C., 1961-87, acting dean medicine, 1976-77, dep. dean, 1977-79, dean, provost, 1980-87; dean Cornell U. Grad. Sch. Med. Scis., 1969-76; v.p. Josiah Macy, Jr. Found., N.Y.C., 1980, pres., 1987—; career scientist Health Research Council, N.Y.C., 1969-71. Served to capt. M.C. AUS, 1955-57, Korea. Markle Found. scholar in acad. medicine, 1963-68. Deceased.

MEISSNER, CHARLES, federal agency administrator. Asst. sec. internat. econ. policy U.S. Dept. Commerce, 1994-96. Home: Washington D.C. Deceased.

MEISSNER, DORIS, federal commissioner; b. Nov. 3, 1941; d. Fred and Hertha H. (Tromp) Borst; m. Charles F. Meissner, June 8, 1963 (dec.); children: Christine M., Andrew D. BA, U. Wis., 1963, MA, 1969. Asst. dir. student fin. aid U. Wis., 1964-68; exec. dir. Nat. Women's Polit. Caucus, 1971-73; asst. dir. office policy and planning U.S. Dept. Justice, 1975, exec. dir. cabinet com. illegal aliens, 1976, dep. assoc. atty. gen., 1977-80, acting commr. immigration and naturalization svc., 1981, exec. assoc. commr. immigration and naturalization svc., 1982-86; sr. assoc., dir. immigration policy project The Carnegie Endowment for Internat. Peace, 1986-93; commr. immigration and naturalization svc., 1993; adv. coun. U.S./Mex. project Overseas Devel. Coun., 1981-86; trustee Refugee Policy Group, 1987-93; adv. bd. Program for Rsch. on Immigration Policy Rand Corp./Urban inst., 1988-92; cons. panel to comptroller gen. GAO, 1989-93; with Coun. Fgn. Rels., 1990—, Washington Office Latin Am., 1990-93. White Ho. fellow, 1973-74. Mem. Nat. Women's Polit. Caucus (nat. adv. bd. 1976—), White House Fellows Alumni Assn. and Found. (sec., exec. com. 1979-82, Assn. Governing Bds. Colls. and Univs. (panel higher edn. issues 1990-92), Phi Kappa Phi, Mortar Board, Alpha Chi Omega.

MEITES, LOUIS, chemist, educator; b. Balt., Dec. 6, 1926; s. Louis and Gertrude (Harand) M.; m. Thelma Steinberg, June 10, 1947 (div. 1979); children: Judith Ann, Norman Louis, Robin Leslie; m. Ruth Schwartz Schaefer, Jan. 10, 1979. B.A., Middlebury Coll., 1945; M.A., Harvard, 1946, Ph.D., 1947. Instr. Princeton U., 1947-48; faculty Yale U., 1948-55, asst. prof., 1952-55; faculty Poly. Inst. Bklyn., 1955-68, prof. chemistry, 1962-68; prof. chemistry Clarkson Coll. Tech., Potsdam, N.Y., 1968-84, chmn. dept. chemistry, 1968-81; prof. chemistry George Mason U., Fairfax, Va., 1984-89, chmn. dept. chemistry, 1984-88. Author: Polarographic Techniques, 1955, 2d edit., 1965, (with Henry C. Thomas) Advanced Analytical Chemistry, 1958, (with Petr Zuman, others) Electrochemical Data, 1974, CRC Handbook Series in Organic Electrochemistry, Vols. 1-6, 1977-83, CRC Handbook Series in Inorganic Electrochemistry, Vols. 1-8, 1980-88, Introduction to Chemical Equilibrium and Kinetics, 1981; also numerous articles; contbg. author, editor: Handbook of Analytical Chemistry, 1963; editorial adv. bd.: Chem. Analysis Series, 1965-76, Talanta, 1966-80, Analytical Letters, 1979-89; editor: Critical Revs. Analytical Chemistry, 1970-74; co-editor: Pergamon Series in Analytical Chemistry, 1978-83. Recipient Benedetti-Pichler award Am. Microchem. Soc., 1983. Avocations: Research thermoanalytical and electroanalytical chemistry, controlled-potential electrolysis and coulometry, differential thermometry and ebulliometry, rates and mechanisms chem. reactions in solutions, theory potentiometric, other titration curves, data-handling techniques, machine interpretation of chem. data. Home: Burke Va. Died July, 1993.

MELAND, BERNARD EUGENE, theologian, educator; b. Chgo., June 28, 1899; s. Erick Bernhard and Elizabeth (Hansen) M.; m. Margaret Evans McClusky, Aug. 6, 1926 (dec.); children: Bernard Eugene (dec.), Richard Dennis. A.B., Park Coll., 1923, D.D., 1956; student, U. Ill., 1918, 23-24, McCormick Theol. Sem., 1924-25; B.D., U. Chgo., 1928; Ph.D., 1929; postgrad., U. Marburg, Germany, 1928-29. Ordained to ministry Presbyn. Ch., 1928; prof. religion and philosophy Central Coll., Fayette, Mo., 1929-36; asso. prof. religion, head dept. Pomona Coll., Claremont, Calif., 1936-43; prof. religion Pomona Coll., 1943-45, Clark lectr., 1947; prof. constructive theology U. Chgo., 1945-64; prof. emeritus U. Chgo. (Div. Sch.), 1964, vis. prof. theology, 1965-68, pastors inst. lectr., 1945; vis. prof. philosophy of religion Union Theol. Sem., N.Y.C., 1968-69; Hewitt vis. prof. humanities Ottawa U., Kans., 1971; Barrows lectr., Calcutta and Bangalore, India, Rangoon, Burma; vis. lectr. Serampore Coll., India, 1957-58; Burrows lectr. U. Calcutta, Poona, 1964-65. Author: Modern Man's Worship, 1934, (with H.N. Wieman) American Philosophies of Religion, 1936, Write Your Own Ten Commandments, 1938, The Church and Adult Education, 1939, Seeds of Redemption, 1947, America's Spiritual Culture, 1948, The Reawakening of Christian Faith, 1949, Higher Education and the Human Spirit, 1953, Faith and Culture, 1953, The Realities of Faith: The Revolution in Cultural Forms, 1962, The Secularization of Modern Cultures, 1966, Fallible Forms and Symbols, 1976; editor, contbr.: The Future of Empirical Theology, 1969; co-editor: Jour. Religion, 1946-64. Served with U.S. Army, 1918. Mem. Am. Theol. Soc. (v.p. 1951-52, pres. Midwest div. 1960-61). Home: Chicago Ill. Died Feb. 8, 1993.

MELLENBRUCH, GILES (JOHNNY) EDWARD, orchestra leader, lyricist; b. Hiawatha, Kans., May 9, 1911; s. William Bill and Mary Alice (Hanson) M.; m. Marie Lorraine Guy (dec. 1964); children: Gail Marie Smith, Joanne Kay Gillon; m. Leah Marie Cook, Feb. 25, 1967. BA in Music, U. Kans., 1932; BA in Econs., U. Kansas City, 1944. Band leader at many Kansas City night clubs and ballrooms in the 1930s, Hollywood, Calif, 1940s; recorded for Atlas Records, Movieland Records and others in 1930s and 40s. Treas. Christian Mission Outreach Inc., Aptos, Calif., 1989-94; founding mem. United We Stand Am., The Heritage Found. Recipient Minuteman Leadership Cert. award Am. Conservative Union, 1994. Mem. ASCAP, Local 47 AFM (life). Died Jan. 1, 1996.

MENIUS, ARTHUR CLAYTON, JR., university dean; b. Salisbury, N.C., Apr. 30, 1916; s. Arthur Clayton and Maud Edna (Webb) M.; m. Lucille Clark Varner, Mar. 31, 1946; 1 son, Arthur Clayton III. A.B. in Physics and Math, Catawba Coll., 1937; PhD in Physics, U. N.C., Chapel Hill, 1942; D.Sc., Catawba Coll., 1969; Ph.D. in Physics, U. N.C., 1942. Sr. physicist Applied Physics Lab., Johns Hopkins, 1944-46, head battery group for proximity fuse project, 1945-46; prof. physics Clemson Coll., 1946-48; mem. faculty N.C. State U., Raleigh, 1949-81; prof. physics N.C. State U., 1949-55, head dept., 1956-60; dean N.C. State U. (Sch. Phys. and Math. Scis.), 1960-81; sec., v.p. Tharrington's Handcrafted 18th Century Furniture, Inc., 1984; cons. govt. agys. pvt. bus., 1950-81; Chmn. Gov. N.C. Bd. Adv. Com., 1961-69, Atomic Energy Adv. Com. N.C., 1963-71; mem. N.C. Sci. and Tech. Bd.; N.C. State council rep. Oak Ridge Asso. Univs., 1963-69, mem. bd., 1969-76; edn. rep. So. Interstate Nuclear Bd. Author numerous monographs, articles profl. jours. Bd. govs. Research Triangle Inst. Fellow Am. Phys. Soc.; mem. N.C. Acad. Sci., Am. Inst. Physics, ; Carolina Country club, Sphinx, Wash. (N.C.) Yacht and Country, Sandwich club; Esso Regional Discussion Group; Sigma Xi, Phi Kappa Phi. Presbyn. Address: For Estate of Dr. A. C. Menius Jr. 541 Hertford St Raleigh NC 27609-6905 Home: Raleigh N.C. Died Oct. 13, 1996, White Memorial, Raleigh, N.C.

MERCER, DOUGLAS, lawyer; b. Sharon, Mass., Feb. 16, 1918; m. Pauline Loring Tobey, 4 children. AB, Harvard U., 1940, LLB, 1947. Bar: Mass. 1947. Ptnr. Ropes & Gray, Boston, 1957-90, of counsel, 1991—; moderator, panelist various Am. Law Inst.-ABA and other investment co. seminars. Former mem. and chmn. Planning Bd., Town of Weston, Mass., also former selectman, former mem. fin. com.; former trustee, treas. Social Law Library; chmn. Harvard Coll. Fund, 1975-77; chmn. Boston area Harvard Campaign for $350 Million; former mem. overseers resources com. Harvard U.; former trustee Groton Sch.; mem. corp. Belmont Hill Sch. Served to lt. comdr. USN, 1942-46, PTO. Mem. ABA, Boston Bar Assn. Clubs: The Country. DIED 02/01/97. .

MEREDITH, BURGESS, actor; b. Cleve., Nov. 16, 1909; s. William George and Ida (Burgess) M.; m. Helen Berrian Derby, 1932 (div. 1935); m. Margaret H. Frueauff (Margaret Perry), 1936 (div. July 1938); m. Paulette Goddard, May 21, 1944 (div. July 1948); m. Kaja Sundsten, 1950; children: Jonathan Sanford, Tala Beth. Student, Amherst Coll., 1927-28, A.M. (hon.), 1939. Reporter, salesman, seaman, 1928-29; exec. dir. Actors Studio West, 1972-97; artistic dir. Merle Oberon Theatre, L.A., 1972-97; v.p. Actors Equity, 1938-97, acting pres., spring 1938; chmn. adv. bd. Fed. Arts Projects, 1937. First small part with, Eva La Gallienne's Student Repertory Group, 1930; theatre appearances include Little Ol' Boy, 1933; She Loves Me Not, 1933, The Barretts of Wimpole Street, (with Katherine Cornell) Flowers of the Forest, 1935, Winterset, 1936 (Drama Critics award), High Tor, 1937 (Drama Critics award), Star Wagon, 1937, Five Kings, 1939, Liliom, 1941, Candida, 1942, Lincoln Portrait, 1943, The Playboy of the Western World, 1947, Winterset, 1947, Harvey, 1950, Let Me Hear the Melody, 1951, Lo and Behold! (dir.), 1951, The Remarkable Mr. Pennypacker, 1953, 58, Macbeth (dir.), 1954, Teahouse of the August Moon, 1955, Major Barbara, 1956, Speaking of Murder (producer), 1957, Ulysses in Nighttown (dir.), 1958, 74, Enrico IV, 1958, God and Kate Murphy (dir.), 1959, The Vagabond King, 1959, A Thurber Carnival (dir.), 1960, An Evening with Burgess Meredith, 1960, Midgie Purvis (dir.), 1961, A Whiff of Melancholy (dir.), 1961, Blues for Mr. Charlie (dir.), 1964, Park Your Car in Harvard Yard, 1984; motion pictures include Winterset, 1936; There Goes the Groom, 1937, Spring Madness, 1938, Idiot's Delight, 1938, Of Mice and Men, 1939, Castle on the Hudson, 1940, Second Chorus, 1941, San Francisco Docks, 1941, That Uncertain Feeling, 1941, Tom, Dick and Harry, 1941, The Forgotten Village, 1941, Street of Chance, 1942, Welcome to Britain, 1943, Salute to France, 1944, The Yank Comes Back, 1945, Story of G.I. Joe, 1945, The Diary of a Chambermaid, 1946, Magnificent Doll, 1946, On Our Merry Way, 1948, Mine Own Executioner, 1948, Jigsaw, 1949, The Man on the Eiffel Tower, 1950, The Gay Adventure, 1953, Joe Butterfly, 1957, Universe, 1961, Advise and Consent, 1962, The Cardinal, 1963, In Harm's Way, 1965, Madame X, 1966, The Crazy Quilt, 1966, A Big Hand for the Little Lady, 1966, Batman, 1966, Hurry Sundown, 1967, Fortune Garden, 1968, Stay Away Joe, 1967, Mackenna's Gold, 1967, There Was a Crooked Man, 1969, The Yin and the Yang (also writer, dir.), 1970, A Fan's Notes, 1970, The Clay Pidgeon, 1970, Such Good Friends, 1971, The Man, 1972, B for Murder, 1973, Golden Needles, 1973, Day of the Locust, 1973, The Hindenburg, 1974, 92 in the Shade, 1975, Burnt Offerings, 1975, Rocky, 1976 (Acad. award nomination), The Sentinel, 1977, Foul Play, 1978, Magic, 1978, The Manitou, 1978, Rocky II, 1979, The Day the World Ended, 1979, Clash of the Titans, 1979, Final Assignment, 1979, The Last Chase, 1979, When Time Ran Out, 1980, True Confessions, 1980, Rocky III, 1982, Wet Gold, 1984, Santa Claus-The Movie, 1984, Outrage, 1986, Mr. Corbett's Ghost, 1986, No Thing, 1988, Full Moon in Blue Water, 1988, State of Grace, 1990, Rocky V, 1990, Grumpy Old Men, 1993, Camp Nowhere, 1994, Tall Tale, 1994, Grumpier Old Men, 1995, Ripper, 1996; producer, writer: Diary of a Chambermaid, 1946; producer, actor: On Our Merry Way, 1947; dir.: Man On The Eiffel Tower, 1948, The Latent Heterosexual, 1969; writer, dir., narrator: film Afterglow (on the life Robert Frost), 1986; various TV appearances, including World of Disney; dir. others; directed, N.Y. Symphony, Carnegie Hall, 1969; narrator numerous commls.; film Houdini, 1979; co-host: Those Amazing Animals, ABC-TV, 1980-81; filmed: documentary Myths of Ancient Greece, 1981; singer, narrator the dragon in Puff the Magic Dragon Part II, 1979; appeared as Penguin in TV series Batman, 1965-66; author; So Far, So Good. Served with AUS, 1942-

44, ETO. Episcopalian. Club: Players (N.Y.C.). Died Sept. 10, 1997.

MERINO CASTRO, JOSÉ TORIBIO, retired Chilean naval officer; b. Dec. 14, 1915; m. Margarita Maria Riofrio Bustos, 1952; children: M. Angelica, Carolina, Teresita. Ed., specialized as gunnery officer, Naval Acad., 1931-35. Naval service Maipo, 1936, Rancagua, 1939; instr. Blanco Encalada, 1940; divsn. officer Almirante Latorre, 1943; asst. officer USS Raleigh CL7, 1944-45; arty. officer DD Serrano, 1945, arty. officer DD Riqueline, 1947; with C&R O'Higgins, 1950-51; comdr. Corvette Papudo, 1952; staff officer Naval War. Coll. Staff Course, 1953-54; tech. adviser of armaments Chile Naval Mission, London, 1955-57; comdr. Navy Chile Transport, Angamos, 1959; prof. Naval War Coll., 1960-61; comdr. Destroyer Williams Chile Naval Mission, 1962, chief staff fleet, 1963, vice chief of gen. staff, 1964-68, head weapons bur., 1969, dir. gen. logistic navy, 1970, comdr. chieffleet, 1971, commdr. chief 1st Naval Zone, 1972-73; commdr. chief Navy, mem. Govt. Junta, 1973—, ret., 1990. Decorated Armed Forces medal III, II, I, Grand Star of Naval Merit, Cross for Naval Merit, Decoration of Pres. of Republic (Chile), Grand Cross Order (Spain), Order of Nat. Merit (South Korea), 1st Class Order of Rising Sun (Japan), Order of Star of South Africa, Legion of Merit (U.S.), Gran Mastre Orden de Mayo (Argentina), Cruz Peruana Naval Merit, (Peru), Grand Medal (Uruguay), Grand Cross Order of Quetzal (Guatemala), Cross Dist. Svcs. (Honduras), Grand Cross and Grand Star of Merit Fuerzas Armadas (Ecuador). Died Aug. 30, 1996.

MERKURIEV, STANISLAV PETROVICH, physics educator; b. Koustanai, Kasakhstan, Russia, Apr. 28, 1945; s. Petr Petrovich and Daria Georgievna (Eschenko) M.; m. Anna Alexandrovna Smirnova, Apr. 11, 1975; children: Irina, Petr. M. Math. Physics, Leningrad U., Russia, 1967, PhD, 1971, ScD, 1978; postgrad. honoris cause, Brunel U., London, 1992. Asst. prof. Leningrad U., 1970-76, sr. rschr., 1976-82, prof., 1982-84, dean physics faculty, 1982-86, head dept. math. and computational physics, 1984—, rector, 1986—; postdoctoral fellow U. Paris XI, Orsay, France, 1973-74; mem. exec. com. Nat. Sci. Found. of Russia, Moscow, 1992—. Author: Quantum Scattering Theory for Few-Particle Systems, 1984; contbr. over 151 papers on sci. and edn. to profl. jours. Mem. Royal Acad. Scis. and Arts (corres.) (Barcelona, Spain), Acad. Scis. Russia, Soviet Assn. of Univs. (v.p. 1990—). Avocations: music, painting.

MERRILL, CHARLES MERTON, federal judge; b. Honolulu, Dec. 11, 1907; s. Arthur M. and Grace Graydon (Dickey) M.; m. Mary Luita Sherman, Aug. 28, 1931 (dec.); children: Julia Booth Stoddard, Charles McKinney. AB, U. Calif., 1928; LLB, Harvard, 1931. Bar: Calif. 1931, Nev. 1932. Sole practice Reno, 1932-50; judge Nev. Supreme Ct., 1951-59, chief justice, 1955-56, 59; judge U.S. Ct. of Appeals (9th cir.), San Francisco, 1959-74, sr. judge, 1974—. Mem. ABA, State Bar Nev. (gov. 1947-50), Am. Law Inst. (council 1960—).

MERRILL, JAMES, poet, playwright; b. N.Y.C., Mar. 3, 1926; s. Charles Edward and Hellen (Ingram) M. B.A., Amherst Coll., 1947. Author works including: Jim's Book: A Collection of Poems and Short Stories, 1942, The Black Swan, 1946, First Poems, 1951, The Bait, 1953, Short Stories, 1954, The Immortal Husband, 1955, The Seraglio, 1957, The Country of a Thousand Years of Peace, 1959, Selected Poems, 1961, Water Street, 1962, The Thousand and Second Night, 1963, Violent Pastoral, 1965, The (Diblos) Notebook, 1965, Nights and Days, 1967 (Nat. Book award poetry 1967), The Fire Screen, 1969, Braving the Elements, 1972, Two Poems: From the Cupola and the Summer People, 1972, Yannina 1973, The Yellow Pages, 1974, Divine Comedies, 1976 (Pulitzer Prize for Poetry 1977), Metamorphosis of 741, 1977, Mirabell: Books of Number, 1978 (Nat. Book award poetry 1979), Scripts for the Pageant, 1980 (Nat. Book Critics Circle award nomination 1980), From the First Nine: Poems 1946-76, 1982, The Changing Light at Sandover, 1982 (Nat. Book Critics Circle award 1983), Santonini Stopping the Leak, 1982, Souvenirs, 1984, Bronze, 1984, Late Settings, 1985, Recitative, 1986, The Image Maker, 1986, The Inner Room, 1988, Three Poems, 1988, A Different Person: A Memoir, 1993, Selected Poems 1946-85, 1993. Served with AUS, 1944-45. Recipient Oscar Blumenthal prize, 1947, Levinson prize Poetry Mag., 1949, Harriet Monroe Meml. prize, 1951, Morton Dauwen Zabel Meml. prize, 1965, Bollingen prize poetry, 1973, Rebekah Johnson Bobbitt Nat. prize poetry, 1990. Mem. Nat. Inst. Arts and Letters, Am. Acad. and Inst. Arts and Letters. Home: Stonington Conn. Died Feb. 6, 1995.

MERRILL, JAMES MERCER, history educator, writer; b. L.A., Apr. 25, 1920; s. Clarence Mercer and Helen Eugenia (Hillman) M.; m. Ann Elizabeth McIntosh, July 7, 1945; children: Eugenia Louise, James McIntosh. BA, Pomona Coll., 1947; MA, Claremont Grad. Sch., 1949; PhD, U. Calif., L.A., 1954. Asst. prof. Whittier Coll., 1952-56, asso. prof., 1957-66; prof. history U. Del., Newark, 1966-95; dir. U. Del. Press. Author: Rebel Shore, 1958, Quarter-Deck and Fo'c'sle, 1962, Uncommon Valor, 1964, Target Tokyo, 1964, Spurs to Glory, 1966, Battle Flags South, 1970, William Tecumseh Sherman, 1972 (Florence Roberts Head Meml. book award), The USA: History of the American Republic, 1975, A Sailors Admiral: William F. Halsey, 1976; DuPont: Making of an Admiral, 1986, Fleet Admiral William F. Halsey Jr., 1992, Men of War: Great Naval Leaders of World War Two. Served to lt. (j.g.) USNR, 1942-46. Recipient Harry E. Pratt Meml. award; John and Dora Haynes grantee, 1958; Guggenheim research fellow, 1958-59; Mershon Nat. Security fellow, 1961-62. Mem. Am. Hist. Assn., So. Hist. Assn., Phi Beta Kappa, Phi Kappa Phi. Home: Newark Del. Died Mar. 22, 1995.

MESGARZADEH, MAMED, radiologist; b. Tabriz, Azarbaijan, Iran, Aug. 30, 1944; came to U.S., 1972; s. Mahmoud and Fatemeh (Sharabianlou) M.; m. Faria Moytahedi; 1 child, Eugene Z. MD, Tehran (Iran) U., 1969. Diplomate Am. Bd. Radiology, Am. Bd. Nuclear Medicine. Intern Germantown Hosp., Phila., 1972-73; resident Temple U. Hosp., Phila., 1973-75, Health Sci. U. Oreg., Portland, 1980-82, Germantown Hosp., 1982-83; instr. diagnostic imaging Temple U. Sch. Medicine, Phila., 1984, from asst. prof. to prof. diagnostic imaging, 1985-93; staff radiologist Shriners Hosp., Phila., 1984—. Com. mem. Phila. Roentgen Ray Soc., Phila., 1989-92; sci. com. mem. Pa. Radiological Soc., 1989-92. Seed grant Radiologicol Soc. N.Am., 1987; recipient 1st place award Pa. Radiological Soc., 1987-88. Mem. Am. Coll. Radiology, Internat. Skeletal Radiology, Radiol. Soc. N.Am. (hon. mention and cum laude award 1987), Assn. U. Radiologist, Am. Roentgen Ray Soc. Avocations: photography, computers, boating, wine collecting. DIED 03/17/97. .

METCALF, ARTHUR GEORGE BRADFORD, electronics company executive; b. Boston, Nov. 1, 1908; s. Franklin B. and Emma A. (Maclachlan) M.; m. Mary G. Curtis, Feb. 22, 1935; children: Anne C., Helen C., Mary Lee, Hope S. Student, Mass. Inst. Tech., 1932; S.B., Boston U., 1935, LL.D., 1974, S.M., Harvard U., 1939; S.D., Franklin Pierce Coll., 1966. Engring. test pilot, 1930—; prof. math., physics Boston U., 1935; pres. Electronics Corp. Am., Cambridge, Mass., 1954—. Mil. editor: Strategic Rev; contbr. articles to profl. jours. Chmn. emeritus, bd. trustees, exec. com. Boston U.; bd. overseers Mus. Fine Arts, Boston; mem. trustee coun. Boston U. Med. Ctr.; chmn. U.S. Strategic Inst., Washington. Served to lt. col. AUS, WWII. Decorated Legion of Merit, Commendation medal.; Benjamin Franklin fellow Royal Soc. Arts London, 1972. Asso. fellow Royal Aero. Soc. (London), Inst. Aero. Scis.; mem. Am. Def. Preparedness Assn. (dir.), Phi Beta Kappa. Clubs: Harvard (Boston, N.Y.C.); Harvard Faculty (Boston), Algonquin (Boston); Edgartown (Mass.) Yacht; Army and Navy (Washington). Died Mar. 16, 1997.

METCALF, LAWRENCE VINCENT, investment executive; b. Berkeley, Calif., Sept. 20, 1919; s. John Brockway and Elizabeth Vincent Huntington M.; m. Susan Stimmel, Jan. 27, 1950; children: Elsie (dec.), John Brockway. B.S., U. Calif.-Berkeley, 1940; postgrad., Stanford U., 1941. Auto dealer, 1947-76; ptnr. Tecolote Fund, San Francisco, 1966-90; v.p. Alpine Meadows of Tahoe, Inc., Tahoe City, Calif., 1971-90; also dir. Alpine Meadows of Tahoe, Inc. Pres. San Francisco Symphony Assn., 1974-80; chmn. bd. trustees Town Sch. Boys, 1969-75; trustee U. Calif. Berkeley Found., Pacific Tropical Botanical Gardens; bd. dirs. San Francisco Ballet, 1975-81, San Francisco Opera, 1975-81. Served to lt. comdr. USNR, 1941-45. Mem. Calif. Hist. Soc. (trustee). Clubs: Pacific Union, Burlingame Country. Home: San Francisco Calif. Died Oct. 25, 1990.

MEYER, CHARLES APPLETON, retailing executive; b. Boston, June 27, 1918; s. George von Lengerke and Frances (Saltonstall) M.; m. Suzanne Seyburn, June 15, 1940; children: Brooke M. Gray, Nancy M. Hovey. BA, Phillips Acad.; B.A., Harvard, 1939. With Sears, Roebuck & Co., 1939-69; beginning in New Haven store, successively mail order buyer Sears, Roebuck & Co., Boston; asst. buyer hdqrs. orgn., staff asst. fgn. stores, mgr. fgn. adminstrn., pres. Sears, Roebuck & Co. (Sears subsidiary), Bogota, Colombia, 1953-55; v.p. fgn. ops. Sears, Roebuck & Co., 1955-60; v.p., dir. southwestern ter. Sears, Roebuck & Co. (Sears subsidiary), 1960-66, v.p., dir. Eastern ter., 1966-69, v.p. corp. planning, 1973-78, sr. v.p. public affairs, 1978-81; ret., 1980; asst. sec. state for inter-Am. affairs, 1969-73; bd. dirs. Addison Capital Shares. Life trustee Children's Meml. Hosp. Chgo., Art Inst. Chgo., Lake Forest (Ill.) Coll.; trustee emeritus Phillips Acad., Andover, Mass. Capt. AUS, World War II. Clubs: Harvard (N.Y.C.); Racquet (Chgo.); Old Elm (Ft. Sheridan, Ill.); Shoreacres (Lake Bluff, Ill.); Metropolitan (Washington). Home: Chicago Ill. Died Aug. 12, 1996.

MEYER, CHARLES EDWARD, art historian, educator; b. Detroit, Sept. 7, 1928; s. Heinz Adolph and Anna (Blunck) M.; m. Marjorie Ellen Keilholz, June 14, 1952; children: Heidi Anna, Katrina Ellen, Karl Victor. BFA, Wayne State U., 1950, MA, 1952; postgrad., Freie U., Berlin, Germany, 1952-54, U. Wurzburg, Germany, 1958-59; Ph.D., U. Mich., 1967. Curator, faculty Detroit Inst. Arts, 1957-58; asst. prof., asso. prof. art history Mich. State U., 1959-66, dir. div. fine arts, 1960-61, acting head art dept., 1960-62; head art dept. Western Mich. U., Kalamazoo, 1966-77; prof. art history Western Mich. U., 1977-83; prof. art history, dir. div. art Bradley U., 1983-90; art cons., 1990-92; juror exhbns. of art. Served with AUS, 1952-54. Recipient Disting. Alumni award Wayne State U., 1967; Fulbright Rsch. grantee, Würzburg, Fed. Republic Germany, 1958-59. Disting. fellow Nat. Assn. Schs. Art and Design; mem. Coll. Art Assn., Midwest Coll. Art Conf., Nat. Assn. Schs. of Art (dir. Div. II schs. 1976-80, accrediting officer 1974-80), Ann Arbor Potters Guild (pres. 1954-57). Home: Kalamazoo Mich. Died Dec. 18, 1992.

MEYER, HANS PAUL, brokerage house executive; b. Vienna, Austria, July 8, 1928; came to U.S., 1938; s. Leo and Julie (Feldman) M.; m. Myrna Spencer, Aug. 22, 1959; children: Robert, Bruce. Student, N.Y. Inst. Arts & Scis., 1947, CCNY, 1948-49, Columbia U., 1951-53, N.Y. Inst. of Fin., 1963-68. Cert. Fin. Planner. Pres. Custom Covers, Inc., New Rochelle, N.Y., 1948-68, Sport Tech., Inc., New Rochelle, N.Y., 1948-68, Air Tech. Industries, Clifton, N.J., 1955-68; v.p. Paine Webber, Inc., N.Y.C., 1968-84, Prudential Securities, Inc., Mount Kisco, N.Y., 1984—; assoc. prof., dir. cert. fin. planner program, Adelphi U., Garden City, N.J., 1977-85. Inventor: inflatable structures (8 patents), 1955-62, automated garage (5 patents), 1973; designer: N.J. Expo Pavilion (2nd prize), 1964, curriculum for AdelphiU. Cert. Fin. Planner degree, Garden City, N.Y., 1977; cons. Prentice Hall's Income Tax Text Book, 1978. Active Charitable Trust, Rockefeller U., N.Y.C., 1978, White Plains (N.Y.) Hosp., White Plains (N.Y.) Sch. Bd., Am. Diabetes Assn., N.Y.C., 1980. Avocations: inventing, traveling, bicycle touring in U.S. and abroad. Died Jan. 1993.

MEYER, SANDRA W(ASSERSTEIN), bank executive, management consultant; b. N.J., Aug. 20, 1937; children—Jenifer Anne Schweitzer, Samantha Boughton Schweitzer. Student, U. Mich.; B.A. cum laude, Syracuse U., 1957; postgrad., London Sch. Econs., 1958. Advt. account exec. London Press Exchange, 1959-63; product mgr. Beecham Products Inc., Clifton, N.J., 1963-66; with Gen. Foods Co., White Plains, N.J., 1966-76; mktg. mgr. coffee div. Gen. Foods Co., 1973-74, dir. corp. mktg. planning, 1975-76; with Am. Express Co., N.Y.C., 1976-84; pres. communications div. Am. Express Co., 1980-84; mng. dir. Russell Reynolds Assocs., N.Y.C., 1985-89; sr. corp. officer corp. affairs Citicorp, N.Y.C., 1989-93; sr. partner Clark & Weinstock, N.Y.C., 1993-98. Trustee Met. Opera Guild, East Hampton Guild Hall; mng. dir. Met. Opera Assn.; bd. dirs. St. Luke's Orch. Home: New York N.Y. Died Dec. 30, 1997.

MICCIO, JOSEPH V., business educator, consultant; b. Bklyn., May 1, 1915; s. Salvatore and Marian (Lauro) M.; m. Lillian Teves Pratt, Oct. 12, 1957; children: Kathryn, Michael. B.B.A. cum laude (econ. award), St. John's U., 1938; M.A. cum laude, NYU, 1940, Ed.D., 1965; LL.D., Fairleigh Dickinson U., 1963. C.P.A., N.Y. Accountant Rockwood & Co., Bklyn., 1932-39; controller Lightfoot, Schultz Co., N.J., 1939-42; controller, asst. to financial v.p. Republic Aviation Corp., L.I., 1942-45; controller-treas. Air-cooled Motors, Inc., Syracuse, N.Y., 1945-50; gen. mgr. electronics div. Curtiss-Wright Corp., 1951-54, v.p. corp., 1953-64; pres., gen. mgr. Curtiss-Wright Corp. (Wright Aero. div.), Wood-Ridge, N.J., 1954-64, sr. v.p., 1964-66, gen. mgr. plastics div., 1953-54; gen. mgr., exec. v.p. Columbia Protektosite Co. (wholly-owned subs.), 1951-54; chmn. bd. Redel Corp., Anaheim, Calif.; adj. prof. Fairleigh Dickinson U.; instr. NYU; prof. mgmt. and bus. policy U. Hawaii, 1966-69, prof., 1969-96, chmn. Grad. Sch. Bus., 1966-69, assoc. dean Coll. Bus. Adminstrn., 1966-69; founder, chmn. bd., CEO, Hawaii Biotech. Group, Inc.; mgr. Hawaiian State Kitechs Bus. Incubator Facility in Honolulu; mem. state com. on employee stock ownership plans, Hawaii Govs. Task Force on Internat. Bus.; bd. dirs. Sun Fashions Inc., Cen. Pacific Supply Inc., IMUA Builders,, Grace Pacific Corp., Hawkins Audio Comm., Inc.; adviser SBA; Hawaii del. Pres.'s Conf. Small Bus., 1980, 87; advisor Hawaii State Com. on E.S.O.P.'s, Hawaii State Spaceport Com. Contbr. articles to profl. jours. Trustee N.J. Symphony; bd. fellows Fairleigh Dickinson U.; mem. coun. St. John's U.; bd. regents Chaminade U., Honolulu. Recipient award of merit Aircraft War Prodn. Coun.; Founders award NYU; Profl. Mgr. award Soc. Advancement Mgmt., 1975; Outstanding Educator award and Excellence in Teaching award U. Hawaii Coll. Bus. Adminstrn., 1985, U. Pres. Citation for Teaching Excellence U. Hawaii, 1986, Bus. Advocate award for Region IX (Calif., Ariz., Nev., Hawaii) U.S. SBA, 1988. Fellow Soc. Advancement of Mgmt.; mem. N.Y. State Soc. CPAs, Fin. Execs. Inst., Am. Arbitration Assn., Am. Mgmt. Assn., Fin. Execs. Inst., Aerospace Industries Assn., Acad. Mgmt., Am. Inst. C.P.A.s, AIAA, Navy League U.S., Conquistadores del Cielo, Honolulu C. of C., Phi Delta Kappa, Phi Delta Epsilon, Beta Gamma Sigma (adv. com. to Hawaii Crime Com.). Clubs: Economic (N.Y.C.); Outrigger Canoe. Died July 13, 1996.

MICHAELIS, GEORGE H., securities executive; b. 1937. BS in Engring. with honors, UCLA, 1958; MBA with distinction, Harvard Bus. Sch., 1960. V.p.

Hohneberg & Assocs., Inc., 1969-71; sr. v.p. Source Capital, Inc., L.A., 1971-76, pres., dir., 1978—; sr. v.p. CMB Investment Counselors, 1976-78; exec. v.p. Paramount Mutual Fund, Inc., L.A.; chmn. bd., CEO First Pacific Advisors, Inc.

MICHAK, HELEN BARBARA, educator, nurse; b. Cleve., July 31; d. Andrew and Mary (Patrick) M. Diploma Cleve. City Hosp. Sch. Nursing, 1947; BA, Miami U., Oxford, Ohio, 1951; MA, Case Western Res. U., 1960. Staff nurse Cleve. City Hosp., 1947-48; pub. health nurse Cleve. Div. Health, 1951-52; instr. Cleve. City Hosp. Sch. Nursing, 1952-56; supr. nursing Cuyahoga County Hosp., Cleve., 1956-58; pub. information dir. N.E. Ohio Am. Heart Assn., Cleve., 1960-64; dir. spl. events Higbee Co., Cleve., 1964-66; exec. dir. Cleve. Area League for Nursing, 1966-72; dir. continuing edn. nurses, adj. assoc. prof. Cleve. State U., 1972-86; asst. regional cons. Ohio Bd. Nursing, 1991-98. Trustee N.E. Ohio Regional Med. Program, 1970-73; mem. adv. com. Dept. Nursing Cuyahoga C.C., 1967-87; mem. long term care com. Met. Health Planning Corp., 1974-76, plan devel. com. 1977; mem. policy bd. Ctr. Health Data N.E. Ohio, 1972-73; mem. Rep. Assembly and Health Planning and Devel. Commn., Welfare Fedn. Cleve., 1967-72, Cleve. Cmty. Health Network, 1972-73, United Appeal Films and Speakers Bur., 1967-73; mem. adv. com. Ohio Fedn. Lic. Practical Nurses, 1970-73; mem. tech. adv. com. No. Ohio Lung Assn., 1967-74, 90-93; mem. Ohio Commn. on Nursing, 1971-74; mem. citizens com. nursing homes Fedn. Community Planning, 1973-77; mem. com. on home health services Met. Health Planning Corp., 1973-75; mem. profl. adv. com. on home care Fairview Gen. Hosp., 1987-91. Mem. Nat. League Nursing (mem. com. 1970-72), Am. Nurses Assn. (accreditation visitor 1977-78, 83-88) Ohio Nurses Assn., (com. continuing edn. 1974-79, 82-87, 89-92, chmn. 1984-86), Greater Cleve. (joint practice com. 1973-74, Greater Cleve. Nurses Assn. (trustee 1975-76) , Cleve. Area Citizens League for Nursing (trustee 1976-79, v.p. 1988-90), Zeta Tau Alpha, Sigma Theta Tau. Democrat.

MICHALKO, JÁN, bishop; b. Važec, East Slovakia, Oct. 16, 1912; s. Ján Michalko and Anna (Duranová) Michalková; m. Alžbeta Škovranová, June 4, 1946; children: Alžbeta Darina, Viera, Ján Vladimír, Ludmila. BA in Theology, Slovak Luth. Sem., Czechoslovakia, 1937, ThD, 1946, ThD (honoris causa), 1989; ThD (honoris causa), Friedrich Schiller U., Fed. Republic Germany, 1963; PhD (honoris causa), Christian Theol. Acad., Poland, 1974, Evang. Theol. Acad., Hungary, 1978, Muhlenberg Coll., 1988, Orthodox Theol. Sem., Czechoslovakia, 1988. Ordained to ministry Slovak Evang. Luth. Ch. Czechoslovakia, 1937. Clergyman Slovak Evang. Luth. Ch. Czechoslovakia, Važec, 1937; clergyman parish office Slovak Evang. Luth. Ch. Czechoslovakia, Bratislava, 1937-38; clergyman Slovak Evang. Luth. Ch. Czechoslovakia, Spišská Nová Ves, 1938-42, Pozdišovce, 1942-47, Myslenice, 1947-54, Rača, 1954-59; clergyman Slovak Evang. Luth. Ch. Czechoslovakia, Bratislava, 1959-70, gen. bishop, 1970-90; prof. systematic and practical theology Slovak Luth. Sem., Bratislava, 1953; chmn. com. of liturgy and spiritual life Luth. World Fedn., Geneva, 1965-77, mem. exec. com., 1970-76; chmn. liturgical com. Slovak Evang. Luth. Ch. Czechoslovakia, Bratislava, 1970-90, mem. com. for preparation of 1st Slovak lang. hymnal; chmn. com. mgmt. Tranoscius pub. house, LiptovskY Mikulás, Czechoslovakia, 1970-90; mem. com. of world's mission and evangelization World Coun. Chs., 1957-90; mem. com. Leuenberg Dialogues. Author: Kážňové smery v evanjelickej cirkvi, 1955; also articles; editor: Evanjelická Postila, Cirkevné listy jour., 1952-64; editor in chief Služba slova, 1952-90; prime leader, mem. com. of 1st transl. of Bible into modern Slovak lang., 1977. Mem. com. Found. Dr. Martin Niemüller, Wiesbaden, Fed. Republic Germany, Theol. Sem. Mem. Societas Ethica, Conf. European Chs. Died Dec. 10, 1990.

MICHALOS, JAMES, educator, consulting engineer; b. Milw., Sept. 12, 1912; s. Peter and Angeline (Metros) M.; m. Claire Pappas, June 4, 1939; children—Kiki, Peter. B.S., U. Wis., 1938; M.Engring., Yale, 1945; Ph.D., Northwestern U., 1949. Designer Chas. S. Whitney (cons. engr.), Milw., 1938; project engr. Chas. W. Cole & Son, Gary, Ind., 1938-40; civil engr. Michael Pontarelli & Sons, Chgo., 1940; asso. structural engr. TVA, 1940-43; designer Carnegie-Ill. Steel Corp., Gary, Ind., 1943; asst. prof. Mont. State Coll., 1944-46, Syracuse U., 1946-47; assoc. prof. Iowa State Coll., 1947-52; prof., 1952-54; prof. civil engring., chmn. dept. N.Y. U., 1954-73; prof. civil engring. Poly. Inst. N.Y., 1973-81; Engring. cons., 1945—. Author: Theory of Structural analysis and Design, 1958, Structural Mechanics and Analysis, 1965, also papers in field.; Editor civil engineering sect.: Sci. Ency, 1958. NSF sr. postdoctoral fellow U. Cambridge, Eng., 1963. Mem. ASCE, Am. Ry. Engring. Assn., Am. Concrete Inst., Art Students League, AAUP, Sigma Xi, Chi Epsilon. DIED 01/07/95. .

MICHELS, EUGENE, physical therapist; b. Cin., May 16, 1926; s. Joseph and Anna (Bauer) M.; m. Genevieve Wilma Readinger, June 28, 1947; children: Karen, Timothy, Donald, Marian, Monica, Martha, David, Ann. B.S., U. Cin., 1950; cert. phys. therapy, U. Pa., 1951, M.A., 1965; Litt.D. (hon.), Thomas Jefferson U., 1985. Phys. therapist Grad. Hosp., U. Pa., Phila., 1951-58, mem. faculty dept. phys. therapy, 1965-96, asst. prof., 1969-75, asso. prof., 1975-77; dir. phys. therapy Magee Meml. Hosp., Phila., 1958-65; assoc. exec. v.p. Am. Phys. Therapy Assn., 1977-88. Served with USNR, 1944-46. Recipient Lindback Found. Disting. Tchg. award, 1972; Pa. Phys. Therapy Assn. ann. achievement award named Carlin-Michels Achievement award in honor of Eleanor J. Carlin and Eugene Michels. Mem. Pa. Phys. Therapy Assn. (past pres.), Am. Phys. Therapy Assn. (past pres., Dorothy Briggs Meml. Sci. Inquiry award 1971, Golden Pen award 1977, Mary McMillan lectr. 1984, Catherine Worthingham fellow 1986, Eugene Michels New Investigator award established in his honor 1989, John Maley award sect. rsch. 1994), World Confedn. Phys. Therapy (pres. 1974-82). Democrat. Roman Catholic. Home: College Park Md. Died Nov. 14, 1996.

MICHENER, JAMES ALBERT, author; b. N.Y.C., Feb. 3, 1907; s. Edwin and Mabel (Haddock) M.; m. Patti Koon, July 27, 1935 (div.); m. Vange Nord, Sept. 2, 1948 (div.); m. Mari Yoriko Sabusawa, Oct. 23, 1955 (dec. 1994). A.B. summa cum laude, Swarthmore Coll., 1929; A.M., U. No. Colo., 1937; research study, U. Pa., U. Va., Ohio State U., Harvard U., U. St. Andrews, Scotland, U. Siena, Italy, Brit. Mus. London; research study (Lippincott Traveling fellow), 1930-33, numerous hon. degrees. Tchr. Hill Sch., 1929-31, George Sch., Pa., 1933-36; prof. Colo. State Coll. Edn., 1936-41; vis. prof. Harvard U., 1939-40; asso. editor Macmillan Co., 1941-49; mem. adv. com. on arts State Dept., 1957; mem. adv. council NASA, 1980-83; mem. U.S. Adv. Commn. on Info., 1971; mem. Citizen's Adv. Stamp Com., 1982-87; mem. Bd. for Internat. Broadcasting. Author: Unit in the Social Studies, 1940, Tales of the South Pacific, 1947 (Pulitzer prize), The Fires of Spring, 1949, Return to Paradise, 1951, The Voice of Asia, 1951, The Bridges at Toko Ri, 1953, Sayonara, 1954, Floating World, 1955, The Bridge at Andau, 1957, Rascals in Paradise, (with A. Grove Day), 1957, Selected Writings, 1957, The Hokusai Sketchbook, 1958, Japanese Prints, 1959, Hawaii, 1959, Report of the County Chairman, 1961, Caravans, 1963, The Source, 1965, Iberia, 1968, Presidential Lottery, 1969, The Quality of Life, 1970, Kent State, 1971, The Drifters, 1971, A Michener Miscellany, 1973, Centennial, 1974, Sports in America, 1976, Chesapeake, 1978, The Covenant, 1980, Space, 1982, Poland, 1983, Texas, 1985, Legacy, 1987, Journey, 1988, Alaska, 1988, Caribbean, 1989; (with John Kings) Six Days in Havana, 1989, The Novel, 1991, The World Is My Home, 1991, Writer's Handbook, 1992, Mexico, 1992, My Lost Mexico, 1992, Creatures of the Kingdom: Stories of Animals and Nature, 1993, Literary Reflections: Michener on Michener, Hemingway, Capote, and Others, 1993, Recessional, 1994, Miracle in Seville, 1995, This Noble Land: My Vision for America, 1996; editor: Future of Social Studies for N.E.A, 1940. With USNR, 1944-46. Recipient U.S. Medal of Freedom, Disting. Svc. medal NASA, Golden Badge of Order of Merit, 1988. Mem. Phi Beta Kappa. Democrat. Mem. Soc. of Friends. Home: Austin Tex. Died Oct. 16, 1997.

MIFUNE, TOSHIRO, actor, film producer; b. Chintago, Japan, Apr. 1, 1920; s. Tokuzo and Sen M.; children: Shiro, Takeshi. Film actor, 1947—; films include These Foolish Times, 1947, Drunken Angel, 1948, The Seven Samurai, Rashamon, 1950, The Legend of Musashi, 1954, The Rickshawman, 1958, The Hidden Fortress, 1958, The Three Treasures, 1959, Yojimbo, 1961, The Storm of the Pacific, Grand Prix, Rebellion, 1965, Admiral Yamamoto, 1968, Hell In The Pacific, 1968, Furinkazan, 1969, Red Sun, 1971, Paper Tiger, 1974, The Battle of Midway, 1975, Shogun, 1981, The Equals, 198, Inchon, 1982, The Challenge, 1982, The Death of Tea Master, 1989, Journey of Honor, 1992, Shadow of the Wolf, 1993, others; pres. Mifune Prodns. Co. Ltd. Clubs: Hunting, Yacht, Flying. Office: Mifune Prodns Co Ltd, 9-30-7 Seijyo Setagaya-ku, Tokyo Japan

MIHALICH, HERMAN, state legislator; b. Monessen, Pa., Aug. 3, 1930; m. Lois E. Mihalich. BA, U. Pitts., 1953; student, Calif. U., Pa., 1971; AA, Westmoreland County Cmty. Coll, 1973. Pa. state rep. Dist. 58, 1990—; real estate broker. Democrat. Died Sept. 30, 1997.

MIKLOWITZ, JULIUS, educator, scientist; b. Schenectady, May 22, 1919; s. Henry and Rebecca (Wolf) M.; m. Gloria Elaine Dubov, Aug. 28, 1948; children—Paul Stephen, David Jay. B.S. in Mech. Engring, U. Mich., 1943; M.S. in Engring. Mechanics, 1948, Ph.D., 1949. Rsch. engr. plasticity Westinghouse Rsch. Labs., 1943-46, 49; asso. prof. engring., head dept. N.Mex. Inst. Mining and Tech., 1949-51; rsch. engr., cons. solid mechanics Naval Ordnance Test Sta., 1951-56; faculty Calif. Inst. Tech., Pasadena, 1956—; prof. applied mechanics Calif. Inst. Tech., 1962-85, prof. emeritus, 1985—; Cons. to industry, govt., 1956—; W.W. Clyde prof. engring. U. Utah, 1970; Mem. U.S. Nat. Com. on Theoretical and Applied Mechanics, 1976-80. Author: Theory of Elastic Waves and Waveguides, 1978; editor: Wave Propagation in Solids, 1969, Modern Problems in Elastic Wave Propagation, 1978, Wave Motion, 1979—. Westinghouse Research Labs. grad. fellow, 1946-49; NSF sr. postdoctoral fellow, 1964-65. Fellow ASME (exec. com. applied mechanics div. 1971-76, chmn. div. 1975-76, Policy Bd. engr. 1979-80); mem. AAAS, AAUP, Internat. Soc. Interaction Mechanics and Math. Research and publs. on wave propagation in solids, yielding, fracture metals, polymers.

MIKULSKI, PIOTR WITOLD, mathematics educator; b. Warsaw, Poland, July 20, 1925; came to U.S., 1957; s. Julian and Zofia (Zalewska) M.; m. Barbara H. Weston, Sept. 2, 1960; 1 son, Antony F. B.S., Sch. Stats., Warsaw, Poland, 1951, M.S., 1952; Ph.D., U. Calif.-Berkeley, 1961. Adj. Sch. Stats., 1950-57, Inst. Math., Warsaw, Poland, 1952-57; teaching and research asst. U. Calif.-Berkeley, 1957-61; asst. prof. math. U. Ill., Urbana, 1961-62; asst. prof. U. Md., College Park, 1962-66, assoc. prof., 1966-70, prof., 1970. Assoc. editor: Am. Jour. Math. and Mgmt. Sci., 1982-97; contbr. articles to profl. jours. Mem. Inst. Math. Stats., Polish Inst. Arts and Scis. Am. Home: Annapolis Md. Died July 24, 1997.

MILBURN, JOHN ANTHONY, botany educator; b. Carlisle, Cumbria, U.K., Aug. 7, 1936; arrived in Australia, 1981; s. Tom and Margaret Agnes (Johnston) M.; m. Anita Sheila Fyfe; children: Dirk Bryon, Erik Alan, Hazel Karen. BSc with honors, U. Durham, U.K., 1958; PhD, U. Aberdeen, U.K., 1964. Lectr. U. Glasgow, U.K., 1964; sr. lectr. U. Glasgow, 1972-79, reader, 1979-80; prof. U. New England, Armidale, Australia, 1981—; dean of sci. U. New England, Armidale, 1982-85; agronomist Bookers Sugar Estates, Georgetown, Guyana, 1958-60; cons. expert Internat. Atomic Energy Assn., Vienna, Sri Lanka, 1988. Author: Water Flow in Plants, 1979; editor (with M.H. Zimmermann) Transport in Plants Phloem Transport, 1975, (with D.A. Baker) Transport of Photoassimilates, 1989; contbr. articles to profl. jours. Overseas Visiting fellow Brit. Coun., U.K./India, 1972; Fulbright Hays scholar Harvard U., 1973-74. Fellow Inst. Biology; mem. Australian Soc. Plant Physiology, Biophys. Soc., Internat. Assn. Wood Anatomists. Humanist. Avocations: squash, scuba, windsurfing, ultralight pilot, photography. Died June 9, 1997; cremated.

MILLER, DONALD MORTON, physiology educator; b. Chgo., July 24, 1930; s. Harry Madison and Anna Loraine (Zeller) M.; 1 son, Tad Michael. A.B. in Zoology, U. Ill., Urbana, 1960, M.A. in Physiology, 1962, Ph.D. (NIH fellow), 1965; NIH postgrad. fellow, UCLA, 1965-66. Insp. Buick Jet div. Gen. Motors Corp., Willow Springs, Ill., 1953-55; sci. asst. Organic Chemistry Lab., U. Ill., 1960-62, counselor residence halls, 1960-63, teaching asst. physiology, 1960-64; mem. faculty So. Ill. U., Carbondale, 1966-97, prof. physiology, 1976-94, retired, 1995, vis. prof., 1995; adj. prof. McKendree Coll., Lebanon, Ill., 1986-88, Queensland U. of Tech., Brisbane, Australia, 1989; Damon lectr., 1973-74; lectr. trauma edn. Ill. Hwy. Div., So. Ill. Health Manpower Consortium, Critical Care Nurse Program; judge Ill. Jr. Acad. Sci; vis. instr. Nakajo, Japan, 1992. Contbr. articles to profl. jours. Treas. Jackson County chpt. ARC, 1973-79; active CAP, 1968-79. Served with USAF, 1955-59. USPHS summer grantee, 1962, 73, NIH grantee, 1968-80, NASA grantee, 1973-85, Coll. Sea Grant Program grantee, 1983-88, U.S. Army Med. Rsch. Inst. grantee, 1987-92. Mem. Am. Physiol. Soc., Biophys. Soc., Am. Microscopic Soc., Neurosci. Soc., Am. Soc. Zoologists, N.Y. Acad. Scis., Am. Soc. Photobiology (charter), Am. Soc. Parasitologists (ednl. policies com.), Am. Midwest Conf. of Parasitologists (pres. 1980-81 sec.-treas. 1985-93), Am. Trauma Soc., Sigma Xi (past chpt. pres.), Chi Gamma Iota. Clubs: Elks, Lions. Died May 27, 1997.

MILLER, FRANKLIN RUSH, internist, educator; b. Bloomington, Ill., Aug. 24, 1902; s. Frank Ira and Sadie Jackman (Kimball) M.; m. Anne McAllister, July 10, 1931 (div. 1940); 1 child, Franklin Rush; m. Ellen Newhall, Apr. 5, 1941; children: Ellen Newhall Lewis, Mary Caroline Miller Thorington, Cushman Newhall. BS, Ill. Wesleyan U., 1923; MD, Harvard U., 1927. Diplomate Am. Bd. Internal Medicine. Resident Huntington Meml. Hosp., Boston, 1927-28; intern Boston City Hosp., 1928-29; asst. and fellow in bacteriology and pathology Rockefeller Inst., N.Y.C., 1929-31; chief med. resident Lakeside Hosp./Univ. Hosps., Cleve., 1931-32; from demonstrator to asst. prof. Western Res. U. Med. Sch., Cleve., 1931-39; asst. prof., then assoc. prof. Jefferson Med. Coll., 1939-55; assoc. prof. medicine, neurology U. Kans., 1957-60; assoc. prof. medicine, then vis. prof. medicine Hahnemann U., Phila., 1960-81; chief of internal medicine Snyder Clinic Assn., Winfield, Kans., 1960-81; chief internal medicine Snyder Clinic, Winfield, 1954-60; acting supt. Winfield State Hosp. and Tng. Ctr., 1958-59, supt., 1959-60. Contbr. articles to profl. jours. Mem. ACP, AAAS, AMA, Am. Assn. Cancer Rsch., Am. Soc. Clin. Investigation, Am. Soc. Exptl. Pathology, Soc. Exptl. Biology and Medicine, Internat. Hematological Assn., Am. Soc. Hematology, Am. Therapeutic Soc., Phila. Coll. Physicians, Am. Assn. Pathologists, Coll. Physicians, Am. Assn. Pathologists, N.Y. Acad. Scis., Alpha Omega Alpha, Sigma Chi, Phi Chi. Home: Winfield Kans. Died Aug. 22, 1995; interred Union Cemetery, Winfield, KS.

MILLER, GAVIN, lawyer; b. N.Y.C., Mar. 8, 1926; s. George Gavin and Catherine (Schurman) M.; m.

Camilla Congreve Strong, Aug. 15, 1959 (dec. Mar. 1982); children: Emily, Louise, Catherine; m. Suzanne Techentin, Feb. 17, 1991. AB, Harvard U., 1950, LLB, 1953. Bar: N.Y. 1955, Calif. 1962. Assoc. Davis, Polk & Wardwell, N.Y.C., 1953-61; assoc. Kindel & Anderson, L.A., 1961-63, ptnr., 1963-66; ptnr. Agnew, Miller & Carlson, L.A., 1966-81, Hufstedler, Miller, Carlson & Beardsley, 1981-90, Heller, Ehrman, Smith & McAuliffe, L.A., 1990—. With AUS, 1944-46. Mem. ABA, State Bar Calif., L.A. County Bar Assn., (trustee 1978-84, v.p. 1980-81, sr. v.p. 1981-82, pres.-elect 1982-83, pres. 1983-84), N.Y. State Bar Assn., Nature Conservancy (trustee So. Calif. chpt. 1974-80), California Club, University Club, (N.Y.C., L.A.), Phi Beta Kappa. DIED 06/15/97. .

MILLER, GLENN, library director, retired; b. Saginaw, Mich., Dec. 5, 1937; s. H.H. and Evelyn Miller; m. Janice Gase, Aug. 11, 1962; children: Anne, Thomas, John. AA, Bay City (Mich.) Jr. Coll., 1960; BA in Polit. Sci., U. Mich., 1962, MLS, 1963. City librarian Southfield, Mich., 1963-66; dir. Genessee County Libr. System, Flint, Mich., 1967-69; asst. dir. Orlando (Fla.) Pub. Libr., 1969-70; dir. Orange County Libr. System, Orlando, 1970-95; ret., 1995; cons. in field. Bd. dirs. Additions of Orange County, 1974-77, Sta. WMFE Pub. TV, Orlando, 1970-76; bd. trustees Lucerne Hosp., Orlando, 1974-79. Mem. ALA (chmn. constitution and by-laws com. 1973-76), Pub. Library Assn. of ALA (bd. dirs. 1974-77), Southeastern Library Assn., Fla. Library Assn. (chmn. edn. com. 1974-76, legis. and planning com. 1978-79, pres. 1977-78). DIED 06/24/96. .

MILLER, JACK BARNETT, retired physician; b. Winslow, Ind., June 17, 1918; s. Lawrence R. and Bess Ellen (Barnett) M.; m. Jeanne Pierson, June 5, 1943; children—John Ross, Jeffrey Allen. A.B., Ind. U., 1939, M.D., 1943. Diplomate: Am. Bd. Otolaryngology. Intern Indpls. City Hosp., 1943-44; fellow in otolaryngology Cleve. Clinic Found., 1946-49; chief dept. otolaryngology Med. Clinic, Portland, Oreg., 1949-85; mem. staffs Emanuel Hosp., Portland, Shrine Hosp., Portland, Portland Adventist Hosp., Physician and Surgeons Hosp., Portland, City of Roses Hosp., Portland, Dwyer Meml. Hosp., Milwaukie, Oreg.; clin. instr. U. Oreg., 1950-61; otolaryngology preceptor for intern-resident tng. program Emanuel Hosp., 1955-85 ; cons. Shriner Hosp., 1954-85. Contbr. articles to profl. jours. Served to capt. M.C. AUS, 1944-46, 51-51. Decorated Combat Med. badge, Bronze Star medal; recipient certificate of acknowledgement Shriners Hosp. for Crippled Children, 1962, certificate of appreciation Chiron Club Phi Beta Pi, 1955, Physicians Recognition award AMA, 1969-95; certificate for participation as active tchr. Am. Acad. Family Physicians, 1976, 78, 79. Mem. AAAS, AMA, Am. Assn. Study Headache, Am. Thoracic Soc., Internat. Corr. Soc. Ophthalmologists and Otolaryngologists, Oreg. Acad. Ophthalmology and Otolaryngology (pres. 1970-71), Oreg. Ifed. Assn., Pacific Coast Soc. Otolaryngology and Ophthalmology, Pan-Pacific Surg. Assn., Am. Acad. Otolaryngology and Ophthalmology, Am. Laryngol., Rhinol., Otolaryn. Soc., Pan-Am. Assn. Oto-Rhinol., Laryngol. and Broncho-Esophaegeal, Pan-Am. Med. Assn., Am., Internat. rhinologic socs., Am. Council Otolaryngology, Delta Upsilon. Republican. Mem. Christian Ch. (Disciples of Christ). Clubs: Internat. Active (appreciation certificate 19—, chmn. com. hearings 1954-55), Portland Active (pres. 1952-53), Multnomah Athletic. Lodge: Masons. Home: Portland Oreg. Died Oct. 1, 1995.

MILLER, LEONARD DAVID, surgeon; b. Jersey City, July 8, 1930; s. Louis Abner and Esther (Levy) M.; children—Steven Lawrence, Jason Lloyd. A.B., Yale U., 1951; M.D., U. Pa., 1955. Intern Hosp. of U. Pa., Phila., 1955-56; resident Hosp. of U. Pa., 1956-57, 59-65; practice medicine, specializing in surgery Phila., 1965—; vice chmn. dept. research and surgery U. Pa., 1972-75, acting chmn., 1975-78, John Rhea Barton prof., 1978-83, chmn. dept. surgery, 1978-83; dir. Harrison Dept. Surgery. Mem. editorial bd.: Annals of Surgery, 1973—. Served to capt., M.C. USAF, 1957-59. Recipient Lindback award for disting. teaching, 1969, Student award for clin. teaching, 1965. Mem. Am. Surg. Assn., AAAS, Soc. for Surgery of Alimentary Tract, Nat. Soc. Med. Research (rep.), Soc. Univ. Surgeons, Am. Soc. Surgery of Trauma, Coll. Physicians of Phila., N.Y. Acad. Sci., Sigma Xi, Alpha Omega Alpha. Died June 24, 1997.

MILLER, MORTON DAVID, retired life insurance company executive; b. N.Y.C., Jan. 4, 1915; s. Samuel A. and Rhea R. (Loewenthal) M.; m. Florence Louis, Feb. 14, 1949; 1 son, Jonathan David. B.S. cum laude, CCNY, 1937. With Equitable Life Assurance Soc. U.S., N.Y.C., 1937-80; dir. Equitable Life Assurance Soc. U.S., 1971, exec. v.p., chief actuary, 1973-80, vice chmn. bd., 1975-80; advisor to chmn. Nat. Exec. Service Corps, N.Y.C., 1980-95; dir. Nat. Found. Life Ins. Co.; Mem. actuarial adv. com. N.Y. State Dept. Audit and Control. Bd. dirs. N.Y. Urban Coalition, Point Lookout Civic Assn., City Coll. Fund; chmn. Nat. Med. Fellowships Inc.; mem. Alumni Devel. Council CUNY; bd. overseers Sch. Medicine; mem. adv. council on Social Security HEW, 1978-79, mem. adv. com. on nat. health ins. issues, 1977; adv. panel on med. tech. Office Technol. Assessment, U.S. Congress. Fellow Soc. Actuaries (pres. 1967-68, bd. govs. 1957-70); mem. Am. Acad. Actuaries (pres. 1973, bd. dirs.), Am. Arbitration Assn. (nat. panel arbitrators), Inst. of Medicine, Nat. Acad. Scis., Nat. Health Council (bd. dirs., pres.), Pilgrims of U.S. Club: Univ. Home: New York N.Y. Died July 8, 1995.

MILLER, NAOMI, art historian; b. N.Y.C., Feb. 28, 1928; d. Nathan and Hannah M. B.S., CCNY, 1948; M.A., Columbia U., 1950, NYU, 1960; Ph.D., NYU, 1966. Asst. prof. art history R.I. Sch. Design, 1963-64; asst. prof. U. Calif.-Berkeley, 1969-70; asst. to assoc. prof. Boston U., 1964—, prof. art history, 1981—; vis. prof. U. B.C., Vancouver, 1967, Hebrew U., Jerusalem, 1980, U. Padua, 1990; vis. scholar I Tatti, 1984-85. Author: French Renaissance Fountains, 1977, Heavenly Caves, 1982, Renaissance Bologna, 1989; co-author: Fons Sapientiae: Garden Fountains in Illustrated Books, 16th-18th Centuries, 1977, Boston Architecture 1975-90, 1990; book rev. editor: Jour. Soc. Archtl. Historians, 1975-81, editor, 1981-84; articles, catalogues. Jr. fellow NEH, 1972-73; sr. fellow Dumbarton Oaks, 1976-77, 83-89; vis. sr. fellow Ctr. for Advanced Study in Visual Arts, 1988, 95. Mem. Coll. Art Assn., Soc. Archtl. Historians, Renaissance Soc. Died Jan. 5, 1996.

MILLER, RICHARD HAMILTON, lawyer, broadcasting company executive; b. Cleve., July 18, 1931; s. Ray Thomas and Ruth (Hamilton) M.; m. Ernestine Bowman, Aug. 25, 1985; children: James M., Suanne R., Elizabeth M., Judith K., William P., Matthew W. A.B., U. Notre Dame, 1953, J.D., 1955. Bar: Ohio 1955. Since practiced in Cleve. as mem. firm Miller & Miller; asst. prosecutor Cuyahoga County, 1957-60; pres. Cleve. Broadcasting, Inc., 1966-70, Searles Lake Chem. Corp., Los Angeles, 1966-69, Miller Broadcasting Co., Cleve., 1970-87, Hollywood Bldg. Systems, Inc., Meridian, Miss., 1974-86; mng. partner Miller & Co., Cleve., 1974—; former owner, dir. Cleve. Profl. Basketball Co., Cleve. Baseball, Inc. Dir. gen. counsel Mail Marketing Inc., 1974—, R.W. Sidley, Inc., 1966—; gen. chmn. N.E. Ohio March of Dimes, 1971-73; adv. council Catherine Horstman Home Retarded Children, 1969-73; mem. Cuyahoga Democratic Exec. Com., 1955-66. Served to capt. AUS, 1956-57. Named Irishman of the Yr., City Counsel of Cleve., 1995. Mem. Ohio, Cuyahoga County, Cleve. bar assns., Cleve. Citizens League. Clubs: K.C. (Cleve.), Variety (Cleve.), Notre Dame (Cleve.) (pres. 1964-65), Cleve. Athletic (Cleve.) (dir. 1971-74); Shaker Heights (Ohio) Country. Died Mar. 15, 1997.

MILLER, TEVIE, supernumary justice, academic administrator; b. Edmonton, Alta., Can., Jan. 1, 1928; s. Abe William and Rebecca (Griesdorf) M.; m. Arliss June Toban, June 24, 1951; children: Catherine Dolgoy, Joshua Miller, Lisa Shadlyn. BA, U. Alta., 1949, LLB, 1950, LLD (hon.), 1991; LLD (hon.), U. Alta., 1991. Bar: Alta. 1951. Sr. ptnr. Miller, Miller, Witten, Edmonton, 1974; judge Alta. Dist. Ct., 1974; dep. judge N.W. territories, 1976; appointed to trial div. Supreme Ct. Alta., 1976; dep. judge Yukon territory, 1978; judge Ct. of Queen's Bench of Alta., 1974-84, assoc. chief justice, 1984-93; chancellor U. Alta., Edmonton, 1986-90; sessional lectr. law U. Alta., bd. govs., 1986-90; chmn. bd. Banff (Alta.) Sch. Advanced Mgmt., 1982-92. Former pres., former conv. chmn. Edmonton Liberal Assn.; liberal candidate Edmonton West Fed. Riding, 1968. Served to sub-lt. Royal Can. Navy. Recipient Torch of Learning award Hebrew U. of Jerusalem, 1992; honoree Edmonton Jewish Community Negev Dinner, 1972, Faculty Club of U. Alta. Avocations: sailing, travel.

MILLS, VICTOR, chemical engineer; b. Milford, Nebr., 1897; m. Grace Riggs. Chem. engr. Procter & Gamble Co., Cin. Inventor Pampers, numerous other products. Home: Tucson Ariz. Died 1997.

MILLS, WILLIS NATHANIEL, architect, consultant; b. Menominee, Mich., Jan. 5, 1907; s. Willis Nathaniel and Elizabeth Butler (Wright) M.; m. Esther Stehle, Jan. 28, 1933 (dec. 1985); children: Willis Nathaniel Jr., Matthew Richard. BArch, U. Pa., 1929. Registered architect, Mass. Draftsman, designer Shreve, Lamb & Harmon, N.Y.C., 1929-32; instr. architecture Columbia U., N.Y.C., 1932-33; pvt. practice architecture N.Y.C., Westchester, 1933-38, N.Y.C., Cape Cod, Mass., 1971-95; ptnr. Sherwood Mills & Smith, Architects, N.Y.C., 1946-71; pres. Sherwood Mills & Smith, Architects, Stamford, Conn., 1946-55. Mem. Hist. Dist. Commn., Cape Cod, 1981, 91. Capt. USMC, 1942-45, PTO. Decorated Bronze Star. Fellow AIA (pres. Conn. chpt. 1950-52, jurist ann. awards 1950); mem. Boston Soc. Architects (emeritus), Archtl. League N.Y.C. (chmn. com. 1934-71), Creative Arts Ctr., Boston Mus. Arts, Eastward Ho Country Club (bd. dirs. 1970). Episcopalian. Avocations: watercolor painting, golf. Home: Chatham Mass. Died Sept. 21, 1995; interred St. James the Less, Philadelphia, PA.

MILSTEN, DAVID RANDOLPH, lawyer; b. Coalgate, Okla., Sept. 29, 1903; s. Morris and Etta (Goldstein) M.; m. Minnie Gottlieb, Nov. 16, 1930 (dec. June 1991); children: Donald E., Suzanne Parelman. BA, U. Okla., 1925, LLB, 1928; postgrad., Yale Law Sch., 1926. Bar: Okla. 1928. Practiced in Tulsa, 1928-90; asst. county atty. Tulsa County, 1930-32. Author: An Appreciation of Will Rogers, 1935, Howdy Folks (Official State of Okla. poem about Will Rogers), 1938; (poetry) Before My Night, 1962, The Morning After, 1968, Thomas Gilcrease, 1969, Will Rogers, The Cherokee Kid, 1987. Pub. spkr., lectr.; founder, chmn. Benevolent and Welfare Fund and conceived establishment of Juvenile Ct. of Tulsa County, 1934; mem. Will Rogers Commn. Okla., 1978-93; chmn. bd. Tulsa Salvation Army, 1954-55; pres. Tulsa Opera, 1953-55, bd. dirs., 1951-96; pres. Thoms Gilcrease Inst. Am. History and Art, Tulsa, 1967-68, chmn. bd., 1969-70, bd. dirs., 1954-72, life bd. dirs. emeritus, from 1972. Recipient Commendation Okla. Hist. Soc., Disting. Svc. award Okla. Heritage Assn. for State of Okla., 1990; inductee Hall of Fame, Tulsa Hist. Soc., 1994. Mem. Sigma Alpha Mu (nat. historian, past supreme prior). Jewish (bd. dirs., past pres. Temple Israel, hon. life pres.), Mason (33 deg., past potentate, Shriner).

MINCHEFF, EDISON ELAINE, construction company executive; b. Winnett, Mont., July 20, 1920; s. Peter and Lota (Hooker) M.; B.S. in Mech. Engring., U. Kans., 1949; m. Evelyn Lee Moore, Nov. 4, 1943; children—Sharon Lee, Claudia Anne, Cristine Marie, Marc Edison. Engr., Bendix Aviation Co., Kansas City, Mo., 1949-51; asst. chief engr. Great Lakes Pipeline Co., Kansas City, 1951-57; engr., v.p. Williams Bros. Co., Tulsa, 1957-75; v.p. Williams Internat. Group, Inc., Tulsa, 1976-84; project mgr. Willbros Butler Engrs., Inc., 1984—; pvt. cons. to oil and gas pipeline industry. Served with USNR, 1942-45. Registered profl. engr., Ill., Fla., Mo., Okla. Mem. ASME, Am. Petroleum Inst., Internat. Pipeline Assn., Pipeline Industries Guild (Eng.), Soc. Am. Mil. Engrs. Club: Masons. Contbr. articles to tech. jours.

MINER, HORACE MITCHELL, anthropology and sociology educator; b. St. Paul, May 26, 1912; s. James Burt and Jessie Leightner (Schulten) M.; m. Agnes Genevieve Murphy, June 12, 1936; 1 child, Denise Miner Stanford. A.B., U. Ky., 1933; A.M., U. Chgo., 1935, Ph.D., 1937; postgrad. (Yale Inst. Human Relations fellow), Colombia, 1941-42. Asso. curator Mus. Anthropology, U. Ky., 1932-33; dir. archeol. field party TVA, 1934; instr. anthropology and sociology Wayne U., Detroit, 1937-39; dir. archeol. field party U. Chgo., summer 1938; sr. social sci. analyst, field research in Ia. Dept. Agr., 1939; cons. Nat. Resources Planning Bd., 1941; asst. prof. sociology U. Mich., Ann Arbor, 1946-47; assoc. prof. sociology, anthropology U. Mich., 1947-51; research asso. Mus. Anthropology, 1948-80, sr. research scientist, 1980-93, prof. sociology, anthropology, 1951-80, prof. emeritus, 1980-93; Fulbright lectr. Makerere U., Uganda, 1961-62; research North African Center, Morocco, 1967-68. Author: St. Denis, a French-Canadian Parish, 1939, 2d edit., 1963, French edit., 1985, Culture and Agriculture, 1949, Principles of Sociology (with others), 1952, 2d edit., 1956, The Primitive City of Timbuctoo, 1953, 2d edit., 1965, Oasis and Casbah: Algerian Culture and Personality in Change, (with G. DeVos), 1960, Rorschachs of Arabs from Algiers and from an Oasis, 1961, Urban Influences on The Rural Hausa, 1965, Le Declindes Corporations de fes, 1968, Community-Society Contnua International Encyclopedia of Social Sciences, 1968, Traditional Mobility Among the Weavers in Fez, 1973, Reflections on Science or Quid Principal in Human Organization, 1978; Editor: Social Science in Action in Sub-Saharan Africa, vol. 19, no. 3 of Human Organization, 1960, The City in Modern Africa, 1967. Mem. com. experts on indigenous labor Internat. Labor Office, 1949-65, conf. on indigenous labor, La Paz, 1951, Geneva, 1954, 62; mem. divisional com. for social scis. NSF, 1962-67. Served to lt. col. AUS, 1942-45, NATOUSA, ETO. Decorated Legion of Merit, Bronze Star.; Recipient Social Sci. Research Council demobilization award, 1945; Soc. Sci. Research Council fellow, 1936-37, 40; Ford Found. grantee, 1956; Rockefeller grantee Nigeria, 1957-58; Fulbright research award, Horace Rackham grant for field research Algeria, 1950; NSF grant for research Nigeria, 1970-71. Fellow Am. Sociol. Assn., Am. Anthrop. Assn.; mem. Am. Philos. Soc., Internat. African Inst. (governing body 1949-64), Soc. Applied Anthropology (pres. 1954-55), Phi Beta Kappa, Sigma Xi, Omicron Delta Kappa, Delta Tau Delta. Home: Ann Arbor Mich. Died Nov. 26, 1993.

MINNICH, VIRGINIA, retired medical researcher, educator; b. Zanesville, Ohio, Jan. 24, 1910; d. Rufus Humphrey and Ollie (Burley) M.; m. Jerry Hajek, Oct. 23, 1987. BS in Home Econs, Ohio State U., 1937; MS in Nutrition, Iowa State Coll., 1938; ScD (hon.), Williams Woods Coll., Fulton, Mo., 1972. Research asst., then research assoc. medicine, div. hematology Washington U. Sch. Medicine, St. Louis, 1939-78; mem. faculty Washington U. Sch. Medicine, 1958—, prof. medicine, 1974-78, prof. emeritus, 1978—. Contbr. articles to profl. jours. Recipient Alumni award home econs. Ohio State U., 1975; named St. Louis Woman of Achievement Group Action Council, 1947; award for founder of thalassemia research in Thailand, Mahidol U. Bangkok, 1985; Fulbright-Hays grantee Turkey, 1964. Mem. Am. Fedn. Clin. Research, Soc. Exptl. Biology and Medicine, Internat., Am. socs. hematology, Sigma Xi, Omicron Nu, Phi Upsilon Omicron. Died Apr. 26, 1996.

MINTOR, ALEXANDER V. (ALEX BLUES), musician; b. Paris, June 27, 1940; came to U.S., 1953; s. Alexander and Helen (Obert) M.; m. Cecile Towers, 1965 (div. 1979); children: Jacqueline, Robert. BA, U. So. Calif., 1962; MFA in Music, UCLA, 1965, MEd, 1966. Lic. tchr., Calif. Tchr. Los Angeles Pub. Schs., 1967-70; instr. music Calif. State U., Chico, 1970-76, asst. prof., 1976-83; instr. guitar, violin Los Pasos (Calif.) Community Coll., 1970-73. Composer: Theme and Variations for guitar and violin, 1980, popular songs including Way Down Blues, Done with You, Take the Long Walk, Glad to See Ya-Hard to Leave Ya. Active Big Bros. Am., Los Angeles, 1966-67. Recipient composition award AGVA, 1983. Mem. AFTRA, ANTA, Am. Soc. Guitar Artists and Performers, Nat. Soc. Blues Musicians, Mensa, Phi Kappa Phi. Democrat. Unitarian. Club: The Univ. Lodge: Rotary. Avocations: jogging and phys. fitness, reading. deceased, 1988.

MINUTILLA, ROSEMARIE JOAN, nursing educator; b. Bayonne, N.J., Sept. 28, 1943; d. Joseph and Mary Angela (Martorano) M. BS in Nursing, Georgetown U., 1966; MA in Nursing, NYU, 1973; PhD, U. Nebr., 1983. RN, N.J. Instr., dept. head, psychiat. nurse Muhlenberg Hosp. Sch. Nursing, Plainfield, N.J., 1967-72; asst. prof. U. Nebr. Coll. Nursing, Omaha, 1973-74, chmn. dept., 1974-78, master tchr. cons., 1978-79; assoc. prof. U. Evansville, Ind., 1980-88, asst. dean, 1980-88; prof. nursing, chmn. dept., co-chmn. health sci. Coll. St. Scholastica, Duluth, Minn., 1988—; peer reviewer HHS, Washington, 1989. Recipient recognition award Ind. Nurses Assn., 1988. Mem. Nat. League for Nursing, Midwest Alliance in Nursing, Minn. Nurses Assn., Sigma Theta Tau. Avocations: travel, reading, handwork. Home: Cranford N.J. Died Jan. 17, 1995.

MISCH, PETER, geology educator; b. Berlin, Aug. 30, 1909; came to U.S., 1946, naturalized 1952; s. Georg and Clara (Dilthey) M.; m. Susan Maier-Leibnitz, 1934 (dec. 1942); 1 child, Hanna French-Misch; m. Nicoletta Rosenthal, 1947; children: Felix George, Anthony Arthur. PhD, U. Göttingen, Fed. Republic of Germany, 1932. Geologist Himalayan Expdn. to Nanga Parbat, 1934; prof. structural geology Nat. Sun Yat-sen U., Canton, Peoples Republic of China, 1935-38; adviser Geol. Surveys, Kwangtung and Yunnan, 1936-46; prof. structural geology Nat. Sun Yat-sen U., Yunnan, Peoples Republic of China, 1938-40; prof. Nat. Peking U. (inc. into Nat. S.W. Assoc. U.), Kunming, Yunnan, 1940-46; asst. prof. U. Wash., Seattle, 1947-48, assoc. prof., 1948-50, prof., 1950-80, prof. emeritus, 1980—. Guggenheim fellow, 1954-55. Mem. Geol. Soc. Am. (past. chmn. Cordilleran sect.), Geol. Assn. Can. (hon. mem. Cordilleran Sect.), Am. Geophys. Union , Am. Assn. Petroleum Geologists (disting. lectr. 1953, assoc. editor 1965-76), Mineral. Soc. Am., Geochem. Soc., Mineral. Assn. Can., Geol. Soc. London, Geologische Vereinigung, N.W. Sci. Assn. (Outstanding Scientist award 1979), Sigma Xi. Club: Am. Alpine. Office: U Wash Dept Geol Scis Seattle WA 98195

MISKOVSKY, GEORGE, SR., lawyer; b. Oklahoma City, Feb. 13, 1910; s. Frank and Mary (Bourek) M.; m. Nelly Oleta Donahue, Dec. 30, 1932; children: George Jr., Gary Phillip, Grover, Gail Marie Trice. LL.B., U. Okla., 1936. Bar: Okla. 1936, U.S. Dist. Ct. (we. dist.) Okla., U.S. CT. Appeals (10th cir.). Sr. ptnr. firm Miskovsky, Sullivan, Miskovsky and Assocs., Oklahoma City, 1936—; pub. defender Oklahoma City, 1936; county atty. Oklahoma County, 1943-44; of counsel the late Col. John Embry. Mem. Okla. Ho. of Reps., 1939-42; mem. Okla. Senate, 1950-60; pres., dir. Economy Square Inc. Mem. Am., Okla., Oklahoma County Bar Assns., Am. Judicature Soc., Am. Trial Lawyers Assn., Nat. Assn. Criminal Def. Lawyers, Am. Acad. Matrimonial Lawyers, U. Okla. Law Assn., Oklahoma City C. of C., Order of Coif, Pi Kappa Alpha, Phi Alpha Delta. Democrat. Episcopalian. Clubs: Lions, Oklahoma City Golf and Country, Sooner Dinner, Masons, Shriners, Pair de la Chaine, Bailli Honoraire d'Okla, Confrerie de la Chaine des Rotisseurs. Home: Oklahoma City Okla. DIED 01/17/95. .

MITCHUM, ROBERT CHARLES DURMAN (CHARLES MITCHUM), actor; b. Bridgeport, Conn., Aug. 6, 1917; m. Dorothy Spence, Mar. 16, 1940; children: Jim, Petrine, Chris. Ed., N.Y.C. pub. schs. Motion picture debut in Hopalong Cassidy film, 1944; producer, actor motion pictures including Nightkill, Thunder Road; film appearances include The Story of G.I. Joe, 1945, Undercurrent, 1946, Till the End of Time, 1946, Pursued Locket, 1947, Til the End of Time, 1946, Desire Me, 1947, Crossfire, 1947, Out of the Past, 1947, Rachel and the Stranger, 1948, Blood on the Moon, 1948, Red Pony, 1949, Where Danger Lives, 1950, My Forbidden Past, 1951, The Racket, 1951, Macao, 1952, The Lusty Men, 1952, One Minute to Zero, 1952, Angel Face, 1953, River of No Return, Track of the Cat, She Couldn't Say No, 1954, Not as a Stranger, 1955, The Night of the Hunter, 1955, The Man with the Gun, 1955, Bandido, 1956, Foreign Intrigue, 1956, Heaven Knows Mr. Allison, 1957, Fire Down Below, 1957, The Enemy Below, 1957, Thunder Road, 1958, The Hunters, 1958, The Angry Hills, 1959, The Wonderful Country, 1959, Home from the Hill, 1960, A Terrible Beauty, 1960, The Grass is Greener, 1960, The Sundowners, 1960, The Longest Day, 1962, Cape Fear, 1962, Two for the Seesaw, 1962, The List of Adrian Messenger, 1963, Rampage, 1963, Man in the Middle, 1964, What a Way to Go, 1964, Mr. Moses, 1965, The Way West, 1967, El Dorado, 1967, Anzio, 1968, Five Card Stud, 1968, Secret Ceremony, 1968, Villa Rides, 1968, Young Billy Young, 1969, The Good Guys and the Bad Guys, 1969, Ryan's Daughter, 1971, Wrath of God, 1972, The Friends of Eddie Coyle, 1973, The Yakusa, 1974, Battle of Midway, 1975, Farewell My Lovely, 1975, The Amsterdam Kill, 1975, The Last Tycoon, 1976, The Big Sleep, 1977, Matilda, 1978, That Championship Season, 1982, Breakthrough, 1984, The Ambassador, 1984, Maria's Lovers, 1985, Mr. North, 1988, Scrooged, 1988, Cape Fear (Martin Scorsese remake) 1991, Tombstone, 1994; TV appearances include The Hearst and Davies Affair, Reunion at Fairborough, Promises to Keep, Thompson's Lost Run, Brotherhood of the Rose, 1989, Jake Spanner, Private Eye, 1989; starring role in TV mini-series The Winds of War, 1983, War and Remberance, 1988; TV series: A Family for Joe, 1990, Family Man, 1990. Subject of book: It Sure Beats Working, 1972. Home: Los Angeles Calif. Died July 1, 1997.

MITFORD, JESSICA, author, singer; b. Batsford Mansion, Eng., Sept. 11, 1917; d. Lord and Lady Redesdale; m. Esmond Romilly, June 1937; 1 dau., Constancia; m. Robert Treuhaft, June 21, 1943; 1 son, Benjamin. Author: Life Itselfmanship, 1956, Daughters and Rebels, 1960, The American Way of Death, 1963, The Trial of Dr. Spock, 1969, Kind and Usual Punishment-The Prison Business, 1973, A Fine Old Conflict, 1977, Poison Penmanship: The Gentle Art of Muckraking, 1979, Faces of Philip: A Memoir of Philip Toynbee, 1984, Grace Had an English Heart: The Story of Grace Darling, Heroine and Victorian Superstar, 1988, The American Way of Birth, 1992; singer with Decca and the Dectones, 1992-95, song's include; Right Said Fred, Maxwell's Silver Hammer, Song of Grace Darling. Died July 23, 1996.

MIXON, ALAN, actor; b. Miami, Fla., Mar. 15, 1933; s. James E. and Matilda (Beers) M. Student, U. Miami, 1951-52. Appeared in: premiere prodn. play Sweet Bird of Youth, Miami, 1956, N.Y.C., 1956; appeared in: premiere prodn. play View from the Bridge, Chgo. and San Francisco, 1957, 59, Royal Hunt of the Sun, Broadway and Hollywood, 1966; New York prodns. include Suddenly Last Summer, 1958, Desire Under the Elms, 1963, Trojan Women, 1963-64, The Alchemist, 1964, Sign in Sidney Brustein's Window, 1964-65, The Child Buyer, 1964-65, The Devils, 1965-66, A Whitman Portrait, 1966, Black Comedy, 1966-67, Unknown Soldier and His Wife, 1967, Iphegenia in Aulis, 1967-68, Love Suicide at Schofield Barracks, 1972, Small Craft Warnings, 1972, Mourning Becomes Electra, 1972, Equus, 1974-75, Benito Cereno, 1976; London prodn. Whitman Portrait, 1969; TV appearances include Theatre in America. Served with AUS, 1953-54. DIED 07/19/97. .

MOBUTU SESE SEKO, president of Zaire; b. Oct. 14, 1930. Ed., Mbandaka and Kinshasa. Sgt.-maj. accountancy dept. Force Publique, Belgian Congo, 1949-56; journalist in Kinshasa; course Inst. Social Studies, Brussels, Belgian, then journalist in Leopoldville; mem. Mouvement Nat. Congolaise; del. Brussels Round Table Conf. on Congo Independence, 1959-60; sec. state for nat. def. Lumunba cabinet, 1960; chief staff Congo Army, 1960; took over supreme power in name of army, suspended all polit. activity for 3 months, 1960; apptd. coll. high commrs. to take over govt.; maj. gen., comdr.-in-chief Congolese forces, 1961-65; lt. gen., pres. of Zaire, 1965—; state commr. for fgn. affairs and internat. cooperation, until 1989; advanced to rank of marshal, 1982. Founder nat. party Mouvement Populaire de la Revolution, 1967; restored name of Zaire to the country. Died Sept. 7, 1997.

MOCK, LAWRENCE EDWARD, finance counsel; b. Zanesville, Ohio, May 2, 1917; s. Clay Madon and Frances Brush (Merrick) M.; m. Mary Ann McCoy, June 2, 1945; children: Lawrence Edward, Martha Mock Ryan, Nelson McCoy, Ann Mock Short. B.S., Ohio State U., 1939; M.B.A., Harvard U., 1943. C.P.A., Pa., Ill., Ga. Auditor Ernst & Young, Pitts., 1939-41; ptnr. Ernst & Young, 1947-49; controller Harbison-Walker Refractories Co., 1949-51, treas., 1951-68, v.p., 1959-68, dir., 1967-68; finance v.p. Royal Crown Cola Co., Columbus, Ga., 1968-76; fin. mgr. Fed. Energy Adminstrn., Washington, 1976-77; treas. Overseas Pvt. Investment Corp., Washington, 1977-79; controller Naval Petroleum and Oil Shale Reserves, Washington, 1979-83. Served from 2d lt. to maj. AUS, 1942-46. Mem. Conf. Bd. (chmn. fin. coun. 1971-72), Harvard Bus. Sch. Assn. (exec. coun. 1964-67), Am. Contract Bridge League (pres. Ga. unit 114 1973, bd. govs. 1975-77, gold life master 1992), Tau Kappa Epsilon. Presbyterian (elder). Home: Largo Fla. Died Oct. 8, 1993.

MOE, EDITH MONROE, author; b. Chgo., Nov. 5, 1895; d. Nelson and Bertha Estelle Conover (Van Couwenhoven) Monroe; m. Henry Allen Moe, Dec. 18 1924; 1 child, Christian Hollis. BA in Philosophy first class honors, U. Calif., Berkeley, 1919; doctorate, La Sorbonne U., Paris; postgrad., Columbia U., Coll. of France; cert. in Italian, Siena, Italy. Marine law average adjustor Johnson & Higgins, San Francisco, 1918-20. Author: The Power of Freedom, The Beauty of hte Silversmith's Craft, The Beauty of Lace, Witness of the Twentieth Century. Benefactor The Glimmerglass Opera, Cooperstown, N.Y., Cooperstown Pub. Library, Sherman (Conn.) Pub. Library, Riverdale (N.Y.) Pub. Library; edower Henry Allen Moe Prize Am. Philosophical Soc., Henry Allen Moe Prize Mary Imogene Bassett Hosp., Cooperstown, Henry Allen Moe Prize N.Y. State Hist. Assn. Mem. DAR, Shakespeare Club (Riverdale), Yacht Club (Riverdale), Garden Club (Riverdale), Country Club (Cooperstown), Mauwehoo Club (Sherman). Fluent in 7 langs. including French, Italian, Greek, and Spanish.

MONDER, CARL, biochemist; b. N.Y.C., Aug. 24, 1928; s. Frank and Jennie (Black) M.; m. Batya Ruth Pais, Dec. 4, 1983; children by previous marriage: Benjamin, Eric; stepchildren: David, Jonathan. B.S., CCNY, 1950; M.S., Cornell U., 1952; Ph.D., U. Wis., 1956. Asst. prof. biochemistry Albert Einstein Coll. Medicine, N.Y.C., 1959-69; assoc. prof. biochemistry Mt. Sinai Coll. Medicine, N.Y.C., 1969-78; assoc. dir. research Research Inst., Hosp. Joint Disease, N.Y.C., 1964-81; prof. biochemistry Mt. Sinai Coll. Medicine, 1978-81; sr. scientist, head div. health and safety Ctr. Biomed. Research Population Council, N.Y.C., 1981-95; cons. Squibb Corp., Can. Research Council. Corr. editor: Jour Steroid Biochemistry, Paris, 1978-95. Editorial bd. Endocrinology, N.Y.C., 1985-95; assoc. editor Steroids, New York, 1985-95. Bd. dirs. Yale Musical Instrument Collection, 1985-95. Quillman fellow, Cornell U., 1951; USPHS fellow, 1956; Career Devel. awardee USPHS, 1969. Mem. Am. Soc. Biol. Chemists, N.Y. Acad. Sci., Harvey Soc., Endocrine Soc., Phi Beta Kappa. Died Jan. 5, 1995. Home: Teaneck N.J.

MONGAN, AGNES, museum curator, art historian, educator; b. Somerville, Mass., 1905. B.A., Bryn Mawr Coll., 1927; spl. student, Fogg Mus., Harvard U., 1928-29; A.M., Smith Coll., 1929, L.H.D. (hon.), 1941; Litt.D. (hon.), Wheaton Coll., 1954; L.H.D. (hon.), U. Mass., 1970; D.F.A. (hon.), LaSalle Coll., 1973, Colby Coll., 1973, U. Notre Dame, 1980, Boston Coll., 1985. Research asst. Fogg Mus., Harvard U., Cambridge, Mass., 1929-37; keeper of drawings Fogg Mus., Harvard U., 1937-47, curator of drawings, 1974-75, asst. dir., 1951-64, assoc. dir., 1964-68, acting dir., 1968-69, dir., 1969-71, cons., 1972-96; Martin A. Ryerson lectr. fine arts Harvard U., 1960-75; vis. dir. Timken Art Gallery, San Diego, 1971-72; Kreeger-Wolf disting. vis. prof. Northwestern U., 1976; Bingham vis. prof. U. Louisville, 1976; Waggoner vis. prof. U. Tex., Austin, 1977, vis. prof. fine arts, 1981; Samuel H. Kress prof.-in-residence Nat. Gallery Art, Washington, 1977-78; vis. prof. fine arts U. Calif.-Santa Barbara, 1979; vis. dir. Met. Mus. and Arts Ctrs., Coral Gables, Fla., 1980; Brazilian Govt. lectr., 1954; Amy Sackler Meml. lectr. Mt. Holyoke Coll., 1966-67; vis. prof. fine arts U. Tex. Austin, 1981; Baldwin lectr. Oberlin Coll., 1966; lectr. throughout U.S., Can., Japan; organized numerous exhbns.; leader, lectr. yearly tours Europe to Friends of the Fogg groups. Former mem. editorial bd. Art Bull.; mem. adv. bd. Arte Veneta, Venice; editor: Heart of Spain (Georgiana Goddard King), 1941; One Hundred Master Drawings, 1949; contbr. to exhbn. and catalogue In Pursuit of Perfection: The Art of J.-A.-D.-Ingres, 1983; contbr. catalogue In Quest of Excellence, 1983; intro. to catalogue The Fine Line, 1985, exhbn. catalogue Ingres and Delacroix, Germany and Belgium, 1986; contbr. Silverpoint Drawings in the Fogg Art Museum, 1987, Some Brief Comments on Left-Handedness for Fogg Old Master Drawings Symposium, 1987; contbr. to books in field. Trustee, mem. corp. Inst. Contemporary Art, Boston, 1940-60; a founder, v.p. Pan-Am. Soc. New Eng., 1940-62; mem. U.S. Nat. Commn. for UNESCO, 1954-57, White House Com. for Edn. in Age of Sci., 1961; trustee Chaplebrook Found.; mem. vis. com. art dept. Wheaton Coll., 1961-68; mem. vis. com. to Art Mus., Smith Coll., to 1970; mem. council for arts MIT; mem. adv. bd. Skowhegan Sch. Painting and Sculpture, 1974-96; mem. exec. com. Save Venice, Council for Villa I Tatti; mem. vis. com. dept. textiles Boston Mus. Fine Arts; bd. dirs. Brit. Inst.; mem. exec. com. Somerville Hist. Soc.; vice chmn. Com. for Restoration of Italian Art. Decorated Palms d'Academie (France), cavaliere ufficiale (Italy); recipient Julius Stratton award Friends of Switzerland, 1978, Signet Soc. Medal for Achevement in the Arts Harvard U., 1986, 350th Harvard medal for Extraordinary Service, 1986, Benemerenti medal Vatican, 1987; honored by Women's Caucus for the Arts, 1987; Benjamin Franklin fellow Royal Acad. Art; Inst. Internat. Edn. grantee, 1935; Fulbright scholar, 1950. Fellow Am. Acad. Arts and Scis.; mem. Coll. Art Assn. (bd. dirs. 1949-54), Am. Assn. Art Mus. Dirs. (assoc.), Academie de Montauban, Phi Beta Kappa (hon.). Died Sept. 15, 1996.

MONROE, STANLEY EDWIN, surgeon; b. Bangor, Mich., June 26, 1902; s. Samuel E. and Ella (Monroe) M.; AB, U. Mich., 1925; MD, U. Chgo./Rush Med. Coll., 1936; m. Ruth Williams, June 14, 1932 (dec. 1981); m. 2d, Flora Doss, Aug. 6, 1982. Intern, Evanston (Ill.) Hosp., 1935-36, resident surgeon, 1936-37, asst. surgeon, 1940-41; clin. asst. surgeon Northwestern U., 1938-39, instr. surgery, 1940-41; asst. to Dr. Frederick Christopher, 1937-41; chief surgery VA Hosp., Tucson, 1947-49; surgeon ARAMCO, Saudi

Arabia, 1950; pvt. practice, Chula Vista, Calif., 1952-82; former chief of septic and plastic surgery, Thayer Gen. Hosp., Nashville; staff Paradise Valley Hosp., Mercy Hosp. (San Diego); founder Monroe Clinic. Maj. AUS Med. Corps 1942-47, PTO. Diplomate Am. Bd. Surgery. Fellow Soc. for Academic Achievement, Internat. Coll. Surgeons; mem. Soc. Gen. Surgeons of San Diego, Am. Med. Writers Assn., Assn. Mil. Surgeons, Am. Soc. Abdominal Surgeons (founding), Alpha Omega Alpha, Phi Beta Pi. Author: Medical Phrase Book with Vocabulary (also Spanish edit.).

MONROE, WILLIAM SMITH, mandolin player, singer; b. Rosine, Ky., Sept. 13, 1911; s. James Buchanan and Malissa (Vandiver) M.; m. Carolyn Brown, 1935 (div.); children: James, Melissa. Worked in oil refinery; mem. WSN Grand Ole Opry, 1939—. Played on, WLS Barn Dance, East Chicago, Ind., 1929-34, formed group, The Monroe Brothers, 1934-38, playing on radio stas. in, N.C. and S.C.; formed group, The Blue Grass Boys, 1938—, nationwide concert and festival appearances; recorded for, Victor Records, 1940-41, Columbia Records, 1945-49, Decca (now MCA), 1950—; songs recorded include My Little Georgia Rose; albums include In The Pines, 1988, Live at The Opry, 1989, The Country Music Hall of Fame, 1991, The Essential Bill Monroe and His Blusgrass Boys (1945-49), 1992, Mule Skinner Blues, 1991, The Music of Bill Monroe 1936-1994, 1994. Elected to County Music Hall of Fame, 1970. Originated term bluegrass and defined its style. Died Sept. 13, 1996.

MONTANA, PATSY See ROSE, RUBYE BLEVINS

MONTEITH, ROBERT, banker; b. Thunder Bay, Ont., Can., Feb. 24, 1930; s. Robert and Nina Bell (Babcock) M.; m. Deanie G. Walker, Mar. 13, 1959; children: Tracey T., Cassie C., Roberta D., Robert, III. Grad., Sch. Banking, So. Methodist U., 1969. Sales rep. Traders Fin. Corp., Thunder Bay, 1951-54; sales adminstr. Chrysler Corp. Can., Winnipeg, Man., 1954-60; gen. mgr. Century Motors Ltd., Winnipeg, 1960-63; sr. v.p. Security Pacific Nat. Bank, Los Angeles, 1963—; pres. SEPAC Acceptance & Lease Services Inc., 1978—; exec. com. Security Pacific Fin. Corp., 1978—. Trustee U. LaVerne (Calif.). Presbyterian. Club: North Ranch Country. DIED 02/13/96. .

MONTGOMERY, DONALD JOSEPH, physicist, educator; b. Cin., June 11, 1917; s. Robert John and Stella (Steffen) M.; m. Mary Miller, July 27, 1951; children—Denis Broyles, Malcolm David, Steven Michael, Laurence Matthew. Chem.E., U. Cin., 1939, Ph.D., 1945; postgrad., Cornell U., 1941-42. Instr. elec. engring. U. Cin., 1942-44; physicist Flight Propulsion Lab., NACA, Cleve., 1944-45; research asso. physics, asst. prof. Princeton, 1945-46; sci. liaison officer Office Naval Research, London, Eng., 1947-48; research fellow physics U. Manchester, Eng., 1947-48; chief spl. problems br. Interior Ballistics Lab., Ballistic Research Labs., Aberdeen Proving Ground, Md., 1948-50; head gen. physics sect. Textile Research Inst., Princeton, N.J., 1950-53; asso. prof. physics Mich. State U., East Lansing, 1953-56; prof. Mich. State U., 1956-61, research prof. physics, prof. engring. research, 1961-66, prof. physics, chmn. dept. metallurgy, mechanics and material sci., 1966-71, research prof. engring. sci., 1971-88, prof. emeritus, 1988; Cons. Chemstrand Research Center, Durham, N.C., 1956-88, Owens-Ill., 1966-88; spl. asst. to dir. Office Grants and Research Contracts, NASA, 1964-65; vis. research physicist Space Sci. Lab., U. Calif.-Berkeley, 1965-66; vis. scholar dept. polit. sci. U. Ill., 1984-87. Author: Cosmic Ray Physics, 1949; also chpts. in books, articles, revs. Recipient Distinguished Faculty award Mich. State U., 1961, Distinguished Alumnus award U. Cin., 1969; Fulbright lectr. in physics; Guggenheim fellow U. Grenoble, France, 1959-60; Fulbright researcher in engring., econs. U. Augsburg, Germany; asso. Internat. Inst. Empirical Socioecons., Leitershofen-Augsburg, 1974-75. Fellow Am. Phys. Soc.; mem. AAAS, Am. Nuclear Soc. (charter), Am. Assn. Physics Tchrs., Biophys. Soc., Am. Acad. Mechanics, Textile Rsch. Inst., Am. Soc. Engring. Edn., Internat. Assn. Impact Assessment, Internat. Soc. Tech. Assessment, Am. Acad. Polit. & Social Sci., Policy Studies Assn., Acad. Polit. Sci., Coun. Applied Social Rsch., Fulbright Alumni Assn., Mich. Acad. Art, Letters & Sci., N.Y. Acad. Scis., Soc. Social Studies of Sci., Sigma Xi, Tau Beta Pi, Phi Kappa Phi, Omicron Delta Kappa. Achievements include development of practical formula for predicting charge transfer in static electrification of solids, of scheme for sociotechnical assessment of consequences of public policy measures as an aid to decision making; research on materials science. Home: East Lansing Mich. Died Jan. 19, 1996.

MONTGOMERY, EDWARD BENJAMIN, physicist, retired educator; b. Louisville, June 15, 1915; s. Thomas Edward and Mary (Nofsinger) M.; m. Mary Louise Lynch, May 30, 1942; children: Mary Patterson Montgomery Cleary, Susan Ellen Montgomery Gartner, Thomas Edward, Margaret Aquin. AB, U. Louisville, 1942. Ballistic physicist Ind. Ordnance Works, E.I. duPont de Nemours & Co., Inc., 1941-42; research asst. Manhattan project. U. Chgo., 1943-44; reactor physicist Hanford Works, 1944-46; with Gen. Electric Co., 1947-63, head spl. irradiations program, 1948-49, group head experimental physics, 1949-51, sect. chief reactor physics and engring., 1951-52, physicist advanced tech., 1953-54, data processing specialist, 1954-56, mgr. computer applications, 1956-57, cons. product planning, 1957-59; cons. physicist sci. applications computer dept. Gen. Electric Co., Phoenix, 1956-61; project engr. ednl. tech. Gen. Electric Co., Syracuse, N.Y., 1961-63; research cons. info. systems Syracuse U., 1963-65; prof., dean Syracuse U. (Sch. Library Sci.), 1965-68; prof. Health Sci. Center, U. Tex., Dallas, 1968-82, also; coordinator council of pres.'s U. Tex. components in North Tex.; Cons. in field, 1965-95. Mem. Gov. Ariz., Com. Arid Lands, 1959-60; Trustee Richland (Wash.) Pub. Library, 1953-55, chmn. bd., 1955. Mem. Am. Phys. Soc., IEEE, AAAS. Home: Dallas Tex. Died May 26, 1995.

MONTGOMERY, ELIZABETH, actress; b. Los Angeles, Apr. 15, 1933; d. Robert and Elizabeth Bryan (Allen) M.; m. Frederick Gallatin Cammann, 1954 (div. 1955); m. Gig Young, 1957 (div. 1963); m. William Asher, 1963 (div. 1974); children: William Jr., Robert, Rebecca Elizabeth. Grad., Spence Sch.; student, Acad. Dramatic Arts. Made TV debut in Top Secret; Broadway debut in Late Love (Daniel Blum Theatre World award); star: TV series Bewitched, ABC-TV, 1964-72; has appeared: over 250 TV shows including Twilight Zone; appeared: motion pictures Court Martial of Billy Mitchell, 1955, Johnny Cool, 1963, Who's Been Sleeping in My Bed, 1964; TV movies The Victim, 1977, A Case of Rape, 1974, Mrs. Sundance, 1974, The Legend of Lizzie Borden, 1975, Dark Victory, 1976, The Awakening Land, 1978, Jennifer: A Woman's Story, 1979, Act of Violence, 1979, Belle Star, 1980, When the Circus Came to Town, 1981, The Rules of Marriage, 1982, Missing Pieces, 1983, Second Sight: A Love Story, 1984, Amos, Between Darkness and Dawn, Face to Face, 1990. Mem. SAG.

MOODY, RICHARD, theatre educator; b. Des Moines, Sept. 30, 1911; s. Carl Eric and Josephine (Peterson) M.; m. Esther Carol Martin, Feb. 26, 1937; children: Pamela Martin Moody Powers, Eric Craig. B.A., Drake U., 1932, M.A., 1934; Ph.D., Cornell U., 1942; student, Yale Sch. Drama, 1932-33, 34-35. Instr. speech, theatre, also tech. dir. theatre U. Ill., 1936-40; asst. prof. speech and theatre Ind. U., 1942-43, asso. prof., 1946-55, prof., 1955-78, prof. emeritus, 1979—; dir. Ind. U. Theatre, 1958-70; vis. asst. prof. speech, theatre Northwestern U., summer 1946; vis. asso. prof. U. Hawaii, 1952; vis. prof. U. Calif.-Davis, 1983; dir. Ind. Theatre Co.; mem. Theatre Communications Group; Green Honors prof. T.C.U., 1986; pres. Internat. PEN Ctr., San Miguel de Allende, Mexico, 1988-91; attended Paul Moriarty performance of Edwin Forrest, Brighton Mus. and Garrick Club, London, 1990. Author: America Takes the Stage, 1955, The Astor Place Riot, 1958, Edwin Forrest. First Star of the American Stage, 1960, Dramas from the American Theatre, 1762- 1909, 1966, Lillian Hellman, Playwright, 1972, Revels History of the Drama in English, Vol. VIII, American Drama, 1978, Ned Harrigan: From Corlear's Hook to Herald Square, 1980; contbr. articles to profl. jours. and encys. Served to lt. (s.g.) USNR, 1943-46. Recipient Disting. Alumni award Drake U., 1961; Nat. Theatre Conf. fellow Cornell U., 1940-42; Guggenheim fellow, 1959-60; NEH sr. fellow, 1973-74. Fellow Am. Theatre Assn. (award 1983); mem. Speech Assn. Am., Am. Soc. Theatre Rsch. (award 1988), Phi Beta Kappa.

MOONEY, JOHN FRED, utilities company executive; b. Chgo., Jan. 21, 1934; s. John A. and Betty Jenkins (Cully) M.; m. Dolores Joyce Tanner, July 28, 1956; children: Cathleen J., Karen J., Sheryl L. BSME, Ill. Inst. Tech., 1955; MBA, U. Chgo., 1972. Registered profl. engr., Ill. Jr. engr. The Peoples Gas, Light and Coke Co., Chgo., 1955-57, various mgmt. and supr. positions, 1958-72, 76-81; adminstrv. asst. to pres. Natural Gas Pipeline Co. of Am., Chgo., 1973-74, exec. ops. engr., 1974-75; asst. v.p., lab relations The Peoples Gas, Light & Coke Co., North Shore Gas Co., Chgo. and Waukegan, Ill., 1981-87; v.p., human resources The Peoples Gas, Light & Coke Co., North Shore Gas Co., Chgo. and Waukegan, 1987-95. Bd. dirs. Leadership Council for Met. Open Communities, Chgo., 1988-90; mem. bus. adv. coun. Banaventure House, Chgo., 1989-95. Capt. USAFR, 1955-63. Mem. Am. Gas Assn., Chgo. Assn. Commerce and Industry. Presbyterian. Home: Lake Forest Ill. Died Oct. 15, 1995.

MOOR, EDGAR JACQUES, management consultant, corporate executive; b. June 6, 1912; came to U.S., 1941, naturalized, 1946; s. Ernest and Henriette Caroline (Goldschmidt) M.; m. Joan Rothwell, Aug. 5, 1950. Student, U. Paris Sorbonne, 1931; diploma ing. cum laude, Tech. U., Berlin, 1937; MBA, Harvard U., 1942. Indsl. engr. Chrysler Corp., Johannesburg, Republic of South Africa, 1938-39; asst. to pres. Holtzer-Cabot div. 1st Indsl. Corp., Boston, 1942-46; v.p. USMC, Internat., Geneva, 1947-64; dir. internat. planning USM Corp., Boston, 1947-64; mng. ptnr. Multinat. Bus. Assocs., Cambridge, Mass., 1966-77, mng. ptnr., 1977-87; spl. appointments U.S. Dept. Commerce, Washington, 1968-70, Overseas Pvt. Investment Corp., Washington, 1971. Contbr. articles on multinat. corp. mgmt. to profl. jours. Mem. commerce com. Alliance for Progress, Washington, 1962-64; mem Gov. Volpe's Task Force, Boston, 1965; bd. dirs. Spanish Cultural Inst., 1978-85, Internat. Inst. Boston. Decorated comendador Order of Isabel la Catolica (Spain). Fellow Internat. Acad. Law Sci., Royal Soc. Arts, Manufacture and Commerce London; mem. Pan Am. Soc. New Eng. (gov. 1971-78, pres. 1971-73), Boston Com. Fgn. Rels., Multinat. Bus. Council (co-chmn. Cambridge 1968-78), World Affairs Coun. (bd. dirs. 1981-83), Cosmos Club (Washington), Harvard Club (Boston). Died July 1, 1994. Home: Cambridge Mass.

MOORE, ARTHUR JAMES, editor; b. San Antonio, May 7, 1922; s. Arthur James and Martha (MacDonald) M. B.A., Emory U., 1947. With N.Y. Daily News, 1947-50; editorial asst. Musical Am., 1950; editor, contbr. encys. other reference books Columbia U. Press, 1951-53; with Methodist Bd. of Global Ministries (formerly Bd. Missions), 1953-87; editor World Outlook, 1964-70; editor New World Outlook, 1970-87, dir. editorial dept. Edn. and Cultivation Div., 1980-87; cons. in field, 1987—; mem. press staff World Council Chs. assembly, Evanston, Ill., 1954, New Delhi, India, 1961; spl. corr. Religious News Service, Vatican Council, 1965, World Conf. Ch. and Soc., 1966. Mem. editorial bd. Christianity and Crisis, 1967-72, bd. dirs., 1971-82, contbg. editor, 1974-93; contbg. author: Religion and Peace, 1966, Ethics in the Present Tense, 1991; contbr. to various nat. mags. Served with USNR, 1942-45. Recipient Citation of Honor Associated Ch. Press, 1990; named to United Meth. Assn. of Communicators Hall of Fame, 1988. Mem. Alpha Tau Omega. Methodist. Died August 22, 1996.

MOORE, ASHER, educator, philosopher; b. Johnstown, Pa., Mar. 7, 1919; s. Charles Asher and Emma Lucinda (Jones) M. A.B., Wesleyan U., Middletown, Conn., 1940; M.A., Harvard, 1942, Ph.D., 1948. Instr. philosophy N.Y.U., 1945-46; teaching fellow Harvard U., 1946-48; mem. faculty dept. philosophy Northwestern U., 1948-60; prof. philosophy U. N.H., 1960—, Donald C. Babcock Found. prof., 1960—, chmn. dept. philosophy, 1973-79; vis. prof. Bowdoin Coll., 1962-63, Pa. State U., 1972; exchange prof. U. Osaka, Japan, 1979-80; lectr. U. P.R., Mayaguez, 1984—. Served with USNR, 1942-45. Ford Found. fellow, 1954-55. Mem. Phi Beta Kappa. DIED 11/08/95. .

MOORE, GARRY (THOMAS GARRISON MORFIT), actor, writer, producer; b. Balt., Jan. 31, 1915; s. Mason Pitner and Mary Louise (Harris) Morfit; m. Eleanor Borum Little, June 5, 1939 (dec. Aug. 1974); children—John Mason Morfit, Thomas Garrison Morfit; m. Mary Elizabeth De Chant, Jan. 16, 1975. Student publ. schs. of Balt. Writer, actor, radio sta. WBAL, Balt., 1935-38; also KWK, St. Louis, 1939. Star and writer: club Matinee, NBC, Chgo., 1939-43; co-star, writer: Jimmy Durante-Garry Moore Show, 1943-48; star: Take It or Leave It, 1948-50, Garry Moore Show, CBS-TV, 1950-64, 1966-67; moderator: TV I've Got a Secret, 1953-64, To Tell The Truth, 1969-77. Nat. chmn. Nat. Soc. Crippled Children and Adults, 1959; bd. govs. Nat. Hosp. Speech Disorders. Selected by TV editors of U.S. as best daytime TV shows, 1953, 62, best master of ceremonies in TV, 1957, 58; recipient Peabody award for radio program Voice Am., 1971. Mem. Nat. Acad. TV Arts and Scis. (past gov.). Club: Northeast Harbor (Maine) Fleet. Died Nov. 28, 1993.

MOORE, JOACHIM MICHAEL, French and German educator, consultant; b. Berlin, Nov. 12, 1914; (parents Am. citizens); s. James Michael and Hedwig (Rosenow) M.; m. Ardath Norcross, 1951 (div. June 1966); children: James, Peter, David; m. Sylvia M. Keller, Nov. 28, 1967. AB, Wagner Coll., 1942; MA, Columbia U., 1944; PhD cum laude, U. Bern, Switzerland, 1951. Cert. life C.C. credential, Calif. Instr. German, Muhlenberg Coll., Allentown, Pa., 1947-49; resettlement dir. Luth. World Fedn., Geneva, 1949-51; instr. German, Queens and Manhattan Coll., N.Y.C., 1950-51; lectr. English and Am. civilization Acad. Rennes and Aix, France, 1951-53; prof. German, Def. Lang. Inst., Monterey, Calif., 1954-55; prof. French and German, San Diego City Coll., 1955-64; fgn. lang. specialist San Diego Bd. Edn., 1964-67; prof. French and German, San Diego Mesa Coll., from 1967, prof. emeritus; fgn. lang. cons. Calif. Dept. Edn., Sacramento, 1962-63, mem. articulation conf., 1966-69; lectr. USIA, Berlin, Munich, Stuttgart, Germany, Vienna, Austria, 1971. Author filmstrips and tapes Paris, Mon Amour, 1977, Wie Regieren Sie Sich, 1982, Hier Spricht Man Deutsch, 1983. Mem. MLA, AAUP, Am. Assn. Tchrs. German (founder San Diego chpt., nat. chmn. Fgn. Lang. in Elem. Sch. com. 1965-67), Am. Assn. Tchrs. French (treas. 1965-66), Am. Coun. for Tchg. Fgn. Langs. (founding), Calif. Tchrs. Assn. Democrat. Lutheran. Avocations: aerobic exercises, travel, photography, reading. Home: San Diego Calif. Died April 18, 1995.

MOORE, NORMAN SLAWSON, physician; b. Ithaca, N.Y., Apr. 17, 1901; s. Veranus A. and Mary Louise (Slawson) M.; m. Bernice A. Barkee, June 28, 1932. A.B., Cornell, 1923, M.D., 1926. Diplomate: Am. Bd. Internal Medicine. Intern Bellevue Hosp., 1926-28; asst. resident Rockefeller Inst., 1928-29; instr. anatomy Cornell Med. Coll., 1929-31, head dept. clin. and preventive medicine, 1943-67; emeritus prof. clin. medicine Cornell U. Sch. Nutrition; clin. dir. Sage Hosp.-Gannett Clinic, 1943-67; pvt. practice internal medicine Ithaca, 1929-40; cons. physician Tompkins

County Meml. Hosp., 1940-72, hon., 1973; Dir., chmn. emeritus Ithaca Savs. and Loan Assn.; Responsible investigator at Cornell for OSRD, 1942-45; mem. nurse adv. council N.Y. State Dept. Edn., 1946-54; mem. Pub. Health Council N.Y. State, 1954-80, chmn., 1969-80; mem. Temporary Health Ins. Bd. N.Y. State, 1956-59; pres. Empire State Med., Sci. and Ednl. Found., 1961-70, dir., 1960-74; chmn. N.Y. State Hosp. Rev. and Planning Council, 1961-70; mem. N.Y. State Health Resources Commn., 1967-74; mem. adv. council N.Y. State Health Planning Commn., 1968-72; mem. N.Y. State Mental Hygiene Council, 1970-75, N.Y. State Commn. on Acupuncture. Contbr. articles med. publs. Fellow A.C.P., N.Y. Acad. Medicine; mem. Am. Coll. Health Assn. (pres. 1954), Med. Soc. State N.Y. (past v.p., past pres. 6th dist. br., council 1955-65, chmn. com. pub. health and edn. 1957-60, pres. 1960-61, trustee 1961-65, dir. sci. activities 1967-74), AMA (del. 1956-70, chmn. council vol. health agys. 1967-70), Tompkins County Med. Soc. (past pres.), Sigma Xi, Phi Sigma Kappa, Omega Alpha Omega, Nu Sigma Nu. Home: Ithaca N.Y. Died Apr. 3, 1995.

MOORE, WALTER EDWARD CLADEK, microbiologist; b. Rahway, N.J., Oct. 12, 1927; s. Rollins Woodward and Anstes Dorinda (Cladek), M.; m. Hester J. Barrus, June 18, 1949 (div.); children—David Rollins, Howard Michael, Jey Edward; m. Lillian V. Holdeman, Apr. 20, 1985. B.S. with honors, U. N.H., 1951; M.S., U. Wis., 1952, Ph.D., 1954. Asst. prof. Va. Poly Tech., Blackburg, Va., 1954-60; assoc. prof. Va. Poly Tech., Blackburg, 1960-64, prof., 1964—, dept. head, 1977-85, univ. distinguished prof., 1981—; vice chmn. Internat. Judicial Commn. on Bacterial Nomen, 1978—. Editor-in-chief: Internat. Jour. of Systematic Bacteriology, 1980—; contbr. articles to profl. jours.; patentee in field. Recipient Kimble award Conf. Pub. Health Lab. Dirs., 1973; Becton-Dickenson lectr. Becton-Dickenson Co., 1983; recipient Bergey's Manual award Bergey's Manual Trust, 1984, Porter award U.S. Fedn. Culture Collections, 1988. Office: Va Poly Inst & State U Dept Anaerobic Microbiology Blacksburg VA 24061 Died Sept. 25, 1996.

MORAN, FRANK SULLIVAN, accounting executive; b. Detroit, Oct. 11, 1918; s. Thomas and Lucy (Sullivan) M.; m. Georgene Stritch, Jan. 4, 1941; children: Frank Jr., Midge, George, Elaine Kelly. AB in Philosophy, U. Detroit, 1940. Ptnr. Plante & Moran, Southfield, Mich., 1950—, mng. ptnr., 1955-82, chmn., 1982—. Died March 26, 1997.

MORFIT, THOMAS GARRISON See MOORE, GARRY

MORGAN, GEORGE JEFFERSON, interior designer; b. Montgomery, Ala., June 21, 1908; s. Platte Jefferson and Margaret Louise (Wagner) M.; m. Frances E. Fitz, Feb. 7, 1937; children—Pamela Fitz Marvin, Leslie Platte Van Der Zee. B.S., Auburn U., 1930. Dir. interior design Mayfair, Inc., Albany, N.Y., 1934—; cons. various historic restorations. Important works include interior, Ten Broeck Mansion. Fellow Am. Soc. Interior Designers, Inst. Profl. Designers (Gt. Britain); mem. Albany Inst. History and Art, Albany County Hist. Assn., Albany Historic Found. Democrat. Presbyterian. Clubs: University, Albany Country. Home and Office: 66 Chestnut St Albany NY 12210-1902 Died Oct. 23, 1997.

MORGAN, THOMAS SELLERS, history professor; b. Jackson, Miss., Dec. 13, 1934; s. Thomas Sellers Sr. and Mabel (Tew) M.; m. Nancy Ann Grondin, June 25, 1960; children: Kevin John, Christopher Thomas, David Vincent. AB, Davidson (N.C.) Coll., 1957; MA, Duke U., 1962; PhD, U. N.C., 1969. Tchr. social studies Edmondson High Sch., Balt., 1959-62; instr. history Wake Forest U., Winston-Salem, N.C., 1964-65, U. N.C., Chapel Hill, 1966-67; with Winthrop Coll., Rock Hill, S.C., 1967—, dean Coll. Arts and Scis., 1978-81, prof. history, 1974—; reader history exams. Ednl. Testing Svc., Princeton, N.J., 1986—, workshop leader, project EQ, 1987—. Author: Study Guide for America A Narrative History, 1984, (with others) 2d edit., 1988, 3d edit., 1992, Study Guide for America: A Narrative History: Brief Edition, 1989; co-editor: Women Leaders in South Carolina, 1984. Mem. exec. com. York County (S.C.) Dem. Party, 1972-79, 86-90. Danforth Found. fellow, 1972-86. Mem. So. Hist. Assn. (chair membership com. 1972-73), Orgn. Am. Historians, Am. Hist. Assn., Kiwanis (bd. dirs. Rock Hill chpt. 1985-88), Phi Alpha Theta (book award com. 1982-89, nat. v.p. 1989-91, pres. 1991—). Presbyterian. Avocation: photography. Died April 23, 1996.

MORLEY, JOHN, actor, playwright; b. Dec. 24, 1924; s. Austin and Patricia (Bray) M. Ed. St. John's Coll., Cambridge. Wrote Coldstream Guards pantomine, Dick Whittington and his kit, 1944; performed in and wrote two revues and pantomines, St. John's Coll., Cambridge, 1947-48; performed in and co-author of Cambridge Footlights Revue, 1948; performed in Private View, Fortune, 1948, Birmingham Rep., 1949, Bob's Your Uncle, Theatre Royal, Stratford, and Music at Midnight, Her Majesty's, 1950, Victorian Music Hall, Players 1951, Fancy Free, Prince of Wales, 1951-53, Northampton Rep., 1953, Call Me Madam tour, 1953-54, After the Ball, Globe, 1954, Jubilee Girl, Victoria Palace, 1956, The Crystal Heart, Saville, and Love a' la Carte, Richmond, 1958, Marigold, Savoy, 1959, Follow that Girl, Vaudeville, 1960; performer and writer: Cafe de Paris, 1955-60; pantomine writer for Howerd and Wyndham, 1964-73; pantomine writer for Triumph of Apollo Ltd., 1973—. Author: Songs for the Art of Living, Criterion, 1960-61, (jointly) Puss in Boots, London Palladium, 1963, Houdini, Man of Magic, Picadilly, 1966, The Littlest Clown, Round House, 1972, Aladdin, BBC Radio, 1980, Big Night Out, (Thames TV variety series), 1963-66 (incl. the Beatles Night Out, Blackpool Night Out, Boxing Night Out); BBC TV pantomines; Babes in the Wood, 1972; The Basil Brush Pantomine, 1980; Aladdin and the Forty Thieves, 1983; BBC Children's TV series: Crazy Bus, 1972, Captain Bonny the Pirate, 1973-74; Children's TV Revue, 1975; Basil Brush, 1979-81; has written 138 pantomines; publs. include jointly: The Magic of Houdini, 1978, The Performing Arts, 1980, Pinocchio, 1983; pantomines: Aladdin, Jack and the Beanstalk, Sinbad the Sailor, Goldilocks and the Three Bears, Robinson Crusoe. Avocations: architecture; furniture; travel; Brit. folklore.

MORRELL, FRANK, neurologist, educator; b. N.Y.C., June 4, 1926; s. Benjamin R. and Rose (Langson) M.; m. Lenore Korkes, Mar. 24, 1957 (div.); children: Seth, Paul, Michael, Suzanna; m. Leyla deToledo, May 25, 1978. AB, Columbia U., 1948, MD, 1951; MS, McGill U., Montreal, Can., 1955. Diplomate Am. Bd. Psychiatry and Neurology. Intern in medicine Montefiore Hosp., Bronx, N.Y., 1951-52, resident in neurology, 1953-54; fellow EEG Nat. Hosp., London, 1952-53; fellow Montreal Neurol. Inst., 1954-55; from asst. prof. to assoc. prof. neurology U. Minn., Mpls., 1955-61; prof., chmn. dept. neurology Stanford (Calif.) U., 1961-69; vis. prof. N.Y. Med. Coll., 1969-72; prof. Rush Med. Coll., Chgo., 1972—; William Lennox lectr. Western Inst. of Epilepsy, Colo., 1980; Hans Berger lectr. Med. Coll. Va., 1987; assoc. neurosci. rsch. program MIT, Boston, 1965-76; cons. in field. Contbr. numerous articles to profl. jours. Served as cpl. USAF, 1944-45. Fellow Royal Soc. Medicine, Am. Acad. Neurology; mem. Am. Electro-encephalographic Soc. (pres.), Am. Epilepsy Soc., Soc. for Neurosci. Jewish. Died Oct. 22, 1996.

MORRIN, VIRGINIA WHITE, retired college educator; b. Escondido, Calif., May 16, 1913; d. Harry Parmalee and Ethel Norine (Nutting) Rising; BS, Oreg. State Coll., 1952; MEd, Oreg. State U., 1957; m. Raymond Bennett White, 1933 (dec. 1953); children: Katherine Anne, Marjorie Virginia, William Raymond; m. 2d, Laurence Morrin, 1959 (dec. 1972). Social caseworker Los Angeles County, Los Angeles, 1934-40, 61-64; acctg. clk. War Dept., Ft. MacArthur, Calif., 1940-42; prin. clk. USAAF, Las Vegas, Nev., 1942-44; high sch. tchr., North Bend-Coos Bay, Oreg., 1952-56, Mojave, Calif., 1957-60; instr. electric bus. machines Antelope Valley Coll., Lancaster, Calif., 1961-73; ret., 1974. Treas., Humane Soc. Antelope Valley, Inc., 1968—. Mem. Nat. Aero. Assn., Calif. State Sheriffs' Assn. (charter assoc.), Oreg. State U. Alumni Assn. (life). Deceased.

MORRIS, DANIEL T., management services executive; b. Denver, Jan. 28, 1950; s. John J. and Virginia Lee (Quisenberry) M.; m. Kathy Jeanne Duckworth, Sept. 2, 1978; children: Sean Patrick, Aron Michael, Ryan Joseph. BA in Bus. Adminstrn., Western State Coll. Colo., 1972, MA in Bus. Adminstrn., 1973; Assoc. in Risk Mgmt., Ins. Sch. Chgo., 1979. CPCU, 1984. Asst. mgr. K-Mart, Inc., Denver, 1973-74; ins. analyst Walgreen Co., Deerfield, Ill., 1974-77; v.p. risk mgmt. and safety Service-Master Co. L.P., Downers Grove, Ill., 1977—, v.p. risk mgmt. adminstrn., 1985-87; tchr. Ins. Sch. Chgo., 1985—. Mem. Risk and Ins. Mgmt. Soc. (bd. dirs. Chgo. chpt. 1980-84), pres. 1983-84), RIMS (dir. nat. soc.), Soc. CPCU Nat. Safety Coun., K.C. (past grand knight). Republican. Roman Catholic. Lodge: KC (chancellor) (Bloomingdale, Ill.). Home: 1379 Rolling Oaks Dr Carol Stream IL 60188-4611 Died Aug. 21, 1997.

MORRIS, PHYLLIS SUTTON, philosophy educator; b. Quincy, Ill., Jan. 25, 1931; d. John Guice and Helen Elizabeth (Provis) Sutton; m. John Martin Morris, Feb. 4, 1950; children: William Robert, Katherine Jill. Student, U. Mich., 1948-51; AB, U. Calif., 1953; MA, Colo. Coll., 1963; PhD, U. Mich., 1969. Instr. humanities Mich. State U., East Lansing, 1968-69; from lectr. to assoc. prof. Kirkland Coll., Clinton, N.Y., 1969-78; assoc. prof. Hamilton Coll., Clinton, 1978-83; adj. assoc. prof. LeMoyne Coll., Syracuse, N.Y., 1983-85; rsch. assoc. in philosophy Oberlin (Ohio) Coll., 1995—; vis. prof. philosophy Oberlin Coll., 1989-91, 93, 94-95, U. Mich., Ann Arbor, 1996. Author: Sartre's Concept of a Person, 1976; revs. editor Sartre Studies Internat. jour., 1995; contbr. articles to profl. jours. Travel grantee Am. Coun. Learned Socs., 1988, Summer Seminar grantee NEH, 1974, 82. Mem. Am. Philos. Assn., Sartre Cir., Sartre Soc. N.Am. (co-founder 1985, exec. com. 1985-91), Soc. for Phenomenology and Existential Philosophy, Soc. for Women in Philosophy. Democrat. Avocations: reading, walking, film watching. Died May 31, 1997.

MORRIS, ROBERT, lawyer, writer; b. Jersey City, Sept. 30, 1915; s. John Henry and Sarah (Williams) M.; m. Joan Russell Byles, Dec. 27, 1951; children: Robert, Paul E., Roger, Joan Byles Barry, William E., John Henry II, Geoffrey. AB, St. Peters Coll., Jersey City, 1936; JD, Fordham U., 1939; LLD, St. Francis Coll., Bklyn., 1954, U. Plano, 1976; LHD, Fujen U., Taipei, Taiwan, 1971. Bar: N.Y. 1939, Tex. 1962, U.S. Supreme Ct. 1952. Newspaper reporter, 1934-36; tchr. Greek, Latin and govt. St. Peters Prep. Sch., Jersey City, 1936-39; with firm Hines, Rearick, Dorr & Hammond, N.Y.C., 1939-40; asst. counsel N.Y. State Investigating Com., 1940-41; sec. to Congressman F. R. Coudert, Jr., 1946-50; sec.-treas. Monrovia Port Mgmt. Co., Africa, 1947-49; with firm Hochwald, Morris & Richmond, N.Y.C., 1946-52; spl. counsel U.S. Senate Internal Security Subcom., 1951-53, chief counsel, 1953, 56-58; judge Mcpl. Ct., N.Y.C., 1954-56; counsel to U.S. senators Hickenlooper and Lodge on U.S. Senate Fgn. Relations Com., 1950; adviser U.S. Senate Rules Com., 1955; pres. U. Dallas, 1960-62; pres. U. Plano, Tex., 1964-71, 73-77, chancellor, 1971-72; observer Zimbabwean parliamentary elections, 1979. Author: No Wonder We Are Losing, 1958, Disarmament, Weapon of Conquest, 1963, What Is Developmental Education?, 1967, Self-Destruct, 1979, Our Globe Under Siege, 1982, vol. II, 1985, vol. III, 1988, also nat. column; contbr. articles to profls. Candidate for Rep. nomination to U.S. Senate from N.J., 1958, 60, 84, from Tex., 1964, 70; chmn. Nat. Com. to Restore Internal Security, 1979—; bd. dirs. Insts. for Achievement Human Potential, 1977-89, bd. govs., 1989—; bd. dirs. Univ. Profs. for Acad. Order, 1988-91, U.S. Coun. World Freedom, 1981-91, Am.'s Future, 1985—, chmn. bd. and pres., 1995—. Lt. comdr. USNR, 1941-46, comdr. ret. Mem. ABA (internat. law sect.), Mil. Order World Wars (comdr. Monmouth chpt. 1984—), Am. Zimbabwean Assn. (chmn. 1978-87), Univ. Club (N.Y.C.), Mantoloking Yacht Club, Shanghai-Tiffin Club, Circumnavigators, Army-Navy Club (Washington), Admirals Club. Died Dec. 29, 1996.

MORRIS, ROBERT CRAWFORD, lawyer; b. Columbus, Ohio, Oct. 29, 1916; s. Charles Leon and Marie Marguerite (Crawford) M.; m. Emma Jones Robinson, Aug. 31, 1942; children: Cynthia Morris Yarmesch, Sylvia Marie. A.B., Princeton U., 1938; LL.B., Harvard U., 1941. Assoc. Arter & Hadden, Cleve., 1941-51, ptnr., 1951-90, ret., 1990. Served to capt. USAAF, 1942-46. Decorated Air medal with six oak leaf clusters. Fellow Am. Coll. Trial Lawyers, Internat. Acad. Trial Lawyers; mem. Internat. Assn. Def. Counsel (exec. com., Yancey Meml. award 1971, 83, 86, editor Def. Counsel Jour. 1988—), ABA, Cleve. Bar Assn., Am. Law Inst., Am. Bar Found. Republican. Episcopalian. Club: Union (Cleve.). Avocations: snow skiing; sailing. Died Sept. 7, 1997.

MORRIS, ROBERT DARRELL, life energy research director; b. Beaver, Pa., Sept. 3, 1914; s. David Earl and Marguerite (Krepps) M.; m. Ina Logan, Apr. 30, 1953 (div. July 26, 1976); children: Heather, Tamara; m. Berniece Henderson; children: R. Jeffrey, Stephen H. BA, Mount Union Coll., 1935; STD, Sch. Theology, Boston, 1938; MPH Sch. Pub. Health, U. Pitts., 1960. Dir. clin. tng. Pa. Hosp., Phila., 1939-40; chaplain, dir. clin. tng. Episcopal Hosp., Phila., 1940-53; lectr. clin. theology Temple U., Phila., 1948-52; intern social biology Pioneer Health Ctr., Peckham, London, 1949; family therapist Craig House for Children, Pitts., 1954-64; dir. social rsch. U. Miami Med. Sch. Family Medicine, Fla., 1966-68; pvt. practice Miami, 1969-89, life energy researcher, 1980—; co-dir. Orgone Biophys. Rsch. Lab., San Francisco, 1984-88. Recipient Jacob Sleeper fellowship Boston U., 1938-39, Doehla fellowship Rust Grant Rust Found., 1963, Durlach Grant Durlach Found., 1953. Mem. AAAS, Occidental Research Found., Upledger Inst. for Cranio-Sacral Therapy, N.Y. Acad. Sci., Coral Reef Yacht. Republican. Episcopalian. Avocations: rowing, sailing, photography, poetry. Died Nov. 25, 1996.

MORRIS, WRIGHT, novelist, critic; b. Central City, Nebr., Jan. 6, 1910; s. William H. and Grace (Osborn) M.; m. Mary E. Finfrock, 1934 (div. 1961); m. Josephine Kantor, 1961. Student, Pomona Coll., 1930-33; hon. degrees, Westminster Coll, U. Nebr., Pomona Coll. Prof. San Francisco State U., 1962-75. Author: My Uncle Dudley, 1942, The Man Who Was There, 1945, The Inhabitants, 1946, The Home Place, 1948, The World in the Attic, 1949, Man and Boy, 1951, The Works of Love, 1952, The Deep Sleep, 1953, The Huge Season, 1954, The Field of Vision, 1956 (Nat. Book award 1957), Love Among the Cannibals, 1957, The Territory Ahead, 1958, Ceremony in Lone Tree, 1960, The Mississippi River Reader, 1961, What a Way to Go, 1962, Cause for Wonder, 1963, One Day, 1965, In Orbit, 1967, A Bill of Rites, a Bill of Wrongs, a Bill of Goods, 1968, God's Country and My People, 1968, Wright Morris: A Reader, 1970, Fire Sermon, 1971, War Games, 1971, Love Affair: A Venetian Journal, 1972, Here is Einbaum, 1973, A Life, 1973, About Fiction, 1975, Real Losses, Imaginary Gains, 1976, The Fork River Space Project, 1977, Earthly Delights, Unearthly Adornments: The American Writer as Image Maker. 1978, Plains Song, 1980 (Am. Book award 1981), Will's Boy, 1981, Photographs and Words, 1982, Solo: An American Dreamer in Europe, 1933-34, 1983, A Cloak of Light, 1985, Collected Stories, 1986, Time Pieces: Word and Image, 1989, Writing My Life: An

Autobiography, 1992, Three Easy Pieces, 1993, Two for the Road, 1994. Recipient Robert Kirsch award for body of work, 1981, Life Achievement award Nat. Endowment for Arts, 1986; Guggenheim fellow, 1942, 46, 54. Mem. Nat. Inst. Arts and Letters, Am. Acad. Arts and Scis. (Whiting award 1982). Office: care Harper & Collins Pubs 10 E 53rd St New York NY 10022-5244 Died May 1998. †

MORRISON, ROY DENNIS, II, philosophy, religion and science educator emeritus; b. Marshall, Tex., Dec. 30, 1926; s. Roy Dennis and Louise (Smith) M.; m. Margaret Cornelia Johnson, July 18, 1959; 1 child, Sylvia Louise. BA, Howard U., 1947; BD, North Bapt. Theol. Seminar, Chgo., 1950; MA, U. Chgo., 1969, PhD with distinction, 1972. Asst. prof. New Collegiate Div., U. Chgo., 1970-73, Divinity Sch., U. Chgo., 1970-73; prof. philosophy, epistemology, religion and sci. Wesley Theol. Sem., Washington, 1973-93; retired, 1993; chmn. Master of Theol. Studies degree program Wesley Theol Sem. Author: Science, Theology and the Transcendental Horizon: Einstein, Kant and Tillich, 1994; contbr. articles to profl. jours. Mem. Am. Acad. Religion, N.Am. Paul Tillich Soc. (pres. 1985), Inst. on Religion in Age of Sci. (acad. fellow 1991), Psi Chi. Unitarian Universalist. Avocations: H.O. scale model railroading, photography, high fidelity radio, high technology computing systems, metal machining. Home: Silver Spring Md. Died Oct. 21, 1995.

MORRISON, WALTON STEPHEN, lawyer; b. Big Spring, Tex., June 16, 1907; s. Matthew Harmon and Ethel (Jackson) M.; m. Mary Lyon Bell, Dec. 19, 1932. Student Tex. A&M U., 1926-28; J.D., U. Tex., 1932. Bar: Tex. 1932. Asso., Morrison & Morrison, Big Spring, 1932-36, ptnr., 1939, 46; atty. County of Howard, 1937-39, judge, 1941-42, 47-48; atty. City of Big Spring, 1949-58; sole practice, Big Spring, 1953—; lectr. Am. Inst. Banking. Served with USAF, 1942-46. Fellow Tex. Bar Found., Am. Coll. Probate Counsel; mem. Tex. City Attys. Assn. (pres. 1955-56), Am. Judicature Soc., Tex. Bar Assn., ABA. Baptist. Clubs: Rotary (pres. 1949), Masons, Shriner. Died March 14, 1997.

MORSE, BRADFORD, academic administrator, educator, former congressman, former UN official; b. Lowell, Mass., Aug. 7, 1921; s. Frank Young and Inez Rice (Turnbull) M.; m. Josephine Anne Neale, Jan. 1, 1981; 1 child, Stephanie Hilary Jennifer; children from previous marriage: Susanna Francesca, Anthony Bradford. BS, Boston U., 1948, LLB cum laude, 1949; DSc (hon.), U. Lowell, 1965; DPA (hon.), Northeastern U., 1967; LLD (hon.), Clark U., 1978, U. Guadalajara, 1986, New Eng. Coll., 1988. Bar: Mass. 1948. Lectr., instr. Boston U. Sch. Law, 1949-53; spl. counsel Senate Com. on Armed Services, 1953-54; exec. sec., chief asst. U.S. Senator Leverett Saltonstall, 1955-58; dep. adminstr. VA, Washington, 1958-60; mem. 87th-92d Congresses from 5th Mass. dist.; under-sec. gen. for polit. and gen. assembly affairs UN, 1972-75, adminstr. UN devel. program, 1976-86; pres. Salzburg Seminar Cambridge, Mass., Salzburg, Austria, 1986—. Trustee Boston U., 1972-88; bd. visitors Georgetown Sch. Fgn. Service; bd. dirs. Panos Found., Population Crisis Com., Save the Children Fedn. Served with AUS, 1942-46. Decorated official de la Gran Cruz de la Order de San Carlos de Columbia; officier de l'Ordre National du Niger; grand commdr. du Lion de Senegal; grand officer of the Republic of Gambia; officer of the Grand Cordon of the Sacred Treasure of Japan; recipient Am. Soc. Pub. Adminstrn. Nat. Pub. Service award, 1984, U.S. Presdl. World without Hunger award, 1985, Inter-Am. Leadership award, 1985, Franklin Delano Roosevelt Freedom award, 1986, ASAID Humanitarian award, 1986, Internat. Devel. Conf. Humanitarian award, 1987, AMVETS Peace award, 1987, Christian A. Herter award Boston World Affairs Council, 1987. Fellow U.S. Inst. of Peace (Disting.), Nat. Acad. Pub. Adminstrn. (sr.); mem. Soc. Internat. Devel. (gov. coun.), Coun. Fgn. Rels., Overseas Devel. Coun., Technoserve, Am. Acad. Diplomacy. Republican. Congregationalist. DIED 12/18/94. .

MORSE, ERSKINE VANCE, veterinarian, educator; b. Peoria, Ill., June 25, 1921; s. Frank T. and Ethel G. (Vance) M.; m. Lucy Anne Howard, Oct. 6, 1945; children—Elizabeth Anne Coffman, Thomas H., James E., William W. D.V.M., Cornell U., 1944, M.S., 1948, Ph.D., 1949. Diplomate: Am. Coll. Vet. Preventive Medicine (charter). Teaching asst. Cornell U., 1947-48; asst. prof., then asso. prof. vet. sci. U. Wis., 1949-55; asso. prof., then prof. microbiology and pub. health Mich. State U., 1955-58; prof. vet. hygiene, asso. dir. Vet. Med. Research Inst., Iowa State U., 1958-60; dean Sch. Vet. Sci. and Medicine, Purdue U., 1960-70; H.W. Handley Disting. prof. vet. medicine and environ. health, assoc. dir. Sch. Vet. Sci. and Medicine, Purdue U. (Environ. Health Inst.), 1970-86, prof. emeritus vet. microbiology, dean emeritus vet. medicine, 1986-95; Gen. chmn Nat. Leptospirosis Research Com., 1958-59; mem. leptospirosis com. U.S. Livestock San. Assn., 1959-60; mem. Ind. Livestock San. Bd., 1960-70, Nat. Bd. Vet. Med. Examiners, 1970-75; del. 4th Pan Am. Vet. Congress, Mexico City, 1962; cons. USPHS, 1963-95; AID cons. vet. medicine, Brazil, S.Am., 1965; FAO/WHO, U.S. del. 2d Internat. Conf. Vet. Edn., Copenhagen, Denmark, 1965; AID cons., Republic Phillippines, 1966; cons. VA, 1966-74; Surgeon Gen. USAF, 1968-70, North Central Assn. Colls. and Secondary Schs.; nat. cons. Purdue Research Found., 1967-95; cons. Am. Assn. for Accreditation Lab. Animal Care, 1976; mem. Bur. Health Manpower, HEW, 1968-70; U.S. Army, Vet. corps. faculty liaison rep., 1973-95; judge Internat. Sci. Fair finals, 1965-68, 74-83; treas., bd. dirs. Am. Vet. Med. Assn. Found., 1965-66; mem. com. on animal health NRC/Nat. Acad. Scis., 1968-71, chmn., 1969-71; chmn. organizing com. Nat. Salmonellosis Symposium, Washington, 1976-77; mem. organizing com. Internat. Symposium on Salmonellosis, New Orleans, 1983-84. Author research papers on infectious diseases of animals and man, environ. health, salmonellosis, seafood poisonings; collaborator manuals and texts. Served to capt. Vet. Corps U.S. Army, 1944-47. Named Sagamore of Wabash State of Ind., 1963, Ind. Master Gardener, 1990. Mem. AVMA (hon., rsch. fellow 1948-49, council on research 1964-69, com. on environmentology 1972-74), Am. Coll. Epidemiology (assoc.), Ind. Vet. Med. Assn., Am. Assn. Vet. Bacteriology (pres. 1959-60), Am. Public Health Assn. (com. environ. health manpower 1972-74), Soc. Exptl. Biology and Medicine, Assn. Tchrs. Vet. Pub. Health and Preventive Medicine, Am. Assn. Lab. Animal Sci. (council on edn. 1971-74), Conf. Research Workers Animal Diseases, Nat. Assn. Standard Med. Vocabulary (cons.), Assn. State Univ. and Land Grant Colls. (chmn. vet. div.), Am. Animal Hosp. Assn. (hon.), Am. Assn. for Lab. Animal Accreditation (vice chmn., exec. bd. 1970-74, chmn. 1974-75), Am. Assn. Vet. Med. Colls. (pres. elect 1971), Internat. Assn. for Aquatic Animal Medicine, U.S. Animal Health Assn. (chmn. com. on salmonellosis 1976-81), Sigma Xi, Phi Zeta (pres. Zeta chpt. 1957-58), Phi Gamma Delta (pres. grad. assn. 1957-58), Gamma Alpha, Alpha Psi. Presbyn. Home: West Lafayette Ind. Died Feb. 7, 1995.

MORSE, KENNETH PRATT, manufacturing executive; b. Cambridge, Mass., Mar. 9, 1905; s. Clifford E. and Jessie C. (Barr) M.; m. Florence Stillwell, June 20, 1931; children—Kenneth P., Peter S. Student, MIT, 1922-26. Asst. chief engr. Lanston Monotype Machine Co., Phila., 1926-37; devel. engr. Standard Register Co., Dayton, 1937, chief engr., 1938, chief engr., works supt., 1938-42, asst. gen. mgr., 1942-45, exec. v.p., gen. mgr., 1945-64, pres., 1964-70, chmn. bd., 1970-71, chmn. emeritus, 1971-95; v.p., dir. Office Equipment Mfg. Inst., 1953-54, pres., dir., 1955-57; pres., dir. Huebner Co., Dayton, 1951-58; dir. emeritus 3d Nat. Bank & Trust Co., Dayton.; Mem. Industry adv. com. continuous forms and adv. com. office equipment U.S. Dept. Commerce and U.S. Dept. Labor Manpower Commn., 1951-95. Mem. budget com. Community Chest, 1948-54; chmn. com. financing devel. Dayton area Mass. Inst. Tech., 1949-95; adv. bd. Salvation Army, 1953-60; Bd. dirs. Goodwill Industries, Dayton, 1957-66, pres., 1960-64; bd. dirs. Community Chest, 1958-95, chmn. campaign, 1961; Trustee Miami Valley Hosp., Dayton, 1958-77, U. Dayton, 1970-75. Recipient Inland Printer award, 1958, Disting. Corp. Leadership award MIT, 1987. Mem. Edn. Council of Graphic Arts (dir. 1959-66, pres. 1964-66), U.S. C of C., Dayton C of C. (pres. 1957-59), Printing Industry Am., Inc. (sec. 1952-53, dir. 1952-54), Dayton Printing Industry Assn. (pres. 1950-53, dir. 1950-95), Graphic Arts Research and Engring. Council (planning com. 1953). Presbyterian. Lodges: Masons, Shriners. Home: Dayton Ohio Died Oct. 1, 1995.

MORSE, LEON WILLIAM, traffic, physical distribution and transportation management executive, consultant; b. N.Y.C., Nov. 13, 1912; s. Benjamin and Leah (Shapiro) M.; m. Goldie Kohn, Mar. 30, 1941; children: Jeffrey W., Saul J. BS, NYU, 1935; grad. Acad. Advanced Traffic, 1937, 1954; DBA, Columbia Pacific U., 1979. Registered practitioner STB, Fed. Maritime Commn. Individual bus., traffic mgmt. cons., Phila., 1950-58; gen. traffic mgr. W.H. Rorer, Inc., Ft. Washington, Pa., 1958-78; adj. prof. econs. of transp., logistics Pa. State U., Ogontz campus, 1960-82; owner Morse Assocs.; course leader seminars in freight traffic mgmt., phys. distbn. mgmt., transp. contract negotiations and freight claims for univs. in the U.S.; bd. dirs. Sr. Security Assocs., Inc.; Bd. trustees Temple B'rith Shalom. Author: Practical Handbook of Industrial Traffic Management, 1980, 87, (manuals) Job of the Traffic Manager, Effective Traffic Management, Fundamentals of Traffic Management, Transportation Contract Negotiations and Freight Claims. Capt. transp. corps, AUS, World War II. Recipient Del. Valley Traffic Mgr. of Yr. award, 1963. Mem. Traffic and Transp. Club of Phila., Traffic Club of Phila., Traffic Club of Norristown, Am. Soc. Internat. Execs. (past pres., bd. dirs., sec., cert.), Assn. Transp. Practitioners, Am. Soc. Transp. and Logistics (emeritus), Council Logistics Mgmt., Transp. Research Forum, Health & Personal Care Distribution Conf. (pres. 1973-75, chmn. bd. 1975-77), Sr. Security Assn., Inc (bd. dirs.), Delta Nu Alpha Transp. Fraternity, Mason, Shriner. Died Aug. 12, 1997.

MOSCOVITZ, ISADORE, editor, publisher; b. Jacksonville, Fla., Sept. 15, 1911; s. Joseph and Anne (Zosim) M.; div., children: David, Howard, m. Ethel Katz; 1 child, Arlene Shainbrown. BS in Journalism, U. Fla., 1933. Editor, publisher So. Jewish Weekly, Jacksonville, 1933—. SE v.p. Zionist Orgn. Am. Served to maj. U.S. Army, 1941-45. Lodge: B'Nai Brith. DIED 02/24/96. .

MOSER, KENNETH MILES, physician, educator; b. Balt., Apr. 12, 1929; s. Simon and Helene Joyce M.; m. Sara Falk, June 17, 1951; children: Gregory, Kathleen, Margot, Diana. BA, Haverford Coll., 1950; MD, Johns Hopkins U., 1954. Diplomate Am. Bd. Internal Medicine. Intern, resident in medicine D.C. Gen. Hosp., Georgetown Hosp., 1954-59; chief pulmonary and infectious disease svc. Nat. Naval Med. Ctr., Bethesda, Md., 1959-61; dir. pulmonary div. Georgetown U. Med. Ctr., Washington, 1961-68; prof. medicine, dir. pulmonary and critical care med. divsn. Sch. Medicine U. Calif., San Diego, 1968-97; dir. Specialized Ctr. Rsch. U. Calif.-San Diego/Nat. Heart Lung and Blood Inst., 1978-97. Author 15 books in field of pulmonary medicine and thrombosis.; contbr. articles to med. jours. Bd. dirs. Am. Lung Assn. of San Diego and Imperial Counties, 1969-76, Am. Lung Assn. of Calif., 1976-80; mem. manpower com. Nat. Heart, Lung and Blood Inst., bd. dirs. 1978-97. With USN, 1959-61. Fellow ACP, AAAS, Am. Coll. Chest Physicians; mem. Am. Thoracic Soc. (exec. bd., pres. 1985-86), Am. Heart Assn. Coun. on Thrombosis, Am. Physiol. Soc. Home: La Jolla Calif. Died June 9, 1997.

MOSER, NORMAN CALVIN, writer, editor, publisher; b. Durham, N.C., Oct. 15, 1931; s. William Monroe and Myrtle Sarah (Jordan) M.; m. Hadassah Haskale, July 1966 (div. 1971); m. Yolanda Ponce Chirinos de Jesus, Nov. 17, 1977 (div. 1982); 1 child, David Preston. Student, U. Md., Ulm, Germany, 1955-56, U. Pacific, spring, 1958; B.A., San Francisco State U., 1961, M.A. in Lang. Arts, 1966; postgrad., U. Wash., 1962, U. B.C., Can., 1963. Co-pub. weekly tabloid Bay Window (name later changed to Bay Area Arts Rev.), San Francisco, 1957-59; editor lit. mag. Transfer, San Francisco State U., 1959-61; editor, pub. Illuminations, Berkeley, Calif., 1965—; freelance writer. Singer-actor, Am. Guild Variety Artists, 1950-53; actor in plays and films; author: Jumpsongs, 1973, A Shaman's Songbook/Poems & Tales, 1975, I Live in the South of My Heart, 1980, Open Season, 1980, The Shorter Plays & Scenarios of Norm Moser, 1981, El Grito del Norte: Stories and Tales, 1984, South by Southwest, 1989; contbr. to: anthologies Because You Talk, 1976, Travols, 1976, Living Underground, 1973, Contemporary Literary Scene, 1974, Red Clay Reader, 1968, Other Side, 1982, Green Isle in the Sea, 1986, The Illuminations Reader: Art & Writing from Illuminations, Pulse & Gar, 1989, others; contbg. editor Grande Ronde Rev., 1969-71; staff editor, writer The Gar, 1972-74, Berkeley Rev. Books, 1989—, others; contbr. numerous articles, stories, poems and revs. to lit. jours., anthologies and newspapers. Recipient prize for Illuminations, Nat. Endowment for Arts, 1966; Coordinating Council Lit. Mags. grantee, 1967, 69, 70, 74, 77; P.E.N. grantee, 1972, 74, 75, 78, 81, 86, 91.

MOSES, GILBERT, film and theatre director; b. Cleve., Aug. 20, 1942; s. Gilbert and Bertha Mae (Jones) M. Student, Oberlin (Ohio) Coll., 1960-63, Sorbonne, Paris, 1963, NYU Sch. Arts, 1966-67. Copy boy N.Y. Post, 1964; mem. staff Free Press, Jackson, Miss., 1963-64; editor Free Press, 1964; co-founder, artistic dir. Free So. Theatre, Jackson, 1963—; bd. dirs. Free So. Theatre, 1966—; stage dir. Arena Stage, 1982-83. Mem. Second City, Chgo., 1967, guitarist, composer, Nick Gravenitis Group, 1967, The Street Choir, 1968; dir.: Slaveship, 1969 (Obie award 1970), The Taking of Miss Janie (Obie award 1977, N.Y. Drama Critics Circle award 1977, N.Y. Drama Critics award 1977), Ain't Supposed to Die a Natural Death, 1973 (Tony nomination), 1600 Pennsylvania Avenue, 1976, The Duplex, 1972, Don't Let it Go To Your Head, 1973, Every Night When the Sun Goes Down, 1975, all in N.Y.C., Bloodknot in San Francisco, 1970, No Place to Be Somebody, 1971, Mother Courage, 1971, all in Washington, Buried Child, Arena Stage Co., all in Washington, Rigoletto at San Francisco Opera House, 1972; dir., composer: music and lyrics for film Willie Dynamite, 1975, The Fish That Saved Pittsburgh; dir.: TV films including Roots (2 segments) (Humanitas award 1977, Emmy nominee 1977), The Greatest Thing That Almost Happened, 1977, The Wiz (prior to Broadway opening), 1976; multicamera episodes Benson, 1985, M.O.W., Fight for Jenny, 1986, The Day They Came to Arrest the Book, 1987 (Humanitas award 1987), Runaway, 1989; dir. episodes TV series: Call to Glory, Paper Chase, Maximum Security (HBO), 1994; producer, dir. Daddy Can't Read, ABC; producer PBS-TV prodn. The Ossie and Ruby Series, 1988. DIED 04/15/95. .

MOSES, JOHNNIE, JR., microbiologist; b. Kinston, N.C., May 24, 1939; s. Johnnie Moses and Lillie Ann (Williams) Dillahunt; m. Mirian Louise Mosely, Aug. 16, 1958; children: Nicholas G., Adrianne D. BA, Fordham U., 1978; MA, NYU, 1982. Lic. clin. lab. tech. Lab. technologist Harlem Hosp. Ctr., N.Y.C., 1962-68, sr. lab. technologist, 1968-80, lab. microbiologist, 1980-90, lab. microbiology cons., 1980-94, assoc. microbiology, 1990-94; hematology instr. Mandl Med. Asst. Sch., N.Y.C., 1983-85; Am. history prof. Malcolm-King Coll., N.Y.C., 1983-88. Mem. editorial rev. bd. Black Chronicle. Adv. mem. N.Y. State Assembly, N.Y.C., 1988; treas., exec. Addicts Rehab. Ctr., 1975-94; treas. Manhattan Christian Reformed Ch.,

1975-94. Recipient Cert. of Appreciation, Harlem Hosp. Pathology Dept., 1990. Mem. Internat. Soc. Clin. Lab. Tech. (certs. of merit 1982, 91), Nat. Sickle Cell Anemia Found., Guitar Found. Am., Fordham U. Alumni Assn., NYU Alumni Assn. Democrat. Avocations: microphotography, classical guitar, art, African-American research. Home: Bronx N.Y. Died Nov. 7, 1994.

MOSS, CHARLES NORMAN, physician; b. L.A., June 13, 1914; s. Charles Francis and Lena (Rye) M.; A.B., Stanford U., 1940; M.D., Harvard U., 1944; cert. U. Vienna, 1947; M.P.H., U. Calif.-Berkeley, 1955; Dr.P.H., UCLA, 1970; m. Margaret Louise Stakias; children—Charles Eric, Gail Linda, and Lori Anne. Surg. intern Peter Bent Brigham Hosp., Boston, 1944-45, asst. in surgery, 1947; commd. 1st lt. USAF, M.C., USAAF, 1945, advanced through grades to lt. col., USAF, 1956; Long course for flight surgeon USAF Sch. Aviation Medicine, Randolph AFB, Tex., 1948-49, preventive medicine div. Office USAF Surgeon Gen., Washington, 1955-59; air observer, med., 1954, became sr. flight surgeon 1956; later med. dir., Los Angeles div. North Am. Rockwell Corp., Los Angeles; chief med. adv. unit Los Angeles County, now ret. Decorated Army Commendation medal (U.S.); Chinese Breast Order of Yun Hui. Recipient Physicians Recognition award AMA, 1969, 72, 76, 79, 82. Diplomate in aerospace medicine and occupational medicine Am. Bd. Preventive Medicine. Fellow Am. Pub. Health Assn., AAAS, Am. Coll. Preventive Medicine, Royal Soc. Health, Am. Acad. Occupational Medicine, Western Occupational Med. Assn., Am. Assn. Occupational Medicine; mem. AMA, Mil. Surgeons U.S., Soc. Air Force Flight Surgeons, Am. Conf. Govt. Hygienests, Calif. Acad. Preventive Medicine, (dir.), Aerospace Med. Assn., Calif., Los Angeles County med. assns., Assn. Oldetime Barbell and Strongmen. Research and publs. in field. Died March 24, 1996.

MOSS, JOHN EMERSON, banker, former congressman; b. Carbon County, Utah, Apr. 13, 1915; s. John Emerson and Della Orta (Mower) M.; m. Jean Kueny, Sept. 15, 1935; children: Jennifer, Allison. In retail bus., 1938-43, real estate broker, 1945-85; mem. 83d-95th congresses 3d Dist. Calif., mem. govt. ops., interstate and fgn. commerce coms., chmn. select com. on govt. info., 1955-68; also chmn. oversight and investigation subcom.; dep. majority whip 2d session 87th-91st congresses; mem. 93d-94th congresses Democratic Policy and Steering Com.; chmn. bd. 1st Comml. Bank, Sacramento, 1979-85; chmn. Capitol Hist. Preservation Soc., 1985-92; Mem. Calif. Assembly, 9th Dist., 1948-52. Served with USNR, 1943-45. Mem. DAV, Laguna Hgts. Coop. Corp. (bd. dirs., v.p. 1993, pres. 1994—), C. of C., Commonwealth of Calif. Club.

MOTHERWAY, JOSEPH EDWARD, mechanical engineer, educator; b. Providence, Jan. 28, 1930; s. Edward John and Josephine Dorothea (Conway) M.; m. Sally Alicia Doherty, June 11, 1955; children: Carmel A., Suzanne M., Joseph Edward, Mavis E., Melita A., Megan L., William D., Edward J., Mara A. Sc.B., Brown U., 1955; M.S., U. Conn., 1961; postgrad., Columbia U., 1965-67; Ph.D., U. Conn., 1970. Mech. engr. Standard Oil (N.J.), Bayway, 1955-56; design engr. Electric Boat div. Gen. Dynamic Corp., Groton, Conn., 1956-58; design group leader Electric Boat div. Gen. Dynamic Corp., 1958-59; sr. project engr. Remington Rand Univac Lab., South Norwalk, Conn., 1959-60; chief engr. C.H.I. div. Textron, Inc., Warwick, R.I., 1960-64; lectr. Brown U., Providence, 1962-64; asst. prof. mech. engring. U. Bridgeport, Conn., 1964-65; assoc. prof. U. Bridgeport, 1965-70, Bullard prof. engring. design, 1970-82, head dept. mech. engring., 1971-75; prof. mech. engring. U. Mass., 1982—; pres. Alpha Engring. Co., 1975-96; Cons. U.S. Navy, 1965-69, Dorr-Oliver Inc., Consol. Controls Corp., Energy Research Corp., Malcolm Pirnie Engrs. Assoc. editor: Jour. Mech. Design, 1978-80; contbr. articles to profl. jours. Served with USMC, 1949-53. Recipient Engring. Service award Brown Engring. Assn., 1962; NSF Sci. Faculty fellow, 1968-69. Mem. ASME, Soc. Exptl. Mechanics, Am. Soc. Engring. Edn., Brown Engring. Assn. (pres. 1968-69), Sigma Xi, Tau Beta Pi. Died, Feb. 8, 1996.

MOTT, NEVILL (FRANCIS MOTT), physicist, educator, author; b. Leeds, Eng., Sept. 30, 1905; s. C.F. and Lilian Mary (Reynolds) M.; m. Ruth Horder, Mar. 21, 1930; children: Elizabeth, Alice. Student, Cambridge (Eng.) U., 1924-29; MA, St. John's Coll., Cambridge, 1929; DSc (hon.), Univs. of Sheffield, London, Louvain, Grenoble, Paris, Poitiers, Bristol, Univs. of Ottawa, Liverpool, Reading, Warwick, Lancaster, Heriot Watt, Bordeaux, Univs. of St. Andrews, Essex, Stuttgart, Sussex, William and Mary, Marburg, Univs. of Bar Ilan, Lille, Rome, Lisbon, Cambridge; D Tech, Linköping. Lectr. math. Cambridge U., 1930-33, Cavendish prof. exptl. physics, 1954-71; master Gonville and Caius Coll., 1959-66; prof. physics U. Bristol, 1933-54, bd. dir. H.H. Wills Phys. Lab., 1948-54; Page-Barbour lectr. U. Va., 1956. Author: An Outline of Wave Mechanics, 1930, (with H.S.W. Massey) The Theory of Atomic Collisions, 1993, (with H. Jones) The Theory of the Properties of Metals and Alloys, 1936, (with R.W. Gurney) Electronic Processes in Ionic Crystals, 1940, Wave (with I.N. Snedden) Wave Mechanics and Its Applications, 1948, Elements of Wave Mechanics, 1952, Atomic Structure and the Strength of Metals, 1956, (with E.A. Davis) Electronic Processes in Noncrystalline Materials, 1971, 2d edit., 1979, Elements of Quantum Mechanics, 1972, Metal-Insulator Transitions, 1974, 2d edit., 1991, Conduction in Noncrystalline Materials, 1987, 2d edit., 1993, (autobiography) A Life in Science, 1986, 2d edit., 1996, Can Scientists Believe?, 1991, (with A. Alexandov) Polaron Theory of High Temperature Superconductors, 1994, Polarons, Bipolorons, 1995. Mem. cen. adv. coun. Ministry of Edn., 1956-59; chmn. com. physics edn. Nuffield Found., 1965-75. Sci. adviser to Anti Aircraft Command, also supt. theoretical rsch. in armaments Armament Rsch. Dept., World War II. Decorated knight bachelor, Companion of Honor, 1995; recipient Nobel prize for physics, 1977. Fellow Royal Soc. (Hughes medalist 1941, Royal medal 1953, Copley medal 1972), Phys. Soc. of Great Brit. (pres. 1956-58); mem. NAS, AAAS (corr.), Inst. Physics (hon. fellow), Internat. Union Pure and Applied Physics (pres. 1951-57), Modern Langs. Assn. (pres. 1955), Société Française de Physique (hon.). Died Aug. 8, 1996.

MOTT, WILLIAM CHAMBERLAIN, lawyer, retired naval officer; b. Maplewood, N.J., Sept. 7, 1911; s. Raymond Louis and Helen (Chamberlain) M.; m. Rosemary Baker, Sept. 17, 1938 (div. 1947); children: Adam S., Janie B.; m. Edith Grace, Nov. 13, 1947; children: Diane B., Lucy A., Sarah G., William Chamberlain. B.S., U.S. Naval Acad., 1933; J.D., George Washington U., 1940; LL.D., John Marshall Law Sch., 1961, Rhode Island Coll., 1964. Bar: D.C. 1940. Patent examiner Washington, 1936-40; commd. lt. (j.g.) U.S. Navy, 1939, advanced through grades to rear adm., 1960; asst. naval aide to Pres. Roosevelt, 1942-43; assigned (Amphibious Forces Pacific), 1944-45; liaison (UN and Dept. of State), 1946-48; legal adviser comdr. in chief (Pacific Area Command), 1948-50; comdg. officer (Sch. Naval Justice), 1950-53; spl. asst., chmn. (Joint Chiefs Staff), 1954-58; dep. judge adv. gen. (Office Judge Adv. Gen., Dept. of Navy), 1958-60, judge adv. gen., 1960-64; exec. dir. (Council on Econs. and Nat. Security). Exec. v.p. U.S. Ind. Telephone Assn., 1964-77; pres. Capital Legal Found.; chmn. adv. com. Nat. Strategic Materials and Minerals Program. Decorated Legion of Merit. Fellow Am. Bar Found.; mem. Am. Soc. Internat. Law, Am. Bar Assn., Fed. Bar Assn. Episcopalian. Clubs: Army and Navy, Farmington, Chevy Chase. Died Nov. 1, 1997.

MOVERLEY, GERALD, bishop; b. Bradford, Yorkshire, Eng., Apr. 9, 1922; s. William Joseph and Irene Mary (Dewhirst) M. D in Canon Law, Angelicum U., Rome, 1954. J.C.D.; ordained Roman Cath. priest Diocese of Leeds, 1946, bishop of Diocese of Hallam, 1980. Priest Diocese of Leeds, Yorkshire, 1946; sec., chaplain Bishop of Leeds, 1946-51; asst. St. Anne's Cathedral, Leeds, 1954-60; chancellor Diocese of Leeds, 1957-80; pastor St. Brigid's Churwell, Leeds, 1960-68; consecrated aux. bishop of Leeds, 1968-96; first bishop Diocese of Hallam, South Yorkshire, 1980-96; mem. Coun. of Univ. of Sheffield. Mem. Canon Law Soc. of Gt. Britain and Ireland (founder, pres. 1980-86). Roman Catholic. Home: Quarters Carrick Hill Way, Sheffield S10 3LT, England Died Dec. 14, 1996.

MOWBRAY, JOHN CODE, state supreme court chief justice; b. Bradford, Ill., Sept. 20, 1918; s. Thomas John and Ellen Driscoll (Code) M.; m. Kathlyn Ann Hammes, Oct. 15, 1949; children: John, Romy, Jerry, Terry. BA, Western Ill. U., 1940, LHD (hon.), 1976, LLD (hon.), 1977; LLD (hon.), Far Eastern Civil Affairs Tng. Sch., Northwestern U., 1945; JD cum laude, U. Notre Dame, 1949; LLD (hon.), U. Nev., 1978. Bar: Nev. 1949, Ill. 1950. Dep. dist. atty. Clark County, Las Vegas, Nev., 1949-53; U.S. referee Fed. Cts. in Nev., 1955-59; dist. judge for Nev., 1959-67; justice Nev. Supreme Ct., Carson City, 1967-97, chief justice, 1986-97; founder 1st pub. defender program in Nev., 1967; mem. faculty Nat. Coll. State Judiciary, 1967. V.p. Boulder Dam Area council Boy Scouts Am., 1960-70; bd. dirs. Nev. Area council, 1967-97; pres. City of Hope, 1963-64, NCCJ, 1965-66; v.p. YMCA, 1964-97; chmn. Nev. Commn. on Bicentennial U.S. Constitution, 1986; nat. trustee Freedoms Found. Valley Forge, Pa. Served to maj. AUS, 1942-46, PTO. Recipient Silver Beaver award Boy Scouts Am., 1966, Outstanding Alumni award Western Ill. U., 1971, Equal Justice award Western regional dept. NAACP, 1970, Minuteman award SAR, 1982, Silver Antelope award Boy Scouts Am., 1983, Jurist of Yr. award Nev. Trial Lawyers Assn., 1986, Judicial Officer of Yr. award State Sheriff and Police Assn., 1986, medal of honor DAR, 1990; Mowbray Hall, Western Ill. U. named in his honor, 1974. Mem. ABA (Liberty Bell award 1991), Nev. Trial Lawyers Assn. (Jurist of Yr. award 1986), Am. Judicature Soc., State Sheriff and Police Assn. (Jud. Officer of Yr. award 1986), SAR (pres. Nev. 1969-70, Nat. Gen. MacArthur medal 1971, nat. trustee 1971-97), VFW. Clubs: Rotarian (hon.), Elk, Knights of Columbus. Home: Las Vegas Nev. Died Mar. 5, 1997.

MOYNIHAN, WALTER RICHARD, lawyer; b. St. Louis, Oct. 6, 1923; s. Walter Richard and Helen Irene (Clancey) M.; m. Marie T. Kilburn, Oct. 20, 1951; children: Richard T., David K. AB, Holy Cross Coll., 1943; JD, Boston U., 1949, LLM in Taxation, 1971. Bar: Mass., 1949. Counsel, contract mgr. GCA Corp., Bedford, Mass., 1959-69; v.p. Electronics Space Systems, Concord, Mass., 1969-75; sole practice Boston, 1972—, Lynnfield, Mass., 1985—; counsel John M. Doukas Law Office, Boston, 1972—, Biotek, Inc., Woburn, Mass, 1980—, Prestige Mktg., Inc., No. Andover, Mass., 1983—; counsel, clk. Computer Genetics Corp., Wakefield, Mass., 1980—. Mem. ABA (publs. Pub. Contract Law Jour., taxation, corp., pub. contract, banking and bus. law sects.), Nat. Contract Mgmt. Assn., Essex County Estate and Bus. Planning Council. Republican. Roman Catholic. Club: Salem Country (Peabody, Mass.). Avocation: tennis. Died Aug. 24, 1996.

MUELLER, HAROLD, flutist, conductor, educator; b. Austin, Tex., Jan. 28, 1920; s. Robert and Leona (Mayer) M.; m. Beatrice J. Baldinger, June 26, 1959; children—Harold Edward, Robert Baldinger. Mus.B., U. Mich., 1941, Mus.M., 1946; Ph.D., Eastman Sch. Music, U. Rochester, 1956; postgrad., Juilliard Sch. Music, 1947, L'Ecole Monteux, summers 1948-51. Instr. Corpus Christi (Tex.) High Sch., 1941; flutist Columbus (Ohio) Philharmon. Orch., 1946-48, New Orleans Symphony Orch., 1948-53; instr. Eastman Sch. Music, Rochester, N.Y., 1953-56; asst. prof. music U. Minn., 1956-57; assoc. prof. Austin Coll., Sherman, Tex., 1958-61; prof. Austin Coll., 1961-67, chmn. music dept., 1958-66, chmn. fine arts area, 1960-66; prof. Marietta (Ohio) Coll., 1967-85, prof. emeritus, 1985-94, head Edward E. MacTaggart dept. music, 1967-75; condr. Marietta Coll. Civic Symphonette, Marietta Oratorio Chorus, 1967-85; mus. dir. Parkersburg (W.Va.) Choral Soc., 1977-79; mus. dir. various prodns. Parkersburg Actors Guild, 1981-85; music commentator WMRT-FM, Marietta, 1976—. editor, pub. compositions of Andreas Hammerschmidt.; composer Rondo for woodwind quintet, 1984; contbr. articles profl. jours.; music arranger for Blennerhassett Drama Assn.'s outdoor prodn. "Eden On the River", 1987, 88. Bd. dirs. Orgn. Ohio Orchs., 1975-85. Served with USAAF, 1941-46. Mem. AAUP, Am. Musicol. Soc. (past chpt. chmn.), Coll. Music Soc., Music Library Assn., Am. Symphony Orch. League, Pi Kappa Lambda, Phi Mu Alpha-Sinfonia, Phi Delta Kappa, Kappa Kappa Psi. Lutheran. Home: Marietta Ohio Died Sept. 21, 1994.

MUELLER, STEPHAN, geophysicist, educator; b. Marktredwitz, Ger., July 30, 1930; s. Hermann Friedrich and Johanna Antonie Fanny (Leuze) M.; m. Doris Luise Pfleiderer, July 31, 1959; children: Johannes Christoph, Tobias Ulrich. Dipl.-Phys., Inst. Tech. Stuttgart, 1957; M.Sc. in Elec. Engring., Columbia U., 1959; Dr.rer.nat., U. Stuttgart, 1962. Lectr. geophysics U. Stuttgart, 1962-64; vis. prof. S.W. Center Advanced Studies, Richardson, Tex., 1964-65; prof. geophysics U. Karlsruhe, 1964-71, dean Faculty Natural Scis., 1968-69; vis. prof. U. Tex., Dallas, 1969-70; prof. Swiss Fed. Inst. Tech., 1971-96, U. Zurich, 1977-96; dean Sch. Natural Scis., Swiss Fed. Inst. Tech., 1978-80; dir. Swiss Earthquake Service, 1971-96; pres. Swiss Geophys. Commn., 1972-93, hon. pres. 1994; pres. European Seismol. Commn., 1972-76, Internat. Commn. Controlled Source Seismology, 1975-83; chmn. governing council Internat. Seismol. Centre, 1975-85; chmn. European-Mediterranean Seismol. Centre, 1976-82; chmn. Swiss Specialist Group of Geophysics, 1993—. German Acad. Interchange scholar, 1954-55. Fellow Royal Astron. Soc. (hon. fgn. assoc.), Am. Geophys. Union, Geol. Soc. London (hon.); mem. Internat. Assn. Seismology and Physics of Earth's Interior (pres. 1987-91), European Geophys. Soc. (pres. 1978-80, hon. mem.), European Union Geoscis. (Alfred Wegener medal 1993), German Geophys. Soc., Soc. Exploration Geophysicists, European Assn. Geoscientists and Engrs., Seismol. Soc. Am., Seismol. Soc. Japan, Acoustical Soc. Am., Swiss Geophys. Soc. (pres. 1977-80), Swiss Acad. Scis., Academia Europaea (founding mem.), German Acad. Leopoldina Researchers in Natural Scis., Internat. Assn. Geodesy (hon. assoc.), Swiss Fed. Comm. Geology, Sigma Xi. Co-editor Pure and Applied Geophysics, 1974-83; editor-in-chief Annales Geophysicae, 1982-87; editorial bd. Jour. Geophysics, 1969-87, Tectonophysics, 1971-77, 84—, Bolletino di Geofisica Teorica ed Applicata, 1978—, Jour. Geodynamics, 1983—, Tectonics, 1988-96; Recipient Medaille de l'Ordre Grand-Ducal Luxembourgois de la Couronne de Chene, 1994, Gustav Steinmann medal, 1995. Died Feb. 17, 1997.

MUENCH, JOHN, artist; b. Medford, Mass., Oct. 15, 1914; s. James Adams and Marjorie (Davie) M.; m. Barbara Davey, Sept. 6, 1941; children: Robin, Anthony, Katherine, Jon. Student, Art Students League, N.Y.C., Academie Julien, Paris; LLD (hon.), Portland Sch. Art, 1987. Dir. Sch. Fine and Applied Art, Portland, Maine, 1958-65; asso. prof. art R.I. Sch. Design, Providence, 1965-76; artist in residence Westbrook Coll., Portland, 1976—; vis. instr. Tamarind Lithography Workshop, Los Angeles, 1962; vis. critic Boston U., 1971-72; vis. artist Tamarind Lithography Workshop U. N.Mex., 1982; bd. dirs. Maine Printmaking Workshop, 1976—. One-man shows include Albany (N.Y.) Inst. History and Art, 1952, Rochester (N.Y.) Meml. Art Gallery, 1953, Portland (Maine) Mus. Art, 1960, 61, Farnsworth Mus., Rockland, Maine, 1954, Nat. Collection of Fine Arts, Smithsonian Instn., Washington, 1954, Detering Galleries Houston, 1956, Bowdoin Coll., 1960, Phila. Art Alliance, Farnsworth Mus., 1982, Joan Whitney Payson Gallery, 1983, Assoc. Am. Artists, N.Y.C., 1984; retrospective exhbn. Westbrook Coll., Portland, Oreg., 1992; represented in permanent collections Bklyn. Mus., Met. Mus. Art, U. So. Calif. Gallery, Dallas Mus. Art, Smith Coll. Mus., Fogg Mus., Cordova Mus., Lincoln, Mass., Victoria and Albert Mus., London, Nat. Mus., Jerusalem, Bibliotheque Nat. France, others; subject of book John Muench Paintings and Prints 1950-1990, 1991. Recipient U.S. Dept. State Specialist grant, 1966, awards Bklyn. Mus., 1947, awards Library Congress, 1951, 54, awards Dallas Mus. Art, 1954, awards U. So. Calif., 1954, awards Soc. Am. Graphic Artists, 1954, 55, awards Portland Soc. Art, 1957, awards Silvermine Guild Artists, 1959, awards N.A.D., 1967, 70, 73, 83, awards Audubon Artists, 1965, 70, 72, Joseph Pennell Meml. medal, Eyre medal Phila. Watercolor Club; Tiffany fellow, 1948, 54, 76. Mem. Phila. Watercolor Club (award 1954), Audubon Artists (medal of honor 1959, John Taylor Arms medal 1960, 64), Soc. Am. Graphic Arts, NAD (asso.).

MUIR, JOHN SCOTT, lawyer; b. San Francisco, June 20, 1930; s. James Hamilton and Edna Elizabeth (Scott) M.; m. Betty Ann Robustelli, Dec. 30, 1966; children: Kenneth Charles, Janet Elaine, Jeffrey Scott. AB, U. Calif., Berkeley, 1952, MA, 1955; JD, Golden Gate U., 1971. Bar: Calif. 1973, U.S. Dist. Ct. (no. dist.) Calif. 1973, U.S. Dist. Ct. Ariz. 1974, U.S. Supreme Ct. 1979. Tchr. Danville (Calif.) Elem. Sch. Dist., 1952-57; cons. Calif. Tchrs. Assn., Burlingame, 1957-88; pvt. practice Castro Valley, Calif., 1988-93, Sun City West, Ariz., 1993-96; lectr. corp. law Francis Yee Bar Rev. Course, San Francisco, 1974-75, lectr. sch. law Calif. State U., Hayward, 1980. Author: Law and the Teacher, 1967, Teachers' Guide to Educational Expenses, 1966, Juvenile Court School Law, 1986, Bilingual Education Law, 1986. Active Dem. Nat. Com., Sun City West program chmn. 1995. Named Commodore Spinnaker Yacht Club, 1973. Mem. Sun City West Model Railroad Club (program chmn.), Sun City Scots. Avocations: magic, sailing, political activities. Died Mar. 1, 1996.

MULCAHY, JOHN J., bishop; b. Dorchester, Mass., June 26, 1922. Student, St. John's Sem., Mass. Ordained priest, Roman Catholic Ch. 1947. Rector Pope John XXIII Sem. for Delayed Vocations, 1969-73; ordained titular bishop of Penafiel and aux. bishop Diocese of Boston, 1975-96. Died 1996.

MULINOS, MICHAEL GEORGE, retired research physician; b. Kefalonia, Kefaloma, Greece, Nov. 24, 1897; came to U.S., 1908; s. George Gerassimos and Helen (Couros) M.; m. Joyce Leora Stevens; 1 child, Stephen Michael. AB, Columbia U., 1921, MA, 1922, MD, 1924, PhD, 1927. Intern St. Vincent's Hosp., Erie, Pa., 1924-25; from asst. prof. to assoc. prof. pharmacology Coll. Physicians and Surgeons, Columbia U., 1929-44; assoc. prof. physiology and pharmacology N.Y. Med. Coll., N.Y.C., 1944-58; med. rsch. dir. Interchem. Corp., N.Y.C., 1945-47; med. dir. Comml. Slvents Corp., N.Y.C., 1953-62; pres. Med. Execs., N.Y.C., 1969-70, sec.-treas., 1970-85; assoc. med. dir. Life Extension Inst., N.Y.C., 1977-85; med. dir., dir. rsch. Unimed, Inc., Somerville, N.J., 1977-87; cons. med. rsch. to the chem. and pharm. industry, 1947-53, to pharm. and advt. industries, 1963-77; rsch. cons. Schmid Labs., Little Falls, N.J., 1977-80. Pres. Hellenic Med. Soc., N.Y., 1924, Assn. Med. Dirs., N.Y., 1956. Sterling Drug Inc. honoree Coll. Physicians and Surgeons, Columbia U., 1985; recipient Cert. of Recognition, Columbia Univ. Fellow AAAS. Republican. Orthodox. Died Nov. 17, 1996.

MULLEN, THOMAS MOORE, lawyer; b. Redding, Calif., June 20, 1915; s. Thomas B. and Enid (Moore) M.; m. Agnes Druecker, July 7, 1941; children: Thomas Moore, Patricia, Cheryl, Kathleen. B.S., U. San Francisco, 1937; J.D., Hastings Coll. Law, 1939. Bar: Calif. 1939. Practice in Redding, 1939-41; ptnr. firm Cavaletto, Webster, Mullen & McCaughey, Santa Barbara, Calif., 1946-82, Mullen, McCaughey & Henzell, Santa Barbara, Calif., 1982—; Bar Examiner State Bar of Calif., 1963-65. Del. Republican Nat. Conv., 1948; chmn. Rep. Central Com. Santa Barbara County, 1946-48. Served to col. AUS, 1941-46, USAR, 1946-75. Mem. Santa Barbara County Bar Assn. (pres. 1968-69). Club: Rotarian (pres. Santa Barbara 1949-50).

MULLINS, BETTY JOHNSON, realtor; b. Killen, Ala., Dec. 29, 1925; d. James E. and Vernie (Muse) Johnson; m. Charles Harvey Mullins, Nov. 18, 1944; children: Charles Harvey Jr., Susan. BS, U. North Ala., 1945. Tchr. Biloxi (Miss.) City Schs., 1945-46, Elizabeth City County Schs., Buckroe Beach, Va., 1946-47, Sheffield (Ala.) City Schs., 1949-58; with family automobile bus., 1958-86; real estate assoc. Neese Real Estate, Inc., Florence, Ala., 1986—. Pres. Project Courtview, Florence, 1980, Heritage Found., Florence, 1994—, Concert Guild, Florence; mem. Tenn. Valley Art Guild, Tuscumbia, Tenn. Valley Art Ctr., Tuscumbia, Friends of Kennedy Douglas Art Ctr., Florence; v.p. Salvation Army Aux., 1991-92; mem., past pres. United Meth. Women, First Meth. Ch., Florence, mem. adminstrv. bds.; bd. dirs. Friends of Libr., Florence, 1993—, Downtown Florence Unltd., Florence Main St., Bd. Rape Response; mem., past pres. Lauderdale-Colbert-Franklin Foster Grandparent Adv. Bd., Russellville, Ala., Ret. Sr. Vol. Program Adv. Bd.; pres. cabinet U. North Ala., mem. found. bd., 1994, 95, 96; trustee United Way, Shoals, 1992—; family built and maintains garden at First Meth. Ch., Florence in memory of Charles Mullins, Jr. Recipient Shoals Area Citizen of Yr., 1984, Shoals Area Top Prodr. Muscle Shoals Area Bd. Realtors, 1991, 92, 93, 94, Realtor of the Yr., 1996-97, Cmty. Svc. award U. North Ala., 1994; named Woman of Yr. Bus. and Profl. Women, 1980. Mem. LWV, Shoals-AAUW (pres. 1990-91), Nat. Bd. Realtors, U. North Ala. Alumni Assn. (past pres., bd. dirs., Alumni of Yr. award 1985, Cmty. Svc. award 1994, Found. Bd. 1994, 95, 96), Internat. Fertilizer Devel. Ctr. Century Club (past pres. Muscle Shoals, Ala. chpt.), Shoals C. of C. (past bd. dirs.), Tenn. Valley Hist. Assn., U. North Ala. Sportsman Club, Muscle Shoals Bd. Realtors, Ala. Bd. Realtors. Republican. Methodist. Avocation: family. Home and Office: PO Box 70 Florence AL 35631-0070 Died Nov. 16, 1997.

MULLINS, RICHARD AUSTIN, chemical engineer; b. Seelyville, Ind., Apr. 22, 1918; s. Fred A. and Ethel (Zenor) M.; B.S. in Chem. Engring., Rose Poly. Inst., 1940; postgrad. Yale, 1942-43; m. Margaret Ann Dellacca, Nov. 27, 1946 (dec. Nov. 1982); children—Scott Alan, Mark Earl. Chemist, Ayrshire Collieries Corp., Brazil, Ind., 1940-49; chief chemist Fairview Collieries Corp., Danville, Ill., 1949-54; preparations mgr. Enos Coal Mining Co., Oakland City, Ind., 1954-72, Enoco Collieries, Inc., Bruceville, Ind., 1954-62; mining engr. Kings Station Coal Corp.; mgr. analytical procedures Old Ben Coal Corp., 1973-84; ret., 1984. Am. Mining Congress cons. to Am. Standards Assn. and Internat. Orgn. for Standards, 1960-74; mem. indsl. cons. com. Ind. Geol. Survey, 1958-72; mem. organizing com. 5th Internat. Coal Preparation Congress, Pittsburgh, 1966. Mem. exec. bd. Buffalo Trace council Boy Scouts Am., also mem. speakers bur. Bd. dirs. Princeton Boys Club. Served with AUS, 1942-46; ETO. Decorated Medaille de la France Liberee (France); recipient Eagle Scout award, Boy Scouts Am., 1935, Silver Beaver award, 1962, Wood Badge Beads award, 1960; Outstanding Community Svc. award Princeton Civitan Club, 1964; Engr. of Year award S.W. chpt. Ind. Soc. Profl. Engrs., 1965; Prince of Princeton award Princeton C. of C., 1981, Sagamore of the Wabash award Ind. gov. R.D. Orr, 1984. Registered profl. engr., Ind., Ill., registered profl. land surveyor. Mem. AIME (life mem.), ASTM (sr. mem., R.A. Glenn award 1985), Am. Chem. Soc., Nat. Soc. Profl. Engrs. (life mem.), Ind., Ill. mining insts., Ind. Coal Soc. (pres. 1958-59), Am. Mining Congress (chmn. com. coal preparation 1964-68), Am. Legion (life, past county comdr.), VFW (life), 40 & 8 (life), Ind. Soc. Profl. Land Surveyors, Rose Tech. Alumni Assn. (pres. 1976-77, Honor Alumnus 1980), Order of Ring, Sigma Nu. Methodist (lay speaker). Mason, Elk. hon. founder, Elks Nat. Found. Contbr. articles to profl. jours. Died Feb. 28, 1997.

MULVIHILL, EDWARD ROBERT, language educator; b. Boulder, Colo., May 20, 1917; s. Edward Robert and Vida E. (Abair) M.; m. Eleanor B. Pittenger, Dec. 20, 1939; children: Michael N., W. Dennis, Patricia E. B.A., U. Colo., 1938; M.A., U. Wis., 1939, Ph.D., 1942. Spl. agt. FBI, 1942-46; asst. prof. Spanish U. Wis., 1946-48, asso. prof., 1948-55, prof., 1955-85, prof. emeritus, 1985-95, chmn. dept. Spanish and Portuguese, 1952-72, chmn. dept. comparative lit., 1978-80, asso. dean coll. Letters and Sci., 1962-85; cons., evaluator North Central Assn., 1970-85; Text editor Oxford U. Press. Decorated Order of Vasco Núñez de Balboa (Panama), Order Isabel la Catølica (Spain); Ford Found. Faculty fellow. Mem. Am. Assn. Tchrs. Spanish and Portuguese, Modern Lang. Assn., Central States Modern Lang. Assn., Wis. Assn. Modern Fgn. Lang. Tchrs. (pres. 1953-54, 57-58), Phi Beta Kappa, Kappa Kappa Psi, Kappa Delta Pi, Sigma Delta Pi, Phi Sigma Iota, Phi Kappa Tau. Home: Allenspark Colo. Died Feb. 21, 1995.

MUMMA, ALBERT G., retired naval officer, manufacturing company executive, management consultant; b. Findlay, Ohio, June 2, 1906; grad. U.S. Naval Acad., 1926; D.Eng. (hon.) N.J. Inst. Tech.; m. Carmen Braley, 1927; children—Albert G. Jr., John S., David B. Commd. ensign USN, 1926, advanced through grades to rear adm.; head tech. intelligence div. Naval Forces Europe, World War II; comdr. David Taylor Model Basin, Mare Island Naval Shipyard, also chief Bur. Ships, U.S. Navy, 1955-59; builder nuclear high speed submarines, U.S.S. Enterprise, Long Beach, Bainbridge and Polaris submarines; ret., 1959; v.p., group exec. Worthington Corp., 1964, exec. v.p., dir. in charge all domestic ops., 1967, pres., chief operating officer, 1967, chmn. bd., 1967-71; chmn. Am. Shipbldg. Commn., 1971-73. Trustee emeritus Drew U., Madison, N.J. Recipient Adm. Jerry Land Gold medal; awarded Knight Grand Officer of Orange Nassau by the Queen of the Netherlands. Fellow Soc. Naval Architects and Marine Engrs. (hon.; past pres.); mem. Am. Soc. Naval Engrs. (hon.; past pres.), Nat. Acad. Scis. (past mem. research council; past chmn. numerous coms.), Nat. Acad. Engring. (life). Clubs: Army and Navy, Army and Navy Country (Washington), Baltusrol Golf (Springfield, N.J.); Mountain Lake (Lake Wales, Fla.). Died July 15, 1997.

MUNDEL, MARVIN EVERETT, industrial engineer; b. N.Y.C., Apr. 20, 1916; s. Maxwell Herbert and Aimee (Baer) M. B.S.M.E., NYU, 1936; M.S. in Indsl. Engring., State U. Iowa, Iowa City, 1938, Ph.D. in Indsl. Engring, 1939. Registered profl. engr., Ind., Wis. Prof. Purdue U., West Lafayette, Ind., 1942-52; dir. U.S. Army Mgmt. Tng., Rock Island, Ill., 1952-53; staff officer U.S. Bur. Budget, Washington, 1963-65; prin. M.E. Mundel & Assocs., Silver Spring, Md., 1953-63, 65-96. Author texts: Motion and Time Study, 7th edit., 1994, (with David L. Danner) Improving Productivity and Effectiveness, 1983. Recipient Gold medal Asian Productivity Orgn., Tokyo, 1980; named Engr. of Yr., Washington Council Engrs., 1980. Fellow Inst. Indsl. Engrs. (pres. 1979-80, Frank and Lillian Gilbreth award 1982), World Acad. Productivity Sci. Died July 7, 1996.

MUNRO, CHARLES ROBERT ORROCK, lawyer; b. Winnipeg, Manitoba, Can., Apr. 8, 1925; s. Hugh Johnson and Isobel Euphemia (Farquharson) M.; m. Joan Kathleen Swallow, May 1, 1950; children: Janice, Eve, Pamela, Ross. BA with honors, U. Toronto, 1949, LLB, 1952. Bar: B.C. 1953, Que. 1981, Alta. 1983. Adv. counsel Dept. Justice, Ottawa, Ont., Can., 1954-63; dir. civil litigation Govt. of Can., 1963-67, asst. dep. atty. gen., 1967-75; asst. v.p. law Can. Pacific Ltd., Montreal, Que., Can., 1975-85, v.p. law, gen. counsel, 1985-90; ret., 1990. Mem. Law Soc. B.C., Alta. Law Soc., Barreau Du Que., Can. Bar Assn., Assn. Can. Gen. Counsel. Anglican. Club: Royal St. Lawrence Yacht. Avocations: amateur radio, boating. Office: Can Pacific Ltd, PO Box 6042 Station A, Montreal, PQ Canada H3C 3E4

MUNSTERBERG, HUGO, author, art educator; b. Berlin, Germany, Sept. 13, 1916; came to U.S., 1935, naturalized, 1941; s. Oskar and Helen (Rice) M.; m. Marjorie Bowen, June 26, 1943; 1 dau., Marjorie. A.B., Harvard, 1938, Ph.D., 1941. Asst. prof. fine arts Mich. State U., 1946-49, assoc. prof., 1949-52; prof. art history Internat. Christian U., Tokyo, 1952-56; prof. art history State U. N.Y. Coll. at New Paltz, 1958-78, chmn. dept., 1968-75; vis. lectr. Bard Coll., 1978-88; adj. prof. Parsons Sch. Design, 1979-91; art critic Arts Mag., 1957-60; cons. Japanese art Sotheby's Auction House. Author: A Short History of Chinese Art, 1949, Twentieth Century Painting, 1951, Landscape Painting of China and Japan, 1955, The Arts of Japan, 1957, The Folk Art of Japan, 1958, The Art of the Chinese Sculptor, 1960, The Ceramic Art of Japan, 1963, Zen and Oriental Art, 1965, Mingei, 1965, Buddhist Bronzes of China, 1967, Art of the Far East, 1968, The Art of India and Southeast Asia, 1970, Oriental Sculpture, 1971, Dragon in Chinese Art, 1972, The Arts of China, 1972, A History of Women Artists, 1975, The Art of Modern Japan, 1977, Die Kunst Asiens, 1980, Dictionary of Chinese and Japanese Art, 1981, Japanese Prints, 1982, The Crown of Life, 1983; Symbolism in Ancient Chinese Art, 1985. Served with AUS, 1942-46. Mem. Japan Soc., Asia Soc., Ukiyo-e Soc. DIED 02/16/95. .

MURCHIE, GUY, author; b. Boston, Jan. 25, 1907; s. Guy and Agnes (Donald) M.; m. Eleanor Forrester Parker, Mar. 1932; m. Josephine Egan, Dec. 27, 1941; m. Barbara Cooney, Dec. 23, 1942; children: Gretel, Barnaby; m. Kathe Luise Rautenstrauch, Jan. 17, 1949; 1 child, Jed (dec.); m. Marie Lyons, May 6, 1987. BS, Harvard U., 1929. Feature writer Chgo. Tribune, 1934-40, war corr. European div., 1940-42; flight instr. navigation under air transport command Am. Airlines, 1942-43, trans-oceanic navigator, 1944; trans-oceanic navigator Seaboard & Western Airlines, 1951-52; faculty Landhaven Sch., Camden, Maine, 1949. Author: Men on the Horizon, 1932, Soldiers of Darkness, 1937, The Veil of Glory, 1994, The Soul School: Confessions of a Passenger on Planet Earth, 1994; author, illustrator: Song of the Sky, 1954 (John Burroughs medal for best nature book 1955), Music of the Spheres, 1961 (Thormod Monsen award Soc. Midland Authors 1962), The Seven Mysteries of Life, 1978 (Am. Book award nomination 1982); editor, contbr.: Mutiny on the Bounty and Other Sea Stories, 1936. Founder, dir. Apple Hill Camp, Pepperell, Mass. and Nelson, N.H., 1945-55; mem. Pepperell (Mass.) Sch. Bd., 1946-50. Mem. Inst. Nav. (council 1956-58, 61-63), United World Federalists, Phi Beta Kappa. Mem. Baha'i World Faith. Archives located at Mugar Meml. Library, Boston U. DIED 07/08/97. .

MURDOCK, STUART LAIRD, banker, investment adviser; b. Hackensack, N.J., July 18, 1926; s. Charles Watson and Mary-Evelyn (Mehrhof) M.; m. Lois Maura Anderson, Aug. 12, 1950; 1 dau., Susan Lynn. AB, Yale U., 1949; MBA, STanford U., 1951. Security analyst Bank of N.Y., 1952-53; portfolio mgr. Brown Bros. Harriman & Co., N.Y.C., 1954-56; trust investment officer United Mo. Bank Kansas City N/A, 1957-62, v.p., 1963-66, sr. v.p., sr. trust investment officer, 1967-70, exec. v.p., sr. trust investment officer, 1971-94. Retired marshal City of Countryside, Kans., 1968-93; past mem. fin. adv. com. to bd. trustees Pub. Sch. Retirement Sys. Kansas City; trustee Kans. Pub. Employees Retirement Sys.; adv. dir., past pres. Friends of the Zoo; bd. dirs. Youth Symphony of Kansas City. With U.S. Army, 1945-46. Mem. Kansas City Soc. Fin. Analysts (past pres.), Inst. Chartered Fin. Analysts, Fin. Analysts Fedn., C. of C., Yale Club (past pres.), Saddle and Sirloin Club (past pres.), Mercury Club, Desert Caballeros, Shriners. Died May 7, 1997.

MURO, JAMES JOSEPH, university official; b. Central City, Pa., Mar. 13, 1934; s. James J. and Mary (Kuna) M.; m. Patricia Ann Hart, Aug. 20, 1960; children: Joel Hart, James Patrick. B.S., Lock Haven State Coll., 1956; M.Ed., Rutgers U., 1961; Ed.D., U. Ga., 1965; cert. inst. ednl. mgmt., Harvard U., 1984. Tchr.-counselor, dir. adult edn. Hackettstown (N.J.) Sch. System, 1958-60; counselor, dir. adult edn., wrestling coach Sparta (N.J.) Sch. System, 1960-63; teaching asst. U. Ga., Athens, 1963-65; faculty U. Maine, Orono, 1965-77; prof. edn. U. Maine, 1972—, dean, 1973-77; prof. edn., dean North Tex. State U., Denton, 1977-85, v.p. for devel., 1985—. Author: (with S. Freeman) Readings in Group Counseling, 1968, Elementary School Guidance: What It Should Be, 1969, (with G. Prescott) The Counselor's Work in the Elementary School, 1970, (with D. Dinkmeyer) Group Counseling—Theory and Practice, 1971, Counseling the Young Child and Preadolescent, 1975, Group Work in the Public Schools, 1972, Youth: New Perspectives on Old Dimensions, 1973; editor: (with D. Dinkmeyer) The Elementary and Middle Schools, 1977, The Humanist Educator, 1977—; contbr. (with D. Dinkmeyer) articles to profl. jours. Served with AUS, 1956-58. Mem. Am., Maine personnel and guidance assns., Am. Sch. Counselors Assn. (chmn. publs. com.), N.E.A., Maine Tchrs. Assn., Assn. for Humanistic Psychology, Assn. for Counselor Edn. and Supervision, Phi Delta Kappa, Kappa Delta Pi. Died April 8, 1996.

MURPHY, ANDREW PHILLIP, JR., lawyer; b. Swampscott, Mass., Sept. 27, 1922; s. Andrew Phillip and Irene Mary (O'Connell) M.; m. Ann Marie O'Hagan, Feb. 13, 1954; children: Sean Francis, Andrew Phillip III, Chrystal Ann, James Byrne, Paul Clarke. AB, Harvard Coll., 1943; LLB, Boston U., 1949. Bar: Mass. 1949, D.C. 1957. Assoc. Hannan and Mayo, Lynn, Mass., 1949-50; atty. Econ. Stabilization Agy., Wage Stabilization Bd., Washington, 1951-52, R.R. and Airline Wage Bd., Washington, 1952; mem. chief counsel Nat. Enforcement Commn., Washington, 1952-53; labor rels. counsel, asst. legis. counsel Nat. Assn. Home Builders, Washington, 1954-60; pvt. practice Washington, 1960—; gen. counsel Western Mortgage Investors, Boston, 1964-83, Southeastern Mortgage Investors, Charlotte, N.C., 1963-70, Universal Investors Trust, Miami, Fla., 1970-72, First Gen. Real Estate Trust, Washington, 1962-78; trustee, counsel Found.for Constitution, N.Y.C., 1987—; counsel Found. for Friends of Museums, Balt., 1990. Co-editor: Research and Development Procurement Law, 1958; editor in chief Fed. Bar Jour., 1954-60. Mem. labor rels. com. U.S. C. of C., Washington, 1956-60; alt. mem. Constrn. Industry Stabilization Com., Washington, 1974-75; mem. Collective Bargaining Com. in Constrn., Washington, 1975-76; mem. Coun. Constrn. Employers, Washington, 1972-76. Lt. (j.g.) USN, 1943-46. Mem. Metropolitan Club (Washington), Metropolitan Club (N.Y.C.), Gibson Island (Md.) Club, Farmington Country Club (Charlottesville, Va.), Eastern Yacht Club (Marblehead, Mass.). Roman Catholic. Avocations: sailing, tennis.

MURPHY, EWELL EDWARD, SR., lawyer; b. Weatherford, Tex., May 12, 1895; s. Robert W. and Maude (Baker) M.; m. Lou Phillips, June 21, 1923; children—Ewell Edward, Mary Lou Murphy Williams. LL.B., Cumberland U. Law, 1916, Nat. U., Washington, 1925; B.F.S. in Internat. Law, Georgetown U., 1926; postgrad. George Washington U., 1928-30. Bar: Tex. 1916, D.C. 1920. Sole practice, San Angelo, Tex., 1916-17, 1919-23, Washington, 1923-30, San Angelo, 1930—; county atty. Tom Green County, Tex., 1919-23; mem. Tex. Commn. Uniform Laws, 1941-45. Tom Green County Democratic chmn., 1940-76; chmn. U.S. Selective Service Appeal Bd., No. Dist. Tex., 1940-75; pres. elector, Tex., 1962. Served to 2d lt. U.S. Army, 1917-1919. Mem. Tex. State Bar, Georgetown U. Cum Laude Alumni Assn., Tom Green County Bar Assn. (pres. 1948), VFW, DAV, Am. Legion (1st comdr. San Angelo 1919). Democrat. Baptist. Lodge: Masons (32 degree).

MURPHY, GORDON LAURENCE, insurance company executive; b. Stamford, Conn., Feb. 2, 1935; s. Dennis Joseph Sr. and Carolyn Gertrude (Fessenden) M.; m. Rosemary Elizabeth Engel; 1 child, Erin Maureen. BA with honors, Williams Coll., 1963; postgrad., Northwestern U., 1964. Group sales Conn. Gen. Life Ins. Co., Bloomfield, 1964-68, group adminstr., 1968-71, asst. sec. group underwriting, 1971-75, sec. corp. controllers, 1975-78; 2d v.p. field ops. Aetna Ins. Co., Hartford, Conn., 1978-82; sr. v.p. agy. div. INA/Aetna-CIGNA P&C Group, Phila., 1982-84; pres. Life Ins. Co. of N.A., Phila., 1984-92; chmn. bd. dirs. INA Life Ins. Co. N.Y., 1992—. Served to sgt. U.S. Army, 1954-59. Avocations: hiking, reading, duplicate bridge, white-water rafting, hunting. Died Feb. 5, 1996.

MURPHY, JOSEPH F., lawyer; b. White Plains, N.Y., Apr. 4, 1915; s. Joseph Francis and Bessie L. (Madden) M.; m. Marion L. Barrett, Oct. 18, 1942; children: Elizabeth Ann, Kevin Barrett, Brian Sean. A.B., Fordham U., 1936, LL.B., 1938. Bar: N.Y. 1938. Eastern counsel Kemper Ins. Group, 1947-52; dep. supt. N.Y. Ins. Dept., 1952-55; with Continental Ins. Cos., 1955-80, v.p., gen. counsel, 1957-74, exec. v.p., 1974-80; exec. v.p. Continental Corp., 1974-80; partner Le Boeuf, Lamb, Leiby & MacRae, N.Y.C., 1980-82, 84-87; vice chmn. Consol. Internat. Ins. Group, 1987—; commr. of ins. State of N.J., 1982-84. Served to lt. comdr. USNR, 1942-45. Decorated Bronze Star. Died Jan. 19, 1997.

MURPHY, THOMAS JOSEPH, archbishop; b. Chgo., Oct. 3, 1932; s. Barthomew Thomas and Nellie M. AB, St. Mary of the Lake Sem., 1954, STB, 1956, MA, 1957, STL, 1958, STD, 1960. Ordained priest Roman Cath. Ch., 1958. Various positions with Archdiocese of Chgo.; bishop of Great Falls-Billings Mont., 1978-87; coadjutor archbishop of Seattle, 1987-91, archbishop of Seattle, 1991—. Died June 26, 1997.

MURRAY, CONSTANCE ANN, college dean; b. N.Y.C., Feb. 24, 1929; d. John Francis and Jeanne (Dur) M. B.S., Villanova U., 1959, M.A. in Secondary Edn, 1961; M.A. in English, Catholic U., 1969; Ph.D. in Higher Edn. Adminstrn, Syracuse U., 1976. Joined Sisters of the Holy Child Jesus; tchr. Oak Knoll Sch., Summit, N.J., 1957-58; prin., tchr. Sch. of the Holy Child, Rosemont, Pa., 1958-67; asst. prin., head English dept. Holy Child High Sch., Old Westbury, N.Y., 1967-69; resident adv. Syracuse U., 1969-71; adv., researcher Office Student Affairs, 1972-73, asst. to v.p. student affairs, 1973-74; student personnel intern Community Coll. of 213245 Lakes, Canandaigna, N.Y., 1971-72; asst. dean students Cornell U., 1974-76, assoc. dean, 1976-78; dean student services N.J. Inst. Tech., Newark, 1978-87 (on leave of absence), 89-90 (on leave of absence); faculty fellow, assoc. dir. project: Integrating the Scholarship on Gender, N.J. Dept. Social Scis. & Policy Studies; spl. lectr. Dept. Social Scis. and Policy Studies, N.J. Inst. Tech., 1993. Grantee Wharton Sch. Finance, 1978, faculty fellow Dept. Higher Edn. Mem. Am. Assn. Higher Edn., Am. Personnel and Guidance Assn., Nat. Assn. Women Deans, Adminstrs. and Counselors, Nat. Assn. Student Personnel Adminstrs., Nat. Womens Studies Assn., Assn. New Student Personnel Adminstrs. (charter), Student Personnel Assn. N.Y. State (charter). Roman Catholic. Home: Southold N.Y. DIED 12/28/94. .

MURRAY, HUGH LEANDER, deacon; b. Galt, Ont., Can., Feb. 27, 1925; came to U.S., 1951; s. Douglas and Nora (Weiler) Murray. BA, Goddard Coll., 1970; MusB, St. Michael's Choir Sch., 1972; D Ministry, United Theol. Sem., 1990. Ordained deacon Roman Cath. Ch., 1980. Dir. music ministry, organist Rosary Cathedral, Toledo, Ohio, 1951—, cons. to restoration cathedral skinner pipe organ, 1991; part time staff Toledo Diocesan Ministry Program, 1981-88, mem. deacon coun. edn. com., 1991. Author: Deacon Ritual Handbook, 1989; also articles; editor, writer Toledo Diocese, 1983-88. Mem. Am. Guild Organists (choirmaster cert. 1956), Deanery Deacon Fraternity.

MURRAY, JAMES D., lawyer; b. Manhattan, Kans., Mar. 19, 1936; s. Edward F. and Esther M. (Stagg) M.; m. Eileen M. Pavlick, Feb. 6, 1965; children: James, Robert, Jennifer. B.S., Kans. State U., 1958; LL.B., Washburn U., 1961. Asst. mgr. advanced underwriting Pacific Mut. Life Ins. Co., 1965; dep. dist. atty. County of Los Angeles, 1965; asst. U.S. atty. Central Dist. Calif., 1965-70; individual practice law, 1970-81; partner Petillon & Murray, Los Angeles, 1983—; lectr. bus. law U. Md., 1962-63. Pres. St. Paul The Apostel Parish Council, 1974. Served to maj. USAF, 1961-64. Mem. Los Angeles Fed. Bar Assn. (pres. 1976), Santa Monica Bay Dist. Bar Assn. (trustee 1972-75), Am. Bar Assn., Calif. Bar Assn., Fed. Bar Assn., Los Angeles County Bar Assn., Sigma Alpha Epsilon, Phi Alpha Delta. Democrat. Roman Catholic. Deceased.

MURRAY, JOHN JOSEPH, historian, educator; b. Bath, Maine, July 2, 1915; s. John Joseph and Ida (King) M.; m. Helen Elizabeth Tomson, Jan. 30, 1942; children: John Joseph III, Michael Tomson. A.B., U. Maine, 1937; M.A., Ind. U., 1938; Ph.D., UCLA, 1942. Editor Douglas Aircraft, 1938-45; instr. history Ohio State U., 1945; instr. Northwestern U., 1945-46; asst. prof. Ind. U., 1946-54, assoc. prof., 1949-54; prof. Coe Coll., 1954-93, chmn. history dept., 1955-93, Henrietta Arnold prof., 1977-80, Arnold prof. emeritus, 1980-93; vis. assoc. prof. UCLA, summer 1949; vis. prof. U. B.C., summer 1956; historian Iowa Light and Power Co., 1980-93. Author: A Student Guidebook to English History, 1947, An Honest Diplomat at the Hague, 1956, Amsterdam in the Age of Rembrandt, 1967, George I, the Baltic and the Whig Split, 1969, Antwerp in the Age of Plantin and Breughel, 1970, It Took All of Us, 1982, Flanders and England: The Influence of the Low Countries on Tudor-Stuart England, 1984, Netherlands Women in Two Centuries, 1990. Collected Verses for Betty, 1992; editor: Essays in Modern European History, 1952, The Heritage of the Middle West, 1958; contbr. articles, book revs. to Am., fgn. hist. jours.; author, narrator TV scripts for comml. TV. Fulbright research scholar U. Leiden, netherlands, 1951-52; fellow Folger Shakespeare Library, Washington, 1954, summer 1959, sr. research fellow, 1973-74; Social Sci. fellow to Eng., 1960-61; fellow Newberry Library, summer 1963; faculty fellow Assoc. Colls. of Midwest-Newberry Library Seminar in Humanities, 1965-66; Guggenheim fellow, 1968-69; Mercator Fonds fellow Belgium, summer 1973; decorated Knight Order Belgian Crown, 1981; U. Maine Alumni Career award, 1989, others. Fellow Royal Hist. Soc. (Eng.), Historisch Genootschop (Netherlands), Karolinska Förbundet (Sweden); mem. Cedar Rapids Art Assn., Am. Hist. Assn., Blue Key, Sr. Skull, Kappa Sigma, Phi Kappa Phi. Congregationalist. Club: Cosmos. Home: San Marcos Calif. Died July 29, 1993; buried Cedar Memorial, Cedar Rapids, IA.

MURRELL, JUDITH ANN, oil service company executive; b. Des Moines, Iowa, Dec. 28, 1940; d. James E. and Shirley (Hardman) Stimson; m. Fred L. Murrell, Nov. 16, 1962 (dec. Oct. 1972). MBA, So. Methodist U., 1980. Investor relations mgr. Dresser Industries, Inc., Dallas, 1975-85; investor relations dir. Lone Star Techs., Inc., Dallas, 1985-87, v.p. corp. relations, 1987—, also treas., 1992—. Mem. Nat. Investor Relations Inst. (bd. dirs. 1982-86, v.p. edn. 1984—, v.p. membership 1985). Republican. Congregationalist. Died April 19, 1996.

MURTAGH, FREDERICK, JR., neurosurgeon, educator; b. Phila., May 16, 1917; s. Frederick and Maude (Rhoad) M.; m. Mary Elizabeth Shaner, Apr. 17, 1943; children—Frederick Reed, Dean Fredric, Merry Jane. Student, U. Pa., 1936-39; M.D., Temple U., 1943, M.Sc. in Neurosurgery, 1951; M.A., U. Pa., 1975. Diplomate: Am. Bd. Neurol. Surgery. Intern U.S. Naval Hosp., Phila., 1943; gen. surgery U.S. Naval Hosp., 1946-47; resident Temple U. Hosp., 1948-51; faculty Temple U. Med. Sch., 1951-74, prof. neurosurgery, 1966-74, chmn. dept. neurosurgery, 1966-74, asso. v.p. health and acad. affairs, 1973; prof., chmn. neurosurgery U. Pa. Med. Sch., Phila., 1975-87; dir. dept. neurosurgery St. Christopher's Hosp. Children, Phila., 1951-74; neurosurgeon-in-chief Hosp. U. Pa., Children's Hosp. Phila., 1975-87; prof. emeritus neurosurgery U. Pa., 1987—; cons. numerous hosps. Served to lt. M.C. USN, 1943-47. Roy R. hornor fellow Lehigh U., 1943-44, Student Chem. Found. fellow Lehigh U., 1945-46. Fellow ACS; mem. AMA (neurosurg. del. interspltу. com. 1968-75), AAAS, Am. Assn. Neurol. Surgeons, Congress Neurol. Surgery, Phila. Neurol. Soc. (pres. 1964), Soc. Neurosurgeons, Coll. Physicians of Phila. (pres. 1994), Temple U. Med. Sch. Alumni Assn. (pres. 1965, Man of Yr. award 1970), Med. Club Phila. (pres. 1967), Mid Atlantic Neurosurg. Soc. (pres. 1970). Republican. Lutheran. DIED 06/16/96. .

MUTH, GEORGE EDWARD, art and drafting supply company executive; b. Washington, July 1, 1906; s. Edward Everhardt and Edna Elizabeth (Cassidy) M.; m. Lydagene Black, Apr. 19, 1930. A.B., George Washington U., 1931, J.D., 1934; LL.D. (hon.), Gallaudet Coll., 1965. Bar: D.C. 1933. With firm Pennie, Davis, Marvin and Edmonds (patent law), Washington, 1924-36; pres., treas. Geo. F. Muth Co., Inc., Washington, 1936-71; pres. Geo. F. Muth Co., Inc., 1971, 72-97; sec., treas. GFM, Inc., Woodville, Va., 1972-82. Past mem. zoning appeal bd. Rappahannock County, Va.; past mem. Rappahannock County Electoral Bd., Rappahannock County Planning Commn.; past chmn. bd. Gallaudet Coll., Washington; past trustee Westbrook Sch., Montgomery County, Md., George Washington U.; trustee Rappahannock County Libr., Washington, Va.; past mem. fine arts com. U.S. Agr. Grad. Sch.; past pres. Boys Club Washington, Travelers Aid Soc. Washington; past v.p. Nat. Travelers Aid Soc., Nat. Capital Area coun. Boy Scouts Am., Washington Soc. for Blind; bd. dirs., past vice chmn. Culpeper (Va.) Meml. Hosp.; past bd. dirs., past chmn. Rappahannock-Rapidan Cmty. Svcs. Bd. Mem. Nat. Art Materials Trade Assn. (past pres., dir.), Arts Club (past pres.), Rotary (past pres.), Rappahannock Hunt Club (past pres. Washington, Va.), Masons, Sigma Alpha Epsilon, Gamma Eta Gamma, Omicron Delta Kappa. Presbyterian (elder). Home: Harrisonburg Va. Died May 17, 1997.

MUWANGA, PAULO, minister of defence, vice president of Uganda. Mem. Uganda Nat. Congress, 1950's, mem. Central Com.; with Fgn. Ministry of Dr. Obote's govt., 1962, Chief of Protocol. 1969-71; ambassador to Paris, 1971-73; in exile, London and Dar es Salaam, 1973-79; mem. exec. com. Uganda Nat. Liberation Front (UNLF), 1979-80; internal affairs Minister in former Pres. Lule's govt., Pres. Binaisa's govt., 1979-80 minister of labor, 1980; chmn. Mil. Commn. UNLF, 1980; minister of def., v.p. of Uganda, 1980—.

MYER, ELIZABETH GALLUP, retired librarian; b. Hyde Park, Mass.; d. Otto John and Edith (Geer) M. Student, Conn. Coll., 1930-32; A.B., Barnard Coll., 1935; B.S. in L.S, Simmons Coll., 1940; M.A., Brown U., 1947; European study tour, Wayne State U., 1956. Asst. Providence Pub. Library, 1935-39; supr. R.I library project WPA, 1940-42; librarian Phoebe Griffin Noyes Meml. Library, Old Lyme, Conn., 1946; bookmobile librarian Enoch Pratt Free Library, Balt., 1948-50; reference librarian Morrill Meml. Library, Norwood, Mass., 1950-53; tchr., librarian Newton (Mass.) Pub. Schs., 1953-57; supr. pub. library services in rural areas R.I. Dept State, 1958-64; dir. dept. R.I. State Library Services, 1964-75; R.I. exec. dir. Nat. Library Week, 1959; mem. sch. library adv. com. to R.I. Bd. Edn., 1959-63; mem. R.I. Legis. Commn. Libraries, 1962-64; mem. adv. com. on U. R.I. Grad. Library Sch., 1962-64 70-75; chmn. com. to Revise Standards for Library Functions at the State Level, ALA, 1970; mem., sec

New Eng. Library Bd., 1972-73, chmn., 1975; mem. governing bd. New Eng. Document Conservation Center (name now Northeast Document Conservation Center), 1973-74; mem. exec. com. New Eng. Library Information Network, 1973-74. Author: The Social Situation of Women in the Novels of Ellen Glasgow, 1978; Contbr. articles to periodicals. Mem. exec. bd. Narragansett council Camp Fire Girls, 1968-70; mem. women's com. R.I. Bicentennial Commn., 1975-76; mem. legis. subcom. Advisory Commn. Women, 1975-76. Served from ensign to lt. USNR, 1942-45. Recipient numerous citations; Vol. Services for Animals award, 1981, 82, 83; cert. of appreciation Bristol County Chpt. for Retarded Citizens, 1981, 82, 83. Mem. ALA, Conn. Library Assn., R.I. Library Assn. (pres. 1962-64, Distinguished Service award 1974), New Eng. Library Assn. (chmn. state library services sect. 1969-71), Assn. State Library Agys. (exec. bd. 1965-67), R.I. Hist. Soc., Audubon Soc. R.I., Vol. Services for Animals, Mass. Soc. for Prevention Cruelty to Animals, Providence Animal Rescue League, Sierra Club, Gungywamp Soc., Barnard Coll., Simmons Coll., Brown U. alumni assns., R.I. LWV, DAR, Smithsonian Assocs. Episcopalian. Home: Barrington R.I. Died July 7, 1993.

MYERS, AL, realtor, property manager, mayor; b. Oakland, Calif., Aug. 6, 1922; s. Alvi A. and Emma (Thoren) M.; student Oreg. Inst. Tech., 1940-41; m. Viola Doreen Wennermark, Sept. 11, 1954; children: Susan Faye, Pamela Ann, Jason Allen. Supt.'s asst. Aluminum Co. Am., Troutdale, Oreg., 1942-44; asst. mgr. Western Auto Supply Co., Portland, 1944-46; owner, operator Al Myers Auto & Electric, Gresham, Oreg., 1946-53; realtor, broker Al Myers Property Mgmt., 1954-96; v.p., sec. Oreg. Country, Inc.; faculty Mt. Hood Community Coll. Chmn., Indsl. and Econ. Devel. Com. for Multonomah County, Oreg. Real Estate Ednl. Program, 1961. Mayor Gresham, Oreg., 1972-83. Pres. East Multonomah County Dem. Forum, 1965-96, mem. exec. com., 1958-96. With AUS, 1943. Mem. Portland Realty Bd., Nat. Assn. Real Estate Bds., Christian Bus. Men's Com. Internat., Internat. Platform Assn., Rho Epsilon Kappa (pres. Oreg.). Mem. Evang. Ch. (trustee, treas.). Died Nov. 3, 1996.

MYERS, IRA THOMAS, physicist; b. Iona, S.D., June 10, 1925; s. Coy Thomas and Elizabeth Ann (Dooley) M.; m. Betty Harrod LaFaver, June 18, 1947; children: Nancy, Sandra, Robert, Alyssa, David, James, Richard, Christopher. BS, Wash. State U., 1948, MS, 1952, PhD, 1958. Cert. health physicist. Chief engr. Radio Sta. KWSC, Pullman, Wash., 1948-49; physicist GE, Richland, Wash., 1949-62, NASA, Cleve., 1962-95; ret., 1995. Author: (with others) Radiation Dosimetry, 1965. Mem. AIAA. Avocations: church work, genealogy. Home: Westlake Ohio Died Oct. 12, 1995.

MYRDAL, ALVA, former Swedish government official, sociologist, educator, author; b. Uppsala, Sweden, Jan. 31, 1902; d. Albert and Lova (Larson) Reimer; B.A., Stockholm U., 1924; M.A., Uppsala U., 1934; Rockefeller fellow, U.S.A., 1929-30; student Geneva U., 1930-31; LL.D. (hon.), Mt. Holyoke Coll., 1950, Edinburgh U., 1964, Columbia, 1965, Temple U., 1968; Ph.D. (hon.), Leeds U., 1962; D.D. (hon.), Gustavus Adolphus U., 1971, Brandeis U., 1974, Gothenburg U., 1975, U. East Anglia, 1976, U. Helsinki, 1981, U. Oslo, 1981, U. Linkö ping (Sweden), 1982; m. Gunnar Myrdal, Oct. 8, 1924; children—Jan, Sissela, Kaj. Tchr., Workers Edn. Assn., Stockholm, 1924-32; psychol. asst. Central Prison at Stockholm, 1932-34; founded Tng. Coll. for Preschool Tchrs., 1936, dir., 1936-48; prin.-dir. UN Dept. Social Affairs, Feb. 1949-Dec. 1950; dir. social sci. UNESCO, 1950-55; Swedish ambassador to India and minister to Ceylon, 1955-61, minister to Burma, 1955-58, also Nepal, 1960-61; mem. Swedish Parliament. 1962-70; ambassador-at-large, 1961-66; cabinet minister in charge disarmament, Swedish Govt. 1966-73, in charge ch. affairs, 1969-73; served on numerous Swedish govt. coms., 1935—; Swedish rep. ILO Conf., Paris, 1945, Geneva, 1947, UNESCO, Paris, 1946, New Delhi, 1956; Swedish del. UN Gen. Assembly, 1962-73; chief Swedish del. to Disarmament Com., Geneva, 1962-73; chmn. UN Expert Group on South Africa, 1964, on Disarmament and Devel., 1972; founder, chmn. Internat. Peace Research Inst., 1966-67, Govt. Commn. Disestablishment Swedish State Ch., 1968-72, Commn. Studies of Future, 1971-72; mem. Swedish Govt. Del. for Expanding Internat. Laws against Brutality in War, 1972-73; cons. Swedish Def. Commn., 1978. Chmn., World Council Early Childhood Edn., 1946-49. Recipient Wateler prize Hague Acad. Internat. Peace, 1973; Albert Einstein Peace prize, 1980; Nehru award for internat. understanding, 1981; Peace prize of Fed. Republic of Germany, 1970; Nobel prize for Peace, 1982. Mem. Internat. Fedn. Univ. Women (chmn. com. on econ. and profl. questions 1946-48), Swedish Civic Orgn. for Cultural Relief in Europe (vice chmn. 1943-48), Swedish Fedn. Bus. and Profl. Women (pres. 1936-38, 40-42, internat. v.p. 1938-47), Am. Philos. Soc. Mem. Social Dem. Party of Sweden (mem. com. charged with postwar program of Labour Party and Trade Union Fedn., 1943; mem. party's Program Commn. 1944-48, Commn. Equality 1968-73). Author: Crisis in the Population Question (with G. Myrdal), 1934; City Children, 1935; author of the official report on Women's Work, 1938; Nation and Family, 2d edit., 1965; Contact with America (with G. Myrdal), 1941; Cross Section of Great Britain, 1942; Postwar Planning, 1944; Comments, 1944; Women in the Community, 1943; Are We Too Many (coll. P. Vincent), UNESCO, 1950; Americas' Role in International Social Welfare (with others), 1954; Women's Two Roles (with V. Klein), rev. edit., 1968; Disarmament-Reality or Illusion, 1965; Towards Equality: The Alva Myrdal Report, 1972; The Right to Conduct Nuclear Explosions, 1975; The Game of Disarmament, 1976, rev., expanded edit., 1982; Wars, Weapons and Everyday Violence, 1977; Dynamics of European Nuclear Disarmament, 1981. Editor: Via Suecia (multi-lingual refugee mag.), 1945-46. Contbr. articles on social, ednl. and internat. problems to newspapers, periodicals, books and reports.

NAFE, JOHN ELLIOTT, geophysicist; b. Seattle, July 22, 1914; s. Arthur Edward and Muriel (Elliott) N.; m. Sarah Gilpin Underhill, Sept. 6, 1941; children—Mary Malcolm (Mrs. Richard L. Chase), Katharine Elliott (Mrs. Christopher Kenah). B.S., U. Mich., 1938; M.S., Wash. U., 1940; Ph.D., Columbia, 1948. Instr. physics Columbia, 1946-49, adj. asso. prof. geology, 1953-58, prof. geology, 1958-80, prof. emeritus, 1980-96, chmn. dept., 1962-65; hon. prof. dept. geophysics and astronomy U. B.C., Vancouver, 1980-96; asst. prof. physics U. Minn., 1949-51; dir. research Hudson Labs., 1951-53; research scientist Lamont Geol. Obs., 1953-55; chief scientist oceanographic cruises, 1951-62; vis. fellow Cambridge (Eng.) U., 1971-72. Served with USNR, 1941-46. Fellow Geol. Soc. Am., A.A.A.S., Am. Phys. Soc., Am. Geophys. Union; mem. Seismol. Soc. Am., Royal Astron. Soc., Soc. Exploration Geophysicists, Am. Assn. Physics Tchrs., Can. Assn. Physicists, Sigma Xi. Research and publs. in physics, geophysics, oceanography. Home: Vancouver Can. Died Apr. 6, 1996.

NAGEL, MARGARET (PEGGY NAGEL), college president; b. Gt. Falls, Mont., July 5, 1952; children: Wilbur Joseph, LuCelia Ann. BS, No. Mont. Coll., 1975; MEd, Mont. State U., 1982. cert. tchr., prin. supt., counselor; lic. practical nurse. Nurse No. Mont. Hosp., Havre, 1972-74; exec. sec. 1st Bank System, Havre, 1974-76; tchr. Twin Buttes Schs., Halliday, N.D., 1976-78; asst. supt. Sch. Dist #87-J, Box Elder, Mont., 1978-80; dir. pers. Pretty Eagle Sch., St. Xavier, Mont., 1980-82; dir. edn. Chippewa-Cree Tribe, Box Elder, 1982-85; founding pres. Stone Child Coll., Box Elder, 1985—; cons. Cree-ations, Rocky Boy, Mont., 1987—; owner, trainer throughbred race horses. Vice chair Chippewa-Cree Devel. Co., Rocky Boy, 1987—; mem. Rocky Boy Dem. Assn., 1986—; bd. dirs. Big Bud Mfg. Inc., Havre, 1988-91, Mont. Progressive Policy, Helena, 1990—. Named Outstanding Educator Chippewa-Cree Tribe, 1989. Mem. Am. Indian Higher Edn. (treas. 1990—, bd. dirs.), Am. Coun. Edn. (bd. dirs.), Nat. Indian Edn. Assn., Mont. Indian Edn. Assn. (pres. 1987-89, treas. 1989—). Democrat. Home: Box Elder Mont. Died Dec. 13, 1994.

NAGLEY, WINFIELD EUGENE, educator; b. Chgo., Mar. 8, 1918; s. Frank Alvin and Mildred (Leach) N.; m. Patrice Penderghast McCarthy, June 19, 1945; children—Pamela Ann, Frederick Eugene. B.A., U. So. Calif., 1940; B.D., San Francisco Theol. Sem., 1943; postgrad., Yale Div. Sch., 1944-45; Ph.D., U. So. Cal., 1947. Instr. philosophy Lewis and Clark Coll., 1947-49; asst. prof. philosophy Wash. State U., 1949-51; asst. prof. philosophy U. Hawaii, 1951-54, asso. prof., 1954-61, prof. philosophy, 1961—, chmn. dept. philosophy, 1957-71. Bd. editors: Philosophy East and West, 1955—. Mem. Mayor Honolulu's Commn. on Conflict of Interest, 1961-65; adv. bd. Found. Thanatology, N.Y.C., 1973—; dir. Hawaii Govt. Employees Assn., 1960-64; chmn. Community Scholarship Program, 1966-71; Bd. dirs. Community Scholarship Found., Inst. for Religion and Social Change; bd. mgrs. Atherton YMCA, 1955-65. Fellow Am. Scandinavian Found., 1964-65. Mem. Am. Philos. Assn. (v.p. Pacific div. 1968-69), East-West Philosophers Conf., Soc. Asian and Comparative Philosophy, Phi Kappa Phi, Pi Kappa Alpha. Club: Waikiki Yacht. Died Sept. 1, 1996.

NAJIBULLAH, S'AYID MOHAMMAD, head of state of Democratic Republic of Afghanistan, army officer and party official; b. Kabul, Afghanistan, 1947; married; 1 dau. Student, Kabul U., 1964. Head of KHAD Secret Police Afghanistan, 1979-80, head security forces and armed forces, 1985-92; mem. Peoples Dem. Party, Afghanistan, 1965, mem. cen. com., 1977-78, gen. sec. cen. com., 1986-92; amb. to Iran Afghanistan, 1979; pres. Republic of Afghanistan, Afghanistan, 1987-92. Died Sept. 27, 1996.

NAJIRA, DICK DOCTOR, librarian; b. Mulanje, Malawi, Dec. 20, 1947; s. Reginald Doctor and Fanny (Chimberenga) N.; m. Bertha Mapinda, Mar. 25, 1972 (div. Sept. 1983); children: Edina, Martha, Masautso; m. Neffa Kalimenti, July 8, 1986; 1 child, Chimwemwe. Libr. cert., Mindolo Tng. Ctr., Kitwe, Zambia, 1973; libr. diploma, U. Botswana, Gaborone, 1986. Libr. asst. Univ. Librs., Blantyre, 1968-71; sr. libr. asst. Univ. Librs., Zomba, Malawi, 1972-74; asst. libr. Nat. Archives of Malawi, Zomba, 1975-81, libr., 1981-90, sr. libr., 1991-96; coord. Nat. ISBN Agy., Zomba, 1991-96. Editor: Malawi National Bibliography, 1994. Mem. Malawi Libr. Assn. (sec. 1980-81), African Standing Conf. on Bibliographic Control (nat. rep. 1983-96). Mem. United Democratic Front. Roman Catholic. Died May 8, 1996.

NAMIAS, JEROME, meteorologist; b. Bridgeport, Conn., Mar. 19, 1910; s. Joseph and Saydie (Jacobs) N.; m. Edith Paipert, Sept. 15, 1938; 1 child, Judith Ellen. Student, MIT, 1932-34, M.S., 1941; M.S., U. Mich., 1934-35; Sc.D. (hon.), U. R.I., 1972, Clark U., 1984. Research asst. Blue Hill Meteorol. Obs., Milton, Mass., 1933-35; research assoc. MIT, Boston, 1936-41, Woods Hole (Mass.) Oceanographic Inst.; mgr. extended forecast br. U.S. Weather Bur., Washington, 1941-64; assoc. dir. Nat. Meteorol. Ctr., 1964-66, chief extended forecast div., 1966-71; vis. scientist NYU, N.Y.C., 1966; research meteorologist Scripps Inst. Oceanography, La Jolla, Calif., 1968-97; vis. scholar Rockefeller Study and Conf. Center, Bellagio, Italy, 1977; frequent cons. USAAF, USN; developer of system for extending time range of gen. weather forecasts up to a season. Author: An Introduction to the Study of Air Mass and Isentropic Analysis, 1936, Extended Forecasting by Mean Circulation Methods; monograph, 1947, Thirty-Day Forecasting, 1953; Short Period Climatic Variations, Collected Works of Jerome Namias, 1934-74, 1975-82, 83, Namias Symposium Volume, 1986; also tech. articles to sci. jours.; Editorial bd.: Geofisica Internacional, Mexico. Recipient citation for weather forecasts North African invasion Sec. of Navy, 1942; Dept. Commerce Meritorious Service award, 1950; Rockefeller Pub. Service award, 1955; Gold medal for disting. achievement Dept. Commerce, 1965; Chancellor's Assocs. award excellence in research U. Calif.-San Diego; Compass award for research Marine Tech. Soc., 1984; Rossby fellow Woods Hole (Mass.) Oceanographic Instn., 1972. Fellow AAAS, Am. Geophys. Union, Washington Acad. Scis., Am. Meteorol. Soc. (Meisinger award 1983, extraordinatry achievement award 1955, Sverdrup Godl medal 1981, Lifetime Achievement award So. Calif. chpt. 1991, councilor 1940-42, 50-53, 60-63, 70-73); mem. NAS, Am. Acad. Arts and Sci., Royal Meteorol. Soc. Great Britain (hon. mem.), Explorers Club. Home: La Jolla Calif. Died Feb. 10, 1997.

NANCE, CECIL BOONE, JR., lawyer; b. Marion, Ark., Feb. 14, 1925; s. Cecil Boone and Virginia (Essary) N.; m. Harriet Jane McGee, Aug. 7, 1948; children: Janet E., Cecil Boone III. J.D., U. Ark., 1951. Bar: Ark. 1951. Since practiced in West Memphis; mem. firm Nance, Nance & Fleming (named changed to Nance & Nance P.A.), 1951—; Chmn. bd. Fidelity Nat. Bank West Memphis, 1966-71; dir., gen. counsel E. Ark. Savs. & Loan Assn., 1970-83; spl. asso. justice Ark. Supreme Ct. Contbr. articles to profl. jours. Mem. Ark. Ho. of Reps., 1957-68; v.p. Ark. Constl. Conv., 1969. Served with AUS, 1943-46, 52-53. Decorated Bronze Star. Mem. Am. Bar Assn., Ark. Bar Assn. (chmn. jr. bar sect. 1957-58, dir. Ark. Law Rev. and Bar Assn. Jour. 1975). Methodist. Club: Rotarian (West Memphis) (pres. 1970-71). Died July 24, 1997.

NANCE, JACK, actor. Studied with, Paul Baker. With Pasadena Playhouse, Circus Theater Co., San Francisco. Actor: (film) Eraserhead, 1978, Dune, 1984, Blue Velvet, 1986, Colors, 1988, Wild at Heart, 1990, Lost Highway, 1997, (tv series) Twin Peaks. Home: South Pasadena Calif. Died Dec. 30, 1996.

NANCE, JOSEPH MILTON, history educator; b. Kyle, Tex., Sept. 18, 1913; s. Jeremiah Milton and Mary Louise (Hutchison) N.; m. Eleanor Glenn Hanover, Mar. 19, 1944; children: Jeremiah Milton, Joseph Hanover, James Clifton. B.A., U. Tex., 1935, M.A., 1936, Ph.D., 1941; cert. in naval communications, Harvard U., 1944. Tex. supr. Am. imprints, manuscripts and newspaper inventories U.S. Hist. Records Survey, 1938-40; instr. history Tex. A&M U., 1941-42, 46-47, asst. prof., 1947-51, assoc. prof., 1951-57, prof., 1957-58, prof., head dept. history and govt., 1958-68, head dept. history, 1968-73, prof., 1973-78, prof. emeritis, 1978-97; instr. U.S. Naval Tng. Sch., College Station, 1942-43; vis. prof. history SW Tex. State Coll., San Marcos, summers 1956, 58. Author: Checklist of Texas Newspapers, 1813-1939, 1941, 3d edit., 1963, The Early History of Bryan and the Surrounding Area, 1962, After San Jacinto: The Texas-Mexican Frontier, 1836-1841, 1963, Attack and Counter-Attack, The Texas Mexican Frontier, 1842, 1964; co-author: Heroes of Texas, 1964; student guide to accompany A History of the American People (Graebner, Fite, White), 1971; also instr.'s man.; editor: Some Reflections upon Modern America, 1969, A Mier Expedition Diary: A Texan Prisoner's Account (Joseph D. McCutchan), 1978, Dare-Devils All: The Texas Mier Expedition, 1842-1844; mem. editl. bd.: Ariz. and the West, 1980-83; sr. editor: Handbook of Texas, 1983-97; co-editor: The Handbook of Texas, 6 vols., 1996. Mem. Hood's Brigade-Bryan Centennial Com., 1960-62; panel participant Tex. Legis. Assembly, 1967; mem. Ann. Faculty seminar Standard Oil Co. Calif., summer 1959, Brazos County Hist. Commn., Tex., 1972-97. Served to lt. (j.g.) USNR, 1943-46. Recipient 15th Ann. Writers Roundup award Theta Sigma Phi, 1963, Tex. Inst. Letters award, 1964, Walter Prescott Webb award in history U. Tex., 1967, AMOCO Disting. Research award Tex. A&M U., 1979, History award and medal DAR, 1985; 3 ann. scholarships established in his name at Baylor U. Coll. Law, 1979-97; ann. lectureship established in his honor Tex. A&M U., 1980-97; named Knight of San Jacinto Sons of Republic, 1983. Fellow Tex. State Hist. Assn. (exec. coun.), East Hist. Assn., East Tex. Hist. Assn. (dir. 1980-83); mem.

Tex. Inst. Letters, Am. Hist. Assn., So. Hist. Assn., W. Tex. Hist. Assn. (exec. coun., book rev. editor 1975-81, v.p. 1978-81, pres. 1981-82), Orgn. Am. Historians, Western History Assn., Am. Heritage Soc., Am. Studies Assn. Tex. (pres. 1969), Southwestern Social Sci. Assn., Central Tex. Area Writers Conf., Nat. Geog. Soc., Phi Beta Kappa, Phi Kappa Phi, Phi Alpha Theta. Home: Westfield Center Ohio Died Jan. 17, 1997; interred Wheelock Cemetery, Wheelock, TX.

NANNEY, HERBERT BOSWELL, musician, educator; b. Whittier, Calif., Aug. 1, 1918; s. Leslie Carson and Edna (Thornburgh) N.; m. Jean Duncan, Aug. 1, 1947; 1 child, Duncan Leslie. BA, Whittier Coll., 1940; artists diploma, Curtis Inst. Music, Phila., 1947, Paris Conservatory, 1946; MA in Music, Stanford U., 1951. Organist First Meth. Ch., Pasadena, Calif., 1937-40; organist, choir dir. Jenkintown, Pa., 1941-42; asst. organist Stanford (Calif.) Univ., 1940-41; mem. faculty Stanford (Calif.) U., 1947-85, prof. music, 1952-85, univ. organist, 1947-85, prof. music and univ. organist emeritus, 1985-96; organist First Congl. Ch., Los Angeles, summer 1942; organist, choir dir. Am. Cathedral, Paris, 1945; minister of music Ninth Presbyn. Ch., Phila., 1946-47; cons. First Congl. Chs., Santa Cruz and Oakland, Calif., 1956-57, St. Mark's Episcopal Ch., Palo Alto, Calif., 1984-85, St. Denis Cath. Ch., Menlo Park, Calif., 1980-87. Composer: Sonata for Organ, 1940, Trio for Oboe, Viola and Piano, 1950, Cantata-The Creation, 1951. Mem. exec. bd. Santa Clara County chpt. Nat. Council Alcoholism, San Jose, Calif., 1976-79. Served with U.S. Army, 1942-46, ETO. Herbert Nanney organ scholarship named in his honor Stanford Univ., 1987. Mem. Am. Guild Organists (chmn. Far Western region 1975-81, nat. council 1975-81, program chmn. nat. conv. 1984), Coll. Music Soc., Am. Musicol. Soc., Music Tchrs. Assn. Calif. Democrat. Presbyterian. Avocations: traveling, photography. Died May 20, 1996.

NASH, BRADLEY DELAMATER, transportation executive; b. Boston, Apr. 7, 1900; s. Edward R. and Allie (DeLamater) N.; m. Ruth B. Cowan, June 30, 1956 (dec. 1993); m. Virginia Josie Ingram, Aug. 3, 1995. A.B. cum laude, Harvard, 1923, postgrad., 1924; LHD (hon.), Shepherd Coll., Shepherdstown, W.Va. Banker N.Y.C., 1929-32, 35-40, Washington, 1949-51; sec. to Herbert Hoover, 1927-29; financial adviser RFC, 1932-35, WPB, 1941-42; cons. Pres.'s Adv. Com. Govt. Orgn., 1953; dep. asst. sec. Dept. of Air Force, 1953-56; dep. under sec. transp. Dept. Commerce, 1957-61; cons. U.S. Weather Bur., 1961-63; historian, cons. Nat. Park Svc., Dept. Interior, 1963-64; mayor of Harper's Ferry, W.Va., 1971-77, 81-86; mem. W.Va. R.R. Maintenance Authority, 1977-97. Author: Investment Banking in England, 1924, A Hook in Leviathan, 1950, Staffing the Presidency, 1952, (with Milton S. Eisenhower et al) Organizing and Staffing the Presidency, 1980. Bd. advs. Nat. Trust for Historic Preservation; trustee Center for Study Presidency, 1975-84, Storer Coll., Alderson Broaddus Coll. Lt. col. AUS, 1942-45, MTO and Italian campaigns. Decorated Bronze Star, Commendation medal War Dept. Mem. Harvard Club (N.Y.C.), Metropolitan Club (Washington), Nat. Press Club (Washington), Chevy Chase Club (Md.). Home: Harpers Ferry W. Va. Died Jan. 1, 1997; interred Harpers Cemetery, Harpers Ferry, WV.

NASH, FRANCIS J., retired obstetrician/gynecologist; b. Boston, Feb. 24, 1925. MD, Jefferson Med. Coll., 1954. Diplomate Am. Bd. Ob-Gyn. Intern St. Elizabeth's Hosp., Boston, 1954-55; resident St. Margaret's Hosp., Boston, 1955-58, Carney Hosp., Boston, 1955-58; sr. gynecol. staff St. Elizabeth's Hosp., Boston; sr. clin. instr. ob-gyn Tufts U. Mem. ACOG. Died Oct. 25, 997.

NATANSON, MAURICE ALEXANDER, philosopher, educator; b. N.Y.C., Nov. 26, 1924; s. Charles and Kate (Scheer) N.; m. Lois Janet Lichenstein, Jan. 21, 1949; children: Charles, Nicholas, Kathy. A.B., Lincoln Meml. U., 1945; M.A., N.Y. U., 1948; Ph.D., U. Nebr., 1950; D.S.Sc. summa cum laude, New Sch. Social Research, 1953; M.A. (hon.), Yale U., 1976. Teaching asst. philosophy U. Neb., Lincoln, 1948-50; instr. U. Neb., 1950-51; lectr. philosophy grad. faculty New Sch. Social Research, N.Y.C., 1952-53; Am. Council Learned Socs. scholar New Sch. Social Research, 1951-53; asst. prof. philosophy U. Houston, 1953-56, asso. prof., 1956-57; assoc. prof. philosophy U. N.C., Chapel Hill, 1957-62; Am. Coun. Learned Socs. fellow, 1961-62; prof. U. N.C., 1962-65; Disting. vis. prof. philosophy, rhetoric Pa. State U., University Park, spring 1963; vis. prof. philosophy U. Calif., Berkeley, 1964-65; prof. philosophy, fellow, Cowell Coll. U. Calif. at Santa Cruz, 1965-76, chmn. bd. philosophy, 1965-67, 68-70, faculty research lectr., 1966; sr. humanities fellow U. Calif., 1967-68; dir. Methuselah, adult edn. program U. Calif., Santa Cruz, summer 1967; prof. philosophy Yale U., 1976-96; Guest prof. sociology U. Konstanz, West Germany, spring 1974; Nat. Endowment Humanities sr. fellow, 1971-72, panelist, 1974, dir. summer seminar, 1976, 77, 79; dir. grad. studies in philosophy Yale, 1991-93. Author: A Critique of Jean-Paul Sartre's Ontology, 1951, The Social Dynamics of George H. Mead, 1956, Literature, Philosophy, and the Social Sciences, 1962, The Journeying Self, 1970, Edmund Husserl, 1973, Phenomenology, Role, and Reason, 1974, Anonymity: A Study in the Philosophy of Alfred Schutz, 1986; editor: The Problem of Social Reality (Alfred Schutz), 1962, Philosophy of the Social Sciences, 1963, Essays in Phenomenology, 1966, Psychiatry and Philosophy, 1969, Phenomenology and Social Reality, 1970, Phenomenology and the Social Sciences, 2 vols., 1973, (with Henry W. Johnstone, Jr.) Philosophy, Rhetoric, and Argumentation, 1965; cons. editor Philosophy and Phenomenological Rsch., 1960-84, Ind.-Northwestern U. Press Studies Phenomenology Existential Philosophy, 1963—, Jour. Value Inquiry, 1967-90, Philosophy and Rhetoric, 1968-94, Medicine and Philosophy, 1975-90; book rev. editor: Man and World, 1968-78, Selected Studies Phenomenology Existential Philosophy, 1973-82; mem. editorial adv. bd. Phenomenology and Human Scis., 1981-96 . Mem. adv. com. Phänomenologische Bibliothek, 1992-96. Recipient Nat. Book award Philosophy and Religion, 1974, Yale Coll. award for disting. undergrad. teaching, 1984. Mem. Am. Philos. Assn. (Alfred Schutz lectr. 1969), Soc. Phenomenology and Existential Philosophy (mem. exec. com. 1964-68). Democrat. Jewish. Died Aug. 16, 1996.

NATHAN, THEODORE READE, author, editor; b. Rouses Point, N.Y., Oct. 3, 1911; s. Harry and Harriette (Steiner) N.; m. Elizabeth Virginia Angelier, Apr. 5, 1934; children: Joy Nathan Stern, Gay Theodora. BA, NYU, 1934; MA, Columbia U., 1936. Exec. dir. Union Jewish Congregations Am., 1934-36; exec. sec. Nat. Coun. Young Israel, 1936-38; mng. editor The Orthodox Union, 1934-36; assoc. editor Opinion mag., 1936-38; v.p. Dreier Hotel Corp., 1938-42, Blackstone Co., 1942-44; assoc. editor The Synagogue Light, 1944-74, exec. asst. to Billy Rose, 1944-47; producer, dir. ABC-TV, 1944-48; editor Theatre Arts mag., 1947-49, Young People's Ency.; exec. editor Hotel Gazette mag., Greater Amusements mag.; pres. Laureate Press; asst. to pres. Bd. Edn., N.Y.C., 1955-65; pres. Pub. Rels. Inst., 1958—; pres. Theodore Reade Nathan Advt., Inc., N.Y.C., 1952—. Author: Best College Verse, 1970, Hotel Promotion, 1941, Promotion Work Book, 1943, The City and Chas. H. Silver, 1979, Hotelmanship, 1980, Modern Hotel Marketing, 1990. Asst. to pres. Beth Israel Med. Ctr.; dir. Lincoln Sq. Acad.; assoc. chmn. bd. U. Settlement; chmn. scholarship com. Religious Edn. Assn. U.S. and Can.; v.p. Wall St. Synagogue, Beth Jacob Schs.; bd. dirs. NCCJ, Consumer Commn. on Accreditation Health Svcs., Am. Shakespeare Theatre.

NATHANSON, TED, television executive; b. Phila.; m. Edith Nathanson; children: Michael, Laura, Carla. With CBS, ABC; former coord. prodr. of football, tennis NBC Sports; former dir. telecast for major league baseball, boxing, college football, hockey, golf NBC Sports. Vol. Am. Field Svc. Recipient Dirs. Guild of Am. Life Achievement award. Home: Manhattan N.Y. Died 1997.

NAYLOR, FRANKLIN LLEWELLYN, JR., financial advisor; b. Arlington, N.J., July 17, 1910; s. Franklin Llewellyn Sr. and Mary H. (Fliedner) N.; m. Edna Anabel Woglom, Sept. 7, 1932 (dec. 1978); children: Marjorie Evelyn Glidden, Franklin III, Virginia Irene Hubacek. Registered profl. engr., gen. bldg. contractor, real estate broker, Calif.; lic. ins. agt., Ariz.; registered fin. adviser SEC. Engaged in various engring. capacities, 1928—; cons. indsl. engr., 1946—; formerly with Indsl. div. S.S. White Dental Mfg. Co., Breeze Corp., Inc., Walker-Turner Corp., Aluminum Co. Am., also U.S. Spring and Bumper Co., Lockhead Aircraft Corp., Pacific div. Bendix Aviation Corp., Grand Central Aircraft Co.; v.p. Baker and Weikel engrs., after 1948; pres. Naylor Engring. & Research Corp., Los Angeles; mng. gen. agt. Nat. Old Line Ins. Co.; pres. Am. Pacific Life Ins. Co., Honolulu, after 1964; owner, operator Ariz. Chem. & Engring. Co., Tucson and Phoenix, Naylor & Assocs., estate and bus. cons., Tucson and Phoenix; lectr. estate preservation and tax planning, also investment planning for retirement; instr. Tucson and Phoenix secondary schs., Burbank and Glendale Unified Sch. Dists., Calif., 1939—, Ariz. Jr. Colls., Ariz. State Colls., Calif. State Colls. Author: Aluminum and Its Alloys; co-author several books on supervisory devel. Contbr. articles to maj. trade jours. Pres. Glendale-Burbank Joint Carpentry Apprentice Com., 1948; mem. War Prodn. Bd., World War II; chmn. trade adv. com. for sheet metal workers Nat. Def. Com., 1943-45, employer rep. trade com. for drafting, lofting and pattern makers, 1943-45.; chmn. SCORE, Phoenix, 1966-86, mem. Hattiesburg, Miss., 1987—; vice chmn. Small Bus. Execs. Clearing House; mem. Internat. Exec. Service Corps.; pres. Greater Phoenix Republican Club, 1962; active Rep. Senatorial Inner Circle, 1963—. Mem. AMSE (life, bd. dirs. profl. mgmt. div.), Am. Ordnance Assn., Bldg. Contractors Assn. Calif., Soc. Advancement Mgmt., Glendale C. of C., Am. Arbitration Assn. (nat. panel arbitrators), Hammond Organ Soc. (pres. Tucson 1955), AIM, Hawaii C. of C. (aero affairs com., vocat. edn. and manpower com., indsl. devel. com.), NSPE, Navy League U.S. Nat. Travel Club, Presidents Club, Phoenix Execs. Club, Statesman's Club. Died Sept. 21, 1997.

NEAL, FRED WARNER, political scientist, educator; b. Northville, Mich., Aug. 5, 1915; s. Frank Stephenson and Bertha (Fendt) N.; m. Grace Irene Repine, Feb. 14, 1952; children: Susan Victoria, Frank Stephenson, Alexander Frederick (dec.); m. Marian Katherine Walker, Jan. 2, 1969; m. Mary Caroline Hall, Jan. 10, 1982. B.A., U. Mich., 1937, Ph.D., 1955; student (Nieman fellow), Harvard U., 1942-43, U. Karlova, Prague, Czechoslovakia, 1949; Fulbright research fellow, U. Paris, 1950. Washington corr. UP and Wall St. Jour., 1938-43; cons. Russian affairs, chief fgn. research State Dept., 1946-48; asst. to pres. Univ. State of N.Y., 1948-49; asst. to chmn. Com. on Present Danger, 1951; asst. prof. polit. sci. U. Colo., 1951-56; asso. prof. UCLA, 1956-57; asso. prof. internat. relations and govt. Claremont (Calif.) Grad. Sch., 1957-60, prof., 1960-83, prof. emeritus, 1983—; Rockefeller prof. internat. rels. U. W.I., 1965-66; vis. lectr. U. Mich., 1950, 53-54; assoc. Am. U. Field Staff, 1954-55; co-dir. Twentieth Century Fund Study on Yugoslavia, 1958-61; Fulbright fellow, Paris, 1961-62; cons. Ctr. for Study of Dem. Instns.; organizer, dir. Pacem in Terris convocations; chmn. Am. Com. on U.S.-Soviet Rels., 1974-77, exec. v.p., 1977-93. Author: Titoism in Action: The Reforms in Yugoslavia after 1948, 1958, U.S. Foreign Policy and the Soviet Union, 1961, War and Peace and Germany, 1962; co-author: Yugoslvia and the New Communism, 1962; editor: Pacem in Terris III: New Opportunities for American Foreign Policy, 1974, Pacem in Terris IV: American Foreign Policy at Home and Abroad, 1976, Detente or Debacle, 1979; author: A Survey of Detente—Past, Present, Future, 1977. Democratic nominee for Congress 24th Dist. Calif., 1968; Pres. Albert Parvin Found., 1969-70. Served with A.C., USNR, 1943-46, Russia, Siberia. Recipient Decoration of Yugoslav Flag with Golden Wreath, highest honor of Yugoslvia, 1987; Japan Found. fellow, 1978. Mem. Am., Internat., Western polit. sci. assns., Internat. Studies Assn., Am. Assn. Advancement Slavic Studies, AAUP, Soc. Nieman Fellows, Los Angeles Com. Fgn. Relations. Died Nov. 21, 1996.

NEBERGALL, ROGER ELLIS, speech educator; b. Davenport, Iowa, July 3, 1926; s. Ellis William and Hilda (Bruhn) N.; m. Nelda Lee Smith, Apr. 10, 1958; 1 dau., Madelon. A.B., Augustana Coll., 1949; M.A., Bradley U., 1951; Ph.D., U. Ill., 1956. Instr., asst. prof. speech Bradley U., 1951-54, 54-55; asst. prof. U. Okla., Norman, 1955-60; assoc. prof. U. Okla., 1960-65, prof. speech, 1965-69, chmn. dept. speech, 1959-69; prof. speech communication U. Ill., Urbana, 1969-86, prof. emeritus, 1986-94, head dept., 1969-78. Author: (with W.R. Carmack) Communication and Supervision, 1960, (with others) Attitude and Attitude Change: The Social Judgment Involvement Approach, 1965; editor: (with others) Dimensions of Rhetorical Scholarship, 1963, Central States Speech Jour., 1967-70, Speech Monographs-Communication Monographs, 1974-77; contbr. (with others) articles to profl. jours. Exec. sec. Missouri Valley Forensic League, 1959-69. Served with AUS, 1946-47, PTO. Recipient Golden Ann. Prize Fund award Speech Assn. Am., 1966. Mem. Speech Commn. Assn. (group chmn.), Central States, Ill. speech assns., Assn. for Communication Adminstrn. (exec. com. 1975-77), Internat. Communication Assn., Pi Kappa Delta, Pi Kappa Alpha, Gamma Alpha Beta. Republican. Lutheran. Home: Norman Okla. Died Apr. 13, 1994.

NEIMAN, LIONEL JOSEPH, sociologist, educator; b. Cleve., May 23, 1921; s. Lionel and Essie (Nyman) N.; m. Edith Blanche Grossman, Dec. 26, 1943. A.B., Ind. State U., 1943, M.A., 1946; postgrad., Ind. U., 1947-52. High sch. tchr., 1943-46; dir. Monroe County Welfare Dept., Bloomington, Ind., 1952-60; parole officer State of Ind., 1952-56; mem. faculty Ball State U., Muncie, Ind., 1962-94, prof. sociology, 1975-94, coordinator criminal justice and corrections program, 1973-76, chmn. dept. criminal justice and corrections, 1976-94, prof. emeritus, 1986-94; lectr. Ind. U., 1972-94; cons. in field. Recipient Sagamore of the Wabash award Ind. Gov. Evan Bayh, 1990; named to Ky. Cols., 1978; grantee Law Enforcement Assistance Adminstrn., 1970-94, Criminal Justice Planning Agy., 1970-73, Lily Endowment, 1974. Mem. Am. Correctional Assn., Ind. Correctional Assn. (Disting. Service award 1974, 86, pres. 1978), Am. Sociol. Assn., AAUP, Am. Judicature Soc., Nat. Council Crime and Delinquency, Acad. Criminal Justice Scis., Am. Soc. Criminology, ACLU, Ind. Conf. Social Welfare. Died Aug. 31, 1994.

NELLEMOSE, KNUD, sculptor; b. Copenhagen, Mar. 12, 1908; s. Aage and Anna Nellemose; m. Pia Bendix, 1950; 3 sons. Educated Royal Acad. Art, Copenhagen, 1928. First exhbn. of sculpture, 1931; represented at Venice Biennale, 1950, other internat. exhbns.; prin. works include: busts of Their Majesties King Frederik, Queen Ingrid and Queen Margrethe II of Denmark; statues of Soren Kierkegaard, King Frederik IX; represented in permanent collections State Gallery of Copenhagen, other Danish museums, Nat. Mus. Stockholm, Nat. Mus. Oslo, Nat. Mus. Auschwitz, Poland; sculptor marble bust of Hans Andersen for 150th anniversary celebrations Nat. Athletics Ground, Copenhagen, 1994. Mem. State Art Found., 1958-64. Decorated knight Order of Dannebrog; recipient Eckersberg medal, 1944; Kai Nielsen Bequest, 1947; Carlsberg Travelling scholar, 1947-48; Thorvaldson medal, 1968. Mem. Royal Acad. (hon.). Died Jan. 14, 1997.

NELSON, ALAN CURTIS, government official, lawyer; b. Oakland, Calif., Oct. 18, 1933; s. Albert C and Martha (Peters) N.; m. JoAnn Wallen, Jan. 31, 1960; children: Kristine Ann, Kathryn Donna, Karin Martha. BS, U. Calif., Berkeley, 1955, JD, 1958. Bar: Calif. 1959, U.S. Dist. Cts. Calif. 1959, U.S. Supreme Ct. 1984. Atty. Rogers, Clark & Jordan, San Francisco, 1959-64; dep. dist. atty. Alameda County (Calif.), 1964-69; asst. dir. State of Calif. Human Resource Dept., Sacramento, 1969-72; dir. State of Calif. Dept. Rehab., Sacramento, 1972-75; gen. atty. Pacific Telephone & Telegraph, San Francisco, 1975-81; dep. commr. Immigration and Naturalization Service, Washington, 1981-82, commr., 1982-89; cons. fed. Am. immigration reform U.S. Dept. Justice, Washington, 1989-90; gen. counsel Employment Devel. Dept. State of Calif., 1990-91; atty. and cons. on immigration Sacramento, 1994—; adj. prof. McGeorge Sch. Law, U. Pacific. Chmn. Calif. Gov. Com. for Employment of Handicapped, 1981-82. Recipient Alumnus of Yr. award Tau Kappa Epsilon, 1987; Border Patrol Sta., Imperial Beach, Calif. dedicated to Commr. Nelson, 1988. Mem. State Bar Calif., Assn. Calif. Tort Reform (dir.), Bar Assn. San Francisco, Legal Aid Soc. San Francisco (dir.), Assn. Fed. Investigators (pres. 1987). Republican. Club: Commonwealth. Died Jan. 29, 1997.

NELSON, DONALD LLOYD, broadcasting executive; b. Mpls., Dec. 30, 1923; s. Carl A. and Eleanor K. (Truax) N.; m. Genevieve Thompson, Dec. 11, 1943; 1 dau. Student, St. Paul Bible Sch., 1951-53. Pres. Calvary's No. Lights Mission, 1955—; missionary Stevens Village, Alaska, 1956-64; dir. Sta. KJNP, North Pole, Alaska, 1967—; missions dir. Evangelistic Missionary Fellowship, 1961—, former v.p. radio. Author: (with Don Leach) Shadows on the Arctic Snow, 1980, In the Army of the Lord: None Dare Call it Desertion, 1985. Mem. Pollution Control Commn., Alaska, 1970-73, Alaska Ednl. Broadcasting Commn., 1970; v.p. Alaska Lung Assn., 1975-78, Alaska Heart Assn., 1976-78; former bd. dirs. Alaska Red Cross; trustee Cath. Parochial Sch. Fund Raising, 1976—. With USAAF, 1943-45. Decorated Air medal with three bronze clusters, Purple Heart; recipient Outstanding Service award Weather Bur., 1976; recipient Spl. Service award Fairbanks (Alaska) Daily News Miner, 1975; named Man of Yr., Internat. Awards Acad., 1987. Mem. Soc. Profl. Journalists, Nat. Religious Broadcasters (bd. dirs. 1985—). Died May 8, 1977.

NELSON, LINDSEY, sportscaster; b. Pulaski, Tenn., May 25, 1919; s. John Lee and Osie (Baker) N.; m. Mildred Murphy Lambert, May 9, 1946 (dec. Jan. 1973); children: Sharon, Nancy Lynne. BA, U. Tenn., 1941. With WKGN and WROL, Knoxville, Tenn., 1947-50, Liberty Broadcasting System, Dallas, 1951-52, NBC, N.Y.C., 1952-62; baseball announcer N.Y. Mets, 1962-78, San Francisco Giants, 1979—; freelance football announcer CBS, NBC, ABC, Notre Dame Network, MBS, 1962—; Conducted baseball clinics for U.S. Army in Europe, 1960. Author: (with Al Hirshberg) Backstage at the Mets, 1966; Hello Everybody, I'm Lindsey Nelson, 1985. Mem. Pres.'s Council on Youth Fitness, 1956. Served to capt., inf. AUS, 1941-45, ETO. Decorated Bronze Star medal; recipient Golden Mike award Nat. Touchdown Club, 1978. Mem. Nat. Sportscasters and Sportswriters Assn. (pres., named Nat. Sportscaster of Yr. 1959-63, named to Hall of Fame 1979), Overseas Press Club Am. Home: San Francisco Calif. Died June 10, 1995.

NELSON, LOWRY, JR., comparative literature educator; b. Provo, Utah, May 1, 1926; s. Lowry and Florence (Newell) N. A.B., Harvard U., 1947; Ph.D., Yale U., 1951. Jr. fellow Soc. Fellows, Harvard U., Cambridge, 1951-54; instr. Harvard U., 1954-56; asst. to assoc. prof. English UCLA, 1956-64; assoc. prof. comparative lit. Yale U., New Haven, 1964-71; prof. Yale U., 1971—, chmn. medieval studies, 1981-86; panelist Fgn. Area Fellowship Program, Ford Found., N.Y.C., 1964-66, NEH, Washington, 1977-82, 88. Author: Baroque Lyric Poetry, 1961; co-editor: Disciplines of Criticism, 1968, Cervantes: A Collection of Essays, 1969, The Poetry of Guido Cavalcanti, 1986, Garland Library of Medieval Literature, 90 vols., 1984—, Thirty-three Sonnets of Guido Cavalcanti Translated by Ezra Pound, 1991, Configurations of Poetry, 1992; co-editor, contbr. (with R.L. Jackson) Ivanov: Poet, Critic, Philosopher, 1986; contbr. articles to profl. jours. Bd. dirs. New Haven Symphony, 1968-74. Guggenheim fellow, 1961; Diploma di Benemerenza Assn. Internat. per gli Studi di Lingua & Letteratura Italiana Rome, 1972, NEH grantee, 1992-93. Mem. Internat. Comparative Lit Assn., PEN Internat., Medieval Acad. Am., Modern Humanities Rsch. Assn., Elizabethan Club, Elapthorne Soc., Yale Club of N.Y.C. Home: Lexington Ky. Died Nov. 12, 1994.

NELSON, LYLE MORGAN, communications educator; b. Yamhill, Oreg., Feb. 28, 1918; s. Guy Calvin and Bessie Alzine (Morgan) N.; m. Corrine Marlis Vignes, Oct. 2, 1941; children: Gayle Kathryn, Judith Lee. AB, U. Oreg., 1941, LHD (hon.), Linfield (Oreg.) Coll., 1981; Dr. honoris causa, U. Autónoma de Guadalajara, Mex., 1981. Acting dir. Univ. News Service, U. Oreg., 1941-43, asst. to pres., asso. prof. journalism, 1947-53; with U.S. Army Ordnance Dept., 1943-45; asst. regional info. officer Bur. Reclamation, Boise, Idaho, 1945-47; asst. to pres., sec. bd. dirs. Ednl. TV and Radio Center, Ann Arbor, Mich., 1953-55; asst. to pres., prof. communications San Francisco State Coll., 1955-57; v.p., prof. journalism U. Mich., 1957-60, v.p., 1960-62; dir. univ. relations Stanford, 1962-72, prof. communications, chmn. dept., 1968-78, dir. John S. Knight profl. journalism fellow program, 1972-86, Thomas M. Storke distinguished prof. emeritus, 1986—; hon. prof. journalism Autonomous U. Guadalajara; cons. edn. Ford Found., 1962-63, 65, Meyer Meml. Trust, 1982—; acad. cons. Xiamen U. Author: (with W. Schramm) Financing of Public Television, Bold Experiment: The Impact of Television on American Samoa; Editor: (with Dan Lerner) Communication Research: A Half Century Appraisal. Exec. dir. White House Conf. Edn., 1965; spl. cons. U.S. Commr. Edn., 1963, 67-70; cons. USIA, 1966-69; cons. higher edn. master plans, Ohio, N.Y., Kans.; mem. Greenbrier Conf. Higher Edn., 1958, U.S. ednl. del. to USSR, 1959; UNESCO ednl. TV Study Team; chmn. UNDP/UNESCO team to Evaluate TV Tng. in India, 1973; 1st vice chmn., bd. govs. Nature Conservancy, 1972-74; chmn. bd. fgn. scholarships State Dept., 1973-76; chmn. bd. trustees Alliance for Devel. of Latin Am. Higher Edn., 1974-79; trustee Hewlett Found., 1975-94. Recipient award for disting. svc. to higher edn. Am. Coll. Pub. Rels. Assn., 1953, 66, award for exceptional svc. to Stanford U., 1984, Disting. Svc. award U. Oreg., 1994; sr. Fulbright scholar, Australia, New Zealand, 1978. Mem. Am. Coll. Pub. Rels. Assn. (bd. dirs. 1956-65, pres. 1959-60), Bohemian Club (San Francisco), Lamplighters Club, Phi Kappa Phi, Sigma Delta Chi, Sigma Chi. Clubs: Bohemian (San Francisco); Lamplighters. Died Sept. 5, 1997.

NELSON, MARY BERTHA, public relations executive; b. Mpls., Aug. 26, 1921; d. Charles and Edna Eva (Wrabek) Ring; m. Roger Anton Nelson, Jan. 4, 1941 (dec. 1981); children: Barbara Leigh, Judith Ann, Ward Anton. BA in Pub. Rels. and Journalism, Columbia Pacific U., 1983, MA, 1984. Reporter East Mpls. Argus, 1949-57, Southtown Economist, Oak Lawn, Ill., 1958-59; columnist-reporter S.W. Messenger Press, Midlothian, Ill., 1959-68; pub. info. dir. Moraine Valley Coll., Palos Hills, Ill., 1968-82; pub. rels. officer Oak Lawn Pub. Libr., 1982-91; owner, pres. Promoplans, Evergreen Park, Ill., 1991—. Contbr. articles to profl. jours. Bd. dirs. Family/Mental Health Svcs., Worth, Ill., 1968-80, Children's Craniofacial Assn., Dallas, 1994-96; exec. dir. Ch. Coun., Chgo., 1982-92; trustee Ednl. Found., Oak Lawn, 1993—, Cmty. Libr. Found., Oak Lawn, 1993—. Mem. South Suburban Programmers, Publicity Club Chgo., Cmty. Coll. Annuitants, Oak Lawn C. of C. (bd. dirs. 1984—). Lutheran. Avocations: reading, overseas travel, crocheting, power walking.

NELSON, PAUL EDWARD, science educator; b. Franklin Township, Wis., May 26, 1927; s. John Richard and Zella Mae (Merritt) N.; m. Barbara Jean Enyeart, June 18, 1950; children: Kathryn, John, Nancy. AA in Plant Sci., Fullerton Jr. Coll., 1949; BS in Plant Pathology, U. Calif., Berkeley, 1951, PhD in Plant Pathology, 1955. Asst. prof. plant pathology Cornell U., Ithaca, 1955-61, assoc. prof., 1961-65; assoc. prof. Pa. State U., University Park, 1965-67, prof., 1967—, interim dept. head, 1981-82; adj. prof. Cornell U., 1975—; hon. assoc. dept. plant pathology and agrl. entomology U. Sydney, Australia, 1981; mem. various coms. Pa. State U.; cons. med. mycology sect. M.D. Anderson Cancer Ctr., Houston; mem. rev. panel USDA, Southeast Area, Agrl. Rsch. rev. culture collection rsch. No. Regional Rsch. Ctr., Peoria, Ill., Coop. States Rsch. Svc. rev. grad. program and rsch. and tng. programs dept. entomology and plant pathology U. Tenn., Knoxville, comprehensive program rev.. Contbr. articles to profl. jours. Recipient Alex & Jessie C. Black award Coll. Agrl. Scis., Pa. State U., 1992. Fellow Am. Phytopathological Soc. (northeastern divsn., mem. various coms., asst. editor Phytopathology 1970, sr. editor 1970-72, Award of Merit 1986); mem. Mycological Soc. Am., U.S. Fedn. Culture Collections, Am. Soc. Microbiology. Died Aug. 15, 1996.

NELSON, RALPH LOWELL, economics educator; b. St. Paul, June 9, 1926; s. Ralph Edward and Beulah (Pierce) N.; m. Ann Eileen Carson, Apr. 18, 1954; children—David Lowell, Rachel Jean. B.S., U. Minn., 1949; M.A., Columbia U., 1953, Ph.D., 1955. Instr. econs. Adelphi Coll., 1950-54; asst. prof. fin. Northwestern U., 1956-59; econ. census monographist Social Sci. Research Council, 1958-59; research staff Nat. Bur. Econ. Research, 1959-72; dir. Found. Investment Study, Found. Library Ctr., 1962-64; assoc. prof. econs. Queens Coll., CUNY, 1964-67, prof. econs., 1968—, acting assoc. dean grad. div., 1969-70; acad. visitor London Sch. Econs. and Polit. Sci., 1970-71; mem. securities industry task force 20th Century Fund, 1972-74; spl. cons. Commn. on Pvt. Philanthropy and Pub. Needs, 1974-76; cons. Dept. Treasury, 1977; mem. rsch. staff Philanthropic Found. rsch. project, program on non-profit orgn. Yale U., 1982-87; cons. Am. Assn. Fund-Raising Counsel, 1984—; bd. dirs. trust for philanthropy, 1985-90. Author: Merger Movements in American Industry, 1959, Concentration in the Manufacturing Industries of the United States, 1963, The Investment Policies of Foundations, 1967, Economic Factors in Corporation Giving, 1970, Total Personal Giving in the United States, 1986, An Economic History of Large Foundations, 1987; contbr. articles to profl. jours. Bd. govs. Caroline Veatch Assistance and Extension Program, 1974-76. Served with USNR, 1944-46. Mem. AAUP, Am. Econ. Assn., Royal Econ. Soc., Phi Beta Kappa, Beta Gamma Sigma. Unitarian. Died, Jan. 1, 1997.

NELSON, RAYMOND JOHN, mathematics and philosophy educator; b. Chgo., Oct. 8, 1917; s. Emil and Florence (Anderson) N.; m. Hendrieka Rinkema, Aug. 11, 1942; children: Susan Nelson McGuire, Steven, Peter. AB, Grinnell Coll., 1941; PhD, U. Chgo., 1949. Prof. philosophy U. Akron, 1946-52; mathematician IBM, 1952-55; staff engr. Link Aviation Corp., 1955-56; prof. math., dir. Computing Ctr. Case Western Res. U., 1956-65, prof. math. and philosophy, 1965-72, Truman P. Handy prof. philosophy, 1972-81; prof. emeritus, 1981-97; Rockefeller Scholar, Belagio, 1982; cons. to industry, 1956-97; spl. rsch. on computer logic, philosophy of sci.; bd. dirs. CHI Corp.; adj. prof. of computer sci. U. N.C., 1986-97. Author: Introduction to Automata, 1967, The Logic of Mind, 1982, 2d edit., 1989, Naming and Reference, 1992; contbr. articles to profl. jours.; patentee electronic switching device, large data processing device. Mem. Ohio Environ. Health Com. Capt. AUS, 1942-46. Mem. AAUP, Am. Philos. Assn., Am. Math. Soc., Assn. Symbolic Logic, Assn. Computing Machinery, Philos. Sci. Assn., Sigma Xi. Died Mar. 17, 1997.

NENNO, ROBERT PETER, physician; b. Buffalo, Mar. 3, 1922; s. Clayton A. and Kathryn L. (Fox) N.; m. Mary Catherine Stasson, Sept. 30, 1950; children: Mary C. Nenno Burke, Ann Nenno Biller, Elizabeth Nenno Howerton, Robert Peter Jr. B.S., U. Notre Dame, 1943; M.D., Loyola U., Chgo., 1947. Diplomate: Nat. Bd. Med. Examiners, Am. Bd. Psychiatry and Neurology. Intern E.J. Meyer Hosp., Buffalo, 1947-48; resident psychiatry VA Hosp., Mpls., 1948-50, Downey, Ill., 1950-51; with CIA, 1953, cons., 1953-58; asst. prof., asst. dir. psychiatry Georgetown U. Sch. Medicine, 1953-56, assoc. prof., 1956-58; assoc. dir. psychiatry div. Georgetown U. Hosp., 1953-56; prof. psychiatry, founding chmn. dept. Seton Hall Coll. Medicine, 1958-63; med. dir., chief exec. officer N.J. State Hosp., Marlboro, 1963-68; clin. prof. psychiatry Rutgers U. Sch. Medicine, 1966-73; prof. psychiatry, dir. div. behavioral sci. N.J. Coll. Medicine, 1973-77, vis. prof., 1977-95; dir. dept. psychiatry Jersey City Med. Center, 1973-76, acting med. dir., 1975-76; cons. mental health services Middlesex County, N.J., 1968-77; clin. prof. psychiatry East Carolina U. Med. Sch., 1977-91, prof. emeritus, 1991-95; med. dir. Pitt County (N.C.) Mental Health Center, 1977-83. Contbr. to profl. jours. Served to lt. (j.g.) M.C. USNR, 1951-53. Fellow psychiatry WHO, 1963; recipient Leadership in Mental Health N.J. Gen. Assembly, 1977. Fellow Am. Psychiat. Assn. (life); mem. Acad. Psychoanalysis. Home: Grimesland N.C. Died Jan. 20, 1995.

NESBITT, LEROY EDWARD, inventor, design specialist; b. Phila., Sept. 14, 1925; s. Lonnie Reynolds and Josephine Elvira N.; student Temple U., 1965-69; m. Vivian Elizabeth Lee, June 27, 1952; 1 son, Warren Eric. Founder, pres. Incentives, Inc., Wilmington, Del., 1975—; design specialist Sperry Corp., Blue Bell, Pa. Served with U.S. Army, 1943-46. Decorated Bronze Star (4). Died July 30, 1996.

NESVOLD, BETTY ANNE KRAMBUHL, political scientist, educator; b. Pensacola, Fla., Aug. 12, 1922; d. Otto G. and Anne P. (Price) Krambuhl; m. Alfred Ole Nesvold, Apr. 3, 1943; children: Alfred Ole, Stephen G., Thomas J., Deborah, Vikki L. B.A., San Diego State Coll., 1961, M.A., 1964; Ph.D. (NDEA fellow), U. Minn., Mpls., 1968. Asst. prof. polit. sci. San Diego State U., 1967-70, assoc. prof., 1970-73, prof., 1973-86, prof. emeritus, 1986-92, chmn. dept., 1977-80, assoc. dean Coll. Arts and Letters, 1980-84; chmn. Inter-Univ. Consortium Polit. Research Council, 1974-92 ; vis. prof. U. Hawaii, 1985-86. Author: Macro-Quantitative Analysis, 1971; contbr. articles on cross-nat. study of polit. conflict for Nat. Commn. Causes and Prevention of Violence to profl. jours. NSF grantee, 1967-72. Mem. Am. Polit. Sci. Assn. (treas. 1974-76), Western Polit. Sci. Assn. (pres. 1975-76), Internat. Studies Assn., Women's Caucus in Polit. Sci. (pres.), NOW. Home: San Diego Calif. Died Jan. 27, 1992.

NETTER, IRENE M., secondary education educator; b. N.Y.C., Oct. 29, 1926; m. Emile Netter Sr., 1951; children: Michael Eliot, Emile Jr.; m. Lance Allan Dohe, 1994. BS summa cum laude, NYU, 1948, MA, 1949; postgrad., Rutgers U., San Diego State U., Sarah Lawrence Coll. Cert. elem. tchr. (life), profl. growth adv., Calif. Bd. dir., writer Copley Press, San Diego; pres. bd. Christian edn., supt. Sunday sch. and Vacation Bible sch. Holy Cross Luth. Ch., San Diego; mentor speech, drama tchr., coach, sponsor San Diego (Calif.) Unified Sch. Dist. Prodr., dir., writer, actress Messiah's Messengers, King's Players, San Diego. Named Tchr. of Yr., San Diego, 1986, Vol. of Yr., San Diego, 1992; recipient EXCEL award for excellence in teaching. Mem. ASCD, Nat. Coun. Tchrs. English, Newspaper in Edn., Optimist Internat. (chmn. optimist oratorical and essay contest), Kappa Delta Pi. Died June 23, 1996.

NEULINGER, JOHN, psychologist, educator; b. Dresden, Germany, Apr. 26, 1924; came to U.S., 1947; s. Rudolph and Julie (Konirsch) N.; 1 child, Ronald. BA summa cum laude, Hunter Coll., 1960;

PhD, NYU, 1965. Lic. psychologist, N.Y. Rsch. assoc. Russell Sage Found., N.Y.C., 1964-65; rsch. asst. prof. NYU, N.Y.C., 1965-67; asst. prof., assoc. prof., then prof. psychology CCNY, 1967-86, prof. emeritus, 1986—; bd. dirs. Leisure Inst., Dolgeville, N.Y., 1983—. Author: The Psychology of Leisure, 1974, 2d edit., 1981, To Leisure: An Introduction, 1981, The Waid, 1986, The Road to Eden, After All, 1990. Mem. Am. Psychol. Assn., Acad. Leisure Scis. (pres. 1982-83), World Fedn. Mental Health, Soc. for Reduction of Human Labor (conductor, editor 1988—). Avocations: carpentry, gardening. Deceased.

NEUMANN, GERHARD, mechanical engineer. Engineering College, Mittweida, Germany, 1939. Gen. Mgr. GE, 1948-74; co-creator CFM Intl., 1974-97. developed variable stators for jet-powered aircraft. Recipient Ordre Nationale de la Legion d'Honour award Govt. France, 1977, Elder Statesman of Aviation award NAA, 1984, R. Tom Sawyer award ASME, 1991, Wright Bros. Meml. award, 1993. Home: Swampscott Mass. Died Nov. 2, 1997.

NEVILLE, EMILY CHENEY, author; b. Manchester, Conn., Dec. 28, 1919; d. Howell and Anne (Bunce) Cheney; m. Glenn Neville; children—Emily Tam, Glenn H.H., Dessie, Marcy, Alec. A.B., Bryn Mawr Coll., 1940; J.D., Albany Law Sch., 1976. Bar: N.Y. bar 1977. Feature writer N.Y. Mirror, 1941-42. Author books including: Seventeen Street Gang, 1966, Traveler from a Small Kingdom, 1968, Fogarty, 1969, Garden of Broken Glass, 1975, The Bridge, 1988, The China Year, 1991. Recipient Newbery award for It's Like This Cat 1964, Jane Addams award for Berries Goodman 1966. Died Dec. 14, 1997.

NEVILLE, LLOYD L., sugar manufacturing executive; b. Ogden, Utah, May 19, 1929; s. Joseph L. and Kathryn (Lemon) N.; m. Catharine Reese, Dec. 22, 1950; children: Scott R., Ted R., Amy K. Palmer, Carol M. Hansen. BS in Chemistry, Coll. Idaho, 1951. Basketball player REA Coop., Artesia, N.Mex., 1952-54; chemist Valley Gas Corp., Artesia, 1954-56, plant supt., 1956-65; research chemist Holly Sugar Corp., Colorado Springs, Colo., 1956-66; chief chemist Holly Sugar Corp., Brawley, Calif., 1966-67; asst. factory mgr. Holly Sugar Corp., Hereford, Tex., 1967-69; factory mgr. Holly Sugar Corp., Santa Ana, Calif., 1969-73; dist. mgr. Holly Sugar Corp., Colorado Springs, 1973-77, sr. v.p. ops., 1977—; Tchr. Beet Sugar Inst., Ft. Collins, Colo., 1973—. Mem. Am. Soc. Sugar Beet Tchrs. (pres. 1987—). Republican. Presbyterian. Died Oct. 5, 1997.

NEWMAN, JOSEPH, journalist, editor; b. Pittsfield, Mass., Dec. 11, 1912; s. Jacob and Ida (Greenberg) N.; m. Lucia Meza Barros, July 22, 1949; children—Lucia Ramona, Consuelo, Pia, Joseph Jr. A.B., Williams Coll., 1935. Mem. editorial staff Japan Advertiser, Tokyo, 1938-40; bur. chief New York Herald Tribune, Tokyo, 1940-41, Buenos Aires, 1943-46, Moscow, 1947-49, Berlin, 1949-50, London, 1950-55, Latin Am. (based in Buenos Aires), 1955-58, UN hdqtrs., N.Y.C., 1958-62, editorial writer New York Herald Tribune, 1962-66; producer/moderator weekly TV program " Editorial Page Conference" , Sta. WOR-TV/RKO, N.Y.C., 1962-64; interviewer Sta. WNET-TV, WNEW-TV, N.Y.C., 1964-66; co-founder (with David Lawrence), directing editor book div. U.S. News and World Report, Washington, 1967-80. Author: Goodbye Japan, 1942; Cuba S.S.R., 1961; A New Look at Red China, 1971; editor: U.S. News and World Report Money Management Library (24 vols.); 200 Years—A Bicentennial Illustrated History of the United States (2 vols.); A Bicentennial Portrait of the American People; Our Country; (with Eleanor Goldstein) A Watch on World Affairs; A Watch on the Economy, A Watch on Government. Recipient award for reports on Russia Overseas Press Club, 1948; award for reports from London English-Speaking Union, 1953; for series on Castro's Cuba Sigma Delta Chi, 1961; Guggenheim fellow, 1957. Clubs: Nat. Press; Overseas Press.

NEWMAN, MELVIN MICKLIN, surgeon; b. Chgo., Dec. 20, 1921; s. Morris and Cecilia (Micklin) N.; m. Joyce Kligerman, Sept. 11, 1949; children: Rebecca, Morris H. BS, U. Chgo., 1942, MD, 1944. Diplomate Am. Bd. Surgery, Am. Bd. Thoracic Surgery. Intern U. Chgo. Clinics, 1944-45, from resident to instr. gen. thoracic surgery, 1946-52; from asst. to assoc. prof. surgery SUNY, Bklyn., 1954-59; chief surgery Nat. Jewish Hosp., Denver, 1959-68; assoc. prof. and attending surgeon U. Colo., Denver, 1968-84; surgeon City of Hope Med. Ctr., Duarte, Calif., 1984-86, CIGNA Med. Group, 1986-92; cons. VA Hosp. Ft. Hamilton, Bklyn., 1957-59; assoc. vis. surgeon Kings County Hosp., Bklyn., 1955-59; clin. assoc. prof. U. So. Calif. Contbr. chpts. to books, articles to profl. jours. Lt. USN, 1945-46, 52-54. Grantee NIH, 1961-64, 64-66, 71-74. Fellow ACS, Am. Coll. Chest Physicians (gov. Colo. chpt. 1972-77); mem. Am. Soc. Artificial Internal Organs (pres. 1960-61), Am. Assn. Thoracic Surgery, Soc. Univ. Surgeons, Phi Beta Kappa, Alpha Omega Alpha. Democrat. Jewish. Avocations: violin and viola music, photography.

NEWMARK, MILTON MAXWELL, lawyer; b. Oakland, Calif., Feb. 24, 1916; s. Milton and Mary (Maxwell) N.; m. Marion Irene Johnson, July 31, 1941 (dec.); children—Mari Newmark Anderson, Lucy Newmark Sammons, Grace Newmark Lucini; m. Aylene Pruett Rosselli, June 21, 1991. A.B., U. Calif.-Berkeley, 1936, J.D., 1947. Bar: Calif. 1940, U.S. Supreme Ct. 1944. Ptnr. Milton Newmark, San Francisco, 1941-56; sole practice, 1956-62; sole practice, Lafayette, Calif., 1962-80, Walnut Creek, Calif., 1980-94; lectr. bankruptcy State Bar of Calif. Continuing Edn. Program. Served with U.S. Army, 1942-46; to lt. col. USAR. Mem. Alameda County Rep. Cen. Com., 1940-41; pres. Alameda County Rep. Assembly, 1950. Mem. Am. Legion, ABA, San Francisco Bar Assn., Contra Costa Bar Assn., Alameda County Bar Assn., Scabbard and Blade. Lodges: Masons, Shriners, Rotary. Died March 11, 1997.

NEWTON, JOHN SKILLMAN, engineering executive; b. Oneonta, N.Y., Sept. 21, 1908; s. Charles E. and Elizabeth (Coats) N.; m. Catherine Strachan, Sept. 23, 1929; children: Ronald, Richard, Bette, Margaret; m. Wannetta Roth, Oct. 24, 1946; children: Barbara, Charles. B.S., Oreg. State U., 1930. Engr., Westinghouse Elec. Corp., 1930-48, asst. mgr. engring., steam div., 1944-48; v.p. charge engring. Baldwin Locomotive Works, 1948-51, v.p. locomotive div., 1951-53; v.p. Baldwin-Lima-Hamilton Corp., Eddystone, 1953; v.p. testing equipment div. Baldwin-Lima-Hamilton Corp., 1954-55; v.p., then exec. v.p. Goodman Mgf. Co., Chgo., 1955-63; pres., chief adminstrv. officer Goodman Mgf. Co., 1963-65; v.p. Westinghouse Air Brake Co., 1965-66; pres., chief exec. officer Portec Inc., Chgo., 1966-74, also dir.; pres. Newton Engring. Co., 1976-94. Contbr. tech. articles to profl. jours. Trustee Goodwill Industries Chgo. Mem. ASME, Fox Valley Electric Auto Assn., Mid-Am. Club (Chgo.), Glen Oak Country Club, Plantation Golf and Country Club. Home: Glen Ellyn Ill. Died Feb. 2, 1994.

NEWTON, ROBERT EUGENE, mechanical engineering educator; b. St. Louis, Oct. 16, 1917; s. H. Melville and Lily C. (Peterson) N.; m. Dorothy M. Fairbank, Jan. 31, 1942; children: Peggy D. (Mrs. Alan L. Rector), Gary Fairbank. B.S. in Mech. Engring, Washington U., St. Louis, 1938, M.S., 1939; Ph.D., U. Mich., 1951. From asst. applied math. to asso. prof. Washington U., 1938-51; head structural methods unit Curtiss-Wright Corp., 1941-45; sr. engr. McDonnell Aircraft Corp., 1945; prof. mech. engring. Naval Postgrad. Sch., Monterey, Calif., 1951-86; prof. emeritus Naval Postgrad. Sch., Monterey, 1986—, chmn. dept., 1953-67; vis. prof. U. Wales, Swansea, 1968-69, Universite de Nantes, 1981-82; cons. to industry, 1938—. Author articles, chpt. in book. Trustee Carmel (Calif.) Unified Sch. Dist., 1961-68, pres., 1962-67; Gov. Cmty. Theatre Monterey Peninsula, 1971-73; dir. Cypress Fire Protection Dist., 1993-96. Recipient Distinguished Service award St. Louis County Jr. C. of C. Fellow ASME (life, Jr. award 1940); mem. Am. Soc. Engring. Edn., Soc. for Exptl. Mechanics, Sigma Xi, Tau Beta Pi, Omicron Delta Kappa. Died Jan. 8, 1998.

NEY, EDWARD PURDY, astrophysicist, astronomer, educator; b. Mpls., Oct. 28, 1920; s. Otto Frederick and Jessamine (Purdy) N.; m. June Felsing, June, 1942; children—Judy, John, Arthur, William. B.S., U. Minn., 1942; Ph.D., U. Va., 1947. Research asst., research asso. U. Va., 1940-46; cons. Naval Research Lab., 1943-44; asst. prof. U. Va., 1947; mem. faculty dept. physics and astronomy U. Minn., Mpls., 1947—; prof. U. Minn., 1955-74, U. Minn. regents prof., 1974—, chmn. dept. astronomy, 1974-78. Author: Electromagnetism and Relativity, 1962; contbr. articles to profl. jours. Recipient Outstanding Teaching award U. Minn., 1963, NASA Exceptional Sci. Achievement medal, 1975. Fellow AAAS, Am. Phys. Soc., Am. Geophys. Union, Am. Acad. Arts and Scis.; mem. Am. Astron. Soc. (council 1976-79), Nat. Acad. Scis., Sigma Xi (pres. Minn. chpt. 1981). Lodges: Masons, Raven Soc. Avocation: fishing. Died July 9, 1996.

NICHOLS, DAVID ARTHUR, mediator, retired state justice; b. Lincolnville, Maine, Aug. 6, 1917; s. George E. and Flora E. (Pillsbury) N. A.B. magna cum laude, Bates Coll., 1942; J.D., U. Mich., 1949. Bar: Maine bar 1949, Mass. bar 1949, U.S. Supreme Ct 1954. Pvt. practice Camden, Maine, 1949-75; justice Maine Superior Ct., 1975-77, Maine Supreme Jud. Ct., 1977-88; mediator, 1988—; Mem. Maine Exec. Council, 1955-57; moderator Lincolnville Town Meeting, 1950-74. Mem. editorial bd. Picton Press, 1989—; contbr. to legal and geneal. publs. Chmn. Maine Republican Com., 1960-64; mem. Rep. Nat. Com., 1960-68; chmn. Maine council Young Reps., 1950-54; New Eng. council Young Reps., 1952-54; trustee, past pres. Penobscot Bay Med. Center. Served with USAAF, 1942-45. Fellow Am. Bar Found., Am. Coll. Trial Lawyers; mem. Am. Law Inst., Camden-Rockport C. of C. (past pres.), Maine Hist. Soc., Camden Hist. Soc. (past pres.), Camden Bus. Men's Assn. (past pres.), ABA (bd. govs. 1960-63, ho. dels. 1957-78), Maine Bar Assn., Am. Judicature Soc. (dir. 1960-64), New Eng. Historic Geneal. Soc. (trustee), Bates Coll. Alumni Assn. (past pres.), Maine Trial Lawyers Assn. (past pres.), Phi Beta Kappa, Delta Sigma Rho. Clubs: Odd Fellows, Rotary (past pres.).

NICHOLS, DAVID LEE, air force officer; b. Iola, Kans., Jan. 18, 1934; s. David Hiram and Evelyn Leota (Coble) N.; m. Janice Elaine Lesan, Feb. 2, 1958; children—Pamela Jo, Terri Lynn, David Brian. Student, Iola Jr. Coll., Kans., 1954; B.S., Okla. State U., 1964; M.S. in Systems Mgmt., U. So. Calif., 1973; grad., Squadron Officer Sch., Maxwell AFB, 1961, Air Command and Staff Coll., Maxwell AFB, 1966, Air War Coll., Maxwell AFB, 1973. Served as enlisted man U.S. Air Force, 1954, commd. 2d lt., 1955, advanced through grades to lt. gen., 1984;, various assignments, 1954-67; assigned to 357th Tactical Fighter Squadron U.S. Air Force, Tahkli Royal Thai AFB, Thailand, 1967 flight comdr. F-105, flight comdr. F-105, 1967; flight comdr. 563rd Tactical Fighter Squadron U.S. Air Force, McConnell AFB, Kans., 1967-68, flight safety officer then chief of safety 23rd Tactical Fighter Wing, 1968-70; chief of safety 18th Tactical Fighter Wing U.S. Air Force, Kadena AFB, Okinawa, 1970-71, comdr. 12th Tactical Squadron, 1971-72; mil. asst. to asst. sec. def. for atomic energy Washington, 1973-75; chief of staff 9th Air Force, Shaw AFB, S.C., 1975-76; vice comdr. 33rd. Tactical Fighter Wing (F-4D) Eglin AFB, Fla., 1976-77, commdr. 33rd Tactical Fighter Wing (F-4E and F-15), 1977-79; dep. dir. ops. and tng. Directorate of Ops. and Readiness U.S. Air Force, Washington, 1979-80, dep. dir. for plans and policy Office of Dep. Chief of Staff, Ops., Plans and Readiness, 1980-81; dep. chief of staff, plans U.S. Air Forces in Europe, Ramstein AFB, W. Ger., 1981-82, chief of staff, 1982-83; asst. dep. chief of staff plans and ops. Hdqrs. U.S. Air Force, Washington, 1983-84; dep. chief of staff, plans and ops. Hdqrs. U.S. Air Force, Washington, 1984—. Decorated D.S.M., Silver Star, Legion of Merit with two oak leaf clusters, D.F.C. with three oak leaf clusters, Air medal with 16 oak leaf clusters, Air Force Commendation Medal with one oak leaf cluster, many other mil. decorations and awards. Mem. Air Force Assn., Order of Daedalians. Died April 5, 1997.

NICHOLS, FREDERICK DOVETON, emeritus architecture educator; b. July 1, 1911. Student, Colo. Coll., 1929-31; MFA, Yale U., 1935. Regional dir. historic bldgs. survey Nat. Pk. Svc., 1935-41; head archtl. studies program U. Hawaii, 1946-50; assoc. prof. art and architecture U. Va., Charlottesville, 1950-60, prof., 1960-67, Cary D. Langhorne prof. architecture, 1967, now emeritus, former chmn. div. archtl. history Sch. Architecture, also univ. designer bldgs. and restoration, restoration cons. Jefferson's bldgs., 1970—; mem. Nat. Adv. Com. for Aeronautics, 1941-46; mem. Monticello Restoration Com., 1956, cons. restoration, 1970—; mem. Va. Historic Landmarks Commn., 1966-88; mem. Nat. Fine Arts Commn., 1976-80; bd. dirs., trustee Thomas Jefferson Meml. Found., 1970; mem. properties com. Nat. Trust for Historic Preservation, 1958-78; mem. Drayton Hall Charleston S.C. Coun.; cons. restorations Harewood, Va., Stratford, Va., Christ Ch., Lancaster County, Va., Jefferson's Poplar Forest, Va., John Marshall House, Richmond, Va., Woodrow Wilson birthplace, Staunton, Va., Tudor Pl., Georgetown, Washington, Oatlands, Hamlet, Va.; guide, lectr. Jefferson's Garden Tour of France and Eng. Smithsonian Instn., 1978; archtl. cons. The Eye of Jefferson Exhbn., 1976; founding mem. adv. bd. Jeffersonian Restoration, 1984—; lectr. in field. Author: Early Architecture of Georgia, 1957 (Alice Davis Hitchcock medal Soc. Archtl. Historians), 2d rev. edit., 1976, (with James Grady and William B. O'Neal) Index of American Architectural Drawings Before 1900, 1957, (with W. O'Neal) Architecture in Virginia, 1776-1858, 1958, Thomas Jefferson's Architectural Drawings, 1959, (with James Bear) Monticello, 1967, (with Ralph Griswold) Thomas Jefferson Landscape Architect, 1978; contbr. archtl. portion Jefferson papers; editor: The Historic American Buildings Survey, 1941; contbr. articles to profl. publs., prefaces to books. With USAAF, 1943-45. Recipient Thomas Jefferson Disting. Teaching award U. Va., 1979, Disting. Faculty award U. Va. Alumni Assn., 1975, Archtl. Spl. Honor award U. Va. and Va. Mus. Fine Arts, 1960, Pub. Svc. award U.S. Dept. Interior; Guggenheim Found. fellow, 1963; grantee NEH, 1979. Fellow AIA (mem. task force preservation West front Capitol bldg. 1978—); mem. Am. Assn. Archtl. Bibliographers (bd. dirs. 1957, founding gov.), Walpole Soc., Century Assn., Colonnade Club. Home: Charlottesville Va. DIED 04/09/95. .

NICHOLS, ROBERT E(DMUND), editor, writer, journalist; b. Daytona Beach, Fla., Feb. 14, 1925; s. Joe D. and Edna A. (Casper) N.; m. Diana R. Grosso children by previous marriage: Craig S., Kim S., Robin K. San Diego State Coll., 1942-43, St. John's Coll. 1944-45. Reporter San Diego Union, 1942-44; corr Washington bur. N.Y. Herald Tribune, 1945-48, CBS, 1948-51, Time, Inc., 1951-61; contbg. editor Time, asst edn. dir. Life mag., N.Y.C., 1951-52; corr. representing Time, Life, Fortune, Sports Illus. mags., San Diego area 1952-61; Sunday editor San Diego Union, 1952-61; fin editor Los Angeles Times, 1961-68, mem. editorial bd. 1965-68; spl. asst. to bd. govs. FRS, 1968-70; v.p., dir editorial svcs. Bank of Am., 1970-85. Mem. U.S Antarctic Expedition, 1946-47. Recipient Loeb Newspaper Spl. Achievement award, 1963, Loeb award disting. fin. reporting, 1964. Fellow Royal Geog. Soc. Explorers Club; mem. Am. Polar Soc., Calif. Scholarship fedn. (hon., life), Soc. Am. Bus. Editors and Writers (hon., life, pres. 1967-68), South Polar Press Club. Home: San Francisco Calif. Died Sept. 30, 1996.

NICHOLS, ROBERT LEE, food company executive; b. Clarksburg, W.Va., Nov. 4, 1924; s. Clarence Garfield and Reatha Maude (Berry) N.; m. Vianne Hope Demaray, Oct. 21, 1973; children: Donna Beth, Michael Alan, Jeffrey Mark. Student, Bus. Coll., 1944, U. Detroit, 1959. Sales rep. Kellogg Sales Co., Battle Creek, Mich., 1944-50; dist. mgr. Kellogg Sales Co., 1950-61, asst. div. mgr., 1961-64, sales promotion dir., 1964-69, exec. v.p., gen. sales mgr., 1969-71, pres., 1976-78; pres. Fearn Internat., 1971-76, dir., 1971-82; group exec. v.p. Kellogg Co., Battle Creek, 1979-82, dir., 1977-89, vice chmn., 1983-89; pres., dir. Mrs. Smith's Frozen Foods Co., 1979-82, McCamly Square Corp., 1983-89; dir., pres. Battle Creek Unltd., 1985-87; bd. dirs. Cereal Inst., 1976-79, Am. Frozen Food Inst., 1979-82, Cereal City Devel. Corp., 1986; bd. govs. Acad. Food Mktg., St. Joseph U., 1976-79. Exec. v.p., bd. dirs. Jr. Achievement, Battle Creek, 1970-71; trustee Mich. Colls. Found., 1985-89, Thomas Jefferson Found., Lakeview Schs., 1986-89, Mich. Biotechnology Inst., 1985-89, Citizens Rsch. Coun. Mich., 1985-90; mem., bd. dirs. United Way of Greater Battle Creek Area, 1984-89, campaign chmn., 1985; pres. Battle Creek Unltd., 1985-87; vice chmn. Battle Creek Airport Adv. Com., 1984-89; mem. Nat. Corp. Coun. Interlochen Ctr for the Arts, 1986-89; mem. adminstrv. bd. 1st United Meth. Ch., Stuart, Fla., 1990-94. Mem. Svc. Core Ret. Execs. (vice chair 1991-93), Snug Harbor Yacht Club (vice commodore 1990-92, commodore 1992-93), First Nat. Bank & Trust of the Treasure Coast (adv. bd. 1993-96), Martin County Coun. for Arts (dir. 1990-96), Masons. Home: Battle Creek Mich. Died Aug. 12, 1996, interred Memorial Park.

NICHOLS, WADE HAMPTON, JR., editorial and publishing consultant; b. Charlotte, N.C., May 31, 1915; s. Wade Hampton and Ora (Calloway) N.; m. Edith Lou Docekal, July 12, 1938 (dec. 1975); children—Wade Hampton III, Nancy Elizabeth. B.S., Northwestern U., 1936. Staff mem. Radio Guide mag., 1936; editor Screen Guide, 1938, Stardom, 1941, Click mag., 1942; free-lance articles, 1946-48, editor Modern Screen mag., 1948, Good Housekeeping Mag., 1958-75; v.p., dir. editorial devel. Mags. Div. Hearst Corp., 1975-76; assoc. pub. Bluebook mag., 1953-55; editor Redbook, 1949-58, assoc. pub., 1953-55, pub., 1955-58; v.p., dir. McCall Corp., 1955-58; editorial and pub. cons., 1976—. Author: (basic orientation handbooks for Army) WAC Life, 1944, Army Life, 1944-45. Served to 1st lt. AUS, 1943-46. Recipient Benjamin Franklin Gold medal, 1955. Member Mag. Pubs. Assn. (chmn. editorial com. 1956-57), Am. Council Edn. Journalism (accrediting com. 1957-60), Am. Soc. Mag. Editors (exec. council, chmn. 1967-68), Phi Gamma Delta, Sigma Delta Chi. Club: Bronxville Field.

NICHOLS, WARREN DE FORREST, engineering company executive, citrus grower; b. Los Angeles, Sept. 9, 1926; s. Forrest Clifford and Gladys Harriet (Hunick) N.; m. Willene Dorothy Pegg, Sept. 3, 1949; children: Anne, Clifford, Charles, Carol. Student, UCLA, 1946-49. Registered profl. engr., Calif. With Hughes Aerospace Groups, Culver City, Calif., 1960-72; lab. mgr. Hughes Space and Communications Group, El Segundo, Calif., 1972-74, asst. mgr. mfg. div., 1974-77; asst. systems div. mgr. Hughes Missile Systems Group, Canoga Park, Calif., 1977-79; asst. co. mgr. Santa Barbara Research Ctr., Goleta, Calif., 1979-81, v.p., 1981—; mem. land remote sensing adv. com. Dept. Commerce, 1982-83. Served with USNR, 1944-46, PTO. Recipient Disting. Pub. Service medal NASA, 1983. Mem. Am. Astron. Soc. (W. Randolph Lovelace III award 1983). Republican. Methodist. Died Dec. 1, 1996.

NICHOLSON, GEORGE ALBERT, JR., financial analyst; b. Baldwin City, Kan., May 7, 1908; s. George Albert and Nellie May (Ruthrauff) N.; m. Elizabeth Farnham, Sept. 1, 1933; children: George Albert III, Edwin F., John R., Elizabeth C. (Mrs. David D. Hamm). A.B., U. Mich., 1928; M.B.A., Harvard U., 1930; LL.D., Carthage Coll., 1972. Chartered fin. analyst. With Hudson Motor Co., 1930-31, Union Guardian Trust Co., 1931-33; fin. analyst Whitlock, Smith & Co., Detroit, 1933-37, Am. Industries, Detroit, 1937-41, Inc. Investors, Boston, 1941; civilian renegotiator USAF, 1942-45; fin. analyst Watling, Lerchen & Co., Detroit, 1945-58; rsch. dir. Smith, Hague & Co. Inc., Detroit, 1958-90; columnist Better Investing Mag.; cons. 1st of Mich. Merger, Detroit, 1990—; chmn. Investment Edn. Inst., Internat. Investment Edn. Inst., World Fedn. Investment Clubs. Nicholson awards for best ann. reports for individual investors established by Nat. Assn. Investors, 1978. Mem. Fin. Analyst Soc. Detroit (pres. 1957), Nat. Assn. Investment Clubs (chmn. adv. bd.), Delta Kappa Epsilon. Republican. Episcopalian. Clubs: Country (Detroit), Indian Village (Detroit). Died July 22, 1996.

NICHOLSON, LUTHER BEAL, financial consultant; b. Sulphur Springs, Tex., Dec. 15, 1921; s. Stephen Edward and Elma (McCracken) N.; B.B.A., So. Meth. U., 1942, postgrad., 1946-47, Tex. U., 1947-48; diploma Southwestern Grad. Sch. Banking, 1967; m. Ruth Wimbish, May 29, 1952; children—Penelope Elizabeth, Stephen David. Controller, Varo, Inc., Garland, Tex., 1946-55, dir., 1947-72, v.p. fin., 1955-66, sr. v.p., 1966-67, exec. v.p., 1967-70, pres., 1970-71, chmn. bd., 1971-72, cons. to bd. dirs., 1972-75; gen. mgr. Challenger Lock Co., Los Angeles, 1956-58; dir. Varo Inc. Electrokinetics div., Varo Optical, Inc., Biometrics Instrument Corp., Varo Atlas GmbH, Micropac Industries, Inc., Gt. No. Corp., Garland Bank & Trust Co. Bd. dirs., exec. v.p. Harriett Stanton-Edna Murray Found. Served with AUS, 1942-46. Mem. Fin. Execs. Inst. (past pres.), Am. Inst. C.P.A.'s, AIM, Am. Mgmt. Assn., NAM. Died Feb. 7, 1996.

NICHOLSON, ROY S., clergyman; b. Walhalla, S.C., July 12, 1903; s. Samuel Dendy and Beulah Young (Lindsay) N.; m. Ethel Macy, June 26, 1924 (dec. Dec. 1985); children: Roy S., Lee Huffman; m. Winifred Bisbing, Oct. 7, 1986. Student, Wesleyan Meth. Acad. and Coll., Central, S.C., 1918-24; D.D., Houghton Coll., 1944; Th.B., Central Sch. Religion, 1956; Litt.D., Central Wesleyan Coll., 1981; L.H.D., Bartlesville Wesleyan Coll., 1985. Ordained to ministry Wesleyan Meth. Ch., 1925; tchr. N.C., 1924; pastor East Radford, Va., 1925-26, Long Shoals, N.C., 1926-30, Kannapolis, N.C., 1930-35, Brooksville, Fla., 1969-74; supt. Wesleyan Youth Work, 1934-35, Sunday sch. sec. and editor, 1935-39, home missionary sec., 1939-43; mem. bd. adminstrn. Wesleyan Meth. Ch., 1935-59, 63-68, chmn., 1947-59; v.p. Wesleyan Meth. Ch. Am., 1939-47, pres., 1947-59, pres. emeritus, 1959-68; prof. Bible Central Wesleyan Coll., 1959-68, chmn. div. religion, 1959-68; Editor Wesleyan Meth., Wesleyan Youth, 1943-47; Am. counselor Immanuel Gen. Mission, Japan, 1964-93; bd. dirs. Wesleyan Bible Conf. Assn., 1970-93; gen. supt. emeritus Wesleyan Ch., 1972-93, Wesleyan Bible Conf. Assn., 1981-93. Author: Wesleyan Methodism in the South, 1933, History of the Wesleyan Methodist Church, 1951, Notes on True Holiness, 1952, Arminian Emphases, 1962, A Valid Theology for Our Day, 1963, Commentary on The Pastoral Epistles, 1965, Commentary on The First Epistle of Peter, 1969, Studies in Church Doctrine, True Holiness: The Wesleyan-Arminian Emphasis (revised edit.), 1985; also articles; contbr. to: Aldersgate Doctrinal Series, 1963; other publs. in field. Chmn. bd. trustees Houghton, Central, Miltonvale and Marion colls., 1947-59; adv. council Ky. Mountain Bible Inst., World Gospel Mission. Recipient Disting. Alumnus of Yr. award Central Wesleyan Coll. Alumni Assn., 1973. Mem. Nat. Holiness Assn. (bd. adminstrn. 1955-64, 70-93, rec. sec. 1960-64). Home: High Point N.C. Died Mar. 2, 1993.

NICKLAUS, CHARLES EDWARD, sales training executive; b. Columbus, Ohio, Nov. 2, 1915; m. Hazel Stine, Aug. 31, 1940; children: Carol Marie, James Frank. BSBA, Franklin U., Columbus, 1980. Dir. rsch. lab. H. Braun Co., Columbus, 1939-41; gen. mgr. Edmont Co. Br., Mt. Sterling, Ohio, 1943-48; internat. sales tng. dir. Warren-Teed Pharm. Co., Columbus, 1948-75; prof. mktg. Columbus State C.C., 1986-90; adj. faculty Franklin U., Columbus, 1975-90, Svc. Corps of Ret. Execs. and Active Corps Execs., U.S. SBA # 285, Charleston, S.C. Mem. Masons (Mt. Sterling, Ohio). Died Mar. 29, 1996.

NIEDERJOHN, RUSSELL JAMES, electrical and computer engineering educator; b. Schenectady, June 13, 1944; s. Russell Kelly and Jeanette Ody (Burnison) N.; m. Susan A Swenson, June 7, 1969; children: Matthew Scott, Jeremy Michael. B.S. in Elec. Engring., U. Mass., Amherst, 1967, M.S. in Elec. Engring., 1968, Ph.D. in Elec. Engring., 1971. Registered profl. engr., Wis. Research asst. elec. engring. dept. U. Mass., Amherst, 1968-71; asst. prof. elec. engring. dept. Marquette U., Milw., 1971-75, assoc. prof., 1975-80, prof. elec. engring. and computer sci., dir. computer sci. and engring., 1980-87, prof., chmn. elec. and computer engring. dept., 1987-94; prof. elec. and computer engring. dept., 1994—; dir. speech and signal processing lab. Marquette U., Milw., 1973—, co-dir. signal processing rsch. ctr., 1991—; cons. William C. Brown Co. Pubs., Dubuque, Iowa, 1981-85, Eaton Corp., Milw., 1978-85, Seaman Nuclear Corp., Milw., 1979-81, 92-93, MacMillan Pubs., Encino, Calif., 1983-86. Contbr. articles to profl. jours. Mem. Milw. Ednl. TV Auction Com., 1978-81. Recipient Dow Outstanding Young Faculty award, 1977, award Western Electric Fund, 1981, Marquette U. Faculty award for teaching excellence, 1988. Fellow IEEE (mem. exec. com. Milw. sect. 1974-75, 76-79, 82-89, treas. 1982-83, sec. 1983-84, vice chmn. 1984-85, chmn. 1985-86, edn. chmn. 1977-80, chmn. nominating com. 1986-87, awards chmn. 1987-89, Meml. award 1979); mem. IEEE Signal Processing Soc., IEEE Computer Soc. (bd. dirs. Milw. chpt. 1981-85), IEEE Ind. Elec. Soc. (adminstrv. com. 1986—, edn. com. 1986-89, soc. chpt. coord. 1989-91, assoc. editor Trans. 1988—, v.p. for confs. 1992, v.p. for pubs. 1993, v.p. adminstrn. 1994-95, pres. 1996—, IEEE Systems, Man and Cybernetics Soc. (bd. dirs. Milw. chpt. 1975-79), Am. Soc. Engring. Edn. (exec. com. North Midwest sect. 1974-89), Acoustical Soc. Am., Milw. Symposium on Automatic Control (program chmn. 1975), Sigma Xi (pres. elect Marquette U. chpt. 1986-87, pres. 1987-88, sci. achievement award 1993), Eta Kappa Nu (C. Holmes MacDonald Outstanding Elec. Engring. Prof. in U.S. 1978, Marquette U. chpt. adv. 1986—, bd. dirs. 1993-95), Tau Beta Pi. Died Nov. 17, 1996.

NIELSEN, ALVIN HERBORG, university dean, physicist; b. Menominee, Mich., May 30, 1910; s. Knud and Maren (Nielsen) N.; m. Jane Ann Evans, Dec. 29, 1942; 1 dau., Margaret Arthur Wayne. B.A., U. Mich., 1931, M.S., 1932, Ph.D., 1934. Research fellow Ohio State U., 1934-35; faculty U. Tenn., 1935—, prof. physics, 1946-80, prof. emeritus, 1980—, head dept., 1956-69, dean Coll. Liberal Arts, 1963-77; dean emeritus U. Tenn. (Coll. Liberal Arts), 1977—, Mace Bearer and Phi Kappa Phi disting. faculty lectr., 1962-63; Research asso. for OSRD Ohio State U. Research Found., 1944-46; cons. Oak Ridge Gaseous Diffusion Plant Labs. and Oak Ridge Nat. Lab., 1947-80. Author articles molecular spectroscopy.; Asso. editor: Jour. Chem. Physics, 1955-57. Mem. Knoxville Symphony Soc. Bd., 1963—, v.p., 1965-68, 75-76, 77-78, pres., 1968-69, 76-77; bd. dirs. Greater Knox Council for the Arts, 1974—, v.p., 1974-77. NRC fellow elect, 1942; Fulbright research scholar Astrophys. Inst., U. Liege, Belgium, 1951-52; Alvin H. Nielsen Physics Bldg., U. Tenn. dedicated Oct. 1980; recipient Mayor's award for support of arts, 1978. Fellow Am. Phys. Soc. (Pegram award S.E. sect. 1980), Optical Soc. Am., AAAS; mem. AAUP, Tenn. Acad. Sci. (exec. com. 1959-61), Coblentz Soc., Am. Inst. Physics, Am. Conf. Acad. Deans (dir. 1968-75, chmn. 1972), Phi Beta Kappa, Sigma Xi, Phi Kappa Phi, Sigma Pi Sigma, Pi Delta Phi, Omicron Delta Kappa. Episcopalian. Clubs: Faculty, Irving. Died Nov. 3, 1994.

NIEMEYER, GERHART, political science educator; b. Essen, Germany, Feb. 15, 1907; came to U.S., 1937, naturalized, 1943; s. Victor and Kaethe (Ley) N.; m. Lucie Lenzner, Sept. 18, 1931; children: A. Hermann, Lucian L., Paul V., Lisa M., Christian B. Student, Cambridge U., 1925-26, Munich U., 1926-27; J.U.D., Kiel U., 1932. Ordained priest Episcopal Ch. 1980, canon, 1987. Lectr., asst. prof. Princeton U., 1937-44; prof., head div. Oglethorpe U., 1944-50; fgn. affairs officer Dept. State, 1950-53; research analyst Council Fgn. Relations, 1953-55; prof. U. Notre Dame, 1955-76, emeritus, 1976—; mem. Bd. Fgn. Scholarships, 1981-84, chmn., 1982-84; vis. prof. Yale U., 1942, 46, 54-55, Columbia U., 1952, Vanderbilt U., 1962-66; faculty Nat. War Coll., 1958-59, 61; Fulbright prof. U. Munich, 1962-63; Distinguished vis. prof. Hillsdale Coll., 1976-82. Author: Law Without Force, 1941, An Inquiry into Soviet Mentality, 1956, Facts on Communism, vol. 1: The Communist Ideology, 1959, Handbook on Communism, 1962, Between Nothingness and Paradise, 1971, Deceitful Peace, 1971, Aftersight and Foresight, 1988, Within and Above Ourselves, 1996; assoc. editor Modern Age, 1965—. Mem. task force on fgn. policy Republican Nat. Com., 1965-68. Mem. Am. Polit. Sci. Assn. Roman Catholic. DIED 06/23/97. .

NIES, HELEN WILSON, federal judge; b. Birmingham, Ala., Aug. 7, 1925; d. George Earl and Lida Blanche (Erckert) Wilson; m. John Dirk Nies; children: Dirk, Nancy, Eric. BA, U. Mich., 1946, JD, 1948. Bar: Mich. 1948, D.C. 1961, U.S. Supreme Ct. 1962. Atty. Dept. Justice, Washington, 1948-51, Office Price Stblzn., Washington, 1951-52; assoc. Pattishall, McAuliffe and Hofstetter, Washington, 1960-66, resident ptnr., 1966-77; ptnr. Howrey & Simon, Washington, 1978-80; judge U.S. Ct. Customs and Patent Appeals, 1980-82; cir. judge U.S. Ct. Appeals Fed. Cir., 1982-96; chief judge U.S. Ct. Appeals (fed. cir.), 1990-94, sr. status, 1995-96; mem. jud. conf. U.S. Com. on Bicentennial of Constn., 1986-92; mem. pub. adv. com. trademark affairs Dept. Commerce, 1976-80; mem. adv. bd. BNA's Patent Trademark and Copyright Jour., 1976-78; mem. bd. visitors U. Mich. Law Sch., 1975-78; adv. for restatement of law and unfair competition Am. Law Inst., 1986-96; speaker World Intellectual Property Orgn., Forum of Judges, Calcutta, 1987, European Judges Conf., Hague, 1991, Kyoto (Japan) Comparative Law Ctr., 1992, others. Recipient Athena Outstanding Alumna award U. Mich., 1987, Jefferson medal N.J. Patent Law Assn., 1991, Judicial Honoree award Bar Assn. D.C., 1992, D. of Laws, Honoris Causa, John Marshall Law Sch., Chgo., 1993. Mem. ABA (chmn. com. 203, 1972-74, com. 504, 1975-76), Bar Assn. D.C. (chmn. patent trademark copyright sect. 1975-76, dir. 1976-78), U.S. Trademark Assn. (chmn. lawyers adv. com. 1974-76, bd. dirs. 1976-78), Am. Patent Law Assn., Fed. Bar Assn., Nat. Assn. Women Lawyers, Women's Bar D.C. (Woman Lawyer of Yr. 1980), Order of Coif, Phi Beta Kappa, Phi Kappa Phi. Died Aug. 7, 1996.

NISBET, ROBERT A., historian, sociologist; b. Los Angeles, Sept. 30, 1913; s. Henry S. and Cynthia (Jenifer) N.; m. Emily P. Heron (div.); children: Martha Rehrman, Constance Field; m. Caroline Burks Kirkpatrick; 1 child, Ann Nash. AB, U. Calif., Berkeley, 1936, MA, 1937, PhD, 1939, Berkeley citation, 1970; LHD (hon.), Hofstra U., 1974. Instr. social instns. U. Calif. at Berkeley, 1939-43; asst. dean U. Calif. at Berkeley (Coll. Letters and Sci.), 1942-43, 46, asst. prof. social instns., 1943-48, asso. prof. sociology, 1948-52; prof. sociology U. Calif., Riverside, 1953-72; vice chancellor U. Calif., 1960-63; dean U. Calif. (Coll. Letters and Sci.), 1953-63; vis. prof. Columbia U., 1949, Albert Schweitzer prof. humanities, 1974-78, emeritus, 1978—; resident scholar Am. Enterprise Inst., Washington, 1978-80, adj. scholar, 1980-86, prof. history and sociology U. Ariz., 1972-74; vis. prof. U. Bologna, Italy, 1956-57; Rieker lectr. U. Ariz., 1956; lectr. all univs., Calif., 1961, Guggenheim fellow, 1963-64; Cooper lectr. Swarthmore Coll., 1966; John Dewey lectr. John Dewey Soc., 1970; William A. Neilson research prof. Smith

Coll., 1971-72; Blazer lectr. U. Ky., 1971; Phi Beta Kappa Nat. vis. scholar, 1971-72; vis. fellow Princeton U., 1963-64; Johns Hopkins Centennial scholar, 1975-76; W.G. Sumner lectr. Yale U., 1976; Leon lectr. U. Pa., 1982; Benjamin Rush lectr. Am. Psychiat. Assn., 1983; Jefferson lectr. in Humanities NEH, 1988. Author: The Quest for Community, 1953, Human Relations in Administration, 1956, Emile Durkheim, 1965, The Sociological Tradition, 1966, Tradition and Revolt, 1968, Social Change and History, 1969, The Social Bond, 1970, The Degradation of the Academic Dogma, 1971, The Social Philosophers, 1973, rev. edit., 1983, The Sociology of Emile Durkheim, 1974, Twilight of Authority, 1975, Sociology as an Art Form, 1976, History of the Idea of Progress, 1980, Prejudices: A Philosophical Dictionary, 1982, Conservatism: Dream and Reality, 1986, The Making of Modern Society, 1986, The Present Age, 1988, Roosevelt and Stalin, 1989, Teachers and Scholars, 1992; editor: Social Change; co-editor: Contemporary Social Problems, 1961, 66, 71, 1976, History of Sociological Analysis, 1978; bd. editors Am. Jour. Sociology, 1970-74; mem. publ. com. The Public Interest, 1976-84; mem. editorial bd. The American Scholar, 1975-80; contbr. articles to profl. jours. Mem. Nat. Council Humanities, 1975-78; mem. N.Y. Gov.'s Health Adv. Council, 1975-76, Parkman Prize Com., 1978-80; bd. dirs. Am. Council Learned Socs., 1974-79, Council Acad. Advisers, Am. Enterprise Inst., Washington, 1972-86, Rockford Inst., 1978-84. Served with AUS, 1943-45, PTO. Decorated cavaliere ufficiale Order of Merit Italy; recipient Ingersoll award in humanities, 1985; Rockefeller Found. grantee, 1975-78. Fellow Am. Acad. Arts and Scis. (councillor 1977-80), Am. Philos. Soc. (councillor 1977-80, Penrose Meml. lectr. 1982), Soc. Am. Historians; mem. Société Europèene de Culture, Columbia Soc. Fellows, Institut Internationale de Sociologie, Phi Beta Kappa. Died Sept. 9, 1996.

NIVEN, WILLIAM JOHN, historian, educator; b. Bklyn., Oct. 26, 1921; s. William John and Marion (Fredricks) N.; m. Elizabeth Thomson, Sept. 11, 1948; children: John Drake, Katherine Pope. BA, U. Conn., 1943; MA, Columbia U., 1947, PhD, 1954. Instr. Mitchell Coll., New London, Conn., 1949-51; supr. employee rels. Electric Boat divsn. Gen. Dynamics Corp., Groton, Conn., 1951-54; asst. to v.p. comm. Gen. Dynamics Corp., N.Y.C., 1954-55, asst. to CEO and pres., 1955-57, dir. pubs., 1955-60; assoc. prof., prof. Claremont (Calif.) Grad. Sch., 1965-90; prof. emeritus, 1990—; cons. in field. Co-author: Dynamic America, 1960; author: Connecticut for the Union, 1965, Years of Turmoil: The Civil War and Reconstruction, 1969, Gideon Welles, Lincoln's Secretary of the Navy, 1973, Connecticut Hero: Israel Putnam, 1977, Martin Van Buren and the Romantic Era of American Politics, 1983, The American President Lines and Its Forebears, 1848-1984: From Paddle Wheelers to Container Ships, 1986, The Coming of the Civil War, 1989, John C. Calhoun and the Price of Union, 1987, Salmon P. Chase, A Study in Paradox, 1995; editor: The Salmon P. Chase Papers,. Lt. USNR, 1942-46, WWII. Grantee Am. Philos. Soc., 1962, Am. Coun. Learned Socs., 1962; recipient Award of Merit, Nat. Assn. State and Local History, 1966, Jules and Frances Landry award, 1987; Commonwealth Club Calif. Silver medal, 1974. Fellow Smithsonian Inst. (sr. 1965-66), Soc. Am. Historians; mem. Am. Hist. Assn. (chmn. Avery Craven award com. 1985, Beveridge-Dunning award com. 1974, 75, chmn. 1976, Pacific Coast Br. award 1966), Orgn. Am. Historians, So. Hist. Assn. (chmn. Charles Sydnor prize com. 1983, 84), Zamorano Club, Coffee House. Avocation: gardening. Died Aug. 14, 1997.

NIXON, ROBERT PLEASANTS, former electric motor manufacturing company executive; b. Rome, Ga., Dec. 5, 1913; s. George Felton and Eunice (Adamson) N.; m. Helen May Hill, June 4, 1942; children: Robert H., Edward H., James R. Grad. summa cum laude, Darlington Sch., 1931; AB in Econs. with honors, Duke U., 1935. CPA. Treas., dir., pub. Bus. News Pub. Co., Detroit, 1935-48; asst. to v.p. Wachovia Bank & Trust Co., Winston-Salem, N.C., 1941; auditor Jacuzzi Bros., Inc., Richmond, Calif., 1948-52; v.p., 1st controller then sec.-treas. Franklin Electric Co., Inc., Bluffton, Ind., 1952-83; also dir. Franklin Electric and subs. in Can., Europe, S. Africa; sec. Oil Dynamics, Inc., Tulsa, 1967-83. Bd. dirs. Caylor-Nickel Hosp., Bluffton, 1974-83; bd. dirs., exec. com. Allen-Wells Red Cross, 1980-82; pres. Wells County Found., 1972; mem. bd. vis. Ball State U., 1968-72. Served with USNR, 1941-45, PTO; lt. comdr. Res. 1949. Mem. NAM (environ. quality com.), Ind. C. of C. (taxation com.), The Garden Conservancy, Detroit Tennis Club, Fort Wayne Racquet Club, Parlor City Country Club, Phi Beta Kappa, Omicron Delta Kappa, Alpha Kappa Psi, Phi Eta Sigma, Sigma Nu. Republican. Presbyterian (elder). Avocation: tree gardening. Home: Bluffton Ind. Died Mar. 4, 1994.

NKUBITO, ALPHONSE MARIE, Rwandan government official; b. Hutu, Rwanda. Former prosecutor Kigali (Rwanda) Appeals Ct.; min. justice Govt. of Rwanda, Kigali, 1994—; human rights worker. Died Feb. 13, 1997.

NOEL, EMILE, university administrator; b. Istanbul, Turkey, Nov. 17, 1922; s. Fernand Edouard and France Marthe (Giraud) N.; m. Lise Durand, 1946 (dec. April 1985); 2 children; m. Madeleine Gobeil, June 1994. Student, Ecole Normale Supérieure, Paris, 1941-45; Degree in Sci. and Math., U. Paris, 1943; D in Law and Polit. Sci. (hon.), Irish Nat. U., 1981, U. Edinburgh, Scotland, 1982, U. Urbino, Italy, 1987, U. Marmara, Turkey, 1988, Ritsumeikan U. of Kyoto, Japan, 1989, Georgetown U., 1992; D (hon.), Minho U., Portugal, 1990. Sec. gen. affairs commn. consultative assembly Coun. of Europe, 1949-52, chief of cabinet to pres. consultative assembly, 1954-56; dir. constl. commn. of assembly European Polit. Community, 1952-54; chief of cabinet, then dep. dir cabinet to pres. Coun. of Ministers, Paris, 1956-57; exec. sec. commn. EEC, Brussels, 1958-67; sec. gen. Commn. European Communities, Brussels, 1968-87; prin. European U. Inst., Florence, Italy, 1987-93; pres. European U. Coun., Jean Monnet Project, 1991—; hon. prof. Free U., Brussells; adv. prof. Fudan U., Shanghai, U. Chengdu, China. Author: Les Rouages de l'Europe, 1976, Working Together, 1975, Le Comité des Reprentants Permanents, 1966, The Single European Act (Government and Opposition - London), 1988, Reflections on the Maastricht Treaty, 1992. Hon. sec.-gen. Commn. of European Communities; hon. prin. European Univ. Inst. Home: 16 rue Gracieuse, 75005 Paris France Died Aug. 24, 1996.

NOEL, JAMES LATANE, JR., retired district judge; b. Pilot Point, Tex., Oct. 28, 1909; s. James Latane Sr. and Ina (Bobbit) N.; m. Virginia Grubbs, Apr. 21, 1942; children: James Latane III, Carol Annelle, Edmund Orr, William David, Robert Cornelius. BSCE, So. Meth. U., 1931, BS in Commerce, 1932, LLB, 1938, LLD, 1966. Bar: Tex. 1937. Asst. budget officer Dallas County, Tex., 1935-37, asst. dist. atty., 1937-38; asst. atty. gen. State of Tex., Austin, 1939-42, 45-46; ptnr. Butler, Binion, Rice and Cook, Houston, 1946-53; pvt. practice law Houston, 1953-61; judge U.S. Dist. Ct. (so. dist.) Tex., 1961-78; mem. U.S. Commn. on Govt. Security, Washington, 1956-58; mem. com. on inter-circuit assignments of judges U.S. Jud. Conf. Author: Shut-in Gas Well Payments, 1961. Bd. dirs. Camp Fire Girls; mem. bd. devel. Sam Rayburn Found.; trustee So. Meth. U., 1966. Named Disting. Alumnus So. Meth. U. Ex-students Assn., Sch. Engring. Ex-students Assn., Sch. of Law Ex-students Assn., 1986. Mem. ABA, SAR, Tex. Bar Assn., Houston Bar Assn., Dallas County Heritage Soc., Galveston Boat Club (Tex.), Houston Country Club, Forum Club, Idlewild and Tojas Club, Terpsichorean Club, Dallas Club. Democrat. Methodist. Died Aug. 15, 1997.

NOGUCHI, TERUO, oil company executive; b. Tokyo, Nov. 5, 1917; s. Eizaburo and Yae (Minakami) N.; m. Michiko Kohama, Oct. 20, 1948; children: Hideo, Yasuo. BSc, Osaka U., 1941, DSc, 1958, postgrad. Pa. State U., 1952-53. With Koa Oil Co., Ltd., Tokyo, 1944—, dir., 1961-64, mng. dir., 1964-67, chief mng. dir., 1967-73, pres., 1973-91, chmn., chief exec. officer, 1991-94, honorary chmn. dir., 1994—. chmn. Rsch. Assn. Residual Oil Processing, 1979—; chmn., pres. Rsch. Assn. Petroleum Devel. Alternatives, 1980—; pres. Japan Cooperation Ctr. Petroleum Industry Devel., 1981-92; chmn. Rsch. Assn. Utilization Light Oil, 1983—; dir. Mitsui Petrochem. Industries. Decorated Order of Blue Ribbon (Japan), Order of Rising Sun, Gold Rays with Neck Ribbon, Mainichi Sci. Bounty award Mainichi Shimbun, 1954. Mem. Keidanren, Japan Petroleum Inst. (hon.), Rotary. Deceased.

NOKES, MARY TRIPLETT, former university president, counselor, artist; b. Weatherford, Okla., Sept. 6, 1920; d. Ernest Carlton and Eva Hannah (Claridge) Triplett; m. George Willis Malcom Nokes, July 11, 1937; 1 child, William Careton. BA, Cen. State U., 1943; Masters Degree, U. Okla., 1949, Doctors Degree, 1969. Tchr., sec. Okla. Edn. Assn., Oklahoma City, 1943-83; advisor Nat. Honor Soc., Oklahoma City, 1955-83; 1st v.p. Internat. Porcelain Artist, 1966-68, pres., 1968-70, sec. bd., 1979-92; pres. Okla. State U., 1975-91; ret., 1991; legis. rep. for Okla. Edn. Assn., 1979-92; presenter seminars on china painting, 1991-97. Sponsor Student Coun., 1955-83; pres. Okla. State China Painting Tchr., 1986-87; dir. Vacation Bible Sch., 1984-95, 96—; pres. Sooner Club, 1995-96, Sooner Art Club, 1996—. Named Vol. Woman of Yr. Salvation Army, Okla., 1992-93, Woman of Yr. Salvation Army, 1995-96, Personality of South, 1994-95, Cmty. Leader for Noteworthy Ams., 1994-95, Cmty. Leader Oklahoma City, 1994-95; recipient proclamation Mayor Oklahoma City, 1994-95, 95-96, named Amb. of Good Will by Governor of Okla. Mem. Internat. Porcelain Art Tchrs. (past v.p., past pres., regional chmn., sec. to internat. bd. dirs.), Intercontinental Biographical Assn., C. of C. (sec.), Les Lefeyetts Home Club (pres. 1941-43), Garden Club (pres.), Sooner Art Club (pres. 1991-97), Kermac Art Club, Alpha Phi Sigma, Kappa Delta Phi, Kappa Kappa Iota. Baptist. Died July 29, 1997.

NOLTE, WALTER EDUARD, retired retirement home executive, foundation counsel, former banker; b. Joplin, Mo., Oct. 28, 1911; s. Ernest Henry and Clara (Meyer) N.; m. Sara Elizabeth Mumford, Oct. 6, 1939 (dec. May 1990); children: Walter Eduard, Craig R. (dec.). AB, U. Nebr., 1934, JD, 1936. Bar: Nebr. 1936, Tex. 1952, U.S. Supreme Ct 1952. With firm Beghtol, Foe & Rankin, Lincoln, Nebr., 1936-48; asst. atty. gen. Neb., 1948-50; dep. atty. gen., 1950-52; pres. Nolte Nat. Bank, Seguin, Tex., 1952-59; v.p. 1st Nat. Bank & Trust Co., Lincoln, 1959-60; exec. v.p. 1st Nat. Bank & Trust Co., 1960-76; pres. Gateway Manor, Inc., 1976-89; dir. Am. Combined Life Ins. Co., Chgo. Co-editor: Nebraska Restatement of Trusts, 1941. Pres. Lincoln Better Bus. Bur., 1964-65; Past pres. Lincoln Gen. Hosp. and Lincoln Hosp. Assn.; gen. chmn. Lincoln United Fund, 1973-74; bd. dirs. Lincoln Symphony Assn.; pres. Tb Assn., 1970. Served to lt. comdr. USNR, 1943-45. Mem. Nebr. Bar Assn., State Bar Tex., Lincoln C. of C. (pres. 1967-68), Nebr. Assn. Commerce and Industry (pres. 1975-76), Lincoln U. Club, Ak-Sar-Ben Club, Lincoln Country Club, Beta Theta Pi, Phi Delta Phi. Republican. Episcopalian. Died Sept. 6, 1996.

NOOJIN, RAY OSCAR, JR., lawyer; b. Durham, N.C., Apr. 26, 1945; s. Ray O. and Martha (Gunning) N.; m. Janice Skinner, May 25, 1966; children: Catherine, Allison, Ronnie. BS, U. Ala., 1967, JD, 1970. Bar: Ala. 1970, U.S. Dist. Ct. (11th cir.) 1970. Assoc. Sadler, Sadler, Sullivan & Sharp, Birmingham, Ala., 1970-73; ptnr. Hardin, Stuart, Moncus & Noojin, Birmingham, 1973-76, Noojin, Haley & Ashford, Birmingham, 1976-79; ptnr. Hare, Wynn, Newell & Newton, Birmingham, 1979—, mng. ptnr., 1985—. Mem. Am. Judicature Soc., ATLA, Ala. Trial Lawyers Assn. (bd. govs. 1980-89, exec. com. 1989—), Ala. Bar Assn. (chmn. task force on legal svcs. to poor 1986—), Birmingham Bar Assn. (exec. com. 1986-91, pres. 1992), U. Ala. Alumni Assn. (pres. Jeff County chpt. 1976, nat. exec. com. 1988-89), Rotary. Avocations: racquetball, jogging, tennis, golf. Died June 17, 1996.

NOREN, RICHARD CARL, superior court judge; b. Putnam, Conn., Oct. 25, 1941; s. Charles William and Millicent Eula (Dodge) N. AB, Harvard U., 1963; JD, George Washington U., 1966. Bar: Conn. 1966, D.C. 1967, U.S. Ct. Mil. Appeals 1973, U.S. Dist. Ct. Conn. 1980. Chief clk. Windham Jud. Dist., Putnam, 1971-80; judge Conn. Superior Ct., Putnam, 1980--. Trustee Woodstock Acad., Ea. States Expn.; chmn. Bradford-Marcy Cemetery Com.; bd. dirs., past v.p. Opera New Eng. Northeastern Conn., Inc. With USN, 1967-71. Mem. ABA, Windham County Bar Assn., Am. Judicature Soc., Antiquarian and Landmarks Soc., Woodstock Agrl. Soc., Naval Res. Assn., Navy and Marine Corps Res. Lawyers Assn., Smithsonian Assocs., Nature Conservancy, Am. Mus. Natural History, Nat. Audubon Soc., Res. Officers Assn., Soc. for Preservation New Eng. Antiquities, Navy League U.S., George Washington U. Law Assn., Nat. Trust for Historic Preservation, Wadsworth Atheneum, Mass. Hort. Soc., Conn. Mus. Natural History, Windham Textile and History Mus., Conn. Hist. Soc., Navy Inst., Les Amis du Vin, Officers Club Conn., Harvard-Radcliffe Club No. Conn., Harvard Club (Boston). Democrat.

NORMAN, EDWARD COBB, psychiatrist, educator; b. Prince George, B.C., Can., Oct. 5, 1913; s. Arthur J. and Lilla E. (Cobb) N.; m. June Marie Morris, Sept. 24, 1949; children: Donald, Cornelia, Sharon. BS, U. Wash., 1935; MD, U. Pa., 1940; MPH, Tulane U., 1965. Intern, Phila. Gen. Hosp., 1940-42; resident, Pa. Hosp., 1942-43; resident Michael Reese Hosp., 1946-49; asst. surgeon, USPHS, 1943-46; pvt. practice psychiatry, Chgo., 1949-53, New Orleans, 1953—; clin. instr. psychiatry U. Ill., Chgo., 1949-53; asst. prof. clin. psychiatry Tulane U., New Orleans, 1953-60, assoc. prof., 1960-64, prof., 1964-79; emeritus, 1979-96; dir. community mental health sect. Tulane U. Sch. Pub. Health Tropical medicine, 1967-79; assoc. dir. Pain Rehab. Unit Hotel Dieu Hosp., 1978—; adminstr. Learning Procedures, Inc., New Orleans, 977-78, v.p., 1978-96; cons. to govt. agys. Fellow APHA, Am. Psychiat. Assn. (life), Am. Acad. Psychoanalysis; mem. N.Y. Acad. Scis., Forum for Improvement of Quality of Life (sec.), Delta Omega (pres. Eta chpt.). Contbr. numerous articles to profl. jours. Died Dec. 18, 1996.

NORMAN, RICHARD ARTHUR, humanities educator; b. Columbus, Ohio, July 11, 1915; s. Norman Oscar and Marie (Falter) Kuhnheim. BA, George Washington U., 1951; MA, Columbia U., 1952, PhD, 1957. Instr. Columbia U., N.Y.C., 1952-57; asst. prof. English Barnard Coll., 1957-64, asso. prof., 1964-72, prof., 1972-81, spl. lectr., 1981-85, prof. emeritus, 1985—; instr. grad. div. Hunter Coll., 1960-62; Speech cons. CBS News, 1971-85; reader Talking Books Am. Found. for Blind, 1973-80. Radio announcer, producer, actor, 1934-50; commentator for chamber music concerts broadcast, from Library of Congress, Washington, 1948-50; Author: (with George W. Hibbitt) A Guide to Speech Training, 1964; radio series The Wonder of Words, 1962. Vice pres. Axe-Houghton Found., now emeritus. Served to capt. USAAF, 1942-45. Died July 25, 1997.

NORTHROP, STUART JOHNSTON, manufacturing company executive; b. New Haven, Oct. 22, 1925; s. Filmer Stuart Cuchow and Christine (Johnston) N.; divorced; children: Christine Daniell, Richard Rockwell Stafford; m. Judith S. Northrop. BA in Physics, Yale U., 1948. Indsl. engr. U.S. Rubber Co., Naugatuck, Conn., 1948-51; head indsl. engring. dept. Am. Cyanamid Co., Wallingford, Conn., 1951-54; mfg. mgr. Linear, Inc., Phila., 1954-57; mgr. quality control and mfg. Westinghouse Electric Co., Pitts., 1957-58; mfg. supt. SKF Industries, Phila., 1958-61; v.p. mfg. Am

Meter Co., Phila., 1961-69; founder, v.p., gen. mgr. water resources div. Singer Co., Phila.; pres., dir. Buffalo Meter Co., Four Layne Cos.; dir. Gen. Filter Co., 1969-72; chmn., CEO Huffy Corp., Dayton, Ohio, 1972-85, chmn. exec. com., 1985-94; bd. dirs. Union Corp., N.Y.C., DSLT, Inc., St. Clair, Mich., Elbit Sys. Am., Ft. Worth. County fin. chmn. George Bush Presdl. campaign, 1980; presdl. appointee Pres.'s Commn. on Ams. Outdoors, 1985-86; chmn. nat. hwy. safety adv. com. Dept. Transp., 1986—; founder, dir. emeritus Recreation Roundtable, Washington. Served with USAAF, 1944-45. Named Chief Exec. Officer of Yr. for leisure industry Wall Street Transcript, 1980. Mem. Del. Valley Investors (past pres.), Interlocutors, Elihu, Am. Bus. Conf. (founding), Fin. Commn. of Funds Am. Future, Boulders Club (Scottsdale), KOA Soc., Delta Kappa Epsilon. Died Sept. 15, 1997.

NOSHPITZ, JOSEPH DOVE, child and adolescent psychiatrist; b. N.Y.C., Aug. 31, 1922; s. Israel Abraham and Sarah (Stolar) N.; m. Charlotte S., Sept. 20, 1956; 1 child, Claude A.S. BA, U. Louisville, 1943, MD, 1945. Diplomate: Am. Bd. Psychiatry and Neurology (psychiatry and child psychiatry). Intern, Morrisania City Hosp., Bronx, N.Y., 1945-46; resident in psychiatry Winter VA Hosp., Topeka, 1948-51; resident in child psychiatry Menninger Found., 1952-54; chief children's service Topeka State Hosp., 1951-56; chief children's unit, child research br. NIMH, 1956-60; mem. faculty dept. psychiatry George Washington U. Sch. Medicine, 1971-77, prof., 1977-88, clin. prof., 1988—; sr. attending staff psychiatrist Children's Hosp. Nat. Med. Center, Washington, 1976-89; dir. psychiatry Crittenton Barrett Program, Washington, 1977-82; cons. in child psychiatry Area B Community Mental Health Center, 1973-82; bd. dirs. Joint Commn. on the Mental Health of Children, 1966-69; mem. Task Force on Financing, Pres.'s Commn. on Mental Health, 1978-79. Editor-in-chief: Basic Handbook of Child Psychiatry, 5 vols., 1979. Psychiatrist-in-chief Am. Health Group Inc., 1989-93. Capt. M.C., AUS, 1943-45, 46-47. Fellow Am. Orthopsychiat. Assn. (life), Am. Acad. Child Psychiatry (life, past pres.); mem. Am. Assn. Children's Residential Ctrs. (life, past pres.), Am. Psychiat. Assn. (life), Group for Advancement of Psychiatry (corr.), Internat. Soc. for Adolescent Psychiatry, Am. Psychoanalytic Assn. Died Jan. 28, 1997.

NOTHMANN, GERHARD ADOLF, engineering executive, research engineer; b. Berlin, Germany, Dec. 9, 1921; came to U.S., 1939, naturalized, 1944; s. Rudolf and Margarete (Caro) N.; m. Charlotte Braude, June 21, 1943; children—Joyce Anne, Ruth Ellen, Barbara Fay. B.S. in Mech. Engring, Purdue U., 1942, M.S. in Mech. Engring, 1942; Ph.D., Cornell U., 1948. Tchr. machine design and kinematics Cornell U., 1942-44, 46-48, instr., 1942-44, 46-48, asst. prof., 1948; engr. for design spl. bindery R. R. Donnelley & Sons, 1946-47; research engr. Armour Research Found., Ill. Inst. Tech., Chgo., 1948-59; successively asst. supr., asst. chmn., chmn., mgr. dept. mech. engring. research Armour Research Found., Ill. Inst. Tech., 1952-59; dir. creative and devel. engring. Miehle div. Miehle-Goss-Dexter, Inc., 1959-62, dir. research and devel., 1962-64, dir. engring., 1964-67, dir. tech. research, 1967-68; dir. engring. Robertson Photo-Mechanix, Inc., 1968-69, v.p. engring., 1969-71; chief engr. duplicators Addressograph Multigraph Corp., 1971-77; dir. engring. Visual Graphics Corp., Tamarac, Fla., 1977-79; prin. engr. Xerox Corp., Pasadena, Calif., 1979-89, ret., 1989; chmn. mechanics colloquim Ill. Inst. Tech., 1953-54; mem. adv. com. Graphic Arts Tech. Found. Author: Nonimpact Printing, 1989. Pres. bd. dirs. Wilmette United Fund, 1963; mem. Wilmette Sch. Bd., 1968-74; pres. Pasadena Jewish Temple and Ctr., 1989-91. With USNR, 1944-46. Named one of six outstanding young men in Chgo. area. Chgo. Jr. Assn. Commerce and Industry, 1954. Mem. ASME, Am. Soc. Engring. Edn., Tech. Assn. for Graphic Arts, Jewish Geneal. Soc. of L.A., Sigma Xi, Tau Beta Pi, Pi Tau Sigma. Home: Buffalo Grove Ill. Died July 3, 1996.

NOTHMANN, RUDOLF S., legal researcher; b. Hamburg, Fed. Republic of Germany, Feb. 4, 1907; came to U.S., 1941, naturalized, 1943; s. Nathan and Henrietta G. (Heymann) N. Referendar, U. Hamburg, 1929, PhD in Law, 1932; postgrad. U. Liverpool Law Sch. (Eng.), 1931-32. Law clk. Hamburg Cts., 1929-31, 32-33; export, legal adviser, adviser ocean marine ins. various firms, Ger., Eng., Sweden, Calif., 1933-43, 46-47; instr. fgn. exchange, fgn. trade Extension div. UCLA, 1947-48, vis. assoc. prof. UCLA, 1951; asst. prof. econs. Whittier Coll., 1948-50, assoc. prof., 1950-51; contract work U.S. Air Force, U.S. Navy, 1953-59; contract negotiator space projects, space and missile systems orgn. USAF, L.A., 1959-77; pvt. researcher in internat. comml. law, Pacific Palisades, Calif., 1977—. With U.S. Army, 1943-45; ETO. Recipient Gold Tape award Air Force Systems Command, 1970. Mem. Internat. Bar Assn. (vice chmn. internat. sales and related comml. trans. com. 1977-82), Am. Econ. Assn., Calif. Bar Assn. (internat. law sect.), Am. Soc. Internat. Law, Uebersee Club (Hamburg, Germany). Author: The Insurance Certificate in International Ocean Marine Insurance Law and Foreign Trade, 1932; The Oldest Corporation in the World: Six Hundred Years of Economic Evolution, 1949. Died Aug. 25, 1997.

NOTTBERG, HENRY, III, construction company executive; b. Kansas City, Mo., Feb. 11, 1949; s. Henry Jr. and Barbara (Bodwell) N.; m. Linda Kay Freeman, June 20, 1971; children: H. Tyler, Jamie Blair. BA in Politics, Washington & Lee U., 1971. Sec.-treas. U.S. Engring. Co., Kansas City, 1971-78, exec. v.p., 1978-82, pres., 1982—; bd. dirs. United Mo. Bank, Kansas City, Dodson Ins. Co., Kansas City. Trustee Research Med. Ctr., Kansas City, 1979—, vice chmn. bd. trustees, 1987—; trustee Pembroke Hill Sch., Kansas City, 1983—, Univ. Kansas City, 1986—; alumni bd. trustees Washington & Lee U., Lexington, Va., 1981-84. DIED 02/03/97. .

NOWAK, LIONEL HENRY, music educator; b. Cleve., Sept. 25, 1911; s. Henry Frederic Nowak and Mascha Sofia (Argelander) Brooks; m. Isabelle Wood, (div. 1945); children: Lionel Augustus, Karen Marie; m. Laura Walton Taylor, May 21, 1945; children: Laura A., Alison Ann, Robert Henry. MusB, Cleve. Inst. Music, 1933, MusM, 1936, MusD, 1988. Music dir. Fenn Coll., Cleve., 1932-38; pianist and composer Humphrey-Weidman Dance Co., N.Y.C., 1938-42; assoc. prof. Converse Coll., Spartanburg, S.C., 1942-46; prof. music Syracuse (N.Y.) U., 1946-48; music prof. Bennington (Vt.) U., 1948-93; condr. Spartanburg Symphony Orch., 1942-45; dir. summer sch. for High Sch. Music Tchrs., Bennington, 1961-63; cons. Manhattanville Curriculum Project, U.S. Office of Edn., 1965-72, Vt. Coun. on the Arts, Montpelier, 1972-74; piano recitalist Assn. of Am. Colls., N.Y.C., 1945-63; visiting music prof. Union Coll., Schenectady, N.Y. 1969-70. Composer Square Dance, 1939, Mexican Dances, 1939, On My Mother's Side, 1940, Flickers, 1941, House Divided, 1945, Story of Mankind, 1947. Fellow Vt. Acad. Arts and Scis. (pres. 1974-76); mem. Am. Composers Alliance, Fed. Musician's Union. Republican. Avocations: poker, horseshoes. Office: Bennington Coll Bennington VT 05201

NOWAK, TADEUSZ, author; b. Sikorzyce, Poland, Nov. 11, 1930; s. Josef and Honorata (Mikkowska) N.; m. Zofia Iwanska, Apr. 27, 1971. Grad. Polish philology, Jagiellonian U., 1954. Author over 20 books of poems and novels. Decorated knight Cross Polonia Restituta Order; recipient Wladystaw Broniewski award, 1964, Stanislaw Pietak award, 1966, City of Krakow award, 1966, Minister of Culture and Art award, 1971, State Prize 2d class, 1974, Koscielscy award, 1967. Died Oct. 8, 1991.

NOYES, RICHARD MACY, physical chemist, educator; b. Champaign, Ill., Apr. 6, 1919; s. William Albert and Katharine Haworth (Macy) N.; m. Winninette Arnold, July 12, 1946 (dec. Mar. 1972); m. Patricia Jean Harris, Jan. 26, 1973 (dec. Nov. 1997). A.B. summa cum laude, Harvard U., 1939; Ph.D., Calif. Inst. Tech., 1942. Research assoc. rocket propellants Calif. Inst. Tech., 1942-46; mem. faculty Columbia U., 1946-58, assoc. prof., 1954-58; Guggenheim fellow, vis. prof. U. Leeds, Eng., 1955-56; prof. chemistry U. Oreg., 1958—, head dept., 1963-68, 75-78, ret., 1984—. Editorial adv. com.: Chem. Revs, 1967-69; editorial adv. com.: Jour. Phys. Chemistry, 1973-80; assoc. editor: Internat. Jour. Chem. Kinetics, 1972-82, Jour. Phys. Chemistry, 1980-82; Contbr. to profl. jours. Fulbright fellow; Victoria U. Wellington, New Zealand, 1964; NSF sr. postdoctoral fellow Max Planck Inst. für Physikalische Chemie, Göttingen, Fed. Republic Germany, 1965; sr. Am. scientist awardee Alexander von Humboldt Found., 1978-79. Fellow Am. Phys. Soc.; mem. NAS, Am. Acad. Arts and Scis., Am. Chem. Soc. (chmn. div. phys. chemistry 1961-62, exec. com. div. 1960-75, mem. coun. 1960-75, chmn. Oreg. sect. 1967-68, com. on nominations and elections 1962-68, com. on publs. 1969-72), Chem. Soc. (London), Wilderness Soc., ACLU, Hungarian Acad. Scis. (hon.), Sierra Club (past chmn. Atlantic and Pacific N.W. chpts., N.W. regional v.p. 1973-74), Phi Beta Kappa, Sigma Xi. Achievements include research mechanisms chemical reactions, developing general theories, intrepretation physical properties chemicals. Died Nov. 25, 1997.

NOZOE, TETSUO, organic chemist, research consultant; b. Sendai, Japan, May 16, 1902; s. Juichi Kinoshita and Toyoko Nozoe; m. Kyoko Horiuchi, Nov. 2, 1927; children: Takako Masamune, Shigeo Nozoe, Yoko Ishikura, Yuriko Higashihara. BS in Chemistry, Tohoku Imperial U., 1926; DSc in Chemistry, Osaka Imperial U., 1936. Asst. prof. Taihoku Imperial U., 1929-37, prof., 1937-45; prof. Nat. Tawian U., Taipei, 1945-48; prof. Tohoku U., Sendai, Japan, 1948-66, prof. emeritus, 1966—; rsch. cons. Kao Corp., Tokyo, 1966—, Takasago Perfumery Co., Tokyo, 1966—, Sankyo (pharm.) Co., Tokyo, 1966—; mem. Found. IUPAC Symposium in Chemistry Nonbenzenoid Aromatic Compounds, 1970—. Author: Nonbenzenoid Aromatic Compounds, 1960, Tamkang Chair Lecture, 1991, American Chemical Society Autobiography (Seventy Years in Organic Chemistry), 1991; editor: Topics in Nonbenzenoid Aromatic Chem. (2 vols.) 1972, Organic Chemistry (2 vols.) 1970; contbr. article to profl. jours. Named hon. citizen Sendai City, 1959, Taipei City, 1982; recipient Majima award Chem. Soc. Japan, 1944, Asahi Cultural award Asahi Newspaper, 1952, Order of Cultural Merit Japanese Govt., 1958, Von Hofman Meml. medal German Chem. Soc., 1981, Grand Prize Soc. Synthetic Org. Chem. Japan, 1984. Mem. AAAS, Royal Swedish Acad. Scis. (fgn. mem.), Japan Acad. (award 1953), N.Y. Acad. Scis., Chinese Chem. Soc. Taiwan, Swiss Chem. Soc.; hon. mem. Chem. Soc. Japan, Japan Soc. Bioscience, Biotechnology, and Agrochemistry, Pharm. Soc. Japan, Soc. Synthetic Organic Chemistry. Achievements include discovery of hinokitiol, having 7-membered aromatic system, structural elucidation of hederagenin and oleanol, novel constituents of wool wax, establishment of a wide area of nonbenzenoid aromatic chemistry, synthesis of representative troponoid compounds, one-pot syntheses of various azulene derivatives, of azulenequinones, of tropocoronands, others. Died Apr. 4, 1996.

NYRO, LAURA, singer, songwriter; b. Bronx, N.Y., Oct. 18, 1947. Ind. singer, songwriter, rec. artist, 1967-97. Composer: And When I Die, Stoney End, Eli's Coming, Stoned Soul Picnic, Lonely Women, December's Boudoir, I Am the Blues, numerous other songs; albums include First Songs, Eli and the Thirteenth Confession, New York Tendaberry, Christmas and the Beads of Sweat, Gonna Take a Miracle, Smile, Seasons of Light, Nested, Mother's Spiritual. Died April 9, 1997.

NYSTROM, HAROLD CHARLES, lawyer, labor consultant; b. White, S.D., Apr. 6, 1906; s. Charles Alfred and Augusta Cornelia (Olson) N.; m. Ruth Greenwood, Sept. 30, 1931 (dec. Jan. 1974); children: Nancy Ann Nystrom Railton, Erik Linfred; m. Martha Ann Harper Pattison, Oct. 13, 1980. Student, S.D. State Sch. Mines and Tech., 1922-23; AB cum laude, U. S.D., 1926; JD with honors, George Washington U., 1931. Bar: S.D. 1931, U.S. Supreme Ct. 1947. Asst. reading room Library of Congress, Washington, 1927-31; ptnr. Nystrom & Nystrom, Rapid City, S.D., 1931-35; editor Am. Jurisprudence Lawyers Coop. Pub. Co., Rochester, N.Y., 1935-41; br. and sect. chief, acting asst. solicitor for legis. and gen. legal services, asst. solicitor U.S. Dept. Labor, Washington, 1941-58, dep. solicitor, 1958-59, acting solicitor, 1959-61, dep. solicitor, 1961-62, assoc. solicitor, 1962-74; pvt. practice, cons. fed. labor standards Bethesda and Rockville, Md., 1975-95; lectr. Labor Law Inst., Southwestern Legal Found., Dallas, 1960, Banking Law Inst., N.Y.C., 1967; speaker sect. labor law Assn. Bar City N.Y., 1967, Labor Relations Inst., Atlanta Lawyers Found., 1969, 73. Contbr. articles to legal publs. Atty. City of New Underwood, S.D., 1934; sec.-treas. Citizen's Com., Oakmont, Md., 1950-59; bd. dirs. Fenwick Island (Del.) Soc. Homeowners, 1974-75; deacon local Presbyn. Ch. Recipient cert. of appreciation Employment Standards Adminstrn., 1975. Mem. ABA (vice chmn. agy. liaison com. adminstrv. law sect. 1960-73), Fed. Bar Assn. (speaker BNA Labor Law briefing conf. 1967), Tenn. Bar Assn. (hon. life mem. labor law sect.), S.D. State Bar (50 Yr. award 1981), Old Georgetown Road Citizens Assn. (exec. bd. 1958-60), Phi Beta Kappa, Phi Alpha Delta. Home: Rockville Md. Died Nov. 11, 1995; interred Parklawn Cemetery, Rockville, MD.

O'BENAR, JOHN DEMARION, research neurophysiologist; b. Chgo., Apr. 10, 1943; s. Jack Jay and Geraldine Agnes (Light) O'B.; m. Mary Caroline Teal, June 18, 1970. BA, Cornell Coll., 1964; MS, U. Ill., 1968, PhD, 1971; postdoctoral study, U. Calif., Berkeley, 1972; postgrad., U. Wis., 1973. Surg. rsch. tech. Billings Hosp. U. Chgo., 1958-61; teaching asst. U. Ill., Urbana, 1968-69; rsch. physiologist Naval Weapons Ctr., Crane, Ind., 1972-75, Naval Aerospace Med. Rsch. Lab., Pensacola, Fla., 1975-78; analytical chemist Army Aviation Ctr., Ft. Rucker, Ala., 1978-80; rsch. physiologist Letterman Army Inst. Rsch., San Francisco, 1980-93, Inst. Surg. Rsch., San Antonio, 1993—; railroad lighting cons. U.S. Dept. Transp., Washington, 1973-74; battlefield target acquisition cons. U.S. Dept. Navy, Washington, 1972-74, cons. Project Sanguine, 1976-78; contracting officers rep. Army Med. R&D Command, 1983-93. Author: Advances in Blood Substitute Research, 1983; contbr. chpts. to books and articles to profl. jours. Co-founder Innerarity Inst., Pensacola, 1976. Fellow NIH, 1967-71, Nat. Eye Inst., 1971-72, Marine Biol. Lab., 1967-68. Mem. Am. Physiol. Soc., Shock Soc., Phi Sigma. Achievements include research in new solutions for shock resuscitation and blood substitutes, mechanisms for information processing in central nervous system. Home: San Antonio Tex. Died March 5, 1997.

OBENHAUS, VICTOR, theology educator, clergyman; b. Superior, Wis., Sept. 26, 1903; s. Herman and Grace (Dexter) O.; m. Marion Pendleton, July 30, 1938; children: Constance, Helen, Mark. A.B., Oberlin Coll., 1925; B.D., Union Theol. Sem., N.Y.C., 1929; Ed.D., Columbia U., 1940; D.D., Chgo. Theol. Sem., 1973. Ordained to ministry Congl. Christian Ch., 1929; asst. Ch. of Covenant Cleve., 1929-36; mem. ministerial staff Riverside Ch., N.Y.C., 1936-38; prin. Pleasant Hill Acad., Tenn., 1938-44; mem. federated theol. faculty Chgo. Theol. Sem., U. Chgo., 1944-94, assoc. prof. ch. in agrl. and indsl. life, 1948-61; prof. Christian Ethics Chgo. Theol. Sem., 1961-73, acting pres., 1973-74; cons. com. on theol. edn. United Ch. Christ, exec. Med Am. sems., 1974-94; bd. dirs. Kobe Coll. Corp., Japan; bd. dirs., co-founder Agropolitan Ministries; chmn. Ill. Prisons and Jails Project. Author: Hebrew Prophets and America's Conscience, 1948, The Responsible Christian, 1957, Church and Faith in Mid-America,

1963; Co-author: Religion in American Culture, 1964, Ethics for An Industrial Age, 1965; Editor: The Church in Our World, 1965, And See The People, 1968, Religion and Ethical Issues, 1991, (with others) Suburban Religion, 1974. Mem. Am., Rural sociol. socs., Religious Research Assn., Soc. for Sci. Study Religion, Ams. for Moral Integrity (chmn., pub. study guide Religion and Ethical Issues 1991), Chgo. Com. To Defend Bill of Rights (co-chmn., Civil Libertarian of Yr. 1979), Am. Soc. Christian Ethics (pres. 1966-67). Home: Chicago Ill. Died Apr. 2, 1994.

O'BRIEN, FRANCIS JOSEPH, lawyer; b. Bklyn., Mar. 25, 1926; s. Francis Casimir and Marjorie (MacKell) O'B.; m. Ellin Carley Amorosi, Feb. 4, 1956; children—Francis, Paul, Matthew, Christopher. B.S., Holy Cross Coll., 1947; LL.B., Fordham U., 1950. Bar: N.Y. 1950, U.S. Dist. Ct. (cen., so. and ea. dists.) N.Y. 1950, U.S. Ct. Appeals (2d cir.) 1951, U.S. Supreme Ct. 1960. Ptnr. Hill Rivkins, Carey, Loesberg, O'Brien & Mulroy, N.Y.C., 1972—; lectr. admiralty Tulane U., Practising Law Inst., ABA; chmn. U.S. del. Comité Maritime Internat. to Rio de Janeiro Charter Party (Laytime) Definitions. Mem. ABA (internat. sect. del. People's Republic of China 1978), Comite Maritime Internat., Assn. Average Adjusters, Maritime Law Assn. (sec., 1st and 2d v.p., chmn. maritime arbitration. pres. 1986—). Assoc. editor Am. Maritime Cases. Died April 1, 1997.

O'BRIEN, ROBERT, company executive. CEO RJ O'Brien & Assocs.

O'BRIEN, ROBERT STEPHEN COX, lawyer; b. Westmount, Que., Can., Oct. 21, 1929. B.A., McGill U., 1951, B.C.L., 1953. Bar: Que. 1954, named Queen's Counsel 1972. Ptnr. Lavery, deBilly, Montreal. Mem. Montreal Bar (treas. 1976-77), Que. Bar, Canadian Bar Assn.

O'CONNOR, DONALD J., environmental engineer, educator, consultant; b. N.Y.C., Nov. 7, 1922; s. William J. and Helen G. O'C.; m. Anita Jane Lordi, Oct. 30, 1948; children—Dennis, Arlene, Jeanette. B.C.E., Manhattan Coll., 1944; M.C.E., Poly. Tech. Bklyn., 1947; Engring. Sc.D., NYU, 1956. Registered profl. engr. N.Y. Engr. Parsons, Brinckerhoff, N.Y.C., 1948-51; asst. prof. to prof. dept. environ. engring. Manhattan Coll., Bronx, N.Y., 1951—; co-founder, ptnr. Hydroscience, Westwood, N.J., 1962-70, prin. cons., 1970-80; prin. HydroQual, Inc., Mahwah, N.J., 1980—; dir. Summer Inst. on Water Pollution, Manhattan Coll.; condr., supr. research projects EPA, NSF, NOAA, U.S. Army Corps. Engrs.; mem. sci. adv. bd. EPA, NEC, NSF; bd. dirs. Water and Sci. Tech., NRC, 1989; nat. and internat. lectr. in field. Author: Biological Waste Treatment, 1960; contbr. more than 100 papers to sci. and engring. jours. Treas., Glen Rock Race and Human Relations Com., N.J. Served to staff sgt. U.S. Army, 1944-46; ETO. Recipient Rudolf Hering award ASCE, 1959, 66, 84, 89. Mem. Nat. Acad. Engring. Died April 18, 1997.

O'CONNOR, JAMES JOSEPH, pathologist, educator; b. Blakely, Pa., Oct. 23, 1924; s. James J. and Mae G. (Kennedy) O'C.; m. Margaret Louise Terrill, Feb. 26, 1952; children: Patricia, Maureen, Karen, Susan, Erin, James III, Jeffrey, Ellen. Student, U. Scranton, 1942-44; MD, Jefferson Med. Coll., 1948. Bd. cert. Am. Bd. Pathology. Intern, pathology resident St. Francis Gen. Hosp., Pitts., 1948-52; resident pathology Med. Coll. Va., Richmond, 1954-55; dir. labs. Scranton (Pa.) State Gen. Hosp., 1955-61; chmn. dept. pathology Mercy Hosp., Scranton, 1958-95; founder, pres. Pathology Assocs. of N.E. Pa. Ltd. and Clin. Labs., Scranton, 1958-95; clin. assoc. prof. pathology Temple U. Sch. Medicine, Phila., 1988-95; dir., sec. Pioneer Am. Bank, Carbondale, Pa., 1961-95. Pres. Lacka Cancer Soc., Scranton, 1964-66; dir. Lacka Red Cross, Scranton, 1976-80, N.E. Philharm., Scranton and Wilkes-Barre, 1988-95. Capt. USAF, 1952-54. Fellow Am. Soc. Clin. Pathologists, Coll. Am. Pathology; mem. AMA, Pa. Assn. Pathologists (exec. com. 1986-92), Lacka County Med. Soc., County Club Scranton. Republican. Roman Catholic. Avocations: golf, music. Home: Clarks Summit Pa. Died Mar. 2, 1995.

O'CONNOR, JOHN CHRISTOPHER, JR., consulting petroleum engineer; b. New Orleans, Feb. 13, 1920; s. John Christopher and Adelaide Pauline (Estopinal) O'C.; m. Olivia Hortense Cazayoux, Dec. 27, 1944; children: Maureen Judith, Karen Inez, Rebecca Frances, Denise Olivia. BS in Petroleum Engring., La. State U., 1941. Registered petroleum engr., La., Tex. Petroleum engr. The Calif. Co., La., Gulf of Mex., Okla., Colo., Wyo. and Utah, 1946-56; v.p. ops. Continental Shelf Drilling Corp., New Orleans, 1956-59; consulting petroleum engr. New Orleans, 1959—. Eucharistic min. St. Edward the Confessor Cath. Ch.; mem. U.S. Com. for Battle of Normandy Mus. With Corps Engrs., U.S. Army, 1941-46, CBI and ETO. Mem. NSPE, Soc. Petroleum Engrs., Am. Petroleum Inst., Am. Assn. Drilling Engrs., La. Engring. Soc., Knights of Columbus, Holy Name Soc., Equestrian Order of Holy Sepulchre of Jerusalem (Knight of Holy Sepulchre), Sovereign Mil. Order of Malta (Knight of Order of Malta), St. Vincent de Paul Soc., China-Burma-India Vets. Assn., Burma Star Assn., Am. Legion, Ret. Officers Assn., Serra Club New Orleans, Petroleum Club New Orleans, Plimsoll Club, Internat. House Club. Republican. Died Feb. 24, 1996.

O'CONNOR, LAWRENCE JOSEPH, JR., energy consultant; b. Tulsa, Dec. 29, 1914; s. Lawrence Joseph and Bess (Yarbrough) O'C. Student, Tulsa U., 1932-33; A.B., Rice U., 1936; M.B.A., Harvard U., 1938. With Haskins & Sells (C.P.A.s), Houston, 1938-45; v.p., treas. Goldston Oil Corp., Houston, 1945-58; oil and gas cons. Houston, 1958-59; asst. dir. Office Oil and Gas, Dept. Interior, 1959-60, adminstr. oil import adminstrn., 1960-61; commr. Fed. Power Commn., 1961-71; v.p. Standard Oil Co. (Ohio), Washington, 1971-74; energy cons. Houston, 1975—. Roman Catholic. Clubs: Congressional Country, Houston Country. Died June 6, 1996.

ODELL, GLENDON TOWNSEND, librarian; b. Mill City, Pa., Apr. 15, 1926; s. Glendon Townsend and Mildred Nanette (Keith) O. B.A., U. Pa., 1950, M.A., 1952; M.L.S., Columbia U., 1966. Sales rep. Mirriam-Webster Co., Oberlin, Ohio, 1952-53; tchr. York Country Day Sch., Pa., 1953-55; asst. librarian U. Pa., Phila., 1955-58; librarian Amstar Corp., N.Y.C., 1958-66, Cities Service Gas Co., Cranbury, N.J., 1966-69; asst. univ. librarian Princeton U., N.J., 1969-80, assoc. univ. librarian, 1980—. Served with USN, 1944-46. Mem. Spl. Libraries Assn. Died July 28, 1997.

ODLAND, GEORGE FISHER, dermatologist; b. Mpls., Aug. 27, 1922; s. Henry O. and Alice Chipman (Fisher) O.; m. Elisabeth Ann Brierley, Sept. 25, 1945; children—Henry II, Peter B., John C. Student, Princeton U., 1940-42; MD, Harvard U., 1946. Diplomate: Am. Bd. Dermatology. Intern Mass. Gen. Hosp., Boston, 1946-47; asst. resident dermatology Mass. Gen. Hosp., 1953-54, chief resident, 1954, clin. and research fellow, 1952-53; research fellow anatomy Harvard U., 1949-51, research fellow dermatology, 1951-52, asst. in dermatology, 1952-54; clin. instr. anatomy U. Wash., Seattle, 1955-60; clin. instr. medicine U. Wash., 1956-60, clin. asst. prof. depts. anatomy and medicine, 1960-62, asst. prof. biol. structure and medicine, 1962-64, asso. prof., 1964-69, prof., 1969—, head div. dermatology, 1962-88; chmn. NIH tng. grants com., 1966-69; chmn. liaison com. ad hoc rev. com. tng. grants NIAMDD; prin. investigator spl. com. analysis of priorities and needs for research in dermatology NIH tng. grants com., 1977-80; adv. council Nat. Insts. Arthritis, Metabolic and Digestive Diseases, 1973-76; mem. med. and sci. com. Dermatology Found., 1968-71, trustee, 1979—; mem. med. adv. bd., trustee Nat. Psoriasis Found., 1972—. Contbr. articles to med. jours. Active United Way of King County, 1971—. Fellow Am. Acad. Dermatology (council govt. liaison, chmn. NIAMDD liaison subcom. 1979—); mem. Am., Pacific dermatol. assns., Pacific N.W., Seattle dermatol. socs., Soc. for Investigative Dermatology (dir. 1966-70, pres. 1978-79), Western Soc. Clin. Research, Seattle Acad. Internal Medicine, Western Assn. Physicians, N.Y. Acad. Scis., King County Med. Soc. (sec.-treas. 1971-72, jud. council 1972-74), Assn. Profs. Dermatology (dir. 1976-78, pres. 1980-82), Sigma Xi. Clubs: Seattle Tennis, University. Died Nov. 21, 1997.

O'DONNELL, JAMES FRANCIS, communications executive; b. Boston, June 15, 1941. BA, Boston Coll., 1965. Account exec. J. Walter Thompson, N.Y.C., 1969-71; pub. relations officer Dow Jones & Co. Inc., N.Y.C., 1971-77; sr. v.p. Ruder Finn & Rotman, N.Y.C., 1977-83; dir. corp. communications The Hearst Corp., N.Y.C., 1983—. Lt. U.S. Army, 1966-69, Vietnam. Mem. Sigma Delta Chi, Deadline Club. Died Aug. 16, 1997.

ODORIZZI, M. EVELYN, educator, author; b. Hurley, Wis., Aug. 17, 1909; d. John Henry and Nora Mae (Shaffer) Colenso; widowed Aug. 1977; children: Carol Rae Dillman, Linda Lee Rudolph, Terri Lynn Latshaw. BA, U. Wis., 1930; postgrad., U. Del., 1981, U. Tex. Tchr. Marquette, Mich., 1930-31; tchr. spl. edn., vol. Sunnyhill Sch., Greenwich Conn., 1956-70; spl. edn. tchr., founder Stepping Stone Sch., Naples, Fla. Author children's books. Recipient Alpha Delta Kappa award, 1981, Naples Women's Club, 1971; named Disting. Woman Fla. Mental Health Dept., Outstanding Woman of Fla., Outstanding Poet of 1994 Nat. Library of Poetry. Republican. Methodist. Avocations: children's choirs and plays. Died Jan. 27, 1996.

OEHMLER, GEORGE COURTLAND, corporate executive; b. Pitts., May 6, 1926; s. Rudolph Christian and Virgia Sylvia (Stark) O.; B.S. in Indsl. Engring, Pa. State U., 1950; m. Martha Jane Swagler, July 3, 1954; children—Wendy Lynn, Christy Ann, Geoffrey Colin. Indsl. engr. Allegheny Ludlum Steel Corp., Pitts., 1953-54, salesman, 1954-60, mgr. export sales, 1960-67, mgr. flat rolled products, 1967-68, asst. to chmn., 1968-73, v.p. internat., 1973-75, v.p. internat. Allegheny Internat., Inc., Pitts., 1975-81, v.p. public and internat. affairs, 1981-86; pres., chief operating officer World Affairs Council, Pitts., 1987-95; dir. Mathews Internat. Corp., 1982-95; Mem. exec. bd. Pa. State U. Alumni Council, 1976-82; bd. dirs. United Way Allegheny County, 1982-84, Pitts. Ballet, 1982-89, Pitts. Pub. Theater, 1986-95, Mendelssohn Choir of Pitts., 1987-95. With U.S. Army, 1944-46, 51-52. Mem. Am. Iron and Steel Inst., Assn. Iron and Steel Engrs., Machinery and Allied Products Inst. (internat. and pub. affairs councils), World Affairs Council Pitts. (chmn. 1980-82, dir.), Pitts. Council for Internat. Visitors (dir. 1975-87, pres. 1976-78), Greater Pitts. C. of C. Republican. Presbyterian. Clubs: Duquesne, Longue Vue (gov. 1982-84). Died Dec. 10, 1995.

OEHSER, PAUL HENRY, editor, writer, conservationist; b. Cherry Creek, N.Y., Mar. 27, 1904; s. Henry Christian and Agnes Theodosia (Abbey) O.; m. Grace M. Edgbert, Oct. 4, 1927; children: Gordon Vincent, Richard Edgbert. Student, U. Iowa, 1924; A.B., Greenville (Ill.) Coll., 1925; postgrad., Am. U., 1926-30. Asst. editor Bur. Biol. Survey, Dept. Agr., 1925-31; editor U.S. Nat. Mus., Smithsonian Instn., 1931-50; chief editorial and publs. div., pub. relations officer Smithsonian Instn., 1950-66, research asso., 1966—; editor sci. publs. Nat. Geog. Soc., 1966-78; mng. editor Jour. Washington Acad. Scis., 1939-59; editor Proc. 8th Am. Sci. Congress, Dept. State, 1941-43. Author: Sons of Science, the Story of the Smithsonian Institution and Its Leaders, 1949, Fifty Poems, 1954, The Smithsonian Institution, 1970; (poems and essays) The Witch of Scrapfaggot Green, 1981; The Smithsonian Institution, 1983; contbr. articles, reviews and verse to mags., jours., encys., news publs.; gen. editor: United States Ency. of History, 1967-68. Bd. dirs. Greater Washington Ednl. TV Assn., Inc., 1958-64. Fellow Washington Acad. Scis.; mem. Philos. Soc. Washington, Am. Ornithol. Union, Biol. Soc. Washington, Wilderness Soc. (mem. governing council 1964-77, hon. council 1977—, asst. treas. 1965-70, 72-76, v.p. 1976-77), History of Sci. Club (Washington), Thoreau Soc. Am. (pres. 1961), Washington Biologists' Field Club (v.p. 1962-64, pres. 1964-67), Literary Soc. of Washington (corr. sec. and treas. 1972-84). Clubs: Cosmos (Washington) (sec. 1950-69, editor Bull. 1951-69, v.p. 1973, pres. 1974), Palaver (Washington). Died Dec. 4, 1996.

OETTINGER, KATHERINE BROWNELL, social worker; b. Nyack, N.Y., Sept. 24, 1903; d. Charles Leonard and Eunice (Bennet) Brownell; m. Malcolm H. Oettinger, July 1, 1931; children—Malcolm H., John Brownell. A.B., Smith Coll., 1925, M in Social Sci., 1926, LL.D., 1957; postgrad., Marywood Coll., Pa. State U., Columbia, U. Pitts.; L.H.D. (hon.), Dickinson Coll., 1966. Social case-worker N.Y.C., 1926-30; mental health cons. Scranton, Pa., 1930-50; chief div. community services Bur. Mental Health, Pa. Dept. Welfare, 1950-54; dean Sch. Social Work, Boston U., 1954-57; chief Children's Bur., HEW, 1957-68, dep. asst. sec. for population and family planning, 1968-70; lectr., cons. population and family planning, 1970—; cons. Internat. Assn. Schs. for Social Work Edn., 1971-76; dir. adolescent studies Inter-Am. Dialogue Center, Airlie, Va., 1976-77; Sec. 1960 White House Conf. on Children and Youth; U.S. rep. to UNICEF, 1957—; vice chmn. Nat. Com. Children and Youth, 1960—; coordinator 1st Inter-Hemisphere Conf. on Adolescent Fertility, 1977; vis. prof. Sch. Social and Behavioral Scis., U. South Fla., 1981. Author: Readers Guide: Population and Family Planning: Analytical Abstracts for Social Work Educators and Related Disciplines, 1972, An Asian Prospective, 1975, Not My Daughter: Facing Up to Adolescent Pregnancy, 1979, An Oral History: A Pioneer in the Twentieth Century; Contbr. articles to profl. jours. Trustee Boston U.; mem. nat. bd. Med. Coll. Pa., 1977—. Fellow Am. Orthopsychiat. Assn.; mem. Nat. Assn. Social Workers, Nat. Conf. Social Welfare, Am. Pub. Welfare Assn., Soc. Projective Techniques, Rorschach Inst., Inc., Council Social Work Edn., Phi Beta Kappa. DIED 10/13/97. .

OFFICER, JAMES EOFF, anthropologist; b. Boulder, Colo., July 28, 1924; s. Forrest Irving and Josephine Emma (Eoff) O.; m. Roberta Mitzel, Feb. 22, 1946; children: Sarah Jean, James Robert. AB, U. Ariz., 1950, PhD, 1964. Radio announcer Kansas City, Kans. and Phoenix, 1942-45; radio announcer, writer various stas. Tucson, 1946-50; intern Dept. State, Washington, 1950-51; info. attache U.S. Embassy Dept. State, Santiago, Chile, 1951-53; radio and TV announcer, writer various stas. Tucson, 1953-60; assoc. commr. Bur. Indian Affairs, Washington, 1961-67; adminstrv. asst. to sec. Dept. Interior, Washington, 1967-69; prof. anthropology U. Ariz., Tucson, 1969-89; U.S. rep. Interam. Indian Inst., Mexico City, 1966-78; bd. dirs. Ariz./Mex. Commn., Tucson, 1976-80. Author: Hispanic Arizona, 1987 (S.W. Books award Border Regional Libr. Assn. 1988), Arizona's Hispanic Perspective, 1981, Anthropology and the American Indian, 1973; collaborator (book) The Hodges' Ruin. Active Tucson-Guadalajara Sister City Commn., 1974-80, Tucson-Pima County Hist. commn., 1989; precinct committeeman Dem. Com., Tucson, 1970-72; bd. dirs. Ariz. Hist. Soc., 1985—, Hospitality Internat. Tucson, 1971-78. Staff sgt. U.S. Army, 1945-46. Recipient Best Article on Ariz. History award Ariz. Hist. Found., Phoenix, 1988. Fellow Am. Anthrop. Assn. (program chmn. 1974), Soc. Applied Anthropology (chmn. local arrangements 1972), Pacific Coast Coun. on Latin Am. Studies (mem. bd. govs. 1987-90), Tucson Press Club (bd. dirs. 1956-59, 91—), Rotary (historian Tucson club 1978—). Avocation: writing. Died May 27, 1996.

OFFNER, HEBE ZONCHELLO, special education educator; b. Easton, Pa., Dec. 30, 1924; d. Costantino and Mercedes (Luppi) Zonchello; m. Harry G. Offner June 15, 1953; children: Lawrence, James, Kenneth. Student, Ohio State U., 1943-47; BA in French, Calif. State U., Northridge, 1970; postgrad., Calif. State U., L.A., 1974, Calif. State U., Carson, 1993. Cert. elem. tchr., spl. edn. of severely handicapped tchr., Calif. Tchr., spl. edn. tchr. Glendale (Calif.) Unified Sch. Dist., 1983-84; spl. edn. tchr. of mentally handicapped and autistic Los Angeles County Office of Edn., Downey, Calif., 1985-96. Mem. Alliance for the Mentally Ill. Died May 17, 1996.

OGANESOFF, IGOR MICHAEL, producer; b. N.Y.C., Sept. 29, 1924; s. Michael Minaitch and Olga Borisovna (Hoppe) O.; m. Maria Tauber, Mar. 22, 1980; children by previous marriages: Eric, Risa, Tina. B.S., Columbia U., 1951, M.S., 1951. Freelance journalist, 1952-57; chief Far East Bur. Wall St. Jour., Tokyo, 1957-64; chief Paris bur. Wall St. Jour., 1964-65; chief corr. Tokyo bur. CBS News, 1966-68; CBS corr. in Vietnam N.E. Asia, 1966-68; wounded in Vietnam, 1968; instr. TV workshop Columbia U. Grad. Sch. Journalism, spring 1983, 84. Producer documentaries, CBS News, TV, N.Y.C., 1968-71; Sixty Minutes, 1971-81, Walter Cronkite's Universe, 1981—; freelance producer: documentaries The Japanese (Nat. Acad. TV Arts and Scis. Emmy award), (George Foster Peabody award for broadcasting, Christopher award 1969), The Catholic Dilemma, 1970, Inflation, 1969, Reischauer on Asia, 1971. Served with U.S. Army, 1943-46. Mem. Dirs. Guild Am., Writers Guild Am., Am. Film Inst. Died April 13, 1996.

OGLE, JOSEPH WOMACK, composer, retired piano teacher; b. Guthrie, Okla., Oct. 25, 1902; s. James Taylor and Ella (Womack) O.; m. Inez Helen Klein, Aug. 9, 1929; 1 child, Dottie Ella. BA, MusB, Phillips U., 1925; postgrad., Columbia U., 1924-28; studied with various teachers. Chmn. piano dept. Lon Morris Coll., Jacksonville, Tex., 1928-29, 30, Milligan (Tenn.) Coll., 1929-32; pvt. studio tchr. Santa Ana, Calif., 1932-91; ret., 1991. Musical compositions published by Boston Music, Schroeder and Gunther, Pro Art Publications, Summy-Birchard and Mills Music, and others; contbr. articles to profl. jours. Cpl. Nat. Guard, 1921-24. Rhodes scholar Oxford U., 1926. Mem. Music Tchrs. Assn. of Calif., Musical Arts Club of Orange County. Democrat. Avocation: golf. Address: 871 S Fairmont Way Orange CA 92869-5025 Died April 25, 1997.

OHL, DONALD CHARLES, news service executive; b. Grand Junction, Iowa, Dec. 19, 1924; s. August and Agnes (Thornburg) O.; m. Evelyn Marie Broadway, Jan. 21, 1955; 1 son, Gary Martin. B.A., U. Iowa, 1950. Formerly mng. editor Guthrie Center (Iowa) Times-Guthrian; Sunday editor Galveston (Tex.) News-Tribune; asst. bur. mgr. UPI, N.Y.C., 1960-64; fgn. editor Copley News Service, San Diego, 1964-69, exec. news editor, from 1969, now gen. mgr. Died May 3, 1997.

OIKAWA, ATSUSHI, pharmacology educator; b. Tokyo, Jan. 27, 1929; s. Yasuo and Tsuya (Yamagishi) O.; m. Masako Hirota, Apr. 4, 1931; children: Hikaru, Kahoru, Akira. BS, U. Tokyo, 1953; PhD, Osaka U., 1961. Research asst. Osaka U., 1957-61, lectr., 1961-62; sect. head Nat. Cancer Ctr. Research Inst., Tokyo, 1962-74; prof. pharmacology Tohoku U., Sendai, 1974-92, prof. emeritus, 1992-97; dir. cancer cell repository Tohoku U., 1988-90; cons. Nihon Biosvc., 1992—; cons. on positron emission tomography Yamanakako Clinic, 1992-95. Editor: Pigment Cells (in Japanese), 1982; author: Cancer: Fundamentals (in Japanese), 1986, What is the Biological Science (in Japanese), 1992. Recipient Seiji Meml. award for pigment research Lydia O'Leary Meml. Fund, 1984. Mem. Japan Radioisotope Assn. (councilor radiation protection suprs. sect. 1992-96), N.Y. Acad. Scis., Planetary Soc. Died May 1997.

O'KEEFE, JOSEPH THOMAS, bishop; b. N.Y.C., Mar. 12, 1919. Ed. Cathedral Coll., N.Y.C., St. Joseph's Sem., Yonkers, N.Y., Cath. U., Washington. Ordained Roman Catholic priest, 1948; ordained titular bishop of Tre Taverse and aux. bishop of N.Y., 1982-87; apptd. and installed bishop of Syracuse, 1987. Died Sept. 2, 1997. Home: Syracuse N.Y.

O'LEARY, WILFRED LEO, retired headmaster; b. Boston, July 3, 1906; s. Daniel Joseph and Frances Marie (O'Hara) O'L.; m. Gertrude Margaret Cashman, June 26, 1938; 1 child, Ann Marie (Mrs. James S. Gessner). Grad., Boston Latin Sch., 1925; A.B., Boston Coll., 1929, A.M., 1930; Ed.M., State Coll. at Boston, 1938; Ed.D., Calvin Coolidge Coll., 1954. Master Boston Latin Sch., 1934-42, 64-76, headmaster, 1948-57; head history dept. Jeremiah E. Burke High Sch., Dorchester, Mass., 1948-57; asst. prof. edn. Calvin Coolidge Coll., 1952-57; head master Roslindale High Sch., Mass., 1957-64; bd. dirs., chmn. fin. com. Roslindale (Mass.) Coop. Bank. Author: (With others) Communism vs. Democracy, 1955, Philosophy of the Mass. Secondary School Principals Assn, 1960. Mem. Mass. Adv. Council on Edn.; public mem. Mass. Bd. Dental Examiners, 1979-85; mem. adv. bd. Scholastic mag., 1960-64; Bd. dirs. Boston chpt. ARC; mem. ho. of dels. Mass. Easter Seal Soc., 1976-78; chmn. founds. com. Pkwy. Boys Club, Boston, 1978; mem. Mass. State-Boston Retirement Bd., 1985-86. Served with USAF, 1942-46; col. Res. (ret.). Recipient Man-Boy award Parkway Boys Club, Boston, 1981. Mem. Boston Headmasters Assn. (pres. 1963-65), Boston Latin Sch. Alumni Assn. (sec., librarian, Man of Year award 1975), Am. Hist. Assn., Boston Athenaeum, Nat. Council Social Studies Tchrs., Nat. Assn. Secondary Sch. Prins. (citation for outstanding contbns. to pub. edn. 1975), Mass. Assn. Secondary Sch. Prins., Bostonian Soc., Mil. Order World Wars U.S., P.M., Boston Head Masters' and Prins. Assn. (pres. 1966-69), Mass. Schoolmasters' Club (pres. 1964-65), The Headmasters Assn. (v.p. 1972-73, pres. 1976-77, Great Head award 1983), Air Force Assn. (charter), N.E. History Tchrs. Assn. (v.p. 1958-59, pres. 1950-60). Home: Walpole Mass. Died July 12, 1995.

OLEJNICZAK, DOMINIC, real estate executive, football executive; b. Green Bay, Wis., Aug. 18, 1908; s. John A.B. and Victoria (Marshall) O.; m. Regina Bettine, Nov. 24, 1938; children: Thomas, Mark. Student, U. Wis., U. Chgo. Owner realty firm Green Bay, 1955-88; pres. Green Bay Packer Football Corp., 1958-81, chmn. bd., 1981-88. Mem. City Coun. Green Bay, 1936-54, mayor, 1945-55; mem. Gov.'s Commn. on Mass Urban Transp., 1953-54.,. Mem. Land Bank Assn. (past sec.), Wis. League Municipalities (past pres.), Elks. Roman Catholic (treas. congregation 1944-88). Home: Green Bay Wis. Died 1988.

OLIN, SPENCER TRUMAN, retired manufacturing executive; b. Alton, Ill., Aug. 20, 1900; s. Franklin W. and Mary (Moulton) O.; m. Ann Whitney, Jan. 12, 1928 (dec. Nov. 11, 1976); children: Mary Dell Olin Pritzlaff, Spencer Truman, Barbara Olin Taylor, Eunice Whitney Olin Higgins. M.E., Cornell U., 1921; D.Sc., So. Ill. U., 1958; LL.D., Washington U., St. Louis, 1969. Chief insp. Western Cartridge Co., East Alton, Ill., 1921-24; works mgr. Western Cartridge Co., 1924-43, sec., 1928-42, sales mgr., 1933-41, treas., 1935-43, v.p., 1942-45; 1st v.p. Olin Industries, Inc. (consolidation Western Cartridge Co., Winchester Repeating Arms Co., Olin Corp., others), 1945-54; dir. Olin Corp. (consolidation of Olin Industries Inc. and Mathieson Chem. Corp.), 1925-72; mem. adv. bd. Centerre Trust Co.; hon. dir. First Nat. Bank & Trust Co., Alton. Chmn. Republican Nat. Fin. Com., 1958-60; treas. Rep. Nat. Com., 1960-62; trustee emeritus Washington U., St. Louis, Cornell U.; emeritus bd. dirs. Barnes Hosp. Recipient Civic award Alton Order DeMolay, 1950; Man of Year award St. Louis chpt. Kappa Sigma, 1953; Distinguished Citizen award Greater Alton Assn. Commerce, 1956. Mem. Kappa Sigma. Clubs: Log Cabin, St. Louis Country, St. Louis (St. Louis); Seminole Golf (Palm Beach, Fla.). Home: Saint Louis Mo. Died Apr. 14, 1995.

OLIN, THOMAS FRANKLIN, food products executive; b. Mpls., Apr. 24, 1928; s. Merton Franklin and Ann Sylvia Roring; m. Gloria Joan Skidmore, Sept. 20, 1952; children: Susan Lee, Deborah Lynn, Thomas Franklin Jr., Rebeccah Anne. BA in Econs., U. Mich, 1952. Gen. contracting F.J. Skidmore & Son, Battle Creek, Mich., 1953-64; with home design and constrn. Olin Constrn. Co., Battle Creek, 1959-64; gen. mgr. Archway Cookies, Inc., Ashland, Ohio, 1964-71, nat. v.p. and regional mgr., 1971-83; chmn. bd. dirs. and co-chief exec. officer Archway Cookies, Inc., Battle Creek, 1983—; bd. dirs. Mich. Nat. Bank, Kalamazoo; bd. trustees Ashland (Ohio) Coll. Pres. Am. Cancer Soc., Battle Creek, 1958-1964; trustee Ashland Pub. Libr., 1970-77; chmn. Sch. Survey "Task Force," Ashland, 1971. Maj. U.S. Army, 1946-47, active in U.S. Intelligence during Korean War. Mem. Mfrs. Coun., Young Men's Bus. Club Ashland, U. Club Ashland, Battle CreekCountry Club, Rotary, Mason. Republican. Presbyterian. Avocations: photography, golf, hunting, fishing, travel. Died Oct. 30, 1996.

ÖLLING, EDWARD HENRY, aerospace engineer, consulting firm executive; b. Zion, Ill., Feb. 18, 1922; s. Edward and Lydia Ester (Amstudz) O.; children—Linda S., Charles R., Carole L. B.S.M.E., Purdue U., 1949; postgrad., UCLA, 1952-54, U. Houston, 1963-66. Registered profl. engr., Tex. Sr. thermodynamics engr. Lockheed Aircraft Corp., Burbank, Calif., 1954-56; project mgr. NASA Project Mercury, Garret Airesearch Corp., Los Angeles, 1956-60; dep. asst. Apollo project mgr., chief Future Projects Office chief advanced earth orbital missions office and space sta. office NASA, Houston, 1960-70; dir. Galaxy Engring. Inc., Captiva Island, Fla., 1971-90; cons. in oceanography, energy, environment, conservation. Pres. Captiva Island Wildlife Sci. Research Found.; pres. Satellite-TV Communications Enterprises; surrogate astronaut, 1962-69; cons.-dir. Orbita Space Sta., 1985-94, revised space sta., 1990-94; pres. Seaboard Stamp Svc., 1980-94; leader Hong Kong-China Progress Studios; cons. People to People Ambassadors, China Space Progress Tour and Survey; delaer rare books and antiques, big band era records; pres. Nouveaux Terra Electic Motion Corp., Generator Electrics. Contbg. author: Enciclopedia Mondadori, Italy; Contbr. articles to profl. jours.; Inventor, developer auto rsch. engring. devel. patent applications; inventor, patentee and devel. APU Electric Car. Bd. dirs. Captiva Seaside Flora and Fauna Research Found. Center; bd. dirs. Concerned Captiva Citizens.; mem. exec. com. Lee County (Fla.) Democratic Party; Nat. campaign worker John Glenn for Pres., 1984 Dem. State Conv.; campaign worker Frank Mann for Fla. Gov., 1986; founder, dir. Restoration of Mars Found., 1975-94; CEO Les Nouveaux Mars Found.; dir. Found. for Restoration Pyramids, Stonehenge. Served with USAAC, 1942-46. Recipient Sustained Superior Performance awards NASA, Inventions and Contbns. awards. Mem. Nat. Space Inst., Nat. Energy Inst., Nat. Audubon Soc. (pres. Theodore Roosevelt chpt.), Am. Assn. Concerned Scientists, Sanibel Captiva Conservation Assn., Captiva Civic Assn., Am., Fla. Stamp Dealers Assns., Am. Topical Assn., Rocket Mail Soc., Tex. Profl. Engring. Soc., Am. Legion, LBJ Space Center Stamp Club, Jack Knight Aerospace Philatelic Assn., Am. Soc. Polar Philatelists, Strengthen Am. Def. Assn., Support Nuclear Energy Soc. (pres.), Purdue Club S. W. Fla., Danish Am. Genealogy Rsch. Assn., High Flight Soc. (search for Noah's Ark divsn.), Scientists So. Fla., Imaginarium Ft. Meyers, Conquest Space Philatelic Soc., Orbital Space Covers, Lea. Co. Edison Philatelic Soc., Alligator Deltrology Soc., Sunshine Postcard Club, Tropical Postcard Club, Edison Inventor Assn. (dir.). Died May 24, 1997.

OLNEY, PETER BUTLER, JR., retired management consulting firm executive; b. N.Y.C., Nov. 29, 1924; s. Peter Butler and Amy (Cruger) O.; m. Elinor Ann Bowman, Sept. 10, 1949; children: Peter B., Ann B., Stephen R. AB, Harvard U., 1949; MA, Boston U., 1951. Cert. mgmt. cons. Credit investigator Shawmut Bank, Boston, 1949-51; tchr. social studies Cohasset (Mass.) Sch., 1951-53; mgmt. trainee Corn Exch. Bank, N.Y.C., 1953-55; job analyst Allied Chem., N.Y.C., 1955-56; pers. adminstr. Avco Corp., Lawrence, Mass., 1956-58; dir. pers. Avco Corp., Cin., 1958-61; dir. human resources United Shoe Corp., Beverly, Mass., 1961-64; mgmt. cons. Frank C. Brown Co., Boston, 1964-66; founder, pres. of mgmt. cons. corp. Olney Assocs., Inc., Boston, 1966-89. Author: (periodical) Meeting the Challenge of Comparable Worth, 1987. Pres. West Andover PTA, Andover, Mass., 1963; bd. dirs. Unitarian Universalist Ch., Andover, 1964-70, Interfaith Counseling, Andover, 1986-93. Named one of Top 100 Cons. Firms in U.S. by Inst. Mgmt. Cons., 1987. Mem. North Andover Country Club (bd. dirs. 1970-74). Democrat. Avocations: traveling, water color painting. Died Apr. 13, 1996.

OLSEN, KURT, investment company executive, adviser; b. Astoria, Oreg., Nov. 2, 1924; s. Matt J. and Irene (Lindholm) O.; m. Lois Helen Giberson, Mar. 23, 1947; children: Kurt F., Eric J., Mark C. BS, U. Oreg., 1949. RR mgr. and ptnr. Foster & Marshall, Eugene, Oreg., 1948-61; mgr., v.p., dir. Harris, Upham Inc., Portland, Oreg., 1961-70; v.p., dir. Foster & Marshall Inc., Portland, 1971-76; pres. Alpen Securities, Inc., Portland, 1977—. Mem. adv. bd. Columbia Pacific coun. Boy Scouts Am., mem. nat. coun., 1966-73; bd. dirs. United Way Columbia and Willamette, 1973-77, Oreg. Law Found., 1986-89. With USNR, 1944-46. Mem. Nat. Assn. Securities Dealers (chmn. dist. 1 1967), Investment Bankers Assn. Am. (bd. govs. 1968-70), Sigma Alpha Epsilon, Rotary. DIED 09/09/97. .

OLSON, CARL WILHELM, construction company executive; b. Lincoln, Nebr., Nov. 16, 1905; s. Charles John and Carolina (Palm) O.; m. Charlotte Angela Joyce, Jan. 28, 1931; children: David Charles, Samuel Palm, Carolyn Joyce. BS in Archtl. Engring., U. Nebr., 1929; LLD (hon.), Midland Luth. Coll., Fremont, Nebr., 1962. V.p. Olson Constrn. Co., Lincoln, Nebr., 1929-45, pres., 1945-75, chmn., 1975-85; bd. dirs., cons. dir. Provident Fed. Savs. Bank, Lincoln. Campaign chmn. Lincoln Community Chest, 1950, pres., 1951; trustee Gustavus Adolphus Coll., St. Peter, Minn., 1967-81. Recipient Disting. Service award U. Nebr. Alumni Assn., 1963, Alumni Achievement award, 1979, Builders award U. Nebr., 1983. Mem. Associated Gen. Contractors Am. (life, bd. dirs. 1947—, chmn. bldg. div. 1960); Lincoln C. of C. (bd. dirs. 1955-58). Republican. Lutheran. Clubs: Country of Lincoln (bd. dirs.), Lincoln Univ. (bd. dirs.), Nebr. (bd. dirs.). Lodges: Masons, Shriners, Royal Order of Jesters. Avocations: golf, travel, spectator sports. Died June 20, 1996.

OLSON, DONALD ERNEST, physician; b. Portland, Oreg., June 22, 1921; s. Ernest S. and Edith (Swanman) O.; m. Alice Curtis Bergh, July 7, 1951; children—Julie Rene, Reid Martin, Kathy Ruth, Marc Ernest. B.A., Reed Coll., 1943; M.S., U. Oreg., 1947, M.D., 1947, Ph.D., 1948. Diplomate: Am. Bd. Internal Medicine (chmn. subsplty. pulmonary disease 1968-70; mem. bd. 1972-79). Intern U. Hosps., Madison, Wis., 1948-49; resident U. Hosps., 1949-51; research fellow dept. medicine U. Wis., 1952-53; staff physician VA Hosp., Madison, 1952-53, Portland Clinic, 1955-92; mem. staff VA Hosp., Portland; assoc. clin. prof. medicine U. Oreg. Served with M.C., AUS, 1953-55. Fellow ACP (master 1992); mem. Am., Oreg. thoracic socs., Am. Coll. Chest Physicians, North Pacific Soc. Internal Medicine, Am., Ore. med. assns., Am. Clin. and Climatol. Assn., Multnomah County Med. Soc., Phi Beta Kappa, Alpha Omega Alpha. Home: Portland Oreg. Died June 6, 1996.

OLSON, HENRY DEXTER, electrical engineer; b. San Mateo, Calif., Sept. 21, 1931; s. Oscar Henry and Bessie (Deyoung) O.; m. Jane Grace McKenzie; 1 child, Dana. BS, Stanford U., MS. Rsch. asst. Stanford (Calif.) U. Elecs. Rsch. Lab., 1956-58; sr. rsch. engr. Stanford Rsch. Inst., Menlo Park, Calif., 1958-87; consulting engr. pvt. practice, Menlo Park, Calif., 1987—;

instr. Foothill Coll., Los Altos Hills, Calif., 1970-85; cons. in field. Contbr. articles to profl. jours. With U.S. Army, 1954-56. Mem. IEEE (sr.), Am. Radio Relay League, Ancient Wireless Assn. (life), Soc. Wireless Pioneers (life). Avocations: ham radio, old sports cars. Died March 9, 1996.

OLSON, KENNETH BARRIE, physician, educator; b. Seattle, Jan. 21, 1908; s. Donald Barrie and Hattie (Palmer) O.; m. Emma Naomi Tallman, Apr. 3, 1937 (dec. Mar. 1986); children: Karen Barrie Mason, Kenneth Barrie Jr. BS, U. Wash., 1929; MD, Harvard U., 1933. Resident in pathology Boston City Hosp., 1933-34; intern in surgery Presbyn. Hosp., N.Y.C., 1934-36, asst. resident and resident surgery, 1936-39; clin. asst. in surgery Columbia U. Sch. Medicine, N.Y., 1939-40, Trudeau Sanatorium, N.Y., 1941; asst. physician, acting pathologist Olive View Sanatorium, Calif., 1941-43; dir. Tb Control and dir. Firland Sanatorium, Seattle, 1943-45; asst. physician Glenridge Sanatorium, Schenectady, 1947-50; from instr. to assoc. prof. Albany Med. Coll., Union U., N.Y., from 1950, prof. medicine and head div. oncology, until 1972, prof. emeritus, 1973—; chief diagnosis br. div. cancer biology and diagnosis Nat. Cancer Inst.; cons. Nat. Cancer Inst., Bethesda, Md., 1973-74, Fla. Cancer Council, Tampa, 1974-88, Halifax Hosp. Med. Ctr., Daytona Beach, Fla., 1974—. Author: One Doctor Learns to be a Patient, 1993; contbr. articles to profl. jours., chpt. to book. Bd. dirs. Am. Cancer Soc., Daytona Beach, 1974-83. Recipient Faculty Research award Albany Med. Sch., 1986, Golden Apple award for teaching, 1958, 66; Kenneth B. Olson Cancer Teaching Day at Albany Med. Coll. named in his honor, 1986. Fellow ACP; mem. Am. Soc. Clin. Oncology (pres. 1971-72), Am. Assn. Cancer Edn. (chmn. 1958, Margaret Hay Edwards award 1987), Am. Assn. Cancer Research, Alpha Omega Alpha. Club: Smyrna Yacht. Current work: Chemotherapy of cancer; tumor markers. Subspecialties: Internal medicine, Chemotherapy, Blood Clotting. Deceased.

OLSON, WALTER THEODORE, research scientist, consultant; b. Royal Oak, Mich., July 4, 1917; s. Oscar Thomas and Edith Margaret (Ketcham) O.; m. Ruth Elisabeth Barker, Oct. 28, 1943; 1 child, David Paul. AB, DePauw U., 1939; MS, Case Inst. Tech., 1940, PhD, 1942. Instr. Case Inst. Tech., 1941-42; research scientist Lewis Research Center, NASA, Cleve., 1942-45; chief combustion br. Lewis Research Center, NASA, 1945-50, chief chemistry and energy conversion research div., 1950-63, asst. dir., 1963-72, dir. tech. utilization and public affairs, 1972-81, disting. research assoc., 1981-82; pvt. cons., 1981—; mem. numerous govt. adv. coms. Editor: (with W.R. Hawthorne) Design and Performance of Gas Turbine Power Plants, 1960; editorial bd.: Combustion and Flame, 1955-65; contbr. articles to profl. jours. Dir. Build Up Greater Cleve. Program, 1981-91; vice chmn. United Appeal Greater Cleve., 1965-73; chmn. legis. affairs Ohio Assn. Gifted Children, 1969-76; trustee Blue Cross N.E., Ohio, 1972-84, N.E. Ohio Transit Coalition, 1992—; mem. industry adv. com. Coll. Engrs., Cleve. State U., 1975-85, chmn., 1975-76; mem. Ohio Pub. Works Commn., 1988-89. Recipient Career Service award Greater Cleve. Growth Assn., 1972, Exceptional Contbns. award NASA, 1981, Excellence award Am. Soc. Assn. Execs., 1987. Fellow AIAA (dir. 1969-75, Disting. Svc. award Cleve.-Akron sect. 1966, 75, Exceptional Svc. award 1981, other awards), AAAS; mem. Combustion Inst. (dir. 1954—), Am. Chem. Soc., Sigma Xi, Phi Gamma Delta. Methodist. Clubs: Cosmos (Washington); City (Cleve.). Patentee in field. Died June 16, 1997.

OLSTOWSKI, FRANCISZEK, chemical engineer, consultant; b. N.Y.C., Apr. 23, 1927; s. Franciszek and Marguerite (Stewart) O.; A.A., Monmouth Coll., 1950; BSCE, Tex. A&M U., 1954; m. Rosemary Sole, May 19, 1952; children: Marguerita Antonina, Anna Rosa, Franciszek, Anton, Henryk Alexander. Research and devel. engr. Dow Chem. Co., Freeport, Tex., 1954-56, project leader, 1956-65, sr. research engr., 1965-72, research specialist, 1972-79, research leader, 1979-87; dir. Tech. Cons. Services, Freeport, 1987—. Lectr. phys. scis. elementary and intermediate schs., Freeport, 1961-85. Vice chmn. Freeport Traffic Commn., 1974-76, chmn., 1976-79, vice-chmn. 1987-89, chmn., 1989-92. With USNR, 1944-46. Fellow Am. Inst. Chemist; mem. AAAS, Am. Chem. Soc., Electrochem. Soc. (sec. treas. South Tex. sect. 1963-64, vice chmn. 1964-65, chmn. 1965-67, councillor 1967-70), N.Y. Acad. Sci, Velasco Cemetery Assn. (sec.-treas. 1992-95). Patentee in synthesis of fluorocarbons, natural graphite products, electrolytic prodn. magnesium metal and polyurethane tech.

O'MAHONEY, ROBERT M., retired lawyer; b. Indpls., Jan. 4, 1925; s. Joseph Francis and Evelyn (O'Connor) O'M.; m. Mary C. Mitchell, Sept. 12, 1953; children: Terrance M., Patrick J., Mary E., Susan M., Sharon A. B.S., Purdue U., 1948; J.D., Georgetown U., 1954. Bar: D.C. 1954, Ind. 1954, U.S. Supreme Ct. 1959. Assoc. Ross McCord, Ice and Miller, Indpls., 1954-55; dep. atty. gen. Ind., 1954-59; gen. counsel Def. Air Transp. Adminstrn., 1959; dep. asst. gen. counsel for transp. Dept. Commerce, 1959-66; adviser to dep. asst. sec. state for transp. and communications, 1966-67; asst. gen. counsel Fed. Hwy. Adminstrn., 1968-69; commr. transp. and telecommunications service GSA, 1969-73; transp. cons. EPA, 1973; atty. Fed. Power Commn., Washington, 1973-77, Fed. Energy Regulatory Commn., Washington, 1977-80; sales assoc. Shannon & Luchs, Potomac, Md., 1980-83, Merrill Lynch Realty, Potomac, Md., 1983-85, Long & Foster Realtors, Rockville, Md., 1985-86. Co-author: Great Lakes Pilotage Act, 1960. Served with USAAF, 1943-45; Served with USAF, 1950-52. Decorated Air medal with oak leaf cluster. Mem. Phi Alpha Delta. Republican. Roman Catholic. Died Oct. 9, 1997.

O'MALLEY, T. E., lumber company executive.

O'MALLEY, TIMOTHY JOHN, broadcasting executive; b. Berkeley, Calif., Jan. 29, 1951; s. John Thomas and Mary (Madigan) O'M. Pres. OMPC Prodn. Co., Richmond, Calif., 1968-73, news dir., 1973; pres. Corp. Community Radio, Richmond, 1969-73, OMPC Wireless Broadcast Co., Inc., Richmond, 1979-81; founder, news anchor, producer NGN Radio Network, 1981-86; chief exec. officer, news anchor, producer, dir. Am. Cities Radio Network, 1986—; lectr. mass. comunications, cons., sr. systems analyst Bank of Am., Blue Cross of Calif., Fireman's Fund Ins. Co.; designer, manufacturer exclusive line of silk and silk jacquard neckwear. Irish tenor; (albums) What Have I, Searching, Love is the Thing; producer 2 gold records; producer, singing host Citynet's "Melody Lane" Radio Broadcasts. Mem. Nat. Assn. Broadcasters (plaque), NorCal Radio/TV News Dirs. Assn. Democrat. Roman Catholic.

OMORI, MORIO, lawyer; b. Maui, Hawaii, Oct. 15, 1921; m. Rachel T. Tanaka, June 29, 1946; children: Sharyn, Colleen. BE, U. Hawaii, 1942, 5th yr. cert., 1943; LLB, U. Colo., 1954. Bar: Hawaii 1955, U.S. Dist. Ct. Hawaii 1955, U.S. Supreme Ct. 1959. Law clk. to chief justice Supreme Ct. Hawaii, Honolulu, 1954-55, dep. atty. gen., 1955-56, spl. dep. atty. gen., 1956-68; pvt. practice law, 1957—; gen. counsel Pacific Savs. & Loan, Honolulu, 1968-76, chmn. bd., 1972-76; gen. counsel Halekulani Corp., Honolulu, 1985—, bd. dirs., 1985—; bd. dirs. Mitsui Real Estate Sales, Inc., Consolidated Amusement Co., Ltd., 1986—. Campaign coord. for U.S. Senator Daniel Inouye, Hawaii, 1959, 62, state rep., 1959-70. With U.S. Army, 1944-46, ETO. Mem. ABA, Hawaii Bar Assn., 442d Vets. Club, Phi Delta Phi. Avocations: golf, landscaping, travel. Deceased.

OMURA, JAMES MATSUMOTO, journalist, editor, publisher; b. Bainbridge Island, Washington, Nov. 27, 1912; m. Karen Haruko; children: Gregg Kiyoshi, Wayne Stanley. English lang. editor New Japanese Am. News, L.A., 1933-34, New World Daily, San Francisco, 1934-36; columnist Passing Show Japanese Am. News, San Francisco, 1938-40; founder Nisei mag. Current Life, San Francisco, 1940-42; English lang. editor, pub. rels. dir. The Rocky Shimpo, Denver, 1944, 47; columnist Plain Speaking Hokubei Mainichi, San Francisco, 1984-88; writer and speaker in field; speaker in protest over eviction/detention of Japanese people before Tolan Congl. Com., San Francisco, 1942. Recipient Cert. of Honor award Status of Liberty/Ellis Island Centennial Commn., 1983, Bicentennial Recognition, Smithsonian Instn., 1988, Lifetime Achievement award Asian Am. Journalists Assn., 1989, Internat. Order of Merit, 1990; inducted Maison Internat. Des Intellectuals (France); honored as Ethnic Benefactor Nat. Coun. Redress/Reparation, 1992, Fighting Spirit award, 1994. Mem. Grand Coun. World Parliament of Chivalry (Sidney, Australia)(life, 20th Century Award of Achievement 1993), World Biographical Hall of Fame. Home: Denver Colo. Died June 20, 1994.

ONASCH, DONALD CARL, business executive; b. New Castle, Pa., July 5, 1927; m. Ruth Ellen Widman; children: Gregory W., Jay W., David R. BA, Washington and Jefferson Coll., 1950; MS in Retailing, U. Pitts., 1952. Div. mgr. mdse. Higbee Co., Cleve., 1953-65, Sibley, Lindsay & Curr, Rochester, N.Y., 1965-70; v.p., gen. mgr. mdse. Liberty House of Hawaii, Honolulu, 1970-72, pres., 1973-77; v.p. Amfac, Inc., Honolulu, 1977-78, exec. v.p., 1978—; bd. dirs. Associated Merchandising Corp. Served with USCG, 1945-46. Club: Oahu Country. Died June 19, 1996.

O'NEIL, JOHN G. A., assemblyman; b. Saranac Lake, N.Y., Jan. 12, 1937; m. Chloe Ann O'Neil; m. John Jr., Beth Ann. B, St. Bonaventure U.; postgrad., SUNY, Albany, SUNY, Pitts., SUNY, Potsdam. Tchr. Orange County, Lake Placid, N.Y.; restaurant mgr. Dew Drop Up Restaurant, Potsdam; tchr. SUNY, Canton, 1966-1980; asst. dir. Inst. Am. Studies at SUNY, Potsdam; assemblyman 112th Assembly Dist., St. Lawrence County, 1980-92; guest lectr. Master Dei, Ogdensburg; cons. North Franklin BOCES; mem. assembly standing coms. aging, commerce, industry and econ. devel., and corps.; mem. authorities and commns. on govt. employees, higher edn., housind, labor, samll bus., energy, and ranking minority mem.; com. on agrl. and ranking minority mem. on small bus.; legis. chmn. United Univ. Professions SUNY, treas., local negotiations chmn. Past sch. bd., past pres. Home and Sch. Assn. of St. Mary's. Mem. Elks, Lions, Phi Delta Kappa. Home: Potsdam N.Y. Died Dec. 10, 1992.

O'NEIL, LEO E., bishop; b. Holyoke, Mass., Jan. 31, 1928. Ed. Mary-knoll Sem., St. Anselm's Coll., Manchester, N.H., Grand Sem., Montreal, Que., Can. Ordained Roman Cath. priest, 1955; ordained titular bishop of Bencenna and aux. bishop of Springfield (Mass.), 1980-89, co-adjutor bishop Manchester, N.H., 1989-90, bishop, diocese of Manchester, 1990—.

ONETO, GEORGE J., retired union executive; b. May 20, 1910; m. Rose. Vice-pres. Distillery, Wine and Allied Workers Internat. Union, AFL-CIO, Englewood, N.J., 1940-57; gen. sec.-treas. Distillery, Wine and Allied Workers Internat. Union, AFL-CIO, 1957-74, gen. pres., 1974-85; pres. Local 1, 1936-85. Served with U.S. Army, World War II. Died Dec. 11, 1996.

OOSTERMEYER, JAN STUART, chemical company executive; b. Mukden, Manchuria, Peoples Republic China, Dec. 20, 1930; came to U.S., 1939; s. Jan and Agnes Kathleen (Robertson) O.; m. Dale Grove, Oct. 1, 1965. BS in Biology, U. San Francisco, 1951. With Shell Chem. Co., 1951—; chemist, tech. salesman various locations, 1951-62; dist. mgr. indsl. chems. Los Angeles, 1961-64; plant supt. polymers Woodbury, N.J., 1964-65; mktg. mgr. ammonia div. San Francisco, 1965-70; gen. mgr. Houston, 1975-80, v.p., 1980—; div. head Shell Internat. Chem. Co., London, 1970-74; chmn. bd. Pecten Chems., Inc., Houston, Western Farms Service, Inc., Walnut Creek, Calif., Triton Bioscis., Inc., Alameda, Calif., Nickerson Am. Plant Breeders, Salida, Kans.; bd. dirs. Scallop Corp., Houston, Saudi Petrochems., Saudi Arabia. Mem. Soc. for Chem. Industry. Club: Heritage (Houston). Avocation: breeder and trainer Arabian horses. Died Aug. 8, 1996.

OPATOSHU, DAVID, actor, writer; b. N.Y.C., Jan. 30, 1918; s. Joseph and Adele (Wolf) O.; m. Nancy Rigler, June 19, 1984; 1 child, Dan. Grad. high sch., N.Y.C., 1935. Actor theatre, film, TV, N.Y.C., Calif., 1935—. Appeared in plays Me and Molly, 1947, Silk Stockings, 1954, The Wall, 1963, Bravo Giovanni, 1965, Does a Tiger Wear A Necktie, 1969, Twelve Angry Men, 1985; films include Exodus, 1960, Cimarron, 1960, The Brothers Karamazov; screen writer Romance of a Horse Thief, 1970. Sgt. USAF, 1942-46. Recipient LAMED award Ctrl. Yiddish Cultural Orgn., 1948, Emmy award for outstanding guest actor, 1990-91. DIED 04/29/96. .

ORGAIN, BENJAMIN DARBY, lawyer; b. Bastrop, Tex., Dec. 26, 1909; s. William Edmund and May (Bolinger) O.; m. Martha Chastain Avery, Apr. 16, 1977; children: Lucy Allen Orgain White, Benjamin Darby. Student, South Park Coll., Beaumont, Tex., 1926-27; B.A., LL.B., U. Tex., 1933; LL.M., Harvard U., 1934. Bar: Tex. bar 1933. Since practiced in Beaumont; of counsel firm Orgain, Bell & Tucker.; Dir. Gulf States Utilities Co., 1963-75, adv. dir., 1975-80. Chmn. Jefferson County Democratic Com., 1940-42; vice chmn. devel. bd. U. Tex., 1966-68, mem., 1963-91; trustee U. Tex. Law Sch. Found., 1991; assoc. mem. bd. visitors U. Tex. Cancer Found.; mem. chancellor's coun. U. Tex. Served to lt. comdr. USNR, 1942-46. Decorated Commendation ribbon. Fellow Am. Bar Found.; mem. Am., Tex., Jefferson County bar assns., Tex. Ornithol. Soc. (pres. 1979-81), Beaumont C. of C., Friar Soc., Phi Delta Phi, Kappa Sigma. Methodist. Clubs: Beaumont Country; Piping Rock (Locust Valley, N.Y.). Died Nov. 22, 1996.

ORMANDY, EUGENE, music director; b. Budapest, Hungary, Nov. 18, 1899; came to U.S., 1921, naturalized, 1927; s. Benjamin and Rosalie O.; student Royal State Acad. Music, 1904-13, B.A., 1913; state diploma for violin as prof., 1915; student U. Budapest, 1917-20; Mus.D. (hon.), Hamline U., 1934, U. Pa., 1937, Phila. Acad. Music, 1939, Curtis Inst. Music, 1946, U. Mich., 1952; LL.D. (hon.), Temple U., 1949; Dr. honoris causa, Clarke U., 1957, Miami U., Oxford, Ohio, 1959, Rutgers U., 1960, L.I. U., 1965; L.H.D. (hon.), Lehigh U., 1952, C. W. Post Coll., 1965; Litt.D. (hon.), Lafayette Coll., 1966, Villanova U., 1968, Peabody Inst., 1968, Rensselaer Poly. Inst., 1968, U. Ill., 1969; m. Steffy Goldner, 1922 (dec.); m. 2d, Margaret Frances Hitch, May 15, 1950. Toured Hungary as child prodigy, later toured Central Europe; apptd. head of master classes State Conservatorium of Music, Budapest at age of 20; substituted for Toscannini as condr. Phila. Orch.; condr. Mpls. Symphony Orch., 1931-36; condr. and music dir. Phila. Orch., 1936-80, condr. laureate, 1980—. Decorated comdr. French Legion of Honor; comdr. Order of Dannebrog (Denmark); comdr. Order of Lion (Finland); Order Merit Juan Pablo Duarte (Dominican Republic); knight Order of White Rose (Finland); recipient citation Disting. Service in music Boston U., 1957; Honor Cross for Arts and Sci. (Austria), 1966; Golden medallion Vienna Philharm., 1967; Presdl. Medal of Freedom, 1970; Phila. award, 1970; Nat. Recognition award Freedoms Found., 1970; Alice M. Ditson Condrs. award, 1977; Broadcast Pioneer award, 1979; Medal of Freedom award City of Phila., 1980.

ORNSTEIN-GALICIA, JACOB LEONARD (JACK ORNSTEIN-GALICIA), foreign language educator, linguist, author; b. Cleve., Aug. 12, 1915; s. Joseph and Bertha (Schwartz) Ornstein; m. Janet Ann Eaton, Dec. 25, 1962 (div. Nov. 1977); 1 child, Dena Hayden. BS in Edn., Ohio State U., 1936, MA, 1937; PhD, U. Wis.,

1940. Cert. tchr., Ohio. Instr. Spanish and Portuguese U. Wis., Madison, 1940-41; asst. prof. Washington U., St. Louis, 1941-42; intelligence officer Office Strategic Svcs., Washington, North Africa and Italy, 1942-45; assoc. prof. Waldorf Coll., Forest City, Iowa, 1947-49, N.Mex. State U., Las Cruces, 1949-51; intelligence officer, sci. linguist CIA, Washington, 1951-68; prof. linguistics and langs. U. Tex., El Paso, 1968-96, emeritus prof.; lectr. Sch. Langs. and Linguistics, Georgetown U., Washington, 1964-68; cons. U.S. Office Edn., Washington, 1968-74, S.W. Coop. Ednl. Lab., Albuquerque, 1970, Ednl. Testing Svc., Princeton, N.J., 1974; reader proposals NSF, Washington, 1975-96; faculty mem. U. Ctr. for Lifelong Learning, 1992-96, prof. continuing edn. U. Tex., El Paso, 1993-96. Author: Slavic and East European Studies: Their Development in the Western hemisphere, 1957, A Sociolinguistic Study of Mexican-American and Anglo Students in a Border University, 1975, Sociolinguistic Foundations of Language Assessment, 1983; also articles; co-author: Elements of Russian, 1964, Programmed Instruction and Educational Technology in the Language Teaching Field, 1971, The New ABC's of Language and Linguistics, 1977, A Problem-Solving Model for Integrating Science and Language in Bilingual-Bicultural Education, 1983; editor: Repetición de amores (Luis de Lucena), 1954, Form and Function in Chicano English: New Insights, 1984, rev. edit., 1988; co-editor: Studies in Language and Linguistics, 1969-70, Studies in Language and Linguistics II, 1970-71, College English and the Mexican-American, 1976, Problems of Standard vs. Non-Standard: Dimensions of Foreign Language Teaching, 1977, Problems in Applied Educational Sociolinguistics: Readings on Language and Cultural Problems of U.S. Ethnic Groups, 1978, Bilingualism and Bilingual Education: New Readings and Insights, 1979, Sociolinguistic Studies in Language Contact: Methods and Cases, 1979, Problems of Loyalty and Accomodation Among Minority Languages and Dialects, 1980, Social and Educational Issues in Bilingualism and Biculturalism, 1981, Politics and Society in the Southwest: Ethnicity and Chicano Pluralism, 1982, Chicano English: An Ethnic Contact Dialect, 1985, Mexican-American Language: Usage, Attitudes, Maintenance, Instruction and Policy, 1986, Chicano Speech in the Bilingual Classroom, 1988, Research Issues and Problems in U.S. Spanish, 1988, Mexican-American Spanish in its Societal and Cultural Context, 1989, Jewish Farmer in America, The Unknown Chronicle, 1992. Adviser Armadillo, Disabled Students' Orgn., U. Tex., El Paso, 1969-81; organizer Town and Gown forum, El Paso, 1975-85. Recipient A. G. Solalinde award U. Wis., 1938, Outstanding Alumnus award Ohio State U. Stadium Scholarship Alumni Assn., 1989. Mem. MLA, Linguistic Soc. Am., Am. Assn. Tchrs. Spanish and Portuguese, Assn. Lingistica y Filologia de America Latina Linguistica. Home: El Paso Tex. Deceased.

ORTH, THOMAS M., energy company executive; b. Kansas City, Mo., Jan. 26, 1927; s. Harry and Irma O.; m. Jacqueline Ann Farrar, Apr. 2, 1954; children—Tam, Scott T., Karey, Kristi, Chad. B.S., U. Wash., 1950; postgrad., South Tex. Law Sch., 1950-52, U. So. Calif., 1959, Stanford U., 1969. With Kirby Forest Industries, Inc., Houston, 1950-81; gen. mgr. Kirby Forest Industries, Inc., 1962-69, pres., 1970-81; chief exec. officer Santa Fe Energy Co., Houston, 1981—. Served with U.S. Navy, World War II. Mem. Nat. Forest Products Assn. (pres. 1976-77, chmn. bd. 1978), Forest Industries Council (chmn. 1980), Am. Petroleum Inst (Domestic Petroleum Council). Presbyterian.

ORTIZ, ALFONSO ALEX, anthropology educator; b. San Juan Pueblo, N.Mex., Apr. 30, 1939; s. Sam and Lupe (Naranjo) O.; m. Margaret Drew Davisson, July 26, 1961; children: Juliana, Elena, Nico. Student, St. Michael's Coll., 1957-58; A.B., U. N.Mex., 1961; postgrad., Ariz. State U., 1961-62; M.A., U. Chgo., 1963, Ph.D., 1967. Asst. prof. anthropology Pitzer Coll., Claremont, Calif., 1966-67; asst. prof. anthropology Princeton, 1967-70, William D. Paterson Bicentennial preceptor, 1969-72; assoc. prof. anthropology Princeton U., 1970-74; prof. anthropology U. N.Mex., Albuquerque, 1974—; disting. bicentennial prof. U. Utah, 1976; Charles Charropin vis. scholar, lectr. Rockhurst Coll., 1977. Author: The Tewa World: Space, Time, Being and Becoming in a Pueblo Society, 1969; editor: New Perspectives on the Pueblos, 1972, Handbook of North American Indians, Vol. 9, 1980, Vol. 10, 1983, American Indian Myths and Legends, 1984. Chmn. Native Am. adv. group Div. Performing Arts, Smithsonian Instn., 1975-76; chmn. selection com. Doctoral Fellowships for Am. Indians, Ford Found., 1975-78; mem. advisory council Nat. Indian Youth Council.; Bd. dirs. Social Sci. Research Council, 1972-74, Inst. Devel. Indian Law; mem. adv. council Center for History of the Am. Indian, Newberry Library, 1972—, chmn., 1978—; mem. Nat. Humanities Faculty, 1972—; mem. nat. council Inst. Am. West, Sun Valley Center Humanities, 1976-83; mem. minority advisory panel Danforth Grad. Fellowship Program, 1976-79; mem. Com. Edn. Women and Minorities in Sci. NRC, 1975—, Nat. Commn. Minorities in Higher Edn., 1979-81. Recipient Roy D. Albert prize U. Chgo., 1964; Guggenheim fellow, 1975-76; Fellow Center Advanced Study in Behavioral Scis., Stanford U., 1977-78; Weatherhead scholar in residence Navajo Community Coll., 1976; MacArthur Found. fellow, 1982-87. Fellow Am. Anthrop. Assn., Royal Anthrop. Inst.; mem. Assn. on Am. Indian Affairs (pres. 1973-88, bd. dirs. 1967—). Died Jan. 28, 1997.

OSBORN, LESLIE ANDREWARTHA, psychiatrist; b. Warrnambool, Victoria, Australia, Aug. 10, 1906; came to U.S., 1931, naturalized, 1938; s. Andrew Rule and Annie (Delbridge) O.; m. Dora Wright, June 12, 1931 (dec.); children: Anne L. Osborn Krueger Henderson, June E.; m. Gwen F. Arnold, Aug. 13, 1960 (dec. Mar. 12, 1976); m. Corinne H. Kirchmaier, June 7, 1985. Student, Wesley Coll., Melbourne, 1920-23; M.B., B.S., Melbourne Med. Sch., 1929; M.D., U. Buffalo, 1945. Diplomate: Am. Bd. Psychiatry and Neurology, 1944. Intern Melbourne Gen. Hosp., 1930-31; postgrad. Post Grad. Hosp., N.Y.C., 1934; in chest diseases Trudeau Sch. Tb, Saranac Lake, 1937; in neurology and psychiatry Columbia U., 1940; gen. practice medicine, physician Endicott-Johnson Med. Dept., Binghamton, N.Y., 1932-38; asst. physician Willard (N.Y.) State Hosp., 1938-41; psychiatrist Meyer Meml. Hosp.; assoc. psychiatry U. Buffalo, 1941-45; attending psychiatrist, dir. psychiatry Edward J. Meyer Meml. Hosp., psychiat. service, 1946-49; prof. psychiatry U. Buffalo Sch. Medicine, 1946, acting dir. dept. psychiatry, 1946-49, head dept., 1949-50; dir. Wis. Psychiat. Inst.; prof. psychiatry U. Wis. Med. Sch., 1950-60; dir. div. mental hygiene Wis. Dept. Pub. Welfare, 1950-60; dir. Walworth County Family Counseling Center, 1960; prof. psychiatry dept. neurology and psychiatry U. Nebr., 1960-66; dir. Swanson Clinic for Multiply Handicapped Children, Nebr. Psychiat. Inst., Omaha, 1960-64; med. dir. Winnebago County Mental Health Clinic, Rockford, Ill., 1966; dir. Mental Health Services, Tompkins County, 1967-68; pvt. practice psychiatry Seneca Falls, N.Y., 1968-74, Scottsdale, Ariz., 1974-96. Author: Psychiatry and Medicine, 1952, Prognosis, A Guide to the Study and Practice of Clinical Medicine, 1966, Foundation Learning and Innumeracy, 1977, King of the Hill: Chess for Children: 1981, Preventing War: A Doctor's Trilogy: Vol. 1 Living in a Changed World, 1994. Fellow Am. Psychiat. Assn. (life). Presbyterian. Died June 16, 1996.

OSBORNE, RAYMOND LESTER, physician; b. N.Y.C., Apr. 20, 1910; s. Nat and Mary (Bellow) O.; AB, Columbia, 1932, MD, 1936, MA, 1936. Intern Roosevelt Hosp., N.Y.C., 1936-37, Bellevue Hosp., 1941; resident nueropsychiatry Rockland State Hosp., Orangeburg, N.Y., 1937-39; fellow neuropsychiatry Neuropsychiat. Inst. of Hartford (Conn.) Retreat, 1939-41; asso. resident, resident neurologist Bellevue Hosp. neurol. and neurosurg. service Cornell U., 1941-42; chief resident neurologist Cornell U., 1942; sr. alienist psychiat. div. Bellevue Hosp., 1942-46; sr. psychiatrist Psychiat. Clinic, Ct of Gen. Sessions, N.Y., 1942-46; asst. vis. neurologist neurol. and neurosurg. service Bellevue Hosp., 1946-50; sr. clin. neuropsychiatrist Lenox Hill Hosp., N.Y., 1946-48; asst. vis. neurologist Mt. Sinai Hosp., N.Y.C., 1946-96, fellow in neurology, 1946-51; cons. surgeon N.Y. Police Dept.; sr. med. examiner FAA. Served from capt. to maj., M.C., AUS, 1942-46. Licensed comml. pilot. Fellow Am. Acad. Neurology, N.Y. Acad. Medicine; mem. Am. Psychiatric Assn., AMA, Am. Psychopathol. Assn., Assn. for Research in Nervous and Mental Diseases, Internat. League Against Epilepsy, Am. Geriatric Soc., N.Y. Acad. Scis., N.Y. Neurol. Soc., N.Y. Soc. Clin. Psychiatry, Am. Assn. Automotive Medicine, Am. Guild Authors and Composers, ASCAP, Flying Physicians Assn., Aerospace Med. Assn., Airplane Owners and Pilots Assn., Nat. Pilots Assn., Nat. Aero. Assn., Civil Aviation Med. Assn., Airplane Owners and Pilots Assn., Quiet Birdmen, Air Force Assn., Nat. Bus. Aircraft Assn. (Million Miler Safety award), Antique Auto Club, Allard Owners Club (London), Internat. Order Characters (v.p.), Wings Club, Sigma Xi. Contbr. papers to profl. publs. Died Feb. 15, 1996.

OSKI, FRANK ARAM, physician, educator; b. Phila., June 17, 1932; s. Aram P. and Sarah (Koshgerian) O.; m. Barbara Fassett, June 22, 1957; children: Jonathan, Jane, Jessica. BA, Swarthmore Coll., 1954; MD, U. Pa., 1958; DSc (hon.), SUNY, 1991. Diplomate Am. Bd. Pediatrics. Intern Hosp. U. Pa., 1958-59, resident, 1959-61; practice medicine specializing in pediatrics Phila., 1962-72; mem. faculty Sch. Medicine, U. Pa., 1963-72, asso. prof. pediatrics, 1968-72; prof. pediatrics, chmn. dept. Upstate Med. Center, SUNY-Syracuse, 1972-85; chmn. dept. pediatrics Johns Hopkins U. Sch. Medicine, Balt., 1985—; former mem. staff State Univ. Hosp., Crouse-Irving Meml. Hosp., Syracuse; physician-in-chief Children's Ctr., Johns Hopkins Hosp., 1985—. Author: Hematologic Problems of the Newborn, 3d edit., 1982, Hematology of Infancy and Childhood, 3d edit., 1987, The Whole Pediatrician Catalog, Vol. 1, 1977, Vol. 2, 1979, Vol. 3, 1981, Don't Drink Your Milk, 1977, Core Textbook of Pediatrics, 1978, 2d edit., 1982, Principles and Practice of Pediatrics, 1994; editor Year Book of Pediatrics, 1979-81, Contemporary Pediatrics, 1984—, Current Opinion in Pediatrics, 1992—; also articles. Recipient E. Mead-Johnson award Am. Acad. Pediatrics, 1972, St. Geme award, 1990, Disting. Grad. award. U. Pa. Sch. Medicine, 1990; named Scientist of Yr., Am. Students Assn., 1972. Mem. Soc. Pediatric Rsch. (pres. 1977-78), Am. Pediatric Soc., Am. Soc. Clin. Investigation, Am. Soc. Clin. Nutrition, Red Cell Club, Am. Soc. Hematology-Oncology (Disting. Career award 1993), Assn. Am. Med. Sch. Pediatric Dept. Chairmen (pres. 1992-93). Died Oct. 24, 1996.

OSLIN, GEORGE POER, writer, telegraph official; b. West Point, Ga., Aug. 5, 1899; s. Reuben Jefferson and Mary (Poer) O.; m. Louise Love, Jan. 31, 1922; children: Louise, Jeanne, Catherine; m. Susanna Meigs, Dec. 22, 1956. Student, Duke U., 1915-19; AB, Mercer U., 1920; postgrad. in journalism, Columbia U., 1921. Reporter Macon (Ga.) Daily Telegraph, 1920-21; fin., real estate and auto editor Newark (N.J.) Ledger, 1922; reporter, feature writer Newark Evening News, 1922-29; dir. pub. rels. Western Union, 1929-64. Author: Talking Wires, 1942, The Story of Telecommunications, 1993, also monograph; contbr. chpts. and sects. to books, artles to profl. jours. and mags.; creator singing telegram. Home: Delray Beach Fla. Died Jan. 15, 1996.

OST, WARREN WILLIAM, minister; b. Mankato, Minn., June 24, 1926; s. William Frederick and Margaret Avery (Denison) O.; m. Nancy Nesbitt, May 15, 1954; 1 child, Laura Margaret. BA, U. Minn., 1948; MDiv, Princeton U., 1951; DD (hon.), Moravian Theol. Sem., Bethlehem, Pa., 1971. Ordained to ministry Presbyn. Ch. (U.S.A.), 1951. Min. parishes, Phila., Scranton, Pa., N.J., 1948-51; resident min. Yellowstone Nat. Park, Wyo., 1950-52; dir. A Christian Ministry in Nat. Parks, N.Y.C., 1951-97; bd. dirs. Ring Lake Ranch, Dubois, Wyo., 1964-97; charter mem. Tourisme-Oecumenique, Geneva, 1967-97; cons. Pontifical Commn. on Migration and Tourism, The Vatican, Rome, 1967-97. Editor: Gospel, Freedom and Leisure, 1965. Bd. dirs. Prescott Neighborhood House, N.Y.C., 1961-97, pres. East 49th Street Assn., N.Y.C., 1961-62. Recipient Pub. Svc. award U.S. Dept. Interior, 1977; named hon. park ranger Nat. Park Svc., 1977. Mem. Assn. Theol. Field Educators, Nat. Park Svc. Employees and Alumni Assn. (life), Conf. Nat. Park Concessioners (life), Denison Soc., Amis du Chemin St. Jacques, Union League Club, Princeton Club, Phi Mu Alpha. Home: New York N.Y. Died Nov. 6, 1997.

OSTENSO, NED ALLEN, oceanographer, government official; b. Fargo, N.D., June 22, 1930; s. Nels Andres and Estella (Temple) O.; m. Grace Elaine Laudon, June 29, 1963. BS, U. Wis., 1952, MS, 1953, PhD, 1962; postgrad., Johns Hopkins U., 1975. Scientist Arctic Inst. N.Am., Washington, 1956-66; asst. prof. geology and geophysics U. Wis., Madison, 1962-66; dir. marine geol. and geophys. programs Office Naval Rsch., Washington, 1966-69, sr. oceanographer, 1970-77; asst. Presdl. sci. advisor White House, Washington, 1969-70; dir. nat. sea grant coll. program NOAA, Washington, 1977-83, dir. Office Oceanic Rsch., 1983-89, chief scientist, 1989-90, asst. adminstr. for rsch., 1990-96, cons., 1996-97; fellow Fed. Execs. Inst., Charlottesville, Va., 1974, Am. Polit. Sci. Assn., Washington, 1975-76. Cotnbr. over 60 articles on polar regions, oceanography and geophysics to sci. jours., chpts. to books. 1st lt. Signal Corps, U.S. Army, 1953-56. Recipient Antarctic Svc. medal Dept. of Def., 1958, Meritorius Svc. citation NAS, 1959, Superior Accomplishment award USN, 1968; Mt. Ostenso named in his honor, 1963, Ostenso Seamount (Arctic Ocean) named in his honor, 1978; recipient Compass Dist. award marine Technol. Soc., 1993. Fellow Geol. Soc. Am., Am. Geophys. Union (Ocean Sci. award 1992, Waldo E. Smith medal 1996), Arctic Inst. N.Am., Marine Tech. Soc., Explorers Club; mem. Acad. Polit. Sci., UN Assn. U.S.A., Cosmos Club. Home: Washington D.C. Died Apr. 13, 1997; interred Forest Hill Cemetery, Chippewa Falls, WI.

OSTERLOH, EVERETT WILLIAM, county official; b. Luxemburg, Mo., June 7, 1919; s. Fred and Esther (Miller) O.; m. Eunice Gramann, Oct. 20, 1940 (dec. Apr. 1983); m. Herta Anna Emery, Oct. 25, 1987. BSME, Washington U., St. Louis, 1958. Registered profl. engr., Mo.; cert. code ofcl. Plant engr. Jasper-Blackburn Corp., St. Louis, 1958-60; equipment engr. Monsanto Chem. Co., St. Louis, 1960-68; pres. Caribean Beach Club, Antigua, West Indies, 1968-73; dep. dir. pub. works St. Louis County Govt., Clayton, Mo., 1973-93; assoc. dir. emergency preparedness pub. works St. Louis County Govt., St. Louis, 1993-96; engring. instr. St. Louis Community Coll., 1986-91; exec. sec. Profl. Code Com. St. Louis, 1975-96, Met. Area Code Com., St. Louis, 1982-96. Staff sgt. USAF, 1942-53. Mem. Mo. Soc. Profl. Engrs. (emergency response task force 1990-92, pres. St. Louis chpt. 1991-92, chmn. disaster response com. 1992-96, Outstanding Engr. in Govt. 1987). Lutheran. Home: Ballwin Mo. Died Aug. 9, 1996.

OSTHEIMER, GERARD WILLIAM, anesthesiology educator; b. Poughkeepsie, N.Y., Feb. 9, 1940; s. Gerard William and Margaret Amelia (Theil) O. BS, St. Francis Coll., Loretto, Pa., 1961; MD, U. Pa., 1965; MS (hon.), Harvard U., 1992. Diplomate Am. Bd. Anesthesiology. Rotating intern Misericordia Hosp., Phila., 1965-66; resident in anesthesiology Hosp. of U. Pa., Phila., 1966-68; instr. U. Pa., 1966-69; fellow in cardiovasc. anesthesiology Mayo Clinic, Rochester, Minn., 1968-69; rsch. fellow dept. anesthesia Mass. Gen. Hosp., Boston, 1969-70; rsch. fellow dept. anesthesia Harvard U. Med. Sch., Boston, 1969-70, instr., 1970, 72-76, asst. prof., 1976-83, assoc. prof., 1983-91, prof., 1991-95; anesthesiologist Brigham and Women's Hosp., Boston, 1972-95, dir. obstetric anesthesia, 1982-88, vice chmn.

dept. anesthesia, 1988-91, 92-95; vis. prof. numerous univs., 1974-95, including U. Md., U. Wis., UCLA, 1990, U. Rochester, Columbia U., 1991, U. Ill., Chgo., 1992, 93, 94, Rush Med. Sch., Chgo., 1992, U. Cin., U. Conn., U. Colo., Denver, Med. Coll. Pa., Cornell U., 1993, Wake Forest U., Med. Coll. Wis., 1994; editl. reviewer Anesthesiology, Anesthesia and Analgesia, Ob-Gyn., Am. Jour. Ob-Gyn.; Astra Pharm. vis. prof., Australia and New Zealand, 1989; 1st Benjamin J. Covino lectr. Maimonides Med. Ctr., 1992, U. Mass. Sch. Medicine, 1992; Henry Ruth lectr. Hanhemann U., Phila., 1993; med. projects advisor Internat. Coun. on Edn., 1977-82; mem. ednl. materials project appraisal panel Assn. Am. Med. Colls., 1977-82; profl. cons. Internat. Childbirth Edn. Assn., 1980-82. Editor: Manual of Obstetric Anesthesia, 1984, 2d edit., 1992, (with S. Datta) Common Problems in Obstetric Anesthesia, 1987, (with Ferrante and Covino) Patient-Controlled Analgesia, 1989, Pain Relief and Anesthesia in Obstetrics, 1995; editor-in-chief Regional Anesthesia, 1990-95; mem. editl. bd. Jour. Cli. Anesthesia, 1988-95, Internat. Monitor, 1990-95, also others; contbr. numerous articles, revs. and abstracts to med. jours., chpts. to books. Maj. M.C., U.S. Army, 1970-72. Fellow Am. Coll. Anesthesiologists; mem. AMA, Am. Soc. Anesthesiologists, Internat. Anesthesia Rsch. Soc., Soc. for Obstetric Anesthesia and Perinatology (bd. dirs. 1973-81, pres. 1980-81), Mass. Soc. Anesthesiologists, New Eng. Soc. Anesthesiologists, Obstetric Anaesthetists Assn., Mass. Med. Soc. (com. on perinatal welfare 1977-95, com. on maternal welfare 1981-95), Norfolk Dist. Med. Soc., New Eng. Perinatal Soc., Assn. Univ. Anesthetists, World Fedn. Scocs. Anaesthesiologists (com. on obstetic anaesthesia and analgesia 1984-92), Am. Soc. Regional Anesthesia (bd. dirs. 1985-94, pres. 1991-92), European Soc. Regional Anesthesia, L.Am. Soc. Regional Anesthesia, Phi Rho Sigma. Avocation: fly fishing. Home: Dover Mass. Died Oct. 1, 1995.

O'SULLIVAN, BRENDAN PATRICK, lawyer; b. N.Y.C., May 26, 1930; s. Patrick Joseph and Rosaleen (McQuillan) O'S.; m. Maria Teresa Colonna, Sept. 8, 1957; children: Leslie, Laurie, James. Bar: N.Y. 1958, Fla. 1961, U.S. Dist. Ct. (so., mid. and no. dists.) Fla. 1961, U.S. Ct. Appeals (5th and 11th cirs.) 1961, U.S. Ct. Internat. Trade 1980, U.S. Supreme Ct. 1975; bd. cert. in civil trial practice and admiralty and maritime law. Staff atty. Maritime Administrn., Washington, 1958-60; assoc. Fowler, White, Gillen, Boggs, Villareal & Banker, P.A., Tampa, Fla., 1960-63, ptnr., 1963—. Coach, mgr. Tampa Bay Little League, Tampa, 1973-78. Lt. Comdr USNR-R, 1951-77. Mem. ABA, Fla. Bar Assn. (chmn. admiralty law com. 1979-80, admiralty and maritime law cert. com. 1995—), Hillsborough County Bar Assn., Maritime Law Assn. (bd. dirs. 1993-96), Fed. Bar Assn., Def. Rsch. Inst. (chmn. admiralty law com., 1988-91, editor newsletter, 1987-95), Civil Trial Lawyer (bd. cert.), Nat. Bd. Trial Advocates, Tampa Bay Mariners Club (skipper 1979-80, speakers trophy, 1976), Gray-Gables-Bon Air Civic Club (pres. 1964-65), Southeastern Admiralty Law Inst. (bd. govs. 1974-77), Tampa Cath. Lawyers Guild (v.p. 1996—), University Club, Centre Club. Democrat. Roman Catholic. Avocations: tennis, swimming, jogging. Deceased.

OTTINGER, RICHARD ESTES, public broadcasting executive, retired; b. Knoxville, Tenn., Apr. 23, 1932; s. Clive Estes and Mary (Groves) O.; m. Phyllis Blevins Dec. 22, 1957; children, Jeannie Elaine Whittington, Richard Estes Jr. BS in Edn., U. Tenn., 1957, MS in Edn., 1958; EDd, Auburn U., 1963. Head coach W. Ga. Coll., Carrollton, 1958-61; assoc. prof. Ga. Southern Coll., Statesboro, 1963-66; learning ctr. dir. Brunswick (Ga.) Pub. Schs., 1966-68; dir. Ga. ETV Network State of Ga., Atlanta, 1968-82; exec. dir. Ga. Pub. Telecommunications Comn. State of Ga., 1982-94; ret., 1994. Served with the U.S. Army, 1954-56. Mem. NATAS, So. Ednl. Communications Assn. (chmn. bd. 1986-87), Nat. Assn. of Pub. TV Stas. (chmn. bd. 1986-89). Persbyterian. Avocations: golf, reading, civic work. Died Nov. 4, 1997.

OUGHTON, JAMES HENRY, JR., corporate executive, farmer; b. Chgo., May 14, 1913; s. James H. and Barbara (Corbett) O.; student Dartmouth Coll., 1931-35; m. Jane Boyce, Jan. 23, 1940 (dec.); children: Diana (dec.), Carol Oughton Biondi, Pamela Oughton Armstrong, Deborah Oughton Callahan. Pres., dir. L.E. Keeley Co., Dwight, Ill., 1936—, Nev. Corp.; past adminstr. The Keeley Inst., Dwight, 1938-66; dir. 1st Nat. Bank of Dwight, Ill., 1939—, Ill. Valley Investment Co., 1945-89; farmer, farm mgr., livestock feeder, Ill.; sec., dir. Dwight Indsl. Assn., 1958-93; past mem. Ill. Ho. of Reps. Co-chmn. 1st Indsl. Conf. on Alcoholism, 1948; chmn. Midwest Seminar on Alcoholism for Pastors, 1957, 58, 59, 60; chmn. adv. bd. Ill. Dept. Corrections; chmn. Gov.'s Task Force on Mental Health Adminstrn., 1971-72; mem. adv. bd. Ill. Dept. Mental Health; dir., mem. exec. bd. W.D. Boyce council Boy Scouts Am.; del. 31st Internat. Congress on Alcoholism and Drug Dependence, Bangkok, 1975; mem. Internat. Council on Alcohol and Addictions, Lausanne, Switzerland, 1977; mem. Ill. Trade and Investment Mission to Japan and Korea, 1985; mem. adv. council Small Bus., Fed. Reserve Bank Chgo., 1985-86. Served as lt. (j.g.) USNR, 1944-46; PTO. Republican. Episcopalian. Clubs: Univ., Union League (Chgo.).

OVIATT, ROSS HANNUM, lawyer; b. Huron, S.D., Apr. 14, 1918; s. Thad Walter and Grace (Hannum) O.; m. Marion Melham, Oct. 12, 1943; children: Timothy M., Jonathan J., Nancy Lou. J.D., U. S.D., 1941. Bar: S.D. 1941. Practiced in Watertown, 1945—; ptnr. Oviatt, Green, Schulz & Roby (and predecessors), 1945-83; assoc. Green, Schulz, Roby & Ford, 1983-89; of counsel Green, Schulz, Roby & Oviatt, 1989—; state's atty. Codington County, 1951-55; mem. S.D. Jud. Council, 1960-68, 73-74. Author: South Dakota Justice-The Judges and the System, 1989; contbr. articles to profl. jours. Mem. S.D. Jud. Qualifications Commn., 1979-83, chmn., 1981-83; chmn. S.D. Senate Screening Com. for U.S. Dist. Judge Applicants; mem. fed. practice com. Dist. S.D. 8th Cir., 1980-86; chancellor S.D. Ann. Conf. United Meth. Ch., 1981-90. Lt. comdr. USNR, 1942-45. Recipient Marshall McKusick award U. S.D. Law Sch., 1974. Fellow Am. Coll. of Trust and Estate Counsel (regent 1975-81), Am. Bar Found. (S.D. chmn. 1979-87), Internat. Soc. Barristers, Am. Bd. Trial Advs. (adv., pres. S.D. chpt. 1981-82); mem. ABA (ho. of dels. 1960-73, gov. 10th Dist. 1968-71, state del. 1978-87), S.D. Bar Assn. (pres. 1973-74), Am. Judicature Soc. (dir. 1971-75), Phi Delta Phi. Methodist. Club: Masons.

OWEN, JOHN PIPKIN, management educator; b. Newport, Ark., Sept. 13, 1919; s. Henry M. and Alice C. (Pipkin) O.; m. Yvonne M. Olinde, Aug. 16, 1947; children: Trina A., Yvonne T., Joan P., J. Elizabeth, John P. B.A., La. State U., 1941, M.B.A., 1944, Ph.D., 1949. Instr. econs. La. State U., 1946-49; prof. econs., dir. grad. studies Coll. Bus. Adminstrn., U. Houston, 1949-67, chmn. dept. econs. and finance, 1949-66; dean Coll. Bus. Adminstrn., U. Ark., 1967-83, disting. prof. mgmt., 1983-85, prof. emeritus, 1986—; Tex. mem. Econ. Stblzn. Planning Task Group; dir. Northwest Nat. Bank, 1975-77. Author: Syllabus and Workbook for Principles of Economics, 1952, What's Wrong With Workmen's Compensation, 1956, Adequacy of the Louisiana Unemployment Compensation Fund, 1949, Survey of Grievance and Arbitration Proceedings in The Houston Industrial Area, 1953, The Determination of Economic Feasibility of Multiple-Purpose Dams, 1957; co-author: Mantrap; The Anatomy of a Workforce Reduction, 1967. Recipient Small Bus. Adminstrn. research grant to Center for Research, U. Houston, 1962. Mem. Am., So. econ. assns., Southwestern Social Sci. Assn., Indsl. Relations Research Assn., Sch. Banking of the South (sec. leader), Am. Arbitration Assn., Fed. Mediation and Conciliation Service, Nat. Acad. Arbitrators, Ark. Hwy. Research Com., Ark. Council on Econ. Edn., Fayetteville C. of C., Southwestern Bus. Adminstrn. Assn. (pres. 1971-72), Alpha Kappa Psi, Sigma Iota Epsilon, Beta Alpha Psi, Phi Kappa Phi, Beta Gamma Sigma. Club: Rotary. Died Nov. 18, 1996.

OWEN, LARRY MALCOLM, electric company executive; b. Lincoln, Nebr., Jan. 1, 1928; s. Leonard J. and Ruth L. (Anderson) O.; m. Marilyn Wilkens, Aug. 6, 1950; children—David L., Sue Ellen. B.S. in Bus. Adminstrn., U. Nebr., 1950; Dr. Bus. Adminstrn. (hon.), S.D. Sch. Mines and Tech., 1984. Mgmt. trainee J.C. Penney Co., Lincoln, 1950-52; with mgmt. Nebr. City C. of C., Nebr., 1952-55, Columbus C. of C., Nebr., 1955-57, Rapid City C. of C., Nebr., 1957-66; exec. v.p. Cedar Rapids C. of C., Iowa, 1967-70; chmn., pres., chief exec. officer Black Hills Corp., Rapid City, 1970—. Chmn. bd. trustees Rushmore Nat. Health, Rapid City, 1984-86. Served with USN, 1945-46. Mem. Edison Electric Inst. (dir. 1984-86), North Central Electric Assn. (pres. 1984), Rocky Mountain Electric League (dir. 1980—). Republican. Presbyterian. Died 7, 1997.

OWEN, WILLIAM HAROLD, JR., academic administrator; b. Stilwell, Okla., Aug. 2, 1933; s. William Harold Sr. and Nellie (Whiteside) O.; m. Mary Ann Fryar, Mar. 10, 1956; children: David G., John F. AA, Jr. Agrl. Coll., Beebe, Ark., 1953; BS, Ark. State Tchrs. Coll., 1957, MS in Edn., 1960. Tchr. Beebe Pub. Schs., 1957-59; asst. prof. social scis. Ark. State U., Beebe, 1959-69, dean students, registrar, 1969-81, chancellor, 1981—; bd. dirs. Beebe Indsl. Devel. Corp. Corp. sec. White County Meml. Hosp., Searcy, Ark., 1987—. With USAF, 1953-55. Mem. Ark. Assn. Two-Yr. Colls. (chmn. bd. dirs. 1989-90), Ark. Higher Edn. Coun., Beebe C. of C. (bd. dirs. 1985—), Beebe Kiwanis (past pres.). Presbyterian. Avocations: hunting, fishing, woodworking. Deceased.

OXLEY, JOHN THURMAN, ranching and investments executive, petroleum company executive; b. Bromide, Okla., July 26, 1909; s. Moses E. and Sallie E. (Cochran) O.; m. Mary K. Yetter, Aug. 17, 1935; children: John C., Mary J., Thomas E. Student, East Central Coll., Okla., Tulsa Bus. Coll., Tulsa Law Sch., U. Tulsa. With Amerada Petroleum Corp., 1927-35; with Warren Petroleum Corp., 1935-48; sec. and mgr. gasoline div., pres., dir. Tex. Natural Gasoline Corp., Tulsa, 1948-60; exec. v.p., dir. Union Tex. Petroleum Corp., 1960-63; cons. Union Tex. Petroleum (merged with Allied Chem. Corp.), 1963; part owner Oxley Petroleum Co., 1963-96; chmn., pres., chief exec. officer, dir. Arkansas Valley Industries, Inc., 1964-69; dir. Apco Oil Corp. Mem. So. Hills Country Club, Royal Palm Polo Sports Club, Boca Raton, Fla. Home: Tulsa Okla. Died Sept. 19, 1996.

OXTOBY, ROBERT BOYNTON, lawyer; b. Huron, S.D., May 8, 1921; s. Frederic Breading and Frieda (Boynton) O.; m. Carolyn Bartholf; children: Michael, Thomas, Susan. Student, Ill. Coll.; B.A., Carleton Coll., 1943; J.D., Northwestern U., 1949. Bar: Ill. 1949. Mem. firm Van Meter, Oxtoby & Funk, 1949—; asst. U.S. atty., 1953-57, spl. asst. atty. gen., 1970—. Chmn. Ill Capital Devel. Bd., 1991-95; bd. dirs. Downtown Park, Inc., Springfield Bd. Edn. Served to 1st lt. USMCR, 1943-46, PTO. Died July 4, 1997.

OZOLINS, KARLIS LOTARS, retired library director; b. Riga, Latvia, Mar. 11, 1923; came to U.S, 1943; s. Karl and Alma (Cukste) O.; m. Sulamit I. Ivask, Nov. 10, 1945; children: Dina Ruth, Andrew Lynn, Peter Charles. BA, Augsburg Coll., 1951; BTh, Augsburg Theol. Sem., 1952; MLS, U. Minn., 1961, MEd, 1966; MDiv, U. Luther Northwestern Sem., 1970; PhD, U. Mich., 1972. Pastor Luth Free Ch., Barronett, Wis., 1951-55; instr. Augsburg Coll., Mpls., 1955-59, libr., 1959-61; lectr. U. Minn., Mpls., 1961-69; Fulbright prof. Nat. Taiwan U., Taipei, 1963-64; lectr. U. Mich., Ann Arbor, 1966-67; dept. head libr. sci. Ill. State U., Normal, 1971-73; dir. libr. Gustavus Adolphus Coll., St. Peter, Minn., 1973-80; dir. libr. U. St. Thomas, St. Paul, 1980-90, ret., 1990—. Editorial advisor Jour. of Baltic Studies; book reviewer in field. Mem. ALA, Minn. Libr. Assn., Am. Latvian Assn., Hist. Luth Conf., Beta Phi Mu. Lutheran. Died June 18, 1997.

PABST, RALPH MALCOM, import-export, publishing and mining executive; b. Macon, Ga., Nov. 2, 1920; s. Eugene Price and Beatrice I. (Kenney) Jernigan; adopted s. George A. Pabst; children: Genevieve A. Martinez, Yvonne M. Pierce, George P. BFA, Bradley U.; postgrad., Brigham Young U., Jones Bus. Coll., Fla.; DO, Anglo-Am. Inst. Drugless Therapy, Eng.; PhD, Hamilton State U. Owner, mgr. Bam's Overseas Treasures; chmn. bd. The Augury Press, Greater Denver-Phoenix Mining Co., Inc., Am. Entertainment Corp., Commodity Exch. U.S.A.; mem. Consular Corps, Washington. Author: Plodding toward Terror, Away and Beyond, Executive Handbook, The Spoofiness Lexicon, Match Wits, I Remember Cuisine's Finest Moments, Zodiac of Life, Renew Your Life through God, The Handiwork of God in the Holy Land, Mental Telepathy, Astral Peer, God's Handwriting, Hitler the Occultist, Top Hat, Bugsy Siegel/Betty Woods Memories, Jacob von Walzer, Facts: Then and Now, J F K, "The Whole Truth...So Help Me...," Kenney and Allied Families, The Cowart/Jernigan Allied Families; pub. God Is Still My Co-Pilot, Gene Austin'-Ole Buddy, The Hereditary Register of USA. Dep. sheriff, Ariz., Nev., Mass. Officer USN, World War II. Decorated knight grand officer Ancient and Imperial Order of Crescent (Eng.), knight Order St. Dennis of Zante, (Greece), King Peter of Yugoslavia; recipient award Freedoms Found. at Valley Forge, Acad. Palms class A, Internat. Am. Inst.; named Ky. col., lt. col. Ala., marshall Phoenix Rep. Com. Mem. Nat. Sheriffs Assn. (life), Navy League (life), SAR (past treas. gen., gold citizenship medal, Patriot's medal, Minute Man award), Mayflower Soc., Sons and Daus. Pilgrims (life), Soc. Colonial Wars, Soc. Founders and Patriots, Desc. Colonial Clergy (life), Huguenot Soc., St. Andrew's Soc., St. George's Soc., Nat. Sojurners (life), Masons (32d degree), Son of a Witch (pres. gen.). Home: Phoenix Ariz. Died Oct. 12, 1995.

PACK, JANE ROBIN, advertising executive; b. Bklyn., Mar. 4, 1955; d. Milton O. and Phyllis J. (Klausner) P.; m. Stephen P. Dessau, Jan. 18, 1981; children: Julianna Sara, David Stephen. BA, SUNY, Albany, 1975; MBA, CUNY, 1982; student, Sch. Visual Arts and New Sch., 1976-77. Spls. programming asst. Grey Advt. Inc., N.Y.C., 1975-76; asst. account exec. new projects devel. Internat. Health Co. div. Rapid Am. Corp., N.Y.C., 1976-77; exec. v.p. Levine Huntley Schmidt & Beaver, N.Y.C., 1977-93. Active radio and TV com. U.N. Anti-Defammation League, 1984-85. Named One of 100 Best and Brightest Advt. and Mktg. Women 1988-89 Advt. Age Mag. Mem. Advt. Women N.Y., Advt. Club N.Y. Home: New York N.Y. Died May 19, 1993.

PACK, ROY SANGHUN, financial analyst; b. Corvallis, Oreg., Oct. 22, 1964; s. Moo Young and Haesun (Shin) P. BS, Boston U., 1986; MBA, Pa. State U., 1990. Registered rep. First Investors Corp., Boston, 1986-87; customer svc. rep. Cambridge (Mass.) Trust Co., 1987-88; fin. analyst Air Products and Chems., Inc., Allentown, Pa., 1990—. Mem. Korean Ch. of Lehigh Valley, Whitehall, Pa., 1990—. Avocation: fostering relationships between Asian community and rest of community. Died Dec. 29, 1996.

PACKARD, VANCE OAKLEY, writer; b. Granville Summit, Pa., May 22, 1914; s. Philip Joseph and Mabel (Case) P.; m. Mamie Virginia Mathews, Nov. 25, 1938; children: Vance Philip, Randall Mathews, Cynthia Ann. BA, Pa. State U., 1936; MS, Columbia U., 1937; LittD, Monmouth Coll., 1975. Reporter Centre Daily Times, State College, Pa., 1936; columnist Boston Record, 1937-38; writer, editor Asso. Press Feature Service, 1938-42; editor, staff writer Am. mag., 1942-56; staff writer Collier's mag., 1956; lectr. reporting, mag.

writing Columbia, 1941-44, N.Y.U., 1945-57; guest lectr. several hundred colls. and univs., U.S. and 13 other countries. Author: Animal IQ, 1950, The Hidden Persuaders, 1957, The Status Seekers, 1959, The Waste Makers, 1960, The Pyramid Climbers, 1962, The Naked Society, 1964, The Sexual Wilderness, 1968, A Nation of Strangers, 1972, The People Shapers, 1977 (Notable Book of 1977, ALA), Our Endangered Children, 1983, The Ultra Rich, 1988;. Mem. planning commn., New Canaan, Conn., 1954-56; pres. Chappaquiddick Island Assn., 1977-78; mem. nat. bd. Nat. Book Com.; Trustee Silvermine Coll. Art. Recipient Distinguished Alumni award Pa. State U., 1961; Outstanding Alumni award Grad. Sch. Journalism, Columbia, 1963. Mem. Soc. Mag. Writers (pres. 1961); mem. Am. Sociol. Assn., Authors' Guild, Am. Acad. Polit. and Social Sci., Population Resource Ctr. (bd. dirs.), Ctr. for Study of Commercialism (bd. advisors). Died Dec. 12, 1996.

PAGEL, WILLIAM RUSH, labor relations executive; b. Egan, S.D., Nov. 4, 1901; s. William Reinhart and Carrie Edith (Rush) P.; m. Dorothy Loretta Johnsen, Aug. 19, 1939; children: William Kingston, Diane Lynette (Mrs. Robert N. Harsh). Student, U. S.D., 1919-21; B.A. cum laude, U. Wis., 1924. With Ill. Bell Telephone Co., 1924-67; geneol. researcher Shawnee Mission, Kans., 1971-93; lectr., author on geneal. subjects. Speaker U. Wyo. Old Time Ranch Tour, 1961, Kansas City Pub. Library Geneal. Seminar, 1974. Author: George Morgan American Hereford Pioneer, 1967, A Mayflower Lineage of Twelve Generations, 1974. Recipient Bicentennial citation D.A.R., 1974. Mem. Telephone Pioneers Am., Soc. Mayflower Descendants (bd. assts. Ill. chpt. 1967-71, gov. Kans. chpt. 1975-78), Sons and Daus. Pilgrims, Descendants Colonial Govs., Descendants Colonial Clergy, Soc. Colonial Wars, Huguenot Soc. (dir. Ill. chpt. 1964-67, v.p. 1965-67), Sons Union Vets. Civil War, S.A.R. (v.p. Ill. chpt. 1963-68, founding mem. George Rogers Clark chpt., Distinguished Service and Patriots awards 1963, 66), Heart of Am., Johnson County, Ill. geneal. socs., S.D., Moody County hist. socs. Club: Aztec. Home: Shawnee Mission Kans. Died Aug. 4, 1993; Johnson County Memorial Gardens Cemetery.

PALEWICZ, RICHARD ALFRED, judge; b. Chgo., June 26, 1927; s. Emil FRanz Witold and Alfreds (Pold) P.; m. Shirley Ann Bauman, July 10, 1954 (dec. Apr. 1993). BA in Econs. and Speech, U. Ill., 1950; JD, Loyola U., Chgo., 1958; diploma, U.S. Army War Coll., Carlisle, Pa., 1979, U.S. Army Command & Staff Coll, Ft. Riley, Kans., 1976. Merchandise sect. head Montgomery Ward & Co., Chgo., 1954-56; oper. mgr. Allied Radio Co., Chgo., 1956-58; gen. office mgr. Win-Chek Products Corp., Addison, Ill., 1959; legal editor labor law Commerce Clearing House, Chgo., 1960-62; sr. ptnr. Bamberger & Palewicz, Chgo., 1959-62; atty. trade regulations FTC, Chgo., 1962-65, sr. trial atty., 1966-74, supervising atty. trade regulations, 1975-80; U.S. adminstrv. law judge Office Hearing & Appeals Health & Human Svcs., Chgo., 1980-81, hearing office chief adminstrv. law judge, 1981-88; U.S. adminstrv. law judge Office Hearings & Appeals HHS & Social Sec. Adminstrn., Chgo., 1989—. Bd. dirs. Jane Adams Hull House-Uptown Ctr., Chgo., 1972—; pres. Truman Coll. Coun., Chgo., 1978-80; chmn. presdl. selection com. Truman Coll., Chgo., 1978, mem. coll. coun., 1979—. Col. Inf., U.S. Army, 1951-54; active res. 1954-80. Recipient Honoree Night award Cook County Vets. Assistance Commn., Chgo. Mem. ABA, FBA, Ill. State Bar Assn., Chgo. Bar Assn., Res. Officers Assn. U.S. (nat. judge advocate 1992-94, pres. Ill. dept. 1988, pres. Cook County chpt. 1986. Eagle award 1993, Brigade of Vols. 1990), Mil. Order World Wars (comdr. Ill. State 1976, chgo. chpt. comdr. 1975, vice-comdr. in chief 1991-93, sr. vice comdr. 1993-94, comdr. in chief 1994-95, Youth Leadership award 1995), Advocate Soc., Chgo. Soc. PNA SARCOM (Sr. Army Res. Comdrs. - Col. & Generals). Roman Catholic. Died Aug. 1, 1997.

PALME, OLOF SVEN JOACHIM, prime minister of Sweden; b. Stockholm, Sweden, Jan. 30, 1927; ed. Kenyon Coll., Gambier, O., U. Stockholm; m. Lisbeth Beck Friis, 1956; 3 sons. Spl. counsel to Swedish prime minister, 1956-63; mem. Parliament, 1958—; minister without portfolio, 1963-65; minister of communications, 1965-67, of edn. and culture, 1967-69; prime minister, 1969-76, 82—; mem. Ind. Commn. on Internat. Devel. Issues; chmn. Ind. Commn. on Disarmament and Security Issues; v.p. Socialist Internat. Mem. Swedish del. to UN, 1961. Mem. exec. Swedish Social Democratic Youth and Workers Ednl. Assn., 1955-61; mem. exec. Swedish Social Dem. Party, 1964—, chmn., 1969—. Chmn., Coms. Student Welfare, 1960-63.

PALMER, LANE MORRIS, magazine publishing executive, editor; b. Park Valley, Utah, Sept. 4, 1921; s. James Watts and Lilis (Morris) P.; m. Anne Ryan, Aug. 21, 1946; children—Cheryl, Kandra, Deems. B.S., Utah State U., 1943; M.S., U. Wis., 1947. Assoc. N.C. State U., 1947-52; assoc. Farm Jour., Phila., 1952-55, mng. editor, 1955-68, editor, 1968-86, editor emeritus, 1986—, sr. v.p., dir., 1974—; vis. prof. U. Wis., 1970. Borough councilman, Hatboro, Pa., 1955-59. Served to capt., arty., inf. AUS, 1943-46. Recipient Disting. Centennial Alumni award Utah State U., 1987. Mem. Pi Kappa Alpha, Sigma Delta Chi. Republican. Unitarian. Home: 410 Continental Rd Hatboro PA 19040-3908 Office: 230 W Washington Sq Philadelphia PA 19106-3522 Died Nov. 9, 1996.

PALMER, ROBERT FRANKLIN, JR., music critic; b. Little Rock, June 19, 1945; s. Robert Franklin and Marguerite (Bowers) P. B.A. in English, U. Ark., Little Rock, 1967. prof. Am. vernacular music Bowdoin Coll., Memphis State U., Yale U., Bklyn. Coll., Smithsonian Instn., 1975-77. Profl. saxophonist and clarinetist with jazz, rock and country music bands, 1965-70; assoc. editor: Changes mag., 1969-70; freelance writer on music, 1970-97; music critic: contemporary and exptl. music, jazz and pop N.Y. Times, 1976-86; now free lance music critic; contbg. editor, jazz columnist: Penthouse; author: Baby, That Was Rock and Roll: The Legendary Leiber and Stoller, 1978, A Tale of Two Cities: Memphis Rock and New Orleans Roll, 1979, Deep Blues, 1981, The Rolling Stones, 1983; rec. artist contemporary and exptl. music, jazz and pop, Capitol, Atco and A&M records. Sr. research fellow Inst. Studies Am. Music, Bklyn. Coll., 1977. Mem. Am. Folklore Soc., Soc. Ethnomusicology. Died Nov. 20, 1997.

PALMORE, JAMES ANDREW, JR., sociologist; b. Birmingham, Ala., Feb. 5, 1940; s. James Andrew and Miriam Grey (Gaines) P.; m. Joung-Im Kim, Jan. 21, 1989; children by previous marriages: Jennifer Grey, Tara Alison. B.A., Antioch Coll., Yellow Springs, Ohio, 1962; M.A., U. Chgo., 1964, Ph.D., 1966. Instr. sociology U. Chgo., 1964-65; asst. prof. U. Mich., 1965-66, 67-70; sr. demographic adv. Govt. of Malaysia, 1966-67; mem. faculty U. Hawaii, 1970—, prof. sociology, 1974—, dir. population studies program, 1976-91; cons. in field. Author: Report on the West Malaysian Family Survey, 1966-67, 1968, Psychological Perspectives: Family Planning in Korea, 1972, Measuring Mortality, Fertility, and Natural Increase: A Self-Teaching Guide to Elementary Measures, 1983, also other books, articles; co-editor: Choosing a Contraceptive: Method Choice in Asia and the United States, 1989. Grantee NIH, Ford Found., AID, others. Mem. Population Assn. Am. (dir.), Com. Comparative Behavioral Studies in Population (exec. bd.), Am. Statis. Assn., Am. Sociol. Assn., Internat. Union Sci. Study Population. Died Fb. 20, 1996.

PAN JIFANG See LIU HAISU

PAPA, ANTHONY EMIL, retired army officer; b. Williamstown, N.J., Mar. 31, 1914; s. Gabriel and Mamie (Rizzo) P.; m. Dorothea Louise Gibson, Oct. 3, 1942. Grad., Mil. Police Advanced Sch., 1954; student, U. Pitts., 1955. Commd. 2d lt. U.S. Army, 1940; dir. pers. Mil. Police Corps, Washington, 1943-45; advisor, chief of staff U.S. Mil. Mission w/Imperial Iranian Gendarmerie, Tehran, Iran, 1945-48; comdg. officer 504th MP Bn., 1954-55; advanced through grades to col. U.S. Army, 1955; asst. chief of staff G-1, I-Corps, Korea, 1955-56; provost marshal thence asst. chief of staff G-1, Fifth U.S. Army, Chgo., 1959-61; dep. provost marshal gen., 1964-66, ret., 1966; v.p. Guardsmark, Inc., Memphis, 1968-69, 77-78; U.S. marshal for D.C. Washington, 1970-73. Decorated Legion of Merit with oak leaf cluster, Army Commendation medal with 3 oak leaf clusters; Iranian medal of merit; Iranian medal of honor. Second in command to late Major General H.N. Schwarzkopf, mission chief and father of General H. Norman Schwarzkopf, former CINC Desert Storm. Mem. Internat. Assn. Chiefs of Police (life). Home: Saint Petersburg Fla. Died Dec. 15, 1994.

PAPPAS, COSTAS ERNEST, aeronautical engineer, consultant; b. Providence, Oct. 14, 1910; s. Ernest and Sofie (Rose) P.; m. Thetis Hero, June 9, 1940; children: Alceste, Conrad. B.S., NYU, 1933, M.S., 1934. Registered profl. engr., N.Y., Calif. Stress analyst, aerodynamicist Republic Aviation Corp. (formerly Seversky Aircraft Corp.), 1935-39, chief aerodynamics, 1939-54, chief aerodynamics and thermodynamics, 1954-57, asst. dir. sci. research, 1957-59, asst. to v.p. research and devel., 1959-64; cons. to aerospace industry, from 1964; cons. sci. adv. bd. USAF-Aero Space Vehicles Panel. Author: Design Concepts and Technical Feasibility Studies of an Aerospace Plane, 1961, (with Thetis H. Pappas, memoirs) To the Rainbow and Beyond, 1992; contbr. articles to profl. jours.; patentee in field. Mem. NYU Alumni Vis. Com.; mem. San Mateo County Devel. Assn.; mem. grievance com. San Mateo-Burlingame Bd. Realtors, 1982-83, mem. legis. com., 1985-86; planning commr. City of Redwood City (Calif.), 1984-87, vice chmn. planning commn., 1986; mem. adv. council Growth Policy Counc., 1985-90. Recipient Wright Bros. award Soc. Automotive Engr., 1943; award Rep. Aviation Corp., 1944; Certificate of Distinction NYU Coll. Engring., 1955. Mem. NASA (subcom. high speed aerodynamics 1947-53, spl. subcom. research problems transonic aircraft design 1948), Inst. Aero Scis. (asso. fellow, mem. adv. bd. and membership com.), Inst. Aerospace Scis. (chmn. vehicle design panel 1960), Am. Inst. Aeros. and Astronautics (mem. ram jet panel, chmn. workshop profl. unemployed), Calif. Soc. Profl. Engrs., Air Force Assn., Tau Beta Pi (founder, 1st pres. San Francisco Peninsula alumnus chpt. 1971, asst. dir. Dist. 15 from 1979), Redwood City-San Mateo County C. of C. (econ. devel. and govtl. rels. com. from 1987), Iota Alpha. Club: Commonwealth of Calif. Home: San Mateo Calif. Deceased.

PARADISE, PHIL(IP HERSCHEL), artist; b. Ontario, Oreg., Aug. 26, 1905; s. Joseph Richard and Bessie Ana (Green) P.; m. Virginia Dare McCormick, Oct. 21, 1934 (dec. 1953); children: Virginia Gail, Philip Lee; m. Alice Hancock Johns, Nov. 5, 1959. Grad., Chouinard Art Inst., Los Angeles, 1927. tchr. Chouinard Art Inst., 1932-40, dir. fine arts dept., 1936-40; summer guest instr. U. Calif. at Santa Barbara, Calif. Arts and Crafts, Oakland, Tex. Western Coll.; lectr. Scripps Coll. Exhibited all prin. invitational and competitive exhbns. in U.S., including, Pa. Acad. Fine Arts, Whitney Mus. Am. Art, Met. Mus. Art, Los Angeles County, Denver, San Diego mus., Nat. Gallery Art, Art. Inst. Chgo.; represented in permanent collections, Library of Congress Print Collection, Pa. Acad. Fine Arts, Cornell U., Spokane Art Assn., Los Angeles County Fair Assns., others; editorial illustrations in True; motion picture prodn. design and art dir. major studios. Recipient award Oakland Ann. Watercolor Exhbn., 1938, award Los Angeles County Fair Assn., 1938, Dana medal Pa. Acad. Fine Arts, 1939, 2d pl. oil Calif. State Fair Assn., 1949, Smithsonian Archives Am. Art award, 1990, Life Time Achievements award Laguna Beach Mus., 1991, others. Mem. Calif. Watercolor Soc. (pres. 1939), Am. Watercolor Soc. (life), NAD, Soc. Motion Picture Art Dirs. Died Feb. 7, 1997.

PARCHER, JAMES VERNON, civil engineering educator, consultant; b. Drumright, Okla., July 21, 1920; s. James Augustus and Pearl (Sharp) P.; m. Martha Hoff Ruckman, Aug. 7, 1943; children: Carol Susan Parcher McLeod, James Robert, David Loris, Dee Ellen Parcher Casey, Kay Elaine Parcher Heiserman. BS, Okla. State U., 1941, MS, 1948; MA, Harvard U., 1967; PhD, U. Ark., 1968. Maintenance engr. Remington Arms Co., Kings Mills, Ohio, 1941-42; instr. Okla. State U., Stillwater, 1947-48; asst. prof. Okla. State U., 1948-54, asso. prof., 1954-67, prof., 1967-85, prof. emeritus, 1985-96, head dept. civil engring., 1969-83. Author: A History of the Oklahoma State University College of Engineering, Architecture and Technology, 1988, (with R.E. Means) Physical Properties of Soils, 1962, Soil Mechanics and Foundations, 1968. Served with C.E. AUS, 1942-46, 50-52. Mem. ASCE, NSPE, Okla. Soc. Profl. Engrs., Res. Officers Assn., Am. Assn. Retired People, Phi Kappa Phi, Sigma Tau, Chi Epsilon. Died May 2, 1996.

PARGETER, EDITH MARY (ELLIS PETERS), writer; b. Horsehay, Shropshire, Eng., Sept. 28, 1913; d. Edmund Valentine and Edith (Hordley) P. Pharmacist's asst., dispenser Dawley, Shropshire, 1933-40. Writings (under Edith Mary Pargeter): Hortensius, Friend of Nero, 1936, Iron-Bound, 1936, The City Lies Foursquare, 1939, People of My Own, 1942, She Goes to War, 1942, The Eighth Champion of Christendom, 1945, Reluctant Odyssey, 1946, Warfare Accomplished, 1947, The Fair Young Phoenix, 1948, By this Strange Fire, 1948, The Coast of Bohemia, 1950, Lost Children, 1950, Fallen into the Pit, 1951, Holiday with Violence, 1952, This Rough Magic, 1953, Most Loving Mere Folly, 1953, The Soldier at the Door, 1954, A Means of Grace, 1956, The Assize of the Dying: The Heaven Tree, 1960, The Green Branch, 1962, The Scarlet Seed, 1963, The Lily Hand and Other Stories, 1965, A Bloody Field by Shrewsbury, 1972, The Marriage of Megotta, 1979, The Brothers of Gwynedd series: Sunrise in the West, 1974, The Dragon at Noonday, 1975, The Hounds of Sunset, 1976, Afterglow and Nightfall, 1977; writings (under Ellis Peters): Death Mask, 1959, The Will and the Deed, 1960, Funeral of Figaro, 1962, The Horn of Roland, 1974, Never Pick up Hitch-Hikers!, 1976, Aunt Helen, 1993; Felse Family detective novel series: Death and the Joyful Woman, 1961 (Edgar Allen Poe award for best mystery novel Mystery Writers Am. 1961), Flight of a Witch, 1964, Who Lies Here?, 1965, The Piper on the Mountain, 1966, Black is the Color of My True-Love's Heart, 1967, The Grass Widow's Tale, 1968, The House of Green Turf, 1969, Mourning Raga, 1969, The Knocker on Death's Door, 1970, Death to the Landlords!, 1972, City of Gold and Shadows, 1973, Rainbow's End, 1978; Chronicles of Brother Cadfael mystery series: A Morbid Taste for Bones, 1977, One Corpse Too Many, 1979, Monk's-Hood, 1980 (Silver daggar Crime Writers Assn. 1981), Saint Peter's Fair, 1981, The Leper of St. Giles, 1981, The Virgin in the Ice, 1982, The Sanctuary Sparrow, 1983, The Devil's Novice, 1983, Dead Man's Ransom, 1984, The Pilgrim of Hate, 1984, An Excellent Mystery, 1985, The Raven in the Foregate, 1986, The Rose Rent, 1987, The Hermit of Eyton Forest, 1987, The Confession of Brother Haluin, 1988, A Rare Benedictine, 1988, The Heretic's Apprentice, 1989, The Potter's Field, 1990, The Summer of the Danes, 1991, The Benediction of Brother Cadfael, 1992, The Holy Thief, 1992, Brother Cadfael's Penance: The 20th Chronicle ot Brother Cadfael, 1994; (non-fiction) Strongholds and Sanctuaries: The Borderland of England and Wales, 1994, (with Roy Morgan) Ellis Peter's Shropshire, 1993. Served Women's Royal Naval Svc., 1940-45. Decorated Order Brit. Empire, Brit. Empire medal; recipient Gold medal Czechoslovak Soc. Internat. Rels., 1968. Mem. Internat. Inst. Arts and Letters, Soc. Authors, Authors League Am., Mystery Writers Am., Authors Guild, Crime Writers Assn.

Avocations: music, opera, reading, theatre, art. Home: Shropshire Eng. Died October 14, 1995.

PARK, MILDRED RUTH, nurse; b. Bklyn., Feb. 18, 1910; d. Charles Peter and Millie (Gaques) Metzroth; m. Charles L. Park (dec. July 1983); 1 child, Richard. Diploma in nursing, Yonkers Gen. Hosp., 1937. RN, N.Y. Charge nurse Yonkers (N.Y.) Gen. Hosp., 1937-40; charge nurse oper. rm. Fordham (N.Y.) Hosp., 1940-41. Mem. women's divsn. Gen. Bd. Global Ministries. Mem. United Meth. Women. Republican. Avocations: gardening, interior decorating. Died Jan. 1996.

PARKANY, JOHN, business educator, international financial consultant; b. Budapest, Hungary, Jan. 28, 1921; came to U.S., 1947; s. Sandor and Renee (Linksz) P.; m. Betty Ruth Baird, Oct. 30, 1954; children: John Stephen, Ann Emily, Nancy. J.D., U. Budapest (Hungary), 1945; M.A., Georgetown U., 1949; Ph.D., Columbia U., 1955. Mktg. research mgr. Formica Corp., Cin., 1956-61; assoc. prof. Xavier U., Cin., 1961-62; mgr. econ. research Weyerhaeuser Co., Tacoma, Wash., 1962-73; v.p., sr. internat. economist Wells Fargo Bank N.A., San Francisco, 1973-80; Richard S. Reynolds Jr. prof. bus. adminstrn. Coll. of William and Mary, Williamsburg, Va., 1980-91; prof. emeritus Coll. of William and Mary, Williamsburg, 1991-97. Mem. council econ. advisors Gov. Wash. State, Olympia, 1967-73; pres. Council Fgn. Affairs, Tacoma, Wash., 1968-69. Mem. Nat. Assn. Bus. Economists (v.p. San Francisco chpt. 1973-74), Am. Econ. Assn. Home: Williamsburg Va. Died June 17, 1997.

PARKER, EDNA G., federal judge; b. Johnston County, N.C., 1930; 1 child, Douglas Benjamin. Student, N.J. Coll. for Women (now Douglass Coll.); B.A. with honors, U. Ariz., 1953; postgrad., U. Ariz. Law Sch.; LL.B., George Washington U., 1957. Bar: D.C. Law clk. U.S. Ct. Claims, 1957-59; atty.-advisor Office of Gen. Counsel, Dept. Navy, 1959-60; trial atty. civil and tax div. Dept. Justice, 1960-69; adminstrv. judge Contract Appeals Bd., Dept. Transp., 1969-77; spl. trial judge U.S. Tax Ct., 1977-80, judge, 1980-96. Mem. ABA, Fed. Bar Assn., D.C. Bar, D.C. Bar Assn., Women's Bar Assn. of D.C., Nat. Assn. Women Lawyers, Nat. Assn. Women Judges. Died Nov. 12, 1996.

PARKER, FRANK S., biochemistry educator, researcher; b. Boston, Jan. 25, 1921; s. Louis J. and Jennie G. Parker; m. Gladys Baker, Sept. 1, 1946; children: Judith Ann, George Edward (dec.). BS in Chemistry, Tufts U., 1942, MS in Chemistry, 1944; PhD in Chemistry, Johns Hopkins U., 1950. Jr. instr. Johns Hopkins U., Balt., 1946-50; asst. prof. Bryn Mawr (Pa.) Coll., 1950-54; from asst. to assoc. prof. SUNY Med. Ctr., Bklyn., 1954-63; from assoc. to full prof. N.Y. Med. Coll., Valhalla, 1963-70, prof., 1970-91, prof. emeritus, 1991—; spectroscopy trainee MIT, Cambridge, Mass., 1957, vis. scientist, 1982-87; lectr. Infrared Inst. Canisius Coll., Buffalo, summers 1965-67; cons. NSF. Author: Applications of IR Spectroscopy in Biochemistry, Biology and Medicine, 1971, Applications of IR, Raman and Resonance Raman Spectroscopy in Biochemistry, 1983; past mem. editorial bd. Applied Spectroscopy, Can. Jour. Spectroscopy; referee several jours. Died Dec. 12, 1996.

PARKER, PIERSON, minister, religion educator; b. Shanghai, China, May 27, 1905; s. Alvin Pierson and Susie Estelle (Williams) P.; m. Mildred Ruth Sorg, June 12, 1933; 1 son, Peter Pierson. A.B., U. Calif., 1927; student, So. Meth. U., 1928-29; M.A., Pacific Sch. Religion, 1933, Th.D. magna cum laude, 1934; S.T.D., Ch. Div. Sch. of Pacific, 1964. Ordained to ministry Congregational Ch., 1936, Episcopal Ch., 1944; instr. Bibl. lang. and lit. Pacific Sch. Religion, 1934-36; pastor North Congl. Ch., Berkeley, Calif., 1936-44; St. Andrew's Episc. Ch., Oakland, Calif., 1944-47; pres. No. Calif. Congl. Conf., 1938-39; lectr. Bibl. lit. Ch. Div. Sch. Pacific, 1940-43, instr., 1943-44, asst. prof., 1944-47, assoc. prof., 1947-49; Glorvina Rossell Hoffman prof. N.T. lit. and interpretation Gen. Theol. Sem., N.Y.C., 1949-74; sub-dean Gen. Theol. Sem., 1972-74; chaplain to seminarians Diocese of Los Angeles, 1974-83; disting. prof.-in-residence Cathedral of St. John the Divine, N.Y.C., 1975; prof. N.T. Grad. Sch. Theology, U. of South, 1951-52, 54-55, 56-57, 58-60, 67-69, 71-74; priest-in-charge Trinity Cathedral, Newark, 1953-54; research scholar Oxford U., 1957; lectr. N.T., St. Augustine's Coll., Canterbury, Eng., 1955; seminar asso. Columbia U.; vis. prof. Pacific Sch. of Religion, Ch. Div. Sch. Pacific, 1965, 1966, Seminario del Caribe, 1970, NT Maryknoll Sem., Ossining, N.Y. 1971-73, U. of South, 1975, Bloy Episc. Sch. Theology, 1978-79; priest-in-charge Ch. of Holy Spirit, Nice, France, 1962, St. Helena's Ch., Istanbul, Turkey, 1969; canon Cathedral Ch. of St. Paul, Los Angeles, 1977-81, Diocese of Los Angeles, 1981-95; assoc. rector St. Ambrose Ch., Claremont, Calif., 1990-95. Author: Interpreters' Bible (vol. on Deuteronomy), 1951, (with H.H. Shires, G.E. WRight) The Gospel Before Mark, 1953, Inherit the Promise, 1957, Christ Our Hope, 1958, Meditations on the Life of Christ, 1959, Good News in Matthew, 1976, A China Childhood, 1993; co-author: New Synoptic Studies, 1983; mem. editorial bd. Anglican Theol. Rev., 1949, Jour. Bibl. Lit., 1960-74; contbr. religious publs., Ency. Am. Mem. Studiorum Novi Testamenti Societas, Soc. Bibl. Lit. (pres. Pacific Coast sect. 1946-48, mem. council 1944, v.p. Middle Atlantic sect. 1959-60, pres. 1960-61, archivist 1976-83, nat. hon. pres. 1978), Pacific Theol. Group, Inst. Antiquity and Christianity, Pacific Sch. Religion Alumni Assn. (pres. 1943-46), Alpha Sigma Phi. Died Dec. 13, 1995.

PARKER, RICHARD ANTHONY, Egyptologist; b. Chgo., Dec. 10, 1905; s. Thomas Frank and Emma Ursula (Heldman) P.; m. Gladys Anne Burns, Feb. 10, 1934; children: Michael (dec.), Beatrice Ann. A.B., Dartmouth Coll., 1930; Ph.D., U. Chgo., 1938. Research asst. Oriental Inst., U. Chgo., 1938-42, research assoc., 1942-46, asst. prof. of Egyptology, 1946-48; Wilbour prof. Egyptology Brown U., 1948-72, prof. emeritus, 1972—; epigrapher, epigraphic and archtl. survey Luxor, Egypt, 1938-40; asst. field dir., epigraphic and archtl. survey, 1946-47, field dir., 1947-49; Trustee Am. Research Center Egypt, 1948-74; mem. vis. com. dept. Middle Eastern civilizations Harvard, 1950-61, dept. Egyptian art Boston Mus. Fine Arts, 1950—. Author: (with Harold H. Nelson and others) Medinet Habu IV. Festival Scenes of Rameses III, 1940, Babylonian Chronology 626 B.C.-A.D. 45, 1942, (with Waldo H. Dubberstein) Babylonian Chronology 626 B.C.-A.D. 45, 1942, 46, rev. edit. 626 B.C.-A.D. 75, 1956, The Calendars of Ancient Egypt, 1950, (with G. R. Hughes and others) The Bubastite Portal, 1953, Medinet Habu V: The Temple Proper, Part I, 1957, Medinet Habu VI: The Temple Proper, Part 11, 1963, A Vienna Demotic Papyrus on Eclipse and Lunar-Omina, 1959, (with O. Neugebauer) Egyptian Astronomical Texts I: The Early Decans, 1960, Egyptian Astronomical Texts II: The Ramesside Star Clocks, 1964, Egyptian Astronomical Texts III: Decans, Planets, Constellations and Zodiacs, 1969, A Saite Oracle Papyrus from Thebes, 1962, Demotic Mathematical Papyri, 1972, (with J. Leclant and J.C. Goyon) The Edifice of Taharqa by the Sacred Lake of Karnak, 1979. Corr. fellow Brit. Acad.; mem. Oriental Soc., Egypt Exploration Soc., Société Française d'Egyptologie, Deutsches Archaologisches Institut, Phi Beta Kappa, Theta Chi. Roman Catholic.

PARKER, VIRGINIA ANNE, ranch administrator; b. Brockton, Mass., Apr. 24, 1918; d. John and Jennie (Krusas) Salus; student Bryant Stratton Coll., Boston, 1938, Columbia U., 1941; computer skills diploma Computer Skills Tng., 1993; m. John Glendon Parker, Feb. 1942 (div. 1952); one dau., Deborah Anne. Sales supr. Reuben H. Donnelley Corp., N.Y.C., 1944-46; traveling sales rep. Elizabeth Arden Inc., N.Y.C., 1946-47; advt. salesperson Park East Pub. Co., N.Y.C., 1947-48; point of sale display work Parker Kleinhans Assos. and V.A. Parker Co., N.Y.C., 1950-55; merchandising coordinator WGBS Radio Sta., Miami, 1957-59; lighting cons. Verd-A-Ray Corp., Miami, 1960-63; string writer, advt. salesperson Palm Beach Post Times, Fla., 1963-65; advt. salesperson Avon Park Sun, Fla., and Sebring News, Fla., 1965-67; sales mgr. radio sta. WJCM, Sebring, and advt. salesperson radio sta. WIPC, Lake Wales, Fla., 1967-69; office mgr., trustee asst., exec. sec. Griffith Ranch Inc., Okeechobee, Fla., 1969-80, semi-ret., 1980, ret. 1992; now vol. worker with retarded and handicapped, also with ret. vol. sr. programs Nu-Hope. Mem. Bus. and Profl. Women Miami (2d v.p., rec. sec. 1958-60, state award for nat. security 1960), Parents Without Ptnrs. Fla. (news editor 1962-63). Club: Advt. Miami.

PARRATT, LYMAN GEORGE, physicist, educator; b. Salt Lake City, May 17, 1908; s. Delbert William and Mary (Wardrop) P.; m. Rhea Gibson, Feb. 11, 1944; children: Carolyn, Portia. A.B., U. Utah, 1928; Ph.D., U. Chgo., 1932. NRC fellow Cornell U., 1933-35, mem. faculty, 1935-43, 46-95, chmn. dept. physics, 1959-69, prof. emeritus physics, Lab. Nuclear Studies, Lab. Atomic and Solid State Physics; with engrng. div. research Naval Ordnance Lab., Washington, 1941-43; physicist, group leader Atomic Bomb Research, Los Alamos, 1943-46. Author: Probability and Experimental Errors in Science, 1961; also articles on X-ray physics and electronics in scientific jours. Mem. UN Assn., Fedn. Am. Scientists, Am. Phys. Soc., Am. Assn. Physics Tchrs., AAAS, Sigma Xi, Gamma Alpha, Sigma Pi Sigma. Home: Redmond Oreg. Died June 29, 1995.

PARRISH, ALVIN EDWARD, university dean, medical educator; b. Washington D.C., Sept. 6, 1922; s. John Edward and Thyrza Carrie (Morse) P.; m. Mary Wharton Votaw, June 2, 1945; children—Karen Marie, Anne Elizabeth. M.D., George Washington U., 1945. Intern D.C. Gen. Hosp., Washington, 1945-46; instr. physiology George Washington U., 1947-48; resident medicine Gallinger Municipal Hosp. and VA Hosp., Washington, 1948-50; chief resident medicine Gallinger Municipal Hosp., 1950-51; asst. chief med. service VA Hosp., Washington, 1951-57; chief metabolic lab. VA Hosp., 1955-57; assoc. dean Sch. Medicine, George Washington U., 1957-66, prof. medicine, 1964-91, prof. medicine emeritus, 1991-96; chief renal lab. George Washington div. D.C. Gen. Hosp., 1957-66, clin. coordinator, 1960-66; dir. div. renal diseases George Washington Univ. Medical Center, 1967-79; dir. office of human rsch. George Washington U. Hosp., 1979-89. Author books, articles. Served to capt., M.C. AUS, 1946-47; lt. col. Res. Mem. A.C.P., AMA, Am. Diabetes Assn., N.Y. Acad. Sci., AAAS, So. Soc. Clin. Investigation, Am. Soc. Nephrology, Am. Fedn. Clin. Research, Flying Physicians Assn., Pi Kappa Alpha. Home: Washington D.C. Died May 18, 1996.

PARR-LECHNER, CAROL CUNNINGHAM, higher education executive; b. Chgo., June 3, 1941; d. John William and Margaret Louise (Boettcher) Cunningham; m. James Floyd Parr Jr., Aug. 29, 1964 (div. 1989); children: Lauren Melissa Parr, James Floyd Parr III; m. Ira Mark Lechner, Dec. 23, 1989. BA, U. Colo., 1962; MA, La. State U., 1970, PhD, 1972. Cert. assn. exec. Exec. dir. Women's Equity Action League Ednl. and Legal Def. Fund, Washington, 1976-80; edn. policy fellow U.S. Dept. Edn., Washington, 1980-81; dir. mgmt. LWV of the U.S., Washington, 1981-82, exec. dir., 1982-85; assoc. v.p. U. Md. Found., Adelphi, 1986-88; dir. devel. Gallaudet U., Washington, 1988-89, v.p., 1989—; adj. faculty Goucher Coll., Balt., 1987-89. Author: (with others) Women in Washington, 1981. Mem. inaugural class Leadership Washington, 1987-88. Mem. Am. Soc. Assn. Execs., Greater Washington Soc. of Assn. Execs., Planned Giving Study Group, Phi Beta Kappa. Democrat.

PARSONS, FREDERICK AMBROSE, retired educator; b. Mpls. Feb. 21, 1916; s. Olof and Volborg (Anderson) P.; B.E., St. Cloud State Coll., 1939; postgrad. Colo. U., 1941; M.A., U. Minn., 1947, Ed.S., 1970; m. Margaret C. Anderson, June 20, 1943; children: Gretchen, Mark, Christine. Tchr., Delano (Minn.) H.S., 1940-43, prin., 1943-47; supt. schs. Delano, 1947-82. Mem. Am., Minn., Assns. Sch. Adminstrs., Met. Supts. Assn., U. Minn. Alumni Assn., Tau Kappa Alpha, Kappa Delta Pi, Phi Delta Kappa. Mason. Deceased.

PARSONS, JAMES JEROME, geographer, educator; b. Cortland, N.Y., Nov. 15, 1915; s. James Jerome and Edith (Gere) P.; m. Betty Rupp, Oct. 30, 1942; children—David, John, Sally. A.B., U. Calif. at Berkeley, 1937, M.A., 1939, Ph.D., 1948. Mem. faculty U. Calif. at Berkeley, 1946-97, prof. geography, 1959-97, chmn. dept. geography, 1960-66, 75-80. Author: Antioqueño Colonization in Western Colombia, 1949, San Andrès and Providencia, 1955, The Green Turtle and Man, 1962, Antioquia's Corridor to the Sea, 1967, Hispanic Lands and Peoples: Selected Writings of James J. Parsons, 1988, Las Regiones Tropicales Americanas: Visión Geografica, 1992. Served to maj. USAAF, 1941-45. Recipient Pedro Justo Berrio medal Dept. Antioquia, Colombia, 1987; Guggenheim fellow in Spain, 1959-60. Mem. AAAS, Assn. Am. Geographers (pres. 1974-75), Am. Geog. Soc. (David Livingstone medal 1985), Assn. Pacific Coast Geographers (pres. 1952), Acad. Colombiana de Historia (hon.). Home: Berkeley Calif. Died Feb. 19, 1997.

PARSONS, KEITH I., lawyer; b. Davenport, Iowa, Apr. 28, 1912; s. Alfred and Cora Pearl (McDowell) P.; m. Lorraine Watson, June 28, 1939; children: Robert, Susan, James. Ph.B., U. Chgo., 1933, J.D., 1937. Bar: Ill. 1938. Asst. to sec. U. Chgo., 1934-37; since practiced in Chgo.; asst. chief, later chief legal div. Chgo. Ordnance Dist., 1942-46; ptnr. firm Milliken, Vollers & Parsons, 1946-64, Ross, Hardies, O'Keefe, Babcock & Parsons, 1965-83; of counsel firm Ross & Hardies, 1983-97. Mem. Hinsdale (Ill.) Bd. Edn., 1957-63, pres., 1959-63; mem. bd. govs. Ill. State Colls. and Univs., 1970-73. Served to lt. col. AUS, 1942-46. Mem. ABA, Ill. Bar Assn., Chgo. Bar Assn. (past chmn. corp. law com., mem. bd. mgrs. 1967-69), Chgo. Law Club, Legal Club (past pres.), Phi Beta Kappa, Psi Upsilon, Hinsdale Golf Club, Chikaming Country Club. Home: La Grange Park Ill. Died May 31, 1996.

PARSONS, ROBERT BRYAN, JR., financial services executive; b. Ann Arbor, Mich., Sept. 23, 1925; s. Robert Bryan and Essye (McArthur) P.; m. Jane Ramey, Apr. 30, 1946; children—Robert B. III, Christy, Deborah, Ralph, John. B.S., U. Ga., 1955; M.S., Ga. Inst. Tech., 1958. With Delta Air Lines, Atlanta, 1946-64; staff v.p. Eastern Airlines, Miami, Fla., 1964-68, v.p., 1968-71; v.p. CIT Fin. Corp., N.Y.C., 1971-84, sr. v.p. computer services, Livingston, N.J., 1984—. Served with U.S. Army, 1950-51. Republican. Presbyterian. Died June 3, 1996.

PARSONS, WILLIAM, lawyer; b. Kennebunk, Maine, July 23, 1909; s. Robert William and Alice (Read) P.; m. Louise Bigelow, June 27, 1936; children—Llewellyn S. Parsons Smith, Louise Parsons Pietsch, William. B.A., Yale U., 1931, LL.B., 1934; LL.D., Buena Vista Coll., Storm Lake, Iowa, 1964. Bar: N.Y. 1935. Practice law N.Y.C., 1934—; partner firm Milbank, Tweed, Hadley & McCloy, 1951—. Author: (with Harrison Tweed) Lifetime and Testamentary Estate Planning, 1949. Trustee Tchrs. Coll., Columbia U., N.Y. Blood Ctr., Cancer Rsch. Inst., N.Y. Presbyn. Found., Environ. Def. Fund; mem. distbn. com. N.Y. Community Trust; mem. Community Funds, Inc. Lt. USNR, 1944-46. Mem. Am., N.Y. State bar assns., Bar Assn. City N.Y. Club: Downtown Assn. (N.Y.C.). also: Kennebunk ME 04043 DIED 12/04/96. .

PARTHENIOS, III, patriarch, religious order leader; b. Port-Said, Egypt, Nov. 30, 1919; s. Minas Coinidis and Heleni Lahanas. Degree in theology, Theol. Sch. Halki

Constantinople, Istanbul, 1939. Ordained to ministry Greek Orthodox Ch. as deacon, 1939, as priest, 1948. Chief sec., patriarchal vicar Greek Orthodox Ch., Alexandria, Egypt, 1954-58; bishop Met. of Carthage, Tripoli-Libya-Tunis and Casablanca, 1958-87; patriarch Greek Orthodox Patriarchate Alexandria, 1987—; rep. World Coun. Chs., main speaker for Orthodox Ch., Canberra, Australia, 1991; mem. for dialogues Roman Cath.-Mid. East Coun. Chs. Died 1997.

PATAI, RAPHAEL, anthropology educator; b. Budapest, Hungary, Nov. 22, 1910; s. Joseph and Edith (Ehrenfeld) P.; children: Jennifer Patai Schneider, Daphne. Ph.D., U. Budapest, 1933, Hebrew U. Jerusalem, 1936. Mem. faculty Hebrew U., 1937-47; dir., founder Palestine Inst. Folklore and Ethnology, 1944-48; prof. anthropology Dropsie Coll., Phila., 1948-57; vis. lectr. Columbia U., 1948, 54-56, 60-61, New Sch. Social Research, 1948; vis. prof. U. Pa., 1948-49, Ohio State U., 1956; lectr. N.Y. U., 1951-53; vis. lectr. Princeton U., 1952-54; dir. research Theodor Herzl Inst., N.Y.C.; editor Herzl Press, 1956-71; prof. anthropology Fairleigh Dickinson U., 1966-76; vis. prof. Judaic studies Bklyn. Coll., 1971-72. Adv. editor Judaism: Ency. Americana, 1959-96; author: numerous books, including The Hebrew Goddess, 1967, 2d edit., 1978, 3rd edit., 1990, The Arab Mind, 1973, 83, (with Jennifer Patai) The Myth of the Jewish Race, 1975, 2d. edit., 89, The Jewish Mind, 1977, rev. edit., 1996, The Messiah Texts, 1979, Gates to the Old City, 1980, 81, The Vanished Worlds of Jewry, 1980, On Jewish Folklore, 1983, The Seed of Abraham: Jews and Arabs in Contact and Conflict, 1986, Nahum Goldmann: His Missions to the Gentiles, 1987, Ignaz Goldziher and His Oriental Diary, 1987, Apprentice in Budapest: Memories of a World That Is No More, 1988, Robert Graves and the Hebrew Myths, 1992, Between Budapest and Jerusalem, 1992, Journeyman in Jerusalem, 1992 , The Jewish Alchemists: A History and Source Book, 1994, The Jews of Hungary: History, Culture, Psychology, 1996, Jadid al-Islam: The Jews of Meshhed, 1997; editor: Herzl Yr. Book, 1958-71, Ency. of Zionism and Israel, 1971, Erich Brauer's The Jews of Kurdistan, 1993, (with Emanuel S. Goldsmith) Thinkers and Teachers of Modern Judaism, 1994, (with Goldsmith) Events and Movements in Modern Judaism, 1995; gen. editor Jewish Folklore and Anthropology Series, 1980-98. Pres. Am. Friends of Tel Aviv U., 1956-68; dir. Syria-Lebanon-Jordan research project Human Relations Area Files, Inc., New Haven, 1955-56. Home: Forest Hills N.Y. Died July 20, 1996.

PATTEN, STANLEY FLETCHER, JR., physician, educator; b. San Diego, June 23, 1924; s. Stanley Fletcher and Dorothy Amine (Bartholomew) P.; m. Cornelia Diane Golding, May 22, 1948; children: Lesley Ann, Pamela Linda, Susan Lynn; m. Florence Esther Woodworth, Oct. 20, 1979. B.S., George Washington U., 1949, M.S., 1950, Ph.D. (USPHS fellow), 1953; M.D., Western Res. U., 1956. Instr. anatomy Western Res. U., 1954-56, sr. instr., 1956-57, USPHS fellow in pathology, 1957-60, sr. instr. pathology, 1960-62, asst. prof., 1962-63; intern Univ. Hosps. Cleve., 1957-58, resident pathology, 1958-60; assoc. prof. U. Rochester, N.Y., 1963-69; prof. pathology and obstetrics and gynecology U. Rochester, 1969—, acting chmn. dept. pathology, 1969-70, chmn. dept., 1970-89; pathologist-in-chief Strong Meml. Hosp., Rochester, 1970-89; chmn. Internat. Bd. Cytopathology; cons. in field. Author: Diagnostic Cytopathology of the Uterine Cervix, 1969, 2d edit., 1978; mem. editorial bd.: Acta Cytologica, Analytical and Quantitative Cytology; contbr. articles to profl. jours. Bd. dirs. Monroe County (N.Y.) Cancer and Leukemia Assn., 1964-71, Monroe County unit Am. Cancer Soc., 1968-70. Served to capt., Med. Adminstrv. Corps AUS, 1943-46, PTO. Fellow Internat. Acad. Cytology (Maurice Goldblatt award 1971), Am. Soc. Clin. Pathologists; mem. Am. Assn. Pathologists, Am. Soc. Cytology (pres. 1970-71, Papanicolaou award 1973), Rochester Area Assn. Pathologists (pres. 1968-69), Sigma Xi, Sigma Nu. Patentee diagnostic equipment. Died Jan. 7, 1997.

PATTERSON, SAMUEL S., endodontist, educator; b. Indpls., Mar. 8, 1917; s. Abraham and Rose (Foreman) P.; m. Eunice Brenner, June 29, 1952; children: Alan B., Steven M. DDS, Ind. U., 1940, MSD, 1960. Diplomate Am. Bd. Endodontists. Instr. Ind. U., Indpls., 1949-52, asst. prof., 1952-55, assoc. prof., 1955-60, prof., dir. grad. endodontis, 1960-73; chmn. dept. endodontics Ind. U., Bloomington, 1973-86, prof. emeritis, 1986—; cons. VA, Indpls., 1977; dentist-in-residence Nat. VA, Washington, 1979-83; mem. active staff St. Vincent Health and Hosp. Ctr. Co-author: Endodontics, 1960, Surgical Endodontics, 1980, Methods of Endodontics, 1952. Maj. AUS, 1941-46. Recipient Maynard K. Hine award Ind. Dental Assn., 1990. Fellow Am. Coll. Dentists, Internat. Coll. Dentists; mem. Am. Assn. Endodontists (nat. pres. 1968-69, Edgar Coolidge award 1989), Ind. Dental Assn. (Maynard K. Hine award 1990), Indpls. Dental Assn. (pres. 1964-65, Honor Dentist of Yr. award 1988), Indpls. Athletic Club, Rotary. Died Oct.15, 1993.

PATTON, RICHARD BOLLING, food company executive; b. Pitts., Jan. 8, 1929; s. Melvin Gerald and Anne (King) P.; m. Mary Ann Bickford, June 8, 1963; children—Pamela Watson, Edward Bickford, Richard Randolph, Jennifer Bolling. B.A., Yale U., 1952; M.B.A., Harvard U., 1954. Product mgr. Heinz U.S.A., Pitts., 1958-62; gen. mgr. mktg. Heinz-Australia, 1964-66; asst. v.p. Ogden Corp., N.Y.C., 1966-68; v.p. passenger sales and services TWA, N.Y.C., 1968-70; pres. N. Am. Cunard Line, Ltd., N.Y.C.; also dir. Cunard Line, Ltd., Cunard Steamship Co., Ltd., Cunard Trafalgar Hotels, Ltd., 1970-73; v.p. mktg. and sales, then v.p. tomato products and condiments div. Heinz U.S.A., 1973-76, pres., 1976-80; area dir. H.J. Heinz Co., Pitts., 1980-82, sr. v.p., dir., 1982—; bd. dirs. Weight-Watchers Internat. Bd. dirs. Pa. Economy League, African-Am. Inst. 1st lt. USMCR, 1954-57. Clubs: Pitts. Golf, Duquesne (Pitts.); Fox Chapel Golf; Yale, The Brook (N.Y.C.); John's Island (Fla.). Lodge: Knights of Malta. Died Nov. 25, 1996.

PATTON, WENDELL MELTON, JR., management educator, consulting psychologist, college president; b. Spartanburg, S.C., July 10, 1922; s. Wendell Melton and Emily Jane (Harris) P.; m. Martha Jane Matthews, July 5, 1944; children: Wendell III, Leland, Melissa, Brooks B. Student, Wofford Coll.; B.S., U. Ga., 1946, M.S., 1948; Ph.D., Purdue U., 1950; grad., Advanced Mgmt. Course, Colgate U.; LL.D., Wake Forest U., 1961. Lic. psychologist, N.C., Ga. Asst. registrar U. Ga., 1946-48, asst. prof., 1946-48; prof. edn. and psychology Lander Coll., 1948, treas., dept. head, 1948-52; sr. asso. Bruce Payne & Assos., Inc., mgmt. cons., 1952-55; v.p. pres. and asst. gen. mgr. Shuford Mills, Inc., Hickory, N.C., 1955-59; pres. High Point U., N.C., 1959-81; prof. mgmt. U. S.C., Conway, Coastal Carolina Coll., 1982-87; past dir. Furniture Library, N.C. Assn. Ind. Colls. and Univs., Piedmont U. Ctr., Guilford Tech. Coll., Wachovia Bank and Trust, Jefferson Pilot Mutual Funds. Contbr. articles to trade and profl. publs. Served as capt. Air Transport Command AUS, 1942-45. Mem. Am. Mgmt. Assn., Am. Psychol. Assn., SAR, Sigma Xi, Phi Kappa Phi, Delta Kappa Pi, Psi Chi. Methodist. Club: Rotarian. Home: Myrtle Beach S.C. Died Oct. 7, 1996.

PATTULLO, ANDREW, former foundation executive; b. Omaha, Feb. 12, 1917; s. Andrew and Dorothy Anna (Askwith) P.; m. Jean Harriet Fralick, May 1, 1941; children: Andrew, Douglas Ernest. B.S. in Bus. Adminstrn, U. Nebr., 1941, D.Sc. (hon.), 1979; M.B.A. in Hosp. Adminstrn, U. Chgo., 1943; D.Adm. (hon.), Can. Sch. Mgmt., 1981; D.Sc. (hon.), U. Alta., 1982, Georgetown U., 1983. Fellow W.K. Kellogg Found., Battle Creek, Mich., 1943-44; assoc. dir. div. hosps. W.K. Kellogg Found., 1944-51, dir. div. hosps., 1951-67, program dir., 1967-71, v.p. programs, 1971-75, v.p., 1975-78, sr. v.p., 1978-82; ret., 1982; trustee W.K. Kellogg Found., 1972-82; non-resident lectr. U. Mich. Sch. Public Health, 1960-88; mem. Fed. Hosp. Council, 1965-73; mem. Nat. Adv. Com. on Nursing Home Adminstrn., 1968-69; mem. com. on health careers Nat. Health Council, 1964-70; cons. USPHS, 1962-64, Bur. Health Services Research, Dept. HEW, 1968-78; mem. vis. com. for sponsored research M.I.T., 1976-79; mem. nat. adv. council Health Services Research Center, U. Mo.-Columbia, 1977-82; mem. adv. council Mich. Health Facilities, 1965-72, Mich. Mental Health Facilities (Gov.'s Action Com. on Health Care), 1963-66; chmn. community betterment award com. (Mich. Welfare League), 1962, 63; mem. (Mich. Adv. Hosp. Council), 1960-72, (Gov.'s Commn. on Govtl. Relations), 1954-56, (Adv. Commn. Prepaid Hosp. and Med. Care), 1962; hon. prof. Cayetana Hereida U. (Lima), Peru, 1982, U. Sao Paulo Sch. Pub. Health (Brazil), 1982. Mem. editorial bd.: Inquiry, 1980-81. Pres. Battle Creek Area United Fund, 1963, chmn. fund drive, 1960; pres. Battle Creek YMCA, 1959-60, Nottawa Trails council Boy Scouts Am., 1957-60; Trustee Calhoun County chpt. ARC, 1962-65; bd. dirs. Great Lakes Health and Edn. Found., 1973-74; bd. dirs. Calhoun County unit Am. Cancer Soc., 1976-78, chmn. com. on founds. Mich. div., 1978-79; trustee Mich. Health Council, 1951-74, pres., 1967; mem. Calhoun County Bd. Social Services, 1982-90; trustee Southwestern Mich. Rehab. Hosp., 1982—, First Congl. Ch., Battle Creek, 1982-89. Recipient Distinguished Service award U. Chgo. Hosp. Adminstrn. Alumni Assn., 1955; Tri-State Hosp. Assembly award, 1963; award of merit Am. Assn. Hosp. Planning, 1966; award for advancement edn. in hosp. adminstrn. Assn. U. Programs in Hosp. Adminstrn., 1968; Key award for meritorious service Mich. Hosp. Assn., 1970; Trustees award Am. Hosp. Assn., 1972; Disting. Service award Mich. Health Council, 1973; Disting. Achievement award Ohio State U. Hosp. Adminstrn. Alumni, 1982; George Findlay Stephens award Can. Hosp. Assn., 1982; named to Mich. Health Hall of Fame, 1978; Disting. Service award Hosp. Mgmt. Systems Soc. of Am. Hosp. Assn., 1974; Silver Beaver award Boy Scouts Am. Fellow Am. Pub. Health Assn., Am. Coll. Hosp. Adminstrs. (hon.); mem. Am. Hosp. Assn. (adv. coun. hosp. rsch. and ednl. trust 1960-67, mem. coun. rsch. and edn. 1959-62, life mem., chmn. adv. com. Ctr. for History of Hosps. and Healthcare Admnistrns., 1985—), Mich. Hosp. Assn. (trustee 1949-55, pres. 1954-55, life mem.), Internat. Hosp. Fedn., Mich. Pub. Health Assn., Can. Coll. Health Service Execs. (hon.), Latin Am. Hosp. Fedn. (hon.), Duke U. Hosp. Adminstrn. Alumni Assn. (hon.), Sao Paulo Hosp. Assn. (hon.). DIED 07/13/96. .

PATTYN, REMI CEASAR, management consultant; b. Chatham, Ont., Can., Jan. 12, 1922; came to U.S., 1927, naturalized, 1932; s. Achille J. and Marie (Simoens) P.; m. Mary Devine, Nov. 10, 1945; children: John Martin, Drew Remi, Lynn Mary, Diane Marie, Carol Anne, Neal Remi. B.S. in Indsl. Engring, Ill. Inst. Tech., 1950; M.B.A., U. Chgo., 1954; postgrad., Ind. U. Law Sch., 1961. Methods engr. Internat. Register Co., Chgo., 1939-44; acting dir. adminstrn. Chgo. Housing Authority, 1950-52; mgmt. cons. Booz, Allen & Hamilton, Chgo., 1952-56; asst. sec., personnel dir. Chgo. Aerial Industries, Inc., Barrington, Ill., 1956-58; v.p. personnel relations Public Service Co. Ind., Inc., 1958-74; v.p. adminstrv. services Public Service Co. Ind., Inc., Plainfield, 1974-77; sr. v.p. ops. Public Service Co. Ind., Inc., 1977-79, sr. v.p. and asst. to pres., 1979-81; pres. Pattyn & Assocs., Inc. (mgmt. cons.), Indpls., 1981—; mem. asso. faculty Ind. U., Purdue U., 1965-77; lectr. Ind. U. Med. Sch., 1967-80, Bus. Roundtable, 1970-84; chmn. coordinating com. Ind. Constrn.-Anti-Inflation Roundtable, 70-76, co-chmn., 1980-84; dir. Istar Corp.; mem. nat. labor relations council State Chambers Commerce, 1971-83; chmn. Ind. Council Econ. Edn., 1973-75; trustee Joint Council on Econ. Edn., 1980-82. Chmn. fund campaign Ind. Mental Health Assn., 1977-79; past bd. dirs. Ind. div. Am. Cancer Soc.; nominee for sec. of labor, Pres. of U.S., 1980; commr. Marion County Met. Devel. Commn., 1982-85; adv. com. bd. trustees Indpls. Mus. Art, 1983-89. Served with USNAF, 1944-47. Recipient Outstanding Indsl. Engr. Alumnus award Ill. Inst. Tech., 1974, Alumni award of merit, 1976; Jefferson award for community svc. State of Ind., 1979, Paul Samuelson Enterprise award for community leaders, 1992. Mem. Am. Soc. Personnel Adminstrn. (past pres. Indpls. chpt., chmn. pres.'s nat. council 1977-79), Ill. Inst. Tech. Alumni Assn. (pres. Indpls. 1963-85), Edison Electric Inst. (past chmn. personnel relations com.), Ind. C. of C. (chmn. personnel and labor relations com. 1984-86), Delta Lambda Xi. Republican. Roman Catholic. Clubs: Ulen Country, Arcadian Shores, Sloane Gardens Ltd. (London). Died Feb. 2, 1996.

PAUL, MARTIN AMBROSE, physical chemist; b. N.Y.C., June 29, 1910; s. Martin and Rosena (Sing) P.; m. Genevieve Wells, June 28, 1935; children: Harriet (Mrs. J. Henry Jonquiere), Dorothy (Mrs. Duvall A. Jones). B.A., CCNY, 1930; M.A., Columbia U., 1931, Ph.D., 1936. Instr. CCNY, 1930-42; research supr. Explosives Research Lab., NDRC, Bruceton, Pa., 1942-45; asst. prof. chemistry Triple Cities Coll., Syracuse U., 1946-48, asso. prof., 1948-50; prof. chemistry Harpur Coll., State U. N.Y. at Binghamton, 1950-65, chmn. dept., 1950-60; exec. sec. div. chemistry and chem. tech. Nat. Acad. Scis.-NRC, Washington, 1965-74; cons., 1974-96; Vis. prof. Cornell U., several summers, U. Calif. at Los Angeles, 1957-58, Columbia, 1960-61; Exec. sec. XXIII Internat. Congress Pure and Applied Chemistry, 1971, sec. commn. on symbols, terminology and units, 1967-71, chmn., 1971-73, sec. com. on nomenclature and symbols, 1975-79. Author: Principles of Chemical Thermodynamics, 1951, Physical Chemistry, 1962, (with King, Farinholt) General Chemistry, 1967; also articles. Recipient Naval Ordnance Devel. award, 1946; John Simon Guggenheim fellow, 1957. Fellow A.A.A.S. (v.p., chmn. chemistry sect. 1972); Benjamin Franklin fellow Royal Soc. Arts; mem. Am. Chem. Soc., AAUP, Phi Beta Kappa, Sigma Xi, Phi Lambda Upsilon. Club: Cosmos (Washington). Research on measurement of acidity in highly acid media, nature of indicators, catalysis by acids, thermodynamic properties of solutions, sci. policy. Home: Merrick N.Y. Died April 22, 1996.

PAUL, SHERMAN, retired English language educator; b. Cleve., Aug. 26, 1920; s. Jacob and Gertrude (Leavitt) P.; m. Grace McDowell, May 1, 1943; children—Jared, Meredith, Erica, Jeremy. B.A., U. Iowa, 1941; M.A., Harvard, 1948, Ph.D., 1950. Instr. English U. Iowa, 1946; teaching fellow Harvard U., 1948-50, instr., tutor, 1950-52; asst. prof. U. Ill., Urbana, 1952-55; assoc. prof. U. Ill., 1955-57, prof., 1957-67; past mem. Center for Advanced Study, U. Ill.; M.F. Carpenter prof. U. Iowa, Iowa City, 1967-74; Carver disting. prof. U. Iowa, 1974-88; vis. prof. U. Vienna, Austria, 1957-58; Fulbright lectr., 1957-58. Author: Emerson's Angle of Vision, 1952, The Shores of America, 1958, Louis Sullivan, 1962, Edmund Wilson, 1965, Randolph Bourne, 1966, The Music of Survival, 1968, Hart's Bridge, 1972, Repossessing and Renewing, 1976, Olson's Push, 1978, The Lost America of Love, 1981, In Search of the Primitive, 1986, In Love with the Gratuitous, 1987, Hewing to Experience, 1989; For Love of the World, 1992; mem. editorial bd. Am. Lit., 1963-65; mem. adv. com. PMLA, 1973-77. Served to capt. USAAF, 1942-46, PTO. Recipient Bowdoin prize Harvard, 1950; Ford Found. fellow, 1952; Guggenheim fellow, 1963-64. Mem. Modern Lang. Assn. Am., Phi Beta Kappa. Home: Bemidji Minn. DIED 05/28/95. .

PAULSEN, PAT (LAYTON PAULSEN), entertainer, vintner; b. South Bend, Wash., July 6, 1927; s. Norman and Beulah (Fadden) P.; children: Terri, Monty, Justin. Student, San Francisco City Coll., 1948-50; PhD (hon.), Eastern Mich. U. Featured entertainer Smothers Bros. Comedy Hour, 1968-69; entertainer Pat Paulsen Half-a-Comedy-Hour (TV), 1970; owner Pat Paulsen Vineyards Winery, Cloverdale, Calif., 1980-90; owner Pat Paulsen Tasting Room, Asti, Calif. Author: Pat Paulsen for President, 1968, How to Wage a Successful

Campaign for the Presidency, 1972; appeared in TV special Pat Paulsen for President, CBS, 1968, Night Patrol, Elly, Harper Valley PTA, They Still Call Me Vruce, Blood SuckersFrom Mars, Where Were You When the Lights Went Out?. Auntie Lee's Meat Pies, (videos) Pat Paulsen's Greatest TV Bits, Pat Paulsen on Wine, Pat Paulsen for President; albums Pat Paulsen for President, 1968, Pat Paulsen Live at the Ice House, 1970, Pat Paulsen...Unzipped, 1996. Mayor Asti Village, Calif., 1986; hon. chmn. Nat. Kidney Found., 1985. Served with USMC, 1945-46. Recipient Emmy award for individual achievement in Smothers Bros. Comedy Hour, 1967-68, Mark Twain award Outstanding Work in Field Comedy, 1992. Home: Santa Rosa Calif. Died Apr. 24, 1997.

PAVLICK, CHARLES RALEIGH, architect, engineer, retired air force officer; b. Chgo., Mar. 28, 1918; s. Charles Harry and Myrtle Mildred (von Meyenberg) P.; m. Hilda Fay vanDeinse, Feb. 8, 1945; children: Ann, Charles, Elizabeth, James. Student, Deforrests Electronics Sch., Chgo. Art Inst., Chgo. Acad. Fine Arts, Air War Coll., Ohio State U. Commd. 2nd lt. USAAC, 1937; advanced through grades to col. USAF, 1968; served in WWII, Korea, Vietnam, USAAF and USAF; supervising arch.-engr. D.C. Dept. Pub. Works, Washington, 1968-93; owner, pres. Pavlick-Restordance, Alexandria, Va., 1993-97; ret., 1968; cons. Met. Washington rea. Decorated Bronze Star, Air medal. mem. NRA, Mil. Order Purple Heart, Ret. Officers Assn., Navy Tailhook Assn., Air Force Assn., Am. Legion, Navy League, U.s. Naval Sailing Assn., Inst. Legis. Affairs, Naval Inst., USCG Aux., Brotherood of St. Andrew. Republican. Episcopalian. Avocations: collecting military memorabilia, antiques, hunting, fishing, political history. Died Sept. 23, 1997.

PAYNTER, GRENVILLE HOWARD, banker; b. N.Y.C., May 20, 1931; s. Richard Kates and Mary Jane (Howard) P.; m. Fay Enger Taft, June 5, 1958 (div. 1960); m. Sally Gooch, Dec. 8, 1962; children—Bradford, Cameron, Nathaniel. A.B., Princeton U. With Chem. Bank, N.Y.C., 1953—, exec. v.p., 1984—. Served to 1st lt. N.H.N.G. 1949-57.

PAZ, OCTAVIO, poet, Mexican diplomat; b. Mex., Mar. 31, 1914; s. Octavio Paz and Josephina Lozano; m. Elena Garro, 1937 (div.); m. Marie José Tramini, 1964. Student, U. Mex.; D (hon.), New Sch. Social Rsch. Sec. Mex. Embassy, Paris, 1945; chargé d'affaires Mex. Embassy, Tokyo, 1951, secretariat external affairs, 1953-58; extraordinary and plenipotentiary minister Mex. Embassy, Paris, 1959-62; Mex. amb. to India, 1962-68; vis. prof. U. Tex., Austin, U. Pitts., 1968-70; Simón Bolívar prof. Latin Am. studies, 1970; fellow Churchill Coll., Cambridge U., 1970-71; Charles Eliot Norton prof. poetry Harvard U., 1971-72; Regent's fellow U. Calif., San Diego; now dir. Revista Vuelta, Mexico City; founder literary rev. Barandal, 1931; mem. editorial bd., columnist El Popular; co-founder Taller, 1938; co-founder, editor El Hijo Prodigo, 1943-46; editor Plural, 1971-75; founder, editor Vuelta, 1976—. Author: (poetry) Luna Silvestre, 1933, No pasarán!, 1936, Raíz del hombre, 1937, Bajo tu clara sombra y otros poemas sobre España, 1937, Entre la piedra y la flor, 1941, A la orilla del mundo y primer dia, 1942, Libertad bajo palabra, 1949, Aguila o sol?, 1951 (pub. as Eagle or Sun?, 1970), Semillas para un himno, 1954, Piedra de sol, 1957 (pub. as Sun Stone, 1963), La estación violenta, 1958, Agua y viento, 1959, Libertad bajo palabra: obra poética 1935-1958, 1960, Salamandra 1958-1961, 1962, Selected Poems, 1935-1957, 1963, Viento entero, 1965, Vrindaban, Madurai, 1965, Blanco, 1967, Disco visuales, 1968, Ladera este (1962-1968), 1969, La centana: poemas 1935-1968, 1969, Configurations, 1958-1969, 1971, Renga, 1971, Topoemas, 1971, Early Poems 1935-1955, 1973, Pasado en claro, 1975, Vuelta, 1976, A Draft of Shadows and Other Poems, 1979, Selected Poems, 1979, Airborn/Hijos del aire, 1981, Poemas 1935-1975, 1981, Poemas recientes, 1981, Instante y revelación, 1982, Selected Poems, 1984, Cuatro chopos/The Four Poplars, 1985, Arbol adentro, 1987 (pub. as A Tree Within, 1988), Nineteen Ways of Looking at Wang Wei, 1987, The Collected Poems of Octavio Paz 1957-1987, 1988, Lo mejor de Octavio Paz: el fuego de cada día, A Tale of Two Gardens: Poems from India 1952-95, 1997; (prose) El laberinto de la soledad, 1950 (pub. as The Labyrinth of Solitude: Life and Thought in Mexico, 1961), Aguila o Sole, 1951, El arco y la lira: el poema, la revelación poética, poésia e historia, 1956 (pub. as The Bow and the Lyre: The Poem, the Poetic Revelation, Poetry and History, 1973), Las peras del olmo, 1957, Tamayo en la pintura mexicana, 1959, Cuadrivio, 1965, Los signos en rotación, 1965, Puertas al campo, 1966, Claude Lévi-Strauss; o, El nuevo festín de Esopo, 1967 (pub. as Claude Lévi-Strauss: An Introduction, 1970), Corriente alterna, 1967 (pub. as Alternating Current, 1973), Marcel Duchamp; o, El castillo de la pureza, 1968 (pub. as Marcel Duchamp; or, The Castle of Purity, 1970), México: la última década, 1969, Conjunciones y disyunciones, 1969 (pub. as Conjunctions and Disjunctions, 1974), Posdata, 1970 (Pub. as The Other Mexico: Critique of the Pyramid, 1972), Las cosas en su sitio: sobre la literatura española del siglo XX, 1971, Los signos en rotación y otros ensayos, 1971, Traducción: literatura y literalidad, 1971, Apariencia desnuda: la obra de Marcel Duchamp, 1973 (pub. as Marcel Duchamp: Appearance Stripped Bare, 1979), El signo y el garabato, 1973, Solo a dos voces, 1973, Teatro de signos/transparencias, 1974, Versiones y diversiones, 1974, Los hijos del limo: del romanticismo a la vanguardia, 1974 (pub. as Children of the Mire: Modern Poetry from Romanticism to the Avant-Garde, 1974), El mono gramético, 1974 (pub. as The Monkey Grammarian, 1981), La búsqueda del comienzo: escritos sobre el surrealismo, 1974, The Siren and the Seashells and Other Essays on Poets and Poetry, 1976, Xavier Villaurrutia en persona y en obra, 1978, El ogro filantrópico: historia y política 1971-1978, 1979, Rufino Tamayo: Myth and Magic, 1979, México en la obra de Octavio Paz, 1979, Rufino Tamayo, 1982, Sor Juana Inés de la Cruz, o, Las trampas de la fe, 1982 (pub. as Sor Juana, or, The Traps of Faith, 1988), Tiempo nublado, 1983 (pub. as One Earth, Four or Five Worlds: Reflections on Contemporary History, 1985), Sombras de obras: arte y literatura, 1983, Günter Gerzo, 1983, Hombres en su siglo y otros ensayos, 1984 (pub. as On Poets and Others, 1986), Pasión crítica: conversaciones con Octavio Paz, 1985, Convergences: Essays on Art and Literature, 1987, Generaciones y semblanzas: escritores y letras de México, 1987, El pelegrino en su patria: historia y política de México, 1987, Los privilegios de la vista: arte de México, 1987, Primeras letras, 1931-1943, 1988, One World or the Other, 1989, Poesía, mito, revolución, 1989, La otra voz: poesía y fin de siglo, 1990 (pub. as The Other Voice, 1992), Essays on Mexican Art, 1993, My Life With the Wave, 1994, The Double Flame, 1995, In Light of India: Essays, 1997; adapter: (plays) La hija de Rappaccini, 1956; editor: Voces de España, 1938, Laurel: antología de la poésia moderna en lengua española, 1941, Anthologie de la poésie mexicaine, 1952, Anthología poética, 1956, Anthology of Mexican Poetry, 1958, Tamayo el la pintura mexicana, 1959, Magia de la risa, 1962, Antología by Fernando Pessoa, 1962, Cuatro poetas contemporáneos de Suecia: Martinson, Lundkvist, Ekelöf, y Lindegren, 1963, Poesía en movimiento: Mexico 1915-1966, 1966, Remedios varo, 1966, Antología by Xavier Villaurrutia, 1980; translator: Sendas de Oku by Basho, 1957, Veinte poemas by William Carlos Williams, 1973, 15 poemas by Guillaume Appollinaire, 1979; writer (film) Yo, la Peor de Todas, 1990. Guggenheim fellow, U.S., 1944; recipient Grand Prix Internat. de Poesie (Belgium), 1963, Jerusalem prize, 1977, Critics prize (Spain), 1977, Nat. prize for letters (Mex.), 1977, Grand Golden Eagle Internat. Festival (Paris) 1979, Grand Aigle d'Or (Nice), 1979, Premio Ollin Yoliztli (Mex.), 1980, Miguel de Cervantes prize (Spain), 1982, Neustadt Internat. prize for literature, 1982, Wilhelm Heinse medal (Germany), 1984, Fedn. German Book Trade Peace prize, 1984, Gran Cruz de Alfonso X el Sabrio, 1986, T.S. Eliot award for creative writing Ingersoll Found., 1987, Alexis de Toqueville prize Inst. France, 1988, Nobel Prize in literature, 1990. Mem. AAAL (hon.). Died April, 1997.

PEAL, JAMES ALBERT, psychiatrist; b. Chgo., Jan. 11, 1922; s. Allen Saunders and Helen (Goines) P.; m. Edithie Ventura Figueroa, Oct. 19, 1951; children: James A. II, Arturo A. BS, Mich. State Coll., 1943; MD, Howard U., 1948. Diplomate Nat. Bd. Med. Examiners, Am. Bd. Psychiatry and Neurology; lic. physician, Md., Conn., Calif., Va. Intern Harlem Hosp., N.Y.C., 1948-49; resident Norwich (Conn.) State Hosp., 1949-51, USN Hosp., Oakland, Calif., 1954-56; staff psychiatrist Napa State Hosp., Imola, Calif., 1955-57, Agnew (Calif.) State Hosp., 1957-58; chief of clin. svcs. Calif. Med. Facility Dept. Corrections, Vacaville, 1958-59; asst. supt. psychiat. svcs. Stockton (Calif.) State Hosp., 1959-63, assoc. supt. clin. svcs., 1963-64; asst. dir. divsn. svcs. to mentally ill Mich. Dept. Mental Health, Lansing, 1964-67; dir. Fresno County (Calif.) Dept. Mental Health, 1967-70; sr. psychiatrist San Joaquin County (Calif.) Mental Health Svcs., 1970-72; pvt. practice Stockton and Sacramento, Calif., 1973-92; staff psychiatrist Tex. Dept. of Mental Health and Mental Retardation, Vernon, 1992-93, Southwestern Va. Mental Health Inst., Marion, 1993-95; civilian cons. psychiatry USAF Hosp., Travis AFB, 1958-64, spl. cons. Calif. Dept. Corrections, 1959-64, cons. Office of Pub. Defender, Sonoma County, Calif., 1973-93; chief psychiat. cons. for prosecution in second Juan Corona trial, 1982; founder, dir. John Hale Mental Health Ctr., San Francisco, 1973-78; med. advisor Social Security Adminstrn., Adminstrv. Law Judges, 1973-93; mem. staff Harbor Gen. Hosp., Torrance, Calif., chief gen. practice, 1951-53; assoc. prof. U. So. Calif., 1968-72; asst. prof. U. Calif., Davis, 1973-78. Cons. Adult Authority, Calif., Dist. Atty.'s Office and Sheriff's Office, San Joaquin County, appt. dep. sheriff; bd. dirs. Family Svc., Stockton, Calif. (pres. 1964). Capt. U.S. Army, 1953; Maj. USAFR. Fellow Am. Psychiat. Assn. (life); mem. AMA, Am. Assn. Group Psychotherapy, Psychiat. Soc. Va., Inc., Mich. State Med. Soc., Mich. Soc. Neurology and Psychiatry, Calif. Med. Assn., Ctrl. Calif. Psychiat. Assn., Ingham County Med. Soc., San Joaquin County Med. Soc., Rotary Internat. Home: Marion Va. Died July 4, 1995.

PEARCE, CHARLES WELLINGTON, surgeon; b. Ballinger, Tex., Nov. 2, 1927; s. Francis Marion and Fannie (Brown) P.; student Rice U., 1945-46, 48-49, U. Tex., 1948; M.D., Cornell U., 1953; m. Dorothy Andree DeLorenzo, Apr. 2, 1955; children—Charles Wellington, Andrew F., Margaret E., John Y., III; m. Patricia Mary Flannery, Dec. 28, 1983; 1 child, Leslie E. Intern, resident N.Y. Hosp.-Cornell U. Med. Center, N.Y.C., 1953-55, 56-60; resident Baylor U. Affiliated Hosps., 1955-56, Charity Hosp., New Orleans, 1960-61; practice medicine specializing in cardiovascular and thoracic surgery, New Orleans, 1961—; mem. staff Touro Infirmary, So. Bapt. Hosp., Hotel Dieu,mem. faculty Tulane U., New Orleans, 1960-83, asso. prof. surgery, 1966-69, head sect. cardiovascular and thoracic surgery, 1967-69, asso. prof. clin. surgery, 1969-83; head cardiothoracic surgery, clin. prof. surgery La. State U., 1983—; vis. surgeon Charity Hosp., New Orleans, 1961-69; cons. surgery Huey P. Long Charity Hosp., Pineville, La., 1961-70, Lallie Kemp Charity Hosp., Independence, La., 1961-70, VA Hosp., Alexandria, La., 1961-69, Keesler Air Force Hosp., Biloxi, Miss., 1967-70; cons. cardiac sect. crippled children program La. Dept. Health. Served with AUS, 1946-48. La. Heart Assn. grantee, 1961-62. Diplomate Am. Bd. Surgery, Bd. Thoracic Surgery. Fellow A.C.S., Am. Coll. Chest Physicians, Am. Coll. Cardiology; mem. Am. Assn. Thoracic Surgery, Soc. for Vascular Surgery, Am. Heart Assn. (established investigator 1962-65), Soc. Thoracic Surgeons, Internat. Cardiovascular Soc., Internat. Surg. Soc., So. Med. Assn., Orleans Parish, La. med. socs., La., New Orleans surg. socs., La. Heart Assn., Soc. Mayflower Descs. (La. gov. 1975-81), SAR, New Orleans Opera House Assn. (dir. 1976—), New Orleans Opera Club, La. Landmark Soc., New Orleans Mus. Art, Internat. Platform Assn., R Assn. Rice U., Phi Chi, Alpha Omega Alpha. Republican. Presbyn. Contbr. articles to profl. jours. Died Sept. 18, 1997.

PEARL, MINNIE (SARAH OPHELIA COLLEY CANNON), entertainer; b. Centerville, Tenn., Oct. 25, 1912; d. Thomas Kelly and Fannie Tate (House) Colley; m. Henry R. Cannon. Ed., Ward-Belmont Coll. Dir. amateur plays, Atlanta and surrounding areas, 1934-40; performer, WSM Grand Ole Opry, Nashville, 1940-95; TV appearances include The World's Largest Indoor Country Music Show, 1978, A Country Christmas, Hee Haw, Johnny Cash and the Country Girls; rec. artist, Everest, RCA, Starday rec. cos.; Records include Story of Country Music, Minnie Pearl, Minnie Pearl at the Party, Answer to Giddyup and Go; Author: Minnie Pearl: Am. Autobiography, 1980. Recipient Woman of the Year award, Billboard; All Time Great award, Billboard; 1987 Roy Acuff Community Service Award, Country Music Found.; named to Country Music Hall of Fame, 1972; Pioneer Award, Acad. of Country Music, 1987. Home: Nashville Tenn. Died Mar. 5, 1996.

PEARSALL, HARRY JAMES, dentist; b. Bay City, Mich., Apr. 12, 1916; s. Roy August and Gladys Agnes (Tierney) P.; m. Betty Almina Dahlke, Oct. 5, 1946 (dec. Nov. 1982); 1 child, Paul Roy. BS, Marquette U., 1937, DDS, 1939. Gen. practice dentistry Bay City, 1939—; cons. Delta Dental Ins., Lansing, Mich., 1975-86. Mem. Bay City chpt. Revision Com., 1965-66; bd. dirs. Downtown Bay City, 1962-73. Served to maj. U.S. Army, MC, 1940-46. Mem. ADA, Am. Coll. Dentists, Internat. Coll. Dentists, Mich. Dental Assn. (pres. 1972-73, spl. com. on life mems.), Saginaw Valley Dental Soc. (pres. 1955-56), Bay County Dental Soc. (pres. 1950-51), Am. Legion. Lodge: Elks. Died Dec. 20, 1996.

PEARSON, BELINDA KEMP, economist, consultant; b. Kansas City, Mo., Apr. 14, 1931; d. William Ewing and Margaret Norton (Johnson) Kemp; m. Carl Erik Pearson, Sept. 15, 1953; children: Erik, Frederick, Margaret. BA, Wellesley Coll., 1952; MA, Tufts U., 1954, PhD, 1958. Rsch. asst. Harvard U., Cambridge, Mass., 1954-55; instr. econs. Suffolk U., Boston, 1956-59; lectr. econs., Wellesley Coll., Mass., 1964-65; econ. analyst, asst. econs. Seafirst Bank, Seattle, 1966-79, v.p., 1974-85; chief economist, 1979-85; dir. Lektor, Inc., Issaquah, Wash., 1984—, pres., 1987—; mem. Wash. Gov's. Coun. Econ. Advisors, Olympia, 1979—; dir. Pacific N.W. Regional Econ. Conf., 1979—, chair, Seattle Conf., 1987; mem. Western Blue Chip Econ. Forecast Panel, 1988—; mem. King County, Wash., Land Capacity Task Force, 1995-96; mem. bd. regents Wash. State U., Pullman, 1985-90, v.p., 1988-90, Regents Found. Investment Com. of Wash. State U., 1987-91; mem. Wash. State Libr. Commn., Olympia, 1976-84. Fulbright scholar London Sch. Econs., 1952-53. Mem. Am. Econ. Assn., Nat. Assn. Bus. Economists (chmn. arrangements 1982 ann. meeting), Seattle Economists Club (pres. 1973-74), Mcpl. League, City Club (Seattle) (chmn. reports com. 1986-88), pres. LWV, Lake Wash. East, 1993-95. Died Oct. 10, 1996.

PEARSON, LOUISE MARY, retired manufacturing company executive; b. Inverness, Scotland, Dec. 14, 1919 (parents Am. citizens); d. Louis Houston and Jessie M. (McKenzie) Lenox; grad. high sch.; m. Nels Kenneth Pearson, June 28, 1941; children: Lorine Walters, Karla Pearson. Dir. Wauconda Tool & Engring. Co., Inc., Algonquin, Ill., 1950-86; reporter Oak Leaflet, Crystal Lake, Ill., 1944-47, Sidelights, Wilmette, Ill., 1969-72, 79-82. Active Girl Scouts U.S.A., 1955-65. Recipient award for appreciation work with Girl Scouts U.S., 1965. Clubs: Antique Automobile of Am. (Hershey, Pa.), Vet. Motor Car (Boston), Classic Car of Am. (Madison, N.J.), Hoseless Carriage Club. Died Dec. 18, 1996; interred Crystal Lake Memorial Park. Died Dec. 18, 1996. Home: Crystal Lake Ill.

PEARSON, PAUL BROWN, nutritionist, educator; b. Oakley, Utah, Nov. 28, 1905; s. Levi and Ada (Brown) P.; m. Emma Snow, June 20, 1933 (dec.); children—Paula (Mrs. Raymond Soller), Marilyn (Mrs. Walter Johnson). B.S., Brigham Young U., 1928; M.S. (Walsh fellow), Mont. State U., 1930; Ph.D. (fellow), U. Wis., 1937. Asst. prof. Mont. State U., 1930-31; research assoc. U. Calif., 1932-35; prof. A&M Coll. Tex., 1937, disting. prof., 1941, dean grad. sch., head dept. biochemistry and nutrition, 1947; chief biology AEC, 1949-58, cons., 1958-70; prof. Johns Hopkins U., 1951-58; with program in sci. and engring. Ford Found., 1958-63; pres., sci. dir. Nutrition Found., 1963-72; chmn. dept. nutrition Drexel U., 1972-73; prof. dept. family and community medicine and dept. nutrition and food sci. U. Ariz., Tucson, 1974—; chief dept. nutrition U. Autónoma de Guadalajara, Mexico, 1974-84; prof. U. Autónoma de Guadalajara, Mexico, 1984—; Collaborator Bur. Animal Industry.; cons. Pres.'s Sci. Adv. Com., Nat. Agr. Rsch. Adv. Com., 1952-58; del. 6th Internat. Zootechnic Congress, Copenhagen, 1952, 2d Internat. Biochem. Congress, Paris, 1952, U.S.-Japan Conf. on Radiobiology, Tokyo, 1954, World Conf. Peaceful Uses Atomic Energy, Geneva, 1955, Internat. Symposium on Biochemistry of Sulphur, Roscoff, France, 1956; mem. exec. com. div. biol. and agrl. NRC, 1950-52; liaison Food and Nutrition Bd.; program com. Internat. Congress on Nutrition, 1960; chmn. adv. com. P.R. Nuclear Ctr., 1962-73; del. White Ho. Conf. Internat. Cooperation, 1965, White Ho. Conf. on Food, Nutrition and Health, 1969; adv. com. McCollum-Pratt Inst.; trustee Food Drug Law Inst., 1967-85, Nutrition Found., 1972-74; mem. com. Internat. Union of Nutrition, 1970-76. Author bulls., NRC, numerous sci. publs. on nutrition and biochemistry. Fellow AAAS, Soc. for Animal Sci., Am. Inst. Nutrition; mem. Biochem. Soc. London, Am. Chem. Soc., Brit. Nutrition Soc., Soc. Biol. Chemists, El Coligeo de Medicos Cirujanos de Jalisco. Clubs: Lochinvar, Cosmos. also: U Autonoma Guadalajara, Faculty Medicine, Apdo Postal 1-440, 44100 Guadalajara Jalisco, Mexico Died May 9, 1997.

PEARSON, WILLARD, army officer; b. West Elizabeth, Pa., July 4, 1915; s. John Alfred and Mary Catherine (Mehrmann) P.; m. Reba E. Barton, Sept. 12, 1947; children: Richard Barton, Joan Louise, Patricia Jean. Student, Douglass Bus. Coll., 1933-35; M.S., Columbia U., 1953; postgrad., Army War Coll., 1956-57; postgrad. in mgmt., U. Pitts., 1962; M.A., George Washington U., 1963. Commd. 2d lt. U.S. Army Res., 1936; advanced through grades to lt. gen. U.S. Army, 1971; comdg. gen. 1st Brigade, 101st Airborne Div. Vietnam, 1966-67; J3, USMACV Saigon, 1967-68; dir. individual tng. ODCSPER, Hdqrs. Dept. Army Washington, 1968-69; comdg. gen. Ft. Lewis, Wash., 1969-71, V Corps U.S. Army Europe, 1971-73; supt. Valley Forge Mil. Acad. and Jr. Coll., Wayne, Pa., 1973-85. Mem. Franklin Inst., Phila. Orchestra Assn., Friends Independence Nat. Hist. Park; bd. advisors Vietnam Veterans Meml. Inst.; trustee Chapel of 4 Chaplains, exec. com., 1984-87; bd. dirs. Citizens Crime Commn. Phila. Decorated D.S.M. with 2 oak leaf clusters, Silver Star medal with two oak leaf clusters, Legion of Merit with two oak leaf clusters, Bronze Star medal with two oak leaf clusters, Combat Inf. badge with star, Air medal with six oak leaf clusters; Republic of Korea Presdl. Commendation; Mil. Order of Merit Korea; Vietnamese Order 4th and 5th Classes; Vietnamese Gallantry Cross with palm; Grand Cross Merit with star Fed. Repub. Germany; Pa. D.S.M. Mem. Accuracy in Media, Am. Legion, Am. Security Coun., Assn. U.S. Army, Coun. for Inter-Am. Security, Mil. Order World Wars, Nat. Assn. Uniformed Svcs., 101st Airborne Divsn. Assn., Olympia Assn., Navy League, VFW, Res. Officers Assn., Nat. Sojourners Inc., Beta Gamma Sigma. Presbyterian. Club: Penn. Lodge: Masons (33 degree), Shriners (knight comdr. ct. honor). Master parachutist. Home: Daly City Calif. Died Mar. 6, 1996; interred Arlington National Cemetery.

PECK, N(EWTON) TENNEY, mathematics educator; b. Honolulu, Feb. 3, 1937; s. Newton Tenney and Caroline Durant (Ziegler) P.; m. Emily Mann, June 23, 1973. BA, Haverford (Pa.) Coll., 1959; PhD, U. Wash., 1964. Instr. Yale U., New Haven, 1964-66; fellow Alexander von Humboldt Stiftung, Frankfurt, Fed. Republic of Germany, 1966-67; lectr. U. Warwick, Coventry, Eng., 1967-68; asst. prof. U. Ill., Urbana, 1968-70, assoc. prof., 1970-82, prof., 1982—. Co-author: An F-space Sampler, 1984; co-editor: Geometry of Normed Spaces, 1986, Analysis at Urbana, 1989; contbr. articles to profl. jours. Australian Rsch. Coun. fellow Monash U., Australia, 1983; grantee NSF. Mem. Am. Math. Soc., Math. Assn. Am., London Math. Soc., Sigma Xi. Achievements include research on the structure of non-locally convex topological vector spaces. Died July 5, 1996.

PECK, TEMPLETON, newspaperman; b. Pomona, Cal., Aug. 26, 1908; s. Austin Hurlbut and Helena (Templeton) P.; m. Catherine Esther Clift, July 1, 1938; children—Templeton Clift, Caroline. A.B., Stanford, 1930; student, U. So. Cal. Law Sch., 1935-37. Reporter San Francisco News, 1930-31, San Diego Sun, 1931-33, Long Beach (Cal.) Press-Telegram, 1934-35, Los Angeles Daily News, 1935-37; lectr. journalism Stanford, 1937-41, lectr. communication, 1963-71; policy editor OWI, N.Y.C. and London, Eng., 1941-45; editorial writer San Francisco Chronicle, 1946-54, editor editorial page, 1954-84. Fellow Wilton Park (Eng.). Republican. Episcopalian. DIED 01/02/96. .

PEDERSEN, BERNARD EDWIN, state legislator; b. Grinnell, Iowa, Nov. 24, 1925; s. Edwin Bernard and Hattie (Jantzen) P.; m. Patricia Jean O'Brien, 1950; children: Christina Pedersen Tinning, Edwin, Andrew. BA, Grinnell Coll., 1949. Ins. broker Palatine and Chgo., Ill., 1949—; mem. Ill. Ho. of Reps. from 54th dist., 1983—; mem. Ins. Com. Ill. Ho. of Reps., Minority Spokesman Consumer Protection, Labor & Commerce, Small Bus., Aging, Vet. Affairs, Citizen Coun on Pub. Aid Coms.; co-chmn. Day Care Task Force; Ill. Chmn. Am. Legis. Exch. Coun.; chmn. Children and Family Svc. Assessor Palatine Twp., Ill., 1966-83, committeeman, 1969—; chmn. Crane for Congress, 1969; sec. Cook County Suburban Rep. Orgn., 1974-82; Cook County coord. Crane for Pres. Com., 1979; chmn. Palatine Twp. Reagan for Pres. Com., 1980. Decorated Purple Heart; recipient Disting. Unit Citation. Mem. KC (4th degree), Am. Coll. Life Underwriters, Chgo. Bd. Underwriters, Jesuit Retreat League of Chgo., Am. Legion. Died Nov. 6, 1996.

PEISER, DONALD EDWARD, business executive; b. Bklyn., May 6, 1919; s. Milton Alfred and Frances Jeannette (Zinman) P.; m. Edith Sutker, Dec. 3, 1967; children by previous marriage—Robert Alan, Marlene Hope Peiser Saltzberg. B.A., Bklyn. Coll., 1940; M.A., Columbia U., 1941; M.B.A., NYU, 1948. Security analyst Merrill Lynch Pierce Fenner & Beane, N.Y.C., 1946-49; v.p. Central Nat. Corp., investments, N.Y.C., 1950-60; partner Andresen & Co., mems. N.Y. Stock Exchange, N.Y.C., 1961-63; investment exec. S.H. Scheuer Co., N.Y.C., 1964-84; chmn. bd. Southdown, Inc., oil, gas and cement, Houston, 1976-86, CLC of Am., barge transp. and trucking, Houston, 1978-86. Trustee Bklyn. Coll. Found. Served with C.E. AUS, 1941-46. Jewish. Clubs: Muttontown (N.Y.); Canadian (N.Y.C.); Broken Sound (Fla.). Died Oct. 15, 1996.

PEKOW, EUGENE, hotel company executive; b. Chgo., Aug. 11, 1930; s. Philip M. and Celia (Katz) P.; m. Esta Bette Epstein, June 29, 1952 (div. 1980); children: Charles Thomas Wayne, Penelope Susan, Cynthia Ann; m. Barbara B. Hirsch, Mar. 16, 1980. AB cum laude, Brown U., 1952; JD, Northwestern U., 1955. Bar: Ill. 1955. Ptnr. Acorn Tire & Supply Co., Chgo., 1955-65; sec.-treas., dir. Acorn Tire & Supply Co. (and subsidiaries), 1965—; v.p. Exec. House Hotels, Chgo., 1957-68; pres. Midland Hotel Co., Chgo., 1969—, Acorn Mgmt. Co., 1974—; bd. dirs., pres. Midland Bldg. Corp., Chgo. Mem. editorial bd. Chgo. Reporter, 1985-91. Mem. nat. council Bus. Execs. Move for Vietnam Peace; bd. dirs. Deerfield Twp. Voters Assn., 1964-68; treas., bd. dirs. Bus. and Profl. People for Pub. Interest; bd. dirs. U. Chgo. Found. for Emotionally Disturbed Children, Community Renewal Soc., Bus. Execs. for Nat. Security; trustee Mt. Sinai Hosp. Med. Center, Schwab Rehab. Inst. (1980-88); chmn. bd. dirs. Sears Roebuck YMCA, 1980-83. Mem. Am. Technion Soc. (dir. 1976-82), Greater Chgo. Hotel and Motel Assn. (bd. dirs.1979-85). Home: Chicago Ill. Died Jan. 15, 1995.

PELADEAU, PIERRE, publishing company executive, b. Montreal, Apr. 11, 1925; s. Henri and Elmire (Fortier) P.; m. Raymonde Chopin, May 26, 1954; children: Eric, Isabelle, Pierre-Karl, Anne-Marie; m. Line Parisien, May 24, 1979; children: Esther, Pierre Jr., Jean; m. Marion Blanchette. L.Ph., U. Montreal, 1945, M.A., 1947; B.C.L., McGill U., Montreal, 1950; Dr honoris cause, U. Que.; Dr honoris causa, U. Sherbrooke, U. Laval, Que. With Quebecor Inc.; pub., printing and forest products holding co. exec. Quebecor Inc., Montreal, 1965-97; editor, pres., chief exec. officer Quebecor Inc., 1965-97; bd. dirs. Donohue Inc., Sodarcan Inc. 1st chancelor Ste.-Anne U., Novia Scotia, 1988. Officer, Legion d'Hooneur, France. Mem. Order of Can., Nat. Order Que. Club: Saint-Denis. Died Dec. 24, 1997.

PELKAUS, EDWARD EGILS, civil engineer; b. Suntazi, Latvia, May 28, 1935; came to U.S., 1950; s. Arthur Pelkaus and Helen (Rodzina) Puga; m. Inese Scherbin, Oct. 20, 1962 (div. 1973); 1 child, Vivian I.; m. Suzanne LaBastie Guy, July 31, 1992. B of Civil Engring., CCNY, 1967; MS in Indsl. Mgmt., Poly. Inst. Bklyn., 1972. Profl. engr., N.Y., N.J., Pa. Hwy. design engr. Parsons, Brinckerhoff, Quade & Douglas, N.Y.C., 1965-71; civil group leader Sverdrup and Parcel & Assocs., N.Y.C., 1971-73; project engr. DeLeuw, Cather & Co., N.Y.C., 1973-75; sr. project engr. Acres Am. Inc., Buffalo, 1976-77; project mgr. Sverdrup and Parcel & Assocs., Washington, 1977-79; chief civil engr., assoc. Envirodyne Engrs., Inc., N.Y.C., 1980-83; resident engr. Seelye, Stevenson, Value & Knecht, S.I., N.Y., 1983-84; facilities engring. mgr. Saudi Svcs. & Oper. Co., Ltd., Dhahran, Saudi Arabia, 1984-86, project & office mgr. Edwards & Kelcey, Inc., Atlantic City, 1986-89; v.p., br. mgr. Blauvelt Engrs., P.C., Phila. and East Orange, N.J., 1989—. With USMCR, 1957-59. Mem. NSPE, Am. Soc. Hwy. Engrs. (bd. dirs.), Soc. Am. Mil. Engrs. Lutheran. Avocations: swimming, canoeing, hiking, classical music.

PELLERZI, LEO MAURICE, lawyer; b. Cumberland, Md., June 14, 1924; s. John and Ida Lezzer (Regis) P.; m. Betty Lou Mearkle, Jan. 17, 1946; children: Jon Lou, Cheryl M., John C., Michele S., Julie A., Laura M., Jeffrey C. LL.B., George Washington U., 1949, LL.M., 1950. Bar: D.C. bar 1949, also U.S. Supreme Ct 1949. Asst. gen. counsel Subversive Activities Control Bd., 1952-56, 1956-59; adminstv. law judge ICC, 1959-65; gen. counsel U.S. Civil Svc. Commn., 1965-68; asst. atty. gen. for adminstrn. Dept. Justice, 1968-73; chmn. bd. Govt. Svcs., Inc., 1971-73; gen. counsel Am. Fedn. Govt. Employees, AFL-CIO, 1973-78; chmn. bd. Flag Filter Corp., 1978-85; pvt. practice law Washington, 1978-90. Gen. counsel Lafayette Fed. Credit Union, 1956-59; pres. Fed. Adminstrv. Law Judges Conf., 1963-65. Served with USAAF, 1943-45; lt. col. Res. Decorated Air medal with 4 oak leaf clusters.; recipient Commrs.'s award U.S. Civil Svc. Commn., 1968, Justice Tom C. Clark award Fed. Bar Assn., 1967. Roman Catholic. Died June 19, 1997.

PELTEKOF, STEPHAN, systems engineer; b. Plovdiv, Bulgaria, Feb. 11, 1929; came to U.S. 1956; s. Peter and Velika (Christova) P.; m. Colette Gringoire, July 6, 1957; 1 child, Brigitte. PhD, U. Santa Barbara, 1978. Cert. profl. mgr. Inst. Cert. Profl. Mgrs. Engr. Lockheed Missile & Space Co., Sunnyvale, Calif., 1967-69; systems analyst Martin-Marietta Aerospace Div., Vandenberg AFB, Calif., 1981-83; systems engr. Lockheed Space Ops. Co., Vandenberg AFB, Calif., 1983-86, Computer Software Analysts, Inc., Camarillo, Calif., 1987-89; sr. analytical specialist ITT Fed. Svcs. Corp., Vandenberg AFB, 1989-91; dir. edn. Cook's Inst. Engring., Jackson, Miss., 1991—. Author: The Conquest of Space, 1967, Commitment to Excellence, 1985, New Era Leadership, 1991, Forty Years in Exile, 1992. Recipient Outstanding Performance award Martin-Marietta Aerospace, 1982, Lockheed Space Ops. Co., 1985, Space Shuttle Directorate, 1986; named Employee of the Yr. Nat. Mgmt. Assn., 1986. Mem. Nat. Mgmt. Assn., Inst. Cert. Profl. Mgrs., N.Y. Acad. Scis. Eastern Orthodox. Achievements include development/ implementation "Vandenberg Launch and Landing Site Excellence Program". DIED 03/06/96. .

PENN, HUGH FRANKLIN, small business owner; b. Morgan County, Ala., Aug. 15, 1917; s. Charles Franklin and Bessie Melinda (Praytor) P.; m. Marynelle Walter, Nov. 12, 1939 (dec. Dec. 1993); children: Hugh Franklin, Charles Phillip, Beverly Ann; m. Martha Ann Jordan Phillips, Feb. 11, 1994. Student, U. Ala., 1936-37. Asst. purchasing agt. for contractors constructing Huntsville Arsenal and Redstone Arsenal, Ala., 1941-43; purchasing agt. U.S. Army Air Force, Courtland Army Air Field, Ala., 1943-46; owner, mgr. Hugh Penn Lumber Co., Hartselle, Ala., 1946-60; owner, mgr. C.F. Penn Hamburgers, Hartselle, 1958-81, chmn. bd., 1981—; postmaster City of Hartselle, 1957-81; office mgr., realtor assoc. Charlie Penn Realty, 1981-85; bd. dirs. Terrell Industries, Inc. Moderator Morgan County Baptist Assn., 1955, 56; chmn. Hartselle Bd. Zoning Adjustment, 1956-76; founder, bd. dirs. Hartselle Downtown Action Com., 1971—; bd. dirs. Morgan County Combined Fed. Campaign, 1971-81, Hartselle Clean City Assn. 1990-93; apptd. to aging adv. coun. North Cen. Ala. Regional Coun. Govt., 1991; bd. dirs., trustee North Cen. Ala. Mental Health Found., 1992. Recipient Hartselle Civitan Unselfish Svc. award, 1995. Mem. Nat. Assn. Post Masters U.S., Hartselle C. of C. (pres. 1976-77); appointed mem. City of Hartselle Industrial Devel. Bd., 1995—. Republican. Baptist. Lodge: Kiwanis (life, Legion of Honor award 1977, Perfect Attendance award 1992). Died June 19, 1997.

PENNINGTON, WELDON JERRY, newspaper executive; b. Tacoma, Mar. 1, 1919; s. Bert Archie and Marguerite Lucille (Heraty) P.; m. Dorothy Grace Kinney, Oct. 6, 1945; children: Susan Diane Merry, Scott Brian, Sally Jane Ringman, Steven Kinney. B.A., U. Wash., 1941. Staff accountant Allen R. Smart & Co. (C.P.A.s), Seattle, 1941-42; spl. agt. FBI, 1942-46; supervising accountant Touche Ross & Co. (C.P.A.s), Seattle, 1946-51; with Seattle Times, from 1951, pres., dir., 1967-82, pres., pub., chief exec. officer, dir., from 1982; pres., dir. Walla Walla (Wash.) Union-Bull., 1971-85, Times Communications Co., 1971, Blethen Corp.; dir. Rainier Nat. Bank, Seattle, Rainier Bancorp., Paccar, Inc.; dir., chmn. fin. com. Safeco Corp.; dir. Westin Hotels, Allied Daily Newspapers., pres., 1982-85. Pres. Seattle King County Community Chest, 1959-60, Seattle King County United Good Neighbor Fund, 1962-63, Downtown Seattle Devel. Assn., 1971-72, Virginia Mason Med. Found., 1980, Corp. Council Arts, 1980; Trustee Seattle Goodwill Industries; bd. dirs. Virginia Mason Hosp.; chmn. Council for Corp. Responsibility, 1982-83; trustee, pres. Seattle Found.; Chmn. adv. bd. U. Wash. Grad. Sch. Bus., 1980-81; treas. Fifth Avenue Theatre Assn., 1981, pres., 1982-83. Named Seattle's First Citizen of 1977 Seattle-King County Bd. Realtors. Mem. Am. Inst. C.P.A.s (Elijah Watts Sells award 1941), Wash. Soc. C.P.A.s (pres. 1951-52), Assn. Former Spl. Agts. FBI, Seattle C. of C. (pres. 1964-65), Sigma Delta Chi, Beta Alpha Psi. Clubs: Rotarian (pres. Seattle 1966-67), Seattle Golf (trustee 1974-77), Rainier (pres. 1968-69), Wash. Athletic, University; Desert Island Country (Palm Springs); Useless Bay Golf and Country. Home: Seattle, Wash. Died Mar. 17, 1985.

PENNOCK, JAMES ROLAND, political scientist, educator; b. Chatham, Pa., Feb. 4, 1906; s. James Levis and Alice Rakestraw (Carter) P.; m. Helen B. Sharpless, Jan. 24, 1931; children: Joan Pennock Barnard, Judith Carter Pennock Lilley. Student, London Sch. Econs., 1925-26; B.A., Swarthmore Coll., 1927; M.A., Harvard U., 1928, Ph.D., 1932. Instr. polit. sci. Swarthmore (Pa.) Coll., 1929-32, asst. prof., 1932-41, asso. prof., 1941-45, prof., 1946-62, Richter prof., 1962-76, Richter prof. emeritus, 1976-95, chmn. dept., 1941-70, acting chmn., 1974-75; vis. prof. Columbia U., 1950; vis. lectr. Harvard U., 1953; lectr. U. Pa., 1976-77; vis. prof. U. Calif., San Diego, 1978; Hill disting. vis. prof. U. Minn., 1979. Author: Administration and the Rule of Law, 1941, Liberal Democracy: Its Merits and Prospects, 1950, (with others) Democracy in the Mid-Twentieth Century: Problems and Prospects, (with David G. Smith) Political Science: An Introduction, 1964, Democratic Political Theory, 1979; editor: Self-Government in Modernizing Nations, 1964, NOMOS (yearbook Am. Soc. Polit. and Legal Philosophy), 1965-86, Equality, 1967, Representation, 1968, Voluntary Associations, 1969, Political and Legal Obligation, 1970, Privacy, 1971, Coercion, 1972, The Limits of Law, 1974, Participation in Politics, 1975, Human Nature in Politics, 1976, Due Process, 1977, Anarchism, 1978, Constitutionalism, 1979, Compromise in Ethics, Law, and Politics, 1979, Property, 1980, Human Rights, 1981, Ethics, Economics, and the Law, 1982, Liberal Democracy, 1983, Marxism, 1983, Criminal Justice, 1985, Justification, 1986, Authority Revisited, 1987, Religion, Morality and the Law, 1988, Markets and Justice, 1989; mem. editorial bd.: Am. Polit. Sci. Rev, 1964-68, 73-76; contbr. articles to profl. jours. and chpts. to books. Adminstrv. specialist U.S. Social Security Bd., 1936-37; prin. divisional asst. Office Fgn. Relief, Dept. State, 1943; panel chmn. Regional War Labor Bd., 1943-44; chmn. com. on fellowships polit. theory and legal philosophy Social Sci. Research Council, 1954-64, bd. dirs., 1960-66; trustee Primitive Hall Found., 1973-95, pres., 1984-86. Guggenheim fellow, 1954-55. Mem. Phi Beta Kappa. Mem. Soc. Friends. Home: Haverford Pa. Died Feb. 19, 1995; interred Friends Meeting, London Grove, PA.

PENZL, HERBERT, German language and linguistics educator; b. Neufelden, Austria, Sept. 2, 1910; came to U.S., 1936, naturalized, 1944; s. Johann and Hedwig (Schmidt) P.; m. Vera Rothmüller, Aug. 21, 1950. Grad., Gymnasium Vienna, Austria, 1929; hon. fellow, Brown U., 1932-34; Ph.D., U. Vienna, 1935. Editorial asst. Linguistic Atlas of U.S., Providence, 1932-34; asst. prof. Rockford (Ill.) Coll., 1936-38, U. Ill., Urbana, 1938-50; assoc. prof. U. Mich., Ann Arbor, 1950-53; prof. German U. Mich., 1953-63; prof. Germanic philology U. Calif., Berkeley, 1963-84; Smith-Mundt prof. gen. linguistics U. Kabul, Afghanistan, 1958-59; vis. prof. Georgetown U., 1951-53, Northwestern U., 1960, 65, U. Calif., Irvine, 1966, U. Colo., Boulder, 1969, Australian Nat. U., Canberra, 1970, SUNY-Buffalo, 1971, U. Vienna, Austria, 1980-81, U. Regensburg, 1981, U. Munich, 1982-83, U. Klagenfurt, Austria, 1986, Ariz. State U., Tempe, 1988. Author: A Grammar of Pashto, 1955, A Reader of Pashto, 1962, Geschichtliche deutsche Lautlehre, 1969, Lautsystem und Lautwandel in den althochdeutschen Dialekten, 1971, Methoden der germanischen Linguistik, 1972, Vom Urgermanischen zum Neuhochdeutschen, 1975, J. Ch. Gottsched's Deutsche Sprachkunst; edition and commentary, 1978; Frühneuhochdeutsch, 1984, Althochdeutsch, 1986, Mittelhochdeutsch, 1989, Englisch: eine Sprachgeschichte nach Texten (350 bis 1992), 1994; assoc. editor American Journal of Germanic Linguistics and Literatures, 1989—; contbr. over 150 articles to profl. jours. Served with AUS, 1943-45. Guggenheim fellow, 1967; Fulbright award to Germany, 1982-83; recipient Berkeley Citation, U. Calif., 1980, Österreichisches Ehrenkreuz für Wissenschaft und Kunst I. Klasse, Govt. Austria, 1981. Mem. MLA, Linguistic Soc. Am. (exec. com. 1981-83), Am. Dialect Soc., Am. Name Soc., Internat. Vereinigung Für Germanistik, Am. Assn. Tchrs. German (hon.), Societas Linguistica Europaea, Soc. for Germanic Philology, Aus. Acad. Scis. (hon.). Died Sept. 1, 1995.

PERETTI, ETTORE ALEX JAMES, emeritus metallurgical engineering educator; b. Butte, Mont., Apr. 5, 1913; s. Charles Ludwig and Mary (Crotto) P.; m. Pierina Helen Giacoletto, June 6, 1937; children: Charlene Pierre, Ettore Alex James. B.S., Mont. Coll. Mineral Sci. and Tech., 1934, M.S., 1935; Sc.D., U. Stuttgart, 1936; Metall. Engr. (hon.), U. Mont., 1963. Inst. Internat. Edn. exchange fellow to Germany, 1935-36; instr. metallurgy Mont. Coll. Mineral Sci. and Tech., 1936-39, asst. prof., 1939-40; asst. prof. Columbia U., 1940-46; assoc. prof. U. Notre Dame, 1946-49, prof., 1949-78, prof. emeritus, 1978—, head dept. metallurgy, 1951-69, asst. dean engring., 1970-78; asst. exec. dir. Nat. Consortium for Grad. Degrees for Minorities in Engring., Inc., 1978-89, assoc. exec. dir., 1989-91; cons. Bd. Econ. Warfare, 1943. Author numerous tech. publs. on metallurgy. Fellow Am. Soc. Metals (past sec.-treas., past chmn. Notre Dame chpt.); mem. AIME (past chmn. com. metallurgy courses, edn. div.), Am. Soc. Engring. Edn., Sigma Xi, Tau Beta Pi, Theta Tau, Alpha Sigma Mu (nat. pres. 1969-70). Died July 28, 1997.

PERKINS, CARL, rock and country western musician; b. Lake City, Tenn., Apr. 9, 1932; m. Valda de Vese; children: Steve, Stan, Greg, Debra. DMus (hon.), Lambeth Coll., 1988. Songs include Turn Around, Let the Jukebox Keep on Playing, Gone Gone Gone, Blue Suede Shoes, 1956, Everybody's Trying to Be My Baby, Honey Don't, Matchbox; albums include The Rocking Guitar Man, 1975, The Original Carl Perkins, 1976, Sun Sound Special, 1978, The Carl Perkins Dance Album, 1981, The Sun Years, 1982, Survivors (with Johnny Cash, Jerry Lee Lewis), 1982, Carl Perkins, 1986, Class of 55 (Sun reunion album with Roy Orbison, Jerry Lee Lewis, Johnny Cash), 1985; band leader, toured England, France and Germany, 1970, appeared at Wembley Festival , Eng., 1982; wrote Silver and Gold (recorded by Dolly Parton, 1996); recorded album Go Cat Go with Paul McCartney Group; currently touring U.S. and England with band. Founder Carl Perkins Child Abuse Ctr., Jackson, Tenn., 1981. Inducted into Rock and Roll Hall of Fame, 1987. Deceased.

PERKINS, EDWARD A., management educator; b. Portland, Oreg., Sept. 23, 1928; s. Edward A. and Blanche (Burkl) P.; m. Marilyn Loyce Apted, Jan. 28, 1955; children: Michael Edward, Jeffrey Craig, Robert Harold, Deana Mae. B.A., U. Wash., Seattle, 1953; M.A., Stanford U., 1956; Ed.D., Oreg. State U., 1963. Public sch. tchr. Seattle and Burlingame, Calif., 1953-58; instr. Oreg. State U., 1958-61; mem. faculty Wash. State U., Pullman, 1961-81; prof. mgmt. and adminstrv. systems Wash. State U., 1969-81, chmn. dept. office adminstrn., 1972-78, acting chmn. dept. mgmt. and adminstrv. systems, 1978-80, dir. grad. programs in bus. adminstrn., 1980-81; dir. Office Occupations Research and Devel. Project, 1965-68; mem. faculty U. Ga., Athens; chmn. and prof. dept. bus. edn. U. Ga., 1981-92, prof. dept. occupational studies, 1993-94; vis. prof. Utah State U., Logan, 1962, 65; cons. in field. Author: Executive Typewriting, 1966, 2d edit., 1981, Practice for Professional Typing, 1968, Typing for the Air Force, 1971, Mimeograph Textbook Curriculum Series, 1971, Fluid Instruction Series, 1972, Reprographics in Business Education, 1972, Vocational Business Education, 1974, Word Processing Applications, 1986, Practical Management Communication, 1987, also articles. Active local Boy Scouts Am., Little League, Am. Legion Baseball. Served with USAF, 1946-49. Mem. Nat. Bus. Edn. Assn., Am. Bus. Communications Assn., Western Bus. Edn. Assn. (historian 1966), Wash. (pres. 1966) Bus. Edn. Assn), So. Bus. Edn. Assn., Acad. of Mgmt., Adminstrv. Mgmt. Soc., Phi Delta Kappa, Delta Pi Epsilon, Kappa Delta Pi. Presbyterian. Home: Athens Ga. Died Apr. 29, 1994.

PERRET, MAURICE EDMOND, geography educator; b. La Chaux-de-Fonds, Switzerland, May 19, 1911; s. Jules Henri and Henriette Marie (Leuba) P.; Gymnase La Chaux-de-Fonds, 1929; Bac. es Lettres, U. Zurich (Switzerland), 1930; Licence es Lettres, U. Neuchatel (Switzerland), 1940; M.A. (Internat. House fellow 1940-42), U. Calif. at Berkeley, 1942; Doctorat es Lettres, U. Lausanne (Switzerland), 1950. Tchr., Petropolis and Lycee Francais, Rio de Janeiro, Brazil, 1935-37; asst. consulate Switzerland, San Francisco, 1942-43; del. internat. com. Red Cross, Washington, 1943-45; del. Aid to Arab Refugees, Palestine, 1949-51; asst. Internat. Telecommunication Union, Geneva, Switzerland, 1951-52; librarian La Chaux-de-Fonds, Switzerland, 1953-54; asst. Oltremare, Rome, Italy, 1955-56; prof. Avenches, Switzerland, 1957-63; prof. geography, map librarian U. Wis., Stevens Point, 1963-81, prof. emeritus, 1981—. Curator Roman Mus., Avenches, Switzerland, 1960-63. Mem. city council Avenches, Switzerland, 1961-63. Served with Swiss Army, 1939-40. Initiator Hist. Mus. of Portage County Hist. Soc., Stevens Pt. Mem. Assn. Am. Geographers, Nat. Council Geog. Edn., Am. Geog. Soc., Wis. Acad. Scis., Arts and Letters, Société vaudoise de geographie (v.p. 1960-63), Fedn. Swiss Geog. Socs. (v.p. 1961-63). Club: Travelers Century. Editorial com. Atlas Switzerland, 1960-63. Pub.: Les Colonies Tessinoises en Californie, 1950, Portage County, Of Place and Time, 1992; contbr. articles to profl. jours. Died Nov. 18, 1996.

PERRINE, LAURENCE, emeritus English educator; b. Toronto, Ont., Can., Oct. 13, 1915; s. Ren Brown and Mary (Dollins) P.; m. Catherine Lee Stockard, Sept. 17, 1949; children: David, Douglas. B.A., Oberlin Coll., 1937, M.A., 1939; Ph.D., Yale, 1948; D.H.L., So. Meth. U., 1988. Mem. faculty So. Meth. U., 1946-81, prof. English, 1960-81, prof. emeritus, 1981—. Author: Sound and Sense: An Introduction to Poetry, 7th edit, 1987, Story and Structure, 7th edit., 1988, (with J.M. Reid, J. Ciardi) Poetry: A Closer Look, 1963, (with J.M. Reid) 100 American Poems of the Twentieth Century, 1966, Literature: Structure, Sound and Sense, 1970, 5th edit., 1988, The Art of Total Relevance: Papers on Poetry, 1976, A Limerick's Always a Verse: 200 Original Limericks, 1990. Served with AUS, 1942-46, ETO. Mem. Tex. Inst. Letters, Nat. Council Tchrs. English (bd. dirs. 1962-65), S. Central Modern Lang. Assn. (pres. 1970-71), Tex. Conf. Coll. Tchrs. English (pres. 1973-74), Phi Beta Kappa. DIED 04/27/95. .

PERRY, ERMA JACKSON MCNEIL, journalist; b. Winthrop, Mass.; d. Hooper Martyn and Henrietta D. (Jackson) McNeil; m. Irving C. Perry, Apr. 29, 1939; children: Dorothy Gayle Perry Toy, Irving C. BS, Boston U., 1936. With Phila. Daily News, 1954-56; feature writer Phila. Inquirer, 1956, Phila. Bull., 1963-93; syndicated writer Copley News Service, San Diego, 1967-93; v.p. Arkwright-Boston Ins. Co.; free-lance contbr. nat. mags., newspapers. Mem. women's com. Internat. House, 1951-56; mem. Friends Social Order Com., 1956-66, Friends Prison Service Com., 1965-67; trustee Phila. Center Older People, 1960-67; mem. bd. Quaker Women, 1964-69; active English Speaking Union. Named hon. citizen Tex., 1972; winner nat. article writing contest Writer's Digest Mag., 1971, 72. Mem. Bucks County Writers (pres. 1970), Soc. Am. Travel Writers (Photography award 1980, 81, Grand prize in Photography 1983, Best Sell of Area Picture award 1987), Am. Soc. Journalists and Authors, World Affairs Club, Focal Planes Foto Club, Rotary. Mem. Soc. of Friends. Home: Jenkintown Pa. Died Sept. 13, 1993.

PERRY, JESSE LAURENCE, JR., investment manager, financier; b. Nashville, Oct. 15, 1919; s. Jesse Laurence and Mamie Lucretia (White) P.; m. Susan Taylor White, Nov. 5, 1949 (dec. Mar. 1972); children: Robert Laurance, Judith Foulds; m. 2d Sarah Kinkead Stockell, Apr. 6, 1974. BA magna cum laude, Vanderbilt U., 1941; MBA, Harvard U., 1943; postgrad. in edn. retarded children George Peabody Coll., summer 1953. Treas., J.L. Perry Co., Nashville, 1947-48; v.p., 1949-54, pres., 1954-73, also dir.; pres., chmn. bd. Perry Enterprises, Nashville, 1973-80, pres., Naples, Fla., 1980—, 1st So. Savs. & Loan, Inc., 1973-80; pres. PortersField, Inc., Nashville, 1973-80, The Jelpee Co., Naples, Fla., 1980—. Pres., Police Assistance League, 1973-74; hon. col., Staff Gov. Tenn., 1962-74; 1st v.p. Tenn. Assn. for Retarded Children, 1954-62; mem. Tenn. Mental Retardation Adv. Coun., 1966-72; bd. advisers Salvation Army, 1958-72; founder, sec. Tenn. Bot. Garden and Fine Arts Ctr., 1958—; chmn. 5th dist. Republican Exec. Com., 1950-54; vice chmn. Tenn. Rep. Exec. Com., 1950-54; Middle Tenn. Campaign mgr., 1956, 60, 66; state mgr. Pub. Service Com. Campaign, 1964; mem. spl. com. on urban devel. Rep. Nat. Exec. Com., 1962; del. Rep. Nat. Exec. Com., 1960, vice chmn. Tenn. del., 1960, alt. del., 1968; dist. mem. Rep. State Exec. Com., 1954-75; state chmn. Rep. Capitol Club, 1971-73; state Rep. committeeman, 1956-74; bd. govs. U. South, Sewanee Acad., 1968-74; trustee Task Force for the Homeless, Naples, St. Matthew's House for Homeless, Naples; bd. dirs. Substance Abuse Ministry, Naples. Served to capt. AUS, 1943-46. Decorated knight Hospitaller Order St. John Jerusalem, chevalier Ordo Constantini Magni knight (comdr.) Order Temple of Jerusalem. Mem. Episc. Churchmen Tenn. (v.p. 1956), Am. Ch. Union (v.p. 1958), SAR (chpt. pres. 1977-79), U.S. C. of C., Nat. Office Mgmt. Assn. (pres. Nashville chpt. 1958-59), Am. Legion, English Speaking Union, Magna Charta Barons, Baronial Order Magna Charta, Gen. Soc. Colonial Wars, Ams. of Royal Descent, Plantagenet Soc., Order Crown Charlemagne, Order of Three Crusades, Phi Beta Kappa, Omicron Delta Gamma, Pi Kappa Alpha. Clubs: Nashville Exchange, Nashville Sewanee, Nashville City, Capitol Hill (Washington), Naples Harvard, Royal Poinciana Golf (Naples), Naples Yacht. Died Jan. 11, 1996.

PETERING, JANICE FAYE, hotel executive; b. Covington, Ky., Feb. 10, 1950; d. Edward Charles Petering Sr. and Shirley Ellen (McKenzie) Petering Brancucci. Student, Eastern Ky. U., 1969; cert., Ramada Mgmt. Inst., 1982. Cert. hotel adminstr. Night auditor Caesars Palace Hotel, Las Vegas, Nev., 1970-77; chief rack clk. Caesars Palace Hotel, Las Vegas, 1979-80, supr. accounts receivable, 1980-82, casino comptr., 1982-83, ops. comptr., 1983-85; exec. asst. to hotel mgr. Tropicana Hotel & Country Club, Las Vegas, 1977-79, hotel mgr., 1985-86; hotel mgr. MGM Marina Casino and Hotel, Las Vegas, 1986-87; dir. hotel ops. MGM MArina Casino and Hotel, Las Vegas, 1987-90; hotel mgr. Vacation Village, Las Vegas, Nev., 1991-93; internal controller, fin. analyst Continental Hotel Casino, Las Vegas, 1993—. Mem. Internat. Assn. Hospitality Accts., Las Vegas Hotel-Motel Assn., Las Vegas Hotel Mgrs. Assn., Network of Exec. Women in Hospitality. Roman Catholic. Avocations: bowling, golf, softball, reading. Died Jan. 28, 1996.

PETERKIN, DEWITT, JR., banker; b. Webster Groves, Mo., June 6, 1913; s. DeWitt and Margaret (O'Brien) P.; m. Jane Parks (dec.); 1 dau., Clare; m. Katharine Urban, Oct. 23, 1948; children: DeWitt III, George Urban, Kate, Christopher (dec.), Patrick. A.B., Yale U., 1937. With J.P. Morgan & Co., Inc. (now Morgan Guaranty Trust Co. N.Y.), N.Y.C., 1937-97; v.p. J.P. Morgan & Co., Inc. (now Morgan Guaranty Trust Co. N.Y.), 1953-64, sr. v.p., 1964-65, exec. v.p., 1965-71, vice chmn., 1971-76, advisor to mgmt., 1976-97, also mem. adv. council. Bd. dirs. Yale Alumni Fund; trustee, past pres. St. Luke's-Roosevelt Hosp. Center.; chmn. emeritus United Hosp. Fund of N.Y. Served to capt. USNR, 1941-45. Decorated Silver Star, Bronze Star (2). Mem. Nat. Audubon Soc. (pres.'s council). Episcopalian. Clubs: Wee Burn Country (Darien); Ekwanok Golf (Manchester, Vt.); Yale (N.Y.C.). Home: Darien Conn. Died Aug. 29, 1997.

PETERS, CHESTER EVAN, sculptor, retired university administrator; b. Mpls., Oct. 15, 1922; s. Robert Earl and Gladys (Kresky) P.; m. Doris Lerene Clow,

Jan. 24, 1943; children—Karen Sue Peters Hartner, Stephen Chester. B.S., Kans. State U., 1947, M.S., 1950; Ph.D., U. Wis., 1953. Asst. dean Kans. State U. Sch. Arts and Sci., Manhattan, 1947-51; dir. placement Kans. State U. Sch. Arts and Sci., 1953-62, dean students, 1962-67, v.p. student affairs, 1967-85, ret., 1985; wood sculptor, 1985-95; Reader U.S. Office Edn.; pres. Coll. Placement Council. Served to capt., inf. AUS, 1943-46. Mem. Nat. Assn. Student Personnel Adminstrs. (pres. 1971-72), Kans. Assn. Student Personnel Adminstrs. (pres.), Nat. Woodcarvers Am., Farmhouse. Methodist. Club: Kiwanian. Home: Manhattan Kans. Died Oct. 1, 1995.

PETERS, ELLIS See PARGETER, EDITH MARY

PETERS, STANLEY W., state legislator; b. Amherst, N.H., July 23, 1927; m. Jean Peters; 8 children. BS, U. N.H., 1950. Mem. Peterborough Sch. Bd., 1963-69, bd. selectman, 1979-85, 89-92; bd. selectman Conval Sch. Bd., 1969-74; N.H. state rep. Dist. 8; mem. sci., tech. and energy coms. N.H. Ho. of Reps.; fuel oil distbr. AW Peters, 1956—. Mem. Peterborough Hist. Soc. (dir. 1985-90). Mem. Peterborough Rotary Club (pres. 1988-89). Died Aug. 17, 1997.

PETERSDORF, ROBERT JAMES, labor union exec.; b. Cannon Falls, Minn., Jan. 9, 1921; s. Willus H. and Cora (Haas) P.; m. Margaret McGregor Hankins, Dec. 28, 1969; children by previous marriage—David, Diana, Sherry, Terry, Denise; stepchildren—Timothy, Daniel. Student pub. schs., Zumbrota, Minn. Painter, 1938-46; bus. rep. Rochester (Minn.) Bldg. Trades Council, 1946-55; sec. Minn. State Bldg. Trades, Rochester, 1952-55; gen. organizer Brotherhood of Painters, Rochester and Mpls., 1955-66; gen. v.p. Brotherhood of Painters, 1966-76; gen. sec.-treas. Internat. Brotherhood Painters and Allied Trades, Washington, 1976—. Editor: Painters and Allied Trades jour, 1976—. Served with U.S. Army, 1941-45. Democrat. Roman Catholic. Office: Internat Brotherhood Painters and Allied Trades 1750 New York Ave NW Washington DC 20006 Died Sept. 16, 1997.

PETERSEN, DAVID LEE, insurance agent; b. Louisville, Dec. 17, 1943; s. Clifford Warren and Martha Lee (Schmidt) P.; m. Edwina Marie Stiles, June 22, 1968; children—Christopher Lee, Jennifer Wood, Joshua Kulk. B.S. in Bus. Adminstrn., Marquette U., 1966; M.B.A., U. Utah., 1971; cert. in personal fin. planning., Am. Coll. Commd. 2d lt. U.S. Air Force, 1967; advanced through grades to maj., 1979; chief maintenance 601st Tactical Control Maintenance Squadron, Sembach AFB, Germany; navigator 437 Mil. Airlift Wing, Charleston AFB, S.C., 1972-73; instr. navigator 374 Tactical Airlift Wing, Clark AB, Philippines, 1973-74; navigator flight examiner 314 Tactical Airlift Wing, Little Rock AFB, Ark., 1974-76; chief ops. programs 61 Mil. Airlift Support Wing, Hickam AFB, Hawaii, 1976-79; asst. chief inspections 317 Tactical Airlift Wing, Pope AFB, N.C., 1979-83; chief plans and policy HQ Tactical Air Command Info. Systems, Langley AFB, Va., 1983-87; retired from USAF, 1987; ins. agt. Met. Life Ins. Co., Newport News, Va., 1987—. Vice pres. Wendwood Assn., Newport News, Va., 1984-85, pres., 1985-86, newsletter editor 1987-88; mem. Framework for the Future Commn., City of Newport News. Decorated 2 Air Force Meritorious Svc. medals, 3 Air medals, 2 Humanitarian Svc. medals. Mem. Internat. Platform Assn., Retired Officers Assn., Kiwanis (bd. dirs., charter pres. Oyster Pt. chpt. 1988-89, Disting. Kiwanian 1988-89). Republican. Roman Catholic. Avocations: woodworking, antique and art collecting, consumer advocate, stamp collecting.

PETERSON, ESTHER, consumer advocate; b. Provo, Utah, Dec. 9, 1906; d. Lars and Annie (Nielsen) Eggertsen; m. Oliver A. Peterson, May 28, 1932; children: Karen Kristine, Eric N., Iver E., Lars E. A.B., Brigham Young U., 1927; M.A., Columbia Tchrs. Coll., 1930; M.A. hon. degrees, Smith Coll., Bryant Coll., Carnegie Inst. Tech., Montclair Coll., Hood Coll., Maryhurst Coll., Simmons Coll., Northeastern U., U South Utah, Western Coll. Women, Oxford, Ohio, Mich. State U., U. Mich., U. Utah, Williams Coll., Georgetown U., Temple U., Goucher Coll., Tufts U. Tchr. Branch Agr. Coll., Cedar City, Utah, 1927-29, Utah State U., Winsor Sch., Boston, 1930-36, Bryn Mawr Summer Sch. for Women Workers in Industry, 1932-39; asst. dir. edn. Amal. Clothing Workers Am., 1939-44, Washington legis. rep., 1945-48; legis. rep. indsl. union dept. AFL-CIO, 1958-61; dir. Women's Bur., U.S. Dept. Labor, 1961-64, asst. sec. labor for labor standards, 1961-69; exec. vice chmn. Pres.'s Commn. on Status of Women, 1961-63, Interdeptl. Com. Status Women, 1963-65; chmn. Pres.'s Com. Consumer Interests, 1964-67, spl. asst. to President for consumer affairs, 1964-67; legis. rep. Amal. Clothing Workers Am., Washington, 1969-70; consumer adviser Giant Food Corp., 1970-77; spl. asst. to Pres. for consumer affairs, 1977-80; chmn. Consumer Affairs Council, 1979-80. Active Internat. Med. Svcs. for Health, 1987, United Srs. Health Coop., 1987, Ctr. Sci. in Pub. Interest, 1964; mem. Women's Nat. Dem. Club; NGO rep. Internat. Orgn. Consumers Union at Econ. and Social Coun. UN, 1985, appointed pub. mem. U.S. Del. to Gen. Assembly, 1993. Decorated Presdl. medal of Freedom, 1981; recipient Food Industry Consumer award, 1986, Mgmt. award Brigham Young U., 1989. Mem. AAUW, Am. Home Econs. Assn. (hon.), Nat. Consumers League (pres. 1974-76, hon. pres. 1981), Cosmos Club, Phi Chi Theta (hon.), Delta Sigma Theta (hon.).

PETERSON, RALPH, financial executive; b. N.Y.C., Jan. 24, 1924; s. James and Mildred (Lebowitz) P.; m. Patricia Bloom, Mar. 18, 1951; children: Jeffrey, Stacey Peterson Evans, Beth Lisa. B.B.A., CCNY, 1948. CPA, N.Y. Sr. acct. S.D. Leidesdorf Co., N.Y.C., 1948-51; mgr. Peat, Marwick, Mitchell, N.Y.C., 1951-70; sr. v.p., treas. Warner Bros., Inc., N.Y.C., 1970—; v.p., treas. Warner Bros., Inc., Burbank, Calif., 1970—, exec. v.p., treas., 1987—, sr. v.p., treas., 1987-89, exec. v.p., 1989—, also bd. dirs., mem. exec. com. Bd. dirs. Arthritis Found., Los Angeles, 1981—. Served with USAF, 1943-46. Mem. Am. Inst. CPA's, N.Y. Soc. CPA's. DIED 10/20/97. .

PETERSON, ROGER TORY, ornithologist, artist; b. Jamestown, N.Y., Aug. 28, 1908; s. Charles Gustav and Henrietta (Bader) P.; m. Mildred Warner Washington, Dec. 19, 1936; m. Barbara Coulter, July 29, 1943; children: Tory, Lee; m. Virginia Westervelt, 1976. Student, Art Students League, 1927-28, NAD, 1929-31; DSc (hon.), Franklin and Marshall Coll., 1952, Ohio State U., 1962, Fairfield U., 1967, Allegheny Coll., 1967, Wesleyan U., 1970, Colby Coll., 1974, Gustavus Adolphus Coll., 1978, Conn. Coll., 1985; HHD (hon.), Hamilton Coll., 1976; LHD (hon.), Amherst Coll., 1977, Skidmore Coll., 1981, Yale U., 1986, So. Conn. State Coll., 1991; DFA (hon.), U. Hartford, 1981, SUNY, 1986, Middlebury Coll., 1986, Long Island U., 1987; DSc (hon.), U. Conn., 1987, Meml. U. Nfld., 1987, Bates Coll., 1991; DFA (hon.), MacMurray Coll., 1989. Decorative artist, 1926; instr. sci. and art River Sch., Brookline, Mass., 1931-34; mem. adminstrv. staff Nat. Audubon Soc.; charge ednl. activities; art editor Audubon mag., 1934-43; Audubon screen tour lectr., from 1946; art dir. Nat Wildlife Fedn ; founder Roger Tory Peterson Inst. Study Natural History, 1986—; distinguished scholar-in-residence Fallingwater-Western Pa. Conservancy, 1968; del. 11th Internat. Ornithol. Congress, Basel, Switzerland, 1954, 12th, Helsinki, 1958, 13th, Ithaca, N.Y., 1962, 14th, Oxford, Eng., 1966, 15th, The Hague, Netherlands, 1970, Internat. Bird Protection Conv., Tokyo, 1960, Cambridge, Eng., 1966; mem. Internat. Galapagos Sci. Project, 1964, USARP-Operation Deepfreeze, Antarctica, 1965; chmn. Am. sect. Internat. Bird Protection Com.; Hon. trustee Uganda (Africa) Nat. Parks; sec. Nat. Audubon Soc., 1960-64; mem. council Cornell Lab. Ornithology, bd. dirs. World Wildlife Fund, 1962-76; 1st v.p. Am. Ornithologists Union, 1962-63. Engaged in bird painting and illustration bird books, 1934—; Author: Field Guide to the Birds, 1934, Junior Book of Birds, 1939, A Field Guide to Western Birds, 1941, Birds Over America, 1948, How to Know the Birds, 1949, Wildlife in Color, 1951, A Bird-Watchers Anthology, 1957, A Field Guide to the Birds of Texas, 1959, Penguins, 1979; illustrator: Birds of South Carolina, 1949, Birds of Newfoundland, 1951, Arizona and Its Bird Life, 1952, Birds of Nova Scotia, 1961, Birds of Colorado, 1965, ltd. edit. prints of birds, Mill Pond Press, 1974; author: The Field Guide Art of Roger Tony Peterson, 1990; co-author: The Audubon Guide to Attracting Birds, 1941, Field Guide to Birds of Europe, 1953, Wild America, 1955, The World of Birds, 1964, The Birds, 1963, Field Guide to Wildflowers, 1968, Field Guide to Birds of Mexico, 1973, Peterson First Guide to Birds, 1986, Peterson First Guide to Wildflowers, 1986, Save the Birds, 1989; editor: American Naturalist series, 1965—, Field Guide to Pacific Coast Fishes, 1983, Field Guide to Beetles, 1983, Field Guide to Moths of Eastern North America, 1984, Field Guide to Southwestern and Texas Wildflowers, 1984, Field Guide to Atlantic Coast Fishes, 1986, Field Guide to Western Butterflies, 1986, Filde Guide to Mushrooms, 1987, Field Guide to Hawks, 1987, Field Guide to Seashores, 1988, Field Guide to Eastern Forests, 1988, Field Guide to Birding by Ear, 1989, Field Guide to Advanced Birding, 1990, Field Guide to Medicinal Plants, 1990 (also illustrator), Field Guide to Birding by Ear: Western, 1990, Field Guide to Freshwater Fishes, 1991; contbr. articles to natural history and popular publs.; lectr. in field. Del. 19th Internat. Ornithological Congress, Quebec, 1986. Served with C.E. U.S. Army, 1943-45. Recipient Brewster Meml. medal Am. Ornithologists Union, 1944; John Burroughs medal exemplary nature writing, 1950; Geoffrey St. Hilaire gold medal French Natural History Soc., 1958; gold medal N.Y. Zool. Soc., 1961; Arthur A. Allen medal Lab. Ornithology, 1967; White Meml. Found. Conservation award, 1968; Gold medal Safari Club Phila., 1968; Paul Bartsch award Audubon Naturalist Soc., 1969; Frances Hutchinson award Garden Club Am., 1970; Gold medal N.J. Garden Club, 1970; Gold medal World Wildlife Fund, 1972; Joseph Wood Krutch medal, 1973; Explorers Club medal, 1974; Tchr. of Year award, 1974; Distinguished Pub. Service award Conn. Bar Assn., 1974; Cosmos Club award, 1976; Linné Gold medal Royal Swedish Acad. Scis., 1976; Green World award N.Y. Bot. Garden, 1976; Sarah Joseph Hale award Richards Library, 1977; Master Bird Artist medal Leigh Yankee Mus., 1978; Presdl. Medal of Freedom, 1980, Gold medal Phila. Acad. Natural Scis., 1980, Ludlow Griscom award Am. Birding Assn., 1980, Smithsonian medal, 1984, Roger Tory Peterson award Thames Sci. Ctr., 1985—, Eisenmann medal Linnaean Soc., 1986, award of Merit Chgo. Field Mus. Natural History, 1986, Disting. Community Citizen award U. Conn. ALumni Assn., 1986, N.Y. State Legis. award, 1987; named Swedish-Am. of 1977, Vasa Order of Am.; officer Order of Golden Ark Holland, 1978; Conn. Citizen of Yr., 1986, hon. pres. Internat. Council Bird Preservation, 1986; Silver Buffalo award Boy Scouts Am., 1986; fellow Davenport Coll., Yale, 1966—; recipient award of merit and naming pf owl, Otis petersonii, Field Mus. Nat. History, Chgo., 1986. Fellow AAAS, N.Y. Zool. Soc., Am. Ornithologists Union, Linnaean Soc. N.Y. (hon.), London Zool. Soc. (hon.); mem. Nat. Audubon Soc. (life; dir. 1958-60, 65-67, Audubon medal 1971, spl. cons. 1972—), Soc. Wildlife Artists (Eng.) (v.p.), Wilson Ornithol. Soc. (life pres. 1964-65), Brit. Ornithologists Union (hon.), Cooper Ornithol. Soc., Nat. Assn. Biology Tchrs. (hon.). Clubs: Nuttall (Cambridge, Mass.); Cosmos, Biologists Field (Washington); Century Assn., Explorers (N.Y.C.); Intrepids (pres.). Died July 28, 1996.

PETERSON, THEODORE BERNARD, retired journalism educator; b. Albert Lea, Minn., June 8, 1918; s. Theodore B. and Emilie (Jensen) P.; m. Helen M. Clegg, Sept. 13, 1946; children: Thane Eric, Kristin, Megan, Daniel Alan. B.A., U. Minn., 1941; M.S., Kans. State Coll., 1948; Ph.D., U. Ill., 1955. Instr., then asst. prof. journalism Kans. State Coll., 1945-48, head coll. news bur., 1945-47; instr. journalism U. Ill., 1948-55, assoc. prof., 1955-57, prof., 1957-87; dean U. Ill. (Coll. Communications), 1957-79; judge Nat. Mag. Awards, 1967-88. Author: Writing Nonfiction for Magazines, 1949, Magazines in the Twentieth Century, 1956, rev., 1964, (with F.S. Siebert, Wilbur Schramm) Four Theories of the Press, 1956, (with J.W. Jensen, Wm. L. Rivers) The Mass Media in Modern Society, 1965, rev., 1971. Recipient award for distinguished research journalism Sigma Delta Chi, Kappa Tau Alpha, 1956, Outstanding Achievement award U. Minn., 1973, Outstanding Undergraduate Teaching award U. Ill., 1987. Mem. Assn. Edn. Journalism (1st v.p. 1962, pres. 1963), Am. Council on Edn. Journalism (accrediting com. 1961-70, 72-81), Am. Assn. Schs. and Depts. Journalism (pres. 1965), Kappa Tau Alpha, Phi Kappa Phi. Died Aug. 27, 1997.

PETRIE, JOHN RICHARD, advertising agency executive, writer; b. Astoria, Oreg., Apr. 5, 1945; s. John Richard and Margot Maxwell (Brown) P.; m. Jo Curie Joffe, Feb. 5, 1987. Student, HB Studio, 1964-65, Bowling Green U., 1966-69. Mgr. Discount Records div. CBS, Ann Arbor, Mich., 1971-73; owner King Pleasure, Ann Arbor, 1973-74; program dir. Sta. WABX-FM, Detroit, 1974-75; mgr. Midwest promotion Motown Records, Inc., Detroit, 1975, Mercury Records, Chgo., 1976; advt. mgr. Sidetracks Chgo. Daily News, 1976-77; mgr. Midwest promotion Arista Records, Inc., Chgo., 1978-79; assoc. creative dir. Leo Burnett U.S.A., Chgo., 1980-85; sr. writer HBM/Creamer-Albert J. Rosenthal, Chgo., 1986-88; copywriter Rynne-House Comm., Evanston, Ill., 1988-89; mgr. mags., jours. & periodicals Guild Books & Guild Complex, Chgo., 1990-93; interpretive svcs. John G. Shedd Aquarium, Chgo., 1994—; freelance advt. writer, prodr., instr. Columbia Coll., Nat.-Louis U., Chgo.; interpreter John G. Shedd Aquarium, Chgo., 1994; sales promotion cons. Contbr. articles to Playboy mag., Circus mag., Kitchen Sink Pub., other newspapers, mags. Democrat. Avocations: music, art, poetry, camping, writing. Died Sept 15, 1996.

PETRUCELLI, R(OCCO) JOSEPH, II, nephrologist; b. Meriden, Conn., Sept. 20, 1943; s. Rocco Joseph and Marguerite Robena (Colwell) P. BA, Yale U., 1965; MD, Harvard U., 1969. Diplomate Am. Bd. Internal Medicine, Am. Bd. Nephrology. Intern, then resident Mt. Sinai Hosp., N.Y.C., 1969-72; fellow in nephrology U. Calif. San Francisco Med. Ctr., San Francisco, 1972-74; asst. prof. Mt. Sinai Sch. Medicine, 1978-92; assoc. prof. N.Y. Med. Coll., 1992—; vis. rschr. Karolinska Inst., Stockholm, 1970-71; exec. com. End Stage Renal Disease, N.Y.C., 1980-90, pres. 1985. Author: Medicine: An Illustrated History, 1978, transl. into fgn. langs., 1978-96. Pres. Bklyn. Opera Soc.; mem. med. adv. bd. Nat. Kidney Found., 1987-94, v.p., 1994; treas. Friends of Rare Book Rm. of N.Y. Acad. Medicine, 1993, sec., 1994. Recipient Richard Cabot prize Harvard Med. Sch., 1969, Boylston prize Boylston Med. Soc., 1969, John P. McGovern prize Baylor Coll. Medicine, Houston, 1993. Fellow N.Y. Acad. Medicine (libr. com. 1975—), Am. Soc. Nephrology, Internat. Soc. Nephrology. Democrat. Episcopalian. Died Jan. 24, 1997.

PETRY, ANN LANE, author; b. 1908. Pharmacist Old Saybrook and Old Lyme, Conn., 1931-38; writer, reporter Amsterdam News, N.Y.C., 1938-41, People's Voice, N.Y.C., 1941-44; vis. prof. English U. Hawaii, Honolulu, 1974-75. Author: The Street, 1946, Country Place, 1947, The Drugstore Cat, 1949, The Narrows, 1953, Harriet Tubman: Conducter of the Underground Railroad, 1955, Tituba of Salem Village, 1964, Legends of the Saints, 1970, Miss Muriel and Other Stories, 1971.

PETTIT, ALBERT W., state legislator; b. Pitts., Oct. 18, 1930; s. Albert W. and Sara (Wakefield) P.; m. Joan

E. Claycomb; children: Sara, Katherine, Albert. BA, Pa. State U., 1952; JD, U. Va., 1957. With Civil Svc. Commn., Upper St. Clair, 1977-82, chmn., 1982-88; commr. Upper St. Clair Twp., 1988-93; rep. dist. 40 State of Pa., 1993—; chmn. Upper St. Clair Human Resource Com., Upper St. Clair Pub. Safety Com. and Budget Com.; past corp. dir. human resources and nat. labor rels. Westinghouse Elec. Corp. Active Friends of the Libr., Upper St. Clair. Mem. Am. Legion, Rotary. Died June 15, 1997.

PETTIT, HORACE, allergist, consultant; b. Jan. 28, 1903; s. Horace and Katherine (Howell) P.; B.S., Harvard Coll., 1927; M.D., 1931; m. Millicent Lewis, Nov. 22, 1924 (dec.); children: Emily Connery, Horace (dec.), Deborah Myers, Norman; m. Jane Mann Hiatt, May 13, 1950 (dec.); 1 adopted child, Barbara Mann Ralph. Intern, Bryn Mawr Hosp., 1933-34; asst. instr., instr., assoc. bacteriology U. Pa. Sch. Medicine, 1932-39, instr. medicine, 1939-53; pvt. practice allergy, 1940-42, 1947-75; cons. in allergy Bryn Mawr Hosp., 1963-79, emeritus staff mem., 1979—; cons. allergist Bryn Mawr Coll., 1963-75. Served from maj. to lt. col. AUS, 1942-46. Fellow Coll. Physicians of Phila.; mem. AMA, Am. Acad. Allergy, Am. Soc. Microbiology, Phila. County, Med. Soc., Pa. Med. Soc., Phila. Allergy Soc. (pres. 1958-59), United World Federalists (mem. nat. exec. coun. 10 years), St. Andrew's Soc. Phila. Unitarian. Clubs: Harvard-Radcliffe (Phila.); Merion Cricket (Haverford, Pa.); Camden (Maine) Yacht. Died September 11, 1995.

PETTIT, T. CHRISTOPHER, investment company executive. Pres., COO Lehman Bros. Inc., N.Y.C. Died Feb. 15, 1997.

PETTY, OLIVE SCOTT, geophysical engineer; b. Olive, Tex., Apr. 15, 1895; s. Van Alvin and Mary Cordelia (Dabney) P.; m. Mary Edwina Harris, July 19, 1921; 1 son, Scott. Student Ga. Inst. Tech., 1913-14; BS in Civil Engring., U. Tex., 1917, CE, 1920. Registered profl. engr., Tex. Adj. prof. civil engring. U. Tex., 1920-23; structural engr. R.O. Jameson, Dallas, 1923-25; pres. Petty Geophys. Engring. Co., Petty Labs., Inc., San Antonio, 1925-52, chmn. bd., 1952-73; chmn. bd. Petty Geophys. Engring. Co. de Mex. S.A. de C.V., 1950-73; ptnr. Petty Ranch Co., 1968-94; ranching, oil, timber and investment interests, 1937-94. Author: Seismic Reflections, Recollections of the Formative Years of the Geophysical Exploration Industry, 1976; A Journey to Pleasant Hill, The Civil War Letters of Capt. E. P. Petty, C.S.A., 1982; patentee geophys. methods, instruments, equipment, including electrostatic seismograph detector in op. on the moon and on Mars and now NASA's standard for space exploration. Benefactor, San Antonio Symphony Soc., McNay Art Mus.; mem. exec. com., founding mem. chancellor's council U. Tex. System, Austin, also founding mem., hon. life mem. Geology Found.; mem. Inst. Texan Cultures, mem. devel and adv. bds; adv. council U. Tex., Austin. Served as lt. Engrs., U.S. Army, 1917-18; AEF in France. Hon. adm. Tex. Navy; recipient Disting. Grad. award U. Tex. Coll. Engring., Austin, 1962; Tex. Acad. Sci. (hon. life), N.Y. Acad. Sci.; mem. ASCE (hon. life), AIME (Legion of Honor), Am. Assn. Petroleum Geologists, AAAS (50-yr. mem.), Am. Petroleum Inst., Nat. Soc. Profl. Engrs. (life), Am. Geophys. Union, Houston Geophys. Soc., San Antonio Geophys, Soc., South Tex. Geol. Soc., Soc. Petroleum Engrs. (Legion of Honor), Am. Assn. Petroleum Geologists (life), Soc. Am. Mil. Engrs. (life), Soc. Exptl. Geophysicists (founding mem.; hon. life), Soc. 1st Inf. Div. (founding), Tex. Soc. Profl. Engrs., Explorers Club (life), Mil. Profl. Engrs. in Pvt. Practice, Wisdom Soc., Am. Geol. Inst. (Centurian Club), Am. Assn. Petroleum Geologists Trustee Assn. (life), Chi Epsilon (hon. life), Theta Xi, Tau Beta Pi. Baptist. Clubs: San Antonio Country, Argyle, St. Anthony, Giraud. Died Mar. 2, 1994.

PFEFFER, LEO, lawyer, educator; b. Hungary, Dec. 25, 1910; came to U.S., 1912; naturalized, 1917; s. Alter Saul and Hani (Yaeger) P.; m. Freda Plotkin, Sept. 18, 1937; children: Alan Israel, Susan Beth. BSS, CCNY, 1930; JD, NYU, 1933; LHD (h.c.), Hebrew Union Coll., 1979; LLD (h.c.), Long Island U., 1988. Bar: N.Y. 1933. Pvt. practice N.Y.C., 1933-90, pvt. tchr. law, 1933-45; lectr. New Sch., 1954-58, Mt. Holyoke Coll., 1958-60; David W. Petergorsky prof. constl. law Yeshivah U., 1962-63; gen. counsel Am. Jewish Congress, 1958-64, spl. counsel, 1964-85; prof. polit. sci. L.I. U., 1964-80, adj. prof., 1981-93, chmn. dept., 1964-79; Vis. prof. constl. law Rutgers U., 1965; frequent radio and TV appearances, 1954-93. Author: Church, State and Freedom, 1953, rev. edit., 1967, The Liberties of an American, 1956, Creeds in Competition, 1958, (with Anson Phelps Stokes) Church and State in the United States, 1964, This Honorable Court, 1965, God, Caesar and the Constitution, 1975, Religious Freedom, 1977; Religion, State and the Burger Court, 1984; editorial bd.: Jour. Ch. and State, 1958-93, Judaism, 1964-93 (honored by Religion and State: Essays in Honor of Leo Pfeffer 1985). Pres. Lawyers Constl. Def. Com., 1964-66, counsel, 1967-82, emeritus counsel, 1982-93; cons. counsel Religious Coalition for Abortion Rights, 1976-93; adv. com. Nat. Project Ctr. for Film and the Humanities, 1974-93; mem. religious liberty com. Nat. Council Chs. of Christ in U.S.A.; mem. nat. legal affairs com. Anti-Defamation League B'nai B'rith, 1985-93; mem. nat. adv. bd. Ams. for Religious Liberty, 1985-93. Recipient Religious Freedom award Ams. United for Separation Ch. and State, 1955, citation contbns. to civil rights Minn. Jewish Community Council, 1962, Thomas Jefferson Religious Freedom award Unitarian-Universalist Ch. N.Y., 1967, Bklyn. Civil Liberties award, 1968, citation for contbns. to pub. edn. Horace Mann League, 1972, Lawyers Constl. Def. Com., 1972, award Com. for Pub. Edn. and Religious Liberty, 1972, Rabbi Maurice N. Eisendrath Meml. award Union of Am. Hebrew Congregations, 1977, George Brussel Meml. award Stephen Wise Free Synagogue, 1978, Ams. United Fund award, 1979, Am. Jewish Congress award, 1980, cert. of merit Coun. Jewish Fedns., 1984, award of recognition Nat. Jewish Community Rels. Adv. Com., 1987, Humanist of Yr. award Am. Humanist Assn., 1988. Fellow Jewish Acad. Arts and Scis.; mem. Am. Jewish Congress, Am. Acad. Religion, Am. Acad. Polit. and Social Scis., AAUP (pres. L.I. U. chpt. 1967-68), Jewish Peace Fellowship (exec. com. 1969-93, counsel 1979-93), ACLU (cons., cooperating atty.), Soc. Sci. Study Religion, NYU Law Rev. Alumni Assn. (pres. 1964-66), Am. Judicature Soc., Am. Polit. Sci. Assn., Am. Arbitration Assn. (panel arbitrators), Nat. Assn. Intergroup Rels. Ofcls., Horace Mann League U.S. (gen. counsel), Am. Soc. for Legal History, Com. for Pub. Edn. and Religious Liberty (founder 1967, gen. counsel 1967-82, counsel emeritus 1982-93, award), Nat. Coalition Pub. Edn. and Religious liberty (founder 1967, gen. counsel 1967-82, counsel emeritus 1982-93). Home: Goshen N.Y. Died June 4, 1993.

PFLUEGER, EDWARD MAXIMILIAN, chemical company executive; b. Frankfurt, W. Ger., June 23, 1905; came to U.S., 1926, naturalized, 1935; s. Heinrich and Amalie (Ude) P.; m. Kathleen Isabel Powers, Sept. 16, 1943. Grad. gymnasium, Frankfurt, 1923. Owner, pres. Metachem, Inc., N.Y.C., 1953—; hon. chmn. (ret.) Mobay Chem. Corp., Pitts., 1975—; chmn. emeritus (ret.) Miles Labs., Elkhart, Ind. Mem. Racquet and Tennis Club (N.Y.C.), Knickerbocker Club (N.Y.C.). Died Jan. 15, 1997.

PFORZHEIMER, CARL HOWARD, JR., investment banker; b. N.Y.C., July 17, 1907; s. Carl H. and Lily Maud (Oppenheimer) P.; m. Carol Jerome Koehler, Sept. 1, 1931; children: Nancy (Mrs. Edgar D. Aronson), Carl Howard III. AB, Harvard U., 1928, MBA, 1930; HHD, Capital U., Columbus, 1969; DCS, Pace U., N.Y.C., 1959. Faculty Centre de Preparation aux Affaires, Paris, 1930; banking apprentice France, Germany, Eng., 1930-32; sr. ptnr. investment banking firm Carl H. Pforzheimer & Co., N.Y.C., 1934-96; chmn. bd., past pres., bd. dirs. Petroleum & Trading Corp. Past bd. dir. Central Park South, Inc., Nat. Acad. Sch. Execs.; mem. N.Y. State Bd. Regents, 1958-78, vice chancellor, 1975-78, emeritus, 1978-96; chmn. Nat. Conf. on Govt., 1979-81; treas. Citizens Forum on Self Govt., Nat. Civic League, 1958-75, pres., 1975-78, chmn. council, 1982-86, hon. life bd. dirs.; hon. chmn., past pres. Carl and Lily Pforzheimer Found.; treas. Neustadter Found., 1950-58; mem. research libraries com. N.Y. Pub. Library, 15 yrs.; mem. exec. com. Nat. Council on Ednl. Research, 1973-80; rep. to Edn. Commn. of States, 1971-74; past pres. Nat. Assn. State Bds. Edn.; vis. com. Harvard U. Grad. Sch. Edn., Univ. Library, Univ. Chapel; mem. N.Y. State Commn. on Campus Unrest, 1969-73, Nat. Reading Council, 1969-74; trustee Mt. Sinai Med. Ctr., 1936-86, hon. trustee, 1986-96; former mem. bd. dirs. Econ. Devel. Corp., N.Y.C.; hon. trustee Horace Mann Sch., Boys Club of N.Y.; mem. council Rockefeller U. Col. War Dept. Gen. Staff, AUS, World War II; expert cons. to sec. war 1947. Decorated Legion of Merit; Medalile de la Reconaissance (France); officier Legion of Honor (France; recipient Harvard U. medal. Mem. N.Y. Chamber Commerce and Industry (past bd. dirs.), Keats-Shelley Assn. (pres. 1969-87, hon. pres.), Am. Assn. Community and Jr. Colls. (past dir.), Harvard U. Alumni Assn. (past pres., now hon. dir.), Signet Soc. (hon. fellow). Clubs: Union Interalliée (Paris); Century Assn., City Midday, Harvard, Grolier (N.Y.C.); Harvard, Union Boat (Boston); Ambassador, Willoughby Golf Club. Home: New York N.Y. Died Nov. 4, 1996.

PFRIEM, BERNARD ALDINE, artist; b. Cleve., Sept. 7, 1914; s. Charles and Amanda (Ketterer) P. Student, John Huntington Poly., 1934-36; diploma, Cleve. Inst. Art, 1940. Tchr. Mus. Modern Art, N.Y.C., 1946-51; chief design U.S. Govt. Program Trade Fairs and World Fairs in Europe, 1953-56; tchr. Cooper Union Sch. Art and Architecture, N.Y.C., 1963-69, Sarah Lawrence Coll., 1969-75; founder, dir. Lacoste Sch. of the Arts, France, 1971-91, dir. emeritus, 1991—. Represented in permanent collections: Mus. of Modern Art, N.Y.C., Met. Mus., N.Y.C., Ark. Art Ctr., Little Rock, Bklyn. Mus., Utah Mus., Salt Lake City, Finch Mus., N.Y.C., Worcester (Mass.) Mus., Corcoran Gallery, Washington, Chase Manhattan Bank, N.Y.C., Columbia Banking, Savs. and Loan Assn., Rochester, N.Y., Atlantic Richfield Corp., Los Angeles, Chgo. Art Inst. Served with USAF, 1942-46. William Copley grantee, 1959; Agnes Gund travelling scholar, 1940; Mary Sugget Ranney travelling scholar. Club: Century. Died March 6, 1996.

PHILIPPS, LOUIS EDWARD, data systems manufacturing company executive; b. Duluth, Minn., Feb. 7, 1906; s. Carl Frederick Ferdin and Sarah Marguerithe (Mortenson) P.; m. Gladys Victoria Monsen, Nov. 13, 1930. Student pub. schs., Duluth. Engr. Cleve. Radioelectric Co., 1946-48; v.p., gen. mgr. Radio Systems, Inc., Cleve., 1948-50, Royal Communications, Inc., Cleve., 1950-56; dir. engring. Auth Electric Co., N.Y.C., 1956-59; chief engr. hosp. products div. Motorola-Dahlberg Co., Mpls., 1959-63; founder, pres., chmn. bd. Medelco Inc., Schiller Park, Ill., 1964-74; founder, 1975; since chmn. bd., dir. Datx Corp., Chgo.; dir. sales, chmn. bd. Smart Controllers, Inc., Skokie, Ill., 1985—; cons. to health care industry. Contbr. to profl. jours. Named Father of Hosp. Systems Industry Am. Hosp. Assn., 1974. Sr. mem. IEEE. Republican. Presbyterian. Clubs: Order Eastern Star (Robbinsdale, Minn.), Masons (Robbinsdale, Minn.); Masons (Chgo.), Shriners (Chgo.). Patentee pulsed audio signaling, radio nurse system, data handling system. Died Feb. 6, 1997.

PHILIPS, JESSE, retired manufacturing company executive; b. N.Y.C., Oct. 23, 1914; s. Simon and Sara (Berkowitz) P.; m. Carol Jane Frank, Dec. 23, 1945 (div. 1971); children: Ellen Jane, Thomas Edwin; m. Caryl Ann Dombrosky, Sept. 11, 1978. AB magna cum laude, Oberlin Coll., 1937; MBA, Harvard U., 1939; DBA (hon.), Hillsdale Coll., 1985; HLD (hon.), U. Dayton, 1986; DH (hon.), Oberlin Coll., 1988. Pres. Philips Industries Inc., Dayton, Ohio, 1957-68, chmn. bd., chief exec. officer, 1968-89, chmn. bd. dirs., founder, chmn. emeritus, 1989-94; dir. Soc. Corp., Cleve. Author: International Stabilization of Currencies, 1936, British Rationalization, 1937; contbg. author: Chief Executive Handbook. Active State Ohio bd. regents, Dayton Found. Ind. Colls., Dayton Jewish Community Devel. Coun.; assoc. chmn. Dayton Community Chest; bd. dirs. Good Samaritan Hosp., Dayton, Dayton Jr. Achievement, Dayton Better Bus. Bur., Miami Valley coun. Boy Scouts Am., Dayton Salvation Army; trustee Oberlin Coll., U. Dayton, Ohio Found. Ind. Colls., Dayton Opera Co., Arthritis Found., Wright State U. Found., Sinclair Coll. Found.; mem. exec. com. President's Council on youth Exchange, Sister Cities Internat.; vis. com. Harvard U. Grad. Sch. Bus. Adminstrn. Mem. Conn. N.G., 1930-33. Served with USAAF, 1942-43. Decorated comdr. Ordre Souvenain de Chypre; recipient Free Enterprise award, 1965; Disting. Svc. award Harvard Bus. Sch.; Exec. of Yr. award Dayton Exec. Club, 1983; Spirit of Am. Free Enterprise award Jr. Achievement and Free Enterprise Found., 1983; Big Bros. and Big Sisters award, 1983; award U. Dayton chpt. Beta Gamma Sigma; recognition award NCCJ; CEO bronze award Fin. World, 1985, 86; Nat. On Behalf of Youth award Camp Fire, 1985; Nat. Trustee of Yr. award Assn. Governing Bds. Univs. and Colls., 1986; Internat. Ambassador's award U.S. Dept. State-Sister Cities Internat., 1986; Jesse Philips Day in Dayton proclaimed Sept. 10, 1978; named Ohio gov. for a day, 1982; Andrew Wellington Cordier fellow Columbia U. Mem. Dayton C. of C. (dir.), Dayton Retail Mchts. Assn. (dir.), Nat. Retail Dry Goods Assn., Joint Distbn. Com., Columbia Yacht Club, Meadowbrook Country Club, St. Moritz Toboganning Club, Motor Yacht Club of Cote D'Azur. Home: Dayton Ohio Died Nov. 29, 1994.

PHILLIPS, DUDLEY COOMBS, lawyer; b. Bartlesville, Okla., July 13, 1922; s. Dudley Collings and Mary Elizabeth (Coombs) P.; m. Nan Elizabeth Burg, Mar. 16, 1944; children: Dudley Collier, Jan Clare, Lynn Elizabeth. B.S., U. Okla., 1947, LL.B., 1949. Bar: Okla. 1949, Kans. 1954, N.Y. 1965, U.S. Supreme Ct., Conn. 1987. Atty. Sinclair Oil & Gas Co., Tulsa, Okla., 1949-54; gen. counsel Sinclair Pipeline Co., Independence, Kans., 1954-64; asso. gen. counsel Sinclair Oil Corp., N.Y.C., 1964-69; chief house counsel BP Oil Co., N.Y.C., 1969-70; v.p., gen. counsel Bangor Punta Corp., Greenwich, Conn., 1970-75; sr. v.p., gen. counsel Bangor Punta Corp., 1975-87; v.p., gen. counsel, dir. Piper Aircraft Corp., 1970-87; sole practice New Cannan, Conn., 1987—; dir. Producers Cotton Oil Co., Fresno, Calif., 1974-84. Served with USAAF. Decorated Air medal. Mem. Okla., Kans., N.Y., Conn. bar assns., Order of Coif, Phi Gamma Delta, Phi Delta Phi. Mem. Ch. Christ Scientist. Died Feb. 6, 1996.

PHILLIPS, ETHEL C. (MRS. LLOYD J. PHILLIPS), writer; b. N.Y.C.; d. Henry and Minnie (Hirshfeld) Cohen; m. Lloyd Jay Phillips, 1930; children: Lloyd James, Anne. B.A., Vassar Coll.; M.A. in Pub. Law, Columbia U. Publs. dir. Am. Jewish Com., Inst. Human Relations, N.Y.C., 1939-65; bd. dirs., mem. exec. com. Nat. Charities Info. Bur., N.Y.C., 1966-90, vice-chmn., 1982-90. Author: Mind Your World, 1964, Record and the Vision, 1965, You in Human Rights, 1968; also pamphlets and media features on civil rights, internat. cooperation, human rights, volunteerism. Mem. N.Y. Soc. for Ethical Culture (trustee 1977-83), Nat. Coun. Women U.S. (pres. 1972-74, hon. pres. 1974-76, UN rep. 1976—), Vassar Club (N.Y.C.), Harvard Club (N.Y.C.), Harvard Club of N.Y. Clubs: Vassar (N.Y.C.), Women's City (N.Y.C.).

PHILLIPS, FRANCES MARIE, history educator; b. Hale Center, Tex., Nov. 8, 1918; d. Clyde C. and Ada (Stutzman) P. B.A., West Tex. State Coll., 1940, M.A., 1946; Ph.D. (Univ. fellow), U. N.Mex., 1956; postgrad.

(Fulbright scholar), U. London, 1954-55. Tchr. public schs. Channing, Tex., Miami, Tex., Palisade, Colo., Tucumcari, N.Mex., 1940-46; supr. State Tchrs. Coll. Campus High Sch., Wayne, Nebr., 1947-51; instr. U. Md. Overseas Program, Eng., 1955; grad. asst. U. N.Mex., 1955-56; asst., assoc. prof. history Sul Ross State Coll., Alpine, Tex., 1956-60; prof. history, dean grad. div. Sul Ross State Coll., 1962-71; program dir. sr. colls. Coordinating Bd. Tex. Coll. and Univ. System, Austin, 1971-85; asst. prof. Mankato (Minn.) State Coll., 1960-62; lectr. Lifetime Learning Ins. of Austin, 1994—. Editor: Dear Mother and Folks at Home: Iowa Farm to Clermont-Ferrand, 1917-1918, 1988. Chmn. bd. Carlsbad dist. Wesley Found., 1962-66; mem. Adv. Council for Ednl. Personnel Devel., 1972—, State Bd. Examiners for Tchr. Edn., 1972-79, Tex. Com. on Early Childhood Devel. Careers, 1976—. Mem. AAUW, N.Mex. Hist. Soc., Am. Assn. Higher Edn., Assn. Tex. Grad. Schs. (v.p. 1967-69, pres. 1969-70), Alpha Chi, Phi Kappa Phi, Phi Alpha Theta, Delta Kappa Gamma. Democrat. Methodist (past mem. N.Mex. Conf. Bd. Edn., mem. ofcl. bd.). Research in Anglo-Am. relations, 1954-56, 1962. Died July 5, 1996.

PHINNEY, EDWARD STERL, JR., classics educator; b. Bryan, Tex., Dec. 15, 1935; s. Edward and Marie Elizabeth (Wilson) P.; m. Mary Catherine Davis, Mar. 20, 1959; 1 child, Edward Sterl III. BA in English, U. Oreg., 1957, MA in Classics, 1959; PhD in Classics, U. Calif., 1963. From instr. to assoc. prof. U. So. Calif., L.A., 1962-69; assoc. prof. U. Mass., Amherst, 1969-73, prof. classics, 1973-96; faculty dir. fgn. lang. resource ctr. U. Mass., Amherst, 1985-96. Author: Salvete!, 1995, Lingo, 1995; editor: Cambridge Latin Course, 3d edit., 1988-91. Recipient Excellence in Teaching award U. So. Calif., 1968, Disting. Teaching award U. Mass., 1977. Mem. Am. Classical League (pres. 1986-90, bd. dirs.), Eta Sigma Phi (chmn. 1988-96). Avocation: computers. Home: Amherst Mass. Died Apr. 11, 1996.

PICA, MARISSA ANN, critical care nurse, administrator; b. Waterbury, Conn., Feb. 25, 1961; d. Vincent John and Jennie (Natale) P. BSN, Mount St. Mary Coll., 1983; MSN, Hunter Coll., 1991. RN, N.Y.; cert. CCRN, CNAA; cert. BCLS. Staff nurse The N.Y. Hosp. Medicine, N.Y.C., 1983-85; staff nurse, sr. staff nurse The N.Y. Hosp.-Med. ICU, N.Y.C., 1985-88, nurse mgr., 1988-92; asst. dir. nursing critical care The N.Y. Hosp., N.Y.C., 1992-97. Author AACN Newsletter, 1993-94; poster presenter in field. Mem. AACN (corr. sec. N.Y.C. chpt. 1992-93, pres.-elect 1993-94, pres. 1994-95, dir. 1995-97), Soc. Critical Care Medicine, Am. Orgn. Nurse Execs., MENSA. Avocations: reading, theatre, dining, working out, music. Died June 5, 1997.

PICHAL, HENRI THOMAS, electronics engineer, physicist, consultant; b. London, Feb. 14, 1923; came to the U.S., 1957; s. Henri and Mary (Conway) P.; m. Vida Eloise Collum Jones, Mar. 7, 1966; children: Chris C., Henri T. III, Thomas William Billingsley. MSc in Engring., U. London, 1953, PhD in Physics, 1955. Registered profl. engr., Wash., Fla. Product engr. John Fluke Mfg. Corp., Everett, Wash., 1970-73; engring. specialist Harris Corp., Melbourne, Fla., 1973-75; pres., prin. Profl. Engring. Co., Inc., Kissimmee, Fla., 1975-91. Contbr. articles to Electronics, Microwaves, and others. Named one of Two Thousand Men Achievement, 1972. Mem. Inst. Physics, Am. Phys. Soc., Fla. Engring. Soc. (sr.), Inst. Environ. Scis. (sr.), IEEE (past chmn. microwave theory and techniques communications systems), Aerospace/Navigational Electronics, Space Electronics and Telemetry, Mil. Electronics. Republican. Achievements include 69 patents in microwave RF, high frequency and high speed analog ultra linear technology, large dynamic range performance and intermodulation phenomena, noise, and congested area systems problems. Died July 15, 1997.

PICKARD, FRANKLIN GEORGE THOMAS, mining company executive; b. Sudbury, Ont., Can., Sept. 10, 1933; s. Chester William and Margaret Christine (Downes) P.; m. Audrey Elaine Bull, Apr. 27, 1967; children: Barbara, Beverly. BA, Queen's U., Kingston, Ont., 1958; D of Bus. Adminstrn. (hon.), Laurenton U., Sudbury, Ont., 1996. With Falconbridge Ltd., Toronto, Ont., 1957-96, concentrator supt., 1967-75, chief metall. engr., 1975-82, v.p., 1982-89, sr. v.p., 1989-90, pres., chief exec. officer, 1991-96; also, bd. dirs.; bd. dirs. Falconbridge Ltd., Falconbridge Nikkelverk A/S (Norway), Falconbridge Dominicana C por A (Dominican Republic). Mem. AIME, Can. Inst. Mining and Metall. Engrs., Mining Assn. Can. (bd. dirs.), Assn. Profl. Engrs. Ont., Nickel Devel. Inst. (bd. dirs., chmn. 1988-90, 95), Ont. Club, Toronto Club, Thornhill Country Club, Keowee Key Golf and Country Club. Avocations: fishing, golf, sports cars. Died Sept. 25, 1996.

PIECHOCINSKI, THOMAS ANTHONY, priest; b. N.Y.C., Apr. 26, 1934; s. Anthony Joseph and Genevieve Bernice (Godlewski) P. BA in History, St. Francis Coll., Loretto, Pa., 1957; MA in Edn., Seton Hall U., 1961; EdD, Pacific States U., 1977. Ordained priest Roman Cath. Ch., 1961; lic. marriage counselor, N.J. Counselor Wildwood Cath. High Sch., North Wildwood, N.J., 1961-65, Camden Cath. High Sch., Cherry Hill, N.J., 1965-66; dir. student personnel svcs. Holy Spirit High Sch., Absecon, N.J., 1966-75; counselor chaplain Cabrini Coll., Radnor, Pa., 1975-77; divorce therapist Diocese of Camden, Ventnor, N.J., 1977-83; clin. con. Diocese of Metuchen, N.J., 1983—; pastor St. Cecilia, Monmouth Junction, N.J.; adj. faculty Seton Hall U., South Orange, N.J., 1973-74. Recipient sports photojournalism award Look mag., 1954, commendation USAF Recruitment Svc., 1965, cert. N.J. Sch. Counselor's Assn., 1975; named Counselor of Yr., N.J. Assn. Coll. Admission Counselors, 1976. Fellow Am. Orthopsychiat. Assn.; mem. Am. Assn. Marriage and Family Therapy (clin.), N.J. Assn. Marriage and Family Therapy, Nat. Coun. Family Rels., AACD (life), Nat. Vocat. Guidance Assn. (profl.), Assn. for Religious and Values Issues in Counseling (assoc.), Am. Coll. Personnel Assn. (assoc.), N.Y. Acad. Sci. Republican. Died March 25, 1997.

PIERCE, LAMBERT REID, architect; b. Evanston, Ill., Apr. 12, 1930; s. Ellsworth Reid and Jessie (Lambert) P.; m. Julia Ellen Sellers, Nov. 20, 1948; children: Kenneth Reid, Rebecca June, Wendy Lynn. BSCE, Northwestern u., 1953, postgrad., 1955. Registered architect, Ill., U.S. Virgin Islands; engr. in tng., Ill. Draftsman Rader & Co. Builders, Skokie, Ill., 1949-58; assoc. architect Richard E. Dobroth & Assoc., Deerfield & Glenview, Ill., 1958-67; v.p. Richard E. Dobroth & Assoc., Glenview, 1967-71; prin. Lambert R. Pierce Architect, Glenview, 1971-78, Lambert R. Pierce & Assocs. Architects, St. Croix, V.I., 1979-95; bd. dirs. Virgin Island Properties, Inc., St. Croix. Prin. works include Pelican Cove Beach Club, St. Croix, Queens Quarter Hotel, St. Croix, Fin. Bldg., St. Croix, Red Cross Bldg, St. Croix, Chase Manhattan Bank, St. Croix. Del. 1st Internat. Congress on Religion Architecture and Visual Ats, N.Y.C. and Montreal, Can., 1967; pres., bd. dirs. Beacon Neighborhhod House, Chgo., 1967; mem. program cabinet Prebytery of Chgo., 1972-73; pres. Glenview C. of C., 1978. Mem. AIA, St. Croix C. of C., Our Town Frederiksted, Nat. Trust Hist. Preservation. Presbyterian. Avocations: reading, woodworking, antiques, snorkeling. Home: Kingshill Saint Croix V.I. Died Feb. 14, 1995.

PIERCE, RICHARD SCOTT, mathematics educator; b. Long Beach, Calif., Feb. 26, 1927; s. Robert Scott and Dorothea Stinson (Bloomfield) P.; m. Mary Elizabeth Ray, June 26, 1953 (div.); 1 child, Eric; m. Marilyn Louise Neher, Nov. 23, 1971. BS, Calif. Inst. Tech., 1950, PhD, 1952. From asst. prof. to prof. math. U. Wash., Seattle, 1955-70; prof. U. Hawaii, Honolulu, 1970-75; prof. U. Ariz., Tucson, 1975-90, ret., 1990. Author: Algebraic Foundations of Math, 1963, Introduction to Abstract Algebras, 1968, Associative Algebras, 1983; contbr. articles to profl. jours. Served with U.S. Army, 1945-46. Fellow Yale U., 1952-53, Harvard U., 1953-55, NSF postdoctoral fellow, 1961-62. Mem. AAAS, Assn. Symbolic Logic, Math. Assn. Am., Am. Math. Soc. (assoc. sec. 1958-74), Sigma Xi. Died Mar. 15, 1992.

PIERSON, HERBERT FLETCHER, musician; b. Trenton, N.J., May 9, 1914; s. John Ewing and Margaret (Fletcher) P.; m. Betty G. Wayda, Aug. 25, 1951; children Herbert, Lisa. B.M., Curtis Inst. Music, 1937. French hornist, Trenton Symphony, 1930-36, Kansas City, 1937-38, Phila., 1938-74. Served with AUS, 1942-46. Home: Trenton N.J. Died Apr. 19, 1995.

PIETRZAK, LEONARD WALTER, accountant; b. Phila., Dec. 6, 1939; s. Walter Chester and Estelle Anne (Libucha) P.; m. Patricia Ann Cole, June 17, 1961; children: Stephen L., Diana L., Jeffrey S., Kristen M. BS, St. Joseph's U., Phila., 1961. Commd. officer USAF, Washington, 1961-64; audit mgr. Ernst & Young, Phila., 1964-77; corp. contr. Kleinert's Inc., Plymouth Meeting, Pa., 1977-81; v.p. fin. Jetronic Industries, Inc., Phila., 1981—; pres. NAA, So. Jersey, 1975-76. Mem. AICPA, Pa. Inst. CPA.

PILLET-WILL, JACQUES FRÉDÉRIC, financial consultant; b. Paris, Mar. 1, 1924; s. Jean Frédéric and Marie Thérèse (Chapelle de Jumilhac) P.-W.; m. Jacqueline de Vassal-Montviel, Mar. 25, 1949 (dec.); children: Elena, Alexis, Yolande; m. Mary Elizabeth Mathew, Mar. 1, 1982. Grad. in Philosophy, U. Paris Sorbonne, 1944; Degree in Law, U. Paris, 1944; Degree in Econs., Ecole Libre Scis. Politiques, Paris, 1944. Insp. Ministry of Fin., Caisse Nationale des Marches de l'Etat, Paris, 1946-48; sr. mgr. Banque Industrielle de l'Afrique du Nord, Paris, Algers, Tunis, Casablanca, 1948-62; vice chmn., CEO Banque Rivaud, Paris, 1962-85; chmn. Banque de Picardie, Compiegne, France, 1976-91, hon. chmn., 1991-96; chmn. Cie. Industrielle et Financiere des Ateliers et Chantiers de la Loire, Paris, 1964-84; bd. dirs. Banque Pallas-Stern, Compagnie Generale des Eaux, CNIM, Pyroindustrie, others. Hon. chmn. CILOVA (social housing), Compiegne, 1993, Found. Pillet-Will, Attichy, 1978. Sgt. French Army, 1944-46. Decorated chevalier Legion of Honor, officer Legion of Honor, Croix de Guerre, Presdl. Unit citation. Mem. Jockey Club, Cercle de l'Union Interalliée. Mem. R.P.R. Party. Roman Catholic. Avocation: playing the organ. Died Nov. 15, 1996.

PINEDA, MARIANNA, sculptor, educator; b. Evanston, Ill., May 10, 1925; d. George and Marianna (Dickinson) Packard; m. Harold Tovish, Jan. 14, 1946; children: Margo, Aaron, Nina. Student, Cranbrook Acad. Art, summer 1942, Bennington Coll., 1942-43, U. Calif.-Berkeley, 1943-45, Columbia U., 1945-46, Ossip Zadkine Sch. Drawing and Sculpture, Paris, 1949-50. instr. sculpture Newton Coll. Sacred Heart, 1972-75, Boston Coll., 1975-77; vis. assoc. prof. Boston U., 1974, 78, annually 83-87, 89-90; vis. sculptor Sch. of Mus. Fine Arts, Boston, 1990-91; vis. critic Boston U., 1992. One-woman shows include Slaughter Gallery, San Francisco, 1951, Walker Art Ctr., Mpls., 1952, Currier Gallery, Manchester, N.H., 1954, De Cordova Mus., Lincoln, Mass., 1954, Premier Gallery, Mpls., 1963, Swetzoff Gallery, Boston, 1953, 56, 64, Honolulu Acad. Art, 1970, Alpha Gallery, Boston, 1972, Newton Coll., (Mass.), 1972, Bumpus Gallery, Duxbury, Mass., 1972, Contemporary Art Ctr., Honolulu, 1982, Hanalei Palace, Kona, Hawaii, 1982, Lyman House Mus., Hilo, Hawaii, 1982, Pine Manor Coll., Mass., 1984, Rotenberg Gallery, Boston, 1990, 93, 94, Coll. of William and Mary, 1992, Wiggin Gallery, Boston Libr., 1993 ; group shows include Oakland (Calif.) Civic Mus., 1944, Village Art Ctr., N.Y.C., 1944, Albright Art Gallery, Buffalo, 1947, Bklyn. Mus., 1947, Galerie 8 Paris, 1950, Met. Mus. Art, N.Y.C., 1951, Art Gallery U. Nebr., 1953, San Francisco Mus. of Art, 1955, Inst. Contemporary Art, Boston, 1958, 59, 61, Whitney Mus. Am. Art, N.Y.C., 1953, 54, 55, 57, 59, Boston Arts Festival, 1957, 58, 60, 62, 63, 65, 85, Silvermine Annual Exhibit, Conn., 1957, Art Inst. Chgo., 1957, 61, Pitts. Internat., 1958, Mus. Modern Art., N.Y.C., 1960 (traveling), Addison Gallery Am. Art, 1959, Dallas Mus. Art, 1961, Nat. Inst. Arts & Letters, 1961, N.Y. World's Fair, 1964, De Cordova Mus., 1963, 64, 1972, 75, 87, Sculptors Guild, N.Y.C., 1967-95, Pine Manor Coll, Mass., Pa. State U., 1974, The Women's Bldg., L.A., 1976, Simmons Coll., Mass., 1980, Helen Schlein Gallery, Boston, 1982, SUNY-Buffalo, 1983, Fitchburg Mus. Art, Mass., 1984, Newton Art Ctr., Mass., 1985, Boston U. Art Gallery, 1986, Shulman Scuplture Pk., White Plains, N.Y., 1986, 87, 88, Alchemie Gallery, Boston, 1987, 93, Nat. Acad. Design, N.Y.C., 1985-89, 91, 92, 93, 94-95, Boston Visual Artist Union Invitational, 1986, Bunting Inst., Fed. Reserve Gallery, Boston, 1986, Port of History, Phila., 1987, Brockton Art Ctr., Mass., 1987, Judi Rotenberg Gallery, Boston, ann. 1987-96, A.I.R. Gallery, N.Y.C., 1988, Boston Pub. Libr., 1988, Nat. Sculpture Soc., N.Y.C., 1986-89, 90-95, Holyoke Mus., Mass., 1989, Washington Art Assn., Conn., 1989, Bumpus Art Gallery, Duxbury, 1989, Page St. Gallery, San Francisco, 1989, Louis Ross Gallery, N.Y.C., 1990, Shidoni Galleries, Santa Fe, N. Mex., 1990, The Contemporary Mus., Honolulu, 1990, Cast Iron Gallery, 1993, Kyoto (Japan) Civic Gallery, 1993, Walsh Art Gallery, Fairfield, Conn., 1991, Wingspread Gallery, Northeast Harbor, Maine, 1991, World Fin. Ctr. Gallery, 1992, Phila. Sculptors Guild, 1992, Kingsborough C.C., Bklyn., 1994, Womens Caucus for Arts, Staten Island, N.Y., 1995, FSS Gallery, N.Y.C., 1995, Danforth Mus., Framingham, Mass., 1995, Rose Art Mus. Brandeis U., Mass., George Washington U., 1996, Washington U., 1996; represented permanent collections, Walker Art Ctr., Mus. Fine Arts, Boston Williams Coll., (Mass.), Dartmouth coll., Hanover, N.H., Addison Gallery, Andover, Mass., Munson-Williams-Proctor Inst., Ithaca, N.Y., Fogg Art Mus., Cambridge, Mass., Radcliff Coll., Boston Pub. Library, Wadsworth Athenaeum, Hartford, Conn. State of Hawaii, NAD, 1983, 84, 85, 87, 88, 90, 91, 92, 93, 94, Muscarelle Mus., Williamsburg, Va., Walker Art Ctr., Mpls., Bowdoin Coll., Lewiston, Me., U. Mass., Perseus Collection, Honolulu, Nat. Acad. Design, N.Y.C., Boston Conservatory Music, Boston U.; commd. work, Twirling, Bronze figure group, East Boston Housing for Elderly, The Spirit of Lili'uokalani bronze, Hawaii State Capitol. Recipient award Oakland Civic Mus., 1944, Mather prize Chgo. Art Inst., 1944, Best of Show award Minn. State Fair, 1954, Margaret Brown award Ins. Contemporary Art, Boston, 1957, Grand prize Boston Arts Festival, 1960, Lampston prize Nat. Sculpture Soc., N.Y.C., 1986, Gold medal Nat. Sculpture Soc., 1988, Herbert Adams Meml. medal, 1996, Taillex award, 1991, Lifetime Achievement award Nat. Womens Caucus Art, 1996; grantee Florsheim Art Fund, 1995, Mass. Found. for Humanities, 1995, Thanks to Grandmother Winnefred Found., 1995; Bunting Inst., Radcliffe Coll. fellow, 1962, 63. Fellow NAD (Gold medal 1987, Artists award 1988, 93). Died Nov. 27, 1996.

PINKERTON, CLAYTON DAVID, artist; b. San Francisco, Mar. 6, 1931; s. David B. and Kathryn Irene (Davies) P. B.A. in Edn, Calif. Coll. Arts and Crafts, 1952, M.F.A., 1953; postgrad., U. N.Mex., 1952, U. Paris, 1957. Former curator and former dir. coll. internship program Richmond Art Ctr.; mem. faculty Calif. Coll. Arts and Crafts. One-man exhbns. include Calif. Palace Legion of Honor, San Francisco, 1960, M.H. de Young Meml. Mus., San Francisco, 1962, Everett Ellin Gallery, Los Angeles, 1961, Esther Robles Gallery, Los Angeles, 1968, San Francisco Mus. Art, 1956, 67, Arleigh Gallery, San Francisco, 1970, Richmond (Calif.) Art Ctr., 1976, Himovitz/Salomon Gallery, Sacramento, 1985, 86, 88, Monterey Penisula Mus. Art, 1988, U. of Pacific, Stockton, 1988, Calif. State U., Chico, 1989, Michael Himovitz Gallery, 1991, 93, Spectrum/Himovitz Gallery, San Francisco, 1991-92, (figurative-narrative works) 1991, Am. Cultural Ctr.,

Brussels, 1991, Spectrum/Himovitz Gallery, San Francisco, 1992; group exhbns. include Mus. Modern Art, N.Y.C., 1962, Whitney Mus. Modern Art, N.Y.C., Mus. Contemporary Art, Chgo., 1971, Mus. Fine Arts, Richmond, Va., 1970, San Francisco Mus. Fine Arts, 1978, Los Angeles County Mus., 1979, Phoenix Art Mus., 1970, Oakland (Calif.) Mus., 1979, Bolles Gallery, 1981, Monterey Peninsula Mus. Art, 1985, 86, Art Bridge, Kobe, Japan, 1986, The Human Form Galeria Mesa, Ariz., 1987, (figurative works) Sierra Coll., Rocklin, Calif., 1989, Calif. Eccentrics U. Ill., 1990, Triton Mus., San Jose, 1992, Am. Cultural Ctr., Brussels, 1992, Am. Embassy, Calcutta, New Delhi, 1993, 3 Painters-4 Decades, Sacramento, 1993, others; represented in permanent collections: Ill. Bell Telephone Co., Chgo., M.H. De Young Meml. Mus., San Francisco, Crocker Art Mus., Sacramento, others. Recipient James D. Phelan award, 1957, 61; Fulbright scholar, 1957-58.

PIPAL, GEORGE HENRY, journalist; b. Lafayette, Ind., Oct. 14, 1916; s. Francis John and Belle (Kadavy) P.; m. Caroline Dunsmore, Aug. 17, 1946; children—John, Susan, Philip, Frank. B.A., U. Nebr., 1937; M.S., Columbia, 1939. Corr. various bureaus UPI, 1937-41; bur. mgr. UPI, Prague, 1946; mgr. for UPI, Eastern Europe, 1947, Germany, 1948; dir. European Services, 1949-51; gen. bus. mgr. Europe, Middle East, Africa, 1952-65; gen. sales exec. computer svcs. N.Y.C., 1966-68; gen. mgr. internat. features div., 1968-78; mng. dir. UPI (U.K.), Ltd., 1964-65; v.p. United Feature Syndicate, 1978-84, United Media Enterprises, 1985-96. Served as lt. USNR, 1942-46. Home: Glen Ellen Calif. Died Nov. 20, 1996.

PIPER, ERNST REINHARD, publisher; b. Munich, Mar. 29, 1952; s. Klaus and Elisabeth (Holthaus) P.; m. Katrin Meschkowski, Apr. 25, 1943; m. Martina Petrik, Apr. 14, 1956; children: Paul David. PhD, Tech. U., Berlin, 1981. Pub. R. Piper & Co. Verlag, Munich, from 1984. Author: Der Aufstand der Ciompi, 1978, Savonarola, 1979, Der Stadtplan als Grundri Der Gesellschaft, 1982, Ernst Barlach und die nationalsozialistische Kunstpolitik, 1983, München, Die Geschichte einer Stadt, 1993.

PIRNIE, MALCOLM, JR., consulting engineer; b. Mount Vernon, N.Y., Mar. 15, 1917; s. Malcolm and Gertrude (Knowlton) P.; m. Jane Purse, Nov. 7, 1942 (dec. July 1981); children—Malcolm III, Pamela.; m. Sarah A. Carter, Sept. 25, 1982. A.B., Harvard U., 1939, S.M., 1941. Diplomate: Am. Acad. Environ. Engrs. With Malcolm Pirnie Engrs., 1946—, assoc., 1948-51, ptnr., 1952-70, chmn. bd., 1970-86, chmn. emeritus, 1987—; Pres. Berkeley Assn., Scarsdale, 1954; mem. non-partisan com., Scarsdale, N.Y., 1954-57. Bd. dirs. White Plains YMCA, 1967-70, Westchester County Assn., 1978-89; mem. Hoover Medal Bd. Award, 1976-82; mem. pres.'s adv. council Coll. of New Rochelle, 1977-80. Served from lt. (j.g.) to lt. comdr. USPHS, 1941-45. Fellow ASCE (dir. Met. sect. 1956-57, v.p. 1960-62, pres. 1962-63, nat. dir. 1967-70, chmn. com. standards of practice 1983-84, chmn. environ. systems policy com. 1985-86); mem. Am. Acad. of Environ. Engrs. (diplomate 1970—), Am. Inst. Cons. Engrs. (councilor 1964-66, v.p. 1965-66, 71-72), Inter-Am. Assn. San. Engrs., Fla. Engring. Soc., Water Resources Congress (project com.), Harvard Engring. soc. (v.p. 1955), Engrs. Joint Coun. (planning com. 1955-58, mem. engring. manpower commn. 1965-70), Am. Cons. Engrs. Coun. (v.p. 1970-72). Clubs: Harvard (N.Y.C.), Town (Scarsdale, N.Y.), Scarsdale Golf. (bd. govs. 1981-86), Bald Peak Colony (Melvin Village, N.H.). Died Jan. 18, 1997.

PIROFSKY, BERNARD, physician, educator; b. N.Y.C., Mar. 27, 1926; s. Hyman and Yetta (Herman) P.; m. Elaine Friedwald, June 19, 1953; children: Daniel Niles, Tandy Ellen, Jillann Yetta. A.B., NYU, 1946, M.D., 1950. Intern Bellevue Hosp., N.Y.C., 1950-51; resident medicine Bellevue Hosp., 1951-52, 54-55; dir. Pacific N.W. Regional Blood Center, 1956-58; rsch. fellow Oreg. Health Sci. U., 1955-56, instr., 1956-59, asst. prof., 1959-63, assoc. prof., 1963-66, prof., 1966-92, prof. microbiology, 1973-92, head div. immunology, allergy and rheumatology, 1965-85, dean for rsch., 1985-92, emeritus prof. medicine and microbiology, 1992-93; mem. med. adv. bd. Leukemia Soc., 1965-69; vis. prof. Nat. Inst. Nutrition, Mexico, 1966-67, Med. Research Council, South Africa, 1977; vis. scientist Nat. Acad. Sci., Japan, 1978-79; head immunology, allergy and rheumatology Portland VA Hosp., 1980-83. Author: Autoimmunization and the Autoimmune Hemolytic Anemias, 1969, Blood Banking Principles, 1973; contbr. articles to profl. jours. Served as capt. USAF, 1952-54. Commonwealth Fund fellow, 1966-67; recipient Gov.'s N.W. Sci. award, 1968; Emily Cooley award Am. Assn. Blood Banks, 1972. Fellow ACP; mem. Internat. Soc. Hematology, Internat. Soc. Blood Transfusions, Am. Soc. Hematology, Mexican Soc. Hematology (hon. mem.), Transplantation Soc., Am. Assn. Immunologists. Research on immunology and hematology. Home: Portland Oreg. Died May 28, 1993.

PITTMAN, G. C., banker; b. Victoria County, Tex., Jan. 22, 1921; s. Edward D. and Willie (McCurry) P.; m. Augusta Maurer, Dec. 25, 1942; children: David Jerome, Sharon Ann, Patricia Ann. Student, Victoria (Tex.) Coll., 1938-40, Southwestern Grad. Sch. Banking, 1959-61. Cert. comml. lender. Various positions Victoria (Tex.) Bank & Trust Co., 1940-62, sr. v.p., 1962-68, exec. v.p., 1969-77, pres., mem. exec. com., 1977-81, chmn. bd. dirs., 1981-84, chmn. bd. exec. com., 1984-95, also bd. dirs.; exec. v.p., founding bd. dirs. Victoria Bankshares, Inc., Victoria, 1974-84, pres., chief operating officer, 1984-95, also bd. dirs.; vice chmn., bd. dirs. Transact Fin. Corp.; Victoria Loan and Investment Co.; bd. dirs. South Tex. Small Bus. Investment Co., Town Plaza Co., VBI, Inc. Trustee St. Joseph High Sch., Victoria, 1970-89; past bd. dirs. Salvation Army; chmn. admission and budget United Fund; chmn. citizens adv. com., 1st v.p., bd. dirs. Victoria C. of C.; pres. bd. mgrs. Citizens Meml. Hosp., 1979-95; mem. exec. com. South Tex. C. of C., 1979-95; mem. Bd. Econ. Devel. Com.; past co-chmn. fund raising campaign, past C.C.D. parish coord., former trustee Our Lady Victory Ch.; bd. dirs. Victoria County Cath. Edn. Corp. With U.S. Army, 1942-46. Recipient St. Thomas More Cath. Action award, 1969, Outstanding Cath. Layman's award, 1969; named Layman Extraordinary, Archbishop San Antonio, 1969, Knight of St. Gregory the Great, Pope Paul VI. Mem. Am. Bankers Assn., Serra Club of Victoria (past pres.), Newman Club (bd. dirs.). Home: Victoria Tex. Died Sept. 13, 1995.

PITZER, KENNETH SANBORN, chemist, educator; b. Pomona, Calif., Jan. 6, 1914; s. Russell K. and Flora (Sanborn) P.; m. Jean Mosher, July 1935; children—Ann, Russell, John. BS, Calif. Inst. Tech., 1935; PhD, U. Calif., 1937; DSc, Wesleyan U., 1962; LLD, U. Calif. at Berkeley, 1963, Mills Coll., 1969. Instr. chemistry U. Calif., 1937-39, asst. prof., 1939-42, asso. prof., 1942-45, prof., 1945-61, asst. dean letters and sci., 1947-48, dean coll. chemistry, 1951-60; pres., prof. chemistry Rice U., Houston, 1961-68, Stanford, Calif., 1968-70; prof. chemistry U. Calif. at Berkeley, 1971—; tech. dir. Md. Rsch. Lab. for OSRD, 1943-44; dir. research U.S. AEC, 1949-51, mem. gen. adv. com., 1958-65, chmn., 1960-62; Centenary lectr. Chem. Soc. Gt. Britain, 1978; mem. adv. bd. U.S. Naval Ordnance Test Sta., 1956-59, chmn., 1958-59; mem. commn. chem. thermo-dynamics Internat. Union Pure and Applied Chemistry, 1953-61; mem. Pres.'s Sci. Adv. Com., 1965-68; dir. Owens-Ill., Inc., 1967-86. Author: (with others) Selected Values of Properties of Hydrocarbons, 1947, Quantum Chemistry, 1953, (with L. Brewer) Thermodynamics, 2d edit., 1961, Activity Coefficients in Electrolyte Solutions, 2d ecit., 1992, Molecular Structure and Statistical Thermodynamics, 1993, Thermodynamics, 3d edit., 1995; editor: Prentice-Hall Chemistry series, 1955-61; contbr. articles to profl. jours. Trustee Pitzer Coll., 1966—; Mem. program com. for phys. scis. Sloan Found., 1955-60. Recipient Precision Sci. Co. award in petroleum chemistry, 1950, Clayton prize Instn. Mech. Engrs., London, 1958, Priestley medal Am. Chem. Soc., 1969, Nat. medal for sci., 1975, Robert A. Welch award, 1984, Clark Kerr award U. Calif., Berkeley, 1991, Robert J. Bernard award, 1996; named to Outstanding Young Men, U.S. Jaycees, 1950; named to Hall of Fame of Alpha Chi Sigma, 1994; Guggenheim fellow, 1951. Fellow Am. Nuclear Soc., Am. Inst. Chemists (Gold Medal award 1976), Am. Acad. Arts and Scis., Am. Phys. Soc.; mem. AAAS, NAS (councilor 1964-67, 73-76), Am. Chem. Soc. (award pure chemistry 1943, Gilbert N. Lewis medal 1965, Williard Gibbs medal 1976), Faraday Soc., Geochem. Soc., Am. Philos. Soc., Chem. Soc. (London), Am. Coun. Edn., Chemists Club (hon.), Bohemian Club, Cosmos Club of Washington. Clubs: Chemists (hon.), Bohemian; Cosmos (Washington). Died Dec. 26, 1997.

PLANTINGA, JOHN EVERETT, mechanical engineer; b. Cleve., July 3, 1923; s. John Gilbert and Ruth Hannah (Davis) P.; m. Eugenia Oglesby Kilpatrick, Mar. 26, 1945 (div. Apr. 1950); m. Virginia Colleen Ball, Aug. 6, 1950; children: John Gilbert, Priscilla King. BS in Mech. Engring., Rensselaer Poly. Inst., 1944; BS in Sci., MIT, 1945. Registered profl. engr., Conn., N.Y., Mass., N.H., Ill., Tex., Ohio; chartered engr., U.K. Engr. Meyer Strong & Jones, N.Y.C., 1946-60, ptnr., 1960-88; ind. cons. Westport, Conn., 1988—. Mem. Pub. Sites and Bldgs. Commn., Westport, Conn., 1992; mem. state Codes and Stds. Commn., Conn. State, 1992. With U.S. Army, 1945. Fellow Chartered Instn. Bldg. Svcs. Engrs. U.K.; mem. ASHRAE, Nat. Fire Protection Assn., Acoustical Soc. Am. (assoc.). Republican. Presbyterian. Avocations: computers, automobiles, photography.

PLEASENCE, DONALD, actor; b. Workshop, Eng., Oct. 5, 1919; s. Thomas Stanley and Alice (Armitage) P.; m. Miriam Raymond (div.); children: Angela Daphne, Jean Denise; m. Josephine Martin Crombie; children: Lucy Maria, Polly Jo, Alexis Helena; m. Meira Shore; 1 child, Miranda; m. Linda Woolham. Made 1st appearance on stage in Wuthering Heights at Playhouse, Jersey, Eng., 1939; 1st London appearance in Twelfth Night; actor on London stage in Ebb Tide, Vicious Circle, Saint's Day, Hobson's Choice, The Rules of the Game, The Lark, The Caretaker, 1991; motion pictures include Manuela, 1957, The Man in the Sky, Heart of a Child, 1958, Tale of Two Cities, 1958, The Shakedown, 1959, Battle of the Sexes, 1959, Hell Is a City, 1960, The Flesh and the Fiends, 1960, The Horsemaster, Spare the Rod, 1961, No Love for Johnnie, 1961, The Hallelujah Trail, 1965, Cul-de-Sac, 1966, Fantastic Voyage, 1966, Matchless, 1966, Night of Generals, 1967, You Only Live Twice, 1967, Will Penny, 1968, Soldier Blue, 1970, Cutback, 1971, THX 1138, 1971, The Jerususalem File, 1972, The Pied Piper, 1972, Henry VIII and His Six Wives, 1972, Goldenrod, Arthur! Arthur, Wedding in White, 1973, Innocent Bystanders, 1973, Death Line, The Rainbow Boys, The Black Windmill, 1974, Journey into Fear, Escape to Witch Mountain, 1975, Hearts of the West, 1975, The Devil Within Her, 1975, Passover Plot, 1976, The Last Tycoon, 1976, Trial by Combat, The Eagle Has Landed, 1977, Oh! God, 1977, Telefon, 1977, Halloween, 1978, Sgt. Pepper's Lonely Hearts Club Band, 1978, Dracula, 1979, Escape from New York, 1981, 1984, A Breed Apart, 1984, The Great Escape, Honour Thy Father, Nothing Underneath, Nosferatu, Catacomb, Ground Zero, Into the Darkness, The Rainbow Four, Gila and Rick, Animale Metropolitani, The Return of Djiango, Imbalances, Prince of Darkness, Commander, Hannah's War, Search and Destroy, Halloween IV, Murder on Safari, River of Death, Buried Alive, Casablanca Express, Haloween V, Women in Arms, Miliardi, Shadows and Fog, Dien Bien Phu, Moi de Gaulle, The Big Freeze, The Hour of the Pig; TV appearances include The Count of Monte Cristo, 1975, The Hatchet Man, The Bandstand, Ambrose, Thou Good and Faithful Servant, Call Me Daddy, Taste, The Fox Trot, Omnibus, Julius Caesar, Occupations, The Joke, The Cafeteria, The French Atlantic Affair, 1979, Witness for the Prosecution, 1982, Colombo, Centennial, The Bastard, Mrs. Colombo, Fate and Mrs. Browne, The Silk Purse, A Home of His Own, The Millionaires, Falklands Factor, The Corsican Brothers, Scoop, Master of the Game, Arch of Triumph, The Room, Punishment Without Crime, A Caribbean Mystery, Barchester Chronicles, Femme Fatal, Signs and Wonders. Served with RAF, 1942-46. Named Stage Actor of Yr. London Variety Club, 1968. Home: London Eng. Died Feb. 1995.

PLEMING-YOCUM, LAURA CHALKER, religion educator; b. Sheridan, Wyo., May 25, 1913; d. Sidney Thomas and Florence Theresa (Woodbury) Chalker; m. Edward Kibbler Pleming, Aug. 25, 1938 (dec. Nov. 1980); children: Edward Kibbler, Rowena Pleming Chamberlin, Sidney Thomas; m. William Lewis Yocum, Dec. 19, 1989 (dec. Apr. 1992). BA, Calif. State U., Long Beach, 1953, MA in Speech and Drama, 1954; postgrad., U. So. Calif., L.A., 1960-63; D Religion, Grad. Sch. Theology, Claremont, Calif., 1968. Internat. lectr. Bibl. studies, 1953—, adult seminar resource person, 1953—; Bibl. lectr. Principia Coll., Elsah, Ill., 1968-90; Bible scholar 1st Ch. of Christ, Scientist, Boston, 1970-75; tchr. adult edn. Principia Coll., summers, 1969-71; tour lectr. to Middle East, 1974—; mem. archaeol. team, Negev, Israel. Author: Triumph of Job, 1979; editor (newsletter) Bibleletter, 1968-84. Mem. AAUP, Am. Acad. Religion, Soc. Bibl. Lit. and Exegesis, Am. Schs. Oriental Rsch., Inst. Mediterranean Studies, Religious Edn. Assn., Internat. Platform Assn., Congress Septuagint and Cognate Studies, Religious Edn. Assn., Zeta Tau Alpha (alumni pres. Long Beach chpt. 1960), Gamma Theta Upsilon (pres. Long Beach chpt. 1952).

PLISKIN, MARVIN ROBERT, lawyer; b. Akron, Ohio, Nov. 7, 1938; s. Abraham David and Roselle (Cohen) P.; m. Suzanne Schreiber, Aug. 27, 1961; children: Daniel, Lawrence. BS, Ohio State U., 1960, JD, 1963. Bar: Ohio 1963. Assoc. Murphey, Young & Smith, Columbus, Ohio, 1963-69; ptnr. Murphey, Young & Smith, Columbus, 1970-88, Squire, Sanders & Dempsey, Columbus, 1988-90, Porter, Wright, Morris & Arthur, Columbus, 1990—. Contbr. articles to profl. jours. Active Columbus Jewish Found. Legal and Tax Adv. Com., 1982—, Columbus Found. Legal Adv. Com., 1991—; mem. planning com. Columbus Estate Planning Coun. II, 1975—. Fellow Am. Coll. Trust & Estate Coun. (state chmn. Ohio 1991-95); mem. ABA, Ohio State Bar Assn. (bd. govs. probate and trust sect. 1979—, state chmn. 1987-88), Columbus Bar Assn. (mem. probate law com. 1971—, chmn. 1975-76, mem. estate and gift tax com. 1975—), Columbus Met. Club (mem. nominating com. 1991-94). Avocations: music, sports, travel. Deceased.

PLUMMER, CHARLES MCDONALD, retired community college administrator; b. Garibaldi, Oreg., Mar. 21, 1934; s. Earl Carlos and Florence Elta (Lamb) P.; m. Diane Hansen, July 7, 1957; children: Jeffrey Earl, Susan Lynn Plummer Johnson. BS in Edn., So. Oreg. State Coll., 1957; MEd, U. Oreg., 1967. Tchr. Canyonville (Oreg.) H.S., 1957-59, Glendale (Oreg.) H.S., 1959-60; tchr. Roseburg (Oreg.) H.S., 1960-66, dir. student activities, pub. info., 1963-66; registrar Umpqua C.C., Roseburg, 1966-68, dean admissions and records, 1968-74, dean instrn., 1974-86, v.p. instructional svcs., 1986-94; ret., 1994; exec. bd. N.W. Student Success Conf., Portland, 1989-92; co-founder, staff Pacific NW Great Tchrs. Seminar, Portland, 1979-94. Pres. Greater Douglas United Way, 1989, bd. dirs. 1983-94; pres Roseburg Concert Chorale, 1982-94; bd. dirs. Roseburg Cmty. Concert Assn., 1989-95. Mem. Kiwanis Club (pres. 1979, bd. dirs. 1973-79), Oreg. Coun. of Instrnl Adminstrs. (chair 1990), Roseburg Area C. of C. (bd dirs. 1982-85, Roseburg First Citizen 1991), Phi Delta Kappa. Presbyterian. Avocations: golf, vintage singers, church choir, community service. Died June 26, 1995.

POGUE, FORREST CARLISLE, retired historian; b. Eddyville, Ky., Sept. 17, 1912; s. Forrest Carlisle and Frances (Carter) P.; m. Christine Brown, Sept. 4, 1954. AB, Murray (Ky.) State Coll., 1931, LLD, 1970; MA, U. Ky., 1932, LittD, 1983; PhD, Clark U., 1939, LHD, 1975; LittD, Washington and Lee U., 1970. Instr. history Western Ky. State Coll., 1933; instr. to assoc. prof. Murray State Coll., 1933-42, prof., 1954-56; with Office Chief Mil. History U.S. Dept. Army, 1946-52; ops. rsch. analyst Johns Hopkins U., U.S. Army Hdqrs., Heidelberg, Fed. Republic of Germany, 1952-54; dir. George C. Marshall Rsch. Ctr., Lexington, Va., 1956-64, George C. Marshall Rsch. Libr., Lexington, 1964-74; Harmon Meml. lectr. U.S. Air Acad., 1968; disting. Bicentennial lectr. U.S. Mil. Acad., 1974; disting. vis. prof. Va. Mil. Inst., 1972; professorial lectr. George Washington U., 1948, 49, 50; past chmn. Am. Com. on History 2d World War; former mem. adv. groups U.S. Army, USAF and Navy Hist. Office; chmn. adv. com. Senate Hist. Office; mem. adv. bd. Former Mems. Congress, Ky. Oral History Commn.; mem. adv. com. on Eisenhower papers; adj. fellow Woodrow Wilson Internat. Ctr. Scholars, 1974-77; mem. Hist. Found., Centennial Adv. Com. on the History of the Eisenhower Era; dir. Dwight D. Eisenhower Inst. Hist. Rsch., Nat. Mus. Am. History, Smithsonian Inst., 1974-84; mem. Marine Corps Hist. Found. Author: The Supreme Command, 1954, George C. Marshall: Education of a General, Vol. 1, 1963, Ordeal and Hope, 1939-42, Vol. 2, 1966, Organizer of Victory, 1943-45, Vol. 3, 1973, Statesman, 1945-59, Vol. 4, 1987; author: (with others) The Meaning of Yalta, 1956; contbr. to books including Command Decisions, 1960, Total War and Cold War, 1962, D Day: The Normandy Invasion in Retrospect, 1970, America's Continuing Revolution, 1975, The War Lords, 1976, Bicentennial History of the United States, 1976, (with others) The Marshall Plan in Germany, 1991; contbg. editor: Guide to American Foreign Relations Since 1700, 1983. Trustee Harry S. Truman Inst. Libr.; mem. adv. com. Nat. Hist. Soc. With U.S. Army, 1942-45, ETO. Decorated Bronze Star, Croix de Guerre, France; recipient Disting. Alumni Centennial award U. Ky., 1965, Samuel Eliot Morison award Am. Mil. Inst., 1988; U. Paris Inst. des Hautes Etudes Internationales Am. Exchange fellow, 1937-38. Fellow U.S. Army History Rsch. Inst. (adv. group), Am. Mil. Inst. (past pres.); mem. Assn. U.S. Army (Disting. Svc. award 1990), Oral History Assn. (past pres.), U.S. Commn. on Mil. History (trustee), Am. Hist. Assn., So. Hist. Assn., Orgn. Am. Historians, Soc. Am. Historians (Francis Parkman medal 1988), NEA (life), English Speaking Union, Am. Legion, Murray State U. Alumni Assn. (past pres.), Cosmos Club. Democrat. Presbyterian. Died Oct 6, 1996.

POIRION, DANIEL, foreign language educator; b. Amiens, France, Jan. 22, 1927; came to U.S., 1987; s. Michel and Marie-Louise (Martigny) P.; m. Jacqueline Dokier, Dec. 11, 1980; children: Jean-Marc, Karen; children from previous marriage: Fabrice, Marie-Christine. Student, Ecole Normale Supérieure, 1947-50; Agrégé des Lettres, Université de Paris-Sorbonne, 1950, Docteur-ès-Lettres, 1965. Prof. Lycée, Nevers, Dijon, France, 1951-53; asst. Faculté des Lettres, Paris, 1953-58; asst. prof. Yale U., New Haven, 1958-61, prof. French, 1970-71, 87—; prof. medieval lit. Université de Grenoble, France, 1961-68; dir. French Inst., Naples, Italy, 1968-70; prof. Université de Paris-Sorbonne, 1974-87; chmn. medieval studies YaleU., New Haven, Conn., 1993—; dir. Département d'Etudes Medievales, Paris, 1981-87; cons. Editions Gallimard, Paris, 1987—, Editions Garnier-Bordas, Paris, 1987-91. Author: Le Poéte et le prince, 1965, Le Lexique de Ch. d'Orléans, 1967, Le Roman de la Rose, 1973, Résurgences, 1986, Tristan et Yseut, 1989; editor: Chrétien de Troyes Oeuvres Completes, 1994. Lt. inf., French Army, 1950-51. Decorated chevalier Légion d'Honneur, Palmes Académiques (France). Fellow Am. Acad. Arts and Scis., Medieval Acad.; mem. Arthurian Soc. (treas. 1974-84), Acad. des Inscriptions et Belles Lettres, Inst. de France (corr.). DIED 03/15/96. .

POKORNY, VIRGINIA ANNE, elementary education educator; b. Ashland, Ky., Sept. 27, 1941; d. Law Gibson and Dorothy (Schleicher) Weiner; children: Juliann, Richard. BEd, Nat. Louis U., Evanston, Ill., 1963; M Guidance and Counseling, Northeastern Ill. U., Chgo., 1982. 1st and 2nd grade tchr. West Elem. Sch., Lake Bluff, Ill., 1963-65, West Ridge Sch., Highland Park, Ill., 1965-68; 5th grade tchr. Sherwood Sch., Highland Park, Ill., 1970-71, tchr. combined 2nd to 4th grades and 3rd grade, 1976-95. Mem. Deerfield Area Hist. Soc. (bd. dirs. 1991-95), Optimist Club Deerfield (bd. dirs. 1992-95, co-v.p. 1992-94, pres. 1995). Avocations: singing, gardening, antiquing, hiking, working with youth. Home: Deerfield Ill. Died April 3, 1995.

POLAK, GEORGE, economics educator emeritus; b. Porubka, Slovak, May 7, 1923; s. Jan and Anna (Danko) P.; m. Mildred Sophia Klucho, Sept. 26, 1953; children: George Gregory, Mark Joseph, John Jerome, Catherine Marie, Suzanne Therese. BSBA, Ohio State U., 1954; MBA, Western Res. U., 1956; PhD, Case Western Res. U., 1974. Assoc. economist Fed. Res. Bank of Cleve., 1956-62; assoc. dir. rsch. Griswold-Eshleman Co., Cleve., 1962-63; prof. econs. West Liberty (W.Va.) State Coll., 1963-89; vis. prof. econs. Spring Hill Coll., Mobile, Ala., 1983-84; ret. West Liberty (W.Va.) State Coll., 1989; adj. prof. econs. U. Pitts., 1976-81. Contbr. articles to profl. jours. Sch. bd. mem. Cath. Diocese of Wheeling, Charleston, W.Va., 1975-83. Mem. Am. Econ. Assn., Alpha Kappa Psi, Omicron Delta Epsilon. DIED 06/06/97. .

POLAN, NANCY MOORE, artist; b. Newark, Ohio; d. William Tracy and Francis (Flesher) Moore; m. Lincoln Milton Polan, Mar. 28, 1934; children: Charles Edwin, William Joseph Marion. AB, Marshall U., 1936. One-man shows include Charleston Art Gallery, 1961, 67, 73, Greenbrier, 1963, Huntington Mus. Art, 1963, 66, 71, N.Y. World's Fair, 1965, W.Va. U., 1966, Carroll Reese Mus., 1967; exhibited in group shows Am. Watercolor Soc., Allied Artists of Am., Nat. Arts Club, 1968-74, 76-77, 86, 87, 91-95, Pa. Acad. Fine Arts, Opening of Creative Arts Center W.Va. U., 1969, Internat. Platform Assn. Art Exhibit, 1968-69, 72-74, 74, 79, 85-86, 88-90, (Gold medal Best of Show 1991, 2d award painting 1994, 1st award watercolor 1995, 96, 97), Allied Artists W.Va., 1968-69, 86, Joan Miro Graphic Traveling Exhbn., Barcelona, Spain, 1970-71, XXI Exhibit Contemporary Art, La Scala, Florence, Italy, 1971, Rassegna Internazionale d'Arte Grafica, Siena, Italy, 1973, 79, 82, Opening of Parkersburg (W.Va.) Art Center, 1975, Art Club Washington, 1992, Pen & Brush, 1992-93, others. Hon. v.p. Centro Studie Scambi Internazionale, Rome, Italy, 1977. Recipient Acad. of Italy with Gold medal, 1979, 86, Norton Meml. award 3d Nat. Jury Show Am. Art, Chautauqua, N.Y., 1960; Purchase prize, Jurors award, Watercolor award Huntington Galleries, 1960, 61, Oil award, 1996; Nat. Arts Club for watercolor, 1969; Gold medal Masters of Modern Art exhbn., La Scala Gallery, Florence, 1975, gold medal Accademia Italia, 1984, 1986, diploma Internat. Com. for World Culture and Arts, 1987, Philip Isenberg Watercolor award Pen & Brush, 1995, many others. Mem. AAUW, DAR, Nat. Mus. Women Artists (charter), Allied Artists W.Va., Internat. Platform Assn. (3rd award-painting in ann. art exhbn. 1977, Gold medal for Best of Show 1991, 1st award for painting 1994), Huntington Mus. Fine Arts (life), Tri-State Arts Assn. (Equal Merit award 1978), Sunrise Found., Composers, Authors, Artists Am., Inc., Pen and Brush, Inc. (Watercolor exhbn. 1993, Grumbacher golden palette mem., Grumbacher award 1978), W.Va. Watercolor Soc. (charter mem.), Nat. Arts Club, Leonardo da Vinci Acad. (Rome), Accademia Italia, Vero Beach Arts Club, Riomar Bay Yacht Club, Guyan Golf and Country Club, Huntington Cotillion (hon., charter mem.), Mass. Hist. Soc. (hon.), Sigma Kappa. Episcopalian. Died Oct. 6, 1997.

POLETTI, UGO CARDINAL, archbishop; b. Omegna, Italy, Apr. 19, 1914. Ordained priest Roman Catholic Ch., 1938. Served in various diocesan offices, Novara, Italy; consecrated titular bishop of Medeli and aux. of Novara, 1958; pres. Pontificial Mission Aid Soc. for Italy, 1964-67; archbishop of Spoleto, 1967-69; titular archbishop of Cittanova, from 1969; served as 2d vice-regent of Rome, 1969-72; pro-vicar gen. of Rome, 1972; elevated to cardinal, 1973; cardinal vicar Diocese and City of Rome, 1973-91; cardinal archpriest Patriarchal Basilica of Santa Maria Maggiore, Vatican City, Italy, 1991. Deceased.

POLIKOFF, BENET, JR., lawyer; b. Winston-Salem, N.C., Nov. 25, 1936; s. Benet and Margaret (New) P.; m. Jean Troubh, June 26, 1959 (div. Mar. 1971); children—Elisabeth, Benet Steven, Lee; m. Florence Davis, June 11, 1971. BA, Yale U., 1959; LLB, Harvard U., 1962. Ptnr. Marshall, Bratter, Greene, Allison & Tucker, N.Y.C., 1969-82; Ptnr. Rosenman and Colin, N.Y.C., 1982-90, of counsel, 1990—. Mem. Assn. Bar City N.Y. (chmn. real property law com. 1981-84), N.Y. State Bar Assn., Am. Coll. Real Estate Lawyers. Died Apr. 22, 1997.

POLLARD, DAVID EDWARD, editor; b. Columbus, Ohio, Oct. 7, 1927; s. James Edward and Marjorie Olive (Pearson) P.; m. Ilse Knack, Dec. 24, 1960; children: Walter Thomas, Marcus Andreas, Michael David, Christopher James. B.S., Ohio State U., 1950; postgrad. in cotton econs, Memphis State U., 1967. With Columbus Citizen, 1943-50; with Army Times Pub. Co., 1952-60; mng. editor U.S. Coast Guard Mag., Washington, 1956-57; asso. editor Am. Weekend, Washington, also Frankfurt, Ger., 1957-60; info. specialist Air Forces Europe Exchange, Wiesbaden, Ger., 1961-63; reporter Comml. Appeal, Memphis, 1963-66; fin. writer Comml. Appeal, 1967-68; news-desk editor U.S. News & World Report, Washington, 1968-76; chief news desk U.S. News & World Report, 1976-91; pres. U.S. Moose Co., Inc., Boothbay Harbor, Maine, 1993-96. Patentee garden implement. Served with USMC, 1945-46, 51-52. Mem. Sigma Delta Chi, Alpha Delta Sigma, Alpha Tau Omega. Roman Catholic. Home: Annandale Va. Died July 5, 1996; interred Quantico National Cemetery.

POLLOCK, JACK PADEN, retired dental educator, consultant, army officer; b. Columbus, Miss., May 12, 1920; s. Samuel Lafayette and Pauline Elizabeth (Pollock) O'Neal; m. Anne Olamae Silbernagel, Aug. 25, 1945; children: Poli A., Elizabeth D. Student, Gulf Coast Mil. Acad., 1936-38, Tulane U., 1938-41; BS, Southeastern La. U., 1942; DDS cum laude, Loyola U., New Orleans, 1945; diploma, Army War Coll., 1965, Indsl. Coll. Armed Forces, 1966; hon. degree, Baylor U., 1974. Asst. prof., Loyola U., New Orleans, 1945-46, prof., 1977-86, U.S.A. Command and Gen. Staff Coll., 1959-60, prof., 1977-86, mem. univ. rank and tenure com., 1982-86, prof. emeritus, 1986-95; commd. 1st lt. U.S. Army, 1946, advanced through the grades to brig. gen., 1972; career officer U.S. Army, 1946-77; dental advisor to Sec. of Def., 1970-73; adj. prof. Naval Grad. Dental Sch., 1972-73; cons. Surgeon Gen. U.S. Army, Washington, 1981-84; active Nat. Adv. Dental Rsch. Coun., NIH, 1970-73. Author: International Communism: Its Future Prospects, 1965. Contbr. numerous articles to profl. jours. Active nat. coun. Boy Scouts Am., 1973-92, Nat. Exploring Com., 1973-92. USAR, 1942-46. Decorated D.S.M., Legion of Merit with 2 oak leaf clusters, Bronze Star with one oak leaf cluster, Master Parachutist badges (U.S. and foreign); recipient Silver Beaver award, Boy Scouts of Am., numerous other military, civilian awards and honors. Recipient Disting. Alumnus award Southeastern La. U., 1974. Fellow Am. Coll. Dentistry (life), Internat. Coll. Dentistry (life); mem. ADA (life), VFW (life), NRA (life), La. Dental Assn. (life), New Orleans Dental Assn. (life), Am. Coll. Dentists (life), Internat. Coll. Dentists (life), Fedn. Dentaire Internationale, Assn. Mil. Surgeons of U.S. (life), Pierre Fauchard Acad., C. Victor Vignes Odontological Soc. (life), Am. Assn. Dental Schs., Assoc. U.S. Army (life), Military Order of World Wars (life), Ret. Officers Assoc. (life), Disabled Am. Vets. (life), Am. Legion, Delta Sigma Delta (life), Kappa Sigma (life), Phi Kappa, Omicron Kappa Upsilon (life). Clubs: Army and Navy (Washington), Univ. (San Antonio). Avocations: writing, travel, conservation, gun collector. Died May 31, 1995.

POLLOCK, JOHN DENTON, education association executive; b. Kilmarnock, Ayrshire, Scotland, Apr. 21, 1926; s. John and Elizabeth Hart (Crawford) P.; m. Joyce Margaret Sharpe, Mar. 30, 1961; children: Gordon Alexander, Carolyn Elizabeth Pollock Sherlock. BSc, Glasgow U., Scotland, 1950; FEIS (hon.), Ednl. Inst. Scotland, 1971, 1988. Cert. tchr., 1951; cert. leader Am. Youth Hostels, 1958. Tchr. Mauchline Sch., Ayrshire, 1951-59; headmaster Kilmaurs Secondary Sch., Ayrshire, 1959-65; rector Mainholm Acad., Ayrshire, 1965-74; gen. sec. Ednl. Inst. of Scotland, 1975-88; mem. Employmen Appeal Tribunal, U.K., 1991—; chmn. Network Scotland Charity, Scotland, 1992—; commrs. Forestry Commn., U.K., 1978-91; mem. Annan Com. on Future of Broadcasting, Brit. Govt., 1974-76; pres. European Tchrs., 1980-90; exec. World Confedn. of Orgns. of Tchg. Profession, 1986-90; mem. Broadcasting Coun. for Scotland, 1985-89. Co-author reports in field. Chmn. Ayrshire Labour Fedn., 1949-74, Scottish Labour Party, 1959, 71; pres. Scottish Trade Union Congress, 1982; v.p. European Trade Union Com. for Edn., Brussels, 1989-90; mem. Manpower Svcs. Com., Scotland, 1977-88. Lt. Royal Engrs., 1945-48, Britain. Recipient Russell award World Confedn. of Orgns. of Tchg. Profession, Stockholm, 1993; hon. mem. Nat. Union Tchrs., England/Wales, 1988; hon. v.p. Ulster Tchrs. Union, Ireland, 1989, Scottish Youth Hostels Assn., S.W. Scotland, 1985. Mem. Labour Party. Avocations: politics, travel and outdoor activities. Deceased.

POLUNIN, NICHOLAS, environmentalist, author, editor; b. Checkendon, Oxfordshire, Eng.; s. Vladimir and Elizabeth Violet (Hart) P.; m. Helen Lovat Fraser, 1939 (dec.); 1 child, Michael; m. Helen Eugenie Campbell, Jan. 3, 1948; children: April Xenia, Nicholas V. C., Douglas H. H. Open scholar, Christ Ch., 1928-32; BA (1st class honors), U. Oxford, 1932, MA, 1935, DPhil, 1935, DSc, 1942; MS, Yale U., 1934. Participant or leader numerous sci. expdns., 1930-65, primarily in arctic regions, including Spitsbergen, Greenland, Alaska, Can. East and West Arctic, North Pole; curator, tutor, demonstrator, lectr. various instns., especially Oxford U., 1933-47; vis. prof. botany McGill U., 1946-47, Macdonald prof. botany, 1947-52; Guggenheim fellow, rsch. assoc. Harvard U., 1950-53; earlier fgn. research asso., USAF botanical Ice-island research project dir., lectr. plant sci. Yale, also biology Brandeis U., 1953-55; prof. plant ecology and taxonomy, head dept. botany, dir. U. Herbarium and Botanic Garden, Baghdad, Iraq, 1955-58; guest prof. U. Geneva, 1959-61, 75-76; adviser establishment, planner permanent campus, founding prof. botany, dean faculty sci. U. Ife, Nigeria, 1962-66; founding editor Plant Sci. Monographs and World Crops Books, 1954-78, Biol. Conservation, 1967-74; instigator, founding editor Plant Sci. Monographs and World Crops Books Environ. Pollution, 1969; founding editor Plant Sci. Monographs and World Crops Books Environ. Conservation, 1974-95; chmn. internat. steering com., organizer, editor procs. Internat. Conf. on Environ. Future, Finland, 1971; chmn. internat. steering com., sec. gen., editor procs. 2d Internat. Conf. on Environ. Future, Reykjavik, Iceland, 1977, 3d Internat. Conf. on Environ. Future, Edinburgh, Scotland, 1987; sec.-gen., joint editor procs. 4th Internat. Conf. Environ. Future, Budapest, Hungary, 1990; pres., CEO Found. for Environ. Conservation, 1975-97; participant Internat. Bot. Congresses, Stockholm, 1950, Paris, 1954, Edinburgh, 1964, Seattle, 1969, Leningrad, 1975, Sydney, 1981; initiator (pres., CEO) World Council For The Biosphere, 1984-97. Author: Russian Waters, 1931, The Isle of Auks, 1932, Botany of the Canadian Eastern Arctic, 3 vols., 1940-48, Arctic Unfolding, 1949, Circumpolar Arctic Flora, 1959, Introduction to Plant

Geography and Some Related Sciences, 1960 (various fgn. edits.), Eléménts de Géographie Botanique, 1967; editor: The Environmental Future, 1972, Environmental Monographs and Symposia (series), 1979-88, Growth Without Ecodisasters?, 1980, Ecosystem Theory and Application, 1986, (with Sir John Burnett) Maintenance of the Biosphere, 1990, Surviving With The Biosphere, 1993; (with Mohammad Nazim) Environmental Challenges I: From Stockholm to Rio and Beyond, 1993, II: Population and Global Security, 1994, 97; founding chmn. editl. bd. Cambridge Studies in Environ. Policy, 1984-97; contbr. articles to various jours. Decorated comdr. of Order Brit. Empire, 1975; recipient undergrad., grad. student scholarships, fellowships, rsch. associateships Yale U., 1933-34, Harvard U., 1936-37, 50-53; Rolleston Meml. prize, 1938; D.S.I.R. spl. investigator, 1938; Leverhulme Rsch. award, 1941; from sr. scholar to sr. rsch. fellow New Coll., Oxford, 1934-47; Guggenheim fellow, 1950-52; recipient Ford Found. award Scandinavia, USSR, 1966-67, Can. Marie-Victorin medal, 1957, Indian Ramdeo medal, 1986, Internat. Sasakawa Environ. prize, 1987, USSR Vernadsky commemoration, 1988, Chinese Academia Sinica medal, 1988, Vernadsky medal USSR Acad. Scis., 1988, 89, Founder's (Zéchenyi) medal Hungarian Acad. Scis., 1990, Russian Diaghilev medal, 1997; named to Netherlands Order of the Golden Ark, 1990 (officer), UN Environ. Programme Global 500 Roll of Honour, 1991. Fellow AAAS, Royal Geog. Soc. (life), Royal Hort. Soc. (life), Linnean Soc. London (life), Arctic Inst. N.Am. (life), INSONA (v.p.), NECA (India), Pierson Coll., Yale U. (assoc.); mem. Internat. Soc. Environ. Edn. (life), Internat. Acad. Environment Geneva (conseil de fondation 1992-96), Torrey Bot. Club (life), Bot. Soc. Am. (life), N.Am. Assn. Environ. Edn. (life), Asian Soc. Environ. Protection (life), Sigma Xi, INTECOL, various fgn. and nat. profl. and sci. socs., Harvard Club (N.Y.C.) (life), Field Naturalists' Club (Ottawa) (life), Torrey Botanical (life), Brit. Ecol. Soc., Reform (London) (life), Oxford U. Exploration Club (v.p.). Achievements include confirming existence of Spicer Islands in Foxe Basin and making world's last major land discovery to their East, Can. Arctic, 1946; past rsch. plant life and ecology of arctic, subarctic, and high-altitude regions; present occupation environ. conservation at the global level; initiator of ann. worldwide Biosphere Day, 1991, plans and seeking funds for major Biosphere Fund and Prizes, 1992, Biosphere Clubs, 1993, and plans for planetary econetwork of environmental/conservational watchdogs collated by revived World Coun. for the Biosphere; initiating and editing World Who Is Who and Does What in Environment & Conservation, 1st edit. pub. 1997. Died Dec. 8, 1997.

POMA, ANTONIO CARDINAL, archbishop of Bologna; b. Villanterio, Italy, June 12, 1910. Ordained priest Roman Catholic Ch., 1933; titular bishop of Tagaste, also aux. bishop of Mantova, 1951; bishop of Mantova, 1954; titular archbishop of Gerpiniano, also coadjutor archbishop of Bologna, 1967-68; archbishop of Bologna, 1969—; elevated to Sacred Coll. of Cardinals, 1969; titular ch. St. Luke (Via Prenestina); mem. Congregation of Clergy, Congregation of Cath. Edn.

POMERANCE, RALPH, retired architect; b. N.Y.C., Sept. 1, 1907; s. Harry and Esther (Perlstein) P.; m. Josephine A. Wertheim, June 8, 1934 (dec. 1980); children: Pamela (Mrs. Henry Steiner), Stephen M., Ralph.; m. Marilyn S. Selver, May 6, 1984. B.Arch., Carnegie Inst. Tech., 1930. Archtl. practice as Ralph Pomerance, 1933-38, Pomerance & Breines, N.Y.C., 1938-93. Prin. works include Bronx Municipal Hosp. Center, N.Y.C., 1955, Rose Fitzgerald Kennedy Research Center at Albert Einstein Coll. Medicine, 1969, Riis Houses Plaza and Amphitheatre, N.Y.C., 1966, Bellevue Hosp, 1970, NYU Dental Coll., 1976, NYU Hosp. offices, 1986. Chmn. Greenwich (Conn.) Housing Authority, 1947-53. Served to capt. AUS, 1942-45. Decorated knight 1st class Royal Order Vasa, Sweden, 1939. Fellow AIA (treas. N.Y. chpt. 1950-51, exec. com. 1954-57). Home: Cos Cob Conn. Died Aug. 23, 1995.

POMERANZ, YESHAJAHU, research chemist, technologist; b. Tlumacz, Poland, Nov. 28, 1922; came to U.S., 1959, naturalized, 1967; s. David and Rysia (Bildner) P.; m. Ada Waisberg, Oct. 27, 1948; children: Shlomo, David. B.S., Israeli Inst. Tech., Haifa, 1946; Chem. Engr., Israeli Inst. Tech., 1947; student, U. London, 1954-55; Ph.D., Kans. State U., 1959-62. Dir. Central Food Testing Lab., Haifa, 1948-59; research chemist Agrl. Research Service, U.S. Dept. Agr., Manhattan, Kans., 1962-69; dir. Barley and Malt Lab. Agrl. Research Service, U.S. Dept. Agr., Madison, Wis., 1969-73; dir. U.S. Grain Mktg. Research Ctr. Agrl. Research Service, U.S. Dept. Agr., Manhattan, 1973-86; research prof. dept. food sci. Wash. State U., Pullman, 1986—; vis. prof. U.S. and abroad. Sci. editor, Am. Assn. Cereal Chemists; author, co-author, editor numerous book, symposia procs. in cereal sci., tech., food sci. tech. analysis; patentee high protein bread lipid syntheses and uses. Von Humboldt awardee, 1981; recipient Wiley award, 1980, Osborne award, 1981, W.F. Geddes medal, 1982, Disting. Svc. award U.S. Dept. Agr., 1983, Nat. Assn. Wheat Growers, 1990. Fellow AAAS, Inst. Food Technologists, Assn. Cereal Chemists; mem. Am. Chem. Soc. (Food Agr. award 1984), Assn. Ofcl. Analytical Chemists, Sigma Xi, Gamma Sigma Delta. Home: Pullman Wash. DIED 07/21/95. .

POND, MARTIN ALLEN, academic dean emeritus; b. Ansonia, Conn., Oct. 17, 1912; s. Clifford A. and A. Louise (Hafner) P.; m. Madeleine Huson Davidson, May 28, 1938; children: Sarah L. (Mrs. Gary K. Williams), Jonathan D., Roger A. Grad., Loomis Sch., 1930; B.S., Yale, 1935, M.P.H., 1936. Successively asst., instr., asst. prof. pub. health Yale, 1936-42; commd. officer USPHS (res.), 1942-46, USPHS (regular), 1948-68; asst. prof. pub. health Yale, 1946-1948; prof. pub. health U. Pitts., 1968-81, assoc. dean, 1969-74, acting dean, 1980-81, dean emeritus, 1981-95; Adviser U.S. delegation WHO, 1965, 67; mem. Nat. Adv. Health Council, 1970-73. Recipient Meritorious service medal USPHS, 1965; spl. citation Sec. Health, Edn. and Welfare, 1968; Disting. Service medal U. Pitts., 1982. Mem. Am. Pub. Health Assn. (Sedgwick Meml. medal 1978). Home: Cranberry Township Pa. Died Jan. 4, 1995.

PONSONBY, MOORE CHARLES GARRETT See DROGHEDA, EARL OF

POOLE, CECIL F., circuit court judge; b. Birmingham, Ala., 1914; children: Gayle, Patricia. LL.B., U. Mich.; LL.M., Harvard U., 1939. Practice of law San Francisco, former asst. dist. atty., 1951-58; clemency sec. to Gov. Brown of Calif., 1958-61; U.S. atty. No. Dist. Calif., 1961-70; regents prof. Law U. Calif., Berkeley, 1970; counsel firm Jacobs, Sills & Coblentz, San Francisco, 1970-76; judge U.S. Dist. Ct., No. Dist. Calif., 1976-79, U.S. Ct. of Appeals for 9th Circuit, 1979-97; adj. prof. Golden Gate U. Sch. Law, 1953-58; mem. adv. com. Nat. Commn. for Reform Fed. Criminal Laws, 1968-70. Served to 2d lt. AUS, World War II. Mem. ABA (chmn. sect. individual rights 1971-72, ho. of dels. 1972-74), San Francisco Bar Assn. (dir. 1975-76). Home: San Francisco Calif. Died Nov. 12, 1997.

POORMAN, PAUL ARTHUR, educator, media consultant; b. Lock Haven, Pa., Aug. 29, 1930; s. Wilson Paul and and Margaret (Heylmun) P.; m. Sylvia Elizabeth Powers, Nov. 22, 1952; children: Pamela (Mrs. Robert Phillips), Cynthia (Mrs. Donald Paul), Peter, Stephen, Thomas, Andrew, Robert, William. B.A., Pa. State U., 1952. Reporter State College (Pa.) Centre Daily Times, 1953-57, news editor, 1957-62; news editor Harrisburg (Pa.) Patriot, 1962-63, Phila. Bulletin, 1963-66; asst. mng. editor Detroit News, 1966-69, mng. editor, 1969-75; vis. prof. Northwestern U., Evanston, Ill., 1975-76; editor Akron (Ohio) Beacon Jour., 1976-86; prof. journalism, spl. asst. to pres. Kent (Ohio) State U., 1986—. Served with USAF 1951-53. Mem. Am. Soc. Newspaper Editors, AP Mng. Editors (regent). Deceased.

POOVEY, WILLIAM ARTHUR, theology educator; b. Balt., Sept. 20, 1913; s. William Arthur and Opal (Holl) P.; m. Mary Virginia Smith, June 29, 1940. B.A., Capital U., Columbus, Ohio, 1934; certificate, Evang. Lutheran Sem., Columbus, 1939; M.A., Northwestern U., 1939; D.D., Wartburg Coll., Waverly, Iowa, 1972. Ordained to ministry Am. Luth. Ch., 1939; instr. speech Capital U., 1935-39; pastor in Monterey Park, Cal., 1939-45, San Antonio, 1945-53, Memphis, 1953-57; prof. homiletics Wartburg Theol. Sem., Dubuque, Iowa, 1957-76; acting pres. Wartburg Theol. Sem., 1970, 71; Mem. commn. research and social action Am. Luth. Ch., 1960-72, chmn., 1963-72, mem. bd. pensions, 1972-83. Author: Hymn Dramatizations, 1942, Questions That Trouble Christians, 1946, Problems That Plague Saints, 1950, No Hands But Ours, 1954, Your Neighbor's Faith, 1961, And Pilate Asked, 1965, Cross Words, 1967, Lenten Chancel Dramas, 1967, What Did Jesus Do?, 1968, Chancel Dramas for Lent, 1968, The Christian in Society, 1969, Mustard Seeds and Wine Skins, 1972, Let Us Adore Him, 1972, Stand Still and Move Ahead, 1973, Signs of His Coming, 1973, Six Faces of Lent, 1974, Banquets and Beggars, 1974, the Power of the Kingdom, 1974, Celebrate with Drama, 1975, The Days Before Christmas, 1975, The Wonderful Word Shalom, 1975, The Days Before Easter, 1976, The Prayer He Taught, 1976, Letting the Word Become Alive, 1977, Six Prophets for Today, 1977, Planning a Christian Funeral, 1978, The Days of Pentecost, 1979, Faith is the Password, 1979, Prodigals and Publicans, 1980, We Sing Your Praise, O Lord, 1980, How to Talk to Christians about Money, 1982. Home: San Antonio Tex. Died Feb. 16, 1995; interred Sunset Memorial Park, San Antonio, TX.

POPOVICH, PETER STEPHEN, lawyer, former state supreme court chief justice; b. Crosby, Minn., Nov. 27, 1920; s. Peter and Rose Mary (Mehelich) P.; children: Victoria, Dorothy, Stephen, Susan Jane; stepchildren: Michelle, Paul, Stephen; m. Gail Prince Javorina, July 5, 1985. AA, Hibbing (Minn.) Jr. Coll., 1940; BA, U. Minn., 1942; LLB, St. Paul Coll. of Law, 1947; LLD (hon.), William Mitchell Coll. Law, 1991. Bar: Minn. 1947, U.S. Dist. Ct. Minn. 1947, U.S. Supreme Ct. 1956, U.S. Ct. Appeals (8th cir.) 1975. Sr. ptnr. Peterson & Popovich, St. Paul, 1947-83; chief judge Minn. Ct. Appeals, St. Paul, 1983-87; assoc. justice Minn. Supreme Ct., St. Paul, 1987-89, chief justice, 1989-90; ptnr. Briggs & Morgan, St. Paul, 1991-96. Chmn. Minn. Statehood Centennial Com., 1955-59; rep. Minn. State Legis., St. Paul, 1953-63. Named Outstanding Minnesotan, Minn. Broadcasters Assn., 1983; recipient Dist. Svc. to Journalism award Minn. Newspaper Assn., 1991, John Finnegan Freedom of Info. award, 1991. Mem. ABA, Minn. Bar Assn. Minn. Hist. Soc. (hon. council). Roman Catholic. Avocations: boating, reading. Home: Lakeland Minn. Deceased.

POPPE, FRED CHRISTOPH, advertising agency executive; b. Bklyn., Dec. 26, 1923; s. Fred G. and Laura (Funk) P.; m. Inez Hanssen, Oct. 2, 1952; children: Steven Hammond, Ellen Jane. Student, Adm. Farragut Acad., Toms River, N.J., 1940-41, Bklyn. Poly. Inst., 1941-42; AB, Princeton U., 1948. Copywriter Fuller & Smith & Ross, Inc., N.Y.C., 1948-51; advt. mgr. Yale & Towne Mfg. Co., 1951-53; group account supr. G.M. Basford Co., N.Y.C., 1953-59; mgr. account devel. Donahue & Coe, Inc., N.Y.C., 1959-60; exec. v.p. T.N. Palmer, Inc., N.Y.C., 1960-63; pres. Complan, Inc., N.Y.C., 1963-74; chmn. Poppe Tepon Inc., 1974-86; pres., chmn. emeritus Poppe Tyson Inc., N.Y.C., 1986-96; bd. dirs. Inter-Ad Ltd., Skills Unlimited Inc. Author: The Hundred Greatest Corporate and Industrial Ads, 1983, 50 Rules to Keep a Client Happy, 1987, 100 New Greatest Corporate Ads, 1993. Served with USNR, 1941-46. Named Advt. Agy. Man of Yr., N.Y. Bus./Mktg. Assn., 1966-67. Mem. Bus./Mktg. Assn. (past pres., G.C. Crain award, Advt. Hall of Fame 1981, Communicator of Yr. 1983), Gt. South Bay Yacht Racing Assn., Princeton Club (N.Y.C.), Stuart Yacht and Country Club (Fla.), Elm Club (Princeton, N.J.), Southward Ho Country Club (Bay Shore, N.Y.), Magoun Landing Yacht Club (West Islip, N.Y.). Republican. Died June 17, 1996.

PORTER, ROBERT GEORGE, labor union executive; b. East St. Louis, Ill., Aug. 11, 1927; s. Joseph and Lillian (Wells) P.; m. Patricia Sue Porter, Aug. 23, 1952; children: Stephen, Paula, Rudolph. Grad., Washington U., St. Louis. Tchr. East St. Louis Sch. Dist. #189, 1952-60; sec.-treas. Am. Fedn. Tchrs., Washington, 1960—. Served as sgt. U.S. Army, 1945-47, ETO.

PORZIO, RALPH, lawyer, lecturer, author, editor; b. Bklyn., Aug. 27, 1914; m. Edith Lori, June 6, 1942; 1 child, Ann Lewis. A.B., Drew U., 1938; J.D., Harvard U., 1942. Bar: N.J. 1943, U.S. Supreme Ct. 1943, N.Y. 1981. Of counsel Porzio, Bromberg & Newman, Morristown and N.Y.C.; counsel, bd. of trustees Internat. Coll. Angiology; lectr., London, Vienna, Copenhagen, Dublin, Rome, Lisbon, Geneva, Ghent, Montreal, U.S. Author: The Transplant Age—Reflections on the Legal and Moral Aspects of Organ Transplants, 1969; editor-in-chief: Internat. Jour. Law and Sci., 1975-80; assoc. editor, 1969-75; contbr. articles to profl. jours. Mem. Boonton Charter Commn., 1952-53, Bd. Edn., 1953-56; trustee emeritus Drew U., N.J. Conservation Found., Holmes Library, Boonton. Recipient Freedoms Found. citation for writings advancing Am. way of life, 1951, Outstanding Achievements award in arts Drew U., 1956. Fellow Internat. Acad. Law and Sci. (pres., bd. regents), Internat. Soc. Barristers; mem. ABA, N.J. Bar Assn., Morris County Bar Assn. (pres. 1970-71), Fed. Bar Assn., Am. Judicature Soc., N.Y. State, N.J. plaintiffs trial lawyers assns., N.J. Soc. Hosp. Attys., World Assn. Med. Law, Law-Sci. Acad. Am., Am. Coll. Legal Medicine, Am. Soc. Law and Medicine, Trial Attys. of N.J. (charter, ann. award for disting. service in cause of justice 1979), Assn. Trial Lawyers Am., N.J. Assn. Sch. Attys., Phi Beta Kappa. Club: Optimist (Morristown) (pres.). DIED 07/01/97. .

POSADAS OCAMPO, JUAN JESUS CARDINAL, archbishop; b. Salvatierra, Mexico, Nov. 10, 1926. Ordained priest Roman Cath. Ch., 1950. Named bishop of Tijuana Mexico, 1970-82, bishop of Cuernavaca, 1982-87, archbishop of Guadalajara, 1987—; named cardinal Roman Cath. Ch., 1991—.

POST, JOSEPH, physician, researcher, consultant; b. N.Y.C., Mar. 6, 1913; s. Charles S. and Mollie P.; m. Anne Bretzfelder, Mar. 1, 1942; children: David Louis, Thomas Charles. BS, CCNY, 1932; MD, U. Chgo. 1937; DMS, Columbia U., 1941. Diplomate Am. Bd. Internal Medicine. Fellow in surgery Billings Hosp. Chgo., 1936; intern Michael Reese Hosp., Chgo., 1937-38; resident in research medicine Coll. Phys. and Sugeons Columbia U., N.Y.C., 1938-42, instr. medicine Coll. Phys. and Surgeons, 1939-46; asst. prof. NYU N.Y.C., 1947-54, assoc. prof., 1954-71, prof. Sch. Medicine, 1971-95; cons. Office Profl. Med. Conduct N.Y. State Dept. Health, 1986-95; cons. medicine VA Hosp., Bronx, N.Y., 1946-54; cons. gastroenterology U.S. Naval Hosp., St. Albans, N.Y., 1948-56; attending physician Lenox Hill Hosp., N.Y.C., 1947-88, Univ. Hosp., 1948-88, Goldwater Meml. Hosp., N.Y.C., 1946-88; vis. prof. medicine U. Hawaii, 1970, Hawaii Cancer Ctr., 1974. Contbr. articles to profl. jours. Maj. AUS 1942-46, PTO. Fellow ACP, N.Y. Acad. Medicine (pres. 1979, 80 plaque for service 1982); mem. Soc. Clin. Investigation, Am. Gastroenterol. Assn., Sci. Scos Emeritus, Am. Assn. Cancer Research, Study Liver Disease, Am. Soc. Cell Biology, Am. Soc. Clin. Oncology, Radiation Research Soc., New York County Med. Soc., N.Y. State Med. Soc. Home: New York N.Y. Died Mar. 25, 1995.

POTTER, HAMILTON FISH, JR., lawyer, consultant, author; b. Bklyn., Dec. 21, 1928; s. Hamilton

Fish and Alma Virginia (Murray) P.; m. Virginia Fox Patterson, Sept. 17, 1953 (div. May 1979); children: Virginia Patterson, Hamilton Fish III, Robert Burnside, Elizabeth Stuyvesant; m. Maureen Ellen Cotter, Nov. 28, 1981; children: Nicholas Fish, Warwick Alonzo. B.A., Harvard U., 1950, LL.B., 1956. Bar: N.Y. 1957, U.S. Supreme Ct. 1961. Assoc. Sullivan & Cromwell, N.Y.C., 1956-65, ptnr., 1965-91, sr. counsel, 1997. Bd. dirs. Berkshire Farm for Boys, N.Y.C., 1962-71, Alice and Hamilton Fish Libr., Garrison-on-Hudson, N.Y., 1980-97, European Am. Bank, 1964-91; mem. Bd. Correction, N.Y.C., 1963-71; warden Ch. of Resurrection, 1972-74; trustee Episcopal Sch. of N.Y., 1969-76, Chapin Sch., 1975-81, Knox Sch., 1985-97; warden All Saints Episcopal Ch., 1982-90; bd. dirs. Dutch Am. West Indies Found., 1984-89, The Netherlands Am. Found., 1989-92. Lt. (j.g.) USN, 1950-53, Korea. Mem. ABA (chmn. banking law com. 1975-80), Am. Bar Found., N.Y. State Bar Assn. (ho. of dels. 1978-80), N.Y. Bar Found., Assn. of Bar of City of N.Y. (chmn. banking law com. 1972-74), Am. Law Inst. (3-4-8 com. 1975-83), Mystery Writers Am. (assoc.). Deceased.

POUNCY, MARVA NELL, elementary education educator; b. Ft. Worth, Dec. 17, 1944; d. Lenzy Kert Pouncy and Lavada Cole. BS, Prairie View A&M U., 1967; student, Tex. Wesleyan Coll., Ft. Worth, 1968-69; MEd, Wayne State U., 1974; EdS, Ea. Mich. U., 1993. Cert. elem. tchr., Tex., Mich. Customer svc. clk. Ft. Worth Water Dept., 1968-69; tchr. Port Huron (Mich.) Area Schs., 1970-78; tchr. 6th grade Detroit Pub. Schs., 1978—. Mem. Justice, Unity, Generosity and Svc., Detroit, 1989; precinct del. Dem. Party, Detroit, 1990. Recipient Dedicted Tchr. award Bd. Edn., Detroit, 1988-89, Cert. of Appreciaiton, Gov. of Mich., 1990; recipient mini-grants, 1989, 90, 91, 92, 93; Renaissance Writign fellow, 1985. Mem. Met. Alliance of Black Sch. Educators, Nat. Assn. Negro Bus. and Profl. Women, Optimist Club, Phi Delta Kappa (exec. bd.), Dalta Kappa Gamma. Avocations: skating, planning social activities, dancing. Deceased.

POVEY, THOMAS GEORGE, office systems company executive; b. Norristown, Pa., Dec. 27, 1920; s. Thomas and Blanche (Groff) P.; B.S., Temple U., 1948; m. Bettina O. Houghton, June 2, 1945; children: Bettina C., Denise E. With Sperry Remington div. Sperry Rand Corp., Phila., also Newark, N.Y.C., 1948-76, eastern regional gen. sales mgr., 1960-63, nat. gen. sales mgr., N.Y.C., 1966-67, dir. mktg., Marietta, Ohio, 1968-71, v.p. mktg., 1972-73, v.p. fed. govt. mktg., Washington, 1973-76; pres. Remco Bus. Systems, Inc., Washington, 1976-95, also chmn. bd.; lectr. Newark High Sch., 1954-56, Belleville (N.J.) High Sch., 1956-58, Fairleigh Dickinson Coll., Paterson, N.J., 1957-58, Pace Coll., N.Y.C., 1965-95, Georgetown U., 1974, ednl. TV, N.Y.C., 1965-95. Dir. Community Fund, Essex Fells, N.J., 1967. Served as 1st lt. with USAF, 1942-45. Decorated Air medal; named Remington Dartnell Salesman of Yr., 1950. Mem. Smithsonian Assocs., Internat. Systems Dealer Assn. (bd. dirs. 1977-78, Founders award 1991), Office Systems Equipment Coop. (pres. 1978-80), Pi Delta Epsilon (pres. 1948). Republican. Methodist. Died Sept. 1, 1995. Home: Annapolis Md.

POWE, RALPH ELWARD, university administrator; b. Tylertown, Miss., July 27, 1944; s. Roy Elward and Virginia Alyne (Bradley) P.; m. Sharon Eve Sandifer, May 20, 1962; children: Deborah Lynn, Ryan Elward, Melanie Colleen. BS in Mech. Engring., Miss. State U., 1967, MS in Mech. Engring., 1968; PhD in Mech. Engring., Mont. State U., 1970. Student trainee NASA, 1962-65; research asst., lab. instr. Miss. State U., 1968, instr. dept. mech. engring., 1968; research asst., teaching asst. Mont. State U., Bozeman, 1968-70, asst. prof. dept. mech. engring., 1970-74; assoc. prof. Miss. State U., 1974-78, prof., 1979-80, assoc. dean engring., dir. engring. and indsl. research sta., 1979-80, assoc. v.p. research, 1980-86, v.p., 1986—; chmn. bd. dirs. Coalition of Experimental Program to Stimulate Competitive Rsch. States, 1994-96; bd. dirs. Gulf Univs. Rsch. Consortium, Tenn.-Tombigbee Project Area Coun.; rep. sch. coun. Nat. Assn. State Univs. and Land Grant Colls., So. Growth Policies Bd., Miss. Mineral Resources Inst., Sci. and Tech. Coun. States. Disting. Engring. fellow Coll. Engring.; active Miss. Univ. Res. Authority, Coun. on Rsch. Policy, So. Growth Policies Bd.; rep. Miss. Mineral Resources Inst.; gov. rep. Sci. and Tech. Coun. of States; cons. energy conservation programs, coal fired power plants, torsional vibrations, accident analysis; dir. Miss. Energy Rsch. Ctr., 1979-81, Ctr. for Environ. Studies, 1980—; univ. rep. on lignite task force, rep. on bd. dirs. Miss.-Ala. Sea Grant Consortium, chmn. of Council Oak Ridge Associated Univs., rep. to Tenn.-Tombigbee project area coun.; chmn. Miss. Rsch. Consortium; mem. S.E. Univs. Rsch. Assn. Named Outstanding Egr., Engring. Socs. Contbr. articles to profl. jours. Mem. Miss. Econ. Coun., univ. coord. United Way, 1983, 85; tchr. adult Sunday Sch. class 1st Bapt. Ch. Recipient Ralph E. Teeter award Soc. Automotive Engrs., Commdr.'s award Pub. Svc. U.S. Dept. Army, 1995; named Outstanding Engr. in No. Miss. Joint Engr. Soc., Pub. Svc. Commdr.'s award U.S. Army. Fellow ASME; mem. Nat. Assn. State Universities and Land Grant Colls., Starkville Cmty. Theatre Wing. Edn., Wind Energy Soc. Am., Miss. Acad. Scis., Miss. Engring. Soc., Toastmasters, Starkville Quarterback Club, Rotary, Starkville C. of C. (bd. dirs.), Blue Key, Sigma Xi (Miss. State U. research award), Tau Beta Pi, Kappa Mu Epsilon, Pi Tau Sigma, Phi Kappa Phi, Omicron Delta Kappa. Baptist. Lodge: Rotary. Avocations: hunting, fishing, gardening. Died Nov., 1996.

POWELL, ALLEN ROYAL, bishop; b. Beaumount, Tex., June 9, 1922; s. Millard and Annie (Surrey) P.; m. Mary Louise Barclay, Dec. 9, 1940; children: Allen R. Jr., Gloria P. Russell, Raymond L., Gwendolyn P. Robinson. Student, Bishop Coll., 1949-51. Pastor Ch. of Living God, Lukin, Tex., 1946-49, Dallas, 1949-51, Kansas City, Kans., 1951-62; dist. overseer Ch. of Living God, Tenn., 1960-66, bishop, 1966-74; bishop Ch. of Living God, Miss., 1974—; pastor Ch. of Living God, Chgo., 1961—, revivalist, counselor, nat. youth instr., exec. bd., Cin., 1966—. Chaplain U.S. Army, 1944-46. Named hon. bishop Five Chs. of Monrovia, 1992. Avocations: printing, singing. Deceased.

POWELL, LOUIS, retail company executive; b. 1923; married. With Alexanders Inc., N.Y.C., 1949—, v.p., then sr. v.p., 1969-82, exec. v.p., 1982-85, co-pres., dir., 1985—. With USN, 1947-49.

POWELL, ROBERT, insurance company executive; b. 1941. With Equitable Life Ins. Co., N.Y.C., 1963-68; sr. v.p. Johnson & Higgins Inc., N.Y.C., 1968-88, pres. A Foster Higgins & Co. Inc. subs., from 1988, chmn. bd., also bd. dirs. died.

POWER, CORNELIUS MICHAEL, archbishop; b. Seattle, Dec. 18, 1913; s. William and Kate (Dougherty) P. Student, St. Patrick Sem., 1933-35, St. Edward Sem., 1935-39; J.C.D., Cath. U. Am., 1943. Ordained priest Roman Catholic Ch., 1939; asst. pastor St. James Cathedral, Seattle, 1939-40; resident chaplain Holy Names Acad., Seattle, 1943-52; adminstr. Parish of Our Lady of Lake, Seattle, 1955-56; pastor Parish of Our Lady of Lake, 1956-69; vice chancellor Archdiocese of Seattle, 1943-51, chancellor, 1951-69; apptd. domestic prelate, 1963, 2d bishop of Yakima, 1969, bishop of Yakima, 1969-74; archbishop Portland, Oreg., 1974-86; ret., 1986. Home: Portland Oreg. Deceased.

POWLEY, GEORGE REINHOLD, electrical engineering educator; b. New London, O., Mar. 7, 1916; s. George Starling and Rose (Maier) P.; m. Beverly Carper, July 20, 1940; children: Rosemary, George, Robert, Ann. B.S. in Elec. Engring, Va. Poly. Inst., 1938, M.S. in Elec. Engring, 1939. Engaged in induction motor design, electro-dynamic works Electric Boat Co., 1939; test engr., control engr. Gen. Electric Co., 1939-41, control engr., 1945-48; prof. elec. engring. Va. Polytech. Inst., 1949-81, head dept., 1958-64, Westinghouse prof. elec. engring., 1964-81, chmn. elec. engring. tech. program, 1974-81; vis. prof. elec. engring. Va. Mil. Inst., 1981, 83-84. Pres. Giles Gideon Camp, Giles County, Va., 1959-60. Served to capt. AUS, 1941-45; lt. col. Res. Recipient W.E. Wine-award for faculty achievement Va. Polytech. Inst., 1957, named to Acad. for Teaching Excellence, 1974. Mem. IEEE (sr.), Virginia Gideons (1st v.p. 1968, state pres. 1971-73), Omicron Delta Kappa, Tau Beta Pi, Eta Kappa Nu, Phi Kappa Phi (local pres. 1960-61). Home: Blacksburg Va. Died July 30, 1992.

POYNER, JAMES MARION, retired lawyer; b. Raleigh, N.C., Sept. 18, 1914; s. James Marion and Mary (Smedes) P.; m. Florence I Chan, Feb. 24, 1945; children: Susan Poyner Moore, Chan Poyner Pike, Margaret Poyner Galbraith, Edythe Poyner Lumdsen, James Marion III. BSChemE, N.C. State U., 1935, MS, 1937; JD, Duke U., 1940. Bar: N.C. 1940. Pvt. practice Raleigh, 1946-51; ptnr. Poyner, Geraghty, Hartsfield & Townsend, Raleigh, 1951-86; of counsel Poyner & Spruill, Raleigh, 1986-95, ret., 1995; co-founder Cameron-Brown Co. (now 1st Union Mortgage Co.); life dir. 1st Union Corp., 1st Union Nat. Bank; chmn. bd. dirs. Eastern Standard Ins. Co., George Smedes Poyner Founds. Inc. Orch. leader, trombonist, arranger, Jimmy Poyner and His Orch., 1933-38. Mem. N.C. Senate, 1955-59; Past chmn. bd. trustees St. Mary's Coll.; past chmn. bd. World Golf Hall of Fame; past chmn. trustees N.C. Symphony Soc. Served with Chem. Warfare Service, AUS, 1942-46. Decorated Legion of Merit. Mem. ABA, N.C. Bar Assn. (pres. 1967-68, dir. 1963-67), Am. Judicature Soc. (dir. 1973-77), Raleigh C. of C. (past pres.), Phi Kappa Phi. Episcopalian. Died Dec. 30, 1997.

PRELOG, VLADIMIR, chemist; b. Sarajevo, Bosnia, Yugoslavia, July 23, 1906; s. Milan and Mara (Cettolo) P.; m. Kamila Vítek, Oct. 31, 1933; 1 child, Jan. Chem. Engring. degree, Inst. Tech. Sch. Chemistry, Prague, Czechoslovakia, 1928, D Chem. Engring., 1929; D honoris causa, U. Zagreb, Yugoslavia, 1954, U. Liverpool, Eng., U. Paris, 1963, Cambridge U., U. Brussels, 1969, U. Manchester, 1971, Inst. Quim. Sarria, Barcelona, 1978, Weizmann Inst., Rehovot, 1985, U. Ljubljana, Yugoslavia, 1989, U. Osijek, Yugoslavia, 1989, U. Chem. Tech., Prague, 1992; U. Sarajevo, 1996. Chemist Lab. G.J. Driza, Prague, 1929-35; docent U. Zagreb, 1935-40, assoc. prof., 1940-41; mem. faculty Swiss Fed. Inst. Tech., Zurich, 1942—, prof. chemistry, 1950—, head Lab. Organic Chemistry,, 1957-65, ret., 1976; bd. dir. CIBA Geigy Ltd., Basel, Switzerland, 1963-78. Recipient Werner medal, 1945, Stas medal, 1962, medal of honour Rice U., 1962, Marcel Benoist award, 1965, A.W. Hofmann medal, 1968, Davy medal, 1968, Roger Adams prize, 1969, Nobel prize for chemistry, 1975, Paracelsus medal, 1976. Fellow Royal Soc.; mem. Am. Acad. Arts and Scis. (hon.), Nat. Acad. Scis. (fgn. assoc.), Acad. dei Lincei (Rome)(fgn.), Leopoldina, Halle/Saale, Acad. Scis. USSR (fgn.), Royal Irish Acad. (hon.), Royal Danish Acad. Scis. (hon.), Acad. Pharm. Scis. (hon.), Am. Philos. Soc., Acad. Scis. (Paris)(fgn.), Pontificia Acad. Sci. (Rome), Russian Acad. Sci. (fgn.). Research, numerous publs. on constn. and stereochemistry alkaloids, antibiotics, enzymes, other natural compounds, alicyclic chemistry, chem. topology.

PRESCOTT, ORVILLE, author; b. Cleve., Sept. 8, 1906; s. Orville Wilbur and Eda (Sherwin) P.; m. Lilias Ward-Smith, Nov. 1, 1933; children: Peter Sherwin, Jennifer (Mrs. Edward C. McLean, Jr.). B.A., Williams Coll., 1930, LL.D., 1963. Mng. editor, sports, art, and book columnist Cleve. Town Tidings, 1931-33; mem. editorial staff Newsweek mag., 1933-36; asso. editor, lit. editor Cue mag., 1936-47; co-editor N.Y. Times Books of the Times, 1942-66; lectr. lit. subjects, 1940-54; fiction reviewer Yale Rev., 1943-49. Author: In My Opinion: An Inquiry into the Contemporary Novel, 1952, The Five-Dollar Gold Piece: The Development of a Point of View, 1956, Mid-Century: An Anthology of Distinguished Contemporary American Short Stories, 1958, The Undying Past, 1961, A Father Reads To His Children, 1965, Princes of the Renaissance, 1969, History as Literature, 1971, Lords of Italy: Portraits from the Middle Ages, 1972. Mem. Authors League, Soc. Am. Historians, Century Assn. Club (N.Y.C.), Country Club New Canaan, Yeamans Hall Club (North Charleston). Home: North Branford Conn. Died April 28, 1996.

PRESS, VOLKER, history educator; b. Erding, Bavaria, Germany, Mar. 28; s. Eugen and Elisabeth (Harsch) P. PhD, U. Munich, 1966. Asst. prof. U. Kiel, Germany, 1967-68, U. Frankfurt, Germany, 1968-71; prof. U. Giessen, Germany, 1971-80, U. Tuebingen, Germany, 1980—. Author: Calvinistitus und Territorial Staat Regierurg dek Kurpfalz, 1970, Kaiser Karl J. Konig Ferdinand und Die Entstehung der Reichsritterschaft, 1976, Das Reichskammergericht in der Deutschen 1600-1775, 1991. Mem. Akademie der Wissenschaften Heidelberg and Erfurt. Mem. Evangelist Ch.

PRESTON, FREDERICK WILLARD, surgeon; b. Chgo., June 27, 1912; s. Frederick Augustus and Margaret (Atwater) P.; m. Gertrude Eldred Bradford, June 23, 1942 (div. 1961); children: Frederick Willard Jr., David E. (dec. 1994), William B.; m. Barbara Gay Hess, July 30, 1961. BA, Yale U., 1935; MD, Northwestern U., 1940, MS, 1942; MS, U. Minn., 1947. Intern Presbyn. Hosp., Chgo., 1940-41; fellow surgery Mayo Clinic, Rochester, Minn., 1941-42, 46-48; pvt. practice surgery Chgo., 1968-75; mem. surg. faculty Northwestern U. Med. Sch., 1949-75, prof. surgery, 1960-75; assoc. attending surgeon Northwestern Meml. Hosp., 1950-75; attending surgeon Skokie Valley Community Hosp., 1964-75, Henrotin Hosp., 1950-75; chief surg. svc. VA Rsch. Hosp., Chgo., 1953-68; mem. Supreme Acad. Coun. Ofcl. U. Congo, Lubumbashi, 1965-71; chmn. dept. surgery Santa Barbara Gen. Hosp., 1975-78; dir. surg. edn. Santa Barbara Cottage Hosp., 1975-83; rsch. physiologist U. Calif., Santa Barbara, 1976-84. Author, editor: Basic Surgical Physiology, Loose-Leaf Practice of Surgery, Manual of Ambulatory Surgery; cons. editor Internat. Surg. Digest, 1969-70, contbr. numerous articles to profl. jours. Bd. dirs. Schweppe Found., Love Med. Rsch., English Speaking Union, Chgo. chpt., 1960-65; gov. mem., mem. planning com. Shedd Aquarium, 1968-75. 1st lt. to maj. M.C., AUS, 1942-46. Fellow ACS (chpt. pres. 1965-66); mem. AMA, AAAS, Chgo. Surg. Soc. (sec. 1961-64, pres. 1968-69), Chgo. Acad. Scis. (sec. 1963-67), Am. Assn. Cancer Research (pres. Chgo. sec. 1963-64), Am. Geriatrics Soc., Am. Fedn. Clin. Research, Am. Surg. Assn., Central Surg. Assn., Western Surg. Assn. (coun.), Pacific Coast Surg. Assn., Pan Pacific Surg. Assn., Société Internationale de Chirurgie, Soc. Surgery Alimentary Tract, Santa Barbara Club, La Cumbre Golf and Country Club, Chgo. Literary Club, Univ. Club (Chgo.), Sigma Xi. Republican. Episcopalian. DIED 02/02/96. .

PREUS, JACOB AALL OTTESEN, former seminary president and church executive; b. St. Paul, Jan. 8, 1920; s. J. A. O. and Idella (Haugen) P.; m. Delpha Holleque, June 12, 1943; children: Patricia (Mrs. Gerhard Bode), Delpha (Mrs. George Harris), Carolin (Mrs. Jerold Misner), Sarah (Mrs. Dennis Schwab), Idella (Mrs. Mark Moberg), Mary (Mrs. William Churchill), Jacob, Margaret (Mrs. Steve Jones). B.A., Luther Coll., 1941; B.D., Luther Sem., 1945; M.A., U. Minn., 1946, Ph.D., 1951. Ordained to ministry Luth. Ch., 1945. Pastor South St. Paul, Minn., 1945-46; prof. Bethany Coll., Mankato, Minn., 1947-50, 56-58; pastor Luverne, Minn., 1950-56; prof. Concordia Theol. Sem., Springfield, Ill., 1958-69; pres. Concordia Theol. Sem., 1962-69, Luth. Ch. Mo. Synod, 1969-81; mem. constituting com. Luth. Coun. in U.S.A. Author: The Second Martin, 1994; translator: Luther Commentary on Romans, Chemnitz: The Lord's Supper, The Two Natures of Christ, On Justification, Loci Theologici, Melanchthon: Loci Communes 1543; contbg. author: The Doctrine of God, 1962; contbr. articles to theol. jours.

PRICE, CHARLES GRATTAN, JR., retired insurance agency executive; b. Harrisonburg, Va., May 31, 1919; s. Charles Grattan and Julia Page (Pleasants) P.; m. Kathleen Violette Nutter Price, Mar. 15, 1940 (dec. 1992); children: Julia Kathleen, Melinda Marshall, Charles Grattan III. BS in Mech. Engring., Va. Poly. Inst., Blacksburg, 1940. Mech. engr. Chesapeake Western Ry., Harrisonburg, Va., 1940-41; officer U.S. Army, 1941-45; cons. pvt. practice, Vt., Pa., 1946; with ins. agy. C.G. Price & Sons, Inc., Harrisonburg, Va., 1946-78; ret., 1978; ind. railroad dieselization survey cons., 1946-47. Author: The Crooked and Weedy, 1992, Reminiscences of a Rambling Railroader, 1993, Robert E. Lee's Railroad, 1994. Maj. USAR, 1947-54. Mem. Rlwy. and Locomotive Hist. Soc., Nat. Rlwy. Hist. Soc., Railroadiana Collectors Assn., Elks (lodge 450), Am. Legion (post 27). Presbyterian. Avocations: reading, historical railroad research and writing. Died June 12, 1996.

PRICE, EDWARD DEAN, federal judge; b. Sanger, Calif., Feb. 12, 1919; s. Earl Trousdale and Daisy Shaw (Biggs) P.; m. Katherine S. Merritt, July 18, 1943; children: Katherine Price O'Brien, Edward M., Jane E. B.A., U. Calif., Berkeley, 1947, LL.B., 1949. Bar: Calif. 1949. Assoc. Cleary & Zeff, Modesto, Calif., 1949-51; assoc. Zeff & Halley, Modesto, Calif., 1951-54; ptnr. Zeff, Halley & Price, Modesto, Calif., 1954-63, Zeff & Price, Modesto, Calif., 1963-65, Price & Martin, Modesto, Calif., 1965-69, Price, Martin & Crabtree, Modesto, Calif., 1969-79; judge U.S. Dist. Ct., Fresno, Calif., 1980-90, sr. judge, 1990—; mem. adv. bd. governing com. Continuing Edn. of Bar, San Francisco, 1963-71, governing bd. Calif. State Bar, 1973-76; v.p. Jud. Council, Calif., 1978-79. Contbr. articles to profl. jours. Served with U.S. Army, 1943-46. Mem. ABA, Am. Coll. Trial Lawyers, Am. Bd. Trial Advocates. Democrat. Methodist. Died Nov. 3, 1997.

PRICE, GEORGE, cartoonist; b. Coytesville, N.J., June 9, 1901; s. George and Camille (Vidal) P.; m. Florence Schwank, Dec. 8, 1927; children: George, Wilfrid, Charles, Susan. Ed high sch., Ft. Lee, N.J. Various positions all branches of advt. art, printing, lithography, art service, agy., and free lance work, 1920-29. Cartoonist, book illustrator.; Author and illustrator: Good Humor Man, 1940, It's Smart to be People, 1942, Who's in Charge Here?, 1943, Is It Anyone We Know?, 1944, Geo. Price's Ice-Cold War, 1951, We Buy Old Gold, 1952, George Price's Characters, 1955, My Dear 500 Friends, 1963, The People Zoo, 1971, Browse At Your Own Risk, 1977, The World of George Price, 1988; Contbr. to: New Yorker mag, 1929-95. Home: Tenafly N.J. Died Jan. 12, 1995.

PRICE, PATRICIA ANNE, artist; b. Tulsa, Feb. 4, 1950; d. Max Edward and Katharine (Jordan) P. BA, Oral Roberts U., 1974. Pvt. practice oil and gas lease broker Burleson County, Tex., 1978-84; rsch. and sale clk. The Kiva Indian Arts, Santa Fe, 1984-90; owner, mgr. Singing Coyote-Southwestern Art, Santa Fe, 1992-96. Exhibited in Romanian Libr., N.Y.C., 1975, Boston (Mass.) Coll., 1975, S.W. Tex. State, San Marcos, 1977, Ohio State U., Columbus, 1977. East European scholar, S.W. Tex. State U., 1977, Romania Ministry of Tourism scholar, 1976. Mem. Women's Divsn. Aux. C. of C. Santa Fe, The Cherokee Nation (tribal mem.), VFW Women's Aux., Am. Legion Women's Aux. Died Jan. 6, 1996.

PRIESTLEY, JOHN BOYNTON, author; b. Bradford, Eng., Sept. 13, 1894; M.A., Trinity Hall, Cambridge; LL.D. (hon.); D.Litt. (hon.). Author: (fiction) Adam in Moonshine, 1927; Benighted, 1927; Farthing Hall (with Hugh Walpole), 1929; The Good Companions, 1929; Angel Pavement, 1930; The Town Major of Miraucourt, 1930; Faraway, 1932; I'll Tell You Everthing (with Gerald Bullett), 1933; Wonder Hero, 1933; Albert Goes Through, 1933; They Walk in the City, 1936; Let the People Sing, 1939; Black-out in Gretley, 1942; Daylight on Saturday, 1943; (plays) (with Edward Knoblock) The Good Companions, 1931; Dangerous Corner, 1932; The Roundabout, 1933; Laburnum Grove, 1934; Eden End, 1934; Cornelius, 1935; Bees on the Boat Deck, 1936; Time and the Conways, 1937; I Have Been Here Before, 1937; When We Are Married, 1938; Music at Night, 1938; Johnson Over Jordan, 1939; The Long Mirror, 1940; Goodnight Children, 1941; They Came to a City, 1943; (miscellaneous), Brief Diversions, 1922; Papers from Lilliput, 1922; I for One, 1923; Figures in Modern Literature, 1924; The English Comic Characters, 1925; Meredith, 1926; Talking, 1926; Peacock, 1927; Open House, 1927; English Humor, 1928; Apes and Angels, 1928; The Balconinny, 1929; English Journey, 1934; Midnight on the Desert, 1937; Rain Upon Godshill, 1939; Postscripts, 1940; Out of the People, 1941; Three Men in New Suits, 1945; Bright Day, 1946; (plays) Desert Highway, 1944; How Are They at Home'9 , An Inspector Calls, Ever Since Paradise, 1946; Arts Under Socialism, Jenny Villiers, Theatre Outlook, (play), The Linden Tree, 1947; (play) Home is Tomorrow, 1948; (play) Summer Days Dream, Delight, (libetto of opera) The Olympians, 1949; Festival, 1951; Last Holiday, 1952; Dragon's Mouth (with J. Hawkes), 1952; The Other Place, 1953; The Magicians, 1954; Low Notes on a High Level, 1954; (plays) Take the Fool Away, Mr. Kettle and Mrs. Moon, 1955; (with J. Hawkes) Journey Down a Rainbow, 1955; (play) The Glass Cage, 1957; The Art of the Dramatist, 1957; Literature and Western Man, 1960; Saturn Over the Water, The Thirty-first of June, 1961; The Shapes of Sleep, 1962; Margin Released, 1962; (play) (with Iris Murdoch) A Severed Head, 1963; Man and Time, 1964; (fiction) Lost Empires, 1965; Salt is Leaving, 1966; The Moment and Other Pieces, 1966; It's An Old Country, 1967; Out of Town (vol. 1 of The Image Men), 1968; London End (vol. 2 of The Image Men); 1968; Trumpet Over the Sea, 1968; Essays of Five Decades, 1969; The Prince of Pleasure, 1969; The Edwardians, 1970; Victoria's Heyday, 1971; (juvenile) Snoogle, 1971; Over the Long High Wall, 1972; A Visit to New Zealand, 1974; Outcries and Asides, 1974; Particular Pleasures, 1975; The Carfitt Crisis, 1975; Found, Lost, Found, 1976; English Humour, 1976; Instead of the Trees, 1977. Club: Savile (London).

PRINCE, ROBERT MASON, financial executive; b. Madison, Wis., Oct. 22, 1914; s. Robert Ellsworth and Florence Elizabeth (Mason) P.; AB, U. Mich., 1936; JD, Detroit Coll. Law, 1939; m. Elizabeth Harvey Sherk, 1937; children: Dana, Kathy; m. Sheila Anna Hoban, 1973. Accountant, Haskins & Sells, CPAs, Am. Surety Co., Detroit, 1937-41; admitted to Mich. bar, 1939, Ill. bar, 1948; mem. exec. and legal dept., atty.-mgr. ins. dept., also mgr. govt. controls Dow Chem. Co., 1941-47; engaged in ins., Chgo., 1947-49; ptnr. firm Norman, Engelhardt, Zimmerman & Prince, and predecessor, Chgo., 1949-57; exec. v.p. Devel. Corp. Am. and subs. Acorn Paint & Chem. Co., 1957-58; v.p., dir. Bankers Life and Casualty Co., Chgo., 1958-61; chmn. bd. Am. Airmotive Corp., Shasta Cattle Co., Greengold Farms, Inc., 1958-61; pres. Datronics, Inc., Nat. Drilling Co., Fla. Aviation Corp., 1958-61; dir. Chgo. City Bank & Trust Co., 1959-61; vice chmn. bd. Diversa, Inc., Dallas, 1959-63; chmn. bd. Prince & Cummins, Inc., Chgo., 1962-65, Prince Roosevelt & Cummins, Miami, Fla., 1962-64; asst. to pres. Dow Chem. Internat., 1963-65; dir. Investment svcs. exec. dept. Dow Chem. Co., 1965-69; v.p. ventures investment, fin. div. Dow Chem., 1969-72; v.p., dir. Dow Chem. Fin. Corp., 1966-72, Dolco Packaging Corp., North Hollywood, Calif., 1967-72; chmn. bd. Austral-Pacific Fertilizers, Ltd., Brisbane, Queensland, Australia, 1968-70; dir. Austral-Pacific Fertilizers, Ltd., 1966-72; with affiliates cos. Valley Nat. Bank Phoenix; v.p., gen. mgr., dir. Concho Investment Corp., Concho Life Ins. Co., 1972-75; mng. dir. Prince & Co., 1975-87; atty., of counsel firm Martin, Craig, Chester and Sonnenschein, Chgo., 1975-85; pres. Phoenix Chem. Co. East Dubuque, Ill., 1987-90, dir., 1987-93; with Internat. Consulting Svcs. Mem. Ill., Mich. bar assns. Club: Union League (Chgo.). Died, Sept. 12, 1995. Home: Scottsdale Ariz.

PRINCE, WARREN VICTOR, mechanical engineer; b. Kansas City, Mo., May 21, 1911; s. Charles William and Bertha (Lybarger) P.; m. Edna Skinner Scott, Aug. 31, 1975; children—Charlotte E. Prince Smith, Leslie Warren (dec.), Charles Allan, Charlene Diane Prince Tercovich. Student engring. Baker U., 1931-34, BA (hon.), 1995. Registered mech. engr., Calif. Design engr. Hoover Co., North Canton, Ohio, 1934-39; tool and machine design Thompson Products, Inc., Cleve., 1939-41; devel. engr. The Acrotorque Co., 1941-42; asst. chief devel. engr. The Weatherhead Co., 1942-45; pres. Prince Indsl. Plastics Corp., 1945-46; cons. engr., mech., plastics and plant prodn. problems, Kansas City and Los Angeles, 1946-50; project engr. Aerojet Gen. Corp., 1950-63, chief engr. Deposilube Mfg. Co., 1963-65; cons., 1965-66; sr. mech. engr. Avery Label Co., 1966-68; sr. project engr. machine design projects AMF, Inc., 1969-72; mech. cons. engr. as machine and product design specialist, 1972-80; pres. Contour Spltys., Inc., 1980-85; v.p. mech. engring. HEP Inc., 1985-88, mechanical cons. engr., 1988-95; evening instr. Mt. San Antonio Coll., 1954-93, alternate pres., mgr. of rsch. and devel. Progressive Household Products, Inc. Recipient Soc. Plastics Engrs. 1948 Nat. award for establishing basic laws of plastic molding process, Commendable Recognition award First Internat. Conf. on Machine Tech., Hong Kong, 1991. Mem. ASME, ASTM (D28 com.), Kappa Sigma. Presbyterian. Lodges: Masons, Shriners, Rotary. Contbr. articles to profl. jours. Patentee in field. Achievements include an explanation of break through performance with a new principle of anti-friction. Died Dec. 6, 1995. Home: Anaheim Calif.

PRINSLOO, WILLEM STERRENBERG, theology educator, minister; b. Vrede, South Africa, Aug. 19, 1944; s. Jakobus Lukas and Magrieta P.; m. Jean Avrille De Klerk, Oct. 1, 1970; children: Jakobus, Karen, Marieta. BA, U. Pretoria, South Africa, 1965, BD, 1968, DD, 1976. Ordained to ministry, Dutch Ref. Ch., 1969. Minister Duth Ref. Ch., Standerton, South Africa, 1971-74; prof. theology U. Pretoria, 1975—, dean faculty of theology, 1989—. Author: The Theology of the Book of Joel, 1985. Alexander Von Humboldt scholar, 1982-83. Mem. Old Testament Soc. South Africa (sec. 1986-89, chmn. 1990—), Soc. of Bibl. Lit. Avocation: tennis. Died Oct. 5, 1997.

PRITCHARD, ARTHUR OSBORN, retired business administrator; b. Scarsdale, N.Y., Oct. 7, 1910; m. Dorothy E. White (dec.); m. Virginia R. Cunningham (div.). AB, Pomona Coll., 1932; MA in Internat. Rels., Columbia U., 1934. With Dept. Agr. and Gen. Acctg. Office U.S. Govt., Washington, 1934-36, Berkeley, Calif., 1936-41; staff sgt., Army Med. Corp. U.S. Army, 1941-45; pub. acctg. pvt. practice, 1945; acct. and office mgr. Talbot Bird & Co., SF, 1946-60; treas. and bus. mgr. No. Calif. Conf. of United Ch. of Christ, 1960-76; ret., 1976; participant UN Film Study Guide project, 1991-93, 94-95. Mem. Outlook Club of Calif. 1948-95, sec., 1967-93; bd. dirs, Berkeley City Club, 1977-83, pres., 1978-82; instr. of adult edn. Berkeley YMCA; pres. 1989 program, City Commons Club of Berkeley; program dir., 1991-95; active mem. First Congl. Ch. of Berkeley, 19380-95; life mem. Commonwealth Club, 1939-95. Decorated Bronze Star; Team Facilitator grantee U.S. Inst. of Peace, Washington, 1991-93. Mem. Am. Assn. for the UN, UN Assn. of the U.S. of Am. (pres. Alameda County chpt., 1956-59, No. Calif. Divsn. of UNA-USA, 1959-65, received citation), World Affairs Coun. of No. Calif. (charter mem. 1947). Home: Berkeley Calif. Died Jan. 31, 1995.

PRITCHARD, JAMES BENNETT, archaeologist, educator, author; b. Louisville, Oct. 4, 1909; s. John Hayden and Mary (Bennett) P.; m. Anne Elizabeth Cassedy, June 30, 1937; children: Sarah Anne (Mrs. Robert F. Hayman), Mary Bennett (Mrs. Clifton Mitchell). AB, Asbury Coll., 1930; BD, Drew U., 1935; PhD, U. Pa., 1942, LHD (hon.), 1991; STD, Phila. Div. Sch., 1961; DD, Ch. Div. Sch. of Pacific, 1962; LHD (hon.), Swarthmore Coll., 1977; DD (hon.), U. Uppsala, Sweden, 1977. Prof. O.T. lit. Crozer Theol. Sem., 1942-54; ann. prof. Am. Sch. Oriental Research, Jerusalem, 1950-51; archeol. dir. expdn. to Jericho, Jordan, 1951; vis. prof. Am. Sch. Oriental Research, 1956-57, 61-62; dir. expdns. to el-Jib, Jordan, 1956-62; to Tell es-Sa'idiyeh, Jordan, 1964-67, Am. Sch. Oriental Research, Sarafand, Lebanon, 1969, 70, 71, 72, 74; prof. O.T. lit. Ch. Div. Sch. Pacific, 1954-62; curator Bib. archeology Univ. Mus., 1962-78, assoc. dir., 1967-76, dir., 1976-77; prof. religious thought U. Pa., 1962-78; Winslow lectr. Gen. Theol. Sem., 1960; Fulbright-Hays vis. prof. archaeology Am. U. Beirut, 1966-67; mem. Inst. Advanced Study, Princeton, N.J., 1978; Sec., Am. Schs. Oriental Research, 1963-71. Author: Palestinian Figurines, 1943, Ancient Near Eastern Texts, 1950, 55, 69, The Ancient Near East in Pictures, 1954, 69, Archaeology and the Old Testament, 1958, The Excavation at Herodian Jericho, 1958, The Ancient Near East, 1958, vol. 2, 1975, Hebrew Inscriptions from Gibeon, 1959, The Water System at Gibeon, 1961, Gibeon, Where the Sun Stood Still, 1962, Bronze Age Cemetery at Gibeon, 1963, Winery, Defenses and Soundings at Gibeon, 1964, Sarepta, 1975, Recovering Sarepta, A Phoenician City, 1978, The Cemetery at Tell es-Sa'idiyeh, 1980, Excavations on the Tell, 1964-66, 1985, The Times Atlas of the Bible, 1987, The Times Concise Atlas of the Bible, 1991, Sarepta IV, 1988, The Harper Concise Atlas of the Bible, 1991; assoc. editor: Jour. Am. Oriental Soc, 1948-52; editor, 1952-54. Trustee Am. U. Beirut, 1970-79. Decorated Order of Istiqlal, 1st Class Jordan, 1964. Mem. Am. Philos. Soc. (Benjamin Franklin medal 1990), Am. Oriental Soc., Archeol. Inst. Am. (pres. 1973, 74, Disting. Archeol. Achievement award 1983). Clubs: Franklin Inn, Penn. Died Jan. 1, 1997.

PRITCHARD, JOEL, state lieutenant governor; b. Seattle, May 5, 1925; children: Peggy, Frank, Anne, Jeanie. Student, Marietta Coll.; PhD (Hon.), Seattle U. Pres. Griffin Envelope Co., Seattle; mem. Wash. Ho. of Reps., Olympia, 1958-66, Wash. State Senate, 1966-70, U.S. Ho. of Reps., Washington, 1972-84; dir. govt. rels. Bogle & Gates, 1985-88; lt. gov. State of Wash., Olympia, 1989—; mem. Merchant Marine and Fisheries Com. U.S. Ho. of Reps., subcom. on Asia and the Pacific Fgn. Rels. Com., Panama Canal Consultative Commn., 1987-88; U.S. del. to UN Gen. Assembly, 1983. With U.S. Army, PTO, WWII. DIED 10/09/97.
.

PRITCHETT, CHARLES HERMAN, political science educator; b. Latham, Ill., Feb. 9, 1907; s. Charles and Anna Margaret (Nottelmann) P.; m. Marguerite A. Lentner, July 27, 1937; children: Jean Charla, Philip Lentner. AB, Millikin U., 1926; PhD, U. Chgo., 1937. Rsch. asst. U. Chgo., 1934, asst. prof. polit. sci., 1940-46, assoc. prof., 1946-52, prof., 1952-69, acting chmn. dept., 1948-49, chmn. dept., 49-55, 58-64; rsch. assoc. TVA, 1934-37; rsch. assoc. pub. adminstrn. com. Social Sci. Rsch. Coun., 1937-38, post-doctoral research fellow, 1938-39; Ford prof. govtl. affairs, 1958-59; Bacon lectr. constn. Boston U., 1957; Dillon lectr. law and govt. U. S.D., 1957; Guy Stanton Ford lectr. U. Minn., 1959; vis. prof. Stanford, 1966; prof. U. Calif. at, Santa Barbara, 1965-67, 69-89; faculty rsch. lectr. U. Calif., 1975, emeritus prof., 1975-89. Author: The Tennessee Valley Authority: A Study in Public Administration, 1943, The Roosevelt Court, 1948, Civil Liberties and the Vinson Court, 1954, The Political Offender and the Warren Court, 1958, The American Constitution, 3d edit, 1977, Congress Versus the Supreme Court, 1960, Courts Judges and Politics, 4th edit, 1986, American Constitutional Issues, 1962, The Third Branch of Government 1963, The American Constitutional System, 5th edit 1981; co-author: The Revolutionary Theme in Contemporary America, 1965, American Government in

World Perspective, 5th edit., 1981, The Presidency Reappraised, 2d edit., 1977, The Federal System in Constitutional Law, 1978, Essays on the Constitution of the United States, 1978, Constitutional Civil Liberties, 1984; Contbr. articles to sci. revs. Dir. Nat. Endowment for Humanities summer seminar, 1975; Residential Fellowships seminar, 1977; adminstrv. analyst Dept. Labor, 1939; Staff Commn. Orgn. Exec. Branch Govt. (Hoover Commn.), 1948. Fellow Am. Acad. Arts and Scis.; mem. Am. Polit. Sci. Assn. (pres. 1963-64), Am. Bar Assn. (com. electoral coll. reform 1966). Home: Santa Barbara Calif. Died Apr. 28, 1995.

PRITCHETT, SIR VICTOR SAWDON, author; b. Ipswich, Eng., Dec. 16, 1900; s. Sawdon and Beatrice (Martin) P.; m. Dorothy Roberts, Oct. 2, 1936; children: Josephine, Oliver. Ed., Alleyn's Sch., Dulwich; D.Litt. (hon.), Leeds U., 1973, Columbia U., 1978, U. Sussex, 1980, Harvard U., 1985. Free-lance journalist France, Ireland, Spain and U.S., 1921-28; lit. critic New Statesman, London, 1928-78; dir. New Statesman, 1951-78; Christian Gauss lectr. Princeton U., 1953; Beckman prof. U. Calif., Berkeley, 1960; writer-in-residence Smith Coll., 1966-71; Zisskind prof. Brandeis U., Waltham, Mass., 1969; vis. prof. Sch. Fine Arts, Columbia U., 1972; Clark lectr. Cambridge (Eng.) U., 1969, Vanderbilt U., 1981. Author: Marching Spain, 1928, Clare Drummer, 1929, The Spanish Virgin, 1930, Elopement into Exile, 1932, Nothing Like Leather, 1935, You Make Your Own Life, 1938, It May Never Happen, 1945, The Living Novel, 1949, Mr. Beluncle, 1951, The Spanish Temper, 1954, Books in General, 1962, In My Good Books, 1953, The Working Novelist, 1965, When My Girl Comes Home, 1961, Dead Man Leading, 1949, The Key to My Heart, 1963, London Perceived, 1962, The Offensive Traveller, 1964, New York Proclaimed, 1965, (with Elizabeth Bowen and Graham Greene) Why Do I Write?, 1948, Dublin: A Portrait, 1967, A Cab at the Door, 1967, Blind Love, 1970, Meredith's English Comedy, 1970, Midnight Oil, 1971, Balzac, 1973, The Camberwell Beauty, 1974, The Gentle Barbarian: Turgenev: Selected Stories, 1978, The Myth Makers, 1979, On the Edge of the Cliff, 1980, The Tale Bearers (essays), 1980, Collected Stories, 1981, More Collected Stories, 1983, The Turn of the Year, 1984, The Oxford Book of Short Stories, 1981, Man of Letters (essays), 1986, Chekhov, 1987, A Careless Widow, 1989, At Home and Abroad, 1989, Lasting Impressions (essays), 1990, Complete Short Stories, 1990, Complete Essays, 1992; contbr. stories to leading mags. Decorated comdr. Order Brit. Empire, 1968, created knight, 1975, Companion of Honor, 1993; recipient Royal Soc. Lit. award, 1969, 87, W.H. Smith award, 1990, Elmer Holmes Bobst award NYU, 1991, Golden Pen award Internat. PEN, 1993. Mem. Soc. Authors (pres. 1978). Clubs: Savile (London), Beefsteak (London). Died Mar. 20, 1997.

PRITIKIN, ROLAND I., ophthalmologic surgeon, writer, lecturer; b. Chgo., Jan. 9, 1906; s. Edward and Bluma (Saval) P.; m. Jeanne DuPre Moore, May 25, 1940 (dec. May 1988); children: Gloria Anne, Karin (Mrs. Craig Howard Heiser). B.S., Loyola U., 1928, M.D., 1930; diploma, U.S. Army Command and Gen. Staff Coll., 1964. Diplomate: Am. Bd. Ophthalmology. Eye department Loyola U. School Medicine, 1933-35; resident Ill. Eye and Ear Infirmary, 1936-38, staff 1939-48; vis. eye surgeon Shikarpur, Sind, Pakistan, under Sir Henry Holland, 1939, 57, 60, 63, 66, 71, vis. eye surgeon Ethiopia, 1972; cons. Rockford industries, 1946-96; pvt. practice ophthalmology Rockford, 1946-96; pres. staff Winnebago County (Ill.) Hosp., 1950; lecture, research tour, Western Europe, Near and Middle East, 1951, vis. eye surgeon, Pakistan, 1960; cons. in ophthalmology IHS; hearing officer Social Security Adminstrn.; vis. eye clinics Vienna, Zurich, Paris, 1934. Author: Essentials of Ophthalmology, 1950, 3d edit., 1975, World War Three Is Inevitable, 1976; contbr. Ency. Commander supplements, 1946-80, reg. vols., 1955-72, articles on ophthalmology various med. jours., also sects. on spectacles and contact lenses to Acad. Am. Ency. Med. Res. Officers; chmn. meeting on computers in ophthalmology Internat. Symposium on Bio-Engring. in Ophthalmology, Haifa, Israel, 1975, Ctr. For Global Security, 1978-96; life mem. Weizmann Inst., Sci. Served s col. M.C. AUS, 1941-45; brig. gen. Ill. N.G. Recipient 1st award World Medical Assn., 1964; Quetta Mission Hosp. medal, 1964; Physician's Recognition award AMA, 1972, 75, 77, 83, 86, 89, 92, Cert. award FW, 1986, Cert. award Chapel of the Four Chaplains, 1980, Super Sr. award Winnebago County Coun. on Aging, 1991, Cert. Appreciation for 25 yrs. vol. cons. ophthalmology U.S. Army Health Svcs. Command; named Commodore State of W.Va., 1980, Ky. Col., 1982; decorated Army Commendation medal, 1965, Order St. John of Jerusalem by Queen Elizabeth II, 1970; promoted to Comdr. by Queen Elizabeth II, 1993. Fellow Indsl. Med. Assn., Am. Med. Writers Assn., soc. Mil. Ophthalmologists (bd. govs., 1st life), AMA, A.C.S., Internat. Coll. Surgeons, AAAS, Am. Geriatrics soc., Royal Soc. Health, Am. Coll. Nuclear Medicine distinguished mem., founding mem.), Instituto Barraquer, Barcelona; assoc. Royal Soc. Medicine London; em. Internat. Assn. Secs. Ophthalmol. and Otoryngol. Socs. (editor ophthalmology 1973-80), Ill., Winnebago County med. socs., Am. Nuclear Soc., Am. cad. Ophthalmology and Otolaryngology, Chgo. phthal. Soc., Assn. Mil. Surgeons U.S., Rock River

Valley Ophthalmology Assn. (sec. 1978-96), World Med. Assn., Pan-Am. Assn. Ophthalmology, Am. Assn. History of Medicine, Assn. Am. Phys. and Surg., Internat. Assn. Prevention of Blindness, Joseph Waring Meml. Library Assn. History of Medicine, Soc. Med. Cons. to Armed Forces, N.Y. Acad. Scis., Contact Lens Soc. of Ophthalmologists, Nat. Soc. Prevention Blindness, Henry Holland Hosps. Alumni Assn. and Fund (pres.), Internat. Assn. Against Trachoma, Assn. Research Ophthalmology, Soc. Nuclear Medicine, Pan Am. Soc. Ophthalmic Microsurgery (charter), Ophthalmol. Soc. Cayman Islands (hon.), Internat. Soc. History Medicine (hon.), Am. Coll. Eye Surgeons (life mem.), C. of C., 33d Div. War Vets. Assn. (surgeon 1975-85), Am. Legion, Res. Officers Assn. U.S., Internat. Agy. Prevention Blindness, Ophthalmol. Soc. Pakistan (life), others. Club: Univ. (Rockford). Inventor surg. and diagnostic equipment for the eye. Home: Oak Park Ill. Died Oct. 31, 1996.

PROCTOR, AMELIA DOLEMAN, mathematics educator; b. Occoquan, Va., Aug. 16, 1913; d. James Upshur and Mary Elveta (White) Doleman; m. Franklin Webster Proctor, Nov. 19, 1941. BS, Miner Tchrs. Coll., 1936; MA, NYU, 1953. Elem. tchr. Prince William County Pub. Sch., Quantico, Hickory Ridge and Dumfries, Va., 1937-40; sta. clk. Cencus Bur., Fed. Govt., Washington, 1940-41; jr. high math. tchr. D.C. Pub. Schs., Washington, 1941-63; spl. tchr. math. improvement program Dept. Math., Washington, 1963-65, asst. dir., 1965-70, ret., 1970; speaker and exhibitor in field. Inventor in field. Hon. fellow John F. Kennedy Libr. Found.; chmn. Girl Scouts U.S., Arlington, Va. and Washington; mem. Civic Assn. D.C. and Va., NAACP; founder Community Libr., Ebenezer Bapt. Ch., Occoquan, Va., 1973. Recipient trophy and cert. Ebenezer Bapt. Ch., 1961, 83, cert. No. Va. Mins. Wives, 1973, plaque Woodlawn United Meth. Ch., 1986, Woodlawn United Meth. Women and Men, 1985, St. James United Meth. Ch., 1989. Mem. Nat. Mus. Women in the Arts (charter 1988-95). Democrat. Home: Hampton Va. Died Sept 27, 1995.

PROVOST, DANIEL EDWARD, III, consumer products company executive; b. Bklyn., June 12, 1919; s. Daniel Edward and Anna Elizabeth (MacGowan) P.; A.B., Dartmouth Coll., 1941; m. Maxine Lorraine Cooper, Dec. 18, 1982; children from previous marriage—Daniel Edward IV, Richard Mark, Peter Michael, Patricia Ellen Voumard. Acctg. supr. Western Electric Co., N.Y.C., 1941-48; account supr. Cunningham & Walsh, N.Y.C., 1948-56; account supr. McCann Erickson, N.Y.C., 1956-61; v.p. pub. affairs GrandMet U.S.A., Inc., (formerly Liggett Group Inc.), Montvale, N.J., 1961—. Bd. dirs. Bergen County United Way; trustee Found. for Free Enterprise; mem. exec. com. Duke Children's Classic; mem. adv. bd. Tobacco History Corp.; mem. nat. communications com. Boy Scouts Am. Served with USNR, 1941-45. Mem. Montvale Bus. Assn. (v.p., dir.), Commerce and Industry Assn. No. N.J. (dir.). Republican.

PROVOST, WALLY (WALLACE B. PROVOST), journalist; b. Lincoln, Nebr., May 20, 1922; s. Orison C. and Irma (Arbogast) P.; m. Irene Peckham, May 19, 1947. Student, U. Nebr., 1940-43, Milw. State Tchrs. Coll., 1943; LL.D., U. Nebr., Omaha, 1980. Rewrite man UPI, Lincoln, 1942; asst. sports editor Nebr. State Jour., Lincoln, 1942-43, Lincoln Evening Jour., 1946-51; sports and courthouse reporter Omaha World-Herald, 1951-54, sports editor, 1955-72, sports columnist, 1955-85; ret.; v.p. Nat. Golden Gloves Assn., 1961-63; mem. nat. boxing com. AAU, 1958-60. Pres. World-Herald Good Fellows Charities, 1964-70. Served with USAAF, 1943-46, CBI. Recipient citizen's award of merit Urban League, 1966, sports writing award Nebr. AP, 1969, 70, Humanitarian award Jewish Fedn. Omaha, 1976, Communications award U. Nebr.-Omaha, 1978, Clarence F. Swanson Service award U. Nebr.-Lincoln, 1979, Sportsman and Humanitarian award B'nai B'rith, 1979; named to Omaha Met. Wrestling Hall of Fame., Nebr. Sportswriter of Yr., 1963-65, 68, 81. Mem. Football Writers Assn., Baseball Writers Assn., Nat. Assn. Sportscasters and Sportswriters, Omaha Sportscasters Assn. Club: Omaha Press. Home: Omaha Nebr. Died Sept. 9, 1996; interred Lincoln Memorial Park, Lincoln, NE.

PUCHTA, CHARLES GEORGE, lawyer; b. Cin., Feb. 19, 1918; s. Charles George and Kate (Carlisle) P.; m. Jean Geary, Dec. 12, 1959; children: Polly Carlisle Puchta Wells, Charles George, Jr. AB, U. Cin., 1940, LLD, 1943. Bar: Ohio 1943, Ky. 1964, U.S. Dist. Ct. (so. dist.) Ohio 1944, U.S. Ct. Appeals (6th cir.) 1960. Assoc. Frost & Jacobs, Cin., 1943-53, ptnr., 1953-83, chmn. exec. com., 1978-83, sr. ptnr., 1983—. Pres. Cin. C. of C., 1978, C. of C. Found., 1978; pres. Cin. Nature Ctr., 1979-81, chmn., 1981-84; trustee U. Cin. Endowment Fund, 1979—; trustee U. Cin. Found., 1978-85, emeritus, 1989—; Greater Cin. Ctr. for Econ. Edn., 1981-93, Cin. Mus. Natural History, 1988-90, Jewish Hosp., 1992-95; chmn. Bus. Mobilized for Xavier campaign, 1976; chmn. exec. com. Hebrew Union Coll. Assoc. Ann. Tribute Dinner, 1988-89; former trustee. sec. Cin. Country Day Sch.; former mem., pres., bd. dirs. Bradley U. Parents Assn.; mem. adv. bd. Juvenile Diabetes Found., 1982—. Mem. ABA, Ohio Bar Assn., Ky. Bar Assn., Cin. Bar Assn., Cin. Country Club,

Queen City Club, Comml. Club (sec. 1983-85), Commonwealth Club (v.p. 1985-86), Queen City Optimists Club (past pres.). Republican. Methodist. Deceased.

PUGSLEY, SIR ALFRED GRENVILE, civil engineer; b. May, 1903; s. H.W. Pugsley; attended London U.; D.Sc. (hon.), Belfast, 1965, Cranfield, 1978, Birmingham, 1982; D.Univ. (hon.), Surrey, 1968; m. Kathleen M. Warner, 1928 (dec. 1974). Civil engring. apprentice Royal Arsenal, Woolwich, Eng., 1923-26; tech. officer Royal Airship Works, Cardington, 1926-31; mem. sci. and tech. staff Royal Aircraft Establishment, Farnborough, Eng., 1931-45; prof. bldg. structural and mech. engring., 1941-45; prof. civil engring. U. Bristol (Eng.), 1944-68, now emeritus prof., pro-vice-chancellor, 1961-64; vis. lectr. on aircraft structures Imperial Coll., London, 1938-40; chmn. Aero. Research Council, 1952-57; mem. Adv. Council on Sci. Policy, 1956-69; mem. Tribunal of Inquiry on Ronan Point, 1968; mem. various sci. and profl. instn., coms.; pres. Inst. Structural Engrs., 1957-58; a v.p. ICE, 1971-73. Decorated Order Brit. Empire; knight bachelor; recipient Structural Engrs. Gold medal, 1968, Civil Engrs. Ewing Gold medal, 1979. Fellow Royal Soc., Royal Acad. Engring., Royal Aero. Soc. (hon.), ICE (hon.), U. Bristol (hon.). Author: The Theory of Suspension Bridges, 1957, 2d edit., 1968; The Safety of Structures, 1966; editor, contbr. The Works of Isambard Kingdom Brunel, 1976; numerous reports and memoranda of Aero. Research Council; contbr. articles, revs. to profl. publs.

PURCELL, EDWARD MILLS, physics educator; b. Taylorville, Ill., Aug. 30, 1912; s. Edward A. and Mary Elizabeth (Mills) P.; m. Beth C. Busser, Jan. 22, 1937; children: Dennis W., Frank B. B.S. in Elec. Engring., Purdue U., 1933, D. Engring. (hon.), 1953; Internat. Exchange student, Technische Hochschule, Karlsruhe, Germany, 1933-34; A.M., Harvard U., 1935, Ph.D., 1938. Instr. physics Harvard U., 1938-40, asso. prof., 1946-49, prof. physics, 1949-58, Donner prof. sci., 1958-60, Gerhard Gade Univ. prof., 1960-80, emeritus, 1980—; sr. fellow Soc. of Fellows, 1949-71; group leader Radiation Lab., MIT, 1941-45. Contbg. author: Radiation Lab. series, 1949, Berkeley Physics Course, 1965; contbr. sci. papers on nuclear magnetism, radio astronomy, astrophysics, biophysics. Mem. Pres.'s Sci. Advisory Com., 1957-60, 62-65. Co-winner Nobel prize in Physics, 1952; recipient Oersted medal Am. Assn. Physics Tchrs., 1968, Nat. Medal of Sci., 1980, Harvard medal, 1986. Mem. NAS, Am. Philos. Soc., Am. Phys. Soc., Am. Acad. Arts and Scis., Royal Soc. (fgn. mem.). Died Mar. 7, 1997.

PURVES, ALAN CARROLL, English language educator, education educator; b. Phila., Dec. 14, 1931; s. Edmund Randolph and Mary Carroll (Spencer) P.; m. Anita Woodruff Parker, June 18, 1960 (dec. 1975); children: William Carroll, Theodore Rehn; m. Anne Hathaway Nesbitt, July 14, 1976. A.B., Harvard U., 1953; M.A., Columbia U., 1956, Ph.D., 1960. Lectr. Hofstra Coll., 1956-58; instr. Columbia U., 1958-61; asst. prof. English Barnard Coll., N.Y.C., 1961-65; examiner in humanities Ednl. Testing Service, 1965-68; assoc. prof. English U. Ill., Urbana, 1968-70, prof., 1970-73, dir. curriculum lab., 1973-86; dir. U. Ill. (Curriculum Lab.), 1976-86; prof. edn. and humanities SUNY, Albany, 1986-96; prof. emeritus, 1996, dir. Ctr. for Writing and Literacy, 1987-96; staff assoc. Ctrl. Midwest Regional Ednl. Lab., St. Ann, Mo., 1968-70; cons. Coll. Entrance Exam. Bd., 1987-90, Grad. Record Exam. Bd., 1988-91, N.Y. State Found. for Sci. and Tech., N.Y. State Edn. Dept. Acad. Sys. Inc., MLA; pres. The Scribes, Inc. Editl. Svcs. Author: The Essays of Theodore Spencer, 1968, The Elements of Writing about a Literary Work, 1968, Testing in Literature, 1971, How Porcupines Make Love, 1972, Literature and the Reader, 1972, Responding, 1973, Literature Education in Ten Countries, 1973, Educational Policy and International Assessment, 1975, Common Sense and Testing in English, 1975, Evaluation in English, 1976, Achievement in Reading and Literature: New Zealand in International Perspective, 1979, Evaluation of Learning in Literature, 1980, Achievement in Reading and Literature: The U.S. in International Perspective, 1981, The Implementation of Language and International Schools, 1981, An International Perspective on the Evaluation of Written Composition, 1982, Experiencing Children's Literature, 1984, How to Write Well in College, 1984, Contrastive Rhetoric, 1988, Cultural Literacy and General Education, 1988, International Study of Writing Achievement, 1988, The Scribal Society, 1989, International Research And Educational Reform, 1989, How Porcupines Make Love II, 1990, The Idea of Difficulty in Literature, 1991, Literate Systems and Individual Lives, 1991, Tapestry: A Multicultural Anthology, 1992, International Study of Writing Achievement 2, 1992, Encyclopaedia of English Studies and Language Arts, 2 vols., 1994, Creating the Writing Portfolio, 1995, How Porcupines Make Love III, 1995, Creating the Literature Portfolio, 1996; editor: Research in the Teaching of English, 1971-77, IMEN Rev., 1986-92. Pres. Wonalancet (N.H.) Corp., 1967-69, 75-77; mem. vestry Episcopalian ch., 1970-73, 77-79, 88-91, 92-94, warden 1994-96). With AUS, 1953-55. Fellow Internat. Assn. Evaluation Edn. Achievement Internat., 1971, Coolidge Colloquium, 1994; recipient Fulbright Hayes award, 1977, 86, Leppert award, 1980, noted lectr. award U. B.C., 1991, disting. rsch. award NCRE,

1994. Mem. MLA, Nat. Coun. Tchrs. English (trustee rsch. found. 1969-72, 83-86, mem. com. rsch. 1968-77, 82-85, v.p. 1977-78, pres. 1979-80), Newcomen Soc. (hon.), N.Y. State Coun., Nat. Conf. Rsch. English, Internat. Assn. for Evaluation of Ednl. Achievement (chmn. 1986-90), Farm Bur. (edn. com. 1991-96), Wonalancet Outdoor Club (pres. 1965-69), Appalachian Mountain Club, Harvard Club. Home: Melrose N.Y. Died Dec. 31, 1996.

PUTNAM, BORDEN ROGER, JR., state agency administrator; b. Washington, Mar. 18, 1922; s. Borden Roger and Mabel Ashley (Ernst) P.; B.S.E. with honors, Princeton U., 1943, Ch.E., 1943; m. Dec. 9, 1950; children—Ashley Elizabeth, Borden Roger III, Andrea Jean. With Cyanamid Corp., Wayne, N.J., 1947—, pres. Lederle Labs. div., 1968-71, v.p. Am. Cyanamid, 1971-72, sr. v.p., dir., 1972-82; commr. N.J. Dept. Commerce, chmn. N.J. Econ. Devel. Authority, 1982—; mem. adv. council dept. chem. engring. Princeton U. Lay leader, trustee Grace Meth. Ch., Wyckoff, N.J.; bd. overseers N.J. Inst. Tech.; vice chmn., trustee Montclair State Coll.; trustee The Valley Hosp. Served with USN, 1943-46; PTO. Mem. Chem. Mktg. Research Assn. (past pres., Disting. Service award 1979), Soc. Chem. Industry (exec. com.), Princeton Club N.Y., Sigma Xi. Republican. Clubs: Arcola Country, Indian Trail. Author publs. on public policy, regulatory affairs, mktg. Office: Dept Commerce Trenton NJ 08625

QADIR, CHAUDRY ABDUL, philosopher, educator, researcher, writer; b. Jullander, Bharat, Nov. 5, 1909; s. Mahbub Alam and Attar Bibi Q.; m. Majida Begum, Apr. 24, 1927; children: Sarwar, Muzaffar, Ashraf, Jamila, Imtiaz, Shakila, Ijaz, Rukhsana, Sajjad. BA with honors, Murray Coll., Sialkot, Pakistan, 1930; MA, Govt. Coll., Lahore, Pakistan, 1932; B of Teaching, Cen. Tng. Coll., Lahore, 1934; DLitt, U. Panjab, Lahore, 1977. Lectr. Govt. Coll., various locations, Pakistan, 1934-52; sr. lectr. Govt. Coll., Lahore, 1952-63; prof., prin. Govt. Evaluators Coll., Lyallpur, Pakistan, 1963-64; Iqbal prof., head dept. philosophy U. of the Panjab, 1964-70, vis. prof. dept. philosophy, 1973—; vis. prof. Ulema Acad., Lahore, 1971-72, Civil Services Acad., Lahore, 1972, Fin. Services Acad., Lahore, 1972; subject specialist West Pakistna Urdu Acad., Lahore, 1972-79; mem. exec. com. West Pakistan Urdu Acad., 1964—, sec.-gen., 1987—; sr. fellow, chmn. several curriculm coms. Univ. Grants Commn. Commn., Islamabad, Pakistan, 1977-79.; convenor bd. studies Univ. of Punjab, 1965-80, Bd. of Intermediate and Secondary Edn., Lahore, 1987—; regional dir., cons. internat. adv. body World Univ., U.S.A., 1973-75; bd. dirs. Mashal (pub. co.), Lahore. Author: (in Urdu) Ethics, 1961, Psychology of Adjustment, 1969, Psychology, 4th edit., 1972, Technical Terms of Applied Psychology, 1972, Industrial Psychology, 1973, Social Psychology, 1973, Sociology, 1974, Developmental Psychology, 1973, Military Psychology, 1975, Sociological Thinkers, 1976, Industrial Sociology, 1977, Human Ecology, 1981, Criminology, 1979, Scientific Method, 1980, Child Psychology, 1980, Sociology of Populations, 1981, Change and Theories of Change, 19981, Philosophy Today and Its Schools, 1981, Robert Malthus and His Teachings, 1984, History of Science, 1985, (in English) Logical Positivism, 1965, The World of Philosophy, 1963, Islamic Philosphy of Life and its Significance, Quest for Truth, 1985, Science and Philosophy in the Islamic World, 1987; editor-in-chief Pakistan Philos. Jour., 1977—; editor research jour. U. Panjab, 1965-70; contbr. 60 articles in English, 15 in Urdu to profl. jours. Sec. Soc. Prevention Cruelty Animals, 1973; hon. cons. Fountain House (half-way house for mental patients), Lahore; v.p. Children Aid Soc., 1974. Recipient Iqbal Gold medal Govt. Pakistan, 1977, Golden Ring and monetary award for 50 yrs. of teaching Ch. of Pakistan, Diocese of Lahore, 1987, numerous others. Mem. Pakistan Philos. Congress (pres. 1977—, Golden Pin award 1985, Festchrift award 1987), Internat. Islamic Philos. Assn. (pres. 1984—), Pakistan Assn. Inter-Religious Dialogue (pres. 1984—), Metaphys. Soc. (pres. 1970-86). Avocations: music, journalism, hiking. Died Dec. 2, 1987.

QUASHA, WILLIAM HOWARD, lawyer; b. N.Y.C., May 19, 1912; BS in Mech. Engring., NYU, 1933, MA, 1935; LLB, St. John's U., 1936; HHD honoris causa, Lyceum of the Philippines, 1995; 1 child: Angelina; m. Isabel Abad Santos, May 22, 1989. Bar: N.Y., 1936, Philippine, 1945, U.S. Supreme Ct., 1947. Pvt. Practice law, N.Y.C., 1936-42, Manila, 1946-96; sr. ptnr. Quasha, Asperilla, Ancheta, Peña, and Nolasco; chmn., bd. dirs. Marcopper Mining Corp., Manila. Faculty, N.Y. U., 1933-35, Santo Tomas U., Manila, 1946-48; vis. assoc. prof. L.I. U., 1966; lectr. Harvard U. Law Sch.,1976, U. Philippines Coll. Law, 1979. Mem. nat. exec. bd. Boy Scouts Philippines, 1955-74, mem. exec. bd. Manila coun., 1949-74, v.p., treas., 1964-74, hon. life pres., 1970; v.p., legal counsel Acacia Mut. Aid Soc., Inc., Manila, 1963-96; mem. exec. bd. Far East coun. Boy Scouts Am., 1973-96; pres., chmn. bd. trustees St. Luke's Med. Ctr., Manila, 1975-96, incorporator, cons. to bd. trustees St. Luke's Coll. Medicine; mem. coun. advisers Jose P. Laurel Meml. Found.; chmn. Reps. Abroad Com., Philippines, 1979-84, chmn. Asia-Pacific region, 1985-86, chmn. adv. com. 1987-90; founder bd. trustees Filipino Am. Meml. Endowment. With AUS, 1942-46, PTO; lt. col. Res. Decorated Bronze Star with oak leaf cluster, Philippine Legion of Honor (officer rank); recipient Silver Tamaraw, Boy Scouts Philippines, 1959, Silver Fir Tree Br., Boy Scouts Austria, 1960; Distinguished Eagle Scout award Boy Scouts Am., 1970, Silver Buffalo award, 1974, Predl. citation Republic of The Philippines, 1995; named Outstanding Manilan City of Manila, 1970, 93; tribute of appreciation U.S. Dept. State, 1983; Conrado Benitez Heritage award Philippine Women's U., 1983. Mem. ABA, Integrated Bar of Philippines (Pioneer of Bar Integration award 1994), Law Asia, Interlaw, Am. Soc. Internat. Law, Am. C. of C. of Philippines, USN League U.S. (judge adv., chartermem.), Am. Assn. Philippines, Propeller Club U.S. (past pres., charter mem. Manila chpt.), Philippine Constn. Assn. (life), Philippine Soc. Internat. Law, Ramon Magsaysay Meml. Soc., Knights of Rizal (knight comdr.), Nat. Sojourners (pres. 1959), Am. Legion (dept. comdr. 1954-55), Manila Jr. C. of C. (assoc., v.p. 1949), Internat. C. of C. (gov. Philippine coun. 1964-86). Episcopalian (sr. warden, chancellor). Lodge: Masons (33 deg., grand master 1962-63, Chevalier of Legion of Honor Supreme Coun. of Order De Molay 1986, dean of preceptory Philippines chpt. 1991-96), regent, trustee Cathedral St. John the Divine, N.Y., 1988-96, Shriner, Elk (bd. dirs. palsy project 1954-69, chmn. 1963-65), Rotarian (past bd. dir. Manila). Clubs: Nat. Lawyers' (Washington); Am. Nat. (Sydney, Australia); Univ. (N.Y.); Army and Navy, Manila Polo, others. Author: (with Rensis Likert) Revised Minnesota Paper Form Board Test. Died May 12, 1996. Home: Metro Manila The Philippines

QUISENBERRY, JOHN ASCUM, investment broker; b. Evanston, Ill., Apr. 5, 1924; s. T. Edwin and Quinlan Hanna Q.; m. Ann F. Cleland, June 21, 1947 (div. 1972); children: Sarah Quisenberry Travis, Peggy; m. Hilda Christine Slight, Nov. 15., 1972; stepchildren: Jonathan Musil, Christopher Musil. Grad., Harvard U., 1948; LLB, George Washington U., 1953. Bar: Ill. 1955. Travel auditor trainee Altantic Coast Line R.R., Wilmington, N.C., 1948, So. Freight Assn., 1949-51; rsch. asst. Assn. Am. R.R.'s, Washington, 1951-54; asst. to compt. C&NW Railway, Chgo., 1955; with security sales and pvt. placement staff A.C. Allyn & Co., Chgo., 1956-60; with inst. sales staff Glore, Forgan & Co., Chgo., 1960-62; with sales and comml. paper staff A.G. Becker & Co., Chgo., 1962-65; with instnl. and individual sales staff Chgo. Corp., 1965-67; with securities sales investment rsch. staff Ill. Co., 1967-90; sr. v.p. Birkelback Investments, Inc., Chgo., 1990—; dir. Neveridle Corp., Wilmette, Ill. Appointed mem. Ill. Pvt. Bus. Sch. Commn., Springfield, Ill.; trustee Roycemore Sch., Evanston, Aid Assn. India; active numerous Dem. orgns.; pres. Community Chest, Highland Pk., Ill., 1958; life mem. Art Inst. Chgo. Lt. U.S. Army, 1943-46, PTO. Mem. Am. Vets. Com. (life), Univ. Club, Bond Club, Harvard Club.

RACZ, ANDRE, artist, engraver, educator; b. Cluj, Rumania, Nov. 21, 1916; came to U.S., 1939, naturalized, 1948; s. Simion and Ana (Rosenmann) R.; m. Claire Enge, May 25, 1962; children by previous marriage: Juan Andres, Maria Simone, Ana Constanza. B.A., U. Bucharest, 1935. Teaching asst. Atelier 17, N.Y.C., 1944; dir. Academia Villavicencio, Santiago, Chile, 1950; lectr. Columbia U., 1951-54, instr., 1954-56, asst. prof., 1956-61, assoc. prof., 1961-67, prof., 1967-94, chmn. dept. painting and sculpture, 1964-73, 75-77, prof. emeritus, 1983-94; vis. prof. U. Ky., 1960. Author: The Flowering Rock, 1943, The Battle of the Starfish, 1944, The Reign of Claws, 1945, XII Prophets of Aleijandinho, 1947, Via Crucis, 1948, Mother and Child, 1949, Voz de Luna, 1951, Sal de Dunas, 1953, Canciones Negras, 1953, Salmos y Piedras, 1955; Editor: Poemas de las Madres by Gabriela Mistral, pub. in 1950 with 63 of his drawings (Nobel prize 1945); one man shows, N.Y.C., 1942-44, 46, 48, 49, 51, 53, 56, 57, 59, 61, 77, 83, Phila., 1945, Washington, 1947, U. Tenn., U. Iowa, 1948, Green Lake, Wis., 1951, Rio de Janeiro, Brazil, 1946, Santiago, 1947-50, Buenos Aires, Argentina, 1949, Cordoba, Argentina, 1949, Valdivia, Valparaiso, Vina, Chile, 1957, one man show circulated by, Am. Fedn. Art, 1948-51, retrospective show graphic work, N.Y. Pub. Library, 1954-55, Museo de Bellas Artes, Santiago, 1957, U. Ky., Lexington, 1960; exhibited group shows, Mus. Modern Art, Whitney Mus., Bklyn. Mus., Carnegie Inst., Phila. Mus., Library Congress San Francisco Mus., N.Y. Pub. Library, also internat. shows., France, Eng., Italy, Spain, Germany, Austria, Norway, Poland, Yugoslavia, Switzerland, Argentina, Peru, Bolivia, Chile, Mexico, Venezuela, Australia; Fifty Years of Am. Art, Mus. Modern Arts show, Paris, London, Barcelona and, Belgrade, 1955, 1st Inter-Am. Biennial in Mexico, 1958, 1st Biennial of Religious Art, Salzburg, Austria, 1958, Internat. Watercolor Biennial, Bklyn. Mus. Art, 1961, Nat. Inst. Arts and Letters, 1968, 25th Anniversary Rockefeller Print Room, Mus. Modern Art, 1975, Surrealism in Am. Art, Rutgers U., 1977, 50th Anniversary Atelier 17, U. Wis., 1978, Mus. Modern Art, Bklyn. Mus., Whitney Mus., N.Y. Pub. Library, Butler Inst., Smithsonian Instn., Library Congress, San Francisco Mus., Rosenwald Collection, Dept. State, Hartford Cath. Library, U. Ky., Albion Coll., Downer Coll., Columbia, Smith Coll., U. St. Louis, U. Minn., New Sch. for Social Research, N.Y.C., Phila. Mus., Tulsa Mus., Museum of Oslo, Norway, Museo de Cordoba, Argentina, Salzburg Mus., Austria, Nat. Gallery, Melbourne, Australia, Bibilotheque Nationale, Paris, U. P.R., Rio Piedras, others., (Recipient Erickson prize for intaglio 1953, Noyes prize, 1st prize for intaglio Soc. Graphic Artists 1955, 1st prize Motive mag. 1957, purchase prize U. Ky. 1959). Guggenheim fellow for printmaking, 1956; Fulbright research scholar Chile, 1957; Ford Found. Award, 1962; Bankroft award for disting. teaching Columbia U., 1983. Mem. Am. Soc. Graphic Artists (past v.p.), Am. Assn. U. Profs. Home: Demarest N.J. Died Sept. 29, 1994.

RADCLIFFE, BEVERLY LOUISE, council director, consultant; b. Reading, Pa., Apr. 26, 1942; d. Frank Edmund and Katherine Emma Mae (Kohler) R.; m. Helmut Franz Pfanner, Sept. 16, 1966 (div. Aug. 1988); children: Heidi Louise, Eric Franz, Marta Katrin. BA, Gettysburg (Pa.) Coll., 1964; MEd, Kutztown (Pa.) U., 1968; PhD, Purdue U., 1985. Cert. secondary edn. tchr., Nebr. Tchr. German Reading Sr. High Sch., 1964-66; tchr. English second lang. HBLA für wirtschaftliche Frauenberufe, Linz, Austria, 1976-78; teaching asst. Purdue U., W. Lafayette, Ind., 1979-82; lectr. U. N.H., Durham, 1983-86; cons. Nebr. Dept. Edn., Lincoln, 1986-88; dir. mediated fng. lang. program Instructional Materials Coun., Lincoln, 1988-94, exec. dir., 1989-94; cons. Nebr. Japanese-by-Satellite Project, Lincoln, 1988-91; student tchr. supr. U. Nebr., Lincoln, 1988-89. Contbr. articles to profl. jours. Fulbright scholar, Austria, 1976-78; Deutscher Akademischer Austauschdienst grantee, 1985. Mem. Computer Assisted Lang. Learning and Instrn. Consortium, Nebr. Fgn. Lang. Assn., Am. Coun. on Teaching Fgn. Langs., Am. Assn. Tchrs. German, Nebr. Assn. Tchrs. German. Avocations: reading, model railroading, gardening, needlework. Home: Lincoln Nebr. Died Aug. 24, 1994.

RAFFO, STEVE, artist; b. Hoboken, N.J., Aug. 21, 1912; s. John and Sadie (Boasi) R. Grad., Cooper Union Sch. Art, 1938. Instr. art Cooper Union Sch. Art, N.Y.C., 1939-43, 47-50, Parsons Sch. Design, N.Y.C., 1956-63. Represented in permanent collections at Delgado Mus., New Orleans, Fla. Gulf Coast Art Ctr., Clearwater, Pa. Acad. Fine Arts, Phila., Legal Aid Offices, N.Y.C.; exhbns. include Whitney Mus. Am. Art, 1947-49, 51, Corocoran Gallery, Washington, 1947, 51, Pa. Acad., Phila., 1948-49, 53, 61-62, 69, Carnegie Inst., Pa., 1949, Am. Acad. and Inst. Arts, N.Y.C., 1951, 58, 60, Art Inst. Chgo., 1952, 61, R.I. Mus. Art, 1955, Nat. Acad. Design, N.Y.C., 1960, 67, 69, 75-76, 88, others. Served with U.S. Army, 1944-47. Recipient Scheidt Meml. prize Pa. Acad., 1948, Prix de Rome, 1952-55, 2 Guggenheim fellowships, 1950-51. Home: New York N.Y. DIED 04/07/95. .

RAINS, HARRY HANO, lawyer, arbitrator, mediator; b. N.Y.C., Jan. 27, 1909; s. Jackson and Rose (Heller) R.; m. Muriel, May 17, 1942; 1 child, Peggy Jane Rains Goodman. LL.B., St. Lawrence U., 1932; M.P.A., NYU, 1947, LL.M. in Labor Law, 1954. Bar: N.Y. 1933, U.S. Supreme Ct. 1965, U.S. Dist. Ct. (so. and ea. dists.) N.Y. 1947. Referee N.Y. State Dept. Labor, 1936-38, unemployment ins. mgr., 1939-42; sole practice Mineola, N.Y., 1933-42; sr. ptnr. firm Rains & Pogrebin, N.Y.C., 1947-81, of counsel, cons., 1982-96; labor arbitrator, mediator, lectr.; prof. labor law CCNY, 1935-37, 46-47; prof. labor law Hofstra U., 1947-54, Harry H. Rains Disting. prof. arbitration and alternative dispute settlement law, 1982-96; mem. faculty L.I. U. 1953; dir. Sealectro Corp., John Hassall Co., Inc. Contbr. articles to profl. jours. Mem. Fed. Mediation and Conciliation Service, 1948-96; mem. N.Y. State Pub Employment Relations Bd. Panel Mediators and Fact Finders, 1968-96. Served to capt. QMC, AUS, 1942-46. Mem. ABA, Fed. Bar Coun., N.Y. State Bar Assn. Nassau County Bar Assn., Nat. Acad. Arbitrators Indsl. Rels. Rsch. Assn., Am. Arbitration Assn. (panel labor arbitrators), L.I. C. of C. (bd. dirs.), Univ. Club (Garden City, N.Y.). Died Dec. 24, 1996.

RAITT, JAMES THOMAS, musical director, arranger b. Santa Ana, Calif., Feb. 21, 1953; s. George Emmet and Harriette Virginia (Johnson) R. BMus., U. So Calif., 1975. Mus. dir. Am. Dance Machine, N.Y.C. 1979-87, Agnes DeMille, N.Y.C., 1982; mus. dir. orchestrator, arranger Stardust Broadway show, N.Y.C. 1987; instr. NYU, 1980-83, Sarah Lawrence Coll. Bronxville, N.Y., 1985-87. Dance arranger shows in cluding Mike, 1988, Late Night Comic, 1988, Meet Me in St. Louis, 1989. Mem. Am. Fedn. Musicians, Am Soc. Composers and Pubs. Avocations: collecting salt and pepper shakers and lunch boxes. Home: New York N.Y. Died Apr. 25, 1994.

RAM, SAMUEL BUCK, composer, record producer song publisher, group musical director; b. Chgo., Nov 21, 1908; s. Phillip R.; m. Lucille; children—Lynn Ram Paul, Melody. Law degree. Saxophonist Benny Goodman's band, Gene Krupa's band; musical arranger for big bands, including Duke Ellington, Glenn Miller Count Basie, Dorsey Bros., and Cab Calloway; composer for motion pictures; rock composer, creator musical dir. The Platters, 1954-91; composer numerous songs, including: Only You, You've Got The Magic Touch, The Great Pretender, I'll Be Home For Christmas, You'll Never Never Know, One In A Million, I'm Sorry, I Wish, Twilight time, Where, Adorable Remember When, Afterglow, Fool That I Am; discovered The Three Suns, 1940s, The Union Gap, 1960s

Winner 16 gold records Nat. Music Pubs.'s Assn., platinum record for The Great Pretender, 1982; Broadcast Music, Inc. Spl. Citation of Achievement; songs recorded by various artists including Bing Crosby, Three Suns, Mario Lanza, Glenn Miller, Mahalia Jackson, The Inkspots, B.B. King, Frank Sinatra, Ella Fitzgerald, and numerous recs. by The Platters. Died Jan. 1, 1991.

RAMANUJAN, A. K., language and literature educator; b. Mysore, India, Mar. 16, 1929. BA in English Lang. and Lit. with honors, Mysore U., 1949, MA in English Lit., 1950; grad. diplomas in descriptive and hist. linguistics, Deccan Coll., India, 1958; PhD in Linguistics, Ind. U., 1963. Lectr. in English various colls., 1950-59; rsch. assoc. U. Chgo., 1961, asst. prof., 1961, asst. prof. linguistics, Tamil and Dravidian langs., 1962-66, assoc. prof. Dravidian studies and linguistics, 1966-68, prof., 1968-93, William E. Colvin prof., 1983-93, chmn. dept. South Asian langs. and civilizations, 1980-85; vis. asst. prof. Indian studies, U. Wis., 1965, vis. prof., 1971; acad. dir. Inter-Univ. Rotating Program in Indian Studies, Chgo., 1966; vis. assoc. prof. dept. speech U. Calif., Berkeley, 1967, vis. prof., 1973; mem. adv. bd. Princeton Libr. Asian Translations Series, 1975-86; vis. Benedict prof. depts. sociology and anthropology Carleton Coll., 1978, Disting. vis. Benedict prof., 1982; cons. Ford Found., India, 1984; vis. prof. Harvard Div. Sch., 1987; lectr. Ecole des Haute Etudes en Scis. Sociales, Paris, 1987, Watumull Disting. Indian lectr. U. Hawaii, Honolulu, 1988, Radhakrishnan Meml. lectr. Oxford U., Eng., 1988, vis. Walgreen prof. Inst. for Humanities, U. Mich., 1989-90; lectr. in field. Author: The Striders: Poems, 1966, Hokkulalli Huvilla, 1969, Relations: Poems, 1971, Selected Poems, 1976, Mattu Itara Padyagalu, 1977, Mattobbana Atmakate, 1978, Second Sight, 1986, Kuntobille, 1990, Folktales from India, 1992; co-author: (with others) The Literatures of India: An Introduction, 1975; editor: Proverbs in Kannada, 1955; co-editor: (with Stuart Blackburn) Another Harmony: New Essays on the Folklore of India, 1986, (with Vinay Dharwadker) The Oxford India Anthology of Modern Indian Poetry, 1993; translator: The Interior Landscape: Translations from a Classical Tamil Anthology (honor Tamil Writers' Assn.), 1967, Speaking of Siva, 1973, Samskara: A Rite for a Dead Man, 1976, Hymns for the Drowning: Poems for Visnu by Nammalvar, 1981, Poems of Love and War, 1985; co-translator: When God Is A Customer: Telugu Courtesan Songs, 1993; contbr. to books, anthologies, profl. jours.; adv. editor The Carleton Miscellany, 1977-81. Decorated Padma Shri (India); recipient Summer award Am. Coun. Learned Socs., 1960, award for poetry Ill. Arts Coun., 1981, Arts and Letters award Fedn. Indians in N.Am., 1982, 84, award Karnataka Sahitya Akademi, 1983, Disting. award Taraknathdas Found., 1984, Chgo. Poets' award City of Chgo., 1985; Deccan Coll. fellow, 1958-59, Fulbright fellow, Smith-Mundt fellow, 1959-60, Ind. U. fellow, 1960-61, 63, Am. Inst. Indian Studies fellow, 1963-64, 75, 83, Fulbright-Hays fellow, 1967, 69, Am. Coun. Learned Socs. fellow, 1973, NEH fellow, 1977, 82, Am. Coun. Learned Socs./Social Sci. Rsch. Coun. fellow, 1979, MacArthur fellow, 1983-88, John M. Olin Ctr. sr. fellow, 1983-93, U. Mich. fellow, 1988, Hebrew U. fellow, 1989; honored by Indian Embassy, Washington, 1979. Fellow Am. Acad. Arts and Scis.; mem. Social Sci. Rsch. Coun./Am. Coun. Learned Socs. (joint com. on south Asia 1975-78, com. on lang. and culture 1985-93), Assn. Asian Studies (bd. dirs., south Asia coun. 1984-87). Home: Chicago Ill. Died July 13, 1993.

RAMU, ANANTHA S., civil engineering educator; b. Mysore, Karnatak, India, Jan. 14, 1941; s. Srinivas Char and Seetha Ramu; m. Vijaya Lakshmi Chari, July 12, 1972; children: Venkatesh, Siddharth. B Engring., U. Mysore, 1960; MSc, Indian Inst. Sci., 1963; PhD, U. Waterloo, Can., 1966. Chartered engr., India. Asst. design engr. Hindustan Steel Ltd., India, 1963-64; rsch. fellow U. Waterloo, 1964-66; staff engr. United Aircraft Ltd., Can., 1966-70; asst. prof. engring. Indian Inst. Sci., Bangalore, 1970-75, prof. engring., 1975-95; vis. prof. U. Hannover, Fed. Republic Germany, 1976-78, Concordia U., Montreal, Que., Can., 1990-91; cons. structural engr. Dept. Aerospace, India, 1975-95, Dept. Atomic Energy, 1975-95. Author: Design of Beams on Elastic Foundation, 1971; contbr. over 100 articles to profl. jours. Alexander von Humboldt Found. sr. fellow, 1976. Fellow Instn. Engrs. India; mem. N.Y. Acad. Scis., Am. Math. Soc. Died Nov. 29, 1995.

RAND, PAUL, graphic designer, educator; b. N.Y.C., Aug. 15, 1914. Student, Pratt Inst., 1929-32, Art Students League, 1934; DFA (hon.), Phila. Coll. Art, Parson Sch. Design, U. Hartford Sch. Visul Arts, Kutztown U.; MA, Yale U.; postgrad., Pratt Inst., 1996. Art dir. Esquire/Apparel Arts; creative dir. William H. Weintraub Advt. Agy., N.Y.; prof. graphic design Sch. Art Yale U., New Haven, 1956-91, prof. emeritus; cons. IBM, 1956-92, Cummins Engine Co., 1962-96, Westinghouse Electric, 1960-81,numerous others; tchr. Yale Summer Sch. Program, Brissago, Switzerland, 1977-96. Author: Thoughts on Design, 1946, Design and the Play Instinct, 1965, The Trademarks of Paul Rand, 1960, A Paul Rand Miscellaney, 1984, Paul Rand: A Designer's Art, 1985, Design, Form and Chaos, 1993, From Lascaux to Brooklyn, 1996; contbr. numerous articles to profl. publs.; represented in permanent collections various museums, U.S., Europe and Japan. Pres.'s fellow RISD; recipient Florence prize for Visual Comm., City of Florence, 1987. Home: Weston Conn. Died Nov. 26, 1996.

RANDALL, JOHN (TURTON), physicist, educator; b. Mar. 23, 1905; s. Sidney and Hannah (Cawley) Randall; M.Sc., U. Manchester, 1926, D.Sc., 1938; m. Doris Duckworth, 1928; 1 son, Christopher John. Research physicist Research Labs., Gen. Electric Co., Ltd., 1926-37; Warren research fellow Royal Soc., 1937-44; research on cavity magnetron for Admiralty, U. Birmingham, 1939-43, hon. mem. staff, 1940-43; temporary lectr. Cavendish Lab., Cambridge, 1943-44; prof. natural philosophy United Coll. of St. Salvator and St. Leonard, U. St. Andrews, 1944-46; Wheatstone prof. physics, 1946-61, prof. biophysics King's Coll., U. London, 1961-70; hon. prof. U. Edinburgh (Scotland), 1970—; hon. dir. med. research council Biophysics Research Unit, 1947-70, chmn. Sch. Biol. Scis., 1964-69. Lectr. Rockefeller Inst. Med. Research, N.Y., 1956-57; Greg y Nog lectr. U. Coll. Wales, Aberystwyth, 1958; vis. prof. biophysics Yale, 1960. Created knight, 1962. Recipient Thomas Gray Meml. prize for discovery cavity magetron Royal Soc. Arts, 1943; Duddell medallist Phys. Soc. London, 1945; Hughes medallist Royal Soc., 1946; John Price Wetherill medal Franklin Inst., 1958; John Scott award City of Phila., 1959; fellow of King's College, London, Eng., 1960. Fellow Royal Soc. Club: Athenaeum (London). Research on scattering of neutrons and synchrotron radiation by biol. systems.

RANDOLPH, JAMES HARRISON, SR., realty company executive; b. Springfield, Tenn., Feb. 17, 1917; s. Bayless Jones and Effie Lee (Cummings) R.; m. Millicent Roma Lincoln, Aug. 14, 1943; 1 child, James Harrison. BSBA, U. Tenn., 1940. Spl. agt., adminstrv. asst. to dir. FBI, Washington, 1942-52; personnel dir. Dallas Housing Authority, 1952-54; real estate broker Bolanz & Bolanz, Dallas, 1954-58; real estate broker, investor Jim Randolph & Co., Dallas, 1958-95. Former bd. govs. U. Tenn. Mem. Soc. Former Spl. Agts. of FBI, Greater Dallas Assn. Realtors (life), Soc. Indsl. and Office Realtors, Dallas C. of C. (hon. life), Scarabbean, Brookhaven Country Club (Dallas), Phi Sigma Kappa. Baptist. Died Apr. 23, 1995. Home: Dallas Tex.

RANKAMA, KALERVO, geology educator; b. Helsinki, Finland, Feb. 22, 1913; m. Riti Narvanen, 1938 (div. 1976); 1 child, Liisa Helen Inkeri. MA, U. Helsinki, 1938, PhD, 1944. Geologist Geol. Survey of Finland, 1938-46; docent of mineral chemistry U. Helsinki, 1945-50, personal prof. mineral chemistry, 1950-80; retired, 1980; rsch. assoc. in geochemistry U. Chgo., 1947-50; vis. prof. U. Buenos Aires, 1971, U. New South Wales, Australia, 1965, U. Toronto, 1972. Author: Isotope Geology, 1954, 2d edit., 1960, Progress in Isotope Geology, 1963, (with T. Sahama) Geochemistry, 1950, 6th edit., 1968, Geoquimica, 1954, 2d edit., 1962; editor: The Precambrian 1, 1963, The Precambrian 2, 1965, The Quaternary 1, 1965, Precambrian 3, 1967, The Quaternary 2, 1967, others. Decorated comdr. Order of the Finnish Lion; recipient Frantisek Posepny Gold medal Czechoslovak Acad. Scis., 1968, Gustav-Steinmann medal Geologische Vereinigung, Germany, 1971. Mem. Helsinki Stock Exch. Club, Sigma Xi. Roman Catholic. Avocations: recorded classical music, reading in science. Deceased.

RAPPING, LEONARD ALLEN, economics educator, consultant; b. Apr. 16, 1934; s. Joseph and Rose (Scharfin) R.; m. Elayne J. Antler, Aug. 15, 1960 (div. May 1973); children—Alison, Jonathan; m. 2d, Judith Alt Wilson, Sept. 12, 1980. B.A., UCLA, 1956; M.A., U. Chgo., 1958, Ph.D., 1961. Research economist Northwestern Transp. Ctr., Evanston, Ill., 1959-60, Rand Corp., Santa Monica, Calif., 1961; prof. econs. Carnegie-Mellon U., Pitts., 1962-73; prof. econs. U. Mass., Amherst, 1974—; disting. vis. prof. U. Nev., Las Vegas, 1978; vis. prof. Brandeis U., Waltham, Mass., 1984, 87, U. Notre Dame, South Bend, Ind., 1985-86; cons. govt. agys., including Fed. Railroad Adminstrn., 1980; mem. hwy. research bd. Nat. Acad. Scis., Washington, 1972, dir. tech.-employment panel, 1985-86. Author: (with others) The Economic Value of the U.S. Merchant Marine, 1961, International Reorganization and American Economic Policy, 1988; author monographs; contbr. articles to profl. jours.; mem. editorial bd. Am. Econ. Rev., 1973-76. Mem. Am. Econ. Assn., Phi Beta Kappa.

RASHISH, MYER, economics consultant; b. Cambridge, Mass., Nov. 10, 1924; s. Aaron Joshua and Pearl (Steinberg) R.; m. Bernice Osheroff, June 20, 1948; children: Peter Seth, Alisa Jessica, Andrea Beth. A.B., Harvard U., 1944, A.M., 1947. Instr. econs. MIT, 1946-47, Williams Coll., 1947-49; asst. prof. Bowdoin Coll., 1949-51; with Dept. State, 1952-53; economist Com. Nat. Trade Policy, 1953-56; staff dir. subcom. fgn. trade policy U.S. Ho. of Reps., 1956-60; asst. to pres., 1960-63, cons. economist, 1963-81; undersec. econ. affairs Dept. State, 1981-82; pres. Rashish Assocs. Inc., Washington, 1982—. Mem. Council Fgn. Relations, Internat. Inst. Strategic Studies, Am. Econ. Assn. Home: Washington D.C. DIED 05/23/95. .

RASKIN, ABRAHAM HENRY, editor; b. Edmonton, Alta., Can., Apr. 26, 1911; came to U.S., 1913, naturalized, 1920; s. Henry and Mary (Slatkin) R.; m. Marjorie Neikrug, Dec. 4, 1990; children from previous marriage: Jane, Donald. B.A., CCNY, 1931. Mem. staff N.Y. Times, 1931-77, mem. editorial bd., 1961-64, asst. editor editorial page, 1964-76, labor columnist, 1976-77; assoc. dir. Nat. News Council, 1978-84; lectr. N.Y. Sch. Social Work, 1947-52; adj. prof. Grad. Sch. Bus. Columbia, 1976, Stanford U., 1984; Woodrow Wilson vis. fellow Union Coll., 1982, Lawrence U., 1983, Gustavus Adolphus Coll., 1985, Trinity U., 1986, Washington Coll., 1988; fellow Employment Studies Inst. Syracuse U., 1986-93; cons. President's Com. Universal Tng., 1947. Co-author: David Dubinsky: A Life with Labor, 1977; contbg. editor Bus. Month, 1988-89. Bd. dirs. Jewish Family Service N.Y., 1950-62, Legal Aid Soc., N.Y.C., 1967-74, UN Assn., 1980-93; trustee Lowell Mellett Fund, 1968-83, James Gordon Bennett Found., 1971-84. Served to lt. col. AUS, 1942-45. Decorated D.S.M.; recipient George Polk Meml. award, 1953, 64, Sidney Hillman Meml. award, 1951, Page One award N.Y. Newspaper Guild, 1961, 64, Soc. Silurians award, 1964, 70, Heywood Broun Meml. citation, 1964, Journalism award Columbia U., 1976. Mem. N.Y. Guild (vice chmn. 1948-62), Indsl. Relations Research Assn. (nat. exec. bd.), Internat. Press Inst., Am. Acad. Polit. Sci., Phi Beta Kappa. Mem. Liberal Party. Jewish. Home: New York N.Y. Died Dec. 22, 1993; interred Martha's Vineyard, MA.

RAY, JEANNE CULLINAN, lawyer, insurance company executive; b. N.Y.C., May 5, 1943; d. Thomas Patrick and Agnes Joan (Buckley) C.; children: Christopher Lawrence, Douglas James. Student, Univ. Coll., Dublin, Ireland, 1963; AB, Coll. Mt. St. Vincent, Riverdale, N.Y., 1964; LLB, Fordham U., 1967. Bar: N.Y. 1967. Atty. Mut. Life Ins. Co. N.Y. (MONY), N.Y.C., 1967-68, asst. counsel, 1969-72, assoc. counsel, 1972-73, counsel, 1974-75, asst. gen. counsel, 1976-80, assoc. gen counsel, 1981-83, v.p. pension counsel, 1984-85, v.p. area counsel group and pension ops., 1985-87; v.p. sector counsel group and pension ops., 1988, v.p., chief counsel exec. and corp. affairs, 1988-89; v.p. law, sec. MONY Securities Corp., N.Y.C., 1980-85; v.p. law, sec. MONY Advisers, Inc., N.Y.C., 1980-88; sec. MONYCO, Inc., N.Y.C., 1980-85; v.p., counsel MONY Series Fund, Inc., Balt., 1984-87; v.p., assoc. gen. counsel Tchrs. Ins. and Annuity Assoc. Coll. Ret. Equities Fund (TIAA-CREF), N.Y.C., 1989-91, v.p., chief counsel ins., 1991—. Contbr. articles to legal jours. Cubmaster, den mother Greater N.Y. coun. Boy Scouts Am., N.Y.C., 1978-84, mem. bd. rev. and scouting com., 1985—. Mem. ABA (chmn employee benefits com. Tort and Ins. Practice sect. 1981-82, vice-chmn. 1983-96), Assn. Life Ins. Counsel (chmn. policyholders tax com. tax sect. 1982-91, vice chmn. tax sect. 1991-93, chmn. 1993—), Assn. Bar City N.Y. (chmn. employee benefits com. 1992-95), Investment Co. Inst. (mem. pension com. 1993—, Am. Coun. Life Ins. (chmn. fiduciary task force of pension com. 1990—), Am. Coun. Life Ins. Democrat. Roman Catholic.

RAYMOND, GUY, actor; b. Niagara Falls, N.Y., July 1, 1911; s. Samuel and Jane (Gross) Guyer; m. Ann Morgan Guilbert, Sept. 8, 1969; stepchildren: Nora Sekowski, Hallie Withrow. Student, Berghoff-Hagen Sch. Drama, 1954-56. Dancer, appearing on Broadway and on tour in leading theatres, nightclubs and hotels, 1930-52; standup comedian in early TV; films include The Undefeated, Gypsy, Marjorie Morningstar, Bandolero, The Reluctant Astronaut, The Russians are Coming; appeared on Broadway with Helen Hayes in Mrs. McThing, 1953; appeared on stage in Hollywood as Gregory Solomon in The Price, 1976; as Pontius Pilate in Absence of Miracles, 1980; as Baylor in Lie of the Mind, Denver, 1988; as Rappaport in I'm not Rappaport, 1988; as Patsy in Three Men on a Horse; mem. Denver Ctr. Theatre Co., 1985-93; actor, tchr., Pacific Conservatory of Performing Arts, Santa Maria, Calif., 1982-83; created role of Milton Perry in The Immigrant, premiering Mark Taper Forum, L.A., Aug. 1986. Mem. SAG, AFTRA, Actors Equity. Home: Pacific Palisades Calif. Died Jan. 26, 1997.

READING, SADIE ETHEL, retired public health nurse; b. Louisiana, Mo., Dec. 16, 1915; d. William M. Reading and Sadie E. Vasconcellos. RN, St. Luke's Hosp. Sch. Nursing, St. Louis, 1937; BSN, Vanderbilt U., 1948; MA, Columbia U., 1956. RN, Mo., Tenn., Fla. Asst. supr. Children's Hosp., Chattanooga, Tenn., 1937-42; sr. staff nurse Chattanooga-Hamilton County Health Dept., Chattanooga, 1948-52; supr. pub. health nursing Gibson County Health Dept., Trenton, Tenn., 1952-55; asst. supr., ednl. dir. Chattanooga-Hamilton County Health Dept., Chattanooga, 1956-59; cons. pub. health nursing Fla. State Bd. Health, Jacksonville, 1959-64, asst. dir. pub. health nursing, 1964-75; pub. health nursing supr. health program office Dept. of Health, Tallahassee, 1975-80; adj. prof. U. Mich. Sch. Pub. Health, Ann Arbor, 1960-74; dist. pres. Tenn. Nurses Assn., 1953; v.p. Fla. Nurses Assn., 1971-72, pres., 1972-73. Author: Blue and Gray: Nursing Outlook, 1962. 1st female lobbyist Fla. State Bd. Health, Jacksonville and Tallahassee, 1974; mem. Common Cause, Hunter Mus., Friends of Chattanooga Pub. Libr., Friends of Signal Mountain Libr., Tenn. Aquarium, Chattanooga. Capt. USAF and Army Nurse Corps, 1942-46, ETO. Mem. AAUW, ANA (vice chair pub. health nursing sect. 1952), LWV, DAR, Fla. Pub. Health Assn. (life, Meritorious Svc. award 1975),

Women in Mil. Svc. for Am. (charter), U.S. Golf Assn., Am. Assn. Ret. People, Fla. Sheriff's Assn., Signal Mountain Golf and Country Club, Vanderbilt Alumni Assn., Sigma Theta Tau. Democrat. Avocations: golf, bowling, volunteer activities. Deceased.

REAGAN, REGINALD LEE, biologist, clinical pathologist; b. Broadford, Pa., July 19, 1910; s. James Blaine and Helen (McLaughlin) R.; PhD, U. Md., 1956; m. Marie Ann Johnson, Mar. 5, 1932 (dec. 1980); children: Nelda (Mrs. Dan Cullivan) (dec.), Helen (Mrs. Bill Savage), Bill Olsen (dec.), Elsa (Mrs. Leo Sullivan). Joined U.S. Army, 1928, advanced through grades to maj., 1946; Rockefeller Found. Research assoc. Rockefeller Inst., N.Y.C., 1936-40; faculty U. Md., College Park, 1946-61, assoc. prof., 1948-52, prof. med. virology, 1952-61; chief virologist Jen-Sal Lab., Kansas City, Mo., 1961-62; biologist Nat. Cancer Inst., Bethesda, Md., 1962-80. Mem. N.Y. Acad. Sci., Soc. Exptl. Biology and Medicine, Electronmicroscopic Soc., Ret. Officers Assn., Soc. Clin. Pathologists, AAUP. Author: One Man's Research, 1980; contbr. over 300 articles to profl. jours. Died Nov. 4, 1996.

REAMES, JAMES MITCHELL, former librarian; b. Rembert, S.C., Aug. 31, 1920; s. James Alex and Carrie (James) R.; m. Mary Beall Hall, July 24, 1948; 1 child, James Alan. BA, Furman U., 1941; BLS, U. N.C., 1942; MLS, U. Mich., 1954. Reference librarian Clemson S.C. State U., 1946-52; from assoc. librarian to assoc. prof. Northwestern State U. La., 1952-58; dir. undergrad. library U. S.C., 1958-66, assoc. dir. libraries, 1966-70; dir. James A. Rogers Library, 1970-83; prof. Francis Marion Coll., Florence, S.C., 1970-83; cons. library devel. Warren Wilson Coll., Erskine Coll., Lander Coll, Coll. of Charleston, U. of N.C. at Asheville; mem. evaluation com. So. Assn. Colls., 1962-86. Contbr. articles to ednl. religious periodicals. Vice-chmn. bd. dirs. Claflin Coll., 1986-87, trustee 1974-87; dir., mem. exec. com. Alston Wilkes Soc., 1968-73; mem. Gov.'s Mansion and Lace House Commn., 1970-71; bd. govs. Christian Action Council, 1968-72; bd. curators S.C. Hist. Soc., 1986-87; bd. govs. Williams-Brice Mus., Sumter, S.C. 1984-87; del. S.C. ann. conf., 1974-79, mem. adminstrv. bd. 1971-79, 82-87. Served with USNR, 1942-46. Recipient Disting. Service award Francis Marion Coll., 1982, S.C. State Library Bd., 1983. Mem S.C. (pres. 1949, 70-71), Southeastern Library Assns., South Caroliniana Soc. Democrat. Methodist. Home: Greenwood S.C. Died Aug. 28, 1987.

RECK, W(ALDO) EMERSON, university administrator, public relations consultant, writer; b. Gettysburg, Ohio, Dec. 28, 1903; s. Samuel Harvey and Effie D. (Arnett) R.; m. Hazel Winifred January, Sept. 7, 1926; children: Phyllis (Mrs. Louis E. Welch, Jr.), Elizabeth Ann (Mrs. Gabriel J. Lada). A.B., Wittenberg U., 1926; A.M., U. Iowa, 1946; LL.D., Midland Coll., 1949. Reporter Springfield (Ohio) News, 1922-26; publicity dir. Midland Coll., Fremont, Nebr., 1926-28; dir. pub. rels., asst. prof. journalism Midland Coll., 1928-40; dir. pub. relations Colgate U., 1940-48; v.p. Wittenberg U., Springfield, Ohio, 1948-70; v.p. emeritus Wittenberg U., 1970-95; pub. relations specialist Cumerford Corp., 1970-78; hist. columnist Springfield Sun, 1973-81; spl. corr. AP, 1928-38; mng. editor Fremont Morning Guide, 1939; vis. lectr. pub. rels. State U. Iowa, summers 1941, 42, U. Wyo., summer 1948; co-dir. Seminar on Pub. Rels. for High Edn., Syracuse U., summers 1944, 45, 46; mem. commn. on ch. papers United Luth. Ch., 1951-62, cons. com. dept. of press, radio and TV, 1955-60; mem. commn. on ch. papers Luth Ch. in Am., 1962-64, 70-72, mem. exec. com., also chmn. com. periodicals of bd. publs., 1962-72; mem. mgmt. com. Office of Communications, 1972-76; chmn. pub. relations com. Council Protestant Colls. and Univs., 1961-65. Author: Public Relations: a Program for Colleges and Universities, 1946, The Changing World of College Relations, 1976, Father Can't Forget, 1982, A. Lincoln: His Last 24 Hours, 1987, 93, When the Nation Said Farewell to Lincoln, 1989, (with others) The American College, 1949; contbg. author: Public Relations Handbook, 1950, 62, 67; editor: Publicity Problems, 1939, College Publicity Manual, 1948; contbr. hist. and pub. rels. articles to gen. ednl., profl. mags. Cons. Gov. Mario Cuomo's Lincoln on Democracy Project, 1989. Recipient award Am. Coll. Pub. Rels. Assn. for Disting. Svc., 1942, Outstanding Achievement award, 1944, 47, Coun. for Advancement and Support of Edn. award, 1977, Medal of Honor, Wittenberg U., 1982, Diploma of Honor, Lincoln Meml. U., 1989, Distinction in Journalism award Midlands, 1991. Mem. Am. Coll. Pub. Relations Assn. (pres. 1940-41, historian 1966-76), Luth. Coll. Pub. Relations Assn. (pres. 1951-53), Pub. Relations Soc. Am. (nat. jud. council 1952), Assn. Am. Colls. (mem. com. on pub. relations 1945-48), AAUP, Nat. Luth. Ednl. Conf. (chmn. com. pub. relations 1949-50), Ohio Coll. Pub. Relations Officers (pres. 1954-55), Clark County Hist. Soc. (pres. 1985-86), Nat. Trust for Hist. Preservation, Archives Assos., Nat. Hist. Soc. (founding asso.), Abraham Lincoln Assn., Blue Key, Sigma Delta Chi, Pi Delta Epsilon, Delta Sigma Phi, Omicron Delta Kappa. Home: Springfield Ohio Died August 22, 1995 in Springfield, Ohio.

RECKARD, EDGAR CARPENTER, JR., minister, educator, college official; b. Huntington, W.Va., Dec. 20, 1919; s. Edgar Carpenter and Nanny Lois (Musselwhite) R.; m. Susanna Laing McWhorter, June 26, 1948; children—Edgar Scott, Francis Laing, Matthew Kinsley, Charles William, Mark Alan. B.A., Yale, 1942, M.Div., 1948; M.A. (ad eundem), Brown U., 1958; D.H.L., Westminster Coll., Mo., 1978; postgrad., U. Cambridge, Eng., U. Edinburgh, Scotland, 1948-50. Ordained to ministry Presbyn. Ch., 1948; chaplain, adviser to overseas students U. Edinburgh, 1948-50; chaplain, prof. Westminster Coll., Mo., 1950-52, Brown U., 1952-58; chaplain, prof.-at-large, gen. sec., dir. Ctr. Ednl. Opportunity Claremont Coll., Calif., 1958-72; v.p., dean of coll., prof. Centre Coll. of Ky., Danville, 1972-85; prof. emeritus Centre Coll. of Ky., 1985-95, provost, 1976-83, pres. pro tem, 1981-82; sr. cons. Council on Founds., 1983-84, Assn. Am. Colls., 1983-84; vis. mem. Sr. Common Room, Mansfield Coll., Oxford, 1964-65; Underwood fellow, 1971-72, ednl. cons., India, 1971-72. Named Claremont, Calif. Citizen of Yr., 1967; recipient Human Rights award Pomona Valley UN Assn., 1968, Golden Goblet award for svcs. to youth Los Angeles County, 1969, Gov.'s citation for outstanding svc. to Ky. Gov.'s scholar program, 1986. Mem. AAUP, Am. Acad. Religion, Am. Inst. Archaeology, Elizabethan Club Yale U., Faculty House of Claremont U. Ctr., Phi Beta Kappa, Omicron Delta Kappa. Home: Claremont Calif. Died July 18, 1995; interred Oak Park Cemetery, Claremont, CA.

RECKTENWALD, HORST CLAUS, economics educator; b. Spiesen, Saarland, Germany, Jan. 25, 1920; s. Jakob and Maria (Bund) R.; m. Hertha Joanni, Mar. 21, 1953. D in Polit. Sci., U. Mainz, Fed. Republic Germany, 1954, Venia Legendi, 1957. Prof. econs. Technische Hochschule, Darmstadt, Fed. Republic Germany, 1958-60, U. Freiburg (Fed. Republic Germany), 1960-63; prof. econs., dir. inst. U. Erlangen-Nürnberg (Fed. Republic Germany), 1963-90, prof. emeritus, 1990—; past mem. adv. couns. Bundesministerium, Bonn, Fed. Republic Germany; pres. German Fakultatentag. Author numerous books, 1966—, latest being Markt und Staat, 1980, Adam Smith Renaissance anno 1976—, 1982, Lexikon der Staats- und Geldwirtschaft, 1983, Ethik, Markt und Staat, 1985, Klassiker der Ntionalökonomie, 1983, Die Nobel-Preisträger der ökonomischen Wissenschaft-Kritische Analyse, 1989. Lt. German Army, 1938-46. Decorated Bundesverdienstkreuz lst class, Grosses Bundesverdienstkreuz (Fed. Republic Germany). Mem. Internat. Inst. Pub. Fin. (pres. 1979-82, hon. pres. 1982—), Internat. Inst. Mgmt. (bd. dirs.), Leibniz-Akanuice der Wiss in der Liberalur, Am. Econ. Assn., Verein fur Socialpolitik, Rotary.

RECLAM, HEINRICH, publisher; b. Leipzig, Ger., Oct. 30, 1910; s. Ernest R. and Marianne (von Zimmermann) R.; m. Brigitte. Ph.D. Trained as bookseller, 1938-39; trainee F. Bruckmann, Munich, 1946-47; trainee Georg Thieme Verlag, Stuttgart, 1948; mng. dir. Reclam Berlag GmbH, 1949-58; with Philipp Reclam jun Verlag GmbH, Phillip Reclam jun Graph Betrieb GmbH, Ditzingen, W.Ger.; chmn. Baden-Wurttember Pubs. Com. Mem. Co. German Book Pubs.

RECTOR, HELEN CAROLYNE, real estate associate; b. Portsmouth, Ohio, Aug. 9, 1929; d. Patrick H. and Norma I. (Massie) Mitchell; m. Ronald F. Rector, Jan. 30, 1948; children: Lucinda E., Jan R. Student, Ohio U., 1947, Shawnee U., M. Miller Real Estate Acad. Realtor C.M. Strickland, Eugene Geary, Neal Hatcher, Portsmouth, 1963—. Vol. ARC, Portsmouth, Am. Cancer Soc., Portsmouth, United Way, Portsmouth; sec. Scioto Meml. Silver Guild; mem. United Meth. Wesley Ch.; officer, Wesley United Meth. Ladies Aux., Raven Rock Ladies Golf Assn. Mem. Portsmouth Bd. Realtors, Assoc. Portsmouth Bd. Realtors (sec.). Republican. Avocations: bridge, golf, sports, antiques.

REDGRAVE, MICHAEL SCUDAMORE, actor, author; b. Bristol, Eng., Mar. 20, 1908; s. G. E. and Margaret (Scudamore) R.; m. Rachel Kempson, 1935; 3 children. Ed. Clifton Coll., Magdalene Coll., Cambridge U., also instns. in Germany and France. With Liverpool Repertory Theatre, 1934-36, Old Vic, 1936-37, 49-50, John Gielgud's Co., 1937-38, Michel St. Denis's Co., 1938-39, Stratford-on-Avon Co., 1951, 53, 58; appeared in Beggar's Opera and Thunder Rock 1940; Appeared in A Month in the Country, 1943, Uncle Harry, 1944, Macbeth, London and N.Y.C., 1947, Hamlet, London, Zurich, Elsinore and Holland Festivals, 1950, Winter Journey, 1952, Merchant of Venice, King Lear, Anthony and Cleopatra, 1953-54, A Touch of the Sun, 1958, The Aspern Papers, 1959-60, The Tiger and the Horse, 1960-61; toured Russia playing Hamlet, 1958-59; appeared in The Complaisant Lover, 1961-62, Out of Bounds, 1962, Uncle Vanya, 1962, 63, National Theatre Co. Hamlet, Hobson's Choice, The Master Builder, 1963-64; dir. opening season of Yvonne Arnaud Theatre, Guildford, 1965; dir. A Month in the Country, 1965, The Old Boys, 1971, Voyage Round My Father, 1972, 73, The Hollow Crown, 1973, Pleasure and Repentance, 1974, Shakespeare's People, 1975, 76, 77, Close of Play, 1979; films acted in include: The Lady Vanishes, The Stars Look Down, Thunder Rock, The Way to the Star, Dead of Night, Fame is the Spur, The Browning Version, The Importance of Being Earnest, The Dam Busters, The Innocents, The Loneliness of the Long Distance Runner, The Heroes of Telemark, The Hill, Oh! What a Lovely War, Battle of Britain, Goodbye Mr. Chips, Connecting Rooms, Goodbye Gemini, The Go-Between, 1971; dir. Werther 1966, LaBoheme, Glyndebourne, 1967; author: The Seventh Man (play), 1936; Actor's Ways and Means, 1953; Mask or Face, 1955; The Mountebank's Tale (novel), The Aspern Papers (play), 1959, Circus Boy (play), 1963. Served with Royal Navy, 1941-42. Decorated comdr. Order of Dannesbrog. Died Mar. 21, 1985.

REES, MINA (SPIEGEL), university administrator; b. Cleve., Aug. 2, 1902; d. Moses and Alice Louise (Stackhouse) R.; m. Leopold Brahdy, June 24, 1955 (dec. Nov. 1977). A.B., Hunter Coll., 1923, Sc.D., 1973; A.M., Columbia U., 1925, LL.D., 1971; Ph.D., U. Chgo., 1931; Sc.D. (hon.), Mt. Holyoke Coll., 1962, Wilson Coll., Wheaton Coll., Norton, Mass., Oberlin Coll., 1964, U. Mich., 1970, Nazareth Coll. of Rochester, 1971, U. Rochester, 1971, Carnegie Mellon U., 1972, Mt. Sinai Sch. Medicine, 1972, U. Ill., 1972, SUNY, 1987; Litt.D. (hon.), Rutgers U., 1965; LL.D. (hon.), Miami U., 1970; L.H.D. (hon.), N.Y. U., 1971, Marymount Coll., 1971, City U. N.Y., 1974; D.Eng. (hon.), Stevens Inst. Tech., 1980. Instr. math. Hunter Coll., 1926-32, asst. prof., 1932-40, assoc. prof., 1940-50, prof., dean faculty, 1953-61; prof., dean grad. studies CUNY, 1961-68, provost Grad. Div., 1968-69, pres. Grad. Sch. and Univ. Center, 1969-72, pres. emeritus, 1972—; Tech. aide, adminstrv. asst. to chief applied math. panel, nat. def. research com. Office Sci. Research and Devel., 1943-46; head math. br. Office Naval Research, 1946-49, dir. math. scis. div., 1949-52, dep. sci. dir., 1952-53; mem. math. div. NRC, 1953-56, mem. exec. com., 1954-56; mem. gen. scis. adv. panel. Dept. Def., 1957-61; mem. adv. bd. Computation and Exterior Ballistics Lab. U.S. Navy, 1958-61; adv. commn. for math. Nat. Bur. Standards, 1954-58, chmn., 1954-57; mem. adv. panel for math. scis. NSF, 1955-58; adv. bd. Sch. Math. Study Group, 1962-64; mem. N.Y. State Adv. Council Grad. Edn., 1962-72, Commn. Humanities, 1963-64, Nat. Sci. Bd., 1964-70; chmn. Council Grad. Schs. in U.S., 1970. Contbr. to math. publs. Mem. exec. com., trustee Woodrow Wilson Nat. Fellowship Found.; trustee Charles Babbage Inst. for History of Info. Processing; bd. dirs. Associated Hosp. Svc. N.Y., 1962-75, Lenox Hill Neighborhood Assn., 1976-81, Health Services Improvement Fund (N.Y. Blue Cross-Blue Shield), 1974-83, Sci. Inst. for Math and Soc., 1986—; vis. com. Coll. U. Chgo., 1973-85; bd. visitors CUNY Grad. Sch. and Univ. Center. Awarded fellowship U. Chgo., 1930-31; recipient King's Medal for Service in Cause of Freedom Eng., Pres.'s Cert. of Merit U.S., Elizabeth Blackwell Gold medal Hobart and William Smith Coll., Mayor's award of Honor for Sci. and Tech., N.Y.C., 1986, N.Y. Pub. Svc. award for profl. achievement, 1964, Achievement award AAUW, 1965, Pres.'s medal Hunter Coll., 1971, Alumni medal U. Chgo., 1971, Chancellor's medal CUNY, 1972, Pub. Welfare medal NAS, 1983, Disting. Svc. medal Tchrs. Coll. Columbia U., 1983; named Profl. Woman of Yr. Bus. and Profl. Women N.Y. State, 1961, Spl. Computer Pioneer award Computer Soc. IEEE, 1989. Fellow AAAS (dir. 1957-60, 66-72, chmn. bd. dirs. 1972, pres.-elect 1970, pres. 1971), N.Y. Acad. Scis.; mem. Am. Math. Soc. (trustee 1955-59), Math. Assn. Am. (2d v.p. 1963-65, recipient 1st award for disting. svc. to math.), Soc. for Indsl. and Applied Math. (dir. Inst. for Math. and Soc. 1973-86), Cosmopolitan Club, Sigma Xi, Phi Beta Kappa (mem. triennial coun. united chpts. 1940-46, senator 1970-88), Pi Mu Epsilon.

REES, PAUL STROMBERG, clergyman; b. Providence, Sept. 4, 1900; s. Seth Cook and Frida Marie (Stromberg) R.; m. Edith Alice Brown, June 3, 1926; children: Evelyn Joy Rees Moore (dec.), Daniel Seth, Julianna Rees Robertson. A.B., U. So. Calif., 1923, D.D. (hon.), 1944; D.D. (hon.), Asbury Coll., 1939, North Park Coll., Chgo., 1965, Warner Pacific Coll., 1982; Litt.D., Houghton Coll., 1953; L.H.D., Seattle Pacific U., 1959. Ordained to ministry Wesleyan Ch., 1921, Evangel. Covenant Ch., 1940. Assoc. pastor Pilgrim Tabernacle, Pasadena, Calif., 1920-23; ministerial supt. Detroit Holiness Tabernacle, 1928-32; pastor 1st Covenant Ch., Mpls., 1938-58; v.p. at large World Vision Internat., Monrovia, Calif., 1958-75; bd. dirs. World Vision Internat., 1960-85, now hon. life mem.; dir. Pastors' Conf. Ministry, 1964-75; editor World Vision Mag., 1964-72, contbg. editor, 1972-74, editor at large, 1974-87; internat. lectr. and preacher; moderator Evang. Covenant Ch. Am., 1948, v.p., 1950-55; v.p. World Evang. Fellowship; minister to ministers Billy Graham Crusades, London, 1954, Glasgow, 1955, N.Y.C., 1957, Sydney, Australia, 1959; columnist Covenant Companion, 1959-72; adviser World Council of Chs. Assembly, New Delhi, India, 1961, Uppsala, Sweden, 1968; speaker World Congress on Evangelism, Berlin, 1966, Nat. Congress on Evangelism, Mpls., 1969; lectr. Staley Disting. Scholar Found.; guest tchr. Congress on Japanese Evangelism, 1985. Author: Seth Cook Rees: The Warrior Saint, 1934, If God Be For Us, 1940, Things Unshakable, 1947, The Radiant Cross, 1949, The Face of Our Lord, 1951, Stir Up the Gift, 1952, Prayer and Life's Highest, 1956, Christian: Commit Yourself, 1957, The Adequate Man, 1958, Stand Up in Praise to God, 1960, Triumphant in Trouble, 1962, Proclaiming the New Testament—Philippians, Colossians, Philemon, 1964, Men of Action in the Book of Acts, 1966, Don't Sleep Through the Revolution, 1969; editor: Nairobi to Berkeley, 1967; assoc. editor: The Herald, 1955-75;

contbg. editor, 1975-81, Christianity Today, 1958-75; cons. editor: Eternity mag, 1960-77; speaker Staley Lectr. Series George Fox Coll., 1972, Olivet Nazarene U., 1973, Houghton Coll., 1976, Mt. Vernon Nazarene Coll., 1977, Warner Pacific Coll., 1977, Asbury Coll., 1977, Cen. Wesleyan Coll., 1984. Trustee Asbury Coll., 1935-65; trustee Asbury Theol. Sem., 1967-80, now hon. life mem.; bd. dirs. William Penn Coll., 1950-58; bd. dirs. Christianity Today, 1958-81, now hon. life mem.; bd. dirs. Paul Carlson Found., 1965-72, Bread for the World, 1974-81, World Vision Inc., 1959-85, now hon. life mem. Recipient Freedoms Found. award, 1951. Mem. Nat. Assn. Evangs. (bd. adminstrn. 1942—, pres 1952-54, now emeritus mem.), Phi Beta Kappa.

REESE, JOHN TERENCE, professional bridge player, writer; b. Epsom, Surrey, Eng., Aug. 28, 1913; s. John and Anne Maria (Hutchings) R.; m. Alwyn Sherrington, Jan. 23, 1970. Student, Bradfield Coll., Berkshire, Eng.; grad., New Coll., Oxford U., Eng. Worldwide profl. bridge player, 1955-96; bridge corr. The London Evening News, 1948-96, The Observer newspaper, 1949-96, The Lady Mag., 1954-96, The London Evening Standard, 1981-96; world champion bridge player, 1955; mem. world team Olympiad, 1980, World Pairs Olympiad, 1962, world par champion, 1961, European champion, 1948, 49, 54, 63; winner all top Brit. championships, including Gold Cup 8 times, Masters Pairs 7 times, also others; an originator of ACOL sys. in the 1930's; considered at one time top-ranking player in world. Author or co-author over 100 books on bridge, poker, backgammon, casino gambling, and canasta, including Reese on Play, 1948, 2d edit., 1975 (transl. into 5 langs.), The Expert Game, 1958, 2d edit., 1973, Teach Yourself Bridge, 1980, 2d edit., 1992; contbr. articles on bridge to mags. and periodicals worldwide. Mem. English Bridge Union (hon. life). Avocation: golf. Died Jan. 28, 1996.

REEVES, CHARLES HOWELL, classics educator; b. Schenectady, Nov. 23, 1915; s. Howell H. and Justina (Smith) R.; m. Lucille Jane Pritchard, Dec. 22, 1945; children—Jane L. Reeves McGee, Frances E. Reeves Herring, Helen Ann Reeves Hanks, Ruth M. Reeves Connell, Justina P. Reeves Byrne, Charles Howell. A.B., Union Coll., Schenectady, 1937; Ph.D. in Classics, U. Cin., 1947. Instr. classics Ind. U., 1946-49; asst. prof. classics Johns Hopkins, 1949-52; asso. prof., then prof. classics U. Okla., 1952-66; prof. classics Case Western Res. U., 1966-86, prof. emeritus, 1986-96, chmn. dept., 1966-77. Author articles on Greek tragedy. Served to lt. USNR, 1942-45. Mem. Am. Philol. Assn., Am. Inst. Archaeology, Classical Assn., Middle West and South, Soc. Ancient Greek Philosophy, Virgilian Soc., N. Am. Patristics Soc., Phi Beta Kappa. Home: Cleveland Ohio Died Nov. 27, 1996; interred Lakeview Cemetery, Cleveland, OH.

REEVES, ROBERT GRIER LEFEVRE, geology educator, scientist; b. York, Pa., May 30, 1920; s. Edward LeGrande and Helen (Baker) R.; m. Elizabeth Bodette Simmons, June 11, 1942; children: Dale Ann, Edward Boyd. Student, Yuba Coll., 1938-40; B.S., U. Nev., 1949; M.S., Stanford U., 1950, Ph.D., 1965. Registered profl. engr., Tex. Geophysicist, geologist U.S. Geol. Survey, 1949-69; with assignments as project chief iron ore deposits of Nev., tech. adviser Fgn. Aid Program; vis. prof. econ. geology U. Rio Grande do Sul, Brazil; staff geologist for research contracts and grants and profl. staffing Washington; prof. geology Colo. Sch. Mines, Golden, 1969-73; staff scientist Earth Resources Observation Systems Data Center, U.S. Geol. Survey, Sioux Falls, S.D., 1973-78; prof. geology U. Tex.-Permian Basin, Odessa, 1978-85, chmn. earth scis., 1978-82; dean Coll. Sci. and Engring. U. Tex. Permian Basin, 1979-84; cons. geologist, engr. ptnr. Orion, Ltd., Midland, Tex., 1984-87, cons. engr., geologist, 1987—; leader People to People Econ. Geology Trip to Brazil and Peru, 1985; co-leader Am. Geol. Inst. Internat. Field Inst. to Brazil, 1966; vis. geol. scientist Boston Coll., Boston U., 1967; sr. Fulbright lectr. U. Adelaide, Australia, 1969. Contbr. articles profl. jours. Served to maj. Signal Corps AUS, 1941-46, ETO. Recipient Outstanding Service award U.S. Geol. Survey, 1965. Fellow Geol. Soc. Am., Soc. Econ. Geologists; mem. Am. Inst. Mining, Metall. and Petroleum Engrs. (sec. Washington 1964), Am. Soc. Photogrammetry (editor-in-chief Manual of Remote Sensing), Soc. Ind. Profl. Earth Scientists. Died Dec. 28, 1995.

REGAN, FRANCIS, mathematics educator; b. West Terre Haute, Ind., Jan. 10, 1903; s. Patrick and Ella Frances (Curley) R. AB, Ind. State U., 1922; MA, Ind. U., 1930; LLB, LaSalle U., Chgo., 1928; PhD, U. Mich., 1932. High sch. math. tchr. Warren County, Williamsport, Ind., 1923-25; prof. math. Columbus Coll., Sioux Falls, S.D., 1925-29; asst. prof. Colo. State U., Ft. Collins, 1929-30; prof. math. St. Louis U., 1932-71, head dept. math., 1949-71, prof. emeritus, head dept. emeritus, 1971—. Contbr. articles to math. jours. Mem. Sigma Xi, Phi Beta Kappa, Pi Mu Epsilon. DIED 02/18/96. .

REGES, MARIE STEPHEN, religion educator; b. Washington, Mar. 27, 1915; d. George Henry and Mary (Gately) R. BA, Trinity Coll., 1937; MA, Catholic U. Am., 1938; BA, Providence Coll., 1952; MA, U. Wis., 1970; LHD (hon.), Rosary Coll., 1984, Edgewood Coll., 1990. Prof. religious studies and math. Rosary Coll., River Forest, Ill., 1947-59, Edgewood Coll., Madison, Wis., 1959-62; prof. religious studies and scriptures Edgewood Coll., Madison, 1962-80; prof. emeritis Madison, Wis., 1980-97; lectr. Outreach Programs, Madison, 1959—. Author: The New Catholic Encyclopedia, 1975, Womens Encyclopedia, 1991. Coord. Jewish-Christian Dialogue, Madison, 1987—; dir. Edn. for Parish Svc., Madison, 1981—; coord., lectr. Continuing Edn. of Edgewood, Madison, 1965—. Recipient City of Jerusalem Peace award Madison Jewish Coun., 1975, Swarsensky Svc. award Rotary, Madison, 1990. Mem. Cath. Bibl. Soc., Assn. Hebrew Lang. Prof., Wis. Acad. Arts and Sci., Hadassah, Sinsinawa Dominicans. Home: Madison Wis. Died 05/25/97.

REICH, JACK EGAN, insurance company executive; b. Chgo., June 17, 1910; s. Henry Carl and Rose (Egan) B.; m. Jean Grady, Apr. 30, 1935; children: Rosemary (Mrs. Jerry Semler), Judith (Mrs. Dan Hoyt). Student, Purdue U., 1928-31; LLD (hon.), Butler U., 1973; PhD (hon.), Marian Coll., 1983; LLD (hon.), Ind. U., 1986; PhD (hon.), Purdue U., 1993. With Inland Steel Co., East Chicago, Ind., 1925-31; field dir. gross income tax and employment security divs. State of Ind., 1933-40; field dir. Ind. C. of C., 1940-52, exec. v.p., 1952-62; pres., chmn. bd. Indpls. Water Co., 1962-67; chmn. bd. emeritus Am. United Life Ins. Co.; mem., past pres. Assn. Ind. Life Ins. Cos. Bd. dirs., past pres. Greater Indpls. Progress Com.; mem. exec. com., past chmn. Ind. Legal Found.; bd. dirs. Ind. Colls. of Ind. Found., Wishard Meml. Found., Indpls. Downtown Inc.; bd. dirs., past campaign chmn., past pres. United Way Cen. Ind.; past mem. bd. lay trustees St. Mary-of-Woods Colls.; mem. adv. bd. St. Vincent Hosp.; bd. regents, past pres. Ind. Acad.; past local and state pres., nat. v.p. Jaycees. Mem. Ind. C. of C. (bd. dir., past chmn. and exec. v.p.), Econ. Club (past pres.), Columbia Club, Indpls. Athletic Club, Indpls. Press Club, Meridian Hills Country Club, Skyline Club (chmn.), Ind. Soc. Club (Chgo.), Pi Kappa Alpha. Home: Indianapolis Ind. Died Sept. 26, 1996.

REICHELDERFER, MARGARET M., technical writer; b. Gary, Ind., Jan. 2, 1946; m. Edward L. Reichelderfer, Oct. 19, 1985. BA, U. N.Mex., 1968; MA, U. Dayton, 1969, postgrad., 1975-76; postgrad., Ill. Inst. Tech., 1980. Lectr. Ohio State U., Columbus, 1969-70; bus. systems specialist Bell Labs. AT&T, Piscataway, N.J., 1970-71; sr. tech. writer AT&T, Naperville, Ill., 1979-84; sr. product planner AT&T, Lisle, Ill., 1984-86; sr. systems analyst 3d Nat. Bank, Dayton, 1972-74, asst. mgr. systems group, 1974-76; sr. tech. writer Digital Equipment Corp., Marlboro, Mass., 1976-77; sr. sales tng. specialist NCR Corp., Dayton, 1977-79; sr. tech. cons. Personnel Scis. Inc., N.Y.C., 1986-87, Profl. Data Res., Dayton, 1987-89. Author: Systems Writing, 1971, Document Converter Guide, 1986, Project Management Guide, 1987, SAMNA: The Basics, 1987. Advisor Explorer Boy Scouts Am., Dayton, 1972-76. Mem. Am. Soc. Tng. Devel. (sec. 1974-75, v.p.), Assn. System Mgmt., Soc. Tech. Writing (judge 1981), Phi Kappa Phi, Phi Beta Kappa. Home: Englewood Ohio Died Nov. 30, 1989; interred Calvary Cemetery.

REICHSTEIN, TADEUS, botanist, scientist, educator; b. Wloclawek, Poland, July 20, 1897; s. Isidor and Gustava (Brokman) R.; m. Luise Henriette Quarles v. Ufford, July 21, 1927; children: Margrit, Ruth. Student, Industrieschule, Zurich, 1914-16; diploma in chem. engring., Eidg. Tech. Hochschule, Zurich, 1920, Dr. Ing.-Chem., 1922; D.Sc. (hon.), U. Sorbonne, Paris, 1947, U. Basel, 1951, U. Geneva, U. Abidjan, 1967, U. London, 1968, U. Leeds, 1970. Prof. Eidg. Techn. Hochschule, 1934-38; prof. U. Basel, Switzerland, 1938-67, prof. emeritus, 1967-96; dir. Pharmacol. Inst., 1938-48, Inst. Organic Chemistry, 1946-67; research botanist on ferns, 1967-96. Contbr. articles to profl. publs. Recipient Marcel-Benoist prize, 1948; co-recipient Nobel prize in physiology or medicine, 1950, various other prizes. Fellow Royal Soc. London, Nat. Acad. Sci. (Washington), Royal Irish Acad., Chem. Soc. London (hon.), Swiss Med. Acad. (hon.), Indian Acad. Sci. (hon.); mem. Mus. Hist. Nat. Paris (corr.), Med. Faculty U. Basel (hon.), Linn. Soc. (London, hon.), Am. Fern Soc. (hon.), Acad. Royale Med. Belg. (hon.), Am. Rheumat. Assn. (hon.), Weizmann Inst. Rehovoth, Pharm. Soc. Japan (hon.), Deutsche Akad. Leopoldina, Am. Soc. Bd. Chem. (hon.). Home: Basel Switzerland Died Aug. 1, 1996.

REINHEIMER, ROBERT, JR., architect; b. Mercury, Tex., Aug. 8, 1917; s. Robert and Frances Curry (Bell) R.; m. Dalma Louise Rawls, July 23, 1938 (dec. 1978); children: Patricia, Frances; m. Lyda McNully, Jan. 6, 1980. AA, Tarleton State U., 1935. Registered architect, Ark., Tex. Draftsman Bayard Witt, Architects, Texarkana, Tex., 1938-44; ptnr. Witt & Reinheimer, Texarkana, Tex., 1944-47, Reinheimer & Cox, Texarkana, Tex., 1947-69; pres. Reinheimer, Cox & Assoc., Inc., Texarkana, Tex., 1969-76, RHB Group, Inc., Texarkana, Tex., 1976—. Chmn. Bldg. Code Bd. of Appeals, City of Texarkana, Ark., 1959-62; vice-chmn. Zoning Bd. Adjustment, City of Texarkana, Tex., 1969-85. Fellow AIA (pres. N.E. Tex. chpt. 1961-62); mem. Tex. Soc. Architects (chmn. profl. devel. com. 1969-72, v.p. 1967-68). Lodge: Rotary. Home: Texarkana Tex. DIED 04/18/95. .

REISSNER, ERIC (MAX ERICH REISSNER), applied mechanics researcher; b. Aachen, Germany, Jan. 5, 1913; came to U.S., 1936, naturalized, 1945; s. Hans and Josephine (Reichenberger) R.; m. Johanna Siegel, Apr. 19, 1938; children: John E., Eva M. Dipl. Ing., Technische Hochschule, Berlin, 1935, Dr. Ing., 1936; Ph.D., MIT, 1938; Dr. Ing. (hon.), U. Hannover, Germany, 1964. Mem. faculty MIT, Cambridge, 1939-69, prof. math., 1949-66; prof. applied math. MIT, 1966-69; prof. applied mechanics U. Calif., San Diego, 1970-78, prof. emeritus, 1978—; aero. rsch. scientist NACA, Langley Field, 1948, 51, Ramo, Wooldridge, 1954, 55, Lockheed, Palo Alto, 1956, 57; vis. prof. U. Mich., Ann Arbor, 1949, U. Calif., San Diego, 1967. Cons. editor Addison-Wesley Pub. Co., 1949-60; mng. editor Jour. Math. and Physics, 1945-67; assoc. editor Quar. Applied Math., 1946-95, Studies Applied Math., 1970—, Internat. Jour. Solids and Structures, 1983-95; contbr. chpts. to books, articles to profl. jours. Recipient Clemens Herschel award Boston Soc. Civil Engrs., 1956, Theodore von Karman medal ASCE, 1964; Guggenheim fellow, 1962. Fellow ASME (hon. mem. 1991; Timoshenko medal 1973, ASME medal 1988), AIAA (Structures and Materials award 1984), Am. Acad. Arts and Scis., Am. Acad. Mechanics; mem. NAE, Internat. Acad. Astronautics, Am. Math. Soc., Gesellschaft für Angewandte Mathematik und Mechanik (hon.). DIED 11/01/96. .

REISTLE, CARL ERNEST, JR., petroleum engineer; b. Denver, June 26, 1901; s. Carl E. and Leonora I. (McMaster) R.; m. Mattie A Muldrow, June 23, 1922; children: Bette Jean (Mrs. George F. Pierce), Mattie Ann (Mrs. James Tracy Clark), Nancy L. (Mrs. Travis Parker), Carl Ernest III. B.S., U. Okla., 1922; postgrad., Harvard Sch. Bus. Adminstrn., 1948. Petroleum chemist U.S. Bur. Mines, 1922-29, petroleum engr., 1929-33; chmn. East Tex. Engring. Assn., 1933-36; engr. in charge Humble Oil & Refining Co., 1936-40, chief petroleum engr., 1940-45, gen. supt. prodn., 1945-46, mgr. prodn. dept., 1946-51, dir., 1948-51, dir. in charge prodn. dept., 1951-55, v.p., 1955-57, exec. v.p., 1957-61, pres., 1961-63, chmn. bd., chief exec. officer, 1963-66, ret., 1966, cons., 1966-69; dir. Eltra Corp.; dir., chmn. exec. com. Olinkraft, Inc., 1967-78. Contbr. numerous articles to profl. jours. Bd. dirs. Tex. Tech Coll., Lubbock, 1966-69, U. Okla. Research Inst., Norman. Recipient Anthony F. Lucas Gold medal Am. Inst. Mining, Metall. and Petroleum Engrs., 1958. Mem. Am. Petroleum Inst., Am. Inst. Mining, Metall. and Petroleum Engrs. (pres. 1956), Sigma Xi, Tau Beta Pi, Sigma Tau, Alpha Chi Sigma. Club: River Oaks Country. Died Oct. 20, 1996.

RELSON, MORRIS, patent lawyer; b. N.Y.C., Apr. 14, 1915; s. Benjamin and Minnie R.; m. Rita L. Rubenstein, Apr. 5, 1941; children—Katherine D., David M., Peter J. BSEE, CCNY, 1935; MA in Math, George Washington U., 1940; JD, NYU, 1945. Bar: N.Y. 1945, U.S. Supreme Ct. 1950. Elec. engr. Nat. Park Svc., Washington, 1936-37; patent examiner U.S. Patent Office, 1937-41; patent agt. and atty. Sperry Gyroscope Co., Gt. Neck, N.Y., 1941-48; ptnr. Darby & Darby P.C., and predecessor, N.Y.C., 1948—; vol. spl. master U.S. Dist Ct. for So. Dist N.Y., 1979-80. Contbr. articles to legal jours. Mem. ABA (patent, trademark and copyright sect.), IEEE, Am. Patent Law Assn., N.Y. Patent Law Assn. (pres. 1976-77, bd. dirs. 1970-78), N.Y. Acad. Sci., Phi Beta Kappa, Sigma Xi., Sigma Pi Sigma. Patentee in field. DIED 05/31/96. .

REPLOGLE, FREDERICK ALLEN, management psychologist; b. Rossville, Ind., Dec. 15, 1898; s. William H. and Elizabeth (Metzger) R.; m. Georgia Miller, Sept. 8, 1926; children—Justin, Carol Ann (Mrs. Christian Nielsen). B.A., Manchester Coll., Ind., 1921, LL.D., 1956; M.A., Northwestern U., 1927; Ph.D., U. Chgo., 1936. Diplomate: Am. Bd. Profl. Psychology. Pub. sch. adminstrn. Ind., 1921-26; asso. dir. research Meth. Bd. of Edn., Chgo., 1928-31; dean, prof. edn. and psychology McPherson Coll., 1931-35; dean, head sociology dept. Oklahoma City U., 1935-38; personnel dir. Macalester Coll., St. Paul, 1938-43; supr. Chgo. region psychol. services Stevenson, Jordan & Harrison, Chgo., 1943-45; founding partner Rohrer, Hibler & Replogle, Inc. (mgmt. psychologists), 1945—, dir. Chgo. region, 1945-68, cons., 1968—. Former pres. bd. trustees, former chmn. bd. YMCA Met. Chgo.; former mem. nat. bd., former vice chmn. YMCA, N.Y.C.; hon. former mem. bd., past chmn. bd. Chgo. Theol. Sem.; former vice chmn. bd. trustees George Williams Coll., Chgo.; hon. trustee Manchester Coll.; bd. dirs. World without War Coun. Inc. Fellow Am. Psychol. Assn., AAAS; mem. Soc. Advancement Mgmt., Mid-Western, Ill., Chgo. psychol. assns., Am. Guidance and Personnel Assn., Religious Edn. Assn. (dir.). Clubs: Execs. (Chgo.), Univ. (Chgo.), Plaza (Chgo.); Rotary.

RESNEKOV, LEON, medical educator; b. Cape Town, South Africa, Mar. 20, 1928; came to U.S., 1967; s. Charles and Alice (Mitchell) R.; m. Carmella Ocheroff, Aug. 28, 1955; children: Orna, Charles Dean. M.B.Ch.B., U. Cape Town, 1951, M.D., 1965. Am. Bd. Internal Medicine. Intern Groote Schuur Hosp., U. Cape Town, 1951-52; registrar Kings Coll. Hosp., U.

London, 1954-61; sr. registrar Inst. Cardiology, Nat. Heart Hosp., London, 1961-67; assoc. prof. medicine U. Chgo., 1967-71, prof. medicine, 1971-81, Frederick H. Rawson prof., 1981-93, dir. myocardial infarction research unit, 1967-75, joint dir. sect. cardiology, 1971-81, dir. spl. ctr. research in ischemic heart disease, 1975-80; attending physician in cardiology U. Chgo. Med. Ctr., 1967-93; Viscount St. Cyres lectr. Inst. Cardiology, London, 1979; Welker vis. prof. medicine U. Kans., Kansas City, 1981; Harry and Anna Borun vis. prof. cardiology UCLA, 1981; Sampson vis. prof. cardiology U. Calif.-San Francisco, 1982. Author: (with A. Gilston) Cardiopulmonary Resuscitation, 1967; contbr. numerous articles to sci. jours.; editor: Year Book of Cardiology, 1980-93; mem. editorial bd.: Circulation, 1981-93. Yearly lectureship and fellowship established in his name U. Chgo., 1993; Wellcome rsch. fellow Karolinska Hosp., Stockholm, 1967. Fellow Royal Soc. Medicine, Royal Coll. Physicians, Am. Coll. Cardiology; mem. Brit. Cardiac Soc., Chgo. Heart Assn. (pres. 1978-79 Heart of Yr. award), Chgo. Cardiology Group (chmn. 1978-80), Am. Coll. Chest Physicians (pres. 1979-80), Assn. Univ. Cardiologists, Am. Fedn. Clin. Research, Central Soc. Clin. Research, Alpha Omega Alpha. Home: Chicago Ill. Died Aug. 17, 1993.

REUMAN, ROBERT EVERETT, philosophy educator; b. Foochow, China, Feb. 16, 1923; s. Otto G. and Martha Lydia (Bourne) R.; m. Dorothy Ann Swan, Sept. 2, 1949; children: Martha Claire, David Alan, Jonathan Robert, Ann Evalyn, Elizabeth Linda. A.B., Middlebury Coll., 1945; M.A., U. Pa., 1946, Ph.D., 1949. Asst. instr. U. Pa., 1946-48; instr. Temple U., 1947-49; mem. Friends' Ambulance Service Unit, China, 1949-51, chmn., 1950-51; dir. Quaker Student House, Freiburg im Breisgau, Fed. Republic Germany, 1951-53; instr. Lafayette Coll., 1953-54, asst. prof., 1954-56; mem. faculty Colby Coll., Waterville, Maine, 1956—, prof. philosophy, 1969—, chmn. social sci. div., 1975-78, chmn. dept. philosophy and religion, 1975-78; Dana prof. philosophy Colby Coll., 1986-91, ret., 1991. Author: Mauern, 1965, (with others) Anatomy of Anti-Communism, 1969; pamphlet Walls, 1966; contbr. articles to profl. jours. New Eng. regional chmn. Danforth Assocs., 1963-64; Quaker internat. affairs rep., Germany, 1964-66; bd. dirs. Am. Friends of Le College Cevenol, 1973-85; mem. Maine Humanities Coun., 1980-85, mem. exec. com., 1981-84. With Civilian Pub. Svc., 1943-46. Harrison fellow, 1945-46; Colby Coll. grantee, 1972, 79, 82. Mem. Am. Philos. Assn., AAUP, Soc. for Values in Higher Edn. Democrat. Unitarian-Quaker. Died Aug. 29, 1997.

REVOLLO BRAVO, MARIO CARDINAL, bishop; b. Genoa, Italy, June 15, 1919. Ordained priest Roman Cath. Ch., 1943. Elected to titular Ch. of Tinisa di Numidia, 1973; consecrated bishop, 1973; prefect Nueva Pamplona, 1978; transferred to Bogota, Colombia, 1984—; created cardinal, 1988.

REY, MARGRET ELIZABETH, writer; b. Hamburg, Germany, May 16, 1906; came to U.S., 1940; d. Felix and Gertrude (Rosenfeld) Waldstein; m. Hans A. Rey (dec. 1977). Art degree, Art Acad., Hamburg, Germany, 1929, Bauhaus, Dessau, Germany, 1931, Acad. Art, Dusseldorf, Germany, 1932. Children's author Houghton Mifflin Co., Boston, 1941-97, Harper & Row, N.Y.C., 1945-97; script cons. Curgeo, Montreal, Quebec, Can., 1977-83; adj. prof. Brandeis U., Waltham, Mass., 1978-84. Author: Pretzel, 1944, Spotty, 1945, Billy's Picture, 1948; co-author: Curious George, 1941, Curious George Takes a Job, 1947, Curious George Rides a Bike, 1952, Curious George Gets a Medal, 1957, Curious George Flies a Kite, 1958, Curious George Learns the Alphabet, 1963, Curious George Goes to the Hospital, 1966. Founder, trustee The Curious George Found., Cambridge, Mass., 1991—; bd. dirs. Phillips Brooks House, Harvard U., Cambridge, Mass., 1989—. Mem. World Wildlife, Smithsonian, Mus. Fine Arts, Audobon Soc., Defenders of Wildlife. Democrat. Avocations: reading, gardening. Home: Cambridge Mass. Died Dec. 21, 1996.

REY, WILLIAM KENNETH, aerospace engineer, educator; b. N.Y.C., Aug. 11, 1925; s. William and Frances Sophia (Sauer) R.; m. Ruth Jeanette Vickery, Nov. 27, 1946; children: Jeanette Rey Todd, William Kenneth. B.S. in Aero. Engring., U. Ala., 1946, M.S. in Civil Engring., 1949; postgrad., U. Ariz., 1961. Registered profl. engr., Ala. Instr. math. U. Ala., 1946-47, instr. engring. mechanics, 1947-49, asst. prof. engring. mechanics, 1949-52, assoc. prof. aero. engring., 1952-58, prof. aero. engring., 1958-60, prof. aerospace engring., 1960-93, acting head dept., 1972, dir. high sch. relations, 1970-93, asst. dean engring., 1976-93; Disting. Engring. fellow U. Ala., 1988; cons. rsch. NACA, NASA, Army and Air Force depts. Contbr. NACA and NASA reports, revs., lab. manual. Recipient Dist. Scouter award Boy Scouts Am., 1970, Penny Allen award 1985 and Keith Woodman award U. Ala., 1991, also Algernon Sidney Sullivan award, 1991; named Tuscaloosa Engr. of Yr., 1983. Assoc. fellow AIAA; mem. NSPE (chpt. v.p. 1982-83, pres. 1983-84), Am. Soc. Engring. Edn., Ala. Soc. Profl. Engrs. (v.p. 1984-85, pres.-elect 1985-86, pres. 1986-87), Capstone Engring. Soc. (exec. dir. 1976-90), Golden Key, Theta Tau (grand regent, nat. pres. 1963-66, grand marshal 1968-72), Tau Beta Pi, Omicron Delta Kappa, Sigma Gamma Tau, Pi Mu Epsilon, Phi Kappa Phi. Baptist (deacon). Clubs: Kiwanis (dir. Tuscaloosa, Ala. 1969-74, 76-84, 88-89, 90-91, 1st v.p. 1976-77, pres. 1978-79, zone chmn. 1975-78, lt. gov.-elect 1984-85, lt. gov. 1985-86, accredited rep. 1990-91, Kiwanian of Yr. award 1991), University (gov. Tuscaloosa 1970-77, pres. 1976). Home: Tuscaloosa Ala. Died April 20, 1993, interred Memory Hills, Tuscaloosa.

REYNOLDS, MARJORIE, actress; b. Buhl, Idaho; m. Jack Reynolds (div.); m. Jon M. Haffen; 1 child, Linda Hinshaw. Appeared in films Holiday Inn, 1942, Ministry of Fear, 1944, Up in Mabel's Room, 1944, Duffy's Tavern, 1945, Monsieur Beaucaire, 1946, That Midnight Kiss, 1949, Box Rhythm, 1959, The Silent Witness, 1962, (tv shows) The Life of Riley, The Millionaire, Leave It to Beaver. Home: Manhattan Beach Calif. Died Feb. 1, 1997.

REYNOLDS, WILLIAM HAROLD, music educator, choral conductor, music critic; b. Hermosa Beach, Calif., July 19, 1925; s. Frank Harold and Elma Katherine (Williams) R.; m. Mary Lee Kingman, June 19, 1949; children: Christopher, Joel, Ellen, Anne Marie, Susan, Martha. B.A. with highest honors, UCLA, 1949; M.F.A., Princeton U., 1952. Asst. music critic L.A. Times, 1948-50; asst. instr. music Princton (N.J.) U., 1951-52; instr. music Vassar Coll., Poughkeepsie, N.Y., 1952-54; asst. prof. U. Calif., Riverside, 1954-60, assoc. prof., 1960-66, prof., 1966-91, chmn. dept. music, 1961-67, 77-82, chmn. acad. senate, 1968-70, mem. statewide acad. coun., 1968-70, assoc. dean Coll. Humanities and Social Scis., 1989-94, prof. emeritus, 1991-95; appointed dir. U. Calif. Scandinavian Study Ctr. at Lund U. (Sweden) and Copenhagen U., 1987-89; asso. Danforth Found., 1958-95. Author: Common Practice Harmony, 1985; contbr. articles on Danish composers to Grove's Dictionary of Music; contbr. articles to New Grove Dictionary of Opera, 1992. Recipient E. Harris Harbison prize for disting. teaching Danforth Found., 1969, Riverside Arts Coun. award for music, 1979; grantee Am. Philos Soc., 1960-61, 75-76, Statewide U. Calif. Humanities Inst., 1967-68, Creative Arts Inst., 1974, Danmarks Nat. Bank, 1975, Am. Scandinavian Found., 1982-83. Mem. Coll. Music Soc. (v.p. 1972-75, pres. 1975-77), Calif. Music Execs. (pres. 1981-82), Internat., Am. musicol. socs., Am. Choral Dirs. Assn., Calif. Choral Condrs. Guild (pres. Riverside-San Bernardino chpt. 1956-57), Phi Beta Kappa (hon., pres. Iota chpt. 1985-86). Democrat. Episcopalian. Home: Riverside Calif. Died Mar. 3, 1995.

RHEA, EDWARD BUFORD, JR., brokerage house executive; b. Kansas City, Kans., Aug. 14, 1934; s. Edward Buford Sr. and Dorothy Marie (Corless) R.; m. M. Maureen Duffin, June 16, 1957 (div. May 1969); m. Joanne H. Pilsl, June 15, 1969; children: Mary Bridget, Marita, Edward. BS Econs., Rockhurst Coll., 1958. Grain buyer Gen. Mills Inc., Mpls., 1958-60; merchandiser Gen. Mills Inc., Kansas City, Mo., 1960-63; salesman Gen. Foods Corp., Kankakee, Ill., 1963-65; sales mgr. Gen. Foods Corp., Kankakee, 1965, purchasing mgr., 1966-67; broker Paine Webber Jackson Curtis, 1967-72; v.p. Paine Webber Jackson Curtis, Chgo., 1972-80, Merrill Lynch, Chgo., 1980-89; sr. v.p. Paine Webber, 1989-92; v.p. Merrill Lynch, Chgo., 1993-95; Mem. Chgo. Bd. of Trade 1971-95. Village trustee Village of Mt. Prospect, Ill., 1975-77; bd. dirs. United Way, 1986-88. With U.S. Army 1953-55. Mem. Lions Club (pres. 1986-87, Mt. Prospect), Rolling Green C. of C., Moose, AM Legion. Republican. Roman Catholic. Avocations: golf, bridge. Deceased.

RHETT, HARRY MOORE, JR., investment executive; b. Huntsville, Ala., Mar. 3, 1912; s. Harry Moore and Marie Louise (Rison) R.; m. Sharon Barbour, June 14, 1952 (dec. May 1972); children: Louise Rhett Orem, Harry Moore III, William Warren Barbour, Leslie Rhett Crosby. AB, Washington & Lee U., 1935; MBA, Harvard U., 1937; LHD (hon.), U. Ala., 1995. Asst. underwriter Accident & Casualty Ins. Co., N.Y.C., 1937-39; spl. agt. Accident & Casualty Ins. Co., L.A., 1939-41; asst. to pres. Rison Banking Co., Huntsville, 1946-48; prin. H. M. Rhett Jr., Huntsville, 1948-96; bd. dirs. emeritus First Ala. Bank, Huntsville, First Ala. Bancshares, Birmingham. Mem. Army Community Rels. Com., Redstone Arsenal, Ala, 1955-96; treas. U. Ala. Huntsville Found., 1979-96; chmn. Hunstville Waterworks Utility Bd., 1954-95, Huntsville Gas Utility Bd., 1954-95. Maj. U.S. Army, 1941-46, ETO. Recipient Outstanding Citizen award Huntsville-Madison County C. of C., 1973; Harry Moore Rhett Jr. Solarium named in his honor Huntsville Hosp., 1987. Mem. Masters of Foxhound Assn. (bd. dirs. Leesburg, Va.), Nat. Steeplechase and Hunt Assn. Md., Huntsville-Madison County C. of C. (pres. 1952), Harvard Club of N.Y.C. (Chatham (Mass.) Beach and Tennis Club (pres. 1977-82), Byrd Spring Rod and Gun Club, Rotary (pres. Huntsville club 1952). Democrat. Episcopalian. Avocations: tennis, fox hunting. Died Feb. 3, 1996.

RHODES, RONDELL HORACE, biology educator; b. Abbeville, S.C., May 25, 1918; s. Leslie Franklin and Pearl Lee (Clinkscales) R.; B.S., Benedict Coll., Columbia, S.C., 1940; M.S., U. Mich., 1950; Ph.D., N.Y.U., 1960. Instr. biology Lincoln U., Jefferson City, Mo., 1947-49; asst. prof. Tuskegee (Ala.) Inst., 1950-55; teaching fellow N.Y.U., 1955-61; mem. faculty Fairleigh Dickinson U., Teaneck, N.Y., 1961-97, prof. biol. scis., 1968-88, prof. emeritus, from 1988; chmn. dept., 1966-70, 73-76, 79-82. Served with AUS, 1942-46. Mem. AAAS, Am. Inst. Biol. Scis., Am. Soc. Zoologists, AAUP, Nat. Assn. Biology Tchrs., N.Y. Acad. Scis., Sigma Xi. Democrat. Episcopalian. Deceased. Home: Brooklyn N.Y.

RIBICOFF, ABRAHAM A., lawyer, former senator; b. New Britain, Conn., Apr. 9, 1910; s. Samuel and Rose (Sable) R.; m. Ruth Siegel, June 28, 1931 (dec.); children: Peter, Jane; m. Lois Mathes, 1972. Student, NYU; LL.B. cum laude, U. Chgo., 1933. Bar: Conn. 1933, N.Y. 1981, U.S. Ct. Appeals (D.C. cir.) 1982, U.S. Supreme Ct. 1981. Mem. Conn. Ho. of Reps., 1939-42; mcpl. judge Hartford, Conn., 1942-43, 45-47; chmn. Conn. Assembly Mcpl. Ct. Judges, 1942; mem. 81st—82d congresses from 1st Conn. Dist., mem. com. fgn. affairs; gov. Conn., 1955-61; sec. HEW, 1961-62; mem. U.S. Senate from Conn., 1963-81, mem. fin., joint econ. coms., chmn. govt. affairs com.; spl. counsel firm Kaye, Scholer, Fierman, Hays & Handler, N.Y.C. and Washington, 1981—; dir. Hartford Ins. Group, United Television, Inc. Author: Politics: The American Way, 1967, America Can Make It, 1972, The American Medical Machine, 1972. Democrat.

RICH, ERIC, plastics company executive; b. Znojmo, Czechoslovakia, Oct. 1, 1921; came to U.S., 1955, naturalized, 1962; s. Sandor and Alice (Shifferes) Reich; m. Ilse L.B. Renard, Nov. 14, 1959; children—Susan Frances, Sally Dora, Charles Anthony. Ed., U. Coll., Wales, Bangor, U.K. Export sales mgr. Pilot Radio, Ltd., London, Eng., 1945-49; dir. Derwent Exports, Ltd., London, 1949-55; export sales mgr. Am. Molding Powder & Chem. Corp., N.Y.C., 1956-58; with Gering Plastics Co. div. Monsanto Chem. Co., Kenilworth, N.J., 1958-67; v.p., gen. mgr. Goldmark Plastics Internat., Inc., New Hyde Park, N.Y., 1967—. Served with RAF, 1941-45. Decorated Gallantry medal, 1939-43, Star Atlantic Star. Home: Garden City N.Y. Died Jan. 4, 1995.

RICHARD, SANDRA CLAYTON, academic administrator, educator; b. Athens, Tex.; d. Chester Armendale and Lola Hybernia (Clayton) R. AA, Trinity Valley Community Coll.; BBA, U. Tex., 1958, MBA, 1959, PhD, 1968. Instr. Am. U. of Beirut, 1959-61, asst. prof., 1968-74, vis. assoc. prof., 1978-81; asst. prof. Haile Selassie I U., Ethiopia, 1965-66, U. Mo., St. Louis, 1966-67; vis. assoc. prof. U. Notre Dame, 1974-77, Calif. State U., Long Beach, 1977-78; assoc. prof., chmn., div. bus. adminstrn. Tex. A&M Internat. Univ., 1981-93, dir. doctoral program, 1993-94; prodn. and inventory control cons. Mathes Mfg. Co., Athens, 1958, U.N. Indsl. Devel. Orgn., Vienna, Austria, 1968; mgmt. devel. programs Pakistan Indsl. Devel. Corp., Karachi, 1963, Beirut, Bahrain, Qatar, 1970-74, 78-81. Contbr. articles to profl. jours. Mem. Leadership Laredo, 1985—; founding bd. mem. Laredo Regional Food Bank, 1982—; bd. mem. Animal Protective Soc., Laredo, 1982—; mem. steering com. Am. for Justice in the Middle East, Beirut, 1980-81. Named Outstanding Ex-Student Trinity Valley Community Coll., Athens, 1983; Fulbright grad. research grantee, Karachi, 1962-63. Mem. Soc. for Internat. Devel., Acad. Internat. Bus., Acad. Mgmt., Internat. Trade and Fin. Assn. (bd. dirs.), Tex. Assn. Mid. East Scholars, AAUP, Animal Air Transp. Assn., Phi Kappa Phi. Avocations: genealogy, animal rescue. Died July 2, 1994.

RICHARDS, DANIEL THOMAS, library director; b. Salisbury, N.C., Dec. 13, 1945; s. Eric Kenneth and Martha Emaline (Camp) R. BS, U. Maine, 1967; MS, U. Wis., 1969; postgrad., U. Md., 1970-71; cert., Nat. Libr. Medicine, Bethesda, Md., 1971. Reference libr. Brown U., Providence, 1969-70; libr. assoc. Nat. Libr. Medicine, 1970-71, collection devel. officer, 1988-91; cataloger UCLA Biomed. Libr., 1971-72, head acquisitions div., 1972-79, asst. to biomed. libr., 1972-78, collection devel. officer, 1979-81; asst. health scis. libr. for resources and reference svcs. Columbia U., N.Y.C., 1981-88, acting health scis. libr., 1982-83; dir. biomed. librs. Dartmouth Coll., Hanover, N.H., 1991-95; lectr. UCLA Grad. Sch. Libr. and Info. Sci., 1973-81, Columbia U. Sch. Libr. Svc., 1982-83, Cath. U. Am. Sch. Libr. and Info. Scis., Washington, 1989; instr. Internat. Fedn. Libr. Assns., Sydney, Australia, 1988; tutor Dartmouth Med. Sch., 1993-95; mem. librs. adv. bd. John Wiley & Sons, Inc., N.Y.C., 1991-95; mem. bd. libr. advisors Doody's Health Scis. Book Rev. Jour., Chgo., 1993-95; cons. Meml. Sloan-Kettering Cancer Ctr., N.Y.C., 1989, U. Ariz., 1991, McGill U., Montreal, 1992, also others. Author: Development and Assessment of Collections in Health Sciences Libraries, 1989, rev. edit., 1991, (with D. Morse) Collection Development Policies for Health Sciences Libraries, 1992, (with others) Collection Development Manual of the National Library of Medicine, 3d edit., 1993, (with D. Eakin) Collection Development in Health Sciences Libraries, 1995; contbr. articles to profl. jours., chpts. to books. Pres., chmn. bd. dirs. Choo-San Goh and H. Robert Magee Found., Washington, 1989-95; pres. Culinary Historians N.Y., N.Y.C., 1987-89. Mem. ALA (chmn, chief collection devel. officers large rsch. librs. discussion group 1990), Med. Libr. Assn. (nat. nominating com. 1987, nat. bd. dirs. 1993-96, Louise Darling medal, 1989, founding chmn. collection devel.

sect. 1986, mem. coms. and bds. for 4 regional chpts. 1971-95), Am. Assn. Acad. Health Scis. Libr. Dirs., Am. Assn. for History Medicine, Coun. Biology Editors, Friends Dartmouth Coll. Libr., Friends Nat. Libr. Medicine. Democrat. Roman Catholic. Avocations: collecting John Updike books, culinary and medical history. Died Dec. 9, 1995.

RICHARDS, FREDERICK EDWARD MAXWELL, school system administrator; b. Detroit, July 11, 1929; s. Albert George and Rose Isabella (Coote) R.; m. Nellie Irene Sims, July 14, 1973. BS, Wayne State U., 1958; MA, U. Detroit, 1977. Cert. tchr., adminstr. Clk. City of Detroit, 1949-51, 54-57; enlisted man U.S. Army, 1951-52; welfare investigator City of Detroit, 1957-58; tchr. Detroit Bd. of Edn., 1958-89, adminstr., 1989—; officer, 1st lt. U.S. Army, 1952-54; bd. dirs. camp and conf. Episcopal Diocese of Mich., Detroit, 1988-92, Emrick Conf. Ctr., 1988—. Appeared in films Detroit 9,000, Collision Course. Community theatre Lafayette Pk. Players, Detroit, 1968-71. Mem. Lafayette Park Players (pres. 1969-71), Jim Dandy Ski club (v.p. 1974-75), Detroit Ski Jets (pres. 1977-78), Motor City Yacht Club (sec. 1976-77), Mt. Brighton ski Patrol (bd. dirs. 1985-86), Nat. Ski Patrol, NAACP, St. Cyprians Episcoal Ch. Episcopalian. Avocations: community theatre, golf, skiing, swimming, travel. DIED 02/22/96. .

RICHARDS, JOHN RAYMOND, lawyer; b. Tulsa, Aug. 25, 1918; s. Chester Raymond and Bertha (Gayman) R.; m. Cecile Little Davis, Mar. 20, 1948; children: Ann Gayman, Barbara Jane, Philip Raymond, Julia Neal. BA, U. Okla., 1942, LLB, 1942. Bar: Okla. 1942. Pvt. practice law Tulsa, 1946-47; asst. county atty. Tulsa County, 1947-49; mem. Houston Klein & Davidson, 1949-71; ptnr. Grigg Richards & Paul, 1971-83, Richards, Paul & Wood, 1983-87, Richards, Paul, Richards & Siegel, Tulsa, 1988—; head dept. law Okla. Sch. Accountancy, 1947-53; judge Ct. on Judiciary, State of Okla., 1966-77. Pres. Young Reps., Tulsa County, 1948; mem. 1st CSC Tulsa, 1954-56, Mayor's Study Com. Civil Svc. Charter Amendment, 1956; chmn., trustee Tulsa Police and Fire Acad. Trust. Served from 2d lt. to capt. AUS, 1942-46. Mem. ABA, Fed. Bar Assn., Okla. Bar Assn. (chmn. com., cert. of merit 1959), Tulsa County Bar Assn. (chmn. com., past v.p., Outstanding Sr. Lawyer award 1958), Am. Judicature Soc., Summit Club, Delta Chi. Presbyterian.

RICHEY, CHARLES ROBERT, federal judge; b. Logan County, Ohio, Oct. 16, 1923; s. Paul D. and Miriam (Blaine) R.; m. Agnes Mardelle White, Mar. 25, 1950; children: Charles R. Jr., William Paul. BA, Ohio Wesleyan U., 1945, LLD, 1996; LLB, Case-Western Res. U., 1948. Bar: Ohio 1949, D.C. 1951, U.S. Supreme Ct. 1952, Md. 1964. Legis. counsel, former congresswoman Frances P. Bolton, Ohio, 1948-49; practice in Washington and Chevy Chase, Md., 1950-71; founding partner firm Richey & Clancy, Washington and Chevy Chase, Md., 1964-71; gen. counsel Md. Pub. Service Commn., 1967-71; judge U.S. Dist. Ct. D.C., 1971-97; sr. judge U.S. Dist Ct. D.C., 1997; sat by designation as mem. U.S. Ct. Appeals for D.C., 1972-75, 77-85; mem. Temporary U.S. Emergency Ct. Appeals, 1983-84, Commn. on Criminal Law and Adminstrn. of Probation Sys. of Jud. Conf. U.S., 1954-55; adj. prof. trial advocacy-practice Georgetown Law Ctr., 1975-94, mem. adv. bd. CLE Program, 1979-85; mem. faculty Nat. Coll. State Judiciary, 1973-75, Fed. Jud. Ctr., 1976-86, U.S. Atty. Gen.'s Advocacy Inst., Washington, 1977-85, 96; spl. counsel councilmanic redistricting Montgomery County Govt., 1965-66; vice chmn. Charter Revision Commn., 1967-68; lectr. ABA and ATLA ann. meetings, CLE programs of Am. Law Inst., ABA, Practicing Law Inst. and other Bar and civic groups throughout U.S.; mem. Jud. Coun., D.C. Cir., 1988-94; co-chair D.C. 1st and 3d cirs. Sentencing Insts., 1984, D.C. 3d and 7th cirs. Sentencing Insts., 1992. Author: Manual on Employment Discrimination and Civil Rights Actions, 1994, Prisoner Litigation in the United States Courts, 1995, 2d edit., 1997; contbr. articles to profl. jours. and law revs. Legal counsel Boys' Clubs Greater Washington, 1966-71; affiliate mem. D.C. Urban Renewal Council and Citizens Housing Commn., 1961-64; chmn. parents assn. Sidwell Friends Sch., Washington, 1968-70; mem. Montgomery County Bd. Appeals, 1965-67, chmn., 1966-67; trustee Immaculata Coll., Washington, 1970-73, Suburban Hosp. Bethesda, Md., 1967-71; pres. PTA, Potomac, Md., 1966-67. Recipient Outstanding and Dedicated Pub. Svc. award Montgomery County, Md., 1966, 68, Cert. Disting. Citizenship award Gov. Md., 1971, Ann. Award of Merit by Adminstrv. Law Judges of U.S., 1979, Outstanding U.S. Fed. Trial Judge, ATLA, 1979, Humanitarian of Yr. award, Howard U. Law Sch. Alumni Assn., 1979, Supreme Ct. Justice Howard Hitz Burton award, Cleveland Club of Washington, 1990, Judge H. Carl Moultrie award for Jud. Excellence, D.C. Area Trial Lawyers Assn., 1990, Outstanding Spkr. award Fla. Bar Assn., 1991, Ben A Arneson Disting. Pub. Career award Ohio Wesleyan U., 1994, Case Western Res. U. Law Sch. medal, 1994. Fellow Am. Bar Found. (life); mem. ABA (ho. of dels. 1981-85, chmn. com. on alcohol and drug abuse 1973-76, chmn. com. on sentencing probation and parole 1975-77, mem. coun. criminal justice sect. 1976-80, chmn. nat. adv. com. Project ADVoCATE 1976-80, chmn. nat. conf. fed. trial judges 1980-81, officer and mem. exec. com. 1975-85, mem. coun. jud. adminstrv. divsn. 1980-81), ATLA (faculty Nat. Coll. Advocacy 1975-77), Am. Judicature Soc., Bar Assn. D.C., Md. Bar Assn., Supreme Ct. Hist. Soc. (founding), Edward Bennett Williams Am. Inn. of Ct. (master, charter), Charlotte E. Ray Am. Inn of Ct. (master, charter), Soc. of Benchers of Case Western Res. U. Sch. Law, Omicron Delta Kappa, Delta Sigma Rho, Pi Delta Epsilon, Phi Delta Phi, Phi Gamma Delta (gen. counsel 1960-63). Methodist. Club: Nat. Lawyers (Washington). Lodge: Masons (33rd degree). Home: Chevy Chase Md. Died Mar. 19, 1997.

RICHTER, SVIATOSLAV THEOFILOVICH, pianist; b. Zhitomir, Russia, Mar. 20, 1915; grad. piano class Moscow Conservatory, 1947; DMus (hon.) Oxford, 1990. m. Nina Dorliak. Rehearsals condr. Odessa Theater Opera and Ballet, 1934-37; debut concert pianist, Odessa, 1935; won 1st prize Third USSR Competition of Executant Musicans, 1945, since has made extensive concert tours of Europe; recordings include Richter Live: Beethoven's Diabella Variations, Wolfgang Amadeus Mozart: Piano Sonatas in E-flat Major, C-Major and A Minor. U.S. Recipient Stalin prize, 1950; Lenin prize, 1961; decorated Order of Lenin; named People's Artist of USSR, 1961. Died Aug. 1, 1997.

RICKS, DON FRANK, artist; b. Teton, Idaho, June 14, 1929; s. Henry Hans Peter and Alice (Dean) R;. m. Iris Viola Hunter, Sept. 17, 1933; children: Douglas, Jeffery, Rebecca, Connie, Russel, Martin, Kristie. Student, Ricks Coll., Utah State U. Freelance comml. artist Salt Lake City, 1953-73; art instr., 1969-89, artist, 1986-96. One man show Charles and Emma Frye Art Mus., Seattle, 1986; represented in numerous permanent collections. Recipient Silver medal Soc. Western Artists, 1982; named Best of Show, Utah State Fair Bd., 1950, Wind River Valley Nat. Art Competition, 1973. Avocations: walking, photography, hiking, basketball, football. Died Jan. 16, 1996.

RIDDER, ERIC, newspaper publisher; b. Hewlett, L.I., N.Y., July 1, 1918; s. Joseph E. and Hedwig (Schneider) R.; m. Ethelette Tucker, 1939 (div.); children: Eric, Susan; m. Madeleine Graham, 1955 (dec. Nov. 1991). Student, Harvard U., 1936-37. Entire career in newspaper work; dir. Seattle Times Co., Knight-Ridder Newspapers, Inc. Trustee South St. Seaport Mus. Republican. Roman Catholic. Clubs: Seawanhaka-Corinthian Yacht (N.Y.C.), Piping Rock (N.Y.C.), N.Y. Yacht (N.Y.C.), India House (N.Y.C.); Royal Swedish Yacht. Home: Locust Valley N.Y. Deceased.

RIDGELY, ROBERT, actor; b. Teaneck, N.J.; m. Patricia Ridgely. Appeared in films Melvin and Howard, Philadelphia, Blazzing Saddles, Robin Hood: Men in Tights, Beverly Hills Cop II, The Ref, Fire Down Below, (tv shows) Get Smart, Sea Hunt, Coach. Home: Toluca Lake Calif. Died Feb. 8, 1997.

RIEBE, NORMAN JOHN, contractor; b. Michigan City, Ind., Mar. 9, 1903; s. William J. and Hattie (Fink) R.; m. Gwendolyn Ester Main (dec. 1924); children: Norman W., Harriet M. Kirchner; m. Eddie Lou Growden, 1978. PhD in Constrn., DSc (hon.). Registered profl. engr., Ind., Ark. Ariz. Draftsman, die designer Haskel and Barker Car Co.; with Steel Fabricating Corp., 1924-26; chief engr. Stefco Steel Co., 1926-36; pvt. practice Michigan City, Ind., 1936-40; v.p. R.E. McKee, Gen. Contractor, Los Alamos, N.Mex., 1947-52; v.p., gen. mgr. C.H. Leavell & Co., El Paso, 1952-61. Contbr. articles to profl. jours. Active Yuma County Bd. Adjustment; past vestryman Episc. Ch. Col. U.S. Army, 1932-62. Decorated Legion of Merit. Mem. Soc. Am. Mil. Engrs. (life), Ret. Officers Assn. (life), Associated Gen. Contractors (past pres. El Paso chpt. 1960), Am. Arbitration Assn., Am. Ordnance Assn. (past pres.), Masons, Shriners, Knights Templar. Republican. Avocation: raising peafowl and peaches. Home: Yuma Ariz. Deceased.

RIESE, MURRAY, real estate and restaurant executive; b. N.Y.C., Nov. 15, 1921; s. Samuel and Minnie R.; m. Anita Roese. Student, DeWitt Clinton Coll. Treas. Riese Orgn., N.Y.C. Patron Lincoln Ctr., N.Y.C.; affiliate Met. Mus. Art, Office Film and TV; organizer ann. Christmas Party Sr. Citizens, N.Y., 1970-95; active Catholic Charities Am., Literacy Vols. Am. Recipient Membership award Nat. Com. Futherance Jewish Edn., 1971. Avocation: charity programs elderly and underpriviledged. Home: Great Neck N.Y. Died July 28, 1995.

RIESEN, AUSTIN HERBERT, psychologist, researcher; b. Newton, Kans., July 1, 1913; s. Emil Richert and Rachel (Penner) R.; m. Helen Haglin, July 29, 1939; children: Carol, Kent. AB, U. Ariz., 1935; PhD, Yale, 1939; DSc (hon.), U. Ariz., 1981. Rsch. assoc. Yale U., New Haven, Conn., 1939; asst. prof. psychobiology Yerkes Labs. Primate Biology, Orange Park, Fla., 1939-49; assoc. prof. U. Chgo., 1949-56, prof. psychology, 1956-62; prof. psychology U. Calif., Riverside, 1962-80, also chmn., 1962-68, prof. emeritus psychology, 1980-96, ann. faculty rsch. lectr., 1974; vis. rsch. prof. U. Rochester, 1951-53; researcher in psychiatry NIMH Found., Bethesda, Md., 1964-69; mem. vision rsch. com. NIH, 1959-63; rsch. lectr. Sigma Xi, U. Ariz., 1961, U. Calif., Riverside, 1975. Author: Development of Infant Chimpanzees, 1952; author, editor: Developmental Neuropsychology of Sensory Deprivation, 1975; editor: Advances in Psychobiology, 1972-76; contbr. numerous articles on visual development. Capt. USAF, 1943-46. Recipient emeritus faculty award U. Calif., 1992. Mem. NAS, APA (pres. divsn. 6 1965-67), Phi Beta Kappa, Sigma Xi, Phi Kappa Phi. Congregationalist. Home: Riverside CA Died Sept. 15, 1996; buried National Cemetary, Riverside, CA.

RIFKIN, HAROLD, physician, educator; b. N.Y.C., Sept. 10, 1916; s. Jack and Rose (Zuckoff) R.; m. Beatrice Weiss, Nov. 25, 1945; children—Janet, Matthew, Phyllis. B.A., U. Mo., 1935; M.D., Dalhousie U., 1940. Diplomate Am. Bd. Internal Medicine. Intern Jewish Hosp., Bklyn, 1940-41; resident in internal medicine Montefiore Hosp., N.Y.C., 1942-43, 46-47; practice medicine specializing in internal medicine and diabetes N.Y.C., 1947—; clin. prof. medicine Albert Einstein Coll. Medicine, N.Y.C., 1974-93, disting. univ. prof. of medicine emeritus, 1993—; prof. clin. medicine NYU Sch. Medicine, 1975—; chief of diabetes svc. emeritus Montefiore Med. Ctr., N.Y.C., 1993—; cons. emeritus Lenox Hill Hosp., N.Y.C., 1992—. With U.S. Army, 1943-46. Fellow ACS, N.Y. Acad. Medicine, N.Y. Acad. Scis.; mem. AMA, Internat. Diabetes Fedn. (chmn. N.Am. region 1985—, assoc. editor-in-chief Bull. 1985-91, v.p. 1988-94, hon. pres. 1994—), Am. Diabetes Assn. (bd. dirs. 1973-79, pres. 1985-86), N.Y. Diabetes Assn. (past pres., bd. dirs. 1970—), N.Y. County Med. Soc., N.Y. State Med. Soc., Am. Soc. Clin. Rsch., Harvey Soc. Home: New York N.Y. Died May 19, 1997.

ŘÍHA, BOHUMIL, writer; b. Vyšetice, Czechoslovakia, Feb. 22, 1907; parents: Josef and Karolina (Říhová) Dušek; m. Věra Patočková, July 7, 1933; children: Eliška, Jitka. Student, Pedagogical Inst., Cáslav, Czechoslovakia, 1925. Tchr. Ministry of Edn., Czechoslovakia, 1926-45, sch. inspector, 1945-52; dir. State Publ. House Children's Books, Prague, 1952-67. Author numerous adult and children's novels including Země dokořán, 1950, Adam a Otka, 1970 (Albatros Publ. Annual prize 1970), Přede Mnou Poklekni, 1971 (Annual prize Czech Union of Writers), Učitel Viktor Pelc, 1984 (Minister of Culture prize 1986). Recipient Order for Outstanding Work, 1965, Marie Majerová prize Minister of Culture, 1972, Order of Labour, 1977, Minister of Culture prize, 1977, Han Christian Andersen medal, 1980, Publ. House Nasza Ksiegarnia Meml. medal, 1981, Order of the Republic, 1982, Ludmila Podjavorinská plaque Minister of Culture, 1987; named Artist of Merit, 1967, Nat. Artist, 1975. Mem. Czech Union of Writers (mem. presidium 1952-87), IBBY (pres. Czech sect. 1964-87). Mem. Communist Party. Avocations: fine arts, traveling. Home: Prague Czechoslovakia

RILEY, JOSEPH HARRY, retired banker; b. Pitts., May 13, 1922; s. Joseph John and Frances P. (Wacker) R.; m. Anna Belle Hepler, May 2, 1957 (dec. May 1994); 1 child, Michelle Patricia. B.C.S., Benjamin Franklin U., 1950; postgrad., Grad. Sch. Banking, Rutgers U., 1954. With Crestar Bank, N.A. (name formerly Nat. Savs. & Trust Co.), Washington, 1947-96; exec. v.p. Crestar Bank, N.A. (name formerly Nat. Savs. & Trust Co.), 1970-73, sr. exec. v.p., 1973-76, pres., 1976-80, chmn., pres., 1980-84, also bd. dirs. Treas. Heroes; bd. dirs. Anthony Francis Lucas Spindletop Found., Anson Mills Found., Jr. Achievement Washington, Boys Club Greater Washington; bd. dirs., pres. Kiwanis Found.; past pres. Met. Washington Bd. Trade. Served with USMCR, 1942-46, 50-51. Mem. D.C. Bankers Assn. (past pres.), Am. Bankers Assn., Mortgage Bankers Assn., Washington Conv. and Visitors Bur. (past pres.), Soc. Friendly Sons St. Patrick (past pres.), Congl. Country Club (Washington), Univ. Club (Washington), Met. Club (Washington), Burning Tree Club, Rolling Rock Club (Ligonier, Pa.). Died Mar. 5, 1996.

RISO, NICHOLAS, retail food chain executive; b. Batavia, N.Y., Nov. 29, 1930; s. Andrew Nicholas and Josephine Rose (Zito) R.; m. Natalie Carol Laskowski, July 4, 1957; children: Andrea Marie, Nicholas Frank. Student, Stamford U. Owner, mgr. B&R Supermarket, LeRoy, N.Y., 1950-60; ops. supr. Peter J. Schmittco, Buffalo, 1960-64; v.p., div. mgr. Allied Supermarkets, Detroit, 1964-70; sr. v.p., chief ops. officer Hillis Supermarkets, Brentwood, N.Y., 1970-72; chief ops. officer Giant Food Stores Inc., Carlisle, Pa., from 1972, pres., 1972—, now also dir.; bd. dirs. Acad. Food Mktg. St. Joseph's U., Phila., 1982—. Bd. dirs. Tri County United Way, Harrisburg, Pa., 1982—, Keystone Sports Found., Harrisburg, 1984-85; vice chmn. Susquehanna Twp., Harrisburg, 1983-84. Mem. Food Mktg. Inst., Heritage Found., Pa. Food Mchts. Assn., Shippensburg U. Found., Greater Harrisburg C. of C. (dir. 1982—). Republican. Roman Catholic. Club: Harrisburg Country (dir. 1983-84). Avocations: golf; art collector. DIED 10/15/97. .

RISON, CLARENCE HERBERT, manufacturing company executive; b. Central Falls, R.I., Feb. 25, 1904; s. Herbert Thomas and Sophie (Raithel) R.; m. Ebba R. Rydberg, Dec. 5, 1931; children—Carolyn Anne, John Brooks. LL.B., Northeastern U., Boston, 1938. Instr. Northeastern U., 1941-42, 1942-43; instr. Tech. Inst.,

Providence YMCA, 1940-41; treas. Grinnell Corp., 1944-64, dir., exec. com., 1948-85, v.p. fin., 1964-68, pres. corp., 1968-70, vice chmn., 1970-85; hon. dir. AMICA Mut. Ins. Co. Mem. NAM (dir. 1958-61), Nat. Assn. Credit Men (dir. 1938-41), R.I. Assn. Credit Men. Baptist (clk. 1945-55). Clubs: Mason, Squantum, Turks Head, Dunes. Died January 1996.

RITCHIE, ROBERT FIELD, lawyer; b. Dallas, July 9, 1917; s. Robert Allan and Sallie Bowen (Field) R.; m. Catherine Canfield, Sept. 14, 1949; children—Allan, Lee, Ann, Kate, Sara, Beth. B.S., So. Meth. U., 1939, LL.B., 1941; LL.M., U. Mich., 1942, S.J.D., 1953. Bar: Tex. 1941. Ptnr. Ritchie Ritchie & Crosland, Dallas, 1946-66; ptnr. Ritchie Crosland & Egan, Dallas, 1966-82, Andrews & Kurth, Dallas, 1982—. Author: Integration of Public Utility Holding Companies, 1954. Elder Presbyn. Ch., Dallas, 1976—. Recipient Silver Beaver award Boy Scouts Am., 1970, Disting. Eagle Scout award, 1975, Order of San Jacinto, Sons Republic of Tex., 1979. Mem. ABA, Dallas Bar Assn., Tex. Bar Found., Crescent Club, Dallas Country Club, Tower Club, Kappa Alpha (Court of Honor 1974). Avocation: photography. Died April 13, 1997.

ROAN, CHARLES THURSTON, management consultant; b. Atlanta, May 15, 1928; s. Augustus Morrow and Margaret Josephine (Zattau) R.; m. Tattie Mae Williams, Mar. 26, 1960; children: Ansley Josephine, Caroline Tabitha. BBA, U. Ga., 1954. Cert. data processing. With Lockheed Ga. Co., Marietta, 1951-73, mgr. materials systems, 1961-64, mgr. indsl. engring. systems, 1965-68, mfg. ops. systems adminstr., 1968-73; pres. Roan & Assocs., Atlanta, 1974—; lectr., chmn. tng. and orientation seminars for various orgns. and computer mfg. cos. Served with U.S. Army, 1946-49. Mem. Am. Mgmt. Assn., Adminstrv. Systems Assn., Am. Prodn. and Inventory Control Soc. Presbyterian.

ROBB, FELIX COMPTON, association executive, consultant; b. Birmingham, Ala., Dec. 26, 1914; s. Felix Compton and Ruth (Nicholson) R.; m. Virginia Lytle Threlkeld. A.B. summa cum laude, Birmingham-So. Coll., 1936; M.A., Vanderbilt U., 1939; postgrad., George Peabody Coll., 1939-40; Ed.D., Harvard U., 1952; D.Ped., W.Va. Wesleyan Coll., 1968; LL.D., Mercer U., 1968, U. S.C., 1978; D.H.L., U. Ala. System, 1975, Jacksonville U., 1981; H.H.D., Birmingham So. Coll., 1979. Tchr. jr. high sch. Irondale, Ala., 1936-37; tchr. Ensley High Sch., Birmingham, 1937-38; instr. English Birmingham-So. Coll., 1940-42, successively alumni sec., registrar, 1946; asst. to pres. Peabody Coll., 1947-51, acting dir. Libr. Sch., 1947-48, acting dean of coll. Libr. Sch., 1948-49, assoc. prof. higher edn. Libr. Sch., 1950-53, prof. Libr. Sch., 1953-66, acting dir. surveys and field svcs. Libr. Sch., 1951, dean instrn. Libr. Sch., 1951-61, coll. pres. Libr. Sch., 1961-66; dir. So. Assn. Colls. and Schs., Atlanta, 1966-79; exec. dir. So. Assn. Colls. and Schs., 1979-82, exec. dir. emeritus, 1982—; pres. Ginge, Inc., 1982-94; interim pres. Tallulah Falls Sch., 1988-89; sec., treas. So. Edn. Exec. Search Assocs., 1989-92; coord. edn. project, Republic of Korea, 1956-58; bd. dirs. Carnegie fellowships in tchg., 1950-60, Peabody Bldg. Fund Campaign, 1958; chief of staff The Study of Coll. and Univ. Presidency, 1958-60; mem. Tenn. Adv. Coun. on Tchr. Edn. and Cert., 1954-58; case writer Inst. for Coll. and Univ. Adminstrs., Harvard, 1955; nat. selection com. Fulbright awards, 1955-57; bd. dirs. workshops in TV, ednl. TV program series, Nashville; chmn. gov.'s conf. Edn. Beyond H.S., 1958; mem. com. specialized pers. Dept. Labor; mem. Tenn. Commn. Human Rels., 1964-66; exec. com. Met. Action Commn., 1965-66; chmn. S.E. Manpower Adv. Com., 1965-68; mem. bd. So. Edn. Reporting Svc., 1961-69; mem. nat. adv. com. Acad. of Sr. Profls. at Eckerd Coll., 1974-76; cons. Profl. Assn. Ga. Educators. Author: America's Urgent Agenda, 1990. Trustee, chmn. scholarship com. Presser Found.; trustee, chmn. fin. com. United Meth. Children's Home, 1985-88; trustee Longview Found., Reinhardt Coll.; mem. Cleve. Conf.; mem. devel. coun. Birmingham-So. Coll., adv. bd. Southall Trust; trustee, chmn. adminstrv. bd. Meth. ch., 1974. Mem. So. Coun. Tchr. Edn. (pres. 1956-57), Am. Soc. Assn. Execs., Loulie Compton Sem. Alumni Assn. (pres.), Phi Beta Kappa, Omicron Delta Kappa, Phi Delta Kappa, Kappa Phi Kappa, Pi Gamma Mu, Kappa Alpha Order, Kappa Delta Pi (Laureate mem., mem. ednl. found.), Rotary. Died June 22, 1997.

ROBBINS, ANDREW JOSEPH, minister; b. Morgantown, W.Va., Nov. 19, 1910; s. Strawn Murphy and Oakie Urbana (Christner) R.; m. Ollie Mae Robertson, July 28, 1931; children: David Bruce, Linda Jean. BTh, Columbia Union Coll., 1931; MA, U. Chgo., 1942. Ordained to ministry Seventh-day Adventist Ch., 1935. Pastor Seventh-day Adventist Ch., Johnstown, Pa., 1931-35; overseas missionary Seventh-day Adventist Ch., China, 1935-41; tchr. Columbia Union Coll., 1942-50; pres. W. Pa. Conf. Seventh-day Adventis, 1950-58, pres. N. Philippine Union Mission, 1958-63, pres. Hong Kong-Macao Mission, 1964-69; dept. sec. Ariz. Conf. Seventh-day Adventists, 1969-71; chaplain Tempe (Ariz.) Community Hosp., 1971-77; vol. Tsuen Wan Adventist Hosp., Hong Kong. Pres. Tempe Ministerial Assn., 1975-76, Ariz. Assn. Hosp. Chaplains, 1976-77; sec.-treas. Tri-City Evangelicals, 1975-76. Died Aug. 3, 1996.

ROBBINS, HAROLD, author; b. N.Y.C., May 21, 1916; m. Lillian Machnivitz (div.); m. Grace Palermo (div.); children: Caryn, Adreana; m. Jann Stapp. Student pub. schs., N.Y.C. In food factoring bus., until 1940; shipping clk. Universal Pictures, N.Y.C., 1940-46. Author: Never Love a Stranger, 1948, The Dream Merchants, 1949, A Stone for Danny Fisher, 1951, Never Leave Me, 1953, 79 Park Avenue, 1955, Stiletto, 1953, The Carpetbaggers, 1961, Where Love Has Gone, 1962, The Adventurers, 1966, The Inheritors, 1969, The Betsy, 1971, The Pirate, 1974, Lonely Lady, 1976, Dreams Die First, 1977, Memories of Another Day, 1979, Goodbye, Janette, 1981, Spellbinder, 1982, Descent for Xanadu, 1984, The Storyteller, 1985, The Piranhas, 1991, The Raiders, 1994, The Stallion, 1996, Tycoon, 1997. Home: New York N.Y. Died Oct. 14, 1997.

ROBBINS, JEROME WALTER, manufacturing company executive; b. N.Y.C., July 26, 1925; s. Mayer and Rose (Reiter) R.; m. Patricia Davis, Oct. 9, 1949; children—Cynthia, Richard. Student, Cornell U., 1943-44; B.S., U.S. Naval Acad., 1947; student, Grad. Sch. Bus., Columbia, 1950-51. Enlisted in USNR, 1943, commd. ensign, 1947, advanced through grades to lt., 1953, ret., 1960; advt. mgr. Norman M. Morris Corp., N.Y.C., 1950-58; nat. sales mgr., marketing dir. Norman M. Morris Corp., 1958-62; asst. to pres., dir. planning Bulova Watch Co., N.Y.C., 1962-65; pres., chief exec. officer Elgin Nat. Watch Co., Ill., 1965-68; also dir.; v.p. Brunswick Corp., Chgo., 1968-70; pres. Brunswick Corp. (Mac Gregor div.), 1970-71; pres., chief exec. officer HMW Industries, Inc. (formerly Hamilton Watch Co.), 1971-95, chmn. bd., dir., 1973-83; chief exec. officer W & J Sloane Corp., 1985-95. Mem. N.Y.C. Sales Execs. Club, Chgo. Econ. Club. Club: Rotary. Home: New Canaan Conn. Died Apr. 15, 1995.

ROBE, LUCY BARRY, editor, educator; b. Boston, Jan. 15, 1934; d. Herbert Jr. and Lucy (Brown) Barry; m. Robert S. Robe Jr., Feb. 6, 1971; 1 child, Parrish C. BA, Harvard U., 1955; MA in Med. Writing, Pacific Western U., 1992. Writer Alcoholism Update Biomed. Info. Corp., N.Y.C., 1979-85; editor newsletter Am. Soc. of Addiction Medicine News, Washington, 1985-95; conf. mgr. Fla. Soc. of Addiction Medicine News; v.p. L.I. Coun. on Alcoholism, Mineola, N.Y., 1978-92. Author: Just So It's Healthy, 1978, Haunted Inheritance, 1982, Co-Starring: Famous Women & Alcohol, 1986; editor numerous books. Mem. Authors Guild of Am., Am. Med. Writer's Assn. Died May 13, 1996.

ROBERT, GILBERT O'DAY, banker; b. Cohoes, N.Y., Sept. 28, 1925; s. Gilbert H. and Marie (O'Day) R.; m. Rosemarie Alice Mitchell, Oct. 1, 1949; children—Alice Marie, Gilbert Mitchell. Student, Dartmouth U., 1943-44; A.B., Siena Coll., 1949. Real estate broker appraiser, 1949-60; appraiser N.Y. State Bd. Equalization and Assessment, 1960-63; asst. treas. Albany Savs. Bank, 1963-68, v.p., 1968-69, sr. v.p., 1969-72, exec. v.p., 1972-74, pres., 1975-85, trustee, 1975—, chmn. bd., chief exec. officer, 1983-90, chmn. exec. com., 1990—; pres. SBNY Mut. Service Corp.; bd. dirs., treas., v.p. Mutual Savs. Banks Fund Inc., 1986, Univ. Found., 1984; dir. Savs. Bank Trust Co., N.Y. Bus. Devel. Corp., 1983, Fed. Home Loan Bank of N.Y., 1986, Instl. Securities Corp.; mem. Albany County Bd. Realtors.; bd. dirs. Savs. Bank Assn. N.Y. State; mem. Albany Local Devel. Corp. Trustee Meml. Hosp., 1976-84, Coll. St. Rose, 1976-84. Served to ensign USNR, 1943-46; to lt. 1950-52. Mem. Mortgage Bankers Assn., Albany Area C. of C. (dir. 1975—). Clubs: Schuyler Meadows Country, Ft. Orange (Albany). Died Dec. 5, 1996.

ROBERTS, BETTY, associate justice state supreme court; b. Arkansas City, Kans., Feb. 5, 1923; d. David Murray and Mary Pearl (Higgins) Cantrell; m. John W. Rice, Sept. 25, 1942 (div. Feb. 1960); children—S. Dian Rice Odell, John W., Jo R., Randall G.; m. Keith D. Skelton, June 15, 1968. BS, Portland State U., 1958; MS, U. Oreg., 1962; JD, Lewis and Clark Coll., 1966, LLD (hon.), 1985. Bar: Oreg. Mem. faculty Mt. Hood Community Coll., Gresham, Oreg., 1967-76; mem. Oreg. Senate, 1969-77, Oreg. Ho. of Reps., 1965-69; ptnr. Skelton & Roberts, Portland, Oreg., 1968-77; judge Oreg. Ct. Appeals, Salem, 1977-82; assoc. justice Oreg. Supreme Ct., Salem, 1982—. Bd. visitors U. Oreg. Law Sch., Eugene, 1985—; mem. McCall Leadership Commn., Oreg. State U., Corvallis, 1984—; mem. Gov.'s Com. on Child Support Enforcement, 1985—; mem. Oreg. Criminal Justice Council, 1985—; candidate for gov. of Oreg., 1974, for U.S. Senate, 1974; state chmn. Carter for Pres., 1976; state co-chmn. McGovern for Pres., 1972. Recipient Disting. Service award Portland State U., 1985; Woman Helping Women award Soroptomists Internat., 1982; Woman of Yr., Oreg. Women's Polit. Caucus, 1975; Edn. Citizen of Yr., Oreg. Edn. Assn., 1975. Mem. ABA, Oreg. Bar Assn., Nat. Assn. Women Judges, LWV, Oreg. Women's Forum. Democrat. Avocations: quilting; golf. DIED 02/16/96. .

ROBERTS, BRUCE EVERETT, engineer, consultant; b. Chanute, Kans., May 22, 1917; s. Everett Earl and Belle M. (Jones) R.; m. Marcelle Braden, Aug. 9, 1941; children: Stephen Kent, Craig Arnold. BS in Civil Engring., Kans. State U., 1939. Registered profl. engr. and land surveyor, Kans. Civil engr. Cheyenne County, Kans., 1939-40; contrn. engr. Frazier-Bruce on Weldon Springs (Kans.) Ordnance Plant, 1940; field engr. Wilson & Co., Salina, Kans., 1946—, project mgr., exec. ptnr., 1959—, also bd. dirs.; pres. Wilson-Murrow Co. (fgn. subs. Wilson & Co.), Salina, Kans., 1963—, also bd. dirs.; bd. dirs. Planters State Bank, Salina; co-owner B&R Ranch; past chmn. Kans. Bd. Engring. Examiners. Lt. USNR, 1942-45. Recipient Disting. Svc. award Kans. State U. Coll. Engring., 1979. Mem. ASCE, NSPE, Jans. Egr. Soc. (Engr. of Yr. 1982), Am. Cons. Engrs. Coun., Am. Rd. and Transp. Builders Assn., Internat. Rd. Fedn., Profl. Engrs. in Pvt. Practice, Am. Water Works Assn., Am. Soc. Photogrammetrists, Salina Country Club, Masons, Elks. Died Feb. 22, 1996.

ROBERTS, JOSEPHINE ANASTASIA, English literature educator; b. Richmond, Va., Nov. 11, 1948; d. John and Anastasia (Leuty) R.; m. James Frederick Gaines, July 19, 1975; 1 child, John Manley. BA, Coll. William and Mary, 1970; MA, U. Pa., 1971, PhD, 1975. Teaching asst. U. Pa., Phila., 1971-75; asst. prof. La. State U., Baton Rouge, 1975-80, assoc. prof., 1980-86, prof., 1986-91, William A. Read chair, 1991—. Author: Architectonic Knowledge in the New Arcadia, 1978, Richard II: Annotated Bibliography, Vols. I, II, 1988; editor: The Poems of Lady Mary Wroth, 1983, The Countess of Montgomery's Urania, Vol. I, 1995. NEH grantee, 1989-91, Newberry Libr. grantee, 1988, Am. Philos. Soc. grantee, 1988, Henry E. Huntington Libr. grantee, 1980. Mem. Renaissance English Text Soc. (exec. coun. 1986—), MLA, Shakespeare Assn. Am., Renaissance Soc. Am., AAUP, South Cen. MLA, South Cen. Renaissance Assn. DIED 08/26/96. .

ROBERTS, JUSTIN, retired journalist; b. N.Y.C., June 10, 1919; s. Louis and Claire (Meyers) R.; m. Lois Elinore Schneider, Sept. 5, 1943; children: Donn Roberts (dec.), Alta Roberts Nelson, Sarah Roberts Jacobson. B.A., Wayne U., 1941. With N.Y. Daily Mirror, 1935-36, INP, 1936-41, Acme Newspictures, N.Y.C., 1941-50; editor Calif. newspapers, 1953-61; editor, writer Contra Costa Times Lesher Newspapers, Walnut Creek, Calif., 1961-86; condr. investigation Bay Area Rapid Transit Dist., 1972-73. Dir. Calif. Alcohol Fuels Commn. Recipient nat. journalism award Nat. Soc. Profl. Engrs., 1972; A.P. Writing award, 1974; Journalism award State Soc. Profl. Engrs., 1976; award for outstanding reporting on conservation Scripps-Howard Found., 1977. Club: Contra Costa Press. Home: Antioch Calif. Died Sept. 30, 1992.

ROBERTS, ROBERT, JR., lawyer; b. Minden, La., Sept. 20, 1903; s. Robert and Olive (Goodwill) R.; m. Mary Hodges Marshall, Apr. 25, 1929 (dec.); children: Robert III, Mary Susan (Mrs. Robert O'Neal Chadwick), Olive G. (Mrs. William H. Forman, Jr.); m. Clara Barney Robinson, Oct. 4, 1980. B.A., La. State U., 1923, LL.B., 1925. Bar: La. 1925. Since practiced in Shreveport; mem. legal dept. Ark. Natural Gas Corp., 1934-53, chief atty., 1939-53; mem. law firm Blanchard, Walker, O'Quin & Roberts (and predecessor), 1953-89, of counsel, 1990—; gen. counsel and dir. emeritus, cons. Arkla, Inc. Chmn. Shreveport Council Social Agys., 1945-46; Pres. bd. trustees Southfield Sch., 1953-54; mem. La. Civil Service League. Mem. ABA, La. Bar Assn. (del. 1957-58), Shreveport Bar Assn. (pres. 1962), La. State U. Found., Order of Coif. Episcopalian (past jr. warden). Clubs: Boston Club (New Orleans); Shreveport (pres. 1973).

ROBERTS, ROBERT FRANKLIN, oil company executive; b. Austin, Tex., Nov. 29, 1924; s. Allen Pickney and Lillian (Lane) R.; m. Leila Crain, Dec. 23, 1951; 1 son, Mark Allen. J.D., U. Tex., 1945. Bar: Tex. 1945. Mem. firm Hamilton, Hamilton, Turner & Hutchison, Dallas, 1945-47; ind. oil producer La., 1947-63; chmn. bd. Crystal Oil Co., Shreveport, 1963—; also dir. Crystal Oil Co.; dir. La. Bank and Trust Co., Shreveport. Episcopalian. Clubs: University (Shreveport) (gov.), Shreveport Petroleum (Shreveport), Shreveport Country. (Shreveport). Died April 14, 1997.

ROBERTS, ROBERT J., neonatologist; b. Centralia, Wash., Sept. 19, 1939; s. Waldo J. and Anna Laura (Von Behren) R.; m. Donna M. Whitney, Mar. 23, 1940; children: Robert J. Jr., CeAnn M. Wambacher. BS, Wash. State U., 1962, B.Pharmacy, 1964; MS in Pharmacology, U. Iowa, 1966, PhD in Pharmacology, 1968, MD, 1970. Diplomate Am. Bd. Pediats.; lic. physician, Iowa, Va. Intern in pediatrics U. Iowa Hosps., Iowa City, 1970-71, pediat. resident, 1971-73; instr. pharmacology U. Iowa, Iowa City, 1968-71, asst. prof., 1971-73, assoc. prof., 1973-77, chmn. divsn. pediat. clin. pharmacology, 1973-87, mem. divsn. neonatology, 1973-87, prof. pharmacology/pediats., 1977-87; prof., chmn. dept. pediats., med. dir. Children's Med. Ctr. U. Va., Charlottesville, 1987-97; adj. prof. dept. pharmacology, clin. prof. dept. pediats. Tulane U. Med. Ctr., New Orleans, 1993-97; vis. prof. Harvard Joint Program in Neonatology/Boston Children's Hosp., 1979; cons. in field; reviewer March of Dimes grants, Can. Heart Assn.; mem. pediat. adv. panel U.S. Pharmacopeial Conv., Inc., 1995-97; bd. dirs. Health Svcs. Found., mem. exec. com., 1987-97, mem. Piedmont Liability Trust bd., 1989-97. Author: Drug Therapy in Infants, 1984; contbr. numerous articles to profl. jours.; editl. bd. Drug Metabolism and Disposition, 1976-82, Jour. Lab. and Clin. Medicine, 1980-84, Develop. Pharmacology and Therapeutics, 1982-97; reviewer Jour. Pediats., Pediat. Rsch., New Eng. Jour. Medicine, Jour. Clin. Investigation, Jour. Pharmacology and Exptl. Therapeutics, Toxicology and Applied Pharmacology, Jour. Clin. Toxicology, Pediats., Sci., Jour. of AMA, Pediat. Pulmonology, Biochem. Pharmacology, Fedn. Procs., Can. Jour. Physiology and Pharmacology, Am. Rev. of Respiratory Disease, Neonatal Pahrmacology Quar. Recipient Faculty Devel. award in clin. pharmacology PMA Found., 1973, Herbert C. Miller Vis. lectr., U. Kans., 1981, Pfizer lectr. in clin. pharmacology Dartmouth Med. Sch., 1985, Tex. Tech. Med. Sch., 1985; grantee NIH, 1985-87, 87-92, 86-92, 86-89, 93-95, 90-95, 92-97, FDA, 1985-87, Proctor and Gamble, 1985-87, 3M Co., 1985-86, IVAC Corp., 1985. Fellow Am. Acad. Pediats.; mem. Am. Soc. Pharmacology and Exptl. Therapeutics, Soc. Toxicology, Am. Acad. Clin. Toxicology, Soc. Pediat. Rsch., Am. Soc. Clin. Pharmacology and Therapeutics, Perinatal Rsch. Soc. (exec. com. 1989-91), Midwest Soc. for Pediat. Rsch., Am. Pediat. Soc., So. Soc. for Pediat. Rsch., Va. Perinatal Soc. Home: Charlottesville Va. Died Jan. 19, 1997.

ROBERTSHAW, JAMES, lawyer, pilot; b. Greenville, Miss., May 19, 1916; s. Frank Newell and Hannah Mary (Aldridge) R.; m. Sylvia Schively, Apr. 26, 1956; children: Mary Nicholson, Sylvia Yale, Frank Paxton. SB, Miss. State U., 1937; JD, Harvard U., 1940, Vet.'s Cert., Harvard Bus. Sch., 1946; postgrad. Command and Gen. Staff Sch., 1943. Bar: Miss. 1940, U.S. Dist. Ct. (no. dist.) Miss. 1951, U.S. Ct. Appeals (5th cir.) 1954, U.S. Tax Ct. 1958, U.S. Supreme Ct. 1967, U.S. Dist. Ct. (so. dist.) Miss. 1984. Sole practice, Greenville, Miss., 1940, 46-62; ptnr. Robertshaw & Merideth, 1962-84; ptnr. Robertshaw, Terney & Noble, Greenville, 1984-95; of counsel, 1995. Chmn. Community and County Devel. Com., Miss. Econ. Council, 1968-70; mem. Miss. Ho. of Reps., 1953-56; chmn. Greenville Airport Commn., 1967-73, Indsl. Found., 1974; mem. com. tech. in the cts., mem. complaint tribunal Miss. Supreme Ct., 1987-93. Served to col. U.S. Army, 1941-46. Decorated Legion of Merit, Croix de Guerre (France). Mem. Am. Judicature Soc., Miss. Bar Found., Univ. Club, Greenville Golf and Country Club, Sigma Alpha Epsilon. Episcopalian.

ROBERTSON, JAMES DAVID, neurobiologist educator; b. Tuscaloosa, Ala., Oct. 13, 1922; s. Floyd Earl and Gladys (Williams) R.; m. Doris Elizabeth Kohler, Oct. 21, 1946; children—Karen Lee, Elizabeth Ann, James David. B.S., U. Ala., 1942; M.D., Harvard U., 1945; Ph.D., Mass. Inst. Tech., 1952. Lab. teaching asst. biology U. Ala., 1940-42; intern 4th Med. Service Harvard, Boston City Hosp., 1945-46; part-time practice medicine, specializing internal medicine Lowndsborough and Hayneville, Ala., 1947-48; asst. physician U.S. VA Hosp., Montgomery, Ala., 1947-48; asst. physician med. dept. Mass. Inst. Tech., 1948-49; research fellow Am. Cancer Soc., 1949-52; asst. prof. pathology and oncology Med. Sch. U. Kans., Kansas City, 1952-55; hon. rsch. assoc. (reader level) dept. anatomy U. Coll. London, Eng., 1955-60; asso. biophysicist, biophysicist rsch. lab. McLean Hosp., Belmont, Mass., 1960-66; asst. prof. neuropathology Med. Sch. Harvard, 1960-64, assoc. prof. (with tenure), 1964-66; prof., chmn. dept. anatomy Duke U., Durham, N.C., 1966-88, James B. Duke prof. anatomy, 1975-88, chmn. emeritus dept. anatomy, 1988-95, James B. Duke prof. neurobiology and cell biology, 1988-92, James B. Duke prof. neurobiology emeritus, 1992-95; vis. prof. Inst. Physiol. Chemistry, U. Wuerzburg, Fed. Republic of Germany, 1978-79, other univs.; chmn. exec. com. Internat. Cell Membrane Confs., Frascati, Italy, 1965-70, mem. exec. com., 1970-95; mem. cell biology study sec. NIH, 1967-71, ad hoc, 1975, 87-95; now cons.; cons. NSF, Avco Corp., 1963-64, Dept. Def.; past mem. panel IV Internat. Cell Rsch. Orgn.; mem. faculty 2d Curso Latinam. de Micros. Electronica, U. Chile, 1974; mem. external vis. com. Lawrence Radiation Lab., U. Calif., Berkeley, 1978; cons. dept def., chmn. search com. for chair anatomy dept. Uniformed Svcs. U. of the Health Scis., 1975; mem. external vis. com. in biology Brookhaven Nat. Lab., 1978-81; 1st Pomerat Meml. lectr. U. Tex., 1966; Ferris lectr. Yale U., 1977; Damon lectr. U. Conn., 1975; Disting. lectr. Tulane U., 1975; Ferris lectr. Yale U., 1977; Otto Mortenson lectr. U. Wis., 1977; Cummings Meml. lectr. Tulane U., 1984; George Harvey Miller Disting. lectr. in anatomy U. Ill. Med. Sch., 1988. Editorial bd.: Anat. Record, 1968-69, Jour. Neurobiology, Lipid Research, 1963-66; editorial bd.: Jour. Cell Biology, 1965-68; editorial cons., 1968-95, cons. editor, Scott Forsman Co., Wiley-Intersci. Charter mem. Searle Scholars Selection Com., 1981-84; mem. external adv. com. High Voltage Electron Microscopy Facility, U. Colo., Boulder, 1985-92; trustee N.C. Sch. Sci. and Math., 1985-86. Served to lt. (j.g.), M.C. USNR, 1942-45, 48-49. Recipient W.B. Saunders award in pathology and bacteriology, 1943, Alexander von Humboldt Soc. Sr. Scientist prize Fed. Republic of Germany, 1978; Kellogg Found. scholar U. Ala., 1942-43. Mem. AAAS, Electron Microscope Soc. Am. (council 1983-85, pres. 1984), Am. Assn. Anatomists, Assn. Anatomy, Cell Biology and Neurol. Biology Chmns. (chmn. founding com.), Anat. Soc. Gt. Britain and Ireland, Physiol. Soc., Research Def. Soc., Internat. Assn. Cell Biology, Biophys. Soc., Neurochem. Soc., Soc. Neurosci., N.C. Soc. Neurosci (pres. 1987-88), Pan Am. Assn. Anatomists, Southeastern Electron Microscopy Soc., So. Soc. Anatomists, Am. Soc. Zoology, Soc. Ind. Scholars, Brit. Biophys. Soc., Am. Soc. Cell Biology, Soc. Devel. Biology, Internat. Neurochem. Soc., Am. Crystal. Assn., Sigma Xi, Phi Beta Kappa, Alpha Omega Alpha, Phi Eta Sigma. Home: Durham N.C. Died Aug. 11, 1995.

ROBERTSON, JEFFREY D., lawyer; b. Jan. 17, 1946. BA, CUNY, Bklyn., 1968, JD, 1973; postgrad., Harvard U., 1987. Bar: N.Y. 1973, U.S. Dist. Ct. (so. and ea. dists.) N.Y. 1973, U.S. Ct. Appeals (2d cir.) 1974. Ptnr. Wilson, Elser, Moskowitz, Edelman & Dicker, N.Y.C.; med. staff cons., lectr. St. Vincent's Med. Ctr., Richmond, N.Y.; lectr. in field; cons. Ladies Home Jour., The Manhattan Lawyer, N.Y. Law Jour. Author: Psychiatric Malpractice, 1988, The Medical Malpractice Manual, 1986, Plastic Surgery Litigation, 1987, Direct and Cross Examination of the Orthopedic Expert, 1987, Plastic Surgery Malpractice, 1989, (with Simon and Smith) The Psychiatric Malpractice Manual, 1984; contbr. chpts. to books; contbr. articles to profl. jours.; editor-in-chief, columnist, bd. contbrs. Med. Malpractice: Law and Strategy Mag. Mem. ABA (tort, ins. and litigation sects.), N.Y. County Assn., Assn. Trial Lawyer Am., N.Y. State Bar Assn., Def. Rsch. Inst., Am. Soc. Law and Medicine. Died July 17, 1997.

ROBERTSON, LUCRETIA SPEZIALE, interior designer, author; b. Pitts., Feb. 23, 1944; d. Louis Albert and Irene (Lavenka) Speziale; m. Ronald Paul Parlato, Aug. 21, 1965 (div. Dec. 1967); m. William Sterling Robertson III, Feb. 3., 1973; children: Evan Alexander, Ian Stewart. BFA in Art History, Fine Arts and Archtl. Design, Smith Coll., 1965. Asst. art dept. Condé Nast-Mademoiselle, N.Y.C., 1965-66; dir. fashion M. Lowenstein and Sons, N.Y.C., 1966-67; fashion coordinator Vogue/Butterick Pattern Co., N.Y.C., 1967-70, creative dir. advt./promotions, 1970-73; prin. Lang/Robertson, Ltd., N.Y.C. and Montclair, N.J., 1975-92; cons., designer Boussac of France, N.Y.C., 1975-92; cons. Burlington Industries, N.Y.C., 1976-79, Levolor/Lorentzen, Parsippany, N.J., 1980-92; designer McCalls Patterns, N.Y.C., 1979-81, AABE Fabrieken, Tillburg, Holland, 1983-85. Author: (ghostwriter) Body and Beauty Secrets of the Superbeauties, 1978, Decorating with Fabric, (with Donna Lang), 1986; contbr. to Am. Psychiat. Press, Inc., presenter paper on vol. work to 5th Nat. Conv. on Pediatric AIDS, L.A., 1989. Decorating wih Paper, (with Donna Lang), 1993. Vol. St. Luke's Ch. Outreach program, Montclair, 1978-92, Whole Theatre Co., Montclair, 1980-92, AIDS Resource Found. for Children, Newark; singer N.J. Oratorio Soc.; vol. pediatric AIDS, Albert Einstein Coll. Medicine, Bronx, N.Y.; devel. bd. Hyacinth Found. AIDS Resources, N.J.; mem. Montclair AIDS Task Force; organizing com. St. Luke's Episcopal Ch. AIDS Task Force. Mem. Smith Club. Democrat. Episcopalian. Avocations: photography, poetry, sailing, gardening, singing. Home: Montclair N.J. Died June 15, 1992.

ROBINS, ELI, psychiatrist, biochemist, educator; b. Houston, Feb. 22, 1921; m. Lee Nelken, Feb. 22, 1946; children: Paul, James, Thomas, Nicholas. BA, Rice U., 1940; MD, Harvard U., 1943; DSc (hon.), Wash. U., St. Louis, 1984. Intern Mt. Sinai Hosp., N.Y.C., 1944; resident Mass. Gen. Hosp., Boston, 1944-45, McLean Hosp., Waverley, Mass., 1945-46, Pratt Diagnostic Hosp., Boston, 1948-49; instr. neuropsychiatry Washington U. Sch. Medicine, St. Louis, 1951-53, asst. prof. psychiatry, 1953-56, assoc. prof., 1956-58, prof., 1958-66, Wallace Renard prof., 1966-91, prof. emeritus, 1991-94, head dept. psychiatry, 1963-75. Author: (with M.T. Saghir) Male and Female Homosexuality: A Comprehensive Study, 1973; editor: (with others) Ultrastructure and Metabolism of the Nervous System, 1962, (with K. Leonhard) Classification of Endogenous Psychoses; The Final Months, A Study of the Lives of 134 Persons Who Committed Suicide, 1981; contbr. to profl. jours. Fellow Am. Psychiat. Assn. (life, Disting. Svc. award 1992), Am. Coll. Neuropsychopharmacology (hon.), Royal Coll. Psychiatrists (hon.); mem. Am. Soc. Clin. Investigation, Am. Soc. Biol. Chemists, Psychiat. Rsch. Soc., Am. Psychopath. Assn. Home: Saint Louis Mo. Died Dec. 21, 1994.

ROBINSON, EMMA CALLOWAY, senior citizen's advocate; b. Red Ash, W.Va., Feb. 19, 1896; d. Anthony Tuschan and Janie Elizabeth (Beasley) Calloway; m. Robert Lee Robinson; children: Geraldine Elizabeth, Evelyn Robinson Jones, Francine Robinson Jackson. Tchr.'s degree, Storer Coll., Harpers Ferry, W.Va., 1917; AB in Edn., W.Va. State Coll., 1940; MA in Edn., W.Va. U., 1949. Cert. elem. tchr., W.Va. Tchr. Fayette (W.Va.) Pub. Schs., Raleigh County (W.Va.) Pub. Schs. Del. White House Conf. on Aging, Washington, 1971—; life mem. Rep. Presdl. Task Force, 1988—; bd. dirs. Martin Luther King, Jr. Community Coll., Mt. Hope, W.Va.; guest speaker numerous orgns. Mem. NEA, W.Va. Edn. Assn., Nat. Caucus and Ctr. on Black Aged, W.V.a Edn. Assn., Am. Assn. Ret. Persons. Baptist. Died February 1996.

ROBINSON, GORDON PRINGLE, forester; b. Vancouver, B.C., Can., Apr. 7, 1911; came to U.S., 1920; s. Laforest George and Sarah Lawrence (Mitchie) R.; m. Adina Wiens, Feb. 7, 1943; children: Charlotte Wiens, Daniel Gordon, Lawrence Pringle. Student, J.C. Marin Jr. Coll., Kentfield, Calif., 1934; BS in Forestry, U. Calif., Berkeley, 1937. Forester So. Pacific Transp. Co., 1939-66; staff forester Sierra Club, 1966-79; cons. Tiburon, Calif., 1966-95. Author: The Forest and the Trees: a guide to Excellent Forestry, 1988. Honored for life and work Lawrence Hall of Sci., Berkeley, 1993. Democrat. Unitarian. Avocation: artist. Died Nov. 27, 1995.

ROBINSON, JAMES HERBERT, physician, educator, surgeon; b. Altoona, Pa., Jan. 27, 1927; s. June and Dora (Potter) R.; m. Soiesette Elaine Furlonge, June 28, 1952; children: James Herbert II, Charles Furlonge, Malcolm Kenneth. B.S., Pa. State U., 1949; M.D., U. Pa., 1953. Diplomate: Am. Bd. Med. Examiners, Am. Bd. Surgery; Pan-Am. Med. Assn. Intern Hosp. of U. Pa., Phila., 1953-54; resident in surgery Hosp. of U. Pa., 1954-58, chief resident, 1958-59, asst. instr. surgery, 1954-57, instr., 1957-59; fellow in Harrison Dept. Surg. Research, 1954-59, assoc. in surgery, 1960-71, lectr., 1971—; clin. asst. prof. surgery Hahneman Med. Coll. and Hosp., Phila., 1971-73; clin. assoc. prof. surgery Jefferson Med. Coll. of Thomas Jefferson U., Phila., 1973-76, assoc. dean, clin. prof. surgery, dir. minority affairs, 1975—, dir. student affairs, 1981—; program dir. Mercy Douglas Hosp., Phila., 1961-67, assoc. med. dir., 1967-70. Vice chmn. United Fund ChCampaign, Phila., 1967; mem. centennial com. Stephen Smith Home for Aged, Phila., 1964, bd. dirs., 1967—; health and safety com. Boy Scouts of Am., 1964, Phila. dist. council, 1965; mem. fellowship commn. Haverford (Pa.) Twp. Civic Council, 1966; bd. dirs. Family Services of Main Line Neighborhood, Havertown, Pa., 1968-71, Sing City Assn., Phila., 1968-74, William Penn Found., 1979—, Nat. Med. Fellowships Inc., 1982—, Opera Ebony, 1983—; v.p., bd. dirs. A Better Chance, Lower Merion, Pa., 1979—; aux. vestry St. Thomas Protestant Episcopal Ch., Phila., 1967-69; trustee Episcopal Acad., 1977—; bd. overseers Phila. Theol. Inst., 1982—. Served with USAAF, 1945-46. Decorated Legion of Honor Chapel of Four Chaplains; John W. White fellow Pa. State U., 1949; recipient distinguished alumnus award Pa. State U., 1978; recognition award AMA, 1976; certificate of merit for service to medicine, 1967; certificate of appreciation Greater Phila. Health Fair, 1976; fellow Am. Cancer Soc., U. Pa. Med. Sch., 1956-58; Nat. Cancer Inst. trainee NIH, 1958-59; rehab. fellow, 1956-57. Fellow A.C.S., Phila. Coll. Physicians, Am. Soc. Abdominal Surgeons; mem. Nat. Assn. Med. Minority Educators, Phila. County Med. Soc. (bd. dirs. 1966-68, bd. censors 1972-77), Pa. State Med. Soc., AMA, Nat. Med. Assn., Ravdin-Rhoads Surg. Soc., AAUP, Assn. Am. Med. Colleges, Am. Med. Writers Assn., Phila. Com. Trauma, Pa. State U. Alumni Assn. (Alumni Council 1982—, bd. dirs. Coll. Sci. 1979—), Group Student Affairs, Alpha Boule of Sigma Pi Phi, ONYX Hon. Soc., Skull and Bones Soc., Phi Eta Sigma, Alpha Epsilon Delta. Episcopalian. Club: Mason. Contbr. cardiovascular research, U. Pa. Died Sept. 23, 1997.

ROBINSON, ORMSBEE WRIGHT, educational consultant; b. Bklyn., June 17, 1910; s. Harry Alexander and Claire (Wright) R.; m. Janet MacNaughton Miller, June 22, 1935; children: Heather (Mrs. Phillips Thorp), John Alexander. AB cum laude, Princeton U., 1932, MSS, New Sch. Social Rsch., 1937; MA, Columbia U. Tchrs. Coll., 1942, EdD, 1949. Exec. sec. Plainfield Inst., N.J., 1934-35; high sch. instr., 1935; dir. adult edn. Soc. Ethical Culture, N.Y.C., 1935-41; tchr. ethics Fieldston Sch., N.Y.C., 1935-42; exec. dir. Assoc. Jr. Work Camps, Inc., 1938-42; assoc. OPA, Region II, 1942-46; dir. admissions and pub. rels. Bard Coll., 1946-50, v.p., 1950-54; ednl. cons. for higher edn. Conn. State Dept. Edn., 1954-55, chief Bur. Higher and Adult Edn., 1955-57; exec. sec. Conn. Coun. Higher Edn., 1954-57; cons. in exec. devel., IBM, 1957-61; program dir. IBM Exec. Sch., 1962; dir. ednl. affairs IBM, 1962-70, dir. univ. rels. planning, 1970-75; dir. internat. program Nat. Coun. on Philanthropy, 1975-79, acting pres., 1977-78; cons. Eugenio Mendoza Found. and Venezuelan Fedn. Pvt. Founds., Caracas, Venezuela, 1979-83, Technoserve, Inc., 1980-83; assoc. Columbia U. seminar on technology and social change, 1962-75; chmn. bus. edn. adv. bd. Com. Econ. Devel., 1963-64, mem. Coun. Devel., Edn., Tng. Nat. Indsl. Conf. Bd., 1960-68; faculty Salzburg Seminar in Am. Studies, 1968; mem. U.S. Nat. Commn. UNESCO, 1971-74, exec. com., 1972-74, chmn. adv. com. on bus. and internat. edn., 1971-72, chmn. membership com., 1974; mem. standards com. Am. Assembly Coll. Schs. of Bus., 1971-72, chmn. internat. affairs com., 1973-75, bd. dirs., 1974-75; mem. task force bus. and internat. edn. Am. Coun. on Edn., 1975-76. Bd. dirs. World Affairs Ctr., Hartford, 1982-83; adv. coun. Am. Ditchley Found., 1969-86, advisor Assn. for Internat. Practical Tng.; mem. Granby Bd. Edn., Conn., 1979-83; bd. founders U. Hartford; bd. dirs. United Way of Chatham County, 1985-91, United Way N.C., 1993-95. Mem. Soc. Internat. Devel., S.R., Soc. Colonial Wars, Fearrington Garden Club. Co-author: Education in Business and Industry, 1966. Editorial adv. bd. Indian Adminstrv. and Mgmt. Rev., New Delhi, 1968-75. Contbr. to profl. jours. Died July 3, 1995. Home: Pittsboro N.C.

ROBINSON, RONALD JAMES, petroleum engineer; b. Pueblo, Colo., Mar. 10, 1946; s. James Claude and Doris Loraine Robinson; B.S. in Math. and Physics, So.

Colo. State Coll., 1968; M.S. in Physics, Baylor U., Waco, Tex., 1971; Ph.D. in Petroleum Engring., Tex. A&M U., 1974; m. Bonnie Lynn Martin, Aug. 31, 1968; children: Kevin James, Kyle Bryant, Kurt David. With Getty Oil Co., 1973-78, dist. reservoir engr., Bakersfield, Calif., 1975-78; mgr. thermal recovery Grace Petroleum Corp., Oklahoma City, 1978-79; sr. cons. INTERCOMP Resource Devel. and Engring., Houston, 1979-80; supr. thermal research Getty Oil Co., Houston, 1980-81; spl. projects coordinator Getty Research Ctr., Houston, 1981-84; mgr. reservoir engring. research Texaco, Inc., 1984-89; mgr. internat. applications Texaco, Inc., 1989-92; mgr. internat. applications & tech. transfer Texaco, Inc., 1992-94; gen. mgr. Texaco Exploration and Prodn. Tech. Dept., 1994-95; pres. tech. divsn. Texaco, 1996-97hmn. RBR Investments, 1988-97; trustee S.W. Rsch. Inst.; bd. dirs. Petroleum Transfer Coun., 1995-96, Sheltering Arms Sr. Svcs., 1996-97, Jr. Achievement, 1996-97; industry adv. bd. U. Md. Balt. County, 1996-97; industry adv. coun. dept. petroleum engring. Tex. A&M U.; appointee Gov.'s Sci. and Tech. Coun., Tex., 1997; NASA fellow, 1968. Mem. Can. Inst. Mining, Indonesian/Am. Bus. Assn. (bd. dirs. 1994-97), pres. 1997), Soc. Profl. Well Log Analysts, Soc. Petroleum Engrs. (dir.), Scientific Rsch. Soc. N.Am., Greater Houston C. of C. (mem. chmn.'s club 1987-97) Sigma Xi. Club: Kiwanis. Author papers in field. Died Jan. 16, 1997.

ROCK, IRVIN, research scientist; b. N.Y.C., July 7, 1922; s. Daniel Joel and Lilian (Weinberger) R.; m. Romola Hardy, Oct. 26, 1945 (div. July 1963); children: Peter, Alice; m. Sylvia Shilling, July 24, 1963; children: Lisa, David. BS, CCNY, 1947, MA, 1948; PhD summa cum laude, New Sch. for Social Rsch., N.Y.C., 1952. From rsch. asst. to assoc. prof. New Sch. for Social Rsch., N.Y.C., 1947-59; assoc. prof. Yeshiva U., N.Y.C., 1959-67; prof. Inst. for Cognitive Studies Rutgers U., Newark, 1967-81; prof. Program in Cognition Rutgers U., New Brunswick, N.J., 1981-87; prof. emeritus Rutgers U., New Brunswick, 1987-95; fellow to instr. CCNY, 1947-49; adj. prof. U. Calif., Berkeley, 1987-95; adv. bd. mem. Perception Jour., Bristol, Eng., 1986-95. Author: The Nature of Perceptual Adaptation, 1966, An Introduction to Perception, 1975, Orientation and Form, 1973, The Logic of Perception, 1983, Perception, 1984; peer reviewer various psychology jours. With U.S. Army, 1943-45, ETO. Fellow AAAS, APA, Soc. Exptl. Psychologists. Achievements include discovery of one trial learning, the effect of perceived orientation on phenomenal shape; co-investigated the moon illusion; co-discovered the dominance of vision over touch; co-inventor new method for studying perception without attention; research includes theoretical analysis of intelligence of perception. Home: Berkeley Calif. Died July 18, 1995.

ROCKEFELLER, MARY FRENCH (MRS. LAURANCE S. ROCKEFELLER), association executive; b. N.Y.C., May 1, 1910; d. John and Mary Montague (Billings) French; m. Laurance Spelman Rockefeller, Aug. 15, 1934; children—Laura Rockefeller Chasin, Marion Rockefeller Weber, Lucy Rockefeller Waletzky, Laurance. Student, Vassar Coll., 1927-29, Art Students League N.Y.C., 1929-34. Mem. nat. bd. YWCA, 1951-88, trustee, 1988—; chmn. Am. Centennial Observance and Celebration, 1955, co-chmn. nat. convocation on racial justice, 1972; chmn. World Service Council, 1958-64, chmn. world relations com., 1964-73. Mem. coun. Found. Child Devel.; trustee Spelman Coll., Atlanta, 1946-70, hon. trustee, 1970—, mem. exec. com.; trustee Whitney Mus. of Am. Art, 1965-89, Gordon-Conwell Theol. Sem., 1976—, United Bd. For Christian Higher Edn. in Asia, 1989—, Woodstock Hist. Soc., Calvin Coolidge Found.; trustee YWCA of City N.Y., 1971-84, hon. bd. dirs., 1984—; trustee Fgn. Policy Assn., 1977-86, hon. trustee, 1986—; mem. distbn. com. N.Y. Community Trust, 1969—; bd. dirs. N.Y. Community Fund, Inc., 1969—; mem. adminstrv. bd. Meml. Sloan-Kettering Cancer Center, 1976—. Recipient Gold medal Nat. Inst. Social Scis., 1972, Ambassador award YWCA of the U.S.A., 1993. Mem. N.Y. Zool. Soc., Hort. Soc. N.Y., Met. Mus. Art, Mus. Modern Art, Philharmonic Symphony, Park Assn. N.Y.C., Women's Nat. Republican Club. Clubs: Women's City (N.Y.C.), Cosmopolitan (N.Y.C.), Colony (N.Y.C.). Died April 17, 1997.

ROCKWOOD, RUTH H., library science educator; b. Chgo., Oct. 15, 1906; d. Charles Edward and Myrtle Isabelle (Wheeler) Humiston; m. George Herbert Rockwood, Apr. 14, 1928 (dec.); children: Charles Edward, Nancy Hoyt Rockwood Haigh, Alice Frances Rockwood Bethke. A.B., Wellesley Coll., 1927; M.S., U. Ill., 1949; Ed.D., Ind. U., 1960. Adminstrv. asst., instr. U. Ill. Library Sch., 1949-52; Fulbright lectr. Chulalongkorn U., Bangkok, Thailand, 1952-53; vis. asst. prof. Ind. U. Library Sch., 1958-59; prof. library sci. Fla. State U., 1953-79, prof. emeritus, 1979-97. Mem. Fla. Trail Assn., Sierra Club, Beta Phi Mu. Club: Pilot (Tallahassee). Died July 5, 1997.

RODMAN, HARRY EUGENE, architect, educator, acoustical and illumination consultant; b. Plainfield, Iowa, Sept. 29, 1913; s. Harry Irwin and Iva (Reade) R.; m. Marion G. Rooney, Feb. 14, 1942; children—Harry Eugene, Bruce Ervin, Gerald Reade, Blair Douglas. B. Archtl. Engring., Iowa State U., 1936; M.Arch., Harvard, 1937. Instr. Wash. State U., 1937-41; designer Austin Co., Cleve., 1941-45; asso. architect U. Ill. at Urbana, 1945-46; mem. faculty Rensselaer Poly. Inst., 1946-78, prof. architecture, 1955-78; vis. prof. Sch. Architecture and Environ. Design, Calif. Poly. State U., 1979-82; profl. practice Troy, N.Y., 1946-78; cons. in field, 1946-96; chmn. N.Y. State Bd. Examiners Architects, 1962-64; bd. dirs. Nat. Council Archtl. Registration Bds., 1964-71, sec., 1967-71, chmn. com. exams., 1965-70; sec. Nat. Archtl. Accrediting Bd., 1969-70; mem. tech. adv. com. Illuminating Engring. Research Inst., 1972-78; mem. U.S. nat. com. Internat. Commn. on Illumination. Contbr. to profl. jours. Mem. exec. bd. Uncle Sam council Boy Scouts Am., 1956-70. Recipient Profl. Achievement citation Iowa State U., 1980. Fellow AIA (pres. Eastern N.Y. chpt. 1952, bd. dirs. 1953), Illuminating Engring. Soc.; mem. N.Y. State Assn. Architects (bd. dirs. 1954); asso. Acoustical Soc. Am.; mem. Allied Arts Com., Illuminating Engring. Soc. (vice chmn. Mohawk-Hudson sect. 1956, bd. mgrs. 1971-74), Am. Arbitration Assn. (panel constrn. arbitrators), Tau Beta Pi, Tau Sigma Delta, Scarab. Home: San Luis Obispo Calif. Died May 24, 1996.

RODNEY, GEORGE ALBERT, federal government agency executive; b. Steelton, Pa., June 3, 1921; s. Frank and Mary (Gearhardt) R.; m. Priscilla Williamson, June 10, 1948 (div. 1973); 1 child, John W.; m. Roberta Cynthia Forsyth-Reid, Sept. 15, 1984. BSME, Carnegie Mellon, 1942; postgrad., USA Exptl. Test Pilot Sch., Dayton, Ohio, 1948. Various positions Martin Marietta, 1946-80; dir. mission success Martin Marietta, Orlando, Fla., 1980-86; assoc. adminstr. for safety, reliability, maintainability and quality assurance NASA, Washington, 1986—. 1st lt. air corps U.S. Army, 1943-46. Mem. AIAA (sr.), Soc. Exptl. Test Pilots. Republican. Episcopalian. Died Oct. 5, 1996.

RODRIGUEZ, CARLOS RAFAEL, economist, Cuban government official; b. Cienfuegos, Cuba, May 23, 1913; s. Pedro Rodriguez Villametide and Antonia Rodriguez R.; m. Mirta Rodriguez, Feb. 12, 1976; children: Anabelle, Dania, Enrique. D. Law, Dr. Social, Polit. and Econ. Scis. magna cum laude, Havana U., 1939. Bar: Cuba 1939. Mayor City of Cienfuegos, 1933-34; minister without portfolio Cuban Govt., 1944; rep. Socialist Popular Party in Sierra Maestra, 1958-59; editor Party newspaper News of Hoy, 1959-62; pres. Nat. Inst. Agrarian Reform, Ministry Agr. and Animal Prodn., 1962-65; pres. Nat. Commn. Econ., Sci. and Tech. Collaboration, 1965-75; permanent rep. Cuba to Council of Mut. Econ. Aid; v.p. Council of State, v.p. coun. mins. charge fgn. affairs, fgn. trade, Nat. Bank Cuba, Com. Econ. Collaboration, 1976—; v.p. Councils of State and Ministers, 1976—; prof. econs. Havana U., 1960-62, dean Sch. Econs., 1961-62; mem. South Commn., Geneva, 1987. Author: Marxism in Cuban History, 1943; Jose de la Luz y Caballero, 1947; Welles Mission, 1957; Four Years of Agrarian Reform, 1962; Lenin and the Colonial Question, 1970; Marti, Contemporary and Companion, 1973; The Cuban Transition Toward Socialism 1959-63, 1978; Letra con Filo 3 vols., 1984, 88; Palabras en los 70, 1985. Contbr. articles to profl. jours. Mem. Revolutionairies Integrated Orgns., United Party Socialist Revolution Cuba; mem. cen. com., mem. secretariat Community Party Cuba, 1975-78, mem. polit. bur., 1975—. Recipient Cuban Nat. González Lanusa award, 1939, Nat. Essay award, 1938, Nat. Journalism award, 1939, XX Ann. Revolution medal, 1973; Orden Frank Pais, 1983; Orden Juan Marinello, 1983; named Prof. emeritus Havano U., 1983; also numerous decorations, Poland, Rumania, Bulgaria, U.S.S.R., Czechislovakia. Mem. Nat. Assn. Econs., Nat. Lawyers Guild.

RODRIGUEZ PEDOTTI, ANDRES, president of Paraguay; b. 1923; m. Nelida Reig. Gen., comdr. 1st Army Corps; former leader Colo. Party; comdr. Cav. Div., Asuncion, Paraguay, 1961—; pres. of Paraguay, Asuncion, 1989—. Died Apr. 21, 1997.

ROEHL, JOSEPH E., lawyer; b. Albuquerque, Feb. 17, 1913; s. H.C. and Elizabeth J. (Walsh) R.; m. Jeanne F. Scott, Nov. 1, 1938. BA, U. N.Mex., 1936; LLB; LL.B., U. Tex., 1946. Bar: Tex. 1946, N.Mex. 1946, U.S. Ct. Appeals (10th cir.). Asst. adminstr. OPA, 1942-44; librarian Supreme Ct. Tex., Austin, 1945-46; practice in Albuquerque, 1946—; law clk. U.S. Circuit Judge Sam G. Bratton, Albuquerque, 1946-47; assoc. Simms & Modrall, 1947-53; mng. partner Modrall, Seymour, Sperling, Roehl & Harris, 1954-74; sr. dir. Modrall, Sperling, Roehl, Harris & Sisk, 1953—; chmn. com. uniform jury instrns. Supreme Ct. N.M., 1962-83; bd. dirs. Mountain States Mut. Casualty Ins. Co., 1977-93; Pres. Rio Grande Lumber Co., 1959-68; pres. Rico, Inc. Co-author, editor: New Mexico Civil Jury Instruction, 1966, 2d edit., 1981; Contbr. articles on law office econs. and mgmt. profl. jours.; speaker before profl. groups. Recipient First Nat. award for state bar activities, 1962. Fellow Am. Bar Found.; mem. ABA, Tex. Bar Assn., N.Mex. Bar Assn. Died May 12, 1996.

ROEMER, MICHAEL, economist, consultant, educator; b. N.Y.C., June 6, 1937; s. David Edwin and Pauline (Herman) R.; m. Linda Cohen, Aug. 27, 1960; children: Margery Roemer McDonald, Brian. BS, Stanford U., 1959, SM in Engring. Sci., 1960; SM in Indsl. Mgmt., MIT, 1962, PhD in Econs., 1968. Fellow in Africa MIT, Nairobi, Kenya, 1962-64; internat. economist, acting chief program and policy divsn. AID, Washington, 1967-70; devel. advisor Harvard Devel. Adv. Svc., Cambridge, Mass., 1971-74; lectr. econs. Harvard U., Cambridge, 1974-84, sr. lectr., 1984—, fellow Inst. for Internat. Devel., 1974—, dep. dir., 1979-80, exec. dir., 1980-84; mem. adv. bd. Internat. Ctr. for Econ. Growth, Inst. for Comtemporary Studies, San Francisco, 1985—. Author: Fishing for Growth: Export-led Development in Peru, 1950-1967, 1970, (with Stern) Appraisal of Development Projects: A Practical Guide with Case Studies from Ghana, 1975, (with Kim) Studies in the Modernization of the Republic of Korea, 1945-1975, 1979 ,(with Stern) Cases in Economic Development, 1981, (with others) Economics of Development, 1983, 2d edit. 1987, 3d edit., 1992; co-editor: Parallel Markets in Developing Countries, 1989, Markets in Developing Countries: Parallel, Fragmented and Black, 1991; co-editor Reforming Economic Systems in Developing Countries, 1991, Asia and Africa: Legacies and Opportunities in Development, 1994, also articles. Exxon Edn. Found. grantee, 1979. Mem. Am. Econ. Assn. (editorial bd. Quar. Jour. Econs. 1981-84). Avocation: bird watching. DIED 12/13/96. .

ROERICK, WILLIAM (GEORGE) (WILLIAM ROEHRICK), actor, author; b. New Jersey, Dec. 17, 1912; s. William George and Josephine (Clark) Roehrick. BS, Hamilton Coll., 1934, DFA (hon.), 1971; student, Berkshire Playhouse Drama Sch., 1935. chmn. fine arts adv. com. Alumni Coun., Hamilton Coll.; bd. dirs. Berkshire Theatre Festival, Stockbridge, Mass. Broadway roles include: Romeo and Juliet, 1935, St. Joan, 1936, Hamlet, 1936, Our Town, 1938, The Land is Bright, 1941, This is the Army, 1942-45, Magnificent Yankee, 1946, Tonight at 8:30, 1948, Right Honourable Gentleman, 1961, Marat/Sade, 1967, The Homecoming, 1967, Waltz of the Toreadors, 1973, Night of the Iguana, 1976-77; film appearances include The Other Side of the Mountain, This is the Army, Day of the Dolphin; numerous TV appearances including role as Henry Chamberlain in TV serial Guiding Light; co-author: (with Thomas Coley) play The Happiest Years, 1949, A Passage to E.M. Forster; dramatic reading, 1970; TV scripts for Climax, Mamma. Served with AUS, 1942-45. Mem. Actors Equity Assn. (council 10 years), Screen Actors Guild. AFTRA, Dramatists Guild, Actors Fund Am., Players Club, Century Club. Died Nov. 30, 1995.

ROGERS, RALPH B., industrial business executive; b. Boston, 1909; married. Ed., Northeastern U. With Cummins Diesel Engine Corp., Edwards Co., Hill Diesel Engine Co., Ideal Power Lawnmower Co., Indian Motocycle Co., Rogers Diesel & Aircraft Corp., Rogers Internat. Corp., Armstrong Rubber Export Corp.; with Tex. Industries Inc., Dallas, 1950—, chmn. bd., pres., CEO, 1951-75, chmn. bd., 1975—; dir. numerous subsidiaries. Chmn. bd. dirs. Tex. Industries Found.; chmn. emeritus Pub. Communication Found. North Tex., Pub. Broadcasting Svc., Univ. Med. Ctr., Inc.; past bd. dirs. Nat. Captioning Inst.; trustee Northeastern U.; trustee, chmn. emeritus St. Mark's Sch. of Tex.; former chmn. bd. mgrs. Dallas County Hosp. Dist.; founding chmn., chmn. emeritus Dallas Arboretum and Bot. Soc.; pres. Dallas Found. for Health, Edn. and Rsch.; co-founder Children's TV Workshop; founder, chmn. Zale Lipshy Univ. Hosp. Mem. Masons. Died Nov. 4, 1997.

ROKKE, DONALD LEIF, aerospace engineer, mechanical engineer; b. Pendleton, Oreg., June 9, 1924; s. Leif R. and Edith Marjorie (Mack) Kraft; divorced; children: Jonathan Leif, Lynn A. BS in Mathematic, U. Wash., 1945; BS in Aerospace Engring., U.S.N.R Midshipman Sch., 1947; BSME, U. Wash., 1948; postgrad., La Salle U., 1996—. Lic. profl. aerospace and mech. engr. Sr. project engr. The Boeing Co., Seattle, 1949-72; sr. engr. Comarco, Ridgecrest, Calif., 1973-74; strategy planner Chemsult A.G., Zug, Switzerland, 1975-79; staff engr. Martin Marietta, Denver, 1980-87; pres., CEO Major Spector Corp., Seattle, 1983—. Contbr. articles to profl. jours. Mem. VFW., received 2 presidential Commendations, 1977, 87, Declared to be Nat. Treas., U.S. Central Intelligence Agy., 1979.Founder & Pres., The Celibacy Found. Seattle, 1991—, pres.,The Endorphn Press, 1995—. Avocations: macroeconomy, parametric studies, tennis, swimming, biking, pysical fitness. Died Feb. 22, 1997.

ROLAND, EMMERETT WILBUR, minister; b. Red Bird, Okla., Oct. 24, 1931; s. Melvin Fred and Maggie Elizabeth (Wright) R.; m. Virginia Mae Bishop, Aug. 5, 1965. BD, St. Matthew U., 1956; DD, Mt. Sinai Theol. Sem., 1970. Ordained to ministry Am. Bapt. Conv., 1956. Pastor First St. Paul Bapt. Ch., North Oakland, Calif., 1961-66, St. Mary's Bapt. Ch., East Oakland, Calif., 1966-68; organizer and pastor Cornerstone Bapt. Ch., East Oakland, 1968-69; pastor 2d Bapt. Ch., Merced, Calif., 1969—. Editor Intermediate Quar., 1967-75; editorial staff writer Nat. Bapt. Publ. Bd., 1965-75. Mem. adv. bd. exec. opportunities program Merced Coll., 1972-74; mem. Koininia Scholarship Found., Oakland, 1964—. Mem. Shiloh Dist. Bapt. Assn. (moderator 1973), Gamma Chi Epsilon. Died Oct. 12, 1997.

ROLLASON, WENDELL NORTON, social services administrator; b. Winsted, Conn., Aug. 21, 1916; s. George Herbert Sanderson and Helen Hotchkiss (Norton) R.; m. Mary Jane Kemp, 1946 (div. 1971); children: Wendell, Frank, Raleigh; m. Barbara Louise Schott, Oct. 29, 1978. Grad. high sch., Winsted. Supr. Dade County Port Authority, Miami, Fla., 1946-51; exec. dir. Inter Am. Affairs Com., Miami, Fla., 1952-64; exec. dir. Redlands Christian Migrant Assn., Immokalee, Fla., 1966-90, exec. v.p., 1990—; chmn. Gov.'s Adv. Coun. on Farmworker Affairs, 1979, 86, 90; mem. Nat. Commn. on Migrant Edn. appt. by U.S. Senate, 1989-92. Vice chmn. Fla. Interagy. Coordinating Coun. for Infants and Toddlers, 1989-93; chmn. dist. adv. coun. Fla. Dept. Health Related Svcs., 1989-91. Petty officer 1st class USN, 1941-45. Recipient various awards, 1952-93; named One of Fla.'s Greatest Humanitarian Assets, Gov. of Fla., 1985; ann. health award created in his name, 1988; scholarship fund created in his name Migrant Parent Orgn., 1992. Mem. Fla. Assn. Community Health Ctrs. Democrat. Episcopalian. Avocations: reading, politics, outdoor activities. Died Jan. 18, 1997.

ROLLINS, HOWARD ELLSWORTH, JR., actor; b. Balt., Oct. 17, 1950; s. Howard E. Sr. and Ruth R. Student, Towson State U. Appearances include (Broadway) We Interrupt This Program, (TV) Eliza: Our Story, 1975, All My Children, Another World (Emmy nomination), King, Roots, The Next Generation, For Us The Living, Moving Right Along, Thornwell, My Old Man, The Neigborhood, Doctor's Story, With Murder in Mind, (series) In the Heat of the Night, 1988-94; (films) The House of God, 1978, Ragtime (Oscar nomination), 1981, A Soldier's Story, 1984, On the Block, 1990, Drunks, 1995, (theatrical prodns.) Streamers, Medal of Honor Rag, G.R. Point, The Mighty Gents. Died Dec. 8, 1996.

ROLSTON, KENNETH STUART, administrative assistant; b. Camden, N.J., Mar. 7, 1928; s. Kenneth Stuart and Miriam (Chew) R.; m. Thelma Ruth McDonald, Jan. 28, 1972; children—Kenneth Stuart III, David Lee, Kelly Chew, Andrew Douglas. B.S. in Forestry, Pa. State U. Conservation forester Kimberly-Clark Corp., Coosa Pines, Ala., 1951-61; truckwood supr. Kimberly-Clark Corp., to 1961; with Am. Pulpwood Assn., Washington, 1961-91, mgr. tech. programs, then exec. v.p., pres., ret., 1991; cons., 1991-92; administrv. asst. NORTIM Corp., 1993-97. Served with USN, 1945-47. Mem. Am. Soc. Assn. Execs. Died April 10, 1997.

ROLSTON, ROBERT JOHN, accountant, consultant; b. N.Y.C., June 28, 1944; s. Robert Joseph and Meta Loretta (Marshall) R.; m. Heide-Maria Aniszewski, Nov. 8, 1969 (div. Mar. 1975); m. Annie Teresa Cryan, Oct. 2, 1982 (div. Apr. 1991). BBA, Hofstra U., 1974. CPA, N.Y. Sr. acct. Fass, Tuchler & Muster, CPAs, Great Neck, N.Y., 1974-77, Seidman & Seidman, CPAs, N.Y.C., 1977-78, Kraft, Fischman & Assocs., CPAs, N.Y.C., 1978-80; supervising acct. David Tarlow & Co., CPAs, N.Y.C., 1980-81; fin. officer Allied Trading Corp., Secaucus, N.J., 1981-82; contr. Konishiroku Photo Industries, Enlwd Cliffs, N.J., 1982-84; mng. acct. Bachman, Schwartz, Abramson, CPAs, N.Y.C., 1984-86; corp. contr. Yarnell Group, N.Y.C., 1986-87; tax mgr. Lazar, Levine & Co., CPAs, N.Y.C., 1987-88; prin. Robert J. Rolston, CPA, Guttenberg, N.J., 1988-95. Co-author (with others): Accounting II, 1974. Mgr. Richmond Hill (N.Y.) Little League, 1978; deacon Second Ref. Ch., Hackensack, N.J., 1986-89, ch. Sunday sch. tchr., 1988-89; mem. leadership group Marble Collegiate Ch., 1993-95; chmn. Condo Govt. Affairs Com., Guttenberg, 1986-87; facilitator Compassionate Friends, Hackensack, 1991-95; music dir. Galaxy Singers, Guttenberg, 1989; asst. music dir. Metrognomes Singing Group, 1988-93, bus. mgr., 1993-95; mem. Univ. Glee Club of N.Y.C. Mem. AICPA, N.Y. State Soc. CPAs, Coop. Stock Brokers and Exchs. Com., Internat. Taxation Com., Beta Gamma Sigma. Democrat. Avocations: music, golf, art, history, coin and stamp collecting. Home: West New York N.J. Died Oct. 8, 1995.

ROMAN, SISTER GLORIA BELLE, nun, educator, educational administrator; b. Jackson, Mich., Dec. 19, 1941; d. Harry and Dorothy (Kracko) R. BA, Nazareth, 1967; MA, Notre Dame U., 1975, Boston Coll., 1988. Joined Sisters of St. Joseph of Nazareth, Roman Cath. Ch., 1960; cert. elem. educator, Mich.; cert. religious educator Diocese of Marquette, Mich. Mid. sch. tchr. St. Rita's Sch., Detroit, 1965; elem. tchr. St. Joseph Sch., Lake Orion, Mich., 1965-67, Our Lady of Fatima Sch., Michigan Center, Mich., 1967-69, St. Joseph Sch., Battle Creek, 1969-72, St. Mary Sch., Williamston, 1972-79, St. Therese Sch, Lansing, Mich, 1979-82; prin. Holy Angels Sch., Sturgis, Mich., 1982-83, St. Joseph the Worker Sch., Beal City, Mich., 1983-87; religious edn. coord., parish adminstr. Holy Name of Mary, Sault St. Marie, Mich., 1988—; com. mem. Pathways to the Chs., Sault Ste. Marie, 1989—. Vol. Kalamazoo (Mich.) COunty Jail, 1987 88. Recipient Grant Cen. Mich. U., 1980. Mem. Holy Name of Mary Parish Coun., Youth Group, Altar Soc. Died Dec. 13, 1993.

ROMERO, CESAR, actor; b. N.Y.C., Feb. 14, 1907; s. Cesar Juelin and Maria Marti Romero. Collegiate Sch., N.Y.C. Appeared in plays including My Three Angels, 1977, The Max Factor, 1981-82; films include The Castillian, Donovan's Reef, The Strongest Man in The World, Simple Justice, 1989; TV series include Cisco Kid, Falcon Crest, The Circus of the Stars, Will Shriner Show; TV guest star include Milton Berle Shows, Dinah Shore, Ironside, Buck Rogers, Fantasy Island, Charlie's Angels, and numerous others. With USCG, 1943.

ROMNEY, GEORGE, organization executive, former government official; b. Chihuahua, Mex., July 8, 1907; s. Gaskell and Anna (Pratt) R.; m. Lenore LaFount, July 2, 1931; children: Lynn Romney Keenan, Jane Romney Robinson, Scott, Willard Mitt. Student, Latter Day Saints High Sch. and Jr. Coll., U. Utah, 1929, George Washington U., 1929-30. Missionary Scotland and Eng., 1927- 28; tariff specialist for U.S. Senator David I. Walsh, 1929-30; apprentice Aluminum Co. Am., 1930; salesman Aluminum Co. Am., Los Angeles, 1931; Washington rep. Aluminum Co. Am., also Aluminum Wares Assn., 1932-38; Detroit mgr. Automobile Mfrs. Assn., 1939-41, gen. mgr. assn., 1942-48; v.p. Nash-Kelvinator Corp., 1950-53, exec. v.p., 1953-54, dir., 1953-54; pres., chmn. bd., gen. mgr. Am. Motors Corp., 1954-62, vice chmn., dir. (on leave), until 1962; gov. Mich., 1963-69; sec. HUD, 1969-72; chmn., chief exec. officer Nat. Center Vol. Action, 1973-79; chmn. Volunteer: Nat. Center, 1979-95; U.S. employer del. to Metal Trades Industry Confs., 1946-49; mng. dir. Automotive Coun. War Prodn., 1942-45; chmn. Citizens for Mich., 1959-62; mgmt. mem. War Manpower Commn., Labor-Mgmt. Commn., Detroit area; also pres. Washington Trade Assn. Execs., 1937-38; pres. Detroit Trade Assn., 1941; dir. Am. Trade Assn. Execs., 1944-47; mng. dir. Nat. Auto. Golden Jubilee Com., 1946. Past mem. bd. dirs. NCCJ, United Fund, Cranbrook Sch.; past pres. Detroit Stake Ch. Jesus Christ of Latter-Day Saints, regional rep., 1973-80; bd. dirs. Points of Light Found., Nat. and Community Commn. Named A.P. Industry Man of Year, 1958-61. Home: Bloomfield Hill Mich. Died July, 1995.

ROOKS, FLOYD JEFFERSON, public relations executive, non-profit corporation executive; b. Umatilla, Fla., June 26, 1923; s. Floyd J. and Bessie (Golden) R.; m. Marjorie Ann Fowler, Oct. 9, 1954; children: Virginia Ann, Sharon Elaine, Deborah Ann, Christina Carol. A.B., U. Fla., 1948, M.A. in Polit. Sci., 1949; M.S., Medill Sch. Journalism, Northwestern U., 1950; postrgrad. Sch. Biblical Studies, Regent U., 1985-87. Account exec. Internat. Nickel Co., Inc., N.Y.C., 1952-56; regional pub. relations Celanese Corp. Am., Charlotte, N.C., 1956-58; prin. Jeff Rooks Assos., Inc., Pub. Relations, Charlotte, 1958-63, Miami, Fla., 1966-76; pres. Christians Afloat, Inc., Palm Bay, Fla., 1976—. Served with AUS, 1943-46. Mem. Pub. Relations Soc. Am., Christian Boaters Assn., Inc. (founder, chmn. 1988—), Christians Afloat, Inc. (founder, pres. 1976—). Democrat. Clubs: Banana River Power Squandron, Indian Harbour Beach (Fla.).

ROOSA, STUART, former astronaut, beverage distributor; b. Durango, Colo., Aug. 16, 1933; s. Dewey R.; m. Joan C. Barrett; children: Christopher A., John D., Stuart Allen, Rosemary D. Ed., Okla. State U., U. Ariz.; B.S. in Aero. Engring, U. Colo.; Litt.D., U. St. Thomas, 1971. Served as commd. officer USAF, 1953-94; advanced through grades to col.; formerly exptl. test pilot USAF, Edwards AFB, Calif.; named astronaut NASA, 1966; mem. support crew (Apollo IX); command module pilot (Apollo XIV), 1971; backup command module pilot (Apollo XVI and XVII); assigned crew tng. space shuttle, until 1976; pres. Gulf Coast Coors, Inc., Gulfport, Miss., 1981-94. Decorated Disting. Service medal NASA, Air Force Command Pilot Astronaut Wings, USAF D.S.M.; recipient Arnold Air Soc.'s John F. Kennedy award, 1971, City N.Y. Gold medal, 1971. Home: Gulfport Miss. Died Dec. 12, 1994.

RORICK, ALAN GREEN, lawyer; b. Seneca, Mich., Oct. 22, 1918; s. John Porter and Bertha (Green) R.; m. Evelyn Edwards, May 10, 1941; children—Emily, Stephen, Josephine, Mark. B.S., U.S. Military Acad., 1940; LL.D., Case Western Res. U., 1947. Bar: Ohio bar 1948. Assoc. Baker & Hostetler, Cleve., 1947-57, ptnr., 1957-83, mng. ptnr., 1974-79. Mem. Bd. Edn., Brecksville, Ohio, 1962-67, pres., 1966. Served to maj. U.S. Army, 1940-45. Mem. Am. Law Inst. Republican. Mem. United Ch. of Christ. Died Jan. 7, 1996.

ROSALES, SYLVIA (SYLVIA ST CLAIR), composer, author, singer; b. N.Y.C., June 14, 1917. BA, NYU, 1937; studies with Helen Mück, Maurice Finnell, Lehman Engel, Fred Silver. Writer/dir. NYU Varsity Show, 1938; writer Columbia Workshop, CBS, 1939; appeared in cabaret revue The Nite Wits, 1939-40; co-writer/producer TV mus. La Ronda Del Monte, This is Puerto Rico; writer/producer/singer Spanish lang. commls.; songs include The Merry Mailman, El Piraguero, Yo Te Tengo A Ti; writer/producer shows explaining rehabilitation programs to convalescent soldiers, 1944. Mem. ASCAP, Am. Fedn. TV and Radio Artists, Am. Fedn. Musicians, Screen Actors Guild, Local 802, Phi Beta Kappa. Died July 31, 1994.

ROSBERG, CARL GUSTAF, political science educator; b. Oakland, Calif., Feb. 28, 1923; s. Carl Gustaf and Ethel (Moore) R.; m. Elizabeth Joanna Wilson, Oct. 23, 1954; children—James Howard, David Nils. B.S., Georgetown U., 1948, M.S., 1950; D.Phil., Oxford (Eng.) U., 1954. Asst. prof., research asso. African studies program Boston U., 1955-58; vis. asst. prof. U. Calif., Berkeley, 1958-59, asst. prof. dept. polit. sci., 1959-63, asso. prof., 1963-67, prof., 1967-91, prof. emeritus, 1991-96, chmn. dept. polit. sci., 1969-74, dir. Inst. Internat. Studies, 1973-89. Author: (with John Nottingham) The Myth of Mau Mau: Nationalism in Kenya, 1966, (with George Bennett) The Kenyatta Election: Kenya, 1960-61, 1961, (with Robert Jackson) Personal Rule in Black Africa: Prince, Autocrat, Prophet, Tyrant, 1982; editor: (with James S. Coleman) Political Parties and National Integration in Tropical Africa, 1964, (with William H. Friedland) African Socialism, 1964, (with Thomas Callaghy) Socialism in Sub-Saharan Africa, 1979, (with Robert M. Price) The Apartheid Regime: Political Power and Racial Domination, 1980, (with David E. Apter) Political Development and the New Realism in Sub-Saharan Africa, 1994. Served with USAAF, 1943-45. Decorated Purple Heart, Air medal, Prisoner of War medal; Ford Found. fellow, 1954-55. Mem. Coun. Fgn. Rels., African Studies Assn. (past pres.). Home: Berkeley Calif. Died Oct. 3, 1996.

ROSE, RUBYE BLEVINS (PATSY MONTANA), singer; b. Hot Springs, Ark., Oct. 30; d. Augustus Marion and Victoria Amanda (Meeks) Blevins; m. Paul Edward Rose, July 3, 1934; children: Beverly Losey, Judy (dec.). Student public schs., Hope, Ark. Country and Western singer with appearances in 49 states, also U.K., The Netherlands, toured Eng. and Europe, 1972, 75, 76, 77, 78; concerts in Paris, Berlin, 1986; composer over 200 pub. songs including I Want to be a Cowboy's Sweetheart; rec. for over 200 pub. songs including Columbia, Decca, RCA, Birch, Look Records, Huddersfield, Eng., 1975, Munich Records, Holland, 1978, Cattle Records, W. Ger., 1981, Flying Fish Records, Chgo.; including million seller I Want to be a Cowboy's Sweetheart; performer: Wake Up and Smile, ABC, 1944 (Recipient Pioneer award Acad. Country and Western Music 1970, awards from Pres. Roosevelt 1937, Gov. Love of Colo. 1973, various from VFW), Library of Congress, Washington, 1987; guest on David Letterman show, NBC. Named Queen of Country and Western Music, 1973; named Ky. col., 1978, Ark. Hall of Fame, 1985, Nat. Cowgirl Hall of Fame, Hereford, Tex., 1987. Mem. VFW Aux., Screen Actor's Guild, AFTRA, ASCAP, Country Music Assn., Acad. Country and Western Music. Republican. First country and western female singer to have a million selling record. Avocations: swimming, music, meeting people. Died May 3, 1996.

ROSE, STANLEY JAY, newspaper executive; b. Kansas City, Mo., June 3, 1918; s. Joseph and Mae (Lund) R.; m. Shirley Mallin, Oct. 7, 1942; children: Roberta Susan Rose Small, Stephen F. AA, Los Angeles City Coll., 1939; BJ, U. Mo., 1941. Chmn. bd., pub. Sun Publs., Inc., Overland Park, Kans., 1950; pub Sun Newspapers, 1950, Kansas City (Mo.) Jewish Chronicle, Inc., 1964, Coll. Blvd. News, 1984, Kansas City Nursing News, 1994, Johnson County Bus. News, 1994; apptd. U.S. Commr. Preservation Am.'s Heritage

Abroad, 1992-95. Author: Memo from Russia, 1986. Past bd. dirs. Kaw Valley Heart Assn., Heart of Am. council Boy Scouts Am.; hon. life dir. Johnson City, Kans., C.C.; past chmn. bd. trustees Humana Med Ctr.; trustee William Allen White Found.; mem. adv. council U. Kans. Med. Center, K.U. Chancellor's Cabinet, 1986. Served to lt. (j.g.) USNR, World War II; PTO. Recipient Sweepstakes, 1st place awards Kans. Better Newspaper Contest, 1968-70, 72, 73, William Allen White News Enterprise award, 1975, Bea Johnson award Am. Cancer Soc., 1st place winner for gen. excellence Suburban Newspapers Am., 1983-84, Chancellor's award U. Kans., 1988; named Philanthropist of Yr. Greater Kans. City, 1991, Johnson Countian of Yr.; honoree Matrix Tabl Table, 1980; honoree NCCJ, 1989; hon. lifetime dir. Johnson County C.C.; past Regional Comdr.; named Kans. Cav., Hon. Commr. Mem. Kans. State C. of C. and Industry (chmn., past bd. dirs.), Sigma Delta Chi. Club: Kansas City (Mo.) Press. Lodges: Masons, Shriners, Rotary (Paul Harris fellow 1985). Died Jan. 11, 1997.

ROSENBAUM, FRED JEROME, electrical engineering educator; b. Chgo., Feb. 15, 1937; s. Meyer G. and Ruth (Graff) R.; m. Carol Phyllis Letwin, Dec. 24, 1960; children: Ellen R., Gail E. BS in Elec. Engring., U. Ill., 1959, MS in Elec. Engring., 1960, PhD in Elec. Engring., 1963. Rsch. asst. U. Ill., Urbana, 1959-63; rsch. scientist McDonnell Aircraft Corp., St. Louis, 1963-65; asst. prof. elec. engring. dept. Washington U., St. Louis, 1965-67, assoc. prof., 1967-73, prof., 1973—; chief scientist Cen. Microwave Co., St. Louis, 1983-85; cons. Microwave Tech., Inc., Fremont, Calif., 1985-90, Varian Assocs., Santa Clara, Calif., 1986—, Litton Industries, UN, PNUD, Sao Paulo, Brazil, 1989, 91, various U.S. cos. and agys. of U.S. Govt., 1965—. Contbr. articles to profl. jours. and encys., chpts. to books; patentee in field. D.E. Evans fellow U. Queensland, Brisbane, Australia, 1980; recipient Alumnus award U. Ill. Elec. Engring. Dept., 1982. Fellow IEEE (pres. microwave theory and techniques soc. 1981, centennial medal 1984, disting. svc. award 1988).

ROSENBERG, MAURICE, lawyer, educator; b. Oswego, N.Y., Sept. 3, 1919; s. Samuel and Diana (Lishansky) R.; m. Ruth Myers, Dec. 7, 1941 (dec. Nov. 1945); 1 child, David Lee; m. Gloria Jacobson, Dec. 19, 1948; children: Joan Myra dec. Sept. 1988), Richard Sam. A.B., Syracuse U., 1940; LL.B. (editor-in-chief Law Rev.), Columbia, 1947. Bar: N.Y. 1947. Law sec. to judge N.Y. Ct. Appeals, 1947-49; asso. firm Cravath, Swaine & Moore, N.Y.C., 1949-53; assoc. firm Austrian, Lance & Stewart, N.Y.C., 1953-56; prof. Columbia U. Law Sch., 1956, Nash prof., Harold R. Medina prof. procedural jurisprudence, 1973-91; on leave, 1978-81; dir. Project Effective Justice, 1956-64, Walter E. Meyer Research Inst. Law, 1965-71; spl. asst. to atty. gen. U.S., 1976; vis. prof. Harvard U., 1969-70; cons. U.S. Dept. Justice, 1977-79, asst. atty. gen. U.S., 1979-81; lectr., U.S., Asia and Europe; mem. faculty Appellate Judges Sems., Nat. Jud. Coll., Fed. Jud. Ctr.; cons. Western Justice Rsch. Ctr., 1992—, Tech. and Govt., 1989—, cons. Long Range Planning Com. on Judicial Conf. U.S.; mem. Mayor N.Y.C. Com. on Judiciary, 1962-77; chmn. Adv. Council Appellate Justice, 1970-75, Coun. on Role of Cts., 1978-80; bd. dirs. Pvt. Adjudication Ctr. Duke Law Sch., 1985—; dir. program for judges on scientific evidence, 1991-92. Author: (with Rochelle Dreyfuss and Hans Smit) Elements of Civil Procedure, 1962, 5th edit., 1990, (with Willis Reese and Peter Hay) Conflict of Laws, 9th edit, 1990, The Pretrial Conference and Effective Justice, 1964, (with Paul Carrington and Daniel Meador) Justice on Appeal, 1976, (with James D. Hopkins and Robert MacCrate) Appellate Justice in New York, 1982; Editor: Dollars, Delay and the Automobile Victim, 1968, (with Lloyd Ohlin) Law and Social Research, 1977. Trustee Practising Law Inst., 1979—. Served with AUS, 1941-45, ETO. Fellow Am. Acad. Arts and Scis., Inst. Jud. Adminstrn.; mem. ABA (commn. to reduce ct. delay and expenses 1979-84, adv. com. on rules of civil procedure to U.S. Supreme Ct. 1980-87, chmn. standing com. on fed. judicial improvements 1990-92), Assn. of Bar of City of N.Y., Am. Bar Found., Assn. Am. Law Schs. (pres. 1972-73), Am. Judicature Soc. Clubs: Century (N.Y.C.); Cosmos (Washington). Home: White Plains N.Y. DIED 08/25/95. .

ROSENFELD, RONALD MARVIN, advertising executive; b. Balt., July 13, 1932; s. Bernard and Bessie (Feinglass) R.; m. Toni Pagane; children: Bonnie, Ned. Student, Balt. City Coll., 1946-49. Copywriter, Applestein, Levinstein & Golnick, Balt., 1955-57; v.p., co-copy chief Doyle Dane Bernbach, N.Y.C., 1957-68; sr. v.p., creative mgmt. supr. J. Walter Thompson, N.Y.C., 1968-69; prin., co-chmn. bd., co-creative dir. Rosenfeld, Sirowitz & Lawson, Inc., N.Y.C., 1970-97. Bd. dirs. Daytop Village, drug program, N.Y.C., 1974-76, Hope for Diabetics Found. Served with U.S. Army, 1953-55. Named to Copywriters Hall of Fame, 1971; recipient numerous awards, including Copy Club N.Y., Art Dirs. Club, Clio awards. Mem. One Show (co-chmn.), Copy Club (pres. 1970-71). Died Sept. 12, 1997.

ROSENFIELD, BRUCE ALAN, lawyer; b. Mpls., Apr. 30, 1951; s. Arnold M. and Phyllis M. (Fruchtman) R.; m. Bonnie S. Brier, Aug. 15, 1976; children: Rebecca, Elizabeth, Benjamin. AB, Dartmouth Coll., 1973; JD, Stanford U., 1976. Bar: Pa. 1976, U.S. Dist. Ct. (ea. dist.) Pa. 1976. Law clk. to Hon. Raymond Broderick U.S. Dist. Ct. (ea. dist.) Pa., Phila., 1976-78; assoc. Schnader, Harrison, Segal & Lewis, Phila., 1978-85, ptnr., 1986—; cons. Pa. Joint State Govt. Adv. Com. on Decedent and Estate Laws, 1991-97, mem., 1997—; bd. dirs. Rittenhouse Trust Co.; counsel Settlement Music Sch. Phila. Fellow Am. Coll. Trust and Estate Coun.; mem. Pa. Bar Assn. (coun. real property and trust law sect. 1995-97), Phila. Bar Assn. (chmn. probate sect. 1993).

ROSENFIELD, RICHARD ERNEST, emeritus medical educator; b. Pitts., Apr. 7, 1915; s. Abe E. and Ernestine (Lowenthal) R.; m. Olive da Costa-Levy, Apr. 5, 1944; children: Richard Ernest, Allan Oliver, Phyllis Ann Rosenfield Steele. BS, U. Pitts., 1936, MD, 1940. Rsch. and clin. asst. Mt. Sinai Hosp., N.Y.C., 1948-53, asst. hematologist, 1953-57, assoc. hematologist, 1957-71, dir. blood bank, 1957-80; prof. medicine Mt. Sinai Sch. Medicine, N.Y.C., 1966-67, 79-85, prof. pathology, 1972-85, emeritus prof. medicine, 1985—; hematologist N.Y.C. Health Dept., 1948-72; mem. sci. adv. com. N.Y. Blood Ctr., N.Y.C., 1964-78; mem. nat. blood rsch. coun. Nat. Acad. Sci., Washington, 1952-62. Contbr. more than 200 articles to profl. jours. Recipient Humanitarian award Nat. Hemophilia Found., 1981, Landsteiner award Am. Assn. Blood Banks, 1972; NIH grantee, 1958-78, 62-77. Mem. AAAS, AMA (emeritus), Am. Acad. Forensic Scis. (emeritus), Am. Assn. Immunologists (emeritus), Am. Soc. Hematology (emeritus), Am. Pub. Health Assn. (emeritus), Am. Soc. Human Genetics (emeritus), Internat. Soc. Blood Transfusion, Internat. Soc. Hematology (emeritus), Am. Soc. Clin. Pathologists (emeritus, Philip Levine award 1975). Died Oct. 3, 1997.

ROSENSWEIG, STANLEY HAROLD, retail executive; b. Phila., May 5, 1918; s. Emanuel Martin and Jennie (Hoffman) R.; m. Elaine Gordon Decker, Dec. 4, 1967; children by previous marriage: Susan, Ellen, Tod, Lisa. BABA, George Washington U., 1939. Chmn. bd. Electronics Wholesalers Co., Washington, 1947-68; chmn. bd. CWF Corp., Washington, 1963-73; pres. Sun Appliance Wholesalers, Washington, 1950-69; pres. Gem Internat. Inc., St. Louis, 1961-65, chmn. exec. com., 1963-66; bd. dirs. St. Louis Blues, 1966-74; chmn. bd. Lewis & Thomas Saltz Clothiers, Inc., Washington, 1977-84; dir. St. Louis Arena Inc., Action Leasing Inc. Trustee Boys Club, Greater Washington Jewish Community Found.; exec. bd. United Jewish Appeal, Washington; bd. dirs. Jewish Social Services Agy., Washington; bd. dirs. Nat. Symphony Orch., Child Guidance Clinic, Washington. Lt. U.S. Navy Res., 1941-45, PTO, 1944-45. Mem. Young Pres. Orgn. Clubs: Standard (Chgo.); Woodmont Country, Circus Saints and Sinners (Washington). Died Aug. 10, 1996.

ROSENTHAL, MACHA LOUIS, author, educator; b. Washington, Mar. 14, 1917; s. Jacob and Ethel (Brown) R.; m. Victoria Himmelstein, Jan. 7, 1939; children: David, Alan, Laura. B.A., U. Chgo., 1937, M.A., 1938; Ph.D., N.Y. U., 1949. Faculty Mich. State U., 1939-45; faculty NYU, N.Y.C., 1945-96; prof. NYU, 1961-87, English prof. emeritus, 1987-96; 1st Moss chair of excellence in English Memphis State U. (now Memphis U.), 1989; founder, dir. NYU Poetics Inst., 1977-79; poetry editor The Nation, 1956-61, Humanist, 1970-78, Present Tense, 1973-91; vis. specialist U.S. Cultural Exch. programs, Germany, 1961, Pakistan, 1965, Poland, Romania, Bulgaria, 1966, Italy and France, 1980, 88; lectr. New Zealand univs., 1989, Italian univs., 1995; vis. prof. U. Pa., 1974, U. Zurich, 1984, U. Bologna, 1995; vis. poet, Israel, 1974, Yugoslavia, 1980, World Poetry Festival, Can., 1993; Disting. Scholar Exch. Program, China, 1982, World Poetry Festival, Toronto, 1993; dir. summer seminar NEH, 1981, 93, dir. NEH Inst., 1985; mem. Bolligen award com., 1968-70; chmn. Delmore Schwartz Meml. award, 1970-96; mem. creative arts awards lit. jury Brandeis U., 1976. Author: (with A.J.M. Smith) Exploring Poetry, 1955, 73, The Modern Poets: A Critical Introduction, 1960, A Primer of Ezra Pound, 1960, Blue Boy on Skates: Poems, 1964, The New Poets: American and British Poetry since World War II, 1967, Beyond Power: New Poems, 1969, The View from the Peacock's Tail: Poems, 1972, Randall Jarrell, 1972, Poetry and the Common Life, 1974, 83, She: A Sequence of Poems, 1977, Sailing into the Unknown: Yeats, Pound, and Eliot, 1978, Poems, 1964-80, 1981, (with Sally M. Gall) The Modern Poetic Sequence: The Genius of Modern Poetry, 1983, 86, The Poet's Art, 1987, As for Love: Poems and Translations, 1987, Our Life in Poetry: Selected Essays and Reviews, 1991, Running to Paradise: Yeats' Poetic Art, 1994, In the World Pub.: A Sequence or Opera Seria (in Exile, 1995); editor: The Macmillan Paperback Poets, 1957-62; Selected Poems and Two Plays of W.B. Yeats, 1962, 73, The William Carlos Williams Reader, 1966, The New Modern Poetry: An Anthology of American and British Poetry since World War II, 1967, 69, 100 Postwar Poems, British and American, 1968, Selected Poems and Three Plays of William Butler Yeats, 1986; co-editor: Chief Modern Poets of Britain and America, 1970; gen. editor Poetry in English: An Anthology, 1987; editor Persea Books Lamplighters Series, 1982-92, Works-in-Progress (issue Ploughshares mag.), 1991; translator: The Adventures of Pinocchio: Tale of a Puppet, 1983; poetry adviser Macmillan Co., 1957-62; contbr. articles and poems to profl. publs. Recipient Explicator Found. award, 1984, 1st Yeats Soc. award for Disting. Contbns. to Yeats Scholarship, 1993; Fellow Am. Coun. Learned Socs., 1942, 50-51, Guggenheim Found., 1960-61, 64-65, Rockefeller Found. Rsch. Ctr., Bellagio, Italy, 1988. Mem. AAUP, MLA, PEN, Poetry Soc. Am. (v.p., bd. govs. 1989-92), Am. Lit. Assn., Yeats Soc., Phi Beta Kappa. Died July 21, 1996.

ROSENTHAL, SOL, architect; b. New Orleans, July 25, 1892; s. Jonas U. and Adele (Weil) R. BArch, Tulane U., 1913. Architect Rosenthal & Grosz, 1915-17, Rosenthal & Vanos, 1919-21; pvt. practice New Orleans, from 1921; assoc. Jack J.H. Kessels, Ernest W. Jones, New Orleans, from 1939, Charles E. Ammen, La., from 1950; chief architect Calliope St., Lafitte Ave housing projects, Bienville Homes, Naval Hosp., Naval Air Base, other army and navy bases, 1942-44; vis. lectr. Sch. Architecture, Tulane U., from 1949; mem. Pres.'s Adv. Com. to Sch. Architecture, from 1959; spl. cons. architect La. fire marshal, from 1942; architect of numerous bldgs. for schs., univs. Author: Public Schools of Jefferson Parish, Louisiana: A Survey Report, A Community Survey of Educational Needs (Charles R. Colbert, assoc.); also articles; contbr. to archtl. publs. in U.S. and fgn. countries. Mem. city fire prevention com., 1944-49, civil, archtl., structural engring br., engring pub. works sect.; tech. div. New Orleans Civil Def., 1951. Sgt. U.S. Army, 1917-18. Recipient W.R. Irby prize Arts and Crafts Club competition, New Orleans, 1922. Fellow AIA (emeritus fellow from 1962), mem. nat. unification com. 1947-49, pres. La. 1948-51; award New Orleans chpt. 1951, chmn. Gulf States regional judiciary com., 1957-59); mem. La. Architects Assn. (pres. 1945-47), Soc. Am. Mil. Engrs., Am. Cryptogram Assn., New Orleans Art Assn., Delgado Mus. Art of New Orleans, Masons (32 degree Shriner), New Orleans Athletic Club, Zeta Beta Tau. Home: New Orleans La.

ROSENWALD, WILLIAM, investment executive, philanthropist; b. Chgo., Aug. 19, 1903; s. Julius and Augusta (Nusbaum) R.; m. Ruth G. Israels, Dec. 1995. B.S., Mass. Inst. Tech., 1924; student, Harvard Coll., 1924-25, London (Eng.) Sch. Econs. and Polit. Sci., 1925-27; hon. Dr. Hebrew Letters, Hebrew Union Coll., 1944; LL.D., Tuskegee Inst., 1964. Dir. Sears, Roebuck & Co., 1934-38; established W.R. Enterprises, 1936. Hon. v.p. Am. Jewish Com., Am. Jewish Joint Distbn. Com., Inc.; hon. pres. United Jewish Appeal-Fedn. Jewish Philanthropies N.Y. Inc.; life trustee, hon. nat. chmn. United Jewish Appeal, Inc.; life mem. bd. dirs. Coun. Jewish Fedns.; hon. v.p. Am. Jewish Com.; life mem., v.p. Hebrew Immigrant Aid Soc.; hon. trustee Tuskegee U.; hon. life trustee Mus. Sci. and Industry, Chgo.; gen. chmn. nat. United Jewish Appeal, 1954, 55, 56 Campaigns. Mem. Harmonie Club (N.Y.C.). DIED 10/31/96. .

ROSICH, DANIEL, computer science and information systems educator; b. N.Y.C., Jan. 26, 1943; s. Taca and Iuliana (Terlaitch) R.; m. Catherine Louise Oldford, Jan. 29, 1951. AB, CUNY, 1963, AM, 1971; PhD, NYU, 1980. CDP, CSP Inst. for Cert. of Computer Profls., CDE Internat. Soc. Computer Info. Systems, COAP Office Automation Soc. Internat. Mem. tech. staff Automation Scis., Inc., N.Y.C., 1963-68; sr. systems engr. Graphical Tech. Corp., N.Y.C., 1968-69; mgr. applications support Intermedia Computer Scis., Inc., N.Y.C., 1969-70; asst. prof. CUNY, N.Y.C., 1970-77; asst. prof. Hofstra U., Hempstead, N.Y., 1977-78, assoc. prof., 1981-84; asst. prof. U. Conn., Storrs, 1978-81; prof. computer sci. and info. sys. Pace U., White Plains, N.Y., 1984-94; vis. prof. Ecole Supérieure Libre des Scis. Comml. Appliquées, Paris, 1981; cons. in field, Sharon, Conn., 1970-84; dir. Coun. Comms. Socs., Balt., 1982-85. Contbr. articles to profl. publs. Fellow Am. Bd. Master Educators, Coll. Preceptors London; mem. IEEE (mem. tech. activities bd. 1983-87, Alfred N. Goldsmith award 1985), Instrument Soc. Am. Avocations: baroque and early classical music, woodworking, gardening. Died Oct. 31, 1994.

ROSNER, JORGE, therapist, institute director, deceased; b. N.Y.C., Mar. 10, 1921; s. Samuel and Anna (Blumental) R.; m. Charlotte Francis Heller, Apr. 22, 1949 (div. Aug. 1979); children: Cindy Ann, Ellen Sue; m. Lisbet Trier, June 1986. Master Mechanic, Acad. Aeros., 1941; student, Cleve. Gestalt Inst., 1967-70. Supt. tng. internat. div. TWA Airlines, Wilmington, Del., 1946-48; mgr. store ops. Darling Shops, Inc., N.Y.C., 1952-53; pres., founder Display by Jorge (displays and designs), Chgo., 1953-67; founding fellow, treas., mem. faculty Gestalt Inst. Chgo., 1968-94; also dir.; pres., founder The Center, Gestalt counseling, Chgo., 1970-94; chmn., exec. dir. Gestalt Inst., Toronto, Ont., Can., 1972-94; chmn., dir. tng. Gestalt Inst., Amsterdam, Netherlands, 1973-94; dir., chmn. tng. Gestalt Inst. Scandinavia, Norway-Denmark-Sweden; mem. faculty Northwestern U. Inst. Psychiatry, 1973-94, Gestalt Inst., Brisbane,, Australia, 1983; founder, exec. dir. Internat. Gestalt Inst., 1981-94; guest faculty Gestalt Inst., Denver, 1970, 71, 72, Trollegen Rehab. Center U. Stockholm, 1973; lectr. in field, U.S. and, Europe; Am. Assn. Psychology, Am. Psychiat. Assn., Ontoanalystical conv., 1969, others; teaching and lectr. tour, Australia, 1980. Actor, theatre dir., Chgo., 1965-68, pres. Theatre of Being, Chgo., 1965-68, dir. Willa Jones City Chgo Passion Play, 1969, 71; author: Peeling the Onion: Gestalt Theory and Methodology, 1990, Heaven Can Wait-Couples Can't: A Gestalt Approach to Couples Counselling, 1992, Notes to Myself, 1993. Mem. Adult Edn. Coun., Chgo., 1970-72; founding fellow, bd. dirs. Oasis Midwest Ctr. Human Potential, 1966-94; founding mem. Inst. Psychiatry Northwestern U., Chgo., 1976. Mem. Contemporary Forum, Inst. of Psychiatry Northwestern U. (founding mem.). Home: Whitewater Wis. Died May 13, 1994.

ROSS, DONNA LEE, auditor; b. San Francisco, Dec. 1, 1956; d. Arthur J. and Myrtle Joan (Haynes) Lee; m. Eugene Ross Sr., Mar. 31, 1990. BS in Acctg., U. San Francisco, 1983. CPA, Calif. Sales supr. Macy's Calif., San Francisco, 1974-84; acctg. clk. 3/33 Ins. Co., San Francisco, 1979-80; advt. acct. San Francisco Newspaper Agy., 1980-83; supervising sr. auditor Arthur Young & Co., San Francisco, 1984-87; corp. auditor Hewlett-Packard Co., Palo Alto, Calif., 1987-90; ea. region audit mgr. Hewlett-Packard Co., Paramus, N.J., 1990-92, sr. internal auditor, 1992—. Author: (classroom tng. material) Understanding Basic Business Controls in a Changing Environment, 1992. Active Hist. Preservation Soc. Mem. Nat. Assn. Black Accts., State Soc. CPAs, Inst. Internal Auditors (mem. N.J. chpt.). Democrat. Roman Catholic. Avocation: restoration of historic house. Died Aprl 10, 1996.

ROSS, JAMES ELMER, economist, administrator; b. Danville, Ill., Jan. 15, 1931; s. Carl Henry and Lura Jane (Witherspoon) R.; m. Barbara Lou Becker, Dec. 24, 1958 (dec. Aug. 1982); 1 child, Candis Anne; m. Erin Elizabeth O'Shea, June 20, 1986. BS, U. Ill., 1953, MS, 1959, PhD, 1966. Agrl. counselor Am. Embassy, Caracas, Venezuela, 1976-78, Cairo, Egypt, 1978-81; asst. adminstr. Fgn. Agrl. Svc., Washington, 1981-83; mem. Sr. Exec. Seminar, Dept. State, 1983-84; alt. permanent rep. U.S. Mission to UN Agys., Rome, 1984-87; agrl. counselor U.S. Embassy, Seoul, Republic of Korea, 1987-88; dir. trade assistance and planning office Fgn. Agrl. Svc., Washington, 1988-92; courtesy prof. U. Fla., 1992-96; v.p. J.E. Ross & Assocs., Inc., 1993-96; cons. Govt. of Ecuador, 1971-72; mem. internat. programs U. Fla., Costa Rica, 1966-69, Ghana, 1969-70; assoc. dir., 1970-72; asst. dean Fla. Coop. Extension Svc., 1972-75; spl. asst. to undersecretary USDA, 1975-76. Author: Cooperative Rural Electrification, 1972; co-author: Rural Electrification and Development, 1978. Col. USAR, Mem. Internat. Assn. Agrl. Economists, Am. Agrl. Econs. Assn., Assn. for Internat. Agriculture and Rural Devel., Assn. for the Study of the Cuban Economy, Internat. Agrl. Trade Rsch. Consortium, Internat. Agribus. Mgmt. Assn., Masons. Republican. Died Jan. 8, 1996.

ROSS, LEABELLE ISAAC (MRS. CHARLES R. ROSS), psychiatrist; b. Lorain, Ohio, Feb. 11, 1905; d. Charles E. and Harriet (Dobbie) Isaac; AB, Western Res. U., 1927, MD, 1930; m. Charles R. Ross, Sept. 23, 1941; children: Charles R., John Edwin. surg. intern Lakeside Hosp., Cleve., 1931-32; resident in ob-gyn. Iowa State U. Hosp., 1932-33; resident obstetrics and surgery N.Y. Infirmary, N.Y.C., 1933-34; pvt. practice, Cleve., 1935-40; staff physician Cleve. State Hosp., 1938-42; dir. student health Bowling Green (Ohio) State U., 1942-45; psychiatrist Bur. Juvenile Rsch., Columbus, Ohio, 1946-47; psychiat. cons., 1948-51; psychiatrist Mental Hygiene Clinic, Columbus, Va., 1951-55; dir. med. svcs. Juvenile Diagnostic Ctr., 1955-59, acting supt., 1958, 61-62, dir. psychiat. svcs., 1959-62, clin. dir., 1962-70. Mem. Am. Psychiat. Assn., Ohio Psychiat. Assn., Am. Group Psychotherapy Assn., Tri-State Group Psychotherapy Soc., Neuropsychiat. Assn. Ctrl. Ohio, Assn. Physicians Divsn. Mental Hygiene and Correction (pres. 1963-64), Soroptomist, Alpha Sigma Rho, Nu Sigma Phi. Died Oct. 6, 1996.

ROSS, LEONARD Q. See **ROSTEN, LEO CALVIN**

ROSS, ROBERT KING, retired educator; b. Manti, Utah, Jan. 27, 1927; s. Clarence King Ross and Annamae Plant Nielson; m. Patsy Ruth Tattu, Dec. 25, 1947 (dec. 1988); children: Scott, Barbara, Richard, Michael. BA in Secondary Edn., Ea. Wash. Coll. Edn., 1951. Cert. master tchr., Wash. Tchr. Reardon (Wash.) High Sch., 1951-52; microphotography specialist U.S. Atomic Energy Commn., Richland, Wash., 1952-54; mgr. St. Paul br. Dakota Microfilm Svc., 1954-61; system specialist 3M Co., Seattle, 1961-64; prin., tchr. U.S. Bur. Indian Affairs, Shungnak, Alaska, 1964-68; tchr. Port Angeles (Wash.) Sch. Dist., 1968-89, ret., 1989; mem. Wash. State Newspaper in Edn. Com., Tacoma, 1970-92; instr. record ann. tchrs. seminars. Contbr. articles to profl. jours. With USMC, 1945-47. Recipient Cert. of Appreciation Seattle P.I. Newspaper, 1980. Fellow Elks; mem. DAV, VFW. Avocations: writing, photography, travel. Home: Port Angeles Wash. Died June 21, 1995.

ROSSBERG, ROBERT HOWARD, psychology educator, university dean; b. Bklyn., Mar. 9, 1926; s. Benjamin William and Mollie (Linn) R.; m. Mary Jo Kogan, June 22, 1947; 1 child, Susan Lea. Student, U. Mich., 1943-44; B.S., CCNY, 1949; M.A., Columbia U., 1951; Ph.D., N.Y. U., 1956. Counselor, Fedn. of, 1950-51; staff psychologist N.Y. U. Med. Center, 1951-53; asst. chief psychologist, 1953-56; asst. prof. edn. and psychology SUNY, Buffalo, 1956-59; assoc. prof. SUNY, 1959-64, prof., 1964-96, dir. grad. programs in counseling and ednl. psychology, 1959-65, assoc. dean, 1965-67; dean Faculty Ednl. Studies, 1978-80, v.p. for acad. affairs, 1980-84, dean faculty of health related profession, 1987-88, chair dept. psychology, 1988-96, disting. svc. prof., 1990; prof. emeritus SUNY, 1995-96; cons. in field. Author: Youth: Myths and Realities, 1972; co-author: Counseling Psychology, Strategies and Services, 1989; co-author: Counseling: Theory and Practice, 1993; contbr. articles to profl. publs.; editorial assoc. Urban Edn., 1961-70. Served with USAAF, 1944-46. Rehab. Counseling grantee, 1956-60; NDEA grantee, 1959-60; Office Edn.; leadership tng. grantee, 1969-70. Mem. Am. Psychol. Assn., AAUP. Died May 4, 1996.

ROSSELOT, MAX B., university administrator; b. West Elkton, Ohio, June 30, 1913; s. Harvey L. and Gertrude (Vance) R.; A.B., Denison U., 1935; A.M., Miami U., Oxford, Ohio, 1950; postgrad. Ind. U., 1953-54, summer 1960; M.A., Columbia U., 1982; Ed.M., Columbia U., 1984; m. Lillian Anna Draut, Oct. 5, 1940; children: Deborah Rosselot Bramlage, Michael T., Keith V. (dec.), Bruce E., Rome H. Sales corr. Armco Internat. Corp., Middletown, Ohio, 1936-43; asst. to pres. E.B. Thirkield & Sons, Franklin, Ohio, 1943-46; pres. M.B. Rosselot Sales Co., Middletown, 1946-47; asst. prin., tchr. Monroe (Ohio) High Sch., 1947-49; mem. faculty Miami U., Oxford, 1949-68, assoc. registrar, asst. prof. office skills and mgmt., 1956-60, registrar and assoc. prof., 1960-68; dir. univ. records and studies SUNY, Stony Brook, from 1968, dean for student adminstrv. svcs., from 1971, dean emeritus student adminstrv. svcs., psychol. counselor in gerontology; case mgr., social worker dept. for aging, City of N.Y. and Queens div. N.Y. Urban League, 1988—; gerontological cons. Coll. Point Sr. Citizens Ctr., Queens, N.Y.; cons. U. Ibadan (Nigeria), 1966-67, vis. registrar, cons. in the registry, 1972-74; cons. N.Y. State Edn. Dept. Bd. dirs. Hamilton County coun. Boy Scouts Am.; mem. Queens Coalition for Pub. Affairs, 1989; designated eucharistic minister Diocese of L.I. All Saints' Ch., Sunnyside, N.Y., 1986—. Grantee SUNY, Rockefeller Found.; Brookdale Inst. fellow, 1982-83; recipient citation U. Ibadan. Mem. Am. Assn. Higher Edn., NEA, Am. Coun. on Edn., Nat. Office Mgmt. Assn. (dir., Butler County chpt. sec. 1958-60), Am. (chmn. rsch. in admissions ann. meeting 1970, chmn. nat. standing com. 1970-72), Ohio (past sec., treas., pres. elect) assns. collegiate registrars and admissions officers, SUNY Registrars Assn. (v.p. 1974-75), AAUP (sec. Miami U. chpt. 1954-55), Common Cause, Am. Acad. Polit. and Social Scis., Nat. Assn. Student Personnel Adminstrs., Am. Acad. Arts and Scis., Assn. Community and Univ. Cooperation (v.p. 1975-76), Am. Mgmt. Assn., L.I. Coll. Student Personnel Assn. (pres. 1978-79), N.Y. Zool. Soc., Am. Mus. Natural History, ACLU, Theta Chi, Delta Pi Epsilon, Phi Delta Kappa, Kappa Delta Pi. Jewish. Clubs: Masons, Rotary, Old Field (gov.).

ROSSTON, EDWARD WILLIAM, lawyer; b. San Francisco, Nov. 14, 1918; s. Ernest William and Goldah Ray (Charmak) R.; m. Maxine Goldmark Aaron, June 28, 1947; children—Edward William, Richard Mark, Ellen Maxine Rosston Neft, Jean Frances. A.B., U. Calif.-Berkeley, 1939, JD, 1947; LL.M., Columbia U., 1948. Bar: Calif. 1947. Assoc. Heller Ehrman White & McAuliff, San Francisco, 1948-58; ptnr. Heller Ehrman White & McAuliff, 1958—; instr. Hastings Coll. Law, U. Calif., San Francisco, 1949-51; bd. dirs. Consumer Credit Counsellors, San Francisco, 1965-95; sec. MPC Ins. Ltd., 1986-93. Nat. trustee Lawyers Com. for Civil Rights, 1977—; co-chmn., mem. exec. com. San Francisco Lawyers Com. for Urban Affairs, 1972-83; trustee The Mechanics Inst. and Chessroom, 1991—, v.p., 1993-97. Lt. USNR, 1941-46, PTO. Mem. ABA, State Bar Calif., Bar Assn. San Francisco (bd. dirs., com. chmn. 1959-65), Am. Arbitration Assn. (arbitrator and mediator, adv. coun. North Calif. chpt. 1988—), Boalt Hall Alumni Assn. (trustee 1977-79). Democrat. Jewish. Club: Commonwealth (San Francisco). Deceased.

ROSTEN, LEO CALVIN (LEONARD Q. ROSS), author, political scientist; b. Lodz, Poland, Apr. 11, 1908; came to U.S., 1911; s. Samuel C. and Ida (Freundlich) R.; m. Priscilla Mead, Mar. 30, 1935 (dec.); children: Philip, Madeline, Margaret; m. Gertrude Zimmerman, Jan. 5, 1960. PhB, U. Chgo., 1930, PhD, 1937; postgrad., London (Eng.) Sch. Econs. and Polit. Sci., 1934; travel, study, Europe, 1928, 34, 45, 51, 53; LHD (hon.), U. Rochester, 1973, Hebrew Union Coll., 1980. Instr. English U. Chgo., 1932-34, rsch. asst. polit. sci. dept., 1934-35; pub. lectr., 1932-35; fellow Social Sci. Rsch. Council, 1935-36; mem. rsch. staff Pres.'s Com. Adminstrv. Mgmt., 1936; dir. Motion Picture Rsch. Project, 1939-41; spl. cons. Nat. Defense Commn., 1939-40; cons. expert to Nat. Def. Adv. Commn. and Office for Emergency Mgmt. (Exec. Office Pres.), 1941; chief motion pictures div. Office Facts and Figures, 1942; dep. dir. OWI, 1942-44; expert cons. Sec. of War's Office, War Dept., 1945, sent to France, Germany, Eng. on spl. mission; sr. staff RAND Corp., 1947-49; lectr. NYU, Stanford, New Sch. Social Rsch., UCLA, Yale, others; faculty assoc. Columbia; Ford vis. prof. polit. sci. U. Calif., 1960-61; cons. Pres.'s Commn. on Nat. Goals, 1960; spl. editorial advisor Look mag., N.Y.C., 1950-74. Writer for motion pictures, 1937; author: The Washington Correspondents, 1937, The Education of Hyman Kaplan, 1937, The Strangest Places, 1939, Dateline: Europe, 1939, Adventure in Washington, 1940, Hollywood: The Movie Colony, the Movie Makers, 1941, The Dark Corner, 1945, 112 Gripes About the French, 1945, Sleep, My Love, 1946, The Return of Hyman Kaplan, 1959, Captain Newman, M.D, 1961, The Story Behind the Painting, 1961, The Many Worlds of Leo Rosten, 1964, A Most Private Intrigue, 1967, The Joys of Yiddish, 1968, A Trumpet for Reason, 1970, People I Have Loved, Known, or Admired, 1970, Rome Wasn't Burned In a Day: The Mischief of Language, 1972, Leo Rosten's Treasury of Jewish Quotations, 1972, Dear Herm, 1974, The 3:10 to Anywhere, 1976, O Kaplan! My Kaplan!, 1976, The Power of Positive Nonsense, 1977, Passions and Prejudices: or, Some of My Best Friends Are People, 1978, Silky!: A Detective Story, 1979, King Silky!, 1980, Hooray for Yiddish: A Book about English, 1982, Leo Rosten's Giant Book of Laughter, 1985, The Joys of Yinglish, 1989, Leo Rosten's Carnival of Wit: From Aristotle to Groucho Marx, 1994; editor: A Guide to the Religions of America, 1955, The Look Book, 1975, Infinite Riches: Gems from a Lifetime of Reading, 1979; screenwriter: All Through the Night, 1942, The Conspirators, 1944, Lured, 1947, Sleep, My Love, 1947, The Velvet Touch, 1948, Where Danger Lives, 1950, Double Dynamite, 1952, Walk East on Beacon, 1952; contbr. to nat. mags. Recipient George Polk Meml. award, 1955, Freedom Found. award, 1955, Profl. Achievement Alumni award U. Chgo., 1969; hon. fellow London Sch. Econs. and Polit. Sci. Mem. Am. Acad. Polit. and Social Sci., Am. Polit. Sci. Assn., AAAS, Authors League Am. (bd.), Authors' Guild Am., Roundtable, Phi Beta Kappa. Died Feb., 1997.

ROTH, HENRY, writer; b. Tysmenica, Galicia, Austria-Hungary, Feb. 8, 1906; s. Herman and Leah (Farb) R.; m. Muriel Parker, Oct. 7, 1939; children: Jeremy, Hugh. BA, CCNY, 1928; LittD (hon.), U. N.Mex., 1994, Hebrew Union Coll. of Cin., 1994. With Works Progress Adminstrn., 1939; substitute high sch. tchr. Bronx, N.Y., 1939-41; precision metal grinder N.Y.C., 1941-45, Boston and Providence, R.I., 1945-46; tchr. Maine, 1947-48; attendant Augusta (Maine) State Hosp., 1949-53; water fowl farmer, 1953-63, tutor math and latin, 1956-65. Author: Call t Sleep, 1934, Nature's First Green, 1979, Shifting Landscape: A Composite, 1925-87, 1987, A Star Shines Over Mount Morris Park, 1994, Mercy of a Rude Stream, vol. 1, 1994, A Diving Rock on the Hudson Vol. II Mercy of a Rude Stream, 1995; contbr. Best American Short Stories 1967, 1967. Recipient Townsend Harris medal CCNY, 1965; Nat. Inst. Arts & Letters grantee, 1965, D.H. Lawrence fellow, 1968. Home: New York N.Y. Died Oct. 1995.

ROTH, JAMES LUTHER AUMONT, physician, educator; b. Milw., Mar. 8, 1917; s. Paul Wagner and Rose Marie (Schulzke) R.; m. Marion S. Main, June 7, 1938 (div. Dec. 1983); children—Stephen Andrew, Kristina Marie, Lisa Kathryn; m. Mary Alice Burns, Dec. 30, 1983. B.A., Carthage Coll., 1938, D.Sc. (hon.), 1957; M.A., U. Ill., 1939; M.D., Northwestern U., 1944, Ph.D., 1945. Intern Mass. Gen. Hosp., Boston, 1944-45; resident (Grad. Hosp.), 1945-46, 49-50, Hosp. U. Pa., Phila., 1948-49; practice medicine specializing in gastroenterology Phila., 1950—; instr. physiology Northwestern U., 1942-44; instr. div. gastroenterology Grad. Sch. Medicine, U. Pa., 1950-52, asso., 1952-54, asst. prof., 1954-56, asso. prof., 1956-59, clin. prof. gastroenterology, 1959-68, dir. div., 1961-69, prof. clin. medicine, 1968—; chief gastroenterology service Grad. Sch. Medicine, U. Pa. (Grad. Hosp.), 1961-69; dir. Inst. Gastroenterology, Presbyn. U. Pa. Med. Center, 1965-85; emeritus prof. clin. medicine U. Pa., 1987—; cons. USN, Bethesda, Md., 1967-75, USAF, 1946-48. Mem. editorial bd. Gastroenterology, 1960-67, Am. Jour. Gastroenterology, 1976-79, Current Therapy, 1972-85, Current Concepts in Gastroenterology, 1976-81; editor: Bockus' 4th edit. Gastroenterology; Contbr. articles to med. jours. Recipient Bronze medal AMA, 1944; certs. of merit Am. Roentgen Ray Soc., AMA, 1958; CINE Golden Eagle award Cannes Film Festival, 1975; Disting. Alumni award Carthage Coll., 1979. Fellow A.C.P.; mem. AMA, Pan Am. Med. Assn., N.Y. Acad. Sci., Am. Physiol. Soc., Am. Fedn. Clin. Research, Am. Gastroent. Assn. (chmn. admissions com.), Am. Coll. Gastroenterology (trustee 1977—, chmn. grad. edn. com. 1978-81, v.p. 1981), Bockus Internat. Soc. Gastroenterology (pres. 1973-75), Digestive Disease Fedn. (dir.), Union League Phila., Sigma Xi, Alpha Omega Alpha; hon. mem. Fla., Colombian, Venezuelian, Dominican Republic socs. gastroenterology. Republican. Lutheran. Died Sept. 12, 1997.

ROTH, ROBERT AUGUST, university administrator; b. Cleve., Jan. 26, 1943; s. August Joseph and Carmel Maria (Narducci) R.; children: Rob Eugene, Todd Jason, Tracy Lynn. BA, Hiram Coll., 1964; MEd, Pa. State U., 1967; PhD, Kent State U., 1970; postgrad., Rutgers U., 1972-73. Cert. tchr. Tchr., coach Kirtland (Ohio) Schs., 1965-67, Cuyahoga Heights High Sch., Cleve., 1968-69; mem. edn. faculty, dir. performance project State of N.J. Rutgers U., New Brunswick, N.J., 1971-73; state supr. State of Mich. Dept. Edn. Certification, Lansing, 1974-79, state dir., 1979-83; dir. Ctr. for Rsch. on Teaching and Human Resources Devel. U.

So. Fla., Tampa, 1985-86; dir., chmn., edn. tchr. Calif. State U., Long Beach, 1987—. Contbr. over 150 books and articles to profl. jours. recipient Resolution of Tribute Mich. Legislature, 1983, Resolution of Recognition of Leadership Mich. State Bd. Edn., 1982, 84; named Disting. Leader in Tchr. Edn. in U.S., 1990, Univ. Disting. Faculty scholar, Calif. State U. at Long Beach, 1990. Mem. Assn. Tchr. Educators of Mich. (Leadership award 1979, past pres.), Nat. Assn. State Dirs. of Edn. (past nat. pres., Disting. Leadership award 1984), Assn. Tchr. Educators (past nat. pres., Leadership award 1985, Disting. mem. 1988, Disting. Tchr. Educator State of Calif. 1992), Phi Delta Kappa. Avocations: photography, sports. Died Feb. 23, 1997.

ROTHFUS, JOHN ARDEN, chemist; b. Des Moines, Dec. 25, 1932; s. Truman Clinton and Beatrice (Keeney) R.; m. Paula Kay Harris, Sept. 26, 1959; children: Lee Ellen, David Merrill. B.A., Drake U., 1955; Ph.D., U. Ill., 1960. Asst. biochemistry U. Ill., Urbana, 1955-59; instr. U. Utah Coll. Medicine, Salt Lake City, 1961-63; asst. prof. U. Calif. Med. Sch., Los Angeles, 1963-65; prin. research chemist U.S Dept. Agr., Peoria, Ill., 1965-70, investigations head, 1970-74, research leader, 1974-90, lead scientist, 1990—. Proctor & Gamble Co. fellow, 1957-58; USPHS postdoctoral fellow, 1959-61, archer Daniels Midland award in chem. & nutrition Am. Oil Chemists Soc., 1996. Mem. Am. Chem. Soc., AAAS, N.Y. Acad. Scis., Am. Oil Chemists Soc., Am. Soc. Plant Physiologists, Jojoba Soc., Phi Beta Kappa, Sigma Xi, Phi Lambda Upsilon, Omicron Delta Kappa, Alpha Chi Sigma. Died Sept. 10, 1996.

ROTHMAN, JULIUS LAWRENCE, English language educator; b. N.Y.C., Sept. 22, 1920; s. Samuel and Bessie (Kantor) R.; m. Stella Lambert, June 23, 1948. BSS, CCNY, 1941; MA, Columbia U., 1947, PhD, 1954. Lectr. Hunter Coll., N.Y.C., 1947-50, Rutgers U., New Brunswick, N.J., 1950-53; tech. writer Olympic Radio & TV, L.I. City, N.Y., 1951-61; prof. English Nassau Community Coll., Garden City, N.Y., 1962-86, prof. emeritus, 1986-96; broadcaster, talk show host weekly program Sta. WHPC, 1974-82; deputy dir. gen. Internat. Biographical Ctr., Cambridge, England, 1992-96. Editor, contbg. author The Cabellian, 1968-72; contbr. sects. to books on folklore and legend; contbr. articles to profl. jours. Mem. Nat. Com. to Preserve Social Security and Medicare, Arthritis Found.; mem. adv. bd. 9th Senatorial Dist. N.Y., 1984-88; seat sponsor Ariz. State U. Sundome Performing Arts Assn. Named Internat. Man of Year 1991-92, Internat. Biographical Ctr., Cambridge. Mem. Cabell Soc. (founder 1967, exec. v.p. 1968-72), Ret. Pub. Employees Assn., Nat. Wildlife Fedn., Nat. Ret. Tchrs. Assn., Columbia U. Alumni Assn. Methodist. Died July 22, 1996.

ROTHWELL, ALBERT FALCON, lawyer, natural resource company executive; b. N.Y.C., Sept. 2, 1926; s. Albert Cyril and Finita Maria (Falcon) R.; m. Jane Thomas, June 4, 1949 (dec. Dec. 1994); children: Susan, Peter, Anne, James. AB, Princeton U., 1948; LLB, Columbia U., 1951, postgrad., 1956-58. Bar: N.Y. Assoc. Sullivan & Cromwell, N.Y.C., 1951-56; chief exec. officer Nat. Potash Co., N.Y.C., 1972-75; v.p. Freeport Minerals Co., N.Y.C., 1975-81; sr. v.p., treas. Freeport-McMoRan Inc., N.Y.C., 1981-86, ret., 1986. Pres. Quioque Assn., Westhampton Beach, N.Y., 1982-83, Citizens for Good Schs., Glen Ridge, N.J., 1973-74; vice chmn. civic conf. com., Glen Ridge, 1970-71. Served with USN, 1944-46. Mem. Quantuck Yacht Club (commodore 1969-70), Quantuck Beach Club (Westhampton Beach, N.y., pres. 1989-92). Avocations: fishing, photography. Died Nov. 6, 1996.

ROUNTREE, ROBERT BENJAMIN, utility executive; b. Burnsville, N.C., Oct. 20, 1924; s. Benjamin F. and Carrie R.; m. Martha Jane McBee, Feb. 23, 1946; 1 dau., Janet Fay Rountree Wilson. B.S.E.E., U. N.Mex., 1946. With Pub. Svc. Co. N.Mex., 1948—; beginning as draftsman successively gen. supt. Pub. Svc. Co. N.Mex., Belen, N.Mex.; mgr. Pub. Svc. Co. N.Mex., Deming, N.Mex.; div. mgr. Pub. Svc. Co. N.Mex., Albuquerque, div. v.p., v.p. div. ops., 1948-72; sr. v.p. Pub. Svc. Co. N.Mex., 1972-86, ret., 1986, dir.; chmn. bd. Meadows Resources, Inc., 1983—, Sunbelt Minig Co., 1983—. Mem. IEEE, Am. Inst. Mgmt., Nat. Soc. Profl. Engrs. Died Nov. 30, 1996.

ROUSAR, IVO, electrochemistry educator; b. Kromeriz, Moravia, Czech Republic, Apr. 22, 1932; s. Zdenek and Bozena (Anderova) R.; m. Iva Kypenova, Feb. 4, 1956; children: Ivo, Sarka. MSc, U. Chem. Tech., Czech Republic, 1956, PhD, 1963, DSc, 1984. Asst. U. Chem. Tech., Czech Republic, 1956-74, assoc. prof., 1974-90, prof. electrochem. engring., 1990—; cons. in field, 1990—. Co-author: Electrochemical Engineering, vols. 1 and 2, 1986; contbr. numerous articles to profl. jours. Mem. Internat. Soc. Electrochemistry, Electrochem. Soc., European Fedn. Chem. Engrs. Died Nov. 10, 1996.

ROWEN, HOBART, journalist; b. Burlington, Vt., July 31, 1918; s. Moses G. and Sarah (Rosenberg) R.; m. Alice B. Stadler, Aug. 5, 1941; children: Judith Diane, James Everett, Daniel Jared. B.S. in Social Sci, CCNY, 1938. Reporter N.Y. Jour. Commerce, N.Y.C., 1938-41; Washington corr. N.Y. Jour. Commerce, 1941-42; with information div. War Prodn. Bd., Washington, 1942-44; corr. Washington bur. Newsweek (mag.), 1944-65, Bus. Trends editor, 1957-65; financial editor, asst. mng. editor Washington Post, 1966-75, econs. editor, 1975-91, syndicated columnist, 1975-95. Contbr. articles and columns to various mags. and newspapers, including New Republic; author: The Free Enterprisers-Kennedy, Johnson and the Business Establishemnt, 1964, Self-Inflicted Wounds: From LBJ's Guns & Butter to Reagan's Voodoo Economics, 1994. Councilman Town of Somerset, Md., 1957-65. Recipient Spl. Achievement award Loeb mag., 1961, Disting. Svc. award for mag. writing Sigma Delta Chi, 1961, John Hancock award for excellence, 1968, A.T. Kearney award, 1968, Gerald Loeb award for best econs. column, 1978, Best Columnist award Population Action Coun., 1982, 85, Best Newspaper Bus. Reporter award Washington Journalism Rev., 1985, Townsend Harris medal CCNY, 1985, Silver medal Film and TV Festival, N.Y.C., 1990, Gerald Loeb award Lifetime Achievement in Bus. and Fin. Journalism, 1992, Profl. Achievement award Soc. Am. Bus. Editors and Writers, 1993. Mem. Soc. Am. Bus. Editors and Writers (pres. 1975-76, Profl. Achievement award 1993), Sigma Delta Chi, Tau Delta Phi. Democrat. Jewish. Clubs: Nat. Press (Washington), Nat. Economists (Washington). Home: Chevy Chase Md. Died, April 13, 1995.

ROWLES, JAMES GEORGE, musician, composer; b. Spokane, Wash., Aug. 19, 1918; s. James Polk Hunter and Eileen Cicely (McCarthy) Hunter-Rowles-Byrd; m. Dorothy Jewel Paden, Aug. 12, 1941; children: Gary Leonard, Stacy Amanda, Stephanie Heather. Student, Gonzaga U., 1937-38. Pianist, rec. artist numerous band leaders, performers including Lester Young, Benny Goodman, Woody Herman, Les Brown. Tommy Dorsey, Billie Holiday, Vic Damone, Peggy Lee, Carmen McRae, Sarah Vaughan, Ella Fitzgerald, Henry Mancini, Hollywood and Los Angeles, Calif., 1940-96. Composer: The Peacocks (rec. Bill Evans, Branford Marsalis), 1973 (Grammy nomination 1978, featured in film 'Round Midnight 1986), various songs with Johnny Mercer. Active wildlife and marine life conservation. Served as sgt. U.S. Army, 1943-46. Recipient 5 Grammy nominations, 1978-82, Peabody award, 1986; honored by Los Angeles Jazz Soc., 1986. Mem. Am. Fedn. Musicians, ASCAP, Songwriters Guild Am., Am. Guild Authors and Composers. Democrat. Roman Catholic. Club: Giraffe (Washington). Avocations: cartooning, tennis, visiting the zoo, swimming, golf. Home: Burbank Calif. Died May 28, 1996.

ROWND, ROBERT HARVEY, biochemistry and molecular biology, molecular medicine and genetics educator; b. Chgo., July 4, 1937; s. Walter Lemuel and Marie Francis (Joyce) R.; m. Rosalie Anne Lowery, June 13, 1959; children: Jennifer Rose, Robert Harvey, David Matthew. BS in Chemistry, St. Louis U., 1959; MA in Med. Scis, Harvard U., 1961, PhD in Biophysics, 1964. Postdoctoral fellow Med. Rsch. Coun., NIH, Cambridge, Eng., 1963-65; postdoctoral fellow Nat. Acad. Scis.-NRC, Institut Pasteur, Paris, 1965-66; prof., chmn. molecular biology and biochemistry U. Wis., Madison, 1966-81; John G. Searle prof., chmn. molecular biology and biochemistry Med. and Dental Schs., Northwestern U., Chgo., 1981-90; leader cancer molecular biology program Cancer Ctr.Northwestern U., Chgo., 1982-89; prof. biochemistry, dir. Ctr. for Molecular Biology Wayne State U., Detroit, 1990-94, interim chair dept. molecular biology and genetics, 1993-94; dir., prof. Ctr. for Molecular Medicine and Genetics Wayne State U. Sch. Medicine, Detroit, 1994-97, prof. internal medicine, 1994-97; vice chmn. Gordon Rsch. Conf. Extrachromosomal Elements, 1984, chmn., 1986; hon. rsch. prof. Biotech. Rsch. Ctr., Chinese Acad. Agrl. Scis., Beijing, 1987-97. Contbr. numerous articles to sci. jours. and books; mem. editorial bd. Jour. of Bacteriology, 1975-81, editor, 1981-90; assoc. editor Plasmid, 1977-87. Mem. troop com., treas. Four Lakes Coun. Boy Scouts Am., Madison, 1973-77, mem. People to People Program del. of microbiologists to China, 1983; mem. Nat. Acad. Scis./Nat. Rsch. Coun. Com. on Human Health Effects of Subtherapeutic Antibiotic Use in Animal Feeds, 1979-81; sr. tech. adv. recruitment cons. UN Devel. Program in China, 1987. NSF fellow, NIH fellow, 1959-66, rsch. grantee, 1966-92, tng. grantee, 1970-79, 83-91; USPHS Rsch. Career Devel. awardee, 1968-73; recipient Alumni Merit award St. Louis U., 1984. Mem. NIH (microbial genetics study sect. 1978-82, spl. study sect. 1971, 73, 74, 75, 78, 79, 82, chmn. 1983, 84-86, 88, 89, 90, 93-95, dir. med. scientist tng. program 1982-90, adv. panel Nat. Rsch. Coun. 1974-77, chmn. 1976-77, adv. panel for devel. biology NSF, 1968-71, NSF adv. panel NATO postdoctoral fellowships in sci. program 1979), Am. Soc. Microbiology, Assn. Harvard Chemists, Am. Soc. Biol. Chemists, Am. Acad. Microbiology, N.Y. Acad. Scis. Deceased.

ROWSE, ALFRED LESLIE, British historian, poet, writer; b. St. Austell, Cornwall, Dec. 4, 1903. Emeritus fellow All Souls Coll., Oxford. Author: Sir Richard Grenville of the Revenge, 1937; Tudor Cornwall, 1941; Poems of a Decade 1931-41, A Cornish Childhood, 1942; The Spirit of English History, 1943, Poems Chiefly Cornish, 1944, The English Spirit, 1944; West Country Stories, 1945; The Use of History, 1946; The End of an Epoch, 1947; The England of Elizabeth, 1950; The English Past (revised edit. entitled Times, Persons, Places 1965), 1951; The Expansion of Elizabethan England, 1955; The Early Churchills, 1956; The Later Churchills, 1958; Poems Partly American, 1959; The Elizabethans and America, 1959; Appeasement: A Study in Political Decline, 1961; Raleigh and the Throckmortons, 1962; William Shakespeare: A Biography, 1963; Christopher Marlowe: A Biography, 1964; A Cornishman at Oxford, 1965; Shakespeare's Southampton, 1965; Bosworth Field and the Wars of the Roses, 1966; Poems of Cornwall and America, 1967; Cornish Stories, 1967; A Cornish Anthology, 1968; The Cornish in America, 1969; The Elizabethan Renaissance: Vol. I The Life of the Society, 1971, Vol. II The Cultural Achievement, 1972; The Tower of London in the History of the Nation, 1972, Shakespeare the Man, 1973 (rev. 1988); Simon Forman: Sex and Society in Shakespeare's Age, 1974; Windsor Castle in the History of the Nation, 1974; Oxford in the History of the Nation, 1975; Discoveries and Reviews from Renaissance to Restoration, 1975; Jonathan Swift, Major Prophet, 1975; A Cornishman Abroad, 1976; Brown Buck: A Californian Fantasy, 1976; Matthew Arnold: Poet and Prophet, 1976; Shakespeare the Elizabethan, 1976; Homosexuals in History: Ambivalence in Society, Literature and the Arts, 1977; Milton the Puritan, 1977; Heritage of Britain, 1977; The Road to Oxford: Poems, 1978; The Byrons and Trevanions, 1978; Night at the Carn: Stories, 1978; A Man of the Thirties, 1979, Portraits and Views, 1979, Story of Britain, 1979, Memories of Men and Women, 1980, A Life: Collected Poems 1981, Eminent Elizabethans, 1983, Shakespeare's Sonnets, with prose versions (rev. edit.), 1983; Stories from Trenarren, 1986; Reflections on the Puritan Revolution, 1986; The Little Land of Cornwall, 1986; Glimpses of the Great, 1986; Hakluyt's Voyages of North America, 1986; The Poet Auden: A Personal Memoir, 1988; Quiller Couch: Portrait of Q, 1988; Froude the Historian, 1988; A.L. Rowse's Cornwall, 1988; Friends and Contemporaries, 1989, Transatlantic: Later Poems, 1989, The Controversial Colensos: South Africa and New Zealand, 1989, Discovering Shakespeare, 1989, Four Caroline Portraits, 1993, All Souls in My Time, 1993, The Regicides and the Puritan Revolution, 1994, Historians I Have Known, 1995, A Shakespeare Calendar, 1996, My View of Shakespeare, 1996; editor: The Poems of Shakespeare's Dark Lady 1978; The Contemporary Shakespeare, Froude's Spanish Story of the Armada, 1988, Selected Poems, 1990, Prompting the Age: Poems Early and Late, The Sayings of Shakespeare, 1989. Fellow British Academy, Royal Soc. Literature. Died Oct. 3, 1997.

ROYCE, MARY WELLER SA'ID, artist, poet; b. Tupper Lake, N.Y., July 9, 1933; d. Gerard Charles and Mary Weller (McCarthy) de Grandpré; m. Majed Farhan Sa'id, Nov. 19, 1960 (dec. 1966); children: Mary Weller Richardson, Emily Ann Bacon; m. William Ronald Royce, Sept. 2, 1974. AA with honors, Georgetown Visitation Jr. Coll., 1953; BS cum laude, Georgetown U., 1960; MA in Italian, Middlebury Coll., 1968. Writer, artist, 1954—; translator, adminstrv. asst. U.S. Army, Orleans, France, 1956-58; tchg. asst. dept. Italian Rutgers U., New Brunswick, N.J., 1968-70; translator N.J., Ariz., 1971-84; owner, designer The Stamp Act, Rockville, Md., 1990-93. Groups shows include Rockville (Md.) Arts Pl., 1992—, Rockville Art League, 1993—, Montpelier Cultural Arts Ctr., Laurel, Md., 1994—, Strathmore Hall Arts Ctr., North Bethesda, Md., 1994—; poetry collected in anthologies. Coord. Equal Rights Coalition, Utah, 1975; ACLU rep. So. Ariz. Coalition for ERA, Tucson, 1975-78; mem. steering com. Ariz. ERA, 1976-78; Md. state activist Caths. for a Free Choice, 1991-93; mem. The Alliance of Rockville Citizens, 1995—. Fulbright grantee, 1960. Mem. Acad. Am. Poets (assoc.), Nat. Mus. Women in Arts (charter), Washington Project for Arts, Rockville Art League, Strathmore Hall Arts Ctr., Rockville Arts Pl., Arlington Arts Ctr., Montpelier Cultural Arts Ctr. Avocations: photography, jazz, swimming. Died Nov. 11, 1996.

ROYKO, MIKE, newspaper columnist; b. Chgo., Sept. 19, 1932; s. Michael and Helen (Zak) R.; m. Carol Joyce Duckman, Nov. 7, 1954 (dec. Sept. 1979); children: M. David, Robert F.; m. Judith Arndt, May 21, 1985; children: Samuel, Katherine. Student, Wright Jr. Coll., 1951-52. Reporter Chgo. North Side Newspapers, 1956; reporter, asst. city editor Chgo. City News Bur., 1956-59; reporter, columnist Chgo. Daily News, 1959-78, assoc. editor, 1977-78; reporter, columnist Chgo. Sun-Times, 1978-84; columnist Chgo. Tribune, 1984-97. Author: Up Against It, 1967, I May Be Wrong But I Doubt It, 1968, Boss-Richard J. Daley of Chicago, 1971, Slats Grobnik and Some Other Friends, 1973, Sez Who? Sez Me, 1982, Like I Was Sayin', 1984, Dr. Kookie, You're Right!, 1989. Served with USAF, 1952-56. Recipient Heywood Broun award, 1968, Pulitzer prize for commentary, 1972, H.L. Mencken award, 1981, Ernie Pyle award, 1982; medal for svc. to journalism U. Mo. Sch. Journalism, 1979, Lifetime Achievement award Nat. Press Club, 1990; named Best Newspaper Columnist in Am., Washington Journalism Rev., 1985, 87, 88, 90; named to Chgo. Press Club Journalism Hall of Fame, 1980. Club: LaSalle St. Rod and Gun. Died Apr. 29, 1997.

ROYSTER, VERMONT (CONNECTICUT), journalist; b. Raleigh, N.C., Apr. 30, 1914; s. Wilbur High and

Olivette (Broadway) R.; m. Frances Claypoole, June 5, 1937; children: Frances Claypoole, Sara Eleanor. Grad., Webb Sch., Bellbuckle, Tenn., 1931; A.B., U. N.C., 1935, LL.D., 1959; Litt.D., Temple U., 1964, Williams Coll., 1979; L.H.D., Elon Coll., 1968; LL.D., Colby Coll., 1976. Reporter N.Y.C. News Bur., 1936; reporter Wall St. Jour., 1936, Washington corr., 1936-41, 45-46, chief Washington corr., 1946-48, editorial writer and columnist, 1946-48, assoc. editor, 1948-51, sr. assoc. editor, 1951-58, editor, 1958-71, contbg. editor, columnist, 1971—, editor emeritus, 1993—; sr. v.p. Dow Jones & Co., Inc., 1960-71; William Rand Kenan prof. journalism and pub. affairs U. N.C., Chapel Hill, 1971-86; regular commentator pub. affairs CBS Radio and TV, 1972-77; appears on pub. affairs programs on TV and radio.; sr. fellow Inst. Policy Scis., Duke, 1973-85; mem. adv. com. Pulitzer prizes Columbia, 1967-76; mem. Nat. Commn. Hist. Publs., 1974-76. Author: (with others) Main Street and Beyond, 1959, Journey Through the Soviet Union, 1962, A Pride of Prejudices, 1967, (memoirs) My Own, My Country's Time, 1983, The Essential Royster (ed. Edmund Fuller), 1985 contbr. numerous articles on financial and econ. subjects to periodicals. Bd. dirs. Newspaper Fund, Inc.; trustee St. Augustine Coll., Raleigh, N.C. Commd. ensign USNR, 1940; active duty 1941-46, Atlantic, Caribbean, Pacific; exec. officer USS LaPrade comdg. officer USS Jack Miller, USS PC-1262 lt. comdr. Res. Recipient Pulitzer prize for editorial writing, 1953, Pulitzer prize for commentary, 1984; medal for distinguished service in journalism Sigma Delta Chi, 1958; William Allan White award for distinguished service to journalism, 1971; Loeb Meml. award for contbn. to econ. journalism UCLA, 1975; Elijah Lovejoy award Colby Coll., 1976; Fourth Estate award Nat. Press Club, Washington, 1978; Presdl. Medal of Freedom, 1986; named to N.C. Journalism Hall of Fame, 1980. Mem. Am. Soc. Newspaper Editors (pres. 1965-66), Nat. Conf. Editorial Writers (chmn. 1957), Phi Beta Kappa Assos., Phi Beta Kappa. Episcopalian. Clubs: University (N.Y.C.); Nat. Press (Washington). Died July 22, 1996.

ROZELLE, PETE (ALVIN RAY ROZELLE), former commissioner athletic league; b. South Gate, Calif., Mar. 1, 1926; s. Raymond Foster and Hazel Viola (Healey) R.; 1 dau., Ann Marie. B.A., U. San Francisco, 1950. Athletic news dir. U. San Francisco, 1948-50, asst. athletic dir., 1950-52; pub. relations dir. Los Angeles Rams Football Club, 1952-55; partner Internat. Bus. Relations (pub. relations), San Francisco, 1955-57; gen. mgr. Los Angeles Rams Football Club, 1957-60; commr. NFL, N.Y.C., 1960-89. Served with USNR, 1944-46. Mem. Pro Football Hall of Fame. Died Dec. 12, 1996.

ROZSA, MIKLOS, composer; b. Budapest, Hungary, Apr. 18, 1907; s. Gyula and Regina R.; m. Margaret Finlason, Aug. 30, 1943; children: Juliet Valerie Alexandra, Nicholas John Reginald. Diploma, Leipzig Conservatory, 1929; student, N.Y. Conservatory of Music, 1941, Coll. of Wooster, 1982, U. So. Calif., 1988. Composer London Films, London, 1936-42, Universal Studios, L.A., 1942-46, Paramount Studios, L.A., 1946-47, MGM, L.A., 1948-62; tchr. Univ. So. Calif. Sch. Music, L.A., 1945-65. Composer numerous musical pieces for 100 movies including Spellbound, 1946 (Acad. award), Double Life, 1948 (Acad. award), Ben-Hur, 1959 (Acad. award); composer 46 orchestral works. Mem. Screen Composer's Guild (pres. for 10 yrs.). Home: West Hollywood Calif. Died July 27, 1995.

RUBENSTEIN, ALBERT IRWIN, real estate developer, lawyer; b. Chgo., Mar. 28, 1927; s. William D. and Regina (Ribaysen) R.; student Herzl City Coll., 1944-46, Roosevelt Coll., 1946-48; LL.B., J.D., John Marshall Law Sch., 1951; m. Joyce Shirley Leeman, June 12, 1954; children—Jeffrey, Lauren, Jan. Bar: Ill. 1951. Sole practice law, Chgo., 1951-64; pres., chief exec. officer Fleetwood Realty Corp., Chgo., 1969—, also dir.; sr. partner Fleetwood Realty Co., Chgo., 1969-83; pres. Fleetwood Devel. Corp., 1983—; dir. Exec. Bus. Center, Inc., Fleetwood Industries; lectr. corp. real estate fin. and devel. Bd. dirs. Feinberg Charitable Found., 1969—, Hebrew Theol. Coll., 1975—; mem. Highland Park (Ill.) Planning Commn., 1980—, Highland Park Econ. Devel. Com., 1984; spl. real estate negotiator by mayoral appointment, Highland Park, 1980. Recipient Outstanding Alumnus award John Marshall Law Sch., 1982; named 1 of top 10 real estate developers Chicago mag., 1981. Mem. ABA, Ill. Bar Assn., Chgo. Bar Assn., Am. Trial Lawyers Assn., Chgo. Assn. Commerce and Industry, Nat. Real Estate Bd., Chgo. Real Estate Bd. (dir. 1980-82), Decalogue Soc. Lawyers, Nat. Realty Com., Inc., Am. Arbitration Soc. Clubs: Covenant, Execs. (Chgo.). Lodge: B'nai B'rith. Contbr. articles in field to profl. jours.

RUBIN, GUSTAV, orthopedic surgeon, consultant, researcher; b. N.Y.C., May 19, 1913; s. William and Rose (Strongin) R.; m. Mildred Synthia Holtzer, July 4, 1946 (dec. Dec. 1964); m. Esther Rosenberg Partnow, July 23, 1965; 1 stepchild, Michael Partnow. B.S., NYU, 1934; M.D., SUNY-Downstate Med. Ctr., 1939. Diplomate Am. Bd. Orthopedic Surgery. Intern Maimonides Hosp., Bklyn., 1939-41; resident in orthopedics Hosp. for Joint Diseases, N.Y.C., 1941-42, 1946; practice medicine specializing in orthopedics Bklyn., 1947-56; from orthopedic surgeon to dir. clinic VA Clinic, Bklyn., 1956-70; chief Spl. Prosthetic Clinic VA Prosthetics Ctr., N.Y.C., 1970-85, dir. spl. team for amputations, mobility, prosthetics/orthotics, 1985-87, mem. chief med. dir. adv. group on prosthetics services, rehab. research and devel., 1985-87, orthopedic cons., 1970-87, ret., 1987; pvt. practice N.Y.C., 1987—; med. advisor prosthetic rsch. com. N.Y. State DAV, 1970—; lectr. prosthetics NYU, 1972-89; clin. prof. orthopedics N.Y. Coll. Podiatric Medicine, 1980—; orthopedic cons. Internat. Ctr. for the Disabled, N.Y.C., 1987—. Contbr. book chpts., articles to profl. jours.; contbr. article on amputations Ency. for Disability and Rehab., 1995. Capt. U.S. Army, 1943-46. Recipient Nat. Comdrs. award DAV, 1968, Amvets award for outstanding service, 1969, award for Service to Veterans Allied Veterans Meml. Com., 1970, Eastern Paralyzed Veterans Assn. award, 1977, award for Service to Israeli Wounded Israeli Govt. Dept. Rehab., 1981, Cert. of Merit, Nat. Amputation Found., 1972, Olin E. Teague award VA, 1984, Physician of Yr. award Pres.'s Commn. on Employment of People with Disabilities, 1984. Fellow Am. Acad. Orthopedic Surgeons, ACS, Am. Acad. Neurol. and Orthopedic Surgeons; mem. Alumni Assn. Hosp. Joint Disease, Sigma Xi. Jewish. Avocations: sculpting; oil painting. DIED 05/18/96. .

RUBY, CHARLES LEROY, law educator, lawyer, civic leader; b. Carthage, Ind., Dec. 28, 1900; s. Edgar Valentine and Mary Emma (Butler) R.; certificate Ball State U., 1921-22; AB, Cen. Normal Coll., 1924, LLB, 1926, BS, 1931, BPE, 1932; MA, Stanford, 1929; JD, Pacific Coll. of Law, 1931; PhD, Olympic U., 1933; m. Rachael Elizabeth Martindale, Aug. 30, 1925; children: Phyllis Arline (Mrs. Norman Braskat), Charles L., Martin Dale. Prin., Pine Village (Ind.) High Sch., 1923-25; Glenwood (Ind.) Pub. Schs., 1925-26; tchr. El Centro (Calif.) Pub. Sch., 1926-27, Fresno Cen. (Calif.) Union High Sch., 1927-29; prof. law Fullerton Coll., 1929-66; prof. edn. Armstrong Coll., summer 1935, Cen. Normal Coll., summers 1929-33; admitted to Ind. bar, 1926, U.S. Supreme Ct. bar, 1970; pres. Ret. Service Vol. Program, North Orange County, Calif., 1973-76, 83-84; dir. North Orange County Vol. Bur., Fullerton Sr. Citizens Task Force. Life trustee, co-founder Continuing Learning Experiences program Calif. State U., Fullerton, hon. chmn. fund com. Gerontology Bldg; founder, dir. Fullerton Pub. Forum, 1929-39; founder Elks Nat. Found.; co-founder, benefactor Gerontology Ctr. Calif. State U., Fullerton; pres. Fullerton Rotary, 1939-40, hon. mem., 1983-97; mem. U.S. Assay Commn., 1968-97; mem. Orange County Dem. Cen. Com., 1962-78; bd. dirs. Fullerton Sr. Multi-purpose Ctr., 1981-97; bd. dirs. Orange County Sr. Citizens Adv. Council; mem. pres.'s com. Calif. State U., Fullerton. Recipient Medal of Merit, Am. Numis. Assn., 1954, Spl. Commendation Calif. State Assembly, 1966, 88, Calif. State Senate, 1978, 86, Commendation Ind. Sec. of State, 1984, Commendation Bd. Suprs. Orange County, 1985, Commendation Fullerton City Council, 1986, 88, Commendation Orange County Bd. Supervisors, 1986, Commendation Calif. State Senate, 1986, Commendation Exec. Com. Pres. Calif. State U., Fullerton, 1986, Commendation Calif. gov., 1988; Charles L. and Rachael E. Ruby Gerontology Ctr. named in his and late wife's honor, Calif. State U., Fullerton. Fellow Ind. Bar Found.; mem. Pres. Assocs. Calif. State U. Fullerton, Fullerton Coll. Assocs. (named Spl. Retiree of Yr. 1986, Commendation 1986), Calif. (life, pres. So. sect. 1962-63, treas. 1964-65, pres. 1960-61, dir. 1956-65), pres. Fullerton Secondary Tchrs. Assn., Orange County Tchrs. Assn. (pres. 1953-55), Fullerton Coll. (pres. 1958-60) Tchrs. Assn., NEA (life), Ind. Bar Assn., Stanford U. Law Soc., Calif. State Council Edn., Am. Numismatic Assn. (gov. 1951-53, life adv. bd.), Ind. Bar Assn. (hon. life, Golden Career award 1983), Calif. Bus. Educators Assn. (hon. life), Calif. Assn. Univ. Profs., Pacific S.W. Bus. Law Assn. (pres. 1969-70, life), Numismatic Assn. So. Calif. (life, pres. 1961), Calif. Numis. Assn., Indpls. Coin Club (hon. life), Los Angeles Coin Club (hon. life), U.S. Supreme Ct. Hist. Soc., Calif. Town Hall, North Orange County Mus. Assn. (life, benefactor dir.), Stanford U. Alumni Assn. (life), Old Timers Assay Commn. (life), Fullerton Archeology (hon. life, benefactor dir.). Methodist. Clubs: Elks, Fullerton Coll. Vets. (hon. life). Contbr. articles in field to profl. jours. Died Aug. 23, 1997.

RUCH, WILLIAM VAUGHN, writer, educator, consultant; b. Allentown, Pa., Sept. 29, 1937; s. Weston H. and Dorothy D. (Daubert) R. BA, Moravian Coll., 1959; MA in Comm., Syracuse U., 1969; MBA, Fairleigh Dickinson U., 1972; PhD, Rensselaer Poly. Inst., 1980; JD, Western State U. Coll. Law, 1983. Reporter Call-Chronicle Newspapers, Allentown, Pa., 1959-60; tchr. English conversation Jonan Sr. High Sch., Matsuyama, Japan, 1960-62; asst. editor Dixie News, Am. Can Co., Easton, Pa., 1964-65; fin. editor Pa. Power & Light Co., Allentown, 1967-69, advt. asst., 1966-67, sales promotion writer, 1965-66; tech. writer, editor Space Tech. Ctr., GE Co., King of Prussia, Pa., 1969; asst. editor Bell System Tech. Jour., Bell Telephone Labs., Murray Hill, N.J., 1969-71; field rep. N.W. Ayer & Son, Inc., N.Y.C., 1972-73; asst. prof. bus. communication Fairleigh Dickinson U., Madison, N.J., 1974-75, Bloomsburg (Pa.) State Coll., 1975-76; lectr. Sch. Bus. and Pub. Adminstrn., Calif. State U., Sacramento, 1977-79; asst. prof. bus. communication Coll. Bus. Adminstrn., San Diego (Calif.) State U., 1979-84; lectr. European div. U. Md., 1984-85; prof. mgmt. Monmouth Coll., West Long Br., N.J., 1985-88; cons. Corp. Communication, 1988-91; pres., owner WVR Assocs., 1991—; founder, exec. dir. Internat. Inst. of Corp. Communication, 1992—; adj. prof. orgnl. commn., N.Y.U., 1993—. Author: Corporate Communications: A Comparison of Japanese and American Practices, 1984, Business Reports: Written and Oral, 1988, International Handbook of Corporate Communication, 1989, Business Communication, 1990, The Manager's Complete Handbook of Communication, 1992, Business Reporting in the Information Age, 1994, (novels) Effective Business Reports, 1995, Infinity/Affinity, 1994, It Takes Great Strive, 1996. Named Outstanding Prof. of Yr. San Diego State U., 1983. Mem. Acad. Mgmt., Assn. for Bus. Communication, Internat. Assn. Bus. Communicators, Internat. Platform Assn. Republican. Mem. United Ch. of Christ. Died Aug. 15, 1997.

RUDD, LEO SLATON, psychology educator, minister; b. Hereford, Tex., Feb. 20, 1924; s. Charles Ival and Susan Leola (Horton) R.; m. Virginia Mae Daniel, Nov. 17, 1943; children: Virginia Kaye, Leo Jr., Bobbie Ann. BA, William Jewell Coll., Liberty, Mo., 1947; MRE, Cen. Bapt. Sem., Kansas City, Kans., 1948; MS, E. Tex. State U., Commerce, 1957; PhD, N. Tex. State U., Denton, 1959. Ordained to ministry, Southern Bapt. Conv., 1936. Bapt. student dir./instr. Smith County Bapt., Tyler, Tex.; psychology instr. Tyler (Tex.) Jr. Coll.; dir. missions, Linn County, Mo. Author: Syllabus for New Testament Studies, Syllabus for Old Testament Studies. With U.S. Army, 1942-43. Named Tchr. of the Yr., Tyler Jr. Coll., 1987, 1986 Best Tchr. Alumni award. Mem. Tex. Jr. Coll. Tchrs. Assn., Southwestern Bible Tchrs. Assn., East Tex. Counselors Assn., Internat. Platform Assn., DAV. Died Nov. 9, 1997.

RUDERMAN, ROBERT, internist, hematologist; b. Bklyn., Aug. 1, 1938; s. Israel Irving and Rebecca (Kochman) R.; m. Elaine Savatsky, June 9, 1962; children—Mindy Lisa, Marchelle Ann. BS cum laude in Chemistry Bklyn. Coll., 1959; MD, SUNY-Syracuse, 1963. Diplomate Am. Bd. Internal Medicine. Intern Syracuse Med. Ctr. Hosp., N.Y., 1963-64; resident Kings County Hosp. Ctr., Bklyn., 1964-65, V.A. Hosp., Washington, 1967-69; fellow hematology, 1969-70; practice medicine specializing in internal medicine-hematology College Park, Md., 1970-84, Riverdale, 1984-97; chief, div. hematology-oncology Med. Ctr. of Prince George Gen. Hosp., Cheverly, Md, 1974-86; v.p. Prince George Found. Med. Care, Landover, Md., 1981-84, pres. 1984-87; chmn. utilization rev. dept. Leland Meml. Hosp., Riverdale, Md., 1986-93; pres. Nat. Frozen Blood Svcs., Inc., 1986-87; med. dir. utilization mgmt. Dr.'s Community Hosp., Lanham, Md., 1992-94, treas., 1993-95. Mem. steering com. ARC (Prince George chpt.) Hyattsville, Md., 1983-87, 94; bd. dirs. Mishkan Torah Synagogue, Greenbelt, Md., 1980; Capt., AUS, 1965-67. Army Commendation medal; recipient Gubernatorial citation State of Md., 1990, Exec. citation Prince George's County, 1990, Citation Senate of State of Md., 1990; N.Y. State Regents scholar, 1955. Mem. Prince George County Med. Soc. (bd. dirs. 1984, treas. 1986, sec. 1987, pres. elect 1988, pres. 1989-90), Med. Surg. Faculty Md., Am. Physician Fellowship, Am. Soc. Internal Med., D.C. Soc. Internal Medicine, Jaycees, Upsilon Lambda Phi (nat. sec. 1956-58, reg. pres. 1955-56). Democrat. Jewish. Club: Prospect Bay Yacht (commodore 1986-87, past-commodore 1988). Deceased.

RUDNICK, ISADORE, physicist; b. N.Y.C., May 8, 1917; s. Joseph A. and Jennie (Siedlecki) R.; m. Mildred Karasik, Sept. 16. 1939; children: Joseph Alan, Charles Franklin, Deborah Ann, Michael Ira, Daniel Lars. B.A., UCLA, 1938, M.A., 1940, Ph.D., 1944. Researcher Duke U., 1942-45; asst. prof. physics Pa. State U., 1945-48; mem. faculty U. Calif., Los Angeles, 1948—; prof. physics U. Calif., 1958—, Faculty research lectr., 1975-76; vis. prof. U. Paris, 1972-73, Technion, Haifa, Israel, 1973, U. Tokyo, fall 1977, U. Nanjing, China, fall 1979. Fulbright fellow to Denmark, Royal Inst. Tech. Copenhagen, 1957-58; Fulbright fellow Israel Inst. Tech. Haifa, 1965; Guggenheim fellow, 1957-58; Recipient Fritz London Meml. award Commn. for Very Low Temperature Physics, Internat. Union Pure and Applied Physics, 1981. Fellow Am. Phys. Soc., Acoustical Soc. Am. (Biennial award 1948, pres. 1969-70, Silver medal 1975, Gold medal 1982); mem. Am. Inst. Physics (governing bd. 1967-69), Nat. Acad. Scis. DIED 08/22/97. .

RUDOLF, MAX, symphony and opera conductor; b. Frankfurt-Am-Main, Germany, June 15, 1902; came to U.S., 1940, naturalized, 1946; student Goethe-Gymnasium, Frankfurt, Hoch Conservatory Music, Frankfurt U.; pvt. mus. instrn.; D.Mus. (hon.), Cin. Conservatory Music; L.H.D. (hon.), U. Cin., 1960, Miami U., 1963, Curtis Inst. Music, 1972; D.Mus., Baldwin-Wallace Coll., 1973, Temple U., 1975; m. Liese Ederheimer, Aug. 4, 1927; children: William, Marianne. Asst. condr. Freiburg (Germany) Municipal Opera, 1922-23; condr. State Opera of Hesse, Darmstadt, Germany, 1923-29, German Opera, Prague, 1929-35; guest condr. Gothenburg (Sweden) Orch. Soc., also choral dir. radio concerts Swedish Broadcasting Corp., 1935-40; mem. faculty Central YMCA Coll., Chgo.,

1941-43; condr. New Opera Co., N.Y.C., 1944; mem. mus. staff Met. Opera Assn., N.Y.C., 1945-58, artistic adminstr., 1950-58; adminstr. Kathryn Long opera courses Met. Opera, N.Y.C., 1949-58; mus. dir. Cin. May Festival, 1963-70; music dir., condr. Cin. Symphony Orch., 1958-70, world-wide concert tour, 1966; condr. Met. Opera Assn., N.Y.C., 1973-75; mem. faculty Curtis Inst. Music, Phila., 1970-73, 83—; tchr. conducting Ford Found. project, Balt., 1962-64, Tanglewood, 1964; Distinguished Service prof. U. Cin., 1966-68; condr. Columbia Records, Book of Month Club Music Appreciation Series, Cetra (Italy), Decca; guest condr. symphony orchs. throughout U.S., Italy; panel mem. Nat. Endowment for Arts, Washington, 1970-73; artistic adviser Dallas Symphony Orch., 1973, N.J. Symphony Orch., 1976-77, Detroit Symphony Orch., 1983, Exxon/Art Endowment Condrs. Program, 1977—. Recipient Alice M. Diston award, 1964; 1st recipient of Theodore Thomas award Conductors' Guild, 1988. Author: The Grammar of Conducting, 1950, 3d edit., 1993. Home: Philadelphia Pa.

RUDOLPH, MALCOLM ROME, investment banker; b. Balt., Sept. 22, 1924; s. Louis and Sara E. (Rome) R.; m. Zita Herzmark, July 1, 1956 (div. 1979); children: Madelon R. II, Margot R.; m. Barbara J. Girson, 1979. AB, Harvard U., 1947; postgrad., Grenoble U., France, 1948, Hayden Stone Mgmt. Sch., 1965. With div. internat. confs. U.S. Dept. State, Paris, 1949; registered rep. trainee Orvis Bros. & Co., N.Y.C., 1949, rep., asst. mgr., acting mgr., 1950-64; mgr. Hayden Stone Inc., Washington, 1964-68, ptnr., 1968-69; chmn. bd. Donatelli, Rudolph & Schoen Inc., Washington, 1970-74; chmn. bd. Multi-Nat. Fin. Group, Inc., Washington, 1974-79, pres., 1979-86; chmn. Multi-Nat. Precious Metals Corp., 1974-75; chmn. bd. Multi-Nat. Money Mgmt. Co. Inc., 1974-79, pres., 1979—; pres. Rudolph & Schoen Inc., 1975-85; sr. v.p., dir. Laidlaw Adams & Peck Inc., 1975-79; pres. Laidlaw Resources Inc., 1976-95, Sutton Energy, Inc., 1976-90, DeRand Resources Corp., 1979-88; sr. v.p., dir. DeRand Corp. Am., 1979-88; chmn. bd. Arlington Energy Corp., 1980-88; mem. Phila.-Balt.-Washington Stock Exch., 1972-75; pres. Rome Resources Corp., 1982—, Investment Bankers and Cons.; assoc. mem. Pitts., Boston, Montreal stock exchs., 1972-75; allied mem. N.Y. Stock Exch., 1975-79. Mem. Presdl. Inaugural Com., 1960, 64; mem. select com. Palm Beach County Coop Ext. Svc., 1993, U. Fla. Inst. Food and Agrl. Scis. ext. 2000 Select Com.; treas. and dir. Friends of the Mounts Bot. Garden, West Palm Beach, 1994; v.p., dir. Hort. Soc. South Fla., 1994. Mem. Assn. Investment Brokers Met. Washington (v.p. 1965-66, pres. 1967), Bond Club Washington, Ohio Oil and Gas Assn., Ind. Oil and Gas Assn. W.Va., Ind. Petroleum Assn. Am., Southeastern Ohio Oil and Gas Assn., Washignton Met. Bd. Trade, Internat. Assn. Fin. Planners, Internat. Club of Washington, Hasty-Pudding Inst. 1770, Harvard Club of Washington (asst. treas. 1957-60, treas. 1960-64, exec. com. 1957-67), Harvard Club Palm Beaches, Nat. Aviation Club, Club Colette (Palm Beach), Palm Beach Yacht Club, Poinsiana Club (Palm Beach). Died July 7, 1997.

RUDULPH, MIMI TERHUNE, journalist, civic worker; b. Boston, Oct. 29, 1923; d. Frank Newell and Frederica (Lord) Terhune; BA, U. N.H., 1944; postgrad. Juilliard Sch. Music, 1944-45, Columbia U., 1945, Boston U., 1948; H.H.O. (hon.), Northwood Inst., Dallas, 1983; m. Burwell Blount Rudulph, Dec. 30, 1948; 1 dau., Frederica Lord Harvey. Founder Sunday Afternoon Concerts, Palm Springs (Calif.) Desert Mus., 1963, mem. performing arts and women's coms.; founder Palm Springs Friends of the Los Angeles Philharmonic, Met. Opera Showcase Concert, 1977; co-founder Palm Springs Opera Guild; producer-host weekly radio interview program: Window to the Arts, 1977-84; coordinator Festival of the Desert, 1980-82; music critic Desert Sun, 1962-83; arts columnist Sand to Sea mag., from 1974; mem. first community adv. bd. sta. KCET (PBS), 1979-82; arts advisor Coll. of the Desert, coordinator MGM lecture series, author People to People Day Proclamation, 1971; founder Walk for Devel., 1968, Freedom From Hunger, 1969, Internat. Friendship Fiesta, 1967-72; pres. Desert Chpt., People to People, 1972-77; chmn. Books and Authors Luncheon, 1973; mem. regional bd. Western Opera Theater, 1973-77; co-chmn. Welcome N.Z., 1972, Welcome Israel, for Conv. and Visitors Bur., 1973; mem. adv. panel Valley Solar Environ. Grant. Named Mother of Yr., recipient C. of C. award, 1961; honored testimonial luncheon, various civic groups, 1967; recipient vol. award Patton Hosp. various yrs., Betty Ford award Coll. of Desert, 1981, B'nai Brith award, 1975, Am. Soc. Interior Designers award, 1977, 20th Year Outstanding Citizen award, Coll. of Desert, 1982; Vol. of Yr. award Palm Springs Women's Press Club, 1982; Woman of Yr. award Women United Internat., 1985. Proclamation Palm Springs Desert Mus., 1986; named Leading Women of Desert in arts category Palm Springs Life mag., 1986; day named in her honor by mayor of Palm Springs, Mar. 16, 1986. Mem. Music Critics Assn., World Affairs Council (bd.), Met. Opera Nat. Council. Clubs: Palm Springs Pathfinders. Writer on the arts; sonnet Two Silent Watchers used by composer Ernst Krenek for his Opus 222, 1975, author: Inside the Iron Lung, 1985. Deceased. Home: Los Angeles Calif.

RUFFIN, CRAIGE, retired lumber-millwork executive; b. Richmond, Va., May 11, 1902; s. Thomas Champion and Grace Helen (Spear) R.; m. Marjorie Belvin, Oct. 20, 1934; 1 child, Marjorie Belvin. BS, U. Va., 1923. Gen. clk. Ruffin & Payne, Inc., Richmond, 1923-25, shipping clk., 1925-28, buyer, 1928-30, v.p., 1930-73, exec. v.p., 1972-79, pres., 1979-83, chmn., pres., 1983-84, chmn. 1984—, chmn. bd. dirs., emeritus; dir. Dominion Nat. Bank, Richmond, 1967-78 (ret.). Past pres. Salvation Army Hosp.; past dir. United Givers Fund, Richmond Community Coun.; former vestryman St. Stephens Episc. Ch. Mem. Archtl. Woodwork Internat. (past dir.), Richmond C. of C. (past dir.), Richmond Retail Mchts. Assn. (past dir.), Va. Forests (past dir.), Va. Bldg. Materials Dealers Assn. (past pres., dir.), Nat. Lumber Dealers Assn. (past dir.), Lumber Dealers Rsch. Coun. (past dir.), Commonwealth Club, Country of Va. Club (past dir.), Masons (past master), Rotary (past pres.). Republican. Died Nov. 7, 1992.

RUGENERA, MARC, Rwandan government official; b. Gitarama, Hutu, Rwanda. Formerly with banking cos.; min. fin. Govt. of Rwanda, Kigali, 1994-97; min. crafts, mines, & tourism Govt. of Rwanda, 1997—. Mem. Social Dem. Party.

RUGGILL, SOLOMON P., psychologist; b. N.Y.C., Sept. 29, 1906; s. Abraham and Sarah (Silverberg) R.; m. Sophie Stock, June 8, 1938; children: Robert Zachary, Peter Alan. BS, CCNY, 1927; MA in Edn., Columbia U., 1930, PhD in Psychology, 1934. Lic. psychologist, N.Y. Tchr. elem. and jr. high sch. Bd. of Edn. of N.Y.C., 1929-59, psychologist, Bur. of Child Guidance, 1959-62; psychologist Baro Civic Ctr. Clinic, Bklyn., 1961-62; assoc. prof. L.I. U., Bklyn., 1962-69, prof., 1969-79, prof. emeritus, 1979—, acting chmn. dept. guidance and counseling, 1972-73; dir. Flatback Progressive Sch., Bklyn., 1943-45, Camp Kinderwelt, Fraternal Order Farband, N.Y.C., 1959-60; lectr. in gerontology to various orgns., Tucson, 1980—, Keeping Mentally Alert classes Sr. Day Ctrs., 1985-97. Pres. Chancy Meml. Found., N.Y.C., 1961-63; mem. adv. council Pima Council on Aging, Tucson, 1987-97. Mem. N.Y. Acad. Pub. Edn., N.Y. State Guidance Assn., Jewish Tchrs. Assn. (life). Jewish.

RUPP, JOHN NORRIS, lawyer; b. Seattle, Mar. 18, 1913; s. Otto Burton and Edith Cornelia (Norris) R.; m. Elizabeth Milner McElroy, Aug. 31, 1937; children: Joanne (Mrs. George Crispin), William John, Elizabeth (Mrs. Brian Fulwiler), James McElroy. A.B., U. Wash., 1934, J.D., 1937. Bar: Wash. 1937. Law clk. to chief justice Wash. State Supreme Ct., Olympia, 1937-38; atty. McMicken, Rupp & Schweppe, Seattle, 1939-62; v.p., gen. counsel Pacific N.W. Bell Telephone Co., 1962-75; of counsel Schweppe, Krug & Tausend, Seattle, 1975-90, Preston Gates and Ellis, Seattle, 1990-95. Mem. Wash. State Bd Edn., 1957-67; mem. Seattle Transit Commn., 1957-62, Wash. State Hwy. Commn., 1967-73. Served from ensign to lt. (j.g.) USNR, 1944-46. Decorated Bronze Star. Mem. ABA (ho. dels. 1964-68), Wash. Bar Assn. (hon., pres. 1966-67), Seattle Bar Assn. (pres. 1956-57), Seattle C. of C. (gen. counsel 1960-62), Mcpl. League of Seattle (pres. 1948-50), Seattle Hist. Soc. (pres. 1978-79), Rainier Club, Monday Club, Harbor Club, Seattle Yacht Club, Order of Coif, Phi Gamma Delta, Phi Delta Phi. Clubs: Rainier, Monday, Harbor, Seattle Yacht. Died Aug. 21, 1996.

RUPPE, LORET MILLER, former ambassador; b. Milw., Jan. 3, 1936; d. Frederick C. Miller and Adele (Kanaley) O'Shaughnessy; m. Philip E. Ruppe, Nov. 30, 1957; children: Antoinette B., Adele E., Loret M., Katherine T., Mary Speed. D Pub. Svc. (hon.), No. Mich. U., 1981; LHD (hon.), Marymount Coll., 1981, Luther Coll., 1990; HHD (hon.), Wheeling Coll., 1982, Loyola U., 1987; DCL (hon.), Marquette U., 1983, U. Notre Dame, 1984; hon. degree, Nebr. Wesleyan U., Augustana Coll., Concordia Coll., 1993, St. Bonaventure, 1994, Pace U., Concordia Coll., 1985. Chair Bush Campaign Com., Mich., 1980; co-chair Reagan-Bush Com., Mich., 1980; dir. Peace Corps, Washington, 1981-89; amb. to Norway U.S. Embassy, Oslo, 1989-93. Chair Vice Presdl. Inaugural Reception, 1981; trustee U. Notre Dame, 1988—; bd. dirs. Save the Children, The Hewlett Found., The Shriver Ctr. Decorated Grand Cross Royal Norwegian Order of Merit, Dame of Sovereign Mil. Order Malta. Mem. LWV, Internat. Neighbor's Club IV, Coun. Am. Ambs., The Explorer's Club, Sons of Norway. Roman Catholic. Avocations: reading, tennis. Died Aug. 3, 1996.

RUSH, KENNETH, lawyer, industrialist, government official; b. Jan. 17, 1910; s. David Campbell and Emma Kate (Kidwell) R.; m. Jane Gilbert Smith, June 12, 1937; children: George Gilbert (dec.), David (dec.), Malcolm, Cynthia Shepherd (Mrs. Thomas J. Monahan), John Randall, Kenneth. AB, U. Tenn., 1930; JD, Yale U., 1932; LLD (hon.), Tusculum Coll., 1961; HHD (hon.), The Citadel, 1982. Assoc. Chadbourne & Parke, N.Y.C., 1932-36; asst. prof. Duke U. Law Sch., 1936-37; with Union Carbide Corp., N.Y.C., 1937-69; v.p. Union Carbide Corp., 1949-61, exec. v.p., 1961-66, pres., 1966-69, dir., 1958-69, mem. exec. com., 1966-69, chmn. gen. operating com., 1965-69; dir. Bankers Trust Co., 1966-69, Amstar Corp., 1962-69, Bankers Trust N.Y. Corp., 1966-69, El Paso Co., El Paso Natural Gas Co., 1977-83; U.S. ambassador to Germany, 1969-72; also Am. negotiator and signer Quadripartite Agreement on Berlin, 1971; dep. sec. def. U.S., 1972-73; dep. sec. of state, 1973-74, sec. ad interim, 1973, mem. cabinets Presidents Nixon and Ford as counsellor for econ. policy, 1974, ambassador to France, 1974-77. Editor: Yale Law Jour, 1930-32. Mem. Pres. Johnson's Pub. Adv. Com. U.S. Trade Policy, 1968-69; chmn. Bd. Fgn. Service, 1973-74; mem. Nat. Security Council, 1973-74; chmn. Council Internat. Econ. Policy, Pres.'s Com. East-West Trade Policy, Pres.'s Food Com., Council Wage and Price Stability, Joint Presdl.-Congl. Steering Com. for Conf. on Inflation, all 1974, Atlantic Council, 1978-85, Exec. Council on Fgn. Diplomats, 1977-78; mem. Commn. on Jud. Fellows, U.S. Supreme Ct.; bd. dirs. Alliance To Save Energy, 1977-88; trustee Taft Sch., 1957-62, Richard Nixon Birthplace and Libr., 1982-94, Inst. Study Diplomacy Georgetown U., 1980-89, Am. Inst. Contemporary German Studies Johns Hopkins, 1983-93; Found. for Commemoration of the Constitution, vice chmn. 1986-94; chmn. Presdl. Com. For German-Am. Tricentennial, 1983-84; vice chmn. Atlantic Treaty Assn., 1981-85; bd. govs. Am. Nat. Red Cross, 1972-74; chmn. personnel com., mem. audit and planning com. Smithsonian Instn., 1978-88; chmn. Council Am. Ambassadors, 1982-89, Youth for Understanding, 1984-89. Recipient Distinguished Pub. Service medal Dept. Def., 1972; gold medal French Senate, 1977; decorated Grand Cross Order Merit Germany, 1972. Mem. Chem. Mfrs. Assn. (chmn. 1966-69), Internat. C. of C. (trustee U.S. coun. 1955-69), Yale Law Sch. Assn. (exec. com. 1952-62), Fgn. Policy Assn. (bd. dirs.1964-69), Coun. Fgn. Rels., Am. Acad. Diplomacy, Supreme Ct. Hist. Soc. (chmn. 1983-89), Phi Beta Kappa. Episcopalian. Home: Delray Beach Fla. Died Dec. 11, 1994.

RUSHING, JANE GILMORE, writer; b. Pyron, Tex., Nov. 15, 1925; d. Clyde Preston and Mabel Irene (Adams) Gilmore; m. James Arthur Rushing, Nov. 29, 1956; 1 son, James Arthur. BA, Tex. Tech U., 1944, MA, 1945, PhD, 1957. Reporter Abilene (Tex.) Reporter-News, 1946-47; tchr. Tex. high schs., 1947-54; instr. U. Tenn., 1957-59; instr. to asst. prof. Tex. Tech U., intermittently, 1959-68. Author: Walnut Grove, 1964, Against the Moon, 1968, Tamzen, 1972, Mary Dove, 1974, The Raincrow, 1977, Covenant of Grace, 1982, Winds of Blame, 1983, Starting from Pyron, 1992; co-author (with Kline A. Nall) Evolution of a University, Texas Tech's First Fifty Years, 1975. Vassie James Hill fellow of AAUW, 1956-57; recipient Emily Clark Balch prize, 1961; LeBaron R. Barker, Jr., Fiction award, 1975; Tex. Lit. award for fiction, 1984. Mem. Tex. Inst. Letters. Methodist. Died July 4, 1997.

RUSK, DEAN, educator, former secretary of state; b. Cherokee County, Ga., Feb. 9, 1909; s. Robert Hugh and Elizabeth (Clotfelter) R.; m. Virginia Foisle, June 19, 1937; children: David Patrick, Richard Geary, Margaret Elizabeth. A.B., Davidson Coll., N.C., 1931; B.S. (Rhodes scholar), St. John's Coll. Oxford (Eng.) U., 1933; M.A., 1934, M.A. various hon. degrees. Asso. prof. govt. and dean faculty Mills Coll., 1934-40; asst. chief Div. Internat. Security Affairs, U.S. Dept. State, 1946; spl. asst. sec. of war, 1946-47; dir. Office UN Affairs, U.S. Dept. State, 1947-49; asst. sec. of state, Feb. 1949, dep. under sec. of state, 1949-50; asst. sec. of state for (Far Eastern Affairs), 1950-51; pres. Rockefeller Found., 1952-60; sec. of state Washington, 1961-69; Sibley prof. internat. law Sch. Law, U. Ga., Athens, 1970-94. Author: (with Richard Rusk) As I Saw It, 1990. Served with AUS, 1940-46. Recipient Cecil Peace Prize, 1933, Legion of Merit with oak leaf cluster. Mem. Am. Soc. Internat. Law, Phi Beta Kappa. Democrat. Presbyn. Home: Athens Ga. Died Dec. 20, 1994.

RUSOFF, MAURICE BORIS, physician; b. Columbus, Ohio, May 30, 1908; s. Boris Simon and Anna (Feldman) R.; m. Jo Ann Fondaw, Feb. 2, 1972; 1 child, Martin Hans. BA, Ohio State U., 1929, MD, 1933. Diplomate in Internal Medicine. Physician in pvt. practice Columbus, 1934-94. Charter mem. Republical Presdl. Task Force, 1982. Capt. U.S. Army, 1942-45. Fellow Am. Coll. Cardiology; mem. Am. Soc. Internal Medicine, Masons. Avocations: swimming, exercise workouts, golf, horseback riding. Died July 18, 1997.

RUSS, ROBERT DALE, air force officer; b. Portland, Oreg., Mar. 7, 1933; s. Walter Vinton and Kathryn Jean (McMillan) R.; m. Jean E. Johnson, Apr. 27, 1957; children: Randall, Robin Russ Lindenmeier, Robert. B.A. in Bus. Adminstrn, Wash. State U., 1955; M.S. in Bus. Adminstrn, George Washington U., 1965; grad., Air Command and Staff Coll., 1964-65, Nat. War Coll., 1972-73. Commd. 2d lt. USAF, 1955, advanced through grades to gen., 1985; fighter pilot 91st Tactical Fighter Squadron Royal Air Force Sta., Bentwaters, Eng., 1957-60; fighter pilot 437th Fighter Interceptor Squadron Oxnard AFB, Calif., 1960-62; chief fighter sect. Directorate Tactical Evaluation 28th Air div. Hamilton AFB, Calif., 1962-64; fighter officer, dir. tactical evaluation and aide to commr. Air Defence Command, Colorado Springs, Colo., 1965-67; F-4 crew training Davis-Monthan AFB, Ariz., 1967-68; pilot 12th tactical fighter wing Cam Ranh Bay Air Base, Republic of Vietnam, 1968-69; fighter plans officer, dep. chief staff plans and ops. Washington, 1969-70; plans officer gen.

purpose forces Office Joint Chiefs Staff, Washington, 1970-72; vice comdr. 68th tactical air support group Shaw AFB, S.C., 1973-74; dep. comdr. ops. 363d Tactical Reconnaissance Wing, Shaw AFB, S.C., 1974; vice comdr. (4th Tactical Fighter Wing), Seymour Johnson AFB, S.C., 1974-75; comdr. 4th Tactical Fighter Wing, 1975-77; asst. dep. chief staff, plans (Hdqrs. Tactical Air Command), Langley AFB, Va., 1977; asst. dep. chief staff ops. and tng. Hdqrs. Tactical Air Command, 1977-78, asst. dep. chief of staff, ops. control and support, 1978-79; dir. operational requirements, dep. chief staff/research, devel. and acquisition Washington, 1979-82; vice comdr. Tactical Air Command, Langley AFB, 1982-83; spl. asst. to vice chief of staff USAF, 1983; dep. chief of staff Research, Devel. and Acquisitions USAF, Washington, 1983-85; comdr. Tactical Air Command, Langley AFB, Va., 1985—. Decorated D.S.M., Silver Star, Legion of Merit with one oak leaf cluster, D.F.C. with two oak leaf clusters, Purple Heart, Air medal with 13 oak leaf clusters, Air Force Commendation medal with one oak leaf cluster; recipient Disting. Grad. Air Command and Staff Coll. award, 1965. Mem. Air Force Assn., Order Daedalians. Died May 22, 1996.

RUSSELL, DAVID L(AWSON), psychology educator; b. Apr. 1, 1921; m. Jean Williams; children: David W., Nancy K. B.A. in Psychology with honors, Wesleyan U., 1942; postgrad., Columbia U., summers 1942, 46; Ph.D. in Psychology, U. Minn., 1953. Lic. psychologist, Ohio. Adminstrv. fellow Office Dean of Students, U. Minn., Mpls., 1947; teaching asst. dept. psychology U. Minn., 1947-48; clin. fellow Student Counseling Bur., 1948-50; dir. student counseling Bowdoin Coll., Brunswick, Maine, 1950-59; instr. Bowdoin Coll., 1950-54, asst. prof. psychology, 1954-59; assoc. prof. Ohio U., 1959-67, prof., 1967-91, asst. chmn. dept. psychology, 1968, chmn., 1969-72, prof. emeritus, 1991—; vis. prof. U. N.H., summer 1958; mem. faculty NDEA Counseling and Guidance Inst. at Ohio U., 1961, 63, 65, 1966-67; pres. Maine Psychol. Assn., 1956-57; chmn. Maine Bd. Examiners Psychologists, 1959; cons. Div. Undergrad. Edn. in Sci., NSF, 1965, 70, 71; sec. Nat. Coun. Chmns. Grad. Depts. Psychology, 1971-72. Author: (with others) Applied Psychology, 1966; contbr. articles to profl. publs. Mem. Superintending Sch. Com., Topsham, Maine, 1953-59, chmn., 1953-54, 56-57, mem. sch. bldg. com., 1953-55, com. chmn., 1953-55; sec. Joint-Com. Maine Sch. Union 46, 1953-59; mem. Topsham Zoning Com., 1956-57; bd. dirs. United Srs. of Athens County, 1987-91; mem. adv. bd. Athens County Dept. Human Services, 1987-94, pres. 1993-94; mem. Buckeye Hills—Hocking Valley Regional Devel. Dist. area agy. on aging, adv. coun. on aging, 1988-94; mem. Athens County Coun. on Aging, 1988-94, pres., 1990-93. Lt. USCGR, 1943-52. Mem. AAUP, VFW, Am. Psychol. Assn., Midwestern Psychol. Assn., Am. Ednl. Rsch. Assn., Mass. Audubon Soc., Hocking Valley Audubon Soc., Buckeye Trail Assn., Vergilian Soc., Athens League of Women Voters, Athens County Humane Soc., Columbus Urban League, Orleans Hist. Soc., Ohio U. Soc. Alumni Friends of Coll. Arts and Scis. (exec. sec. 1985-90), Athens County Hist. Soc., Sierra Club, Appalachian Mountain Club, Sigma Xi (pres. Ohio U. chpt. 1972-73), Psi Chi, Sigma Phi Omega. Died May 15, 1996.

RUSSELL, DOUGLAS ANDREW, fine arts educator; b. Berkeley, Calif., Feb. 9, 1927; s. Foster Douglas and May Inez (Donnell) R.; m. Marilyn Carol Nelson, Dec. 26, 1953; children: Malcolm Lewis, Andrea Susan. BA, Stanford U., 1949, MA, 1950; MFA, Yale U., 1961. Instr. Carnegie Mellon, Pitts., 1950-51, Fla. State U., Tallahassee, 1951-54; asst. prof. U. Kansas City, Mo., 1955-59; from assoc. prof. to prof. Stanford (Calif.) U., 1961—; Fulbright sr. lectr. U. Vienna, Austria, 1989; Disting. Vis. Prof., Tex. Christian U., Ft. Worth, Tex., 1990; costume dir. Oreg. Shakespeare Festival, Ashland, Oreg., 1948-61; costume designer various West Coast profl. theatres, 1964-87. Author: Stage Costume Design, 1973, Theatrical Style, 1976 (West Coast Bookmaker award 1976), Period Style for Theatre, 1980, Costume History and Style, 1982. Style cons. Am. Conservatory Theatre, San Francisco, 1973—; costume hist. cons. Salinger Sch. of Fashion, San Francisco, 1982—. Recipient Fulbright grant Stratford Shakespeare Inst., Eng., 1954-55, Costume Design award Bay Area Theatre, San Francisco, 1980. Mem. U.S. Inst. Theatre Tech. (bd. dirs. 1980-86, vice comr. costumes), Amnesty Internat., Greenpeace, ACLU. Democrat. Unitarian. Avocations: travel, art galleries, photography.

RUSSELL, HAROLD LOUIS, lawyer; b. Abingdon, Va., July 1, 1916; s. Harold L. and Bess N. (Kinzel) R.; m. Katherine C. (Thompson) May 19, 1939; 1 child, Katherine T. Russell Prophet; m. Mildred Baggett Roach, Sept. 5, 1970. AB, Hendrix Coll., 1937; JD, Columbia U., 1940. Bar: N.Y. 1941, Ga. 1942, U.S. Ct. Appeals (1st, 2d, 3d, 5th, 11th and D.C. cirs.), U.S. Supreme Ct. 1950, D.C. 1972. Assoc. Gambrell & Russell and predecessors, Atlanta and N.Y.C., 1941-47, ptnr., 1947-84; ptnr. Smith, Gambrell & Russell, 1984-97. Bd. dirs. Atlanta Fed. Defender Program, 1973-80, pres. 1978-79; bd. visitors, Columbia Law Sch., 1959-97; mem. council Adminstrv. Conf. of U.S., 1968-76; bd. legal advisers Southeastern Legal Found., 1976-97. Recipient Alumni Fedn. medal Columbia U., 1965; Disting. Alumnus award, Hendrix Coll., 1969. Fellow Am. Coll. Trial Lawyers, Am. Bar Found.; mem. ABA (past chmn. pub. utilities law sect., past chmn. spl. com. on legal service procedure, past chmn. administrv. law sect., ho. of dels. 1983-96), D.C. Bar Assn., Fed. Bar Assn., Atlanta Bar Assn., Atlanta Lawyers Club, Assn. Bar City of N.Y., Columbia Law Sch. Assn. (nat. pres. 1973-75), Atlanta C. of C., Phi Delta Phi. Democrat. Clubs: Capital City, Piedmont Driving. Died Aug. 15, 1997.

RUSSELL, JOSIAH COX, historian, educator; b. Richmond, Ind., Sept. 3, 1900; s. Elbert and Lieuetta (Cox) R.; m. Ruth Winslow, Sept. 15, 1924 (dec. Apr. 1966); children: Elbert Winslow, Walter Howard, Joan (dec.). A.B., Earlham Coll., 1922; M.A., Harvard U., 1923, Ph.D., 1926. Asst. in history Radcliffe Coll., 1923-24, Harvard U., 1924-26; asst. prof. Colo. Coll., 1927-29; prof. history and head social sci. dept. N.Mex. Highlands U., 1929-31; instr. to assoc. prof. U. N.C., 1931-46; chmn. history dept. U. N.Mex., 1946-53, prof., 1946-65; prof. emeritus U. N. Mex., 1965-96; prof. Tex. A & I U., 1965-71, Piper prof. (hon.), 1971. Author: Dictionary of Writers of Thirteenth Century England, 1936, British Medieval Population, 1948, Late Ancient and Medieval Population, 1958, Medieval Regions and Their Cities, 1972, Twelfth Century Studies, 1978, Control of Late Ancient and Medieval Population, 1985, Medieval Demography, 1987; contbr. chpt. to Fontana Economic History of Europe, Historia Universal, Salvat, vol. IV; author: (with others) Ever Since Eve: Archaeology, 1994; contbr. numerous articles to profl. jours. Chmn. Orange Dist. com. Boy Scouts Am., 1945-46. Fulbright lectr. Univ. Coll., Wales, 1952-53; research grantee Guggenheim Found., 1930-31, Am. Council Learned Socs., summers 1933, 34, Social Sci. Research Council, summers 1938, 49, 51, Am. Philos. Soc., 1938-39, 61; fellow Islamic Seminar Princeton, summer 1935; cons. Fulbright Brit. Empire Prof. Selection, 1955. Fellow Mediaeval Acad. Am.; mem. Am. Hist. Assn. (mem. Pacific Coast council 1964-65), Soc. of Friends, AAUP (state chmn. 1951-52, nat. council 1953-56), Phi Alpha Theta. Home: Jacksonville Fla. Died Nov. 12, 1996.

RUSSELL, KEITH P(ALMER), obstetrician, gynecologist, educator; b. Baker, Oreg., May 23, 1916; s. Linwood Burt and Gertrude (O'Bryant) R.; m. Betty Jane Stratton, Nov. 20, 1940; children—Susan Carroll Russell Judd, Keith Palmer, Jr., Donna Lynne. Student, North Pacific Coll. Pharmacy, 1932-33; B.S., Oreg. State Coll., 1936; M.D., U. Oreg., 1939. Diplomate Am. Bd. Ob-Gyn. (examiner 1965-83). Intern Multnomah County Hosp., Portland, Oreg., 1939-40; instr. U. Oreg. Med. Sch., Portland, 1940-42; fellow in surgery Portland Clinic, Oreg., 1941-43; assoc. in ob-gyn. Moore-White Med. Clinic, Los Angeles, 1943-45, practice medicine specializing in ob-gyn., mem., 1945—; mem. Calif. Hosp. Med. Ctr., chief of staff, 1961-63; sr. attending obstetrician and gynecologist Los Angeles County -U. So. Calif. Med. Ctr.; clin. prof. ob-gyn. U. So. Calif., L.A.; trustee Audio Digest Found., subs. Calif. Med. Assn., 1968-72, Moore-White Med. Found., 1969—; trustee Pacific Coast Ob-Gyn. Meml. Found., 1963-78, pres. bd. trustees, 1971-73. Author: Eastman's Expectant Motherhood, 8th edit., 1989; contbr. chpts., numerous articles to profl. publs.; mem. editorial bd. Audio-Digest Found., 1965—; cons. editor, mem. adv. editorial bd., adv. editorial com. profl. jours.; editorial bd. Ob/Gyn News, 1970—. Fellow Royal Australian Coll. Obstetricians and Gynaecologists, Italian Soc. Ob-Gyn. (hon.), Soc. Ob-Gyn. Nigeria (hon.), Fedn. Ob-Gyn. Socs. Brazil (hon.), Soc. Obstetricians and Gynecologists Can. (hon.), Wash. State Obsterical Assn., Long Beach Ob-Gyn Soc., S.W. Ob-Gyn Soc., Former Residents Ob-Gyn Los Angeles County Hosp.; mem. AMA (chmn. sect. ob-gyn 1961-62, chmn. com. on maternal and child care 1973-74), Calif. Med. Assn. (chmn. sect. ob-gyn 1957-59, chmn. com. maternal and child care 1965-70), Los Angeles County Med Assn., Am. Gynecol. Soc., Am. Assn. Obstetricians and Gynecologists (exec. council 1971-74, pres. 1975-76, pres. Found. 1976-77), Nat. Med. Commn. Planned Parenthood Fedn. Am., ACS (chmn. council ob-gyn 1963-64, bd. govs. 1960-63), Am. Coll. Obstetricians and Gynecologists (chmn. Calif. sect. 1960-63, chmn. Dist. VIII 1963-66, 2d v.p. 1967-68, 1st v.p. 1968-69, pres. 1969, 73-74), Pacific Coast Obstetrical and Gynecol. Soc. (sec.-treas. 1959-66, pres. 1968), Obstetrical and Gynecol. Assembly So. Cailf. (exec. com. 1955-67, gen. chmn. 1960-62), Los Angeles Obstetrical and Gynecol. Soc. (pres. 1962-63), Med. Symposium Soc. Los Angeles (pres. 1965), Liaison Com. Ob-Gyn, Internat. Fed. Ob-Gyn (pres. 1979-82), U. Oreg. Med. Sch. Alumni Assn. (v.p. 1958-59), Alpha Omega Alpha. Died Sept. 2, 1996.

RUSSELL, RICHARD SHERMAN, insurance company executive; b. Worchester, Mass., Nov. 10, 1931; s. Conrad Arthur and Mildred (Walls) R.; m. Catherine Elizabeth Quinn, Aug. 2, 1931; children: David, Debra, Steven, Linda, Jeffrey. BS, Springfield Coll., Mass., 1953; MEd, Springfield Coll., 1954. Personnel asst. Mass. Mut. Life Ins. Co., Springfield, 1956-60, mgmt. cons. Cole & Assocs., Boston, 1960-63; v.p. Lincoln Nat. Life, Ft. Wayne, Ind., 1963-79; chmn., pres. Guardsman Life, Des Moines, 1979-84; sr. v.p. New England Mut., Boston, 1984-86; exec. v.p. Conn. Nat. Life, Simsbury, 1986—. Contbr. articles to profl. jours. Served as sgt. U.S. Army, 1951-56. Mem. Adminstrv. Soc., Am. Mgmt. Assn., Am. Council Life Ins. Died Aug. 25, 1997.

RUSSELL, ROBERT GILMORE, lawyer; b. Detroit, May 22, 1928; s. William Gilmore and Esther Marion (Redmond) R.; m. Martha Jones, July 9, 1955; children: Robin Russell Millstein, Julie Russell Smith. AB, U. Mich., 1951, JD, 1953. Bar: Mich. 1954. Atty. Kerr, Russell & Weber (and predecessors), Detroit, 1953—; ptnr. Kerr, Russell & Weber (and predecessors), 1959-93, of counsel, 1994—; instr. Wayne State U. Law Sch., 1954-60. Assoc. editor Mich. Law Rev., 1952-53. Fellow Am. Coll. Trial Lawyers, Am. Bar Found. (sustaining life), Mich. Bar Found. (charter); mem. ABA, ABOTA (advocate, charter mem. Mich. chpt.), Mich. Bar assn. (chair negligence coun. 1988-89), Detroit Bar Assn. (dir. 1977—, pres. 1981-82), Am. Judicature Soc., Am. Arbitration Assn., Internat. Assn. Def. Counsel, Assn. Def. Trial Counsel Detroit (pres. 1973-74), U.S. Supreme Ct. Hist. Soc., Mich. Supreme Ct. Hist. Soc., Nat. Conf. State Trial Cts. (mem. lawyers com.), Def. Rsch. Inst. Barristers, Order of Coif, Mimes, Theta Xi, Phi Delta Phi, Phi Eta Sigma, Thomas Cooley Club. Died Nov. 10, 1997.

RUSSELL, VALERIE EILEEN, social service executive; b. Winchester, Mass., Apr. 28, 1941; d. John Randolph Russell and Carrie Belle (Finley) Jones. BA in Sociology, Suffolk U., 1967; postgrad., Columbia U.; D in Theology (hon.), LaFayette Coll., 1985. Program dir. Blue Hill Christian Ctr., Roxbury, Mass., 1965-67; racial justicestaff mem. Nat. Bd. YWCA, N.Y.C., 1967-72; cons. Riverside Ch., N.Y.C., 1972-73, nat. conf. organizer, 1980-81; asst. to pres. United Ch. of Christ, N.Y.C., 1973-79; pres., exec. dir. City Mission Soc., Boston, 1981-90; adj. prof. Union Theol. Sch., N.Y.C., 1976, Harvard U. Div. Sch., Cambridge, Mass., 1983—; bd. dirs. Ctr. Ministry of the Laity, Newton, Mass. Author: Laity in the Church, 1987; inventor simulation game on pluralism, 1973; regular panelist weekly TV program A Show of Faith, Boston; lectr. in field. Bd. dirs. United Way Mass. Bay, Boston, 1984-88, Women and Poverty Network, Boston, 1984—; co-founder Christians for Justice Action, United Ch. of Christ, 1980—. Named Outstanding Young Women in N.Y., 1969; Recipient Outstanding Alumni award Suffolk U., 1981, Outstanding Social Work award The Girl Friends, Boston, 1985, Outstanding Human Services award Delta Sigma Phi, Boston, 1986. Uniter Ch. of Christ. Avocation: writing. Died Feb. 23, 1997.

RUSSELL, WALLACE ADDISON, college dean; b. Windsor, Vt., June 22, 1922; s. Jay Harold and Nina Laura (Thrasher) R.; m. Marjorie Ann Nelson, May 23, 1944; 1 dau., Pamela Jaye. B.S., U. N.H., 1944, M.A., 1947; Ph.D., U. Iowa, 1949. Asst. prof. psychology U. Minn., 1949-55, assoc. prof., 1955-59, prof., 1959-72; assoc. dean U. Minn. (Coll. Liberal Arts), 1971-72; dean Coll. Scis. and Humanities Iowa State U., 1972-82; dean Coll. Social and Behaviorial Scis. U. South Fla., 1982—; Mem. Commn. on Arts and Scis., Nat. Assn. State Univs. and Land Grant Colls., 1974-80, chmn., 1976-78; pres. Council Colls. Arts and Scis, 1978-79. Author: (with M. Tinker) Introduction to Methods in Experimental Psychology, 3d edit, 1958; editor: Milestones in Motivation, 1970; contbr. articles to profl. jours. Served with AUS, 1943-46. Decorated Bronze Star, Purple Heart with one oak leaf cluster.; guest prof., sr. research grantee Fulbright Commn., U. Wuerzburg, W.Germany, 1957-58. Fellow Am. Psychol. Assn.; mem. AAAS, Psychonomic Soc., La Confrérie de la Chaîne des Rôtisseurs, Sigma Xi, Phi Beta Kappa, Alpha Gamma Rho. Died July 26, 1997.

RUSSER, MAXIMILIAN F., religious studies educator, writer; b. Rochester, N.Y., Oct. 5, 1939; s. Max Oren and Marion Helen (Hampel) R.; m. Edna Rita Russer, May 22, 1976. AA, St. Michael's Coll., 1960; psotgrad., St. Mary's Sem., 1960-61, Genesee Abbey, 1961-63; BA in Sacramental Theology, St. Bernard's Sem., 1967; PhD in Religion, 1992. Registered investment adviser, health underwriter. Trappist monk Genesee Abbey, Piffard, N.Y., 1961-63; asst. dir. St. Martin De Porres Ctr., Rochester, N.Y., 1965-67; cantor Assumption Ch., Jacksonville, Fla., 1977-85; tchr., bibl. theology Assumption Ch., 1977-89; writer, lectr., author freelance, Jacksonville, 1989-94; seminarian, St. Joseph's Sem., Bordentown, N.J., 1955-56, St. Michael's Ch., Conesus, N.Y., 1956-58, St. Michael's Coll., 1958-60. Author: Authority in the Roman Catholic Church: The Corporate Rejection of Jesus, 1991, The Mary-Christ: Idolatry in the Roman Catholic Church, 1995. Named to Million Dollar Round Table, 1978; listed in Who's Who in Sales and Marketing and Who's Who in Religion. Mem. Nat. Assn. Life Underwriters (bd. dirs. 1986, Nat. Sales Achievement 1977-90), Nat. Assn. Securities Dealers, Nat. Small Bus. Assn., Jacksonville Life Underwriters Assn. (chmn. 1987), Life Underwriters Tng. Coun., Chmn.'s Coun. (leader 1985-91), Jacksonville C. of C., Toastmasters (bd. dirs. Rochester chpt. 1968-70). Republican. Home: Jacksonville Fla. Died Aug. 25, 1994.

RUST, EDWARD BARRY, ins. exec.; b. Bloomington, Ill., Sept. 5, 1918; s. Adlai H. and Florence Fifer (Barry) R.; A.B. cum laude in Econs., Stanford U., 1940; m. Harriett B. Fuller, Aug. 7, 1940; children—Florence M.,

Harriett H., Edward B. Asst. sec. State Farm Mut. Automobile Ins. Co., 1941, dir. br. offices, 1946-51, v.p., 1951-58, pres., 1958—, chmn. bd., 1983—, also chief exec. officer, dir., exec. com.; pres., chief exec. officer, dir. State Farm Life Ins. Co., State Farm Fire & Casualty Co., State Farm Life & Accident Assurance Co., State Farm Gen. Ins. Co., State Farm Lloyds, State Farm Life & Annuity Co.; pres., chief exec. officer State Farm County Mut. Ins. Co. Tex. Trustee Ill. Wesleyan U. Served as lt. USNR, 1943-46. Mem. U.S. C. of C. (dir., pres. 1972-73), Phi Beta Kappa.

RUTLEDGE, FELIX NOAH, physician, gynecology educator; b. Anniston, Ala., Nov. 20, 1917; s. Felix and Ethel (Smith) R.; m. Dorothy Wood, June 29, 1980; 1 child, Donald. AB, U. Ala., 1937; MD, Johns Hopkins U., 1947. Diplomate Am. Bd. Ob-Gyn., Am. Bd. Gynecol. Oncology. Intern Johns Hopkins Hosp., Balt., 1943-44, resident in pathology, 1944-45, resident in urology, 1946-47; resident in ob-gyn. Hosp. for Women of Md., Balt., 1945-46; prof. gynecology U. Tex., Houston, 1954—, chief dept. gynecology M.D. Anderson Hosp., 1954-87; nat. cons. USAF, 1972-78. Mem. River Oaks Club, Houston, 1960-85. Named Clinician of Yr. Am. Cancer Soc., 1986. Mem. Am. Radium Soc. (pres.), Pelvic Surgeons (pres.), Tex. Ob-Gyn. Soc. (pres.), Houston Ob-Gyn. Soc. (pres.). Deceased.

RUUD, MILLARD HARRINGTON, legal association administrator, educator; b. Ostrander, Minn., Jan. 7, 1917; s. Mentor L. and Helma M. (Olson) R.; m. Barbara W. Dailey, Aug. 28, 1943; children: Stephen D., Christopher O., Michael L. B.S. in Law, U. Minn., 1942, LL.B., 1947; LL.D., Georgetown U., 1980, U. Pacific, 1981, New Eng. Sch. Law, 1981, Southwestern U., 1983, Widener U., 1987, John Marshall Law Sch., 1987. Bar: Minn. 1947, Tex. 1956. Asst. prof. law U. Kans., Lawrence, 1947-48; assoc. prof. U. Tex., Austin, 1948-52, prof., 1952-78, 80-83, prof. emeritus, 1983—; asst. exec. dir. Tex. Legis. Council, 1950-52; exec. dir. Assn. Am. Law Schs., Washington, 1973-80, 83-87; mem. Tex. Commn. Uniform State Laws, 1967—; cons. legal edn. Am. Bar Assn., 1968-73; chmn. Law Sch. Admission Council, 1966-69, Council on Legal Edn. Opportunity, 1968. Bd. visitors U. Miami, 1980-94, McGeorge Sch. Law, U. of Pacific, 1985-92, U. Minn., 1994—. Recipient Disting. Grad. award U. Minn., 1980. Mem. ABA (Robert J. Kutak award for disting. svc. to legal edn. and profession 1988), Tex. Bar Assn., Am. Law Inst., Order of Coif (nat. sec.-treas. 1981-83). Club: Cosmos. Died Feb. 10, 1997.

RUZE, JOHN, electronics engineer; b. N.Y.C., May 24, 1916; s. John and Marie (Valenta) R.; m. Rose L. Perry, Oct. 6, 1956; children: Elizabeth, Patricia, Katherine, John. B.S. in Elec. Engring., CCNY, 1938; M.S., Columbia U., 1940; D.Sc., M.I.T., 1952. Head antenna design sect. Signal Corps Engring. Lab., Belmar, N.J., 1939-46; asst. head antenna lab. Air Force Cambridge Research Lab., 1946-52; pres. Radiation Engring. Lab., Maynard, Mass., 1952-59; sr. staff mem. Lincoln Lab., M.I.T., Lexington, Mass., 1959—. Author chpts. in books.; editor IEEE Trans. Antennas and Propagation, 1966-68. Fellow IEEE (life), Inst. Radio Engrs. Democrat. DIED 09/06/97. .

RYAN, KEVIN DURWOOD, retail executive; b. Syracuse, N.Y., Jan. 9, 1961; s. William Durwood and Sally Ann (Foelker) R. AA in Bus., Allen Hancock Coll., 1983, AS in Mgmt., 1986, AS in Acctg., 1986. Recreation supr. Santa Maria (Calif.) Recreation Dept., 1975-81; sales mgr. Bulders Emporium, Santa Maria, 1979-84; mgr. Los Padres Theatres, Inc., Santa Maria, Calif., 1980-90; gen. mgr. Grossmans Inc., Novato, Calif., 1987-92; mgr. Mrs. Fields Co., San Ramon, Calif., 1992; gen. mgr. Hollywood Entertainment Corp., Pleasant Hill, Calif., 1993-95; pres. Ryan Enterprises, San Francisco, 1993—. Recipient award Dept. Social Svcs. for Handicapped, Archdiocese L.A., 1978, Home Improvement Specialist award Wickes Corp., 1980, 82, 84. Mem. KTEH Founders Soc., Vallejo Police and Fireman Benefit Assn., Diablo Valley AIDS Soc., Solano County AIDS Task Force, K.C. Republican. Roman Catholic. Died Jan. 13, 1996.

RYAN, PETER JOHN, lawyer; b. N.Y.C., Sept. 13, 1922. BS, U.S. Mil. Acad., 1943; LLB, NYU, 1953, LL.M., 1963. Bar: N.Y. 1953, U.S. Dist. Ct. (so. dist.) N.Y. 1953. Commd. 2d lt. U.S. Army, 1943, advanced through grades to lt. col., 1951; ret., 1953; assoc. Fried, Frank, Harris, Shriver & Jacobson, N.Y.C., 1953-60, ptnr., 1960-87; pres. Alfred Harcourt Found., White Plains, N.Y., 1985—; bd. dirs. Harcourt, Brace, Jovanovich, Inc. Mem. Assn. Bar City N.Y., N.Y. State Bar Assn., ABA. Democrat. Died July 18, 1997.

RYLE, JOSEPH DONALD, public relations executive; b. Stamford, Conn., Aug. 19, 1910; s. Joseph P. and Vivian (Sander) R. B.S., NYU, 1933. With pub. relations dept. Joseph D. Ryle, N.Y.C., 1933-41; dir. pub. relations Am. Overseas Airlines, London, 1946-50, Am. Airlines, N.Y.C., 1950-52; exec. v.p. Fedn. Ry. Progress, Washington, 1953-55, vice chmn., 1955—; pres. Nat. Transit Ads., 1955-57; exec. v.p. pub. relations Thomas J. Deegan Jr., Inc., now dir.; pub. relations cons., N.Y.C.; promotion cons. Met. Mus. Art. Exec. dir. Gov.'s Com. for the Centennial of Thoroughbred Racing at Saratoga; v.p., bd. dirs. East Side Settlement House; adv. com. Am. Folk Art Mus.; chmn. emeritus Winter Antiques Show; trustee Hancock (Mass.) Shaker Village; bd. dirs. Isabel O'Neil Sch., N.Y.C. Served with USAAF, 1942-45; dep. to Gen. H. H. Arnold, pub. relations. Decorated Legion of Merit. Mem. Air Transport Assn. (past chmn. pub. relations com.), Newcomen Soc., Irish Georgian Soc. (bd. dirs.). Clubs: Nat. Press (Washington), Army Navy (Washington); Overseas Press (N.Y.C.), Wings (N.Y.C.); Squadron A; Reading Room (Saratoga, N.Y.). Died July 26, 1997.

RYLE, MARTIN, physicist; b. Sept. 27, 1918; s. J.A. and Miriam (Scully) R.; ed. Oxford U.; m. Ella Rowena Palmer, 1947; 1 son, 2 daus. ICI fellow Cavendish Lab., Cambridge, Eng., 1945-48, Univ. lectr. in physics, 1948-59; fellow Trinity Coll., Cambridge U., 1949—, prof. radio astronomy, 1959-82, now prof. emeritus, dir. Mullard Radio-Astronomy Obs., 1957-82; astronomer royal, 1972-82. Recipient Hughes medal, 1954; Royal medal, 1973; Gold medal Royal Astron. Soc., 1964; Henry Draper medal Nat. Acad. Scis. (U.S.), 1965; Nobel prize for physics, 1974. Mem. Russian Acad. Scis. (fgn.) Am. Acad. Arts and Scis. (hon. fgn.), Nat. Acad. Scis. Washington (asso. fgn.), Pontifical Acad. Scis. (Vatican). Contbr. articles to profl. jours.

RYSANEK, LEONIE, soprano; b. Vienna, Austria, Nov. 14, 1926; d. Peter and Josefine (Hoeberth) R.; m. Ernst-Ludwig Gausmann, Dec. 23, 1968. Student, Vienna Conservatory, 1947-49. First singing engagements include Bayreuth, (Sieglinde-Die Walkure), 1951, San Francisco Opera, (Senta-Der Fliegende Hollaender), 1956, Met. Opera, (Lady Macbeth), 1959; now appears in world's foremost opera houses, N.Y.C., Vienna, Milan, San Francisco, London, Paris, (Chrysothemis-Elektra 1973), Berlin, (Gioconda 1974), Munich, Hamburg, Budapest, Moscow, (Parsifal 1975), and festivals of Salzburg, (Kaiserin-Die Frau Ohne Schatten 1974), Bayreuth, Orange, (Salome 1974), Sieglinde-Die Walkuere, 1975, Aix en Provende, Athens, (Medea 1973), Edinburgh recordings for RCA Victor, Deutsche Grammophon, London Records, EMI and Phillips, Kundry, Parsifal (Stuttgart 1978), Kammersangerin of Austria and Bavaria, Kostelnicka, Jenufa, Australian Opera, 1985, Vienna, 1986, San Francisco, 1986, N.Y. Carnegie Hall, 1988; only artist to sing three major roles in opera Elektra on videocassette; debut Spain, Sieglinde in Die Walküre, Kostelnicka in Janufa, Carnegie Hall, 1988, Liceo, Barcelona, Spain, 1989, Kabanicha in Katya Kabanova, Paris and L.A., 1988, Klytaemnesha in Elektra, Marseille, France, 1989, Orange, 1991, Met. Opera, N.Y.C., 1992, 95-96, Old Countess, Queen of Spades, Barcelona, 1992, San Francisco, 1994, S.Am. Teatro Color, Buenos Aires, 1995, Rio de Janeiro, 1996, Operate Farewell Salzburg Festival, Elektra, 1996; Met. Farewell, 1996. Recipient Chappel Gold medal of singing London; Silver Rose Vienna Philharmonic; Austrian Gold Cross 1st class for arts and scis.; San Francisco medal. Hon. mem. Vienna Staatsoper. Died March 1998.

SABECK, ROBERT V., banker; b. St. Louis, Nov. 6, 1920; s. H.T. and Clara (Mahl) S.; m. Ruth Mary Enyeart, Aug. 1, 1942; children: Pamela (Mrs. Tom Fitzgerald), Deanne (Mrs. William Hardwick), Debra (Mrs. Marvin Moore). Student, Phoenix Coll., 1938-40, Pacific Coast Banking Sch., 1960. With Valley Nat. Bank, Phoenix, 1941—; br. mgr. Valley Nat. Bank, 1953-60, v.p., 1960-68, v.p., met. div. mgr., 1968-71, sr. v.p., met. div. mgr., 1971-74, sr. v.p., br. adminstr., 1974-77, exec. v.p., br. adminstr., 1977-78, exec. v.p., mgr. systems planning and ops. group, 1978-83, exec. v.p., mgr. systems, ops. and personnel group, 1983—. Pres. Greater Phoenix United Fund, 1969; pres. Boys' Clubs Phoenix, bd. dirs., 1982-83; treas. Beatitudes Campus of Care, 1978. Served with USAAF, 1941-46. Mem. Ariz. Bankers Assn., Am. Bankers Assn. (bd. dirs. 1982-83), Am. Inst. Banking, Robert Morris Assn. Republican. Congregationalist (pres.). Clubs: Arizona (treas., bd. dirs.), Kiwanis (pres. 1963).

SACKS, JEAN WEBER, publisher; b. Freeport, Ill., Apr. 25, 1918; d. Anchor Christian and Laura (Hoefer) Weber; m. Sheldon Sacks, June 2, 1967 (dec. 1979); children by previous marriage—Sheila Koons Tabakoff, George Benton Koons, Jeffrey Lee Koons. B.A., U. Chgo. Editorial asst. to dir. U. Chgo. Press, 1962-63, asst. jours. mgr., 1963-64, jours. mgr., 1966—, asst. dir. and jours. mgr., 1971—. Author: History of Journals From Chicago, 1962. Founder acad. jour. Signs: Jour. of Women in Culture and Soc., 1975. Mem. Soc. Scholarly Publishing, Assn. Learned and Profl. Scholarly Pubs., Internat. Fedn. Scholarly Edn. Assn., Council Biology Editors, Assn. Am. Pubs. (exec. council), Am. Assn. Univ. Presses. Died March 4, 1996.

SAGAN, CARL EDWARD, astronomer, educator, author; b. N.Y.C., Nov. 9, 1934; s. Samuel and Rachel (Gruber) S.; m. Ann Druyan; children: Alexandra, Samuel; children by previous marriages: Dorion, Jeremy, Nicholas. AB with gen. and spl. honors, U. Chgo., 1954, BS, 1955, MS, 1956, PhD, 1960; ScD (hon.), Rensselaer Poly. Inst., 1975, Denison U., 1976, Clarkson Coll. Tech., 1977, Whittier Coll., 1978, Clark U., 1978, U. S.C., 1984, Hofstra U., 1985, L.I. U., 1987, Tuskegee U., 1988, Lehigh U., 1990, Wheaton Coll., 1993, SUNY, Albany, 1994; DHL (hon.), Skidmore Coll., 1976, Lewis and Clark Coll., 1980, Bklyn. Coll., CUNY, 1982; LLD (hon.), U. Wyo., 1978, Drexel U., 1986, Queens U., 1993; DScL (hon.), U. Ill., 1990; LHD (hon.), U. Hartford, 1991. Miller research fellow U. Calif.-Berkeley, 1960-62; vis. asst. prof. genetics Stanford Med. Sch., 1962-63; astrophysicist Smithsonian Astrophys. Obs., Cambridge, Mass., 1962-68; asst. prof. Harvard U., 1962-67; mem. faculty Cornell U., 1968—, prof. astronomy and space scis., 1970—, David Duncan prof., 1976—, dir. Lab. Planetary Studies, 1968—, assoc. dir. Center for Radiophysics and Space Research, 1972-81, Johnson Disting. lectr. Johnson Grad. Sch. Mgmt., 1985; pres. Carl Sagan Prodns. (Cosmos TV series), 1977—; nonresident fellow Robotics Inst., Carnegie-Mellon U., 1982—; NSF-Am. Astron. Soc. vis. prof. various colls., 1963-67, Condon lectr., Oreg., 1967-68; Holiday lectr. AAAS, 1970; Vanuxem lectr. Princeton U., 1973; Smith lectr. Dartmouth Coll., 1974, 77; Wagner lectr. U. Pa., 1975; Bronowski lectr. U. Toronto, 1975; Philips lectr. Haverford Coll., 1975; Disting. scholar Am. U., 1976; Danz lectr. U. Wash., 1976; Clark Meml. lectr. U. Tex., 1976; Stahl lectr. Bowdoin Coll., 1977; Christmas lectr. Royal Instn., London, 1977; Menninger Meml. lectr. Am. Psychiat. Assn., 1978, Adolf Meyer lectr., 1984; Carver Meml. lectr. Tuskegee Inst., 1981; Feinstone lectr. U.S. Mil. Acad., 1981; Pal lectr. Motion Picture Acad. Arts and Scis., 1982; Dodge lectr. U. Ariz., 1982; Disting. lectr. USAF Acad., 1983; Lowell lectr. Harvard U., 1984; Poynter fellow, Schultz lectr. Yale U., 1984; Disting. lectr. Fla. State U., 1984; Jack Disting. Am. lectr., Ind. U., Pa., 1984; Keystone lectr. Nat. War Coll., Nat. Def. U., Washington, 1984-86; Marshall lectr. Nat. Resources Def. Coun., Washington, 1985; Gifford lectr. in natural theology U. Glasgow, 1985; Lilenthal lectr. Calif. Acad. Sci., 1986;, Dolan lectr. Am. Pub. Health Assn., 1986; von Braun lectr. U. Ala., Huntsville, 1987; Gilbert Grosvenor Centennial lectr. Nat. Geog. Soc., Washington, 1988; Murata lectr., Kyoto, Japan, 1989; Bart Bok Centennial lectr. Astron. Soc. of the Pacific, 1989, James R. Thompson Leadership lectr. Ill. Math. and Sci. Acad., 1991, Nehru Meml. lectr. New Delhi, 1991, Boyer lectr. Stanford U., 1993, Robert Resnick lectr. in physics Rensselaer Poly. Inst., 1993; other lectureships; mem. various adv. groups NASA and Nat. Acad. Scis., 1959—; mem. council Smithsonian Instn., 1975-80; vice chmn. working group moon and planets, space orgn. Internat. Council Sci. Unions, 1968-74; lectr. Apollo flight crews NASA, 1969-72; chmn. U.S. del. joint conf. U.S. Nat. and Soviet Acads. Sci. on Communication with Extraterrestrial Intelligence, 1971; responsible for Pioneer 10 and 11 and Voyager 1 and 2 interstellar messages; judge Nat. Book Awards, 1975; mem. fellowship panel Guggenheim Found., 1976—; disting. vis. scientist Jet Propulsion Lab., Calif. Inst. Tech., 1986—; researcher physics and chemistry of planetary atmospheres and surfaces, origin of life, exobiology, Mariner, Viking, Voyager amd Galileo spacecraft observations of planets, long-term consequences nuclear war. Author: Atmospheres of Mars and Venus, 1961, Planets, 1966, Intelligent Life in the Universe, 1966, Planetary Exploration, 1970, Mars and the Mind of Man, 1973, The Cosmic Connection, 1973, Other Worlds, 1975, The Dragons of Eden, 1977, Murmurs of Earth: The Voyager Interstellar Record, 1978, Broca's Brain, 1979, Cosmos, 1980, (novel) Contact, 1985, (with Ann Druyan) Comet, 1985, (with Richard Turco) Path Where No Man Thought: Nuclear Winter and the End of the Arms Race, (with Ann Druyan) Shadows of Forgotten Ancestors: A Search for Who We Are, 1993, Pale Blue Dot, 1994; also numerous articles; editor: Icarus: Internat. Jour. Solar System Studies, 1968-79, Planetary Atmospheres, 1971, Space Research, 1971, UFOs: A Scientific Debate, 1972, Communication with Extraterrestrial Intelligence, 1973; editorial bd.: Origins of Life, 1974-84, Icarus, 1962—, Climatic Change, 1976-90, Science 80, 1979-82. Mem. bd. advisors Children's Health Fund, N.Y.C., 1988—. Recipient Smith prize Harvard U., 1964, NASA medal for exceptional sci. achievement, 1972, Prix Galabert, 1973, John W. Campbell Meml. award, 1974, Klumpke-Roberts prize, 1974, Priestley award, 1975, NASA medal for disting. pub. service, 1977, 81, Pulitzer prize for lit., 1978, Washburn medal, 1978, Rittenhouse medal, 1980, Peabody award, 1981, Hugo award, 1981, Seaborg prize, 1981, Roe medal, 1981, Enivironment Programme medal UN, 1984, SANE Nat. Peace award, 1984, Regents medal Bd. Regents Univ. of State N.Y., 1984, Ann. award Physicians for Social Responsibility, 1985, Disting. Svc. award World Peace Film Festival, 1985, Honda prize Honda Found., 1985, Nahum Goldmann medal World Jewish Congress, 1986, Ann. award of merit Am. Cons. Engrs. Coun., 1986, Maurice Eisendrath award Cen. Conf. Am. Rabbis and Union Am. Hebrew Congregations, 1987, In Praise of Reason award Com. for Sci. Investigation of Claims of the Paranormal, 1987, Konstantin Tsiolkovsky medal Soviet Cosmonautics Fedn., 1987, George F. Kennan Peace award SANE/Freeze, 1988, Roger Baldwin award Mass. Civil Liberties Union, 1989, Oersted medal Am. Assn. Physics Tchrs., 1990, Ann. award for Outstanding TV Script Writers Guild Am., 1991, UCLA medal UCLA, 1991, Disting. Leadership award Nuclear Age Peace Found., 1993, 1st Carl Sagan Pub. Understanding of Sci. award Coun. Sci. Soc. Pres., 1993, 1st Isaac Asimov award Com. Sci. Investigation of Claims of Paranormal, 1994, Public Welfare medal NAS, 1994, award for Pub. Understanding of Sci. and Tech. AAAS

1995; named Humanist of Yr. by Am. Humanist Assn., 1981; NSF fellow, 1955-60, Sloan research fellow, 1963-67. Fellow AAAS (chmn. astronomy sect. 1975, John Wesley Powell Meml. lectr. Tucson, 1992, Award for Public Understanding of Science and Technology, 1995), AIAA, Am. Geophys. Union (pres. planetology sect. 1980-82), Am. Astronautical Soc. (council 1976-81, Kennedy award 1983), Brit. Interplanetary Soc., Explorers Club (75th Anniversary award 1980); hon. mem. NAS, mem. Am. Phys. Soc. (Leo Szilard award 1985), Am. Astron. Soc. (councillor, chmn. div. for planetary scis. 1975-76, Masursky award 1991, Annenberg Found. prize 1993), Fedn. Am. Scientists (council 1977-81, bd. sponsors 1988—, Ann. award 1985), Soc. Study of Evolution, Genetics Soc. Am., Internat. Astron. Union, Internat. Acad. Astronautics, Internat. Soc. Study Origin of Life (council 1980—), Planetary Soc. (pres. 1979—), Authors Guild, Astron. Soc. of the Pacific, Coun. Fgn. Rels., Coun. Econ. Priorities, Phi Beta Kappa, Sigma Xi. Died Dec. 20, 1996.

SAGE, MILDRED DEVEREUX, foundation administrator; m. Henry M. Sage (div. 1972); children: Linn Sage Jackson, Henry M. Jr. and Reginald D. (twins), David C.; m. William E. Barlow, July 16, 1987. Grad., Radcliffe Coll., 1951; postgrad., Yale U., Harvard U. Ptnr. AHF Assocs., Inc. indsl. psychologists, S.Am., 1957-62; pres., chief exec. officer Internat. Univ. Found. (formerly Interam. Univ. Found.), N.Y.C., 1962—, now chmn., chief exec. officer; cons. Agribus. Council, Ednl. Testing Service, Internat. Assn. Univ. Pres., UN U. in Costa Rica, Fund for Higher Edn., Friedrich Naumann Found.; trustee Accion, Inc.; advisor, assoc. Royal Acad. Trust; mem. nominating com. N.Y. Stock Exchange; formerly cons. AID, Battelle Inst., Council of Ams., Experiment for Internat. Living, Johnson Research Inc., Peace Corps, also various univs.; advisor Mus. Modern Art; bd. dirs. MIN Pub., Priorities, Inc. Adviser to White House on Latin Am., 1961-68; adviser Brazilian Cultural Found.; trustee, mem. acad. com. Am. U. in Cairo; trustee Women's Econ. Roundtable, Internat. U. Found., Mohonk Environ. Council; past trustee, mem. Western hemisphere exec. com. Internat. Planned Parenthood Fedn.; past trustee Inst. Contemporary Hispanic Art; fellow Morgan Library. Decorated Order So. Cross Brazil; named hon. citizen City of São Paulo, Brazil; recipient award Americas Found. Mem. Americas Soc., Council Fgn. Relations, Internat. Assn. Univ. Pres., Soc. Internat. Devel. Clubs: Colony, Radcliffe; L.I. Wyandanch.

SAGER, RUTH, geneticist; b. Chgo., Feb. 7, 1918; married, 1973. BS, U. Chgo., 1938; MS, Rutgers U., 1944; PhD, Columbia U., 1948. Merck fellow Nat. Research Council, 1949-51; asst. in biochemistry Rockefeller Inst., 1951-55; research assoc. in zoology Columbia U., N.Y.C., 1955-60, sr. research assoc. in zoology, 1961-65; prof. biology Hunter Coll., CUNY, 1966-75; prof. cellular genetics Harvard Med. Sch., 1975-88, prof. emeritus, 1988—; chief cancer genetics div. Dana-Farber Cancer Inst., from 1975; mem. sci. adv. bd. Friedrich Miescher Inst., Basle, 1990—; mem. coun. Nat. Inst. Aging NIH, 1993—. Author: (with F.J. Ryan) Cell Heredity, 1961, Cytoplasmic Genes and Organelles, 1972. Recipient Gilbert Morgan Smith medal Nat. Acad. Scis., 1988, Alumni medal U. Chgo. Alumni Assn., 1994; Guggenheim fellow, 1972-73. Fellow AAAS; mem. Am. Acad. Arts and Sci., Nat. Acad. Scis., Inst. of Medicine, Am. Soc. Cell Biologists, Genetics Soc. Am., Am. Assn. Cancer Rsch., Am. Soc. Biol. Chem., Sigma Xi, Phi Beta Kappa. DIED 03/29/97. .

SAIDENBERG, DANIEL, cellist, conductor; b. Winnipeg, Man., Can., Oct. 12, 1906; s. Albert and Minnie (Sokoloff) S.; m. Eleanore Block, Apr. 15, 1934; children: Lawrence Daniel, Robert Paul. Student, Paris Conservatory, 1921-22, Juilliard Music Found., 1926-30. Pres. Saidenberg Art Gallery, Inc. Began as concert cellist, 1918; with Phila. Symphony Orch., 1926-29, solo cellist, Chgo. Symphony Orch., 1930-36; engaged in chamber music activities; head cello dept., Chgo. Musical Coll., 1930-37; condr. small, large groups, 1933—, Cin. Symphony Orch., summer 1936, Chgo. Opera Orch., fall 1937; formed Saidenberg Chamber Orch., 1937, Saidenberg Sinfonietta Series, Chgo. and on tour, 1937-42; guest condr. Ill. Symphony Orch., 1937, 38, 39; created Saidenberg Little Symphony, 1940; concert series Town Hall, N.Y.C., 1940, 41, 42; condr. Alka Seltzer radio series, NBC; condr. artistic dir., Town Hall Music Forum, N.Y.C., 1943; chief music dept.: overseas radio O.W.I, 1944; music dir. Ballet Theatre, 1945; cellist Coolidge String Quartet, 1944; Pablo Casals Festival Concerts, 1950, 51; condr. Saidenberg Little Symphony, N.Y. Times Hall, 1944; guest condr., CBS, 1945, 46, 47, Phila. Orch., 1946; condr., Conn. Symphony Orch., 1947, Concert Hall Soc.; condr. Chamber Music series of The New Friends of Music, Town Hall, N.Y., 1948-49, ann. series concerts, Kaufman Auditorium, 1948-57; performed concerts with Budapest String Quartet, Library of Congress, Washington; Recordings, Saidenberg Little Symphony. Clubs: Cliff Dwellers (Chgo.); Lotos (N.Y.C.). DIED 05/18/97. .

SAINI, T.S., economics educator; b. June 17, 1921; came to U.S., 1954; naturalized, 1957; s. Puran Singh and Kishan Kaur; m. Betty A. Stein, Jan. 4, 1962; children: Kiranjit Kaur, Maninder. BA in Econs., Punjab U., Lahore, India, 1941, MA in Econs., 1943; D Forestry, Duke U., 1958; PhD in Econs., New Sch. for Social Rsch., 1972. Lectr. in econs. G.N. Tutorial Inst., 1941-42; with range forest office Punjab, 1945-54; grad. fellow, rsch. asst. Duke U., 1954-58; forest economist FAO, UN, Africa, Mid. East, Europe, 1962-65; assoc. prof., chmn. dept. bus. and econs. Bluffton (Ohio) Coll., 1966-68; prof. econ. Bloomsburg (Pa.) U., 1968-94, chmn. econ. dept., 1968-77; lectr. New Sch. Social Rsch., 1961-62; vis. scholar, mem. High Table, Kings Coll., Cambridge (Eng.) U., 1982-83; assoc. v.p. for acad. affairs Bloomsburg U., 1981-82; dir. rsch. project on solid waste mgmt. Pa. Sci. and Engring. Found.; v.p. Pa. Conf. Economists, 1971-73, pres., 1973-74, editor procs. ann. meetings, 1971, 73, 74; mem. exec. coun. Internat. Forum for Improvement of Quality of Life, chair goals and objectives com.; bd. dirs. Area Coun. Econ. Edn. Founder, mng. editor Ea. Econ. Jour.; contbr. articles to profl. jours. Mem. Gov.'s Sci. Adv. Com. Task Force on Economy, 1974-77; nat. co-chair badminton tournament 1st Sr. Olympics, St. Louis, 1987; mem. Pa. Task Force on Solid Waste Mgmt., 1976-77; mem. Pa. Gov.'s Econ. Adv. Com., 1976-78; mem. steering com. Pa. Coun. Econ. Edn. Recipient Hind Rattan award former Pres. of India, 1990, COPE honor, 1993, Recognition plaque Assn. Indians in Am., 1990. Mem. Assn. Indian Econ. Studies (co-founder, exec. bd. 1974-94), Congress of Polit. Economists, Internat. (founder, chair 1989-94), Ea. Econ. Assn. (founder, editor procs. inaugural conv., exec. v.p., v.p. fin. 1976-80, pres. 1979-80, exec. dir. 1981-83, Recognition award 1983), North Indian Studies Assn. (sec.-treas. 1985-86, ptrs. 1985-86), Columbia Montour Torch Club (v.p. 1988-89, pres. 1989-90), Internat. Assn. Torch Clubs (bd. dirs. 1991-94). Home: Bloomsberg Pa. Died Feb. 14, 1994.

ST CLAIR, SYLVIA See ROSALES, SYLVIA

SALABOUNIS, MANUEL, computer information scientist, mathematician; b. Salonica, Greece, Apr. 15, 1935; came to U.S., 1954; s. Anastasios and Matrona (Pevaskevaidou) Tsalabounis; children from previous marriage: Stacy, Mary E., John; m. Baerbel Thekla Steinbach-Rushford, July 2, 1988. Cert., Anatolia Coll., Salonica, Greece, 1954; student, Morris Harvey Coll., 1954-56; BS in Engring. Sci., Cleve. State U., 1960; MS in Math., Akron U., 1964. Master Univ. Sch., Shaker Heights, Ohio, 1960-62; mathematician Babcock and Wilcox, Alliance, Ohio, 1962-66; dir. computer ctr. John Carroll U., University Heights, Ohio, 1966-68; pres. Electronic Service Assocs. Corp., Euclid, Ohio, 1968-73; v.p. North Am. Co., Chgo., 1974-79; sr. project leader Hibernia Bank, New Orleans, 1979-83; project mgr. Compuware Corp., Farmington Hills, Mich., 1984—, mgr. spl. projects, 1990-91, MIS planning mgr., 1991—. Accomplishments include work in internat. banking applications, 3 dim. thermostress analysis, generic tool definitions and design, law office info. systems, software delivery system, and other. Vol. Sts. Constantine and Helen Ch., Cleve., 1960-74, St. Nicholas, Detroit, 1986-92, Annunciation Ch., Detroit, 1992—. Avocations: classical music, opera, golf, fishing, cooking. DIED 09/05/95. .

SALAM, ABDUS, physicist, educator; b. Jhang, Pakistan, Jan. 29, 1926. Student, Govt. Coll., Lahore, Pakistan, 1938-46, St. John's Coll., Cambridge (Eng.) U., 1946-49; BA, Cambridge U., 1949, PhD, 1952; 46 DSc hon. degrees including, Panjab U., 1957, U. Edinburgh, 1971, Hindu U., U. Chittagong, U. Bristol, U. Maiduguri, 1981, U. Khartoum, U. Complutense de Madrid, 1983; U. Cambridge, U. Glasgow, U. Exeter, U. Gent, 1985-88, U. Ghana, U. Dakar, U. Tucuman, U. Lagos, U.S.C., U. West Indies, U. St.Petersburg, 1990-93; 46 DSc hon. degrees including, U. Gulbanga, U, Dhaka, 1990-93. Prof. Govt. Coll., Lahore, 1951-54; prof., head math. dept. U. Panjab, Lahore, 1951-54; fellow St. John's Coll. Cambridge, 1951-56; prof. theoretical physics Imperial Coll., London, 1957-93, sr. rsch. fellow, 1994—; founder, dir. Internat. Ctr. for Theoretical Physics, Trieste, Italy, 1964-93, pres., 1994—; mem. AEC Pakistan, 1958-74, Pakistan Nat. Sci. Coun., 1963-75, South Commn., 1987; hon. sci. adviser to Pres. of Pakistan, 1961-74; mem. sci. and tech. adv. com. UN, 1964-75; gov. Internat. Atomic Energy Agy., Vienna, 1962-63; developer new physics ctrs. and schs. Pakistan, Peru, Jordan, Sudan, Colombia; hon. life fellow St. John's Coll., Cambridge, 1971—; hon. prof. Beijing Univ., 1987. Author: Symmetry Concepts in Modern Physics, 1965, Aspects of Quantum Mechanics, 1972; (with E. Sezgin) Supergravity in Diverse Dimensions, Vols. I and II, 1988, Unification of Fundamental Forces: The First of the 1988 Dirac Memorial Lectures, 1990, Science and Technology: Challenge for the South, 1992, Selected papers of Abadus Salam (with commentary), 1994, Renaissance of Sciences in Islamic Countries, 1994. Mem. sci. coun. Stockholm Internat. Peace Rsch. Inst., 1970—; mem. coun. Univ. for Peace, Costa Rica, 1981-86. Recipient Hopkins prize Cambridge U., 1957, Adams prize, 1958, Maxwell medal and prize London Phys. Soc., 1961, Atoms for Peace prize, 1968, Oppenheimer prize and medal, 1971, Guthrie medal and prinze Inst. Physics, London, 1976, Sir D. Sarvadhikary Gold medal Calcutta U., 1977, Matteucci medal Acad. Nat. dei XL, Rome, 1978, John Torrence Tate medal Am. Inst. Physics, 1978, Nobel prize in Physics, 1979, Einstein medal UNESCO, 1979, Shri R.D. Birla award Indian Physics Assn., 1979, Josef Stefan Inst. medal Ljublijana, Yugoslavia, 1980, Peace medal Charles U., Prague, 1981, Gold medal for outstanding contbns. to physics Czechoslovak Acac. Scis., 1981, Lomonosov gold medal USSR Acad. Scis., 1983, Dayemi Internat. Peace award, Bangladesh, 1986, Premio Umberto Biancamano, Italy, 1986, 1st Edinburgh medal and prize, 1989, Internat. Devel. of Peoples prize, Genoa, Italy, 1988, Ettore Meijorana-Erice Sci. for Peace prize, 1989, Erice Science Peace prize (Italy), 1989, Catalunya Internat. prize, 1990, Medal of 260th Anniversary of Havana, Cuba, 1991, Gold medal Slovak Acad. Scis., 1992, Mazhar-Ali Applied Sci. medal Pakistan League of Am., 1992, Internat. Leoncino d'Oro prize Italy, 1993; named Hon. Knight Comdr. Order of Brit. Empire, 1989; also numerous decorations. Fellow Am. Physical Soc., Royal Soc. London (Hughes medal 1964, medal 1978, Copley medal 1990), Royal Swedish Acad. Scis. (bd. dirs. Beijir Inst. 1986-89), Pakistan Acad. Sci., Bangladesh Acad. Scis.; mem. U.S. Nat. Acad. Scis. (fgn. assoc.), Am. Acad. Arts and Scis. (fgn.), Acad. dei Lincei (Rome, fgn. assoc.), European Acad. Sci., Arts and Humanities, Acad. Scis. USSR, Third World Acad. Scis. (founding, pres. 1983-94, hon. pres. 1995—), Third World Network Sci. Orgns. (founding, pres. 1988-94, hon. pres. 1995—), Club of Rome, also hon. mem. or hon. fellow numerous other worldwide sci. orgns. Died Nov. 21, 1996.

SALE, EDWIN WELLS, lawyer; b. Fisher, Ill., June 29, 1912; s. Leslie Oscar and Margaret Laurinda (Moore) S.; m. Esther E. Sale, Aug. 1, 1936; 1 dau., Margaret Sale Hubbard. B.S., Northwestern U., 1934; J.D., U. Ill., 1937. Bar: Ill. 1937, U.S. Supreme Ct. 1944, U.S. Dist. Ct. (ea. dist.) Ill. 1959, U.S. Ct. Appeals (7th cir.) 1960. Legal researcher Claims dept. Lumbermen's Mut. Ins. Co., Chgo., 1937-38; sole practice, Champaign, Ill., 1938-42, Kankakee, Ill., 1946-13 . Served with U.S. Army, 1942-46. Decorated Army Commendation medal. Mem. Kankakee Bar Assn. (pres.), C.of C., Am. Arbitration Assn., Ill. Bar Assn., Chgo. Bar Assn., ABA, Judge Advocates Assn., Am. Coll. Probate Counsel, Appellate Lawyers Assn., Am. Judicature Soc., Am. Legion, Delta Upsilon, Phi Delta Phi. Republican. Methodist. Clubs: Kankakee Country. Lodge: Rotary. Contbr. articles to profl. jours. Died Dec. 20, 1996.

SALISBURY, ARTHUR J., physician, found. adminstr.; b. North Platte, Nebr., June 13, 1924; s. Arthur J. and Katherine Frances (Clark) S. B.S., Yale U., 1948; M.D., Harvard U., 1952, M.P.H., 1963. Diplomate: Am. Bd. Pediatrics. Intern Johns Hopkins Hosp., Balt., 1952-53; resident in pediatrics Children's Hosp. Med. Center, Boston, 1953-55; practice medicine specializing in pediatrics Boston, 1955-62; med. dir. Mass. Com. on Children and Youth, 1963-70; v.p. med. services March of Dimes Birth Defects Found., White Plains, N.Y., 1970-86, retired. Contbr. articles to med. jours. Served with AUS, 1943-46. Fellow Am. Public Health Assn.; mem. Am. Acad. Pediatrics. Democrat. Episcopalian. Died July 13, 1997.

SALISBURY, FRANKLIN CARY, foundation executive, lawyer; b. Cleve., Sept. 29, 1910. B.A., Yale U., 1932; J.D., Case Western Res. U., 1937; LL.D. (hon.), U. Wales, 1985. Bar: Ohio 1937, D.C. 1947. Adminstrv. asst. to commr. FCC, 1939-40; chief legal div. ammunition br. Office Chief Ordnance, U.S. Army, 1941-45; chief clearance div. WPB, Army Service Forces, 1945; dir. legal div. Office Fgn. Liquidation Commn., Rio de Janeiro, Brazil, 1945-46; asst. solicitor Indian legal activities Dept. Interior, 1956-61; gen. counsel Ams. United for Separation Ch. and State, 1963-72; pres., chief exec. officer Nat. Found. Cancer Research, Bethesda, Md., 1973-97; hon. pres., hon. dir. Assn. for Internat. Cancer Research, St. Andrews, Scotland, 1973-95; chmn. Krebsforschung Internat., Dusseldorf, Federal Republic Germany; trustee, counsel Latin Am. Inst., 1943-75; sec., dir. Atlantic Research Corp., 1949-64, Dryomatic Corp., 1950-59; chmn. bd., sec., dir. Orbit Industries, Inc., 1960-68; co-founder, dir. Internat. Sch. Law (now George Mason Law Sch.), 1975-77. Named Pro Universitate Med. U. Debrecen, 1982; recipient Quantum Biology award Internat. Soc. Quantum Biology, 1983, Medal of Merit U. Turin, Italy, 1984; decorated Order of Leopold II (Belgium). Mem. Fed. Bar Assn.; associated fgn. mem. Institut de Biologie Physico-Chimique (Fondation Edmond de Rothschild). Office: NFCR 7315 Wisconsin Ave Ste 500W Bethesda MD 20814-3206 Died Mar. 12, 1997.

SALKIND, ALEXANDER, film producer; b. Gdansk, Poland., June 2, 1921; s. Michael and Maria S.; m. Berta Dominguez, Oct. 18, 1946; 1 child, Ilya. Began career as asst. to father, Miguel Salkind; first solo film Buster Keaton comedy Boom in the Moon, 1945; prodr.: numerous films in Europe and U.S. including Black Jack, 1950, Austerlitz, 1960, Rape of the Sabines, 1962, The Trial, 1963, Ballad in Blue, 1965, The Hot Line, 1965, Servantes, 1967, The Light at the Edge of the World, 1970, Kill, Kill, Kill, 1971, Bluebeard, 1972, The Three Musketeers, 1973, The Four Musketeers, 1975, The Prince and the Pauper, 1977, Superman, 1978. Died Mar. 8, 1997.

SALLEE, FRANK, securities and investment executive; b. Manhattan, Mont., Mar. 29, 1930; s. Frank and

Mildred (Easton) S.; m. Nancy Ann Foster, Jan. 27, 1952; children: Debra Ann Cook, Linda Gail Robbins, Frank F., David R. BS in Agr., U. Mo., 1951. Dist. mgr. Investors Diversified Svcs., St. Joseph, Mo., 1956-62; pres., chmn. Camden County Bank, Camdenton, Mo., 1962-88; fin. cons. Merrill Lynch Pierce Fenner & Smith, Camdenton, 1989-91; gen. securities prin. Sentra Securities Corp., Camdenton, 1991—; pres. Frank Sallee and Assocs., Inc., Camdenton, 1993—; pres., chmn. loan rev. com. Cen. Ozarks Devel., Inc., Camdenton, 1993—. Adv. dir. Great Rivers Coun. Boy Scouts Am., Columbia, 1975—; dir. Nat. Bd. U. Mo. Alumni Assn., Columbia, 1994—; trustee Mo. 4-H Found., Columbia, 1988-97. 1st lt. U.S. Army, 1951-55, ETO. Mem. Mo. Bankers Assn. (assoc., bd. dirs. 1976-78), Lake of the Ozarks Assn. (disting. bd. mem., disting. svc. dir. 1963-93, bd. dirs., pres. chmn. 1975-77), Kansas City Club, Country Club of Mo. Disciples of Christ. Avocations: fly fishing, horse packing, canoeing, bird hunting.

SALTARELLI, EUGENE A., engineering and construction company executive, consultant; b. Buffalo, Feb. 22, 1923; s. Joseph A. and Mary (Cataldo) S.; m. Jean Marie Cray, Nov. 25, 1950; children—Margaret, Joseph, Thomas, Paul, Mary, John. B.Mech. Engring., U. Detroit, 1949; M.S. in Mech. Engring., Northwestern U., 1951. Registered profl. engr. Calif., Md., Mich., N.Y., Pa. Tex., Ariz., Ga. Design engr. Bell Aircraft Corp., Buffalo, 1950-56; sr. mgr. Bettis Atomic Power Lab., Pitts., 1956-67; group v.p. NUS Corp., Gaithersburg, Md., 1967-80; sr. v.p., chief engr. power Brown & Root, U.S.A., Inc., Houston, 1980-88; now pvt. cons.; expert witness in power plant engring. and constrn. litigation. Contbr. articles to profl. jours.; patentee in field. Served to 1st lt. USAAF, 1942-46. Mem. ASME (George Westinghouse Gold medal 1985), Atomic Indsl. Forum, Am. Nuclear Soc. (exec. com. power divsn. 1975). Roman Catholic. Club: Montgomery Country Club, Laytonsville, Md. Avocations: woodworking; piano and organ; golf. Home: Gaithersburg Md. Died June 15, 1996; interred Gate of Heaven, Rockville, MD.

SALTON, GERARD, computer science educator; b. Nuremberg, Germany, Mar. 8, 1927; s. Rudolf and Elisabeth (Tuchmann) S.; m. Mary Birnbaum, Aug. 31, 1950; children: Mariann, Peter. B.A. magna cum laude, Bklyn. Coll., 1950, M.A., 1952; Ph.D., Harvard U., 1958. Mem. staff computation lab. Harvard U., 1952-58, instr., then asst. prof. applied math., 1958-65; prof. computer sci. Cornell U., 1965—, chmn. dept., 1971-77; cons. to industry. Author: Automatic Information Organization and Retrieval, 1968, The Smart System-Experiments in Automatic Document Processing, 1971, Dynamic Information and Library Processing, 1975, Introduction to Modern Information Retrieval, 1983, Automatic Text Processing, 1989; editor-in-chief ACM Comm., 1966-68, ACM Jour., 1969-72; editor ACM Transactions on Info. Systems. Guggenheim fellow, 1963; recipient Alexander von Humboldt Sr. Scientist award, 1988. Fellow AAAS, Assn. Computing Machinery (coun. 1972-78, Outstanding Contbn. award 1983); mem. Am. Soc. for Info. Sci. (award of merit 1989), Phi Beta Kappa. Home: Ithaca N.Y. DIED 08/28/95. .

SALVADORI, MARIO, mathematical physicist, structural engineer; b. Rome, Italy, Mar. 19, 1907; came to U.S., 1939; s. Riccardo and Ermelinda (Alatri) S.; m. Giuseppina Tagliacozzo, July 30, 1935 (div. June 1975); 1 child, Vieri R.; m. Carol B. Salvadori, Apr. 5, 1975. DCE, U. Rome, 1930, D of Math. Physics, 1933; DSc, Columbia U., 1977; D of Fine Letters, New Sch. for Social Rsch., 1990; LHD, Lehman Coll., 1994. Prof. U. Rome (Italy) Sch. Engring., 1932-38, Columbia U., N.Y.C., 1940-90; chmn. Weidlinger Assocs., N.Y.C., 1957-90, hon. chmn, 1991-97; founder, chmn. Salvadori Ednl. Ctr. on Built Environment, 1975-91, hon. chmn., 1993-97. Author of 25 books; contbr. articles to profl. jours. Recipient Founders award NAE, 1997, more than 20 awards from univs., engring. and archtl. socs. and ednl. assns., 1970-95. Fellow ASME, Am. Concrete Inst.; mem. ASCE (hon.), AIA (hon.). Democrat. Achievements include research in applied mathematics and engineering structures; 27 new routes and 3 virgin peaks climbed in the Eastern Alps. Home: New York N.Y. Died June 25, 1997.

SAMENT, SIDNEY, neurologist; b. Zagaré, Lithuania, Apr. 25, 1928; came to the U.S., 1964; s. Bernard and Mina Sament; children: Hilary, David, Brian. MB, BCh, Witwatersrand U., 1952. Intern Baragwanath Hosp., Johannesburg, 1953-55, resident, 1955-60; postgrad. tng. various hosps., Great Britain, 1960-64; resident in neurology Jersey City Med. Ctr., 1964-65, New Eng. Med. Ctr., Boston, 1965-67; EEG fellow, asst. in enurology Mass. Gen. Hosp., Boston, 1967-69; in charge EEG Lab. VA Hosp., Boston, 1969-70; asst. prof. neurology Hahnemann Hosp., Phila., 1970-73; pvt. practice Easton, Pa., 1973-88, Visalia, Calif., 1988-97. Mem. Calif. Med. Soc. Home: Visalia Calif. Died Jan. 6, 1997.

SAMERS, BERNARD NORMAN, fund raising organization executive; b. N.Y.C., Jan. 25, 1934; s. Abraham and Edith (Slomack) S.; m. Edith Maralyn Rosenblum, Sept. 7, 1958; children: Audrey Meryl, Michael Eric, William David. BS, Queens Coll., 1956; BSIE, Columbia U., 1956; MBA, Harvard U., 1958; Profl. Indsl. Engr., Columbia U., 1968. Registered profl. engr., Calif; Cer: CFRE. Cons. S.B. Littauer & Assocs., N.Y.C., 1956; asst. dir. spl. studies Hudson Pulp & Paper Corp., N.Y.C., 1957; sr. mgmt. scientist Dunlap & Assocs., Inc., Darien, Conn., 1958-66; v.p. Cooper & Co., Mgmt. Cons., Stamford, Conn., 1966-82; v.p. adminstrn. and regional ops. Am. Technion Soc., N.Y.C., 1982-86; exec. v.p. Am. Com. for the Weizmann Inst. of Sci., N.Y.C., 1986-96; exec. v.p. emeritus Am. Soc. Future Weizman Inst. Sci., N.Y.C., 1996-97; adj. asst. prof. mgmt. engring. U. Bridgeport, 1972-88; lectr. MBA program U. Conn., 1980-82. Pres. Jewish Edn. in media, N.Y.C., 1978-97, United Jewish Fedn. of Stamford, 1978-79; dir. Coun. of Jewish Fedn., 1979-80; committeeman Dem. City Com., Stamford, 1980-82. Mem. Nat. Assn. Fund Raising Execs., Assn. Jewish Community Orgn. Pers., Ops. Rsch. Soc. of Am. Democrat. jewish. Avocation: abstract painting. Died Apr. 13, 1997.

SAMORA, JULIAN, sociologist; b. Pagosa Springs, Colo., Mar. 1, 1920; 5 children. B.A. (Frederick G. Bonfils Found. scholar 1938-42), Adams State Coll., Alamosa, Colo., 1942; M.S., Colo. State U., 1947; Ph.D. (Herman fellow 1950), Washington U., St. Louis, 1953; LL.D. (hon.), Incarnate Word Coll., 1980. Tchr. Huerfano County High Sch., Walsenburg, Colo., 1942-43; research fellow Colo. State U., 1943-44; mem. faculty Adams State Coll., 1944-45; teaching asst. U. Wis., 1948-49, Washington U., 1949-50; asst. prof. preventive medicine and public health U. Colo. Med. Sch., Denver, 1955-57; assoc. prof. sociology and anthropology Mich. State U., 1957-59; prof. sociology U. Notre Dame, 1959-85, head dept., 1963-66, emeritus, 1985—; vis. prof. U. N.Mex., 1954, U. Nacional de Colombia, Bogotá, 1963, UCLA, 1964, U. Tex., Austin, 1971, U. Mich., Ann Arbor, 1988; vis. scholar U. Wash., Seattle, spring 1990; fieldwork in, Colo., N.Mex., Mich., Denver, Bogotá, East Chicago, Ind., U.S.-Mex. border; program adv. population Ford Found. in, Mex. and C.A.; mem. President's Commn. Rural Poverty, President's Commn. Income Maintenance Program, Ind. Civil Rights Commn.; cons. in field. Author: Los Mojados: The Wetback Story, 1971; co-author: Mexican-Americans in the Southwest, 1969, A History of the Mexican American People, 1977, Gunpowder Justice: A Reassessment of the Texas Rangers, 1979; editor: LaRaza: Forgotten Americans, 1966. Recipient La Raza award Nat. Council LaRaza, 1979, hon. alumni award Colo. State U., 1981, Emily M. Schossberger award U. Notre Dame Press, 1981, Spl. Presdl. award U. Notre Dame, 1985, cert. of achievement Adams State Coll., Colo., 1985, medal of honor Nat. Hispanic U., Calif., 1985, award Midwest Latino Council Higher Edn., 1985, also numerous citations; Office Inter-Am. Affairs scholar, 1943; Inst. Internat. Edn. fellow, 1943-44; Nat. Endowment Humanities scholar, 1979; fellow Whitney Found., 1951-52; fellow Am. Sociol. Assn., 1978; Nat. Assn. Chicano Studies scholar, 1983; Julian Samora Rsch. Inst., Mich. State U., East Lansing, established in his name, 1989. DIED 02/02/96. .

SAMPOLINSKI, ANTHONY THOMAS, family practice physician; b. Chgo., Jan. 16, 1926; s. Anthony Zigmund and Anna Julia (Wroblewski) S.; m. Joan Charlotte Lundy, Jan. 23, 1960; children: Richard Thomas, Wendy Ann Sampolinski Stannard, Thomas Matthew. MD, Loyola U., Chgo., 1948. Diplomate Am. Bd. Family Practice. Intern, resident Cook County Hosp., Chgo., 1948-50; pvt. practice Chgo., 1953-77, Lindenhurst, Ill., 1977-96; mem. staff N.W. Hosp., Chgo., 1954-78, Condell Hosp., Libertyville, Ill., 1978-96, St. Therese Hosp., Waukegan, Ill., 1980-96; mem., past chmn. bd., med. assisting adv. com. Lake County Area Vocat. Sch., Grayslake, Ill., 1972-96; mem. Am. Bd. Utilization Rev., 1983-88. Bd. dirs. Dist. 41 Scholarship Fund, Lake County, Ill., 1985-88; mem. profl. rev. orgn. Crescent Found, State Ill. Recipient letters of award Am. Bd. Utilization Rev., 1983-87, marble plaque Midwest Claims Conf., 1985. Fellow Internat. Coll. Medicine and Surgery, Am. Coll. Utilization Rev. Physiciains (pres. Gt. Lakes chpt. 1989—), ABQUARP; mem. Am. Acad. Family Practice, Am. Bd. Utilization (mem. exec. com.), Ill. Acad. Family Practice, Lake County Health Care Assn., Lindenhurst C. of C. (bd. dirs.), Reef Point Yacht Club (Racine, Wis.). Republican. Roman Catholic. Avocation: yachting. Died July 26, 1996.

SAMUEL, ATHANASIUS YESHUE, archbishop; b. Hilwah, Syria, Dec. 25, 1907; s. Sowmey Malkey and Khatoun Malkey (Hido) S. Student, St. Mark's Sem., 1923-27, 29-31, Cairo Theol. Coll., 1927-29; DD (hon.), Gen. Theol. Sem., N.Y.C., 1989. Ordained priest Syrian Orthodox Ch. of Antioch, 1932; sec. to Syrian orthodox patriarch of Antioch, 1931-32; father superior St. Mark's Monastery, Jerusalem, 1933-43; patriarchal vicar of Jerusalem, 1943-46; archbishop, 1946-52; patriarchal del. to U.S.A. and Can., 1949-57; archbishop to U.S.A. and Can., 1957-95. Author: Treasure of Qumran, 1966, Liturgy of St. James, 1967, Rites of Baptism, Holy Matrimony and Burial, 1974, Book of Church Festivals, 1984, Anaphoras, The Book of the Divine Liturgies, 1991, The Shorter Daily Prayer Book for the Faithful, 1993, Prayer Book for Various Occasions for the Use of the Clergy, 1993. Decorated by Emperor Haile Selassie I gold cross and papal medallion Pope Paul VI, cross Knights of St. John of Jerusalem., Grand Cross of St. Ignatius Theophoros; proclaimed Dean of Bishops of the Holy See of Antioch, 1989. Mem. World Council Chs., Nat. Council Chs. of Christ in U.S.A. Home: Lodi N.J. Died Apr. 16, 1995.

SAMUEL, JOSIE HARRIS, secondary educator; b. Camden, S.C., Sept. 6, 1934; d. Willie English and Bertha (Smith) Harris; m. Theodore Samuel, Nov. 29, 1957; 1 child, Angela C. BS, Bennett Coll., 1955. Cert. tchr., S.C. Math. tchr. Mayo High Sch., Darlington, S.C., 1955-92, girls basketball coach, 1955-76, girls cheerleader advisor, 1955-84, chair math., 1960-90. Sec. Sunday sch. St. James Ch., Darlington. Grantee NSF, 1958, 60, 70. Mem. NAACP, S.C. Ednl. Assn., Darlington County Ednl. Assn., Nat. Coun. Tchrs. Math., S.C. Coun. Tchrs. Math. Democrat. Methodist. Avocations: singing, working with students, yard work, sewing. Died Feb 15, 1997.

SÁNCHEZ, RICARDO, poet, educator English, Chicano studies, cultures; b. El Paso, Tex., Mar. 29, 1941; s. Pedro Lucero Sánchez and Adelinas (Gallegos-Campbell) Sánchez; m. Maria Teresa Silva, Nov. 28, 1964; children: Rikard-Sergei, Libertad-Yvonne, Jacinto-Temilotzin. GED, U.S. Army, 1959; PhD, Union Inst., 1974. Prison inmate Tex., Calif. Systems, 1960-69; poet, activist, performer U.S., 1969-73; poet in residence El Paso (Tex.) C.C., 1975-76; vis. asst. prof. U. Wis., Milw., 1977, U. Utah, Salt Lake City, 1977-80; free lance writer, performance poet U.S., Mex., Can., Europe, 1980-91; prof. comparative Am. cultures Wash. State U., Pullman, 1991—; founder Mictla Publs., Inc., El Paso, Tex., 1971, Los Desboradados, El Paso, Tex. and Juarez, Mex., 1988; mem. lit. panel NEA, Washington, 1978-81, lit. panel, Tex. Coun. for the Arts, 1978-81; only U.S. Invitee to 1st Meeting of Poets of Latin World, Palace of Fine Arts, Mexico City, 1986. Author: 12 books including Cantoy Gr. to Milibracidos, 1973, Hechinzospells, 1976, Selected Poems, 1987, Am. Journeys, 1994; also 800 columns and articles. Named Outstanding Prof., Chicano Students Assn. U. Utah, Salt Lake City, 1979, Best of Summer Inst., Western States Summer Inst. Couer d'Alene, Idaho, 1993. Mem. Nat. Assn. for Chicano Studies (editor, chmn. edn. com. 1993—), Internat. Poetry Festival. Avocations: chess, readings, fighting my cancer. DIED 09/03/95. .

SANDEFUR, THOMAS EDWIN, JR., tobacco company executive; b. Cochran, Ga., Dec. 4, 1939; s. Thomas Edwin and Elsie (Camp) S.; m. Annette Crawford Meginniss, May 8, 1965. B.S. in Bus. Acctg., Ga. So. U., 1963. Sales and mktg. positions R.J. Reynolds Tobacco Co., Winston-Salem, N.C., 1964-76, sr. v.p. advt. and brand mgmt., 1976-79; sr. v.p. R.J. Reynolds Internat., Winston-Salem, N.C., 1979-81; exec. v.p. Europe, Geneva, 1981-82; sr. v.p. internat. mktg. Brown & Williamson Tobacco Corp., Louisville, 1982-84, exec. v.p., 1984-85, pres., COO, 1985-93, chmn., CEO, 1993—; bd. dirs. Bank Louisville. Bd. dirs. Wesleyan Coll., L.A. Bantle Inst., Greater Louisville Fund for Arts, Cathedral Heritage Found., Boy Scout coun. Louisville; bd. overseers U. Louisville; bd. adv. coun. Ga. So. Coll., Nat. Assn. Mfrs. Mem. Am. Wholesale Marketers Assn. Died July 14, 1996.

SANDGREN, FIND, mech. engr.; b. Copenhagen, June 15, 1922; came to U.S., 1949, naturalized, 1955; s. August Oswald and Marie Charlotte (Peterman) S.; m. Jytte Rubak Larsen, Mar. 5, 1949; children—Kim, Eric, Glenn, Karen. B.S. in Mech. Engring, Copenhagen Teknikum, 1942; postgrad., Poly. Inst. Denmark, 1947; M.B.A., U. Chgo., 1955. Registered profl. engr., Ill. Gen. mgr. indsl. automation RCA, Detroit, 1957-59; dir. research and devel. Ideal Industries, Sycamore, Ill., 1959-61, Wabash Inc., Ind., 1961-64; exec. v.p., gen. mgr. Midwest Applied Sci. Corp., West Lafayette, Ind., 1964-69; prof. mech. engring. Purdue U., West Lafayette, 1969—; dir. coop. engring. edn. Purdue U., 1969—; propr. Find Sandgren (Cons. to Industry), 1969—. Served with Motorized Arty. Danish Army, 1943. Mem. IEEE, ASME, Am. Soc. Engring. Edn., Am. Soc. Metals. DIED 10/04/97. .

SANDOR, GEORGE NASON, mechanical engineer, educator; b. Budapest, Hungary, Feb. 24, 1912; came to U.S., 1938, naturalized, 1949; s. Alexander S. and Maria (Adler) S.; m. Magda Breiner, Dec. 5, 1964; stepchildren: Stephen Gergely, Judith Patricia Gergely (Mrs. J. Peter Vernon). Diploma in Mech. Engring, Poly. U. Budapest, 1934; D. Eng. Sci., Columbia U., 1959; D (hon.), Budapest Technol. U., 1986. Registered profl. engr., Fla., N.J., N.Y., N.C., cert. of qualification Nat. Council Engring. Examiners. Asst. to chief engr. Hungarian Rubber Co., Budapest, 1935-36; mfg. dept. head Hungarian Rubber Co., 1936-38; design engr. Babcock Printing Press Corp., New London, Conn., 1939-44; v.p., chief engr. H.W. Faeber Corp., N.Y.C., 1944-46; chief engr. Time Inc. Graphic Arts Research Labs., Springdale, Conn., 1946-61, Huck Co., Inc., N.Y.C., 1961; assoc. prof. mech. engring. Yale, 1961-66; prof. mech. engring. Rennselaer Poly. Inst., Troy, N.Y., 1966-67; Alcoa Found. prof. mech. design, chmn. machines and structures div. Rennselaer Poly. Inst., 1967-75; rsch. prof. mech. engring. U. Fla., Gainesville, 1976-89, rsch. prof. emeritus, 1989-96; dir. mech. engring. design and rotordynamics labs. U. Fla., 1979-87; instr. engring. U. Conn. Extension, New London and Norwich, 1940-44; lectr. mech. engring. Columbia U., N.Y.C., 1961-62; dir.

Huck Design Corp., Huck Co., Inc., Montvale, N.J., 1964-70; cons. engr., printing equipment and automatic machinery, mech. engring. design, 1961-96; cons. NSF Departmental and Instl. Devel. Program, 1970-72; cons. nat. materials adv. bd. Nat. Acad. Scis., 1974; cons. Xerox Corp., Burroughs Corp., Govt. Products div. Pratt & Whitney Aircraft Co., Time Inc., also others, 1961-92; prin. investigator, co-investigator NSF, U.S. Army Research Office and NASA sponsored research at Yale U.; dir. and co-dir. NSF, U.S. Army Research Office and NASA sponsored research at Rensselaer Poly. Inst. and; U. Fla. at Gainesville; chief U.S.A. del. to Internat. Fedn. for Theory Machines and Mechanisms, 1969-75; cons. for materials conservation through design Office Tech. Assessment, Congress U.S., 1977. Author: (with others) Mechanical Design and Systems Handbook, 1964, 2d edit., 1985, Linkage Design Handbook, 1977, Mechanism Design-Analysis and Synthesis, vol. 1, 1984, 2d edit., 1991, Advanced Mechanism Design, Analysis and Synthesis, vol. 2, 1984; mem. editorial bd. Jour. Mechanism, 1966-72, Machine and Mechanism Theory, 1972-96, Robotica, 1982-96; contbr. articles to profl. jours. Recipient Outstanding Achievement awrd Northctrl. sect. Fla. Engring. Soc., 1983; Fla. Blue Key Leadership award for disting. faculty mem. U. Fla., 1985; elected hon. mem. Internat. Fedn. for Theory Machines and Mechanisms, 1987, Hungarian Acad. Scis., Budapest, 1993. Fellow ASME (life, Machine Design award 1975, mechanisms com. award 1980, hon. mem. 1991); mem. NSPE, Am. Soc. Engring. Edn. (Ralph Coats Roe award 1985), N.Y. Acad. Scis., Am. Acad. Mechanics, Hungarian Acad. Scis. (hon. mem. 1993), Flying Engrs. Internat., Sigma Xi, Tau Beta Pi, Pi Tau Sigma. Achievements include patent for rotary-linear actuator for robotic manipulators, and 5 others. Home: Highlands N.C. Died April 22, 1996.

SANDQUIST, ELROY CHARLES, JR., lawyer; b. Chgo., Dec. 18, 1922; s. Elroy Carl and Lillian (Peterson) S.; m. Sally Patricia Dunham, Mar. 15, 1945; children: Deirdre, Elroy Charles III, Peter, Ellen. BS, U.S. Naval Acad., 1943; JD, Northwestern U., 1950. Bar: Ill. 1950. Assoc. Peterson, Ross, Schloerb & Seidel, Chgo., 1950-57, ptnr., 1960-96; asst. state's atty. County of Cook, Ill., 1957-60; mem. Ho. of Reps. State of Ill., Springfield, 1977-83; legis. coord. County of Cook, 1983-91. Pres. Child Svc., Park Ridge, Ill., 1985-88. Lt. USN, 1943-46. Mem. City Club Chgo. (pres. 1966-68). Republican. Methodist. Died April 7, 1996.

SANFORD, JAY PHILIP, internist, educator; b. Madison, Wis., May 27, 1928; s. Joseph Arthur and Arlyn (Carlson) S.; m. Lorraine Burklund, Apr. 7, 1950; children—Jeb, Nancy, Sarah, Philip, Catherine. M.D., U. Mich., 1952; D of Mil. Medicine (hon.), Uniformed Svcs. U. Health Sci., 1991. Intern Peter Bent Brigham Hosp., Boston, 1952-53; research fellow Harvard Med. Sch., Boston, 1953-54; resident Duke U. Hosp., Durham, N.C., 1956-57; practice medicine specializing in internal medicine Dallas, 1957-75; mem. faculty U. Tex. Southwestern Med. Sch. at Dallas, 1957-75; prof. internal medicine, 1965-75; dean F. Edward Hebert Sch. Medicine, Uniformed Services U. Health Scis., Bethesda, Md., 1975-90; pres. Uniformed Services U. Health Scis., 1981-90, dean emeritus, 1990-96; clin. prof. internal medicine U. Tex. Southwestern Med. Sch., 1992-96; chief microbiology lab. Parkland Meml. Hosp., Dallas, 1957-75, pres. med. staff, 1968-69, mem. attending staff; mem. adv. coun. Dallas Health and Sci. Mus., 1968-75; chmn. Am. Bd. Internal Medicine, 1978-79, Gov.'s Commn. Phys. Fitness, 1971-75; bd. regents Nat. Libr. Medicine, 1984-90; mem. Accreditation Coun. on Grad. Med. Edn., 1987-92, chmn. transitional year residency rev. com., 1989-92, chmn., 1990-91; mem. bd. on army sci. and tech. NRC, 1995-96; cons. Dallas VA Ctr. Contbr. articles to profl. jours. With M.C., U.S. Army, 1954-56; col. Res., 1983-96. Decorated Medal of Honor du Service de Sante des Armees, France, 1991; recipient cert. of award Div. Health Moblzn. USPHS, 1963, 64, Prizer award for CD, 1965, Presdl. citation for Health Moblzn. Planning, 1970, Disting. Pub. Svc. medal Dept. Def., 1982, 91. Fellow Am. Acad. Microbiology, ACP (master); mem. Inst. Medicine of NAS, Assn. Am. Physicians, Nat. Inst. Allergy and Infectious Diseases (chmn. tng. grant com. 1971, adv. coun. 1979-90), Am. Fedn. Clin. Research (pres. 1968-69), Am. Soc. Microbiology, Central Soc. Clin. Rsch., Soc. Exptl. Biology and Medicine, Am. Soc. Clin. Investigation, Soc. Med. Consultants to Armed Forces (pres. 1976-77, John R. Seal award 1988, 91), Am. Thoracic Soc., Infectious Disease Soc. Am. (pres. 1978-79, Bristol award 1981, E.H. Kass lectr. 1994), Sigma Xi, Alpha Omega Alpha, Phi Kappa Phi. Home: Dallas Tex. Died Oct. 23, 1996.

SANFORD, TERRY, lawyer, educator, former United States Senator, former governor, former university president; b. Laurinburg, N.C., Aug. 20, 1917; s. Cecil and Elizabeth (Martin) S.; m. Margaret Rose Knight, July 4, 1942; children: Elizabeth Knight, Terry. AB, U. N.C., 1939, JD, 1946; 30 hon. degrees from colls. and univs. Bar: N.C. 1946, D.C. 1979. Asst. dir. Inst. Govt., U. N.C., 1940-41, 46-48; spl. agt. FBI, 1941-42; pvt. practice Fayetteville, 1948-60; ptnr. Sanford, Adams, McCullough & Beard, Raleigh, N.C. and Washington, 1965-86; gov. State of N.C., 1961-65; pres. Duke U., Durham, N.C., 1969-85; mem. U.S. Senate 99th-102d Congresses from N.C., 1986-93; ptnr. The Sanford-Holhouser Law Firm, PLLC, Raleigh, 1993—; pub. gov. Am. Stock Exchange, 1977-83; dir. Study of Am. States, Duke U., 1965-68; mem. Carnegie Commn. Ednl. TV, 1964-67; pres. Urban Am., Inc., 1968-69; chmn. ITT Internat. Fellowship Com., 1974-86, Am. Coun. Young Polit. Leaders, 1976-86; pres. U.S. Del. Inter-Parliamentary Union, 1988-90. Author: But What About the People?, 1966, Storm Over the States, 1967, A Danger of Democracy, 1981, Outlive Your Enemies, 1996. Sec.-treas. N. C. Port Authority, 1950-53; mem. N.C. Senate, 1953-54; pres. N.C. Young Dem. Clubs, 1949-50; del. Nat. Dem. Conv., 1956, 60, 64, 68, 72, 84, 88, 92; chmn. Nat. Dem. Charter Commn., 1972-74; mem. governing bd. Nat. Com. for Citizens in Edn., Am. Art Alliance; trustee Am. Council Learned Socs., 1970-73, Nat. Humanities Center, 1978-86, Meth. Coll., 1958-94, chmn., 1958-68, Howard U., 1968-86; chmn. N.C. Mus. Art, 1993—; bd. dirs. Children's TV Workshop, 1967-71, Council on Founds., 1971-76, N.C. Outward Bound, 1981-88; chmn. bd. trustees U. N.C., 1961-65; chmn. So. Regional Edn. Bd., 1961-63, Sta. ACSN (The Learning Channel), 1980-86, Assn. Am. Univs., 1980-81, Nat. Civic League, 1985-86. Served to 1st lt. AUS, 1942-46. Mem. ABA, Am. Acad. Polit. and Social Sci., Coun. Fgn. Rels., Am. Judicature Soc., Nat. Acad. Pub. Adminstrn., AAAS, Phi Beta Kappa. Methodist. Died April 1998.

SANNO, ALFRED ROBERT, advertising executive; b. N.Y.C., Aug. 25, 1925; s. John D. and Elizabeth (Corrado) S.; m. Yolanda Ciccarelli, Apr. 1, 1951; children: Laura, Lisa. B.A., Dartmouth Coll., 1946. Sr. v.p. broadcast services Batten, Barton, Durstine & Osborn, Inc., N.Y.C., 1963—. Died Nov. 18, 1996.

SANTIAGO, JULIO VICTOR, medical educator, researcher, administrator; b. San German, Puerto Rico, Jan. 13, 1942. BS, Manhattan Coll., 1963; MD, U. Puerto Rico, 1967. Diplomate Am. Bd. of Internal Medicine, 1975. Fellow in metabolism and endocrinology Washington U., St. Louis, 1972-74; chief resident Barnes Hosp., St. Louis, 1974-75; dir. divsn. of endocrinology and metabolism Dept. of Pediatrics, 1984—; program dir., Diabetes Rsch. and Tng. Ctr. Wash. U. Sch. Medicine, 1987—, prof. of medicine, pediatrics, 1983—. Assoc. editor Diabetes, 1977-79, 91-95, editor, 1995—. Mem. Am. Soc. for Clin. Investigation, Soc. for Pediatric Rsch., Am. Diabetes Assn. Home: 4 Forest Parkway Dr Ballwin MO 63021-5553 Died Aug. 10, 1997.

SANTULLI, THOMAS VINCENT, surgeon; b. N.Y.C., Mar. 16, 1915; s. Frank and Amalia (Avagliano) S.; m. Dorothy Muriel Beverly, Apr. 10, 1941 (dec.); children: Thomas Vincent Jr., Robert B.; m. Patricia Rita, May 28, 1982. B.S., Columbia, 1935; M.D., Georgetown U., 1939. Intern N.Y. Polyclinic Hosp., 1939-41, resident, 1941-44; prof. surgery Columbia U., N.Y.C., 1967-81, prof. emeritus, 1981—; chief pediatric surg. service emeritus Babies Hosp., Columbia-Presbyn. Med. Center, N.Y.C., 1955-81; attending surgeon emeritus Presybn. Hosp., Columbia-Presbyn. Med. Center. Mem. Am. Surg. Assn., Am. Pediatric Surg. Assn. (pres. 1980-81), A.C.S., British Assn. Pediatric Surgeons, N.Y. Pediatric Surg. Soc. (pres. 1967-69). Died June 2, 1997.

SAPERSTON, HOWARD TRUMAN, SR., lawyer; b. Buffalo, Oct. 30, 1899; s. Willard W. and Julia (Wilson) S.; m. Nan Basch, Oct. 5, 1937; children: Howard Truman, Willard B. Student, Cornell U., 1917; LLB, Syracuse U., 1921, LLD (hon.), 1969. Bar: N.Y. 1922. Since practiced in Buffalo; mem. Saperston and Day, P.C. Assoc. editor: Cornell U. Daily Sun, 1918. Mem. Nat. coun., mem. exec. com. Buffalo coun. Boy Scouts Am.; pres., gov. United Jewish Fedn., 1948-51; pres. Community Vol. Svc. Bur., 1946-47; bd. dirs. United Fund, 1950-68, 1973-74, trustee, 1950—; bd. dirs. Buffalo chpt. ARC, 1948—; gen. chmn. Community Chest-ARC campaign United Fund, 1955; v.p. Federated Health Fund Buffalo, 1948-49; mem. adv. bd. Cerebral Palsy Assn. Western N.Y., 1953-68; bd. dirs. Buffalo Tennis Found., 1970-72; mem. exec. bd., co-chmn. Buffalo chpt. NCCJ, 1962-65; v.p. Coun. Jewish Fedns. and Welfare Funds for N.Y., Ont., 1935-50; bd. dirs. Jr. Achievement of Niagara Frontier, 1960—, Arthritis Found., 1978-88; pres. United Jewish Fedn., 1952-55, Community Chest, 1956-57; trustee Union of Am. Hebrew Congregations, 1956; pres. Temple Beth Zion, 1953-55; hon. chmn. Temple Beth Zion Endowment Fund; nat. coun. Joint Def. Appeal, Am. Jewish Joint Distbn. Com.; del. bd. Community Welfare Coun.; dir. Western N.Y. Traffic Coun.; N.Y. State assoc. chmn. U.S. Olympic Com., 1976; regent Canisius Coll., 1955-70, trustee, 1970-77; mem. coun. U. Buffalo, 1957-63; chmn. bd. dirs. Chmns. Club of Erie County Rep. Party, 1965-72, pres., 1978-80; bd. visitors Syracuse U. Coll. Law, 1960-96; mem. deans adv. com. U. Buffalo Coll. Law, 1955-65; bd. dirs. Bradley Sch. Music, 1960-85; trustee Buffalo Gen. Hosp., pres., 1969-72; trustee, mem. adv. com. Children's Hosp., 1962-69; mem. governing com. Buffalo Found., 1960-77, chmn., 1972-75; chmn. United Negro Coll. Fund, 1951-52, gen. chmn., 1953; bd. dirs. Greater Buffalo Devel. Found., 1960-68, Buffalo Urban League, 1942-65, Meals on Wheels, 1981-87; mem. devel. bd. U. Buffalo, 1957-62; mem. Pres.' Assocs. State U. N.Y. at Buffalo; dir. Jewish Ctr. Buffalo, 1940-43; mem. adv. bd. Camp Lakeland, 1950-75; chmn. Erie County Republican Fin. Com., 1954-73, 78-79. Officer U.S. Army, World War I, Officers Tng. Camp. Named one of 6 outstanding citizens Buffalo Eve. News, 1955; recipient Brotherhood award NCCJ, 1956, President's medal Canisius Coll., 1963, Silver Beaver award Boy Scouts Am., 1964, Nat. award NCCJ, 1966, Disting. Citizen's award Canisius Coll., 1968, Chancellor's award SUNY-Buffalo, 1982, Outstanding Citizen's award Syracuse U. Club of Buffalo, 1982, Outstanding Citizen Am. Jewish Comm. 1987, Lawyer of Yr. award Erie County Bar Assn., 1986, Citizen of Yr. award Am. Jewish Com., 1987, Lifetime Svc. award Jr. Achievement of Western N.Y., 1989, Bronze Leadership award, 1989. Mem. Am., N.Y., Erie County bar assns., Lawyers Club Buffalo, Greater Buffalo Advt. Club (sec.-treas. 1934), 100 Club of Buffalo, Am. Legion, C. of C., Am. Arbitration Assn. (dir. 1960-70), Buffalo Hist. Soc., Buffalo Pub. Libr. (life), Buffalo Fine Arts Acad. (life), Buffalo Soc. Natural Scis., Grovesnor Soc., The Soc. of the Buffalo (Ann. award 1989), Cornell Spike Shoe Soc., Zeta Beta Tau. Jewish (temple pres., trustee). Clubs: Mason (Shriner); Wilmont Country (pres. 1936-38, 43), Buffalo, Westwood Country (pres. 1948), Cornell, Syracuse, Automobile, 100, Marshall, Mid-Day, Capitol Hill, Saturn. Home: Buffalo N.Y. Died Aug. 22, 1996.

SARGENT, DIANA RHEA, corporate executive; b. Cheyenne, Wyo., Feb. 20, 1939; d. Clarence and Edith (de Castro) Hayes; grad. high sch.; m. Charles Sargent, Apr. 17, 1975 (div. 1991); children: Rene A. Coburn, Rochelle A. Rollins, Clayton R. Weldy, Christopher J. IBM proof operator Bank Am., Stockton, Calif., 1956-58, gen. ledger bookkeeper, Modesto, Calif., 1963-66; office mgr., head bookkeeper Cen. Drug Store, Modesto, 1966-76; pres. Sargent & Coburn, Inc., Modesto, 1976-96, sec.-treas., v.p. Mem. Stanislaus Women's Ctr., NOW, San Francisco Mus. Soc., Modesto Women's Network, Stanislaus County Commn. for Women, Yerba Buena Art Ctr. Died Oct. 17, 1996.

SARICKS, AMBROSE, retired history educator; b. Wilkes-Barre, Pa., May 12, 1915; s. Ambrose and Barbara (Hauze) S.; m. Reese Pyott, Mar. 4, 1945 (dec. Mar. 1984); children: Christopher Lee, Alison Barbara; m. Margaret Byrne, Sept. 7, 1985. B.A., Bucknell U., 1937, M.A., 1941; Ph.D., U. Wis., 1950. Tchr. social studies Muncy Creek (Pa.) Pub. Schs., 1938-39; salesman Liberty Mut. Ins Co., Bklyn., 1939-40; grad. teaching asst. U. Wis., 1940-42, 46, instr. history, 1946; instr. history Ohio State U., Columbus, 1947-50; asst. prof. U. Kans., Lawrence, 1950-56, assoc. prof., 1956-62, prof., 1962-83, prof. emeritus, 1983-93, assoc. dean Grad. Sch., 1966-70, vice chancellor for acad. affairs, 1972-75; assoc. dean faculties, dean grad. sch. Wichita (Kans.) State U., 1970-72. Author: A Bibliography of the Frank E. Melvin Collection of Pamphlets of the French Revolution in the University of Kansas Libraries, 2 vols, 1960, Pierre Samuel DuPont de Nemours, 1965. Served with USAAF, 1942-46. Mem. Am. Hist. Assn., Soc. for French Hist. Studies, Soc. for 18th Century Studies, AAUP. Unitarian. Club: Kiwanian. Home: Lawrence Kans. Died Oct. 24, 1993.

SARNOFF, ROBERT W., television executive; b. N.Y.C., July 2, 1918; s. David Sarnoff and Lizett Hermant; m. Anna Moffo; children: Rosita, Serena Benenson, Claudia Parrot. B in Govt. and Philosophy, Harvard U., 1939; postgrad., Columbia Law Sch. Asst. to the pub. The Des Moines Register and Tribune, Look Mag.; account exec. sales dept. RCA, pres., 1965-67, chief. exec., 1967-70, chmn.; pres. NBC. With USN. Home: Manhattan N.Y. Died Feb. 22, 1997.

SARTON, MAY, author, poet; b. Wondelgem, Belgium, May 3, 1912; came to U.S., 1916, naturalized, 1924; d. George Alfred Leon and Eleanor Mabel (Elwes) Sarton. Grad., Cambridge High and Latin Sch., Brussels, 1929; Litt.D. (hon.), Russell Sage Coll., Troy, N.Y., 1959, Clark U., 1975, U. N.H., 1976, Bates Coll., 1976, Colby Coll., 1976, Thomas Starr King Sch. Ministry, 1976, U. Maine, 1981, Bowdoin Coll., 1983, Bucknell U., 1985, Providence (R.I.) Coll., 1989, Centenary Coll., 1990. Lectr. poetry U. Chgo., Harvard U., U. Iowa, Colo. Coll., Wellesley Coll., Beloit Coll., U. Kans., Denison U., others; Briggs-Copeland instr. composition Harvard U., 1950-52. Author: The Single Hound, 1938, The Bridge of Years, 1946, Shadow of a Man, 1950, A Shower of Summer Days, 1952, Faithful Are the Wounds, 1955, The Birth of a Grandfather, 1957, The Fur Person (fiction), 1957, The Small Room, 1961, Joanna and Ulysses, 1963, Mrs. Stevens Hears the Mermaids Singing, 1965, Miss Pickthorn and Mr. Hare, 1966, The Poet and the Donkey, 1969, Kinds of Love, 1970, Journal of a Solitude, 1973, As We Are Now, 1973, Punch's Secret, 1974, Crucial Conversations, 1975, A Walk Through the Woods, 1976, A Reckoning, 1978, Anger, 1982, The Magnificent Spinster, 1985, The Education of Harriet Hatfield, 1989; (poems) Encounter in April, 1937, Inner Landscape, 1939, The Lion and The Rose, 1948, The Leaves of the Tree, 1950, The Land of Silence, 1953, In Time Like Air, 1957, Cloud, Stone, Sun, Vine, 1961, A Private Mythology, 1966, As Does New Hampshire, 1967, A Grain of Mustard Seed, 1971, A Durable Fire, 1972, Collected Poems, 1974, Selected Poems of May Sarton, 1978, Halfway to Silence, 1980, A Winter Garland, 1982, Letters from Maine, 1984, The Phoenix Again, 1988, The Silence Now, 1988, Collected Poems, 1993, Coming Into Eighty, 1994; (autobiographies) I Knew a Phoenix, 1959, Plant Dreaming Deep, 1968, A World of Light, 1976, May Sarton: a Self Portrait, 1986, Honey in the Hive, 1988; (jours.) The House by the Sea, 1977, Recovering, 1980, After the Stroke, 1988, Endgame, 1992; (essays) Writings on Writing, 1981; (play) The Underground River: A Play in Three Acts, 1947; (anthology) Sarton Selected: An Anthology of Novels, Journals and Poetry, 1991; editor: Letters to May, 1986. Recipient Golden Rose award for poetry, 1945, Edward Bland Meml. prize Poetry Mag., 1945, Alexandrine medal Coll. St. Catherine, 1975, Deborah Morton award, Westbrook, 1981, Ministry to Women award Unitarian Universalist Women's Fedn., 1982, Avon/COCOA Pioneer Woman award, 1983, Fund for Human Dignity award, 1984, Human Rights award, 1985, Am. Book award, 1985, Maryann Hartman award U. Maine, 1986, N.E. Author award N.E. Booksellers Assn., 1990; Bryn Mawr fellow in poetry, 1953-54, Guggenheim Found. fellow, 1954-55; Nat. Found. Arts and Humanities grantee, 1967. Fellow Am. Acad. Arts and Scis.; mem. N.E. Poetry Soc., Poetry Soc. Am. (Reynolds lyric award 1953). Home: York Maine Died July 16, 1995.

SAUDEK, ROBERT, film, television producer; b. Pitts., Apr. 11, 1911; s. Victor and Fedora (Wolff) S.; m. Elizabeth Koch, Nov. 2, 1935; children: Richard H., Christopher D., Robert E., Mary Elizabeth Jaffee, Stephen Low. AB, Harvard U., 1932; postgrad., Duquesne U., 1935-38. Jr. exec. NBC-TV, N.Y.C., 1938-42; v.p. ABC-TV, N.Y.C., 1942-51; dir. TV workshop Ford Found., N.Y.C., 1951-57; pres. Robert Saudek & Assocs., N.Y.C., 1957-75, Museum Broadcasting, N.Y.C., 1975-81; chief motion picture and TV Libr. Congress, Washington, 1983-91, ret., 1991—; lectr. Harvard U., Cambridge, Mass., 1969-76. Exec. producer TV series Omnibus, 1952-61, Leonard Berskin and N.Y. Philharm., 1958-64, Profiles in Courage, 1964-65, and other series and Tv spls. Pres. Bronxville (N.Y.) Bd. Edn., 1950's. Recipient 11 Emmy awards, 4 Peabody awards U. Ga., Silver Gavel award ABA. Mem. Century Assn., Marlboro Music Assn. (bd. dirs., trustee), Harvard Club (N.Y.C.), New England Historic Film Soc., Boothbay Harbor (Maine) Yacht Club. Democrat. Episcopalian. DIED 03/13/97. .

SAUDER, ERIE JOSEPH, manufacturing executive; b. Archbold, Ohio, Aug. 6, 1904; s. Daniel D. and Anna (Schrock) S.; m. Leona Short, June 23, 1927 (dec. Nov. 1974); children: Delmar, Maynard, Myrl; m. Orlyss Alline Short, Feb. 1, 1976. PhD (hon.), Defiance (Ohio) Coll., 1985, North Tech. Coll., Archbold, 1987. Chmn. bd. Sauder Woodworking, Archbold; v.p., bd. dirs. F&M Bank; founder Sauder Farm & Craft Village. Trustee Defiance Coll.; overseer Goshen Coll; treas. Ohio-Eastern Mission Bd., 1978—; pres., bd. trustees Sunshine Children's Home, others. Home: PO Box 261 Archbold OH 43502-0261 Died June 15, 1997.

SAULSBURY, RUTH EVA, special education educator; b. Madison County, Miss., Mar. 26, 1920; d. Samuel Paul and Sarah Libby (Thomas) Johnson; m. Otis Samuel Saulsbury; children: Byron Henry, Nelda Kaye, Onwin Samuel. BS, Tougaloo Coll., 1944; MEd, DePaul U., 1981. Cert. tchr., Miss., Ill., Del., La. Tchr. Sts. Indsl. Sch., Lexington, Miss., 1944-46, Union Parish Sch., Farmerville, La., 1946-47, Dunbar High Sch, Chgo. Elem. Schs., 1948-50, Delena Day Elem., Chgo., 1963-65, Garfield Elem. Sch., Chicago Heights, Ill., 1965-81, Chipman Jr. High Sch., Harrington, Del., 1981-93; vol. tchr. So. Area Lit. Coun., Ill., 1994—. Adult Sun. Sch. tchr. Calvary Assembly of God, Dover, Del., 1985-91; Sunday sch. tchr. Evangelistic Crusaders Ch. of God in Christ, Chgo. Mem. ASCD, Coun. Exceptional Children, Smithsonian Assoc. Democrat. Pentecostal. Avocations: reading, flower gardening, fishing. Died July 1, 1996.

SAVAGE, HENRY, JR., lawyer, writer; b. Camden, S.C., Aug. 1, 1903; s. Henry and Helen (Alexander) S.; m. Elizabeth C. Anderson, Aug. 21, 1929 (dec. Apr. 1932); 1 child, William Henry; m. Elizabeth Clarke Jones, Oct. 7, 1933; children: Carroll J., Elizabeth Hope, Virginia B., Samuel P., Henry III, Helen A. BS, U. Va., 1926, LLB, 1926; LHD (hon.), U. S.C., 1976, Med. U. S.C., 1976. Bar: S.C. 1926. Practice law Camden, 1926-90; presently sr. ptnr. Savage, Royall, Kinard, Sheeheen & Byars, Camden; mayor City of Camden, 1948-58; tree farmer, 1928-90; bd. dirs. Companion Life Ins. Co. Author: America Goes Socialistic, 1934, River of the Carolinas: The Santee, 1956, Seeds of Time, The Background of Southern Thinking, 1959, Lost Heritage, Wilderness America as Seen Through the Eyes of Seven Pre-Audobon Naturalists, 1970, Discovering America 1700-1875, 1979, The Mysterious Carolina Bays, 1982; (with Elizabeth J. Savage) André and François Michaux, 1987. Former pres. S.C. Mcpl. Assn., S.C. Forestry Assn.; former trustee Med. U. S.C., Ashley Hall Sch. for Caroliniana Soc.; former v.p. Camden Hosp.; former dir., treas. Am. Forestry Assn.; former dir. S.C. Heritage Trust Bd.; former vice chmn. Carolina Cup Racing Assn. Recipient Charles H. Flory award for outstanding contbns. to forestry in S.C. and local community svc. awards, 1974, William B. Greely award Am. Forestry Assn., 1986; named Conservationist of the Yr. S.C. Wildlife Fedn., 1985; Henry Savage chair estab. in honor U. S.C. Sch. Pub. Health, 1985. Mem. Raven Soc., Phi Beta Kappa, Phi Delta Phi, Phi Sigma Kappa. Home: Camden S.C. Died Sept. 26, 1990.

SAVAGE, MANUEL D., lawyer; b. N.Y.C., Nov. 4, 1950. AB cum laude, Duke U., 1972; JD, U. Denver, 1976; LLM, NYU, 1978. Bar: N.Y. 1979, Colo. 1983. Jud. clk. to Hon. Charles Donaldson Idaho Supreme Ct., 1976-77; mem. Sherman & Howard, Denver; adj. prof. law U. Denver Coll. Law Grad. Tax Program, 1982—. Mem. N.Y. State Bar Assn., Order of St. Ives. Died May 13, 1997.

SAVAGE, WILLIAM WOODROW, education educator; b. Onley, Va., Jan. 9, 1914; s. Frank Howard and Florence Elmira (Twyford) S.; m. Margaret Jane Clarke; children—Earl R., William W. A.B., Coll. William and Mary, 1937; M.A., U. Chgo., 1946, Ph.D., 1955; student, U. Va., summer 1951. Research editor, div. rural research Fed. Emergency Relief Adminstrn., Richmond, Va., 1935-36; div. mgr. Montgomery Ward & Co., Newport News, Va., 1937-38; statis. worker WPA, Richmond, 1938-39; counselor Va. Consultation Service, Richmond, 1939-42; acting dir. Va. Consultation Service, 1942-45; asst. state supr. guidance and consultation services Va. Dept. Edn., 1946-47; dean Longwood Coll., Farmville, Va., 1947-52; project coordinator, asso. dir. Midwest Adminstrn. Center, U. Chgo., 1952-56; dean Coll. Edn., U. S.C., 1956-65, prof. edn., 1956-79; curator U. S.C. Mus. Edn., 1973-85. Author: Interpersonal and Group Relations, 1968; Coauthor: Readings in American Education, 1963; Editor: Work and Training, monthly Va. Bd. Edn, 1941-47, Administrator's Notebook, monthly Midwest Adminstrn. Center, 1954-56, U. S.C. Edn. Report, 1957-65, 67-85; adv. com.: Sch. Rev, 1954-56; Contbr. articles to jours. Mem. visitation and appraisal com. Nat. Coun. for Accreditation Tchr. Edn., 1964-67. Mem. S.C. Assn. Sch. Adminstrs., U. S.C. Soc., Wardlaw Club (pres. 1974-75), Order of White Jacket, Phi Delta Kappa. Methodist. Died May 20, 1997.

SAVELLI, ANGELO, artist; b. Pizzo Calabria, Italy, Oct. 30, 1911; came to U.S., 1954; s. Giorgio and Maria (Barone) S.; m. Elizabeth Fisher Friedman, Jan. 10, 1953; 1 stepdau., Ellen. Student, Ginnasio Vibo Valentia, C.Z., 1928, Maturitá Artistica Liceo Artistico, Rome, 1932; diploma, Acad. diBelle Arti, Rome, 1936. Prof. Liceo Artistico, Rome, 1940, 43, 48, 54; instr. New Sch. Social Research, 1959-65; assoc. prof. fine arts Grad. Sch. Fine Arts, U. Pa., 1960-70; vis. artist Cornell U., 1974, U. Tex.-Arlington, 1977-82. Exhibited one man shows, Galleria Roma, 1941, Galleria Cairola, Genoa, Italy, 1942, Galleria del Naviglio, Milan, Italy, 1947, 54, 61, Centre d'Art Itallienne, Paris, 1952, The Contemporaries, N.Y.C., 1955, Castelli Gallery, N.Y.C., 1958, Galleria del Cavallino, Venice, Italy, 1958, Tweed Mus., U. Minn., Duluth, 1960, Peter Deitsch Gallery, N.Y.C., 1962, Art Alliance, Phila., 1963, D'Arcy Galleries, N.Y.C., 1963, XXXII Internat. Biennale, Venice, 1964, Henri Gallery, Washington, 1969, Peale Gallery, Phila., 1969, Lorenzelli Arte, Milano, 1981, L'Arco Studio Internazionale d'Arte Grafica, Roma, 1981, Editalia, Roma, 1981, Gimpel-Hanover-Andre Emmerich Gallery, Zurich, 1981; group shows Quadriennale di Roma, 1943, 49, 60, Biennale of Venice, 1950, 52, 64, Castelli Gallery, Balt. Mus. Art Gallery, 1957, De Cordova Mus., Lincoln, Mass., 1963, White Chapel Gallery, London, 1963, Bklyn. Mus., 1957, 60, 62, 64, 66, Library of Congress, 1959, 63, 66, U.S.A. Cultural Exchange in 5 Russian Cities, 1963, Whitney Rev., 1965, Whitney Mus. Ann., 1966, Internat. Graphic Show, Yugoslavia, 1964, Janis Gallery, N.Y.C., 1964, Jewish Mus., N.Y.C., 1964, Internat. de Gravure, Tokyo, 1964, Mus. Modern Art, 1966, 67, Galleria Naz D'Arts Moderna, Rome, Museo Civico, Phila. Mus. Art, 1966, Everson Mus., Syracuse, N.Y., 1972, Tweed Mus., Duluth, 1973, Stout U. Art Gallery, Menomonie, 1973, Zoller Gallery Pa. State U., 1975, Hutchinson Gallery, N.Y.C., 1978, Parson-Dreyfuss Gallery, N.Y.C., 1978, Padiglione d'Arte Comtemporanea, Milano, 1984, Studio Bonifacio, Genova, 1986, Castello Murat, Pizzo Calabro, 1986, Pinacoteca Comunale, Arona, 1986, Art Coop. Palladio, Zurich, 1987, Studio Brazzani, 1987, Torino, Studio d'Ars, Milano, 1987; represented in permanent collections Torino, Italy, Mus. Modern Art, N.Y.C., Cin. Mus. Art, Tweed Mus., Chase Manhattan Bank, Nelson Rockefeller Collection, Arnold Maremont Collection, N.Y. Pub. Library, Art Mus., Helsinki, Finland, Victoria and Albert Mus., London, Phila. Mus. Art, Nat. Collection Fine Arts, Smithsonian Instn, Wichita (Kans.) Art Mus., Contemporary Art Mus. Milano, Contemporary Art Mus. Gibellina, Italy. Recipient Fellowship for study in Paris, 1948; recipient Grand Prize per L'Incisione XXXII Venice Biennale, 1964, Am. Acad. of Arts and Letters award, 1983, Silver trofy Cittá Della Magna Graecia, 1987; Guggenheim fellow, 1979-80; grant Pollock-Krasner, 1987. DIED 04/28/95. .

SAW MAUNG, Myanmar (formerly Burma) government official. Chmn. State Law and Order Restoration Coun., Yangon, Myanmar, 1988—; min. def. and fgn. affairs Govt. of Myanmar, Yangon, 1988—. Died July 24, 1997.

SAX, STANLEY PAUL, manufacturing company executive; b. Cin., Sept. 1, 1925; s. Ben Philip and Goldie (Quitman) S.; children: Steven Jay, David Jay; m. Patricia Moran Leach, June 14, 1970; children: Cathy, Carolyn. A.B., U. Wis., 1948. Researcher Market Research Co. Am., Chgo., 1942; instr. U. Wis., 1948; v.p., dir. Am. Buff Co., Detroit, 1948-57; exec. v.p., dir. Am. Buff Co., Chgo., 1957—; pres. Speedway Buff Co.; pres., chmn. bd., dir. J.J. Siefen Co., 1961—; chmn. bd., pres. Sax Abrasive Corp., 1961—, Sax Cal. Corp., 1962—, Klem Chem. Corp., 1963—, Stan Sax Corp., Seco Chems., Inc., 1965—; chmn. bd. Buckingham Products Co., McAleer Mfg. Co., 1968—, Sax Realty Investment Corp., 1967—, Globe Compound Corp., 1971—, Goodison Mfg. Co., 1972—, Ana, Inc., 1974—; partner S & D Leasing Co. Contbr. articles to profl. jours. Trustee Sax Family Found.; nat. trustee Balt. Mus. Art; bd. dirs. Met. Soc. Crippled Children and Adults. Served to lt. AUS, 1943-46; to lt. col. Res. 1946—. Recipient Wis. scholar award. Mem. Mil. Order World Wars, Metal Finishing Suppliers Assn. (trustee), Detroit C. of C., Detroit Inst. Arts (patron), Friends of Am. Wing (Founders Soc.), Friends of Henry Ford Mus., Pres.'s Soc., Am. Electroplaters Soc., Am. Soc. for Abrasives, Soc. Mil. Engrs., Young President's Orgn., World Presidents Orgn., Chief Execs. Orgn., Amateur Athletic Union, Soc. Die Casting Engrs., Res. Officers Assn., V.F.W., Wis. Alumni Assn., Winterhur Collectors Circle Mt. Vernon 100, Phi Beta Kappa, Alpha Phi Omega, Phi Kappa Phi, Psi Chi, Phi Eta Sigma. Clubs: Elk (Detroit), Rotarian. (Detroit), Economic (Detroit), Renaissance (Detroit); Recess, Army-Navy. Lender furnishings to diplomatic reception rooms, Nat. Portrait Gallery, Smithsonian Inst.; benefactor fine arts com. Dept. State. Died July 17, 1997.

SAYER, JOHN SAMUEL, retired information systems consultant; b. St. Paul, July 27, 1917; s. Arthur Samuel and Genevieve (Ollis) S.; m. Elizabeth Hughes, June 9, 1940; children: Stephen, Susan, Kathryn, Nancy. BSME, U. Minn., 1940. Registered profl. engr., Del. Sect. mgr. E.I. Du Pont de Nemours & Co, Wilmington, Del., 1940-60; exec. v.p. Documentation, Inc., Washington, 1960-63; v.p. corp. devel. Aurbach Corp., Phila., 1963-65; exec. v.p. Leasco Systems & Rsch., Bethesda, Md., 1966-70, Leasco Info. Products, Silver Spring, Md., 1971-74; pres. Remac Info. Corp., Gaithersburg, Md., 1975-82; cons. John Sayer Assocs., Gaithersburg, 1983-94, ret., 1994; numerous presentations in field. Contbr. numerous articles to profl. jours. Recipient Info. Product of Yr. award Info. Industries Assn., 1973. Mem. ASME, Assn. Info. and Image Mgmt., Am. Inst. Info. Sci. Achievements include direction of work leading to critical path method of planning and scheduling, technical word thesarus, microfiche, data base publishing. Died Dec. 14, 1997.

SCAFE, LINCOLN ROBERT, JR., sales executive; b. Cleve., July 28, 1922; s. Lincoln Robert and Charlotte (Hawkins) S.; student Cornell U., 1940-41; m. Mary Anne Wilkinson, Nov. 14, 1945; children—Amanda Katharine, Lincoln Robert III. Service mgr. Avery Engring. Co., Cleve., 1946-51; nat. service mgr. Trane Co., LaCrosse, Wis., 1951-57; service and installation mgr. Mech. Equipment Supply Co., Honolulu, 1957-58; chief engr. Sam P. Wallace of Pacific, Honolulu, 1958-62; pres. Air Conditioning Service Co., Inc., Honolulu, 1962-84; sales engr. G.J. Campbell & Assocs., Seattle, 1984-89. Served with USNR, 1942-45; PTO. Mem. ASHRAE, Alpha Delta Phi. Clubs: Cornell Hawaii (past pres.); Outrigger Canoe. Republican. Author tech. service lit. and parts manuals; contbr. articles to trade publs. Died Dec. 8, 1997.

SCAGGS, HOWARD IRWIN, savings and loan association executive, lawyer; b. Balt., July 4, 1921; s. Howard Irwin and Margaret Anna (Mitchell) S.; m. Grace Briscoe Brawner, Aug. 16, 1941; children—Howard Irwin III, Gordon B., Robert Mark. LL.B., U. Balt., 1941. Clk.-teller Am. Nat. Bldg. & Loan Assn., Balt., 1945-61; pres. Am. Nat. Bldg. & Loan Assn., 1961-81, chmn. bd., 1968-89, chmn. emeritus, 1989—; pvt. law practice, 1948-85; vice chmn., dir. Fed. Home Loan Bank, Atlanta, 1973-78; past mem. adv. council Fed. Home Loan Bank Bd., Washington. Mem. policy com., center for met. planning and research Johns Hopkins U.; Chmn. Commn. Forests and Parks Md., 1963-68; Chmn. bd. Neighborhood Housing Services Balt., Inc., 1974-78; mem. Balt. Conv. Center Com., Md. Gov.'s Salary Commn., Mayor's Adv. Council; chmn. bd. trustees Md. Acad. Sci., 1980-85, chmn. emeritus, 1985—. Served with AUS, 1943; served to lt. USNR, 1943-46. Mem. U.S. Savs. and Loan League (chmn. urban affairs com.), Md. Savs. and Loan Leagues (past dir.), Advt. Club Balt. (past pres.), C. of C. Met. Balt. (past dir.), Sigma Delta Kappa. Democrat. Episcopalian. Died June 26, 1996.

SCANLAN, JOHN JOSEPH, bishop; b. Ihiscarra, County Cork, Ireland, May 24, 1906; came to U.S., 1930; s. Peter Scanlan and Katherine Coleman. Student, Hallows Coll., Dublin, Ireland, 1923-30; LLD (hon.), Portland U., 1966; LHD (hon.), Chaminade U. Hawaii, 1980. Ordained priest Roman Cath. Ch., 1930. Asst. pastor Archiodese of San Francisco, 1930-50, pastor, 1950-54; aux. bishop Diocese of Honolulu, 1954-67, ordinary bishop, 1968-81, adminstr., 1981-82, ret., 1982; dir. archdiocesan coun. cath. men Archdiocese of San Francisco, 1952-54; mem.

Cath. Philosophic Assn., San Francisco, 1940-50. Mem. Nat. Coun. Cath. Bishops. Died Feb. 5, 1997.

SCHAAB, WILLIAM COLSON, lawyer; b. Wildwood, N.J., Dec. 28, 1927; s. William Louis and Lillian (Colson) S.; divorced; children: William Colson, Sarah, Susan; m. Judith C. Schaab. BA, Conn. Wesleyan U., 1949, MA, 1951; JD, Yale U., 1952. Bar: N.Y. 1954, N.Mex. 1956. Assoc., Cravath, Swaine & Moore, N.Y.C., 1952-56; assoc. Rodey, Dickason, Sloan, Akin & Robb P.A., Albuquerque, 1956-59, mem. firm, 1959-72, v.p., dir., 1972-96. Editorial bd. Yale Law Jour. Mem. ABA, Albuquerque Bar Assn., Phi Beta Kappa. Democrat. Episcopalian. Contbr. articles to profl. jours. Died Feb. 20, 1996.

SCHAAF, JAMES LEWIS, church history educator, registrar; b. Sharon, Pa., July 28, 1932; s. Lewis Christian and Helen Louise (Weimer) Schaaf; m. Phyllis Ann Reeck, Sept. 13, 1959; children: Karen Elizabeth, Susan Ann. BA, Capital U., 1954, BD, 1958; ThD, Universität Heidelberg, Germany, 1961. Instr. Trinity Luth. Sem., Columbus, Ohio, 1961-62; prof. ch. history Trinity Luth. Sem., Columbus, 1965—; pastor St. John Luth. Ch., Ottawa, Ontario, Can., 1962-65; registrar Trinity Luth. Sem., Columbus, 1988—. Mem. Am. Soc. Ch. Hist., Am. Assn. Collegiate Registrars and Admissions Officers, Am. Translators Assn., Luth. Hist. Conf. (treas. 1972-78, newsletter editor 1978—, membership sec. 1982—, v.p. 1990—). Republican. Lutheran. Died Nov. 30, 1996.

SCHACHTER, STANLEY, psychology educator; b. N.Y.C., Apr. 15, 1922; s. Nathan and Anna (Fruchter) S.; m. Sophia Thalia Duckworth, June 2, 1967; 1 child, Elijah. BS, Yale U., 1942, MA, 1944; postgrad., MIT, 1946-48; PhD, U. Mich., 1949. From asst. prof. to prof. U. Minn., Mpls., 1949-61; Niven prof. psychology Columbia U., N.Y.C., 1961—; dir. research Orgn. for Comparative Social Research, Amsterdam, The Netherlands, 1952-54; vis. prof. U. Amsterdam, 1952-53, Stanford (Calif.) U., 1960. Author: (with others) Social Pressure Informal Groups, 1950, (with others) When Prophecy Fails, 1956, Psychology of Affiliation, 1959 (AAAS award 1959), Emotion, Obesity and Crime, 1971, (with others) Obese Humans and Rats, 1980; editor (with others): Extending Psychological Frontiers, 1989. Sgt. USAF, 1944-46. Fulbright fellow, 1952, Guggenheim fellow, 1967, Cattell Found. fellow, 1974; hon. research fellow U. London, 1975. Fellow Am. Psychol. Assn. (Disting. Scientific Contbr. award 1969), AAAS (Socio-Psychol. prize 1959), Am. Acad. Art and Scis., Nat. Acad. Sci., Soc. Exptl. Social Psychology (Disting. Scientist award 1984); mem. Cognitive Neurosci. Inst. (bd. dirs. 1980—), Internat. Soc. Emotion (bd. dirs. 1980—), Commn. Behavioral and Social Scis., Century Club (N.Y.C.). Jewish. Club: Century (N.Y.C.). Home: 175 Riverside Dr New York NY 10024-1616 DIED 06/07/97. .

SCHAEFER, GEORGE, obstetrician-gynecologist, consultant; b. N.Y.C., May 30, 1913. MD, Cornell U., 1937. Intern Jewish Hosp., N.Y.C., 1937-38; resident ob-gyn. Sea View Hosp., 1938-40; ob-gyn. Mercy Hosp. Med. Ctr., San Diego; prof. emeritus ob-gyn. Cornell U. Fellow ACS; mem. ACOG. Home: La Mesa Calif. Died Sept. 27, 1997.

SCHAEFER, GEORGE LOUIS, theatrical producer and director, educator; b. Wallingford, Conn., Dec. 16, 1920; s. Louis and Elsie (Otterbein) S.; m. Mildred Trares, Feb. 5, 1954. BA magna cum laude, Lafayette Coll., 1941, LittD, 1963; postgrad., Yale Drama Sch., 1942; LHD, Coker Coll., 1973. Producer, dir. TV series Hallmark Hall of Fame, 1955-68; freelance producer, dir., 1945—; assoc. dean sch. theater, film and TV UCLA, 1986-91; artistic dir. N.Y.C. Ctr. Theatre Co., 1949-52; dir. Dallas State Fair Musicals, 1952-58; pres. Compass Prodns., Inc., 1959-86. Dir. Broadway prodns. G.I. Hamlet, 1945, Man and Superman, 1947, The Linden Tree, 1948, The Heiress (revival), 1949, Idiot's Delight (revival), 1950, Southwest Corner, 1955, The Apple Cart, 1956, The Body Beautiful, 1958, Write Me a Murder, 1961, The Great Indoors, 1966, The Last of Mrs. Lincoln, 1972, Mixed Couples, 1980; co-prodr. Broadway and London prodns. The Teahouse of the August Moon, 1953; dir., co-prodr. Zenda for L.A. Civic Light Opera Co., 1963; prodr. To Broadway with Love for N.Y. World's Fair, 1964; prodr., dir. TV spls. Do Not Go Gentle Into That Good Night, 1967, A War of Children, Sandburg's Lincoln, 1974-76, In This House of Brede, 1975, Truman at Potsdam, Amelia Earhart, 1976, Our Town, 1977, First You Cry, Orchard Children, 1978, Blind Ambition, Mayflower, 1979, The Bunker, 1981, Jean Harris Trial, 1982, A Piano for Mrs. Cimino, 1982, Deadly Game, 1983, Answers, 1983, Right of Way, 1983, Children in the Crossfire, 1984, Stone Pillow, 1985, Mrs. Delafield Wants to Marry, 1986, Laura Lansing Slept Here, 1988, Let Me Hear You Whisper, 1990, The Man Upstairs, 1992, Harvey, 1996; dir. films An Enemy of the People, Generation, Doctor's Wives, Pendulum, Macbeth, dir. L.A. prodn. Leave It To Jane, 1987; author: From Live to Tape to Film, 1996. Mem. Nat. Council on the Arts, 1983-88. Recipient Emmy awards, 1959, 60, 61, 68, 73, Dirs. Guild Am. TV awards, 1961, 64, 67, 68, Dinneen award Nat. Cath. Theatre Conf., 1964; named Dir. of Yr., Radio-TV Daily, 1957, 60, 63, 65; Am. Theatre fellow, 1995. Mem. Dirs. Guild Am. (v.p. 1961-79, pres. 1979-81), Phi Beta Kappa. Died Sept. 10, 1997.

SCHAFER, FAY TILLMAN, farmer, association executive; b. Jadwin, Mo., Dec. 10, 1920; s. William Orville and Allie Gertrude (McDonald) S.; m. Peggy Marie Judd, July 19, 1947; children: Marsha Ann, Joan Lea. Grad. high sch., Salem, Mo. Farm owner Salem; pres., v.p. Sho-Me Power Corp., Marshfield, Mo., 1977—; v.p. Rural Electric Coop. Assn., Licking, Mo., 1966—; v.p., bd. dirs. Intercounty Electric Coop., Licking, 1966—; com. chmn. Agrl. Stabilization & Conservation Service, Salem, 20 yrs., mem. county com., 1958-73; mgr. Dent County (Mo.) Coop. Feeder Pig Sales, Salem, 1958-73. Mem. Dist. Sch. Bd. Salem, 1956-62; leader 4-H Club, 1962-67; bd. dirs. Indsl. Bd. Dent County, 1979-83, Dent County Health Ctr., 1972—, Dent County Mut. Ins. Bd., Salem OEO; chmn. Dent County Welfare Commn., 1975-83; chmn., bd. dirs. ABC Meml. Cemetery Orgn., Salem, 1977—; adv. com. B.O. Brown Agriculture Scholarship Fund. Served with M.C. and M.P. U.S. Army, 1943-46. Recipient Univ. Extension Service award, 1962, Future Farmers Am. award, 1966, Farm Family Mgmt. award, 1974, Dent County Citizenship award, Forestry Tree Farm System award, 1972. Mem. Mo. Farmers Assn., Dent County Livestock Assn. (bd. dirs. 1952-77). Democrat. Mem. Ch. of Christ. Lodge: Odd Fellows (officer 1956-81). Fay Schafer scholarship initiated in 1987 to enable Future Farmers Am. students (3 per yr.) to attend Washington Conf. Program for development of leader confidence and skills. Home: HC 81 Box 72 Salem MO 65560-8519 Died Aug. 5, 1997.

SCHAFLER, SAMUEL, academic administrator; b. N.Y.C., Feb. 20, 1929; s. Benjamin Moses and Ethel (Schnapp) S.; m. Sara R. Edell, Sept. 4, 1951; children: Eilel, Gila, Daniel, Seth, Perry, Rena. BS, CCNY, 1950; M in Hebrew Lit., Jewish Theol. Sem., 1952, DHL, 1973, DDiv, 1983. Ordained rabbi Jewish Ch., 1952. Assoc. dir. dept. edn. United Synagogue of Am., N.Y.C., 1955-61; rabbi Temple Gates of Prater, Flushing, N.Y., 1961-76; supt. Chgo. Bd. of Jewish Edn., 1976-87; pres. Hebrew Coll., Brookline, Mass., 1987—; adj. asst. prof. Jewish history Queens (N.Y.) City Coll., 1974-75; fellow in community planning N.Y.C. Bd. Jewish Edn., 1974-86. Book rev. editor Jewish Edn. mag., 1982—. Bd. dirs. Ramah Israel Community Program, 1968-76; ednl. dir. Camp Ramah in the Berkshires, 1964-67. Avocations: architecture, military history.

SCHAPIRO, MORRIS A., investment banker; b. Lithuania, Apr. 9, 1903; came to U.S., 1907, naturalized, 1914; s. Nathan M. and Fanny (Adelman) S.; m. Alma Binion Cahn, Mar. 28, 1929; children: Linda S. Collins, Daniel E. BA, Columbia U., 1923, Engr. Mines, 1925, LLD (hon.), 1987. Engr. geologist Am. Metal Co., 1925-27; bank analyst Hoit, Rose & Troster, 1928-31; ptnr. Monahan, Schapiro & Co., 1931-39; chmn. bd. dirs., CEO M.A. Schapiro & Co., Inc., N.Y.C., 1939—; pres. SD Securities, N.Y.C., 1944—; chmn. adv. com. N.Y. State Joint Legis. Com. to Revise Banking Law, 1957-60. Contbr. articles on banking to profl. jours. Mem. Am. Inst. Mining and Metall. Engrs., N.Y. Soc. Security Analysts, Securities Industry Assn. Died Dec. 23, 1996.

SCHATZ, ARTHUR HERSCHEL, lawyer; b. Hartford, Conn., Dec. 31, 1918; s. Nathan A. and Dora (Goldberg) S.; m. Cecil Ruskay, Feb. 11, 1945; children: Ellen Levine, Robert F., Daniel N. A.B., Cornell U., 1940, J.D., 1942. Bar: Conn. 1942, Fed. Ct 1946. Sr. partner Schatz & Schatz, Hartford, 1945-78, Schatz & Schatz, Ribicoff & Kotkin, Hartford, 1978-87; trial counsel, cons. in forensic sci.; lectr. Cornell Law Sch., 1959-72, U. Conn., 1959-72, New Eng. Law Inst., 1960-76; faculty Law Sci. Inst., U. Tex.; del. Internat. Congress on Forensic Sci., 1960, 63, 66, 69, 72, 75, 78; v.p., gen. counsel, 1975-78; del. Congress Internat. Assn. Traffic Accident Medicine, 1963, 66, 69, 72, 75; mem. Conn. Commn. on Medicolegal Investigations, 1969-85, vice chmn., 1972-79. Mem. council Cornell U., 1970-77; trustee Forensic Sci. Found., 1969-72, Law-Sci. Found Am.; trustee, v.p., gen. counsel Internat. Reference Orgn. in Forensic Medicine, 1969-87. Fellow Am. Acad. Forensic Scis. (chmn. jurisprudence sect., mem. exec. council 1959-71, sec.-treas. 1969-71); mem. Brit. Acad. Forensic Scis., Am. Assn. Automotive Medicine, Cornell Law Assn. (exec. com. 1958-62), Am., Conn., Hartford County bar assns., New Eng. Law Inst. (exec. com. 1960-76), Soc. Med. Jurisprudence. Died May 3, 1997.

SCHAUMBERG, WILLIAM LLOYD, retired banker; b. Lincoln, Nebr., May 4, 1923; s. Edward George and Claire Elizabeth (Barentsen) S.; m. Patricia Louise Ward, Sept. 4, 1948; children: DeeAnn, William Ward, Denise Lynn, Kirstin. B.S., U. Nebr., 1947, LL.B., 1949. Bar: Nebr. 1949, Oreg. 1953. Dep. county atty. Lancaster County, Nebr., 1949-51; v.p. 1st Nat. Bank of Oreg., 1952-69, Columbia Mgmt. Co., Portland, Oreg., 1970-73; exec. v.p., mgr. capital mgmt. div. Rainier Nat. Bank, Seattle, 1973-87; dir. Pacific Coast Depository Trust, San Francisco, 1980-88, Pacific Clearing Corp., L.A., 1985-88, BHC Corp., Phila., 1985-88. Bd. dirs. Willamette Valley Camp Fire Girls, 1955-62, pres., 1960-61; bd. dirs. Ind. Colls. Wash.; bd. dirs. Multnomah County chpt. Nat. Found. March of Dimes, 1963-70, pres. Multnomah County chpt., 1968; bd. visitors Puget Sound U.; mem. Trustees Assn. Wash., pres., 1975, 84; mem. adv. com. Fred Hutchinson Cancer Research Ctr., 1983-87. Served with U.S. Army, 1943-46, 51-52. Recipient Gullick award Nat. Campfire Girls, 1961. Mem. Seattle Estate Planning Council, Assn. Corp. Trustees Wash., Beta Theta Pi. Republican. Episcopalian. Clubs: Broadmoor Golf, D'Anza Country. Died June 23, 1997.

SCHECKNER, SY, former greeting card company executive; b. N.Y.C., Aug. 8, 1924; s. Morris and Bella S.; m. Georgene W. Carrigan, Aug. 17, 1974; children: Barry David, Michael Matthew, Jeri Bella,. Student, CCNY, U. Pitts., U. Ill. Sr. v.p., dir. Papercraft Corp., Pitts, 1956-75, Am. Greetings Corp., Cleve., 1975-85; pres. Knomark, Inc., Plus Mark, Inc.; gen. ptnr. Doubletree Investments. Vice chmn. bd. trustees Tusculum Coll., Greeneville, Tenn. Served with U.S. Army, 1942-45. Decorated Purple Heart. DIED 07/19/97. .

SCHEFFER, ROBERT PAUL, botany educator; b. Newton, N.C., Jan. 26, 1920; s. Paul and Mary Alice (Shuford) S.; m. Beulah J. Spoolman, June 12, 1952; children: Thomas J., Mary Karen. BS, N.C. State U., 1947, MS, 1949; PhD, U. Wis., 1952. Rsch. assoc. U. Wis., Madison, 1952-53; asst. prof. botany and plant pathology Mich. State U., East Lansing, 1953-58, assoc. prof., 1958-63, prof., 1968—; rsch. assoc. Rockefeller U., N.Y.C., 1960-61; prof. emeritus Mich. State U., East Lansing, 1988; cons./panel mem. NSF, Washington, 1963-66. Assoc. editor: Phytopathology, 1965-68 (fellow 1979), Plant Physiology, 1980-88; contbr. over 150 articles to sci. jours. With USAAF, 1941-45. Named Disting. Prof. Mich. State U., 1985. Fellow Am. Phytopathol. Soc. (bd. dirs. APS Press 1975-78, counselor 1965-68), Explorer's Club; mem. Am. Soc. Plant Physiologists (assoc. editor 1980-87). Avocations: travel, reading, gardening, photography. Died April 24, 1996.

SCHERBER, CATHERINE A. (KIT SCHERBER), state legislator, trainer persons with disabilities; b. St. Cloud, Minn., Feb. 18, 1947; d. John J. and Delphine (Danzl) Watercott; m. Kenneth Paul Scherber, July 19, 1969; children: Dzul, Charles. BA in English, St. Cloud State U., 1969. State rep. N.D. State Legislature, Bismarck, 1986—. Vol. U.S. Peace Corps, Malaysia, 1971-73; v.p. Lake Agassiz Habitat for Humanity, Fargo, N.D., 1992—. Named Woman of Yr., Fargo Moorhead YWCA, 1980, Legislator of Yr., N.D. Children's Caucus, 1989, Citizen of Yr., N.D. Assn. Social Workers, 1991; recipient Ruth Meiers award N.D. Mental Health Assn., 1990, N.D. Martin Luther King Jr. award N.D. Holiday Commn. for the Martin Luther King Jr. Holiday, 1992. Mem. LWV (pres. Fargo area 1981-83), Gate City Toastmasters (v.p. membership, pres. 1992—, ATM award 1992). Democrat. Roman Catholic. Avocations: reading, golf. Home: Fargo N.D. DIED 11/12/95. .

SCHEWEL, STANFORD, lawyer; b. Lynchburg, Va., June 1, 1918; s. Abraham M. and Anna R. (Temko) S. LL.B., Washington and Lee U., 1940. Bar: Va. bar 1939, N.Y. bar 1947. Atty. O.P.A., Washington, 1941-42; asso. firm Davis, Polk, Wardwell, Sunderland & Kiendl, N.Y.C., 1940, 46-50; with Neil P. Cullom, 1950-56; practiced in N.Y.C., 1956—; Vice consul, econ. analyst U.S. Diplomatic Service; financial attaché U.S. Consulate Gen., Amsterdam, The Netherlands, 1945-46; cons. Hoover Commn., 1948. Author: The Development of Governmental Powers in the United States, 1948. Trustee Bar Harbor Music Festival, Va., Center for Creative Arts. Served as cpl. AUS, 1941; with 1942-45, OSS, Egypt, Ethiopia, Palestine. Clubs: Harmonie (N.Y.C.) (gov.), City (N.Y.C.). Home: New York N.Y. DIED 10/00/94. .

SCHIEDER, JOSEPH EUGENE, clergyman; b. Buffalo, Sept. 23, 1908; s. Robert and Mary Loretta (Quinn) S. B.A., Niagara U., 1931; M.A., St. Bonaventure U., 1935; Ph.D., U. Ottawa, Ont., Can., 1943; LL.D., St. Vincent's Coll., 1951; Litt.D. (hon.), Seaton Hall U., 1954; L.H.D. (hon.), LaSalle Coll., 1956, Canisius Coll., 1986; D. in Pedagogy, Niagara U., 1987, Doctor (hon.). Ordained priest Roman Catholic Ch., 1935; dir. Youth Retreats Diocese of Buffalo, 1939-48; diocesan dir. Confraternity of Christian Doctrine, Buffalo, 1941-48; dir. youth bur. Buffalo Police Dept., 1942-48; nat. dir. Cath. Youth Am., Washington, 1948-61; also dir. youth dept. Nat. Cath. Welfare Conf., Washington; apptd. Papal Chamberlain, 1950, Domestic Prelate, 1953, Prothonatary Apostolic, 1968; pastor St. Andrew's Ch., Buffalo, 1963-76; founder, 1st dir. St. Andrew's Montessori Sch., 1973; mem. Mental Health Bd., 1968—; dean theology Marymount Coll., Arlington, Va., 1961-63; diocesan consultor, 1969—; regional coordinator Diocese of Buffalo, procurator diocesan properties, 1977—; founder Nat. Cath. Youth Week; chmn. Permanent Com. Pub. Decency, Buffalo, 1941-48; diocesan dir. financial drive Diocese of Buffalo, 1971; mem. White House Conf. Children and Youth, 1950; adviser on Youth Spl. Mission to Germany USAF, 1952; Spl. Mission to Tokyo, Japan for UNESCO, 1953; adviser on youth U.S. Sec. Labor, 1951-60; adviser on fitness of youth to Pres. Eisenhower, 1955-60; chmn. task force founding Stella Niagara Ednl.

Parks, Niagara Falls, N.Y.; mem. exec. bd. Cantalician Center, Buffalo; mem. adv. bd. ARC, Kenmore Mercy Hosp. Author: Talks to Parents, 1954, Spiritual Lifts for Youth, 1956; Editor of: Youth mag, 1949-61. Mem. ho. of dels. United Way, 1973—, vice chmn., 1975; bd. dirs. Oral Sch., Ft. Lauderdale, Fla., 1977; vice chmn. Bicentennial Celebration; bd. trustees Erie County Library Assn., 1979—; bd. fin. Diocese of Buffalo, 1979—; chmn. Buffalo div. Christian Bros. Tricentennial World Anniversary, 1981; Founder, past bd. dirs. various Cath. youth assns.; bd. founders St. Andrew's Country Day Sch.; chmn. Drug Abuse Program, Ft. Lauderdale, Fla., 1981—; mem. adv. bd. Project Korle Bu Accra Ghana, West Africa, 1983. Served as adviser to Cath. chief chaplain USAF, 1953; chief chaplain AUS, 1954. Recipient award Christian Bros., 1947, award Mayor of Rome, Italy, 1950, Archdiocese award Hartford, Conn., 1954, De la Salle medal Manhattan Coll., 1958, Padre Youth award for U.S., 1961, Star Solidarity from Pres. Italy, 1969, Bishop McNulty Meml. award, 1973, Pres.'s medal St. John's Coll., Washington, 1973; also awards dioceses Charleston, S.C.; also awards dioceses Wichita, Kans.; Man of Yr. award Town of Tonawanda, 1977; award for prestigious service Buffalo Fire Dept., 1980; 1st recipient Signum Fidei Outstanding Alumni award St. Joseph's Collegiate Inst., 1984; Spl. Gift award for outstanding service to Diocese of Buffalo, 1986; Outstanding Service to Diocese of Buffalo citation Office Bishop of Buffalo, Oustanding Assistance and Help citation United Cerebral Palsy Assn., 1987; named Man of Yr., Marian Guild St. Andrew's Ch., Kenmore, N.Y. Clubs: University (Washington); Niagara Falls Country; Park Country (Buffalo), Saturn (Buffalo); Amherst (N.Y.) Country; Tower (Ft. Lauderdale, Fla.). Lodge: K.C. (4th deg.). Died June 12, 1996.

SCHIFF, SHELDON KIRSNER, psychiatrist; b. Bklyn., Sept. 29, 1931; s. Albert and Judith (Kirsner) S.; m. Louise Antoinette Latsis, June 29, 1957; 1child, Nicholas. BA, NYU, 1952; MD, U. Chgo., 1956. Diplomate Am. Bd. Neurology and Psychiatry (examiner 1969), Nat. Bd. Med. Examiners, Pan Am. Med. Assn. Intern Kings County Hosp., Bklyn., 1956-57; psychiat. resident Yale U. Sch. Medicine, New Haven, 1957-60, instr. psychiatry, 1962-63; chief psychiat. resident Grace-New Haven Hosp., 1959-60; Div. Psych. U.S. Army, Bad Kreuznach, Germany, 1960-62; asst. prof. psychiatry U. Ill. Sch. Medicine, Chgo., 1963-66; assoc. prof. psychiatry U. Chgo., 1967-71; practice medicine specializing in psychiatry Chgo., 1971-98; mental health instr. City New Haven Police Dept., 1959; co-founder and co-founder Woodlawn Metal Health Ctr., Chgo, 1963-70; examiner N.Y. State Dept. Mental Hygiene, 1970; pres. Children's Ctr. Learning Capacities, Chgo., 1970-98; dir. sch. intervention and tng. program dept. pyschiatry Chgo. Med. Sch., 1970-71, clin. prof. psychiatry, 1974-76; chief of psychiatry Downey (Ill.) VA Hosp., 1973-98; cons. in field. Contbr. articles to profl. jours. Mem. Woodlawn Urban Progress Ctr. Adv. Bd., City of Chgo. Com. Urban Opportunity, 1964, Greater Chgo. Com. Rehab. Welfare Council Met. Chgo., 1964-66; mem. systems analysis com. Ill. Mental Health Planning Bd., Ill. State Dept. Mental Health, 1966-67; adv. health com. City of Chgo. Commn. Human Relations, 1966-70; chmn. Service Agys. Council on Woodlawn, 1967-69. Served to capt. USMC, 1960-62. Grantee Ill. State Dept. Mental Health, 1964-65, Research Authority, 1965-68, NIMH, 1966-70, van Amerigen Found., 1968-69, Wieboldt Found., 1968-69, Field Found., 1968-69, Maurice Falk Med. Fund, 1968-69, 70, Iowa State Mental Health Authority, 1971. Fellow Am. Psychiat. Assn. (sec. task force on poverty 1968-70), Am. Orthopsychiat. Assn. (mem. com. community mental health ctrs. 1967-71, children's mental health services com. 1968-70), Am. Pub. Health Assn.; mem. AAUP (pres. U. Chgo. chpt. 1967-70, com. accrediting colls. and univs. 1969-71, ad hoc investigating com. U. Fla. 1969), Am. Acad. Polit. and Social Sci., Am. Ednl. Research Assn., Am. Sch. Health Assn., NY. Acad. Sci., Organisation Mondiale pour l'Education Prescholaire, U.S. Nat. Com. Early Childhood Edn., World Fedn. Mental Health, Phi Chi. Home: Chicago Ill. Died March 11, 1998; interred Evergreen Cemetery, Chicago, IL.

SCHIFF, STEVEN HARVEY, congressman, lawyer; b. Chicago, Ill., Mar. 18, 1947; s. Alan Jerome and Helen M. (Ripper) S.; m. Marcia Lewis, Nov. 8, 1968; children: Jaimi, Daniel. BA, U. Ill., Chgo., 1968; JD, U. N.Mex., 1972. Bar: N.Mex. 1972, U.S. Dist. Ct. N.Mex. 1972, U.S. Ct. Appeals (10th cir.) 1980. Asst. dist. atty. Dist. Atty.'s Office, Albuquerque, 1972-77, sole practice, 1977-79; asst. city atty. City of Albuquerque, 1979-81; dist. atty. State of N.Mex., Albuquerque, 1981-89; mem. 101st-104th Congresses from 1st N.Mex. dist., Washington, D.C., 1989—; mem. govt. reform & oversight com. U.S. House of Reps., mem. judiciary com. and standards of ofcl. conduct com., chmn. sci. subcom. on basic rsch.; lectr. U. N.Mex., Albuquerque, 1981—. Chmn. Bernalillo County Rep. Party Conv., Albuquerque, 1984, 87, staff judge adv. N.Mex. Air N.G. Col. JAGC, USAFR. Recipient Law Enforcement Commendation medal SR, 1984. Mem. ABA, Albuquerque Bar Assn., N.Mex. Bar Assn. Republican. Jewish. Club: Civitan. Lodge: B'nai Brith (pres. 1976-78). Died March, 1998.

SCHILLER, ALFRED GEORGE, veterinarian, educator; b. Irma, Wis., Dec. 5, 1918; s. Adam and Bertha Schiller; m. Carolyn Capps, Apr. 14, 1944; children: James, Charles. DVM, Mich. State U., 1943; MS, U. Ill., 1956. Bd. cert. vet. surgery. Gen. practice vet. medicine Mpls., 1947-52; from instr. to prof. U. Ill., Urbana, 1952-87, head small animal clinic, 1954-74, asst. head dept. vet. medicine, 1974-76, acting dept. head vet. medicine, 1976-78, acting assoc. dean acad. affairs, 1978-79, acting dir. lab. animal care, 1979-80, asst. dept. head vet. clin. medicine, from 1980, prof. emeritus, 1987-96. Contbr. articles to profl. jours. Served to capt. U.S. Army, 1944-47. Recipient Alumni award Mich. State U., 1978. Mem. Am. Vet. Medicine Assn. (various coms.), Ill. State Vet. Medicine Assn. (various coms., Meritorious Svc. award 1972), Am. Coll. Vet. Surgeons (recorder 1968-69, v.p. 1970-71, pres.-elect 1971-72, pres. 1972-73, chmn. 1973-74, exec. sec. 1975-90, Disting. Svc. award 1985). Home: Champaign Ill. Died July 4, 1996.

SCHILLING, CHARLES HENRY, army officer, civil engineer; b. Louisville, June 3, 1918; s. Henry M. and Caroline (Ravenscroft) S.; m. Martha Hunter Wall, Sept. 2, 1945; children: Carolyn Hunter, Charles Henry, Mary Kathryn, Stephen Thomas, Robert Herschel. B.S., U.S. Mil. Acad., 1941; M.S. in Civil Engring, U. Calif., Berkeley, 1947; Ph.D., Rensselaer Poly. Inst., 1959. Registered profl. engr., N.Y., Tenn., Ky., Ind., Ala. Commd. 2d lt. U.S. Army, 1941, advanced through grades to brig. gen.; served with engr. troops, 1941-43; bn. comdr. 284th Engr. Bn., 1943-44, 165th Engr. Combat Bn., XV Corps, ETO, 1944-45, 831st and 862d Engr. Aviation Bns., Germany, 1947-50; instr., then asso. prof. mil. art and engring. U.S. Mil. Acad., 1951-55; area engr. Iceland, 1955-56; prof. mil. art and engring., 1956-69, head dept., 1963-69, prof. engring., head dept., 1969-80, chmn. acad. computer com., 1960-80, mem. chapel bd., 1962-63, 69-80, ret., 1980; civil engr. Allen & Hoshall Engrs., 1981-83, R.W. Beck Engrs., 1987—; modern engring participant UCLA, summer 1963; vis. prof. chem. and metall. engring. U. Mich., summer 1965; vis. prof. Inst. Stats. and Dynamics, U. Stuttgart, Fed. Republic Germany, 1968-69; mem. computer graphics task force, waterways expt. sta. C.E., 1974-75. Co-author: Application of Matrix Methods, in Structural Theory, 1969; contbg. author: History of Public Works in the United States, 1974; contbr. to encys. Pres. bd. edn. West Point elementary schs., 1960-63. Decorated D.S.M., Legion of Merit, Bronze Star, Croix de Guerre with silver star France). Fellow Soc. Am. Mil. Engrs.; mem. NSPE, ASCE, Am. Soc. Engring. Edn. (computers in edn. div.), Assn. Grads. U.S. Mil. Acad. (trustee 1959-62), Tech. Council on Computer Practices (com. on state-of-art computer tech.), ASCE (chmn. subcom. on computer graphics 1973-80), Sigma Xi, Phi Kappa Phi. Died Nov. 5, 1996.

SCHIRMER, HENRY WILLIAM, architect; b. St. Joseph, Mo., Dec. 8, 1922; s. Henry William and Asta (Hansen) S.; m. Jane Irene Krueger; children: Andrew Lewis, Monica Sue, Daniel F. Carr. AS, St. Joseph Jr. Coll., 1942; BArch Design, U. Mich., 1949. Staff architect Eugene Meier, Architect, St. Joseph, 1939, Neville, Sharp & Simon, Kansas City, Mo., 1946, 49, Ramey & Himes, Wichita, Kans., 1950-57; ptnr. Schaefer & Schirmer, Wichita, 1957-60, Schaefer, Schirmer & Eflin, Wichita, 1960-72, Schaefer, Schirmer & Assocs. P.A., Wichita, 1972-76; prin. Henry W. Schirmer, Topeka, 1976-92, Green Valley, 1993-96. Editor: Profile Ofcl. Directory of AIA, 1978, 80, 83, 85, 87, 89-90, 91-92, pub., 1985-92; contbr. AIA Handbook; works include Burn Ctr. U. Kans. Med. Ctr., Allen County Community Jr. Coll., Iola, Kans., Rainbow Mental Health Ctr., Kansas City, Kans., Capitol Area Plaza Project, Topeka. Pres. East Br. YMCA, 1954-96; bd. dirs. Wichita YMCA, 1956-73, San Ignacio Heights Home Owners Assn., 1995-96. With C.E. U.S. Army, ETO. Decorated Purple Heart. Fellow AIA (past pres. Kans. chpt., seminar leader, chmn. nat. com. office mgmt.1976, nat. bd. dirs. 1979-81, treas. 1982-86, fin. com. 1988, nat. documents com. 1978, chmn. nat. com. on project mgmt. 1977, Edward C. Kemper medal 1990); mem. Kans. Bd. Tech. Professions (chmn. bd. 1985, 87), Nat. Coun. Archtl. Registration Bds. (profl. conduct com. 1986-89, procedures and documents com. 1990), Tau Sigma Delta. Lutheran. Died June 16, 1996.

SCHLAIFER, CHARLES, advertising executive; b. Omaha, July 1, 1909; s. Abraham Schlaifer; m. Evelyn Chaikin, June 10, 1934 (dec. Oct. 1978); children: Arlene Lois Silk, Roberta Semer; m. Ann Mesavage, July 31, 1980. Privately ed.; LittD (hon.), John F. Kennedy Coll., 1969. Newspaper reporter Omaha, 1926-29; advt. dir. Publix Tri-States Theatres, Nebr., Iowa, 1929-37; mng. dir. United Artists Theatres, San Francisco, 1937-42; nat. advt. cons. United Artists Prodrs., 1937-42; nat. advt. mgr. 20th Century-Fox Film Corp., N.Y.C., 1942-45; v.p. charge advt. and pub. rels. 20th Century-Fox Film Corp., 1945-49; pres. Charles Schlaifer & Co., Inc., N.Y.C., 1949—; vis. prof. New Sch. Social Rsch.; expert witness U.S. Congl. and Senatorial coms. on mental health, 1949—. Author: Advertising Code, Motion Picture Assn., 1948; co-author: Action for Mental Health, 1961, Heart's Work, 1991; contbr. articles to psychiat. jours. Mem. Pres.'s Com. Employment Handicapped, 1960—; founder, co-chmn. Nat Mental Health Com., 1949-57, mem. nat. mental health adv. council Surgeon Gen. U.S., 1950-54; sec.-treas. Joint Commn. Mental Illness and Health, 1955-61; vice chmn. Found. Child Mental Welfare, 1963; mem. Gov.'s Youth Coun. State N.Y.; chmn. N.Y. State Mental Hygiene Facilities Improvement Corp., 1963—, White House Conf. Children, 1970; sec.-treas., bd. dirs. Joint Commn. Mental Health Children; chmn. N.Y. State Facilities Devel. Corp., 1963-78; mem. adv. council NIMH, 1976—; bd. dirs. Hillside Hosp., League Sch. For Seriously Disturbed Children, Menninger Found., Nat. Mental Hygiene Com. Recipient Social Conscience award Karen Horney Clinic, 1972; Hon. fellow Postgrad. Ctr. Mental Health. Fellow Am. Psychiat. Assn. (hon.), Brit. Royal Soc. Health (hon.), Am. Orthopsychiat. Assn. (hon.); Mem. Nat. Assn. Mental Health (founder), Acad. for Motion Picture Arts and Scis., Harmonie Club. Home and Office: 150 E 69th St New York NY 10021-5704 DIED 05/05/97. .

SCHLESINGER, DAVID HARVEY, medical educator, researcher; b. N.Y.C., Apr. 28, 1939; s. Philip T. and Fay (Margolis) S.; m. Joan M. Aurelia; children: Sarah Jane, Karen Louise. BA, Columbia U., 1962; MS, Albany Med. Coll., 1965; PhD, Mt. Sinai Med. and Grad. Sch., 1972. Research fellow in medicine Mass. Gen. Hosp., Harvard Med. Sch., Boston, 1972-75, instr., 1975-77; asst. in biochemistry Mass. Gen. Hosp., Harvard Med. Sch., 1975-77; rsch. assoc. prof. U. Ill. Med. Ctr., Chgo., 1977-81; rsch. prof. exptl. medicine NYU Med. Ctr., N.Y.C., 1981-95, co-dir. neuroscis. sect. mental health clin. rsch. ctr., 1981-90; dir. microsequency and sythesis facility Kaplan Cancer Ctr., 1983-91; co-dir. neuroscis. sect. mental health clin. rsch. ctr., dir. microsequencing and synthesis faculty Kaplan Cancer Ctr., N.Y. med. Ctr., 1983-92; cons. Ortho Pharm. Co., 1977-91, Armour Pharm., 1971-81, Emisphere Techs., Inc., 1987-93; cons. in drug delivery systems. Editor: monograph Neurobyphysical Peptide Hormones and Other Biological Active Peptides, 1981; editor and contbg. author: Macromolecular Sequencing and Synthesis: Selected Methods and Application, 1988. Recipient Lectureship award Fundacion Gen. Mediterranean, Madrid, 1975. Mem. N.Y. Acad. Scis., Am. Physiol. Soc., Am. Soc. Biol. Chemists, Am. Chem. Soc. Died Apr. 18, 1996.

SCHLESINGER, EDWARD BRUCE, neurological surgeon; b. Pitts., Sept. 6, 1913; s. Samuel B. and Sara Marie (Schlesinger) S.; m. Mary Eddy, Nov. 1941; children—Jane, Mary, Ralph, Prudence. B.A., U. Pa., 1934, M.D., 1938. Diplomate Am. Bd. Neurosurgery. Mem. faculty Columbia Coll. Phys. and Surg., N.Y.C., 1946-97; prof. clin. neurol. surgery Columbia Coll. Phys. and Surg., 1964-97, Byron Stookey prof., chmn. dept. neurol. surgery, 1973-80, Byron Stookey prof. emeritus, 1980-97; dir. neurol. surgery Columbia Presbyn. Hosp., 1973-80, pres. med. bd., 1976-79; cons. in neurosurgery Presbyn. Hosp., 1980-87, cons. emeritus, 1987—. Author rsch. publs. on uses, effects of curare in disease, lesions of central nervous system, localization of brain tumors using radioactive tagged isotopes, genetic problems in neurosurgery and spinal disorders. Trustee Matheson Found., Sharon (Conn.) Hosp. Recipient emeritus rsch. award Presbyn. Hosp. Fellow N.Y. Acad. Scis., N.Y. Acad. Medicine; mem. AAAS, AMA, Am. Assn. Neurol. Surgeons, Harvey Soc., Neurosurg Soc. Am. (pres. 1970-71), Soc. Neurol. Surgeons, Am. Assn. Surgery of Trauma, Am. Rheumatism Soc., Am. Coll. Clin. Pharmacology and Chemotherapy, Ea. Assn. Electroencephalographers, Sigma Xi. Achievements include investigation of clinical pathological markers of genetic disorders and the syndromes created. Home: Lakeville Conn. Died June 2, 1997.

SCHLESINGER, RUDOLF BERTHOLD, lawyer, educator; b. Munich, Germany, Oct. 11, 1909; s. Morris and Emma (Aufhauser) S.; m. Ruth Hirschland, Sept. 4, 1942; children: Steven, June, Fay. Dr. Jur., U. Munich, 1933; LLB, Columbia U., 1942; Dr. Jur. (hon.), U. Trento, 1994. Bar: N.Y. 1942, U.S. Supreme Ct. 1946. Law sec. to Chief Judge Irving Lehman, N.Y. Ct. Appeals, 1942-43; confidential law sec. Judges N.Y. Ct. Appeals, 1943- 44; asso. Milbank, Tweed, Hope & Hadley, N.Y.C., 1944-48; asso. prof. Cornell U., 1948-51, prof., 1951-75, William N. Cromwell prof. internat. and comparative law, 1956-75; prof. Hastings Coll. Law, U. Calif., 1975—, vis. prof., 1974; Cons. N.Y. State Law Rev. Commn., 1949—; mem. adv. com. internat. rules of jud. procedure, 1959-66; vis. prof. Columbia, 1952, Salzburg Seminar, 1964; Charles Inglis Thomson disting. vis. prof. U. Colo., summer 1976. Author: Cases, Text and Materials on Comparative Law, 4th edit., 1980, (with Baade, Damaska and Herzog) 5th edit., 1988, (with Baade, Herzog and Wise) Supplement to 5th edit., 1994; Formation of Contracts: A Study of the Common Core of Legal Systems, 2 vols., 1968, others; editor-in-chief Columbia Law Rev., 1941-42; bd. editors Am. Jour. Comparative Law; author articles on legal topics. Trustee Cornell U., 1961-66. Carnegie Corp. Reflective year fellowship, 1962-63. Mem. Am. Law Inst. (life), Am. Bar Assn., Internat. Acad. Comparative Law, Phi Beta Kappa, Order of Coif. Died Nov. 10, 1996.

SCHLESINGER, RUTH HIRSCHLAND, art curator, consultant; b. Essen, Germany, Mar. 11, 1920; came to U.S., 1936; d. Kurt M. and Henriette (Simons) Hirschland; m. Rudolf B. Schlesinger, Sept. 4, 1942; children: Steven, June, Fay. BA cum laude, Wheaton Coll.,

Norton, Mass., 1942; intern, Met. Mus. of Art, N.Y.C., 1941. Dir. Upstairs Gallery, Ithaca, N.Y., 1960-67; curatorial asst. Andrew D. White Mus. Cornell U., Ithaca, N.Y., 1967-70; curator of prints Herbert F. Johnson Mus. Cornell U., 1970-75; art curator Hastings Coll. of the Law U. Calif., San Francisco, 1978-96. Author: (mus. catalog) 15th and 16th Century Prints of No. Europe from the Nat. Gallery of Art-Rosenwald Collection, 1973, other catalogs. Mem. UN World Centre founding com., 1979-84; mem. art adv. com. N.Y. State Fair, Syracuse, 1973; cons. Gallery Assn., State of N.Y., 1972-74. Recipient History of Art prizes Wheaton Coll., 1941, 42. Home: San Francisco Calif. Died Nov. 10, 1996.

SCHMIDT, JOHN WESLEY, agronomy educator; b. Moundridge, Kans., Mar. 13, 1917; s. John J. and Kathrina (Sperling) S.; m. Olene Lucile Hall, June 23, 1943; children: Karen, Vicki, Wesley, Loren, Jerold. BA, Tabor Coll., Hillsboro, Kans., 1947; MS, Kans. State U., 1949, DSc, 1984; PhD, U. Nebr., 1952. Asst. agronomist Kans. State U., Manhattan, 1951-54; assoc. agronomist Kans. State U., 1954; assoc. prof. agronomy U. Nebr., Lincoln, 1954-62; prof. U. Nebr., 1962-80, Regents prof., 1980-85, prof. emeritus, 1986—. Recipient Outstanding Rsch. and Creativity award U. Nebr.-Lincoln, 1979, Nat. award for excellence in agrl. sci. Nat. Agrl.-Mktg. Assn., 1984. Fellow Am. Soc. Agronomy (Agronomic Rsch. award 1989), Crop Sci. Soc. Am. (Crop Sci. award 1975, DeKalb Crop Sci. career award 1982); mem. Sigma Xi, Phi Kappa Phi, Gamma Sigma Delta (Internat. award for disting. svc. in agr. 1969). Republican. Methodist. Died July 15, 1997.

SCHMIDT, STEPHEN ROBERT, lawyer; b. Louisville, Jan. 29, 1948; s. Adolph William and Olivia Ann (Hohl) S.; m. Wanda Jean Owen, Aug. 17, 1974; children: Johannes, Kathryn. AB, St. Louis U., 1969; Fulbright scholar, Universität Hamburg, Germany, 1969-70; MA, Ohio State U., 1971, JD, 1974. Assoc. Brown, Todd & Heyburn PLLC, Louisville, 1974-79, mem, 1980-97. Co-author: Bad Faith Litigation in Kentucky, 1992, Insurance Coverage Law in Kentucky, 1996, Insurance Law: Third Party Coverage in Kentucky, 1996; editor Ohio State Law Jour., 1973-74; contbr. articles to profl. jours. Named one of Outstanding Young Men of Am. Jaycees, 1983. Mem. ABA (chair comml. torts com., torts and ins. practice sect. 1995-96, speaker ann. meeting 1993, 94), Ohio State U. Alumni Club (pres. Louisville 1983, 86, 93, treas. 1987-97), Fulbright Assn., Order of the Coif, Phi Beta Kappa. Avocations: photography, computers, playing cards, golf. Died Feb. 25, 1997.

SCHNACK, GAYLE HEMINGWAY JEPSON (MRS. HAROLD CLIFFORD SCHNACK), corporate executive; b. Mpls., Aug. 14, 1926; d. Jasper Jay and Ursula (Hemingway) Jepson; student U. Hawaii, 1946; m. Harold Clifford Schnack, Mar. 22, 1947; children: Jerrald Jay, Georgina, Roberta, Michael Clifford. Skater, Shipstad & Johnson Ice Follies, 1944-46; v.p. Harcliff Corp., Honolulu, 1964—, Schnack Indsl. Corp., Honolulu, 1969—, Nutmeg Corp., Cedar Corp.; ltd. ptnr. Koa Corp. Mem. Internat. Platform Assn., Beta Sigma Phi (chpt. pres. 1955-56, pres. city council 1956-57). Established Ursula Hemingway Jepson art award, Carlton Coll., Ernest Hemingway creative writing award, U. Hawaii. Deceased.

SCHNAPF, ABRAHAM, aerospace engineer, consultant; b. N.Y.C., Aug. 1, 1921; s. Meyer and Gussie (Schaeffler) S.; m. Edna Wilensky, Oct. 24, 1943; children: Donald J., Bruce M. BSME, CCNY, 1948; MSME, Drexel Inst. Tech., 1953. Registered profl. engr., N.J. Devel. engr. on lighter-than-air aircraft Goodyear Aircraft Corp., Akron, Ohio, 1948-50; mgr. fire control system def. electronics RCA, Camden, N.Y., 1950-55, mgr. airbourne navigation system, aerospace weapon system, 1955-58; program mgr. TIROS/TOS weather satellite systems RCA Astro-Electronics, Princeton, N.J., 1958-70, mgr. satellite programs, 1970-79, prin. scientist, 1979-82; cons. Aerospace Systems Engring., Willingboro, N.J., 1982—; lectr., presenter on meteor. satellites, space tech., communication satellites. Sgt. USAF, 1943-46. Recipient award Nat. Press Club Washington, 1975, award Am. Soc. Quality Control-NASA, 1968, Pub. Svc. award NASA, 1969, cert. of appreciation U.S. Dept. Commerce, 1984, RCA David Sarnoff award; inducted into Space Tech. Hall of Fame, 1992; named to 5000 Personalities of the World, named Internat. Man. of Yr. 1992-93. Fellow AIAA; mem. Am. Astro. Soc., Am. Meterol. Soc., Space Pioneers, N.Y. Acad. Scis. (mem. think tank week sessions 1980's), N.J. Arbitration Soc.

SCHNEIDER, JURGEN, dancer, ballet master; b. Berlin, May 2, 1936. First studied in East Berlin, student of Tarasov and Gerdt in Moscow at Bolshoi Ballet, student of A. Pushkin at Kirov Sch., Leningrad; grad. as tchr. and ballet master, Theater Inst., Moscow. guest tchr. Royal Ballet and Sch. of London;. Solo dancer, Nat. Theater, Weimar, solo dancer, ballet master, East Berlin Comic Opera, 1968-71; ballet master: Stuttgart Ballet, 1971-73; co-dir.: Munich State Opera Ballet, 1973-74; ballet master, American Ballet Theatre; former pvt. coach to Mikhail Baryshnikov, N.Y.C., 1975. DIED 08/15/95. .

SCHNEIDER, MELVIN FREDERICK, secondary music educator; b. Lark, Wis., Mar. 7, 1904; s. Charles Phillip and Amelia (Thiele) S.; m. Naomi Jessie Manshardt, Sept. 14, 1940. BMus, U. Wis., 1930, MA, 1948, postgrad., to 1955. Tchr. orch., chorus and math. high sch., South Beloit, Ill., 1930-32; tchr. orch., band and social studies high sch., Oregan, Wis., 1932-35, Wisconsin Dells, Wis., 1935-37, Prairie du Sac, Wis., 1937-40; rschr. in music edn. U. Wis., Madison, 1940-45, U. No. Iowa, Cedar Falls, 1945-60; ind. rschr. in music edn. Cedar Falls, 1960—; kindergarten instr. string quartets; 1st grade orch. instr.; instrument repair instr. Mem. String Tchrs. Assn. (a founder), Music Educators Nat. Conf. (award for 50 yrs. of svc.), Cedar Falls C. of C., Phi Delta Kappa. Republican. Congregationalist. Died Jan. 11, 1997.

SCHNUR, JEROME, television producer; b. N.Y.C., July 30, 1923; s. Irving I. and Frances (Buchsbaum) S. Grad., Carnegie Inst. Tech., 1944. Assoc. producer feature films, until 1950, dir., producer network tV, 1950-93; pres. Schnur-Chastain Prodns. Inc., N.Y.C., 1963-93; cons. in field; spl. lectr. TV film dept. U. Miami. Producer, dir. numerous TV shows, including PBS spls. The Joffrey Ballet, The Am. Ballet Theatre, over a dozen music and ballet spls. for CBS-TV. With USAAF, 1943-46. Recipient Peabody award, 1970, Emmy citation, 1971, Ohio State award, 1975, others. Mem. Acad. Motion Pictures Arts and Scis., Acad. Television Arts and Scis., Dirs. Guild Am. Home: New York N.Y. Deceased.

SCHOBER, CHARLES COLEMAN, III, psychiatrist, psychoanalyst; b. Shreveport, La., Nov. 30, 1924; s. Charles Coleman and Mabel Lee (Welsh) S.; B.S., La. State U., 1946, M.D., 1949; m. Martha Elizabeth Welsh, Dec. 27, 1947 (dec.); children—Irene Lee, Ann Welsh; m. 2d, Argeree Maburl Stiles, Feb. 4, 1972; 1 son, Charles Coleman. Intern, Phila. Gen. Hosp., 1949-51; resident in psychiatry Norristown (Pa.) State Hosp., 1953-57; practice medicine specializing in psychiatry and psychoanalysis, Phila., 1957-71; asso. clin. dir. Inst. Pa. Hosp., Phila., 1957-60, clin. dir., 1960-64, attending psychiatrist, 1960-68, sr. attending psychiatrist, 1968-71; mem. faculty Phila. Psychoanalytic Inst., 1966-71; clin. instr. U. Pa. Sch. Medicine, 1957-62, clin. asso., 1962-68, clin. asst. prof., 1968-71; prof., chmn. dept. psychiatry La. State U. Med. Center, Shreveport, 1971-73, chief psychiatry service, 1971-73; chief psychiatry service VA Hosp., Shreveport, 1971-73; faculty New Orleans Psychoanalytic Inst., 1972-73; mem. faculty St. Louis Psychoanalytic Inst., 1973-78; clin. prof. psychiatry St. Louis U. Med. Sch., 1973-78; clin. prof. psychiatry St. Louis U. Med. Sch., 1973-78; active med. staff psychiatry St. Louis U. Hosp., 1973-78; cons. psychiatry Jefferson Barracks VA Hosp., St. Louis, 1973-78; pvt. practice medicine, specializing in psychiatry and psychoanalysis, Shreveport, 1978-93; clin. prof. psychiatry, mem. med. staff psychiatry La. State U. Med. Center Hosp., Shreveport, 1978-97; chief psychiatry service Schumpert Med. Center, 1982-84; med. and clin. dir. psychiatry Willis Knighton Med. Ctr., 1986-89; dir. adult psychiatric treatment program Charter Forest Hosp., Shreveport, 1989-97, prof. psychiat. La. State U. Med. Ctr., Shreveport, 1992-97; dir. in-patient svc. psychiat., psychoanalysis out patient clinic, 1992-97. Served to capt. M.C., USAF, 1951-53. Diplomate Am. Bd. Psychiatry and Neurology (examiner). Fellow Am. Coll. Psychiatrists, Am. Psychiat. Assn.; mem. Am. Psychoanalytic Assn., AMA, La. Psychiat. Soc., La. Med. Soc., New Orleans Psychoanalytic Soc., Phila. Psychoanalytic Soc. Club: Rotary. Contbr. articles to profl. and med. jours. Died Sept. 6, 1997.

SCHOCKWEILER, FERNAND, judge; b. Luxembourg, June 15, 1935; m. Colette Collignon, 1960; 2 children. Student, Faculté de Droit, Paris. Govt. official Ministry Justice, 1961-85; judge Ct. Justice European Communities, 1985-96. Contbr. articles to profl. jours. Died June 1, 1996.

SCHOFIELD, JOHN-DAVID MERCER, bishop; b. Somerville, Mass., Oct. 6, 1938; s. William David and Edith Putnam (Stockman) S. BA, Dartmouth Coll., 1960; MDiv, Gen. Theol. Sem., N.Y.C., 1963, DD (hon.), 1989. Joined Monks of Mt. Tabor, Byzantine Cath. Ch., 1978; ordained priest Episcopal Ch. Asst. priest Ch. of St. Mary the Virgin, San Francisco, 1963-65, Our Most Holy Redeemer Ch., London, 1965-69; rector, retreat master St. Columba's Ch. and Retreat House, Inverness, Calif., 1969-88; bishop Episcopal Diocese of San Joaquin, Fresno, Calif., 1988—; aggregate Holy Transfiguration Monastery, 1984—; bishop protector Order Agape and Reconciliation, Chemainus, B.C., Can., 1990—. Episcopal visitor to Community of Christian Family Ministry, Vista, Calif., 1991—; trustee Nashotah House Sem., Wis., 1991—; bd. dirs. Fresno Leadership Found., 1996—. Mem. Episcopal Synod of Am. (founder 1989), Episcopalians United (bd. dirs. 1987—). Republican. Died Oct. 11, 1997.

SCHOMAKER, VERNER, chemist, educator; b. Nehawka, Nebr., June 22, 1914; s. Edwin Henry and Anna (Heesch) S.; m. Judith Rooke, Sept. 9, 1944; children: David Rooke, Eric Alan, Peter Edwin. B.S., U. Nebr., 1934, M.S., 1935; Ph.D., Calif. Inst. Tech., 1938. With Union Carbide Research Inst., 1958-65, asst. dir., 1959-63, assoc. dir., 1963-65; prof. chemistry U. Wash., Seattle, 1965-84; prof. emeritus U. Wash., 1984-97, chmn. dept., 1965-70; vis. assoc. Calif. Inst. Tech., 1984-92, faculty assoc., 1992-97. Contbr. articles on molecular structure to chem. jours. John Simon Guggenheim Meml. Found. fellow, 1947-48; Recipient Am. Chem. Soc. award in pure chemistry, 1950. Fellow AAAS, N.Y. Acad. Scis.; mem. Am. Chem. Soc., Am. Crystallographic Assn. (pres. 1961-62), Sigma Xi. Home: Pasadena Calif. Died Mar. 30, 1997.

SCHÖN, DONALD ALAN, urban planner, educator; b. Newton, Mass., Sept. 19, 1930; s. Marcus David Henry and Ann (Mason) S.; m. Nancy Quint, Dec. 20, 1952; children: Ellen, Andrew, Elizabeth, Susan. Student, Conservatoire Nationale de Paris, 1950; B.A., Yale U., 1951; M.A., Harvard U., 1952, Ph.D. in Philosophy, 1955. Staff assoc. Arthur D. Little, Inc., Cambridge, Mass., 1957-63; dir. Inst. Applied Tech., Nat. Bur. Standards, Washington, 1963-66; pres. Orgn. Social and Tech. Innovation, Boston, 1966-72; Ford prof. urban studies and planning MIT, Cambridge, 1972-92, prof. emeritus, sr. lectr., 1993—; bd. dirs. Community Systems Found., Ann Arbor, Mich.; Reith lectr. BBC, Eng., 1970; Cecil Green disting. vis. prof. U. B.C., Can., 1979; advisor F.A. Rodet, Stockholm, 1985—; Queens lectr. Queens U., Can., 1985; Leatherbee lectr. Harvard U. Sch. Bus. Adminstrn., 1986; Cubitt lectr. Royal Soc. Arts, Eng., 1986; John Dewey lectr. Am. Assn. Ednl. Rsch., 1990. Author books including: Displacement of Concepts, 1963, Beyond the Stable State, 1971, (with Chris Argyris) Theory in Practice, 1974, Organizational Learning, 1978, The Reflective Practitioner, 1983 (Oustanding Book award 1983), Educating the Reflective Practitioner, 1987, (with Martin Rein) Frame Reflection, 1994; editor: The Reflective Turn, 1990; contbr. numerous articles to profl. jours. Served with U.S. Army, 1955-57. Recipient 1st prize Conservatoire Nationale de Paris, 1950; Woodrow Wilson fellow Harvard U., 1952, fellow Royal Soc. Arts, 1986. Fellow Royal Inst. Brit. Architects (hon. 1985), mem. Commn. on Sociotech. Systems, Nat. Acad. Scis. Democrat. Jewish. Died Sept. 13, 1997.

SCHORRE, LOUIS CHARLES, JR., artist; b. Cuero, Tex., Mar. 9, 1925; s. Louis Charles and Anna (Barthlome) S.; m. Margaret Phipps Storm, July 17, 1948; children—Alice Ann Schorre Stultz, Martha Schorre Jackson, Robin Elisabeth Schorre Glover. B.F.A., U. Tex., 1948. Instr. art Mus. Fine Arts, Houston, 1950-55; prof. Sch. Architecture, Rice U., 1962-72. One-man shows: Tex. Gallery, Meredith Long Gallery, Contemporary Arts Mus.; paintings and drawings in numerous publs. also pvt. and corp. collections throughout U.S.; Author, editor, art dir.: Life Class, 1968 (gold medals in N.Y.C. and abroad); author: Drawings and Notes, 1975, Drawing and Notes II, 1983. Served with USMCR, 1943-46. Died July 20, 1996.

SCHOTTELKOTTE, ALBERT JOSEPH, broadcasting executive; b. Cheviot, Ohio, Mar. 19, 1927; s. Albert William and Venetta (Mentrup) S.; m. Elaine Green, Jan 2, 1988; children: Paul J., Carol A., Matthew J., Joseph G., Louis A., Mary J., Ellen E. Noble, William E., Michael H., Linda Brewer, Martha Schottelkotte, Amy Wholeber. Student pub. and parochial schs. With Cin. Enquirer, 1943-61, successively copy boy, city-wide reporter, columnist, 1953-61; news broadcaster Sta. WSAI, Cin., 1953-59; news broadcaster Sta. WCPO-TV, 1959-94, dir. news-spl. events, 1961-83, sta. dir., 1983-88; gen. mgr. news div. Scripps-Howard Broadcasting Co., 1969-81, v.p. for news, 1971-81, sr. v.p., 1981-93; pres., chief exec. officer, trustee Scripps Howard Found., 1986—. Served with AUS, 1950-52. Recipient Nat. CD award for reporting on subject, 1958, Disting. Broadcaster award Alpha Epsilon Ro, 1990, Carr Van Anda award E.W. Scripps Sch. Journalism Ohio U., 1996—; charter inductee Cin. Journalism Hall of Fame Soc. Profl. Journalists, 1990; inducted into Cin. Broadcasting Hall of Fame, 1992. Mem. Bankers Club, Maketewah Country Club (Cin.), Sea Pines Country Club (Hilton Head, S.C.), Hidden Valley Country Club (Lawrenceburg, Ind.), Hidden Valley Golf Club. Roman Catholic. Died Dec. 15, 1996.

SCHOTTLAND, CHARLES IRWIN, retired legal educator; b. Chgo., Oct. 29, 1906; s. Harry and Millie (Lustberg) S.; m. Edna Lilyan Greenberg, June 7, 1931 (dec.); children: Richard R., Mary Elizabeth (dec.). AB, UCLA, 1927; postgrad., N.Y. Sch. Social Work, 1928-29, U. So. Calif. Law Sch., 1929-33; DHL, Boston U., 1969; LLD, Western Mich. U., 1970; DH, Centro Escolar U., Manila, Philippines, 1970, Washington U., 1976; LLD, Emerson Coll., 1972, Brandeis U., 1972; DHL, Adelphi U., 1986. Bar: Calif. 1933. Dir. Modern Social Ctr., L.A., 1929-33; adminstr. Calif. Relief Adminstrn., 1933-36; exec. dir. Fedn. Jewish Welfare Orgns., L.A., 1936-41; asst. to chief children's bur. Dept. Labor, 1941-42; asst. dir. UNRRA for Germany, 1945; pvt. practice law L.A., 1948-50; dir. Calif. Dept. Social Welfare, 1950-54; lectr. UCLA, 1949-54; commr. social security HEW, 1954-59, dean Florence Heller Grad. Sch. for Advanced Studies in Social Welfare Brandeis U., Waltham, Mass., 1959-70, pres., 1970-72, prof., 1972-79; prof. Ariz. State U., Tucson, 1980-82; Pres. Internat. Coun. Social Welfare, 1968-72, chmn. U.S. com., 1961-66; mem. com. social security experts Internat. Labor Office, 1956-59; prin. adv. U.S. del. UN Social Commn., 1955, 57; mem. adv. bd. Dept. Social Welfare, Commonwealth of Mass., 1964; mem.-at-large Nat. Social Welfare Assembly, 1964-71; mem. task force on financing community health svcs. and facilities Nat. Commn. on Community Health, 1964; mem. Citizens Crusade Against Poverty, 1964; cons. pub. health service Nat. Inst. Mental Health, 1964, chmn. rsch. cons. com., 1973-75; chmn. subcom. on retirement income Nat. Council on Aging, 1964; chmn. task force on social svcs. HEW, 1968; mem. pub. health svcs. Nat. Adv. Mental Health Coun., 1968-72; mem. Milbank Commn. on Pub. Health, 1972-76. Author: The Social Security Program in the United States, 1963, The Welfare State, 1967; mem. editl. bd.: Social Policy and Adminstrn, 1978-95, Adminstrn. in Social Work, 1978-95. Bd. dirs. Big. Bros. Assn. L.A., 1945-95, Nat. Big Bros. Assn., 1975-80, Coun. Internat. Programs, 1980-82; bd. dirs., pres. Nat. Sr. Citizens Law Ctr., 1979-86, 89-92, bd. dirs., 1986-88; chmn. Ariz. del. White House Conf. on Aging, 1980-81, Ariz. Gov.'s Adv. Coun. on Aging, 1983-89; bd. dirs. Pima Coun. on Aging, 1983-95; bd. dirs. Nat. Coun. on Aging, 1983-95, sec., mem. exec. com., 1988-95. Lt. col. AUS, 1942-45, ETO. Decorated by govts. of France, Czechoslovakia, Holland, Greece, Poland; recipient Koshland award Calif. Conf., Social Work, 1954. Mem. Am. Public Welfare Assn., Nat. Assn. Social Workers (chmn. div. social policy and action 1962-66, pres.-elect 1966-67, pres. 1967-68), Nat. Conf. Social Welfare (pres. 1953, 59-60), Am. Public Welfare Assn. (dir.), Western Gerontol. Assn. (dir. 1981-83), Am. Soc. on Aging (pres. 1985-88), Calif. State Bar, Am. Legion, Mil. Order World Wars, Mil. Govt. Assn., Zeta Beta Tau, Pi Sigma Alpha, Pi Kappa Delta. Died June 27, 1995.

SCHRAMM, DAVID NORMAN, astrophysicist, educator; b. St. Louis, Oct. 25, 1945; s. Marvin M. and Betty Virginia (Math) S.; m. Judith J. Gibson, 1986; children from previous marriage: Cary, Brett. SB in Physics, MIT, 1967; PhD in Physics, Calif. Inst. Tech., 1971. Rsch. fellow in physics Calif. Inst. Tech., Pasadena, 1971-72; asst. prof. astronomy and physics U. Tex., Austin, 1972-74; assoc. prof. astronomy, astrophysics, physics Enrico Fermi Inst. and Coll. U. Chgo., 1974-77, prof., 1977-97, Louis Block prof. phys. scis., 1982-97, prof. conceptual founds. of sci., 1984-96, acting chmn. dept. astronomy and astrophysics, 1977, chmn., 1978-84, v.p. for rsch., 1995-97, Louis Block disting. svc. prof. in phys. scis., 1996-97; resident cosmologist Fermilab, 1982-84; cons., lectr. Adler Planetarium, Lawrence Livermore Lab., Los Alamos Nat. Lab.; organizer sci. confs.; frequent lectr. in field; chmn. bd. trustees Aspen Ctr. for Physics 1992-97, honorary trustee, 1997; bd. on physics and astronomy, exec. com. NRC, 1990-97, chair, 1993-97, mem. com. aviation weather systems aeronautics and space engring. bd., 1994-97; bd. dirs. Astron. Rsch. Consortium, 1990-97; pres. Big Bang Aviation, Inc.; bd. overseers Fermi Nat. Accelerator Lab., 1990-97. Co-author: The Advanced Stages of Stellar Evolution, 1977, From Quarks to the Cosmos: Tools of Discovery, 1989, The Shadows of Creation: Dark Matter and the Structure of the Universe, 1991; author: The Big Bang and Other Explosions in Nuclear & Particle Astrophysics, 1996; co-editor: Supernovae, 1977, Fundamental Problems of Stellar Evolution, 1980, Essays in Nucleosynthesis, 1981, Gauge Theory and the Early Universe, 1988, Dark Matter in the Universe, 1990, The Big Bang and Other Explosions in Nuclear and Particle Astrophysics, 1996; editor profl. jours.; columnist Outside mag.; contbr. over 350 articles to profl. jours. Recipient Gravity Rsch. Found. prize, 1980, Humboldt award Fed. Republic Germany, 1987-88, Einstein medal Evotos U., Budapest, Hungary, 1989, Grad. Teaching award U. Chgo., 1994. Fellow Am. Acad. Arts and Scis., Am. Phys. Soc. (Lilienfeld prize 1993), Meteor. Soc.; mem. Nat. Acad. Sci., Am. Astron. Soc. (Helen B. Warner prize 1978, exec. com. planetary sci. divsn. 1977-79, sec.-treas. high energy astrophysics divsn. 1979-81), Am. Assn. Physics Tchrs. (Richtmeyer prize 1984), Astron. Soc. Pacific (Robert J. Trumpler award 1974), Internat. Astron. Union (commns. on cosmology, stellar evolution, high energy astrophysics), Aircraft Owners and Pilots Assn., British-N Am. Com., Hungarian Acad. Scis. (hon.), Alpine Club, Sigma Xi. Achievements include development of the cosmological interface with particle physics and the use of cosmological arguments to constrain fundamental physics; use of big bang to form the principle argument regarding the cosmological density of normal matter. Died Dec. 19, 1997.

SCHRAMM, JOHN CLARENDON, foundation executive; b. Tarrytown, N.Y., July 5, 1908; s. Emil and Vera Victoria (Ormsby) S.; m. Loraine Tonjes, Sept. 18, 1936; children: Judith (Mrs. John Lee Westrate), Linda (Mrs. Donald Bergquist), Ellen Christie (Mrs. Sherwin C. Day). A.B., Columbia, 1929, A.M., 1943, student, 1945-46. Asst. to merchandising mgr. N.Y. Edison Co., 1929; asst. chief of program supply NBC, N.Y.C., 1929-33; radio announcer WOR, WNEW, WBNX, N.Y.C., 1933-35; program dir. WOV, N.Y.C., 1935-41; radio stage coordinator Met. Opera Broadcast, seasons 1942-44; asst. ednl. dir., prodn. dir. Blue Network, Radio City, 1942-44; instr. in charge of radio prodn. and workshop Queens Coll., 1943; radio dir. Christian Herald Mag., 1944; radio dir. and alternate moderator Wake Up America, nat. radio forum, 1944-47; tchr. English Patchogue (L.I.) High Sch., 1947-48; asst. prof. speech radio U. Fla., 1948-49; mng. dir. Calvin K. Kazanjian Econs. Found., Inc., 1949-50, mng. trustee, 1950-85; spl. lectr. econs. So. Conn. State Coll., New Haven, 1973, 74, 77, 78; chmn. consortium on gen. systems edn. S.C. State Coll., New Haven. Trustee Conn. Joint Council on Econ. Edn. John C. Schramm Leadership Award Program in Econ. Edn. established in his honor Joint Coun. on Econ. Edn., 1986, recipient Disting. Svc. placque, 1984; recipient Marvin Bower medal exemplary svc. econ. edn. Nat. Coun. Econ. Edn., 1992. Mem. Am. Econ. Assn. Acad. Polit. and Social Soc., Acad. Polit. Sci., Acad. Ind. Scholars U. Colo. Episcopalian. Home: West Redding Pa. Died Mar. 22, 1994; buried Redding Ridge (Conn.) Cemetery.

SCHRAUT, KENNETH CHARLES, mathematician, educator; b. Hillsboro, Ill., May 19, 1913; s. Charles Frederick and Theresa (Panska) S.; m. Virginia Haury, Feb. 5, 1952; 1 dau., Marilyn Szorc. A.B. with honors, U. Ill., 1936; M.A., U. Cin., 1938, Ph.D., 1940. Vis. instr. U. Notre Dame, summer 1940; instr. dept. math. U. Dayton, (Ohio), 1940-41; asst. prof. U. Dayton, 1941-44, assoc. prof., 1944-48, prof., 1948-72, chmn. dept. math., 1954-72, Disting. Service prof., 1972—, project dir. Research Ctr., 1951-54; vis. lectr. Ohio State U. Grad. Sch., 1946-49; acting prof. U. Cin. Grad. Sch., 1958-60; dir. NSF Math. Inst., Cath. U., Ponce, P.R., summer 1959, U. Dayton, 1961-69, 72; chmn., bd. dirs. Honor Seminars of Met. Dayton, 1987-93. Recipient Lackner award, 1987. Mem. Am. Math. Soc., Math. Assn. Am., Am. Soc. Engring. Edn. (chmn. math. sect. 1967-68, 78-79, mem. exec. com. 1969-73, 76, program chmn. 1977-78), Sigma Xi, Pi Mu Epsilon. Home: 4200 Michael Dr Kokomo IN 46902-4730 Died Oct. 29. 1997.

SCHREIBER, ANN, federal agency administrator; b. July 2, 1936; m. Sol Schreiber, Mar. 25, 1964. AB magna cum laude, Bklyn. Coll., 1957; postgrad., Columbia U., 1957-59. Regional tng. officer Social Security Adminstrn., 1972-73, sr. planning officer, 1973-76, dep. asst. regional commr., 1978-80, regional adminstr. family assistance, 1980-87; exec. asst. to regional dir. HHS, 1976-78; regional adminstr. adminstrn. for children and families region II HHS, N.Y.C., 1991-94; regional adminstr. Family Support Adminstrn., 1987-91. Mid Career fellow Princeton U., 1970-71. Mem. Phi Beta Kappa. Home: Brooklyn N.Y. Died Sept. 18, 1994.

SCHUHMANN, REINHARDT, JR., metallurgical engineering educator, consultant; b. Corpus Christi, Tex., Dec. 16, 1914; s. Reinhardt and Alice (Shuford) S.; m. Betsy Jane Hancock, Aug. 29, 1937; children—Martha Schuh, Alice Bishop. Student, Calif. Inst. Tech., 1929-31; B.S. in Metall. Engring., Mo. Sch. Mines, 1933; M.S. in Metall. Engring., Mont. Sch. Mines, 1935; Sc.D. in Metallurgy, MIT, 1938; DEng (hon.), Purdue U., 1993. Instr. to assoc. prof. MIT, Cambridge, 1938-54; prof. metall. engring. Purdue U., West Lafayette, Ind., 1954-64, head Sch. Metall. Engring., 1959-64, Ross prof. engring., 1964-81, Ross prof. engring. emeritus, 1981—; Battelle vis. prof. Ohio State U., Columbus, 1966-67; Kroll vis. prof. Colo. Sch. Mines, Golden, 1977; metall. engring. cons., 1946—. Author: Metallurgical Engineering, 1952; contbr. articles to profl. jours.; co-inventor Q-S oxygen process, oxygen sprinkle smelting. Fellow Metall. Soc. of AIME (charter, James Douglas Gold medal 1970, Mineral Industry Edn. award 1975, Extractive metallurgy lectr. 1965, Extractive metallurgy Sci. awards 1959, 77), Am. Soc. for Metals, AAAS; mem. Nat. Acad. Engring., Am. Chem. Soc. Democrat. Episcopalian. Club: Parlor (pres. 1963-64)(Lafayette). Lodge: Rotary. Avocations: classical music; hiking. Died July 7, 1996.

SCHUKNECHT, HAROLD FREDERICK, physician, educator; b. Chancellor, S.D., Feb. 10, 1917; s. J.G. and Dena (Weeldreyer) S.; m. Anne Bodle, June 30, 1941; children—Judith, James. Student, U. S.D., 1934-36; B.S., S.D. Sch. Med. Scis., 1938; M.D., Rush Med. Coll., 1940; M.S. (hon.), Harvard, 1961; D.Sc. (hon.), U. S.D., 1972. Diplomate: Am. Bd. Otolaryngology. Intern Mercy Hosp., Des Moines, 1940-41; resident U. Chgo. Clinics, 1946-49; asst. prof. otolaryngology U. Chgo., 1949-53; assoc. surgeon Henry Ford Hosp., Detroit, 1953-61; Walter A. Le Compte prof. otology, prof. laryngology Harvard Med. Sch., Boston, 1961-87, prof. emeritus otology, 1987-96; chief otolaryngology Mass. Eye and Ear Infirmary, 1961-84, emeritus chief otolaryngology, 1984-96. Author nearly 300 jour. articles, more than 70 revs., chpts., editorials, 7 books on anatomy, surgery, pathology of the ear. Recipient Achievement award Deafness Rsch. Found., N.Y.C., Beltone award, Shambaugh prize Collegium ORL, Disting. Alumnus award Rush Med. Coll.; named to S.D. Hall of Fame. Fellow Acoustical Soc. Am., Royal Coll. Surgeons (Glasgow) (hon.), Royal Coll. Surgeons (Edinburgh) (hon.); mem. AMA, Am. Acad. Ophthalmology and Otolaryngology(Disting. award contbns. clin. otology), Am. Triological Soc., Am. Otol. Soc. (award merit), Mass., Suffolk County med. socs., New Eng. Otolaryn. Soc., Soc. Univ. Otolaryngologists, Collegium ORL Amicitiae Sacrum, Deutsche Akademie der Naturforscher Leopoldina, Am. Neurotology Soc., Assn. for Research in Otolaryngology(Award of Merit), Phila. Laryngol. Soc., Sigma Xi; hon. mem. S.D. Acad. Ophthalmology and Otolaryngology, Royal Soc. Medicine (London) (hon.), also otolaryn. socs. in South Africa, Panama, Australia, Nicaragua, Colombia, Japan, Egypt, Austria, Germany. Spl. research pathology ear and physiology hearing. Home: Boston Mass. Died Oct. 19, 1996.

SCHULMAN, EVELINE DOLIN, psychologist, author, consultant; b. N.Y.C.; d. George and Fannie (Simon) Dolin; m. Sol Schulman, June 3, 1941; children: Mark H., Ken S. BS, CCNY, 1939, postgrad., 1940-42; postgrad., State U. Iowa, 1939-40, Am. U., 1947; MEd, U. Md., 1954, EdD, 1957, postgrad., 1979-81. Tchr. Children's Colony, N.Y.C., 1941-42; registrar-tchr. Rockwood Nursery Sch., N.Y.C., 1942-43; asst. dir. Settlement House, Juanita Kauman Nye Council House; dir./tchr. nursery sch., Washington, 1947-48; dir.-tchr. Greenway Co-op. Nursery Sch., Washington, 1947-48, Fairfax Co-op. Nursery Sch., Washington, 1948-50, Community Nursery Sch., Silver Spring, Md., 1952-54; grad. asst. U. Md., 1954-55; psychologist, cons. Prince Georges County Council of Kindergarten and Nursery Schs., 1955-57; psychologist, lectr. Am. U., Washington, 1957; instr. psychology Community Coll. Balt., 1958-62, chmn. dept., 1962-73, prof. psychology, 1964-73, dir. mental health tech. program, 1967-73; lectr. human devel. Inst. for Child Study, U. Md., 1967-68, 69-71; prof. mental health Morgan State Coll., Towson, 1971-77; dir. evaluation and tng. Md. Mental Retardation Adminstrn., Balt., 1974-76, asst. dir. adminstrn., 1976-77; dir., cons. human services Ctr. for Devel. Inter-Personal Skills, Silver Spring, 1977-96; cons. Nat. Disabilities Assn., 1980. Author: Intervention in Human Services—A Guide to Skills and Knowledge, 1974, 4th edit., 1991, Focus on the Retarded Adult, 1980; contbr. articles in field to profl. jours. Active Montgomery County Com. for Cmty. Edn., about Mentally Ill, 1982-86, Clifton T. Perkins Adv. Bd., 1972-80, chmn., 1974-80; chmn. Montgomery County Coun. Adult Pub. Guardianship Rev. Bds. Md., 1986-96, Wheaton Cmty. Mental Health Adv. Com., 1978-96. Fellow, U. Md., 1954-55. Mem. ACA, Am. Psychol. Assn., Am. Assn. Mental Health Counselors Assn., Gerontol. Soc., Nat. Coun. on Aging, Md. Assn. Jr. Colls. (pres. 1967-69). Home: Pasadena Calif. Died Aug. 9, 1996.

SCHULTZ, THEODORE WILLIAM, retired economist, educator; b. Arlington, S.D., Apr. 30, 1902; s. Henry Edward and Anna Elizabeth (Weiss) S.; m. Esther Florence Werth; children: Elaine, Margaret, T. Paul. Grad., Sch. Agr., Brookings, S.D., 1924; B.S., S.D. State Coll., 1927, D.Sc. (hon.), 1959; M.S., U. Wis., 1928, Ph.D., 1930; LL.D. (hon.), Grinnell Coll., 1949, Mich. State U., in 1962, U. Ill., 1968, U. Wis., 1968, Cath. U. Chile, 1979, U. Dijon, France, 1981; LL.D., N.C. State U., 1984. Mem. faculty Iowa State Coll., Ames, 1930-43; prof., head dept. econs. and sociology Iowa State Coll., 1934-43; prof. econs. U. Chgo., 1943-72, chmn. dept. econs., 1946-61, Charles L. Hutchinson Disting. Service prof., 1952-72, prof. emeritus, 1972—; econ. adviser, occasional cons. Com. Econ. Devel., U.S. Dept. Agr., Dept. State, Fed. Res. Bd., various congl. coms., U.S. Dept. Commerce, FAO, U.S. Dept. Def., Germany, 1948, Fgn. Econ. Adminstrn., U.K. and Germany, 1945, IBRD, Resources for the Future, Twentieth Century Fund, Nat. Farm Inst., others.; dir. Nat. Bur. Econ. Research, 1949-67; research dir. Studies of Tech. Assistance in Latin Am.; bd. mem. Nat. Planning Assn.; chmn. Am. Famine Mission to India, 1946; studies of agrl. developments, central Europe and Russia, 1929, Scandinavian countries and Scotland, 1936, Brazil, Uruguay and Argentina, 1941, Western Europe, 1955. Author: Redirecting Farm Policy, 1943, Food for the World, 1945, Agriculture in an Unstable Economy, 1945, Production and Welfare in Agriculture, 1950, The Economic Organization of Agriculture, 1953, Economic Test in Latin America, 1956, Transforming Traditional Agriculture, 1964, The Economic Value of Education, 1963, Economic Crises in World Agriculture, 1965, Economic Growth and Agriculture, 1968, Investment in Human Capital: The Role of Education And of Research, 1971, Human Resources, 1972, Economics of the Family: Marriage, Children, and Human Capital, 1974, Distortions of Agricultural Incentives, 1978, Investing in People: The Economics of Population Quality, 1981, Restoring Economic Equilibrium: Human Capital in the Modernizing Economy, 1990, The Economics of Being Poor, 1993, Origins of Increasing Returns, 1993; co-author: Measures for Economic Development of Under-Developed Countries, 1951; editor: Jour. Farm Econs., 1939-42; contbr. articles to profl. jours. Research fellow Center Advanced Study in Behavioral Sci., 1956-57; recipient Nobel prize in Econs., 1979. Fellow Am. Acad. Arts and Scis., Am. Farm Econs. Assn., Nat. Acad. Scis.; mem. Am. Agrl. Econ. Assn., Am. Econ. Assn. (pres. 1960, Walker medal 1972), Am. Philos. Soc., Royal Econ. Soc., Nat. Acad. Edn., others. Died Feb. 26, 1998.

SCHUMAN, CLIFFORD RICHARD, lawyer; b. N.Y.C., June 11, 1913. s. Samuel and Bertha (Schiff) S.; m. Charlotte Suchman; 1 child, Bonnie. BA, N.Y. U., 1932; JD, Columbia U. Law Sch., 1935. Bar: N.Y. 1935, U.S. Dist. Ct. (so. dist.) N.Y. 1938, U.S. Dist. Ct. (ea. dist.) N.Y. 1938, U.S. Tax Ct. 1940, U.S. Ct. Appeals (2d cir.) 1960, U.S. Supreme Ct. 1939. Sole practice N.Y.C., 1980—; dir. Bolivia R.R. Co., 1938-42; adj prof. Law Baruch Coll., City U. N.Y., 1971—; mem. law faculty Adelphi U. 1977-78; cons. revision ins. law N.Y. State Law Revision Commn., 1980-81; adj. prof. law Pace U., N.Y., 1987—; legal adv. N.Y.C. Selective Service Bd., Harlem Area, 1939-42. Served with JAGC, AUS, 1942-44. Recipient Alumni Meritorious Service award N.Y. U., 1972, Sesquicentennial Crystal award, 1982. Mem. ABA, N.Y. State Bar Assn., Assn. Bar City N.Y. (mem. com. on uniform state laws 1966-84, chmn. 1981-84), N.Y. County Lawyers Assn., NYU Alumni Assn.-Heights Coll. (pres. 1967-69, dir. 1965—), Alumni Fedn. NYU (dir. 1967-90, dir. emeritus 1990—), B'nai B'rith, Masons (N.Y. state grand dir. ceremonies 1966-67), Phi Beta kappa, Pi Lambda Phi. Editor Columbia Law Rev., 1933-35; contbr. articles to profl. jours.

SCHUMANN, MAURICE, writer, politician; b. Paris, Apr. 10, 1911; m. Lucie Daniel, 1944; 3 children. With Havas News Agy., 1932-40; chief ofcl. broadcaster BBC French Service, 1940-44; liaison officer Allied Expeditionary Forces from D-Day until liberation of Paris; mem. French Provisional Consultative Assembly, 1944-45; mem. Constituent Assembly, 1945-46, 46; chmn. Mouvement Republicain Populaire, 1945-49; dep. for Nord, Nat. Assembly, 1945, 58, 67, 68; sec. of state for fgn. affairs, 1951-54; pres. fgn. affairs com. Nat. Assembly, 1969; minister of state, Prime Minister's Office, 1962; minister of state for sci. research, 1967-68; minister of Social Affairs, 1968-69; minister of Fgn. Affairs, 1969-73; senator for Nord, 1974—, v.p. Senate, 1977—. Author: (fiction) Le Rendez-vous avec Quelqu'un, 1962, Les flots roulant auloin, 1973, La Communication, 1974, Le Concerto en Ut Majeur, 1982, La Victoire et la Nuit; (non-fiction) La Mort nèe de leur propre Vie, 1974; Le Vrai Malaise des Intellectuels de Gauche, 1957, Angoisse et Certitude, 1978, Un Certain 18 Juin (Prix Aujourd'hui 1980), Qui a Tuè le duc d'Enghien, 1984, Bergson ou le Retour de Dieu, 1995. Recipient Grand Prix Catholique de Litterature, 1978; decorated Compagnon de la Liberation; Chevalier Legion d'honneur, Order of Leopold, Croix de Guerre. Mem. Acad. Française.

SCHUTTE, WILLIAM METCALF, English language educator; b. New Haven, May 9, 1919; s. Louis Henry and Anna (Metcalf) S.; m. Susan Roberts McDowell, May 15, 1943 (dec. Sept. 1965); children: Scott, Kirk, Kim; m. Anne Cole Jacobson, Dec. 21, 1967 (div. Jan. 1990). Grad., Hotchkiss Sch., 1937; B.A., Yale U., 1941; M.A., Yale, 1947, Ph.D., 1954. Mem. faculty Carnegie Inst. Tech., 1947-60, asso. prof. English, 1955, asst. to pres., 1956-60; mem. faculty Lawrence U., 1960-84, Lucia R. Briggs prof. English, 1965-84, prof. emeritus, 1984—; dir. London Center, 1975-76; faculty fellow Newberry Library Seminar Asso. Colls. Midwest, Chgo., 1969-71; cons. in communications. Author: Joyce and Shakespeare: A Study in the Meaning of Ulysses, 1957, (with E.R. Steinberg) Communication in Business and Industry, 1960, rev. edit., 1983, Personal Integrity, 1961, Twentieth Century Interpretations of Joyce's A Portrait of the Artist as a Young Man, 1968; Index to Recurrent Elements in Joyce's Ulysses, 1982, Rumsey Hall School: The First Forty Years, 1992; contbr. articles to profl. jours. Bd. govs. Attic Theatre, Appleton, 1961-66, pres., 1963-66. Served with AUS, 1941-45. Recipient Carnegie Corp. Teaching award Carnegie Inst. Tech., 1954. Mem. MLA, Renaissance Soc. Am., Wis. Hist. Soc., Shakespeare Assn. Am. Home: 10 N Green Bay Rd Appleton WI 54911-5625 Died Aug. 23, 1997.

SCHWAN, JUDITH ALECIA, photographic researcher; b. Middleport, N.Y., Apr. 16, 1925; d. James William and Mary Alecia (Wythers) S. BSChemE, U. Cin., 1948; MS, Cornell U., 1950. Research scientist Eastman Kodak Co., Rochester, N.Y., 1950-65, lab. head, 1965-68, asst. div. dir. emulsion research div., 1968-71, div. dir. emulsion research div., 1971-75, asst. dir. research labs., 1975-86, dir. photographic research labs., photographic products group, 1986-87, ret., 1987; bd. trustees Eastman Savs. & Loan Assn., Rochester, 1977-87. Patentee in field. Trustee St. John Fisher Coll., Rochester, 1975—; active Meml. Art Gallery, Rochester, Rochester Philharm. Orch., Rochester Mus. and Sci. Ctr., George Eastman House, Rochester; mem. task force Women in Ch. of Rochester Cath. Diocese; mem. econ. pastoral steering com. Rochester Cath. Diocese; mem. parish coun. St. Stephen's Ch., Middleport, N.Y.; mem. Diocesan Pastoral Coun., Buffalo. Recipient Disting. Alumnus award U. Cin. Coll. of Engring., 1976. Fellow Soc. Motion Picture and TV Engrs. (Herbert T. Kalmus Meml award for Outstanding Contbn. in Color Films, 1979); mem. Am. Chem. Soc., Nat. Acad. Engring. Soc. Photographic Scientists and Engrs. Clubs: Shelridge Country (Medina, N.Y.). Home: 107 Crosby Ave Kenmore NY 14217-2453 Died March 19, 1996.

SCHWARTING, ARTHUR ERNEST, pharmacognosy educator and university dean; b. Waubay, S.D., June 8, 1917; s. John Ernest and Johanna Martha (Boelte) S.; m. Roberta L. Mitchell, June 14, 1941; children: Jon Michael, Stephen Arthur (dec.), Gerald Allen. B.S., S.D. State U., 1940; Ph.D., Ohio State U., 1943. Instr. U. Nebr., 1943-45, asst. prof., 1945-49; assoc. prof. U. Conn., Storrs, 1949-53, prof. pharmacognosy, 1953-81, prof. emeritus, 1981—, dean Sch. Pharmacy, 1970-80; vis. prof. U. Munich, 1968-69. Author: (with others) Introduction to Chromatography, 1968, 2d edit., 1985; editor: Jour. Natural Products, 1960-76. Mem. Mansfield Bd. Edn., Conn., 1965-70; bd. dirs. Am. Found. Pharm. Edn., 1974-80. Recipient Research Achievement award Am. Pharm. Assn. Found., 1964; U. Conn. Alumni Assn. award for faculty excellence, 1965, Centennial Achievement award Ohio State U., 1970, Disting. Alumnus award S.D. State U., 1986. Fellow AAAS; mem. Am. Assn. Colls. Pharmacy (pres. 1971-72, pres. council deans 1977-78), Am. Pharm. Assn., Am. Soc. Pharmacognosy (hon. mem. 1981), Sigma Xi, Phi Lambda Upsilon, Phi Kappa Phi, Rho Chi. Lutheran. Research and publs. on chemistry and biochemistry of natural drug products. Died Oct. 22, 1996.

SCHWARTZ, BERNARD, law educator; b. N.Y.C., Aug. 25, 1923; s. Isidore and Ethel (Levenson) S.; m. Aileen Haas, Apr. 18, 1950; 1 child, Brian Michael. BSS, CCNY, 1944; LLB, NYU, 1944; LLM, Harvard U., 1945; PhD, Cambridge (Eng.) U., 1947, LLD, 1956; Doctorat d'Universite, U. Paris, 1963. Bar: N.Y. 1945. Mem. law faculty NYU, 1947-92, Edwin D. Webb prof. law, 1963-92; Chapman Disting. prof. law U. of Tulsa, 1992-97; cons. Hoover Commn., 1955; chief counsel, staff dir. spl. subcom. legislative oversight U.S. Ho. Reps., 1957-58; Tagore Law lectr., Calcutta, India, 1984; corr. mem. Nat. Acad. Law and Social Scis., Argentina, 1986-97. Author: French Administrative Law and the Common Law World, 1954, The Supreme Court, 1957, The Professor and the Commissions, 1959, Introduction to American Administrative Law, 1962, The Reins of Power, 1963, Commentary on the Constitution of the U.S., 5 vols., 1963-68, The Roots of Freedom, 1967, Legal Control of Government, 1972, Constitutional Law: A Textbook, 1972, 2d edit., 1979, The Law in America, 1974, Administrative Law, 1976, 3d edit., 1991, The Great Rights of Mankind, 1977, expanded edit., 1992, Administrative Law: A Casebook, 1977, 4th edit., 1994, Super Chief: Earl Warren and His Supreme Court, 1983, Inside the Warren Court, 1983, The Unpublished Opinions of the Warren Court, 1985, Some Makers of American Law, 1985, Swann's Way: The School Busing Case and the Supreme Court, 1986, Behind Bakke: The Supreme Court and Affirmative Action, 1988, The Unpublished Opinions of the Burger Court, 1988, The Ascent of Pragmatism: The Burger Court in Action, 1990, The New Right and the Constitution, 1990, Constitutional Issues: Freedom of the Press, 1992, Main Currents in American Legal Thought, 1993, A History of the Supreme Court, 1993, The Unpublished Opinions of the Rehnquist Court, 1996, Decision: How The Supreme Court Decides Cases, 1996, A Book of Legal Lists, 1997, Thomas Jefferson and Bolling v. Bolling, 1997. Ann. Survey Am. Law dedicated in his name, 1988. Mem. ABA. Died Dec. 23, 1997.

SCHWARTZ, IRVING LLOYD, retired history educator; m. Rosanne S. Schwartz; children: Barth D., Regina Mara. BA, U. Dayton, 1942; Diplomate, U. Florence, Italy, 1946, Coll. Armed Forces; MA in History, Miami U., 1948. Instr. U.S. Office Edn., Wright-Patterson AFB, Ohio, 1940-43; historian USAF, 1946-47; edn. and tng. specialist, chief spl. rehab. unit VA, Ohio, 1947-50; chief of protocol aeronautical systems USAF, Wright Patterson AFB, 1950-78; prof. history Sinclair Community Coll., Dayton, Ohio, 1978-93, prof. emeritus, 1993—; mem. faculty history dept. U. Dayton, 1953-56. Contbr. articles to profl. jours. Chmn. Gov.'s Help a Disabled Vet. Com., 1945; mem. Mayor's Sister City Com., 1969—; head Dayton com. Bicentennial French Revolution Observances; head Dayton Columbus Quincentary Celebration, 1992; sec. City Plan Bd., Dayton, 1970—; chmn. bd. trustees Dayton and Montgomery County Pub. Libr. System, 1971—; trustee Nat. Aviation Hall of Fame; bd. dirs. Dayton Coun. World Affairs, 1982—. Decorated Chevalier L'Ordre des Palmes Academiques, French Govt., 1990; recipient 2 USAF Exceptional Civilian Svc. award, 1988-89. Mem. Am. Hist. Assn.

SCHWARTZ, JACK THEODORE, publisher; b. N.Y.C., Aug. 24, 1914; s. Nathan and Vera Ida (Rosovsky) S.; m. Pearl Tarnower, May 20, 1941; children: Harriet (Mrs. Tod Johnson), Deborah (Mrs. Gary Raizes). Student, Columbia Coll., 1932-34. Founder, pres. Syndicate Mags., Inc., N.Y.C., 1939-83; founder, pres. Beacon Advt. Assos., Inc., 1950-76; founding partner Beacon Mktg. Consultants, 1959-81; pub. Better Nutrition, Today's Living, Art Material Trade News. Trustee, mem. exec. com. Lesley Coll., Cambridge, Mass.; bd. dirs. Orgn. for Health Initiatives, White Plains, N.Y. Served to 1st lt. AUS, 1943-45. Died Oct. 31, 1996.

SCHWARZSCHILD, MARTIN, astronomer, educator; b. Potsdam, Germany, May 31, 1912; came to U.S., 1937, naturalized, 1942; s. Karl and Else (Rosenbach) S.; m. Barbara Cherry, Aug. 24, 1945. Ph.D., U. Goettingen, 1935; D.Sc. (hon.), Swarthmore Coll., 1960, Columbia U., 1973; DSc, Princeton U., 1992. Research fellow Inst. Astrophysics, Oslo (Norway) U., 1936-37, Harvard U. Obs., 1937-40; lectr., later asst. prof. Rutherfurd Obs., Columbia U., 1940-47; prof. Princeton U., 1947-50, Higgins prof. astronomy, 1950-79. Author: Structure and Evolution of the Stars. Served to 1st lt. AUS, 1942-45. Recipient Dannie Heineman prize Akademie der Wissenschaften zu Goettingen, Germany, 1967, Albert A. Michelson award Case Western Res. U., 1967, Newcomb Cleveland Prize AAAS, 1957, Rittenhouse Silver medal, 1966, Prix Janssen Société astronomique de France, 1970, Medal from l'Assn. Pour le Developpement Internat. de l'Observatoire de Nice, 1986, Gerlach-Adolph von Muenchhausen Medaille Goettingen U., 1987, Dirk Brouwer award Am. Astron. Soc., 1991, Balzan prize, 1994, Nat. Medal Sci., 1997 (posthumous). Fellow Am. Acad. Arts and Scis.; mem. Internat. Astron. Union (v.p. 1964-70), Akademie der Naturforscher Leopoldina, Royal Astron. Soc. (asso., Gold medal 1969, Eddington medal 1963), Royal Astron. Soc. Can. (hon.), Am. Astron. Soc. (pres. 1970-72), Nat. Acad. Scis. (Henry Draper medal 1961), Soc. Royale des Sciences de Liege (corr.), Royal Netherlands Acad. Sci. and Letters (fgn.), Royal Danish Acad. Sci. and Letters (fgn.), Norwegian Acad. Sci. and Letters, Astron. Soc. Pacific (Bruce medal 1965), Am. Philos. Soc., Royal Soc. (fgn.), Sigma Xi. DIED 04/10/97. .

SCHWARZWALDER, JOHN CARL, television executive; b. Columbus, Ohio, June 21, 1917; s. S. John and Alice (Enright) S.; m. Ruth Marie Dierker, July 10, 1945 (dec. May 1991); children: Joan Dierdre, Raymond John. A.B., Ohio State U., 1937; Mus.M., U. Mich., 1940, A.M., 1941; Ed.D., U. Houston, 1953. Assoc. dir. Wall Sch. of Music, Assoc. Republic Prodns., 1946-48; prof. U. Houston, 1948, chmn. radio-TV dept., 1950; pioneer mgr. nation's first ednl. TV sta.; became mgr. radio sta. KUHF, 1950, KUHT-TV, 1953; gen. mgr. KTCA-TV, St. Paul, 1956-76, KTCI-TV, 1965-76; trustee Twin City Area ETV Corp., 1975-78, exec. cons., 1976-81; mgr. KOKH-TV, Oklahoma City, 1977-78, Denton (Tex.) Channel Two Found., 1977-85; music dir. U. Tex. Madrigal Dinner, 1988-92; pres. DLBS, Inc.; bd. dirs. Sta. KMFA-FM. Author: ETV in Controversy: We Caught Spies; also numerous articles on pub. TV. Former bd. dirs. Am. Heart Assn., Minn. Humanities com., Afro-Am. Music Assn., Council State Ednl. TV Commns.; former pres. Minn. Planning Commn., former chmn. research com. Served to maj. AUS, 1941-46. Mem. Nat. Assn. Better Radio-TV (dir.), Nat. Assn. Ednl. TV (sec.-treas.), Nat. Assn. Ednl. Broadcasters (former dir.), Nat. Assn. for Electronic Teaching (pres. 1981-86), Nat. Assn. for Better Broadcasts (dir.), Rotary, Phi Mu Alpha, Kappa Phi Kappa, Alpha Epsilon Rho. Democrat. Episcopalian. Home: Austin Tex. Died May 8, 1992.

SCHWEBEL, ANDREW I., psychology educator; b. N.Y.C., Feb. 5, 1943; s. Milton and Bernice Lois (Davison) S.; m. Carol Rose Lubinsky, May 25, 1969; children David, Sara. B.A., Antioch Coll., 1965; M.S., Yale U., 1967; Ph.D., 1969. Lic. psychologist, Ohio; cert. family therapist, Ohio. Asst. prof. psychology Ohio State U., Columbus, 1969-73; assoc. prof. Ohio State U., 1973-79, prof., 1979-96; pvt. practice clin. psychology Columbus, 1977-96; psychol. cons. SE Ohio Comprehensive Planning Agy., Cambridge, Ohio, 1970-73; adj. prof. Union for Experimenting Colls. and Univs., Yellow Springs, Ohio, 1971-96; cons. Social Ecology Equity Change Quest, Baton Rouge, 1973-75; host Let's Talk It Over, WBNS-AM Radio, Columbus, 1980-81; v.p for human relations New Communities Corp., Columbus; columnist Suburban News Press. Author: Student Teacher's Handbook, 1979, 3rd rev., 1996, Personal Adjustment and Growth: A Life-Span Approach, 1983, 2d rev. edit., 1990, A Guide to a Happier Family: Overcoming the Anger, Frustration and Boredom that Destroy Family Life, 1989; co-author: Understanding and Helping Families: A Cognitive-Behavioral Approach; co-editor: Mental Health of Ethnic Minorities, 1991; assoc. editor Family Rels., 1993-96, Jour. Personal and Interpersonal Loss, 1995-96. Bd. dirs. Urban Alternatives, 1976-87, Columbus Fathers, 1977-89, New Communities, 1981-96; edn. com. The Wellington Sch.; mem. profl. adv. bd. Peers Unlimited, 1993-96; chmn. Gov.'s Com. on Child Support. Recipient award City of Columbus Dept. Devel., 1979, Ohio Dept. Mental Health, 1980-82. Fellow APA; mem. Cmty. Devel. Soc., Internat. Personal Rels. Network, Nat. Coun. for Therapy and Rehab. through Horticulture, Authors Guild, N.Y. Acad. Scis., Nat. Acad. for Cert. Family Therapists (adv. bd. 1995-96), Sigma Xi. Home: Columbus Ohio Died June 4, 1996.

SCHWENDINGER, CHARLES JOSEPH, public administration educator, researcher; b. Dubuque, Iowa, July 2, 1931; s. Leo James and Loretta Lucille (Meyers) S.; m. Marion Jean Blain, June 11, 1957 (div. 1981); 1 child, Julieanne Schwendinger Wattles; m. Chieko Ikeda, Oct. 13, 1982. BA in History, Va. Mil. Inst., 1957; MPA, U. Okla., 1980, D Pub. Adminstrn., 1991. Commd. 2d lt. U.S. Army, 1957, advanced through grades to lt. col., 1971, served in various locations including Vietnam, 1957-78, ret., 1978; asst. prof. pub. adminstrn. Troy (Ala.) State U., 1986-88, asst. prof., 1989, 91—; lectr. in field. Contbr. to profl. publs. Sgt. U.S. Army, 1949-53. Decorated Bronze Star medal with 2 oak leaf clusters, Air medal. Fellow Pi Alpha Alpha (chpt. pres. 1980-86, 89-90), Pi Sigma Alpha; mem. DAV, VFW, NRA, Am. Soc. Pub. Adminstrn. (coun. mem. Okla. chpt. 1989-90), Internat. City Mgmt. Assn., Am. Legion, Ret. Officers Assn. Roman Catholic. Died Oct. 25, 1996.

SCHWEPPE, JOHN SHEDD, research physician, educator, author; b. Chgo., May 8, 1917; s. Charles H. and Laura Abbie (Shedd) S.; m. Lydia Hibbard Elliott, July 17, 1943; children: Leigh Elliott Schweppe Buettner, Charles Hibbard, David Porter. A.B. cum laude, Harvard U., 1939; M.D., Northwestern U., 1943, M.S., 1947. Intern St. Luke's Hosp., Chgo., 1943-44; fellow in internal medicine Mayo Found., Rochester, Minn., 1947-50; researcher Menninger Found., Topeka, 1950-56; research assoc. in medicine and biochemistry Northwestern U. Med. Sch., Chgo., 1956-60, asst. prof. medicine and biochemistry, 1960-64, assoc. prof., 1964-78, prof., 1978—; chmn. edn. com. Cancer Ctr. Northwestern U. Med. Sch., Chgo, 1974—. Author: Man, a Remarkable Animal, 1969, Man in a Changing World, 1986; contbr. articles on carcinogenesis, biochemistry of cancer cells to biochem. jours.; research in control of gene expression, phosphorylation of nucleoproteins in normal, aging and cancer cells. Pres. Schweppe Found., Chgo., 1947—; bd. dirs. United Charities Chgo., 1962—; fellow Aspen Inst. Humanistic Studies, (Colo.), 1964—; trustee Shedd Aquarium, Chgo., 1965—, Inst. for Living, Winnetka, Ill., Nat. Acad. for Families, N.Y.C., 1982-85. Served to capt. M.C. U.S. Army, 1944-46. Recipient Merit award Northwestern U. Alumni Assn., 1973. Fellow ACP, Am. Heart Assn. council on arteriosclerosis); mem. Am. Assn. Cancer Research, Am. Chem. Soc., Am. Soc. Internal Medicine, Drs. Mayo Soc., Mayo Alumni Assn., Endocrine Soc., Inst. Medicine Chgo. (chmn. com. on health care 1983—), Soc. Exptl. Biology and Medicine, Chgo. Med. Soc. (chmn. com. on health care delivery 1979-83). Republican. Episcopalian. Clubs: Chicago, Indian Hill, Shoreacres. Home: 30 Indian Hill Rd Winnetka IL 60093-3940 Office: Northwestern U Med Sch 845 N Michigan Ave Suite 949W Chicago IL 60611 Died Sept. 4, 1996.

SCHWIMMER, DAVID, physician, educator; b. Gödényháza, Hungary, Dec. 8, 1913; came to U.S., 1921; s. George and Laura (Green) S.; m. Gertrude Alpha Dounn, Nov. 12, 1939; children: Betty Laura, Georgia, Mark Ian. B.S. cum laude, Lafayette Coll., 1935; M.D., N.Y. U., 1939; M.Med. Sci., N.Y. Med. Coll., 1944. Diplomate: Am. Bd. Internal Medicine. Intern Met. Hosp., N.Y.C., 1939-41; resident Met. Hosp., 1942-44; practice medicine specializing in internal medicine N.Y.C., 1944—; attending physician Flower Fifth Avs. Hosp., pres. med. bd., 1970-71; attending physician Met., Bird S. Coler, Doctors, Manhattan Eye, Ear and Throat, Lenox Hill hosps.; mem. faculty N.Y. Med. Coll., 1944—, clin. prof. medicine, 1966—; dir. U.S. Quatermaster Survival Rations Study, 1945-48, 50-51; rsch. staff war rsch. div. Met. Hosp., Columbia U., 1944-46; dir. Pvt. Teaching Svc., mem., dir. multiple med. sch. exec. coms.; cons. internist Monmouth Med. Center, Long Branch, N.J., 1950—; cons. St. Luke's-Roosevelt Hosp. Med. Ctr., 1985—; spl. lectr. in medicine Columbia U. Coll. Physicians and Surgeons, 1980—; participant rsch. confs. including Gordon Rsch. Conf. 1948, NATO adv. study Inst.1962, Internat. Symposium 1967. Author: (with Morton Schwimmer) Role of Algae and Plankton in Medicine, 1955; Contbr. to profl. jours.; patentee in field. Research fellow N.Y. Med. Coll., 1944-51; fellow internal medicine, 1941-44. Fellow ACP, Royal Soc. Medicine, N.Y. Acad. Medicine, N.Y. Acad. Scis., Am. Coll. Angiology, N.Y. Cardiol. Soc.; mem. Endocrine Soc., Harvey Soc., AAAS, AAUP, Am. Soc. Internal Medicine, Alpha Omega Alpha. Home: Teaneck N.J. Died Apr. 16, 1995.

SCOTT, FRANK MAXWELL, engineering executive, consultant; b. McCook, Nebr., Dec. 27, 1916; s. Rex Ernest and Hazel Ruth (Barbazette) S.; m. Edna May Lundy, June 7, 1940 (dec. May 1983); children: Ronald, Linda, Suzanne. B.S.E.E., U. Nebr., 1940. Registered profl. engr., Ill., Ind., N.Y., Va., Wis. Design engr. Allis Chalmers, Milw., 1940-42, head spl. application group, 1946-50; regional specialist, mgr. West Central area Allis Chalmers, Chgo., 1958-68; head electric utilities div. Harza Engring. Co., Chgo., 1968-73, assoc., sr. assoc., 1973-76, v.p., 1976—; mem. industry com. Am. Power Conf., Chgo., 1960-82; chmn. Washington Award Com., Chgo., 1965; bd. govs. Am. Assn. Engring. Socs., N.Y.C., 1983-84. Contbr. articles to profl. jours. Scoutmaster Boy Scouts Am., Western Spring, Ill., 1954-59; pres. Western Springs Park Dist., 1958-63; nat. v.p. Camp Fire Girls, Inc., N.Y.C., 1974-75, bd. dirs., 1974-76. Served to lt. col. U.S. Army, 1942-46, PTO. Decorated Bronze Star with oak leaf cluster; decorated Air Medal; recipient Meritorious Service medal Chgo. Heart Fund, 1958, 61, 63, award of merit Chgo. Assn. Tech. Socs., 1980. Fellow ASME (pres. 1983-84 Centennial medallion); mem. Nat. Soc. Prof. Engrs., Western Soc. Engrs. (pres. 1962-63), IEEE (sr., chmn. Chgo. sect. 1963-64), Ill. Engring. Council (dir. 1972-73), Tau Beta Pi. Club: Union League (Chgo.). Died Oct. 9, 1996.

SCOTT, HENRY LAWRENCE, concert pianist, humorist; b. Tivoli on Hudson, N.Y., Jan. 20, 1908; s. Walter and Mary Wigram (Keeney) S.; m. Mary Bell Bard, Aug. 28, 1938; children: Barbara Bell, Henry Lawrence. Student, Syracuse (N.Y.) U., class 1930; L.H.D., Bard Coll., Annandale, N.Y., 1964. head Henry Scott Sch. Modern Piano, N.Y.C.; mem. faculty Champlin Sch., 1940-42; pres., chmn. bd. Solo Theater of Am. Corp., 1948; asst. to pres. Bard Coll., Annandale-on-Hudson, 1966; investment adviser Johnson Lane Space and Smith, 1978-89, Interstate Johnson Lane, 1989-94. Teaching and radio, screen, stage and TV work, 1931-41; concert work, throughout U.S., 1939—, debut, Town Hall, 1941, Carnegie Hall, 1945-46, 27 transcontinental concert tours, Carnegie Hall, N.Y.C. (2), Town Hall, N.Y.C. (2), Detroit Town Hall, Kansas City Town Hall, West Point Mil. Academy (12), Akron Concert Course, Fine Arts Series, Worcester, U. Minn. (8), U. Tex. (3), U. Notre Dame (2), Miss Porters Sch., Conn. (2), St. Mark's Sch., Southborough, Mass. (5), So. Ill. U. (10), USAF Acad., 1960, Mt. Mary Coll., Milw., Emanuel Missionary Coll., Mich., Pacific Union Coll., Calif., U. So. Calif., Amherst (Mass.) U., Dartmouth Coll., Purdue U., U. N.C., U. Oreg., Med. Coll. Va., Union Coll., Lincoln, Nebr., U. N.Mex., Teaching and radio, screen, stage and TV work, Woman's Inst., Knoxville Friday Morning Musicales, Syracuse, Meml. Auditorium, Lowell, Mass., Eaton Auditorium, Toronto, Met. Opera House, N.Y.C., U. Wash., U. Utah, U. Fla. (3), U. Ga., Artists Series, San Diego, U. N.C. (3), North-Western State Coll. (7), 6th tour, Can., 1966-67, Hawaiian Islands, Saudi Arabia, 1963; guest artist various orchs. and symphonies; indsl. concerts for, General Electric Co., Eastman Kodak, IBM Corp., others, 1958-61; pioneer concert humor; now presenting humorous and ednl. lecture recitals in schs., colls., univs. and concert halls; producer, star: Concerto for Fun, 1949; introduced: Fun at the Philharmonic, 1952; guest appearance: TV show Be Our Guest, 1960; Composer: Clavichord Joe; inventor Technic Mittens for piano practice. Trustee Bard Coll., Annandale, N.Y., 1969-70, Charleston Symphony Orch., 1971-75, Charleston Concert Assn., 1971-78, pres., 1979-84; trustee, 2d v.p. Dock St. Theater, Charleston, 1981-83; founder, chmn. Stockholder Adv. Found., 1975-83, Stockholder Adv. Assn., Inc., 1976-79; bd. visitors Kanuga Episcopal Conf. Ctr., Henderson, N.C., 1985-88; trustee, treas. Dockside Assn., Charleston, 1986-87, pres., 1989-91; life mem. Dutchess County (N.Y.) Hist. Soc. Mem. Carolina Yacht Club (Charleston), Old Town Club (Charleston, pres. 1981-82). Republican. Episcopalian. Died Apr 27, 1997.

SCOTT, IRENE FEAGIN, federal judge; b. Union Springs, Ala., Oct. 6, 1912; d. Arthur H. and Irene (Peach) Feagin; m. Thomas Jefferson Scott, Dec. 27, 1939 (dec.); children: Thomas Jefferson, Irene Scott Carroll. A.B., U. Ala., 1932, LL.B., 1936, LL.D., 1978; LL.M., Catholic U. Am., 1939. Bar: Ala. 1936. Law libr. U. Ala. Law Sch., 1932-34; atty. Office Chief Counsel IRS, 1937-50, mem. excess profits tax coun., 1950-52, spl. asst. to head appeals div., 1952-59, staff asst. to chief counsel, 1959-60; judge U.S. Tax Ct., 1960-82, sr. judge serving on recall, 1982—. Contbr. articles to Women Lawyers Jour. Bd. dirs. Mt. Olivet Found., Arlington. Mem. ABA (taxation sect.), Ala. Bar Assn., Fed. Bar Assn., D.C. Bar Assn. (hon.), Nat. Assn. Women Lawyers, Nat. Assn. Women Judges, Kappa Delta, Kappa Beta Pi. Died April 10, 1997.

SCOTT, JAMES J., mining engineer; b. Wiota, Wis., Apr. 22, 1928; m. Edna M. Kettler, 1947 (dec. May 1995); 5 children; m. Ingeborg Kalinski, June 6, 1996. BS, Mo. Sch. of Mines, 1950; MS, U. Wis., 1959, PhD in Mining Engring., 1962. Mine engr. Bethlehem (Pa.) Steel Co., 1950-53, mine foreman, 1953-57; from instr. to asst. prof. mining U. Wis., 1957-63; assoc. prof. U. Mo., Rolla, 1963-65, prof. mining, 1965-80, chmn. depts. mining & petroleum, 1970-76; gen. mgr. Black River Mine, Marble Cliff Quarries Co., 1967; asst. dir. mining rsch. US Bur. Mines, 1970—; adj. prof. mining engring. U. Mo., Rolla, 1980—; pres. Scott Mine Tech. Svc. Inc. Recipient Rock Mechanics award Soc. Mining Engrs. Mem. Am. Inst. Mining, Metall. and Petroleum Engrs. (Daniel C. Jackling award 1990), Can. Inst. Mining and Metallurgy. Achievements include research in field rock mechanics, mine operational problems, experimental stress analysis, photoelasticity, model studies, stress distribution problems, mine and research management; patentee in field. Died April 11, 1997.

SCOTT, JAMES WHITE, newspaper editor; b. Lebanon, Kans., Feb. 22, 1926; s. James Malcolm and Bernice (White) S.; m. Sammy Peete, June 9, 1950; children: James Peete, Thomas Whiteford, Edward English. B.J., U. Kans., 1950. Reporter Kansas City (Mo.) Times, 1950-54; editorial writer Kansas City (Mo.) Star, 1954-93, nat. affairs writer, arts and entertainment assoc. editor, 1968-77, v.p., 1987-93; editor editorial pages Star and Times, 1977-93, sr. editor, 1993-96. Served with AUS, 1944-46, ETO. Mem. Delta Upsilon. Episcopalian. Home: Kansas City Mo. Died Dec. 14, 1995; buried Corinth cemetery.

SCOTT, RODERIC MACDONALD, former optical scientist; b. Sandusky, Ohio, Apr. 9, 1916; s. William Charles and Margaret Carol (Scott) S.; m. Joyce Ris Komanec, Dec. 22, 1938; children: Roderic MacDonald, Jeffrey Anderson, Dane Chapman. B.S. in Physics, Case Sch. Applied Sci., 1938; M.A., Harvard U., 1939, Ph.D. in Astronomy, 1945. Instr. physics Vanderbilt U., 1941; rsch. assoc. Harvard U., 1942-45; rsch. physicist Sharples Corp., Phila., 1946-48; with Perkin Elmer Corp., 1948-80, v.p., 1965-80, chief scientist, 1965-69; tech. dir. optical tech. div. Perkin Elmer Corp., Danbury, Conn., 1969-76; prin. scientist Perkin Elmer Corp., 1976-80; ret., 1980; cons. in optics, 1980-90. Bd. dirs. Perkin Fund. Fellow Optical Soc. Am. (dir., David Richardson medal 1973, 76); mem. U.S. Nat. Com. Internat. Commn. Optics (v.p. 1970-72), Phys. Soc., Soc. Photogrammetry, Soc. Photo-Optical Engrs. (dir., exec. v.p. 1975-76, George W. Goddard award 1977, Pres.'s award 1986).

SCOTT, WILLIAM LLOYD, lawyer, senator, investor; b. Williamsburg, Va., July 1, 1915; s. William David and Nora Bell (Ingram) S.; m. Ruth Inez Huffman, Feb. 5, 1940; children: Gail Ann (Mrs. Charles Eldred), William Lloyd Jr., Paul Alvin. J.D., George Washington U., 1938, LL.M., 1939. Bar: Va. Trial atty. Dept. Justice, 1942-60; spl. asst. to solicitor Dept. Interior, 1960-61; practiced in Fairfax, Va., 1961-66, Springfield, Va., 1979-80; former mem. 90th-92d Congresses from 8th dist. Va.; mem. U.S. Senate from Va., 1973-79, mem. armed services and judiciary coms.; ret., 1979; Mem. Va. Republican Central Com., 1964-68; del. Rep. Nat. Conv., 1968, 72, 76. Served with AUS, World War II. Mem. Va., Fairfax County bar assns., Am. Legion, Sigma Nu Phi (past chancellor). Methodist. Clubs: Masons (33 deg.); Shriners. Died Feb. 14, 1997.

SCRIPPS, EDWARD WYLLIS, newspaper publisher; b. San Diego, May 21, 1909; s. James G. and Josephine (Stedem) S.; m. Betty Jeanne Knight McDonnell, Jan. 31, 1950; children: Edward Wyllis III, Barry Howard. Student, Pomona Coll. Chmn. bd. Scripps Enterprises, Inc., 1931—. Mem. St. Francis Yacht Club, Lyford Cay (Nassau, Bahamas), Boars Head Sports Club, Farmington Country Club, Everglades Club, Bath and Tennis Club, Colony Club, Mrs. Club (N.Y.C.). Died Sept. 4, 1997.

SCUDDER, DAVID BENJAMIN, economist, foundation administrator; b. Evanston, Ill., July 30, 1923; s. Guy and Ruth Marilla (Benjamin) S.; m. Marjorie Adell Buckland, Dec. 27, 1946; children: David Foster, Rexford Guy. BS, Bowling Green State U., 1948; AM, U. Chgo., 1950, postgrad., 1950-51. Economist CIA, Washington, 1951-81, econ. cons., 1981-84; editor, copub. World Amateur Dancer, McLean, Va., 1982-84; treas. The Scudder Assn., Inc., Arlington, Va., 1990-92, Boise, Idaho, 1992-96. Editor quarterly newsletter The Scudder Assn. Inc, 1989-96; contbr. articles and reports to jours. Active Springfield Civic Assn., Fairfax County, Va., 1956-61. With USAF, 1943-45, ETO. Avocations: tennis, ballroom dancing, golf, amateur theater. Died Jan. 15, 1997.

SCULLY, MICHAEL ANDREW, pharmaceutical company executive, writer, editor; b. Bridgeport, Conn., Apr. 26, 1949; s. Michael Richard and Mary-Louise (McQueeney) S.; m. Mary Agnes Tortora, July 29, 1995; 1 child, Grace Mary. BA, Colgate U., 1971; MA, Boston Coll., 1977. Legis. aide U.S. Senate Staff, Washington, 1975-77; mng. editor The Pub. Interest, N.Y.C., 1978-81; editor This World mag., N.Y.C., 1981-86; asst. to amb. U.S. Embassy, London, 1989-91; sr. advisor to dir. U.S. Info. Agy., Washington, 1991-92; dir. policy comms. Pfizer Inc., N.Y.C., 1992—; speechwriter, editl. cons. Fortune 500 cos. including Contel, Pfizer, also presdl. cabinet secs., 1978-89. Editor: Best of This World, 1986; contbr. articles and revs. to popular mags. and newspapers. Recipient Meritorious Honor award U.S. Dept. State, 1991. Mem. Nat. Press Club, Reform Club (London). Republican. Roman Catholic. Died Dec. 17, 1996.

SEACREST, JOE RUSHTON, retired publishing executive, postal historian, stamp dealer; b. Lincoln, Nebr., Feb. 3, 1920; s. Joe W. and Alice (Rushton) S.; m. Beatrice H. Costello, May 21, 1944; children—Eric, Theodore, Gary, Kent, Shawn. Grad. cum laude, Phillips Acad., Exeter, N.H., 1938; B.S., Yale U., 1942; J.D., U. Nebr., 1949. Bar: Nebr. Past editor Lincoln Jour.; dir., past pres. State Jour. Co.; past chmn. bd., exec. v.p., dir. Jour. Star Printing Co.; past sec.-treas., dir. Western Pub. Co., Star-Herald Publishing Co., Western Computer Services, Inc., Western Video Inc.; dir. State Communication Co.; past co-mng. ptnr. Jour. Ltd. Partnership; past pub. consumer mem., past mem. exec. com. Nebr. Blue Cross-Blue Shield; past dir Cayman Water Co., Grand Cayman B.W.I., State Jour Co.; past chmn., dir. Anchorage Condominium, Grand Cayman; past mem. Nat. Hwy. Safety Adv. Com. Past mem. dirs. Nebraskaland Found.; trustee Nebr. State Hist. Soc. Found., U. Nebr. Found.; dir. Nebr. Game and Parks Found.; co-trustee J.C. Seacrest Trust. Served with USNR, World War II. Mem. Nebr. Bar Assn (joint press-bar free press-free trial com.), Nebr. Press Assn. (Masler Editor-Pub. award 1984), Am. Soc Newspaper Editors, Media of Nebr. (past chmn.), Am Newspaper Pub. Assn., Am. Philatelic Soc., Am. Stamp Dealers Assn. (dealer), Lincoln C. of C. (past v.p., dir.) Nebr. State C. of C. (past dir.), Sigma Delta Ch (freedom of information com.). Home: Lincoln Nebr Died Mar. 28, 1995.

SEAGER, FLOYD WILLIAMS, medical educator; b. Ogden, Utah, July 1, 1921; s. Roy Alfred and Florence (Williams) S.; m. Beth Anne Seager, Feb. 6, 1943 (div June 1965); m. Dauna Gayle Olson, July 7, 1973; children: Stephen, Nancy, Candice, Pamela, Kevin, Karen stepchildren: Jeff Stokes, John Stokes, Jeannette Memmott. AS, Weber State U., 1941; BS in Chemistry

U. Utah, 1943; MD, Hahnemann U., 1947. Diplomate Nat. Bd. Med. Examiners. Pvt. practice Ogden, 1949-51; founder Ogden Clinic, 1951; chief of staff McKay Hosp., Ogden, 1979-81, trustee, 1989—; clin. prof. medicine U. Utah Med. Sch., Salt Lake City, 1990—. Editor: (med. jours.) Sub Q, 1980—, Ad Libitum, 1989. Capt. USMC, 1951-53, Korea. Decorated 6 Battle Stars, Bronze Star; Dr. Seager Day named in his honor Mayor of Ogden, 1991; named Dr. of Yr., Utah State Med. Soc., 1993, Quiet Pioneer, Gov. Utah, 1991; recipient Point of Light award Pres. Bush, 1992. Mem. Am. Legion, Dixieland Jazz Soc. (chmn. bd. dirs.), Rotary Club Ogden, Elks. Republican. Mormon. Avocations: playing piano, chess and bridge tournaments. Died Oct. 17, 1996.

SEARS, RALPH WESTGATE, mayor; b. Grand Island, Nebr., Oct. 8, 1922; s. Mark P. and Alma Elizabeth (Westgate) S.; m. Marcia Janis Mockett, June 19, 1948; children: Steven Ralph, Sara Joan Sears Belcher, Randall Jane Sears Rosenberg. BS, U. Nebr., 1948; postgrad., U. So. Calif., 1949-51. Mem. staff Sta. KOLN-Radio, Lincoln, Nebr., 1947-48, Sta. KUSC-Radio, L.A., 1949-51, Sta. KUOA-Radio, Tuscaloosa, Ala., 1951-52; dir. pub. rels. U. Montevallo, Ala., 1956-74; owner Sears Properties, Montevallo, 1980-96; asst. prof. Ala. Coll., Montevallo, 1948-56; pres., owner Sta. WBYE-Radio, Calera, Ala., 1959-84; pres., pub. Shelby County Reporter, Columbiana, Ala., 1967-84. Mem. Montevallo City Coun., 1956-72; mayor City of Montevallo, 1972—; chmn. bd. dirs. Shelby Youth Attention Home; mem. adv. com. Salvation Army, Shelby County. 1st sgt. U.S. Army, 1942-45. Mem. Montevallo C. of C. (past pres., Outstanding Civic Leader award 1982). Avocations: golf, boating. Died Feb. 14, 1996.

SECONDINI, OLINDO, chemist, consultant; b. Marsala, Trapani, Italy, Oct. 29, 1914; came to U.S., 1953, naturalized, 1956; s. Edward and Adeline Defunt; m. Anna Katya, Oct. 31, 1951; children: Adeline, Rosalinda. D. Langs., Lit. and Insts., State Oriental U. Inst., Naples, Italy, 1946; D. Healing Arts, U. Health Sci., L.A., 1978; D. Medicine and Surgery, U. Palermo (Italy), 1982. Prof. langs., acting supt. Niksic and Savinik Dists., Yugoslavia, 1941-43; cons. chemist, chem. engr. Petrizzio Labs., Santiago, Chile, 1949-50, Inst. Indsl. Devel., Guatemala, 1950-53; prof. chemistry Ind. of Pa. State U., 1959-61; prof. fgn. langs. Northwestern State U., Natchitoches, La., 1961-63, Midwestern State U., Wichita Falls, Tex., 1963-64, U. So. Miss., Hattiesburg, 1964-66; prof. Spanish and German Hiram Scott Coll., Scottbluff, Nebr., 1966-67, Dillard U., New Orleans, 1968-69; prof. French Jackson (Miss.) State U., 1969-72, prof. chemistry, 1969-72; cons. chemist, chem. engr. Office Econ. Opportunity, Washington, 1966; prof. chem. engring.R&D natural resources for govt. Khartoum State U. Sudan, Kampala, Uganda, 1972-74; intern Khartoum (Sudan) Civil and U. Hosp., 1976-78; prof. chemistry, chem. engring., R&D natural resources for govt. Kumasi State U. Sci. Tech., Ghana, 1974-76; pvt. practice Jeddah (Saudi Arabia) Med. Ctr., 1979-80, Palermo, Naples, Italy, 1980-85; cons. chemist, chem. engr. Kunerol Natural Products, Hamburg, Flensburg, Fed. Republic Germany, 1986-87; cons. Petrizzio Labs., Santiago, Chile, S.Am ., 1959-50, Inst. Industial Devel., Guatemala, Cen. Am., 1950-53, OEO, 1966, Kamena Products Corp., Cairo, 1984, Kunerol Natural Products, Hamburg and Flensburg, Fed. Republic Germany, 1986-87. Author: The Pillars of the Chemical Industry, vols. 1, 2, 3,4, Industrial Chemistry Laboratory Manual, Industrial Chemistry, Orientative Course, The Basic Concepts of Physical Chemistry, Theory and Practice of Qualitative Analysis, Theory and Practice of Quantitative Analysis, other handbooks and textbooks; contbr. articles, poetry to profl. jours. Recipient Telamone prize, Agrigento, Italy, 1989. Mem. Am. Inst. Chemists (emeritus), Med. Assn. of Agrigento Italy. Achievements include research on the application of acupuncture and oriental medicine to physical theraphy, psychosomatic theraphy, and treatment of syndromes, the disease of the thyroid gland and their treatment, the application of crenotherapy to diseases and syndromes, chemistry, biochemistry and pharmacology of drugs mostly employed in the treatment of the human body. Home: 39 65 51st St Woodside NY 11377 DIED 02/23/97. .

SEDWICK, (BENJAMIN) FRANK, language educator; b. Balt., Apr. 7, 1924; s. Benjamin Frank and Louise (Lambert) S.; m. Alice Elvira Magdeburger, June 4, 1949; children: Eric, Lyn, Coralie, Daniel. A.B., Duke, 1945; M.A., Stanford, 1947; Ph.D., U. So. Cal., 1953. Instr. Spanish U. Md., College Park, 1947-49; asst. prof. Spanish and Italian U.S. Naval Acad., 1951-53; asst. prof. Spanish U. Wis.-Milw., 1953-58; prof. Spanish and Italian Ohio Wesleyan U., Delaware, 1958-63; prof. Spanish, head dept. fgn. langs. Rollins Coll., Winter Park, Fla., 1963-80; dir. overseas programs Rollins Coll., 1963-80; freelance writer, 1980-96. Author: The Tragedy of Manuel Azaña and the Fate of the Spanish Republic, 1963, A History of the Useless-Precaution Plot in Spanish and French Literature, 1964, El otro and Raquel encadenada, 1960, La forja de los sueños, 1960, La gloria de don Ramiro, 1966, Selecciones de Madariaga, 1969, Conversation in Spanish (co-author French, Italian, English and German edits.), 5th edit., 1988, Conversaciones con madrileños, 1973, Spanish for Careers, 1980 (co-author French and German edits.), The Practical Book of Cobs, 1987, 3d edit., 1995, The Gold Coinage of Gran Colombia, 1991; contbr. articles to profl. jours. Served to lt. USNR, 1942-46, PTO. Recipient Heath Lit. award Am. Numismatic Assn., 1994. Home: Winter Park Fla. Died Mar. 7, 1996.

SEELEY, RUDOLPH GERALD, real estate developer and investment officer; b. Berlin, Federal Republic of Germany, Feb. 9, 1915; came to U.S., 1934; s. Karl and Else (Sinai) Seelig; m. Martha Ulfelder, Feb. 26, 1949; children: John N., Margaret Ruth, Julie Ann. Student, NYU, 1938-40, Md. U., 1951-53. Enlisted U.S. Army, 1939; advanced through grades to col. U.S. Army Intelligence, mainly ETO; ret. U.S. Army, 1951; mgr. dairy farm Faifax County, Va., 1951-62; exec. v.p., co-owner, chmn. bd. West Gate and West Park, Inc., Faifax County, Va., 1962—; gen. ptnr. various real estate ventures, McLean, Va.; bd. dirs. Dominion Bankshares, Roanoke, Va., Dominion Bank of No. Va., Vienna. Trustee Va. Mus., Richmond, 1983—, George Mason U. Found., Fairfax, 1984—; bd. dirs. Fairfax Symphony, McLean, 1983—; pres. Fairfax C. of C., 1973,74. Died Jan. 4, 1988.

SEGAL, BERNARD GERARD, lawyer; b. N.Y.C., June 11, 1907; s. Samuel I. and Rose (Cantor) S.; m. Geraldine Rosenbaum, Oct. 22, 1933; children: Loretta Joan Segal Cohen, Richard Murry. A.B., U. Pa., 1928, LL.B., 1931, LL.D., 1969; LL.D., Franklin and Marshall Coll., 1953, Temple U., 1954, Dropsie U., 1966, Jewish Theol. Sem. Am., 1977, Vt. Law Sch., 1978, Villanova U., 1980, Georgetown U., 1983; J.S.D., Suffolk U., 1969; D.H.L., Hebrew Union Coll., 1970. Bar: Pa. 1932, D.C. 1976. Mem. faculty U. Pa., 1928-35, 45-47; Am. reporter on contracts Internat. Congress of Law, The Hague, The Netherlands, 1932; asst. dep. atty. gen. Commonwealth of Pa., 1932-33, dep. atty. gen., 1933-34; co-founder Schnader Harrison Segal & Lewis, Phila., 1935-97; instr. grad. bus., govt. Am. Inst. Banking, 1936-39; chmn. Schnader Harrison Segal & Lewis, Phila., 1968-86, sr. ptnr., 1986-88, of counsel, 1988-94; mem. Bd. Law Examiners, Phila., 1940-46; chmn. Commn. Jud. and Congl. Salaries, U.S. Govt., 1953-55; mem. Atty. Gen.'s Nat. Com. to Study Anti-trust Laws, 1953-55; mem. exec. com. Atty. Gen.'s Nat. Conf. on Ct. Congestion, 1958-61; mem. standing com. on rules of practice and procedure Jud. Conf. U.S., 1959-76; co-chmn. Lawyers Com. on Civil Rights Under Law, 1963-65 (Founder award, 25th Anniversary, 1988); chmn. Pa. Jud. Nominating Commn., 1964-66; mem. Nat. Citizens Com. on Community Rels., 1964-74; mem. adv. com. U.S. mission to UN, 1967-68; mem. adv. panel internat. law U.S. Dept. State, 1967-79; mem. Adminstrv. Conf. U.S., 1968-74; chmn. nat. adv. com. on legal svcs. U.S. OEO, 1968-76, chmn. exec. com., 1971-74; chmn. bd. Coun. Legal Edn. Opportunities, 1968-71; mem. Jud. Coun. Pa., 1968-71; coun. World Peace Through Law Ctr., chmn. 1st demonstration trial, Belgrade, Yugoslavia, 1971, coun., 1973-94, participant world confs., Athens, Greece, Washington, Geneva, Bangkok, Abidjan, Ivory Coast, Manila and Cairo, chmn. com. on internat. communications, world chmn. World Law Day, Madrid, 1979, Berlin, 1985; mem. U.S. Commn. on Exec., Legis. and Jud. Salaries, 1972-73, 76-77; mem. Appellate Ct. Nominating Commn., 1973-79; mem. U.S. Commn. Revision Fed. Ct. Appellate System, 1974-75; chmn. World Conf. on Peace and Violence, Jerusalem, 1979. Editor in chief: Pennsylvania Banking and Building and Loan Law, 3 vols., 1941; editor: The Belgrade Spaceship Trial, 1972; mem. internat. hon. bd. Ency. Judaica; contbr. articles to law revs., other publs. Life trustee, mem. exec. bd. U. Pa., 1959-77, life trustee emeritus, 1977-97; emeritus mem. bd. overseers U. Pa. Law Sch., 1959-97; mem. Commn. on Anti-Poverty Program for Phila., 1967-71, Bus. Leadership Organized for Cath. Schs., 1979-92, Commonwealth Commn. on Bicentennial of U.S. Constn., 1986-87; chmn. bd. Coun. Advancement Legal Edn., 1972-77; coun. trustees Hebrew U. Jerusalem; bd. dirs. So. Africa Legal Svcs. and Legal Edn. Project, 1979-97, NAACP Legal Def. and Ednl. Fund, Found. Fed. Bar Assn.; bd. govs. emeritus, past. v.p., past treas. Dropsie Coll.; trustee emeritus, former exec. com. Albert Einstein Med. Ctr.; trustee Phila. Martin Luther King, Jr. Ctr. Nonviolent Social Change (Drum Major award for legal justice, 1984), 1984-97, Found. for the Commemoration of the U.S. Constn., 1986-88, Found. for U.S. Constn., 1988-97, bd. dirs. Chapel of Four Chaplains; mem. planning commn. Miracle at Phila., 1986-87. Recipient Arthur von Briesen medal Nat. Legal Aid and Defender Assn., 1970, Nat. Human Rels. award NCCJ, 1972, Herbert Lewis Harley award, Am. Judicature Soc., 1974, World Lawyer award World Peace through Law Ctr., 1975, Judge William H. Hastie award NAACP Legal Def. Fund, 1986, Legion Honor Gold Medallion award Chapel of Four Chaplains, 1988, Nat. Civil Rights award U.S. Atty. Gen. and Lawyers Com. for Civil Rights Under Law, 1969, Ford Found. award to our Counselor on Pub. Interest, 1979, Nat. Award of Merit Fed. Adminstrv. Law Judges Conf., 1984, Pa. Bar Assn. award for Dedicated and Disting. Service, Field of Jurisprudence and Admin. of Justice, 1962, 10th Anniversary award Pub. Interest Law Ctr. Phila., 1984; co-recipient Nat. Neighbors Disting. Leadership in Civil Rights award, 1988, ACLU Civil Liberties award, 1991, U. Pa. Law Alumni award of Merit, 1991. Fellow Am. Coll. Trial Lawyers (pres. 1964-65), ABA (pres. 1969-70, Gold medal 1976), Inst. Jud. Adminstrn. (bd. dirs. 1968-86), Am. Bar Found. (pres. 1976-78); mem. Jewish Fed. Greater Phila. (mem. emeritus exec. com.), Pa. Bar Assn., Phila. Bar Assn. (chancellor 1952, 53), Pa. Urban Affairs Partnership, Fed. Bar Assn. (nat. coun.), Assn. of Bar of City of N.Y., D.C. Bar Assn., Am. Arbitration Assn. (former dir.), Am. Law Inst. (1st v.p. 1976-86, 2nd v.p. 1970-75, treas. 1955-69, counselor emeritus 1987-97), Am. Judicature Soc. (chmn. 1958-61, bd. dirs. 1956-97), Coun. Legal Edn. for Profl. Responsibility (dir.), Fed. Juc. Conf. 3d Cir. (life), World Assn. Lawyers (pres. for Ams. 1976-86), Nat. Conf. Bar Pres., Taxpayers Forum Pa. (past pres.), Allied Jewish Appeal (past pres., hon. pres.), Legal Aid Soc. Phila.)bd. dirs.), Jewish League Israel (nat. bd.), Jewish Pub. Soc. Am. (life trustee, mem. exec. com.), Jewish Family Svc. (hon. dir.), Order of Coif, Tau Epsilon Rho, Delta Sigma Rho. Republican. Clubs: Locust, Union League, Faculty, Metropolitan (Washington). Home: Philadelphia Pa. Died June 1, 1997; interred Roosevelt Memorial Park, Trevose, PA.

SEGAL, HAROLD LEWIS, biochemistry educator; b. N.Y.C., Nov. 18, 1924; s. Charles and Rachel (Finn) S.; m. Norma Caplan, June 15, 1945; children: Robin Ann, Deborah Claire. BS, Carnegie Mellon U., 1947; MS, U. Minn., 1949, PhD, 1952. Rsch. assoc. UCLA, 1952-54; asst. prof. biochemistry U. Pitts., 1954-59; assoc. prof. St. Louis U., 1959-64; prof. SUNY, Buffalo, 1964-69, emeritus prof., 1989—; vis. prof. pharmacology Stanford U., 1970-71; prof., fellow U. Coll. Cardiff, Wales, 1971. Contbr. numerous articles to profl. jours. Dir. Biochem. Program, NSF, 1987-88. Served as sgt. USAAF, 1943-46, PTO. Recipient Career Devel. award NIH, 1961-64; Sr. rsch. fellow NSF, 1961, Sr. fellow in sci. NSF/NATO, 1969. Mem. Am. Soc. Molecular Biology and Biochemistry, Am. Soc. Cell Biology, Am. Inst. Nutrition. Deceased.

SEGHERS, PIERRE (PAUL) CHARLES, writer, literary critic; b. Paris, Jan. 5, 1906; s. Charles and Marthe (Lebbe) S.; m. Colette Peugniez, 1968; 2 children by previous marriage. Ed., Coll. deCarpentras, U. Paris; LL.D. (hon.), U. Paris, 1969; D.honoris causa, U. St. Andrews (Scotland), 1984. Founder, pub. mag. Poetes Casques, pub. as Poesie, 1940, 41-48; active in prodn. and distbn. of clandestine publs., 1940-44; founding mem. Comite National des Ecrivains; early collaborator in French Liberation; founder Autour du monde (anthology of fgn. poets), 1952; producer two films, numerous radio and TV prodns.; producer of shows at la Comedie des Champs-Elysees, Theatre de la Ville, others. Author: Bonne esperance, 1939; L'homme du commun ou Jean Dubuffet, 1944; Le domaine public, 1945; Le futur anterieur, 1947; Poemes choisis, 1952; Le coeur-volant, 1954; Racines, 1957; Las Pierres, 1957; Chansons et complaintes, 4 vols., 1959-70; Piranese, 1960; Le Livre d'Or de la poesie francaise, 1962; Dialogues, 1967; Les mots couverts, 1970; Clave, 1972; Les poetes maudits, 1972; Dis-moi ma vie, 1973; La resistance et ses poetes, 1974; Le mur de son, 1976; Au seuil de l'oubli, 1976; Saadi le jardin des roses (transl.), 1977; Le temps des merveilles (complete poetry collection), 1978; Haifiz le divan, 1978; Monsu Desiderio, 1981; Omar Khayyam, les Ruba'iyat (transl.), 1982; Victor Hugo Visionnaire, 1983. Decorated officer Legion d'honneur (France); officer de l'Ordre de Leopold (Belgium); officer Order of So. Cross (Brazil); comdr. des Arts et des Lettres; recipient Prix Apollinaire, 1958; Aigle d'or la poesie, 1971; Grand Prix Internat. Christo Botev, Sofia, 1976; Grand Prix du Disque, 1976; Grand Prix Poesie, Ville de Paris, 1979.

SEID, RUTH (JO SINCLAIR), author; b. Bklyn., July 1, 1913; d. Nathan and Ida S. Grad., John Hay High Sch., Cleve. Various clerical jobs, publicity work, 1943-46; asst. dir. publicity dept. Greater Cleve. chpt. A.R.C., 1945-46. Author: Wasteland, 1946 (exerpts, revs. and notes included in Gay/Lesbian Almanac 1983), reissued, 1987, Sing at My Wake, 1951, (play) The Long Moment, 1951, The Changelings, 1955, reissued, 1985, Anna Teller, 1960, reissued 1992, The Seasons: Death and Transfiguration; A Memoir, 1993; (short stories anthologies) Theme and Variation in the Short Story, 1938, Of the People, 1942, America in Literature, 1944, This Way to Unity, 1945, Social Insight Through Short Stories, 1946, Cross Section, 1947, This Land, These People, 1950; contbr. short stories to anthologies A Treasury of American Jewish Stories, 1958, The American Judaism Reader, 1967, Tales of Our People, 1969, (anthology) Scrittori Ebrei Americani, 2 vols., 1989, America and I. Short Stories by American Jewish Women Writers, 1990, Anthology of Western Reserve Literature, 1992; contbr. to mags. including Readers Digest. Recipient Harper's Prize novel award 1946, 2d prize nat. TV competition Fund for Republic 1956, Ann. Fiction award Jewish Book Council Am. 1956, ann. award Ohioana Library 1956, 61, Brotherhood Week certificate of recognition NCCJ 1956, Lit. award Cleve. Arts prize 1961, Wolpaw Play Writing grant Jewish Community Centers, Cleve. 1969. Mem. Authors Guild Am., P.E.N. Jo Sinclair collection in Mugar Meml. Library, Boston U. Home: Jenkintown Pa. Died 1995.

SEIDEL, GLENDA LEE, newspaper publisher; b. Pitts., Feb. 21, 1936; d. Howard Arthur and Elizabeth

Jean (Peters) Jackson; m. Frederick Rex Seidel, Jan. 19, 1963; children: Paula Jean, Carol Ann. Grad. high sch., Ft. Myers, Fla., 1976. Editorial asst. Success Unltd. Mag., Chgo., 1953-54; sec. various cos., Chgo. and Skokie, Ill., 1955-68; editorial asst. Popular Sci. mag., Chgo., 1959-68; reporter, columnist, photographer weekly Suburban Reporter, Ft. Myers, 1975-76; editor Lehigh (Fla.) News, 1977-78, mng. editor, 1979-84, publisher, 1984-92, also columnist, 1977-92; pres., pub. The Lehigh Acres News-Star, 1992; v.p. Lehigh Corp., Lehigh Pub. Co., 1985-91, pres., 1991-92. Past sec. Lehigh Players; past mem. Lehigh Acres Community Council. Named Best Actress of Yr. Lehigh Players, 1970, Best Supporting Actress, 1975. Mem. Nat. League Am. Pen Women, Fla. Press Assn., Nat. Newspaper Assn., Lehigh C. of C. (Community Service award). Republican. Died Dec. 3, 1996.

SEIDMAN, HERTA LANDE, international trade and information company executive; married. BA in Econs. and Lit., McGill U. and U. Miami, 1959; MA, Cornell U., 1960. Mgr. shipping and internat. trade bus. devel. firm, 1962-76; dep. commr. N.Y. State Dept. of Commerce, 1976-79; asst. sec. for trade U.S. Dept. of Commerce Carter Adminstrn., 1979; mng. dir. Philipp Bros. (thereafter Phibro & Phibro-Salomon and Solomon Brothers), 1981-85; co-founder, chmn. Tradenet Corp., N.Y.C., 1985—; dir Atlantic Coun. of U.S.; chmn. Soros Bus. and Mgmt. Found.; vice chair N.Y. Gov.'s Coun. Internat. Bus. Bd. dirs. Jr. Achievement Internat., Albania Am. Enterprise Fund. Woodrow Wilson fellow, 1960. Mem. Coun. Fgn. Rels. Died Jan. 3, 1997.

SEITZ, HOWARD ALEXANDER, lawyer; b. Bklyn., Nov. 14, 1907; s. Louis A. and Elizabeth A. (Ternan) S.; m. Mary V. Cunningham, Sept. 7, 1933; children: Mary Virginia Seitz Gallagher, Howard G. A.B., Fordham U., 1930; LL.B., Columbia U., 1933. Bar: N.Y. 1934, Fla. 1978. Practiced in N.Y.C., 1934-95; mem. Paul, Weiss, Rifkind, Wharton & Garrison, 1943-78, counsel, 1978-95. Chmn. Cardinal's Task Force on Aging, 1977-82; chmn. N.Y. State Catholic Conf. Commn. on Elderly, 1983-87; bd. dirs. Bklyn. Bur. Community Service, Community Council Greater N.Y., Inner City Scholarship Fund, Inc. Decorated knight of Malta, knight Holy Sepulchre. Mem. ABA, N.Y. State Bar Assn., Fla. Bar, Assn. Bar City N.Y. Roman Catholic. Club: Lost Tree. Home: Rye N.Y. Died Sept. 15, 1995.

SELBY, ROGER LOWELL, museum director; b. Phila., July 4, 1933; s. Willard Lowell and Margaret Anne (Gray) S.; 1 child, Christine. A.B., U. Md., 1960; postgrad., Claremont Grad. Sch., 1960-61, Ind. U., 1963-65; doctoral studies in fine arts, U. N.Mex., 1983—. Curator edn. Nat. Gallery Art, Washington, 1961-62, Corcoran Gallery Art, Washington, 1965-68; head edn. Wadsworth Atheneum, Hartford, 1968-74; dir. Winnipeg (Man., Can.) Art Gallery, 1974-83, Boca Raton Mus. Art., Fla., 1984-95; instr. Corcoran Sch. Art, 1965-68, Hartford Art Sch., 1969-71; Asst., gen. fellow Claremont Grad. Sch., 1960-61; asst. Ind. U., 1963-65; hon. prof. U. Winnipeg, 1979-82. Served with U.S. Army, 1953-55. Recipient Queen's Silver Jubilee medal, 1978. Mem. Assn. Art Mus. Dirs., Canadian Art Mus. Dirs. Orgn. (pres. 1979-81), Can. Mus. Assn. (chmn. fin./exec. com. 1980-81). Home: Boca Raton Fla. Died Apr. 5, 1995.

SELDES, GEORGE, author; b. Alliance, N.J., Nov. 16, 1890; s. George Sergius and Anna (Saphro) S.; m. Helen Larkin Wiesman. Student, Harvard, 1912-13. Reporter Pitts. Leader, 1909-10; night editor Pitts. Post, 1910-16; war corr. with AEF, 1918-19; head Berlin bur. Chgo. Tribune, 1920-25, Rome bur. Chgo. Tribune, 1924-25; war corr. French campaign in Syria, 1926-27; corr. Chgo. Tribune, Mex., 1927-28; war corr. N.Y. Post in, Spain, 1936-37; author, 1928—; editor weekly newsletter In Fact, 1940-50. Author: numerous books including You Can't Print That, 1929, Sawdust Caesar, 1935, Lords of the Press, 1938, Facts and Fascism, 1943, 1000 Americans, 1947, The People Don't Know, 1949, Tell the Truth and Run, 1953, Never Tire of Protesting, 1968, Even the Gods Cannot Change History, 1976, Witness To A Century, 1988; editor, compiler: The Great Quotations, 1961,, Great Thoughts, 1985. Recipient award for profl. excellence Assn. Edn. in Journalism, The George Polk Ann. award, 1982, Sigma Delta Chi Soc. Profl. Journalists, Temple U. award, 1982, ann. C.L. award ACLU Vt., 1989, Vt. Outstanding Citizen award, 1990. Democrat. Died July 2, 1995.

SELF, EDWIN FORBES, editor, publisher; b. Dundee, Scotland, June 15, 1920; came to U.S., 1921; s. Robert Henry and Agnes (Dick) S.; m. Dorothy McCloskey, Nov. 1, 1942; children—Joan, Robert; m. Gloria Eileen Winke Wade, Aug. 18, 1951; children—Winke, Carey. A.B. Magna cum laude with distinction in Polit. Sci, Dartmouth, 1942. Advertising manager La Jolla (Calif.) Light, 1946; pub. North Shores Sentinel, Pacific Beach, Calif., 1947-48; bus. manager Frontier Magazine, Los Angeles, 1949-55; founder, editor, publisher San Diego Magazine, 1948—; publisher cons. for San Francisco mag., 1961-63; pub. cons. Washingtonian Mag., 1965-66. Recipient Telesu award Am. Inst. Planners, San Diego, 1963, Pub. Info. award Calif. AIA, 1970, spl. award 1st Ann. City and Regional Mag. Conf., 1977, William Allen White award. Mem. San Diego C. of C., City and Regional Mag. Assn. U.S. (Gold medal for gen. excellence 1986, Life Time Achievement award 1990), Phi Beta Kappa, Delta Tau Delta, Soc. Profl. Journalsists. Clubs: La Jolla Country, Tennis. Died April 16, 1996.

SELL, KENNETH WALTER, pathologist, educator; b. Valley City, N.D., Apr. 29, 1931; s. Walter Robert and Patricia Haldora (Gottskalkson) S.; Dec. 20, 1950; children—Gregory, Thomas, Barbette, Susan. B.A., U. N.D., 1953, B.S., 1954; M.D., Harvard U., 1956; Ph.D., Cambridge (Eng.) U., 1968. Diplomate Am. Bd. Pediatrics, Am. Bd. Pathology. Commd. capt. M.C. U.S. Navy, 1956; intern Nat. Naval Med. Center, Bethesda, Md., 1956-57; resident, pediatrician Nat. Naval Med. Center, 1956-65, dir. Navy tissue bank, 1965-70, chmn. dept. clin. and exptl. immunology, 1970-74, inst. comdg. officer, 1974-77; ret., 1977; sci. dir. Nat. Inst. Allergy and Infectious Diseases, Bethesda, 1977-85; prof. and chmn. dept. pathology Emory U., Atlanta, 1985—; dir. Emory Cancer Ctr., 1985-92. Editor: Tissue Banking for Transplantation, 1976. Decorated Legion of Merit. Fellow Am. Acad. Pediatrics, Am. Acad. Pathology; mem. AMA, Soc. Cryobiology, Transplantation Soc., Am. Assn. Immunologists, Soc. Exptl. Hematology, Am. Assn. Tissue Banks (pres.), Am. Coll. Pathology, Am. Soc. Microbiology, Phi Beta Kappa, Sigma Xi, Phi Beta Pi. Home: 2860 Greystone Ln Atlanta GA 30341-5860 Office: Dept Pathology 703 WMB Emory U Sch Medicine Atlanta GA 30322 Died Oct. 17, 1996.

SELLERS, JAMES EARL, theological educator; b. Lucedale, Miss., Nov. 1, 1926; s. Lucius Earl and Grace (McVicar) S. BEE, Ga. Inst. Tech., 1947; MS, Fla. State U., 1954; PhD (Kent fellow), Vanderbilt U., 1958. Asst. prof. Christian ethics and theology Div. Sch. Vanderbilt U., Nashville, 1958-61; assoc. prof. Vanderbilt U., 1961-64, prof., 1964-71, dean Div. Sch., 1964-67; David Rice prof. ethics Rice U., Houston, 1971-93, prof. emeritus, 1993—; retired, 1993. Author: The Outsider and the Word of God, 1961, The South and Christian Ethics, 1962, Theological Ethics, 1966, Public Ethics, 1970, Warming Fires, 1975, The Polis in America as Imago Dei, 1984, Tensions in the Ethics of Interdependence, 1986, Medical Ethics and the Civil Rights Movement, 1989, Love and Justice Reconsidered, 1990, Essays in American Ethics, 1991; co-author: The Health-Care Community as a Reservoir of Potential Subjects, 1984; editor-at-large The Christian Century, 1971-86; contbr. articles to Ethical Issues in Am. Life, Lifeboat Ethics. Lt. USNR, 1944-54. Recipient Danforth Rsch. award, France, 1966. Mem. Soc. for Values in Higher Edn., Group for Research in Med-Ethics, AAUP. Died March 23, 1997.

SELOSSE, JACQUES PAUL, psychology educator; b. Lestrem, Nord, France, Apr. 12, 1923; s. Paul Louis and Zulma (De Jans) S.; m. Genevieve Jeanne Charle, Aug. 11, 1944; children: Jacques-Alain, Bruno. BS, Lycée Armentiéres, France, 1941; M Psychology, U. Sorbonne, Paris, 1951, PhD, 1969. Dir. Svc. for Maladjusted Children, Rabat, Morocco, 1952-58; rschr. Ctr. Nat. Rsch. Sci., Vaucresson, France, 1958-72; prof. psychology U. Lille, France, 1972-75; dir. Ctr. Formation & Rsch. Edn., Surveillée-Vaucresson, France, 1975-81; prof. U. Paris-Nord et Inst. Psychology, Paris, 1981-90; prof. emeritus U. Paris - XIII, 1988; prof. Instituto Superior de Psicologia Aplicada, Lisbon, Portugal, 1991-96; prof. Inst. Crimology, Paris, 1972-85; head Svc. Rsch. Edn. Surveillée, 1958-81; expert in field, Strasbourg, France, 1963-81; dir. informational meeting for study of deviant behavior Fonctions des deviances, 1977; organizer meetings in field. Mem. editl. bd. Jour. of Adolescence, 1978-89; co-author, rschr. Que deviennent-ils Enquete sur le devenir des jeunes delinquants, 1974; assoc. editor Annales de Vaucresson, 1963-81. Cons. Conseil Technique de Clubs et Equipes de Prévention, Paris, 1991-96, Ctr. Technique Nat. d'Etudes et Rsch. Handicaps and Inadaptations, Paris, 1978-96; expert Haut Comité d'Etudes et d'Information sur l'Alcoolisme, Paris, 1985-91. Lt. Compagnie Militaire d'Adminstrn., 1944-45. Recipient Légion d'Honneur Chevalier, French Ministry of Justice, 1979. Mem. French Soc. Psychology, Internat. Soc. Criminology. Roman Catholic. Avocations: music, photography, travel. Died Nov. 9, 1996.

SELSKY, SAMUEL, film producer, consultant; b. Chgo., Nov. 11, 1909; arrived in France, 1947.; s. Abraham and Sonia S.; m. Marcella Siegel (div.); m. Lillian Hopkins (dec.); m. Liliane Stoumon (div.). BA, Johns Hopkins U., 1929, postgrad., 1930-32; MA, U. Md., 1942. Sci. tchr. Balt. Sch. Sys., 1935-41; Geologist State Geodetic Survey, Md., D.C., 1930-31; geologist Columbian Mining Enterprises, Colombia, 1933-34; dep. dir. dist. 4 Nat. Youth Adminstrn., Washington, 1942-43; placement officer War Manpower Commn., Washington, 1943-45; dir. War Relocation Authority, L.A., 1945-46; adminstr. UN, 1946-47; dir. pers. UNESCO, Paris, 1947-51; European prodr. "You Asked for It", Paris, 1951-58; film prodr. Les Films ABC, Paris, 1959—; dep. dir. Gen. Inst. Internat. de Biologie Humaine, Paris, Brussels, 1963-65. Editor: Sci. Trade Jour. Assn. U.S.; contbr. articles to profl. jours.; author radio scripts for nat. edn. U.S., 1942. Vol. USCGR, 1944-45. Recipient Medaille Argent Arts Scis. Lettres, Paris, 1966. Phi Delta Kappa. Jewish. Avocations: bridge, golf, travel, dramatics. DIED 06/06/96. .

SELTIN, RICHARD JAMES, natural science educator, vertebrate paleontologist; b. Chgo., Nov. 4, 1927; s. Alfred David Seltin and Ruth Elfreda (Engebrigtsen) S.; m. Edith Hulet, July 4, 1953; children: Kyle Richard, Cristofer Daniel, Jason Andrew. B.A., U. Wyo., 1949; M.S., U. Chgo., 1954, Ph.D., 1956. From instr. to prof. Mich. State U., East Lansing, 1956—, asst. chmn. dept. natural sci., 1968-74, chmn., 1974-84, adj. curator museum, 1957—. Contbg. author: Biology, 1982; contbr. articles to profl. jours. Served with U.S. Army, 1950-52. Mem. Soc. Vertebrate Paleontology, Soc. Study Evolution, Nat. Sci. Tchrs. Assn. Office: Mich State U East Lansing MI 48824 Died June 22, 1997.

SENGSTACKE, JOHN HERMAN HENRY, publishing company executive; b. Savannah, Ga., Nov. 25, 1912; s. Herman Alexander and Rosa Mae (Davis) S.; 1 son, Robert Abbott. B.S., Hampton (Va.) Inst., 1933; postgrad., Ohio State U., 1933. With Robert S. Abbott Pub. Co. (publishers Chgo. Defender), 1934-97, v.p., gen. mgr., 1934-40, pres., gen. mgr., 1940-97; chmn. bd. Mich. Chronicle, Detroit; pres. Tri-State Defender, Defender Publs., Amalgamated Pubs., Inc.; pub. Daily Defender; pres. Sengstacke Enterprises, Inc., Sengstacke Publs., Pitts. Courier Newspaper Chain; dir. Ill. Fed. Savs. & Loan Assn., Golden State Mut. Life Ins. Co. Mem. exec. bd. Nat. Alliance Businessmen; bd. govs. USO; mem. Ill. Sesquicentennial Commn., Pres.'s Com. on Equal Opportunity in Armed Services; mem. pub. affairs adv. com. Air Force Acad.; trustee Bethune-Cookman Coll., Daytona Beach, Fla., Hampton Inst.; bd. dirs. Washington Park YMCA, Joint Negro Appeal; chmn. bd. Provident Hosp. Recipient Two Friends award Nat. Urban League, 1950; Hampton Alumni award, 1954; 1st Mass. Media award Am. Jewish Com. Mem. Negro Newspaper Pubs. Assn. (founder), Nat. Newspaper Pubs. Assn. (founder, pres.), Am. Newspaper Pubs. Assn., Am. Soc. Newspaper Editors (dir.). Congregationalist. Clubs: Royal Order of Snakes, Masons, Elks, Econs, Chgo. Press. Home: Chicago Ill. Died May 28, 1997.

SENKIER, ROBERT JOSEPH, foundation administrator, educator; b. Poughkeepsie, N.Y., May 31, 1916; s. Michael J. and Mary Gilberta (Perrin) S.; m. Mary Theresa Kelly, Mar. 21, 1941; children—Pamela Jeanne Senkier Scott, Deborah Ann. A.B., Columbia U., 1939, M.A., 1940, Ed.D., 1961. Mem. bus. faculty Columbia U., 1948-61; asst. dean Columbia U. (Sch. Bus.), 1958-61; prof. mgmt., dean Sch. Bus. Adminstrn. Seton Hall U., South Orange, N.J., 1962-74; prof. mgmt., dean Grad. Sch. Bus., Fordham U., N.Y.C., 1975-79; exec. dir. Mathers Found., 1982-84; found. cons., 1985-96. Author: Revising a Business Curriculum—The Columbia Experience, 1961; contbr. articles to profl. jours. Mem. alumni bd. dirs. Columbia Coll.; mem. John Jay Assocs.; Holy See del. to U.N., 1980-83; trustee Marymount Coll. Va., 1983-85, Molloy Coll., 1986-89. Served to lt. comdr. USNR, 1940-45. Mem. Acad. Internat. Bus., Columbia Alumni Assn., Phi Delta Kappa, Alpha Kappa Psi, Alpha Sigma Phi, Beta Gamma Sigma. Republican. Roman Catholic. Club: Princeton (N.Y.C.). Died June 1, 1996.

SENTER, WILLIAM JOSEPH, publishing company executive; b. N.Y.C., Dec. 4, 1921; s. Joseph and Sarah (Greenglass) S.; m. Irene Phoebe Marcus, Aug. 3, 1952; children: Adam Douglas, Caren Amy. B.B.A., CCNY, 1947. Chmn. bd., mng. editor Deadline Data, Inc., N.Y.C., 1962-66; pres. Unipub, Inc. (merged with Xerox Corp. 1971), N.Y.C., 1966-72; v.p. planning and devel. Xerox Info. Resources Group (includes AutEx Systems, R.R. Bowker Co., Ginn & Co., Univ. Microfilms Internat., Unipub Inc., Xerox Edn. Publs., Xerox Learning Systems, Xerox Computer Services), Greenwich, Conn., 1973-74; v.p. info. pub. Xerox Info. Resources Group, Greenwich, 1974-75; pres. Xerox Info. Resources Group, 1976-80, chmn., 1980-86; v.p. Xerox Corp., Stamford, Conn., 1978-86; pres. R.R. Bowker Co., N.Y.C., 1974-75. Served with U.S. Army, 1942-46. Mem. Assn. Am. Pubs. (dir. 1978-81), Info. Industry Assn. (dir. 1980-83). Office: PO Box 364 Cos Cob CT 06807-0364 Died Nov. 20, 1997.

SERAFIM, JOAQUIN LAGINHA, retired civil engineering educator; b. Loulé, Algarve, Portugal, Dec. 1, 1921; s. Jose Leal and Antonia (Laginha) S.; m. Maria Jose Diniz Garcia, Dec. 18, 1949; children: Maria Joao, Maria Margarida. CE, Lisbon (Portugal) Tech. U., 1944; D (hon.), U. Rio de Janeiro, U. Liege, Belgium, 1979. Engr. Zezere Hydroelectric Co., Lisbon, 1946-57; founder, head dams dept. Nat. Civil Engring. Lab., Lisbon, 1948-63; pres. bd. dirs. COBA S.A.R.L., internat. cons., Lisbon, 1962—; prof. civil engring Coimbra (Portugal) U. Sci. and Tech. Faculty, 1972-91 ret., 1991; vis. prof. MIT, Cambridge, 1964-65 Eduardoo Mondlane U., Maputo Mozambique, 1976-77 vice pres. Internat. Commn. Large Dams, 1988, mem Nat. Portuguese Commn., hon. mem. Greek Commn. Contbr. numerous articles to profl. jours. Sub-lt. Portugese Army, 1944-45. Decorated officer Order Santiago de Espada, Order Civil Merit (Spain); recipien Aladeadavila, Almendra and Atazar medals Spanish Ministry Pub. Works, Dr. Camacho prize Lisbon Tech U., overseas premium Instn. Civil Engrs., London, investigation premium Manuel Rocha, 1985; sr. fgn scientist fellow NSF, 1964-65. Fellow ASCE, Instn Civil Engrs., Am. Concrete Inst.; mem. AAAS, Por tuguese Order Engrs., Soc. Civil Engrs. France, Internat. Soc. Rock Mechanics, Internat. Assn. Bridges and Structural Engring., Internat. Soc. Applied Solar Energy, Mediterranean Coop. for Application Solar Energy, Reunion Internat. Labs. Essais et Materiaux, Internat. Assn. Shell Structures, Am. Geophys. Union, Am. Seismol. Soc., Portuguese Soc. Structures (hon.), Gabinete Português de Leitura do Rio de Janeiro (hon.).

SERALNICK, MARK, political consultant; b. N.Y.C., Dec. 26, 1954; s. Herman L. and Shirley M. Seralnick. BA, U. Vt., 1976; MA, U. Calif., Santa Barbara, 1978; PhD, U. Tokyo, 1987. Japanese Ministry Edn. rsch. fellow U. Tokyo, 1978-84; researcher James Capel and Co., Tokyo, 1986-88; mgr. corp. strategy office Motorola Inc., Schaumburg, Ill., 1990—. Mem. Am. Polit. Sci. Assn., Assn. Asian Studies. Avocations: tennis, skiing, photography. DIED 01/06/97. .

SERGIEVSKY, OREST, ballet dancer, teacher, choreographer; b. Kiev, USSR, Aug. 21, 1911; s. Boris and Ella S. Pvt. study ballet including, Bronislava Nijinskaya, 1920, 40, Olga Preobrajenskaya, Paris, France, 1927-47, Michael Fokine, 1932-42, others; grad. drama dept., Columbia. Tchr. ballet arts own sch. Theatre Studio of Dance and Carnegie Hall Internat. Ballet Sch., 1950-71. Performed with, Art of Musical Russia, 1935, Salmagi Opera, 1937, Fokine ballets, 1936-38, Met. Opera Co., 1938, 39, Ballet Theatre, 1939-41, Original Ballet Russe, 1941, 45-48, solo concerts, 1936-50; dir., choreographer, Dance Varieties, now free-lance tchr., choreographer.; Author: autobiography Shadows-Memories, 1977. Served with USAAF, World War II.

SERRA-BADUE, DANIEL FRANCISCO, artist, educator; b. Santiago de Cuba, Sept. 8, 1914; came to U.S., 1962; s. Daniel Serra and Eloisa Badue; m. Aida Betancourt, Mar. 8, 1944; 1 dau., Aida Victoria. Licenciate in Law, U. Barcelona, 1936; LL.D., U. Havana, 1938, Dr. in Social, Polit. and Econ. Scis., 1949; M.F.A., Nat. Sch. Fine Arts, Havana, 1943. Prof. Sch. Fine Arts, Santiago de Cuba, 1945-60, Nat. Sch. Fine Arts, Havana, 1960-62; lectr. Columbia U., N.Y.C., 1962-63; instr. Bklyn. Mus. Art Sch., N.Y.C., 1962-85; prof. St. Peter's Coll., Jersey City, 1967-96; asst. dir. culture Ministry Edn., Havana, 1959-60. Exhibited over 40 one-man shows and over 250 group shows. Bd. dirs. Cintas Found., N.Y.C. Recipient Pa. Acad. prize, 1941; recipient Bienal Hispano Americana prize, 1954; Guggenheim Found. fellow, 1938, 39; Cintas Found. fellow, 1963, 64. Mem. AAUP, Coll. Art Assn. Am. Home: New York N.Y. Died July 15, 1996.

SERVAY, KENNETH JOHN, lawyer; b. New Orleans, Jan. 5, 1953; s. John Thomas and Leatrice (Query) S.; m. Olga Marie Stone, June 30, 1983; children: Olga Mae, Anna Marie. BA, U. New Orleans, 1974; JD, Loyola U., New Orleans, 1978. Bar: La. 1978, U.S. Dist. Ct. (ea. dist.) La. 1981, U.S. Ct. Appeals (5th and 11th cirs.) 1981, U.S. Dist. Ct. (mid. dist.) La. 1983, U.S. Supreme Ct. 1983, U.S. Dist. Ct. (we. dist.) la. 1985, Tenn. 1995. Law clk. La. Supreme Ct., New Orleans, 1978-79; staff atty. U.S. Ct. Appeals (5th cir.), New Orleans, 1979-81; assoc. Chaffe, McCall, Phillips, Toler & Sarpy, New Orleans, 1981—; adj. lectr. law Tulane U. Sch. Law, New Orleans, 1990-92, Disting. fellow in appellate advocacy, 1992-94. Contbr. articles to profl. jours. Mem. ABA, Maritime Law Assn., Bar Assn. (fed. 5th cir.). Roman Catholic. Avocations: automobiles, computers. Died Oct. 27, 1996.

SESSOMS, STUART MCGUIRE, physician, educator, insurance company executive; b. Autryville, N.C., July 16, 1921; s. Edwin Tate and Lillian Olive (Howard) S.; m. Thelma Ernestine Call, June 21, 1944; children: Stuart McGuire, Cristi Kay. B.S., U. N.C., 1943; M.D., Med. Coll. Va., 1946; postgrad., Johns Hopkins U. Diplomate: Am. Bd. Internal Medicine. Intern U.S. Marine Hosp., Balt., 1946-47; resident internal medicine U.S. Marine Hosp., 1947-50, asst. chief med. service, charge med. outpatient dept., 1950-52; asst. resident medicine Meml. Center Cancer and Allied Diseases, N.Y.C., 1952-53; with NIH, Bethesda, Md., 1953-68; mem. clin. medicine, surgery Nat. Cancer Inst., 1953-54, acting chief gen. medicine, 1954, asst. dir., 1958, asso. dir. collaberative research, 1961-62; chief cancer chemotherapy Nat. Service Center, 1958-62; asst. dir. clin. center NIH, 1955-57, dep. dir., 1962-68; clin. instr. medicine George Washington U., 1953-54; asso. dean, prof. medicine Duke Sch. Medicine, Durham, 1968-75; dir. Duke U. Hosp., 1968-75, prof. health adminstrn., 1973-75; sr. v.p. Blue Cross and Blue Shield of N.C., 1976-87. Contbr. articles to profl. jours. Active PTA. Recipient Distinguished Service award U.S. Jr. C. of C., 1957. Mem. AMA, Assn. Mil. Surgeons U.S., Am. Hosp. Assn., Am., N.C. hosp. assns., Am. Pub. Health Assn., N.Y. Acad. Sci., Phi Delta Chi, Rho Chi, Alpha Kappa Kappa. Presbyterian. Died April 24, 1997.

SETH, OLIVER, federal judge; b. Albuquerque, May 30, 1915; s. Julien Orem and Bernice (Grefe) S.; m. Jean MacGillivray, Sept. 25, 1946; children: Sandra Bernice, Laurel Jean. AB, Stanford U., 1937; LLB, Yale U., 1940. Bar: N.Mex. 1940. Practice law Santa Fe, 1940, 46-62; judge U.S. Ct. Appeals 10th Circuit, 1962-96, chief judge, 1976-96, sr. judge, 1996; dir. Santa Fe Nat. Bank, 1949-62; chmn. legal com. N.Mex. Oil and Gas Assn., 1956-59, mem. regulatory practices com., 1960-62; counsel N.Mex. Cattlegrowers Assn., 1950-62, N.Mex. Bankers Assn., 1952-62; govt. appeal agent SSS, 1948-52. Mem. bd. regents Mus. of N.Mex., 1956-60; bd. dirs. Boys Club, Santa Fe, 1948-49, New Mex. Land Resources Assn., 1956-60, Ghost Ranch Mus., 1962-96; mng. bd. Sch. Am. Rsch., 1950-96. Served from pvt. to maj. AUS, 1940-45, ETO. Decorated Croix de Guerre (France). Mem. N.Mex. Bar Assn., Santa Fe County Bar Assn., Santa Fe C. of C. (dir.), Phi Beta Kappa. Presbyterian. Home: Santa Fe N.Mex. Died Mar. 26, 1996.

SEWELL, JAMES LESLIE, engineering company executive; b. Coleman, Tex., Nov. 23, 1903; s. James McCord and Pearle (Davis) S.; m. Charlotte Barnard, Aug. 27, 1929; children—George Barnard, Frederic Dana, James McCord, John Charles. BME, Tex. A&M Coll., 1927. Refinery supt. Taylor Refining Co., 1933-35, gen. supt., 1939-47, v.p., 1947-52; refinery supt. Coastal Refineries, Inc., 1935-39; v.p., mem. exec. com., dir. Petroleum Heat & Power Co., 1946-50; pres., dir. Taylor Oil & Gas Co., 1952-55, Delhi-Taylor Oil Corp., Dallas, 1955-68, Standard Lumber Co. of Costa Rica, 1968-95; dir., mem. exec. com. dirs. Aztec Oil & Gas Co., 1969-76; dir. Canyon Resources Inc. Mem. Tex. Mid-Continent Oil and Gas Assn. (pres. 1963-65), Mid-Continent Oil and Gas Assn. (dir., pres. 1967-69), Am. Petroleum Inst., ASME, Soc. Automotive Engrs., Tau Beta Pi. Presbyterian. Clubs: Dallas Petroleum, Dallas Country, Willow Bend Polo and Hunt. Home: Dallas Tex. Died Aug. 3, 1995.

SEXTON, VIRGINIA STAUDT, retired psychology educator; b. N.Y.C., Aug. 30, 1916; d. Philip Henry and Kathryn Philippa (Burkard) Staudt; m. Richard J. Sexton, Jan. 21, 1961. B.A., Hunter Coll., 1936; MA, Fordham U., 1941, PhD, 1946; LHD, Cedar Crest Coll., 1980. Elem. tchr. St. Peter and St. Paul's Sch., Bronx, N.Y., 1936-39; clk. N.Y.C. Dept. Welfare, 1939-44; lectr., asst. prof., assoc. prof. psychology Notre Dame Coll. of S.I., 1944-52; instr. Hunter Coll. of CUNY, 1953-56, asst. prof., 1957-60, assoc. prof., 1961-66, prof., 1967-68; prof. psychology Herbert H. Lehman Coll., 1968-79, prof. emeritus, 1979-97; disting. prof. St. John's U., Jamaica, N.Y., 1979-92; mem. profl. conduct rev. bd. N.Y. State Bd. for Psychology, 1971-78; mem. adv. bd. Archives of History Am. Psychology, 1966—. Author: (with H. Misiak) Catholics in Psychology; A Historical Survey, 1954, History of Psychology: An Overview, 1966, Historical Perspectives in Psychology: Readings, 1971, Phenomenological, Existential and Humanistic Psychologies: A Historical Survey, 1973, Psychology Around the World, 1976. Editor: (with J. Dauben) History and Philosophy of Science: Selected Papers, 1983, (with R. Evans, T. Cadwallader) 100 Years: The American Psychology Assn., 1992, (with J. Hogan) International Psychology: Views From Around The World, 1992; mem. editorial bd. Jour. Phenomenological Psychology, 1977-97, Jour. Mind and Behavior, 1979-97, Interamerican Jour. Psychology, 1982—, The Humanistic Psychologist, 1984-97, Professional Psychology: Research and Practice, 1984-89, Clinician's Research Digest, 1984-92. Contbr. articles to profl. jours. Recipient Margaret Floy Washburn award N.Y. State Psychol. Assn., 1995. Fellow Am. Psychol. Assn., AAAS, N.Y. Acad. Scis., Charles Darwin Assocs.; mem. Am. Hist. Assn., AAUP, AAUW, Am. Assn. for Advancement Humanities, Internat. Assn. Applied Psychology, Internat. Council Psychologists (pres. 1981-82), Interam. Soc. Psychology, Internat. Soc. History of Behavioral and Soc. Scis., Eastern Psychol. Assn., N.Y. Soc. Clin. Psychologists, N.Y. Psychol. Assn., N.Y. Assn. Applied Psychologists, Assn. for Women in Psychology, N.Y. Acad. Scis. (Charles Darwin Assocs. award 1995), Psychologists Social Responsibility, Phi Beta Kappa, Psi Chi (v.p. eastern region 1982-86; pres. 1986-87). Roman Catholic. Avocation: stamp collecting. Died May 24, 1997.

SEYMOUR, JOHN, psychologist, educator; b. Bronx, N.Y., Oct. 21, 1917; s. Anthony Knepper and Sophie Slomowitz; m. Charlotte Rose Seymour, Oct. 11, 1958; children: Linda, Claire. BA, William Paterson Coll., 1951; MA, NYU, 1952, PhD, 1956. Lic. psychologist, N.J. Prof. and chmn. Montclair State Coll., Upper Montclair, N.J., 1967-87; dir. intern tng. program State of N.J., Princeton, 1965-67; chief psychologist North Essex Child Guidance, Belleville, N.J., 1958-60, Essex County Guidance Ctr., East Orange, N.J., 1960-65; pvt. practice Psychol. Growth Svcs., Montclair, 1965—; field supr. Grad. Sch. Applied & Profl. Psychology Rutgers U., New Brunswick, N.J., 1985—; clin. asst. prof. of psychology N.J. Sch. Medicine & Dentistry, Newark, 1963-80. Contbr. chpt. to book, articles to profl. jours. Pres. N.J. Psychol. Assn., 1975, N.J. Acad. Psychology, 1991. Recipient Psychologist of the Yr. award N.J. Psychol. Assn., 1985, Outstanding Recognition award N.J. Acad. Psychology, 1993. Fellow Am. Orthopsychiatric Assn.; mem. APA (coun. mem., rep. N.J. APA), Psychologists in Pvt. Practice (pres. 1967). Avocations: listening to music, vocalist, playing tennis, literature. Died Mar. 2, 1997.

SHAFER, JOSEPH ERNEST, economics educator emeritus, writer; b. Bluffton, Ind., Apr. 25, 1903; s. Otis Ernest and Ida March (Taylor) S.; m. Emily Cornell Marine, June 10, 1926 (dec.); children: Sue Elizabeth (Mrs. Harlow G. Farmer, Jr.), Thayer Cornell; m. Wilda Swango Jones, Feb. 14, 1993. A.B., DePauw U., 1925; M.A., U. Wis., 1929, Ph.D., 1932. Spl. study labor problems, working incognito as factory laborer, 1925-26; asst. instr. econs. U. Wis., 1929-32; assoc. prof. econs., head dept., coll. mines br. U. Tex., 1932-35; asso. prof. econs. Bowling Green State U., 1935-46; economist dist. office OPA, 1943-44; restaurant price br. OPA, Washington, 1944-46; prof. econs. U. N.H., 1946-60, chmn. dept., 1946-49; prof. econs., bus. adminstrn. Alaska Meth. U., 1960-70, dir. summer sessions, 1961-65, dean Coll. Bus. Adminstrn. and Econs., 1965-70, prof. emeritus, 1970-94; Vis. research prof. econs. N.Y. U. Grad. Sch. Bus. Adminstrn., summer 1956. Author: Explanation of the Business Cycle, 1928, The Trend of Non-Monetary Consumption of Gold, 1932, Analysis of the Business System, 1956, Alaska's Economy in Case of a National Economic Pause, 1968, Chrematistics-Economics, 1969, To Forestall the Imminent Super-Depression..., 1988. Trustee Alaska Mut. Savs. Bank, 1963-73. Alfred P. Sloan Found. research grantee, 1953; W. Alton Jones Found. research grantee, 1959. Mem. Am. Econs. Assn., Congress Polit. Economists, Soc. for Advancement Socio-Econs., Rotary. Methodist. Home: San Diego Calif. Died Nov. 9, 1994.

SHAFER, ROBERT EUGENE, English educator; b. Beloit, Wis., Mar. 30, 1925; s. James Vaughn and Harriet (Sewards) S.; m. Susanne Mueller, June 19, 1953. A.B., U. Wis., 1950, M.A., 1953; Ed.D., Columbia U., 1958. Instr., then asst. prof. English San Francisco State U., 1955-58; assoc. prof. Wayne State U., Detroit, 1958-62, Columbia U. Tchrs. Coll., 1962-66; prof. English Ariz. State U., Tempe, 1966-90. Author: Success, 1964, Personal Values, 1975; co-author: Ends and Issues in English, 1966, Success in Reading, vols. 1-8, 1973, Developing Reading Efficiency, 1975, Decisions About the Teaching of English, 1976, Applied Linguistics and Reading, 1979, Language Functions and School Success, 1983, Teaching and Learning English Worldwide, 1990. Served with USMCR, 1943-46. Mem. Internat. Reading Assn., MLA, Am. Linguistic Soc., Nat. Council Tchrs. English (v.p. 1968), Am. Dialect Soc., Am. Assn. Applied Linguistics, English-Speaking Union (pres. Phoenix br. 1985-86). Died April 26, 1997.

SHAFFER, LOUIS RICHARD, engineering research adminsistrator, civil engineering educator; b. Sharon, Pa., Feb. 28, 1955; m. 1955; 3 children. BS, Carnegie-Mellon U., 1950; MS, U. Ill., 1957, PhD in Syss. Civil Engring., 1961. Asst. to master mechanic Nat. Castings Co., Pa., 1950-52; asst. to dir. engring. Sharon (Pa.) Steel Corp., 1953-54; instr. civil engring. U. Ill., Urbana, 1955-61, from asst. prof. to assoc. prof., 1961-65, prof. civil engring., 1965—; tech. dir. constrn. engring. rsch. lab. U.S. Army, 1969—; asst. dir. Tech. Direction Constrn. Engring. Rsch. Lab. U.S. Army, 1969-70, dep. dir., 1970-76; coord. Internat. Working Commn. on Orgn. and Mgmt. Constrn., 1974—; chmn. U.S. Nat. Com. Internat. Coun. Bldg. Rsch., 1977-83. Mem. Am. Soc. Civil Engrs. (chmn. tech. coun. rsch. 1976-77, Walter L. Hubaer rsch. prize, 1967, Constrn. Mgmt. award, 1978, Constrn. Rsch. award, 1987), Soc. Am. Mil. Engrs. Achievements include rsch. on modern constrn. mgmt. with emphasis on tech. innovation to increase productivity of mgmt. on all levels. Died May 16, 1994.

SHAHBENDER, RABAH, electrical engineer, consultant; b. Damascus, Syria, July 23, 1924; came to U.S., 1948.; s. Abd-el-Rahman and Sarrah (Azem) S.; m. Eileen Vera Ogden, Jan. 21, 1954; children: Leila Mayyadah, Tarik Rabah, Randa Sarrah. BEE, Cairo (Egypt) U., 1946; MSEE, Washington U., 1949; PhDEE, U. Ill., 1951. Engr. Anglo-Egyptian Oilfields, Ltd., Cairo, 1946-48; rsch. engr. controls divsn. Honeywell, Phila., 1951-55; devel. engr. RCA Devel. Labs., Camden, N.J., 1955-58; sr. mem. tech. staff rsch. RCA Labs., Princeton, N.J., 1958-87; cons. Princeton, 1987—; evening divsn. chmn. dept. physics LaSalle Coll., Phila., 1960-67. Contbr. articles to profl. jours. Recipient Competition award Materials in Design Engring., 1963, IR 100 award, Indsl. Rsch. Inc., 1964, 69, Best Paper award Am. Fedn. Info. Soc., 1963; fellow U. Ill., 1949, 50. Fellow IEEE; mem. AAAS, Sigma Xi, Eta Kappa Nu. Nine patents in field. DIED 07/27/95. .

SHALLECK, MILTON, lawyer, retired judge; b. N.Y.C., June 8, 1905; s. Morris and Dora (Sussman) S.; m. Rosalyn Baron, June 24, 1934; children: Alan Bennett, Peter Blair. A.B., U. Pa., 1927; LL.B., Fordham U., 1930, LL.D. Bar: N.Y. 1931, also fed. cts 1931, U.S. Supreme Ct 1931. Pvt. practice N.Y.C., 1932-33; sec. to Justice Samuel I. Rosenman, N.Y. Supreme Ct., 1934-43; head atty. Office Lend Lease Adminstrn., Washington, 1943; spl. counsel Fgn. Econ. Adminstrn., 1943-45; pvt. practice with Oscar Cox, N.Y.C. and Washington, 1945-46; with Samuel I. Rosenman, 1946-48; partner Shalleck & Krakower, 1948-53; pvt. practice, 1953-62; counsel to Gainsburg, Gottlieb, Levitan & Cole, 1976—; judge Criminal Ct. of City of N.Y., 1962-76; acting civil and supreme ct. judge. U.S. commr. on South Pacific Commn., 1948-53; spl. dep. supt. of ins. State of N.Y., 1955-59; Sec. Franklin D. Roosevelt Meml. Found., Inc., 1947-48. Author: The Evolution of a Court, 1949, articles legal jours. Mem. Am., Fed. N.Y. State bar assns., Bar Assn. City N.Y., Tau Delta

Phi. Clubs: Mason, Elk. Home: Roslyn N.Y. DIED 05/01/95. .

SHAMBLIN, DARRELL RAY, lay worker; b. Elkhurst, W.Va., Dec. 3, 1927; s. Holly Orville and Claris Marie (Gray) S.; m. Suzanne Jane Perkins May 17, 1958 (dec. Oct. 1990); children: Bryan Drake, Kevin Gray, Holly Anne. Student, W.Va. Wesleyan Coll., 1946-48; BA in Journalism, Marshall U., 1950; M Letters, U. Pitts., 1957; postgrad., Northwestern U., 1958-62, United Theol. Sem., 1974. Dir. Meth. info. Meth. Ch., Pitts., 1953-55; dir. Meth. Info. and Pub. Rels. Meth. Ch., Chgo., 1955-57; mng. editor The Meth. Story, Chgo., 1957-64, editor, 1967-68; editor The Interpreter, Dayton, Nashville, 1969-87; dir. publs., assoc. pub. United Meth. Communications, Nashville, 1988—; lay mem. No. Ill. Ann. Conf., United Meth. Ch., 1960-68, W. Ohio Ann. Conf., United Meth. Ch., 1969-86; mem. communications com. Calvary United Meth. Ch., Nashville, 1990—. Contbr. articles to religious jours. With U.S. Army, 1950-52. Mem. Associated Ch. Press (bd. dirs., treas. 1986-89), Religious Pub. Rels. Coun., United Meth. Assn. Communicators. Deceased.

SHANK, CLARE BROWN WILLIAMS, political leader; b. Syracuse, N.Y., Sept. 19, 1909; d. Curtiss Crofoot and Clara Irene (Shoudy) Brown; m. Frank E. Williams, Feb. 18, 1940 (dec. Feb. 1957); m. Seth Carl Shank, Dec. 28, 1963 (dec. Jan. 1977). B in Oral English, Syracuse U., 1931. Tchr., 1931-33, merchandising exec., 1933-42; Pinellas County mem. Rep. State Com., 1954-58; life mem. Pinellas County Rep. Exec. Com.; exec. com. Fla. Rep. Com., 1954-64; Fla. committeewoman Rep. Nat. Com., 1956-64, mem. exec. com., 1956-64, asst. chmn. and dir. women's activities, 1958-64; alt., mem. exec. arrangements com., major speaker Rep. Nat. Conv., Chgo., 1960; alt., program and arrangement coms. Rep. Nat. Conv., 1964. Pres. St. Petersburg Women's Rep. Club, 1955-57; Mem. Def. Adv. Com. on Women in Services, 1959-65; trustee St. Petersburg Housing Authority, 1976-81. Recipient George Arents medal Syracuse U., 1959; citation for patriotic civilian service 5th U.S. Army and Dept. Def.; 1st woman to preside over any part of nat. polit. conv., Rep. Nat. Conv., Chgo., 1960. Mem. AAUW, DAR, Gen. Fedn. Women's Clubs, Colonial Dames 17th Century, Fla. Fedn. Women's Clubs (dist. pres. 1976-78), Women's Club (St. Petersburg, pres. 1974-76, Yacht Club, Lakewood Country Club (St. Petersburg). Methodist. Deceased Feb. 18, 1996.

SHANKER, ALBERT, labor union official; b. N.Y.C., Sept. 14, 1928; s. Morris and Mamie S.; m. Edith Gerber, 1960; children: Carl, Adam, Jennie, Michael. B.A., U. Ill., 1949; postgrad., Columbia U.; Dr. Pedagogy (hon.), R.I. Coll., 1980; D.H.L. (hon.), CUNY Grad. Sch., 1983, Adelphi U., 1985; LL.D., U. Rochester, 1985. Tchr. elementary schs., jr. high sch. math. pub. schs. N.Y.C., 1952-59; pres. United Fedn. Tchrs., N.Y.C., 1964-86, Am. Fedn. Tchrs., Washington, 1974-97; founding pres. Edn. Internat.; v.p. AFL-CIO, Washington, 1973-97; chair dept. profl. employees, chmn. bd. AFL-CIO; chmn. bd. AFL-CIO; v.p. N.Y. State AFL-CIO, 1973—, mem. N.Y.C. Ctrl. Labor Coun., sec. Jewish Labor Com., 1965—; assoc. Univ. Seminar on Labor Columbia U.; hon. vice chmn. Am. Trade Union Coun. for Histradrut; mem. exec. com. Workers Def. League; mem. group Nat. Bd. Profl. Teaching Stds., 20th Century Fund; mem. labor adv. com. U.S. Holocaust Mus.; tchr. Hunter Coll., Harvard Grad. Sch. Edn.; scholar-in-residence U. Chgo., Claremont Coll., UCLA; apptd. White House Competitiveness Policy Coun., 1990; elected Ind. Sectr. Bd., 1990. Columnist (weekly) Where We Stand; contbr. articles to profl. and popular publs. Mem. labor com. Boy Scouts Am., 1969; bd. dirs. A. Philip Randolph Inst., 1965-97, Internat. Rescue Com., 1973-97, Com. for the Free World, 1980-97; mem. internat. adv. coun. Population Inst., 1976-97. Recipient Disting. Svc. medal Columbia U. Tchrs. Coll., Annual Labor Mgmt. award The Work Am. Inst., 1990. Mem. Nat. Acad. Edn., Nat. Bd. Profl. Teaching Standards. Democrat. Jewish. Avocations: reading, music, gardening, gourmet cooking. Home: Washington D.C. Died Feb., 1997.

SHANKS, EUGENE BAYLIS, mathematician, educator; b. Sumrall, Miss., Nov. 17, 1913; s. James William and Minnie Elnora (Baylis) S.; m. Mary Olivia Harris, June 13, 1940; children: Judith Olivia Shanks Denton, Eugene Baylis Jr. B.A., Millsaps Coll., 1938; M.A., Vanderbilt U., 1940; Ph.D., U. Ill., 1947. Faculty math. Wallace Univ. Sch., Nashville, Tenn., 1938-39; summer sch. faculty Millsaps Coll., Jackson, Miss., 1941; teaching fellow U. Ill., Urbana, 1941, 46-47; teaching fellow Vanderbilt U., Nashville, 1939-40, instr., 1940-41, asst. prof. math., 1947-1949, assoc. prof., 1949-1954, prof., 1954-79, chmn. math. dept., 1956-69, prof. emeritus, 1979-92; dir. summer insts. for high sch. tchrs. sci. and math. NSF and Vanderbilt U., 1959, 60; civilian instr. Air Force Preflight Nav. Sch., Maxwell Field, 1942; cons. to computation div. George C. Marshall Space Flight Center, Huntsville, Ala., NASA, 1962-69; instr. summer sch. George Peabody Coll., Nashville, 1948-55. Author numerous monographs on original solutions of differential equations by evaluations of functions through Runge-Kutta type procedures, including first developed formulas of orders seven, eight, nine and ten. Mem. holding bd. Am. Bapt. Theol. Sem. Served from 2d lt. to capt. USAAF, 1942-46. Recipient Wisdom award, 1970. Fellow Tenn. Acad. Sci. (chmn. math. sect.); mem. AAAS, Am. Math. Soc., Math. Assn. Am. (chmn. Southeastern sect. 1961-62, cons. 1962-92, lectr. 1962-63), Tenn. Math. Tchrs. Assn. (pres. 1955, past chmn. finance com.), Alumni Assn. Millsaps Coll. (dir.), Sigma Xi, Pi Mu Epsilon. Baptist (trustee, deacon). Club: Kiwanis. Achievements include development of Shank's Formulas for Differential Equations. Home: Nashville Tenn. Died Dec. 9, 1992.

SHANNON, EDGAR FINLEY, JR., English language educator; b. Lexington, Va., June 4, 1918; s. Edgar Finley and Eleanor (Duncan) S.; m. Eleanor H. Bosworth, Feb. 11, 1956; children—Eleanor, Elizabeth, Lois, Susan, Virginia. A.B., Washington and Lee U., 1939, Litt.D., 1959; A.M., Duke U., 1941, Harvard U., 1947; Rhodes scholar, Merton Coll., Oxford, 1947-50; D.Phil., Oxford U., 1949, D.Litt., 1996; LL.D., Rhodes Coll., 1960, Duke U., 1964, Hampden-Sydney Coll., 1971; H.H.D., Wake Forest U., 1964; D.H.L., Thomas Jefferson U., Phila., 1967, U. Hartford, 1981, Ohio State U., 1981; Litt.D., Centre Coll., 1968, Coll. William and Mary, 1973; L.H.D., Bridgewater Coll., 1970. Assoc. prof. naval. sci. and tactics Harvard U., 1946, instr. English, 1950-52, asst. prof. English, 1952-56; assoc. prof. English U. Va., Charlottesville, 1956-59; prof. English U. Va., 1959-74, pres., 1959-74, pres. emeritus, 1988—, Commonwealth prof. English, 1974-86, Linden Kent Meml. prof. English, 1986-88, prof. emeritus, 1988—, chmn. dept. English, 1980-81; mem. state and dist. selection coms. Rhodes scholars; pres. Council So. Univs., 1962-64, 71-72; pres. State Univs. Assn., 1963-64; exec. com. Nat. Assn. State Univs. and Land-Grant Colls., 1964-67, chmn. exec. com., 1966-67, pres., 1965-66; mem. So. Regional Edn. Bd., 1963-71; bd. govs. Nat. Commn. on Accrediting, 1961-67; mem. U.S. Nat. Commn. for UNESCO, 1966-67, Pres.'s Commn. on CIA Activities within U.S., 1975. Author: Tennyson and the Reviewers, 1952; editor: (with Cecil Y. Lang) The Letters of Alfred, Lord Tennyson, vol.I, 1981, vol. II, 1987, vol. III, 1990; contbr. articles to various jours. Bd. visitors U.S. Naval Acad., 1962-64, USAF Acad., 1965-67; bd. cons. Nat. War Coll., 1968-71; bd. dirs. Am. Council on Edn., 1967-70, vice chmn., 1971-72; trustee Thomas Jefferson Meml. Found., 1973-88, hon. trustee, 1988—, pres., 1980-83, chmn. 1987-88; trustee Washington and Lee U., 1973-85, Darlington Sch., 1966-76, Mariners Mus., 1966-75, Colonial Williamsburg Found., 1975-88; chmn. Va. Found. Humanities and Pub. Policy, 1973-79; v.p. Oceanic Edn. Found., 1968-83; bd. adminstrs. Va. Inst. Marine Sci., 1963-71; hon. v.p. Tennyson Soc., 1960—; mem. council White Burkett Miller Center for Pub. Affairs, 1975—; mem. Gov. Va.'s Task Force on Sci. and Tech., 1982-83. Served from midshipman to lt. comdr. USNR, 1941-46; capt. Res. ret. Decorated Bronze Star, Meritorious Service medal; Distinguished Eagle Scout, 1973; named Va. Cultural Laureate, 1987; recipient Distinguished Service award Va. State C. of C., 1969; Medallion of Honor Virginians of Md., 1964; Thomas Jefferson award U. Va., 1965; Algernon Sydney Sullivan award Washington and Lee U., 1939; Algernon Sydney Sullivan award U. Va., 1975; Jackson Davis award Va. chpt. AAUP, 1977, Disting. Alumnus award Darlington Sch., 1986; Guggenheim fellow, 1953-54; Fulbright research fellow Eng., 1953-54. Mem. MLA, Assn. Va. Colls. (pres. 1969-70), Raven Soc., Signet Soc., Jefferson Soc., Soc. Cin., Am. Soc. Order of St. John of Jerusalem, Phi Beta Kappa (senator 1967-85, vis. scholar 1976-77, v.p. 1976-79, pres. 1979-82, chmn. Coun. Nominating Com. 1988-94), Omicron Delta Kappa (Laurel Crowned Cir. award 1980), Phi Eta Sigma, Beta Theta Pi, Century Assn. Club, University Club (N.Y.C.). Presbyterian. Died Aug. 24, 1998.

SHARP, AARON JOHN, botanist, educator; b. Plain City, Ohio, July 29, 1904; s. Prentice Daniel and Maude Katharine (Herriott) S.; m. Cora Evelyn Bunch, July 25, 1929; children: Rosa Elizabeth, Maude Katharine, Mary Martha (dec.), Fred Prentice, Jennie Lou. AB, Ohio Wesleyan U., 1927, DSc, 1952; MS, U. Okla., 1929; PhD, Ohio State U., 1938. Instr. botany U. Tenn., Knoxville, 1929-37, asst. prof., 1937-40, assoc. prof., 1940-46, prof., 1946-65, Disting. Service prof., 1965-74, prof. emeritus, 1974—, curator herbarium, 1949-68, assoc. curator herbarium, 1968-80, head dept. botany, 1951-61; assoc. editor The Bryologist, 1938-42, 45-53, acting editor, 1943-44; assoc. editor Castanea, 1947-66; trustee Highlands (N.C.) Biol. Lab., 1934-38, 48-64, bd. mgrs., 1946-52; Cecil Billington lectr. Cranbook Inst. Sci., 1947; sec. sect. Inter-Am. Conf. on Conservation of Renewable Natural Resources, Denver, 1948; vis. prof. Stanford U., 1951, U. Mich. Biol. Sta., 1954-57, 59-64, U. Minn. Biol. Sta., 1971, U. Mont. Biol. Sta., 1972, Nat. U. Taiwan, 1965, Instituto Universitario Pedagógico Experimental, Maracay, Venezuela, 1976, U. Va. Biol. Sta., 1980; mem. staff Hattori (Japan) Bot. Lab., 1956—; vis. lectr. Am. Inst. Biol. Scis., 1967-70; mem. nat. adv. bd. Ministry of Ecology, 1975-81; cons. Time-Life Books, 1975, Brit. Broadcasting Corp., 1984, Nat. Geog. Books, 1985; hon. curatorship in the Inst. of Systematic Botany of the N.Y. Bot. Garden, 1994; hon. life mem. Save-the-Redwoods League, 1995. Assoc. editor: Hattori Bot. Jour., Nichinan, Japan, 1961—; contbr. articles to sci. jours. and Ency. Britanica. Bd. dirs. Nature Conservancy, 1955-61, Gt. Smoky Mountains Nat. Hist. Assn., 1979-81. Decorated officer Order of Rising Sun (Japan); Guggenheim Found. fellow, 1944-46; recipient Merit award Tenn. Environ. Edn. Assn., 1991, Disting. Achievement award Ohio Wesleyan U., 1992, Eloise Payne Luquer medal Garden Club Am., 1983, Appreciation cert. Great Smoky Mountains Nat. Park, 1994. Fellow AAAS (v.p. 1963), Linnean Soc. London; mem. AAUP, New Eng. Bot. Club, Internat. Soc. Phytomorphologists, Internat. Assn. Plant Taxonomy, So. Appalachian Bot. Club (pres. 1946-47), Sullivant Moss Soc. (pres. 1935), Am. Bryol. and Lichen. Soc., Am. Fern Soc., Bot. Soc. Am. (editorial com. 1948-53, treas. 1957-62, v.p. 1963, pres. 1965, Merit award 1972), Soc. for Study Evolution, Soc. Botánica de México (hon.), Soc. Mexicana de Historia Natural, Tenn. Acad. Sci. (exec. com. 1943-44, v.p. 1952, pres. 1953), Am. Soc. Plant Taxonomists (pres. 1961), Assn. Southeastern Biologists (v.p. 1956, Meritorious Tchr. award 1972, Bartholomew award 1989), Ecol. Soc. Am. (v.p. 1958-59), Torrey Bot. Club, Nature Conservancy (gov. 1955-61), Am. Soc. Naturalists, Bot. Brit. Bryol. Soc., Internat. Soc. Tropical Ecology, Internat. Phycolog. Soc., Nat. Assn. Biology Tchrs., Palynolog. Soc. India, Phycolog. Soc. Am., Systematics Assn., Am. Assn. Stratigraphic Palynol., Soc. Latino-Americano de Briologia (hon.), Tenn. Nat. Plant Soc. (hon.), Gt. Smoky Mountains Conservation Assn., (bd. dirs. 1960—), U. Tenn. Arboretum Soc. (bd. dirs. 1979—), Explorers Club, Phi Beta Kappa, Phi Kappa Phi, Sigma Xi, Phi Sigma, Phi Epsilon Phi, Sigma Delta Pi. Died Nov. 16, 1997.

SHARPLESS, RICHARD KENNEDY, lawyer; b. Springdale, Pa., Mar. 30, 1911; s. Charles Thomas and Luella Lincoln (Kennedy) S.; m. Eleanor Ridgway Crowther, Mar. 4, 1946; m. Nancy Jean Sleight, July 23, 1948; children: Kendall Deborah, Richard Kennedy, Lincoln Kennedy. AB, Boston U., 1932; LLB, Harvard U., 1935, JD, 1969. Bar: Pa. 1936, Calif. 1947, Hawaii 1949, U.S. Ct. Appeals (9th dist.) 1964, U.S. Supreme Ct. 1960. With firm Dalzell, McFall & Pringle, Pitts., 1936-42; mem. legal sect. trust dept. Bank of Am., Los Angeles, 1946-48; atty. Office Dist. Engr., Honolulu, 1948-49; with Office Atty. Gen., T.H., 1949-55, atty. gen., 1956-57; mem. Lewis, Saunders & Sharpless (and predecessor firm), 1957-68; mng. dir. City and County of Honolulu, 1968-72, 75-78, corp. counsel, 1973-75, 78-80; of counsel firm Case, Kay & Lynch, Honolulu, 1980-81. Mem. Planning Commn. City and County of Honolulu, 1966-68, chmn., 1968; asst. to Town Atty. of Chapel Hill, 1984-93; bd. dirs. United Way, 1982-85, Pub. Sch. Found., 1984-89, Village Cos. Found., 1987-89; mem. exec. com. PTA Thrift Show, 1986-90. Capt. C.E., AUS, 1942-46. Mem. Bar Assn. Hawaii (pres. 1960-61), Chapel Hill-Carrboro C. of C. (v.p. 1982-85), SAR (pres. Hawaii 1961), Kiwanis. Episcopalian. Died May 10, 1997.

SHAVER, JESSE MILTON, JR., manufacturing company executive; b. Nashville, Nov. 16, 1919; s. Jesse M. and Daisy (Rule) S.; m. Ludmilla B. Tilton, Aug. 26, 1992; children: Jesse Milton III, John Warren. B.S. in Engring, Purdue U., 1942; M.B.A., U. Chgo., 1955. Mgmt. cons. Booz, Allen & Hamilton, 1952-58; div. mgr. Wells-Gardner Electronics Corp., 1958-62; exec. v.p. Am. Air Filter Co., Inc., Louisville, 1962-67; pres., chief operating officer Am. Air Filter Co., Inc., 1967, chmn. bd., pres. chief exec. officer, 1968-80; exec. v.p. Allis-Chalmers Corp., 1978-81, cons., 1981-85; pres. JMS Corp., 1985—, also dir. Bd. dirs. Air Conditioning and Refrigeration Inst., pres., 1972. Served to maj. F.A. AUS, 1942-47, ETO. Decorated Bronze Star medal. Mem. IEEE, ASHRAE, Sigma Chi, Beta Gamma Sigma. Episcopalian. Clubs: Economic (Chgo.), University (Chgo.); Louisville Country (Louisville), Pendennis (Louisville); Metropolitan (N.Y.C.). Died Sept. 2, 1997.

SHAW, WILLIAM VAUGHAN, architect; b. Los Angeles, Apr. 12, 1924; s. Norman Tooker and Elizabeth Allison (Kennedy) S.; m. Mary Morse, Sept. 14, 1967; stepchildren: Susan Osborne, Charles D. Osborne, Polly Osborne, Ellen Osborne. BA in Architecture, U. Calif. at Berkeley, 1950. Practice architecture Carmel, Calif., 1951-55; partner Walter Burde, Burde Shaw & Assos., Carmel, 1955-69; founder, prin. Will Shaw & Assos., Monterey, Calif., 1969—; trustee Monterey Bay Aquarium. (Recipient Calif. Gov.'s award in environmental design for Shell Ser. Sta., Carmel 1964, Urban Renewal Design Award Progressive Architecture mag. 1973). Pres. Calif. 7th Agr. Dist., 1964-65; founder, pres. Monterey County Citizens Planning Assn., 1960-65; chmn. design adv. com. Monterey County, 1960-65; exec. dir. Found. Environmental Design, 1963-69; chmn. exec. com. Monterey Found., 1965-67, pres., 1972-73; bd. dirs. Pebble Beach Corp., 1976—; pres., founding mem. Big Sur Found., 1977—. Served to lt. USNR, 1944-47, PTO. Fellow Am. Acad. in Rome, 1968. Fellow AIA (pres. Monterey chpt. 1964, AIA Honor award for Merchant Built houses 1968). Clubs: Old Capital (Monterey), Pacific Biol. Lab. (Monterey). Office: 225 Cannery Row Ste A Monterey CA 93940-1434 Died July 12, 1997.

SHEA, EDWARD FITZGERALD, JR., lawyer; b. Balt., July 24, 1925; s. Edward Fitzgerald and Marceline Agnes (Lathroum) S.; m. Mary Lou Dean, Aug. 19, 1950; children: Kathleen, Edward III, Michael, Mary, Kevin, Dennis, Patricia, Brian. AB, Loyola U., 1949;

JD, U. Md., 1953. Bar: Md. 1952, U.S. Dist. Ct. Md. 1952, U.S. Ct. Appeals (4th dist.) 1954, U.S. Supreme Ct. 1960. Assoc. Sherbow & Sherbow, Balt., 1952-57; ptnr. Sherbow & Sherbow and Sherbow, Shea & Doyle, Balt., 1957-79, Sherbow, Shea & Tatelbaum, P.A., Balt., 1979-83; pvt. practice Balt., 1983-84; ptnr. Kaplan, Heyman, Greenberg, Engelman & Belgrad, P.A., Balt., 1984—. Mem. Com. to Revise Annotated Code of Md., 1982—, Standing Com. on Rules of Practice and Procedure, Md., 1991-94. Staff sgt. USMC, 1943-46. Fellow Am. Bar Found., Md. Bar Found.; mem. ABA (del. ho. of dels.), Md. State Bar Assn. (bd. govs. 1990-95, pres.-elect 1992-93, pres. 1993-94), Bar Assn. Balt. City. Office: 20 S Charles St Fl 10 Baltimore MD 21201-3220 Died March 30, 1996.

SHEA, JOHN MARTIN, JR., business executive; b. Santa Barbara, Calif., Nov. 14, 1922; s. John Martin and Karmel Kathryn (Knox) S.; m. Marion Abbie; children: Michael Knox, Patrick Campbell, Katherine Martin. B.A., U. Wash., 1944. Vice pres., gen. mgr. Yaras & Co., Far East, Manila, P.I., Hong Kong, Tokyo, Japan, 1946-52; pres. Shea Oil Co., Pasadena, Calif., 1953-57; v.p., dir. Am. Petrofina, Inc.; sr. v.p. mktg., refining, transp., crude oil, dir. Am. Petrofina Co. of Tex., 1957-64; pres. Colonial Oil Products Co., Des Moines, Osmond Oil Co., Waco, Tex., 1958-64; chmn. bd. Freeman, Gossage & Shea (advt. and cons.), San Francisco, 1964-65; chmn. bd., chief exec. officer Beacon Bay Enterprises Inc., Newport Beach, Calif., 1964—, Shea (S.A.), Buenos Aires, Argentina, 1968—; dir. Commercebank, Newport Beach. Trustee Newport Harbor Art Mus., Newport Beach, Calif., 1975—, chmn. bd.trustees 1986-88; pres. bd. trustees Valle Padrinos, Palm Springs, Calif., 1988—. Lt. (j.g.) USNR, World War II. Died Feb. 5, 1997.

SHEAR, NATHANIEL, physicist; b. Bklyn., Dec. 20, 1908; s. Victor Jacob and Henrietta Leah (Robinson) S. A.B. with honors, Columbia U., 1930, M.A., 1932. Physicist U.S. Navy, Civil Service, Washington, Phila., Lakehurst, N.J., 1937-44; research physicist div. war research Columbia U., N.Y.C., 1944-46; ops. research analyst MIT Ops. Evaluation Group, U.S. Navy, Washington, 1946-48; physicist Bur. Ships, U.S. Navy, Washington, 1948-51; cons. physics, Alexandria, Va., 1951-60; cons. physicist U.S. Naval Research Lab., Washington, 1954-60; physicist Emerson Research Lab., Silver Spring, Md., 1960-62; sr. physicist Johns Hopkins U. Applied Physics Lab., Laurel, Md., 1962-66; cons. in physics, Silver Spring, Md., 1966-69; ops. research analyst Def. Spl. Projects Group, Washington, 1969-72; retired, 1972. Author sci. reports for U.S. Navy. Mem. Va. Acad. Sci., Ops. Research Soc. Am., Am. Phys. Soc., U.S. Naval Inst. (Silver mem.), Phi Beta Kappa. Subspecialties: Operations research (mathematics); Oceanography. Home: 9307 Biltmore Dr Silver Spring MD 20901-2921

SHEETZ, RICHARD SMEDLEY, manufacturing executive; b. Phila., June 18, 1924; s. John Wesley and Marian (Smedley) S.; m. Ebba Jean Sterner, Jan. 2, 1954; children—Marian Christine, Rebecca Jane, Laura Jean, Sarah Elizabeth, Constance Smedley. Grad., Episcopal Acad., Phila., 1942; student, Pa. State Coll., 1943-44; B.S. in Elec. Engring, Bucknell U., 1946; M.B.A., Harvard U., 1955. With Westinghouse Electric Corp., 1946-61; gen. mgr. Westinghouse Electric Corp. (E. Springfield plant), 1959-61; exec. v.p. Ohio Crankshaft Co., Cleve., 1961-67; chmn. bd. Park Ohio-Industries, Inc., Cleve., 1967—; bd. dirs. Cedar Fair Mgmt. Co., Cleve.-Cliffs Inc. Past chmn. bd. N.E. Ohio affiliate Am. Heart Assn. Served with USNR, 1943-46. Clubs: Union (Cleve.); Kirtland Country. Died June 12, 1997.

SHELESNYAK, MOSES CHAIM, biodynamicist, physiologist; b. Chgo., June 6, 1909; s. Jonas and Fay (Leavitt) S.; m. Roslyn Benjamin, Jan. 28, 1942 (dec. July 1987); children: Betty Jane (Mrs. Franz Sondheimer), Henry Lawrence (dec.). BA, U. Wis., 1930; PhD (U. fellow), Columbia, 1933; postgrad., Alliance Francaise, Paris, summer 1929, N.Y. Sch. Social Work, 1938-39. Instr. physiology, pharmacology Chgo. Med. Sch., 1935-36; lectr. human growth New Coll., Tchrs. Coll., Columbia, 1936-37; research asso. Mt. Sinai Hosp., N.Y.C., 1936-40; research asso. Friedsam fellow Beth Israel Hosp., N.Y.C., 1940-42; acting head biophysics br. U.S. Office Naval Research, Washington, 1946-47; head human ecology br. U.S. Office Naval Research, 1946-49; lectr. ecology Johns Hopkins U., 1949-50; dir. Arctic Inst. N.Am., Balt.-Washington, 1949-50; sr. scientist Weizmann Inst. Sci., Rehovoth, Israel, 1950-58; asso. prof. Weizmann Inst. Sci., 1958-59, prof., 1959, head dept. biodynamics, 1960-68; assoc. dir. Interdisciplinary Communications Program, Office Asst. Sec. Sci., Smithsonian Instn.-N.Y. Acad. Scis., 1967-68; exec. sec. Council Communication, 1968-72; dir. Interdisciplinary Communications Program, Smithsonian Instn., 1968-77, research assoc., 1977-94; dir. Internat. Program Population Analysis, 1972-77; pres., chmn. bd. Interdisciplinary Communication Assocs., 1969-84; vis. lectr. geography McGill U., 1948; vis. prof. Coll. de France, 1960; mem. bd. human ecology arid zones UNESCO, 1954-72; rsch. com. Internat. Planned Parenthood Fedn., 1959-72; selection and adv. com. Internat. Tng. Program Physiology Reprodn., Worcester, Mass., 1959-70; neuroendocrinology panel Interdisciplinary Brain Rsch. Orgn., 1961-94; expert adv. panel WHO, 1965-70, more. Editor: Ovum Implantation, 1969, Growth of Population, 1969; co-editor: Frontiers in Teaching of Physiology: Computer Literacy and Simulation; editorial bd.: Contraception; contbr. articles to profl. jours. bd. dirs. Santa Ynez Valley Hosp., Solvang, Calif. Served to lt. comdr. USNR, 1942-46. Gen. Edn. Bd. fellow, 1936-38, Sir. Simon Marks Fellow Birmingham (Eng.) U., 1957-58, univ. rsch. fellow, 1957-58. Fellow AAAS, Arctic Inst. N.Am., Eugenics Soc.; mem. Aerospace Med. Assn., AAUP, Israel, Am. chem. socs., Am. Inst. Biol. Sci., Am. Physiol. Soc. (dir. task force centennial commemorative com., exec. editor The Physiology Tchr. 1977-83, exec. editor hist. sect. The Physiologist 1979-83), Am. Polar Soc., Am. Soc. Study Sterility, Animal Behavior Soc., Arctic Circle, Biochem. Soc. Israel, Brit. Glaciological Soc., Ecol. Soc. Am., Endocrine Soc. Am., Endocrine Soc. Israel, European Soc. Drug Toxicity, History Sci. Soc., Inst. Aero. Scis., Soc. Exptl. Biology and Medicine, Israel Fertility Soc., Israel Soc. Exptl. Biology and Medicine, Israel Soc. Undersea Exploration, N.Y. Acad. Scis., Internat. Soc. Research in Reprodn. (founding), Soc. Internat. Devel., Soc. Research Child Devel., Soc. Gen. Systems Research, Am. Acad. Polit. and Social Sci., Acad. Polit. Scis., Population Assn. Am., World Future Soc., Acad. Medicine Washington, Soc. Study Reproduction, Sigma Xi; fgn. mem. La Sociedad Chilena d'Obstetricia y Ginecologia, Societa Italiana per il progresso della zootecnica, Societe Royale Belge de Gynecologie et d'Obstetrique. Clubs: Cosmos (Washington); Explorers (N.Y.C.). Home: Santa Barbara Calif. Died Sept. 12, 1994.

SHELTON, MALCOLM WENDELL, biblical studies educator; b. Eckmansville, Ohio, Aug. 26, 1919; s. Charles Edward and Mary Ina (Suffron) S.; m. Muriel Payne Moore, Aug. 9, 1987. BS in Edn., Olivet Nazarene Coll., 1951, BTh, 1952; M in Religion, Pasadena Nazarene Coll., 1952; BD, Nazarene Theol. Sem., Kansas City, 1954, MDiv, 1972; MS in Edn., Cen. Mo. State U., 1965; D in Ministry, Philips U. Grad. Sem., 1977; postgrad., U. Kans., 1966-67, Hebrew U., Jerusalem, 1979, 81, Wheaton Coll., 1982. Prof. old testament So. Nazarene U., Bethany, Okla., 1967-85, Mid-Am. Bible Coll., Oklahoma City, 1985—; tchr. various pub. schs., Kansas City, Mo., 1954-65. Staff sgt. U.S. Army, 1941-45. Mem. Soc. Bibl. Lit., Am. Sch. Oriental Rsch., Brit. Sch. Archaeology, Wesleyan Theol. Soc., Evang. Theol. Soc., Am. Rsch. Ctr. in Egypt. Republican. Died March 7, 1997.

SHELTON, REID LEROY, actor; b. Salem, Oreg., Oct. 7, 1924; s. Roy Van and Jennie (White) S. Mus.B., Willamette U., 1948; Mus.M., U. Mich., 1951. mem. Inst. Advanced Studies in Theater Arts, 1962-65. Appeared in: Broadway shows Wish You Were Here, 1953, Saint of Bleeker Street, 1954-55, My Fair Lady, 1956-57; toured from 1957-60 including Cultural Exchange to USSR: Broadway shows Oh What a Lovely War, 1964; Carousel, Lincoln Ctr., 1965, Canterbury Tales, 1968-69, Rothschilds, 1971-72, 1600 Pennsylvania Avenue, 1976, Annie, 1977; off-Broadway shows include Phedre, 1966; also tour to, Festival of Arts, Am. Embassy, London; Man With a Load of Mischief, 1966, Beggar's Opera, 1972, Contractor, 1973; TV prodns. include: Remington Steele, 1982, Cheers, 1983, St. Elsewhere, 1983, First and Ten series, 1985, 90, Hunter, 1986, Golden Girls, 1986, Amen, 1986, Family Ties, 1986, Spies, 1986, Scarecrow and Mrs. King, 1986, Me and Mrs. C, 1986, Duet, 1987, L.A. Law, 1990. Served with cav. AUS, 1943-46, PTO. Named Best Actor in a musical for Man with a Load of Mischief, Jersey Jour., 1966; nominated for Drama Desk award for Man with a Load of Mischief, 1966, Annie, 1977; nominee Best Actor in a musical for Annie; Antoinette Perry award, 1977. Mem. AFTRA, Actors Equity Assn., Screen Actors Guild. Democrat. Club: Players. Died June 8, 1997.

SHEPARD, PAUL HOWE, ecology educator, author, lecturer; b. Kansas City, Mo., July 12, 1925; s. Paul Howe and Clara (Grigsby) S.; m. Melba Wheatcroft, 1950 (div.); children: Kenton, Margaret, Jane; m. Florence Krall, 1988. A.B., U. Mo., 1949; M.S., Yale U., 1952, Ph.D., 1954. From instr. to asso. prof. biology and dir. Green Oaks, Knox Coll., 1954-64; lectr. biology Smith Coll., 1965-70; vis. prof. environ. perception Dartmouth Coll., 1971-73; Avery prof. natural philosophy and human ecology Pitzer Coll. and Claremont Grad. Sch., 1973-94, emeritus, 1994—; nat. lectr. Sigma Xi, 1984-86; NSF in-svc. inst. program dir., 1959. Author: The Pictorial History of the 493d Armored Field Artillery Battalion, 1945, Man in the Landscape: A Historic View of the Esthetics of Nature, 1967, 2d edit., 1990, The Subversive Science: Essays Toward an Ecology of Man, 1969, Environmental: Essays on the Planet as a Home, 1971, The Tender Carnivore and the Sacred Game, 1973, Thinking Animals, 1977, Nature and Madness, 1982, The Sacred Paw, The Bear in Nature, Myth and Literature, 1985, 2d edit., 1992, the Others, How Animals Made Us Human, 1995, Subject: The Company of Others: Essays in Celebration of Paul Shepard, 1995, The Only World We've Got: A Paul Shepard Reader, 1996, Traces of an Omnivore, 1996; mem. editorial adv. bd. Landscape and Urban Planning. Served with AUS, 1943-46. Fulbright rsch. scholar Wellington, N.Z., 1961; Guggenheim fellow, 1969; USPHS grantee, 1962; fellow Rockefeller Found., 1977, Coun. for Internat. Exch. Scholars, India, 1989; Disting. Vis. Lectr., India, 1985. Fellow Inst. Human Ecology. Died June 16,1996.

SHEPHERD, JUDY CARLILE, retired government and communication official; b. Kansas City, Mo.; d. John Mercer and Mary Almeda (Chapin) Ellis; student Okla. State U., Tulsa U.; BA, Am. U., Washington, 1960; m. Joseph Elbert Shepherd; 1 child from previous marriage, John Philip Carlile. Chief probation officer Tulsa County Ct., 1947-50; real estate broker United Farm Agy., 1952-58; bldg. fund campaign mgr. AAUW, Washington, 1958-59; govt. and pub. rels. ofcl. Nat. Counsel Assos., Washington, 1959-61; congressional liaison Dept. Agr., Washington, 1961-65; public info. officer OEO, 1965-70, spl. asst. to dep. dir. ops. Head Start, elderly, Indian and migrant programs, 1970-73; dir. pub. rels. Nat. Assn. Social Workers, Washington, 1973-74; social sci. analyst Congressional Rsch. Svc., Libr. Congress, Washington, 1976-85. Author: The Statutory History of the United States Capitol Police Force, 6 vols., 1985. Pres. bd. govs. Agr. Symphony Orch., 1961-64; bd. dirs. ARC, Boy Scouts Am., 1948-50; bd. dirs. Little Theatre, 1956-57. Recipient 1st place Fed. Editors Blue Pencil award, 1967; cert. humanist counselor. Mem. Nat. Press Club, Pub. Rels. Soc. Am., Nat. Assn. Govt. Communicators, Am. Humanist Assn., Assn. Humanistic Psychology, Am. U. Alumni Assn., Okla. State Soc., Mo. State Soc., Ark. State Soc., Library Congress Profl. Assn., Humanist Assn. Nat. Capital Area (pres. 1977-78), Nat. Congress Am. Indians, DAR, Am. Soc. Access Profls. (charter). Club: Woman's Nat Democratic. Coordinator, Am. Discovers Indian Art exhibit, Smithsonian Instn., 1967.

SHEPPARD, HAROLD LLOYD, gerontologist, educator; b. Balt., Apr. 1, 1922; s. Joseph and Anna Leslie (Levy) S.; children: Mark, Jenny. MA, U. Chgo., 1945; PhD, U. Wis., Madison, 1949. Assoc. prof. sociology Wayne State U., Detroit, 1947-59; rsch. and staff dir. spl. com. on aging U.S. Senate, Washington, 1959-61; asst. adminstr. area redevel. adminstrn. U.S. Dept. Commerce, Washington, 1961-63; staff social scientist W.E. Upjohn Inst. Employment Rsch., Washington, 1963-75; sr. rsch. fellow Am. Inst. Rsch., Washington, 1975-80; counselor on aging to Pres. Carter Washington, 1980-81; assoc. dir. Nat. Coun. on Aging, Washington, 1981-82; dir. Internat. Exchange Ctr. Gerontology U. South Fla., Tampa, 1983-91; prof. Dept. Gerontology U. South Fla., Tampa, 1983—; cons. U.S. Dept. Labor, Washington, Senate Com. on Unemployment and Poverty, Washington, ILO, Geneva, OECD, Paris. Author, editor: Towards an Industrial Gerontology, 1970; co-author: Where Have all the Robots Gone?, 1972, The Graying of Working America, 1979; editor: Poverty and Wealth in America, 1972, Future of Older Workers, 1990. Fulbright scholar, France, 1957-58. Fellow Gerontol. Soc. Am. Avocation: sailing. Died July 10, 1997.

SHERMAN, JOHN CLINTON, geography educator; b. Toronto, Ont., Can., May 3, 1916; s. Harold C. and Grace (Ubbes) S.; m. Helen Jean Loyd, Mar. 15, 1941; children: Constance Sherman Newell, John Harold (dec.), Mary Helen (Mrs. Stephen Wood), Barbara Lillian (Mrs. David Graves). B.A., U. Mich., 1937; M.A., Clark U., 1942; Ph.D., U. Wash., 1947. Mem faculty U. Wash., Seattle, 1942-96; prof. geography U. Wash., 1963-86, prof. emeritus, 1986-96, chmn. dept., 1963-73; Mem. sub-com. on geography adv. to U.S. Geol. Survey space programs for earth observation Nat. Acad. Sci.-NRC, 1965-96. Author: Atlas of a Single ERTS Image, 1975, (with others) Atlas of Marine Use for the North Pacific; Adv. co-editor: (with others) Oxford Regional Economic Atlas of U.S. and Can, 1967; visual and tactile map of met. Washington, tactile atlas of The Mall, Washington. Mem. Wash. State Bd. on Geog. Names. Mem. Assn. Am. Geographers, Assn. Pacific Coast Geographers, Internat. Cartographic Assn. (mem. U.S. com.). Research and publs. on maps for the blind, maps and graphics for partially seeing children. Home: Seattle Wash. Died Oct. 21 1996; interred Holyrood Cemetery, Seattle, WA.

SHERMAN, JOSEPH HOWARD, clergyman; b. Marion, S.C., June 14, 1923; s. Samuel and Alma (Cannon) S.; m. Daisy Lee Littles; children: Joseph Howard Jr., Beatrice Sherman Boone. D.D. (hon.), Trinity Hall Coll.; LL.D. (hon.), New Haven Theol. Appointed Jurisdictional Bishop of N.C., 2d Jurisdiction, 1963. Founder, pastor Pentecostal Temple Ch. of God in Christ, Charlotte, N.C.; pres. N.C. Youth Dept.; dist. supt. N.C. Jurisdiction, Wadesboro; chmn. Council of Bishops, Memphis, 1976—; pres. C. H. Mason System of Bible Colls., Charlotte, N.C., 1975; mem. Nat. Hymnal Com. Author: (book) Weapons of the Righteous; (phamplet) Witchcraft, The Work of the Devil; (album) Peace That Only Christ Can Give; editor The Mighty Voice That Crieth mag. pres., founder J. Howard Sherman Scholarship Fund, Charlotte, 1974—; bd. dirs. C. H. Mason Scholarship Found., Memphis, Saints Ctr.; mem. NAACP, Charlotte, Hiring of the Handicapped, Charlotte, 1984, Ch. of God in Christ Hosp. Fund; mem. grievance com. Housing Authority, Charlotte, 1983, 84; mem. steering com. Democratic Governorship, N.C., 1984. Named Knight of Queen City, Charlotte, 1976, hon. citizen City of Balt., 1981, hon. atty. gen. N.C., 1983; J.H. Sherman Day named in his honor, Charlotte, 1980-84. Mem. Ministerial Alliance (sec. Charlotte chpt. 1983—). Died Sept. 12, 1996.

SHERMAN, SAMUEL S., JR., lawyer; b. Wilmette, Ill., Jan. 22, 1909. Student, U. Colo.; A.B., U. Mich., 1931; LL.B. cum laude, U. Denver, 1935. Bar: Colo. 1935. Mem. firm Sherman & Howard, Denver. Mem. ABA, Colo. Bar Assn., Denver Bar Assn., Phi Delta Phi. Home: Denver Colo. Died Nov.21, 1988; buried Denver, Colo.

SHERROD, ROBERT LEE, writer; b. Thomas County, Ga., Feb. 8, 1909; s. Joseph Arnold and Victoria Ellen (Evers) S.; m. Elizabeth Hudson, Oct. 8, 1936 (dec. Dec. 1958); children: John Hudson, Robert Lee; m. Margaret Carson Ruff, May 5, 1961 (div. 1972); m. Mary Gay Labrot Leonhardt, Aug. 26, 1972 (dec. July 1978). A.B., U. Ga., 1929. Reporter Atlanta Constn., Palm Beach (Fla.) Daily News, and others, 1929-35; with Time and Life mags. as Wash. corr., assoc. editor, war and Far East corr., 1935-52; Far East corr. Sat. Eve. Post, 1952-55, mng. editor, 1955-62; editor, 1962, editor-at-large, 1963-64; v.p., editorial coordinator Curtis Pub. Co., 1965-66; writing on fgn. affairs and history, 1966—; contract writer Life Mag., N.Y.C., 1966-68; mem. history adv. com. USMC, 1973-76; bd. dirs. Marine Corps Hist. Found., 1979-86; mem. U. Ga. Pres.'s Adv. Council, 1975-78; mem. bd. judges nat. mag. awards Columbia U., 1979-86. Author: Tarawa, the Story of a Battle, 1944, 5th edit., 1985, On to Westward, 1945, rev. edit., 1990, History of Marine Corps Aviation in World War II, 1952, rev. edit., 1987; text for Life's Picture History of World War II, 1950, also Kobunsha's Picture History of the Pacific War (in Japanese), 1952; (with others) Apollo Expeditions to the Moon, 1975. Trustee Corrs. Fund, 1963-93. Commended by USN Dept., Battle of Attu, May 1943, Battle of Tarawa, Nov. 1943; recipient Headliners Club award for war reporting, 1944, Benjamin Franklin award U. Ill., 1954, Overseas Press Club certificate, 1955, Honor award Mil. Order of Carabao, 1984, Disting. Service award USMC Found., 1987, Disting. Alumnus award U. Ga. Sch. Journalism, 1987. Episcopalian. Clubs: Nat. Press (Washington); Overseas Press, Century Assn. (N.Y.C.).

SHERRY, SOL, physician, scientist, educator; b. N.Y.C., Dec. 8, 1916; s. Hyman and Ada (Greenman) S.; m. Dorothy Sitzman, Aug. 7, 1946; children: Judith Anne, Richard Leslie. A.B., NYU, 1935, M.D., 1939; D.Sc. (hon.), Temple U., 1980. Successively fellow, intern, resident 3d med. div. Bellevue Hosp., N.Y.C., 1939-42, 46; asst. prof. medicine NYU Coll. Medicine, 1946-51; dir. May Inst. Med. Research, Cin., 1951-54; dir. medicine Jewish Hosp., St. Louis, 1954-58; prof. medicine Washington U. Sch. Medicine, St. Louis, 1958-68; co-chmn. dept. Washington U. Sch. Medicine, 1964-68; chmn. dept. Temple U. Sch. Medicine, 1968-84, disting. univ. prof., 1983-87, Disting. prof. emeritus, 1987-93, dean, 1984-86; dir. Thrombosis Research Center, 1970-79, dir. emeritus, 1979-93; cons. emeritus surgeon gen. army; past chmn. com. thrombolytic agts., past chmn. com. on thrombosis USPHS; chmn. council on thrombosis Am. Heart Assn.; past mem. com. blood, past chmn. task force on thrombosis NRC; mem. Internat. Commn. on Hemostasis and Thrombosis; past chmn. and pres. Internat. Socs. on Thrombosis and Hemostasis; past mem. sci. adv. com. St. Louis Heart Assn., also St. Louis Multiple Sclerosis Soc. Contbr. articles to profl. jours. Mem. bd. Hillel, 1961-67; pres. S.E. Pa. chpt. Am. Heart Assn., 1978-79. Served as flight surgeon USAAF, 1942-46, ETO. Recipient medal for typhus control Lower Bavaria U.S. Army Typhus Commn., 1946; Rsch. Career award USPHS, 1962; Disting. Achievement awards Modern Medicine, 1963, ACP, 1968, Am. Coll. Cardiology, 1971, Internat. Soc. Thrombosis and Haemostasis, 1978, Tex. Heart Inst., 1990, Phila. County Med. Soc., 1985, Assn. Program Dirs. Internal Medicine, 1992, Gold medal Internat. Soc. Thrombosis and Hemostasis, 1983. Fellow Royal Coll. Physicians; mem. AMA (past mem. and chmn. council drugs, chmn. sect. exptl. medicine and therapeutics), Assn. Am. Physicians, Assn. Profs. Medicine (council 1973-75, pres. 1976), Am. Soc. Clin. Investigation, Am. Heart Assn., Central Soc. Clin. Research (council 1962-64), Am. Physiol. Soc., Soc. Exptl. Biology and Medicine, A.C.P. (master), Phi Beta Kappa, Sigma Xi (pres. Washington U. chpt. 1962-63), Alpha Omega Alpha. Home: Voorhees N.J. Died Jan. 28, 1993.

SHERRY, WILLIAM JAMES, oil producer; b. Salamanca, N.Y., Aug. 13, 1899; s. William and Bridget (Dunn) S.; m. Margaret Harrington, Oct. 2, 1928; children: Patricia, Margaret, Mary, William James, Anne , Jane, Teresa, Richard J. Student, U. Notre Dame, 1917-19; B.S., MIT, 1921. Petroleum geologist Shaffer Oil & Refining Co., 1921-23; oil producer, 1923—; pres., dir. Sherry Petroleum Corp., Tulsa, 1931—, Rock Creek Oil Co., 1953-59; Mem. Tulsa Utility Bd., 1950-53. Pres. Eastern Okla. Arthritis Found., 1949-53; pres. Tulsa Cath. Community Center, 1951-70, St. John's Hosp., Tulsa, 1969-72; v.p. Nat. Council Alcoholism, 1966; Trustee MIT, 1954-59; trustee St. Gregory's Coll.; bd. govs. U. Notre Dame Found., Okla. State U. Found. Served with U.S. Army, 1918. Created Papal Knight, 1943; chancellor Equestrian Order of Holy Sepulchre Western Lietenantcy, 1950-56. Mem. Am. Assn. Petroleum Geologists., AIME, Am. Petroleum Inst., Ind. Petroleum Assn., Tulsa Geol. Soc., U. Notre Dame Alumni Assn. (dir. 1951-53, v.p. 1953), MIT Alumni Assn. (v.p. 1966), Am. Legion. Republican. Roman Catholic. Clubs: KC, Tulsa. Died June 14, 1997.

SHERWOOD, AARON WILEY, aerodynamics educator; b. St. Louis, Jan. 13, 1915; s. Charles Vliet and Amelia Pauline (Kappler) S.; m. Helene M. Gysin, 1944; children—Susan Helene, Mark Wiley. M.E., Rensselaer Poly. Inst., 1935; M.S., U. Md., 1943. Exptl. engr. Wallace & Tiernan Co., Inc., 1936-38; devel. engr. Assoc. Engring., 1938-39; layout engr. Glenn L. Martin Co., 1939-40; instr. U. Md., 1940-44; aero. project engr. David Taylor Model Basin, 1944-46, prof. aerodynamics, 1946—, acting head dept. aero. engring., 1950-58, head dept. aerospace engring., 1958-67, prof. dept. aerospace engring., 1967-77; in charge wind tunnel lab. Glenn L. Martin Inst. Tech., 1946-55; owner, engring. cons. Aerolab. Author: Aerodynamics, 1946. Fellow ASME (chmn. Washington sect. 1954-55); mem. Am. Inst. Aeros and Astronautics (sect. chmn.), Am. Soc. Engring. Edn., Sigma Xi, Tau Beta Pi, Phi Kappa Phi, Phi Kappa Tau. Deceased.

SHERWOOD, BETTE WILSON, artist; b. Sheffield, Ala., Nov. 1, 1920; d. Hardison S. and Jennie M. (Gaut) Wilson; m. Sidney James Sherwood; children: Bette Anne, Sidney James III. Grad., Miss. Synodical Jr. Coll., M.S., 1940; student, Corcoran Sch. of Art, 1939-40, Art Inst. Chgo., 1940-43. Jr. engr. TVA, Sheffield, Ala., 1941; photographer, reporter Reynolds Aluminum Co., Listerhill, Ala., 1942-45; lectr. art and poetry Sam Houston Book Store, 1972, Galleria, Houston, 1972, Jr. League, Houston, 1973, Lakeside Country Club, 1974, numerous others; judge numerous art shows, 1967—; il rettore Nicolo Pampinto, Univ. Delle Arti, Italy. One-woman shows include Miss. Synodical Coll., 1937, Heath & Brown Gallery, Houston, 1968, Lynn Kottler Galleries, N.Y.C., also Houston Oaks Hotel; exhibited in group shows at Nat. League Am. Pen Women, Art League Houston, Briar Club, Houston, Unitarian Fellowship Hall, numerous others; represented in permanent collections at River Oaks Bank & Trust, Kirby at San Filepe, numerous others; painter Gov. Mark White's wife Linda Gale White, LRC founder Adele Looscan, Spanish Consul Gen. Javier Jimenez-Ugarte, German Vice Consul Christa-Barbara Wilson; painter 1st Houston Library Bldg. with 26 hist. figures, last one artist show at the Coll. of Medicine at Tex. A & M Univ. Fine arts dir. Found. for Children, Houston Med. Ctr., 1971—, Children to Children, Inc., med. found., Washington; chmn. Houston Revolution Centennial Com., 1982; chmn. 1985 Centennial LRC; mem. adv. bd. Children to Children; mem. pres.'s adv. bd. Houston Bapt. U. Recipient numerous awards including 2d and 3d pl. Nat. League Show Houston, 1968, Best in Show, 1969, 2d and 3d pl., 1975; citation city of Houston and Bicentennial Commn.; award from Houston Bicentennial Commn., 1976; Diploma di Merito, 1982. Mem. Nat. League Am. Pen Women (founder meml. br. 1970, state bicentennial chmn. 1974—, Best of Show in Portraiture award 1970, Biennial award 1976), Am. Security Coun. (nat. adv. bd.), Visual Arts and Galleries Assn., Internat. Soc. Artists, Mus. Fine Arts, Nat. Hist. Soc., Nat. Portrait Soc. Republican. Mem. Berachah Ch. Died Jan. 22, 1996.

SHERWOOD, THORNE, architect; b. Montclair, N.J., Dec. 3, 1910; s. William Carman and Lida Crawford (Ramsey) S.; m. Nancy Davol Chapman, June 23, 1934; children: Thorne, Nancy Frost (Mrs. C.M. O'Hearn, Jr.), Michael. A.B., Williams Coll., 1932; M. Arch., Columbia, 1936, Perkins Boring travelling fellow study in Europe, 1937-39. Founding partner Sherwood Mills & Smith, Stamford, Conn., N.Y.C., New Canaan, Conn., 1946-69. Works include Ramapo Regional High Sch, Franklin Lakes, N.J. (awards AIA, Am. Assn. Sch. Architects), Rehab. Center of S.E. Conn, Stamford, Dorr Oliver exec. hdqrs (Boston Fine Arts Festival medal 1957), Olmsted Hall, Vassar Coll., Poughkeepsie, N.Y., Covenant Group Ins. Co. Hdqrs. (formerly Mut. Ins. Co), Hartford, Conn., (1st honor award AIA 1960); also pub. and private schs., coll. and univ. bldgs., residential, indsl., comml. and religious architecture U.S. and abroad. Former park commr., Stamford, mem. planning bd., chmn. joint com. parks and recreational facilities; mem. pub. adv. panel on archtl. services, region 1-Boston Gen. Services Adminstrn., 1967-69; Bd. dirs. Stamford Mus. and Nature Center. Served as lt. USNR, 1942-45. Fellow AIA; mem. NAD, Nat. Inst. Archtl. Edn. (past bd. trustees), Archtl. League N.Y., Mcpl. Art. Soc., Conn. Soc. Architects, Columbia U. Fedn. Alumni Assos. (past dir.), Stamford Good Govt. Assn. (past dir.), Soc. Colonial Wars, Alumni Assn. Columbia Sch. Architecture (pres. 1957-59), NAD (asso.), Alpha Delta Phi, St. Andrews Soc., Litchfield (Conn.) Hist. Soc. (bd. dirs.), Mil. Order Loyal Legion U.S. Episcopalian. Club: Century Assn. (N.Y.C.). Died Dec. 27, 1994.

SHIFLEY, RALPH LOUIS, retired naval officer, retired business executive; b. Mounds, Ill., Oct. 26, 1910; s. Marion Monroe and Elizabeth Alice (Hawkins) S.; m. Frances Ellen Norman, Sept. 8, 1936; 1 dau., Susan Elizabeth. Student, U. Ill., 1928; B.S., U.S. Naval Acad., 1933. Commd. ensign U.S. Navy, 1933, advanced through grades to vice adm., 1967; designated naval aviator, 1937, various assignments in ships, 1933-40, comdg. officer Bombing Squadron 8, 1943-44, comdr. Air Group 8, 1944; supt. tng. Naval Air Sta. Jacksonville, Fla., 1945-47; assigned U.S.S. Randolph, 1947, assigned U.S.S. Leyte, 1948-49, ops. officer to comdr. Air Force, Atlantic Fleet, 1949-51, grad. Naval War Coll., 1952, mem. staff chief naval ops. in aviation plans div., 1952-54, staff comdr. 6th Fleet, 1954-56; comdg. officer Badoeng Strait, 1956-57; sr. aide to chief naval ops., 1957-58, comdg. officer U.S.S. Franklin D. Roosevelt, 1958-59, asst. dir., then dir. aviations plans div., staff chief naval ops., 1959-62, comdr. Carrier Div. 7, 1962-63, vice chief naval material, 1963-67, dep. chief naval operations (logistics), 1967-71, ret., 1971; exec. v.p., treas. Stanwick Corp., Arlington, Va., 1971-78; pres., treas. Stanwick Corp., 1978-80; pres. Stanwick Internat., Inc., Arlington, 1971-78. Decorated Navy Cross, D.S.M., Legion of Merit, DFC with 3 gold stars, Air medal with 2 gold stars. Clubs: Army and Navy (Washington); Army-Navy Country (Arlington, Va.). Home: Washington D.C. Died Jan. 5, 1995.

SHILLINGBURG, C. GORDON, animal nutritionist, quarter horse breeder; b. Gallup, N.Mex., Mar. 12, 1924; s. Condon Gordon and Ruth (Reid) S.; m. Margaret Jean Smith, Aug. 18, 1946 (div. Jan. 1970); children: Robert Gordon, Charles Lester, Bartley Thomas. BS in Agriculture, U. Ariz., 1949, MS in Animal Nutrition, 1951; advanced grad. study animal nutrition, Okla. State U., 1968. Cert. nutritional consulting. Gen. ranch worker Granite Peaks Ranch, Bayfield, Colo., 1946-49; instn.-on-farm instr. Fremont Union High Sch., Sunnyvale, Calif., 1950-51; feed sales and nutritional cons. Producers Cotton Oil Co., Phoenix, 1951-60; owner San Marcos Rsch., Scottsdale, Ariz., 1960—; summer ranch mgr., owner Granite Peaks Ranch, Bayfield, Colo., 1970—; pres. The Equine Sci. Found., 1982—; nutritional cons. Producers Cotton Oil Co., 1960-71, West Coast Land and Cattle Co., 1962-71; pres. Ariz. Feed Yards, Inc., 1967-68; formation of horse care and mgmt. class U. Calif., San Diego, 1970; instr. equine sci. program Ariz. State U., Tempe, 1970-72; instr. Glendale, Phoenix and Scottsdale C.C., 1970-73; coord., dept. chmn. equine sci. dept. Scottsdale (Ariz.) C.C., 1973-88; mem. Coun. of Agrl. Sci. and Tech.; asst. to supt. Ariz. Nat. Livestock Show; others. Author: How Chemical Analysis Can Help You, Beef Cattle Science Handbook, 1964; contbr. articles to profl. jours. Mem. alumni adv. bd. U. Ariz., Tucson, 1970; judging com. mem. Ariz. Nat. Livestock Show; faculty senate mem. Scottsdale C.C.; chmn. agrl. coun. Maricopa County C.C. Dist.; leader 4-H Horse Div.; chmn. Cub Scout and Boy Scouts Am., Scottsdale; PTA organizer, Tempe; pres. bd. deacons Valley Presbyn. Ch., Scottsdale; treas. Meth. Ch., Tempe; others. Mem. Nat. Cottonseed Products Assn. (rsch. subcom. 1957-62), Ariz. Cattle Feeders' Assn. (rsch. co-chmn. 1963-70), Ariz. Cattle Growers' Assn. (rsch. and edn. com. 1957-72), Am. Alfalfa Dehydrators' Assn. (nat. survey team 1968), Alpha Zeta, Am. Registry Cert. Animal Scientists, Ariz. State Horseman's Assn. (bd. dirs.), Pacific Coast Quarter Horse Assn., Am. Horse Shows Assn., Am. Soc. Agrl. Cons. (charter sec.), Ariz. Cattle Feeders' Assn. (rsch. co-chmn.), and others. Republican. Presbyterian. Avocations: fishing, hunting, photography. DIED 11/12/96. .

SHIMAOKA, KATSUTARO, oncologist, researcher; b. Nara, Japan, Sept. 4, 1931; came to U.S., 1956; s. Shigekichi and Shizue (Kishimoto) S.; m. Tomoko Suzuki, Dec. 3, 1931; children: Julia E. and Eva E. MD, Keio U. Sch. Medicine, Tokyo, 1955. Resident Louisville Gen. Hosp., 1957-58; fellow Roswell Park Meml. Inst., Buffalo, 1958-61, assoc. chief cancer rsch. clinician, 1963-86; rsch. asst. U. Coll. Hosp. Med. Sch., London, 1961-63; assoc. chief rsch. Radiation Effects Rsch. Found., Nagasaki, Japan, 1986-94; faculty Harbor-UCLA Med. Ctr., Torrance, Calif., 1994—; rsch. assoc. prof. physiology SUNY, Buffalo, 1972-86, rsch. prof. medicine, 1971-94; cons. in medicine VA Med. Ctr., Buffalo, 1979-94; cons. in endocrine oncology, Ito Hosp., Tokyo, 1987—. Supt. A-Bomb Casualty Coun., Nagasaki, 1986-94. Mem. Endocrine Soc., Japan Endocrine Soc. Coun., Am. Soc. Clin. Oncology, 11 other profl. orgns. Avocation: contract bridge. DIED 05/25/97. .

SHIMBO, OSAMU, engineering consultant; b. Nagaoka, Japan, Aug. 11, 1931; came to U.S., 1969; s. Seiichiro and Yoshie (Kanda) S.; m. Chieko Chiba, Apr. 1, 1956; children: Shizue, Daichi. BS, Tohoku U., Sendai, Japan; PhD, Hokkaido (Japan) U., 1965. Mgr. Oki Elect. Engring. Co. Ltd., Tokyo, 1956-65; sr. engr. GE in Eng., London, 1965-67; sr. scientist No. Electric in Can., Ottawa, 1967-69, COMSAT, Washington, 1969-74; dir. Am. Satellite Corp., Washington, 1974-76; sr. scientist Computer Sci.Corp., Washington, 1976-77; mgr. Satellite Bus. Systems, Washington, 1977-79, Intelsat, Washington, 1979-91; sr. cons. Mitsubishi Elec. Corp., Tolyo, 1991—. Author: Transmission Analysis in Communication Systems, Vols. I and II, 1988; contbr. articles to profl.jours.; patentee in field. Recipient Okabe Meml. award Inst. Elec. Communication Engrs. Japan, 1964, Paper award Inst. Elec. Communications Engrs., 1965, Presdl. award Satellite Bus. Systems, 1979, Creativity award Dir. Gen. Intelsat, 1991. Fellow IEEE . Home: 201 E 80th St Apt 4F New York NY 10021-

0513 Office: Mitsubishi Electric Corp, Kamachiya Japan DIED 03/26/96. .

SHIRPSER, CLARA, former Democratic national committeewoman; b. San Francisco, Aug. 25, 1901; d. Leo and Alexandra (Shragge) Garfinkle; m. Herman Rosenberg, 1921 (dec. 1938); 1 dau., Barbara (Mrs. Robert De Liban); m. Adolph Shirpser, Nov. 10, 1940 (dec. 1970); m. Nat Levy, Dec. 14, 1978 (dec. 1984). Student, U. Calif., 1919-21. Owner, mgr. retail bus. Berkeley, Calif., 1938-45; mem. Alameda County, Calif. State Dem. central coms., 1950-56; Mem. Dem. Nat. Com., 1952-56; vice chmn. nat. and Calif. Kefauver primary campaign for pres., 1952, 56; co-chmn. nat. exec. com. Stevenson-Kefauver Presdl. Campaign gen. election, 1956, del. to Dem. nat. conv., 1952, 56, 60; Dem. nominee for Assembly Calif. Legislature, 1950; Calif. Campaign Com. Brown for Gov., 1958; mem. Kennedy Presdl. Campaign Com., Kennedy Nat. Inaugural Com., 1960, 61; chmn. Alameda County Women for Johnson and Humphrey, 1964; mem. No. Calif. Com. Cranston for U.S. Senator Campaign, 1980, 85; active Congl. campaign, 1983; mem. Dem. Nat. Conv. Host Com., 1984; mem. Dianne Feinstein's Campaign Com. for mayor of San Francisco, 1984, Feinstein for Gov. Campaign Com., 1990—; mem. adv. com. No. Calif. Conf. on Substance Abuse and Family Issues, San Francisco U., 1987; mem. Roger Boas' campaign com. for Mayor of San Francisco, 1987. Subject oral history, Clara Shirpser - One Woman's Role in Democratic Politics- National, California and Local, 1950-73, in Bancroft Libr. U. Calif., Berkeley, 1975, and 16 univ. rsch. librs.; author: Behind the Scene in Politics-Memoirs of Clara Shirpser, 1981 (based on oral history), included in Libr. of Congress, Smithsonian Instn.; pub. American Lives Endowment. Mem. Merola Opera Ctr., San Francisco Opera, 1960-91; chmn. women's div. Herrick Meml. Hosp., Berkeley, 1956-74, hon. trustee, 1968-78; mem. franchise, taxation, charter amendment coms. Berkeley City Council, 1948-50, Alameda County County Dem. Cen. Com., 1952-58; mem. Menninger Found., 1970-91; past mem. nat. bd. Atlantic Union; chmn. Bldg. Fund East Bay Rehab. Center, Women's Div., 1958; mem. Gov.'s Adv. Com. to Calif. Consumers Counsel, 1959-67; pres. Arch Herrick Hosp. Guild, 1957-74; past bd. dirs. Calif. Heritage Council, Planned Parenthood San Francisco and Alameda Counties; chmn. viewpoints com. Center for Learning in Retirement, U. Calif. Extension Div., 1975-76; pres. League Women Voters Berkeley, 1948-49, Town Meeting chmn., 1949-50; mem. nat. bd. Women's Crusade for a Common Sense Economy, 1985.; bd. dirs. San Francisco Outlook, 1985-87; mem. U. Calif. Alliance, UN Assn. U.S.; San Francisco Edn. Childrens Fund, 1987, San Francisco Edn. Sch. Vols., 1988, ACLU, Common Cause, Nat. Council Jewish Women, 1991; past bd. dirs. World Affairs Coun. DIED 05/29/96. .

SHOEMAKER, EUGENE MERLE, geologist; b. L.A., Apr. 28, 1928; s. George Estel and Muriel May (Scott) S.; m. Carolyn Jean Spellmann, Aug. 18, 1951; children: Christine Carol, Patrick Gene, Linda Susan. B.S., Calif. Inst. Tech., 1947, M.S., 1948; M.A., Princeton U., 1954, Ph.D., 1960; Sc.D., Ariz. State Coll., 1965, Temple U., 1967, U. Ariz., 1984. Geologist U.S. Geol. Survey, 1948-93, scientist emeritus, 1993-97, exploration uranium deposits and investigation salt structures Colo. and Utah, 1948-50, regional investigations geochemistry, volcanology and structure Colorado Plateau, 1951-56, research on structure and mechanics of meteorite impact and nuclear explosion craters, 1957-60, with E.C.T. Chao, discovered coesite, Meteor Crater, Ariz., 1960, investigation structure and history of moon, 1960-73, established lunar geol. time scale, methods of geol. mapping of moon, 1960, application TV systems to investigation extraterrestrial geology, 1961-97, geology and paleomagnetism, Colo. Plateau, 1969-97, systematic search for planet-crossing asteroids and comets, 1973-94; with C.S. Shoemaker and D.H. Levy discovered Periodic Comet Shoemaker-Levy 9, 1993; with C.S. Shoemaker discovered 46 Trojan asteroids, 1985-94; geology of satellites of Jupiter, Saturn, Uranus and Neptune, 1978-97, investigating role of large body impacts in evolution of life, 1981-97, impact craters of Australia,, 1983-97; organized br. of astrogeology U.S. Geol. Survey, 1961; co-investigator TV expt. Project Ranger, 1961-65; chief scientist, center of astrogeology U.S. Geol. Survey, 1966-68; prin. investigator geol. field investigations in Apollo lunar landing, 1965-70, also television expt. Project Surveyor, 1963-68; prof. geology Calif. Inst. Tech., 1969-85, chmn. div. geol. and planetary scis., 1969-72; sci. team leader Clementine Mission to the Moon, 1993-94; staff mem. Lowell Observatory, Flagstaff, Ariz., 1993-97. Recipient (with E.C.T. Chao) Wetherill medal Franklin Inst., 1965, Arthur S. Flemming award, 1966, NASA medal for exceptional sci. achievement, 1967, 96, Honor award for meritorious svc. U.S. Dept. Interior, 1973, Disting. Svc. award, 1980, Disting. Alumni award Calif. Inst. Tech., 1986, Space Sci. award AIAA, 1996; co-recipient with C.S. Shoemaker Rittenhouse medal, 1988, Nat. medal of Sci. Pres. Bush, 1992, McGovern award with C.S. Shoemaker Cosmos Club Found., 1995. Mem. NAS, Internat. Astron. Union, Am. Acad. Arts and Scis., Geol. Soc. Am. (Day medal 1982, Gilbert award 1983), Mineral Soc. Am., Soc. Econ. Geologists, Geochem. Soc., Am. Assn. Petroleum Geologists (Spl. award 1997), Am. Geophys. Union (Whipple award 1993, Bowie medal 1996), Am. Astron. Soc. (Kuiper prize 1984), Meteoritical Soc. (Barringer award 1984, Leonard medal 1985). Shoemaker Award with C.S. Shoemaker, Am. Inst. Prof. Geol. 1997; James Craig Watson Medal, 1998. Home: Flagstaff Ariz. Died July 18, 1997.

SHOR, JONATHAN, lawyer; b. N.Y.C., May 8, 1948. BA summa cum laude, Columbia U., 1970; JD cum laude, Harvard U., 1973. Bar: N.Y. 1974. Mem. Proskauer Rose Goetz & Mendelsohn, N.Y.C. Articles editor Harvard Civil Rights—Civil Liberties Law Review, 1972-73. Mem. Phi Beta Kappa. Died 1995.

SHORE, FERDINAND JOHN, physicist, educator; b. Bklyn., Sept. 23, 1919; s. Ferdinand John and Magdalene (Schwarz) S.; m. Paulina Barbara Pucko, May 25, 1946; children: Gregory, David, Carolyn, Pamela, Jonathan. B.S., Queens Coll., 1941; M.A., Conn. Wesleyan U., 1943; Ph.D., U. Ill., 1952. Lab. asst. War Research, NDRC Project, Conn. Wesleyan U., 1941-45; research asst. U. Ill., 1946-51; asso. physicist Brookhaven Nat. Lab., 1952-60; with Queens Coll., Flushing, N.Y., 1960-95; prof. physics Queens Coll., 1964-86, prof. emeritus, 1986-95, chmn. dept., 1980-81; cons. physics dept. Brookhaven Nat. Lab., 1961-72, cons. dept. applied sci., 1976-80; mem. Nat. Council on Radiation Protection and Measurements, 1962-71. Mem. Nat. Council on Radiation Protection and Measurements (consociate mem.), Sigma Xi. Home: Patchogue N.Y. Died Apr. 4, 1995.

SHORE, SAMUEL, lawyer, physician; b. Phila., June 21, 1924; s. Joseph and Freda (Warshilewsky) S.; children: Dale Martin, Cheryl Ann, Andrea Joy. B.S., LaSalle Coll., 1945; M.D., Hahnemann Med. Coll., 1949; J.D., U. So. Calif., 1962. Bar: Calif. 1962. Intern Los Angeles County/Harbor Gen. Hosp., 1949-50, resident in gen. surgery, 1950-54; pvt. practice gen. surgery, L.A., Los Angeles, 1954-62; mem. firm, sr. atty. Samuel Shore, Inc., Los Angeles, 1962—; lectr. advocacy UCLA, U. So. Calif., Pepperdine U.; prof. San Fernando Coll. Law; cons. in law, medicine and med. malpractice litigation. Contbr. articles to profl. jours. Served with U.S. Army, 1942-44. Fellow Roscoe Pound-Am. Trial Lawyers Found., Am. Bd. Profl. Liability Attys. (diplomate, pres. 1982), Am. Coll. Abdominal Surgeons, Am. Bd. Trial Advocates, Am. Coll. Legal Medicine, Am. Acad. Forensic Scis.; mem. L.A. Trial Lawyers Assn. (dir. 1968-77, pres. 1977, Ted Horn meml. award 1979), Calif. Trial Lawyers Assn. (dir. 1973-83, 85, exec. com. 1978-79, 85-87, v.p. 1985-88), Nat. Bd. Trial Advocacy (trustee), Assn. Trial Lawyers of Am. (Calif. del. 1985-90), Am. Bar Assn., L.A. County Bar Assn. Democrat. DIED 06/15/96. .

SHORNEY, MARGO KAY, art gallery owner; b. Great Falls, Mont., July 5, 1930; d. Angus Vaughn McIver and Loneta Eileen Kuhn; m. James Thomas Shorney, Apr. 17, 1954; 1 child, Blair Angus. Student, Coll. Edn., Great Falls, Mont., 1948-50, U. Denver, 1950-53. Owner, dir. Shorney Gallery Fine Art, Oklahoma City, 1976—; pres. Mont. Inst. Arts, Great Falls, 1953-54, Okla. Art Gallery Owners Assn., Oklahoma City, 1981-83; lectr. Norman (Okla.) Art League, 1987-91; judge fine arts Ponca City (Okla.) 12th Ann. Fine Arts, 1986, Edmond (Okla.) Art Assn. Expo 1995, Fine Arts Festival 22nd Ann., 1996; appraiser Globe Life, Oklahoma City, Ponca City Juried Art Assn. 22nd Ann. Fine Arts. Works exhibited in group shows, various orgns., 1953-90. Mentor South Oklahoma City Coll., 1990; active Okla. Mus. Art, 1973-78. Mem. Nat. Assn. Women Bus. Owners, Okla. Sculpture Soc. (charter), Okla. Art Guild (bd. dirs. 1979-82, lectr. 1981, 82, 83, 92). Republican. Episcopalian. Avocations: swimming, figure skating, horseback riding, landscaping. Died Nov. 6, 1996.

SHORT, BYRON ELLIOTT, engineering educator; b. Putnam, Tex., Dec. 29, 1901; s. Samuel W. and Florence Gertrude (Sublett) S.; m. Mary Jo Fitzgerald, June 1, 1937; children: Mary Aileen Short Gauntt, Byron Elliott Jr. B.S., U. Tex., 1926, M.S., 1930; M.M.E., Cornell U., 1936, Ph.D., 1939. Cadet engr. Tex Co., summers 1926-27, mech. engr., summers 1928-30; instr. U. Tex., 1926-29, asst. prof., 1929-36, charge heat-power, fluid mechanics lab., 1930-65, mech. engr., summers 1932-36, 40, asso. prof., 1936-39, prof. mech. engring., 1939-73, prof. emeritus, 1973-96, chmn. dept., 1945-47, 51-53; acting dean U. Tex. (Coll. Engring.), 1948-49; teaching fellow Cornell, 1935-36; cons. Oak Ridge Nat. Lab., research participant, 1956, 57. Author: Flow, Measurement and Pumping of Fluids, 1934, Engineering Thermodynamics, (with H.L. Kent, B.F. Treat), 1953, Pressure Enthalpy Charts (with H.L. kent and H.A. Walls), 1970; assoc. editor Design Volume, Am. Soc. Refrigerating Engrs. Databook, 1953-55, editor, 1957; contbr. articles to engring. Named Outstanding Alumnus, Mech. Engring. Dept., U. Tex., Austin, 1995, Disting. Grad., Coll. Engring., U. Tex., Austin, 1997. Fellow ASME (life; chmn. South Tex. sect. 1938-39, mem. heat transfer and power test code com.), fellow ASHRAE (life); mem. SAR, Am. Soc. Engring. Edn., Huguenot Soc. Am. (state pres. 1983-85), Masons (33d degree SR & KT), Shriners, Sigma Xi, Tau Beta Pi, Phi Kappa Phi, Pi Tau Sigma. Baptist. Home: Austin Tex. Died Oct. 31, 1996; interred Austin Memorial Park, Austin, TX.

SHOUSE, CATHERINE FILENE, philanthropist, cultural organization administrator; b. Boston, June 9, 1896; d. Lincoln and Therese (Weil) Filene; m. Alvin E. Dodd, 1921 (div. 1930); 1 child, Joan Tolley; m. Jouett Shouse, Dec. 10, 1932 (dec.). Grad., Bradford Acad., 1913; student, Vassar Coll., 1913-14; BA, Wheaton Coll., Norton, Mass., 1918; MEd, Harvard U., 1923; postgrad., U. Colo., 1928; HHD (hon.), Tufts U., 1963, Wheaton Coll., 1964; LLD (hon.), Am. U., 1971; HHD (hon.), George Washington U., 1975; HHD, Bucknell U., 1975; MusD, New England Conservatory Music, 1975; HHD (hon.), Catholic U., 1977, Coll. William and Mary, 1977, Skidmore Coll., 1979, U. Md., 1979, Hood Coll., 1981; LittD, Gonzaga U., 1983; MusD, Shenandoah Coll. and Conservatory Music, 1984; HHD (hon.), Marymount Coll. of Va., 1986. Asst. to chief women's div. U.S. Employment Service U.S. Dept. Labor, Washington, 1918-19. Author: Careers for Women, 1920, 3d edition, 1974. 1st woman appointed to Nat. Dem. Com. Mass., 1919-20; founder with Mrs. Borden Harriman Women's Nat. Dem. Club, 1925; 1st woman chmn. appointed by Pres. Coolidge Fed. Prison for Women, 1926; founder, chmn. Inst. Women's Profl. Relations, 1929-45; trustee Filene Found., Boston, 1947-94; organized Gen. Clay Fund to aid German Youth Activities, 1949-56; elected to bd. dirs. Nat. Symphony Orch. Assn., 1949-68, v.p., 1951-68, hon. v.p., 1968-94; bd. dirs. Nat. Arbitration Assn., 1952-63; bd. dirs. Lincoln Filene Ctr. for Citizenship and Pub. Affairs Tufts U., 1955-94; organizer Washington Hungarian Relief Fund at request Pres. Hoover, 1956; bd. trustees National Cultural Ctr. which later became known as John F. Kennedy Ctr. for Performing Arts, 1958-80, hon. trustee, 1980-94; appointed by Pres. Nixon to Pa. Ave. Devel. Commn., 1973; appointed by Pres. Ford to Commn. on Presdl. Scholars, 1975; mem. Am. Com. on The French Revolution, 1989-94. Recipient City of Paris awrd 1949, Vienna Medal of Honor, 1949, Patriotic Civilian award U.S. Army, 1954, Gold Baton award Am. Symphony Orch. League, 1968, Medal of Honor, Music Nat. Arts Club, 1971; decorated Comdr.'s Cross of Merit, Fed. Rep. Ger., 1954, Dame Comdr. of Brit. Empire, Eng., 1976, H.S. Medal of Freedom, 1977, Officer dans l'Ordre des Arts et des Lettres, France, 1985, Nat. Medal of the Arts, 1994. Sigma Alpha Iota. Clubs: 1925 F St.; Am. Newspaper Woman's; Kollegewidgwok Yacht. Home: Vienna Va. Died Dec. 14, 1994.

SHROCK, ROBERT RAKES, geologist; b. Waupecong, Ind., Aug. 27, 1904; s. Andrew and Stella (Glassburn) S.; m. Theodora Antoinette Weidman, Feb. 2, 1933; children: Wendolyn Theodora, Robert Ellsworth. A.B., Ind. U., 1925, A.M., 1926, Ph.D., 1928, D.Sc. (hon.), 1971. Asst. in geology U. Wis., 1928-29, instr., 1929-31, asst. prof., 1931-37; asst. prof. geology Mass. Inst. Tech., 1937-43, asso. prof., 1943-49, exec. officer dept. geology, 1946-49, acting chmn., 1949-50, chmn., 1950-65, prof. of geology, 1949-70, emeritus prof. geology, 1970-93; vis. lectr. geology Harvard, 1948-49, asso. in invertebrate paleontology, 1950-70; cons. various mining and petroleum cos. and engring. groups, 1925-93; sr. indsl. specialist WPB, 1943; cons. Research and Devel. Bd., 1946-52. Author: (with W.H. Twenhofel) Invertebrate Paleontology, 1935, (with H.W. Shimer) Index Fossils of North America, 1944, Sequence in Layered Rocks, 1948, (with W.H. Twenhofel) Principles of Invertebrate Paleontology, 1953, The Geologists Crosby of Boston, 1972, Geology at MIT 1865-1965, 1977, Vol. II, 1982, Cecil and Ida Green, Philanthropists Extraordinary, 1989; contbr. articles to sci. jours. Mem. corp., hon. trustee, hon. mem. Woods Hole Oceanographic Instn. Fellow Geol. Soc. Am., Paleontol. Soc. (patron 1977), AAAS (chmn. sci. 1957, v.p.); mem. Am. Acad. Arts and Scis., Soc. Econ. Paleontologists and Mineralogists (pres. 1956-57, Twenhofel medal 1976), Am. Assn. Petroleum Geologists, Nat. Assn. Geology Tchrs. (pres. 1959), Phi Beta Kappa, Sigma Xi, Sigma Gamma Epsilon. Home: Lexington Mass. Died June 22, 1993.

SHUBIN, HARRY, internist; b. Phila., Mar. 17, 1914; s. Sam and Hannah (Pisner) S.; BS, Temple U., 1933, MD, 1937; m. Celia Fierman, July 8, 1938 (dec. June 1995); children: Charles I., Elliot B. Intern Frankford Hosp., Phila., 1937-38; chief resident Rush Hosp., Phila., 1938-41; pvt. practice internal medicine specializing in, diseases of chest, pulmonary diseases, psychosomatic and occupational medicine, Phila., 1938—; asst. vis. physician dept. chest diseases, Phila. Gen. Hosp., 1938-44, chief vis. physician, 1944-69, chmn. dept. pulmonary diseases, 1950-59, pres. med. staff No. div., 1956-58, cons. 1969-77; med. dir. Broad St. Hosp. and Med. Ctr., 1962-69; med. dir., adminstr. Ctr. City Hosp., Phila., 1969-81; med. advisor SSI., DHEW Region III, 1974-80; cons. in pulmonary diseases Frankford Hosp., Germantown Hosp., Valley Forge Med. Ctr. and Hosp.; fed. judiciary, med. adv. 1976—; clin. ast. prof. Hahnemann U., 1986-87. Contbr. to numerous profl. jours. Mem. exec. com. South Phila. High Sch. Alumni, 1950—; bd. dirs. Oak Lane Day Sch., Blue Bell, Pa.; med. advisor Pa. chpt. Asbestos Victims Edn. Info.; co-founder Asbestos Victims of World. Recipient Selective Service medal SSS, 1944. Fellow AAAS, Royal Coll. London, Royal Soc. Health London, Royal Soc. Medicine London, Am. Coll. Chest Physicians (emeritus 1982), Am. Acad Family Physicians, Am. Acad. Med. Administrs. (nat.

sec., diplomate 1987, Merit award), Am. Pub. Health Assn., Am. Acad. Psychosomatic Medicine, Am. Coll. Occupational/Environ. Medicine, Am. Coll. Angiology, Am. Coll. Sports Medicine, Am. Geriatrics Soc., Coll. Physicians of Phila., Gerontological Soc., Internat. Coll. Angiology, Pa. Pub. Health Assn.; mem. AMA, ACP (life mem.), Royal Soc. Health, Am. Trudeau Soc., Am. Geriatric Soc., Am. Coll. Health Care Adminstrs., World Med. Assn. (founder), Am. Acad. Tb Physicians (pres. 1948-50), 50th Ward Community Ambulance Assn. (med. adviser), Lions, Masons (32 deg.). Contbr. articles to profl. jours.

SHULMAN, IRVING, novelist, educator; b. Bklyn., May 21, 1913; s. Max and Sarah (Ress) S.; m. Julia Grager, July 9, 1938; children: Joan, Leslie. AB magna cum laude, Ohio U., 1937; AM, Columbia U., 1938; PhD, UCLA, 1972. Personnel technician, statistician, adminstrv. officer, info. specialist various govt. agys., 1941-47; mem. faculty dept. English, George Washington U., 1943-47; teaching asst. UCLA, 1962-64; asst. prof. English, Calif. State Coll., Los Angeles, 1964-65. Author: novel The Amboy Dukes, 1947, Cry Tough, 1949, The Big Brokers, 1951; film City Across the River, 1951; novel The Square Trap, 1953; also film version The Ring, 1955; author: novel Children of the Dark, 1956; also treatment, first draft of film version Rebel Without a Cause, 1957, The Velvet Knife, 1959; short stories The Short End of the Stick, 1959; biography The Roots of Fury, 1961, Harlow, 1964, Valentino, 1967; social study Jackie: The Exploitation of a First Lady, 1970; novel The Devil's Knee, 1973, Saturn's Child, 1976. Mem. MLA, English Grad. Assn., AAUP, Writer's Guild Am., Acad. Motion Picture Arts and Scis., Am. Film Inst., Ohio U. Alumni Assn. (cert. of merit 1958), Columbia U. Alumni Assn., UCLA Alumni Assn., Phi Beta Kappa, Phi Epsilon Pi, Zeta Beta Tau. Home: Sherman Oaks Calif. Died March 23, 1995.

SHULTZ, MARTHA JANE See **DIETRICH, MARTHA JANE**

SHURRAGER, PHIL SHERIDAN, psychologist, educator; b. Erie, Pa., Dec. 26, 1907; s. Frederick and Margaret (Lautersbach) S.; m. Harriett Cantrall, Dec. 11, 1937; 1 child, Margaret Lynn. B.S., Muskingum Coll., 1930; A.M., Ohio U., 1932; research fellow, U. Ill., 1936-38, Ph.D., 1939. Diplomate: indsl. psychology Am. Bd. Profl. Psychology. Dept. zoology and physiology Ohio U., 1931-35; research fellow Clark U., 1935-36; research fellow U. Rochester and Rochester Sch. Medicine, 1938-39, NRC fellow, 1938-39; vis. asst. prof. psychology U. Pa., 1940-41, St. Lawrence U., 1941-42; dep. asst. dir. and design engr. Brit. Ministry of Supply, U.S., 1942-44; indsl. cons. and psychologist Stevenson, Jordon and Harrison, Inc., engrs., 1944-46; prof. psychology and chmn. dept. psychology and edn. Ill. Inst. Tech., Chgo., 1946-73; prof. emeritus Ill. Inst. Tech., 1973-94; psychologist neurophysiol. labs. Northwest Inst. Med. Research, 1973-94; cons. bus. and industry, 1946-94. Contbr. articles in biology and exptl. psychology to profl. jours.; co-author occupational aptitude test series. Mem. curriculum council Chgo. Bd. Edn. Fellow Am. Acad. Neurology; mem. Am., Ill., Midwest psychol. assns., Soc. Exptl. Biology and Medicine, Royal Soc. Medicine, N.Y. Acad. Scis. (life mem.), Ill. Acad. Scis. (hon.), AAAS, Soc. Advancement of Engring. Edn., AAUP, Sigma Xi (pres. chpt. 1958-59), Pi Gamma Mu. Clubs: Chgo. Psychology, Chgo. Literary. Lodge: Shriners. Originator of spinal conditioning and learning at a motor neurone synapse; co-discoverer biochem., phys. changes paralleling light and dark adaptation in vitreous humor of mammalian eyes and subphotonal vision. Home: Cape Coral Fla. Died May 30, 1994.

SIAU, JOHN FINN, wood scientist, educator; b. Detroit, Mar. 30, 1921; s. Robert H. and Marguerite L. (Finn) S.; children: John E., Mary M. B.S., Mich. State Coll., 1943; M.S., SUNY, Syracuse, 1964; Ph.D., SUNY-, Syracuse, 1968. Engr. Utah Radio Products, Huntington, Ind., 1946-48; design engr. vacuum tubes Gen. Electric Co., Schenectady, 1948-58; prof. physics Paul Smith's (N.Y.) Coll., 1958-66; prof. wood products engring. SUNY Coll. Environ. Sci. and Forestry, Syracuse, 1966-85, emeritus prof., 1985-93; adj. prof. wood physics VPI, State U., Blacksburg, Va., 1993—; vis. prof. U. Aberdeen, U.K., 1978, Tech. U., Zvolen, Slovakia, 1994. Author: Flow in Wood, 1971, Transport Processes in Wood, 1984, Wood: Influence of Moisture and Physical Properties, 1995; editor Wood and Fiber Sci., 1994-95. Served with USNR, 1943-46. Recipient Wood award 2d pl. Forest Products Research Soc., 1968. Fellow Internat. Acad. Wood Sci.; mem. Forest Products Soc., Internat. Assn. Wood Anatomists, Soc. Wood Sci. and Tech., Tau Beta Pi. Roman Catholic. Club: Adirondack Mountain. Died April 15, 1996.

SIEGAN, HAROLD AARON, county judge, educator; b. Chgo., Oct. 3, 1914; s. Joseph and Bertha (Paster) S.; m. Bernice Rubinoff, June 19, 1938; children—Elayne Siegan Feder, Kenneth R., Jerold N. Student Crane Jr. Coll., 1932-33, YMCA Jr. Coll., 1933-34; J.D., DePaul U., 1938. Bar: Ill. 1938. Ptnr. Siegan & Rubinoff, Chgo., 1941-71; master in chancery Cir. Ct. Cook County, 1955-71, assoc. judge, 1971-73, supervising judge land title sect., 1973-79, judge chancery div., 1979—; adj. prof. Loyola U. Sch. Law, 1974—; lectr. various ednl. instns. and Bar assns.; faculty Ill. Inst. Continuing Legal Edn., 1975—. Author: Mechanic's Liens-Cases, Comments, and Materials, 1976; Illinois Mechanics' Lien Book, 1974, rev. edits., 1977, 81; IICLE Creditors Rights, 1980; Chancery and Special Remedies, 1978-80; contbr. articles to law jours. Bd. govs. Israel Bonds, 1955—; v.p. Gold Coast Chamber Orchestra, 1976-80; chmn. organizing com. Council Traditional/Orthodox Synagogues Greater Chgo., 1976-77, chmn. exec. com., 1977-79; bd. dirs. Bernard Horwich Ctr. Jewish Community Ctrs. Chgo., 1960-67; cubmaster Boy Scouts Am., 1949-50; vice-chmn. Chgo. Com. for Weizman Inst. Sci., 1968-69; bd. dirs. P.R. Congress of Mut. Aid, Inc.; spl. observer Adolph Eichman Trial in Israel, 1961. Mem. ABA, Chgo. Bar Assn. (mem. real property com.), Ill. State Bar Assn., Decalogue Soc. Lawyers (bd. mgrs.), Am. Judicature Soc. Lawyers, Am. Acad. Matrimonial Lawyers, Assn. Trial Lawyers Am., Northwest Suburban Bar Assn. Republican.

SIEGEL, LAURENCE, human resources executive, former psychology educator; b. N.Y.C., Feb. 11, 1928; s. Jacob Maurice and Carolyn (Blum) S.; m. Betty S. Smith, Oct. 2, 1971; 1 son, Brent G. A.B., N.Y.U., 1946, M.A., 1948; Ph.D., U. Tenn., 1952. Asst. prof. Wash. State U., 1950-53; research asso. Ohio State U., 1954-55; asso. prof. Miami U., Oxford, Ohio, 1956-61; prof. Miami U., 1961-65, dir. instructional research service, 1960-66; prof., chmn. dept. psychology La. State U., 1966-84; pres. Human Resource Mgmt. Assn., Inc., 1985—; indsl. and ednl. cons. Author: Industrial Psychology, 1962, 69, 74, Instruction—Some Contemporary Viewpoints, 1967, Personnel and Organizational Psychology, 1982, 2d revised edit., 1987. Served with AUS, 1955-56. Fellow Am. Psychol. Assn.; mem. Southeastern Psychol. Assn. (pres. 1976-78), La. Psychol. Assn. DIED 12/17/94. .

SIEGEL, MILTON P., health foundation executive, international executive, educator, management consultant; b. Des Moines, July 23, 1911; s. Barney and Sylvy (Levinson) S.; m. Rosalie Rosenberg, May 25, 1934 (dec. Jan. 1991); children: Betsy Lee, Larry (dec.), Sally (dec.). Dir. fin. and stats. Iowa Emergency Relief Adminstrn., also treas.; Iowa Rural Rehab. Adminstrn., 1933-35; regional fin. and bus. mgr. Farm Security Adminstrn., U.S. Dept. Agr., 1935-41, chief fiscal officer, 1942-44; asst. treas., dir. Office for Far East, UNRRA, 1944-45; asst. dir. fiscal br. prodn. and mktg. adminstrn. U.S. Dept. Agr., 1945-47; asst. dir.-gen. WHO, Geneva, 1947-71; prof. internat. health Sch. Pub. Health, U. Tex. Health Scis. Center, Houston, 1971-75, prof. internat. health, mgmt. and policy scis., 1988-89, prof. emeritus, 1989; health mgmt. cons. Imperial Govt. of Iran, Nat. Health Ins. Orgn., 1975-76; sr. cons. to adminstr. UN Devel. Program, 1976-77; chmn. bd. trustees Mgmt. Planning Systems Internat., Inc., 1977-95; pres., CEO Fedn. World Health Founds, 1978-95; mem. permanent scale contbns. commn. League Red Cross Socs., 1967-81; sr. mgmt. scientist Children's Nutrition Rsch. Ctr., Baylor Coll. Medicine, Houston, 1979-80; cons. Sch. Pub. Health, U. N.C., Chapel Hill, 1970, Carolina Population Ctr., 1970; vis. prof. Sch. Pub. Health, U. Mich., 1967; awarded acad. chair U. Tex. Health Sci. Ctr., Houston, 1984. Chmn. bd. trustees World Health Found., U.S.A., 1976-89. Recipient Sam Beber award, 1960. Mem. Am. Public Health Assn. Home: Houston Tex. Died Oct. 29, 1995.

SIGLER, WILLIAM FRANKLIN, environmental consultant; b. LeRoy, Ill., Feb. 17, 1909; s. John A. and Bettie (Homan) S.; m. Margaret Eleanor Brotherton, July 3, 1936; children: Elinor Jo, John William. BS, Iowa State U., 1940, MS, 1941, PhD, 1947; postdoctoral studies, UCLA, 1963. Conservationist Soil Conservation Svc., Ill., 1935-37; cons. Cen. Engring. Co., Davenport, Iowa, 1940-41; rsch. assoc. Iowa State U., 1941-42; 1945-47; asst. prof. wildlife sci. Utah State U., 1947-50, prof., head dept., 1950-74; pres. W.F. Sigler & Assocs. Inc., 1974-86; cons. U.S. Surgeon Gen., 1963-67, FAO, Argentina, 1968. Author: Theory and Method of Fish Life History Investigations, 1952, Wildlife Law Enforcement, 1956, 4th edit., 1995, Fishes of Utah, 1963, (with R.R. Miller) Fishes of the Great Basin, 1987, (with J.W. Sigler), Recreational Fishing: Management, Theory and Application, 1990, Fishes of Utah: A Natural History Review, 1995; contbr. numerous articles to profl. jours. Mem. Utah Water Pollution Control Bd., 1957-65, chmn., 1963-65. Lt. (j.g.) USNR, World War II. Named Wildlife Conservationist of Yr., Nat. Wildlife Fedn., 1970, Outstanding Educator of Yr., 1971; recipient Disting. Svc. cert of recognition Iowa Coop. Wildlife Rsch. Unit, 1982, Alumni Achievement award Coll. Natural Resources Utah State U., 1987. Fellow AAAS, Internat. Acad. Fishery Scientists; mem. AAUP, Ecol. Soc. Am., Wildlife Soc. (hon.), Am. Fisheries Soc. (award of merit Bonneville chpt. 1990), Outdoor Writers Am., Sigma Xi, Phi Kappa Phi. Home: Logan Utah Died June 25, 1995.

SIHVONEN, OLI, artist; b. Bklyn., Jan. 31, 1921; s. Toivo Eliel and Elli (Forsman) S.; m. Joan Couch, June 27, 1946; children: Kimry, Jennifer, Conor. Student, Art Students League, N.Y.C., 1938-41, Black Mountain (N.C.) Coll., 1946-48. Mem. faculty Hunter Coll., N.Y.C., 1953-56, U. N.Mex., 1964, U. Denver, 1966; vis. artist La. State U., 1977. Commd. works for South Mall, N.Y. State Art Collection, 1970, Northwestern U., City Bank, N.Y.C., 1973; one-man exhbns. include Jonson Gallery, U. N.Mex., 1952, Stable Gallery, N.Y.C., 1963, Rice U., Houston, 1967, Burpee Mus. Art, Rockford, Ill., 1969, Roswell (N.Mex.) Mus. and Art Ctr., 1978, Katonah (N.Y.) Gallery, 1980, Hoshour Gallery, Albuquerque, 1983, Craig Cornelius, N.Y.C.; group exhbns. include Whitney Mus., N.Y.C., 1962, 63, 65, 67, Mus. Modern Art, N.Y.C., 1965, Corcoran Gallery, Washington, 1967, Albright-Knox Gallery, Buffalo, 1968, Am. Abstract Artists Exhbn., 50th Anniversary, Bronx County Mus., 1986; represented in permanent collections Mus. Modern Art, Corcoran Gallery Art, Whitney Mus., Chase Manhattan Bank, N.Y.C., Midland Fed. Savs. and Loan Assn., Denver, U. N.Mex. Art Mus., Albuquerque, Dallas Mus. Fine Art, N.Y. State Art Collection, Albany, Rockefeller U., N.Y.C., U. Mich., Midland Marine Bank, Buffalo, 1st. Nat. City Bank, N.Y.C., numerous others throughout U.S.; touring Ea. Europe, 1988— via USIA. With C.E., U.S. Army, 1942-45. Nat. Endowment for Arts. grantee, 1967, 76, Gottlieb grantee, 1984, Pollock-Krasner grantee, 1987-88. Mem. Am. Abstract Artists Assn.

SILBAUGH, PRESTON NORWOOD, lawyer, consultant; b. Stockton, Calif., Jan. 15, 1918; s. Herbert A. and Della Mae (Masten) S.; m. Maria Sarah Arriola; children: Judith Ann Freed, Gloria Stypinski, Ximena Carey Braun, Carol Lee Morgan. A.B. in Philosophy, U. Wash., 1940; J.D., Stanford U., 1953. Bar: Calif. With Lockheed Aircraft Corp., 1941-44, Pan Am. World Airways, 1944, Office Civilian Personnel, War Dept., 1944-45; engaged in ins. and real estate in Calif., 1945-54; mem. faculty Stanford Law Sch., 1954-59, assoc. prof. law, 1956-59, assoc. dean, 1956-59; chief dep. savs. and loan commr. for Calif., 1959-61, bus. and commerce adminstr., dir. investment, savs. and loan commr., mem. gov.'s cabinet, 1961-63; dir. Chile-Calif. Aid Program, Sacramento and Santiago, 1963-65; chmn. bd. Beverly Hills Savs. & Loan Assn., Calif., 1965-84; bd. dirs. Wickes Cos., Inc.; chmn. bd., pres. Simon Bolivar Fund, San Diego, Calneva Land and Cattle Co., San Diego; of counsel firm Miller, Boyko & Bell, San Diego. Author: The Economics of Personal Insurance, 1958; also articles. Mem. pres.'s real estate adv. com. U. Calif., 1966—; mem. Beverly Hills Pub. Bldg. Adv. Com., 1970—. Served with USMCR, 1942-43. Mem. ABA, San Diego County Bar Assn., Soc. Internat. Devel., Inter-Am. Savs. and Loan Union, Internat. Union Building Socs., U. Wash., Stanford, Calif. Aggie alumni assns., Order of Coif, Phi Alpha Delta. Clubs: Commonwealth (San Francisco), Town Hall (Los Angeles). Deceased.

SILBER, MAURICE, artist, painter; b. Bklyn., Apr. 12, 1922; s. Leiser and Sylvia (Ehrlich) S. Student Pratt Inst., 1940, Cooper Union, 1940-42, Art Students League, 1945, Queen's Coll., Empire State Coll., SUNY, 1979-81, M.A., NYU, 1984; m. Lillian Lowy, Dec. 23, 1950; children: Roger, Rona. Designer, modelmaker fine jewelry Select Jewelry Co., N.Y.C., 1945-46; founder Jewel Arts Inc., N.Y.C., 1947, pres., 1947-69, exec. v.p. (Jewel Arts Inc. purchase by Jewelcor Inc.), 1969-71; founder Maurice Silber, Inc., 1972-75. Exhibited paintings in one-man shows Casa de Portugal, N.Y.C., 1971, Salmagundi Club, N.Y.C., 1974, Soc. Illustrators, 1972, 75, Instituto Hondureno de Cultura Interamericana, Teguiciagalpa, Honduras, 1978, Empire State Coll., SUNY, 1981, Teatro Nacional, San Jose, Costa Rica, 1977, 78, 79, 80, 81, 83, East Hampton Hist. Soc., Marine Mus., L.I., 1980, French Cultural Ctr., 1983, Knickerbocker Artists, N.Y.C., 1980, 81, 82, 88 Gallery 80, Venice, 1983, NYU, 1984, Wanamaker, Gallery of Centro-Cultural Costarricense Norteamericano, San Jose, Costa Rica, 1975, 76, 84, 88, 89, Echandi Gallery of Museo d'Arte de Costa Rica, 1986, Monge Gallery, San Jose, Calif., 1985; exhibited in group shows Malverne Art Assn. Annual, 1974, Soc. Illustrators, N.Y.C., 1973, 74, 75, 78, Hudson Valley Art Assn., 1975, Genesis Gallery, N.Y.C., 1978, World Trade Ctr., N.Y.C., 1979, Nat. Art League Ann., 1977, 79, Artists Equity, N.Y.C., 1977, Hobe Sound Gallery, Fla., 1977, 78, St. John's U., 1979, Long Beach (N.Y.) Mus., 1979, Am. Artists Profl. League Grand Nat., 1979, Port Washington Ann., N.Y.C., 1975, Salmagundi Club, 1971-90, Pacem in Terris Gallery, N.Y.C., 1975, Nat. Art League, 1977-78, Am. Embassy, San Jose, 1978, Allied Artists Am., 1981, Fordham U., 1982, Alliance Queens Artists, 1984, Chung Cheng Gallery, St. John's U., N.Y., 1984, Guild Hall, East Hampton, N.Y., 1985, Queensborough Community Coll., N.Y., 1986, Soc. Illustrators, 1990; represented in permanent collections East Hampton Hist. Soc., Marine Mus., Teatro Nacional, San Jose, Costa Rica, Nat. Park Svc., USAF Art Collection, USN Collection, Alianza France, San Jose, numerous others; vis. prof. U. Costa Rica, 1984, Queensboro Community Coll.; condr. workshops. With USAAF, 1942-45, ETO. Decorated Air medal with 6 oak leaf clusters; recipient various awards, including 1st prize and specially created award for dramatic value Am. Inst. of City N.Y., 1939; E. W. Graham Meml. award Washington Sq., 1976; Anco award, 1978; others. Mem. Salmagundi Club (admissions chmn. 1975-76, jury of awards 1976-77, art com. 1978), Soc. Illustrators, Nat. Art League, Am. Artists Profl. League, Artists Equity, Artists Fellowship, Art League of Nassau County, Knickerbocker Artists (Anco award

1977), Am. Soc. Marine Artists., San Diego Watercolor Soc. Patentee in field; designer chess pieces. Died Nov. 29, 1995.

SILES ZUAZO, HERNAN, former president of Bolivia; b. 1914. Grad., U. San Andres. Practice law, La Paz, Bolivia, 1939; M.P. for La Paz, 1943-46; in exile in Argentina and Chile, translator U.S. News agys., 1946-51; candidate v.p., Bolivia, 1951; leader revolution, 1952; v.p. Bolivia, 1952-56, pres., 1956-60, 82-85; ambassador to Uruguay, 1960-63, Spain, 1963-64; in exile, 1964-78. Pres. Movimiento Nacionalista Revolucionario-Izquierdo, 1978—.Died Aug. 6, 1996.

SILKIN, JON, poet, writer, editor; b. London, Dec. 2, 1930; s. Joseph and Dora (Rubenstein) S.; m. Lorna Tracy, Mar. 9, 1974 (div. 1995); 4 children. Student, Wycliffe Coll., 1940-45, Dulwich Coll., 1945-47; BA in English with honors, Leeds U., 1947, Leeds U., 1962. Founder, editor Stand Mag., London, 1952—; vis. tchr. Writer's Workshop, U. Iowa, Iowa City, 1968-69, 91, Coll. Idaho, Caldwell, 1978, Mishkenot Sha'ananim, Jerusalem, 1980; vis. lectr. Denison U., Granville, Ohio, 1968; vis. writer U. Sydney, Australia, 1974; Bingham vis. poet U. Louisville, 1981; poet-in-residence Am. U., 1989, U. Iowa Writer's Workshop, 1991, U. Tsukuba, 1991-94; writer-in-residence Dumfries and Galloway Arts. Author: Out of Battle: Poets of the First World War, 1972, 79, 97, Penguin Book of First World War Poetry, 1979, The Psalms with Their Spoils, 1980, Selected Poems, 1980, 88, 94, The War Poems of Wilfred Owen, 1994, The Penguin Book of First World War Prose, 1989, The Lens-Breakers, 1992, Gurney, A Play in Verse, 1985, The Ship's Pasture, 1986, The Life of Metrical and Free Verse in Twentieth Century Poetry, 1997, Making a Republic, 1997. Gregory fellow, 1958-60, C. Day Lewis fellow, 1976-77; recipient Geoffrey Faber award 1966. Fellow Royal Soc. of Lit. Died Nov. 21, 1997.

SILLIN, LELAN FLOR, JR., utility executive; b. Tampa, Fla., Apr. 19, 1918; s. Lelan Flor and Ruth (Berry) S.; m. Joan Outhwaite, Sept. 26, 1942; children: Lelan Flor, John Outhwaite, Andrew Borden, William Berry. AB with distinction, U. Mich., 1940, JD, 1942; LLD (hon.), Wesleyan U., 1969. Bar: N.Y. 1946. With Gould & Wilkie, N.Y.C., 1945-51; with Central Hudson Gas & Electric Corp., Poughkeepsie, N.Y., 1951-68, v.p., asst. gen. mgr., 1955-60, pres., 1960-68, chief exec. officer, 1964-67, also trustee; pres. Northeast Utilities, Hartford, Conn., 1968-70, chmn. bd., 1970-83, chief exec. officer, chmn. bd., 1968-83, also trustee; chmn. bd. Conn. Yankee Atomic Power Co., 1971-83, Northeast Energy, 1970-83; former chmn., dir. Fuel Cell User Group; bd. dirs. Waterbury Rep & Am.; past chmn. nat. power survey exec. adv. com. FPC, 1965-72; dir. Inst. Nuclear Power Ops., 1979-85, chmn., 1982-84; chmn. utility nuc. power oversight task com., 1986. Former mem. steering com. Nat. Urban Coalition; former mem. Pres.'s Adv. Com. Environ. Quality; former bd. dirs. Nat. Office Social Responsibility, New Eng. Council; trustee emeritus Edwin Gould Found. for Children, Woodrow Wilson Nat. Fellowship Found., New Eng. Natural Resources Ctr.; trustee emeritus Wesleyan U., former vice-chmn. bd. trustees; past mem. adv. com. White House Conf. on Balanced Nat. Growth and Econ. Devel.; past mem. Pub. Com. on Mental Health; former mem. Am. Arbitration Assn.; former bd. dirs. Conn. Bus. and Industry Assn.; trustee emeritus Vassar Bros. Hosp., Poughkeepsie. Maj. USMCR, 1942-45. Recipient Raymond E. Baldwin medal Wesleyan U., 1986, Oliver Townsend award Atomic Indsl. Forum, 1986. Former mem. Conf. Bd. (sr.). Clubs: Hartford; Dauntless (Essex, Conn.); Century Association, University (N.Y.C.). Died Jan. 3, 1997.

SILVESTRONE, MARIO, utilities company executive; b. Niagara Falls, N.Y., May 19, 1923; s. Amante and Luigina S.; m. Jeanne Silvestrone, Jan. 26, 1947; children: Kathy Jeanne Postma, Paula Lee, Judy Marie Silvestrone McCarthy. BS in Metall. Engring., Rensselaer Poly. Inst., 1950; MBA, U. Rochester, 1970. Registered profl. engr., N.Y. Engr. consumer and indsl. sales Rochester (N.Y.) Gas & Electric Corp., 1950-60, supr. consumer and indsl. sales, 1960-63, asst. mgr. consumer and indsl. sales, 1963-66, asst. gen. sales mgr., 1969-72, gen. mgr. mktg., 1972-75, v.p. mktg., 1975-76, v.p. consumer service, 1976-80, sr. v.p. gen. services, 1980—. Bd. dirs. N.Y. State Bus. Council, Albany, 1979—, Rochester Downtown Devel. Council, 1976-87, St. John's Home, Rochester, 1975-82, Jr. Achievement, Rochester, 1977-82; chmn. bd. Jr. C. of C., Rochester, 1957. Served to lt. comdr. USN, 1943-45. Recipient Disting. Service award Rochester Jaycees, 1957; Westinghouse Achievement scholar Westinghouse-Rensselaer Poly. Inst., 1949. Mem. Am. Gas Assn. (com. chmn. 1963, 72, I-C Achievement award 1972), AIA (Rochester chpt.), Am. Inst. Plant Engrs. (pres. 1968-69), Elec. Assn. of Rochester (pres. 1972), Profl. Engrs. Soc., Am. Soc. Metals. Republican. Episcopalian. Lodge: Rotary (com. chmn. local chpt.). DIED 07/20/97. .

SIMARD, RODNEY, literature and communications educator, media consultant; b. Ft. Smith, Ark., June 18, 1952; s. Houston H. and Dorothy (Turner) S. BA, U. Memphis, 1974; MA, Miss. State U., 1976; PhD, U. Ala., 1982. Instr. lit. Birmingham-So. Coll., 1981-82; instr. lit. and communications Calif. State U., Bakersfield, 1982-86; asst. prof. lit. Calif. State U., San Bernardino, 1986-92, assoc. prof., coord. Am. Studies program, 1992—. Author: Postmodern Drama, 1984, The Whole Writer's Catalog: An Introduction to Advanced Composition, 1992; gen. editor series American Indian Studies, 1989-93, Studies in American Indian Literatures, 1993; assoc. editor Furniture Methods and Materials, 1973-74; editor Black Warrior Review, 1979-80, Showtime, 1983-84, Tribal Discourse: Proceedings of the Symposium on the Status of American Indians in the CSU; cons. editor Elan, 1988-89; faculty editor Pacific Review, 1988-89; contbg. editor The Variorum Edition of the Poetry of John Donne, 1982-88; contbr. articles to profl. jours., anthologies, other publs. Tribal mem. Cherokee Nation of Okla.; bd. dirs., v.p., mem. profl. adv. coun. Riverside (Calif.) and San Bernardino County Am. Indian Ctr. Mem. MLA, Inland Area Native Am. Assn. (adv. coun., cons. editor assn. newsletter), NAACP, ACLU, Gay Am. Indians, Sigma Tau Delta, Phi Gamma Delta. DIED 03/31/97. .

SIMMONS, HOWARD ENSIGN, JR., chemist, research administrator; b. Norfolk, Va., June 17, 1929; s. Howard Ensign and Marie Magdalene (Weidenhammer) S.; m. Elizabeth Anne Warren, Sept. 1, 1951; children: Howard Ensign III, John W. BS in Chemistry, MIT, 1951, PhD in Organic Chemistry, 1954; DSc (hon.), Rensselaer Poly. Inst., 1987. Mem. rsch. staff cen. rsch. and devel. dept. E.I. du Pont de Nemours & Co., Wilmington, Del., 1954-59, rsch. supr., 1959-70, assoc. dir., 1970-74, dir. rsch., 1974-79, dir., 1979-83, v.p., 1983-90, v.p., sr. sci. advisor, 1990—; adj. prof. chemistry U. Del., 1974—; Sloan vis. prof. Harvard U., 1968; Kharasch vis. prof. U. Chgo., 1978; mem. Nat. Sci. Bd., 1990. Author: (with R.E. Merrifield) Topological Methods in Chemistry, 1989. Trustee Gordon Rsch. Confs., 1974-77; elected trustee U. Del., 1994. Recipient Chandler medal Columbia U., 1991, Nat. medal of sci. NSF, 1992. Fellow N.Y. Acad. Scis., Am. Acad. Arts and Scis.; mem. NAS, AAAS, Soc. Chem. Industry, Am. Chem. Soc. (Priestley medal 1994), Indsl. Rsch. Inst., Nat. Sci. Bd., Am. Philos. Soc., Delta Kappa Epsilon. Died April 26, 1997.

SIMMS, SUSAN FAYE, nursing administrator; b. Bklyn., Nov. 25, 1939; d. Sol and Freda (Leventhal) Simms. Diploma in Nursing, Jewish Hosp. Bklyn. Sch. Nursing, 1956-59; BSN, Tchrs. Coll., Columbia U., N.Y.C., 1964; M. Profl. Svcs. in Health Care Adminstrn., C. W. Post Coll., Long Island U., Greenvale, N.Y., 1975-77. Cons. Norman Jaspan Assocs., N.Y.C., 1968-69; asst./dir. nursing Peninsula Hosp. Ctr., Queens, N.Y., 1969-72; asst. dir. nursing Kingsbrook Jewish Med. Ctr., Bklyn., 1973-76, assoc. dir. nursing, 1976-77; asst. prof. St. Francis Coll., Bklyn., 1976-77; v.p. nursing Arlington Hosp., Va., 1977-87; asst. adminstr. nursing Fresno (Calif.) Community Hosp., 1987-90; prin. Veritas Cons. Group, Madera, Calif., 1990—; instr. U. Phoenix Coll. of Nursing, 1994—; DON Kingsburg (Calif.) Dist. Hosp.; asst. prof. U. Phoenix, Sacramento Campus; cons. nursing edn. State Bd. Higher Edn. Ga., 1979; mem. govs. adv. com. Medicare and Medicaid, Va., 1982; adj. prof. George Mason U., Annandale, Va., 1980-81. Mem. Com. of 100, Arlington, Va., 1977-79; chmn. curriculum adv. com. nursing program No. Va. Community Coll., 1980—. Capt. USAF, 1964-66. Regents scholar N.Y. State U., 1956, 60. Named Honoree Va. div. AAUW, 1985. Mem. ANA, Va. Nurses Assn. (lobbyist 1984; pres. 1984—), Nat. League Nursing, Nat. Forum Adminstrs. Nursing Service, Va. Assn. Nursing Execs. (bd. dirs.), Am. Assn. Nurse Execs. Republican. Jewish. Club: Great Dane Rescue League (v.p. 1981-84) (Vienna, Va.). Avocations: cooking; traveling; gardening; writing. Died Feb. 9, 1996.

SIMON, JEWEL WOODARD, artist; b. Houston, July 28, 1911; d. Chester Arthur and Rachel (Williams) Woodard; m. Edward Lloyd Simon, Feb. 19, 1939 (dec. Sept. 1984); children: Edward Lloyd Jr., Margaret Jewel Simon Summerour. AB summa cum laude, Atlanta U., 1931; BFA, Atlanta Coll. of Art, 1967. Head math. dept. Jack Yates High Sch., Houston, 1931-39; lectr. in field. One-woman shows at Clark Coll., 1973, Carver Mus., 1974, Huntsville Mus., 1979, Internat. Soc. Artists, 1979, Ariel Gallery, Soho, N.Y., 1990, 91; exhibited in group shows at Ringling Mus., Sarasota, Fla., Atlanta U. Gallery, Du Sable Mus., Chgo., Carver Mus., Tuskegee; sculpture "The Tusi Princess" exhibited in Art U.S.A. 58, N.Y., "Paula-Paulina" exhibited in Internat. Artists Show, N.Y.; numerous others; author: (poems) Flight-Preoccupation with Death, Life and Life Eternal, 1990. Chair, vice-chair, emeritus deaconess bd. First Congl. Ch., Atlanta, chmn. social club, 1948; v.p. bd. dirs. Nat. Girls Clubs; pres. E. R. Carter Elem. Sch. PTA, Atlanta, 1946, Jack & Jill Nat. Projects, Atlanta. Recipient Arts Svc. award Phoenix Arts and Theater Co., 1978, Bronze Jubilee award, 1981, James Weldon Johnson award in art, 1977, Golden Poets award, 1985-92, Golden Poet award, 1990, 91, Golden Seal award Nat. Assn. Chiefs of Police, 1994, Editors Choice award, Nat. Libr. Poetry, 1994. Mem. Alpha Kappa Alpha (Golden Girl award, Gold Dove Heritage award 1979). Died Dec. 16, 1996.

SIMON, RALPH, rabbi; b. Newark, Oct. 19, 1906; s. Isaac and Yetta (Biddleman) S.; m. Kelsey Hoffer, June 30, 1931; children—Matthew, Tamar (Mrs. Tamar Hoffs), Jonathan Carmi. B.A., Coll. City N.Y., 1927; M. in Hebrew Lit, Jewish Theol. Sem., 1931; M.A., Columbia, 1943; postgrad., Oriental Inst. U. Chgo., 1944-47; D.D., Jewish Theol Sem., 1964; D.H.L., Spertus Coll. Judaica, 1972. Ordained rabbi, 1931. Rabbi Congregation Rodef Sholom, Johnstown, Pa., 1931-36, Jewish Center, Jackson Heights, N.Y., 1937-43, Congregation Rodfei Zedek, Chgo., 1943—; dir. Jewish Fedn. Met. Chgo., 1949-61; founder Camp Ramah, Conover, Wis., 1947; Pres. Chgo. Bd. Rabbis, 1952-54, Chgo. Council Rabbinical Assembly, 1943-45, Council Hyde Park and Kenwood Churches and Synagogues, 1956; mem. Ill. Bd. Mental Health Commrs., 1957-67, Chgo. Commn. on Human Resources, 1958-71; gen. chmn. Combined Jewish Appeal Met. Chgo., 1967, Bonds for Israel Campaign Greater Chgo., 1965-66; v.p. Rabbinical Assembly Am., 1966-67, pres., 1968-69; v.p. Bur. for Careers in Jewish Service, 1969-70; bd. dirs. World Council Synagogues, 1974—. Author: Challenges and Responses-Messages for the High Holy Day Period, 1985. Editorial writer: Sentinal Mag, 1976—. Recipient Julius Rosenwald award Jewish Fedn. Met. Chgo., 1991; named Man of Yr., Israel Bonds, 1976; named to Sr. Citizens Hall of Fame, 1979; Jewish Theol. Sem. created professorship, Ralph Simon chair in Jewish Ethics and Mysticism, 1959. Clubs: Standard (Chgo.), Idlewild Country (Chgo.). DIED 03/29/96. .

SIMON, SIDNEY, sculptor; b. Pitts., May 21, 1917; s. James and Minnie (Lipman) S.; m. Joan E. Lewisohn, May 26, 1945 (div. Aug. 1964); children: Mark, Teru, Rachel, Nora, Juno; m. Renee Lane Adriance, June 16, 1968; children: John Nicholas, James Anthony. Student, Barnes Found., 1938-40; BFA, Pa. Acad. Fine Arts and U. Pa., 1941; postgrad., Grand Chaumiere, Paris, 1948-49. Instr. New Sch. for Social Rsch., 1963-84, Art Students League, 1973—, Castle Hill, Truro, Mass., 1973—; instr. Skowhegan (Maine) Sch. Painting and Sculpture, 1945-58, 75-76, dir., 1981-83; mem. N.Y.C. Art Commn., 1975-78; artist-in-residence Am. Acad. Rome, 1968-69. One man shows include Branford Coll. of Yale, 1967, Sarah Lawrence Coll., Manhattanville, N.Y., 1972, Graham Gallery, N.Y.C., 1974, Sculpture Ctr., 1978, Long Point Gallery, 1978, 80, 84, 87, 89, 91, 93, numerous others; group shows include State U. N.Y., Binghamton, 1973, many others; represented in permanent collections, Prospect Park, Bklyn., Downstate Med. Ctr., N.Y.C., Williams Coll. Mus., Smith Coll. Mus., Colby Coll. Mus., Met. Mus., N.Y.C., NAD, Art Students League, numerous others; sculpture commns. include West Point Jewish Chapel, N.Y., 1985-86, St. Lukes in the Fields, N.Y.C., 1987, fountain for Graham Bldg., Phila., 1987, fountain sculpture for World Wide Plaza, N.Y.C., 1988, 89, designed Grand Prix Florence Gould medal, 1987. Bd. dirs. Skowhegan Sch. Painting and Sculpture, 1946-87, 93. Capt. C.E., U.S. Army, 1941-45. Decorated Bronze Star; recipient Acad. Arts and Letters award, 1976, Silver medal Nat. Arts Club, 1978, Hakone Outdoor Sculpture award, Japan, 1991, Prosker prize Nat. Sculpture Soc., 1991, Gov.'s medal Skowhegan Sch. Painting and Sculpture, 1993, Benjamin Kleindist medal Artist Fellowship. Mem. NAD (Gold medal 1980, coun. mem. 1987-89), Artists Equity, Sculptors Guild (v.p. 1974-80), Sculpture Ctr. (v.p., trustee 1987-89), Century Assn. Club. Died Aug. 15, 1997.

SIMON, WILLIAM GEORGE, lawyer; b. Douglas, Ariz., Apr. 17, 1913; s. George Elias and Mary (Shamas) S.; m. Alice Van Hecke, Feb. 22, 1941; children—Gregory, Stephanie (Mrs. William Branon), Douglas, Suzette. A.B., St. Mary's Coll., 1937; J.D., U. Calif. at Berkeley, 1940. Bar: Calif. bar 1940. Insp. FBI, Washington and N.Y.C., 1952; spl. agt. in charge maj. cities FBI, 1954-64; practice law Los Angeles, 1964—; partner law firm Simon & Sheridan, Los Angeles, 1964—; pres., dir. Fidelity TV, Inc., Los Angeles, 1967—. Del. 9th Circuit Jud. Conf., 1966, mem. com. on rules criminal procedure, 1967-76; Bd. dirs., exec. v.p. Damon Runyon-Walter Winchell Cancer Fund, N.Y.C., 1966-86; regent Mt. St. Mary's Coll., Los Angeles, 1967-75; bd. dirs., pres. J. Edgar Hoover Found., Washington, 1964—; trustee Alumni Found., U. Calif. at Berkeley, 1974—; bd. dirs. L.A. Oncologic Inst.; bd. regents St. Mary's Coll., Moraga, Calif.; mem. adv. bd. Am. Arbitration Assn., 1967, St. Vincent's Hosp., Los Angeles, 1971—. Mem. Los Angeles County Bar Assn. (chmn. law office mgmt. sect. 1971-72), Cal., Bar Assn., ABA, Boalt Hall Alumni Assn. (trustee 1973—), Phi Delta Phi. Died Aug. 8, 1997.

SIMPSON, ROBERT WILFRED LEVICK, composer; b. Leamington, Warwicks, Eng., Mar. 2, 1921; s. Robert Warren and Helena Hendrika (Govaars) S.; D.Mus., Durham U., 1951; m. Bessie Fraser, 1946 (dec. 1981); m. 2d Angela Musgrave, 1982. Music producer BBC, 1951-80; composer 11 symphonies, 3 concertos for piano, flute and cello, 15 string quartets. Recipient Carl Nielsen gold medal, Denmark, 1956; also Bruckner Medal of Honor. Mem. ISM. Author: Carl Nielsen, Symphonist, 1952, 2d edit. 1979, The Essence of Bruckner, 1967, 77, rev. edit., 1992; editor. The Symphony, from 1966, contbr. articles in field to profl. publs.

SIMPSON, ZACHARY A., surgeon; b. Grensboro, N.C., 1925. MD, Duke U., 1948. Diplomate Am. Bd. Surgery. Intern Duke U. Hosp., Durham, N.C., 1948-

49; resident in surgery Germantown Hosp., Phila., 1950, 52-54; fellow in surg. rsch. U. Pa., Phila., 1948; Chief of surgery Doylestown Hosp., Doylestown, PA. Home: Destin FL Died May 3, 1996.

SIMS, IVOR DONALD, steel company executive; b. Coquimbo, Chile, Mar. 14, 1912; s. George and Florence Kate (Johns) S.; m. Christine Buchman, June 19, 1937; 1 dau., Christine. B.S., Lehigh U., 1933, LL.D., 1970; LL.D., U. Liberia, 1967. With Bethlehem Steel Corp., Pa., 1933-73; successively jr. buyer, buyer, asst. purchasing agt., purchasing agt. Bethlehem Steel Corp., 1933-57, asst. v.p., 1957-63, v.p. adminstrn., 1963-66, exec. v.p., 1966-73, also dir., 1957-73. Trustee Lehigh U. Decorated knight comdr. Liberian Humane Order African Redemption, Liberia; comdr. Star Equatorial Africa Gabon; recipient L in Life award Lehigh Club N.Y., 1970. Mem. Am. Iron and Steel Inst., C. of C., NAM (dir. 1969-73), Newcomen Soc. N.Am. Episcopalian. Clubs: Saucon Valley Country (Bethlehem); Mid Ocean (Bermuda); Sky Top (Pa.). Home: Bethlehem Pa. Died March 1, 1993.

SINATRA, FRANK (FRANCIS ALBERT SINATRA), singer, actor; b. Hoboken, N.J., Dec. 12, 1915; s. Anthony and Natalie (Garaventi) S.; m. Nancy Barbato, Feb. 4, 1939 (div.); children: Nancy, Frank Wayne, Christine; m. Ava Gardner (div.); m. Mia Farrow, 1966 (div.); m. Barbara Marx, 1976. Student, Demarest High Sch., Hoboken, Drake Inst.; hon. doctorate, Stevens Inst. Tech., Hoboken, 1985. Sang with sch. band and helped form sch. glee club; worked after sch. on news truck of Jersey Observer; copy boy on graduation with sports div. covering coll. sports events (won first prize on Maj. Bowes Amateur Hour, touring with co. for 3 months); sustaining programs on 4 radio stas. and in Rustic Cabin, N.J., toured with Harry James Band, then Tommy Dorsey's, solo night club and concert appearances; starred on radio program Lucky Strike Hit Parade; appeared in motion pictures From Here to Eternity (Acad. award as best supporting actor 1953), Las Vegas Nights, 1946, Ship Ahoy, 1942, Miracle of the Bells, 1948, Kissing Bandit, 1949, Take Me Out to the Ball Game, 1949, Higher and Higher, 1942, Step Lively, 1944, Anchors Aweigh, 1945, It Happened in Brooklyn, 1947, Guys and Dolls, 1956, Not as a Stranger, 1955, The Tender Trap, 1955, The Man with the Golden Arm, 1955, Johnny Concho, 1956, The Pride and the Passion, 1957, Pal Joey, 1957, Some Came Running, 1959, Never So Few, 1960, Can-Can, 1960, Oceans 11, 1960, Pepe, 1960, The Devil at 4 O'Clock, 1961, The Manchurian Candidate, 1962, Come Blow Your Horn, 1963, Robin and the Seven Hoods, 1963, None But the Brave, 1964, Assault on a Queen, 1965, Von Ryan's Express, 1966, Tony Rome, 1966, Lady in Cement, 1967, The Detective, 1968, Dirty Dingus McGee, 1970, Who Framed Roger Rabbit (voice), 1988, (TV film) Sinatra: 80 Years My Way, 1995, Listen Up: The Lives of Quincy Jones, 1991; actor, producer motion picture The First Deadly Sin, 1980, TV movie Contract on Cherry Street, 1977; hit songs include Night and Day, 1943, Nancy, 1945, Young at Heart, 1954, Love and Marriage, 1955, The Tender Trap, 1955, How Little We Know, 1956, Chicago, 1957, All The Way, 1957, High Hopes, 1959, It Was a Very Good Year, 1965, Strangers in the Night, 1966, My Way, 1969, (with Nancy Sinatra) Somethin' Stupid, 1969; albums include Songs for Swingin' Lovers, 1956, Come Dance with Me, 1959, Come Fly with Me, 1962, September of My Years (Grammy award for best album), 1965, Moonlight, 1966, Greatest Hits, 1968, My Way, 1969, Greatest Hits, Volume 2, 1970, L.A. is My Lady, 1984, The Very Good Years, 1991, Where Are You, 1992, The World We Knew, Duets, 1993, Duets II, 1994, You Make Me Feel So Young, 1995, Hello Young Lovers, 1996, Sinatra sings Rodgers & Hammerstein, 1996; (with Bing Crosby) All the Best, 1995; (with Luciano Pavarotti) Live in Concert, 1995; (with Tommy Dorsey Orch.) There Are Such Things, 1996; author: A Man and His Art, 1990. Recipient Spl. Oscar award Acad. Motion Picture Arts and Scis., 1945, Sylvania TV award, 1959, Grammy awards for album of yr., 1959, 65, 66, best vocalist, 1959, 65, 66, rec. of yr., 1966, Peabody and Emmy awards, 1965, Jean Hersholt award Acad. Motion Picture Arts and Scis., 1971, Golden Apple award as male star of yr., Hollywood Women's Press Club, 1977, Humanitarian award Variety Clubs Internat., 1980, Cross of Sci. and the Arts, Austria, 1984, Presdl. Medal of Freedom, 1985, Kennedy Ctr. honor, 1986, Life Achievement award NAACP, 1987, Grammy Lifetime Achievement award, 1994. Club: Friars (abbot). Home: Beverly Hills Calif. Died *May 14, 1998.*

SINCLAIR, MADGE, actress; b. Kingston, Jamaica, Apr. 28, 1940; d. Herbert and Jemima (Austin) Walters; m. Royston Sinclair (div. 1969); children: Garry, Wayne; m. Dean Compton, 1971. Degree in teaching, Shortwood Women's Coll.; hon. doctorate, Sierra U. Chairwoman Madge Walters Sinclair, Inc.; mfr. of women's wear; art dealer; owner Action Income Tax Service. Appeared in (stage prodns.) Dark of the Moon, Kumaliza, 1969, Iphigenia, 1971, Division Street, 1980, Tartuffe, 1986, (films) Conrack, 1974, Leadbelly, 1975, Convoy, 1979, Star Trek IV, 1986, (TV) Roots, 1977 (Emmy award nomination), Grandpa Goes to Washington, 1978-79, Trapper John M.D., 1980-86 (Best Supporting Actress, 3 Emmy award nominations, Best Actress in a Dramatic Series award NAACP, 1981, 83), O'Hara, 1987, Medical Center, The Waltons, Executive Suite, Medical Story, Serpico, The White Shadow, All in the Family, TV series Gabriel's Fire (Emmy award for Supporting Actress in a Drama Series 1991). Bd. dirs. African Am. Art, Gwen Bolden Found. Recipient Mother of Yr. award Nat. Mother's Day Com., 1984. Mem. Actors' Equity Assn., Screen Actors Guild, AFTRA, Acad. TV Arts and Scis., Acad. Motion Picture Arts and Scis. Avocations: traveling, skiing, bicycling, piano, yoga.

SINGH, GANESH MAN, former congressman; b. Kathmandu City, Bagmati, Nepal, Nov. 9, 1915; s, Subba Gyan Man and Sanu Nani (Shrestha) S.; Mangala Devi, June 26, 1939; children: Rita Singh Vaidya, Pradeep Man, Prakash Man, Kanta, Mita. Grad., Vidya Safar Coll., India, 1939; student, Vidya Sagar Coll., Calcutta, India, 1935. Min. industry and commerce Govt. of Nepal, 1950-53, min. works and transport, 1958-60; mem. ctrl. com. Nepali Congress Party, 1953-57; incarcerated, 1950; supreme leader Nepali Congress Party, 1992-94, mem.ctrl. com., 1953; min. works and transport Govt. of Nepal, 1968; removed from position by King, incarcerated in exile, 1968-76; Sarba Mannya leader, commdr. Movement for Democracy, 1990; supreme leader Nepali Congress Party, 1992-95; retired, 1995. Author: Mera Katha Ka Pana Haru, 1994. Comdr. All Party Movement, 1990; all party leader Non-Violent Movement, 1985; leader in exile Nepali Congress Party, 1968-76; active Anti-Rana movement Praja Parishad Party, 1939-44. Recipient Human Rights award UN, 1993, U Thant Peace award, 1991, U.S. Peace award U.S. Govt., 1990; named Iron Man of Nepal, 1950-95. Nepali Congress. Avocations: playing tabala, music, jokes. Died Sept. 18, 1997.

SINNINGER, DWIGHT VIRGIL, engineer; b. Bourbon, Ind., Dec. 29, 1901; s. Norman E. and Myra (Huff) S.; student Armour Inst., 1928, U. Chgo., 1942, Northwestern U., 1943; m. Coyla Annetta Annis, Mar. 1, 1929; m. Charlotte M. Lenz, Jan. 21, 1983. Registered profl. engr., Ill. Electronics rsch. engr. Johnson Labs., Chgo., 1935-42; chief engr. Pathfinder Radio Corp., 1943-44, Rowe Engring. Corp., 1945-48, Hupp Electronics Co. div. Hupp Corp., 1948-61; dir. rsch. Pioneer Electric & Research Corp., Forest Park, Ill., 1961-65, Senn Custom, Inc., Forest Park and San Antonio, 1967-97. Patentee in field. Mem. IEEE. Died Nov. 4, 1997.

SINYAVSKY, ANDREI (ABRAM TERTZ), writer; b. Moscow, 1925; m. Mariya Rozanova. Ed., Moscow U. Tchr., writer articles Novy Mir, 1965; arrested for distbg. anti-soviet propaganda, 1965, sentenced to forced labor camps,, 1966-71; left USSR, settled in Paris, 1973; mem. faculty U. Paris, 1973—. Author: On Socialist Realism, 1959, The Begins, 1960, The Icicle and Other Stories, 1961, The Poetry of the Revolutionary Era, 1964, Introduction to Pasternak's Poetry, 1965 (novel) Lyubimov, 1964 (English transl. The Makepeace Experiment 1965), Unguarded Thoughts, 1965, The Fantastic World of Abram Tertz, 1967, A Voice for the Chorus, 1974 (English transl. 1976), Strolling with Pushkin, 1975, In the Shadow of Gogol, 1975, Goodnight!, 1983, also others. Mem. Gorky Inst. World Lit. Died Feb. 25, 1997.

SIRAGUSA, ROSS DAVID, electronics appliance manufacturing executive; b. Buffalo, June 12, 1906; s. John A. and Maria (Barreca) S.; m. Mary Irene O'Brien, Apr. 24, 1929 (dec. Apr. 1969); children: Ross David Jr., John, Richard Donald, Mary Irene; m. Martha Ellen Peace Reibman, Aug. 28, 1973. Student, Loyola U., Chgo. Founder, pres. Admiral Corp. (merged with Rockwell Internat. Corp. 1974), Chgo., 1934-63, ret., 1974; founder RDS Enterprises, Rosemont, Ill., 1974-96. Mem. Pres. Lyndon B. Johnson's bd. visitors USAF, 1970-71; mem. bd. lay trustees, citizens bd. Loyola U., 1950-55. Decorated knight of Malta, Order Holy Sepulchre. Mem. Conseil Internat. Club, De La Chasse Club, Chgo. Club, The Casino Club, Jockey Club. Home: Chicago Ill. Died Mar. 30, 1996.

SISK, ZENOBIA ANN, secondary school educator; b. Johnson City, Tenn., Sept. 5, 1938; d. Lone L. and Alberta (Garrett) S. AB, Milligan Coll., 1960; postgrad., East Tenn. State U., 1961-62. Tchr. chemistry, biology Washington College (Tenn.) Acad., 1962-71; tchr. chemistry, physics, biology David Crockett High Sch., Jonesborough, Tenn., 1971—. Mem. Am. Chem. Soc., Am. Inst. Chemists, NEA, Tenn. Edn. Assn., Washington County Edn. Assn. (bd. dirs.), DAR, Delta Kappa Gamma (2d v.p., sec.). Republican. Baptist. Died Oct. 8, 1997.

SKALAK, RICHARD, engineering mechanics educator, researcher; b. N.Y.C., Feb. 5, 1923; s. Rudolph and Anna (Tuma) S.; m. Anna Lesta Allison, Jan. 24, 1953; children: Steven Leslie, Thomas Cooper, Martha Jean, Barbara Anne. BS, Columbia U., 1943, CE, 1946, PhD, 1954; MD (hon.), Gothenburg U., Sweden, 1990. Instr. civil engring. Columbia U., N.Y.C., 1948-54, asst. prof., 1954-60, assoc. prof., 1960-64, prof., 1964-77, James Kip Finch prof. engring. mechanics, 1977-88, emeritus, 1988-97, dir. Bioengring. Inst., 1978-88; prof. bioengring. U. Calif., San Diego, 1988-97, dir. Inst. for Mechs. and Materials, 1992-96; Hunter lectr. Clemson U., 1994; mem. panel Gov.'s Conf. on Sci. and Engring., R&D, 1989-90. Contbr. articles to sci. jours. Bd. dirs. Biotech. Inst., Gothenburg, Sweden, 1978-97; mem. adv. bd. Ctr. for Biomed. Engring., N.Y.C., 1994-97. Recipient Great Tchr. award Columbia Coll. Soc. of Older Grads., 1972, Merit medal Czechoslovakian Acad. Scis., 1990. Applied Mechanics Award, 1997. Fellow AAAS, ASME (Centennial medal 1980, Melville medal 1990, editor jour. 1984), Am. Acad. Mechanics, Soc. Engring. Sci., Am. Inst. Med. and Biol. Engring. (founding); mem. NAE, Soc. Rheology, Am. Heart Assn., Microcirculatory Soc., Internat. Soc. Biorheology (Poiseuille medal 1989), Biomed. Engring. Soc. (Alza medal 1983), Cardiovascular System Dynamics Soc., Am. Soc. for Engring. Edn., Tau Beta Pi, Sigma Xi. Democrat. Presbyterian. Home: San Diego Calif. Died Aug. 17, 1997.

SKELTON, JOHN EDWARD, computer technology consultant; b. Amarillo, Tex., May 10, 1934; s. Floyd Wayne and Lucille Annabelle (Padduck) S.; m. Katherine Dow, Mar. 22, 1959; children: Laura Ann, Jeanette Kay, Jeffrey Edward. BA, U. Denver, 1956, MA, 1962, PhD, 1971. Mathematician U.S. Naval Ordnance Lab., Corona, Calif., 1956-59; various sales support and mktg. positions Burroughs Corp., Denver, Detroit, Pasadena, Calif., 1959-67; asst. prof. U. Denver, 1967-74; dir. Computer Ctr., U. Minn., Duluth, 1974-85; prof., dir. computing svcs. Oreg. State U., Corvallis, 1985-94; computer tech. cons., Corvallis, 1995-96; cons. World Bank, China, 1988, Educom Cons. Group, 1985. Author: Introduction to the Basic Language, 1971; coauhtor: Who Runs the Computer, 1975; also articles. Mem. Assn. for Computing Machinery (pres. Rocky Mountain chpt. 1971, faculty advisor U. Minn. 1980-82, peer rev. team 3 regions 1981-90), Assn. for Spl. Interest Group on Univ. Computing (bd. dirs. 1987-91), Rotary (dist. youth exch. com. 1991-96), Sigma Xi (chpt. pres. 1983-84), Phi Kappa Phi (chpt. pres. 1989-90). Episcopalian. Avocations: travel, photography, hiking. Home: Corvallis Oreg. Died Nov. 16, 1996.

SKELTON, RED (RICHARD SKELTON), comedian, artist; b. Vincennes, Ind., July 18, 1913; s. Joseph and Ida (Mae) S.; m. Edna Marie Stillwell, June 1932 (div. 1940, dec.); m. 2d, Georgia Maureen Davis, Mar. 1945 (dec.); children: Valentina Maureen Alonso, Richard Freeman (dec.); m. 3d, Lothian Toland, Oct., 1973. HHD, Ball State U., 1986. Began acting career at age of 10 yrs.; successively with a tent show, a minstrel show, on a show boat, a clown in Hagenbeck & Wallace Circus, on burlesque in the Midwest, Walkathon contests (as master of ceremonies); appeared at Loew's Montreal Theatre in vaudeville (developed the doughnut dunking pantomime), 1936; made Broadway debut, June 1937; first motion picture appearance in Having a Wonderful Time, 1939; has since appeared in Flight Command, 1940, The People vs. Dr. Kildare, 1941, Dr. Kildare's Wedding Day, 1941, Lady Be Good, 1941, Whistling in the Dark, 1941, Whistling in Dixie, 1942, Maisie Gets Her Man, 1942, Panama Hattie, 1942, Ship Ahoy, 1942, I Dood It, 1943, Whistling in Brooklyn, 1943, DuBarry Was A Lady, 1943, Thousands Cheer, 1943, Bathing Beauty, 1944, Ziedfield Follies, 1946, The Show Off, 1946, Merton of the Movies, 1947, The Fuller Brush Man, 1948, A Southern Yankee, 1948, Neptune's Daughter, 1949, The Yellow Cab Man, 1950, Three Little Words, 1950, Watch the Birdie, 1950, The Fuller Brush Girl, 1950, Dutchess of Idaho, 1950, Excuse My Dust, 1950, Texas Carnival, 1951, Lovely to Look At, 1952, The Clown, 1952, Halfa Hero, 1953, The Great Diamond Robbery, 1953, Susan Slept Here, 1954, Around the World in 80 Days, 1956, Public Pigeon Number One, 1957, Ocean's Eleven, 1960, Those Magnificent Men in Their Flying Machines, 1965, Eighteen Again, 1988; had first own radio program, 1937, Red Skelton's Scrpabook of Satire, 1942; The Red Skelton Show on TV, 1951-71; nightclub performer, also writer and composer for radio, TV, movies; entertained service men World War II and Korea as pvt. in F.A.; artist original oil paintings and hand sketched linens. Bd. dirs. Red Skelton Needy Children's Fund. Recipient AMVETS Silver Helmet Americanism award, 1969, Freedom's Found. award, 1970, Nat. Comdrs. award Am. Legion, 1970; winner 3 Emmy awards, Golden Globe award, 1978, Ann. Achievement award SAG, 1987, Am. Comedy Hall of Fame award, 1993, Gourgas Gold medal Masonic Order, 1995. Died Sept. 17, 1997.

SKERNICK, ABRAHAM, musician; b. N.Y.C., June 4, 1923. Mem. faculty Peabody Conservatory, 1948-49, Cleve. Inst. Music, 1963-76, Blossom Music Sch., 1968-76; prof. music Ind. U., 1976—. Asst. first violist, St. Louis Symphony, 1946-48, first viola, Balt. Symphony, 1948-49, first viola Cleve. Orch., 1949-76, first violist, Aspen Music Festival, Casals Festival, Chautauqua Music Festival; violist Cleve. Orch. String Quartet, Berkshire Quartet. Mem. Pi Kappa Lambda. Office: Sch Music Ind U Bloomington IN 47405 DIED 12/13/96. .

SKEWES-COX, BENNET, accountant, educator; b. Valparaiso, Chile, Dec. 12, 1918; came to U.S., 1919, naturalized, 1943; s. Vernon and Edith Page (Smith) S-

C.; B.A., U. Calif., Berkeley, 1940; M.A., Georgetown U., 1947; B.B.A., Golden Gate Coll., 1953; m. Mary Osborne Craig, Aug. 31, 1946; children: Anita Page McCann, Pamela Skewes-Cox Anderson, Amy Osborne Skewes-Cox (Mrs. Robert Twiss). Asst. to press officer Am. Embassy, Santiago, Chile, 1941-43; state exec. dir. United World Federalists of Calif., 1948-50; pvt. practice acctg., San Francisco, 1953—; asst. prof. internat. relations San Francisco State U., 1960-62; grad. researcher Stanford (Calif.) U., 1962-63, Georgetown U., Washington, 1963-65; pres. Acad. World Studies, San Francisco, 1969—; sec. Alpha Delta Phi Bldg. Co., San Francisco, 1957—; lectr. in field. Mem. Democratic state central com. Calif., 1958-60, fgn. policy chmn. Calif. Dem. Council, 1959-61, treas. Marin County Dem. Central Com., 1956-62; founder, 1st. chmn. Calif. Council for UN Univ., 1976—; compiler World Knowledge Bank; bd. dirs. Research on Abolition of War; treas. Marin Citizens for Energy Planning. Served as lt. (j.g.), USNR, 1943-46. Mem. Assn. for World Edn. (internat. council 1975—), Am. Soc. Internat. Law, Am. Polit. Sci. Assn., San Francisco Com. Fgn. Relations, Am. Acctg. Assn., Calif. State Univ. Profs., AAUP, Nat. Soc. Public Accts., Fedn. Am. Scientists, UN Assn., Internat. Polit. Sci. Assn. World Federalists Assn., World Govt. Orgns. Coalition (treas.). Clubs: University, Commonwealth of Calif., Lagunitas Country. Author: The Manifold Meanings of Peace, 1964; The United Nations from League to Government, 1965; Peace, Truce or War, 1967.

SKIDMORE, DUANE RICHARD, chemical engineering educator, researcher; b. Seattle, Mar. 5, 1927; s. Everett Sylvester and Ruth (Butler) S.; m. Joann Rebecca Mataleno, Feb. 24, 1962; children: David Louis, Carla Marie, Lara Marie, Richard Duane. B-SChemE, U. N.D., 1949; MSChemE, U. Ill., 1951; PhD in Phys. Chemistry, Fordham U., 1960. Rsch. chemist E. I. DuPont, Wilmington, Del., 1961-64; from asst. to assoc. prof. U. N.D., Grand Forks, 1964-72; prof. mineral processing engring. W.Va. U., Morgantown, 1972-78; prof. chem. engrng. Ohio State U., Columbus, 1978-90, prof. emeritus, 1990-94; cons. DuPont, Occidental Petroleum, 1964-90. Contbr. chpts. to books. Dist. co-chmn. Rep. Com., Wilmington, 1962-64. With U.S. Army, 1945-46. Recipient Victory medal, 1945. Mem. Am. Chem. Soc., AICE (nat. program com. 1973-77). Republican. Roman Catholic. Achievements include development of coal liquefaction, coal gasification, coal desulfurization processes. Died Apr. 15, 1994.

SKOKAN, WILLIAM, retired otolaryngologist; b. Verdigre, Nebr., 1912. MD, U. Nebr., 1942. Intern Nebr. Hosp., Omaha, 1942-43; resident ears, nose and throat medicine Knoxville Gen. Hosp., 1947-48, Jefferson Davis Hosp., Houston, 1948-49; ret. Mem. AMA, Am. Acad. Otolaryngology, Head and Neck Surgery, Am. Laryngological, Rhinological and Otological Soc. Died Jan. 31, 1996.

SLACK, DERALD ALLEN, plant pathology educator; b. Cedar City, Utah, Dec 22, 1924; s. Fredrick Allen and Marsella (Perry) S.; m. Betty Lue Stevens, Aug. 30, 1925; children: Steven A., Bonnie Lue Brown. BS, Utah State U., 1948, MS, 1949; PhD, U. Wis., 1952. Asst. prof. U. Ark., Fayetteville, 1952-54, assoc. prof., 1954-59, prof., 1959-64, prof., head dept., 1964—; bd. mem. Ark. State Plant Bd., Little Rock, 1964—. Author: Plant Pathology Laboratory Manual, 1960; contbr. articles to profl. jours. 2d lt. USAAF, 1943-46. Named Disting. Faculty, Ark. Alumni Assn., Fayetteville, 1961. Mem. Am. Phytopath. Soc. (sec. 1979-80, councilor-at-large 1980-83, outstanding plant pathologist 1989), Soc. Nematologists, Can. Phytopath. Soc., Lions (pres. 1963-64), Gamma Sigma Delta. Avocation: golf. Died May , 1996.

SLIPYJ, JOSEPH, archbishop of Lwow; b. Zazdrist, West Ukraine, Feb. 17, 1892; s. Ivan Kobernycky and Anastasia (Dychkowskyj) S.; S.T.D., Canisianium, Innsbruck, Austria; postgrad. Angelicum U., Gregorianum U., Oriental Inst. Ordained priest Ukrainian Catholic Ch., 1917; prof. Greek Cath. Ecclesiastic Sem., Lwiw, West Ukraine, from 1922; rector Greek Cath. Theol. Acad., from 1926; archbishop of Lwow, 1939-44; now maj. archbishop of Lwow for the Ukrainians; arrested by Russians, 1946; imprisoned for 18 yrs.; released through efforts Pope John XXIII, 1963; elevated to cardinal Roman Catholic Ch., 1965; established Ukrainian Cath. U., Rome; participant Christian unity conv., confs. and meetings in Velehrad, Prague, Pinsk and Lwow. Author numerous sci. articles.

SLOAN, GEORGE B., trade association executive; b. Franklin, N.C., Sept. 6, 1915; s. William Neville and Beulah (Bidwell) S.; m. Mary Plimpton, Sept. 7, 1978; children: Mary Margaret, Barbara Ann, George Bidwell. BS, U.S. Mil. Acad., 1937; student, Army War Coll., 1953, DOD Strategic Intelligence Sch., 1956, Heidelberg U., 1956; MA in Internat. Affairs, Washington U., 1963, postgrad., 1965. Commd. 2d lt. U.S. Army, 1937; advanced through grades to Au.S. Army; retired U.S. Army, 1964; sr. analsyt advanced product planning McDonnell Aircraft Corp., 1964, mgr. environment forecasts, 1967; dir. environment and strategic planning McDonnell Douglas Corp., 1968, dir. bus. environment analysis and forecasts, 1977-80; dir. sci. and engring. St. Louis Regional Commerce and Growth Assn., 1981, v.p. research and technology, 1984—; adjunct prof. mgmt. services St. Louis U., 1981, Webster Coll. 1981. Mem. St. Louis Com. on Fgn. Relations; bd. dirs. World Affairs Council of St. Louis, 1969-74, 76—, v.p. and program chmn. 1970-71, 77-80, chmn. bd. 1980-81, pres. 1982-83. Mem. Assn. U.S. Army (chpt. pres. 1965, bd. dirs. 1968, nat. chmn. resolutions com. 1968, nat. adv. council 1971-74), AIAA (chmn. program com. 1967, chpt. awards com. 1968), MDC Mgmt. Club (chmn. program com. 1965-66, bd. dirs. 1967-68), Assn. Grads. U.S. Mil. Acads. (chpt. v.p. 1968, pres. 1969), St. Louis Japan Am. Soc. (v.p. and program chmn. 1975-80, pres. 1980-81, chmn. bd. 1982-83), Nat. Assn. Bus. Economists (chpt. sec. 1979-80, treas. 1980-81, pres. 1982-83), Mo. Corp. for Sci. and Technoology.

SLOANE, THOMAS CHARLES, lawyer; b. Wilkes-Barre, Pa., Oct. 27, 1922; s. Charles Benedict and Marie Agnes (McHugh) S.; m. Virginia Louise French, June 28, 1952; children: Thomas Henry, Sarah Jane. BA, Pa. State U., 1947; LLB, Columbia U., 1951. Bar: N.Y. 1951. Practice law N.Y.C., 1951-63; dep. gen. counsel Fed. Res. Bank of N.Y., N.Y.C., 1963-76, sr. v.p., sr. advisor, 1976-83; chmn. Com. on Fiscal Agy., 1973-76, Joint Task Force on Planning, 1978-81; mem. Com. on Internat. Monetary Law, 1942-46. Served to 1st lt. USAAF. Democrat. Died Nov. 17, 1996.

SLONIM, ARNOLD ROBERT, biochemist, physiologist; b. Springfield, Mass., Feb. 15, 1926; s. Sam and Esther (Kantor) S.; married, 1951; 3 children; m. 1984. BS, Tufts Coll., 1947; AM, Boston U., 1948; PhD, Johns Hopkins U., 1953. Rsch. asst. nutrition Sterling-Winthrop Rsch. Inst., Rensselaer, N.Y., 1948-49; rsch. asst. pharmacology George Washington U. Med. Sch., Washington, 1949-50; rsch. asst., jr. instr. biology Johns Hopkins U., Balt., 1950-53; rsch. assoc. chemotherapy Children's Cancer Rsch. Found. Harvard U., Boston, 1953-54; head chem. lab. Lynn (Mass.) Hosp., 1955-56; various positions including chief applied ecology, supervisory rsch. biologist, physiologist & biochemist, phys. sci. adminstr., biotech. mgr. Aerospace Med. Rsch. Lab., Wright-Patterson AFB, Ohio, 1956-86; cons., pres. ARSLO Assocs., Columbus, Ohio, 1987—; lectr. Mass. Sch. Physiotherapy, Boston, 1955-56, Antioch U., 1984-85; mem. internat. bioastronautics com. Internat. Astronautical Fedn., 1966 ; mem. environ. carcinogens program Internat. Agy. for Rsch. on Cancer/WHO, Paris, 1981—. Mem. com. for biol. handbooks Fedn. Am. Socs. for Exptl. Biology, 1966-71; mem. editorial bd. Aerospace Medicine, 1967-71; contbr. articles to profl. jours. Served with USN, 1944-46. Mem. Aerospace Med. Assn., Am. Soc. Biochemistry and Molecular Biology, Am. Physiol. Soc., N.Y. Acad. Sci., Internat. Acad. Aviation and Space Medicine, Sigma Xi, Masons, Scottish Rite, Shriners. Died Jan. 10, 1997.

SLOOPE, BILLY WARREN, physicist, educator; b. Clifton Forge, Va., Jan. 4, 1924; s. Guy Heamon and Jessie Josephine (Surratt) S.; m. Anne Carey Phelps, June 9, 1951; children—Billy Warren, Terry Wayne. B.S., U. Richmond, 1949; M.S., U. Va., 1951, Ph.D., 1953. Asst. prof. physics Clemson (S.C.) U., 1953-55; asst. prof., assoc. prof. physics U. Richmond, Va., 1955-61; sr. research physicist, head physics div. Va. Inst. for Sci. Research, Richmond, 1961-68; assoc. prof., then prof. physics Va. Commonwealth U., Richmond, 1968—; chmn. dept. physics Va. Commonwealth U., 1968-79; cons. Materials Research Lab., Philip Morris, 1968-70. Contbr. writings in field to profl. jours., U.S. and Japan. Active Avalon Recreation Assn., 1958-79, pres., 1966-67, bd. dirs., 1964-68; v.p. Maybury Elem. Sch. PTA, 1962. Served with USAF, 1944-45. Decorated Air Medal with four oak leaf clusters. Mem. Am. Assn. Physics Teachers, Am. Vacuum Soc., Va. Acad. Sci. (J.S. Horsley research award 1961), Physics Club of Richmond, Phi Beta Kappa, Sigma Pi Sigma. Republican. Methodist. Died May 14, 1997.

SLOSS, LAURENCE LOUIS, geologist; b. Mountain View, Calif., Aug. 26, 1913; s. Joseph and Edith (Esberg) S.; m. Berenice Loeb, June 20, 1937; children: Laurence J., Peter W.; m. 2d, Marion Stone, Oct. 19, 1979. AB, Stanford U., 1934; PhD, U. Chgo., 1937; DEng (hon.), Colo. Sch. Mines, 1989. From instr. to assoc. prof. geology Mont. Sch. Mines, 1937-46; geologist Mont. Bur. Mines and Geology, 1937-46, Carter Oil Co. and Phillips Petroleum Co., summers 1946-51; faculty Northwestern U., Evanston, Ill., 1947—, prof. geology, 1954-71, William Deering prof., 1971-81, prof. emeritus, 1981—; sci adv. bd. Atlantic Richfield Co., 1981-86; mem. U.S. Nat. Acad. Scis. Com. on Paleontology, 1962-68. Author: (with W.C. Krumbein) Stratigraphy and Sedimentation, 1951, 2d edit., 1963; (with E.C. Dapples and W.C. Krumbein) Lithofacies Maps: An Atlas of the U.S. and Southern Canada, 1960. Mem. Ill. Bd. Nat. Resources and Conservation, 1954-86, U.S. Nat. Com. Geology, 1968-71, U.S. Nat. Com. Internat. Correlations Programme, 1978-80, U.S. Nat. Com. UNESCO, 1973-75, Bd. Radioactive Waste Mgmt. 1983-85. Recipient Hedberg award in Energy Rsch. Inst. Study of Earth and Man, Dallas, 1989. Fellow AAAS, Geol. Soc. Am. (pres. 1979-80, Penrose medal 1986); mem. Am. Geol Inst. (pres. 1968), Am. Geophys. Union, Am. Inst. Profl. Geologists (hon. mem. 1985), Am. Assn. Petroleum Geologists (pres. award 1946, hon. mem. 1981), Soc. Econ. Paleontologists and Mineralogists (pres. 1961-62, hon. mem. 1974, Twenhofel medal 1980), Paleontol. Soc. Died Nov. 2, 1996.

SMALL, S(AUL) MOUCHLY, psychiatrist, educator; b. N.Y.C., Oct. 11, 1913; s. Joseph and Esther (Mouchly) S.; m. Sophie Scholl, June 13, 1937; children: Susan Steinhart, Laurie Block, Jonathan, Cynthia McDonald. BS, CCNY, 1933; MD cum laude, Cornell U., 1937. Diplomate Am. Bd. Psychiatry and Neurology. Instr. psychiatry Cornell Med. Coll., N.Y.C., 1940-43; lectr. psychiatry Columbia U., N.Y.C., 1948-51; adj. and assoc. attending psychiatrist Mt. Sinai Hosp., N.Y.C., 1946-51; prof., chmn. dept. psychiatry SUNY, Buffalo, 1951-78; prof. emeritus dept. psychiatry SUNY, 1978—; dir. psychiatry Meyer Meml. Hosp., Buffalo, 1951-78; attending psychiatrist Erie County Med. Ctr., Buffalo, 1951—, Buffalo Gen. Hosp., 1963—; chief psychiatric cons. VA Hosp., Buffalo, 1952—; neuropsychiat. cons. Surgeon Gen. U.S. Army, Washington, 1947-70; cons. U.S. DOD, Washington, 1966—; mem. N.Y. State Bd. Profl. Med. Conduct, Albany, 1985—; emeritus dir. Am. Bd. Psychiatry and Neurology, 1986—. Co-author textbook: Handbook of Psychiatry, 1943; contbr. articles to profl. jours., chpts. to books. Acting dir. Erie County Mental Health Bd., Buffalo, then mem. bd. dirs.; pres. Muscular Dystrophy Assn., N.Y.C., 1980-89, bd. dirs., chmn. exec. com., 1989—, pres. emeritus, 1989—. Fellow Am. Psychiat. Assn. (Disting. Svc. citation 1978, Psychiatrist of Yr. award 1975), Am. Coll. Psychiatrists (Bowis gold medal 1975), Am. Coll. Psychoanalysts, Am. Assn. Social Psychiatry; mem. AMA, N.Y. Acad. Medicine. Avocations: photography, swimming. Died Dec. 20, 1996.

SMALL, WILLIAM ANDREW, mathematics educator; b. Cobleskill, N.Y., Oct. 16, 1914; s. James Arner and Lois (Patterson) S.; m. Bela Small; children: Lois (Mrs. Paul Gindling), James (dec.). B.S., U.S. Naval Acad., 1936; A.B., U. Rochester, 1950, M.A., 1952, Ph.D., 1958. Commd. ensign U.S. Navy, 1936, advanced through grades to lt. comdr., 1944; comdt. cadets, instr. DeVeaux Sch., Niagara Falls, N.Y., 1945-48; instr. U. Rochester, 1951-55; Alfred (N.Y.) U., 1955-56; asst. prof. math. Grinnell (Iowa) Coll., 1956-58, assoc. prof., chmn. dept., 1958-60; prof. math. Tenn. Tech. U., 1960-62, State Univ. Coll., Geneseo, N.Y., 1962-85; chmn. dept. math. State Univ. Coll., 1962-78; prof. emeritus, disting. service prof. SUNY, 1985—; Fulbright-Hays lectr. math. Aleppo U., Syrian Arab Republic, 1964-65. Contbr. articles to profl. jours. Mem. Math. Assn. Am., U.S. Naval Inst., Mil. Order World Wars, Ret. Officers Assn., Seneca Army Depot Officers Club, Am. Legion, Rotary (pres. Geneseo club 1990-91), Phi Beta Kappa. Episcopalian. Died Nov. 2, 1997.

SMELLIE, ROBERT HENDERSON, JR., chemistry educator; b. Glasgow, Scotland, June 2, 1920; came to U.S., 1928, naturalized, 1934; s. Robert Henderson and Mary Clegg (Armour) S.; m. Dorothy Lee Jones, Nov. 30, 1945; children: Margaret, Mary, Robert. B.S., Trinity Coll., Hartford, Conn., 1942, M.S., 1944; Ph.D., Columbia U., 1951. Analysis supr. Tenn. Eastman Co., Oak Ridge, 1944-46; instr. chemistry Trinity Coll., 1948-51, asst. prof., 1951-53, assoc. prof., 1953-58, prof., 1958-65, Scovill prof., 1965-86, Scovill prof. emeritus, 1986—, chmn. dept. chemistry, 1963-71; cons. AEC project, N.Y.C., 1951-62, FMC Corp., 1963-64, IBM, 1965-66. Contbr. articles to profl. jours.; patentee in field; mem. editorial bd.: Jour. Colloid Sci., 1954-63. Recipient Alumni medal for Excellence Trinity Coll., 1962. Mem. Am. Chem. Soc., Phi Beta Kappa, Sigma Xi. Am. Baptist. Died Nov. 4, 1997.

SMITH, ALBERT MATTHEWS, animal science educator; b. Bangor, Maine, Dec. 25, 1927; s. Albert William and Helen (Matthews) S.; m. Patricia Anne Gray, Sept. 10, 1950; children: Margaret Anne, Kathryn Smith Haslam. BS, U. Maine, 1952; MS, Cornell U., 1954, PhD, 1956. Asst. prof. animal sci. Cornell U., Ithaca, N.Y., 1956-57; asst. prof. animal sci. U. Vt., Burlington, 1957-61, assoc. prof., 1961-67, prof., 1967—, dept. chair, 1962-79, assoc. dean coll., 1978-89, dir. agrl. expt. sta., 1978-89. Fellow AAAS; mem. Am. Dairy Sci. Assn., Am. Assn. Animal Sci., Vt. Feed Dealers and Mfr. Assn. (sec.-treas. 1987—), Masons, Kiwanis Internat. (sec. 1989—), Sigma Xi, Alpha Zeta, Alpha Gamma Rho. Avocations: golf, outdoor activities. Died April 18, 1997.

SMITH, APOLLO MILTON OLIN, aerodynamics engineer; b. Columbia Mo., July 2, 1911; s. Orsino Cecil and Blanche Alice (Whitaker) S.; m. Elisabeth Caroline Krost, Dec. 5, 1943; children: Tove Anne, Gerard Nicholas, Kathleen Roberta. BS in Mech. Engring., Calif. Inst. Tech., 1936, MS, 1937, MS in Aero. Engring., 1938; DSc (hon.), U. Colo., 1975. Asst. chief aerodynamicist Douglas Aircraft Co., El Segundo, Calif., 1938-42, 1944-48, supr. design rsch., 1948-54; supr. aerodynamic rsch. McDonnell Douglas Corp., Long Beach, Calif., 1954-69; chief engr. Aerojet Engring. Corp., Pasadena, Calif., 1942-44; chief aerodynamics engr. rsch. McDonnell Douglas Corp., Long Beach, 1969-75; adj. prof. UCLA, 1975-80; cons. aerodyn. engr., San Marino, Calif., 1975-86. Author: (with others) Analysis of Turbulent Boundary Layers, 1974, contbr. over 65 tech. papers. Recipient Robert H. Goddard award Am. Rocket Soc., 1954, Engring. Achievement award Douglas Aircraft Co., 1958, Casey Baldwin award Can. Aeros. and Space Inst., 1971, Fluids Engring. award ASME, 1985. Fellow AIAA (hon.); Wright Bros. lectr. 1974); mem. NAE. Died May 1, 1997. Home: San Marino Calif.

SMITH, BETTY FAYE, textile chemist; b. Magnolia, Ark., June 29, 1930; d. Carl Excel and Nannie (Nall) S. B.S., U. Ark., 1951; M.S., U. Tenn., 1957; Ph.D., U. Minn., 1960, 65. Home agt. Ark. Agrl. Extension Service, 1951-56; mem. faculty Cornell U., 1965-70, assoc. prof. textiles, 1965-70, chmn. dept., 1968-69; prof. textiles, chmn. dept. U. Md., 1970-91, prof. textiles, 1991-92; prof. materials engring., 1992—. Author papers in field. Fellow Textile Inst.; mem. Fiber Soc., Am. Chem. Soc., Am. Assn. Textile Chemists and Colorists, Soc. Dyers and Colourists, AAUP, Sigma Xi, Omicron Nu, Phi Upsilon Omicron, Iota Sigma Pi. Democrat. Methodist. Died Dec. 23, 1996.

SMITH, CHARLES PHILIP, government official, social scientist; b. Phila., June 12, 1932; s. Frank Folsom and Ernestine Marion (Bell) S.; m. Martha Elizabeth Austin, June 6, 1953 (div. June 1959); children: Charles Burroughs, Ellen Elizabeth; m. Robyn Ryder, Sept. 19, 1959; children: Shannon Dickenson, Shelly Ryder, Taylor Compton, Tucker Freeman, Tia Tomlin. B.A. in Polit. Sci., U. Ariz., 1958, M.A. in Sociology, 1961; Ph.D. in Pub. Adminstrn., U. So. Calif., 1970. Human factors scientist System Devel. Corp., Santa Monica, Calif., 1961-67; dir. mgmt. services State of Calif., Sacramento, 1967-71; project dir. Am. Justice Inst., Sacramento, 1971-81; dep. dir. planning and evaluation White House, Washington, 1981-82; sec. dep. asst. U.S. HUD, Washington, 1982-86; domestic policy advisor White House, 1986-87; dir. bur. justice assistance U.S. Dept. Justice, Washington, 1988-90; dep. dir. Dept. Gen. Svcs., State of Calif., Sacramento, 1990-91; cons., 1991—; mem. adv. com. HEW, Washington, 1968-69; mem. transition task force Pres.-Elect Reagan, Washington, 1980-81; issues analyst Reagan for Pres. Campaign, Sacramento, 1980, Reagan-Finch for Gov.-Lt. Gov., Pacific Palisades, Calif., 1966. Co-author: Serious Crime and the Juvenile Justice Systems, 1980, Impact of Social Trends on Crime and Criminal Justice, 1976, Role Performance and the Criminal Justice System, 1976. Pres. Ariz. Young Republican League, Tucson, 1956; mem. adv. bd. Am. River Health Care Ctr., Sacramento, 1971; vice chmn., bd. dirs. Calif. Crime Tech. Research Found., 1968-72; mem. U. S. Delegation People to People Internat., China, 1982; prin. speaker Hong Kong Computer Conf., 1983. Served with USN, 1952-53. Mem. Am. Soc. Pub. Adminstrn., Am. Sociol. Assn., Sigma Alpha Epsilon. Republican. Presbyterian. Died Jan. 19, 1997.

SMITH, CHARLES ROGER, veterinary medicine educator; b. Hartville, Ohio, Mar. 31, 1918; s. Charles Roger and Ethel Olive (Seeman) S.; m. Genevieve Lorraine Taylor, Aug. 9, 1946; children—Ronald Roger, Debra Smith Beckstett, Eric William. Student, Ohio U., 1936-38, 40-41; D.V.M., Ohio State U., 1944, M.Sc., 1946, Ph.D., 1953. Diplomate: in cardiology Am. Coll. Veterinary Internal Medicine. Instr. veterinary medicine Ohio State U., 1944-53, asst. prof., 1953-55, asso. prof., chmn. dept. veterinary physiology and pharmacology, 1955-59, prof., 1957-69, research prof., chmn. dept. veterinary edn., 1969-71; acting dean Ohio State U. (Coll. Veterinary Medicine), 1972-73, dean, 1973-80, asst., prof., dean emeritus, 1980—; research asso. dept. dairy sci. U. Minn., summer 1947; asst. research veterinarian Purdue U. Agrl. Expt. Sta., summers 1949, 50, 51; vis. scholar dept. physiology Coll. Medicine, U. Wash., summer 1960; cons. Morris Animal Found.; mem. nat. adv. com. Bur. Veterinary Medicine, FDA, 1968-74; mem. com. veterinary med. rev. NIH, 1970-73. Contbg. author: Duke's Physiology of Domestic Animals, 9th edit, 1977; reviewer: Am. Jour. Veterinary Research, 1959-73; contbr. numerous articles to profl. jours. Served with ASTP, 1943-44. Recipient Gamma award Omega Tau Sigma, 1964, Disting. Alumnus award Coll. Vet. Medicine, Ohio State U., 1981; named Ohio Veterinarian of Yr., 1980. Fellow Am. Coll. Vet. Pharmacology and Therapeutics (hon. mem. 1982); mem. Ohio Heart Assn., Am. Heart Assn. (chmn. affiliate com. research 1976-81, rev. and adv. com. 1975—, chmn. 1976—), AVMA (council on research 1959-69, chmn. 1967—), Am. Acad. Vet Physiologists and Pharmacologists ((disting fellow) 1982), Sigma Xi, Phi Zeta. Republican. Methodist. Club: Ohio State Faculty (Columbus Maennerchor). Lodge: Masons. Died July 24, 1996.

SMITH, CLIFFORD NEAL, business educator, writer; b. Wakita, Okla., May 30, 1923; s. Jesse Newton and Inez Lane (Jones) S.; m. Anna Piszczan-Czaja, Sept. 3, 1951; children: Helen Inez Smith Barrette. BS, Okla. State U., 1943; AM, U. Chgo., 1948; postgrad. Columbia U., 1960. Selector, U.S. Displaced Persons Commn., Washington and Munich, Germany, 1948-51; auditor Phillips Petroleum Co., Caracas, Venezuela, 1951-58; planning analyst Mobil Internat. Oil Co., N.Y.C., 1960, 65-66, Mobil Oil A.G., Deutschland, Hamburg, Germany, 1961-63; asst. to v.p. for Germany, Mobil Inner Europe, Inc., Geneva, 1963-65; asst. prof. No. Ill. U. Sch. Bus., DeKalb, 1966-69, part-time prof. internat. bus., 1970—; owner Westland Publs.; lectr. in field. Author: Federal Land Series, vol. 1, 1972, vol. 2, 1973, vol. 3, 1980, vol. 4, part 1, 1982, vol. 4, part 2, 1986, Encyclopedia of German-American Genealogical Research, American Genealogical Resources in German Archives, 1977, numerous monographs in German-Am., Brit.-Am., French-Am. geneal. research series, German and Central European Emigration Series, Selections from the American State Papers; contbg. editor Nat. Geog. Soc. Quar., Geneal. jour. (Utah); contbr. articles to profl. jours. Mem. at large exec. com. Friends Com. on Nat. Legis., 1968-75; mem. regional exec. com. Am. Friends Service Com., 1969-76; v.p. Riverside Dem., N.Y.C., 1959-61; precinct committeeman, 1984—; mem. Ariz. State Central Com. of Dem. Party, 1984—; sec. Dem. Cen. Com. of Cochise County; mem. com. to Re-Elect Clinton for Pres. Recipient Distinguished Service medal Ill. Geneal. Soc., 1973, award for outstanding service to sci. genealogy Am. Soc. Genealogists, 1973; court appointed arbitrator for civil cases, 1992. Fellow Geneal. Soc. of Utah; mem. S.R., SAR, Soc. Descs. Colonial Clergy, Soc. Advancement Mgmt., Ill. Genealogic Soc. (dir. 1968-69), Phi Eta Sigma, Beta Alpha Psi, Sigma Iota Epsilon. Mem. Soc. of Friends. Club: American of Hamburg (v.p. 1962-63); contbr. articles to profl. jours.

SMITH, DONALD F(OSS), chemistry educator; b. Athens, Tenn., Feb. 14, 1913; s. Foss and Mabel Meredith (Osburn) S.; m. Marion Wright Smith, Aug. 31, 1940; children: Marion Berkeley, Donald F. B.S., U. Chattanooga, 1934; M.S., U. Tenn.-Knoxville, 1936; Ph.D., U. Va.-Charlottesville, 1939. Asst. prof. chemistry Judson Coll., Marion, Ala., 1939-40; asst. prof. The Citadel, 1940-43; explosives chemist U.S. Bur. Mines, Pitts., 1943-44; asst. prof. Pa. Coll. Women, Pitts., 1944-45; asst. prof. U. Vt., Burlington, 1945-49, assoc. prof., 1949-51; assoc. prof. U. Ala., University, 1951-56, prof., 1956-83, ret., 1983; cons. Thiokol, Huntville, Ala. Fellow Am. Inst. Chemists; mem. Am. Chem. Soc., Sigma Xi, Gamma Sigma Epsilon, Sigma Pi Sigma. Presbyterian. Home: 25 Ridgeland Tuscaloosa AL 35406-1607 Died June 11, 1997.

SMITH, DONALD MACLEAN, broadcasting executive; b. Toronto, Ont., Can., June 25, 1930; s. Donald MacLean and Annie Winnifred S.; m. Lorraine Henderson, Oct. 23, 1955; children: Mary-Catherine, Susan Anne, Donald James. Radio transcription traffic All Can. Radio Facilities Ltd., Toronto, 1951-54; time salesman All-Can. Radio & TV Ltd., Toronto, 1954; group mgr. All-Can. Radio & TV Ltd., 1962-66, Toronto sales mgr., 1966-70; v.p. All-Can. Radio & TV Ltd. (TV), 1970-73; v.p. sales B.C. TV Ltd., Vancouver, B.C., Can., 1973-78; exec. v.p. B.C. TV Ltd., 1978-82, pres., 1982-90; pres. Westcom TV Grp. Ltd., 1990—; bd. dirs. Sta. CHBC-TV, Western Internat. Communications, Can. Satellite Communications. Mem. Advt. Guild Toronto (past pres.), TVB Can. (chmn. 1976-78, 88), Can. Assn. Broadcasters (chmn. 1979-81), Advt. Standard Council B.C. (chmn.). Anglican. Clubs: Holyburn Country, Broadcast Execs. Soc., Variety, Celebrity, Capilano Golf. Office: 1960 505 Burrard St, Vancouver, BC Canada V7X 1M6 Died Sept. 4, 1996.

SMITH, DONN L., university dean; b. Denver, Nov. 1, 1915; s. Arthur M. and Elizabeth (Setzer) S.; m. Ruth E. Perrin, Apr. 3, 1937; children: Eileen Smith Burg, Darlene Louise Smith Osterholt. A.B., U. Denver, 1939, M.S. (Upjohn scholar 1941), 1941; Ph.D., U. Colo., 1948, M.D., 1958. Asst. prof. physiology U. Denver, 1948-50; asso. prof. physiology U. Colo. Sch. Medicine, 1950-60, asso. dean, 1960-63; prof. physiology, dean Sch. Medicine, U. Louisville, 1963-70; dir. (Med. Center); dean Coll. Medicine, U. South Fla., Tampa, 1970-76; prof. comprehensive medicine and pharmacology Coll. Medicine, U. South Fla., 1976-88; interim v.p., dean U. So. Fla., 1986-88; prof., dean emeritus Coll. Medicine, U. So. Fla., 1988-95; Med. adv. Ky. SSS. Author: (with Philip Ellis) Handbook of Ocular Therapeutics and Pharmacology, 4th edit, 1973; also numerous articles. Served with Inf. AUS, 1942-46. Fellow Am. Coll. Clin. Pharmacology; mem. AMA (council on drugs 1965-72), Fla. Med. Assn., AAAS, Soc. Exptl. Biology and Medicine, Am. Soc. Pharmacology and Exptl. Therapeutics (AMA rep to U.S. Adopted Names Coun.), Alpha Omega Alpha. Home: Tampa Fla. Died Sept. 24, 1995.

SMITH, FRANK EDWARD, publisher, editor; b. Easton, Pa., Oct. 1, 1912; s. Frank Edward and Ella (Heavener) S.; m. Arlene K. Mumbower, Sept. 9, 1937; 1 child, Nancy Joan, m. Lena June Popenciu, Sept. 16, 1950; m. Margaret Zimmer, Oct. 21, 1989. BS, East Stroudsburg (Pa.) U., 1934; MA, NYU, 1946; D Hypnotherapy (hon.), Brodheadsville U., 1981; grad., Pasco County Sheriff's Office Citizens Police Acad., 1991. Cert. hypnologist; cert. hypnotherapist. Tchr., coach pub. schs. Easton, 1934-36; supervising prin., 1936-38; dir. employee activities Riegel Paper Co., Milford, N.J., 1938-43; nat. field rep. ARC, 1943-44; recreation dir. Gen. Electric Co., Erie, Pa., 1947-50; adminstrv. asst. C. J. La Roche Advt. Agy., N.Y.C., 1950-52; promotion mgr. McFadden Publs., N.Y.C., 1952-54; mgr. Buttenheim Pub. Co., Cleve., 1954-62; pub. School Product News; editor Changing Sch. Market Indsl. Pub. Co., Cleve., 1962-77; editorial cons., staff columnist Peter Li Inc., Dayton, Ohio, 1977-79; staff columnist 18 mags. Sieber Pub., New Port Richey, Fla., 1979—; chmn. Frank E. Smith Inc., 1978-79; mem. faculty Black Hills Mgmt. Seminar, 1983. Chief co-author: It Doesn't Pay to Work Too Hard; Monthly columnist: Ednl. Dealer, Money Making Magic Mag., Service Business Mag., 1980-81; contbr. articles to profl. jours. Bd. dirs. Beacon Woods (Fla.) Civic Assn., 1979-85, 1987-88, publicity chmn. 1979-85; warrant officer U.S. Mcht. Marines, 1945-46; mem. exec. com. Rep. Party, 1991. Recipient Spl. award Nat. Sch. Supply and Equipment Assn., 1971, Black Hills Gang plaque, 1976, Spl. Pres.'s award, 1976, Alumni award East Stroudsburg State U., 1979, cert. of appreciation Assn. Sch. Bus. Ofcls., 1975-76, Disting. Svc. award Pasco County, 1992. Mem. Nat. Sch. Supply Assn. (hon. life mem.; dir., exec. com. 1973-74, com. long range planning 1975-79), Internat. Assn. Counselors and Therapists, Nat. Audio Visual Assn. (cert. media specialist; faculty U. Ind. Inst. 1970-79, Spl. award 1973, 77, profl. devel. bd. 1974-80, public relations com. 1976-79, Inst. cert. 1970-75, vice chmn. continuing edn. com., disting. service award 1981), Edn. Industries (dir., sec.-treas. 1974—), Assn. Ednl. Communications and Tech. (exhibitors com. 1971—), Edn. Mgmt. Council (chmn. 1976), Internat. Communications Industries Assn. (communications tech. specialist), Fla. Free-lance Writers Assn., Phi Delta Kappa, Kappa Delta Pi. Clubs: High Twelve Internat, Masons. Died Nov. 10, 1997.

SMITH, FRANK WINFRED, clergyman; b. Redding, Calif., May 2, 1909; s. Chester Otis and Lena C. (Whitmore) S.; m. F. Rose Jolly, June 22, 1930 (dec. Apr. 1944); children: Ronald, David; m. Marie C. Christensen, Aug. 15, 1945; children: Joyce, Janice, Jonathan. BTh, Life Bible Coll., Los Angeles, BA; postgrad., Drake U., Des Moines; LittD (hon.), Eugene Bible Coll., 1989. Ordained to ministry, Internat. Ch. Foursquare Gospel, 1930, Open Bible Standard Chs., 1934. Pastor Foursquare Ch., Hollywood, Calif., 1930-34, Open Bible Ch., Ft. Des Moines, Iowa, 1934-38; pastor 1st Ch. Open Bible, Des Moines, 1939-76, pastor emeritus, 1989—; chmn. Pentecostal Fellowship N. Am., Springfield, Mo., 1979-83; chmn. Open Bible Standard Chs., Des Moines, 1976-79, dir., 1983—; chmn. Pentecostal Fellowship N. Am., 1980-83; pres. Midwest Nat. Assn. Evangelicals, 1955-57. Author: Pentecostal Positive, 1975. Recipient Disting. Christian award Midwest region Nat. Assn. Evangelicals, 1966. Mem. Des Moines Council Chs. (chmn. 1940), Iowa Assn. Evangelicals (pres. 1945). Republican. Died Nov. 3, 1997.

SMITH, G. E. KIDDER, architect, author; b. Birmingham, Ala., Oct. 1, 1913; s. F. Hopkinson and Annie (Kidder) S.; m. Dorothea Fales Wilder, Aug. 22, 1942; children: G.E. Kidder, Hopkinson Kidder. A.B., Princeton U., 1935, M.F.A., 1938; student, Ecole Americaine, Fontainbleau, France, 1935. Registered architect, N.Y., Ala., N.C. Architect Princeton Expdn. to, Antioch, Syria, 1938; designer, site planner, camoufleur with Caribbean Architect-Engr. on Army bases, Caribbean, 1940-42; own archtl. practice, 1946-97; lectr. numerous European archtl. socs., also many Am. univs. and museums; archtl. critic Yale U., 1948-49; vis. prof. MIT, 1955-56; guest arch. Archtl. Inst. Japan, 1988. Author: (with P.L. Goodwin) Brazil Builds, 1943, Switzerland Builds, 1950, Italy Builds, 1955, Sweden Builds, 1950, rev. edit., 1957, The New Architecture of Europe, 1961, The New Churches of Europe, 1963, A Pictorial History of Architecture in America, 1976, The Architecture of the United States, 3 vols, 1981, The Beacon Guide to New England Churches, 1989, Looking at Architecture, 1990, Source Book of American Architecture, 1995; also contbr. articles to encys.; exhibits, Stockholm Builds, 1940, Brazil Builds, 1943; installed: Power in the Pacific, USN, 1945 (all at Museum Modern Art, N.Y.C); New Churches of Germany, Goethe House, N.Y.C., and Am. Fedn. Arts, 1957-58, Masterpieces of European Posters (donated), Va. State Mus., Richmond, 1958; Work of Alvar Aalto, Smithsonian Instn., 1965-82, Am.'s Archtl. Heritage for, Smithsonian Instn., 1976, Smithsonian, 1976, photographs in collection, Mus. Modern Art, Met. Mus., N.Y.C. Served to lt. USNR, 1942-46. Recipient Butler prize Princeton, 1938; fellow Am. Scandinavian Found., 1939-40; Guggenheim Found. fellow, 1946-47; President's fellow Brown U., 1949-50; research Fulbright fellow Italy, 1950-51; research Fulbright fellow India, 1965-66; Samuel H. Kress grantee India, 1967 Brunner scholar, 1959-60; Graham Found. for Advanced Study in Arts-Nat. Endowment on Arts joint fellowship, 1967-69; Nat. Endowment Arts fellow, 1974-75; Ford Found. grantee, 1970-71, 75-76; decorated Order So. Cross Brazil; Premio ENIT gold medal Italy recipient gold medal (archtl. photography) AIA, 1964 E.M. Conover award, 1965; subject of public TV spl. 1976. Fellow AIA, Internat. Inst. Arts and Letters (life Switzerland); mem. Soc. Archtl. Historians, Assn. Collegiate Schs. of Architecture, Municipal Art Soc N.Y.C., Coll. Art Assn. Episcopalian. Clubs: Century Assn. (N.Y.C.); Cooperstown Country. Home: New York N.Y. Died Oct. 8, 1997.

SMITH, HALLETT DARIUS, English literature educator; b. Chattanooga, Aug. 15, 1907; s. Charles Wilson and Elizabeth Russell (Atkinson) S.; m. Mary Elizabeth Earl, Dec. 30, 1931; children—Diana Russell Smith Gordon, Hallett Earl. A.B., U. Colo., 1928, L.H.D

1968; Ph.D., Yale U., 1934. Instr. English Williams Coll., Williamstown, Mass., 1931-36, asst. prof., 1937-40, assoc. prof., 1940-45, prof., 1946-49; prof. Calif. Inst. Tech., Pasadena, 1949-75, chmn. div. humanities, 1949-70; Guggenheim fellow, 1947-48; vis. prof. Columbia U., summer 1949; sr. research asso. Huntington Library, 1970—; Henry W. and Albert A. Berg prof. Eng. lit. N.Y. U., spring 1977; vis. prof. U. B.C., Spring 1980; Mem. Commn. English. Author: The Golden Hind, 1942, The Critical Reader, 1949, Elizabethan Poetry, 1951, Renaissance England, 1956, Twentieth Century Interpretations of The Tempest, 1970, Shakespeare's Romances, 1972, The Tension of the Lyre: Poetry in Shakespeare's Sonnets, 1981; contbr. articles to ednl. jours. Trustee Am. Univs. Field Staff, Poly. Sch.; mem. adv. com. Guggenheim Found. Recipient Poetry Chapbook prize Poetry Soc. Am., 1952; Phi Beta Kappa vis. scholar, 1959-60. Fellow Am. Acad. Arts and Scis.; mem. Modern Lang. Assn. Am., Phi Beta Kappa (senator at large). Died Aug. 15, 1996.

SMITH, HUESTON MERRIAM, engineer, consultant; b. Almeta, Tex., Dec. 19, 1912; s. Harry Merriam and Ruth Alice (Vansconcellos) S.; m. Edith Adele Fort, Dec. 12, 1970; 1 child, Joseph Hueston. BSEE, U. Mo., Rolla, 1938; profl. degree of electrical engring., U. Mo., 1982. Registered profl. engr. Mo., Tex., Kans., Ark. Asst. engr. Mo. Pub. Service Commn., Jefferson City, 1938-40; indsl. engr. Union Electric Co., St. Louis, 1947-50; chief engr. Fruin-Colnon Co., St. Louis, 1950-54; pres. Smith-Zurhelde & Assocs. Inc., St. Louis, 1954-65; sr. v.p. Thatcher & Patient Inc., St. Louis, 1965-69; prin. Hueston M. Smith & Assocs. Inc., St. Louis, 1969—. Mem. editorial adv. bd. Cons. Engr. mag., 1958-77, Bldg. Constrn. mag., 1960-74. City engr. Frontenac, Mo., 1957-59; chief of police City of Fontenac, 1952-54. Served to col. C.E. U.S. Army, 1940-46. Decorated Bronze Star. Mem. Cons. Engrs. Council U.S. (pres. 1960-61, bd. dirs. 1963-64), Cons. Engrs. Mo. (pres. 1965-67, bd. dirs. 1962-63), Mo. Soc. Profl. Engrs. (Outstanding Achievement award 1962), Soc. Am. Mil. Engrs., Res. Officers Assn. U.S., Ret. Officers Assn., Mil. Order of World Wars, Mo. Real Estate Assn., Nat. Rifle Assn., U. Mo.-Rolla Alumni Assn., Acad. Elec. Engrs. of U. Mo.-Rolla, Eta Kappa Nu. Club: Mo. Athletic. Lodge: Masons.

SMITH, JACK CLIFFORD, journalist, author; b. Long Beach, Calif., Aug. 27, 1916; s. Charles Franklin and Anna Mary (Hughes) S.; m. Denise Bresson, June 17, 1939; children: Curtis Bresson, Douglas Franklin. Student, Bakersfield (Calif.) Coll., 1937-38. Reporter Bakersfield Californian, 1937-38, Honolulu Advertiser, 1941-42, UPI, Sacramento, 1943, Los Angeles Daily News, 1946-49, Los Angeles Herald-Express, 1950-52; reporter Los Angeles Times, 1953-58, columnist, 1958-95. Author: Three Coins in the Birdbath, 1965, Smith on Wry, 1970, God and Mr. Gomez, 1974, The Big Orange, 1976, Spend All Your Kisses, Mr. Smith, 1978, Jack Smith's L.A, 1980, How to Win a Pullet Surprise, 1982, Cats, Dogs and Other Strangers at My Door, 1984, Alive in La La Land, 1989. Served with USMC, 1944-45. Club: Sunset. Died Jan. 9, 1996.

SMITH, JOACHIM, artist; b. Grand Island, Nebr., Apr. 3, 1929; s. Victor Bordwell and Vesta Marie (Houf) S.; children—Melanie, Therese. B.A., Calif. State U., Long Beach, 1953, M.A., 1954. From instr. to assoc. prof. art Calif. State U., Long Beach, 1955-62; mem. faculty Calif. State U., Fullerton, 1962—; prof. art Calif. State U., 1968-81, prof. emeritus, 1981—, chmn. dept., 1976-77, vice chmn. dept., 1977-79. One-man exhbns. include, Comara Gallery, Los Angeles, 1960, 62, 66, 67, 69, Long Beach (Calif.) Mus. Art, 1959, Santa Barbara (Calif.) Mus. Art, 1962, Pasadena (Calif.) Art Mus., 1963, Los Angeles Mcpl. Art Gallery, 1968, Newport Harbor (Calif.) Art Mus., 1975, group exhbns. in, U.S., abroad; represented in numerous permanent collections. (Recipient over 70 awards for drawing and painting.). Office: Calif State U Art Dept Fullerton CA 92634 DIED 11/17/94. .

SMITH, KENNETH BLOSE, financial executive; b. Monmouth, Ill., Jan. 29, 1926; s. Elmer Edwin and Florence (Logan) S.; m. Julia M. Stupp, June 17, 1950; children: Donald E., Paul C., Marilyn D. B.S., U. Iowa, 1947. Internal auditor Deere & Co, Moline, Ill., 1947-52; treas. John Deere Chem. Co., Pryor, Okla., 1952-65; fin. mgr. Deere & Co., Moline, Ill., 1965-71, asst. treas., 1971-81, treas., 1981-85. Republican. Lutheran. Died Dec. 15, 1996.

SMITH, LAWRENCE W., surgeon; b. Racine, Wis., Nov. 24, 1923. MD, Marquette Sch. Medicine, 1946. Diplomate Am. Bd. Surgery. Intern Boston City Hosp., 1947-48, resident in surgery, 1948-52; staff St. Marys Med. Ctr., Racine. Mem. Wis. Med. Soc., Wis. Soc. Surgeons. Died Dec. 29, 1996.

SMITH, LEON POLK, artist; b. Chickasha, Okla., May 20, 1906. BA, East Cen. State U., 1934; MA, Columbia U., 1938. Lectr. Brandeis U., 1968; resident artist U. Calif., Davis, 1972; lectr. SUNY-Old Westbury, 1978, Yale U., 1983, East Cen. U., Ada, Okla., 1986. One-man shows include San Francisco Mus. and Rose Mus. Retrospective, 1968, Musèe Nat. d'Art Modern, Georges Pompidou (Beaubourg), Paris, Washburn Gallery, N.Y.C., 1981-82, Nat. Galerie, Berlin, 1983, Burnett Miller Gallery, L.A., 1985, Hoffmann Galerie, Friedberg, Germany, 1987, Venice Biennale, 1987, Cleve. Mus. Art, Inyedian Art Gallery, Lausanne, Switzerland, Schlègl Gallery, Zurich; exhibited in group shows at Haus der Kunst, Munich, 1982, Nat. Gallery, Washington, 1984, Nat. Mus., Berlin, 1984, Wilhelm-Hack-Mus., Ludwigshafen, Germany, 1988, U. Okla. Mus. Art, 1989, Grenoble Mus., France, 1989, Bklyn. Mus., 1995; represented in permanent collections Guggenheim Mus., N.Y.C., Met. Mus. Art, N.Y.C., Mus. Modern Art, N.Y.C., Birmingham Mus. Art, Whitney Mus. Art, N.Y.C., Hirshhorn Mus., Nat. Gallery, Berlin, Peter Ludwig, Vienna, Austria, Nürnberg Kunsthalle, Germany, Wilhelm Hack Mus., Ludwigshafen-an Rhein, Germany, Wiesbaden Mus., Germany, Nurnberg Mus. Art, Germany, Grenoble Mus., France, Wiesbaden Mus. Germany, Bklyn. Mus. Solomon R. Guggenheim fellow, 1943; recipient Hassum Speicher Fund Purchase Exhbn. award Am. Acad. and Inst. Arts and Letters, 1979, Disting. Alumnus award East Ctrl. U., 1986; grantee Nat. Coun. Arts, 1967, Tamarind, 1968, Longview grantee, 1958. Home: New York N.Y. Died Dec. 4, 1996.

SMITH, MARY LOUISE, politics and public affairs consultant; b. Eddyville, Iowa, Oct. 6, 1914; d. Frank and Louise Anna (Jager) Epperson; BA, U. Iowa, 1935; LHD (hon.), Drake U., 1980; LLD (hon.), Grinnell Coll., 1984; m. Elmer Milton Smith, Oct. 7, 1934; children: Robert C., Margaret L., James E. Mem. Eagle Grove (Iowa) Bd. Edn., 1955-60; Republican precinct committeewoman, Eagle Grove, 1960-62, vice-chairwoman, Wright County, Iowa, 1962-63; mem. Rep. Nat. Com., 1964-84, mem. exec. com., 1969-84, mem. conv. reforms com., 1966, vice-chairwoman Steiger com. on conv. reform, 1973, co-chmn. nat. com., 1974, chmn. Com., 1974-77; vice-chairwoman U.S. Commn. on Civil Rights, 1982-83; vice-chairwoman Midwest region Rep. Conf., 1969-71; del. Rep. Nat. Conv., 1968, 72, 76, 80, 84, alt. del., 1964, hon officer, 1988, 92, organized and called to order, 1976; vice-chairwoman Iowa Presdl. campaign, 1964; nat. co-chmn. Physicians Com. for Presdl. Campaign, 1972; co-chairwoman Iowa Com. to Reelect the Pres., 1972; mem. Nat. Commn. on Observance Internat. Women's Year, 1975-77, del. Internat. Women's Yr. Conf., Houston, 1977; vis. fellow Woodrow Wilson Fellowship Found., 1979. Mem. U.S. del. to Extraordinary Session of UNESCO Gen. Conf., Paris, 1973; mem. U.S. del. 15th session population commn. UN Econ. and Social Council, Geneva, 1969; mem. Pres.'s Commn. for Observance of 25th Anniversary of UN, 1970-71; mem. Iowa Commn. for Blind, 1961-63, chairwoman, 1963; mem. Iowa Gov.'s Commn. on Aging, 1962; trustee Robert A. Taft Inst. Govt., 1974-84, Herbert Hoover Presdl. Libr. Assn., Inc., 1979-91. Pres. Eagle Grove Cmty. Chest; bd. dirs. Mental Health Center North Iowa, 1962-63, YWCA of Greater Des Moines, 1983-87, Orchard Place Resdl. Facility for Emotionally Disturbed Children, 1983-88, Learning Channel, cable TV, 1984-87, Iowa Peace Inst., 1985-90, Planned Parenthood of Greater Iowa, 1986-92, U. Iowa Found., 1987-97; trustee Drake U., 1990-97; bd. dirs. U.S. Inst. Peace, 1990-97, Chrysalis Womens Found., 1994-97; bd. dirs., nat. co-chair Rep. Mainstream Com.; bd. dirs. Alliance for Arts and Understanding, 1993-96, The Interfaith Alliance of Iowa, 1996-97; mem. adv. coun. U. Iowa Hawkeye Fund Women's Program, 1982-87, co-founder Iowa Women's Archives, 1991; chairperson UN Day for Iowa, 1987; polit. communication ctr. conf. U. Okla., 1987; disting. vis. exec. Coll. Bus. Adminstrn. U. Iowa, 1988; co-chmn. select com. on drug abuse City of Des Moines, 1989-90; mem. bipartisan legislative com. on govt. ethics and procedures, 1992; mem. Gov.'s Blue Ribbon Task Force on Campaign Fin. Disclosure Law, 1989; mem. Des Moines Human Rights Commn., 1995—; hon. chmn. Iowa Student/Parent Mock Election, 1995-96. Named hon. col., mil. staff Gov. Iowa, 1973; Iowa Women's Hall of Fame, 1977; named to Iowa City H.S. Hall of Fame, 1995; recipient Disting. Alumni award U. Iowa, 1984, Hancher Medallion award, 1991; Cristine Wilson medal for equality and justice Iowa Commn. on Status of Women, 1984, Elinor Robson award Coun. for Internat. Understanding, 1992, Pres. award Midwest Archives Conf., 1994; Mary Louise Smith award named in her honor, YWCA, 1988; Mary Louise Smith endowed chair in Women and Politics, Iowa State U., 1995; Brotherhood/Sisterhood award Iowa region NCCJ, 1996. Mem. Women's Aux. AMA, UN Assn., Nat. Conf. Christians and Jews, Nat. Women's Polit. Caucus (adv. bd. 1978-97), PEO, Kappa Alpha Theta. Died Aug. 22, 1997.

SMITH, MAURICE FREDERIK, business consultant, conservationist; b. Fort Wayne, Ind., Nov. 24, 1908; s. George Levi and Lou Emma (Pierce) S.; m. Vivian Weston, 1932; 1 son, Christopher F.; m. Catherine Hanley, Aug. 22, 1941; children: Michaele, Mark, Frederik, Drusilla, Francesca. Student, U. Mich., 1924-26, Coll. William and Mary, 1927-29, Dayton Art Inst., 1926-30. Advt. mgr. Hobart Mfg. Co., 1924-30; dir. pub. relations Batten, Barton, Durstine & Osborn, N.Y.C., 1931-36; partner Selvage & Smith, 1937-40; dir. pub. relations Young & Rubicam, 1941-42; v.p. ABC, 1944-45; dir. advt. Simon & Schuster, 1945-46, Book-of-the-Month Club, 1946-48; pres. Fred Smith & Co., N.Y.C., 1948-56; v.p. Prudential Ins. Co., Newark, 1956-64; asso. Rockefeller Family & Assos., N.Y.C., 1964—; dir. Am. Motors, Howard Johnson Co., Perini Corp., George Rogers Constrn. Co., UN Devel. Corp., Grand Teton Lodge Co.; trustee Jackson Hole Preserve Inc.; asst. to sec. Treasury, 1942-44; asst. to U.S. Pres., Bretton Woods Conf., 1944; mem. Nat. Outdoor Recreation Resources Rev. Commn., 1958-60; mem. adv. bd. Nat. Parks, 1945—. Author: The Story of Grand Coulee Dam, 1938; contbr. articles to profl. jours. Recipient award Trustees of Reservations, 1956. Fellow Rochester (N.Y.) Mus.; mem. Explorers Club. Republican. Clubs: Boone and Crockett, Sky, Rockefeller Center Luncheon, Whitehall, Johns Island. Died March 12, 1997.

SMITH, MICHAEL ANTHONY, professional hockey team manager; b. Potsdam, N.Y., Aug. 31, 1945; s. James Michael and Helen Francis (Codner) S.; m. Judith Ann Smith; 1 child, Jason. BS, Clarkson U., 1968; MS and PhD, Syracuse U., 1975. Asst. coach N.Y. Rangers, N.Y.C., 1976-78, Colo. Rockies, Denver, 1978-79; coach Tulsa Oilers, 1979-80; coach Winnipeg (Man., Can.) Jets Hockey Club, 1981, dir. recruiting, 1981-84, asst. gen. mgr., 1984-88, gen. mgr., 1988—, also alt. gov., v.p.; owner Codner Books, St. Paul, 1978-89. Author: Life After Hockey, 1988, also several books on coaching. Democrat. Roman Catholic. Avocation: American Indian art. Home: 15-1430 Maroons Rd, Winnipeg, MB Canada R3G 0L5 Died Jan. 31, 1997.

SMITH, MONCRIEFF HYNSON, psychology educator; b. St. Louis, Sept. 21, 1917; s. Moncrieff Hynson and Nell Drane (Galbraith) S.; m. Malvene Parker Grimshaw, Sept. 12, 1941 (div. Oct. 1959); children: Mason, Virginia, Parker; m. Mary Mildred Devine, June 12, 1960; children: MacKenzie, Laurie. AB, U. Mo., 1940, MA, 1941; postgrad., U. Iowa, 1941-42; PhD, Stanford U., 1947. Instr. Harvard U., Cambridge, Mass., 1947-49; from asst. prof. to prof. U. Wash., Seattle, 1949-88, prof. emeritus, 1988-95, chmn. joint PhD program in physiology and psychology, 1960-85; cons. USAF, Sacramento, 1949, San Antonio, 1950, Rsch. Lab. Electronics, MIT, Cambridge, 1951-53. Capt. U.S. Army, 1942-46. Fellow Am. Psychol. Assn. Avocations: photography, bridge. Home: Seattle Wash. Died April 28, 1995.

SMITH, OPAL WHETSALL, school system administrator; b. Park Springs, Tex., Oct. 27, 1923; d. William Edward and Myrtle Erwin Whetsall; m. McClain G. Smith, June 4, 1944 (dec. Aug. 1979); children: Gareth McClain, Ivan Mitchell, Rebecca Diana. AA, Decatur Bapt., 1943; MA, East Tex. State, 1972, postgrad. With youth div. East Tex. United Meth. Chs., 1944-80; coordinator Girl Scouts Am. and Boy Scouts Am., Tex., 1944-87; elem. tchr. Park Springs (Tex.) Ind. Sch. Dist., 1942-44; tchr. Sulphur Bluff (Tex.) Ind. Sch. Dist., 1944-45, Murry Ind. Sch. Dist., 1971-73, Fanendale Schs., Ladonin, Tex., 1973-76; elem. tchr. Crandell (Tex.) Schs., 1976-80, sch. system adminstr., 1980—; supr. curriculum pub. schs. Crandell Ind. Sch. Dist. Active City of Crandall Planning and Zoning, 1984; chmn. Pastor/Parish relations com. Meth. Ch., Crandall, 1986-88; mem. Tex. Sesquecentennial Com., Crandall, 1985-86; v.p. Com. on Aging, Kaufman County, Tex., 1986; vol. coordinator Kaufman-Crandall Meals-on-Wheels Com. Recipient Outstanding Community Service award Future Farmers of Am., 1985, Cert. Appreciation Wadley Blood Ctr., 1986-87, Cert. Merit Faufman County Sr. Citizen Services, Terrell, Tex., 1987, Proclamation award County Judge Kaufman, Tex., 1987, Cert. Appreciation Support of Community Edn., Ennis, Tex. Mem. Crandell-Combine Bus. and Profl. Women (1st v.p., Women of Yr. 1987), PTA (Life Service award 1980), Phi Delta Kappa. Democrat. Lodge: Order Eastern Star.

SMITH, PHILIP WAYNE, writer, communications company executive; b. Fayetteville, Tenn., Sept. 2, 1945; s. Clyde Wilson and Chastain (Finch) S.; m. Susan Jones, June 22, 1968; 1 child, Alan Wayne. Student, U. So. Miss., 1963-64, Athens Coll., 1964-65, 69-70. Reporter The Huntsville (Ala.) Times, 1964-66, The Elk Valley Times, Fayetteville, 1969-70; edn. reporter The Huntsville Times, 1970-71; Washington corr. The Huntsville Times, Washington, 1971-76; White House corr. Newhouse News Svc., Washington, 1977-80, Pentagon corr., 1981-84; writer Huntsville, 1984—; pres. P.S. Comms., Huntsville, 1994—; pub. rels. cons. Teledyne Brown Engring., Huntsville, 1984—; safety film producer VECO, Inc., Prudhoe Bay, Alaska, 1991. Co-author: Protecting the President, 1985 (Lit. Guild alt. selection 1986); screenwriter Our Land Too, 1987, Chemicals in War, 1989, Security: Everyone's Job, 1990, Face to Face Prospecting, 1992, Investigating Child Abuse, 1992, Lead Generation, 1993, Telephone Prospecting, 1993, Delayed Enlistment Program Management, 1993, Recruiter Sales Presentation, 1994, Duties and Responsibilities of Recruiting Station Commanders, 1994, Training Future Leaders, 1994, Rehabilitative Training Instructor Program, 1994, U.S. Army Program Executive Office for Tactical Missiles, 1995, Training: The Army Advantage, 1995, National Environmental Policy Act Compliance, 1996, Operations of the M21 Remote Sensing Chemical Agent Alarm, 1996, Buying Green: Purchasing Environmentally Friendly Products, 1997, Introduction to Terrorism, 1997, Terrorist Operations, 1997, Individual Protective Measures, 1997, Hostage Survival, 1997, Detecting Terrorist Surveillance, 1997, Buying Green: Using Environmentally Friendly Products, 1997. Sgt. USMC, 1966-69, Vietnam. Decorated Navy Achievement medal with combat V; named for Reporting Without Deadline, Ala. Press Assn., 1972, News Feature Writing, Ala. AP, 1975. Mem. Tenn. Screenwriting Assn., VFW. Democrat. Episcopalian. Avocations: tennis, swimming. Died Aug. 1, 1997.

SMITH, RANKIN MCEACHERN, SR., insurance company executive, professional football team executive; b. Atlanta, GA, Oct. 29, 1925; married; 5 children. Ed., Emory U., U. Fla., U. Ga. With Life Ins. Co. of Ga., 1943—, agy. asst. v.p., 1954, corp. sec., 1954-57, agy. v.p., 1957-63, exec. v.p., 1963-68, sr. v.p., 1968-70, pres., chief exec. officer, from 1970; later chmn., now dir.; owner Atlanta Falcons football team, 1965—, past pres., now chmn. bd.; dir. Greyhound, Inc., Trust Co. Ga. Assos. Div. chmn. United Way, Atlanta, 1973-74; Ga. sightsaving chmn. Nat. Soc. for Prevention Blindness, 1973-74; mem. exec. com. Central Atlanta Progress, Inc.; mem. exec. bd. Atlanta Area Council Boy Scouts Am.; Bd. dirs. Better Bus. Bur. Atlanta; trustee U. Ga. Found., Reinhardt Coll., Waleska, Ga., Lovett Sch., Atlanta. Mem. Atlanta C. of C., Commerce Club, Chi Pi. Methodist. Clubs: Capitol City (gov.), Piedmont Driving. Lodges: Masons; Shriners; Rotary. Died Oct. 26, 1997.

SMITH, RICHARD JOYCE, lawyer; b. Hartford, Conn., July 28, 1903; s. Clarence H. and Anne M.B. (Horan) S.; m. Sheila Alexander, Sept. 6, 1932 (dec. Aug. 1984); children: Peter, Timothy, Christopher, Andrew, Wilford, Joyce. B.A., Cath. U. Am., 1924; LL.B., Yale U., 1927; LL.D. (hon.), Am. Internat. Coll., 1970. Bar: Conn. 1927, N.Y. 1934. Instr., asso. prof. law Yale, 1927-33, vis. lectr., 1945-48; social sci. research fellow London and Dublin, 1929-30; mem. law firm Whitman & Ransom, 1934-83, counsel, 1983-95, ret. sr. ptnr., 1984-95; reorgn. trustee New York, New Haven & Hartford Railroad Co., 1961-80; Member Conn. State Board Pardons, 1937-43. Member Fairfield bd. edn., 1941-51; member Conn. State Bd. Edn., 1951-57; adv. com. U.S. Alien Property Custodian, 1943-44; chief counsel Petroleum Resources Com., U.S. Senate, 1944-45; Del. Dem. Nat. Conv., Chgo., 1940; Trustee Nat. Citizens Commn. Pub. Schs., 1951-56; mem. exec. com. Yale Law Sch. Assn. Mem. Am., Conn., N.Y. State bar assns., Association Bar City N.Y., Phi Delta Phi. Clubs: Graduates (New Haven); Yale (N.Y.C.), Century Assn. (N.Y.C.); Fairfield Country, Pequot Yacht, N.Y. Yacht. Home: Southport Conn. Died Apr. 5, 1995.

SMITH, ROBERT B., hospital administrator; b. Downey, Calif., Feb. 9, 1937; m. Judith Smith; 2 children. B.S., Calif. State U.-Northridge, 1963; M.B.A., Calif. State U.-Long Beach, 1970; Cert. in Hosp. Adminstrn., Ohio State U., 1978. Adminstrv. trainee Los Angeles County Chief Adminstrv. Office, 1963-64, adminstrv. aid, 1964-66, adminstrv. analyst, 1966; mem. staff Los Angeles County-Harbor-UCLA Med. Ctr., 1966-71; adminstr. Los Angeles County Wesley Hosp., 1971-72; adminstr. UCLA Med. Ctr., 1972-74; exec. dir. Los Angeles County-U. So. Calif. Med. Ctr., 1974-75; dir. hosp. and clinics U. Calif.-Davis Med. Ctr., 1975-79, assoc. clin. prof., 1975-79; chief exec. officer U. Mo.-Columbia Hosp. and Clinics, 1979-96 ; cons. and lectr. in field. Contbr. articles to profl. jours. Mem. Am. Coll. Hosp. Adminstrs., Mo. Hosp. Assn. (vice chmn. research policy com.), C. of C. (bd. dirs. Columbia, Mo. 1982-84), Calif. Hosp. Assn., Sacramento-Sierra Hosp. Assn. (treas. exec. com. 1975-79), Hosp. Council So. Calif. (com. chmn. 1971-74). Died April 6, 1996.

SMITH, ROBERT JUNIUS, accounting educator; b. Snowflake, Ariz., Dec. 25, 1920; s. Samuel Francis and Lulu Jane (Hatch) S.; m. Lola Nielson, Nov. 5, 1945; children—Junola (Mrs. Charles D. Bush), Lynette (Mrs. Gregory L. Lyman), Lynn Robert, Shirley (Mrs. Stephen D. Ricks), LaRae (Mrs. Benjamin L. Blake), Jeanine (Mrs. Stanley A. Denton), Larry Kay, Sheldon Ray. B.S., Brigham Young U., 1948; M.B.A., Northwestern U., 1949; D.B.A., Ind. U., 1957. With Brigham Young U., 1949-85, asst. to assoc. prof. accounting, 1949-57, prof., 1957-85, chmn. dept., 1951-55, 59-62, acting dean Coll. Business, 1963-64, asst. acad. v.p., 1968-70, assoc. acad. v.p., 1970-78, fin. v.p., 1978-85, comptroller Jeruslaem Ctr. Near Ea. Studies, 1984-88; ptnr. Burton, Tenney, Smith & Lewis Co. (C.P.A.'s), 1961-65; cons. ptnr. Main Lafrentz & Co. (C.P.A.'s), 1966-67. Author: Preparing for the CPA Examination, 1960, 2d edit., 1967. V.p. Utah County United Fund, 1970-71, pres., 1972; comptr. Nat. Parks coun. Boy Scouts Am., 1981-84. Served with USNR, 1944-46. Recipient gold medal Ill. Soc. C.P.A.s, 1949, Elijah Watt Sells gold medal Am. Inst. Accts., 1949, Alumni Disting. Service award Brigham Young U., 1982, Presdl. citation Brigham Young U., 1988. Mem. Alpha Kappa Psi, Beta Gamma Sigma, Beta Alpha Psi, Phi Kappa Phi. Mem. LDS Ch. Died Nov. 28, 1996.

SMITH, ROBERT LEO, ecologist, wildlife biologist; b. Brookville, Pa., Mar. 23, 1925; s. Leo F. and Josephine Elizabeth (Ferguson) S.; m. Alice Elizabeth Casey, Nov. 15, 1952; children: Robert Leo, Thomas Michael, Pauline Ann, Maureen Elizabeth. B.S., Pa. State U., 1949, M.S., 1954; Ph.D., Cornell U., 1956. Asst. prof. biology SUNY, Plattsburgh, 1956-58; prof. wildlife ecology W.Va. U., Morgantown, 1958—; cons. in ecology to pubs. and govt. Author: Ecology and Field Biology, 5th edit, 1995, The Ecology of Man: An Ecosystem Approach, 1976, 2d edit., Russian transl., 1982, Elements of Ecology and Field Biology, 1977, Elements of Ecology, 1985, 3d edit., 1992; contbr. to: Ency. Brit. and World Book Ency., also profl. jours. and books; adv. bd., contbr.: Funk and Wagnalls Ency. Served with U.S. Army, 1950-52. Mem. Ecol. Soc. Am., Am. Ornithologists Union, Wildlife Soc., Am. Soc. Mammalogists, Am. Soc. Naturalists, Am. Inst. Biol. Scis., Outdoor Writers Assn. Am., Wilson Ornithol. Soc., Cooper Ornithol. Soc., Sigma Xi. Republican. Roman Catholic. Office: Div Forestry WVa U Morgantown WV 26506 Died Oct. 24, 1997.

SMITH, ROBERT SELLERS, lawyer; b. Samson, Ala., July 31, 1931; s. Abb Jackson and Rose (Sellers) S.; m. June Claire West, Feb. 2, 1963; children-Robert Sellers, David West, Rosemary True, Adam Douglas. BS, U. Va., 1953, LLB, 1958, LLM, 1990. Bar: Ala. 1959. Asst. counsel spl. com. to investigate campaign expenditures U.S. Ho. of Reps., 1960; counsel U.S. Senate Labor and Pub. Welfare Com., 1961-63; ptnr. firm Smith, Huckaby & Graves (P.A.), Huntsville, 1963-85, Bradley, Arant, Rose & White, Huntsville, 1985-95; ptnr. Foley, Smith & Mahmood, Huntsville, 1995—; instr. econs., Am. econ. history U. Ala., 1963-64; Mem. industry adv. com., select com. small bus. U.S. Senate. Author: West's Tax Law Dictionary and 11 other books; mem. bd. editors Ala. Lawyer, 1994—. Pres. Madison County (Ala.) Legal Aid Soc., 1971-75; pres. North Ala. Estate Planning Council, 1974. Served with U.S. Navy, 1953-57. Mem. ABA, Am. Immigration Lawyers Assn., Internat. Bar Assn., Ala. Bar Assn., Huntsville-Madison County Bar Assn. (pres. 1988). Episcopalian. Died Nov. 9, 1996.

SMITH, R(OBERT) SMITH, lawyer; b. South Bend, Ind., June 29, 1929; s. Lloyd Franklin and Florence (Yerly) S.; m. Barbara L. Stech, Sept. 29, 1956; children: Dana, Linda, Robbin. BA, Carleton Coll., 1951; JD, U. Chgo., 1956. Bar: Ill. 1956, U.S. Supreme Ct. 1975. Assoc. Ross & Hardies, Chgo., 1956-65, ptnr., 1966—; spl. counsel Village of Mt. Prospect, Ill., 1966-79, gen. counsel, 1979-81; village atty., corp. counsel Village of Bolingbrook, Ill., 1967-77; gen. counsel Village of Barrington Hills, Ill., 1977-83; adj. prof. Coll. Urban Sci., U. Ill., 1974-81, Northwestern U. Sch. Law, 1983; co-chmn. Chgo. Lawyers Com. for Civil Rights Under Law, 1979-81. Mem. Mayor's Task Force on Neighborhood Land Use, Chgo., 1986. Mem. ABA, Ill. State Bar Assn., Chgo. Bar Assn., Nat. Inst. Mcpl. Law Officers, Am. Planning Assn. (chmn. planning and law div. 1986—).

SMITH, RUSSELL L., film critic; b. Dallas, Nov. 11, 1956. BJ, U. Tex., Arlington, 1983. Pop music critic Dallas Morning News, 1984-89, film critic, 1989—. Recipient First Pl. award criticism Tex. AP Mng. Editors, 1989, awards of merit Gay and Lesbian Assn. Against Defamation, Dallas, 1992, Tex. Lesbian and Gay Journalists Assn., Austin, 1993.

SMITH, SCOTT BENNETT, author and publishing executive; b. Indpls., June 5, 1940; s. Donald Maxwell and Elsie Ann (Wilson) S.; divorced; children: Don, Laura, Jessie, Huntley. AB in English, Lafayette Coll., 1962. Reporter Allentown (Pa.) Morning Call, 1961-64; prin. asst., nat. editor, metro editor Wash. Star, Washington, 1964-73; prof. journalism U. Ariz., Tucson, 1974-76; mgr. Mgmt. Recruiters, San Francisco and Menlo Park, Calif., 1978-83; pres., pub. San Jose (Calif.) Bus. Jour., 1983-86; nat. editor Am. City Bus. Jours. Inc., Kansas City, Mo. Columnist Living Bus.; editor: The Insider (San Jose), 1988; contbr. articles to profl. publs. Bd. dirs. San Jose Symphony, Jr. Achievement, San Jose, Civic Light Opera, San Jose, Convention and Visitors Bur., San Jose, O'Connor Hosp. Found., San Jose, San Jose Shelter, County Arts Council, San Jose. Stanford U. fellow, 1970-71. Republican. Avocation: golf. Died Aug. 18, 1997.

SMITH, THOMAS CLAYTON, architect; b. Wesson, Miss., Nov. 30, 1927; s. Willard and Mattie Irene (Lowery) S.; m. Dorothy Emily Davenport, June 5, 1940; children: Marsha Ann, Clayton Brent, Brenda Faye. BArch, Tex. A&M U., 1952. Registered architect, La., Miss. Intern Easterwood and Easterwood, Waco, Tex., 1951; draftsman Goodman and Miller, Baton Rouge, 1952; architect Geroge Dahl and Assocs., Dallas, 1952-53, Stanley Brown, Dallas, 1953, Goodman and Miller, Baton Rouge, 1954-57; v.p. Miller, Smith and Champagne, Baton Rouge, 1957-85; pres. Smith and Champagne, Inc., Baton Rouge, 1985—; guest speaker, jury mem. La. State U. Mem. sch. curricula and planning com. East Baton Rouge Parish, 1968-70; mem. Chem. Abuse Com., 1979—, I Care Program, 1981; ; mem. long range planning com. St. John the Bapt. Parish Sch. Bd., 1970-76, Judson Bapt. Assn., 1972-83, State of La., 1976-80; bldg. official West Baton Rouge Parish, 1977-80; advisor Adolescent Chem. Dependency Unit, 1979—; bd. dirs. Baton Rouge Youth, Inc., 1983; mem. Baton Rouge Goals Congress, 1972-75. Served with USN, 1945-46, PTO. Fellow AIA (sec. Baton Rouge chpt. 1953-54, exec. com. 1953-58, treas. 1954-55, v.p. 1955-56, program chmn. 1958-60, govtl. affairs com. 1956-62, chmn. office practice com. 1956-58, 79-81, chmn. pub. relations com. 1960-62, pres. 1965-67, 74-75); mem. La. Architects Assn. (chmn. continuing edn. com. 1964-66, govtl. affairs com. 1966-81, chmn. 1979-81, sec.-treas. 1967-68, 75-76, bd. dirs. 1966-71, 73-80, v.p. 1975-76, pres. 1978-79), Gulf States Region Architects Assn. (exec. com. 1966-67, 74-75, 78-79, chmn. com. to rev. structure and future of region 1979, nat. state and local govtl. affairs com. 1980, chmn. nat. AIA/PAC fund raising 1981), Baton Rouge C. of C., Baton Rouge Roundtable. Club: Exchange. Democrat. Baptist. Avocations: woodworking, camping, fishing. Home: 656 Magnolia Wood Ave Baton Rouge LA 70808-6052 Died May 25, 1996.

SMITH, THOMAS WOODWARD, cardiologist, educator; b. Akron, Ohio, Mar. 29, 1936; s. Luther David and Beatrice Pearl (Woodward) S.; m. Sherley Louise Goodwin, Sept. 13, 1958; children: Julia Goodwin, Geoffrey Woodward, Allison Lloyd. A.B., Harvard U., 1958, M.D., 1965. Diplomate: Am. Bd. Internal Medicine; Am. Bd. Cardiovascular Diseases. Intern in medicine Mass. Gen. Hosp., Boston, 1965-66, asst. resident in medicine, 1966-67, clin. and research fellow in cardiology, 1967-69, Nat. Heart and Lung Inst. spl. fellow, 1969-71, asst. in medicine, 1969-72, assoc. program dir. myocardial infarction research unit, 1972-74, asst. physician, 1972-77, cons. in medicine, 1977—; asst. prof. medicine Harvard U. Med. Sch., 1971-73, assoc. prof., 1973-79, prof., 1979—; physician Peter Bent Brigham Hosp. (now Brigham and Women's Hosp.), Boston, chief cardiovascular div.; cons. in cardiology Children's Hosp. Med. Ctr. and Sidney Farber Cancer Inst. (now Dana-Farber Cancer Inst.); prof. medicine MIT div. Health Scis. and Tech.; Hall vis. prof., Sydney, Australia, 1977; Sir Henry Hallett Dale vis. prof. Johns Hopkins U. Med. Sch., 1979; Nahum lectr. Yale U. Sch. Medicine, 1979. Reviewer med. jours.; contbr. articles to profl. publs. Mem. Am. Heart Assn. (council clin. cardiology, council basic sci., council on circulation, established investigator 1971-76 Rosenthal award), Am. Fedn. Clin. Research, Paul Dudley White Soc., AAAS, Am. Soc. Pharmacology and Exptl. Therapeutics, Am. Soc. Clin. Investigation, Am. Coll. Cardiology, ACP, Assn. Univ. Cardiologists, Am. Physiol. Soc., Assn. Am. Physicians, Soc. Gen. Physiologists, Alpha Omega Alpha. Died Mar. 23, 1997.

SMITH, VIRGINIA LESUEUR CARTER, retired educational association executive; b. Bristol, Va., Nov. 15, 1932; d. Homer Crockett and Jennie (Phillips) LeSueur; m. William Joseph Carter, Aug. 28, 1954 (div. Nov. 1973); children: Jennie L., Laura Ann; m. Robert Gerald Smith Jan. 29, 1982; stepchildren: Lynn Beaber, Donald, Michele Willis, Paul, Gregory. BA in Polit. Sci., U. Richmond, 1953, LittD (hon.), 1990; postgrad., Columbia U., 1953-54. Info. officer Va. Dept. Agrl., Richmond, 1954-55, 61-62; dir. pub. info. ARC, Roanoke, Va., 1958-59; dir. info., publs. Hollins Coll., Va., 1960-61, 65-72; edit. cons., dir. publs. U. Richmond, 1972-73; editor, coordinator univ. publs. U. Md., College Park, 1973-75; v.p., editor jour. Council for Advancement and Support of Edn., Washington, 1975-86; sr. v.p. Coun. for Advancement and Support Edn., Washington, 1986-91, interim pres., 1990, pres. emeritus, 1991—; Cons. in field. Editor: Update on Publications, 1978, Annual Fund Ideas, 1979, A Marketing Approach to Student Recruitment, 1979, How To Survey Your Readers, 1981; co-editor: Planned Giving Ideas, 1979, Involving Volunteers in Your Advancement, 1983, How To Cut Publications Costs, 1984; editor Case Currents mag., 1975-86 (Golden Lamp award 1982, Am. Soc. Assn. Execs. award 1987, 88). Trustee Md. Coll. Art and Design, Silver Spring, 1982-92, chmn. bd., 1984-86; trustee U. Richmond, 1974-78, chmn. bd. assocs., 1982-84; bd. visitors U. N.C., Asheville, 1992—. Recipient Total Publs. Program 1st prize Am. Coll. Pub. Rels. Assn., 1968, 71, Mag. Edited by Woman award Va. Press Women, 1970, 71, 72, Time-Life Direct Mail award Am. Alumni Coun., 1973, 74, Frank L. Ashmore award Coun. for Advancement and Support Edn., 1991. Mem. LWV (bd. dirs. 1968, 71), Sigma Delta Chi. Democrat.

SMITH, WATSON, anthropologist; b. Cin., Aug. 21, 1897; s. Samuel Watson and Olive (Perkins) S.; m. Lucy May Cranwell, Sept. 30, 1943; 1 child, Benjamin. Ph.B., Brown U., 1919, LL.D., 1964; LL.B., Harvard U., 1924; student, U. Calif.-Berkeley, 1934-35. Bar: R.I. 1925, Ohio 1931. With Hinckley, Allen, Tillinghast & Phillips, Providence, 1924-30; pvt. practice law Cin., 1930-33; anthrop. and archeol. research, direction and writing Mus. No. Ariz., 1935-38, 48, trustee, 1956-79; staff Rainbow Bridge-Monument Valley Expdn., Ariz., 1935-37; curator Southwestern archeol. Peabody Mus., Harvard U., 1936-93; research assoc. U. Ariz., 1952-93. Contbr. articles profl. jours. Board advisers Arizona-Sonora Desert Mus., Tucson, 1957-60, 74-81, trustee, 1960-74, pres., 1968-70; Trustee Brown U., 1950-64, fellow, 1964-70; past trustee Howard Found., Providence, Sch. Am. Research Santa Fe. Served as maj. USAAF, 1942-45. Fellow Am. Anthrop. Assn. (A.V. Kidder award 1983); mem. Soc. Am. Archeology (50th anniversary award 1985), Ariz. Archaeol. and Hist. Soc. (Byron S. Cummings award 1987), S.W. Parks and Monuments Assn. (Emil W. Haury award 1987), Am. Ethnol. Soc., Sigma Xi. Home: Tucson Ariz. Died July 29, 1993.

SMITS, THEODORE RICHARD, newspaperman; b. Jackson, Mich., Apr. 24, 1905; s. Bastian and Helen (Hull) S.; m. Anna Mary Wells, Sept. 10, 1931 (div. 1952); children—Jean Smits Miles, Helen Smits LeCompte, Gerrit (dec.); m. Pamela Seward, Sept. 22, 1952; 1 son, Richard. Student, Mich. State U., 1922-24. State and telegraph editor Lansing (Mich.) State Jour., 1924-29; city editor Internat. News Service, N.Y.C., 1929-31; bur. mgr. Internat. News Service, Los Angeles, 1931-34; with AP, Los Angeles, 1934-37; chief bur. AP, Salt Lake City, 1937-39, Detroit, 1939-46; gen. sports editor AP, N.Y.C., 1946-69; charge world coverage 1948 Olympics in, St. Moritz, Switzerland and London, 1952 Olympics in, Oslo and Helsinki, Finland, 1956 Olympics in, Cortina, Italy and Melbourne, Austrailia, 1960 Olympics in, Squaw Valley, Calif. and Rome, 1964 Olympics in, Innsbruck, Austria and Tokyo, 1968 Olympics, Mexico City; editorial adviser Leisure Time Products, AMF, Inc., 1969-74; editor The Armchair Quarterback, 1976-78, AP Cleartime, 1984-96; Dir. Hertz Number One award, 1977-84. Author: Soccer For The American Boy; editor: The Year in Sports, 1958. Died Sept. 12, 1996.

SMOKE, RICHARD, political scientist, political psychologist; b. Huntington, Pa., Oct. 21, 1944; s. Kenneth Ludwig and Lillian Duerer (Harbaugh) S. B.A., Harvard Coll., 1965; Ph.D., MIT, 1972. Asst. dean, lectr. Kennedy Sch. Govt. Harvard U., Cambridge, Mass., 1971-73; postdoctoral fellow Inst. Personality Assessment and Research U. Calif.-Berkeley, 1973-74; fellow Ctr. Advanced Study Behavioral Scis., Palo Alto, Calif., 1974-75, 94-95; rsch. assoc., prof. Wright Inst., Berkeley, 1975-81; interim dean Wright Inst., 1981-82; exec. dir., co-founder Peace and Common Security, San Francisco, 1982-84; prof. polit. sci., rsch. dir. Ctr. for Fgn. Policy Devel. Brown U., Providence, 1984—. Author: National Security and the Nuclear Dilemma, 1984, 3d edit., 1992, War: Controlling Escalation, 1977; co-author: (with Alexander L. George) Deterrence in American Foreign Policy: Theory and Practice, 1974 (winner Bancroft prize 1974); (with Willis Harman) Paths to Peace, 1987; editor: (with Andrei Kortunov) Mutual Security, 1991; assoc. editor Polit. Psychology, 1978-81. Mem. Internat. Soc. Polit. Psychology (governing council 1980-82), Am. Polit. Sci. Assn. (Helen Dwight Reid award), Am. Psychol. Assn. Died May 23, 1995.

SMOLENS, BERNARD J., lawyer; b. Phila., May 15, 1916; s. Maxwell and Anna (Rosenman) S.; m. Dorothy M. Hoyt, June 5, 1943 (div. Oct. 1981). A.B., U. Pa., 1938, LL.B., 1941. Bar: Pa. 1946. Ptnr. Schnader, Harrison, Segal & Lewis, Phila., 1960—. Author: Court is in Session, 1953. Served to 1st lt. USAAF, 1941-45, ETO. Fellow Am. Coll. Trial Lawyers; mem. ABA, Pa. Bar Assn., Phila. Bar Assn., Pi Gamma Mu. Avocations: tennis; sailing; skiing. Died May 20, 1997.

SMYTH, BERNARD JOHN, newspaper editor; b. Renovo, Pa., Nov. 16, 1915; s. John Bernard and Alice C. (Russell) S.; m. Eva Mae Stone, Dec. 31, 1936; children: Constance, Joe, Pamela, Lisa. Grad., Dickinson Jr. Coll., 1935. Machinist helper Pa. R.R. Renovo Shops, 1936-39; mgr. Smyth Bros., Renovo, 1939-45; editor, pub., owner Renovo Daily Record, 1946-53; owner, editor, pub. Del. State News, Dover, 1953-70; chmn. bd. Independent Newspapers Inc., 1970-85; pres. Valley Newspapers Inc., Tempe, Ariz., 1971-85. Served with AUS, 1944-45. Mem. Soc. Profl. Journalists, Ariz. Newspaper Assn., Sigma Delta Chi. Died April 29, 1996.

SNIDER, JOHN JOSEPH, lawyer; b. Seminole, Okla., July 25, 1928; s. George Nathan and Katherine (Harris) S.; m. Harriet Jean Edmonds, June 14, 1952; children—John Joseph, Dorothy Susan (Mrs. Mark E. Blohm), William Arnold. A.B., U. Okla., 1950, LL.B., 1955. Bar: Okla. bar 1955. Since practiced in Oklahoma City; atty. Fellers, Snider, Blankenship, Bailey & Tippens, 1964-93, counsel to, 1993—; mem. Okla. adv. council Nat. Legal Services Corp., 1976-77. Pres. Okla. Soc. to Prevent Blindness, 1965-71; bd. dirs. Hosp. Hospitality House, Okla., 1978-86; bd. dirs. Nat. Soc. Prevention Blindness, 1971-75; vice chmn. Oklahoma City Crime Prevention Council, 1976-77. Served to 1st lt. USAF, 1950-53. Fellow Am. Bar Found. (Okla. chmn. 1986-88); mem. Oklahoma City C. of C., Okla. Bar Assn., Okla. County Bar Assn., Am. Judicature Soc., Phi Delta Phi, Phi Kappa Psi. Methodist. Office: First Nat Bldg Oklahoma City OK 73102 Died April 3, 1997.

SNIVELY, WILLIAM DANIEL, JR., physician, emeritus educator; b. Rock Island, Ill., Feb. 9, 1911; s. William Daniel, Sr. and Mary (Wills) S. Student, Augustana Coll., 1930-32; AB, U. Ill., 1934; MB, MD, Northwestern U., 1938; DSc (hon.), U. Evansville, 1989. Intern Cin. Gen. Hosp., 1937-38; resident Children's Meml. Hosp., Chgo., 1938-39; pvt. practice limited to internal medicine and pediatrics Rock Island, 1939-41; med. cons. Mead Johnson & Co., 1947-49, med. dir., 1949-54, v.p., med. dir., 1954-60, exec. v.p., 1960-65, v.p. med. affairs, 1965-69; prof. life scis. U. Evansville, 1970-76, prof. emeritus, 1976—; clin. prof. pediatrics Ind. U., 1973-83; staff St. Mary's Hosp., Evansville.; prof. emeritus Ind. U., 1983—. Author: (with others) Fluid Balance Handbook for Practitioners, 1956, Sea Within, 1960, Pageantry of the English Language, 2d edit., 1983, Profile of a Manager, 1965, Nurse's Fluid Balance Handbook, 1967, 3d edit., 1978, 4th edit., 1983, Satan's Ferryman, 1968, Sea of Life, 1969; textbook Pathophysiology, 1973, Healing Beyond Medicine, 1973; co-author: Fluids and Electrolytes, Pharmacologic Aspects of Nursing, 1986; also articles in med. and history jours.; Editor, contbr.: (with others) Body Fluid Disturbances, 1962. Founder Ohio Wabash Valley Hist. Soc.; bd. trustees Willard Library, Evansville, Ind. Served from lt. (j.g.) to comdr. USNR, 1941-46; flight surgeon in Okinawa operation, air war in Japan, later Japanese occupation resigned comdr. USNR. Recipient Gold medal AMA, 1956; sci. exhibit medal Am. Acad. Gen. Practice, 1965. Fellow Am. Med. Writers Assn. (bd. dirs. 1957-66, pres. 1964), ACP; mem. AMA, Ind. Med. Assn., Vanderburgh County Med. Soc., Ind. Acad., Sigma Xi, Phi Beta Kappa, Phi Kappa Phi. Roman Catholic. Club: Evansville Petroleum.

SODEMAN, WILLIAM ANTHONY, SR., cardiologist; b. Charleroi, Pa., June 13, 1906; s. William Joseph Carl and Anna (Dietz) S.; m. Lucile Marie Kadle, Sept. 23, 1989; children: William Anthony, Thomas Michael. BS, U. Mich., 1928, MD, 1931; ScD, Villanova U., 1959; LHD, Thomas Jefferson U., 1967. Diplomate Am. Bd. Internat. Medicine, Am. Bd. Preventive Medicine. Intern St. Vincent's Hosp., Toledo, 1931-32; instr. medicine Tulane U. Sch. Medicine, New Orleans, 1932-40, 1940-41, prof., head dept. preventive medicine, 1941-46, prof., chmn. dept. tropical medicine, 1946-53; prof., chmn. dept. internal Medicine U. Mo., Columbia, 1953-57; Magee prof., chmn. dept. internal Medicine Jefferson Med. Coll., Phila., 1957-58, dean, prof. medicine, 1958-67; sci. dir. Life Ins. Med. Rsch. Fund, Rosemont, Pa., 1967-70; exec. dir. Commn. on Fgn. Med. Grads., Phila., 1970-73; clin. prof. medicine Med. Coll. Ohio, Toledo, 1974-86; Kellogg scholar Navajo Health Authority, Ariz., 1974-77; cons. U.S. Bur. Hearings and Appeals, Dept. Health; cons. cardiology Sch. Dist. Phila., 1959-63; cons. med. USPHS Hosp. Leprosarium, Carville, La., 1939-53; cons. ICA, State Dept. for Med. Sch. in Ghana, 1961. Author: Patholic Physiology, 1953; contbr. articles on internal medicine to profl. jours. Recipient Disting. Alumni award Med. Ctr. Alumni, U. Mich., Ann Arbor, 1968, Strittmatter award Phila. County Med. Soc., 1975, Disting. Svc. award AMA, 1979. Fellow Am. Coll. Cardiology (pres. 1970-71, disting. fellow 1973); mem. ACP (pres. 1972-73, pres. emeritus 1985), Ccsmos Club (Washington). Republican. Lutheran. Home: Tampa Fla. Died June 10, 1995.

SOLOMON, JOSEPH, lawyer; b. N.Y.C., Mar. 11, 1904; s. Abraham and Rebecca (Rubin) S.; m. Rita Schwartz, Aug. 31, 1929; children: Alan, Diane Solomon Kempler. LL.B., N.Y. Law Sch., 1927, LL.D. with honors, 1976; L.H.D. (hon.), Bar-Ilan U., 1986. Bar: N.Y. 1928. With Leventritt, Cook, Nathan & Lehman, N.Y.C., 1919-22; asst. to mng. clk. Leventritt, Cook, Nathan & Lehman, 1922-28, mem. legal staff, 1928-45; partner firm Lehman, Rohrlich & Solomon (and predecessor firms), 1945-63, sr. partner, 1963-79; sr. ptnr. firm Pincus, Ohrenstein, Bizar, De Alessandro and Solomon, 1980-83; counsel Ohrenstein & Brown, 1983-87, Milman, Stone, Poltarak, Finell & Solomon, N.Y.C., 1987-90, Gallet, Dreyer & Berkey, N.Y.C., 1990—; mem. com. on character and fitness of applicants for admission to bar appellate div. 1st Jud. Dept., 1977—. Author: Jewish Rights in a Jewish Land, 1987; bd. editors N.Y. Law Jour. Mem. Dr. Alfred Meyer Found. Mt. Sinai Hosp., 1951—; trustee Milton Helpern Libr. Legal Medicine Award, 1980; hon. trustee N.Y. Law Sch., 1985; bd. visitors Columbia U. Sch. Law, 1993—. Decorated cavaliere dell' Ordine al Merito (Italy); recipient Horatio Alger Nat. award, 1978, Disting. Alumnus award N.Y. Law Sch., 1986; Joseph Solomon chair in wills, trusts and estates named in his honor Columbia U. Sch. Law, 1974, Joseph Solomon Fund for arts law internship, Joseph Solomon Presdl. Scholars and Fellows Fund; Joseph Solomon chair in law N.Y. Law Sch., 1975, Rita and Joseph Solomon prof. wills, trusts and estates, 1983, Joseph Solomon Pub. Svc. Scholarship and Endowment Fund N.Y. Law Sch., 1990; Joseph Solomon chair in medicine Mt. Sinai Sch. Medicine, 1976. Mem. ABA, New York County Lawyers Assn. (bd. dirs. 1974-78, certification of appreciation), New York County Lawyers Assn. Found., Assn. Bar City N.Y., Lawyers Club (bd. govs. 1975-79), Am. Soc. Italian Legions of Merit, Phi Delta Phi (hon.). DIED 10/08/96. .

SOLOMON, MARGARET CLAIRE BOYLE, English literature educator; b. Enid, Okla., Nov. 27, 1918; d. David H.M. and Ida Candace (Morrison) Boyle; m. Marland R. Solomon (div.); children—Stephen L., Stuart G. Student, San Diego State Coll., 1956-58; B.A., U. Hawaii, 1960; M.A. (Woodrow Wilson nat. fellow), U. Calif., Berkeley, 1961; Ph.D. (univ. grantee), Claremont Grad. Sch., 1966. Various acctg. and office mgmt. positions, 1940-56; instr. English U. Hawaii, Honolulu, 1961-64, asst. prof., 1966-69, assoc. prof., 1969-74, prof., 1974-81, prof. emeritus, 1981 , chmn. grad. studies in English, 1974-75; sr. guest lectr. St. Peter's Coll., Oxford, Eng., 1971. Author: Eternal Geomater, 1969. Juliette M. Atherton Trust grantee, 1960, 64; U. Hawaii Found. grantee, 1967; Am. Council Learned Socs. grantee, 1975. Died Dec. 30, 1996.

SOLOMONS, DAVID, emeritus accounting educator; b. London, Oct. 11, 1912; came to U.S., 1959; s. Louis and Hannah (Isaacs) S.; m. Miriam Kate Goldschmidt, Sept. 14, 1945; children: Jane N., Jonathan P. BCom, London Sch. Econs., 1932; DSc in Econs., U. London, 1966; LHD (hon.), Widener U., 1986; DSc (hon.), Buckingham U., 1987. Audit asst. Robson Rhodes, London, 1936-39, 45-48; lectr., reader London Sch. Econs., 1946-55; prof. acctg. U. Bristol, Eng., 1955-59; prof. acctg. U. Pa., Phila., 1959-74, Arthur Young prof. acctg., 1974—, now Ernst & Young emeritus prof.; mem. Fin. Acctg. Stds. Adv. Coun., 1982-86. Author: Divisional Performance, 1965, Making Accounting Policy, 1986, Guidelins for financial Reporting Standards, 1989; author, editor: Collected Papers (2 vols.), 1984. Capt. U.K. Army, 1939-45, North Africa. Named to Acctg. Hall of Fame, Ohio State U., 1992. Fellow Inst. Chartered Accts. Eng. and Wales (Internat. award 1989); mem. Am. Acctg. Assn. (pres. 1977-78, Outstanding Acctg. Educator award 1980), Swarthmore Rotary Club (auditor 1990). DIED 02/12/95. .

SOLOW, MARTIN, copywriter, creative director; b. N.Y.C., May 19, 1920; s. John and Ruth (Nelson) S.; m. Rita N. Solow, Dec. 12, 1943; children: Ellen, Peter, Michael, Steven. AB, Franklin Marshall Coll., 1942. Asst. editor Nat. CIO News, Washington, 1946-47; freelance editor, 1948-53; assoc. pub. The Nation Mag., N.Y.C., 1953-56; pres. Creative Advtg. Promotion Svc., N.Y.C., 1956-58; exec. v.p. The Wexton Co., N.Y.C., 1958-61; pres., creative dir. Solow/Wexton, N.Y.C., 1961-73; sr. v.p. copy chief Kenyon & Eckhardt, N.Y.C., 1973-74; pres. Martin Solow Creative Svc., N.Y.C., 1975-81, Durfee & Solow Advtg., N.Y.C., 1981-88; chmn. The Solow Agy., N.Y.C., 1988—; assoc. prof. Hofstra U., Hempstead, N.Y.; lectr. New Sch., N.Y.C. Author: Effective Advertising, 1963, Second Love, 1973; numerous short stories and articles; creator The Herring Maven. Sgt. AUS, 1942-46. Recipient numerous awards including Clios and Gold Keys. Mem. One Club (pres.). Democrat. Avocations: writing, photography.

SOLTESZ, JAMES A., marketing executive; b. Cleve., Feb. 24, 1942; s. Elmer S. and Mildred (Zupancic) S.; m. Margaret Anne Schuchaid, July 23, 1945; children: Deborah Loren, Jeffrey James. BS in Econs., Marietta Coll., 1965. Claims adjuster Liberty Mutual Ins. Co., Poughkeepsie, N.Y., 1965-67; sales rep. Standard Register Co., Pitts., 1967-68, Dun & Bradstreet, Boston, 1968-71; owner, CEO Creative Profl. Svcs., Woburn, Mass., 1971-94. Sec. Cohasset (Mass.) Gridiron Club, 1983-88. Mem. Mail Advt. Svcs. Assn. (pres. 1987-89). Roman Catholic. Avocations: tennis, golf, skiing, fishing. Died Jan., 1994.

SOLTI, SIR GEORG, conductor; b. Budapest, Hungary, Oct. 21, 1912; naturalized Brit. citizen, 1972; s. Mor Stern and Theres (Rosenbaum) S.; m. Hedi Oechsli, Oct. 29, 1946; m. Anne Valerie Pitts, Nov. 11, 1967; 2 daus. Ed., Budapest Music High Sch.; MusD (hon.), Leeds U., 1971, Oxford U., 1972, DePaul U., Yale U., 1974, Harvard U., 1979, Furman U., 1983, Sussex U., 1983, London U., 1986, Rochester U., 1987, Bologna (Italy) U., 1988, Roosevelt U., Chgo., 1990, U. Durham, 1995. Music dir. Chgo. Symphony Orch., 1969-91, music dir. laureate, 1991—. Mus. asst. Budapest Opera House, 1930-39, pianist, Switzerland, 1939-45; gen. music dir. Munich (Germany) State Opera, 1946-52, Frankfurt (Germany) City Opera, 1952-60; mus. dir. Royal Opera House Covent Garden, London, 1961-71, Orchestre de Paris, 1972-75; prin. condr. and artistic dir. London Philharm., 1979-83; condr. emeritus London Philharm., 1983-90, music dir. laureate Royal Opera House Covent Garden, London, 1992—; pianist Concours Internat., Geneva, 1942; guest condr. various orchs. including N.Y. Philharm., Vienna Philharm., Berlin Philharm., London Symphony, Bayerischer Rundfunk, Norddeutscher Rundfunk, Salzburg, Edinburgh, Glyndebourne, Ravinia and Bayreuth Festivals, Vienna State, Met. Opera; condr. concert tours with Chgo. Symphony to Europe, 1971, 74, 78, 81, 85, 89, 90, Chgo. Symphony to Japan, 1977, 86, 90, Chgo. Symphony to Australia, 1988; artistic dir. Salzburg Easter Festival and Whitsun Concerts, 1992-93; prin. guest condr. Paris Opera Bicentennial Tour, 1976, rec. artist for London Records. Recipient 31 Grammys, Lifetime Achievement Grammy award, 1996, Gold medal Royal Philharm. Soc., Gt. Britain, 1992, honored by John F. Kennedy Ctr. for Performing Arts, Washington, for lifetime achievement in music. Hon. fellow Royal Coll. Music (London). Died Sept. 5, 1997.

SOMERS, ROBERT VANCE, state senator, lawyer; b. Statesville, N.C., Nov. 21, 1937; s. Walter Vance and Ethel (Owens) S.; m. Denise Lingelbach; children: Jordan, Allison, Garren. BS, E. Tenn. State, 1960; JD, U. N.C., 1963. Pros. atty. Randolph County Ct., Asheboro, N.C., 1964, judge, 1965-66; pros. atty. Rowan County Ct., Salisbury, N.C., 1967-68; senator State of N.C., Salisbury, 1973-74, 77-78, 85-86, 87-88. Rep. candidate for U.S. Senate, N.C., 1968. Mem. N.C. Bar Assn., N.C. Acad. Trial Lawyers. Died July 23, 1997.

SOMERSON, NORMAN LEONARD, medical microbiologist; b. Phila., Dec. 17, 1928; s. David and Gertrude (Marcus) S.; m. Janet Patricia Oren, July 31,

1955; children: Michele, Steven, Lisa, Amy, Mark, Wendy. BS, Marietta (Ohio) Coll., 1950; MS, U. Pa., Phila., 1952, PhD, 1954. Bacteriologist Phila. Gen. Hosp., 1955; asst. prof. Bucknell U., Lewisburg, Pa., 1955-56; rsch. microbiologist Merck & Co., Danville, Pa., 1956-62; commd. officer USPHS, Bethesda, Md., 1962-66; prof. med. microbiology Ohio State U Coll. Medicine, Columbus, 1966—; cons. Ohio Dept. Health, Columbus, 1975—. Contbr. articles to profl. jours.; patentee in field. With USPHS, 1962-66. NIH grantee, 1968-73. Mem. Am. Soc. Microbiology (chmn. div. 1987), AAAS, Soc. Exptl. Biology and Medicine. Democrat.

SOPINKA, JOHN, Canadian supreme court justice; b. Broderick, Sask., Can., Mar. 19, 1933; s. Metro and Nancy (Kikcio) S.; m. Marie Wilson, 1956; children: Randall, Melanie. BA, U. Toronto, 1955, LLB, 1958; JD (hon.), Ukrainian Free U., Munich. Bar: Nfld. 1973, N.B. 1975, Sask. 1984, Alta. 1987, Y.T. 1987, N.W.T.1987. Assoc. Fasken & Calvin, Barristers and Solicitors, Toronto, 1960-66, ptnr., 1966-77; ptnr., head litigation dept. Stikeman, Elliott, Barristers & Solicitors, Toronto, 1977-88; puisine judge Supreme Ct. of Can., Ottawa, Ont., 1988—; apptd. Queen's Counsel, 1975; lectr. civil procedure Osgoode Hall Law Sch., 1974-82, U. Toronto Law Sch., 1976-84; mem. Commns. of Inquiry into Royal Can. Mounted Police relationship with Dept. Nat. Revenue, into Certain Deaths Hosp. for Sick Children and Related Matters, into Facts of Allegations of Conflict of Interest Concerning Hon. Sinclair M. Stevens; chief counsel Commn. on Aviation Safety; counsel Commn. of Inquiry into Cessation of Ops. Can. Comml. Bank and Northland Bank; mem. Task Force on Equality of Opportuniy in Athletics; former bencher Law Soc. Upper Can., frequent lectr. continuing edn. series. Author: (with Lederman and Bryant) The Law of Evidence in Canada, 1992, The Trial of an Action, 1981, (with Gelowitz) The Conduct of an Appeal, 1993; contbr. articles to profl. jours. Bd. dirs. Hockey Can., 1960—; mem. Bd. Edn. Town of Oakville, 1967-69; co-chmn. Acad. Tribunal U. Toronto, 1975-80; mem. Police Complaints Bd. Met. Toronto; mem. bd. fgn. advisors Ukranian Legal Found. Fellow Am. Coll. Trial Lawyers (jud.); mem. Advocate's Soc. (bd. dirs., chmn. subcom. adminstrn. Ont. cts., lectr.), Can. Bar Assn. (chmn. Ont. subsect. comparative law sect. 1967-68, nat. chmn. of sect. 1970, lectr.), County of York Law Assn., Univ. Club, Blvd. Club, Lawyer's Club. Avocations: squash, skiing, tennis, music. Home: 161 Carleton St, Rockcliffe Pk, Ottawa, ON Canada K1M OG6

SORENSEN, THOMAS CHAIKIN, financial executive; b. Lincoln, Nebr., Mar. 31, 1926; s. Christian and Annis (Chaikin) S.; m. Mary Barstler (div.); children: Ann Christine Sorensen Ketter, Alan Thomas, Jens Christian.; m. Pamela A. Berse; children—Matthew Thomas, Adam Lincoln. B.A., U. Nebr., 1947, LHD (hon.), 1996. Radio announcer, 1943-44, newspaper reporter, 1945-46; asst. night editor Nebr. State Jour., 1946-49; dir. news and pub. affairs radio sta. KLMS, Lincoln, 1949-51; instr. U. Nebr. Sch. Journalism, 1948-50; info. officer, press attaché Am. Embassy, Beirut, Lebanon, 1952-56, Baghdad, Iraq, 1956, Cairo, Egypt, 1957-59; program officer for Near East USIA, Washington, 1959-61; dep. dir. for policy USIA, 1961-65; v.p. U. Calif., 1966-68; sr. fellow Adlai Stevenson Inst., 1968-69; v.p. Leasco Corp., 1969-70; ptnr. Sartorius & Co., N.Y.C., 1971-74; sr. v.p., dir. Advest Inc., 1974-80; v.p. Capital Rsch. Internat., 1980-90; cons. Capital Group Inc., 1990-96; lectr. govt. and fgn. affairs U. Va., 1995-96. Author: The Word War, 1968. Named one of 10 Outstanding Young Men in Fed. Service, 1961. Mem. Washington Inst. of Fgn. Affairs, Va. Inst. Polit. Leadership, Phi Beta Kappa, Sigma Delta Chi, Delta Sigma Rho. Died Nov. 5, 1997.

SORIANO, ANDRES, JR., corporate executive; b. Manila, May 3, 1926; s. Andres Soriano y Roxas and Carmen de Montemar y Martinez; m. Maria Natividad Loinaz; children—Andres III, Cristina Herrera, Eduardo J., Carlos T. B.S. in Econs., Wharton Sch. Fin., U. Pa., 1950; Ph.D. in Econs. (hon.), U. San Carlos, Philippines, 1968; Ph.D. in Bus. Mgmt. (hon.), U. Santo Tomas, Philippines, 1980. Chmn., chief exec. officer Soriano Corp., Manila; chmn. bd. Phelps Dodge Philippines Inc., Ramie Textiles Inc., Anscor Capital and Investment Corp., Anscor Fin. Corp.; dir. Anscor Container Corp., Anscor Transport and Terminals Inc.; pres., chmn. bd. Atlas Consolidated Mining and Devel. Corp.; chmn., chief exec. officer Atlas Fertilizer Corp., Indsl. Textiles Mfg. Co. of Philippines, Paper Industries Corp. of Philippines; pres., dir. Nin Bay Mining Co. Inc.; chmn. bd., chief exec. officer Philippine Oil Devel. Co. Inc.; chmn., chief exec. officer San Miguel Corp.; dir. West Palawan Consolidated Nickel Mines Inc.; also fgn. bus. affiliations in Australia, Belgium, Canada, Hong Kong, Indonesia, New Guinea, Spain, and the U.S. Pres., mem. bd. trustees Andres Soriano Cancer Research Found. Inc., Andres Soriano Found. Inc.; bd. trustees Andres Soriano Cancer Research Fund; bd. trustees Andres Soriano Meml. Found. Inc., Cultural Ctr. of Philippines, Philippine Bus. for Social Progress; chmn. bd. Tondo Youth Found. Inc. Served with AC, U.S. Army, 1944-46. Recipient Bus. Exec. of Yr. award Bus. Writers Assn. Philippines, 1964; Condecoration award Spanish Govt., 1971; Condecoration award Pope Paul VI, 1973; Plaque of Appreciation, Bur. Internal Revenue, Philippines, 1981, Archdiocese of Manila, 1981. Roman Catholic. Clubs: Alabang Country, Baguio Country, Calatagan Golf, Canlubang Golf and Country, Casino Españ ol de Manila, Filipino, Las Rocas Tennis and Country, Manila Club, Manila Golf and Country, Manila Polo, Manila Yacht, Nielson Tower and Restaurant, University of Manila, Valley Golf, Valle Verde Country, Vintage Car of the Philippines, Wack Wack Golf and Country, West Side Tennis, Wharton of the Philippines; American (Hong Kong); Mark's (London); Pole de Paris; Mission Hills Country (U.S.); University of Pa. Office: A Soriano Corp, 8776 Paseo de Roxas, Makati Metro Manila Philippines

SOTH, LAUREN KEPHART, journalist, economist; b. Sibley, Iowa, Oct. 2, 1910; s. Michael Ray and Virginia Mabel (Kephart) S.; m. Marcella Shaw Van, June 15, 1934; children: John Michael, Sara Kathryn, Melinda. BS in Journalism, Iowa State U., 1932, MS in Econs., 1938; LHD (hon.), Grinnell Coll., 1990. From instr. to assoc. prof. journalism and econs. Iowa State U., Ames, 1933-46; from editorial writer to editorial page editor Des Moines Register and Des Moines Tribune, 1947-75; columnist Des Moines Register/Extra Newspaper Features syndicate, 1976-94; chmn. agr. com., bd. dirs. Nat. Planning Assn., Washington, 1953-76; bd. dirs. Resources for the Future, Washington, 1956-76; mem. Am. Soc. Newspaper Editors, 1954-75. Author: Farm Trouble, 1957, An Embarrassment of Plenty, 1965, The Farm Policy Game--Play by Play, 1989. Maj. U.S. Army, 1942-46, PTO. Decorated Bronze star medal; recipient Pulitzer prize for editorial writing, 1956. Mem. Nat. Conf. Editorial Writers (pres. 1961), Am. Agrl. Econs. Assn. Episcopalian. Avocations: golf, fishing.

SOUTHWICK, ARTHUR FREDERICK, legal educator; b. Pitts., Nov. 22, 1924. BA, Coll. of Wooster, 1947; MBA, U. Mich., 1950, JD, 1951. Bar: Ohio 1951. Atty. trust dept. Nat. City Bank, Cleve., 1951-56; asst. prof. law U. Mich., Ann Arbor, 1956-61, assoc. prof., 1961-66, prof. bus. law, health svcs. mgmt. and policy, 1966-90, prof. emeritus, 1990—. Author: The Law of Hospital and Health Care Administration, 1988; contbr. articles to legal publs. and med. jours. Elder 1st Presbyterian Ch., Ann Arbor, 1963—. Mem. Am. Acad. Health Care Attys., Acad. of Legal Studies in Bus., Nat. Health Lawyers Assn., Am. Soc. Law, Medicine and Ethics. Died Mar. 3, 1998.

SOUTHWICK, HARRY WEBB, surgeon; b. Grand Rapids, Mich., Nov. 21, 1918; s. G. Howard and Jessie (Webb) S.; m. Lorraine Hinsdale, June 27, 1942; children: Harry Webb Jr., Sandra, Charles Howard, Gay. B.S., Harvard U., 1940, M.D., 1943. Intern Presbyn. Hosp., Chgo., 1944-45, resident in surgery, 1945-46; surg. resident U. Ill. Research and Ednl. Hosps., 1948-50; chmn. dept. gen. surgery Rush-Presbyn.-St. Luke's Med. Center, Chgo., 1970-84; pvt. practice surgery Chgo., 1950-84; clin. assoc. prof. surgery U. Ill. Med. Sch., 1957-63, clin. prof., 1963-71; Helen Shedd Keith prof. surgery Rush Med. Coll., 1971-84; bd. dirs. Howard Young Med. Ctr., sec., 1987-89, vice-chmn., 1989-90, chmn., 1990—; bd. dris. Howard Young Health Care, Eagle River Meml. Hosp. Contbr. articles to med. jours. Pres. Chgo. unit Am. Cancer Soc., 1964-66, pres. Ill. div. 1972-73; bd. dirs. Eagle River Meml. Hosp., 1989—. Lt. (j.g.) M.C., USNR, 1946-48. Fellow ACS; mem. Am. Surg. Assn., Pan Am. Surg. Soc., Minn. Surg. Soc. (hon.), Western Surg. Soc., Cen. Surg. Soc., Chgo. Surg. Soc. (pres. 1979-80), Soc. Head and Neck Surgeons (sec.-treas. 1956-63, pres. 1964-65), Soc. Surgery Alimentary Tract, Soc. Surg. Oncology, Plum Lake Golf Club. Died Jan. 7, 1997.

SOUTTER, LAMAR, physician, educator; b. Boston, Mar. 9, 1909; s. Robert and Helen E. (Whiteside) S.; m. Norah Goldsmith, 1939 (div. 1945); 1 son, Nicholas B.; m. Mary C. Bigelow, 1946; children: Elizabeth P., Sarah B. A.B. cum laude, Harvard U., 1931, M.D., 1935; D.Sc. (hon.), U. Mass., 1975. Diplomate: Am. Bd. Surgery, Am. Bd. Thoracic Surgery. Intern gen. surgery Presbyn. Hosp., N.Y.C., 1936-38; intern gynecology Free Hosp. for Women, 1939-40; chief resident 1st surg. div. Bellevue Hosp., 1938-39; 1st asst. resident surgery Mass. Gen. Hosp., 1940-41, organized Blood Bank, 1942, dir. Blood Bank, 1942-52; prof. surgery Boston U., 1959-64; dean Boston U. (Sch. Medicine), 1959-61; dean, chancellor (Worcester campus); prof. surgery U. Mass., 1964-75; cons. to chancellor State U. and Community Coll. System of Tenn., 1976—; acting dean East Tenn. Coll. Medicine, 1980; chief surgery N.Y.-New Eng. Area VA, 1961-63; area cons. thoracic surgery VA; chmn. blood Mass. Civil Def. Agy., 1950-53. Bd. dirs. Nat. Easter Seal Soc., 1971-78, pres., 1975-77; Trustee Faulkner Hosp., Boston, 1975—; vol. Internat. Exec. Service Corps, 1979. Served to maj. AUS, 1943-45; head surg. team ETO. Decorated Silver Star. Fellow A.C.S.; mem. Am. Assn. Thoracic Surgery, AMA, AAUP, Bostonian Soc., Suffolk Dist. Med. Soc. (pres. 1960-63), Eastern Surg. Soc., New Eng. Surg. Soc., Boston Surg. Soc. (exec. council 1957-61), Halsted Soc., Mass. Med. Soc. (pres. 1970-71), Mass. Easter Seal Soc. (pres. 1970-71, 77-79), Sigma Xi, Alpha Omega Alpha. Clubs: Harvard (N.Y.C.); Somerset, Cohasset Yacht. DIED 10/12/96. .

SOWA, WALTER D., educator, lawyer; b. McKeesport, Pa., Jan. 17, 1907; s. Peter and Anna (Jankowska) S.; A.B., U. Pitts., 1928, Litt.M., 1940; J.D., Duquesne U., 1933; m. Eva Ingersoll Long, Apr. 4, 1942; children—Peter William, Thomas Michael. Tchr. elementary sch., Alliquippa, Pa., 1928-30, high sch., Pa., 1930-42; probation officer Juvenile Ct., Allegheny County, Pa., 1940-41; joined U.S. Army, 1942, advanced through grades to lt. col., 1962; acad. coordinator Baylor U., 1943-44, Tex. A. and M. Coll., 1944-46; judge adv. Korea Base Command, 1946-48; at Pa. State Coll., 1948-50; asst. judge adv. X Corps, Korea, 1950-51; sec. gen. staff X Corps, 1951-52; chief contracting div. Hdqrs. 3d Army, 1952-56; legal assistance adviser, 1956-60; trial observer-lawyer, 1960-62, prof. criminal law Cumberland Law Sch. Howard Coll., Birmingham, Ala., 1963-89; prof. criminal law and evidence Samford U., Birmingham, 1963-77, adj. prof. law, 1977-89 . Decorated Bronze Star. Mem. Am., Ga., Ala. bar assns., Pa. Edn. Assn. Methodist. Mason. Died in 1989. Died Aug. 19, 1989; interred Point Clear Cemetery, Point Clear, AL. Home: Birmingham Ala.

SOWERS, GEORGE FREDERICK, civil engineer; b. Cleve., Sept. 23, 1921; s. George Bloomer and Marie (Tyler) S.; m. Frances Adair Lott, Apr. 29, 1944; children—Carol Adair, Janet, Nancy, George. B.S. in Civil Engring, Case Inst. Tech., 1942; M.S. in Civil Engring, Harvard, 1947. Registered civil engr., Ohio, Ga., N.C., Fla., Tenn., Va., Ala., Ariz.; registered geologist, Ga. Pvt. practice engring. with G. B. Sowers, Cleve., 1939-42; hydraulic engr. TVA, 1942-44, U.S. Navy, 1944-46; co-founder Law Engring. Inc., Atlanta, 1947-66; cons. engr., sr. v.p. Law Cos. Group, Inc.; Regents prof. civil engring. Ga. Inst. Tech., 1966-88, Regents prof. emeritus, 1988-96; lectr. in field; cons. Resources Devel. Center of South East Asia, Roorkee, India, 1959, AID, 1966, Nat. Power Co. Indonesia, Duke Power Co., Ga. Power Co. Author: Soil Laboratory Manual, 1955, Earth and Rockfill Dam Engineering, 1961, Introductory Soil Mechanics and Foundations, 1951, 4th edit., 1979; co-author: Foundation Engineering, 1961; contbr. 140 articles to profl. jours. Recipient, Richard R. Torrens award American Soc. of Civil Engineers, 1995. Fellow Geol. Soc. Am.; mem. ASCE (hon.), Seismol. Soc. Am., Earthquake Engring. Inst., U.S. Nat. Soc. Soil Mechanics, Internat. Soc. Soil Mechanics (v.p.), Ga. Acad. Sci., Nat. Acad. Engring., Sigma Xi, Tau Beta Pi, Beta Theta Pi, Tau Kappa Alpha, Theta Tau. Home: Atlanta Ga. Died Oct. 23, 1996.

SPAETH, CARL F., JR., bank holding company executive. Pres. CB Fin. Corp., Jackson, Mich.

SPALDING, JAMES COLWELL, minister, educator; b. Kansas City, Mo., Nov. 6, 1921; s. John W. and Helen Muriel (Kerr) S.; m. Virginia Esther Burford, Oct. 21, 1945; children: Paul Stuart, Helen Harriet, Peter Marshall, Mary Christine, Ann Louise. BA, U. Ill., 1942; BD, Hartford Theol. Sem., 1945; PhD, Columbia U., 1950. Ordained to ministry Presbyn. Ch. (U.S.A.). Asst. pastor Ft. Peck Larger Parish, Poplar, Mont., 1945-46; chaplain, prof. Mo. Valley Coll., Marshall, 1948-53; pastor 1st Presbyn. Ch., Slater, Mo., 1950-53; assoc. prof. religion Trinity U., San Antonio, 1953-56; prof. U. Iowa, Iowa City, 1956—; moderator Presbytery of Kansas City, Presbyn. Ch. (U.S.A.), 1953, Presbytery of Austin (Tex.), 1956, mem. theology and worship ministry unit, Louiseville, 1985—, mem. com. on theol. edn., Louisville, 1987—. Co-author: Piety, Politics, and Ethics, 1984; contbr. articles to profl. publs. Folger Shakespeare Libr. fellow, 1968. Fellow Swiss-Am. Soc. for Cultural Rels.; mem. Am. Soc. on Ch. History (chmn. program com. 1971), Coun. on Grad. Studies in Religion (sec./treas. 1968-81), Am. Acad. Religion, Presbyn. Hist. Soc., 16th Century Studies Conf. (pres. 1975-76, Leadership award 1977). Democrat. Died Nov. 5, 1996.

SPALDING, VERNON BENJAMIN, consulting civil engineer; b. Ingram, Wis., Jan. 30, 1922; s. Benjamin Bacon and Cassie Gertrude (Baker) S.; m. Ardis Adele Engler, Feb. 27, 1943; children: Patricia, Gail, Craig, Thom, Jill, Kay, Chris. B.C.E., U. Minn., 1949. Office engr. C.E., Ft. Randall, S.D., 1949; design engr. Consoer, Townsend & Assos., Chgo., 1950-51; chief engr. D.L. Briegal Assos., Detroit, 1952-54; part owner, pres. Spalding, DeDecker & Assos., Madison Heights, Mich., 1955—; also dir.; past dir. Design Profls. Ins. Co. Chmn. Southfield (Mich.) Bldg. Code Bd. Appeals, 1977; trustee Eads Gen. Trust. Served with USAAF, 1940-45. Fellow Am. Cons. Engrs. Council (past sr. v.p.); mem. Cons. Engrs. Council Mich. (past pres., dir.), Am. Arbitration (panel arbitrators), ASCE, Am. Water Works Assn. Died Sept. 3, 1997.

SPANGLER, DAISY KIRCHOFF, educator, educational consultant; b. Lancaster, Pa., Jan. 27, 1913; d. Frank Augustus and Lida Flaharty (Forewood) Kirchoff; BS, Millersville State Coll., 1963; MEd, Pa. State U., 1966, EdD, 1972; PhD, Stanton U., 1974; m. Francis R. Cosgrove Spangler, June 3, 1939 (dec.); children: Stephen Russell, Michael Denis. Tchr. rural sch., Providence, Pa., 1933-35, Rapho Twp., Pa., 1935-42, Mastersonville, Pa., 1942-51; elem. sch. prin. Manheim Cen., Pa., 1952-66; tchr., Manheim, Pa., 1967-68; assoc. prof. elem. edn. Millersville U., Pa., 1968-78, prof. emeritus, 1978-96, advisor Kappa Delta Phi, 1968-

88; tchr. Buckview Parachiol Sch., 1989-93; ednl. cons., 1978-96. Author: Teacher Daisy, 1994, Good Morning Teacher Daisy, 1994. Dist. chmn. ARC, 1965-66; mem. Hempfield PTA, 1966-67. Mem. Pa. Edn. Assn., Pa. Elem. Prins. Assn., Assn. Pa. State Coll. and Univ. Profs., Nat. Prin. Assn., Lancaster Prin. Assn. (pres. 1963-64), Pa. Assn. Ret. State Employees, Pa. Assn. State Retirees, Lancaster Area Ret. Pub. Sch. Employees Assn., Am. Ednl. Rsch. Assn., Manheim Tchrs. Assn. (pres. 1964-65), Hempfield Profl. Women, Am. Assn. Ret. Persons (chpt. pres. 1983-85, 89-90), Pi Lambda Theta (nat. com. 1980, advisor Millersville U. 1968-78, named outstanding advisor 1988, 89), Delta Kappa Gamma (pres. 1976-78), Order Eastern Star. Lutheran (pres. Luth. Women 1966-67, 79-81). Died Feb. 6, 1996.

SPARKMAN, ROBERT SATTERFIELD, surgeon, educator; b. Brownwood, Tex., Feb. 18, 1912; s. Ellis Hugh and Ola (Stanley) S.; m. Willie Ford Bassett, Feb. 21, 1942. B.A., Baylor U., 1935, M.D., 1935, LL.D., 1974. Diplomate Am. Bd. Surgery. Intern Cin. Gen. Hosp., 1935-36, resident in surgery, 1938-40; intern Good Samaritan Hosp., Lexington, Ky., 1936-37; resident in pathology Baylor Hosp., Dallas, 1937-38; practice medicine specializing in surgery Dallas, 1946—; chief dept. surgery Baylor U. Med. Center, Dallas, 1969-81; emeritus chief Baylor U. Med. Center, 1982-97; mem. staff Parkland Meml. Hosp., Dallas; clin. prof. surgery U. Tex. Southwestern Med. Sch., Dallas, 1963-97; chief civilian surg. cons. 5th U.S. Army Area, 1950-73. Editor, also prin. author: The Texas Surgical Society—The First Fifty Years, 1965; editor: Essays of a Louisiana Surgeon, 1977, Minutes of the American Surgical Association, 1880-68, 1972, The Southern .Surgical Association; The First 100 Years, 1887-1987, 1989—; mem. editorial bd.: Am. Jour. Surgery; Contbr. articles to profl. jours. Bd. dirs. Friends of Dallas Pub. Libr., 1968—. Served to col. M.C. AUS, 1940-46, PTO. Decorated Bronze Star medal; recipient Disting. Alumnus award Baylor U., 1976, Disting. Alumnus award Coll. Medicine, 1976, Disting. Alumnus award Tex. Beta chpt. Alpha Epsilon Delta, A.C. Greene award Friends of Dallas Pub. Libr., 1993; commd. hon. Ky. col., 1980. Fellow ACS (bd. govs. 1962-70); mem. AMA, Am. Surg. Assn. (2d v.p. 1977-78), So. Surg. Assn. (pres. 1978, hon. mem. 1983), Okla. Surg. Assn. (hon.), Tex. Surg. Soc. (pres. 1965), Dallas Gen. Surgeons Soc. (pres. 1961), Internat. Soc. Surgery, Tex. Med. Assn., Soc. Med. Cons. to Armed Forces, James D. Rives Surg. Soc., Soc. Surgery Alimentary Tract, Internat. Biliary Assn., Philos. Soc. Tex., Parkland Surg. Soc. (hon. mem.), Petroleum Club, Dallas Country Club, Phi Beta Kappa, Alpha Omega Alpha. Died Mar. 22, 1997.

SPARLING, REBECCA HALL, retired materials engineer, energy consultant; b. Memphis, June 7, 1910; d. Robert Meredith and Kate Wallace (Sampson) Hall; m. Edwin Kinmonth Smith, Oct. 30, 1935 (div. 1947); 1 child, Douglas Kinmonth; m. Joseph Sparling, July 10, 1948; B.A., Vanderbilt U., 1930, M.S., 1931. Registered profl. engr., Calif. Design specialist Gen. Dynamics, Pomona, Calif., 1951-68, Northrop Aircraft, Hawthorne, Calif., 1944-51; cons. engr., Detroit, 1936-44; tech. writer William H. Baldwin, N.Y.C., 1934-35; metallurgist Lakeside Malleable, Racine, Wis., 1933-34, Am. Cast Iron Pipe, Birmingham, Ala., 1931-32; energy cons., Laguna Hills, Calif., 1973-85. Author; contbr. articles to profl. jours. Officer, leader Fgn. Policy Assn. of Leisure World, Laguna Hills, 1980-84; bd. dirs. AAUW, 1974-84; mem. Air Pollution Control Bd., San Bernardino County, 1973; cons., intervenor Calif. Energy Commn., 1975-82. Recipient Engring. Merit award Orange County Council Engrs. Soc., 1978; named Outstanding Engr. Inst. Advancement of Engring., 1978, Los Angeles Engrs. Week, 1965. Fellow Soc. Woman Engrs. (Achievement award 1957), Inst. Advancement Engring.; mem. Am. Soc. Metals, Am. Soc. Nondestructive Testing, Delta Delta Delta. Republican. Religious Sci. Ch. Died Nov. 24, 1996.

SPAZIANI, JOANN, national sales manager; b. Monogehela, Pa., Dec. 26, 1952; d. Oscar Antonio and Ellen Rose (Franks) S. Assoc., Pa. State U., 1972. Buyer Gimbels Bros., Pitts., Pa., 1974-78, Emporium Capwell, Oakland, Calif., 1978-81; co-op sales dir. Sta. KNEW/KSAN, Oakland, Calif., 1981-83; acct. exec. Sta. KITS-FM, San Francisco, 1983-86, Sta. KYUU-FM, San Francisco, 1986-87; nat. sales mgr. Sta. KOIT-AM-FM, Calif., 1987-91. Volunteer, Cystic Fibrosis Found, San Francisco, 1987-89, Am. Heart Assn., 1987-89, Gerry Lewis Telethon Multiple Sclerosis, 1987-91, March of Dimes Bid for Bachelors, 1988. Fellow: Northern Calif. Broadcasters Assn., Soc. of TV and Radio. Avocations: water skiing, snow skiing, mountain biking, skating, swimming, tennis. Home: Mill Valley Calif. Died Jan. 11, 1991.

SPEAKER, FRED, lawyer; b. Williamsport, Pa., Apr. 16, 1930; s. Frederick and Helen (Collins) S.; m. Jo Ann Dunn, June 7, 1952; children—Mark, Paul, Peter, Joseph, Andrew, Thomas. Student, U. Pa., 1948-50, 54; LL.B., St. John's U., 1957. Bar: Pa. bar 1957. Counsel to majority leader Pa. Ho. of Reps., Harrisburg, 1967; atty. gen. State of Pa., Harrisburg, 1970-71; partner firm Morgan, Lewis & Bockius, Harrisburg, 1968-70, 71; dir. Office of Legal Services, OEO, Washington, 1971-72; ptnr. Pepper, Hamilton & Scheetz, Harrisburg, 1972-93; pvt. practice Harrisburg, 1993—; mem. lawyers adv. com. U.S. Ct. Appeals (3d crct.), 1986-89; mem. nominating com. Pa. Appellate Ct., 1987—; mem. Fed. Jud. Nominating Commn., Pa., 1986-90; mem. Tuskegee Syphilis ad hoc panel HEW, Washington, 1972. Editor-in-chief: St. John's U. Law Rev, 1954. Mem. Pa. State Bd. Edn., 1974-77; bd. dirs. Gaudenzia, 1972-75, Pa. Legal Svcs. Ctr., 1973-80, Defender Assn. Phila., 1973-76, Diagnostic and Rehab. Ctr., Phila., 1983—, Law Coord. Ctr., Harrisburg, 1988—; mem. Citizens Com. on Basic Edn., 1972-73, Pa. Joint Coun. on Criminal Justice System, 1972-74; treas., bd. dirs. Harristown Devel. Corp., Harrisburg, 1984—. With Counterintelligence Corps, U.S. Army, 1951-54. Mem. Am. Law Inst. Republican. Roman Catholic. DIED 09/10/96. .

SPEARE, ALDEN, JR., sociology educator; b. Hartford, Conn., Dec. 25, 1939; s. Alden and Elizabeth (George) S.; m. Mary Elizabeth Chapmen, May 21, 1966; children: Philip Alden, Laura Elizabeth. B. Engring. Physics, Cornell U., 1963; M.S. in Nuclear Sci., U. Mich., 1964, M.A. in Sociology, 1967, Ph.D. in Sociology, 1969. Field assoc. Population Council, Jakarta, Indonesia, 1974-76; prof. sociology Brown U., Providence, 1969-94, chmn. dept. sociology, 1979-84; vis. researcher Bur. Census, Washington, 1984-85. Author: Residential Mobility Migration, 1975, Urbanization and Development: The Rural-Urban Transition in Taiwan, 1988, Regional and Metropolitan Growth and Decline in the U.S., 1988; contbr. articles to profl. jours. also chpts. to books in field. Mem. Population Assn. Am., Internat. Union Sci. Study Population, Am. Sociol. Assn., Am. Statis. Assn. Unitarian. Avocations: sailing; amateur radio. Home: Providence R.I. Died Jan. 1994.

SPEARS, FRANKLIN SCOTT, supreme court justice; b. San Antonio, Aug. 20, 1931; s. Jacob Franklin and Lois Louise (Harkey) S.; m. Rebecca Nell Errington, Dec. 4, 1977; children: Franklin Scott, Carleton Blaise, John Adrian. Student, So. Meth. U., 1948-50; B.B.A., U. Tex., 1954, J.D., 1954. Bar: Tex. bar 1954, U.S. Dist. Ct. bar for Western Dist. Tex 1956, 5th Circuit Ct. bar 1961, U.S. Supreme Ct. bar 1966. Practiced law San Antonio, 1956-68; mem. Tex. Ho. of Reps., 1958-61, Tex. Senate, 1961-67; dist. judge 57th Jud. Dist. Tex., 1968-78; justice Tex. Supreme Ct., 1979-91; ret. Tex. Supreme Ct., San Antonio, 1991; of counsel Branton & Hall, San Antonio, 1991—. Exec. com. Frontier dist. Boy Scouts Am., 1964-68. Served with U.S. Army, 1955-56. Mem. State Bar Tex., San Antonio Bar Assn., Soc. Preservation and Encouragement Barbershop Quartet Singing in Am., SAR, Masons, Shriners. Democrat. Presbyterian. Died April 10, 1996.

SPECTER, MELVIN HAROLD, lawyer; b. East Chicago, Ind., July 12, 1903; s. Moses and Sadie (Rossuck) S.; A.B., U. Mich., 1925; J.D., U. Chgo., 1928; m. Nellie Rubenstein, Feb. 1, 1927; children—Lois, Michael Joseph. Admitted to Ind. bar, 1928; individual practice law, East Chicago, Ind. 1928—. Bd. dirs. ARC (chpt. chmn. 1940-46), Community Chest Assn., Salvation Army Adv. Bd., pres., 1930-35; bd. dirs. Vis. Nurse Assn., pres., 1943-44; bd. dirs. East Chgo. Boys Club, 1958-65; trustee East Chicago Pub. Library, 1956-80, pres., 1957-67; pres. Anselm Forum, 1957-58; chmn. Brotherhood Week NCCJ, East Chicago, 1958-61; exec. bd. Twin City council Boy Scouts Am.; city chmn. U. Chgo. Alumni Found. Fund, 1951-55. Awarded James Couzen Medal for Inter-collegiate debate, U. Mich., 1924; citation for distinguished pub. service, U. Chgo. Alumni Assn., 1958. Citizenship award Community Chest Assn., 1965. Mem. Am. Ind. (del.), East Chicago (pres. 1942-44) bar assns., Am. Judicature Soc., Comml. Law League Am., Community Concert Assn. (dir. 1950-55), Wig and Robe Frat., Phi Beta Kappa, Delta Sigma Rho. Elk (exalted ruler 1945), K.P., Kiwanian (dir. 1946, 49-51, 52-55, pres. 1961); mem. B'nai B'rith.

SPEER, HUGH W., education educator; b. Olathe, Kans., May 28, 1906; s. Henry W. and Amelia (Shonehair) S.; m. Catherine Edwards (dec. May 1995); children: Marcia Speer Snook, Mary Lynn Shea. AB, Am. U., 1928; MA, George Washington U., 1933; PhD, U. Chgo., 1950. From tchr. to prin. Fredonia (Kans.) H.S., 1928-36; prin. Hays (Kans.) Jr.-Sr. H.S., 1936-42; Am. field dir. ARC, Italy, 1943-45; from dir. veterans advisement to prof. U. Mo., Kansas City, 1945-76; trustee, chmn. Johnson County C.C., Overland Park, Kans., 1967—; trustee Faith Village, Overland Park, 1979-84; columnist Olathe Daily News, 1988-95. Author: Case of the Century, 1968, Funny Things on the Way to the Supreme Court, 1988. Fulbright grantee, 1951, 61, 64. Democrat. Avocations: woodworking, farming. Died June 21, 1996.

SPENCE, JOHN DANIEL, real estate broker, educator; b. Lethbridge, Alberta, Can., May 18, 1915; came to U.S., 1915, naturalized, 1943; s. Benjamin Abner and Clara May (Fullerton) S.; m. Phyllis Saxton Johnson, Feb. 4, 1939; children: Susan Kathleen Spence-Glassberg, John Daniel. A.B., Grinnell (Iowa) Coll., 1938; LL.D. (hon.), Rockford Coll., 1979. With Container Corp. Am., 1938-54, v.p., 1949-54; exec. Lanzit Corrugated Box Co., Chgo., from 1954; v.p. Consol. Paper Co., 1963; dir. devel. Rockford Coll., 1964-65, v.p., 1965-77, acting pres., 1977-79, cons., 1979-80; bus. and edn. cons., 1980-85; bus. and ednl. cons., 1980—. Pres. Woodcrest Assn., Rockford, 1974-78; adv. com. Forest Preserve Dist. Winnebago County, 1974-91; chmn. adv. coun. Severson Dells Forest Preserve, 1976-78; bd. dirs. John Howard Assn., 1974-76; trustee Keith Country Day Sch., 1971-81, Children's Home Rockford, 1973-76, Pecatonica Prairie Path, 1975-85, Rockford Art Assn., 1980-83, Ctr. for Sight and Hearing Impaired, 1986-87; trustee Highview Retirement Home, 1983-90, pres., 1986-88; community adv. bd. WNIU-FM, No. Ill. U., 1984-90. Recipient Karl L. Williams award Rockford Coll. Alumni Assn., 1980, Service Above Self award Rockford Rotary Club, 1980. Mem. Rockford C. of C. (bd. dirs. 1966-71, v.p.), Lions. Home and Office: PO Box 729 West Tisbury MA 02575-0729 Died Jan. 8, 1997.

SPENCER, HARRY CHADWICK, minister; b. Chgo., Apr. 10, 1905; s. John Carroll and Jessie Grace (Chadwick) S.; m. Mary Louise Wakefield, May 26, 1935; children: Mary Grace Spencer Lyman, Ralph Wakefield. B.A., Willamette U., 1925, D.D. (hon.), 1953; M.Div., Garrett Bibl. Inst., 1929; M.A., Harvard U., 1932. Ordained to ministry Meth. Ch., 1931; pastor Washington Heights Ch., Chgo., 1931-33, Portage Park Ch., Chgo., 1933-35; rec. sec. bd. missions Meth. Ch., 1935-40, asst. exec. sec., 1940-45, sec. dept. visual edn., 1945-52, exec. sec. radio and film commn., 1952-56, gen. sec. TV, radio and film commn., 1956-68, asso. gen. sec. program council div. TV, radio and film communication, 1968-72; asso. exec. sec. joint commn. on communications United Meth. Ch., 1972, ret., 1973; mem. exec. com. Nat. Council Chs. Broadcasting and Film Commn., 1952-73, chmn., 1960-63; mem. exec. com. Nat. Council Chs., 1960-63, mem. gen. bd., 1967-72, v.p. Cen. div. communications, 1969-72; chmn. constituting assembly World Assn. for Christian Broadcasting, 1963; mem. constituting assembly World Assn. Christian Communication, 1968, dir. assembly, 1975; mem. adminstrv. com. Ravemco, 1950-70, Intermedia, 1970-72; vis. prof. Garrett Evang. Theol. Sem., 1975; lectr. in field. Exec. producer: TV series Learning to Live; radio series Night Call; motion pictures John Wesley, etc.; Contbr. articles on films to ch. publs. Trustee Scarritt Coll., 1967-74, emeritus, 1974-88; bd. dirs. Outlook Nashville, 1977-83, sec., 1980; bd. dirs. Nashville chpt. UN Assn., 1976-83. Recipient award excellence art communications Claremont Sch. Theology, 1973, The Pioneer in Religious Communications award World assn. for Christian Communication, 1989; inducted into United Meth. Communicators Hall of Fame, 1983. Mem. United Meth. Assn. Communicators, World Assn. Christian Communications (award). Clubs: Kiwanis (Woodmont); Harvard (Nashville). Died Dec. 18, 1996.

SPENCER, ROBERT WILFORD, education educator, administrator; b. Logan, Utah, May 19, 1938; s. Farrell J. and Bertha (Farnsworth) S.; m. Alice Marie Anderson; children: Catherine, Douglas, Steven, David, Deborah. BS, Utah State U., 1963, MS, 1965; EdD, Brigham Young U., 1971. Cert. tchr., counselor, Utah. Tchr., counselor Tooele (Utah) Sch. Dist., 1963-64, dir. pupil personnel, 1964-67; admissions counselor, then dir. admissions, asst. dean Brigham Young U., Provo, Utah, 1967-70, assoc. prof. ednl. psychology, chair counselor edn., 1970-71, dean admissions and records, 1971-90, prof. instructional sci., 1990—. With U.S. Army, 1956-57, 61-62, Berlin. Mem. Pacific Assn. of Admissions Officers and Collegiate Registrars (past. officer, pres.). Republican. Mem. LDS Ch. Avocations: boating, all-terrain-vehicle exploration, snowmobiles, poetry, music. Died May 5, 1996.

SPENCER, SAMUEL, lawyer; b. Washington, Dec. 8, 1910; s. Henry Benning and Katharine (Price) S.; children from previous marriage: Henry B., Janet Spencer Dougherty, Richard A.; m. June Byrne, May 29, 1982. Student, Milton (Mass.) Acad., 1924-29; A.B. magna cum laude, Harvard U., 1932, LL.B., 1935. Bar: N.Y. 1937, D.C 1938, U.S. Supreme Ct 1950. Assoc. Shearman & Sterling, N.Y.C., 1935-37, Covington, Burling, Rublee, Acheson & Shorb, Washington, 1937-40, 45-47; ptnr. Spencer, Graham & Holderman, 1947—; pres. bd. commrs., D.C., 1953-56; pres., chmn. bd. Tenn. R.R. Co., 1956-73. Bd. dirs. Nat. Symphony Orch., 1949-51, Garfield Hosp., 1947-53, 56-62; bd. dirs. Children's Hosp., 1948-53, sec., 1951-53; trustee Potomac Sch., 1947-53; pres. Washington Hosp. Ctr., 1958-60, bd. dirs., 1958-65; mem. Washington Nat. Monument Soc., 1958-91. Served to comdr. USNR, 1940-45. Decorated Bronze Star with combat V. Mem. ABA, Bar Assn. D.C., Am. Cancer Soc. (trustee D.C. chpt. 1951-53), AIA (hon.), Washington Inst. Fgn. Affairs (bd. dirs. 1961-89, sec. 1961-81), Jud. Council D.C. Circuit (com. on adminstrn. of justice 1966-70), Soc. of Cincinnati, Phi Beta Kappa. Episcopalian (sr. warden). Clubs: Metropolitan of Washington (bd. govs. 1949-53, 56-61, pres. 1959-60); Chevy Chase (Md.). DIED 03/23/97. .

SPIEGEL, FRANCIS HERMAN, JR., pharmaceutical company executive; b. Bethlehem, Pa., Apr. 25, 1935; s. Francis H. and Elizabeth (Redding) S.; m. Nancy Starner; children: Todd, Tadd, Thomas. B.A. in Acctg., Lehigh U., 1957. C.P.A., Pa. Account analyst Merck & Co., Inc., Rahway, N.J., 1966, mgr. internal auditing, 1967-70, dir. acctg., 1970-72, asst. controller, 1972-76, controller, 1976-79, treas., 1979-81, v.p. corp. planning, 1981-82; v.p. planning and devel. Merck & Co., Inc., 1983-84, v.p. fin., 1985-87, sr. v.p., 1987—, exec. v.p., 1992—; bd. dirs. Arkwright Ins. Co. Chmn. vis. com. Lehigh U., Bethlehem, Pa., 1980-83, now trustee; trustee Fin. Execs. Rsch. Found. Served to capt. USMC, 1958-61. Mem. AICPA, Fin. Execs. Inst., Conf. Bd. Coun. Fin. Execs.

SPIEGEL, HENRY WILLIAM, economics educator; b. Berlin, Oct. 13, 1911; came to U.S., 1936; naturalized, 1943; s. Isaac and Augusta (Fuld) S.; m. Cecile E. Wassermann, May 2, 1947; children: Robert, Richard. JUD, U. Berlin, 1933; PhD, U. Wis., 1939. Asst. prof. econs. Duquesne U., Pitts., 1939-42; mem. faculty Cath. U. Am., Washington, 1943-95; prof. econs. Cath. U. Am., 1950-77, prof. emeritus, 1977-95; part-time/summer lectr. Mich. State U., East Lansing, 1942, U. Wis., 1947, Johns Hopkins U., Balt., 1950, Howard U., Washington, 1954-63, Dumbarton Coll., 1955-59, Trinity Coll., 1956-62, Indsl. Coll. Armed Forces, 1957, 59, 61, U. Idaho, 1958, U. Md. 1959, 62-68, U. Wash. 1961, U. Calif., Santa Barbara and Berkeley, 1962, U. Va., 1965; economist U.S. Dept. State, 1945; cons. Pres.'s Materials Policy Commn., 1951, Pub. Adv. Bd. on Mut. Security, 1952, Com. on Pub. Works, U.S. Ho. of Reps, 1962; advisor Villanova U., Havana, 1954; mem. nat. panel Am. Arbitration Assn. 1959-95; dist. judge Fed. Republic of Germany Restitution. Assoc. editor Internat. Social Sci. Rev., 1984-95; bd. editors Handbook of Latin Am. Studies, 1946-60. Social Sci., 1953-84, History of Polit. Economy, 1974-85; author: Land Tenure Policies at Home and Abroad, 1941, The Economics of Total War, 1942, The Brazilian Economy, 1949, Current Economic Problems, 1949, 3d edit. 1961, Introduction to Economics, 1951, Development of Economic Thought, 1952, Japanes translation, 1953, Du Pont on Economic Curves, 1955, Rise of American Economic Thought, 1960, Growth of Economic Thought, 1971, Spanish translation, 1973, 3d edit., 1991; co-editor: Contemporary Economists in Perspective, 1984; contbr. The New Palgrave, 1987. With U.S. Army, 1942-45. Guggenheim fellow, 1945-46. Mem. AAUP, Am. Econ. Assn., Royal Econ. Soc., Am. Polit. Sci. Assn., History of Econs. Soc. (exec. com. 1974-77), Order of Artus, Pi Gamma Mu (chancellor Atlantic region 1955-65), Phi Beta Kappa. Home: Washington D.C. Died July 24, 1995; interred Maryland Veterans Cemetery, Cheltenham, MD.

SPIKES, JOHN JEFFERSON, SR., forensic toxicologist, pharmacologist; b. Grand Prairie, Tex., Jan. 30, 1929; s. George W. and Madge (Ballard) S.; m. Marilyn Ruth Tomlimson, Apr. 17, 1949; children: Juli Spikes Jensen, John J. Jr., James M., Jay S., Jerry D. BS, Union Coll., 1951; MS, George Washington U., 1959; PhD, U. Tex., Galveston, 1971. Diplomate Am. Bd. Forensic Toxicologists. Instr. U. Tex. Med. Br., Galveston, 1971-72; toxicologist Pathology Labs. Houston, 1972-73, Biochemical Procedures, North Hollywood, Calif., 1973-75; chief toxicologist Ill. Dept. Pub. Health, Chgo., 1975-85; forensic toxicologist Nat. Med. Svcs., Willow Grove, Pa., 1985—; mem. drug abuse adv. com. FDA, Washington, 1984-87; cons. U.S. Postal Svc., 1982-84, Chgo. Transit Authority, 1978-86; presenter in field. Co-author: (chpt.) Progress in Clinical Pathology, vol. III, 1981; contbr. articles to profl. jours. Cpl. U.S. Army Med. Corp 1952-54. Fellow Am. Acad. Forensic Scientists; mem. Soc. Forensic Toxicologists, Assn. Clin. Scientists, Sigma Xi. Died Jan. 4, 1997.

SPILHAUS, ATHELSTAN, meteorologist, oceanographer; b. Cape Town, Union of South Africa, Nov. 25, 1911; came to U.S., 1931, naturalized, 1946; s. Karl Antonio and Nellie (Muir) S.; m. Kathleen Fitzgerald, 1978; children by previous marriage: Athelstan F., Mary Muir, Eleanor (dec.), Margaret Ann, Karl Henry. B.Sc., U. Cape Town, 1931, D.Sc., 1948; M.S., Mass. Inst. Tech., 1933; D.Sc., Coe Coll., 1961, Hahnemann Med. Coll., 1968, U. R.I., 1968, Phila. Coll. Pharmacy and Sci., 1969, Hamilton Coll., 1970, U. S.E. Mass., 1970, U. Durham, Eng., 1970, U. S.C., 1971, Southwestern U. at Memphis, 1972; LL.D., Nova U., 1970, U. Md., 1978. Research asst. Mass. Inst. Tech., 1934-35; asst. dir. tech. services Union of South Africa Def. Forces, Pretoria, 1935-36; research asst. Woods Hole (Mass.) Oceanographic Instn., and Cambridge, Mass., 1936-37; investigator in phys. oceanography Woods Hole (Mass.) Oceanographic Instn., and Cambridge, 1938, phys. oceanographer, 1940—; asst. prof. meteorology N.Y. U., 1937, asso. prof., 1937-42, prof., 1942, dir. research, 1946; meteorol. adviser to Union S. Africa Govt., 1947; dean Inst. Tech. U. Minn., 1949-66, prof. physics, 1966-67; pres. Franklin Inst., Phila., 1967-69, Aqua Internat. Inc., 1969-70; fellow Woodrow Wilson Internat. Center for Scholars, 1971-74; with NOAA, Dept Commerce, Washington, 1974-80; disting. scholar Annenberg Center, U. So. Calif., 1981; vis. scholar Inst. Marine and Coastal Studies, U. So. Calif., 1982-83; pres. Pan Geo, Inc., 1984—; Dir. Sci. Service, Inc., Am. Dynamics Corp., Donaldson Co., Minn.; trustee Aerospace Corp., Los Angeles; U.S. commr. Seattle World's Fair, 1961-62; chmn. nat. fisheries center and aquariam adv. bd. U.S. Dept. Interior; mem. adv. coms. for armed forces; mem. nat. com. IGY; mem com. on oceanography, com. on polar research Nat. Acad. Scis.; mem. exec. bd. UNESCO, 1955-58; mem. sci. adv. com. Am. Newspapers and Pubs. Assn.; sr. summer fellow Woods Hole Oceanographic Instn., 1990. Contbr.: numerous articles to profl. jours. including Jour. of Meterology; author: numerous articles to profl. jours. including The Ocean Laboratory. Trustee Woods Hole Oceanographic Instn., St. Paul Inst.; mem. Nat. Sci. Bd., 1966-72; vice chmn. Invest-in-America. Served from capt. to lt. col. USAAF, 1943-46. Decorated Legion of Merit, Exception Civilian Service medal USAF; recipient Patriotic Civilian Service award Dept. Army. Fellow AAAS (pres. 1970, chmn. 1971), Am. Geog. Soc., Geog. Soc., Royal Meteorol. Soc., Am. Geophys. Union; mem. AIAA, NAS (mem. com. pollution), Am. Philos. Soc. Episcopalian. Clubs: Cosmos (Washington); Bohemian (San Francisco). Inventor of Bathythermograph, 1938. Died Apr. 1998.

SPIRO, WALTER ANSELM, advertising and public relations agency executive; b. Berlin, Germany, Aug. 10, 1923; came to U.S., 1940, naturalized, 1945; s. Harry L. and Kate (Loewenstein) S.; children: Karen Leslie, Pamela Anne, Paul David, Amy Eloise. Student, Athelton Coll., affiliate Cambridge U., Folkestone, Eng., 1938-40. Display dir. Allied Stores, N.Y.C., 1947-51; advt. dir. Gimbel Bros., Phila., 1951-58; exec. v.p. Lavenson Bur. Advt., Phila., 1958-64; chmn. Spiro & Assocs. (now Earle Palmer Brown & Spiro), Phila., 1964—; now CEO Earle Palmer Brown & Spiro, Philadelphia, PA. Bd. dirs. Pa. Ballet, 1982—; bd. dirs. Pa. Hosp., 1984—; trustee Phila. United Fund, 1973—, Phila. Orch. Assn., 1981—, Phila. Mus. Art, 1981—; bd. dirs., mem. exec. com. Urban Affairs Partnership; mem. founding group Global InterDependence Center, 1978—; mem. leadership com. Bus. Leaders Organized for Catholic Schs., 1981—; founding mem. Bus. Execs. for Nuclear Arms Control, 1983—; bd. dirs. Greater Phila. First Corp., 1983—, WHYY-TV & FM radio broadcasting stas. Mem. World Affairs Council Phila. (dir. 1971—, vice-chmn. 1974-78), Am. Assn. Advt. Agys. (com. of bd. agy. mgmt.). Clubs: Downtown, Urban, Vesper, Peale, Sunday Breakfast. Died Sept. 16, 1997.

SPITZER, LYMAN, JR., astronomer; b. Toledo, June 26, 1914; s. Lyman and Blanche C. (Brumback) S.; m. Doreen D. Canaday, June 29, 1940; children: Nicholas, Dionis, Lutetia, Lydia. AB, Yale U., 1935, DSc, 1958; Henry Fellow, Cambridge (Eng.) U., 1935-36; PhD, Princeton U., 1938; Nat. Rsch. fellow, Harvard U., 1938-39; DSc, Case Inst. Tech., 1961, Harvard U., 1975, Princeton U., 1984; LLD, Toledo U., 1963. Instr. physics and astronomy Yale U., 1939-42; scientist Spl. Studies Group, Columbia U. Div. War Research, 1942-44; dir. Sonar Analysis Group, 1944-46; assoc. prof. astrophysics Yale U., 1946-47; prof. astronomy, chmn. dept. and dir. obs. Princeton U., 1947-79, Charles A. Young prof. astronomy, 1952-82, chmn. rsch. bd., 1967-72, dir. project Matterhorn, 1953-61, chmn. exec. com. Plasma Physics Lab., 1961-66, sr. rsch. astronomer, 1982-97; trustee Woods Hole Oceanographic Inst., 1946-51; mem. Com. on Undersea Warfare, NRC, 1948-51; mem. Yale U. Council, 1948-51; chmn. Scientists Com. on Loyalty Problems, 1948-51; chmn. Space Telescope Inst. Council, Assoc. Univs. Rsch. Astronomy, 1981-90. Author: monograph Physics of Fully Ionized Gases, 1956, rev., 1962; Diffuse Matter in Space, 1968, Physical Processes in the Interstellar Medium, 1978, Searching Between The Stars, 1982, Dynamical Evolution of Globular Clusters, 1987, Dreams, Stars and Electrons-Selected Writings of L. Spitzer, 1997; editor: Physics of Sound in the Sea, 1946; contbr. articles to Astrophysical Jour., Physics of Fluids, Phys. Rev., others. Recipient Rittenhouse medal, 1957, Exceptional Sci. Achievement medal NASA, 1972, Bruce Gold medal, 1973, Henry Draper Gold medal, 1974, James C. Maxwell prize, 1975, Karl Schwarzschild medal, 1975, Disting. Pub. Svc. medal NASA, 1976, Gold medal Royal Astron. Soc., 1978, Nat. medal sci., 1980, Janssen medal, 1980, Franklin medal Franklin Inst., 1980, Crafoord prize Royal Swedish Acad. Scis., 1985, Madison medal Princeton U., 1989, Franklin medal Am. Philos. Soc., 1991. Mem. NAS, Am. Acad. Arts and Scis., Am. Philos. Soc., Am. Astron. Soc. (past pres.), Royal Soc. (London, fgn.), Royal Astron. Soc. (assoc.), Royal Soc. Scis. Liège (fgn. corr.), Am. Phys. Soc., Astron. Soc. Pacific, Am. Alpine Club, Alpine Club (London). Unitarian. Research on interstellar matter, space astronomy, stellar dynamics, broadening of spectral lines, conductivity of ionized gases, controlled release of thermonuclear energy. Home: Princeton N.J. Died Mar. 31, 1997; buried Princeton Cemetery.

SPOCK, BENJAMIN MCLANE, physician, educator; b. New Haven, Conn., May 2, 1903; s. Benjamin Ives and Mildred Louise (Stoughton) S.; m. Jane Davenport Cheney, June 25, 1927 (div. 1976); children: Michael, John Cheney; m. Mary Morgan Councille, Oct. 24, 1976. B.A., Yale U., 1925, student Med. Sch., 1925-27; M.D., Columbia U., 1929. Intern in medicine Presbyn. Hosp., N.Y.C., 1929-31; in pediatrics N.Y. Nursery and Child's Hosp., 1931-32; in psychiatry N.Y. Hosp., 1932-33; practice pediatrics N.Y.C., 1933-44, 46-47; instr. pediatrics Cornell Med. Coll., 1933-47; asst. attending pediatrician N.Y. Hosp., 1933-47; cons. in pediatric psychiatry N.Y. City Health Dept., 1942-47; cons. psychiatry Mayo Clinic and Rochester Child Health Project, Rochester, Minn.; asso. prof. psychiatry Mayo Found., U. Minn., 1947-51; prof. child devel. U. Pitts., 1951-55, Western Res. U., 1955-67. Author: Baby and Child Care, 1946, (with J. Reinhart and W. Miller) A Baby's First Year, 1954, (with M. Lowenberg) Feeding Your Baby and Child, 1955, Dr. Spock Talks with Mothers, 1961, Problems of Parents, 1962, (with M. Lerrigo) Caring for Your Disabled Child, 1965, (with Mitchell Zimmerman) Dr. Spock on Vietnam, 1968, Decent and Indecent, 1970, A Teenagers Guide to Life and Love, 1970, Raising Children in a Difficult Time, 1974, Spock on Parenting, 1988, (with Mary Morgan) Spock on Spock: A Memoir of Growing Up With the Century, 1989, A Better World for Our Children, 1994. Presdl. candidate Peoples Party, 1972, advocator Nat. Com. for a Sane Nuclear Policy (SANE), co-chmn., 1962 . Served to lt. comdr. M.C., USNR, 1944-46. Home: PO Box 1268 Camden ME 04843-1268

SPOHN, BEATRICE EVELYN, education educator; b. Backus, Minn., Sept. 4, 1907; d. George Lawrence and Carolyn Jean (Hart) S. BS, U. Nebr., 1973, MEd, 1980. Profl. life Cert. in Teaching, Nebr. Tchr. Plattsmouth, Nebr., 1927-28, Cook, Nebr., 1929-32, Weeping Water, Nebr., 1932-50, Sutton, Nebr., 1950-68; tchr. Campo Coll., 1968-72. Trustee Cedars Home for Children, Lincoln, Nebr., 1978; mem. Burnett Soc. of U. Nebr. Found., Lincoln, 1990. Mem. nat., state and local edn. orgns., AAUW, Pi Lambda Theta, Phi Delta Gamma (historian 1978-88). Republican. Mem. United Ch. Christ. Avocations: travel. reading. Home: Lincoln Nebr. Died Mar. 27, 1995.

SPONG, WILLIAM BELSER, JR., lawyer, educator; b. Portsmouth, Va., Sept. 29, 1920; s. William Belser and Emily (Nichols) S.; m. Virginia Wise Galliford, June 3, 1950 (dec. May 1993); children: Martha Kingman, Thomas Nichols. Student, Hampden-Sydney Coll., 1937-40, LLD (hon.), 1968; LLB, U. Va., 1947; post-grad., U. Edinburgh, Scotland, 1947-48; LLD (hon.), Roanoke Coll., Washington and Lee U. and Coll. William and Mary. Bar: Va. 1947. Lectr. law Coll. William and Mary, 1948-49, 75-76; practice law Portsmouth, 1949-76; mem. Va. Ho. Dels., 1954-55, Va. Senate, 1956-66, U.S. Senate, 1966-73; gen. counsel Comm. for Conduct Fgn. Policy, 1973-75; dean Marshall-Wythe Sch. Law Coll. William and Mary, 1976-85, Woodbridge prof. emeritus, 1985—; pres. Old Dominion U., 1989-90; spl. master Va. Electric & Power Co., et al vs. Westinghouse Corp., 1977-80, re Dalkon Shield litigation, 1983-85, Smith vs. Morton-Thiokol, 1988; ptnr. Cooper, Spong & Davis, Portsmouth, 1990—; guest scholar Woodrow Wilson Center Smithsonian Instn.; vis. scholar U. Va. Sch. Law, 1973; adj. prof. law U. Richmond, 1974-75, Salzburg Seminar, 1979; sr. visitor Inst. Advanced Legal Studies, U. London, 1985; vis. prof. Washington and Lee U., 1986; Ewald Disting. vis. prof. U. Va. Sch. Law, 1987; Menzies lectr. Australian Nat. U., 1990. Chmn. Va. Commn. Pub. Edn., 1958-62, Gov.'s Commn. on Va.'s Future, 1982-84; mem. Va. Coun. Higher Edn., 1985-89; trustee Hampden-Sydney Coll., 1951-72, Va. Hist. Soc., 1990-96; mem. bd. visitors Air Force Acad., 1970, Naval Acad., 1971, Coll. William and Mary, 1992-96. With USAAF, 1942-45. Mem. Va. Bar Assn. (pres. 1976), Portsmouth Bar Assn. (past pres.), Order of Coif, Phi Beta Kappa, Phi Alpha Delta, Omicron Delta Kappa, Pi Kappa Alpha. Home: 351 Middle St Portsmouth VA 23704-2826 Died Oct. 8, 1997.

SPRAGUE, NORMAN FREDERICK, JR., surgeon, educator; b. L.A., June 12, 1914; s. Norman F. and Frances E. (Ludeman) S.; m. Caryll E. Mudd, Dec. 27, 1941 (dec. Apr. 1978); children: Caryll (Mrs. Mingst), Norman Frederick III, Cynthia Sprague Connolly, Elizabeth (Mrs. Day); m. Erlenne Estes, Dec. 31, 1981. AB, U. Calif., 1933; MD, Harvard U., 1937. Intern Bellevue Hosp., N.Y.C., 1937, house surgeon, 1938-39; pvt. med. practice L. A., 1946—; mem. hon. staff Hosp. of Good Samaritan, L. A.; mem. staff St. Vincent Med. Ctr., L. A.; asst. clin. prof. surgery UCLA, 1951—; dir. emeritus Western Fed. Savs. & Loan Assn.; chmn. bd. dirs. Western Pioneer Co., 1961-63, Pioneer Savs. & Loan Assn., 1959-63; dir. Arden-Mayfair, Inc., 1966-69; also chmn. exec. com.; dir., mem. exec. com. Cyprus Mines Corp., 1959-79; trustee Mesabi Trust, 1964-76. Chmn. exec. com., v.p. Harvard Sch., 1954-65; mem. Cmty. Redevel. Agy. City of L.A., 1966-69, vice-chmn., 1967-69; mem. Calif. Regional Med. Programs Area IV Coun., 1970-75; bd. dirs., v.p. Calif. Inst. Cancer Rsch., 1974-80, pres., 1980-82; bd. dirs. Cancer Assoc., 1975-80; trustee UCLA Found., Marlborough Sch., 1981-90, Mildred E. and Harvey S. Mudd Found., Hollywood Bowl Assn., 1962-66; hon. trustee Calif. Mus. Found.; mem. exec. com., trustee Youth Tennis Found., 1960-70; trustee, pres., mem. exec. com. S.W. Mus.; founding trustee Harvey Mudd Coll.; chmn. bd. trustees Caryll and Norman Sprague Found., 1957—, Harvard Sch.; mem. bd. visitors UCLA Med. Sch.; nat. bd. dirs. Retonitis Pigmentosa Internat.; mem. adv. com. Univs. Space Rsch. Assn., Divsn. Space Biomedicine, 1982-94. Maj. M.C. AUS, 1941-46. Decorated Bronze Star; recipient Bishop's award of Merit Episc. Diocese L.A., 1966, Highest Merit award So. Calif. Pub. Health Assn., 1968. Mem. AMA, SAR, Calif. Med. Assn., L.A. County Med. Assn., Univ. Space Rsch. Assn. (mem. adv. com. divsn. space biomedicine 1982-94), Am. Cattlemen's Assn., Symposium Soc., Tennis Patrons Assn. (dir. 1960-70), Calif. Club,

Harvard Club, L.A. Country Club, Delta Kappa Epsilon. Died April 5, 1997.

SPRINGER, AXEL, publisher; b. Hamburg-Altona, May 2, 1912; s. Hinrich and Ottilie Springer; ed. Realgymnasium, Hamburg-Altona; L.H.D. (hon.), Temple U., Phila.; Dr.Phil. (hon.) Bar Ilan U., Tel Aviv; div.; 2 sons, 1 dau. Apprentice printing and pub. with provinical newspapers; journalistic tng. with news agy. WTB and father's paper Altonaer Nachrichten (discontinued by Nazi decree); founded own pub. co. after 1945; now sole propr. Axel Springer Pub. Group, consisting of Axel Springer Verlag AG (publishing dailies WELT, BILD, Hamburger ABENDBLATT, Berliner Morgenpost, BZ, Sunday papers BILD am. SONNTAG, WELT am SONNTAG, weekly Bild der Frau, radio-TV program mags. HÖRZU and FUNK-UHR, also Ullstein and Propyläen book pub. branches and Ullstein AV (audio-visual prodn. and distbn.). Decorated Grand Cross Order Merit German Fed. Republic; Bavarian Order of Merit. Hon. fellow Weizmann Inst., Israel. Author: Von Berlin aus gesehen, 1971; Aus Sorge um Deutschland, 1979; also numerous articles, speeches.

SPRINGER, EDWIN KENT, mechanical engineer; b. Bellingham, Wash., Sept. 17, 1912; s. George Edwin and Abbie (Kent) S.; m. Frances Stewart, Oct. 19, 1940; children: Ann Bogue, Robert Edwin, Bruce Kent. BS in Mech. Engring., U. So. Calif., 1936; MS in Mech. Engring., U. Wis., 1945. Registered profl. engr., Calif., Wis. Draftsman Fluid Packed Pump Co., Los Nietos, Calif., 1935-36, plant engr., 1936-39; mech. engr. Preco, L.A., 1939-41, Consol. Western Steel Co., L.A., 1941; instr., asst. prof. U. Wis., Madison, 1941-46; successively asst. prof. mech. engring., assoc. prof., and prof. U. So. Calif., Los Angeles, 1946-77, dir. Fedn. for Cross-Connection Control and Hydraulic Research, 1965-85; emeritus dir. Fedn. for Cross-Connection Control and Hydraulic Research, 1985-95; bd. dirs. Western States Symposium, Cypress, Calif., 1980-95; assoc. bd. mem. So. Calif. Water Utility Assn., San Dimas, 1975-95. Mem. Utility Adv. Commn. City of Pasadena, Calif., 1979-86; mem. Linda Vista Property Owners Assn., Barton Flats Cabin Owners Assn. Recipient Disting. Emeriti award U. So. Calif., 1986. Fellow ASME (life, Charles Russ Richards award 1986); mem. AAUP, Am. Soc. Engring. Edn., Am. Backflow Prevention Assn. (life), Am. Water Works Assn. (hon., George Warren Fuller award 1986). Republican. Episcopalian. Avocations: gardening, fishing. Died Dec. 4, 1995.

SQUIER, LESLIE HAMILTON, psychology educator; b. San Francisco, Nov. 17, 1917; s. Leslie Hamilton and Alma Ida (Bergmann) S.; m. Anne Frances Wood, Dec. 12, 1959; children—Renata, Leslie III, Stafford, Kurt. B.A., U. Calif.-Berkeley, 1950, Ph.D., 1953. From instr. to prof. psychology Reed Coll., Portland, Oreg, 1953-88, dean of students, 1955-61, prof. emeritus, 1988—; vis. scientist Oceanic Inst., Makapuu, Oahu, Hawaii, 1969-70, 71; vis. prof. Paine Coll., Augusta, Ga., 1984; NSF fellow U. Oreg. Med. Sch., Portland, 1976, U. Hawaii Med. Sch., Honolulu, 1977. Trustee Portland Zool. Soc., 1962-68. Served with USAF, 1942-46. Mem. AAAS, APA, Am. Psychol. Soc., Oreg. Psychol. Assn. (pres. 1965), Western Psychol. Assn., Assn. for the Study of Dreaming, Phi Beta Kappa, Sigma Xi. Deceased.

SQUIRE, LUCY FRANK, radiology educator; b. Washington, May 10, 1915; d. Leslie Carl and Ethelwyn (Harris) Frank; 1 child, Gordon. MD, Woman's Med. Coll. of Pa., Phila., 1940; DSc, SUNY, Bklyn., 1993. Resident in radiology Mass. Gen. Hosp., Boston, 1942-44; fellow New Eng. Med. Ctr., Boston, 1944-45; lectr. radiology Harvard Med. Sch., 1965—; cons. in tchg. Mass. Gen. Hosp., 1965—; prof. radiology SUNY Health Sci. Ctr., Bklyn., 1970—. Author: (textbook) Fundamentals of Radiology, 1964, 4th edit., 1988; co-author: Living Anatomy, Exercises in Diagnostic Radiology, 1987. Recipient Gold medal Radiol. Soc. N.Am., 1972, Assn. U. Radiologists, 1982. Avocation: piano. Died Sept. 15, 1996.

SQUIRE, RUSSEL NELSON, musician, emeritus educator; b. Cleve., Sept. 21, 1908. B.Mus. Edn., Oberlin Coll., 1929; A.M., Case Western Res. U., 1939; Ph.D., NYU, 1942; postgrad. U. So. Calif. Dir. Oberlin Summer Music Sch., Ohio, 1929; dir. instrumental music instrn. Chillicothe Pub. Schs., Ohio, 1929-37; faculty Pepperdine U., Malibu, Calif., 1937-56, prof. music, 1937-56, now prof. emeritus, also chmn. fine arts div., 1940-56; faculty Calif. State U.-Long Beach, 1956-72, prof. music, 1964-72, now prof. emeritus; vis. prof. Pacific Christian Coll., 1970-74; prof. philosophy Sch. Edn., Pepperdine U., 1972-78; profl. theater orch. pianist, 1926-28; founder/propr./dir. Ednl. Travel Service involving study residencies in Europe, the Near East, China, India, Australia, Africa; Service: Agoura, Calif., 1958-84. Author: Studies in Sight Singing, 1950; Introduction to Music Education, 1952; Church Music, 1962; Class Piano for Adult Beginners, 1964, 4th edit., 1990; also contbr. articles to profl. jours. Founder/pres. Council for Scholarship Aid to Fgn. Students, Inc.; mem. Los Angeles County Music Commn., 1948-60; bd. dirs. Opera Guild So. Calif., 1948-60; pres. Long Beach Symphony Assn., 1963-64 (bd. dirs 1961-64). Mem. Music Tchrs. Assn. Calif. (br. pres. 1948-51), AAUP (chpt. founding pres. 1948-49), Rotary, Phi Mu Alpha Sinfonia (life). Club: Twenty (Los Angeles), Bohemians (Los Angeles). Died Nov. 17, 1997.

SRIVASTAVA, AWDHESH CHANDRA, physician, health facility administrator, researcher; b. Rai Bareli, India, Apr. 12, 1934; s. Iqbal Bahadur and Leela Devi Srivastava; m. Sandra Bayliss, Apr. 10, 1976; children: Avadh, Atul, Kiron, Nisha. MBBS, U. Lucknow, India, 1961; MD, U. Lucknow (India), 1971; PhD, U. Wales, Cardiff, 1983; LLB, Somerset U., 1993, LLM, 1994. Med. officer Provincial Med. Svcs., India, 1961-62, 63-72; Indian Army, 1962-63; registrar Health Authority, Birmingham, Eng., 1972-73; registrar Health Authority, Cardiff, 1973, sr. registrar, 1974-80; cons. Health Authority, Truro-Cornwall, Eng., 1980-92, clin. dir., 1992-95; mem. Gen. Med. Coun., London, 1989-95. Editor-in-Chief (jour.) Medical Times, 1987-95. Mem. AIDS action group, Truro-Cornwall, 1989-95, Nat. Coun. Med. Practitioners, 1989-95, Physicians for Human Rights, 1991-95, Nat. Coun. Civil Liberties, 1992-95. Mem. British Med. Assn. (sec. Truro-Cornwall divsn. 1992-95), Socialist Health Assn., Overseas Doctors' Fedn. Ltd. (pres. 1985-95), AIDS Care Ethnic Minority, AIDS Rsch. Fund Ltd. (chmn. 1986-95). Avocations: travel, cooking. Home: Truro England Died June 24, 1995.

STABILE, ROSE K. TOWNE (MRS. FRED STABILE), building and management executive, public relations consultant; b. Sunderland, Eng.; d. Stephen and Amelia Bergman; student English schs., Tchrs. Coll., Columbia; m. Wilfred Kermode (dec. Feb. 1934); m. 2d, Arthur Whittlesey Towne, May 29, 1936 (dec. 1954); m. 3d, Norbert Le Veillie, June 10, 1961 (div. Feb. 1969); m. 4th, Fred Stabile, May 30, 1970. Formerly auditor Brit. Govt., Whitehall, London; activities and membership dir. N.Y. League of Girls Clubs, N.Y.C.; real estate exec., now semi-ret. bldg. mgr. State Tower Bldg., Syracuse, N.Y.; cons. public relations, office designer and decorator; lectr. real estate dept. Syracuse U. An initiator Syracuse Peace Council; mem. area sponsoring com. Assn. for Crippled Children and Adults; mem. Met. Mus., N.Y.C., The Met. Opera, N.Y.C. Mem. English Speaking Union (membership com.), Nat. N.Y. Assn. Real Estate Bd., Nat. Assn. Bldg. Owners and Mgrs., Syracuse C. of C., LWV, Assn. UN, Women of Rotary, Bus. and Profl. Women's Clubs, Everson Mus. Art Friends of Reading, Mus. Modern Art (N.Y.C.), Internat. Center of Syracuse, Hist. Soc. Syracuse, Opera Club of Syracuse, Corinthian Club. Unitarian (chmn. service com. 1956-57.). Died, Oct. 28, 1996.

STAFFORD, JOSEPHINE HOWARD, lawyer; b. San Antonio, July 27, 1921; d. Joseph and Olive Maeblume (Goodson) Howard; m. Harry B. Stafford (div. 1958); 1 child, Julie. BA, U. N.C., 1942, LLB, 1952. Bar: N.C. 1952, Fla. 1953, U.S. Dist. Ct. (mid. dist.) Fla. 1954, U.S. Ct. Appeals (11th cir.), U.S. Ct. Appeals (5th cir.); lic. real estate broker; cert. arbitrator, Hillsborough County Cir. Ct. Assoc. Fowler, White, Gillen, Yancey and Humkey, Tampa, Fla., 1952-54; pvt. practice Tampa, 1954-57, 69-72; exec. dir., atty. Legal Aid Bur., Tampa, 1957-69; atty. City of Tampa, 1972—; instr. U. South Fla., Tampa, 1971-72; adj. prof. Hillsborough Community Coll., Tampa, 1980-86; lectr. U. South Fla., Tampa, 1973, U. Tampa, U. Fla., Gainesville, 1959; atty. Housing Authority City of Tampa, 1970-72; substitute judge mcpl. ct., 1958-71, interim mcpl. ct. judge, 1971-72; mem. Grievance Com. "13C". Author: Amendments to Search Warrant Law; Tax Laws, Agencies and Divorce, 1979; author Mayor's Proclamation Commemorating D-Day, 1994. Precinct committeewoman Hillsborough County Dem. Exec. Coun., Tampa, 1991, co-chmn., 1970; bd. mem., past pres., chmn. com. Travelers Aid Soc., Tampa, 1971-93, life mem., 1994; bd. mem., fin. com. Girl Scouts Am., Tampa, 1991-95; bd. mem., exec. com., past pres. Police Athletic League, Tampa, 1984-88, 90—; mem. Fla. Commn. on Status of Women; co-chmn. Selective Svc. System, 1971-76; bd. dirs. ARC, Tampa chpt., 1964-79, Am. Cancer Soc., Hillsborough County unit, 1982-84. Recipient Svc. to Mankind award Sertoma Internat., Tampa, 1969, Outstanding Bus. and Profl. Woman of Yr. award Bus. and Profl. Women, Tampa, 1959, 69, Women Helping Women award Soroptimist Club, Tampa, 1979, Excellence award Hillsborough County Dem. Women's Club, 1991. Mem. ABA (Nat. Conf. Lawyers and Social Workers, Nat. Conf. Lawyers and Realtors, Standing Com. on Nat. Conf. Groups), Fla. Bar assn. (chmn., legal aid com.), Tampa and Hillsborough County Bar Assn. (dir. 1958-63, chmn. elder law com. 1991-93, mem Liberty Bell award com. 1996), Nat. Legal Aid and Defender Assn. (nat. bd. dirs.), Fla. Assn. Women Lawyers (pres.), Tampa Assn. Women Lawyers (pres., named Outstanding Women Lawyers of Achievement 1993), Fla. Fedn. Social Workers (pres. Hillsborough County chpt. 1964, pres. state bd. 1969), Tampa Legal Sec. Assn., U.S. Navy League. Democrat. Methodist. Avocations: poetry, art, theatre, pottery, gardening, swimming. Home: Tampa Fla. Died Dec. 5, 1996.

STAFFORD, WILLIAM TALMADGE, English language educator; b. Marianna, Fla., Oct. 31, 1924; s. William H. and Lovie L. (Lamb) S.; m. Frances Marie McKeown, June 12, 1949 (div. 1981); children: Melinda, Jocelyn, Kathleen; m. Ruth Ann Miller, Sept. 17, 1981. B.A. with honors, U. Fla., 1948; M.A., Columbia U., 1950; Ph.D., U. Ky., 1956. Research asst. Columbia U. Press, 1950; part-time instr. U. Ky., 1950-53; mem. faculty Purdue U., 1953—, prof. English, 1966-90; vis. prof. U. Ky., 1966, Columbia U., 1967, Tulsa Grad. Inst. Modern Letters, 1973; Fulbright prof., Finland, 1963-64, Yugoslavia, 1970-71; cons. Ednl. Testing Service, 1958-70, Coll. Entrance Exam. Bd., 1964-70. Author: A Name, Title and Place Index to the Critical Writings of Henry James, 1975, Books Speaking to Books, 1981; also articles, revs.; editor: Melville's Billy Budd and the Critics, 2d edit., 1968, James's Daisy Miller, 1963, Twentieth Century American Writing, 1965, Perspectives on James's The Portrait of a Lady, 1967, Studies in The American, 1971, Henry James Novels, 1871-1880, 1983, Henry James Novels, 1881-1886, 1985; editor Modern Fiction Studies, 1956-90. Served with AUS, 1943-46. Am. Council Learned Socs. grantee, 1978. Mem. Internat. Assn. Univ. Profs. English, Henry James Soc. (pres. 1984-85), Phi Beta Kappa (alumni mem.).

STALNAKER, JOHN HULBERT, physician; b. Portland, Oreg., Aug. 29, 1918; s. William Park II and Helen Caryl (Hulbert) S.; m. Louise Isabel Lucas, Sept. 8, 1946; children: Carol Ann, Janet Lee, Mary Louise, John Park, Laurie Jean, James Mark. Student, Reed Coll., Portland, 1936-38; AB, Willamette U., Salem, Oreg., 1941; MD, Oreg. Health Scis. U., 1945. Diplomate Am. Bd. Internal Medicine. Intern Emanuel Hosp., Portland, 1945-46; resident in internal medicine St. Vincent Hosp., Portland, 1948-51; clin. instr. U. Oreg. Med. Sch., 1951-54, 60-62; staff physician VA Hosp., Vancouver, Wash., 1970-79; cons. in internal medicine, 1951-79. Contbr. articles to profl. jours. Pianist various civic and club meetings, Portland; leader Johnny Stalnaker's Dance Orch., 1936-39. Lt. (j.g.) USNR, 1946-48. Fellow ACP; mem. AMA, Multnomah County Med. Soc., Oreg. State Med. Assn., N.Am. Lily Soc., Am. Rose Soc. Avocations: music, photography, horticulture. Home: 2204 SW Sunset Dr Portland OR 97201-2068 Died Nov. 7, 1997.

STAMOS, THEODOROS, artist; b. N.Y.C., 1922. Student, Am. Artists Sch. One-man shows of paintings and drawings, most recently at Athens (Greece) Gallery, 1974, Louis K. Meisel Gallery, N.Y.C., 1977, 79, Galerie Le Portail, Heidelberg, Fed. Republic of Germany, 1977, Tomasulo Gallery, Union Coll., N.J., 1978, Edwin Ulrich Mus., Wichita, Kans., 1979, SUNY, New Paltz, 1980, Munson Williams-Proctor Inst., Utica, N.Y., 1980, Hokin Gallery, Chgo., 1980, Pierides Gallery Modern Art, Athens, Greece, 1987, Mus. Morsbroich, Leverkusen, Ger., 1988, Ileana Tounta Contemporary Art Ctr., Athens, 1991-92, ACA Galleries, N.Y.C., 1991-92; group shows, most recently at Solomon Guggenheim Mus., N.Y.C., 1977, Herbert F. Johnson Mus., Cornell U., Ithaca, N.Y., 1978, Whitney Mus. Modern Art, N.Y.C., 1978, Washington Internat. Art Fair, 1978, Louis K. Meisel Gallery, 1978, Gallery 700, Milw., 1979, Hokin Gallery, Chgo., 1980, DuBose Gallery, Houston, 1980, Munson-Williams-Proctor Inst., Utica, 1980, Mus. Knoedler, Zurich, Switzerland, 1983-85, Ericson Gallery, 1985, Kouros Gallery, 1985-86, Studio d'arte Zanuzzi, Milan, Italy, 1988, Ileana Tounta Gallery, Athens, 1989; represented in numerous collections including Met. Mus. Art, N.Y.C., Corcoran Gallery Art, Washington, Mus. Modern Art, N.Y.C., San Francisco Mus. Art, Va. Mus. Fine Arts, Norfolk, Art Inst. Chgo., Whitney Mus. Am. Art, N.Y.C., Smith Coll. Mus. Art, Northhampton, Mass., Museo d'Arte Moderno, Rio de Janiero, Balt. Mus. Art, Bklyn. Mus. Art, Tel Aviv Mus., Wadsworth Athenuem, Hartford, Conn., Fogg Art Mus., Harvard U., Cambridge, Mass., Nat. Picture Gallery, Athens, Nat. Mus. Greece, Wilhelm-Hack Mus., Ludwigshafen, Fed. Republic Germany, Mus. Moderner Kunst, Vienna, Austria, Guggenheim Mus., N.Y.C., others; retrospective exhbn. Mus. Morsbroich, Lever Kusen, Fed. Republic Germany, 1988; illustrator Sorrows of Cold Stone, 1951, The Hidden Airdome & Uncollected Poems, 1956. Tiffany Found. fellow, Brandeis U. Creative Arts award. Died Feb. 2, 1997.

STANCIU, LUCA, medical educator; b. Buzau, Romania, May 20, 1924; s. Ioan and Angela (Avramescu) S.; m. Magdalena Bobu, July 31, 1949 (div. Oct. 1983); children: Angelica, Alexandra. MD, Inst. Medicina, Timisoara, Romania, 1949, D in Med. Sci., 1960. Extern Spitalul Central, Timisoara, 1947-48; intern Clinica Pediatrica, Timisoara, 1948-49; asst. prof. Inst. Medicina, 1949-63, assoc. prof., 1963-72, prof., 1972—; dean facultatea de medicina Inst. Medicina, 1976-81; chief outpatient dept. Spitalul Clinic #2, 1974—. Author: Tulburarile de Ritm Cardiac, 1958, Policlinica Medicala, 1983, Cardiomiopatiile Cronice, 1987; editor: Medicul Salvarii, 1983. Recipient Ordinul Muncii cl. III, State Council Romania, 1967, Ordinul Meritul Sanitar, 1972. Fellow Roumanian Soc. Med. Scis.; mem. Internat. Soc. Cardiology. Avocation: music. Office: Policlinica Medicala Univ, bv 23 August no 12, Timisoara, Timis 1900, Romania Died Oct. 1983.

STANDAERT, FRANK GEORGE, medical research administrator, physician; b. Paterson, N.J., Nov. 12, 1929; s. George Joseph and Ethel Mirene (Miller) S.; m. Joan Frances Cairns, Feb. 7, 1959; children: David,

Robert, Christopher. AB, Harvard Coll., 1951; MD, Cornell U., 1955. Lic. physician Ohio, Md., D.C., N.Y. Intern in medicine Johns Hopkins Hosp., Balt., 1955-56; rsch. fellow Cornell U. Med. Coll., N.Y.C., 1956-57, instr. pharmacology, 1959-60, from asst. to assoc. prof. pharmacology, 1960-67; Schering Found. Prof., chmn. dept. pharmacology Georgetown U. Schs. Medicine and Dentistry, Washington, 1967-86, acting chmn. dept. biochemistry, 1985-86; v.p. acad. affairs, dean Coll. Medicine Med. Coll. Ohio, Toledo, 1986-89, prof. pharmacology and anesthesiology, 1986-91; assoc. v.p. for rsch. Med. Coll. Ohio, 1990-91; dir. rsch. Toledo Hosp., 1990—; adj. prof. anesthesiology U. Mich. Sch. Medicine, 1993—; active various coms. NIH, 1968-86; mem. merit rev. bd. neurobiology VA, 1974-77, chmn., 1976-77, cons., 1977; mem. Commn. Fed. Drug Approval Process U.S. Congress, 1981-82; discussion leader toxicology and safety evaluation Gordon Rsch. Conf., 1983; cons. FTC, 1971-74, 78, Occupational Safety and Health Adminstrn., 1974, FDA, initial rev. group orphan products devel., 1984—; del. U.S. Pharmacopeial Conv., 1970-86; adj. prof. anesthesiology Med. Sch. U. Mich., 1992—. Contbr. over 75 articles to profl. jours. Served to lt. USN, 1957-59. Recipient Career Devel. award USPHS, 1961-65, 66-67, Golden Apple award Georgetown Med. Sch., 1968. Fellow AAAS; mem. AMA, Am. Soc. Clin. Pharmacology and Therapeutics, Drug Info. Assn., Soc. Neurosci., The Peripatetic Soc., Am. Soc. Pharmacology and Exptl. Therapeutics (active various coms., 1966—, pres. 1990—), Fedn. Am. Socs. for Exptl. Biology (treas. 1982-84, bd. dirs. 1991—, various coms.), Assn. Med. Sch. Pharmacology (councilor 1974-75, sec. 1975-76, pres. 1982-84), Am. Assn. Med. Colls. (audit com. 1984), Soc. Toxicology (sect. mechanisms, founding mem. Nat. Capital Area chpt., 1982), Georgetown Inst. Neurosci. (bd. dirs. 1985-90, bd. scientific advisors 1985-90), Pharm. Mfr.'s Assn. Found., Nat. Bd. Med. Examiners (pharmacology com. 1983-86, comprehensive part II com. 1986-89), Nat. Research Council (div. biology and agr., various coms.), Am. Heart Assn. (nat. capital affiliate, bd. dirs. 1972-78, Exceptional Service award 1983), Sigma Xi, Alpha Omega Alpha. Clubs: Cosmos (Washington), Toledo Country. Died Mar. 17, 1994.

STANLEY, EDWARD LANE, insurance company executive; b. Phila., Jan. 19, 1916; s. Edwin C. and Edith (Worsham) S.; m. Mary Gaylord, June 25, 1938; children: Peter G., Linda. Grad., Episcopal Acad., 1933; A.B., Williams Coll., 1937. C.L.U. Asst. mgr. mortgage loans Provident Mut. Life Ins. Co., Phila., 1949-58; v.p. mortgage loans and real estate Provident Mut. Life Ins. Co., 1958-67, sr. v.p. fin., 1967-69, pres., dir., 1969-76, chmn., chief exec. officer, 1976-78, chmn. exec. com., 1978-86; chmn., trustee Mortgage and Realty Trust; bd. dirs. Meritor Fin. Cos. Trustee emeritus Chestnut Hill Hosp., Williams Coll., Episcopal Acad. Served to lt. USNR, 1943-46. Fellow Life Office Mgmt. Inst. Clubs: Phila. Cricket, Sunnybrook Golf, Phila. Died Jan. 6, 1997.

STANLEY, JOEL FRANCIS, postal employee, labor union administrator; b. Houston, Dec. 7, 1934; s. Earl Rogers and Joyce Frances (Buntyn) S.; m. Betty Sue Boatman, Nov. 13, 1954; children: Joel Lynn, Debra Cheryl. AS, North Harris Community Coll., 1980. Mail clk. Lykes Bros. Steamship Co., Houston, 1952-53; lathe operator Oil Ctr. Tool Co., Houston, 1958-59; machine operator Continental Can Co., Houston, 1959-65; mail distbn. U.S. Postal Svc., Houston, 1965-69, maintenance control clk., 1969—; chmn. bd. trustees Am. Postal Workers Union, Houston, 1989—. With Tex. Air N.G., 1950-51, USAF, 1954-58. Mem. nat. Postal Workers Union (officer Houston chpt. 1965-70), Am. Postal Workers Union (chartered, chmn. bd. trustees 1991-92), Tex. Postal Workers Union (officer Houston chpt. 1989—), DAV, Am. Legion, Tex. State Polio Survivors Assn., Masons (chaplain 1975, v.p. local chpt. 1980), Shriners (sec., v.p., pres. Conroe, Tex. chpt. 1970, maj. Houston chpt. 1982, amb. Livingston, Tex. chpt. 1983—, amb. Montgomery County chpt. 1991, amb. Lake Houston club 1990, mem. past pres.' assn. Arabia Shrine Temple). Democrat. Avocation: music. Home: Spring Tex. Deceased.

STANLEY, JUSTIN ARMSTRONG, lawyer; b. Leesburg, Ind., Jan. 2, 1911; s. Walter H. and Janet (Armstrong) S.; m. Helen Leigh Fletcher, Jan. 3, 1938; children: Janet Van Wie Hoffmann, Melinda Fletcher Douglas, Justin Armstrong, Harlan Fletcher. AB, Dartmouth Coll., 1933, AM (hon.), 1952, LLD (hon.), 1983; LLB, Columbia U., 1937; LLD (hon.), John Marshall Law Sch., 1976, Suffolk U., 1976, Vt. Law Sch., 1977, Norwich U., 1977, Ind. U., 1981, Oklahoma City U., 1981, IIT-Chgo.-Kent Coll. Law, 1988, William Mitchell Coll. Law, 1989. Bar: Ill. 1937. Practiced in Chgo.; assoc. Isham, Lincoln & Beale, 1937-48, ptnr., 1948-66; ptnr. Mayer, Brown & Platt, 1967-91; of counsel, 1991-96; v.p. Dartmouth Coll., 1952-54; asst. prof. law Chgo.-Kent Coll. Law, 1938-43, prof., 1943-46; pub. mem. disputes sect. Nat. War Labor Bd., 1943-44. Trustee Presbyn.-St. Luke's Hosp., Wells Coll., 1960-69, Rockford Coll., 1962-70; trustee Ill. Childrens Home and Aid Soc., pres., 1963-64. Served as lt. USNR, 1944-46. Recipient medal for excellence Columbia U. Law Sch., 1984, Disting. Svc. award, 1994, Lux in Deserto award Dartmouth Coll., 1996. Fellow Am. Bar Found., Am. Coll. Trial Lawyers; mem. ABA (chmn. pub. utility sect. 1970-71, ho. of dels. 1973-96, pres. 1976-77, chmn. commn. on professionalism 1985-86, ABA medal 1986), Fed. Energy Bar Assn., Chgo. Bar Assn. (pres. 1967-68), Ill. Bar Assn. (Disting. Svc. award 1986), Alumni Coun. Dartmouth (pres. 1952), Am. Law Inst., Am. Judicature Soc., Supreme Ct. Hist. Soc. (pres. 1987-91, chmn. 1995-96), Alpha Delta Phi. Episcopalian. Died Sept. 25, 1996.

STANLEY, THOMAS BAHNSON, JR., investor; b. Martinsville, Va., Jan. 9, 1927; s. Thomas B. and Anne (Bassett) S.; m. Ruth Barnes, Sept. 10, 1949; children: Thomas Bahnson III, Susan Walker, Andrew. B.S. in C.E., Va. Mil. Inst., 1946; B.S.C., U. Va., 1948; grad., Advanced Mgmt. Program, Harvard U., 1970. With Stanley Furniture Co., Stanleytown, Va., 1948-79, dir., 1950-79, exec. v.p., 1952-62, pres., 1962-71, chmn., 1971-79; pres. Mead Interiors, Stanleytown, 1969-74; group v.p. Mead Corp., Dayton, Ohio, 1969-74; also dir. Mead Corp.; bd. dirs. Main Street Bank Group, Martinsville, Va., Stanley Land & Lumber Co., Drakes Branch, Va. Mem. Henry County Sch. Bd., 1957-80; chmn. bd. trustees Ferrum Coll., 1977-79. Mem. So. Furniture Mfrs. Assn. (dir., pres. 1966, chmn. 1967). Methodist. Lodge: Masons (32 deg.). Died Oct. 29, 1997.

STANLEY, TIMOTHY WADSWORTH, economist; b. Hartford, Conn., Sept. 28, 1927; s. Maurice and Margaret Stowell (Sammond) S.; m. Nadia Leon, June 7, 1952; children: Timothy Wadsworth III, Alessandra Maria, Christopher Maurice, Flavia Margaret. Student, Choate Sch., 1943-45; B.A., Yale, 1950; LL.B., Harvard, 1955, Ph.D., 1957. Bar: Conn. 1956, U.S. Supreme Ct. 1971. Mem. staff Office Sec. Def., 1955; teaching fellow Harvard U., 1955-56; spl. asst. White House staff, 1957-59, spl. asst. to asst. sec. def. for internat. security affairs, 1959-62; vis. research fellow Council on Fgn. Relations, N.Y.C., 1962-63; div. dir. policy planning staff Office Sec. Def., 1963-64; asst. to sec. def. for NATO force planning, Paris, 1965-67; def. adviser (minister) U.S. Mission to NATO, Paris and Brussels, 1967-69; vis. prof. internat. relations Johns Hopkins Sch. Advanced Internat. Studies, 1969-70; exec. v.p. Internat. Econ. Policy Assn., Washington, 1970-74; pres. Internat. Econ. Policy Assn., 1974-84, chmn., 1984-87; pres. Internat. Econ. Studies Inst., 1974-96; profl. lectr. George Washington U., 1957-60; cons. to various govt. agys., univs., bus. orgns., 1969-70; spl. rep. ACDA in negotiations for East-West Mut. Balanced Force Reductions, 1973-74, cons., 1974-80; mem. U.S. Govt. Adv. Com. on Investment, Tech. and Devel., 1974-93; mem. Nat. Strategic Materials and Minerals Program Adv. Com., 1984-88. Author: American Defense and National Security, 1955, NATO in Transition, 1965, Detente Diplomacy, 1970; co-author: U.S. Troops in Europe, 1971, The United States Balance of Payments, 1972, Raw Materials and Foreign Policy, 1977, Technology and Economic Development, 1979, U.S. Foreign Economic Strategy for the Eighties, 1982, Mobilizing U.S. Industry: A Vanishing Option for National Security?, 1987, To Unite our Strength: Enhancing the United Nations Peace and Security System, 1992; contbr. articles to profl. jours. Bd. dirs. Atlantic Coun. U.S., UN Assn. U.S., Nat. Capital Area, v.p., 1992-96; mem. transition team Pres.-elect George Bush, 1988-89. Served to 1st lt. AUS, 1946-48, 51-52. Recipient Distinguished Civilian Service medal Dept. Def., 1969. Mem. Met. Club. Congregationalist. Died Sept. 21, 1997.

STANLEY, WILLIAM ROBERT, federal agency official; b. Bklyn., Dec. 22, 1932; s. William and Mabel Christine (Stark) S.; m. Edith Joyce Stafford, July 4, 1956 (div. July 1983); children: Donna Lynne, Susan Carole, Christopher Robert; m. Marian Kasica, Mar. 24, 1984. Student, Upsala Coll., 1951-52; BA, St. Lawrence U., 1955. With credit dept. Chase Manhattan Bank, N.A., N.Y.C., 1956-58, Fedn. Bank and Trust Co., N.Y.C., 1959-62; bank examiner State of N.Y., N.Y.C., 1962-71, sr. bank examiner, 1971-75, prin. bank examiner, 1975-86, supervising bank examiner, 1986-89; sr. trust analyst bd. govs. Fed. Res. System, 1989-94, supervisory trust analyst, 1994—; coordinator employee assistance program State of N.Y., N.Y.C., 1984-86. Vol. fireman Jackson Twp. Vol. Fire Co., N.J., 1965-67. Mem. Fundamental Christian Ch. Avocations: racquetball, swimming, reading, hiking. Office: Fed Res System Washington DC 20551 Died March 31, 1996.

STANS, MAURICE HUBERT, retired business consultant, former government official; b. Shakopee, Minn., Mar. 22, 1908; s. J. Hubert and Mathilda (Nyssen) S.; m. Kathleen Carmody, Sept. 7, 1933 (dec. Oct. 1984); children: Steven, Maureen (dec.), Theodore, Terrell. Student, Northwestern U., 1925-28, Columbia U., 1929-30; LL.D., Ill. Wesleyan U., 1954, Northwestern U., 1960, DePaul U., 1960; D.P.A., Parsons Coll., 1960; LL.D., Grove City Coll., St. Anselm's Coll., 1969, U. San Diego, Gustavus Adolphus Coll., 1970, Pomona Coll., 1971, Maryville Coll., 1971, Rio Grande Coll., 1972, Nat. U., 1979, Pepperdine U., 1984. C.P.A. With Alexander Grant & Co. (C.P.A.'s), Chgo., 1928, exec. ptnr., 1940-55; pres., dir. Moore Corp. (stove mfrs.), Joliet, Ill., 1938-45; dir., mem. exec. com. James Talcott, Inc., N.Y.C., 1941-55; fin. cons. to postmaster gen. U.S., 1953-55, dep. postmaster gen. U.S., 1955-57; dep. dir. U.S. Bur. Budget, 1957-58, dir., 1958-61; pres. Western Bancorp., Los Angeles, 1961-62; also vice chmn. United Calif. Bank; sr. ptnr. William R. Staats & Co., 1963-64; pres. William R. Staats Co., Inc., 1964-65, Glore Forgan, William R. Staats, Inc., N.Y.C., 1965-69; syndicated columnist, 1961-62; sec. of Commerce Washington, 1969-72; Bd. dirs. Uniglobe Travel (Internat.), Vancouver; pres., bd. dirs. Farmont Corp., L.A.; bd. dirs., treas. Electronic Town Hall Meetings, Inc., 1992-93; bd. dirs., chmn. AT&D Inc., 1992-93; bus. cons., L.A., 1975-92; chmn., bd. dirs. Weatherby, Inc., 1986-91. Author: The Terrors of Justice, 1978, One of the Presidents' Men, Twenty Years With Eisenhower and Nixon, 1995; contbr. numerous articles on govt. fin., fgn. trade and bus. to profl. publs. Founder, past pres., dir. Stans Found., Chgo.; chmn. Nixon Finance Com., 1968, Republican Nat. Finance Com., 1968-69, 72-73, Finance Com. to Re-Elect Pres., 1972-73; fin. chmn., bd. dirs. Nixon Presdl. Library, 1985—; trustee Pomona Coll., 1962-69; bd. dirs. Huntington Med. Rsch. Inst.; bd. dirs. Arnold and Mabel Beckman Found., Irvine, Calif., 1988-92, Eisenhower World Affairs Inst., Washington, 1991-93; chmn. Minority Enterprise Devel. Adv. Coun., Washington, 1989-91; founding dir. African Wildlife Found., Washington, 1958. Recipient Great Living Am. award U.S. C. of C., 1961, Tax Found. award, 1960, Free Enterprise award Internat. Franchise Assn., 1988; named to Acctg. Hall of Fame, 1968; creator Stans African Halls sect. Mus. York County, Rock Hill, S.C., 1980; financed and constructed Stans Hist. Ctr. Shakopee, Minn., 1988, deeded to Scott County Hist. Soc. Mem. NAM (dir. 1968-69), AICPA (pres. 1954-55, Pub. Service award 1954), Ill. Soc. CPAs (dir. 1944-46), D.C. Soc. CPAs (hon.), Hawaii Soc. CPAs (hon.), Am. Acctg. Assn. (nat. Alpha Kappa Psi award 1952), Fed. Govt. Accts. Assn., Nat. Assn. Postmasters (hon.), Iron Molders and Foundry Workers Union (hon.). Clubs: Union League, Adventurers (Chgo.), California (Los Angeles), Athenaeum (Pasadena), Shikar-Safari Club Internat. (founding 1952, trustee internat. found.), Safari Club Internat., East African Profl. Hunters (hon.), Explorers (N.Y.C.), African Safari (Washington, founding bd. dirs. 1957), Jamhuri of Garissa (Kenya) (hon.), Valley Hunt (Pasadena). Died April 1998.

STAUFFER, CHARLES HENRY, chemistry educator; b. Harrisburg, Pa., Apr. 17, 1913; s. Charles C. and Hannah (Henry) S.; m. Eleanor Ramsdell, July 8, 1939; children—Charles R., Anne Elizabeth, John E. A.B., Swarthmore Coll., 1934; M.A., Harvard U., 1936, Ph.D., 1937. Instr. Worcester (Mass.) Poly. Inst., 1937-43, asst. prof., 1943-52, assoc. prof., 1952-58; assoc. prof. affiliate Clark U., Worcester, 1941; prof., chmn. dept. chemistry St. Lawrence U., Canton, N.Y., 1958-65; prof. chemistry, chmn. div. natural scis. math. Bates Coll., Lewiston, Maine, 1965—, Charles A. Dana prof. chemistry, 1968-77, prof. emeritus, 1977—; dir. chem. kinetics data project Nat. Acad. Scis., 1954-64; mem. adv. com. Office Critical Constants, 1961-64. Fellow AAAS, Am. Chem. Soc. (sec., chmn. No. N.Y. sect., councilor Maine sect.); mem. Sigma Xi, Phi Beta Kappa (Swarthmore Coll. chpt.). Clubs: Mason, Searsport Yacht. Died Sept. 30, 1997.

STAUFFER, ROBERT ALLEN, research company executive; b. Dayton, Ohio, Jan. 26, 1920; s. John G. and Verna G. (Theobald) S.; m. Justine M. Wells, Mar. 20, 1943 (div. 1969); children—Susan, Nancy; m. Ruth Stanley Munro, Oct. 30, 1969. B.A. in Chemistry, Harvard, 1942. With Nat. Research Corp., Cambridge, 1942-67; gen. mgr. research div. Nat. Research Corp., 1949-63, dir., 1954-67, v.p., 1949-67; with Norton Co., Worcester, Mass., 1963-71; v.p. research Norton Co., 1963-71; v.p., gen. mgr. Norton Research Corp., Cambridge, 1968-71; v.p. NRC Metals Corp., 1955-56, Environ. Research and Tech., Concord, Mass., 1971-80. Patentee in field. Died Nov. 1997.

STAUFFER, SARAH ANN, political worker; b. Lancaster, Pa., June 13, 1915; d. Charles F. and Gertrude (Frantz) S. Student, Franklin and Marshall Coll., 1957-58, Wharton Sch. Bus. Adminstrn., U. Pa., 1958-62. Office mgr. aircraft div. Armstrong Cork Co., 1941-43; mem., then capt. 45th div. Clubmobile unit ARC, Anzio, Italy and Munich, Germany, 1943-45; dir. personnel and operations U.S. Occupied Ty. ETO Clubmobile div., 1945-46; bd. dirs. Lancaster (Pa.) chpt. ARC, 1947-51, treas., 1949-51; past mem. bd. Lancaster Symphony Assn.; mem. exec. com. Pa. Health Council, 1954-55; del.-at-large Community Chest Council, 1958-72; regional dir. Assn. Jr. Leagues Am., 1951-55, treas., 1955-57; del. gov.'s conf. White House Conf. on Children and Youth, 1960; del. to U.S. Dept. Labor Women's Bur. Nat. Conf., 1970; mem. friends adv. com. Scheie Eye Inst., 1980-93; Mem. bd. Young Republicans of Pa., 1937-39, 45-47; mem. Rep. Nat. Com. for Pa., 1964-74; exec. com. Rep. Nat. Com., 1964-68; mem. bd. Pa. Council Rep. Women, 1957-96, hon. pres.; alt. del. Rep. Nat. Conv., 1960, del.-at-large, 1964, 68, 72, 80. Pres. Commonwealth Bd. Med. Coll., 1973-75; mem. exec. com. Nat. Bd. Med. Coll Pa., 1978; bd. visitors Franklin-Marshall Coll., 1972-84; sec. Pa. Electoral Coll., 1972; bd. dirs. Rehab. Internat. U.S.A., 1981-85, del. to world congress, Portugal, 1984; fellow Lancaster Country Day Sch., 1989. Named Disting. Dau. of Pa., 1965; mem. Legion of Honor-Chapel of Four Chaplains, 1979. Former assoc. mem. Acad. Polit. and Social Sci., Acad. Polit. Sci; charter mem. Historic Preservation

Trust of Lancaster County. Clubs: Colony (N.Y.C.); Acorn (Phila.); Soroptimist (Lancaster, Pa.) (hon.), Bus./Profl. Women (Lancaster, Pa.). Home: Rohrerstown Pa. Died Jan. 20, 1996.

STAVROPOULOS, GEORGE PETER, designer; b. Tripolis, Greece, Jan. 22, 1920; s. Peter Dmitri and Dmitra (Paraskereopoulos) S.; m. Nancy Angelakos, Oct. 31, 1960; 1 child, Peter George. Formerly designer, owner Haute Couture, Athens; now designer, prin. Stavropoulos Corp., N.Y.C. Mem. Doubles Club. Greek Orthodox.

STEADMAN, CHARLES WALTERS, lawyer, corporate executive, writer; b. Falls City, Nebr., July 25, 1914; s. William Sherman and Marie (Walters) S.; m. Dorothy Marie Fawick, Feb. 14, 1942 (dec. Sept. 1974); children: Suzanne Louise Steadman Hoerr (dec.), Carole Elaine Steadman Kinney, Charles T. W., Dorothy M. (Diana); m. Consuelo Matthews Artini, May 10, 1986. A.B., U. Nebr., 1935; J.D., Harvard U., 1938. Bar: Ohio 1939, D.C. 1956, U.S. Supreme Ct. 1950, U.S. Ct. Claims 1958. Partner Marshman, Hornbeck, Hollington, Steadman & McLaughlin, Cleve., 1946-65, Steadman, Jones & Baxter, 1956-70; chmn. bd. St. Regis Hotel Corp., 1960-63; vice chmn. Leaseway Intercontinental, 1961-65; prin. Charles W. Steadman Counselor-at-Law, 1970; chmn. com. to end govt. waste Nat. Taxpayers Union, 1979; chmn. bd., pres. Steadman Security Corp., Steadman Technology and Growth Fund, Steadman Investment Fund, Steadman Associated Fund, Steadman American Industry Fund; chief counsel Select U.S. Senate Com., 1956; spl. master commr. Matter of Dissolution of Cleve. Savs. Soc., 1959-62; spl. presdl. rep. to Oman, 1980. Author: Steadman's Revision of the Ohio Civil Practice Manual, 1950, The National Debt Conclusion: Establishing the Debt Repayment Plan, 1993; also legal and econ. articles.; editor: Charles W. Steadman Economic Review. Bd. govs. Investment Co. Inst., 1969-72; chmn. Washington met. area Rep. Nat. Fin. Com., 1980-81; mem. exec. com. Presdl. Inaugural Com., 1981; founder Presdl. Trust, 1981; trustee Tex. Wesleyan Coll., 1982-84; founder, chmn. Nat. Debt Repayment Found, 1982. Served as lt. col. AUS, World War II; chief counsel legal div. Cleve. Ordnance Dist. Recipient Disting. Service award U. Nebr., 1960. Mem. ABA (coun. corp., banking and bus. law 1958-60), Ohio Bar Assn., Cleve. Bar Assn., Ohio Bar, Bar Assn. D.C., Internat. Bar Assn., Am. Law Inst. (life), Am. Judicature Soc., 1925 F Street Club, Union Club (Cleve.), Beach Club (Palm Beach, Fla.), Everglades Club (Palm Beach, Fla.), Racquet and Tennis Club (N.Y.C.), Sky Club (N.Y.C.). Died Dec. 4, 1997.

STEARNS, LLOYD WORTHINGTON, investment adviser, Oriental artifact consultant; b. Somerville, Mass., Feb. 16, 1910; s. Charles Victor and Flora D. (Liscom) S.; B.S. in Indsl. Engring., N.Y. U., 1934; m. Adelaide Church, Nov. 23, 1932; 1 child, Adelaide Liscom Stearns McRae. Indsl. security analyst Adminstrv. and Research Corp., 1934-38; asst. to treas., v.p. Northam Warren Corp., 1938-41; with Met. Life Ins. Co., 1941-75, sr. procedure analyst, mgmt. cons., exec. asst. to sr. v.p., to exec. v.p., 1941-60, to pres., 1960, sec., emergency com., 1950-75; coll. relations cons.; dir. Soundscriber, Inc.; pres., dir. Dispoz Sani Products, Ltd. Bd. dirs. Mil. Pub. Inst., Inc.; sec. N.Y. State Life Ins. Civil Def. Adv. Com., 1954-64; corp. mem. N.Y. World's Fair 1964-65 Corp.; mem. nat. def. com. U.S. C. of C. and NAM; mem. joint com. emergency operation Am. Life Conv.-Life Ins. Assn. Am.; mem. corps com. Lincoln Center for Performing Arts, 1959-62; v.p., treas., dir., vice chmn. N.Y. com. Nat. Strategy Seminars, Inc.; dir. Nat. Inst. Disaster Moblzn., Inc., Battery Park Colonnade Assocs., Inc.; sec. French-Polyclinic Fund, Inc. Trustee French Hosp., N.Y.C., N.Y. Polyclinic Med. Sch. and Hosp. Served to col. AUS, 1933-70; sec. gen. to chief commr. Allied Commn. Rome, Mediterranean Theater Opers., WWII, 1941-46, NATOUSA; with Res. 1946-70. Decorated Legion of Merit; recipient Outstanding Civilian Service medal U.S. Army; decorated comdr. Crown of Italy, comdr. Sts. Maurice and Lazarus (Italy); War Cross Commemorative Royal Yugoslav Army. Mem. Am. Ordnance Assn. (dir., chmn. programs), Am. Legion, Vet. Fgn. Wars, Soc. Colonial Wars (council), SAR (bd. mgrs.), N.Y. Soc. Mil. and Naval Officers World Wars (sec.), Mil. Order of World Wars, Assn. U.S. Army (pres. N.Y. chpt. 1961-62, regional pres. 1963-64), Def. Orientation Conf. Assn., N.Y. Chamber Commerce, Newcomen Soc., New Eng. Hist. and Geneal. Soc., U.S. Naval Inst., Statue of Liberty Found., Gateway Civic Assn (pres., sec., treas. 1983—), Phi Gamma Delta. Episcopalian. Clubs: University (N.Y.C.); Army and Navy (Washington); Masons. Deceased Oct. 12, 1997.

STEARNS, STEPHEN RUSSELL, civil engineer, forensic engineer, educator; b. Manchester, N.H., Feb. 28, 1915; s. Hiram Austin and Elisabeth Scribner (Brown) S.; m. Eulalie Moody Holmes, Jan. 1 1939; children: Marjorie Elisabeth, Stephen James, Jonathan David. A.B., Dartmouth Coll., 1937; C.E., Thayer Sch. Engring., 1938; M.S., Purdue U., 1949. Civil engr. Gannett, Eastman, Fleming, Harrisburg, Pa., 1938-40; marine egr. Bur. Ships, Phila. Navy Yard, 1940-41; engr. Dry Dock Assocs., Phila Navy Yard, 1941-43; instr. Thayer Sch. Engring., Dartmouth, 1943-45, asst. prof., 1945-53, prof. civil engring., 1953-80; UN cons., Poland, 1974, 78; engr. Ops. Research, Inc., Washington., 1962-64; phys. reconnaisance in Alaska Boston U. Phys. Research Labs., 1953; chief applied snow and ice research br. Snow, Ice, Permafrost Research Establishment, U.S. Army Engrs., 1954-55; Mem. Sch. Bd., Hanover, N.H., 1951-60, chmn., 1957-59; mem. N.H. Gov.'s Transp. Com., 1966-67, Task Force, 1969; chmn. Lebanon (N.H.) Regional Airport Authority, 1966-69; mem. N.H. Bd. Registration Profl. Engrs., 1975-83. Mem. ASCE (dir. 1978-81, pres. 1983-84), NSPE, Am. Soc. Engring. Edn., Nat. Soc. Profl. Engrs., Dartmouth Soc. Engrs. (Robert Fletcher award), Sigma Chi. Congregationalist.

STEEL, DAWN, motion picture producer; b. N.Y.C., Aug. 19; m. Charles Roven; 1 child, Rebecca. Student in mktg., Boston U., 1964-65, NYU, 1966-67. Sportswriter Major League Baseball Digest and NFL, N.Y.C., 1968-69; editor Penthouse Mag., N.Y.C., 1969-75; pres. Oh Dawn!, Inc., N.Y.C., 1975-78; v.p. merchandising, cons. Playboy mag., N.Y.C., 1978-79; v.p. merchandising Paramount Pictures, N.Y.C., 1979-80; v.p. prodn. Paramount Pictures, L.A., 1980-83, sr. v.p. prodn., 1983-85, pres. prodn., 1985-87; pres. Columbia Pictures, 1987-90; formed Steel Pictures, 1990—; (with Charles Raven and Bob Cavallo) formed Atlas Entertainment (with exclusive movie prodn. agreement with Turner Pictures), 1994. Bd. dirs. Claremont Coll., Home Edn. Network; mem. dean's adv. bd. UCLA Sch. Theater, Film and TV, 1993—. Recipient Crystal award Women in Film, L.A., 1989. Mem. Acad. Motion Picture Arts and Scis., Am. Film Inst. (bd. dirs. 1988-90), NOW Legal Def. Fund. Democrat. Jewish. Avocations: skiing, tennis, gardening. Died Jan. 1998.

STEELE, HILDA BERNEICE HODGSON, farm manager, home economics supervisor; b. Wilmington, Ohio, Mar. 24, 1911; d. George Sanders and Mary Jane (Rolston) Hodgson; m. John C. Steele, Jan. 10, 1963 (dec. Jan. 1973). BS, Wilmington Coll., 1935; MA, Ohio State U., 1941; postgrad., Ohio U., 1954, Miami U., Oxford, Ohio, 1959. Cert. elem. and high sch. gen. tchr. and vocat. supr., Ohio. Part-time tchr. Wilmington Pub. Schs., Midland Elem. Sch., 1931-32; tchr. Brookville (Ohio) Pub. Schs., 1932-37, Dayton (Ohio) Pub. Schs., Lincoln Jr. High Sch., 1937-40; tchr. practical arts, coord. home econs. Dayton Pub. Schs., 1940-45, supr. home econs., 1945-81; mgr. Steele's Farm, Xenia, Ohio, 1972—; mem. home econs. adv. com. Cen. State U., Wilburforce, Ohio, 1941-92, Miami Valley Hosp. Nursing Sch., Dayton, 1951-63; mem. adv. bd. Dayton Sch. Practical Nursing, 1951-92. Mem. adv. com. Montgomery County ARC, Dayton, 1940-80; mem. town and country career com. Miami Valley Br. YMCA, Dayton, 1948-59; mem. Ohio Electrification Com., Dayton, 1964-66; mem. corp. com. United Way, Dayton, 1970-96; bd. dirs. Ohio Future Homemakers of Am.-Home Econs. Related Occupations, Columbus, 1979-81; chmn. home econs. adv. com. Ohio Vets. Children Home, 1987-95. Recipient Outstanding Contbns. award Girls Scouts U.S., 1987, Appreciation award Dayton Practical Nursing Program, 1989; named Ohio Vocat. Educator of the Yr., 1981. Mem. NEA, Ohio Edn. Assn., Am. Home Econs. Assn. (Appreciation award 1990), Am. Vocat. Assn., Ohio Home Econs. Assn. (various coms., Friend of Family award 1994), Ohio Vocat. Assn. (life), Ohio Dist. C Home Econs. Assn., Ohio Ret. Tchrs. Assn. (life), Montgomery County Ret. Tchrs. Assn., Dayton Pub. Schs. Adminstrv. Assn., Met. Home Econs. Assn. (pres. 1949-50, 60-61), Greene County Landmark Assn., Electric Womens Roundtable Assn. (Dayton-Cin. chpt. 1951-72, mem.-at-large 1972—), U.S. C. of C., Phi Upsilon Omicron (hon.), Ea. Star, Zonta (pres. Dayton chpt. 1950-52). Mem. Ch. of Christ. Avocations: gardening, sewing, helping others. Died Sept. 26, 1997.

STEHLING, KURT RICHARD, physical scientist, administrator; b. Giessen, Germany, Sept. 19, 1919; came to Can., 1929; s. Wilhelm and Ernestine Diane (de Partier) S.; m. Helen Niess Bauer, Dec. 29, 1945; children: Wendy Joan, Andrew Alan. BA, U. Toronto, 1948; MA, Georgetown U., 1957; DSc (hon.), Tech. U., Berlin, 1977. Group leader rocket research Bell Aerospace Corp., Buffalo, 1948-55; research assoc. Princeton U., N.J., 1953-54; div. chief Project Vanguard U.S. Naval Research Lab., Washington, 1955-59; sr. scientist NASA, Washington, 1959-62; v.p. electro-optical Xerox Corp., Pasadena, Calif., 1963-67; sr. staff scientist Office of Pres., Washington, 1967-71; sr. project mgr. NOAA, Rockville, Md., 1971-86, sr. scientist emeritus, 1986—. Author: Project Vanguard, 1960; Skyhooks, 1962; Lasers and Applications, 1966; Computers and You, 1968; Bags Up, 1970; also numerous articles. Patentee in field. Mem. zoning com. Chevy Chase, Md., 1963-79; mem. com. Maria Mitchell Assn. Recipient Liebig medal U. Giessen, 1977, Space Pioneer medal Nat. Space Club, 1966, Galbraith award Engring. Inst. Can., 1948, Golden Pin of Honour, Hermann Oberth Space & Rocket Soc., Germany, 1989. Fellow AIAA (bd. dirs., Disting. Svc. award 1980), Explorers Club, Marine Tech. Soc. (coun.); mem. Internat. Acad. Astronautics, Lighter-Than-Air Soc. (hon. life), Cosmos Club (libr. com.), Press Club (Washington). Congregationalist. Avocations: hiking; dramatics; astronomy. Died March 19, 1997.

STEIDEL, ROBERT FRANCIS, JR., educator; b. Goshen, N.Y., July 6, 1926; s. Robert Francis and Edna (Terry) S.; m. Jean Ann McKissick, Nov. 13, 1946; children—John Robert, Mark Howard, David William, Steven James. B.S. (Pulitzer Nat. scholar, Regents scholar), Columbia U., 1948, M.S., 1949; D.Eng. (NSF fellow), U. Calif.-Berkeley, 1955. Instr., asst. prof. mech. engring. Oreg. State U., 1949-52; asst. prof., assoc. prof., prof. mech. engring. U. Calif.-Berkeley, 1955—, asso. dean Coll. Engring., 1981-86, chmn. dept., 1969-74, U. Calif. rep. Pacific-10 Conf., 1972-89, pres., 1973-74, 83-84; cons. Lawrence Radiation Lab., 1955-87, Jet Propulsion Lab., 1962-68; mem. mech. engring. adv. bd. John Wiley & Sons, N.Y.C., 1974-87. Served with USNR, 1944-46. Fellow Inst. Mech. Engrs. Gt. Britain, ASME (past chmn. San Francisco); mem. Am. Soc. Engring. Edn. (Western Electric Fund award 1973, Chester F. Carlson award 1974), Sigma Xi, Tau Beta Pi, Pi Tau Sigma. Office: U Calif 5138 Etcheverry Hall Berkeley CA 94720 Died March 2, 1997.

STEIN, BRUNO, economist; b. Vienna, Austria, July 19, 1930; s. Leo and Paula (Lindenbaum) S.; m. Judith A. Paris, Dec. 26, 1969; 1 child, Elizabeth P. AB, NYU, 1950, AM, 1952, PhD, 1959. Fellow NYU Ctr. for Internat. Studies, 1973-74; instr. NYU, 1956-59, asst. prof., 1959-63, assoc. prof., 1963-68, prof. econs. and dir. Inst. Labor Rels., 1968—; vis. fellow Policy Studies Inst., London; acad. visitor London Sch. Econs., 1972-73; lectr. Columbia U. Grad. Sch. Bus., summer 1958; vis. lectr. Cornell U., 1976; labor arbitrator, mediator; cons. in field; panel mem. Am. Arbitration Assn., Fed. Mediation and Conciliation Svc., others. Author: On Relief: The Economics of Poverty and Public Welfare, 1971, Work and Welfare in Britain and the USA, 1976, Social Security and the Private Pension System, 1979, Social Security and Pensions in Transition: Udnerstanding the American Retirement System, 1980, 2d edit., 1983, Japanese edit., 1984, Contemporar Issues in Labor and Employment Law; contbr. articles to profl. jours. Grantee, U.S. Dept. Labor, 1964-66, 66, 72-73, N.Y. C. Dept. Social Svcs., 1968, U.S. HEW, 1969-70, others. Mem. Am. Arbitration Assn., Am. Econ. Assn., History of Econs. Soc., Internat. Indsl. Rels. Assn., Indsl. Rels. Rsch. Assn. (N.Y.C. chpt. pres. 1980-81), Metro. Econ. Assn. N.Y.C. (sec. 1959-63, pres. 1976-77), Soc. of Profls. in Dispute Resolution, Soc. of Fed. Labor Rels. Profls., Nat. Acad. Social Ins. DIED 03/15/96.

STEIN, RITA F., hospital administrator, educator; b. Buffalo, July 25, 1922; d. Samuel I. and Mary (Resnick) Fish; m. Jacob B. Stein, Dec. 21, 1947. Diploma, Edward J. Meyer Meml. Hosp. Sch. Nursing, 1942; B.S. with distinction in Pub. Health Nursing, U. Buffalo, 1952; M.S. in Pub. Health, SUNY-Buffalo, 1957; Ph.D. with distinction in Social Psychiatry, Med. Sociology; Ph.D. (USPHS fellow), 1966. Pub. health nurse Vis. Nurse Assn., Hartford, Conn., 1942-43; med., surg., neurol. nurse U.S. Army Nurse Corps, 1943-47; psychiat. nurse Dr. H.E. Favor, 1954-66; psychiat. nursing instr. Buffalo State Hosp., 1959-66; assoc. prof., dir. research Sch. Nursing, Ind. U., Indpls., 1966-81; prof., dir. research Sch. Nursing, Ind. U., 1968-81; adminstr. LaRue Carter Mental Hosp., 1981-86; cons. in field. Contbr. articles to profl. jours. Mem. Am. Sociol. Assn., Am. Psychol. Assn., Nat. League Nurses, Am. Nurses Assn., Nat. Assn. Study Edn., Midwest Regional Med. Library and Coop. Info. Services (council), AAUP (mem. exec. com.), Ind. State Nurses Assn. (council on edn.), Am. Pub. Health Assn., Sigma Theta Tau. Jewish. Clubs: Hadassah, Sisterhood of Temple of Hebrew Congregation. Office: LaRue Carter Hosp Indianapolis IN 46202 Died April 14, 1996.

STEINBERG, MARVIN BERNARD, judge; b. Balt., Sept. 10, 1929; s. Israel and Dorothy (Pinkner) S.; m. Ilene Abel, Aug. 3, 1952 (div. 1975); children: John, Jill, Scott; m. Kathryn Burch, Aug. 29, 1975. AA, U. Balt., 1949, LLB cum laude, 1952. Bar: Md. 1952, U.S. Supreme Ct. 1960. Ptnr. Hyman Rubenstein, Balt., 1954-56, Steinberg & Steinberg, Balt., 1961-70, Gomborov, Steinberg, Schlachman & Harris, Balt., 1971-77, Steinberg, Schlachman, Potler & Belsky, Balt., 1978-79, Steinberg, Schlachman, Potler, Belsky & Weiner, Balt., 1980-85; judge Cir. Ct. of Balt., 1985—; mem. Jud. Nominating Commn., 1974-78. Bd. dirs. Alzheimer's Assn., Zionists Am., 1984-86. Served with USAF, 1953-54. Mem. ABA (adminstrv. div., com. standards of jud. adminstrn.), Md. State Bar Assn. (bd. govs. 1971-72, chmn. section legal edn. and adminstrn. 1971, chmn. sect. jud. adminstrn. 1988—), Balt. City Bar Assn (chmn. workmen's compensation com. 1964,). Democrat. Jewish. Avocations: traveling, mountain climbing, camping. Died Oct. 14, 1996.

STEINMAN, NEAL, lawyer; b. Mar. 10, 1942. Home: Philadelphia Pa. Died Jan. 28, 1993.

STENEHJEM, LELAND MANFORD, banker; b. Arnegard, N.D., May 25, 1918; s. Odin N. and Lillie (Moe) S.; m. Judith H. Johnson, July 21, 1944; children—Leland Manford, Stephen Leslie, Joan Marie. B.S., N.D. State U., 1941; grad., U. Wis. Grad. Sch. Banking, 1948. With First Internat. Bank, Watford City, N.D., 1943-96; exec. v.p. First Internat. Bank, 1961-66, pres., 1966-96; chmn. bd. dirs. First Internat. Bank and Trust, 1992-96; chmn. First Nat Bank of Fessenden, N.D., 1983-96; Mem. N.D. Banking Bd., 1958-63; mem. N.D. adv. council Farmers Home Adminstrn., 1957-60; bd. dirs. N.D. State U. Found. Pres. Good Shepherd Home, 1963-96; bd. dirs. N.D. State U. Alumni Assn.; pres., bd. trustees First Luth. Ch. 2d lt. USMCR World War II. Recipient Singular Achievement award Greater N.D. Assn. Mem. Am. Bankers Assn. (past mem. exec. coun.), N.D. Bankers Assn. (past pres.), Ind. Bankers Assn. Am. (past pres.), Watford City Assn., Commerce Club (pres.), Viking Club (Mesa, Ariz.; pres.), Masons, Shriners, Elks, Lions (pres. Watford City), Rotary (pres.), Alpha Tau Omega. Lutheran. Lodges: Mason, Elk, Lion (pres. Watford City), Rotarian (pres.), Shriners. Died Sept. 15, 1996.

STEPHAN, EDMUND ANTON, lawyer; b. Chgo., Oct. 7, 1911; s. Anton Charles and Mary Veronica (Egan) S.; m. Evelyn Way, July 3, 1937; children: Miriam, Edmund Anton, Martha (Mrs. Robert McNeill), Donald, Christopher, Evelyn, Gregory, Joan (Mrs. David Nelson). AB, U. Notre Dame, 1933; LLB, Harvard, 1939. Bar: N.Y. 1940, Ill. 1945. Assoc. Carter, Ledyard & Milburn, N.Y.C., 1939-42; atty. charge N.Y. office U.S. Alien Property Custodian, 1943-45; assoc. Mayer, Brown & Platt (and predecessors), Chgo., 1945-47; ptnr. Mayer, Brown & Platt (and predecessors), 1947-90, sr. counsel, 1991—; dir. (hon.) Brunswick Corp., Marsh & McLennan Cos. Emeritus chmn. bd. trustees U. Notre Dame. Mem. ABA, Ill. Bar Assn., Chgo. Bar Assn., Legal Club, Mid-Day Club, Chgo. Club, Law Club, Michigan Shores Club, Westmoreland Country Club, Harvard Club (N.Y.C.), Bob-O-Link Golf Club (Highland Park, Ill.). Roman Catholic. Deceased.

STERN, JOSEPH AARON, services contracting executive; b. N.Y.C., Apr. 24, 1927; s. Charles M. and Anna (Robinson) S.; m. Phyllis A. Swett, Aug. 26, 1950; children: Carole, Beth, Charles. BS in Food Tech., MIT, 1949, MS in Food Tech., 1950, PhD in Food Tech., 1953. Food technologist Davis Bros. Fisheries Inc., Gloucester, Mass., 1948-49; teaching and research asst. Dept. Food Tech. MIT, Cambridge, 1950-53; assoc. prof. U. Wash. Coll. of Fisheries, Seattle, 1953-55; chief biochemistry unit, chief life scis. sect., mgr. interplanetary mission support and advanced exploration systems Boeing Co., Seattle, 1958-66; assoc. prof. U. Wash. Coll. of Fisheries, Seattle, 1963-68; asst. sect. mgr. Jet Propulsion Lab., Pasadena, Calif., 1966-69; pres. The Bionetics Corp., Hampton, Va., 1969—. Contbr. articles to profl. jours. Recipient cert. appreciation Viking Project Office, NASA, 1975, pub. svc. award NASA, 1977. Mem. Am. Inst. Biol. Sci., AIAA, Nat. Contract Mgmt. Assn., N.Y. Acad. Scis., Sigma Xi. Died Jan. 31, 1996.

STEVENS, BROOKS, industrial designer, educator; b. Milw., June 7, 1911. Arch. degree, Cornell U. Founder Brooks Stevens Design Assocs., 1933; now tchr. Milw. Inst. Art and Design. Designer numerous consumer products including Harley Davidson motorcycles, Evinrude outboard motors, Petipoint irons. Brooks Stevens Design Ctr. named in his honor, 1992. Coined the term 'planned obsolescence'. DIED 01/04/95. .

STEVENS, ROGER LACEY, theatrical producer; b. Detroit, Mar. 12, 1910; s. Stanley and Florence (Jackson) S.; m. Christine Gesell, Jan. 1, 1938; 1 child, Christabel. Student, Choate Sch., 1928, U. Mich., 1928-30; DHL, U. Mich., 1964; HHD (hon.), Wayne State U., 1960; DHL, Tulane U., 1960; LLD, Amherst Coll., 1968; hon. degrees, Skidmore Coll., 1969, U. Ill., 1970, Boston U., 1970, Am. U., 1979, Boston U., 1979, Miami U., 1983, Phila. Coll. Art, 1986. Former real estate broker specializing in hotels and investment properties, 1934-60; spl. asst. to the Pres. on the arts, 1964-68; chmn. Nat. Coun. on the Arts, 1965-69, Nat. Endowment for the Arts, also trustee; pres. Nat. Inst. for Music Theater; chmn. Am. Film Inst., 1969-72; chmn. adv. com. Nat. Book Award, 1970-75, 1988-89; mem. Coun. for Arts, Mass. Inst. Tech.; chmn. Fund for New Am. Plays, 1986—; mem. Pres.'s Com. on Arts and Humanities, 1982-93. Producing partner in more than 200 theatrical prodns. including Old Times, West Side Story, Cat on a Hot Tin Roof, Bus Stop, The Visit, Mary, Mary, A Man for all Seasons, The Best Man, Deathtrap, Death of a Salesman; Kennedy Ctr. prodns. include Annie, First Monday in October, On Your Toes, Mass, Jumpers, Night and Day, Wings, Texas Trilogy, Bedroom Farce, Cocktail Hour, Love Letters, Metamorphosis, A Few Good Men, Artist Descending a Staircase, Shadowlands, She Loves Me. Chmn. fin. com. Dem. Party, 1956; chmn. bd. trustees John F. Kennedy Ctr. Performing Arts, 1961-88; trustee Am. Shakespeare Theater and Acad., Choate Sch., 1982-93, Ballet Theatre Found., 1977-94; bd. dirs. Met. Opera Assn., 1958—, Nat. Symphony Orch., 1981-93, Filene Ctr./Wolf Trap Farm Park for Performing Arts, 1969-92, The Washington Opera, 1988-94, Peabody Conservatory, 1979-82, Folger Libr., Acad. Am. Poets. Decorated knight comdr. Brit. Empire; Royal Order of Vasa, Sweden; grand ufficiale Order of Merit Italy; comdr.'s cross Order of Merit Fed. Republic Germany; recipient award contbn. theatre Nat. Theater Conf., 1970, , Presdl. Medal of Freedom, 1988, Nat. Medal of Arts, 1988; Kennedy Ctr. honoree, 1988. Fellow Royal Soc. Arts; mem. ANTA (exec. com.), Pilgrims Club (N.Y.C.), Century Club (N.Y.C.), Cosmos Club (Washington), Phi Gamma Delta.

STEVENSON, JOHN REESE, lawyer; b. Chgo., Oct. 24, 1921; s. John A. and Josephine R. S.; m. Patience Fullerton, Apr. 10, 1943 (dec. 1982); children: Elizabeth F., Sally H. Stevenson Fischer, John R. Jr., Patience Stevenson Scott; m. Ruth Carter Johnson, May 21, 1983. AB summa cum laude, Princeton U., 1942; LLB, Columbia U., 1949, DJS, 1952. Bar: N.Y. 1949, U.S. Supreme Ct. 1964, D.C. 1971. Assoc. Sullivan & Cromwell, N.Y.C., 1950-55, ptnr., 1956-69, 75-87, chmn., sr. ptnr., 1979-87, counsel, 1987-92; legal adv. with rank of asst. sec. U.S. Dept. State, 1969-72, chmn. adv. com. on pub. internat. law, 1986-90, mem. com. 1993-97; adviser U.S. del. Gen. Assembly UN, 1969-74; chmn. U.S. del. Internat. Conf. on Air Law, The Hague, The Netherlands, 1970; mem. U.S. del. Internat. Conf. on Law of Treaties, Vienna, 1969; amb., spl. rep. of Pres. Law of the Sea conf., 1973-75; U.S. mem. Permanent Ct. of Arbitration, The Hague, 1969-79, 84-90; U.S. rep. Internat. Ct. Justice Namibia (S.W. Africa) case, 1970; spl. counsel U.S. del. Delimitation of Martime Boundary in Gulf of Maine (Can. vs. U.S.A.), 1984; mem. OAS Inter-Am. commn. on Human Rights, 1987-90; dir. Ctr. for Strategic and Internat. Studies; prin. Ctr. Excellence in Govt.; bd. dirs. Americas Soc. Author: The Chilean Popular Front, 1952; editor-in-chief Columbia Law Rev.; contbr. articles to legal and State Dept. jours. Fellow ABA (hon.); mem. Am. Soc. Internat. Law (pres. 1966-68, hon. v.p. 1968-92, 93-97, hon. pres. 1992-93), N.Y. State Bar Assn. (chmn. com. on internat. law 1963-65), Internat. Law Assn., Inst. de Droit Internat. (v.p. 1987-89), Assn. of Bar of City of N.Y. (chmn. com. on internat. law 1958-61), Am. Arbitration Assn. (bd. dirs. 1984-92, exec. com., chmn. internat. sect. law com.), Coun. Fgn. Rels., Am. Law Inst., Phi Beta Kappa. Home: Fort Worth Tex. Died Oct. 26, 1997.

STEWART, ALLEN WARREN, lawyer; b. Manchester, N.H., Dec. 12, 1938; s. Ellwyn F. and Aelene W. (Harriman) S.; children: William, Paul, Geoffrey. BS, U.S. Naval Acad., 1961; MS, George Washington U., 1967; JD, U. Pa., 1970. Bar: Pa. 1970, U.S. Ct. Appeals (3d cir.) 1971, U.S. Supreme Ct. 1980. Morgan, Lewis & Bockius, Phila., 1970-77, ptnr., 1977-94; chmn. bd. dirs. Am. Sentinel Ins. Co., Conestoga Life Assurance Co., Tartan Mgmt. Corp. Editor: Reinsurance, 1991; contbr. articles to legal and ins. jours. Naval aviator, lt. comdr. USN, 1961-66. Mem. ABA, Pa. Bar Assn., Phila. Bar Assn. Club: Phila. Racquet. Avocations: sailing, fishing. Died Jan. 24, 1997.

STEWART, JAMES MAITLAND, actor; b. Indiana, Pa., May 20, 1908; s. Alexander Maitland and Elizabeth Ruth (Jackson) S.; m. Gloria McLean, Aug. 9, 1949 (dec. Feb. 1994); children: Michael, Ronald (dec.), Judy and Kelly (twins). BS in Architecture, Princeton U., 1932; hon. degree, Indiana U. of Pa., U. S.C., Chapman Coll.; 7 other hon. degrees. Appeared in N.Y.C. in: Goodbye Again, 1932, Yellow Jack, Divided by Three and Page Miss Glory, 1934; motion pictures include Mr. Smith Goes to Washington, 1939, The Philadelphia Story, 1940, It's a Wonderful Life, 1946, Rear Window, 1954, Far Country, 1955, Man from Laramie, 1955, Strategic Air Command, 1955, The Man Who Knew too Much, 1956, Night Passage, 1957 Spirit of St. Louis, 1957, Vertigo, 1958, Bell, Book and Candle, 1959, It's a Wonderful World, 1959, Anatomy of Murder, 1959, The FBI, 1959, The Mountain Road, 1960, Two Rode Together, 1961, Mr. Hobbs Takes a Vacation, 1962, How the West Was Won, 1962, Take Her, She's Mine, 1963, Cheyenne Autumn, 1964, The Rare Breed, 1966, Flight of the Phoenix, 1966, Firecreek, 1968, Bandolero, 1968, Cheyenne Social Club, 1970, Fool's Parade, 1971, That's Entertainment, 1974, The Shootist, 1976, Airport '77, 1977, The Big Sleep, 1978, The Magic of Lassie, 1978, Right of Way, 1983, (voice) An American Tail: Fivel Goes West, 1991; TV show The Jimmy Stewart Show, 1971-72, Hawkins Murder, 1973-74, Marlene Dietrich: Shadow and Light, 1996; author: Jimmy Stewart and His Poems, 1989 (Recipient N.Y. Critics award for best male performance of 1939 in Mr. Smith Goes to Washington, Acad. award for performance in Philadelphia Story 1940, Berlin Film award 1962, Life Achievement award Am. Film Inst. 1980). Col. A.C., U.S. Army, World War II; brig. gen. USAFR, 1959. Decorated D.F.C. with oak leaf cluster, Air medal, Croix de Guerre with palm; recipient Lifetime Achievement award Screen Actors Guild, 1968, Disting. Performance award Drama League, 1970, Nat. Artist award Am. Nat. Acad. and Theatre, 1981, Kennedy Ctr. medal for lifetime achievement, 1983, Lifetime Achievement Award Oscar, Nat. Acad. of Motion Picture Arts and Scis., 1984, Presdl. medal of Freedom, 1985, Lifetime Achievement award Santa Barbara Film Festival, 1987, Lifetime Achievement award Monterey Film Festival, 1988, Lifetime Achievement award Am. Mus. of the Moving Image, 1988, Master Screen Artist award Dallas Film Festival, 1989, Ann. Spencer Tracy award UCLA, 1989, Woodrow Wilson medal Princeton U., 1990, Ann. Tribute N.Y. Film Soc., 1990, Ann. Tribute Film soc. of Lincoln Ctr., 1990, Career Achievement award Nat. Bd. Rev., 1991, Lifetime Achievement award Internat. Film Festival, 1992, Palm award Palm Springs Internat. Film Festival, 1992. Presbyterian. Died July 2, 1997.

STEWART, MARK ARMSTRONG, child psychiatrist, medical educator; b. Yeovil, Somerset, Eng., July 23, 1929; came to U.S., 1957; s. Francis Hugh and Violet Beaumont (Knight) S.; m. Pamela Mary Finlow, Mar. 19, 1955; children: Sarah G. Stewart Tallman, R. Anne Stewart Hefner, Duncan R. B.A., Cambridge (Eng.) U., 1952, M.A. (hon.), 1957; M.R.C.S., L.R.C.P., St. Thomas Hosp. Med. Sch., London, 1956. Diplomate Am. Bd. Psychiatry and Neurology, Am. Bd. Gen. and Child Psychiatry. Intern St. John's Gen. Hosp., (NewFoundland), 1956-57; resident in psychiatry Barnes Hosp., St. Louis, 1956-61; faculty mem. Washington U. Sch. Medicine, St. Louis, 1961-72, prof. dept. psychiatry, 1970-72, assoc. prof. pediatrics, 1963-72; Ida P. Haller prof. child psychiatry U. Iowa Coll. Medicine, Iowa City, 1972—. Author: (with Sally Olds) Raising a Hyperactive Child, 1973 (1st place media award Family Sevice Assn. 1974), (with Ann Gath) Psychological Disorders of Children, 1978; contbr. many chpts. to textbooks, numerous articles to profl. jours. Served with M.C. Royal Brit. Army, 1947-49. Brit. Govt. math. scholar; NIMH Research Career awardee, 1961-71. Fellow Am. Psychiat. Assn., Am. Acad. Child Psychiatry; mem. Psychiat. Research Soc., Soc. for Research in Child Devel., Internat. Soc. Research in Aggression. Democrat. Died May 20, 1997.

STIFEL, LAURENCE DAVIS, agricultural development administrator; b. Cleve., Aug. 29, 1930; s. Richard Ernest and Loretta Ann (Davis) S.; m. Dell C. Chenoweth, June 16, 1962; children: Laura Chenoweth, David Calvert. A.B. in Econs., Harvard U., 1952, M.B.A., 1954; LL.B., Cleve. Marshall Law Sch., 1960; Ph.D. in Econs., Western Res. U., 1962; L.H.D., Urbana Coll., 1976. Bar: Ohio 1960. Asst. prof. econs. Willamette U., Salem, Oreg., 1961-62; program economist AID, Rangoon, Burma, 1962-64; econ. adviser Nat. Econ. Devel. Bd., Bangkok, 1964-67; social sci. project leader Rockefeller Found. in Thailand, also vis. prof. econs. Thammasat U., Bangkok, 1967-74; vis. fellow Econ. Growth Center, Yale U., 1969-70; sec. Internat. Agrl. Devel. Service, N.Y.C., 1975-79, Rockefeller Found., N.Y.C., 1974-83; asso. dir. social scis. Rockefeller Found., 1977-78, v.p., 1977-85; dir. gen. Internat. Inst. Tropical Agr., Ibadan, Nigeria, 1985-90; vis. fellow Cornell Internat. Inst. Food, Agr. & Devel., Ithaca, N.Y., 1990-93; dir. gen. Internat. Ctr. Living Aquatic Resources Mgmt, Manila, Philippines, 1993-95; vis. fellow Cornell U., Ithaca, 1993-95; trustee Gen. Edn. Bd., N.Y.C., 1974-85, Princeton-in-Asia, 1976-85, Thailand Devel. Research Inst., Bangkok, 1985-95; mem. governing council, exec. com. Rockefeller Archive Center; chmn. mgmt. rev. of West Africa Rice Devel. Assn. for Consultative Group for Internat. Agrl. Research, 1983. Author: The Textile Industry-A Case Study of Industrial Development in the Philippines, 1963, Methodology for Preparation of the Second Economic and Social Development Plan of Thailand, 1967; also articles.; co-editor: Education and Training for Public Sector Management in the Developing Countries, 1977, Social Sciences and Public Policy in Developing Areas, 1982. Fulbright fellow Philippines, 1959-60. Mem. Asia Soc. (chmn. Thai council 1975-77), Siam Soc. (council 1969-72), Soc. Internat. Devel. (v.p., co-founder Bangkok chpt. 1968-70), Council Fgn. Relations, Am. Econs. Assn., Assn. Asian Studies. Club: Harvard, Century Assn. (N.Y.C.). Home: Ithaca N.Y. Died Apr. 19, 1995.

STIFF, JOHN STERLING, development company executive; b. McKinney, Tex., Feb. 14, 1921; s. James Harrison and Elva (Boone) S.; m. Harriet Raschig, May 21, 1946; children—Mark, Justin. Student, Tex. A&M Coll., 1938-41; B.E., Yale U., 1947. Registered profl. engr., Tex. Mgmt. trainee City of Big Spring, Tex., 1938-39, 41-42; city engr. Abilene, Tex., 1947-51; city mgr. Irving, Tex., 1953-57; gen. mgr. Hardee-Pipkin Constrn.Co., Irving, 1957-58; city mgr. Garland, Tex., 1958-63, Amarillo, Tex., 1963-83; pres. Quail Creek Devel. Co., Amarillo, Tex., 1983-95. Pres. Amarillo Area Found., 1988; bd. dirs. Harrington Found., 1989. Served with USNR, 1942-46, 51-52. Mem. Internat. City Mgrs. Assn. (past pres.), Tex. City Mgrs. Assn. (past pres.), Panhandle Home Builders Assn. (past bd. dirs.), Garland Home Builders Assn., Amarillo Exec. Assn. (pres. 1988-89), Amarillo C. of C., Dallas C. of C., Amarillo A & M Club, Amarillo Yale Club, Rotary. Methodist. Home: Amarillo Tex. Died June 10, 1996.

STILES, MERVIN, clergyman; b. Cazadero, Calif., Oct. 27, 1917; s. Earl and Katherine (Ancel) S.; m. Beulah May Matteson, Aug. 3, 1943; children: Enid Ruth Bundy, Steven Eugene S., L. Margaret DeMers. BA, Simpson Bible Coll., San Francisco, 1959. Pastor Bapt. City Mission Soc., Portland, Oreg., 1947-51, First Christian Ch., Mansfield, Wash., 1951-52; tchr., mem. adv. bd. New Life Ctr., Santa Cruz, Calif., 1972-90; contbr. SBL Regional Meetings, 1973-90. Author, editor: Shofar, Vols. I to XX, 1973-90. DIED 08/26/96. .

STILLMAN, GEORGE, artist; b. Laramie, Wyo., Feb. 25, 1921; s. Herman and Estelle (Heimlich) S.; m. Lillian Lucille Blitz, Dec. 1, 1942; children: David, Anthony. Cert. of completion, Calif. Sch. Fine Art,

1949; MFA, Ariz. State U., 1970. Prof. art U. Guadalajara, Mex., 1950-51; chief map reprodn. Inter Am. Geodetic Survey U.S. Army, Panama C.Z., 1951-58; comm. officer AID, L.Am., 1958-66; prodr. and dir. TV, Ariz. State U., Tempe, 1966-70; chmn. art dept. Columbus (Ga.) Coll., 1970-72; prof., chmn. dept. Ctrl. Wash. U., Ellensburg, 1972-88, prof. emeritus, from 1988. One-man shows include Guild Gallery, San Francisco, 1947, Lucien Labaudt Gallery, San Francisco, 1949, Ariz. State U. Mus., Tempe, 1970, Foster/White Gallery, Seattle, 1986, Ctrl. Wash. U., Ellensburg, 1991, Tacoma Libr. Handforth Gallery, Tacoma, 1995; exhibited in group shows at Palace of the Legion of Honor, San Francisco, 1947, San Francisco Mus. Art, 1949, Bklyn. Mus. Art, 1952, Ga. Artists, High Mus., Atlanta, 32d Spokane (Wash.) Ann. Nat., 1980, Art for the Parks, Jackson, Wyo., 1989, 100 Yrs. of Washington Art, Tacoma, Wash., 1990, Art Mus. Santa Cruz, Calif., 1993, Laguna Art Mus., 1996, San Francisco Mus. of Modern Art, 1996; represented in permanent collections Met. Mus. Art, N.Y.C., Nat. Mus. Am. Art, Smithsonian, Washington, Oakland (Calif.) Mus. Art, High Mus. Art, Atlanta, Tacoma Mus. Art, Washington State Arts Commn., British Mus. Art, London, Laguna (Calif.) Mus. Art, Worcester (Mass.) Mus. Art. Recipient Bender award San Francisco Art Assn., 1949, Nat. Endowment for Arts, 1990. Mem. Coll. Art Assn., Nat. Watercolor Soc. Deceased.

STINE, GEORGE HARRY, consulting engineer, author; b. Phila., Mar. 26, 1928; s. George Haeberle and Rhea (Matilda) (O'Neill) S.; m. Barbara Ann Kauth, June 10, 1952; children: Constance Rhea, Eleanor Anne, George Willard. B.A. in Physics, Colo. Coll., 1952. Chief controls and instruments sect., propulsion br. White Sands (N.Mex.) Proving Grounds, 1952-55; chief range ops. div. U.S. Naval Ordnance Missile Test Facility at proving grounds, 1955-57; design specialist Martin Co., Denver, 1957; chief engr., pres. Model Missiles, Inc., Denver, 1957-59; design engr. Stanley Aviation Corp., Denver, 1959-60; asst. dir. research Huyck Corp., Stamford, Conn., 1960-65; sci. cons. CBS-TV, 1969, CBC, Toronto, 1969; sci. reporter Metromedia Radio News, N.Y.C., 1968; cons. Young & Rubicam Inc., N.Y.C., also Gen. Electric Co., Valley Forge, Pa., 1966-69; lectr. Franklin Inst., Phila., 1966-72; mktg. mgr. Flow Technology, Inc., Phoenix, 1973-76; cons. curator Internat. Space Hall of Fame, 1976; cons. astronautical history Nat. Air and Space Museum, Smithsonian Instn., 1965-97; cons. mktg. research and surveys Talley Industries, Inc., Mesa, Ariz., 1977; cons. mktg. and comm. Flow Tech., Inc., 1976-79; cons. Sci. Applications, Inc. 1976-81, Visions of the Future, 1982-86, McDonnell Douglas Corp., 1988-90, Sci. Applications Internat. Corp., 1990, Quest Aerospace Edn., Inc., 1992-97, Aero Tech., Inc., 1991; expert witness fireworks injury cases, 1984-97; pres. The Enterprise Inst., Inc., 1987-97; cons., writer Discover Space Computer Program, Broderbond Software, Inc., 1992-93; moderator aviation and sport rocketry conf., Bix on-line computer network, 1986-97. Freelance writer, 1951-97; author more than 50 books on astronautics and sci., including The Model Rocketry Manual, 1975, The Third Industrial Revolution, 2d edit., 1979, The New Model Rocketry Manual, 1977, Shuttle Into Space, 1978, The Space Enterprise, 1980, Space Power, 1981, Confrontation in Space, 1981, The Hopeful Future, 1983, The Untold Story of the Computer Revolution, 1984, The Silicon Gods, 1984, Handbook for Space Colonists, 1985, The Corporate Survivors, 1986, Thirty Years of Model Rocketry, A Safety Report, 1988, Mind Machines You Can Build, 1991, ICBM, The Making of the Weapon That Changed the World, 1991, The Handbook of Model Rocketry 6th edit., 1994, Halfway to Anywhere, 1996; author: (as Lee Correy) sci. fiction novels and stories, including Starship Through Space, 1954, Rocket Man, 1955, Contraband Rocket, 1956, Star Driver, 1980, Shuttle Down, 1981, Space Doctor, 1981, The Abode of Life, 1982, Manna, 1984, A Matter of Metalaw, 1986, (under own name) Warbots, 1988, Operation Steel Band, 1988, The Bastaard Rebellion, 1988, Sierra Madre, 1988, Operation High Dragon, 1989, The Lost Battalion, 1989, Operation Iron Fist, 1989, Force of Arms, 1990, Blood Siege, 1990, Guts and Glory, 1991, Warrior Shield, 1992, Judgement Day, 1992, Starsea Invaders # 1, First Action, 1993, Star-sea Invaders # 2, Second Contact, 1994, Star-sea Invaders # 3, Third Encounter, 1995, Living in Space, 1997; contbr. numerous articles to jours. Charter mem. citizen's adv. coun. Nat. Space Policy, 1981-97; mem. Ariz. Space Commn., 1992-97, NASA Tech. and Commercialization Adv. Com., 1995. Recipient Silver medal Assn. U.S. Army, 1967, Spl. award Hobby Industry Assn., 1969; Paul Tissandier diploma Fedn. Aeronautique Internationale, 1985, Lifetime Space Activist award Space Access Soc., 1995. Fellow AIAA (assoc.)Explorers Club, Brit. Interplanetary Soc., Am. Rocket Soc.; mem. Nat. Assn. Rocketry (hon. trustee 1978-81, founder 1957, pres. 1957-67, trustee 1978-81, Spl. Founder's award 1967, Howard Galloway Svc. award 1978, 83, 85, 87), Nat. Fire Protection Assn. (chmn. com. pyrotechnics 1974-94, Svc. award 1993, emeritus mem. 1994), N.Y. Acad. Scis., Aircraft Owners and Pilots Assn., Ariz. Pilots Assn. (dir. 1980-93, v.p. 1981-84), L-5 Soc. (v.p. 1984). Home: Phoenix Ariz. Died Nov. 2, 1997.

STINEBRING, WARREN RICHARD, microbiologist, educator; b. Niagara Falls, N.Y., July 31, 1924; s. Clifford Thomas and Signe (Arvidson) S.; m. Delores Jean Zakes, June 12, 1948; children: Dan R., Beth E., Eric. B.A., U. Buffalo, 1948; M.S., U. Pa., 1949, Ph.D., 1951. With U. Pa., Phila., 1949-55; asso. U. Pa., 1953-55; asst. prof. U. Tex. Med. Br., Galveston, 1955-57; asso. research prof. Inst. Microbiology, Rutgers U., New Brunswick, N.J., 1957-60; asst. prof. U. Pitts. Coll. Medicine, 1960-65, asso. prof., 1965-66; prof., chmn. med. microbiology U. Calif. Coll. Medicine at Irvine, 1966-68; prof. U. Vt. Coll. Medicine, Burlington, 1968-86, prof. emeritus, 1986—; chmn. med. microbiology U. Vt. Coll. Medicine, 1968-78; sabbatical leave Royal Postgrad. Med. Sch., London, 1974-75. Served with inf. AUS, 1943-45, ETO. Decorated Purple Heart.; Recipient Golden Apple award Student AMA, 1966-67, award for outstanding research and diagnosis in brucellosis eradication in Vt. Vt. Vt. Med. Assn., 1983. Mem. AAAS, Tissue Culture Assn. (ednl. com. 1970-72, chmn. 1970-72), Reticuloendothelial Soc., Am. Soc. Microbiology, Am. Soc. Mammalogy, Soc. Exptl. Biol. Medicine, Brucellosis Research Conf. (hon. patron). Research on host-parasite interactions delayed hypersensitivity, interferon stimulation by non-viral agts., brucellosis. Died Sept. 26, 1996.

STIPP, JOHN EDGAR, financial consultant, lawyer; b. Watseka, Ill., Feb. 10, 1914; s. George Y. and Stella M. (Tubbs) S.; m. Janet E. Miller, June 4, 1938; 1 child, Thomas John. J.D., Drake U., 1936; LL.D., Lincoln Coll., 1961. Bar: Ill., Iowa, U.S. Supreme Ct. Practiced in Danville, Ill., 1936-50; dir. Bldg. & Loan Dept., Ill. State, 1949; gen. claims atty. Continental Casualty Co., Chgo., 1950, v.p., sec., mem. fin. com., dir.; v.p., sec., mem. fin. com., dir. Continental Assurance Co., Chgo.; pres. Fed. Home Loan Bank of Chgo., 1953-74; fin. cons., 1974—; bd. dirs., mem. fin. com. CNA Fin. Corp.; trustee retirement fund Fed. Home Loan Bank System, 1953-74; bd. dirs., mem. fin. investment coms. Chgo. Title, Chgo. Title Ins., 1961-78; bd. dirs. Transp. Ins. Co. Speaker, author articles on econs., fin. Mem. Chgo. Crime Commn., Fed. Savs. and Loan Adv. Council, created by 74th Congress, 1951; commr. Vermillion Co. Airport Authority, 1946-49; bd. govs., sec., treas., chmn. fin. and investment com. Alpha Tau Omega Found., 1978—; bd. dirs. Goodwill Industries, Cook County chpt. ARC; mem. Mayor's Com. on Econ. and Cultural Devel. Chgo. Served as lt. USNR, 1943-45. Mem. Chgo. Hist. Soc., Chgo. Mus. Natural History, Newcomen Soc., Alpha Tau Omega (past nat. treas.). Lutheran. Clubs: Elks; Executives (Chgo.) (past pres.), Economic (Chgo.), Tavern (Chgo.), University (Chgo.); Restless Weasels of Lac du Flambeau (Wis.); Wisconsin (Milw.); Minocqua (Wis.) Country (Minocqua). Died Mar. 8, 1994.

STIREWALT, EDWARD NEALE, chemist, scientific analyst; b. Hartsville, S.C., Nov. 29, 1918; s. Neale Summers and Evelyn (Fraser) S.; m. Marcia Marvin Winton, Nov. 21, 1947; children: James Neale, Evelyn Fraser, Marcia Winton. AB, High Point U., 1938; MA, U. N.C., 1942. Staff scientist U.S. AEC, Washington, 1948-53; physicist, supr. U.S. Naval Rsch. Lab., Washington, 1953-57; br. chief Analytic Svcs., Inc., Arlington, Va., 1957-63; ind. cons. def. and energy fields Washington, 1963-77; sr. assoc. Planning Rsch. Corp., McLean, Va., 1977-86; assoc. editor PV News, Casanova, Va., 1984-95; mem. Fairfax (Va.) County Air Pollution Control Bd., 1980-85; bd. dirs. Fairfax Hosp., 1963-66. Co-author: Photovoltaics--Sunlight to Electricity in One Step, 1981, A Guide to the Photovoltaic Revolution, 1985. Chmn. Fairfax County Hosp. Commn., 1963-66; mem. Herndon (Va.) Planning Commn., 1989-95; bd. dirs. Assn. to Unite Dems., Washington, 1992. Lt. (j.g.) USNR, Manhattan Project, PTO, 1944-46. Mem. AAAS, Washington Philos. Soc., Masons, Sigma Xi. Presbyterian. Home: Herndon Va. Died Feb. 19, 1995, interred Chestnut Grove Cemetery, Herndon, Va.

STOCKS, CHESTER LEE, JR., health care executive; b. Montgomery, Ala., Oct. 8, 1928; s. Chester Lee and Evelyn (Cooley) S.; m. Mary Gwendoline Hase, June 5, 1954; children: Susan, Bradley Hase, Charles Lee, Sally. B.S., Auburn U., 1949; M.H.A., Washington U., St. Louis, 1955. Resident Baylor U. Med. Center, Dallas, 1954-55; adminstrv. asst. Baylor U. Med. Center, 1955-57, asst. adminstr., 1957-63; exec. v.p. Good Samaritan Hosp. and Med. Center, 1963, Portland, Oreg., 1963-89; pres. Legacy Health System, Portland, 1989-90; Preceptor grad. programs in hosp. adminstrn. U. Calif., U. Iowa, Washington U.; lectr., participant programs on health care; mem. exec. com. Oreg. Regional Med. Programs, 1966-74, v.p., 1969-76; mem. Oreg. Commn. on Nursing, 1969-75, Oreg. Health Manpower Commn., 1966-73, Comprehensive Health Planning Assn. Met. Portland, 1969-76, Oreg. Health Commn. Siting Com., 1974-77; dir. Oreg. Med. Polit. Action Com., 1974-77; Oreg. chmn. Wash. U. devel. program, 1967-70. Trustee Fred Hutchison Cancer Center, Seattle, 1972-79, Oreg. Comprehensive Cancer Center, 1973-75, Blue Cross Oreg., 1965-90 ; pres. Oreg. Hosp. Found., 1979; mem. vestry Trinity Episc. Ch., 1983-86. Served to 1st lt. USAF, 1950-53. Recipient Disting. Alumnus award Washington U., 1989. Fellow Am. Coll. Health Care Execs. (regent 1969-75, gov. 1975-78, chmn. 1979); mem. Assn. Western Hosps. (trustee, pres. 1973-74), Am. Hosp. Assn. (trustee 1984-87, various coms. 1965-90), Oreg. Assn. Hosps. (pres. 1967-68, trustee 1973-76), Portland Council of Hosps. (pres. 1966-67), Greater Portland Area Hosp. Council (pres. 1983), NW Oreg. Council Hosps. (exec. com. 1980-83), Tex. Hosp. Assn. (hon.), Portland C. of C. (bd. dirs. 1967-69), Nat. Assn. for Practical Nurse Edn. and Service (trustee 1960-86), Voluntary Hosps. Am. (bd. dirs. 1988-89), Am. health Care Systems (bd. dirs. 1989-90), Voluntary Hosps. Am. Enterprises (bd. dirs. 1986-89), Protestant Hosp. Assn., Nat. League for Nursing, Pi Kappa Alpha. Episcopalian (dir. William Temple House 1965-70). Clubs: Rotarian. (Portland), Multnomah Athletic (Portland), Arlington (Portland). Home: Portland Oreg. Died Dec. 5, 1990.

STOCKTON, RALPH MADISON, JR., lawyer; b. Winston-Salem, N.C., June 22, 1927; s. Ralph Madison and Margaret (Thompson) S.; m. Frances Bowles, July 15, 1950 (dec. Apr. 27, 1994); children: Mary Ellen Sartin, Ralph Madison III, David Anderson, James Alexander; m. Margaret Norfleet, Mar. 3, 1995. B.S., U. N.C., 1948, LL.B. cum laude, 1950; LL.D. (hon.), Winston-Salem U., 1983. Bar: N.C. 1950. Assoc. firm Dwight, Royal, Harris Koeger & Caskey, Washington, 1950-51; with Petree Stockton, Winston-Salem, Charlotte, N.C. and Raleigh, N.C., 1951—, ptnr., 1956—, chmn. exec. com., 1980—; permanent mem. jud. conf. U.S. Ct. Appeals (4th cir.), 1958—. Trustee Winston-Salem State U., 1958-84, vice chmn., 1973-84; trustee Forsyth County Legal Aid Soc., 1966-70, pres., 1969; trustee Meth. Children's Home, 1966-84, chmn. exec. com., 1969-75, pres. bd. trustees, 1975-84; bd. mgrs. Meth. Home, Charlotte, N.C., 1967-70; bd. dirs. Winston-Salem Found., 1979-86, chmn. bd., 1985-86; mem. Leadership Winston-Salem, 1984-85, alumni council, 1987-88; co-chmn. N.C. Legis. Com. on Evidence and Comparative Negligence, 1980-82; mem. Gov.'s Jud. Nominating Com., 1982-85; chmn. adminstrv. bd. local United Meth. Ch., 1984-86. Mem. ABA (Ho. of Dels. 1986-91, standing com. fed. judiciary 1989-92), N.C. Bar Assn. (bd. govs. 1957-60, chmn. comml. banking and bus. law com. 1958-60, chmn. appellate rules study com. 1973-75, pres. 1976-77, named to Hall of Fame 1993), Forsyth County Bar Assn. (pres. 1965-66), Am. Coll. Trial Lawyers (state chmn. 1984-86), regent 1987-91), Nat. Conf. Bar Presidents, Fellows of Am. Bar Found., Supreme Ct. Hist. Soc. (state chmn. 1989-91, cir. rep. nat. membership 1991-93), Law Alumni Assn. U. N.C. (pres. 1964, dir. gen. 1970-73, Disting. Alumni award 1994), Order of Coif, Phi Delta Phi. Democrat. Methodist. Lodge: Rotary (pres. Winston-Salem 1965-66).

STOCKWELL, EUGENE LOUDON, international religious organization administrator; b. Boston, Sept. 28, 1923; s. Bowman F. and Vera L. (Loudon) S.; m. Margaret E. Smyres, June 3, 1950; children—William John, Robert Foster, Martha Ellen, Richard Roy. B.A., Oberlin Coll., 1943; J.D., Columbia U., 1948; M.Div., Union Theol. Sem., 1952. Ordained to ministry United Methodist Ch., 1952. Student pastor, Maybrook and Montgomery, N.Y., 1950-52; missionary, Uruguay, 1953-62; Latin Am. exec. sec., div. world missions Meth. Ch., N.Y.C., 1962-64; asst. gen. sec. world div. United Meth. Bd. Missions, 1964-72; assoc. gen. sec. for overseas ministries Nat. Council Chs. of Christ in U.S.A., N.Y.C., 1972-83; dir. commn. world mission and evangelism World Council of Chs., Geneva, 1984-96; v.p. United Bd. Christian Higher Edn. in Asia, 1970-73. Author: Claimed by God for Mission, 1966. Democrat. Died Oct. 8, 1996.

STOCKWELL, RICHARD E., journalist, business executive; b. Neillsville, Wis., Mar. 12, 1917; s. Arthur Raymond and Ella (Stelloh) S. B.S., U. Wis., 1940; M.A., U. Minn., 1945; Nieman fellow, Harvard U., 1945-46. Farm editor Sta. WIBA, Madison, Wis., 1939-40; news staff WLW, Cin., 1940-41; program dir. Wis. Network, Wisconsin Rapids, 1941-42; asso. news editor WMT, Cedar Rapids, Iowa, 1942-43, WCCO-CBS, Mpls., 1943-45; editorial writer Mpls. Star, 1946-49; editor Aviation Age, N.Y.C., 1949-52, Monsanto Mag., Monsanto Internat. Mag., St. Louis, 1952-54; editorial dir. Am. Aviation Publs., Inc., Washington, 1954-55; cons., mgmt. information analyst Flight Propulsion Lab., Gen. Electric Co., Cin., 1956-58; group dir. pub. relations and advt., electronics, ordnance and aerostructures divs. Avco Corp., Cin., 1958-68; v.p. comml. and indsl. products group Avco Corp., Nashville, 1968-74; v.p. products and research group Avco Corp., 1974-76. Author: Soviet Air Power, 1956; also numerous mag. articles. Sta. WLW scholar, 1940. Mem. Royal, Am. econs. assns., Am. Polit. Sci. Assn. Clubs: Wings (N.Y.C.); Nat. Press (Washington). Deceased.

STOKELY, HUGH LAWSON, economist, publisher; b. Newport, Tenn., Jan. 6, 1933; s. Hugh Lawson and Nellie Roberta (Runnion) S.; children: David Kerr, George Seligman. A.B., U. Tenn., 1952; postgrad., NYU Grad. Sch. Bus., 1966-67. Chartered fin. analyst, Washington. Assoc. economist, cons. Far and Middle East-Chase Manhattan Bank, N.Y.C., 1962-67, chief economist Keystone Custodian Funds, Boston, 1967-70; sr. v.p., dir. investment research and econs. Girard Bank, Phila., 1970-75; v.p., dir. econs. Bradley Woods & Co. Inc., Washington, 1975-78; pres. Hugh Stokely Assocs., Washington, 1978—; mem. econ. adv. bd. U.S.

Dept. Commerce, 1973-74; pub. Washington Economist, 1975—, Washington Investor, 1979—, Washington Strategist, 1979—; mgr. asset rsch. Chalke Inc., 1994—; mem. Com. on Data Analysis, 1991—. Served to comdr. USNR. Mem. Assn. Investment Mgmt. and Rsch., Fed. City Club. Died Dec. 18, 1996.

STOKES, DONALD ELKINTON, political science educator; b. Phila., Apr. 1, 1927; s. Joseph, Jr. and Frances Deborah (Elkinton) S.; m. Sybil Langbaum, May 18, 1955; children—Elizabeth Ann, Susan Carol. A.B., Princeton, 1951; Ph.D., Yale, 1958. Purser Grace Line, Inc., 1946-47; instr. polit. sci. Yale, 1952-54; prof. polit. sci. U. Mich., Ann Arbor, 1958-74; program dir. U. Mich. (Inst. Social Research), 1958-74, chmn. dept. polit. sci., 1970-71; dean U. Mich. (Grad. Sch.), 1971-74, Woodrow Wilson Sch. Pub. and Internat. Affairs Princeton U., N.J., 1974-92; prof. pub. and internat. affairs Princeton U., 1974—; vis. prof. Australian Nat. U., U. W.I., 1969. Author: Pasteur's Quadrant, 1996; co-author: The American Voter, 1960, Elections and the Political Order, 1966, Political Change in Britain, 1969. Assoc. mem. Nuffield Coll., Oxford, 1963-64; Sr. Fulbright scholar to Britain, 1963; fellow Social Sci. Rsch. Coun., 1955-57; fellow Guggenheim Found., 1964-65; vis. rsch. fellow Royal Inst. Internat. Affairs, 1980, Brookings Inst., 1987, 89. Fellow Am. Acad. Arts and Scis., AAAS, Nat. Acad. Pub. Adminstrn.; mem. Am. Polit. Sci. Assn. (Woodrow Wilson award 1970), Coun. Fgn. Rels., Am. Assn. Pub. Opinion Rsch., Phi Beta Kappa. Mem. Soc. Friends. Died Jan. 26, 1997.

STONE, DAVID ULRIC, management executive; author; b. Santa Cruz, Calif., Feb. 4, 1927; s. Ernest Marshall and Grace (Stone) S.; student Theol. Ministry Sch., San Jose, Calif., 1945-48; grad. Real Estate Inst., Nat. Inst. Real Estate, 1964; m. Iva Dell Frazier, July 20, 1947; children: Katherine LaVerne, Russell Keith, Susan Marie. With E.M. Stone Realty, San Jose, 1945-48; mgr. Broadway-Hale Co., San Jose, 1948-52; sales mgr. William Perry Co., San Francisco, 1952-56; gen. mgr., ptnr. Stone & Schulte, Inc., San Jose, 1956-66; pres., chmn. bd. dirs. Stone Inst., Los Gatos, Calif., 1966-95; pres. Sunchoke Internat., Inc., San Juan Bautista, Calif., 1983-84, chmn. bd. 1985-92; chmn. bd. Custom One Internat. Inc., 1986-90; pres. The Mktg. Forum, Inc., Mpls., 1986-92; dir. Realty Programming Corp. St. Louis. Named Realtor of Yr. Homes for Living Network, 1982. Mem. Nat. Inst. Real Estate Brokers (faculty mem. 1965-82), Nat. Assn. Real Estate Bds. (chmn. joint task force 1966-68), Builder's Mktg. Soc. (founder, chmn. 1985), Calif. Real Estate Assn. (dir.), Nat. Assn. Home Builders (Sales Mgr. of Year award 1960, Bill Molster award, 1990, chmn. joint task force 1966-68, faculty mem. Inst. Residential Mktg. 1982-95). Author: How to Operate a Real Estate Trade-In Program, 1962; Training Manual for Real Estate Salesmen, 1966; Guaranteed Sales Plan for Realtors and Builders, 1968 New Home Sales Training Course; The Professional Approach To Selling Real Estate; How To Communicate with Persuasive Power; How to Sell New Homes and Environmental Communities; How to Market and Sell Condominiums; How to Hire, Train and Motivate Real Estate Salespeople, How to Profitably Manage a Real Estate Office, 1977; The Road to Success in Real Estate, 1978; New Horizons in Real Estate, 1980; New Home Sales, 1982, Sales Power: American Sales Masters, 1986, The Gold Series, 1986, New Home Marketing, 1988. Died July 1, 1995. Home: Los Gatos Calif.

STONE, DONALD CRAWFORD, public administrator, educator; b. Cleve., June 17, 1903; s. Alfred William and Mary Rebecca (Crawford) S.; m. Alice Kathryn Biermann, June 10, 1928; children: Nancy Leland Stone Dickinson, Alice Crawford Stone Ilchman, Elizabeth Stone, Donald Crawford Stone Jr. AB, Colgate U., 1925, LLD (hon.), 1960; MS, Syracuse U., 1926; postgrad., U. Cin., 1927-28, Columbia, 1928-30; LLD (hon.), George Williams Coll., 1953. Asst. to city mgr. City of Cin., 1926-28; mem. staff Inst. Pub. Adminstrn., N.Y.C., 1928-29; dir. research internat. city mgmt. assn., research assoc. U. Chgo., 1930-33; exec. dir. Pub. Adminstrn. Service, 1933-39; asst. dir. Bur. of Budget, Exec. Office of Pres., 1939-48; dir. adminstrn. ECA (Marshall Plan), 1948-51, Mut. Security Agy., 1951-53; pres. Springfield (Mass.) Coll., 1953-57; dean Grad. Sch. Pub. and Internat. Affairs, U. Pitts., 1957-69, prof., 1969-74; Disting. Pub. Service prof. Carnegie-Mellon U., Pitts., 1975-92; dir. coalition to improve mgmt. in state/local govt., 1984-92; coalition sr. advisor Ind. U., Indpls., 1992-95; Green Honors Chair prof. Tex. Christian U., 1976; exec. dir. Am. Pub. Works Assn., 1934-36; spl. asst. to Fed. WPA adminstr., 1935; lectr. pub. adminstrn. Syracuse U., 1933-37; adj. prof. Am. U., 1943-53; pres. Internat. Assn. Schs. and Insts. of Adminstrn., 1962-82; cons. Fed. PWA, 1932, Civil Works Adminstrn., 1933, Fed. Relief Adminstrn., 1934-36, TVA, 1934, Fed. Social Security Bd., 1936, U.S. Pub. Housing and R.E.A., 1938, Fgn. Ops. Agy., 1954, Nat. Council Chs., 1956, Am. Council on Edn., 1957, OAS, 1957-58, 60-61, Nat. Security Orgn., 1957-58, NASA, 1960, 73, 74-75, Com. for Econ. Devel., 1966-74, UN, 1969-73, NSF, 1974-75, 79-80, OMB, 1974; cons. Saudi Arabia, 1976, Kuwait, 1977-80; cons. GAO, 1977-80; adviser U.S. del. to UN confs., San Francisco, 1945, London, 1945-46, Lake Success, 1947, Paris, 1948; mem. UN Gen. Assembly standing com. on budget and adminstrn., 1946-48; U.S. rep. to UNESCO Preparatory Commn., London, 1945-46; Mem. Commn. on Edn. and Internat. Affairs, Am. Coun. on Edn., 1954-63; com. on internat. affairs Nat. Coun. Chs., 1960-67; past pres. Am. Consortium for Internat. Pub. Adminstrn. Author books, monographs, articles in profl. jours. Recipient numerous nat. pub. svc. awards. Mem. Cosmos Club (Washington). Mem. Disciples of Christ Ch. Home: Indianapolis Ind. Died Oct. 19, 1995.

STONE, JAMES MICHAEL, medical educator; b. Oct. 30, 1952. BS in Psychology magna cum laude, U. Ill., 1974; MD, Northwestern U., Chgo., 1978. Diplomate Nat. Bd. Med. Examiners, Am. Bd. Surgery, Am. Bd. Colon and Rectal Surgery; lic. physician, Calif. Intern surgery Michael Reese Hosp. & Med. Ctr., Chgo., 1978-79, resident, 1979-83, adminstrv. chief resident, 1982-83; trauma rsch. fellow U. Calif.-San Francisco, San Francisco Gen. Hosp., 1980-81; asst. prof. surgery U. Ill., 1983-85; attending surgeon, co-dir. hyperalimentation svc. Cook County Hosp., Chgo., 1983-85; clin. asst. prof. Stanford U. Med. Ctr., 1986-89, asst. prof. surgery, divsn. surg. oncology, 1990—, chief divsn. trauma, 1992—; chief gen. surgery Palo Alto VA Med. Ctr., 1986-89; med. fellow dept. colon and rectal surgery U. Minn., 1989-90; mem. staff U. Ill. Hosp. and Clinics, Cook County Hosp., 1983-85, Stanford U. Med. Ctr., Palo Alto VA Med. Ctr., 1985-89, U. Minn. Med. Ctr., 1989-90, Stanford U. Med. Ctr., 1990—. Contbr. articles to profl. jours., chpts. to books. James scholar U. Ill., Urbana, 1970-74, Paul M. Cherementa award Paralyzed Vets. Am., 1988, grant Spinal Cord Rsch. Found., 1988-90. Mem. Phi Beta Kappa, Phi Kappa Phi. Deceased.

STONE, JON, television producer, director, writer; b. New Haven, Apr. 13, 1931; s. Emerson Law and Grace Elizabeth Stone; m. Beverly Owen, June 1966 (div. 1986); children: Polly Diantha, Katherine Winter. BA, Williams Coll., 1952, LHD (hon.), 1976; MFA, Yale U., 1955. With prodn. dept. CBS-TV, N.Y.C., 1955-59; producer Captain Kangaroo, N.Y.C., 1959-63; head-writer, producer Sesame Street, N.Y.C., 1968-71, exec. producer, dir., 1971-77, dir., cons., 1977—; exec. producer, writer, dir. Children's TV Workshop, N.Y.C., 1971—; guest lectr. various univs., 1981—. Author various children's books; producer, writer (TV spls.) Christmas Eve on Sesame Street, 1977 (Emmy award), Big Bird in China, 1983 (Emmy award, Writers Guild Am. award). Recipient 13 Emmy awards Nat. Acad. TV Arts and Scis., 1969-88, Monitor award Videotape Prodn. Assn. Mem. Dirs. Guild Am., Writers Guild Am. Home: New York N.Y. DIED 03/30/97. .

STONE, KIRK HASKIN, geographer, educator; b. Bay Village, Ohio, Apr. 27, 1914; s. Charles Henry and Katherine Stockwell (Haskin) S.; m. Vera Grace Erwin, Nov. 26, 1936; 1 child, Martha Stone Werth. B.A., U. Mich., 1935, Ph.D., 1949; M.A., Syracuse (N.Y.) U., 1937. Prof. geography U. Wis., Madison, 1947-65; research prof. geography U. Ga., Athens, 1965-80; Fulbright sr. research fellow Oslo, 1955-56; geographer U.S. Bur. Land Mgmt., 1941, 45-46, 48; cons. Bur. Census, Dept. Def.; geographer Lincoln Lab., MIT, 1952-53. Author: Alaskan Group Settlement, 1950, Norway's Internal Migration, 1971, Northern Finland's Post-War Colonizing, 1974, (with E.E. Melvin) The South's Nonmetropolitan Counties, 1981; contbr. articles to profl. jours. Served to lt., geographer OSS, USNR, 1942-46. Mem. Assn. Am. Geographers (Meritorious Service citation 1965). Died Nov. 7, 1997.

STONE, ROBERT FREDERICK, advertising agency executive, marketing educator; b. Chgo., Sept. 5, 1918; s. Irving John and Theresa Grace (Baier) S.; m. Dorothy Joan Hebner, Apr. 17, 1948; children: Karen, Jeffrey, Richard, William, Lawrence. Student, Northwestern U., 1936-41. V.p. Nat. Rsch. Bur., 1945-60; pres. Nat. Communications Corp., Chgo., 1960-66; pres. Stone & Adler, Inc., Chgo., 1966-78, chmn., 1978-84, chmn. emeritus, 1984—; bd. dirs. Baldwin Cooke Co., Chgo., Alan Drey Co., Hunter Bus. Direct, Milw.; prof. direct mktg. Northwestern U. Author: Successful Direct Mail Advertising and Selling, 1955, Successful Direct Marketing Methods, 1975, 79, 84, 88, Successful Telemarketing, 1985; feature writer: Advertising Age, 1967-74. Chmn. bd. Cath. Guild for the Blind, Chgo., 1985—. Recipient Irving Wunderman award Direct Mktg. Creative Guild, 1989. Mem. Direct Mktg. Assn. (trustee Ednl. Found. 1965—, Hall of Fame 1978), Chgo. Assn. Direct Mktg. (pres. 1948-49, Charles Downes award 1983), Direct Mktg. Ednl. Found. (bd. dirs. 1983—, Edward N. Mayer award 1975, 79). Roman Catholic. Died Oct. 6, 1997.

STONE, WILLARD JOHN, lawyer; b. Toledo, May 19, 1913; s. Willard John and Charlotte Hall (Walker) S.; m. Mabel-June Lindauer, June 15, 1940 (div. Jan. 1952); 1 child, Arthur Walter (dec. May 1991); m. Juanita Marian Hammond, June 22, 1952 (dec. Apr. 1976); children: Willard Andrew, Stewart Hall, Marian Louise Stone Neuhouser; m. Charlotte Deane Haas, Jan. 2, 1977 (dec. June 1995). A.B., U. Mich., 1936, J.D. cum laude, 1936. Bar: Calif. 1937, U.S. Supreme Ct. 1942; cert. specialist in taxation law. Sole practice Los Angeles, 1937-41, 45-51; sole practice Pasadena, Calif., 1951-86; mem. firm Stone & Doyle and predecessor firms, 1975-86; atty. war div. Dept. Justice, 1941-43; asst. prof. law Southwestern U., 1937-41. Mem. editorial bd. Mich. Law Rev., 1934-36. Contbr. articles to profl. jours. Bd. dirs. San Gabriel Valley council Boy Scouts Am. Served as lt. USNR, 1943-46. Decorated Bronze Star. Fellow Am. Coll. Trust and Estate Counsel; mem. ABA, L.A. County Bar Assn., Pasadena Bar Assn., State Bar Calif., Am. Arbitration Assn. (nat. panel arbitrators 1963—), Am. Judicature Soc., Order of Coif. Republican. Episcopalian. Clubs: Fine Arts (pres. 1969-70), University (Pasadena); Oneonta. Lodge: Masons.

STORKE, WILLIAM FREDERICK JOSEPH, film producer; b. Rochester, N.Y., Aug. 12; s. Legrand Frederick Sommerfeldt and Patricia Louise S.; children: Victoria Jane, Adam John, William MacKenzie; m. Georgette MacKenzie Edwards, Feb. 22, 1970. B.A. in Econs., UCLA, 1948. With NBC, N.Y.C., 1948-96, comml. editor, then comml. supr. network sales West Coast and participating program sales, dir. participating program sales, dir. program adminstrn., v.p. program adminstrn., 1948-57, v.p. programs East Coast, 1967-68, v.p. spl. programs East Coast, 1968-96; pres. Claridge Group, Ltd. div. Trident TV Ltd., London, 1979-96; exec. v.p. Entertainment Ptnrs., Inc., N.Y.C., 1982-87; pres. Storke Enterprises Inc., 1987-96. Producer: (films) Oliver Twist, 1982, To Catch a King, 1983, A Christmas Carol, 1984, The Last Days of Patton, 1985, The Ted Kennedy Jr. Story, 1986, A Special Friendship, 1986, (TV series) Buck James, 1987, The Old Man and the Sea, 1989, Hands of a Murderer (Sherlock Holmes), 1990. Served with USNR, 1943-46. Mem. University Club, Nat. Endowment for Arts (theatre panel 1976-78). Home: New York N.Y. Died May 30, 1996.

STOVER, WILLIAM RUFFNER, insurance company executive; b. Washington, Aug. 31, 1922; s. Daniel I. and Carrie E. (Brubaker) S.; m. Carolyn McKean, July 19, 1947; children—Deborah Ann Stover Bowgren, Wendi Lee Stover Mirretti, Sheree Kay. Student, Northwestern U., 1941-45. Sales rep. Old Republic Life Ins. Co., 1945-1949, v.p., 1949-60, sr. v.p., 1960-68, pres., 1968-69, also bd. dirs.; ret., 1994; pres. Old Republic Internat. Corp., 1969-90, chmn. bd., chief exec. officer, 1990—; dir. Old Republic Life N.Y., Old Republic Ins. Co., Internat. Bus. and Merc. Reassurance Co., Home Owners Life Ins. Co. and subs., Minn. Title Fin. Corp., Bitco Corp., Founders Title Group, Inc., Republica Mortgage Ins. Co. Republican. Died Aug. 30, 1996.

STOWE, DAVID HENRY, arbitrator; b. New Canaan, Conn., Sept. 10, 1910; s. Ansel Roy Monroe and Marjorie (Henry) S.; m. Mildred Walker, June 7, 1932; children—David H., Richard W. Student, Washington and Lee U., 1927-30; A.B., Duke, 1931, M. Ed., 1934. Tchr. N.C., 1931-37; asst. state dir. N.C. state Employment Service, 1937-41; chief examiner Bur. Budget, Washington, 1943-47; dep. to asst. to Pres. U.S., 1947-49; adminstrv. asst. to Pres., 1949-53; arbitrator Washington, 1953-70; mem. Nat. Mediation Bd., 1970-79, chmn., 1972-75, 78; mem. atomic energy-labor mgmt. relations panel, 1962—; pub. mem. Pres.'s Missile Sites Labor Commn., 1961-67; mem. bd. Harry S. Truman Library Inst., 1981—. Recipient distinguished service award Dept. Labor, 1965. Mem. Nat. Acad. Arbitrators, Lambda Chi Alpha, Alpha Kappa Psi. Democrat. Episcopalian. Deceased.

STRADLEY, DAVID COWAN, lawyer; b. Columbus, Ohio, Oct. 10, 1922; s. Bland Lloyd and Elizabeth (Cowan) S.; m. Barbara Thornberry, Nov. 15, 1943; children: Sara, Daniel, Jane. A.B., Ohio Wesleyan U., 1943; LL.B., U. Cin., 1948. Bar: Ohio 1948. Ptnr. McConnaughey, McConnaughey & Stradley, Columbus, 1957-62; ptnr. Laylin, McConnaughey & Stradley, Columbus, 1962-67, George, Greek, King, McMahon & McConnaughey, Columbus, 1967-79, McConnaughey, Stradley, Mone & Moul, Columbus, 1979-81, Thompson, Hine & Flory (merger McConnaughey, Stradley, Mone & Moul), Columbus, 1981-92; pres. Mt. Perry Coal Co., Columbus, 1968-81; owner, mgr. Cowan & McCarty Farms, Franklin County, Ohio, 1961-92; mgr. Winding Hollow Farms, Coshocton County, Ohio, 1967-92; entrance examiner Ohio State Med. Bd., Columbus, 1950-78; trustee Robert B. Hurst Charitable Trust, Columbus, 1967-92. Served as aerial gunner Army Air Corps, 1943-45. Mem. ABA, Ohio State Bar Assn., Columbus Bar Assn. Republican. Clubs: Ohio State U. Faculty, Columbus, Scioto Country. Lodges: Rotary, Masons. Home: Columbus Ohio Died Aug. 21, 1992.

STRATTNER, LAWRENCE WENZ, JR., life insurance company executive; b. Mechanicville, N.Y., Nov. 28, 1917; s. Lawrence Walderman and Marie (Wenz) S.; m. Ruth Marie Dillon, Aug. 28, 1941; children: Lawrence J., Gregory P., Timothy J., Martha M., Anthony O, Maria A. A.B. SUNY, Albany, 1939, A.M., 1941. High sch. tchr., 1940-44; with Reader's Digest, 1946-48, Prudential Life Ins. Co., 1948-55, Berkshire Life Ins. Co., Pittsfield, Mass., 1955—; pres. Berkshire Life Ins. Co., 1967-82, chmn. bd., 1982—, also dir. Trustee, Berkshire Med. Center, 1967—, Berkshire Retirement Community, 1983—. Roman Catholic. Died May 29, 1997.

STRAUBEL, JAMES HENDERSON, education consultant; b. Green Bay, Wis., Apr. 11, 1915; s. Otto C. and Alice (Henderson) S.; m. Bette Lee, May 9, 1942; 1 dau., Gay; m. Arlene Hanon, Sept. 9, 1955; children: Jean, Judie. A.B., Lawrence U., 1937. Reporter Green Bay Press Gazette, 1937-40, Milw. Jour., 1940; mag. editor Am. Aviation mag., 1941; editor, pub. dir. Air Force mag., 1947-57, pub., 1957-78; exec. dir. Air Force Assn., Washington, 1958-80; exec. dir. Aerospace Edn. Found., 1956-80. Author: Crusade for Airpower, 1982; Editor: Official Guide to AAF, 1944, Air Force Diary, 1947. Mem. nat. bd. trustees Aerospace Edn. Found.; exec. dir., mem. nat. bd. dirs. Flight Found., 1986—. With USAAF, 1941-46. Mem. Air Force Assn. (nat. bd. dirs.), Phi Delta Theta. Died Dec. 15, 1990.

STRAUS, KENNETH HOLLISTER, retail store executive; b. N.Y.C., Feb. 18, 1925; s. Jack Isidor and Margaret (Hollister) S.; m. Elizabeth Browne, Apr. 14, 1945 (dec. 1991); children: Melinda Straus Schwartz, Timothy; m. Brenda Neubauer Murphy, June 28, 1993. Grad., Milton Acad., 1943; student, NYU Sch. Retailing, 1945-46; grad. advanced mgmt. program, Harvard Bus. Sch., 1957. With R.H. Macy & Co., Inc., N.Y.C., 1947-85, v.p. men's and boy's wear, 1963-67, sr. v.p. domestic and internat. corp. buying, 1967-78, pres. corp. buying, 1978-80, chmn., chief exec. officer corp. buying, 1980-85, also dir., ret., 1985; cons. Nat Exec. Svc. Corp., 1985-96. Hon. dep. commr., 1985-93, trustee, hon. commr. 1993-96, honor emergency fund N.Y.C. Fire Dept., 1966-96, chair, hon. officer adv. com., 1988-96; bd. dirs. N.Y. Fire Safety Found., 1984-96; pres. Fire Found. of N.Y. Inc., 1968-96; mem. adv. bd. John Jay Coll. Criminal Justice, 1987-96; mem. pub. safety com. The Partnership, 1987-89; bd. dirs. Police Found. 1987-96, chair crime stoppers program, 1987-96; vestryman St. James' Ch., 1988-94, chmn. bldgs. and grounds com., 1988-94, grants com., Michel Fund com., 1989-90; trustee St. Luke's/Roosevelt Hosp. Ctr., 1988-96, mem. exec. com., 1994-96; trustee, v.p. Bd. Fgn. Parishes, 1988-96, exec. com., 1989-96; mem. coun. Episcopal Diocese of N.Y., 1988-91, chair comm. task force, 1989-90; bd. dirs. Episcopal Mission Soc., 1989-91, Crime Stoppers Internat., 1993-96; v.p., bd. dirs. Eastside Community Ctr., Inc., 1988-91. With AUS, 1943-45. Decorated Order of Crown (Belgium); recipient Good Scout award Boy Scouts Am., 1965; named to Soc. St. John Jerusalem, 1987-96. Mem. Piping Rock Club, Union Club, Harvard Club, Honor Legion FDNY (hon. 1992-96). Home: New York N.Y. Died July 24, 1996; interred Woodlawn Cemetery, Bronx, NY.

STRAWBRIDGE, G. STOCKTON, retail executive; b. 1913; married. With Strawbridge and Clothier, Phila., 1934 , v.p., 1948-51, exec. v.p., 1951-55, pres., 1955-67, chmn., chief exec. officer, 1967-79, chmn. exec. com., 1979—, also bd. dirs. Lt. comdr. USN, 1941-46.

STRONG, DONALD RUSSELL, librarian; b. Homer City, Pa., Mar. 2, 1931; s. Donald Holton and Laura Louella (Kunkle) S.; m. Mabel Villetta McKelvey, Aug. 6, 1960; children: Russell, Nancy. BA, U. Pitts., 1959; MLS, Carnegie Mellon U., 1958. Reader's adv. libr. Carnegie Libr., Pitts., 1958-60; head ready reference, bookmobile Young Adult Svcs. Dayton (Ohio) & Montgomery Pub. Libr., 1960-64; libr. dir. West Liberty (W.Va.) State Coll., 1964—. Author: (book reviews) Library Journal; contbr. articles to profl. jours. Mem. W.Va. Libr. Assn. (1st v.p. 1966). Democrat. Avocations: music, gardening, walking. Office: West Liberty State Coll Libr West Liberty WV 26074

STRUBBE, JOHN LEWIS, food chain store executive; b. Cin., June 27, 1921; s. John August and Emma Katherine (Coleman) S.; m. Nancy Richards Baer, Sept. 16, 1950; children: William Burrows, Laura, John Charles, Mary. B.S. in Gen. Engring, U. Cin., 1947, J.D., 1948. Bar: Ohio 1948, U.S. Supreme Ct. 1960, U.S. Patent Office 1950. Assoc. Wood, Arey, Herron & Evans, Cin., 1948-50; with The Kroger Co., Cin., 1950-86, sec., 1959-65, gen. atty., 1956-62, v.p., 1961-77, group v.p., 1977-85, sr. v.p., 1985-86. Gen. chmn. United Appeal Greater Cin., 1967; mem. Food Industry Productivity Task Force, 1972; past pres. Dan Beard coun. Boy Scouts Am.; past pres. bd. trustees Cmty. Chest and Coun. of Cin. Area; past trustee Greater Cin. Found., James Gamble Inst. Med. Rsch., Meth. Union; trustee Cin. Ballet Co.; vice chmn. emeritus, trustee U. Cin. Found.; past chmn. bd. The Christ Hosp., Elizabeth Gamble Deaconess Home Assn.; mem. bd. advisors to dean U. Cin. Coll. Bus. Adminstrn. With USMCR, 1943-46, 50-52. Recipient U. Cin. Distinguished Alumnus award, chmn. award for devel. new food tech. Supermarket Inst., 1976, Brotherhood citation NCCJ, 1982; named Great Living Cincinnatian, Greater Cin. C. of C., 1986. Mem. Cincinnatus Assn. (past pres., chmn.), Uniform Grocery Products Code Coun., Queen City Club (past trustee), Cin. Country Club (past trustee), Commonwealth Club, Delta Tau Delta. Methodist. Died Dec. 14, 1996.

STRYPE, FREDERICK CULVER, JR., paper industry executive; b. Bklyn., Nov. 25, 1918; s. Frederick Culver and Claire (Williams) S.; m. Louise Marie Schweinler, Oct. 25, 1947; children: Susan, Elizabeth, Kathleen Marie, Frederick, Margaret. Student, U. Maine, 1940, Harvard U., 1941; grad., U. Pa., Wharton, 1941. Sec. Fred. C. Strype, Inc., N.Y.C., 1946, pres. and treas., 1960-95; cons. paper and pulp div. ECA, Wash., 1950-51. Co-author: Guide for the Export Packing of Paper, 1949. Pres. Dem. Club, Ho-Ho-Kus, 1964-67. Served as lt. comdr. Supply Corps, USN, 1941-46. Named Ky. Col. Mem. U.S. Paper Exporters Council (v.p. 1950-52, pres. 1952-54, 69-70), Tech. Assn. Pulp and Paper Industry (assoc.). Roman Catholic. Clubs: Pathfinders (London); Channel, Monmouth Beach (N.J.) (trustee). Home: Spring Lake N.J. Died May 31, 1995.

STUCKEY, WALTER JACKSON, physician, educator; b. Fairfield, Ala., Mar. 6, 1927; s. Walter Jackson and Lena (Brackin) S.; m. Mildred Creel Roberts, Nov. 27, 1952; children: Walter Jackson, III, John Hamlin, James Allan. B.S., U. Ala., 1947; M.D., Tulane U., 1951. Intern Charity Hosp. La., New Orleans, 1951-52; resident in gen. practice Lafayette (La.) Charity Hosp., 1952; resident in internal medicine Tulane med. service Charity Hosp. La., VA Hosp., New Orleans, 1955-57; fellow, instr. dept. medicine Tulane U. Sch. Medicine, 1958-60, asst. prof., 1960-62, asso. prof., 1962-68, prof., 1968-92, prof. emeritus, 1992—, chief sect. hematology/med. oncology, 1963-92; ret.; cons. Charity Hosp., 1968—; active staff Tulane Med. Center Hosp.; practice medicine specializing in hematology and oncology New Orleans; cons. VA, Mercy; East Jefferson; Highland Park, St. Tammany Hosp., (Covington, La.). Served with USNR, 1952-54. Fellow ACP; mem. AMA, AAAS, Am. Assn. Cancer Edn., Am. Soc. Internal Medicine, La. Parish Med. Soc., Orleans Parish Med. Soc., New Orleans Acad. Internal Medicine, N.Y. Acad. Scis., Internat. Soc. Hematology, Am. Soc. Hematology, Am. Soc. Clin. Oncology. Methodist. Died Feb. 20, 1997.

SUDBEY, GERALD ANTHONY, photographic company executive; b. Boston, Dec. 31, 1935; s. Frederick Chester and Lucy Madeline (Sears) S.; m. Margaret Frances Geary, June 1, 1957; children: Karen, Jeff. AB, Boston U., 1971. Various positions Polaroid Corp., Cambridge, Mass., 1958-64, resident rep., 1964-66, prodn. mgr., 1966-69, sr. mgr. quality control, 1969-72, dir. program office, 1972-79, dir. mfg., 1979-81, v.p. camera mfg., 1981-84, group v.p. worldwide mfg., 1984-87, group v.p. elec. imaging, 1987—; pres. Polaroid Found., Cambridge, 1987—; bd. dirs. Inner City Corp., Boston, 1982—. Pres. Family Counseling Region West, Newton, Mass., 1986—. Roman Catholic. Died June 11, 1997.

SUGDEN, THEODORE MORRIS, educational administrator; b. Halifax, Yorkshire, Eng., Dec. 31, 1919; s. Frederick Morris and Florence (Chadwick) S.; M.A., U. Cambridge, 1944, Ph.D., 1949, Sc.D., 1962; D.Tech. (hon.), U. Bradford, 1967; D.Sc. (hon.), York U., 1974, U. Liverpool, 1977, U. Leeds, 1978; m. Marain Florence Cotton, Sept. 4, 1945; 1 son, Andrew Morris With Shell Research Ltd., 1964-76, dir. Thornton Research Center, 1964-74, chief exec., 1974-76, later cons.; demonstrator phys. chemistry dept. U. Cambridge (Eng.), 1946-51, lectr., 1951-59, reader, from 1959, master Trinity Hall, 1976—. Chmn. adv. com. Safety in Nuclear Installations, 1978—. Fellow Royal Soc. (v.p. 1973-74, 78—, phys. sec. 1978—); mem. Royal Soc. Chemistry (pres. 1978-79), Combustion Inst. (internat. v.p. 1974-82). Contbr. articles to sci. jours. Deceased.

SUHRBIER, KLAUS RUDOLF, hydrodynamicist, naval architect; b. Gnoien, Germany, Sept. 12, 1930; arrived in U.K., 1966; s. Ulrich Julius and Dora Auguste (Elsaesser) S.; m. Inge Ursula Koepke, Oct. 1, 1955; children: Andreas, Karin. Dipl. Ing., U. Rostock, Germany, 1955; Dr. Ing., Tech. U., Berlin, 1995. Chartered engr. Hydrodynamicist Institut fuer Schiffbau, Berlin, 1955-60, Versuchsanstalt fuer Binnenschiffbau e.V., Duisburg, Fed. Republic of Germany, 1960-63; sci. officer Inst. fuer Schiffbau U. Hamburg, Fed. Republic of Germany, 1963-66; sr. hydrodynamicist Vosper Ltd., Portsmouth, Eng., 1966; chief hydrodynamicist Vosper Thornycroft (U.K.) Ltd., Portsmouth, Eng., 1966-92; cons. ship hydrodynamics, 1992—; mem. cavitation com. 16th and 17th Internat. Towing Tank Conf., Leningrad, USSR, 1978-81, Gothenburg, Sweden, 1981-84; chmn. cavitation com. 18th Internat. Towing Tank Conf., Kobe, Japan, 1984-87; chmn. high speed marine vehicles com. Internat. Towing Tank Conf., Madrid, 1987-90. Co-author: (book) Dhows to Deltas, 1971; inventor reduction of cavitation erosion, 1974, 92; contbr. numerous articles and papers to profl. jours. and procs. Fellow Royal Soc. Naval Architects; mem. Soc. Naval Architects and Marine Engrs., Schiffbautechnische Ges. e.V. Avocations: sailing, skiing, history. Deceased.

SULKIN, SIDNEY, editor, writer; b. Boston, Feb. 2, 1918; s. Frank Sam and Celia (Glazer) S.; m. Naomi Ann Levenson, Oct. 4, 1950; 1 child, Jonathan Leigh. Grad., Boston Pub. Latin Sch., 1935; B.A. cum laude, Harvard Coll., 1939. Editorial asst. Howell-Soskin Pub. Co., N.Y.C., 1940-41; chief World Wide English Programs, Voice of Am., N.Y.C., 1943-44; chief news Am. Broadcasting Sta. in Europe, SHAEF, London, 1945; with psychol. warfare divsn. SHAEF, The Hague, The Netherlands, 1945; dir. No. and Eastern Europe U.S. Internat. Book Assn., N.Y.C. and Stockholm, 1945-47; spl. Scandinavian corr. CBS-News, Stockholm, 1945-47; cons. U.S. Mil. Govt. in Germany, 1947; commentator Sta. WCCO, Mpls., 1947; chief Washington bur. Voice of Am., 1949-53; editorial dir. Nat. Issues Com., Washington, 1953-55; asso. editor Changing Times Mag., Washington, 1955-62; sr. editor Changing Times Mag., 1962-71, mng. editor, 1971-75, editor, 1975-81; dir. Kiplinger Washington Editors, 1975-81; playwright-in-residence Shakespeare-under-Stars festival, Tucson, 1981; instr. creative writing Writer's Ctr., Bethesda, Md., 1987—, U. Md., College Park, 1989-91. Author: (novel) The Family Man, 1962, Complete Planning for College, 1962, rev. edit., 1968, (play) Gate of the Lions, 1976 (Quar. Rev. Lit. Contemporary Poetry Publ. award 1980), (play) The Other Side of Babylon, 1979, (play) No More to Prophesy, 1981, (play) Summer Storm, (play) If I Lie, 1992, (stories and poems) The Secret Seed, 1983; included in anthologies: O. Henry Prize Stories, 1948, Best American Short Stories, 1948, These Your Children, Fiction of the Eighties, 1990; co-editor: For Your Freedom and Ours, 1943; co-translator: Matthew the Young King (by Korczak), 1945; contbr. short stories, articles, poetry to numerous periodicals. One-man show (paintings) Friendship Gallery, 1991; exhibited in group show at Provincetown Art Mus., 1990. Adv. com. Jewish Pub. Libr.; bd. mem. Writers Ctr. Mem. PEN, Authors Guild, Poetry Soc. Am., Dramatists Guild, Writers Watch (past pres.), Provincetown Art Assn., Nat. Press Club, Harvard Club. Democrat. Jewish. Died June 29, 1995.

SULLIVAN, JOHN PATRICK, classics educator; b. Liverpool, Eng., July 13, 1930; came to U.S., 1961; s. Daniel and Alice (Long) S.; m. Mary Frances Rock, July 20, 1954 (div. 1963); m. Judith Patrice Eldridge, Apr. 7, 1967 (div. Apr. 1972); m. Judith Lee Godfrey, Apr. 21, 1973. B.A., St. John's Coll., Cambridge (Eng.) U., 1955, M.A., 1957; M.A., Oxford (Eng.) U., 1957. Jr. research fellow Queen's Coll., Oxford U., 1954; fellow, tutor classics Lincoln Coll., 1955-62, dean, 1960-61; vis. prof. U. Tex., 1961-62, asso. prof. classics, 1962-63, prof. classics, 1963-69, chmn. dept., 1963-65; sr. fellow. Nat. Endowment for the Arts and Humanities, 1967-68; prof. arts and letters SUNY, Buffalo, 1969-78, provost arts and letters, 1972-75; prof. classics U. Calif., Santa Barbara, 1978-93, chmn. dept., 1990-93; vis. fellow Clare Hall, Cambridge (Eng.) U., 1975-76, Gray lectr., 1978; vis. prof. U. Hawaii, 1977; Martin lectr. Oberlin Coll., 1976; vis. fellow Wolfson Coll., Oxford (Eng.) U., 1981; Guggenheim fellow, 1984. Author: Ezra Pound and Sextus Propertius: A Study in Creative Translation, 1965, The Satyricon of Petronius: A Literary Study, 1968, Propertius: A Critical Introduction, 1976, The Jaundiced Eye, poems, 1977, Literature and Politics in the Age of Nero, 1986, Martial: The Unexpected Classic, 1991; also various classical, philosophical and lit. articles.; editor: Critical Essays on Roman Literature: Elegy and Lyric, 1962, Critical Essays on Roman Literature: Satire, 1963, Penguin Critical Anthologies: Ezra Pound, 1970, Women in the Ancient World: The Arethusa Papers, 1984, Epigrams of Martial Englished by Divers Hands, 1987, Roman Poets of the Early Empire, 1991; editor: Arion mag., 1961-70, Arethusa Mag., 1972-75; translator: Satyricon (Petronius), 1978. Served with Brit. Army, 1948-49. Home: Santa Barbara Calif. Died Apr. 9, 1993.

SUMMERFIELD, MARTIN, physicist; b. N.Y.C., Oct. 20, 1916; s. Jacob and Augusta (Tobias) S.; m. Eileen Budin, Aug. 31, 1945; 1 child, Jacqueline. BS, Bklyn. Coll., 1936; MS, Calif. Inst. Tech., 1938, PhD, 1941. Asst. chief Air Corps Jet Propulsion Project, Calif. Inst. Tech., 1940-43, chief, rocket rsch. divsn., 1945-49; chief, rocket devel. divsn. Aerojet Engring. Corp., Azusa, Calif., 1943-45; mem. subcom. on fuels NACA, 1948-49, subcom. on combustion, 1949-50; prof. jet propulsion Princeton U., 1951-78, prof. emeritus, 1978—; Astor prof. applied sci. NYU, 1978-80; tech. dir. Project Squid, 1949-51; chief scientist Flow Industries Inc., 1975-78; pres. Princeton Combustion Research Labs., 1978-94; editor Aeros. Publ. Program, 1949-52; editor in chief Jour. Am. Rocket Soc., 1951-57; editor Jet Propulsion; also tech. editor Astronautics, 1957-63; editor in chief AIAA series on Progress in Astronautics and Aeros., 1960-90, mem. editorial bd., 1990—; editor in chief Astronautica Acta, 1964-69; cons. U.S. Army Rsch. Office, 1968-71; mem. adv. com. chem. propulsion NASA, 1968-71, Inst. of Aerospace and Astronautics, Cheng-Kung Univ., Tainan, Taiwan, 1985—; chmn. com. on toxicity hazards of materials NRC, 1984-86, mem. com. on energetic materials, 1984-87. Patentee on rocket motors and related devices. Recipient Pendray award, 1954; Wyld award, 1977. Fellow AAAS, AIAA (v.p. 1963-65), Am. Rocket Soc. (pres. 1962-63), Inst. of Advanced Tech., U. Texas, 1991—; mem. Inst. Aeronautics and Astronomy, Internat. Acad. Astronautics, Nat. Acad. Engring., ASME (Heat Transfer award 1978), Internat. Astronautical Fedn. (v.p. 1963-65), Sigma Xi. Home: Highest N.J. Died July 18, 1996.

SUMMERILL, JOHN FREDERICK, mortuary science college dean and educator; b. Long Beach, Calif., Aug. 25, 1917; s. Theo Samuel and Nellie May (Goodall) S.; m. Edna Bull (div. 1962); 1 child, Adrianne Summerill Burton; m. Betty Ohlstrom, June 1988 (div.). BS, Calif. Maritime Acad., 1938, San Francisco Coll. Mortuary Sci., 1945; D Mortuary Sci. (hon.), San Francisco Coll. Mortuary Sci., 1962. 3d, 2d and chief mate U.S. Mcht. Marines, 1938-40; commandent midshipment, exec. officer tng. Calif. Maritime Acad., Vallejo, 1940; chief dep. coroner Marin County, San Rafael, Calif., 1947-48; locum tenens mng. and funeral dir. Calif., 1948-49; owner, funeral dir. Chapel of Lake Mortuary, Lakeport, Calif., 1949-62; dean students, prof. pathology, adminstrn. and pub. rels. San Francisco Coll. Mortuary Sci., 1962-82. Author: West Coast Piloting, 1940, Training Tanker Manual, 1947, Ancient Funeral Customs, 1960. Post leader, dist. chmn. Boy Scouts Am., Lakeport and Lake County, 1958-61; county gen. chmn., state dist. chmn. Am. Cancer Soc., 1959-60; dist. chmn. Calif. Tb Assn., Lake County. Lt. comdr. USN, 1941-45, mem. Res. ret. Recipient hon. award Boy Scouts Am., 1960, Am. Cancer Soc., Calif. Tb Assn. Mem. Funeral Dirs. and Doctors Soc., Redwood Empire Funeral Dirs. Assn. (past pres.), Lake County Officers Assn., Am. Mensa Soc. (dist. and nat. judge scholarship awards), Internat. Mark Twain Soc., Masons, Lions, Rotary, KP (past sec., chancellor comdr.), Clearlake Grange (past master), Elks (chmn. events com.). Avocations: flying light planes, trout fishing, power boating, foreign travel, oriental art. Died Aug. 7, 1997.

SUMNERS, WILLIAM GLENN, JR., lawyer; b. Pueblo, Colo., Feb. 23, 1928; s. William Glen Sr. and Ruth Priscilla (Carmody) S.; 1 child from previous marriage, William Glenn III; m. Virginia Christine Thomson, June 16, 1985. BA, MA, U. Colo., 1951; postgrad., Colo. Sch. of Mines, 1954; LLB, U. Denver, 1954. Bar: Colo. 1954, U.S. Dist. Ct. Colo. 1954, U.S. Supreme Ct. 1962, U.S. Ct. Appeals (10th cir.) 1963, U.S. Ct. Claims 1982. Sole practice Denver, 1954-75; ptnr. Sumners & Fowler, Denver, 1975-80, Sumners & Miller, Denver, 1980-85, Sumners & Eppich, Denver, 1985-88, William G. Sumners Jr., P.C., 1988-95; ret., 1995. Contbr. articles to profl. jours. Judge Denver Mcpl. Ct., 1962. Served with U.S. Army, 1945-47, PTO. Mem. ABA (chmn. internat. ins. law com. 1980-81, ins., negligence and compensation sect., internat. energy law sect.), Rocky Mountain Mineral Law Found. (trustee 1960-63, 80-85), Mountain States Legal Found. (bd. of litigation 1977-95), Colo. Mining Assn. (bd. dirs. 1962-95, pres. 1977), Internat. Bar Assn., Internat. Assn. Ins. Counsel, Ind. Petroleum Assn. Mountain States (bd. dirs. 1975). Died July 9, 1995.

SUMRALL, LESTER FRANK, missionary, evangelist; b. Feb. 15, 1913; s. George William and Betty Elizabeth (Chandler) S.; m. Louise Margaret Layman, Sept. 30, 1944; children: Frank Lester Jr., Stephen Philip, Peter Andrew. DD, Berea Bible Co., 1964; LittD, Ind. Christian U., 1974; PhD in Religious Studies, Golden State U., 1983; DD (hon.), Oral Roberts U., 1983. Founder, chmn. LeSEA Ministries, South Bend, Ind., 1959-96; founder, pastor Christian Ctr. Cathedral of Praise, South Bend, 1965-96; founder, owner 9 TV stas., South Bend, 1972-96, LeSea Brodcasting, South Bend, 1972-96; founder, pres. World Harvest Bible Coll., South Bend, 1975-96; pres. Ind. Christian U., South Bend, 1989-96. Author numerous books; pub., founder World Harvest Mag., WHRI Short Wave Radio, 1988. Founder Feed the Hungry, 1987-96. Named Hon. Citizen of Knoxville, Tenn., Mayor of Knoxville, 1984, Leader of Yr., Internat. Christian Bus. Leaders, 1988; recipient Congl. award U.S. Ho. of Reps., 1980, Honor Citation Nat. Religious Broadcasters, 1982, award of merit Nat. Religious Broadcasters, 1983, Meritorious Achievement award Internat. Assn. Christian Clin. Counselors, 1983, Meritorious Hoosier award Ind. Sec. State, 1983, Outstanding Community Svc. award FaithAm. Found, 1984.. Mem. Full Gospel Ch. Died Apr. 28, 1996.

SUNDBERG, OVE, chemical company executive; b. Ornskoldsvik, Sweden, Mar. 18, 1933; s. Gustaf and Nanny (Johansson) S.; m. Hélène Thofelt, Jan. 5, 1982; children-Johan, Maria. M of Chem. Engring., 1957, Licentiate in Engring., 1960. Rsch. engr., 1957-60; with Korsnas-Marma AB, 1960-62; chief engr. Wifstavarfs AB, 1962-66; asst. v.p. Swedish Match Co., 1966-67, v.p., head paper div. and corp. devel., 1967-70, v.p., head corp. div., 1970-72; pres., CEO KemaNobel Corp., Stockholm, 1972-92; prin. Sundberg Invest, Stockholm, 1992—; dir. Saléninvest AB, Swedish Petroleum AB, others. Served to 2d lt., Swedish Army. Mem. Assn. Swedish Chem. Industries (chmn.), Swedish Employers Fedn. (dir.), Fedn. Swedish Industries. Died May 5, 1994.

SUOMI, VERNER EDWARD, meteorologist, administrator, inventor; b. Eveleth, Minn., Dec. 6, 1915; s. John E. and Anna Emelia (Sundquist) S.; m. Paula Meyer, Aug. 10, 1941; children: Lois, Stephen, Eric. BE, Winona Tchrs. Coll., 1938; PhD, U.Chgo., 1953; DS (hon.), SUNY, Albany, 1983. Tchr. sci. and math. Minn. Schs., 1938-42; instr. meteorology U. Chgo., 1943-45; prof. meteorology U. Wis., Madison, 1948-86, prof. emeritus, 1986-95, founder, dir. Space Sci. and Engring. Ctr., 1966-88, Wexler prof. meteorology, 1972-87; dir. Coop. Inst. for Meteorological Satellite Studies, 1980-84; assoc. program dir. for atmospheric sci. NSF, Washington, 1962; chief scientist U.S. Weather Bur., 1964. Patentee in field; developed flat-plate radiometer, 1957-60, satellite spin-scan weather camera, 1963, balloon-borne radioaltimeter (with N. Levanon), 1968, video display/processing computer system (with staff Space Sci. and Engring. Ctr.), 1972; contbr. articles, books. Recipient Am. Meteorological Soc. awards, 1961, 1968-69, 1980, 88, Losey award AIAA, 1971 NSF Nat. Medal of Sci., 1977, NASA Exceptional Scientist Achievement medal, 1980, Franklin Inst. medal, 1984, NOAA silver medallion, 1985, commemorative medal Soviet Geophysical Comm., 1985, Nat. Scholar award Phi Kappa Phi, 1986, Nev. medal, 1988, Walter Ahlstrom prize Finnish Acads. Tech., 1990, 38th Internat. Meteorological prize WMO, 1993; named Sr. Disting. Research Prof. Wis. Alumnae Research Found., 1984; recognized by Soc. of Exploration Geophysicists/Pecora for application of remote sensing, 1980. Fellow Acad. Arts and Scis.; mem. Am. Meteorol. Soc. (hon., pres. 1969-70, Meisinger award 1961, Carl-Gustav Rossby Research medal 1968, Charles Franklin Brooks award 1980; hon.), Nat. Acad. Engring., Am. Fedn. Scientists, Am. Geophys. Union, AAUP, Wis. Acad. Sci., Arts and Letters (hon.), Am. Philos. Soc., Finnish Acad. Sci. Deutsch Akademie der Naturforscher Internat. Acad. Astronautics Paris, Phi Beta Kappa, Sigma Xi, Phi Kappa Phi, Sigma Pi Sigma. Died July, 1995.

SUPER, ROBERT HENRY, English educator; b. Wilkes-Barre, Pa., June 13, 1914; s. John Henry and Sadie (Rothermel) S.; m. Rebecca Ragsdale, Jan. 25, 1953; children: David Allen, Paul Eric. A.B., Princeton U., 1935, Ph.D., 1941; B.Litt., U. Oxford, Eng., 1937. Instr. English Princeton, 1938-42; asst. prof. Mich. State Normal Coll., Ypsilanti, 1942-47; from asst. prof. to prof. U. Mich., Ann Arbor, 1947-84, prof. emeritus, from 1984; vis. prof. Rice U., 1965-66, U. Chgo., summer 1954, UCLA, 1967, U. Calif., Berkeley, 1973, Tex. A&M U., Winter 1984; field intelligence officer Fgn. Econ. Adminstrn., 1945; Harris Found. lectr. Northwestern U., 1968. Author: Walter Savage Landor: A Biography, 1954, The Publication of Landor's Works, 1954, The Time-Spirit of Matthew Arnold, 1970, Trollope in the Post Office, 1981, The Chronicler of Barsetshire: A Life of Anthony Trollope, 1988; Editor: The Complete Prose Works of Matthew Arnold, 11 vols, 1960-77, Anthony Trollope's Marion Fay, 1982, (with Miriam Allott) The Oxford Arnold, 1986, Anthony Trollope's The Fixed Period, 1990, Anthony Trollope's The Landleaguers, 1992. Fulbright research fellow, 1949-50; Am. Council Learned Socs. fellow, 1959-60; Guggenheim fellow, 1962-63, 70-71; NEH fellow, 1978-79. Fellow Brit. Acad. (corr.). Home: Ann Arbor Mich. Died March 29, 1996.

SURBECK, LEIGHTON HOMER, lawyer; b. Jasper, Minn., Oct. 8, 1902; s. James S. and Kathryn (Kilpatrick) S.; m. Margaret H. Packard, 1976. B.S., S.D. State Sch. Mines, 1924; J.D. magna cum laude, Yale, 1927; L.H.D., S.D. Sch. Mines and Tech., 1957; LL.D., Central Coll., 1973; D.Humanitarian Services, Northwestern Coll., Iowa, 1980; LL.D., Hope Coll., 1986; DHL (hon.), Judson Coll., Elgin, Ill., 1995. Bar: N.Y. 1929. Law sec. to Chief Justice Taft, 1927-28; assoc. Hughes, Schurman & Dwight, N.Y.C., 1928-34; mem. firm Hughes, Schurman & Dwight, 1934-37; mem. firm Hughes, Hubbard & Reed, N.Y.C., 1937-70, counsel, 1970-97. Author: Success on the Job, 1957, The Success Formula that Really Works, 1986. Trustee Pacific Sch. Religion, Berkeley, Calif., 1962-80, Golden Gate U., San Francisco, 1979-91, Central Coll., Pella, Iowa, 1966-78, Collegiate Boy's Sch., N.Y.C., 1975-78; chmn. Yale Law Sch. Fund, 1971-75. Served as col. AUS, 1942-45; chief econ. br. M.I. 1944-45. Recipient Yale medal Yale Alumni, 1975, Distinguished Service award Yale Law Sch., 1976; Horatio Alger award, 1977; named Centennial Alumnus State of S.D., 1989. Mem. ABA, N.Y. State Bar Assn., N.Y. County Bar Assn., Assn. of Bar of City of N.Y., Siwanoy Country Club, Univ. Club (N.Y.C.), Menlo Country Club (Woodside, Calif.), Masons, Order of Coif, Sigma Tau., Delta Theta Phi. Mem. Marble Collegiate Ch. (elder 1962-78). Home: Atherton Calif. Died Sept. 5, 1997; interred Oak Hill Cemetery, San Jose, CA.

SURO, DARIO, artist, diplomat; b. La Vega, Dominican Republic, June 13, 1917; s. Jaime and Isabel Emilia (Garcia-Godoy) S.; m. Ada Maruxa Franco; children: Federico, Rosa. Studied with, Enrique Garcia Godoy, 1935-37, Diego Rivera, Agustin Lazo, Mexico City, 1943-46. Cultural attache Embassy of Dominican Rep., Mexico City, 1943-47, Madrid, 1950-63; cultural attache Embassy of Dominican Rep., Washington, 1963-65, cultural counselor, 1965-67, minister counselor of cultural affairs, 1967-70, minister plenipotentiary, dep. chief of mission, 1970—; delegate Congress of Latin Am. Intellectual Cooperation, Madrid, 1947; dir. gen. of fine arts Govt. of the Dominican Rep., Santo Domingo, 1947-50; attache permanent mission of the Dominican Rep. to the OAS, 1963-65, minister counselor, 1967-80; counselor permanent mission of the OAS, Washington, 1965-67; ambassador, alternate rep. of the Dominican Rep. to the OAS, Washington, 1980—; mem. jury 1st Caribbean Biennial, 1992; lectr. in art. Author: Arte Dominicano, 1969, several other books and catalogues; one-man shows include Palace Fine Arts, Mexico City, 1946, Galería Caralt, Barcelona, 1952, Poindexter Gallery, N.Y.C., 1962, Nat. Gallery Modern Art, 1981, La Galeria, Santo Domingo, 1985, 87, numerous others; exhibited in numerous group shows, including Salon de los Once, Madrid, 1951, Carnegie Inst., Pitts., 1952, Martin Luther King Meml. Libr., Washington, 1981, Casa de Bastidas, Santo Domingo, 1982, La Galeria, 1986, Cuban Mus., Miami Fla., 1988, Montclair Mus., 1992, Noyes Mus., 1993; paintings reproduced in numerous publs. Recipient Silver medal 2d Nat. Bienniel Fine Arts, Santo Domingo, 1944, Gold medal, 1946, Eloy Alfaro Internat. Found. medal Panama, 1954, First Nat. Fine Arts Achievement award Santo Domingo, 1993. Roman Catholic. DIED 01/18/97. .

SURWILL, BENEDICT JOSEPH, JR., college dean, educator; b. Chgo., Oct. 8, 1925; s. Benedict Joseph and Emily (Zemgolis) S.; m. Frances May Welling, Oct. 16, 1948; children: Thomas, Benedict, Robert, Patricia; m. Charlene R. McClintock, Feb. 17, 1990; 1 child, Michael McClintock. BS in Edn., Ariz. State Coll., 1951, MS in Edn., 1954; EdD, U. Colo., 1962. Elem. tchr. Winnetka (Ill.) Pub. Schs., 1958-61; jr. high sch. prin. Champaign (Ill.) Pub. Schs., 1961-63; dir. Campus Sch. SUNY, Buffalo, 1963-68; dean. Sch. Edn. Ea. Mont. Coll., Billings, 1968-88, asst. to pres., 1988-91, dean Sch. Edn., prof. edn. emeritus, 1991-96; chmn. dean's coun. Mont. Univ. System, 1974; mem. Mont. Supts. Adv. Com. on Tchr. Edn. and Cert., 1969-76, chmn., 1972-73; mem. ednl. forum State Supt. Pub. Instrn., 1977-83, Mont. Rural Youth Adv. Coun., Billings, 1979-81; lectr. in field. Editor: A Critical Examination of American Education, 1985; mem. editorial bd., contbg. editor Jour. Creative Behavior, 1966-93. Co-chmn. cancer drive Billings chpt. Am. Cancer Soc., 1988-89, Mont. State Cancer Crusade, 1989. With inf. U.S. Army. Recipient Am. Assn. of Coll. for Tchr. Edn. award, 1972, Presdl. citation Ill. Assn. Sch. Adminstrs., 1973. Mem. Nat. Coun. Accreditation Tchr. Edn. (mem. standards com., mem. multicultural edn. com. 1977, bd. appeals 1980-83, bd. examiners 1988-90), Elks, Yellowstone Country Club, Phi Delta Kappa, Kappa Delta Pi. Died Oct. 2, 1996.

SUTTER, HARVEY MACK, engineer, consultant; b. Jennings, La., Oct. 5, 1906; s. Josiah Harvey and Effie Relief (Murray) S.; AB, U. Wichita, 1932; m. Julia Genevieve Wright, Sept. 19, 1936; children: James Houston, Robert Mack, Julia Ann Boyd, John Norman. Design and prodn. engr. Boeing Aircraft, Wichita, Kans., 1936-38; supr. arts, crafts and coop. activities Bur. Indian Affairs, U.S. Dept. of Interior, 1938-42, chief procurement br. Bur. of Reclamation, Washington, 1946-54, chief div. procurement and property mgmt., 1954-58; asst. to adminstr. Bonneville Power Adminstrn., 1958-61, asst. to chief engr., 1962-66; cons. engr., 1967—; analyst, chief prodn. service WPB, Denver, 1942-44; chief div. supply C.E., Denver, 1944-46. Mem. exec. bd. Portland area Boy Scouts Am. Recipient Silver Beaver award. Presbyterian. Mem. Nat., Western woodcarvers assns., Internat. Wood Collectors Soc., Electric of Oreg. Author or co-author books and articles on woodcarving. Died June 19, 1997.

SUTTON, FREDERICK ISLER, JR., realtor; b. Greensboro, N.C., Sept. 13, 1916; s. Fred I. and Annie (Fry) S.; m. Helen Sykes Morrison, Mar. 18, 1941; children: Fred Isler III, Frank Morrison. Grad. Culver (Ind.) Mil. Acad., 1934; AB, U. N.C., 1939, student Law Sch., 1939-41. Lic. in real estate; cert. property mgr. Propr. Fred I. Sutton, Jr., realtor, Kinston, N.C., 1946-95; comml. pilot, 1949-95. Chmn. Kinston Parking Authority, Kinston Water Resources, Kinston Hist. Commn.; pres. Lenoir County United Fund, 1969-70; trustee, dean U. N.C. Realtors Inst.; trustee Florence Crittenton Services; v.p. N.C. Real Estate Edn. Found.; deacon Presbyn. Ch.; bd. dirs. Pride of Kinston. Served to lt. comdr. USNR, 1940-46. Named Kinston Realtor of Yr., 1963. Mem. Kinston Bd. Realtors (pres.), N.C. Bd. Realtors (v.p. 1957), N.C. Assn. Realtors (regional v.p., chmn. ednl. com., dir. Realtors Ednl. Found.), N.C. Assn. Real Estate Bds. (bd. dirs., v.p. 1958-60, 61, 63), Newcomen Soc., Am. Power Boat Assn. (7 Liter Hydroplane Nat. Champion 1951, Region 4 Champion 1976, 78-80, 82, Nat. High Point Champion 1982, Eastern Div. Champion 1982), U.S. Power Squadron (navigator, Kinston comdg. officer, adminstrv. officer dist. 27 1987), Kinston C. of C. (v.p.), SR. Lodges: Kiwanis (pres. Kinston chpt., bd. dirs.), Masons (32 deg.), Shriners, Elks. Died Jan. 15, 1995. Home: Kinston N.C.

SUTTON, JOHN ROBERT, biological sciences educator; b. Sydney, Australia, Mar. 31, 1941; s. Thomas Alysosius and Philomena Gladys (Conlon) S.; m. Yvonne Joan Harman, Feb. 21, 1967; children: Dianne Joan, Caroline Anne, Joanne Louise. MB, BS in Medicine & Surgery, U. Sydney, 1965, MD, 1991, DSc, 1993. Resident med. officer St. Vincents Hosp., Sydney, 1965, 66, med. registrar, 1968-72; from rsch. fellow to prof. McMaster U., Hamilton, Ont., Can., 1972-89; chair biol. scis., prof. medicine, med. dir. Sports Clinic U. Sydney, 1989—; founder, med. dir. Sydney Human Performance Lab., 1970; v.p. Can. Acad. Sports Medicine, Ont., 1987-89. Author: Hypoxia: Man at Altitude, 1980, Hypoxia and Cold, 1985, Hypoxia: The Adaptations, 1990, Hypoxia and Molecular Medicine, 1993 and 16 other books. Fellow Royal Australasian Coll. Physicians, Royal Coll. Physicians and Surgeons of Can., Am. Coll. Sports Medicine (v.p. 1983-85, pres. 1986-87), Australian Coll. Sports Physicians, Australian Sports Fedns. (v.p. 1970-72), Royal Geog. Soc.; mem. Internat. Soc. for Mountain Medicine (pres.-elect 1994—), Internat. Hypoxia Symposium (chmn. 1980—).

Roman Catholic. Avocations: mountaineering, canoeing, running, mountain biking, skiing. Died Feb. 7, 1996.

SUZUKI, SHINICHI, education institute executive; b. Nagoya, Aichi, Japan, Oct. 17, 1898; s. Masakichi and Ryoh (Fujie) S.; m. Feb. 8, 1928. Studied in Germany under Prof. Karl Klingler, 1921; D.Mus. (hon.), New Eng. U., Boston, 1966, Louisville U., 1967, Eastman Music Sch., 1971, Rochester U., 1972. Founder, pres., dir. Talent Edn. Inst., Matsumoto, Japan, 1946—; founder, pres. Suzuki Method Presch., Matsumoto, N.Y., 1949—; hon. disting. prof., Northeast La. U., 1982. Author: Suzuki Violin, Flute, Cello and Piano Music Books, 1959; Nurtured by Love, 1966; Ability Development From Age Zero, 1969. Paul Harris fellow Found. Rotary Internat., 1976; named Hon. Citizen, City of Winnipeg, 1972, City of Matsumoto, 1979, City of Atlanta, 1978, City of Monroe (La.), 1982; recipient Chunichi Culture award, Japan, 1951; Shinmai Culture award, Japan, 1961; Ysayi award, Belgium, 1969; Mobil Mus. award, Japan, 1976, Kohl Internat. Ach. award, U.S.A., 1994; Palmes Academiques, The French Gov., 1982; award The Japan Found., 1983; decorated Order of Sacred Treasure, 3d Class (Japan). Mem. Internat. Suzuki Assn. (pres. 1983—), European Suzuki Assn., Suzuki Assn. Ams. (hon. Pres.), Suzuki Talent Edn. Assn. Australia, New Zealand Suzuki Inst. Roman Catholic.

SVANHOLM, BERT-OLOF, electro-technical company executive; b. Nordmaling, Sweden, Mar. 11, 1935; s. Jonas S. and Elisabeth (Andersson) S.; m. Laila Klintberg; children: Jonas, Mattias. MS, Royal Inst. Tech., Stockholm, 1961. Project mgr. Nya Asalt AB, 1961-69; mgr. project dept. Fosfatbolaget AB, 1969-73; tech. dir. Nitro-Nobel AB, 1973, div. gen. mgr., 1973-77, pres., 1977; pres. Katrinefors Group (Swedish Match), 1978-82; exec. v.p. Asea AB, Västeras, Sweden, 1982-87; pres. Asea Brown Boveri AB, Sweden, 1988—; exec. v.p. ABB Asea Brown Boveri Ltd., Zurich, 1988—; chmn. AB Volvo, 1994—; chmn. Fedn. Swedish Industires, 1995—; bd. dirs. A. Ahlström Corp., Helsinki. Chmn. Chalmers U. Tech., 1994—. Avocations: skiing, golf. Office: Asea Brown Boveri AB, S-721 83 Västeras Sweden Died Mar. 18, 1997.

SWAEBE, GEOFFREY, foreign service officer; b. London, Mar. 23, 1911; s. Daniel and Deborah Dora (Abhrams) S.; m. Mary Angeline Mossman, Jan. 1942; 1 child, Geoffrey Jr. Exec. Florsheim Shoe Co., Chgo., 1935-38; divisional merchandise mgr. Thalhimers, Richmond, Va., 1938-48; gen. merchandise mgr. Pizitz Dept. Store, Birmingham, Ala., 1948-50; v.p., gen. mgr./dir. Hecht Co., Balt., 1950-62; chmn. bd., pres. May Dept. Stores Calif., 1962-72; bus. and mgmt. cons., 1972-81; ambassador UN, Geneva, Switzerland, 1981-83, U.S. Embassy, Brussels, Belgium, 1983—. Bd. dirs. Community Redevel. Agy. Commn., Los Angeles, Better Bus. Bur. Los Angeles, Greater Los Angeles Plans, Inc., Hollywood Bowl Symphony Assn. Served to capt. AUS, 1942-45. Decorated Bronze Star, Order of Merit Italian Republic. Republican. Died Feb. 18, 1997.

SWAN, HENRY, retired surgeon; b. Denver, May 27, 1913; s. Henry and Carla (Denison) S.; m. Mary Fletcher Wardwell, June 25, 1937 (div. Jan. 25, 1964); children: Edith, Henry, Gretchen; m. Geraldine Morris Fairchild, Mar. 21, 1964. AB magna cum laude, Williams Coll., 1935, DSc (hon.), 1958; MD cum laude, Harvard U., 1939. Diplomate Nat. Bd. Med. Examiners, Am. Bd. Surgery. Pathology fellow Colo. Gen. Hosp., Denver, 1939-40; intern surgery Peter Bent Brigham Children's Hosp., Boston, 1940-42; pathology fellow Children's Hosp., Boston, 1942-43; asst. in surgery Harvard Med. Sch., Boston, 1942-43; from asst. to assoc. prof. surgery U. Colo. Med. Sch., 1946-50, prof. surgery, head dept. surgery, 1950-61, prof. surgery, rsch., 1963-82, prof. emeritus, 1985—. Author: Thermoregulation and Bioenergetics, 1974; assoc. editor Jour. Cardiovasc. Surgery, 1956-70, AMA Archives Surgery, 1956-66; contbr. articles to profl. jours. With AUS, 1943-45, ETO. Mem. ACS, AMA (Gold medal for original rsch. 1955), AAAS, Acad. Surg. Rsch. (medallion for exptl. surgery 1996), Am. Surg. Assn., Am. Assn. Thoracic Surgery, Soc. for Cryobiology, Soc. Univ. Surgeons, Soc. Vascular Surgery, Halsted Soc., Surgery Biology Club, Ctrl. Surg. Assn., Western Surg. Assn., Internat. Cardiovasc. Soc., Internat. Soc. Surgery, Assn. Surgery Costa Rica, Soc. Surgeons Chile, Soc. Cardiology Chile, Soc. Pediat. Mex., Denver Acad. Surgery, Denver Clin. and Path. Soc., Phi Beta Kappa, Alpha Omega Alpha. Republican. Episcopalian. Avocations: sailing, tennis, fly fishing, duck hunting, golf. DIED 07/13/96. .

SWAN, ROY CRAIG, anatomist; b. Bklyn., June 7, 1920; s. Roy Craig and Ruth (Paxton) S.; m. Marian Evalyn Morse, Mar. 26, 1949 (div. 1970); children—R. Craig, Kyle, Brian; m. Beatrice Gremaud, May 27, 1977; children—Chantal, Malcolm. A.B., Cornell U., 1941, M.D., 1947. Intern, then asst. resident medicine N.Y. Hosp., 1948-49, resident endocrinology and metabolism, 1949-50; research fellow medicine Harvard Med. Sch., 1950-52; asst. medicine Peter Bent Brigham Hosp., Boston, 1950-52; research asso. physiology Cambridge (Eng.) U., 1955-56; instr. to asso. prof. physiology Cornell U. Med. Coll., N.Y.C., 1952-59; prof. anatomy, chmn. dept. Cornell U. Med. Coll., 1959-78, Hinsey prof. anatomy, 1966-87, mem. univ. council, 1961-70; vis. prof. anatomy Boston U. Sch. Medicine, 1977-78; cons. USPHS, 1960-64, Office Sci. and Tech., 1964-65, Health Research Council City N.Y., 1960-65, mem., 1965-71; Mem. Nat. Bd. Med. Examiners, 1971-86, mem. exec. bd., 1979-86. Mem. editorial bd. Physiol. Revs., 1964-70, Circulation Rsch, 1965-70; sect. editor Biol. Abstracts, 1970-96; contbr. articles to profl. jours. Served to lt. (j.g.), Submarine Service USNR, 1943-46, PTO. Markle scholar med. scis., 1954-59. Mem. Am. Physiol. Soc., Am. Soc. Clin. Investigation, Am. Assn. Anatomists, Assn. Anatomy Chairmen (sec.-treas. 1974-77), Am. Assn. Med. Colls. (coun. acad. socs. 1974-77, adminstrv. bd. 1976-77), Alpha Omega Alpha. Home: Camden Maine Died Apr. 26, 1996.

SWANEY, RUSSEL ALGER, economic consultant; b. Detroit, June 24, 1907; s. Clark Alva and Mae Eva (Perkins) S.; m. Marian Theresa Chinnick, Sept. 11, 1930; children—Shirley Anne (Mrs. Gene P. Eyler), Russel Perkins, Sandra Lou (Mrs. Courtney A. Lecklider), William Chinnick, Richard George. Student, Grand Rapids (Mich.) Jr. Coll.; student banking, U. Wis. (financial pub. relations), Northwestern U. Security salesman Chase Securities Corp., Chgo., 1929-30; investment banker Grand Rapids, Mich., 1931-40; asst. to pres. and dir. Vento Steel Products Co., Muskegon, Mich., 1941-42; dep. mgr. war finance div. U.S. Treasury, Detroit, 1943-45; Mich. rep. Fed. Res. Bank of Chgo., 1945-48, asst. cashier, 1948-52, asst. v.p., 1952-53; v.p. charge Fed. Res. Bank of Chgo. (Detroit br.), 1953-68, sr. v.p. in charge, 1968-69; treas., dir. Econ. Club Detroit, 1953-67, sr. v.p., dir., 1968-69, pres., 1969-81, dir., 1969—, leader 11 study tours meeting with bus. and govt. leaders in 41 countries; dir. Detroit Market Opinion Research Inc., Americal Devel. Corp., Detroit, Mich. Blue Cross-Blue Shield. Gen. chmn. Mich. Week., 1956; mem. Holland Bd. Pub. Works, Mich.; chmn. study com. Birmingham (Mich.) Sch. System, 1970; past bd. dirs. YMCA Met. Detroit; hon. trustee Children's Hosp. Mich. Mem. Fin. Analysts Soc., Alpha Kappa Psi. Episcopalian. Clubs: Holland Country; Circumnavigators, Detroit Athletic, Detroit, Bankers (pres. 1956-57 (Detroit); Econ. (dir.) (Grand Rapids, Mich.). Died Dec. 29, 1996.

SWARTZ, HARRY, biomedical communications consultant; b. Detroit, June 21, 1911; s. Isaac and Anne (Srere) S.; m. Eve Sutton, Oct. 3, 1942 (dec. Mar. 1980); 1 child, Mark (dec.); m. Marie Marchowsky, Apr. 26, 1987. AB, U. Mich., 1930, MD, 1933. Diplomate Am. Bd. Clin. Immunology and Allergy. Assoc. dir. Allergy Testing Lab., N.Y.C., 1986-88; cons., science advisor Mundo Medico, Mexico, 1979-96; cons. Biomedical Communications, N.Y.C., 1984-96, Editioni Scientifiche Internat., Milan, Italy, 1984-96. Editor-in-chief, cofounder Invetigacion Medica Internac, 1974-96; author 10 books, over 100 jour. articles. Served. to maj. M.C. AUS, 1942-46. Recipient Award of Merit, Am. Coll. Allergists, 1982. Fellow Am. Acad. Allerty (emeritus), Am. Coll. Allergists (emeritus), am. Assn. Clin. Immunology and Allergy (emeritus), Royal Soc. Health; mem. AAAS, N.Y. State Med. Soc. (life mem.), Med. Soc. County N.Y. (life mem.), Fgn. Press Ctr., Fgn. Press Assn. Avocation: sculpture. Home: New York N.Y. Died Feb. 20, 1996.

SWENSON, JOHN WILLIAM, government official; b. Worcester, Mass., Nov. 9, 1917; s. Andrew W. and Ellen M. (Lindstrom) S.; m. Priscilla A. Atwood, Feb. 7, 1941; children—Peter J., Susan A. (Mrs. Niederjohn). B.S., Mass. State Coll., 1940. Personnel mgr. Leland-Gifford Co., Worcester, 1944-46; with VA, 1946-95; personnel adminstr. Rutland Heights (Mass.) VA Hosp., 1946-65; personnel dir. VA Hosp., Northampton, Mass., 1965-66; asst. adminstr. The Meml. Hosp., Worcester, Mass., 1966-70; dep. regional adminstr. Region I SBA, Boston, 1970-95; Mem. Nat. Health Council, 1961-95. Bd. dirs. U. Mass. Found., 1950-52; chmn. alumni fund U. Mass., 1968-70. Served to capt. AUS, World War II. Mem. Worcester County Health Assn. (pres. 1962-64), Mass. Tb and Respiratory Disease League (pres. 1964-66), Nat. Tb Assn. (sec. 1964-68), U. Mass. Alumni Assn. (pres. 1950-52), Nat. Tb and Respiratory Disease Assn. (v.p. 1968-70), Internat. Personnel Mgmt. Assn., Sr. Execs. Assn., Am. Arbitration Assn. (panel of arbitrators 1970-95), Lambda Chi Alpha (pres. local chpt. 1939-40). Home: Yarmouth Port Mass. Died June 4, 1995.

SWIDLER, JOSEPH CHARLES, lawyer; b. Chgo., Jan. 28, 1907; s. Abraham and Dora (Cromer) S.; m. Gertrude Tyrna, 1944; children: Ann, Mark. Student, U. Ill., U. Fla.; PhB, U. Chgo., 1929, JD, 1930. Pvt. law practice Chgo., 1930-33; asst. solicitor U.S. Dept. Interior, 1933; mem. legal dept. TVA, 1933-57; gen. counsel, sec., chmn. bd. TVA Retirement System, 1945-57; counsel Alien Property Bur., Dept. Justice, 1941, Power Div., War Prodn. Bd., 1942; pvt. practice law Knoxville and Nashville, 1957-61; chmn. FPC, 1961-65; mem. Water Resources Council, 1964-65, Swidler & Belnap, Washington, 1966-70; chmn. N.Y. State Pub. Service Commn., Albany, 1970-74; dir. Inst. Pub. Policy Alternatives, SUNY, Albany, 1974-75; ptnr. Leva, Hawes, Symington, Martin & Oppenheimer, Washington, 1975-82; counsel Swidler & Berlin, Washington, 1982-97; bd. dirs. Nat. Regulatory Rsch. Inst.; mem. adv. coun. Electric Power Rsch. Inst., 1973-80, Gas Rsch. Inst. Served with USNR, 1943-45. Fellow Nat. Acad. Pub. Adminstrn. Died May 1, 1997.

SWOPE, GEORGE WENDELL, minister, educator; b. Norfolk, Va., Feb. 2, 1916; s. Dr. George W. and Nellie (Guthrie) S.; student Drexel U., 1940-41, U. Pa., 1941-42, Marshall U., 1960-63; AB, Eastern Coll., 1945; ThB, Eastern Bapt. Theol. Sem., 1945, DD, 1958, M. in Divinity, 1972; STB, Temple U., 1946; m. Winifred A. Devlin, June 26, 1940; children: George Wendell, Gregory Willard, Winifred Ruth. Ordained to ministry Bapt. Ch., 1945; pastor, Essington, Pa., 1940-43, Camden, N.J., 1943-46; dir. evangelism, Christian edn. Am. Bapt. Conv., 1946-54; pastor East Orange, N.J., 1954-58, Kenova, W.Va., 1958-63, Port Chester, N.Y., 1963-70; registrar Westchester Community Coll., 1970-74, asst. dir. guidance services, 1975-84; founder, owner Maplecroft Realty Ltd., 1988-90; pastor, Sutton, N.H., 1989-91. Pres. Nat. Alumni Assn., Ea. Bapt. Theol. Sem., 1956-58; pres. N.J. Bapt. Ministers Council, 1955-57, East Orange Protestant Council, 1955-56; mem. pastor's adv. com. Am. Bapt. Publs., 1957-62; vice chmn. press relation com. Am. Bapt. Conv., 1958-62, chmn. nominations com., 1962; chmn. commn. on Christian unity W.Va. Council Chs., 1958-60; pres. Port Chester Council Chs., 1969-70; mem. dept. evangelism Fed. Council of Chs., Nat. Council Chs. Chaplain East Orange His. Soc., 1957-58, mem. moderator council ordination Met. N.Y. Bapt. City Soc., also v.p.; chmn. ministers div. Planned Parenthood Assn. So. Westchester County; mem. Port Chester Anti-Poverty Commn.; chmn. mayor's commn. on community improvement Port Chester; chmn. Nat. Com. Engaged in Freeing Minds, 1976-79; exec. dir. Am. Family Found., 1979-81; minister-at-large Am. Bapt. Ch., 1985—; chmn. adminstrv. bd., min. of visitation Christ United Meth. Ch.; chmn. Bradford Bicentennial Meml. Day Program, Bradford, N.H.; hospice vol., 1986-91; mem. Rep. Presdl. Citizens Adv. Commn. Mem. SAR (v.p. Savaman chpt.), Sunapee Region Bd. Realtors, Nat. Assn. Realtors, Religious Liberty Coun. (charter 1990—), New London Country Squires, Rangely Country Squires, Plantation Golf And Country Club, Masons (past master), Rotary (past pres.). Died Jan. 25, 1998.

SYNAR, MICHAEL LYNN (MIKE LYNN), congressman; b. Vinita, Okla., Oct. 17, 1950; s. Edmond and Virginia Anne (Gann) S. B.B.A., U. Okla., 1972, J.D., 1977; M.A. in Econs., Northwestern U., 1973; postgrad., U. Edinburgh, 1973-74. Farmer, rancher Muskogee, Okla.; real estate broker Muskogee, 1968-78; mem. 96th-103rd Congresses from 2nd Okla. dist., Washington, D.C., 1979-96; chmn. subcom. environ., energy and natural resources; mem. com. on govt. opers.; chmn. Dem. Study Group. Del. White House Conf. on Aging, 1971. Democrat. Episcopalian. Home: Arlington Va. Died Jan. 9, 1996.

SZALAY, LAJOS, graphic artist; b. Ormezo, Hungary, Feb. 26, 1909; came to U.S., 1960,; naturalized, 1965; s. Nandor and Karolin (Sike) S.; m. Julieta Hering, Oct. 2, 1939; 1 child, Clara. Grad., Acad. Fine Arts, Budapest, Hungary, 1935. Prof. drawing U. Nacional de Tucumán, Argentina, 1949-55; prof. drawing Escuela Superior de Bellas Artes, Buenos Aires, Argentina, 1955-59. One-man exhibitions include Tucumán, 1949, Buenos Aires, 1955, 56, 57, 59, Pan Am. Union, Washington, 1958, Budapest, 1972, 84, Paris, 1975, N.Y., 1984; represented in permanent collections U. Chgo. Mus., Mus. of U. Notre Dame, Fogg Mus., Cambridge, Mass., museums in Budapest, Buenos Aires and Tucumán; contbr. drawings to various publs. Served to cpl. Hungarian Army, 1938-42. Recipient Order of Hungarian Nat. Flag, 1979, 3 additional awards; scholar Hungarian Govt., Budapest, 1941, UNESCO, Paris, 1948. Roman Catholic. Avocation: reading. Home: New York N.Y. Died Apr. 1, 1995.

SZATHMÁRY, LOUIS ISTVÁN, II, former restaurateur, writer; b. Rakospalota, Hungary, June 2, 1919; came to U.S., 1951, naturalized, 1963; s. Louis Istvan and Irene (Strauss) S.; m. Sadako Tanino, May 9, 1960; 1 dau., Magda. Ph.D., U. Budapest, 1944. Chef New Eng. Province Jesuits, Manresa Island, Conn., 1952-55; exec. chef Mut. Broadcasting System, N.Y.C., 1955-58; plant supt. Reddi Fox, Inc., Darien, Conn., 1958-59; exec. chef Armour & Co., Chgo., 1959-64; chef, owner Bakery Restaurant, Chgo., 1962-89; owner Louis Szathmáry Assocs.; chef laureate Johnson and Wales U., Providence. Author: The Bakery Restaurant Cookbook; author-editor: Cookery Americana, 16 vols. Mem. AFTRA, Chgo. Acad. Scis. (trustee emeritus), Internat. Food, Wine and Traveel Writers Assn., Soc. Profl. Mgmt. Cons., Coun. on Hotel, Restaurant and Instnl. Edn., SAG, Acad. Chefs U.S.A., Nat. Space Soc. (bd. govs.), Grolier Club (N.Y.C.), Caxton Club, Cliff Dwellers Club.

SZEBEHELY, VICTOR G., aeronautical engineer; b. Budapest, Hungary, Aug. 10, 1921; s. Victor and Vilma (Stockl) S.; m. Jo Betsy Lewallen, May 21, 1970; 1 dau., Julia. M.E., U. Budapest, 1943, Ph.D. in Engring, 1945; Dr. (hon.), Eotvos U. Budapest, 1991. Asst. prof. U. Budapest, 1945-47; research asso. State U. Pa., 1947-48; asso. prof. Va. Poly. Inst., 1948-53; research asso.

Model Basin, U.S. Navy, 1953-57; research mgr. Gen. Electric Co., 1957-62; asso. prof. astronomy Yale U., 1962-68; prof. aerospace engring. U. Tex., Austin, 1968-97; chmn. dept. U. Tex., 1977-81, R.B. Curran Centennial chair in engring., 1983-97; cons. NASA-Johnson Space Center, U.S. Air Force Space Command, Lawrence Berkeley Lab., U. Calif. Author 18 books; contbr. over 200 articles on space research, celestial mechanics and ship dynamics to profl. jours. Knighted by Queen Juliana of Netherlands, 1956. Fellow AIAA, AAAS; mem. Am. Astron. Soc. (Brouwer award div. dynamical astronomy 1977), Internat. Astron. Union (pres. commn. on celestial mechanics), NAE, European Acad. Arts, Scis., Lit. Home: Austin Tex. Died Sept. 13, 1997.

TAGGART, LESLIE DAVIDSON, lawyer; b. Glasgow, Scotland, Aug. 28, 1910; came to U.S. (from Can.), 1920, naturalized, 1934; s. Frederick James and Petrina W. (Paterson) T.; m. Mary Mason Kerr, Sept. 27, 1940; children: Georgia M. Taggart Brackett, William K., Patricia A. Taggart Shepherd, Douglas G. A.B., Columbia U., 1931, LL.B., 1934. Bar: N.Y. 1934. Practiced in N.Y.C.; former sr. partner Watson Leavenworth Kelton & Taggart; dir. Magnetic Analysis Corp., Mt. Vernon, N.Y.; lectr. Practising Law Inst. Past sec., bd. mgrs. St. Andrews Soc. N.Y. State. Mem. N.Y. Patent Law Assn., Am. Patent Law Assn. (past dir.), U.S. Trademark Assn. (past dir.), ABA, Am. Coll. Trial Lawyers, Phi Beta Kappa, Phi Sigma Kappa. Congregationalist. Clubs: Univ. (N.Y.C.); Patterson (Fairfield, Conn.).

TAKAL, PETER, artist; b. Bucharest, Romania, Dec. 8, 1905; emigrated to U.S., 1939, naturalized, 1944; s. Gustave and Renee (Vassal) T.; m. Charlotte Tournerie, 1933; 1 dau., Anne; m. Susy Laytha, 1945; 1 son, Kim; m. Jean Mali Noyes, Aug. 8, 1956; 1 son, Pierre. Student schs. of, Paris, France, also Berlin, Germany. One-man shows include Gallery Gurlitt, Berlin, 1932, Gallery Zak, Paris, 1933, Gallery Jeanne Castel, 1935, 37, Katherine Kuh Gallery, Chgo., 1937, 39, 43, Santa Barbara Mus. Art, 1941, Gallery Charpentier, 1939, The Cleve. Mus. Art, 1958, Palazzo Strozzi, Florence, Italy, 1960, Gallery Benador, Geneva, 1977, Smithsonian Instn., 1959-60, Kestner Mus. Hanover, throughout West Germany, 1961-62, others; group exhbn. White House, 1966, 70, Whitney Mus. Art, 1955-74, Bklyn. Mus., 1954-64, Libr. Congress, 1955-62, Mus. Modern Art Print Coun. Am.; retrospective exhbns. Geneva, 1970, 90, Kresge Art Mus., 1986, Pfalzgalerie Kaiserslautern, Germany, 1993 (illus. catalogue); works in over 100 permanent collections in Berlin, Bremen, Kassel, Zurich, Geneva, Florence, Montreal, Hamburg, Copenhagen, Stockholm, Hanover, Stuttgart, Darmstadt, USIS, Cleveland Mus. Art, Hunt Bot. Libr., Pitts., Art Inst., Chgo., San Francisco Mus. Art, L.A. County Mus., Met. Mus. Art, N.Y., Pa. Acad. Fine Arts, Nat. Gallery, Washington, Libr. Congress, Victoria and Albert Mus., London, Whitney Mus. Am. Art, Mus. Modern Art, Bklyn. Mus., Phila. Mus. Art, E.B. Crocker Art Gallery, Sacramento, Dallas Mus. Fine Art, Balt. Mus. Art, John Herron Art Inst., Indpls., Musee de l'Art Moderne, Paris, others; author: portfolio drawings and poems Takal, 1945, About The Invisible Art, Theodore Lyman Wright Art Ctr., Beloit, 1965, Takal Dessins, 1930-90, Danses (portfolio drawings), 1992, others; contbr. illustrations to mags., U.S., Paris, Stockholm; catalogue raisonne of prints by Peter Takal published by Kresge Art Mus., 1986; print commns.: Print Club Cleve., 1956-57, Internat. Graphic Art Soc., 1956, 59, 63, 64, Associated Am. Artists, 1958, 75, Pratt, 1969, Hollander Workshop, 1969, and numerous others. Recipient award for drawing biennial exhbn. Bklyn. Mus., 1954, 8th ann. Knickerbocker art exhbn. Riverside Mus., N.Y.C., 1955, Print Club award Ball State Tchrs. Coll., 1958, drawing prize Providence Pint Club, 1963; fellow Yaddo Found., 1961; grantee Ford Found., Tamarind Workshop, 1963, Ford Found. grantee, artist-in-residence mus. Beloit (Wis.) Coll., 1965. Home: Geneva Switzerland Died Mar. 12, 1995.

TAKAYAMA, AKIRA, economics educator; b. Yokohama, Japan; came to U.S., 1957; s. Tsunaki and Shoko (Takeuchi) T.; m. Machiko Onabe, Jan. 31, 1970 (dec. Jan. 1996). B.A., Internat. Christian U., Tokyo, 1957; M.A., U. Rochester, 1960, Ph.D., 1962; Ph.D., Hitotsubashi U., Tokyo, 1964. Instr., then asst. prof. econs. Internat. Christian U., Tokyo, Japan, 1962-64; fellow in econ. stats. U. Manchester, Eng., 1964-65; vis. assoc. prof. econs. U. Minn.-Mpls., 1965-66; assoc. prof. econs. Purdue U.-West Lafayette, 1967-68, prof. econs., 1968-80; prof. econs. Tex. A&M U., College Station, 1978-82, Kyoto U., Japan, 1982-85; Vandeveer prof. econs. So. Ill. U., Carbondale, 1983-96; vis. prof. econs. U. Rochester, 1969-70, Australian Nat. U., 1968, 77, U. Hawaii, 1971-72, U. Tokyo, 1974-75, Doshisha U., Japan, 1989, Tulane U., New Orleans, 1991, Internat. Christian U., Japan, 1993, 94; J. Fish Smith profl. Brigham Young U., Provo, Utah, 1976. Author: Mathematical Economics, 1974, 2d edit. 1985, International Trade, 1972, Analytical Methods in Economics, 1994; co-editor: Economic Development in East and Southeast Asia, 1990, Trade, Policy and International Adjustments, 1991; contbr. articles to profl. jours. Mem. Am. Econs. Assn., Econometric Soc., Econ. Rsch. Ctr. Japan, Japan Assn. Econs. and Econometrics. Deceased Jan. 2, 1996.

TALEBIAN, ABDOL HOSSEN, chemistry educator; b. Dezful, Iran, Mar. 21, 1952; came to the U.S., 1976; s. Ahmad and Fatemah (Kajforoosh) T.; m. Sedighah Izadpanah; children: Bobak, David Ali. BS in Chemistry, Tehran U., 1976; MS in Organic Chemistry, George Washington U., 1979, PhD, 1983; postdoctoral study, Georgetown U., 1983-86. Asst. prof. George Mason U., Fairfax, Va., 1981-82; postdoctoral rsch. assoc. Georgetown U., Washington, 1983-86, rsch. scientist, assoc. rsch. prof., 1987—; cons. Delta Mgmt. Group, Bethesda, Md., 1983—, US Biosci. Inc., Conshohocken, Pa., 1986—, Unimed Inc., Summersville, N.J., 1983-92; chem. nomenclator Nat. Cancer Inst., Bethesda, 1983-87; com. me. Nat. Tchr. Exams., 1981. Contbr. articles to profl. jours. Recipient Alan Berman Rsch. Publ. award Dept. of Navy, 1988. Mem. Am. Chem. Soc., Am. Assn. for Cancer Rsch., Sigma Xi. Avocations: camping, reading, photography, bicycling. Deceased.

TAMM, IGOR, biomedical scientist, educator; b. Tapa, Estonia, Apr. 27, 1922; s. Alexander and Olga Tamm; m. Olive Pitkin, May 9, 1953; children: Carol, Eric, Ellen. Student, Tartu U. Med. Faculty, Estonia, 1942-43; med. candid. exam., Karolinska Mediko-Kirurgiska Inst., Stockholm, 1945; MD cum laude, Yale U., 1947. Intern, asst. resident Grace-New Haven Community Hosp., 1947-49; asst. in medicine Yale U. Sch. Medicine, 1947-49; asst. and asst. physician The Rockefeller Inst., N.Y.C., 1949-53, assoc. and assoc. physician, 1953-56, assoc. prof., assoc. physician, 1956-58, assoc. prof. and physician, 1958-64; prof. and sr. physician The Rockefeller U., N.Y.C., 1964-86, Abby Rockefeller Mauzé prof. and sr. physician, 1986-92, emeritus, 1992-95; assoc. mem. Commn. on Acute Respiratory Diseases, Armed Forces Epidemiol. Bd., 1961-73; mem. virology and rickettsiology study sect. NIH, 1964-68; mem. bd. sci. cons. Sloan-Kettering Inst. Cancer Research, 1966-75, vice chmn., 1971-72, chmn., 1972-73; mem. study panel for allergy and infectious diseases Health Research Council of City of N.Y., 1968-75; mem. Am. Cancer Soc. adv. com. on virology and cell biology, 1969-74; gen. chmn. task force on virology Nat. Inst. Allergy and Infectious Diseases, 1976-78. Contbr. 255 sci. papers on biology of viruses and cells; assoc. editor Jour. Immunology, 1957-59, procs. Soc. for Exptl. Biology and Medicine, 1963-66; adv. editor Jour. Exptl. Medicine, 1971-81; hon. editorial bd. Biochem. Pharmacology, 1974-84; mem. editorial bd. Jour. Interferon Rsch., 1980-88; editor symposium on viruses Am. Jour. Medicine, 1965; editor: (with F.L. Horsfall) Viral and Rickettsial Infections of Man, 4th edit., 1965. Recipient Alfred Benzon prize, 1967; Centennial lectr. U. Ill., 1968. Fellow AAAS, N.Y. Acad. Scis. (Sarah L. Poiley award 1977); mem. NAS, Am. Soc. Microbiology, Am. Assn. Immunologists, Soc. for Exptl. Biology and Medicine, Am. Soc. Clin. Investigation, Am. Acad. Microbiology, Am. Soc. Cell Biology, Soc. Gen. Microbiology, Assn. Am. Physicians, Deutsche Gesellschaft für Hygiene und Mikrobiologie (corr.), Am. Soc. Virology, Internat. Cell Cycle Soc., Internat. Soc. Interferon Research, Harvey Soc., Alpha Omega Alpha. Achievements include discovery and detailed characterization of the urinary (Tamm-Horsfall) glycoprotein; discovery of double-stranded RNA as the genetic material of reovirus and wound tumor virus; discovery of selective inhibitors of mRNA synthesis; discoveries regarding growth factor and cytokine action. Home: Watch Hill R.I. Died Feb. 6, 1995.

TANG, THOMAS, federal judge; b. Phoenix, Jan. 11, 1922. B.S., U. Santa Clara, 1947, law student, 1948-50; LL.B. with distinction, U. Ariz., 1950. Bar: Ariz. 1950, Calif. 1951. Dep. county atty. Maricopa County, Ariz., 1953-57; asst. atty. gen. State of Ariz., 1957-58; judge Ariz. Superior Ct., 1963-70; mem. firm Sullivan, Mahoney & Tang, Phoenix, 1971-77; councilman City of Phoenix, 1960-62, vice mayor, 1962; judge U.S. Ct. of Appeals 9th Circuit, Phoenix, 1977-93, sr. status judge, 1993-95. Mem. State Bar Ariz. (bd. govs. 1971-77, pres. 1977), State Bar Calif. Died July 18, 1995.

TANKSLEY, RAYMOND RICHARD, JR., judge; b. Spokane, June 9, 1931; s. Raymond Richard and Frances Josephine (Demigne) T.; m. Kathleen Sorensen, Aug. 6, 1960; children: Claire, Michael, Edward, Ann Marie. JD, Gonzaga U., 1955. Bar: Wash. 1955, U.S. Dist. Ct. (ea. and we. dist.) Wash. 1956. Sole practice Spokane, 1957-85; judge Spokane County Dist. Ct., 1985-95. state committeeman Wash. Rep. Party, 1968-72. Mem. Assn. Trial Lawyers Am., Wash. State Bar Assn., Spokane County Bar Assn., Wash. State Dist. and Mcpl. Ct. Judges Assn. Died Jan., 1995.

TARAPATA, PETER, architect; b. Detroit, July 24, 1919; s. Elias and Ahafia (Fedune) T.; m. Helen Louise Cook, June 29, 1946; children—Susan Karyl, Karen Ann. B.S. in Engring, U. Mich, 1940, B.S. in Architecture, 1943, M.Arch., 1947. Registered architect Mich., Ohio, N.Y., Ill., Ind., N.J., Minn. Prin. Eberle M. Smith & Assocs., Detroit, 1949-56; prin. Smith, Tarapata, MacMahon, Birmingham, Mich., 1956-59; prin. Tarapata, MacMahon, Paulsen (name now TMP Assoc., Inc.), Bloomfield Hills, Mich., 1959—, chmn., 1959. Prin. works include campus plan Washtenaw Community Coll., 1968-70, Downtown Urban Renewal, Canton, Ohio, 1962, sch. planning Bloomfield Hills Jr. High Sch., 1964, high sch. planning Aldena High Sch., 1966. Mem. adv. com. Region 5 GSA, 1970-73. Served to 1st lt. C.E., U.S. Army 1943-46, CBI. Recipient award Am. Assn. Sch. Adminstrn. 1966. Fellow AIA (Gold medal 1978, Nat. award 1962, 70, Detroit chpt. award 1964), Engring. Soc. Detroit; mem. Council for Ednl. Facilities Planners, Soc. Coll. and Univ. Planners, Mich. Soc. Architects, Nat. Research Guild. Democrat. Lodge: Rotary (pres. Bloomfield Hills chpt. 1979-80). Avocations: ship models; cabinetry; coach models. DIED 10/22/96. .

TARTIKOFF, BRANDON, broadcast executive; b. L.I., N.Y., Jan. 13, 1949; m. Lilly Samuels, 1982; children: Calla Lianne, Elizabeth Justine. B.A. with honors, Yale U., 1970. With promotion dept. ABC TV, New Haven, Conn., 1971-73; program exec. dramatic programming Sta. WLS-TV (ABC), Chgo., 1973-76; mgr. dramatic devel. ABC TV, N.Y.C., 1976-77; writer, producer Graffiti; dir. comedy programs NBC Entertainment, Burbank, Calif., 1977-78, v.p. programs, 1978-80, pres., 1980-90; chmn. NBC Entertainment Group, 1989-91, Paramount Pictures, 1991-92, New World Entertainment, Ltd., 1994—. Co-author: The Last Great Ride,1992. Named 1 of 10 Outstanding Young Men Am. U.S. Jaycees, 1981; recipient Tree of Life award Jewish Nat. Found., 1986. Home: Los Angeles Calif. DIED 08/27/97. .

TATARIAN, HRACH ROGER, journalist; b. Fresno, Calif., Dec. 25, 1916; s. Edward Y. and Rose (Yegishian) T.; m. Eunice E. Krauchi, Aug. 1, 1939; 1 son, Allan Roger. B.A., Fresno State Coll., 1938; Litt.D. (hon.), Windham Coll., 1967; LL.D. (hon.), Colby Coll., 1980. With UPI, 1938-72; assigned Fresno, San Francisco and Phoenix, 1938-43; overnight news editor Washington, 1943-48; mgr. London, 1949-51; mgr. for Italy, 1951-53; gen. European news mgr., London, 1953-59; mng. editor N.Y.C., 1959-62; exec. editor, 1963-65, v.p., 1963, editor, 1965-72; prof. journalism Calif. State U., Fresno, 1972-87; dir. McClatchy Newspapers, 1982-95; cons. UNESCO, Paris, 1978, U.S. Nat. Commn. for UNESCO, 1978-81; mem. adv. bd. Ctr. Fgn. Journalists. Recipient Distinguished Journalism award Ohio U., 1968; named Outstanding Journalism Prof. Calif. Newspaper Pubs. Assn., 1979; mem. 20th Century Fund Task Force on Internat. News Flow, 1978; Recipient Elijah Parish Lovejoy award for achievement in journalism, 1980. Fellow Sigma Delta chi (Hall of Fame N.Y. chpt.). Home: Fresno Calif. Died June 25, 1995.

TATE, MERZE, educator; b. Blanchard, Mich., Feb. 6, 1905; d. Charles H. and Myrtle Katora (Lett) T.; BA Western Mich. U. 1927; MA Columbia U. 1930, BLitt Oxford U. 1935, PhD Harvard U. 1941; LLD (hon.) Morgan State U., Bowie State Coll. 1977, Lincoln U. 1978; DHL, Havard U., 1986. Tchr., Crispus Attucks High Sch., Indpls. 1927-32, Barber Scotia Coll. Concord, N.C. 1935-36, Bennett Coll. 1936-41, Morgan State U. 1941-42; faculty Howard U. 1942-74, now prof. emeritus; Fulbright prof. India 1950-51. Fellow and grantee in field; recipient Nat. Urban League Disting. Achievement award 1948; Western Mich. U. Disting. Alumna award 1970; Mayor of Detroit award 1978; Am. Black Artist's Pioneer award 1978; award The Prometheans, Inc., 1980; Am. Assn. State Colls. and Univs. award, 1982. Mem. Am. Hist. Assn., Assn. Study Afro-Am. History, AAUW (Disting. Mem. award D.C. chpt. 1983), Phi Beta Kappa, Alpha Kappa Alpha (3d fgn. fellow), Pi Gamma Mu, Radcliffe Club of Washington, Harvard Club of Washington, Writers Club, Howard U. Women's Club, Howard U. Retirees Club, Bridge Builders Club, Bridge Eights Club. Roman Catholic. Author: The Disarmament Illusion—The Movement for a Limitation of Armaments to 1907, 1942, The United States and Armaments, 1948, The United State and the Hawaiian Kingdom, 1965, Hawaii: Reciprocity or Annexation 1968, Diplomacy in the Pacific, 1973; contbr. numerous articles to profl. jours.

TATSUOKA, MAURICE MAKOTO, psychology educator; b. Shanghai, People's Republic of China, Feb. 1, 1922; came to U.S., 1949; s. Noboru and Yuri (Pratt) T.; m. Hisako Tanahashi, Apr. 10, 1946 (div. Mar. 1964); 1 child, Francis; m. Kikumi Kim Kanemitsu, Nov. 5, 1965; children: Kay, Curtis. BS, Nagoya U., Japan, 1945; MA, George Peabody Coll., 1951; EdD, Harvard U., 1956. Lectr. Kinjo Women's Coll., Nagoya, 1945-49; asst. prof. U. Hawaii, Hilo, 1956-61; assoc. prof. U. Ill., Urbana, 1961-64, prof. ednl. psychology, 1964-88, prof. psychology, 1988—; cons. Inst. for Personality and Ability Testing, Champaign, Ill., 1965—; cons. Ednl. Testing Svcs., princeton, N.J., 1990—. Author: Multivariate Analysis, 1971, 87. Mem. Am. Statis. Assn., Am. Ednl. Research Assn. Democratic. Unitarian.

TAVOULAREAS, WILLIAM PETER, oil co. exec.; b. Bklyn., Nov. 9, 1919; s. Peter William and Mary (Palisi) T.; B.B.A., St. John's U., 1941, J.D., 1948; m. Adele Maciejewska, Aug. 13, 1941; children: Peter, Patrice, William. Admitted to N.Y. bar, 1948; with Mobil Oil Corp. 1947-96, v.p. plans and programs Mobil Internat. Oil Co., 1961-63, v.p. charge supply and distbn. and internat. sales parent co., 1963-65, sr. v.p., dir., mem. exec. com., 1965-67, v.p. charge supply, transport and Middle East and Indonesian affairs, pres. N. Am. div., 1967-69, corp. pres., vice chmn. exec. com., dir., 1976-

96; dir. Gen. Foods Corp., Bankers Trust Co., Bankers Trust N.Y. Corp., Bendix Corp. Trustee St. John's U., Athens Coll., St. Paul's Sch.; bd. govs. N.Y. Hosp.; bd. dirs. Georgetown U., Near East Coll. Assn. Served with U.S. Army, World War II. Mem. Harbor Acres Assn., Beta Gamma Sigma. Knights of Malta. Clubs: Royal Palm Yacht and Country, Pinnacle, North Hempstead Country. Died Jan. 13, 1996. Home: Boca Raton Fla.

TAX, SOL, anthropologist, educator; b. Chgo., Oct. 30, 1907; s. Morris Paul and Kate (Hanwit) T.; m. Gertrude Jospe Katz, July 4, 1933; children: Susan Margaret, Marianna. PhB, U. Wis., 1931, DHL (hon.), 1969; PhD, U. Chgo., 1935; LLD (hon.), Wilmington Coll., 1974; DSc (hon.), U. Del Valle De Guatemala, 1974, Beloit Coll., 1975. Mem. Logan Mus. N. Africa Expdn., 1930; mem. field party Lab. Anthropology Mescalero Apache, 1931; research among Fox Indians, 1932-34; ethnologist Carnegie Instn., Washington, 1934-48; field research Indians, Guatemala, 1934-41, Chiapas, Mexico, 1942-46; vis. prof. Nat. Inst. Anthropology and History, Mexico, 1942-43; research assoc. U. Chgo., 1940-44, assoc. prof., 1944-48, prof., 1948—, assoc. dean div. social scis., 1948-53, chmn. dept. anthropology, 1955-58, dean univ. extension, 1963-68; dir. Fox Indian Project, 1948-62; research assoc. Wenner-Gren Found. Anthrop. Research, 1957—; co-ordinator Am. Indian Chgo. Conf., U. Chgo., 1961, Carnegie Cross-Cultural Edn. Program, 1962-67; mem. exec. com. U.S. Nat. Commn. UNESCO, 1963-65; mem. com. internat. relations anthropology Nat. Research Council, 1956-66, com. internat. relations behavioral scis., 1966—; spl. adv. anthropology to sec. Smithsonian Instn., 1965—; dir. Ctr. Study Man; cons. U.S. Office Edn., 1965—; mem. Community Activities and Continuing Edn. Council Ill., 1965-67; sec. Ill. Mus. Bd., 1958-70; bd. dirs. Council Study Mankind, exec. com., 1965—; bd. advs. Council Internat. Communications, 1966—; bd. dirs. Am. Indian Devel., Inc.; trustee Native Am. Ednl. Svcs. Coll. Author: Heritage of Conquest: The Ethnology of Middle America, 1952, Penny Capitalism: A Guatemalan Indian Economy, 1953; editor: Civilization of Ancient America, 1951, Acculturation in the Americas, 1952, Indian Tribes of Aboriginal America, 1952, An Appraisal of Anthropology Today, 1953, 29th Internat. Congress Americanists, 1949-52, Evolution after Darwin, 3 vols., 1960, Anthropology Today-Selections, 1962, Horizons of Anthropology, 1964, Viking Fund Publs. in Anthropology, 1960-68, The People vs. The System: A Dialogue in Urban Conflict; assoc. editor Am. Anthropologist, 1948-53, editor, 1953-56; contbg. editor Handbook Latin Am. Studies, 1947-52; founder, editor Current Anthropology-A World Jour. of Scis. of Man; gen. editor World Anthropology, 91 vols., 1975-79. Pres. Hyde Park Community Council, 1952-53. Viking medalist, 1961-65; fellow Ctr. Advanced Study Behavioral Scis., 1969-70; decorated Govt. Czechoslovakia, 1969. Fellow Am. Anthrop. Assn. (pres. 1958-59, Disting. Service award 1977), AAAS, Am. Folklore Soc., Soc. Applied Anthropology (Bronislaw Malinowski award 1977); hon. mem. Slovakian Anthrop. Soc., Slovak Acad. Scis., Royal Anthrop. Inst. Great Britain, Hungarian Anthrop. Inst., Chilean Anthrop. Inst.; mem. Mexican Anthrop. Soc., Nat. Research Council, Internat. Union Anthrop. and Ethnol. Scis. (pres. 1968-73), Sigma Xi. Club: Quadrangle. Home: Chicago Ill. DIED 01/04/95.

TAYLOR, HAROLD, educator; b. Toronto, Ont., Can., Sept. 28, 1914; came to U.S., 1939, naturalized, 1947; s. Charles W. and Elizabeth (Wilson) T.; m. Grace Muriel Thorne, 1941; children: Mary Elizabeth, Jennifer Thorne. A.B., U. Toronto, 1935, M.A. in Philosophy and Lit., 1936; Ph.D. in Philosophy, U. London, 1938. Instr., research fellow philosophy U. Wis., 1939-42, asst. prof., 1942-45, armed forces rep., 1943; research asso. psychology, war project OSRD, 1944; pres. Sarah Lawrence Coll., Bronxville, N.Y., 1945-59; faculty New Sch. Social Research, 1947-48, 48-49; co-founder, vice chmn. Nat. Com. for Support of Pub. Schs., 1963; vis. lectr. univs. in Australia, Denmark, Finland, Greece, India, Indonesia, Iran, Italy, Japan, Malaysia, Norway, USSR, Sweden, Thailand, Turkey, U.S., 1959-75; dir. pilot project in world coll., 1963; dir. tchr. edn. study U.S. Office of Edn., 1967-68; host ABC TV series, Meet the Professor, 1962-63; disting. prof. CUNY, 1975-76; founder, dir. Ctr. for Internat. Svc., Coll. S.I., 1976-82. Author: On Education and Freedom, 1954, Art and the Intellect, 1960, Students without Teachers, 1969, The World As Teacher, 1969, How To Change Colleges, 1971, Art and the Future, 1971; editor, co-author: Essays in Teaching, 1950; Editor, co-author: Humanities in the Schools, 1968; editor: The Idea of a World University, 1967; contbr.: articles to N.Y. Times Mag., Saturday Rev., also ednl. jours. Chmn. NRC on Peace Strategy; chmn. U.S. com. for UN Univ., 1971-73; trustee Inst. World Order; trustee N.Y. Studio Sch., Coll. Human Services, Inst. Shipboard Edn., Agnes deMille Dance Theatre; pres. Am. Ballet Theatre, 1965-67; vice chmn. Martha Graham Sch. Contemporary Dance, 1965-73. Moss scholar U. Toronto, 1935-36. Club: Century Assn. (N.Y.C.). Home: New York N.Y. Died Feb. 9, 1993.

TAYLOR, HOWARD MELVIN, soil scientist, educator, researcher; b. Pride, Tex., Jan. 20, 1924; s. Clifton Patrick and Dona Margaret (Faulkner) T.; m. Marjorie Claire Joplin, Mar. 25, 1948; children: Carl Stephen, Scott Richard. BSc, Tex. Tech. U., 1949; PhD, U. Calif., Davis, 1957. Soil scientist USDA Soil Conservation Svc., Tex., 1949-54; rsch. asst. U. Calif., Davis, 1954-57; soil scientist USDA Agrl. Rsch. Svc., Amarillo, Tex., 1957-65, Auburn, Ala., 1956-72, Ames, Iowa, 1972-80; prof. agronomy Iowa State U., Ames, 1980-82; Rockwell prof. Tex. Tech. U., Lubbock, 1982—. Author: Soil Plant Interrelationships, 1989; editor: Efficient Water Use In Crop Production, 1983, Modifying the Root Environment, 1981, Minirhixotron Observation Tubes, 1987. 1st lt. USAF, 1943-45, 52-53, ETO. Fellow Crop Sci. Soc. Am., Soil Sci. Soc. Am. (div. chair 1969), Am. Soc. Agronomy, AAAS; mem. Soil & Water Conservation Soc. of Am.

TAYLOR, MILLARD BENJAMIN, concertmaster, educator; b. Crete, Nebr., Aug. 9, 1913; s. Joseph Elbert and Anna Blodgett (Bennett) T.; m. Marie Jeanne Capasso, Jan. 2, 1939; children: Virginia Ann (Mrs. James Edward Smith), Jeanne Taylor Hernandez. MusB, Eastman Sch. Music, 1935; MusD, Doane Coll., 1967; DLitt, Nebr. Wesleyan U., 1975. Prof. violin Eastman Sch. Music, Rochester, N.Y., 1944-79; prof. emeritus Eastman Sch. Music, 1979—, chmn. string dept., 1950-76; Edward F. Arnold vis. prof. music Whitman Coll., 1979-80; head string dept. Chautauqua Summer Music Schs. Concertmaster Nat. Symphony Orch., 1938-44, Rochester Philharm. Orch., 1944-67, Pro-Musica Chamber Orch. of Columbus, 1980-89, Naples (Fla.) Philharm., 1983-92; concertmaster Dallas Symphony Orch., N.J. Symphony Orch.; violinist Eastman Piano Quartet, 1967-79, Eastman String Trio, New Eng. Piano Quartet, 1992-96; 1st violinist, leader Chautauqua String Quartet; contbr. articles to Instrumentalist mag. Bd. dirs. Rochester Civic Music Assn., 1969-72. Named Musician of Year Rochester chpt. Mu Phi Epsilon, 1966. Mem. Pi Kappa Lambda, Phi Mu Alpha Sinfonia. Died Dec. 12, 1996.

TAYLOR, PETER MURRAY, judge; b. May 1, 1930; s. Herman Louis and Raie Helena (Shockett) T.; m. Irene Shirley, 1956; 4 children. Grad., Cambridge U.; LLD (hon.), Newcastle upon Tyne U., 1990, Liverpool U., 1993, Northumbria U., 1993, Nottingham U., 1994, Leeds U., 1995. called to Bar, Inner Temple, 1954, bencher, 1975; QC, 1967. Recorder Huddersfield, 1969-70, Tesside, 1970-71; recorder Crown Ct., 1972-80; dep. chmn. Northumberland QS, 1970-71; judge High Ct. Justice, 1980-88; n. ea. cir. leader, 1975-80, presiding judge, 1984-88, lord justice of appeal, 1988-92; lord chief justice Eng., 1992—; vice chmn. Bar, 1978-79, chmn. 1979-80; pres. Inns of Ct. Coun., 1990-92. Controller Royal Opera House Devel. Land Trust, 1990—; chmn. bd. dirs. Trinity Coll. Music, 1991-92. Mem. ABA (hon.), Can. Bar Assn. (hon.). Avocation: music.

TEICHERT, CURT, geologist, educator; b. Koenigsberg, Germany, May 8, 1905; came to U.S., 1952, naturalized, 1959; s. Richard and Luise (Zander) T.; m. Gertrud Margarete Kaufmann, Dec. 28, 1928. Student, U. Munich, Germany, 1923-25, U. Freiburg, Germany, 1925, U. Koenigsberg, 1925-28; Ph.D., Albertus U., 1928; D.Sc., U. Western Australia, Perth, 1944. Rockefeller fellow U.S., 1930; privatdozent Tech. U., Berlin, 1931-35; research paleontologist U. Copenhagen, Denmark, 1933-37; research lectr. U. Western Australia, 1937-45; asst. chief govt. geologist Dept. Mines, Melbourne, Australia, 1946-47; sr. lectr. U. Melbourne, 1947-53; Fulbright scholar U. Kans., Lawrence, 1951-52; prof. geology N.Mex. Sch. Mines, 1953-54; geologist U.S. Geol. Survey, 1954-64; chief Petroleum Geology Lab., 1954-58, research geologist, 1958-61; AID adviser Geol. Survey, Pakistan, 1961-64; Regents Distinguished prof. geology, dir. Paleontol. Inst. U. Kans., Lawrence, 1964-75; prof. emeritus U. Kans., 1975—; adj. prof. geol. scis. U. Rochester, N.Y., 1977—; geologist Danish N.E. Greenland Expdn., 1931-32; guest prof. U. Bonn, Germany, U. Goettingen, U. Freiburg, 1958, U. Tex., 1960, Free U. Berlin, 1974; U.S. coordinator AID-CENTO Stratigraphic Working Group, 1965-76; Cons. to oil cos., 1940-53, Australian Bur. Mineral Resources, 1948-52. Author: Ordovician and Silurian Faunas from Arctic Canada, 1937, (with Clarke, Prider) Elements of Geology, 1944, 4th edit., 1967, Elementary Practical Geology, 1946, 4th edit., 1968, (with others) Treatise on Invertebrate Paleontology, Park K, 1964; several book size monographs; editor: (with others) Treatise on Invertebrate Paleontology, 1964-80; also miscellaneous symposia; contbr. articles to profl. jours. Recipient David Syme Prize sci. research U. Melbourne, 1950, R.C. Moore medal for excellence in paleontology Soc. Econ. Paleontologists and Mineralogists, 1982. Fellow Geol. Soc. Am., Geol. Soc. London (hon.), AAAS; mem. Internat. Geol. Congress (past sec. internat. com. Gondwana sys.), Soc. Geol. France (fgn. assoc.), Paleontol. Soc. (past corr., pres. 1971-72, medal 1984), Palaeont. Gesellschaft (hon.), Soc. Geol. Belgique (hon.), Royal Soc. Western Australia (hon.), Paleontol. Soc. India (fgn. corr.), Geol. Soc. Australia (hon.), Senckenberg. Naturforsch. Gesellschaft (corr. mem., Curt Teichert Festschrift 1989), Internat. Paleontol. Union (1st v.p. 1968-72), Internat. Paleontol. Assn. (pres. 1976-80). Home: Arlington Va. Died May 10, 1996.

TEJEDA, FRANK, congressman; b. San Antonio, Tex., Oct. 2, 1945; 3 children. BA in Government, St. Mary's U., 1970; JD, U. Calif., Berkeley, 1974; MPA, Harvard U., 1980; LLM, Yale U., 1989. Lawyer; mem. Tex. Ho. of Reps., 1977-87, Tex. State Senate from Dist. 19, 1987-93; mem. house armed svcs. com., mem. house vets. affairs com. 103rd-104th Congress from 28th Tex. dist., Washington, D.C., 1993—; chmn. com. judicial affairs Tex. Ho. Reps., 1983; chmn. sub-com. Urban Affairs Tex. Senate, 1991; mem. senate fin. com. Tex. Senate, 1991; mem. nat. security com., vets affairs com.; chmn. intergovernmental rels. com. urban affairs Tex. Senate, 1991. Maj. USMCR, Vietnam. Decorated Bronze Star, Purple Heart. Mem. Cath. War Vets., Marine Corps. League. Democrat. Roman Catholic. Home: San Antonio Tex. Died Jan. 30, 1997.

TEMMER, GEORGES MAXIME, physicist; b. Vienna, Austria, Apr. 10, 1922; came to U.S., 1939; s. Frederic M. and Margaret D. (Jeiteles) T.; m. Odette Fluchere (div., 1978); m. Sylvia Bjornberg, Feb. 25, 1979. BS in Physics, Queens Coll., 1943; MA in Physics, U. Calif., Berkeley, 1944, PhD in Physics, 1949; ScD (hons.), Queens Coll., 1994. Rsch. assoc. U. Rochester, N.Y., 1949-51; physicist Nat. Bur. Standards, Washington, 1951-53; staff mem. Carnegie Instn. of Washington, 1953-63; prof., dir. Nuclear Physics Lab., Fla. State U., Tallahassee, Fla., 1960-63; dir. Nuclear Physics Lab., Rutgers U., New Brunswick, N.J., 1963-85; prof. of physics Rutgers U., New Brunswick, 1963-85, univ. prof., 1985-91, prof. emeritus, from 1991; mem. adv. bd. Nat. SANE/freeze campaign for global security, 1990-97, physics panel NSF; vis. prof., scholar, Denmark, France, Switzerland, Germany, Austria, China, Mexico, Italy. Translator (from Italian) Fundamentals of Atomic Mech., E. Persico; (from French) Quantum Mechanics, AML Messiah, 1960, Atomic Rivals, B. Goldschmidt, 1990; editor Chinese Physics Am. Inst. of Physics, 1985-92; contbr. more than 100 articles on nuclear and atomic physics to profl. jours. Vice chmn. Coalition for Nuclear Disarmament, Princeton, N.J., 1988-97; With U.S. Navy, 1944-46. Recipient John S. Guggenheim Meml. fellowship, 1956-57, Lindback award Rutgers Univ., 1975, Alexander von Humboldt prize, Humboldt Found., Bonn, Germany, 1984; named Sr. Exchange Fellow, Nat. Acad. of Sci., People's Republic of China, 1980. Fellow Am. Physical Soc.; mem. Cosmos Club. Achievements include discoveries in basic experimental nuclear physics. Home: Skillman N.J. Died Jan. 12, 1997.

TENNSTEDT, KLAUS, conductor; b. Merseburg, Germany, June 6, 1926. Formerly gen. music dir. Dresden Opera, and dir., State Orch. and Theatre in Schwerin, Ger.; gen. music dir. and resident condr. Buehnen der Landeshauptstadt Kiel, Ger., N.Am. debut, Toronto Symphony, U.S. debut, Boston Symphony, 1974; named prin. guest condr. Minn. Orch., 1978, has since conducted all major orchs. of world including Cleve. Symphony, Phila. Orch., N.Y. Philharm., Chgo. Symphony, Berlin Philharm., Israel Philharm., Swedish Radio Orchestra,, Metropolitan Opera; prin. guest condr. The London Philharm., music dir. 1983-87, condr. laureate, 1987—; chief condr. Norddeutscher Rundfunk Orchestra, 1979; recordings include Complete Symphonies of Mahler.

TERESA, MOTHER (AGNES GONXHA BOJAXHIU), nun, missionary; b. Skopje, Yugoslavia, Aug. 26, 1910. D.D. (hon.), U. Cambridge, 1977; Dr. med. (hon.), Cath. U. of Sacred Heart, Rome, 1981, Cath. U. Louvain, Belgium, 1982. Joined Sisters of Loreto, Roman Cath. Ch., 1928. Came to India; founder, head Missionaries of Charity, Calcutta, India, 1950-90, re-elected, 1990-97; opened Nirmal Hriday Home for Dying Destitutes, 1952; started leper colony, West Bengal, 1964; founder Missionary Bros. of Charity, 1963, Contemplative Brothers, 1979, Contemplative Sisters, 1976. Recipient Pope John XXIII Peace prize, 1971, Templeton Found. prize, 1973, Nobel Peace prize, 1979, Bharat Ratna (Star of India), 1980, U.S. Presdl. medal of Freedom, 1985, Notre Dame U. award, 1992, U Thant Peace award, 1994; named hon. citizen of Assisi 1982, Woman of Yr. award, 1989; Hon. fellow Royal Coll. Surgeons Ireland, 1992. Died Sept. 5, 1997.

TERRELL, DOMINIQUE LARA, dramatic soprano, actress, real estate and marketing executive; b. South Bend, Ind., Apr. 26; d. Harold J. Metzler and Margaret Terrell (Whiteman) Metzler Fogarty. BA, Ithaca Coll., 1960; diploma, Brown's Bus. Coll., Decatur, Ill., 1960; postgrad. in real estate sales, NYU, 1984. Lic. securities dealer, real estate salesperson. Exec. legal asst. Carb Luria Glassner Cook & Kufeld, N.Y.C., 1962-64; Exec. legal asst. Graubard Moskovitz McGoldrick Dannett & Horowitz, N.Y.C., 1964-79; opera and concert singer N.Y.C.; real estate salesperson Rosemary Edwards Realty, N.Y.C., 1985, Kenneth D. Laub & Co., Inc., N.Y.C., 1987-89, GSW Realty, Inc., N.Y.C., 1990-91, Kuzmuk Realty, Inc., 1992-94, Gala 72 Realty, Inc., 1994-97; bd. dirs., singer Broadway-Grand Opera, 1992-97; pres. Mystique of Dominique, Whiteman and Stewart Prodns., DharMacduff Publs.; corr. sec., bd. dirs. Community Opera, Inc., N.Y.C., 1984-97. Mem. internat. affairs com. and other coms. Women's Nat. Rep. Club, N.Y.C., 1968-82; active Rep. County Vols., N.Y.C., 1976-82; mem nominating com. Ivy Rep. Club, N.Y.C., 1983-87; bd. dirs. Am. Landmark Festivals, 1986-97. Named Female Singer of Yr., Internat. Beaux Arts, Inc., 1978-79, Princess Nightingale, Allied Indian Tribes N.Am. Continent-Cherokee Nation, 1985. Mem. Wagner Internat. Instn. (dir. pub. rels. 1982-84), Navy

League U.S. (life, mem. N.Y. coun.), Assn. Former Intelligence Officers (assoc.), Friends of Spanish Opera (bd. dirs. 1982-97), Finlandia Found., Inc. (life), The Bohemians, Nat. Arts Club (music com. 1983-87), N.Y. Opera Club. Avocations: tennis, swimming, dancing, travel, antiques. Died May 4, 1997.

TERTZ, ABRAM See SINYAVSKY, ANDREI

TESCHNER, RICHARD REWA, lawyer; b. Milw., Feb. 5, 1908; s. Bruno A. and Thekla (Rewa) T.; m. D. Joy Griesbach, Sept. 24, 1932; 1 son, Richard Vincent. B.A., U. Wis., 1931, LL.B., 1934; L.H.D. (hon.), Carroll Coll., 1976. Bar: Wis. 1934, U.S. Supreme Ct. 1944. Tax counsel Wis. Dept. Taxation, 1938-45; ptnr. Quarles & Brady, 1945-87. Mem. Milwaukee County War Meml. Devel. Com., chmn., 1960-70; mem. Greater Milw. Com.; past mem. Wis. Arts Bd.; chmn. Milw. Performing Arts Center, 1969-74; co-chmn. United Performing Arts Fund drive, 1977; past pres. Will Ross Meml. Found.; chmn. Milw. Found., 1978-79; bd. dirs. Second Harvesters of Wis., Inc., 1980-91, Ice Age Park and Trail of Wis. Found., 1980-89. Mem. ABA, Wis. Bar Assn., Milw. Bar Assn. (pres. 1964-65), Pi Kappa Alpha, Phi Delta Phi. Presbyterian. Lodge: Rotary. Home: Milwaukee Wis. Died April 13, 1997.

TETLEY, GLEN, choreographer; b. Cleve., Feb. 3, 1926; s. Glenford and Eleanor (Byrne) T. Student, Franklin and Marshall Coll., 1944-46; BS, NYU, 1948; student contemporary dance with, Hanya Holm, Martha Graham, 1946; student classical ballet with, Margaret Craske, Anthony Tudor at Met. Opera Ballet Sch., 1949. guest instr. Yale Dramatic Workshop, 1947-48, Colo. Coll., 1946-49, Hanya Holm Sch. Contemporary Dance, 1946-52, Ballet Rambert, 1966-68, Netherlands Dance Theatre, 1962-65, B. De Rothschild Found., Israel, 1965-67. Featured dancer in Broadway musical Kiss Me Kate, 1949, Out of This World, 1950, Juno, 1958; premiered in Broadway musical Menotti's Amahl and the Night Visitors, NBC Opera, 1951; soloist with Broadway musical, N.Y.C. Opera, 1951-54, John Butler's Am. Dance Theatre, 1951-55, Robert Joffrey Ballet, 1955-56, Martha Graham Dance Co., 1957-59, Am. Ballet Theatre, 1959-61, Jerome Robbins: Ballets USA, 1961-62, Netherlands Dance Theater, 1962-65, own co., 1962-69; made govt.-sponsored tour of Europe, 1969, appearances at Spoleto Festival, all maj. Am. dance festivals; guest choreographer, Netherlands Dance Theatre; artistic dir.: Netherlands Dance Theatre, 1969; guest choreographer, Am. Ballet Theatre, Ballet Rambert, Batsheva Co. Israel, Robert Joffrey Ballet, Alvin Alley Co., U. Utah Repertory Dance Theatre, Vancouver Festival, Royal Danish Ballet, 1969, Royal Ballet Covent Garden, Royal Swedish Ballet, Den Norske Opera, Hamburg State Opera, Stuttgart Ballet; former artistic dir., Stuttgart Ballet Co.; artistic assoc., Nat. Ballet of Canada, Toronto, 1987-89; ballets include Pierrot Lunaire, 1962, Birds of Sorrow, 1962, The Anatomy Lesson, 1964, Sargasso, 1964, Field Mass, 1965, Mythical Hunters, 1965, Ricercare, 1966, Chronochromie, 1966, Tehilim, 1966, Freefall, 1967, The Seven Deadly Sins, 1967, Dithyramb, 1967, Ziggurat, 1967, Circles, 1968, Embrace Tiger and Return to Mountain, 1968, Arena, 1968, Imaginary Film, 1970, Mutations, 1970, Field Figures, 1971, Rag Dances, 1971, Small Parades, 1972, Threshold, 1972, Laborintus, 1972, Strophe-Antistrophe, 1972, The Moveable Garden, 1973, Gemini, 1973, Voluntaries, 1973, Sacre du Printemps, 1974, Tristan, 1974, Strender, 1974, Daphnis and Chloe, 1975, Greening, 1975, Alegrias, 1975, Poeme Nocturne, 1977, Sphinx, 1978, Praeludium, 1979, The Tempest, 1979, Contredances, 1979, Summer's End, 1980, Dances of Albion-Dark Night: Glad Day, 1980, Firebird, 1981, Murderer Hope of Women, 1983, Revelation and Fall, 1984, Pulcinella, 1984, Dream Walk of the Shaman, 1985, Alice, 1986, Orpheus, 1987, La Ronde, 1987, Tagore, 1989, Dialogues, 1991, Oracle, 1994, Amorew, 1997; off-Broadway choreographer-dir. ballets including Fortuna, 1961, Ballet Ballads, 1961. Patron Benesh Inst. Choreology; bd. dirs. Tag Found., N.Y.C. Served with USNR, 1944-46. Recipient German critics award for Die Feder; Queen Elizabeth II Coronation award Royal Acad. Dancing, 1981; recipient Prix Italia Rai prize, 1982, Tennant Caledonia award Edinburgh Festival, 1983, Ohioana Career Medal, 1986, achievement award N.Y.U., 1988; named knight Order Merit, 1997.

THEISZ, ERWIN JAN, scientist; b. Velky Slavkov, Slovakia, Oct. 20, 1924; s. Jan and Julia Maria (Copus) T.; m. Lydia Margrete Kracht, Aug. 3, 1963; 1 chld, Christine. MSPE, Wiesbaden (Germany) State U., 1975; dipl. engr., Kassel (Germany) Coll., 1983. R&D chem. engr. U.S. Civil Svc. Commn. (GS12), Newark, 1960-65; chemist Sloan Kettering Cancer Inst., N.Y.C., 1964-65; chem. R&D mgr. Beech Nut Life Savers, Port Chester, N.Y., 1966-67; chemist quality control York Rsch., Stamford, Conn., 1968-71; chemistry mgr. Ducon Co., Mineola, N.Y., 1972; quality control chemist Air Pollution Industry, Engelwood, N.Y., 1973; analytical chemist Riverside Engring., N.Y.C., 1974; analytical chemist R&D Westchester County Health Dept., White Plains, N.Y., 1975—. Contbr. numerous articles to profl. jours. Lutheran. Achievements include patent for a method for inhibiting the growth of tumorous tissue cells in mammals such as humans.

THERMENOS, NICHOLAS, engineering company executive; b. Honolulu, Dec. 30, 1939; s. Nicholas and Helen Mae (Rhine) T.; m. Panagiota Economou, Oct. 14, 1967 (dec. Aug. 1985); children: Nicholas John, Jennifer Lee; m. Gloria Gravel, June 14, 1987. Student, Lafayette Coll., 1963-66; AS in Mech. Engring., Waterbury (Conn.) State Tech. Coll., 1982. Cert. mfg. engr., engring. tech. Sr. designer Harris Intertype Corp., Easton, Pa., 1966-68; design engr. Packer Industries, Meriden, Conn., 1968-71; project engr. Ridson Mfg. Co., Naugatuck, Conn., 1971-75, Cushman Industris, Inc., Hartford, Conn., 1976-79; mgr. spl. products Cushman Industries, Inc., Hartford, Conn., 1986-87; mgr. sales and engring. Powerhold, Inc., Middlefield, Conn., 1979-85; mgr. engring. svcs. Huron Machine Products, Inc., Ft. Lauderdale, 1987-90; pres. ASW Techs., Inc., Middlefield, 1991—; speaker, cons. Workholding Tech., 1981-88, author treatise, 1982. Chmn. Boy Scouts Am., Cheshire, Conn., 1974; coun. mem. Holy Trinity Greek Orthodox Ch., Waterbury, Conn., 1980-84. Mem. Nat. Inst. for Certification in Engring. Techs., Soc. Mfg. Engrs. (charter, sr., program chmn. Hartford chpt. # 7, 1974-76), Computer and Automated Sys. Assn. (charter mem.). Republican. Avocation: running, remodeling, tennis, skiing, photography. Died Dec. 21, 1996.

THIMANN, KENNETH VIVIAN, biology educator; b. Ashford, Eng., Aug. 5, 1904; came to U.S., 1930, naturalized Am. citizen; s. Israel Phoebus and Muriel Kate (Harding) T.; m. Ann Mary Bateman, Mar. 20, 1929; children—Vivianne Thimann Nachmias, Karen Thimann Romer, Linda Thimann Dewing. Student, Caterham Sch., Eng., 1915-21; B.Sc., Imperial Coll. Sci and Tech. London Royal Coll. Sci., 1924, A.R.C.S., 1924, Ph.D., 1928; A.M. (hon.), Harvard U., 1938; Ph.D. (hon.), U. Basel, Switzerland, 1960, U. Clermont-Ferrand, France, 1961; DSc (hon.), Brown U., 1989. Demonstrator bacteriology Kings Coll., London, 1927-29; instr. biochemistry and bacteriology Calif. Inst. Tech., Pasadena, 1930-35; lectr. botany Harvard U., 1935-36, asst. prof. plant physiology, 1936-39, assoc. prof., 1939-46, prof., 1946-62, Higgins prof. biology, 1962-65, prof. emeritus, 1965-97; dir. Biol. Labs., Harvard U., 1946-50, tutor in biology Eliot House, 1936-52, assoc., 1952-65; master East House, Radcliffe Coll., 1962-65; exch. prof. U. Paris, 1954-55; prof. biology U. Calif., Santa Cruz, 1965-84, prof. emeritus, 1984-97; provost Crown Coll., 1965-72; vis. prof. U. Mass., 1974, U. Tex., 1976; pres. XI Internat. Bot. Congress, 1969; pres. 2d Nat. Biol. Congress, Miami, 1970, Internat. Plant Growth Substance Assn. Triennial Meeting, Tokyo, 1973. Author: (with F. W. Went) Phytohormones, 1937, L'Origine et les Fonctions des Auxines, 1956, The Life of Bacteria, 2d edit., 1963, The Natural Plant Hormones, 1972, Hormones in the Whole Life of Plants, 1977, (with J.H. Langenheim) Botany: Plants and Human Affairs, 1982; author (with others) and editor Senescence in Plants, 1981; editor (with R.S. Harris) Vitamins and Hormones (ann.) Vol. 1, 1943, to Vol. 20, 1962, (with G. Pincus) The Hormones, 5 vols., 1948, 55, 63; mem. editorial bd. Archives of Biochemistry and Biophysics, 1949-70, Canadian Jour. Botany, 1966-73, Plant Physiology, 1974-85; contbr.over 300 articles to tech. jours. Bd. dirs. Found. Microbiology, Biol. Scis. Info. Services. Served as civilian scientist, USN, 1942-45. Recipient Stephen Hales prize research Am. Soc. Plant Physiologists, 1936; Guggenheim fellow, Eng., 1950-51, Italy, 1958; medallist Internat. Plant Growth Substance Assn., 1976, Balzan prize, 1982. Fgn. mem. Royal Soc. (London), Soc. Nazionale dei Lincei (Rome), Akad. Leopoldina (Halle), Acad. Nat. de Roumanie (Bucharest), Acad. des Sci. (Paris), Acad. d' Agr. de France, Bot. Soc. Netherlands, Bot. Soc. Japan, Indian Soc. Plant Physiology; mem. Am. Soc. Biol. Chemists, Am. Philos. Soc. (council 1973-76), Am. Acad. Arts and Scis., Nat. Acad. Scis. (chmn. botany sect. 1962-65, mem. council 1967-71, exec. com. assembly life scis. 1972-76), Bot. Soc. Am. (pres. 1960), AAAS (dir. 1968-72), Am. Soc. Plant Physiologists (pres. 1950-51), Soc. Gen. Physiologists (pres. 1949-50), Biochem. Soc., Am. Soc. Naturalists (pres. 1954-55), Am. Inst. Biol. Scis. (pres. 1965), Soc. Study Devel. and Growth (pres. 1955-56). Died Jan. 15, 1997.

THOMAS, E. C., clergyman, religious organization executive; b. Lulu, Fla., Dec. 13, 1920; s. Elver E. and Essie Thomas; m. Alice Douglas, July 19, 1941; children—Charmaine, Cheryl. D.D., Lee Coll, Cleveland, Tenn.; D.Litt., Am. Div. Sch., Chgo. Ordained to ministry Ch. of God, 1945. Pub., Ch. of God, Cleveland, Tenn., 1954-70; state overseer Ch. of God, Va., Ala. and N.C., 1970-78; gen. sec., treas. Ch. of God, Cleveland, 1978-82, gen. overseer, 1982—. Mem. Nat. Assn. Evangs., Pentecostal Fellowship N.Am.

THOMAS, PATRICIA GRAFTON, secondary school educator; b. Michigan City, Ind., Sept. 30, 1921; d. Robert Wadsworth and Elinda (Oppermann) Grafton; student Stephens Coll., 1936-39, Purdue U., summer 1938; BEd magna cum laude, U. Toledo, 1966; post-grad. (fellow) Bowling Green U., 1968; m. Lewis Edward Thomas, Dec. 21, 1939; children: Linda T., Stephanie A. (Mrs. Andrew M. Pawuk), I. Kathryn (Mrs. James N. Ramsey), Deborah (Mrs. Edward Preissler). Lang. art and art tchr. Toledo Bd. Edn., 1959-81, tchr. lang. arts Byrnedale Sch., 1976-81; pres. Jr. High Coun., 1963. Dist. capt. Planned Parenthood, 1952-53, ARC, 1954-55; mem. lang. arts curriculum com. Toledo Bd. Edn., 1969, 73, mem. grammar curriculum com., 1974, pres. Jr. High Coun. Toledo Pub. Schs.; bd. dirs. Anthony Wayne Nursery Sch., 1983—; bd. dirs. Toledo Women's Symphony Orch. League, 1983—, sec., 1985—; co-chmn. Showcase of the Arts, 1990-92. Adolf Dehn fellow, 1939. Mem. AAUW, Toledo Soc. Profl. Engrs. Aux., Helen Kreps Guild, Toledo Artists' Club, Spectrum, Friends of Arts (bd. dirs. 1989—), Phi Kappa Phi, Phi Delta Kappa, Kappa Delta Pi, Pi Lambda Theta (chpt. pres. 1978-80), Delta Kappa Gamma (chpt. pres. 1976-78, area membership chmn. 1978-80, 1st place award for exhbn. 1985). Republican. Episcopalian. Died Nov. 8, 1997.

THOMPSON, (JAMES) BRADBURY, graphic designer; b. Topeka, Mar. 25, 1911; s. James Kay and Eunice (Bradbury) T.; m. Della Deen Dodge, Aug. 28, 1939; children—Leslie Dodge Keller, Mark Bradbury, David Dodge, Elizabeth Thompson Riley. AB, Washburn U., 1934, DFA (hon.), 1965; DFA (hon.), R.I. Sch. Design, 1983, Parsons Sch. Design, 1989. Dir. art Capper Publs., Inc., 1934-38, Rogers-Kellogg-Stillson, 1938-42; assoc. chief art sect. OWI State Dept., 1942-45. Art dir., Mademoiselle mag., 1945-59, Living for Young Homemakers, 1947-49; editor-designer, Westvaco Inspirations, 1938-62; design dir., Art News mag., Art News Ann., 1945-72; designer Smithsonian, 1967; design cons., Westvaco Corp., 1951-95, Yale U. Sch. Art, 1956-95, Famous Artists Schs., 1959-71, Pitney-Bowes, 1959-84, McGraw-Hill mags., 1960-77, Time-Life Books (Library of Art, 1965, Library of America, 1966, Foods of the World, 1966, The Swing Era, 1970), Field Enterprises Ednl. Corp., 1965-78, Harvard Bus. Rev., 1965-67, Cornell U., 1965-73; exhibited one man shows: AIGA Gallery, N.Y.C., 1959, 75, Washburn U., 1964, Cornell U., 1969, Rochester Inst. Tech., 1983, Internat. Typeface Corp., N.Y.C., 1988, Soc. Typographic Artists, 1988, Aspen Internat. Design Conf., 1988, Calif. Coll. Arts and Crafts, San Francisco, 1988, Kans. U., 1988, Dallas, 1988, Atlanta, 1989, Pitts., 1989, Cranbrook, 1989, Balt. U., 1989, Pacific Design Ctr., 1990, Art Inst. Chgo., 1990, Yale U. Libr., 1992, Yale U. Book Show, 1992; exhibited group shows: Alliance Graphique Internationale, Europe, 1955-67, Harvard, 1965, Yale, 1976, 87, Mus. Modern Art, N.Y.C. Faculty, Yale Sch. Art and Architecture, 1956-95. Author: Modern Painting and Typography, 1947, The Monalphabet, 1945, Alphabet 26, 1950; designer for: books including Painting Toward Architecture, 1948, Photo-Graphic, 1949, Abstract Painting, 1951, Annual of Advt. Art, 1943, 54, Graphic Arts Prodn. Yearbook, 1948, 50, The Fiction Factory, 1955, Westvaco Am. Classics, 1958-83, The First 300 Years, 1967, Homage to the Book, 1968, The Quality of Life, 1968, The American Revolution: Three Views, 1975, the Washburn College Bible, 1979, Oxford edit., 1980; The Art of Graphic Design (Yale) 1988; designer over 100 U.S. Postage Stamps, 1958-92. Mem. Citizens Stamp Adv. Com., 1969-92, 1st Fed. Design Assembly, 1973; bd. advisers Parsons Sch. Design, 1949-55; bd. govs. Phila. Mus. Coll. Art, 1956-59; bd. dirs. Perrot Meml. Library, 1966-95, Am. Arbitration Assn., 1976-78; trustee Washburn U., 1972-95. Recipient numerous medals, awards from art orgns., Power of Print award Pimny, 1980, Silver medal Leipzig Internat. Book Design Exhbn., 1982, Gold medal, 1989, Disting. Kansan award, 1983, Fredric Goudy award Rochester Inst. Tech., 1983, medals , Nat. Soc. Art Dirs., 1950, Type Dirs. Club, 1986, Soc. Publ. Designers, 1986, Master Tchr. award Graphic Design Edn. Assn., 1990, Laureate award Greenwich Artist, 1991; named to Art Dirs. Hall of Fame, 1977, N.Y. Printers Wall of Fame, 1983. Mem. Art Dirs. Club N.Y. (v.p., dir.), Am. Inst. Graphic Arts (dir., gold medal 1975), Alliance Graphique Internationale, Soc. of Publication Designers (ann. medal), Soc. Illustrators, Type Dirs. Club (ann. medal), Alpha Delta, Delta Phi Delta. Clubs: Dutch Treat, Riverside Yacht. Home: Riverside Conn. Died Nov. 1, 1995.

THOMPSON, EDWARD KRAMER, editor, publisher; b. Mpls., Sept. 17, 1907; s. Edward T. and Bertha E. (Kramer) T.; m. Marguerite M. Maxam, May 14, 1927 (div.); children—Edward T. Colin R.; m. Lee Eitingon, Apr. 1, 1963. A.B., U. N.D., 1927, H.H.D., 1958. Editor Foster County Independent, Carrington, N.D., 1927; city editor Fargo (N.D.) Morning Forum, 1927; picture editor, asst. news editor Milw. Jour., 1927-37; asso. editor Life, 1937-42, asst. mng. editor, 1945-49, mng. editor, 1949, editor, 1961-68; spl. asst. to sec. state, 1968; editor, pub. Smithsonian mag., 1969-81, cons. to sec., 1981-83, cons. to editor, pub., 1983-96. Author: A Love Affair with Life and Smithsonian, 1995. Served to lt. col. USAAF, 1942-45. Decorated Legion of Merit Order Brit. Empire; named to N.D. Hall of Fame, 1968; named Editor of Yr. Nat. Press Photographers Assn., 1968; recipient Joseph Henry medal Smithsonian Instn., 1973, Lifetime Achievement award Internat. Ctr. of Photography, 1986, Sioux Achievement award U. N.D., 1987, Dumke award for achievement in visual comm. Wis. News Photographers Assn., 1988; named to Pub. Hall of Fame, 1987, U. N.D. Mil. Hall of Fame, 1988. Mem. Phi Beta Kappa, Sigma Delta Chi, Phi Delta Theta. Died Oct. 7, 1996.

THOMPSON, ROBIN JILL, special education educator; b. Massena, N.Y., Apr. 2, 1958; d. Ronald Michael Thompson and Lucille Joy (Smith) Blinzinger; m. Jon Lavern Spindler, Nov. 1, 1980 (div. Dec. 1985); m. Gregory Ray Savage, May 16, 1992 (div. Nov. 1995). BS, Ind. State U., 1980, MS, 1982. Tchr. autistic adolescents Evansville (Ind.)-Vanderburgh Sch. Corp., 1980-81, tchr. seriously emotionally handicapped, 1981—, gymnastics coach, 1982-85, mgr. athletic equipment, 1985-88, acting asst. athletic dir., 1988-89, homebound tchr., 1984-89; chairperson spl. edn. dept. F.J. Reitz High Sch., Evansville, 1989-97; instr. in community living Res-Care Community Alternatives, S.W., Evansville, 1986-90, asst. athletic dir., 1995—. Scholar Rotary Internat., 1990. Mem. Coun. for Exceptional Children, Coun. for Children with Behavior Disorders, Ind. Interscholastic Athletic Adminstrs. Assn. (bd. dirs. 1996—), World Wildlife Fedn., R-Men's Varsity Club, So. Ind. Athletic Conf. (bd. dirs. 1982-83), Pi Lambda Theta (v.p. 1988-90), Phi Kappa Phi, Kappa Delta Pi. Avocations: needlework, hiking, golf, reading. Died Sept. 21, 1997.

THOMPSON, TINA LEWIS CHRYAR, publisher; b. Houston, Dec. 31, 1929; d. Joshua and Mary Christine (Brown) Thompson; m. Joseph Chryar, May 25, 1943; 1 child, Joseph Jr. Cosmotologist, Franklin Coll., Houston, 1950; student, Crenshaw Coll., L.A., 1961. Pubr., composer, author B.M.I., N.Y.C., 1964-74; pubr. ASCAP, N.Y.C., 1974-86, The Fox Agy., N.Y.C., 1986-96, Tech. World, L.A., 1990-96; v.p. music Asset Records, L.A., 1978-96; music dir., v.p. Roach Records, L.A., 1968; music dir. Rendezvous Records, Hollywood, 1950; v.p. Assoc. Internat., L.A., 1973; bd. govs. ABI, Inc., 1994; pres. Cling Music Pub., Soprano Music; pub. processor music catalogs Broadcast Music Inc. Author: Soprano Poems, 1985; creator/designer Baby Napin brand form-fitting, no-leak, no pins baby diaper, 1967, Saver Belt, 1993; patentee/pub. Letter's Tech in Word, used by TV stas. to advertise, 1972. Recipient recognition award IBC, Cambridge, Eng., 1991, cert. of proclamation Internat. Woman of Yr., 1991-92, Merit award Pres. Ronald Reagan, 1986; named Most Admired Woman of Decade, ABI, 1993. Mem. AAUW, NARAS, NOW, ABI (bd. govs. 1994), Am. Soc. Authors and Composers, Nat. Mus. Pubs. Assn., Songwriters Guild Am. (Cert. of Ranks of Composers and Lyracists 1991), Am. Fedn. Label Co. Unions, Am. Theatre Assn. Broadcast Music Inc. (pres. Soprano Music Publ. 1968), Rec. Acad. Country Music Acad., Internat. Platform Assn., L.A. Women in Music.

THOMPSON, WARREN, state official; b. Clarkston, Utah, Dec. 28, 1920; s. George and Esther K. (Godfrey) T.; m. Ivagene Olson, Dec. 21, 1943; children: Marilyn, Paul, Janice, Julie, Mark, Charlene, Bradley. B.S., U. Utah, 1943, grad. cert. in Social Work, 1947; postgrad., NYU, 1951. Rehab. counselor Utah Dept. Edn., 1947-50; asst. state dir. div. Utah Dept. Edn. (Vocational Rehab.), 1950-55; rehab. specialist HEW, Washington, 1955; asst. regional rep. Office Vocat. Rehab., Denver, 1955-59; dir. Colo. Dept. Rehab., Denver, 1959-63, Calif. Dept. Rehab., Sacramento, 1963-67; asst. regional dir. HEW, Denver, 1967-82; regional commr. Rehab. Services Adminstrn., Dept. Edn., Region 8, Denver, 1980-82; dir. div. services for visually handicapped Utah State Office Edn., Salt Lake City, 1982-86; instr. sociology U. Utah, 1946-47; Chmn. Western region workshop, spl. edn. and rehab. Ho. of Reps., 1959. Served to 1st lt. AUS, 1943-45. Mem. Nat. Rehab. Assn. (nat. pres. 1966-67), Phi Kappa Phi, Phi Delta Kappa. Mem. Ch. Jesus Christ of Latter-day Saints. Home: Salt Lake City Utah DIED 06/25/95. .

THOMPSON, WILLIAM BELL, physicist, educator; b. Belfast, No. Ireland, Feb. 27, 1922; s. Herbert Ginnif and Mary (Bell) T.; m. Gertrude Helene Goldschmidt, Mar. 24, 1954 (div. 1971); children—Kathleen Susan, Graham Jonathan; m. Johanna Elzelina Ladestein Korevaar, Jan. 29, 1972. B.A., U. B.C., 1945, M.A., 1947; Ph.D., U. Toronto, 1950; M.A. (hon.), Oxford (Eng.) U., 1962. With U.K. AEC, Harwell, Eng., 1950-60; sr. prin. sci. officer, head plasma theory group U.K. AEC, 1959-60; head plasma theory div. Culham Lab. Plasma Physics and Controlled Fusion Research, Culham, Eng., 1960-62; prof. plasma physics U. Oxford, 1962-65; prof. physics U. Calif. at San Diego, 1965-90, prof. emeritus, 1990, chmn. dept., 1969-72; cons. in field. Contbr. papers in field.; Joint editor: Advances in Plasma Physics, 1967-95; asso. editor: Jour. Plasma Physics, 1966-95. Recipient Hulton award achievement Brit. sci., 1958; fellow St. Peters Coll., U. Oxford, 1962-65. Fellow Am. Phys. Soc., Royal Astron. Soc.; mem. Can. Assn. Physics, Am. Geophys. Union. Home: La Jolla Calif. Died Oct. 17, 1995.

THONNARD, ERNST, internist, researcher; b. Aachen, Germany, May 19, 1898; s. Jean and Anna (Schoddart) T.; m. Constanza Marotti, Jan. 24, 1932; children: Claudia, Ingrid, Norbert. MD, U. Frankfurt, Germany. Intern Mcpl. Hosp., Frankfurt-Hoechst, Germany, 1923, asst., 1924-26; extern Inst. of Tropical Diseases, Hamburg, Germany, 1926-27; docent U. Berlin, Germany, 1942-48; asst. United Fruit Co. Hosp., Panama, 1928-29; asst. supt. United Fruit Co. Hosp., Santa Marta, Colombia, 1929-32; pvt. practice, rsch. on nutrition Barranguilla, Colombia, 1948-58; guest sci. St. Elizabeth Hosp., Washington, 1962—; dir. Inst. Nutrition Universidad del Atlantico, Barrianguilla, Colombia, 1956-58. Contbr. articles to profl. jours. NIH grantee, 1964. Mem. AMA, Sigma Xi. Roman Catholic. DIED 12/30/96. .

THORNTON, J. EDWARD, lawyer; b. Starkville, Miss., Nov. 25, 1907; s. Marmaduke Kimbrough and Annie (Knox) T.; m. Mary Belle Quinn. A.B., Miss. Coll., 1928; LL.B., Harvard, U., 1933. Bar: Ala. bar 1934, Mass. bar 1936. Asst. prosecutor Jefferson County, 1936-39; asst. gen. counsel Ala. Dept. Revenue, 1939-42; mem. firm Thornton & McGowin, Mobile.; Mem. Spl. Supreme Ct. Ala., 1967-68, Ala. Ct. of Judiciary, 1984, 87, Jud. Conf. 5th Cir. U.S., 1951-78; mem. adv. com. on proposed new appellate rules Ala. Supreme Ct., 1972-74, mem. standing com. on appellate rules, 1974-80; chmn. sect. on practice and procedure Ala. State Bar, 1969-72, 73-75. Contbr. articles to prof. publs. Pres. Mobile Chamber Music Soc., 1972-73; adv. coun. home health svcs. Mobile County Bd. Health, 1969-74; Mem. Ala. Democratic Com., 1950-54. Lt. comdr. USNR, 1942-45. Fellow Am. Bar Found.; mem. ABA (ho. dels., state del. for Ala. 1958-59), Ala. Bar Assn. (chmn. com. on jurisprudence and law reform 1951-63, pres. 1963-64), Mobile Bar Assn. (pres. 1955, founder, editor Mobile Bar Bull. 1966-91), Selden Soc., Am. Law Inst., Ala. Law Inst., Mobile Arts Coun. (pres. 1956), English Speaking Union (pres. Mobile 1960-61), Mobile Opera Guild (pres. 1963-65), Mobile C. of C., Scribes. Baptist. Clubs: Athelstan, Bienville (dir.), International Trade. Died Jan. 11, 1997.

THORNTON, SUE BONNER, former librarian; b. nr. Fairfield, Tex.; d. John Carder and Mary (Bonner) T. A.B., U. Okla., 1920, A.B. in L.S, 1938, Mus.B. in Piano, 1921; M.A., Columbia U., 1932; postgrad., U. Hawaii, summer 1936. Music supr. Okla. pub. schs., 1921-25; head music dept. Northeastern State Coll., Tahlequah, Okla., 1925-32; librarian Northeastern State Coll., 1932-64. Author: The Bonner Family History. Mem. Central Area, Freestone County, B-RI museums; chmn. bd. trustees Freestone County (Tex.) Mus. Mem. NEA, ALA, Daus. Am. Colonists, Colonial Dames of 17th Century, Tahlequah C. of C., League Women Voters, United Ch. Women Tahlequah (chmn. 1960), D.A.R. (chmn. good citizens com. for Okla. 1958-60), Magna Charta Dames, Ams. Royal Descent, Plantagenet Soc., Soc. Descs. Knights Garter, Nat. Soc. U.S. Daus. 1812, Huguenot Soc. S.C., P.E.O., Order Washington Daus. Colonial Wars, Colonial Order of Crown, Tex. and Southwestern Cattle Raisers Assn., Pan Am. Round Table, Alpha Gamma Delta. Democrat. Presbyn. Clubs: History (Fairfield, Tex.); Harvey Woman's (Palestine, Tex.); Soroptimist, Freestone County Country. Home: Fairfield Tex. Died Feb. 10, 1993.

THORNTON, WILLIAM JAMES, JR., composer, music educator; b. Birmingham, Ala., July 31, 1919; s. William James and Ada Blanche (Gray) T.; m. Vivian Quine Dyer, Nov. 11, 1939 (dec. 1981); m. Alice Marilyn Dutcher, Mar. 3, 1984 (dec. 1993); m. Katherine Cornell, Nov. 26, 1993. B.Mus., La. State U., 1941, Mus.M., 1948; B.A., Birmingham-So. Coll., 1949; Ph.D., U. So. Calif., 1953. Instr. music U. Minn., 1955-56; prof., chmn. div. fine arts Parsons Coll., Fairfield, Iowa, 1956-60; prof., chmn. music dept. Trinity U., San Antonio, 1960-80, prof. music theory and composition, 1980-88, prof. emeritus, 1988—; tchr. music Pointe Coupee Parish, La., 1939-40; tchr. music St. James Parish, La., 1942, San Juan Capistrano, Calif., 1952-54, Pleasanton, Calif., 1954-55; prof. emeritus Trinity U. San Antonio, 1988; lectr. music composition U. Tex., San Antonio, 1991-93. Performer double bass, 1939-54; composer: major mus. works including String Quartet 1, 1949, Sonata for Cello and Piano, 1950, Serenade for Winds, 1950, Symphony 1, 1953, Sonata for Piano, 1955, Festive Music for Orchestra, 1962, Ceremony of Psalms for Soloists, Choir, Percussion, Organ, 1969, Sinfonía Bejar, Bicentennial commn. San Antonio Symphony, 1976, Sonata for piano, 4 hands, 1982, Solomon Songs, 1983, Sonata for Saxophone and Piano, 1985, Sonata for Harp, 1986, Spirit Divine for chorus and organ, 1986, Fanfare for brass, 1986, Homage for Chamber Orch. commd. Tex. Fedn. Music Clubs Manuscript Archives Com., 1987, Fanfare for Band commd. Trinity U. Wind Symphony and Tex. Composers Forum, 1987, The Grasshopper for chorus, 1987, Psalm No. 1 for mezzo-soprano, harp and flute, 1988, Then in Thy Mercy for mezzo-soprano and organ, 1988, Elegy for Trumpet and Piano, 1989, Woodwind Quintet commd. The King William Winds, 1991, Elegy for Trumpet and Strings to the Memory of Halsey Stevens, 1992, Jambalaya for Four Guitars, 1992, Te Deum Laudamus for organ, 1993, also others. Served with USAAF, 1942-46, PTO. Recipient composition commns. from San Antonio Symphony, Parsons Coll., La. State U., Trinity U., Manuscript Archives Commn., Manor Baptist Ch. (San Antonio) for dedication of new organ: Festive Music for Organ, 1995. Mem. Phi Mu Alpha Sinfonia, Phi Kappa Phi, Phi Sigma Iota, Sigma Nu. Home: San Antonio Tex. Died Sept. 15, 1996.

THUERING, GEORGE LEWIS, industrial engineering educator; b. Milw., Sept. 2, 1919; s. Louis Charles and Elsie (Luetzow) T.; m. Lillian May Cline, Dec. 7, 1945 (dec.); 1 child; m. Betty L. McBride, Aug. 9, 1975. B.S., U. Wis., 1941, M.E., 1954; M.S., Pa. State U., 1949. Registered profl. engr., Pa. Mfg. engr. Lockheed Aircraft Corp., Burbank, Calif., 1941-47; supr. plant layout Lockheed Aircraft Corp., Marietta, Ga., 1951-52; mem. faculty Pa. State U., University Park, 1947—; assoc. prof. indsl. engring. Pa. State U., 1952-56, prof., 1956-82, prof. emeritus, 1982—, dir. mgmt. engring., 1961-82; cons. engring. Contbr. articles to profl. jours. Fellow Soc. Advancement Mgmt.; mem. ASME (chmn. mgmt. div. 1976-77, mem. exec. com. mgmt. div. 1973-77, chmn. papers rev. com. 1969-73, v.p. gen. engring. 1982-84), Am. Inst. Indsl. Engrs. (dir. students affairs 1972-74), Am. Soc. Engring. Edn. (chmn. indsl. engring. div. 1956-57), Sigma Xi, Tau Beta Pi, Pi Tau Sigma, Alpha Pi Mu. Died Aug. 23, 1997.

THURLBECK, WILLIAM MICHAEL, retired pathologist, retired medical educator; b. Johannesburg, South Africa, Sept. 7, 1929; s. William and Enid Muriel (Mears) T.; m. Elizabeth Anne Tippett, Oct. 28, 1955; children—Sarah Margaret, David William, Alison Mary. B.Sc., U. Cape Town, 1951, M.B., Ch.B., 1953. Intern Groote Schuur Hosp., Cape Town, 1955; research fellow resident in pathology Mass. Gen. Hosp. and Harvard U., 1955-61; asst. prof. to prof. pathology McGill U., 1961-73; sr. investigator Midhurst Med. Research Inst. and Royal Postgrad. Med. Sch., Eng., 1973-75; prof. pathology, head U. Man. and Health Scis. Centre, Winnipeg, 1975-80; prof. pathology U. B.C., 1981—, asso. dean research and grad. studies, 1981—, pathologist Children's Hosp., 1985—, acting head med. microbiol., 1992—; examiner in pathology Royal Coll. Physicians and Surgeons Can., 1964-70; mem. McGill Interdisciplinary Com. on Air Pollution, 1967-73; cons. Cardiovascular Research Inst., San Francisco; pulmonary diseases adv. com. Nat. Heart and Lung Inst., 1971-74; task force research planning in environ. health scis. NIH, mem. respiration and applied physiology study sect., 1981—; adv. fellow Indsl. Hygiene Found., Pitts., 1967-71, Paul Dudley White fellow in cardiology, 1960-61; Med. Research Council vis. scientist Oxford (Eng.) U., 1970-71; Schering travelling fellow Canadian Soc. Clin. Investigation, 1971. Author: Chronic Airflow Obstruction in Lung Disease, 1976, The Lung: Structure, Function and Disease, 1978; Contbr. articles to med. jours. Fellow Royal Coll. Physicians, Royal Coll. Pathologists, Am. Coll. Chest Physicians (medalist), Royal Coll. Pathology; mem. Am. Assn. Pathologists, Internat. Acad. Pathology, Path. Soc. Gt. Britain and Ireland, Canadian Soc. Clin. Investigation, Am. Thoracic Soc., Fleischner Soc. Clubs: Rondebosch Old Boys, Pluto. Deceased.

THURMAN, SAMUEL DAVID, legal educator; b. Washington, Dec. 7, 1913; s. Samuel D. and Henrietta (Young) T.; m. Emeline Nebeker, June 16, 1939 (div. Dec. 17, 1977); children: David, Sally Thurman Ware, Susan Thurman Hart, Walter; m. Enid Ryberg, Feb. 25, 1981. A.B., U. Utah, 1935; J.D., Stanford U., 1939; LL.D., U. Pacific McGeorge Sch. Law, 1984, U. Utah, 1988. Bar: Utah 1939. Assoc. Irvine, Skeen, Thurman, Salt Lake City, 1939-42; assoc. prof. law Stanford U., 1942-47, prof. law, 1947-62, Marion Rice Kirkwood prof. law, 1961-62, assoc. dean Law Sch., 1947-49, acting dean Law Sch., 1952-53; dean Coll. Law U. Utah, Salt Lake City, 1962-75; disting. prof. law U. Utah, 1975-95; advisory bd. Found. Press U. Casebook Series, 1962-95; vis. prof. law U. Mich., summer 1949, NYU, 1955-56, U. Tex., 1976, La. State U., 1977, U. Calif. Hastings Coll. Law, 1984-95; vis. prof. law Pepperdine U., 1981-82; Hugo L. Black lectr. U. Ala., 1980. Coauthor: The Study of Federal Tax Law, (with Phillips and Cheatham) The Legal Profession; adviser: Restatement of Torts, Second, Am. Law Inst; Contbr. articles to law revs., bar assn. jours. Commr. Calif. Law Revision Commn., 1954-59; chmn. Utah appeals bd. SSS; mem. Council Legal Edn. for Profl. Responsibility, 1968-73; Sec.-treas. Assn. Am. Law Schs., 1959-61, pres., 1962; Bd. dirs. Nat. Legal Services Corp., 1975-78. Recipient Stanford Law Sch. Merit award, 1992. Fellow Am. Bar Found.; mem. ABA (sec. council legal edn. and admission to bar 1965-70, 74-80, chmn. 1978-79, com. on evaluation of profl. standards, Kutak award 1990), Utah Bar Assn., San Francisco Bar Assn., State Bar Calif., Am. Law Inst. (life), Order of Coif (nat. exec. com. 1964-67, nat. pres. 1977-80), Phi Beta Kappa, Phi Kappa Phi, Sigma Chi, Delta Theta Phi. Mem. Ch. of Jesus Christ of Latter-day Saints. Clubs: Commonwealth (quar. chmn. San Francisco 1955), Timpanogos. Home: Salt Lake City Utah Died Feb. 4, 1995.

TIERNEY, JOHN JAMES, advertising agency executive; b. Detroit, Oct. 13, 1934; s. Edward and Rose (DeLargy) T.; m. Bernice Claire Kaminski, Nov. 12, 1978; children—Erica Lynn, John Vincent, Bradley Edward. B.A. in Bus. Adminstrn., Wayne State U., 1956, B.A. in Advt., 1956. Regional sales mgr. Rox Paint Co., Detroit, 1956-60; asst. advt. dir. Detroit Free Press, 1960-65; dir. mktg. Fretter Appliance, Livonia, Mich., 1965-70; exec. v.p. Northgate Advt., Detroit, 1970-73; 1st sr. v.p. Mars Advt., Southfield, Mich., 1973—. Sgt. U.S. Army, 1956-57. Mem. Detroit Advt. Assn., Adcraft Club of Detroit. Roman Catholic. Died Oct. 6, 1996.

TIERNEY, MICHAEL P., lawyer; b. Port Chester, N.Y., Feb. 18, 1944. BA, Manhattan Coll., 1966; JD cum laude, Columbia U., 1969. Bar: N.Y. 1969.

Writing and rsch. editor Columbia Jour. Law and Social Problems, 1967-69. Died Nov. 5, 1997.

TIKHONOV, NIKOLAY ALEKSANDROVICH, government official; USSR; b. May 14, 1905; ed. Dniepropetrovsk Metall. Inst. Asst. locomotive dirver, technician, 1927-30; engr., chief engr., dir. metall. plant, Dniepropetrovsk; chief main bd. USSR Ministry Ferrous Metallurgy, 1930-55; dep. minister ferrous metallurgy, 1955-57; chmn. Council of Dniepropetrovsk Econ. Region, 1957-60; vice chmn. USSR Sci. Econ. Council, 1960-63; vice chmn. State Planning com., 1963-65; vice chmn. USSR Council Ministers, 1965, 1st vice chmn., 1966-80, chmn., 1980-85; candidate mem. Politburo, Communist Party Soviet Union, 1978-79, 1979-85; dep. to USSR Supreme Soviet, from 1958. Decorated Order of Lenin (7); Order of October Revolution; recipient Nat. prize (2). Died June 1, 1997.

TIKKO, HENNO, surgeon; b. Viljandi, Estonia, July 4, 1936; s. Herman and Helene Tikko;m. Carmen Peikre, Mar. 27, 1973; children: Jaak, Katrin. MD, Tartu (Estonia) U., 1960, PhD, 1965, DSc, 1973. Surgeon City Hosp. Tartu, 1960-62; asst. Tartu U., 1965-71, asst. prof., 1971-76, prof., 1976-96, dean faculty postgrad. med. edn., 1978-89; mem. internat. editl. bd. Angiology and Vascular Surgery; contbr. articles to profl. jours. Recipient Estonian Sci. award vascular surgery Estonian Govt., Tallinn, 1982. Mem. European Soc. Cardiovascular Surgery, Russian Soc. Angiology and Vascular Surgery, Baltic Soc. Thoracic and Cardiovascular Surgery. Died June 7, 1996.

TILBURY, ROGER GRAYDON, lawyer, rancher; b. Guthrie, Okla., July 30, 1925; s. Graydon and Minnie (Lee) T.; m. Margaret Dear, June 24, 1952; 1 dau., Elizabeth Ann. B.S., U. So. Calif., 1945; J.D., U. Kans., 1949; LL.M., Columbia, 1950; postgrad., Oxford (Eng.) U., 1949. Bar: Mo. bar 1950, Oreg. bar 1953. Pvt. practice Kansas City, Mo., 1950-53, Portland, Oreg., 1953-96; assoc. firm Rogers, Field, Gentry, Kansas City, Mo., 1950-53, Stern, Reiter & Day, Portland, 1953-56; ptnr. firm Roth & Tilbury, 1956-58, Tilbury & Kane, 1970-72, Haessler, Tilbury & Platten, 1978-81; pvt. practice Portland, 1981-96; circuit judge pro tem., Oreg., 1972-96, arbitrator and fact finder, 1973-96; sec. Barrington Properties; mem. nat. panel arbitrators U.S. Mediation and Conciliation Svc.; arbitrator for N.Y. Stock Exch., Pacific Stock Exch. and Nat. Assn. Security Dealers; mediator U.S. Dist. Ct.; atty. Animal Defender League, 1969-73. Dep. election commr. Kansas City, Mo., 1952-53; bd. dirs. Multnomah Bar Found. Served to lt. (j.g.) USNR, 1943-45. Battenfeld scholar, 1943. Mem. Oreg. State Bar, Soc. Barristers, Am. Arbitration Assn., Save the Redwoods League, East African Wildlife League, Nat. Wildlife Found., Am. Trial Lawyers Assn., Delta Tau Delta, Phi Delta Phi. Died Dec. 29, 1996.

TILLEY, WILLIAM JESSE, steel and iron works company executive; b. Pulaski, Va., Aug. 11, 1908; s. James Garfield and Mabel Love (Stone) T.; m. Annette Ferguson, June 29, 1928 (div. 1974); children—Sally Ann, William J., Jr., Anthony F., Michael S.; m. Barbara Kemper, Nov. 11, 1974. With Bristol Steel & Iron Works, Inc., Bristol, Va, 1926—; now chmn. bd. Episcopalian.

TILMOUTH, MICHAEL, music educator; b. Grimsby, Lincolnshire, Scotland, Nov. 30, 1930; s. Herbert George and Amy (Hall) T.; m. Mary Jelliman, Sept. 17, 1966; children: Andrew Michael, Penelope Jane, Christopher Dominic James. BA, Christ's Coll., Cambridge, 1954; MA, Christ's Coll., 1958, PhD, 1960. Lectr. U. Glasgow, Scotland, 1959-71; Tovey prof. music U. Edinburgh, Scotland, 1971—. Editor: Musica Britannica, 1971-86; contbr. articles to profl. jours. Bd. dirs. Scottish Opera, Glasgow, 1975—; chmn. Purcell Soc., London, 1983—. Mem. Royal Musical Assn. (council mem. 1970-76); Purcell Soc. (chmn. London 1983—, jour. editor 1976, 81, 87). Avocations: hill walking, gardening, reading. Office: U Edinburgh, Old College South Bridge, Edinburgh EH8 9YL, Scotland

TIMBERS, WILLIAM HOMER, federal judge; b. Yonkers, N.Y., Sept. 5, 1915; s. Harley Homer and Florence (Birmingham) T.; m. Charlotte MacLachlan Tanner, June 21, 1941; children: John William, Nancy Joan, Dwight Edward, William Homer Jr. A.B. magna cum laude, Dartmouth Coll., 1937; LL.B., Yale U., 1940; LL.D. (hon.), Fairfield U., 1977. Bar: N.Y. 1940, U.S. Supreme Ct 1946, also other fed. cts 1946, Conn. 1948, D.C. 1954. Assoc. firm Davis, Polk, Wardwell, Sunderland & Kiendl, N.Y.C., 1940-48; mem. firm Cummings & Lockwood, Stamford, Conn., 1948-53; gen. counsel SEC, Washington, 1953-56; mem. firm Skadden, Arps, Slate & Timbers, N.Y.C., 1956-60; judge U.S. Dist. Ct., Dist. Conn., 1960-71, chief judge, 1964-71; judge U.S. Ct. Appeals, 2d Circuit, 1971-94. Mem. alumni council Dartmouth Coll., 1967-71, pres., 1969-71, Yale Law Sch. Alumni Assn., 1953-61, sec. 1959-61, Pres.'s Adv. Com. on Fitness of Am. Youth, 1958-60. Mem. Phi Beta Kappa, Phi Kappa Psi. Presbyterian (elder, trustee). Clubs: Am. Kennel (dir. 1968-84, chmn. bd. 1982-84), Norwegian Elkhound Assn. Am. (pres. 1961-71, dir. 1961-71), Ox Ridge Kennel (pres. 1958-68, dir. 1958-85), Westminster Kennel. Home: Darien Conn. Died Nov. 26, 1994.

TIPPETT, MICHAEL KEMP, composer; b. London, Eng. Jan. 2, 1905; s. Henry William and Isabel (Kemp) T.; ed. Royal Coll. Music; MusD (hon.) Cambridge U., 1964, Trinity Coll., Dublin, 1964, Oxford U., 1967, Dublin U., Wales U., Leeds U., 1965, London U., 1975, U. Keele, 1986, U. York, 1966; DLitt U. Warwick, 1974. Formerly mus. dir. chorus and orch. soc., Oxted, Eng., tchr. French, Hazelwood Sch., until 1931; tchr. adult edn. dept. London County Council, Royal Arsenal Coop. Soc. Edn., 1932; music dir. Morley Coll., London, 1940-51; artistic dir. Bath Festival, 1969-74. Pres. Kent Opera Co., 1979—, London Coll. of Music, 1983—. Composer numerous orchestral works, including 4 symphonies, 1945, 58, 72, 77, 5 string quartets, 1935, 42, 46, 78, 91, Fantasia for piano, orch., 1942, orch. suite, 1948, Little Music for string orch., 1952, Fantasia Theme by Correlli for string orch., 1953, piano concerto, 1955, 4 piano sonatas, 1937, 62, 73, 84, Symphony No. 4, 1977, String Quartet No. 4, 1978, Triple Concerto, 1979, Piano Sonata #4, 1984, The Rose Lake, 1992-93; works for organ, choral works including A Child of our Time, 1944, The Vision of St. Augustine, 1966, Crown of the Year, The Mask of Time, 1983; (operas) The Midsummer Marriage, 1952, King Priam, 1958-61, The Knot Garden, 1970, The Ice Break, 1977, New Year, 1988, also songs include Boyhoods End, 1943, Heart's Assurance, 1951, Byzantium, 1990; author: Tippett on Music, 1995, Created knight, 1966; (autobiography) Those 20th Century Blues, 1991; decorated comdr. Order Brit. Empire, Order of Merit. Mem. Am. Acad. Arts and Letters (hon.), Akad. der Kunste (extraordinary).

TOBIN, JOHN EVERARD, retired lawyer; b. Utica, N.Y., Sept. 28, 1923; s. Michael and Julia Theresa (O'Brien) T.; m. Margaret T. Swope, June 17, 1944; children: John E. Jr., Catherine J. (dec.), Brian D., Paul C. A.B., Hamilton Coll., 1947; LL.B., Columbia U., 1950. Bar: N.Y. 1950, U.S. Supreme Ct. 1966. Practiced law N.Y.C., 1950-94; assoc. Donovan, Leisure, Newton & Irvine, 1950-59, ptnr., 1959-84; ptnr. Dorsey & Whitney, 1984-94; chief counsel subcom. administrn. internal revenue laws, ways and means com. U.S. Ho. of Reps., 1952-53; dir. Alleghany Corp. Bd. dirs. Legal Aid Soc., N.Y., 1979-85; trustee Hamilton Coll., 1974-97; mem. exec. com. Lawyers Com. for Civil Rights under Law. 1st lt. USAF, 1942-46. Mem. Assn. of Bar of City of N.Y., Am. Judicature Soc., Century Assn. (N.Y.C.). Died Jan. 19, 1997.

TODD, ALEXANDER ROBERTUS (BARON TODD OF TRUMPINGTON), chemistry educator; b. Glasgow, Scotland, Oct. 2, 1907; s. Alexander and Jane (Lowrie) T.; m. Alison Sarah Dale, Jan. 30, 1937 (dec. 1987); children: Alexander Henry, Helen Todd Brown, Hilary Alison. B.Sc. (Carnegie Research scholar 1928-29), U. Glasgow, 1928, D.Sc., 1938; Dr.phil.nat., U. Frankfurt am Main, 1931; D.Phil., Oxford U., Eng., 1933; M.A., U. Cambridge, Eng., 1944; LL.D. (hon.), univs. of Glasgow, Melbourne, Edinburg, Cal., Manchester, Hokkaido, Melbourne, Edinburh, Cal., Manchester, Hokkaido; Dr.rer.nat. (hon.), U. Kiel; D.Litt. (hon.), U. Sydney; D.Sc. (hon.), univs. of London, Exeter, Warwick, Sheffield, Liverpool, Oxford, Leicester, Durham, Eng., Univ. of Wales, U. Madrid, Spain, U. Aligarh, India, U. Strasbourg, France, Harvard U., Yale U.,U. Mich., U. Paris, U. Adelaide, Australia, U. Strathclyde, Scotland, Australian Nat. U., U. Cambridge, U. Philippines, Tufts U., Chinese U. Hong Kong, Hong Kong U. Mem. staff Lister Inst. Preventive Medicine, London, 1936-38; reader biochemistry U. London, 1937-38; prof., dir. chem. labs. U. Manchester, Eng., 1938-44; prof. organic chemistry U. Cambridge, Eng., 1944-71, fellow Christ's Coll.,, 1944—, master, 1963-78; chancellor U. Strathclyde, 1963-91; dir. Fisons Ltd., London, 1963-78, Nat. Rsch. Devel. Corp., London, 1968-76; vis. prof. Calif. Inst. Tech., 1938, U. Chgo., 1948, U. Sydney, 1950, MIT, Cambridge, 1954, U. Calif., 1957, Tex. Christian U., 1980; chmn. adv. Coun. Sci. Policy, 1952-64, Royal Commn. Med. Edn., 1965-68. Contbr. articles to profl. jours. Chmn. Nuffield Found., London, 1936-80; chmn. govs. United Cambridge Hosps., 1969-74; chmn. trustees Croucher Found., Hong Kong, 1980-87, pres., 1988—. Created knight, 1954, baron (life peer), 1962; Order of Merit (U.K.); Order Rising Sun (Japan); recipient Nobel prize for chemistry, 1957; Pour le Merite (W. Germany), 1966; Lomonosov medal U.S.S.R. Acad. Sci., 1978; medals various chem. socs., sci. orgns., including Royal Copley medals Royal Soc., 1949; named master Salter's Co., 1961. Fellow Royal Soc. (pres. 1975-80), Australian Chem. Inst. (hon.), Manchester Coll. Tech. (hon.), Royal Soc. Edinburgh (hon.), Royal Coll. Physicians London (hon.), Royal Coll. Physicians, Surg. Glasgow; mem. AAAS, NAS, French Chem. Soc. (hon.), German Chem. Soc. (hon.), Spanish Chem. Soc. (hon.), Belgian Chem. Soc. (hon.), Swiss Chem. Soc. (hon.), Japanese Chem. Soc. (hon.), Australian Acad. Sci., Austrian Acad. Sci., Ghana Acad. Sci., Polish Acad. Sci., Russian Acad. Sci., Acad. Natural Philosophy Halle (Germany), Am. Philos. Soc., N.Y. Acad. Sci., Chem. Soc. (pres. 1960-62), Internat. Union Pure and Applied Chemistry (pres. 1963-65), Soc. Chem. Industry. Died Oct. 1, 1996.

TODD, JAMES S., surgeon, educator, medical association administrator; b. Hyannis, Mass., 1931. Intern Presbyn. Hosp., N.Y.C., 1957-58, resident in surgery, 1959-63; resident in surgery Delafield Hosp., N.Y.C., 1963; resident ob-gyn. Sloane Womens Hosp., N.Y.C., 1958-59; resident Valley Hosp., Ridgewood, N.J.; clin. asst. prof. surgery U. Medicine and Dentistry N.J., Newark; exec. v.p. AMA, 1993; pres. AMA. Home: Chicago Ill. Deceased.

TODOROV, STANKO, politician; b. Pernik region, Bulgaria, Dec. 10, 1920; m. Sonya Todorova, 1947; 2 sons. Active Resistance Movement, 1941-44; mem. Nat. Assembly; minister of agr. Govt. of Bulgaria, 1952-58; sec. cen. com. Bulgarian Communist Party, 1958-59, 66-71, full mem. politburo, 1961-88; dep. prime minister, 1959-66; permanent Bulgarian rep. to Council for Mut. Econ. Assistance, 1962-66; chair Council of Ministers, 1971-81, Nat. Assembly, 1981—; dep. chmn. Supreme Council Bulgarian Socialist Party, 1990—. Decorated Order of the October Revolution, 1981. Died Dec. 17, 1996.

TOLLE, DONALD JAMES, education educator; b. Roxbury, Kans., May 29, 1918; s. Edgar Earl and Sadie M. (Lott) T.; m. Mary Alice McNeill, July 24, 1945; children: Donald MacDavid, Louise Margaret Tolle Huffman, Theresa Love Pohlman. A.B., Fla. So. Coll., 1940; M.A., U. Fla., 1947; Ed.D., Fla. State U., 1957. Tchr. Palmetto (Fla.) Jr.-Sr. High Sch., 1940-42, Winter Haven (Fla.) High Sch., 1946-47, Monticello (Fla.) Jr. High Sch., 1947-48; prin. Jefferson County High Sch., Monticello; also supervising prin. Monticello Pub. Schs. (W), 1949-51; instr. St. Petersburg (Fla.) Jr. Coll., 1951-55, dean of men, 1953-58, dean instrn., 1958-66; dean acad. studies Fla. Jr. Coll., Jacksonville, 1966-67; assoc. prof. higher edn., assoc. dir. community coll. coop. internship program So. Ill. U., Carbondale, 1967-71; prof. higher edn. So. Ill. U., 1971-84, prof. emeritus, 1984—; vis. prof. Appalachian State U., summer 1964; acting prof. U. South Fla., 1965-66; mem. exec. com. Fla. Assn. Colls. and Univs., 1958-66, sec.-treas., 1960-61. Co-author book; contbr. articles to profl. jours. Mem. Fla. Gov.'s Adv. Com. Law Enforcement Edn., 1964-66; mem. exec. com. Fla. Ctr. for Edn. in Politics, 1958-66; cons. to several community colls. Served with USAAF, 1942-45. Recipient John E. King award Post-doctoral Acad. Higher Edn., So. Ill. U., 1989, Disting. Commendation award Ednl. Coun. of 100/So. Ill. U., 1989. Died Aug. 9, 1993.

TOLLEY, WILLIAM PEARSON, university chancellor, airline executive; b. Honesdale, Pa., Sept. 13, 1900; s. Adolphus Charles and Emma Grace (Sumner) T.; m. Ruth Marion Canfield, July 3, 1925; children: Nelda Tolley Price, William Pearson, Katryn Tolley Fritz. A.B., Syracuse U., 1922, A.M., 1924; B.D., Drew Theol. Sem., 1925; A.M., Columbia, 1927, Ph.D., 1930; D.D., Mt. Union Coll., Alliance, Ohio, 1931; LL.D., Dickinson Coll., Carlisle, Pa., 1933, Bucknell U., 1943, Rensselaer Poly. Inst., 1954, Marshall Coll., Huntington, W.Va., 1957, Pratt Inst., Bklyn., 1959, Northeastern U., 1943, Allegheny Coll., 1943, Villanova Coll., 1943, Temple U., 1944, Juniata Coll., Colgate U., 1944, Boston U., 1950, U. Chattanooga, 1951, Oklahoma City U., Columbia U., 1955, St. Lawrence U., 1956, Lycoming Coll., 1962, Drew U., 1966, Concord Coll., 1967; Litt.D., Grove City (Pa.) Coll., 1938; L.H.D., Hamilton Coll., 1943, Albion Coll., 1945, Hobart Coll., 1946, Union Coll., 1946, Alfred U., 1951, Pace Coll., 1963, Japan Internat. Christian U., 1966, Elmira Coll., 1970; Ed.D., Fla. So. U., 1948; D.P.A., U. Puget Sound, 1963; H.H.D., Bowling Green State U., 1964; L.H.D., Rosary Hill Coll., 1967; Ped.D., Baldwin-Wallace Coll., 1967; LL.D., Syracuse U., 1969. Ordained to ministry Meth. Episcopal Ch., 1923; alumni sec. Drew Theol. Sem., 1925-27, instr. systematic theology, 1926-28, asst. to pres., 1927-28, acting dean Brothers Coll., instr. in philosophy, 1928-29; dean Drew Theol. Sem. (Brothers Coll.), 1929-31, prof. philosophy, 1930-31; pres. Allegheny Coll., 1931-42; chancellor Syracuse (N.Y.) U., 1942-69, chancellor emeritus, 1969-96; chmn. bd. Mohawk Airlines Inc., 1970-71, chmn., pres., 1971-72; dir. First Trust & Deposit Co.; Vice pres. Japan Internat. Christian U. Found., Inc.; dir. U.S. Air. Author: The Idea of God in St. Augustine, 1930, Preface to Philosophy, 1946, The Transcendent Aim, 1967, The Meaning of Freedom, 1969, The Adventure of Learning, 1977, At The Fountain of Youth, 1988; editor: Alumni Record of Drew Theological Seminary (1867-1925), 1926, Preface to Philosophy, 1945. Pres. Assn. Colls. and Univs. State N.Y.; mem. U. Senate of Meth. Ch., 1932-36, 38-96, pres., 1960-70; pres., dir. Assn. Am. Colls., 1942-43; chmn. exec. com. Coop. Study in Gen. Edn., Am. Council of Edn., 1940-46; pres. Nat. Meth. Found. for Christian Higher Edn., 1969-73, Pi Kappa Alpha Meml. Found., 1975-76. Served with U.S. Army, 1918. Decorated chavalier Legion of Honor France; recipient George Arents Alumni medal, Salzberg medal in transp. Syracuse U. Mem. Newcomen Soc. Eng., Phi Beta Kappa, Beta Gamma Sigma, Delta Sigma Rho, Phi Kappa Phi, Pi Delta Epsilon, Pi Kappa Alpha, Omicron Delta Kappa, Phi Delta Kappa. Republican. Clubs: Cosmos (Washington); Iron City Fishing (Pittsburgh); Century (Syracuse); Grolier (N.Y.C.); University (N.Y.C.); Oswelewgois, Sedgwick Farm Tennis. Home: Manlius N.Y. Died Jan. 26, 1996.

TOMBAUGH, CLYDE WILLIAM, astronomer, educator; b. Streator, Ill., Feb. 4, 1906; s. Muron D. and Adella Pearl (Chritton) T.; m. Patricia Irene Edson,

June 7, 1934; children: Annette Roberta, Alden Clyde. AB, U. Kans., 1936, MA, 1939; DSc (hon.), No. Ariz. U., 1960. Asst. Lowell Obs., Flagstaff, Ariz., 1929, asst. astronomer, 1938; instr. sci. Ariz. State Coll., Flagstaff, 1943-45; vis. asst. prof. astronomy UCLA, 1945-46; astronomer Aberdeen Ballistics Labs. Annex/White Sands Missile Range, Las Cruces, N.Mex., 1946-97, chief optical measurement sect., 1948, chief research and evaluation br. planning dept. Flight Determination div., 1948-53, chief investigator search for natural satellites project, 1953-58, planetary astrophys. researcher, 1958-97; research assoc. prof. astronomy N.Mex. State U., 1955-59, prof., 1965-73, prof. emeritus, 1973-97, with planetary astrophysics research program, 1959-97; discoverer planet Pluto, 1930, 1 globular star cluster, 1932, 5 galactic star clusters, variable stars, asteroids, clusters of galaxies; extensive search for distant planets and natural earth's satellites, studies in apparent distbn. extragalactic galaxies, geol. studies Mars' and Moon's surface features, prodn. telescope mirrors; mem. expdn. extension satellite research project, Quito, Ecuador, 1956-58; lectr. in field. Author: Out of the Darkness: the Planet Pluto, 1980; contbr. articles to profl. jours. Paul Harris fellow Rotary Internat.; Edward Emory Slosson scholar in sci. U. Kans., 1932-36; recipient Jackson-Guilt medal and gift Royal Astron. Soc. Eng., 1931, Fairbanks award Soc. Photog. Instrument Engrs., 1968, Bruce Blair award, 1965, Disting. Svc. citation U. Kans., 1966, Rittenhouse award, Phila., 1990, Golden Plate award Am. Acad. Achievement, 1991; named to White Sand Missile Range Hall of Fame, 1980, Internat. Space Hall of Fame; Clyde Tombaugh Scholars Endowment Fund established in his honor at N.Mex. State U., 1987. Fellow Soc. for Research on Meteorites, AIAA; mem. Am. Astron. Soc., Internat. Astron. Union, Astron. Soc. Pacific, Sigma Xi. Mem. Unitarian Ch. Avocations: grinding telescope mirrors, designing small telescopes. Died Jan. 17, 1997.

TOMPSETT, RALPH, physician; b. Tidioute, Pa., Oct. 8, 1913; s. William Charles and Madora Selena (Foster) T.; m. Jean MacEwen, June 30, 1942; children: Joan, William, Polly, Selene. AB, Cornell U., Ithaca, N.Y., 1934; MD, Cornell U., N.Y.C., 1939. Intern in internal medicine N.Y. Hosp., 1939-40, resident, 1940; instr. to assoc. prof. internal medicine Cornell U. Med. Coll., N.Y.C., 1946-57; chief internal medicine Baylor U. Med. Ctr., Dallas, 1957-79; prof. internal medicine U. Tex. Southwestern Med. Sch., Dallas, 1957—. Contbr. numerous articles to profl. jours. Maj. U.S. Army, 1942-46. Master ACP; mem. Am. Soc. Clin. Investigation, Am. Clin. and Climatol. Assn., Assn. Am. Physicians. Home: Dallas Tex. DIED 01/18/95. .

TONEY, EDNA, playwright, actress; b. N.Y.C., Mar. 22, 1914; d. Henry and Frieda (Berger) Greenfield; m. Anthony Toney, Apr. 8, 1947; children: Anita Karen, Adele Susan. Student New Theatre Sch., 1936; Columbia U., 1953-55, New Sch. Social Research, 1975. Actress WPA Theatre Project, N.Y.C., 1937; writer Kraft Music Hall, N.Y.C., 1946; writer, producer, actress schs., community ctrs., colls., libraries, etc., 1972-82; playwright Meet Miss Lucy Stone (video prodn. written by and starring Edna Toney 1988), Lincoln Ctr. Library's Museum of the Performing Arts, 1977, Baby Brother Prodn., Mid-Hudson Arts and Sci. Ctr., Poughkeepsie, N.Y., 1980; writer, dir., actress, producer Katonah Community Theatre, N.Y., 1984; columnist Queries and Theories. Author: Once Told Tales, 1967, How to Become a Famous Playwright, 1987, Stuff and Nonsense, 1992; featured in The Rosenbergs: Collected Visions of Artists & Writers by Rob Okun, 1988, Book of Spoofs, edited by Norman Cousins, 1989. Benefit performance Meet Miss Lucy Stone, North Westchester-Putnam County Women's Resource Ctr., Mahopac, N.Y., 1986; featured performer Sane/Freeze of No. Westchester Hiroshima Day meeting, 1989; performer for Rosenberg Commemoration Program, NYU Law Sch., 1990; writer, performer Pound Ridge Players, 1991. Recipient acting awards 10th Annual Arts Festival, 1976. Mem. NOW, Women's Internat. League Peace and Freedom, SANE, Katonah Gallery. Democrat. Avocation: swimming.

TOOLEY, CHARLES FREDERICK, communications executive, consultant; b. Seattle, Sept. 29, 1947; s. Creath Athol and Catherine Ella (Wainman) T.; m. Valerie Adele Gose, Mar. 7, 1981 (dec. Feb. 1991); children: Paige Arlene Chytka, Marni Higdon Tooley; m. Joan Marie Stapleton, Feb. 21, 1998. BA, Lynchburg Coll., 1968. Producer, stage mgr., tech. dir. various theatre cos. and performing arts orgns., 1965-74; field underwriter N.Y. Life Ins. Co., Billings, Mont., 1974-77; market adminstr. Mountain Bell Telephone Co., Butte and Billings, Mont., 1978-83; pres. BCC Inc., Billings, Mont., 1983—. Active Mont. Arts Coun., 1982-92, Billings/Yellowstone County Centennial, 1981-82, Mont. Cultural Advocacy, 1982-92; bd. dirs. Yellowstone 89ers, 1987-89, Christian Chs. in Mont., 1983—, divsn. of overseas ministries Christian Ch. Disciples of Christ, 1997—; elder Ctrl. Christian Ch., Billings, 1983—, chmn. trustees, 1983-85; mem. Mont. Dem. Exec. Bd., 1982-87; mem. adv. bd. Salvation Army, Billings, 1984—; del. Dem. Nat. Conv., 1980; Dem. candidate Mont. Ho. of Reps., 1986; mem. Billings City Coun., 1988-94, mayor pro tem, 1992-94; mayor City of Billings, 1996—; mem. Common Global Missions Bd., 1997—. Sgt. U.S. Army, 1969-72, Vietnam. Mem. Billings Coun. Fgn. Rels., Toastmasters (Div. Gov.'s Cup 1978), Kiwanis (bd. dirs. 1981-88), Masons, Shriners, Elks. Mem. Disciples of Christ. Avocations: theatre productions.

TOONE, ELAM COOKSEY, JR., physician, educator; b. Richmond, Va., Nov. 4, 1908; s. Elam C. and Elizabeth (Ryl) T.; m. Marion Van Nostrand, July 20, 1964 (dec. 1983); 1 child, Elam Cooksey III. B.A. magna cum laude, Hampden Sydney Coll., 1929, LL.D., 1973; M.D., Med. Coll. Va., 1934. Diplomate: Am. Bd. Internal Medicine. House officer Hillman Hosp., Birmingham, Ala., also; Med. Coll. Va. Hosp., Richmond, 1934-38; from asst. to prof. medicine Med. Coll. Va., 1936-60, chmn. div. connective tissue diseases, 1966-74; dir. sect. rheumatology McGuire VA Hosp., 1975-83, cons., 1983-93; prof. emeritus Med. Coll. Va., 1984. Contbr. papers dealing with arthritis and related subjects to profl. jours. Pres., chmn. bd. trustees Richmond Acad. Med., 1957-58; bd. advisers Family Service Soc., 1950, Dept. Pub. Welfare, Richmond, 1961-63; Bd. govs., dir. Nat. Arthritis Found., 1958-60, chpts., 1955-93, chmn. inter-chpt. advisory com., 1957; bd. dirs. Charles W. Thomas Arthritis Research Fund, 1965-74; trustee MCV Found., 1970-80. Served to lt. col. AUS, 1942-46, MTO. Decorated Bronze Star medal; recipient Disting. Service award Nat. Arthritis Found., 1966, Disting. Service award Med. Coll. Va., 1980, Disting. Faculty award, 1985, Laureate award Va. chpt. ACP, 1986, Louise Obici Hosp. Med. Staff award, 1988; mem. Va. Cultural Laureate Soc., 1986. Fellow ACP; mem. Am. Coll. Rheumatology (Master 1989, v.p. 1963), AAAS, Richmond Soc. Internal Medicine (pres. 1963), Va. Med. Soc. (program chmn. 1957), AMA, Clin. and Climatol. Assn., Am. Fedn. Clin. Research, Phi Beta Kappa, Alpha Omega Alpha, Kappa Sigma. Republican. Episcopalian. Club: Commonwealth (Richmond). Elam Toone Endowed Professorship of Rheumatology established in his honor, 1986. Home: Richmond Va. Died Oct. 3, 1993.

TOPPING, NORMAN HAWKINS, former university chancellor; b. Flat River, Mo., Jan. 12, 1908; s. Moses H. and Charlotte Amanda (Blue) T.; m. Helen Rummens, Sept. 2, 1930 (dec. Aug. 1989); children—Brian, Linda. A.B., U. So. Calif., 1933, M.D., 1936. Diplomate: Am. Bd. Preventive Medicine and Pub. Health. Intern USPHS marine hosps., San Francisco, Seattle; mem. staff NIH, Bethesda, Md., 1937-52; asst. chief div. infectious diseases NIH, 1946-48; asst. surgeon gen. USPHS; asso. dir. NIH, 1948-52; v.p. for med. affairs U. Pa., 1952-58; pres. U. So. Calif., 1958-70, chancellor, 1970-80, chancellor emeritus, 1980-97; engaged in med. research, viral and rickettsial diseases, 1937-48; mem. com. on virus research and epidemiology Nat. Found. Infantile Paralysis, 1950-56, chmn., 1956-58; mem. research com. Nat. Found., chmn., 1958-77; pres. Am. Soc. Tropical Medicine, 1949. Author articles on typhus, Rocky Mountain spotted fever, Q fever, pub. health. Pres. So. Calif. Rapid Transit Dist., 1971-73. Recipient Bailey K. Ashford award, 1943; Wash. Acad. Sci. award, 1944; U.S.A. Typhus Commn. medal, 1945. Mem. A.A.A.S., Assn. Am. Physicians, Am. Epidemiological Soc., Soc. Exptl. Biology and Medicine. Home: Burbank Calif. Died Nov. 18, 1997.

TORRE, DOUGLAS PAUL, dermatologist; b. New Orleans, Feb. 6, 1919; s. Peter and Jeanne Renee (Mottram) T.; m. Sylvia Elizabeth Stenmark, Apr. 22, 1954 (div. May 1977); children—Eric, Jeanne; m. Catherine Babcock, May 28, 1977. BS, Tulane U., 1940, MD, 1943; postgrad., Cornell U., 1946-50. Intern Phila. Gen. Hosp., 1943-44; fellow Cornell U. Med. Coll.-N.Y. Hosp., 1946-50; practice medicine, specializing in dermatology N.Y.C., 1946—; instr. Cornell U. Med. Coll., N.Y.C., 1950-55; from asst. to assoc. prof. Cornell U. Med. Coll., 1956-65, clin. prof. dermatology, 1966-95, clin. prof. emeritus dermatology, 1995-96; attending physician N.Y. Hosp.; cons. Meml. Hosp. Contbr. articles to profl. jours. and chpts. to textbooks. Served to lt., M.C. USNR, 1944-46, PTO. Mem. AMA, Am. Acad. Dermatology, Soc. Investigative Dermatology, Atlantic Dermatology Assn (pres. 1969), N.Y. Dermatology Assn. (pres. 1969, 79), Am. Soc. Dermatol. Surgery (v.p. 1979, pres. 1980-81), Am. Coll. Cryosurgery (pres. 1982-83), N.Y. Acad. Medicine, Phi Beta Kappa, Delta Tau Delta. Club: University (N.Y.C.). Died Sept. 21, 1996.

TOUSEY, RICHARD, physicist; b. Somerville, Mass., May 18, 1908; s. Coleman and Adella Richards (Hill) T.; m. Ruth Lowe, June 29, 1932; 1 dau., Joanna. A.B., Tufts U., 1928, Sc.D. (hon.), 1961; A.M., Harvard, 1929; Ph.D., 1933. Instr. physics Harvard, 1933-36, tutor div. phys. scis., 1934-36; research instr. Tufts U., 1936-41; physicist U.S. Naval Research Lab. optics div., 1941-58, head instrument sect., 1942-45, head micron waves br., 1945-58, head rocket spectroscopy br., atmosphere and astrophysics div., 1958-67, space sci. div., 1967-78, cons., 1978—; Mem. com. vision Armed Forces-NRC, 1944-97; line spectra of elements com. NRC, 1960-72; mem. Rocket and Satellite Research Panel, 1958-97; mem. astronomy subcom. space sci. steering com. NASA, 1960-62, mem. solar physics subcom., 1969-71; prin. investigator expts. including Skylab; mem. com. aeronomy Internat. Union Geodesy and Geophysics, 1958-97 ; U.S. nat. com. Internat. Commn. Optics, 1960-66; mem. sci. steering com. Project Vanguard, 1956-58; mem. adv. com. to office sci. personnel Nat. Acad. Scis.-NRC, 1969-72. Contbr. articles to sci. jours. and books. Bayard Cutting fellow Harvard, 1931-33, 35-36; recipient Meritorious Civilian Service award U.S. Navy, 1945; E.O. Hulburt award Naval Research Labs., 1958; Progress medal photog. Soc. Am., 1959; Prix Ancel Soc. Francaise de Photographie, 1962; Henry Draper medal Nat. Acad. Scis., 1963; Navy award for distinguished achievement in sci, 1963; Eddington medal, 1964; NASA medal for exceptional sci. achievement, 1974; George Darwin lectr. Royal Astron. Soc., 1963. Fellow Am. Acad. Arts and Scis., Am. Phys. Soc., Optical Soc. Am. (dir. 1953-57, Frederic Ives medal 1960), Am. Geophys. Union; mem. Internat. Acad. Astronautics, Nat. Acad. Scis., Am. Astron. Soc. (v.p. 1964-66, Henry Norris Russell lectr. 1966, George Ellery Hale award 1992), Soc. Applied Spectroscopy, AAAS, Am. Geophys. Union, Philos. Soc. Washington, Internat. Astron. Union, Nuttall Ornithol. Club, Audubon Naturalists Soc., Phi Beta Kappa, Sigma Xi, Theta Delta Chi. Home: Tucson Ariz. Died Apr. 15, 1997.

TOWERS, (AUGUSTUS) ROBERT, JR., English educator, writer; b. Richmond, Va., Jan. 21, 1923; s. Augustus Robert Sr. and Miriam (Reynolds) T.; m. Patricia Constance Locke, May 13, 1967; 1 child, Sarah Constance. AB summa cum laude, Princeton U., 1945, PhD, 1952. English instr. Princeton (N.J.) U., 1951-54; English instr. CUNY, Queens, 1954-58, asst. prof., 1958-62, assoc. prof., 1962-68, prof., 1968-84, chmn. dept. of English, 1970-73, assoc. dean faculty, arts div., 1974-75; prof. writing, chmn. writing div. Columbia U. Sch. Arts, N.Y.C., 1984-89; bd. dirs. Corp. Yaddo, Saratoga Springs, N.Y., 1981—, vice chmn., 1989—; judge PEN-Faulkner Fiction award, 1985, Irish Times-Aer Lingus Internat. Fiction award, 1992. Author: The Necklace of Kali, 1960, The Monkey Watcher, 1964, The Summoning, 1983; contbr. more than 150 critical revs. and articles to profl. jours. Recipient Proctor fellow, Princeton U., 1950-51. Mem. P.E.N. Am. Ctr. (bd. dirs. 1979-83, 89-91), Phi Beta Kappa. Democrat. Club: Century. Avocation: country life. Home: New York N.Y. DIED 05/02/95. .

TRAPP, MARIA AUGUSTA VON, musician, author; b. Vienna, Austria, Jan. 26, 1905; came to U.S., 1939, naturalized, 1948; d. Karl and Augusta (Rainer) Kutschera; m. Baron Georg von Trapp, Nov. 26, 1927 (dec. May 30, 1947); children: Rupert, Agathe, Maria, Werner, Hedwig, Johanna Trapp Winter, Martina, Rosemarie, Eleanor Trapp Campbell, Johannes. Student, State Tchrs. Coll. Progressive Edn., Vienna; LL.D., St. Mary's Coll., Notre Dame, Ind., 1957; Mus.D., St. Anselms Coll., Manchester, N.H., 1966, St. Michael's Coll., Winooski, Vt., 1971. organizer Trapp Family Austrian Relief, Inc., pres., 1947; mgr. Trapp Family Lodge, Stowe, Vt., until 1967; dir. Trapp Family Music Camp, 1940-56. Author: The Story of the Trapp Family Singers, 1948, Yesterday, Today and Forever, 1952, Around the Year with the Trapp Family, 1955, A Family on Wheels, 1959, Maria, 1972, When the King Was Carpenter, 1976; concert tours with family, Trapp Family Singers, Europe, S.Am., C.Am., Can., Hawaii, U.S., Australia, N.Z., 1938-56. Decorated Papal decoration, Bene Merenti medal, 1949, Gold Cross for Meritorious Service Austria, Austrian Cross of Honor; recipient St. Francis de Sales award Cath. Writers Guild, Gold Medal award Nat. Cath. Family Life Conf.; named Cath. Mother of Year, 1957, Lady of Holy Sepulchre, 1951. Club: Cath. Women's of Stowe. Home: Stowe Vt. Died Mar. 28, 1987.

TREAT, LAWRENCE, author; b. N.Y.C., Dec. 21, 1903; s. Henry and Daisy (Stein) Goldstone; m. Rose Ehrenfreund, 1943. BA cum laude, Dartmouth Coll., 1924; LLB, Columbia U., 1927. Author: fiction Run Far, Run Fast, 1937, B as in Banshee, 1940, D as in Dead, 1941, H as in Hangman, 1942, O as in Omen, 1943, The Leatherman, 1944, V as in Victim, 1945, H as in Hunted, 1946, Q as in Quicksand, 1947, Over the Edge, 1948, F as in Flight, 1948, Trial and Terror, 1949, Big Shot, 1951, Weep for a Wanton, 1956, Lady, Drop Dead, 1960, Venus Unarmed, 1961, P as in Police, 1970, True Crime With Judge Norbert Ehrenfreund: You're the Jury, 1992; originator of police procedurals and pictorial mysteries, Bringing Sherlock Home, 1931, Crime and Puzzlement, 1981, Crime and Puzzlement 2, 1982, You're the Detective, 1983, The Clue Armchair Detective, 1983, Crime and Puzzlement 3, 1988, Cherchez le Coupable, 1 and 2, 1989, Crime and Puzzlement, My Cousin Phoebe, 1991, Crime and Puzzlement on Martha's Vineyard, 1993; editor: Murder in Mind, 1967; The Mystery Writer's Handbook, 1976, A Special Kind of Crime, 1982; contbr. short stories to mags. including Alfred Hitchcock's Mystery Mag., Ellery Queen's Mystery Mag., Red Book, others. Recipient Ceremonial sword Mystery Writers Japan, 1961, Edgar Allan Poe award Mystery Writers of Am., 1965, 78, Spl. Edgar Allan Poe award for story in Alfred Hitchcock TV Hour, 1986; prize Internat. Crime Writer's Conv., Stockholm, 1981. Mem. Mystery Writers Am. (founder, past pres.), Phi Beta Kappa. Died Jan. 7, 1998.

TREFETHEN, EUGENE E., JR., insurance company executive; b. 1909. Grad., U. Calif., Harvard Sch. Bus.

Officer, dir. Kaiser Co., Oakland, Calif., 1953-96; chmn. bd. emeritus Kaiser Found. Health Plan, Oakland, Calif. Home: Napa Calif. Died Jan. 31, 1996.

TREICHLER, HARVEY ALBERT, financial planner; b. Annandale, Minn., Sept. 19, 1927; s. Rudolph and Hedwig (Zeidler) T.; m. Delores Dorothy Streich, Aug. 21, 1948; children: Shirley Susan, Bruce Brian, Jana Jolene. CLU, ChFC. Agt. Prudential Ins. Co., Mpls., 1955-57; divsn. mgr. Prudential Ins. Co., Grand Forks, N.D., 1957-62, Mfr.'s Fin., Tucson, Ariz., 1962-67; asst. br. mgr. Mfr.'s Fin., Phoenix, 1967-68; owner H.A. Treichler, CLU, Phoenix, 1968-89; pres. Treichler-Brannon, Inc., Phoenix, 1989—; instr. (part time) Phoenix Coll., 1979-85. Bd. dirs. Valley of the Sun United Way, Phoenix, 1986-87, Tempe (Ariz.) United Way, 1981-86 (divsn. leader 1979-80), Luth. Ch. Ext. Fund, St. Louis, 1984—. Named Employer of Yr. Life Ins. Office Mgr.'s Assn., 1986. Mem. CLU (organizing pres. Tucson 1966), Life Underwriters (v.p. N.D. Assn. 1962, Nat. Quality award 1971-90, Nat. Sales Achievement award, 1980-90), Estate Planning Study Group. Republican. Lutheran. Avocations: golf, fishing. Died June 28, 1996.

TREICHLER, RAY, agricultural chemist; b. Rock Island, Ill., Sept. 10, 1907; s. Wallace and Pearl (Cushman) T.; B.S., M.S., Pa. State U., 1929; Ph.D., U. Ill., 1939; m. Kathryn Amelia Blakeley, June 13, 1942. Asst. state chemist Tex. Agrl. Expt. Sta., Tex. A&M Coll., College Station, 1929-40; chief, chemistry and biochemistry research Fish & Wildlife Service Labs., U.S. Dept. Interior, Laurel, Md., 1941-44; chief, biol. activities Office of Quartermaster Gen., U.S. Army, Washington, 1945-53; asst. chief, toxic agents br. Rand D. Command, Army Chem. Center, Md., 1953-56, asst. to dir. med. research Chem. Warfare Labs., 1956-58; research adminstr. USAF, Bolling Field, Washington, 1958-68; tech. services mgr. H.D. Hudson Mfg. Co., Washington, 1968—. Fellow N.Y. Acad. Scis.; mem. Am. Chem. Soc., Entomol. Soc. Am., Am. Soc. Tropical Medicine and Hygiene, Am. Mosquito Assn., Am. Soc. Agrl. Engrs., ASTM, Sigma Xi, Gamma Sigma Delta. Club: Masons. Developed pesticide application equipment, prevention deterioration, chemistry and formulations pesticides, pesticide dissemination systems. Contbr. articles on vitamins, basal energy and endogenous nitrogen metabolism, nutrition, composition fishery products, toxic compounds, prevention material deterioration. Died Nov. 29, 1997.

TREINEN, SYLVESTER WILLIAM, bishop; b. Donnelly, Minn., Nov. 19, 1917; s. William John and Kathryn (Krausert) T. Student, Crosier Sem., Onamia, Minn., 1935-41; B.A., St. Paul's Sem., 1943. Ordained priest Roman Cath. Ch., 1946; asst. pastor Dickinson, N.D., 1946-50; sec. to bishops Ryan and Hoch, 1950-53; asst. pastor Cathedral Holy Spirit, Bismarck, N.D., 1950-57; chancellor Diocese Bismarck, 1953-59; asst. pastor St. Anne's Ch., Bismarck, 1957-59; pastor St. Joseph's Ch., Mandan, N.D., 1959-62; bishop Boise, Idaho, 1962-88; retired bishop Diocese of Boise, Idaho, 1988—. DIED 09/30/96. .

TRILLING, DIANA, writer; b. N.Y.C., July 21, 1905; d. Joseph and Sadie Helene (Forbert) Rubin; m. Lionel Trilling, June 12, 1929; 1 son, James Lionel. A.B., Radcliffe Coll., 1925. Fiction critic: The Nation, 1941-49; free-lance writer on lit., social and polit. subjects, 1949—; author: Claremont Essays, 1964, We Must March My Darlings, 1977, Reviewing The Forties, 1978, Mrs. Harris: The Death of the Scarsdale Diet Doctor, 1981, The Beginning of the Journey: The Marriage of Diana and Lionel Trilling, 1993; contbr. numerous articles to mags.; Editor: Viking Portable D. H. Lawrence, 1947, Selected Letters of D. H. Lawrence, 1958, Uniform Edition of the Works of Lionel Trilling, 1978-80. Guggenheim fellow, 1950-51, 91-92; Rockefeller-NEH grantee, 1977-79. Fellow Am. Acad. Arts and Scis.; mem. Phi Beta Kappa (hon.). Home: New York N.Y. Deceased.

TRUEBLOOD, DAVID ELTON, philosophy educator; b. Pleasantville, Iowa, Dec. 12, 1900; s. Samuel and Effie (Crew) T.; m. Pauline Goodenow, Aug. 24, 1925 (dec.); children: David M., Arnold, Samuel J. II, Elizabeth; m. Virginia Zuttermeister, Aug. 5, 1956. A.B., Penn Coll., Oskaloosa, Iowa, 1922; student, Brown U., 1922-23, Hartford Theol. Sem., 1923-24; S.T.B., Harvard, 1926; Ph.D., Johns Hopkins, 1934; Litt.D., Washington and Lee U., 1949, U. Vt., 1951, William Penn Coll., 1959, Tarkio Coll., 1963, Friends U., 1973, John Brown U., 1977; LL.D., Miami U., 1951; S.I.D., Ripon Coll., 1954, McKendree Coll., 1969; L.H.D., Simpson Coll., 1955, Otterbein Coll., 1960; D.D., Kenyon Coll., 1964, Pepperdine U., 1971. Prof. philosophy and dean men Guilford (N.C.) Coll., 1927-30; exec. sec. Balt. Yearly Meeting of Friends, 1930-33; asst. prof. philosophy Haverford (Pa.) Coll., 1933-36; acting chaplain Harvard, summer 1935; prof. philosophy religion and chaplain Stanford U., 1936-45; fellow of Woodbrooke, 1939; Swarthmore lectr. Eng., 1939; acting prof. Harvard U., 1944, Garrett Bibl. Sem., 1944, 45, 46; prof. philosophy Earlham Coll., 1946-66, prof.-at large, 1966-94; Purington lectr. Mt. Holyoke Coll., 1970; chief religious info. USIA, 1954-55; pres. Yokefellows Internat.; clk. Ind. Yearly Meeting Friends, 1955-60. Author: books relating to field including The Yoke of Christ, 1958; books relating to field The Idea of College, 1959, Confronting Christ, 1960, The Company of the Committed, 1961, General Philosophy, 1963, The Humor of Christ, 1964, The Lord's Prayers, 1965, The People Called Quakers, 1966, The Incendiary Fellowship, 1967, Robert Barclay, 1968, A Place to Stand, 1969, The New Man for our Time, 1970, The Future of the Christian, 1971, The Validity of The Christian Mission, 1972, Abraham Lincoln, Theologian of American Anguish, 1973, While It's Day: An Autobiography; Editor: books relating to field The Friend, 1935-47. Bd. overseers William Penn Coll., 1980-94. Named Churchman of Year Am. Heritage, 1960; Doan Disting. Prof. award Earlham Coll., 1964; Doan Disting. Prof. award Ind. Acad., 1971. Mem. Soc. of Friends. Home: Lansdale Pa. Died Dec. 20, 1994.

TRUEMAN, WALTER, retired advertising agency executive; b. N.Y.C., Oct. 20, 1928; s. David Frank and Bertha H. T.; m. Enid Prussman, Nov. 7, 1953; children—Beth, Deborah, Glenn, Richard. B.A., N.Y. U., 1951. Advt. services dir. Pepsi-Cola Co., Purchase, N.Y., 1966-74; advt. dir. Royal Crown Cola Co., Columbus, GA., 1974-76; sr. v.p., creative mgr. SSC&B, Inc., N.Y.C., 1976-81; sr. v.p., dir. creative ops. McCann-Erickson, N.Y.C., 1981-87; seminar leader, guest speaker in field. Exec. v.p. H.S. Richards Boys Club, Yonkers, N.Y., 1972-74. Served with AUS, 1946-48. Jewish. Home: Yonkers N.Y. Died October 31, 1996.

TRUMBULL, RICHARD, psychologist; b. Johnstown, N.Y., Apr. 6, 1916; s. Milton Elmer and Hazel (Busse) T.; m. Alice Esther McDaniel, June 17, 1939; children—Judith Trumbull Townsend, Joanne Trumbull Titus, Janice Trumbull Smith, Joyce Ellen Trumbull Setzer. A.B., Union Coll., 1937; M.S., Union U., 1939; Ph.D., Syracuse U., 1951. Asst. prof. psychology Green Mountain Jr. Coll., Poultney, Vt., 1939-41; chmn. dept. psychology, 46-49; lectr. Syracuse U., 1941-43; chmn. undergrad. program psychology, 49-51; mem. research staff Sch. Aviation Medicine, U.S. Navy, 1951-53, asst. head physiol. psychology br., Office of Naval Research, 1953-54, head, 1954-61, dir. psychol. scis., 1961-67; dir. research Office Naval Research, Washington, 1967-70; dep. exec. officer AAAS, 1970-74; exec. dir. Am. Inst. Biol. Scis., Arlington, Va., 1974-79, Renewable Natural Resources Found., Bethesda, Md., 1979-80; chmn. adv. group on human factors NATO; research advisory com. NASA; surgeon gen. advisory com. FAA. Author: Research and Its Management, 1984; joint editor: Sensory Deprivation, 1961, Psychological Stress: Issues in Research, 1966, The Dynamics of Stress, 1986, Scientific Freedom and Responsibility in Psychology, Science and Human Affairs, 1994; contbr. articles to profl. jours. Trustee Green Mountain Jr. Coll., Biol. Scis. Info. Service. Served with USNR, 1943-46, 51-53. Recipient Navy Distinguished Civilian Service award, 1961, Longacre award in aerospace medicine, 1966; Sustained Super Accomplishment award, 1966. Mem. AAAS, Aerospace Med. Assn., Natural Resources Council Am. (sec. 1977), Sigma Xi. DIED 05/21/97. .

TRUMBULL, ROBERT, journalist; b. Chgo., May 26, 1912; s. Oliver Morton and Sydney (Farmer) T.; m. Jean Magnier Musson, Sept. 30, 1934; children: Suzanne, Joan, Stephanie. Student, U. Wash., 1930-33. Reporter, city editor Honolulu Advertiser, 1933-43; war corr. Pacific area N.Y. Times, 1941-45; fgn. corr. Pacific area N.Y. Times, Japan, Philippines, South and S.E. Asia, 1945-54; chief bur. Pacific area N.Y. Times, Tokyo, 1954-61, 64-68; chief corr. Pacific area N.Y. Times, China-S.E. Asia, 1961-63; chief S. Pacific bur., corr. N.Y. Times, Australia-N.Z.-Pacific Islands, 1968-73; chief corr. Pacific area N.Y. Times, Can., 1974-78; Pacific corr. N.Y. Times, Honolulu, 1978-93; cons. editor Asia Mail. Author: The Raft (Book-of-the-Month Club selection), 1942, Sol Pluvius' Hawaiian Communiques, 1942, Silversides, 1945, India Since Independence, 1954, As I See India, 1956, Nine Who Survived Hiroshima and Nagasaki, 1957, Paradise in Trust, 1959, The Scrutable East, 1964 (Overseas Press Club Am. award), Tin Roofs and Palm Trees, 1977; contbr. on Asian and Pacific affairs various publs.; Editor: This Is Communist China, 1968. Former mem. U.S. Ednl. Commn. in, Japan; former mem. bd. dirs. U.S. Ednl. Found. in, India. Decorated Commendations, Pacific Theatre Ribbon Navy).; Recipient Better Understanding award English Speaking Union, 1951. Mem. Authors Guild, Authors League Am., Japan-Am. Soc., Pacific-Asia Affairs Council, Honolulu Com. Fgn. Relations, Phi Sigma Kappa, Sigma Delta Chi. Clubs: Overseas Press Am. (N.Y.C.); Fgn. Corrs. Japan; Am. Nat. (Sydney, Australia), Journalists (Sydney, Australia); Gymkhana (New Delhi, India); Rideau (Ottawa), Nat. Press Canada (Ottawa). Home: Honolulu Hawaii Died Oct. 1992.

TRUSTMAN, BENJAMIN ARTHUR, lawyer; b. June 14, 1902; s. Israel and Pessie (Rubin) T.; m. Julia Bertha Myerson, July 31, 1927; children: Alan Robert, Phyllis Anne (Mrs. Robert W. Gelfman). A.B summa cum laude, Harvard U., 1922, J.D., 1925; Sc.D. (hon.), Lowell Coll., 1964; fellow, Brandeis U. Bar: Mass. 1925, Fla. 1953. Asso. Nutter, McClennen & Fish (and predecessor), Boston, 1925-34; mem. firm Nutter, McClennen & Fish (and predecessor), 1934-77; past dir. Wm. Filene's Sons Co., Shawmut Corp., Shawmut Bank of Boston N.A. Co-author: Town Meeting Time, 1962, 2d edit., 1964. Former hon. life dir. Lincoln and Therese Filene Found.; former mem. corp. Eye Research Inst. of Retina Found.; former trustee Met. Mus., Coral Gables, Fla.; former dir. John F. Kennedy Ctr. Performing Arts, Washington; hon. life mem., patron bd. visitors dept. prints and drawings, life overseer, donor Prints and Drawings Gallery, Boston Mus. Fine Arts; donor Daumier Print Dept. Brandeis U.; former elective town moderator, Brookline, Mass.; donor Trustman Art Gallery and Trustman travelling fellowships, Simmons Coll., Boston; past chmn. Brookline Housing Authority; past mem. nat. adv. council Am. Assn. Jewish Edn.; past mem. adv. council Lincoln Filene Ctr. Law in Social Studies Project, Tufts U.; former dir. United Community Services Met. Boston; founder Trustman Travelling Fellowships Harvard U., donor Trustman Scholarship Fund, Harvard Law Sch.; life trustee, past pres. Hebrew Coll., Boston; donor Trustman Lecture Hall, John F. Kennedy Sch. Govt., Harvard U.; life trustee, past chmn. bd. mgrs., past pres. Combined Jewish Philanthropies Greater Boston; life trustee, past chmn. bd. mgrs., former v.p., donor, bd. dirs. meeting rm. Beth Israel Hosp. Assn., Boston; founding mem. Mass. Council Arts and Humanities; past mem. bd. visitors Lowell Coll. Recipient Nat. Brotherhood award NCCJ, 1964; Benjamin A. Trustman Apts. dedicated by Brookline Housing Authority, 1975. Mem. Harvard U. Law Sch. Assn. (life), Am., Mass., Fla. Boston bar assns., Am. Law Inst. (life), Am. Jewish Hist. Soc. (patron, life), Nat. Phi Beta Kappa Assos. (life), Phi Beta Kappa (Harvard Alpha chpt.). Jewish (trustee temple). Clubs: Miami Shores Country; Harvard (Miami) (dir.). Leading collector works of Honoré Daumier.

TSONGAS, PAUL EFTHEMIOS, lawyer, former senator; b. Lowell, Mass., Feb. 14, 1941; s. Efthemios and Katina Tsongas; m. Nicola Sauvage, Dec. 21, 1969; children: Ashley, Katina, Molly. BA, Dartmouth Coll., 1962; LLB, Yale U., 1967. Bar: Mass. Tng. coord. Peace Corps, W.I., 1967-68; mem. Gov.'s Com. on Law Enforcement, 1968-69; dep. asst. atty. gen. Mass., 1969-71; pvt. practice, 1971-74; mem. 94th-95th Congresses from 5th Mass. dist., 1975-79; U.S. senator from Mass., 1979-85; ptnr. Foley, Hoag & Eliot, Boston, 1985-97; Dem. candidate for U.S. pres., 1992; mem. energy and natural resources com., mem. com. on small bus., mem. fgn. rels. com., co-chmn. ad-hoc Congl. monitoring group on So. Africa. Author: The Road From Here, 1981, Heading Home, 1984, A Call to Economic Arms, 1992, Journey of Purpose, 1996. Vol. Peace Corps, Ethiopia, 1962-64; city councillor City of Lowell, 1969-72; county commr. Middlesex County, 1973-74; chmn. Mass. Bd. Regents of Higher Edn., 1989-91; bd. govs. Am. Stock Exch. Democrat. Greek Orthodox. Home: Lowell Mass.

TULL, DONALD STANLEY, marketing educator; b. Mo., Oct. 28, 1924; s. Raymond Edgar and Ethel (Stanley) T.; m. Marjorie Ann Dobbie, May 15, 1948; children: Susan Margaret, David Dobbie, Brooks William. S.B., U. Chgo., 1948, M.B.A., 1949, Ph.D., 1956. Analyst U.S. Steel Corp., 1949-50; instr. U. Wash., 1950-52; mgr. adminstrn. N.Am. Aviation, 1954-61; prof. mktg. Calif. State U., Fullerton, 1961-67; dean Sch. Bus. Adminstrn. and Econs., 1966-67; prof. mktg. Coll. Mgmt. and Bus. U. Oreg., 1967-90, chmn. dept. mktg., transp. and bus. environment, 1967-69, 73-81. Author: (with P.E. Green and G.S. Albaum) Research for Marketing Decisions, 1987, (with G.S. Albaum) Survey Research, 1973, (with L.R. Kahle) Marketing Management, 1989, (with D.I. Hawkins) Marketing Research: Measurement and Method, 1993, Essentials of Marketing Research, 1994. Served to lt. (j.g.) USNR, 1943-46. Mem. AAUP (pres. 1978-79), Beta Gamma Sigma. Home: Eugene Oreg. Died Aug. 24, 1996.

TULLY, ANDREW FREDERICK, JR., writer; b. Southbridge, Mass., Oct. 24, 1914; s. Andrew F. and Amelia (Mason) T.; m. Mary Dani, Apr. 15, 1939 (div.); children: Martha Hardy, Mary Elizabeth, Sheila, Andrew Frederick III, Mark; m. Barbara Witchell, Sept. 5, 1960 (div.); m. Mary Ellen Wood, Dec. 19, 1964; 1 child, John Spaulding. Grad. high sch. Reporter Worcester (Mass.) Post, 1936-38, Southbridge Evening News, 1933-36; editor, owner Southbridge Press, weekly, 1939-42; war corr. Boston Traveller, ETO, 1944-45; rewrite, feature N.Y. World Telegram, 1945-47; free-lance, 1947-48; with Washington bur. Scripps-Howard Newspapers, 1948-61; Washington columnist McNaught Syndicate, 1961-67; dir. United Dairy Equipment Co., West Chester, Pa., 1967-87. Author: Era of Elegance, 1947, Treasury Agent, 1958, A Race of Rebels, 1960, When They Burned the White House, 1961, CIA: The Inside Story, 1962, Capitol Hill, 1962, Berlin: Story of a Battle, 1963, Supreme Court, 1963, (with Milton Britten) Where Did Your Money Go?, 1964, The FBI's Most Famous Cases, 1965, The Time of the Hawk, 1967, White Tie and Dagger, 1967, The Super Spies, 1969, The Secret War Against Dope, 1973, The Brahmin Arrangement, 1974, Inside the FBI, 1979, also articles in mags. Recipient Ernie Pyle award for series on Soviet Russia, 1955; Headliners award, 1956. Mem. White House Corrs. Assn. Club: Cosmos. Home: Washington D.C. Died Sept. 27, 1993.

TURNBULL, FRED GERDES, electronics engineer; b. Oakland, Calif., Apr. 12, 1931; s. Fred and Gertrude Turnbull; m. Nancy Greene, Aug. 22, 1959; children: Fred, David. BSEE, U. Calif., Berkeley, 1953, MSEE, 1959. Electronics engr. corp. rsch. devel. ctr. GE, Schenectady, N.Y., 1959-93; cons. Scotia, N.Y., 1993-97. Co-author: Power Electronic Control Of AC Motors, 1988. Lt. (j.g.) USN, 1954-57. Fellow IEEE; assoc. mem. Sigma Xi. Home: Scotia N.Y. Died Feb. 24, 1997.

TURNBULL, WILLIAM, JR., architect; b. N.Y.C., Apr. 1, 1935; s. William and Elizabeth (Howe) T. A.B., Princeton U., 1956, M.F.A. in Architecture, 1959; student, Ecole des Beaux Arts Fontainebleau, France, 1956. With Skidmore, Owings & Merrill, San Francisco, 1960-63; founding ptnr. Moore, Lyndon, Turnbull, Whitaker, 1962; partner-in-charge Moore, Turnbull (San Francisco office), 1965-69; mem. design group Pres.'s Adv. Coun. Pennsylvania Ave., 1963; lectr. U. Calif.-Berkeley, Berkeley, 1965-69; vis. prof. U. Oreg., 1966-68; dir. MLTW/Turnbull Assocs., 1970-83; dir. William Turnbull Assocs. William Turnbull Assocs., 1983—; lectr. Stanford U., 1974-77, vis. design critic MIT, 1975, U. Calif., Berkeley, 1977-81, 95; Mobil vis. design critic Yale U., 1982, Bishop vis. prof. archtl. design, 1986; Hyde prof. excellence U. Nebr., 1994; design cons. Formica Corp., 1977-84, World Savs. and Loan, 1976-95; mem. design rev. bd. U. Calif., San Diego, 1988-93, City of Sausalito, Calif., 1976-77; mem. fgn. bldgs. adv. bd. Dept. of State, 1991—; design critic Calif. Coll. Arts & Crafts, 1997. Author: Global Architecture Series: Moore, Lyndon, Turnbull & Whitaker: The Sea Ranch, The Sea Ranch Details, The Poetics of Gardens, 1988; illustrator: The Place of Houses; prin. works include Sea Ranch Condominium I, 1965, Sea Ranch Swim Tennis Club, 1966, Lovejoy Fountain Plaza, Portland (assoc. architect), Faculty Club at U. Calif.-Santa Barbara, Kresge Coll. at U. Calif.-Santa Cruz, Biloxi (Miss.) Library, Am. Club, Hong Kong, Ariz. State U. Sonora Ctr., Tempe, Foothill Student Housing, U. Calif., Berkeley, Mountain View City Hall and Community Theater, Calif., Grace Cathedral Close, San Francisco, St. Andrews Ch., Sonoma, Calif.; mem. editl. adv. bd. Architecture California, 1986-92. Mem. tech. adv. com. Calif. Legislature Joint Com. Open Space Lands, 1968-71; mem. regional honor awards (90) jury AIA, 1968—, nat. honor awards jury, 1969, chmn. jury, 1977, 1988; chmn. jury C.E. honor award, 1973, 79; mem. Progressive Architecture Honor Awards Jury, 1975, Pres.'s Jury for Nat. Design Excellence, 1984; bd. dirs. Pub. Sculpture Pub. Places, 1981-85. Served with AUS, 1959-60. Recipient Calif. Gov. award Planned Communities, 1966, citation Progressive Architecture Design awards, 1962-66, 68-70, 81, 1st honor award, 1971, 74, 1st honor award Homes for Better Living, 1963, Merit award, 1966; Honor award Western Home awards, 1961-62, 62, 63, 66-67, 88, 89, 93, 95; Merit award, 1966-67; House of Yr. award Archtl. Record, 1961, 67, 69, 70, 72, 83; award of Honor San Francisco Art Commn., 1982; Am. Wood Coun. Design award, 1984, Honor award, 1985, 89, 92, 93, 94; Firm of Yr. award Calif. Coun. AIA, 1986, Maybeck award, 1993, cited for continuous distinctive practice of architecture in Calif. by an individual; Am. Wood Coun. Merit award, 1991; Honor award San Francisco AIA, 1988, 91, 93. Fellow AIA (dir. chpt. 1981, Nat. Honor award 1967, 68, 73, 79, 90, 91, 95, award of merit Bay Region honor awards 1963, 67, 7, 78, 82, Nat. 25 Yr. Honor award 1991), Am. Acad. in Rome. DIED 06/26/97.

TURNER, ALAN FORBES, publishing company executive; b. N.Y.C., Dec. 14, 1929; s. Kenneth Burlen and Helen Forbes (McIlvaine) T.; m. Jeanne Rita Magee, Mar. 25, 1961; children—Kenneth Burlen II, Kate Fitzpatrick. B.A., Yale U., 1951. Various positions Holt, Rinehart and Winston, N.Y.C., 1954-66; editor-in-chief coll. div. Holt, Rinehart and Winston, 1966-68; asst. v.p. Acad. Press, N.Y.C.; v.p. Intext, N.Y.C., Thomas Y. Crowell, N.Y.C., 1973-77; editorial dir. Chilton Book Co., Radnor, Pa., 1977—. Served to 1st lt. U.S. Army, 1951-53, Korea. Democrat. Roman Catholic.

TURNER, MARY ANN THORNBURG, nurse; b. Tulsa, Nov. 15, 1933; d. B. Ralph and Helen E. (Morin) Thornburg; children: Dan, Elaine, Randy. Student, St. Paul Sch. Nursing, Dallas, 1955, U. Rochester, 1951-52, Amber U., 1990-91. RN, Tex.; cert. ins. rehab. specialist; cert. case mgr. Operating rm. staff HCA South Arlington Med. Ctr., Arlington, Tex., 1986-88; rehab. coord. Profl. Rehab. Manage, Dallas, 1988-89; 7-3 supr. Dallas Meml. Hosp., 1989-90; ind. ins. rehab. Dallas, 1990-95; mgr. disability med. case Metra Health Conservco, Dallas, 1995—. Died Oct. 17, 1995.

TURRELL, EUGENE SNOW, retired psychiatrist; b. Hyattsville, Md., Feb. 27, 1919; m. Denise Deuprey, Dec. 26, 1942 (div. Jan. 1976); children: David Hillyer, Gregory Sherman (dec.); m. Zenobia A. Hopper, Apr. 16, 1988; stepchildren: Elizabeth Ann Crofoot, Mary Jane Cooper. BS, Ind. U., 1939, MD, 1947. Diplomate Am. Bd. Psychiatry and Neurology. Intern Peter Bent Brigham Hosp., Boston, 1947-48; resident physician Kandakee (Ill.) State Hosp., 1948-49; clin. asst. psychiatry U. Calif., San Francisco, 1949-51; asst. prof. Ind. U. Sch. Medicine, 1952-53, assoc. prof., 1953-58; prof., chmn. dept. psychiatry Marquette U. Sch. Medicine, 1958-63, clin. prof. psychiatry, 1963-69; lectr. U. Calif., San Francisco, 1969-75; assoc. prof. Ind. U., 1975-80, prof., 1980-89, prof. emeritus, 1989-96; dean emeritus San Diego County Psychiat. Hosp., 1995-96, 1995-96; assoc. clin. prof. U. Calif., San Diego, 1991-95; ret., 1995; mem., bd. dirs. Community Addictions Svcs. Agy, Indpls., 1975-79, pres. bd., 1976-77. Contr. articles to profl. jours. Lt. USNR, 1950-52. Recipient Certs. of Appreciation Office Sci. Rsch. and Devel., 1945, VA, 1964, Ind. U. Found., 1966. Fellow Am. Psychiat. Assn. (life); mem. AMA (Physician's Recognition award 1978-96), AAAS, Calif. State Med. Assn., Calif. State Psychiat. Assn., San Diego County Med. Soc., San Diego County Soc. Psychiat. Physicians, Sigma Xi, Alpha Omega Alpha. Democrat. Episcopalian. Avocations: tennis, motorcycling, bridge, literature, arts. Died July 8, 1996.

TUTHILL, JOHN WILLS, former diplomat, educator; b. Montclair, N.J., Nov. 10, 1910; s. Oliver Bailey and Louise Jerolomen (Wills) T.; m. Erna Lueders, July 3, 1937; children: Carol Anne (dec.), David. SB, Coll. William and Mary, 1932, LLD, 1978; MBA, NYU, 1936; AM, Harvard U., 1943; LLD, MacMurray Coll., 1967. Teller First Nat. Bank, Paterson, N.J., 1932-34; corporate trust adminstr. Bankers Trust Co. N.Y., 1934-36; investment counsel Fiduciary Counsel, N.Y.C., 1936-37; instr. Northeastern U., 1937-39, asst. prof. banking and finance, 1939-40; apptd. fgn. service officer Dept. State, 1940; served as vice counsul Windsor, Ont., Can., 1940-41, Mazatlan, Mexico, 1942; 3d sec. embassy Ottawa, Ont., 1942-44; sec. mission Office U.S. Polit. Adviser SHAEF, 1944-45; sec. mission and Am. Mil. Govt. for Germany, 1945-47, Am. consul, 1947; asst. chief shipping div. Dept. State, 1948, adviser, 1949; counselor of embassy Stockholm, 1949-51; spl. asst. ambassador London, 1952; dep. dir. Office Econ. Affairs, Bonn, W. Ger., 1952-54, USOM, Bonn, 1954; dir. USOM, 1954-56, counselor of embassy for econ. affairs, 1955-56; counselor embassy for econ. affairs with personal rank of minister Paris, 1956-59; dir. Office European Regional Affairs, Dept. State, 1959; minister-counselor econ. affairs U.S. Mission to NATO, European Regional Orgns., U.S.; rep. prep. com. for OECD; also dep. U.S. rep. OEEC, 1960; U.S. rep. OECD with personal rank of ambassador, 1960-62; U.S. ambassador to European Communities, 1962-66, Brazil, 1966-69; prof. internat. politics Johns Hopkins U., Bologna Center, Italy, 1969; pres. Salzburg Seminar in Am. Studies, Cambridge, Mass., 1977-85; vis. fellow Woodrow Wilson Nat. Fellowship Found., Princeton, 1978-80; exec. dir., trustee The Am.-Austrian Found., 1985-88. Author: Some Things to Some Men: Serving in the Foreign Service, 1995. Gov. Atlantic Inst. for Internat. Affairs, Paris, 1969-86, dir. gen. 1969-76. Recipient All Am. Silver Anniversary award Sports Illustrated, 1956; named to Athletic Hall of Fame Coll. William and Mary, 1979; Dir. Gen.'s Cup Dept. State, 1983. Mem. N.Y. Coun. Fgn. Rels., Washington Inst. Fgn. Policy, Am. Acad. Diplomacy (bd. dirs.), Jean Monnet Coun. (bd. dirs. 1985-95), Harvard Club (N.Y.C.), Cosmos Club (Washington), Flat Hat of William and Mary, Omicron Delta Kappa, Theta Delta Chi. Died Sept. 9, 1996.

TUTT, CHARLES LEAMING, JR., educational administrator, former mechanical engineering educator; b. Coronado, Calif., Jan. 26, 1911; s. Charles Leaming and Eleanor (Armit) T.; m. Pauline Barbara Shaffer, Aug. 16, 1933 (dec. Aug. 1981); children: Charles Leaming IV, William Bullard; m. Mildred Dailey LeMieux, Aug. 7, 1982; stepchildren: Linda Dailey LeMieux, Leslie Evans LeMieux. BSE, Princeton U., 1933, ME, 1934; D in Engring., Norwich U., 1967. Student engr. Buick Motor div. GM, Flint, Mich., 1934-36; engr. chassis unit sect. Buick Motor div. GM, 1936-38, spl. assignment engr., 1938-40; asst. prof. mech. engring. Princeton U., 1940-46; staff asst. ASME, N.Y.C., 1940-44; assoc. editor Product Engring. mag. McGraw-Hill Pub. Co., N.Y.C., 1944-46; asst. to pres. Gen. Motors Inst., Flint, 1946-50; adminstrv. chmn. Gen. Motors Inst., 1950-60, dean engring., 1960-69, dean acad. affairs, 1969-75; pres. Sunnyrest Sanitarium, Colorado Springs, Colo., 1982-93, chmn., 1989-93. Contbr. articles to profl. jours. Mem. adv. com. Sloan Mus., Flint, 1965-82; trustee Norwich U., Northfield, Vt., 1963-76; bd. dirs. Engring. Found., N.Y.C., 1963-75, chmn., 1967-73; v.p. Friends of Pike Peak Libr. Dist., 1985-88, pres., 1986-88; mem. adv. bd. Pikes Peak Community Coll., 1986-93. Fellow ASME (life, v.p. 1964-66, pres. 1975-76); mem. Soc. Mfg. Engrs. (dir. 1972-78), Am. Soc. Engring. Edn., Soc. Automotive Engrs., Colo. Soc. Profl. Engrs., Engrs. Coun. for Profl. Devel. (dir. 1975-80), Am. Soc. Metals, Soc. of Cin. in State of Va., Sigma Xi, Delta Tau Delta, Tau Beta Pi. Clubs.: Flint City, University (Flint), Wigwam (Deckers, Colo.), Princeton (N.Y.C.), Cooking, Cheyenne Mountain Country (Colorado Springs), Broadmoor Golf. Home: Colorado Springs Colo. Died Nov. 3, 1993.

TUTT, RUSSELL THAYER, investment company executive; b. Coronado, Calif., July 27, 1913; s. Charles Leaming and Eleanor (Armit) T.; m. Margaret Louise Honnen, Aug. 12, 1950 (dec. Nov. 1974); children: Margaret Honnen Tutt Steinegger, Russell Thayer. B.S. in Engring., Princeton U., 1935. With buying dept. Halsey, Stuart & Co., Inc., N.Y.C., 1935-40; v.p., gen. mgr. Garden City (Kans.) Co., 1946-56; pres. S.W. Kans. Power, Inc., Garden City, 1946-56; v.p. El Pomar Investment Co., Colorado Springs, Colo., 1956-61; pres. El Pomar Investment Co., 1961-82; chmn. El Pomar Investment Co., Colo. Springs, 1982-86, now pres.; chmn. bd. Holly Sugar Corp., 1977-81; chmn. exec. com. Affiliated Bank Shares of Colo., Inc., 1970-84, CENTEL Corp.; pres. Garden City Co., 1956-92; pres. Broadmoor Hotel, Inc., 1977-82, chmn., 1982-91; chmn. bd. First Nat. Bank Colorado Springs., 1975-84. Trustee Cheyenne Mountain Mus. and Zool. Soc., 1956—, pres., 1963-74, chmn. bd., 1974-80, hon. chmn. bd., 1980—; chmn., trustee El Pomar Found., 1982-89, chmn. exec. com. 1989-92; trustee Colo. Coll., 1957—, chmn., 1966-84; life trustee Fountain Valley Sch. of Colo., Nat. Recreation Found., N.Y.C. Maj. AUS, 1940-45. Decorated Bronze Star. Republican. Episcopalian. Clubs: Cheyenne Mountain Country (Colorado Springs), Broadmoor Golf (Colorado Springs), El Paso (Colorado Springs), Country of Colo. (Colorado Springs), Cooking (Colorado Springs). Deceased.

TUTTLE, M(ARGARET) DIANE, infosystems executive; b. Kansas City, Mo., Aug. 11, 1945; d. Allen T. and Vernia Margaret (Pugh) Ashbaugh; m. Robert Stephen Tuttle; 1 child, Robert Stephen II. BBA, Baker U. Supr. bus. officer South Cen. Bell Tel. Co., 1975-80, supr. network adminstrn., 1980-81, project mgr. billing adminstrn. and contracts, 1981-83, mgr. data telecommunications data systems, 1983-85; sr. mgr. telecommunications, mgmt. infosystems Fed. Express, Memphis, 1985—. Active Alcohol and Drug Coun., Memphis, 1987. Fellow Data Processing Mgmt. Assn.; mem. Christian Bus. Women's Club. Republican. Baptist. Avocations: aerobics, running, gardening. Deceased.

UHL, VINCENT WILLIAM, chemical engineer, consultant, educator emeritus; b. Phila., May 16, 1917; s. Joseph and Anna Elizabeth (Schuck) U.; m. Frances Kathryn Crowe, Nov. 28, 1940; children—Ann Marie Uhl Judson, Vincent William, Christopher, Frances Theresa (dec.), Monica Uhl Oat. B.Sc., Drexel U., 1940; M.S., Lehigh U., 1949, Ph.D., 1952. Registered profl. engr., Pa. Devel. engr. The Sun Co., Marcus Hook, Pa., 1940-44; asst. mgr. heat transfer div. Downingtown Iron Works, Pa., 1944-46; instr. chem. engring. Lehigh U., Bethlehem, PA., 1947-51; mgr. process equipment div. The Bethlehem Corp., Pa., 1951-54; assoc. prof. chem. engring. Villanova U., Pa., 1954-57; assoc. prof. chem. engring. Drexel U., Phila., 1957-60, prof., 1960-63; prof. chem. engring. U. Va., Charlottesville, 1963-84, prof. emeritus, 1985—, chmn. dept., 1963-74; sr. chem. engring. advisor EPA, Research Triangle Park, N.C., 1966-68; cons. in field. Author: Technical Economics for Engineers, 1971. Sr. editor, contbg. author: Mixing: Theory and Practice, 1966, 67, 86. Contbr. articles to profl. jours. NSF fellow 1962-63. Fellow Am. Inst. Chem. Engrs.; mem. Am. Chem. Soc., Sigma Xi, Tau Beta Pi, Phi Kappa Phi. Democrat. Roman Catholic. Avocations: tennis; cooking; travel. Office: Univ Va Dept Chem Engring Charlottesville VA 22901

ULLRICH, JOHN FREDERICK, diversified manufacturing company executive; b. Kalamazoo, Aug. 27, 1940; s. Frederick John and Opal Louise (Confer) U.; m. Susan K. Brundage, July 16, 1962; children: Frederick, Kathryn, Amy. BS in Engring. Physics, U. Mich. 1962, MS in Nuclear Engring., 1963, PhD in Nuc. Engring., 1967. Mgr. ignition systems dept. Ford Motor Co., Dearborn, Mich., 1975-76, mgr. vehicle evaluation, 1976-77, exec. engr. elec. and electronics div., 1977-79; v.p. sci. and tech. Internat. Harvester Co., Hinsdale, Ill., 1979-81, v.p. components engring. and devel., 1981-82, v.p. quality and reliability, 1982-83, v.p. mfg. engine and foundry div., 1983-86; v.p. strategic mgmt. Ex-Cell-o Corp., Troy, Mich., 1986, group v.p. Textron, Inc., Providence, R.I., 1987, v.p. ethics and environ. affairs, 1987-88; v.p. tech. and support svcs. Masco Corp., Taylor, Mich., 1988-96. Mem. Mich. Rep. State Ctrl. Com., 1971-75; chmn. Reps. of Dearborn, 1972-74; alt. del. Rep. Nat. Conv., 1972; mem. bd. regents Ea. Mich. U., 1974-79, trustee Ea. Mich. U. Found., 1990-96; mem. nat. adv. bd. Coll. Engring., U. Mich., corp. rels. and nat. campaign coms. U. Mich., 1981-96, alumni mem. Coll. Engring. planning com., 1993-94, mem. bd. govs., 1995-96; divsn. chmn. Chgo. United Way, 1983, Detroit United Way, 1986; mem. guarantor's com. Goodman Theatre, Chgo., 1980-83; mem. editorial adv. bd. Mfg. Engring. Mag., 1983-90; mem. nat. adv. bd. Nat. Kidney Found., 1989-95; mem. corp. devel. com., Univ. Mich. Mus. Art, Rackham Grad. Sch., 1990-96; pres. Ann Arbor Art Assn., 1993-95, bd. dirs. 1993-96; bd. dirs. Ind. Tech. Inst., 1993-96, Ann Arbor Hands on Mus., 1994-96, Mich. Artrain, 1995-96, ERIM, 1995-96. Named Outstanding Alumnus, 1984, Alumni Soc. award, 1992; recipient Cmty. Svc. award Ford Motor Co., 1969, 73. Mem. Soc. Automotive Engrs., Soc. Mfg. Engrs., Engring. Soc. Detroit (chmn. membership com. 1989-90, Cmty. Svc. award 1991, bd. dirs. 1992-96, treas. 1994-95, gen. chair IPC 1995, v.p. 1995-96), Barton Hills Country Club, Hinsdale Golf Club, L'Arbre Croche Club, Sigma Xi, Tau Beta Pi, Kappa Kappa Psi. Republican. Presbyterian. Died March 7, 1996; buried Riverside Cemetery, Kalamazoo, MI. Home: Ann Arbor Mich.

UMEZAWA, HIROOMI, physics educator, researcher; b. Saitama-ken, Japan, Sept. 20, 1924; came to Can., 1975; s. Junichi and Takako (Sato) U.; m. Tamae Yamagami, July 30, 1958; children: Rui, Ado. B of Engring., U. Nagoya, Japan, 1947, DSc in Physics, 1952. Research asst. U. Nagoya, 1947-53, assoc. prof., 1953; assoc. prof. U. Tokyo, 1955, prof., 1960-64; prof. U. Napoli Inst. Theoretical Physics, Italy, 1964-66; prof. U. Wis., Milw., 1967-67, disting. prof., 1967-75; dir. Inst. Theoretical Physics, Helsinki, Finland, 1965; group leader on structure of matter Centre of Nat. Research Naples div., Italy, 1964-66; Killam Meml. prof. sci., prof. physics U. Alta., Edmonton, Can., 1975-92, Killam prof. emeritus, 1992—; vis. prof. U. Wash., Seattle, 1956, U. Md., College Park, 1957, U. Iowa, Iowa City, 1957, U. Marseille, France, 1959. Mem. editorial bd. Physics Essays, NRC Can.; contbr. numerous articles to profl. jours. ICI fellow U. Manchester, Eng., 1953-55; Lady Davis Sr. scholar, Israel, 1989; Two books published in honor of his 60th birthday, 1985, 86; several internat. workshops held in his honor. Fellow N.Y. Acad. Scis., Am. Phys. Soc., Royal Soc. Can.; mem. Japan Phys. Soc. (life). Home: Edmonton Can. DIED 03/00/95. .

UPTON, RICHARD F., lawyer; b. Bow, N.H., Sept. 3, 1914; s. Robert W. and Martha G. U.; m. Marie Audibert, Sept. 23, 1950 (dec. 1970); children: William W., Mathew H.; m. Shirley D. Knowland, May 17, 1975. Grad., Phillips Exeter Acad., 1931; A.B., Dartmouth, 1935; LL.B., Harvard, 1938. Bar: N.H. 1938. Practice law Concord, 1938—; Dir. Concord Nat. Bank, Concord Group Ins. Cos. Author: Revolutionary New Hampshire, 1936, drafted N.H. Presidential Primary Law, 1949. Mem. N.H. State Housing Bd., 1946-48, N.H. War Records Com., 1946-51, N.H. Commn. Alcoholism, 1951-63, N.H. Commn. Interstate Cooperation, 1951-55; chmn. N.H. Civil Rights Adv. Commn., 1958-62, N.H. Lincoln Sesquicentennial Com., 1958-60; mem. N.H. Com. Study Pub. Schs., 1961-63; mem. N.H. Hist. Commn., 1963-68, chmn., 1965-68; chmn. N.H. Fish and Game Commn., 1968-74; chmn. com. environ. systems N.H. Citizens' Task Force, 1969-70; mem. N.H. Interstate Wetlands Commn., 1969-70; chmn. N.H. Environ. Council, 1970-71; mem. N.H. Boundary Commn., 1971-73, N.H. Am. Revolutionary Bicentennial Com., 1969-75, Mem. N.H. Legislature, 1941, 47, 49, maj. floor leader, 1947, speaker, 1949; pres. 15th N.H. Constl. Conv., 1964 (pres.), 17th N.H. Constl. Conv., 1984; trustee N.H. Hosp., 1946-48. Served to capt. AUS, 1942-46. Fellow Am. Bar Found.; mem. ABA, N.H. Bar Assn. (pres. 1964-65), N.H. Hist. Soc. (pres. 1974-80, trustee 1980—). Died Aug. 12, 1996.

UZE, IRVING, automotive executive; b. Chelsea, Mass., June 21, 1918; s. Philip and Ann (Connoers) U.; m. Rosalynn Siegel, Apr. 6, 1941 (dec. May 1985); m. Meriam Breitholz, July 17, 1990; children: Martin Andrew, Beth Ellen, Vicki Jean. Grad., N.E. Conservatory of Music, Boston, 1939. Pres. ESCO Corp., Waterloo, Iowa, 1946-83, Cen. States Distbn. Warehouse, Waterloo, 1961-83, Royal Oaks Co., Cedar Falls, Iowa, 1969-91; pres., treas., sec. BANVIR Corp., Waterloo, 1961—; pres. Banyan Pt., Inc., PGI. Solicited Iowa rep. for Richard Nixon, 1961, Ronald Reagan, 1979-80. With USN, 1943-45. Mem. Seminole Lakes Country Club, Sunnyside Country Club, Burnt Store Country Club, Shriner, Mason (32 degree). Avocation: physical activities. Home: Delray Beach Fla. Died Mar. 3, 1997.

VAILLE, LORRAINE LA CAVA, educator; b. San Francisco, Sept. 2, 1924; d. Rocco Anthony and Anne Marie (Bernhard) La Cava; m. Alexander Vladimiroff Vaille, Mar. 6, 1945; children: Alexander, John, Christopher, David. BA in Edn., Calif. State U., San Francisco, 1958; MA in Edn., Calif. State U., Turlock, 1976. Cert. gen. edn., learning handicapped specialist, resource specialist, adminstrv. svcs. Asst. dir. Modesto (Calif.) Adult Edn. Nursery Sch., 1953-57; dir., founder Aid Retarded Children Nursery Sch., Modesto, 1957-58; tchr. Sylvan Union Sch. Dist., Modesto, 1960-61; asst., tutor, cons. Modesto Rehab. Svcs., 1968-87; tchr. Stanislaus County Dept. Edn., Modesto, 1978—; dir. Small Talk Child Ctr., Modesto, 1980-84; resource specialist Stanislaus County Dept. Edn., Modesto, 1970—; instr. in-svc. tng., assessments and teaching techs.; cons. in field. Author: (video) A Multi-Sensory Classroom; contbr. articles to profl. jours.; singer various orgns. Life mem. PTA, pres. 1970; singer Stockton Chorale. Mem. NEA, Calif. Tchrs. Assn., Calif. Assn. Resource Specialists (founder Stanislaus chpt.), Stanislaus Reading Assn., Orton Dyslexia Soc., Phi Delta Kappa. Republican. Roman Catholic. Avocation: singing, travelling. Home: Modesto Calif. Deceased.

VALENCY, MAURICE, educator, playwright; b. N.Y.C., Mar. 22, 1903; s. Jacques and Mathilde (Solesme) V.; m. Janet Cornell, Dec. 25, 1936. A.B., CCNY, 1923; A.M., Columbia U., 1924, LL.B., 1927, Ph.D., 1939; Litt.D., L.I. U., 1975. Bar: N.Y. 1928. Instr. philosophy CCNY, 1931-33; instr. English Bklyn. Coll., 1933-42, asst. prof., 1942-46; assoc. prof. comparative lit. Columbia U., 1946-54, prof., 1954-71, Brander Matthews prof. dramatic lit., 1968-71, emeritus prof., 1971—; vis. prof. Grad. Ctr., CUNY, 1985-87, Hunter Coll., 1987-89; dir. acad. studies Juilliard Sch., N.Y.C., 1971-85; over-all adviser text-film div. McGraw-Hill Co. Author: The Tragedies of Herod, 1939, In Praise of Love, 1958, The Flower and the Castle, 1963, The Breaking String, 1966, The Cart and the Trumpet, 1973, The End of the World, 1980, Ashby, 1983, Julie, 1988, Tragedy, 1990, The Linden Tree, 1992; playwright: The Thracian Horses, 1940, Battleship Bismarck, 1945, The Reluctant Virgin, 1948, The Madwoman of Chaillot (after Giraudoux), 1949, The Enchanted, 1950, Ondine, 1954, The Virtuous Island, 1955, Feathertop, 1959, The Queen's Gambit, 1956, The Apollo of Bellac, 1954, The Visit (after Duerrenmatt), 1958, Savonarola, 1974, Electra, 1975, Conversation with a Sphinx, 1976; librettist: La Perichole, 1957, The Gypsy Baron, 1959, The Reluctant King, 1974, Feathertop, 1979; editor: The Palace of Pleasure, 1960, Giraudoux, Four Plays, 1958; adv. editor for humanities: Ency. Americana. Recipient award Sigma Tau Found., 1991; Ford Found. rsch. fellow, 1958; Guggenheim fellow, 1961, 65. Mem. Internat. Assn. U. Profs. English, Authors League (council, sec. 1968-75, v.p. 1967, dir. Authors League Fund), Dramatists League Fund (v.p.), Dramatists Guild, MLA, Acad. Lit. Studies, Renaissance Soc., Asia Soc., A.S.C.A.P. (awards 1964—), Am. Comparative Lit. Assn. (adv. bd.), Dante Soc., Writers Guild East. Club: Century Assn. (N.Y.C.). also: Point Salines Grenada DIED 09/28/96. .

VAN ACKEREN, MAURICE EDWARD, college administrator; b. Cedar Rapids, Nebr., Aug. 21, 1911; s. Edward M. and Frances (O'Leary) Van A. B.A. in Chemistry, Creighton U., 1932; M.A. in Edn., St. Louis U., 1946; LL.D. (hon.), Benedictine Coll., 1976. Ordained Jesuit priest Roman Cath. Ch., 1943. Tchr. Campion High Sch., Prairie du Chien, Wis., 1937-40; prin. St. Louis U. High Sch., 1946-51; pres. Rockhurst Coll., Kansas City, Mo., 1951-77, chancellor, 1977-97. Recipient Knight of Holy Sepulchre award Catholic Ch., Chgo., 1968, Chancellor's medal U. Mo.-Kansas City, 1981, Mr. Kansas City award Greater Kansas City C. of C., 1983; named to Creighton U. Athletic Hall of Fame, Omaha, 1971; named Mktg. Exec. of Yr., Sales and Mktg. Club Kansas City, 1979. Mem. C. of C. of Greater Kansas City. Lodge: Rotary (Paul Harris fellow 1983). Avocations: fishing; golf; baseball; football. Died May 12, 1997.

VAN ARSDELL, PAUL MARION, economics and finance educator; b. Indpls., Sept. 25, 1905; s. Marion and Katherine (Palmer) Van A.; m. Sophia Wilsford Smith, Sept. 15, 1946; children: Paul Marion, Stephen Cottrell. Student, Ind. U., 1923-24; B.S., U. Ill., 1927, M.S., 1929, Ph.D., 1935. Mem. faculty U. Ill., Urbana, 1927-94; successively asst. examiner Office of Registrar U. Ill., teaching staff dept. econs., vice chmn. dept. econs., assoc. dean Coll. Commerce and Bus. Adminstrn., 1927-57, prof. finance and head dept., 1957-71, prof. finance emeritus, 1971-94; distinguished prof. finance Fla. Atlantic U., 1971-75; Armco alumni prof. finance Miami U., Oxford, Ohio, 1975-80; cons. analysis of risk and profitability in Bell Telephone System AT&T, 1955-59, 64-65, 69-70; prin. bus. economist, iron and steel price br. OPA, 1942-43; mem. adv. bd. Urbana-Champaign div. Champion Fed. Savs. and Loan Assn., 1983-92. Author: Problem Manual in Security Analysis, 1940, Problem Manual in Corporation Finance, rev. edit, 1958, Corporation Finance: Policy, Planning, Administration, 1968; mem editorial bd.: Quar. Rev. Econs. and Bus, 1962-77; contbr. articles to profl. jours. Chmn. U. Ill. YMCA, 1949-54; dir. Citizens Bldg. Assn., Urbana, 1967-82; trustee Millikin U., 1970-73; exec. com. Urbana-Champaign chpt. State Univs. Annuitants Assn., 1981-83. Served from lt. (j.g.) to lt. comdr. USNR, 1943-46. Mem. Am. Fin. Assn. (editorial bd. 1955-56, dir. investments 1957-58, pres. 1960, dir. and mem. adv. com. 1961-64), Midwest Fin. Assn., So. Fin. Assn. (exec. com. 1972-73), U.S. Savs. and Loan League (exec. com. ann. conf. on savs. and residential financing 1958-71), Fin. Mgmt. Assn., Phi Kappa Phi, Beta Gamma Sigma, Beta Alpha Psi, Sigma Iota Epsilon, Omicron Delta Epsilon, Sigma Alpha Epsilon, Alpha Kappa Psi. Presbyn. (elder). Lodges: Masons, Kiwanis (pres. Champaign-Urbana club 1966). Home: Urbana Ill. Died Oct. 10, 1994; buried Woodlawn Cemetery, Urbana, Ill.

VAN ATTA, ROBERT ERNEST, chemistry educator; b. Ada, Ohio, Feb. 29, 1924; s. Ernest A. and Agnes (Klingler) Van A.; m. Mary Ellen Koons, Jan. 20, 1946; children: John Robert, Richard Lewis, Matthew Ernest. Student, Ohio No. U., 1941-43, B.A., 1948; M.S., Purdue U., 1950; Ph.D., Pa. State U., 1952. Asso. prof. dept. chemistry Ohio No. U., Ada, 1952-54; also chmn. dept., dir. div. natural scis. Ohio No. U., 1953-54; mem. faculty So. Ill. U., Carbondale, 1954-69; asso. prof. So. Ill. U., 1959-67, prof., 1967-69; prof. chemistry Ball State U., Muncie, Ind., 1969-86; retired Ball State U., 1986, head dept., 1969-79; dir. Inst. Environmental Studies, 1973-74; cons. bus., local govt. Author: Introduction to Analytical Chemistry, 1964, Experimental Chemical Analysis, 1973, Instrumental Methods of Analysis for Laboratory Technicians, 1978; rev. edit., 1979, Instrumental Techniques for Food Analysis, 1979, An Introduction to Inorganic Qualitative Analysis, 1980, Quantitative Operations and Chemical Analysis, 1981, rev. edit., 1983; Contbr. profl. jours. Served to 2d lt. AUS, 1943-46. Recipient numerous fed. agy. research grants; recipient Alumni Founder's Day award Ohio No. Univ., 1972. Fellow Am. Inst. Chemists, Ind. Acad. Sci. (sec. 1975-79); mem. Am. Chem. Soc., ASTM, AAAS, AAUP, Sigma Xi, Phi Lambda Upsilon, Phi Mu Delta. Republican. Mem. Ch. Christ. Clubs: Masons, KOA (Billings, Mont.); Good Sam (Calabasas, Calif.); NCHA (Buffalo).

VAN BERGEN, FREDERICK HALL, physician, educator; b. Mpls., Sept. 21, 1914; s. Frederick S. and Jeannette (Hall) Van B.; m. Nancy Thiel, July 9, 1964. Student, St. Thomas Coll., St. Paul, 1933-37; M.B., U. Minn., 1941, M.D., 1942, M.S., 1952. Intern Bremerton (Wash.) Naval Hosp., 1941-42; resident U. Minn. Hosp., 1946-48; practice medicine, specializing in anesthesiology Mpls., 1948—; instr. anesthesiology Med. Sch. U. Minn., 1948-53, asst. prof., asso. dir. anesthesiology, 1953-54, acting dir. anesthesiology, 1955-57, prof., chmn. dept. anesthesiology, 1957-78, emeritus, 1978—, Van Bergen lectr. in anesthesiology, 1978—; regional VA cons. Served to lt. comdr. M.C. USNR, 1941-46. Recipient Cert. of Merit Am. Soc. Anesthesiologists, 1955. Mem. Am. Soc. Anesthesiologists (past dir.), Minn. Soc. Anesthesiologists (past pres.), Assn. Univ. Anesthetists, Acad. Anesthesiology (pres. 1968), Am. Therapeutic Soc., Minn. Acad. Medicine (sr.), N.Y. Acad. Scis., Phi Chi. Club: University of Minnesota Alumni, Ocean Reef. Developed Van Bergen Respirator. also: Ocean Reef Club Key Largo FL 33037 DIED 09/11/96. .

VANCE, DON KELVIN, baking industry consultant; b. Detroit, Jan. 3, 1935; s. George Paul and Marie Jo (Nichols) V.; children—James Delano, Sarah Elizabeth, David Paul. B.B.A., U. Mich., 1957, M.B.A., 1958. Various positions ITT Continental Baking Co., 1958-72; v.p. ITT Continental Baking Co., Rye, N.Y., 1972-83; sr. v.p., div. pres. Am. Bakeries Co., N.Y.C., 1983-86; cons. to baking industry; pres., chief oper. officer Country Home Bakers, Bridgeport, Conn., 1991-94; COO Quality Bakers of Am., Greenwich, Conn., 1994—. Served with USAFR, 1958-64. Methodist. Club: Pensacola (Fla.) Country. Avocations: sailing; skiing; golfing.

VANDEKIEFT, RUTH MARGUERITE, English literature educator; b. Holland, Mich., Sept. 12, 1925; d. John Martin and Cornelia (Bogard) Vande K. BA, Meredith Coll., 1946; MA, U. Mich., 1947, PhD, 1957. Instr. English Calvin Coll., Grand Rapids, Mich., 1947-50, Wellesley (Mass.) Coll., 1956-59; assoc. prof. English Fairleigh Dickinson U., Madison, N.J., 1959-60; asst. prof., assoc. prof., then prof. English lit. Queens Coll.-CUNY, 1961-90, prof. emeritus, from 1990. Author: Eudora Welty, 1962, 2d edit., 1988; editor: Thirteen Stories by Eudora Welty, 1965. Minnie Cummock Blodgett fellow AAUW, 1960-61. Mem. MLA, Soc. Study So. Lit. (pres. 1980-82). Democrat. Presbyterian. Home: New York N.Y. Deceased.

VAN DEMARK, ROBERT EUGENE, SR., orthopedic surgeon; b. Alexandria, S.D., Nov. 14, 1913; s. Walter Eugene and Esther Ruth (Marble) Van D.; m. Bertie Thompson, Dec. 28, 1940; children: Ruth Elaine, Robert, Richard. B.S., U. S.D., 1936; A.B., Sioux Falls (S.D.) Coll., 1937; M.B., Northwestern U., 1938, M.D., 1939; M.S. in Orthopedic Surgery, U. Minn., 1943. Diplomate Am. Bd. Orthopedic Surgery; cert. addl. qualifications surgery of the hand. Intern Passavant Meml. Hosp., Chgo., 1938-39; fellow in orthopedic surgery Mayo Found., 1939-43; 1st asst. orthopedic surgery Mayo Clinic, 1942-43; orthopedic surgeon Sioux Falls; hon. mem. past pres. staff McKennan Hosp.; hon. mem. Sioux Valley Hosp., past pres. staff; clin. prof. orthopedic surgery U. S.D., Sioux Falls, 1953-95, adj. prof orthopedic anatomy, 1983-95; med. dir. Crippled Children's Hosp. and Sch., 1956-84; chief hand surgery clinic VA Hosp., Sioux Falls., 1978-90; bd. dir. S.D. Blue Shield, 1976-88. Editor: S.D. Jour. Medicine, 1958-90; contbr. articles to med. jours. Bd. dirs. S.D. Found. for Med. Care, 1976-83; hon. chmn. S.D. Lung Assn., 1982. Maj. U.S. Army, 1943-46. Recipient citation for outstanding svc. Pres.'s Commn. for Employment Physically Handicapped, 1960; Svc. to Mankind award Sertoma Internat., 1963; award for dedicated svcs. to handicapped S.D. Easter Seal Soc., 1969; Robins award for outstanding community svc., 1971; Humanitarian Svc. award United Cerebral Palsy, 1976; Alumni Achievement award U. S.D., 1977, Disting. Alumnus award, 1992; Disting. Citizen award S.D. Press Assn., 1978; U. S.D. Med. Sch. Faculty Recognition award, 1980; outstanding contbns. to Handicapped Children award S.D. State Dept. Health, 1985, Community Svc. Health award Sioux Valley Hosp. Found., 1991; named Humanitarian of Yr. S.D. Human Svcs. Forum, 1987; Robert E. Van Demark Inst. Anat. Rsch. at U. S.D. named in his honor, 1989; named Disting. Alumnus U. S.D. Med. Sch. Fellow ACS (first pres. S.D. chpt. 1952-53); mem. Am. Acad. Orthopedic Surgery, Am. Soc. Surgery Hand, Am. Assn. Hand Surgery (cert.), Am. Coll. Sports Medicine, Mid-Am. Orthopedic Assn., Am. Soc. Surgery Hand, Am. Acad. Cerebral Palsy, Clin. Orthopedic Soc., Doctors Mayo Soc., S.D. Med. Assn. (pres. 1974-75, Disting. Svc. award 1987, Spl. Presdl. award 1991), Sioux Falls Dist. Med. Soc., SAR, 500 First Families, Optimists, Minnehaha Country Club, Sigma Xi, Alpha Omega Alpha, Phi Chi. Lutheran. Died Aug. 25, 1995.

VAN FLEET, JO, actress; b. Oakland, Calif., 1922; d. Roy H. and Elizabeth (Gardner) Van F.; m. William Bales; 1 child. BA, Coll. of the Pacific, DFA (hon.); studies with Sanford Meisner, Elia Kazan, Lee Strasberg. Actress: (Broadway debut) The Winter's Tale, Cort Theatre, 1946, (stage prodns.) The Whole World Over, 1947, The Closing Door, 1949, King Lear, 1950, Flight into Egypt, 1952, Camino Real, 1953, The Trip to Bountiful, 1953 (Antoinette Perry award 1954, Donaldson award 1954, Show Bus. award 1954), My Aunt Daisy, 1954, Look Homeward Angel, 1957 (N.Y. Drama Critics award 1958), The Glass Menagerie, 1959, The Alligators, 1960, Rosemary, 1960, The Visit, 1961, I Rise in Flame Cried the Phoenix, 1961, The Lady of Larkspur Lotion, 1961, Oh Dad, Poor Dad, Mom's Hung You in the Closet and I'm Feeling So Sad, 1962, The Effect of Gamma Rays on Man-in-the-Moon Marigolds, 1971, The Gingerbread Lady, 1971, Death of a Salesman, 1972, (feature films) East of Eden, 1955 (Acad. award 1956), I'll Cry Tomorrow, 1955, The Rose Tatoo, 1955, The King and Four Queens, 1956, Gunfight at the O.K. Corral, 1957, This Angry Age, 1958, Wild River, 1960, Cool Hand Luke, 1967, I Love You Alice B. Toklas, 1969, Eighty Steps to Jonah, 1969, The Gang that Couldn't Shoot Straight, 1971, The Tenant, 1976, (TV movies) The Family Rico, 1972, Satan's School for Girls, 1973, Power, 1980. Mem. AFTRA, SAG, Actors Equity Assn. Died June 10, 1996.

VAN GAASBECK, HARRY ROBERT, investment company executive; b. Chemung, N.Y., Nov. 26, 1919; s. Harry Sage and Jessie (Lenox) Van G.; m. Martha Clark Newton, May 6, 1944; children: Robert Clark, Margaret Newton. A.B., Middlebury Coll., 1941; student (fellow), Babson Inst., 1941-42; M.B.A., Harvard U., 1947. Asst. treas. investment sec. Springfield Ins. Co., Mass., 1951-65; investment sec., v.p. investment stocks, v.p. securities Monarch Life Ins. Co. and Springfield Life Ins. Co., Springfield, 1960-84; pres., dir. Monarch Securities, Inc., 1968-84; sr. v.p., dir. Monarch Investment Mgmt. Corp., Springfield, 1974-84; v.p., treas., dir. Variable Stock Fund Inc., 1977-84. Served with USAAF, 1942-46. Mem. Nat. Assn. Security Dealers, Boston Security Analysts Soc., Chi Psi. Republican. Congregationalist. Lodge: Rotary. Home: Longmeadow Mass. Died Jan. 1, 1991.

VAN METRE, THOMAS EARLE, physician, allergist; b. Newport, R.I., Jan. 11, 1923; s. Thomas Earle and Anne Heap (Gleaves) Van M.; m. Mary Rosalie Evans, Sept. 7, 1947 (dec. Jan., 1967); children: Rosalie Van Metre Baker, Anne Gleaves Van Metre Kibbe, Mary Evans Van Metre Chodroff, Elizabeth Bowyer Van Meter Domowski, Helen Jenkins Van Metre Weary; m. Adéla Bell Hurst Winand, June 29, 1968; stepchildren: William Thomas Winand III, Bruce Hurst Winand. BS cum laude, Harvard U., 1943; MD cum laude, Harvard Med. Sch., 1946. Diplomate Am. Bd. Internal Medicine, Am. Bd. Allergy. Intern in internal medicine Johns Hopkins Hosp., 1946-47, resident in internal medicine, 1947-48, 50, 1951-52, Am. Cancer Soc. fellow virology and bacteriology, 1952-53, physician diagnostic clin., asst. physician allergy clinic, 1954-56, physician, 1956-96, physician OPD, allergy and infectious disease clinic, 1956-96, pediatrician, 1957-66, physician-in-charge allergy clinic, 1966-84; pvt. practice in internal medicine and allergy Balt., 1954-96; asst. in medicine Johns Hopkins U. Med. Sch., 1947-48, 51-52, 54-56, part-time instr. in medicine 1953-63, part time asst. prof. medicine 1963-70, part-time assoc. prof. medicine, 1970-94, part-time prof., 1994—; attending physician Balt. City Hosp. (now Johns Hopkins Bayview Med. Ctr.), 1954—; active staff The Union Meml. Hosp., 1959—; courtesy staff Church Home and Hosp., 1956-66. Contbr. numerous articles to profl. jours. John Harvard fellowship Harvard Med. Sch., 1945. Fellow ACP, Am. Acad. of Allergy and Immunology (pres. 1978-79, exec. com. 1973-81, other coms., Disting. Svc. award 1986, Disting. Clinician award 1994), Am. Acad. of Allergy; mem. Am. Assn. for Certified Allergists (co-chmn. allergen and immunotherapy com. 1973-77), Am. Bd. of Internal Medicine, Am. Clin. and Climatol. Assn., Am. Fedn. for clin. Rsch., Am. Soc. of Internal Medicine, Asthma and Allergy Found. of Am. (coms.), Balt. City Med. Soc. (coms.), Joint Coun. of Allergy and Immunology (bd. dirs. 1975-84, tres. 1976-84), Md. Blue Cross and Blue Shield, Md. Found. for Health Care, Md. Soc. of Allergy (pres. 1973-74), Md. Soc. of Internal Medicine (pres. elect 1971-73, pres. 1973-75), So. Med. Assn., U.S. FDA (adv. com.), Sigma Xi. Achievements include contributions to understanding risk factors for pneumococcal pneumonia, longitudinal growth of children treated with corticosteroids, inflammatory diseases of eye, severe asthma and immunotherapy for hay fever and asthma. Died Oct. 8, 1996.

VAN WOERKOM, DOROTHY O'BRIEN, author; b. Buffalo, June 26, 1924; d. Peter Simon and Helen Elizabeth (Miller) O'Brien; m. John Van Woerkom, Feb. 22, 1961. Student, Canisius Coll., 1948-50. Author: children's books including Stepka and the Magic Fire, 1974 (Best Religious Children's Book, Cath. Press Assn.), Journeys to Bethlehem, 1974, Meat Pies and Sausages, 1976, A Hundred Angels, Singing, 1976, The Queen Who Couldn't Bake Gingerbread, 1974, Abu Ali, 1976, Tit for Tat, 1977, Harry and Shellburt, 1977, The Friends of Abu Ali, 1978, Donkey Ysabel, 1978, Alexandra the Rock-Eater, 1978, When All the World Was Waiting, 1979, Hidden Messages, 1979 (named an outstanding sci. trade book), Lands of Fire and Ice, 1980, Pearl in the Egg, 1980, Something to Crow About, 1982, Old Devil is Waiting, 1985, Tall Corn/A Tall Tale, 1987; series editor: children's books including I Can Read a Bible Story, Concordia Pub. House, 1975. Mem. Authors Guild, Mystery Writers Am. Home: Houston Tex. Died May 23, 1996; buried Veterans Cemetery.

VARGAS, FERNANDO RODOLFO, recording studio executive; b. San Jose, Costa Rica, Sept. 22, 1928; came to U.S., 1946; s. Elias and Elena (Zamora) V. Student, RCA Inst., 1954. Engr. Audiosonic Rec., N.Y.C., 1953-61; exec. dir. Variety Sound Corp., N.Y.C., 1961-88; co-owner, engr. Variety Rec. Studio, N.Y.C., 1961-88; v.p. AAA Record Plating, N.Y.C., 1986-88; co-owner AAA Rec. Studio, 1980-88. Avocations: electrical engineering, astronomy.

VARNUM, LAURENT KIMBALL, lawyer; b. Chgo., Oct. 31, 1895; s. Clark and Irene (Galloway) V.; m. Maryellen Brown, June 7, 1930 (dec. Oct. 1955); children: Irene Varnum Honn, Catherine Varnum Beaman (dec.); m. Zoe Shippen, Feb. 28, 1959. A.B., U. Mich., 1925, J.D., 1927. Bar: Mich. 1927. Since practiced in Grand Rapids; mem. Varnum, Riddering, Schmidt & Howlett, and predecessors, 1935—; spl. counsel City of Grand Rapids, 1943-44; mem. Little Hoover Commn.; chmn. com. for balanced legislature and co-author constnl. amendment on reapportionment, adopted in Mich., 1952; chmn. Alien Enemy Hearing Bd., 1941-45; mem. bd. Kent County Dept. Aeros., 1958-67. Bd. dirs. Grand Rapids Symphony Soc., pres., 1955-56; Mem. citizens adv. commn. on Reorgn. State Govt. Fellow Am. Coll. Trial Lawyers; mem. Am. Law Inst., Am. Judicature Soc., ABA (ho. dels. 1947-50), Mich. Bar Assn. (pres. 1946- 47), Grand Rapids Bar Assn., Internat. Assn. Ins. Counsel, Jud. Council Mich., Sixth Circuit Jud. Conf. (life mem.), Better Govt in Mich., Order of Coif, Phi Beta Kappa. Club: Beach (Palm Beach, Fla.).

VARTANIAN, ARAM, French literature educator, researcher, writer; b. N.Y.C., Nov. 14, 1922; s. Vahan and Sirane (Casparian) V.; m. Irka Eitingon, Jan. 28, 1948 (div. 1961); 1 child, Michael; m. Anne Darrow, June 28, 1979 (div. 1984); m. Susanne Schroeder, June 28, 1990. B.A., Columbia U., 1944, M.A., 1947, Ph.D., 1951. Asst. prof. French Tulane U., 1951-52, Harvard U., 1952-57; assoc. prof. then prof. French U. Minn., Mpls., 1957-64; prof. French NYU, 1964-81; William R. Kenan prof. French lit. U. Va., Charlottesville, 1981-93; emeritus, 1993. Author: Diderot and Descartes, 1953, La Mettrie's L'Homme Machine, 1960, Critical Edition of Diderot's Les Bijoux Indiscrets, 1978; adv. editor Jour. History of Ideas, 1977, Continuum, 1987. Served with AUS, 1943-46. Recipient Gold medal City of Paris, 1988; fellow Ford Found., 1951-52, Fulbright rsch. fellow, 1962-63, Guggenheim Found. fellow, 1962-63. Mem. MLA, Am. Soc. 18th Century Studies (pres. 1990-91), Societe Francaise d'Etude du XVIIIe Siecle. DIED 01/18/97. .

VASARELY, VICTOR, artist; b. Pecs, Hungary, 1908. Student medicine; Dr. honoris causa in Humanities, State U. Cleve., 1977. Mem. Budapest Bauhaus; moved to Paris, 1930. One-man shows include Rose Fried Gallery, N.Y.C., World House Gallery, N.Y.C., Met. Mus. Art, Montevideo, Hanover Gallery, London, Pace Gallery, Boston, Papal Palace, Avignon, France, 1985, French Inst., Budapest, 1985, Galerija S. Dubrownik, Sombor, Yugoslavia, Jazz Acad., Budapest, 1985, Villeurbanne City Hall, France, 1985, Galerie der Stadt Esslingen am Neckar, Fed. Republic Germany, 1986, Musée Nat. des Beaux-Arts d'Alger, 1986, Heimatsmus. Gablitzhalle, Austria, 1986, Galerie Guigné, Paris, 1987, Maison de Culture de Berlin, 1987, Galerie Richard, Zurich, 1987, Galerie Abisz de Stuttgart, 1987, numerous others; major group exhbns. Paris Salons, Stadelijk Mus., Amsterdam, Documenta III Kassel, Carnegie Inst., Gallery Chalette, N.Y.C., Sidney Janis Gallery, N.Y.C., Guggenheim Mus., Sao Paolo, Rio de Janeiro, Montevideo, State Gallery Esslingen, French Embassy Thailand; rep. permanent collections Mus. Modern Art, N.Y.C., Mus. St. Etienne, Paris, Mus. Modern Art, Paris, Albright-Knox Gallery, Harvard U., Buenos Aires Mus., Montivideo Mus., Brussels Mus., Reykjavik Mus., Carnegie Inst., Stedelijk Mus., Sao Paulo Mus., Tate Gallery, London, Vienna Mus., Tel Aviv Mus., Guggenheim Mus., Rockefeller Found., Helsinki Mus., Dallas Mus., others; study, followed by sculpture for XXIVth Olympic Games, Seoul, Korea; subject numerous bibliographies. Decorated officer Legion of Honor, officer Nat. Order of Arts and Letters, France; grand ribbon honor Order Andre Bello, Venezuela; medal Order of Flag, Hungary; recipient Guggenheim Internat. award Merit, 1964; named to Order Arts and Letters France, 1965; named hon. citizen of New Orleans, 1966; prize 9th Biennal Minister Fgn. Affairs, Tokyo, 1967; grand prize 8th Biennal Art Sao Paulo, Brazil, 1965; cert. of distinction NYU, 1978; Art prize City of Goslar, 1978; décoration du chéquier de la Caisse d'Epargne Ecureuil, 1986; mem. Com. d'Honneur de Compétition Industrie, Paris, 1987; pres. d'Honneur du Prix Départemental d'Architecture contemporaine au Moulin de Guérard, Montreuil; médaille de la Ville de Clermont-Ferrand, 1987. Mem. France-Hungary Assn. (hon. pres. 1977—), Internat. Inst. Nuclear Engrs. (corres. mem.). Citoyen d'Honneur de la Ville d'Aix en Provence. Musèe Vasarely at Château de Gordes, France, dedicated, 1971; Fondation Vasarely á Aix-en-Provence, opened 1976; inauguration of Musée Vasarely, Château Zichy, Budapest, 1987. Died March 15, 1997.

VATCHENKO, ALEKSEY FEDOSEYEVICH, government official; Ukraine; b. Yelizaveto-Kameneto, Feb. 25, 1914; ed. Dnieprpetrovsk U. Mem. Central Com., Communist Party Ukraine, 1960—, candidate mem., 1961-66, mem., 1966—; mem. econs. com. Soviet of Nationalities, 1962-66; dep. to USSR Supreme Soviet, 1962—; mem. com. for industry, transport and communications Soviet of the Union, 1966-70, mem. com. for edn. sci. and culture, 1970-74, mem. com. for industry, 1974-76; 1st sec. Dnepropetrovsk regional com. for agr. Communist Party Ukraine, 1963-64, 1st sec. Cherkessy regional com., 1964-65, 1st sec. Dnepropetrovsk regional com., 1965-76, mem. Politburo, 1966—; dep. chmn. presidium Supreme Soviet Ukraine, 1976—. Decorated Hero of Socialist Labor, Order of Lenin (5), Order of October Revolution.

VELTMAN, PETER, college dean; b. Muskegon, Mich., Jan. 29, 1917; s. Douglas and Minnie (Achterhof) V.; m. Marian Waalkes, Aug. 20, 1940; children: Virginia Veltman Rice, Donna Veltman Garcia, Marian Veltman Gardner, Michelle Veltman. A.B., Hope Coll., Holland, Mich., 1938; M.A., Western Res. U., 1939; student, U. Chgo., 1939-40, U. Amsterdam, Netherlands, 1949-50; Ph.D., Northwestern U., 1959. Tchr. Chgo. Christian High Sch., 1939-40, Holland (Mich.) pub. schs., 1940-48; mem. English dept. Wheaton (Ill.) Coll., 1948-57, chmn. edn. dept., 1957-66, dean. coll., 1966-82, dean emeritus, 1984—, interim curator Marion E. Wade (C.S. Lewis) Collection, 1982-83; chmn. Associated Colls. Chgo. Area, 1966-67; exec. dir./dean Am. Inst. Holy Land Studies, Jerusalem, 1984-86; cons. European Media Acad., Altensteig, Fed. Republic Germany, Chgo.-Wheaton Billy Graham Telephone Ministry. Author: (with others) Modern Journalism, 1962; Reviewer: (with others) Dutch and Belgian lit. for Books Abroad. Mem. Wheaton Pub. Library Bd., 1955-70, pres., 1967-70; mem. adv. com. Honey Rock Camp, Wis., 1966—, Ill. Bd. Higher Edn., 1974-75; mem. Wheaton Sister City Commn., 1974-84; bd. dirs. Grace Bible Coll., Grand Rapids, Mich.; bd. dirs., mem. exec. com. Inst. Holy Land Studies, Israel; commr. North Cen. Accrediting Assn., 1979-82. Fulbright grantee, 1949-50; Danforth grantee, 1957-58. Mem. Phi Delta Kappa (past pres. Du Page County chpt.), Pi Kappa Delta (hon.). Mem. Wheaton Bible Ch. (chmn. bd. 1980-84). Club: Exchange (Wheaton) (pres. 1969-70). DIED 05/30/97. .

VERDUIN, JACOB, botany educator; b. Orange City, Iowa, Nov. 19, 1913; s. Peter and Jennie (Lagestee) V.; m. Bethy Albertha Anderson, July 3, 1942; children: Lans, Jan, Charlotte (dec.), Leslie, Bethy. B.S., Iowa State Coll., 1939, M.S., 1941, Ph.D., 1947. Farmer, 1933-35; head botany dept. S.D. State U., 1946-48; asso. prof. hydrobiology F. T. Stone Lab., Ohio State U., 1948-54; head biology dept. Bowling Green State U., 1955-64; prof. botany So. Ill. U., Carbondale, 1964-84, prof. emeritus, 1984-97; Cons. NIH, summer 1954; cons. water pollution control sect. TVA, summer 1957, Commonwealth Edison, 1972-86, EPA, 1975-79. Mem. editorial bd.: Ecology, 1954-57, Limnology and Oceanography, Ohio Jour. Sci, Trans. Am. Fisheries Soc. Served to ensign USNR, 1942-45. Fellow Ohio Acad. Sci. (exec. v.p. plant sci. sect. 1958), AAAS; mem. Am. Inst. Biol. Scis., Societas Internationalis Limnologiae, Ecol. Soc. Am., Am. Fisheries Soc., Am. Assn. Limnologists and Oceanographers, Sigma Xi, Phi Kappa Phi, Beta Beta Beta, Gamma Sigma Delta, Omicron Delta Kappa. Episcopalian. Home: Carbondale Ill. Deceased.

VERITY, GEORGE LUTHER, lawyer; b. Oklahoma City, Jan. 3, 1914; s. George H. and Mae (Tibbals) V.; m. Ellen Van Hoesen, Mar. 18, 1939; children: George Luther II, Grover Steven, David Webster, Mark Sidney. LLB, Okla. U., 1937; M of Theol. Studies, So. Meth. U., 1989. Bar: Okla. 1937, Tex. 1939, N.Mex. 1957. Practice in Shawnee, Okla., 1937-39, Wichita Falls, Tex., 1939-40, 46-48, Oklahoma City, 1948-57, Farmington, N.Mex., 1957-64, Oklahoma City, 1964-96; ptnr. Verity, Brown & Verity (and predecessor), 1964-77; of counsel Bay, Hamilton, Lee, Spears & Verity, 1978-96; chmn. bd., dir. Big D Industries; pres., dir. Okla. Mgmt. Co., Okla. Ind. Exploration Co.; former chmn. bd., dir. Progress Life & Accident Ins. Co. Author: The Modern Oil and Gas Lease, From Bataan to Victory, An Agnostic Finds God in Jananese Prison Camp. Trustee Rocky Mountain Mineral Law Found. Capt. USAAF, 1941-46, PTO; prisoner of war. Decorated Purple Heart. Mem. ABA, Okla. Bar Assn., State Bar N.Mex. (chmn. mineral sect.), State Bar Tex., Assn. Trial Lawyers Am., Okla. Trial Lawyers Assn., Acacia. Lodges: Masons; Elks. Died Sept. 4, 1996.

VERNON, DAVID LYLE (DAVID COREY), actor, dancer, singer, choreographer; b. Greensboro, N.C., Feb. 7, 1959; s. Brenda K. (Richardson) V. Grad. high sch., Greensboro. Artist in residence, tchr. Dayton (Ohio) Dance Theatre, 1981-82. Actor: (plays) Robin

Hood, 1982, A Chorus Line, Guys and Dolls, Oklahoma!, Pippin, Shenandoah, George M!, (films) 9 1/2 Weeks, A Chorus Line, (TV shows) The Guiding Light, Search for Tomorrow, As the World Turns, Geraldo, One Life to Live, Merv Griffin; dancer Cole Porter, A Day in Hollywood/A Night in the Ukraine. Mem. Actors' Equity Assn., Screen Actors Guild, AFTRA. Avocations: psychology, collecting Marilyn Monroe memorabilia, writing. Home: High Point N.C. Died May 14, 1995.

VERSACE, GIANNI, fashion designer; b. Reggion Calabria, Italy, Dec. 2, 1946; s. Antonio and Francesca Versace. Student, pub. sch., Italy. Designer: Complice, Genny and Callaghan, Milan, Italy, 1972-78; 1st signature women's wear collection, Milan, Italy, 1978—, menswear collection, Versaci Signature exhbn., Berlin, 1995; founder 1st of 80 exclusive boutiques, Milan, 1979—; developer namesake fragrance, Italy, France, Switzerland, Austria and U.S.A., 1981—; costume designer for ballets Leib und Leid, Josephlegende, Dyonisos, for opera Don Pasquale (La Scala), 1984; collaborator South Beach Stories, 1992; author: Designs, 1994. Recipient Golden Eye award for best fashion designer of women's wear for fall-winter, 1982-84, Cutty Sark award, 1983, International award, CFDA, 1992, Oscar award Coun. Fashion Designers Am., 1993, VH1 Fashion and Music award, 1995; decorated Commendatore delle Repubblice Italiane Govt. Italy, 1986. Died July 15, 1997.

VICKREY, ROBERT EDWARD, JR., petroleum engineer; b. Cooper, Ky., Nov. 20, 1912; s. Robert Edward and Idell (Wade) V.; m. Ruth LaVerne Chambers, Nov. 30, 1935 (div. 1965); children: Jeanie, Paul; m. Dixie Doyle Richards, June 5, 1971. BS, Okla. State U., 1934; postgrad., U. Dallas, 1971. Registered petroleum engr., Tex. Prodn. engr. Sun Oil Co., Tulsa, 1934-41; natural gas engr. Sun Oil Co., Dallas, 1942-46; prodn. supt. Sun Oil Co., Carthage, Tex., 1947-49; mgr. gas measurement Sun Oil Co., Dallas, 1950-71; advisor pipeline ops. Nat. Iranian Gas Co., Tehran, 1972-74; cons. Sun Exploration & Prodn. Co., Dallas, 1975-85; pres. Vickrey Engring., Inc., Dallas, 1986-95; part-time instr. U. Okla., Norman, 1956-95, U. Tex. Extension, Kilgore, 1955-82; supr. Dept. of Energy/U. Okla. Petroleum Data System, Dallas, 1977-82; chmn. working groups Measurement Standards, Am. Petroleum Inst., 1982-92. Contbr. articles to profl. jours.; chmn. working groups Measurement Standards, 1982-95. Presdl. commn. Nat. Rep. Senatorial Com., Washington, 1992. Recipient Citation for Svc. Am. Petroleum Inst., 1975, 92, Presdl. Order of Merit Nat. Rep. Senatorial Com., 1991. Mem. Soc. Petroleum Engrs. (North Tex. chmn. 1961-62), Soc. of Petroleum Evaluation Engrs., Dallas Geol. Soc., Petroleum Engrs. Club of Dallas (pres. 1960-61, Permian Pot award 1982), Instrument Soc. Am. (North Tex. pres. 1955-56), Nat. Soc. Profl. Engrs., Tex. Soc. Profl. Engrs., North Tex. Measurement Soc. (pres. 1968-69), Exchange Club of Oak Cliff (pres. 1958). Republican. Ch. of Christ. Avocations: computers, gardening, golf, hunting. Home: Dallas Tex. Died July 11, 1995.

VICKREY, WILLIAM SPENCER, economist, educator; b. Victoria, B.C., Can., June 21, 1914; came to U.S., 1914; s. Charles Vernon and Ada Eliza (Spencer) V.; m. Cecile Montez Thompson, July 21, 1951. B.A. in Math. with high honors (scholar), Yale, 1935; M.A., Columbia, 1937, Ph.D., 1947; D.H.L., U. Chgo., 1979; Social Sci. Research Council predoctoral field fellow, 1938-39. Jr. economist Nat. Resources Com., Washington, 1937-38; research asst. 20th Century Fund, 1939-40; economist OPA, 1940-41; sr. economist, div. tax research Treasury Dept., 1941-43; civilian pub. service assignee, 1943- 46, tax cons. to gov. P.R., 1946; mem. faculty Columbia U., N.Y.C., 1946-81; prof. econs. Columbia U., 1958-81; chmn. dept. Columbia, 1964-67, McVickar prof. polit. economy, 1971-81, prof. emeritus, from 1981; Cons. to govt. and industry, 1949-96; participant numerous confs., seminars; Ford research prof. Columbia, 1958-59; instr. IBM Systems Research Inst., 1964; vis. lectr. Monash U., Melbourne, Australia, 1971; inter-regional adviser UN, 1974-75. Author: Agenda for Progressive Taxation, 1947, Microstatics: Metastatics and Macroeconomics, 1964, Public Economics, 1994. Clk. Scarsdale (N.Y.) Friends Meeting, 1959-62. Fellow Inst. Advanced Study Behavioral Scis., Stanford, 1967-68. Fellow Am. Econ. Assn. (pres. 1992), Econometric Soc.; mem. Met. Econ. Assn., Am. Statis. Assn., Royal Econ. Soc., Ea. Econ. Assn., Atlantic Econ. Soc. (pres. 1992-93). Died Oct. 11, 1996.

VINE, ALLYN COLLINS, oceanographer; b. Garrettsville, Ohio, June 1, 1914; s. Elmer James and Lulu (Collins) V.; m. Adelaide Ruth Holton, Nov. 16, 1940; children: Vivian (Mrs. Carl F. Dreisbach), Norman, David. B.A., Hiram (Ohio) Coll., 1936; M.S., Lehigh U., 1938, D.Sc. (hon.), 1973. Oceanographer Woods Hole (Mass.) Oceanographic Instn., 1940-79, scientist emeritus, 1979-94; part-time oceanographer Bur. Ships, Dept. Navy, 1947-50; Mem. panel engring. aids for oceanography Nat. Acad. Scis., 1958-64; Trustee Ocean Resources Inst., 1952-64; Internat. Oceanographic Found., 1960-94. Recipient David B. Stone award New Eng. Aquarium, 1977; Garfield scholar Hiram Coll., 1972, Turner award, 1989. Fellow AAAS, Marine Tech. Soc. (founder, bd. dirs. 1964-65, Compass award 1969, Lockheed award 1987), Soc. Naval Architects and Marine Engrs. (Elmer Sperry award 1989, Blakely Smith award 1991); mem. NAE, Acoustical Soc. Am., Am. Geophys. Union. Home: Woods Hole Mass. Died Jan. 4, 1994.

VON ECKARDT, WOLF, design critic, educator; b. Berlin, Germany, Mar. 6, 1918; came to U.S., 1936, naturalized, 1943; s. Hans Felix and Gertrude (Lederer) E.; m. Marianne Horney, June 28, 1941 (div.); children: Barbara, Marina Von Eckardt Gilman; m. Nina ffrench-frazier, Feb. 14, 1987. Student, New Sch. Social Research, 1936-38; L.H.D. (hon.), The Md. Inst., 1983. Info. officer Dept. State, Washington, 1945-53; free-lance pub. info. specialist Washington, 1953-59; dir. pub. info. AIA, 1959-63; architecture critic Washington Post, 1963-81; design critic Time mag., 1981-85; guest prof. dept. city and regional planning Cornell U., Ithaca, N.Y., 1986; Albert A. Levin prof. urban studies and pub. service Coll. Urban Affairs, Cleve. State U., 1978-80; lectr. Harvard U., 1966, MIT, 1967. Graphic artist, book designer, N.Y.C., 1936-41; Author: Eric Mendelsohn, 1960, The Challenge of Megalopolis, 1964, A Place to Live-The Crisis of the Cities, 1968, (with Sander Gilman) Bertolt Brecht's Berlin, 1975, Back to the Drawing Board! Planning Livable Cities, 1979, (with Sander Gilman) Oscar Wilde's London, 1987, Please Write, How To Improve Your Handwriting for Business and Pleasure in Ten Quick and Easy Lessons, 1988; also articles. Served with AUS, World War II. Hon. mem. AIA; mem. Am. Inst. Graphic Arts (pres. Washington chpt. 1962-65), Soc. Archtl. Historians. Died Aug. 27, 1995.

VON FRIESEN, STEN, former physicist; b. Uppsala, Sweden, Mar. 18, 1907; s. Otto and Vendla (Ohlsson) von F. FM, U. Uppsala, 1930, FL, 1933, FD, 1936. Mem. faculty U. Uppsala, 1935-37; mem. staff Nobel Inst. Physics, Stockholm, 1937-39; with Rsch. Inst. Nat. Def., 1940-44; mem. faculty U. Lund, 1946-72, prof. physics, 1948-72, prof. emeritus, 1972-96; mem. Swedish Atomic Energy Commn., 1949-59, organizing com. Lund Inst. Tech., 1960-69, physics Nobel Prize Com., 1965-71. Author: Om Mått och Män (transl. to Of Measures and Men); mem. editorial bd. (ency.) Bra Böckers Lexikon (25 vols.); contbr. articles to profl. jours. Recipient Angstrom medal 1935. Fellow Am. Phys. Soc.; mem. Royal Physiographic Soc. Lund, Royal Swedish Acad. Scis., Royal Soc. Sci. Uppsala. Died Sept. 9, 1996.

VONNEGUT, BERNARD, chemist, scientist, educator; b. Indpls., Aug. 29, 1914; s. Kurt and Edith Sophia (Lieber) V.; m. Lois Gloria Bowler, Dec. 25, 1943; children: Peter, Scott, Terry, Kurt, Alex. BS in Chemistry, MIT, 1936, PhD in Chemistry, 1939. Rsch. sci. Hartford (Conn.) Empire Co., 1939-41, MIT, Cambridge, Mass., 1941-46, Gen. Electric Co., Schenectady, N.Y., 1946-54, Arthur D. Little Inc., Cambridge, 1954-67; prof. U. Albany, N.Y., 1967, prof. emeritus, 1985-97. Fellow Am. Meteorol. Soc., Am. Geophys. Union. Home: Albany N.Y. Died Apr. 1997.

VON SANDOR, COUNT ROBERT, optometrist, educator, researcher; b. Budapest, Hungary, Apr. 16, 1929; s. Louis and Irene (Bauer) von S.; m. Anita Bernice Johansson, Apr. 4, 1952; children: Jan-Douglas, Helen Bernice. PhD, U. Ariz., 1987; LittD (hon.), U. Found., Del., 1987; HHD (hon.), Albert Einstein Acad. Found., Kans., 1990. Diplomate in social anthropology, diplomate in visual optics and physiology. Dean Coll. of Optometry, Stockholm, 1954-67; head of info. Coun. of Info. of Visual Scis., Stockholm, 1967-85; sr. lectr., rschr. Coll. Applied Visual Scis., Sigtuna, Sweden, 1985—; head of info. Hoya-Optikslip, Stockholm, 1985-96; bd. dirs. Optichistorical Mus. Sweden, 1996—; chief rsch. Inst. Japanology, Teckomatorp, Sweden, 1991—, adj. prof. clin. optometry, visual scis. and physiol. optics, 1992. Author 5 textbooks in visual optics and optometry and 16 handbooks in Japanology, 1952—; contbr. more than 270 articles to profl. jours. Pres. The Japanese The-Ceremony Found., Stockholm, 1990-96, Japanese Token and Bijutsu Ctr., Stockholm, 1980—. Recipient Gullstrand medal, 1979, Peace medal Albert Einstein Acad. Found., 1988, Alfred Nobel medal Internat. Acad. Found., 1991, Gold medal of merits Swedish Sport Fedn., 1980, Swedish Judo Assn., 1964, Medal of merit U. Medicine, Budapest, 1947, The Einstein Acad. Cross of Merit, 1992. Fellow Am. Acad. Optometry, N.Y. Acad. Scis.; mem. Swedish Optometric Assn. (bd. dirs. 1985-90, Medal of Merit 1985), Internat. Fedn. Japanese Fencing (v.p. 1970-80, Gold medal 1989), European Kendo Fedn. (h. pres. 1982, Medal of Merit 1982), Judo Club Stockholm (pres. 1960-74, Gold medal 1974), Budo Club Lidingo (pres. 1970-96, Medal of Merit 1990), European Assn. Japanese Fencing (pres. 1970-82), Swedish Budo Fedn. (pres. 1980-82, Medal of Merit 1985), Stockholm-Sergel Rotary Club (pres. 1990-91). Avocations: Japanese antiques and martial arts, Japanology, optical history. Died June 1, 1997.

VORIS, CLYDE ANDREW, marketing educator, management consultant; b. Rockbridge, Ohio, May 22, 1911; s. Asbury Shady and Maud Jenny (Beougher) V.; m. Margaret Anne Radebaugh, Jan. 1936 (dec. June 1963); children: Michael Jay, Clyde Andrew Jr.; m. Martha Rose Weichold, May 10, 1968. BS, Ohio U., 1934; MS, Akron U., 1951; PhD, U. Palm Beach, 1970. Cert. adminstrv. mgr. Personnel dir. B.F. Goodrich Co., Akron, Ohio, 1941-49; corp. mgr. personnel and labor rels. Albers-Colonial Stores, Cin., 1950-65; prof. mktg. and mgmt. U. Cin., 1965-95, coord. pub. rels. and mgmt. subjects, cons. retailing program, 1965-81; mgmt. cons. AT&T, Cin., 1970-72, Dayton (Ohio) Tire & Rubber Co., 1972-73, Thai Feed Co., Bangkok, 1977, Manpower, Inc.; examiner Bus. Schs. Accrediting Commn., Washington, 1970-85; v.p. W.E. Shell & Co., Cin., 1970-73. Contbr. articles to profl. jours. and newspapers. Mem. Westwood Civic Assn., Cin.; founder Bob Hope House, Cin., 1963; active YMCA, Cin., 1950-95. Named Ky. col. Commonwealth of Ky., 1988. Mem. Adminstrv. Mgmt. Soc. (cert., bd. dirs. 1950-95, coll. faculty advisor 1973-95, Merit Key award 1985), Sales and Mktg. Execs. (v.p., bd. dirs. 1970-88), Pub. Rels. Soc. Am. (bd. dirs. 1955-70), Cin. Mgmt. Assn. (lectr. 1965-70), Masons, Shriners, Elks, Rotary (pres. Cin. club 1980-95). Republican. Avocations: walking, swimming. Home: Cincinnati Ohio Died March 1, 1995.

VOSS, CARL HERMANN, clergyman, humanities educator, author; b. Pitts., Dec. 8, 1910; s. Carl August and Lucy (Wilms) V.; m. Dorothy Katherine Grote, Nov. 25, 1940 (div. 1957); 1 dau., Carlyn Grote (Mrs. Harold Iuzzolino); m. Phyllis MacKenzie Gierlotka, May 9, 1959; 1 dau., Christina Elisabeth Gierlotka (Mrs. Russell P. Wynings Jr.). AB, U. Pitts., 1931, PhD, 1942; student, Internat. People's Coll., Elsinore, Denmark, U. Geneva, Switzerland, 1931, Chgo. Theol. Sem., 1931-32; M.Div., Union Theol. Sem., N.Y.C., 1935; postgrad., Yale Div. Sch., 1938-40; postgrad. in Hebrew studies, Oxford U., 1977-79; postgrad., Ecumenical Inst. Bossey, World Council Chs., Geneva, 1980-81; L.H.D., Hebrew Union Coll.-Jewish Inst. Religion, N.Y.C., 1981. Minister United Ch. (Congl.-Christian-Friends), Raleigh, N.C., 1935-38; chaplain Cheshire (Conn.) Acad., 1938-40; assoc. minister Smithfield United Ch., Pitts., 1940-43; extension sec. Ch. Peace Union and World Alliance for Internat. Friendship Through the Chs., 1943-49; editor World Alliance News Letter, 1944-49; exec. sec. Christian Council on Palestine, 1943-46; chmn. exec. council Am. Christian Palestine Com., 1946-57; minister Flatbush Unitarian Ch., Bklyn., 1953-57, N.E. Congl. Ch., Saratoga Springs, N.Y., 1957-64; Merrill research asso. Brandeis U., 1965-67; lectr. New Sch. for Soc. Research, 1948-56; lectr. dept. philosophy and religion Skidmore College, Saratoga Springs, 1960-61, 65-66; vis. prof. theology and history religions Theol. Sch. St. Lawrence U., Canton, N.Y., 1964-65; prof. humanities Edward Waters Coll., Jacksonville, Fla., 1973-76; chmn. humanities div. Edward Waters Coll., 1974-76; NCCJ ecumenical-scholar-in-residence; resident scholar Ecumenical Inst. Advanced Theol. Studies, Tantur, Jerusalem, 1976-77; Centre Postgrad. Hebrew Studies Oxford U., 1977, 79; conducted European tours, 1930, 31, 35, (Arab countries and Israel), 1949, 51, 53, 55, 58, 63, 66, 70, 73, 75, 79; (lectr. tour), Rhodesia, South Africa under auspices Good Will Council S.Africa, 1947. Author: The Palestine Problem Today, 1953, (with Theodore Huebner) This Is Israel, 1956, Rabbi and Minister: The Friendship of Stephen S. Wise and John Haynes Holmes, 1964, In Search of Meaning: Living Religions of the World, 1968, Stephen S. Wise: Servant of The People-Selected Letters, 1969, A Summons unto Men: An Anthology of the Writings of John Haynes Holmes, 1971, Living Religions of the World: Our Search for Meaning, 1977, (with David A. Rausch) Protestantism: Its Modern Meaning, 1987; editor: The Universal God: An Interfaith Anthology, 1953, Excalibur Books, 1964-95, Quotations of Courage and Vision: A Source Book for Speaking, Writing and Meditation, 1972, (with David A. Rausch) World Religions: Our Quest for Meaning, 1989; contbr. to mags. and religious jours. Recipient Nat. Brotherhood award NCCJ, 1978; hon. fellow Hebrew U., Jerusalem, 1979; Carl Hermann Voss scholarship named in honor by Ctr. for Hebrew Studies Oxford U., Eng., 1990. Mem. United Ch. of Christ. Home: Jacksonville Fla. Died Mar. 14, 1995.

VUCKOVICH, DRAGOMIR MICHAEL, neurologist, educator; b. Bileca, Herzegovina, Yugoslavia, Oct. 27, 1927; came to U.S., 1957; s. Alexander John and Anka Mia (Ivanisevich) V.; m. Brenda Mary Luther, Aug. 23, 1958; children: John, Nicholas, Adrian. M.D., U. Birmingham, Eng., 1953. Diplomate Am. Bd. Psychiatry and Neurology, Am. Bd. Pediatrics. Intern United Birmingham Hosps., Eng., 1953-54, resident in pediatrics, 1954-55; resident med. officer Princess Beatrice Hosp., London, 1955; sr. resident Hosp. for Sick Children, London, 1955; sr. resident in neurology Atkinson Morley br. St. George's Hosp., London, 1955-56; resident in neurology Nat. Hosp. Queens Sq., London, 1956-57, VA Hosp., Chgo., 1958-59; resident in psychiatry Wesley Meml. Hosp., Chgo., 1959-60; fellow in neurology Northwestern U. Med. Sch., Chgo., 1960; resident in pediatrics Children's Meml. Hosp., Chgo., 1961; asst. prof. neurology, psychiatry and pediatrics Northwestern U. Med. Ctr., Chgo., 1967-70; assoc. clin. prof. neurology and pediatrics Stritch Sch. Medicine, Chgo., 1970-77, clin. prof. neurology and pediatrics, 1977-93; chmn. Columbus Hosp., Chgo., 1981-88; chief of neurology svc. N. Chgo. VAMC, 1992-94; prof. neurology and pediatrics Finch U. Health Sch. Chgo. Med. Sch., 1994-96; prof. clin. psychiatry Chgo. Med.

Sch., 1995-96; dir. EEG Lab. Columbus Hosp., Chgo., 1969-89, chief neurology and psychiatry, 1971-81; chief of child neurology Loyola U., Maywood, Ill., 1970-79; cons. Trinity House, 1988-92; acting chmn. neurology FUHS/CMS, 1993-96; program dir. neurology residency program FUHS/CMS affiliated hosp., 1993-96. Co-author: Psychoanalysis and the Two Cerebral Hemispheres, 1983; contbr., co-contbr. articles in field to profl. jours. Lt. col. MC, USAR, 1983-87. Decorated Army Achievement medal, Army Commendation medal, 1986; recipient Physician Recognition award AMA, 1971; named Best Attending Physician Med. House Staff, Columbus Hosp., 1979. Fellow Am. Acad. Pediatrics, Am. Acad. Neurology, Royal Soc. Health Eng.; mem. Am. Med. Electroencephalographic Assn., Profs. of Child Neurology, Cen. Neuropsychiat. Assn. Republican. Serbian Orthodox. Clubs: Beefeaters (N.Y.C.); Les Gourmet's (Chgo.). Avocations: music, reading, writing, tennis, swimming. Home: Deerfield Ill. Died May 2, 1996; interred St. Sava Monastery, Libertyville, IL.

WACHTEL, HARRY H., lawyer, chain store executive; b. N.Y.C., Mar. 26, 1917; s. Samuel and Minnie (Herzhaft) W.; m. Leonora Golden, July 30, 1939; children: Alan B., Susan M., William B. B.S. in Social Sci, CCNY, 1938; LL.B., Columbia U., 1940. Bar: N.Y. bar 1940. Since practiced in N.Y.C.; sr. partner firm Rubin, Wachtel, Baum & Levin, until 1975; counsel Gold and Wachtel, N.Y.C., 1985—; exec. v.p., gen. counsel, dir. McCrory Corp., 1959-75, exec. asst. to pres., 1975-83; vice chmn., exec. v.p. Rapid Am. Corp., 1960-65; gen. counsel, dir. Lerner Stores Corp., 1961-75; Vis. prof. polit. sci. Hofstra U., 1967-71; adj. prof. polit. sci. Columbia, 1973-85; fellow Urban Center, 1972-80; dir. Vanguard Nat. Bank, Hempstead, N.Y., 1972-74. Mem. exec. com. N.Y. State Com. Am. Vets. Com., 1947; bd. dirs. North Shore Cmty. Arts Ctr., Roslyn, N.Y., 1960-72; v.p., counsel Martin Luther King Jr. Ctr. for Nonviolent Social Change, 1969-82, bd. dirs., 1969-92, mem. bd. advisors, 1992—; exec. v.p., counsel Am. Found. Nonviolence, 1964-72; trustee SCLC, 1970-72; past mem. coun. Hofstra U. With AUS, 1942-45. Decorated Bronze Star medal. Mem. Phi Beta Kappa. Died Feb. 3, 1997.

WADLIN, GEORGE KNOWLTON, JR., professional engineering consultant; b. New Haven, Sept. 20, 1923; s. George Knowlton and Laura (Mason) W.; m. Nora Elizabeth Thompson, July 29, 1944 (div. Dec. 1974); children: Gail Thompson, George Knowlton III, Lela Mason; m. Josephine C. Perkins, Aug. 2, 1975 (div. Apr. 1977); m. Ruth Feldman Schwartz, Oct. 1977. B.S. in Civil Engring, Pa. State U., 1948; M.S., U. Maine, 1953; Ph.D., Carnegie Inst. Tech., 1959. Registered profl. engr., Maine. Mem. faculty U. Maine, 1948-69, prof. civil engring., 1961-69, head dept., 1958-69; research prof. engring. George Washington U., 1967-68; prof., head dept. civil engring. Mich. Tech. U., 1969-78; dir. edn. services and continuing edn. ASCE, N.Y.C., 1978-86; cons. civil and structural engr., 1953—. Contbr. articles to profl. jours. Served with AUS, 1942-46, ETO. Fellow ASCE, Am. Soc. Engring. Edn. (chmn. civil engring. div. 1970-71, chmn. profl. interest council I 1976-78, v.p. 1978, bd. dirs. 1982-83); mem. Order of Engr., Sigma Xi, Lambda Chi Alpha, Tau Beta Pi, Chi Epsilon, Phi Kappa Phi.

WAGNER, PHILIP MARSHALL, writer; b. New Haven, Feb. 18, 1904; s. Charles Philip and Ruth (Kenyon) W.; m. Helen Crocker, Apr. 16, 1925; children: Susan, Philip; m. Jocelyn McDonough, Sept. 4, 1940. A.B., U. Mich., 1925. With publicity dept. Gen. Electric Co., Schenectady, 1925-30; editorial writer Balt. Evening Sun, 1930-36; London corr. Balt. Sun, 1936-37; editor Evening Sun, 1938-43, Balt. Sun, 1943-64; writer syndicated newspaper column, 1964—; lectr. U. Calif., 1961, 64; Am. del. Federation Nationale de la Viticulture Nouvelle. Author: American Wines and How to Make Them, 1933, Wine Grapes and How to Grow Them, 1937, The Wine-Grower's Guide, 1945, 3d rev. edit., 1985, American Wines and Wine Making, 1963, H.L. Mencken, 1966, Grapes into Wine, 1976; editor: (with Dr. Sanford V. Larkey) Turner on Wines, 1941; contbr. articles to numerous mags. Named officier Ordre du Merite Agricole (France). Mem. N.Y. Fruit Testing Coop. Assn. Democrat. Clubs: National Press (Washington), Overseas Writers (Washington); Hamilton St. (Balt.). Maintains an experimental vineyard and nursery devoted to adaptation of wine grapes to Am. conditions. Died Dec. 29, 1996.

WAITE, SCOTIA BALLARD KNOUFF, criminal justice specialist; b. Willis Wharf, Va., Apr. 8, 1909; d. Warren Alan and Lotta Mondora (Chard) Ballard; B.L.I., Emerson Coll., 1931; M.Ed., Boston U., 1933; diploma Sch. Social Work, Columbia U., 1939; m. William Francis Knouff, Oct. 9, 1943 (dec. Jan. 1968); children—Mary Francis Knouff Linn, Warren Irving Knouff; m. 2d Frederick Waite, Jan. 3, 1976. Dir., Mathews County (Va.) Relief Office, 1932-35, Rappahanock County Relief Office, 1935-36, dir. relief offices Norfolk County and City of S. Norfolk (Va.), 1936-37, case worker Henry Watson Children's Aid Soc., Balt., 1937, with New Orleans Council Social Agys., 1938-40, dir. Council Social Agenices, Syracuse, NY, 1940-44, asst. dir. Detroit Council Social Agys., 1944-45, tech. cons. juvenile delinquency Dept. Justice, Washington, 1948-50, instr., dir. Sociology Research Lab. CCNY, 1950-55, faculty dept. Sociology Adelphi U., 1955-63; dir. research and staff devel. Nassau County (N.Y.) Probation Dept., 1963-78; co-dir. Improving Victim Services Through Probation project Am. Probation and Parole Assn. of Aberdeen (N.C.) and Blackstone Inst. of Washington, 1978-80; cons. criminal justice, Pinehurst, N.C., 1980—; examiner Nat. Commn. on Accreditation for Corrections, 1979—; adj. asso. prof. Sch. Criminal Justice, C.W. Post Coll., L.I.U., 1967—; tech. cons. Nat. Inst. Corrections, 1983; mem. Child Placement Rev. Com. Moore County, N.C.; chmn. Youth Services Commn. Moore County. Mem. Nat. Republican Com. Recipient Outstanding Achievement award C.W. Post Coll. Sch. Criminal Justice, 1977, Spl. award Nassau County Probation Dept., 1978. Mem. Am. Probation and Parole Assn. (Walter Dunbar award 1977), Am. Correctional Assn., Northeastern Assn. Correctional Educators, Tex. Correctional Assn., AAUW. Episcopalian. Clubs: Pinehurst Country. Author numerous reports in corrections, victim services.

WALD, GEORGE, biochemist, educator; b. N.Y.C., N.Y., Nov. 18, 1906; s. Isaac and Ernestine (Rosenmann) W.; m. Frances Kingsley, May 15, 1931 (div.); children: Michael, David; m. Ruth Hubbard, 1958; children: Elijah, Deborah. B.S., NYU, 1927, D.Sc. (hon.), 1965; M.A., Columbia U., 1928, Ph.D., 1932; M.D. (hon.), U. Berne, 1957, U. Leon, Nicaragua, 1984; D.Sc. (hon.), Yale U., 1958, Wesleyan U., 1962, McGill U., 1966, Amherst Coll., 1968, U. Rennes, 1970, U. Utah, 1971, Gustavus Adolphus U., 1972, Hamline U., 1977, Columbia U., 1990; D.H.L. (hon.), Kalamazoo Coll., 1984. NRC fellow at Kaiser Wilhelm Inst. Berlin and Heidelberg, U. Zurich, U. Chgo., 1932-34; tutor biochem. scis. Harvard U., 1934-35, instr. biology, 1935-39, faculty instr., 1939-44, assoc. prof. biology, 1944-48, prof., 1948-77, Higgins prof. biology, 1968-77, prof. emeritus, 1977-97; vis. prof. biochemistry U. Calif., Berkeley, summer 1956; Nat. Sigma Xi lectr., 1952; chmn. divisional com. biology and med. scis. NSF, 1954-56; Guggenheim fellow, 1963-64; Overseas fellow Churchill Coll., Cambridge U., 1963-64; participant U.S.-Japan Eminent Scholar Exchange, 1973; guest China Assn. Friendship with Fgn. Peoples, 1972; v.p. Permanent Peoples' Tribunal, Rome, 1980-97. Co-author: General Education in a Free Society, 1945, Twenty Six Afternoons of Biology, 1962, 66, also sci. papers on vision and biochem. evolution. Recipient Eli Lilly prize Am. Chem. Soc., 1939, Lasker award Am. Pub. Health Assn., 1953, Proctor medal Assn. Rsch. in Opthalmology, 1955, Rumford medal Am. Acad. Arts and Scis., 1959, Ives medal Optical Soc. Am., 1966, Paul Karrer medal in chemistry U. Zurich, 1967, T. Duckett Jones award Helen Hay Whitney Found., 1967, Bradford Washburn medal Boston Mus. Sci., 1968, Max Berg award, 1969, Priestley medal Dickinson Coll., 1970, Columbia U. award for Disting. Achievement, 1991; co-recipient Nobel prize for physiology or medicine, 1967. Fellow NAS, Am. Acad. Arts and Scis., Am. Philos. Soc.; mem. Optical Soc. Am. (hon.). Home: Cambridge Mass. Died Apr. 12, 1996; interred Church of the Messiah, Woods Hole, MA.

WALDEN, MATTHIAS (OTTO EUGEN WILHELM FREIHERR VON SASS), author, journalist; b. Dresden, Germany, May 16, 1927; s. Eugen and Elisabeth (Risse) F. von S.; m. Edelgard von Müller, Dec. 21, 1950; children: Gabriele, Angelika, Bettina. Ed., Dresden. With RIAS, Berlin, 1950-56, Sender Freies Berlin, 1956-80, Die Welt, Welt am Sonntag, Bonn, Hamburg, Fed. Republic Germany, 1956-80, Die Welt, Bonn, 1980, Axel Springer Gesellschaft für Publzistik GmbH & Co., Berlin, 1981—. Author: (TV programs) Ich rufe Dresden, 1960, Schwarz-Rot-Gold in Asien, 1961, Vor unserer eigenen Tür, 1962, Einige Tage im Leben des Mischael Rosenberg, 1975; (books) Ostblind-Westblind, 1962, Berlin-Symphonie im Farben, 1963, Politik im Visier, 1965, Kassandra-Rufe, 1975, Die Fütterung der Krokodile, 1980, Wenn Deutschland rot wird, 1983, Von Wölfen und Schafen, 1983. Recipient Jacob Kaiser prize, Heinrich Stahl prize, Bundesverdienstkreuz, Adenauer prize, Goldene Kamera award.

WALDSTEIN, SHELDON SAUL, physician, educator; b. Chgo., June 23, 1924; s. Herman S. and Sophia (Klapper) W.; m. Jacqueline Sheila Denbo, Apr. 2, 1952; children: Sara Jean, Peter Denbo, David John. Student, Harvard U., 1941-43; M.D., Northwestern U., 1947. Diplomate: Am. Bd. Internal Medicine. Intern Cook County Hosp., 1947-48, resident in internal medicine, 1948-51; chief Northwestern Med. Service, 1954-62, exec. dir. dept. medicine, 1962-64, chmn. dept. medicine, 1964-69; exec. dir. North Suburban Assn. Health Resources, 1969-72; mem. faculty Northwestern U. Med. Sch., 1954-61, assoc. prof. medicine, 1961-66, prof. medicine, 1966—, assoc. dean health services, dir. Northwestern U. Med. Assos., 1974-77; exec. v.p. Nat. Ctr. for Advanced Med. Edn., Chgo., 1977-91; pres. Nat. Ctr. Advanced Med. Edn., Chgo., 1961-96. Contbr. articles to med. jours. Trustee Nat. Ctr. Advanced Med. Edn., Chgo., 1961-96. Served to capt. M.C., AUS, 1952-54. Fellow Am. Coll. Physicians, Am. Coll. Endocrinology; mem. AMA, Chgo. Med. Soc., Cen. Soc. Clin. Rsch., Endocrine Soc., Am. Assn. Clin. Endocrinology, Am. Fedn. Med. Rsch., Chgo. Soc. Internal Medicine, Alpha Omega Alpha. Office: 541 N Fairbanks Ct Chicago IL 60611-3319 Died Apr. 28, 1997.

WALES, HAROLD WEBSTER, lawyer; b. Seattle, June 23, 1928; s. John Harold and Clara (Webster) W.; m. Dorothy C. Kotthoff, July 15, 1955; children—Elizabeth Marie, Mary Celine. B.C.S. cum laude, Seattle U., 1950; J.D., U. San Francisco, 1958. Bar: Calif. 1959, Ariz. 1959. Pvt. practice Phoenix, 1959-96; pres. Central Ariz. Estate Planning Council, 1964-65; lectr. Tax Inst., Ariz. State U., 1962, 64, Nat. Automobile Dealers Assn., 1975-76; lectr., income tax Scottsdale (Ariz.) C.C., 1971-96. Pres. Cath. Social Svc., Phoenix, 1964; Ariz. chmn. Nat. Found. March of Dimes, 1969; bd. dirs. Camelback Hosp., 1984-90, ARC, Maricopa County, Cath. Family and Cmty. Svcs., 1960-86; mem. exec. com. Friends of Orphans, 1990. With USAF, 1950-54. Mem. ABA, Maricopa County bar assns., State Bar Calif., State Bar Ariz. (chmn. taxation sect. 1966-67), Am. Coll. Trust and Estate Counsel, Ariz. Acad., Order of Malta, We. Assn., Alpha Sigma Nu. Republican. Club: Serra of Phoenix (pres. 1964-65, 86-87). Lodge: Rotary of Scottsdale. Home: Phoenix Ariz. Died June 1, 1996.

WALES, HUGH GREGORY, marketing educator, business executive; b. Topeka, Feb. 28, 1910; s. Raymond Otis and Nola V. (Chestnut) W.; m. Alice Fulkerson, June 11, 1938. A.B., Washburn Coll., 1932; M.B.A., Harvard U., 1934; Ph.D., Northwestern U., 1944; D.Sc., Washburn Municipal U., 1968. Dean men N.W. Mo. State Tchrs. Coll., 1935-38, dean students, head dept. econs., 1938-39; dean students, dir. summer sch., vets. bur., head dept. econs. Washburn U., 1939-46; assoc. prof. marketing U. Ill., 1946-53, prof., 1953-70, prof. emeritus, dir. micro-precision projects, 1970-95; prof. marketing and mgmt., head dept. Roosevelt U., 1970-75; pres. Decisions, Evaluations & Learning, Internat. Assocs.; vis. prof. marketing U. South Africa, Pretoria, 1962; lectr. U. Stellenbosch, South Africa, 1973, 75, 76; cons. South African Govt., Pretoria, 1974; participant internat. confs.; bus., marketing research cons.; internat. pres. Micro-precision Miniaturization Inst., 1970-95, dir., program chmn., Chgo., 1970-95. Author: Changing Perspectives in Marketing, 1951, Marketing Research, 1952, 4th edit., 1974, Marketing Research-Selected Literature, 1952, Cases and Problems in Marketing Research, 1953, (with Robert Ferber) Basic Bibliography in Marketing Research, 1956, 3d edit., 1974, Motivation and Market Behavior, (with Ferber), 1958, Advertising Copy, Layout, and Typography, (with Gentry and M. Wales), 1958, (with R. Ferber) The Champaign-Urbana Metropolitan Area, (with Engel and Warshaw) Promotional Strategy, 1967, 3d edit., 1975, (with Dik Twedt and Lyndon Dawson) Personality Theory in Marketing Research: A Basic Bibliography, 1976, (with Sharon Abrams) English as a Second Language in Business, 1978, (with Luck, Taylor and Rubin) Marketing Research, 1978; numerous others, works transl. several langs.; Contbr. (with Luck, Taylor and Rubin) articles to profl. jours. Pres. Civic Symphony Soc., 1964-65. Mem. Am. Econ. Assn., Am. Marketing Assn. (sec., acad. v.p.), Am. Watchmakers Inst. (dir. research and edn. 1963-66), Nat. Assn. Watch and Clock Collectors (chpt. pres. 1981, 83), Arizonans for Nat. Security (chmn. visual aids com. 1979-95), Internat. Alliance Theatrical Stage Employees and Moving Picture Machine Operators, Internat. Platform Assn., Internat. TV Assn., Assn. Edn. Internat. Bus., Soc. Internat. Devel., Am. Statis. Assn., Nat. Assn. for Mgmt. Educators., Acad. Mgmt. Home: Tempe Ariz. Died Sept. 29, 1995.

WALKER, HENRY GARY, real estate developer; b. Alta., Can., Oct. 1, 1921; s. Henry and Amalia (Nagel) W.; m. Alam Jane Eichinger, Oct. 1, 1951; children: Cynthia Louis Zeigler, Henry Gary III, Catherine Ann Walker Eure. Ed. pub. schs. Photographer Silver Screen mag., 1939-41, San Francisco Examiner, 1941; White House photographer Life mag., 1949-59; fgn. corr. in Life mag., Berlin, U.K., Paris, Japan and Korea, 1948, 51, 60; with Curtis Pub. Co., 1962-65, mem. editorial bd., 1963-65, mng. dir. Photography, 1963-65; asst. mng. editor Sat. Eve. Post, 1962-65; pres. Walker Broadcasting Co., Ft. Pierce, Fla.; owner radio sta. WARN AM-FM, 1965-68; coord. Manned Spaceflight Still Photo Pool, Cocoa Beach, Fla., 1965-68; sr. v.p. C.V.R. Industries, Inc.; pres. Scottie Craft Boat Corp. Am., 1968-72, Congress Industries; v.p., dir. Outdoor Supply Corp., Servinational Inc., 1972-79; owner I&W Properties Ltd., 1972-84, W & W Properties Ltd., 1984-96. Served with USMCR, World War II. Home: Bal Harbour Fla. Died Oct. 13, 1996.

WALKER, ROBERT MIKE, federal agency administrator; m. Romy Patterson. Student, U. Tenn. Page Washington; asst., budget analyst U.S. Rep. Joe L. Evins, 1969-76, nat. security & appropriations advisor U.S. Sen. Jim Sasser, 1977-94; mem. staff Senate's Com. on Appropriations, Washington, 1979-81, mem. staff Subcom. on Mil. Constrn., 1981-87, staff dir. Subcom. on Mil. Constrn., 1987-94; asst. sec. Army for Installations, Logistics and Environment, 1994—; head Senate Task Forces on Persian Gulf and Cen. Am.; mil. affairs advisor Senate dels. to former Yugoslavia, Ea. Europe, Somalia, Korea, and Antarctica. With Tenn. and D.C. Army N.G., 1969-75.

WALKER, VINCENT HENRY, lawyer, former government official; b. Lowell, Mass., Oct. 14, 1915; s. Daniel Henry and Annie Jane (Gookin) W.; m. Irene Iris Johnson, Nov. 16, 1946; children: Patricia Anne (Mrs. John Armstrong III), Johnnie Melinda. J.D., Boston Coll. Law, 1939; B.C.S., Benjamin Franklin U., 1951. Bar: Mass. 1940, Fed. Tax Ct. 1952, U.S. Supreme Ct. 1965, D.C. 1980. Partner firm, 1940-42; gen. mgr., counsel, joint venture land and subdiv. devels. and sales South and Southwestern U.S., 1946-60; FHA regional atty. Southeastern U.S. and Virgin Islands; then regional atty. FHA Washington Hdqrs. for Mid Atlantic region, 1960; asst. for zone ops. Southwestern U.S., 1960-61; AID State Dept. contract specialist, chief comml. contracts br., adviser to Govt. of Sudan for contract negotiations, developed conversion of AID contracts to automatic data processing system in Vietnam AID Office of Contract Services, Washington, 1961-69; internat. trade policy specialist, chief trade policy br., dir. (acting) indsl. resources div. AID Office of Procurement, 1969-72; internat. trade specialist, agrl. commoditiies mgr., procurement support div. Office of Commodity Mgmt., AID, 1972-75; contract specialist, interagy. rep., mem. interagy. procurement policy com. Office Contracts Mgmt., 1975-85; ind. legal, fin. cons., 1985-93. Author and interagy. collaborator AID govt. and world-wide legal and regulatory publs., export program directives, notices to U.S. industry, internat. posts and orgns., 1970-85; author: pub. Agrl. Commodity Supply, Price, Trends, Report, 1972-75; photog. works published various media in, U.S. and fgn. countries., 1970-93. Hon. mem. bd. dirs. Am. Opera Scholarship Soc.; mem. men's com. Internat. Eye Found.; contbr. incorporating atty. Lowell Light Opera Guild, 1942. Served to lt. comdr. USNR, Overseas, 1942-46. Named hon. citizen City of Lexington (Ky.), 1970. Mem. Lowell, Middlesex County, Mass., D.C. bar assns., Nat. Trust for Historic Preservation, Smithsonian Assos., Wolf Trap Assos. Home: Bethesda Md. Died Jan. 12, 1993.

WALL, FRED WILLARD, agricultural products supplier; b. 1923. With Porterville (Calif.) Drug Co., 1946-49; with Walco Internat. Inc., 1950—, now pres., chmn. bd., CEO. With USN., 1946. Died Sept. 14, 1996.

WALLACE, ALLEN, arts administrator; b. Detroit, Sept. 20, 1953; s. Stanley John and Julia Ann (Srock) W. BA, Wayne State U., 1976; MA, Boston U., 1981. Curator Cummings Collection, Detroit, 1977-79; founder, dir. Preservation Wayne, Detroit, 1975-79, cons., 1983-92; dir. spl. projects Martha Graham Dance Co., N.Y.C., 1980-86; pres. New Old World Products, Inc., N.Y.C., 1984-87; dir. pub. rels. The Dance Gallery, Lewitzky Dance Co., L.A., 1987-92; cons. Opera Ensemble N.Y., N.Y.C., 1981, Manhattan Ensemble, N.Y.C., 1983-92; pub. rels. and arts mgmt. cons. Calif. State U., L.A., Dance Kaleidoscope, Occidental Coll., L.A. Theatre Ctr., Westside Ballet; chmn. bd. L.A. Performance Exch.; bd. dirs. Shirley Kirkes Ballet, 1990, Dance Resource Ctr. of Greater L.A., 1991. Pub. Martha Graham Jour., Frankfurt Ballet Jour., Michigan History, Los Angeles Today. Active animal rights groups, 1989-92. Resolution of Tribute Mich. Senate, Honor award Nat. Trust Hist. Preservation; Wayne State U. Bd. Govs. scholar, Detroit, 1974, 75, 76. Mem. Polish-Am. Congress, Polish-Am. Cultural Network. Home: Los Angeles Calif. Died Dec. 12, 1992.

WALLACE, JANE YOUNG (MRS. DONALD H. WALLACE), editor; b. Geneseo, Ill., Feb. 17, 1933; d. Worling R. and Margaret C. (McBroom) Young; m. Donald H. Wallace, Aug. 24, 1959; children: Robert, Julia. BS in Journalism, Northwestern U., 1955, MS in Journalism, 1956; LittD (hon.), Johnson and Wales U., 1990. Diplomate Nat. Restaurant Assn. Edn. Found., 1991. Editor house organ Libby McNeill & Libby, Chgo., 1956-58; prodn. editor Instns. Mag., Chgo., 1958-61; food editor Instns. Mag., 1961-65, mng. editor, 1965-68, editor-in-chief, 1968-85; editor Restaurants and Instns., 1970-85, editorial dir., 1985-89, assoc. pub., 1985-89, pub., 1989-94; pub. R & I Market Pl., 1989-94, v.p., editor/pub. emeritus, 1994-96; editorial dir. Hotels and Restaurants Internat. Mag., 1971-89; v.p., editor/pub. emeritus Restaurants and Instns., 1994-96; editorial dir. Foodservice Equipment Specialist Mag., 1975-89; v.p. Cahners Pub. Co. (Reed USA), 1982; mem. editorial quality audit bd. Reed USA, 1993-96; cons. Nat. Restaurant Assn., dir., 1977-82; cons. Nat. Inst. for Food Svc. Industry; vis. lectr. Fla. Internat. U., 1980. Editor: The Professional Chef, 1962, The Professional Chef's Book of Buffets, 1965, Culinary Olympics Cookbook, 1980, 3d edit., 1988, Academy of American Culinary Foundation Cookbook, 1985, American Dietetic Associaton Foundation Cookbook, 1986; contbr. restaurant chpt. World Book Ency., 1975, 94, Food Service Trends, American Quantity Cooking, 1976. Mem. com. investigation vocat. needs for food svc. tng. U.S. Dept. Edn., 1969; mem. Inst. Food Editors' Conf., 1959-88, pres., 1967; mem. hospitality industry edn. adv. bd. Ill. Dept. Edn., 1976, mem. adv. bd. Ill. sch. foodsvc., 1978; mem. corp. adv. bd. Am. Dietetic Assn. Found., 1981-92, bd. dirs., 1996; trustee Presbyn. Ch., Barrington, Ill., 1983-85; bd. trustees Culinary Inst. Am., 1987-96. Recipient Jesse H. Neal award for best bus. press editorial, 1969, 70, 73, 76, 77, 79, 82, 87, Diplomate award Nat. Restaurant Assn. Edn. Found., 1991; named Outstanding Woman Northwood Inst., 1983. Fellow Soc. for Advancement Foodservice Rsch. (dir. 1975-77, sec. 1980); mem. Internat. Foodservice Mfrs. Assn. (Spark Plug award 1979), Nat. Assn. Foodservice Equipment Mfrs., Am. Bus. Press Assn. (chmn. editl. com. 1978), Am. Inst. Interior Designers (assoc.), Women in Comms. (v.p. Chgo. 1957-58), Ivy Soc. Restauranteurs of Distinction (co-founder 1970-96), Am. Dietetic Assn. (hon., bd. dirs. 1996), Roundtable for Women in Food Service (bd. dirs. 1980-84; Foodservice Woman of Yr. 1988, Lifetime Recognition award 1994), Les Dames d'Escoffier (charter mem.), Culinary Inst. of Am. (ambassador 1986, trustee 1987-96), Brotherhood of Knights of Vine (Gentlelady award 1980, 81), Disting. Restaurateurs of N.Am. (Hall of Fame award 1994), Internat. Assn. Cooking Profls., Gamma Phi Beta, Kappa Tau Alpha. Home: Barrington Ill. Died May 16, 1996.

WALLACE, RICHARD S., academic administrator, economics educator; b. Washington, June 24, 1934. AB, Wofford Coll., 1956; PhD in Econs., U. Va., 1965. Economist Fed. Res. Bank Richmond, Va., 1963-66; asst. prof. econs. Ga. State Coll., 1966-67, assoc. prof., 1966-70; prof. econs., dean sch. bus. adminstrn. Winthrop Coll., Rock Hill, S.C., from 1970; v.p. for acad. affairs Augusta (Ga.) Coll., pres., 1987—. Served to lt. U.S. Army, 1957-60.

WALLER, WILLIAM, lawyer; b. Nashville, Oct. 28, 1898; s. Claude and Martha Armistead (Nelson) W.; m. Elizabeth Warner Estes, Dec. 31, 1924; 1 son, William; m. Milbrey Warner, Sept. 11, 1935; 1 dau., Mrs. Thomas G. Andrews, Jr. Student, Wallace U. Sch., 1911-14; B.S., Vanderbilt U., 1918; LL.B. magna cum laude, Yale, 1922. Bar: Tenn. bar 1922. Asst. to gen. counsel N.C. & St.L Ry., 1922-27; gen. practice law Nashville, 1927—; mem. firm Waller, Lansden, Dortch & Davis and predecessor firms, now of counsel; lectr. Vanderbilt Law Sch., 1925-26, 50-56. Editor, compiler: Nashville in the 1890's, 1970, Nashville, 1900 to 1910, 1972. Trustee Vanderbilt U., 1956—, Harpeth Hall Sch., 1950-66, Ladies Hermitage Assn., 1959—. Served as 2d lt., C.A.C. U.S. Army, 1918-19, AEF. Mem. Am. Law Inst., Mont Pelerin Soc., Tenn. Hist. Commn., Order of Coif, Phi Beta Kappa, Phi Delta Theta, Phi Delta Phi. Clubs: Round Table (Nashville), Belle Meade Country (Nashville), University (Nashville). Home: Nashville Tenn. DIED 08/10/95. .

WALLERSTEIN, DAVID B., business consultant; b. Richmond, Va., May 13, 1905; s. David B. and Hattie (Pfaelzer) W.; m. Caroline Rieser, Dec. 28, 1931 (dec.); children: John M., Michael R. (dec.), David L. B.S., U. Va., 1924; M.B.A., Harvard U., 1926. With Balaban & Katz Corp., Chgo., 1926-66; v.p., gen. mgr. Balaban & Katz Corp., 1950-57, pres., 1957-66; past dir.; dir. Am. Broadcasting Cos., 1962-66; cons. Bell & Howell Corp., 1968-69; dir. McDonald's Corp. Chmn., dir. State St. Council, Chgo., 1952-65; dir., mem. exec. com. Theatre Owners Am., 1950-65; bd. dirs. Chgo. Better Bus. Bur., 1958-64, Chgo. Assn. Commerce, 1959-66; Pres., chmn. bd. Francis W. Parker Sch., Chgo., 1951-58, trustee, 1946-62, life trustee, 1962-93; life trustee Michael Reese Hosp. and Med. Center. Club: Standard (Chgo.). Home: Chicago Ill. Died Jan. 4, 1993.

WALLERSTEIN, HARRY, retired hematologist; b. N.Y.C., Dec. 11, 1906; s. Jacob Mordecai and Lena (Goldberg) W.; m. Gussie Arnold, June 29, 1926; children: Sally W. Sedler, Caryl W. Sands. AB, George Washington U., 1927, MD, 1930. Intern Sydenham Hosp., N.Y.C., 1930-31; assoc. pathologist to dir. rsch. Jewish Meml. Hosp., 1964-83; from dir. blood bank to vis. pathologist Bronx Mcpl. Hosp. Ctr., 1956-83; cons. in hematology St. Elizabeth Hosp., 1954-93, Fordham City Hosp., 1951-93, Morrisania City Hosp., 1948-93, St. Clare's Hosp. and Health Ctr., 1971-93; lectr. pathology Albert Einstein Coll. Medicine, 1956-59, vis. asst. prof. pathology, 1959-76; dir. labs., pathologist Jewish Meml. Hosp., 1933-37, assoc. hematologist, 1937-50; assoc vis. pathologist Bronx Mcpl. Hosp., 1956-58; asst./assoc. vis. pathologist Queens Cen. Hosp., 1942-56; assoc. pathologist Sea View Hosp., 1933; dir. Marcia Slater Lab. for Rsch. in Leukemia. Contbr. articles to profl. jours. Mem. Blood Bank and Transfusion Adv. Bd. to Dept. Health, N.Y.C., 1967-93. Recipient Hon. Mention Med. Soc. State N.Y., 1948, 3d award for Meritorious Individual Investigation, 1948, 1st award for Sci. Rsch., 1964; received posthumously Award for lifetime of Dedication to Transfusion Medicine, Coun. of Hosp. Blood Bank Dirs. of Greater N.Y. Region, Cert. of Merit in exptl. medicine and therapuetics AMA, 1963; Dept. HEW grantee. Fellow N.Y. Acad. Medicine, N.Y. Acad. Sci., AMA (cert. merit 1962), Am. Soc. Clin. Pathologists, Internat. Soc. Hematology (founder); mem. AAAS, Am. Assn. Blood Banks, Blood Bank Assn. N.Y. State, Internat. Soc. Blood Transfusions, Am. Soc. Hematology, N.Y. Pathol. Soc. (life), Am. Soc. Human Genetics, N.Y. Acad. Scis. (life), N.Y. Soc. for Study of Blood, N.Y. State Soc. Pathologists, Am. Eugenics Soc., Am. Assn. Cancer Rsch., Albert Gallatin Assocs. of NYU (life), Luther Rice Soc. George Washington U. (life). Died June 26, 1993.

WALLINGFORD, DANA R(IO), financial consultant; b. Long Beach, Calif., Jan. 19, 1948; s. Richard Keller and Faith (Gribell) W.; m. Susan C. Kollmar, Oct. 21, 1978; children: Sidney Miller, Melissa Miller. BA in Bus. Adminstrn., U. Wash., 1971. Cert. fin. mgr., 1988, comml. underwater diver. Comml. underwater diver Seattle, 1975-76; asst. mgr. loss prevention Seattle Stevedore Co., Seattle, 1976-78; asst. mgr. loading ops. Sea Star Stevedore Co., Anchorage, 1978-80; asst. v.p. pvt. client group Merrill Lynch, Anchorage, 1981-87; v.p. pvt. client group Merrill Lynch, Phoenix, Ariz., 1987—; charter mem. Master Network, Merrill Lynch, Phoenix, 1990—, mem. Chmn.'s Club, 1992, 93, 94; charter founding mem. Phoenix Forum, 1994—. Com. mem. Fiesta Bowl, Tempe, Ariz., 1987-94; charter mem. Anchorage Sr. Ctr. Endowment, 1985-86; mem. Sheriff's Posse, Maricopa County, Ariz., 1994—. Capt. U.S. Army, 1971-75. Mem. Mason (Master, Phonecia # 58, sgt. at arms 1992-93), El Zaribah Temple (Shrine Noble 1992—), U. Wash. Alumni Assn. (geographic coord. Ariz. chpt., chmn. 1992—), Rotary Internat. (Paul Harris fellow 1986). Republican. Avocations: horseback riding, scuba diving, classic car collecting, hiking, traveling. Died, June 9, 1996.

WALSH, JAMES LOUIS, retired lawyer, insurance company executive; b. Parsons, Kan., Feb. 24, 1909; s. James Louis and Catharine (Nolan) W. A.B., U. Notre Dame, 1930; LL.B., So. Meth. U., 1933. Bar: Tex. bar 1933. Asst. counsel Home Owners Loan Corp., Dallas, 1934-35; counsel Home Owners Loan Corp., 1935-40, div. counsel, 1940-44; asso. law firm Hamilton, Lipscomb, Wood & Swift, Dallas, 1944-45; with legal dept. Southwestern Life Ins. Co., Dallas, 1945-92; asso. gen. counsel Southwestern Life Ins. Co., 1951-65, v.p., 1965-70, gen. counsel, 1965-74, sr. v.p., 1970-73, exec. v.p., gen. counsel, 1973-74. Mem. Dallas Estate Council, 1947-92, pres., 1955-56; pres. Catholic Charities, Dallas, 1962-63; Dir. Community Council Greater Dallas, 1962-68. Decorated knight grand cross Order Holy Sepulchre, Knight of Malta. Mem. Am., Tex., Dallas bar assns., Assn. Life Ins. Counsel (mem. emeritus), Phi Alpha Delta. Roman Catholic. Home: Dallas Tex. Deceased, April 1992.

WALSH, WILLIAM BERTALAN, physician; b. Bklyn., Apr. 26, 1920; s. Joseph W. and Irene (Viola) W.; m. Helen Rundvold, Dec. 19, 1943; children: William Bertalan, John Thomas, Thomas Stephen. BS, St. John's U., 1940; MD, Georgetown U., 1943, DSc (hon.), 1962; LHD (hon.), Beaver Coll., Pa., 1967; DSc, St. John's U., 1968, Howard U., 1969; LLD, Trinity Coll., 1969; DHL (hon.), Clarkson Coll. Tech., 1975, Carthage Coll., 1970, N.Y. Med. Coll., 1983; HHD (hon.), Duquesne U., 1983; LHD (hon.), Copernicus Med. Acad., Jagiellonian U., Krakow, Poland, 1990. Intern L.I. Coll. Hosp., 1943-44; resident internal medicine Georgetown U. Hosp., 1946-48; practice medicine specializing in internal medicine Washington, 1946-64; clin. prof. internal medicine Georgetown U. Med. Sch., 1958-70; bd. dirs. GenCorp; chief exec. officer, pres. People-to-People Health Found., 1958-91; founder Project HOPE, 1958—; pub. Health Affairs; cons. surgeon gen. USAF, surgeon gen. USPHS; mem. Pres.'s Adv. Com. Physical Fitness Youth, 1956-59; vice chmn. Pres.'s Adv. Com. Selection Doctors and Dentists and Allied Specialists for SSS, 1959-60; vice chmn. health resources adv. com. OCDM, 1956-59, chmn., 1960; cons. diseases chest NIH, 1954-61; former mem. Pres.'s Com. on Employment Handicapped; former vice chmn. Fedn. People-to-People Programs; former mem. directing program Nat. Council on Patient Info. and Edn.; former mem. pub. liaison bd. Nat. Ctr. for Allied Health Leadership; former mem. adv. com. on vol. fgn. aid AID; mem. exec. com. President's Pvt. Sector Survey on Cost Control; former chmn. Pres.'s Adv. Com. on Health; bd. dirs. Marimed Found.; mem. pvt. sector book and library com. U.S. Info. Agy.; former mem. Presdl. Bd. Advisors on Pvt. Sector Initiatives; mem. Am. del. to World Health Assembly, 1986, 87-88, 89, 90; mem. adj. faculty Shenandoah Coll. and Conservatory Music; bd. dirs. Advanced Tissue Scis., Inc.; mem. Am. com. Internat. Red Cross Mus. Author: A Ship Called HOPE, 1964, Yanqui, Come Back, 1966, HOPE in the East: The Mission to Ceylon; co-author: Medicine and the Satellite, 1974; vice chmn. med. adv. bd. Med. Source Book Series, 1991—. Bd. govs. John Carroll Soc.; mem., life regent emeritus Georgetown U.; trustee Landon Sch. Boys, Washington.; mem. President's Commn. on Exec. Exchange, Nat. Bipartisan Commn. on C.Am.; mem. Presdl. Commn. on the Human Immunodeficiency Virus Epidemic; bd. councillors Am. Assn. of Sovereign Mil. Order of Malta; former chmn. Sharing Internat. Served to lt., M.C. USNR, 1943-46, PTO. Decorated Knight Magisterial Palms, Knight Order Daniel A. Carrion Peru; Star of October; Al Merito Ecuador; Order of Ruben Dario; Grand Ofcl. Grade Nicaragua; officer Order Tunisian Republic; Gold medal (Medallo de Oro) City of Trujillo, Peru; Order San Carlos Colombia; Order So. Cross Brazil; Order of Merit Poland; comdr. Cross of Merit, So. Assn. Sovereign Mil. Order Malta, Papal Knighthood of St. Gregory, Nat. Order of Merit France, Nat. Order of Merit with star, rank commr., Poland, Order of Vasco Nunez de Balboa in rank of Comdr. (Govt. Panana), others; named to Internat. Pediatrics Hall of Fame Miami Children's Hosp., 1989; recipient Georgetown U. Alumni award, 1961; Health U.S.A. award, 1961; Distinguished Service award USIA, 1961; Detroit Internat. Freedom Festival award, 1961; Humanitarian of Year award Lions, 1961; Sertoma Internat. Service to

Mankind award, 1962; Nat. Citizenship award Mil. Chaplains Assn., 1963; Theodore Roosevelt Distinguished Service medal, 1967; Americas award Americas Found., 1967; Freedom Leadership medal Freedom Founds. at Valley Forge, 1968; Lawrence C. Kline World Peace award, 1968; Stritch medal Stritch Sch. Medicine, Loyola U., 1970; Laetare medal U. Notre Dame, 1970; Simon Le Moyne award Le Moyne Coll., 1970; Distinguished Service award Am. Coll. Cardiology, 1971; Good Samaritan award St. Joseph Hosp., Albuquerque, 1972; Distinguished Service medal People-to-People Program, 1967; Alumni Achievement award Georgetown U. Alumni Club of Met. Washington, 1967; Magna Charta award Baronial Order Magna Charta, 1974; Bellarmine Coll. medal, 1974; Sovereign Mil. Order Malta, 1975; gold medal Nat. Inst. Social Scis., 1977; Walter F. Patenge medal Mich. State U., 1982, cert. recognition Shenandoah U., 1990; Commemorative medal Inst. for Further Edn. of Medicine Doctors and Pharmacists Govt. Czech and Slovak Republics, 1990; named to St. John's U. Alumni Hall of Fame, 1970; award of recognition for humanitarian services, 1982; Best of Va. award, 1983; Nat. Service award Environ. Mgmt. Assn., 1983; named Washingtonian of Yr., 1983; Presdl. Pvt. Sector Initiative Commendation, 1986; Knight of Order of Arts and Letters, Ministry of Culture, France, 1986; Presdl. Medal of Freedom, 1987; Commemorative medal Inst. for Further Edn. of Medicine Doctors and Pharmacists in Prague, 1990; named to Internat. Pediatrics Hall of Fame, Miami Children's Hosp., 1989. Fellow Internat. Coll. Dentists (hon.); mem. AMA (mem. council nat. def. 1954-56), Am. Soc. Internal Medicine (exec. com., chmn. legislative com. 1957-59), D.C. Med. Soc., Nat. Med. Vets. Soc. (pres. 1952), ADA (hon.), Am. Soc. Assn. Execs.(key philanthropic orgns. com. 1991—), U.S. Pharmacopoeial Conv. Inc. Adv. Panel. Clubs: University (Washington); Columbia Country (Chevy Chase, Md.); Circumnavigators (Magellan medal 1965) (N.Y.C); Union League (N.Y.C.). Died Dec. 27, 1996.

WALTERS, C. GLENN, college dean, marketing educator; b. Americus, Ga., Apr. 20, 1929; s. Johnny B. and Eunice Dorothy Walters; m. Patricia Jean Mohelnitzky, Sept. 27, 1952; children: Michael, David, Greg, Julie. BS in Bus., Auburn U., 1955, MS in Econs., 1957; PhD in Mktg., U. Ill., Carbondale, 1963. Asst. prof. mktg. La. State U., Baton Rouge, 1961-66, acting asst. dean, 1963, coordinator mktg., 1969-70; prof. mktg. Miss. State U., Starksville, 1970-77; chmn. mktg. dept. So. Ill. U., Carbondale, 1977-81; disting. prof. mktg. Nicholls State U., Thibodaux, La., 1982—, dean Coll. of Bus., 1984—. Author: Marketing Channels, 1982, Consumer Behavior: Theory and Practice, 1984, Basic Marketing: A Situational Orientation, 1988. Bd. dirs. Bayou Council on Alcoholism, Parish Council, Thibodaux, 1986-88; bd. trustees La. Council on Econ. Edn., Baton Rouge, 1986-87. Served with USN, 1948-52. Mem. Acad. Mktg. Sci., Am. Acad. Advt., Am. Mktg. Assn., Mid-South Mktg. Conf., Southwestern Fedn. Adminstrv. Disciplines, Thibodaux C. of C. Roman Catholic. Avocations: reading, writing, gardening. DIED 09/26/95. .

WALTERS, EVERETT, retired university official, author; b. Bethlehem, Pa., Apr. 4, 1915; s. Raymond and Elsie (Rosenberg) W.; m. Jane C. Schrader, Apr. 23, 1938; children: Diane Colley (Mrs. Patrick B. Hearne), Everett Garrison. A.B., U. Cin., 1936; M.A., Columbia U., 1940, Ph.D., 1947. Instr. Finch Jr. Coll., 1940-43; rep. U.S. Civil Service Commn., 1943-44; instr. history Ohio State U., 1946-48, asst. prof., 1948-54, assoc. prof., 1954-63, asst. dean Grad. Sch., 1954-55, acting dean Grad. Sch., 1956-57, dean Grad. Sch., 1957-63, chmn. editorial bd. Ohio State U. Press; Vis. prof. Whittier Coll., summer 1950; dir. grad. fellowship program U.S. Office Edn., 1962-63; v.p. acad. affairs Boston U., 1963-69, sr. v.p., dean faculties, 1969-71; dean faculties U. Mo.-St. Louis, 1971-75, vice chancellor community affairs, 1975-79, prof., 1979-80, interim chancellor, 1972-73; Chmn. Grad. Conf. on Grad. Study and Research, 1961-62. Author: Joseph Benson Foraker; An Uncompromising Republican, 1948; Editor, contbr: Graduate Education Today, 1965; Contbr. articles to hist., ednl. jours. Bd. dirs. Sta. KETC-TV, St. Louis, 1973-80, chmn., 1979-80; chmn. bd. dirs. St. Louis Bach Soc., 1977-78. Served as lt. USNR, 1944-46; Naval Officers Candidate Sch. 1950-52, Newport, R.I. Recipient Centennial Achievement award Ohio State U., 1970. Mem. Am. Hist. Assn., Ohio Hist. Soc. (trustee 1961-63, 82-87), Ohio Hist. Found. (trustee, sec. 1987-91), Assn. Grad. Schs. (sec.-treas. 1960-61, editor Procs. Jour. 1959-63), St. Louis Council World Affairs (chmn. bd.), Columbus Met. Club, University Club (Columbus), Phi Delta Theta. Episcopalian. Home: Columbus Ohio Died Mar. 15, 1997.

WALTERS, WANDA LENK, choreographer, educator, artistic director; b. Nashville, Apr. 27, 1944; d. Walter Albert and Wanda (Lewis) Lenk; m. Edward Rehfeldt, 1963 (div. 1974); 1 child, Edward John Rehfeldt IV; m. Bayard Harding Walters, Nov. 23, 1977. Student, Chgo. Conservatory Music, 1962-63, Taipei Lang. Inst., Taiwan, 1965-68; BA, U. Md.-Far East br., Taiwan, 1973. Profl. dancer Edna McCrae Dance Co., Chgo., 1962-64; tchr. classical ballet Am. Club, Taipei, Taiwan, 1966-68; prof. classical ballet Chinese Cultural Coll., Taipei, 1966-73; tchr., owner Wanda Lenk Sch. Ballet, Nashville, 1974-91; artistic dir. Nashville Contemporary Ballet Co., 1983-91; choreographer Shrewsbury (Eng.) Internat. Music Festival, 1987, Tenn. Gov's. Sch. Arts, 1986. Dance panelist Tenn. Arts Commn., 1983-84. Subject of Tribute to Miss Wanda, Nashville Contemporary Ballet Co., 1991. Mem. Dance Alliance (pres. 1987-89), Internat. Ballet Coun. (regional membership chmn. 1990-91), Nashville Ballet Soc. (artist 1958-62), Nat. Assn. Broadcasters (founder Encore club 1988, Recognition award 1991), Dance Educators Am., Tenn. Assn. Dance. Democrat. Methodist. Avocation: working with children. Home: Nashville Tenn. Died Feb. 2, 1991.

WALZER, WILLIAM CHARLES, church administrator, religious publisher; b. Rochester, N.Y., July 20, 1912; s. William Frederick and Mable Beatrice (McElroy) W.; m. Dorothy Mae Kramer, Aug. 28, 1938; children—Carolyn Walzer Dennis, Lorraine Walzer Harbaugh, William T. B.A., U. Rochester, 1935; M.A., 1937; B.D., Colgate-Rochester Div. Sch., 1941; Ph.D., U. Chgo., 1944; postgrad., Syracuse U. Sch. Journalism, 1951. Ordained to ministry United Meth. Ch., 1941, United Ch. of Christ, 1985, Christian Ch. (Disciples of Christ), 1986. Tchr. high sch., 1935-38; pastor Stafford (N.Y.) Meth. Ch., 1938-41; asst. pastor Hyde Park Meth. Ch., Chgo., 1941-43; asst. prof. Garrett Theol. Sem., Evanston, Ill., 1943-45; prof. Scarritt Coll. for Christian Workers and Vanderbilt U. Div. Sch., Nashville, 1945-51; mem. staff Bd. Missions, Presbyn. Ch. in U.S.A., N.Y.C., 1951-54; exec. dir. dept. edn. for mission Nat. Council Chs., N.Y.C., 1954-77; exec. dir. Friendship Press, N.Y.C., 1954-77; interim pastor Westminster Presbyn. Ch., N.Y.C., 1955-59, 66-68, 75-77; minister Community Ch. of Great Neck, N.Y., 1979-85; treas. Eastern Ecumenical Conf. Christian World Mission, 1985-92; interim minister Fairfax (Va.) Christian Ch., 1987-88, 92-93; dec., 1995; cons. div. world mission and ecumenism Luth. Ch. in Am., N.Y.C., 1978-79; chmn. Eastern Ecumenical Conf. on World Mission, Silver Bay, N.Y., 1978-80; pres. Religious Pub. Relations Council, 1959-61; bd. dirs. Religion in Am. Life, 1965-68; del. World Council Christian Edn., Tokyo, 1958, Lima, Peru, 1971; cons. Pacific Council of Chs., Suva, Fiji, Joint Bd. Christian Edn., Australia and N.Z., 1972; staff World Council Chs. Assembly, New Delhi, 1961, Uppsala, Sweden, 1968. Author: American Denominations, 1953, Your World, Your Mission, 1963, Great Protestant Leaders, 1965. Mem. U.S. Nat. Commn. for UNESCO, 1972-78; chmn. Potomac assn. stewardship and mission com. United Ch. of Christ, 1991-92. Mem. Am. Soc. Ch. History, Internat. Soc. Missiology, Gray Panthers, Phi Beta Kappa, Phi Sigma Iota. Home: Reston Va. Died Feb. 21, 1995.

WANG, HAO, logician; b. Tsinan, Shantung, China, May 20, 1921; s. Chuchen and Tsecheng (Liu) W.; m. Yenking Kan, June 22, 1948 (div.); children: Sanyok, Yiming, Jane Hsiaoching. B.Sc., Southwestern Asso. U., China, 1943; M.A., Tsing Hua U., China, 1945; M.A. (by decree), Balliol Coll., Oxford, 1956; Ph.D., Harvard, 1948; postdoc., Zurich, 1950-51. Tchr. math. China, 1943-46; research engr. Burroughs Corp., 1953-54; asst. prof. philosophy Harvard, 1951-56, Gordon McKay prof. math. logic, applied math., 1961-67; John Locke lectr. philosophy U. Oxford, 1954-55, reader philosophy of math., 1956-61; prof. Rockefeller U., 1967—; pres. Kurt Gödel Soc., Vienna, 1987-89; cons. U. Mich., summers 1956, 57, IBM, summers, 1957, 58, MIT, summer 1960, Bell Tel. Labs., 1962-64, mem. tech. staff, 1959-60; vis. prof. Rockefeller U., 1966-67; hon. prof. Peking U., 1985—, Tsinghua U., 1986—; vis. scientist IBM Research Labs., 1973-74; visitor Inst. for Advanced Study, 1975-76; lectr. on math. logic Academia Sinica, Beijing, 1977, Taipei, 1987. Author: A Survey of Mathematical Logic, 1962, reissued as Logic, Computers and Sets, 1970, (Rumanian edit. 1972), Reflections on China (in Chinese), 1973, From Mathematics to Philosophy, 1974 (Italian edit. 1984), Popular Lectures on Mathematical Logic, English and Chinese edits., 1981, reissued, 1992, Beyond Analytic Philosophy 1985, Reflections on Kurt Gödel, 1987, French edit., 1990, Spanish edit., 1991, Computation, Logic, Philosophy, 1990; contbr. numerous articles to math. and philos. jours. Recipient 1st Mileston prize Joint Internat. Conf. on Artificial Intelligence, 1983; Jr. fellow Soc. of Fellows, Harvard, 1948-51; fellow Rockefeller Found., 1954-55. Fellow Am. Acad. Arts and Sci., mem. Assn. Symbolic Logic, Brit. Acad. (corr. fellow). DIED 05/13/95. .

WANG, SHIH C., physiologist, educator; b. Tientsin, China, Jan. 25, 1910; came to U.S., 1937, naturalized, 1949; s. Yen Sun and Hsi (Han) W.; m. Mamie Kwoh, Jan. 10, 1939; children: Phyllis M., Nancy E. B.S., Yenching U., 1931; M.D., Peking Union Med. Coll., 1935; Ph.D., Northwestern U., 1940. Specialist in neurophysiology and neuro-pharmacology N.Y.C., 1940-93; faculty Columbia Coll. Phys. and Surgs., 1941-93, prof. physiology, 1954-56, prof. pharmacology, 1956-93, Pfeiffer prof., 1975-79, Pfeiffer prof. emeritus, 1979-93; vis. prof. China Med. Bd. Rockefeller Found., Taiwan, 1958. Author monograph; contbr. chpts. to Handbook of Physiology, 1965, Physiological Pharmacology, 1965, Physiology and Pharmacology of the Brain Stem, 1980. John Guggenheim fellow, 1951; Commonwealth fellow U. Gäteborg, Sweden, 1966. Mem. Am. Physiol. Soc., Am. Pharmacol. Soc., N.Y. Acad. Scis., N.Y. Acad. Medicine, Assn. for Research on Nervous and Mental Diseases, Soc. Exptl. Biology and Medicine, Harvey Soc., AAAS, N.Y. State Med. Soc., Sigma Xi. Research, numerous publs. primarily in field physiology and pharmacology of automatic nervous system. Home: Tenafly N.J. Died June 6, 1993.

WARBURTON, (NATHANIEL) CALVIN, JR., state legislator, retired clergyman; b. Lynn, Mass., May 28, 1910; s. Nathaniel Calvin and Susan Blanche (Dillihunt) W.; m. Janice Orene Fitch, Sept. 18, 1935 (dec. 1991); children: David Calvin, Natalie Rae Warburton Sable, Mary Susan Warburton Ward, Ellen Orena Warburton Levesque, Edward James. BS, Boston U., 1932, STB, 1935; postgrad., U. N.H., 1946-47; ThM, Sch. Theology, Colorado Springs, Colo., 1960. Ordained elder Meth. Ch., 1937. Pastor Fremont (N.H.) Meth. Episcopal Ch., 1935-36, Moultonville (N.H.) and Tuftonboro Meth. Episcopal Ch., 1936-38, 1st Meth. Ch., Hampton, N.H., 1938-42, Pleasant Street Meth. Ch., Salem, N.H., 1945-48, 1st Meth. Ch., Bushton, Kans., 1957-63, Trinity Heights Meth. Ch., Newton, Kans., 1963-65, Contoocook and Bow Mills United Meth. Ch., Hopkinton, N.H., 1965-71, Grace United Meth. Ch., Haverhill, Mass., 1971-75; ret., 1975; rep. N.H. Gen. Ct., Concord, 1978-94; sec. bd. Christian edn. Ctrl. Kans. Conf. Meth. Chs., 1960-65, treas., trustee bd. hosp. and homes, 1963-65; chmn. bd. pensions N.H. Ann. Conf., 1971-75, conf. sec., 1972-76; exec. sec., treas. N.H. Preachers Aid Soc., 1984-93. Mem. Gt. Bend (N.Y.) Sch. Bd., 1953. Lt. col. U.S. Army, 1942-45, 48-57; chaplain Kans. Army N.G., 1958-64, mem. USAR ret. Mem. VFW (surgeon), Am. Legion, Heroes of '76 (comdr. 1990-91), Sojourners (pres. 1989-90, 94-95), Masons, Kiwanis, Demolay (master councillor 1930, Legion of Honor 1995). Libertarian. Home: Raymond N.H. DIED 10/16/95. .

WARD, SYLVAN DONALD, music conductor, educator; b. Rock Springs, Wyo., July 7, 1909; s. Samuel and Hannah (Davis) W.; m. Beatrice Dorrell Stackhouse, June 27, 1936; children: Dorrell Deen (Mrs. Gordon H. Williams), Susan Diane (Mrs. William D. Johnston), Jill Dawn (Mrs. George L. Manderino), Jack Donald, Nancy Deborah (Mrs. Dennis P. Orgill). BMus, Chgo. Mus. Coll., 1931, MMus, 1932; MS in Edn., Northwestern U., 1934, MEdn, 1946; DMusEdn, Chgo. Mus. Coll., 1954; student violin, John Brueggemann, Leon Sametini. Advt. mgr. Edn. Music mag., Chgo., 1931-36; asso. editor edn. Edn. Music mag., 1937-43; asst. gen. mgr. edn. Music Bur., 1936-37; tchr. instrumental, vocal music Farragut High Sch., Chgo., 1936-49; instr. music Chgo. Mus. Coll., 1946-51, Chgo. Tchrs. Coll., 1949-58, Wilson Jr. Coll., part-time 1951-63, Crane Jr. Coll., Loop Jr. Coll., 1965; vis. prof. U. Ill., summers 1959-61; prof. music Chgo. State U., 1958-77, chmn. dept., 1958-71; tchr. Vandercook Coll. Music, 1975-81. Dir., Chgo. Regional Mormon Choir, 1935-91, condr., mus. dir., Chgo. Bus. Men's Orch., 1963-68, 77-82, Chgo. Met. Symphony Orch., 1982-84, mem., Chgo. State Coll. String Quartet, 1952-77, stage orch., Chgo. Lyric Opera Co., 1960-69; author: Instrumental Director's Handbook, Methods for Viola, Cello and String Bass; contbr. articles to profl. jours. Bishop Ch. of Jesus Christ of Latter-day Saints, 1963-72; mem. high council Chgo. Heights Stake, 1973, music chmn., 1973-91. Served with USAAF, 1943-45. Mem. NEA (life), Music Educators Nat. Conf., Ill. Music Educators Assn. (life), Am. Fedn. Musicians (life), Am. String Tchrs. Assn. (pres. Ill. unit 1959-63, editor Scroll 1961-63), Phi Mu Alpha (life). Home: Rockford Ill. Died May 26, 1995.

WARD, WALLACE DIXON, medical educator; b. Pierre, S.D., June 30, 1924; s. Edmund Dixon and Thelma Marie (Hill) W.; m. Edith Marion Bystrom, Dec. 27,1949; children: Edith Marion IV, Laurie Elizabeth, Kathryn Christine, Holly Lydene. BS in Physics, S.D. Sch. Mines and Tech., 1944, DSc, 1971; PhD in Exptl. Psychology, Harvard U., 1953. Research engr. Baldwin Piano Co., Cin., 1953-54; research assoc. Cen. Inst. for Deaf, St. Louis, 1954-57; assoc. dir. research Noise Research Ctr., Am. Acad. Ophthalmology and Otolaryngology, Los Angeles, 1957-62; prof., depts. communication disorders, otolaryngology, pub. health and psychology U. Minn., Mpls., 1962-96; mem. com. on hearing, bioacoustics and biomechanics NRC, 1960-92, mem. exec. coun., 1970-75, chmn., 1971-73; mem. communicative scis. study sect. div. rsch. grants NIH, 1969-73; sci. adviser Callier Hearing and Speech Ctr., Dallas, 1968-86; cons. U.S. Army, 1972-88, EPA Office Noise Abatement and Control, 1973; mem., co-chmn. Internat. Sci. Noise Teams, 1973-96. Editor: Noise as a Public Health Hazard, 1969, Noise as a Public Health Problem, 1974, Noise and Hearing Conservation Manual, 1986; contbr. articles to tech. jours. Served with USNR, 1944-46. Recipient Research Career Devel. award NIH, 1962. Fellow Acoustical Soc. Am. (mem. exec. coun. 1978-81, pres. 1988), Am. Speech and Hearing Assn.; mem. AAAS, Am. Audiology Soc. (v.p. 1973-75, pres. 1976), Internat. Soc. Audiology (governing bd., pres. 1978-80), Am. Otol. Soc., Am. Indsl. Hygiene Assn., Mensa, Triangle, Soc. for Music Perception and Cognition (v.p. 1992), Sigma Xi, Sigma Tau. Libertarian. Home: Falcon Heights Minn. Died Dec. 19, 1996; interred Lakewood Cemetery, Minneapolis, MN.

WARD-MCLEMORE, ETHEL, research geophysicist, mathematician; b. Sylvarena, Miss., Jan. 22, 1908; d. William Robert and Frances Virginia (Douglas) Ward; m. Robert Henry McLemore, June 30, 1935; 1 child, Mary Frances. BA, Miss. Woman's Coll., 1928; MA, U. N.C., 1929; postgrad., U. Chgo., 1931, Colo. Sch. Mines, 1941-42, So. Meth. U., 1962-64. Head math. dept. Miss. Jr. Coll., 1929-30; instr. chemistry, math. Miss. State Coll. for Women, 1930-32; rsch. mathematician Humble Oil & Refining Co., Houston, 1933-36; ind. geophys. rsch., Tex. and Colo., 1936-42, Ft. Worth, 1946—; geophysicist United Geophys. Co., Pasadena, Cal., 1942-46; tchr. chemistry, physics, Hockaday Sch., Dallas, 1958-59, tchr. math., 1959-60, tchr. chemistry, 1968-69; tchr. chemistry Ursuline Acad., Dallas, 1964-67; geophys. cons., Dallas, 1957—; with Eugene McDermott Libr., U. Tex., rsch. geophysicist. Author: China, 1983, Bibliography of the Publications of the Texas Academy of Science, 1929-87, 1989, The Academies of Science of Texas (1880-1987), 1989, also annotated bibliographies of sedimentary basins, 1981; contbr. articles to profl. jours. Mem. AAAS, Am. Math. Soc., Acads. of Sci. Tex., Math. Assn. Am., Am. Geophys. Union (40 yr. Mem. Rsch. Silver Pin award 1988), Seismol. Soc. Am., Soc. Exploration Geophysicists (50 yr. Gold cert. 1986, Hon. Membership award 1989, hon. life), Soc. Indsl. and Applied Math., Am. Chem. Soc., Inst. Math. Statis., Tex Acad. Sci. (Appreciation cert. 1985), Dallas Geophys. Soc. (hon. life 1986, Disting. Svc. award 1988), Sigma Xi.

WARE, MARCUS JOHN, lawyer; b. Yakima, Wash., Mar. 17, 1904; s. Marcus Clark and Ruby Marie (Cross) W.; m. Helen Gorton, June 6, 1933; children: Robert Gorton, Donald Frank (dec.), Barbara Jean (Mrs. Wray W. Featherstone, Jr.), Mary Elizabeth (Mrs. James H. Rathlesberger). LL.B., U. Idaho, 1927. Bar: Idaho 1927. Since practiced in Lewiston; with firm Ware, O'Connell & Creason, and predecessors, 1927-87, sr. ptnr., 1955-87; pros. atty. Nez Perce County, Idaho, 1943, 44. Chmn. Lewis-Clark Sesquicentennial Celebration, Lewiston, also Clarkston, Wash., 1955-56; chmn. Lewiston Centennial Celebration, 1961; former vice chmn. Lewis and Clark Trail Commn.; mem. Idaho Hist. Sites Rev. Bd., 1969-91, Idaho Bicentennial Commn., 1972-76, Lewiston Bicentennial Commn., 1973-76, Idaho TV History series adv. bd., 1988-91; mem. nat. adv. coun. on ethnic heritage studies Office Edn., HEW, 1975-76; bd. dirs. Pacific N.W. Nat. Parks Assn., 1976-82, Pacific N.W. Nat. Parks and Forests Assn., 1985-91; past dir. Lewis and Clark Trail Heritage Found. Recipient award of merit Am. Assn. State and Local History, 1961, citation Idaho Recreation and Park Soc., 1973, Disting. Service award Lewis and Clark Trail Heritage Found., 1983. Mem. ABA, Idaho State Bar Assn. (commr. 1959-62, pres. 1961-62, Outstanding Svc. award 1988, Idaho Disting. Lawyer award Idaho State Bar 1991), Clearwater Bar Assn., Am. Coll. Trial Lawyers, SAR (past state pres.), Soc. Mayflower Descendants (past gov. Idaho soc., past dep. gov. gen.), Nez Perce County Hist. Soc. (past pres.), James Willard Schultz Soc., Scottish Gaelic Texts Soc., Gaelic Soc. Inverness, An Comunn Gaidhealach, Mont. Hist. Soc., Nev. HIst. Soc., Idaho State Hist. Soc. (trustee 1971-91), The Nature Conservancy, Outlook Club (Lewiston), Ind. Order Odd Fellows, Masons (33 deg., Blue Lodge, Nez Perce #10 , grand master Idaho 1945-46), Scottish Rite, 33d Degree, York Rite, Red Cross Constantine, Shrine, Elks, Kiwanis (past pres.). Home: Lewiston Idaho Died Sept. 27, 1996.

WARNER, JEROME, state legislator; b. Waverly, Nebr., Nov. 23, 1927; s. Charles J. Warner and Esther Anderson Warner; m. Betty Person; children: Jamie, Elizabeth. BS, U. Nebr., 1952. Mem. Nebr. State Senate, 1962—, sprk., 1969-71, vice chair edn. com., 1962-65, 73-75, chmn. govt. & mil. affairs com., 1965-67, mem. legis. coun. exec. bd., 1967-69, appropriations com., 1977-91, exec. bd., com. on coms. Mem. Lancaster County Extension Bd., Lincoln-Lancaster County Planning Commn., Nebr. State Agr. Bd., Lancaster County Com. Reorganization Sch. Dist. Mem. Lancaster County Agr. Soc. (treas.), Nebr. State Grange, Order Eastern Star, Scottish Rite, Alpha Zeta, Gamma Sigma Delta. Office: State Legislature State Capitol Lincoln NE 68516 DIED 04/20/97. .

WARREN, KENNETH S., medical educator, physician; b. N.Y.C., June 11, 1929; m. Sylvia Marjorie Rothwell, Feb. 14, 1959; children: Christopher Harwood, Erica Marjorie. (dec.). AB, Harvard U., 1951, MD, 1955; DSc (hon.), Mahidol U., Thailand, 1990. Intern, Harvard service Boston City Hosp., 1955-56; research assoc. Lab. Tropical Diseases, NIH, Bethesda, Md., 1956-62; asst. prof. medicine Case Western Res. U., 1963-68, asso. prof., 1968-75, prof., 1975-77, prof. library sci., 1974-77; dir. health scis. Rockefeller Found., N.Y.C., 1977-87, assoc. v.p., 1988-89; adj. prof. Rockefeller U., 1977-89; prof. medicine NYU, 1977-96; dir. sci. Maxwell Communication Corp., Maxwell Found., N.Y.C., 1989-92; Heath Clark lectr. London Sch. Hygiene and Tropical Medicine, 1988; adj. prof. medicine Tufts U., 1990-96; cons. ed. Charles Scribner's Sons, 1992-93; CEO Comprehensive Med. Sys., Inc., 1992-94; v.p. acad. affairs Picower Inst. Med. Rsch., 1993-96; chmn. Harvard Internat. Med. Libr., Inc. 1994-96; mem. Inst. Medicine, Nat. Acad. Scis.; bd. dirs. Immunotherapy, Inc.; cons. WHO. Author: Schistosomiasis: The Evolution of a Medical Literature, Selected Abstracts and Citations, 1852-1972, 1973, Geographic Medicine for the Practitioner, 2d edit., 1985, Scientific Information Systems and the Principle of Selectivity, 1980, Coping with the Biomedical Literature, 1981, Tropical and Geographical Medicine, 2d edit., 1990, Immunology and Molecular Biology of Parasitic Infections, 1993, Doing More Good Than Harm, 1993; founding editor: Jour. Molecular Medicine; contbr. numerous articles to profl. jours. Recipient Career Devel. award NIH, 1966-71, Mary Kingsley medal Liverpool Sch. Tropical Med., 1987, Frohlich award N.Y. Acad. Sci., 1988, Van Thiel medal Dutch Soc. Parasitology, 1989. Fellow ACP, Royal Coll. Physicians, N.Y. Acad. Scis. (bd. govs. 1991-93); mem. Am. Soc. Clin. Investigation, Assn. Am. Physicians, Am. Assn. Immunologists, Am. Assn. Study Liver Diseases, Am. Soc. Tropical Medicine and Hygiene (Bailey K. Ashford award 1974), Infectious Diseases Soc. Am. (Squibb award 1975), Royal Soc. Tropical Medicine and Hygiene, Internat. Fedn. Sci. Editors (exec. bd.), N.Y. Acad. Scis. (bd. govs. 1991-93), Royal Soc. Medicine Found. (bd. dirs. 1992-96, treas. 1994-96), Internat. Molecular Medicine Soc. (founding sec., treas.). Patentee diagnostic methods, drugs. Office: Picower Inst Med Rsch 350 Community Dr Manhasset NY 11030-3849 Died Sept. 18, 1996.

WARREN, L. D., editorial cartoonist; b. Wilmington, Del., Dec. 27, 1906; s. Robert L. and Annie (Melvin) W.; m. Julianne Bussert Baker, May 9, 1958; children: Joy Warren Haines, L.D. II. Ed. pub. schs. Cartoonist Camden (N.J.) Courier Post, 1925-28, Phila. Record, 1928-47; Cartoonist Cin. Enquirer, 1947-78, ret., 1978; guest instr. cartooning Art Acad. Cin., 1957. Illustrator: Penny Penguin, 1935, Terry and Bunky Play Baseball, 1947, Japanese edit., 1949, Terry and Bunky Play Basketball series, 1945-51, (with Walter C. Langsam) The World and Warren's Cartoons, 1977 (Martha Kinney Cooper Ohioana Book award 1977); one-man show Cin. Art Mus., 1974; numerous cartoon illustrations for books, mags. and brochures; exhibited in group shows at Met. Mus. Art, N.Y.C., 1954, Internat. Pavillion of Humor, Montreal, Que., Can., 1968-74, World Cartoon Gallery, Skopje, Yugoslavia, 1969, 71, Nat. Portrait Gallery, London, 1970; represented in permanent collections Pub. Library Cin. and Hamilton County, U. Cin., Lyndon B. Johnson Library, Austin, Tex., Mus. Cartoon Art, Port Chester, N.Y.; Smithsonian Instn., also numerous univs., librs., mus. in U.S., and pvt. collections of Pres. Truman, Eisenhower, Kennedy, Johnson, Nixon, and Ford, numerous others; 2-man exhbn. Cin. Hist. Soc., Cin. and Hmailton County Pub. Libr., 1989; exhbn. in honor L. D. Warren's 85th birthday, Ohio State U., 1991. Recipient over 25 awards Freedoms Found., 1949-73, award Nat. Headliners Club, 1961, Best Cartoon of Sixties award Nat. Found. Hwy. Safety, 1971, Mass Media Brotherhood awards NCCJ, Nat. Comdr.'s citation Am. Legion, 1974. Mem. Assn. Am. Editorial Cartoonists (v.p. 1960, 75), Nat. Cartoonists Soc., Cin. Art Mus. Home: Cincinnati Ohio Died May 14, 1992; interred Spring Grove Cemetery, Cincinnati, OH.

WARREN, MARY ALICE, health science association administrator; b. Lorain, Ohio, Apr. 12, 1931; d. Howard Edson and Emma Grace (Warren) Dulmage; m. Grant Harland Muse, Oct. 21, 1950 (div. July 1963); children: Howard Lee, George Harland, Michele Adrienne; m. Joe Sherman Warren, Dec. 21, 1981. Ed. pvt. schs., Oberlin, Ohio and Berkeley, Calif. Dir. Midwest Celiac Sprue Assn., Des Moines, 1985-86, Celiac Sprue Assn., Omaha, 1986-89; dir., founder Celiacs of the Desert, Palm Springs, Calif., 1988-89; co-dir., founder Gluten Intolerance Group of Fla., Cocoa Beach, Fla., 1990-95; founder Celiac Experience, Cocoa Beach, 1991-95; facilitator Celiac Experience II, Cocoa Beach, 1992; co-facilitator Celiac Experience III, Cocoa Beach, 1994. Editor Celiac ActionLine, 1990-95. Civic coord. Vols. Against Drugs and Alcohol, Palm Springs, 1988-89; campaign coord. Bono for Palm Springs Mayor, 1988; vol. hydrotherapist Crippled Children's Ctr., Merritt Island, Fla., 1989-95. Mem. Celiac Disease Found., Can. Celiac Soc., Gluten Intolerance Group of N.Am. Home: Titusville Fla. Died Jan. 10, 1995.

WARREN, ROBERT CARLTON, manufacturing company executive; b. Portland, Oreg., Apr. 13, 1918; s. Floyd Carlton and Ethel (Wright) W.; m. Nani Marie Swigert, June 23, 1945; children: Catharine K., Robert Carlton, Wendy W., William S., Elizabeth B. Grad., Stanford U., 1940. With U.S. Steel Corp., Portland, 1940, Esco Corp., Portland, 1941, Oreg. Shipbldg. Corp., 1941-43; gen. mgr., dir. Cascade Corp., Portland, 1943-54; pres., CEO Cascade Corp., 1954-71, chmn., CEO, 1971-83, chmn., 1983-93, chmn. emeritus, 1993-97; chmn., CEO Stair Assist Corp., 1983-93, chmn. emeritus, CEO, 1993-97. Pres. Portland Art Assn., 1979-80; Mem. Pres.'s Export Council, 1981-84. Mem. NAM (dir. 1958-83), Chi Psi. Home: Portland Oreg. Died Feb. 21, 1997.

WARREN, WILLIAM GERALD, lawyer; b. Detroit, Apr. 22, 1930; s. William Grant and Margaret Kathryn (Matthews) W.; m. Martha Elsie Artz, Apr. 20, 1974; children: Mary Katharine, Elizabeth Bogo. A.B. with honors, U. Mich., 1952, LL.B. (Frederick L. Leckie scholar), 1955. Bar: Mich. 1956. Assoc. firm Dickinson, Wright, Moon, Van Dusen & Freeman, Detroit, 1955-63, ptnr., 1964—; bd. dirs. Mackinac Fin. Corp., Mackinac Corp., V.G. Nahrgang Co.; gen. counsel, sec. bd. Detroit Savs. Bank. Contbr. articles to profl. jours. Mem., chmn. Wayne County (Mich.) Grievance Com., 1966—; spl. counsel 4-H Found. Mich., 1966-68. Recipient Henry M. Campbell award, 1954, Roberts P. Hudson award State Bar Mich., 1978. Fellow Am. Coll. Trial Lawyers, Internat. Soc. Barristers, Am. Bar Found., Mich Bar Found.; mem. Phi Beta Kappa, Phi Kappa Phi, Pi Sigma Alpha, Phi Alpha Delta. Republican. Roman Catholic. Clubs: Detroit, University, Otsego Ski, Grosse Pointe, Witenagemote. Died Jan. 8, 1997.

WARRINER, DAVID DORTCH, judge; b. Brunswick County, Va., Feb. 25, 1929; s. Thomas Emmett and Maria Clarke (Dortch) W.; m. Barbara Ann Jenkins, Jan. 31, 1959; children: Susan Wells, David Thomas Dortch, Julia Cotman. B.A. in Polit. Sci., U. N.C., 1951; LL.B., U. Va., 1957. Bar: Va. 1957, U.S. Supreme Ct. 1970. Partner Warriner & Outten, Emporia, Va., 1957-74; judge U.S. Dist. Ct. Eastern Dist. Va., Richmond, from 1974. Mem. Va. Republican Central Com., 1963-74, gen. counsel, 1972-74. Served as lt. USNR, 1951-54. Mem. Am., Va. bar assns. Home: Richmond Va. Deceased.

WARTLUFT, DAVID JONATHAN, librarian, clergyman; b. Stouchsburg, Pa., Sept. 22, 1938; s. Cleaver Milvard and Dorothy (Stump) W.; m. Joyce Claudia Dittmer, June 15, 1963 (div. Sept. 1988); children: Elizabeth Marie, Deborah Joy, Rebecca Janet, Andrew Jonathan. A.B. (Trexler scholar), Muhlenberg Coll., 1960; Div.M. (Danforth scholar), Lutheran Theol. Sem., Phila., 1964; A.M. (scholar), U. Pa., 1964; M.S. (Lilly Found. scholar), Drexel U., 1968. Asst. chaplain, instr. religion Springfield (Mass.) Coll., 1962-63; ordained minister Luth. Ch., 1964; pastor Jerusalem Luth. Ch., Allentown, Pa., 1964-66; cataloger, reference librarian Luth. Sem. Phila., 1966-68, asst. librarian, 1968-77, dir. library and archives, 1977—, chaplain, 1978-79, dir. 1st yr. field edn., 1979-81, 82-83, faculty sec., 1985—; archivist Northeastern Pa. Synod, Luth. Ch. Am., 1970-87, mem. comms. com., 1967-78, sec., 1975-78, mem. conv. com., 1976; archivist Northeastern Pa. Synod, Evang. Luth. Ch. Am., 1988-91; v.p. Luth. Archives Ctr. at Phila., 1979-85, bd. dirs., 1979—; libr. cons. Gurkul Luth. Ch., Madras, India, 1989, Huria Kristen Batak Protestant Sem., Pematang Siantar, Sumatra, Indonesia, 1989, Luther Sem., Adelaide, Australia, 1996. Editor: Teamwork, 1970-84, The Periodical, 1979-84, Luth. Hist. Soc. Eastern Pa.; author: (index) Luther in Mid-Career (H. Bornkamm), 1983, Theodicy in the Old Testament (J. Crenshaw), 1983, The Roots of Anti-Semitism (H. Obermann), 1984, The Book of Revelation: Justice and Judgment (E.S. Fiorenza), 1985, Rediscovering Paul (N.R. Peterson), 1985, The Opponents of Paul in Second Corinthians (D. Georgi), 1986, Psychological Aspects of Pauline Theology (G. Theissen), 1986, Ethics of the New Testament (W. Schragg), 1987, Israel's Praise (W. Brueggemann), 1987, Commitment to Unity (W.K. Gilbert), 1988, Paul and His Letters (L. Keck), 2d rev. edit., 1988, Finally Comes the Poet (W. Bruggemann), 1989, Community and Commitment (G. Rupp), 1989, Protest and Praise (J.M. Spenser), 1990, After the Absolute (L. Swidler), 1990, Greeks, Romans and Christians, 1990, The New Era in Religious Education (P. Babin), 1991, A Commentary on the Book of Amos (S.M. Paul), 1992, The Book of Revelation (J. Roloff), 1993, What is Scripture? (W.C. Smith), 1993, Jesus in the Gospels (R. Schnackenburg), 1995; contbr. articles to profl. jours. Active Boy Scouts Am., 1964-66. Mem. ALA, Am. Theol. Libr. Assn. (exec. sec. 1971-81, editor procs. 1971-81, bd. dirs. 1991-94, sec. 1992-94, recording sec. 1995-97), Southeastern Pa. Theol. Librs. Assn. (sec. 1970-73, chair 1982-85, chair planning com. 1986-89), Coun. Nat. Libr. and Info. Assn. (counselor 1978-81), Coun. on Study Religion (liaison com. 1974-77, 81-82, nominating com. 1978-80), Luth. Hist. Conf. (com. on scholarly rsch. and pub. 1981—, constl. revision com. 1984-86, bd. dirs. 1988-94, 96—, treas. 1988-94, 96—, membership chair 1994—), Assn. Theol. Schs. in U.S. and Can. (selection panel for libr. grants), Paradise Falls Luth. Assn. (bd. dirs. 1985-87, chmn. religious activities 1985-86), Assn. Uniting Religion and Art (chmn. membership com., treas. 1995—), Mid. States Assn. (accreditation visitor), Luth. Hist. Soc. Ea. Pa. (lie, bd. dirs. 1991-94, v.p. 1994—), Drexel U. Grad. Sch. Libr. and Info. Sci. Alumni Assn. (bd. dirs. 1978-80), Eta Sigma Phi, Phi Sigma Tau, Beta Phi Mu. Democrat.

WASHBURN, WILCOMB EDWARD, historian, educator; b. Ottawa, Kans., Jan. 13, 1925; s. Harold Edward and Sidsell Marie (Nelson) W.; m. Lelia Elizabeth Kanavarioti, July 14, 1951 (div. June 1981); children: Harold Kitsos, Edward Alexandros; m. Kathryn Lafler Cousins, Jan 2, 1985. Grad., Phillips Exeter Acad., 1943; AB summa cum laude, Dartmouth Coll., 1948; MA, Harvard U., 1951, PhD, 1955; HHD (hon.), St. Mary's Coll. Md., 1970, Assumption Coll., 1983, St. Lawrence U., 1991, Salisbury State U., 1996. Teaching fellow history and lit. Harvard, 1954-55; fellow Inst. Early Am. History and Culture, Williamsburg, Va., 1955-58; instr. Coll. William and Mary, 1955-58; curator div. polit. history Smithsonian Instn., U.S. Nat. Mus.,

Washington, 1958-65; dir. Am. studies program Smithsonian Instn., 1965-97; Professorial lectr. Am. U., 1961-63, adj. prof., 1963-69; cons. in research Grad. Sch. Arts and Scis., professorial lectr. in Am. civilization George Washington U., 1966-97; adj. prof. U. Md., 1975-97; Civil info. and edn. officer Toyama Mil. Govt. Team, Toyama Prefecture, Japan, 1946-47. Author: The Governor and the Rebel: A History of Bacon's Rebellion in Virginia, 1957, Red Man's Land/White Man's Law: A Study of the Past and Present Status of the American Indian, 1971, revised edit., 1995, The Assault on Indian Tribalism: General Allotment Law (Dawes Act) of 1887, 1975, The Indian in America, 1975, (with others) The Federal City: Plans and Realities, The Exhibition, 1976; editor: (with others) The Indian and the White Man, 1964, Proc. of the Vinland Map Conf., 1971, The American Heritage History of the Indian Wars, 1977; contbr. articles to profl. jours. Past pres. Hist. Soc. of Washington; active Am. Hist Assn., Va. Hist. Assn., Md. Hist. Assn., Mass. Hist. Soc. With USMCR, 1943-45, 51-52. Fellow Am. Anthropol. Assn.; mem. AAAS, Am. Soc. Ethnohistory (past pres.), Am. Studies Assn. (past pres.), Colonial Soc. Mass., Am. Antiquarian Soc., Orgn. Am. Historians, Japan-Am. Soc. Washington (past trustee), Instituto Histórico e Geográfico Brasileiro, Anthropol. Soc. Washington, Phi Beta Kappa, Cosmos Club. Club: Cosmos (Washington). Died Feb. 1, 1997.

WATANABE, KOUICHI, pharmacologist, educator; b. Manchuria, Japan, Aug. 26, 1942; s. Tetsuya and Mine W.; m. Harumi Miyamoto; children: Toshikazu, Yoshihiro, Motohiro. BS, Tokyo Coll. Pharmacy, 1966; MS, Osaka U., 1968; PhD, 1971; LPIBA, 1986; DSc (hon.) Internat. U. Found., 1987, World U. Roundtable, 1988. Vis. fellow reprodn. rsch. br. Nat. Inst. Child Health and Devel., NIH, Bethesda, Md., 1971-73; vis. scientist dept. pharmacology Coll. Medicine, Howard U., Washington, 1973-75, asst. prof., 1975-83; asst. prof. pharmacology U. Hawaii, 1983-96; drug info. mgr. med. info. dept. Minophagen Pharm. Co., Tokyo, 1993-96. Contbr. articles to sci. jours. Am. Cancer Soc. grantee, 1980-81. Hon. mem. adv. coun. Internat. Biog. Ctr. (named man of year 1991,92); hon. mem. rsch. bd. advisors Am. Biog. Inst. (named man of year 1991,93,95), Mem. Am. Soc. Pharmacology and Exptl. Therapeutics, N.Y. Acad. Scis. (inaugural mem.), Am. Soc. Hypertension (charter). Subspecialties: Chemotherapy; Molecular pharmacology. Current work: Mechanism of action of various antineoplastic agts. on calmodulin. Vinca alkaloids found to be calmodulin inhibitors. Suggested that amounts of calmodulin or its binding proteins may be endogenous regulators of antineoplastic action or transport of these drugs. Died Mar. 20, 1996. Home: Tokyo Japan

WATANABE, YASUSHI, banker; b. Chiba, Japan, Oct. 10, 1919; s. Itsuro and Chiyoko Watanabe; m. Tomoko Nakatsuji, Feb. 8, 1948; children—Hisashi, Yuko, Yoko. B. Laws, Tokyo Imperial U., 1944. With Yokohama Specie Bank, 1944-47; with Bank of Tokyo, Ltd., 1947—, dir., gen. mgr. internat. investment div., 1972-73, dir., gen. mgr. N.Y. Agy., 1973-74, mng. dir., regional exec., N.Y., 1974-75, managing dir., Tokyo, 1975-77, sr. managing dir., 1977-79, dep. pres., 1979-82, pres., 1982—; chmn. com. internat. fin. Fedn. Econ. Orgn., 1982—, Bank of Tokyo, Ltd., Zurich, Switzerland, 1982—, Bank of Tokyo Internat., Ltd., London, 1982—; permanent rep., dir. Banque Europeene de Tokyo S.A., Paris, 1982—. Home: 4-10 Kami-Ikedai 3-chome, Ohtaku, Tokyo 145,, Japan Office: Chuo-ku,, Bank of Tokyo Ltd,, 6-3 Nihombashi,, Hongoku-cho 1-chome,, Tokyo 103, Japan

WATERMAN, JOHN THOMAS, foreign language educator; b. Council Bluffs, Iowa, Aug. 1, 1918; s. Charles Murray and Edith (Clark) W.; m. Mary Catherine Adams, Oct. 10, 1942; children—John Robert, Teresa Kathleen. Abitur, Concordia Coll., 1934-38; B.A., Concordia Theol. Sem., 1940; M.A., Washington U., 1945; Ph.D., U. Cal. at Los Angeles, 1949; postgrad., Yale, 1947. Prof. linguistics U. So. Cal., 1948-68, dept. head, 1958-67; vis. prof. linguistics U. B.C., 1967; prof. German, chmn. dept. Germanic and Slavic langs. U. Calif., Santa Barbara, 1968-82, prof. emeritus, 1983—; Linguistic cons. CBS, 1963—; lang. cons. Los Angeles City Sch. System, 1955—, Ventura County Sch. System, 1958—. Author: Sayri Dar Zaban Shinasi, 1969, Perspectives in Linguistics, 2d edit, 1970, Spanish edit., 1971, Die Linguistik und ihre Perspektiven, 1966, Breve Storia della linguistica, 1968, A History of the German Language, 2d edit, 1975, Gendei Gengogaku No Haikeli—Tenbo to Genjo, 1975, Leibniz and Ludolf on Things Linguistic, 1978. Served with USAAF, 1941-44. Recipient award for creative research and scholarship U. So. Calif., 1967. Mem. Modern Lang. Assn. Am., Linguistic Soc. Am., Philol. Assn. Pacific Coast, Order St. Lazarus of Jerusalem, Delta Phi Alpha (hon.). Republican. Anglo-Catholic.

WATKINS, ELTON, JR., biomedical research administrator, surgeon; b. Portland, Oreg., Aug. 16, 1921; s. Elton and Daniela Ruth (Sturges) W.; married; children: Elton III, Sturges Benjamin. BA, Reed Coll., 1941; MD, U. Oreg., 1944. Diplomate Am. Bd. Surgery, Am. Bd. Thoracic Surgery. Rotating intern U. Oreg. Med. Sch. Hosps. and Clinics, 1944-45, asst. resident in thoracic surgery, 1945-47, chief resident in thoracic surgery, 1947-48, dir., 1948-49, asst. resident in gen. surgery, 1949-50, chief resident in gen. surgery, 1950-51; instr. in physiology U. Oreg., 1948-49; various positions including sr. staff surgeon Children's Hosp. Med. Ctr., Boston, 1951-75; sr. staff surgeon to chmn. div. rsch. Lahey Clinic Found., Burlington, Mass., 1957—; various teaching positions Harvard U. Med. Sch., 1953—; mem. staff New Eng. Deaconess Hosp., Boston, New Eng. Baptist Hosp.; lectr. First Brit. Acad. Conf. in Otolaryngology, Royal Coll. Surgeons, London, 1963; ann. orator Danish Surg. Soc., Copenhagen, 1967. Contbr. numerous articles to profl. jours. Chmn. bd. dirs. Pub. Responsibility in Medicine and Rsch., Inc., Boston, 1977-79. Comdr. M.C. USNR, 1954-56. Nat. Cancer Inst. grantee, 1975-81; Nat. Inst. Heart, Lung and Blood grantee, 1957-75. Fellow ACS, Am. Heart Assn. Coun. Cardiovascular Surgery; mem. Am. Assn. Thoracic Surgery, Am. Assn. Cancer Rsch., New Eng. Surg. Soc., Soc. Vascular Surgery, Mass. Med. Soc., AMA, AAAS, Am. Fedn. Clin. Rsch., Am. Soc. Clin. Oncology, Soc. Surg. Oncology, Transplantation Soc. (charter), Tissue Culture Assn., Am. Assn. Med. Instrumentation, Tumor Registrars Assn. New Eng. (hon.), Soc. Internat. de Chirugie, Brit. Assn. Surg. Oncology (fgn. corr.), Brit. Assn. Cancer Rsch., Sigma Xi, others. Democrat. Episcopalian.

WATSON, BILLY, publishing executive, newspaper; b. Pitts, Ga., Sept. 7, 1938; m. Helen Turk; children: Kevin, Kim Holland. Degree in Journalism, U. Ga., 1960; postgrad., Ga. State U. With Cordele Dispatch, Wilcox County Chronicle, 1960-61; with Macon Telegraph, 1963, 67-78, bur. chief Atlanta, 1963-67; exec. editor Telegraph and News, 1978-83, gen. mgr., 1983-87; pres., pub. Columbus Ledger-Enquirer, 1987—; vis. instr. journalism Mercer U.; mem. journalism bd. U. Ga.; pres. Ga. AP, chmn. News Coun. AP. Founding chmn. Columbus Literate Community Program, Inc.; past chmn. Ga. Coun. Adult Literacy; bd. dirs. UPtown Columbus, Columbus Tech. Inst., Creek Indian Meml. Assn. With US Army. Mem. Ga. Press Assn. (former pres.), U. Ga. Journalism Alumni Assn. (former pres.), Columbus Rotary Club, Columbus Country Club, Chattahoochee River Club, Columbus C. of C. (bd. dirs.). Avocations: swimming, running, fishing, bluegrass music. Deceased.

WATSON, THOMPSON See MCCORD, DAVID

WATTS, DANIEL THOMAS, university dean, pharmacologist; b. Wadesboro, N.C., July 31, 1916; s. James Cyrus and Blanche (Rogers) W.; m. Margaret Montgomery, Sept. 12, 1942 (dec. 1963); children: Daniel Thomas, Margaret Peyton; m. Ann M. Brewbaker, June 12, 1965; stepchildren: Carol Kay, Susan. A.B., Elon Coll., 1937; Ph.D., Duke, 1942. High sch. tchr. Yanceyville, N.C., 1937-38; grad. asst. Duke, 1938-42; physiologist Naval Air Expt. Sta., 1946-47; mem. faculty U. Va., 1947-53, asso. prof. pharmacology, 1949-53; prof. pharmacology, chmn. dept. W.Va. U., 1953-66; dean Sch. Basic Scis. Med. Coll. Va., Va. Commonwealth U., 1966-82, dean emeritus, 1982-94; cons. pharmacology Walter Reed Army Med. Center, 1959-69. Pres. Morgantown Planning Commn., 1963-66. Served with USNR, 1942-46; capt. Res. Mem. Am. Soc. Pharmacology and Exptl. Therapeutics, Soc. Exptl. Biology and Medicine. Democrat. Presbyn. Club: Rotarian (pres. Morgantown 1958, Richmond 1977). Home: Richmond Va. Died May 11, 1994.

WAX, NELSON, electrical engineering educator; b. Phila., Apr. 2, 1917; s. Samuel and Anna (Kaminker) W.; m. Bernice Schwartz, June 21, 1942; children: Ruth, Saul, David. B.S. in Elec. Engring., U. Pa., 1937, M.S. in Elec. Engring., 1938; Ph.D., Ohio State U., 1942. Mem. tech. staff Bell Telephone Labs., N.Y.C., 1942-48; asst. prof. elec. engring. U. Ill., Urbana, 1948-49; assoc. prof. U. Ill., 1949-53; prof. U. Ill., Urbana, 1953-92, research prof., 1953-92; prof. U. Colo., 1963, U. Tex., 1965; vis. scholar dept. applied math. Weizmann Inst., Rehovoth, Israel, 1978; cons. Rand Corp., 1958-62. Editor Noise and Stochastic Processes, 1954. Fellow Moore Sch., 1937-48; fellow Stillman W. Robinson, 1941, Guggenheim Found., 1954-55. Home: Champaign Ill. Died Jan. 13, 1992.

WEATHERBEE, ARTEMUS EDWIN, federal government official; b. Bangor, Maine, Feb. 9, 1918; s. Ray Wellman Sherman (stepfather) and Lola (Yelland) W.; m. Pauline Jellison, June 18, 1940; children: Sue Weatherbee Adams, Richard Charles, Steven Sherman. A.B. with honors, U. Maine, 1939; intern, Nat. Inst. Pub. Affairs, 1939-40. Chief of classification, chief of placement F.C.A., 1941-42; sr. personnel officer Office Emergency Mgmt., 1942-43; dir. personnel Nat. War Labor Bd., 1943; W.S.B., 1946; chief exec. selection War Assets Adminstrn., 1946; chief fgn. service recruitment Dept. State, 1946-48, asst. chief allowances staff, 1948-49, chief, 1949-50, asst. chief deptl. personnel div., 1950-51, spl. asst. to dir. personnel, 1951-52, dep. dir. personnel, 1952-53; exec. dir., dep. asst. postmaster gen. Bur. Personnel, P.O. Dept., 1954-59; adminstrv. asst. sec., asst. sec. for adminstrn. Treasury Dept., 1959-70; U.S. dir. Asian Devel. Bank-Manila with personal rank of ambassador, 1970-73; exec. dir. Kennebunk-Kennebunkport C. of C., 1975-78; corporator Kennebunk Savs. Bank, 1978-81; cons. Maine Mgmt. and Cost Survey Commn., 1974. Mem. nat. adv. com. Am. Security Coun., 1978-80; mem. Nat. Tax Limitation Com., 1979-80; chmn. U. Maine Devel. Coun., 1975-77; mem. Gov.'s adv. com. on U. Maine, 1975-78, Kennebunk Budget Bd., 1974-77; bd. dirs. Kennebunk Area Indsl. Corp., 1976-79, York County Community Concert Assn., 1978-80; mem. Nat. Rights to Work Com., 1975-80; trustee U. Maine, 1975-80; deacon United Community Ch., 1984-85, trustee, 1985-88; candidate for Maine Senate, 1978; bd. dirs. Security Patrol, 1982-83. Served to lt. (j.g.) USN, 1943-45; ret. comdr. Res. 1978. Recipient Meritorious Service award Dept. State, 1950, Arthur S. Flemming award U.S. Junior C. of C., 1956; Exceptional Service award Treasury Dept., 1965; Career Service award Nat. Civil Service League, 1965; Rockefeller Pub. Service award, 1968; Alexander Hamilton award Treasury Dept., 1970; Alumni Career Service award U. Maine, 1972. Mem. U. Maine Alumni Assn., Sun City Center C. of C. (exec. dir. 1981-83, pres. 1982), Naval Res. Assn., Nat. Assn. Retired Fed. Employees (bd. dirs. Sun City Ctr. chpt. 1985-88, pres. 1986-87), Cape Arundel Golf Club, Sun City Ctr. Golf and Country Club, Lions (dir. 1975-77), Rotary (Paul Harris fellow 1978-95), Phi Beta Kappa, Beta Theta Pi, Phi Kappa Phi, Sigma Mu Sigma. Republican. Home: Sun City Center Fla. Died Nov. 11, 1995.

WEATHERFORD, WILLIS DUKE, JR., college president emeritus; b. Biltmore, N.C., June 24, 1916; m. Anne Smith, 1954; children: Edith, Julia, Willis III, Susan, Alice. B.A., Vanderbilt U., 1937; B.D., Yale U., 1940; postgrad., U. N.C., 1940-41; M.A., Harvard U., 1943, Ph.D. in Econs., 1952; LL.D., Carleton Coll., 1969, Swarthmore Coll., 1981; L.H.D., Blackburn U., 1983, Transylvania U., 1983, Berea Coll., 1984; L.L.D., Tusculum Coll., 1987. Dir. youth work Methodist Commn. World Peace, 1943-44; relief worker Am. Friends Service Com., Europe, 1944-47; asst. prof. econs. Swarthmore Coll., 1948-54, asso. prof., 1954-64; acad. dean Carleton Coll., 1965-67; pres. Berea Coll., Ky., 1967-84; pres. emeritus, asst. to pres. Berea Coll., 1984-91. Author: Geographic Differentials in Agricultural Wages, 1957; co-author: Economies of the World Today, 1962, 65, 76; contbg. author: Labor in Developing Countries, 1962; Editor: The Goals of Higher Education, 1960. Rural devel. specialist Am. Friends Svc. Com., India, 1950-51, UN, Malaya, 1959-60, Rotary Club, India, 1993; bd. chmn. Pine Mountain Settlement Sch., 1967-84; pres. Black Mountain Pairing Project, 1988-89, 92-93; bd. dirs. Frontier Nursing Svc., Warren Wilson Coll., Blue Ridge YMCA Assembly N.C., The Morgan Sch., Black Mountain Rotary Club. Recepient Chevalier de la Santé Publique award by French government, 1946; Ford Found. fellow India, 1954-55. Mem. Am. Econ. Assn., Assn. Asian Studies, AAUP (pres. chpt. 1965), Grace Episcopal Ch., Phi Beta Kappa, Omicron Delta Kappa, Phi Kappa Phi.

WEAVER, ARTHUR GORDON, retired financial services consultant; b. Toronto, Ont., Can., June 21, 1915; s. S. Roy and Edith (Pratt) W.; m. Melba L. Trombley., Sept. 27, 1941; children: David Roy, Arthur Bruce. B.A. with honours in Math, McGill U., 1936; grad., Advanced Mgmt. Program, Harvard U., 1959. With Prudential Assurance Co., 1936-39, Montreal Life Ins. Co., 1945-49; various positions to v.p. John Hancock Mut. Life Ins. Co., 1949-70; pres., chief exec. officer, dir. Eaton-Bay Fin. Services Ltd. and affiliated cos., 1970-78; dir. Eaton's of Can., 1977-79; cons. Exec. Services Ltd., 1974-79; dir. HFC Corp. of Can., 1980-87. Served to flight lt. RCAF, 1939-45. Fellow Soc. Actuaries, Canadian Inst. Actuaries, Am. Acad. Actuaries. Baptist. Home: Sutton West Can. Died July 26, 1993.

WEAVER, CHARLES STEELE, investments consultant; b. Bluefield, W.Va., Nov. 17, 1918; s. Edward H. and India (Spencer) W.; m. Louise Marsh, Jan. 30, 1954; 1 dau., Leslie J. Student, U. Cin., 1938-41. Vocat. tng. elec. design Appalachian Electric Power Co., 1936-38, developing, installation and maintenance carrier telephone and telemetering system, 1938-41; chief electronics and sci. equipment sect. tech. indsl. intelligence div. U.S. Dept. Commerce, Germany, 1947; indsl. engr. reparations br. Office Mil. Govt., Germany, 1948-49; intelligence specialist Dept. Def., 1949-70; dir. Office Fgn. Programs, Office Asst. Sec. Def. for Research and Engring., 1957-62; dep. asst. dir. (planning) Office of Dir. Def. Research and Engring., 1962-67, spl. asst. (policy planning) to dir. def. research and engring., 1967-70; pvt. cons. and investment bus., 1970-94. Served from 2d lt. to maj. AUS, 1942-46; electronics engr. Air Def. Research and Devel. Establishment, Brit. Ministry and Supply 1942-43; U.S. Army engring. rep. to signal planning com. SHAEF 1943-45; electronics engring. officer Field Information Agy. 1945-46, Technical Germany. Home: Falls Church Va. Died Dec. 15, 1994.

WEAVER, RITA MARGARET, art association executive; b. N.Y.C., Oct. 28, 1925; d. Newcomb and Lucy Elizabeth (Roche) Gaylord; B.A., N.Y. U., 1945; postgrad Lady Margaret Hall, Oxford (Eng.) U., 1945-46; m. Robert A. Weaver (dec.); children—Richard L.N., Michael Cameron. Concert pianist, 1940; reporter Nuremberg trials, 1946-48; syndicated columnist Fashions from New York, Escort Publs., London, 1949-51; actress, Off Broadway productions and summer stock, 1952-56; pres. Empire State chpt. Nat. Soc. Arts and Letters, N.Y.C., 1978-80, chmn. ballet career awards conv., 1980, v.p. and chmn. lit. career awards dinner and music career awards dinner, 1980-82, ways and means chmn. nat. bd., 1982-84, credentials chmn., 1986-84, credentials chmn., 1986-88, v.p., career awards chmn.; chmn. liaison internat. consulates, 1982-84, v.p. chmn. by laws, 1984-86, nat. dance com., 1984-86; producer Off-Broadway Musical, 1980; bd. dirs. Eleanor Gay Lee Gallery Found., N.Y.C., 1977, membership chmn., 1978-80, chmn. benefit com., 1981-82; Died June 22, 1991. Home: New York N.Y.

WEAVER, ROBERT CLIFTON, economist, educator, public administrator; b. Washington, Dec. 29, 1907; s. Mortimer G. and Florence (Freeman) W.; m. Ella V. Haith, July 19, 1935 (dec.); 1 child, Robert (dec.). B.S., Harvard U., 1929, M.A., 1931, Ph.D., 1934,, LL.D.; L.H.D. (hon.), Temple U., Pratt Inst.; LL.D. (hon.), Howard U., Morehouse Coll., Amherst Coll., Boston Coll., Rutgers U., So. Ill. U., Columbia U., Harvard U., U. Mich., U. Pa.; D.C.L. (hon.), U. Ill.; D.S.S. (hon.), Duquesne U. Adviser Negro affairs U.S. Dept. Interior, Washington, 1933-37; spl. asst. to adminstr. U.S. Housing Authority, Washington, 1937-40; adminstrv. asst. OPM, WPB, Washington, 1940-44; vis. prof. Columbia U. Tchrs. Coll., N.Y.C., 1947, NYU Sch. Edn., N.Y.C., 1947-49; dir. opportunity fellowships J.H. Whitney Found., 1949-54; dep. commr. N.Y. State Div. Housing, Albany, 1954-55; rent adminstr. N.Y. State, Albany, 1955-59; cons. Ford Found., 1959-60; vice-chmn. Housing and Redevel. Bd. N.Y.C., 1960-61; adminstr. HHFA, 1961-66; sec. HUD, Washington, 1966-68; pres. Bernard M. Baruch Coll., N.Y.C., 1969-70; Disting. prof. urban affairs Hunter Coll., N.Y.C., 1970-78; Disting. prof. emeritus Hunter Coll., 1978—, dir. urban programs Brookdale Ctr. on Aging, 1978; pres. Nat. Com. Against Discrimination in Housing, Inc., 1973-87; mem. conciliation and appeals bd. N.Y.C. Rent Stblzn. Bd., 1974-84; mem. Mcpl. Assistance Corp., N.Y.C., 1975—; mem. com. transp. NRC; lectr. Northwestern U., Evanston, Ill., 1947-48; dir. Met. Life Ins. Co., 1969-78; trustee Bowery Savs. Bank, N.Y.C., 1969-80; adminstr. Hunter Coll. Inst. Trial Judges, 1973-78; cons. GAO, 1973—; mem. housing policy task force AIA, 1974-75; chmn. Gov. Carey's Task Force on Housing and Community Devel., 1975. Author: Negro Labor: A National Problem, 1946; The Negro Ghetto, 1948; The Urban Complex 1964; Dilemmas of Urban America, 1965; contbr. over 175 articles to jours. and mags. Exec. sec. Chgo. Mayor's Com. on Race Relations, 1944-45; bd. dirs. Nat. Acad. Pub. Adminstrn., 1969, Mt. Sinai Hosp. and Sch. Medicine, 1969—; vice-chmn. N.Y. State Temp. Commn. on Powers of Local Govts., 1970-73; mem. vis. com. Sch. Urban and Pub. Affairs, Carnegie-Mellon U., Pitts., 1984-85 , Sch. Design, Harvard U., 1978-82; chmn. nat. bd. emeritus NAACP, 1978—; mem. exec. com. bd. dirs. NAACP Legal Def. Fund, 1978—; bd. overseers Sch. Fine Arts, U. Pa., 1962; hon. trustee Com. for Econ. Devel. Recipient Springarn medal NAACP, 1962, Pub. Svc. award U.S. Gen. Acctg. Office, 1975; M. Justice Herman Meml. award, Nat. Assn. Housing and Redevel. Officials, 1986, Equal Opportunity award Nat. Urban League, 1987; named to Nat. Assn. Homebuilders Hall of Fame, 1982. Fellow Am. Acad. Arts and Scis. (emeritus), Nat. Acad. Pub. Adminstrn. (sr. fellow, bd. dirs.). Died July 17, 1997.

WEAVER, WARREN, JR., writer; b. Madison, Wis., Feb. 7, 1923; s. Warren and Mary (Hemenway) W.; m. Barbara J. Woodall, July 8, 1950 (div. Feb. 1975); children: Carolyn, Sally, Melissa, Anne; m. Marianne Means, Feb. 10, 1977. B.A., Amherst Coll., 1943; M.S., Columbia U., 1947; J.D., Albany (N.Y.) Law Sch., 1958. Bar: N.Y. bar 1959, D.C. bar 1980. Reporter, then asst. state editor Watertown (N.Y.) Daily Times, 1947-48; mem. staff N.Y. Times, 1948-89; bur. chief N.Y. Times, Albany, 1959-62; mem. staff Washington bur. N.Y. Times, 1962-89, nat. polit. corr., 1966-68, Congressional corr., 1969-72, 79-81, Supreme Ct. corr., 1973-75, 77-78, columnist, 1982-87. Author: Making Our Government Work, 1964, Both Your Houses, 1972; contg. author: The Kennedy Years, 1964, The New York Times Election Handbook, 1964, 2d edit., 1968, The Road to the White House, 1965, Washington D.C.: Guide to the Nations Capital, 1967. Mem. N.Y. State Legis. Corrs. Assn. (pres. 1957). Clubs: Washington Press (dir. 1980-81), Nat. Press, Gridiron. Home: Washington D.C. Died Feb. 19, 1997.

WEBB, HARRY CHARLES, consultant; b. Felsenthal, Ark., Sept. 30, 1905; s. Victor Leach and Lillian Zenobia (Stinnett) W.; m. Ruth Alene Brown, July 5, 1929; children: Harry Charles, Richard C. Student, U. Tex. With Tex. Gulf Sulpher Co., Houston, 1929-53; exec. asst., asst. to v.p., dir. pub. relations; pres. Pan Am. Sulphur Co., Houston, 1954-70; dir. Pan Am. Sulphur Co., 1953-70, ret.; now cons. Mem. Am. Inst. M.E. Clubs: Houston Country, Petroleum, Coronado River Oaks Country. Home: Houston Tex. Died May 21, 1995.

WEBB, LANCE, bishop; b. Boaz, N.Mex., Dec. 10, 1909; s. John Newton Shields and Delia (Lance) W.; m. Mary Elizabeth Hunt, June 30, 1933 (dec. Mar. 1990); children—Gloria Jeanne (Mrs. David B. Davis), Mary M. (Mrs. Lee Edlund), Ruth Elizabeth (Mrs. Allan Lindstrom); m. Marie S. White, June 22, 1991. B.A. with highest honors, McMurry Coll., 1931, D.D., 1948; B.D., So. Meth. U., 1934, M.A., 1934; summer student, Union Theol. Sem., 1939, 47, 54, 57, 59, 60, 63; D.D., Ohio Wesleyan, U., 1960, MacMurray Coll., 1967, McKendree Coll., 1970; Litt.D., Morningside Coll., 1977; H.H.D., Ill. Wesleyan U., 1966; LL.D., So. Meth. U., 1966; Litt.D., Simpson Coll., 1979; Litt.D. (hon.), Wiley Coll., 1986. Ordained to ministry Meth. Ch., 1935; pastor McCullough-Harrah Meth. Chs., Pampa, Tex., 1934-37; chaplain prof. religion McMurry Coll., Abilene, Tex., 1937-38; pastor Shamrock, Tex., 1938-40, Eastland, Tex., 1940-41; pastor University Park Meth. Ch., Dallas, 1941-52, North Broadway Meth. Ch., Columbus, Ohio, 1953-64; bishop Meth. Ch., 1964-80; resident bishop Meth. Ch., Ill. area, 1964-76, Iowa area, 1976-80; retired Meth. Ch.; Ann. Endowed Lance Webb lectr. on spiritual formation Cen. Ill. Conf., 1976—, cons. on spiritual formation for the upper rm., Nashville, 1980—; chmn. com. on worship Meth. Ch., 1964-72, mem. gen. and jurisdictional confs., 1956, 60, 64, co-chmn. world Meth. com. worship and liturgy, 1966-71; mem. World Meth. Council, 1966-81, sec., vice chmn. com. worship and liturgy, 1971-76 , chmn. com., 1976-81; mem. gen. bd. higher edn. United Meth. Ch., 1972-80; pres. north central jurisdiction Coll. of Bishops, 1979-80; conducted goodwill tours Middle East and Round the World, 1961, 63; Nat. Council Chs. interchange preacher Britain, 1959; chancellor Discipled Order of Christ, 1964-89, chancellor emeritus, 1989—. Author: Conquering the Seven Deadly Sins, 1955, Discovering Love, 1959, Point of Glad Return, 1960, Art of Personal Prayer, 1962, On the Edge of the Absurd, 1965, When God Comes Alive, 1968, Disciplines for Life in the Age of Aquarius, 1971, God's Surprises, 1976, Onesimus, 1980, Making Love Grow, 1983, How Bad Are Your Sins, 1983, How Good Are Your Virtues, 1983, Disciplines for Life, 1986, Onesimus-Rebel and Saint, 1988; Sin and the Human Predicament, Vol. I, When Virtues Become Sins: God's Love and Human Transformation, Vol. II, 1988; A Traveller in the Company of God's Friends, 1991, Escape from Ephesus: A Novel of the First Century, 1991, Rebel and Saint, 1992 (sequel to Escape from Ephesus). Mem. Mayor's Com. on Human Relations, Columbus, 1953-64; chaplain Ohio Senate, 1963; internat. chaplain Civitain Internat., 1951; trustee Meth. Sch. Theology in Ohio, Garrett Evang. Theol. Sch., Evanston, Ill., McKendree Coll., Lebanon, Ill., Ill. Wesleyan U., MacMurray Coll., 1964-76; trustee Wiley Coll., 1972-87, emeritus, 1987—; chmn. bd. Wesley Found., U. Ill., 1964-76, Morningside Coll., Simpson Coll., Cornell Coll., Iowa Wesleyan Coll., Westmar Coll., 1976-80, Rust Coll., 1976-80. Clubs: Masons (Scottish Rite) (33 deg.), Torch (Columbus). Home: Dallas Tex. Died Sept. 9, 1995.

WEBB, WILLIAM HESS, lawyer; b. Scottdale, Pa., Sept. 10, 1905; s. Austin Allison and Gertrude (Hess) W.; m. Marian Elizabeth Wellings, Nov. 26, 1931; children: John M., Patricia Ann (Mrs. Terence S. Small). BS, U. Pitts, 1926, LLB, 1929. Bar: Pa. 1929. Practiced in Pitts., 1929—; sr. ptnr. Webb, Ziesenheim, Bruening, Logsdon, Orkin & Hanson, Pitts., 1948—. Bd. dirs., v.p., treas. Pitts. Opera, Inc.; mem. Pitts. Symphony Soc. Served to lst lt. U.S. Army Res., 1926-34. Mem. ABA (ho. of dels. 1961-65), Am. Intellectual Property Law Assn. (bd. mgrs. 1953-62, pres. 1959-60), Pa. Bar Assn., Allegheny County Bar Assn., Am. Law Inst., Duquesne Club, Univ. Club (Pitts.), Edgeworth Club (Sewickley, Pa.), Allegheny Country Club, Delta Theta Phi, Theta Chi. Deceased.

WEEKS, FRANCIS WILLIAM, business communications educator emeritus; b. E. Orange, N.J., Jan. 26, 1916; s. Caleb Ora and Daisy (Tack) W.; m. Dorothy Anne Skiles, July 23, 1942; children: Hilda Jean, Alice Anne, Virginia Lueze, Sara Elizabeth, Marjorie Estelle, Cynthia Grace, Janet Christine. B.A. with honors, Swarthmore Coll., 1937; A.M., Columbia U., 1939. Mem. faculty U. Ill., 1939-93, prof. English, chmn. div. bus. and tech. writing, 1964-82, prof. emeritus, 1983-93; vis. prof. bus. communication U. Houston, 1967-68. Author: (with C.R. Anderson) Business Reports, 1957, (with D. Jameson) Principles of Business Communication, 1979, (with K. Locker) Business Writing Cases and Problems, 1980; editor: Readings in Communication from Fortune, 1961, Jour. Bus. Communication, 1963-64. Fellow Assn. for Bus. Communication (exec. dir., treas. 1964-82, exec. dir. emeritus 1982-93); mem. Japan Bus. English Assn. (hon.), Rotary (pres. Urbana club 1978), Phi Sigma Kappa (dir. Ill. assn. 1962-71, pres. 1964-66, nat. v.p. scholarship 1965-70, nat. chmn. scholarship 1974, trustee Phi Sigma Kappa Found). Mem. Soc. of Friends (clk. Urbana-Champaign meeting 1951-53, 55-57, 68-70). Home: Urbana Ill. Died Oct. 30, 1993.

WEIL, HERMAN, psychology educator; b. Regisheim, Alsace Lorraine, Dec. 15, 1905; came to U.S., 1938, naturalized, 1944; m. Bertha Weiler, July 26, 1931; 1 son, Gunther M. Ph.D. in Psychology, U. Marburg, Germany, 1929, state exam. in math., chemistry, physics, 1929, state exam. in edn., 1931; D.Pub. Service (hon.), U. Wis.-Milw., 1986. Instr. Realgymnasium for Girls, Hersfeld, Germany, 1931-33; instr., studienrat Philanthropin Realgymnasium, Frankfurt on Main, Germany, 1933-38; postdoctoral scholar U. Iowa, 1939; prof. sci. Nebr. Central Coll., 1939-40; prof. Milw. Sch. Engring., 1940-43; prof. edn. and psychology, head dept. Wis. State Coll., Milw., 1943-56; prof. psychology U. Wis., Milw., 1956-76; prof. emeritus U. Wis., 1976—, chmn. dept., 1956-61, chmn. honors program superior students Coll. Letters and Scis., 1960-74, asso. dean, 1967-71, faculty retirement counselor, 1973-75; vis. prof. Northwestern U., summers 1947, 48, 51; cons. Human Relations Workshop, U. Mich., summers 1952-56; dir. Workshops on Human Relations, Wis. State Coll., summers 1952-56; lectr. Milw. Downer Coll., 1943-47; cons. Dept. State, also U.S. Office Edn., Jugenheim, Ger., 1954; Disting. Service fellow Temple Emanu-El B'ne Jeshurun, 1976-78, 79-84, emeritus, 1984—, dean adult Jewish studies, 1978-79; Disting. scholar-in-residence Milw. Jewish Community Ctr., 1977-80; invited speaker dedication ceremonies of permanent edn. exhbt. in former Jewish Gymnasium Philanthropin, as sole Holocaust survivor of tenured faculty, Frankfurt, Fed. Republic Germany, 1988; curator Rubenstein Ctr. for 20th Century Jewry, 1992-93. Author: In Quest of Excellence, 1975, University of Wisconsin-Milwaukee Faculty Retirement Guidebook, 1975, 2d edit., 1976; contbr. chpts. and sects. to books on psychol. subjects. Co-chmn. Wis. region NCCJ, 1952-72, mem. commn. on ednl. orgns., 1955-60, nat. bd. dirs., 1977-84, nat. co-chmn. schs. and colls. com. observance of Nat. Brotherhood Week, 1957; mem. Gov.'s Commn. on Human Rights, 1953-56; counselor Milw. B'nai B'rith Hillel Found., 1950-60; pres. New Home Club, Inc., 1940-57, hon. pres., 1977-87; chmn. Milw. chpt. Am. Jewish Com., 1973-75, mem. nat. exec. com., 1973-80. Recipient citation of merit for work in human rels. Milw. B'nai B'rith Couns., 1952, Brotherhood award Wis. region NCCJ, 1959, Citation award Internat. Inst. Milwaukee County, 1960, Disting. Merit citation NCCJ, 1973, Disting. Merit citation Wis. Soc. Jewish Learning, 1973, Disting. Svc. award U. Wis.-Milw. chpt. AAUP, 1975, Disting. Merit citation Coll. Letters and Sci., U. Wis.-Milw., 1976, Am. Jewish Com. Inst. Human Rels. award, 1978, Spl. Lifetime Svc. award Milw. Assn. for Jewish Edn., 1989; guest of honor Mayor and Senate, City of West Berlin, 1979; linden tree planted in his honor near courtyard of Gold Meir Libr., U. Wis., Milw., 1990; named as one of Milw. Ret. profs. who have made significant, enduring and institution wide contbns., U. Wis.-Milw., 1994. Mem. AAUP (pres. Wis. conf. 1973-74), Wis. Soc. Jewish Learning (past pres.), Wis. Psychol. Assn. (past pres.), Milwaukee County Psychol. Assn. (past pres.), Nat. Collegiate Honors Council (mem. exec. com. 1972-73), Ret. Faculty Assn. U. Wis.-Milw. (pres. 1977-79), Phi Kappa Phi (hon.). Jewish (past v.p., trustee temple). Died Aug. 6, 1995.

WEINBERG, EDWARD, lawyer; b. Whitewater, Wis., Sept. 5, 1918; s. Bernhard and Molly (Schotzky) W.; m. Anne Goldsmith, June 13, 1943; children—Mark, Robert. B.A., U. Wis.-Madison, 1939, LL.B., 1941. Bar: Wis. 1941, D.C. 1964, U.S. Supreme Ct. 1965. Atty., then asst. chief counsel Bur. Reclamation, 1944-54; asst. solicitor Dept. Interior, 1955-61, assoc. solicitor, 1962-63, dep. solicitor, 1963-68, solicitor, 1968-69; practiced in Washington, 1969—; mem. firm Duncan, Weinberg, Miller & Pembroke, P.C., 1974—; prin. cons. Nat. Water Commn., 1969-73. Author: Intrastate, Interstate and International Problems of Large-scale Water Transfer, 1969, The Colorado River Salinity Dispute, 1973; co-author: Meandering Through the Interior Maze, 1985, Federal Reserved Water Rights, 1990. Mem. Am., Fed., D.C. bar assns., Order of Coif, Artus, Tau Epsilon Rho. Democrat. Jewish. Home: Washington D.C. Died May 1, 1995.

WEINSTEIN, LEWIS H., lawyer; b. Vilna, Lithuania, Apr. 10, 1905; came to U.S., 1906; s. Jacob Menahem and Kuna (Romanow) W.; m. Selma Yeslawsky, Sept. 2, 1932 (dec. Apr. 20, 1986); children: David J., Louise W. Dozois. AB magna cum laude, Harvard U., 1927, JD, 1930; DHL (hon.), Brandeis U., 1986; D Hebrew Laws (hon.), Hebrew Coll., Boston, 1987. Bar: Mass. 1930, Fed. 1932, U.S. Supreme Ct. 1933. Assoc., then ptnr. Rome & Weinstein, 1930-45; asst. corp. counsel Boston, 1934-45; ptnr. Foley, Hoag & Eliot, Boston, 1946-79; sr. ptnr. Foley, Hoag & Eliot, 1979-93; lectr. law Harvard U., 1960-75; sr. vis. lectr. dept. city and regional planning MIT, 1960-68; occasional lectr. Practising Law Inst., N.Y.C., New England Law Inst.-ABA-Am. Law Inst., Mass. Continuing Legal Edn.; past clk. Spencer Cos.; mem. faculty Nat. Inst. Trial Advocacy, Boulder, Colo.; mem. fin. com., bd. dirs. B&M R.R., 1960-74, LTV Corp., 1973; trustee Boston 5 Cent Savs. Bank, 1964-78; cons. U.S. Housing Authority, 1940-42. Author: Masa: Odyssey of an American Jew, 1989, My Life at the Bar: Six Decades as Lawyer, Soldier, Teacher, Pro Bono Activist, 1993; contbr. articles to law and other jours., chpts. to law books; author plays, biog. articles. Chmn. Mass. Emergency Housing Commn., 1946-47; chmn. Mass. Bd. Housing, 1947-48, Mass. Housing Council, 1948-52; mem. rent control and housing coms. Nat. Def. Commn., 1941-42; chmn. Nat. Jewish Community Relations Adv. Council, 1960-64, Armed Forces Adv. Com. Greater Boston, 1946-48; pres., Combined Jewish Philanthropies Greater Boston, 1954-57, gen. campaign chmn., 1957, mem. exec. com.; past pres. Jewish Community Relations Council Met. Boston, 1952-54; former mem. nat. council Jewish Welfare Bd.; chmn. Conf. Presidents Maj. Am. Jewish

Orgns., 1964-66; chmn. Nat. Conf. Soviet Jewry, 1968-70; mem. nat. com. Harvard Center for Jewish Studies; past lay rep. Nat. Assembly for Social Policy and Devel.; former mem. exec. com. City of Boston Civic Unity Com.; former mem. adv. council Mass. Dept. Edn.; Mass. Dept. Mental Health; mem. human rights com. housing and urban renewal com. World Peace Through Law Center; former mem. exec. com., bd. dirs. New Eng. region, nat. bd. dirs. NCCJ; exec. com. Pres.'s Com. Equal Opportunity Housing, 1961-68; past chmn. Gov.'s Task Force to Establish Mass. Dept. Community Affairs; pres., 1965-66, now mem. exec. com. Council Jewish Fedn.; mem. nat. council Am. Jewish Joint Distbn. Com.; past v.p. Nat. Fedn. Jewish Men's Clubs.; hon. trustee United Israel Appeal; past trustee Social Law, Library Ct. House Boston; past v.p. Am. Jewish League for Israel; past trustee Mass. Fedn. Taxpayers' Assn., Meml. Found. Jewish Culture; past bd. overseers Hiatt Inst.; past mem. bd. overseers Lown Inst. Contemporary Jewish Studies, Heller Grad. Sch. Pub. Welfare; fellow Brandeis U.; past mem. vis. com., bd. overseers Middle Eastern Ctr. and Near Eastern Langs. and Civilizations, Harvard U.; mem. steering com. capital fund campaign, past class agt., vice chmn. '27 Coll. Law Sch. Class of '30; mem. steering com. Divinity Sch. Fund for Christian-Jewish Relations; hon. life trustee Nat. Found. Jewish Culture; trustee Hebrew Rehab. Ctr. for Aged, Boston, 1955-96, Beth Israel Hosp., 1956-96, Inst. for Jewish Life; pres. Hebrew Coll., Boston, 1946-53, now trustee; mem. assembly Jewish Agy. for Israel; founding trustee Ency. Judaica Found.; mem. exec. Seminar program Aspen (Colo.) Inst., 1978; mem. Mass. Ward Commn. To Investigate Corruption and Malfeasance in State and County Constrn., 1978-80; hon. life trustee Temple Emanuel; bd. dirs. Temple Mishkan Tefila, Newton, Mass. Served to col. AUS, World War II. Decorated Legion of Merit, Bronze Star with oak leaf clusters, Legion of Honor, Croix de Guerre with palm (France); recipient Nat. Citation, NCCJ, Heritage award Jewish Theol. Sem., FDR Day award Ams. Dem. Action, Mass., Harvard Ctr. Jewish Studies award, 1986, Tree of Life award Jewish Nat. Fund, 1989, Heritage award Yeshire U., 1971; named Disting. Bostonian C. of C., 1988, Humanitarian of Yr., Alzheimer's Disease Mass. Assn., 1988. Fellow Am. Coll. Trial Lawyers; mem. Am. Bar Found., Am. Assn. Jewish Edn. (v.p., mem. adv. panel on Alzheimer's disease to Congress and exec. depts. 1988-96); mem. ABA (past mem. standing com. fed. judiciary), Mass. Bar Assn. (past chmn. grievance com.), Boston Bar Assn. (past mem. coun., chmn. real estate and eminent domain com.), Am. Jewish Hist. Soc. (past mem. exec. coun.), Assn. of U.S. Army (bd. dirs. Bay State chpt.), Mil. Govt. Assn. (past pres. Mass. chpt.), Harvard Club Boston, Phi Beta Kappa. Address: For Estate of Mr. Lewis Weinstein c/o Louise Dozois 196 White St Belmont MA 02178-4724 Died Oct. 23, 1996.

WEINTRAUB, HENRY, advertising agency executive; b. Bronx, N.Y., July 31, 1937. B.B.A., CCNY, 1959. Asst. advt. mgr. 20th Century Fox, 1964-66; acct. exec. Diener Hauser Greenthal, 1966-67; advt. mgr. NBC-TV, 1967-68; with Diener/Hauser/Bates Co. Inc. (now AC & R Advt. Inc.), 1968—; acct. exec. Diener/Hauser/Bates Co. Inc., N.Y.C., 1968-74, v.p., acct. supr., 1974-77; pres. Diener/Hauser/Bates Co. Inc., then AC & R/DHB & Bess Advt., Inc., N.Y.C.; chmn. AC & R Advt. Inc., N.Y.C., 1988—, also chmn. entertainment div. DIED 08/24/97. .

WEISGALL, HUGO DAVID, composer, conductor; b. Ivancice, Czechoslovakia, Oct. 13, 1912; came to U.S., 1920, naturalized, 1926; s. Adolph Joseph and Aranka (Stricker) W.; m. Nathalie Shulman, Dec. 28, 1942; children: Deborah, Jonathan. Student, Johns Hopkins, 1929-31, Ph.D., 1940; musical edn., Peabody Conservatory, Baltimore, 1927-30, Curtis Inst., Phila., 1936-39; studied composition with, Roger Sessions. Instr. composition Cummington Sch. Arts, 1948-51; instr. Julliard Sch. Music Arts, 1957-69; Disting. prof. composition CUNY, 1960-83; disting. vis. prof. Penn State U., 1959-60; disting. prof. Peabody Inst., Balt., 1974-75; chmn. faculty Sem. Coll. of Jewish Music, Jewish Theol. Sem. of Am.; pres. Am. Music Ctr., 1964-73; assoc. Lincoln Ctr. Fund, 1965-68; dir. Hilltop Mus. Co., Balt., 1951-54. Condr. Har Sinai Temple Choir, 1931-42, Y-Alliance Orch., 1935-42, Balt. String Symphony, 1936-38, Md. N.Y.A. Orch., 1940-41; guest condr. London Symphony, London Philharmonic, BBC Symphony orchs., Orchestre de la Chapelle Musicale de la Reine Elizabeth, Belgium, Radio National Belge, dir. Balt. Inst. Mus. Arts, 1949, composer in residence Am. Acad. in Rome, 1966-67, 84; composer Songs, 1929, Quest; ballet, 1937, One Thing Is Certain, ballet, 1939, Hymn for chorus and orch, 1941; Overture in F, 1942, Soldier Songs, 1944-45, Outpost, 1947; opera The Tenor, 1949-50, The Stronger, 1952, Three Symphonic Songs for high voice and orch, 1952, Six Characters in Search of an Author, 1956, Purgatory, 1958, Athaliah, 1963, Nine Rivers from Jordan, 1968; song cycle Fancies and Inventions, 1970, Translations, 1971, End of Summer, 1974; cantata for soprano, tenor, chorus and orch. Song of Celebration, 1976; (opera) Jenny or the Hundred Nights, 1976, The Golden Peacock, 1976; song cycle Liebeslieder, 1979; opera The Gardens of Adonis, 1981, Piano Sonata, 1982, Prospect, 1983, 4 Birthday Cards, 1983, Lyrical Interval, song cycle for low voice and piano, 1984, Tekiatot: Rituals for Rosh Hashannah for orch., 1985, Tangents, 4 episodes for flute and marimba, 1985, Arioso and Burlesca for cello and piano, 1983, Loves Wounded 2 songs for baritone and orch., 1986, opera Will You Marry Me?, 1987, opera Esther, 1992, Evening Liturgies, 1994; Ditson Opera commn., Columbia, 1952, Koussevitzky commn., 1961, Psalm of the Distant Dove canticle for mezzo soprano and piano, 1992, Evening Liturgies for baritone, chorus and organ, 1995. Enlisted as pvt. AUS, 1942; asst. mil. attache to govts. in exile, London, later to Czechoslovakia cultural attache Am. embassy 1946-47, Prague. Awarded Bearns prize Columbia, 1931, William Schuman award, 1994; traveling fellow Curtis Inst., 1938; Ditson fellow Columbia, 1944; grantee Nat. Inst. Arts and Letters, 1952; Guggenheim fellow, 1955-56, 61-62, 66-67. Mem. Nat. Inst. Arts and Letters, Am. Acad.-Inst. Arts and Letters (pres. 1990-93), Phi Beta Kappa.

WEISS, EDWIN, mathematics educator; b. Bklyn., Aug. 23, 1927; s. Paul and Clara Ida (Rodman) W.; m. Janice S. Gopen, May 25, 1952; children: S. Ariel, Rena R. B.S., Bklyn. Coll., 1948; Ph.D., Mass. Inst. Tech., 1953. Instr. U. Mich., Ann Arbor, 1953-54, mem. Inst. Advanced Study, 1954-55; Benjamin Peirce instr. math. Harvard U., Cambridge, Mass., 1955-58; asst. prof. UCLA, 1958-59; staff mem. Lincoln Lab., MIT, Cambridge, 1959-65; prof. math. Boston U., 1965-91; Vis. prof. Weizmann Inst. Sci., 1970-71, summer 1974. Author: Algebraic Number Theory, 1963, Cohomology of Groups, 1969, First Course in Algebra and Number Theory, 1971; co-author: Modern Elementary Mathematics: A Laboratory Approach, 1972. Home: Brookline Mass. Died Oct. 7, 1991.

WEISS, IRA FRANCIS, banker; b. Providence, R.I., Oct. 19, 1909; s. Abraham and Minnie (Chernoff) W.; m. Gladys Abbott (div. 1966); children: Abbott, Michael, John. Student, CCNY, 1926-28; LL.B., St. Lawrence U., 1931; postgrad., Columbia U., 1931-33, St. John's Coll., Annapolis, 1975-78; B.A., Seminar Coll., New Sch., 1980, M.A., 1982; postgrad., CUNY Grad. Ctr. Bar: N.Y. 1934. Pvt. practice N.Y.C., 1934-37; asst. sec. Credit Utility Co., Inc., N.Y.C., 1937-42; successively asst. sec., asst. v.p., v.p., adminstrv. v.p., sr. v.p. Trade Bank & Trust Co., 1926-33, 45-70; sr. v.p. Nat. Bank N. Am., N.Y.C., 1970-74; sr. cons. Nat. Bank N.Am. (now Fleet Bank), 1975. Mem. Jewish Com. on Scouting, N.Y.C., 1950-53; asst. mgr. United Fund, Glen Ridge, N.J., 1959; mem. Civic Conf. Com., 1961-64, Mayor's Transp. Com., 1962-65, Speakers Bur. of United Cerebral Palsy Soc., N.Y.C., 1946-50; treas., exec. bd. N.Y. chpt., mem. nat. exec. council Am. Jewish Com., 1962-75; mem. Nat. Com. on Am. Fgn. Policy. Sgt. U.S. Army, 1942-45. Mem. AIM, N.Y. Credit and Financial Mgmt. Assn., Am. Arbitration Assn. (nat. panel), Robert Morris Assocs., Fgn. Policy Assn., Carnegie Council on Ethics and Internat. Affairs, Ctr. for Study Presidency, Acad. Polit. Sci. Died Dec. 13, 1996.

WEISS, JEROME PAUL, lawyer; b. Binghamton, N.Y., May 16, 1934; s. Milton I. and Irene (Freeman) W.; m. Marion Levitt, June 30, 1963; children: Jonathan Peter, Andrew Stephen. AB magna cum laude, Princeton U., 1956; JD, Harvard U., 1961. Bar: N.Y. 1962, D.C. 1975. Assoc., Hiscock, Cowie, Bruce, Lee & Mawhinney, Syracuse, N.Y., 1961-64; asst. gen. counsel Agway, Inc., Syracuse, 1964-72; dep. gov. and gen. counsel Farm Credit Adminstrn., Washington, 1972-73; assoc. Hamel, Park, McCabe & Saunders, Washington, 1974-76, ptnr., 1976-78, sr. ptnr., 1978-83, mng. ptnr., 1983-86; mng. ptnr. Sonnenschein, Nath & Rosenthal, Washington, 1986-96; adj. prof. Syracue U. Sch. Law, 1970-74, Antioch Sch. Law, 1974-76. Trustee Landon Sch., Bethesda, Md., 1982-88. Lt. USNR, 1956-58. Mem. ABA, N.Y. State Bar Assn., D.C. Bar Assn. Clubs: Riverbend Country (Great Falls, Va.); Naples (Fla.) Bath and Tennis. Contbr. articles to legal jours. Died July 6, 1996. Home: Great Falls Va.

WEISS, LEONARD, international economics consultant; b. Chgo., June 5, 1918; s. Ben and Esther (Tepper) W.; m. Mary L. Barker, Sept. 21, 1946; children: Susan R., David A. B.A., U. Chgo., 1939; M.A., Fletcher Sch. Law and Diplomacy, 1940. Rsch. asst. Ill. Tax Commn., 1938, Carnegie Endowment for Internat. Peace, 1940; fellow Brookings Instn., 1941-42; economist Office Inter-Am. Affairs, 1942-43, 46; ofcl. Dept. of State, 1946-56, fgn. svc. officer, 1956-74; asst. chief trade agreements div., alt. chmn. inter-departmental trade agreements com., until 1957; dep. dir. and acting dir. USOM, Belgrade, Yugoslavia, 1957-60; also 1st sec. Am. Embassy, Belgrade, 1957-58; then counselor econ. affairs Am. embassy, Belgrade, 1959-60; with Dept. State, Washington, 1960-63; dep. dir., then dir. Office Internat. Trade and Fin. Dept. State, 1960-63; counselor econ. affairs Am. embassy, New Delhi, 1963-65; also minister-counselor polit. and econ. affairs Am. embassy, New Delhi, India, 1965-67; minister econ. and comml. affairs Am. embassy Bonn, 1968-70; dep. dir. Bur. Intelligence and Research Dept. State, Washington, 1970-74; chief World Bank Mission, Bangladesh, 1974-78; internat. econs. cons., mem. trade policy group U.S. Atlantic Council, 1978-88; U.S. del. ECOSOC, 1951, GATT, 1950, 53-54, 55, 61, 62, 63, OEEC Council of Ministers meeting, 1954; vice chmn. U.S. del. to ECAFE, 1965, 66, 67, alt. U.S. rep., 1966-67; spl. rep. for Offset Talks, 1968; mem. U.S. del. to Offset Talks, 1969, Sr. Seminar Fgn. Policy, State Dept., 1967-68, World Bank del. to Bangladesh Aid Group meeting, 1974, 75, 76, 77. Contbr. articles and monographs on internat. trade to profl. publs. Served to lt. (j.g.) USNR, 1943-46. Recipient Superior Service award Dept. State, 1963. Mem. Am. Econ. Assn., Am. Soc. Internat. Law (research and study panel on internat. trade issues 1982-83), Am. Fgn. Service Assn., Diplomatic and Consular Officers Ret., Alumni Assn. Fletcher Sch. Law and Diplomacy, U. Chgo. Alumni Assn., 1818 Soc. (World Bank), Phi Beta Kappa. DIED 09/30/96. .

WEITZMANN, KURT, archaeologist, educator, art historian; b. Klein Almerode, Germany, Mar. 7, 1904; came to U.S., 1935, naturalized, 1940; s. Wilhelm and Antonie (Keiper) W.; m. Josepha Fiedler, Jan. 13, 1932. Student univs., Munster, Wurzburg, Vienna, Berlin, 1923-29; PhD, U. Berlin, 1929; Doctor honoris causa, U. Heidelberg, 1967, Freie Universitat Berlin, 1982; LHD, U. Chgo., 1968. Stipend German Archaeolog. Institut, Greece, 1931; with Archaeol. Institut, Berlin, 1932-35; permanent mem. Inst. Advanced Study, Princeton, 1935-72; assoc. prof. art and archaeology Princeton U., 1945-50, prof. art and archaeology, 1950-72, prof. emeritus, 1972-93; vis. prof. Yale, 1954-55, U. Alexandria, Egypt, 1960; guest prof. U. Bonn, 1962; bd. scholars Dumbarton Oaks Rsch. Libr. and Collection, Harvard, 1949-72; vis. scholar Dumbarton Oaks, 1972-73; hon. trustee Met. Mus., consultative curator, 1973-82. Author: (with Adolph Goldschmidt), 2 vols.) Die Byzantinischen Elfenbeinskulpturen, 1930-34, Die Armenische Buchmalerei, 1933, Die Byzantinische Buchmalerei des 9. und 10. Jahrhunderts, 1935, Illustrations in Roll and Codex, 1947, The Joshua Roll, 1948, Greek Mythology in Byzantine Art, 1951, The Fresco Cycle of S. Maria Di Castelseprio, 1951, Ancient Book-illumination (Martin Classical Lectures Volume XVI), 1959, Geistige Grundlagen und Wesen der Makedonischen Renaissance, 1963, Studies in Classical and Byzantine Manuscript Illumination, 1971, (with George H. Forsyth) The Monastery of St. Catherine at Mount Sinai: The Church and Fortress of Justinian, 1973, The Icons, Vol. I: From the Sixth to the Tenth Century, 1976, Late Antique and Early Christian Book Illumination, 1977, The Icon, Holy Images: Sixth to Fourteenth Century, 1978, The Miniatures of the Sacra Parallela, 1979, Byzantine Book Illumination and Ivories, Var. Repr., 1980, Byzantine Liturgical Psalters and Gospels, Var. Repr., 1980, Classical Heritage in Byzantine and Near Eastern Art, Var. Repr., 1981, Art in the Medieval West and Its Contacts with Byzantium, Var. Repr., 1982, Studies in the Arts at Sinai, 1982, (with H. L. Kessler) The Cotton Genesis, 1986, (with H.L. Kessler) The Frescoes of the Dura Synagogue and Christian Art, 1990, (with George Galavaris) The Illuminated Manuscripts of St. Catherine's Monastery at Mt. Sinai, vol. I, 1990; editor The Illustrations in the Manuscripts of the Septuagint, 1941-93, Studies in Honor of A.M. Friend, Jr, 1955, Studies in Manuscript Illumination, Age of Spirituality: Catalogue Metropolitan Museum Exhibition, 1979, Expedition Mt. Sinai, 1956, 58, 60, 63, 65; contbr. articles profl. publs. Recipient Prix Schlumberger Academie des Inscriptions et Belles-Lettres, Paris, 1969, Great Cross of Merit, Fed. Republic Germany, 1986. Fellow Medieval Acad. Am. (Haskins medal 1974), Pierpont Morgan Library (hon.); mem. German Archaeol. Institut Berlin, Acad. Scis. Goettingen (corr.), Acad. Athens (corr.), Am. Acad. Arts and Scis., Mediterranean Acad. Scis. (Catania), Brit. Acad. (corr.), Am. Philos. Soc., Coll. Art Assn. (Charles Rufus Morey Book award), Archaeol. Inst. Am., Assn. Internationale des Etudes Byzantines (v.p.), Acad. Scis. Heidelberg (corr.), Pontificia Accedemia Romana di Archeologia (corr.), Am. Acad. Arts and Scis., Austrian Acad. Scis. (corr.). Home: Princeton N.J. Died June 3, 1993.

WELCH, KEASLEY, surgeon; b. Bridgeport, Conn., June 3, 1920; s. James M. and Hazel (Keasley) W.; m. Elizabeth MacRae, May 15, 1948; children: Elizabeth, Mary, Anne, Joan, Stephanie. Student, Duquesne U., 1937-38; B.S., U. Pitts., 1940; M.D., Yale, 1943; M.Sc., McGill U., Can., 1947; M.A. (hon.), Harvard, 1971. Diplomate: Am. Bd. Neurol. Surgery. Intern New Haven Hosp., 1944-45; asst. resident neurosurgery Montreal (Que.) Neurol. Inst., 1945-46, fellow neuropathology, 1946-47, resident neurosurgery, 1947-48; practice medicine specializing in neurosurgery Montreal, Detroit, Denver, Boston; demonstrator in neuropathology McGill U., 1947-48, lectr. neurosurgery, 1949-50; asso. neurosurgeon Henry Ford Hosp., Detroit, 1950-51; attending neurosurgeon Colo. Gen. Hosp., Denver, 1953-70, Denver Gen. Hosp., 1953-61; cons. neurosurgeon VA Hosp., Denver, 1953-70, Fitzsimmons Army Hosp., Denver, 1955-70; from asst. prof. to prof. neurosurgery U. Colo., Denver, 1953-63; neurosurgeon-in-chief Children's Hosp. Med. Center, Boston, 1971-96; div. chief Brigham and Women's Hosp., Boston, 1971-96; cons. neurosurgery various hosps. in, Mass., 1973-96; hon. research asso. U. Coll. London, 1969 70; Franc D. Ingraham prof. neurosurgery Harvard Med. Sch., Boston, 1971-96. Contbr. articles to profl. jours. Served as capt. M.C. U.S. Army, 1952-53. Fellow A.C.S.; mem. Am. Acad. Neurol. Surgery, Soc. Neurol. Surgeons, Am. Neurol. Assn., Am. Assn. Neurol. Surgeons, Am. Acad. Neurology, Neurosurg. Soc. Am., World Fedn. Neurology, New Eng. Neurosurg. Soc.,

Boston Surg. Soc., Am. Physiol. Soc., Soc. for Reserach into Hydrocephalus and Spina Bifida, Royal Soc. Medicine, Boston Soc. Psychiatry and Neurology. Home: Waban Mass. Died Feb. 2, 1996.

WELLER, RALPH ALBERT, retired elevator company manufacturing executive; b. Cleve., Sept. 8, 1921; s. Ralph A. and Aileen (Fitzpatrick) W.; m. Martha Early, Oct. 10, 1950 (div.); children: Michael F., John A., Robert O. B.S., Va. Mil. Inst., 1942; M.B.A., Harvard U., 1947. With Otis Elevator Co., N.Y.C., 1947-84; regional v.p. Otis Elevator Co., San Francisco, 1964-66; v.p. engring., prodn. and purchasing Otis Elevator Co., N.Y.C., 1966-68; pres. Otis Elevator Co., 1968-69, chief exec. officer, 1969-75, chmn. bd., 1975-80, chmn. emeritus, 1980-95. Served with USMC, 1942-46. Mem. Council on Fgn. Relations. Clubs: Olympic (San Francisco); Sky (N.Y.C.); Blind Brook (Port Chester, N.Y.). Home: New York N.Y. Died Mar. 31, 1995.

WELLS, ALEXANDER FRANK, chemist, educator; b. London, Eng., Sept. 2, 1912; came to U.S., 1968; s. Alexander Edward and Emma Isabel (Wilks) W.; m. Ada Squires, Dec. 30, 1939; children: Alexander John, Janet (Mrs. John Bray). M.A., Oxford (Eng.) U., 1937; Ph.D., Cambridge (Eng.) U., 1937, Sc.D., 1956. Research univs Cambridge and Birmingham, 1937-44; sr. research asso. Imperial Chem. Industries Ltd., 1944-68; prof. chemistry U. Conn., 1968-80, prof. emeritus, 1980—; hon. reader chemistry U. Manchester, Eng., 1966-68; NSF vis. sr. fgn. scientist, 1965-66. Author: Structural Inorganic Chemistry, 5th edit., 1984, The Third Dimension in Chemistry, 1956, Models in Structural Inorganic Chemistry, 1970, Three-dimensional Nets and Polyhedra, 1977; also articles, monographs. Fellow Chem. Soc., Inst. Physics; mem. Am. Chem. Soc. Home: Mansfield Center Conn. DIED 11/28/94. .

WELLS, CHARLES MARION, lawyer; b. Lawrenceburg, Ind., Mar. 15, 1905; s. Charles Lewis and Leona (Rogers) W.; m. Elizabeth Cooper, Oct. 25, 1950; 1 son, John. A.B., Butler U., 1927; LL.B., Ind. U., 1929; LL.M., Harvard U., 1932. Bar: Ind. 1929, U.S. Supreme Ct 1935. Practice in Indpls., 1929-90; mem. firm Barnes, Hickam, Pantzer & Boyd, 1940-81; of counsel Barnes & Thornburg, 1982-90; spl. counsel Ind. Dept. Financial Instns., 1935-37. Served to lt. col. USAAF, 1943-46. Mem. Am., Ind., Indpls. bar assns., Am. Judicature Soc., Delta Tau Delta, Delta Theta Phi. Republican. Methodist. Clubs: Indpls. Athletic (Indpls.), Lawyers (Indpls.), Woodstock (Indpls.). Lodge: Masons (Indpls.). Died 1991.

WENSTROM, FRANK AUGUSTUS, state senator, city and county official; b. Dover, N.D., July 27, 1903; s. James August a1d Anna Petra (Kringstad) W.; student public schs., Carrington, N.D.; LLD (hon.), U. N.D., 1990. m. Mary Esther Pickett, June 10, 1938. In oil bus., Carrington, 1932-38, Williston, N.D., 1938-45; mgr. Williston C. of C., 1945-51; pub. rels. officer 1st Nat. Bank, Williston, 1951-53, mng. officer real estate mortgage dept., 1953-60; exec. officer Northwestern Fed. Savs. and Loan Assn. Williston, 1964-68; spl. cons. Am. State Bank Williston, 1968-73; mem. N.D. Senate, 1957-60, 67—, pres. pro tem, 1973-74; lt. gov. State of N.D., 1963-64; dir., sec. Williston Cmty. Hotel Co., 1950—; chmn. subscriber's com. N.W. dist. N.D. Blue Cross-Blue Shield, 1972—. Mem. Williston Public Housing Authority, 1951—, Williams County Park Bd., 1951—, N.D. Yellowstone-Ft. Union Commn., 1957-64, Legis. Rsch. Coun., 1957-60, Legis. Coun., 1969-70; del. N.D. 2d Constl. Conv., 1970, pres., 1971-72; Williams County chmn. U.S. Savs. Bonds Com., 1958-69; creator Frank A. Wenstrom Libr. for Student Rsch., Grank Forks, N.D., 1984; co-chair N.D. Constitution subcom. for developing and displaying hist. papers pertaining to U.S. constitution; mem. Constitutional Celebration com., 1985; pres. N.D. 2d Constitutional Conv., 1971-72; co-chair archives search com. N.D. Const. Conv., 1971-72; bd. dirs. N.D. Easter Seals Soc., 1960-75, state pres., 1970-71; bd. advisors Salvation Army, 1960-75; bd. dirs. Univ. Found., U. N.D., Williston Center, 1965—; mem. joint legis. com. Nat. Assn. Ret. Tchrs.-Am. Assn. Ret. Persons, 1975—, chmn., 1979-80. Recipient Liberty Bell award N.D. Bar Assn., 1977, Disting. Svc. award Bismarck Jr. Coll., 1981; award Nature Conservancy, 1982; Svc. award Greater N.D. Assn., 1983, C.P. Lura award Disting. Service to Edn. Minot State Coll., 1986, Award of Excellence Com. of Gov.'s Council on Human Resources, 1986. Mem. Upper Missouri Purebred Cattle Breeders Assn. (sec.-treas. 1947-62), N.D. Wildlife Fedn. (state pres. 1947-48), Greater N.D. Assn. (dir. 1955-56, mem. Roosevelt Nat. Meml. Park com. 1957-63), U.S. Savs. and Loan League (legis. com. 1965-67). Republican. Congregationalist. Clubs: Rotary, Elks, Masons (hon. grand master), Shriners, Order Eastern Star. Died May 12, 1997.

WENTZ, THEODORE EMORY, heavy equipment manufacturing company executive; b. Pitts., Aug. 10, 1931; s. Welker Wallace and Kathryn Ebberts) W.; B.A. cum laude, Amhest Coll., 1953; B.S. magna cum laude, U. Buffalo, 1958, M.B.A., 1960; m. Eleanor Frances Donald, July 23, 1955; 1 child, Donald Richard. Asso. cons. Touche Ross & Co., San Francisco, 1960-65; div. controller Varian Assos., Palo Alto, Calif., 1965-69; dir. fin. Symbolic Control, Inc., San Mateo, Calif., 1969-70; controller Clementina Ltd., San Francisco, 1971-73; dir. fin. Probe Systems, Inc., Sunnyvale, Calif., 1973-76; v.p. fin. Viking Industries, Inc., Chatsworth, Calif., 1976-78; chief fin. officer Calavar Corp., Santa Fe Springs, Calif., 1979-80; v.p. fin. Web Press Corp., Seattle. Served with USNR, 1953-55. C.P.A., Calif. Mem. Calif. Soc. C.P.A.s, Calif. C.P.A. Found. Edn. and Research. Died May 15, 1995. Home: Redmond Wash.

WERNER, SIDNEY CHARLES, physician, educator; b. N.Y.C., June 29, 1909; s. Max A. and Sadie (Hoffberg) W.; m. Shirley Benczer, Aug. 18, 1947; children: Pamela Anne Werner Bortoletto, Mady Jo Werner Jaquin, Russell Seth, Morgan Simon. AB, Columbia U., 1929, MD, 1932, DSc in Medicine, 1937. Intern medicine Presbyn. Hosp., N.Y.C., 1932-34, mem. staff, 1934-94, asst. resident medicine, 1936-38, attending physician, 1964-74, chief thyroid, 1947-77, chief combined endocrine clinics, 1947-74, cons. in medicine, 1974-86; cons. emeritus in medicine, 1986-94; mem. faculty Columbia Coll. Phys. & Surg., 1932-94, prof. clin. medicine, 1964-74, prof. emeritus, 1974-94; vis. prof. medicine U. Ariz. Med. Ctr., 1978-85; Smelo lectr. U. Ala., Birmingham, 1980; cons. NIH, 1955-63; endocrinology Roosevelt Hosp., N.Y.C., 1954-77, Greenwich (Conn.) Hosp., 1953-77, Grasslands Hosp., Valhalla, N.Y., 1946-77. Editor: The Thyroid, 4th edit., 1955-78, 5th edit., 1986, 6th edit., 1992, contbr. 6th, 7th edits., Thyrotropin, 1963; contbr. 190 articles to profl. jours., chpts. to books. Jacobaeus lectr. Nordinsulin Found., Sweden, 1968; recipient Thornton Wilson award Eastern Psychiat. Assn., 1960, Stevens Triennial award Columbia Coll. Phys. & Surg., 1966, disting. thyroid scientist VII Internat. Thyroid Conf., 1975; gold medal Alumni Assn. Columbia Coll. Phys. and Surg., 1976; Sidney C. Werner Lectureship (ann.) established at Columbia Coll. Phys. and Surg., 1977. Fellow AMA, AAAS, N.Y. Acad. Medicine; mem. Assn. Am. Physicians (emeritus), Am. Soc. Clin. Investigation, Endocrine Soc. (council 1961-65), Am. Thyroid Assn. (1st v.p. 1967, bd. dirs. 1967-74, pres. 1972-73, Disting. Service award 1969), Soc. Exptl. Biology and Medicine, Harvey Soc., N.Y. Thyroid Club (founder), Phi Beta Kappa, Alpha Omega Alpha; hon. mem. Endocrine Soc. Haiti, Argentine Med. Assn. Soc. Endocrinology and Nutrition, Colombian Soc. Endocrinology, Med. Soc. Finland. Home: Tucson Ariz. Died Apr. 21, 1994.

WESLAGER, CLINTON ALFRED, historian, writer; b. Pitts., Apr. 30, 1909; s. Fred H. and Alice (Lowe) W.; m. Ruth G. Hurst, June 9, 1934; children: Ruth Ann (Mrs. George G. Tatnall), Clinton Alfred, Thomas Hurst. BA, U. Pitts., 1933; LHD, Widener U., 1986; LittD (hon.), Wesley Coll., 1993. Vis. prof. Am. history Wesley Coll., 1969, U. Del., 1971-73; vis. prof. Am. history Brandywine Coll., 1970-82, prof. emeritus, 1983-94. Author: Delaware's Forgotten Folk, 1943, Delaware's Buried Past, 1944, Delaware's Forgotten River, 1947, The Nanticoke Indians, 1948, Brandywine Springs, 1949, Indian Place-Names in Delaware, 1950, Red Men on the Brandywine, 1953, Richardsons of Delaware, 1957, Dutch Explorers, Traders and Settlers, 1961, Garrett Snuff Fortune, 1965, English on the Delaware, 1967, Log Cabin in America, 1969, The Delaware Indians, A History, 1972, Magic Medicines of the Indians, 1973, The Stamp Act Congress, 1976, The Delaware Indian Westward Migration, 1978, The Delawares, A Critical Bibliography, 1978, The Nanticoke Indians, Past and Present, 1983, Swedes and Dutch at New Castle, 1987, New Sweden on the Delaware, 1988, A Man and His Ship: Peter Minuit and the Kalmar Nyckel, 1990; editor: Historic Red Clay Valley, Inc, 1961-69. Pres. trustees Richardson Park Sch., 1953-57. Recipient Merit award Am. Assn. State and Local History, 1965, 68, Christian Lindback award for teaching excellence, 1977, Trustee award Hist. Soc. Del., 1987, Medal of Distinction, U. Del., 1988, History medal DAR, 1990, del Tufo award Del. Humanities Forum, 1991. Fellow Archaeol. Soc. N.J., Holland Soc. N.Y.; mem. AAUP, Hist. Soc. Pa., Soc. Pa. Archaeology, Am. Name Soc., Archaeol. Soc. Del. (Archibald Crozier award 1987, pres. 1942-48), Ea. States Archaeol. Fedn. (pres. 1954-58), Dupont Country Club, Masons, Sigma Delta Chi. Died Aug. 5, 1994.

WESSEL, ROBERT HOOVER, economist, educator; b. Cin., Apr. 22, 1921; s. Herman Henry and Bessie (Hoover) W.; m. Helen Ann Mueller, July 26, 1952. Student, Harvard, 1940, 42; A.B., U. Cin., 1942, M.A., 1946, Ph.D., 1953. With drug products div. Proctor & Gamble Co., 1943-45; mem. faculty U. Cin., 1945-56, 57-96, prof. econs., 1960-77, David Sinton prof. econs., chmn. dept., 1962-68, vice provost for grad. studies, 1967-73, prof. polit. economy and adminstrn., 1973-91; prof. emeritus, 1991-96; assoc. prof. Northeastern U., 1956-57; vis. prof. Boston U., 1960; cons. to industry and govt., 1955-96. Author: Statistics Applied to Economics, rev. edit, 1973, Principles of Financial Analysis, 1961; also articles. Trustee Ohio Council for Econ. Edn.; bd. dirs. Ctr. for Research Libraries, 1973-80, chmn., 1976-77. Mem. Am. Econ. Assn., Ohio Assn. Economists and Polit. Scientists (pres. 1969-70), Missouri Valley Econ. Assn. (asst. editor), Midwest Econ. Assn., Nat. Assn. Bus. Economists, Phi Beta Kappa, Beta Gamma Sigma, Omicron Delta Kappa. Died Mar. 18, 1996.

WESTBROOK, JOEL WHITSITT, III, lawyer; b. San Angelo, Tex., June 19, 1916; s. Lawrence Whittington and Minnie Frances (Millspaugh) W.; m. Elaine Frances Summers, Feb. 13, 1943; 1 son, Jay Lawrence. Student, U. Va., 1934-35; B.A., U. Tex., 1937, J.D., 1940. Bar: Tex. 1940. 1st asst. U.S. Atty., San Antonio, 1946-51; 1st asst. dist. atty. Bexar County, San Antonio, 1951-52; dist. atty. pro tem, 1956; pvt.practice San Antonio, 1952-54; partner Trueheart, McMillan, Russell & Westbrook, San Antonio, 1954-61; ptnr. Jones, Boyd, Westbrook & Lovelace, Waco, Tex., 1962-68, Sheehy, Cureton, Westbrook, Lovelace & Nielsen, Waco, 1968-74, Trueheart, McMillan, Westbrook & Hoffman, San Antonio, 1974-80, Westbrook & Goldston, 1980-81, Westbrook Schroeder & Piker, San Antonio, 1981-84; pvt. practice San Antonio, 1984—; adj. prof. criminal law, legal ethics and evidence St. Mary's Sch. Law, San Antonio, 1957-61, 74-76; adj. prof. med. malpractice U. Tex. Law Sch., Austin, 1985, 86. Author: (with others) Texas Torts and Remedies, 1987; contbr. articles to legal and mil. jours. Chmn. San Antonio Crime Prevention Com., 1954-56; pres. Action Planning Coun., Waco, 1966-68; chmn. Waco-McLennan County Mental Health-Mental Retardation Bd. Trustees, 1967-70; pres. adv. bd. Providence Hosp., Waco, 1969-70, Model City com., Waco, 1969-72, chmn., 1971-72. Served to maj., inf. AUS, 1940-46, ETO, MTO. Decorated Combat Inf. badge, Silver Star, Bronze Star, Purple Heart. Fellow Tex. Bar Found. (life sustaining, charter); mem. Waco-McLennan County Bar Assn. (bd. dirs. 1963-66), San Antonio Bar Assn. (pres. 1957-58), State Bar of Tex. (bd. dirs. 1965-68, chmn. com. for local bar svcs. 1968-76, chmn. com. for legal svcs. to elderly 1976-79, mem. com. for ct. costs and delay 1980-81, mem. coll. bd. 1981-83, vice chmn. membership rels. 1981-83, mem. history and traditions of bar 1983—, chmn. spl. projects), Tex. Assn. Def. Counsel (v.p. 1970-71), U. Tex. Law Sch. Alumni Assn. (dir. 1969-72), Mil. Order World Wars (comdr. San Antonio chpt. 1952-53), Delta Theta Phi, Sigma Alpha Epsilon. Episcopalian. Clubs: Giraud (San Antonio); Army-Navy (Washington). Episcopalian. Deceased.

WESTERFIELD, LOUIS, law educator; b. Dekalb, Miss., July 31, 1949; s. Louis Sr. and Helen (Clayborne) W.; m. Gelounder, June 19, 1971; children: Anthony, Anika, Anson. BA, So. La. U., 1971; JD, Loyola U., 1974; LLM, Columbia U., 1980; LHD (hon.), So. U. New Orleans, 1992; LLD (hon.), Dillard U., 1995. Bar: La. Instr. Am. govt. So. U., New Orleans, 1973-75; asst. dist. atty. City of New Orleans, 1974-75; staff atty. sch. law, dir. law ctr. La. Legis. Coun., Baton Rouge, 1977; prof. law Loyola U. Sch. Law, New Orleans, 1978-83, U. Miss. Sch. Law, Oxford, 1983-86; prof. law, dean N.C. Ctrl. U. Sch. Law, Durham, 1986-90, Loyola U. Sch. Law, 1990-94; prof. law, dean sch. law, dir. law ctr. U. Miss. Sch. LAw, 1994—; vis. prof. Loyola U. Sch. Law, 1977-78, U. Miss. Sch. Law, 1989, disting. vis. prof., 1980; mem. expedited arbitration panel United Steel Workers and Continental and Am. Can Cos., 1975-83; mem. bd. arbitrators New Orleans Longshoremen Union and New Orleans Steamship Assn., 1982-85; judge pro tem La. Ct. Appeals (2d cir.), 1994; barrister Am. Inns of Ct., 1994—. Author: Westerfield, Louisiana Evidence, 1986, Westerfield and Harges, Louisiana Evidence, 1992; contbr. articles to law reviews. Bd. trustees Lawyers Com. Civil Rights Under Law, Washington, 1992—; mem. La. task force racial and ethnic fariness in cts., La. Supreme Ct., 1993—; mem. La. Ctr. Law-Related Edn., New Orleans; chmn. Miss. adv. com. U.S. Commn. Civil Rights, 1985-86; mem. evidence com. La. State Law Inst., 1991—; mem. vis. bd. Loyola U. Sch. Law, 1989-90; bd. dirs. New Orleans Legal Assistancr Corp., 1981-82, La. Civil Liberties Union, 1982-83; mem. adv. com. Criminal Procedure of La. Law Inst.; govs. task force New Goals La., 1977; govs. constitutional study commn. Staet of Miss., 1986; mem. adv. bd. Loyola U. Upward Bound, New Orleans, 1992—; chair L.B. Landry High sch. task force com. New Orleans Pub. Sch. Bd., 1992; bd. dirs. Bur. Govtl. Rsch., New Orleans, 1991—, Urban LEague of Greater New Orleans, 1991—, Children's Bus., New Orleans, 1991-93, bd. advisors, 1993—; mem. World Trade Ctr. New Orleans, 1992—; bd. dirs. So. U., New Orleans Found., 1987—, Big Bros. Greater New Orleans, 1982, Druades St. YMCA, 1981-83; vice chmn. bd. dirs. Loyola Inst. Human Rels., 1980-83. Recipient Ella Roy award Outstanding Cmty. Svc. Tenant Coun. of Fisher Housing Project New Orleans, 1982, Alexander P. Tureaud Black Citizenship medal, 1994, Disting. African Am. Alumnus of Yr. award Black Student Union Loyola U. Law Sch., New Orleans, 1995; named Outstanding Jaycee, Baton Rouge, 1977. Mem. ABA (chair rapportuer conf. law deans, pres. and provosts 1992, Law Student award 1994), Assn. Am. Law Schs. (libr. com. 1992—), Am. Soc. Writers in Legal Subjects (bd. dirs. of scribes 1991—), La. Bar Assn., La. Bar Found. (bd. dirs. 1991—), La. Orgn. Judicial Excellence, New Orleans Bar Assn. (long range planning com. 1991-92), Greater New Orleans Found. (devel. com. 1992—), Rotary, Phi Beta Sigma, Sigma Pi Phi. DIED 08/24/96.
.

WESTFALL, RICHARD SAMUEL, historian; b. Fort Collins, Colo., Apr. 22, 1924; s. Alfred Rensselaer and Dorothy (Towne) W.; m. Gloria Marilyn Dunn, Aug. 23, 1952; children: Alfred, Jennifer, Kristin. B.A., Yale U., 1948; M.A., 1949, Ph.D., 1955; postgrad., London

U., 1951-52. Instr. history Calif. Inst. Tech., Pasadena, 1952-53; instr., asst. prof. history State U. Iowa, Iowa City, 1953-57; asst. prof. history Grinnell Coll., 1957-60, assoc. prof., 1960-63; prof. history of sci. Ind. U., Bloomington, 1963-89; prof. history Ind. U., 1965-89, disting. prof. of history and philosophy of sci., 1976-89, chmn. dept., 1967-73; prof. emeritus Ind. U., Bloomington, 1989-96. Author: Science and Religion in Seventennth Century England, 1958, Force in Newton's Physics, 1971, Construction of Modern Science, 1971, Never at Rest: A Biography of Isaac Newton, 1980, Essays on the Trial of Galileo, 1990, Life of Isaac Newton, 1993; editor: (with V. E. Thoren) Steps in the Scientific Tradition, 1969, (with I. B. Cohen) Newton, 1995. Mem. United Ministry Bd., Bloomington, 1964-73; elder First Presbyterian Ch., Bloomington. Served with USNR, 1944-46. Fellow Am. Acad. Arts and Scis., Royal Soc. Lit.; mem. AAUP, Am. Hist. Assn. (Leo Gershoy award 1981), History of Sci. Soc. (2d v.p. 1973-74, v.p. 1975-76, pres. 1977-78, Pfizer award 1972, 83, Sarton medal 1985), Societe internationale d'histoire des sciences. Home: Bloomington Ind. Died Aug. 21, 1996.

WESTPHAL, ARNOLD CARL, religious publishing company executive, minister; b. Michigan City, Ind., June 23, 1897; s. Henry H. and Friederika (Laborn) W.; m. Esther Helen Dysard, Sept. 21, 1918 (dec. Dec. 1954); children: Rex, Juanita, Arlo; m. Addie Dysard, May 10, 1957 (dec. 1980); stepchildren: John, Wilbert, Marjory, Phyllis, Warren. Grad., Valparaiso U., 1922, Moody Bible Inst., Chgo., 1924, No. Bapt. Sem., Chgo., 1926, Harvard Mil. Chaplain's Sch., 1944. Lic. to ministry Bapt. Ch., 1918, ordained, 1922. Pastor 1st Bapt. Ch., Royal Ctr., Ind., 1922-23, Epiphany Bapt. Ch., Chgo., 1923-26, Eastside Bapt. Ch., Evansville, Ind., 1926-28; sr. pastor 1st Bapt. Ch., Salem, Ohio, 1928-37, Greensburg, Ind., 1937-40, Michigan City, 1940-44, Valparaiso, Ind., 1955-61; pres. Visual Evangels Pubs., Michigan City, 1922—. Author 29 visual aid books. With U.S. Army, 1918, capt. chaplain, 1944-46, ETO. Died Dec. 30, 1991.

WETZEL, CARROLL ROBBINS, lawyer; b. Trenton, N.J., Apr. 5, 1906; s. William and V. Caroline (Wieand) W.; m. Phoebe Meade Francine, June 21, 1935; children: Anne F., Phoebe Wetzel Griswold, Carroll Robbins. A.B., Wesleyan U., Middletown, Conn., 1927; LL.B., U. Pa., 1930, Gowen fellow, 1931. Bar: Pa. 1931, N.J. 1931, U.S. Suprene Ct. 1962. Since practiced Phila.; partner firm Dechert, Price & Rhoads, 1934-73, of counsel, 1973-96; mem. adv. com. to Comptroller of Currency, 1962. Bd. dirs. Libr. Co. Phila., 1952-83, pres., 1975-83; trustee Phila. Gen. Hosp., 1958-67; bd. dirs. Bok Tower Gardens, 1962-88, bd. dirs. emeritus, 1989-96; bd. dirs. Phila. Maritime Mus., 1976-86, U. Pa. Law Sch., 1978-83. With USAAF, 1942-45, ETO. Mem. ABA (chmn. sect. bus. law 1966-67, editor Bus. Lawyer 1964-65), Pa. Hort. Soc. (bd. dirs. 1954-70, pres. 1967-70), Phila. Club. Democrat. Episcopalian. Home: Ambler Pa. Died Nov. 27, 1996.

WHEAT, JOSIAH, lawyer; b. Tyler County, Tex., Dec. 21, 1928; s. James E. and Ruby R. Wheat; m. Glendale Richter, July 12, 1952; children—Julia Roberts, Elizabeth Seale, Josiah, Jennifer Wheat Pariseau. B.A., U. Tex., 1951, J.D., 1952. Bar: Tex. 1952, U.S. Dist. Ct. (ea. dist.) Tex. 1955, U.S. Supreme Ct. 1961, U.S. Ct. Appeals (5th cir.) 1969. Ptnr. Wheat & Wheat, Woodville, Tex., 1952-67; ptnr. Wheat & Stafford, Woodville, Tex., 1967-83, of counsel, 1983-86; counsel Wheat, Stafford & Allison, 1986—; legal counsel Tex. Water Quality Bd., 1971-73, Sam Houston Elec. Coop., 1988—; gen. counsel Lower Neches Valley Authority, 1974—; city atty. City of Woodville, 1959—; county judge Tyler County, 1987-89; ptnr. Wheat Abstract/Woodville Abstract and Title Combined Cos., Woodville, F, W&S and The Timber Co., Woodville; dir. August C. Richter, Inc., Laredo, Tex.; dir. Citizens State Bank, Woodville; trustee Goolsbee Mineral Trust, Wheat Mineral Trust. Contbr. articles to legal jours. Mem. Nat. Water Commn. U.S., 1969-73; life mem. bd. visitors, past mem. adv. council astronomy dept. and McDonald Obs., U. Tex., 1978-83; mem. exec. com. U. Tex. Centennial Commn.; mem. adminstrv. bd. Woodville United Methodist Ch.; mem. exec. com. Trinity Neches council Boy Scouts Am.; bd. dirs. Tyler County Indsl. Corp., Tyler County Devel. Corp., Scottish Rite dormitory U. Tex., 1990—; pres. Tyler County Dogwood Festival Assn., Inc.; vice-chmn. Tex. med. disclosure panel Tex. Dept. Health; sec. Gov.'s Water Task Force, chmn. subcom. on water fin., 1980-83; bd. mgrs. Tyler County Hosp., 1987—. Served with U.S. Army, 1953-54. Recipient Silver Beaver award Boy Scouts Am., 1976. Mem. ABA (state bar del. 1972-78, state del. 1978-83, bd. govs. 1983-86, ho. of dels. 1972-88, spl. and standing coms. on environ. law 1969-76, 82-83, bd. edns. gen. practice sect., commn. on interest on lawyers trusts accounts 1986-90), State Bar Tex. (pres. 1969-70, acting exec. dir. 1972-73, chmn. sect. environ. law 1973-74, Disting. Service award 1973), Tyler County Bar Assn. (pres. 1989-90), Jefferson County Bar Assn., Nat. Water Resources Assn. (resolutions com. 1988—), East Tex. C. of C. (bd. dirs. 1960-63), Beaumont C. of C. (waterways com.), Gulf Intercoastal Canal Assn. (bd. dirs.), Tex. Water Conservation Assn. (bd. dirs., pres. 1968-70, chmn. bd. dirs. 1970-72), Deep East Tex. Council Govts. (pres. 1970-72), Deep East Tex. Devel. Assn. (water resources com.), Tex. Ex-Students Assn. (life). Lodges: Masons (York and Scottish Rites, 32 deg., Red Cross of Constantine). Home: 304 Westmont Dr Laredo TX 78041-2744 DIED 11/19/97. .

WHEELER, HAROLD ALDEN, retired radio engineer; b. St. Paul, May 10, 1903; s. William Archie Wheeler and Harriet Maria Alden; m. Ruth Gregory, Aug. 25, 1926 (dec. Feb. 1986); children: Dorothy, Caroline, Alden Gregory. BS in Physics, George Washington U., 1925, DSc (hon.), 1972; DEngring. (hon.), Stevens Inst. Tech., 1978, Polytechnic U., 1992. Engr. Hazeltine Service Corp., N.Y.C. and Bayside, N.Y., 1929-39; v.p., chief cons. engr. Hazeltine Service Corp., Little Neck, N.Y., 1940-45; cons. radio physicist Great Neck, N.Y., 1946-59; pres. Wheeler Labs Inc., Great Neck, 1947-68; dir. Hazeltine Corp., Little Neck, 1959-70, v.p., 1959-65, chmn., 1965-70; dir. Hazeltine Corp., Greenlawn, N.Y., 1971-83, chmn., 1971-77, chmn. emeritus, 1977-87, chief scientist, 1971-87; cons. Office of Sec. of Def., Washington, 1950-53; mem. Def. Sci. Bd., Washington, 1961-64. About 180 patents in field, including diode automatic volume control, 1932; author: Wheeler Monographs, Vol. 1, 1953, Hazeltine the Professor, 1978, Early Days of Wheeler and Hazeltine Corporation, 1982, Hazeltine Corporation in World War II, 1993; numerous papers in, procs. and transactions of IRE and IEEE. Recipient Modern Pioneer award Nat. Assn. Mfrs., 1940. Fellow IEEE (medal of honor 1964), IRE (Morris Liebmann prize 1940), Radio Club Am. (Armstrong medal 1964); mem. Nat. Acad. Engring., Inst. Elec. Engrs. (U.K.), Sigma Xi, Tau Beta Pi, Gamma Alpha. Republican. Unitarian. Died Apr. 25, 1996.

WHEELER, LEONARD, lawyer; b. Worcester, Mass., July 20, 1901; s. Leonard and Elizabeth (Cheever) W.; m. Cornelia Balch, Oct. 5, 1929; children: Cornelia Wheeler Lanou, Leonard, Penelope Wheeler Pi-Sunyer, John B. A.B. magna cum laude, Harvard U., 1922, LL.B., 1925. Bar: Mass. 1926. Practiced in Boston; assoc. Goodwin, Procter & Hoar, 1925-72, ptnr., 1932-72, of counsel, 1972-95; dir., clk. Harold Cabot & Co., Inc., 1930-80; past corporator Cambridge Savs. Bank. Grad. treas. Harvard Law Rev., 1956-71; bd. dirs., past treas., pres. Cambridge Family and Children's Service; past treas., dir. Cambridge council Boy Scouts Am., Internat. Student Assn. Greater Boston; past pres., bd. overseers Shady Hill Sch., Cambridge; past bd. dirs. Boston Legal Aid Soc.; past bd. dirs., past v.p. Cambridge Community Services; past bd. dirs., past pres. Chocorua (N.H.) Lake Assn.; past trustee Tamworth (N.H.) Found., Social Law Library, Boston. Served to col. AUS, 1942-46; mem. pros. staff first Nuremberg War Crimes Trial 1945-46. Mem. ABA, Mass. Bar Assn., Cambridge Bar Assn. (past pres.), Am. Law Inst., Phi Beta Kappa. Republican. Unitarian-Universalist (past mem. standing com. 1st parish, Cambridge). Clubs: Union, Union Boat (past pres.), St. Botolph (Boston); Cambridge (past pres.), Cambridge Boat (past sec.). Home: Cambridge Mass. Died Apr. 4, 1995.

WHITE, DAVID MANNING, author, educator; b. Milw., June 28, 1917; s. Max A. and Mary (Kazan) W.; m. Catherine Wallerstein, Apr. 20, 1944; children: Steven, Richard, Max. A.B., Cornell Coll., Mt. Vernon, Iowa, 1938, L.H.D., 1964; M.S., Columbia U., 1939; Ph.D., U. Iowa, 1942. Teaching fellow English U. Iowa, 1940-42; instr. English Coll. William and Mary, 1945-46; mem. faculty Bradley U., 1946-49, assoc. prof. journalism, chmn. dept., 1947-49; research prof. journalism Boston U., 1949-75, chmn. div. journalism, 1964-72; prof. mass communication Va. Commonwealth U., Richmond, 1975-82, prof. emeritus, 1982-86; pres. Internat. Council Religions, Inc., 1982-85, Marlborough House Pub. Co., Richmond, 1982-93; vis. prof. Centro Internat. de Estudios Superiores de Periodismo Am. Latina, Quito, Ecuador, Oct. 1970, 71; news commentator Sta. WBZ-TV, Boston, 1949-50; project dir. Center Internat. Studies, Mass. Inst. Tech., 1951, Newspaper Comics Council 3 year study, 1959-93; research dir. N.Y. Office Internat. Press Inst., 1952-53; research adviser Sarpay Beikman Inst., Rangoon, Burma, 1957-58; corr. NBC News, Rangoon, 1957-58; supr. Gallup Poll in, Boston area, 1952-56; spl. elections editor AP, Boston, 1954-62; mem. UNESCO relations com. State Dept., 1954-56; cons. dept. mass communications UNESCO, Paris, 1954-62; lectr. Burma Sch. Journalism, 1957-58, Centre Internationale d'Enseignement Superieur de Journalisme, U. Strasbourg, France, 1957, 60, 61, 62, Inst. fur Publizistik, Free U., Berlin, 1962, 66; gen. editor Beacon Press contemporary communication series, 1966-93; chmn. Gov.'s Com. on Communication, 1965-70. Co-author: Elementary Statistics for Journalists, 1954, Mass Culture: The Popular Arts in America, 1957, (with Al Capp) From Dogpatch to Slobbovia, 1964; author: Journalism in the Mass Media, 1970; (with Richard Averson) The Celluloid Weapon: Social Comment in the American Film, 1972; author: The Search for God, 1983, the Affirmation of God, 1985; co-editor: Introduction to Mass Communications Research, 1958, (with Richard Averson) Publishing for the New Reading Audience, 1959; editor: Identity and Anxiety: Survival of the Individual in Mass Society, 1960, The Funnies, An American Idiom, 1963, People, Society and Mass Communications, 1964, Sight, Sound and Society, 1968, Pop Culture in America, 1970, Electronic Drama: Television Plays of the 1960's, 1971, Mass Culture Revisited, 1971, Popular Culture; Mirror of American Life, 1977; TV Quar., 1969-71; commentator, Nat. Pub. Radio Network, 1976-78. Served to ensign USNR, 1943-44. Decorated chevalier d'Honneur et de Mérite Ordre Souverain de Saint-Jean de Jerusalem; Order of Polonia Restituta; recipient Yankee Quill award, 1970; inducted into Va. Communications Hall of Fame, 1992. Mem. Ill. Acad. Sci., Boston Authors Club, Hist. Soc. Iowa, Assn. Edn. Journalism, Council Communications Research (chmn. 1954-57), New Eng. Acad. Journalists (hon.), Phi Beta Kappa, Eta Sigma Phi, Kappa Tau Alpha, Tau Kappa Alpha, Sigma Delta Chi. Democrat. Home: Richmond Va. Died Dec. 17, 1993.

WHITE, ETHYLE HERMAN (MRS. S. ROY WHITE), artist; b. San Antonio, Apr. 10, 1904; d. Ferdinand and Minnie (Simmang) Herman; ed. pvt. schs., instrs.; m. S. Roy White, Mar. 3, 1924 (dec.); children: Mrs. William Marion Mohrle, Patsyruth Wheeler. Exhibited numerous one-man, group shows, Tex.; represented pub. collections in U.S., pvt. collections in Switzerland, Germany, Sweden. Del. Internat. Com. Centro Studi E. Scambi Internationali. Mem. Anahuac Fine Arts Group, San Antonio, Beaumont, Galveston, Houston art leagues, Daus. Republic Tex., UDC, Pastel Soc. Tex., Watercolor Soc., Nat. League Am. Pen Women, Dallas Tex. Sumie Soc. of Am., Baytown (Tex.) Porcelain Guild. Episcopalian. Mem. Order Eastern Star. Clubs: Fine Arts (Anahuac); Artist and Craftsmen (Dallas). Author, illustrator: Arabella. Author: Poet's Hour. Died Sept. 30, 1996.

WHITE, JESSE MARC, actor; b. Buffalo, Jan. 3; s. Elias and Freda Weidenfeld; m. Cecelia Kahn, Jan. 18, 1942; children—Carole, Janet. Appeared in: 17 Broadway plays including Harvey, 1944; appeared in 64 movies; TV series Ann Sothern Show, 1956-62, Danny Thomas' Make Room for Daddy, 1952-58, Marlo Thomas Show, 1969-71; numerous dramatic and comedy TV shows, 1945—; TV spokesman, Maytag Co., 1967-89, Acura automobiles, 1990—. Mem. AFTRA, SAG, Actors Equity Assn. Club: Friars of Calif. Died Jan. 9, 1997.

WHITE, MERIT PENNIMAN, engineering educator; b. Whately, Mass., Oct. 25, 1908; s. Henry and Jessie (Penniman) W.; m. Jarmila Jaskova, 1965; children: Mary Jessie, Irene Helen, Elisabeth Cecelia, Ellen Patricia. A.B. cum laude, Dartmouth Coll., 1930, C.E., 1931; M.S., Calif. Inst. Tech., 1932, Ph.D. magna cum laude, 1935. With U.S. Dept. Agr., 1935-37; postdoctoral fellow Harvard U., 1937-38; research asso. Calif. Inst. Tech., 1938-39; asst. prof. Ill. Inst. Tech., 1939-42; cons. OSRD, 1942-45, War and Navy Depts., 1945-47; prof., head civil engring. dept. U. Mass., 1948-96, Commonwealth head of dept., 1961-77, Commonwealth prof., 1977-94, Commonwealth prof. emeritus, 1994-96. Contbr. articles to engring. jours. Recipient Pres.'s certificate of merit, 1948. Fellow ASME; mem. ASCE (hon.), Instn. Mech. Engrs. (chartered), Rèunion Internat. Laboratoires d'Essais et de Recherches sur les Matériaux (founding), Boston Soc. Civil Engrs. (hon.), Phi Beta Kappa, Sigma Xi, Tau Beta Pi. Died Dec. 1, 1996.

WHITE, PAUL DUNBAR, lawyer; b. LaGrange, Ky., Oct. 20, 1917; s. Isham Forrest and Florence (Harris) W.; m. Marion Loutenas Stallworth, Sept. 2, 1949; children: Paulette, Ronald. A.B., Ky. State Coll., 1940; LL.B., Western Res. U., 1950. Bar: Ohio 1950, U.S. Supreme Ct. 1972. Supr. Ind. State Boys Sch., 1940-41; group worker spl. projects Karamu, Cleve., 1941-43; visitor Cuyahoga County Agy., 1946-47; individual practice law Cleve., 1950-51; police prosecutor City of Cleve., 1951-59, 1st asst. prosecutor, 1960-63, dir. law, 1967-68; judge Cleve. Mcpl. Ct., 1964-67; assoc. Baker & Hostetler, Cleve., 1968-70; ptnr. Baker & Hostetler, 1970—; mem. State of Ohio Bd. Examiners, 1972-78. Trustee NCCJ, Cleve., 1972-86; trustee Ohio Law Opportunity Fund, 1975-87, Cleve. Urban League, 1975-78, Dyke Coll., Cleve., 1976-86; bd. commrs. Cleve. Met. Park, 1975-78. Served with U.S. Army, 1943-46. Mem. ABA, Ohio Bar Assn., Greater Cleve. Bar Assn. (trustee 1976-79, del. 8th Jud. Dist. Ohio conf. 1985—), Nat. Bar Assn., Soc. Benchers (Case Western Res. U.), Norman S. Minor Bar Assn.

WHITE, STEPHEN, writer, consultant; b. Boston, Nov. 22, 1915; m. Miriam Wheeler, Nov. 19, 1942 (dec. Sept. 8, 1980); children: Lawrence, Geoffrey. Student, Harvard U., 1933-34, 38-39. Reporter Boston Herald, 1942-43; mem. staff N.Y. Herald Tribune, 1943-50, roving European corr., 1948-50; European editor Look mag., 1950-51, asst. mng. editor, 1951-54; screen writer Twentieth-Century Fox, 1954-55; dir. film div. Edn. Services, Inc., Cambridge, Mass., 1956-60; dir. spl. projects Edn. Services, Inc., 1960-64; producer CBS News, N.Y.C., 1964-65; asst. to chmn. Carnegie Commn. Ednl. TV, 1965-67; dir. spl. projects Salk Inst., La Jolla, Calif., 1967-69; program officer Alfred P. Sloan Found., N.Y.C., 1969-70; v.p. Alfred P. Sloan Found., 1970-80, dir. spl. projects, 1980-83; cons. in field. Author: Goals for School Mathematics, 1963, Students, Scholars and Parents, 1964, Medical Education Reconsidered, 1965, Public Television, 1967, Should We Now Believe the Warren Report?, 1968, On the Cable, 1972, The Written Word, 1984. Home: Southbury Conn. Died Mar. 27, 1993.

WHITENER, JEAN VERONICA, psychotherapist; b. Bklyn.; d. Alexander and Zenobia A. (Mann) W. BA, Cen. State U., Wilberforce, Ohio, 1960; MSW, Howard U., 1966. Diplomate in Clin. Social Work. Clinic administr. Bklyn. Psychiat. Ctrs., 1970-77; cons. D.H.M.H., State of Md., Balt., 1978-79; psychotherapist D.C. Inst. Mental Hygiene, Washington, 1979-81, Community Mental Health Activity, Ft. Meade, Md., 1981-83; pvt. practice psychotherapy Columbia, Md., 1984-87; exec. dir., owner Columbia Inst. Psychotherapy, 1987-95; regional coord. Md. Soc. Clin. Social Work, Balt., 1995; v.p. Howard County Mental Health Assn., Columbia, 1989-91. Mem. NASW, Assn. Mental Health Adminstrs., Md. Register Clin. Social Workers, Am. Orthopsychiat. Assn., Acad. Cert. Social Workers, Howard County Mental Health Assn., Alpha Kappa Alpha. Democrat. Episcopalian. Died Aug. 27, 1995.

WHITNEY, MARVIN EDWARD, adult education educator; b. Spokane, Wash., Dec. 9, 1920; s. Edward Ruthland and Rena Belle (Dornberger) W.; m. Annie Louise Lacy, Nov. 16, 1943. BSBA, D.C. Tchrs. Coll., 1969. Page U.S. Ho. of Reps., Washington, 1940-41; watch and chronometer maker U.S. Naval Obs., Washington, 1941-50; tchr. D.C. Pub. Schs., Washington, 1950-63, prin., 1963-77; tchr. Fairfax County Pub. Schs. Adult Edn., Alexandria, Va., 1977-95; mem. vocat. sch. adv. bd. VA, Washington, 1948-55; cons. to watchmakers of Switzerland, N.Y.C., 1958-63; curriculum cons. Ont. (Can.) Watchmakers Assn., 1978-80. Co-author: Questions and Answers for Clock-Making Profession, 1981; author: History of the American Watchmakers Institute, 1985, The Ship's Chronometer, 1985, Military Timepieces, 1992. Chmn. Anacostia area Boy Scouts Am., Washington, 1963; block capt. Am. Heart Assn., Alexandria, 1987-92. With U.S. Army, 1945-46, ETO. Recipient Outstanding Svc. to Watchmaking Profession, Ont. Watchmaking Assn., 1981, Outstanding Tchr. award Fairfax County Pub. Schs. Adult Edn., 1992, Henry B. Fried Watch Excellence award Nat. Assn. Watch and Clock Collectors, 1992. Fellow Am. Watchmakers Inst. (pres. 1973-75, tech. editor 1977-95), Nat. Assn. Watch and Clock Collectors; mem. NEA, Am. Vocat. Assn., D.C. Vocat. Assn. (pres. 1959-61, Outstanding Vocat. Educator award 1982), Fed. Schoolmen's Club (pres. 1976-77), Horological Assn. Va. (treas. 1975-83, Watchmaker of Yr. award 1980), Nat. Assn. Secondary Sch. Prins. (sec. D.C. 1970-71). Avocations: gardening, collecting military watches and clocks, swimming, travel. Home: Alexandria Va. Died May 25, 1995.

WIDDER, WILLARD GRAVES, retired banker; b. Kansas City, Kans., June 21, 1924; s. George A. and Dorothy B. (Graves) W. B.S. in Mech. Engring, U. Kans., 1946, LL.B., 1949. Bar: Kans. 1949. Pvt. practice Kansas City, Kans., 1949-53; with First Nat. Bank Kansas City, Mo., 1953-84; trust officer First Nat. Bank Kansas City, 1961-66, v.p., 1966-71, sr. v.p., 1971-84. Sec., dir. 1st Nat. Found., Kansas City Estate Planning Coun.; sec. Edward F. Swinney Found. With USNR, 1943-46. Mem. Masons (master 1958-95), Phi Alpha Delta. Republican. Methodist. Died Oct. 7, 1995.

WIDERBERG, BO, film director, writer; b. Malmö, Sweden, June 8, 1930; s. Arvid Widerberg and Margaretha Gustafsson; m. Ann Mari Björklund, 1953 (div.); m. Vanja Nettelbladt, 1957 (div.). Director: (films) The Pram, 1962, Raven's End, 1963 (nom. academy award, 1964), Love 65, 1965, Elvira Madigan, 1967(Golden Palm Best Actress Cannes Internat. Film Festival: Pia Degermark), Adalen '31, 1969 (Best Fgn. Film U.S. Film Critics Guild, Cannes Internat. Film Festival Grand Prize, nom. academy award, 1970), The Ballad of Joe Hill, 1971 (Cannes Internat. Film Festival Jury Prize), Stubby, 1974, Man on the Roof, 1977, Victoria, 1979, Mannen Fran Mallorca, 1985, The Serpent's Way Up The Naked Rock, 1987, All Things Fair, 1995 (Silver Bear Berlin Internat. Film Festival, 1996, nom. academy award, 1996); author: Kyssas, 1952, Erotikon, 1957, Den gröna draken, 1959, Vision in svensk film, 1962.

WIEHL, JOHN JACK, foundry executive; b. Bklyn., May 4, 1920; s. Ferdinand and Theresa (Kogut) W.; m. Ruth Dorothy Anderson, May 11, 1946; children: John R., Edward, Robert, Fred. Grad. high sch., Elmhurst, N.Y. Cert. molder. Pres. Wiehl Bros. Brass Foundry, Bklyn., 1946-53, Hoboken (N.J.) Bronze Foundry, 1968-72, Franklin (N.H.) Non-Ferrous Foundry, 1981-96; owner Wiehl Dairy Farm, Milford, N.Y., 1954-67; foundry mgr. Perkins Marine, Miami, Fla., 1973-74, Watts Regulator, Lawrence, Mass., 1974-76, Samuel Eastman, Concord, N.H., 1976-78, Hayes Fluid Control, Gastonia, N.C., 1978-79, Jenkins Bros., Bridgeport, Conn., 1979-81. With USN, 1944-46, ETO, PTO. Mem. Am. Legion, Elks (brother). Avocation: music. Home: Franklin N.H. Died July 11, 1996.

WIGGERS, HAROLD CARL, physiologist; b. Ann Arbor, Mich., Sept. 1, 1910; s. Carl John and Minerva (Berry) W.; m. Virginia B. Balay, Nov. 21, 1935; children—Kathrine B., Janet H. B.A., Wesleyan U., Middletown, Conn., 1932; Ph.D., Western Res. U., 1936; Porter fellow, Harvard Med. Sch., 1936-37; Sc.D. (hon.), Union Coll., 1959, Union U., 1975. Instr. physiology Coll. Physicians and Surgeons, Columbia U., 1937-42; asst. prof. Western Res. U., 1942-43; asso. prof. Coll. Medicine, U. Ill., 1943-47; prof. Albany (N.Y.) Med. Coll., Union U., 1947—, chmn. dept. physiology, 1947-53, dean, 1953-74, exec. v.p., dean, 1966-74, pres. and dean emeritus, 1974-94; acting dean and sr. cons. Eastern Carolina U. Sch. Medicine, 1974-77; dir. Bankers Trust Co. Albany; cons. div. physician manpower HEW, 1967-71; cons. to chmn. VA Instl. Research Program, 1968-70; trustee Regional Hosp. Rev. and Planning Council Northeastern N.Y., Inc., 1962-74; mem. adv. council Ednl. TV; mem. adv. staff, senate and assembly coms. health, mental health and retardation N.Y. State Legislature, 1966-67; regents adv. com. Regionalism Northeastern N.Y., 1972-74; adv. council N.Y. State Health Planning Commn., 1968-70, chmn. com. organizational planning coordination, 1969-70; mem. ad hoc panel rev. specialized centers research applications in hypertension Nat. Heart and Lung Inst., 1971. Bd. dirs. Albany County Heart Assn., 1965-66, Albany Blue Cross, 1953-74; adj. trustee Rensselaer Poly. Inst., 1971-74; bd. visitors Capital Dist. Psychiat. Center, 1974—. Recipient Wesleyan U. Distinguished Alumnus award, 1972, Theobald Smith Lecture award Albany Med. Coll., 1980; named First Disting. Dean Albany Med. Coll., 1988. Mem. AAAS, Am. Heart Assn., Asso. Med. Schs. N.Y. and N.J. (trustee 1973-75), Am. Physiol. Soc., Central Soc. Clin. Research, Assn. Am. Med. Colls. (exec. com. council deans), Nat., N.Y. State socs. med. research, Albany Area C. of C. (dir. 1974—). Unitarian. Clubs: Albany (dir. 1968-74), Vero Beach Country. Home: Greenville N.C. Died Mar. 16, 1994.

WIGHT, JAMES ALFRED See HERRIOT, JAMES

WILBUR, DWIGHT LOCKE, physician; b. Harrow-on-the-Hill, Eng., Sept. 18, 1903; came to U.S., 1904; s. Ray Lyman and Marguerite May (Blake) W.; m. Ruth Esther Jordan, Oct. 20, 1928; children: Dwight L., Jordan R., Gregory F. AB, Stanford U., 1923; MD, U. Pa., 1926; MS in Medicine, U. Minn.-Mpls., 1933; DSc (hon.), Dartmouth Coll., 1973. Diplomate Am. Bd. Internal Medicine. Intern, U. Pa. Hosp., Phila., 1926-28; resident, Mayo Found., Rochester, Minn., 1929-31; staff Mayo Clinic, Rochester, 1931-37; clin. prof. medicine Stanford U., Calif., 1937-68; pvt. practice medicine, San Francisco, 1937-83; physician U.S. Naval Res., Oakland, Calif., 1942-46; clin. prof. medicine emeritus Stanford U. from 1968. Editor, Calif. Medicine, 1946-67. Author (with J.R. Gamble): Chemistry of Digestive Diseases, 1961, Current Concepts of Clinical Gastroenterology, 1965. Contbr. articles to profl. jours. Trustee Mayo Found., 1951-71, emeritus from 1971. Served to comdr., USNR, 1942-46. Recipient Julius Friedenwald medal, Am. Gastronenterol. Assn., 1961; Spl. Commendation for Outstanding Achievement, U. Minn., 1964; Outstanding Civilian Service medal, Dept. Army, 1966; First Disting. Internist award, Am. Soc. Internal Medicine, 1970. Mem. Calif. Med. Assn. (hon. past pres.), Inst. Medicine Nat. Acad. Scis. (charter), ACP (charter, Alfred Stengel Meml. award 1964, pres. 1958-59, fellow), AMA (pres. 1968-69), Am. Gastroenterologic Assn. (pres. 1954-55). Republican. Club: Commonwealth, Bohemian. Died March 9, 1997. Home: San Francisco Calif.

WILBUR, JAMES BENJAMIN, III, philosopher, educator; b. Hartford, Conn., Feb. 21, 1924; s. James Benjamin, Jr. and Martha (Shekosky) W.; m. Margie Mattmiller, July 9, 1949; children: James Benjamin IV, Ann Elizabeth. B.A., U. Ky., 1948; postgrad., Harvard, 1948-50; M.A., Columbia, 1951, Ph.D., 1954. Mem. faculty Adelphi U., Garden City, N.Y., 1952-64; chmn. philosophy dept. Adelphi U., 1954-64, asst. prof., 1954-59, assoc. prof., 1959-64; assoc. prof. U. Akron, Ohio, 1964-66; prof. U. Akron, 1966-68, chmn. philosophy dept., 1964-68; prof. philosophy SUNY Coll. Arts and Sci., Geneseo, 1968-90; chmn. philosophy dept. SUNY Coll. Arts and Sci., 1968-78; founder, co-dir. Confs. on Value Inquiry, 1967-90; vis. prof. U. Kent, Canterbury, Eng., spring 1971; faculty adviser Empire State Coll., 1972-74. Author: (with H.J. Allen) The Worlds of Hume and Kant, 1967, 2d rev. edit., 1981, The Worlds of Plato and Aristotle, 1962, 2d rev. edit., 1979, The Worlds of the Early Greek Philosophers, 1979, The Moral Foundations of Business Practice, 1992; editor, contbr.; (with B. Magnus) Cartesian Essays (M. Nijhoff), 1969, Spinoza's Metaphysics (Van Gorcum), 1976; co-editor: (with E. Laszlo) Human Values and Natural Science, 1970, Values and the Mind of Man, 1971, Value Theory in Philosophy and Social Science (Gordon and Breach), 1971, Value and the Arts, 1978, The Dynamics of Value Change, 1978; editor: Human Value and Economic Activity, 1979, The Life Sciences and Human Values, 1979, Human Values and the law, 1980, Values in the Law, 1980, Ethics and Management, 1983, Integration of Ethics into Business Education, 1984, Integrating Ethics into Business Education, 1983; contbn. Self-interest Dictionary of Business Ethics, 1995, others. Served with AUS, 1943-45. SUNY grantee, 1969, 70; NEH grantee, 1981; Western Electric Fund awardee, 1983. Mem. AAUP, Am. Metaphys. Soc., L.I. Philos. Soc. (founder 1963), Creighton Club (pres. 1970-72), Rochester Oratorio Soc., Am. Soc. Value Inquiry (sec.-treas. 1971, pres. 1973-74, founder Jour. Value Inquiry 1967, exec. editor 1967-90, assoc. editor 1990-96), Vt. Hist. Soc., Manchester Hist. Soc. (pres. 1991-94), Hudson (Ohio) Country Club (founding trustee, hon. life mem.), Ekwanok Country Club (Manchester), Harvard Club (N.Y.C.). Home: Manchester Vt. Died Sept. 29, 1996.

WILDEBUSH, JOSEPH FREDERICK, economist; b. Bklyn., July 18, 1910; s. Harry Frederick and Elizabeth (Stolzenberg) W.; AB, Columbia, 1931, postgrad Law Sch., 1932; LLB, Bklyn. Law Sch., 1934, JD, 1967; m. Martha Janssens, July 18, 1935; children: Diane Elaine (Mrs. Solon Finkelstein), Joan Marilyn (Mrs. Bobby Sanford Berry); m. Edith Sorensen, May 30, 1964. Admitted to N.Y. State bar, 1934, Fed. bar, 1935; practice law, N.Y.C., 1934-41; labor relations dir. Botany Mills, Passaic, N.J., 1945-48; exec. v.p. Silk and Rayon Printers and Dyers Assn. Am., Inc., Paterson, N.J., 1948-70; exec. v.p. Textile Printers and Dyers Labor Rels. Inst., Paterson, 1954-70; mem. panel labor arbitrators Fed. Mediation and Conciliation Svc., N.Y. State Mediation Bd., N.J. State Mediation Bd., N.J. Pub. Employment Relations Commn., Am. Arbitration Assn.; co-adj. faculty Rutgers U., 1948-90; lectr. Pres. Pascack Valley Hosp., Westwood, N.J., 1950-64, chmn. bd., 1964-67, chmn. emeritus, 1967-80; dir. Group Health Ins. N.Y., 1950-56. Served as maj. Engrs. Corps, U.S. Army, 1941-43. Mem. N.Y. County Lawyers Assn., Am. Acad. Polit. and Social Sci., Indsl. Rels. Rsch. Assn., Ret. Officers Assn., Nat. Geog. Soc. Lutheran. Contbr. articles profl. jours. Died Aug. 26, 1997.

WILENTZ, ROBERT NATHAN, retired state supreme court justice; b. Perth Amboy, N.J., Feb. 17, 1927; children: James Robert, Amy, Thomas Malino. Student, Princeton U., 1944-45; AB, Harvard U., 1949; LLB, Columbia U., 1952. Bar: N.J. 1952. Ptnr. Wilentz, Goldman & Spitzer, Perth Amboy, 1952-79; mem. N.J. legislature, 1966-69; chief justice N.J. Supreme Ct., 1979-96. With USN, 1945-46. Died July 5, 1996.

WILEY, WILLIAM RODNEY, microbiologist, administrator; b. Oxford, Miss., Sept. 5, 1931; s. William Russell and Edna Alberta (Threlkeld) W.; m. Myrtle Louise Smith, Nov. 10, 1952; 1 child: Johari. B.S., Tougaloo Coll., Miss., 1954; M.S., U. Ill., Urbana, 1960; Ph.D., Wash. State U., Pullman, 1965. Instr. electronics and radar repair Keesler AFB-U.S. Air Force, 1956-58; Rockefeller Found. fellow U. Ill., 1958-59; research assoc. Wash. State U., Pullman, 1960-65; research scientist dept. biology Battelle-Pacific N.W. Labs., 1965-69, mgr. cellular and molecular biology sect. dept. biology, 1969-72, inst. coordinator, life scis. program, assoc. mgr. dept. biology, 1972-74, mgr. dept. biology, 1974-79, dir. research, 1979-84; dir. Pacific Northwest Lab., Richland, Wash., 1984-94; sr. v.p. for sci. & tech. policy Battelle Meml. Inst., Richland, Wash., 1994—; adj. assoc. prof. microbiology Wash. State U., Pullman, 1968—; found. assoc. Pacific Sci. Ctr., Seattle, 1989—; bd. dirs. Sta. KCTS Channel 9, Seattle, 1990-94; trustee Oreg. Grad. Ctr., 1990-95; cons. and lectr. in field. Contbr. chpts. to books, articles to profl. jours. Co-author book in microbiology. Bd. dirs. Wash. Tech. Ctr., 1984-88, sci. adv. panel Wash. Tech. Ctr., 1984-88, Fed. Res. Bank of San Francisco (Seattle br.) 1991—; mem. adv. com. U. Wash. Sch. Medicine, 1976-79; trustee Gonzaga U., 1981-89, bd. regents, 1968-81; bd. dirs. MESA program U. Wash., Seattle, 1984-90, United Way of Benton & Franklin Counties, Wash., 1984—, Tri-City Indsl. Devel. Coun., 1984-94; mem. Wash. Coun. Tech. Advancement, 1984-85; bd. dirs. Forward Wash., The Voice for Statewide Econ. Vitality, 1984-95, N.W. Coll. and Univ. Assn. for Sci., 1985—; mem. Tri-City Univ. Ctr. Citizens Adv. Coun., 1985—; apptd. Wash. State Higher Edn. Coord. Bd., 1985-89, Wash. State U. Found., 1986—; mem. Wash. State U. bd. Regents, 1989—, bd. dirs. Washington Roundtable, 1989—, Goodwill Games, 1989-90; mem. adv. coun. Mont. State Sci. and Tech., 1990-91; mem. bd. overseers Whitman Coll., 1990—; mem. external adv. bd. Clark Atlanta U., 1991—; mem. Ctrl. Wash. U. Inst. for Sci. and Soc. Bd. of Advisors, 1991—, Engring. exec. com. So. U., Baton Rouge, La., 1992—; mem. Coun. Govt. Univ. Industry Rsch. Roundtable, 1993—; trustee Fred Hutchinson Cancer Rsch. Ctr., 1992—; engring. exec. com. Southern U., 1992—. With U.S. Army, 1954-56. Named Black Engr. of Yr., 1994. Mem. AAAS, Am. Soc. Biol. Chemists, Am. Soc. Microbiology, Soc. Exptl. Biology and Medicine, Sigma Xi (pres.-elect 1995).

WILKINSON, GEOFFREY, chemist, educator; b. Todmorden, Eng., July 14, 1921; s. Henry and Ruth (Crowther) W.; m. Lise Schou, July 17, 1951; children: Anne Marie, Pernille Jane. BSc, Imperial Coll., London, 1941, PhD, 1946; DSc (hon.), U. Edinburgh, U. Granada, 1977, Columbia U., 1979, U. Bath, 1980, Essex U., 1989. With NRC, Can., 1943-46; staff Radiation Lab. U. Calif., Berkeley, 1946-50; mem. faculty MIT, 1950-51; faculty chemistry dept. Harvard U., 1951-55; faculty Imperial Coll. Sci., Tech. and Medicine, U. London, 1955-88; prof. emeritus Imperial Coll. Sci. and Tech., U. London, 1988; Falk-Plaut vis. lectr. Columbia, 1961; Arthur D. Little vis. prof. MIT, 1967; Hawkins Meml. lectr. U. Chgo., 1968; 1st Mond lectr. Royal Soc. Chemistry, 1981; Chini lectr. Italian Chem. Soc., 1981; Tovborg Jensen lectr. U. Copenhagen, 1992. Author: (with F.A. Cotton) Advanced Inorganic Chemistry: A Comprehensive Text, 5th edit., 1988; Basic Inorganic Chemistry, 2d edit., 1987. John Simon Guggenheim fellow, 1954; recipient award inorganic chemistry Am. Chem. Soc., 1966, Centennial Fgn. fellow, 1976, Royal Soc. Chem. Transition medal chemistry, 1972; Lavoisier medal French Chem. Soc., 1968; Nobel prize in chemistry, 1973; Hiroshima U. medal, 1978; Royal medal, 1981; Galileo medal U. Pisa, 1983; Longstaff medal, 1987; Royal Soc. Chem. 1st Polyhedron prize, 1989; hon. fellow Inst. Tech. U. Manchester, Eng., 1989; Messel medal Soc. Chem. Industry, 1990. Fellow Royal Soc., Imperial Coll. Sci. and Tech. (hon.); fgn. mem. Royal Danish Acad. Sci., Am. Acad. Arts and Scis., Nat. Acad. Scis., Spanish Sci. Rsch. Coun. Home: London Eng. Died Sept. 26, 1996.

WILLCOX, FREDERICK PRESTON, engineer; b. L.A., Aug. 1, 1910; s. Frederick William and Kate Lillian (Preston) W.; m. Velma Rose Gander, 1935; 1 child, Ann Louise. Grad. high sch. Pvt. practice rsch. and devel. engr. and cons., 1939-51, govt. cons., 1949-50, 61-65; tech. v.p. Fairchild Camera & Instrument Corp., 1951-60; inventor R&D lab. New Canaan, Conn., 1960-96. Patentee in field of photog. sci. and data communications; photography work exhibited Smithsonian Gallery. Maj. U.S. Army, 1940-45. Recipient Sherman Fairchild Photogrammetric award Am. Soc. Photogrammetry, 1951. Fellow AAAS; mem. ASME, AIAA (sr. mem.), Am. Soc. Photogrammetry and Remote Sensing, Soc. Photographic Scientists and Engrs., Optical Soc. Am., Am. Def. Preparedness Assn. Avocations: machine sculpture, photography. Home: New Canaan Conn. Died Oct. 26, 1996.

WILLEMS, PAUL, playwright; b. Missembourg, Edegem, Belgium, Apr. 4, 1912; m. Elsa de Groodt, 1942; 2 children. LLD, Free Univ., Brussels, 1936. Atty. Antwerp, Belgium, 1937-40; dir. maritime fishing Ministry of Rationing, Brussels, 1941-46; sec. gen., then dir. gen. Palais des Beaux-Arts, Brussels, 1947-84; sec. gen. Fedn. Internat. des Jeunesses Musicales; founder with Baron de Voghel Europalia Festival, 1969. Writings include: (plays) Le Bon Vin de Monsieur Nuche, 1949, Lamentable Julie, 1949, Peau d'ours, 1951, Off et la lune, 1955, Il pleut dans ma maison, 1958, La Plage aux anguilles, 1959, Warna, 1962, Le Marché des petites heures, 1964, La Ville à voile, 1967, Le Soleil sur la mer, 1970, Les Miroirs d'Ostende, 1974, Nuit avec ombres en couleurs, 1983, Elle disait dormir pour mourir, 1983, La Vita breve, 1991, Dreams and Reflections: Plays of Paul Willems, 1992, The Drowned and La Vita breve, 1994, (theatre) Off et La Lune, La Place Aux Anguilles, Marceline, 1995; (radio play) Plus de danger pour Berto, 1966; (teleplay) L'Écho, 1963; (fiction) Tout est réel ici, 1941, Blessures, 1945, La Chronique du cygne, 1949, La Cathédrale de brume, 1983, Le Pays noyé, 1990; (other writings) L'Herbe qui tremble, 1942, Le Monde de Paul Willems, 1984, Un Arrière-pays, 1989, Le Vase de Delft, 1995. Served in Belgian Army, 1937-40. Decorated comdr. Order Brit. Empire, officier de Orde van Oranje-Nassau (Pays-bas), grand-officer l'Ordre de Léopold (Belgium), Das grosse Verdienstkreuz der Bundesrepublik Deutscheland (Germany); recipient Belgian State prize, 1963, 70, 80, Latin Theatre prize Spain, 1965, Marzotto prize, 1966. Mem. l'Acad. Royale (Belgium). Died Nov. 27, 1997.

WILLERMAN, LEE, psychologist, educator; b. Chgo., July 26, 1939; s. Israel and Anna Willerman; m. Benne Secter, Jan. 21, 1962; children: Raquel, Amiel. BA, Roosevelt U., Chgo., 1961, MA, 1964; PhD, Wayne State U., 1967. Research psychologist NIH, Bethesda, Md., 1967-70; NIH postdoctoral fellow dept. human genetics U. Mich. Med. Sch., Ann Arbor, 1970-71; asst. prof. psychology U. Tex., Austin, 1971-74, assoc. prof., 1974-81, prof., 1981—, Sarah M. and Charles E. Seay Regents prof. clin. psychology, 1985—; vis. Scheinfeld prof. Hebrew U. Jerusalem, 1983. Author: Psychology of Individual and Group Differences, 1979; co-author: Psychopathology, 1990. Fellow Am. Psychol. Assn., Internat. Soc. Twin Studies; mem. AAAS, Soc. Study Social Biology, Behavior Genetics Assn. Jewish. Died Jan. 10, 1997.

WILLIAMS, GEORGE RAINEY, surgeon, educator; b. Atlanta, Oct. 25, 1926; s. George Rainey and Hildred (Russell) W.; m. Martha Vose, June 16, 1950; children: Bruce, Alden, Margaret, Rainey. Student, U. Tex., 1944-46; B.S., Northwestern U., 1948; M.B., 1950, M.D., 1950. Intern Johns Hopkins Hosp., 1950-51, William Stewart Halsted fellow surgery, 1951-52, asst. resident surgery, 1952-53, asst. resident surgeon, 1955-57, resident surgeon, 1957-58; practice medicine specializing in gen. and thoracic surgery Oklahoma City, 1958-96; asst. prof. surgery U. Okla. Health Scis. Center, Oklahoma City, 1958-61; assoc. prof. U. Okla. Health Scis. Center, 1961-63; prof. surgery U. Okla. Health Scis. Center Coll. of Medicine, 1963-96, chmn. dept. surgery, 1974-96; interim dean U. Okla. Coll. Medicine, 1981-82, 85-86, 88-89; dir. Am. Bd. Surgery, 1975-81, vice chmn., 1979-81. Contbr. articles on gen. and thoracic surgery to profl. jours. Served lt., MC, 3d Inf. Div. AUS, 1953-55. Recipient Disting. Service citation U. Okla., 1982; named to Okla. Hall of Fame, 1986. Fellow ACS (sec. bd. govs. 1985-87, 1st v.p. 1989-90), Soc. Univ. Surgeons, Am. Assn. Thoracic Surgery, So. Surg. Assn., Am. Surg. Assn., Phi Beta Kappa, Delta Kappa Epsilon, Phi Beta Pi, Alpha Epsilon Delta, Alpha Omega Alpha, Pi Kappa Epsilon. Home: Oklahoma City Okla. Died Apr. 20, 1997.

WILLIAMS, GORDON ROLAND, librarian; b. Ontario, Oreg., July 26, 1914; s. Herbert Harrison and George Lola (Davis) W.; m. Jane Margaret Smith, Apr. 25, 1942; 1 dau., Megan Davis. AB, Stanford U., 1936; AM, U. Chgo., 1952. Vice pres. Brentano's Inc., Calif., 1945-49; chief asst. librarian UCLA, 1952-59; dir. Center for Research Libraries, Chgo., 1959-80; bd. dirs. Napa Valley Wine Libr., 1984-95; Mem. 1st Japan-U.S. Conf. on Libraries in Higher Edn., Tokyo, 1969, 2d Japan-U.S. Conf. on Libraries in Higher Edn., Wingspread, 1972, Internat. Conf. on Library Automation, Brasenose Coll., Oxford U., 1966; mem. archives and library com. Nat. Conservation Advisory Council, 1973—; Trustee, vice chmn. Bioscis. Info. of Biol. Abstracts, 1977-83; chmn. Conf. Cataloging and Info. Sers. for Machine-Readable Data Files, 1978; mem. Study Com. Libraries and Archives Nat. Conservation Advisory Council, 1973—; chmn. adv. com. McCune Rare Book Collection, 1989—. Author: Ravens and Crows, 1966, Bewick to Dovaston, Letters 1824-1828, 1968, Cost of Owning vs. Borrowing Serials, 1969; hon. editorial adv. Interlending Rev., Eng. Served with USNR, 1942-45. Decorated Commendation medal. Mem. ALA (chmn. com. nat. union catalogue 1960-85), Internat. Inst. Conservation Historic and Artistic Works, Assn. Research Libraries (com. on preservation of research library materials 1960-68, dir. 1964-67), Soc. Am. Archivists (chmn. com. on paper preservation 1970-77). Clubs: Caxton (Chgo., hon.); Rounce and Coffin, Zamorano (Los Angeles); Roxburghe (San Francisco).

WILLIAMS, JACK BYRON, anesthesiologist, retired; b. Atlanta, Feb. 19, 1924. MD, Med. Coll. S.C., 1953. Diplomate Am. Bd. Anesthesiology. Intern D.C. Gen. Hosp., Washington, 1953-54; resident anesthesiology U. Iowa Hosp., Iowa City, 1956-58; anesthesiologist E Talmadge Meml. Hosp., Augusta, Ga.; prof. Med. Coll. Ga., Augusta. Mem. AMA, Am. Coll. Angiology, Am. Soc. Anesthesiologists, Soc. Critical Care Medicine. Died Aug. 8, 1997.

WILLIAMS, LOUIS BOOTH, college president emeritus; b. Paris, Tex., Oct. 15, 1916; s. William Louis and Maggie Jo (Booth) W.; m. Mary Lou Newman, Oct. 15, 1938; children: Joanne Williams Click, Louis Booth, Jr. AA, Paris (Tex.) Jr. Coll., 1935; BBA, U. Tex., 1951; MBA, E. Tex. State U., 1961; LLD (hon.), Tex. Wesleyan U., 1976. Profl. local C. of C. exec., Austin, Navasota and Paris, Tex., 1938-44; mgr. Bireley's Beverages, Denison, Tex., 1946-49; asst. to pres. Paris Jr. Coll., 1949-52; pers. mgr. Paris Works, Babcock & Wilcox Co., 1952-67; pres. Paris Jr. Coll., 1968-83, pres. emeritus, 1983-94; dir. Liberty Nat. Bank, Paris, McCuistion Regional Med. Ctr., pres. bd. govs.; co-chmn. Am. 2000 Lamar County Coalition of Edn. Bus. and Industry, 1990-93; apptd. by Gov. of Tex. for State Tng. Coord. Coun., 1989-91; mem. U. Tex. Coll. Edn. Found. Adv. Bd. With USNR, 1944-46, lt. comdr. ret., 1976. Recipient Silver Beaver award Boy Scouts Am., 1956; named I Love Paris honoree Paris Edn. Found., 1993; Paul Harris fellow Rotary Internat., 1974. Mem. Am. Assn. Community Jr. Colls., Tex. Assn. Colls. and Univs. (pres. 1981), Assn. Tex. Jr. Colls. (pres. 1976), Rotary (dist. gov. 1985-86, meritorious svc. citation, 1991, Disting. Svc. award 1994), Theta Kappa Omega, Delta Sigma Pi, Phi Theta Kappa (hon.). Democrat. Methodist. Author: The Organization, Administration and Functions of a Local Chamber of Commerce, 1937. Died Oct. 24, 1994. Home: Paris Tex.

WILLIAMS, MURAT WILLIS, retired government official; b. Richmond, Va., June 11, 1914; s. Lewis Catlett and Maria Ward (Williams) W.; m. Eda Louise Burke, May 2, 1942 (dec. July 29, 1944); m. Joan Cunningham, Jan. 24, 1946; children: Kathleen, Brigid, Nicholas, Michael. Student, Woodberry Forest Sch., 1928-31; A.B., U. Va., 1935; B.A., Oxford U.; B.A. (Rhodes Scholar, 1936-39), 1938, M.A., 1943. Reporter Richmond News Leader, 1935-36, asst. to editor, 1940; asst. Dept. of State, 1946-47; pvt. sec. to U.S. ambassador to Spain, 1939-40, apptd. fgn. service officer, 1947; 1st sec. San Salvador, 1947-49; 1st sec. and sometime charge d'affaires Bucharest, 1949-51; asst. to dep. undersec. of state, 1951-53; student Nat. War Coll., 1953-54; consul gen. Salonika, 1954-55; fgn. service insp., 1955-56; dep. dir. Office of Greek, Turkish, Iranian Affairs, Dept. State, 1956-59; counselor of embassy Tel Aviv, Israel, 1959-61; ambassador to San Salvador, 1961-64; dep. dir. coordination Bur. Intelligence and Research, Washington, 1964-65; vis. scholar Mary Washington Coll. Contbr. to Va. Quar. Rev. Chmn. Va. State Com. for McCarthy for Pres., 1968; Dem. nominee for Ho. of Reps. from 7th Dist. Va., 1970, 72; pres. Va. Ctr. for Creative Arts, 1974-75; bd. dirs. Pub. Welfare Found., 1972-93; mem. Am. Com. on East-West Accord, Internat. Inst. Strategic Studies; advisor Washington Office on L.Am.; chmn. adv. bd. Sch. Internat. Svc., Am. U., 1977-79. Lt. comdr. USNR, 1940-45. Decorated Sec. of Navy's Commendation ribbon. Mem. U. Va. Soc. of Fellows, Phi Beta Kappa, Delta Psi. Episcopalian. Club: Metropolitan (Washington). Home: Charlottesville Va. Died Mar. 31, 1994.

WILLIAMS, ROBERT LEEDWARD, academic administrator, dean; b. Flora, Miss., Feb. 17, 1947; s. Albert and Paralee (Henry) W.; m. Virginia Williams, Dec. 10, 1966; children: Zealyne, Marchelle, Keisha. BA, Jackson (Miss.) State U., 1970; MBA, Atlanta U., 1981, EdD, 1985; postdoctoral, U. Ala., 1987-88, Harvard U., 1989, MIT, UCLA, 1990. Bus. mgr. Saints Coll., Lexington, Miss., 1974-76; purchasing mgr. Pineywoods (Miss.) Sch., 1976-77; asst. prof. bus. Jarvis Christian Coll., Hawkins, Tex., 1977-78; chief acct. Atlanta Ga., 1979-81; asst. prof. bus. Tuskegee (Ala.) U., 1981-88; dir. bus. adminstr. Fisk U., Nashville, 1988-91; now assoc. v.p. for acad. affairs, dean Sch. Bus. Alcorn State U., Lorman, Miss.; cons. Cons. and Developers of Bus. Enterprises, Atlanta, 1979—; assoc. v.p. acad. affairs, dean sch. bus. Alcorn State U., Lorman, Miss. Author: Organizational Management, 1986, Instructional Case Guide, 1986; editor The Rsch. Jour., 1988, Organizational Behavior and Institutional Effectiveness in Higher Edn.; contbr. articles to profl. jours. Pres. One-Way Boys' Mission, Jackson, Miss., 1976—. Nat. Dean scholar Ednl. Com. Inc., 1983-84. Mem. Researchers Assn. (pres. 1985—), Case Rsch. Assn., Nat. Bus. League, Acad. Mgmt., Alpha Kappa Psi, Delta Mu Delta, Alpha Phi Alpha. Avocation: singing. Deceased.

WILLIAMS, ROSS EDWARD, physicist; b. Carlinville, Ill., June 28, 1922; s. Cyrus Hillis and Mildred Denby (Ross) W.; m. Carolyn Chenoweth Williams, July 5, 1958 (div. June 12, 1986); children: Robert H. (dec.), Katherine J., Ross E. Jr.; m. Madeline D. Peters, Sept. 21, 1996. BS in Physics and Math., Bowdoin Coll., Brunswick, Maine, 1940-43; MS in Physics, Columbia U., 1947; PhD in Physics, 1955. Instr. in Physics Bowdoin Coll., Brunswick, Maine, 1942-43; project engr. Spl. Devices Ctr. ONR, Sands Point, L.I., 1946; sr. rsch. engr. Sperry Products, Inc., Danbury, Conn., 1947-49; cons., govt. and indsl. pvt. practice, 1953-60; sr. rsch. assoc. Hudson Labs Columbia U., Dobbs Ferry, N.Y., 1960-65; assoc. dir., 1965-68; prof. Engring. and Applied Sci. Columbia U., N.Y.C., 1968-74; pres., CEO Ocean and Atmospheric Scis., Inc., Dobbs Ferry, N.Y., 1974—; cons. Nat. Acad. Scis., Washington, 1967—, Naval Rsch. Lab., Washington, 1968-78; dir. Ocean and Atmospheric Sci. Inc., Dobbs Ferry, N.Y., 1968—, Optimum Applied Systems, Inc., Dobbs Ferry, N.Y., 1974—, Valleywood Realty, Inc., Yonkers, N.Y., 1991—, Esthetic Challenges, Inc., Exeter, N.H., 1993—. Lay leader, 1976-79, trustee, 1985-94, Asbury United Meth. Ch., Tuckahoe, N.Y., 1976-79. Lt. USNR, 1943-46. Fellow Acoustical Soc. Am., 1994. Mem. Am. Phys. Soc., Phi Beta Kappa, Sigma Xi. Avocations: hiking, ice skating. Died Nov. 8, 1997.

WILLIAMS, SYLVIA HILL, museum director; b. Lincoln University, Pa., Feb. 10, 1936; m. Charlton E. Williams. AB, Oberlin Coll., 1957; Cert. de Francais Parle, Ecole Pract. de l'Alliance Francaise, Paris, 1963; MA in Primitive Art, NYU Inst. of Fine Arts, 1975; LHD honoris causa, Amherst Coll., 1989. Program cons. Nat. Assembly for Social Policy and Devel., N.Y.C., 1963-68; account exec. Harry L. Oram, Inc., N.Y.C., 1968-71; Mellon research fellow The Bklyn. Mus., 1971-73, asst. curator, 1973-76, assoc. curator, 1976-78, curator, 1978-83; dir. Nat. Museum of African Art, Smithsonian Inst., Washington, 1983-96; lectr. African art New Sch. for Social Rsch., N.Y.C., 1979-80; adj. asst. prof. NYU, 1980; mem. vis. com. Allen Meml. Art Mus. Oberlin Coll. Author: Black South Africa: Contemporary Graphics, 1976, Mohammad Omer Khalil, Etchings/Amir I. M. Nour, Sculpture, 1994; contbg. author: African Art as Philosophy, 1974; contbr. articles to Apollo mag., African Arts, also others; curator, organizer major exhbns. Bklyn. Mus., Nat. Mus. African Art. Trustee Oberlin Coll., 1990-96; mem. pvt. sect. arts com. USIA, 1990-92. Nat. Mus. Act grantee (Paris, Tervuren, London), 1974. Mem. Assn. Art Mus. Dirs. (pres. 1994-95), Am. Assn. Museums. Home: Washington D.C. Died Feb. 28, 1996.

WILLIAMS, TONY, jazz drummer; b. Chgo., Dec. 12, 1945. Played with Sam Rivers, Boston, Jackie McLean, N.Y.C., 1962, mem. Miles Davis quintet, 1963-69, founder group Lifetime (with John McLaughlin and Larry Young), 1969, re-formed Lifetime (with Miles Davis), 1975; albums include: Nefertiti, Believe It, Emergency, Turn It Over, Ego, Million Dollar Legs, The Joy of Flying, Foreign Intrigue, Old Burn's Rush, Miles Smiles, Sorcerer, Nefertiti, Civilization, 1987, Angel Street, 1988, Native Heart, 1990; albums include (with Gil Evans) There Comes a Time, Spring, 1985, Tokyo Live, 1993. Died Feb. 23, 1997.

WILLIAMSON, SAM, lawyer; b. Detroit, Aug. 15, 1910; s. Solomon and Minnie (Nichamin) W.; m. Sophie Ann Kaplan, May 6, 1943; children: Peter D., Jane Williamson Kessler, Marianne Williamson. B.A., U. Ill., 1937, J.D., 1940. Bar: Ill. 1940, Tex. 1946. Since practiced in Houston. Maj. U.S. Army, 1942-46. Mem. ABA, Fed. Bar Assn. (pres. Houston chpt. 1956), Houston Bar Assn., Am. Immigration Lawyers Assn. (past chmn. Tex.), State Bar Tex., Am. Soc. Internat. Law, Nat. Lawyers Guild, Am.-Arab Anti-Discrimination Com. Home: Houston Tex. Died Oct. 31, 1995.

WILLIFORD, RICHARD ALLEN, oil executive, flight simulator company executive; b. Galveston, Tex., Dec. 24, 1934; s. Walter Hamilton and Marian Lela (Heartfield) W.; m. Mollie Marie Blansett, Feb. 16, 1957; children: Richard Allen Jr., Monica Marie Williford Powell. BS in Petroleum Engring., Tex. A&M U.,

1956, BS in Geol. Engring., 1956. Registered profl. engr., Tex. Petroleum/reservoir engr. Gulf Oil Co., La., Tex., 1956-61; mgr. prodn. Tenneco Oil Co., Lafayette, La., and Denver, 1961-73; exec. v.p. Samson Resources Co., Tulsa, 1973-79; owner, chmn. Williford Energy Co., 1979—; chmn., CEO Safety Tng. Systems, Inc., Tulsa, 1984—, Williford Bldg. Corp., Tulsa, 1990—; chmn. Engineered Equipment Systems, Tulsa, 1989—; past bd. dirs. Samson Resources Co., Tulsa, Tilco, Inc., Tulsa, Intersci. Capital Mgmt. Corp., Tulsa, W-R Leasing Co., Fourth Nat. Bank Tulsa, Sun Belt Bank & Trust Tulsa, Union Nat. Bank Tulsa. Patentee in field. Bd. dirs. OIPA, 12th Man Found., College Station, Tex., 1983-85, Tulsa Opera, Inc., 1985—, Thomas Gilcrease Mus. Assn., Tulsa, 1987-93, Tex. A&M Assn. Former Students, College Station, 1985-91, pres., 1989; bd. dirs. Inst. Nautical Archaeology, 1993—, chmn., 1996; trustee River Parks Authority, Tulsa, 1987-93, chmn. bd. trustees, 1993-94; trustee, chmn. Tex. A&M Devel. Found., 1991—, Verde Valley Sch., Sedona, Ariz., 1983-86; pres. exec. bd. Indian Nations coun. INA (pres. 1996)., Boy Scouts Am. Recipient Disting. Achievement medal Geoscis. and Resource Coun., Tex. A&M U., 1991, Humanitarian award Nat. Jewish Ctr. for Immunology, 1994. Mem. Ind. Petroleum Assn. Am., Soc. Petroleum Engrs., Okla. Ind. Producers Assn., Tex. Ind. Producers and Royalty Owners Assn., Masons, Shriners, Royal Order Jesters, So. Hills Country Club, The Golf Club Okla., Philcrest Tennis Club, The Summit Club, Tex. A&M Faculty Club, Tau Beta Pi. Republican. Methodist. Avocations: golf, hunting, fishing, flying, scuba diving.

WILLMAN, ALLAN ARTHUR, musician, composer, educator; b. Hinckly, Ill., May 11, 1909; m. Regina Hansen (dec.). MusB, Knox Coll., 1928; MusM, Chgo. Music Coll., 1930; studied with Nadia Boulanger, Thomas de Hartmann, Paris, 1935-36. Prof. emeritus dept. music U. Wyo. Dept. Music, 1974—. Pianist numerous appearances in U.S., Austria, Switzerland, France, U.K., Ireland, Germany; compositions include works performed by Boston Symphony Orch., other major orchs., chamber groups, artists; author: I Am a Composer. Recipient Paderewski award for Orchestral Work, 1935. Mem. Nat. Assn. Music Execs. in State Univs., Wyo. Music Tchrs. Assn. (founder, pres.), Pi Kappa Lambda. Avocation: collecting old music books. Deceased.

WILLS, HELEN, professional tennis player; b. Oct. 6, 1905. Author: 15-30: The Story of a Tennis Player, 1937. Winner 31 Grand Slam titles, 19 single titles including eight at Wimbledon, seven at the U.S. Open, four at the French Open; from 1927 to 1933 she won 180 consecutive singles matches. Died Jan. 1, 1998.

WILSON, ALICE HORNBUCKLE, retired physician; b. Pittsburg, Kans., Apr. 10, 1909; d. Alfred Rice and Ica Leola (Justice) Hornbuckle; widowed. RN, Wesley Meml. Sch. Nursing, 1929; student, U. Chgo., 1930-36; BA, Pittsburg (Kans.) State U., 1946; MD, U. Kans., 1949. RN N.W. Univ. Clinic, Chgo., 1930-36; supr. health clinic Pittsburg State Tech. Coll., 1944-46; intern U. Kans. Sch. Medicine, Kansas City, 1949-50; pvt. practice Joplin, Mo., 1950-87; dir. Ozark Mental Health, Joplin, 1962-68, Parkinson and other neurol. disorders, Joplin, 1969-94; retired emeritus med. staff St. Johns Regional Med. Ctr., 1950-94, Freeman Hosp. Med. Staff, 1950-94. Mem Boys Club, Joplin, 1950-94, Girls Club, Joplin, 1950-94; med. cons. vocat. rehab., Joplin, 1970-85. Named Woman of Yr., Bus. and Profl. Women, 1965, Woman of Yr. in medicine, 1975; recipient commendation Mo. Assn. for Mental Health, 1966, Quality in Medicine award Freeman Hosp., 1994; U. Kans. Med. Ctr. Alice Wilson award named in her honor. Mem. AMA, AAUW, Mo. Med. Assn., Jasper County Med. Assn., Am. Acad. Family Practice, Parkinson's and Other Neurol. Diseases Assn., Nat. Arbor Day Found., Order Ea. Star, Elks. Avocations: horse training and showing, music. Home: Neosho Mo. Died Nov. 8, 1994.

WILSON, EDWARD GEORGE, lawyer; b. Richmond, Ind., Mar. 23, 1909; s. Harvey T. and Ruth (Wiggins) W.; m. Jane Hunt Johnson, Nov. 19, 1932; 1 child, Edward Folger. A.B., Earlham Coll., 1930, LL.D. (hon.), 1976; J.D., N.Y. U., 1934. Bar: N.Y. bar 1935. With J. Walter Thompson Co., N.Y.C., 1930-36, 38-71; assoc. Donovan, Leisure, Newton & Lumbard, 1936-38; gen. counsel J. Walter Thompson Co., 1946-61, treas., 1959-62, v.p., 1954-62, exec. v.p., 1962-71, sec., 1965-71, dir., 1957-72. Hon. life trustee Earlham Coll., former chmn.; bd. dirs., sec. Assn. Governing Bds. Univs. and Colls., 1973-81, hon. dir., 1981-84, trustee; trustee AFTRA Pension and Welfare Funds, 1954-62, Common Fund, 1973-77; bd. dirs. Sharon Land Trust. Served as lt. USNR, 1943-45. Decorated Legion of Merit; recipient Disting. Service award Assn. Governing Bds. Univ. and Colls., 1987. Mem. Mil. Order Fgn. Wars, Assn. Bar City N.Y., ABA. Episcopalian. Clubs: Pilgrims (N.Y.C.), University (N.Y.C.); Metropolitan (Washington). Home: Sharon Conn. Died July 24, 1993.

WILSON, MARJORIE PRICE, physician, medical commission executive. Student, Bryn Mawr Coll., 1942-45; M.D., U. Pitts., 1949. Intern U. Pitts. Med. Ctr. Hosps., 1949-50; resident Children's Hosp. U. Pitts.,

1950-51, Jackson Meml. Hosp., U. Miami Sch. Medicine, 1954-56; chief residency and internship div. edn. svc. Office of Rsch. and Edn., VA, Washington, 1956, chief profl. tng. div., 1956-60, asst. dir. edn. svc., 1960; chief tng. br. Nat. Inst. Arthritis and Metabolic Disease NIH, Bethesda, Md., 1960-63, asst. to assoc. dir. for tng. Office of Dir., 1963-64, assoc. dir. program devel. OPPD, 1967-69, asst. dir. program planning and evaluation, 1969-70; assoc. dir. extramural programs Nat. Libr. Medicine, 1964-67; dir. dept. instl. devel. Assn. Am. Med. Colls., Washington, 1970-81; sr. assoc. dean U. Md. Sch. Medicine, Balt., 1981-86, vice dean, 1986-88, acting dean, 1984; pres., CEO, Ednl. Commn. Fgn. Med. Grads., Phila., 1988-95, emeritus, 1995—; mem. Inst. Medicine Nat. Acad. Scis.,1974—; bd. visitors U. Pitts. Sch. Medicine, 1974—; mem. Nat. Bd. Med. Examiners, 1980-87, 89—; mem. adv. bd. Fogarty Internat. Ctr., 1991—. Contbr. articles to profl. jours. Mem. adv. bd. Robert Wood Johnson Health Policy Fellowships, 1975-87; trustee Analytic Services, Inc., Falls Church, Va., 1976—. Fellow Am. Coll. Physician Execs., AAAS; mem. Assn. Am. Med. Colls., Am. Fedn. Clin. Research, IEEE. Died 1997.

WIMBERLY, GEORGE JAMES, architect; b. Ellensburg, Wash., Jan. 16, 1915; s. George Welch and Eurma (Bezdechek) W.; m. Janet Harrietta Brebner, July 7, 1939 (div. Sept. 1969); 1 child, Heather Mary; m. Walton Jeffords, Dec. 12, 1969. B.Arch., U. Wash., 1937; student in. Mex., 1938. Draftsman, designer Seattle, Los Angeles, Phoenix, 1938-40; architect U.S. Civil Service, Pearl Harbor, 1940-45; practice architecture Honolulu, 1945—; partner Wimberly & Cook, 1945-59; pres., dir. Wimberly, Whisenand, Allison, Tong & Goo, Architects, Ltd., 1959-87; con.s Wimberly, Allison, Tong & Goo, Inc., 1987—; cons. for tourist facilities, Western Samoa, 1967-69, Ceylon, 1968, New Zealand, 1968, Australia, 1969, Singapore, 1970, 85, Taiwan, 1971, Malaysia, 1971, Fiji, 1972, India, 1972, Nepal, 1975; mem. Hawaii Bd. Registration Profl. Architects and Engrs., 1959-67; pres. Waikiki Assn., 1951-53. Prin. works include Keelikolani State Bldg., Honolulu, 1950, Canlis Restaurant, Seattle, 1951, Coco Palms Hotel, Kauai, Hawaii, 1952, First Nat. Bank, Waikiki, 1953, Canlis Restaurant, Honolulu, 1954, Honolulu Gas Co. Bldg., 1955, Hawaiian Trust Co. Bldg., Honolulu, 1956, Windward City Shopping Ctr., Kaneohe, Hawaii, 1957, First Nat. Bank, Kapiolani br., Honolulu, 1958, Fin. Factors home office bldg., Honolulu, 1958, Home Ins. Bldg., Honolulu, 1959, Princess Kaiulani Hotel Waikiki, 1960, Hotel Tahiti, 1960, 3019 Kalakaua Ave. Apt., 1961, Sheraton Maui Hotel, 1962, Civic Auditorium, American Samoa, 1963, Pago Pago Intercontinental Hotel, American Samoa, 1965, Bank of Hawaii Bldg., Waikiki, 1967, Visitor Ctr., Mt. Rainier Nat. Park, 1967, Kona-Hilton Hotel, 1968, Taharaa's Intercontinental Hotel, Tahiti, 1968, Fijian Hotel, Nadi, Fiji, 1968, Sheraton Kauai Hotel, Kauai, 1968, Mauna Kea Beach Hotel South Wing, Kamuela, Hawaii, 1968, New Surfrider Hotel, Waikiki, 1969, Royal Hawaiian Diamond Head Wing, Waikiki, 1969, Tokyu Djakarta Hotel, Indonesia, 1971, Sheraton Waikiki Hotel, Honolulu, 1971, Hawaiian Telephone Office Bldg., Honolulu, 1972, Ibusuki Kanko Hotel, Tokyo, 1972, Maui Land and Pineapple Co. Bldg., 1972, Mauna Kea Beach Hotel Addition, Kamuela, 1972, First Hawaiian Bank, Waianae, Oahu, 1972, Hayashida Onsen Hotel, Japan, 1973, Iwasaki Hotel, Japan, 1973, Wailea Golf Clubhouse, Maui, 1973, Hanalei Beach and Racquet Club, 1975, Hyatt Regency at Hemmeter Ctr., Waikiki, 1976, Aloha Towers Condominium, Waikiki, 1977, Sheraton Molokai Hotel, 1977, Tangjong Jara Beach Hotel, Malaysia, 1978, Shangri-La Hotel Addition, Singapore, 1978, Hyatt Maui Hotel, 1980, Hilton Tapa Tower, 1982, Bangkok Peninsula Hotel, 1983, Arcadia Condominiums, Singapore, 1984, Ritz-Carlton Hotel, Laguna Niguel, Calif., 1985, Four Seasons Hotel, Newport Beach, Calif., 1986. Bd. dirs. Honolulu Community Theatre, 1961-64, 80-84, Honolulu Theatre for Youth, 1960-63; mem. Hawaii Visitors Bur., 1952—, bd. dirs., 1973-77; mem. U.S. Dept. Commerce Hawaii/ Pacific Dist. Export Council, 1979-83. Recipient Institutions Mag. Design awards; Holiday Mag. Design award; White Cement award of excellence Portland Cement Assn., 1972; Aga Kahn award for architecture Tanjong Jara Beach Hotel and Rantau Abang Visitor Ctr., 1983; Platinum Circle award Restaurant and Hotel Design mag., 1989. Fellow AIA (pres. Hawaii 1953, hon. awards Hawaii chpt. 1955, 60 (3), 1962, 64, 66, 68 (2), 1972, 73-75, 79, 82, 84); mem. Pacific Area Travel Assn. (life mem., contbg. mem., alt. dir. 1972-77, chmn. Devel. Authority 1979-81, award of merit 1979), Honolulu C. of C., Waikiki Improvement Assn., Tau Sigma Delta (pres. 1936). Clubs: Sports Car Club Am, Les Chevaliers du Deuxième Hemisiècle, Le Grand Chevalier Intérimaire (sr. steward); Pacific (Waikiki), Outrigger Canoe (Waikiki). Died Dec. 30, 1995.

WINER, HAROLD, retired federal agency administrator, educator; b. S.I., N.Y., Mar. 31, 1910; s. Leonard and Lillian (Block) W.; m. Elizabeth G. Jensen, Apr. 21, 1934; children—Peter D., Susan A., Jane L. B.S., Cornell U., 1932, student summers, 1933-36; student, Sch. Advanced Internat. Studies, Johns Hopkins, 1958. Tchr. vocational agr. Richmondville, N.Y., 1933-39; tchr. vocational agr., farm mgr. Canaan, N.Y., 1939-41; chief edn. and tng. sect. VA, Albany, 1946-53; chief vocational adviser Govt. of Iran, U.S. Operations Mis-

sion, Tehran, 1953-55; dep. chief edn. adviser Govt. of Iran, U.S. Operations Mission, 1955-58; chief edn. adviser Govt. of Nepal, U.S. Operations Mission, Kathmandu, Nepal, 1959- 64; chief Instnl. Devel. div. Bur. Near East and So. Asia, AID, Dept. State, Washington, 1964-65; chief edn. adviser to Govt. South Vietnam, U.S. AID, Saigon, 1965-69; ret. Dept. State, 1970. Served from 2d lt. to maj., inf. AUS, 1941-46. Decorated Legion of Merit, Silver Star, Bronze Star, Philippine Liberation medal; conspicuous service medal State of N.Y.; Ministry Edn. medal of Culture and Edn.; Medal of Merit; Ministry of Vets. Affairs medal 1st class Vietnam; U.S. medal for Civilan Service in Vietnam. Mem. Am. Fgn. Service Assn., Diplomatic and Consular Officers Ret., Am.-Nepal Soc., 77th Div., Assn. Am. Legion, Ret. Officers Assn., Nat. Assn. Ret. Fed. Employees, U.S. Capitol Hist. Soc., Am. Jewish Hist. Soc., Cornell U. Alumni Assn. Jewish. Clubs: Officers, Cornell (Washington). Lodge: Masons (Albany). Home: 2096 Kedge Dr Vienna VA 22181-3210 DIED 07/02/97. .

WINGERT, ROBERT IRVIN, obstetrician, gynecologist; b. Canistota, S.D., Jan. 31, 1934; s. Mathias Jacob and Lyda Adelaide (Doeden) W.; m. Karen Frances Bollinger, July 16, 1960; children: Robert, Scott, Mark, Jon. BA, U. S.D., 1957; MD, Marquette U., 1959. Commd. capt. USAF, 1960, advanced through grades to col., 1974-81; prof. ob-gyn. U. S.D. Sch. Medicine, Vermillion, 1982-94, prof. emeritus, 1994-95; cons. ob-gyn Pub. Health Service/Indsl. Health Service Pine Ridge, Sioux San and Eagle Butte, S.D., 1982-95. Fellow ACOG; mem. S.D. Med. Soc., S.D. Perinatal Assn. (Man of Yr. 1991), Black Hills Med. Soc. Ret. Officers Assn. (pres. 1982-84), Air Force Assn., Elks. Roman Catholic. Avocations: skiing, hiking, waterskiing, motorcycle riding, camping. Home: Rapid City S.D. Died June 13, 1995.

WINOKUR, GEORGE, psychiatrist, educator; b. Phila., Feb. 10, 1925; s. Louis and Vera P. Winokur; m. Betty Stricklin, Sept. 15, 1951; children: Thomas, Kenneth, Patricia. A.B., Johns Hopkins U., 1944; M.D., U. Md., 1947. Intern Church Home and Hosp., Balt., 1947-48; asst. resident Seton Inst., Balt., 1948-50; assoc. in neuropsychiatry Washington U., St. Louis, 1950-51; resident in neuropsychiatry Barnes Hosp., St. Louis, 1950-51; asst. prof. psychiatry Washington U., St. Louis, 1955-59, assoc. prof., 1959-66, prof., 1966-71; assoc. psychiatrist Barnes Hosp., 1963-71; cons. in psychiatry Homer G. Phillips Hosp., 1954-64; instr. psychiatry Meharry Med. Coll., Nashville, 1954-55; prof. U. Iowa, Iowa City, 1971-96, head dept. psychiatry, 1971-90; dir. Iowa Psychiat. Hosp.; acad. guest U. Zurich, 1984; Louis H. Hohler Meml. lectr. St. Mary's Health Ctr., St. Louis, 1985. Author: Manic Depressive Illness, 1969, Depression: The Facts, 1981, Mania and Depression, A Classification of Syndrome and Disease, 1991, The Natural History of Mania, Depression and Schizophrenia, 1996; mng. editor European Archives of Psychiatry and Neurol. Scis.; chief Am. editor Jour. Affective Disorders, 1979-96; mem. editl. bd. 8 profl. jours.; contbr. numerous articles on clin. genetics of affective disorders, alcoholism and schizophrenia to profl. jours. Served to capt. M.C. USAF, 1952-54. Recipient Anna-Monika 1st prize award, 1973, Hofheimer prize, 1972, Samuel W. Hamilton award, 1977, Leonard Crammer Meml. award, 1980, Paul Hoch award, 1981, Vol. Svc. award Nat. Coun. Alcoholism, 1974, Achievement award Am. Acad. Clin. Psychiatrists, 1987, Nelson Urban Rsch. award Mental Health Assn., Iowa, 1988, Lifetime Rsch. award Nat. Depressive and Manic Depressive Assn., 1990, Lifetime Achievement award Internat. Soc. Psychiat. Genetics, 1993, Regents award U. Iowa, 1994, Paul Huston award Iowa Psychiat. Soc., 1994, Gold medal Soc. Biol. Psychiatry, 1984, Lapinlahti medal Helsinki Finland Lapinlahti Hosp. Fellow Am. Psychiat. Assn. (life), Royal Coll. Psychiatrists (hon.); mem. Am. Psychopath. Assn. (pres. 1975-77, Joseph Zubin award 1992), Am. Soc. Human Genetics, Assn. Am. Physicians (hon.), Internat. Group Study of Affective Disorders, Psychiat. Rsch. Soc., Am. Fedn. Clin. Rsch., Assn. Rsch. in Nervous and Mental Disorders, Am. Coll. Neuropsychopharmacology, Societat Catalana de Psiquiatra, Sigma Xi, Tudor and Stewart Club (Balt.). Home: Iowa City Iowa Died Oct. 12, 1996.

WINPISINGER, WILLIAM, labor union official; b. Cleve., Dec. 10, 1924; married; 5 children. Ed. pub. schs., Cleve. Automotive mechanic, 1942-51; with Internat. Assn. Machinists and Aerospace Workers, 1947—, grand lodge rep., 1951-58, air transp. dept., 1958-64, automotive coordinator, 1965-67, gen. v.p., 1967, now pres., also co-chmn. and union trustee pension fund; mem. exec. council AFL-CIO; mem. Fed. Com. on Apprenticeship. Co-chmn. Machinists Non-Partisan Polit. League; council N.Y. State Sch. Indsl. and Labor Relations, Cornell U. Served in USN, 1942-45. Mem. Nat. Planning Assn. (planning com.).

WINSTEN, ARCHER, retired newspaper and movie critic; b. Seattle, Sept. 18, 1904; s. Harry Jerome and Nell (Archer) W.; m. Sheila Raleigh, Feb. 6, 1931 (div.); children: Kezia, Stephen, Martha. Student, Augusta Mil. Acad., 1916-18, Univ. Sch., Cleve., 1918-22; A.B., Princeton U., 1926. Reporter Phila. Evening Pub. Ledger, 1928, New Yorker mag., 1930; columnist (In the Wake of the News) New York Post, 1933-35, motion picture critic, 1936-86, also ski editor, 1947-86; motion picture documentary script writer Princeton Film Center, 1944-48, for R.K.O. Pathe, 1946; lectr., asso. in journalism Columbia U., 1946, 47. Recipient 1st prize Harper's 1st Intercollegiate Short Story prize contest, 1926. Mem. Am. Newspaper guild. Home: Gansevoort N.Y. Died Feb. 21, 1997.

WINTER, MAX, retired professional football team executive; b. Ostrava, Austria, June 29, 1904; came to U.S., 1913, naturalized, 1920; s. Jacob and Bertha (Kuker) W.; m. Helen Horovitz, Dec. 5, 1939; children: Susan (Mrs. Robert Diamond), Nancy (Mrs. Dennis Ditlove), Diane (Mrs. Richard Cohen). Student, Hamline U., 1925-26, U. Chgo., 1927. Co-owner, gen. mgr. Mpls. Lakers Basketball Team, 1947-56; originator Minn. Vikings (Nat. Football League), Mpls., 1960; pres. Minn. Vikings (Nat. Football League), 1960—; pres. Max Winter Enterprises, Hawaii; v.p. Income Guarantee, Aloha C.A.T.V.; dir. Downtown Bank of St. Paul, Bank of Mpls., Viking Enterprise Mpls., Mpls. Bank and Trust Co., Gambles Continental Bank. Author: Sports Books for Children, 1957. Mem. County Park Bd., 1959-64; chmn. Muscular Dystrophy, 1961; mem. Gov.'s Bus. Adv. Com., 1965; chmn. Nat. Govs. Conf., 1965. Recipient Hon. Scout award, 1946, 47, 48. Mem. Mpls. C. of C. (pres. 1969). Jewish. Clubs: Rotary, Optimist, Mpls. Athletic, Oak Ridge Country; Waialae Country (Honolulu), Outrigger (Honolulu). DIED 07/26/96. .

WISSNER, JOHN KARL, lawyer; b. Evansville, Ind., Nov. 11, 1951; s. Gustave A. and Emma K. (Winiger) W.; m. Maridawn Dempsey, June 23, 1973; children: John Andrew, Matthew Karl, Ryan Patrick. BS in Acctg., Ind. U., 1973, JD, 1976. Assoc. Clark, Statham & McCray, Evansville, Ind., 1976-78; ptnr. Scales, Wissner & Krantz, Boonville, Ind., 1978—; counsel Warrick County, 1995—. Mem. Boonville Kiwanis, Ducks Unltd. (treas. Pigeon Creek chpt. 1992-95), Outboard Boating Club Evansville (commodore). Avocations: boating, hunting. Died Apr. 8, 1996.

WITHERSPOON, JIMMY, blues singer; b. Gurdon, Ark., 1923. Ind. blues singer, 1943—. Sang with Teddy Weatherford's band in Far East, 1943; mem. Jay McShannon Orch. until 1948; solo hits include Ain't Nobody's Business, Big Fine Girl, The Wind Is Blowing, No Rollin' Blues; solo albums include Ain't Nobody's Business, A Spoonful of Blues, The Spoon Concerts, Witherspoon at the Renaissance, Buck Clayton and Jinny Witherspoon Live in Paris, Evenin' Blues, Blue Spoon, Jimmy Witherspoon and Ben Webster, Spoonful, Love Is a Five Letter Word. Served with U.S. Mcht. Marines, 1941-43, PTO. Died Sept. 18, 1997.

WIXON, RUFUS, retired accounting educator; b. Cherokee County, Iowa, Nov. 27, 1911; s. Rufus and Stella Maude (Mathews) W.; m. Doris Elizabeth Hunter, Oct. 28, 1939; children: Marjorie Jeanne, Joanne Elizabeth, Kathryn Ann. B.S.C., U. Iowa, 1933, M.A., 1935; Ph.D., U. Mich., 1945. Staff accountant I.B. McGladrey & Co., Cedar Rapids, Iowa, 1933-34; instr. accounting U. N.D., 1935-36; staff accountant Edward Gore & Co., Chgo., 1936-37; instr. accounting Wayne U., 1937-41; lectr. econs. U. Mich., 1941-45, asst. prof. econs., 1945-47; prof. accounting, chmn. dept. U. Buffalo, 1947-49, U. Pa., 1949-65; prof. accounting Fla. Inst. chair accountancy U. Fla., Gainesville, 1965-66; prof. accounting U. Pa., Phila., 1966-80, emeritus prof., 1980-96; assoc. chief, specialist accounting U. Pa.-U. Karachi Project, Karachi, Pakistan, 1955-57; Cons. Office Asst. Sec. Def. (comptroller), 1958-60; prof. IMEDE, Mgmt. Devel. Inst., Lausanne, Switzerland, 1961-62; accounting editorial bd. Found. Press. Author: (with W.A. Paton, R.L. Dixon) Problems and Practise Sets for Essentials of Accounting, 1949, Budgetary Control, 1952, rev., 1961, Principles of Accounting, (with R.G. Cox), 1961, 2nd edit., 1969; Editor: Accountant's Handbook, 5th edit, 1970. Mem. Am. Acad. Polit. and Social Sci., Am. Accounting Assn. (chmn. com. standards accounting instrn., v.p. 1959), Am. Econ. Assn., Controllers Inst. Am., Order of Artus, Beta Gamma Sigma, Beta Alpha Psi. Phi Kappa Phi, Alpha Kappa Psi, Alpha Tau Omega. Club: Springhaven. Home: Philadelphia Pa. Died June 6, 1996.

WOIT, ERIK PETER, corporate executive, lawyer; b. Riga, Latvia, Mar. 10, 1931; s. Walter E. and Sigrid (Radzins) W.; m. Bonnie Jean Ford, June 16, 1953; children: Peter Gordon, Steven Ford. A.B., Allegheny Coll., 1953; J.D., Harvard U., 1956. Bar: N.Y. 1959, U.S. Supreme Ct., 1971. Asso. firm Mudge, Stern, Baldwin & Todd, N.Y.C., 1956-57, 60-62; asst. sec., internat. counsel Richardson-Merrell, Inc., 1962-71; sec., gen. counsel Amerace Corp., N.Y.C., 1971-73, v.p., group exec., 1973-74, pres. ESNA div., 1974-77, sr. v.p. adminstrn., chief adminstrv. and chief fin. officer, 1977-83; sr. v.p. Orient Express Hotels, Inc., N.Y.C., 1983—, also bd. dirs.; chmn. Sea Containers Am. Inc., 1984—; sr. v.p. Sea Containers Ltd., 1987—, participant Dept. Def. Joint Civilian Orientation Conf., 1994. Served to capt. USMCR, 1957-60. Recipient Maj. Gen. John H. Russell leadership award USMC Command and Staff Coll. Found., 1996. Mem. ABA, Assn. Bar City N.Y., Sigma Alpha Epsilon. Clubs: Harvard, Sky (N.Y.C.), 21 Club Inc. (N.Y.C.) (pres. 1995—). Died Aug. 9, 1997.

WOLANIN, SOPHIE MAE, civic worker, tutor, scholar, lecturer; b. Alton, Ill., June 11, 1915; d. Stephen and Mary (Fijalka) W. Student Pa. State Coll., 1943-44; cert. secretarial sci. U. S.C., 1946, BSBA cum laude, 1948; PhD (hon.), Colo. State Christian Coll., 1972. Clk., stenographer, sec. Mercer County (Pa.) Tax Collector's Office, Sharon, 1932-34; receptionist, social sec., nurse-technician to doctor, N.Y.C., 1934-37; coil winder, assembler Westinghouse Electric Corp., Sharon, 1937-39, duplicator operator, typist, stenographer, 1939-44, confidential sec., Pitts., 1949-54; exec. sec., charter mem. Westinghouse Credit Corp., Pitts., 1954-72, hdqrs. sr. sec., 1972-80, reporter WCC News, 1967-68, asst. editor, 1968-71, asso. editor, 1971-76; student office sec. to dean U. S.C. Sch. Commerce, 1944-46, instr. math., bus. adminstrn., secretarial sci., 1946-48. Publicity and pub. relations chmn., corr. sec. South Oakland Rehab. Council, 1967-69; U. S.C. official del. Univ. Pitts. 200th Anniversary Bicentennial Convocation, 1986; mem. nat. adv. bd. Am. Security Council; mem. Friends Winston Churchill Meml. and Library, Westminster Coll., Fulton, Mo.; active U. S.C. Ednl. Found. Fellow; charter mem. Rep. Presdl. Task Force, trustee; sustaining mem. Rep. Nat. Com.; permanent mem. Nat. Rep. Senatorial Com.; patron Inst. Community Service (life), U. S.C. Alumni Assn. (Pa. state fund chmn. 1967-68, pres. council 1972-76, ofcl. del. rep. inauguration Bethany Coll. pres. 1973); mem. Allegheny County Scholarship Assn. (life), Allegheny County League Women voters, AAUW (life), Internat. Fedn. U. Women, N.E. Historic Geneal. Soc. (life), Hypatian Lit. Soc. (hon.), Acad. Polit. Sci. (Columbia) (life), Bus. and Profl. Women's Club Pitts. (bd. dirs. 1963-80, editor Bull. 1963-65, treas. 1965-66, historian 1969-70, pub. relations 1971-76, Woman of Year 1972), Met. Opera Guild, Nat. Arbor Day Found., Kosciuszko Found. (assoc.), World Literary Acad., Missionary Assn. Mary Immaculate Nat. Shrine of Our Lady of Snows; charter mem. Nat. Mus. Women in Arts, Statue Liberty Ellis Island Found. Inc., Shenago Conservancy (life); supporting mem. Nat. Woman's Hall of Fame; Recipient numerous prizes Allegheny County Fair, 1951-56; citation Congl. Record, 1969; medal of Merit, Pres. Reagan, 1982; named WPIC Sweetheart-of-the-Day Mercer County's Info. and Entertainment Radio Sta. 790, 1991. Fellow Internat. Inst. Community Service (founder); mem. World Inst. Achievement (rep.), Liturgical Conf. N. Am. (life), Westinghouse Vet. Employees Assn., Nat. Soc. Lit. and Arts, Early Am. Soc., Am. Acad. Social and Polit. Sci., Societe Commemorative de Femmes Celebres, Nat. Trust Historic Preservation, Am. Counselors Soc. (life), Am. Mus. Natural History (asso.), Nat. Hist. Soc. (founding mem.), Anglo-Am. Hist. Soc. (charter), Nat. Assn. Exec. Secs., Internat. Platform Assn., Smithsonian Assos., Asso. Nat. Archives, Nat., Pa., Fed. bus. and profl. women's clubs, Mercer County Hist. Soc. (life), Am. Bible Soc., Polish Am. Numismatic Assn., Polonus Philatelic Soc., UN Assn. U.S., Polish Inst. Arts and Scis. Am. Inc. (assoc.), N.Y. Acad. Scis. (assoc.), Am. Council Polish Cultural Clubs Inc. Roman Catholic (mem. St. Paul Cathedral Altar Soc., patron organ recitals). Clubs: Jonathan Maxcy of U. S.C. (charter); Univ. Catholic of Pitts.; Key of Pa., Fedn. Bus. and Profl. Women (hon.); Coll. (hon.) (Sharon). Contbr. articles to newspapers.

WOLD, FINN, biochemist, educator; b. Stavanger, Norway, Feb. 3, 1928; came to U.S., 1950, naturalized, 1957; s. Sverre and Herdis (Rasmussen) W.; m. Bernadine Moe, June 13, 1953; children—Eric Robert, Marc Sverre. Student, U. Oslo, 1946-50; M.S., Okla. State U., 1953; Ph.D., U. Calif. at Berkeley, 1956. Research asso. U. Calif. at Berkeley, 1956-57; asst. prof. biochemistry U. Ill., Urbana, 1957-62; asso. prof. U. Ill., 1962-66; prof. biochemistry U. Minn. Med. Sch., Mpls., 1966-74; prof. biochemistry U. Minn., St. Paul, 1974-81, head dept., 1974-79; Robert A. Welch prof. chemistry U. Tex. Med. Sch., Houston, 1981—; vis. prof. Nat. Taiwan U., 1971, Rice U., 1974, Amademia Sinica, Taiwan, 1990, U. Tromso, Norway, 1991-94; cons. in field. Author, contbg. author books; mem. editl. bd. Jour. Biol. Chemistry, 1974-79, 81-86, Biochemistry, 1974-83, Protein Sci., 1995—; contbr. articles to profl. jours. Fulbright fellow, 1950; John Simon Guggenheim fellow, 1960-61; recipient Lalor Found. Research award, 1958, NIH research career devel. award, 1961-66. Mem. AAAS, Am. Soc. Biochemistry and Molecular Biology (councilor 1978-81, sec. 1992-95), Am. Chem. Soc. (councilor 1980-83, chmn. divsn. biol. chemistry 1985-86), Protein Soc. (pres. 1989-91), Biochem. Soc. (London). DIED 04/14/97. .

WOLF, CLARENCE, JR., stockbroker; b. Phila., May 11, 1908; s. Clarence and Nan (Hogan) W.; m. Alma C. Backhus, Sept. 11, 1942. Student, Pa. Mil. Prep. Sch., Chester, Pa., 1921; grad., Swarthmore (Pa.) Prep. Sch., 1923. Bar: Phila.-Balt. Stock Exch. 1937. Founder French-Wolf Paint Products Corp., Phila., 1926, pres., until 1943; assoc., v.p. investments Reynolds Securities, Inc. (now Dean Witter Reynolds Inc.), Miami Beach, Fla., 1944-86, spl. rep., 1946-86; v.p. investments E.F. Hutton, 1987-95; registered investment advisor Miami, 1986-95; pres. $even Letter$ Corp. Author: $even Letter$-An Investment Primer, 1980, $even Letter$ Inve$tment Guidebook, 1988. Pres. Normandy Isles Improvement Assn., Miami Beach, 1952-53; mem. Pres. Coun., Miami Beach, 1952-95. Mem. Alumnus Pa. Mil. Coll. (bd. dir. Fla. chpt. 1961-64), Jockey Club (Miami), Com. of 100 Club. Home: Miami Fla. Died Aug. 14, 1995.

WOLF, LEWIS ISIDORE, lawyer; b. Bklyn., June 8, 1933; s. Ephraim and Rachel (Dunajevsky) W.; m. Ruth Ullmann; children: Sara S., Joseph J. BA, Bklyn. Coll., 1954; JD cum laude, Bklyn. Law Sch., 1957; LLM, NYU, 1967. Bar: N.Y. 1958, U.S. Dist. Ct. (so. and ea. dists.) N.Y. 1961, U.S. Ct. Appeals (2d cir.) 1964, U.S. Supreme Ct. 1964. Pvt. practice law, N.Y.C., 1958—; atty. and mng. atty. Cosmopolitan Mut. Ins. Co., 1958-77, atty. of record, 1977-81; mem. Smith, Mazure, Director, Wilkins, Young, Yagerman & Tarallo, P.C., N.Y.C., 1981—; arbitrator N.Y. County Civil Ct. With N.Y. N.G., 1957-63. Mem. ABA, N.Y. State Bar Assn., N.Y. County Lawyers Assn., Am. Arbitration Assn. (arbitrator accident claims tribunal). Died May 11, 1996.

WOLFERMAN, ADOLPH, physician, otolaryngologist; b. Hamburg, Germany, Feb. 24, 1916; came to U.S., 1946; s. Markus and Bella (Jonas) W.; m. Pierrette Perrin, Oct. 21, 1944 (dec. July 1986); children: Marc, Sondra, Eric; m. Irene Thorner, June 8, 1991. MD, U. Geneva, 1941. Diplomate Am. Bd. Otolaryngology. Prof. N.Y. State U., Bklyn., 1965-97; chief ear nose-throat Bklyn. Ey and Ear Hosp., 1970-75, Brookdale (N.Y.) Hosp., 1975-81; cons. N.Y. Eye and Ear, N.Y.C., 197597; guest tchr. ear surgery Humboldt U., Berlin, 1972, Hosp. San Camillo, Rome, 1971, Hosp., Tunis, Tunisia, 1968. Author: Reconstructive Surgery of the Middle Ear, 1970; co-author: Atlas of Ear Surgery, 1974; author (motion picture) Ear Surgery, 1968. Fellow Am. Acad. of Otolarygology; mem. Soc. of Univ. Otolarygologists. Avocation: bridge (sr. master). Home: New York N.Y. Died May 22, 1997.

WOLFSON, SAMUEL, anesthesiologist; b. N.Y.C., July 3, 1911. MD, U. Sheffield, 1937. Intern Franklyn Sq. Hosp., Balt., 1937-39; resident Bellevue Hosp. Ctr., N.Y.C., 1940-42; anesthesiologist New Britain (Conn.) Gen. Hosp. Maj. U.S. Army Med. Corps, 1942-46. Mem. AMA, Am. Soc. Anesthesiology. DIED 07/24/97. .

WOLLMAN, LEO, physician; b. N.Y.C., Mar. 14, 1914; s. Joseph and Sara (Samrick) W.; m. Eleanor Rakow, Aug. 16, 1936 (dec. 1953); children: Arthur Lee, Bryant Lee; m. Charlotte Kornberg Seidman, Oct. 6, 1954 (div. 1969); m. Ellen Hershenson, Mar. 25, 1985. BS, Columbia U., 1934; MS, NYU, 1938; MD, Royal Coll. Edinburgh, 1942; PhD (hon.), Rochdale, 1972; DSc (hon.), U. Mich., 1973. Diplomate Am. Bd. Hypnosis in Ob-Gyn, Nat. Bd. Acupuncture Medicine, Am. Acad. Pain Mgmt., Am. Bd. Psychiatry and Neurology, Am. Bd. Sexology. Intern Cumberland Hosp., Bklyn., 1942-43; resident Leith Gen. Hosp., 1942; practice medicine specializing in ob-gyn Bklyn., 1944-72; in psychiatry, 1972-97; mem. staff Maimonides, Coney Island hosps., Bklyn. Hosp. Ctr., Bklyn., Park East, Mt. Sinai hosps., N.Y.C.; med. dir. acupuncture dept. Lexington Health Facility, N.Y.C. Author: Write Yourself Slim, 1976, Eating Your Way to a Better Sex Life, 1983, numerous articles in profl. jours.; editor-in-chief: Jour. Am. Soc. Psychosomatic Dentistry and Medicine, 1968-83; editor newsletter: Soc. Sci. Study Sex; editor: News Bull. of Inst. for Comprehensive Medicine; assoc. editor: Jour. Sex Research; internat. editor: Latin Am. Jour. Clin. Hypnosis; films I Am Not This Body, 1970, StrangeHer, 1971, Let Me Die a Woman, 1978. Pres. Jewish Com. Coun. Greater Coney Island, 1989-97. Recipient Jules Weinstein Ann. Pioneer in Modern Hypnosis award, 1964. Fellow Am. Geriatrics Soc., N.Y. Acad. Scis., Acad. Psychosomatic Medicine (sec. 1965), Soc. Clin. and Exptl. Hypnosis, Am. Soc. Clin. Hypnosis , Soc. Sci. Study Sex (pres. Eastern region 1979-81), Am. Soc. Psychical Research, Am. Med. Writers Assn.,Internat. Soc. Comprehensive Medicine, Am. Acad. Psychiatry and Neurology, Am. Coll. Sexology; mem. Nat. Geog. Soc.,AAAS (council 1971-73), Am. Assn. Social Psychiatry, Am. Soc. Abdominal Surgeons, Internat. Soc. Nonverbal Psychotherapy, N.Y. State Soc. Med. Research, Royal Medico-Psychol. Assn. (Eng.), N.Y. Soc. for Gen. Semantics, Nat. Assn. on Standard Med. Vocabulary (sec. 1964-97), Am. Assn. History Medicine, Am. Assn. Study Headache, Am. Acad. Dental Medicine, Am. Assn. Marriage Counselors, Soc. Med. Jurisprudence, Bklyn. Psychol. Assn., Canadian Soc. for Study Fertility, Am. Fertility Soc., Internat. Fertility Assn., Internat. Soc. for Clin. and Exptl. Hypnosis, Am. Soc. Psychosomatic Dentistry and Medicine (pres. 1969-72, exec. dir. 1973-83), Assn. Advancement Psychotherapy, Pan-Am. Med. Assn., Andalusian Soc. Sophrology and Psychosomatic Medicine, Brit. Med. Assn., Bklyn. Acad. Medicine, Internat. Soc. Psychoneuroendocrinology, L.I. Hist. Soc.; also hon. mem. numerous fgn. orgns. Home: Brooklyn N.Y. Died April 22, 1997.

WOLPER, MARSHALL, insurance and financial consultant; b. Chgo., Nov. 19, 1922; s. Harry B. and Bessie (Steiner) W.; m. Thelma R. Freedman, April 15, 1957 (div. Oct. 1968); m. Jacqueline N. Miller, Sept. 19, 1969 (div. Jan. 1976); m. Lucee I. G. Lee, Mar. 20, 1985; stepchildren—Robert Insinga, Cyndi Wolper. BA in

Polit. Sci. and Econs., U. Ill., 1942. Chartered fin. cons. With Kent Products, Chgo., 1946; pres. Marshall Industries, Chgo., 1947-52; with Equitable Life Assurance Soc., 1953-89, nat. honor agt., 1966, nat. sales cons., 1967—; sr. ptnr. Wolper & Katz, 1958—; ptnr. Wolper and Katz Thoroughbred Racing Stable, 1977-86; instr. life underwriting and pensions U. Miami, 1959—; pres. Marshall Wolper Co., 1953—; chmn. bd. M.W. Computer Systems, Inc., 1971-80; pres. Marshall Wolper Pension Sers. Inc., 1978-80, Wolper Ross & Co., 1980-87; lectr. life ins., employee benefit plans, pensions, estate planning to various univs. and spl. meetings; pres. Greater Miami Tax Inst., 1963, Estate Planning Coun. Greater Miami, 1969-70; faculty Practicing Law Inst., 1967—; mem. adv. com., lectr. Inst. on Estate Planning. Author: Medical Entities Taxed as Corporations, 1961, Tax and Business Aspects of Professional Corporations and Associations, 1968; contbr. articles to profl. jours. Bd. dirs. Dade County chpt. ARC, Profl. Selling Inst. Served to 1st lt. AUS, Parachute Infantry, World War II, ETO. Decorated Bronze Star, Purple Heart; recipient Paragon award Equitable Life Assurance Soc., 1972; C.L.U. Mem. Am. Soc. CLUs (pres. Miami chpt. 1963, inst. faculty 1963-65, dir. 1966-67, regional v.p. 1968), The Am. Coll. (joint com. on continuing edn. 1965—), Nat. Assn. Life Underwriters (lectr. 1963, 66, 81), Million Dollar Round Table (life mem., speaker 1962-81, exec. com. 1974-78, pres. 1977), Assn. Advanced Life Underwriting (lectr. 1966, pres. 1972), Am. Soc. Pension Actuaries (dir.), Nat. Assn. Pension Consultants and Adminstrs. (treas.). Home: Miami Fla. Died July 10, 1997.

WOOD, BEATRICE, potter, writer; b. San Francisco, Mar. 3, 1893; d. Benjamin and Carrara Wood. Student, Shipley's Sch., 1910, Finch Sch., 1911. Author: I Shock Myself, 1985, Pinching Spaniards, 1988, The Angel Who Wore Black Tights, 1982, The 33rd Wife of the Maharajah, 1990. Exhibited in group shows at L.A. County Mus. Art, 1947, Honolulu Acad. Art, 1951, Am. Gallery, L.A., 1955, Pasadena Art Mus., 1959, Takashimaya Dept. Store, Japan, 1962, Santa Barbara Mus. Art, 1964-65, Phoenix Art Mus., Tucson, Art Ctr., 1973, Del. Art Mus., Wilmington, 1975, Everson Mus. Art, Syracuse, N.Y., 1978, Phila. Mus. Art, 1978, Hadler Galleries, N.Y.C., 1978, EversonMus. Art, Syrafuse, 1979, Garth Clark Gallery, L.A., 1984, Philbrook Mus. Art, 1987, Oakland Mus., 1989, many others. Recipient Women's Internat. Ctr. Living Legacy award, 1989, Inst. for Ceramic History Ceramics Symposium award, 1983, others. Mem. Nat. Coun. on Edn. for The Ceramic Arts. Died March 1998.

WOOD, HARLESTON READ, retired manufacturing executive; b. Phila., Oct. 18, 1913; s. Alan and Elizabeth Fitz Simons (Read) W.; m. Emily Newbold Campbell, June 21, 1942; children—Harleston R., Alan IV, Ross G., Morrow, Anthony. Student, Haverford Sch., 1929-31; A.B., Princeton, 1936. Various positions Alan Wood Steel Co., 1938-52, asst. v.p., 1952-54, v.p., 1954, pres., 1955-72, chmn., 1962-79. Gen. chmn. Phila. United Fund Torch drive, 1972; bd. dirs. Ursinus Coll.; Del. Rep. Nat. Conv., 1972; mem. Council on Fgn. Relations, 1961-84. Episcopalian. Home: Stuart Fla. Died Apr. 21, 1995.

WOODHULL, NANCY JANE, foundation executive; b. Perth Amboy, N.J., Mar. 1, 1945; d. Harold and May (Post) Cromwell; m. William Douglass Watson, Sept. 24, 1976; 1 child, Tennessee Jane. Student, Trenton State Tchrs. Coll., 1963-64. Dept. editor News Tribune, Woodbridge, N.J., 1964-73; reporter Detroit Free Press, 1973-75; mng. editor Times-Union, Rochester, N.Y., 1975-80, Democrat & Chronicle, Rochester, 1980-82; mng. editor USA Today, Arlington, Va., 1982-83, sr. editor, 1983-87; pres. Gannett New Media, Washington, 1986-90, Gannett News Svc., Washington, 1988-90; exec. v.p., editor-in-chief So. Living Mags., Birmingham, Ala., 1990-92; pres. Nancy Woodhull & Assoc., Inc., Washington and Pittsford, N.Y., 1991-96; scholar-in-residence U. Rochester, N.Y., 1992-96; chmn. bd. Peabody Radio and TV awards; trustee The Freedom Forum, 1989-96; co-chair Women, Men & Media, Washington, 1989—; mem. adv. bd. New Direction For News U. Mo., 1989—; mem., pres. Nat. Women's Hall of Fame, Seneca Falls, N.Y., 1990-96, chair adv. bd., 1996—; mem. adv. bd. Knight Ctr. for Specialized Journalism U. Md., 1993—; vice chair Internat. Women's Media Found., Washington, 1996—; exec. dir. Media Studies Ctr., N.Y., 1996—; sr. v.p. The Freedom Forum, Arlington, Va., 1996—. Deceased.

WOODMAN, WILLIAM E., theater, opera and television director; b. N.Y.C.; s. William E. and Ruth (Cornwall) W. BA, Hamilton Coll.; MFA, Columbia U. Stage mgr. Am. Shakespeare Festival, Stratford, Conn., 1957-61; co-producer Robin Hood Theater, Arden, Del., 1961-64; drama educator (founding mem.) Julliard Sch. Lincoln Ctr. Drama Div., N.Y.C., 1968-73; artistic dir. Goodman Theater, Chgo., 1973-78; drama educator U. So. Calif., 1993, Hamilton Coll., 1994, Circle in the Square Theatre Sch., 1995. Dir. The Freedom of the City (Brian Friel) on Broadway and at the Goodman Theatre, Chgo.; producer, dir. premieres by Edward Bond, Sam Shepard, Christopher Hampton, David Rabe, Studes Terkel, others; dir. ABC ARTS Cable TV Long Day's Journey into Night, 1982, Shakespeare Video Richard II, Romeo and Juliet, The Tempest 1981-83, Phila. Drama Gild, 1981-94, Dramski Teatar, Skopje, Yugoslavia, Buried Child, 1987, Man & Superman, Roundabout Theatre, N.Y.C., 1988, (PBS American Playhouse) The Diaries of Adam & Eve, 1988, Saint Joan, Repertory Theatre of St. Louis, 1989, The Lighthouse, Chgo. Opera Theatre, 1990, Die Fledermaus, June Opera Festival of N.J., 1990, Moon for the Misbegotten, Mo. Repertory, 1990, Cocktail House, Syracuse Stage, 1990, The Miser, Who's Afraid of Virginia Woolf, Playmaker's Repertory Co., 1991-92, The Gigli Concert, Court Theatre, 1992, The Tempest, Shakespeare in the Park, Westerly, R.I., 1992, The Glass Menagerie, Vt. Stage Co., 1994, Twelfth Night, Syracuse Stage, 1995. Served with U.S. Army, 1954-56. Mem. Dirs. Guild of Am., Soc. Stage Dirs. and Choreographers. Died Dec. 19, 1995.

WOODRING, MARGARET DALEY, architect, planner; b. N.Y.C., Mar. 29, 1933; d. Joseph Michael and Mary (Barron) Daley; m. Francis Woodring, Oct. 25, 1954 (div. 1962); m. Robert Bell, Dec. 20, 1971 (dec.); children: Ward, Lissa, Gabrielle, Phaedra. Student, NYU, 1959-60; BArch, Columbia U., 1966; MArch, Princeton U., 1971. Registered architect; cert. planner. Architect, planner various firms, N.Y.C.; environ. design specialist Rutgers U., New Brunswick, N.J., 1966-68; programming cons. Davis & Brody, N.Y.C., 1968-71; planning cons. William H. Liskamm, San Francisco, 1971-74; mgr. planning Met. Transp. Commn., Oakland, Calif., 1974-81; dir. Internat. Program for Housing and Urban Devel. Ofcls. Ctr. for Environ. Design Rsch. U. Calif., Berkeley, 1981-89; prin. Woodring & Assocs., San Rafael, Calif., 1989—; adj. lectr. dept. architecture U. Calif., Berkeley, 1974-84; founder New Horizons Savs. Assn., San Rafael, 1977-79; cons. U.S. Agy. for Internat. Devel., Washington, 1981-89; mem. jury Nat. Endowment Arts, others. Chair Bicentennial Com., San Rafael, 1976; bd. dirs. Displaced Homemakers Ctr., Oakland, 1981-84; pres. Environ Design Found., San Francisco, 1984-90. William Kinne Travel fellow Columbia U., 1965-66; Richard King Mellon fellow Princeton U., 1968-70. Mem. AIA (chair urban design com. San Francisco chpt. 1980-81), Am. Inst. Cert. Planners, Urban Land Inst., Soc. for Internat. Devel. (pres. San Francisco chpt. 1980-83), World Affairs Coun., Internat. World Congress on Land Policy. Avocations: hiking, gardening, reading, race walking.

WOODS, LUCIUS EARLE, lawyer; b. Yonkers, N.Y., Oct. 14, 1921; s. Henry Earle and Esther May (Potter) W.; m. Ruth Claybourne, May 27, 1950; children: Samuel (dec.), Henry, Beverly Woods Bravo. BS, Columbia U., 1943, LLB, 1948. Bar: N.Y. 1949, Colo. 1952, U.S. Supreme Ct. 1955. Assoc. Duke & Landis, N.Y.C., 1948-51; assoc. Holme Roberts & Owen, Denver, 1953-55, ptnr., 1955-79; asst. atty. gen.nat. resources State of Colo., Denver, 1979-81; prin. Wade Ash Woods Hill & Farley, P.C., Denver, 1982-95; chmn. Gov.'s Task Force on Mental Retardation, 1964-65; cons. on guardianship Pres.'s Com. Retardation, 1970; bd. examiners Colo. Supreme Ct., 1979-82; lectr. Minn. Bar Assn., Mpls.,1976, U. Denver Coll. of Law, 1981-83, Continuing Legal Edn. Colo. Bar Assn. Contbr. articles to profl. jours. Lt. (j.g.) USN, 1943-46. Fellow Am. Coll. Trust and Estate Counsel; mem. ABA (natural resources, real property, probate and trust, taxation, administrv. law sects.), ACLU (Colo. founding bd.), Colo. Bar Assn. (chmn. special com. on uniform probate code 1972-73, mem. statutory revision com.), Columbia U. Alumni Assn. Died Oct. 10, 1995.

WOODS, SYLVANIA WEBB, SR., judge; b. Ft. Gaines, Ga., Aug. 4, 1927; s. Andrew Lee and Cora Mae (Mathis) W.; m. Geneva Holloway; children: Sylvania W. Jr., Sebrena W. BS in Bus. Adminstrn., Morris Brown U., 1949; student, Atlanta U., 1950-51; JD, Am. U., 1960; grad., Jericho Christian Coll., 1997. Bar: Md. 1969. Pvt. practice Washington, 1962-69, Prince Georg'e Co, Md., 1969-76; dist. ct. judge 5th Dist. Ct., Upper Marlboro, Md., 1976-94; cir. ct. judge 7th Cir., Upper Marlboro, Md., 1994-97. Deacon, bd. trustee Upper Room Bapt. Ch., Washington, 1965-97; vice chmn. Dem. Ctrl. com., Prince George's Co., 1976. With U.S. Navy, 1943-45, Korea. Named Top 10 Area Judges The Washingtonian, 1996, Man of Yr. Bus. & Profl. Woman, 1990, Upper Room Bapt. Ch., 1985. Mem. Nat. Bar Assn., D.C. Bar Assn., J. Frankyn Bourne Bar Assn., Am. Univ. Law Alumni Assn., Morris Brown Alumni Assn., Am. Legion (judge adv. 1976-80), Felix Lodge, Masons. Democrat. Baptist. Avocations: computers, christian study, public speaking. Home: Lanham Md. Died June 21, 1997.

WOODYARD, HARRY, state legislator; b. Danville, Ill., Dec. 3, 1930; s. Lewis J. and Lucile (Holden) W.; m. Mary D. Hester, 1952; children: Leslie, Kirk. Student, Wesleyan U. State rep. Dist. 106, 1979-87; Ill. state senator Dist. 53, 1987—; mem. agrl. and conserv. Ill. State Senate, internat. trade and port promotion coms., joint coms. on adminstrn. rules, local govt., revenue coms., state employees suggestion award bd. coms., appropriations I & II, com. econ. devel. coms.; chmn. bd. Ridgefarm State Bank; farmer. Named Outstanding Legislator for Cmty. Colls.; recipient John M. Lewis Outstanding Legislator award Ill. Cmty. Coll. Trustees Assn., 1982, Svc. award Ill. Land Improvement Contractors Assn., 1983, Meritorious Svc. award Ill. Cmty. Coll. Trustees Assn., 1987. Mem. VFW, Kiwanis, Shriners, Farm Bur., Masons, Am. Legion (life mem.), Sigma Chi. Republican. DIED 01/31/97. .

WOOTAN, GUY, lawyer; b. Caserta, Italy, Nov. 19, 1938; came to U.S., 1941;. BBA, Tulane U., 1960, JD, 1963. Bar: La. 1963, U.S. Dist. Ct. La. 1964, U.S. Ct. Appeals (5th and Fed. cirs.) 1964, U.S. Supreme Ct. 1973. Tchr. bus. law Tulane U., New Orleans, 1965-76, mem. curriculum adv. com., 1972-76; ptnr. Chaffe, McCall, Phillips, Toler & Sarpy, New Orleans; lectr. La. State U. Sch. Dentistry, Tulane U. Law Sch., La. State Med. Soc., Nat. Notary Assn. Author: Louisiana's Unique Notaries - A Blend of Old and New, 1975. Mem. New Orleans Track Club, New Orleans Opera Guild Assn., 1975, New Orleans Symphony, 1980, United Way, 1968; bd. dirs. Audubon Park Commn., 1973-82, Friends of the Zoo, 1982-84; bd. govs. New Orleans City Club, 1988-95. Roman Catholic. Avocations: jogging, biking, reading. Home: New Orleans La. Died Feb. 19, 1995.

WORNER, LLOYD EDSON, retired college president; b. Mexico, Mo., Sept. 13, 1918; s. Lloyd Edson and Letitia (Owen) W.; m. Mary Haden, Aug. 24, 1945; children: Linda Lou, Mary Susan. Student, Washington and Lee U., 1936-38, LL.D., 1972; A.B., Colo. Coll., 1942, LL.D., 1981; postgrad., Princeton U., 1942-43; M.A., U. Mo., 1944, Ph.D., 1946, L.H.D. (hon.), 1983; L.H.D. (hon.), U. No. Colo., 1975. Instr. history Colo. Coll., 1946-47, asst. prof., 1947-50, assoc. prof., 1950-55, prof., dean coll., 1955-63, pres., 1963-81, pres. emeritus, 1981—. Trustee emeritus Fountain Valley Sch.; bd. visitors Mo. Mil. Acad. Congregationalist. Deceased.

WORTZEL, LAWRENCE HERBERT, marketing educator; b. Newark, Sept. 28, 1932; s. Charles and Sadie (Bornstein) W.; m. Heidi Pamela Vernon, Dec. 23, 1956; children: Joshua Charles, Jennifer Rachel. BS, Rutgers U., 1954; MBA with distinction, Harvard U., 1963, D.B.A., 1967. Ptnr., owner two pharmacies N.J., 1957-61; rsch. asst., then rsch. assoc. Harvard U., 1963-65; mem. faculty Boston U., 1965—, prof. mktg., 1969—, chmn. dept., 1968-72, 73-75; faculty assoc. Mgmt. Analysis Ctr., Group/Gemini, 1978—; faculty assoc. in residence Mgmt. Analysis Ctr., 1982-83, 89-90; vis. rsch. prof. Mktg. Sci. Inst., 1976; cons. World Bank, 1976—, Inst. for Internat. Econ. Mgmt., Beijing and Shanghai, People's Republic of China, 1981—; sr. faculty mem. Prasetiya Mulya Grad. Sch. Bus., Jakarta, Indonesia, 1994—. Co-author: The Development of Financial Managers, 1971; co-editor: Marketing to the Changing Household, 1984, Strategic Managment of Multinational Corporations: The Essentials, 1984, Global Strategic Management: The Essentials, 1991. Bd. dirs. Boston Concert Opera Assn., 1981-87; pres. Boston U. Hillel Found., 1985-87. Served with U.S. Army, 1956-57. Mem. Am. Mktg. Assn., Assn. Consumer Rsch. Acad., Acad. Internat. Bus., Am. Econ. Assn., Strategic Mgmt. Soc., Acad. Mgmt. Jewish.

WRIGHT, GORDON KENNEDY, lawyer; b. St. Louis, Feb. 19, 1920; m. Frances Willis (dec. Dec. 12, 1992), Dec. 11, 1948; children: Geoffrey, Robert. B.A., U. So. Calif., 1941, LL.B., 1948. Bar: Calif. 1948, U.S. Dist. Ct. 1948, U.S. Ct. Appeals (9th cir.) 1955, U.S. Supreme Ct. 1971. Mem. Lillick & McHose (and predecessor firm), Los Angeles, 1949-92, ptnr., 1956-92. Served as lt. comdr. USN, 1941-45. Decorated Legion of Merit with combat V. Fellow Am. Bar Found.; mem. Am. Coll. Trial Lawyers, ABA, Calif. Bar Assn., Los Angeles Bar Assn., Internat. Acad. Trial Lawyers. Clubs: Annandale Golf, Chancery, 5000.

WRIGHT, IRVING SHERWOOD, physician, retired educator; b. N.Y.C., Oct. 27, 1901; s. Harry J. and Cora Ann (Hassett) W.; m. Grace Mansfield Demarest, Oct. 15, 1927; children: Barbara Mansfield, Alison Sherwood; m. Lois Elliman Findlay, Oct. 31, 1953. A.B., Cornell U., 1923, M.D., 1926. Diplomate: Am. Bd. Internal Medicine (mem. adv. bd. 1940-49), subcert. in cardiovascular diseases. Intern N.Y. Post Grad. Med. Sch. and Hosp. of Columbia, 1927-29, asst. and assoc. vis. physician, 1929-39, prof. clin. medicine, dir. and exec. officer dept. medicine, 1939-46; asst. physician Bellevue Hosp. (Cornell Div.), 1931-34, assoc., 1934-37; assoc. prof. Cornell Med. Coll. and assoc. attending physician N.Y. Hosp., 1946-48; prof. clin. medicine Cornell Med. Coll., 1948-68, emeritus clin. prof., 1968-97; attending physician Drs. Hosp., N.Y.C., 1934-80, N.Y. Hosp., 1948-80; investigator into biomed. problems of aging; hon. staff dept. medicine N.Y. Hosp., 1980-97; physician Met. Opera, 1935-62; dir. medicine Cornell Div.) Welfare Hosp. Chronic Disease, 1937-40 (1st pres. its med. bd. 1937-39), cons. physician, 1940-46; cons. to Orange Meml. Hosp., East Orange, N.J., Monmouth Meml. Hosp., Long Branch, N.J., Hackensack (N.J.) Hosp., Mt. Vernon (N.Y.) Hosp.; chief of med. service Army and Navy Gen. Hosp., Hot Springs (Ark.) Nat. Park, 1942-43; cons. in medicine U.S. Army, 6th Service Command, 1944-45, 9th Service Command, 1945; coordinator health survey Am. prisoners of war from Far East, 1945; chmn. Internat. Com. on Blood Clotting Factors, 1954-63, sec. gen., 1963-68; chmn. com. on cerebral vascular diseases NIH, 1961-65; mem. Pres.'s Comm. Heart Disease, Cancer and Stroke, 1966-68; nat. chmn. Commn. Heart Disease Resources, 1968-76. Author and editor numerous books on cardiovascular diseases.; Editor-in-chief: Modern Medical Monographs;

Contbr. articles to med. jours. Chmn. Josiah Macy, Jr. Found. Conf. Blood Clotting, 1947-52; Trustee Cornell U., 1960-65. Served as lt. comdr. USNR, 1935-39; lt. col. to col. AUS, 1942-46; civilian cons. in medicine to surgeon gen. U.S. Army, 1946-74; mem. civilian adv. com. to sec. navy, 1946-47. Recipient Albert and Mary Lasker award Am. Heart Assn., 1960, Gold Heart award, 1958, Disting. Service award, 1976; Irving Sherwood Wright professorship in geriatrics at Cornell U. Med. Coll., 1976. Fellow Royal Coll. Physicians (London), ACP (regent, pres. 1965-66, pres. emeritus 1987-97), Acad. Medicine (chmn. geriatrics sect. 1976-79, outstanding Contbns. to Sci. and Medicine award medal 1986); mem. Am. Assn. Physicians, AMA (chmn. sect. exptl. med. and therapeutics 1939-40), Am. Heart Assn. (chmn. sect. for study peripheral circulation 1939-40, mem. exec. com., bd. dirs. 1935-57, pres. 1952-53, mem. Nat. Adv. Heart Council 1954-58, 60-61), Cornell U. Med. Coll. Alumni Assn. (pres 1953), NRC (subcom. cardiovascular diseases 1947-51), Am. Soc. Clin. Investigation, Soc. Exptl. Biology and Medicine, N.Y. Acad. Scis., Am. Geriatrics Soc. (pres. 1971-72, Henderson award 1970, Thewlis award 1974), Am. Fedn. for Aging Research (founding pres. 1980-86, AFAR Distinction award 1987), Harvey Soc., Sigma Xi, Alpha Omega Alpha; corr. mem. of Acad. Columbian de Ciencas Exactas Fisico-Quimicas Y Naturales (Bogota); hon. mem. Royal Soc. Medicine of London, med. socs. Brazil, Chile, Peru, Argentina, Cuba, Switzerland, Sweden and USSR; also hon. faculty of U. Chile. Presbyn (bd. sessions 1935-36). Club: St. Nicholas Society (N.Y.). Died Dec. 8, 1997.

WU, CHIEN SHIUNG, physicist; b. Shanghai, May 31, 1912; naturalized citizen, U.S.; married, 1942; 1 child. BS, Nat. Cent. U., China, 1934; PhD, U. Calif., 1940; DSc (hon.), Princeton U., 1958, Smith Coll., 1959, Goucher Coll., 1960, Rutgers U., 1961, Yale U., 1967, Russell Sage Coll., 1971, Harvard U., 1974, Bard Coll., 1974, Adelphi U., 1974, Dickinson Coll., 1975; LLD (hon.), Chinese U., Hong Kong, 1969. Rsch. fellow, lectr. U. Calif., 1940-42; asst. prof. Smith Coll., 1942-43; instr. Princeton U., 1943-44; sr. scientist Columbia U., 1944-47, assoc., 1947-52, from assoc. to full prof., 1952-72, Pupin prof. physics, 1972-81; mem. adv. com. to dir. NIH, 1975-82; hon. prof. Nanking U., Sci. & Tech. U., Beijing U., Tsing Hwa U., Nan Kai U., People's Republic China & Padua U., Italy; Nishina Meml. lectr. Univs. Tokyo, Osaka and Kyoto, 1983. Recipient Rsch. award Rsch. Corp., 1959, AAUW award, 1960, Achievement award Chi-Tsin Cult Found., 1965, Nat. Sci. Medal, 1975, Wolf Prize in Physics, 1978, Pupin medal Columbia Engring. Sch. Alumni Assn., 1991, Ettore Majorana-Erice-Sci. for Peace prize, 1992; named Scientist of Yr., Indsl. Rsch. Mag., 1974; asteroid named in honor, 1990. Fellow AAAS, Royal Soc. Edinburgh (hon.); mem. NAS (Comstock award 1964), Am. Phys. Soc. (pres. 1975, Tom Bonner prize 1975), Chinese Acad. Sci., Am. Acad. Arts & Sci. Achievements include research in nuclear physics, non-conservation of parity in beta decay. Home: New York N.Y. Died Feb. 16, 1997.

XHUMARI, ARIAN, neurosurgeon, educator; b. Tirana, Albania, June 21, 1941; s. Kol and Antigoni (Sallabanda) X.; m. Silvia Tashko, May 26, 1968; children: Florian, Artur. Grad. medicine, Tirana State U., 1963, grad. neurosurgery, 1967. Med. diplomate. Gen. surgery Hosp. Number 2, Tirana, 1963-67, neurosurgeon, 1967-85; prof. U. Hosp. Ctr., Tirana, 1985—; chief Neurosurg. Clinic, 1985-96; pres. Albanian Neurosurg. Union, 1994-96; founding mem. Balkan Union Oncology, 1995. Recipient Medal for Good Svc. to the People, Presidency of the People's Assembly, 1969, The Order for Good Svc. to the People, Presidency of the People's Assembly, 1987. Mem. European Assn. Neurosurg. Socs. Avocations: classical music, literature. Died July 5, 1996.

YAMABE, SHIGERU, medical educator; b. Tokyo, July 7, 1923; s. Hiroshi and Jyo (Mihara) Y.; m. Takako Naoi, Apr. 2, 1967; 1 child, Yoko. MS, Osaka (Japan) U., 1946, MD, 1952. Lectr. Osaka U. Med. Sch., 1953-58; prof. Kobe Coll., Nishinomiya, Japan, 1958-89, hon. prof., 1989—; system dir. Drug Rsch. System Internat., Kobe, 1989—; rsch. exec. mbr. Osaka Seijinbyo Med. Ctr., Higashinariku, Osaka, Japan, 1991—; vis. lectr. Tokyo U., Kyoto (Japan) U., 1966-84; vis. prof. dept. microbiology London Hosp. Med. Coll., 1978—, Case Western Res. U., Cleve., 1982, 84, Harvard Med. Sch., Boston, 1988-89; hon. vis. lectr. London Hosp. Med. Coll., 1990—; invited lectr. U. Paris VI, 1992—; vis. sr. scientist Inst. Pathology, Oxford, 1992—; vis. prof. Grad. Sch. Pub. Health U. Pitts., 1993—; sr. sci. advisor Taiho Pharm. Co., Tokyo, 1991—. Author: Bioenergetics, 1968 (award 1970); editor: Research and Development of New Drugs, 1994; editor: Drug Designing, Planning and Management, 1997; internat. jour. editor Antiviral Chemistry and Chemotherapy, 1993—, Jour. Chemotherapy, 1988—; drug designer, inventor Tazobactam antibiotic, 1991, Zaltoprofen anti-inflammatory drug, 1993; 40 patents for cancer and AIDS drugs. Fellow Royal Soc. Medicine; active mem. N.Y. Acad. Sci. Avocation: poetry. Died Apr. 25, 1997.

YAMAOKA, MICHIAKI, law educator; b. Ochi-gun Tamagawa-cho, Ehime, Japan, Sept. 9, 1901; s. Benji and Tune (Seno) Y.; m. Uta Takiya, Feb. 20, 1945; children: Arihiro, Michihiro. BA, Meiji U., Chiyoda-ku, Tokyo, 1926. Cert. patent atty. Instr. comml. law Senshu U., Chiyoda-ku, 1929-37; instr. law Meiji U., Chiyoda-ku, 1952-78; prof. law Econs. Faculty of Daitobunka U., Itabashi-ku, Tokyo, 1962-71, Law Faculty of Soka U., Hachioji-shi, Tokyo, 1971-85; adviser Law Faculty of Soka U., Hachioji-shi, 1971-88; dir. Soka U., Hachioji-shi, 1973-86, adviser, 1986—, hon. prof., 1988—; dir. alumni assn. Meiji U., Chiyodakku, 1960—. Author: The Principles of Law, 1980, An Introduction to Law, 1981, 2d edit., 1984, Principles of Will Law, 1988. Census com. Prime Minister's Office, 1955, promoting com. Japan-Korea Friendship Treaty, 1965, commr. civil rights com., 1978; commr. Japan-China Human Social Sci. Interchange Soc., 1981. Recipient Cultural medal Prime Min.'s Office, 1985. Mem. Civil Law Soc. Japan, Autonomous Constn. Soc. Japan. Avocations: Haiga, Haiku, Sho-do, photography. Died Feb. 3, 1997.

YATSEVITCH, GRATIAN MICHAEL, retired army officer, diplomat, engineer; b. Kiev, Russia, Nov. 16, 1911; s. Michael Gratian and Margaret (Thomas) Y.; A.B., Harvard U., 1933, M.A., 1934, postgrad. (J.B. Woodworth fellow), 1935-40; m. Barbara Stewart Franks, July 2, 1973; children by previous marriage—Gael Yatsevitch McKibben, Peter, Kara, Gratian. Mining engr. Zlot Mines Ltd., also Beshina Gold Mines Ltd. of London in Yugoslavia, 1935-40, mgr. gold mine, 1936-40; commd. 2d lt. field arty.-U.S. Army, 1933, advanced through grades to col., 1951; chief cannon and aircraft armament br. devel. prodn. cannon, Office of Chief of Ordnance, 1940-45; mil. attache, Moscow, 1945-46; U.S. del. Allied Control Commn., Sofia, Bulgaria, 1946-47; mil. attache, Sofia, 1947-49; attache and spl. asst. to U.S. Amb., Turkey, 1952-53, Iran, 1957-63; sr. staff officer, Washington, 1950-52, 53-57; ret., 1969; hon. chmn. Star Trading and Marine Co., Washington; econ. cons. Middle E. Decorated Legion of Merit with oak leaf cluster. Clubs: Met. (Washington); Carlton, Lansdowne (London); Camden Yacht. Contbr. articles on arty. and mineral subjects to mags. Died Sept. 26, 1997.

YEH, CHAI, electrical engineer, educator; b. Hangchow, China, Sept. 21, 1911; came to U.S., 1933, naturalized, 1956; s. Yun Ching and Ai Hwa (Ho) Y.; m. Ida Chiang, June 20, 1936; children—Yin, Jen. B.S., Chekiang U., Hangchow, 1931; Ph.D., Harvard U., 1936. Prof. elec. engring. Pei Yang U., Tientsin, China, 1936-37, Tsing Hwa U., Peking, China, 1937-48; chmn. dept. elec. engring. Tsing Hwa U., 1945-47; vis. prof. elec. engring. U. Kans., 1948-56; prof. elec. and computer engring. U. Mich., Ann Arbor, 1956-81, prof. emeritus, 1981-97. Author: Handbook of Fiber Optics, Theory and Applications, 1990, Applied Photonics, 1994; contbr. articles to profl. jours. Elected to Internat. Directory Disting. Leadership, 1994. Mem. IEEE, Sigma Xi. DIED 02/15/97. .

YERBY, ALONZO SMYTHE, health services administrator, educator; b. Augusta, Ga., Oct. 15, 1921; s. Rufus Garvin and Wilhelmina Ethlyn (Smythe) Y.; m. Monteal Monica May, Sept. 17, 1943; children—Mark, Lynne, Kristen. B.S., U. Chgo., 1941; M.D., Meharry Med. Coll., 1946; M.P.H., Harvard, 1948. Diplomate: Am. Bd. Preventive Medicine. Intern Coney Island Hosp., Bklyn.; resident in preventive medicine Health Ins. Plan N.Y., 1950-53; exec. dir. med. services N.Y.C. Dept. Health; med. welfare adminstr. N.Y.C. Dept. Welfare, 1960-65; commr. of hosps. N.Y.C., 1965-66; prof. health services adminstrn. Harvard Sch. Pub. Health, Boston, 1966-82; dep. asst. sec. health for intergovtl. affairs Dept. Health and Human Services, Washington, 1980-81; prof., dir. div. health services adminstrn. Uniformed Services U. of Health Scis., Bethesda, Md., 1982-96; cons. Bur. Family Services, Nat. Center Health Services Research, HEW, WHO; mem. Nat. Adv. Commn. on Health Manpower, 1966-67, HEW Adv. Com. on Relationships with State Health Agys., 1963-66, Nat. Profl. Standards Rev. Council, 1978-80; vis. scientist USA-USSR Exchange Program, 1967, 79. Author: Community Medicine in England and Scotland, 1976. Served with AUS, 1943-46. Fellow Am. Pub. Health Assn.; mem. Am. Coll. Preventive Medicine, Inst. Medicine of Nat. Acad. Scis., N.Y. Acad. Medicine. Club: Harvard (N.Y.C.).

YODER, AMOS, university research official; b. Falls City, Nebr., Mar. 2, 1921; s. Amos Howard and Mildred Ann (Johnson) Y.; m. Janet Lee Tatman, June 15, 1946; children: James Amos, Barbara Ann Yoder Gorga, Sally Irene Yoder Ramseyer. BA, Ohio Wesleyan U., 1942; PhD, U. Chgo., 1949. Jr. econs. editor Bd. of Econ. Warfare, Washington, 1942-43; fgn. svc. officer Dept. of State, U.S. Embassies in Thailand and Israel., Washington, 1949-74; Borah Disting. prof. polit. sci. U. Idaho, Moscow, 1974-91; Fulbright prof. Lajos Kossuth U., Debrecen, Hungary, 1991; rsch. assoc. Mershon Ctr., Ohio State U., Columbus, 1993—; vis. lectr. U. Calif., Davis, 1964-65; Fulbright prof. Fgn. Affairs Coll., Beijing, 1986-87. Author: International Politics and Policymakers Ideas, 1982, The Conduct of American Foreign Policy Since World War II, 1986, World Politics and the Causes of War Since 1914, 1986, The Evolution of the United Nations, 1989, rev. edit., 1996, Communist Systems and Challenges, 1990, Communism in Transition, 1993; guest editor Terrorism-An Internat. Jour., summer 1983; contbr. articles to profl. jours. With USAF, 1943-46. Recipient Commendation ribbon War Dept., 1946, Merit Honor award Dept. State, 1967. Mem. Internat. Studies Assn., Idaho Polit. Sci. Assn. (v.p., pres. 1980-81), Amnesty Internat., Kiwanis (pres. Moscow, Idaho chpt. 1981-82). Democrat. Presbyterian. Home: Westerville Ohio Died Feb. 9, 1997.

YOEL, JOSE, physician, surgeon; b. Valparaiso, Chile, Nov. 26, 1913; s. Aaron and Raquel (Esquenazi) Y.; m. Sara Croizet; children: Claudia, Gerardo, Adriana. BS, Colegio Nacional, Rio Cuarto, Argentina, 1930; MD, U. Cordoba, Argentina, 1937, Doctorado, 1963; M Maxilo facial surgery, Maimonides U., 1995. Mem. staff Hosp. Rawson, Buenos Aires, 1950-77; prof. maxillofacial surgery Faculty of Odontologia, Buenos Aires, 1960-68; mem. staff Escuela Finochietto, Buenos Aires, 1963-77; mem. maxillofacial staff Hosp. Municipal Oncologia, Buenos Aires, 1977-79; mem. staff Inst. Municipal J. Mendez, Buenos Aires, 1981-84; cons. Sanatorio Guemes, Buenos Aires, 1984-93; prof. facial surgery U. Salvador, Buenos Aires, 1989-96; maxillofacial cons. Centro Oncologico Mainetti, Buenos Aires, 1992-96; docent Facultad Medicina, Buenos Aires; apptd. pres. XXXI World Biennial Congress, Buenos Aires, 1998. Author: Infecciones Maxilares, 1955, Atlas Cirugia Del Bocio, 1969, Pathology and Surgery of Salivary Glands, 1975, Atlas Cir. Gebezaly Cuello, 1986. Recipient numerous awards. Fellow Soc. Head and Neck Surgery, Internat. Coll. Angiology, Internat. Coll. Surgeons (pres. Argentine sect. 1993, world v.p. 1995-96); mem. Academia Argentina Cirugia, Soc. Internat. Chirurgie. Died Sept. 27, 1996.

YOSELOFF, MARTIN, writer; b. Sioux City, Iowa, July 26, 1919; s. Morris and Sarah (Rosansky) Y. B.A., State U. Iowa, 1941. Tchr. Drake Sch., N.Y.C.; writer various Iowa newspapers; editorial staff pub. houses N.Y.C., 1941-43, 47-49; contbg. writer Bank Street Coll. publs. Author: No Greener Meadows, 1946, The Family Members, 1948, The Girl in the Spike-Heeled Shoes, 1949, The Magic Margin, 1954, Lily and the Sergeant, 1957, A Time to Be Young, 1967, Remember Me to Marcie, 1973, What Are Little Girls Made Of?, 1979, The Wednesday Game, 1988; also narrative for sketch books City of the Mardi Gras, City on the Potomac, 1946. Served with AUS, 1943-46. Mem. Authors League Am., P.E.N. DIED 03/27/97. .

YOSHIMOTO, SHINJI, researcher; b. Osaka, Japan, July 17, 1909; s. Ichiro and Yae (Matta) Baba; m. Yasu Yoshimoto, Feb. 3, 1935; children: Noriko, Hiroko, Ritsuko (dec.). Degree in econs., U. Tokyo, 1932. Jr. official Ministry of Fin., Tokyo, 1932-34; chief Ujiyamada Tax Office, Ise, 1934-35; sr. researcher Office of Prime Minister, Tokyo, 1935-38, Ministry of Fin., Tokyo, 1938-41, 46-61; several adminstrv. positions Minstry of Fin., Tokyo, 1941-46, 61-70; spl. researcher Nat. Diet Libr., Tokyo, 1972-75; chief rep. Japanese Govt., ECAFE workshop on fin., Bankok, 1954. Author: The Rate of Interest, 1962, Equilibrium Analysis of the Rate of Interest, 1981, (summary in English), 1982. Mem. Internat. Ho. of Japan (life), Japan Assn. of Econs. and Econometrics, Japan Soc. of Internat. Econs. Avocations: jogging, light training, swimming.

YOSHIO, BAN, pharmacy educator; b. Tokyo, Apr. 15, 1921; s. Tsuneo and Takako Ban; m. Miwa Hara, Nov. 20, 1948; children: Yumiko, Takashi. B, U. Tokyo, 1945, PhD, 1955. Postdoctoral fellow U. Calif., Berkeley, 1955-56; instr. U. Tokyo, 1945-56; assoc. prof. Hokkaido U., Sapporo, Japan, 1956-57, prof., 1957-85, prof. emeritus Pharm. Inst., 1985—, pres., 1987-91; prof. Toho U., Funabashi, Chiba, Japan, 1985-87. Editor: Heterocycles, 1973—, Medicinal Rsch. Rev., 1988—, Natural Product Letters, 1991—, Heterocyclic Comm., Jaipur, India, 1993—; contbr. articles to profl. jours. Dir. Naito Sci. Found.,Tokyo, 1969—, Akiyama Life Sci. Found., Sapporo, Japan, 1987—; trustee Uehara Meml. Found., Tokyo, 1984—; bd. mem. Nat. Sci. Mus., Tokyo, 1993—. Recipient award Pharm. Soc., Tokyo, 1963, Grant award NIH, Bethesda, Md., 1963, Acad. Prize Japan Acad., Tokyo, 1984, Spl. award Soc. Synthetic Organic Chemistry, Tokyo, 1993. Mem. Pharm. Soc. Japan (pres. 1981-83), Internat. Soc. Heterocyclic Chemistry (pres. 1989-91), Pharm. Soc. and Soc. Cynthetic Organic Chemistry (hon.).

YOUNG, COLEMAN ALEXANDER, mayor; b. Tuscaloosa, Ala., May 24, 1918; s. Coleman and Ida Reese (Jones) Y. Hon. degrees, Eastern Mich. U., Wayne State U., U. Detroit, Stillman Coll., U. Mich. Del. Mich. Constl. Conv., 1961-62; mem. Mich. Senate, 1964-73; also Dem. floor leader Mich. Senate, Detroit; mayor City of Detroit, 1974-93; Del. to Dem. Nat. Conv., 1968, 72, 76, 80, 84, 88, 92; Dem. nat. committeeman from Mich.; vice chmn. Nat. Dem. Party, 1977-81; chmn. Dem. Conv. Platform Com., 1980; pres. U.S. Conf. of Mayors, 1982-83, Dem. Conf. of Mayors, 1986—; also mem. tech. adv. panel on adminstrn. of programs on aging; mem. nat. adv. com. Whit Ho. Conf. on Aging, 1981; mem. Nat. Adv. Commn. on Resource Conservation and Recovery. Bd. dirs. Ferndale Coop., Credit Union, Kirwood Hosp., Detroit, Detroit Renaissance, Detroit Econ. Growth Corp. Served to 2d lt. USAAF, World War II. Recipient Jefferson award Am. Inst. for Pub. Service, 1976. Mem.

NAACP (Spingarn medal 1981), Booker T. Washington Bus. Men's Assn., Trade Union Leadership Council, Assn. for Study Negro Life and History, AFL-CIO Council (spl. rep.). Baptist.

YOUNG, DON J., district judge; b. Norwalk, Ohio, July 13, 1910; s. Don J. and Elaine (Dennis) Y.; m. Seville Beatrice Shagrin, June 27, 1936; children—Don J., Patricia C. A.B. cum laude, Western Res. U., 1932, LL.B., 1934; student, Cleve. Art Sch., 1932-34. Bar: Ohio bar 1934. Pvt. practice Norwalk, 1934-52; judge Ct. Common Pleas, Huron County, Ohio, 1952-53, Probate and Juvenile Ct., Huron County, 1953-65; U.S. judge No. Dist. Ohio for Western Div., 1965-96; instr., lectr. juvenile ct. laws at seminars and insts. for judges, 1959-96; v.p. Ohio Assn. Probate Ct. Judges, 1958-60; pres. Ohio Assn. Juvenile Ct. Judges, 1960-62; law reporter Nat. Juvenile Ct. Found., 1959-73, sec.-treas., 1960-61, sec., 1961-62; sec. Nat. Council Juvenile Ct. Judges, 1962-65, exec. com., 1966-69. Contbr. articles to profl. jours.; exhibited jewelry, Cleve. Mus. Art, Butler Art Inst., Nat. Ceramic Exhbn. Exec. dir. Norwalk CD Corps, 1942-46; pres. Firelands Hist. Soc., 1945-46, Norwalk Cemetery Assn., 1951-57; sec. Norwalk Recreation Com., 1946-53; trustee Young Men's Library and Reading Room Assn., 1955-65, 86-96, Whittlesey Acad. Arts and Scis., 1955-65. Mem. ABA, Ohio Bar Assn., Order of Coif, Phi Beta Kappa, Pi Epsilon Delta. Episcopalian. Died May 10, 1996.

YOUNG, FARON, entertainer; b. Shreveport, Feb. 25, 1932; s. Harlan Ray and Doris (Birtch) Y.; m. Hilda Margot Macon, July 1, 1954 (div. 1986); children—Damion Ray, Robyn Ferrel, Kevin Robert, Alana Denise. Student public schs., Shreveport. Pres. Faron Young Enterprises., 1952—. Singer radio programs La. Hayride, 1951-52, Grand Ole Opry, 1952-64; numerous appearances on TV and 14 movies; recorded over 60 albums, 105 single records, 32 No. 1 records, 79 top ten records, million sellers; composer: Hello Walls, Goin Steady, Sweet Dreams, I Miss You Already, Alone With You, Four in the Morning. Served with AUS, 1953-54. Decorated Commendation medal; named No. 1 Country Singer, 1956. Mem. VFW, Am. Legion. Baptist. Club: Moose. Home: Franklin Tenn. Died Dec. 12, 1996.

YOUNG, MAHONRI SHARP, author; b. N.Y.C., July 23, 1911; s. Mahonri Mackintosh and Cecilia (Sharp) Y.; m. Elizabeth Chamberlain, July 23, 1932 (div. 1940); m. Rhoda Satterthwaite, Dec. 7, 1940 (dec. May 1989); 1 son, Mahonri Mackintosh II. A.B., Dartmouth Coll., 1933; M.A., N.Y. U., 1951. Mem. art dept. Sarah Lawrence Coll., 1941-50; acting dir. community arts program Munson-Williams-Proctor Inst., Utica, N.Y., 1951-53; dir. Columbus (Ohio) Gallery of Fine Arts, 1953-76; Am. corr. for Apollo mag., 1966-90. Author: Old George, 1940, George Bellows, 1973, The Eight, 1973, Early American Moderns, 1974, American Realists: Homer to Hopper, 1977, The Golden Eye, 1983. Served with USAAF, 1942-46. Mem. Phi Beta Kappa. Club: Century Assn. (N.Y.C.). Home: Water Mill N.Y. Died June 16, 1996.

YOUNG, RICHARD STUART, technical services executive; b. Southampton, N.Y., Mar. 6, 1927; s. P. Stuart and Myrtle F. (Terrell) Y.; m. Nancy J. Mayer, June 7, 1955; children: Dee Ann, Sandra, Mark. A.B., Gettysburg Coll., 1948, Sc.D., 1966; postgrad., U. N.C., 1951-53; Ph.D., Fla. State U., 1955. With FDA, Washington, 1956-58; with NASA, Army Ballistic Missile Agency, Huntsville, Ala., 1958-59, NASA-Ames Research Center, Moffett Field, Calif., 1960-67; chief exobiology program-hdqrs., chief program scientist Viking NASA, Washington, 1969-77; chief of bioscis. div. NASA Hdqrs., 1975-79; v.p. Rockefeller U., N.Y.C., 1979-82; exec. dir. Am. Soc. Cell Biology, Bethesda, Md., 1982-85; mgr. Mgmt. and Tech. Svcs. Co., Washington, 1985-96; sr. scientist Kennedy Space Ctr., Fla., 1987-96. Contbr. articles to profl. jours., also books. Served with USN, 1944-46. Mem. Internat. Soc. for Study Origin of Life (sec. 1970-77, v.p. 1977-82). Home: Cocoa Beach Fla. Died Oct. 6, 1996.

YOUNG, THOMAS DANIEL, retired humanities educator, author; b. Louisville, Miss., Oct. 22, 1919; s. William Allen and Lula (Wright) Y.; m. Arlease Lewis, Dec. 21, 1941; children: Thomas Daniel, Terry Lewis, Kyle David. B.S., Miss. So. Coll., 1941; M.A., U. Miss., 1948; Ph.D., Vanderbilt U., 1950; postgrad., U. Oxford, 1962, The Sorbonne, 1974. Instr. English U. Miss., 1946-48; asst. Vanderbilt U., Nashville, 1948-50, dean admissions, asst. to vice-chancellor, 1961-64, prof., chmn. dept. English, 1964-72, Gertrude C. Vanderbilt prof. English, 1972-85, Gertrude C. Vanderbilt prof. emeritus, 1985—; asst. prof. English Miss. So. Coll., 1950-51, prof., chmn. dept., 1951-54, dean basic coll., 1954-57; prof. English, dean Delta State Coll., Cleveland, Miss., 1957-61; Pres. So. Lit. Festival Assn., 1952-53; chmn. English commn. Miss. Assn. Coll., 1952-55; coordinator Gen. Edn. Conf., 1953. Author: Jack London and the Era of Social Protest, 1950, The Literature of the South, 1952, rev. edit., 1968, Donald Davidson: An Essay and a Bibliography, 1965, American Literature: A Critical Survey, 1968, John Crowe Ransom; Critical Essays and a Bibliography, 1968, John Crowe Ransom, 1970, Donald Davidson, 1971, The Literary Correspondence of Allen Tate and Donald Davidson, 1974, The New Criticism and After, 1976, Gentleman in a Dustcoat: A Biography of John Crowe Ransom, 1977, The Past in the Present: Studies in the Modern American Novel, 1981, Tennessee Writers, 1981, John Crowe Ransom: An Annotated Bibliography, 1982, The Vocation of Letters in America: The Literary Correspondence of Allen Tate and John Peale Bishop, 1982, Selected Essays of John Crowe Ransom, 1983, Selected Letters of John Crowe Ransom, 1985, Singin' Billy, 1985, (with Louis D. Rubin and others) The History of Southern Literature, Conversations with Malcolm Cowley, 1986, The Lytle-Tate Letters, 1987, Fabulous Provinces: A Memoir, 1988, Modern American Fiction, 1989, Selected Essays, 1990; gen. editor: The Fugitive Bibliographies. Mem. AAUP, South Atlantic MLA (chmn. Am. lit. sect. 1971, chmn. lit. criticism sect. 1969, mem. exec. com. 1969-72), MLA (chmn. So. Lit. sect. 1969, 80, 82), Am. Studies Assn. Lower Miss. (pres. 1956-57), Phi Delta Kappa, Omicron Delta Kappa. Died Jan. 29, 1997.

YOUNGBLOOD, J. CRAIG, lawyer; b. Ft. Worth, July 6, 1947; s. Angus O'Neal and Kathleen (Hill) Y.; m. Linda Gilman, Apr. 17, 1982; children: Jesica Caye, Jaclyn Cristine. Student, Rice U., 1965-66; BA in Polit. Sci. and Math, U. Tex., San Antonio, 1977; JD, U. Tex., Austin, 1980. Bar: Tex. 1982, U.S. Dist. Ct. (so. dist.) Tex. 1982, U.S. Ct. Appeals (D.C., 3rd, 5th and 11th cirs.) 1982, U.S. Ct. Appeals (10th cir.) 1983. Assoc. Vinson & Elkins, Houston, 1981-87, ptnr., 1988-96; adv. bd. grad. program in energy and natural resources U. Houston Law Ctr. Mem. Tex. Law Rev.; contbr. chpt. to book; contbr. articles to profl. jours., lectr. in field. Mem. ABA, Tex. Bar Assn., Houston Bar Assn., Fed. Energy Bar Assn., Tex. Law Rev. Assn. Republican. Avocations: hunting, fishing, snow skiing, personal computers. Died Dec. 29, 1996.

YOUNGMAN, HENNY, comedian; m. Sadie Cohen (dec.); children: Gary, Marilyn. Appeared regularly on: radio show Kate Smith, during 1930's, now nightclub and concerts comedian; appears on TV; appeared in: TV series Henny and Rocky, 1955, Joey and Dad, 1975; film Silent Movie, 1976, History of the World, Part I, 1981, The Comeback Trial, 1982, Goodfellows, 1990; recs. include Take My Album...Please, 1978, 128 Greatest Jokes, In Concert, 1987, Bits & Pieces, 1992; author 10 books including: How Do Youe Like ME So Far?, Take My Wife Please, 400 Travelins Salesmen's Jokes, 500 All Time Greatest One-Liners, Don't Put My Name on This Book, Take My Life, Please, Big Book of Insults, 1995, Big Big Book of Insults. Died Feb. 24, 1998.

YOUNGMAN, WILLIAM STERLING, lawyer; b. Boston, May 25, 1907; s. William Sterling and Helen Isabel (Yerxa) Y.; m. Elsie Hooper Perkins, Apr. 17, 1937; children: William Sterling, 3d, Robert, Elsie Youngman Hull. Student, Middlesex Sch., 1919-25; A.B. magna cum laude, Harvard U., 1929, J.D. magna cum laude, 1932; LL.D. (hon.), Middlebury Coll., 1978. Bar: Mass. 1934, U.S. Supreme Ct. 1939, D.C. 1941, N.Y. 1951, N.H. 1969. Law sec. to Judge Learned Hand, N.Y.C., 1932-33; with law firm Palmer, Dodge, Barstow, Wilkins & Davis, Boston, 1933-38; counsel Nat. Power Policy Commn., Washington, and; chief counsel power div. PWA, 1939-40; gen. counsel FPC, 1940-1941; exec. v.p. and dir. China Def. Supplies, Inc., 1941-42, pres., 1942-45; gen. counsel in U.S., Nat. Resources Commn. of China, 1944-47; partner Corcoran and Youngman, 1949-68; pres. C.V. Starr & Co., Inc., 1949-68; chmn. bd. Am. Home Asssurance Co., Ins. Co. of State of Pa., 1952-69, Am. Internat. Assurance Co., Ltd., Hong Kong, 1958-67, Philippine Am. Life Ins. Co., 1958-68, Am. Internat. Underwriters Corp., 1959-68, Am. Internat. Reins. Co., 1967-68, Am. Internat. Group, 1968; Vice chmn. Council for Latin Am., 1967-69. Trustee emeritus Middlebury Coll.; Mem. Council Fgn. Relations. Clubs: Metropolitan, Chevy Chase (Washington); St. Botolph (Boston); Harvard, River, (N.Y.C.); Varsity (Harvard U.), Manchester (Mass.) Yacht; Essex County (Mass.). Home: Vero Beach Fla. Died Oct. 10, 1994.

YOUNKIN, C. GEORGE, archivist; b. Great Bend, Kan., Oct. 13, 1910; s. Charles Franklin and Nannie Sylvia (Wilson) Y.; student Washburn U., 1932-35, Southeastern U., Washington, 1936-37; m. Ruth Ward, Dec. 27, 1939 (dec. 1980); children: Karen (Mrs. John R. Postma), Eleta (Mrs. Stephen B. McElroy), Cheryl (Mrs. Thomas R. Gamble), Chip G. With U.S. Dept. Agr., Washington, 1935-51; with Nat. Archives, Ft. Worth, 1951-75, regional archivist for Ark., La., N.Mex., Okla. and Tex., 1968-75; ret., 1975; pres. S.W. Archives Cons., 1975—; archive cons. Kiowa Hist. and Research Assn., Carnegie, Okla. Mem. council exec. com. and historian Boy Scouts Am., Ft. Worth, 1975-80; mem. Gov.'s Adv. Com. on Aged for Tarrant County, 1976-80; mem. Tarrant County Hist. Commn.; trustee Ch. of Good Shepherd, 1980-83; pres. Sr. Citizens Alliance Tarrant County, Inc., 1992-94; legis. chmn. Nat. Assn. Retired Fed. Employees, Arlington, Tex., 1978-93; mem. NEH, 1986-94; mem. Am. Indian Vet.'s Soc. North Tex., 1992—. Served with AUS, 1943-45. Recipient Silver Beaver award Boy Scouts Am., 1966, Order of Arrow, Boy Scouts Am., 1966; pub. service award GSA, 1967, spl. service award Fed. Bus. Assn., 1967, Cross and Flame award United Meth. Ch. and Boy Scouts Am., 1988. Fellow Tex. State Geneal. Soc.; mem. Soc. S.W. Archivists (sec.-treas. 1971-80), Internat. Council Archives, Soc. Am. Archivists (regional activities com.), Nat. Trust Historic Preservation, Kiowa Tia-Piah Soc. Carnegie (Okla.), Westerners Internat., Western History Assn., Tex. Hist. Assn. Dir., Llano Estacado Heritage Quar., 1974-82.

YOW, JOHN STUART, JR., retired internist; b. Mt. Vernon, Ind., Sept. 15, 1926; s. John Stuart and Helen (Keck) Y.; m. Cecelia McGowin, June 6, 1950 (dec. Aug. 14,1 988); children: Tere, Cecelia, John III. Student, Newberry Coll., 1944-45, Ga. Tech, 1945-46; BS, Auburn U., 1948; MD, U. Ala. Sch. Medicine, 1953. Chief resident internal medicine U. Ala., Birmingham, 1958-59; asst. chief internal medicine 3380 USAF Hosp., Biloxi, Miss., 1955-56; chief internal medicine St. Margaret's Hosp., Montgomery, Ala., 1965-67; internist Montgomery, Ala., 1959-93; ret., 1993; standing com. Episcopal Diocese of Ala., Birmingham, 1989—, commn. of ministry, 1989—; admissions com. U. Ala. Sch. Medicine, 1979—. Capt. USAF, 1955-57. Mem. AMA, Med. Soc. Ala., So. Med. Soc., Am. Soc. Internal Medicine, Ala. Soc. Internal Medicine, Am. Coll. Sports Medicine, Montgomery Country Club, Capital City Club. Episcopalian. Avocations: photography, music. Died Oct. 1, 1994.

ZABEL, EDWARD, economist, educator; b. Orange, N.J., Oct. 17, 1927; s. Otto and Helen (Katzenberger) Z.; m. Norma Nicholson, June 23, 1956; children: Jeffrey, David, Richard. B.A., Syracuse (N.Y.) U., 1950; M.A., Princeton U., 1953, Ph.D., 1956. Research asst. Princeton U., 1954-56; economist Rand Corp., Santa Monica, Calif., 1956-58; mem. faculty U. Rochester, N.Y., 1958-81; prof. econs. U. Rochester, 1967-81; prof. econs. U. Fla., Gainesville, 1981-83, Matherly prof. econs. and decision scis., 1983—; assoc. editor Mgmt. Sci., 1969-73; bd. editors Applied Econs., 1973—, Applied Econs. Letters, 1993—. Contbr. to profl. jours. Served with AUS, 1945-47. Ford Found. fellow, 1964-65; NSF rsch. grantee, 1960-81. Mem. Am. Econ. Assn., Econometric Soc., Internat. Soc. Inventory Rsch., Western Econ. Assn., Inst. mgmt. Scis., AAUP, Phi Beta Kappa. Democrat. DIED 04/25/97. .

ZAKARIA, IBRAHIM, international organization administrator. Pres. World Fedn. of Trade Unions, Prague.

ZAMARAEV, KIRILL ILYICH, chemist; b. Moscow, Russia, 1939; married; 2 children. BS, Moscow Inst. Physics and Tech., 1963, PhD in Chem. Physics, 1966, DS in Phys. Chemistry, 1972. Head lab. Inst. Chem. Physics, Moscow, 1966-76; asst. prof. Moscow Inst. Physics and Tech., 1966-76; dir. Boreskov Inst. Catalysis Novosibirsk, Russia, 1984—; prof. chemistry, chmn. dept. phys. chemistry Novosibirsk State U., 1977—. Rsch. fellow Inst. Chem. Physics Moscow, 1966-76. Mem. Internat. Union Pure and Applied Chemistry (pres. 1993—). Avocations: music, poetry, camping. Died June 26, 1996.

ZANDIER, FRED F., special education educator; b. Pitts., Jan. 21, 1924; s. Fred A. and Anna G. (Little) Z.; children: Lin A., William T., Jan M., David F., Julie P. BPE, U. Ill., 1949, MPE, 1950. Cert. spl. edn. (learning disabled, emotionally disabled, behavior disorders). Tchr., coord. McHenry County (Ill.) Rural Schs., 1949; supt., prin. Riley Twp., Ill., 1953-54; athletic dir. Cary, Ill., 1955-60; coach, tchr. Hampshire, Ill., 1961-62; spl. edn. tchr. Sch. Dist. 300, Alqonquin, Ill., 1962-68; dir. career devel. program, spl. studies tchr. Barrington (Ill.) Sch. Dist. 220, 1968-93; edn. cons. Psychol. & Edn. Assocs., Crystal Lake, Ill., 1963-66, Palatine (Ill.) Child Guidance Clinic, 1968-72, pvt. practice, 1972-95; owner, pub. weekly newspaper, Wonder Lake, Ill. Author: Citizens' Guide, 1989. Past mem. bd. dirs. Salvation Army, Wonder Lake, Ill., United Cerebal Palsy, McHenry County, Ill.; founder/pres. Wonder Lake Little League, McHenry County Lighweight Football league. S/sgt. USAF, 1942-45, ETO. Mem. NEA, Ill. Edn. Assn., Barrington Edn. Assn., Kiwanis (past sec., pres.). Home: Palatine Ill. Died July 17, 1995.

ZARAFONETIS, CHRIS JOHN DIMITER, physician, emeritus educator; b. Hillsboro, Tex., Jan. 6, 1914; s. James and Helen (Skouras) Z.; m. Sophia Levathes, Mar. 27, 1943; 1 child, John Christopher. AB, U. Mich., 1936, MS, 1937, MD, 1941. Diplomate: Am. Bd. Internal Medicine. Extern Simpson Meml. Inst., U. Mich., 1940-41, research asso., 1947-50; also asst. prof. medicine at univ.; intern Harvard IV Med. Service, Boston City Hosp., 1941-42; research fellow internal medicine U. Mich. Med. Sch., 1946-47; faculty Temple U. Med. Sch., 1950-60, prof. clin. and research medicine, 1957-60; chief hematology sect. Temple U. Hosp., 1950-60; dir. Simpson Meml. Inst. Med. Research, 1960-78; prof. internal medicine U. Mich., 1960-80, emeritus, 1980-95; coord. med. edn. for nat. def., 1966-71; mem. com. on naval med. rsch. NRC-NAS, 1970-74, med. com. on problems of drug dependence, 1970-74; sci. adv. bd. Armed Forces Inst. Pathology, 1970-74; dir. rsch. and engring. Def. Dept., chmn. joint med. rsch. conf., 1968-75; mem. Army Sci. Adv. Panel, 1974-78, Army Sci. Bd., 1978-86; bd. dirs. Medicine in the Pub. Interest, 1973-89, Gorgas Meml.

Inst. Tropical and Preventive Medicine, 1982-92. Author numerous articles in field.; asst. editor: Am. Jour. Med. Scis, 1951-60; editor Procs. Internat. Conf. on Leukemia-Lymphoma, 1968; Procs. Internat. Conf. Drug Abuse; mem. editorial adv. bd.: History of U.S. Army Medical Service in Vietnam and South Asia. Served to maj. M.C. AUS, 1942-46, col. Res. ret. Decorated Order Ismail Egypt; Legion of Merit U.S.; recipient Sternberg medal U. Mich., 1941, U.S.A. Typhus Commn. medal, 1946, Henry Russel award U. Mich., 1950; Disting. Service award Am. Soc. Clin. Pharmacology and Therapeutics, 1980, Dept. Def. medal for disting. pub. service, 1984. Fellow ACP (Physician Laureate award Mich. chpt. 1988), Internat. Soc. Hematology; mem. Am. Soc. Hematology, Am. Micros. Soc. (editorial bd. trans. 1956-65), AMA (vice chmn. sect. exptl. medicine 1968-69, chmn. sect. clin. pharmacology and therapeutics 1969-71, alt. del. 1971-73, del. 1973-75), Am. Fedn. Clin. Research, Am. Soc. Tropical Medicine, Soc. Exptl. Biology and Medicine, N.Y. Acad. Scis., Soc. Med. Cons. to Armed Forces (v.p. 1968-69, pres. 1969-70, alt. del. to AMA 1978-83, del. 1984-88, John R. Seal award, 1986), AAAS, Am., Internat. socs. internal medicine, Midwest Blood Club, Am. Soc. Clin. Pharmacology and Chemotherapy (regent, pres. 1968-69), Internat. Soc. Blood Transfusion, Med. Mycol. Soc. Ams., Assn. Mil. Surgeons U.S., Am. Therapeutic Soc. (pres. 1968-69), Internat. Soc. Toxinology, Asociación Médica Argentina, Sociedad de Farmacología y Terapeútica (hon.), Phi Beta Kappa, Sigma Xi, Alpha Omega Alpha, Phi Kappa Phi. Home: Ann Arbor Mich. Died June 27, 1995.

ZAREMBO, LEV KONSTANTINOVICH, physicist; b. Moscow, Ukraine, Mar. 18, 1925; s. Konstantin Stanislavovich and Yanina Adamovna (Jvirblis) A.; m. Renata Ipolitovna Sitkovskaya, May 25, 1952; children: Elena, Konstantin. Dr.phys.mat.sci., Moscow State U., 1971. Physicist, researcher Acad. Sci. USSR, Moscow, Russia, 1953-58, Acad. Sci. USSR Acoustical Inst., Moscow, Russia, 1958-61; physicist, researcher, prof. Moscow State U. Phys. Dept., 1961-96. Author: Introduction in Nonlinear Acoustics, 1966, Nonlinear Acoustics, 1984, Spin-Phonon Interactions in Crystals, 1991; co-author: Power Ultrasonic Fields, 1968. Mem. Acad. Natural Sci., Russian Assn. Acoustics, Internat. Acad. Info. Died Sept. 16, 1996.

ZEBLEY, JOSEPH WILDMAN, JR., management consultant; b. Appleton, Md., July 9, 1914; s. Joseph Wildman and Annie May (Benjamin) Z.; m. Edith Sophie Schubel, July 4, 1947 (dec. Sept. 1972); children: Joseph Wildman III, Charles Schubel. AA, U. Balt., 1947, LLB, 1949; BS in Mil. Studies, U. Md., 1963; BS in Indsl. Mgmt., U. Balt., 1964, JD, 1970; MEd, Johns Hopkins U., 1973; PhD in Human Behavior, Newport U., 1984; cert. advanced study in edn., Johns Hopkins U., 1978. Cert. tchr. supr./administrator edn., Md. Operator Nat. Vulcanized Fibre Co., Newark, Del., 1934-36; owner, operator Clover Valley Produce, Elkton, Md., 1936-39; engring. asst. E.I. duPont de Nemours & Co., Seaford, Del., 1939-41; owner, operator Clover Valley Farms and Zebley Assocs., Balt. and Elkton, Md., 1946—; coord., bd. dir. Balt. Met. Area Manpower Tng. Skills Ctr., 1965-82; adj. prof. Balt. Coll. Commerce (now U. Balt. U. Md. System), 1966-70; exec. sec. Coun. Affiliate Orgns., Am. Assn. Adult Continuing Edn., Washington, 1983—; co-chmn., mem. Avd. Coun. Adult and Community Svcs., Md. State Dept. Edn., 1976—; chmn., mem. Adv. Com. Apprenticeship Info., Md. State Employment Svc., 1978—; com. chmn. Adv. Coun. Adult Continuing Edn. Community Coll. Balt., 1987—; cons. Adv. Com. Adult Literacy, Cecil C.C., 1987—. Author: Battlefield Tour of Metz, France Area, 1961 (Citation 1961), Family Zublin ou Zobel in America, 1736-1976, 1976, Scribbling With My Pen, 1980. Mem. exec. com., dist. chmn. Balt. area coun. Boy Scouts Am., 1970—; chmn., mem. devel. com. Balt. Sherwood Gardens in Guilford, 1970—. Maj. U.S. Army, 1941-46, ETO, ret. Recipient Silver Beaver award Boy Scout Am., 1979, Meritorious Svc. award Am. Assn. Adult and Continuing Edn., Washington, 1984; named Outstanding Adult Educator Lit. Tng. Office Mayor, Balt., 1986. Mem. ASTD, Soc. Advancement Mgmt. (pres. Greater Balt. chpt. 1974-75, Leadership award 1975), Md. Assn. Adult Community and Continuing Edn. (pres. 1982-83, Outstanding Svc. award 1987), Cecil County C. of C., Internat. Platform Assn., Sigma Delta Kappa, Phi Delta Gamma, Advt. and Profl. Club of Balt., Ea. Shore Soc. of City of Balt. (pres. 1989-91), Horticulturists/Foresters, Phi Delta Gamma (pres. Gamma chpt. 1990-93), Phi Delta Kappa (editor newsletter Hopkins chapt. 1980-86), Masons, Shriners. Democrat. Avocations: arts and music, world travel, writing, pub. speaking, hist. trust conservation. Died Dec. 9, 1993.

ZELDITCH, BERNICE OSMOLA, English language educator; b. Detroit, May 19, 1929; d. Steven M. and Mary (Skrompulska) Osmola; m. Morris Zelditch, Jr., June 2, 1950; children: Miriam Lea, Steven Morris. BA, Oberlin Coll., 1951; MA, Stanford U., 1965. Cert. tchr., Calif. Indexer, picture editor 11 pub. firms including Random House, Knopf, McGraw Hill, N.Y.C., 1955 61; instr., asst. prof., assoc. prof. English, Foothill Coll., Los Altos Hills, Calif., 1966-69, prof., 1969-96; vis. prof. Stanford (Calif.) U. Sch. Edn., 1974-76, mem. adv. bd. Friends of Mary Schofield Collection, 1985-90. Contbr. poems to lit. publs. Info. officer Internat. Yr. of Child, UNICEF, Palo Alto, Calif., 1978-80. Conf. grantee Calif. Coun. for Humanities, NEH, 1975. Mem. MLA, NOW, AAUW, Children's Lit. Assn., also local art and music guilds. Democrat. Avocations: writing, gardening, attending concerts. Home: Stanford Calif. Died May 10, 1996.

ZELLER, ROBERT HENRY, former university president; b. St. Louis, May 24, 1926; s. Albert C. and Allie M. (Durbin) Z.; m. Barbara J. Estes, May 31, 1948; children: David, John. BS, Shurtleff Coll., Alton, Ill., 1948; MS in Edn., U. Ill., 1951, Adv. Edn. Specialist, 1955; EdD, Washington U., St. Louis, 1959. Tchr., adminstr. Pub. Schs., Alton, 1948-59; dean students Carthage (Ill.) Coll., 1959-60; state adminstr. Ill. Dept. Edn., Springfield, 1960-63, 64-71; adminstr. Maine Twp. High Schs., Park Ridge, Ill., 1963-64; prof., adminstr. Sangamon State U., Springfield, 1971-84; pres. U. Sarasota (Fla.), 1984-92. With USN, 1943-46. Mem. Masons, Scottish Rite, Shriners. Presbyterian. Avocations: reading, bridge, travel. Died Dec. 2, 1995.

ZERMAN, MAXINE LORAINE, mathematics and science braille consultant; b. Menomonie, Wis., Oct. 18, 1927; d. James and Celia May (Dunahee) Beaver; m. R. P. Allan, Feb. 11, 1945 (div. Aug. 1956); children: Darlene, David (dec.), Daniel; m. Arnold Elwood Zerman, Oct. 29, 1967 (dec. Nov. 1993); stepchildren: Patricia, Gary, Karen (dec.). Student, Milw. Conservatory of Music, 1950-51. Cert. literary braille, math. and sci. braille, math. and sci. braille proofreading. Math. and sci. braille advisor Libr. of Congress/Nat. Libr. Svc. for the Blind and Physically Handicapped, Washington, 1986-96; cons. All Braillists, 1985-96. Contbr. articles to profl. jours. Named Innovator of the Yr., Fla. Assn. Educators and Rehabilitators, 1991. Mem. Nat. Braille Assn. (math. chmn. 1985-88), Visual Aid Vols. Fla. (pres. 1989-91, editor newsletter 1988-90), Sarasota County Braille Transcribers (pres. 1991-95). Avocations: travel, reading, playing organ, volunteering. Died Sept. 3, 1996.

ZHU, WUHUA, electronics and water acoustics educator; b. Yangzhou, Jiangsu, China, Jan. 3, 1902; s. Hongjun and Qitong (Zhou) Z.; m. Qin Tao, Aug. 1930; children: Zhensheng, Songsheng, Pingsheng. BSc, Jiao Tong U., Shanghai, 1923; MSc, MIT, 1924, Harvard U., 1925; DSc, Harvard U., 1926. Prof. Zhongshan U., Guangzhou, China, 1927-30; prof. Jiao Tong U., Tangshan, China, 1930-33; prof. Jiao Tong U., Shanghai, 1946-55, 61—, v.p., 1961-66, pres., 1978-80; prof. Beijing (China) U., 1933-37, Kunming, China, 1937-46; prof., v.p. Harbin (China) Inst. Tech., 1955-61; mem. electronics and acoustics group of Nat. Sci. Com., China, 1962. Contbr. articles to profl. jours. Mem. Chinese People's Polit. Cons. Conf., 1978-88. Mem. Chinese Inst. Elec. Engring., Chinese Acad. Scis., Chinese Soc. Electronics (v.p. 1963-66). Mem. Communist party.

ZIFF, LLOYD RICHARD, lawyer; b. N.Y.C., Mar. 9, 1942; s. George and Lillian (Gisnet) Z.; m. M. Morrow Cox, Jan. 28, 1967; children: Tina Marie, M. Courtney, Robert G. Grad., Peekskill Mil. Acad.; BA, U. Pa., 1968, JD magna cum laude, 1971. Bar: Pa. 1971, U.S. Supreme Ct. 1975; cert. as arbitrator, 1982—, as mediator, 1992— U.S. Dist. Ct. (ea. dist.) Pa. Assoc. Pepper, Hamilton & Scheetz, Phila., 1971-77, ptnr., 1977-92; founding ptnr. Harkins Cunningham, Phila. and Washington, 1992—; tchg. fellow Sch. Law U. Pa., 1971, lectr., 1981-82; mem. faculty Acad. Advocacy, 1980—; mem. DeVitt implementation com. U.S. Dist. Ct. (ea. dist.) Pa., 1980-84, mem. CLE com., 1985—, chmn. local civil rules adv. com., 1991—, apptd. to adv. group under Civil Justice Reform Act, 1995—; co-chmn. Seminar on Complex Litigation, 1983; invitee Jud. Conf. of 3d Cir., 1986, 89, 91. Contbr. articles to legal jours. Mem. Kent State U. Task Force, Pres.'s Commn. on Campus Unrest, Ohio, 1970; mem. Inter-disciplinary Com. on Child Abuse S.E. Pa., 1973-75; mem. adv. com. Family Resources Ctr., St. Christopher's Hosp. for Children, Phila., 1976; chmn. Phila. Bail Project, 1969; counsel Phila. Vietnam Vets. Meml. Fund, 1985—; mem., bd. dirs. Penndelphia Scholarship Found., 1995—. With U.S. Army, 1965-67. Warwick Found. scholar U. Pa., 1971; Salzburg Seminar fellow Am. Studies-Am. Law and Legal Instns., (Austria), 1978. Mem. ABA, Pa. Bar Assn., Phila. Bar Assn. (chmn. election procedures com. 1976, chmn. spl. com. on admission attys. to fed. practice 1986, chair Fidelity award com. 1987, chair fed. bench bar conf., 1988, chmn. fed. cts. com. 1989), Am. Judicature Soc., U.S. Supreme Ct. Hist. Soc., U.S. Ct. Appeals for the 3d Cir. Hist. Soc., U.S. Dist. Ct. for Ea. Dist. Pa. Hist. Soc., Order of Coif, Chapel of the Four Chaplains, Legion of Honor. Died Sept. 5, 1996.

ZIKORUS, ALBERT MICHAEL, golf course architect; b. Needham, Mass., Apr. 9, 1921; s. Walter Peter and Rose Mary (Smith) Z.; m. Charlene Bradstreet Aldrich; 1 child, Michael; m. Joan Gayle Boone, 1979. Student, Mass. State Coll., 1941. Greenskeeper Ould Newbury Golf Course, Newburyport, Mass., 1942, Wellesley (Mass.) Golf Course, 1946, Woodbridge (Conn.) Golf Course, 1948-51; assoc. William F. Mitchell Architect, 1951-52, Orin E. Smith Architect, Southington, Conn., 1953-58. Designed Tunxis Plantation Country Club, Farmington, Conn., Twin Hills Country Club, Longmeadow, Mass., Timberlin Golf Course, Berlin, Conn., Tashua Golf Course, Trumbull, Conn., Segalla Country Club, Amenia, N.Y., others. Sgt. USAF, 1942-46. Mem. Am. Soc. Golf Course Architects. Avocations: swimming, fishing, hiking, hunting, golf. Died June 11, 1997.

ZIMMER, BASIL GEORGE, sociologist, educator; b. Smith Creek, Mich., June 29, 1920; s. Walter Nicholas and Mary Alice (Martin) Z.; m. Janet Mae Jackson, Nov. 3, 1942; children: Basil George, Linda Jean. Student, Port Huron (Mich.) Jr. Coll., 1939-41, Shrivenham Am. U., Eng., 1945; B.A., U. Mich., 1947, M.A., 1949, Ph.D., 1954. Teaching fellow U. Mich., 1948-50, research asst. dept. corrections, 1948; lectr., resident dir. Social Sci. Research Project, 1953-59; asso. prof. U. Mich.-Flint Coll., 1957-59, Brown U., Providence, 1959-61; prof. Brown U., 1962-90, chmn. urban studies, 1974-90; fellow Human Resources Research Inst. U.S. Dept. Air Force, 1952-53; instr. Eastern Mich. U., 1950-51, U. Mich., 1951-52; asst. prof. Fla. State U., 1952-53; cons. Met. Area Problems, Flint, 1956-59, Research Med. Research Council U. Aberdeen, Scotland, 1965, 70, 72, Demographic Tng. Center U. Kerala, India, 1964, Div. Vocational Rehab. Spl. Sch. Project, 1964-90 ; vis. scholar Australian Nat. U., 1973. Author: Rebuilding Cities: The Effects of Displacement and Relocation on Small Business, 1964, (with A. H. Hawley) Resistance to Reorganization of School Districts in Metropolitan Areas, 1966, Resistances to Government Unification in Metropolitan Areas, 1967, The Metropolitan Community: Its People and Government, 1970, Migration in the United States, 1971, The Urban Centrifugal Drift, 1975, Urban Family Building Patterns, 1977; Editor: Directory of Population Study Centers, Population Assn. Am., 1971, Demography, 1971-72; Contbr. to profl. jours. Mem. Urban League, 1955-90 ; chmn. Gen. Plan, Providence, 1963-90 ; bd. dirs. Flint Youth Bd., Center for Urban Studies, 1974-90 ; mem. exec. com. Mayor's Adv. Com. Urban Renewal; mem. com. urban transp. research Hwy. Research Bd., 1961-63; pres. Urban Obs. of R.I., 1978-90. Served with AUS, 1941-45, ETO. Fellow Am. Sociol. Assn.; mem. Population Assn. Am., Eastern Sociol. Soc., Internat. Union Sci. Study Population. Home: Rumford R.I. Died June 12, 1990; interred Hillside Cemetery, St. Clair, MI.

ZIMMERMAN, EDWARD KLINE, management consultant; b. Elizabeth City, N.C., Oct. 13, 1936; m. Carol DeSilvio; children: Joanne Burgess, Edward William, Carson Freas. Student in radio, TV and motion pictures, U. N.C., 1954-58. Research asst. Research Computation Center, U. N.C., 1959; systems programmer Sperry Univac, beginning 1960; later staff cons. Sperry Univac (Sperry Internat.), until 1965; gen. mgr. Computer Services Ltd. (became subs. University Computing Co.), Birmingham, Eng., beginning 1965; later became mgr. info. systems for edni. subs. of University Computing Co., in U.S.; cons. info. processing N.Y.C., 1969, Washington, 1970; from customer systems mgr. to sr. tech. cons. Nat. Teleprocessing Service, Info. Network div. Computer Sci. Corp., 1970-73; dir. Master Calendar Services for Am. Revolution Bicentennial Commn., 1973-77; spl. asst. to dir Office Adminstrn., Exec. Office of Pres., 1977-79; dep. asst. sec. of commerce for communications and info., dep. adminstr. Nat. Telecommunications and Info. Adminstrn., Dept. Commerce, Washington, 1979-80; spl. asst. to dir. Office Planning and Evaluation, White House, 1981; exec. dir. Nat. Computer Graphics Assn., 1981-82; mgmt. cons. Washington, 1982-90; chmn. Inter-Agy. Com. on Automatic Data Processing, 1980-81; exec. dir. adv. com. on info. network structure and function for Exec. Office of Pres., 1979; co-chmn. Domestic Info. Display System Steering Com., 1978-81; exec. sec. Adv. Group on White House Info. Systems, 1977; mem. steering com. Nat. Computer Conf., 1976; mem. public-pvt. sector task force Nat. Commn. on Library and Info. Sci., 1979-81. Mem. editorial bd. Info. Soc., 1983-90. Bd. dirs. Holmes Run Acres Civic Assn., 1974-77, pres., 1976. Served with U.S. Army, 1960-62. Recipient Disting. Service award Am. Revolution Bicentennial Adminstrn., 1977. Mem. Assn. for Computing Machinery, Nat. Computer Graphics Assn., World Computer Graphics Assn. (dir. 1981). Home: Oakton Va. Died Dec. 19, 1990.

ZINNEMANN, FRED, film director; b. Austria, Apr. 29, 1907; emigrated to U.S., 1929, naturalized, 1937; s. Oskar and Anna (Feiwel) Z.; m. Renee Bartlett, Oct. 9, 1936; 1 child, Tim. Student law, Vienna U., 1925-27; student, Sch. Cinematography, Paris, France, 1927-28; DLitt (hon.), Durham U., U.K., 1994. Asst. cameraman Paris and Berlin, Germany, 1928; asst. dir. to Berthold Viertel, Fox Studio, Hollywood, 1929-30; asst. to Robert Flaherty, 1931. 1st directorial assignment: documentary on Mexican fishermen The Wave, 1934; dir. 16 short subjects for Metro-Goldwyn-Mayer, including Story of Dr. Carver, a series on great physicians including Dr. Semmelweis (Acad. award), also several anti-crime shorts, 1937-41, features including The Seventh Cross, The Search, 1946-47 (Screen Dirs. Guild award), Act of Violence, 1948, The Men, 1949, Teresa, 1950, High Noon, 1951 (Screen Dirs. Guild, N.Y. Film Critics awards), The Member of the Wedding, 1952, Benjy, 1951 (Acad. award best documentary), From

Here to Eternity, 1953 (Acad. awards including best picture, best dir., N.Y. Film Critics' Screen Dirs. Guild), Oklahoma !, 1956, A Hatful of Rain, 1957, The Nun's Story, 1958 (N.Y. Film Critic's award), The Sundowners, 1959, Behold a Pale Horse, 1964, A Man for All Seasons, 1966 (Acad. awards best picture, best dir., Dir.'s Guild ann. award , N.Y. Film Critics' award for best film, best dir.); dir. The Day of the Jackal, 1972, Julia, 1976 (3 Oscars, Donatello award 1978), Five Days One Summer, 1982; author: A Life in The Movies, 1992; contbr. to: Ency. Brit.; photo exhibition Victoria & Albert Mus., London, 1992. Co-founder, hon. trustee Artists' Rights Found., 1994. Recipient Golden Thistle award Edinborough Film Festival, 1965, award Moscow Film Festival, 1965, Gold medal City of Vienna, 1967, D. W. Griffith award Dirs. Guild Am., 1971, Donatello (Italy) award, 1976, 3 Golden Globe awards, U.S. Congl. Lifetime Achievement award, 1987, John Huston award Artists Rights Found., 1994; named to Order Arts and Letters, France, 1982. Fellow Brit. Acad. Film and TV (Fellowship award 1978), Brit. Film Inst.; mem. Acad. Motion Picture Arts and Scis., Am. Film Inst. (co-founder 1961, former trustee). Co-founder sch. of neo-realism in Am. motion pictures. Strongly involved in battle for federal laws protecting moral rights of authors. Home: London Eng. Died March 14, 1997.

ZIPPER, HERBERT, symphony conductor; b. Vienna, Austria, Apr. 27, 1904; came to U.S., 1946; s. Emil and Regina (Westreich) Z.; m. Trudl Dubsky, Oct. 1, 1939 (dec. July, 1976). Master diploma, Vienna State Acad. for Music and Drama, Vienna, 1926. Prof. Conservatory of Düsseldorf, Fed. Republic Germany, 1931-33; apptd. by Pres. Sergio Osmeñ-a of Philippines as mem. com. for cultural rehab. of Philippines, 1946; lectr. New Sch. for Social Research in opera, symphony, and composition, 1947-52; exec. dir. Nat. Guild Community Mus. Schs., 1967-72; music cons. JDR 3d Fund, N.Y.C.; projects dir. U. So. Calif. Sch. Performing Arts, Los Angeles, 1972-80; invited guest condr. and tchr. conducting and composition People's Republic of China, 1981. Asst. condr. Wiener Burgtheater, 1923-25, condr. Vienna Madrigal Assn., 1927-29, opera condr. Stadtheater Ingolstadt, Bavaria, 1929-30, condr. Mcpl. Music Soc., 1931-33; guest condr. in various cities of Europe, 1933-37; instrumental in found. and orgn. of Vienna Concert Orch., composed mainly of musicians who fled Germany, 1934; composed music for polit. satires in Paris, 1939; mus. dir. Manila Symphony Orch. and head Acad. Music of Manila, 1939-42; gave 130 symphony concerts for armed forces and civilians, 1945-46; mus. dir. Bklyn. Symphony Orch., 1947-50; Fine Arts Quartet Concert series, Chgo., Wilmette, Ill., 1960-67; condr. summer season, Manila Symphony Orch., 1951-69; dir. Community Music Ctr. North Shore, 1953-67, condr. Chgo. Businessmen's Orch., 1955-62, condr. 26 symphony concerts in Beijing, Tienjin and Guangzhou, Peoples Republic China, 1981, 4 months 1982, condr. orchs. in 4 cities, Peoples Republic China, 4 months, 1984; condr. concerts in Beijing, Jinan, Tianjin, Qingdao, Peoples Republic China, 1986, Beijing and Shenyang, China, 1988, Beijing and Changchun, 1989, Beijing Cen. Philharm., Orch. Concerts, 1990; condr. Cen. Philharm. of China, Philharm. Chamber Orch., Radio Broadcast Orch., Beijing, 1991, concerts with Tianjin Philharmonic, 1993; opened Styrian Automn, Graz, Austria, 1988, Zipper's Biography, 1992, Chinese edition, 1992, German edition, 1993; composer revision of choral works by old masters and own choral arrangements, 1948-49; German version of Ernst Toch's opera The Last Tale, 1964. Chmn. Philippine fellowship project, 1966; pres. Nat. Guild Community Music Schs., 1957-62, exec. dir. 1967-72; project dir. U. So. Calif. Sch. of Performing Arts, 1972-80. Prisoner Dachau and Buchenwald concentration camps, 1938-39. Recipient Louis S. Weiss Meml. prize New Sch. of Social Research, N.Y., 1954, Presdl. award medal and citation Pres. of Philippines, 1959, Austrian Cross Honor for Sci. and Art, 1966, Silangan award U. East Manila, Philippines, 1977, Samuel Rosenbaum Meml. award Nat. Guild Community Schs. Arts, Golden Honor Insignia for important achievements Govt. Vienna, Austria, 1993. Reorganized orch. after imprisonment by Japanese and work in underground, 1945. Home: Los Angeles Calif. Died April 21, 1997.

ZMUDA, SHARON LOUISE, construction executive; b. Chgo., May 31, 1942; d. Theodore Edward and Virginia (Fleig) Z. Student, Sch. Art Inst. Chgo., 1961-62; BA, Mundelein Coll., Chgo., 1964. In student services dept. La Salle Extension U., Chgo., 1965-69; sales coordinator S.K. Smith Co., Chgo., 1969-71; customer service specialist Am. Express Co., Chgo., 1971-73; office mgr. North Shore Cement, Inc., Chgo., 1975-84; pres. Abacor Rd. Constrn., Inc., Chgo., 1984—; program host, Consumers' Counter, CRIS Radio, 1983—. Fundraiser Sch. Art Inst. of Chgo., 1987—. Mem. Women's Bus. Devel. Ctr., Nat. Assn. Women in Constrn. Roman Catholic. Avocations: interior decorating, catering, collecting.

ZOLA, IRVING KENNETH, sociology educator, consultant; b. Boston, Jan. 24, 1935; s. Bernard and Betty (Weinberg) Z.; m. Leonora Katz, Nov. 14, 1957 (div. June 1973); children: Warren Keith, Amanda Beth; m. Judy Norsigian, Oct. 23, 1981; 1 child, Kyra. B.A., Harvard U., 1956, Ph.D., 1962. Research and cons. sociologist Mass. Gen. Hosp., Boston, 1959-94; asst.

prof. sociology Brandeis U., Waltham, Mass., 1963-68, assoc. prof., 1968-71, prof., 1972-94, prof. Florence Heller Grad. Sch. for Advanced Studies in Social Welfare, 1979-94, chmn. sociology dept., 1972-74, 79-84; exec. dir. Boston Self Help Ctr., Brookline, Mass., 1982-87; cons. in resident WHO, Geneva, Switzerland, 1968-69, Netherlands Inst. for Preventive Medicine, Leiden, 1972. Author: Missing Pieces, 1982, Socio-Medical Inquirires, 1983; co-author: Independent Living for Physically Disable People, 1983; editor: Ordinary Lives (anthology), 1982; editor/pub. Disability Studies Quar., 1982-94. Grantee Ford Found., 1960-61, NIMH, 1963-66, Nat. Inst. Gen. Med. Sci., 1963-68; Mary Switzer scholar in rehab., 1983; recipient Apple award, Mass. Sociol. Assn., 1986, cert. of recognition, Sociol. Practice Assn., 1986. Fellow AAAS; mem. Am. Sociol. Assn. (med. sociology sect. chmn. 1982-83), Soc. for Med. Anthropology, Soc. for the Psychol. Study of Social Issues, Soc. For Study of Social Problems, Am. Congress of Rehab. Medicine, Am. Pub. Health Assn. (social sci. conf.), Soc. for Disability Studies. Home: Chestnut Hill Mass. Died Dec. 1, 1994.

ZSCHIESCHE, WOLFGANG, pathologist, immunohistochemistry consultant; b. Merseburg, Germany, Mar. 14, 1933; s. Hans Kurt and Anna E. Gertraud (Pietzker) Z.; Annelies Bott Löber, 1960 (div. 1971); 1 child, Eckhardt Zschiesche; m. Waltraud Heppner, Aug. 25, 1978; 1 child, Runa Löber. MD, U. Halle, Germany, 1957. Med. asst. U. Halle, Germany, 1957-62; med. asst. Acad. of Scis. GDR, Jena, Germany, 1962-71, dept. head, 1971-79; prof. Acad. of Scis. GDR, Berlin, Germany, 1976, dir. inst., 1980-84, head of lab., 1985-90; head of lab. Ctr. of Molecular Medicine, Berlin, Germany, 1991-96. Co-author: (book) Immunopathology of Viral Diseases, 1977; co-author and editor: (book) Immune Modulation by Infectious Agents, 1991. Mem. Deutsche Akademie der Naturforscher Leopoldina. Home: Lindenberger Weg 74, D-13125 Berlin Germany Died Oct. 29, 1996.

ZULU, MTHEMBENI MACPHERSON, chemistry educator; b. Nquthu, Kwa-Zulu, S. Africa, Nov. 24, 1947; s. Ambrose and Josephina Thembekile (Mtshali) Z.; m. Philile Roseline Sibiya, Aug. 21, 1976; children: Bonga, Ntuthuko, Mandla, Sphelele. BS, Zululand U., 1974, BS with hons., 1979; MS, Binghamton U., 1985, PhD, 1988. Sr. lab. asst. U. Zululand, Empangeni, S. Africa, 1975-83, sr. lectr., 1989, assoc. prof., 1990-92, prof., head, vice-dean faculty of sci., 1993—; grad. rsch. asst. U. Binghamton, N.Y., 1986-87; vis. lectr. U. Natal, Durban, S. Africa, 1991—. Contbr. articles to profl. publs. Recipient Alexander von Humboldt award Fed. Rep. of Germany, 1993, Zappert award Am. Chem. Soc., N.Y., 1988; fellowship Found. for Rsch. Devel., Pretoria, 1986-88; scholarship UN, N.Y., 1983-88; grantee FRD-UK Royal Soc., 1996—. Mem. Internat. Union of Pure and Applied Chem. Com. on The Nomenclature of Inorganic Chem., Internat. Coun. of Sci. Unions Nat. bd., Coun. Found. Edn. Sci. and Tech. (vice chmn. 1996—), Found. for Rsch. Devel. (coun. mem.), Assn. Black Scientists, Engrs. and Technologists, South African Chem. Inst., Matriculation Bds. Maths and Scis., Acad. Scis. South Africa (elected founder mem. 1994—). Anglican.

ZWERLING, ISRAEL, psychiatrist, educator; b. N.Y.C., June 12, 1917; s. Max and Anna (Greidinger) Z.; m. Florence Erdtrachter, Nov. 16, 1940; children: Matthew Henry, Sara Kay. BS, CCNY, 1937, MS, 1938; PhD, Columbia U., 1947, diploma psychoanalytic medicine, 1960; MD, SUNY Downstate Med. Ctr., 1950. Diplomate Am. Bd. Psychiatry and Neurology. Intern Maimonides Hosp., Bklyn., 1950- 51; resident research fellow psychiatry Cin. Gen. Hosp., 1951-54; dir. SUNY Alcohol Clinic, Downstate Med. Ctr., Bklyn., 1954-56; lectr. Ctr. Alcohol Studies Yale U., 1955-60; mem. faculty Albert Einstein Coll. Medicine, 1955-73, prof. psychiatry, 1964-73, exec. officer dept. psychiatry, 1970-72; dir. Bronx State Hosp., 1966-73; prof., chmn. dept. mental health scis. Hahnemann Med. Coll., Phila., 1973-85; dean sch. medicine Hahnemann Med. Coll., 1985-87. Maj. USAAF, 1942-46. Decorated Bronze Star; recipient Strecker award Inst. Pa. Hosp., 1965, Disting. Contbn. award Am. Family Assn., 1983, Lifetime Achievement award Phila. Psychiat. Soc., 1990. Fellow Am. Psychiat. Assn.; mem. AMA, Group Advancement Psychiatry (chmn. com. family 1964-68), Jewish Acad. Arts and Scis., Phila. Med. Soc., Am. Psychosomatic Soc., Am. Psychoanalytic Assn., Am. Psychol. Assn., Sigma Xi, Alpha Omega Alpha. Home: Philadelphia Pa. Died Nov. 12, 1993.

ZWICKEL, WALTER, athletic wear manufacturing executive; b. Phila., Dec. 21, 1927; s. Benjamin and Sarah (Tellem) Z.; m. Myra Coverman, Dec. 24, 1955 (dec. 1963); children—Ellyn, Benjamin; m. Leda Volov, Mar. 26, 1964; children—Ellen, Bruce, Jayne. B.S., Temple U., Phila., 1948. Mgr., apprentice designer Zwickel Tailoring, Phila., 1948-52; prodn. mgr., designer Alcon Mfg., Miami, Fla., 1952-56; gen. mgr. Zwickel Clothing Stores, Phila., 1956-69; pres. Zwickel Mfg., Phila., 1969-95; guest lectr. West Chester State Coll., Pa., 1979-82; mem. bd. gymnastic com. Maccabiah Games, 1962-95. Fashion editor Modern Gymnast Mag., Los Angeles, 1968-79; contbr. chpts. to books, articles to profl. jours.; designer items for Olympic

Games, 1968, 72, 76, 80, 84, 5 Pan Am Games, 6 Maccabiah Games; inventor numerous protective devices for gymnasts. Chmn., Columbia Ave. Businessmen's Assn., 1960-69; past pres. Susquehanna Ave. Businessmen's Assn. Named to Gymnastics Hall of Fame, NCAA Gym Coaches Assn., 1973. Mem. AAHPERD (guest speaker 1970, mem. bd. assoc. exhibitors), Temple U. Gym Team Alumni Assn., U.S. Gymnastics Fedn., U.S. Rowing Assn., Nat. Rifle Assn. (life mem.). Republican. Jewish. Avocations: target shooting; sculpting; cabinet making; fishing. Home: Philadelphia Pa. Died Nov. 6, 1995.